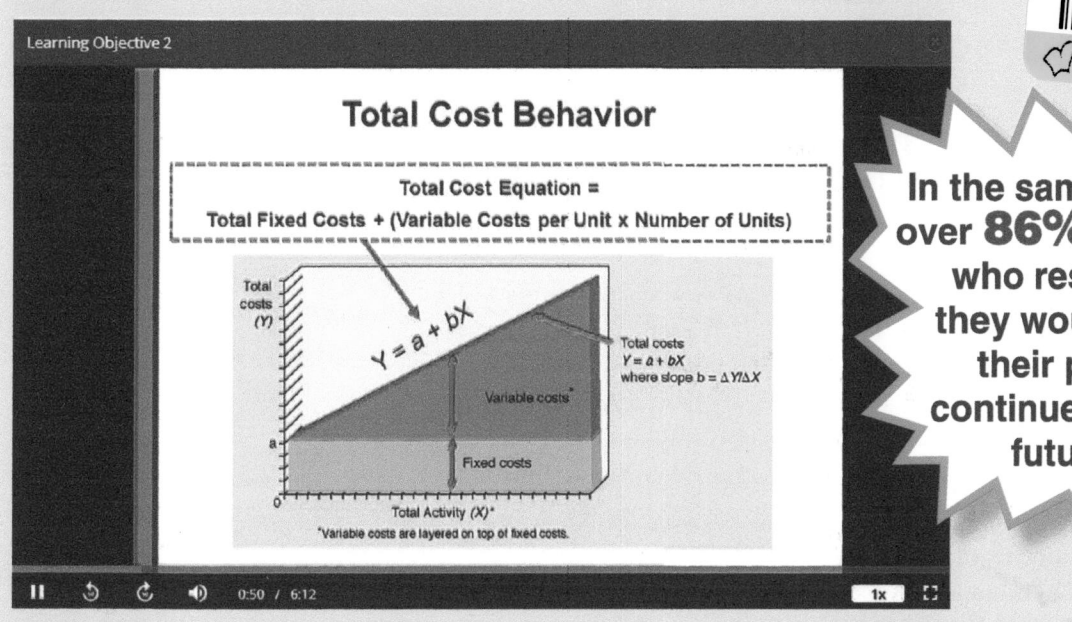

Make Instruction Needs-Based

◆ Identify where your students are struggling and customize your instruction to address their needs.

◆ Gauge how your entire class or individual students are performing by viewing the easy-to-use gradebook.

◆ Ensure your students are getting the additional reinforcement and direction they need between class meetings.

Provide Instruction and Practice 24/7

◆ Assign homework from your Cambridge Business Publishers' textbook and have myBusinessCourse grade it for you automatically.

◆ With our eLectures, your students can revisit accounting topics as often as they like or until they master the topic.

◆ Guided Examples show students how to solve select problems.

◆ Make homework due before class to ensure students enter your classroom prepared.

◆ For an additional fee, upgrade MBC to include the eBook and you have all the tools needed for an online course.

LMS Integration

*my*BusinessCourse integrates with many learning management systems, including **Canvas**, **Blackboard**, **Moodle**, **D2L**, **Schoology**, and **Sakai**. Your gradebooks sync automatically.

Getting Started is as EASY as 1, 2, 3 . . . 4!

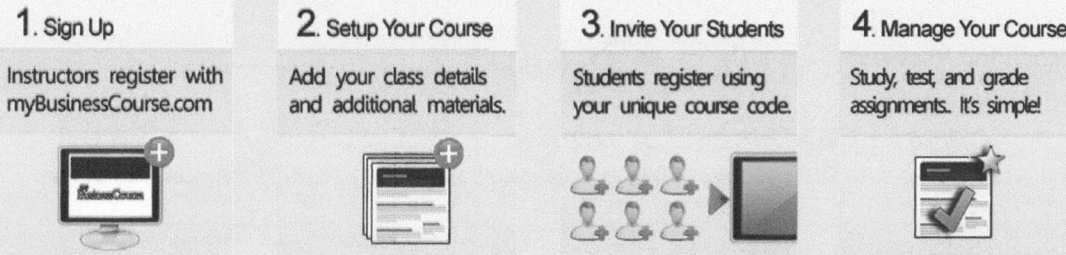

1. Sign Up
Instructors register with myBusinessCourse.com

2. Setup Your Course
Add your class details and additional materials.

3. Invite Your Students
Students register using your unique course code.

4. Manage Your Course
Study, test, and grade assignments. It's simple!

Want to learn more about myBusinessCourse?

Contact your sales representative or visit **www.mybusinesscourse.com**.

Series in Accounting

Financial Accounting
- **Financial Accounting for Decision Makers, 2e** by DeFond
- **Financial Accounting for Undergraduates, 4e** by Wallace, Nelson, and Christensen
- **Financial Accounting, 6e** by Dyckman, Hanlon, Magee, and Pfeiffer
- **Financial Accounting for MBAs, 8e** by Easton, Wild, Halsey, and McAnally
- **Financial Accounting for Executives & MBAs, 5e** by Simko, Wallace, and Comprix
- **Financial Accounting Using IFRS, 2e** by Wong, Dyckman, Hanlon, Magee, and Pfeiffer

Managerial Accounting
- **Managerial Accounting for Undergraduates, 2e** by Christensen, Hobson, Wallace, and Matthews
- **Managerial Accounting, 8e** by Hartgraves & Morse
- **Management Accounting: Information for Decision Making, 7e** by Atkinson, Kaplan, Matsumura, and Young

Combined Financial & Managerial Accounting
- **Financial & Managerial Accounting for Undergraduates, 2e** by Wallace, Nelson, Christensen, Hobson, and Matthews
- **Financial & Managerial Accounting for Decision Makers, 4e** by Hanlon, Magee, Pfeiffer, and Dyckman
- **Financial & Managerial Accounting for MBAs, 6e** by Easton, Halsey, and McAnally

Intermediate Accounting
- **Intermediate Accounting, 2e** by Hanlon, Hodder, Nelson, Roulstone, and Dragoo
- **Guide to Intermediate Accounting Research, 2e** by Collins

Cost Accounting
- **Cost Accounting: Foundations and Evolutions, 10e** by Kinney, Raiborn, and Dragoo

Auditing
- **Alpine Cupcakes Audit Case, 2e** by Dee, Durtschi, and Mindak

Financial Statement Analysis & Valuation
- **Financial Statement Analysis & Valuation, 6e** by Easton, McAnally, and Sommers
- **Corporate Valuation, 2e** by Holthausen & Zmijewski
- **Valuation Using Financial Statements, 2e** by Sommers, Easton, and Drake

Advanced Accounting
- **Advanced Accounting, 4e** by Hamlen
- **Advanced Accounting, 4e** by Halsey & Hopkins

Taxation
- **Scholes & Wolfson's Taxes and Business Strategy, 6e** by Erickson, Hanlon, Maydew, and Shevlin

Governmental and Not-For-Profit Accounting
- **Accounting for Governmental and Nonprofit Organizations, 1e** by Patton, Patton, and Ives
- **Governmental and Not-for-Profit Accounting: An Active Learning Workbook, 2e** by Convery

FASB Codification and eIFRS
- **Skills for Accounting Research: Text & Cases, 4e** by Collins

Computerized Accounting
- **QuickBooks Online:** *2020 Update*, by Williams & Johnson
- **Computerized Accounting with QuickBooks® 2019** and **QuickBooks 2020** *(Desktop version)*, by Williams

Casebooks
- **Cases in Financial Reporting, 8e** by Drake, Engel, Hirst, and McAnally
- **Cases in Managerial and Cost Accounting, 1e** by Allen, Brownlee, Haskins, and Lynch

www.CambridgePub.com
www.myBusinessCourse.com

# myBusinessCourse

FREE WITH NEW COPIES OF THIS TEXTBOOK*

Start using myBusinessCourse Today: www.mybusinesscourse.com

myBusinessCourse is a web-based learning and assessment program intended to complement your textbook and faculty instruction.

Student Benefits

- **eLectures**: These videos review the key concepts of each Learning Objective in each chapter.
- **Guided examples**: These videos provide step-by-step solutions for select problems in each chapter.
- **Auto-graded assignments**: Provide students with immediate feedback on select assignments. **(with Instructor-Led course ONLY)**.
- **Quiz and Exam preparation**: myBusinessCourse provides students with additional practice and exam preparation materials to help students achieve better grades and content mastery.

You can access myBusinessCourse 24/7 from any web-enabled device, including iPads, smartphones, laptops, and tablets.

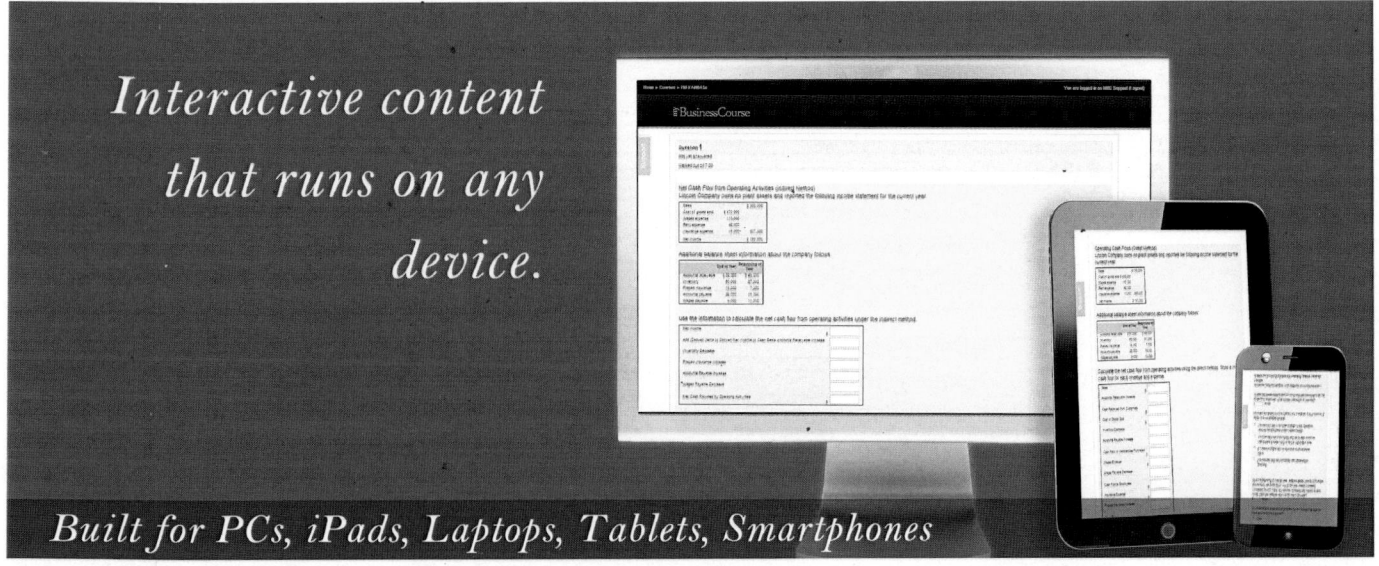

Interactive content that runs on any device.

Built for PCs, iPads, Laptops, Tablets, Smartphones

Financial & Managerial Accounting for MBAs

Sixth Edition

Peter D. Easton
University of Notre Dame

Robert F. Halsey
Babson College

Mary Lea McAnally
Texas A&M University

Cambridge
BUSINESS PUBLISHERS

To my daughters, Joanne and Stacey
—PDE

To my wife, Ellie, and children, Grace and Christian
—RFH

To my husband, Brittan, and my children, Loic, Cindy, Maclean, Lacey, Quinn, and Kay
—MLM

Cambridge Business Publishers

FINANCIAL & MANAGERIAL ACCOUNTING FOR MBAs, Sixth Edition, by Peter D. Easton, Robert F. Halsey, and Mary Lea McAnally.

Student Edition ISBN 978-1-61853-359-3

Bookstores & Faculty: to order this book, call **800-619-6473** or email **customerservice@cambridgepub.com.**

Students: to order this book, please visit the book's website and order directly online.

Printed in the United States of America.
10 9 8 7 6 5 4 3 2

Preface

Welcome to *Financial & Managerial Accounting for MBAs*. Our main goal in writing this book was to satisfy the needs of today's business manager by creating a contemporary, engaging, and user-oriented textbook. This book is the product of extensive market research including focus groups, market surveys, class tests, manuscript reviews, and interviews with faculty from around the world. We are grateful to the students and faculty who provided us with useful feedback during the preparation of this book.

Target Audience

Financial & Managerial Accounting for MBAs is intended for use in full-time, part-time, executive, and evening MBA programs that include a combined financial and managerial accounting course as part of the curriculum, and one in which managerial decision making and analysis are emphasized. This book easily accommodates mini-courses lasting several days as well as extended courses lasting a full semester.

Innovative Approach

Financial & Managerial Accounting for MBAs is managerially oriented and focuses on the most salient aspects of accounting. It teaches MBA students how to read, analyze, and interpret accounting data to make informed business decisions. This textbook makes accounting **engaging, relevant,** and **contemporary.** To that end, it consistently incorporates **real company data,** both in the body of each module and throughout assignment material.

Flexible Structure

The MBA curricula, instructor preferences, and course lengths vary across colleges. Accordingly and to the extent possible, the 25 modules that make up *Financial & Managerial Accounting for MBAs* were designed independently of one another. This modular presentation enables each college and instructor to "customize" the book to best fit the needs of their students. Our introduction and discussion of financial statements constitute Modules 1, 2, and 3. Module 4 presents the analysis of financial statements with an emphasis on profitability analysis. Modules 5 through 10 highlight major financial accounting topics including assets, liabilities, equity, and off-balance-sheet financing. Module 11 details the process for preparing and analyzing the statement of cash flow. Module 12 explains forecasting financial statements, and Module 13 introduces simple valuation models. At the end of each financial accounting module (Modules 1 through 13), we present an ongoing analysis project that can be used as a guide for an independent project. Like the rest of the book, the project is independent across the various modules. Module 14 introduces managerial accounting and is followed by a discussion of cost behavior and cost estimation in Module 15. Module 16 explains cost-volume-profit analysis while Module 17 focuses on using relevant costs to make business decisions. Job and process costing are covered in a single module, Module 18, followed by activity-based costing in Module 19 and the assignment of indirect costs in Module 20. The remaining modules, 21 through 25, highlight managerial accounting topics ranging from operational budgets and variance analysis to segment reporting, product pricing, and capital budgeting. At the end of the book, we include several useful resources. Appendix A contains compound interest tables and formulas. Appendix B is a chart of accounts used in the book. Appendix C is an illustrative case that applies the techniques described in Modules 1 through 13 to an actual company, Harley-Davidson. Appendix C can be used as a guide, in conjunction with the module-end project questions, by students required to prepare a company analysis.

Managerial Emphasis

As MBA instructors, we recognize that the core MBA accounting course is not directed toward accounting majors. *Financial & Managerial Accounting for MBAs* embraces this reality. This book highlights **reporting, analysis, interpretation,** and **decision making.** In the financial accounting modules, we incorporate the following **financial statement effects template** when relevant to train MBA students in understanding the economic ramifications of transactions and their impact on all key financial statements. This analytical tool is a great resource for MBA students in learning accounting and applying it to their future courses and careers. Each transaction is identified in the "Transaction" column. Then, the dollar amounts (positive or negative) of the financial statement effects are recorded in the appropriate balance sheet or income statement columns. The template also reflects the statement of cash flow effects (via the cash column) and the statement of stockholders' equity effects (via the contributed capital and earned capital columns). The earned capital account is immediately updated to reflect any income or loss arising from each transaction (denoted by the arrow line from net income to earned capital). This template is instructive as it reveals the financial impacts of transactions, and it provides insights into the effects of accounting choices.

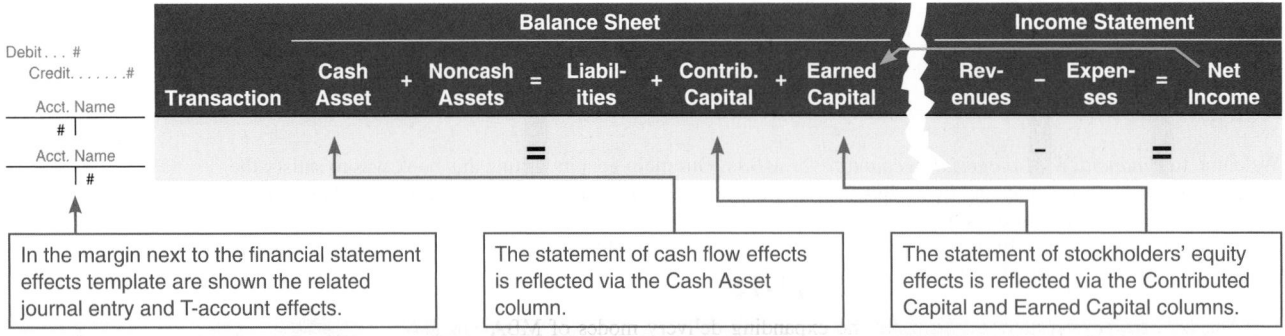

In the margin next to the financial statement effects template are shown the related journal entry and T-account effects.

The statement of cash flow effects is reflected via the Cash Asset column.

The statement of stockholders' equity effects is reflected via the Contributed Capital and Earned Capital columns.

Innovative Pedagogy

Focus Companies for Each Module

In the financial accounting portion of the book, each module's content is explained through the accounting and reporting activities of real companies. To that end, each module incorporates a "focus company" for special emphasis and demonstration. The enhanced instructional value of focus companies comes from the way they engage MBA students in real analysis and interpretation. Focus companies were selected based on the industries that MBA students typically enter upon graduation. We apply a similar approach to the managerial accounting modules, but limited access to internal accounting information prevents us from illustrating all managerial accounting topics using real company data. We do, however, incorporate real-world examples throughout each module. Each managerial accounting module is presented in context using real-world scenarios from a variety of service, retail, and manufacturing companies. The following table lists focus companies by module.

MODULE 1	Apple	MODULE 10	Microsoft, Deere, HP	MODULE 19	Unilever
MODULE 2	Apple	MODULE 11	Starbucks	MODULE 20	Whole Foods
MODULE 3	Apple	MODULE 12	Procter & Gamble	MODULE 21	Roku
MODULE 4	Boston Scientific	MODULE 13	Procter & Gamble	MODULE 22	Pinterest
MODULE 5	Pfizer	MODULE 14	Primark	MODULE 23	Southwest Airlines
MODULE 6	Home Depot	MODULE 15	Square	MODULE 24	Volkswagen
MODULE 7	Verizon	MODULE 16	Razor USA, LLC	MODULE 25	Amazon
MODULE 8	Johnson & Johnson	MODULE 17	Uber	APPENDIX C	Harley-Davidson
MODULE 9	Google	MODULE 18	Samsung		

Real Company Data Throughout

Market research and reviewer feedback tell us that one of instructors' greatest frustrations with other MBA textbooks is their lack of real company data. We have gone to great lengths to incorporate real company data throughout each module to reinforce important concepts and engage MBA students. We engage nonaccounting MBA students specializing in finance, marketing, management, real estate, operations, and so forth, with companies and scenarios that are relevant to them. For representative examples, **SEE PAGES 2-6, 4-16, 6-23, 7-3, 8-4, 9-10, 10-4, 11-6, and 12-17.**

Decision-Making Orientation

One primary goal of an MBA accounting course is to teach students the skills needed to apply their accounting knowledge to solving real business problems and making informed business decisions. With that goal in mind, **Managerial Decision** boxes in each module encourage students to apply the material presented to solving actual business scenarios. For representative examples, **SEE PAGES 4-26, 5-4, 8-11, 10-8, and 11-15.** Each financial module also includes **Analysis Insight** boxes that provide insight into data analysis techniques and models that financial analysts typically use. For representative examples, **SEE PAGES 2-11, 6-13, 7-15, 9-17, 10-9, 11-28, and 12-24.**

Reviews for Each Learning Objective

Accounting can be challenging—especially for MBA students lacking business experience or previous exposure to business courses. To reinforce concepts presented in each module and to ensure student comprehension, we include reviews that require students to recall and apply the accounting techniques and concepts described in each module.

Excellent, Class-Tested Assignment Materials

Excellent assignment material is a must-have component of any successful textbook (and class). In keeping with the rest of the book, we used real company data extensively. We also ensured that assignments reflect our belief that MBA students should be trained in analyzing accounting information to make business decisions, as opposed to working on mechanical bookkeeping tasks. Assignments encourage students to analyze accounting information, interpret it, and apply the knowledge gained to a business decision.

New Edition Changes

Based on classroom use and reviewer feedback, a number of substantive changes have been made in this edition to further enhance the MBA students' experiences:

Financial Accounting Modules (1-13)

- **Digital delivery enhanced**   To serve the expanding delivery modes of MBA education, we updated our in-chapter Reviews and Guided Example videos for all chapters (each Learning Objective has a Review/Guided Example, as well as a corresponding eLecture).

- **Data visualization and analytics**   Companies are increasingly using data visualization (charts, pictures, and graphs) to more effectively convey financial information. To support student learning, each module opens with a data dashboard and includes end-of-chapter assignments that present data graphically and require students to analyze and interpret the data visualizations. We provide students with online access (via MBC) to author-created PowerBI dashboards where they can interact with the data and learn how to create their own data visualizations.

- **Content reflects new standards**   This edition covers new standards on Revenue Recognition, Leases, and Marketable Securities. It also includes in-depth discussion of the Tax Cuts and Jobs Act and how new tax law impacts financial analysis.

- **Revenue, Operating Expenses, and Receivables**   We expanded the discussion of revenue recognition following the new standard and included an illustration and analysis of Microsoft's revenue recognition. We also discuss sales returns and allowances and the effects of foreign currency exchange rates. Our operating expenses discussion introduces the effects of the Tax Cuts and Jobs Act, with a deeper discussion in Module 10.

- **Inventories**   Our discussion of cash conversion cycle includes an illustration of management actions undertaken by Home Depot to streamline its supply chain to reduce days inventory outstanding.

- **Bond rating**   A new section in Module 7 discusses Credit Analysis, including how bond ratings are determined. We provide an example of S&P Global's ratings for Verizon, following its purchase of Vodafone's interest in Verizon Wireless. We also simplify our discussion of bond pricing.

- **Share-based compensation**   Module 8 includes an expanded discussion of share-based compensation, and Tesla's use of convertible debt.

- **Investments**   We include a deeper discussion of the determination of fair value, including an expanded discussion of Level 3 inputs to value securities with limited markets and the accounting for those securities. Module 6 includes a new, expanded discussion of the new goodwill impairment standard.

- **Derivatives**   We markedly revised our discussion of derivatives to simplify the exposition while maintaining the analysis coverage.

- **Equity Carve-Outs**   The discussion of equity carve-outs is simplified and we provide examples of the accounting for Sell-offs, IPOs, Spin-offs, and Split-offs. We also discuss the deconsolidation of a subsidiary.

- **Leasing**   Module 10 reflects the new lease standard including the analysis of right-of-use assets and differences between operating and financial leases. We discuss retrospective and prospective adoption, using Microsoft and Delta Airlines.

- **Pension disclosures**   We markedly revised our discussion of pension accounting with a detailed illustration of the pension footnote disclosures. We include a section on fair valuation of pension obligations and the accounting for plan settlements.

- **Taxes**   We provide an in-depth, completely revised, discussion of income tax expense, including the effects of the Tax Cuts and Jobs Act and the analysis implications during the transition period.

- **Updated Assignments**   We updated all data and financial statements throughout the book to reflect each company's latest available financial statement filings and disclosures. Assignments include current financial statement excerpts and reflect new standards for Revenue Recognition, Leases, and Marketable Securities and the Tax Cuts and Jobs Act.

Managerial Accounting Modules (14-25)

- **Contemporary Topics and Examples:** The authors have revised and added new *Business Insight* boxes throughout each module to bring the accounting to life for students using current, real-world examples. Several new *Research Insight* boxes have been incorporated throughout the text to emphasize the important relationship between research and modern business.

- **Real Company Examples:** Dozens of new, real company examples have been integrated throughout the text.

- **Revised Assignments:** Nearly two-thirds of the assignments in each module have been revised and updated.

Fundamentals of Financial Accounting Tutorial

This interactive tutorial is intended for use in programs that either require or would like to offer a pre-term tutorial that creates a baseline of accounting knowledge for students with little to no prior exposure to financial accounting. Initially developed as a pre-term tutorial for first-year MBA students, this product can be used as a warm-up for any introductory-level financial accounting course. It is designed as an asynchronous, interactive, self-paced experience for students.

Available Learning Modules (You Select)

1. Introducing Financial Accounting (approximate completion time 2 hours)
2. Constructing Financial Statements (approximate completion time 4 hours)
3. Adjusting Entries and Completing the Accounting Cycle (approximate completion time 4 hours)
4. Reporting and Analyzing Cash Flows (approximate completion time 3.5 hours)
5. Analyzing and Interpreting Financial Statements (approximate completion time 3.5 hours)
6. Excel and Time-Value of Money Basics (approximate completion time 2 hours)

This is a separate, saleable item. Contact your sales representative to receive more information or email customerservice@cambridgepub.com.

Supplement Package

For Instructors

myBusinessCourse: A web-based learning and assessment program intended to complement your textbook and classroom instruction. This easy-to-use course management system grades homework automatically and provides students with additional help when you are not available. In addition, detailed diagnostic tools assess class and individual performance. **myBusinessCourse** is ideal for online courses or traditional face-to-face courses for which you want to offer students more resources to succeed. Assignments with the 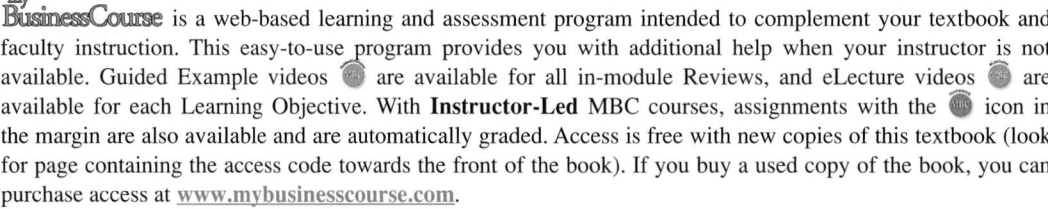 icon in the margin are available in myBusinessCourse. eLecture videos are available for the module Learning Objectives, and Guided Examples for the in-module Reviews are available for you to assign students.

Solutions Manual: Created by the authors, the *Solutions Manual* contains complete solutions to all assignments.

PowerPoint: Created by the authors, the PowerPoint slides outline key elements of each module.

Test Bank: Written by the authors, the test bank includes multiple-choice items, matching questions, short essay questions, and problems.

Website: All instructor materials are accessible via the book's website (password protected) along with other useful links and information. www.cambridgepub.com

For Students

myBusinessCourse is a web-based learning and assessment program intended to complement your textbook and faculty instruction. This easy-to-use program provides you with additional help when your instructor is not available. Guided Example videos are available for all in-module Reviews, and eLecture videos are available for each Learning Objective. With **Instructor-Led** MBC courses, assignments with the icon in the margin are also available and are automatically graded. Access is free with new copies of this textbook (look for page containing the access code towards the front of the book). If you buy a used copy of the book, you can purchase access at www.mybusinesscourse.com.

eLectures: Each Learning Objective within a module includes an eLecture video available in our online learning management system, myBusinessCourse (see above for more information).

Guided Examples: Guided Example videos are available for each in-module Review, also in myBusinessCourse (see above for more information).

Website: Useful links are available to students free of charge on the book's website.

Technology That Improves Learning and Complements Faculty Instruction

myBusinessCourse is an online learning and assessment program intended to complement your textbook and faculty instruction. Access to **myBusinessCourse** is FREE ONLY with the purchase of a new textbook, but can be purchased separately. MBC is ideal for faculty seeking opportunities to augment their course with an online component. MBC is also a turnkey solution for online courses. The following are some of the features of MBC.

Increase Student Readiness

- **eLectures** cover each chapter's learning objectives and concepts. Consistent with the text and created by the authors, these videos are ideal for remediation and online instruction.
- **Guided Examples** are narrated video demonstrations created by the authors that show students how to solve the Review problems from the textbook.
- Immediate feedback with **auto-graded homework**.
- **Test Bank** questions that can be incorporated into your assignments.
- Instructor **gradebook** with immediate grade results.

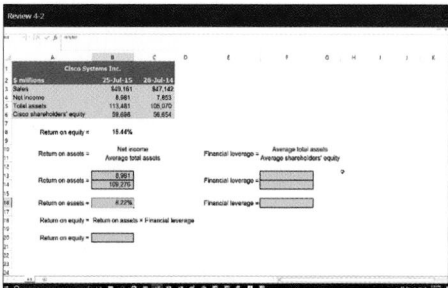

95% students who used MBC, responded that MBC helped them learn accounting.*

Make Instruction Needs-Based

- Identify where your students are struggling and customize your instruction to address their needs.
- Gauge how your entire class or individual students are performing by viewing the easy-to-use gradebook.
- Ensure your students are getting the additional reinforcement and direction they need between class meetings.

Provide Instruction and Practice 24/7

- Assign homework from your Cambridge Business Publishers' textbook and have MBC grade it for you automatically.
- With our videos, your students can revisit accounting topics as often as they like or until they master the topic.
- Make homework due before class to ensure students enter your classroom prepared.
- For an additional fee, upgrade MBC to include the eBook and you have all the tools needed for an online course.

86% of students said they would encourage their professor to continue using MBC in future terms.*

Integrate with LMS

myBusinessCourse integrates with many learning management systems, including **Canvas**, **Blackboard**, **Moodle**, **D2L**, **Schoology**, and **Sakai**. Your gradebooks sync automatically.

Acknowledgments

This book benefited greatly from the valuable feedback of focus group attendees, reviewers, students, and colleagues. We are extremely grateful to them for their help in making this project a success.

Helen Adams, *University of Washington*
Akinloye Akindayomi, *UT—Rio Grande Valley*
William Albrecht, *Bowling Green University*
Ashiq Ali, *University of Texas—Dallas*
Beverley Alleyne, *Belmont University*
Dan Amiram, *Tel Aviv University*
Walter Austin, *Mercer University*
Steve Baginski, *University of Georgia*
Eli Bartov, *New York University*
Dan Bens, *INSEAD*
Denny Beresford, *University of Georgia*
Richard Bernstein, *The University of Toledo*
James Biagi, *Marywood University*
James Bierstaker, *Villanova University*
Dennis Bline, *Bryant University*
Susan Borkowski, *LaSalle University*
A. Faye Borthick, *Georgia State University*
Mark Bradshaw, *Boston College*
Gary Bridges, *University of Texas—San Antonio*
John Briginshaw, *Pepperdine University*
Stephen Brown, *University of Maryland*
Gene Bryson, *University of Alabama—Huntsville*
Thomas Buchman, *University of Colorado—Boulder*
Brian Cadman, *The University of Utah*
Edgar Carter, *University of Massachusetts—Lowell*

Mary Ellen Carter, *Boston College*
Judson Caskey, *UCLA*
Sandra Cereola, *James Madison University*
Sumantra Chakravarty, *CSU—Fullerton*
Betty Chavis, *CSU—Fullerton*
Agnes Cheng, *Louisiana State University—Lafayette*
Tom Clausen, *The University of Illinois—Springfield*
Douglas Clinton, *Northern Illinois University*
Gary Colbert, *University of Colorado—Denver*
Joseph Comprix, *Syracuse University*
Carmen Cook, *Baker University*
Ellen Cook, *University of Louisiana*
David Cooper, *Baker University*
Michael Coyne, *Fairfield University*
Araya Debessay, *University of Delaware*
Roger Debreceny, *University of Hawaii*
Carol Dee, *University of Colorado—Denver*
Rosemond Desir, *Colorado State University*
Vicki Dickinson, *University of Mississippi*
Jeffrey Doyle, *University of Utah*
Donald Drake, *Georgia State University*
Phil Drake, *Arizona State University*
Joanne Duke, *San Francisco State University*
Cindy Durtschi, *DePaul University*
Craig Emby, *Simon Fraser University*

Gerard Engeholm, *Pace University*
Kathryn Epps, *Kennesaw State University*
Connie Fajardo, *National University*
Andrew Felo, *Nova Southeastern University*
Bud Fennema, *Florida State University*
Mark Finn, *Northwestern University*
Carol Fischer, *St. Bonaventure University*
Paul M. Fischer, *University of Wisconsin—Milwaukee*
Tim Fogarty, *Case Western Reserve*
Benjamin P. Foster, *University of Louisville*
Karen Foust, *Tulane University*
Nate Franke, *University of California—Irvine*
Richard Frankel, *Washington University*
David P. Franz, *San Francisco State University*
Mark Friedman, *University of Miami*
Peter Frischmann, *Idaho State University*
Margaret Gagne, *Marist College*
Andy Garcia, *Bowling Green State University*
Maclean Gaulin, *Rice University*
Karen Geiger, *Arizona State University*
John Giles, *North Carolina State University*
Dan Givoly, *Pennsylvania State University*
Julia Grant, *Case Western Reserve*
Kris Gulick, *University of Iowa*
Karl Hackenbrack, *Vanderbilt University*

* These statistics are based on the results of two surveys in which 2,330 students participated.

Michelle Hanlon, *MIT*
John Hassell, *Indiana University—Indianapolis*
Bob Hartman, *University of Iowa*
Carla Hayn, *UCLA*
Frank Heflin, *University of Georgia*
Michele Henney, *University of Oregon*
Elaine Henry, *University of Miami*
Eleanor Henry, *Southeast Missouri State University*
James Hesford, *Cornell University*
Clayton Hock, *Miami University*
Jay S. Holmen, *University of Wisconsin—Eau Claire*
David R. Honodel, *University of Denver*
Judith Hora, *University of San Diego*
Herbert Hunt, *CSU—Long Beach*
Richard Hurley, *University of Connecticut*
Ross Jennings, *University of Texas*
Eric N. Johnson, *Indiana University—Indianapolis*
Greg Jonas, *Case Western Reserve*
Bill Joyce, *Bemidji State University*
Paul Juras, *Wake Forest University*
Sanjay Kallapur, *Indian School of Business*
Greg Kane, *University of Delaware*
Victoria Kaskey, *Ashland University*
Anthony Craig Keller, *Missouri State University*
Zafar Khan, *Eastern Michigan University*
Saleha Khumawala, *University of Houston*
Suzanne Kiess, *Jackson College*
Charles Kile, *Middle Tennessee University*
Larry N. Killough, *Virginia Tech Univeristy*
Marinilka Kimbro, *University of Washington*
Ron King, *Washington University*
Michael Kirschenheiter, *University of Illinois*
John Koeplin, *University of San Francisco*
Phillip J. Korb, *University of Baltimore*
Susan Kulp, *George Washington University*
Krishna Kumar, *George Washington University*
Lisa Kutcher, *University of Oregon*
William Lathen, *Boise State University*
James Ledwith, *San Diego State University*
Brian Leventhal, *University of Illinois—Chicago*
Elliot Levy, *Bentley College*
Pierre Liang, *Carnegie Mellon University*
Cathy Zishang Liu, *University of Houston*
Josh Livnat, *New York University*
Frank Longo, *Centenary University*
Donna Losell, *University of Toronto*
Barbara Lougee, *University of San Diego*
Yvonne Lu, *Lehigh University*
Luann Lynch, *University of Virginia—Darden*
Jason MacGregor, *Baylor University*
Lois Mahoney, *Eastern Michigan University*
Michael Maier, *University of Alberta*
Ron Mano, *Westminster College*
Ronald Marcusson, *DePaul University*
Ariel Markelevich, *Suffolk University*
Linda M. Marquis, *Northern Kentucky University*
Otto B. Martinson, *Old Dominion University*

Katie Matt, *SUNY Polytechnic*
Jason Matthews, *University of Georgia*
Brian McAllister, *UC—Colorado Springs*
Bruce McClain, *Cleveland State University*
Karen McDougal, *St. Joseph's University*
James McKinney, *University of Maryland*
Gregory Merrill, *Saint Mary's University*
Michael J. Meyer, *University of Notre Dame*
Greg Miller, *University of Michigan*
Donald Minyard, *University of Alabama—Tuscaloosa*
Jose Miranda-Lopez, *CSU—Fullerton*
Melanie Mogg, *University of Minnesota*
Steve Monahan, *INSEAD*
John Morris, *Kansas State University*
Philip Morris, *Sam Houston University*
Dale Morse, *University of Oregon*
Dennis Murray, *University of Colorado—Denver*
Sandeep Nabar, *Oklahoma State University*
Suresh Nallareddy, *Columbia University*
Ramesh Narasimhan, *Montclair State University*
Siva Nathan, *Georgia State University*
Joshua Neil, *Colorado University—Boulder*
Doron Nissim, *Columbia University*
Jeanie O'Laughlin, *Pepperdine University*
Gary Olsen, *Carroll University*
Stephen Owusu-Ansah, *Houston Baptist University*
Shail Pandit, *University of Illinois—Chicago*
Larry Paquette, *Francis Marion University*
Susan Parker, *Santa Clara University*
William Pasewark, *Texas Tech*
Stephen Penman, *Columbia University*
Mark Penno, *University of Iowa*
Gary Peters, *University of Arkansas*
Kathy Petroni, *Michigan State University*
Christine Petrovits, *New York University*
Kirk Philipich, *University of Michigan—Dearborn*
Matthew Pickard, *University of New Mexico*
Morton Pincus, *UC—Irvine*
Lincoln Pinto, *Concordia University*
Kay Poston, *University of Indianapolis*
Gordon Potter, *Cornell University*
Grace Pownall, *Emory University*
Ram Ramanan, *University of Notre Dame*
David Randolph, *Xavier University*
Paul Recupero, *Newbury College*
Barbara Reider, *University of Montana*
Laura Rickett, *Kent State University*
Susan Riffe, *Southern Methodist University*
Maryanne Rouse, *University of South Florida*
Jack Ruhl, *Western Michigan University*
Jane Saly, *University of St. Thomas*
Bruce Samuelson, *Pepperdine University*
Diane Satin, *CSU—East Bay*
Shahrokh Saudagaran, *University of Washington*
Jeffrey Schatzberg, *University of Arizona*
Andrew Schmidt, *Columbia University*
Chandra Seethamraju, *Washington University*

Stephen Sefcik, *University of Washington*
Galen Sevcik, *Georgia State University*
Kenneth Shaw, *University of Missouri*
Lewis Shaw, *Suffolk University*
Todd Shawver, *Bloomsburg University*
Evan Shough, *UNC—Greensboro*
Robin Shuler, *Seattle Pacific University*
Paul Simko, *University of Virginia—Darden*
Andreas Simon, *Pepperdine University*
Henry Smith, III, *Otterbein College*
Kevin Smith, *University of Kansas*
Pam Smith, *Northern Illinois University*
Rod Smith, *California State University—Long Beach*
Hakjoon Song, *The University of Akron*
Xiaofei Song, *Saint Mary's University*
Sri Sridharan, *Northwestern University*
Charles Stanley, *Baylor University*
Jens Stephan, *Eastern Michigan University*
Phillip Stocken, *Dartmouth College*
Jerry Strawser, *Texas A&M University*
Sherre Strickland, *University of Massachusetts—Lowell*
Chandra Subramaniam, *University of Texas*
K.R. Subramanyam, *USC*
Ziad Syed, *Texas A&M University*
Audrey Taylor, *Western Washington University*
Gary Taylor, *University of Alabama*
Mark Taylor, *Case Western Reserve*
Therese Tiggeman, *University of the Incarnate Word*
Sam Tiras, *Louisiana State University*
Pamela Trafford, *University of Massachusetts*
Suzanne Traylor, *SUNY—Albany*
Leslie Turner, *Northern Kentucky University*
Jerry Van Os, *Westminster College*
Mark Vargus, *University of Texas—Dallas*
Lisa Victoravich, *University of Denver*
Sheila Viel, *University of Wisconsin—Milwaukee*
Marcia Vorholt, *Xavier University*
Charles Wasley, *University of Rochester*
Greg Waymire, *Emory University*
Andrea Weickgenannt, *Xavier University*
Daniel Weimer, *Wayne State University*
Edward Werner, *Drexel University*
Lourdes White, *University of Baltimore*
Jonathan M. Wild, *Oklahoma State University*
Jeffrey Williams, *University of Michigan*
Peter Wilson, *Babson College*
Wallace Wood, *University of Cincinnati*
David Wright, *University of Michigan*
Michelle Yetman, *UC—Davis*
Tzachi Zack, *Ohio State University*
Kimberly Zahller, *UC—Colorado Springs*
Xiao-Jun Zhang, *UC—Berkeley*
Yuan Zhang, *Columbia University*
Yuping Zhao, *University of Houston*
Elisa Zuliani, *University of Toronto*

Special thanks is extended to Gayle Williams for her contribution to this edition. We are grateful to Vicki Dickinson and Brian Cadman for their contributions in previous editions. We would also like to thank Susan Hamlen and Paul Hutchison for their thorough accuracy checking. In addition, we are grateful to George Werthman, Jocelyn Mousel, Lorraine Gleeson, Marnee Fieldman, Beth Nodus, Debbie McQuade, Terry McQuade, and the entire team at Cambridge Business Publishers for their encouragement, enthusiasm, and guidance.

Peter   *Bob*   *Mary Lea*

February 2020

Brief Contents

Preface   iii

MODULE 1

Financial Accounting for MBAs **1-1**

MODULE 2

Introducing Financial Statements **2-1**

MODULE 3

Transactions, Adjustments, and Financial Statements **3-1**

MODULE 4

Analyzing and Interpreting Financial Statements **4-1**

MODULE 5

Revenues, Receivables, and Operating Expenses **5-1**

MODULE 6

Inventories, Accounts Payable, and Long-Term Assets **6-1**

MODULE 7

Current and Long-Term Liabilities **7-1**

MODULE 8

Stock Transactions, Dividends, and EPS **8-1**

MODULE 9

Intercorporate Investments **9-1**

MODULE 10

Leases, Pensions, and Income Taxes **10-1**

MODULE 11

Cash Flows **11-1**

MODULE 12

Financial Statement Forecasting . . . **12-1**

MODULE 13

Using Financial Statements for Valuation **13-1**

MODULE 14

Managerial Accounting for MBAs . . . **14-1**

MODULE 15

Cost Behavior, Activity Analysis, and Cost Estimation **15-1**

MODULE 16

Cost-Volume-Profit Analysis and Planning **16-1**

MODULE 17

Relevant Costs and Benefits for Decision Making **17-1**

MODULE 18

Product Costing: Job and Process Operations **18-1**

MODULE 19

Activity-Based Costing, Customer Profitability, and Activity-Based Management **19-1**

MODULE 20

Additional Topics in Product Costing **20-1**

MODULE 21

Pricing and Other Product Management Decisions **21-1**

MODULE 22

Operational Budgeting and Profit Planning **22-1**

MODULE 23

Standard Costs and Performance Reports **23-1**

MODULE 24

Segment Reporting, Transfer Pricing, and Balanced Scorecard . . . **24-1**

MODULE 25

Capital Budgeting Decisions **25-1**

APPENDIX A

Compound Interest Tables **A-1**

APPENDIX B

Chart of Accounts (with Acronyms) **B-1**

APPENDIX C

Comprehensive Case **C-1**

Glossary   G-1

Index   I-1

Contents

Preface v

MODULE 1

Financial Accounting for MBAs 1-1

Preview. 1-1
Reporting on Business Activities 1-3
Review 1-1 1-4
Financial Statements: Demand and Supply 1-4
    Demand for Information **1-4**
    Supply of Information **1-7**
    International Accounting Standards **1-8**
Review 1-2 1-9
Structure of Financial Statements 1-9
    Balance Sheet **1-10**
    Income Statement **1-13**
    Statement of Stockholders' Equity **1-14**
    Statement of Cash Flows **1-15**
    Information Beyond Financial Statements **1-16**
    Managerial Choices in Financial Accounting **1-17**
Review 1-3 1-18
Analysis of Financial Statements 1-18
    Return on Assets **1-18**
    Components of Return on Assets **1-18**
    Return on Equity **1-20**
    Are Financial Statements Relevant? **1-20**
Review 1-4 1-21
Financial Statements and Business Analysis 1-22
    Analyzing the Competitive Environment **1-22**
    SWOT Analysis of the Business Environment **1-23**
    Analyzing Competitive Advantage **1-24**
Review 1-5 1-25
Book Road Map 1-25
Global Accounting 1-26
Appendix 1A: Financial Statement Data and Analytics 1-26
    Data Analytics **1-29**
Appendix 1B: Accounting Principles and Governance 1-30
    Financial Accounting Environment **1-30**
    Audit Report **1-31**
Guidance Answers 1-34
Assignments 1-34
IFRS Applications 1-46
Management Applications 1-47
Ongoing Project 1-48
Solutions to Review Problems 1-48

MODULE 2

Introducing Financial Statements 2-1

Preview. 2-1
Balance Sheet 2-3
    Balance Sheet and the Flow of Costs **2-3**
    Assets **2-4**
    Liabilities and Equity **2-6**
Review 2-1 2-13
Income Statement 2-13
    Recognizing Revenues and Expenses **2-14**
    Reporting of Transitory Items **2-15**
    Analyzing the Income Statement **2-16**

Review 2-2 2-17
Statement of Stockholders' Equity 2-17
Review 2-3 2-18
Statement of Cash Flows 2-18
    Statement Format and Data Sources **2-18**
Review 2-4 2-20
Articulation of Financial Statements 2-20
    Retained Earnings Reconciliation **2-20**
    Financial Statement Linkages **2-20**
Review 2-5 2-22
Additional Information Sources. 2-22
    Form 10-K **2-22**
    Form 20-F and Form 40-F **2-24**
    Form 8-K **2-25**
    Analyst Reports **2-25**
    Credit Services **2-26**
    Data Services **2-26**
Review 2-6 2-26
Global Accounting 2-26
Guidance Answers 2-27
Assignments 2-27
IFRS Applications 2-38
Management Applications 2-38
Ongoing Project 2-39
Solutions to Review Problems 2-40

MODULE 3

Transactions, Adjustments, and Financial Statements 3-1

Preview. 3-1
Basics of Accounting 3-3
    Four-Step Accounting Cycle **3-3**
    Financial Statement Effects Template **3-3**
Review 3-1 3-5
Accounting Cycle Step 1—Analyze Transactions and Prepare
    Entries. 3-6
    Apple's Transactions **3-6**
    Applying the Financial Statement Effects Template **3-6**
    Applying the Journal Entry and T-Account **3-6**
Review 3-2 3-8
Accounting Cycle Step 2—Prepare Accounting Adjustments 3-9
    Prepaid Expenses **3-10**
    Unearned Revenues **3-10**
    Accrued Expenses **3-11**
    Accrued Revenues **3-12**
    Accounting Adjustments for Apple **3-12**
Review 3-3 3-13
Accounting Cycle Step 3—Prepare Financial Statements 3-13
    Income Statement **3-13**
    Balance Sheet **3-14**
    Statement of Stockholders' Equity **3-15**
Review 3-4 3-16
Accounting Cycle Step 4—Close the Books. 3-16
Review 3-5 3-18
Global Accounting 3-18
Appendix 3A: FASB's Financial Statement
                 Presentation Project 3-19
Guidance Answers 3-19

Assignments. 3-20
IFRS Applications. 3-32
Management Applications 3-33
Solutions to Review Problems 3-35

MODULE 4

Analyzing and Interpreting Financial Statements 4-1

Preview. 4-1
Return on Equity (ROE) 4-3
Review 4-1 4-3
ROE Disaggregation: DuPont Analysis 4-4
Review 4-2 4-5
Return on Assets and Its Disaggregation 4-6
    Analysis of Profitability and Productivity 4-7
    Analysis of Profitability 4-8
    Analysis of Productivity 4-9
    Analysis of Financial Leverage 4-12
Review 4-3 4-14
Balance Sheet Analysis with an Operating Focus 4-14
    Net Operating Assets (NOA) 4-15
    Net Nonoperating Obligations (NNO) 4-17
Review 4-4 4-18
Income Statement Analysis with an Operating Focus 4-19
Review 4-5 4-22
Return on Net Operating Assets (RNOA) 4-23
Review 4-6 4-25
RNOA Disaggregation into Margin and Turnover 4-25
    Net Operating Profit Margin 4-25
    Net Operating Asset Turnover 4-26
    Trade-Off between Margin and Turnover 4-27
Review 4-7 4-29
Global Accounting 4-29
Appendix 4A: Operating versus Nonoperating Classification . . 4-30
Appendix 4B: Nonoperating Return Component of ROE 4-31
    Nonoperating Return 4-31
    Nonoperating Return—With Substantial Net Nonoperating
        Assets: Amazon 4-33
    Nonoperating Return—With Noncontrolling Interest: AT&T 4-34
Review 4-8 4-35
Appendix 4C: Liquidity and Solvency Analysis. 4-35
    Liquidity Analysis 4-36
    Current Ratio 4-36
    Quick Ratio 4-36
    Solvency Analysis 4-37
    Liabilities-to-Equity 4-37
    Times Interest Earned 4-38
    Vertical and Horizontal Analysis 4-38
    Limitations of Ratio Analysis 4-40
Review 4-9 4-41
Guidance Answers 4-41
Assignments. 4-42
IFRS Applications. 4-57
Management Applications 4-57
Ongoing Project 4-58
Solutions to Review Problems 4-59

MODULE 5

Revenues, Receivables, and Operating Expenses 5-1

Preview. 5-1
Revenue 5-3
    Revenue Recognition Rules 5-4
    Complications of Revenue Recognition 5-5
    Performance Obligations Satisfied Over Time 5-7
Review 5-1 5-11
Sales Allowances 5-11
    Accounting for Sales Allowances 5-11
    Reporting Sales Allowances 5-12

    Analysis of Sales Allowances 5-13
Review 5-2 5-13
Unearned (Deferred) Revenue 5-14
Review 5-3 5-15
Foreign Currency Effects on Revenue, Expenses, and
    Cash Flow 5-15
    Foreign Currency and Cash Flows 5-16
    Foreign Currency and Income 5-17
    Foreign Currency and Future Results 5-17
Review 5-4 5-18
Accounts Receivable 5-19
    Aging Analysis of Receivables 5-19
    Accounting for Accounts Receivable 5-20
    Analysis of Accounts Receivable–Magnitude 5-21
    Analysis of Accounts Receivable—Quality 5-22
Review 5-5 5-24
Expenses and Losses 5-25
    Deductions from Income 5-25
    Research and Development Expense 5-26
    Provision (Benefit) for Taxes on Income 5-28
    Discontinued Operations 5-28
Review 5-6 5-30
Pro Forma Income Reporting 5-31
    Regulation G Reconciliation 5-31
    SEC Warnings about Pro Forma Numbers 5-32
    Disclosures and Market Assessments 5-32
Review 5-7 5-34
Global Accounting 5-35
Guidance Answers 5-35
Assignments. 5-35
IFRS Applications. 5-53
Management Applications 5-54
Ongoing Project 5-54
Solutions to Review Problems 5-55

MODULE 6

Inventories, Accounts Payable, and Long-Term Assets 6-1

Preview. 6-1
Inventory—Costing Methods 6-3
    First-In, First-Out (FIFO) 6-4
    Last-In, First-Out (LIFO) 6-5
    Average Cost (AC) 6-5
    Financial Statement Effects of Inventory Costing 6-7
Review 6-1 6-8
Inventory—Reporting 6-8
    Lower of Cost or Market (LCM) 6-8
    LIFO Reserve Adjustments to Financial Statements 6-9
    LIFO Liquidations 6-11
Review 6-2 6-11
Inventory—Analysis Tools 6-12
    Gross Profit Analysis 6-12
    Days Inventory Outstanding and Inventory Turnover 6-13
    Days Payable Outstanding 6-15
    Cash Conversion Cycle 6-16
Review 6-3 6-17
PPE Assets—Capitalization and Depreciation 6-17
    Plant and Equipment 6-18
    Research and Development Facilities and Equipment 6-19
Review 6-4 6-20
PPE Assets—Sales, Impairments, and Restructuring 6-20
    Asset Sales 6-20
    Asset Impairments 6-21
    Restructuring Costs 6-22
Review 6-5 6-24
PPE Assets—Analysis Tools 6-25
    PPE Turnover 6-25
    PPE Useful Life 6-26
    PPE Percent Used Up 6-27

Review 6-6 6-27
Global Accounting 6-27
Guidance Answers 6-28
Assignments 6-29
IFRS Applications 6-40
Management Applications 6-42
Ongoing Project 6-42
Solutions to Review Problems 6-43

MODULE 7

Current and Long-Term Liabilities 7-1

Preview 7-1
Accrued Liabilities 7-3
    Accrued Liabilities Defined **7-3**
    Accruals for Contractual Liabilities—Wages Payable
       Example **7-4**
    Accruals for Contractual Liabilities—Deferred
       Revenue Example **7-4**
    Accruals for Contingent Liabilities **7-5**
    Accruals for Contingent Liabilities—Warranties Example **7-5**
Review 7-1 7-7
Short-Term Debt 7-7
    Accounting for Short-Term Debt **7-7**
    Current Maturities of Long-Term Debt **7-8**
Review 7-2 7-9
Long-Term Debt—Pricing 7-9
    Pricing of Bonds Issued at Par **7-10**
    Pricing of Bonds Issued at a Discount **7-10**
    Pricing of Bonds Issued at a Premium **7-11**
    Effective Cost of Debt **7-11**
Review 7-3 7-13
Long-Term Debt—Reporting 7-13
    Balance Sheet Reporting **7-13**
    Income Statement Reporting **7-14**
    Financial Statement Effects of Bond Repurchase **7-14**
    Fair Value Disclosures **7-15**
Review 7-4 7-16
Quality of Debt 7-16
    Credit Analysis **7-16**
    What Are Credit Ratings? **7-18**
    What Determines Credit Ratings? **7-18**
    Verizon Credit Rating Example **7-21**
    Why Credit Ratings Matter **7-23**
Review 7-5 7-24
Global Accounting 7-24
Appendix 7A: Time Value of Money 7-25
    Present Value Concepts **7-25**
    Present Value of a Single Amount **7-25**
    Time Value of Money Tables **7-25**
    Present Value of an Annuity **7-26**
    Bond Valuation **7-27**
    Time Value of Money Computations Using a Calculator **7-28**
    Time Value of Money Computations Using Excel **7-28**
    Future Value Concepts **7-30**
    Future Value of a Single Amount **7-30**
    Future Value of an Annuity **7-30**
Review 7-6 7-30
Appendix 7B: Amortization of Debt 7-31
    Amortization of Discount **7-31**
    Amortization of Premium **7-32**
Guidance Answers 7-32
Assignments 7-32
IFRS Applications 7-46
Management Applications 7-47
Ongoing Project 7-47
Solutions to Review Problems 7-48

MODULE 8

Stock Transactions, Dividends, and EPS 8-1

Preview 8-1
Stockholders' Equity and Classes of Stock 8-3
    Stockholders' Equity Accounts **8-3**
    Statement of Stockholders' Equity **8-5**
    Preferred Stock **8-6**
    Common Stock **8-7**
Review 8-1 8-8
Stock Transactions 8-9
    Stock Issuance **8-9**
    Stock Repurchase (Treasury Stock) **8-10**
Review 8-2 8-12
Stock-Based Compensation 8-13
    Accounting for Stock-Based Compensation **8-14**
    Footnote Disclosures for Stock-Based Compensation **8-15**
Review 8-3 8-16
Dividends and Stock Splits 8-16
    Cash Dividend Disclosures **8-17**
    Dividend Payout and Yield **8-17**
    Cash Dividends Financial Effects **8-17**
    Stock Split **8-18**
Review 8-4 8-19
Accumulated Other Comprehensive Income 8-19
    AOCI Components **8-19**
    AOCI Disclosures and Interpretation **8-20**
Review 8-5 8-21
Convertible Securities 8-22
Review 8-6 8-23
Earnings per Share (EPS) 8-23
Review 8-7 8-25
Global Accounting 8-25
Appendix 8A: Stock-Based Compensation: Reporting and
              Analyzing 8-26
    Employee Stock Purchase Plans (ESPP) **8-26**
    Stock Awards **8-27**
    Stock Options **8-27**
    Stock Appreciation Rights (SAR) **8-28**
    Summary of Share-Based Compensation **8-28**
    Analysis Implications **8-28**
Guidance Answers 8-29
Assignments 8-30
IFRS Applications 8-48
Ongoing Project 8-50
Solutions to Review Problems 8-51

MODULE 9

Intercorporate Investments 9-1

Preview 9-1
Intercorporate Investments 9-3
    Passive Investments in Equity Securities **9-4**
    Investments in Debt Securities **9-8**
Review 9-1 9-11
Equity Investments with Significant Influence 9-12
    Accounting for Investments with Significant Influence **9-12**
    Equity Method Accounting and ROE Effects **9-14**
Review 9-2 9-17
Equity Investments with Control 9-17
    Accounting for Investments with Control **9-18**
Review 9-3 9-27
Global Accounting 9-28
Appendix 9A: Accounting for Derivatives 9-29
    Analysis of Derivatives **9-30**
Review 9-4 9-31
Appendix 9B: Equity Carve-Outs 9-32
    Analysis of Equity Carve-Outs **9-36**
Guidance Answers 9-36
Assignments 9-36
IFRS Applications 9-52

Management Applications 9-53
Ongoing Project 9-54
Solutions to Review Problems 9-55

MODULE 10

Leases, Pensions, and Income Taxes 10-1

Preview 10-1
Leases 10-3
   New Lease Reporting Standard 10-3
   Lessee Reporting Example—Microsoft Corporation 10-4
   Lease Accounting 10-5
   Summary of Lease Accounting and Reporting 10-9
   Analysis Issues Relating to Leases 10-10
Review 10-1 10-11
Pensions 10-11
   Defined Benefit Pension Plans on the Balance Sheet 10-12
   Analysis Issue—Sufficiency of Plan Assets to Pay Pension
      Obligations 10-13
   Defined Benefit Pension Plans on the Income Statement 10-15
   Pension Expense Smoothing 10-16
   Fair Value Accounting for Pensions 10-19
   Footnote Disclosure—Key Assumptions 10-21
   Analysis Implications 10-22
   Other Post-Employment Benefits (OPEB) 10-23
Review 10-2 10-23
Income Taxes 10-24
   Timing Differences Create Deferred Tax Assets and
      Liabilities 10-24
   Disclosures for Income Taxes 10-29
   Analysis of Income Tax Disclosures 10-30
   Expanded Explanation of Deferred Taxes 10-31
Review 10-3 10-33
Global Accounting 10-35
Appendix 10A: Lease Accounting Example—
             Finance and Operating Leases 10-35
Assignments 10-36
IFRS Applications 10-59
Ongoing Project 10-61
Solutions to Review Problems 10-61

MODULE 11

Cash Flows 11-1

Preview 11-1
Framework for Statement of Cash Flows 11-3
   Relation Among Financial Statements 11-3
   Statement of Cash Flows Structure 11-4
   Operating Activities Preview 11-5
   Investing Activities Preview 11-8
   Financing Activities Preview 11-8
Review 11-1 11-8
Cash Flow from Operating Activities 11-9
   Steps to Compute Net Cash Flow from Operating
      Activities 11-10
   Java House Case Illustration 11-11
Review 11-2 11-15
Computing Cash Flows from Investing Activities 11-16
   Analyze Remaining Noncash Assets 11-16
   Java House Case Illustration 11-16
Review 11-3 11-18
Cash Flows from Financing Activities 11-18
   Analyze Remaining Liabilities and Equity 11-18
   Java House Case Illustration 11-18
Review 11-4A 11-19
   Computing Cash Flows from Balance Sheet Accounts 11-19
   Supplemental Disclosures for the Indirect Method 11-20
Review 11-4B 11-21
Analysis of Cash Flow Information 11-21
   Cash Flow Components 11-21

   Cash Flow Patterns 11-23
   Usefulness of the Statement of Cash Flows 11-25
Review 11-5 11-27
   Ratio Analyses of Cash Flows 11-27
   Free Cash Flow 11-28
Review 11-6 11-29
Appendix 11A: Direct Method Reporting for Statement of Cash
           Flows 11-29
   Cash Flows from Operating Activities 11-29
   Converting Revenues and Expenses to Cash Flows 11-29
   Java House Case Illustration 11-29
   Convert Sales to Cash Received from Customers 11-30
   Convert Cost of Goods Sold to Cash Paid for Merchandise
      Purchased 11-30
   Convert Wages Expense to Cash Paid to Employees 11-31
   Convert Insurance Expense to Cash Paid for Insurance 11-31
   Eliminate Depreciation Expense and Other Noncash Operating
      Expenses 11-31
   Convert Income Tax Expense to Cash Paid for Income Taxes 11-31
   Omit Gains and Losses Related to Investing and Financing
      Activities 11-31
   Cash Flows from Investing and Financing 11-32
   Supplemental Disclosures 11-32
Review 11-7 11-32
Guidance Answers 11-32
Assignments 11-33
IFRS Applications 11-55
Solutions to Review Problems 11-56

MODULE 12

Financial Statement Forecasting 12-1

Preview 12-1
Forecasting Process 12-3
   Company Guidance 12-5
Review 12-1 12-6
Forecasting the Income Statement 12-8
Review 12-2 12-11
Forecasting the Balance Sheet 12-12
Review 12-3 12-16
Building Forecasts from the Bottom Up 12-16
   Segment Data 12-16
Review 12-4 12-18
Appendix 12A: Forecasting the Statement of Cash Flows . . . 12-19
Review 12-5 12-20
Appendix 12B: Multiyear Forecasting with Target Cash
           and New Debt Financing 12-20
Review 12-6 12-22
Appendix 12C: Parsimonious Method for Forecasting
           NOPAT and NOA 12-22
   Multiyear Forecasting with Parsimonious Method 12-22
Review 12-7 12-23
Appendix 12D: Morgan Stanley's Forecast Report on
           Procter & Gamble 12-23
Assignments 12-31
Ongoing Project 12-51
Solutions to Review Problems 12-51

MODULE 13

Using Financial Statements for Valuation 13-1

Preview 13-1
Equity Valuation Models 13-3
   Dividend Discount Model 13-3
   Discounted Cash Flow Model 13-3
   Residual Operating Income Model 13-3
   Valuation Model Inputs 13-4
Review 13-1 13-5
Discounted Cash Flow (DCF) Model 13-5
   DCF Model Structure 13-5

Steps in Applying the DCF Model **13-6**
Illustrating the DCF Model **13-6**
Review 13-2 . . . . **13-8**
Residual Operating Income (ROPI) Model **13-9**
ROPI Model Structure **13-9**
Steps in Applying the ROPI Model **13-9**
Illustrating the ROPI Model **13-10**
Review 13-3 . . . . **13-11**
Further Considerations Involving Valuation Models **13-11**
Managerial Insights from the ROPI Model **13-11**
Assessment of Valuation Models **13-12**
Review 13-4 . . . . **13-13**
Global Accounting **13-14**
Appendix 13A: Derivation of Free Cash Flow Formula **13-14**
Appendix 13B: Deutsche Bank Valuation of Procter &
Gamble **13-14**
Qualitative and Quantitative Summary **13-14**
Concluding Observations of Analyst Report **13-25**
Guidance Answers **13-25**
Assignments **13-25**
Management Applications **13-36**
Ongoing Project **13-37**
Solutions to Review Problems **13-38**

MODULE 14
Managerial Accounting for MBAs **14-1**
Preview **14-1**
Uses of Accounting Information **14-3**
Financial Accounting **14-3**
Managerial Accounting **14-4**
Review 14-1 . . . . **14-5**
Strategic Cost Management **14-5**
Review 14-2 . . . . **14-6**
Missions, Goals, and Strategies **14-6**
An Organization's Mission and Goals **14-6**
Strategic Position Analysis **14-7**
Managerial Accounting and Goal Attainment **14-9**
Planning, Organizing, and Controlling **14-10**
Review 14-3 . . . . **14-11**
Changing Environment of Business **14-12**
Global Competition and Its Key Dimensions **14-12**
Big Data and Analysis **14-12**
Robotics and Cognitive Technologies **14-12**
Enterprise Risk Management (ERM) **14-13**
Review 14-4 . . . . **14-13**
Ethics in Managerial Accounting **14-13**
Codes of Ethics **14-15**
Corporate Governance **14-15**
Sustainability Accounting and Corporate Social
Responsibility **14-16**
Review 14-5 . . . . **14-17**
Cost Drivers **14-17**
Structural Cost Drivers **14-18**
Organizational Cost Drivers **14-19**
Activity Cost Drivers **14-19**
Review 14-6 . . . . **14-20**
Guidance Answers **14-20**
Assignments **14-21**
Management Applications **14-24**
Solutions to Review Problems **14-26**

MODULE 15
Cost Behavior, Activity Analysis, and Cost Estimation **15-1**
Preview **15-1**
Cost Behavior Analysis **15-3**
Four Basic Cost Behavior Patterns **15-3**
Factors Affecting Cost Behavior Patterns **15-5**
Review 15-1 . . . . **15-5**

Total Cost Function for an Organization or Segment **15-6**
Relevant Range **15-7**
Additional Cost Behavior Patterns **15-8**
Committed and Discretionary Fixed Costs **15-10**
Review 15-2 . . . . **15-11**
Cost Estimation **15-11**
High-Low Cost Estimation **15-11**
Scatter Diagrams **15-13**
Least-Squares Regression **15-14**
Review 15-3 . . . . **15-16**
Additional Issues in Cost Estimation **15-17**
Changes in Technology and Prices **15-17**
Matching Activity and Costs **15-17**
Identifying Activity Cost Drivers **15-18**
Review 15-4 . . . . **15-18**
Alternative Cost Driver Classifications **15-18**
Manufacturing Cost Hierarchy **15-19**
Customer Cost Hierarchy **15-20**
Review 15-5 . . . . **15-21**
Guidance Answers **15-21**
Assignments **15-22**
Management Applications **15-29**
Solutions to Review Problems **15-32**

MODULE 16
Cost-Volume-Profit Analysis and Planning **16-1**
Preview **16-1**
Cost-Volume-Profit Analysis **16-3**
Key Assumptions **16-3**
Profit Formula **16-5**
Review 16-1 . . . . **16-6**
Contribution and Functional Income Statements **16-7**
Contribution Income Statement **16-7**
Functional Income Statement **16-7**
Analysis Using Contribution Margin Ratio **16-8**
Review 16-2 . . . . **16-8**
Break-Even Point and Profit Planning **16-9**
Determining Break-Even Point in Units **16-9**
Profit Planning **16-10**
Cost-Volume-Profit Graph **16-11**
Profit-Volume Graph **16-11**
Impact of Income Taxes **16-13**
Review 16-3 . . . . **16-14**
Multiple-Product Cost-Volume-Profit Analysis **16-15**
Determining Break-Even and Target Profit Sales Dollars **16-15**
Sales Mix Analysis **16-15**
Review 16-4 . . . . **16-18**
Analysis of Operating Leverage **16-18**
Review 16-5 . . . . **16-20**
Appendix 16A: Profitability Analysis with Unit and
Nonunit Cost Drivers **16-21**
Multi-Level Contribution Income Statement **16-21**
Variations in Multi-Level Contribution Income Statement **16-23**
Review 16-6 . . . . **16-24**
Guidance Answers **16-24**
Assignments **16-24**
Management Applications **16-35**
Solutions to Review Problems **16-36**

MODULE 17
Relevant Costs and Benefits for Decision Making **17-1**
Preview **17-1**
Identifying Relevant Costs **17-3**
Relevance of Future Revenues **17-4**
Relevance of Outlay Costs **17-4**
Irrelevance of Sunk Costs **17-4**
Sunk Costs Can Cause Ethical Dilemmas **17-5**
Relevance of Disposal and Salvage Values **17-5**

Relevance of Opportunity Costs **17-5**
Review 17-1 .... **17-6**
Differential Analysis of Relevant Costs **17-7**
Review 17-2 .... **17-8**
Applying Differential Analysis **17-8**
Multiple Changes in Profit Plans **17-8**
Review 17-3 .... **17-9**
Special Orders **17-10**
Review 17-4 .... **17-12**
Outsourcing Decisions (Make or Buy) **17-13**
Review 17-5 .... **17-16**
Sell or Process Further **17-16**
Review 17-6 .... **17-18**
Use of Limited Resources **17-18**
Single Constraint **17-19**
Multiple Constraints **17-19**
Theory of Constraints **17-20**
Limitations of Decision Analysis Models **17-21**
Review 17-7 .... **17-21**
Guidance Answers **17-21**
Assignments **17-22**
Management Applications **17-33**
Solutions to Review Problems **17-36**

MODULE 18
Product Costing: Job and Process Operations **18-1**

Preview 18-1
Inventory Costs in Various Organizations **18-3**
Review 18-1 .... **18-3**
Inventory Costs for Financial Reporting **18-4**
Product Costs and Period Costs **18-4**
Three Components of Product Costs **18-5**
A Closer Look at Manufacturing Overhead **18-6**
Review 18-2 .... **18-8**
The Production Environment **18-9**
Production Files and Records **18-10**
Review 18-3 .... **18-10**
Job Costing for Products and Services **18-11**
Job Costing Illustrated **18-12**
Statement of Cost of Goods Manufactured **18-16**
Overapplied and Underapplied Overhead **18-17**
Job Costing in Service Organizations **18-18**
Review 18-4 .... **18-19**
Process Costing **18-20**
Cost of Production Report **18-21**
Weighted Average and First-In, First-Out Process Costing **18-24**
Process Costing in Service Organizations **18-25**
Review 18-5 .... **18-25**
Appendix 18A: Absorption and Variable Costing **18-26**
Basic Concepts **18-26**
Inventory Valuations **18-26**
Income Under Absorption and Variable Costing **18-27**
Production Equals Sales **18-27**
Production Exceeds Sales **18-28**
Sales Exceed Production **18-29**
Evaluating Alternatives to Inventory Valuation **18-30**
Review 18-6 .... **18-31**
Guidance Answers **18-31**
Assignments **18-32**
Management Applications **18-44**
Solutions to Review Problems **18-46**

MODULE 19
Activity-Based Costing, Customer Profitability, and Activity-Based Management **19-1**

Preview 19-1
Activity-Based Costing (ABC) **19-3**
Changing Cost Environment **19-3**

Review 19-1 .... **19-4**
Activity-Based Costing Concepts **19-4**
ABC Product Costing Model **19-5**
Review 19-2 .... **19-6**
Traditional Product Costing and ABC Compared **19-6**
Applying Overhead with a Plantwide Rate **19-7**
Applying Overhead with Department Rates **19-7**
Applying Overhead with Activity-Based Costing **19-9**
Review 19-3 .... **19-12**
Implementation of ABC **19-13**
Limitations of ABC Illustration **19-13**
Comparing Traditional and Activity-Based Costing **19-13**
ABC Implementation Issues **19-14**
Review 19-4 .... **19-15**
ABC and Customer Profitability Analysis **19-16**
Customer Profitability Profile **19-16**
ABC Customer Profitability Analysis Illustrated **19-16**
Review 19-5 .... **19-19**
Activity-Based Management **19-19**
The Difference Between ABC and Activity-Based
Management **19-19**
Review 19-6 .... **19-20**
Guidance Answers **19-20**
Assignments **19-21**
\Management Applications **19-33**
Solutions to Review Problems **19-37**

MODULE 20
Additional Topics in Product Costing **20-1**

Preview **20-1**
Production and Service Department Costs **20-3**
Review 20-1 .... **20-3**
Service Department Cost Allocation **20-4**
Direct Method **20-5**
Step Method **20-6**
Linear Algebra (Reciprocal) Method **20-7**
Dual Rates **20-9**
Review 20-2 .... **20-9**
Lean Production and Just-in-Time Inventory Management **20-10**
Reducing Incoming Materials Inventory **20-10**
Reducing Work-in-Process Inventory **20-11**
Reducing Finished Goods Inventory **20-12**
Review 20-3 .... **20-12**
Performance Evaluation and Recordkeeping with Lean
Production and JIT **20-13**
Performance Evaluation **20-13**
Simplified Recordkeeping **20-14**
Review 20-4 .... **20-15**
Increased Focus on Data-Driven Decision Making **20-15**
Review 20-5 .... **20-16**
Guidance Answers **20-17**
Assignments **20-17**
Management Applications **20-26**
Solutions to Review Problems **20-27**

MODULE 21
Pricing and Other Product Management Decisions **21-1**

Preview **21-1**
Understanding the Value Chain **21-3**
Usefulness of a Value Chain Perspective **21-5**
Value-Added and Value Chain Perspectives **21-6**
Review 21-1 .... **21-7**
The Pricing Decision **21-7**
Economic Approaches to Pricing **21-7**
Cost-Based Approaches to Pricing **21-8**
Review 21-2 .... **21-11**
Target Costing **21-12**
Target Costing Is Proactive for Cost Management **21-12**

Target Costing Encourages Design for Production 21-13
Target Costing Reduces Time to Introduce Products 21-14
Target Costing Requires Cost Information 21-14
Target Costing Requires Coordination 21-14
Target Costing Is Key for Products with Short Life Cycles 21-15
Target Costing Helps Manage Life-Cycle Costs 21-16
Review 21-3 .... **21-17**
Continuous Improvement Costing **21-17**
Review 21-4 .... **21-18**
Benchmarking... **21-18**
Review 21-5 .... **21-20**
Guidance Answers **21-20**
Assignments.. **21-20**
Management Applications **21-26**
Solutions to Review Problems **21-27**

MODULE 22

Operational Budgeting and Profit Planning 22-1

Preview... **22-1**
Reasons for Budgeting.................................. **22-3**
Compel Planning 22-3
Promote Communication and Coordination 22-3
Provide a Guide to Action and Basis of Evaluation 22-3
Aid in Risk Management 22-3
Review 22-1 .... **22-4**
General Approaches to Budgeting **22-4**
Output/Input Approach 22-5
Activity-Based Approach 22-5
Incremental Approach 22-5
Minimum Level Approach 22-5
Review 22-2 .... **22-6**
Master Budget **22-7**
Sales Budget 22-9
Purchases Budget 22-10
Selling Expense Budget 22-10
General and Administrative Expense Budget 22-11
Cash Budget 22-11
Budgeted Financial Statements 22-13
Finalizing the Budget 22-14
Review 22-3 .... **22-15**
Budget Development in Manufacturing Organizations **22-16**
Production Budget 22-16
Manufacturing Cost Budget 22-16
Review 22-4 .... **22-19**
Budget Development and Manager Behavior............... **22-20**
Employee Participation 22-20
Budgeting Periods 22-21
Forecasts 22-21
Ethics 22-22
Open Book Management 22-22
Review 22-5 .... **22-23**
Guidance Answers **22-23**
Assignments.. **22-23**
Management Applications **22-35**
Solutions to Review Problems **22-37**

MODULE 23

Standard Costs and Performance Reports 23-1

Preview... **23-1**
Responsibility Accounting............................... **23-3**
Performance Reporting and Organization Structures 23-4
Types of Responsibility Centers 23-4
Financial and Nonfinancial Performance Measures 23-5
Review 23-1 .... **23-6**
Performance Reporting for Cost Centers................. **23-6**
Development of Flexible Budgets 23-6
Flexible Budgets Emphasize Performance 23-7
Standard Costs and Performance Reports 23-8
Review 23-2 .... **23-8**

Variance Analysis for Costs **23-9**
Components of Standard Cost Analysis 23-9
Establishing and Using Standards for Direct Materials 23-10
Review 23-3 .... **23-13**
Establishing and Using Standards for Direct Labor 23-13
Review 23-4 .... **23-15**
Establishing and Using Standards for Variable Overhead 23-15
Fixed Overhead Variances 23-17
Review 23-5 .... **23-18**
Performance Reports for Revenue Centers............... **23-18**
Inclusion of Controllable Costs 23-19
Revenue Centers as Profit Centers 23-20
Review 23-6 .... **23-21**
Appendix 23A: Fixed Overhead Variances **23-21**
Review 23-7 .... **23-23**
Appendix 23B: Reconciling Budgeted and Actual Income ... **23-23**
Review 23-8 .... **23-24**
Guidance Answers **23-25**
Assignments.. **23-25**
Management Applications **23-35**
Solutions to Review Problems **23-38**

MODULE 24

Segment Reporting, Transfer Pricing, and Balanced Scorecard 24-1

Preview... **24-1**
Strategic Business Segments and Segment Reporting **24-3**
Multilevel Segment Income Statements 24-5
Interpreting Segment Reports 24-5
Review 24-1 .... **24-7**
Transfer Pricing **24-7**
Management Considerations 24-8
Determining Transfer Prices 24-10
Review 24-2 .... **24-13**
Investment Center Evaluation Measures **24-13**
Return on Investment 24-13
Investment Center Income 24-15
Investment Center Asset Base 24-16
Other Valuation Issues 24-16
Residual Income 24-17
Economic Value Added 24-17
Which Measure Is Best? 24-18
Review 24-3 .... **24-20**
Balanced Scorecard.................................... **24-20**
Balanced Scorecard Framework 24-20
Balanced Scorecard and Strategy 24-22
Review 24-4 .... **24-24**
Guidance Answers **24-24**
Assignments.. **24-24**
Management Applications **24-36**
Solutions to Review Problems **24-38**

MODULE 25

Capital Budgeting Decisions 25-1

Preview... **25-1**
Long-Range Planning and Capital Budgeting **25-3**
Review 25-1 .... **25-6**
Capital Budgeting Models That Consider Time Value of Money ... **25-6**
Expected Cash Flows 25-6
Manager Behavior and Expected Cash Flows 25-8
Net Present Value 25-8
Internal Rate of Return 25-9
Cost of Capital 25-10
Review 25-2 .... **25-11**
Capital Budgeting Models That Do Not Consider Time
Value of Money **25-11**
Payback Period 25-12
Accounting Rate of Return 25-13
Review 25-3 .... **25-13**

Evaluation of Capital Budgeting Models 25-14
Review 25-4 25-16
Additional Aspects of Capital Budgeting 25-16
    Using Multiple Investment Criteria **25-16**
    Evaluating Risk **25-17**
    Differential Analysis of Project Cash Flows **25-17**
    Predicting Differential Costs and Revenues for
       High-Tech Investments **25-19**
Review 25-5 25-20
Taxes in Capital Budgeting Decisions 25-20
    Depreciation Tax Shield **25-21**
    Investment Tax Credit **25-22**
Review 25-6 25-23
Appendix 25A: Time Value of Money 25-23
    Future Value **25-24**
    Present Value **25-24**
    Annuities **25-25**
    Unequal Cash Flows **25-26**
    Deferred Returns **25-28**
Review 25-7 25-28
Appendix 25B: Table Approach to Determining
              Internal Rate of Return 25-29
    Equal Cash Inflows **25-29**
    Unequal Cash Inflows **25-29**
Review 25-8 25-30
Guidance Answers 25-30
Assignments 25-31
Management Applications 25-37
Solutions to Review Problems 25-42

APPENDIX A
Compound Interest Tables **A-1**

APPENDIX B
Chart of Accounts with Acronyms **B-1**
    Assets **B-1**
    Liabilities **B-1**
    Equity **B-1**
    Revenues and Expenses **B-1**

APPENDIX C (Online)
Comprehensive Case **C-1**
Preview C-1
Reviewing Financial Statements C-3
    Business Environment for Financial Reporting **C-3**
    Income Statement Reporting and Analysis **C-3**
    Balance Sheet Reporting and Analysis **C-9**
    Statement of Cash Flows Reporting and Analysis **C-21**
    Independent Audit Opinion **C-22**
Assessing Profitability and Creditworthiness C-23
    ROE Disaggregation—DuPont Analysis **C-23**
    ROE Disaggregation—Operating Focus **C-24**
    Disaggregation of RNOA—Margin and Turnover **C-25**
    Credit Analysis **C-26**
    Summarizing Profitability and Creditworthiness **C-26**
Forecasting Financial Statements C-27
Valuing Equity Securities C-30
    Discounted Cash Flow Valuation **C-31**
    Residual Operating Income Valuation **C-32**
    Assessment of the Valuation Estimate **C-32**
    Summary Observations **C-33**

Index **I-1**

Module 1

Financial Accounting for MBAs

Module Organization visually depicts key topics and their sequence.

Financial Accounting for MBAs

Information Environment	Financial Statements	Profitability Analysis	Business Environment	Regulatory and Legal Environment
■ Reporting on Business Activities ■ Demand for Information ■ Supply of Information	■ Balance Sheet ■ Income Statement ■ Statement of Stockholders' Equity ■ Statement of Cash Flows	■ Measuring Return on Assets ■ Disaggregating Return on Assets ■ Measuring Return on Equity ■ Relevance of Accounting	■ Competitive Analysis ■ Business Analysis ■ Analyzing Competitive Advantage	■ Financial Accounting Environment ■ Audits and Governance ■ SEC and the Courts
Review 1-1	Review 1-2	Review 1-3	Review 1-4	Review 1-5

A **Preview** *introduces each module.*

PREVIEW

We introduce four financial statements

■ Balance sheet ■ Income statement ■ Statement of stockholders' equity ■ Statement of cash flows

We provide a simple, powerful set of metrics to analyze financial statements

■ Return on assets (ROA) ■ Net profit margin ■ Total asset turnover ■ Return on equity (ROE)

We discuss the broad context for analyzing a company's business

■ Porter's five forces ■ SWOT analysis ■ Analysis of competitive advantage

Each module lays out Learning Objectives and maps them to the module's eLectures, guided examples, and end-of-chapter problem assignments. Use the roadmap in each module to track your learning. Consider looping back to the Learning Objectives as we work through each module and ask whether we have learned that content.

A **focus company** *in each module provides a real-world application.*

Apple Inc. is the Module 1 focus company and we refer to its financial statements to illustrate key financial accounting issues. The dashboard here conveys information about Apple's balance sheet, income statement, and statement of cash flows over the past nine years.

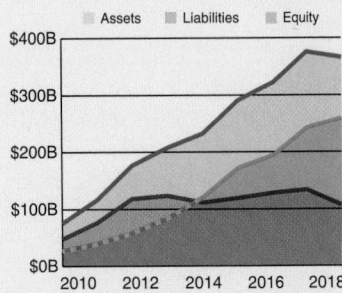

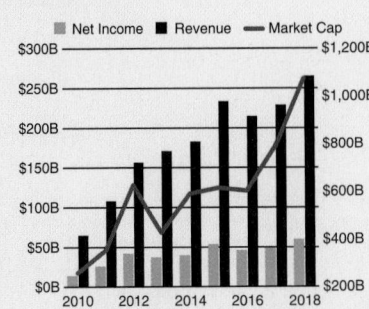

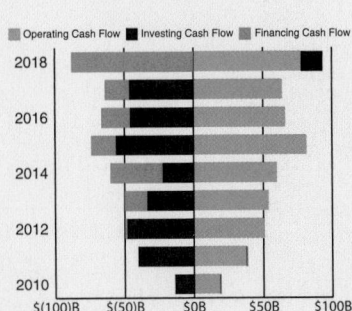

Road Maps *visually organize the topics, eLecture videos, Guided Example videos, and assignments by Learning Objective.*

Road Map

LO	Learning Objective | Topics	Page	eLecture	Guided Example	Assignments
1-1	**Explain and assess the four main business activities.** Planning :: Operating :: Investing :: Financing	1-3	e1-1	Review 1-1	1, 21, 58
1-2	**Identify and discuss the users and suppliers of financial statement information.** Information Demand :: Information Supply :: Global Setting	1-4	e1-2	Review 1-2	8, 9, 13, 17,18, 22, 35, 39, 60
1-3	**Describe and examine the four financial statements, and define the accounting equation.** Balance Sheet :: Income Statement of Stockholders' Equity :: Statement of Cash Flows	1-9	e1-3	Review 1-3	2, 3, 4, 5, 6, 7, 21, 23, 24, 25, 26, 27, 28, 33, 34, 36, 42, 43, 44, 45, 46, 52, 56, 58, 59
1-4	**Explain and apply basic profitability analysis.** Return on Assets :: Return on Equity :: Relevance of Financial Statements	1-18	e1-4	Review 1-4	19, 20, 31, 37, 38, 40, 41, 42, 43, 44, 47, 48, 49, 50, 51, 57, 59
1-5	**Assess business operations within the context of a competitive environment.** Competitive Environment :: Business Environment :: Competitive Advantage	1-22	e1-5	Review 1-5	10, 11, 30
1-6	**Access and analyze financial datasets.** Datasets :: www.SEC.gov :: Data Analytics :: Excel :: Data Visualization	1-26	e1-6		12, 26, 27, 31
1-7	**Describe the accounting principles and regulations that frame financial statements (Appendix 1B).** Accounting Environment :: Auditing :: Regulatory and Legal	1-30	e1-7		14, 15, 16, 29, 32, 53, 54, 55, 61, 62

Reporting on Business Activities

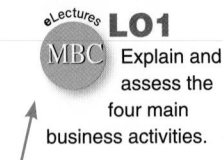

eLectures **LO1**

MBC Explain and
assess the
four main
business activities.

eLecture *icons identify
topics for which there
are instructional videos
in* **myBusinessCourse**
*(MBC). See the Preface
for more information on
MBC.*

The main objective of financial reporting is to provide users with information that supports investment and management decisions. Although there are many users of financial statements provided by companies, there are three main user groups:

- *Investors and equity analysts* who use financial statement information to judge the company's profitability and financial strength and to make reasonable estimates of the value of the company's equity securities.

- *Lenders and credit analysts* who use financial statement information to assess the company's ability to repay its debts and to determine how to manage credit risk associated with the company's debt securities.

- *Company managers* who use financial statements to inform decisions such as where to invest scarce resources, how to finance those investments, how to maximize the company's profitability, and how much cash to maintain.

Business Activities   To effectively analyze and use accounting information, we must consider the larger business context—see Exhibit 1.1. The yellow circle at the center of the exhibit captures the three types of ongoing business activities at every firm.

1. **Operating activities:** companies hire and train employees, manufacture products, deliver services, market and sell their products and services, and manage after-sale customer support.

2. **Investing activities:** companies acquire land, buildings and equipment, grow the business with new products and services, or acquire other companies to expand into new markets.

3. **Financing activities:** companies raise cash to fund the operating and investing activities. This includes selling stock to equity investors and borrowing from banks and other lenders.

Business activities occur within a particular business environment characterized by a number of **business forces**, including market conditions, competitive pressures, and regulations. These forces affect the way the company does business and shapes the company's overarching goals and objectives along with the company's strategy and its strategic planning process. Exhibit 1.1 depicts these forces and strategic plans in the outer (purplish) ring.

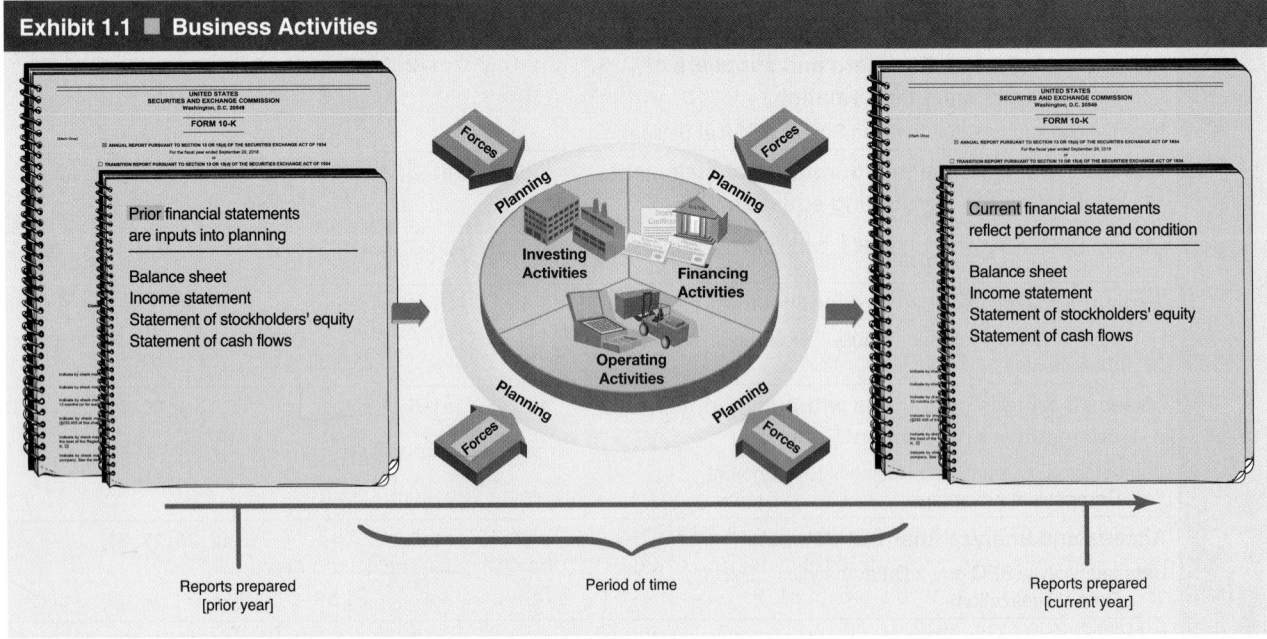

Exhibit 1.1 ■ Business Activities

Business Strategy   A company's *strategic* (or *business*) *plan* reflects how it plans to achieve its goals and objectives. A plan's success depends on an effective analysis of market demand and supply.

Infographics *are used
to convey concepts and
procedures.*

Specifically, a company must assess demand for its products and services and assess the supply of its inputs (both labor and capital). The plan must also include competitive analyses, opportunity assessments, and consideration of business threats. We discuss competitive forces later in the module.

Past financial statements (depicted on the left of Exhibit 1.1) are an important input into the planning process. They provide information about the relative success of past strategic plans. Managers use that information to take corrective action and make new operating, investing, and financing decisions. These new actions yield the current financial statements (on the right hand side of Exhibit 1.1) and the process starts anew. Understanding a company's strategic plan helps focus our analysis of financial statements by placing them in proper context.

LO1 Review 1-1

Complete the statements by filling in the blanks.
1. Companies engage in the following three types of ongoing business activities: _____ activities, _____ activities, and _____ activities.
2. A company's _____ reflects how it plans to achieve its goals and objectives.
3. Investors use financial statement information to make reasonable estimates of the value of _____.
4. Lenders use financial statement information to assess the company's ability to _____.
5. Company managers use financial statements to decide where to invest _____ resources.
6. Indicate whether the following business activities are operating, investing, or financing activities.

- Manufacturing products
- Issuing stock to investors
- Repaying a mortgage
- Selling services to a client
- Acquiring land
- Engaging in after-sales support

- Constructing new manufacturing facilities
- Hiring and training employees
- Gaining control of the voting stock of a supplier to secure the supply chain
- Entering into a bank loan

Solution on p. 1-48.

Financial Statements: Demand and Supply

Demand for financial statements has existed for centuries as a means to facilitate efficient contracting and risk-sharing. Decision makers and other stakeholders demand information on a company's past and prospective returns and risks. Supply of financial statements is driven by companies' wish to lower financing costs and other costs such as political, contracting, and labor. Managers decide how much financial information to supply by weighing the costs of disclosure against the benefits of disclosure. Regulatory agencies intervene in this process with various disclosure requirements that establish a minimum supply of information.

eLectures **LO2**
MBC Identify and discuss the users and suppliers of financial statement information.

Learning Objectives are highlighted at the start of the section covering that topic.

Demand for Information

The following broad classes of users demand financial accounting information.

- Managers and employees
- Investment analysts and information intermediaries
- Creditors and suppliers

- Stockholders and directors
- Customers and strategic partners
- Regulators and tax agencies
- Voters and their representatives

Managers and Employees

Managers and employees are interested in the company's current and future financial health. This leads to a demand for accounting information on the financial condition, profitability, and prospects of their companies as well as comparative financial information on competing companies and business opportunities. This permits them to benchmark their company's performance and condition. Managers and employees also demand financial accounting information for use in compensation and bonus contracts that are tied to such numbers. The popularity of employee profit sharing and stock ownership plans has further increased demand for financial information. Other sources of demand include union contracts that link wage negotiations to accounting numbers and monitor pension and benefit plans whose solvency depends on company performance. Financial statements provide useful information to company managers to address the following types of questions.

■ What product lines, geographic areas, or other segments are performing well compared with our peer companies and our own benchmarks?

■ Should we consider expanding or contracting our business?

■ How will current profit levels impact incentive and share-based compensation?

Investment Analysts and Information Intermediaries

Investment analysts and other information intermediaries, such as financial press writers and business commentators, are interested in predicting companies' future performance. Expectations about future profitability and the ability to generate cash impact stock price and a company's ability to borrow money at favorable terms. Financial reports reflect information about past performance and current resources available to companies. These reports also provide information about claims on those resources, including claims by suppliers, creditors, lenders, and stockholders. This information allows analysts to make informed assessments about future financial performance and condition so they can provide stock recommendations or write commentaries. Financial statements provide useful information to investment analysts to address the following types of questions.

■ What are expected future profits, cash flows, and dividends for input into stock-price models?

■ Is the company financially solvent and able to meet its financial obligations?

■ How do expectations about the economy, interest rates, and the competitive environment affect the company?

Excerpts of reports from agencies such as Credit Suisse, Moody's, and Deutsche Bank illustrate how accounting information is used by financial services.

Analysts use financial information to prepare research reports similar to the one issued in 2019 by **Credit Suisse** on **Apple Inc.** (below). Analysts use balance sheet numbers, including debt and equity along with income statement numbers, including revenue, earnings per share (EPS), and earnings before interest, tax, depreciation, and amortization (EBITDA) to compute ratios that inform their price target ($209) and their stock rating (Neutral). We will discuss analysts and their activities in more depth later. For now, know that accounting information is a bedrock for equity analysis.

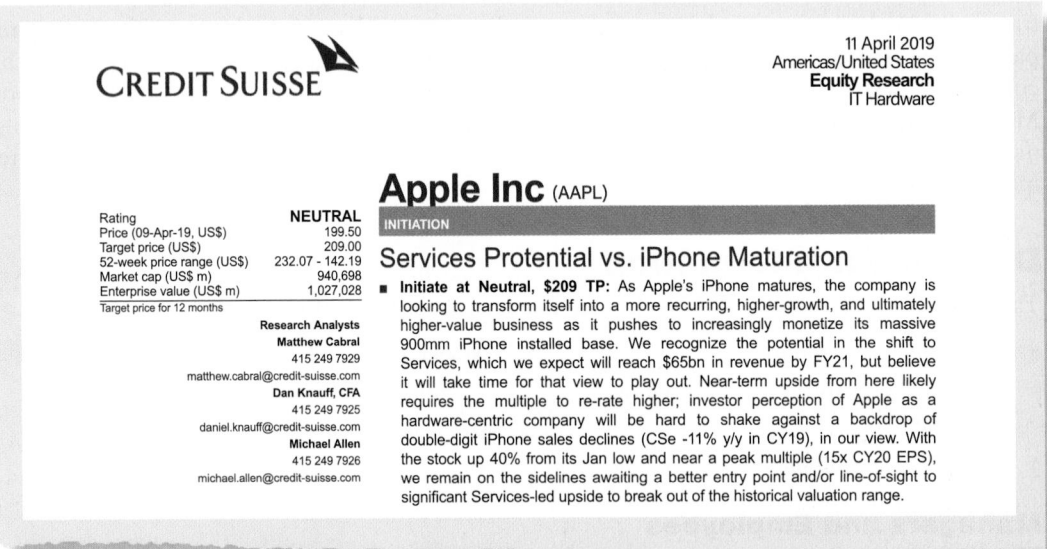

Creditors and Suppliers

Banks and other lenders demand financial accounting information to help determine loan terms, loan amounts, interest rates, and required collateral. Loan agreements often include contractual requirements, called **covenants**, that restrict the borrower's behavior in some fashion. For example, loan covenants might require the loan recipient to maintain minimum levels of working capital, retained earnings, and interest coverage to safeguard lenders. If covenants are violated, the lender can demand early payment or other compensation. Suppliers demand financial information to establish credit terms and to determine their long-term commitment to supply-chain relations. Both creditors and suppliers use financial information to monitor and adjust their contracts and commitments with a company. Financial statements provide useful information to creditors and suppliers to address the following types of questions.

▪ Should we extend credit in the form of a loan or line of credit for inventory purchases?

▪ What interest rate is reasonable given the company's current debt load and overall risk profile?

▪ Is the company in compliance with the existing loan covenants (loan conditions that restrict the borrower's behavior in some fashion, such as minimum levels of working capital, retained earnings, and cash flow, which safeguard lenders)?

Excerpts from recent financial statements are used to illustrate and reinforce concepts.

Following is Apple, Inc's disclosure of loan covenants on its credit facility (a line of credit) from a recent annual report.

> **Credit Facility**   We are party to a credit agreement that provides revolving commitments for up to $1.25 billion of borrowings, as well as term loan commitments, in each case maturing in January 2021. . . . The credit agreement contains negative covenants that, subject to significant exceptions, limit our ability to, among other things, incur additional indebtedness, make restricted payments, pledge our assets as security, make investments, loans, advances, guarantees and acquisitions, undergo fundamental changes and enter into transactions with affiliates. We are also required to maintain a ratio of consolidated EBITDA, as defined in the credit agreement, to consolidated interest expense of not less than 3.50 to 1.00 and are not permitted to allow the ratio of consolidated total indebtedness to consolidated EBITDA to be greater than 3.25 to 1.00. . . . As of December 31, 2018, we were in compliance with these ratios.

Stockholders and Directors

Stockholders and directors and others (such as investment analysts, brokers, and potential investors) demand financial accounting information to assess the profitability and risks of companies and other information useful in their investment decisions. **Fundamental analysis** uses financial information to estimate company value and to form buy-sell stock strategies. Both directors and stockholders use accounting information to evaluate managerial performance. Outside directors are crucial to determining who runs the company, and these directors use accounting information to help make leadership decisions. Financial statements provide useful information to stockholders and directors to address the following questions.

▪ Is company management demonstrating good stewardship of the resources that have been entrusted to it?

▪ Do we have the information we need to critically evaluate strategic initiatives that management proposes?

Customers and Strategic Partners

Customers (both current and potential) demand accounting information to assess a company's ability to provide products or services and to assess the company's staying power and reliability. Strategic partners wish to estimate the company's profitability to assess the fairness of returns on mutual transactions and strategic alliances. Financial statements provide useful information to customers and strategic partners to address the following questions.

▪ Will the company be a reliable supplier?

▪ Is the strategic partnership providing reasonable returns to both parties?

Regulators and Tax Agencies

Regulators (such as the Securities and Exchange Commission [SEC], the Federal Trade Commission, and the Federal Reserve Bank) and tax agencies demand accounting information for antitrust assessments, public protection, setting prices, import-export analyses, and setting tax policies. Timely and reliable information is crucial to effective regulatory policy, and accounting information is often central to social and economic policies. For example, governments often grant monopoly rights to electric and gas companies serving specific areas in exchange for regulation over prices charged to consumers. These prices are mainly determined from accounting measures.

Voters and Their Representatives

Voters and their representatives to national, state, and local governments demand accounting information for policy decisions. The decisions can involve economic, social, taxation, and other initiatives. Voters and their representatives also use accounting information to monitor government spending. Contributors to nonprofit organizations also demand accounting information to assess the impact of their donations.

Supply of Information

In general, the quantity and quality of accounting information that companies supply are determined by managers' assessment of the benefits and costs of disclosure. Managers release information provided the benefits of disclosing that information outweigh the costs of doing so. Both *regulation* and *bargaining power* affect disclosure costs and benefits and thus play roles in determining the supply of accounting information. Most areas of the world regulate the minimum levels of accounting disclosures. In the United States, publicly traded firms must file financial accounting information with the SEC. There are two main compulsory SEC filings.

- Form **10-K**: the audited annual report that includes the four financial statements, discussed below, with explanatory notes and the management's discussion and analysis (MD&A) of financial results.

- Form **10-Q**: the unaudited quarterly report that includes summary versions of the four financial statements and limited additional disclosures.

Forms 10-K (which must be filed within 60 [90] days of the year-end for larger [smaller] companies) and 10-Q (which must be filed within 40 [45] days of the quarter-end for larger [smaller] companies, except for the fourth quarter, when it is part of the 10-K) are available electronically from the SEC website (see Appendix 1A). The minimum, regulated level of information is prescribed by SEC regulations, but both the quantity and quality of information differ across companies and over time. We need only look at several annual reports to see considerable variance in the amount and type of accounting information supplied. For example, differences abound on disclosures for segment operations, product performance reports, and financing activities. Further, some stakeholders possess ample bargaining power to obtain accounting information for themselves. These typically include private lenders and major suppliers and customers.

There are a number of datasets that aggregate financial statement data (including SEC data), to aid access to financial statement information for a single firm or for large sets of firms. Most university libraries have subscriptions to one or more of the following datasets that we can access without charge.

- Compustat   - Mergent Online   - EMIS (for emerging-market companies)

Datasets consist of data that are "scrubbed" and formatted. Yet, we can use computer languages such as Python, R, or Java to gather data directly from the SEC website. This makes it possible to perform more-sophisticated textual analyses. For analyses in this text we use existing datasets and simpler programs such as Excel and Power BI, which are widely available Microsoft tools. We discuss this in more detail in Appendix 1A.

Benefits of Disclosure

The benefits of supplying accounting information extend to a company's capital, labor, input, and output markets. Companies must compete in these markets. For example, capital markets provide debt and equity financing; the better a company's prospects, the lower is its cost of capital (as reflected in lower interest rates or higher stock prices). The same holds for a company's recruiting efforts in labor markets and its ability to establish superior supplier-customer relations in the input and output markets.

A company's performance in these markets depends on success with its business activities *and* the market's awareness of that success. Companies reap the benefits of disclosure with good news about their products, processes, management, and so forth. That is, there are real economic incentives for companies to disclose reliable (audited) accounting information, enabling them to better compete in capital, labor, input, and output markets.

What inhibits companies from providing false or misleading good news? There are several constraints. An important constraint imposed by stakeholders is that of audit requirements and legal repercussions associated with inaccurate accounting information. Another relates to reputation effects from disclosures as subsequent events either support or refute earlier news.

Costs of Disclosure

Costs of supplying financial information include the following.

- **Preparation and dissemination costs**. Even though companies might already have gathered information for internal use, the cost of auditing the information and complying with the SEC's rules can be time consuming and costly.

- **Competitive disadvantages**. Disclosing product or segment successes, strategic alliances or pursuits, technological or system innovations, and product or process quality improvements could reduce or eliminate a company's competitive advantage.

- **Litigation**. Risk of litigation increases if companies disclose information that creates expectations that are not met. The cost of defending against customer or investor lawsuits in not inconsequential even for cases that are dismissed.

- **Political costs**. Highly visible companies can face political and public pressure. For example, government defense contractors, large software conglomerates, and oil companies are favorite targets of public scrutiny. Extra disclosure can increase this scrutiny.

The SEC adopted Regulation Fair Disclosure (FD), or Reg FD for short, to curb the practice of selective disclosure by public companies (called *issuers* by the SEC) to certain stockholders and financial analysts. In the past, many companies disclosed important information in meetings and conference calls that excluded individual stockholders. The goal of this rule is to level the playing field for all investors. Reg FD reads as follows: "Whenever an issuer discloses any material nonpublic information regarding that issuer, the issuer shall make public disclosure of that information . . . simultaneously, in the case of an intentional disclosure; and . . . promptly, in the case of a non-intentional disclosure." Reg FD increased the cost of voluntary financial disclosure and led some companies to curtail the supply of financial information to all users.

International Accounting Standards

Companies in more than 120 countries, including the European Union, the United Kingdom, Canada, and Japan use International Financial Reporting Standards (IFRS) for their financial reports. Headquartered in London, the International Accounting Standards Board (IASB) oversees the development of IFRS. While the IASB and the Financial Accounting Standards Board (FASB) operate as independent standard-setting bodies, the two boards work together cooperatively, often undertaking joint projects. Consequently, IFRS and U.S. GAAP (generally accepted accounting principles) are generally more alike than different for most transactions.

Currently, there is no formal plan for the U.S. to transition to IFRS or for the IASB and FASB to converge; however, both boards believe comparable global accounting standards are desirable because comparability would

- Improve the quality of financial reports.

- Benefit investors, companies, and other market participants who make global investment decisions.

- Reduce costs for both users and preparers of financial statements.

- Make worldwide capital markets more efficient.

Evidence of increasing "comparability" of U.S. GAAP and IFRS includes the following.

- Since 2007, the SEC has permitted foreign companies to file IFRS financial statements without requiring reconciliation to U.S. GAAP. Currently, more than 500 companies with a cumulative market capitalization of trillions of dollars report to the SEC using IFRS.

- The FASB participates actively in the development of IFRS, providing input on IASB projects through the IASB's Accounting Standards Advisory Forum (ASAF).

- Recent joint projects between the two boards relate to leases, financial instruments, revenue recognition, and insurance contracts.

We might ask: are financial statements prepared under IFRS substantially different from those prepared under U.S. GAAP? At a broad level, the answer is no. Both are prepared using accrual accounting and utilize somewhat similar conceptual frameworks. Both require the same set of financial statements: a balance sheet, an income statement, a statement of cash flows, a statement of stockholders' equity, and a set of explanatory footnotes. That does not mean that no differences exist. However, the differences are typically technical in nature, and do not differ on broad principles discussed in this book.

Review Problems are self-study tools that require the application of accounting topics covered in each section. To aid learning, solutions are provided at the end of the module.

At the end of each module, we summarize key differences between U.S. GAAP and IFRS. Also, there are a variety of sources that provide more detailed and technical analysis of similarities and differences between U.S. GAAP and IFRS. The FASB, the IASB, and each of the "Big 4" accounting firms also maintain websites devoted to this issue. Search under IFRS and PwC, KPMG, EY, and Deloitte. The two standard-setting bodies also provide useful information. See: FASB (**www.fasb .org/intl/**) and IASB (**www.ifrs.org**).

Review 1-2 LO2

MBC GuidedExamples

Required

Match the users of financial statement information with the types of questions they would typically ask and answer using accounting data.

_____ I. Managers and employees	*a.* Is company management demonstrating good stewardship of the resources that have been entrusted to it?
_____ II. Investment analysts and information intermediaries	*b.* What product lines have performed well compared with competitors?
_____ III. Creditors and suppliers	*c.* What regulated price is appropriate given the company's financial condition?
_____ IV. Stockholders and directors	*d.* Is the strategic partnership providing reasonable returns to both parties?
_____ V. Customers and strategic partners	*e.* What expectations about the company's future profit and cash flow should we use as input into the pricing of its stock?
_____ VI. Regulators and tax agencies	*f.* Is the company in compliance with the contractual terms of its existing loan covenants?

Solution on p. 1-49.

Structure of Financial Statements

eLectures **LO3**
MBC Describe and examine the four financial statements, and define the accounting equation.

Companies use four financial statements to periodically report on business activities. These statements are the balance sheet, income statement, statement of stockholders' equity, and statement of cash flows. Exhibit 1.2 shows how these statements are linked across time. A balance sheet reports on a company's financial position at a *point in time*. The income statement, statement of stockholders' equity, and the statement of cash flows report on performance over a *period of time*. The three statements in the middle of Exhibit 1.2 (period-of-time statements) link the balance sheet from the beginning to the end of a period.

A one-year, or annual, reporting period is common and is called the *accounting (fiscal) year*. Of course, firms prepare financial statements more frequently; semiannual, quarterly, and monthly financial statements are common. *Calendar-year* companies have reporting periods beginning on January 1 and ending on December 31. Some companies choose a fiscal year ending on a date other than December 31. Sometimes the fiscal year end coincides with a time when inventory is at a low point or at the end of a natural business cycle. Other times, the fiscal year is an industry standard. Most companies end their fiscal year on the same date each year (such as May 31). Other companies select a fiscal year that ends on the same week day each year. For example, many U.S. retailers have a fiscal year ending on the Saturday closest to February 1—some years that will be in late January, other years in early February. **Apple, Inc.** ends its fiscal year on the last Saturday in September.

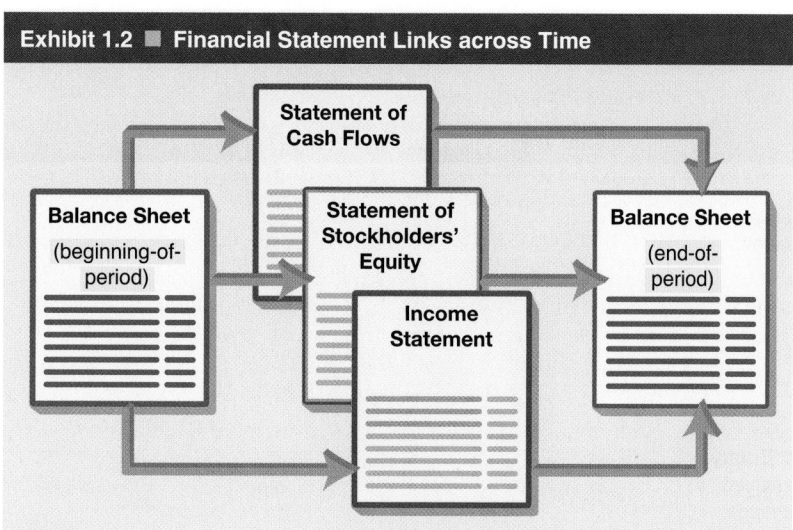

Exhibit 1.2 ■ Financial Statement Links across Time

Balance Sheet

A balance sheet reports a company's financial position at a point in time. The balance sheet reports the company's *resources* (*assets*), namely, what the company owns. The balance sheet also reports the *sources* of asset financing. There are two ways a company can finance its assets. It can raise money from stockholders; this is *owner financing*. It can also raise money from banks or other creditors and suppliers; this is *nonowner financing*. This means both owners and nonowners hold claims on company assets. Owner claims on assets are referred to as *equity,* and nonowner claims are referred to as *liabilities* (or debt). Since all financing must be invested in something, we obtain the following basic relation: *investing equals financing*. This equality is called the **accounting equation**, which follows.

Investing	=	Nonowner Financing	+	Owner Financing
Assets	=	Liabilities	+	Equity

The accounting equation works for all companies at all points in time.

Apple's balance sheet (condensed) is in Exhibit 1.3. Its accounting equation follows ($ millions).

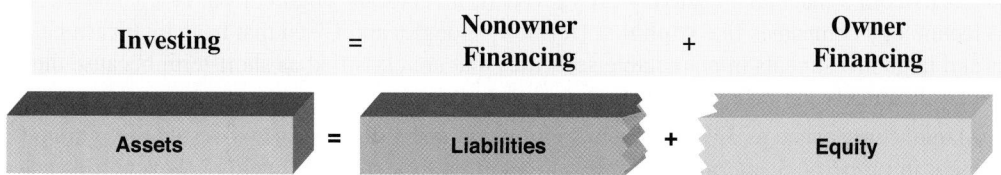

Assets	=	Liabilities	+	Equity
$365,725	=	$258,578	+	$107,147

Investing Activities

Balance sheets are prepared at a point in time and are organized like the accounting equation. Investing activities are represented by the company's assets. These assets are financed by a combination of nonowner financing (liabilities) and owner financing (equity).

Apple's condensed balance sheet in Exhibit 1.3 categorizes assets into short-term and long-term assets (Module 2 explains the composition of assets in more detail). Assets are listed on the balance sheet in order of their nearness to cash, with short-term assets (also called current assets) expected to generate

Real financial
data *for focus
companies
illustrate key
concepts of each
module.*

cash within one year from the balance sheet date. For example, the first short-term asset listed is cash, then accounts receivable (amounts owed to Apple by its customers that will be collected in cash in the near future), and then inventories (goods available for sale that must first be sold before cash can be collected). Land, buildings, and equipment (often referred to as property, plant, and equipment or just PPE) will generate cash over a long period of time and are, therefore, classified as long-term assets.

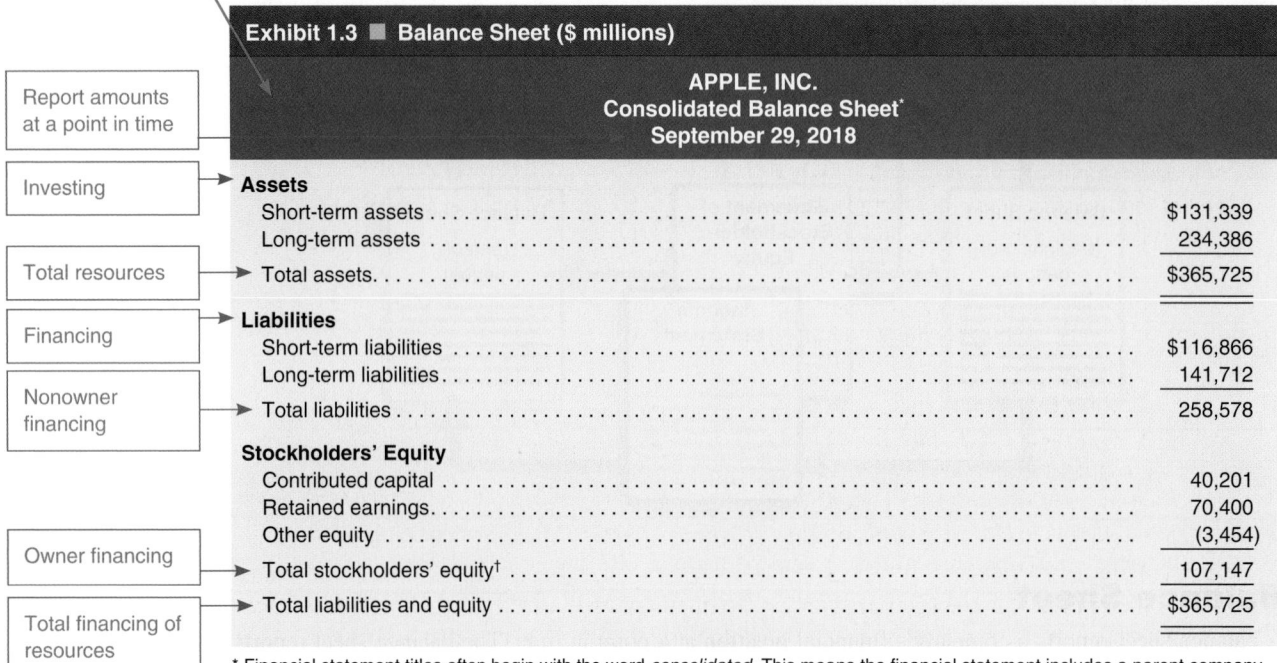

Report amounts
at a point in time

Investing

Total resources

Financing

Nonowner
financing

Owner financing

Total financing of
resources

Exhibit 1.3 ■ Balance Sheet ($ millions)

APPLE, INC.
Consolidated Balance Sheet*
September 29, 2018

Assets	
Short-term assets	$131,339
Long-term assets	234,386
Total assets	$365,725
Liabilities	
Short-term liabilities	$116,866
Long-term liabilities	141,712
Total liabilities	258,578
Stockholders' Equity	
Contributed capital	40,201
Retained earnings	70,400
Other equity	(3,454)
Total stockholders' equity†	107,147
Total liabilities and equity	$365,725

* Financial statement titles often begin with the word *consolidated*. This means the financial statement includes a parent company and one or more subsidiaries, which are companies the parent company controls.

† Components of equity are explained as part of Exhibit 1.5.

The relative proportion of short- and long-term assets is largely determined by a company's industry and business model. This is evident in the graph to the side that depicts the relative proportion of short- and long-term assets for a number of well-known companies.

■ Larger investments in short-term assets occur at companies such as Best Buy, Starbucks, and Nordstrom's that carry relatively high levels of inventories. High current assets also occur for technology companies like Alphabet (formerly Google) and Cisco that have high cash balances and large investments in marketable securities that are classified as short-term because they can be sold quickly in financial markets.

■ Manufacturers such as 3M, Johnson & Johnson, and Colgate-Palmolive require more investment in property, plant, and equipment in addition to large investments in inventories and accounts receivable from customers.

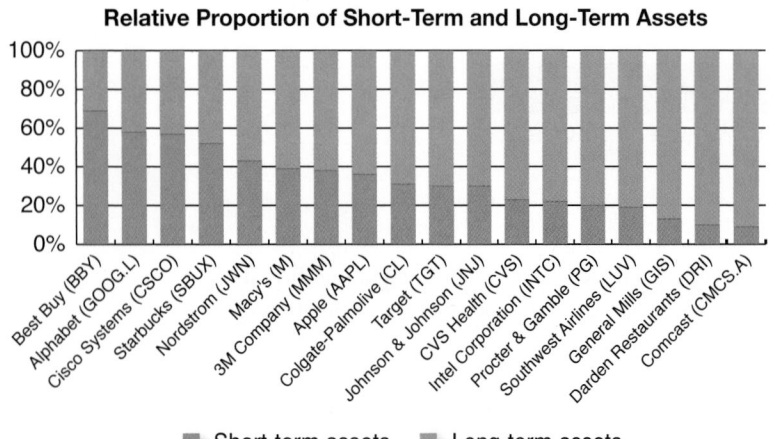

Relative Proportion of Short-Term and Long-Term Assets

■ Short-term assets   ■ Long-term assets

■ At the other end of the spectrum are transportation companies like Southwest Airlines and communications companies like Comcast whose business models require significant investment in long-term equipment, such as planes and telecom infrastructure.

Although managers can influence the relative amounts and proportion of assets, their flexibility is somewhat limited by the nature of their industries.

Financing Activities

To pay for assets, companies use a combination of owner (or equity) and nonowner financing (liabilities or debt). Owner financing has two components: resources (mostly cash, but sometimes noncash assets) contributed to the company by its owners, and profits retained by the company. Nonowner financing is borrowed money. We distinguish between these two financing sources for a reason: borrowed money must be repaid, and failure to do so can result in severe consequences for the borrower. Equity financing entails no such obligation for repayment.

The relative proportion of nonowner and owner financing is largely determined by a company's industry and business model. This is evident in the graph to the side.

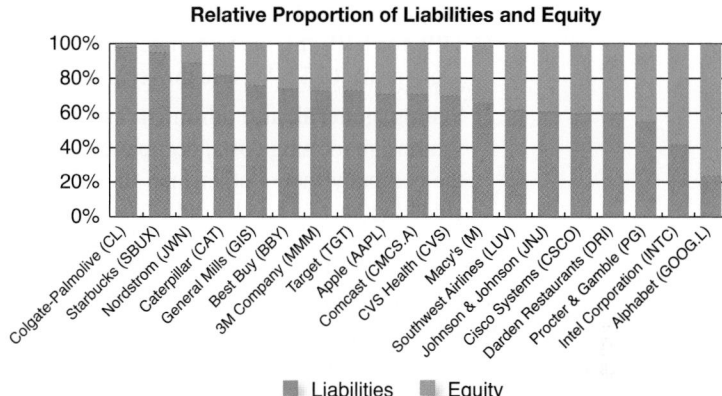

- Companies with relatively stable cash flows can operate more comfortably with a higher level of debt. Caterpillar, for example, sells much of its equipment on lease and the predictability of lease payments allows CAT to carry more debt. General Mills operates in the relatively stable consumer staples industry.

- Colgate-Palmolive, Starbucks, and Best Buy have used their stable cash flow to repurchase significant amounts of their common stock in order to boost returns for their shareholders. This has the effect of increasing debt relative to equity.

- At the other end of the spectrum are companies like Alphabet, and Intel that, like most technology companies, have higher levels of business risk. To offset the higher business risk, these companies reduce the level of financial risk by substituting equity capital for borrowed funds.

Most public companies tend to use slightly more debt than equity in their capital structures.

Manager Insights challenge us to think like a manager and consider the company's accounting choices and their consequences.

Manager Insights ■ Balance sheet considerations

We have provided a sneak preview into the interplay among financial statements, managerial decisions, economic conditions, and the competitive landscape. We have used terms and concepts that might be unfamiliar to you. We might start thinking about the following sorts of questions from a manager's perspective.

- Alphabet reports $109.1 billion of cash on its 2018 balance sheet, nearly half of its total assets. Many high-tech companies do likewise. Why is that? Is it costly to carry too much cash?

- A company's business model largely dictates the relative proportion of short- and long-term assets. Why is this the case? Why is the composition of assets similar for companies in the same industry?

- What are the trade-offs in financing a company by owner versus nonowner financing? If nonowner financing is less costly, why don't companies finance themselves entirely with borrowed money?

- How might stockholders influence the strategic direction of a company? What about bankers and other lenders —can they influence strategic direction?

- Most assets and liabilities are reported on the balance sheet at the price the company paid to acquire them (called historical cost). Would reporting assets and liabilities at fair values be more informative? What problems might that cause?

IFRS Insights examine issues related to similarities and differences in accounting practices of U.S. and other countries.

IFRS Insight ■ Balance Sheet Presentation and IFRS

Balance sheets prepared under IFRS often classify accounts in reverse order of liquidity (lack of nearness to cash), which is the opposite of what U.S. companies do. For example, intangible assets are typically listed first, and cash is listed last among assets. Also, equity is often listed before liabilities, where liabilities are again listed in order of decreasing liquidity. These choices reflect convention and *not* IFRS requirements.

Income Statement

An **income statement** reports on a company's performance over a period of time and lists amounts for its *top line* revenues (also called sales) and its expenses. Revenues less expenses equals the *bottom-line* net income amount (also called *profit* or *earnings*). Apple, as is typical of companies that sell products, reports two basic kinds of operating expenses.

■ **Cost of goods sold** (COGS, also called cost of sales). While revenues represent the retail selling price of the goods sold to customers, cost of goods sold is the amount Apple paid to purchase or manufacture the goods (inventories) that it sold. Manufacturing and merchandising companies typically include a subtotal called *gross profit*, which is revenues less cost of goods sold. For example, if it costs a company $7 to purchase or manufacture an item of inventory and the item sells for $10, the income statement reports revenues of $10, cost of goods sold of $7, and a gross profit of $3. We use the term *gross* to mean the profit available to cover all other expenses.

■ **Selling, general, and administrative expenses (SG&A).** This is Apple's overhead and includes salaries, marketing costs, occupancy costs, HR and IT costs, and all the other operating expenses the company incurs other than the cost of purchasing or manufacturing inventory (which is included in cost of goods sold).

Apple's income statement is in Exhibit 1.4. Refer to the income statement to verify the following: revenues of $265,595 million, cost of goods sold of $163,756 million, and operating expenses of $30,941 million. After interest income, net and income taxes, the company reports net income of $59,531 million. Net income reflects the profit (or earnings) to the company's shareholders for the period.

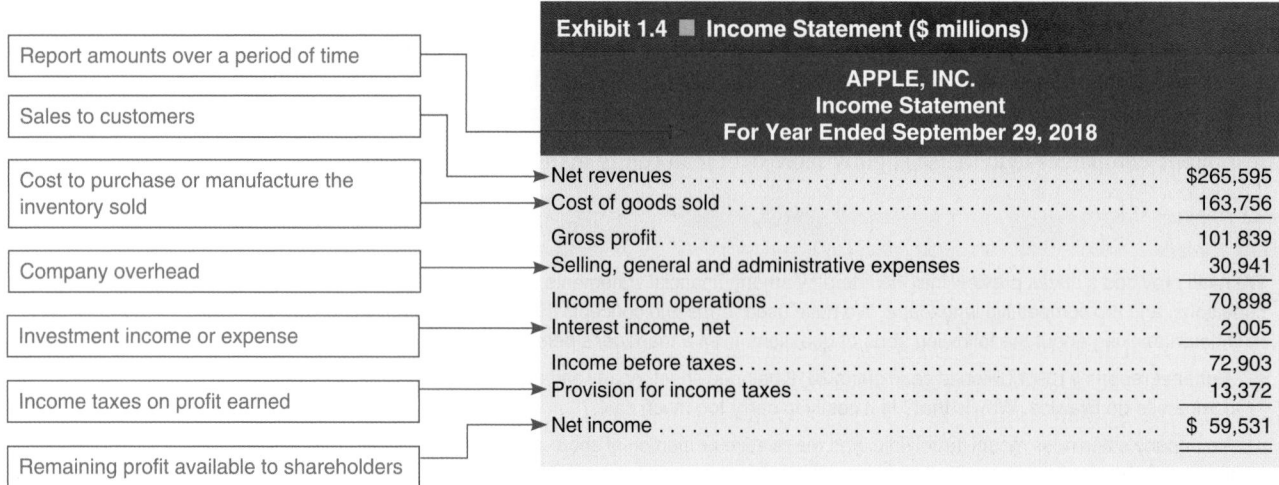

Exhibit 1.4 ■ Income Statement ($ millions)

APPLE, INC. Income Statement For Year Ended September 29, 2018	
Net revenues	$265,595
Cost of goods sold	163,756
Gross profit	101,839
Selling, general and administrative expenses	30,941
Income from operations	70,898
Interest income, net	2,005
Income before taxes	72,903
Provision for income taxes	13,372
Net income	$ 59,531

Left-side labels:
- Report amounts over a period of time
- Sales to customers
- Cost to purchase or manufacture the inventory sold
- Company overhead
- Investment income or expense
- Income taxes on profit earned
- Remaining profit available to shareholders

To generate net income, companies engage in operating activities that use company resources to produce, promote, and sell products and services. These activities extend from input markets involving suppliers of materials and labor to a company's output markets, involving customers of products and services. Input markets generate most *expenses* (or *costs*) such as inventory, salaries, materials, and logistics. Output markets generate *revenues* (or *sales*) to customers. Output markets also generate some expenses such as marketing and distributing products and services to customers. Net income arises when revenues exceed expenses. A net loss occurs when expenses exceed revenues.

Relative profitability (net income as a percent of sales) differs widely across industries and even among companies in the same industry. Although effective managers can increase their company's profitability, business models play a large part in determining profit levels. These differences are illustrated in the graph (below) of net income as a percent of sales for several companies.

■ Retailers such as **Best Buy**, **CVS**, **Target**, **Nordstrom** and **Macy's** operate in a mature industry and have difficulty differentiating their products. Hence, their net income as a percent of sales is low.

■ At the other end of the spectrum are companies like **Intel**, **Apple**, **Johnson & Johnson**, **Cisco**, and **Alphabet** that enjoy higher levels of operating profit resulting from patent protection for their intellectual property and companies like Colgate-Palmolive, Procter & Gamble, and 3M whose brands are well-established and command higher market prices and yield higher levels of profitability.

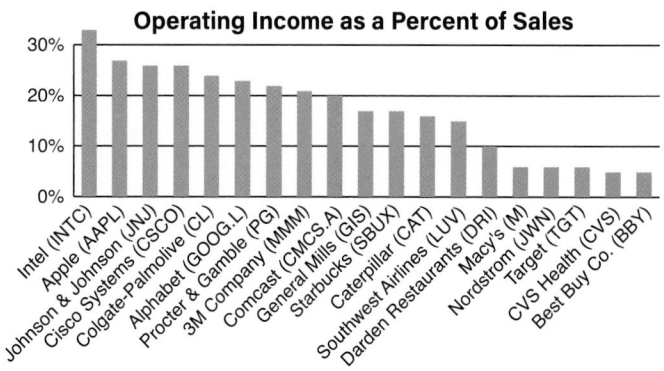

Companies' ability to create barriers to competitive pressure, either by patent protection, effective marketing, or otherwise, is a key factor in determining their level of profitability. Those that compete in highly competitive markets with little product differentiation must concentrate on controlling operating expenses to offset lower gross profits.

Manager Insights ■ Income statement considerations

Put yourself in the position of a senior company manager and think about the following situations.

- You sell to customers who promise to pay in 30 days. When should you (the seller) recognize the sale—when it is made or when cash is collected?

- Your company purchases a new building and reports the cost on the balance sheet as a long-term asset. What do you think of recording the entire cost of the building as an expense on the income statement in the year it is acquired?

- As a manufacturer, your company reports the cost of a product as an expense when the product is sold. How might you measure that cost? What sorts of items might be included in the calculation?

- If a piece of land increases in value, that increase is not reported as income until the land is sold. What consequences can you imagine if land appreciation *was* reported as income each year?

- Most of your employees are paid with a two-week lag. When should your company (the employer) record wages expense—in the period the employees worked or when you eventually pay the wages?

- Companies are not allowed to report profit when they sell their own shares of stock. Nor do they report an expense when dividends are paid to stockholders. Why do you suppose this is the case?

Statement of Stockholders' Equity

The **statement of stockholders' equity** reports on year-over-year changes in the equity accounts that are reported on the balance sheet. For each type of equity, the statement reports the beginning balance, a summary of the activity in the account during the year, and the ending balance. Apple's statement of stockholders' equity is in Exhibit 1.5. During the recent period, its equity changed because Apple issued shares and retained a profit. The company classifies these changes into three categories.

■ *Contributed capital*, the stockholders' net contributions to the company.

■ *Retained earnings*, net income over the life of the company minus all dividends ever paid.

■ *Other equity*, consists of amounts we explain later in the book.

Exhibit 1.5 reconciles the activity in each of the equity accounts from the balance sheet in Exhibit 1.3. We briefly discuss the two larger accounts here and explain the accounts in depth in Module 8.

■ **Contributed capital** represents assets the company received from issuing stock to stockholders (also called shareholders). The balance of this account at the beginning of the year was $35,867 million. During the year, Apple sold additional shares for $4,334 million to yield a year-end balance of $40,201 million.

■ **Retained earnings** (also called *earned capital* or *reinvested capital*) represent the cumulative total amount of income the company has earned and that has been retained in the business; that is, not distributed to stockholders in the form of dividends. The change in retained earnings links consecutive balance sheets via the income statement:

> Beginning retained earnings
> + Net income for the period
> − Dividends for the period
> Ending retained earnings

Apple's retained earnings increased by the $59,531 million of net income reported in its income statement and decreased by the $13,735 million of dividends paid to shareholders. These dividends are *a distribution* of the shareholders' investment in the company and are not treated as an *expense* in the income statement. That is why they are included as a separate row in the computation of ending retained earnings. The table also reveals a decrease of ($73,056 + $670) million in retained earnings. This represents another distribution to the shareholders: the amount Apple paid to repurchase common stock from shareholders (Apple retired those shares, which we explain in Module 8).

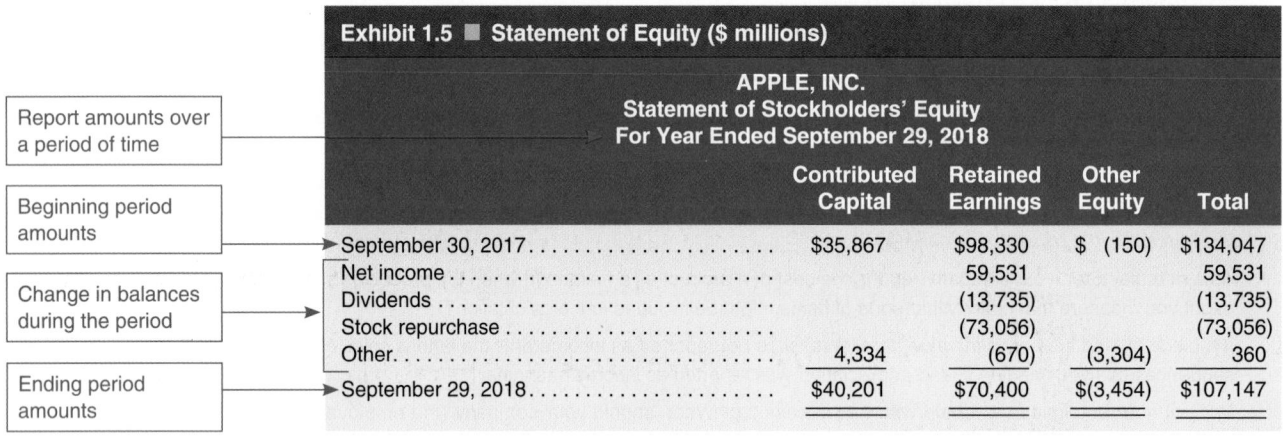

Exhibit 1.5 ■ Statement of Equity ($ millions)

APPLE, INC.
Statement of Stockholders' Equity
For Year Ended September 29, 2018

	Contributed Capital	Retained Earnings	Other Equity	Total
September 30, 2017.	$35,867	$98,330	$ (150)	$134,047
Net income		59,531		59,531
Dividends		(13,735)		(13,735)
Stock repurchase		(73,056)		(73,056)
Other.	4,334	(670)	(3,304)	360
September 29, 2018.	$40,201	$70,400	$(3,454)	$107,147

Annotations on the left (aid learning):
- Report amounts over a period of time
- Beginning period amounts
- Change in balances during the period
- Ending period amounts

Annotations are used to aid learning.

Statement of Cash Flows

The **statement of cash flows** reports the change (either an increase or a decrease) in a company's cash balance over a period of time. The statement reports cash inflows and outflows from operating, investing, and financing activities over a period of time. Apple's statement of cash flows is shown in Exhibit 1.6.

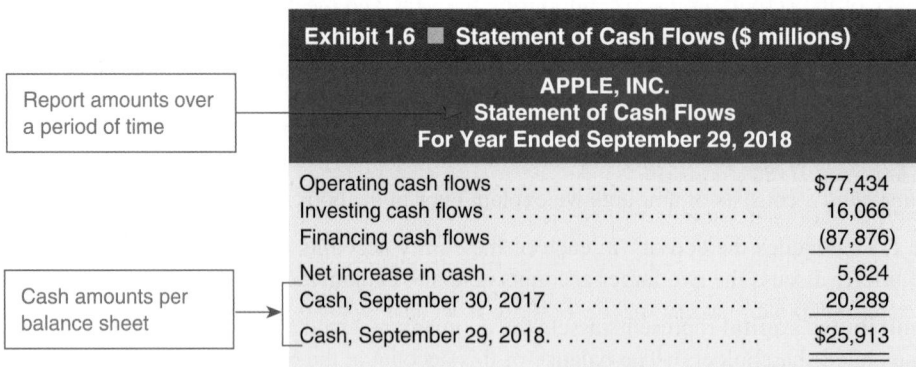

Exhibit 1.6 ■ Statement of Cash Flows ($ millions)

APPLE, INC.
Statement of Cash Flows
For Year Ended September 29, 2018

Operating cash flows	$77,434
Investing cash flows	16,066
Financing cash flows	(87,876)
Net increase in cash.	5,624
Cash, September 30, 2017.	20,289
Cash, September 29, 2018.	$25,913

Annotations on the left:
- Report amounts over a period of time
- Cash amounts per balance sheet

Apple's cash balance increased by $5,624 million in fiscal 2018 owing to the following three activities:

■ **Operating activities.** The increase of $77,434 million from operating activities represents the net cash that Apple generated from its core business activities of making and selling products and services to its customers.

■ **Investing activities.** Investing cash flows include cash outflows for the purchase of property, plant and equipment (PPE assets) and inflows and outflows of cash for sales and purchases of marketable securities. In 2018, Apple reduced its investments in marketable securities, which generated cash.

■ **Financing activities.** Financing cash flows relate to borrowing and repayment of debt, sales and repurchases of stock, and the payment of dividends. During 2018, Apple's most significant items included a cash outflow of $13,712 million for dividends paid to shareholders and a cash outflow of $72,738 million to repurchase common stock from Apple shareholders.

It is important to reinforce one point that we cite above: Apple's cash flow from operating activities of $77,434 million does not equal its net income of $59,531 million. This is typical and is due to timing differences between when revenue and expense items are recognized on the income statement and when cash is received and paid. (We discuss this concept further in subsequent modules.)

Both cash flow and net income numbers are important for business decisions. Each is used in security valuation models, and both help users of accounting reports understand and assess a company's past, present, and future business activities.

Manager Insights   ■   Statement of cash flows considerations

Put yourself in the position of a senior company manager and consider the following issues.

• Your accounting department prepares the statement of cash flows. Aren't the balance sheet and income statement sufficient?

• What types of information, disclosed in the statement of cash flows, can help you make important decisions?

• Is it critical for your company to report positive operating cash flow? What are the implications if operating cash flows are negative for an extended period of time?

• Why is it important for your company to report its investing cash flows? Which is more favorable, positive or negative investing cash flows?

• Is it useful to know the cash implications of your company's financing activities? What questions might that information help you answer?

• How might the composition of operating, investing, and financing cash flows change over your company's life cycle?

Review the Apple statement of cash flows summarized in Exhibit 1.6, and think about these questions. We provide answers for each of these questions as we progress through the book.

Information Beyond Financial Statements

Important financial information about a company is communicated to various decision makers through means other than the four financial statements. These include the following.

■ Management Discussion and Analysis (MD&A)

■ Independent auditor report

■ Financial statement footnotes

■ Regulatory filings, including proxy statements and other SEC filings

We describe and explain the usefulness of these additional information sources throughout the book.

Managerial
Decisions require
us to assume
various roles within
a business and
use our accounting
knowledge to
address an issue.
Solutions are
provided at the end
of the module.

Managerial Decision   ■   You Are the Product Manager

There is often friction between investors' need for information and a company's desire to safeguard competitive advantages. Assume you are a key-product manager at your company. Your department has test-marketed a potentially lucrative new product, which it plans to further finance. You are asked for advice on the extent of information to disclose about the new product in the MD&A section of the company's upcoming annual report. What advice do you provide and why? [Answer, p. 1-34]

Managerial Choices in Financial Accounting

Some people mistakenly assume financial accounting is an exact discipline—that is, companies select the one proper accounting method to account for a transaction and then follow the rules. The reality is that GAAP allows companies choices in preparing financial statements. The choice of methods can yield financial statements that are markedly different from one another in terms of reported income, assets, liabilities, and equity amounts.

People often are surprised that financial statements comprise numerous estimates. For example, companies must estimate the amounts that will eventually be collected from customers, the length of time that buildings and equipment will be productive, the value impairments of assets, the future costs of warranty claims, the eventual payouts on pension plans, and numerous other estimates.

Historically, the FASB has promulgated standards that were quite complicated and replete with guidelines. In recent years, the pendulum has begun to swing away from such rigidity. Now, once financial statements are prepared, company management is required to step back from the details and make a judgment on whether the statements taken as a whole "fairly present" the financial condition of the company as is asserted in the company's audit report (see below).

Moreover, since the enactment of the *Sarbanes-Oxley Act* (SOX) in 2002, the SEC requires the chief executive officer (CEO) of the company and its chief financial officer (CFO) to personally sign a statement attesting to the accuracy and completeness of the financial statements. This requirement is an important step in maintaining confidence in the integrity of financial accounting. The statements signed by both the CEO and CFO contain the following declarations.

- Both the CEO and CFO have personally reviewed the annual report.

- There are no untrue statements of a material fact that would make the statements misleading.

- Financial statements fairly present in all material respects the financial condition of the company.

- All material facts are disclosed to the company's auditors and board of directors.

- No changes to its system of internal controls are made unless properly communicated.

SOX also imposed fines and potential jail time for executives for untrue statements or omissions of important facts. Presumably, the prospect of personal losses is designed to make these executives more vigilant in monitoring the financial accounting system. More recently, Congress passed the *Wall Street Reform and Consumer Protection Act* of 2010 (or the Dodd-Frank Act). Among the provisions of the act are rules that strengthened SOX by augmenting "claw-back" provisions for executives' ill-gotten gains.

Research Insight ▪ Quality of Earnings

A recent study conducted a survey of nearly 400 CFOs on the definition and drivers of earnings quality, with an emphasis on the prevalence and detection of earnings misrepresentation. The CFOs cited the hallmarks of earnings quality as sustainability, absence of one-time items, and backing by actual cash flows. However, they also believe that, in any given period, a remarkable 20% of companies intentionally distort earnings, even while adhering to GAAP. The magnitude of the average misrepresentation is large: 10% of reported earnings.

Research Insights introduce relevant research findings on the topics presented.

What are the lessons for us? We can become informed and critical readers of financial reports by first understanding how reports are constructed and the types of assumptions and estimates that are used in their preparation. Much of this information is contained in the footnotes to the financial statements. This textbook will help you acquire the knowledge needed to become an informed and critical reader of financial reports.

Source: Ilia Dichev, John Graham, Campbell R. Harvey, and Shiva Rajgopal. 2016. "The Misrepresentation of Earnings" by *Financial Analyst Journal*, vol. 72, no. 1, pages 22–35.

LO3 Review 1-3

The following financial information is from Samsung Electronics, a competitor of Apple, for December 31, 2018 (in billions Korean won).

Short-term liabilities	₩ 69,082	Cost of goods sold	₩132,394
Cash flows from financing	(14,996)	Cash, beginning-year	30,545
Revenues	243,771	Income tax expense	16,815
Stockholders' equity	247,752	Short-term assets	174,697
Cash flows from operations	67,032	Long-term liabilities	22,523
SG&A expenses	52,490	Cash, end of year	30,341
Long-term assets	164,660	Cash flows from investing	(52,240)
Interest income, net	2,273		

Required

1. Prepare an income statement and statement of cash flows for Samsung Electronics for the year ended December 31, 2018. Prepare Samsung Electronics's balance sheet as of December 31, 2018.
2. Compare the balance sheet and income statement of Samsung Electronics with those of Apple, Inc. in Exhibits 1.3 and 1.4. What differences do we observe?

Guided Examples icons denote the availability of a demonstration video in **myBusinessCourse** (MBC) for each Review Problem— see the Preface for more on MBC.

Solution on p. 1-49.

Analysis of Financial Statements

This section previews the analysis framework of this book. This framework is used extensively by market professionals who analyze financial reports to evaluate company management and value the company's debt and equity securities. Analysis of financial performance is crucial in assessing prior strategic decisions and evaluating strategic alternatives.

eLectures LO4
MBC Explain and apply basic profitability analysis.

Return on Assets

Suppose we learn that a company reports a profit of $10 million. Does the $10 million profit indicate the company is performing well? Knowing a company reports a profit is certainly positive as it indicates customers value its goods or services, and its revenues exceed expenses. However, we cannot assess how well it is performing without considering the context. To explain, suppose we learn this company has $500 million in assets. We now assess the $10 million profit as low because, relative to the size of its asset investment, the company earned a paltry 2% return ($10 million/$500 million). A 2% return on assets is what a lower-risk investment in government-backed bonds might yield. The important point is that a company's profitability must be assessed with respect to the size of its investment. This is done with a common metric: the *return on assets* (ROA)—defined as net income for that period divided by the average total assets during that period.

Components of Return on Assets

To further isolate components that are driving return on assets, we can separate ROA into two components: profitability and productivity.

- **Profitability relates profit to sales.** This ratio is called the *profit margin* (PM), and it reflects the net income (profit after tax) earned on each sales dollar. Management wants to earn as much profit as possible from sales.

- **Productivity relates sales to assets.** This component, called *asset turnover* (AT), reflects sales generated by each dollar of assets. Management wants to maximize asset productivity to achieve the highest possible sales level for a given level of assets (or to achieve a given level of sales with the smallest level of assets).

Exhibit 1.7 depicts the disaggregation of ROA into these two components. Profitability (PM) and productivity (AT) are multiplied to yield the ROA. Average assets are commonly defined as (beginning-year assets + ending-year assets)/2.

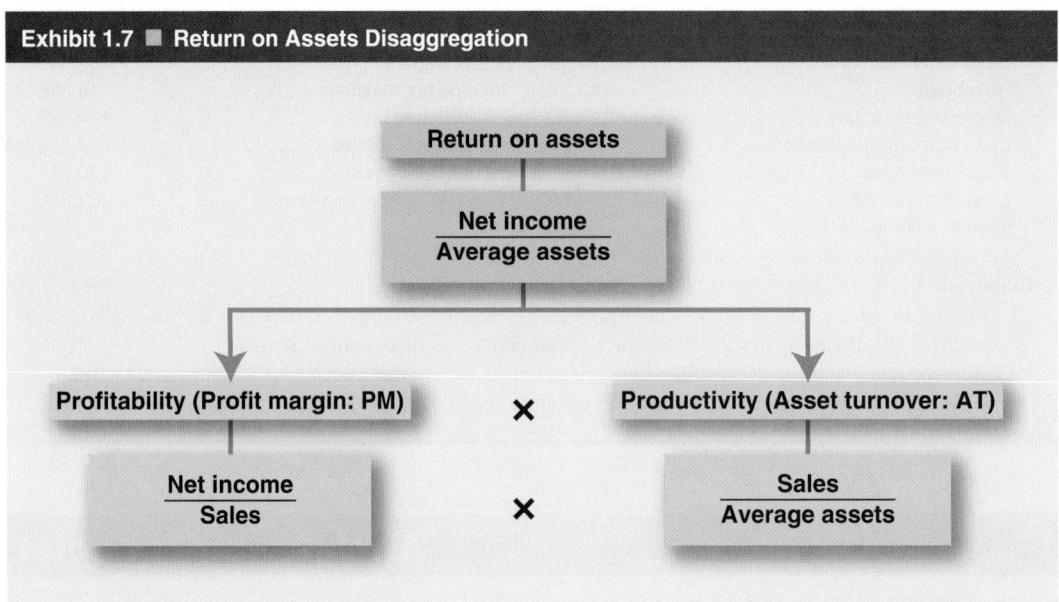

Exhibit 1.7 ■ Return on Assets Disaggregation

There are an infinite number of combinations of profit margin (PM) and asset turnover (AT) that yield the same ROA. To illustrate, Exhibit 1.8 graphs actual combinations of these two components for companies we highlight in this book (each is identified by its ticker symbol). The graph's green line represents possible combinations of margin and turnover to yield the 7.7% median ROA for the companies graphed here. The 7.7% ROA is higher than the 5.7% median ROA for all of the Standard & Poor's 500 companies for this same year. (Exhibit 1.8 focuses on core operating profit where we use earnings before unusual items and apply standardized tax rates to reduce variations from unusual activities.) Following are some general observations on Exhibit 1.8.

- **High margin and Low turnover.** Technology companies like Intel (INTC), Cisco (CSCO), Johnson & Johnson (JNJ), and Apple (AAPL) are characterized by high net profit margins resulting from patent protection that increase barriers to entry and reduce competition. These companies also report substantial assets, typically in the form of marketable securities and intangible assets that arise when these companies acquire other companies (a typical method of expansion in the high-tech industry). Because these securities and intangible assets do not generate "sales," the productivity ratio (AT) is decreased by the inflated assets in the denominator.

- **Low margin and High turnover.** At the other end of the spectrum, retailers like Nordstrom (JWN) and Target (TGT), Macy's (M), CVS (CVS), and Darden Restaurants (DRI) find it difficult to differentiate their products. This open competition keeps prices down, which yields lower profit margins. These retailing companies must focus on increasing AT to maintain an acceptable ROA. To do this, they watch inventory and PPE assets carefully and rarely have accounts receivable because most of their trade is cash-and-carry.

- **High performance.** The return on assets (ROA) is the product of profit margin and asset turnover and is higher as we move further away from the origin. Companies like Intel (INTC), Apple (AAPL), Colgate Palmolive (CL), Starbucks (SBUX), and Home Depot (HD) have higher ROAs than other companies. As we see, to achieve a high level of ROA, companies need to manage *both* profit margin and asset turnover. This is an important point—companies must manage both the income statement and the balance sheet to achieve high levels of financial performance. Managing one, but not the other, is generally not sufficient.

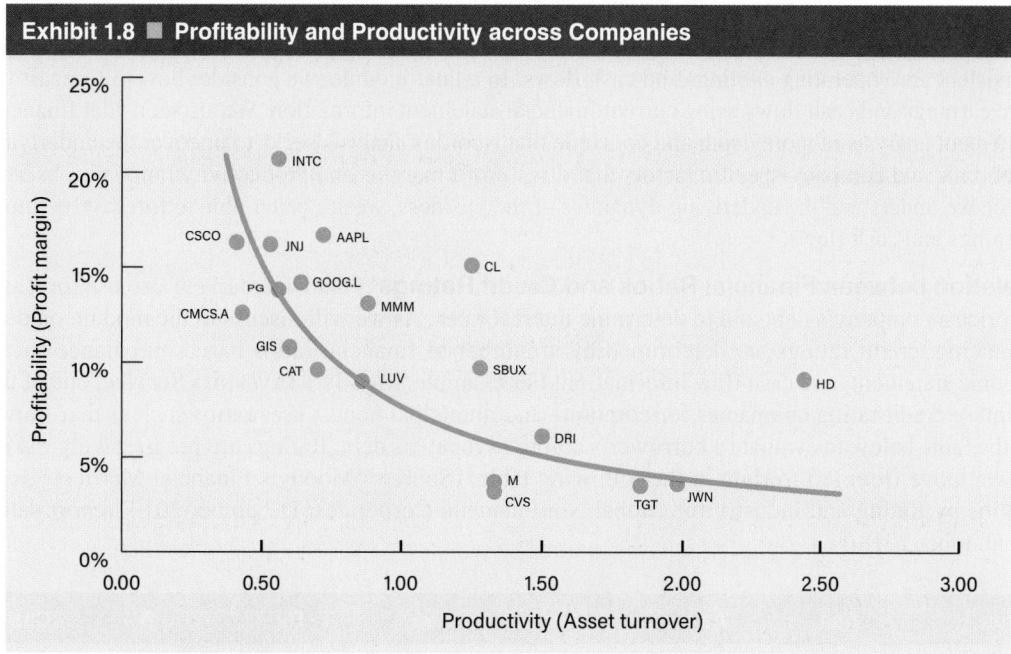

Exhibit 1.8 ■ Profitability and Productivity across Companies

Return on Equity

Another important analysis measure is return on equity (ROE), which is defined as net income divided by average stockholders' equity, where average equity is commonly defined as (beginning-year equity + ending-year equity)/2. In this case, company earnings are compared to the level of stockholder investment. ROE reflects the return to stockholders, which is different from the return for the entire company (ROA). We return to ROE in more detail in Module 4.

Are Financial Statements Relevant?

Accounting, finance, and economic researchers have long investigated the role of financial statement data in capital markets.

Relation between Earnings and Stock Prices   Early research focused on whether and how reported earnings are related to stock prices. There is a natural positive relation between expected earnings and stock prices, because stockholders expect dividends, which are paid out of earnings. Early research by Ball and Brown confirmed this expected relation, and the study produced the seminal graph shown here. (Source: Ball, R., and P. Brown. 1968. "An Empirical Evaluation of Accounting Income Numbers." *Journal of Accounting Research* (Autumn): 159–178.) It shows stock returns trending up during the year for companies that subsequently reported higher earnings (as compared with the prior year) and trending down for companies that subsequently reported lower earnings.

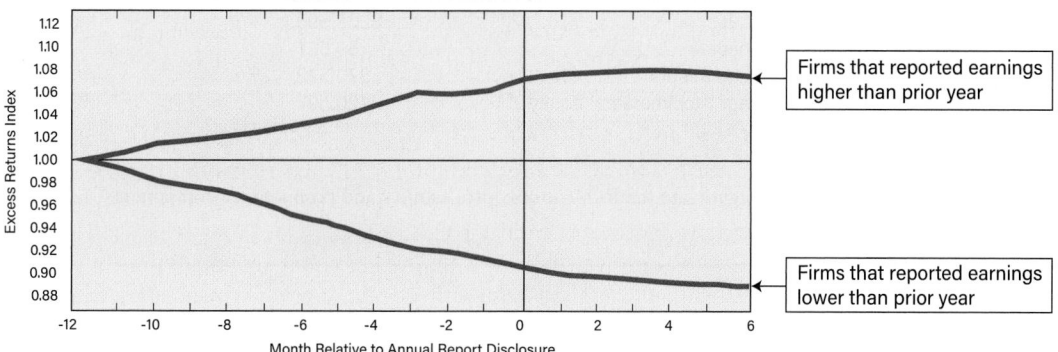

Subsequent research would show that persistent core earnings have the highest predictive ability for future earnings and cash flows. Rigorous financial statement analysis seeks to uncover a company's persistent core operating earnings and cash flows. In a later module, we consider how to forecast future earnings and cash flows using current financial statement information. We also consider financial statement analysis in more depth and conclude that rigorous analysis seeks to uncover the underlying economic and company-specific factors that drive profit margins and productivity ratios we observe. Once we understand the underlying dynamics of the business, we are better able to forecast its future earnings and cash flows.

Relation between Financial Ratios and Credit Ratings   Financial markets also use forecasts to price a company's debt and to determine interest rates. As we will discuss in the module on debt financing, credit ratings are determined by a number of financial ratios based on balance sheet, income statement, and cash flow information. For example, Moody's Investors Service, one of the primary credit rating companies for corporate and municipal bonds, uses ratios such as that shown in the table below to evaluate a borrower's ability to repay its debt. Ratings are progressively riskier as we move from left to right in the following table. (Source: 'Moody's Financial Metrics™ Key Ratios by Rating and Industry for Global NonFinancial Corporates: December 2017' report dated 25 October 2018.)

Moody's Financial Ratios	Aaa	Aa	A	Baa	Ba	B	Caa
Debt/EBITDA	1.9	1.7	2.2	2.7	3.6	5.2	7.2
FCF/Debt	40.4%	45.9%	35.7%	28.2%	21.5%	13.2%	5.7%
EBITDA/Interest expense..........	12.0	20.7	11.4	6.4	3.7	2.0	0.7

These ratios use debt, EBITDA (earnings before interest, taxes, and amortization expense), and FCF (free cash flow, which is defined as operating cash flow less purchases of PPE). The table indicates that as the company credit ratings decline (Aaa, Aa, A, Baa, etc.), each ratio becomes progressively "weaker." So, to answer the question: Are financial statements relevant? Yes. They provide critical input into the pricing of equity and debt securities and, therefore, the creation of shareholder wealth. For that reason, they are also essential in the development and monitoring of corporate strategy.

Managerial Decision   ■   You Are the Chief Financial Officer

You are reviewing your company's financial performance for the first six months of the year and are unsatisfied with the results. How can you disaggregate ROA to identify areas for improvement? [Answer, p. 1-34]

Review 1-4 LO4

Following are selected data from Apple's 2018 10-K.

$ millions	2018
Net sales.........................	$265,595
Net income	59,531
Average assets...................	370,522
Average stockholders' equity	120,597

Required

Solution on p. 1-50.

a. Compute Apple's ROA. Disaggregate the ROA into its profitability and productivity components.

b. Compute Apple's ROE.

Financial Statements and Business Analysis

Analysis and interpretation of financial statements must consider the broader business context in which a company operates. This section describes how to systematically consider those broader business forces to enhance our analysis and interpretation. This business analysis can sharpen our insights and help us better estimate future performance and company value.

eLectures **LO5**
MBC Assess business operations within the context of a competitive environment.

Analyzing the Competitive Environment

Financial statements are influenced by five important forces that determine competitive intensity: (A) industry competition, (B) buyer power, (C) supplier power, (D) product substitutes, and (E) threat of entry (for further discussion, see Porter, *Competitive Strategy: Techniques for Analyzing Industries and Competitors,* 1980 and 1998).

These five forces are depicted graphically in Exhibit 1.9 and are key determinants of profitability.

(A) **Industry competition** Competition and rivalry raise the cost of doing business as companies must hire and train competitive workers, advertise products, research and develop products, and engage in other related activities.

(B) **Bargaining power of buyers** Buyers with strong bargaining power can extract price concessions and demand a higher level of service and delayed payment terms; this force reduces both profits from sales and the operating cash flows to sellers.

(C) **Bargaining power of suppliers** Suppliers with strong bargaining power can demand higher prices and earlier payments, yielding adverse effects on profits and cash flows to buyers.

(D) **Threat of substitution** As the number of product substitutes increases, sellers have less power to raise prices and/or pass on costs to buyers; accordingly, threat of substitution places downward pressure on profits of sellers.

(E) **Threat of entry** New market entrants increase competition; to mitigate that threat, companies expend monies on activities such as new technologies, promotion, and human development to erect *barriers to entry* and to create *economies of scale.*

Exhibit 1.9 ■ Competitive Forces within the Broader Business Environment

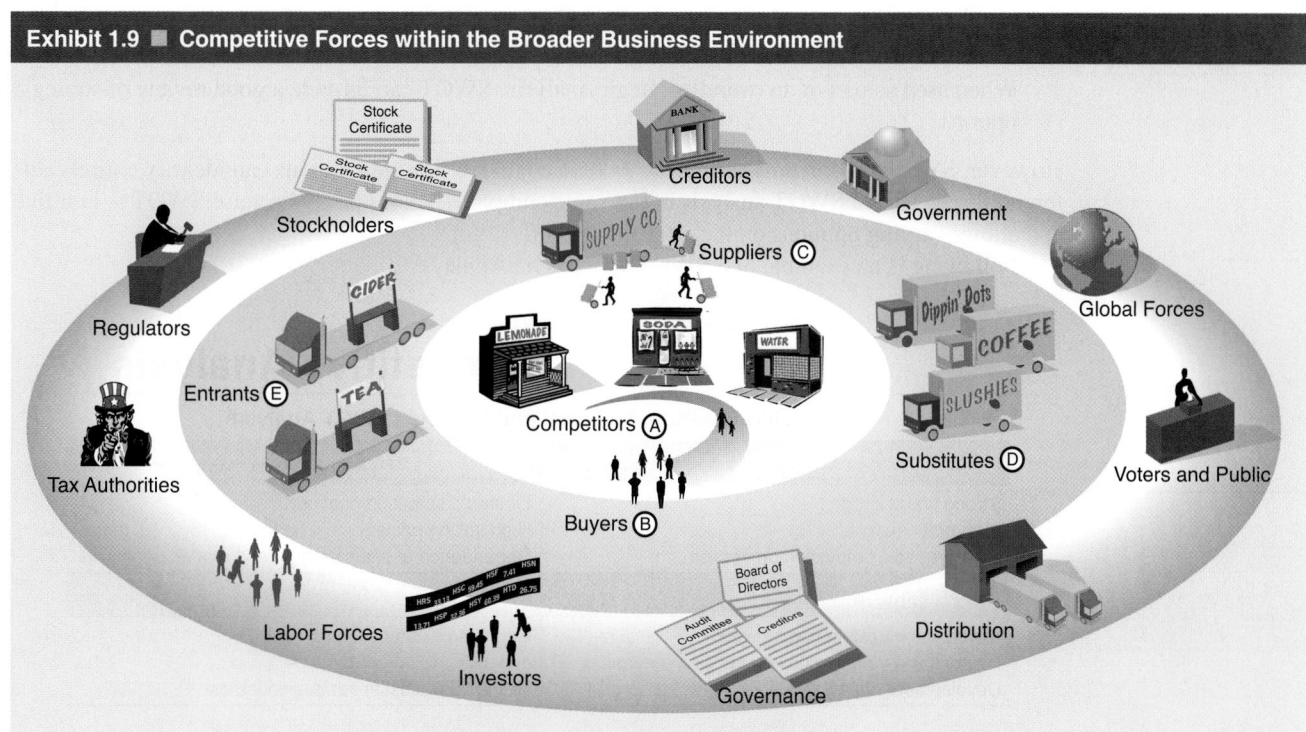

The relative strength of companies within their industries, and vis-à-vis suppliers and customers, is an important determinant of both their profitability and the structure of their balance sheets. As competition intensifies, profitability likely declines, and the amount of assets companies need to carry on their balance sheet likely increases in an effort to generate more profit. Such changes are revealed in the income statement and the balance sheet.

SWOT Analysis of the Business Environment

As an alternative to Porter-based competitive analysis, some prefer a SWOT analysis of a company. SWOT is an acronym that stands for strengths, weaknesses, opportunities and threats. This analysis can be applied to almost any organization. This approach is universally applicable and easy to apply, and it can be graphically portrayed as follows:

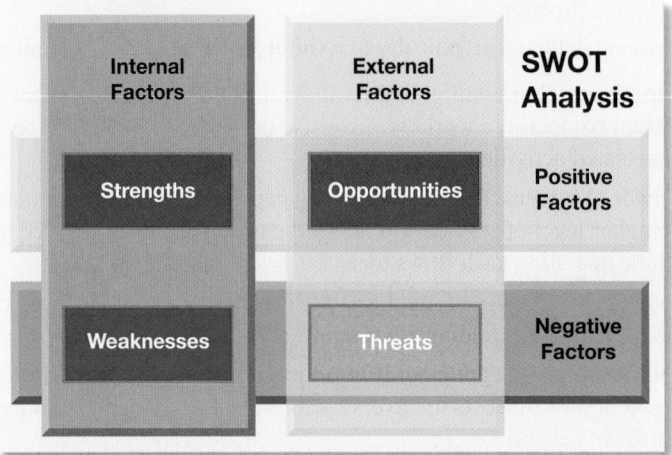

SWOT analysis has two parts.

- Looking internally, we review a company's strengths and weaknesses, while for external purposes, we review the opportunities of and threats to the company. SWOT analysis tries to understand particular strengths and weaknesses that give rise to specific opportunities (to exploit the strengths) and threats (caused by the weaknesses).

- When used as part of an overall strategic analysis, SWOT can provide a good review of strategic options.

However, SWOT is sometimes criticized as too subjective. Two individuals can identify entirely different factors from a SWOT analysis of the same company. This is partly because SWOT is intuitive and allows varying opinions on the relevant factors.

Following is an example of a SWOT analysis on Apple.

Competitive Analysis »

Apple, Inc. (AAPL) – Financial and Strategic SWOT Analysis

Strengths	Weaknesses
Strong brand image	Limited distribution network
High profit margins	High selling prices
Effective rapid innovation processes	Dependence of sales on high-end market segments
Opportunities	**Threats**
Expansion of distribution network	Aggressive competition
Higher sales volumes based on rising demand	Imitation
Development of new product lines	Rising labor cost in various countries

Analyzing Competitive Advantage

The goal of our analysis is to identify sustainable operating income and cash flow. This is true whether our analysis is focused on valuation of equity securities as a current or prospective investor or on a company's ability to repay its debt as a current or prospective creditor or on trying to grow company value as part of management. This analysis is much deeper than merely eliminating transitory (nonrecurring) items from financial statements. It is an exploration of the following two lines of thought.

1. Does the company have a competitive advantage, and, if so, what factors explain it? Further, is the competitive advantage sustainable?

2. If the company has no competitive advantage, does its management have a plan to develop a sustainable competitive advantage that can be implemented in an acceptable period of time and with a reasonable amount of investment?

Answers to these questions impact forecasts of the company's future performance.

Barriers to Entry Patents and other protections of intellectual property create **barriers to entry** that allow a company to achieve a competitive advantage and charge higher prices for their products or services and thereby earn excess returns. These legal barriers typically have a finite life, however, and a company must maintain a pipeline of innovations to replace intellectual property that loses patent protection.

Product Differentiation **Product differentiation** also allows companies to earn excess returns. Typically, differentiation is achieved from technological innovation that produces products and services with attributes valued by customers and not easily replicated by competitors. Differentiation along the dimensions of product design, marketing, distribution, and after-sale customer support are examples. Such differentiation has costs such as research and development, advertising, and other marketing expenses.

Cost Leader Another approach to achieve excess returns is to become a **cost leader**. Cost leadership can result from a number of factors, including access to low-cost raw materials or labor (while maintaining quality), manufacturing or service efficiency in the form of cost-efficient processes and manufacturing scale efficiencies, greater bargaining power with suppliers, sophisticated IT systems that permit timely collection of key information, and other avenues.

Other Factors In the absence of a competitive advantage, our analysis focuses on the likelihood that a company develops such an advantage. Management often discusses strategy with stockholders and equity analysts, which are recorded in conference calls that are readily available or reported in the financial press. In the case of a turnaround situation, our focus is on viability of the plan; that is, can it be achieved at an acceptable cost given the current state of the industry? Moreover, our focus is long term. Companies can often achieve short-term gains at long-term cost, such as by selling profitable segments. Such actions do not create long-term value.

Creating a sustainable competitive advantage that yields excess returns is difficult, and we are wary of forecasted excess returns for an extended period. Through a critical and thorough investigation of financial statements, and the footnotes, the MD&A, and all publicly available information, we can identify drivers of a company's competitive advantage. We then test the sustainability and validity of those drivers. This is an important step in assessing competitive advantage.

Review 1-5 LO5

Required

1. Match each of the following statements *a* through *f* with the category to which it relates.

    I. Analyzing the competitive environment

    II. SWOT analysis of the business environment

    III. Analyzing competitive advantage

    _____ *a.* Internal factors include a company's strengths and weaknesses.

    _____ *b.* Buyers with strong bargaining power can extract price concessions and demand a higher level of service and delayed payment terms; this force reduces both profits and operating cash flows to sellers.

    _____ *c.* The goal of our analysis is to identify sustainable operating income and cash flow.

    _____ *d.* New market entrants increase competition; to mitigate that threat, companies expend monies on activities such as new technologies, promotion, and human development to erect barriers to entry and to create economies of scale.

    _____ *e.* External factors include opportunities and threats.

    _____ *f.* If the company has no competitive advantage, does its management have a plan to develop a sustainable competitive advantage that can be implemented in an acceptable period of time and with a reasonable amount of investment?

2. Following are selected balance sheet and income statement accounts for Apple Inc. and Samsung Electronics. For both companies, compute ROA and its two components, PM and AT. Which company is performing better on these three measures?

	Apple ($ millions)	Samsung Electronics (Korean won billions)
Average assets.	$370,522	₩320,555
Revenue.	265,595	243,771
Net income	59,531	44,345

Solution on p. 1-50.

Book Road Map

The book can be broken into four parts—see figure below.

▪ **Part 1** consists of Modules 1, 2, and 3 and offers an introduction of accounting fundamentals and the business environment.

▪ **Part 2** consists of Module 4, which introduces analysis of financial statements. Analysis of financial statements is aided by an understanding of how those statements are prepared.

▪ **Part 3**, which consists of Modules 5 through 11, describes the accounting for assets, liabilities, and equity; this includes accounting for cash flows.

▪ **Part 4** consists of Modules 12 and 13, which explain the forecasting of financial statements and the valuation of equity. Appendix C is a comprehensive case, which applies many of the analysis tools introduced in this book.

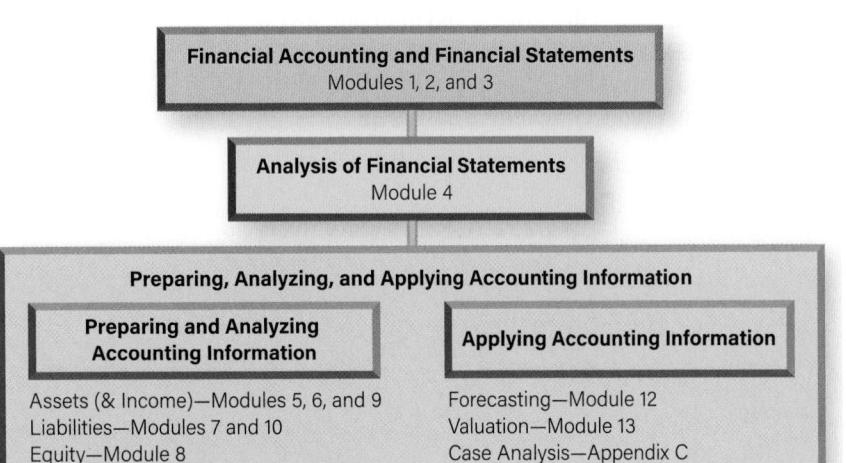

Global Accounting

As we discussed, the United States is among only a few economically developed countries that do not use IFRS. While laws and enforcement mechanisms vary across countries, the demand and supply of accounting information are governed by global economic forces. Thus, it is not surprising that IFRS and U.S. GAAP both prescribe the same set of financial statements. While account titles and note details differ, the underlying principles are the same. That is, U.S. GAAP and IFRS both capture, aggregate, summarize, and report economic activities on an accrual basis.

Given the global economy and liquid transnational capital markets, along with the fact that many non-U.S. companies file IFRS financial statements with the SEC, it is useful for us to be conversant with both U.S. GAAP and IFRS. For this purpose, the final section of each module includes a summary of notable differences between these two systems of accounting for topics covered in that module. Also, each module has assignments that examine IFRS companies and their financial statements.

Global Accounting *sections summarize notable differences between IFRS and U.S. GAAP for topics covered in the module.*

Appendix 1A: Financial Statement Data and Analytics

SEC Filings

LO6 Access and analyze financial statement data.

As noted in the chapter, all publicly traded companies are required to file various reports with the SEC, two of which are the 10-Q (quarterly financial statements) and the 10-K (annual financial statements). Following is a brief tutorial to access these electronic filings. The SEC's website is **https://www.sec.gov/edgar/searchedgar/companysearch.html**.

1. In the Company name box, type in the name of the company we are looking for. In this case, we are searching for Apple, Inc. (AAPL). Then click Search.

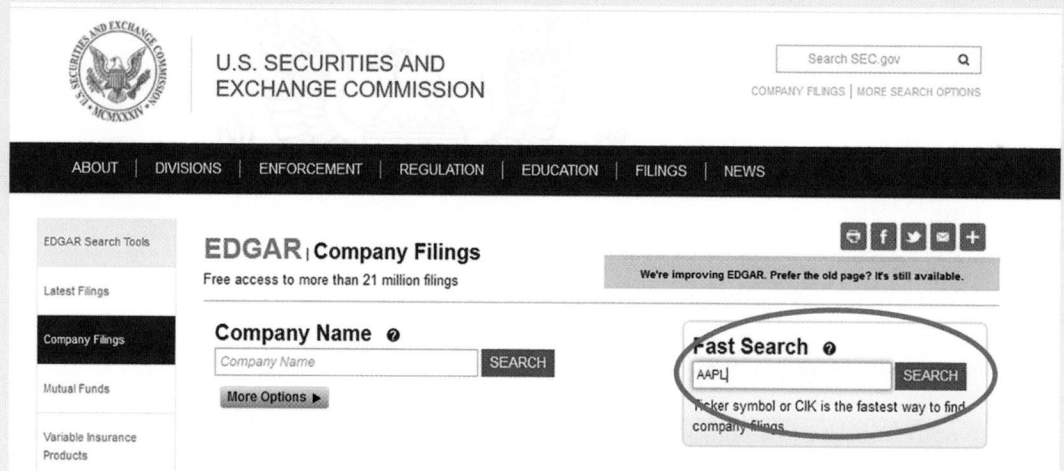

2. Enter the form number under "filing type" we want to access. Click the Search button. In this case, we are looking for the 10-K.

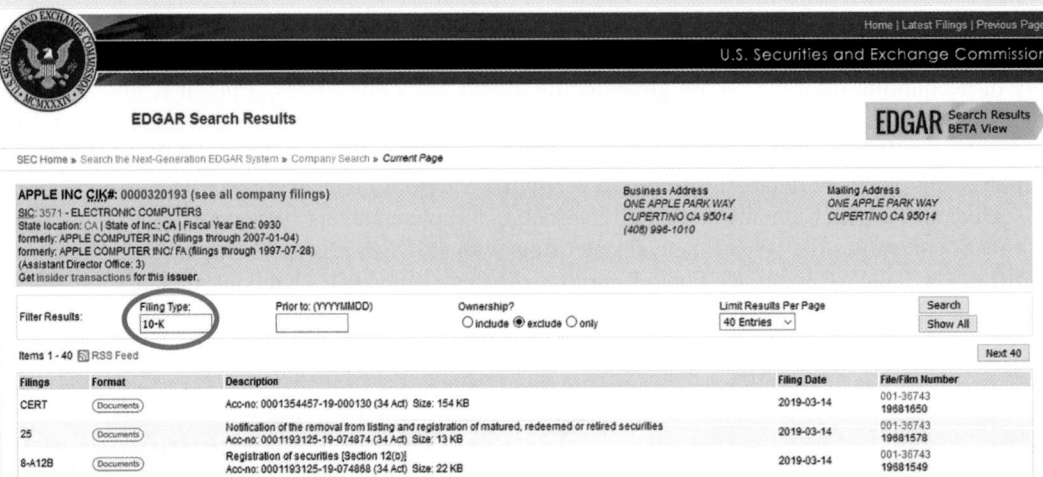

3. Click on the document link for the year we want to access. The filing date listed (2018-11-05 for Apple) is about 5 weeks after the fiscal year end.

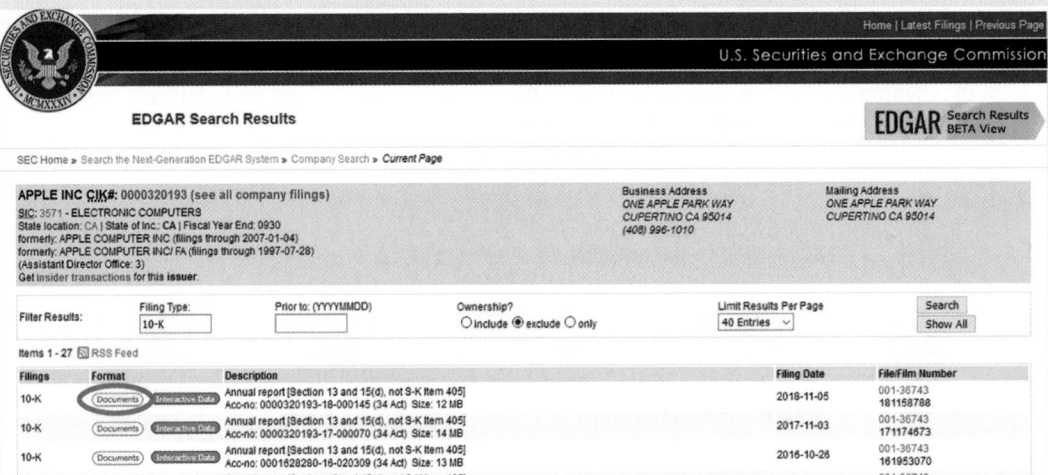

4. Exhibits relating to Apple's 10-K filing appear; click on the 10-K document.

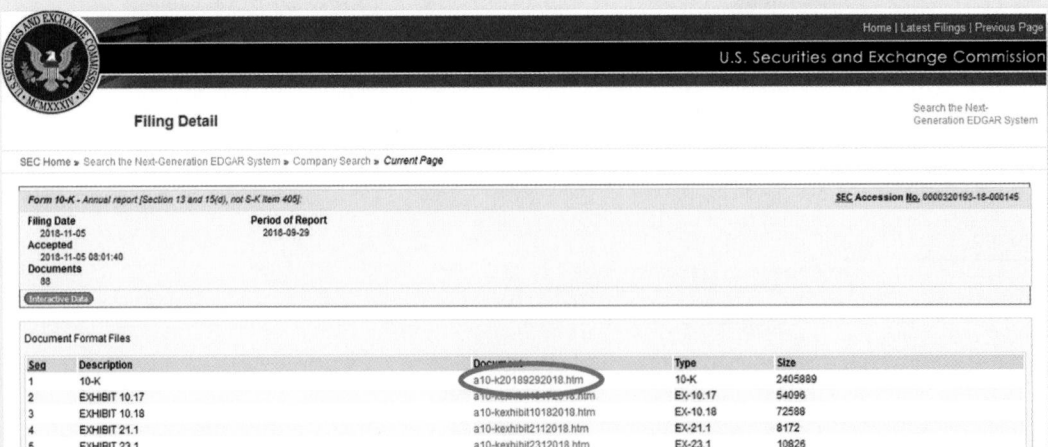

5. The Apple 10-K will open; the file is searchable.

6. An alternative is to download an Excel file of the financial statement data. From the Search Results page, click on "Interactive Data."

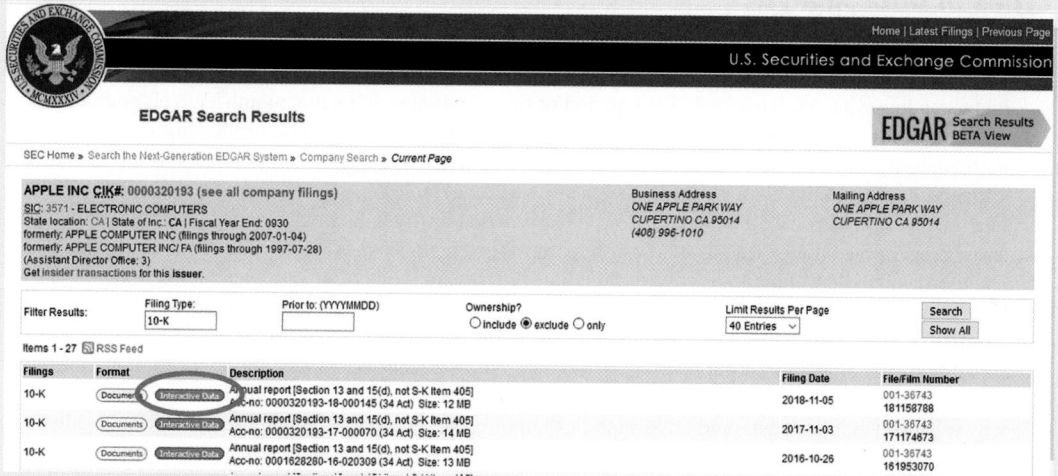

7. Click on "View Excel Document" to view or download as a spreadsheet. Or, to quickly view the financial statements or notes, use the links in the yellow box on the left.

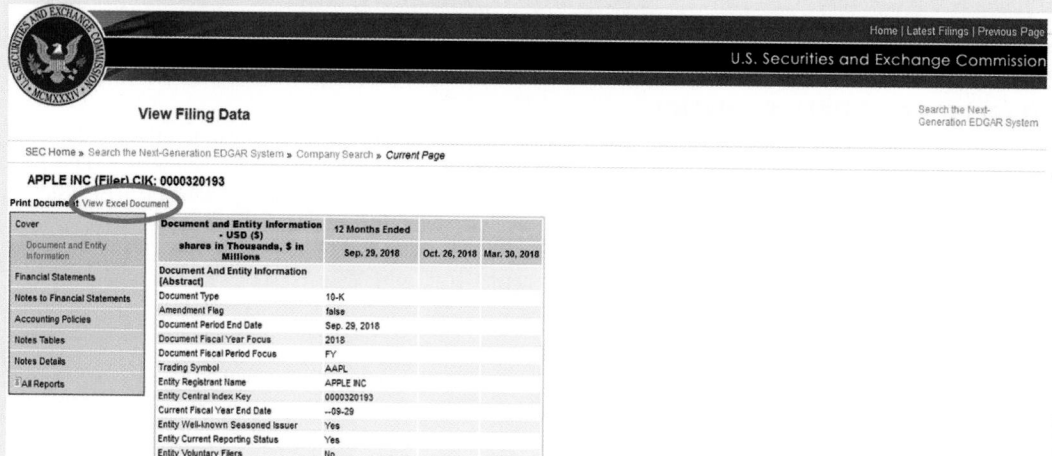

Data Analytics

Data analytics is an umbrella term for diverse activities that gather, organize, and analyze raw data. Fueled by advances in computing power, mass storage, and machine learning, we have seen data analytics applications skyrocket in the past decade. Business has benefited greatly—consider the following:

- Data analytics can be applied to any type of information including structured data (such as spreadsheets and databases) and unstructured data (such as 10-K footnotes and transcripts of earnings calls). In the business realm, leaders use data analytics techniques to better understand and manage data related to customers, input costs, production, employees, operations, risks, prices, and other aspects.

- Data analytics provide the business intelligence that informs critical firm-level decisions such as lending at banks, production optimization at manufacturing plants, new product development at biotech firms, and commodity sales by agriculture cooperatives, and many additional applications.

- Financial information intermediaries have developed sophisticated data analytics techniques. Debt and equity analysts rely on data analytics, using large datasets (structured and unstructured) and writing algorithms to create industry benchmarks, assess firms' performance, forecast earnings, predict bankruptcy, and assign credit scores.

- Auditors—both internal and external—increasingly rely on data analytics to identify irregular accounts or activities that warrant closer inspection.

- Regulators including tax authorities and securities exchanges analyze disparate datasets to deter and detect fraud.

Types of Data Analytics

There are at least four types of data analytics.

1. **Descriptive analytics** summarize data and describe observable patterns. These analyses focus on understanding what has happened over a period of time. Did sales go up this month? Which product lines account for the biggest change in revenues? What proportion of sales of a new service line came from a particular sales region? Descriptive analytic techniques include statistics (such as totals, averages, and variances) and cross-tabulating the data (such as using pivot tables).
2. **Diagnostic analytics** seek to understand what happened and why. This involves more diverse data inputs and a deeper dive into the data. A hunch or hypothesis often guides the direction for a diagnostic analysis. Diagnostic analytic techniques involve correlations, regressions, and often culminate in dashboards that capture meaningful outcomes. Google Analytics is a prime example of diagnostic analytics.
3. **Predictive analytics** enable an understanding of what is likely going to happen or what will happen "if" something else happens. Sales forecasts depend on predictive analytics as do equity valuation models that financial analysts use. To be able to predict what will happen, we first need to understand how and why it happened in the past: predictive analytics builds on descriptive and diagnostic analytics. Predictive analytic techniques involve building models using past data and statistical techniques including regression and a deep understanding of cause and effect.
4. **Prescriptive analytics** address the question of what "should" be done and suggests next steps or complete courses of action. A classic example is the Waze navigation app that analyzes traffic and road data and recommends the best driving route. In the business domain, prescriptive analytics can be tremendously valuable for a company, but requires a deep knowledge of the company's objectives and values.

Importance of Data Analytics

Data analytics can provide fodder for well-informed, data-driven decisions. Understanding relevant data at a deeper level can give a firm a competitive advantage and help business leaders better meet their goals. At the firm level, consider for example the vast quantities of data generated by enterprise resource planning (ERP) systems, customer relationship management (CRM) systems, and point-of-sale (POS) systems.

Data analytics is especially relevant to financial statement analysis because there exist many large structured datasets of financial statement data including the SEC's XBRL data.

Data Visualization

Data visualization, the graphical display of numbers with charts, figures, and bars, is often a very effective way to convey meaning and trends vis-à-vis tabular data arrays. This is especially true for big data sets that can be so complex that visualization is a necessary first step for analyzing raw data. Companies and analysts used data visualization for descriptive and diagnostic data analytics, and to prepare reports that inform business decisions. A wide range of data visualization software packages is available, including Sisense, Microsoft PowerBI, Tableau, and IBM Watson Analytics, among others. These packages can accommodate structured and unstructured data and are user friendly; and most have a drag-and-drop user interface. A powerful feature of these data visualization tools is the "dashboard" that simultaneously displays a number of charts and graphics to capture key insights in one view.

In each module, we will encounter data visualization of competitor metrics, industry benchmarks, or time trends for critical accounting numbers. End-of-chapter exercises also present data graphically to create experiential learning opportunities. The text's MyBusinessCourse website provides online access to author-created PowerBI dashboards where we can interact with the data and learn how to create data visualizations of our own.

Appendix 1B: Accounting Principles and Governance

Financial Accounting Environment

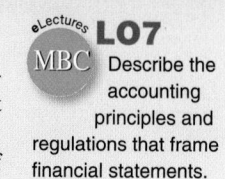

LO7
Describe the accounting principles and regulations that frame financial statements.

Information in financial statements is crucial to valuing a company's debt and equity securities. Financial statement information can affect the price the market is willing to pay for the company's equity securities and interest rates attached to its debt securities.

The importance of financial statements means their reliability is paramount. This includes the crucial role of ethics. To the extent that financial performance and condition are accurately communicated to business decision makers, debt and equity securities are more accurately priced. When securities are mispriced, resources can be inefficiently allocated both within and across economies. Accurate, reliable financial statements are also important for the effective functioning of many other markets, such as labor, input, and output markets.

To illustrate, recall the consequences of a breakdown in the integrity of the financial accounting system at Enron. Once it became clear Enron had not faithfully and accurately reported its financial condition and performance, the market became unwilling to purchase Enron's securities. The value of its debt and equity securities dropped precipitously, and the company was unable to obtain cash needed for operating activities. Within months of the disclosure of its financial accounting irregularities, Enron, with revenues of more than $100 billion and total company value of more than $60 billion, the fifth largest U.S. company, was bankrupt!

Further historical evidence of the importance of financial accounting is provided by the Great Depression of the twentieth century. This depression was caused, in part, by the failure of companies to faithfully report their financial condition and performance.

Oversight of Financial Accounting

The stock market crash of 1929 and the ensuing Great Depression led Congress to pass the 1933 Securities Act. This act had two main objectives: (1) to require disclosure of financial and other information about securities being offered for public sale; and (2) to prohibit deceit, misrepresentations, and other fraud in the sale of securities. This act also required that companies register all securities proposed for public sale and disclose information about the securities being offered, including information about company financial condition and performance. This act became and remains a foundation for contemporary financial reporting.

Congress also passed the 1934 Securities Exchange Act, which created the **Securities and Exchange Commission** (SEC) and gave it broad powers to regulate the issuance and trading of securities. The act also provides that companies with more than $10 million in assets and whose securities are held by more than 500 owners must file annual and other periodic reports, including financial statements that are available for download from the SEC's database (**www.sec.gov**).

The SEC has ultimate authority over U.S. financial reporting, including setting accounting standards for preparing financial statements. Since 1939, however, the SEC has looked primarily to the private sector to set accounting standards. One such private sector organization is the American Institute of Certified Public Accountants (AICPA), whose two committees, the Committee on Accounting Procedure (1939–59) and the Accounting Principles Board (1959–73), authored the initial body of accounting standards.

The **Financial Accounting Standards Board (FASB)** sets U.S. financial accounting standards. The FASB is an independent body overseen by a foundation whose members include public accounting firms, investment managers, academics, and corporate managers. The FASB has published about 200 accounting standards governing the preparation of financial reports. This is in addition to more than 40 standards that were written by predecessor organizations to the FASB, numerous bulletins and interpretations, Emerging Issues Task Force (EITF) statements, AICPA statements of position (SOP), and direct SEC guidance, along with speeches made by high-ranking SEC personnel, all of which form the body of accounting standards governing financial statements. Collectively, these pronouncements, rules, and guidance create what is called **Generally Accepted Accounting Principles (GAAP)**. In 2009, the FASB rolled out the Accounting Standards Codification, to simplify user access to all authoritative U.S. GAAP. The Codification changed the structure of how GAAP are organized, from a standards-based model (with thousands of individual standards) to a topically based model (with roughly 90 topics). The Codification streamlined GAAP research for auditors, analysts, company managers, and students alike.

The standard-setting process is arduous, often lasting a decade and involving extensive comment by the public, public officials, accountants, academics, investors, analysts, and corporate preparers of financial reports. The reason for this involved process is that amendments to existing standards or the creation of new standards affect the reported financial performance and condition of companies. Consequently, given the widespread impact of financial accounting, there are considerable economic consequences as a result of accounting changes. To influence the standard-setting process, special interest groups often lobby members of Congress to pressure the SEC and, ultimately, the FASB, on issues about which constituents feel strongly.

Audits and Corporate Governance

Even though key executives must personally attest to the completeness and accuracy of company financial statements, markets demand further assurances from outside parties to achieve the level of confidence necessary to warrant investment, credit, and other business decisions. To that end, companies engage external auditors to provide an opinion about financial statements. Further, companies implement a system of checks and balances that monitor managers' actions, which is called *corporate governance*.

Audit Report

Financial statements for each publicly traded company must be audited by an independent audit firm. There are a number of large auditing firms that are authorized by the SEC to provide auditing services for companies that issue securities to the public: PwC, EY, KPMG, Deloitte, BDO, and RSM, to name a few. These firms provide opinions about financial statements for the large majority of publicly traded U.S. companies. A company's board of directors hires the auditors to review and express an opinion on its financial statements. The audit opinion expressed by Ernst & Young, LLP, on the financial statements of Apple Inc. is reproduced in Exhibit 1.10.

Exhibit 1.10 ■ Audit Report for Apple Inc.

Report of Independent Registered Public Accounting Firm

To the Shareholders and Board of Directors of Apple Inc.

Opinion on the Financial Statements

We have audited the accompanying consolidated balance sheets of Apple, Inc. as of September 29, 2018 and September 30, 2017, and the related statements of operations, comprehensive income, Shareholders' equity and cash flows for each of the three years in the period ended September 29, 2018, and the related notes (collectively referred to as the "financial statements"). In our opinion, the financial statements present fairly, in all material respects, the financial position of Apple, Inc. at September 29, 2018 and September 30, 2017, and the results of its operations and its cash flows for each of the three years in the period ended September 29, 2018, in conformity with U.S. generally accepted accounting principles.

We also have audited, in accordance with the standards of the Public Company Accounting Oversight Board (United States) (the "PCAOB"), Apple, Inc.'s internal control over financial reporting as of September 29, 2018, based on criteria established in *Internal Control—Integrated Framework* issued by the Commitee of Sponsoring Organizations of the Treadway Commission (2013 framework) and our report dated November 2, 2018 expressed an unqualified opinion thereon.

Basis for Opinion

These financial statements are the responsibility of Apple, Inc.'s management. Our responsibility is to express an opinion on Apple, Inc.'s financial statements based on our audits. We are a public accounting firm registered with the PCAOB and are required to be independent with respect to Apple, Inc. in accordance with the U.S. federal securities laws and the applicable rules and regulations of the U.S. Securities and Exchange Commission and the PCAOB.

We conducted our audits in accordance with the standards of the PCAOB. Those standards require that we plan and perform the audit to obtain reasonable assurance about whether the financial statements are free of material misstatement, whether due to error or fraud. Our audits included performing procedures to assess the risks of material misstatement of the financial statements, whether due to error or fraud, and performing procedures that respond to those risks. Such procedures included examining, on a test basis, evidence regarding the amounts and disclosures in the financial statements. Our audits also included evaluating the accounting principles used and significant estimates made by management, as well as evaluating the overall presentation of the financial statements. We believe that our audits provide a reasonable basis for our opinion.

/s/ Ernst & Young LLP

We have served as Apple, Inc.'s auditor since 2009.

San Jose, California
November 5, 2018

The basic "clean" audit report is consistent across companies and includes these assertions.

- Financial statements are management's responsibility. Auditor responsibility is to express an *opinion* on those statements.

- Auditing involves a sampling of transactions, not investigation of each transaction.

- Audit opinion provides *reasonable assurance* the statements are free of *material* misstatements, not a guarantee.

- Auditors review accounting policies used by management and the estimates used in preparing the statements.

- Financial statements *present fairly, in all material respects* a company's financial condition, in conformity with GAAP.

If the auditor cannot make all of these assertions, the auditor cannot issue a clean opinion. Instead, the auditor issues a "qualified" opinion and states the reasons a clean opinion cannot be issued. Financial report readers should scrutinize with care both the qualified audit opinion and the financial statements themselves.

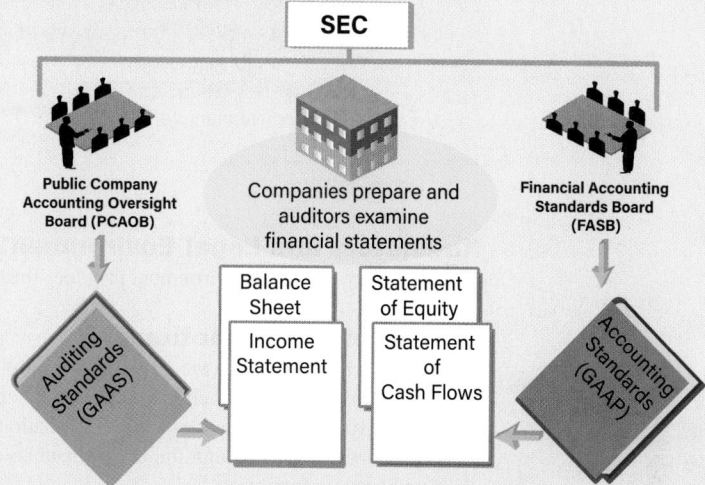

The audit opinion is not based on a test of each transaction. Instead, auditors usually develop statistical samples to make inferences about the larger set of transactions. The audit report is not a guarantee that no misstatements exist. Auditors only provide reasonable assurance that the statements are free of material misstatements. Their use of the word *reasonable* is deliberate, as they do not want to be held to an absolute standard should problems be subsequently uncovered. The word *material* is used in the sense that an item must be of sufficient magnitude to change the perceptions or decisions of the financial statement user (such as a decision to purchase stock or extend credit).

The requirement of auditor independence is the cornerstone of effective auditing and is subject to debate because the company pays the auditor's fees. Regulators have questioned the perceived lack of independence of auditing firms and the degree to which declining independence compromises the ability of auditing firms to challenge a client's dubious accounting.

SOX contains several provisions designed to encourage auditor independence.

1. It established the **Public Company Accounting Oversight Board** (PCAOB) to oversee the development of audit standards and to monitor the effectiveness of auditors.
2. It prohibits auditors from offering certain types of consulting services, and requires audit partners to rotate clients every five years.
3. It requires audit committees to consist of independent members.

Audit Committee

Law requires each publicly traded company to have a board of directors where stockholders elect each director. This board represents the company owners and oversees management. The board also hires the company's executive management and regularly reviews company operations.

The board of directors usually establishes several subcommittees to focus on particular governance tasks, such as compensation, strategic plans, and financial management. Governance committees are commonplace. One of these, the audit committee, oversees the financial accounting system. Exhibit 1.11 illustrates a typical organization of a company's governance structure.

The audit committee must consist solely of outside directors, and cannot include the CEO. As part of its oversight of the financial accounting system, the audit committee focuses on **internal controls**, which are the policies and procedures used to protect assets, ensure reliable accounting, promote efficient operations, and urge adherence to company policies.

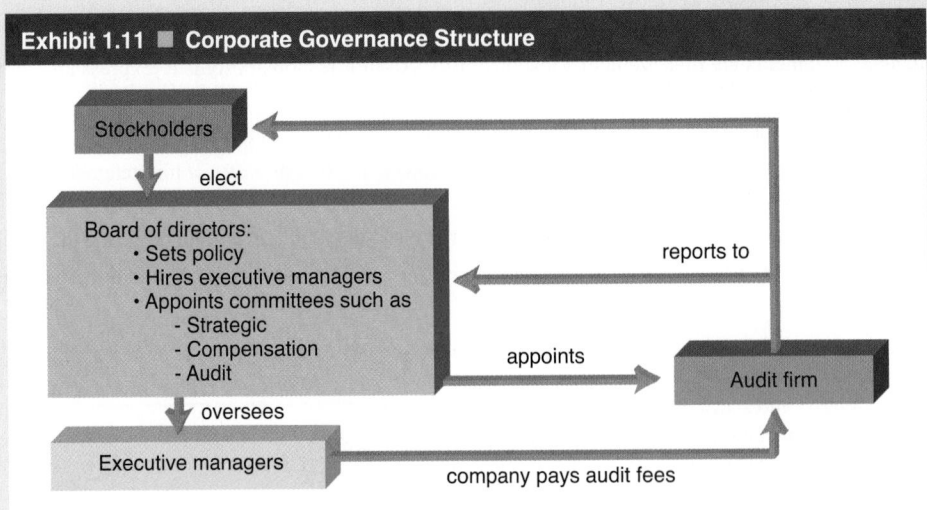

Exhibit 1.11 ■ Corporate Governance Structure

Regulatory and Legal Environment

The regulatory and legal environment provides further assurance financial statements are complete and accurate.

SEC Enforcement Actions

Companies whose securities are issued to the public must file reports with the SEC (see **www.sec.gov**). One of these reports is the 10-K, which includes the annual financial statements (quarterly statements are filed on report 10-Q). The 10-K report provides more information than the company's glossy annual report, which is partly a marketing document (although the basic financial statements are identical). We prefer to use the 10-K because of its additional information.

The SEC critically reviews all the financial reports companies submit. If irregularities are found, the SEC has the authority to bring enforcement actions against companies it believes are misrepresenting their financial condition (remember the phrase in the audit opinion that requires companies to "present fairly, in all material respects, the financial position of . . ."). One such action was brought against Celadon Group Inc. and its executives. Following are excerpts from the SEC's press release 2019-60.

SEC Charges Truckload Freight Company with Accounting Fraud

Washington D.C., April 25, 2019—The Securities and Exchange Commission today charged Indianapolis-based Celadon Group Inc. with an accounting fraud that allowed the truckload freight company to avoid disclosing substantial losses and misrepresent its financial condition.

In a complaint filed in federal court in Indianapolis, the SEC charged that between mid-2016 and April 2017, Celadon avoided recognizing at least $20 million in impairment charges and losses—almost two-thirds of its 2016 pre-tax income—by selling and buying used trucks at inflated prices from third parties. According to the complaint, as a result of the alleged scheme, Celadon overstated its pre-tax and net income and earnings per share in its annual report for the period ending June 30, 2016, and in its subsequent public filings for the first two fiscal quarters of 2017.

"We allege that Celadon knowingly engaged in a multi-faceted scheme to hide at least $20 million in losses from its investors, and lied to its auditors to conceal the scheme," said Joel R. Levin, Director of the SEC's Chicago Regional Office. "We will continue to hold issuers accountable for such serious breaches of trust to the investing public."

The SEC's complaint charges Celadon with fraud and with reporting, books and records, and internal control violations. Celadon admitted to those violations and agreed to a permanent injunction and to remediate the material weaknesses in its internal control over financial reporting. Celadon has also agreed to pay $7 million in disgorgement, which will be deemed satisfied by Celadon's payment of restitution in an action announced today by the Department of Justice. The settlement is subject to court approval.

Courts

Courts provide remedies to individuals and companies that suffer damages as a result of material misstatements in financial statements. Typical court actions involve stockholders who sue the company and its auditors, alleging the company disclosed, and the auditors attested to, false and misleading financial statements. Stockholder lawsuits are chronically in the news, although the number of such suits has declined in recent years. Stanford Law School's Securities Class Action Clearinghouse commented, "Two factors are likely responsible for the decline. First, lawsuits arising from the dramatic boom and bust of U.S. equities in the late 1990s and early 2000s are now largely behind us. Second, improved corporate governance in the wake of the Enron and WorldCom frauds likely reduced the actual incidence of fraud." Nevertheless, courts continue to wield considerable power.

Business Insight ◼ Warren Buffett on Audit Committees

"Audit committees can't audit. Only a company's outside auditor can determine whether the earnings that a management purports to have made are suspect. Reforms that ignore this reality and that instead focus on the structure and charter of the audit committee will accomplish little. As we've discussed, far too many managers have fudged their company's numbers in recent years, using both accounting and operational techniques that are typically legal but that nevertheless materially mislead investors. Frequently, auditors knew about these deceptions. Too often, however, they remained silent. The key job of the audit committee is simply to get the auditors to divulge what they know. To do this job, the committee must make sure that the auditors worry more about misleading its members than about offending management. In recent years auditors have not felt that way. They have instead generally viewed the CEO, rather than the shareholders or directors, as their client. That has been a natural result of day-to-day working relationships and also of the auditors' understanding that, no matter what the book says, the CEO and CFO pay their fees and determine whether they are retained for both auditing and other work. The rules that have been recently instituted won't materially change this reality. What will break this cozy relationship is audit committees unequivocally putting auditors on the spot, making them understand they will become liable for major monetary penalties if they don't come forth with what they know or suspect."

—Warren Buffett, Berkshire Hathaway Annual Report

Business Insights offer examples from the business news and popular press.

Guidance Answers

You Are the Product Manager

Pg. 1-16 As a manager, you must balance two conflicting objectives—namely, mandatory disclosure requirements and your company's need to protect its competitive advantages. You must comply with all minimum required disclosure rules. The extent to which you offer additional disclosures depends on the sensitivity of the information; that is, how beneficial it is to your existing and potential competitors. Another consideration is how the information disclosed will impact your existing and potential investors. Disclosures such as these can be beneficial in that they inform investors and others about your company's successful investments. Still, there are many stakeholders impacted by your disclosure decision, and each must be given due consideration.

You Are the Chief Financial Officer

Pg. 1-21 Financial performance is often measured by ROA, which can be disaggregated into the profit margin (profit after tax/sales) and AT (sales/average assets). This disaggregation might lead you to review factors affecting profitability (gross margins and expense control) and to assess how effectively your company is utilizing its assets (the turnover rates). Finding ways to increase profitability for a given level of investment or to reduce the amount of invested capital while not adversely impacting profitability contributes to improved financial performance.

Superscript $^{A(B)}$ denotes assignments based on Appendix 1A (1B).

Questions

Q1-1. Firms engage in four basic types of activities. List the activities. Describe how financial statements can provide useful information for each activity. How can subsequent financial statements be used to evaluate the success of each of the activities?

Q1-2. The accounting equation (Assets = Liabilities + Equity) is a fundamental business concept. Explain what this equation reveals about a company's sources and uses of funds and the claims on company resources.

Q1-3. Companies prepare four primary financial statements. What are those financial statements, and what information is typically conveyed by each?

Q1-4. Does a balance sheet report on a period of time or at a point in time? Explain the information conveyed in the balance sheet.

Q1-5. Does an income statement report on a period of time or at a point in time? Explain the information conveyed in the income statement.

Q1-6. Does a statement of cash flows report on a period of time or at a point in time? Explain the information and activities conveyed in the statement of cash flows.

Q1-7. Explain how a company's four primary financial statements are linked.

Q1-8. Financial statements are used by several interested stakeholders. List three or more potential external users of financial statements. Explain how each constituent on your list might use financial statement information in their decision-making process.

Q1-9. What ethical issues might managers face in dealing with confidential information?

Q1-10 What are the five important forces that confront the company and determine its competitive intensity?

Q1-11 What are the components of a SWOT analysis? For each component, indicate whether it is an internal or external environmental factor.

Seagate Technology
(STX)

Q1-12.[A] Access the 2018 10-K for Seagate Technology plc at the SEC's database of financial reports (**www.sec.gov**). Who is the company's auditor? What specific language does the auditor use in expressing its opinion, and what responsibilities does it assume?

Q1-13. Business decision makers external to the company increasingly demand more financial information from the company. Discuss the reasons why companies have traditionally opposed the efforts of regulatory agencies like the SEC to require more disclosure.

Q1-14.[B] What are generally accepted accounting principles, and what organizations presently establish them?

Enron

Q1-15.[B] Corporate governance has received considerable attention since the collapse of Enron and other accounting-related scandals. What is meant by corporate governance? What are the primary means by which sound corporate governance is achieved?

Q1-16.[B] What is the primary function of the auditor? In your own words, describe what an audit opinion says.

Q1-17. Describe a decision that requires financial statement information, other than a stock investment decision. How is financial statement information useful in making this decision?

Q1-18. Users of financial statement information are vitally concerned with the company's strategic direction. Despite their understanding of this need for information, companies are reluctant to supply it. Why? In particular, what costs are companies concerned about?

Q1-19. One of Warren Buffett's acquisition criteria is to invest in businesses "earning good return on equity." The ROE formula uses both net income and stockholders' equity. Why is it important to relate net income to stockholders' equity? Why isn't it sufficient to merely concentrate on companies with the highest net income?

Q1-20. One of Warren Buffett's acquisition criteria is to invest in businesses "earning good return on equity while employing little or no debt." Why is Buffett concerned about debt?

Assignments with the ⊚ logo in the margin are available in BusinessCourse.
See the Preface of the book for details.

Mini Exercises

LO1

AT&T (T)

M1-21.   Understanding How the Four Business Activities Are Related
In its November 2018 press release, AT&T revealed that CAPEX for fiscal 2019 (capital expenditures for additional property, plant and equipment) was expected to be in the $23 billion range. How will this planned expenditure affect operating, investing, and financing activities in 2019?

M1-22. Understanding What Information Financial Statement Users Demand

Match each of the financial statement users listed to the question they are most likely to ask.

LO2

Financial Statement User	Questions
_____ A. Current shareholders	1. What is the expected net income for next quarter?
_____ B. Company CEO	2. Will the company have enough cash to pay dividends?
_____ C. Banker	3. Has the company paid for inventory purchases promptly in the past?
_____ D. Equity analyst	4. Will there be sufficient profits and cash flow to pay bonuses?
_____ E. Supplier	5. Will the company have enough cash to repay its loans?

Homework icons indicate which assignments are available in **myBusinessCourse** *(MBC). This feature is only available when the instructor incorporates MBC in the course.*

M1-23. Balance Sheet Equation and Financing Sources

In a recent year, the total assets of Microsoft Corporation equal $258,848 million, and its equity is $82,718 million.

LO3
Microsoft (MSFT)

Required

a. What is the amount of its liabilities?

b. Does Microsoft receive more financing from its owners or nonowners?

c. What percentage of financing is provided by Microsoft's owners?

M1-24. Balance Sheet Equation and Financing Sources

Best Buy's financial statements, dated February 2, 2019, report total assets of $12,901 million and total liabilities of $9,595 million.

LO3
Best Buy (BBY)

Required

a. Why might Best Buy have chosen February 2 as a year-end date? Select all that apply.

1. February is after the holiday season when sales are high. Best Buy wants to include those holiday sales in its results.

2. A non-December year end will help reduce federal income taxes.

3. In early February, inventory will be lower because of the holiday season sales and Best Buy can more easily (and inexpensively) count its inventory.

4. Other retailers pick late January or early February, and so there is an industry standard that Best Buy wants to use.

b. What is the amount of Best Buy's equity at February 2, 2019?

c. Does Best Buy receive more financing from its owners or nonowners?

d. What percentage of financing is provided by Best Buy's nonowners?

LOs link assignments to the Learning Objectives of each module.

M1-25. Applying the Accounting Equation and Computing Financing Proportions

Use the accounting equation to compute the missing financial amounts (a), (b), and (c). Which of these companies is more owner-financed? Which of these companies is more nonowner-financed?

LO3

$ millions	Assets	=	Liabilities	+	Equity
Hewlett-Packard	$106,882	=	$78,731	+	$ (a)
General Mills	$ 21,712	=	$ (b)	+	$ 5,307
Target	$ (c)	=	$27,305	+	$12,957

Hewlett-Packard (HPQ)
General Mills (GIS)
Target (TGT)

M1-26.ᴬ Identifying Key Numbers from Financial Statements

Access the September 30, 2018, 10-K for Starbucks Corporation at the SEC's database for financial reports (www.sec.gov).

LO3, 6
Starbucks (SBUX)

Required

a. Fill in the amounts for Starbucks for fiscal year ended September 30, 2018.

Total assets $_____   Total liabilities $_____   Total equity $_____

b. Confirm that the balance sheet equation holds.

c. What percent of Starbucks' assets is financed by owners?

M1-27.ᴬ Analyzing Retained Earnings

Access the 2018 10-K for Symantec Corp. at the SEC's database of financial reports (www.sec.gov). Use the March 30, 2018, consolidated statement of stockholders' equity to fill in the blanks below to prepare a statement of retained earnings for the year ($ millions).

LO3, 6
Symantec Corp (SYMC)

Symantec Corp. Statement of Retained Earnings For Year Ended March 30, 2018	
Balance, beginning of year..........	$
Net income (loss)...............	
Cash dividends..................	
Balance, end of year.............	$

LO3 **M1-28. Identifying Financial Statement Line Items and Accounts**

Several line items and account titles are listed below. For each, indicate in which of the following financial statement(s) we would likely find the item or account: income statement (IS), balance sheet (BS), statement of stockholders' equity (SE), or statement of cash flows (SCF).

a. Cash asset	d. Contributed capital	g. Cash inflow for stock issued
b. Expenses	e. Cash outflow for capital expenditures	h. Cash outflow for dividends
c. Noncash assets	f. Retained earnings	i. Revenue

LO7 **M1-29. Identifying Ethical Issues and Accounting Choices**

Assume you are a technology services provider and you must decide on whether to record revenue from the installation of computer software for one of your clients. Your contract calls for acceptance of the software by the client within six months of installation. According to the contract, you will be paid only when the client "accepts" the installation. Although you have not yet received your client's formal acceptance, you are confident it is forthcoming. Failure to record these revenues will cause your company to miss Wall Street's earnings estimates. What stakeholders will be affected by your decision, and how might they be affected?

LO5 **M1-30. Assessing the Competitive Environment**

For each of the following companies, briefly explain what type of competitive advantage(s) they have, if any. Select from: barriers to entry, product differentiation, cost leader, or buyer power.

a. Apple	c. Pfizer	e. American Airlines	g. McDonald's
b. Walmart	d. Uber	f. UPS	

LO4, 6 **M1-31.[A] Accessing SEC reports and Calculating Ratios**

Medtronic (MDT)

Boston Scientific (BSX)

Access the financial reports for the fiscal year ending in 2018 at the SEC website for **Medtronic** and **Boston Scientific**, two competitors in the medical device industry.

a. Use data from the companies' balance sheets and income statements to complete the following table.

$ millions	Medtronic	Boston Scientific
Total assets, beginning of fiscal year		
Total assets, end of fiscal year		
Average total assets..................		
Net income (consolidated)		
Revenue...........................		

b. Calculate the following ratios for each company.

$ millions	Medtronic	Boston Scientific
Return on assets (ROA)...............		
Profit margin (PM)		
Asset turnover (AT)..................		

c. Which company has the better ROA?

d. Which of the following is true?

    1. As compared to Boston Scientific, Medtronic has a better profit margin and a weaker asset turnover.

    2. As compared to Boston Scientific, Medtronic has a weaker profit margin and a weaker asset turnover.

3. As compared to Boston Scientific, Medtronic has a better profit margin and a better asset turnover.

4. As compared to Boston Scientific, Medtronic has a weaker profit margin and a better asset turnover.

M1-32. Understanding Internal Controls and Their Importance   **LO7**

SOX legislation requires companies to report on the effectiveness of their internal controls. The SEC administers SOX, and defines internal controls as follows.

Why would Congress believe internal controls are such an important area to monitor and report on?

> A process designed by, or under the supervision of, the registrant's principal executive and principal financial officers . . . to provide reasonable assurance regarding the reliability of financial reporting and the preparation of financial statements for external purposes in accordance with generally accepted accounting principles.

Exercises

E1-33. Composition of Accounts on the Balance Sheet   **LO3**

Answer the following questions about Target.   Target (TGT)

a. Briefly describe the types of assets Target is likely to include in its inventory.

b. What kinds of assets would Target likely include in its property and equipment?

c. Target's balance sheet reports about two-thirds of its total assets as long term. Given Target's business model, why do we see it report a relatively high proportion of long-term assets?

Ticker symbols are provided for companies so one can easily obtain additional information online.

E1-34. Applying the Accounting Equation and Assessing Financial Statement Linkages   **LO3**

The following information is available for Advanced Micro Devices (AMD) and Intel for the current year.

- AMD's assets increased by $1,004 million and its liabilities increased by $334 million.
- Intel's assets increased by $4,714 million and its liabilities decreased by $830 million.

Advanced Micro Devices (AMD) Intel (INTC)

a. Complete the following table.

$ millions	Assets, beginning of year	Assets, end of year	Liabilities, beginning of year	Liabilities, end of year	Stockholders' Equity, end of year
Advanced Micro Devices......	_____	$4,556	$2,956	_____	_____
Intel	$123,249	_____	_____	$53,400	_____

b. Calculate average assets for each company.

$ millions	Average Assets
Advanced Micro Devices..........	_____
Intel	_____

c. Which company has the larger proportion of its assets financed by the company's owners at year-end?

E1-35. Specifying Financial Information Users and Uses   **LO2**

Financial statements have a wide audience of interested stakeholders. Identify two or more financial statement users who are external to the company. For each user on your list, specify two questions that could be addressed with financial statement information.

LO3

Norfolk Southern
(NSC)

MBC

E1-36.   Applying Financial Statement Relations to Compute Dividends

a. Fill in the amounts for the Norfolk Southern statement of changes in retained earnings.

Norfolk Southern Inc.
Consolidated Statements of Changes in Retained Income

Beginning Balance at Dec. 31, 2015	$10,191
Net income	☐
Dividends on Common Stock	(695)
Share repurchases	(731)
Other.	(8)
Ending Balance at Dec. 31, 2016.	10,425
Net income	5,404
Dividends on Common Stock	☐
Share repurchases	(945)
Other.	(5)
Ending Balance at Dec. 31, 2017.	14,176
Net income	2,666
Dividends on Common Stock	(844)
Share repurchases	☐
Other.	81
Ending Balance at Dec. 31, 2018.	$13,440

b. Is it true (or false) that Norfolk Southern purchased its own shares back during each year from 2016 to 2018?

LO4

Norfolk Southern
(NSC)

MBC

E1-37.   Computing and Interpreting Financial Statement Ratios

Following are selected ratios of Norfolk Southern for 2018 and 2017.

Return on Assets (ROA) Component	2018	2017
Profitability (Net income/Sales)	23.3%	51.2%
Productivity (Sales/Average assets).	0.318	0.299

a. Was the company profitable in 2018?

b. Was the company more profitable in 2018 or 2017?

c. Is the change in productivity a **positive** or **negative** development?

d. Compute the company's ROA for 2018 and for 2017.

e. From the information provided, which of the following best explains the change in ROA during 2018?

    1. The company's profitability weakened considerably.

    2. The company's profitability weakened considerably and its productivity fell.

    3. The company had markedly more assets in 2018.

    4. The company had a marked drop in revenue in 2018.

LO4

Nordstrom Inc. (JWN)

MBC

E1-38.   Computing Return on Assets and Applying the Accounting Equation

Nordstrom Inc. reports net income of $564 million for its fiscal year ended February 2019. At the beginning of that fiscal year, Nordstrom had $8,115 million in total assets. By fiscal year ended February 2019, total assets had decreased to $7,886 million. What is Nordstrom's ROA?

LO2

E1-39.   Assessing the Role of Financial Statements in Society

Financial statement information plays an important role in modern society and business.

a. Identify two or more external stakeholders who are interested in a company's financial statements and what their particular interests are.

b. What are *generally accepted accounting principles*? What organizations have primary responsibility for the formulation of GAAP?

c. What role does financial statement information play in the allocation of society's financial resources?

d. What are three aspects of the accounting environment that can create ethical pressure on management?

E1-40. Computing Return on Equity

Starbucks reports net income for 2018 of $4,518.3 million. Its stockholders' equity is $5,450.1 million and $1,169.5 million for 2017 and 2018, respectively.

a. Compute its return on equity for 2018.
b. Starbucks repurchased over $7,208.7 million of its common stock in 2018. Did this repurchase increase or decrease Starbucks' ROE?
c. If Starbucks had not repurchased common stock in 2018, what would ROE have been?

LO4
Starbucks (SBUX)

Problems

P1-41. Computing Return on Equity and Return on Assets

The following table contains financial statement information for Walmart Inc.

LO4
Walmart Inc. (WMT)

$ millions	Total Assets	Net Income	Sales	Equity
2018	$219,295	$ 6,670	$510,329	$72,496
2017	204,522	9,862	495,761	77,869
2016	198,825	13,643	481,317	77,798

Required

a. Compute return on equity (ROE) for the two recent years.
b. Compute return on assets (ROA) for the two recent years.
c. Compute profit margin (PM) for the two recent years.
d. Compute asset turnover (AT) for the two recent years.
e. Which of the following best explains the change in ROA during 2018?
   1. The company's profitability weakened considerably.
   2. The company's asset productivity weakened considerably.
   3. The company had higher sales in 2018.
   4. The company had higher assets 2018.

P1-42. Formulating Financial Statements from Raw Data and Calculating Ratios

Following is selected financial information from General Mills Inc. for its fiscal year ended May 27, 2018 ($ millions).

LO3, 4
General Mills Inc. (GIS)

Cost of goods sold (COGS)	$10,312.9	Cash from operating activities	$ 2,841.0
Cash from investing activities	(8,685.4)	Noncash assets, end of year	30,225.0
Cash, end of year	399.0	Cash from financing activities*	5,477.3
Income tax expense	57.3	Total assets, beginning of year	21,812.6
Revenue	15,740.4	Total liabilities, end of year**	24,131.6
Total expenses, other than COGS and income tax	3,207.2	Stockholders' equity, end of year	6,492.4

* Cash from financing activities includes the effects of foreign exchange rate fluctuations.
** Total liabilities includes redeemable interest.

Required

a. Prepare the income statement for the year ended May 27, 2018.
b. Prepare the balance sheet as of May 27, 2018.
c. Prepare the statement of cash flows for the year ended May 27, 2018.
d. Compute ROA.
e. Compute profit margin (PM).
f. Compute asset turnover (AT).

LO3, 4

Five Below, Inc. (FIVE)

P1-43. **Formulating Financial Statements from Raw Data and Calculating Ratios**

Following is selected financial information from Five Below for its fiscal year ended February 2, 2019 ($ thousands).

Noncash assets, end of year	$ 700,516	Stockholders' equity, end of year	$615,094
Cash from investing activities. . . .	(39,472)	Cash from financing activities.	(5,582)
Cash, end of year.	251,748	Total assets, beginning of year.	695,708
Total liabilities, end of year	337,170	Cost of goods sold (COGS)	994,478
Revenue.	1,559,563	Cash, beginning of year	112,669
Stockholders' equity, beginning		Total expenses, other than COGS	
of year.	458,558	and income tax	373,278
Cash from operating activities . . .	184,133	Income tax expense	42,162

Required

a. Prepare the income statement for the year ended February 2, 2019.

b. Prepare the balance sheet as of February 2, 2019.

c. Prepare the statement of cash flows for the year ended February 2, 2019.

d. Compute ROA.

e. Compute profit margin (PM).

f. Compute asset turnover (AT).

g. Compute ROE.

LO3, 4

JM Smucker Co.
(SJM)

P1-44. **Formulating Financial Statements from Raw Data and Calculating Ratios**

Following is selected financial information from JM Smucker Co. for the year ended April 30, 2018 ($ millions).

Current assets, end of year	$1,555.0	Long-term liabilities, end of year.	$ 6,376.3
Cash, end of year.	192.6	Stockholders' equity, end of year	7,891.1
Cash from investing activities.	(277.6)	Cash from operating activities	1,218.0
Cost of product sold	4,521.0	Total assets, beginning of year.	15,639.7
Total liabilities, end of year	7,410.1	Revenue.	7,357.1
Cash from financing activities*	(914.6)	Total expenses, other than cost of	
Stockholders' equity, beginning of		product sold	1,497.5
year.	6,850.2	Dividends paid	350.3

* Cash from financing activities includes the effects of foreign exchange rate fluctuations.

Required

a. Prepare the income statement for the year ended April 30, 2018.

b. Prepare the balance sheet as of April 30, 2018.

c. Prepare the statement of cash flows for the year ended April 30, 2018.

d. Compute ROA.

e. Compute profit margin (PM).

f. Compute asset turnover (AT).

g. Compute ROE.

LO3

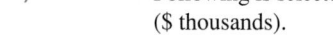

P1-45. **Formulating a Statement of Stockholders' Equity from Raw Data**

Crocker Corporation began calendar-year 2019 with stockholders' equity of $150,000, consisting of contributed capital of $120,000 and retained earnings of $30,000. During 2019, it issued additional stock for total cash proceeds of $30,000. It also reported $50,000 of net income and paid $25,000 as a cash dividend to stockholders.

Required

Prepare the 2019 statement of stockholders' equity for Crocker Corporation.

P1-46. Formulating a Statement of Stockholders' Equity from Raw Data

Winnebago Industries Inc. reports the following selected information for its fiscal year ended August 25, 2018 ($ thousands).

Contributed capital, August 26, 2017	$ 106,289
Treasury stock, August 26, 2017	(342,730)
Retained earnings, August 26, 2017	679,138
Accumulated other comprehensive (loss) income, August 26, 2017	(1,023)

During fiscal year 2018, Winnebago reported the following.

Issuance of stock	$ 5,822	Cash dividends	$12,738
Repurchase of stock for resale	4,644	Other comprehensive income (loss)	1,915
Net income	102,416		

Required

Use this information to prepare the statement of stockholders' equity for Winnebago's fiscal year ended August 25, 2018.

P1-47. Computing, Analyzing, and Interpreting Return on Equity and Return on Assets

Following are summary financial statement data for Logitech International for 2016 through 2018.

$ thousands	2018	2017	2016
Sales	$2,566,863	$2,221,427	$2,018,100
Net income	208,542	205,876	119,317
Total assets	1,743,157	1,498,677	1,324,147
Equity	1,050,557	856,111	759,948

Required

a. Compute the return on assets (ROA) for 2018 and 2017.
b. Compute the profit margin (PM) for 2018 and 2017.
c. Compute the asset turnover (AT) for 2018 and 2017.
d. Which component of ROA (profit margin or asset turnover or both) drives the change in ROA in 2018?
e. Compute the return on equity (ROE) for 2018 and 2017.
f. Logitech repurchased common shares in 2018 at a cost of $30 million. Did this repurchase increase or decrease the company's ROE?

P1-48. Computing, Analyzing, and Interpreting Return on Equity and Return on Assets

Following are summary financial statement data for Nordstrom Inc. for fiscal years ended 2017 through 2019.

$ millions	2019	2018	2017
Sales	$15,860	$15,478	$14,757
Net income	564	437	354
Total assets	7,886	8,115	7,858
Equity	873	977	870

Required

a. Compute the return on assets (ROA) for fiscal years ended 2019 and 2018.
b. Compute the profit margin (PM) or fiscal years ended 2019 and 2018.
c. Compute the asset turnover (AT) or fiscal years ended 2019 and 2018.
d. Which component of ROA (profit margin or asset turnover or both) drives the change in ROA in 2018?
e. Compute the return on equity (ROE) for fiscal years ended 2019 and 2018.
f. Nordstrom has a large negative balance in retained earnings (a retained deficit). How does this affect the company's ROE: does it increase it or decrease it?

LO4

Capri Holdings (CPRI)
Five Below (FIVE)

P1-49.   Comparing Ratios for Luxury and Budget Retailers

Following are selected financial statement data from Capri Holdings (a retailer that owns upscale brands Michael Kors, Jimmy Choo, and Versace) and Five Below (a value-priced toy and novelty retailer).

	Capri Holdings ($ millions)		Five Below ($ thousands)	
	2018	**2017**	**2018**	**2017**
Sales.	$4,718.6	$4,493.7	$1,559,563	$1,278,208
Cost of sales.	1,859.3	1,832.3	994,478	814,795
Net income	592.1	551.5	149,645	102,451
Average equity	1,805	1,794	536,826	394,982

Required

a. Calculate the gross profit for each company for both years. Gross profit is equal to sales minus the cost of sales.

b. Calculate gross profit as a percentage of sales for each company for both years.

c. Compute the return on equity for each company for both years.

d. Which of the following best explains why the ratios for Five Below and Capri Holdings differ.

1. Capri Holdings is much larger than Five Below and so its ratios are naturally larger.

2. Five Below is a younger company and so its ratios are naturally lower.

3. Capri Holdings' brand recognition creates a competitive advantage, which allows the company to add a bigger markup to the products it sells.

4. Five Below imports its products from Southeast Asia, which allows the company to keep product costs down.

LO4

McDonald's (MCD)

P1-50.   Computing and Interpreting Return on Assets and Its Components

McDonald's Corporation (MCD) reported the following balance sheet and income statement data for 2016 through 2018.

$ millions	Total Assets	Net Income	Sales
2018	$32,811.2	$5,924.3	$21,025.2
2017	33,803.7	5,192.3	22,820.4
2016	31,023.9	—	—

Required

a. What is McDonald's return on assets for 2018 and 2017?

b. Determine the profit margin for 2018 and 2017.

c. Calculate the asset turnover for 2018 and 2017.

d. What factor is mainly responsible for the change in McDonald's ROA over this period? Is it profit margin or asset turnover or both?

LO4

3M Company (MMM)

P1-51.   Disaggregating Return on Assets over Multiple Periods

Following are selected financial statement data from 3M Company for 2015 through 2018.

$ millions	Total Assets	Net Income	Sales
2015	$32,883	$4,841	$30,274
2016	32,906	5,058	30,109
2017	37,987	4,869	31,657
2018	36,500	5,363	32,765

Required

a. What was 3M Company's return on assets (ROA) for 2016, 2017, and 2018?

b. Determine profit margin (PM) for each of the three years 2016–2018.

c. Determine asset turnover (AT) for each of the three years 2016–2018.

d. What factor is mainly responsible for the change in 3M's ROA from 2016 to 2017? Is it profit margin or asset turnover or both?

e. What factor is mainly responsible for the change in 3M's ROA from 2017 to 2018? Is it profit margin or asset turnover or both?

P1-52. **Data Visualization for Insights into Financial Statements**

LO3
Thermo Fisher
Scientific (TMO)

The following graphics relate to Thermo Fisher Scientific for 2009 through 2018. Access the dashboard at the text MyBusinessCourse website to answer the requirements.

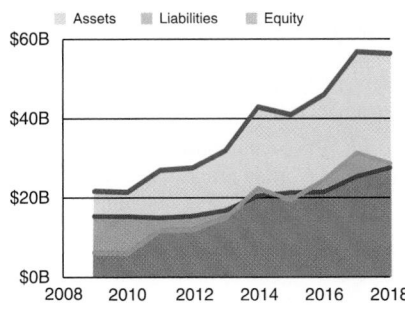 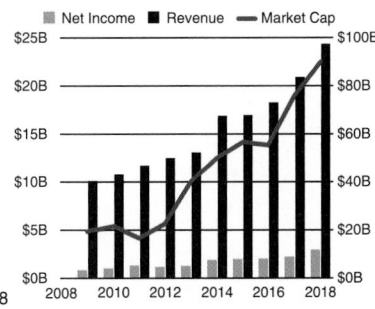 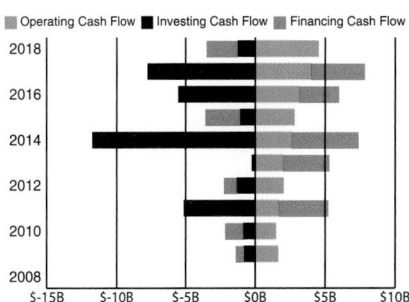

Required

a. The graphic on the left shows balance sheet data.
- i. Which year has the largest assets?
- ii. What general trend do we observe for Thermo Fisher's assets?
- iii. Which tracks more closely with total assets: liabilities or equity?
- iv. Over the 10-year period, how often did liabilities exceed equity?

b. The middle graphic shows income statement data and Thermo Fisher's market capitalization (the value of all the company's stock) each year.
- i. From 2009 to 2017, revenue roughly doubled from $10,110 million to $20,918 million. What was the growth in net income over that period?
- ii. What general pattern do we observe for revenue?
- iii. Which year had the biggest percentage increase in revenue?
- iv. Which year has a better profit margin (PM), 2017 or 2018?
- v. What is the company's market cap in 2018?

c. The graphic on the right shows cash flow data.
- i. Which year has the smallest operating cash flow?
- ii. In how many years were financing cash flows negative?
- iii. In all years but one, cumulative positive cash flows were about equal to cumulative negative cash flows. What year was the exception? Explain what the graphic shows for that year.

d. Use data from the left and middle graphics to calculate return on assets (ROA) and return on equity (ROE) for 2018.

e. Compare the data in all three graphics for 2014. What might explain the relation between the investing cash flow and the increase in revenue and assets for that year?

P1-53.[A] **Reading and Interpreting Audit Opinions**

LO7
Twitter Inc. (TWTR)

Twitter Inc. financial statements include the following audit report from Pricewaterhouse Coopers LLP.

Report of Independent Registered Public Accounting Firm

To the Board of Directors and Stockholders of Twitter, Inc.

Opinions on the Financial Statements and Internal Control over Financial Reporting

We have audited the accompanying consolidated balance sheets of Twitter, Inc. and its subsidiaries (the "Company") as of December 31, 2018 and 2017, and cash flows for each of the three years in the period ended December 31, 2018, including the related notes and financial statement schedule listed in the index appearing under Item 15.2 (collectively referred to as the "consolidated financial statements"). We also have audited the Company's internal control over financial reporting as of December 31, 2018, based on criteria established in Internal Control—Integrated Framework (2013) issued by the Committee of Sponsoring Organizations of the Treadway Commission (COSO).

continued

continued from previous page

In our opinion, the consolidated financial statements referred to above present fairly, in all material respects, the financial position of the Company as of December 31, 2018 and 2017, and the results of its operations and its cash flows for each of the three years in the period ended December 31, 2018, in conformity with accounting principles generally accepted in the United States of America. Also in our opinion, the Company maintained, in all material respects, effective internal control over financial reporting as of December 31, 2018, based on criteria established in Internal Control—Integrated Framework (2013) issued by the COSO.

/s/ Pricewaterhouse Coopers LLP
San Francisco, California
February 20, 2019
We have served as the Company's auditor since 2009.

Required

a. To whom is the audit report addressed?

b. Which of the following accurately describes the audit process or audit report? Select as many as apply.

1. Auditors express an opinion as to whether Twitter's financial statements present a fair picture and are free from material misstatement.
2. Auditors express an opinion that there was not fraudulent activity at Twitter.
3. Auditors' opinion is that there are no misstatements in the related notes to Twitter's financial statements.
4. Auditors separately audited Twitter's internal controls over the financial reporting process.
5. Auditors examined most of Twitter's financial transactions to ensure they were accurate and not misstated.

c. What sort of opinion, *qualified* or *unqualified*, did PricewaterhouseCoopers provide?

d. PricewaterhouseCoopers provides two types of opinions in their report above. Which of the following accurately describes the scope of the two opinions?

1. Financial statements and related footnotes.
2. Material and nonmaterial respects.
3. Financial statements and internal controls over financial reporting.
4. Financial and nonfinancial information.
5. Generally Accepted Accounting Principles (GAAP) and Committee of Sponsoring Organizations of the Treadway Commission (COSO).

LO7

Twitter, Inc. (TWTR)

P1-54.   Reading and Interpreting CEO Certifications

Following is the CEO certification required by the Sarbanes-Oxley Act and signed by Twitter CEO Jack Dorsey. Twitter's Chief Financial Officer signed a similar form.

CERTIFICATIONS

I, Jack Dorsey, certify that:

1. I have reviewed this Annual Report on Form 10-K of Twitter, Inc.

2. Based on my knowledge, this report does not contain any untrue statement of a material fact or omit to state a material fact necessary to make the statements made, in light of the circumstances under which such statements were made, not misleading with respect to the period covered by this report;

3. Based on my knowledge, the financial statements, and other financial information included in this report, fairly present in all material respects the financial condition, results of operations and cash flows of the registrant as of, and for, the periods presented in this report;

4. The registrant's other certifying officer and I are responsible for establishing and maintaining disclosure controls and procedures (as defined in Exchange Act Rules 13–15(e) and 15d–15(e)) and internal control over financial reporting (as defined in Exchange Act Rules 13a–15(f) and 15d–15(f)) for the registrant and have:

    (a) Designed such disclosure controls and procedures, or caused such disclosure controls and procedures to be designed under our supervision, to ensure that material information relating to the registrant, including its consolidated subsidiaries, is made known to us by others within those entities, particularly during the period in which this report is being prepared;

continued

continued from previous page

(b) Designed such internal control over financial reporting, or caused such internal control over financial reporting to be designed under our supervision, to provide reasonable assurance regarding the reliability of financial reporting and the preparation of financial statements for external purposes in accordance with generally accepted accounting principles;

(c) Evaluated the effectiveness of the registrant's disclosure controls and procedures and presented in this report our conclusions about the effectiveness of the disclosure controls and procedures, as of the end of the period covered by this report based on such evaluation; and

(d) Disclosed in this report any change in the registrant's internal control over financial reporting that occurred during the registrant's most recent fiscal quarter (the registrant's fourth fiscal quarter in the case of an annual report) that has materially affected, or is reasonably likely to materially affect, the registrant's internal control over financial reporting; and;

5. The registrant's other certifying officer and I have disclosed, based on our most recent evaluation of internal control over financial reporting, to the registrant's auditors and the audit committee of the registrant's board of directors (or persons performing the equivalent functions):

(a) All significant deficiencies and material weaknesses in the design or operation of internal control over financial reporting which are reasonably likely to adversely affect the registrant's ability to record, process, summarize and report financial information; and

(b) Any fraud, whether or not material, that involves management or other employees who have a significant role in the registrant's internal control over financial reporting.

Date: February 20, 2019

/s/ Jack Dorsey

Jack Dorsey
Chief Executive Officer

Required

a. Summarize the assertions that Jack Dorsey made in this certification.
b. Why did Congress feel it important that CEOs and CFOs sign such certifications?
c. What potential liability do you believe the CEO and CFO are assuming by signing such certifications?

P1-55. **Assessing Corporate Governance and Its Effects**

LO7
General Electric (GE)

Review the corporate governance section of **General Electric**'s website (**http://www.ge.com**). Find and click on "investor relations"; then, find and click on "governance," and open the "Governance Principles" PDF.

Required

a. Briefly describe General Electric's governance structure.
b. What is the main purpose of its governance structure?

IFRS Applications

I1-56. **Applying the Accounting Equation and Computing Financing Proportions**

LO3
OMV Group
Ericsson
BAE Systems

Following is fiscal 2018 information for three companies that report under IFRS.

Required

a. Apply the accounting equation to compute the missing financial amounts (a), (b), and (c).
b. Which of the companies has the highest proportion of financing from owners?
c. Which of the companies has the highest proportion of financing from nonowners?

In millions	Assets	=	Liabilities	+	Equity
OMV Group (Austria)....	€ 36,961		€21,619		(a)
Ericsson (Sweden)	SEK 268,761		(b)		SEK 87,770
BAE Systems (UK)	(c)		£24,746		£5,618

I1-57. **Computing Return on Equity and Return on Assets**

The following table contains financial statement information for OMV Group, which is a petrochemical company headquartered in Vienna.

euros millions	2018	2017	2016	2015
Sales.	€22,930	€20,222	€19,260	—
Net profit (Loss)	3,298	1,486	(230)	—
Assets.	36,961	31,576	32,112	€32,664
Equity	15,342	14,334	13,925	14,298

Required

a. What was OMV Group's return on assets (ROA) for 2016, 2017, and 2018?

b. Determine its profit margin (PM) for each of the three years 2016–2018.

c. Determine its asset turnover (AT) for each of the three years 2016–2018.

d. What factor is mainly responsible for the change in OMV's ROA from 2016 to 2017? Is it profit margin or asset turnover or both?

e. What factor is mainly responsible for the change in OMV's ROA from 2017 to 2018? Is it profit margin or asset turnover or both?

f. Determine OMV Group's return on equity (ROE) for each of the three years 2016–2018.

Management Applications

LO1, 3   **MA1-58.** **Strategic Financing**

You and your management team are working to develop the strategic direction of your company for the next three years. One issue you are discussing is how to finance the projected increases in operating assets. Your options are to rely more heavily on operating creditors, borrow the funds, or to sell additional stock in your company. Discuss the pros and cons of each source of financing.

LO3, 4   **MA1-59.** **Statement Analysis**

You are evaluating your company's recent operating performance and are trying to decide on the relative weights you should put on the income statement, the balance sheet, and the statement of cash flows. Discuss the information each of these statements provides and its role in evaluating operating performance.

LO2   **MA1-60.** **Analyst Relations**

Your investor relations department reports to you that stockholders and financial analysts evaluate the quality of a company's financial reports based on their "transparency," namely, the clarity and completeness of the company's financial disclosures. Discuss the trade-offs of providing more or less transparent financial reports.

LO7   **MA1-61.** **Ethics and Governance: Management Communications**

Many companies publicly describe their performance using terms such as *EBITDA* or *earnings purged of various expenses* because they believe these terms more effectively reflect their companies' performance than GAAP-defined terms such as *net income*. What ethical issues might arise from the use of such terms, and what challenges does their use present for the governance of a company by stockholders and directors?

LO7   **MA1-62.** **Ethics and Governance: Auditor Independence**

The SEC has been concerned with the "independence" of external auditing firms. It is especially concerned about how large nonaudit (such as consulting) fees might impact how aggressively auditing firms pursue accounting issues they uncover in their audits. Congress passed legislation that prohibits accounting firms from providing both consulting and auditing services to the same client. How might consulting fees affect auditor independence? What other conflicts of interest might exist for auditors? How do these conflicts impact the governance process?

Ongoing Project

An important part of learning is application. To learn accounting, we must practice the skills taught and apply those skills to real-world problems. To that end, we have designed a project to reinforce the lessons in each module and apply them to real companies. The goal of this project is to complete a comprehensive analysis of two (or more) companies in the same industry. We will then create a set of forecasted financial statements and a valuation of the companies' equity. This is essentially what financial analysts and many creditors do. We might not aspire to be an analyst or creditor, but by completing a project of this magnitude, we will have mastered financial reporting at a sufficient level to be able to step into any role in an organization. The goal of Module 1's assignment is to obtain and begin to explore the financial reports for two publicly traded companies that compete with each other.

- Select two publicly traded companies that compete with each other. They must be publicly traded, as private company financial statements will not be publicly available. While the two companies do not need to be head-to-head competitors, their main lines of business should broadly overlap.

- Download the annual reports for each company and peruse them. At this stage, choose companies that are profitable (net income is positive) and that have positive retained earnings and stockholders' equity. Select companies whose financial statements are not overly complicated. (Probably avoid the automotive, banking, insurance, and financial services industries. Automotive companies have large financial services subsidiaries that act like banks for customers, which complicates the analysis. Banking, insurance, and financial services have operations that differ drastically from the usual industrial companies common in practice. While these companies can be analyzed, they present challenges for the beginning analyst.)

- Use the SEC EDGAR website to locate the recent Form 10-K (or other annual report such as 20-F or 40-F) (**www.sec.gov**). Download a spreadsheet version of financial statements. Use Appendix 1A as a guide.

- Use the annual report and the financial statements, along with any websites, to assess the companies' business environment. Use Porter's five forces or a SWOT analysis to briefly analyze the competitive landscape for the two companies. The aim is to understand the competitive position of each company so we can assess their financial statements in a broader business context.

- Explore the financial statements, and familiarize yourself with the company basics. The following give an indication of some questions that guide us as we look for answers.

  ❏ What accounting standards are used, U.S. GAAP, IFRS, or other?

  ❏ What is the date of the most recent fiscal year-end?

  ❏ Determine the relative proportion of short- and long-term assets.

  ❏ Determine the relative proportion of liabilities and equity.

  ❏ Calculate the return on assets (ROA) for the most recent year.

  ❏ Disaggregate ROA into the two component parts as shown in Exhibit 1.7. Compare the numbers/ratios for each company.

  ❏ Find the companies' audit reports. Who are the auditors? Are any concerns raised in the reports?

  ❏ Do the audit reports differ significantly from the one for Under Armour in this module?

Solutions to Review Problems

Review 1-1—Solution

1. Companies engage in the following three types of ongoing business activities: <u>operating</u> activities, <u>investing</u> activities, and <u>financing</u> activities.
2. A company's <u>strategic plan</u> reflects how it plans to achieve its goals and objectives.
3. Investors use financial statement information to make reasonable estimates of the value of the <u>company's stock</u>.
4. Lenders use financial statement information to assess the company's ability to <u>repay its debt</u>.
5. Company managers use financial statements to decide where to invest <u>scarce</u> resources.

6.
• Manufacturing products	OPERATING		• Constructing new manufacturing facilities	INVESTING
• Issuing stock to investors	FINANCING		• Hiring and training employees	OPERATING
• Repaying a mortgage	FINANCING		• Gaining control of the voting stock of a	
• Selling services to a client	OPERATING		supplier to secure the supply chain	INVESTING
• Acquiring land	INVESTING		• Entering into a bank loan	FINANCING
• Engaging in after-sales support	OPERATING			

Review 1-2—Solution

 I. b
 II. e
 III. f
 IV. a
 V. d
 VI. c

Review 1-3—Solution

1.

SAMSUNG ELECTRONICS Balance Sheet (billions Korean won) December 31, 2018			
Short-term assets.....	₩174,697	Short-term liabilities..........	₩ 69,082
Long-term assets.....	164,660	Long-term liabilities...........	22,523
		Stockholders' equity..........	247,752
Total assets.........	₩339,357	Total liabilities and equity......	₩339,357

SAMSUNG ELECTRONICS Income Statement (billions Korean won) For the Year Ended December 31, 2018	
Revenues......................................	₩243,771
Cost of goods sold..........................	132,394
Gross profit.................................	111,377
SG&A expenses..............................	52,490
Income from operations......................	58,887
Interest income, net.........................	2,273
Income before taxes.........................	61,160
Provision for income taxes..................	16,815
Net income..................................	₩ 44,345

SAMSUNG ELECTRONICS Statement of Cash Flows (billions Korean won) For the Year Ended December 31, 2018	
Cash flows from operations...................	₩67,032
Cash flows from investing....................	(52,240)
Cash flows from financing...................	(14,996)
Net increase (decrease) in cash..............	(204)
Cash, beginning year........................	30,545
Cash, ending year...........................	₩30,341

2. Both companies are very profitable. Samsung reports net income that is 18% of revenue while Apple's is 22%. Samsung's balance sheet reports about half of its assets as current, while Apple's balance shows a smaller proportion (about one-third). Samsung relies less on borrowed money; its stockholders' equity comprises 73% of total assets for Samsung compared to 29% for Apple. These are both financially strong companies and formidable competitors.

Review 1-4—Solution

a.

$ millions	
Net sales.	$265,595
Net income	59,531
Average assets.	370,522
ROA = Net income / Average assets = $59,531 / $370,522	16.1%
Asset turnover (AT) = Net sales / Average assets = $265,595 / $370,522 . . .	0.72
Profit margin (PM) = Net income / Net sales = $59,531 / $265,595	22.4%

b. ROE = Net income/Average stockholders' equity = $59,531/$120,597 = 49.4%.

Review 1-5—Solution

1. *a.* II
   b. I
   c. III
   d. I
   e. II
   f. III

2. Both of these companies are strong, but Apple's ROA is higher than Samsung's. While asset turnover rates are comparable, Apple's profitability is higher.

$ millions	Apple	Samsung
Average assets.	$370,522	₩320,555
Revenue	265,595	243,771
Net income	59,531	44,345
ROA = Net income / Average assets	16.1%	13.8%
Asset turnover (AT) = Revenue / Average assets.	0.72	0.76
Profit margin (PM) = Net income / Revenue.	22.4%	18.2%

Module 2

Introducing Financial Statements

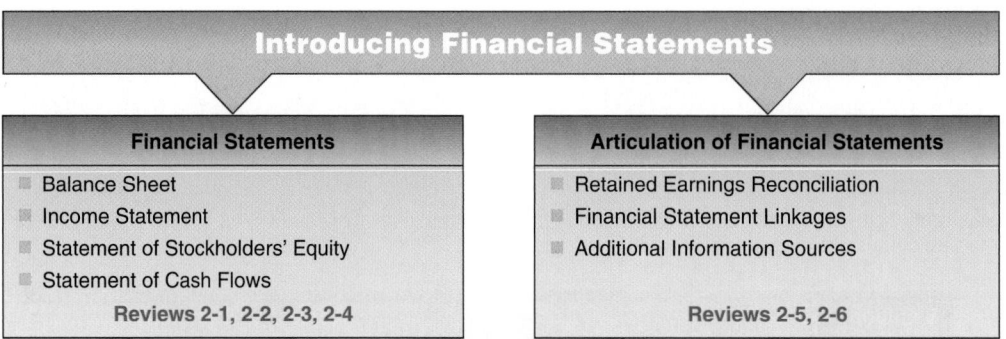

Introducing Financial Statements

Financial Statements	Articulation of Financial Statements
▪ Balance Sheet	▪ Retained Earnings Reconciliation
▪ Income Statement	▪ Financial Statement Linkages
▪ Statement of Stockholders' Equity	▪ Additional Information Sources
▪ Statement of Cash Flows	
Reviews 2-1, 2-2, 2-3, 2-4	Reviews 2-5, 2-6

We examine, in detail, the

- ○ balance sheet
- ○ income statement
- ○ statement of stockholders' equity
- ○ statement of cash flows

We explain how financial statements are linked over time.

We use **Apple Inc.** as the focus company for this module. The following dashboard conveys key information from its balance sheet, income statement, and statement of cash flows.

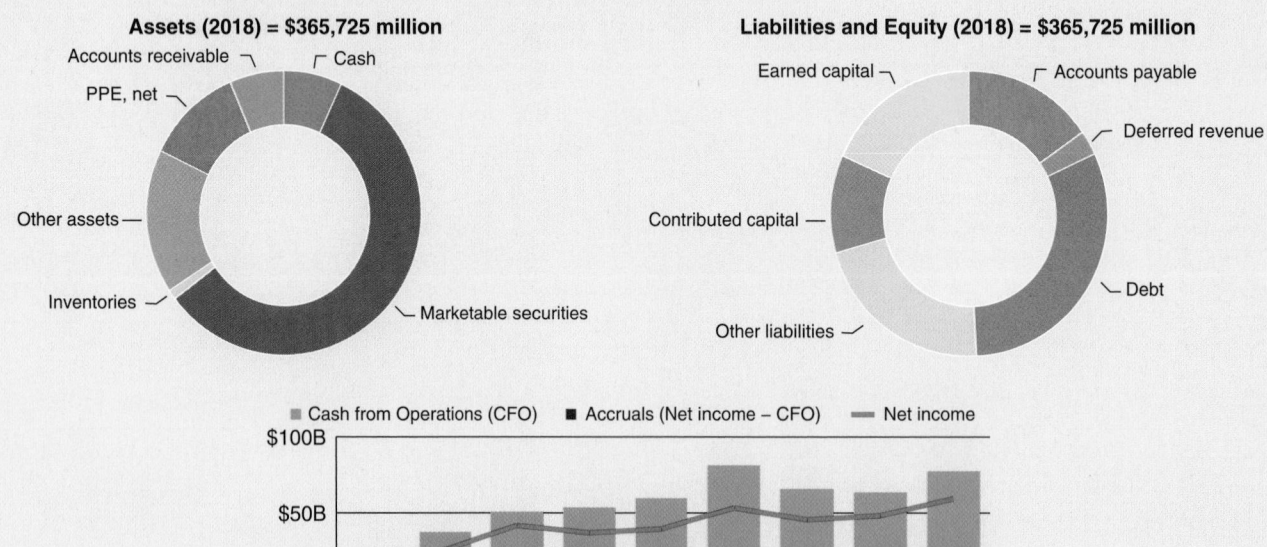

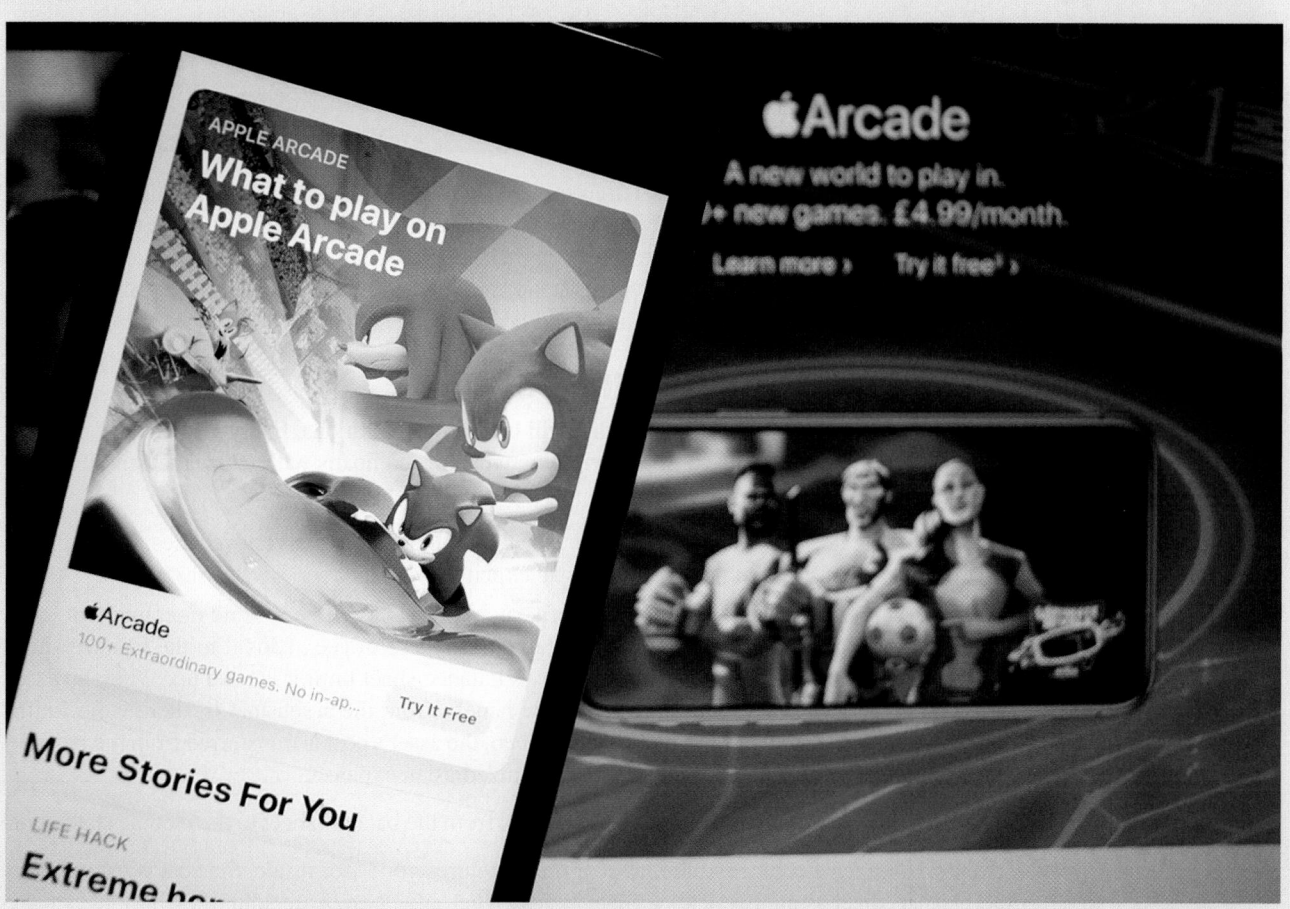

Road Map

LO	Learning Objective | Topics	Page	eLecture	Guided Example	Assignments
2-1	**Examine and interpret a balance sheet.** Cost Flows :: Assets :: Liabilities :: Equity	2-3	e2–1	Review 2-1	1, 2, 8, 9, 10, 11, 12, 13, 14, 15, 16, 17, 19, 20, 22, 26, 27, 28, 29, 30, 31, 32, 33, 34, 35, 36, 37, 38, 39, 41, 44, 45
2-2	**Examine and interpret an income statement.** Statement Format :: Revenue and Expense Recognition :: Analysis	2-13	e2–2	Review 2-2	3, 4, 8, 19, 20, 27, 28, 29, 30, 31, 32, 33, 34, 35, 36, 37, 39, 41, 42, 44, 46
2-3	**Examine and interpret a statement of stockholders' equity.** Statement Format :: Interpretation	2-17	e2–3	Review 2-3	5, 23, 24, 29, 30, 37
2-4	**Describe a statement of cash flows.** Statement Format :: Operating :: Investing :: Financing	2-18	e2–4	Review 2-4	6, 29, 30, 37, 42, 45
2-5	**Construct and apply linkages among the four financial statements.** Retained Earnings :: Linkages :: Articulation	2-20	e2–5	Review 2-5	7, 18, 29, 30, 37, 39
2-6	**Locate and use additional financial information from public sources.** Forms 10-K, 20-F, 40-F and 8-K :: Analyst Reports :: Credit and Data Services	2-22	e2–6	Review 2-6	21, 25, 26, 39, 40, 43

Balance Sheet

LO1
Examine and interpret a balance sheet.

The balance sheet is divided into three sections: assets, liabilities, and stockholders' equity. It provides information about the resources available to management and the claims against those resources by creditors and stockholders. The balance sheet reports the assets, liabilities, and equity at a *point* in time. Balance sheet accounts are called "permanent accounts" in that they carry over from period to period; that is, the ending balance from one period becomes the beginning balance for the next.

Balance Sheet and the Flow of Costs

Companies incur costs to acquire resources that will be used in operations. Every cost creates either an immediate or a future economic benefit. Determining when the company will realize the benefit from a cost is important.

- When a cost creates an *immediate* benefit, such as gasoline used in delivery vehicles, the company records the cost in the income statement as an expense.

- When a cost creates a *future* economic benefit, such as inventory to be resold or equipment to be later used for manufacturing, the company capitalizes the cost (i.e., adds it to the balance sheet as an asset). An asset remains on the company's balance sheet until it is used up. When an asset is used up, the company realizes the economic benefit from the asset; that is, there is no future economic benefit left, so there is no asset left. Then, the asset's cost is transferred from the balance sheet to the income statement, where it is recognized as an expense.

Two examples illustrate how asset costs are transferred from the balance sheet to the income statement.

- Inventory—when a company purchases or manufactures goods for resale, the cost is recorded on the balance sheet as an asset called *inventories*. When inventories are sold, they no longer have an economic benefit to the company, and their cost is transferred to the income statement in an expense called *cost of goods sold*.

- Equipment—when a company acquires equipment, the cost is recorded on the balance sheet in an asset called *equipment* (often included in the general category of property, plant, and equipment, or PPE). As the equipment is used in operations, a portion of the acquisition cost is transferred to the income statement as an expense. To illustrate, if an asset costs $100,000, and 10% is used up during the period in operating activities, then 10% of the asset's cost ($10,000) is transferred from the balance sheet to the income statement. This systematic allocation process is called *depreciation*.

Sometimes, however, companies immediately expense costs that are expected to provide future benefits because their future economic benefits cannot be reliably measured. Advertising and salary costs are examples. We expect, for example, that advertising will produce future benefits in the form of increased sales, but we cannot reliably measure those uncertain benefits. For that reason, we do not recognize an advertising asset; we expense that cost immediately. We immediately expense salaries for the same reason.

The point is that all costs are eventually recognized in the income statement as an expense. Those that create an immediate benefit are recognized as an expense immediately, and those that create a future benefit are added to the balance sheet as an asset (capitalized) and recognized as an expense in the future as the benefit is realized.

Exhibit 2.1 illustrates how costs flow from the balance sheet to the income statement.

Exhibit 2.1 ■ Flow of Costs

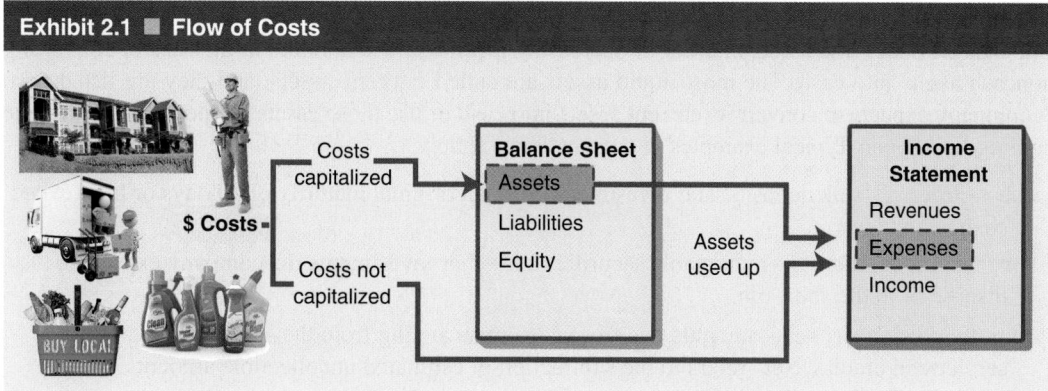

Assets

Companies acquire assets to yield a return for their shareholders. Assets are expected to produce economic benefits in the form of revenues, either directly, such as with inventory, or indirectly, such as with a manufacturing plant that produces inventories for sale. To create stockholder value, assets must yield income that is in excess of the cost of the funds used to acquire the assets.

The asset section of the **Apple** balance sheet is shown in Exhibit 2.2. Apple reports $365,725 million in total assets as of September 29, 2018, its year-end. Amounts reported on the balance sheet are at a *point in time*—that is, the close of business on the day of the report. An asset must possess two characteristics to be reported on the balance sheet.

1. It must be owned (or controlled) by the company.

2. It must confer expected future economic benefits that result from a past transaction or event.

The first requirement, owning or controlling an asset, implies that a company has legal title to the asset, such as the title to property, or has the unrestricted right to use the asset, such as a lease on the property. The second requirement implies that a company expects to realize a benefit from the asset. Benefits can be cash inflows from the sale of an asset or from sales of products produced by the asset. Benefits also can refer to the receipt of other assets, such as an account receivable from a credit sale; or benefits can arise from future services the company will receive, such as prepaying for a year-long insurance policy.

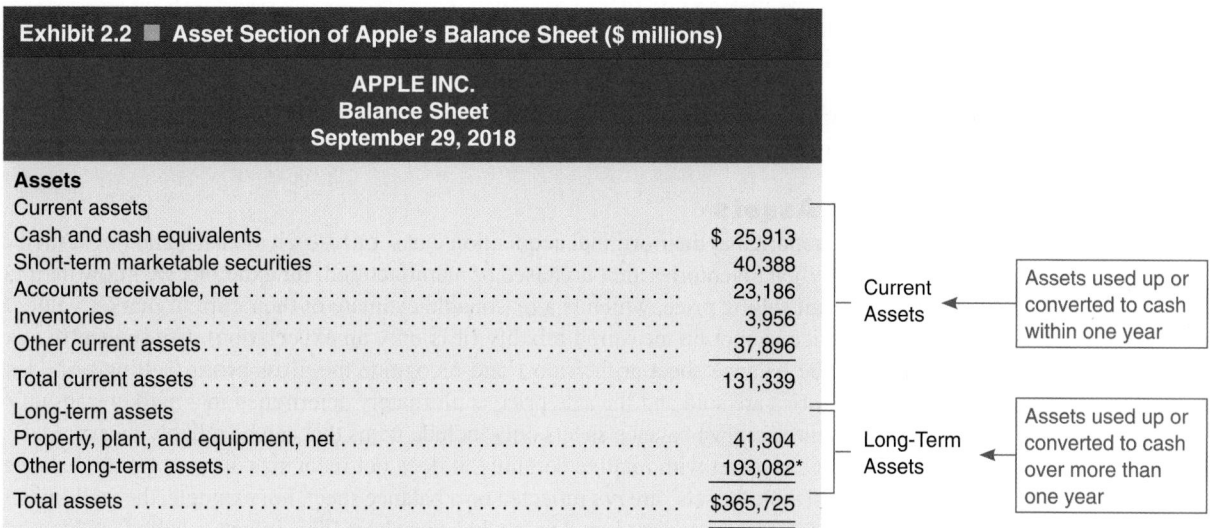

Exhibit 2.2 ■ Asset Section of Apple's Balance Sheet ($ millions)

APPLE INC.
Balance Sheet
September 29, 2018

Assets		
Current assets		
Cash and cash equivalents	$ 25,913	
Short-term marketable securities	40,388	
Accounts receivable, net	23,186	Current Assets — Assets used up or converted to cash within one year
Inventories	3,956	
Other current assets	37,896	
Total current assets	131,339	
Long-term assets		
Property, plant, and equipment, net	41,304	Long-Term Assets — Assets used up or converted to cash over more than one year
Other long-term assets	193,082*	
Total assets	$365,725	

*Includes $170,799 million of long-term marketable securities

Current Assets

The balance sheet lists assets in order of decreasing **liquidity**, which refers to the ease of converting noncash assets into cash. The most liquid assets are called **current assets**, and they are listed first. A company expects to convert its current assets into cash or use those assets in operations within the coming fiscal year. Typical examples of current assets follow.

Cash—currency, bank deposits, and investments with an original maturity of 90 days or less (called *cash equivalents*).

Short-term investments—marketable securities and other investments the company expects to dispose of in the short run.

Accounts receivable, net—amounts due from customers arising from the sale of products and services on credit. "Net" refers to the subtraction of estimated uncollectible amounts. Also called Trade receivables.

Inventories—goods purchased or produced for sale to customers.

Prepaid expenses—costs paid in advance for rent, insurance, advertising, and other services.

Apple reports current assets of $131,339 million in 2018, which is 36% of its total assets. The amount of current assets is an important measure of liquidity, which relates to a company's ability to make short-term payments. Companies require a degree of liquidity to operate effectively, as they must be able to respond to changing market conditions and take advantage of opportunities. However, current assets such as receivables and inventories are expensive to hold (they must be stored, insured, monitored, financed, and so forth)—and they typically generate relatively low returns. As a result, companies seek to maintain only just enough current assets to cover liquidity needs, but not so much to unnecessarily reduce income.

Long-Term Assets

The second section of the balance sheet reports long-term (noncurrent) assets. Long-term assets include the following.

Property, plant, and equipment (PPE), net—land, factory buildings, warehouses, office buildings, machinery, motor vehicles, office equipment, and other items used in operating activities ("net" refers to the subtraction of accumulated depreciation, the portion of the assets' cost that has been expensed).

Long-term investments—investments the company does not intend to sell in the next fiscal year.

Intangible and other assets—assets without physical substance, including patents, trademarks, franchise rights, goodwill, and other costs the company incurred that provide future benefits.

Long-term assets are expected to generate economic benefits over a longer period of time and are, therefore, listed after current assets.

Measuring Assets

Most assets are reported at their original acquisition costs, or **historical costs**, and not at their current market values. When inventories are purchased or manufactured, for example, we know their cost and the expected retail selling price, which is a reasonable estimate of their current market value. But the actual selling price cannot be measured reliably (it is only an expectation). Consequently, we report inventories on the balance sheet at their cost and recognize the gross profit (selling price less cost) when the inventories are sold and the sale price is ultimately determined in a market transaction.[1]

It is important to realize balance sheets only include items that can be reliably measured. If a company cannot value an asset with relative certainty, it does not recognize an asset on the balance sheet. This means that sizable "assets" are *not* reflected on a balance sheet. For example, the well-known apple image is not among the assets listed on Apple's balance sheet. This image is called an "unrecognized

---

[1] However, one class of assets, marketable securities, is reported on the balance sheet at fair (market) value if the securities are frequently traded in organized markets with sufficient liquidity. Under those conditions, the fair value can be reliably measured. We discuss accounting for marketable securities in a later module.

intangible asset." While Apple owns the image and expects to realize future benefits from it, its value is not reliably measured. Other intangible assets missing from companies' balance sheets include the Coke bottle silhouette, the iPhone brand name, and the Nike swoosh. Companies only report intangible assets on the balance sheet when the assets are *purchased*. Any *internally created* intangible assets are not reported on a balance sheet.

Excluded intangible assets often relate to *knowledge-based* (intellectual) assets, such as a strong management team, a well-designed supply chain, or superior technology. Although these intangible assets confer a competitive advantage to the company and yield above-normal income (and clear economic benefits to those companies), they cannot be reliably measured. This is one reason why companies in knowledge-based industries are so difficult to analyze and value.

Presumably, however, companies' market values reflect these excluded intangible assets. This can yield a large difference between the market value of a company and the reported amount (book value) of stockholders' equity. This is illustrated in the following graph of Apple's market value per share (stock price) to book value per share from 2006 through 2019. Each year, market value is greater than book value but the difference between the two measures has widened over time. To put this into context, the ratio of Apple's market value to book value at fiscal 2019 year-end is 10.0 (computed as $225.74/$22.53) compared to a ratio of 3.3 for Target (computed as $71.17/$21.82 million).

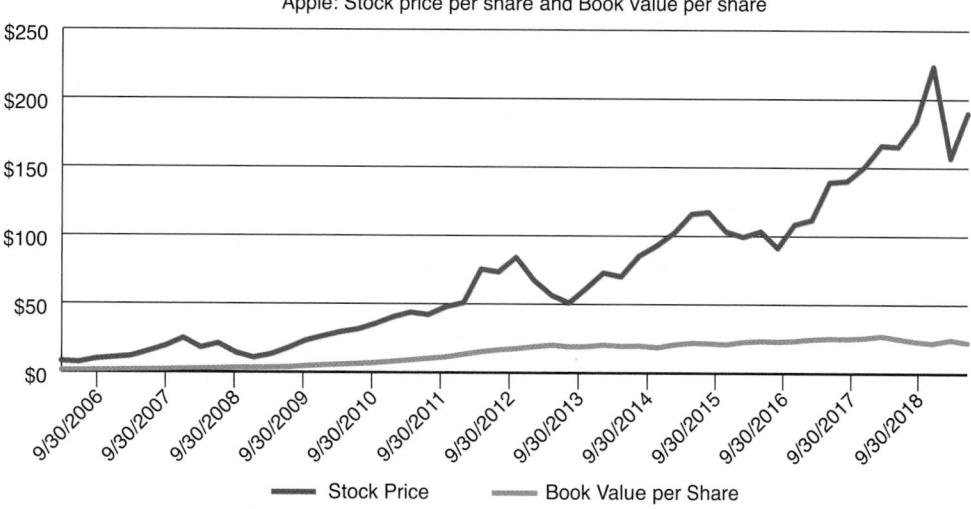

These market-to-book values (ratios) are greater for companies with large knowledge-based assets that are not reported on the balance sheet but are reflected in company market value (such as with Apple). Companies such as Target have fewer of these assets. Hence, their balance sheets usually reflect a greater portion of company value.

Liabilities and Equity

Liabilities and stockholders' equity (also called shareholders' equity) represent the sources of capital the company uses to finance the acquisition of assets.

- Liabilities represent a company's future economic sacrifices. Liabilities are borrowed funds, such as accounts payable and obligations to lenders. They can be interest-bearing or non-interest-bearing.

- Stockholders' equity represents capital that has been invested by the stockholders, either directly via the purchase of stock, or indirectly in the form of *retained earnings* that reflect profits that are reinvested in the business and not paid out as dividends.

The liabilities and stockholders' equity sections of the Apple balance sheet are reproduced in Exhibit 2.3. Apple reports $258,578 million of total liabilities and $107,147 million of stockholders' equity as of its 2018 year-end.

Why would Apple obtain capital from both borrowed funds and stockholders? Why not just one or the other? The answer lies in their relative costs and the contractual agreements Apple has with each.

Creditors have the first claim on the assets of the company. As a result, their position is not as risky and, accordingly, their expected return on investment is less than that required by stockholders. Also, interest is tax deductible, whereas dividends are not. This makes debt a less expensive source of capital than equity. So, then, why should a company not finance itself entirely with borrowed funds? The reason is that companies must repay the principal and interest on the debt. If a company cannot make these payments when they come due, creditors can force the company into bankruptcy and potentially put the company out of business. Stockholders, in contrast, cannot require a company to repurchase its stock or even to pay dividends. Thus, companies take on a level of debt they can comfortably repay at reasonable interest costs. The remaining balance required to fund business activities is financed with more costly equity capital.

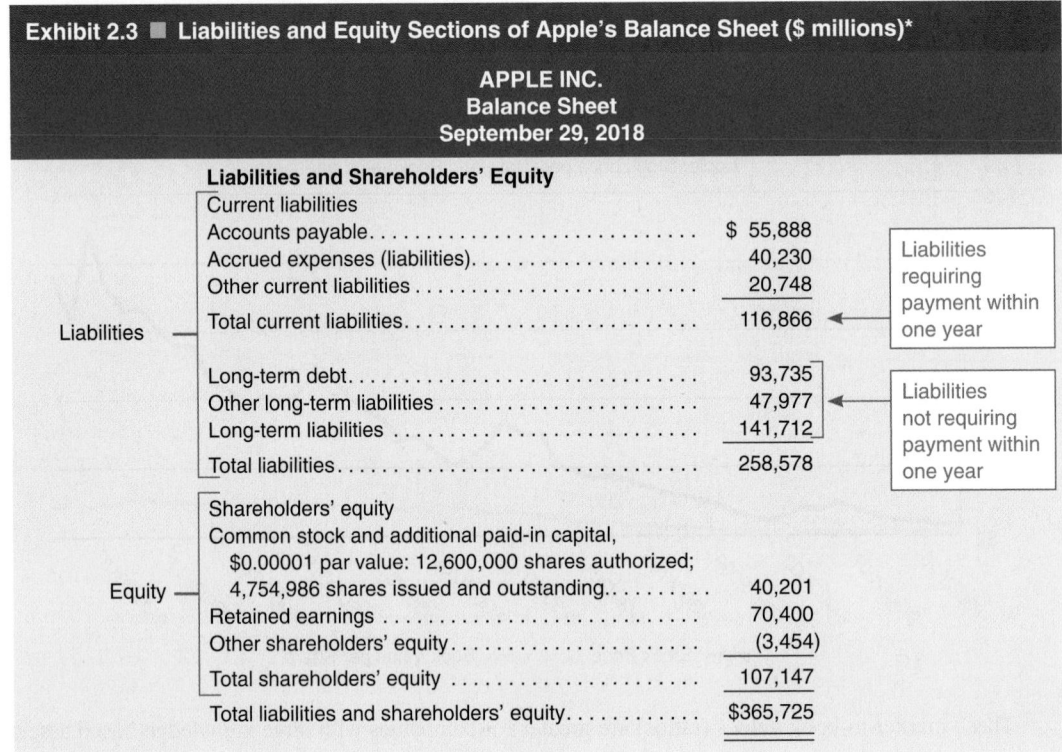

Exhibit 2.3 ■ Liabilities and Equity Sections of Apple's Balance Sheet ($ millions)*

APPLE INC.
Balance Sheet
September 29, 2018

Liabilities and Shareholders' Equity

Current liabilities		
Accounts payable............................	$ 55,888	
Accrued expenses (liabilities)..................	40,230	*Liabilities requiring payment within one year*
Other current liabilities	20,748	
Total current liabilities........................	116,866	
Long-term debt............................	93,735	
Other long-term liabilities	47,977	*Liabilities not requiring payment within one year*
Long-term liabilities	141,712	
Total liabilities...............................	258,578	
Shareholders' equity		
Common stock and additional paid-in capital, $0.00001 par value: 12,600,000 shares authorized; 4,754,986 shares issued and outstanding..........	40,201	
Retained earnings	70,400	
Other shareholders' equity.....................	(3,454)	
Total shareholders' equity	107,147	
Total liabilities and shareholders' equity...........	$365,725	

* In millions, except number of shares in thousands and par value.

Current Liabilities

The balance sheet lists liabilities in order of maturity. Obligations that must be settled within one year are called **current liabilities**. Examples of common current liabilities follow.

Accounts payable—amounts owed to suppliers for goods and services purchased on credit; also called trade payables or trade credit.

Accrued liabilities—obligations for expenses that have been incurred but not yet paid; also called accrued expenses.

Unearned revenues—cash the seller receives in advance from customers for goods or services it will deliver in the future; also called advances from customers, customer deposits, or deferred revenues.

Short-term debt—loans from banks or other creditors; includes short-term notes and commercial paper.

Current maturities of long-term debt—principal portion of long-term debt that is due to be paid within one year.

Apple reports current liabilities of $116,866 million on its 2018 balance sheet.

Accounts payable arise when one company purchases goods or services from another company. Typically, sellers offer credit terms when selling to other companies rather than expecting cash on delivery. The seller records an account receivable, and the buyer records an account payable. Apple reports accounts payable of $55,888 million as of the balance sheet date. Accounts payable are relatively uncomplicated liabilities. A transaction (say, an inventory purchase) occurs, a bill is sent by the seller, and the amount owed is reported on the buyer's balance sheet as a liability.

Accrued liabilities refer to incomplete transactions. For example, employees work and earn wages but usually are not paid until later, such as several days after the period-end. Wages must be reported as expense in the period employees earn them because those wages payable are obligations of the company, and a liability (wages payable) must be set up on the balance sheet. This is an *accrual*. Other common accruals include the recording of liabilities such as rent and utilities payable, taxes payable, and interest payable on borrowings. All of these accruals involve recognition of expense in the income statement and a liability on the balance sheet.

Apple has substantial unearned revenue because the company promises to provide after-sales support for each device or computer sold. These promises create obligations for the company that extend over the product's expected life. In its 2018 balance sheet, Apple reports current deferred revenue of $7,543 million and long-term deferred revenue of $2,797 million, which is cash Apple has received from its customers for future services, and therefore, represents revenue that has not yet been earned. Unearned revenue also arises for companies that sell gift cards, or offer subscription services, or take advance deposits from customers.

Net working capital, or simply working capital, reflects the difference between current assets and current liabilities and is defined as follows.

$$\text{Net working capital} = \text{Current assets} - \text{Current liabilities}$$

We usually prefer to see more current assets than current liabilities to ensure that companies are liquid. That is, companies should have sufficient funds to pay their short-term obligations as they come due. The net working capital required to conduct business depends on the company's **operating (or cash) cycle**, which is the time between paying cash for goods and receiving cash from customers—see Exhibit 2.4.

Exhibit 2.4 ■ Operating Cycle

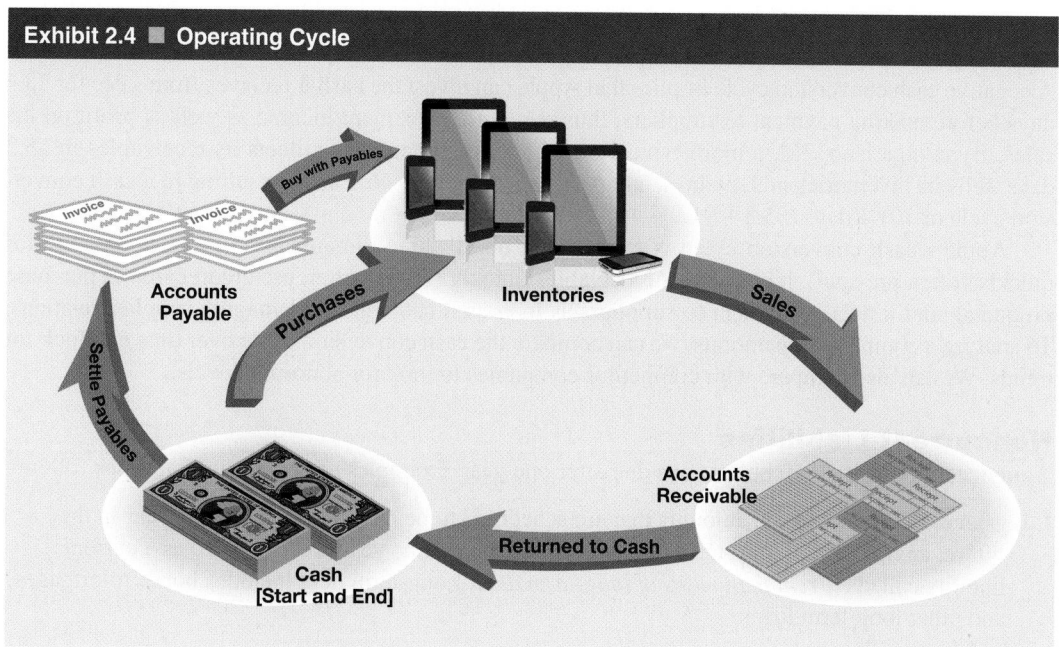

Companies, for example, use cash to purchase or manufacture inventories. Inventories are usually purchased on credit from suppliers (accounts payable). This financing is called **trade credit**. Inventories are sold either for cash or on credit (accounts receivable). When accounts receivable are ultimately collected, a portion of the cash received is used to repay accounts payable, and the remainder goes to the cash account for the next operating cycle.

When cash is invested in inventory, the inventory can remain with the company for 30 to 90 days or more. Once inventory is sold, the resulting accounts receivable can remain with the company for another 30 to 90 days. Assets such as inventories and accounts receivable are costly to hold because they tie up cash. As companies complete one operating cycle, sales and gross profit are reported in the income statement, and cash is generated (equal to the sales proceeds less the purchase cost of the inventory sold). A prime objective is to shorten the operating cycle in order to complete as many cycles as possible during the year. Doing so maximizes profit and cash flow. To shorten the operating cycle, managers can undertake any or all of the following actions.

- Decrease accounts receivable with tighter credit-granting policies and more assertive collection procedures.
- Reduce inventory levels by improved production systems and management of the depth and breadth of inventory.
- Increase accounts payable (supplier credit) to minimize the cash invested in inventories.

Cash Conversion Cycle Analysts often use the "cash conversion cycle" to evaluate company liquidity. The cash conversion cycle is the number of days the company has its cash tied up in receivables and inventories less the number of days of trade credit provided by company suppliers.

Following are the cash conversion cycles for **Apple Inc.** and **3M Company** (a manufacturing company).

Numbers in Days	Apple Inc.	3M Company
Average Days Sales Outstanding.	28.2 days	55.3 days
+ Average Days Inventory Outstanding.	9.8 days	91.9 days
− Average Days Payable Outstanding.	111.6 days	46.1 days
= Average Cash Conversion Cycle	(73.6) days	101.1 days

On average, Apple collects its receivables in 28.2 days, sells its inventories in 9.8 days, and pays its accounts payable in 111.6 days, resulting in a cash conversion cycle of (73.6) days (28.2 + 9.8 − 111.6). A negative cash conversion cycle implies that Apple can invest the cash it receives from sales for 73.6 days before making payment to suppliers, thus realizing investment income as well as profit on the sales. By comparison, 3M, a more typical manufacturing company, collects its receivables in 55.3 days, sells its inventories in 91.9 days, and pays its suppliers in 46.1 days, resulting in a cash conversion cycle of 101.1 days (55.3 + 91.9 − 46.1).

Apple's cash conversion cycle is exceptional on all three dimensions: it sells its inventories quickly (often pre-sold), it collects its receivables quickly (buyers often use credit cards to purchase products), and it delays payment to suppliers as long as it can without damaging supplier relations. To analyze a company's operations, we can compare the cash conversion cycle over time and look for trends. We can also compare with competitor companies to look for abnormal levels.

Noncurrent Liabilities

Noncurrent liabilities are obligations due after one year. Examples of noncurrent liabilities follow.

Long-term debt—borrowed amounts that are scheduled to be repaid more than one year in the future; any portion of long-term debt that is due within one year is reclassified as a current liability called *current maturities of long-term debt*. Long-term debt includes bonds, mortgages, and other long-term loans.

Other long-term liabilities—various obligations, such as pension liabilities and long-term tax liabilities, that will be settled a year or more into the future.

Apple reports $141,712 million of noncurrent liabilities. Apple's noncurrent liabilities include long-term debt, deferred revenue, and deferred tax liability for income taxes the company will pay in the future. Deferred (unearned) revenue arises when a company receives cash in advance of providing a good or service.

Apple reports total assets of $365,725 million and liabilities of $258,578 million. This means that Apple finances 71% of its assets with borrowed funds ($258,578 million/$365,725 million), which is somewhat higher than average. For example, in 2018, the S&P 500 companies financed about 64% of assets with borrowed funds. Given Apple's level of profitability and the amount of cash it generates, this level of liabilities is less concerning than it would be for another company with lower and more volatile levels of cash flow. Companies must monitor their financing sources and amounts. Too much borrowing is risky in that borrowed money must be repaid with interest. The level of debt a company can effectively manage is directly related to the stability and reliability of its operating cash flows.

Stockholders' Equity

Stockholders' equity reflects financing provided from company owners. Equity is often referred to as *residual interest*. That is, stockholders have a claim on any assets in excess of what is needed to meet company obligations to creditors. The following are examples of items typically included in equity.

Common stock—par value received from the original sale of common stock to investors.

Additional paid-in capital—amounts received from the original sale of stock to investors in excess of the par value of stock.

Preferred stock—value received from the original sale of preferred stock to investors; preferred stock has fewer ownership rights than common stock.

Treasury stock—amount the company paid to reacquire its common stock from shareholders.

Retained earnings—accumulated net income (profit) that has not been distributed to stockholders as dividends or as stock repurchases.

Accumulated other comprehensive income or loss—accumulated changes in asset and liability fair values that are not reported in the income statement.

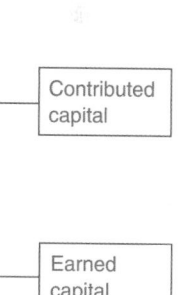

Contributed capital

Earned capital

The equity section of a balance sheet consists of two basic components: contributed capital and earned capital.

Contributed Capital **Contributed capital** is the net funding a company received from issuing and reacquiring its shares; that is, the funds received from issuing shares less any funds paid to repurchase such. Apple reports $107,147 million in total stockholders' equity. Its contributed capital is $40,201 million. Apple's common stock has a par value of $0.00001 per share (see Exhibit 2.3). This means that, when Apple sells shares of stock, its Common stock account increases by the number of shares sold multiplied by $0.00001, and its Additional paid-in capital account increases by the remainder of the proceeds from the sale (Apple's balance sheet aggregates the common stock and additional paid-in capital accounts, which is acceptable under GAAP). Apple's stockholders (via its board of directors) have authorized the company to issue up to 12.6 billion shares of common stock. As of September 29, 2018, Apple has sold (issued) 4,754,986,000 shares for total proceeds of $40,201 million, or $8.45 per share, on average.

Earned Capital **Earned capital** primarily includes Retained earnings, which is the cumulative net income (loss) that the company has earned but not paid out to stockholders as dividends. Retained earnings also includes the cost of repurchased stock that the company has retired. Apple's Retained earnings totals $70,400 million as of its 2018 year-end. Its other earned capital accounts total $(3,454) million.

One tool for analyzing a company's balance sheet is the *common-size balance sheet*. This is a balance sheet where each item is recast as a percent of total assets. It is called *common size* because each item is scaled by a common denominator. *Vertical analysis* and *"right-sized" balance sheet* are other phrases for common-size balance sheets. Common sizing the balance sheet enables us to perform the following types of analyses:

- Compare a company's balance sheets across two or more years. Companies provide side-by-side balance sheets for two years, and the 10-K often includes an 11-year history of key balance sheet accounts. If the company has grown or shrunk in size over time, comparing dollars (or other currency) masks shifts in relative size of balance sheet items. Percentages reveal a more accurate picture.

- Compare two or more companies' balance sheets. The common sizing eliminates size differences among companies—we can compare a small firm with a large firm because each asset, liability, and equity account is expressed in percentage terms. The other benefit is that common sizing is unit free, so we can compare companies that report in different currencies.

- Compare balance sheets with an industry average or some other benchmark. The percentages create a common basis for comparison, and this can help assess a particular company's financial position relative to others in the same industry.

Retained Earnings

There is an important relation for retained earnings that reconciles its beginning balance and its ending balance as follows. (Some might view stock repurchases and cancellations as a form of dividend.)

> Beginning retained earnings
> + Net income (or − Net loss)
> − Dividends
> − Stock repurchased and retired
> = Ending retained earnings

This is a useful relation to remember. Apple's retained earnings increases (or decreases) each year by the amount of its reported net income (loss) minus its dividends, and the cost of any shares the company repurchases and then retires. (There are other items that can impact retained earnings that we discuss in later modules.) After we explain the income statement, we will revisit this relation and show how retained earnings link the balance sheet and income statement.

Apple's market value has historically exceeded its book value of equity (see graph). Much of Apple's market value derives from intangible assets, such as brand equity, that are not fully reflected on its balance sheet and from favorable expectations of future financial performance (particularly in recent years). Apple has incurred many costs, such as research and development (R&D), advertising, and promotion, that will yield future economic benefits. However, Apple expensed these costs (did not capitalize them as assets) because their future benefits were uncertain and, therefore, could not be reliably measured. Companies capitalize intangible assets only when those assets are purchased, and not when they are internally developed. Consequently, Apple's balance sheet and the balance sheets of many knowledge-based companies are, arguably, less informative about company value.

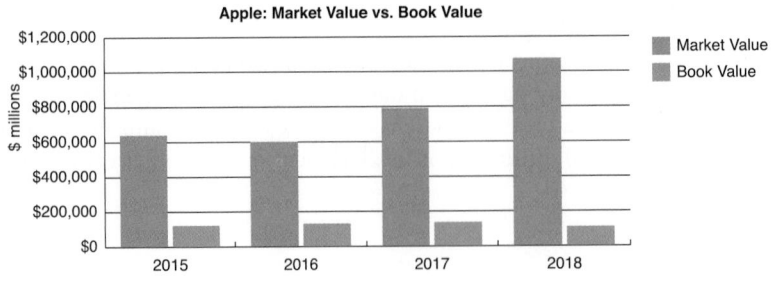

Market Value vs. Book Value Stockholders' equity is the "value" of the company determined by generally accepted accounting principles (GAAP) and is commonly referred to as the company's **book value**. This book value is different from a company's **market value** (market capitalization or *market cap*), which is computed by multiplying the number of outstanding common shares by the company's stock price. To compute Apple's market cap, we multiply the number of outstanding shares at September 29, 2018 (4,754,986,000 shares), by stock price on that date ($225.74). This equals $1,073,391 million, which is considerably larger than Apple's book value of equity of $107,147 million on that date. Book value and market value can differ for several reasons, mostly related to the following.

- GAAP generally reports assets and liabilities at historical costs, whereas the market attempts to estimate fair market values.

- GAAP excludes resources that cannot be reliably measured (due to the absence of a past transaction or event), such as talented management, employee morale, recent innovations, and successful marketing, whereas the market attempts to value these.

- GAAP does not consider the business environment in which companies operate, such as competitive conditions and expected changes, whereas the market attempts to factor in these differences in determining value.

- GAAP does not usually capture expected future performance, whereas the market attempts to predict and value future performance.

As of the end of 2018, the median market-to-book ratio for U.S. companies included in the Russell 3000 Index is 1.8. (The Russell 3000 Index consists of the 3,000 largest public companies incorporated in the U.S. as measured by total market capitalization, and represents approximately 98% of the U.S. public equity market.) The 1.8 ratio value exceeds 1.0, which implies the market has drawn on information in addition to that provided in the balance sheet and income statement in valuing companies' stock. Some of this additional value-relevant information is in financial statement notes, but not all. It is important to understand that, eventually, factors determining company market value are reflected in financial statements and book value. Assets are eventually sold, and liabilities are settled. Moreover, talented management, employee morale, technological innovations, and successful marketing are eventually recognized in reported profit. The difference between book value and market value is one of timing.

<table>
<tr><td>Research Insight   ■   Market-to-Book Ratio</td></tr>
</table>

The market-to-book ratio is computed as a company's market value divided by the book value to total equity. It can also be computed as stock price per share divided by book value or equity per share. The market-to-book ratio varies considerably over time, reflecting the variability in the global economy. Specifically, over the past ten years, the median market-to-book ratio for the S&P 500 companies has ranged from a low of 2.05 to a high of 3.23.

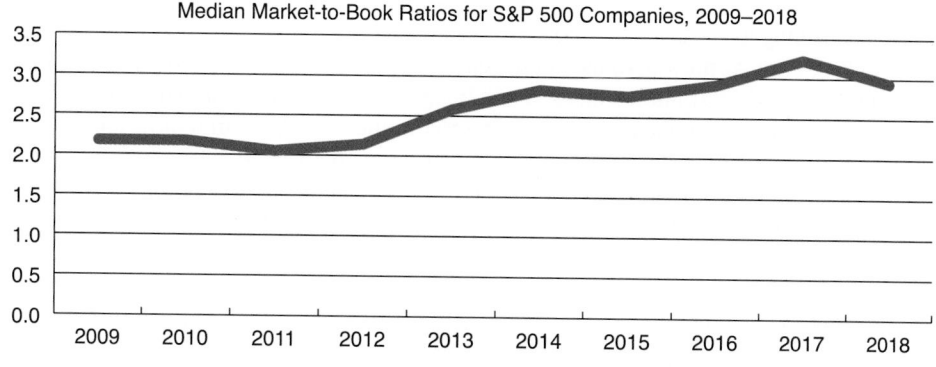

Median Market-to-Book Ratios for S&P 500 Companies, 2009–2018

Review 2-1 LO1

Following are account balances ($ millions) for Microsoft Corporation as of the fiscal year ended June 30, 2018. Prepare Microsoft's balance sheet as of June 30, 2018.

Total revenue	$110,360	Cash flows for financing activities	$ (33,540)
Accounts payable	8,617	Other current assets	6,751
Cash and short-term investments	133,768	Accrued expenses	6,103
Cash flows from operating activities	43,884	Other stockholders' equity	(2,187)
Other current liabilities	43,768	Accounts receivable	26,481
Inventories	2,662	Long-term liabilities	117,642
Cost of goods sold	38,353	Cash at beginning of year	7,663
Cash flows for investing activities	(6,061)	Other long-term assets	59,726
Retained earnings	13,682	Other income	1,416
Income tax expense	19,903	Property, plant, and equipment, net	29,460
Operating expenses (other than COGS)	36,949	Common stock and paid-in capital	71,223

Solution on p. 2-40.

Income Statement

LO2
Examine and interpret an income statement.

The income statement reports revenues earned from products sold and services provided during a period, the expenses incurred to produce those revenues, and the resulting net income or loss. The general structure of the income statement follows.

	Revenues
–	Cost of goods sold
	Gross profit
–	Operating expenses
	Operating profit
–	Nonoperating expenses (+ Nonoperating revenues)
–	Income tax expense
	Income from continuing operations
+/–	Discontinued operations, net of tax
=	Net income

On some income statements we see two lines after the net income line. These lines apportion "consolidated" net income between *net income attributable to noncontrolling interests* and *net income attributable to the parent company shareholders* (also called the controlling interest). Noncontrolling interests arise when a subsidiary company is partially owned by shareholders other than the parent company. We discuss noncontrolling interests in later modules.

See Exhibit 2.5 for Apple's 2018 income statement (titled *statement of operations* by Apple). Apple reports net income of $59,531 million on sales of $265,595 million. This means about $0.22 of each dollar of sales is brought down to the bottom line ($59,531 million/$265,595 million). Apple's net income margin is higher than that of the average publicly-traded company (Russell 3000 companies) that reports about $0.065 in profit for each sales dollar. For Apple, the remaining $0.78 ($1.00 – $0.22) is consumed by expenses incurred to generate sales, including costs to manufacture Apple products (cost of sales), as well as wages, advertising, R&D, equipment costs (such as depreciation), and taxes.

Operating expenses are the usual and customary costs a company incurs to support its operating activities. Those include cost of goods sold, selling expenses, depreciation expense, and research and development expense. Not all of these expenses require a cash outlay; for example, depreciation expense is a noncash expense, as are many accrued expenses, such as wages payable, that recognize the expense in advance of cash payment.

Nonoperating income and expenses relate to the company's financing and investing activities and include interest expense, interest or dividend income, and gains and losses from the sale of securities. We see, for example, that Apple reports $2,005 million of other income. This is nonoperating income. It's important to understand that it is a company's operating activities that create value for shareholders. Granted, investments do earn additional returns, but only at the going market rate, and shareholders could invest at that rate themselves. Apple holding the investments does not create additional shareholder value. It is for this reason our analysis seeks to isolate the core (or sustainable) operating profit and cash flows. We discuss operating profit more thoroughly in a later module.

> **Alert** The FASB has released a preliminary draft of a proposal to restructure financial statements to, among other things, better distinguish operating and nonoperating activities.

Exhibit 2.5 ■ Apple's Income Statement ($ millions)

APPLE INC.
Income Statement
For Year Ended September 29, 2018

Income statement	
Net sales.	$265,595
Cost of sales.	163,756
Gross margin	101,839
Operating expenses	
Research and development	14,236
Selling, general, and administrative	16,705
Total operating expenses	30,941
Operating income	70,898
Other income, net.	2,005
Income before provision for income taxes	72,903
Provision for income taxes	13,372
Net income	$ 59,531

Managerial Decision ■ You Are the Securities Analyst

You are analyzing the performance of a company that hired a new chief executive officer (CEO) during the current year. The current year's income statement includes an expense labeled "asset write-offs." Write-offs represent the accelerated transfer of costs from the balance sheet to the income statement. Are you concerned about the legitimacy of these expenses? Why or why not? [Answer, p. 2-27]

Recognizing Revenues and Expenses

An important consideration in preparing the income statement is *when* to recognize revenues and expenses. For many revenues and expenses, the decision is easy. When a customer purchases an item, pays with cash, and walks out of the store with the item, we know the sale is made and revenue should be recognized. Or when companies receive and pay an electric bill, they have clearly incurred an expense that should be recognized.

However, should Apple recognize revenue when it sells products to a retailer that does not have to pay Apple for 60 days? Should Apple recognize an expense for employees who work this week but will not be paid until the first of next month? The answer to both of these questions is yes.

Two fundamental principles guide recognition of revenues and expenses.

Revenue recognition principle—recognize revenue when a performance obligation is satisfied by transferring to a customer a promised good or service.[2]

Expense recognition (matching) principle—recognize expenses when *incurred*.

---

[2] Revenue recognition follows the standard "Revenue from Contracts with Customers (Topic 606)," *Accounting Standards Update No. 2014-09*. The precise language follows: *An entity should recognize revenue when (or as) it satisfies a performance obligation by transferring a promised good or service to a customer. A good or service is transferred when (or as) the customer obtains control of that good or service. For each performance obligation, an entity should determine whether the entity satisfies the performance obligation over time by transferring control of a good or service over time. If an entity does not satisfy a performance obligation over time, the performance obligation is satisfied at a point in time.* We discuss revenue recognition more fully in Module 5.

These two principles are the foundation of **accrual accounting**, which is the accounting system used to prepare all GAAP-based financial statements. The general approach is this: first, recognize revenues in the time period when the company satisfies the performance obligations of the sales contract at the amount expected to be received; then, record all expenses *incurred* to generate those revenues during that same time period (this is called matching expenses to revenues). Net income is then correctly reported for that period.

Recognizing revenues does not necessarily imply the receipt of cash. Revenue is *recognized* when the company has done what it is obligated to do under the sales contract, such as when goods have been transferred or services performed for the customer. This means a sale of goods on credit would qualify for recognition as long as the goods have been transferred to the customer as laid out in the sales contract. The company records revenue but receives no cash; instead, it records an accounts receivable. Likewise, companies recognize an expense when it is *incurred*, even if no cash is paid. For example, companies recognize as expenses the wages earned by employees, even though they will not be paid until the next pay period. The company records an expense but pays no cash; instead, it records an accrued liability for the wages payable.

Accrual accounting requires estimates and assumptions. Examples include estimating how much revenue has been earned on a long-term contract, the amount of accounts receivable that will not be collected, the degree to which equipment has been "used up," and numerous other estimates. All of these estimates and assumptions affect both reported net income and the balance sheet. Judgments affect all financial statements. This is an important by-product of accrual accounting. We discuss these estimates and assumptions, and their effects on financial statements, throughout the book.

> **Managerial Decision** ■ **You Are the Operations Manager**
>
> You are the operations manager on a new consumer product that was launched this period with very successful sales. The chief financial officer (CFO) asks you to prepare an estimate of warranty costs to charge against those sales. Why does the CFO desire a warranty cost estimate? What issues must you address in arriving at such an estimate? [Answer, p. 2-27]

Reporting of Transitory Items

From time to time, companies will divest a segment of their business as their strategy changes. When they do, we see an additional component of net income located at the bottom of the statement called **discontinued operations**—see Exhibit 2.6. Discontinued operations has two components.

1. Net income (loss) from the discontinued segment's business activities prior to sale.
2. Any gain or loss on the actual sale of the discontinued segment.

The income statement separately reports the per share effects with two EPS numbers.

■ Earnings per share from continuing operations.
■ Earnings per share from discontinued operations.

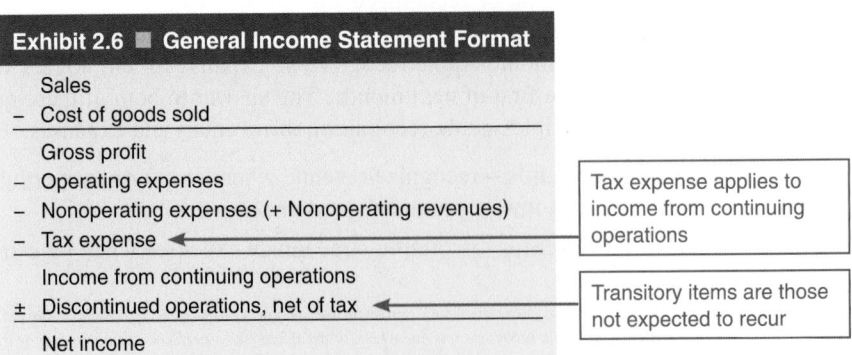

Exhibit 2.6 ■ **General Income Statement Format**

Sales	
– Cost of goods sold	
Gross profit	
– Operating expenses	
– Nonoperating expenses (+ Nonoperating revenues)	
– Tax expense ◄———	Tax expense applies to income from continuing operations
Income from continuing operations	
± Discontinued operations, net of tax ◄———	Transitory items are those not expected to recur
Net income	

To be classified as a discontinued operation, the disposal of the business unit must represent a strategic shift that has, or will have, a major effect on the company's financial results. Because these divestitures represent strategic shifts with material financial effects, the reporting of discontinued operations is relatively infrequent.

Discontinued operations are segregated from "Income from continuing operations" because the discontinued operations affect the current and prior periods but will not recur. Many financial statement users analyze current-year financial statements to help predict future performance. One good example is a company's stock price, which is heavily influenced by expected future profits and cash flows. Although transitory items help us understand past performance, they are largely irrelevant to predicting future performance. Consequently, investors and other financial statement users focus on income from continuing operations because it represents the profitability that is likely to persist (continue) into the future. Likewise, the financial press tends to focus on income from continuing operations when it discloses corporate earnings (often described as earnings before one-time charges, or street earnings).

In addition to segregating the results of operations of the discontinued operation in the current and previous two years' income statements reported, companies are also required to segregate the discontinued operation's assets and liabilities that remain at year-end, on its current year's and prior year's balance sheets.

Analyzing the Income Statement

In the prior module, we described an analytical framework to disaggregate return on assets (ROA) into two important components: (1) profit margin, computed as Net income/Sales, and (2) asset turnover, computed as Sales/Average total assets. To augment the ROA analysis, we look at two additional profitability measures.

- Gross profit margin (Gross profit/Sales).
- Operating expense margins (Operating expense/Sales).

The **gross profit margin** is influenced by both the selling price of the company's products and the cost to make or buy those products. For example, if we purchase a product for $6 and sell it for $10, our gross profit margin is 40% ([$10 − $6]/$10). We analyze the gross profit margin by comparing the ratio over time and with peer companies' ratios. Typically, a high and/or increasing gross profit margin is a positive sign. A low or declining margin signals more intense competition or a lessening of the desirability of the company's product line or increasing inventory costs.

Analysis of **operating expenses** focuses on each expense category reported by the company as a percentage of sales over time and compared with peer companies. Any deviations from historical trends or significantly higher or lower levels from peer companies should be investigated to uncover causes. A particularly worrisome sign is when margins for operating expenses are declining in the face of falling profits. The concern is that the company has tried to address declining profits by reducing critical expenses such as R&D, marketing, or compensation costs. This generally leads to a short-term improvement at a long-term cost as market share declines and employee morale suffers. We discuss the analysis of the income statement in much more detail in Module 4.

Analysis Insight   ■   Common-Size Income Statement

Analysts typically prepare common-size income statements as a starting point for their analysis; each income statement item is expressed as a percent of net sales. As with the common-size balance sheet, a common-size income statement facilitates the same three types of comparisons: one company across years (called time-series analysis), many companies across one year (called cross-sectional analysis), and to a benchmark such as an industry average. Common-size analysis is also referred to as "vertical analysis" because the percentages in the column on the income statement add up vertically to 100% of total sales (the top-line number on the income statement). A common-size balance sheet adds up vertically to 100% of total assets, and for that reason, is also called a vertical analysis.

Review 2-2 LO2

Refer to the data in Review 2-1 to answer the following requirement.

Required

Prepare Microsoft's income statement for the fiscal year ended June 30, 2018. *Hint:* Refer to Exhibits 2.5 and

Solution on p. 2-40.   2.6 for presentation guidance.

Statement of Stockholders' Equity

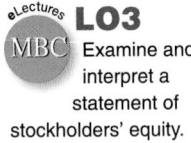

eLectures **LO3**

MBC Examine and
interpret a
statement of
stockholders' equity.

The statement of stockholders' equity reconciles the beginning and ending balances of stockholders' equity accounts. The statement of stockholders' equity for Apple is shown in Exhibit 2.7.

Exhibit 2.7 ■ **Apple's Statement of Stockholders' Equity ($ millions)**

	Common Stock and Additional Paid-in Capital	Retained Earnings	Accumulated Other Comprehensive Income (Loss)	Total Equity
APPLE INC. Statement of Shareholders' Equity For Year Ended September 29, 2018				
September 30, 2017......................	$35,867	$98,330	$ (150)	$134,047
Stock issuance, net	4,334	(948)		3,386
Net income................................		59,531		59,531
Dividends and dividend equivalents declared		(13,735)		(13,735)
Repurchase of common stock		(73,056)		(73,056)
Other.....................................		278	(3,304)	(3,026)
September 29, 2018.......................	$40,201	$70,400	$(3,454)	$107,147

Common stock and additional paid-in capital increase by the proceeds from the sale of stock. Retained earnings increase by the net income (or decrease by the net loss) reported in the income statement and decrease by the dividends to shareholders. Retained earnings also decrease if a company repurchases shares from stockholders and then retires the repurchased shares. These "buybacks" are another form of distribution to shareholders similar to the payment of dividends (which also decreases retained earnings).[3] Accumulated other comprehensive income (loss) increases and decreases by changes in asset and liability fair values that are not reported in the income statement (we discuss accumulated other comprehensive income in Module 8).

In sum, Apple's stockholders' equity begins the year at $134,047 million and ends fiscal 2018 with a balance of $107,147 million for a net decrease of $26,900 million. Stock issuances and net income increase total equity, whereas dividends, common stock repurchased and retired, and other adjustments decrease total equity.

---

[3] During the year, Apple paid $73,056 million to repurchase common stock from its shareholders and then retired those shares, which decreased retained earnings. Had Apple not retired the shares, they would have been reported in an account called *Treasury stock*, a stockholders' equity account that has a negative balance. Whether Apple retires repurchased shares or not, total stockholders' equity decreases by the buyback amount. Treasury shares that are not retired can be resold. Module 8 discusses treasury stock in more detail.

IFRS Insight ■ Balance Sheet and Income Statement under IFRS

U.S. GAAP and IFRS require a similar set of financial statements with similar formats. Both standards require current and long-term classifications for assets and liabilities, and both recognize revenues when earned (meaning when performance obligations are satisfied) and expenses when incurred. Although differences between U.S. GAAP and IFRS do exist at the "detailed level," there are two broader differences worth mention.

▪ SEC requires three years of comparative income statements, whereas IFRS requires only two.

▪ GAAP income statements categorize expenses by their function (e.g., cost of sales, selling, or administrative). For IFRS, expenses can be shown either by function or by nature (e.g., materials, labor, or overhead), whichever provides more reliable and relevant information.

LO3 Review 2-3

Use the data below to prepare **Microsoft**'s statement of stockholders' equity for the fiscal year ended June 30, 2018.

$ millions	Common Stock and Additional Paid-In Capital	Retained Earnings	Accumulated Other Comprehensive Income
Beginning balance	$69,315	$17,769	$627

Additional information for fiscal year 2018:
- Stock issuances, net increased common stock and additional paid-in capital by $1,908 million and decreased retained earnings by $(7,699) million.
- Accumulated other comprehensive income decreased by $2,814 million.
- Net income was $16,571 million.
- Dividends were $12,917 million.
- Other decreases in retained earnings total $42 million.

Solution on p. 2-40.

Statement of Cash Flows

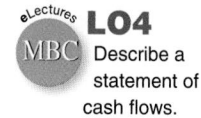

The balance sheet and income statement are prepared using accrual accounting, in which revenues are recognized when earned and expenses when incurred. This means companies can report income even though no cash is received. Cash shortages—due to unexpected cash outlays or when customers refuse to or cannot pay—can create economic hardships for companies and even cause their demise.

LO4 Describe a statement of cash flows.

To evaluate company performance, we must assess a company's cash management in addition to its profitability. Obligations to employees, creditors, and others are usually settled with cash. Illiquid companies (those lacking cash) are at risk for failure. Given the importance of cash management, companies must report a statement of cash flows in addition to the balance sheet, income statement, and statement of equity.

The income statement provides information about the economic viability of the company's products and services. It tells us whether the company can sell its products and services at prices that cover its costs and provide a reasonable return to lenders and stockholders. On the other hand, the statement of cash flows provides information about the company's ability to generate cash from those same transactions. It tells us from what sources the company has generated its cash (so we can evaluate whether those sources are persistent or transitory) and what it has done with the cash it generated.

Statement Format and Data Sources

The statement of cash flows is formatted to report cash inflows and cash outflows by the three primary business activities. To distinguish positive from negative cash flow, the statement of cash flows uses brackets to indicate cash *outflows*.

■ **Cash flows from operating activities** Cash flows from the company's transactions and events that relate to its operations.

■ **Cash flows from investing activities** Cash flows from acquisitions and divestitures of investments and long-term assets.

■ **Cash flows from financing activities** Cash flows from issuances of and payments toward borrowings and equity.

The combined cash flows from these three sections yield the net change in cash for the period as illustrated by the following condensed cash flow statement for **Apple**.

Exhibit 2.8 ■ Apple's Statement of Cash Flows ($ millions)

APPLE INC.
Statement of Cash Flows
For Year Ended September 29, 2018

Cash generated by operating activities	$77,434
Cash from investing activities.	16,066
Cash used in financing activities	(87,876)
Net change in cash.	5,624
Cash balance, September 30, 2017.	20,289
Cash balance, September 29, 2018.	$25,913

Apple generated $77,434 million of cash from its operating activities. It generated $16,066 million of cash from investing activities, such as the purchase of PPE assets or marketable securities (Apple reported a net investing cash inflow because proceeds from the sale of marketable securities were greater than the outflow for the purchase of PPE). Apple used $(87,876) million of cash for financing activities, such as paying dividends, repurchasing common stock from the market, or reducing debt. The three types of cash flow together generated $5,624 million of cash during the year, thereby increasing the cash account from $20,289 million at the beginning of fiscal 2018 to $25,913 million at fiscal-year-end. Apple's cash flow picture is healthy: the company generated substantial cash from operating activities and from the sale of investments, and used that cash to invest in PPE infrastructure, reduce debt, and return cash to stockholders in the form of dividends and stock repurchases.

Our analysis of cash flows focuses on the sources and uses of cash.

■ Is the company generating cash from operating activities?

■ Is the operating cash flow sustainable?

■ Is the company investing its cash to grow its infrastructure (PPE) or to enter new markets by acquiring other companies?

■ Is the company using its excess cash to build liquidity (purchase of marketable securities)?

■ Is the company paying down debt or paying dividends?

■ Is the company repurchasing stock?

Ultimately, a company's ending cash balance must be positive. So, if operating cash flow is negative, the company must raise cash from investing activities (the sale of PPE assets or marketable securities) or financing activities (borrowing money, selling stock, or cutting dividends and share repurchases). In the long run, the amount of cash that can be raised from investing and financing activities is finite. Although companies can usually sustain a short-term negative operating cash flow, long-term operating cash outflows are a serious concern. We discuss the statement of cash flows in detail in a later module.

LO4 Review 2-4

Refer to the data in Review 2-1 to answer the following requirement.

Required
Prepare Microsoft's statement of cash flows for the fiscal year ended June 30, 2018.

Solution on p. 2-41.

Articulation of Financial Statements

The four financial statements are linked with each other and linked across time. This section demonstrates the linkages (articulation) of financial statements using Apple.

eLectures **LO5**
MBC Construct and apply linkages among the four financial statements.

Retained Earnings Reconciliation

One of the most important articulations between financial statements involves the balance sheet and income statement. The two statements are linked via retained earnings. Recall that retained earnings is updated each period as follows.

	Beginning retained earnings
±	Net income (loss)
–	Dividends
–	Shares repurchased and retired
=	Ending retained earnings

Retained earnings reflect cumulative income that has not yet been distributed to shareholders. Exhibit 2.9 shows Apple's retained earnings reconciliation for 2018.

Exhibit 2.9 ■ Apple's Retained Earnings Reconciliation ($ millions)

APPLE INC.
Retained Earnings Reconciliation
For Year Ended September 29, 2018

Retained earnings, September 30, 2017	$98,330
Net income	59,531
Dividends declared	(13,735)
Repurchase and retirement of common stock	(73,056)
Other adjustments	(670)
Retained earnings, September 29, 2018	$70,400

This reconciliation of retained earnings links the balance sheet and the income statement.

In the absence of transactions with stockholders—such as stock issuances and repurchases, dividend payments, and other adjustments—the change in stockholders' equity equals income or loss for the period. The income statement, thus, measures the change in company value as measured by *GAAP*. This is not necessarily company value as measured by the *market*. Of course, all value-relevant items eventually find their way into the income statement. So, from a long-term perspective, the income statement does measure change in company value. This is why stock prices react to reported income and to analysts' expectations about future income.

Financial Statement Linkages

Exhibit 2.10 lays out the linkages among the four financial statements. Apple begins fiscal 2018 with assets of $375,319 million, consisting of cash of $20,289 million and noncash assets of $355,030 million. These investments are financed with $241,272 million from nonowners and $134,047 million

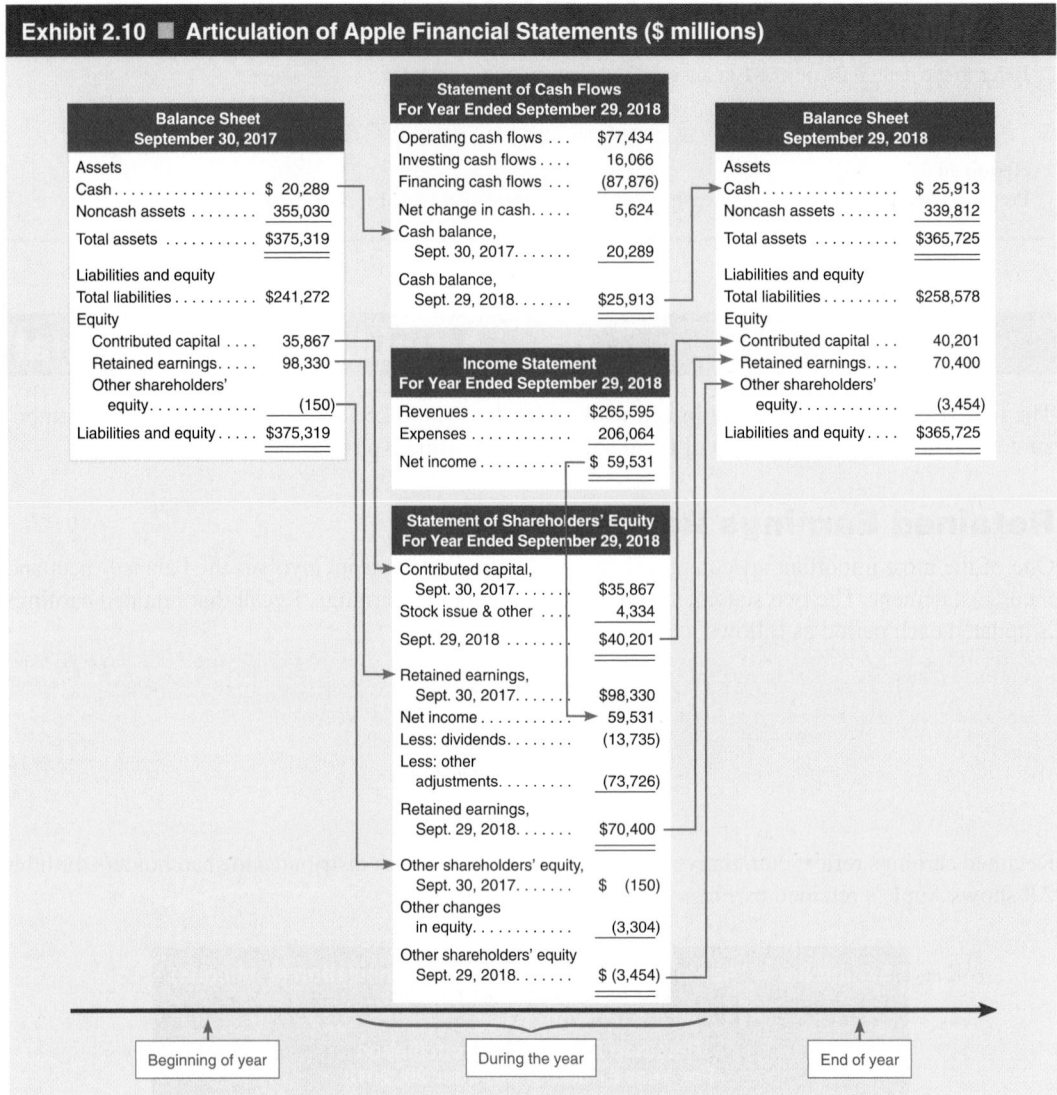

Exhibit 2.10 ■ Articulation of Apple Financial Statements ($ millions)

from stockholders. Owner financing consists of contributed capital of $35,867 million, retained earnings of $98,330 million, and other shareholders' equity of $(150) million.

Exhibit 2.10 shows balance sheets at the beginning and end of Apple's fiscal year on the left and right columns, respectively. The middle column reflects annual operating activities. The statement of cash flows explains how operating, investing, and financing activities increase the cash balance by $5,624 million from $20,289 million at the beginning of the year to $25,913 million at year-end. The ending balance in cash is reported in the year-end balance sheet on the right.

Apple's $59,531 million net income reported on the income statement is linked to the statement of shareholders' equity. Apple's retained earnings increases by net income of $59,531 million and decreases by dividend payments of $(13,735) million, by the repurchase of stock of $(73,056) million, and by other items of $(670) million.

Understanding these linkages gives managers as well as external financial statement users a keener ability to assess the impact transactions have on the financial statements. Every transaction has at least two effects on the financial statements. For example, purchasing new PPE increases non-cash assets and decreases cash on the balance sheet, which in turn affects the statement of cash flows. Many other transactions have more than two effects. For example, consider the cash sale of inventory. This transaction has the following income statement effects: (1) revenue increases, (2) expenses increase, and (3) net income increases (assuming the sales price exceeded the cost of the inventory). The balance sheet is affected as follows: (1) cash increases, (2) inventory decreases, and (3) retained earnings increases. Cash from operations increases on the statement of cash flows, and the statement of stockholders' equity is affected via retained earnings. With such an understanding, we can more accurately answer questions such as the following.

- What are the financial statement effects of purchasing new PPE versus renting it?
- How is ROA affected when the company discontinues certain operations?
- What are the income statement and balance sheet effects of outsourcing production?
- How will a proposed merger affect profit margin and asset turnover?

LO5 Review 2-5

Assume Microsoft Corporation reports the following balances for the prior-year balance sheet and current-year income statement ($ millions). Prepare the articulation of Microsoft's financial statements for fiscal years 2017 and 2018 following the format of Exhibit 2.10.

Balance Sheet, June 30, 2017	
Assets	
Cash	$ 7,663
Noncash assets	242,649
Total assets	$250,312
Liabilities and equity	
Total liabilities	$162,601
Equity	
Contributed capital	69,315
Retained earnings	17,769
Other stockholders' equity	627
Liabilities and equity	$250,312

Income Statement, For Year Ended June 30, 2018	
Revenues	$110,360
Expenses	93,789
Net income	$ 16,571

Statement of Cash Flows, For Year Ended June 30, 2018	
Operating cash flows	$43,884
Investing cash flows	(6,061)
Financing cash flows	(33,540)
Net change in cash	4,283
Cash balance, June 30, 2017	7,663
Cash balance, June 30, 2018	$11,946

Notes: 1. Stock issuances for the year are $1,098.
   2. Dividends for the year are $12,917.
   3. Other decreases in retained earnings are $7,741.
   4. Change in other stockholders' equity for the year is $(2,814).
   5. Total assets at June 30, 2018 are $258,848.

Solution on p. 2-41.

Additional Information Sources

The four financial statements are only a part of the information available to financial statement users. Additional information from a variety of sources provides useful insight into company operating activities and future prospects. This section highlights additional information sources.

LO6 Locate and use additional financial information from public sources.

Form 10-K

Companies with publicly traded securities must file with the SEC a detailed annual report and discussion of their business activities in their Form 10-K (quarterly reports are filed on Form 10-Q). Many of the disclosures in the 10-K are mandated by law and include the following general categories:

- **Item 1**, Business
- **Item 1A**, Risk Factors
- **Item 2**, Properties
- **Item 3**, Legal Proceedings
- **Item 4**, Submission of Matters to a Vote of Security Holders
- **Item 5**, Market for Registrant's Common Equity and Related Stockholder Matters

- **Item 6**, Selected Financial Data
- **Item 7**, Management's Discussion and Analysis of Financial Condition and Results of Operations
- **Item 7A**, Quantitative and Qualitative Disclosures About Market Risk
- **Item 8**, Financial Statements and Supplementary Data
- **Item 9**, Changes in and Disagreements with Accountants on Accounting and Financial Disclosure
- **Item 9A**, Controls and Procedures
- **Item 10**, Directors, Executive Officers, and Corporate Governance
- **Item 11**, Executive Compensation
- **Item 12**, Security Ownership of Certain Beneficial Owners and Management and Related Stockholder Matters
- **Item 13**, Certain Relationships and Related Transactions, and Director Independence
- **Item 14**, Principal Accountant Fees and Services

Description of Business (Item 1)

Companies must provide a general description of their business, including their principal products and services, the source and availability of required raw materials; all patents, trademarks, licenses, and important related agreements; seasonality of the business; any dependence upon a single customer; and competitive conditions, including particular markets in which the company competes, the product offerings in those markets, and the status of its competitive environment. Companies must also provide a description of their overall strategy. Apple's partial disclosure follows.

> **Business Strategy**   The Company is committed to bringing the best user experience to its customers through its innovative hardware, software and services. The Company's business strategy leverages its unique ability to design and develop its own operating systems, hardware, application software and services to provide its customers products and solutions with innovative design, superior ease-of-use and seamless integration. As part of its strategy, the Company continues to expand its platform for the discovery and delivery of digital content and applications through its Digital Content and Services, which allows customers to discover and download or stream digital content, iOS, Mac, Apple Watch and Apple TV applications, and books through either a Mac or Windows personal computer or through iPhone, iPad and iPod touch® devices ("iOS devices"), Apple TV, Apple Watch and HomePod. The Company also supports a community for the development of third-party software and hardware products and digital content that complement the Company's offerings. The Company believes a high-quality buying experience with knowledgeable salespersons who can convey the value of the Company's products and services greatly enhances its ability to attract and retain customers. Therefore, the Company's strategy also includes building and expanding its own retail and online stores and its third-party distribution network to effectively reach more customers and provide them with a high-quality sales and post-sales support experience. The Company believes ongoing investment in research and development ("R&D"), marketing and advertising is critical to the development and sale of innovative products, services and technologies.

Management's Discussion and Analysis (Item 7)

The management discussion and analysis (MD&A) section of the 10-K contains valuable insight into the company's results of operations. In addition to an executive overview of company status and its recent operating results, the MD&A section includes information relating to critical accounting policies and estimates used in preparing the financial statements, a detailed discussion of sales activity; year-over-year comparisons of operating activities; analysis of gross margin, operating expenses, taxes, and off-balance-sheet and contractual obligations; assessment of factors that affect future results; and financial condition.

Item 7A reports quantitative and qualitative disclosures about market risk. For example, Apple makes the following disclosure relating to its Mac operating system and its iPods, iPhones, iPads, and other products.

Competition The markets for the Company's products and services are highly competitive and the Company is confronted by aggressive competition in all areas of its business. These markets are characterized by frequent product introductions and rapid technological advances that have substantially increased the capabilities and use of mobile communication and media devices, personal computers and other digital electronic devices. Many of the Company's competitors that sell mobile devices and personal computers based on other operating systems seek to compete primarily through aggressive pricing and very low cost structures. The Company's financial condition and operating results can be adversely affected by these and other industry-wide downward pressures on gross margins. Principal competitive factors important to the Company include price, product and service features (including security features), relative price and performance, product and service quality and reliability, design innovation, a strong third-party software and accessories ecosystem, marketing and distribution capability, service and support and corporate reputation.

Schedule II—Valuation and Qualifying Accounts

In addition to the 10-K sections described above, the SEC requires companies to report additional information about certain balance sheet accounts. That information explains reserves and allowances the company establishes to reflect expected losses or uncollectible amounts. (We explain these accounts in later modules.) Many companies comply with this requirement by including the required information in notes to financial statements or as additional information at the end of the 10-K. Exhibit 2.11 shows a typical disclosure from Cisco Inc. from its 2018 10-K.

Exhibit 2.11 ■ Cisco's Schedule II from 2018 10-K

SCHEDULE II VALUATION AND QUALIFYING ACCOUNTS	Allowances for	
Year Ended July 28, 2018 ($ millions)	Financing Receivables	Accounts Receivable
Balance at beginning of fiscal year..	$295	$211
Provisions (benefits)...	(89)	(45)
Write-offs net of recoveries..	(6)	(37)
Foreign exchange and other...	5	—
Balance at end of fiscal year	$205	$129

Cisco provides information relating to its reserves for anticipated losses on its financing receivables (leases and loans), and on its accounts receivable. Companies often provide similar analysis on estimated sales returns and deferred tax accounts. Our objective in reviewing these accounts is to determine if they are reasonable in amount and, if not, the extent to which our estimate of core operating income differs from that reported in the company's income statement. We discuss this analysis in later modules.

Form 20-F and Form 40-F

Non-U.S. companies that are publicly traded in the United States also file annual reports with the SEC. These foreign companies must furnish, within four months after the fiscal year-end, the same audited financial statements required on Form 10-K. The filing, labeled Form 20-F, requires that firms provide financial statements prepared according to U.S. GAAP or IFRS. If the company uses accounting standards other than GAAP or IFRS, Form 20-F must discuss major differences between the accounting principles used and GAAP and provide a table that reconciles net income as reported to U.S. GAAP net income. In addition, substantive balance sheet and cash flow items that differ from U.S. GAAP must be reconciled. Canadian companies file their annual reports, prepared under IFRS, using Form 40-F.

Form 8-K

Another useful report that is required by the SEC and is publicly available is the Form 8-K. This form must be filed within four business days of any of the following events.

- Quarterly earnings press release
- Entry into or termination of a material definitive agreement (including petition for bankruptcy)
- Exit from a line of business or impairment of assets
- Change in the company's certified public accounting firm
- Change in control of the company
- Departure of the company's executive officers
- Changes in the company's articles of incorporation or bylaws

Outsiders typically use Form 8-K to monitor for material adverse changes in the company.

Analyst Reports

Sell-side analysts provide their clients with objective analyses of company operating activities. Frequently, these reports include a discussion of the competitive environment for each of the company's principal product lines, strengths and weaknesses of the company, and an investment recommendation, including financial analysis and a stock price target. For example, RBC Capital Markets provides the following in its October 8, 2018, report to clients on Apple.

 **RBC Capital Markets**

EQUITY RESEARCH

ROC Capital Markets, LLC
Amit Daryananl, CFA
(Analyst)
(415) 633-8659
amit.daryanani@rbccm.com
Amitesh Bajad (Senior Associate)
(415) 633-8795
amitesh.bajod@rbccm.com

Irvin Llu (AVP)
(415) 633-8539
irvin.liu@rbccm.com

October 8, 2018
Apple Inc.

Data Download—Upside Ahead

Our view: We think AAPL should post strong Sep-qtr results helped by multiple factors including new products, ASP uplift , benign memory costs, Services tailwind, and continued buybacks.

Key points:
All You Need to Know: Heading into Sep-qtr earnings, we think investor sentiment is largely neutral to even slightly negative toward new iPhones and ability to maintain flat to up units in FY19. We expect AAPL to post Sep-qtr results slightly above Street expectations driven by revenues, modest upside to GMs, and continued buyback tailwinds. We think new iPhone launch will boost ASPs as well as units and note that last year iPhone X's delay should imply somewhat easier comps in Sep-qtr. Carrier promotions, which are more attractive this year, could be a driver of units upside. In addition, we think that the Others product segment could surprise positively given the new Apple Watch and rising AirPods attach rate. Overall, we see Sep-qtr revenues up mid/high teens vs. Sep-2017. While FX could be a slight headwind, AAPL's hedging program should largely offset that. On the GM side, in addition to ASP dynamic, we should start seeing impact of lower memory prices flowing through, particularly with the launch of new iPhones. Finally, services momentum should remain strong and we think AAPL's stock repurchase momentum remains strong. **Net/Net:** Maintaining Outperform rating and $250 price target.

Data Download: 1) On 9/12, AAPL announced its new lineup of phones: iPhone XS Max (6.5" OLED), iPhone XS (5.8" OLED), and iPhone XR (6.1" LCD). 2) For August, the contract price for 64Gb TLC wafer was flat m/m, for 128Gb TLC wafer declined –5.5% m/m, and for 256Gb TLC declined –12.8% m/m. 3) Aug DRAM contract prices were largely flat but spot was beginning to show some signs of softness. 4) On 9/25, JBL reported an Aug-qtr beat with revenue/EPS of $5.77B/$0.70 vs. Street at $5.41B/$0.68. 5) On 9/6, AVGO reported Jul-qtr revs/EPS of $5.07B/$4.98 vs. Street at $5.06B/$4.83.

Sector: IT Hardware

Outperform
NASDAQ : AAPL; USD 224.29
Price Target USD 250.00

WHAT'S INSIDE	
☐ Rating/Risk Change	☐ Price Target Change
☐ In-Depth Report	☐ Est. Change
☐ Preview	☑ News Analysis

Scenario Analysis*

	Downside Scenario	Current Price	Price Target	Upside Scenario
	190.00	224.29	250.00	280.00
	↓14%		↑12%	↑26%

*Implied Total Returns
Key Statistics

Shares O/S (MM):	4,926.6	Market Cap (MM):	1,104,987
Dividend:	2.28	Yield:	1.0%
BVPS:	23.78	P/BVPS:	9.43x
		Avg. Daily Volume:	32,936,934

RBC Estimates

FY Sep	2016A	2017A	2018E	2019E
EPS, Ops Diluted	8.28	9.19	11.75	13.77
P/E	27.1x	24.4x	19.1x	16.3x
Revenue	215.6	229.2	264.9	286.4

EPS, Ops Diluted	Q1	Q2	Q3	Q4
2017	3.36A	2.10A	1.67A	2.07A
2018	3.89A	2.73A	2.34A	2.80E
2019	4.94E	3.16E	2.56E	3.11E
Revenue				
2017	78.4A	52.9A	45.4A	52.6A
2018	88.3A	61.1A	53.3A	62.2E
2019	95.2E	66.2E	57.9E	67.2E

All values in USD unless otherwise noted.

Credit Services

Several firms, including S&P Global Ratings (**StandardAndPoors.com**), Moody's Investors Service (**Moodys.com**), and Fitch Ratings (**FitchRatings.com**), provide credit analysis that assists potential lenders, investors, employees, and other users in evaluating a company's creditworthiness and future financial viability. Credit analysis is a specialized field of analysis, quite different from the equity analysis illustrated here. These firms issue credit ratings on publicly issued bonds as well as on firms' commercial paper.

Data Services

A number of companies supply financial statement data in easy-to-download spreadsheet formats. Thomson Reuters Corporation (**ThomsonReuters.com**) provides a wealth of information to its database subscribers, including the widely quoted *First Call* summary of analysts' earnings forecasts. S&P Global Ratings provides financial data for all publicly traded companies in its *Compustat* database. This database reports a plethora of individual data items for all publicly traded companies or for any specified subset of companies. These data are useful for performing statistical analysis and making comparisons across companies or within industries. Finally, Capital IQ (**CapitalIQ.com**), a division of Standard & Poor's, provides "as presented" financial data that conform to published financial statements, as well as additional statistical data and analysis.

LO6 Review 2-6

Use the SEC website (**www.sec.gov/edgar/searchedgar/companysearch.html**) to download Microsoft's 2018 10-K, and answer the requirements.

Required

1. On what date did Microsoft file its 2018 10-K with the SEC? Compare this date with the company's fiscal year-end. Why do the two dates differ?
2. Item 1 of the 10-K lists the company's executive officers. What are the names of the CEO and CFO?
3. As of June 30, 2018, how many people worked for Microsoft, and where were they located?
4. Review the fiscal year highlights reported in the Overview (Part II, item 7). What specific products and services drive the company's 2018 revenue growth?
5. Who are the company's auditors?

Solution on p. 2-42.

Global Accounting

Both GAAP and IFRS use accrual accounting to prepare financial statements. Although there are vastly more similarities than differences, we highlight below a few of the more notable differences for financial statements.

Balance Sheet The most visible difference is that many IFRS-based balance sheets are presented in reverse order of liquidity. The least liquid asset, usually goodwill, is listed first, and the most liquid asset, cash, is last. The same inverse liquidity order applies to liabilities. There are also several detailed presentation and measurement differences that we explain in other modules. As one example, for GAAP-based balance sheets, bank overdrafts are often netted against cash balances. IFRS does not permit this netting on the balance sheet. However, the IFRS statement of cash flows *does* net the cash balance with any bank overdrafts and, thus, the cash balance on the statement of cash flows might not match the cash amount on the balance sheet.

Income Statement The most visible difference is that GAAP requires three years' of data on the income statement whereas IFRS requires only two. Another difference is that GAAP income statements classify expenses by *function* and must separately report cost of goods sold, whereas IFRS permits expense classification by *function* (cost of sales, selling and administrative, etc.) or by *type* (raw materials, labor, depreciation, etc.). This means, for example, there is no requirement to report a cost of sales figure under IFRS.

Guidance Answers

You Are the Securities Analyst

Pg. 2-14 Of special concern is the possibility that the new CEO is shifting costs to the current period in lieu of recording them in future periods. Evidence suggests such behavior occurs when a new management team takes control. The reasoning is that the new management can blame poor current period performance on prior management and, at the same time, rid the balance sheet (and the new management team) of costs that would normally be expensed in future periods.

You Are the Operations Manager

Pg. 2-15 The CFO desires a warranty cost estimate that corresponds to the sales generated from the new product. To arrive at such an estimate, you must estimate the expected number and types of deficiencies in your product and the costs to repair each deficiency per the warranty provisions. This is often a difficult task for product engineers because it forces them to focus on product failures and associated costs.

Questions

Q2-1. The balance sheet consists of assets, liabilities, and equity. Define each category, and provide two examples of accounts reported within each category.

Q2-2. Explain how we account for a cost that creates an immediate benefit versus a cost that creates a future benefit.

Q2-3. GAAP is based on the concept of accrual accounting. Define and describe accrual accounting.

Q2-4. Analysts attempt to identify transitory items in an income statement. Define transitory items. What is the purpose of identifying transitory items?

Q2-5. What is the statement of stockholders' equity? What useful information does it contain?

Q2-6. What is the statement of cash flows? What useful information does it contain?

Q2-7. Define and explain the concept of financial statement articulation. What insight comes from understanding articulation?

Q2-8. Describe the flow of costs for the purchase of a machine. At what point do such costs become expenses? Why is it necessary to record the expenses related to the machine in the same period as the revenues it produces?

Q2-9. What are the two essential characteristics of an asset?

Q2-10. What does the concept of liquidity refer to? Explain.

Q2-11. What does the term *current* denote when referring to assets?

Q2-12. Assets are recorded at historical costs even though current market values might, arguably, be more relevant to financial statement readers. Describe the reasoning behind historical cost usage.

Q2-13. Identify three intangible assets that are likely to be *excluded* from the balance sheet because they cannot be reliably measured.

Q2-14. Identify three intangible assets that are recorded on the balance sheet.

Q2-15. What are accrued liabilities? Provide an example.

Q2-16. Define net working capital. Explain how increasing the amount of trade credit can reduce the net working capital for a company.

Q2-17. What is the difference between company *book value* and *market value*? Explain why these two amounts differ.

Q2-18. Describe the linkage between the income statement and the equity section of the balance sheet. Describe the linkage between the statement of cash flows and the equity section of the balance sheet when a company pays dividends.

Mini Exercises

M2-19. Identify and Classify Financial Statement Items
For each of the following items, indicate whether they would be reported in the balance sheet (B) or income statement (I).

LO1, 2

_____ *a.* Net income _____ *d.* Accumulated depreciation _____ *g.* Interest expense
_____ *b.* Retained earnings _____ *e.* Wages expense _____ *h.* Interest payable
_____ *c.* Depreciation expense _____ *f.* Wages payable _____ *i.* Sales

M2-20. Identify and Classify Financial Statement Items
For each of the following items, indicate whether they would be reported in the balance sheet (B) or income statement (I).

LO1, 2

_____ *a.* Machinery _____ *e.* Common stock _____ *i.* Taxes expense
_____ *b.* Supplies expense _____ *f.* Factory buildings _____ *j.* Cost of goods sold
_____ *c.* Inventories _____ *g.* Receivables _____ *k.* Long-term debt
_____ *d.* Sales _____ *h.* Taxes payable _____ *l.* Treasury stock

M2-21. Collect and Use Information from Form 8-K
On February 28, 2019, Kraft Heinz filed a Form 8-K Current Report with the SEC. What important announcement did Kraft make that day? *Hint:* Use the SEC website (www.sec.gov/edgar/searchedgar /companysearch.html) to find the Form 8-K.

LO6
Kraft Heinz (KHC)

M2-22. Assign Accounts to Sections of the Balance Sheet
Identify each of the following accounts as a component of assets (A), liabilities (L), or equity (E).

LO1

_____ *a.* Cash and cash equivalents _____ *e.* Long-term debt
_____ *b.* Wages payable _____ *f.* Retained earnings
_____ *c.* Common stock _____ *g.* Additional paid-in capital
_____ *d.* Equipment _____ *h.* Taxes payable

M2-23. Determine Missing Information Using the Accounting Equation
Use knowledge of accounting relations to complete the following table for Boatsman Company.

LO3

	2020	2019
Beginning retained earnings...........	$189,089	$?
Net income (loss)..................	?	48,192
Dividends........................	0	15,060
Ending retained earnings............	169,634	?

M2-24. Reconcile Retained Earnings
Following is financial information from Johnson & Johnson for the year ended December 30, 2018. Prepare the retained earnings reconciliation for Johnson & Johnson for the year ended December 30, 2018 ($ millions).

LO3
Johnson & Johnson (JNJ)

Retained earnings, Dec. 31, 2017	$101,793	Dividends	$9,494
Net earnings....................	15,297	Retained earnings, Dec. 30, 2018	?
Other retained earnings changes.....	(1,380)		

Exercises

E2-25.   Use Information from Form 20-F

Stock of Credit Suisse Group trades on the New York Stock Exchange as well as in various European stock markets. The company's Form 20-F reported the following.

> The accompanying consolidated financial statements of Credit Suisse Group AG (the Group) are prepared in accordance with accounting principles generally accepted in the US (US GAAP) and are stated in Swiss francs (CHF). The financial year for the Group ends on December 31.
>
> A major focus of US policy and regulation relating to financial institutions has been to combat money laundering and terrorist financing. These laws and regulations impose obligations to maintain appropriate policies, procedures and controls to detect, prevent and report money laundering and terrorist financing, verify the identity of customers and comply with economic sanctions. Any failure to maintain and implement adequate programs to combat money laundering and terrorist financing, and violations of such economic sanctions, laws and regulations, could have serious legal and reputational consequences. We take our obligations to prevent money laundering and terrorist financing in the US and globally very seriously, while appropriately respecting and protecting the confidentiality of clients. We have policies, procedures and training intended to ensure that our employees comply with "know your customer" regulations and understand when a client relationship or business should be evaluated as higher risk for us.

Required

a. Why would Credit Suisse prepare its financial statements in accordance with U.S. GAAP?

b. Credit Suisse discusses various criminal activities and explains its anti-corruption policies. Why might this be the case?

E2-26.   Use Information from Form 20-F

H&R Block reports the following information in Schedule II of its 2018 Form 10-K. Accounts receivable represents the amount customers owe the company at year-end. The balance in the allowance for doubtful accounts is the company's best estimate of the amount customers will not repay.

VALUATION AND QUALIFYING ACCOUNTS				
For Year Ended April 30 ($ millions)	Balance at Beginning of Period	Additions Charged to Costs and Expenses	Deductions	Balance at End of Period
Allowance for doubtful accounts, April 30, 2016...	$54,527	$73,682	$(71,198)	$57,011
Allowance for doubtful accounts, April 30, 2017...	57,011	52,776	(54,491)	55,296
Allowance for doubtful accounts, April 30, 2018...	55,296	74,489	(47,972)	81,813

Required

The balance in the allowance account increased during 2018 (from $55,296 million to $81,813 million) after decreasing during 2017 (from $57,011 million to $55,296 million). What additional information would an analyst want to use to determine if this variability is of concern?

E2-27.   Construct Financial Statements from Account Data

Barth Company reports the following year-end account balances at December 31, 2019. Prepare the 2019 income statement and the balance sheet as of December 31, 2019.

Accounts payable	$ 16,000	Inventory	$ 36,000
Accounts receivable	30,000	Land	80,000
Bonds payable, long-term	200,000	Goodwill	8,000
Buildings	151,000	Retained earnings	160,000
Cash	148,000	Sales revenue	500,000
Common stock	150,000	Supplies inventory	3,000
Cost of goods sold	180,000	Supplies expense	6,000
Equipment	70,000	Wages expense	40,000

E2-28. Construct Financial Statements from Transaction Data

Baiman Corporation commences operations at the beginning of January. It provides its services on credit and bills its customers $40,000 for January sales, which are unpaid at month-end. Its employees also earn January wages of $12,000 that are not paid until the first of February. Complete the following statements for the month-end of January.

LO1, 2

Income Statement	
Sales	$
Wages expense	
Net income (loss)	$

Balance Sheet	
Cash	$
Accounts receivable	
Total assets	$
Wages payable	$
Retained earnings	
Total liabilities and equity	$

E2-29. Apply Financial Statement Linkages to Understand Transactions

Consider the effects of the independent transactions, *a* through *g*, on a company's balance sheet, income statement, and statement of cash flows. Complete the table below to explain the effects and financial statement linkages. Use "+" to indicate the account increases and "−" to indicate the account decreases. Refer to Exhibit 2.10 as a guide for the linkages.

LO1, 2, 3, 4, 5

	a.	b.	c.	d.	e.	f.	g.
Balance Sheet							
Cash							
Noncash assets							
Total liabilities							
Contributed capital							
Retained earnings							
Other equity							
Statement of Cash Flows							
Operating cash flow							
Investing cash flow							
Financing cash flow							
Income Statement							
Revenues							
Expenses							
Net income							
Statement of Stockholders' Equity							
Contributed capital							
Retained earnings							

a. The company issued common stock in exchange for cash and property and equipment.
b. The company paid cash for rent of office furnishings and facilities.
c. The company performed services for clients and immediately received cash earned.
d. The company performed services for clients and sent a bill with payment due within 60 days.

e. The company compensated an office employee with cash as salary.

f. The company received cash as partial payment on the amount owed from clients in transaction *d*.

g. The company paid cash in dividends.

LO1, 2, 3, 4, 5   **E2-30.**   **Apply Financial Statement Linkages to Understand Transactions**

Consider the effects of the independent transactions, *a* through *g*, on a company's balance sheet, income statement, and statement of cash flow. Complete the table below to explain the effects and financial statement linkages. Use "+" to indicate the account increases and "−" to indicate the account decreases. Refer to Exhibit 2-10 as a guide for the linkages.

	a.	b.	c.	d.	e.	f.	g.
Balance Sheet							
Cash							
Noncash assets							
Total liabilities							
Contributed capital							
Retained earnings							
Other equity							
Statement of Cash Flows							
Operating cash flow							
Investing cash flow							
Financing cash flow							
Income Statement							
Revenues							
Expenses							
Net income							
Statement of Stockholders' Equity							
Contributed capital							
Retained earnings							

a. Owners invested cash in the company in exchange for shares of common stock.

b. The company received cash from the bank for a loan.

c. The company purchased equipment to manufacture goods for sale and paid with cash.

d. The company manufactured a custom piece of inventory and paid cash for materials and labor. The company sold the inventory for more than cost, and the customer promised to pay for the inventory in 30 days.

e. The company paid monthly rent for a manufacturing space.

f. The company paid cash dividends to the owners.

g. The company received cash from the customer in transaction *d*.

LO1, 2   **E2-31.**   **Identify and Classify Balance Sheet and Income Statement Accounts**

Best Buy, Inc. (BBY)

Following are selected accounts for Best Buy Inc. for the fiscal year ended February 2, 2019.

a. Indicate whether each account appears on the balance sheet (B) or income statement (I).

b. Using the following data, compute total assets and total expenses.

$ millions	Amount	Classification
Sales	$42,879	
Accumulated depreciation	6,690	
Depreciation expense	770	
Retained earnings	2,985	
Net income	1,464	
Property, plant, and equipment, net	2,510	
Selling, general, and administrative expense	8,015	
Accounts receivable	1,015	
Total liabilities	9,595	
Total stockholders' equity	3,306	

E2-32. **Identify and Classify Balance Sheet and Income Statement Accounts**

Following are selected accounts for Terex Corp for the fiscal year ended December 31, 2018.

LO1, 2
Terex Corp (TEX)

 a. Indicate whether each account appears on the balance sheet (B) or income statement (I).

 b. Using the following data, compute total assets and total expenses.

$ millions	Amount	Classification
Total revenues	$5,125.0	_____
Accrued compensation and benefits	152.2	_____
Depreciation and amortization expense.......	59.7	_____
Retained earnings	749.0	_____
Net income............................	113.7	_____
Property, plant, and equipment, net	345.6	_____
Selling, general, and administrative expense...	673.5	_____
Inventory..............................	1,212.0	_____
Total liabilities	2,624.9	_____
Total stockholders' equity	861.0	_____

E2-33. **Compare Income Statements and Balance Sheets of Competitors**

Following are selected income statement and balance sheet data from two retailers, Abercrombie & Fitch (clothing retailer in the high-end market) and TJX Companies (clothing retailer in the value-priced market), for the fiscal year ended February 2, 2019.

LO1, 2

Abercrombie & Fitch
(ANF)
TJX Companies (TJX)

Income Statement ($ thousands)	ANF	TJX
Sales.........................	$3,590,109	$38,972,934
Cost of goods sold	1,430,193	27,831,177
Gross profit.....................	2,159,916	11,141,757
Total expenses	2,081,108	8,081,959
Net income	$ 78,808	$ 3,059,798

Balance Sheet ($ thousands)	ANF	TJX
Current assets	$1,335,950	$ 8,469,222
Long-term assets	1,049,643	5,856,807
Total assets	$2,385,593	$14,326,029
Current liabilities.................	$ 558,917	$ 5,531,374
Long-term liabilities...............	608,055	3,746,049
Total liabilities...................	1,166,972	9,277,423
Stockholders' equity	1,218,621	5,048,606
Total liabilities and equity	$2,385,593	$14,326,029

 a. Express each income statement amount as a percentage of sales. Comment on any differences observed between these two companies, especially as they relate to their respective business models.

 b. Express each balance sheet amount as a percentage of total assets. Comment on any differences observed between these two companies, especially as they relate to their respective business models.

 c. Which company has a lower proportion of debt? What do the ratios tell us about the relative riskiness of the two companies?

E2-34. **Compare Income Statements and Balance Sheets of Competitors**

Following are selected income statement and balance sheet data from two pharmaceutical companies, Pfizer and Dr. Reddy's, for their respective 2018 fiscal years.

LO1, 2
Pfizer, Inc (PFE)

Dr. Reddy's
Laboratories (RDY)

Income Statement ($ millions)	Pfizer	Dr. Reddy's
Sales..........................	$53,647	$2,181
Cost of goods sold	11,248	1,009
Gross profit......................	42,399	1,172
Total expenses	31,211	1,021
Net income.....................	$11,188	$ 151

Balance Sheet ($ millions)	Pfizer	Dr. Reddy's
Current assets	$ 49,926	$1,684
Long-term assets	109,496	1,781
Total assets	$159,422	3,465
Current liabilities..................	$ 31,858	$1,070
Long-term liabilities...............	63,806	453
Total liabilities	95,664	1,523
Stockholders' equity..............	63,758	1,942
Total liabilities and equity	$159,422	$3,465

a. Express each income statement amount as a percentage of sales. Comment on any differences observed between the two companies, especially as they relate to their respective business models. (*Hint:* Pfizer's gross profit as a percentage of sales is considerably higher than Dr. Reddy's. What aspect of Pfizer's business do we believe is driving its profitability?)

b. Express each balance sheet amount as a percentage of total assets. Comment on any differences observed between the two companies. Pfizer has chosen to structure itself with a lower proportion of equity (and a higher proportion of debt) than Dr. Reddy's. How does this capital structure decision affect our evaluation of the relative riskiness of these two companies?

LO1, 2
Comcast (CMCSA)
Verizon (VZ)

E2-35.   Compare Income Statements and Balance Sheets of Competitors
Following are selected income statement and balance sheet data for two communications companies, Comcast and Verizon, for the year ended December 31, 2018.

Income Statement ($ millions)	Comcast	Verizon
Sales..........................	$94,507	$130,863
Operating costs	75,498	108,585
Operating profit...................	19,009	22,278
Nonoperating expenses	7,147	6,239
Net income.....................	$11,862	$ 16,039

Balance Sheet ($ millions)	Comcast	Verizon
Current assets	$ 21,848	$ 34,636
Long-term assets	229,836	230,193
Total assets	$251,684	$264,829
Current liabilities..................	$ 27,603	$ 37,930
Long-term liabilities...............	151,579	172,189
Total liabilities	$179,182	210,119
Stockholders' equity*	72,502	54,710
Total liabilities and equity	$251,684	$264,829

*Includes noncontrolling interest

a. Express each income statement amount as a percentage of sales. Comment on any differences observed between the two companies.

b. Express each balance sheet amount as a percentage of total assets. Comment on any differences observed between the two companies, especially as they relate to their respective business models.

   c. Both Verizon and Comcast have chosen a capital structure with a higher proportion of liabilities than equity. How does this capital structure decision affect our evaluation of the riskiness of these two companies? Take into consideration the large level of capital expenditures that each must make to remain competitive.

E2-36. Compare Financial Information Across Industries

Use the data and computations required in parts *a* and *b* of exercises E2-33 and E2-34 to compare TJX Companies and Pfizer, Inc.

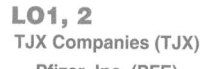

LO1, 2
TJX Companies (TJX)
Pfizer, Inc. (PFE)

   a. Compare gross profit and net income as a percentage of sales for these two companies. How might differences in their respective business models explain the differences observed?

   b. Compare sales versus total assets. What do observed differences indicate about the relative capital intensity of these two industries?

   c. Which company has the higher percentage of total liabilities to stockholders' equity? What do these ratios imply about the relative riskiness of these two companies?

E2-37. Apply Financial Statement Linkages to Understand Transactions

Consider the effects of the independent transactions, *a* through *h*, on a company's balance sheet, income statement, and statement of cash flow. Complete the table below to explain the effects and financial statement linkages. Use "+" to indicate the account increases and "−" to indicate the account decreases. Refer to Exhibit 2-10 as a guide for the linkages.

LO1, 2, 3, 4, 5

	a.	b.	c.	d.	e.	f.	g.	h.
Balance Sheet								
Cash								
Noncash assets								
Total liabilities								
Contributed capital								
Retained earnings								
Other equity								
Statement of Cash Flows								
Operating cash flow								
Investing cash flow								
Financing cash flow								
Income Statement								
Revenues								
Expenses								
Net income								
Statement of Stockholders' Equity								
Contributed capital								
Retained earnings								

   a. Wages are earned by employees but not yet paid.
   b. Inventory is purchased on credit.
   c. Inventory purchased in transaction *b* is sold on credit (and for more than its cost).
   d. Collected cash from transaction *c*.
   e. Equipment is acquired for cash.
   f. Paid cash for inventory purchased in transaction *b*.
   g. Paid cash toward a note payable that came due.
   h. Paid cash for interest on borrowings.

Problems

P2-38. Construct and Analyze Balance Sheet Amounts from Incomplete Data

Selected balance sheet amounts for 3M Company, a manufacturer of consumer and business products, for three recent years follow.

LO1

3M Company (MMM)

$ millions	Current Assets	Long-Term Assets	Total Assets	Current Liabilities	Long-Term Liabilities	Total Liabilities	Stockholders' Equity*
2018	$13,709	$?	$36,500	$?	$19,408	$26,652	$ 9,848
2017	14,277	23,710	?	7,687	18,678	?	11,622
2016	?	21,180	32,906	6,219	16,344	22,563	?

* Includes noncontrolling interest

Required

a. Compute the missing balance sheet amounts for each of the three years shown.

b. Which of the following would not be included among 3M's current assets? Select all that apply.

1. Cash and cash equivalents
2. Property plant & equipment
3. Inventory
4. Accounts payable
5. Marketable securities
6. Goodwill
7. Accrued expenses
8. Prepaid expenses

c. Which of the following would be included among 3M's long-term assets? Select all that apply.

1. Property plant & equipment
2. Accounts payable
3. Intangible assets
4. Work in process
5. Goodwill
6. Accrued expenses
7. Prepaid expenses
8. Long-term notes payable

LO1, 2, 5, 6
Community Health
Systems (CYH)

P2-39.   Use Additional Information from 10-K to Explain Linkages Among Financial Statements

Community Health Systems operates general acute care hospitals in communities across the United States. The company reports the following information in Schedule II of its 2017 10-K.

$ millions	Balance at Beginning of Year	Acquisitions and Dispositions	Bad Debt Expense	Write-Offs	Balance at End of Year
SCHEDULE II—VALUATION AND QUALIFYING ACCOUNTS					
December 31, 2017, allowance for doubtful accounts . . .	$3,773	$ (21)	$3,054	$(2,936)	$3,870
December 31, 2016, allowance for doubtful accounts . . .	4,110	(365)	2,849	(2,821)	3,773
December 31, 2015, allowance for doubtful accounts . . .	3,504	(17)	3,168	(2,545)	4,110

Accounts receivable represents the amount customers owe Community Health Systems for services rendered. The balance in the allowance for doubtful accounts is the company's best estimate of the amount that customers will not repay.

Community Health Systems' balance sheet and income statements reported the following.

$ millions	2017	2016	2015
Revenue.	$18,398	$21,275	$22,564
Operating income (loss) before tax	(1,878)	(860)	1,337
Total assets	17,450	21,944	26,861

Required

a. Compute the common-size allowance for doubtful accounts for each year. Compare 2017 to the prior years; what do we observe? What is one conclusion analysts might draw from this analysis?

b. On average, the firms in the S&P 500 report common-size allowance for doubtful accounts between 3% and 5%. Why might Community Health Systems' ratio be so much higher? How could an analyst verify this inference?

c. Compute the common-size bad debt expense for each year. Interpret the ratio for 2017. What trend do we observe?

d. If the company had recorded bad debt expense of $2,554 in 2017 (which is $500 less than actually recorded), which of the following would be true? (Ignore taxes for this question.)

1. The company would have reported operating loss of $1,378 and cash flow would have been $500 higher.
2. The company would have reported operating loss of $2,378 and cash flow would have been $500 higher.
3. The company would have reported operating loss of $1,378 and cash flow would have been unchanged.

4. The company would have reported operating loss of $1,878 and cash flow would have been unchanged.

P2-40. Collect and Use Additional Information from 10-K

Use the SEC website (www.sec.gov/edgar/searchedgar/companysearch.html) to download the 2018 10-K for Facebook Inc. and answer the following questions.

a. On what date did Facebook file its 2018 10-K with the SEC? Compare this date to the company's fiscal year-end. Why do the two dates differ?
b. Item 1 of the 10-K reports the company's mission. What is its mission?
c. Who does Facebook see as its main competition? See Item 1 of the 10-K.
d. As of December 31, 2018, how many people worked for Facebook?
e. How many daily active users did Facebook have in December 2018? How does this compare with December 2017?
f. Many companies file Schedule II with the 10-K. One of the components of Schedule II is an estimate of the amount owing from customers that will not be collected (allowance for doubtful accounts). What does Facebook report concerning this schedule? Explain.
g. Who are the company's auditors?

P2-41. Compare Operating Characteristics Across Industries

Following are selected income statement and balance sheet data for companies in different industries.

$ millions	Sales	Cost of Goods Sold	Net Income	Assets	Liabilities	Stockholders' Equity
Target Corp.	$75,356	$53,299	$ 2,937	$ 41,290	$29,993	$11,297
Nike Inc.............	36,397	20,441	1,933	22,536	12,724	9,812
Harley-Davidson......	5,717	3,352	531	10,666	8,892	1,774
Pfizer	53,647	11,248	11,188	159,422	95,664	63,758

Required

a. Compute the following ratios for each company.
   1. Gross profit/Sales
   2. Net income/Sales
   3. Net income/Stockholders' equity
   4. Liabilities/Stockholders' equity
b. Comment on any differences among the companies' gross profit-to-sales ratios and net income as a percentage of sales. Do differences in the companies' business models explain the differences observed?
c. Which company reports the highest ratio of net income to equity? Suggest one or more reasons for this result.
d. Which company has financed itself with the highest percentage of liabilities to equity? Suggest one or more reasons why this company can take on such debt levels.

P2-42. Compare Cash Flows Across Retailers

Following are selected accounts from the income statement and the statement of cash flows for several retailers, for their fiscal years ended in 2018.

$ millions	Sales	Net Income	Cash Flows from Operating	Cash Flows from Investing	Cash Flows from Financing
Macy's	$ 25,739	$ 1,108	$ 1,735	$ (456)	$ (1,544)
Home Depot Inc.....	108,203	11,121	13,038	(2,416)	(12,420)
Best Buy	42,879	1,464	2,408	508	(2,018)
Target Corp.	75,356	2,937	5,973	(3,416)	(3,644)
Walmart Stores.....	511,729	6,670	27,753	(24,036)	(2,537)

Required

a. Compute the ratio of net income to sales for each company. Rank the companies on the basis of this ratio. Do their respective business models give insight into these differences?

b. Compute net cash flows from operating activities as a percentage of sales. Rank the companies on the basis of this ratio. Does this ranking coincide with the ratio rankings from part *a*? Suggest one or more reasons for any differences observed.

c. Compute net cash flows from investing activities as a percentage of sales. Rank the companies on the basis of this ratio. Does this ranking coincide with the ratio rankings from part *a*? Suggest one or more reasons for any differences observed.

LO6 **P2-43** **Interpret Data Visualization to Interpret Balance Sheet Data**

Access the Power BI dashboard on **MyBusinessCourse** to use the data visualization for Apple's balance sheet and cash flow data.

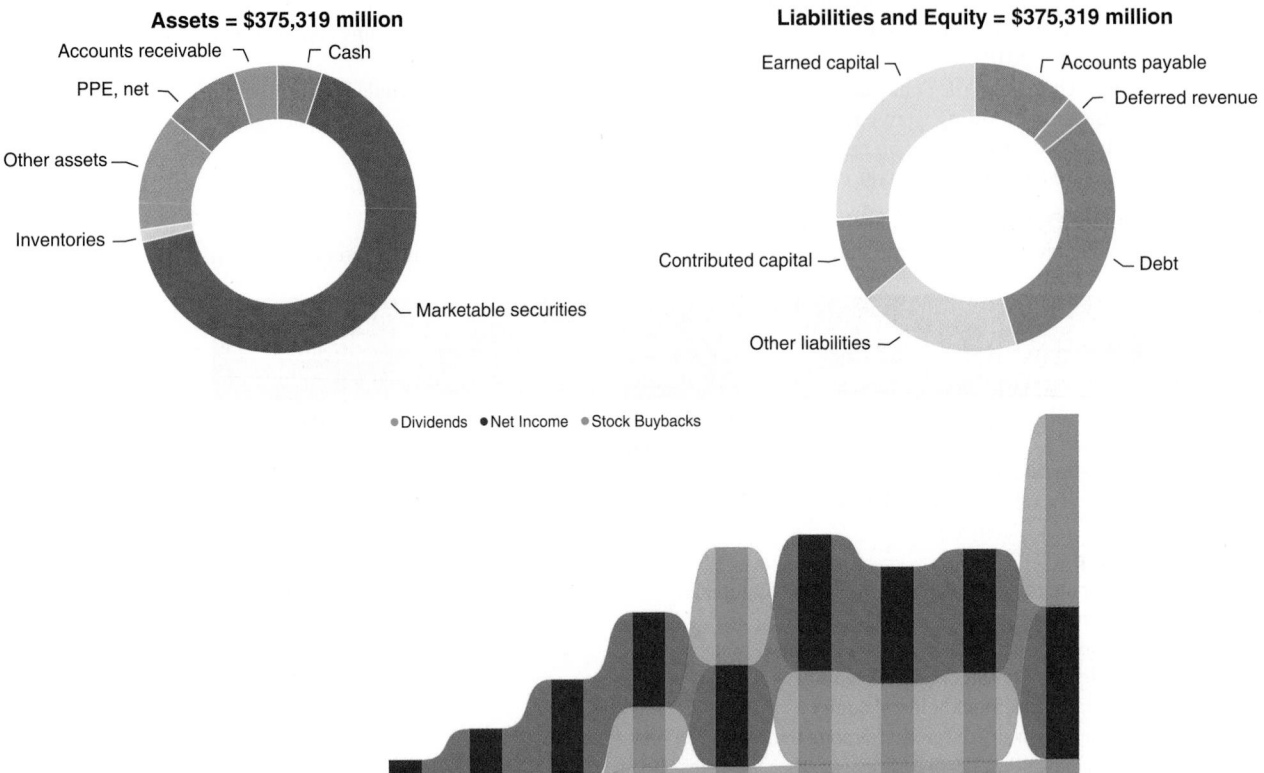

Required

a. Using this visualization, what is the largest asset? The smallest? What is the largest liability? Of the two equity components, which is smaller?

b. Compare this visualization of Apple's balance sheet (for 2017) with the Apple graphics on page 2-1 (for 2018).
   1. What do we observe about the relative size of Apple's balance sheet? How did the asset composition change across these years?
   2. Compare the liability and equity side of the balance sheet. How did the composition change during the year?

c. Consider the ribbon graph that depicts net income, dividends, and stock buybacks. In which year did Apple initiate dividends? What pattern do we observe with respect to dividends?

d. Compare net income and stock buybacks in the ribbon graph. What do we observe? What distinguishes 2014 and 2018 compared to all other years in this graphic?

e. From the ribbon graph, what can we conclude about the change in retained earnings between 2017 and 2018?

IFRS Applications

I2-44. **Compare Income Statements and Balance Sheets of Competitors**

LO1, 2

Following are selected income statement and balance sheet data from two European grocery chain companies: **Tesco PLC** (UK) and **Ahold** (the Netherlands).

Income Statements For Fiscal Year Ended	Tesco February 24, 2019 (£ millions)	Carrefour Group December 31, 2018 (€ millions)
Sales.	£63,911	€77,917
Cost of goods sold	59,767	60,850
Gross profit.	4,144	17,067
Total expenses	2,824	17,411
Net income	£ 1,320	€ (344)

Balance Sheet	Tesco February 24, 2019 (£ millions)	Carrefour Group December 31, 2018 (€ millions)
Current assets	£12,668	€18,670
Long-term assets	36,379	28,708
Total assets	£49,047	€47,378
Current liabilities.	£20,680	€23,162
Long-term liabilities.	13,533	12,930
Total liabilities	34,213	36,092
Stockholders' equity	14,834	11,286
Total liabilities and equity	£49,047	€47,378

Required

a. Prepare a common-size income statement. To do this, express each income statement amount as a percent of sales. Comment on any differences observed between the two companies.

b. Prepare a common-size balance sheet. To do this, express each balance sheet amount as a percent of total assets. Comment on any differences observed between the two companies.

c. Which company has chosen to structure itself with a higher proportion of equity (and a lower proportion of debt)? How does this capital structure decision affect our assessment of the relative riskiness of these two companies?

Management Applications

MA2-45. **Explain the Company Operating Cycle and Management Strategy**

LO1, 4

Consider the operating cycle as depicted in Exhibit 2.4 to answer the following questions.

a. Why might a company want to reduce its cash conversion cycle? (*Hint*: Consider the financial statement implications of reducing the cash conversion cycle.)

b. How might a company reduce its cash conversion cycle?

c. Examine and discuss the potential impacts on *customers* and *suppliers* of taking the actions identified in part b.

MA2-46. **Ethics and Governance: Understand Revenue Recognition and Expense Recording**

LO2

Revenue should be recognized when the performance obligation is satisfied and expense when incurred. Given some lack of specificity in these terms, companies have some latitude when applying GAAP to determine the timing and amount of revenues and expenses. A few companies use this latitude to manage reported earnings. Some have argued that it is not necessarily bad for companies to manage earnings in that, by doing so, management (1) can better provide investors and creditors with reported earnings that are closer to "core" earnings (i.e., management purges earnings of components deemed irrelevant or distracting so that share prices better reflect company performance) and (2) can present the company in the best light, which benefits both shareholders and employees—a Machiavellian argument that "the end justifies the means."

a. Is it good that GAAP is written as broadly as it is? Explain. What are the pros and cons of defining accounting terms more strictly?

b. Assess (both pro and con) the Machiavellian argument above that defends managing earnings.

Ongoing Project

(This ongoing project began in Module 1 and continues through most of the book; even if previous segments were not completed, the requirements are still applicable to any business analysis.) The goal of this module's project is to perform vertical analysis of the balance sheet and income statement, assess cash flows, and determine market capitalization.

1. *Balance Sheet Analysis.*   Prepare a common-size balance sheet. To facilitate this, obtain the balance sheet in spreadsheet form from the SEC website at the the "Interactive Data" link on the search results page. Look for major differences over time. Some questions to consider:
   - What are the company's largest assets? Largest liabilities?
   - What proportion of total assets is financed by owners? (*Hint:* Compare with total equity.)
   - What proportion of total assets is financed by nonowners?

2. *Income Statement Analysis.*   Prepare a common-size income statement. Express each item on the income statement as a percent of total sales or revenue. Do this for all years on the income statement. Look for major differences over time and between the companies. Do any patterns emerge? Some questions to consider:
   - What are the major expenses?
   - Are there any unusual or discontinued items? Are they large in magnitude?
   - Was the company more or less profitable when compared with the prior year?

3. *Statement of Cash Flows Analysis.*   Determine the size and direction (cash source or use) of cash flows from operations, investing, and financing. One goal is to understand the company's pattern of cash flows and to form an opinion about the general strength of its cash flows. Some questions to consider:
   - What were the cash flows from operations? Were they positive?
   - Were operating cash flows smaller or larger than net income?
   - Did the company generate or use cash from investing activities?
   - Did the company generate or use cash from financing activities?

4. *Market Capitalization.*   Determine the market capitalization at the most recent year-end. Determine the number of shares outstanding from the balance sheet. Recall that shares outstanding is total shares issued less any treasury shares. Obtain the year-end stock price from an investment website such as Seeking Alpha or Yahoo Finance. Compare market cap with the book value (total equity) of the company.

Solutions to Review Problems

Review 2-1—Solution ($ millions)

MICROSOFT CORPORATION Balance Sheet June 30, 2018			
Cash and short-term investments	$133,768	Accounts payable	$ 8,617
Accounts receivable	26,481	Accrued expenses	6,103
Inventories	2,662	Other current liabilities	43,768
Other current assets	6,751	Total current liabilities	58,488
Total current assets	169,662	Long-term liabilities	117,642
Property, plant, and equipment, net	29,460	Total liabilities	176,130
Other long-term assets	59,726		
		Common stock and paid-in capital	71,223
		Retained earnings	13,682
		Other stockholders' equity	(2,187)
		Total stockholders' equity	82,718
Total assets	$258,848	Total liabilities and equity	$258,848

Review 2-2—Solution ($ millions)

MICROSOFT CORPORATION Income Statement For Year Ended June 30, 2018	
Total revenue	$110,360
Cost of goods sold	38,353
Gross profit	72,007
Operating expenses	36,949
Operating income	35,058
Other income	1,416
Income before income tax	36,474
Income tax expense	19,903
Net income	$ 16,571

Review 2-3—Solution ($ millions)

MICROSOFT CORPORATION Statement of Stockholders' Equity For Year Ended June 30, 2018				
	Common Stock and Paid-in Capital	Retained Earnings	Accumulated Other Comprehensive Income (Loss)	Total Equity
Beginning bal., June 30, 2017	$69,315	$17,769	$ 627	$87,711
Stock issuance, net	1,908	(7,699)		(5,791)
Net income		16,571		16,571
Dividends		(12,917)		(12,917)
Other		(42)	(2,814)	(2,856)
Ending bal., June 30, 2018	$71,223	$13,682	$(2,187)	$82,718

Review 2-4—Solution ($ millions)

MICROSOFT CORPORATION Statement of Cash Flows For Year Ended June 30, 2018	
Cash flows from operating activities..........	$43,884
Cash flows used for investing activities	(6,061)
Cash flows used for financing activities	(33,540)
Net change in cash......................	4,283
Cash balance, beginning of year	7,663
Cash balance, end of year	$11,946

Review 2-5—Solution

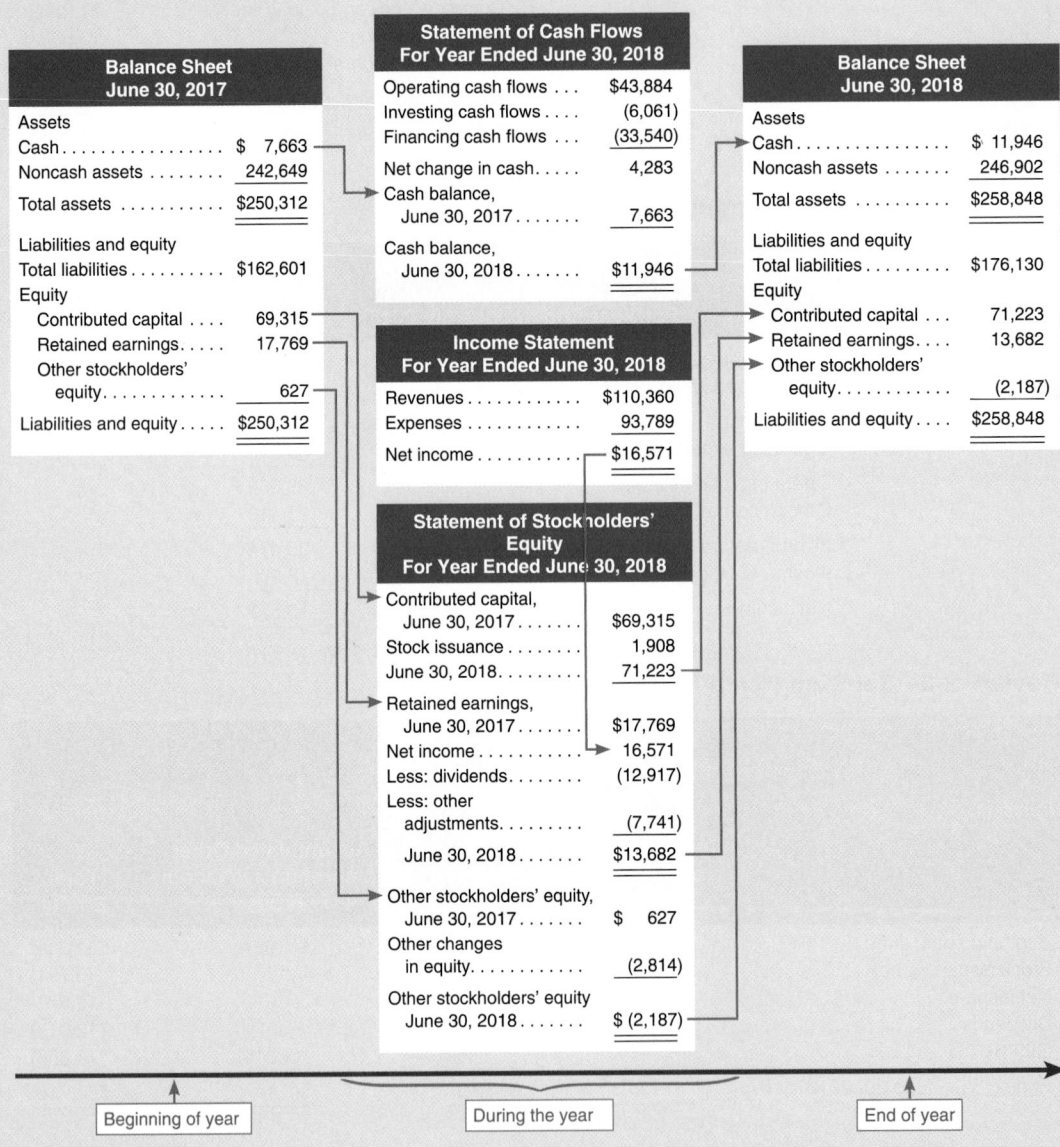

Balance Sheet June 30, 2017	
Assets	
Cash.................	$ 7,663
Noncash assets	242,649
Total assets	$250,312
Liabilities and equity	
Total liabilities..........	$162,601
Equity	
Contributed capital	69,315
Retained earnings.....	17,769
Other stockholders' equity.............	627
Liabilities and equity.....	$250,312

Statement of Cash Flows For Year Ended June 30, 2018	
Operating cash flows ...	$43,884
Investing cash flows	(6,061)
Financing cash flows ...	(33,540)
Net change in cash.....	4,283
Cash balance, June 30, 2017.......	7,663
Cash balance, June 30, 2018.......	$11,946

Income Statement For Year Ended June 30, 2018	
Revenues	$110,360
Expenses	93,789
Net income	$16,571

Statement of Stockholders' Equity For Year Ended June 30, 2018	
Contributed capital, June 30, 2017.......	$69,315
Stock issuance	1,908
June 30, 2018.........	71,223
Retained earnings, June 30, 2017.......	$17,769
Net income	16,571
Less: dividends........	(12,917)
Less: other adjustments........	(7,741)
June 30, 2018.......	$13,682
Other stockholders' equity, June 30, 2017.......	$ 627
Other changes in equity...........	(2,814)
Other stockholders' equity June 30, 2018.......	$ (2,187)

Balance Sheet June 30, 2018	
Assets	
Cash.................	$ 11,946
Noncash assets	246,902
Total assets	$258,848
Liabilities and equity	
Total liabilities..........	$176,130
Equity	
Contributed capital ...	71,223
Retained earnings....	13,682
Other stockholders' equity............	(2,187)
Liabilities and equity....	$258,848

Beginning of year   During the year   End of year

Review 2-6—Solution

1. The 10-K was filed on August 3, 2018, and the company's fiscal year-end was June 30, 2018. The SEC filing is a month after year-end because the auditors took a month to complete the audit.
2. The company's CEO is Satya Nadella, and the CFO is Amy E. Hood.
3. As of June 30, 2018, Microsoft employed approximately 131,000 people on a full-time basis, roughly 78,000 in the United States and 53,000 internationally.
4. The MD&A reports the growth in revenues is due to growth in "Productivity and Business Processes" and "Intelligent Cloud" segments and not from Personal Computing as we might have expected.
5. The company is audited by Deloitte and Touche out of the Seattle office.

Module **3**

Transactions, Adjustments, and Financial Statements

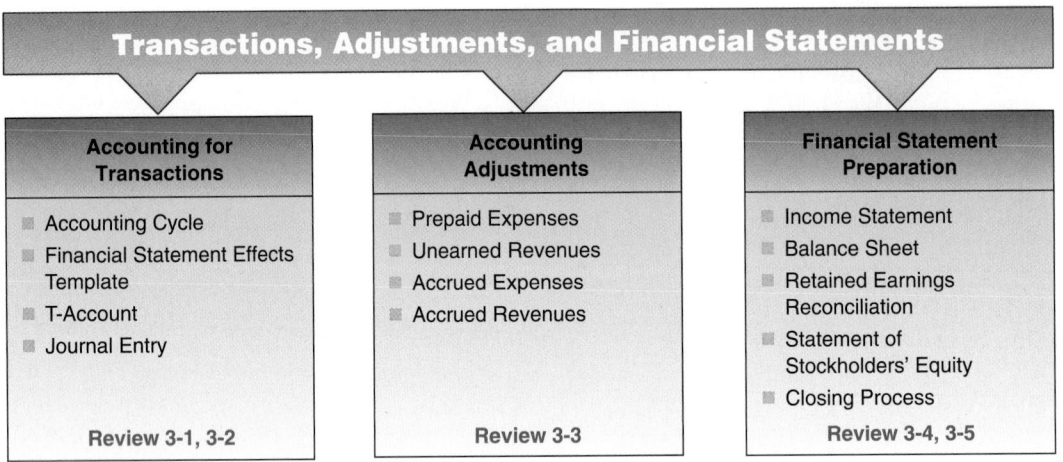

Transactions, Adjustments, and Financial Statements		
Accounting for Transactions	**Accounting Adjustments**	**Financial Statement Preparation**
■ Accounting Cycle ■ Financial Statement Effects Template ■ T-Account ■ Journal Entry	■ Prepaid Expenses ■ Unearned Revenues ■ Accrued Expenses ■ Accrued Revenues	■ Income Statement ■ Balance Sheet ■ Retained Earnings Reconciliation ■ Statement of Stockholders' Equity ■ Closing Process
Review 3-1, 3-2	Review 3-3	Review 3-4, 3-5

- We describe how companies enter transactions into their financial records.
- We explain the adjustments companies make to their financial records after all transactions have been recorded and before the company issues financial statements.
- We show how financial statements are prepared from transactions and adjustments data.
- We describe how the books are closed at the end of each period to get ready for the next period.
- We use Apple Inc. as the focus company and the dashboard below conveys its revenue and expense information for 2018.

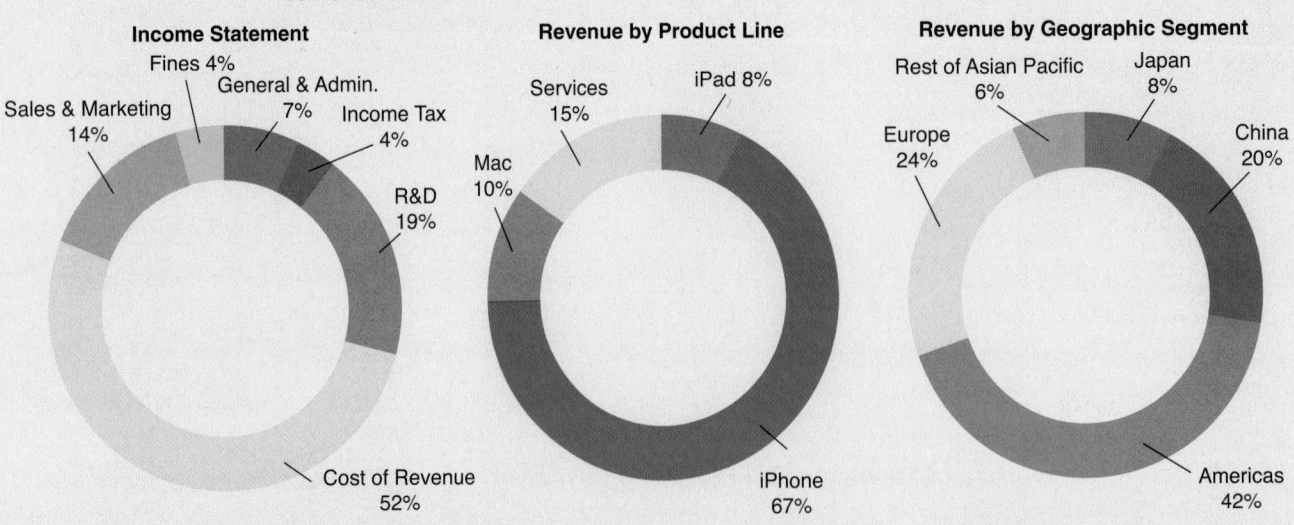

Income Statement
- Fines 4%
- General & Admin. 7%
- Sales & Marketing 14%
- Income Tax 4%
- R&D 19%
- Cost of Revenue 52%

Revenue by Product Line
- Services 15%
- iPad 8%
- Mac 10%
- iPhone 67%

Revenue by Geographic Segment
- Rest of Asian Pacific 6%
- Japan 8%
- Europe 24%
- China 20%
- Americas 42%

Road Map

LO	Learning Objective | Topics	Page	eLecture	Guided Example	Assignments
3–1	**Explain the accounting cycle, and construct the financial statement effects template.** Accounting Cycle :: Template :: T-Account :: Journal Entry	3-3	e3–1	Review 3-1	1, 2, 3
3–2	**Apply the financial statement effects template to analyze accounting transactions.** Transactions :: Applying the Template :: Applying the T-Account and Journal Entry	3-6	e3–2	Review 3-2	7, 8, 12, 13, 14, 15, 16, 17, 20, 21, 24, 28, 36, 37, 39, 40, 42, 44, 47, 48, 49, 50, 56, 57, 58, 59, 60, 62, 63
3–3	**Prepare and explain accounting adjustments and their financial statement effects.** Prepaid Expenses :: Unearned Revenues :: Accrued Expenses :: Accrued Revenues	3-9	e3–3	Review 3-3	4, 5, 6, 7, 8, 9, 10, 16, 17, 18, 19, 26, 27, 29, 30, 31, 32, 33, 34, 35, 44, 45, 46, 47, 48, 49, 50, 51, 52, 53, 54, 55, 57, 58, 60, 62, 63, 64, 65
3–4	**Construct financial statements from accounting records.** Income Statement :: Retained Earnings Reconciliation :: Balance Sheet :: Statement of Equity	3-13	e3–4	Review 3-4	22, 26, 27, 41, 43, 55, 56, 58, 59, 60, 63
3–5	**Explain and apply the closing process.** Revenue Accounts :: Expense Accounts :: Dividend Account	3-16	e3–5	Review 3-5	11, 23, 25, 32, 38, 41, 55, 61

Basics of Accounting

eLectures
MBC
LO1
Explain the accounting cycle, and construct the financial statement effects template.

Financial statements report on the financial performance and condition of a business. Those statements are tied to a period or point in time. The period of time is referred to as the accounting cycle, and each cycle consists of four activities.

Four-Step Accounting Cycle

The *accounting cycle* is illustrated in Exhibit 3.1.

- **Step 1** Record transactions in the accounting records. Each transaction is the result of an external or internal transaction or event, such as a sale to a customer or the payment of wages to employees.

- **Step 2** Prepare accounting adjustments, which recognize a number of events that have occurred but that have not yet been recorded. These might include the recognition of wage expense and the related wages payable for those employees who have earned wages but have not yet been paid or of depreciation expense for buildings and equipment.

- **Step 3** Prepare financial statements.

- **Step 4** Close the books in anticipation of the start of a new accounting cycle.

Exhibit 3.1 ■ Accounting Cycle

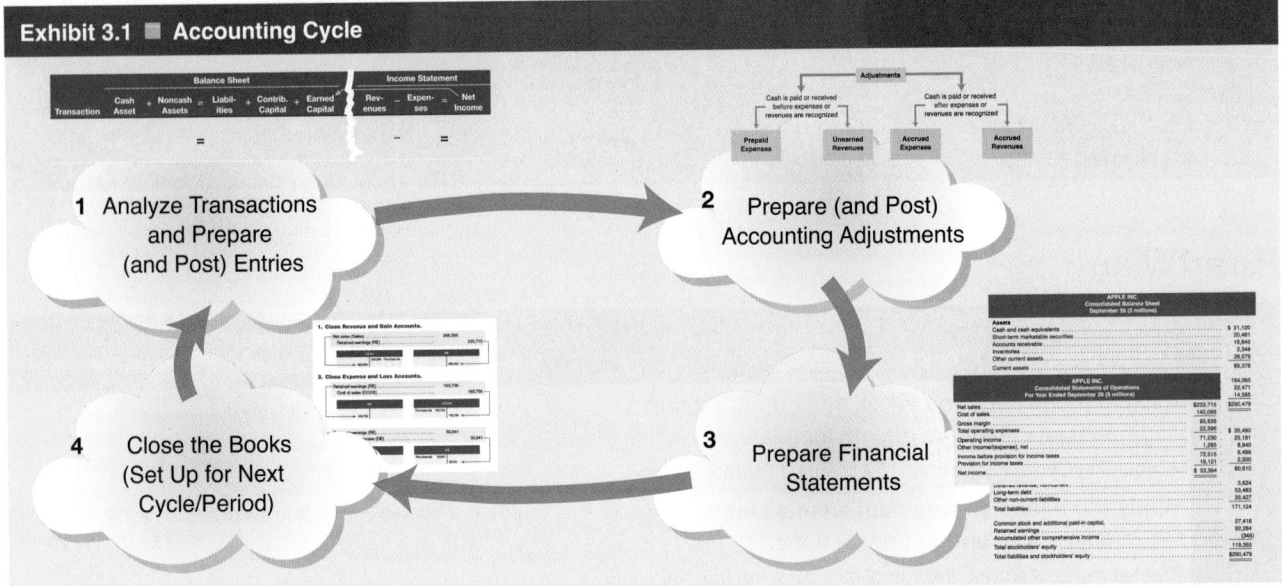

The purpose of this module is to explain the accounting cycle. We use Apple's financials to illustrate the four steps in the accounting cycle. Understanding the financial statement preparation process requires an understanding of the language used to record business transactions in accounting records. The recording and statement preparation processes are readily understood once we learn that language (of financial statement effects) and its mechanics (entries and posting). Even if we never post a transaction or prepare a financial statement, understanding the accounting process aids us in analyzing and interpreting accounting reports. Understanding the accounting language also facilitates our communication with business professionals within a company and with members of the business community outside of a company.

Financial Statement Effects Template

As of its 2018 year-end, Apple reports total assets of $365,725 million, total liabilities of $258,578 million, and equity of $107,147 million. The accounting equation for Apple follows ($ millions).

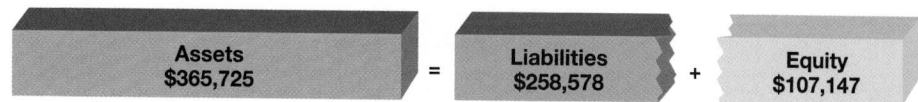

As financial statement users, we often draw on this relation to assess the effects of transactions and events, different accounting methods, and choices that managers make in preparing financial statements. For example, we are interested in knowing the effects of an asset acquisition or sale on the balance sheet, income statement, and statement of cash flows. Or, we might want to understand how the failure to recognize a liability would understate liabilities and overstate profits and equity. A useful tool to perform these sorts of analysis is the following **financial statement effects template.**

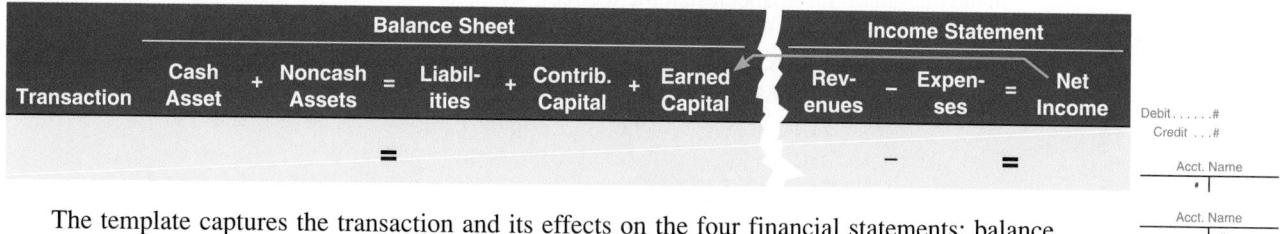

The template captures the transaction and its effects on the four financial statements: balance sheet, income statement, statement of stockholders' equity, and statement of cash flows. For the balance sheet, we differentiate between cash and noncash assets so as to identify the cash effects of transactions. Likewise, equity is separated into the contributed and earned capital components. Finally, income statement effects are separated into revenues, expenses, and net income (the updating of retained earnings is denoted with an arrow line running from net income to earned capital). This template provides a convenient means to represent relatively complex financial accounting transactions and events in a simple, concise manner for both analysis and interpretation.

In addition to using the template to show the dollar effects of a transaction on the four financial statements, we also include each transaction's *journal entry* and *T-account* representation in the margin. We explain journal entries and T-accounts in the next section; these are part of the bookkeeping aspects of accounting. The margin entries can be ignored without any loss of insight gained from the template.

T-accounts

The **T-account**, named for its likeness to a "T," is used to reflect increases and decreases to individual accounts. When a transaction occurs, it is recorded (*journalized*); once recorded, the specific accounts affected are updated in the accounting books (*general ledger*) of the company, and the affected accounts are increased or decreased. This process of continuously updating individual account balances is referred to as *posting* transactions to accounts. A T-account provides a simple illustration of the financial effects of each transaction.

Specifically, one side of the T-account is used for increases and the other for decreases. A convenient way to remember which side records increases is to recall the accounting equation: **Assets = Liabilities + Equity.** Assets are on the left side of the equation. So, the left side of an asset T-account records increases in the asset (referred to as the *normal balance* side), and the right side records decreases. Liabilities and equity are on the right side of the accounting equation. So, the right side of a liability and an equity T-account records increases (the *normal balance* side), and the left side records decreases. This relation is represented graphically as follows.

Assets		=	Liabilities		+	Equity	
+	−		−	+		−	+
Increases	Decreases		Decreases	Increases		Decreases	Increases
Normal bal.				Normal bal.			Normal bal.

Journal Entries

Journal entries also capture the effects of transactions. Journal entries reflect increases and decreases to accounts using the language of debits and credits. Debits and credits simply refer to the left or right side of a T-account, respectively.

Account Title	
Debit (Left side)	Credit (Right side)

The left side of the T-account is the debit side, and the right side is the credit side. This holds for all T-accounts. Thus, to record an increase in an asset, we enter an amount on the left, or debit, side of the T-account—that is, we *debit* the account. Decreases in assets are recorded with an entry on the opposite (credit) side. To record an increase in a liability or equity account, we enter an amount on the right, or credit, side of the T-account—we *credit* the account. Decreases in liability or equity accounts are recorded on the left (debit) side.

In the margin of our financial statement effects template, we show the journal entry first, followed by the related T-accounts. In accounting jargon, this sequence relates to *journalizing* the entry and *posting* it to the affected accounts. The T-accounts represent the financial impact of each transaction on the respective asset, liability, or equity accounts.

Review 3-1 LO1

The table below shows account names (in alphabetical order) from the balance sheet and income statement for Apple Inc.

Required

Solution on p. 3-35.

Indicate the column where each item best fits. The seven columns correspond to the seven account categories in the financial statement effects template.

	Cash Asset	Noncash Asset	Liabilities	Contributed Capital	Earned Capital	Revenues	Expenses
Accounts payable	——	——	——	——	——	——	——
Accounts receivable, less allowances	——	——	——	——	——	——	——
Accrued expenses	——	——	——	——	——	——	——
Acquired intangible assets, net	——	——	——	——	——	——	——
Cash and cash equivalents	——	——	——	——	——	——	——
Common stock and additional paid-in capital	——	——	——	——	——	——	——
Cost of sales	——	——	——	——	——	——	——
Current portion of long-term debt	——	——	——	——	——	——	——
Deferred revenue	——	——	——	——	——	——	——
Deferred tax assets	——	——	——	——	——	——	——
Goodwill	——	——	——	——	——	——	——
Inventories	——	——	——	——	——	——	——
Long-term debt	——	——	——	——	——	——	——
Long-term marketable securities	——	——	——	——	——	——	——
Net sales	——	——	——	——	——	——	——
Other current assets	——	——	——	——	——	——	——
Other noncurrent liabilities	——	——	——	——	——	——	——
Property, plant, and equipment, net	——	——	——	——	——	——	——
Provision for income taxes	——	——	——	——	——	——	——
Research and development	——	——	——	——	——	——	——
Retained earnings	——	——	——	——	——	——	——
Selling, general, and administrative	——	——	——	——	——	——	——

Accounting Cycle Step 1—Analyze Transactions and Prepare Entries

This section uses Apple Inc. to illustrate the accounting for selected business transactions. The assumed time frame is one fiscal year. We will begin with the account balances for Apple at the start of the 2018 fiscal year and illustrate the four steps in the accounting cycle. We construct its 2018 financial statements and close its books.

eLectures LO2
MBC Apply the financial statement effects template to analyze accounting transactions.

Apple's Transactions

This section provides a comprehensive two-part illustration using the financial statement effects template with a number of transactions underlying Apple's 2018 financial statements.

- These summary transactions are described in the far left column of Exhibit 3.2, with their financial statement effects shown to the right-hand-side.

- Detailed explanations for each of the 16 fiscal year transactions are provided in Exhibit 3.3.

Applying the Financial Statement Effects Template

To illustrate Step 1 of the accounting cycle, we consider 16 transactions for Apple. Once details of each transaction are known to Apple's accounting department, entries are made in the company's accounting system. For our learning purposes, we use the financial statement effects template to record these transactions. (Adjusting entries 12 through 16 are described in the next section.)

In the first two rows of Exhibit 3.2, we present each of Apple's balance sheet accounts and related balances as of September 30, 2017. (The end of its 2017 fiscal year is the beginning of its 2018 fiscal year.) We have aggregated some accounts from the Apple balance sheet to keep the size of the financial statement effects template presentable.

Applying the Journal Entry and T-Account

Although we will not repeatedly refer to journal entries and T-accounts, we will describe them for the first transaction in Exhibit 3.2. Specifically, the $4,334 debit equals the $4,334 credit in the journal entry: assets ($4,334 cash) = liabilities ($0) + equity ($4,334 common stock). This balance in transactions is the basis of *double-entry accounting*. For simplicity, we use acronyms (such as CS for common stock) in journal entries and T-accounts. (A listing of accounts and acronyms is located in Appendix B near the end of the book.) The journal entry for this transaction is

Cash.....................	$4,334
CS (common stock)	$4,334

Convention dictates that debits are listed first, followed by credits—the latter are indented.[1] The total debit(s) must always equal the total credit(s) for each transaction. The T-account representation for this transaction follows.

Cash		**CS**	
$4,334			$4,334

Cash is an asset; thus, a cash increase is recorded on the left or debit side of the T-account. Common stock (CS) is an equity account; thus, a common stock increase is recorded on the right or credit side.

---

[1] There can be more than one debit and one credit for a transaction. To illustrate, assume that Apple raises $300 cash, with $200 from investors and $100 borrowed from a bank. The resulting journal entry is

Cash.......................300	
CS (common stock).........	200
NP (note payable)	100

Exhibit 3.2 ■ Financial Statement Effects Template for Apple ($ millions)

Transaction	Balance Sheet					Income Statement		
	Cash Asset	+ Noncash Assets	= Liabil- ities	+ Contrib. Capital	+ Earned Capital*	Rev- enues	– Expen- ses	= Net Income
Balance, September 30, 2017	$ 20,289	$355,030	$241,272	$35,867	$ 98,180			
Step 1—Analyze Transactions, and Prepare Entries								
1. Issue common stock for $4,334 million cash	4,334			4,334 Common stock				
2. Purchase $162,857 million of inventories on account.		162,857 Inventory	162,857 Accounts payable					
3. Sell inventories that cost $163,756 million for $265,551 million, on account.		(163,756) Inventory 265,551 Accounts receivable			101,795 Retained earnings	$265,551 Sales	$163,756 Cost of sales	$101,795
4. Receive $260,239 million cash on account.	260,239	(260,239) Accounts receivable						
5. Pay $151,211 million cash toward accounts payable	(151,211)		(151,211) Accounts payable					
6. Pay $13,137 million cash for operating expenses and $13,372 million cash for income taxes	(26,509)				(26,509) Retained earnings		13,137 Operating expenses 13,372 Income tax expenses	(26,509)
7. Pay cash to purchase current assets of $6,161 million, PPE of $16,821 million, and other long-term assets of $9,683 million.	(32,665)	6,161 Current assets 16,821 PPE 9,683 Other long-term assets						
8. Sell for cash, $13,504 million short-term and $23,915 million long-term marketable securities at the amount reported on the balance sheet	37,419	(13,504) Short-term Marketable Securities (23,915) Long-term Marketable Securities						
9. Repay with cash, short-term debt of $13 million and long-term debt of $1,184 million	(1,197)		(13) Short-term debt (1,184) Long-term debt					
10. Pay $86,791 million cash for dividends and stock buybacks (Apple retired the shares)	(86,791)				(86,791) Retained earnings			
11. Receive $2,005 million cash for net investment income	2,005				2,005 Retained earnings		(2,005) Other income	2,005
Step 2—Prepare Accounting Adjustments								
12. Accrue operating expenses of $2,136 million (current liabilities) and $4,765 million (long-term liabilities)			2,136 Current accrued expenses 4,765 Long-term accrued expenses		(6,901) Retained earnings		6,901 Operating expenses	(6,901)
13. Record depreciation expense of $9,300 million		(9,300) PPE			(9,300) Retained earnings		9,300 Depreciation expense	(9,300)
14. Record amortization expense of $1,603 million on intangible assets		(1,603) Intangible assets			(1,603) Retained earnings		1,603 Amortization expense	(1,603)
15. Apple earns previously deferred revenue of $44 million			(44) Unearned Revenue		44 Retained earnings	44 Sales		44
16. Miscellaneous transactions		(3,974) Other long-term assets			(3,974) Other compre-hensive loss			
Balance, September 29, 2018	$ 25,913	$339,812	$258,578	$ 40,201	$ 66,946	$265,595	$206,064	$ 59,531

* Earned capital includes retained earnings and accumulated other comprehensive loss, another earned capital account.

Exhibit 3.3 ■ Details of Transactions for Apple ($ millions)	
Transaction	**Description**
1. Issue common stock for $4,334 million cash.	Cash, common stock, and additional paid-in capital all increase by the proceeds from issuance. (Apple combines common stock and additional paid-in capital on its balance sheet.) The sale of stock is not revenue. It is a financing transaction between the company and its owners (stockholders). Neither the sale or repurchase of stock, nor the payment of dividends to shareholders, affects revenue or expense. Transactions with stockholders never affect net income.
2. Purchase $162,857 million of inventories on account.	Inventories are often purchased *on account* (also called *on credit*), meaning that suppliers give the company a period of time in which to pay for the purchase. Inventory increases by the purchase price. Because the company has not yet paid for the purchase, accounts payable (a liability) also increases by the purchase price. Note that inventories are not recorded at their expected retail selling price.
3. Sell inventories that cost $163,756 million for $265,551 million on account.	The sale of inventory has two distinct parts: a) **Recognize revenue.** Revenue (net sales) can be recognized because ownership of inventory has transferred to the customer. Because the customer has not yet paid for the inventory, the amount owed to Apple is reported as an account receivable. To recognize revenue, Apple has to have performed its part of the sales contract (given possession of the inventory to the customer). The receipt of cash is not required to recognize revenue; an agreement to pay later is sufficient. b) **Record expense.** The cost of inventory is recognized as an expense at the time of sale. An asset remains on the balance sheet until it is used, at which time its cost is transferred to the income statement as an expense. Because Apple has now sold (used) the inventory, its cost is moved from the inventory account on the balance sheet to the income statement as an expense called cost of goods sold.
4. Receive $260,239 million cash on account.	Cash increases when customers settle their accounts and the accounts receivable balance decreases. Collection of a receivable is not revenue. Instead, revenue is recognized when earned, as in transaction 3.
5. Pay $151,211 million cash toward accounts payable.	Cash and accounts payable both decrease by the amount paid to suppliers to settle the account. Note that payment of a payable is not an expense. The expense was recognized when it was incurred, as in transaction 3.
6. Pay $13,137 million cash for operating expenses and $13,372 million cash for income taxes.	Operating expenses are costs incurred to earn revenue and do business. An example is salaries expense. Cash decreases when employees are paid and salaries expense is recorded in the income statement. Provision for income taxes (or tax expense) is also recognized in the income statement.
7. Pay cash to purchase current assets of $6,161 million, PPE of $16,821 million, and other long-term assets of $9,683 million.	Cash decreases and the company adds the purchase price to the balance sheet as assets. Purchasing assets does not generate an immediate expense because assets generate future economic benefits. But as the assets are consumed and the company realizes the intended benefits, the asset cost is transferred to the income statement as an expense. For example, the cost of PPE is transferred to the income statement as depreciation expense over the assets' useful lives.
8. Sell for cash, $13,504 million short-term and $23,915 million long-term marketable securities.	Apple invests its excess cash in marketable securities. This means cash decreases, and marketable securities accounts increase. The company plans to hold some of the investments for a year or less (short-term) and some for longer (long-term), depending on anticipated future cash needs. In the interim, the investments allow the company to earn interest, dividends, and any appreciation in value.
9. Repay with cash, short-term debt of $13 million and long-term debt of $1,184 million.	Cash decreases as Apple repays its short-term and long-term debt. As with the sale of stock, neither borrowing of money, nor its repayment, is recognized as revenue or expense. Only the interest related to the debt is an expense.
10. Pay $86,791 million cash for stock buybacks (Apple retired the shares) and dividends to stockholders.	Dividends reduce both cash and retained earnings. The payment of dividends is not an expense. It is a transaction with the company's owners (the stockholders), not with its customers, and no expense is recognized in the income statement. When Apple cancels the repurchased shares, it reduces retained earnings by the cost of the shares.
11. Receive $2,005 million cash for net investment income.	Cash increases, as does other income on the income statement. This income includes dividends, interest, and capital gains Apple earns on its short-term and long-term marketable securities. This is not classified as revenue because it is not earned from customers. We recorded other income as a negative expense, which lets us know it is an income item and not an expense.

LO2 Review 3-2

Prestige Inc. experienced the following 12 transactions during the month of January 2020.

1. Issue common stock for $3,000 cash.
2. Purchase inventory for $8,000 on credit.
3. Sell inventory costing $8,000 for $15,000 on credit.
4. Issue long-term debt for $10,000 cash.
5. Pay $15,000 cash for property, plant, and equipment (PPE).
6. Pay $500 cash for salaries.
7. Receive $300 cash in advance from client for future consulting services.

continued

continued from previous page

8. Pay $50 cash for interest on long-term debt.
9. Receive $3,000 cash from accounts receivable.
10. Pay $2,500 cash toward accounts payable.
11. Perform consulting services for client who previously paid in transaction 7.
12. Pay $100 cash for dividends.

Required

Record each transaction in the financial statement effects template. The beginning balances for each account are entered into the template. *Note:* The template includes rows for transactions 13 through 16, which are covered in Review 3-3, later in the module.

Solution on p. 3-36.

	Balance Sheet					Income Statement		
	Cash Assets +	Noncash Assets =	Liabil- ities +	Contrib. Capital +	Earned Capital	Rev- enues −	Expen- ses =	Net Income
Balance January 1, 2020	10,000	41,000	26,000	10,000	15,000	0	0	0
Transactions								
1. Issue common stock for $3,000 cash								
2. Purchase inventory for $8,000 on credit								
3. Sell inventory costing $8,000 for $15,000 on credit								
4. Issue long-term debt for $10,000 cash								
5. Pay $15,000 cash for PPE								
6. Pay $500 cash for salaries								
7. Receive $300 cash in advance for future consulting services								
8. Pay $50 cash for interest on long-term debt								
9. Receive $3,000 cash from accounts receivable								
10. Pay $2,500 cash toward accounts payable								
11. Perform consulting services for client who previously paid in 7								
12. Pay $100 cash for dividends								
Accounting Adjustments								
13. Record depreciation of $600								
14. Accrue salaries of $1,000								
15. Advertising costing $1,300 is aired								
16. Accrue income taxes of $1,200								
Balance January 31, 2020								

Accounting Cycle Step 2—Prepare Accounting Adjustments

LO3
MBC Prepare and explain accounting adjustments and their financial statement effects.

Recognizing revenue when products and services are delivered at an amount expected to be received (even if not received in cash) *and* recording expenses when incurred (even if not paid in cash) are cornerstones of **accrual accounting**, which is required under GAAP. In addition, understanding accounting adjustments, commonly called *accruals*, is crucial to effectively analyzing and interpreting financial statements.

In this module's Apple illustration, we recorded inventory as a purchase even though no cash was paid, and we recognized the sale as revenue even though no cash was received. Both of these transactions reflect accrual accounting. Some accounting transactions affect the balance sheet alone (as with purchasing inventory on account in Exhibit 3.2, transaction 2). Other transactions affect the balance sheet *and* the income statement (as with selling inventory on account in Exhibit 3.2, transaction 3). Accounting transactions can affect asset, liability, or equity accounts and can either increase or decrease net income.

Companies record *adjustments* to more accurately report their financial performance and condition. For example, employees might not have been paid for wages earned at the end of an accounting period. Failure to recognize this labor cost would understate the company's total liabilities (because wages payable would be too low) and would overstate net income for the period (because wages expense would be too low). Thus, neither the balance sheet nor the income statement would be accurate without accounting adjustments.

Four Types of Accounting Adjustments Exhibit 3.4 identifies four general types of accounting adjustments, which are briefly described here.

- **Prepaid expenses** Prepaid expenses reflect advance cash payments that will ultimately become expenses. An example is the payment for radio advertising that will not be aired until sometime in the future.
- **Unearned revenues** Unearned revenues reflect cash received from customers before any services or goods are provided. An example is cash received from patrons for tickets to an upcoming concert.
- **Accrued expenses** Accrued expenses are expenses incurred and recognized on the income statement even though they are not yet paid in cash. An example is wages owed to employees who performed work but who have not yet been paid.
- **Accrued revenues** Accrued revenues are revenues earned and recognized on the income statement even though cash is not yet received. Examples include sales on credit and revenue earned under a long-term contract.

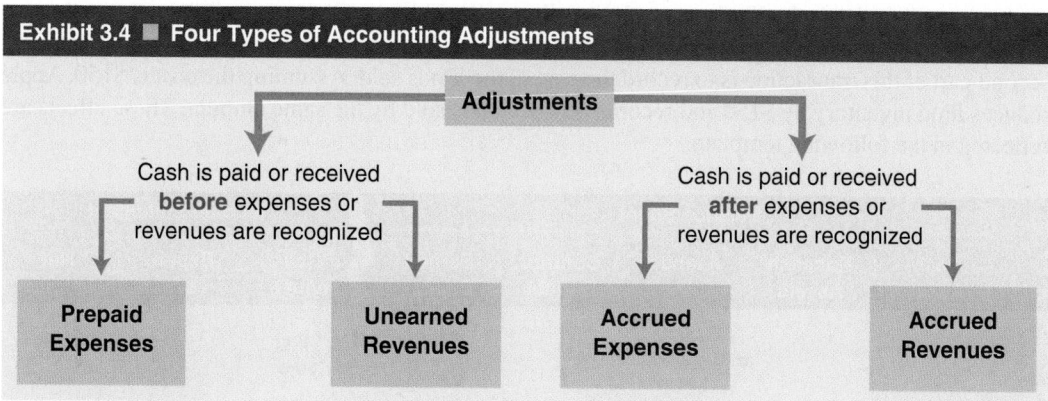

Exhibit 3.4 ■ Four Types of Accounting Adjustments

The remainder of this section illustrates how **Apple**'s financial statements would reflect each of these four types of adjustments.

Prepaid Expenses

Assume Apple pays $200 to purchase time on **MTV** for iPod ads. Apple's cash account decreases by $200. Should the $200 advertising cost be recorded as an expense when Apple pays MTV, when MTV airs the ads, or at some other point? Under accrual accounting, Apple must record an expense when it is incurred. That means Apple should expense the cost of the ads when MTV airs them. When Apple pays for the advertisement, it records an asset; Apple "owns" air time that will presumably provide future benefits when the ads air. In the interim, the cost of the ads is an asset on the balance sheet. Apple's financial statement effects template follows for this transaction. There is a decrease in cash and an increase in the advertising asset, called prepaid advertising, when the ad time is paid for. At period-end, $50 of advertisements had aired. At that point, Apple must record an accounting adjustment to reduce the prepaid advertising account by $50 and transfer the cost to the income statement as advertising expense.

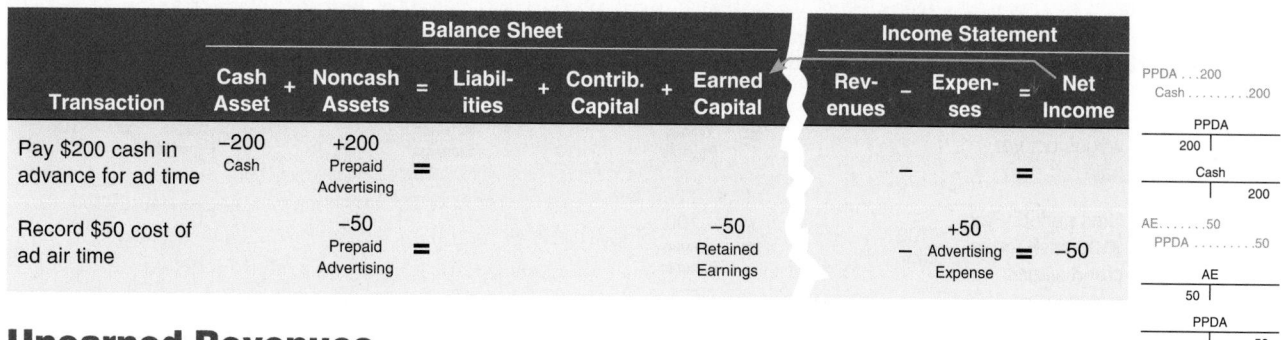

Unearned Revenues

Assume Apple receives $400 cash from a customer as advance payment on a multi-unit iPod sale to be delivered next month. Apple must record cash received on its balance sheet but cannot recognize revenue from the order until earned, which is generally when iPods are delivered to the customer. Until then, Apple must recognize a liability called unearned, or deferred, revenue that represents Apple's obligation to fulfill the order at some future point. The financial statement effects template for this transaction follows.

Cash....400
UR.........400

Cash
400	

UR
	400

	Balance Sheet							Income Statement		
Transaction	Cash Asset	+ Noncash Assets	= Liabil- ities	+ Contrib. Capital	+ Earned Capital		Rev- enues	− Expen- ses	= Net Income
Receive $400 cash in advance for iPod sale	+400 Cash		= +400 Unearned Revenue					−	=

Assume Apple delivers the iPods a month later (but still within the fiscal quarter). Apple must recognize the $400 as revenue at delivery because it is now earned. Thus, net income increases by $400. The second part of this transaction is to record the cost of the iPods sold. Assuming the cost is $150, Apple reduces iPod inventory by $150 and records cost of goods sold by the same amount. These effects are reflected in the following template.

UR 400
Sales........400

UR
400	

Sales
	400

COGS... 150
INV 150

COGS
150	

INV
	150

	Balance Sheet							Income Statement		
Transaction	Cash Asset	+ Noncash Assets	= Liabil- ities	+ Contrib. Capital	+ Earned Capital		Rev- enues	− Expen- ses	= Net Income
Deliver $400 of iPods paid in advance			= −400 Unearned Revenues		+400 Retained Earnings		+400 Sales	−	= +400
Record $150 cost of $400 iPod sale		−150 Inventory =			−150 Retained Earnings			− +150 Cost of Goods Sold	= −150

Accrued Expenses

Assume Apple's sales staff earns $100 of sales commissions this period that will not be paid until next period. The sales staff earned the wages as they made the sales. However, because Apple pays its employees twice a month, the related cash payment will not occur until the next pay period. Should Apple record the wages earned by its employees as an expense even though payment has not yet been made? The answer is yes. The expense recognition principle requires Apple to recognize wages expense when it is *incurred*, even if not paid in cash. It must record wages expense incurred as a liability (wages payable). In the next period, when Apple pays the wages, it reduces both cash and wages payable. Net income is not affected by the cash payment; instead, net income decreased in the previous period when Apple accrued the wage expense.

WE 100
WP 100

WE
100	

WP
	100

WP 100
Cash 100

WP
100	

Cash
	100

	Balance Sheet							Income Statement		
Transaction	Cash Asset	+ Noncash Assets	= Liabil- ities	+ Contrib. Capital	+ Earned Capital		Rev- enues	− Expen- ses	= Net Income
Current period: Incur $100 of wages not yet paid			= +100 Wages Payable		−100 Retained Earnings			− +100 Wages Expense	= −100
Next period: Pay $100 cash for ac- crued wages	−100 Cash		= −100 Wages Payable					−	=

As another example of accrued expenses, assume Apple rents office space and that it owes $25 in rent at period-end. Apple has incurred rent expense in the current period, and that expense must be recorded this period. Failing to make this adjustment would mean Apple's liabilities (rent payable) would be understated and its income would be overstated. The entry to record the accrual of rent expense for office space follows.

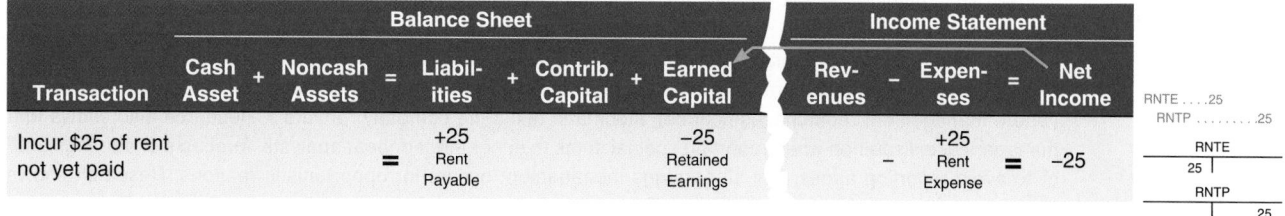

	Balance Sheet						Income Statement		
Transaction	Cash Asset	+ Noncash Assets	= Liabilities	+ Contrib. Capital	+ Earned Capital		Revenues	− Expenses	= Net Income
Incur $25 of rent not yet paid		=	+25 Rent Payable		−25 Retained Earnings			− +25 Rent Expense	= −25

RNTE 25
RNTP 25

RNTE	
25	

RNTP	
	25

Accrued Revenues

Assume Apple delivers iPods to a customer in Boston, Massachusetts, who will pay next quarter. The sales price for those units is $500, and the cost is $400. Apple has completed its revenue earning process with this sale and must accrue revenue from the Boston customer even though Apple received no cash. Like all sales transactions, Apple must record two parts, the sales revenue and the cost of sales. The financial effects template for this two-part transaction follows.

	Balance Sheet						Income Statement		
Transaction	Cash Asset	+ Noncash Assets	= Liabilities	+ Contrib. Capital	+ Earned Capital		Revenues	− Expenses	= Net Income
Sell $500 of iPods on credit		+500 Accounts Receivable =			+500 Retained Earnings		+500 Sales	−	= +500
Record $400 cost of $500 iPod sale		−400 Inventory =			−400 Retained Earnings			− +400 Cost of Goods Sold	= −400

AR 500
Sales 500

AR	
500	

Sales	
	500

COGS . . .400
INV 400

COGS	
400	

INV	
	400

Accounting Adjustments for Apple

Entries 12 through 16 in Exhibit 3.2, which are explained in Exhibit 3.5, reflect the accounting adjustments Apple makes during its fiscal year. These accounting adjustments occur at the end of the accounting period, prior to the preparation of the financial statements. The purpose of accounting adjustments is to adjust balance sheet assets and liabilities so that the financial statements fairly present the company's financial performance and position.

Exhibit 3.5 ■ Details of Accounting Adjustments for Apple ($ millions)	
Adjustment	**Description**
12. Accrue operating expenses of $2,136 million (current liabilities) and $4,765 million (long-term liabilities)	Accrued expenses represent liabilities that have been incurred before the end of the accounting period but have not been recorded. The accrual simultaneously increases liabilities on the balance sheet and expenses in the income statement. Failure to properly accrue expenses would understate liabilities and overstate profit (and retained earnings).
13. Record depreciation expense of $9,300 million	Each period that PPE is used, a portion of the cost of the PPE is transferred to the income statement as *depreciation expense* to reflect the fact that the PPE assets have been used during the period. Failure to record depreciation expense would overstate assets and net income (and retained earnings) for the period.
14. Record amortization expense of $1,603 million	Similar to PPE, certain intangible assets (those that have a limited useful life) are used up over time and amortized. This concept is the same as depreciation, but the word *amortization* is used instead. The accounting adjustment to amortize the intangible assets reduces the balance sheet value of the intangible assets and records an expense. Note that goodwill is not amortized because we assume it has an unlimited useful life. (We discuss intangible assets, including the goodwill asset, in Module 9.)
15. Apple earns previously deferred revenue of $44 million	When customers pay in advance, Apple records the cash pre-payment as a liability. Once Apple transfers the products or delivers the services to its customers, it can recognize revenue from the sale, typically with an accounting adjustment. The adjustment reduces the unearned revenue liability on the balance sheet and increases revenue in the income statement.
16. Miscellaneous transactions	Apple recognizes other comprehensive loss of $3,974 million, which reduces both earned capital and other long-term assets. We discuss other comprehensive income and loss in Modules 8 and 9.

Researchers examine accounting accruals to study the effects of earnings management on financial account-ing. Earnings management is broadly defined as the use of accounting discretion to distort reported earnings. Managers have incentives to manage earnings in many situations. For example, managers have tendencies to accelerate revenue recognition to increase stock prices prior to equity offerings. In contrast, other research shows that managers decelerate revenue recognition to depress stock prices prior to a management buyout (where management repurchases common stock and takes the company "private"). Research also shows that managers use discretion when reporting special items to either meet or beat analysts' forecasts of earnings and/ or to avoid reporting a loss. Not all earnings management occurs for opportunistic reasons. Research shows managers use accruals to communicate private information to outsiders about future profitability. For example, management might signal future profitability through use of income-decreasing accruals to show investors the company can afford to apply conservative accounting. This "signaling" through accruals is found to precede stock splits and dividend increases. In sum, we must look at reported earnings in conjunction with other earn-ings' quality signals (such as levels of disclosure, degree of corporate governance, and industry performance) to interpret information in accruals.

Review 3-3 LO3

Refer to the information in Review 3-2 for Prestige Inc., which is preparing to record its accounting adjustments for month-end January 2020.

Required
Enter the following accounting adjustments in the financial statement effects template, included in Review 3-2.

13. Record depreciation expense of $600.
14. Accrue salaries of $1,000.
15. Advertising costing $1,300 is aired. Prestige had previously paid cash for the advertising and recorded an asset labeled "Prepaid expense."

Solution on p. 3-36.   16. Accrue income taxes of $1,200.

Accounting Cycle Step 3—Prepare Financial Statements

eLectures **LO4**
MBC Construct financial statements from the accounting records.

Once we enter all of the transactions and adjustments into the financial statement effects template, we sum each column to obtain ending balances for the accounts. This is shown on the bottom row of Ex-hibit 3.2, and reflects ending balances of accounts after all of the transactions have been recorded during the accounting period in Step 1 and all of the period-end adjustments have been entered into the ac-counting records in Step 2. With the accounts totaled, we can prepare the financial statements (Step 3).

There is an order to financial statement preparation.

■ First, a company prepares its income statement using the income statement accounts. It then uses the net income number and dividend information to update the retained earnings account.

■ Second, it prepares the balance sheet using the updated retained earnings account along with the remaining balance sheet accounts.

■ Third, it prepares the statement of stockholders' equity.

■ Fourth, it prepares the statement of cash flows using information from the cash account (and other sources).

Income Statement

Our financial statement effects spreadsheet in Exhibit 3.2 summarizes Apple's income statement ac-counts in the last three columns. We use the data from those columns to prepare the income statement in proper form. Apple aggregates its many operating expenses on a line labeled "Total operating expenses." Apple also combines interest expense with other nonoperating income and reports a line labeled "Other income/(expense), net." Apple's income statement for 2018 follows.

APPLE INC. Consolidated Statements of Operations For Year Ended September 29, 2018 ($ millions)	
Net sales.	$265,595
Cost of sales.	163,756
Gross margin	101,839
Total operating expenses	30,941
Operating income.	70,898
Other income/(expense), net	2,005
Income before provision for income taxes	72,903
Provision for income taxes	13,372
Net income	$ 59,531

Apple's income statement includes a subtotal for gross margin, which is a common reporting practice that helps us evaluate company performance and profitability. Apple also reports a subtotal for operating profit. As we will discuss in Module 4, operating profit isolates those activities that create shareholder value and, for that reason, companies frequently report a subtotal for operating profit.

Retained Earnings Reconciliation

Once the income statement is prepared, companies update the retained earnings balance by adding net income and subtracting dividends. We can do likewise using the net income and dividend information from the financial statement effects spreadsheet in Exhibit 3.2. Apple's retained earnings reconciliation for 2018 follows.

APPLE INC. Retained Earnings Reconciliation For Year Ended September 29, 2018 ($ millions)	
Retained earnings, September 30, 2017	$98,330
Add: Net income.	59,531
Deduct: Dividends	(13,735)
Deduct: Repurchase and retirement of common stock	(73,056)
Miscellaneous adjustments[1]	(670)
Retained earnings, September 29, 2018	$70,400

[1] This retained earnings reconciliation, also called *retained earnings statement*, is consistent with Apple's statement of shareholders' equity. The reconciliation here differs from Exhibit 3.2 where we combined retained earnings and AOCI into one account called Earned capital.

Balance Sheet

Once Apple computes the ending balance in retained earnings, it can prepare its balance sheet. Balance sheet accounts are called **permanent accounts** because their respective balances carry over from one period to the next. For example, the cash balance at the end of the current accounting period (ended September 29, 2018) is $25,913 million, which will be the balance at the beginning of the next accounting period (beginning September 30, 2018).

To prepare the balance sheet, we use the ending balances from the last row in the financial statement effects spreadsheet in Exhibit 3.2, along with specific details for accounts within several of the columns. We then apply proper balance sheet format that has subtotals for current assets, current liabilities, total liabilities, and equity to produce Apple's consolidated balance sheet for 2018 as follows.

APPLE INC. Consolidated Balance Sheet September 29, 2018 ($ millions)	
Assets	
Cash and cash equivalents	$ 25,913
Short-term marketable securities	40,388
Accounts receivable.	23,186
Inventories	3,956
Other current assets.	37,896
Current assets	131,339
Long-term marketable securities	170,799
Property, plant, and equipment, net	41,304
Other assets.	22,283
Total assets	$365,725
Liabilities and equity	
Accounts payable.	$ 55,888
Accrued expenses	32,687
Deferred revenue	7,543
Commercial paper	11,964
Current portion of long-term debt	8,784
Current liabilities.	116,866
Deferred revenue, noncurrent	2,797
Long-term debt.	93,735
Other noncurrent liabilities	45,180
Total liabilities	258,578
Common stock and additional paid-in capital.	40,201
Retained earnings	70,400
Accumulated other comprehensive income	(3,454)
Total shareholders' equity.	107,147
Total liabilities and shareholders' equity.	$365,725

Statement of Stockholders' Equity

We use the information from the financial statement effects template pertaining to contributed capital and earned capital to prepare the statement of stockholders' equity, as follows. (The final financial statement is the statement of cash flows, which we cover in detail in a later module.)

APPLE INC. Statement of Shareholders' Equity For Year Ended September 29, 2018				
$ millions	Common Stock and Additional Paid-In Capital	Retained Earnings	Accumulated Other Comprehensive Income	Total Shareholders' Equity
Balance, September 30, 2017	$35,867	$98,330	$ (150)	$134,047
Stock issuance	4,334			4,334
Net income (loss)		59,531		59,531
Dividends		(13,735)		(13,735)
Common stock repurchased and retired . .		(73,056)		(73,056)
Other.		(670)	(3,304)	(3,974)
Balance, September 29, 2018	$40,201	$70,400	$(3,454)	$107,147

LO4 Review 3-4

Refer to the information in Reviews 3-2 and 3-3 for Prestige Inc., which is preparing its financial statements for month-end January 2020. In addition, the financial statement effects template included the following (beginning) account balances at January 1, 2020.

Accounts receivable	$12,000	Accounts payable	$ 3,800
Inventory	7,200	Unearned revenue	200
Prepaid advertising	1,800	Long-term debt	22,000
PPE	20,000	Salaries payable	0
		Taxes payable	0

Required
1. List the 14 accounts, and determine the ending balance for each.
2. Prepare the income statement, retained earnings reconciliation, and balance sheet at the end of the period.   **Solution on p. 3-37.**

Accounting Cycle Step 4—Close the Books

The **closing process** (or *closing the books*) refers to "zeroing out" the temporary accounts by transferring their ending balances to retained earnings. Income statement accounts—revenues and expenses—and the dividend account are **temporary accounts** because their balances are zero at the start of each accounting period so that only the current period's activities are included. Balance sheet accounts carry over from period to period and are called permanent accounts. The closing process is typically carried out via a series of journal entries that successively zero out each revenue and expense account and the dividend account, transferring those balances to retained earnings. The result is that all income statement accounts and the dividend account begin the next period with zero balances. The balance sheet accounts do not need to be similarly adjusted because their balances carry over from period to period.

eLectures LO5
MBC Explain and apply the closing process.

Closing with the Template It is important to distinguish our financial statement effects template from companies' accounting systems. The financial statement effects template and T-accounts are pedagogical tools that represent transactions' effects on financial statements. The template is highly stylized, but its simplicity is instructive.

Closing with Journal Entries In practice, managers use journal entries to record transactions and adjustments. The template captures these in summarized fashion. However, in practice, income statement transactions are not automatically transferred to retained earnings, and retained earnings is not continuously updated. Instead, companies have a formal "closing process" at the end of each reporting period—someone or some program must transfer the temporary account balances to retained earnings. Thus, it is important to understand the closing process and why companies "close" the books each period. We describe the mechanical details of the closing process.

Following are the journal entries, along with the T-account entries, Apple would make to close out its income statement accounts and dividend account to retained earnings (in millions).

1. Close Revenue and Gain Accounts.

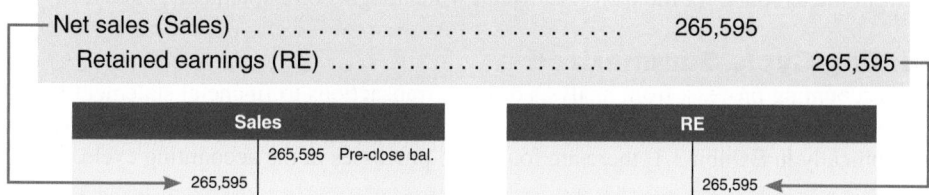

2. Close Expense and Loss Accounts.

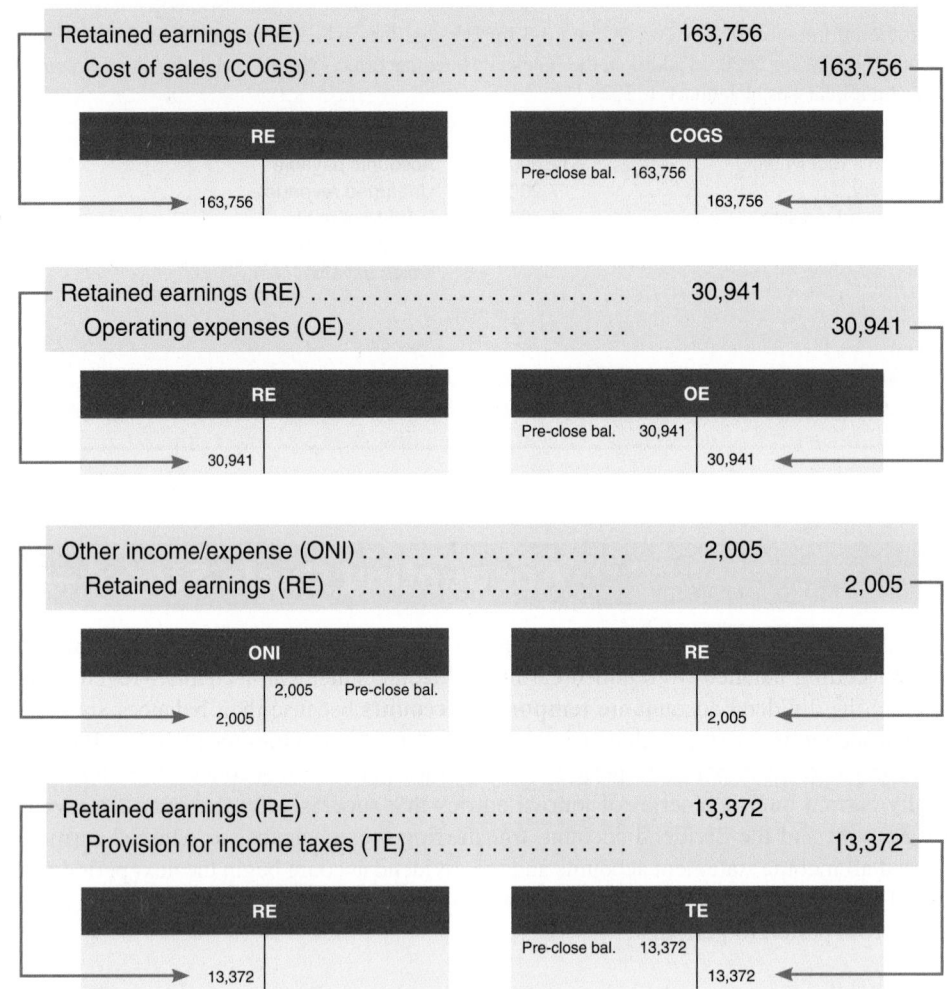

3. Close Dividend Account.

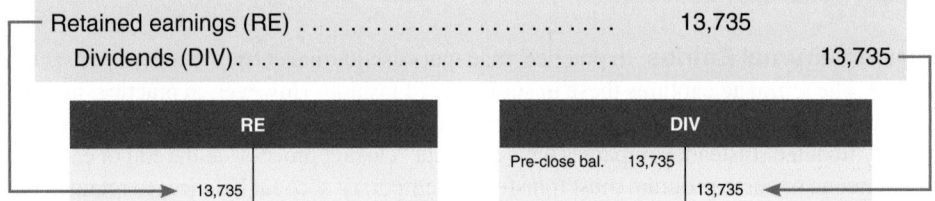

The closing process reduces all of the income statement accounts and the dividend account to zero to begin the next accounting period with a zero balance. This means revenues, expenses, and dividends are accumulated during a period so that the income statement only reflects activities for the period. In contrast, balance sheet accounts carry over from period to period. We can see this from our financial statement effects template for Apple where the bottom row balances as of September 29, 2018, become the top row in the template for the next fiscal year, which begins on September 30, 2018.

Accounting Cycle Summarized

The entire accounting process, from analysis of basic transactions to financial statement preparation to the closing process, is called the **accounting cycle**. As we discuss at the outset of this module and portray graphically in Exhibit 3.1, there are four basic processes in the accounting cycle.

❶ Analyze transactions and prepare (and post) entries.

❷ Prepare (and post) accounting adjustments.

❸ Prepare financial statements.

❹ Perform the closing process.

The analysis and posting of transactions are done regularly during each accounting period. However, the preparation of accounting adjustments and financial statements is only done at the end of an accounting period. At this point, we have explained and illustrated all aspects of the accounting cycle.

Managerial Decision ■ You Are the Chief Financial Officer

Assume that you learn of the leakage of hazardous waste from your company's factory. It is estimated that cleanup could cost $10 million. Part 1: What effect will recording this cost have on your company's balance sheet and its income statement? Part 2: Accounting rules require you to record this cost if it is both probable and can be reliably estimated. Although the cleanup is relatively certain, the cost is a guess at this point. Consequently, you have some discretion whether to record it. Discuss the parties that are likely affected by your decision on whether or not to record the liability and related expense and the ethical issues involved. (Answer, p. 3-19)

L05 Review 3-5

Refer to the information in Reviews 3-2, 3-3, and 3-4 for Prestige Inc. It has prepared its financial statements and is ready to close its books for month-end January 2020.

Required

Prepare the entries required to close the temporary accounts for Prestige Inc. at the end of January 2020.   Solution on p. 3-37.

Global Accounting

The manner in which accounting data are gathered and recorded does not differ across accounting standards. Thus, the accounting cycle in Exhibit 3.1 applies in countries using IFRS in the same manner as in the United States. The difference is that companies create information systems that conform to the specific accounting rules in that country. For example, the rules for recording research and development (R&D) costs are different in the United States vis-à-vis Germany. Thus, the U.S. company and the German company would each tailor their accounting systems to properly record R&D costs so that each company's financial statements comply with their respective countries' accounting standards. The accounting cycle of each company still involves transactions and adjustments and a closing process. The result is that identical R&D expenditures are classified differently and the resulting financial statements diverge.

Large multinational companies often have subsidiaries in different countries. If a U.S. company has a foreign subsidiary, the foreign laws require a domestic set of financial statements for tax, regulatory, banking, or other purposes. For example, **Apple**'s Form 10-K reports it has three subsidiaries incorporated in Ireland. The Irish subsidiaries must prepare IFRS financial statements to file with the Irish Revenue Commission (the Irish equivalent of the IRS). During the closing process of the accounting cycle, Apple Inc. (the U.S. parent) must consolidate the subsidiaries, which means all assets and liabilities of the subsidiaries are included on Apple Inc.'s balance sheet. Similarly, all of the revenues and expenses of the subsidiaries are included on Apple Inc.'s income statement. It would not be appropriate for a simple summing of accounts because of differences between IFRS and U.S. GAAP. Instead, Apple Inc. must convert IFRS financial statements to U.S. GAAP equivalent (as well as convert euros to U.S. dollars). To accomplish this, Apple Inc. keeps two sets of accounting records for subsidiaries, one set in GAAP and the other in IFRS. This is not as complicated as it might seem. Companies like Apple use sophisticated computer accounting systems and enterprise resource planning (ERP) systems that are capable of supporting multiple sets of accounting standards.

Appendix 3A: FASB's Financial Statement Presentation Project

Preparers and users of financial statements have long expressed concern that existing accounting standards provide too little guidance on financial statement presentation. Popular opinion is that U.S. GAAP permits too many presentation formats and is silent on specific line items and on the level of detail required in financial statements. This lack of uniformity impairs comparability across companies. For example, some companies disaggregate product costs (such as materials and labor) as well as general and administrative costs (such as rent and utilities) in their income statements, and other entities present highly aggregated product costs and general and administrative expenses. Due to these concerns, there is broad support for a FASB project on financial statement presentation.

Under current accounting standards, the statement of cash flows categorizes a company's cash flows into three categories: operating, investing, and financing. The proposal under consideration at the FASB would require similar classification on the balance sheet and the income statement. The following table illustrates the proposed sections, categories, and subcategories in each financial statement. (Summarized from "Staff Draft of an Exposure Draft JULY 2010" © IFRS Foundation and made available by the FASB [FASB.org/cs/BlobServer?blobkey=id&blobnocache=true&blobwhere=1175820952961&blobheader=application%2Fpdf&blobheadername2=Content-Length&blobheadername1=Content-Disposition&blobheadervalue2=60259&blobheadervalue1=filename%3DIntroduction_Summary_Staff_draft_1_July.pdf&blobcol=urldata&blobtable=MungoBlobs].)

Statement of Financial Position (Balance Sheet)	Statement of Comprehensive Income	Statement of Cash Flows
Business section	**Business section**	**Business section**
Operating category	Operating category	Operating category
Operating finance subcategory	Operating finance subcategory	
Investing category	Investing category	Investing category
Financing section	**Financing section**	**Financing section**
Debt category	Debt category	
Equity category		
	Multi-category transaction section	**Multi-category transaction section**
Income tax section	**Income tax section**	**Income tax section**
Discontinued operation section	**Discontinued operation section**, net of tax	**Discontinued operation section**
	Other comprehensive income, net of tax	

The proposed presentation format is consistent with the approach we describe in Module 4—the separation of operating and nonoperating items on the income statement and balance sheet. The Module 4 approach extends the traditional DuPont analysis of return on equity (ROE) by isolating the operating activities of the business in order to evaluate what truly creates shareholder value. While the Module 4 approach sharpens our analysis of ROE, it requires additional effort at present because we must first parse operating from nonoperating components on the financial statements. Under the FASB proposal, financial statements would be formatted along these operating and nonoperating dimensions and standardized across companies. If adopted, the new format will make analysis less effortful.

Guidance Answers

You Are the Chief Financial Officer

Pg. 3-18 Part 1: Liabilities will increase by $10 million for the estimated amount of the cleanup, and an expense in that amount will be recognized in the income statement, thus reducing both income and retained earnings (equity) by $10 million. Part 2: Stakeholders affected by recognition decisions of this type are often much broader than first realized. Management is directly involved in the decision. Recording this cost can affect the market value of the company, its relations with lenders and suppliers, its auditors, and many other stakeholders. Further, if recording this cost is the right accounting decision, failure to do so can foster unethical behavior throughout the company, thus affecting additional company employees.

Q3-1. List the four steps in the accounting cycle.

Q3-2. What is the purpose of a general ledger?

Q3-3. Explain the process of posting.

Q3-4. What four different types of adjustments are frequently necessary before financial statements are prepared at the end of an accounting period? Give at least one example of each type.

Q3-5. On January 1, prepaid insurance was increased for $1,896 related to the cost of a two-year premium, with coverage beginning immediately. How should this account be adjusted on January 31 before financial statements are prepared for the current month?

Q3-6. At the beginning of January, the first month of the accounting year, the supplies account (asset) had a normal balance of $875. During January, purchases of $260 worth of supplies were added to the account. At the end of January, $630 of supplies were still available. How should this account be adjusted? If no adjustment is made, describe the impact on (a) the income statement for January and (b) the balance sheet prepared at January 31.

Q3-7. The publisher of *Accounting View*, a monthly magazine, received $9,768 cash on January 1 for new subscriptions covering the next 24 months, with service beginning immediately: (*a*) Use the financial statement effects template to record the receipt of the $9,768; and (*b*) use the template to show how the accounts should be adjusted at the end of January before financial statements are prepared for the current month.

Q3-8. Refer to Q3-7. Prepare journal entries for the receipt of cash and the delivery of the magazines.

Q3-9. Trombley Travel Agency pays an employee $950 in wages each Friday for the five-day work week ending on Friday. The last Friday of January falls on January 27. How should Trombley Travel Agency adjust wages expense on January 31, its fiscal year-end?

Q3-10. The Basu Company earns interest amounting to $720 per month on its investments. The company receives the interest revenue every six months, on December 31 and June 30. Monthly financial statements are prepared. Which accounts should Basu adjust on January 31?

Q3-11. What types of accounts are closed at the end of the accounting year? What are the three major steps in the closing process?

Assignments with the 🔘 **logo in the margin are available in** BusinessCourse.
See the Preface of the book for details.

M3-12. Assessing Financial Statement Effects of Transactions

LO2

K. Daniels started Daniels Services, a firm providing art services for advertisers, on June 1. The following accounts are needed to record the transactions for June: Cash, Accounts Receivable, Supplies, Office Equipment, Accounts Payable, Common Stock, Dividends, Service Fees Earned, Rent Expense, Utilities Expense, and Wages Expense. Record the following transactions for June using the financial statement effects template.

June   1   K. Daniels invested $12,000 cash to begin the business in exchange for common stock.

      2   Paid $950 cash for June rent. *Hint:* Record rent expense on June 2.

      3   Purchased $6,400 of office equipment on credit.

      6   Purchased $3,800 of art materials and other supplies; the company paid $1,800 cash with the remainder due within 30 days.

    11   Billed clients $4,700 for services rendered.

    17   Collected $3,250 cash from clients on their accounts billed on June 11.

    19   Paid $5,000 cash toward the account for office equipment (see June 3).

    25   Paid $900 cash for dividends.

    30   Paid $350 cash for June utilities.

    30   Paid $2,500 cash for June wages.

LO2   M3-13.   Preparing Journal Entries and Posting

Refer to the information in M3-12. Prepare a journal entry for each transaction. Create a T-account for each account, and then post the journal entries to the T-accounts (use dates to reference each entry).

LO2   M3-14.   Assessing Financial Statement Effects of Transactions

B. Fischer started Fischer Company, a cleaning services firm, on April 1. The company created the following accounts to record the transactions for April: Cash; Accounts Receivable; Supplies; Prepaid Van Lease; Equipment; Notes Payable; Accounts Payable; Common Stock; Dividends; Cleaning Fees Earned; Wages Expense; Advertising Expense; and Van Fuel Expense. Record the following transactions for April using the financial statement effects template.

April 1 B. Fischer invested $9,000 cash to begin the business in exchange for common stock.
     2 Paid $2,850 cash for six months' lease on a van for the business.
     3 Borrowed $10,000 cash from a bank and signed a note payable, agreeing to repay it in one year plus 10% interest.
     4 Purchased $5,500 in cleaning equipment; the company paid $2,500 cash with the remainder due within 30 days.
     5 Paid $4,300 cash for cleaning supplies.
     7 Paid $350 cash for advertisements to run in the area newspaper during April.
   21 Billed customers $3,500 for services performed.
   23 Paid $3,000 cash toward the account for cleaning equipment (see April 4).
   28 Collected $2,300 cash from customers on their accounts billed on April 21.
   29 Paid $1,000 cash for dividends.
   30 Paid $2,750 cash for April wages.
   30 Paid $995 cash for gasoline used during April.

LO2   M3-15.   Preparing Journal Entries and Posting

Refer to the information in M3-14. Prepare a journal entry for each transaction. Create a T-account for each account, and then post the journal entries to the T-accounts (use dates to reference each entry).

LO2, 3   M3-16.   Assessing Financial Statement Effects of Transactions and Adjustments

Schrand Services offers janitorial services on both a contract basis and an hourly basis. On January 1, Schrand collected $26,100 cash in advance on a six-month contract for work to be performed evenly during the next six months.

   a. Prepare the entry on January 1 to reflect the receipt of $26,100 cash for contract work; use the financial statement effects template.
   b. Adjust the appropriate accounts on January 31 for the contract work done during January; use the financial statement effects template.
   c. At January 31, a total of 30 hours of hourly rate janitor work was performed but unbilled. The billing rate is $19 per hour. Prepare the accounting adjustment needed on January 31 using the financial statement effects template. (The firm uses the fees receivable account to reflect revenue earned but not yet billed.)

LO2, 3   M3-17.   Preparing Accounting Adjustments

Refer to the information in M3-16. Prepare a journal entry for each of parts *a*, *b*, and *c*.

LO3   M3-18.   Assessing Financial Statement Effects of Adjustments

Selected accounts of Portage Properties, a real estate management firm, are shown below as of January 31, before any accounts have been adjusted. All accounts have normal balances.

Prepaid insurance..............	$ 3,240	Unearned rent revenue.........	$ 5,550
Supplies	1,540	Salaries expense	2,325
Office equipment	6,240	Rent revenue	13,250

Portage Properties prepares monthly financial statements. Using the following information, adjust the accounts as necessary on January 31 using the financial statement effects template.

   a. Prepaid insurance represents a two-year premium paid on January 1.
   b. Supplies of $710 were still available on January 31.
   c. Office equipment is expected to last eight years (or 96 months).
   d. On January 1, Portage collected $5,550 for six months' rent in advance from a tenant renting space for $925 per month.
   e. Salaries of $490 have been earned by employees but not yet recorded as of January 31.

M3-19. Preparing Accounting Adjustments

Refer to the information in M3-18. Prepare journal entries for each of parts *a* through *e*.

M3-20. Inferring Transactions from Financial Statements

Fitbit Inc. is a technology company that designs, manufactures, and sells wearable devices with software and services to help customers reach their health and fitness goals. During fiscal 2018, Fitbit purchased inventory costing $909,380 thousand. Assume Fitbit makes all purchases on credit and its accounts payable is only used for inventory purchases. The following T-accounts reflect information contained in the company's fiscal 2017 and 2018 balance sheets ($ thousands).

Inventories			Accounts Payable	
2017 Bal.	123,895		212,731	2017 Bal.
2018 Bal.	124,871		251,657	2018 Bal.

a. Use the financial statement effects template to record Fitbit's 2018 purchases.

b. What amount did it pay in cash to its suppliers during fiscal year 2018? Explain.

c. Use the financial statement effects template to record cost of goods sold for its fiscal year 2018.

M3-21. Preparing Journal Entries

Refer to the information in M3-20. Prepare journal entries for each of parts *a, b,* and *c*.

M3-22. Preparing a Statement of Stockholders' Equity

On December 31, 2019, the accounts of Leuz Architect Services showed credit balances in its common stock and retained earnings accounts of $30,000 and $18,000, respectively. The company's stock issuances for 2020 totaled $6,000, and it paid $9,700 in cash dividends. During 2020, the company had net income of $27,900. Prepare a 2020 statement of stockholders' equity for Leuz Architect Services.

M3-23. Preparing Closing Journal Entries

KLA-Tencor provides process control and yield management solutions for the semiconductor industry. Selected financial information for the year ended June 30, 2018, follows.

$ millions	Debit	Credit
Net sales.		$4,036,701
Cost of sales.	$1,447,369	
Selling, general, and administrative expense and other.	1,019,025	
Interest expense, net	114,376	
Income tax expense	653,666	
Retained earnings at June 30, 2017.		848,457

Assume the company has not yet closed any accounts to retained earnings. Prepare journal entries to close the temporary accounts above. Set up the needed T-accounts, and post the closing entries. After these entries are posted, what is the balance of the retained earnings account?

M3-24. Inferring Transactions from Financial Statements

Lowe's is the second-largest home improvement retailer in the world, with 2,002 stores. During its fiscal year ended in February 2019, Lowe's purchased merchandise inventory at a cost of $49,569 ($ millions). Assume all purchases were made on account and accounts payable is only used for inventory purchases. The following T-accounts reflect information contained in the company's February 2018 and 2019 balance sheets.

Merchandise Inventories			Accounts Payable	
Feb. 2018 Bal.	8,911		5,124	Feb. 2018 Bal.
Feb. 2019 Bal.	9,458		5,633	Feb. 2019 Bal.

a. Use the financial statement effects template to record Lowe's purchases during the fiscal year ended February 2019.

b. What amount did Lowe's pay in cash to its suppliers during the fiscal year ended February 2019? Explain.

c. Use the financial statement effects template to record cost of sales for the fiscal year ended February 2019.

LO5   **M3-25. Closing Process**

At December 31, Hanlon Consulting's financial records show the following selected account information.

	Debit	Credit
Service fees earned		$80,300
Rent expense	$20,800	
Salaries expense	48,700	
Supplies expense	5,600	
Depreciation expense	10,200	
Retained earnings		67,000

Prepare entries to close these accounts in journal entry form. Set up T-accounts for each account and post the closing entries to the T-accounts. After these entries are posted, what is the balance of the retained earnings account?

LO3, 4   **M3-26. Computing and Comparing Income and Cash Flow Measures**

Penno Corporation recorded service revenues of $200,000 in 2020, of which $170,000 were on credit and $30,000 were for cash. Moreover, of the $170,000 credit sales for 2020, Penno collected $20,000 cash on those receivables before year-end 2020. The company also paid $25,000 cash for 2020 wages. Its employees also earned another $15,000 in wages for 2020, which were not yet paid at year-end 2020. (*a*) Compute the company's net income for 2020; and (*b*) how much net cash inflow or outflow did the company generate in 2020? Explain why Penno's net income and net cash flow differ.

LO3, 4   **M3-27. Analyzing Transactions to Compute Net Income**

Wasley Corp., a start-up company, provided services that were acceptable to its customers and billed those customers for $350,000 in 2019. However, Wasley collected only $280,000 cash in 2019, and the remaining $70,000 was collected in 2020. Wasley employees earned $225,000 in 2019 wages that were not paid until the first week of 2020. How much net income does Wasley report for 2019? For 2020 (assuming no additional transactions)?

LO2   **M3-28. Analyzing Transactions Using the Financial Statement Effects Template**

Report the effects for each of the following transactions using the financial statement effects template.

a. Issue stock for $1,000 cash.
b. Purchase inventory for $500 cash.
c. Sell inventory in transaction *b* for $3,000 on credit.
d. Receive $2,000 cash toward the transaction *c* receivable.

Exercises

LO3   **E3-29. Assessing Financial Statement Effects of Adjustments**

For each of the following separate situations, prepare the necessary accounting adjustments using the financial statement effects template.

a. Unrecorded depreciation on equipment is $720.
b. The supplies account has a balance of $3,870. Supplies still available at the end of the period total $1,100.
c. On the date for preparing financial statements, an estimated utilities expense of $430 has been incurred, but no utility bill has yet been received or paid.
d. On the first day of the current period, rent for four periods was paid and recorded as a $3,200 increase to prepaid rent and a $3,200 decrease to cash.
e. Nine months ago, a one-year service policy was sold to a customer, and the seller recorded the cash received by crediting unearned revenue for $1,872. No accounting adjustments have been prepared during the nine-month period. The seller is now preparing annual financial statements.
f. At the end of the period, employee wages of $965 have been incurred but not paid or recorded.
g. At the end of the period, $300 of interest has been earned but not yet received or recorded.

E3-30. **Preparing Accounting Adjustments**

Refer to the information in E3-29. Prepare journal entries for each accounting adjustment.

LO3

E3-31. **Assessing Financial Statement Effects of Adjustments Across Two Periods**

Oakmont Company closes its accounts on December 31 each year. The company works a five-day work week and pays its employees every two weeks. On December 31, Oakmont accrued $4,700 of salaries payable. On January 9 of the following year, the company paid salaries of $15,000 cash to employees. Prepare entries using the financial statement effects template to (a) accrue the salaries payable on December 31, and (b) record the salary payment nine days later on January 9.

LO3

E3-32. **Preparing Accounting Adjustments**

Refer to the information in E3-31. Prepare journal entries to accrue the salaries in December, close salaries expense for the year, and pay the salaries in January of the following year. Assume there is no change in the pay rate during the year and no change in the company's workforce.

LO3, 5

E3-33. **Financial Analysis Using Adjusted Account Data**

Selected T-account balances for Bloomfield Company are shown below as of January 31, which reflect its accounting adjustments. The firm uses a calendar-year accounting period but prepares *monthly* accounting adjustments.

LO3

Supplies			Supplies Expense	
Jan. 31 Bal.	900		Jan. 31 Bal.	960

Prepaid Insurance			Insurance Expense	
Jan. 31 Bal.	574		Jan. 31 Bal.	82

Wages Payable			Wages Expense	
	700 Jan. 31 Bal.		Jan. 31 Bal.	3,200

Truck			Accumulated Depreciation—Truck	
Jan. 31 Bal. 8,700				2,610 Jan. 31 Bal.

a. If the amount in supplies expense represents the January 31 adjustment for the supplies used in January, and $620 worth of supplies were purchased during January, what was the January 1 beginning balance of supplies?

b. The amount in the insurance expense account represents the adjustment made at January 31 for January insurance expense. If the original insurance premium was for one year, what was the amount of the premium, and on what date did the insurance policy start?

c. If we assume that no beginning balance existed in either wages payable or wages expense on January 1, how much cash was paid as wages during January?

d. If the truck has a useful life of five years (or 60 months), what is the monthly amount of depreciation expense, and how many months has Bloomfield owned the truck?

E3-34. **Assessing Financial Statement Effects of Adjustments**

L. Burnett began Burnett Refinishing Service on July 1. Selected accounts are shown below as of July 31, before any accounting adjustments have been made.

LO3

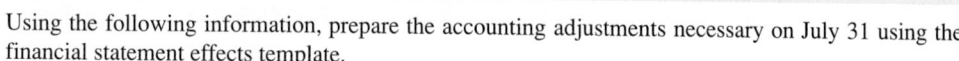

Prepaid rent	$6,900	Unearned refinishing fees	$ 600
Prepaid advertising	630	Refinishing fees revenue	2,500
Supplies	3,000		

Using the following information, prepare the accounting adjustments necessary on July 31 using the financial statement effects template.

a. On July 1, the firm paid one year's rent of $6,900 in cash.

b. On July 1, $630 cash was paid to the local newspaper for an advertisement to run daily for the months of July, August, and September.

c. Supplies still available at July 31 total $1,100.

d. At July 31, refinishing services of $800 have been performed but not yet recorded or billed to customers. The firm uses the fees receivable account to reflect amounts due but not yet billed.

e. In early July, a customer paid $600 in advance for a refinishing project. At July 31, the project is one-half complete.

LO3 **E3-35. Preparing Accounting Adjustments and Posting**

Refer to the information in E3-34. Prepare adjusting journal entries for each transaction. Set up T-accounts for each of the ledger accounts, and post the journal entries to them.

LO2 **E3-36. Inferring Transactions from Financial Statements**

The Gap Inc. (GPS)

The GAP is a global clothing retailer for men, women, children, and babies. The following information is taken from The Gap's annual report for the fiscal year ended February 2, 2019.

Selected Balance Sheet Data ($ millions)	February 2019	February 2018
Merchandise inventory	$2,131	$1,997
Accounts Payable	1,126	1,181

a. The Gap purchased inventories totaling $10,392 for the fiscal year ended February 2, 2019. Use the financial statement effects template to record cost of goods sold for The Gap's fiscal year ended February 2, 2019. (Assume accounts payable is used only for recording purchases of inventories and all inventories are purchased on credit.)

b. What amount did the company pay to suppliers during the year? Record this with the financial statement effects template.

LO2 **E3-37. Inferring Transactions and Preparing Journal Entries**

The GAP Inc. (GPS)

Refer to the information in E3-36. Prepare journal entries for each transaction.

LO5 **E3-38. Preparing Closing Journal Entries**

The GAP Inc. (GPS)

The following selected accounts appear in The GAP Inc.'s financial statements for the fiscal year ended February 2, 2019.

$ millions	Debit	Credit
Net sales		$16,580
Cost of goods sold	$10,258	
Operating expenses (other than COGS)	4,960	
Interest expense, net	40	
Income tax expense	319	
Retained earnings (beginning of year)		3,081

Prepare entries to close these accounts in journal entry form. Set up T-accounts for each of the accounts, and post the entries to them. After these entries are posted, what is the balance of the retained earnings account?

LO2 **E3-39. Inferring Transactions from Financial Statements**

Costco Wholesale Corporation (COST)

Costco Wholesale Corporation operates membership warehouses selling food, appliances, consumer electronics, apparel, and other household goods at 762 U.S. and international locations. As of its fiscal year-end 2018, Costco had approximately 94.3 million members. Selected fiscal-year information from the company's balance sheets follows.

Selected Balance Sheet Data ($ millions)	2018	2017
Merchandise inventories	$11,040	$9,834
Deferred membership income (liability)	1,624	1,498

a. During fiscal 2018, Costco collected $3,268 million cash for membership fees. Use the financial statement effects template to record the cash collected for membership fees.

b. Costco recorded merchandise costs (cost of goods sold) of $123,152 million in fiscal 2018. Record this transaction in the financial statement effects template.

c. Determine the value of merchandise Costco purchased during fiscal 2018. Use the financial statement effects template to record these merchandise purchases. Assume all of Costco's purchases are on account, and recorded in accounts payable.

E3-40.   **Inferring Transactions and Preparing Journal Entries**

Refer to the information in E3-39. Prepare journal entries for transactions in parts *a* through *c*.

E3-41.   **Preparing Financial Statements and Closing Process**

Beneish Company has the following account balances at December 31, the end of its fiscal year.

	Debit	Credit
Cash.	$ 8,000	
Accounts receivable	6,500	
Equipment	78,000	
Accumulated depreciation		$ 14,000
Notes payable.		10,000
Common stock		43,000
Retained earnings		20,600
Dividends	8,000	
Service fees earned		75,000
Rent expense	18,000	
Salaries expense	37,100	
Depreciation expense.	7,000	
Totals	$162,600	$162,600

a.   Prepare Beneish Corporation's income statement and statement of stockholders' equity for year-end December 31 and its balance sheet as of December 31. There were no stock issuances or repurchases during the year.

b.   Prepare journal entries to close Beneish's temporary accounts.

c.   Set up T-accounts for each account and post the closing entries.

E3-42.   **Analyzing and Reporting Financial Statement Effects of Transactions**

M. E. Carter launched Carter Company, a professional services firm on March 1. The firm will prepare financial statements at each month-end. In March (its first month), Carter executed the following transactions. Enter the transactions, *a* through *g*, into the financial statement effects template shown in the module.

a.   Carter (owner) invested in the company $100,000 cash and $20,000 in property and equipment. The company issued common stock to Carter.

b.   The company paid $3,200 cash for rent of office furnishings and facilities for March.

c.   The company performed services for clients and immediately received $4,000 cash for these services.

d.   The company performed services for clients and sent a bill for $24,000 with payment due within 60 days.

e.   The company compensated an office employee with $4,800 cash as salary for March.

f.   The company received $10,000 cash as partial payment on the amount owed from clients in transaction *d*.

g.   The company paid $935 cash in dividends to Carter (owner).

E3-43.   **Analyzing Transactions Using the Financial Statement Effects Template**

Refer to transactions *a* through *g* from E3-42. Prepare an income statement for Carter Company for the month of March.

E3-44.   **Analyzing Transactions and Adjustments Using the Financial Statement Effects Template**

Record the effect of each of the following transactions for Hora Company using the financial statement effects template.

a.   Wages of $500 are earned by employees but not yet paid.

b. $2,000 of inventory is purchased on credit.

c.   Inventory purchased in transaction *b* is sold for $4,000 on credit.

d.   Collected $3,000 cash from transaction *c*.

e.   Equipment is acquired for $5,000 cash.

f.   Recorded $1,000 depreciation expense on equipment from transaction *e*.

g.   Paid $10,000 cash toward a note payable that came due.

h.   Paid $2,000 cash for interest on borrowings.

Problems

LO3   **P3-45.**   **Assessing Financial Statement Effects of Adjustments**

The following information relates to December 31 accounting adjustments for Fulton Fast Print Company. The firm's fiscal year ends on December 31.

1. Weekly salaries for a five-day week total $3,600, payable on Fridays. December 31 of the current year is a Tuesday.
2. Fulton Fast Print has $20,000 of notes payable outstanding at December 31. Interest of $200 has accrued on these notes by December 31 but will not be paid until the notes mature next year.
3. During December, Fulton Fast Print provided $900 of printing services to clients who will be billed on January 2. The firm uses the fees receivable account to reflect amounts earned but not yet billed.
4. Starting December 1, all maintenance work on Fulton Fast Print's equipment is handled by Richardson Repair Company under an agreement whereby Fulton Fast Print pays a fixed monthly charge of $400. Fulton Fast Print paid six months' service charge of $2,400 cash in advance on December 1 and increased its Prepaid maintenance account by $2,400.
5. The firm paid $900 cash on December 15 for a series of radio commercials to run during December and January. One-third of the commercials aired by December 31. The $900 payment was recorded in its prepaid advertising account.
6. Starting December 16, Fulton Fast Print rented 800 square feet of storage space from a neighboring business. The monthly rent of $0.80 per square foot is due in advance on the first of each month. Nothing was paid in December, however, because the neighboring business agreed to add the rent for one-half of December to the January 1 payment.
7. Fulton Fast Print invested $5,000 cash in securities on December 1 and earned interest of $38 on these securities by December 31. No interest will be received until January.
8. Annual depreciation on the firm's equipment is $2,175. No depreciation has been recorded during the year.

Required

Prepare Fulton Fast Print Company's accounting adjustments required at December 31 using the financial statement effects template.

LO3   **P3-46.**   **Preparing Accounting Adjustments**

Refer to the information in P3-45. Prepare accounting adjustments required at December 31 using journal entries.

LO2, 3   **P3-47.**   **Assessing Financial Statement Effects of Transactions and Adjustments Across Two Periods**

Sloan Company has the following account balances at December 31, the end of its fiscal year (all accounts have normal balances).

Prepaid advertising............	$ 1,200	Unearned service fees..........	$ 5,400
Wages expense	43,800	Service fees earned............	87,000
Prepaid insurance.............	3,420	Rental income................	4,900

Required

a. Prepare Sloan Company's accounting adjustments at December 31 using the financial statement effects template and the following additional information.
   1. Prepaid advertising at December 31 is $800.
   2. Unpaid wages earned by employees in December are $2,600.
   3. Prepaid insurance at December 31 is $2,280.
   4. Unearned service fees at December 31 are $3,000.
   5. Rent revenue of $1,000 owed by a tenant is not recorded at December 31.

b. Use the financial statement effects template to record the following transactions on January 4 of the following year:
   1. Payment of $4,800 cash in wages.
   2. Cash receipt from the tenant of the $1,000 rent revenue.

P3-48. **Preparing Accounting Transactions and Adjustments**

Refer to the information in P3-47. Prepare journal entries for parts *a* and *b*.

P3-49. **Journalizing and Posting Transactions and Adjustments**

D. Roulstone opened Roulstone Roofing Service on April 1. Transactions for April follow.

Apr.	1	Roulstone contributed $11,500 cash to the business in exchange for common stock.
	2	Paid $6,100 cash for the purchase of a used truck.
	2	Purchased $6,200 of ladders and other equipment; the company paid $1,000 cash, with the balance due in 30 days.
	3	Paid $2,880 cash for a two-year (or 24-month) premium toward liability insurance.
	5	Purchased $1,200 of supplies on credit.
	5	Received an advance of $1,800 cash from a customer for roof repairs to be done during April and May.
	12	Billed customers $5,500 for roofing services performed.
	18	Collected $4,900 cash from customers toward their accounts billed on April 12.
	29	Paid $675 cash for truck fuel used in April.
	30	Paid $100 cash for April newspaper advertising.
	30	Paid $4,500 cash for assistants' wages earned.
	30	Billed customers $4,000 for roofing services performed.

Required

a. Set up T-accounts for the following accounts: cash, accounts receivable, supplies, prepaid insurance, trucks, accumulated depreciation—trucks, equipment, accumulated depreciation—equipment, accounts payable, unearned roofing fees, common stock, roofing fees earned, fuel expense, advertising expense, wages expense, insurance expense, supplies expense, depreciation expense—trucks, and depreciation expense—equipment.

b. Record these transactions for April using journal entries.

c. Post the journal entries from part *b*. to their T-accounts (reference transactions in T-accounts by date).

d. Prepare journal entries to adjust the following accounts: insurance expense, supplies expense, depreciation expense—trucks, depreciation expense—equipment, and roofing fees earned. Supplies still available on April 30 amount to $200. Depreciation for April was $125 on the truck and $35 on equipment. One-fourth of the roofing fee received on April 5 was earned by April 30.

e. Post the adjusting journal entries from part *d*. to their T-accounts.

P3-50. **Assessing Financial Statement Effects of Transactions and Adjustments**

Refer to the information in P3-49.

Required

a. Use the financial statement effects template to record the transactions for April.

b. Use the financial statement effects template to record the adjustments at the end of April (described in part *d* of P3-49).

P3-51. **Preparing Accounting Adjustments**

Pownall Photomake Company, a commercial photography studio, completed its first year of operations on December 31. Account balances before year-end adjustments follow; no adjustments have been made to the accounts at any time during the year. Assume that all balances are normal.

LO3

Cash.	$ 4,300	Accounts payable.	$ 4,060
Accounts receivable	3,800	Unearned photography fees.	2,600
Prepaid rent	12,600	Common stock	24,000
Prepaid insurance.	2,970	Photography fees earned.	34,480
Supplies	4,250	Wages expense	11,000
Equipment	22,800	Utilities expense.	3,420

An analysis of the firm's records discloses the following (business began on January 1).

1. Photography services of $1,850 have been rendered, but customers have not yet paid or been billed. The company uses the fees receivable account to reflect amounts due but not yet billed.

2. Equipment, purchased January 1, has an estimated life of 10 years.

3. Utilities expense for December is estimated to be $400, but the bill will not arrive or be paid until January of next year. (All prior months' utilities bills have been received and paid.)

4. The balance in prepaid rent represents the amount paid on January 1 for a two-year lease on the studio it operates from.
5. In November, customers paid $2,600 cash in advance for photos to be taken for the holiday season. When received, these fees were credited to unearned photography fees. By December 31, all of these fees are earned.
6. A three-year insurance premium paid on January 1 was debited to prepaid insurance.
7. Supplies still available at December 31 are $1,020.
8. At December 31, wages expense of $375 had been incurred but not yet paid or recorded.

Required
Prepare the required adjusting entries using the financial statement effects template.

LO3   P3-52.   Recording Adjustments with Journal Entries and T-accounts
Refer to the information in P3-51.

Required
a. Prepare journal entries to record the accounting adjustments.
b. Set up T-accounts for each account, and post the journal entries to them.

LO3   P3-53.   Preparing Accounting Adjustments
BensEx, a mailing service, has just completed its first year of operations on December 31. Its account balances before year-end adjustments follow; no adjusting entries have been made to the accounts at any time during the year. Assume all balances are normal.

Cash.......................	$ 1,700	Accounts payable..............	$ 2,700
Accounts receivable............	5,120	Common stock................	9,530
Prepaid advertising............	1,680	Mailing fees earned	86,000
Supplies	6,270	Wages expense	38,800
Equipment	42,240	Rent expense.................	6,900
Notes payable................	7,500	Utilities expense	3,020

An analysis of the firm's records reveals the following (business began on January 1).

1. The balance in prepaid advertising represents the amount paid for newspaper advertising for one year. The agreement, which calls for the same amount of space each month, covers the period from February 1 of this first year to January 31 of the following year. BensEx did not advertise during its first month of operations.
2. Equipment, purchased January 1, has an estimated life of eight years.
3. Utilities expense does not include expense for December, estimated at $325. The bill will not arrive until January of the following year.
4. At year-end, employees have earned $2,400 in wages that will not be paid until January.
5. Supplies available at year-end amount to $1,520.
6. At year-end, unpaid interest of $450 has accrued on the notes payable.
7. The firm's lease calls for rent of $575 per month payable on the first of each month, plus an amount equal to 0.75% of annual mailing fees earned. The rental percentage is payable within 15 days after the end of the year.

Required
Prepare the required adjusting entries using the financial statement effects template.

LO3   P3-54.   Recording Accounting Adjustments with Journal Entries and T-accounts
Refer to information in P3-53.

Required
a. Prepare journal entries to record the accounting adjustments.
b. Set up T-accounts for each account, and post the journal entries to them.

LO3, 4, 5   P3-55.   Preparing Accounting Adjustments
Wysocki Wheels began operations on March 1 to provide automotive wheel alignment and balancing services. On March 31, accounting records revealed the following account balances.

	Debit	Credit
Cash..................................	$ 2,900	
Accounts receivable......................	3,820	
Prepaid rent...........................	4,770	
Supplies...............................	3,700	
Equipment............................	36,180	
Accounts payable......................		$ 3,510
Unearned service revenue................		1,000
Common stock........................		38,400
Service revenue.......................		12,360
Wages expense........................	3,900	
Totals................................	$55,270	$55,270

The following information is also available.

1. The balance in prepaid rent was the amount paid on March 1 to cover the first six months' rent.
2. Supplies available on March 31 amounted to $1,360.
3. Equipment has an estimated life of nine years (or 108 months).
4. Unpaid and unrecorded wages at March 31 were $1,560.
5. Utility services used during March were estimated at $390; a bill is expected early in April.
6. The balance in unearned service revenue was the amount received on March 1 from a car dealer to cover alignment and balancing services on cars sold by the dealer in March and April. Wysocki Wheels agreed to provide the services at a fixed fee of $500 each month.

Required

a. Prepare the accounting adjustments at March 31 in journal entry form.
b. Set up T-accounts, and post the accounting adjustments to them.
c. Prepare the income statement for March and its balance sheet at March 31.
d. Prepare entries to close the temporary accounts in journal entry form. Post the closing entries to the T-accounts.

P3-56. **Analyzing Transactions Using the Financial Statement Effects Template**
Sefcik Company began operations on the first of October. Following are the transactions for its first month of business.

LO2, 4

1. S. Sefcik launched Sefcik Company and invested $50,000 into the business in exchange for common stock. The company also borrowed $100,000 from a local bank.
2. Sefcik Company purchased equipment for $95,000 cash and inventory of $40,000 on credit (the company still owes its suppliers for the inventory at month-end).
3. Sefcik Company sold inventory costing $30,000 for $50,000 cash.
4. Sefcik Company paid $12,000 cash for wages owed employees for October work.
5. Sefcik Company paid interest on the bank loan of $1,000 cash.
6. Sefcik Company recorded $500 of depreciation expense related to its equipment.
7. Sefcik Company paid a dividend of $2,000 cash.

Required

a. Record the effects of each transaction using the financial statement effects template.
b. Prepare the income statement and balance sheet at the end of October.

P3-57. **Analyzing Transactions and Adjustments Using the Financial Statement Effects Template**
Following are selected transactions of Mogg Company. Record the effects of each using the financial statement effects template.

LO2, 3

1. Shareholders contribute $10,000 cash to the business in exchange for common stock.
2. Employees earn $500 in wages that have not been paid at period-end.
3. Inventory of $3,000 is purchased on credit.
4. The inventory purchased in transaction 3 is sold for $4,500 on credit.
5. The company collected the $4,500 owed to it per transaction 4.
6. Equipment is purchased for $5,000 cash.

7. Depreciation of $1,000 is recorded on the equipment from transaction 6.
8. The supplies account had a $3,800 balance at the beginning of this period; a physical count at period-end shows that $800 of supplies are still available. No supplies were purchased during this period.
9. The company paid $12,000 cash toward the principal on a note payable; also, $500 cash is paid to cover this note's interest expense for the period.
10. The company received $8,000 cash in advance for services to be delivered next period.

LO2, 3, 4   **P3-58.**   **Analyzing Transactions and Adjustments Using the Financial Statement Effects Template**

On March 1, S. Penman launched AniFoods Inc., an organic foods retailing company. Following are the transactions for its first month of business.

1. S. Penman contributed $100,000 cash to the company in return for common stock. Penman also lent the company $55,000. This $55,000 note is due one year hence.
2. The company purchased equipment in the amount of $50,000, paying $10,000 cash and signing a note payable to the equipment manufacturer for the remaining balance.
3. The company purchased inventory for $80,000 cash in March.
4. The company had March sales of $100,000, of which $60,000 was for cash and $40,000 on credit. Total cost of goods sold for its March sales was $70,000.
5. The company purchased future advertising time from a local radio station for $10,000 cash.
6. During March, $7,500 worth of radio spots purchased in transaction 5 are aired. The remaining spots will be aired in April.
7. Employee wages earned and paid during March total $17,000 cash.
8. Prior to disclosing the financial statements, the company recognized that employees had earned an additional $1,000 in wages that will be paid in the next period.
9. The company recorded $2,000 of depreciation for March relating to its equipment.

Required
a. Record the effect of each transaction using the financial statement effects template.
b. Prepare a March income statement and a balance sheet as of the end of March for AniFoods Inc.

LO2, 4   **P3-59.**   **Analyzing Transactions Using the Financial Statement Effects Template**

Hanlon Advertising Company began the current month with the following balance sheet.

Cash.....................	$ 80,000	Liabilities..................	$ 70,000
Noncash assets	135,000	Contributed capital	110,000
		Earned capital...............	35,000
Total assets	$215,000	Total liabilities and equity	$215,000

Following are summary transactions that occurred during the current month.

1. The company purchased supplies for $5,000 cash; none were used this month.
2. Services of $2,500 were performed this month on credit.
3. Services were performed for $10,000 cash this month.
4. The company purchased advertising for $8,000 cash; the ads will run next month.
5. The company received $1,200 cash as partial payment on accounts receivable from transaction 2.
6. The company paid $3,400 cash toward the accounts payable balance reported at the beginning of the month.
7. The company paid $3,500 cash toward this month's wages expense.
8. The company declared and paid dividends of $500 cash.

Required
a. Record the effects of each transaction using the financial statement effects template.
b. Prepare the income statement for this month and the balance sheet as of month-end.

LO2, 3, 4   **P3-60.**   **Analyzing Transactions and Adjustments Using the Financial Statement Effects Template**

Werner Realty Company began the month with the following balance sheet.

Cash.....................	$ 30,000	Liabilities..................	$ 90,000
Noncash assets	225,000	Contributed capital	45,000
		Earned capital...............	120,000
Total assets	$255,000	Total liabilities and equity	$255,000

Following are summary transactions that occurred during the current month.

1. The company purchased $6,000 of supplies on credit.
2. The company received $8,000 cash from a new customer for services to be performed next month.
3. The company paid $6,000 cash to cover office rent for two months (the current month and the next).
4. The company billed clients for $25,000 of work performed.
5. The company paid employees $6,000 cash for work performed.
6. The company collected $25,000 cash from accounts receivable in transaction 4.
7. The company recorded $4,000 depreciation on its equipment.
8. At month-end, $2,000 of supplies purchased in transaction 1 are still available; no supplies were available when the month began.

Required

a. Record the effects of each transaction using the financial statement effects template.
b. Prepare the income statement for this month and the balance sheet as of month-end.

IFRS Applications

I3-61.   **Preparing Closing Journal Entries**

On June 30, 2018, Qantas Airlines reports the following balances.

LO5
Qantas Airlines

In AUD millions	Debit	Credit
Total passenger and freight revenue		A$17,060
Manpower and staff related	A$4,300	
Fuel	3,232	
Aircraft operating variable	3,596	
Depreciation and amortization	1,528	
Other expenses	2,831	
Finance costs, net	182	
Income tax expense	411	
Retained earnings, beginning of year		1,084

Assume the company has not yet closed any accounts to retained earnings. Prepare journal entries to close the temporary accounts above. Set up the needed T-accounts, and post the closing entries. After these entries are posted, what is the balance of the retained earnings account?

I3-62.   **Inferring Transactions and Adjustments from Financial Statements**

Rio Tinto is a British-Australian multinational metals and mining corporation with headquarters in London, England, and a management office in Melbourne, Australia. Assume the following amounts have not been recorded for fiscal 2018 ($ millions).

LO2, 3
Rio Tinto

Sales revenue	$18,485
Depreciation and amortization expense	4,015
Income taxes paid	4,242

Use the financial statement effects template to record the following transactions for Rio Tinto for fiscal 2018.

a. Sales revenue. Assume 100% of the company's revenue is credit sales (meaning its sales are on accounts receivable).
b. Depreciation expense.
c. Income taxes paid. Assume this represents the portion of income tax expense paid in cash.

Management Applications

LO2, 3, 4   **MA3-63.** **Preparing Accounting Transactions and Adjustments and Financial Statements**

Stocken Surf Shop began operations on July 1 with an initial investment of $50,000. During the first three months of operations, the following cash transactions were recorded in the firm's checking account.

Deposits	
Initial investment by owner........	$ 50,000
Collected from customers.........	81,000
Borrowings from bank...........	10,000
	$141,000

Checks Drawn	
Rent	$ 24,000
Fixtures and equipment	25,000
Merchandise inventory...........	62,000
Salaries.....................	8,000
Other expenses	13,000
	$132,000

Additional information:

1. Most sales were for cash; however, the store accepted a limited amount of credit sales; at September 30, customers owed the store $9,000.
2. Rent was paid on July 1 for six months. (The company recorded prepaid expense, an asset, on July 1.)
3. Salaries of $4,000 per month were paid on the first of each month for salaries earned in the month prior.
4. Inventories were purchased for cash; at September 30, inventory of $28,000 was still available.
5. Fixtures and equipment were expected to last five years (or 60 months), with zero salvage value.
6. The bank charges 12% annual interest (1% per month) on the $10,000 bank loan. Stocken took out the loan on July 1.

Required

a. Record all of Stocken's cash transactions, and prepare any necessary adjusting entries at September 30. You may either use the financial statement effects template or journal entries combined with T-accounts.
b. Prepare the income statement for the three months ended September 30 and the balance sheet at September 30.
c. Analyze the statements from part b, and assess the company's performance over its initial three months.

LO3   **MA3-64.** **Analyzing Adjustments, Impacts on Financial Ratios, and Loan Covenants**

Kadous Consulting, a firm started three years ago by K. Kadous, offers consulting services for material handling and plant layout. Its balance sheet at the close of the current year follows.

KADOUS CONSULTING
Balance Sheet
December 31

Assets		Liabilities	
Cash.....................	$ 3,400	Notes payable.............	$30,000
Accounts receivable	20,875	Accounts payable..........	4,200
Supplies	13,200	Unearned consulting fees....	11,300
Prepaid insurance..........	6,500	Wages payable............	400
		Total liabilities.............	45,900
Equipment, gross	68,500		
Less: Accumulated		**Equity**	
depreciation	23,975	Common stock............	8,000
Equipment, net............	44,525	Retained earnings	34,600
Total assets	$88,500	Total liabilities and equity	$88,500

Earlier in the year, Kadous obtained a bank loan of $30,000 cash for the firm. A provision of the loan is that the year-end debt-to-equity ratio (total liabilities to total equity) cannot exceed 1.0. Based on the above balance sheet, the ratio at December 31 of this year is 1.08. Kadous is concerned about being in violation of the loan agreement and requests assistance in reviewing the situation. Kadous believes she might have overlooked some items at year-end. Discussions with Kadous reveal the following.

1. On January 1 of this year, the firm paid a $6,500 insurance premium for two years of coverage; the amount in prepaid insurance has not yet been adjusted.
2. Depreciation on equipment should be 10% of cost per year; the company inadvertently recorded 15% for this year.
3. Interest on the bank loan has been paid through the end of this year.
4. The firm concluded a major consulting engagement in December, doing a plant layout analysis for a new factory. The $8,000 fee has not been billed or recorded in the accounts.
5. On December 1 of this year, the firm received an $11,300 cash advance payment from Dichev Corp. for consulting services to be rendered over a two-month period. This payment was credited to the unearned consulting fees account. One-half of this fee was earned but unrecorded by December 31 of this year.
6. Supplies costing $4,800 were available on December 31; the company has made no adjustment of its Supplies account.

Required
a. What is the correct debt-to-equity ratio at December 31?
b. Is the firm in violation of its loan agreement? Prepare computations to support the correct total liabilities and total equity figures at December 31.

MA3-65. Ethics, Accounting Adjustments, and Auditors   **LO3**

It is the end of the accounting year for Anne Beatty, controller of a medium-sized, publicly held corporation specializing in toxic waste cleanup. Within the corporation, only Beatty and the president know the firm has been negotiating for several months to land a large contract for waste cleanup in Western Europe. The president has hired another firm with excellent contacts in Western Europe to help with negotiations. The outside firm will charge an hourly fee plus expenses but has agreed not to submit a bill until the negotiations are in their final stages (expected to occur in another three to four months). Even if the contract falls through, the outside firm is entitled to receive payment for its services. Based on her discussion with a member of the outside firm, Beatty knows its charge for services provided to date will be $150,000. This is a material amount for the company.

Beatty knows the president wants negotiations to remain as secret as possible so competitors will not learn of the contract the company is pursuing in Europe. In fact, the president recently stated to her, "This is not the time to reveal our actions in Western Europe to other staff members, our auditors, or the readers of our financial statements; securing this contract is crucial to our future growth." No entry has been made in the accounting records for the cost of contract negotiations. Beatty now faces an uncomfortable situation. The company's outside auditor has just asked her if she knows of any year-end adjustments that have not yet been recorded.

Required
a. What are the ethical considerations Beatty faces in answering the auditor's question?
b. How should Beatty respond to the auditor's question?

Solutions to Review Problems

Review 3-1—Solution

	Cash Asset	Noncash Asset	Liabilities	Contributed Capital	Earned Capital	Revenues	Expenses
Accounts payable			X				
Accounts receivable, less allowances		X					
Accrued expenses			X				
Acquired intangible assets, net.		X					
Cash and cash equivalents	X						
Common stock and additional paid-in capital. . . .				X			
Cost of sales.							X
Current portion of long-term debt			X				
Deferred revenue			X				
Deferred tax assets		X					
Goodwill		X					
Inventories		X					
Long-term debt			X				
Long-term marketable securities		X					
Net sales.						X	
Other current assets.		X					
Other noncurrent liabilities			X				
Property, plant, and equipment, net		X					
Provision for income taxes							X
Research and development							X
Retained earnings					X		
Selling, general and administrative.							X

Review 3-2—Solution

	Cash Assets +	Noncash Assets =	Liabil-ities	+ Contrib. Capital	+ Earned Capital	Rev-enues −	Expen-ses =	Net Income
Balance January 1, 2020	10,000	41,000	26,000	10,000	15,000	0	0	0
Transactions								
1. Issue common stock for $3,000 cash.	3,000			3,000				
2. Purchase inventory for $8,000 on credit.		8,000 Inventory	8,000 Accounts payable					
3. Sell inventory costing $8,000 for $15,000 on credit		(8,000) Inventory 15,000 Accounts receivable			7,000 Retained earnings	15,000 Revenue	8,000 Cost of goods sold	7,000
4. Issue long-term debt for $10,000 cash.	10,000		10,000 Long-term debt					
5. Pay $15,000 cash for PPE	(15,000)	15,000 PPE						
6. Pay $500 cash for salaries	(500)				(500) Retained earnings		500 Salaries expense	(500)
7. Receive $300 cash in advance for future consulting services . . .	300		300 Unearned revenue					
8. Pay $50 cash for interest on long-term debt.	(50)				(50) Retained earnings		50 Interest expense	(50)
9. Receive $3,000 cash from accounts receivable.	3,000	(3,000) Accounts receivable						
10. Pay $2,500 cash toward accounts payable	(2,500)		(2,500) Accounts payable					
11. Perform consulting services for client who previously paid in 7 . . .			(300) Unearned revenue		300 Retained earnings	300 Revenue		300
12. Pay $100 cash for dividends	(100)				(100) Retained earnings			

Review 3-3—Solution

	Cash Assets +	Noncash Assets =	Liabil-ities	+ Contrib. Capital	+ Earned Capital	Rev-enues −	Expen-ses =	Net Income
Accounting Adjustments.								
13. Record depreciation of $600		(600) PPE			(600) Retained earnings		600 Depreciation expense	(600)
14. Accrue salaries of $1,000.			1,000 Salaries payable		(1,000) Retained earnings		1,000 Salaries expense	(1,000)
15. Advertising costing $1,300 is aired.		(1,300) Prepaid expense			(1,300) Retained earnings		1,300 Advertising expense	(1,300)
16. Accrue income taxes of $1,200			1,200 Taxes payable		(1,200) Retained earnings		1,200 Tax expense	(1,200)
Balance January 31, 2020	**8,150**	**66,100**	**8,150**	**13,000**	**17,550**	**15,300**	**12,650**	**2,650**

Review 3-4—Solution

1.

Cash	$ 8,150	Taxes payable	$ 1,200
Accounts receivable	24,000	Unearned revenue	200
Inventory	7,200	Long-term debt	32,000
Prepaid advertising	500	Common stock	13,000
PPE	34,400	Retained earnings	17,550
Accounts payable	9,300	Revenues	15,300
Salaries payable	1,000	Expenses	12,650

2.

PRESTIGE INC. Income Statement For Month Ended January 31, 2020	
Revenues	$15,300
Cost of goods sold	8,000
Gross profit	7,300
Salaries expense	1,500
Depreciation expense	600
Advertising expense	1,300
Operating profit	3,900
Interest expense	50
Profit before tax	3,850
Tax expense	1,200
Net income	$ 2,650

PRESTIGE INC. Retained Earnings Reconciliation For Month Ended January 31, 2020	
Beginning retained earnings	$15,000
Net income	2,650
Dividends	(100)
Ending retained earnings	$17,550

PRESTIGE INC. Balance Sheet January 31, 2020			
Cash	$ 8,150	Accounts payable	$ 9,300
Accounts receivable	24,000	Wages payable	1,000
Inventories	7,200	Taxes payable	1,200
Prepaid advertising	500	Unearned revenue	200
Current assets	39,850	Current liabilities	11,700
		Long-term debt	32,000
Property, plant, and equipment	34,400	Total liabilities	43,700
		Common stock	13,000
		Retained earnings	17,550
		Total stockholders' equity	30,550
Total assets	$74,250	Total liabilities and stockholders' equity	$74,250

Review 3-5—Solution

1. Close revenue account.

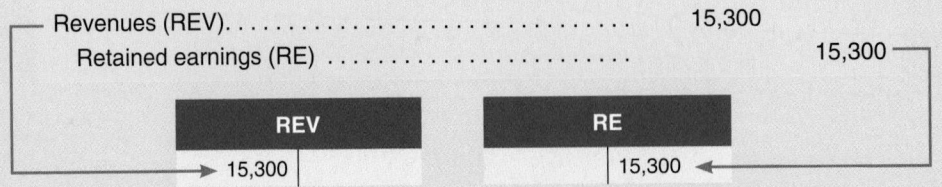

Revenues (REV) 15,300

    Retained earnings (RE) 15,300

REV		RE	
	15,300		15,300

2. Close expense accounts.

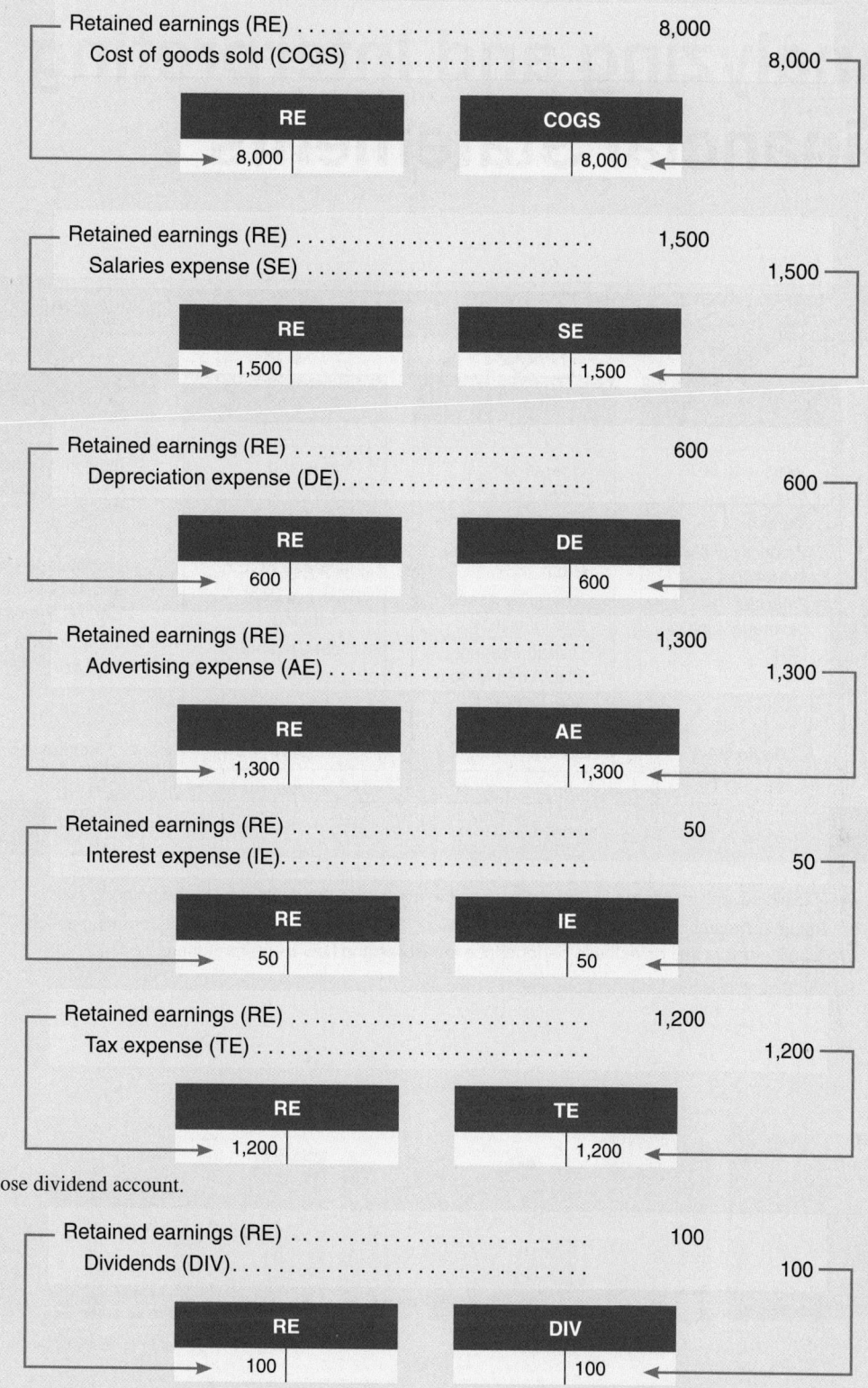

Retained earnings (RE) 8,000
  Cost of goods sold (COGS) 8,000

RE	COGS
8,000	8,000

Retained earnings (RE) 1,500
  Salaries expense (SE) 1,500

RE	SE
1,500	1,500

Retained earnings (RE) 600
  Depreciation expense (DE) 600

RE	DE
600	600

Retained earnings (RE) 1,300
  Advertising expense (AE) 1,300

RE	AE
1,300	1,300

Retained earnings (RE) 50
  Interest expense (IE) 50

RE	IE
50	50

Retained earnings (RE) 1,200
  Tax expense (TE) 1,200

RE	TE
1,200	1,200

3. Close dividend account.

Retained earnings (RE) 100
  Dividends (DIV) 100

RE	DIV
100	100

Module 4

Analyzing and Interpreting Financial Statements

Analyzing and Interpreting Financial Statements

Return on Equity (ROE)

- Measuring ROE
- Disaggregating ROE with DuPont Analysis
- Components: Return on Assets and Financial Leverage

Review 4-1, 4-2

Return on Assets (ROA)

- Measuring ROA
- Profitability (Profit Margin)
- Productivity (Asset Turnover)
- Financial Leverage: Link to ROE

Review 4-3

Operating Focus

- Operating Revenues and Expenses
- Tax on Operating Profit
- Operating Assets and Liabilities
- Disaggregating RNOA into Margin and Turnover

Review 4-4, 5, 6, 7

Nonoperating Return

- Measuring Nonoperating Return
- Leveraging Debt to Increase ROE
- Risks of Debt Financing
- Debt Covenants

Review 4-8

Liquidity and Solvency

- Liquidity: Current Ratio and Quick Ratio
- Solvency: Liabilities-to-Equity and Times Interest Earned Ratios
- Limitations of Ratio Analysis

Review 4-9

PREVIEW

BSX

- We explain several measures of performance that relate the income statement to the balance sheet:
  - Return on assets (ROA)
  - Return on equity (ROE)
  - Return on net operating assets (RNOA)
- We identify factors that drive these performance measures and how to interpret them.
- Boston Scientific is the focus company of this module.

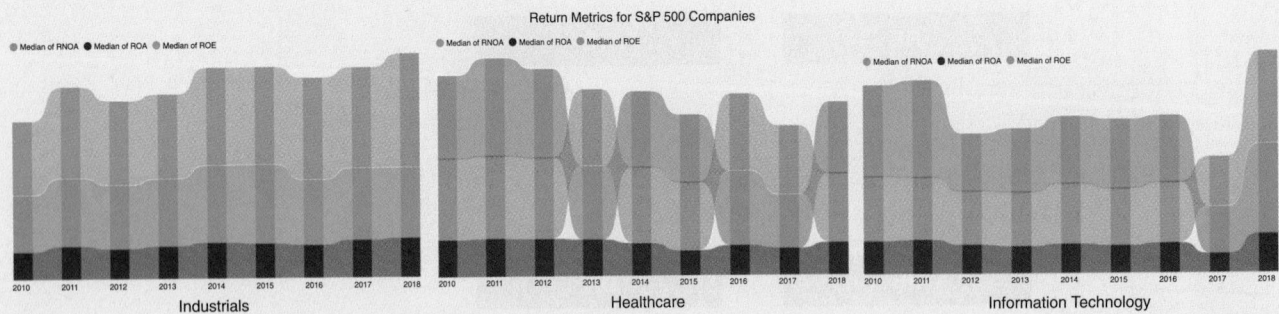

Return Metrics for S&P 500 Companies

Industrials

Healthcare

Information Technology

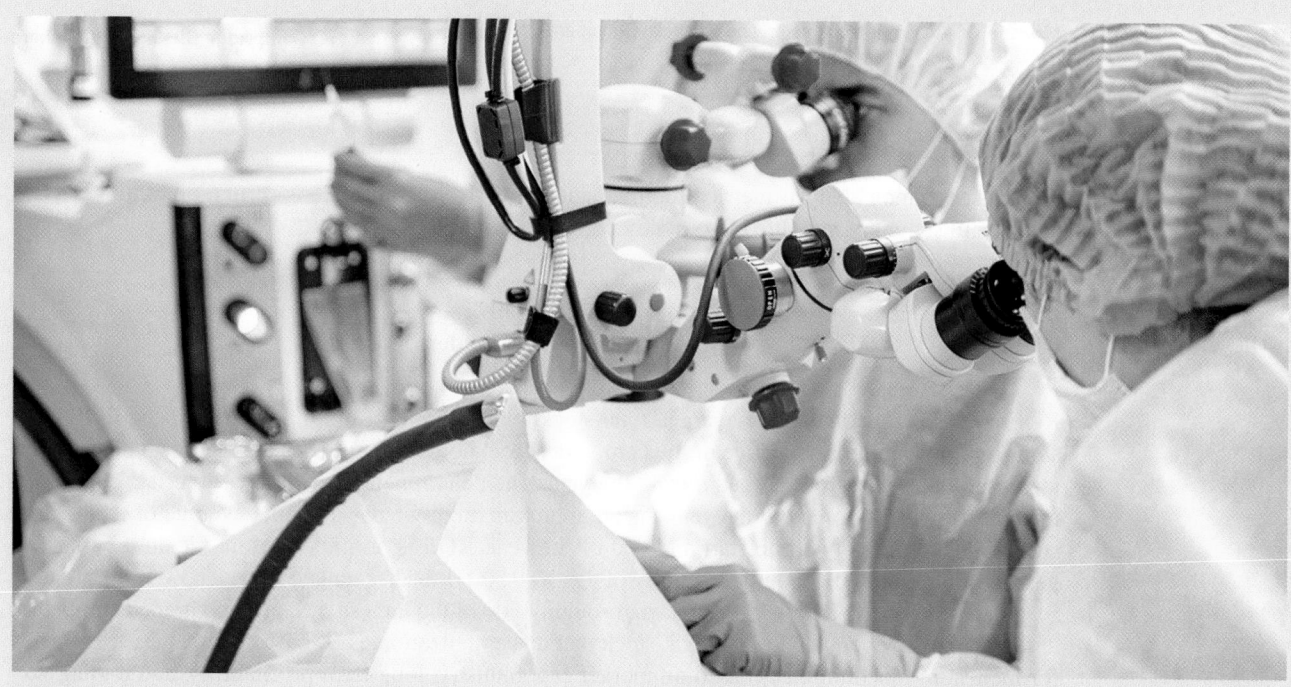

Road Map

LO	Learning Objective | Topics	Page	eLecture	Guided Example	Assignments
4–1	**Compute and interpret return on equity (ROE).** ROE Definition :: ROE Computation :: ROE Interpretation	4-3	e4–1	Review 4-1	1, 18, 26, 32, 34, 35, 36, 42, 48, 49, 51, 54
4–2	**Apply DuPont disaggregation of ROE into return on assets (ROA) and financial leverage.** ROE Disaggregation :: Return on Assets :: Financial Leverage	4-4	e4–2	Review 4-2	2, 19, 26, 32, 34, 36, 42, 51
4–3	**Disaggregate ROA into profitability and productivity and analyze both.** ROA Disaggregation :: Profitability :: Productivity :: Financial Leverage	4-6	e4–3	Review 4-3	3, 4, 5, 16, 19, 26, 31, 32, 34, 42, 51, 53, 56, 57, 58
4–4	**Identify balance sheet operating items and compute net operating assets.** Operating Focus on Balance Sheet :: RNOA Motivation :: NOA Computation	4-14	e4–4	Review 4-4	9, 14, 20, 24, 41, 45, 48, 50
4–5	**Identify income statement operating items and compute net operating profit after tax.** Operating Focus on Income Statement :: Operating vs Nonoperating :: NOPAT Computation :: Income Tax Expense	4-19	e4–5	Review 4-5	3, 7, 8, 14, 21, 25, 29, 40, 41, 45, 48, 50
4–6	**Compute and interpret return on net operating assets (RNOA).** RNOA Computation :: ROA vs RNOA :: ROA components :: Key Definitions	4-23	e4–6	Review 4-6	6, 22, 23, 27, 29, 33, 35, 36, 41, 45, 48, 50, 54
4–7	**Disaggregate RNOA into net operating profitability and net operating asset turnover.** RNOA Disaggregation :: Net Operating Profit Margin :: Net Operating Asset Turnover :: Trade-Off of Margin and Turnover	4-25	e4–7	Review 4-7	3, 4, 10, 11, 15, 22, 23, 27, 29, 33, 35, 41, 45, 48, 50, 52, 54
4–8	**Compute and interpret nonoperating return (Appendix 4B).** Nonoperating Return Components :: FLEV and Spread	4-31	e4–8	Review 4-8	37, 38, 41, 44, 47, 49
4–9	**Compute and interpret measures of liquidity and solvency (Appendix 4C).** Liquidity Analysis :: Solvency Analysis :: Vertical and Horizontal Analysis :: Limitations of Ratios	4-35	e4–9	Review 4-9	12, 13, 17, 28, 30, 39, 43, 46, 55

Return on Equity (ROE)

LO1
Compute and interpret return on equity (ROE).

The most common analysis metric used by managers and investors alike is **return on equity (ROE)**, a powerful summary measure of company performance defined as:

$$\text{ROE} = \frac{\text{Net income}}{\text{Average stockholders' equity}}$$

ROE relates net income to the average total stockholders' equity from the balance sheet. ROE measures return from the perspective of the company's stockholders. ROE uses net income, in the numerator, that represents profit earned *during* the year. The denominator would ideally reflect equity that the company had *throughout* the year. As an approximation, we use a simple average of the balance sheet values for equity at the start and end of the year. ROE is an important metric and, in the five years from 2014 to 2018, return on equity of the S&P 500 firms has ranged from 13.5% to 15.6%. The Standard & Poor's (S&P) 500 consists of roughly 500 of the largest U.S. publicly traded companies and accounts for about 75% of the U.S. stock market capitalization. U.S.-based companies are selected for inclusion (by committee) based on market cap, industry, long-term profitability, and trading volume, and other factors. In 2019, Boston Scientific was #97 on the S&P 500. The S&P 500 Index is a market-capitalization-weighted index of the S&P 500 firms. Exhibit 4.1 includes the income statement and balance sheet data for Boston Scientific Corporation, our focus company for this module. We use these data to compute the ROE for 2018 of 21.24%.

Exhibit 4.1 ■ Financial Statement Data for Boston Scientific Corporation

$ millions	Dec. 29, 2018	Dec. 30, 2017
Sales..................................	$ 9,823	
Net income............................	1,671	
Total assets	20,999	19,042
Total stockholders' equity.................	8,726	7,012

$$\text{ROE} = \frac{\$1,671}{(\$8,726 + \$7,012)/2} = 21.24\%$$

ROE is a summary return metric that measures the return the company has earned on the book (reported) value of the shareholders' investment. It is one measure of how effective management has been in its role as stewards of the capital invested by shareholders. In our analysis of company performance, we seek to uncover the *drivers* of ROE and how those drivers have trended over time so that we are better able to predict future performance.

Review 4-1 LO1

Following are selected income statement and balance sheet data for Stryker Corporation.

$ millions	2018	2017
Sales.........................	$13,601	
Net income.....................	3,553	
Total assets	27,229	22,197
Stockholders' equity..............	11,730	9,980

Required

Solution on p. 4-59. Compute return on equity (ROE) for Stryker Corp. for 2018.

ROE Disaggregation: DuPont Analysis

There are two methods for disaggregating ROE into its components; each provides a different perspective that can inform our analysis.

■ The first method is the traditional **DuPont analysis** that disaggregates return on equity into components of profitability, productivity, and leverage.

■ The second method extends the traditional DuPont analysis by taking an **ROE analysis with an operating focus** that separates operating and nonoperating activities. Operating activities are the drivers of shareholder value. This method, which focuses on operating or core activities, provides insight into the factors that drive value creation.

Disaggregation of return on equity (ROE) was initially introduced by the **E.I. DuPont de Nemours and Company** to aid its managers in performance evaluation. DuPont realized that management's focus on profit alone was insufficient because profit can be increased simply by the purchase of additional investment in low-yielding, but safe, assets. DuPont wanted managers to think like investors and to manage their portfolio of activities using investment principles that allocate scarce investment capital to competing projects in descending order of return on investment (the capital budgeting approach). The DuPont model incorporates this investment perspective into performance measurement by disaggregating ROE into two components.

eLectures   **LO2**

MBC   Apply DuPont disaggregation of ROE into return on assets (ROA) and financial leverage.

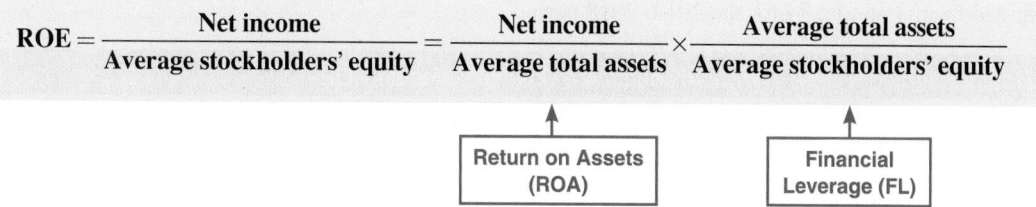

$$\text{ROE} = \frac{\text{Net income}}{\text{Average stockholders' equity}} = \underbrace{\frac{\text{Net income}}{\text{Average total assets}}}_{\substack{\text{Return on Assets} \\ \text{(ROA)}}} \times \underbrace{\frac{\text{Average total assets}}{\text{Average stockholders' equity}}}_{\substack{\text{Financial} \\ \text{Leverage (FL)}}}$$

Return on equity takes the perspective of a company's shareholders and measures rate of return on shareholders' investment—how much net income is earned relative to the equity invested by shareholders. It reflects *both* company performance (as measured by return on assets) *and* how assets are financed (relative use of liabilities and equity). ROE is higher when there is more debt and less equity for a given level of assets (this is because the denominator in ROE, equity, is smaller). There is, however, a trade-off: while using more debt and less equity results in higher ROE, the greater debt means higher risk for the company.

Return on Assets

Return on assets (ROA) measures return from the perspective of the entire company. This return includes both profitability (numerator) and total company assets (denominator). To earn a high return on assets, the company must be profitable *and* manage assets to minimize the assets invested to the level necessary to achieve its profit.

Most operating managers understand the income statement and the focus on profit. However, many of the same managers fail to manage the balance sheet (the denominator in ROA). ROA analysis encourages managers to focus on the profit achieved from the invested capital under their control. This means that managers seek to increase profits with the same level of assets *and* to decrease assets without decreasing the level of profit. It is this dual focus that makes return on assets a powerful performance measure—focusing managers' attention on *both* the income statement and balance sheet.

Boston Scientific's net income is $1,671 million, and its total assets are $20,999 million in 2018 and $19,042 million in 2017 (data from Exhibit 4.1). The company's 2018 return on assets is 8.35%, computed as follows ($ millions).

$$\text{ROA} = \frac{\$1,671}{(\$20,999 + \$19,042)/2} = 8.35\%$$

By comparison, the median return on assets of the S&P 500 companies for 2018 was 6.1% and ranged from 5.2% to 6.1% for the 2014–2018 period.

Financial Leverage

Financial leverage, the second component of ROE, measures the degree to which the company finances its assets with debt versus equity. There are many ways to measure financial leverage. In the DuPont analysis, we measure financial leverage (labeled FL) as the ratio of average total assets to average stockholders' equity. (In a later section of this module we show a different definition of financial leverage that excludes operating liabilities; we label that ratio FLEV.) An increase in this ratio implies an increase in the relative level of debt. This is evident from the accounting equation: assets = liabilities + equity. For example, if assets are financed equally with debt and equity, the accounting equation, expressed in percentage terms is: 100% = 50% + 50%, and financial leverage is 2.0 (100%/50%). If debt increases to 75%, the accounting equation is: 100% = 75% + 25%, and financial leverage is 4.0 (100%/25%).

Measuring financial leverage is important because debt is a contractual obligation and a company's failure to repay principal or interest can result in legal repercussions or even bankruptcy. As financial leverage increases so does the level of debt payments, which all else equal, increases the probability of default and possible bankruptcy. For 2018, Boston Scientific's financial leverage is 2.54, computed as ($ millions):

$$\text{Financial leverage (FL)} = \frac{(\$20{,}999 + \$19{,}042)/2}{(\$8{,}726 + \$7{,}012)/2} = 2.54$$

By comparison, the median financial leverage (FL) of the S&P 500 companies for 2018 was 2.66 and ranged from 2.46 to 2.74 for the 2014–2018 period.

Business Insight ■ Which Accounts Are Used to Compute ROE?

Return on equity has net income in the numerator and stockholders' equity in the denominator. The complexity of company financial statements, however, presents some complications: which net income and stockholders' equity accounts should we use?

- **Preferred Stock.** The ROE formula takes the perspective of the *common* stockholder in that it relates the income available to pay common dividends to the average common stockholder. The presence of preferred stock on the balance sheet requires two adjustments to ROE.

  1. Preferred dividends are subtracted from net income in the numerator.
  2. Preferred stock is subtracted from stockholders' equity in the denominator.

  This modified return on equity is labeled *return on common equity* (ROCE).

$$\text{ROCE} = \frac{\textbf{Net income} - \textbf{Preferred dividends}}{\textbf{Average stockholders' equity} - \textbf{Average preferred equity}}$$

- **Noncontrolling interests.** Many companies have two sets of stockholders: those that own the common stock of the parent company whose financial statements are under analysis (called *controlling interest*) and those that own shares in one or more of the parent company's subsidiaries (called *noncontrolling interest*). Balance sheets separately identify the stockholders' equity relating to each group and, likewise, income statements separately identify net income attributable to each. ROE is computed from the perspective of the controlling (parent company) stockholders and, thus, the ratio is defined as:

$$\text{ROE} = \frac{\textbf{Net income attributable to company shareholders}}{\textbf{Average equity attributable to company shareholders}}$$

  We explain controlling and noncontrolling interest in a later module and ROE computations with noncontrolling interests in Appendix 4B.

Review 4-2 LO2

Refer to the financial information for **Stryker Corp.** reported in Review 4-1.

continued

continued from previous page

Required

Compute return on assets (ROA) and financial leverage following the DuPont disaggregation of ROE for 2018. Confirm that ROA × Financial leverage (FL) = ROE.

Solution on p. 4-59.

Return on Assets and Its Disaggregation

Return on assets (ROA) includes both profitability (in the numerator) and total assets (in the denominator). Managers can increase ROA by increasing profitability for a given level of asset investment or by reducing assets invested to generate a given level of profitability, or both. We gain insight into these two drivers by disaggregating return on assets into two components to isolate its profitability and asset investment levels as:

LO3 Disaggregate ROA into profitability and productivity and analyze both.

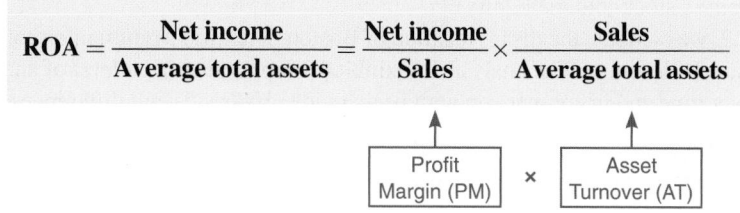

$$\text{ROA} = \frac{\text{Net income}}{\text{Average total assets}} = \frac{\text{Net income}}{\text{Sales}} \times \frac{\text{Sales}}{\text{Average total assets}}$$

Profit Margin (PM) × Asset Turnover (AT)

Return on assets is the product of profit margin and utilization of assets in generating sales (asset turnover). This is the insight that DuPont analysis offers as it focuses managers' attention on both profitability *and* management of the balance sheet. The two drivers of return on assets are:

- **Profit margin (PM).**   PM is what the company earns on each sales dollar; a company increases profit margin by increasing its gross profit margin (Gross profit/Sales) and/or reducing its operating expenses as a percent of sales.

- **Asset turnover (AT).**   AT is the sales level generated from each dollar invested in assets; a company increases asset turnover (*productivity*) by increasing sales volume with no increase in assets and/or by reducing assets invested without reducing sales.

Business Insight   Adjusted ROA

Return on assets is typically under the control of operating managers while the capital structure decision (the relative proportion of debt and equity) is not. Accordingly, a common adjustment is made to the numerator of ROA by adding back the after-tax net interest expense (net of any interest revenue or other nonoperating expense or revenue reported after operating income). The adjusted ROA for Boston Scientific is as follows ($ in millions).

$$\text{Adjusted ROA} = \frac{\text{Net income} + [\text{Net interest expense} \times (1 - \text{Statutory tax rate})]}{\text{Average total assets}}$$

$$\frac{\$1,671 + [(\$241 - \$156) \times (1 - 0.22)]}{(\$20,999 + \$19,042)/2} = 8.68\%$$

Net interest expense for Boston Scientific is interest expense less "other" nonoperating income (see Exhibit 4.6) "Statutory tax rate" in the adjusted ROA formula is the federal statutory tax rate *plus* the state tax rate net of any federal tax benefits; we use the assumed 22% federal and state tax rates as explained in the NOPAT computation later in this module. This adjusted numerator better reflects the company's operating profit as it measures return on assets exclusive of net nonoperating expense (or income) as we describe later in this module.

The goal is to increase the productivity of the company's assets in generating sales and then to bring as much of each sales dollar to the bottom line (net income). Managers usually understand product pricing, management of production costs, and control of overhead costs. Fewer managers understand the role of the balance sheet. The ROA approach to performance measurement encourages managers to focus on returns achieved from assets under their control, and ROA is maximized with a joint focus on both profitability and productivity.

Analysis of Profitability and Productivity

The complete DuPont return on equity disaggregation follows.

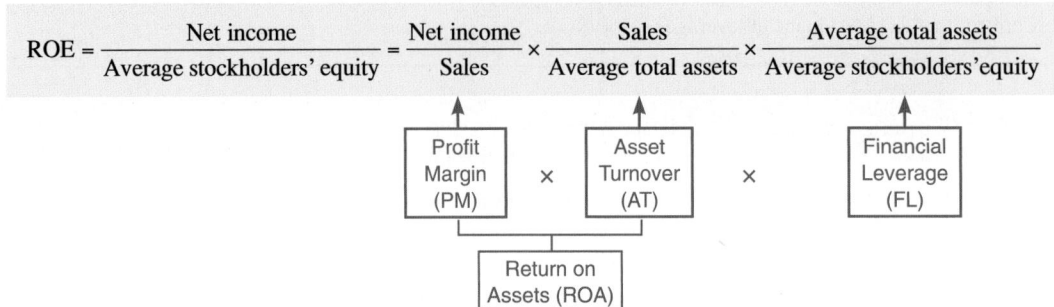

Return on equity increases with each of the three components (provided the company is profitable and reports a positive stockholders' equity).

In Exhibit 4.2, we compute the disaggregation of Boston Scientific's return into profit margin, asset turnover, and financial leverage. The analysis in Exhibit 4.2 represents a *first level* of analysis where we examine ROE over time and in comparison with peers to identify trends and differences from the norm.

Exhibit 4.2 ■ Disaggregation of Boston Scientific's ROE ($ millions)

Profit margin (PM)	Net income / Sales	$1,671 / $9,823	= 17.01%
×			×
Asset turnover (AT)	Sales / Average total assets	$9,823 / ($20,999 + $19,042)/2	= 0.49
=			=
Return on assets (ROA)	Net income / Average total assets	$1,671 / ($20,999 + $19,042)/2	= 8.35%
×			×
Financial leverage (FL)	Average total assets / Average stockholders' equity	($20,999 + $19,042)/2 / ($8,726 + $7,012)/2	= 2.54
=			=
Return on equity (ROE)	Net income / Average stockholders' equity	$1,671 / ($8,726 + $7,012)/2	= 21.24%

The *second level* analysis of the components of return on equity seeks to identify factors driving profitability (profit margin) and productivity (asset turnover) and to assess whether financial leverage increases the risk of default and bankruptcy beyond acceptable levels. The framework for second-level analysis is in Exhibit 4.3 and we explain each component in this module.

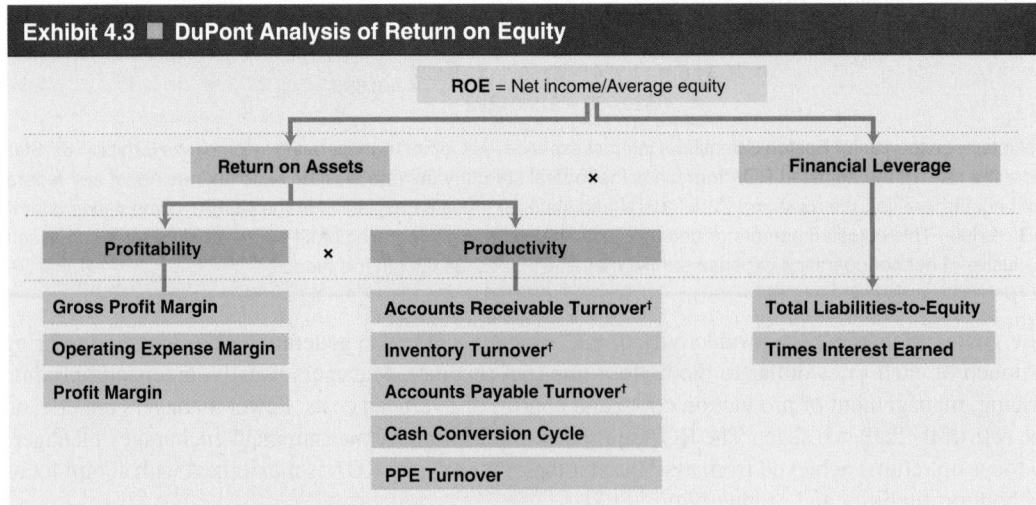

Exhibit 4.3 ■ DuPont Analysis of Return on Equity

† This metric is also commonly measured "in days"—see discussion below.

Analysis of Profitability

Profit margin (Net income/Sales) reflects the profit in each dollar of sales. For 2018, the median profit margin for the S&P 500 companies was 11.2%. During 2009–2018, profit margin ranged from 7.1% in 2009 to 11.2% in 2018.

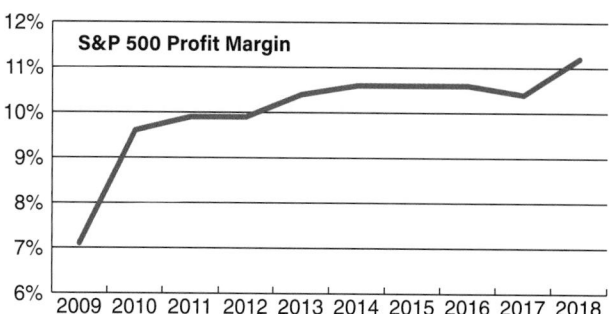

Profit margin, while an important measure of profitability, is influenced by *both* gross profit on sales and SG&A expenses. Consequently, we gain insight into profitability by separately examining gross profit margin and the SG&A expense margin.

Gross Profit Margin

Gross profit margin (Gross profit/Sales) is influenced by *both* the selling price of a company's products and the cost to make or buy those products. For 2018, the median gross profit margin for S&P 500 companies was 43.4% and it has trended upward over the past 10 years from a low of 40.4% in 2009. Gross profit margins differ greatly by industry and depend on a company's specific business model. Consequently, we must be careful in identifying peers for benchmarking to make sure their business models are similar.

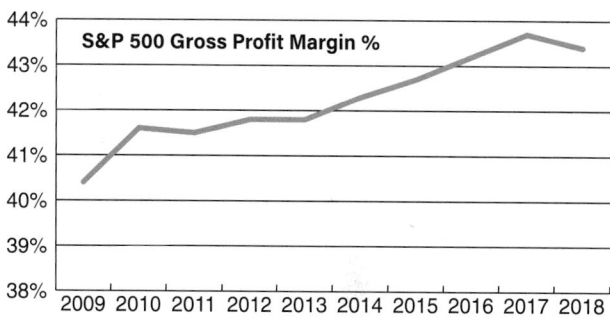

We generally prefer gross profit margin to be high and increasing as the opposite usually signals more competition or less appeal for the company's product line. When analyzing gross profit margin, it is often helpful to view it on a unit basis, that is, as gross profit for one product unit. If, for example, we purchase a product for $6 and sell it for $10, the gross profit margin is 40% ([$10 − $6]/$10). A decline in gross profit margin, then, signals that the spread between the cost to make or buy the product and its selling price has narrowed. This narrowing could be due to several factors, all of which warrant investigation.

■ Perhaps competitive intensity increased and selling prices have dropped to remain competitive.

■ Perhaps the company's product line has lost appeal or its technology is not cutting edge.

■ Perhaps the cost to make or buy products has increased due to increases in material or labor costs and the company cannot pass on that cost increase to customers.

■ Perhaps there is a change in product mix away from high margin products to lower margin products (remember that sales and gross profit include *all* of the company's products, including both high margin and low margin products).

■ Perhaps the volume of products sold has declined, resulting in an increase in manufacturing cost as factory overhead is spread out over a smaller number of units produced.

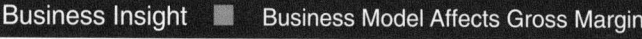

Business Insight　　■　　Business Model Affects Gross Margin

The past few years have seen a sharp increase in the number of firms that use a subscription model—customers sign up for a monthly or annual payment plan. A wide variety of goods and services are now available by subscription, including apparel (such as Stitch Fix and Le Tote), healthcare and grooming (such as Bulu Box and Dollar Shave Club), entertainment (such as Netflix and PlayStation Vue), food and beverages (such as Blue Apron and WSJWine), and fitness (ClassPass and Fitocracy). More reliable revenue streams from subscribed customers and attractive margins drive this evolution. The largest shift, however, has been in the software sector with many vendors migrating to the "SaaS" (Software as a Service) business model, abandoning the traditional licensing model. The effects of this shift impact both revenues and cost of goods or services. In comparing margins over time, we need to keep in mind this dynamic business environment.

It is not enough for our analysis to reveal that a company's gross profit margin has increased or decreased. Instead, we must uncover the *reasons* for the change. It is only with analysis of the underlying cost and pricing structure of a company's products that we are able to predict future levels of gross profit. Many believe that a serious analysis should focus on the *individual product* level and the costs to make or buy those products along with the pricing strategy for the different markets served. That level of granularity is important for effective analysis of gross profit margin.

Operating Expense Margin

The operating expense margin, also referred to as SG&A expense margin (SG&A expense/Sales), measures general operating costs for each sales dollar. These costs include all costs other than those to make or buy the company's products. For 2018, the median SG&A expense margin for S&P 500 companies was 16.3% and that margin has declined steadily from a high of 19% since the economy emerged from recession in 2009.

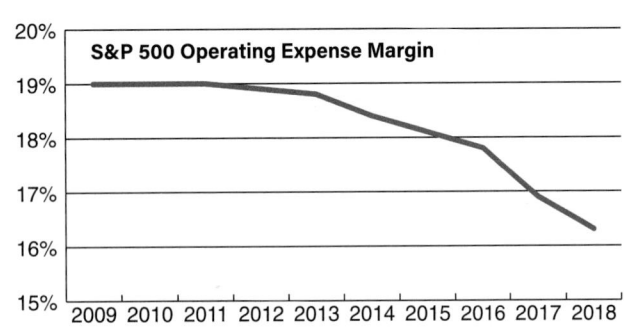

Analysis of operating expense margin focuses on each expense in whatever detail the company provides in its income statement. We compare the operating expense margin, and the margins for each of its components, over time and against peers (making sure that peers have similar business models). We investigate deviations from historical trends or benchmarks to uncover the cause. We are inclined to judge lower expense levels as favorable, but caution is advised. Perhaps a lower expense level happens because the company has tried to mitigate declining profits by reducing R&D, marketing, or compensation costs. Such activities tend to result in short-term improvements at long-term costs such as reduced market share and damaged employee morale.

Analysis of Productivity

Productivity is reflected in return on assets via turnover of total assets (Sales/Total assets). While a useful measure to gauge overall trend, a more rigorous analysis examines the productivity of each major asset category.

Analysis of Working Capital Components

All turnover ratios compare the activity on the income statement to the related balance sheet amount. The three most widely used turnover ratios follow.

Ratio	Computation
Accounts receivable turnover............	Sales/Average accounts receivable
Inventory turnover.....................	Cost of goods sold/Average inventories
Accounts payable turnover..............	Cost of goods sold/Average accounts payable

We discuss these turnover ratios in more detail in later modules; for now, know that they measure productivity, or efficiency, or throughput.

Turnover, while widely reported, has limited usefulness. For example, it is not easy to see how much cash is generated if accounts receivable turnover improves. It is more intuitive to think of the average number of days to collect accounts receivable, the average number of days to sell inventory, or the average number of days to pay accounts payable. Accordingly, a good analysis computes the "days" measures for working capital accounts. We compute annual measures as follows. When using quarterly financial statement data, use 90 or 91 days instead of 365.

Ratio	Computation
Days sales outstanding (DSO)..........	365/Accounts receivable turnover
+ Days inventory outstanding (DIO)........	365/Inventory turnover
− Days payables outstanding (DPO).......	365/Accounts payable turnover
= Cash conversion cycle	DSO + DIO − DPO

Cash Conversion Cycle

The three measures from the table above can be combined to yield the **cash conversion cycle** (Days sales outstanding + Days inventory outstanding – Days payables outstanding). The cash conversion cycle measures the average time (in days) to sell inventories, collect the receivables from the sale, pay the payables incurred for the inventory purchase, and return to cash. This is the same cash conversion cycle we describe in Module 2 (we use the term "operating cycle" in Exhibit 2.4 to describe the same concept). Each time a company completes one cash conversion cycle, it generates profit and cash flow. Managers aim to shorten the cash con-

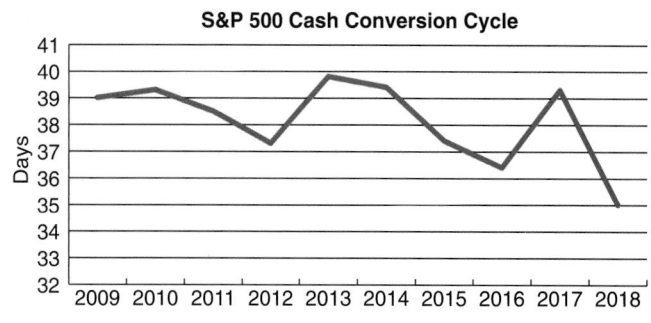

version cycle. The median cash conversion cycle for S&P 500 companies was 35 days in 2018 and has declined from a high of 39 days since the economy emerged from recession in 2009.

Cash conversion cycle depends on the business model of the company, which dictates:

- Credit terms offered to customers.

- Types of inventory carried and depth and breadth of product lines (which influence the time inventories remain unsold).

- Time period in which suppliers are paid for goods and services.

Diversity across business models is evident in the following graphic for medians of the cash conversion cycle for selected industries in 2018.

The variability in the cash conversion cycle across industries reflects fundamental differences in business models. Cash conversion cycle for the healthcare industry, for example, is much longer as a result of the extended period of time to collect receivables from third-party payers such as insurance companies and the government. In contrast, the utilities industry's quick cash conversion results from lower levels of inventory, and rapid collection of receivables from customers who typically pay their utility bill within a month.

Generally companies prefer a lower cash conversion cycle. This means that the operating cycle is generating profit and cash flow quickly. Our analysis of this measure focuses on trends over time and comparisons to peers (with similar business models).

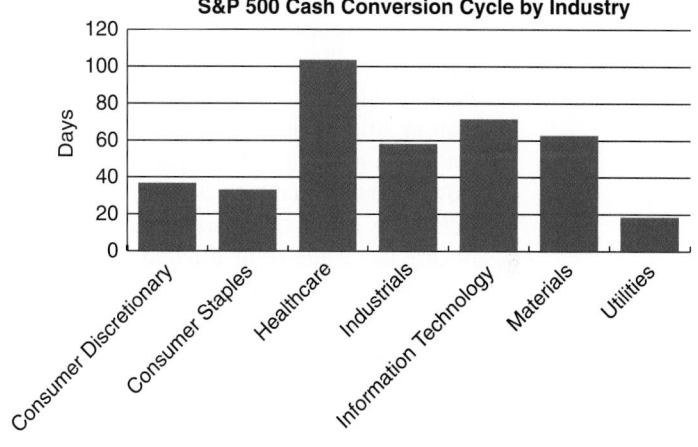

Sometimes, companies have a *negative* cash conversion cycle. Apple's 2018 cash conversion cycle is one example.

Days sales outstanding (DSO).	28.2
+ Days inventory outstanding (DIO)	9.8
− Days payables outstanding (DPO). . . .	(111.6)
= Cash conversion cycle (CCC)	(73.6)

Apple carries little inventory as its products are pre-sold and shipped when manufactured. Consequently, its quick sale of inventory and relatively longer time to pay suppliers result in a negative cash conversion cycle of (73.6) days. The negative number means that Apple is able to invest the cash it receives from the sale of its products for 73.6 days on average before that cash is needed to pay suppliers. This allows Apple to generate both profit from the sale *and* profit from investing cash. A negative cash conversion cycle is generally viewed positively.

A good analysis includes a review of cash conversion cycle over time. Merck & Co., for example, reports improvement in its cash conversion cycle over the 2016–2018 period.

Amounts in Days	2018	2017	2016
Days sales outstanding (DSO).......	61.0	63.4	62.1
+ Days inventory outstanding (DIO)	142.6	143.8	129.3
− Days payables outstanding (DPO)....	(86.9)	(85.3)	(72.2)
= Cash conversion cycle (CCC)	116.7	121.9	119.2

The improvement in Merck's cash conversion cycle from 2017 to 2018 reflects improvement in all three working capital accounts.

- It is collecting receivables more quickly (an improvement).
- It is selling inventories faster (an improvement).
- It is delaying payment on payables (an improvement).

Each improvement generated additional cash during the period. To compute the amount of cash generated (or used) by changes in each of the measures, multiply the change in the the number of days by the related income statement account measured per day: Sales/365 for DSO, and COGS/365 for DIO and DPO. The table here illustrates these measures.

$ millions	Amounts in Days			Sales (or COGS) per day		Cash savings
	2018	2017	Change			
Days sales outstanding (DSO).......	61.0	63.4	2.4	×	$115.9	= $278.2
+ Days inventory outstanding (DIO)	142.6	143.8	1.2	×	37.0	= 44.4
− Days payables outstanding (DPO)....	(86.9)	(85.3)	1.6	×	37.0	= 59.2
= Cash conversion cycle (CCC)	116.7	121.9				$381.8

In 2018, Merck's sales per day were $115.9 million such that collecting receivables 2.4 days sooner than in 2017 increased Merck's cash balance by $278.2 million ($115.9 × 2.4). In 2018, Merck recorded an average COGS of $37 million and sold inventory more quickly and paid suppliers more slowly as compared with 2017. These actions generated $44.4 million and $59.2 million, respectively. In total, by employing working capital more efficiently, Merck generated an additional $381.8 million of cash that could be invested in operating activities or in marketable securities or used to reduce interest-bearing debt, all of which increased profitability.

Although these trends for Merck are favorable, we must investigate whether they are *too* favorable. Companies can generate cash by restricting credit policies, by reducing the depth and breadth of their product offerings, and by delaying payment to suppliers ("leaning on the trade"). All of these actions can generate a short-term inflow of cash at a longer-term cost of market position and supplier relations if not managed properly. These questions must be answered by a review of nonfinancial information in the MD&A section of the 10-K, listening to conference calls with manaagement (on the Investor Relations portion of a company's website), reading the financial press, and reviewing analysts' reports.

Analysis of Plant, Property and Equipment (PPE)

The asset class for which analysis of turnover is most useful is PPE assets (Sales/Average PPE, gross). Lower levels of PPE turnover indicate a higher level of capital intensity. PPE asset turnover differs by industry as revealed in the graph for 2018 shown below for S&P 500 companies. The utilities industry requires high levels of capital investment and, consequently, reports low PPE turnover.

Because investment in PPE assets is often a large part of the balance sheet, improvement in plant asset turnover can greatly impact the company's return on assets and cash flow. Improvements in PPE turnover are not easy to achieve, however, often requiring:

- Divestiture of unproductive assets or entire business segments.
- Joint ventures with other companies to jointly use PPE assets such as distribution networks, information technology, production facilities, and warehouses.

■   Divestiture of production facilities with agreements to purchase finished goods from the facilities' new owners.

■   Sale and leaseback of administrative buildings.

Each of these activities is a strategic and financial event, often requiring integration within the supply chain, new financing, and relationship building. As such, improvements in PPE turnover can be difficult to achieve. If properly structured, however, they can markedly increase asset returns and cash flow.

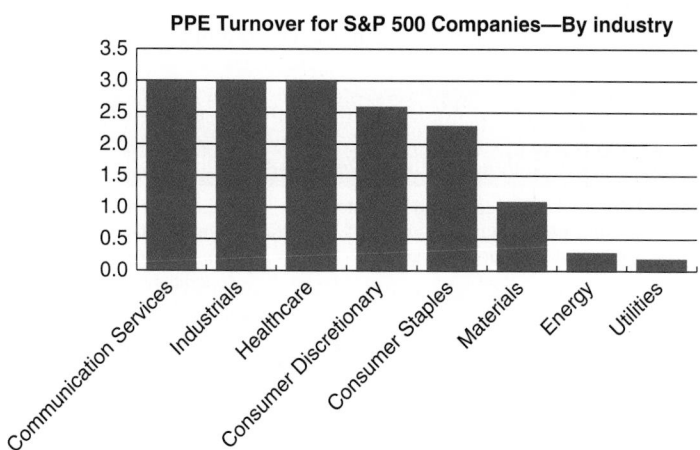

Analysis of Financial Leverage

As companies utilize a larger proportion of borrowed money in their capital structures, they incur obligations for interest payments and the repayment of the amount borrowed (the principal). Those obligations are typically evidenced by a loan agreement (or bond indenture) that contains some or all of the following.

■   Restrictions on certain activities, such as mergers or acquisitions of other companies without approval of lenders.

■   Prohibitions against dividend payments or the repurchase of common stock without approval of lenders.

■   Covenants to maintain required levels of financial ratios, such as a maximum level of financial leverage, minimum levels of the current and quick ratios, minimum level of equity, and minimum level of working capital.

■   Prohibitions against the pledging of assets to secure new borrowings.

■   Remedies to lenders in event of default (failure to make required interest and principal payments when due). These remedies can include seizing company assets or, possibly, forcing the company into bankruptcy and requiring liquidation.

Judicial use of financial leverage is beneficial to stockholders (it is a relatively inexpensive source of capital), but the use of borrowed money adds risk as debt payments are contractual obligations. Analysis typically involves ratios that investigate the *level* of borrowed money relative to equity capital and the level of profitability and *cash flow* relative to required debt payments. Although there are dozens of financial leverage-related ratios in commercial databases, the following two ratios capture the spirit of such analysis.

■   Total liabilities-to-equity ratio (Total liabilities/Stockholders' equity).

■   Times interest earned ratio (Earnings before interest and taxes/Interest expense, gross).

As for all ratios, analysis of financial leverage ratios must consider ratios over time and comparisons with peers. Appropriate financial leverage varies across industries because different business models generate cash flow streams that differ in amount and variability over time. Generally, business models that generate high and stable levels of cash flow can support a higher level of debt.

The median liabilities-to-equity ratio for S&P 500 companies in 2018 was 1.69, indicating that companies typically report about 1.69 times more borrowed money than equity in their capital structures. The median financial leverage ratio for these companies has ranged from 1.56 to 1.76 from 2014 to 2018. Times interest earned ratios for S&P 500 companies was 7.7 in 2018, down markedly from a high of 9.3 in 2014. Again, we stress the importance of remembering that these (and all) ratios differ across industry and company size.

Exhibit 4.4 shows a summary of ratios used in the DuPont disaggregation of return on equity.

Exhibit 4.4 ■ Summary of Ratios in DuPont Disaggregation of Return on Equity

Ratio	Computation	What the Ratio Measures	Positive Indicators Include
Return on equity	Net income ÷ Avg. stockholders' equity, or Return on assets × Financial leverage	ROE measures accounting return to shareholders using net income and the book value of stockholders' equity.	• Improvement over time and favorable comparison to peers. • Greater proportion of ROE from ROA (operations) than financial leverage (risk).
Return on assets	Net income/Avg. total assets or Profit margin × Asset turnover	ROA measures the accounting return on total assets using net income and total assets.	• Improvement over time in both profit margin and asset turnover. • Improvement in gross margins and not solely from expense reduction.
PROFITABILITY			
Gross profit margin	Gross profit / Sales	Gross profit measures the difference between selling price and the cost to make or buy the products sold for the year.	• Improvement over time due to increases in selling prices and/or reductions in cost to make or buy without compromising product quality. • Favorable comparison to peers.
Operating expense margin (or SG&A expense margin)	SG&A expense / Sales	Operating expense margin measures total overhead expense (SG&A) as a percent of sales.	• Improvement over time. • Favorable comparison to peers. • No short-term gains at long-term cost (such as unusual reductions in marketing and R&D expenses).
Profit margin (or net profit margin)	Net income / Sales	Profit margin includes effects of both gross profit margin, the operating expense margin, and net nonoperating expenses.	• Improvement over time. • Favorable comparison to peers.
PRODUCTIVITY			
Accounts receivable turnover	Sales / Avg. accounts receivable	AR turnover reflects how effective a company manages the credit issued to customers.	• Improvement over time. • Favorable comparison to peers.
Days sales outstanding (DSO)	365/Accounts receivable turnover	DSO reflects how well a company's accounts receivables are managed.	• Maintain sales while reducing days to collect receivables.
Inventory turnover	COGS/Avg. inventory	Inventory turnover reflects the number of times inventory is sold or used during the period.	• Improvement over time. • Favorable comparison to peers.
Days inventory outstanding (DIO)	365/Inventory turnover	DIO reflects how many days it takes for a company to sell its inventory.	• Maintain sales while reducing days to sell inventory.
Accounts payable turnover	COGS/Avg. accounts payable	AP turnover reflects how many times a company pays off its suppliers during the period.	• Improvement over time. • Favorable comparison to peers.
Days payables outstanding (DPO)	365/Accounts payable turnover	DPO reflects how long it takes a company to pay its invoices from suppliers.	• Maintain supplier relations while delaying payment to suppliers.
Cash conversion cycle	DSO + DIO – DPO	Cash conversion (operating) cycle measures the days to convert cash to inventories, receivables to cash, cash to payables.	• Improvement over time. • Favorable comparison to peers.
PPE turnover	Sales/Avg. PPE assets	Plant asset turnover is a productivity measure, comparing the volume of sales generated by plant assets.	• Improvement over time. • Favorable comparison to peers.

continued

Exhibit 4.4 ■ Summary of Ratios in DuPont Disaggregation of Return on Equity (cont.)			
Ratio	**Computation**	**What the Ratio Measures**	**Positive Indicators Include**
FINANCIAL LEVERAGE			
Total liabilities-to-equity	Total liabilities/Stockholders' equity	Proportion of liabilities vs. equity in the capital structure.	• Improvement over time. • Favorable comparison to peers. • Relatively lower levels are preferable.
Times interest earned	Earnings before interest and taxes/Interest expense, gross	Pool of operating profit before tax that a company earns relative to its interest expense, gross.	• Improvement over time. • Favorable comparison to peers. • Higher levels are preferable to lower levels.

LO3 Review 4-3

Refer to the income statement and balance sheet data for Stryker Corp. from Review 4-1 along with the following additional information.

$ millions	2018	2017
Cost of sales.	$ 4,663	$ 4,264
Accounts receivable	2,332	2,198
Inventories	2,955	2,465
Accounts payable	646	487
Liabilities.	15,499	12,217

Required

a. Disaggregate 2018 ROA into components of profitability margin (PM) and asset turnover (AT). Then, prove that their product (multiplication) results in ROA.
b. Compute the gross profit margin.
c. Compute the cash conversion cycle.
d. Compute the total liabilities-to-equity ratio for 2018.

Solution on p. 4-59.

Balance Sheet Analysis with an Operating Focus

ROE analysis with an operating focus recognizes that companies create value mainly through core operations of the business. Operating activities involve the manufacturing and selling of company products and services to customers. Nonoperating activities involve nonstrategic investments of cash into marketable securities and debt financing activities. The balance sheet and income statement include both operating and nonoperating items. Because operating activities affect company value much more than do nonoperating activities, our analysis of a company can, arguably, be improved if we separately identify these two components of the business and analyze them separately.

eLectures **LO4**
MBC Identify balance sheet operating items and compute net operating assets.

Operating and Nonoperating Returns Return on equity, computed using net income and total equity, reflects a blend of the return on the company's operating activities and the return that arises from the nonoperating activities. Specifically:

$$\text{ROE} = \text{Operating return} + \text{Nonoperating return}$$

This shows that ROE consists of two returns: (1) return from the company's operating activities, linked to revenues and expenses from the company's sale of products or services, and (2) return from financing and investing (nonoperating) activities. Companies can use debt to increase their return on equity, but this increases risk because the failure to make required debt payments can yield many legal consequences, including bankruptcy. This is one reason why many top investors such as Warren Buffett focus on acquiring companies whose return on equity is derived primarily from operating activities.

Operating and Nonoperating Liabilities A second, more subtle, issue arises in computing return on equity. In the traditional DuPont analysis, ROE is the product of the return on assets and financial leverage. Financial leverage is the ratio of total assets to stockholders' equity, which increases as the proportion of liabilities increases relative to equity. The problem is that the "liabilities" used in this computation includes *all* of the company's liabilities. However, there is a difference between borrowed money and operating liabilities such as accounts payable and accrued liabilities. Accounts payable and accruals are interest free and are *self-liquidating*, meaning that they are paid when receivables are collected as part of the cash conversion cycle. On the other hand, borrowed money is interest-bearing and often contains severe legal repercussions in the event of nonpayment, possibly risking bankruptcy. The operating focus treats these two types of liabilities differently for ROE analysis, treating borrowed money (debt) as a nonoperating item.

> The FASB released a draft of a proposed new format for financial statements to, among other things, distinguish operating and nonoperating activities.

Return on Net Operating Assets (RNOA)

Operating returns can be measured by the **return on net operating assets (RNOA)**.

$$\text{RNOA} = \frac{\text{Net operating profit after tax (NOPAT)}}{\text{Average net operating assets (NOA)}}$$

To implement this formula, we must first classify the balance sheet and income statement into operating and nonoperating components so that we can assess each separately. We first consider operating activities on the balance sheet and explain how to compute NOA. Second, we consider operating activities on the income statement and explain how to compute NOPAT. We summarize the classification method in Appendix 4A.

Net Operating Assets (NOA)

The balance sheet includes both operating and nonoperating assets and liabilites. NOA includes only operating items and we define NOA as follows.

> **Net operating assets = Operating assets – Operating liabilities**

To compute NOA, we must partition the balance sheet into operating and nonoperating items.

Operating Assets

Operating assets are those assets directly linked to the company's ongoing (continuing) business operations of bringing its products or services to the market. The company needs these assets to operate normally and they typically include the following:

- Accounts receivable
- Inventories
- Prepaid expenses and supplies
- Property, plant, and equipment (PPE) including both assets that are owned outright and those that are leased[1]
- Intangible assets and Goodwill
- Deferred income tax assets
- "Equity method" investments, which are strategic investments with partners, associated companies, and joint ventures

Operating Liabilities

Operating liabilities are liabilities that arise from operating revenues and expenses, that is, relating to the core business activities of the company. Examples include:

---

[1] Leasing is a way to acquire an asset for use without the upfront cash outlay. If the leased asset is used for operations, then it is an operating asset and we categorize it as such regardless of how it is financed.

- Accounts payable
- Accrued expenses (for unpaid wages and other operating expenses)
- Unearned or deferred revenue (because it relates to operating revenue)
- Income taxes payable (both short-term and long-term)
- Deferred income tax liabilities
- Pension and other post-employment obligations (that relate to employee retirement and health-care, which are operating activities)

"Other" Assets and Liabilities

Companies typically report "Other" assets and liabilities, both as current and long-term items. We *assume* that these are operating items *unless* information suggests otherwise. For example, details in footnotes might reveal that "other" consists of nonoperating items. In that case, we would classify the "other" as nonoperating. Or if the footnote revealed that "other" includes both operating and nonoperating items, we could consider partitioning the "other" line item into separate operating and nonoperating items.

Exhibit 4.5 shows Boston Scientific's balance sheet with operating assets and operating liabilities highlighted.

Exhibit 4.5 ■ Operating and Nonoperating Items in Boston Scientific's Balance Sheet

December 31, $ millions	2018	2017
Current assets		
Cash and cash equivalents	$ 146	$ 188
Trade accounts receivable, net	1,608	1,548
Inventories	1,166	1,078
Prepaid income taxes	161	66
Other current assets	921	942
Total current assets	4,002	3,822
Property, plant and equipment, net	1,782	1,697
Goodwill	7,911	6,998
Other intangible assets, net	6,372	5,837
Other long-term assets	932	688
Total assets	$20,999	$19,042
Current liabilities		
Current debt obligations	$ 2,253	$ 1,801
Accounts payable	349	530
Accrued expenses	2,246	2,456
Other current liabilities	412	867
Total current liabilities	5,260	5,654
Long-term debt	4,803	3,815
Deferred income taxes	328	191
Other long-term liabilities	1,882	2,370
Stockholders' equity		
Preferred stock	—	—
Common stock	16	16
Treasury stock, at cost	(1,717)	(1,717)
Additional paid-in capital	17,346	17,161
Accumulated deficit	(6,953)	(8,390)
Accumulated other comprehensive income (loss), net of tax:		
Foreign currency translation adjustment	(53)	(32)
Unrealized gain (loss) on derivative financial instruments	111	1
Unrealized gain (loss) on available-for-sale securities	0	(1)
Unrealized costs associated with defined benefit pensions and other items	(25)	(27)
Total stockholders' equity	8,726	7,012
Total liabilities and stockholders' equity	$20,999	$19,042

Operating assets
2018 = $20,853
2017 = $18,854

Operating liabilities
2018 = $5,217
2017 = $6,414

Net Operating Assets (NOA)

Using the classifications in Exhibit 4.5, Boston Scientific's net operating assets follow.

$ millions	2018	2017
Operating assets	$20,853	$18,854
Less operating liabilities	5,217	6,414
Net operating assets (NOA)	$15,636	$12,440

Net Nonoperating Obligations (NNO)

All balance sheets include nonoperating liabilities and/or nonoperating assets, although they are typically less numerous than the operating items. Generally, nonoperating refers to assets and liabilities that are not used as part of the core business activities of the company. As a rule of thumb, if the liability requires the payment of interest expense or if the asset earns interest or dividend income, it is classified as nonoperating. We compute net nonoperating obligations (NNO) as follows.

> **Net nonoperating obligations (NNO) = Nonoperating liabilities – Nonoperating assets**

See that NNO is net "obligations" whereas NOA is net "assets." We subtract any nonoperating assets from nonoperating liabilities to arrive at NNO. For most companies, NNO is a positive amount, meaning that nonoperating obligations are greater than nonoperating assets. We discuss situations where this is not the case in Appendix 4B.

Nonoperating Liabilities

Common nonoperating liabilities include:

- Short-term and long-term debt, regardless of the purpose of the borrowing
- Lease obligations, which are de facto debt liabilities, tied to major capital equipment or other long-term assets
- Interest payable
- Dividends payable
- Discontinued or held-for-sale liabilities[2]
- Derivative liabilities[3]

Nonoperating Assets

Common nonoperating assets are:

- Cash and cash equivalents
- Marketable securities (both current and noncurrent)
- Discontinued or held-for-sale assets
- Derivative assets

It might seem odd that we classify cash and cash equivalents as a nonoperating asset, but this account frequently consists almost totally of "cash equivalents," which are short-term investments with a

---

[2] **Discontinued operations** on the balance sheet represent assets and liabilities that the company no longer operates or has sold off. Companies separately disclose discontinued assets and liabilities on the balance sheet or in footnotes, to distinguish them from continuing items. Similarly, assets and liabilities "held for sale" are categorized as nonoperating because the company has formally decided to sell them to another party but has not yet concluded the sale. Thus, we categorize as nonoperating, all assets and liabilities that are labeled as discontinued or held-for-sale. We discuss discontinued operations in Modules 2 and 9.

[3] Companies use **derivatives** (including futures, forward contracts, options, swaps, and other derivative securities) to hedge (mitigate) risk or to speculate. Balance sheets report derivatives that are in loss positions as liabilities and those in gain positions as assets. For analysis purposes, we treat all derivatives as nonoperating items. Admittedly, some derivatives are operating assets or liabilities; for example, a forward contract on a company's manufacturing raw materials. Some derivatives are clearly nonoperating; for example, interest rate swaps. However, distinguishing between the two is complicated and often impossible for an external analyst. Accordingly, we treat all derivatives as nonoperating, both assets and liabilities. We discuss derivatives in Module 9.

scheduled maturity of 90 days or fewer. Technically, the cash needed to support routine business transactions is an operating asset. However, companies do not separately report that information and it is probably a small portion of the cash and cash equivalents line item. Therefore, we consider the entire cash and cash equivalents account as a nonoperating asset. This is consistent with current practice among external financial analysts.

Using the classified balance sheet for Boston Scientific in Exhibit 4.5, we can calculate net nonoperating obligations as follows.

$ millions	2018	2017
Nonoperating liabilities	$7,056	$5,616
Less nonoperating assets.	146	188
Net nonoperating obligations (NNO)	$6,910	$5,428

LO4 Review 4-4

Refer to the following balance sheet for **Stryker Corporation**.

$ millions	Dec. 31, 2018	Dec. 31, 2017
Current assets		
Cash and cash equivalents.	$ 3,616	$ 2,542
Marketable securities	83	251
Accounts receivable	2,332	2,198
Inventories	2,955	2,465
Prepaid expenses and other current assets	747	537
Total current assets.	9,733	7,993
Property, plant and equipment, net.	2,291	1,975
Goodwill	8,563	7,168
Other intangibles, net	4,163	3,477
Noncurrent deferred income tax assets	1,678	283
Other noncurrent assets.	801	1,301
Total assets	$27,229	$22,197
Current liabilities		
Accounts payable	$ 646	$ 487
Accrued compensation	917	838
Income taxes.	158	143
Dividend payable	192	178
Accrued expenses and other liabilities	1,521	1,207
Current maturities of debt	1,373	632
Total current liabilities	4,807	3,485
Long-term debt, excluding current maturities	8,486	6,590
Income taxes	1,228	1,261
Other noncurrent liabilities	978	881
Total liabilities	15,499	12,217
Shareholders' equity		
Common stock, $0.10 par value.	37	37
Additional paid-in capital.	1,559	1,496
Retained earnings	10,765	8,986
Other equity	(631)	(539)
Total shareholders' equity.	11,730	9,980
Total liabilities and shareholders' equity.	$27,229	$22,197

Required

a. Determine operating assets and operating liabilities for fiscal year-end 2017 and 2018.

b. Compute net operating assets (NOA) for fiscal year-end 2017 and 2018.

Solution on p. 4-60.

Income Statement Analysis with an Operating Focus

LO5 Identify income statement operating items and compute net operating profit after tax.

The income statement reports on both operating and nonoperating activities. Operating activities are those that relate to bringing a company's products or services to market and any after-sales support. The income statement captures operating revenues and expenses, yielding operating profit. Operating profit less income tax on operating profit results in net operating profit after tax (NOPAT). This measure of a company's operating performance warrants special attention because it is the lifeblood of a company's value creation and growth.

Net income (an after-tax measure) is not equivalent to net operating profit after tax because the income statement often includes nonoperating activities. These activities relate to such items as borrowed money that creates interest expense and nonstrategic investments in marketable securities that yield interest or dividend revenue. To more precisely analyze a company's operating activities, we separate the income statement into operating and nonoperating activities, as we did with the balance sheet.

To compute NOPAT, we start with net operating profit before tax from the income statement and use the following formula:

Net operating profit after tax = Net operating profit before tax − Tax on operating profit

To measure net operating profit before tax (NOPBT), we classify the line items on the income statement as either operating or nonoperating.

Operating Line Items on the Income Statement

Operating activities relate to bringing a company's products or services to market and providing after-sales support. These include:

- Revenues
- Costs of goods sold (COGS)
- Selling, general, and administrative expense (SG&A) including wages, advertising, occupancy, insurance, depreciation and amortization, litigation, and restructuring expenses
- Research and development—often reported as part of SG&A
- Impairments of operating assets such as goodwill
- Income from strategic investments (*not* marketable securities)—including joint ventures, partnerships, associated companies, and equity-method investments
- Gains and losses on disposals of operating assets such as PPE and strategic investments
- "Other" operating expenses or income—unless footnote disclosures indicate that the items are nonoperating or they are included in the nonoperating portion of the income statement

Exhibit 4.6 presents Boston Scientific's income statement with operating revenues and expenses highlighted. We use this classified income statement to calculate the 2018 net operating profit before tax (NOPBT) as follows.

$$NOPBT = Net\ sales - Cost\ of\ products\ sold - Operating\ expenses$$

$$NOPBT = \$9,823 - \$2,813 - \$5,504 = \$1,506.$$

Boston Scientific reports NOPBT as a separate line item labeled "Operating income," but this is not required disclosure, and sometimes, a company's reported operating income is not equivalent to the NOPBT we calculate. The lesson here is that line-item classification and careful analysis are required.

Nonoperating Line Items on the Income Statement

Nonoperating income and expense items relate to nonoperating assets and liabilities. These items include:

- Interest expense on debt and lease obligations
- Loss or income relating to discontinued operations

- Debt issuance and retirement costs
- Interest and dividend income on nonstrategic investments (marketable securities)
- Gains or losses on the sale of nonstrategic investments
- "Other" income or expense *if reported separately* from operating income (usually following the operating section of the income statement)

Exhibit 4.6 ■ Operating and Nonoperating Items in Boston Scientific's Income Statement

For Year Ended December 31, $ millions	2018	2017	2016
Net sales	$9,823	$9,048	$8,386
Cost of products sold	2,813	2,593	2,424
Gross profit	7,010	6,455	5,962
Operating expenses			
Selling, general and administrative expenses	3,569	3,294	3,099
Research and development expenses	1,113	997	920
Royalty expense	70	68	79
Amortization expense	599	565	545
Intangible asset impairment charges	35	4	11
Contingent consideration expense (benefit)	(21)	(80)	29
Restructuring charges	36	37	28
Litigation-related charges	103	285	804
Operating expenses	5,504	5,170	5,515
Operating income	1,506	1,285	447
Other expense (income)			
Interest expense	241	229	233
Other expense (income), net	(156)	124	37
Income before income taxes	1,422	932	177
Income tax expense (benefit)	(249)	828	(170)
Net income	$1,671	$ 104	$ 347

For most companies, nonoperating activities create a pretax net nonoperating "expense" (meaning that interest expense exceeds interest and other nonoperating income). When the reverse is true (interest and other nonoperating income is greater than interest expense), then the net nonoperating item is "income" as depicted in the following examples.

	Pretax Nonoperating Expense	Pretax Nonoperating Income	Pretax Nonoperating Net
Company A	$100	$ 10	Expense = $ 90
Company B	50	300	Income = $250

Using Boston Scientific's classified income statement, we calculate 2018 pretax net nonoperating **expense** as $85 million (Interest expense of $241 million less Other income of $156 million).

Tax on Operating Profit   The tax expense that companies report on their income statements pertains to both operating *and* nonoperating activities. To compute NOPAT, we need to compute the tax expense relating solely to operating profit as follows.

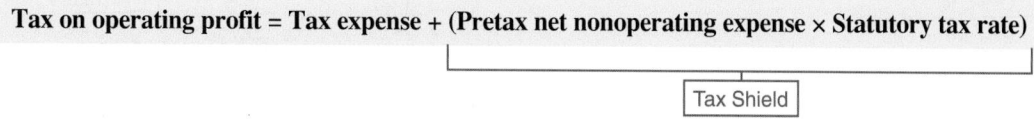

$$\text{Tax on operating profit} = \text{Tax expense} + (\text{Pretax net nonoperating expense} \times \text{Statutory tax rate})$$

Tax Shield

The amount in parentheses is called the tax shield, which are the taxes that a company saves by having tax-deductible nonoperating expenses (see Tax Shield box below for details). By definition, the taxes saved (by the tax shield) do not relate to operating profits; thus, we must add back the tax shield to total tax expense to compute the tax on operating profit.

For companies with nonoperating revenue and gains greater than nonoperating expenses, so-called nonoperating income, the "pretax net nonoperating expense" is a negative number which yields a negative tax shield. A negative tax shield implies that the company is paying more tax than it would have paid if not for the additional nonoperating income. Tax on operating profit is computed in the same manner as in the equation above: we add the negative tax shield to tax expense.

The Tax Cuts and Jobs Act (TCJA) of 2017 reduced the federal income tax rate for corporations from 35% to 21%. Most states and some local jurisdictions also impose an income tax on corporate income. On average, this adds 1% to the tax bill such that the combined statutory tax rate on operating profits is about 22%. Prior to the TCJA, the combined statutory rate was about 37%.

Applying the equations above to Boston Scientific for 2018, we calculate tax on operating profit and obtain NOPAT as follows ($ millions).

Net operating profit before tax (NOPBT)		$1,506
Less tax on operating profit		
Tax expense (benefit) per income statement	$(249)	
Plus tax shield $85 x 22%	19	(230)
Net operating profit after tax (NOPAT)		$1,736

Caveat In addition to lowering tax rates, the TCJA made sweeping changes to many aspects of tax law. Some companies benefitted greatly from the new tax rules while other companies came out behind. Many companies (including Boston Scientific) witnessed large swings in their overall tax bills in 2017 and 2018. This potential effect of the TCJA on the income statement necessitates caution when we compare after-tax profits over years that include 2017 and 2018. Module 10 further discusses the TCJA.

Boston Scientific	2018	2017
Income (loss) before income taxes.	$1,422	$932
Income tax (benefit) expense	$ (249)	$828
Average tax rate (effective rate)	(17.5)%	88.8%

Business Insight ■ Tax Rates for Computing NOPAT

In our examples and assignments, we *assume* the statutory tax rate is 22% as this is the approximate average combined federal and state tax rate for public companies. We can, as an alternative, compute a company specific tax rate using the income tax footnote from the 10-K. For example, Colgate-Palmolive provides the following table in its 10-K for the year ended December 28, 2018. The federal statutory rate is 21.0%, and Colgate pays additional state taxes, net of 1% for a total of 22%.

Percentage of Income Before Income Taxes (For Fiscal Years Ended)	Dec. 28, 2018	Dec. 27, 2017	Dec. 26, 2016
Tax at United States statutory rate	21.0%	35.0%	35.0%
State income taxes, net of federal benefit	1.0	0.5	0.5
Earnings taxed at other than United States statutory rate	4.5	(3.4)	(2.7)
Charge for U.S. tax reform	2.3	7.9	—
Excess tax benefits from stock-based compensation.	(0.3)	(1.4)	—
Foreign tax credit carryback	(1.7)	—	—
(Benefit) charge for foreign tax matters	(0.4)	—	(0.8)
(Benefit) from Venezuela remeasurement	—	—	(5.6)
Tax charge on incremental repatriation of foreign earnings	—	—	5.6
Other, net	(0.2)	(0.9)	(1.2)
Effective tax rate.	26.2%	37.7%	30.8%

For forecasting purposes later in the text we look for a persistent effective tax rate. In 2018, Colgate paid additional taxes amounting to 4.2% of profit before tax, yielding an effective tax rate of 26.2%. When we forecast Colgate's future profitability (see Module 12), we must consider whether these additional taxes are likely to persist. In this case, the charge for U.S. tax reform (2.3%), foreign tax credit carryback (–1.7%), and the (benefit) charge for foreign tax matters (–0.4%) might be considered transitory items, and largely offsetting, leaving an effective tax rate of 26% for use in forecasting, computed as 21.0% + 1.0% + 4.5% – 0.3% – 0.2%.

Business Insight   ■   Tax Shield

Persons with home mortgages understand well the beneficial effects of the "interest tax shield." To see how the interest tax shield works, consider two individuals, each with income of $50,000 and each with only one expense: a home. Assume that one person pays $10,000 per year in rent; the other pays $10,000 in interest on a home mortgage. Rent is not deductible for tax purposes, whereas mortgage interest (but not principal) is deductible. Assume that each person pays taxes at 25%, the personal tax rate for this income level. Their tax payments are as follows.

	Renter	Homeowner
Income before interest and taxes....................	$50,000	$50,000
Less interest deduction...........................	0	(10,000)
Taxable income	$50,000	$40,000
Taxes paid (25% rate)...........................	$12,500	$10,000

The renter reports $50,000 in taxable income and pays $12,500 in taxes. The homeowner deducts $10,000 in interest, which lowers taxable income to $40,000 and reduces taxes to $10,000. By deducting mortgage interest, the homeowner's tax bill is $2,500 lower. The $2,500 is the *interest tax shield*, and we can compute it directly as the $10,000 interest deduction multiplied by the 25% tax rate.

Net Nonoperating Expense (NNE)

Pretax nonoperating expense creates a tax shield. We can calculate net nonoperating expense, **after tax**, which we label, NNE.

> NNE = Pretax net nonoperating expense − Tax shield
>   = Pretax net nonoperating expense − (Pretax net nonoperating expense × Tax%)
>   = Pretax net nonoperating expense × (1 − Tax%).

For Boston Scientific this yields NNE of $66 million, calculated as $85 × (1 − 22%).

Recall that net income includes both operating and nonoperating items, all measured after-tax. This means that Net income is equal to Net operating profit after tax (NOPAT) less Net nonoperating expense after tax (NNE). This is another way to calculate NOPAT.

$$\textbf{NOPAT = Net income + NNE}$$

Applying this to Boston Scientific, we compute NOPAT as $1,671 + $66 = $1,737. We see that this is off by $1 as compared to the NOPAT of $1,736 previously calculated ($ in millions). But recall, Boston Scientific's income statement suffers from a rounding discrepancy of $1 and this causes the two NOPAT calculations to deviate. Ordinarily, the two methods yield identical NOPAT numbers.

LO5 Review 4-5

Refer to the following income statement for Stryker Corporation to answer the requirements.

Stryker Corporation, $ millions	2018
Net sales.	$13,601
Cost of sales.	4,663
Gross profit.	8,938
Research, development and engineering expenses	862
Selling, general and administrative expenses	5,099
Recall charges, net of insurance proceeds	23
Amortization of intangible assets	417
Total operating expenses	6,401
Operating income.	2,537
Nonoperating expense, net	181
Earnings before income taxes	2,356
Income tax expense (benefit).	(1,197)
Net earnings.	$ 3,553

continued

continued from previous page

Required

a. Determine net operating profit before tax (NOPBT) for fiscal 2018.

b. Compute tax on operating profit for fiscal 2018, assuming a 22% statutory tax rate.

c. Compute NOPAT using the formula: NOPBT – Tax on operating profit.

d. Compute after-tax net nonoperating expense, NNE.

Solution on p. 4-60.   e. Calculate NOPAT using the formula: Net income + NNE

Return on Net Operating Assets (RNOA)

eLectures **LO6**
MBC Compute
and interpret
return on net
operating assets
(RNOA).

To determine average NOA, we take a simple average of two consecutive years' numbers. Return on net operating assets (RNOA) for Boston Scientific for 2018 is computed as follows ($ millions).

$$\text{RNOA} = \frac{\text{Net operating profit after tax}}{\text{Average net operating assets}} = \frac{\$1,737}{(\$15,636 + \$12,440)/2} = 12.37\%$$

Boston Scientific's 2018 RNOA is 12.37%. By comparison, the average RNOA for S&P 500 companies is 11.3% in 2018 and has ranged from 9.3% to 12.5% over the 2010-2018 period (see the Research Insight titled "Ratio Behavior over Time").

RNOA vs ROA A comparison of Boston Scientific's RNOA of 12.37% with the ROA of 8.35%, computed earlier, yields insight into the benefits of an operating focus.

DuPont vs Operating Focus, $ millions	DuPont	Operating	Computation
Net income	$ 1,671		
Net operating profit after tax (NOPAT)		$ 1,737	
Average assets.	$20,021		($20,999 + $19,042)/2
Average net operating assets (NOA)		$14,038	($15,636 + $12,440)/2
ROA	8.35%		$1,671/$20,021
RNOA.		12.37%	$1,737/$14,038
ROE	21.24%	21.24%	$1,671/[($8,726 + $7,012)/2]
ROE / ROA (or RNOA):			
DuPont (ROE/ROA)	2.54		21.24%/8.35%
Operating (ROE/ RNOA).		1.72	21.24%/12.37%

Boston Scientific's RNOA of 12.37% is larger than its ROA of 8.35% derived from the DuPont analysis. The reason for the difference is twofold.

1. **Numerator effect** RNOA focuses on NOPAT, which is $66 million higher than net income used in the DuPont ROA. The larger numerator in RNOA vis-a-vis the numerator in ROA pushes RNOA higher.

2. **Denominator effect** The operating approach focuses on net operating assets (NOA) while the DuPont analysis uses total assets. NOA is lower than total assets because operating liabilities have been subtracted to arrive at NOA. This creates a smaller denominator in the RNOA calculation ($14,038) as compared to ROA ($20,021), which makes the RNOA ratio higher.

We can disaggregate ROE into operating and nonoperating components.

ROE = Operating return (via NOPAT) + Nonoperating return

Boston Scientific's ROE of 21.24% consists of an operating return of 12.37% (via NOPAT) and nonoperating return of 8.87% (ROE – NOPAT).

Financial leverage. As we discussed earlier in the module, financial leverage relates to the degree to which the company uses borrowed money, rather than shareholder equity investment, to fund operations and the acquisition of assets. The accounting equation (Assets = Liabilities + Equity) highlights the concept well. Holding total assets constant, as the amount of liabilities increases, means that stockholders' equity decreases, and consequently, financial leverage increases.

We are interested in financial leverage because it is an important measure of the risk a company is incurring with its reliance on debt. As debt increases so does the risk that the company is unable to pay the interest and principal payments on the debt. Financial leverage quantifies this risk.

While financial leverage increases risk, it also increases the return to shareholders *but only if the borrowing rate on the debt is less than the yield on the assets.* Thinking again about the accounting equation, if assets are yielding 12% and liabilities (debt) cost 10%, leverage is a positive force. If the spread between the asset returns and the debt cost is high, then, stockholders benefit even more from the borrowed money (debt). There is a trade-off, however, between the added return and the added risk created by debt. At some level of debt, the risk of default is too high and lenders will demand a higher rate and stockholders will no longer benefit from financial leverage. Continuing with the example, if the assets continue to yield 12% and additional debt costs 13%, leverage is a negative force.

While both the DuPont and Operating approaches consider the impact of financial leverage on ROE, they measure that impact in markedly different ways:

- **DuPont** approach measures the impact of financial leverage on ROE using only balance sheet numbers:

$$FL = \frac{\text{Average total assets}}{\text{Average stockholders' equity}} \quad (\text{and ROE} = \text{ROA} \times \text{FL})$$

- **Operating** approach measures the impact of financial leverage on ROE using **nonoperating returns**, which captures effects from both the balance sheet and the income statement. Recall, ROE– RNOA = Nonoperating returns. Nonoperating returns, therefore, provide a way to measure the impact of financial leverage on ROE. (In Appendix 4B we discuss financial leverage with an operating focus; that definition of financial leverage is labeled FLEV.)

In the table above, the DuPont approach measures the ratio of ROA/ROE as 39.3% and the Operating approach measures the ratio of RNOA/ROE as 58.2%. The DuPont approach ascribes a much smaller proportion of ROE to operating activities (as the effect of financial leverage is greater) than does the Operating approach. The Operating approach shows that much more of Boston Scientific's ROE is due to operating activities that make up its core business.

Divergent conclusions about the drivers of ROE are a key difference between the two approaches. While the difference between the DuPont approach and the Operating approach is moderate for Boston Scientific, for other companies the difference can be large. This is especially true for companies with large investments in marketable securities (such as big technology and pharmaceutical companies) where we come to opposite conclusions about ROE drivers when we use the Operating versus the DuPont approach. We discuss this concept further using Amazon as an example in Appendix 4B.

Exhibit 4.7 ■ Key Ratio and Acronym Definitions		
Ratio		**Definition**
ROE:	Return on equity	Net income attributable to controlling interest/Average equity attributable to controlling interest
NOA:	Net operating assets	Operating assets less operating liabilities
NOPBT:	Net operating profit before tax	Revenue – Operating expenses including COGS
NNE:	Net nonoperating expense after tax . . .	Pretax net nonoperating expense × (1 – Tax%)
NOPAT:	Net operating profit after tax	NOPBT – Tax on operating profit Or: Net income + NNE
RNOA:	Return on net operating assets	NOPAT / Average NOA

Research Insight   ■   Ratio Behavior over Time

How do RNOA and ROE behave over time? Following is a graph of average RNOA and ROE for the S&P 500 companies from 2010 to 2018. The spread between ROE and RNOA has increased in recent years as many companies have utilized excess cash to invest in marketable securities and for stock buy-backs. Yet, in all periods for the S&P 500 companies, ROE exceeds RNOA. This is evidence of the positive effect of leverage on ROE. However, this relation varies by industry; the graphics at the start of this module show some industries where ROE is less than RNOA.

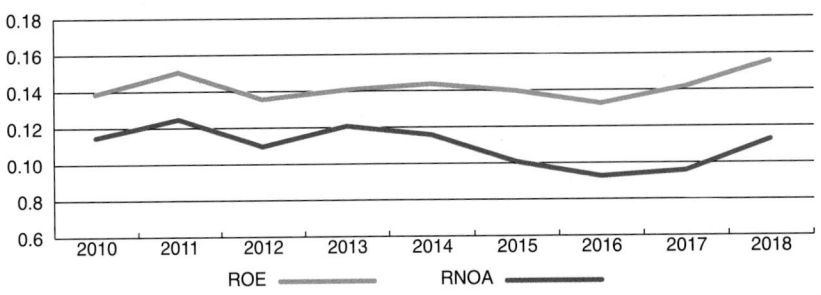

Review 4-6 **LO6**

Refer to Review 4-4 (for NOA) and 4-5 (for NOPAT) for Stryker Corporation to complete the following requirements.

Required

a. Compute and interpret return on net operating assets (RNOA) for fiscal year 2018.

b. Compare RNOA to the company's ROE of 32.73%. What proportion of the total return to shareholders comes from operations versus the effects of financial leverage?

Solution on p. 4-60.

RNOA Disaggregation into Margin and Turnover

LO7
MBC Disaggregate RNOA into net operating profitability and net operating asset turnover.

Similar to the components of ROA, we can disaggregate RNOA into net operating profit margin and net operating asset turnover to gain further insights into a company's performance.

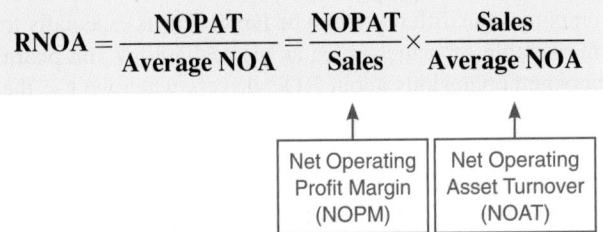

Net Operating Profit Margin

Net operating profit margin (NOPM) reveals how much operating profit the company earns from each sales dollar. All things equal, a higher net operating profit margin is preferable. Net operating profit margin is affected by

■ **Gross profit** (revenues – cost of goods sold) that the company earns on its products, which depends on product prices, manufacturing or purchase costs, and level of competition (that affects product pricing)

■ Other operating expenses and all overhead costs that the company incurs to support its operating activities

Boston Scientific's net operating profit margin for 2018 follows ($ millions).

$$\text{Net operating profit margin (NOPM)} = \frac{\text{Net operating profit after tax}}{\text{Sales}} = \frac{\$1,737}{\$9,823} = 17.68\%$$

This result means that for each dollar of sales, the company earns almost 18¢ profit after all operating expenses and taxes. As a reference, the median NOPM for the S&P 500 companies in 2018 is about 12¢.

Analysis of net operating profit margin examines the ratio over time and in comparison with peers. As with net profit margin in the DuPont analysis, the net operating profit margin includes effects from the gross profit margin (Gross profit/Sales) and the operating expense margin (Operating expenses/Sales). A second-level analysis of net operating profit margin examines these components to uncover underlying trends that drive this ratio.

Net Operating Asset Turnover

Net operating asset turnover (NOAT) measures the productivity of the company's net operating assets. This metric reveals the level of sales the company realizes from each dollar invested in net operating assets. All things equal, a higher NOAT is preferable. Boston Scientific's net operating asset turnover ratio follows ($ millions).

$$\text{Net operating asset turnover} = \frac{\text{Sales}}{\text{Average net operating assets}} = \frac{\$9,823}{(\$15,636 + \$12,440)/2} = 0.70$$

This result means that for each dollar of net operating assets, Boston Scientific realizes $0.70 in sales. As a reference, the median NOAT for S&P 500 companies in 2018 is $0.96.

Companies can increase net operating asset turnover by either increasing sales for a given level of investment in operating assets, or by reducing the amount of operating assets necessary to generate a dollar of sales, or both. Reducing operating working capital (current operating assets less current operating liabilities) is usually easier than reducing long-term net operating assets. For example, companies can implement strategies to collect their receivables more quickly, reduce their inventories, and delay payments to their suppliers. All of these actions reduce operating working capital and, thereby, increase NOAT. These strategies must be managed, however, so as not to negatively impact sales or supplier relations. Working capital management is an important part of managing the company effectively.

It is usually more difficult to reduce the level of long-term net operating assets. The level of PPE required by the company is determined more by the nature of the company's business model than by management action. For example, telecommunications companies require more capital investment than do retail stores. Still, there are several actions that managers can take to reduce capital investment. Some companies pursue novel approaches, such as corporate alliances, outsourcing, and use of special-purpose entities; we discuss some of these approaches in later modules.

Analysis of net operating asset turnover examines the ratio over time and in comparison with peers. As with asset turnover in the DuPont analysis, the net operating asset turnover includes effects from the turnovers (and corresponding days) of each of the working capital accounts (accounts receivable, inventory, accounts payable) and effects from the long-term operating assets turnover. A second-level analysis of net operating profit margin examines these components to uncover underlying trends that drive this ratio.

Managerial Decision ■ You Are the CEO

You are analyzing the performance of your company. Your analysis of RNOA reveals the following (industry benchmarks in parentheses): RNOA is 16% (10%), NOPM is 18% (17%), and NOAT is 0.89 (0.59). What interpretations do you draw that are useful for managing your company? [Answer, p. 4-41]

Trade-Off between Margin and Turnover

Net operating profit margin and turnover of net operating assets are largely affected by a company's business model. This is an important concept. Specifically, an infinite number of combinations of net operating profit margin and net operating asset turnover will yield a given RNOA. This relation is depicted in Exhibit 4.8 (where the curved line reflects the median RNOA of 13.7% in 2018 for the S&P 500 companies included in this graphic).

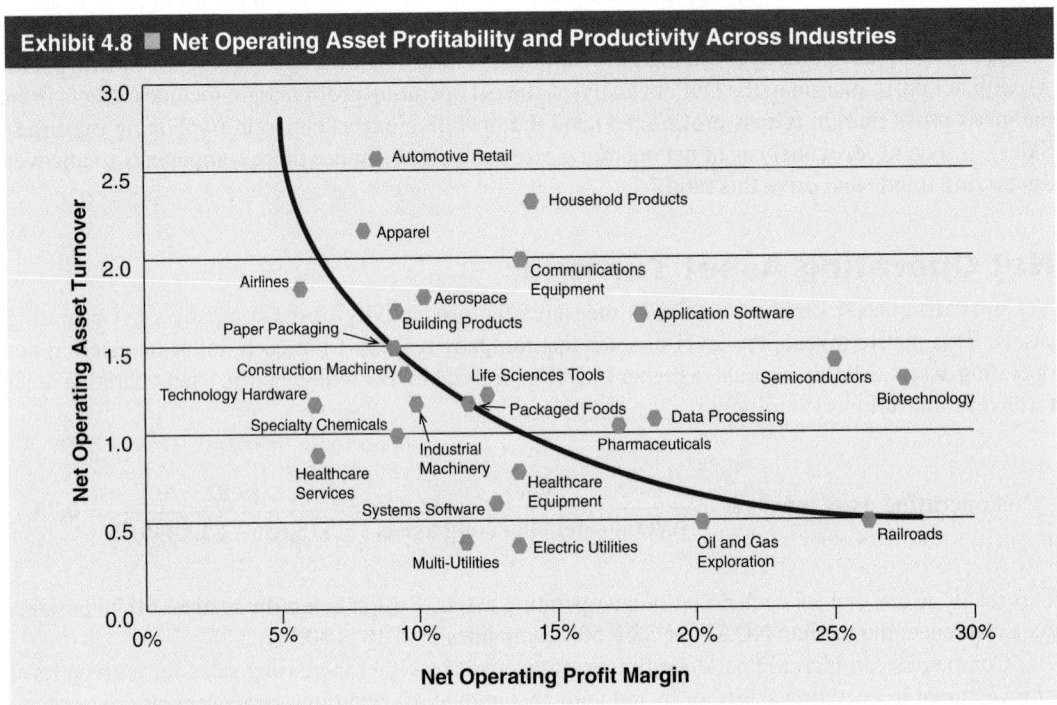

Exhibit 4.8 ■ Net Operating Asset Profitability and Productivity Across Industries

This exhibit reveals that some industries, such as railroads, oil and gas exploration, and utilities, are capital intensive with relatively low net operating asset turnover. For such industries to achieve an adequate RNOA (to be competitive in the overall market), they must obtain a higher profit margin. On the other hand, companies such as automotive retailing, apparel, and household products companies hold fewer assets and, therefore, can operate on lower net operating profit margins to achieve an adequate RNOA. This is because net operating asset turnover is greater.

This exhibit also warns of blindly comparing the performance of companies across different industries. For instance, a higher profit margin (NOPM) in the semiconductor and biotechnology industries compared with apparel and household products is not necessarily the result of better management. Instead, the semiconductor and biotechnology companies have higher operating assets (typically intangibles related to intellectual property) and thus, to achieve an equivalent RNOA, these companies must earn a higher profit margin (NOPM) to offset their lower asset turnover (NOAT). Economics suggests that all industries must earn an adequate return on investment (ROE and RNOA) if they are to continue to attract investors and survive.

The trade-off between margin and turnover is relatively straightforward when comparing companies that operate in one industry (*pure-play* firms). Analyzing conglomerates that operate in several industries is more challenging. The margins and turnover rates for companies that operate in more than one industry are a weighted average of the margins and turnover rates for the various industries in which they operate. For example, Caterpillar Inc. is a blend of a manufacturing company and a financial institution (Caterpillar Financial Services Corp.); thus, the margin and turnover benchmarks for Caterpillar on a consolidated basis are a weighted average of those two industries.

Research shows that stock returns are positively associated with earnings—when companies report higher than expected earnings, stock returns rise. Research also reports that the RNOA components (NOPM and NOAT) are more strongly associated with stock returns and future profitability than earnings (or return on assets) alone. This applies to the short-term market response to earnings announcements and long-term stock price changes. Thus, disaggregating earnings and the balance sheet into operating and nonoperating components is a useful analysis tool.

Source: Soliman, Mark T., "Use of DuPont Analysis by Market Participants," *The Accounting Review*, May 2008, 83(3): 823–853.

Business Insight ■ Return on Invested Capital (ROIC)

Many companies report alternative return metrics in their SEC filings (via their proxy statement or their MD&A in the 10-K). One common metric is the Return on Invested Capital (ROIC). Home Depot provides an example in the following excerpt from its 2019 10-K.

Return on Invested Capital We believe ROIC is meaningful for investors and management because it measures how effectively we deploy our capital base. We define ROIC as NOPAT, a non-GAAP financial measure, for the most recent twelve-month period, divided by average debt and equity. We define average debt and equity as the average of beginning and ending long-term debt (including current installments) and equity for the most recent twelve-month period. The calculation of ROIC, together with a reconciliation of NOPAT to net earnings (the most comparable GAAP measure), follows.

Dollars in millions	Fiscal 2018	Fiscal 2017	Fiscal 2016
Net earnings	$11,121	$ 8,630	$ 7,957
Interest and other, net	974	983	936
Provision for income taxes	3,435	5,068	4,534
Operating income	15,530	14,681	13,427
Income tax adjustment	(3,665)	(5,432)	(4,874)
NOPAT	$11,865	$ 9,249	$ 8,553
Average debt and equity	$26,492	$27,074	$27,203
ROIC	44.8%	34.2%	31.4%

At first glance, it might not be apparent but this definition of ROIC is nearly identical to the RNOA we use. Note that NOPAT can be computed as Net income + After-tax nonoperating expenses; if interest is the only nonoperating expense, then the ROIC and RNOA numerators are identical. As for the denominator, Home Depot sums average debt and average stockholder equity. Consider the accounting equation: Assets = Liabilities + Stockholders' equity, which can be rewritten as:

$$\frac{\text{Operating}}{\text{assets}} + \frac{\text{Nonoperating}}{\text{assets}} = \frac{\text{Operating}}{\text{liabilities}} + \frac{\text{Nonoperating}}{\text{liabilities}} + \frac{\text{Stockholders'}}{\text{equity}}$$

By rearranging terms we see:

$$\frac{\text{Operating}}{\text{assets}} - \frac{\text{Operating}}{\text{liabilities}} = \frac{\text{Nonoperating}}{\text{liabilities}} - \frac{\text{Nonoperating}}{\text{assets}} + \frac{\text{Stockholders'}}{\text{equity}}$$

On the left is net operating assets (the denominator in RNOA). The right has debt and stockholders' equity (the denominator in ROIC) less any nonoperating assets. Thus, RNOA and ROIC are nearly identical. Because companies generally report metrics that they adapt for their industry, it is important that we understand the exact definition of the metric before comparing metrics across different companies and industries.

Review 4-7 LO7

Use the income statement provided in Review 4-5 for Stryker Corporation and the RNOA computed in Review 4-6 to complete the following requirement.

Required
Disaggregate RNOA into components of net operating profit margin and net operating asset turnover for 2018.

Solution on p. 4-60.

Global Accounting

An important aim of this module is to distinguish between operating and nonoperating items for the balance sheet and income statement. U.S. GAAP and IFRS generally account for items similarly, but there are certain disclosure differences worth noting.

The IFRS balance sheet is similar to its U.S. GAAP counterpart, with the visible exception for the frequent, but not mandatory, reverse ordering of assets and liabilities. However, one notable difference is that IFRS companies routinely report "financial assets" or "financial liabilities" on the balance sheet. We must assess these items. IFRS defines financial assets to include receivables (operating item), loans to affiliates or associates (can be operating or nonoperating depending on the nature of the transactions), securities held as investments (nonoperating), and derivatives (nonoperating). IFRS notes to financial statements, which tend to be more detailed than U.S. GAAP notes, usually detail what financial assets and liabilities consist of. This helps us accurately determine NOA and net nonoperating obligations (NNO).

The IFRS income statement usually reports fewer line items than U.S. GAAP income statements and, further, there is no definition of "operating activities" under IFRS. This means we must devote attention to classify operating versus nonoperating income components. Following is a table that shows common U.S. GAAP income statement items and their classification as operating (O) or nonoperating (N). This table also indicates which items are required for IFRS income statements.

Income Statement Line Items	Operating (O) or Nonoperating (N)	Required on IFRS Income Statement
Net sales.	O	YES
Cost of sales.	O	—
Selling, general and administrative (SG&A) expense.	O	—
Provisions for doubtful accounts.	O	—
Nonoperating income.	N	—
Interest revenue and interest expense.	N	YES
Nonoperating expenses.	N	—
Income before income taxes	O and N	—
Income tax expense.	O and N	YES
Earnings on equity investments (associates and joint ventures).	O	YES
Income from continuing operations	O	—
Discontinued operations.	N	YES
Net income.	O and N	YES
Net income attributable to noncontrolling interest	N	YES
Net income attributable to controlling interest	O and N	YES
Earnings per share (Basic EPS and Diluted EPS).	O and N	YES

There is no requirement to report income from operations, yet many IFRS companies do so. However, items that are considered operating such as gains and losses on disposals of operating assets, or income from equity method investments, are often reported below the operating income line. We must examine IFRS income statements and their notes to make an independent assessment of what is operating. IFRS income statements usually report separately the other nonoperating revenues and expenses even though this is not required. We can better assess the nature of these items by reading the accompanying notes.

Appendix 4A: Operating versus Nonoperating Classification

Typical Balance Sheet Operating Items Highlighted in Green

Assets
Current Assets
Cash and cash equivalents
Short-term investments
Accounts receivable
Credit card and other financing receivables†
Unbilled revenues
Inventories
Prepaid expenses
Deferred income tax assets
Other current assets
Current assets of discontinued operations
Current assets held for sale
Loans receivable

Long-Term Assets
Long-term investments in securities
Property, plant and equipment, net
Capitalized lease assets‡
Natural resources
**Equity method investments (including joint
    ventures, associated companies, and partnerships)**
Goodwill and intangible assets
Deferred income tax assets
Other long-term assets
Long-term assets of discontinued operations
Long-term assets held for sale
Derivative assets

Liabilities and Equity
Current Liabilities
Short-term notes and interest payable
Current maturities of long-term debt
Interest payable
Dividends payable
Accounts payable
Accrued liabilities (Accrued expenses)
Unearned (deferred) revenue
Deferred income tax liabilities
Current liabilities of discontinued operations
Current liabilities related to assets held for sale

Long-Term Liabilities
Bonds and notes payable
Capitalized lease obligations
Pension and other post-employment liabilities
Deferred income tax liabilities
Long-term liabilities of discontinued operations
Long-term liabilities related to assets held for sale
Derivative liabilities

Stockholders' Equity
All equity accounts
Noncontrolling interest

† Some companies have their own financing arm (like Ford and Caterpillar) and many retailers have credit cards (including Kohls). Because these are integral to the company's operations, we consider these to be operating assets.

‡ Capitalized leases are recorded as assets (the term capitalized means added to the balance sheet) and are often called "right of use" assets because the lease allows the company to use or control some asset. For example, a long-term land lease would create a right of use asset.

Typical Income Statement Operating Items Highlighted in Green

Revenues
Cost of sales
Gross profit
Operating expenses
   Selling, general and administrative
   Depreciation and amortization expense
   Restructuring expense
   Research and development
   Asset impairment expense
   Gains and losses on PPE and other operating asset disposal
   Total operating expenses
Operating income
Interest expense

continued

continued from previous page

Typical Income Statement Operating Items Highlighted in Green
Gains and losses on debt retirement
Interest and dividend revenue
Investment gains and losses
Income from equity method investments (including joint ventures, associated companies, and partnerships)
Total nonoperating expenses (income), net
Income from continuing operations before taxes
Tax expense (**Tax on operating profit** ± Tax shield from net nonoperating expense)
Income from continuing operations
Income (loss) from discontinued operations, net of tax
Consolidated net income
Less: Consolidated net income attributable to noncontrolling interest
Consolidated net income attributable to controlling interest (parent company stockholders)

Appendix 4B: Nonoperating Return Component of ROE

LO8
Compute and interpret nonoperating return.

Nonoperating Return

Recall that ROE can be written as:

$$\text{ROE} = \text{Operating return (RNOA)} + \text{Nonoperating return}$$

In simple form, return on nonoperating activities measures the extent to which a company is using debt to increase its return on equity.

We can infer the nonoperating return indirectly as the difference between ROE and RNOA. We can also compute the nonoperating return directly as follows.

$$\text{Nonoperating return} = \text{Financial Leverage (FLEV)} \times \text{Spread}$$

Conceptually Financial leverage and Spread can be understood as follows.

Financial leverage (FLEV):   level of net debt (debt net of cash and investments) relative to the shareholders' investment

Spread: difference between what operating assets earn and what the net debt costs.

This means return on equity can be disaggregated as:

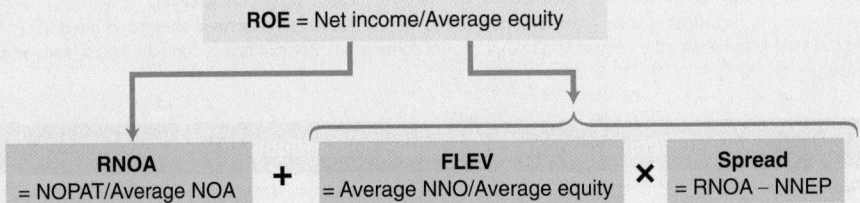

We see that the ratio definition of financial leverage here (labeled FLEV) differs from the definition in the ROA disaggregation (labeled FL). The main distinction is that FLEV uses NNO in the numerator instead of total assets. There are many ways to measure the concept of financial leverage; FL and FLEV are two distinct ways. Exhibit 4B.1 provides definitions for each of the terms required in this computation.

Exhibit 4B.1 ■ Nonoperating Return Definitions	
NNO: **Net nonoperating obligations**	Nonoperating liabilities less nonoperating assets
FLEV: **Financial leverage**	Average NNO/Average total stockholders' equity
NNE: **Net nonoperating expense**	NOPAT – Consolidated net income; or Nonoperating expenses × (1 – Statutory tax rate)
NNEP: **Net nonoperating expense percent**	NNE/Average NNO
Spread:	RNOA – NNEP

This disaggregation of ROE explicitly recognizes that ROE can be increased by judicious use of debt (the non-operating component of ROE). The idea is for a given level of RNOA, there are two ways a company could increase ROE.

1. **Increase FLEV**—the company would need to borrow more (proportionately), which would increase NNO relative to equity and increase FLEV
2. **Increase Spread**—the company (with RNOA held constant) would need to borrow at a lower cost, which would decrease NNEP and increase Spread

The upshot is that if the company can borrow more funds at the same rate of interest or borrow at a lower rate of interest, then stockholders will enjoy a higher ROE.

There is a limit: nonoperating return can only be increased as long as the company does not take on too much debt. Credit risk (the risk of default or bankruptcy) increases with the level of debt. As the company takes on more debt, lenders will mitigate the increased credit risk by charging higher interest rates. Further, as borrowing costs increase, there will be fewer investment opportunities (assets that the company can acquire) that earn an adequate return to justify the increased borrowing. At some point, further borrowing will not be cost-effective. This explains why we do not often see companies with excessive levels of financial leverage, or at least not over the long term.

BUSINESS INSIGHT ■   Financial Leverage and Spread Create Nonoperating return

$$\text{Nonoperating return} = \frac{\text{Average net nonoperating obligations (NNO)}}{\text{Average stockholders' equity (EQ)}} \times (\text{RNOA} - \text{NNEP})$$

Financial Leverage (FLEV)   Boston Scientific reports net nonoperating obligations as follows (see Exhibit 4.5 for balance sheet details).

$ millions	2018	2017	Average
Current debt obligations	$2,253	$1,801	
Long-term debt	4,803	3,815	
Cash and cash equivalents	(146)	(188)	
Net nonoperating obligations . . .	$6,910	$5,428	$6,169

Boston Scientific's average stockholders' equity in 2018 is $7,869 million, calculated as ([$8,726 million + $7,012 million]/2), and its financial leverage is 0.784, computed as follows.

$$\text{Financial leverage (FLEV)} = \frac{\text{Average net nonoperating obligations}}{\text{Average stockholders' equity}} = \frac{\$6,169}{\$7,869} = 0.784$$

That the denominator in FLEV includes all equity and not just the equity to the parent company; that is, the denominator includes the equity of any noncontrolling interests.

Spread   We first calculate net nonoperating expense in percentage terms (NNEP) as follows (see Exhibit 4.6 for income statement details). Recall that the company's operating return RNOA for 2018 is 12.37%.

Interest expense.	$241
Other expense (income), net	(156)
Pretax net nonoperating expense.	85
Less: Tax shield (at 22%)	(19)
Net nonoperating expense (NNE)	$ 66

Then: NNEP = NNE/Average NNO   and   Spread = RNOA − NNEP
                = $66/$6,169 = 1.07%   = 12.37% − 1.07% = 11.3%

Nonoperating Return   The benefit of financial leverage creates a nonoperating return of 8.86%.

Benefit (in %) of financial leverage = FLEV × Spread
                                = 0.784 × 11.3%
                                = 8.86%

Nonoperating Return—With Substantial Net Nonoperating Assets: Amazon

In 2018, nonoperating assets (cash and investments in marketable securities) comprised 10% of total assets for the average S&P 500 firm with over a third of firms reporting nonoperating asset balances exceeding 20% of total assets. About 35% of the S&P 500 have a negative NNO because nonoperating assets exceed nonoperating liabilities, which creates negative financial leverage (FLEV).

Two factors explain this. First, operating cash flows as a percentage of total revenues has increased steadily from 17% to 20% over the past decade, which has created large cash balances. The second factor relates to U.S. income tax law (before 2018) that compels firms to pay taxes only when they bring foreign earnings back to the U.S. in the form of dividends. To avoid these **repatriation taxes** over the past decade, firms left more and more international profits abroad and cash balances ballooned. For example, because of the way it structured its operations, Apple's earnings are generated primarily by it Irish subsidiaries. Worldwide profits have accumulated on the Irish subsidiaries' balance sheets such that in 2018, Apple reported $237,100 million in cash and investments, or 65% of its total assets. For all companies, this "trapped cash" was freed up somewhat when Congress passed the TCJA in 2017, reducing the tax rate from 35% to 21% and creating other incentives for firms to repatriate foreign profits.

How does negative FLEV affect the relation between ROE and RNOA? The short answer is that ROE is reduced as a consequence of the firm holding relatively low-earning financial assets that are financed by higher-cost debt. Negative FLEV companies typically report an acceptable level of ROE, but have foregone the opportunity to increase ROE even further. Amazon provides an example and its data follow.

Amazon (AMZN)	2018	2017	Average	Computation
Nonoperating assets: Cash and marketable securities	$ 41,250	$ 30,986		
Total assets	$162,648	$131,310		Reported on 2018 balance sheet
Current operating liabilities.	$ (68,391)	$ (57,883)		
Long-term operating liabilities. . . .	$ (27,213)	$ (24,743)		
NOA	$ 25,794	$ 21,466	$ 23,630	
NNO	$ (17,755)	$ (6,243)	$(11,999)	Equity – NOA
Equity	$ 43,549	$ 27,709	$ 35,629	Reported on 2018 balance sheet
Pretax NNE.	$ 1,160			Reported on 2018 income statement
Tax rate.	22%			Assumed rate
NNE	$ 905			Pretax NNE × (1 – 0.22)
Net income	$ 10,073	—	—	Reported on 2018 income statement
NOPAT	$ 10,978	—	—	Net income + NNE
FLEV.	(0.337)	—	—	$(11,999)/$35,629
RNOA.	46.46%	—	—	$10,978/$23,630
NNEP	(7.54)%	—	—	$905/$(11,999)
Spread	54.00%	—	—	46.46% – (7.54%)
ROE	28.26%	—	—	$10,073/$35,629

We can disaggregate Amazon's ROE for 2018 as follows.

$$\begin{aligned} ROE &= RNOA + [\ FLEV \times Spread] \\ &= 46.46\% + [-0.337 \times 54.0\%] \\ &= 46.46\% + [-18.20\%] \\ &= 28.26\% \end{aligned}$$

Amazon's ROE is lower than its RNOA because of its large investment in marketable securities. That is, its excessive liquidity is reducing shareholder returns. Amazon's operating assets are providing an outstanding return (46.46%), much higher than the cost of its debt net of the return on its marketable securities (7.54%). Holding liquid assets that are less productive means that Amazon's stockholders are funding a mountain of cash and sacrificing returns in the process. (The graphic on the first page of this module shows that the median ROE for information technology companies exceeds the median RNOA in eight of the last 10 years.)

Why does Amazon hold so much cash? Many companies feel the need to maintain excessive liquidity to gain flexibility—the flexibility to take advantage of opportunities and to react quickly to competitor maneuvers. Amazon's management, evidently, feels that the investment of costly equity capital will reap future rewards for its stockholders. Its robust ROE of 28.26% provides some evidence that this strategy is not necessarily misguided.

While the Operating approach to ROE provides insight into the effects of financial leverage, it also offers deeper insight into the firm's operating performance than what we learn from the traditional Dupont approach.

The table below compares Amazon's ROA (from the DuPont approach) to its RNOA (from the Operating approach). The ROA for 2018 is 6.85% whereas RNOA is 46.46%, about seven times larger.

Analysis Approach, $ millions	DuPont	Operating	Computation
Net income	$ 10,073		
Net operating profit after tax (NOPAT)		$10,978	
Average assets.	$146,979		($162,648 + $131,310)/2
Average net operating assets (NOA)		$23,630	($25,794 + $21,466)/2
ROA	6.85%		($10,073/$146,979)
RNOA		46.46%	($10,978/$23,630)

While both the numerator and denominator in the RNOA calculation reveal why ROA is so much smaller, the main reason for the drastic difference is in the denominator: ROA includes all of Amazon's assets whereas RNOA includes net operating assets (NOA). Specifically:

1. NOA excludes Amazon's sizable investment in cash marketable securities
2. NOA reveals the power of non-debt (interest-free) liabilities such as supplier credit and operating accruals such as payables for utilities, wages, and so forth

For all companies, NOA ≤ Total assets. However, for Amazon, this difference is dramatic as Amazon holds such sizeable investments in marketable securities. RNOA arguably measures Amazon's operating performance more accurately than does ROA. This is important because it is operating activities that drive shareholder value, not investment in marketable securities. In this case, the operating approach is a critical (and superior) measure of Amazon's company's financial performance.

Nonoperating Return—With Noncontrolling Interest: AT&T

When a company acquires controlling interest of the outstanding voting stock of another company, the parent company must consolidate the new subsidiary in its balance sheet and income statement. This means that the parent company must include 100% of the subsidiary's assets, liabilities, revenues, and expenses. If the parent acquires less than 100% of the subsidiary's voting stock, the remaining claim of noncontrolling stockholders is reported on the balance sheet as a component of stockholders' equity called noncontrolling interest, and net income is separated into income attributable to company stockholders and that attributable to noncontrolling interests. We need to amend the ROE calculation to measure the return to the parent company shareholders only, as follows.

$$\text{Return on equity (ROE)} = \frac{\text{Income attributable to parent company}}{\text{Average equity attributable to parent company}}$$

We compute RNOA as usual because NOPAT is operating income before any noncontrolling interest on the income statement, and NOA is unaffected by noncontrolling interest on the balance sheet. Similarly, we compute Spread and FLEV as usual.

However, we must modify the ROE = RNOA + [FLEV × Spread] formula slightly. Recall that a company's operating and nonoperating activities generate returns to both the controlling interest (labeled CI, which is the parent company's stockholders' equity) and the noncontrolling stockholders (labeled NCI). To account for this, we must multiply the ROE equation, RNOA + [FLEV × Spread], by a ratio that captures the relative income statement and balance sheet effects of the noncontrolling interest. This ratio is called the *noncontrolling interest ratio*, and is computed as follows.

$$\text{Noncontrolling interest ratio} = \left[\frac{\left(\dfrac{\text{Net income attributable to controlling interest (NI}_{\text{CI}})}{\text{Net income (NI)}} \right)}{\left(\dfrac{\text{Average equity attributable to controlling interest (CI)}}{\text{Average total equity (EQ)}} \right)} \right]$$

Hence, for companies with a noncontrolling interest (NCI), the disaggregated return on equity is expressed as:

$$\text{ROE} = [\text{RNOA} + (\text{FLEV} \times \text{Spread})] \times \text{NCI ratio}$$

To illustrate the calculation of ROE, FLEV, and Spread in the presence of noncontrolling interest, we consider the balance sheet and income statement items from AT&T ($ millions).

AT&T	2018	2017	Average
Balance sheet items			
Net operating assets (NOA)	$369,039	$258,925	$313,982
Net nonoperating obligations (NNO)	$175,155	$116,918	$146,037
Noncontrolling interest (NCI)	9,795	1,146	5,471
AT&T stockholders' equity (CI)	184,089	140,861	162,475
Total equity (EQ = NCI + CI)	193,884	142,007	167,946
Total net nonoperating obligations and Total equity (NNO + EQ)	$369,039	$258,925	$313,982
Income statement items			
Net operating profit after tax (NOPAT)	$ 19,037		
Net nonoperating expense (NNE)	(917)		
Net income (NOPAT + NNE)	19,953		
Net income attributable to noncontrolling interest (NI_{NCI})	583		
Net income attributable to AT&T stockholders (NI_{CI})	$ 19,370		

We compute AT&T's ROE for 2018 using the formula above (computations are in right column).

RNOA = NOPAT/Average NOA	6.06%	$19,037/$313,982
ROE = NI_{CI}/Average CI	11.92%	$19,370/$162,475
FLEV = Average NNO/Average EQ	0.8695	$146,037/$167,946
NNEP = NNE/Average NNO	(0.63)%	$(917)/$146,037
Spread = RNOA − NNEP	6.69%	6.06% − (0.63)%
Noncontrolling interest (NCI) ratio	1.0035	$\dfrac{\$19,370}{\$19,953}\Big/\dfrac{\$162,475}{\$167,946}$
ROE = [RNOA + (FLEV × Spread)] × NCI ratio	11.92%	[6.06% + (0.8695 × 6.69%)] × 1.0035

Review 4-8 LO8

Refer to Stryker Corporation's balance sheet from Review 4-4 and its income statement from Review 4-5, along with its ROE and RNOA computations from Reviews 4-1 and 4-6, respectively, to complete the requirements.

Required

a. Use ROE and RNOA ratios to determine the nonoperating return for 2018.
b. Compute net nonoperating obligations (NNO) for 2017 and 2018 and FLEV for 2018.
c. Compute net nonoperating expense (NNE) and net nonoperating expense as a percentage of NNO (NNEP).
d. Determine Spread using the formula: RNOA − NNEP.

Solution on p. 4-60.   e. Demonstrate that ROE = RNOA + (FLEV × Spread).

Appendix 4C: Liquidity and Solvency Analysis

LO9 Compute and interpret measures of liquidity and solvency.

Companies can effectively use debt to increase return on equity via nonoperating return. We might further ask: if a higher ROE is desirable, why don't companies use the maximum debt possible? The short answer is that lenders, such as banks and bondholders, charge successively higher interest rates for increasing levels of debt relative to the amount of equity investment. At some point, the cost of the additional debt exceeds the return on the additional assets acquired from the debt financing. Thereafter, further debt financing does not make economic sense. The market, in essence, places a limit on the level of debt that a company can effectively acquire. In sum, stockholders benefit from increased use of debt provided that the assets financed with the debt earn a return that exceeds the cost of the debt.

Creditors usually require a company to execute a loan agreement that places varying restrictions on the company's operating activities. These restrictions, called *covenants*, help safeguard debtholders in the face of increased risk. Covenants exist because debtholders do not have a voice on the board of directors like stockholders do. These debt covenants impose a "cost" on the company beyond that of the interest rate, and these covenants are more stringent as a company increases its reliance on debt financing.

In this appenedix, we explore how much debt a company can reasonably manage. We examine a number of liquidity and solvency metrics that lenders use to assess the default risk and set interest rates. Credit analysts typically use the same ratios to develop credit ratings, which are key determinants of bond prices and cost of debt financing for public companies.

Liquidity Analysis

Liquidity refers to cash availability: how much cash a company has, and how much it can raise on short notice. Two of the most common ratios used to assess the degree of liquidity are the current ratio and the quick ratio. Both of these ratios link required near-term payments to cash available in the near-term.

Current Ratio

Current assets are assets that a company expects to convert into cash within the next operating cycle, which is typically a year. *Current liabilities* are liabilities that come due within the next year. An excess of current assets over current liabilities (Current assets − Current liabilities) is known as *net working capital* or simply *working capital*.[4] Positive working capital implies that cash generated by "liquidating" current assets would be sufficient to pay current liabilities. The current ratio expresses working capital as a ratio and is computed as follows.

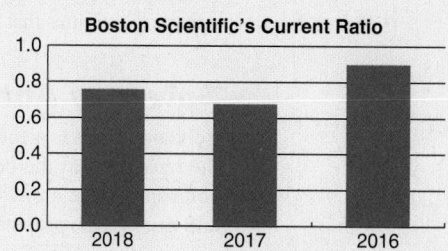

Boston Scientific's Current Ratio

$$\text{Current ratio} = \frac{\text{Current assets}}{\text{Current liabilities}}$$

A current ratio greater than 1.0 implies positive working capital. Both working capital and the current ratio consider existing balance sheet data only and ignore cash inflows from future sales or other sources. The current ratio is more commonly used than working capital because ratios allow comparisons across companies of different size. Generally, companies prefer a higher current ratio; however, an excessively high current ratio indicates inefficient asset use. Furthermore, a current ratio less than 1.0 is not always bad for at least two reasons:

1. A cash-and-carry company with comparatively fewer accounts receivable (like Walmart for example) can have potentially few current assets (and a low current ratio), but consistently large operating cash inflows ensure the company will be sufficiently liquid.
2. A company can efficiently manage its working capital by minimizing receivables and inventories and maximizing payables. Walmart, for example, uses its buying power to exact extended credit terms from suppliers. Consequently, because it is essentially a cash-and-carry company, its current ratio is less than 1.0 and is sufficiently liquid.

Boston Scientific's current ratio has declined over the recent past, mainly because it has initiated a program to reduce the level of accounts receivable and is paying its suppliers more quickly. In addition, the company's products are relatively slow-moving as they are technical and relatively high-priced in nature. The company reports that 40% of its finished goods inventory was at customer locations pursuant to consignment arrangements or held by sales representatives. Further, the company does not maintain large investments in marketable securities. All of these factors combine to reduce the level of current assets and the current ratio. Although its current ratio is not particularly high, Boston Scientific generates large cash inflows from operating activities that are more than sufficient to cover its operations, its investment in infrastructure, and its contractual obligations. We would not be concerned with the current ratio or its recent decline.

Quick Ratio

The quick ratio is a variant of the current ratio. It focuses on quick assets, which are assets likely to be converted to cash within a relatively short period of time. Specifically, quick assets include cash, marketable

---

[4] Both operating assets and operating liabilities can be either current or long-term. "Current" means that the asset is expected to be used, or the liability paid, within the next operating cycle or one year, whichever is longer, which for most companies means a year. Using the current versus long-term nature of operating assets and liabilities, we derive two types of net operating assets: net operating working capital (NOWC), and net long-term operating assets. Net operating working capital is defined as:

Net operating working capital (NOWC) = Current operating assets − Current operating liabilities

For Boston Scientific, NOWC is $849 million for 2018 ($1,608 million + $1,166 million + $161 million + $921 million − $349 million − $2,246 million − $412 million).

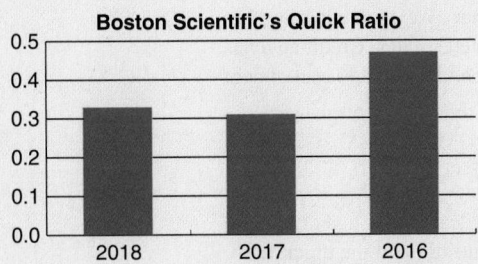

Boston Scientific's Quick Ratio

securities, and accounts receivable; they exclude inventories, prepaid assets, and other current assets. The quick ratio is defined as follows.

$$\text{Quick ratio} = \frac{\text{Cash} + \text{Marketable securities} + \text{Accounts receivable}}{\text{Current liabilities}}$$

The quick ratio reflects on a company's ability to meet its current liabilities without liquidating inventories. It is a more stringent test of liquidity than the current ratio. Boston Scientific's 2018 quick ratio is 0.33 ($146 million + $1,608 million)/ $5,260 million. Like the current ratio, Boston Scientific's quick ratio has declined slightly over the past three years mainly because the company is collecting accounts receivable and paying suppliers more quickly. It is not uncommon for a company's quick ratio to be less than 1.0. Again, Boston Scientific generates large cash inflows from operating activities that are more than sufficient to keep the company liquid.

Solvency Analysis

Solvency refers to a company's ability to meet its debt obligations, including both periodic interest payments and the repayment of the principal amount borrowed. Solvency is crucial because an insolvent company is a failed company. There are two general approaches to measuring solvency. The first approach uses balance sheet data and assesses the proportion of capital raised from creditors. The second approach uses income statement data and assesses the profit generated relative to interest payment obligations. We discuss each approach in turn.

Liabilities-to-Equity

The liabilities-to-equity ratio is a useful tool for the first type of solvency analysis. It is defined as follows.

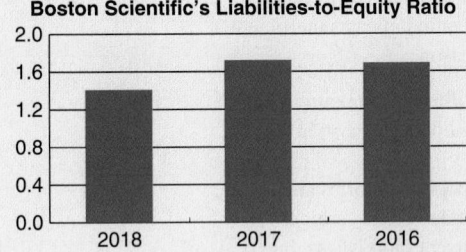

Boston Scientific's Liabilities-to-Equity Ratio

$$\text{Liabilities-to-equity ratio} = \frac{\text{Total liabilities}}{\text{Stockholders' equity}}$$

This ratio conveys how reliant a company is on creditor financing compared with equity financing. A higher ratio indicates less solvency, and more risk. Boston Scientific's 2018 liabilities-to-equity ratio is 1.41 ($5,260 million + $4,803 million + $328 million + $1,882 million)/$8,726 million). This ratio has steadily declined from 1.69 to 1.41 over the past three years, and is similar to the 1.67 average for S&P 500 firms in 2018.

As we would expect, the relative use of debt varies considerably across industries as illustrated in Exhibit 4C.1.

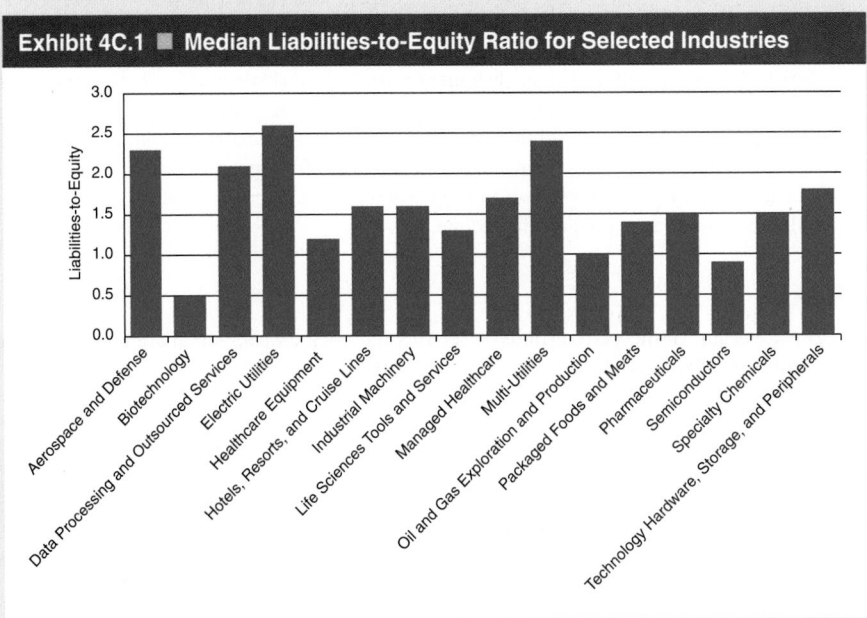

Exhibit 4C.1 ■ Median Liabilities-to-Equity Ratio for Selected Industries

Two factors explain why industries such as Aerospace, Data processing ("Cloud" companies), and Utilities have a larger proportion of debt. First, these industries are capital intensive, and second, they have relatively stable cash flows to cover higher interest costs and principal repayment.

A variant of the liabilities-to-equity ratio considers a company's long-term debt divided by equity. This ratio assumes that current liabilities are repaid from current assets (so-called self-liquidating). It assumes that creditors and stockholders need only focus on the relative proportion of long-term capital. In 2018, Boston Scientific's long-term debt divided by equity is 0.55, somewhat lower than the average of 0.62 for S&P 500 companies.

Times Interest Earned

The second type of solvency analysis compares profits to liabilities. This approach assesses how much operating profit is available to cover debt obligations. A common measure for this type of solvency analysis is the times interest earned ratio, defined as follows.

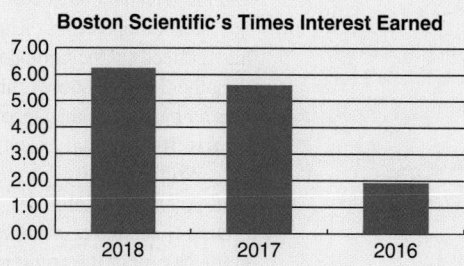

Boston Scientific's Times Interest Earned

$$\text{Times interest earned} = \frac{\text{Earnings before interest and taxes}}{\text{Interest expense, gross}}$$

The times interest earned ratio reflects the operating income available to pay interest expense. The underlying assumption is that only interest needs to be paid because the principal will be refinanced. This ratio is sometimes abbreviated as EBIT/I. The numerator is similar to net operating profits after tax (NOPAT), but it is *pretax* instead of after tax. We use earnings before net interest expense, that is, net of any other nonoperating income or expenses. We use gross interest, which does not include interest income or other investment income or expenses. If the income statement reports Interest, net, the line item likely includes interest income. Footnotes or the MD&A section of Form 10-K typically report interest expense, gross.

The higher this ratio, the lower the risk of default. Boston Scientific's 2018 times interest earned is 6.25 ($1,506 million/$241 million), a large increase from the 1.92 reported two years prior. The level of this ratio implies that Boston Scientific could suffer a fairly large decline in profitability and still be able to service its interest payments when due. Notice that the times interest earned ratio uses interest expense in the denominator and analysts typically do not include "other" nonoperating income in this statistic. The ratio is also called a "coverage" ratio.

There are many variations of solvency and liquidity analysis and ratios. The basic idea is to construct measures that reflect a company's credit risk exposure. There is not one "best" financial leverage ratio. Instead, as financial statement users, we want to use measures that capture the risk we are most concerned with. It is also important to compute the ratios ourselves to ensure we know what is included and excluded from each ratio.

Vertical and Horizontal Analysis

Companies come in all sizes, which presents difficulties when making comparisons among firms, or between a firm and an industry benchmark, or over time. There are several methods that attempt to overcome this obstacle.

Vertical analysis expresses financial statements in ratio form. Specifically, we express income statement items as a percent of net sales, and balance sheet items as a percent of total assets. Such *common-size, or right-size, financial statements* facilitate comparisons *across companies* of different sizes and comparisons of accounts within a set of financial statements.

Horizontal analysis is the scrutiny of financial data *across time*. Comparing data across two or more consecutive periods assists in analyzing trends in company performance and in predicting future performance. There are two ways to perform a horizontal analysis.

▪ Compare the vertical analysis over time. Once the balance sheet or income statement is expressed in percentage terms, we can look for trends or changes year over year. This level of analysis points out areas that warrant additional research. We use footnotes, the MD&A section of the Form 10-K, and external sources to explain unusual changes or concerning trends.

▪ Compute the percentage change, for each line item, as follows.

(Current balance − Previous balance)/Previous balance

Special attention is required when the previous balance is a negative number. Consider the example of a company that reports a net loss of $100 in 2017 and net income of $150 in 2018. Using the definition above, percentage change is *negative* 250%, calculated as $250/$(100), and we might erroneously conclude that the company's performance worsened in 2018. One fix is to adjust the denominator, as follows.

(Current balance − Previous balance)/Absolute value of previous balance

Using this approach, we calculate a change of positive 250% and conclude that the company is improving.

Exhibits 4C.2 and 4C.3 report Boston Scientific's common-size balance sheets and income statements for the past three years. This presentation allows us to compare companies of different sizes by focusing on the relative proportions of balance sheet and income statement accounts. The vertical analysis also helps us more easily identify trends and changes. For example, looking at the balance sheet in dollars, we might conclude that trade accounts receivables increased during 2018 from $1,548 million to $1,608 million. But the vertical analysis reveals that trade receivables decreased in relative size from 8.1% to 7.7%.

Boston Scientific's asset composition has remained largely unchanged from 2016 to 2018. The most substantial assets are intangibles (Goodwill and other intangible assets), which comprise 68% of total assets in 2018 and are a testament to the company's long-standing strategy of growth by acquisition.

The composition of liability and equity has changed somewhat over the past three years. Boston Scientific has reduced the percentage of accounts payable and accrued expenses from 15.3% to 12.4% of total assets. On the other hand, its debt (current plus long-term) has increased. While it appears that treasury stock is stable, there was no balance in this account in 2016. The company repurchased sizeable amounts of its common stock in 2017 (nearly 10% of total assets).

While liquidity (as measured by the current ratio) has declined, Boston Scientific financed its 58.4% of its total assets with liabilities, down from 62.8% two years prior. This improvement in solvency (along with an improved times interest earned ratio) has improved the company's risk profile and its debt is rated as "investment grade" by all of the credit ratings companies (see Module 7 for a discussion of the credit rating analysis process).

From the vertical income statement, we see that Boston Scientific's cost of sales has decreased slightly from 28.9% in 2016 to 28.6% in 2018, for marginal increases to an already healthy gross profit margin. This margin reveals that Boston Scientific's product costs comprise relatively small amounts of materials and labor. Instead the company incurs sizeable research and development costs (11.3% of sales in 2018), which are not capitalized into inventory and, therefore, do not flow to the income statement as cost of products sold.

Over this three-year period, Boston Scientific's operating profit margin has increased from 5.3% to 15.3%, but much of this improvement is due to the steep drop in litigation expense.

Net income is 17% of sales in 2018, which seems to be a marked improvement from the 1.1% of sales reported in the prior year. However, the 2017 tax legislation and the consequent wild swings in tax expense make this line item nearly uninterpretable (see Modules 5 and 10 for a discussion of income tax expense). Better to consider pretax income where we observe steady improvement over the three-year period.

Bottom line, Boston Scientific is a profitable and well-capitalized company. It continues to invest in the future with research and development expenses and large corporate acquisitions to enhance its technology portfolio.

Exhibit 4C.2 ■ Boston Scientific Common-Size Balance Sheets

	2018	2017	2016
Current assets			
Cash and cash equivalents.	0.7%	1.0%	1.1%
Trade accounts receivable, net.	7.7%	8.1%	8.1%
Inventories	5.6%	5.7%	5.3%
Prepaid income taxes	0.8%	0.3%	0.4%
Other current assets	4.4%	4.9%	3.0%
Total current assets.	19.1%	20.1%	17.9%
Property, plant and equipment, net.	8.5%	8.9%	9.0%
Goodwill	37.7%	36.8%	36.9%
Other intangible assets, net	30.3%	30.7%	32.5%
Other long-term assets.	4.4%	3.6%	3.7%
Total assets	100.0%	100.0%	100.0%
Current liabilities			
Current debt obligations	10.7%	9.5%	0.4%
Accounts payable	1.7%	2.8%	2.5%
Accrued expenses	10.7%	12.9%	12.8%
Other current liabilities	2.0%	4.6%	4.2%
Total current liabilities	25.0%	29.7%	19.8%
Long-term debt.	22.9%	20.0%	30.0%
Deferred income taxes	1.6%	1.0%	0.1%
Other long-term liabilities	9.0%	12.4%	12.9%
Total liabilities.	58.5%	63.1%	62.8%

continued

continued from previous page

Exhibit 4C.2 ■ Boston Scientific Common-Size Balance Sheets (cont.)			
	2018	**2017**	**2016**
Stockholders' equity			
Preferred stock	—	—	—
Common stock	0.1%	0.1%	0.0%
Treasury stock	(8.2)%	(9.0)%	0.0%
Additional paid-in capital	82.6%	90.1%	0.0%
Accumulated deficit	(33.1)%	(44.1)%	(47.4)%
Accumulated other comprehensive income (loss), net of tax	0.0%	0.0%	0.0%
Foreign currency translation adjustment	(0.3)%	(0.2)%	(0.4)%
Unrealized gain (loss) on derivative financial instruments	0.5%	0.0%	0.6%
Unrealized gain (loss) on available-for-sale securities	0.0%	0.0%	0.0%
Unrealized costs associated with defined benefit pensions and other items	(0.1)%	(0.1)%	(0.1)%
Total stockholders' equity	41.6%	36.8%	37.2%
Total liabilities and stockholders' equity	100.0%	100.0%	100.0%

Exhibit 4C.3 ■ Boston Scientific Common-Size Income Statements			
	2018	**2017**	**2016**
Net sales	100.0%	100.0%	100.0%
Cost of products sold	28.6%	28.7%	28.9%
Gross profit	71.4%	71.3%	71.1%
Operating expenses			
Selling, general and administrative expenses	36.3%	36.4%	37.0%
Research and development expenses	11.3%	11.0%	11.0%
Royalty expense	0.7%	0.8%	0.9%
Amortization expense	6.1%	6.2%	6.5%
Intangible asset impairment charges	0.4%	0.0%	0.1%
Contingent consideration expense (benefit)	(0.2)%	(0.9)%	0.3%
Restructuring charges (credits)	0.4%	0.4%	0.3%
Litigation-related charges (credits)	1.0%	3.1%	9.6%
Operating expenses	56.0%	57.1%	65.8%
Operating income (loss)	15.3%	14.2%	5.3%
Other income (expense)			
Interest expense	(2.5)%	(2.5)%	(2.8)%
Other, net	1.6%	(1.4)%	(0.4)%
Income (loss) before income taxes	14.5%	10.3%	2.1%
Income tax (benefit) expense	(2.5)%	9.2%	(2.0)%
Net income (loss)	17.0%	1.1%	4.1%

Limitations of Ratio Analysis

The quality of financial statement analysis depends on the quality of financial information. We ought not blindly analyze numbers; doing so can lead to faulty conclusions and suboptimal decisions. Instead, we need to acknowledge that current accounting rules (GAAP) have limitations, and be fully aware of the company's environment, its competitive pressures, and any structural and strategic changes. This section discusses some of the factors that limit the usefulness of financial accounting information for ratio analysis.

GAAP Limitations Several limitations in GAAP can distort financial ratios. Limitations include:

1. **Measurability.** Financial statements reflect what can be reliably measured. This results in nonrecognition of certain assets, often internally developed assets, the very assets that are most likely to confer a competitive advantage and create value. Examples are brand name, a superior management team, employee skills, and a reliable supply chain.

2. **Noncapitalized costs.** Related to the concept of measurability is the expensing of costs relating to "assets" that cannot be identified with enough precision to warrant capitalization. Examples are brand equity costs from advertising and other promotional activities, and research and development costs relating to future products.

3. **Historical costs.** Assets and liabilities are usually recorded at original acquisition or issuance costs. Subsequent increases in value are not recorded until realized, and declines in value are only recognized if deemed permanent.

Thus, GAAP balance sheets omit important and valuable assets. Our analysis of ROE and our assessment of liquidity and solvency must consider that assets can be underreported and that ratios can be distorted. We discuss many of these limitations in more detail in later modules.

Company Changes Many companies regularly undertake mergers, acquire new companies, and divest subsidiaries. Such major operational changes can impair the comparability of company ratios across time. Companies also change strategies, such as product pricing, R&D, and financing. We must understand the effects of such changes on ratios and exercise caution when we compare ratios from one period to the next. Companies also behave differently at different points in their life cycles. For instance, growth companies possess a different profile than do mature companies. Seasonal effects also markedly impact analysis of financial statements at different times of the year. Thus, we must consider life cycle and seasonality when we compare ratios across companies and over time.

Conglomerate Effects Few companies are a pure-play; instead, most companies operate in several businesses or industries. Most publicly traded companies consist of a parent company and multiple subsidiaries, often pursuing different lines of business. Most heavy equipment manufacturers, for example, have finance subsidiaries (Ford Credit Corporation and Caterpillar Financial Services Corporation are subsidiaries of Ford and Caterpillar, respectively). Financial statements of such conglomerates are consolidated and include the financial statements of the parent and its subsidiaries. Consequently, such consolidated statements are challenging to analyze. Typically, analysts break the financials apart into their component businesses and separately analyze each component. Fortunately, companies must report financial information (albeit limited) for major business segments in their 10-Ks.

Fuzzy View Ratios reduce, to a single number, the myriad complexities of a company's operations. No scalar can accurately capture all qualitative aspects of a company. Ratios cannot meaningfully convey a company's marketing and management philosophies, its human resource activities, its financing activities, its strategic initiatives, and its product management. In our analysis we must learn to look through the numbers and ratios to better understand the operational factors that drive financial results. Successful analysis seeks to gain insight into what a company is really about and what the future portends. Our overriding purpose in analysis is to understand the past and present to better predict the future. Calculating and analyzing ratios are crucial first steps in that process.

Review 4-9 LO9

Use the income statement and balance sheet for Stryker Corporation from Reviews 4-4 and 4-5.

Required

a. Compute measures of liquidity for 2018.

Solution on p. 4-61.   *b.* Compute liabilities-to-equity ratio and the times interest earned for 2018.

Guidance Answers

You Are the CEO

Pg. 4-26 Your company is performing substantially better than its competitors. Namely, your RNOA of 16% is markedly superior to competitors' RNOA of 10%. However, RNOA disaggregation shows that this is mainly attributed to your NOAT of 0.89 versus competitors' NOAT of 0.59. Your NOPM of 18% is essentially identical to competitors' NOPM of 17%. Accordingly, you will want to maintain your NOAT as further improvements are probably difficult to achieve. Importantly, you are likely to achieve the greatest benefit with efforts at improving your NOPM of 18%, which is only marginally better than the industry norm of 17%.

Superscript ᴮ⁽ᶜ⁾ denotes assignments based on Appendix 4B (4C).

Questions

Q4-1. Explain in general terms the concept of return on investment. Why is this concept important in the analysis of financial performance?

Q4-2.ᴮ (a) Explain how an increase in financial leverage can increase a company's ROE. (b) Given the potentially positive relation between financial leverage and ROE, why don't we see companies with 100% financial leverage (entirely nonowner financed)?

Q4-3. Gross profit margin (Gross profit/Sales) is an important determinant of NOPAT. Identify two factors that can cause gross profit margin to decline. Is a reduction in the gross profit margin always bad news? Explain.

Q4-4. When might a reduction in operating expenses as a percentage of sales denote a short-term gain at the cost of long-term performance?

Q4-5. Describe the concept of asset turnover. What does the concept mean and why is it so important to understanding and interpreting financial performance?

Q4-6. Explain what it means when a company's ROE exceeds its RNOA. What about when the reverse occurs?

Q4-7. Discontinued operations are typically viewed as a nonoperating activity in the analysis of the balance sheet and the income statement. What is the rationale for this treatment?

Q4-8. Describe what is meant by the "tax shield."

Q4-9. What is meant by the term "net" in net operating assets (NOA)?

Q4-10. Why is it important to disaggregate RNOA into net operating profit margin (NOPM) and net operating assets turnover (NOAT)?

Q4-11. What insights do we gain from the graphical relation between profit margin and asset turnover?

Q4-12. Explain the concept of liquidity and why it is crucial to company survival.

Q4-13. Identify at least two factors that limit the usefulness of ratio analysis.

Q4-14. Define (1) net nonoperating obligations and (2) net nonoperating expense.

Q4-15. What is the chief difference between the traditional DuPont disaggregation of ROE and the disaggregation based on RNOA?

Q4-16. What is meant by the term "cash conversion cycle"?

Q4-17. What insights can be gained from a common-size income statement or balance sheet?

Assignments with the 🕓 logo in the margin are available in ᵐʸBusinessCourse.
See the Preface of the book for details.

Mini Exercises

M4-18. **Compute ROE**

Selected balance sheet and income statement information for Facebook Inc. follows. Compute the return on equity for the year ended December 31, 2018.

LO1
Facebook Inc. (FB)

$ millions	Dec. 31, 2018	Dec. 31, 2017
Total assets	$97,334	$84,524
Total liabilities	13,207	10,177
Revenue	55,838	
Net income	22,112	

© Cambridge Business Publishers

LO2, 3
Facebook Inc. (FB)

M4-19. Apply DuPont Disaggregation of ROE

Refer to the balance sheet and income statement information for Facebook Inc. from M4-18.

a. Compute ROE and disaggregate the ratio into its DuPont components of ROA and financial leverage.

b. Disaggregate ROA into profitability and productivity components.

LO4
Home Depot (HD)

M4-20. Compute Net Operating Assets (NOA)

Refer to the balance sheet information below for Home Depot. Compute net operating assets for the years ended February 3, 2019, and January 28, 2018.

$ millions	Feb. 3, 2019	Jan. 28, 2018
Operating assets	$ 42,225	$40,934
Nonoperating assets	1,778	3,595
Total assets	$ 44,003	$44,529
Operating liabilities	$ 16,679	$16,047
Nonoperating liabilities	29,202	27,028
Total liabilities	$ 45,881	$43,075
Net sales	$108,203	
Operating expense before tax	92,673	
Net operating profit before tax (NOPBT)	15,530	
Other expense	974	
Income before tax	14,556	
Tax expense	3,435	
Net earnings	$ 11,121	

LO5
Home Depot (HD)

M4-21. Compute Net Operating Profit after Tax

Refer to the income statement information for Home Depot from M4-20.
Assume a statutory tax rate of 22%.

a. Compute NOPAT using the formula: NOPAT = Net income + NNE

b. Compute NOPAT using the formula: NOPAT = NOPBT – Tax on operating profit

LO6, 7
Home Depot (HD)

M4-22. Compute RNOA with Disaggregation

Refer to the balance sheet and income statement information for Home Depot from M4-20.

a. Compute return on net operating assets (RNOA).

b. Disaggregate RNOA into components of profitability and productivity and show that the product of the two components equals RNOA.

LO6, 7
Netflix, Inc. (NFLX)

M4-23. Compute RNOA, Net Operating Profit Margin, and NOA Turnover

Selected balance sheet and income statement information for Netflix Inc. the world's leading Internet entertainment service, follows.

Company ($ thousands)	Ticker	2018 Revenue	2018 NOPAT	2018 Net Operating Assets	2017 Net Operating Assets
Netflix, Inc.	NFLX	$15,794,341	$1,506,681	$11,804,340	$7,258,593

a. Compute return on net operating assets (RNOA).

b. Disaggregate RNOA into net operating profit margin (NOPM) and net operating asset turnover (NOAT). Confirm that RNOA = NOPM × NOAT.

LO4
Lowe's Companies Inc. (LOW)

M4-24. Identify and Compute Net Operating Assets

Following is the balance sheet for Lowe's Companies Inc. Identify and compute net operating assets (NOA) as of February 1, 2019. Assume that long-term investments are nonoperating.

LOWE'S COMPANIES INC.	
Consolidated Balance Sheet	
$ millions, except par value	**Feb. 1, 2019**
Current assets	
Cash and cash equivalents.	$ 511
Short-term investments.	218
Merchandise inventory—net.	12,561
Other current assets.	938
Total current assets.	14,228
Property, less accumulated depreciation	18,432
Long-term investments.	256
Deferred income taxes—net.	294
Goodwill.	303
Other assets.	995
Total assets	$34,508
Current liabilities	
Short-term borrowings	$ 722
Current maturities of long-term debt.	1,110
Accounts payable.	8,279
Accrued compensation and employee benefits	662
Deferred revenue	1,299
Other current liabilities	2,425
Total current liabilities.	14,497
Long-term debt, excluding current maturities.	14,391
Deferred revenue—extended protection plans.	827
Other liabilities	1,149
Total liabilities.	30,864
Shareholders' equity	
Preferred stock—$5 par value, none issued	0
Common stock—$0.50 par value.	401
Capital in excess of par value.	0
Retained earnings	3,452
Accumulated other comprehensive loss.	(209)
Total shareholders' equity.	3,644
Total liabilities and shareholders' equity.	$34,508

M4-25. Identify and Compute NOPAT

Following is the income statement for Lowe's Companies Inc. Compute its net operating profit after tax (NOPAT) for the 12 months ended ended February 1, 2019, assuming a 22% total statutory tax rate.

LO5
Lowe's Companies
Inc. (LOW)

LOWE'S COMPANIES INC.	
Consolidated Statement of Earnings	
Twelve Months Ended (In millions)	**Feb. 1, 2019**
Net sales.	$71,309
Cost of sales.	48,401
Gross margin	22,908
Expenses	
Selling, general and administrative.	17,413
Depreciation and amortization	1,477
Operating income.	4,018
Interest expense, net	624
Pretax earnings	3,394
Income tax provision.	1,080
Net earnings.	$ 2,314

M4-26. Compute DuPont Analysis Ratios

Selected balance sheet and income statement information for Humana Inc., a health and well-being company, follows.

LO1, 2, 3
Humana Inc. (HUM)

Company ($ millions)	Ticker	2018 Revenue	2018 Net income	2018 Assets	2017 Assets	2018 Stockholders' Equity	2017 Stockholders' Equity
Humana Inc	HUM	$56,912	$1,683	$25,413	$27,178	$10,161	$9,842

Compute the following 2018 ratios for Humana.
a. Return on equity (ROE)
b. Profit margin (PM)
c. Financial leverage (FL)

LO6, 7
Abercrombie &
Fitch Co. (ANF)
TJX Companies Inc.
(TJX)

MBC

M4-27.   Compute RNOA, Net Operating Profit Margin, and NOA Turnover for Competitors

Selected balance sheet and income statement information for the fiscal year ended February 2, 2019, for **Abercrombie & Fitch Co.** and **TJX Companies Inc.**, clothing retailers in the high-end and value-priced segments, respectively, follows.

Company ($ millions)	Ticker	Sales	NOPAT	Current Year Net Operating Assets	Prior Year Net Operating Assets
Abercrombie & Fitch.	ANF	$ 3,590.1	$ 87.4	$ 792.3	$ 877.3
TJX Companies	TJX	38,972.9	3,066.7	4,252.0	4,114.3

Compute the following ratios for both companies for the fiscal year ended February 2, 2019.
a. Return on net operating assets (RNOA)
b. Net operating profit margin (NOPM)
c. Net operating asset turnover (NOAT)

LO9
Verizon
Communications Inc.
(VZ)

MBC

M4-28.   Compute Liquidity and Solvency Ratios

Selected balance sheet and income statement information from **Verizon Communications Inc.** follows.

$ millions	2018	2017
Current assets	$ 34,636	$ 29,913
Current liabilities.	37,930	33,037
Total liabilities.	382,308	391,875
Equity.	54,710	44,687
Earnings before interest and taxes.	22,278	27,425
Interest expense, gross	4,833	4,733
Net cash flow from operating activities.	34,339	24,318

Compute the following ratios for Verizon for both 2018 and 2017.
a. Current ratio
b. Times interest earned
c. Liabilities-to-equity

LO5, 6, 7
Home Depot Inc. (HD)
Lowe's Companies
Inc. (LOW)

MBC

M4-29.   Compute NOPAT

Selected income statement information for 2018 is presented below for **Home Depot Inc.** and **Lowe's Companies Inc.** Assume the statutory tax rate is 22%.

Company ($ millions)	Ticker	Sales	NOPBT	Pretax Net Nonoperating Expense	Tax Expense	Average Net Operating Assets
Home Depot.	HD	$108,203	$15,530	$974	$3,435	$25,217
Lowe's	LOW	71,309	4,018	624	1,080	20,326

a. Compute the following measures for both companies.

	Home Depot	Lowe's
1. Net operating profit (NOPAT)	_____	_____
2. Return on net operating assets (RNOA)	_____	_____
3. Net operating profit margin (NOPM)	_____	_____
4. Net operating asset turnover (NOAT)	_____	_____

b. Indicate which of these two companies:

	Home Depot	Lowe's
1. Is more profitable (in $s).	____	____
2. Produces the higher profit margin (in %).	____	____
3. Uses its NOA more efficiently.	____	____
4. Produces the higher return on NOA.	____	____

Exercises

E4-30. Compute Liquidity and Solvency Ratios for Competing Firms

Halliburton and Schlumberger compete in the oil field services sector. Refer to the following 2018 financial data for the two companies to answer the requirements.

LO9
Halliburton (HAL)
Schlumberger (SLB)

$ millions	HAL	SLB
Cash and equivalents	$ 2,008	$ 1,433
Short-term investments	0	1,344
Accounts receivable	5,234	7,881
Current assets	11,151	15,731
Current liabilities	4,802	13,486
Total liabilities	16,438	33,921
Total equity	9,544	36,586
Earnings before interest and tax (EBIT)	2,467	3,050
Interest expense, gross	554	537

a. Compute the following measures for both companies.

	HAL	SLB
1. Current ratio	____	____
2. Quick ratio	____	____
3. Times interest earned	____	____
4. Liabilities-to-equity	____	____

	HAL	SLB
b. Which company appears more liquid?	____	____
c. Which company appears more solvent?	____	____

E4-31. Compute Cash Conversion Cycle for Competing Firms

Halliburton and Schlumberger compete in the oil field services sector. Refer to the following 2018 financial data for the two companies to answer the requirements.

LO3
Halliburton (HAL)
Schlumberger (SLB)

$ millions	HAL	SLB
Total revenue	$23,995	$32,815
Cost of sales and services	21,009	28,478
Average accounts receivable	5,135	7,983
Average inventory	2,712	4,028
Average accounts payable	2,786	10,130

a. Compute the following measures for both companies.

	HAL	SLB
1. Days sales outstanding (DSO)	____	____
2. Days inventory outstanding (DIO)	____	____
3. Days payables outstanding (DPO)	____	____
4. Cash conversion cycle (CCC)	____	____

	HAL	SLB
b. Which company better manages its accounts receivable?	____	____
c. Which company uses inventory more efficiently?	____	____
d. Which company better manages its accounts payable?	____	____

LO1, 2, 3

3M Company (MMM)

Homework
MBC

E4-32.   Compute and Interpret Measures for DuPont Disaggregation Analysis

Use the information below for 2018 for **3M Company** to answer the requirements (perform these computations from the perspective of a 3M shareholder).

$ millions	2018	2017
Sales.	$32,765	
Net income, consolidated	5,363	
Net income attributable to 3M shareholders.	5,349	
Pretax interest expense, net.	207	
Assets.	36,500	$37,987
Total equity	9,848	11,622
Equity attributable to 3M shareholders.	9,796	11,563

a. Compute return on equity (ROE).

b. Compute the DuPont model components for profit margin (PM), asset turnover (AT), and financial leverage (FL).

c. Compute ROA.

d. Compute adjusted ROA. Assume a statutory tax rate of 22%.

LO6, 7

Halliburton (HAL)

Schlumberger (SLB)

Homework
MBC

E4-33.   Compute, Disaggregate, and Interpret RNOA of Competitors

Halliburton and **Schlumberger** compete in the oil field services sector. Refer to the following 2018 financial data for the two companies to answer the requirements.

$ millions	HAL	SLB
Total revenue	$23,995	$32,815
Pretax net nonoperating expense.	653	426
Net income	1,657	2,177
Average operating assets.	23,361	67,836
Average operating liabilities	5,888	16,499
Marginal tax rate.	22%	19%
Return on equity.	18.56%	5.86%

a. Compute return on net operating assets (RNOA) for each company.

b. Disaggregate RNOA into net operating profit margin (NOPM) and net operating asset turnover (NOAT) for each company.

c. Discuss any differences in these ratios for each company. Identify the factor(s) that drives the differences in RNOA observed from your analyses in parts *a* and *b*.

LO1, 2, 3

KLA-Tencor
Corporation
(KLAC)

Homework
MBC

E4-34.   Disaggregate Traditional DuPont ROE

Graphical representations of the **KLA-Tencor** 2018 income statement and average balance sheet numbers (2017–2018) follow ($ thousands).

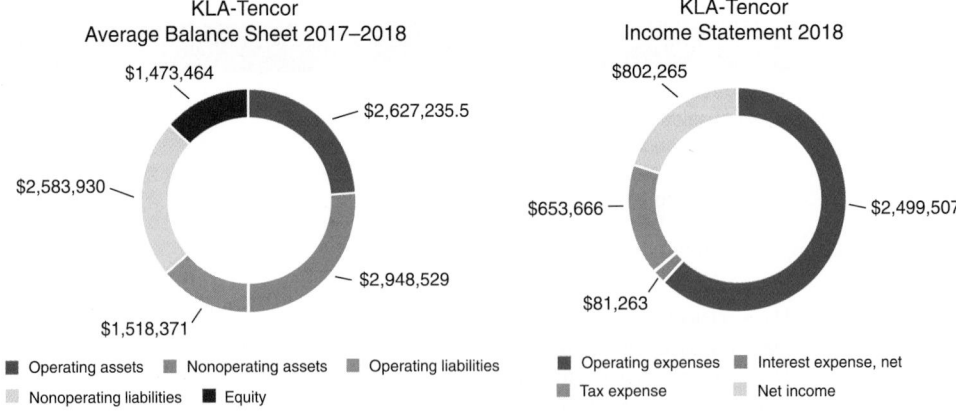

a. Compute return on equity (ROE).

b. Apply the DuPont disaggregation into return on assets (ROA) and financial leverage.

c. Calculate the profitability and productivity components of ROA.

d. Confirm the ROE from part *a.* above with the full DuPont disaggregation: ROE = PM × AT × FL.

E4-35. Compute, Disaggregate, and Interpret ROE and RNOA

LO1, 6, 7
Ingersoll Rand (IR)

Graphical representations of the Ingersoll Rand 2018 income statement and average balance sheets (2017–2018) follow.

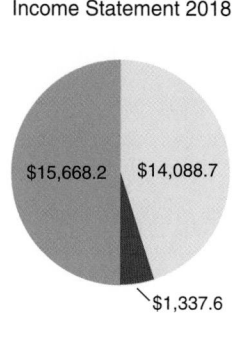

Ingersoll Rand
Income Statement 2018

$15,668.2 $14,088.7

$1,337.6

- Operating expenses including tax on operating profit
- Earning attributable to company shareholders
- Sales

Ingersoll Rand
Average Balance Sheet 2017–2018

$54.4

$7,081.5

$4,077.7 $16,817.7

$6,830.6

$1,226.4

- Operating assets
- Operating liabilities
- Company sharheolders' equity
- Nonoperating assets
- Nonoperating liabilities
- Noncontrolling interest

a. Compute the 2018 return on equity (ROE) and 2018 return on net operating assets (RNOA).

b. Disaggregate RNOA into net operating profit margin (NOPM) and net operating asset turnover (NOAT). What observations can we make about NOPM and NOAT?

c. Compute nonoperating return for 2018.

E4-36. Compute and Compare ROE, ROA, and RNOA

LO1, 2, 6
KLA-Tencor (KLAC)

Refer to the balance sheet and income statement information for KLA-Tencor Corporation in E4-34.

a. Compute return on equity (ROE).

b. Compute return on net assets (ROA).

c. Compute return on net operating assets (RNOA).

d. Compare the three return metrics and explain what each one measures.

E4-37. Directly Compute Nonoperating Return with Noncontrolling Interest

LO8
Abbott Laboratories (ABT)

Selected balance sheet and income statement information from Abbott Laboratories for 2018 follows ($ millions).

Net income	$ 2,368
Net income attributable to Company shareholders	2,368
Net operating profit after tax (NOPAT)	2,940
Net nonoperating expense (NNE)	572
Average net operating assets (NOA)	48,222
Average net nonoperating obligations (NNO)	17,312
Average total equity	30,910
Average equity attributable to Company shareholders	30,711

Compute the following measures a through h.

a. Return on equity = (Net income attributable to Company shareholders/Average equity attributable to Company shareholders)

b. RNOA = NOPAT/Average NOA

c. Nonoperating return = ROE − RNOA

d. NNEP = NNE/Average NNO

e. Spread = RNOA − NNEP

f. FLEV = Average NNO/Average total equity

g. NCI ratio = (Net income attributable to Company shareholders/Net income)/(Average equity attributable to Company shareholders/Average total equity)

h. ROE = (RNOA + (Spread × FLEV)) × NCI ratio

E4-38.   Directly Compute Nonoperating Return with Negative NNO

Selected balance sheet and income statement information from Amgen Inc. for 2018 follows ($ millions).

Net income	$ 8,394
Net operating profit after tax (NOPAT)	8,954
Net nonoperating expense (NNE)	560
Average net operating assets (NOA)	18,015
Average net nonoperating obligations (NNO).	(856)
Average total equity	18,871

Compute the following measures.

a.   Return on equity = Net income/Average total equity
b.   RNOA = NOPAT/Average NOA
c.   Nonoperating return = ROE − RNOA
d.   NNEP = NNE/Average NNO
e.   Spread = RNOA − NNEP
f.   FLEV = Average NNO/Average total equity
g.   ROE = RNOA + (Spread × FLEV)

E4-39.   Compute and Interpret Solvency Ratios

Selected balance sheet and income statement information from TWDC Enterprises from its 2018 Form 10-K follows.

$ millions	2018	2017
Cash and equivalents.	$ 4,150	$ 4,017
Short-term investments	—	—
Accounts receivable	9,334	8,633
Current assets	16,825	15,889
Current liabilities.	17,860	19,595
Total liabilities*	45,766	50,785
Total equity	52,832	45,004
Earnings before interest and tax (EBIT).	14,804	13,775
Interest expense, gross	682	507

*Includes redeemable noncontrolling interests

a.   Compute the following measures for both years.

Measure	2018	2017
1. Current ratio	_____	_____
2. Quick ratio	_____	_____
3. Times interest earned	_____	_____
4. Liabilities-to-equity	_____	_____

	2018	2017
b. In which year does the company appear more liquid?	_____	_____
c. In which year does the company appear more solvent?	_____	_____

E4-40.   Compute NOPAT

The income statement for TJX Companies follows.

TJX COMPANIES	
Consolidated Statement of Income	
Fiscal Year Ended ($ thousands)	**February 2, 2019**
Net sales.	$38,972,934
Cost of sales, including buying and occupancy costs	27,831,177
Selling, general and administrative expenses	6,923,564
Pension settlement charge.	36,122
Interest expense, net	8,860
Income before provision for income taxes	4,173,211
Provision for income taxes	1,113,413
Net income	$ 3,059,798

a. Compute NOPAT using the formula: NOPAT = Net income + NNE.
b. Compute NOPAT using the formula: NOPAT = NOPBT − Tax on operating profit.

Problems

P4-41.   Analysis and Interpretation of Profitability

Balance sheets and income statements for **3M Company** follow.

LO4, 5, 6, 7, 8

3M Company (MMM)

MBC

3M COMPANY Consolidated Statements of Income		
For Years Ended December 31 ($ millions)	**2018**	**2017**
Net sales.	$32,765	$31,657
Operating expenses		
Cost of sales.	16,682	16,055
Selling, general and administrative expenses	7,602	6,626
Research, development and related expenses	1,821	1,870
Gain on sale of businesses	(547)	(586)
Total operating expenses	25,558	23,965
Operating income.	7,207	7,692
Other expense, net*	207	144
Income before income taxes	7,000	7,548
Provision for income taxes	1,637	2,679
Net income including noncontrolling interest	5,363	4,869
Less: Net income attributable to noncontrolling interest.	14	11
Net income attributable to 3M.	$ 5,349	$ 4,858

* Interest expense, gross is $350 million in 2018 and $322 million in 2017.

3M COMPANY Consolidated Balance Sheets		
At December 31 ($ millions)	**2018**	**2017**
Current assets		
Cash and cash equivalents.	$ 2,853	$ 3,053
Marketable securities	380	1,076
Accounts receivable	5,020	4,911
Total inventories	4,366	4,034
Prepaids	741	937
Other current assets	349	266
Total current assets.	13,709	14,277
Property, plant and equipment, net.	8,738	8,866
Goodwill	10,051	10,513
Intangible assets—net	2,657	2,936
Other assets.	1,345	1,395
Total assets	$36,500	$37,987
Current liabilities		
Short-term borrowings and current portion of long-term debt.	$ 1,211	$ 1,853
Accounts payable	2,266	1,945
Accrued payroll.	749	870
Accrued income taxes.	243	310
Other current liabilities	2,775	2,709
Total current liabilities	7,244	7,687
Long-term debt.	13,411	12,096
Pension and postretirement benefits	2,987	3,620
Other liabilities	3,010	2,962
Total liabilities.	26,652	26,365

continued

continued from previous page

3M COMPANY Consolidated Balance Sheets		
At December 31 ($ millions)	2018	2017
3M Company shareholders' equity		
Common stock par value	9	9
Additional paid-in capital.	5,643	5,352
Retained earnings	40,636	39,115
Treasury stock	(29,626)	(25,887)
Accumulated other comprehensive income (loss)	(6,866)	(7,026)
Total 3M Company shareholders' equity	9,796	11,563
Noncontrolling interest	52	59
Total equity	9,848	11,622
Total liabilities and equity	$36,500	$37,987

Required

a. Compute net operating profit after tax (NOPAT) for 2018. Assume that the combined federal and state statutory tax rate is 22%.

b. Compute net operating assets (NOA) for 2018 and 2017.

c. Compute and disaggregate 3M's RNOA into net operating profit margin (NOPM) and net operating asset turnover (NOAT) for 2018. Demonstrate that RNOA = NOPM × NOAT.

d. Compute net nonoperating obligations (NNO) for 2018 and 2017. Confirm the relation: NOA = NNO + Total equity.

e. Compute return on equity (ROE) for 2018.

f. What is the nonoperating return component of ROE for 2018?

g. Comment on the difference between ROE and RNOA. What inference can we draw from this comparison?

LO1, 2, 3

Facebook Inc. (FB)

P4-42. **Compute the DuPont Disaggregation of ROE**

Refer to the balance sheets and income statement below for Facebook Inc.

FACEBOOK INC. Consolidated Statement of Income	
For Year Ended December 31, $ millions	2018
Revenue.	$55,838
Costs and expenses	
Cost of revenue	9,355
Research and development	10,273
Marketing and sales	7,846
General and administrative.	3,451
Total costs and expenses.	30,925
Income from operations	24,913
Interest and other income (expense), net.	448
Income before provision for income taxes	25,361
Provision for income taxes	3,249
Net income	$22,112

FACEBOOK INC. Consolidated Balance Sheet		
At December 31, $ millions	2018	2017
Current assets		
Cash and cash equivalents.	$10,019	$ 8,079
Marketable securities	31,095	33,632
Accounts receivable, net.	7,587	5,832
Prepaid expenses and other current assets	1,779	1,020
Total current assets.	50,480	48,563
Property and equipment, net	24,683	13,721
Intangible assets, net	1,294	1,884
Goodwill	18,301	18,221
Other assets	2,576	2,135
Total assets	$97,334	$84,524
Current liabilities		
Accounts payable	$ 820	$ 380
Partners payable.	541	390
Accrued expenses and other current liabilities	5,509	2,892
Deferred revenue and deposits.	147	98
Total current liabilities	7,017	3,760
Other liabilities	6,190	6,417
Total liabilities	13,207	10,177
Stockholders' equity		
Common stock and additional paid-in capital.	42,906	40,584
Accumulated other comprehensive loss.	(760)	(227)
Retained earnings	41,981	33,990
Total stockholders' equity	84,127	74,347
Total liabilities and stockholders' equity	$97,334	$84,524

Required

a. Compute return on equity (ROE).

b. Apply the DuPont disaggregation into return on assets (ROA) and financial leverage.

c. Calculate the profitability and productivity components of ROA.

d. Confirm the full DuPont disaggregation: ROE = PM × AT × FL.

P4-43.   **Analysis and Interpretation of Liquidity and Solvency**

Refer to the financial information of **3M Company** in P4-41 to answer the following requirements.

LO9
3M Company (MMM)

Required

a. Compute the current ratio and quick ratio for 2018 and 2017. Comment on any observed trends.

b. Compute times interest earned and liabilities-to-equity ratios for 2018 and 2017. Comment on any noticeable changes.

c. Summarize your findings about the company's liquidity and solvency. Do you have any concerns about its ability to meet its debt obligations?

P4-44.   **Direct Computation of Nonoperating Return**

Refer to the financial information of **3M Company** in P4-41 to answer the following requirements. In 2018, 3M's return on equity (ROE) is 50.09% and its return on net operating assets (RNOA) is 25.89%.

LO8
3M Company (MMM)

Required

a. Compute net nonoperating expense (NNE) and net operating profit after tax (NOPAT).

b. Compute net nonoperating obligations (NNO).

c. Compute financial leverage (FLEV).

d. Compute NNEP and Spread.

e. Compute the noncontrolling interest ratio (NCI ratio).

f. Confirm the relation: ROE = [RNOA + (FLEV × Spread)] × NCI ratio.

g. What does the breakdown of nonoperating return imply about the company's use of borrowed funds?

LO4, 5, 6, 7

Costco Wholesale
Corporation (COST)

P4-45.   Analysis and Interpretation of Profitability

Balance sheets and income statements for Costco Wholesale Corporation follow.

COSTCO WHOLESALE CORPORATION Consolidated Statement of Income	
For Fiscal Years Ended ($ millions)	**September 2, 2018**
Total revenue	$141,576
Operating expenses	
Merchandise costs	123,152
Selling, general and administrative	13,876
Preopening expenses	68
Operating income	4,480
Other (income) expense	
Interest expense	159
Interest income and other, net	(121)
Income before income taxes	4,442
Provision for income taxes	1,263
Net income including noncontrolling interests	3,179
Net income attributable to noncontrolling interests	(45)
Net income attributable to Costco	$ 3,134

COSTCO WHOLESALE CORPORATION Consolidated Balance Sheets		
$ millions, except par value and share data	**September 2, 2018**	**September 3, 2017**
Current assets		
Cash and cash equivalents	$ 6,055	$ 4,546
Short-term investments	1,204	1,233
Receivables, net	1,669	1,432
Merchandise inventories	11,040	9,834
Other current assets	321	272
Total current assets	20,289	17,317
Net property and equipment	19,681	18,161
Other assets	860	869
Total assets	$40,830	$36,347
Current liabilities		
Accounts payable	$11,237	$ 9,608
Accrued salaries and benefits	2,994	2,703
Accrued member rewards	1,057	961
Deferred membership fees	1,624	1,498
Other current liabilities	3,014	2,725
Total current liabilities	19,926	17,495
Long-term debt	6,487	6,573
Other liabilities	1,314	1,200
Total liabilities	27,727	25,268
Equity		
Preferred stock $.01 par value	0	0
Common stock $0.01 par value	4	4
Additional paid-in capital	6,107	5,800
Accumulated other comprehensive loss	(1,199)	(1,014)
Retained earnings	7,887	5,988
Total Costco stockholders' equity	12,799	10,778
Noncontrolling interests	304	301
Total equity	13,103	11,079
Total liabilities and equity	$40,830	$36,347

Required

a. Compute net operating profit after tax (NOPAT) for 2018. Assume that the combined federal and state statutory tax rate is 22%.

b. Compute net operating assets (NOA) for 2018 and 2017.

c. Compute and disaggregate Costco's RNOA into net operating profit margin (NOPM) and net operating asset turnover (NOAT) for 2018; confirm that RNOA = NOPM × NOAT.

d. Compute net nonoperating obligations (NNO) for 2018 and 2017. Confirm the relation: NOA = NNO + Total equity.

e. Compute return on equity (ROE) for 2018.

f. Infer the nonoperating return component of ROE for 2018.

g. Comment on the difference between ROE and RNOA. What does this relation suggest about Costco's use of equity capital?

P4-46. **Analysis and Interpretation of Liquidity and Solvency**

Refer to the financial information of Costco Wholesale Corporation in P4-45 to answer the following requirements.

Required

a. Compute Costco's current ratio and quick ratio for 2018 and 2017.

b. Compute Costco's times interest earned and its liabilities-to-equity ratios for 2018 and 2017. In 2017, Costco reported earnings before interest and tax (EBIT) of $4,111 million and interest expense of $134 million.

c. Summarize your findings about the company's liquidity and solvency. Do you have any concerns about Costco's ability to meet its debt obligations?

LO9

Costco Wholesale
Corporation (COST)

P4-47. **Direct Computation of Nonoperating Return with Noncontrolling Interest**

Refer to the financial information of Costco Wholesale Corporation in P4-45 to answer the following requirements. In 2018, Costco's return on equity (ROE) is 26.59% and its return on net operating assets (RNOA) is 26.52%.

Required

a. Compute net nonoperating expense (NNE) and net operating profit after tax (NOPAT).

b. Compute net nonoperating obligations (NNO) for 2018 and 2017.

c. Compute financial leverage (FLEV).

d. Compute NNEP and Spread.

e. Compute the noncontrolling interest ratio (NCI ratio).

f. Confirm the relation: ROE = [RNOA + (FLEV × Spread)] × NCI ratio.

g. What does the breakdown of nonoperating return imply about the company's use of borrowed funds?

LO8

Costco Wholesale
Corporation (COST)

P4-48. **Analysis and Interpretation of Ratios When RNOA Exceeds ROE**

The balance sheets and income statement for Facebook Inc. are found in P4-42. Use these financial statements to answer the requirements.

Required

a. Compute net operating profit after tax (NOPAT) for 2018. Assume that the combined federal and state statutory tax rate is 22%.

b. Compute net operating assets (NOA) for 2018 and 2017.

c. Compute RNOA and disaggregate it into net operating profit margin (NOPM) and net operating asset turnover (NOAT) for 2018.

d. Compute return on equity (ROE) for 2018.

e. Comment on the difference between ROE and RNOA. What is causing this difference?

LO1, 4, 5, 6, 7
Facebook Inc. (FB)

P4-49. **Compute ROE and Nonoperating Return with Negative NNO and No Noncontrolling Interest**

Refer to the balance sheets and income statement for Facebook Inc. in P4-42. Use these financials to answer the requirements. For the 2018 fiscal year, Facebook had a return on net operating assets (RNOA) of 57.54%.

a. Compute ROE.

b. Compute net nonoperating obligations (NNO) for 2018 and 2017, net nonoperating expense (NNE), and the NNE as a percentage of NNO (NNEP), assuming a 22% statutory tax rate.

c. Compute FLEV and Spread.

d. Show that ROE = RNOA + (FLEV × Spread).

e. What is the nonoperating return for the year? Why is it negative? Is Facebook returning as much value to shareholders as possible? Explain.

LO1, 8
Facebook Inc. (FB)

LO4, 5, 6, 7   **P4-50.**   **Analysis and Interpretation of ROE and RNOA with No Noncontrolling Interest**

Netflix Inc. (NFLX)

The 2018 balance sheets and income statement for Netflix Inc. follow. Refer to these financial statements to answer the requirements.

NETFLIX INC. Consolidated Statement of Earnings	
For Year Ended December 31, $ thousands	**2018**
Revenues.	$15,794,341
Cost of revenues	9,967,538
Marketing	2,369,469
Technology and development.	1,221,814
General and administrative.	630,294
Operating income.	1,605,226
Other income (expense)	
Interest expense.	(420,493)
Interest and other income.	41,725
Income before income taxes	1,226,458
Provision for income taxes	15,216
Net income.	$ 1,211,242

NETFLIX INC. Consolidated Balance Sheets		
in thousands, except par value	**2018**	**2017**
Current assets		
Cash and cash equivalents.	$3,794,483	$2,822,795
Current content assets, net.	5,151,186	4,310,934
Other current assets	748,466	536,245
Total current assets.	9,694,135	7,669,974
Noncurrent content assets, net.	14,960,954	10,371,055
Property and equipment, net	418,281	319,404
Other noncurrent assets.	901,030	652,309
Total assets	$25,974,400	$19,012,742
Current liabilities		
Current content liabilities.	$ 4,686,019	$ 4,173,041
Accounts payable	562,985	359,555
Accrued expenses	477,417	315,094
Deferred revenue	760,899	618,622
Total current liabilities	6,487,320	5,466,312
Noncurrent content liabilities	3,759,026	3,329,796
Long-term debt.	10,360,058	6,499,432
Other noncurrent liabilities	129,231	135,246
Total liabilities.	20,735,635	15,430,786
Stockholders' equity		
Preferred stock, $0.001 par value	0	0
Common stock, $0.001 par value.	2,315,988	1,871,396
Accumulated other comprehensive loss.	(19,582)	(20,557)
Retained earnings	2,942,359	1,731,117
Total stockholders' equity.	5,238,765	3,581,956
Total liabilities and stockholders' equity	$25,974,400	$19,012,742

Required

a. Compute net operating profit after tax (NOPAT) for 2018. Assume that the combined federal and state statutory tax rate is 22%.

b. Compute net operating assets (NOA) for 2018 and 2017.

c. Compute RNOA and disaggregate it into net operating profit margin (NOPM) and net operating asset turnover (NOAT) for 2018; confirm that RNOA = NOPM × NOAT.

d. Compute net nonoperating obligations (NNO) for 2018 and 2017. Confirm the relation: NOA = NNO + Shareholders' equity.

e. Compute return on equity (ROE) for 2018.

f. Infer the nonoperating return component of ROE for 2018.

g. Comment on the difference between ROE and RNOA. What does this relation suggest about Netflix's use of equity capital?

P4-51. **Compute and Analyze Measures for DuPont Disaggregation Analysis**

Refer to the 2018 financial data of Netflix Inc. in P4-50 to answer the following requirements.

LO1, 2, 3

Netflix Inc. (NFLX)

Required

a. Compute ROE and ROA for 2018.

b. Confirm that ROE equals ROE computed using the component measures for profit margin, assets turnover, and financial leverage: ROE = PM × AT × FL.

c. Compute adjusted ROA (assume a statutory tax rate of 22%).

P4-52. **Analysis and Interpretation of Profit Margin, Asset Turnover, and RNOA**

Net operating profit margin (NOPM) and net operating asset turnover (NOAT) for several selected companies for the most recent year follow.

LO7

Abbott Laboratories (ABT)

Costco (CSCO)

Netflix (NFLX)

Pfizer (PFE)

3M (MMM)

Halliburton (HAL)

Logitech (LOGI)

TJX (TJX)

Home Depot (HD)

	NOPM	NOAT		NOPM	NOAT
Abbott Laboratories . . .	9.61%	0.63	Halliburton	9.03%	1.37
Costco	2.27%	11.70	Logitech	8.05%	7.16
Netflix	9.54%	1.66	TJX	7.87%	9.32
Pfizer	23.93%	0.60	Home Depot	10.98%	4.29
3M	16.86%	1.54			

Required

a. Use Excel or some other visualization software to graphically represent NOPM and NOAT for each of these companies. Do you see a pattern that is similar to that shown in this module? Explain. (The graph in the module is based on medians for selected industries; the graph for this problem uses fewer companies than in the module and, thus, will not be as smooth.)

b. Consider the trade-off between profit margin and asset turnover. How can we evaluate companies on the profit margin and asset turnover trade-off? Explain.

P4-53. **Compute Cash Conversion Cycle for Competing Firms**

Kellogg's Company and General Mills compete in the consumer packaged goods (CPG) sector. Refer to the following 2018 financial data for the two companies to answer the requirements.

LO9

Kellogg's Company (K)

General Mills (GIS)

$ millions	K	GIS
Total revenue	$13,547.0	$15,740.4
Cost of sales and services	8,821.0	10,312.9
Average accounts receivable	1,382.0	1,557.2
Average inventory	1,273.5	1,562.9
Average accounts payable	2,348.0	2,433.0

a. Compute the following measures for both companies.

	K	GIS
1. Days sales outstanding (DSO)	_____	_____
2. Days inventory outstanding (DIO)	_____	_____
3. Days payables outstanding (DPO)	_____	_____
4. Cash conversion cycle (CCC)	_____	_____

	K	GIS
b. Which company better manages its accounts receivable?	_____	_____
c. Which company uses inventory more efficiently?	_____	_____
d. Which company better manages its accounts payable?	_____	_____

IFRS Applications

LO1, 6, 7
Husky Energy Inc.
(HUSKF)

I4-54.   **Compute, Disaggregate, and Interpret ROE and RNOA**
Headquartered in Calgary, Alberta, Husky Energy Inc. is a publicly traded, integrated energy company. Selected fiscal year balance sheet and income statement information for Husky Energy follow (Canadian $ millions).

C$ millions	2018	2017
Revenues, net	$22,252	
Net income attributable to Husky	1,457	
Pretax NNE	236	
Operating assets	32,231	$30,222
Operating liabilities	9,864	9,520
Equity attributable to Husky shareholders	19,602	17,956
Tax rate	27.20%	

a. Compute the 2018 return on equity (ROE) and the 2018 return on net operating assets (RNOA).
b. Disaggregate RNOA into net operating profit margin (NOPM) and net operating asset turnover (NOAT).
c. Compute the percentage of RNOA to ROE, and compute Husky's nonoperating return for 2018.

LO9
Husky Energy Inc.
(HUSKF)

I4-55.   **Analysis and Interpretation of Liquidity and Solvency**
Headquartered in Calgary, Alberta, Husky Energy Inc. is a publicly traded, integrated energy company. Selected fiscal year balance sheet and income statement information for Husky Energy follow (Canadian $ millions).

C$ millions	2018	2017
Cash and equivalents	$2,866	$2,513
Short-term investments	0	0
Accounts receivable	1,355	1,355
Current assets	5,688	5,616
Current liabilities	4,994	3,507
Total liabilities	15,611	14,960
Total equity	19,614	17,967
Earnings before interest and tax (EBIT)	2,095	724
Interest expense, gross	314	392

Required
a. Compute the current ratio and quick ratio for 2018 and 2017. Comment on any observed trends.
b. Compute times interest earned and liabilities-to-equity ratios for 2018 and 2017. Comment on any noticeable changes.
c. Summarize the findings about the company's liquidity and solvency. Do we have any concerns about Husky Energy's ability to meet its debt obligations?

Management Applications

LO3   **MA4-56.**   **Gross Profit and Strategic Management**
One way to increase overall profitability is to increase gross profit. This can be accomplished by raising prices and/or by reducing manufacturing costs.

Required
a. Will raising prices and/or reducing manufacturing costs unambiguously increase gross profit? Explain.
b. What strategy might you develop as a manager to (i) increase product prices, or (ii) reduce product manufacturing cost?

MA4-57. Asset Turnover and Strategic Management   **LO3**

Increasing net operating asset turnover requires some combination of increasing sales and/or decreasing net operating assets. For the latter, many companies consider ways to reduce their investment in working capital (current assets less current liabilities). This can be accomplished by reducing the level of accounts receivable and inventories, or by increasing the level of accounts payable.

Required

a. Develop a list of suggested actions that you, as a manager, could undertake to achieve these three objectives.

b. Describe the marketing implications of reducing receivables and inventories, and the supplier implications of delaying payment. How can a company reduce working capital without negatively impacting its performance?

MA4-58. Ethics and Governance: Earnings Management   **LO3**

Companies are aware that analysts focus on profitability in evaluating financial performance. Managers have historically utilized a number of methods to improve reported profitability that are cosmetic in nature and do not affect "real" operating performance. These methods are subsumed under the general heading of "earnings management." Justification for such actions typically includes the following arguments:

- Increasing stock price by managing earnings benefits stockholders; thus, no one is hurt by these actions.
- Earnings management is a temporary fix; such actions will be curtailed once "real" profitability improves, as managers expect.

Required

a. Identify the affected parties in any scheme to manage profits to prop up stock price.

b. Do the ends (of earnings management) justify the means? Explain.

c. To what extent are the objectives of managers different from those of stockholders?

d. What governance structure can you envision that might inhibit earnings management?

Ongoing Project

(This ongoing project began in Module 1 and continues through most of the book; even if previous segments were not completed, the requirements are still applicable to any business analysis.)

Analysis of financial statements commonly includes ROE disaggregation and scrutiny of its components as explained in this module.

1. Compute ROE for all three years reported on the income statement. (*Hint:* Do your companies report noncontrolling interest on the income statement and balance sheet? If so, make certain to use income available to the controlling interest (NICI) in the numerator and equity of the controlling interest (CI) in the denominator. To compute ROE for three years, we must determine average stockholders' equity for three years, which means we need four balance sheet amounts. Because the balance sheets of each company will report only two years, we must collect prior years' financial statements.)

2. Compute RNOA and its two components (NOPM and NOAT) for all three years reported on the income statement. We must use balance sheet numbers for four years to obtain three averages of net operating assets. Examine the income statements and balance sheets to determine the operating and nonoperating items. (*Hint:* Use an online source to understand any line items not described in the textbook. Use cell references in the spreadsheet to compute NOPAT and NOA and the various ratios.)

Compare ROE and RNOA and identify differences over time and between the companies. Evaluate the companies' returns and answer questions such as the following:

- Which company is more profitable?
- How do the operating and nonoperating portions of ROE compare?
- Compare the ROE and RNOA with the graph on page 4-25. If the ratios for the companies under analysis differ from the graph, is there an explanation?
- Is the net operating profit margin similar for the two companies? Given that they are roughly in the same industry, major differences should prompt further exploration.
- Are the companies' net operating asset turnover ratios similar or markedly different? Calculate and compare the cash conversion cycle for each year.

3. Determine FLEV and Spread and the noncontrolling interest ratio (if applicable). Show that:

$$\text{ROE} = [\text{RNOA} + (\text{FLEV} \times \text{Spread})] \times \textbf{Noncontrolling interest ratio}$$

Compare the components of the equation for each company over time and follow up on any differences.

4. Compute the four ratios from Appendix 4C for the recent three years for each company: current ratio, quick ratio, liabilities-to-equity, and times interest earned. Compare the ratios for the companies under analysis and identify differences over time and between companies. Evaluate each company's ability to pay its debts in the short term (liquidity) and the long term (solvency), and in the process address the following:

- Which company is more liquid? More solvent?
- Look at the bar chart in Exhibit 4C.1. If the ratios differ from the industry norm, is there an explanation(s)?
- Do the ratios change over time? If yes, does the change make sense given the economic and competitive factors that affect the industry and the companies?

Solutions to Review Problems

Review 4-1—Solution ($ millions)

$$\text{ROE} = \frac{\$3,553}{(\$11,730 + \$9,980)/2} = 32.73\%$$

Review 4-2—Solution ($ millions)

ROE = Return on assets (ROA) × Financial leverage

$$\text{ROA} = \frac{\$3,553}{(\$27,229 + \$22,197)/2} = 14.38\% \qquad \text{Financial leverage (FL)} = \frac{(\$27,229 + \$22,197)/2}{(\$11,730 + \$9,980)/2} = 2.28$$

ROE = 14.38% × 2.28 = 32.79% (.0006 rounding difference)

Review 4-3—Solution ($ millions)

a. $\text{ROA} = \dfrac{\$3,553}{(\$27,229 + \$22,197)/2} = 14.38\%$

$\text{PM} = \dfrac{\$3,553}{\$13,601} = 26.12\%$

$\text{AT} = \dfrac{\$13,601}{(\$27,229 + \$22,197)/2} = 0.55$

ROA = Profit Margin (PM) × Asset Turnover (AT)

ROA = 26.1% × 0.55 = 14.35% (0.0002 rounding difference)

b. Gross profit margin = ($13,601 − $4,663)/$13,601 = 65.72%

c. Days sales outstanding = 365 × [($2,332 + $2,198)/2]/$13,601 = 60.8

Days inventory outstanding = 365 × [($2,955 + $2,465)/2]/$4,663 = 212.1

Days accounts payable outstanding = 365 × [($646 + $487)/2]/$4,663 = 44.3

Cash conversion cycle = 60.8 + 212.1 − 44.3 = 228.6

d. $15,499/$11,730 = 1.32

Review 4-4—Solution ($ millions)

a.

$ millions	2018	2017
Accounts receivable	$ 2,332	$ 2,198
Inventories	2,955	2,465
Prepaid expenses and other current assets	747	537
Property, plant and equipment, net.	2,291	1,975
Goodwill	8,563	7,168
Other intangibles, net	4,163	3,477
Noncurrent deferred income tax assets	1,678	283
Other noncurrent assets	801	1,301
Total operating assets	$23,530	$19,404
Accounts payable	$ 646	$ 487
Accrued compensation	917	838
Income taxes	158	143
Accrued expenses and other liabilities	1,521	1,207
Income taxes	1,228	1,261
Other noncurrent liabilities	978	881
Total operating liabilities	$ 5,448	$ 4,817

b.

$ millions
2018 NOA = $23,530 − $5,448 = $18,082
2017 NOA = $19,404 − $4,817 = $14,587

Review 4-5—Solution ($ millions)

a. NOPBT = Sales − Cost of Sales − Operating expenses = $13,601 − $4,663 − $6,401 = $2,537

b. Tax on operating profit = Tax expense or benefit + [Pretax net nonoperating expense × Statutory tax rate]
= $(1,197) + [181 × 22%] = $(1,197) + $40 = $(1,157).

Because of the new tax act changes, the company has a tax benefit (which is why it's a negative number).

c. NOPAT = NOPBT − Tax on operating profit = $2,537 − $(1,157) = $3,694

d. NNE = Pretax net nonoperating expense × (1 − Tax rate) = $181 × (1 − 22%) = $141

e. NOPAT = Net income + NNE = $3,553 + $141 = $3,694

Review 4-6—Solution ($ millions)

a. $\text{RNOA} = \dfrac{\$3,694}{(\$18,082 + \$14,587)/2} = 22.62\%$

b. RNOA/ROE = 22.62%/32.73% = 69.11%.

Nearly 70% of the return to shareholders comes from the company's operating activities. Thus, about 30% is the effect of financial leverage.

Review 4-7—Solution ($ millions)

$\text{NOPM} = \dfrac{\$3,694}{\$13,601} = 27.16\%$

$\text{NOAT} = \dfrac{\$13,601}{(\$18,082 + \$14,587)/2} = 0.833$

RNOA = Net Operating Profit Margin (NOPM) × Net Operating Asset Turnover (NOAT)

$= 27.16\% \times 0.833 = 22.62\%$

Review 4-8—Solution ($ millions)

a. ROE = Operating return (RNOA) + Nonoperating return
32.73% = 22.62% + 10.11%

b.

	2018	2017
Dividend payable	$ 192	$ 178
Current maturities of debt	1,373	632
Long-term debt, excluding current maturities	8,486	6,590
Nonoperating liabilities	$10,051	$7,400
Cash and cash equivalents	$ 3,616	$2,542
Marketable securities	83	251
Nonoperating assets	$ 3,699	$2,793
NNO = Nonoperating liabilities − Nonoperating assets	$ 6,352	$4,607
Equity	$11,730	$9,980

$\text{FLEV} = \text{Average NNO/Average Total Equity}$

$$= \frac{[\$6,352 + \$(4,607)]/2}{(\$11,730 + \$9,980)/2} = 0.505$$

c.

Pretax net nonoperating expense	$181
Less Tax shield @ 22%	40
NNE	$141

$$\text{NNEP} = \frac{\$141}{(\$6,352 + \$4,607)/2} = 2.57\%$$

d. Spread = RNOA − NNEP

$\qquad$ = 22.62% − 2.57%

$\qquad$ = 20.05%

e. ROE = RNOA + (FLEV × Spread)

$\qquad$ = 22.62% + (0.505 × 20.05%)

$\qquad$ = 32.74% (0.001 rounding difference)

Review 4-9—Solution ($ millions)

a. Current ratio 2018: $9,733/$4,807 = 2.02

$\quad$ Quick ratio 2018: ($3,616 + $83 + $2,332)/$4,807 = 1.25

b. Liabilities-to-equity ratio 2018: $15,499/$11,730 = 1.32

$\quad$ Times interest earned ratio 2018: $2,537/$181 = 14.02

Module 5

Revenues, Receivables, and Operating Expenses

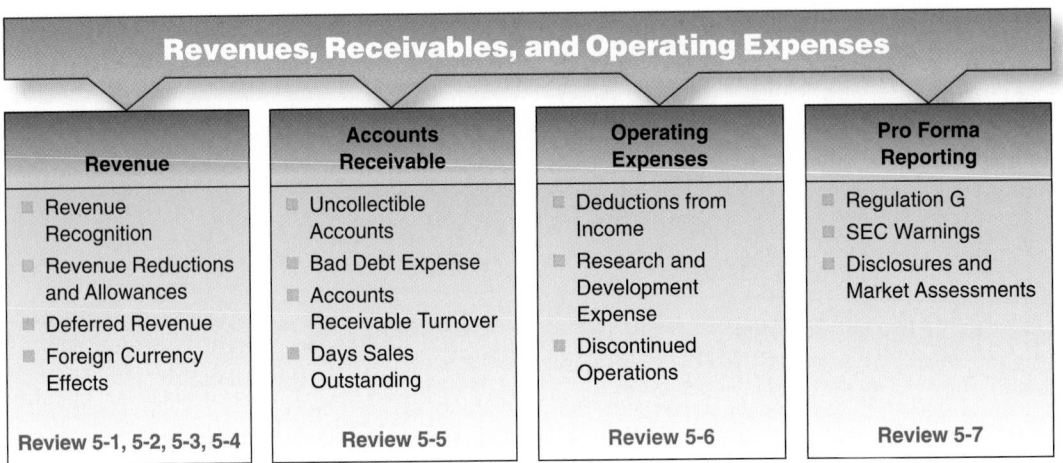

Revenues, Receivables, and Operating Expenses			
Revenue	**Accounts Receivable**	**Operating Expenses**	**Pro Forma Reporting**
■ Revenue Recognition ■ Revenue Reductions and Allowances ■ Deferred Revenue ■ Foreign Currency Effects	■ Uncollectible Accounts ■ Bad Debt Expense ■ Accounts Receivable Turnover ■ Days Sales Outstanding	■ Deductions from Income ■ Research and Development Expense ■ Discontinued Operations	■ Regulation G ■ SEC Warnings ■ Disclosures and Market Assessments
Review 5-1, 5-2, 5-3, 5-4	Review 5-5	Review 5-6	Review 5-7

■ We examine how companies recognize revenue and account for sales returns and allowances, revenue paid in advance, and the effects of foreign currency exchange rates.

■ We describe the accounting for and analysis of accounts receivable, the account most closely related to revenue.

■ We discuss the typical expenses in income statements, including:

- Cost of sales
- Selling, general and administrative (SG&A) expense
- Research and development (R&D) expense
- Amortization of intangible assets
- Restructuring expenses
- Income tax expense

■ We explain discontinued operations and the reporting of them.

■ We examine income attributable to noncontrolling interests.

■ We review pro forma income reporting.

■ We use Pfizer Inc. as the focus company and the dashboard below conveys some key financial results.

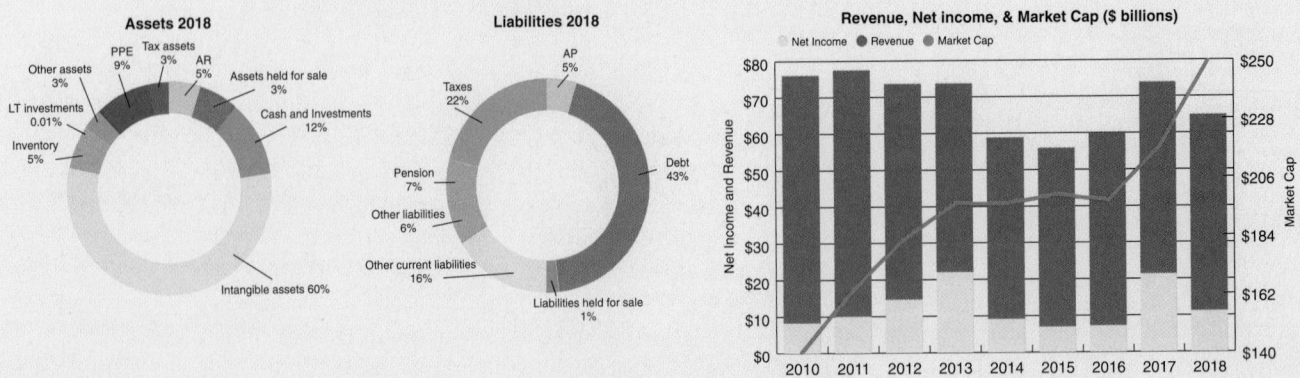

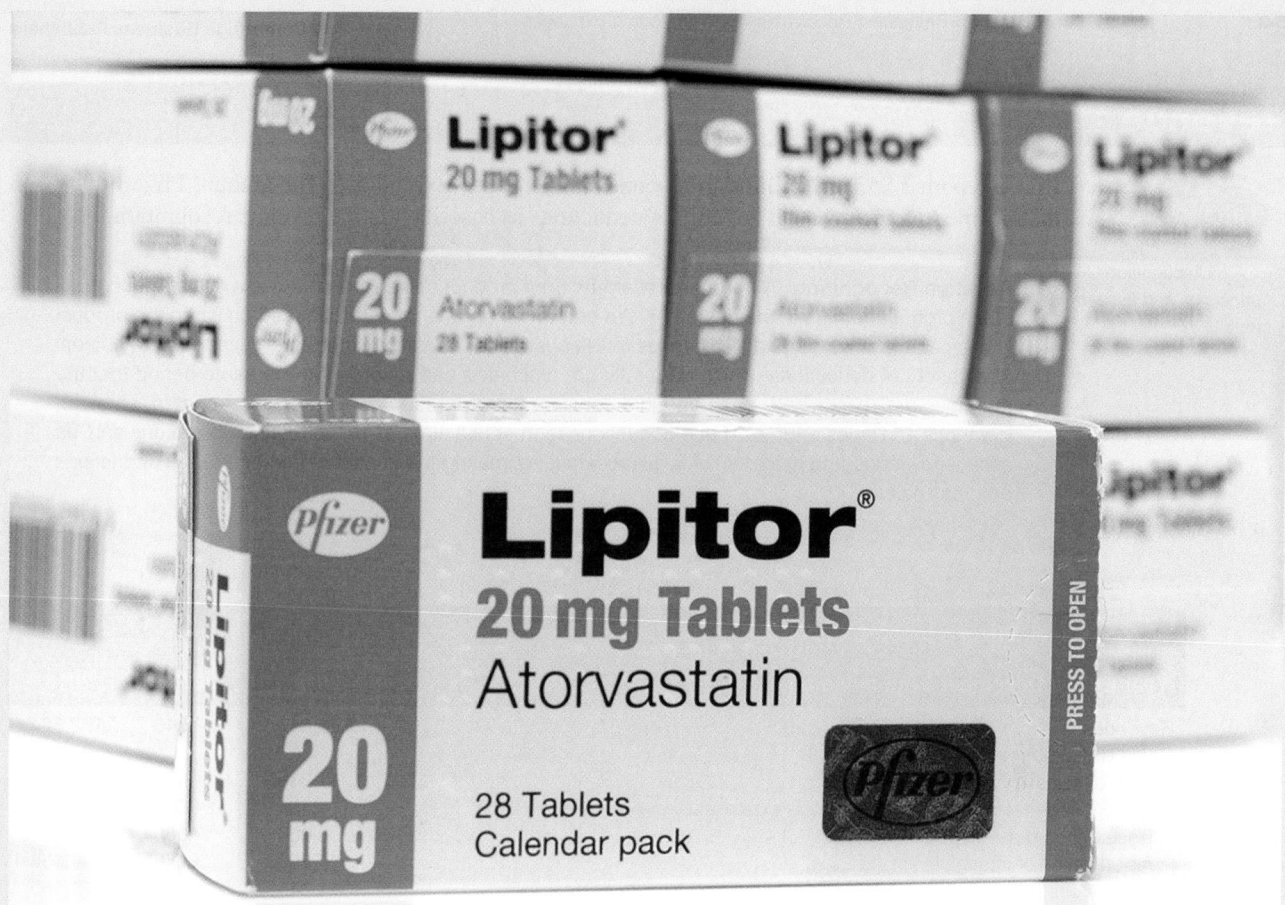

Road Map

LO	Learning Objective | Topics	Page	eLecture	Guided Example	Assignments
5-1	**Apply revenue recognition principles and assess results.** Recognition Rules :: Complications :: Long-Term Contracts :: Reporting	5-3	e5–1	Review 5-1	1, 8, 12, 13, 14, 15, 17, 29, 31, 32, 33, 34, 35, 40, 49, 51, 53, 54, 55, 56, 59, 61
5-2	**Examine and evaluate sales allowances.** Accounting :: Reporting & Disclosure :: Analysis	5-11	e5–2	Review 5-2	3, 17, 25, 51
5-3	**Analyze deferred revenue.** Accounting :: Illustrations :: Disclosure and Interpretation	5-14	e5–3	Review 5-3	10, 23, 24, 26, 29, 47, 55
5-4	**Evaluate how foreign currency exchange rates affect revenue.** Economics :: Cash Flows :: Income :: Forecasting	5-15	e5–4	Review 5-4	5, 6, 22, 27, 36, 39, 60
5-5	**Analyze accounts receivable and uncollectible amounts.** Aging :: Accounting :: Magnitude Analysis :: Quality Analysis	5-19	e5–5	Review 5-5	2, 7, 18, 19, 20, 21, 42, 43, 44, 45, 46, 49, 56, 58
5-6	**Evaluate operating expenses and discontinued operations.** Cost of Sales :: SG&A :: R&D :: Discontinued Operations	5-25	e5–6	Review 5-6	4, 11, 28, 30, 37, 38, 41, 48, 52, 57, 59
5-7	**Interpret pro forma and non-GAAP disclosures.** Regulation G :: SEC Warnings :: Market Assessments	5-31	e5–7	Review 5-7	9, 16, 39, 50

Revenue

eLectures
MBC

LO1
Apply revenue recognition principles and assess results.

Pfizer reported $53,647 million in revenues in 2018; see Exhibit 5.1. The amount Pfizer reports on the income statement is "net" of certain deductions as described in the revenue recognition footnote.

> **Revenue Recognition**   We record revenues from product sales when there is a transfer of control of the product from us to the customer. We determine transfer of control based on when the product is shipped or delivered and title passes to the customer. . . Our gross product revenues are subject to a variety of deductions, which generally are estimated and recorded in the same period that the revenues are recognized. Such variable consideration represents chargebacks, rebates, sales allowances and sales returns. These deductions represent estimates of the related obligations and, as such, knowledge and judgment is required when estimating the impact of these revenue deductions on gross sales.

Exhibit 5.1 ■ Pfizer's Income Statement

Year Ended December 31 ($ millions)	2018	2017	2016
Revenues	$53,647	$52,546	$52,824
Costs and expenses			
Cost of sales	11,248	11,228	12,322
Selling, informational, and administrative expenses	14,455	14,804	14,844
Research and development expenses	8,006	7,683	7,892
Amortization of intangible assets	4,893	4,758	4,056
Restructuring charges and certain acquisition-related costs	1,044	351	1,565
Other deductions—net	2,116	1,416	3,794
Income from continuing operations before provision (benefit) for taxes on income	11,885	12,305	8,351
Provision (benefit) for taxes on income	706	(9,049)	1,123
Income from continuing operations	11,179	21,353	7,229
Discontinued operations			
Income from discontinued operations—net of tax	10	(1)	16
Gain/(loss) on disposal of discontinued operations—net of tax	0	3	0
Discontinued operations—net of tax	10	2	17
Net income before allocation to noncontrolling interests	11,189	21,355	7,246
Less: Net income attributable to noncontrolling interests	36	47	31
Net income attributable to Pfizer Inc.	$11,153	$21,308	$ 7,215

The revenue recognition footnote shown above raises a number of issues related to revenue.

- **Revenue recognition.** Should revenue be recognized when an order is received? When products are shipped? When they are paid for? How should we recognize revenue for long-term contracts spanning more than one year?

- **Sales and related allowances.** How should we treat the various revenue deductions Pfizer references in its revenue footnote?

- **Deferred revenue.** How should we treat advance payments made by customers? Should we only recognize revenue when we receive cash?

- **Foreign currency exchange rates.** How do we account for revenues that are denominated in foreign currencies? In what way do fluctuations in exchange rates affect Pfizer's income statement?

Revenue (or sales) is the "top line" on the income statement and it includes transactions between the company and its customers during the past year (or, in the case of quarterly reports, during the prior three months). Revenue does not include gains or losses on the sale of assets such as property, plant and equipment (PPE) or investments (or the divestiture of a subsidiary company), nor does it include interest and dividend income on investments or gains or losses on their sale. Those items appear in different sections of the income statement.

Revenue Recognition Rules

New revenue recognition rules from the Financial Accounting Standards Board (FASB) went into effect for financial reporting periods beginning after December 15, 2017. The new rules modify the way in which companies recognize revenue (see the details in the text box below) but the core revenue recognition principles remain the same.

■ Recognize revenue when the company transfers a good or service to a customer; that is, when the customer obtains control of that good or service.

■ It is not necessary to receive cash to recognize revenue.

Every sale involves a contract (express or implied) between the customer and the company whereby the company agrees to transfer a good or service to the customer and the customer agrees to pay for it. All that is necessary for the company to recognize revenue is for the good to be transferred or the service performed. It is at that point the company's *performance obligation* under the contract is satisfied and revenue can be recognized.

Many sales are *on credit* (with accounts receivable), meaning the customer has agreed to pay the company in the future. The company still recognizes revenue when the good or service is transferred to the customer, and it records an account receivable that it will collect at a later date. The recognition of revenue is unaffected by the delayed receipt of cash if the company has fulfilled its performance obligation. (We discuss accounting for accounts receivable later in this module.)

When is the good or service transferred to the customer and the performance obligation satisfied? GAAP provides examples of evidence; a transfer is likely when:

■ The customer has legal title to the goods or services purchased.

■ The company has physically transferred the goods sold or has performed the service.

■ The risks and rewards of ownership of the goods or service purchased transfer to the customer.

■ The customer has accepted the goods or service and has agreed to pay the seller.

Manager Insights ■ Revenue Recognition in Practice

Revenue recognition can get complicated in practice, especially if the company sells a bundle of goods for a single price or delivers the goods over a period of time. **Microsoft** provides an example from its 2018 10-K.

> Revenue is recognized upon transfer of control of promised products or services to customers in an amount that reflects the consideration we expect to receive in exchange for those products or services. . . Our contracts with customers often include promises to transfer multiple products and services to a customer.

To recognize revenue, Microsoft first identifies each product and service that it sells and, then, sets a market price for that product or service. Although this may seem simple, Microsoft's contracts with customers often include the sale of multiple products and services for one contract price. This raises a number of product and service identification issues.

- When a cloud-based service includes both on-premises software licenses and cloud services, judgment is required to determine whether the software licenses are considered distinct (and accounted for separately) or not distinct and accounted for together with the cloud service and recognized over time.
- Certain cloud services depend on a significant level of integration, interdependency, and interrelation with the desktop applications. Consequently, the cloud services and desktop apps are accounted for together as one performance obligation even if the products or services can be separately identified.
- Some revenues are not recognized all at once. Revenues from the Office 365 software, for example, are recognized ratably over the period in which the cloud services are provided.

continued

continued from previous page

There are also issues with determining the selling price, where judgment is required to determine the stand-alone selling price for each distinct performance obligation. If the products are sold separately, the price is usually determinable. But, in instances where stand-alone selling price is not directly observable, such as when Microsoft does not sell the product or service separately, the company must estimate the value of each product sold. Following is Microsoft's discussion of how it determines selling prices.

> Judgment is required to determine the stand-alone selling price ("SSP") for each distinct performance obligation. We use a single amount to estimate SSP for items that are not sold separately. . . We use a range of amounts to estimate SSP when we sell each of the products and services separately and need to determine whether there is a discount to be allocated based on the relative SSP of the various products and services.
>
> In instances where SSP is not directly observable, such as when we do not sell the product or service separately, we determine the SSP using information that may include market conditions and other observable inputs. We typically have more than one SSP for individual products and services due to the stratification of those products and services by customers and circumstances. In these instances, we may use information such as the size of the customer and geographic region in determining the SSP.

The FASB issued *Accounting Standards Update 2014-09 Revenue from Contracts with Customers (Topic 606)* that changed the way revenue is recognized starting in 2018 for most firms. The core principle of the new standard is that companies should recognize revenue relating to the transfer of promised goods or services to customers in an amount that reflects *the consideration to which the company expects to be entitled* in exchange for those goods or services. To achieve that core principle, companies need to apply the following steps.

1. **Identify the contract(s) with a customer.** The parties to the contract should be identifiable and the terms of the sale should be specified (including the items sold, the delivery terms, and the payments required).
2. **Identify the performance obligation(s) in the contract.** A performance obligation is the company's contractual promise to transfer a good or service to the customer. If the contract involves the transfer of more than one good or service to the customer, the company needs to account for each promised good or service as a separate performance obligation and recognize revenue separately for each.
3. **Determine the transaction price.** If the purchase price is variable, say dependent upon contingencies, the company should estimate revenue using the *expected* purchase price.
4. **Allocate the transaction price to the performance obligation(s).** For contracts with more than one performance obligation, the company must allocate the transaction price to *each* performance obligation at its *fair value*, that is, the standalone selling price of the distinct goods or services underlying each performance obligation. If published, standalone prices are not available, the company must use a reasonable estimate of the selling price.
5. **Recognize revenue when the performance obligation is satisfied.** Companies should recognize revenue when they satisfy the performance obligation—that is, when the customer obtains control of the goods or services. This will generally be when the company transfers the goods or services to the customer. Performance obligations that are satisfied over a period of time should be recognized as revenue over time.

Complications of Revenue Recognition

In retail settings, revenue recognition is straightforward: revenue is recognized at the point of sale. The customer takes physical possession of the purchased goods and the store immediately satisfies its performance obligation. In other settings, it can be more challenging. Following are some common types of transactions with complicated revenue recognition. Even though each of these situations is a bit more involved than a retail sale, the basic requirement for revenue recognition is the same: recognize revenue when the good or service is transferred to the customer.

■ **Nonrefundable up-front fees.** In some industries, companies charge a fee at or near inception of the contract. These fees could be for setup, access, activation, initiation, or membership. In many cases, even though a nonrefundable up-front fee compels the company to undertake an activity at or near contract inception, that activity does not result in the transfer of the goods or service. Instead, the fee is an advance payment for future goods or services and, therefore, would be recognized as revenue when those future goods or services are provided.

■ **Bill-and-hold arrangements.** Bill-and-hold arrangements arise when a customer is billed for goods that are ready for delivery, but the company "holds" the goods for shipment later. Revenue is recognized at the later date, when control of the goods transfers to the customer.

■ **Consignment sales.** If the seller acts as an *agent* for another company, such as to sell another company's product on its website, it does not recognize the gross amount of the sale as revenue. Instead, it only recognizes its *commission* from the sale. Indicators that the seller is an agent include when the seller:

- Is not responsible for fulfilling the contract.
- Does not bear any risk associated with the inventory being sold.
- Does not have full control over the selling price.
- Does not bear the risk of loss for uncollectible accounts receivable.
- Receives commission or another fee from the sale.

■ **Licenses.** Software sales can take the form of licensing arrangements of intellectual property (IP). Revenue recognition depends on whether the arrangement confers a right to *use* the IP (arguing for recognition of revenue when the customer can first use the IP) or whether the contract promises to provide *access* to the company's IP (arguing for revenue recognition over a period of time).

■ **Franchises.** Franchisors often sell both goods and consulting and other administrative services. The franchisor must separate the sale into separate components for goods and services and recognize the appropriate revenue for each component. The goods component is recognized when the goods are transferred to the buyer. The services component might involve use of a trade name or a license or other services that are provided over time. In such cases, revenue should be recognized as the services are delivered.

■ **Variable consideration.** Portions of the selling price may depend upon future events, such as incentive payments, royalties, and volume discounts. If the good or service has been transferred to the customer and the payment is likely and can be reasonably estimated, the seller should estimate the expected amount to be received and recognize that amount in current revenue.

■ **Multiple-element-contracts.** Many companies bundle multiple products and services together for one price. The added complication is that the seller might deliver some products and services at the point of sale and others in the future. In such cases, the seller must first separate the sale into distinct goods or services (components) that can each be valued on a stand-alone basis. Then, revenue is recognized separately on each distinct component (see the Manager Insight box for a discussion of how Microsoft deals with its multi-element contracts). Components are generally viewed as distinct if the:

- Customer can use the good or service on its own.
- Good or service is not highly interrelated with other goods or services sold per the contract.

■ **Right of return.** Retailers typically offer a right of return if the customer is not satisfied with the product. Companies estimate the dollar amount of goods that are likely to be returned and deduct that amount from gross sales to arrive as the net sales reported in the income statement. We discuss rights of return and other sales allowances later in this module.

■ **Gift cards.** When cash is received from the customer, the company records the receipt of cash and a deferred revenue liability. Then, revenue is recognized when the gift card is used by the customer to purchase goods or services. We discuss deferred revenue later in this module.

Performance Obligations Satisfied Over Time

Many companies enter into long-term contracts that obligate them to future performance. For example:

- **Spitz Inc.** enters into a construction contract with Disney World to design, manufacture, and install massive projection domes in the new Guardians of the Galaxy roller coaster experience.

- **Boeing** enters into a contract with domestic and international airlines and the U.S. military to construct planes.

- **Tata Consultancy Services** enters into long-term contracts with companies to design IT services, implement systems, and provide cloud-based services.

For these types of contracts, companies must determine the point at which their performance obligations have been satisfied so that revenue can be recognized. For a multiple-year contract, waiting to recognize revenue until the good is delivered would be problematic because the expense of constructing the product would be recognized as incurred whereas the revenue recorded only at the end of the contract. Although total revenue, expense, and profit would be accurate over the life of the contract, financial statements issued during the interim would report losses with a substantial profit at the end, making evaluation of the company's financial performance difficult during the interim.

Cost-to-Cost Method An accepted practice for many years has been to recognize revenue over the life of a long-term contract in amounts that track the percentage of completion of the contract. Companies typically use the percentage of projected contract costs that have been incurred to estimate the contract's percentage of completion. This method is called the *cost-to-cost method*. (There are other ways to determine percentage of completion, but cost-to-cost is the most common.) For example, if a company incurred 15% of the total expected cost to create the product in the current period, it would recognize revenues equal to 15% of the contract amount. **Raytheon**, a U.S. conglomerate ranked 114 among the Fortune 500, specializes in aerospace, defense, civil government, and cybersecurity. The company describes its revenue recognition practice as follows.

> Because of control transferring over time, revenue is recognized based on the extent of progress towards completion of the performance obligation. . . We generally use the cost-to-cost measure of progress for our contracts because it best depicts the transfer of control to the customer which occurs as we incur costs on our contracts. Under the cost-to-cost measure of progress, the extent of progress towards completion is measured based on the ratio of costs incurred to date, to the total estimated costs at completion of the performance obligation. Revenues, including estimated fees or profits, are recorded proportionally as costs are incurred.

To illustrate accounting for long-term contracts using the *cost-to-cost* approach, assume Raytheon signs a $10 million contract to develop a prototype for a defense system. Bayer estimates construction will take two years and will cost $7,500,000. This means the contract yields an expected gross profit of $2,500,000 over two years. The following table summarizes costs incurred each year and the revenue Raytheon recognizes.

	Costs Incurred	Percentage Complete	Revenue Recognized
Year 1	$4,500,000	$\frac{\$4,500,000}{\$7,500,000} = 60\%$	$10,000,000 × 60% = $6,000,000
Year 2	$3,000,000	$\frac{\$3,000,000}{\$7,500,000} = 40\%$	$10,000,000 × 40% = $4,000,000

This table reveals Raytheon would report $6 million in revenue and $1.5 million ($6 million − $4.5 million) in gross profit on the project in the first year; it would report $4 million in revenue and $1 million ($4 million − $3 million) in gross profit in the second year.

The following template captures the recognition of revenue and expense over this two-year period (M indicates millions).

	Balance Sheet						Income Statement				
Transaction	Cash Asset	+ Noncash Assets	= Liabil- ities	+ Contrib. Capital	+ Earned Capital		Rev- enues	− Expen- ses	= Net Income		
Year 1: Re- cord $4.5M costs	−4.5M Cash	=			−4.5M Retained Earnings			− +4.5M Cost of Sales	= −4.5M		COGS.... 4.5M Cash ....4.5M COGS 4.5M | Cash | 4.5M
Year 1: Recognize $6M revenue on partly completed contract		+6M Accounts Receivable =			+6M Retained Earnings		+6M Revenue	−	= +6M		AR...... 6M REV.......... 6M AR 6M | REV | 6M
Year 2: Re- cord $3M costs	−3M Cash	=			−3M Retained Earnings			− +3M Cost of Sales	= −3M		COGS... 3M Cash .... 3M COGS 3M | Cash | 3M
Year 2: Rec- ognize $4M revenue for completed contract		+4M Accounts Receivable =			+4M Retained Earnings		+4M Revenue	−	= +4M		AR...... 4M Rev .... 4M AR 4M | Rev | 4M

Cost-to-Cost Reporting Raytheon's reported revenues and expenses for years 1 and year 2 follow.

At December 31	Year 1	Year 2
Revenues	$6,000,000	$4,000,000
Expenses	4,500,000	3,000,000
Gross profit	$1,500,000	$1,000,000

Over the two-year period, Raytheon recognizes total revenues of $10 million, contract expenses of $7.5 million, and a contract gross profit of $2.5 million.

How Raytheon recognizes profit on long-term contracts affects its income statements. In addition, there are often timing differences between when contract costs are paid and when the customer is billed for work performed. These timing differences affect the balance sheet. Raytheon describes the accounting for these timing differences in the following footnote.

> Under the typical payment terms of our U.S. government fixed-price contracts, the customer pays us either performance based payments (PBPs) or progress payments ... Because the customer retains a portion of the contract price until completion of the contract, our U.S. government fixed-price contracts generally result in revenue recognized in excess of billings which we present as contract assets on the balance sheet. Amounts billed and due from our customers are classified as receivables on the balance sheet. ... For non-U.S. government contracts, we typically receive interim payments as work progresses, although for some contracts, we may be entitled to receive an advance payment. We recognize a liability for these advance payments in excess of revenue recognized and present it as contract liabilities on the balance sheet.

When Raytheon receives cash in advance of incurring costs under the contract, it records a liability that represents the obligation to deliver the product for which it has been paid. When Raytheon incurs costs to construct the product in excess of the amount it bills the customer, it recognizes that excess as a current asset, contracts in process, as illustrated in the "current assets" section of Raytheon's 2018 balance sheet.

At December 31 ($ millions)	2018	2017
Current assets		
Cash and cash equivalents.	$ 3,608	$ 3,103
Short-term investments.	—	297
Receivables, net.	1,648	1,324
Contract assets.	**5,594**	**5,247**
Inventories	758	594
Prepaid expenses and other current assets	528	761
Total current assets.	$12,136	$11,326

The cost-to-cost method of revenue recognition requires an estimate of total costs. This estimate is made at the beginning of the contract and is typically the one used to bid the contract. However, estimates are inherently inaccurate. If the estimate changes during the construction period, the percentage of completion is computed as the total costs incurred to date divided by the *current* estimate of total anticipated costs (costs incurred to date plus total estimated costs to complete).

If total construction costs are underestimated, the percentage of completion is overestimated (the denominator is too low) and revenue and gross profit to date are overstated. The estimation process inherent in this method has the potential for inaccurate or even improper revenue recognition. In addition, estimates of remaining costs to complete projects are difficult for the auditors to verify. This uncertainty adds additional risk to financial statement analysis.

Business Insight   Disney's Revenue Recognition

The Walt Disney Company uses a percentage of completion method similar to the cost-to-cost method to determine the amount of production cost to match against film and television revenues. Following is an excerpt from its 10-K.

> **Film and Television Revenues and Costs**   We expense film and television production, participation and residual costs over the applicable product life cycle based upon the ratio of the current period's revenues to the estimated remaining total revenues (Ultimate Revenues) for each production... For film productions, Ultimate Revenues include revenues from all sources that will be earned within ten years from the date of the initial theatrical release. For television series, Ultimate Revenues include revenues that will be earned within ten years from delivery of the first episode, or if still in production, five years from delivery of the most recent episode, if later.

As Disney pays production costs, it records those costs on the balance sheet as inventory. Then, as film and television revenues are recognized, the company matches a portion of production costs (from inventory) against revenues in computing income. Each period, the costs recognized are equal to the proportion of total revenues recognized in the period to the total revenues expected over the "product life cycle" of the film or television show. Thus, estimates of both costs and income depend on the quality of Disney's revenue estimates, which are, likely, imprecise.

Business Insight   Impacts of New Revenue Recognition Standard

There was widespread concern that the new revenue recognition standard could significantly impact a company's reported financial performance. To address this, **PwC** surveyed more than 700 finance executives to learn details about the impact, asking this question: Do you expect the new revenue recognition standard to have a material impact on your company's income statement and/or balance sheet?

continued

continued from previous page

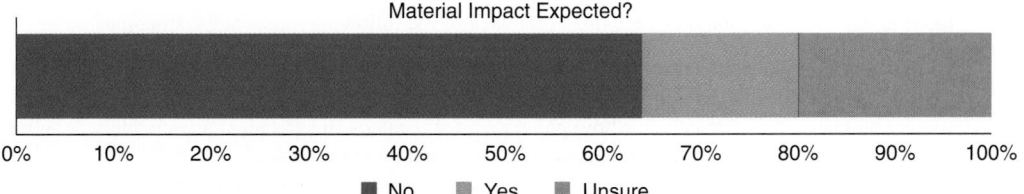

Material Impact Expected?

No   Yes   Unsure

While the new standard's impact varies by industry, and is high for companies with licensing or complex revenue arrangements, the overall impact is not expected to be material. However, the impact extends beyond accounting. Consider the responses to the following PwC survey questions (for those responding "Somewhat difficult" to "Very difficult"):

How difficult will it be to implement the new standard in the following areas?	
Reviewing customer contracts	78%
Documenting the conversion process	76%
Quantifying the revenue adjustments	72%
Managing projects	71%
Revising processes and information systems	68%

An important characteristic of financial statements is comparability. By adopting the new standard, companies changed how they measure revenue beginning in 2018, thereby impairing the comparability of the 2016 and 2017 numbers reported on the 2018 income statement. To avoid this, companies can choose to restate all comparative numbers shown on the 2018 income statement but are not required to do so. For example, consider the following disclosure by Amazon.com.

> We adopted (the standard) on January 1, 2018 for all revenue contracts . . . The adjustment primarily relates to the unredeemed portion of our gift cards, which are now recognized over the expected customer usage period rather than waiting until gift cards expire or when the likelihood of redemption becomes remote. We changed the recognition and classification of Amazon Prime memberships, which are now accounted for as a single performance obligation and recognized ratably over the membership period as service sales. Previously, Prime memberships were considered to be arrangements with multiple deliverables and were allocated among product sales and service sales. Other changes relate primarily to the presentation of revenue. Certain advertising services are now classified as revenue rather than a reduction in cost of sales, and sales of apps, in-app content, and certain digital media content are presented on a net basis. Prior year amounts have not been adjusted and continue to be reported in accordance with our historic accounting policy.

While a more detailed discussion of the transition for accounting is beyond the scope of this text, three important things to remember are:

1. Footnotes will describe the impact of the new standard on 2018 revenue and we can use those disclosures to determine the size and direction of the effect.
2. Comparative years presented in the income statement (2017 and prior) may or may not reflect the new revenue recognition standard. We must use caution when we calculate growth and any ratios that include balance sheet numbers from prior years.
3. We will observe "cumulative adjustments" to firms' retained earnings balances in the statement of equity to reflect the catch-up effect of the new standard on prior years' numbers. As an example, Amazon.com reported a significant cumulative effect related to several new accounting standards (including revenue recognition adjustment of $650 million) in its 2018 Form 10-K.

Retained Earnings Balance as of December 31, 2017.	$ 8,636
Cumulative effect of changes in accounting principles related to revenue recognition, income taxes, and financial instruments.	916
Net income	10,073
Retained Earnings Balance as of December 31, 2018.	$19,625

Review 5-1 LO1

Part I Indicate how revenue should be recognized for each of the following independent situations.

1. A clothing store sells goods to customers who use the store's proprietary (captive) credit card. The store estimates that 2% of the clothes will be returned.
2. A customer purchases a copy machine whose purchase price includes an agreement under which the seller will provide monthly service of the machine for two years at no additional cost.
3. A health club charges an up-front fee to join. Customers are entitled to use the club for one year.
4. A company lists products of other companies on its website and receives a commission equal to a percentage of the selling price when the goods are sold.
5. A franchisor sells franchisees product for sale and provides accounting services on a monthly basis.

Part II A construction company expends $500,000 for work performed under a contract with a total contract price of $3,000,000 and estimated costs of $2,500,000. It sends a bill to the customer for $400,000 under the terms of the contract.

1. How much revenue and gross profit should the company recognize in the income statement?
2. How is the $400,000 billing reported on the balance sheet?

Solution on p. 5-55.

Sales Allowances

LO2

Examine and evaluate sales allowances.

Many companies offer customers a variety of sales allowances, including rights of return, sales discounts for volume purchases, and retailer promotions (point-of-sale price markdowns and other promotions). Sales allowances are especially prevalent in industries with undifferentiated, commoditized products. For example, Levi Strauss discusses allowances in its 2018 10-K.

> The apparel industry is characterized by low barriers to entry for both suppliers and marketers, global sourcing through suppliers located throughout the world, trade liberalization, continuing movement of product sourcing to lower cost countries, regular promotional activity, and the ongoing emergence of new competitors with widely varying strategies and resources. These factors have contributed, and may continue to contribute in the future, to intense pricing pressure and uncertainty throughout the supply chain. Pricing pressure has been exacerbated by the variability of raw materials in recent years. This pressure could have adverse effects on our business and financial condition, including:
> - reduced gross margins across our product lines and distribution channels;
> - increased retailer demands for allowances, incentives and other forms of economic support; and
> - increased pressure on us to reduce our production costs and operating expenses.

Levi Strauss is actively growing its direct-to-consumer (DTC) sales channel because e-commerce sites typically yield higher gross margins than retail-outlet sales. In 2018, Levi Strauss generated 35% of its total revenues through the DTC channel, which increased overall gross margin by 1.5 percentage points to 53.8%.

Accounting for Sales Allowances

GAAP requires companies to report sales revenue at the net amount the company expects to receive. This means companies are to deduct from gross sales the expected sales returns and other allowances. For example, Levi Strauss reports the following in its revenue recognition footnote.

> We recognize allowances for estimated returns in the period in which the related sale is recorded. We recognize allowances for estimated discounts, retailer promotions and other similar incentives at the later of the period in which the related sale is recorded or the period in which the sales incentive is offered to the customer.

When Levi Strauss recognizes revenue, it increases both sales and cash or accounts receivable, by the gross amount of the sale and then reduces the gross sales amount by two specific types of sales allowance: returns and discounts/incentives. To illustrate the allowance for sales returns, assume Levi Strauss sells jeans costing $80 to a customer for $130 on account. Levi Strauss recognizes $130 as revenue and $80 as cost of goods sold (COGS). Because Levi Strauss has offered its customers a right of return, and because prior experience leads the company to expect that returns will occur, Levi Strauss must also set up a reserve for estimated returns. Let's assume Levi Strauss expects returns to amount to 3% of sales. In the same period in which Levi Strauss records the revenue, it also records the estimated returns as follows.

	Balance Sheet							Income Statement		
Transaction	Cash Asset	+	Noncash Assets	=	Liabil- ities	+	Contrib. Capital	+	Earned Capital	Rev- enues	−	Expenses	=	Net Income
Establish allowance for sales returns (3% × $130)			−3.90 Allowance for Sales Returns						−3.90 Retained Earnings	−3.90 Sales Returns and Allowances			−3.90
Adjust COGS ([$80/$130] × $3.90)			2.40 Inventory Adj. for Estimated Returns						2.40 Retained Earnings		−2.40 COGS Adj. for Estimated Returns		2.40

In the first entry, Levi Strauss reduces sales by $3.90 to reflect expected merchandise returns with a corresponding reduction of accounts receivable (similar to the allowance for uncollectible accounts). The second entry reduces COGS by the COGS percentage ($80/$130) and increases inventory for the expected returns. Levi Strauss income statement (through gross profit) follows for the illustration above.

Sales, net ($130 − $3.90)	$126.10
Cost of goods sold ($80 − $2.40)	77.60
Gross profit	$ 48.50

Levi Strauss will also report accounts receivable of $126.10, and the estimated product returns of $2.40 will be reported in its inventory account.

Reporting Sales Allowances

Levi Strauss provides a reconciliation of the beginning and ending balances for the past three years for its allowance for sales returns and for its sales discounts and incentives in its 2018 10-K. This is a typical disclosure for companies with sales returns, discounts, and other sales allowances.

Sales Returns ($ thousands)	Balance at Beginning of Period	Additions During the Year	Deductions	Balance at End of Period
November 25, 2018	$47,401	$245,665	$239,382	$53,684
November 26, 2017	36,457	211,741	200,797	47,401
November 27, 2016	34,021	195,718	193,282	36,457

Sales Discounts ($ thousands)	Balance at Beginning of Period	Additions During the Year	Deductions	Balance at End of Period
November 25, 2018	$135,139	$357,929	$372,364	$120,704
November 26, 2017	105,477	342,169	312,507	135,139
November 27, 2016	86,274	325,843	306,640	105,477

Analysis of Sales Allowances

We use data in the table below to calculate three metrics to analyze sales allowances.

1. **"Additions charged during the year" as compared with gross sales for both sales returns and sales discounts.** This ratio reveals any effects of the pricing pressure on net sales and we would expect the percentage of sales allowances to gross sales to increase (thus reducing net sales) as pricing pressure increases. Over the three-year period, Levi Strauss has reduced the sales returns and discounts given to customers, from 10.3% to 9.8% of gross sales. The company attributes this favorable trend to an increase in its direct-to-consumer (DTC) channel: "Sales directly to consumers generally have higher gross margins than sales through third parties, although these sales typically have higher selling expenses." Although it may not seem like much of an impact, an increase in net sales by 50 basis points (½ percentage point change from 10.3% to 9.8%), for a company with a net profit margin of 5.1% in 2018, is substantial. This explains why analysts focus on the sales allowances, monitoring and following up on any material changes.

2. **Allowances as a percentage of gross sales.** The allowance balance has fluctuated over the three-year period, increasing fairly significantly in 2017 (up from 2.8% to 3.3%) but returning to prior levels in 2018.

$ thousands	2018	2017	2016
Net sales.	$5,575,440	$4,904,030	$4,552,739
Additions charged during the year			
Sales returns	245,665	211,741	195,718
Sales discounts	357,929	342,169	325,843
Total additions charged during the year	603,594	553,910	521,561
Gross sales.	$6,179,034	$5,457,940	$5,074,300
Additions charged during the year/Gross sales . . .	9.8%	10.1%	10.3%
Allowance balance at year-end			
Sales returns	$ 53,684	$ 47,401	$ 36,457
Sales discounts	120,704	135,139	105,477
Total allowances.	$ 174,388	$ 182,540	$ 141,934
Allowances/Gross sales	2.8%	3.3%	2.8%

3. **Adequacy of the allowance account.** This analysis compares the dollar amount Levi Strauss estimates for future sales returns with the amount actually realized during the year. If the company's estimates are 100% accurate, the two amounts will be roughly the same (with some variance due to sales and returns that cross a fiscal year-end). If the amount charged to sales is greater than the cost incurred, the company has reduced sales more than is needed and has reduced its profit accordingly. If the amount charged to sales is less than the cost incurred, the company has under-reserved the allowance account, thus increasing profit. There is not much concern for the adequacy of Levi Strauss's allowance account—the ratio is near 1.0 each year with a moderate amount of variation. We would conclude that Levi Strauss is accurately estimating its sales returns and discounts.

$ thousands	2018	2017	2016
Estimated (total additions charged in the year) . . .	$603,594	$553,910	$521,561
	($245,655 + $357,929)	($211,741 + $342,169)	($195,718 + $325,843)
Actual (total deductions in the year).	611,746	513,304	499,922
	($239,382 + $372,364)	($200,797 + $312,507)	($193,282 + $306,640)
Adequacy (Estimated/Actual).	98.7%	107.9%	104.3%

Review 5-2 LO2

Tiffany & Co. reports the following in its 2019 annual report.

Years Ended January 31 (in millions)	2019	2018	2017
Net sales.	$4,442.1	$4,169.8	$4,001.8

continued

continued from previous page

Revenue Recognition. The Company's performance obligations consist primarily of transferring control of merchandise to customers. Sales are recognized upon transfer of control, which occurs when merchandise is taken in an "over-the-counter" transaction or upon receipt by a customer in a shipped transaction, such as through the Internet and catalog channels. Sales are reported net of returns, sales tax and other similar taxes. . . The Company maintains a reserve for potential product returns and records (as a reduction to sales and cost of sales) its provision for estimated product returns, which is determined based on historical experience.

The company reports the following data related to Tiffany's sales return allowance ($ millions).

Year ended January 31	Balance at Beginning of Period	Charged to Costs and Expenses	Deductions	Balance at End of Period
2019	$15.0	$12.6	$10.1	$17.5
2018	9.6	7.5	2.1	15.0
2017	8.3	2.5	1.2	9.6

Required

1. The reconciliation includes "Charged to costs and expenses" of $12.6 million for the year ended January 31, 2019. What does this item refer to?
2. The reconciliation includes "Deductions" of $10.1 million. What does this item refer to?
3. Compute the following metrics for the past three years and comment on the results.
   a. Sales returns allowance/Gross sales.
   b. Charged to costs and expenses/Gross sales.
   c. Adequacy of the allowance account.

Solution on p. 5-55.

Unearned (Deferred) Revenue

In some industries, it is common to receive cash before recording revenue. Customers might pay in advance for special orders, make deposits for future services, or buy concert tickets, subscriptions, or gift cards. In those cases, companies must record unearned revenues, and only record revenue when those products and services are provided. Specifically, deposits or advance payments are not recorded as revenue until the company performs the services owed or delivers the goods. Until then, the company's balance sheet shows the advance payment as a liability (called unearned revenue or deferred revenue) because the company is obligated to deliver those products and services.

eLectures **LO3**
MBC Analyze deferred revenue.

Unearned revenue is particularly common among retailers that:

▪ Receive advance payments from customers for products that are not yet delivered.

▪ Offer gift cards.

▪ Sell extended-protection plan contracts.

Lowe's Companies, the home improvement company, provides several examples of transactions that require revenue to be deferred, as illustrated in the following excerpts from the revenue recognition footnote in its 10-K for the 2018 fiscal year ended February 1, 2019.

In-store and on-line sales. Revenues from in-store and online merchandise purchases are recognized at the point in time when the customer obtains control of the merchandise, which is at the time of in-store purchase or delivery of the product to the customer. A provision for anticipated merchandise returns is provided through a reduction of sales and cost of sales in the period that the related sales are recorded.

continued

continued from previous page

Service revenue. Revenues from services primarily relate to professional installation services the Company provides through subcontractors related to merchandise purchased by a customer. The Company recognizes revenue associated with services as they are rendered, and the majority of services are completed less than one week from initiation.

Stored-value cards. The Company defers revenues from stored-value cards, which include gift cards and returned merchandise credits, and recognizes revenue into sales when the cards are redeemed.

Extended protection plans. The Company also defers revenues for its separately-priced extended protection plan contracts. The Company recognizes revenue from extended protection plan sales on a straight-line basis over the respective contract term.

As we evaluate profitability for companies that report substantial amounts of deferred revenue, we must be aware of changes in deferred revenue liabilities on the balance sheet. Should deferred revenue liabilities decrease, we infer the company's *current* reported revenue was collected from customers in a *prior* accounting period and there have been fewer new prepayments for which revenue will be recognized in future periods. Such a trend could predict future declines in revenue and profit.

The following schedule allows us to track the deferred revenue liability related to Lowe's extended protection plan contracts.

$ millions	FY2018	FY2017	FY2016
Deferred revenue—extended protection plans, beginning of year	$803	$763	$729
Additions to deferred revenue	414	398	387
Deferred revenue recognized.	(390)	(358)	(353)
Deferred revenue—extended protection plans, end of year.	$827	$803	$763

During the 2018 fiscal year ended February 1, 2019, Lowe's received cash from customers of $414 million for new extended protection plan contracts and recognized revenue of $390 million that related to cash received in prior years. As a result, the balance in the deferred revenue liability account increased from $803 million to $827 million at the end of fiscal year 2018.

From this reconciliation, we would have no reason to predict future revenue declines.

Review 5-3 LO3

Microsoft reports a significant amount of unearned revenue mainly from cloud-services subscriptions. During 2018, Microsoft included the following information in a footnote ($ millions).

Deferred revenue balance, beginning of period	$26,656
Deferred revenue balance, end of period.	32,720
Previously unearned revenue, recognized in 2018	(55,078)

Required

Determine the amount of cash Microsoft collected from customers in advance of recognizing revenue during 2018.

Solution on p. 5-56.

Foreign Currency Effects on Revenue, Expenses, and Cash Flow

eLectures **LO4**

Evaluate how foreign currency exchange rates affect revenue.

Exhibit 5.1 shows Pfizer's income statement that reports an increase in revenues of $1.1 billion from 2017 to 2018. Pfizer explains that changes in foreign exchange rates during 2018 accounted for $310 million of the $1.1 billion total. A footnote describes Pfizer's foreign currency exposure.

Significant portions of our revenues, costs and expenses, as well as our substantial international net assets, are exposed to changes in foreign exchange rates. 53% of our total 2018 revenues were derived from international operations, including 21% from Europe and 22% from China, Japan and the rest of Asia. As we operate in multiple foreign currencies, including the euro, the Japanese yen, the Chinese Renminbi, the U.K. pound, the Canadian dollar and approximately 100 other currencies, changes in those currencies relative to the U.S. dollar will impact our revenues and expenses. If the U.S. dollar were to weaken against another currency, assuming all other variables remained constant, our revenues would increase, having a positive impact on earnings, and our overall expenses would increase, having a negative impact on earnings. Conversely, if the U.S. dollar were to strengthen against another currency, assuming all other variables remained constant, our revenues would decrease, having a negative impact on earnings, and our overall expenses would decrease, having a positive impact on earnings. Therefore, significant changes in foreign exchange rates can impact our results and our financial guidance. . . Revenues in 2018 increased by $1.1 billion, or 2%, compared to 2017, which reflects operational growth of $791 million, or 2%, and the favorable impact of foreign exchange of $310 million.

Increased revenue was not the only foreign exchange impact. The weakening U.S. dollar ($US) also increased Pfizer's COGS and other operating expenses. Because Pfizer is profitable (revenues > expenses), the foreign currency fluctuations had the net effect of increasing Pfizer's net income for 2018.

Companies routinely conduct business in foreign currencies. Although Pfizer's U.S.-based companies may write purchase and sales contracts that are denominated in foreign currencies, Pfizer's foreign subsidiaries likely transact business almost entirely in foreign currencies. These foreign subsidiaries not only conduct business in foreign currencies, they also maintain their accounting records in currencies other than the $US. Before the financial statements of those subsidiaries can be consolidated with the U.S. parent company, they must first be translated into $US.

As the $US weakens vis-à-vis other world currencies in which Pfizer conducts its business, each foreign currency buys more $US. When Pfizer translates a subsidiary's foreign-currency denominated income statement into $US, the income statement grows: reported revenues, expenses, and profit are all larger than before the dollar weakened. In the consolidation process, Pfizer must also translate the foreign subsidiary's balance sheet and, with a weaker $US, the foreign currency-denominated balance sheet grows as well, reporting higher assets, liabilities, and equity. We examine the income statement and cash flow effects of foreign currency here, and we defer our discussion of the balance sheet effects to Module 9, when we discuss the consolidation process.

Foreign Currency and Cash Flows

Following are three examples of the ways in which foreign currency gains and losses may affect *cash flow*.

1. **When the $US company transacts business denominated in foreign currencies.** A U.S. company might denominate a sales contract in Euros, for example. If the $US weakens between the date of the sale and the ultimate collection of the Euro-denominated account receivable, the U.S. company realizes a foreign currency transaction gain. Conversely, if the U.S. company purchases goods, the foreign currency denominated account payable would grow and more $US would be required to settle the obligation, resulting in a foreign currency transaction loss.
2. **When the U.S. parent company borrows money that is denominated in a foreign currency.** If the U.S. parent company borrows in foreign currencies and the $US weakens, it will require more in $US to repay the foreign currency-denominated liability. If the company planned to repay the loan with $US, the company will realize a loss as it repays the foreign currency-denominated loan.
3. **When the foreign subsidiary's cash is repatriated to the United States.** Most foreign subsidiaries maintain cash in foreign bank accounts (local to the subsidiary) for use in ongoing operations. If the U.S. parent repatriates that cash, however, say, by a cash dividend from the subsidiary to the U.S. parent company, a foreign currency transaction gain may arise if the dollar weakens before the foreign currency is converted into $US to pay the dividend.

The difference between these three situations and the translation adjustment that arises solely from the consolidation of Pfizer's foreign subsidiaries' profits is that these three transactions describe *realized* losses, whereas the translation losses that Pfizer reports above are *unrealized*.

Regarding contracts denominated in foreign currencies (#1 above) and borrowing in foreign currencies (#2 above), companies frequently hedge their exposures to these potential realized losses by using financial derivative securities. These derivative securities act like an insurance policy to offset the income statement effects of realized gains and losses by transferring some of the risk for foreign currency fluctuations to other parties who are willing to accept that risk for a fee. An effective hedging process reduces the effects of realized gains and losses and greatly reduces the impact on net income. We discuss hedging in more detail in Appendix 9A .

Accordingly, the *realized* foreign currency translation effects of #1 and #2 above are likely small, and the foreign currency translation gains (the increase in revenues, expenses, and profit Pfizer discusses above) are, therefore, likely to be primarily *unrealized* noncash losses.

Regarding the repatriation of foreign earnings (#3 above), until recently, firms infrequently repatriated foreign earnings (or repatriated only small proportions). Recent estimates are that U.S. companies hold $1 trillion of overseas earnings, mostly invested in U.S. marketable securities. However, the Tax Cuts and Jobs Act (TCJA) removed a major tax barrier to repatriation. From 2017 onward, companies must pay a one-time tax of 15.5% (down from 35%) on repatriated earnings. Since the new tax law was passed, many companies have started to bring foreign profits back to the U.S. One study finds that companies repatriated more earnings in the first sixth months of 2018 than in 2015, 2016, and 2017 combined.

Foreign Currency and Income

So, how should we treat the foreign currency translation effects on the income statement given that the currency fluctuations reduced Pfizer's revenues, expenses, and profit? When we use the income statement numbers, as reported, to calculate metrics such as NOPAT and ratios such as ROE and RNOA, we implicitly include the effects of foreign currency translation. One approach would be to back out the revenue and expense effects to yield income statements that are not affected by these foreign currency fluctuations. Pfizer identifies numerous effects on its 2018 income statement in the management discussion and analysis (MD&A) section of its 10-K, including the following.

1. Revenues were increased by $310 million.
2. COGS was increased by $153 million.

Backing out these foreign currency translation effects on the 2018 income statement (with similar adjustments to prior year financial statements) would allow us to better isolate Pfizer's operating profit without the distortion of foreign currency exchange rate effects. The impact on Pfizer's gross profit for 2018 is $157 million ($310 million − $153 million). This amounts to 1.4% of net income ($157 million/$11,153 million). A thorough analysis computes ratios and numbers with and without the effect of foreign currency.

Foreign Currency and Future Results

Companies frequently provide guidance for analysts to forecast future income statements. Pfizer's 2018 10-K includes the following guidance to analysts for 2019.

Our Financial Guidance for 2019 The following table provides our financial guidance for full-year 2019:

Revenues	$52.0 to $54.0 billion
Adjusted cost of sales as a percentage of revenues	20.8% to 21.8%
Adjusted selling, informational and administrative expenses	$13.5 to $14.5 billion
Adjusted research and development expenses	$7.8 to $8.3 billion
Adjusted other (income) deductions	Approximately $100 million of income
Effective tax rate on adjusted income	Approximately 16.0%
Adjusted diluted EPS	$2.82 to $2.92

Pfizer also includes a footnote to its guidance relating to foreign currency effects (on revenue only).

> Exchange rates assumed are as of mid-January 2019. Reflects the anticipated unfavorable impact of approximately $0.9 billion on revenues and approximately $0.06 on adjusted diluted EPS as a result of changes in foreign exchange rates relative to the U.S. dollar compared to foreign exchange rates from 2018.

Because foreign currency effects are unpredictable and out of the company's direct control, we exclude these effects to better forecast operating cash flow.

LO4 Review 5-4

Alphabet Inc. (Google) reports the following in the notes to its 2018 10-K. EMEA is the acronym for Alphabet's operations in Europe, the Middle East, and Africa.

> The effect of currency exchange rates on our business is an important factor in understanding period-to-period comparisons. Our international revenues are favorably affected as the U.S. dollar weakens relative to other foreign currencies, and unfavorably affected as the U.S. dollar strengthens relative to other foreign currencies. Our international revenues are also favorably affected by net hedging gains and unfavorably affected by net hedging losses. We use non-GAAP constant currency revenues and constant currency revenue growth for financial and operational decision-making and as a means to evaluate period-to-period comparisons. We believe the presentation of results on a constant currency basis in addition to GAAP results helps improve the ability to understand our performance because they exclude the effects of foreign currency volatility that are not indicative of our core operating results. Our revenues and revenue growth from 2017 to 2018 were favorably affected by changes in foreign currency exchange rates, primarily due to the U.S. dollar weakening relative to the Euro and British pound.

Year Ended December 31 ($ millions)	2016	2017	2018
EMEA revenues	$30,304	$36,046	$44,567
Exclude foreign exchange effect on current period revenues using prior year rates.	1,291	(5)	(1,325)
Exclude hedging effect recognized in current period	(479)	190	172
EMEA constant currency revenues	$31,116	$36,231	$43,414
EMEA revenue growth		19%	24%
EMEA constant currency revenue growth		21%	20%

Required
1. Explain how fluctuations in foreign currency exchange rates affected Google's EMEA revenues in 2018 and 2017. Why do these fluctuations occur?
2. What other portions of the income statement are likely affected by these exchange rate fluctuations?
3. How do these fluctuations in foreign exchange rates affect Google's cash flow?   Solution on p. 5-56.

Accounts Receivable

eLectures **LO5**
MBC Analyze
accounts
receivable and
uncollectible amounts.

Pfizer reports $8,025 million of net trade accounts receivable in the current asset section of its balance sheet.

As of December 31 ($ millions)	2018	2017
Cash and cash equivalents	$ 1,139	$ 1,342
Short-term investments	17,694	18,650
Trade accounts receivable, less allowance for		
doubtful accounts: 2018—$541; 2017—$584	**8,025**	**8,221**

Selling goods on account carries the risk that some customers encounter financial difficulty and are unable to pay the amount due. GAAP recognizes this possibility and requires companies to estimate the dollar amount of receivables that are likely to be uncollectible and to report only the net collectible amount on the balance sheet. Pfizer reports net receivables of $8,025 million and estimates that $541 million of its total accounts receivable are uncollectible. From this, we can determine that the gross accounts receivable (the total amount customers owe to Pfizer) is $8,566 million ($8,025 million + $541 million). Pfizer estimates, therefore, that 6.3% ($541 million/$8,566 million) of the total amount of receivables owed is likely uncollectible.

Aging Analysis of Receivables

Companies frequently employ an **aging analysis** of their accounts receivable to estimate the uncollectible amounts. An aging analysis groups accounts receivable by number of days past due (days after the scheduled due date). A common grouping method uses 30-day or 60-day intervals, as shown in the following.

Age of Accounts	Receivable Balance	Estimated Percent Uncollectible	Estimated Uncollectible Accounts
Current	$ 50,000	2%	$1,000
1–60 days past due	30,000	3%	900
61–90 days past due	15,000	4%	600
Over 90 days past due	5,000	8%	400
Total	$100,000		$2,900

In this example, we assume the seller's credit terms are a typical "2/10, net 30" (customers receive a 2% discount from the amount owed if they make payment within 10 days of the invoice date; or the full amount owed is due 30 days from the invoice date). Accounts listed as 1–60 days past due are those 1 to 60 days past their due date. This would include an account that is 45 days outstanding for a net 30-day invoice. Given this aging schedule, the company draws upon its previous experience of uncollectible accounts of that age. The company has experience that if an account is 1–60 days past due, about 3% of the balance is not collected. Based on that past experience, the company estimates a potential loss of $900 for the $30,000 in the 1–60 days past due group. As expected, the percent uncollectible increases with the age of the account.

The company estimates that $2,900, or 2.9% of its $100,000 of gross accounts receivable, is likely uncollectible. The net amount, $97,100, represents the company's best estimate of what it expects to ultimately collect from its customers.

Accounting for Accounts Receivable

To account for uncollectible amounts, companies use an allowance account similar to the ones discussed above for sales returns and other allowances. The *allowance for uncollectible accounts* (also called the allowance for doubtful accounts) reduces the gross amount of receivables that are reported on the balance sheet.

To illustrate, assume the company sells goods on account for $100,000 and, at the end of the accounting period, performs an aging analysis and establishes the allowance for uncollectible accounts in the amount of $2,900. Our financial statement effects for the sale and the estimate of uncollectible accounts receivable are as follows.

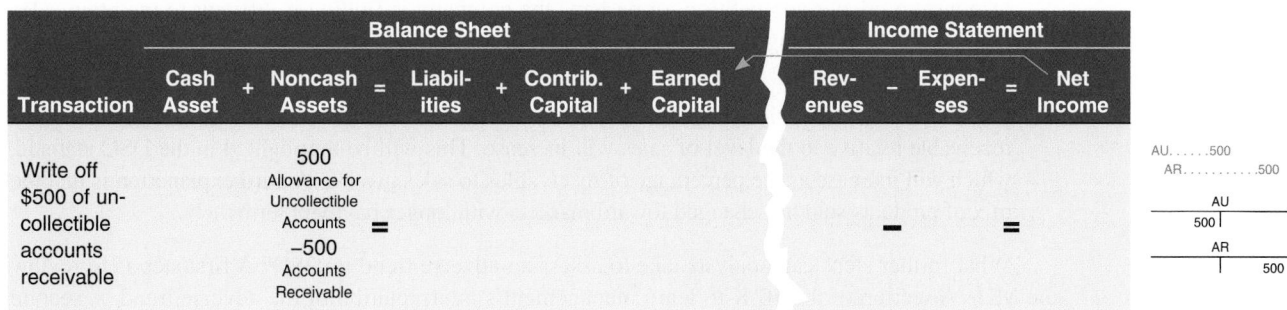

The allowance for uncollectible accounts is subtracted from the gross accounts receivable, and the net amount collectible is reported on the balance sheet.

Accounts receivable (gross amount owed).................................	$100,000
Less: Allowance for uncollectible accounts	(2,900)
Accounts receivable, net (reported on balance sheet).....................	$ 97,100

Companies typically report the allowance for uncollectible accounts along with accounts receivable as follows.

Accounts receivable, less allowance for uncollectible accounts of $2,900........	$97,100

By setting up the allowance, the company has established a reserve, or a cushion, that it can use to absorb credit losses as they occur. To see how this works, assume a customer who owes $500 files for bankruptcy. If the company determines the receivable is now uncollectible, it must write off the receivable. This is absorbed by the allowance for uncollectible accounts as follows.

	Balance Sheet							Income Statement		
Transaction	Cash Asset	+ Noncash Assets	= Liabil- ities	+ Contrib. Capital	+ Earned Capital			Rev- enues	− Expen- ses	= Net Income
Write off $500 of un- collectible accounts receivable		500 Allowance for Uncollectible Accounts = −500 Accounts Receivable							−	=

AU......500
    AR...........500

AU
500 |

AR
| 500

The write-off of the uncollectible account receivable results in the following balances at the end of the period.

Accounts receivable (gross amount owed)...................	$99,500	($100,000 – $500)
Less: Allowance for uncollectible accounts	(2,400)	($2,900 – $500)
Accounts receivable, net (reported on balance sheet)...........	$97,100	

We see that the net amount of accounts receivable the company will report at the end of the period is the same $97,100 balance it reported *before* the write-off of the uncollectible account (i.e., because the write-off was completely absorbed by the allowance account established in the previous period). This leaves the reported amount of net accounts receivable on the balance sheet unchanged. The write-off used up some of the reserve as the allowance decreased from $2,900 to $2,400. Future write-offs will reduce the allowance further. Each period, the company replenishes the allowance account and then draws it down for write-offs.

Analysis of Accounts Receivable–Magnitude

An important analysis tool for accounts receivable is to determine the magnitude and quality of the receivables. The relative magnitude of accounts receivable is usually measured with respect to sales volume using either of the following ratios. (Average accounts receivable is a simple average: (Current year balance + Prior year balance)/2.

■ **Accounts receivable turnover**

$$\text{Accounts receivable turnover} = \frac{\text{Sales}}{\text{Average accounts receivable}}$$

■ **Days sales outstanding (DSO)**

$$\text{Days sales outstanding} = \frac{365 \text{ days}}{\text{Accounts receivable turnover}} = \frac{365 \times \text{Average accounts receivable}}{\text{Sales}}$$

DSO is, arguably, the most intuitive of the ratios, and it reveals the number of days, on average, that accounts receivable are outstanding before they are paid. The DSO statistic can be:

■ Compared with the company's established credit terms to investigate if the company's customers are conforming to those credit terms.

■ Computed over several years for the same company to investigate trends.

■ Compared with peer companies.

A lower accounts receivable turnover, a higher percentage of accounts receivable to sales, and a lengthening of the DSO all provide a signal that accounts receivable have grown more quickly than sales. Generally, such a trend is not favorable for two possible reasons.

■ **The company is becoming more lenient in granting credit to its customers.** Perhaps this is in response to greater competition, or perhaps the company is finding it difficult to maintain sales volume and is reaching for additional volume by selling to new customers with weaker credit scores.

■ **Credit quality is deteriorating.** If existing customers are not paying on time, the level of accounts receivable relative to the level of sales will increase. This will be highlighted in the DSO statistic, which will increase as the percentage of receivables to sales grows. (A third explanation is that the mix of products sold has changed toward markets with longer payment terms.)

What further steps can analysts take to assess an adverse trend in DSO? A first step is to review the MD&A section of the 10-K to learn management's interpretation of the adverse trend. A second step is to review the financial press, analyst reports, and other external reports about the company to glean additional insight.

The ratios we highlight above are often reported in commercial databases that are regularly used by analysts. For example, Standard & Poors' Capital IQ reports the following data for Pfizer.

Pfizer Inc. (NYSE:PFE) Financial Ratios					
Ratios for Fiscal Period Ending	2018	2017	2016	2015	2014
Asset turnover					
Total asset turnover	0.3	0.3	0.3	0.3	0.3
Fixed asset turnover.	3.9	3.9	3.9	3.8	4.1
Accounts receivable turnover.	6.6	6.4	6.4	5.9	5.6
Inventory turnover.	1.5	1.5	1.7	1.4	1.5
Short-term liquidity					
Current ratio	1.6	1.4	1.3	1.5	2.6
Quick ratio	1.0	1.0	0.9	1.2	2.2
Cash from operations to current liabilities	0.5	0.6	0.5	0.5	0.8
Average days sales outstanding.	55.3	57.1	56.8	61.9	65.3
Average days inventory outstanding	247.4	247.8	219.5	256.9	239.0
Average days payable outstanding	154.0	147.5	133.4	111.2	137.9
Average cash conversion cycle	148.7	157.4	142.9	207.6	166.5

We have highlighted the accounts receivable turnover and days sales outstanding (DSO). To compute these ratios for 2018, Capital IQ uses Pfizer's 2018 sales of $53,647 million and its accounts receivable, net of $8,025 million and $8,221 million for 2018 and 2017, respectively:

$$2018 \text{ accounts receivable turnover} = \frac{\$53,647}{(\$8,025 + \$8,221)/2} = 6.6 \text{ times}$$

$$2018 \text{ days sales outstanding} = \frac{365 \text{ days}}{6.6 \text{ times per year}} = 55.3 \text{ days}$$

A review of the Capital IQ data reveals that Pfizer's accounts receivable turnover has increased over the past five years—a good sign. The downward trend for DSO is another way to measure the positive trend. The metric has declined by 10 days from 65.3 days in 2014 to 55.3 days in 2018. Generally, the analysis of accounts receivable focuses on the levels of the turnover and DSO ratios compared with peer companies (shedding evidence on the company's ability to collect its receivables relative to competitors) and trends in these ratios (providing a bigger picture and insight into the company's cash-collection patterns).To assess the 10-day decrease, we would compare to a set of Pfizer's peers.

Collecting receivables more quickly increases operating cash flow. At the current sales volume of $53,647 million, the average sales per day is $147 million ($53,647 million/365), and collecting receivables 10 days more quickly generated an additional (one-time) $1.47 billion of cash in 2018 ($147 million per day × 10 days).

Data Analytics Insight   ■   Reducing Days to Collect Accounts Receivable

A company can generate cash by reducing the days to collect receivables from its customer. On the other side of the transaction, customers that pay earlier will see their cash position reduced. Consequently, efforts to collect receivables more quickly must be done with care so as not to damage customer relationships. One approach is to become smarter about credit decisions. Companies maintain extensive data on their customers and can use data analytics to identify customer profiles and behaviors. Armed with these insights, companies can make more-informed credit decisions, for example, to extend credit on a more selective basis, to offer more generous terms to faster-paying customers, and to reduce credit to slow payers. Thanks to this sort of data analytics, we have FICO credit scores that banks and credit card companies use to determine consumer lines of credit and loan amounts and terms.

Analysis of Accounts Receivable—Quality

To analyze the quality of accounts receivable, we focus on the allowance for uncollectible accounts. Companies are required to report on their balance sheet the amount of accounts receivable they expect to collect (the gross amount of accounts receivable less the estimated uncollectible accounts). Levi Strauss reports its accounts receivable as follows in its 2018 balance sheet.

$ thousands	Nov. 25, 2018	Nov. 26, 2017
Current assets		
Cash and cash equivalents......................	$713,120	$633,622
Trade receivables, net of allowance for doubtful accounts of $10,037 and $11,726	**534,164**	**485,485**

The company also includes Schedule II in its 10-K, where it reports a "roll forward" of the allowance for uncollectible accounts that shows movements in the account.

Allowance for Doubtful Accounts ($ thousands)	Balance at Beginning of Period		Additions Charged to Expenses		Deductions		Balance at End of Period
November 25, 2018	$11,726	+	$2,284	–	$3,973	=	$10,037
November 26, 2017	$11,974	+	$1,645	–	$1,893	=	$11,726
November 27, 2016	$11,025	+	$2,195	–	$1,246	=	$11,974

Reconciling the allowance account from the beginning to the end of the year yields useful insights (in $000s). The allowance account began 2018 with a balance of $11,726. Levi Strauss increased the allowance by $2,284 and recognized bad debt expense (included in selling, general and administrative expense) equal to that amount. The allowance was reduced by $3,973 to absorb the write-off of uncollectible accounts receivable during 2018 and ended the year with a balance of $10,037. The decrease in the account during the year means that Levi Strauss wrote off more than it added to its allowance account. We observe the same pattern in 2017, when the company added $1,645 and wrote off $1,893. However, in 2016, the opposite holds true, additions to the allowance were greater than the write-offs. Over the three-year period, the company wrote off $7,112 ($3,973 + $1,893 + $1,246) while only increasing the allowance account by $6,124 ($2,284 + $1,645 + $2,195).

Because Levi Strauss has not replenished the allowance account for the amount of the write-offs for three years, the balance of the allowance account has declined from $11,025 at the beginning of 2016 to $10,037 at the end of 2018. This would not be an issue if gross receivables had declined proportionately, but this is not the case. Instead, the allowance account as a percentage of gross accounts receivable has declined.

$ thousands	2018	2017
Accounts receivable (net)................................	$534,164	$485,485
Allowance account	10,037	11,726
Accounts receivable (gross).............................	$544,201	$497,211
Allowance account / Accounts receivable (gross)	1.84%	2.36%

There are two possible interpretations for this change.

1. **Credit quality has improved.** If Levi Strauss believes the collectability of its remaining receivables has improved, it can feel confident in allowing the allowance for uncollectible accounts to decline. An improvement in credit quality might be plausible given that the recession ended during this period and customers are in better financial condition.

2. **Levi Strauss is underestimating the allowance account.** This is the more troubling of the two possibilities. Remember, Levi Strauss reports bad debt expense in its income statement when it *increases* its allowance account. Write-offs have no effect on profit; only the estimation of the loss affects income. So, Levi Strauss might be attempting to increase its profitability by not *adding* to the allowance account, and, thus, avoiding more bad debt expense.

How can we determine which of these two possibilities is more likely? We might compare Levi Strauss with its peer companies to determine if its ratio of allowance account to gross accounts receivable is higher or lower. If Levi Strauss's ratio exceeds industry or peer benchmarks, then the decrease might be reasonable. If Levi Strauss's ratio is lower than industry or peer benchmarks, Levi Strauss may be attempting to inflate its earnings by avoiding the additional drag on profits from bad debt expense (maybe to meet analyst forecasts or to avoid a default in loan covenants). All we know for certain is the allowance account has declined, both in absolute dollar amount and as a percentage of gross accounts receivable. It is difficult to know the reasons unless the company discusses those reasons in its MD&A section of the 10-K or in conference calls with analysts.

Managerial Decision ▇ You Are the Receivables Manager

You are analyzing your receivables for the period and you are concerned that the average collection period is lengthening. What specific actions can you take to reduce the average collection period? [Answer, p. 5-35]

L05 Review 5-5

Coca-Cola reports the following in its 2018 10-K about its credit policy for accounts receivable.

> We record trade accounts receivable at net realizable value. This value includes an appropriate allowance for estimated uncollectible accounts to reflect any loss anticipated on the trade accounts receivable balances and charged to the provision for doubtful accounts. We calculate this allowance based on our history of write-offs, the level of past-due accounts based on the contractual terms of the receivables, and our relationships with, and the economic status of, our bottling partners and customers.

Assume that Coca-Cola's customers owe the company $3,885 million as of December 31, 2018, and that an aging analysis of accounts receivable reveals the following.

$ millions	Accounts Receivable	% Uncollectible
Current	$1,554	1.5%
1–30 days past due	971	5.0%
31–60 days past due	544	14.0%
61–90 days past due	427	25.0%
91–120 days past due	272	54.0%
Over 120 days past due	117	75.0%
Total	$3,885	

Required

1. Compute the dollar amount that Coca-Cola should report in its December 31, 2018, balance sheet for the allowance for doubtful accounts and the net balance of accounts receivable it will report on its balance sheet as of that date.
2. Assume that Coca-Cola's estimated uncollectible accounts on December 31, 2017, were $477 million and that the company wrote off $17 million of accounts receivable during 2018. What dollar amount of expense will Coca-Cola report in its 2018 income statement?
3. Coca-Cola's 2017 balance sheet reported accounts receivable, net of $3,667 million. Are Coca-Cola's accounts receivable of higher or lower quality in 2018 as compared with 2017?

Solution on p. 5-57.

Expenses and Losses

LO6
Evaluate operating expenses and discontinued operations.

Pfizer's income statement in Exhibit 5.1 reports a number of expense and loss items.

Deductions from Income

The following expense and loss items reported by Pfizer are typical of many companies.

- **Cost of sales.** This is the cost Pfizer incurred to make or buy the products it sold during the year. As goods are manufactured or purchased, the cost is recognized as inventory on the balance sheet. The inventory remains there until the product is sold, at which time the cost is transferred from the balance sheet into the income statement as cost of goods sold. Given that the product is sold, revenue from the sale of the product is also added to the income statement. The difference between revenue and cost of sales is the gross profit on the sale. We discuss this cost together with inventories in Module 6 and the analysis of the gross profit margin (Gross profit / Sales) in Module 4.

- **Selling, informational and administrative expense.** Usually, this expense category is labeled Selling, general and administrative (SG&A) expense, and it includes a number of general overhead expense categories, such as:
  - Salaries and benefits for administrative personnel and executives.
  - Rent and utilities for office facilities.
  - Marketing and selling expenses.
  - IT, legal, and accounting expenses.
  - Depreciation for Pfizer's depreciable assets that are used for administrative purposes (we discuss this expense together with property, plant, and equipment in Module 6).

- **Research and development expense.** This is the amount Pfizer incurs to conduct research for new products. We discuss this cost in a separate section below.

- **Amortization of intangible assets.** When Pfizer acquires an intangible asset, such as a patent, it amortizes that cost over the useful life of the patent (the period of time Pfizer expects the patent to produce cash flow). Amortization expense is a noncash expense, similar to depreciation expense. Often, it is included with the SG&A expense.

- **Restructuring charges.** This represents the cost Pfizer has incurred and expects to incur to restructure its operations, say, by the elimination of lines of business, consolidation of operations, reduction of the number of employees, and the like. We discuss restructuring charges in Module 6.

- **Provision for taxes on income.** The tax provision shown on the income statement relates to Pfizer's profit. These are taxes that will be paid to federal and state taxing authorities as well as income taxes levied by foreign governments and municipalities. We discuss income tax expense in a separate section below and, in greater depth, in Module 10. Other types of taxes, such as sales tax or employment taxes, are included in SG&A and not with the income tax expense.

- **Discontinued operations.** This represents the operating profit (or loss) plus the gain (or loss) on the sale of businesses Pfizer has decided to divest. We discuss discontinued operations in a separate section below.

- **Income attributable to noncontrolling interest.** Noncontrolling interest arises because Pfizer has one or more subsidiaries where Pfizer does not own 100% of the voting stock. So, while Pfizer owns the controlling interest, other shareholders own the balance of the stock (the noncontrolling interest). The income attributable to the noncontrolling interest is their portion of the subsidiary's income (and is added to the noncontrolling interest equity account on Pfizer's balance sheet). The remainder of the subsidiary's net income is credited to Pfizer's shareholders and is added to retained earnings on Pfizer's balance sheet. We discuss noncontrolling interest in greater depth in Module 9.

Research and Development Expense

Companies in many industries depend heavily on research and development (R&D) for new and improved products and services. For these companies, R&D is critical because failure to offer "cutting edge" technology can lead to loss of market share and even bankruptcy. R&D costs broadly consist of the following.

- Salaries and benefits for researchers and developers.
- Supplies needed to conduct the research.
- Licensing fees for intellectual property or software used in the R&D process.
- Third-party payments to collaborators at other firms and universities.
- Laboratory and other equipment.
- Property and buildings to be used as research facilities. As we discuss in a later module, research facilities are included in PPE and the depreciation on research facilities is included in R&D expense each year.

Accounting for R&D is straightforward: R&D costs are expensed as incurred.

R&D Spending

Exhibit 5.2 shows the median level of R&D spending in 2018 for the S&P 500 firms that report R&D expense on the income statement.

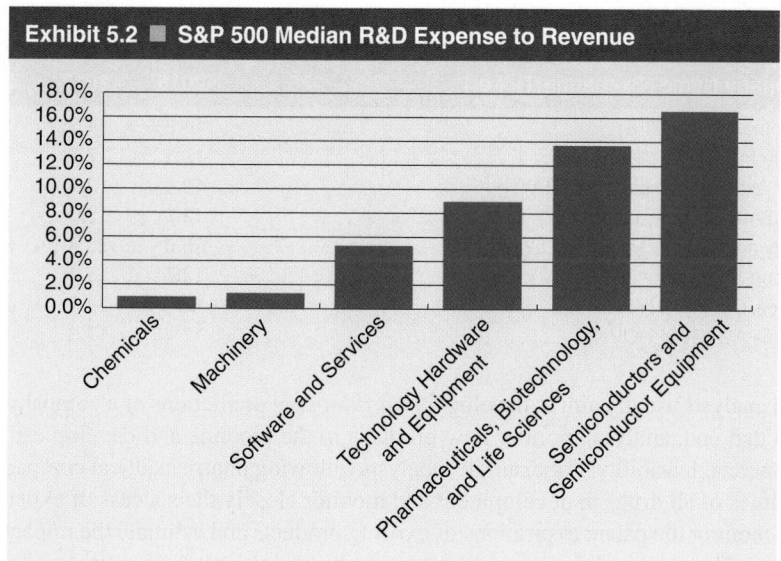

Exhibit 5.2 ■ S&P 500 Median R&D Expense to Revenue

Analysis of R&D

Our analysis of R&D starts with measuring R&D expense in dollars and as a percentage of total revenues. It is important to compare a company's R&D spending to its peers.

R&D is a significant expense for Pfizer as it seeks new compounds and drugs to bring to market. In 2018, Pfizer's R&D expense is $8,006 million or 14.9% of total revenues. As Exhibit 5.3 shows, Pfizer's R&D expense has ranged between 13% and 16% of total revenues over the past six years, in line with the 13.7% median for the pharmaceutical and biotech sector.

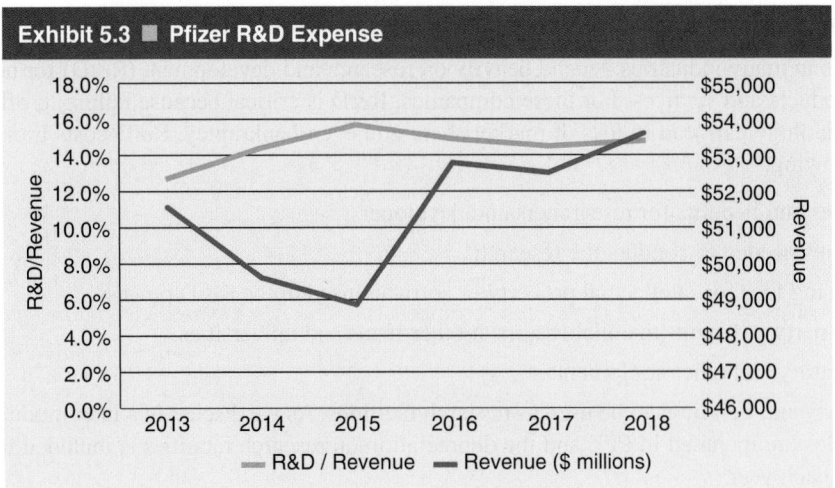

Exhibit 5.3 ■ Pfizer R&D Expense

Among Pfizer's peers there are significant differences in the percentage of revenues devoted to R&D expenditures (see Exhibit 5.4). Pfizer's R&D is about average among its peers. Our analysis focuses on trends over time and whether other firms are experiencing the same trends. As we saw in Exhibit 5.3, R&D spending might vary in percentage terms due to changes in revenue; our analysis needs to consider both dollar levels and percentages.

Exhibit 5.4 ■ R&D Expenditures to Revenue			
Company Name (Exchange:Ticker)	2016	2017	2018
Pfizer Inc. (NYSE:PFE)	14.9%	14.5%	14.8%
AbbVie Inc. (NYSE:ABBV)	17.1	17.7	16.1
Bayer Aktiengesellschaft (DB:BAYN)	12.4	12.8	12.3
GlaxoSmithKline plc (LSE:GSK)	12.7	13.0	12.3
Eli Lilly and Company (NYSE:LLY)	25.0	23.4	21.6
Johnson & Johnson (NYSE:JNJ)	12.7	13.9	13.2
Merck & Co. Inc. (NYSE:MRK)	17.4	24.5	22.8
Novartis AG (SWX:NOVN)	17.4	17.3	17.1

Financial analysts usually aim to develop *forward-looking* predictions of a company's income and cash flow. To that end, analysts monitor new products in the pipeline and develop estimates of their ultimate commercial feasibility. For example, analysts following pharmaceutical companies frequently prepare schedules of all drugs in development and monitor closely the success of experimental trials. Analysts also monitor the patent expirations of existing products and estimate the impact on sales after a patent expires. The challenge for analysts is two-fold; not only must we estimate the magnitude of future revenues, but we must estimate revenue timing as well. There is often a considerable lag between when R&D expenditures occur and when the resulting revenue is earned. But while the income statement might suffer from such lags, the company's market cap reflects at least some of the future revenue related to current period R&D expenditure. This is one reason why we observe market-to-book ratios much greater than 1.0 for R&D intensive firms.

Manager Insights ■ R&D Projects

Company managers aim to maximize return on R&D investments by selecting projects to fund. Managers have a considerable amount of proprietary information about each R&D project, which they can use to make investment decisions. The goal is to maximize the return on the R&D investment by focusing on the following areas:

R&D Costs. Companies can reduce R&D costs by strategically managing the procurement of raw materials and equipment as they do for other business units, by monitoring closely the investment at each stage of the research process (reducing investment cost in high-risk areas and increasing that investment if and when the risk level

continued

continued from previous page

falls), by outsourcing portions of the research process as they do for other production and business processes, by identifying failed research ventures early and cutting their losses, by partnering with other companies interested in the research to share the investment cost and the risk, and a variety of other measures.

Speed of research effort.   Companies can reduce the period of time over which the research is conducted (and thus the cost of the research) with careful planning and control. Some of the same production and scheduling techniques that companies have applied to their manufacturing processes can be applied to the research units. These include project management techniques, parallel processing, and a number of other techniques discussed in operations courses.

Quality of decisions.   Each R&D project requires constant monitoring and numerous decisions relating to a succession of investments and go versus no-go decisions. Failed projects need to be identified early and culled from the research portfolio and managers need to continually analyze the extent to which the research is creating knowledge that will lead to commercially feasible products.

It is important for managers to adopt the mindset that each R&D project is a separate investment decision similar to other capital-budgeting decisions and one which typically involves a series of related investment decisions. It is only with this degree of discipline that the R&D process will achieve maximum returns on investment. Ultimately, firms invest in R&D to earn future revenues. There is an argument to be made that R&D investments create an asset that should be added to the balance sheet and then depreciated over the expected life of the new product.

Provision (Benefit) for Taxes on Income

The tax expense reported on the income statement (also called *tax provision*) relates to taxes the company expects to pay to federal, state and municipal taxing authorities as well as income taxes levied by foreign governments. In 2016, Pfizer reported an income tax provision of $1,123 million, or 13.4% of the $8,351 million reported pretax income. This "effective" tax rate of 13.4% is lower than the 20%–30% rate the company reported in years before 2016.

Oddly, in 2017, Pfizer reported a tax *benefit* of $9,049 million that actually *increased* its net income. This unusual tax activity arose as a result of the U.S. Tax Cuts and Jobs Act (TCJA) of 2017. The TCJA made sweeping changes that significantly impacted companies' income statements. In particular, the new tax law:

- Reduced the corporate tax rate from 35% to 21%.

- Imposed tax on all *future* income earned outside of the U.S. even if the cash profits remain abroad.

- Reduced the repatriation tax on *prior* foreign earnings to 15.5% (from 35%).

In the two years after the TJCA passed, the tax provision line on U.S. companies' income statements gyrated wildly. Some companies reported significant spikes in tax expense in 2017 while others reported dramatic decreases. More than a few, including Pfizer, experienced tax benefits (a *negative* tax expense), which served to increase reported profits in 2017. The effects of the TJCA continued into 2018 as companies responded to the new rules by realigning operations and repatriating past foreign earnings. For example, Pfizer's effective tax rate in 2018 dipped to 5.9% (tax expense of only $706 million on pretax income of $11,885).

Neither the income tax benefit of $9,049 million in 2017 nor the relatively low tax expense of $706 million in 2018 accurately represent the income tax expense that Pfizer will report in future years. Pfizer's guidance for 2019 to analysts (presented earlier in this module) projects a 16% tax rate. We discuss income taxes more fully in Module 10. For now, we should recognize that the forecast of future tax rates is critical to an effective forecast of profit and cash flow. To forecast as accurately as possible, we must carefully read the information the company provides about its current and future income tax expense.

Discontinued Operations

From time to time, as strategy changes, companies will divest a segment of their business. When this occurs (or when there is a definitive agreement to sell the segment), the company reports the event at the bottom of the income statement by segregating income from continuing versus **discontinued operations**. The line item for discontinued operations has two distinct components.

■ Net income (or loss) from the segment's business activities prior to the divestiture or sale.

■ Any gain (or loss) on the sale of the business.

Following is the portion of Pfizer's income statement that reports on its discontinued operations.

Year Ended December 31 ($ millions)	2018	2017	2016
Income from continuing operations	$11,179	$21,353	$7,229
Discontinued operations			
Income from discontinued operations—net of tax	10	(1)	16
Gain on disposal of discontinued operations—net of tax	—	3	—
Discontinued operations—net of tax	10	2	17
Net income before allocation to noncontrolling interests	$11,189	$21,355	$7,246

In addition to segregating the results of operations of the discontinued operation in the current and previous two years' income statements reported, companies are also required to segregate the discontinued operation's assets and liabilities on the current and prior year's balance sheets.

Although the financial effects of Pfizer's discontinued operations were not significant in the most recent years, they have been in the past. In 2013 for example, Pfizer sold its animal health business to a newly formed company, Zoetis. Prior to the sale, the animal health business reported a net income of $308 million. Pfizer reported these operating results as "Income from discontinued operations—net of tax" in the 2013 income statement excerpt below. The sale of the animal health business created a gain on sale of $10,354 million, net of tax. That gain represents the difference between the sales proceeds Pfizer received from Zoetis and the amount at which the animal health business was reported on Pfizer's balance sheet on the date of the sale, that is, its net book value or carrying value.

Footnotes to Pfizer's 2013 10-K provide data relating to both the income earned by the animal health business through the date of sale along with the gain realized when the business was sold.

Year Ended ($ millions)	December 31, 2013
Revenues	$51,584
⋮	
Pretax income from discontinued operations	408
Provision for taxes on income	100
Income from discontinued operations—net of tax	308
Pretax gain on disposal of discontinued operations	10,446
Provision for taxes on income	92
Gain on disposal of discontinued operations—net of tax	10,354
Discontinued operations—net of tax	$10,662

Discontinued operations are segregated in the income statement because they represent a *transitory* item; that is, transactions or events that affect the current period (and in prior periods while the operation was owned by the company) but will not recur. Many readers of financial statements analyze current-year financial statements to gain clues to better predict *future* performance (stock prices, for example, are based on a company's expected profits and cash flows). Although the segregation of transitory items can help us analyze past performance to uncover core operating profit, they are largely irrelevant to predicting future performance. This means investors and other users tend to focus on income from continuing operations because that is the level of profitability that is likely to *persist* (continue) into the future. Likewise, the financial press tends to focus on income from continuing operations when it discloses corporate earnings (often described as "earnings before one-time charges").

Accounting standards relating to discontinued operations have recently changed and have restricted the types of disposals that will be accounted for as discontinued operations. Under the new accounting standard, in order to be classified as a discontinued operation, the disposal of the business unit must represent a *strategic shift* for the company that has or will have a *major effect* on a company's financial results. This represents a substantial hurdle because the company will have to demonstrate that a divestiture represents a strategic shift *and* creates large financial effects. Consequently, the reporting of discontinued operations is likely to be less frequent in the future.

LO6 Review 5-6

Hewlett-Packard Enterprise Co. (HPE) reports the following income statement for 2018 and 2017.

HEWLETT-PACKARD ENTERPRISE COMPANY AND SUBSIDIARIES Consolidated Statements of Earnings		
For fiscal years ended October 31 (in millions)	2018	2017
Net revenue		
Products	$19,504	$17,597
Services	10,901	10,878
Financing income	447	396
Total net revenue	30,852	28,871
Costs and expenses		
Cost of products	14,079	12,715
Cost of services	7,203	7,197
Financing interest	278	265
Research and development	1,663	1,486
Selling, general and administrative.	4,851	5,006
Amortization of intangible assets	294	321
Impairment of goodwill	88	—
Restructuring charges	19	417
Transformation costs	425	359
Disaster charges.	—	93
Acquisition and other related charges	82	203
Separation costs.	12	248
Defined benefit plan settlement charges and remeasurement (benefit). . . .	—	(64)
Gain on H3C and MphasiS divestitures	—	—
Total costs and expenses.	28,994	28,246
Earnings from continuing operations	1,858	625
Interest and other, net.	(274)	(327)
Tax indemnification adjustments	(1,354)	(3)
Earnings (loss) from equity interests	38	(23)
Earnings from continuing operations before taxes.	268	272
Benefit (provision) for taxes	1,744	164
Net earnings from continuing operations	2,012	436
Net loss from discontinued operations	(104)	(92)
Net earnings.	$ 1,908	$ 344

Required

1. Which of the following expenses would **not** be included in selling, general, and administrative expense on the income statement?
   - Salary for the chief executive officer
   - Office supplies
   - Utilities for the research laboratories
   - Depreciation on the company jet
   - Wages for manufacturing employees
   - Shipping costs for products delivered to customers
   - License fees for software used to develop new products
   - Depreciation on machines that package and label finished goods

2. Compare R&D expense for 2017 and 2018. (*Hint:* First determine the common-size expense.) List three types of activities that are included in total R&D expense for HPE.

3. Explain the item on the income statement labeled "Earnings from discontinued operations."   **Solution on p. 5-57.**

Pro Forma Income Reporting

LO7
Interpret pro forma and non-GAAP disclosures.

In its fourth quarter earnings release for 2018, Pfizer described its financial performance as follows.

 **PFIZER REPORTS FOURTH-QUARTER AND FULL-YEAR 2018 RESULTS PROVIDES 2019 FINANCIAL GUIDANCE**

- Full-Year 2018 Revenues of $53.6 Billion, Reflecting 2% Operational Growth; Fourth-Quarter 2018 Revenues of $14.0 Billion, Reflecting 5% Operational Growth
- Full-Year 2018 Reported Diluted EPS of $1.87, **Adjusted Diluted EPS** of $3.00; Fourth-Quarter 2018 Reported Loss Per Share of $0.07, Adjusted Diluted EPS of $0.64
- Returned $20.2 Billion Directly to Shareholders in 2018 Through Share Repurchases and Dividends; Anticipates Repurchasing Approximately $9 Billion of Shares in 2019

The company reports revenue growth and specifically highlights "adjusted diluted EPS" (boldface emphasis added). What is this metric, and why does Pfizer report it? To arrive at the adjusted EPS number, Pfizer made a number of deductions and additions to its published GAAP financials because company management believes doing so provides a better measure of Pfizer's financial performance. These adjusted income statements (sometimes referred to as *pro forma* income statements or non-GAAP numbers) are increasingly common.

Regulation G Reconciliation

The Securities and Exchange Commission (SEC), which oversees all publicly traded companies in the United States, requires that companies reconcile such non-GAAP information to GAAP numbers so financial statement readers can have a basis for comparison and can evaluate the excluded items (Regulation G). To comply with the regulation, Pfizer provides the following adjusted income statement in the management discussion and analysis (MD&A).

Twelve Months Ended December 31, 2018 (In millions, except per common share data)	GAAP Reported	Purchase Accounting Adjustments	Acquisition-Related Costs	Discontinued Operations	Certain Significant Items	Non-GAAP Adjusted
Revenues	$53,647	$ —	$ —	$—	$ —	$53,647
Cost of sales	11,248	3	(10)	—	(110)	11,130
Selling, informational and administrative expenses	14,455	2	(2)	—	(222)	14,232
Research and development expenses	8,006	3	—	—	(47)	7,962
Amortization of intangible assets	4,893	(4,612)	—	—	—	281
Restructuring charges and certain acquisition-related costs	1,044	—	(299)	—	(745)	—
Other (income) deductions—net	2,116	(182)	(7)	—	(3,181)	(1,253)
Income from continuing operations before provision (benefit) for taxes on income	11,885	4,786	318	—	4,305	21,294
Provision (benefit) for taxes on income	706	915	54	—	1,625	3,301
Income from continuing operations	11,179	3,871	264	—	2,680	17,994
Discontinued operations—net of tax	10	—	—	(10)	—	—
Net income attributable to noncontrolling interests	36	—	—	—	—	36
Net income attributable to Pfizer Inc.	11,153	3,871	264	(10)	2,680	**17,958**
Earnings per common share attributable to Pfizer Inc.—diluted	1.87	0.65	0.04	—	0.45	3.00

Adjusted income is an alternative view of performance used by management . . . Because Adjusted income is an important internal measurement for Pfizer, we believe that investors' understanding of our performance is enhanced by disclosing this performance measure . . . We have defined Adjusted income as Net income attributable to Pfizer Inc. before the impact of purchase accounting for acquisitions, acquisition-related costs, discontinued operations and certain significant items.

Pfizer's "adjusted" net income is $17,958 million (as compared with GAAP net income of $11,153 million), and excludes costs primarily relating to transitory items, such as costs relating to acquisitions completed during the year, discontinued operations, and other one-time nonrecurring items.

Pfizer's management appears to be thorough in its reporting of "adjusted" income statement items, but other companies may not be. It is important to remember that a company's purpose for making a non-GAAP disclosure is to portray its financial performance the way that management would like us to analyze it. Unscrupulous companies can attempt to lower the bar for analysis by presenting financial results in the best possible light.

SEC Warnings about Pro Forma Numbers

The SEC is very mindful of the potential for abuse in pro forma income statements and cautions investors as follows. (Excerpted from Securities and Exchange Commission (Release Nos. 33-8039, 34-45124, FR-59) "Cautionary Advice Regarding the Use of 'Pro Forma' Financial Information in Earnings Releases," https://www.sec.gov/rules/other/33-8039.htm.)

> We believe it is appropriate to sound a warning to public companies and other registrants who present to the public their earnings and results of operations on the basis of methodologies other than Generally Accepted Accounting Principles ("GAAP"). This presentation in an earnings release is often referred to as "pro forma" financial information. In this context, that term has no defined meaning and no uniform characteristics. We wish to caution public companies on their use of this "pro forma" financial information and to alert investors to the potential dangers of such information.
>
> "Pro forma" financial information can serve useful purposes. Public companies may quite appropriately wish to focus investors' attention on critical components of quarterly or annual financial results in order to provide a meaningful comparison to results for the same period of prior years or to emphasize the results of core operations. To a large extent, this has been the intended function of disclosures in a company's Management's Discussion and Analysis section of its reports. There is no prohibition preventing public companies from publishing interpretations of their results, or publishing summaries of GAAP financial statements. . .
>
> Nonetheless, we are concerned that "pro forma" financial information, under certain circumstances, can mislead investors if it obscures GAAP results. Because this "pro forma" financial information by its very nature departs from traditional accounting conventions, its use can make it hard for investors to compare an issuer's financial information with other reporting periods and with other companies.
>
> For these reasons . . . we encourage investors to compare any summary or "pro forma" financial presentation with the results reported on GAAP-based financials by the same company. Read before you invest; understand before you commit.

When we read adjusted (pro forma) income statements, it is important to remember they represent management's interpretation of the company's financial performance. We must view those representations as such, not as statements of fact.[1]

Disclosures and Market Assessments

Pro forma income statements must be read and analyzed within the context of the GAAP statements. It is only by a thorough analysis of the GAAP financial statements that we can understand the reasons for, and the implications of, the adjustments management is making with the pro forma statements. We recommend the following steps for a thorough reading of the GAAP financials.

- Read the reports from the external auditor, and take special note of any deviation from boilerplate language.

- Peruse the footnote on accounting policies (typically footnote 1), and compare the company's policies with its industry peers. Deviations from the norm can signal opportunism.

- Examine changes in accounting policies. What would the company have reported absent the change? Did the new policy help it avoid reporting a loss or violating a debt covenant?

- Compare key ratios over time. Follow up on marked increases or decreases in ratios, read footnotes and the MD&A to see how management explains such changes. Follow up on ratios that do not change when a change is expected. For example, during the tech bubble, Worldcom Inc. reported an

---

[1] For a good discussion of the issue of accounting *quality*, see Dechow, P., and C. Schrand. "Earnings Quality," The Research Foundation of CFA Institute. Charlottesville, VA 2004.

expense-to-revenue ratio (ER ratio) of 42% quarter after quarter, despite worsening economic conditions. Later, it was discovered that managers had deliberately underreported expenses to maintain the ER ratio. The lesson is that sometimes no change signals managerial intervention.

- Review ratios of competitors, and consider macroeconomic conditions and how they have shifted over time. Are the ratios reasonable in light of current conditions? Are changes in the income statement aligning with changes on the balance sheet?
- Identify nonrecurring items, and separately assess their impact on company performance and position.
- Recast financial statements as necessary to reflect an accounting policy(ies) that is more in line with competitors or one that better reflects economically relevant numbers. We illustrate recasting at several points in future modules.

Business Insight ▪ Creative Accounting

Pfizer calls its non-GAAP earnings "Adjusted earnings." Other companies use more creative labels. Consider the following examples of pro forma metrics and their effects reported during 2018 and 2019.

UBER *Core-platform contribution margin*, which changed a $3 billion loss to a non-GAAP profit of $940 million.
WeWork *Community-adjusted EBITDA*, which allowed the company to report non-GAAP profit of $467 million instead of a *loss* of $1.9 billion.
Lyft *Adjusted contribution margin*, which was $384.9 million versus a GAAP loss of $1,138.5 million.

Other recent creative non-GAAP measures include:

- Annual recurring revenue
- Bookings
- Cumulative billings
- Adjusted consolidated segment operating income (ACSOI)
- Profit including back-log sales

These pro forma reporting practices are reminiscent of the dot-com bubble of the early 2000s and, like then, are most prevalent among tech and start-up companies. It remains to be seen if investors are any savvier this time around, or whether the rosier non-GAAP profits hold sway.

The purported motive for reporting pro forma income is to eliminate transitory (one-time) items to enhance year-to-year comparability. Although this might be justified on the basis that pro forma income has greater predictive ability, important information could be lost in the process. One role for accounting is to report how effective management has been in its stewardship of invested capital. Asset write-downs, liability accruals, and other charges that are eliminated in calculating pro forma income often reflect outcomes of poor management decisions. Our analysis must not blindly eliminate information contained in nonrecurring items by focusing solely on pro forma income. Critics of pro forma income also argue that the items excluded by managers from GAAP income are inconsistent across companies and time. They contend that a major motive for pro forma income is to mislead stakeholders. Legendary investor Warren Buffett puts pro forma in context: "When companies or investment professionals use terms such as 'EBITDA' and 'pro forma,' they want you to unthinkingly accept concepts that are dangerously flawed." (Berkshire Hathaway, Annual Report)

Research Insight ▪ Assessing Earnings Quality

It is no secret that corporate executives can and do make choices to deliberately influence reported earnings. GAAP permits choices so that each company can make its financial reports as relevant as possible. But the latitude granted by GAAP opens the door for potential abuse that reduces the quality of financial reports in general and of net earnings in particular. But how prevalent is such deliberate intervention? Can it be detected?

Recently, a team of accounting researchers surveyed and interviewed chief financial officers (CFOs) and other finance executives at 400 firms (169 public and 231 private). The research aimed to uncover CFOs' thinking about earnings quality and reasons for deliberate intervention in the reporting process. According to the CFOs, nearly 20% of public companies and 25% of private companies use allowable discretion in GAAP to misrepresent earnings with average misrepresentations of 12 cents on the dollar. Interestingly, 33% of the misrepresentations *decreased* earnings.

When asked about potential motivations for deliberately misrepresenting earnings, CFOs almost unanimously agreed it was "to influence stock price," "to hit earnings benchmarks," and "to influence executive compensation." The researchers compiled a list of 20 red flags that suggest earnings misrepresentation according to the CFOs.

continued

1. GAAP earnings and cash flow from operations move in different direction for 6–8 quarters.
2. Deviations from industry norms on critical metrics, including cash cycle, average profitability, revenue growth, asset impairment, level of disclosure.
3. Consistently meeting or beating earnings targets.
4. Large or frequent one-time items, such as restructuring charges, write-downs, or gains and losses on asset sales.
5. Large changes in accruals or capitalized costs and insufficient explanation of such changes.
6. Too smooth of an earnings progression (relative to economy, market).
7. Frequent changes in significant accounting policies.
8. Using non-GAAP metrics.
9. High executive and employee turnover, sudden change in top management.
10. Inventory buildup and mismatch between inventory and COGS.
11. Wide swings in earnings, especially without real change in business.
12. Buildups of receivables, deterioration of days sales outstanding.
13. Aggressive use of long-term estimates and lack of explanatory detail on estimates.
14. SEC filings becoming less transparent, uninformative MD&A, complex footnotes.
15. Major jumps or turnarounds or breaks with historical performance.
16. Large incentive compensation payment and management turnover after bonus payments.
17. Repeated restatement of earnings and prior period adjustments.
18. Accruals, assets, and working capital growing faster or slower than revenue.
19. Increased debt and high liabilities.
20. Weak sales growth or declining performance versus the industry.

Source: Dichev, I. D., Graham, J. R., Harvey, C. R., and Rajgopal, S., "Earnings Quality: Evidence from the Field" (2013). Available at SSRN: http://ssrn.com/abstract=2103384 or http://dx.doi.org/10.2139/ssrn.2103384.

L07 Review 5-7

In its SEC 10-K filing for 2018, Merck & Co. Inc. provided the proforma disclosures below. Use this information to answer the requirements.

A reconciliation between GAAP financial measures and non-GAAP financial measures is as follows: ($ in millions)	2018	2017	2016
Income before taxes as reported under GAAP	$ 8,701	$ 6,521	$ 4,659
Increase (decrease) for excluded items:			
Acquisition and divestiture-related costs	3,066	3,760	7,312
Restructuring costs	658	927	1,069
Other items:			
Charge related to the formation of an oncology collaboration with Eisai	1,400	—	—
Charge related to the termination of a collaboration with Samsung	423	—	—
Charge for the acquisition of Viralytics	344	—	—
Charge related to the formation of an oncology collaboration with AstraZeneca	—	2,350	—
Charge related to the settlement of worldwide Keytruda patent litigation	—	—	625
Other	(57)	(16)	(67)
Non-GAAP income before taxes	14,535	13,542	13,598
Taxes on income as reported under GAAP	2,508	4,103	718
Estimated tax benefit on excluded items	535	785	2,321
Net tax charge related to the enactment of the TCJA	(160)	(2,625)	—
Net tax benefit from the settlement of certain federal income tax issues	—	234	—
Tax benefit related to the settlement of a state income tax issue	—	88	—
Non-GAAP taxes on income	2,883	2,585	3,039
Non-GAAP net income	$11,652	$10,957	$10,559

Required

1. Why do firms, including Merck, publicly report non-GAAP information?
2. What are the significant items and the effect of the proposed adjustments on non-GAAP net income?　　　**Solution on p. 5-58.**

Global Accounting

Revenue Recognition

The new revenue recognition standard, as discussed in this module, eliminates many prior differences between U.S. GAAP and IFRS. That is, the accounting for revenue is now nearly identical between the two systems.

Accounts Receivable

Accounts receivable are accounted for identically with one notable exception. Under IFRS, all receivables are treated as financial assets. This means future cash flows from accounts receivable must be discounted and reported at net present value. This measurement applies to both short- and long-term receivables, assuming the effect of discounting is material. For analysis purposes, we review the notes to determine the discount rate used by the company using IFRS and assess the significance of any discounting. Ratios using accounts receivable (such as turnover ratios and current ratios) can be affected.

Research and Development

Accounting for R&D represents an ongoing difference between U.S. GAAP and IFRS. International standards required that all research expenditures be expensed in the period in which they are incurred. This is consistent with U.S. GAAP. The two standards diverge when it comes to development costs. Under IFRS standard 38, companies *shall capitalize and recognize* as intangible assets, all development costs related to products and services when the company can demonstrate the following:

- Intangible asset's technical feasibility;
- Intention to complete the development of the intangible asset;
- Ability to use or sell the intangible asset;
- How the intangible asset will generate probable future economic benefits (for example, the existence of a market for the output of the intangible asset or for the intangible asset itself);
- Availability of resources to complete the development; and
- Ability to reliably measure the related expenditures (costs pertaining to the intangible asset).

These *internally generated intangible assets* are amortized over their useful lives and periodically assessed for impairment. As such, we observe larger intangible assets on the balance sheets of IFRS companies.

Guidance Answers

You Are the Receivables Manager

Pg. 5-24 First, we must realize that extending credit is an important tool in the marketing of your products, often as important as advertising and promotion. Given that receivables are necessary, there are certain ways to speed their collection. (1) We can better screen the customers to whom we extend credit. (2) We can negotiate advance or progress payments from customers. (3) We can use bank letters of credit or other automatic drafting procedures that obviate billing. (4) We can make sure products are sent as ordered, to reduce disputes. (5) We can improve administration of past-due accounts to provide for more timely notices of delinquencies and better collection procedures.

Questions

Q5-1. What is a performance obligation and how is it related to revenue recognition?

Q5-2. Explain how management can shift income from one period into another by using the allowance for uncollectibles account.

Q5-3. Why do companies allow sales returns, and how does this business practice affect reported revenue?

Q5-4. The income statement line item "Discontinued operations" typically comprises two distinct components. What are they?

Q5-5. What effect, if any, does a weakening $US have on reported sales and net income for subsidiaries of U.S. companies?

Q5-6. Explain why analysts might remove foreign exchange gains or losses when analyzing revenue and expenses for the year.

Q5-7. What is meant by "aging" of accounts receivable?

Q5-8. Under what circumstances is it appropriate to use the cost-to-cost method to measure revenue?

Q5-9. What is the concept of pro forma income and why has this income measure been criticized?

Q5-10. What is unearned revenue? Provide three examples of unearned revenue.

Q5-11. What is the current U.S. GAAP accounting treatment for research and development costs?

Q5-12. How would a company recognize revenue on a sale that includes equipment and a multi-year service contract all for one price?

Assignments with the 🌐 logo in the margin are available in BusinessCourse.
See the Preface of the book for details.

Mini Exercises

M5-13. Computing Revenues under Long-Term Contracts   LO1

Camden Corporation agreed to build a warehouse for a client at an agreed contract price of $900,000. Expected (and actual) costs for the warehouse follow: 2016, $202,500; 2017, $337,500; and 2018, $135,000. The company completed the warehouse in 2018. Compute revenues, expenses, and income for each year 2016 through 2018, and for all three years combined, using the cost-to-cost method.

M5-14. Applying the Financial Statement Effects Template   LO1

Refer to the information for Camden Corporation in M5-13.

a. Use the financial statement effects template to record contract revenues and expenses for each year 2016 through 2018 using the cost-to-cost method.

b. Prepare journal entries and T-accounts to record contract revenues and expenses for each year 2016 through 2018 using the cost-to-cost method. Assume Camden does not receive payment until the contract is completed. All costs are paid in cash.

M5-15. Assessing Revenue Recognition of Companies   LO1

Match each of the following companies, to the appropriate revenue recognition policy, listed below.

a. The GAP: The GAP is a retailer of clothing items for all ages.

b. GlaxoSmithKline: GSK develops, manufactures, and markets pharmaceutical products. It sells its drugs (many of which have regulated expiry dates) to retailers such as CVS and Walgreens.

c. Deere & Company: Deere manufactures heavy equipment. It sells equipment to a network of independent distributors, who in turn sell the equipment to customers. Deere provides financing and insurance services both to distributors and customers.

d. Bank of America: Bank of America is a banking institution. It lends money to individuals and corporations and invests excess funds in marketable securities.

e. Johnson Controls: Johnson Controls manufactures products for the government under long-term contracts.

The GAP (GPS)

GlaxoSmithKline (GSK)

Deere & Company (DE)

Bank of America (BAC)

Johnson Controls (JCI)

1. The performance obligation is to build and complete projects for specific customers. Revenue is recognized for long-term construction contracts under the percentage-of-completion method, typically using cost-to-cost method to identify the percentage of the project that is complete.

2. The performance obligation is fulfilled when the customer takes delivery of the merchandise and the right of return period for regulated products has expired or costs of returns can be reasonably estimated. The company will also establish an allowance for uncollectible accounts receivable when revenue is recognized.

3. The performance obligation is recorded when the customer takes the merchandise (for in-store sales) or when the goods are delivered (for online sales). The company estimates product returns and records an allowance at the time of sale.

4. The performance obligation is fulfilled when the customer takes the merchandise. The company will also establish allowances for product returns, uncollectible accounts, and a reserve for anticipated warranty costs. Revenues for financial or insurance services are recognized when the services are provided.

5. The performance obligation is fulfilled with the passage of time. Interest is earned by the passage of time. Each period income is accrued on loans even if customers have not yet paid the interest.

LO7
OptimizeRx (OPRX)

M5-16. **Non-GAAP Disclosure**

OptimizeRx provides digital health messaging via electronic health records to provide a direct channel for pharmaceutical companies to communicate with healthcare providers and patients. The company reported the following in its 2018 earnings release.

Reconciliation of Non-GAAP to GAAP Financial Measures	For the Three Months Ended Dec. 31, 2018	For the Twelve Months Ended Dec. 31, 2018
Net income (loss)	$(109,914)	$ 226,344
Depreciation and amortization	153,085	316,502
Stock-based compensation	798,866	2,520,852
Non GAAP net income	$ 842,037	$3,063,698

    a. Explain in plain language the two adjustments that OptimizeRx makes to arrive at non-GAAP net income.

    b. How did the adjustments affect non-GAAP net income for the fiscal quarter ended December 31, 2018? For the 2018 fiscal year? Are these effects significant?

LO1, 2
ModCloth Inc.

M5-17. **Estimating Revenue Recognition with Right of Return**

ModCloth Inc. offers an unconditional return policy. It normally expects 2% of sales at retail selling prices to be returned before the return period expires. Assuming ModCloth records total sales of $10 million for the current period, what amount of *net* sales should it record for this period?

LO5

M5-18. **Estimating Uncollectible Accounts and Reporting Accounts Receivable**

Mohan Company estimates its uncollectible accounts by aging its accounts receivable and applying percentages to various aged categories of accounts. Mohan computes a total of $2,100 in estimated uncollectible accounts as of its current year-end. Its accounts receivable has a balance of $86,000, and its allowance for uncollectible accounts has an unused balance of $700 before any year-end adjustments.

    a. What amount of bad debt expense will Mohan report in its income statement for the current year?

    b. Determine the net amount of accounts receivable reported in current assets at year-end.

LO5

M5-19. **Interpreting the Allowance Method for Accounts Receivable**

At a recent board of directors meeting of Bismark Corp., one of the directors expressed concern over the allowance for uncollectible accounts appearing in the company's balance sheet. "I don't understand this account," he said. "Why don't we just show accounts receivable at the amount owed to us and get rid of that allowance?" Respond to the director's question; include in your response (a) an explanation of why the company has an allowance account, (b) what the balance sheet presentation of accounts receivable is intended to show, and (c) how accrual accounting (as opposed to the cash-basis accounting) affects the presentation of accounts receivable.

LO5
Mondelēz
International (MDLZ)

M5-20. **Analyzing the Allowance for Uncollectible Accounts**

Following is the current asset section from the Mondelēz balance sheet.

$ millions	Dec. 31, 2018	Dec. 31, 2017
Cash and cash equivalents	$ 1,100	$ 761
Trade receivables (net of allowances of $40 at 2018 and $50 at 2017)	2,262	2,691
Other receivables (net of allowances of $47 at 2018 and $98 at 2017)	744	835
Inventories, net	2,592	2,557
Other current assets	906	676
Total current assets	$ 7,604	$ 7,520
Total assets	$62,729	$62,957

    a. What is the common-size trade receivables, net, at year-end 2018?

        i. 29.75%   iii. 3.61%

        ii. 3.94%   iv. 4.79%

    b. What do Mondelez's customers owe the company at December 31, 2018 ($ millions)?

        i. $2,262   iii. $2,222

        ii. $2,302   iv. $3,006

    c. What does Mondelez expect to collect from its customers as of December 31, 2017 ($ millions)?

         i. $2,691   iii. $2,641

         ii. $2,741   iv. $3,526

    d. What is the GROSS Receivables at year-end 2018 ($ millions)?

         i. $2,302   iii. $3,006

         ii. $3,093   iv. $2,919

    e. What percentage of trade receivables does the company deem uncollectible as of year-end 2018?

         i.   1.77%   iii.   1.80%

         ii.   3.85%   iv.   1.74%

    f. Based on the analysis above, in which year does the company have higher quality trade receivables?

         i.   2018   ii.   2017

M5-21.   **Evaluating Accounts Receivable Turnover for Competitors**

    The Procter & Gamble Company and **Colgate-Palmolive Company** report the following sales and accounts receivable balances.

LO5

The Procter & Gamble Company (PG)

Colgate-Palmolive Company (CL)

$ millions	Procter & Gamble	Colgate-Palmolive
2018 Net sales	$66,832	$15,544
2018 Accounts receivable	4,686	1,400
2017 Accounts receivable	4,594	1,480

    a. Compute the accounts receivable turnover and DSO for both companies for 2018.

    b. Identify and discuss a potential explanation for the difference between these competitors' accounts receivable ratios.

M5-22.   **Interpreting Foreign Currency Translation Disclosure**

    Procter & Gamble reports the following table in its 10-K report relating to the change in sales from 2017 to 2018.

LO4

Procter & Gamble Company (PNG)

Net Sales Change Drivers 2018 vs. 2017	Volume	Foreign Exchange	Price	Mix	Net Sales Growth
Beauty	2%	2%	—	5%	9%
Grooming	—	3%	(3)%	(1)%	(1)%
Health care	3%	3%	(1)%	—	5%
Fabric & home care	3%	1%	(1)%	—	3%
Baby, feminine & family care	(1)%	1%	(1)%	—	(1)%
Total company	1%	2%	(1)%	1%	3%

    a. Did total company net sales increase or decrease during the year? By what percentage? How much of this change is attributable to volume versus price changes?

    b. What was the effect of foreign exchange rates on sales during the year? From this result, what can we infer about the relative strength of the $US during the period?

    c. The Grooming and the Baby, Feminine & Family Care segment sales both decreased by 1%. From this result, can we conclude that the dollar decrease in sales was the same for both segments? Explain.

M5-23.   **Assessing Revenue Recognition for Advance Payments**

    Hamilton Company operates a performing arts center. The company sells tickets for its upcoming season of six Broadway musicals and receives $630,000 cash. The performances occur monthly over the next six months.

    a. When should Hamilton record revenue for the Broadway musical series?

    b. Use the financial statement effects template to show the $630,000 cash receipt and recognition of the first month's revenue.

LO3

M5-24.   **Reporting Unearned Revenue**

    Target sells gift cards that can be used at any of the company's Target stores or on Target.com. Target encodes information on the card's magnetic strip about the card's value and the store where it was purchased. Target gift cards do not have expiration dates.

    a. When does Target record revenue from the gift card?

         i.   Two years after the date of the sale, which is when the gift card expires.

         ii.   When the gift card is sold.

LO3

Target Corporation (TGT)

      iii. When the customer uses the gift card, at which point, Target also records an allowance for estimated product returns.

      iv. 90 days after the date the customer uses the gift card, which is when the product return period expires.

  b. How will Target's balance sheet reflect the gift card when it is initially sold?

    i. As an asset: cash and cash equivalents.   iii. As sales revenue.

    ii. As an asset: allowance for product sales.   iv. As a liability: unearned revenue.

LO2

M5-25. **Sales Returns**

Which of the following statements is true relating to the allowance for sales returns?

  a. Sales returns are treated as an expense in the income statement and, therefore, reduce profit for the period.

  b. An excess of the amount by which the allowance for sales returns is increased compared with the actual returns for the period indicates the company may have inflated profit for the period.

  c. The amount by which the allowance for sales returns is reduced during the period is recognized as a reduction of sales for the period, thus reducing profit.

  d. Increasing the allowance for sales returns by an amount that is less than the actual returns recognized for the period may indicate either the company is attempting to increase profit for the period or it estimates that less of its products will be returned in the future.

LO3

M5-26. **Deferred Revenue**

True or false: A reduction of the deferred revenue account can be interpreted as a leading indicator of lower future revenues. Explain.

LO4

M5-27. **Foreign Exchange Effects on Sales**

True or false: A multinational company reports that a large amount of its sales is generated in foreign currencies that have strengthened vis-à-vis the $US. Consolidated revenues are likely lower than would have been reported in the absence of such a shift in exchange rates.

LO6

M5-28. **Operating Expenses**

Indicate whether each of the following is true or false.

  a. Amortization expense is a noncash expense similar to depreciation, except it applies to intangible assets.

  b. Income attributable to noncontrolling interests is an expense item that reduces net income.

  c. Discontinued operations relate to any segment of the business a company is selling.

  d. The income (loss) of Discontinued operations and gain (loss) on their sale are reported in the income statement like other revenue and expense items.

LO1, 3

American Airlines (AMR)

M5-29. **Revenue Disclosure and Unearned Revenue**

American Airlines disclosed the following in its Form 10-Q for the first quarter ended March 31, 2019.

> On March 13, 2019, the Federal Aviation Administration (FAA) grounded all U.S.-registered Boeing 737 MAX aircraft. Our fleet currently includes 24 Boeing 737 MAX aircraft with an additional 76 aircraft on order. As a result, we canceled approximately 1,200 flights in the first quarter of 2019.
>
> In aggregate, we estimate that these grounded aircraft and associated flight cancellations decreased our first quarter 2019 pre-tax income by approximately $80 million.
>
> We have removed all Boeing 737 MAX flying from our flight schedule through August 19, 2019, which is approximately 115 flights per day. These flights represent approximately 2% of our total capacity each day this summer. Although these aircraft represent a small portion of our total fleet, its financial impact is disproportionate as most of the revenue from the cancellations is lost while the vast majority of the costs remain in place. In total, we currently estimate the Boeing 737 MAX cancellations, which are assumed to extend through August 19, 2019, to decrease our 2019 pre-tax income by approximately $350 million.

  a. Why does American Airlines disclose this information?

  b. What would be the effect on deferred revenue on the March 31, 2019, balance sheet (relative to the prior year-end December 31, 2018) because of these flight cancellations?

LO6

Campbell Soup (CPB)

M5-30. **Discontinued Operations**

Campbell Soup reported discontinued operations in its Form 10-Q for the third quarter ended April 28, 2019. The company reported that, during the third quarter, it sold its Garden Fresh Gourmet business for approximately $55 million and also signed a definitive agreement for the sale of Bolthouse Farms for $510 million and expects to close the deal before July 2019. The company disclosed the following related to these discontinued operations ($ millions).

For the Nine Months Ended	April 28, 2019
Net sales.	$ 666
Earnings (loss) from operations, after-tax	$(279)
Loss on sale of businesses, net of tax	(52)
Loss from discontinued operations.	$(331)

a. Which of the following best describes how Campbell Soup reported the Bolthouse transaction?
   i. Campbell Soup will report the Bolthouse unit as discontinued operations in the quarter in which the unit is formally sold.
   ii. Campbell Soup reported the Bolthouse unit as discontinued operations in the April 28, 2019, income statement even though the unit had not been formally sold by then.
   iii. Campbell Soup will retroactively report the Bolthouse unit as discontinued operations in the year in which the unit is formally sold.
   iv. Campbell Soup will pro-rate the effects of the Bolthouse unit sale (as discontinued operations) event among the fiscal quarters in year in which the unit is formally sold.
b. What amount of sales revenue did Campbell Soup earn from Garden Fresh Gourmet and Bolthouse for the first three quarters of fiscal 2019?
c. What amount of earnings did Campbell Soup report from Garden Fresh Gourmet and Bolthouse for the first three quarters of fiscal 2019?
d. What was the combined selling price for Garden Fresh Gourmet and Bolthouse Farms?
e. Ignoring tax effects, what is the approximate combined net book value of Garden Fresh Gourmet and Bolthouse Farms at the date of their respective disposals?

Exercises

E5-31. Assessing Revenue Recognition Timing

LO1

Explain when each of the following businesses fulfills the performance obligations implicit in the sales contract.

a. A clothing retailer like **American Eagle Outfitters Inc.**
b. A contractor like **Raytheon Company** that performs work under long-term government contracts.
c. A grocery store like **Supervalu Inc.**
d. A producer of television shows like **MTV** that syndicates its content to television stations.
e. A residential real estate developer that constructs only speculative houses and later sells these houses to buyers.
f. A banking institution like **Bank of America Corp.** that lends money for home mortgages.
g. A manufacturer like **Harley-Davidson Inc.**
h. A publisher of magazines such as **Time-Warner Inc.**

American Eagle Outfitters Inc. (AEO)
Raytheon Company (RTN)
Supervalu Inc. (SVU)
MTV
Bank of America Corp. (BAC)
Harley-Davidson Inc. (HOG)
Time-Warner Inc. (TWX)

E5-32. Assessing Revenue Recognition Timing and Income Measurement

LO1

Explain when each of the following businesses fulfills the performance obligations implicit in the sales contract and recognizes revenue. Identify any revenue measurement issues that could arise.

a. RealMoney.Com, a division of **TheStreet Inc.**, provides investment advice to customers for an up-front fee. It provides these customers with password-protected access to its website, where they can download investment reports. RealMoney has an obligation to provide updates on its website.
b. **Oracle Corp.** develops general ledger and other business application software that it sells to its customers. The customer pays an up-front fee for the right to use the software and a monthly fee for support services.
c. **Intuit Inc.** develops tax preparation software that it sells to its customers for a flat fee. No further payment is required, and the software cannot be returned, only exchanged if defective.
d. **Electronic Arts** develops and sells computer games. The company will provide a full refund within 24 hours after the game is first launched or within 14 days from the date of sale, if the game has not been launched. After that, there is no refund.

TheStreet Inc. (TST)

Oracle Corp. (ORCL)

Intuit Inc. (INTU)

Electronic Arts (EA)

LO1

GE Hitachi Nuclear
Energy (GEH)

E5-33. **Constructing and Assessing Income Statements Using Cost-to-Cost Method**

Assume **GE Hitachi Nuclear Energy** agreed in May 2019 to construct a nuclear generator for NSTAR, a utility company serving the Boston area. GE Hitachi estimated that its construction costs would be $600 million. The contract price of $750 million is to be paid as follows: $250 million at the time of signing; $250 million on December 31, 2019; and $250 million at completion in May 2020. GE Hitachi Nuclear Energy incurred the following costs in constructing the generator: $240 million in 2019 and $360 million in 2020.

a. Compute the revenue, expense, and income for both 2019 and 2020, and for both years combined, under the company's cost-to-cost revenue recognition method.

b. Discuss whether or not we believe the cost-to-cost method provides a good measure of the company's performance under the contract.

LO1

E5-34. **Constructing and Assessing Income Statements Using Cost-to-Cost Method**

On March 15, 2019, Gilbert Construction contracted to build a shopping center at a contract price of $220 million. The schedule of expected (which equals actual) cash collections and contract costs follows.

Year	Cash Collections	Cost Incurred
2019	$ 55 million	$ 36 million
2020	88 million	81 million
2021	77 million	63 million
Total	$220 million	$180 million

a. Calculate the amount of revenue, expense, and net income for each of the three years 2019 through 2021, and for all three years combined, using the cost-to-cost revenue recognition method.

b. Discuss whether or not the cost-to-cost method provides a good measure of this construction company's performance under the contract.

LO1

Beyond Meat, Inc.
(BYND)

E5-35. **Analyzing Segment Revenue Disclosures from Quarterly Data**

Beyond Meat disclosed the following in its Form 10-Q for the first quarter ended March 30, 2019. The company had its initial public offering (IPO) in May 2019.

The Company's net revenues by platform and channel are included in the tables below:

For Three Months Ended (in thousands)	March 30, 2019	March 31, 2018
Net revenues		
Fresh platform.	$38,806	$ 9,596
Frozen platform.	4,512	4,748
Less: discounts	(3,112)	(1,568)
Net revenues	$40,206	$12,776

For Three Months Ended (in thousands)	March 30, 2019	March 31, 2018
Net revenues		
Retail.	$19,579	$ 9,288
Restaurant and foodservice	20,627	3,488
Net revenues	$40,206	$12,776

Two distributors each accounted for approximately 21% of the Company's gross revenues in the three months ended March 30, 2019; and three distributors accounted for approximately 34%, 14% and 11%, respectively, of the Company's gross revenues in the three months ended March 31, 2018.

a. Calculate the average discount given to customers for the two quarters presented. Why might a company like Beyond Meat grant such generous discounts? What do we observe about the level of the discounts across the two quarters?

b. Beyond Meat's revenue grew tremendously between March 2018 and March 2019. Determine growth rates for each of the platforms and channels disclosed (Fresh, Frozen, Retail, and Restaurant). Use these ratios to explain overall revenue growth.

c. Explain why the company disclosed the proportion of sales to its major distributors. Why would investors care to know this information?

E5-36.   **Foreign Currency Impact**

LO4

Kellogg Company (K)

Kellogg included the following note in its fiscal 2018 10-K report ($ millions).

Adjusted net income attributable to Kellogg......................	$1,510
Foreign currency impact.......................................	4
Currency-neutral adjusted net income attributable to Kellogg...........	$1,506

a. Assume the foreign currency impact related entirely to foreign sales. Determine whether the $US strengthened or weakened vis-à-vis the currencies in which Kellogg conducts business.

b. Assume the foreign currency impact related entirely to purchases of goods from foreign vendors. Determine whether the $US strengthened or weakened vis-à-vis the currencies in which Kellogg conducts business.

c. As an analyst, how would we treat this foreign currency impact in our analysis of Kellogg?

E5-37.   **Identifying Operating Income Components**

Following is the income statement information from Apollo Medical Devices. Identify the components that we would consider operating.

LO6

Homework

MBC

$ thousands	2020
Net sales..	$4,163,770
Cost of sales before special charges	1,382,235
Special inventory obsolescence charge......................	27,876
Total cost of sales......................................	1,410,111
Gross profit..	2,753,659
Selling, general and administrative expense	1,570,667
Research and development expense.........................	531,086
Merger and acquisition costs	46,914
In-process research and development charges	12,244
Litigation settlement	16,500
Operating profit.......................................	576,248
Interest expense.......................................	(57,372)
Interest income.......................................	2,076
Gain on disposal of fixed assets...........................	4,929
Impairment of marketable securities.........................	(5,222)
Other income (expense), net	(2,857)
Earnings before income taxes	517,802
Income tax expense.....................................	191,587
Net earnings..	$ 326,215

E5-38.   **Identifying Operating Income Components**

Following is the Deere & Company income statement for 2018.

LO6

Deere & Company
(DE)

Homework

MBC

$ millions	2018
Net sales and revenues	
Net sales..	$33,350.7
Finance and interest income.............................	3,106.6
Other income	900.4
Total	$37,357.7
Costs and expenses	
Cost of sales.......................................	$25,571.2
Research and development expenses	1,399.1
Selling, administrative and general expenses................	1,657.6
Interest expense	3,455.5
Other operating expenses..............................	1,203.6
Total	33,287.0

continued

continued from previous page

$ millions	2018
Income of consolidated group before income taxes...............	4,070.7
Provision for income taxes.......................................	1,726.9
Income of consolidated group	2,343.8
Equity in income of unconsolidated affiliates	26.8
Net income..	2,370.6
Less: Net income attributable to noncontrolling interests.........	2.2
Net income attributable to Deere & Company	$ 2,368.4

Notes:
- The income statement includes John Deere commercial and consumer tractor segment, a finance subsidiary that provides loan and lease financing relating to the sales of those tractors, and a healthcare segment that provides managed healthcare services for the company and certain outside customers.
- Equity in income of unconsolidated affiliates refers to income John Deere has earned on investments made for strategic purposes.

a. Identify the components in its income statement that we would consider operating.

b. Discuss our treatment of the company's finance and interest income and the income from the unconsolidated affiliates. Would these items be treated as operating or nonoperating?

LO4, 7 **E5-39. Analyzing and Interpreting Foreign Currency Translation Effects and Non-GAAP Disclosures**

Kellogg Co. (K)

Kellogg Co. reports the following table and discussion in its 2018 10-K for its reportable segments.

The following table provides an analysis of operating profit for the year ended December 29, 2018.

$ millions	U.S Morning Foods	U.S. Snacks	U.S. Specialty	North America Other	Europe	Latin America	Asia Pacific	Corporate	Kellogg Consolidated
2018 Reported operating profit......	$446	$478	$251	$222	$297	$102	$128	$(218)	$1,706
Mark-to-market...................	—	—	—	—	—	—	—	7	7
Project K and cost-reduction activities ...	(28)	(50)	(4)	(25)	(33)	(15)	(11)	(7)	(173)
Brexit impacts....................	—	—	—	—	(3)	—	—	—	(3)
Business and portfolio realignment	(3)	—	—	—	—	—	—	(2)	(5)
Adjusted operating profit...........	477	528	255	247	333	117	139	(216)	1,880
Foreign currency impact.............	—	—	—	(2)	6	(3)	(7)	3	(3)
2018 Currency-neutral adjusted operating profit.................	$477	$528	$255	$249	$327	$120	$146	$(219)	$1,883
2017 Reported operating profit......	$138	$567	$312	$229	$276	$108	$84	$(327)	$1,387
2017 Currency-neutral adjusted operating profit.................	$447	$585	$314	$245	$316	$116	$95	$(239)	$1,879
Operating Profit 2018 vs. 2017									
Reported growth....................	224.4%	(15.7)%	(19.8)%	(3.0)%	7.8%	(5.2)%	50.7%	33.1%	22.9%
Mark-to-market....................	—	—	—	—	—	—	—	25.2%	7.3%
Project K and cost-reduction activities ...	218.3%	(6.0)%	(0.7)%	(3.9)%	3.1%	(5.6)%	6.1%	(0.5)%	16.1%
Brexit impacts....................	—	—	—	—	(0.9)%	—	—	—	(0.2)%
Business and portfolio realignment	(0.8)%	—	—	—	—	—	—	(0.8)%	(0.3)%
Adjusted growth	6.9%	(9.7)%	(19.1)%	0.9%	5.6%	0.4%	44.6%	9.2%	—
Foreign currency impact.............	—	—	—	(0.4)%	1.9%	(2.8)%	(7.2)%	0.6%	(0.1)%
Currency-neutral adjusted growth	6.9%	(9.7)%	(19.1)%	1.3%	3.7%	3.2%	51.8%	8.6%	0.1%

Brexit: We recognize that there are still significant uncertainties surrounding the ultimate resolution of Brexit negotiations, and we will continue to monitor any changes that may arise and assess their potential impact on our business.

Project K restructuring: Since inception, Project K has reduced the Company's cost structure, and is expected to provide enduring benefits, including an optimized supply chain infrastructure, an efficient global business services model, a global focus on categories, increased agility from a more efficient organization design, and improved effectiveness in go-to-market models. These benefits are intended to strengthen existing businesses in core markets, increase growth in developing and emerging markets, and drive an increased level of value-added innovation.

continued

continued from previous page

> **Foreign currency risk:** Our company is exposed to fluctuations in foreign currency cash flows related primarily to third-party purchases, intercompany transactions, and when applicable, non-functional currency denominated third-party debt. Our company is also exposed to fluctuations in the value of foreign currency investments in subsidiaries and cash flows related to repatriation of these investments. Additionally, our company is exposed to volatility in the translation of foreign currency denominated earnings to U.S. dollars. Primary exposures include the U.S. dollar versus the euro, British pound, Australian dollar, Canadian dollar, Mexican peso, Brazilian real, Nigerian naira, Russian ruble and Egyptian pound.

a. Complete the following table that summarizes the information that Kellogg reports in the excerpt above. Confirm the % change that Kellogg reports.

Kellogg Consolidated	2018	2017	% change (2017 to 2018)
Reported operating profit			
Currency-neutral adjusted operating profit			

b. Kellogg reports "Adjusted growth" that shows various adjustments to reported growth numbers. Explain why Kellogg provides this information in its financial statements. Briefly explain how Project K and Brexit impacted operating profits in 2018.

c. How did foreign currency exchange rates affect operating profit at each of the geographic segments? What can we infer about the strength of the $US vis-à-vis the currencies in Kellogg's segments?

d. Describe how the accounting for foreign exchange translation affects reported operating profit.

e. What are the three sources of Kellogg's foreign exchange exposure?

E5-40. Interpreting Revenue Recognition Disclosure for Multi-channel Retailer

Amazon.com reports the following in footnotes to its 2018 financial statements.

LO1
Amazon.com (AMZN)

> We serve consumers through our online and physical stores and focus on selection, price, and convenience. We design our stores to enable hundreds of millions of unique products to be sold by us and by third parties across dozens of product categories. Customers access our offerings through our websites, mobile apps, Alexa, and physically visiting our stores. We also manufacture and sell electronic devices, including Kindle e-readers, Fire tablets, Fire TVs, and Echo devices, and we develop and produce media content. In addition, we offer Amazon Prime, a membership program that includes unlimited free shipping on over 100 million items, access to unlimited streaming of thousands of movies and TV episodes, and other benefits.

For each of the following revenue streams, list the nature of the performance obligation and when Amazon would recognize revenue for that performance obligation.

a. Online sale of merchandise owned by Amazon
b. Online sale of merchandise owned by third parties
c. Sale of a Kindle e-reader
d. Collecting cash for an Amazon Prime membership
e. Sale of media content such as a movie available for download

E5-41. Operating Expenses

Target Corporation's footnote from a recent annual report table illustrates the primary items classified in each major expense category: cost of sales (COS), or selling, general and administrative (SG&A). For each expense, indicate whether the item would be included in COS or SG&A.

LO6
Target Corp. (TGT)

a. Advertising expenses . . . . _____
b. Compensation and benefits costs for headquarters employees. . . . . _____
c. Compensation and benefits costs for store employees . . . . _____
d. Compensation and benefits costs for distribution center employees . . . . _____
e. Distribution center costs . . . . _____
f. Freight expenses associated with moving merchandise from our vendors to our
distribution centers and our retail stores . . . . _____
g. Freight expenses associated with moving merchandise among our distribution and retail
stores . . . . _____

continued

continued from previous page

h. Import costs	....	___
i. Inventory shrink and theft	....	___
j. Litigation and defense costs and related insurance recovery.	....	___
k. Markdowns on slow moving inventory	....	___
l. Occupancy and operating costs for headquarters facilities	....	___
m. Occupancy and operating costs of retail locations.	....	___
n. Outbound shipping and handling expenses associated with sales to our guests.	....	___
o. Payment term cash discounts to our vendors	....	___
p. Pre-opening costs of stores and other facilities	....	___
q. U.S. credit cards servicing expenses	....	___
r. Vendor reimbursement of specific, incremental, and identifiable advertising costs	....	___

LO5 **E5-42.** **Estimating Uncollectible Accounts and Reporting Accounts Receivable**

Collins Company analyzes its accounts receivable at December 31 and arrives at the age categories below along with the percentages that are estimated as uncollectible. The balance of the allowance for uncollectible accounts is $1,100 on December 31, before any adjustments.

Age Group	Accounts Receivable	Estimated Loss %
0–30 days past due	$110,000	1%
31–60 days past due	40,000	2
61–120 days past due	27,000	5
121–180 days past due	14,000	10
Over 180 days past due	9,000	25
Total accounts receivable	$200,000	

a. What amount of bad debts expense will Collins report in its income statement for the year?
b. Use the financial statement effects template to record Collins's bad debts expense for the year.
c. What is the balance of accounts receivable on its December 31 balance sheet?

LO5 **E5-43.** **Analyzing and Reporting Receivable Transactions and Uncollectible Accounts Using Percentage-of-Sales Method to Estimate Bad Debt Expense**

At the beginning of the year, Penman Company had the following account balances.

Accounts receivable	$356,000
Allowance for uncollectible accounts	21,400

During the year, Penman's credit sales were $2,008,000, and collections on accounts receivable were $1,963,000. The following additional transactions occurred during the year.

Feb. 17 Wrote off Bava's account, $8,200.
May 28 Wrote off Reed's account, $4,800.
Dec. 15 Wrote off Fischer's account, $2,300.
Dec. 31 Recorded the bad debts expense assuming Penman's policy is to record bad debts expense as 0.9% of credit sales. (*Hint*: The allowance account is increased by 0.9% of credit sales regardless of write-offs.)

Compute the ending balances in accounts receivable and the allowance for uncollectible accounts. Show how Penman's December 31 balance sheet reports the two accounts.

LO5 **E5-44.** **Interpreting the Accounts Receivable Footnote**

HP Inc. (HPQ)

HP Inc. reports the following in its 2018 10-K report.

October 31 ($ millions)	2018	2017
Accounts receivable	$5,113	$4,414

Footnotes to the company's 10-K provide the following additional information relating to its allowance for doubtful accounts.

For Fiscal Years Ended October 31 ($ millions)	2018	2017	2016
Allowance for doubtful accounts—accounts receivable			
Balance, beginning of period	$101	$107	$ 80
Provision for doubtful accounts..........................	57	30	65
Deductions, net of recoveries	(29)	(36)	(38)
Balance, end of period	$129	$101	$107

a. What is the gross amount of accounts receivables for HP in fiscal 2018 and 2017?

b. What is the percentage of the allowance for doubtful accounts to gross accounts receivable for 2018 and 2017?

c. What amount of bad debts expense did HP report each year 2016 through 2018? How does bad debts expense compare with the amounts of its accounts receivable actually written off? (Identify the amounts and explain.)

d. Explain the changes in the allowance for doubtful accounts from 2016 through 2018. Does it appear that HP increased or decreased its allowance for doubtful accounts in any particular year beyond what seems reasonable?

E5-45. Estimating Bad Debts Expense and Reporting Receivables   LO5

At December 31, Barber Company had a balance of $420,000 in its accounts receivable and an unused balance of $2,600 in its allowance for uncollectible accounts. The company then aged its accounts as follows.

Current	$346,000
1–60 days past due	48,000
61–180 days past due	17,000
Over 180 days past due	9,000
Total accounts receivable..........	$420,000

The company has experienced losses as follows: 1% of current balances, 5% of balances 1–60 days past due, 15% of balances 61–180 days past due, and 40% of balances over 180 days past due. The company continues to base its allowance for uncollectible accounts on this aging analysis and percentages.

a. What amount of bad debts expense does Barber report on its income statement for the year?

b. Show how Barber's December 31 balance sheet will report the accounts receivable and the allowance for uncollectible accounts.

E5-46. Estimating Uncollectible Accounts and Reporting Receivables over Multiple Periods   LO5

Weiss Company, which has been in business for three years, makes all of its sales on credit and does not offer cash discounts. Its credit sales, customer collections, and write-offs of uncollectible accounts for its first three years follow.

Year	Sales	Collections	Accounts Written Off
2018	$733,000	$716,000	$5,300
2019	857,000	842,000	5,800
2020	945,000	928,000	6,500

a. Weiss recognizes bad debts expense as 1% of sales. (*Hint:* This means the allowance account is increased by 1% of credit sales regardless of any write-offs and unused balances.) What does Weiss's 2020 balance sheet report for accounts receivable and the allowance for uncollectible accounts? What total amount of bad debts expense appears on Weiss's income statement for each of the three years?

b. Comment on the appropriateness of the 1% rate used to provide for bad debts based on our analysis in part a.

E5-47. Interpreting Graphical Data to Analyze Deferred Revenue   LO3

Use the graphic below that depicts common size deferred revenue for several industries from 2010 to 2018 to answer the requirements.

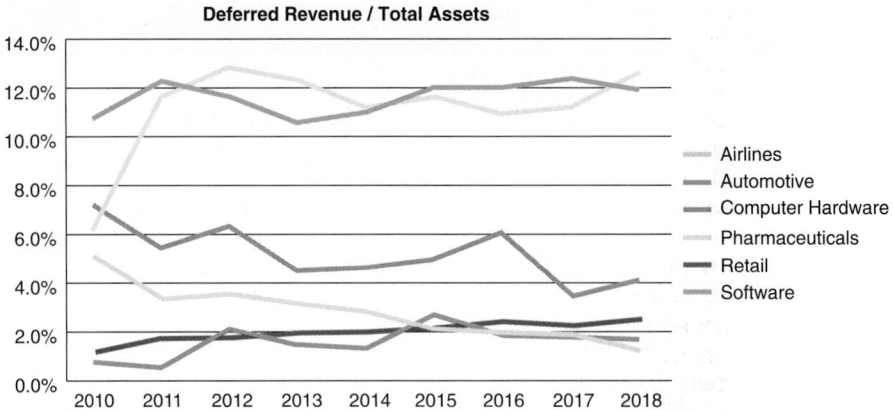

a. Explain how deferred revenue arises for firms in each industry.
b. What might explain the relative size of the deferred revenue of Airlines and Software compared to Pharmaceuticals?

LO6　**E5-48.**　**Interpreting Graphical Data to Analyze R&D and Market Capitalization**
Consider the graphic below that depicts common-size R&D expense and the market-to-book ratio for several industries in 2018.

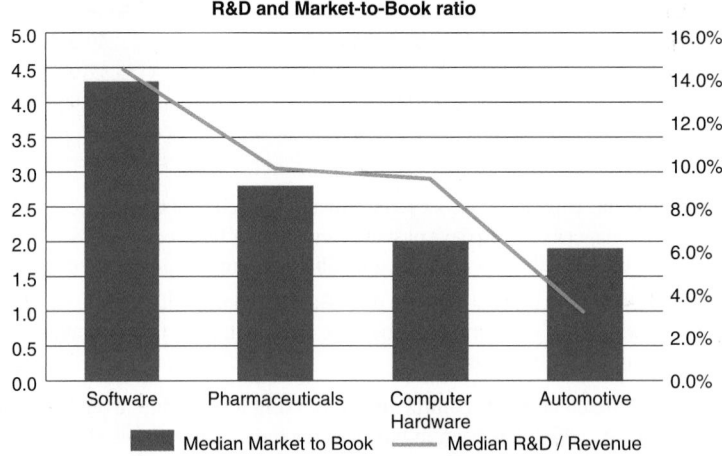

a. What explains the common-size R&D expense across the four industries?
b. What relation do we observe between common-size R&D expense and the market-to-book ratio? Explain.

Problems

LO1, 5　**P5-49.**　**Analyzing Segment Disclosures**
Raytheon Company
(RTN)
Raytheon Company disclosed the following data related to segment sales and operating profits for fiscal 2018.

$ millions	Total Net Sales			Operating Income		
	2018	2017	2016	2018	2017	2016
Integrated defense systems	$ 6,180	$ 5,804	$ 5,529	$1,023	$ 935	$971
Intelligence, information and services	6,722	6,177	6,169	538	455	467
Missile systems	8,298	7,787	7,096	973	1,010	921
Space and airborne systems	6,748	6,430	6,182	884	862	808
Forcepoint	634	608	586	5	33	90
Eliminations	(1,514)	(1,423)	(1,361)			
Total net sales	$27,068	$25,383	$24,201			

The company also reported the following on its balance sheet.

$ millions	2018	2017
Receivables, net of allowance for doubtful accounts of $12 and $8.	$1,648	$1,324

Required

a. Which segment is largest in 2018? Has this ranking changed over the three-year period?

b. Calculate the operating profit margin for each segment and determine which segment is most profitable in 2018 by this measure.

c. Which segment's sales grew the most in 2018? How does this compare to 2017 sales growth?

d. Calculate the company's accounts receivable turnover and its days sales outstanding (DSO) for 2018. Does this seem reasonable? What might explain the DSO?

e. Assess the size of the receivables allowance. Does it seem reasonable?

P5-50.   **Non-GAAP Disclosures**

General Electric (GE) disclosed the following non-GAAP reconciliation for its Industrial segment from its 2018 Form 10-K.

LO7
General Electric (GE)

$ millions	2018	2017	2016
GE Industrial earnings (loss)	$(20,587)	$(1,841)	$ 9,048
Less: Nonoperating pension benefit costs (net of tax)	(2,184)	(1,550)	(1,527)
Less: Gains and impairments for disposed or held for sale businesses (net of tax)	974	864	2,374
Less: Restructuring and other (net of tax)	(2,948)	(2,778)	(2,483)
Less: Goodwill impairments (net of tax)	(22,371)	(1,156)	—
Less: GE Industrial U.S. tax reform enactment adjustment	(38)	(4,905)	—
Adjusted GE Industrial earnings (loss) (Non-GAAP)	$ 5,980	$ 7,685	$10,684

Required

a. Explain how the non-GAAP items (in total) affected adjusted earnings each year. Are the adjustments significant?

b. GE makes five specific adjustments. Are any of the adjustments likely beyond the company's control?

c. Calculate the year-over-year change (in % terms) in reported net income for 2017 and 2018. Calculate the year-over-year change (in % terms) in the non-GAAP net income. Which trend do we believe more accurately depicts GE's performance over this period?

P5-51.   **Revenue Recognition and Sales Allowances**

Target Corporation reported the following on its income statement.

LO1, 2
Target Corp. (TGT)

For 12 Months Ended ($ millions)	Feb. 2, 2019	Feb. 3, 2018	Jan. 28, 2017
Total revenue	$75,356	$72,714	$70,271
Cost of sales.	53,299	51,125	49,145

The revenue recognition footnote from the 10-K for the year ended February 2, 2019, includes the following.

- We record almost all retail store revenues at the point of sale.
- Digital channel sales include shipping revenue and are recorded upon delivery to the guest or upon guest pickup at the store.
- Total revenues do not include sales tax because we are a pass-through conduit for collecting and remitting sales taxes.
- Generally, guests may return national brand merchandise within 90 days of purchase and owned and exclusive brands within one year of purchase. Revenues are recognized net of expected returns, which we estimate using historical return patterns as a percentage of sales and our expectations of future returns.
- Revenue from gift card sales is recognized upon gift card redemption. Our gift cards do not expire. Based on historical redemption rates, a small and relatively stable percentage of gift cards will

continued

continued from previous page

> never be redeemed, referred to as "breakage." Estimated breakage revenue is recognized over time in proportion to actual gift card redemptions.
>
> • Guests receive a 5 percent discount on virtually all purchases and receive free shipping at Target.com when they use their REDcard. This discount is included as a sales reduction in our Consolidated Statements of Operations and was $953 million, $933 million, and $899 million in the fiscal years ended February 2019, 2018, and 2017 respectively.

Required

a. Use the financial statement effects template to record retail cash sales of $1,000 in a state with a sales-tax rate of 8%. For this question, assume 10% of all merchandise sold is returned within 90 days.

b. Use the financial statement effects template to record the following transaction: On March 4, an internet customer places an order for $2,000 and pays online with a credit card (which is equivalent to cash for accounting purposes). The goods are shipped from the warehouse on March 6, and FedEx confirms delivery on March 7. Ignore shipping costs, sales tax, and returns.

c. Use the financial statement effects template to record the gift card activity during the fiscal year ended February 2, 2019. Ignore sales tax and returns. Details are as follows.

$ millions	
Gift card liability, February 3, 2018.	$727
Gift cards issued during current period but not redeemed.	645
Revenue recognized from beginning liability	(532)
Gift card liability, February 2, 2019.	$840

d. Determine the amount of revenue Target collected from customers who used their loyalty card (REDcard™) for each of the fiscal years reported above. What proportion of total revenues come from REDcard™ customers each year? Does the loyalty program seem to be working? Explain.

P5-52.   Research and Development Expense

International Business Machines Corporation (IBM) reported the following on its 2018 form 10-K.

$ millions	2018	2017	2016
Total revenue	$79,591	$79,139	$79,919
Research, development and engineering expense	5,379	5,590	5,726
Number of new patents awarded	9,100	9,043	8,088

Required

a. Calculate IBM's common-size research, development and engineering expense for each year. What pattern do we observe? Is this of potential concern to investors?

b. Compute the research, development and engineering expense per new patent for each year. What pattern do we observe? What flaw is there in this metric?

c. What other data might analysts and investors collect to form an opinion about the level and effectiveness of IBM's R&D endeavors?

P5-53.   Analyzing and Interpreting Revenue Recognition Policies and Adoption of the New Standard

Barnes & Noble provides the following explanation of its gift card liabilities.

> **Gift Cards**   The Company sells gift cards, which can be used in its stores, on **www.barnesandnoble**
> **.com**, on NOOK® devices and at Barnes & Noble Education, Inc. (B&N Education) stores. Upon the purchase of a gift card, a liability is established for its cash value. Revenue associated with gift cards is deferred until redemption of the gift card. Over time, a portion of the gift cards issued is typically not redeemed. This is referred to as gift card breakage. Effective April 29, 2018, the Company adopted Topic 606. The adoption of Topic 606 resulted in changes in the timing of revenue recognition for gift card breakage. The Company estimates the portion of the gift card liability for which the likelihood of redemption is remote based upon the Company's historical redemption patterns. Prior to adoption of Topic 606, the Company recorded this amount in revenue on a straight-line basis over a 12-month period beginning in the 13th month after the month the gift card was originally sold. Upon adoption, the Company now recognizes estimated gift card

continued

continued from previous page

breakage as revenue proportionately as redemption occurs. Below is a summary of the changes to the company's gift card liability during fiscal 2019 (in thousands):

Gift card liabilities balance as of April 28, 2018	$323,465
Adoption of Topic 606 Revenue Recognition	(90,147)
Gift card breakage	(42,282)
Gift card redemptions	(247,231)
Gift card issuances	271,654
Gift card liabilities balance as of April 27, 2019	$215,459

Required

a. Explain in plain language "breakage" of gift cards.

b. The company adopted the new revenue recognition standard effective April 29, 2018. Explain how the company accounted for breakage (i) before adopting the new standard and (ii) after adoption.

c. Did the new revenue recognition standard slow down or speed up revenue recognition?

d. What effect did the new revenue recognition standard have on Barnes & Noble's unearned revenue account? Explain.

P5-54.   **Analyzing and Interpreting Income Disclosures**

Sales information for Tesla Inc. follows.

LO1

Tesla Inc. (TSLA)

Year Ended December 31 ($ thousands)	2018	2017	2016
Automotive sales	$17,631,522	$8,534,752	$5,589,007
Automotive leasing	883,461	1,106,548	761,759
Total automotive revenues	18,514,983	9,641,300	6,350,766
Services and other	1,391,041	1,001,185	467,972
Total automotive & services and other segment revenue.	19,906,024	10,642,485	6,818,738
Energy generation and storage segment revenue	1,555,244	1,116,266	181,394
Total revenues	$21,461,268	$11,758,751	$7,000,132

Automotive sales revenue includes revenues related to sale of new Model S, Model X and Model 3 vehicles, including access to our Supercharger network, internet connectivity, Autopilot, full self-driving and over-the-air software updates.

Automotive leasing revenue includes the amortization of revenue for Model S and Model X vehicles under direct lease agreements as well as those sold with resale value guarantees accounted for as operating leases under lease accounting. We do not yet offer leasing for Model 3 vehicles.

Services and other revenue consists of non-warranty after-sales vehicle services, sales of used vehicles, sales of electric vehicle components and systems to other manufacturers, retail merchandise, and sales by our acquired subsidiaries to third party customers.

Energy generation and storage revenues consists of the sale of solar energy systems and energy storage systems to residential, small commercial, and large commercial and utility grade customers.

Required

a. Tesla reports several sources of revenue. How should revenue be recognized for each of these business activities? Explain.

b. Compute the relative size of sales revenue from the four types of revenue Tesla discloses. (*Hint:* Scale each type of revenue by total revenue.) What observations can be made about the different sources of revenue?

c. Compute the growth in sales revenue for both years from each of the four types of revenue. What do we observe?

P5-55.   **Analyzing Unearned Revenue Disclosures**

The following disclosures (excerpted) are from the September 2, 2018, annual report of Costco Whole-sale Corporation.

> The Company generally recognizes sales, net of returns, at the time the member takes possession of merchandise or receives services.
>
> When the Company collects payments from members prior to the transfer of ownership of merchandise or the performance of services, the amounts received are generally recorded as deferred sales, included in other current liabilities in the consolidated balance sheets, until the sale or service is completed.
>
> The Company reserves for estimated sales returns based on historical trends in merchandise returns and reduces sales and merchandise costs accordingly.
>
> The Company accounts for membership fee revenue, net of refunds, on a deferred basis, ratably over the one-year membership.
>
> The Company's Executive members qualify for a 2% reward on qualified purchases (up to a maximum reward of approximately $1,000 per year), which can be redeemed only at Costco warehouses. The Company accounts for this reward as a reduction in sales. The sales reduction and corresponding liability (classified as accrued member rewards in the consolidated balance sheets) are computed after giving effect to the estimated impact of non-redemptions, based on historical data. The net reduction in sales was $1,394, $1,281, and $1,172 in 2018, 2017, and 2016, respectively.

Revenue ($ millions)	Sept. 2, 2018	Sept. 3, 2017	Aug. 28, 2016
Net sales.	$138,434	$126,172	$116,073
Membership fees	3,142	2,853	2,646
Total revenue	$141,576	$129,025	$118,719

Current Liabilities ($ millions)	Sept. 2, 2018	Sept. 3, 2017
Accounts payable.	$11,237	$9,608
Accrued salaries and benefits	2,994	2,703
Accrued member rewards	1,057	961
Deferred membership fees.	1,624	1,498
Other current liabilities	3,014	2,725
Total current liabilities.	$19,926	$17,495

Required

a. Explain in layman's terms how Costco accounts for the cash received for membership fees.

b. Use the balance sheet information on Costco's deferred membership fees liability account and its income statement revenues related to membership fees earned during fiscal 2018 to compute the cash Costco received during fiscal 2018 for membership fees.

c. Use the financial statement effects template to show the effect of the cash Costco received during fiscal 2018 for membership fees and the recognition of membership fees revenue for fiscal 2018.

d. Explain in plain language the "accrued member rewards" liability.

e. Complete the following sentence. Costco recorded sales of at least $_____ from the Company's Executive members, during fiscal 2018.

P5-56.   **Interpreting Accounts Receivable and Related Footnote Disclosure**

Following is information from the Fitbit Inc. financial statements.

$ thousands	Dec. 31, 2018	Dec. 31, 2017	Dec. 31, 2016
Revenue.	$1,511,983	$1,615,519	$2,169,461
Accounts receivable, net	414,209	406,019	477,825

continued

continued from previous page

Allowance for Doubtful Accounts ($ thousands)	2018	2017	2016
Beginning balance	$9,229	$ 282	$1,825
Increases	56	30,551	339
Write-offs	(5,543)	(21,604)	(1,882)
Ending balance.	$3,742	$ 9,229	$ 282

Customer Bankruptcy   In September 2017, Wynit Distribution filed for bankruptcy protection under Chapter 11 of the United States Bankruptcy Code. Wynit was the Company's largest customer, historically representing 11% of total revenue during the six months ended July 1, 2017 and 19% of total accounts receivables as of July 1, 2017. In connection with Wynit's bankruptcy filing, the Company believed that the collectability of the product shipments to Wynit during the third quarter of 2017 was not reasonably assured. However, as of July 1, 2017, collectability of accounts receivables from Wynit was reasonably assured. The Company ceased to recognize revenue from Wynit, which totaled $8.1 million during the third quarter of 2017. Additionally, the Company recorded a charge of $35.8 million during the third quarter ended September 30, 2017 comprised of cost of revenue of $5.5 million associated with shipments to Wynit in the third quarter of 2017 and bad debt expense of $30.3 million associated with all of Wynit's outstanding accounts receivables.

Required

a. What amount do customers owe Fitbit at each of the year-ends 2016 through 2018?

b. What percentage of its total accounts receivable does Fitbit deem uncollectible? (*Hint:* Percentage of uncollectible accounts = Allowance for uncollectible accounts/Gross accounts receivable.)

c. What amount of bad debts expense did Fitbit report in its income statement for each of the years 2016 through 2018? Is this a significant expense? (*Hint:* Calculate the common-size expense.)

d. Consider the information about Wynit Distribution. How might we adjust our analyses in parts *a* through *c* to reflect this information?

e. Calculate the average number of days that it took Fitbit to collect its receivables during 2018 and 2017.

f. Overall, what is our assessment of the quality of Fitbit's accounts receivable?

P5-57.   **Analyzing and Interpreting Operating Expenses for an Early Stage Company**

LO6

Tesla Inc. (TSLA)

The graphic below depicts revenue, cost of goods sold, and R&D expense for Tesla Inc. for 2010 through 2018 ($ in millions).

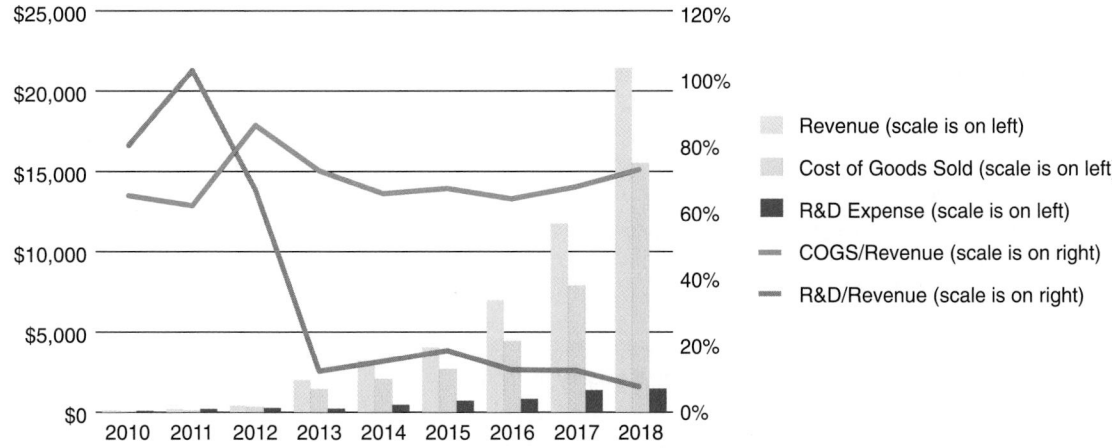

a. What pattern do we observe for revenue over the eight years?

b. What pattern do we observe for COGS and R&D expense over the eight years?

c. What explains the volatile pattern of cost of goods sold and R&D expense relative to revenue in the earlier years? How would analysts interpret the declining R&D as a % of revenue over time?

IFRS Applications

LO5

Lupin
Pharmaceuticals
(LUPIN)

Homework
MBC

I5-58.   Analyzing Accounts Receivable

Lupin Pharmaceuticals, an Indian transnational pharmaceutical company, develops and markets a wide portfolio of branded and generic products. The company reported the following in its 2018 annual report.

INR millions	2018	2017	2016
Trade receivables	52,229.0	43,391.8	45,946.3
Less provision for doubtful receivables	306.9	318.4	448.2
Trade receivables, net	51,922.1	43,073.4	45,498.1
Total assets	140,958	146,544	127,375
Revenue from operations	158,042	174,943	142,555

Required

a. Calculate days sale outstanding (DSO) for 2018 and 2017.
b. Determine the total amount that customers owe Lupin each year.
c. What proportion of trade receivables is doubtful each year? From this ratio, what do we conclude about the quality of its trade receivables over time?

LO1, 6

Repsol S.A. (REPYY)

I5-59.   Identifying Operating Income Components

Repsol S.A. is a Spanish energy company based in Madrid. It carries out upstream and downstream activities throughout the entire world.

Repsol, S.A. and investees comprising the Repsol Group Consolidated income statement for years ending December 31, 2018 (€ Million)	
Sales	€49,701
Income from services rendered and other income	172
Changes in inventories of finished goods and work in progress	130
Reversal of impairment provisions and gains on disposal of assets	277
Other operating income	1,073
Operating income	51,353
Supplies	(38,056)
Amortization of noncurrent assets	(2,140)
Personnel expenses	(1,874)
Transport and freights	(1,114)
Supplies	(739)
Impairment loss provisions recognized and losses on disposal of assets	(1,281)
Other operating expenses	(3,696)
Operating costs	(48,900)
Operating income	2,453
Net interest	(230)
Change in fair value of financial instruments	200
Exchange gains (losses)	467
Impairment of financial instruments	(370)
Other finance income and expenses	(240)
Financial result	(173)
Income investments accounted for using the equity method	1,053
Net income before tax	3,333
Income tax	(1,386)
Profit from continuing operations	1,947
Income from continuing operations attributed to noncurrent interests	(18)
Income from continuing operations attributed to the parent	€ 1,929

Required

a. Identify the components considered operating for each year.

b. Identify the nonrecurring operating items for 2018 and explain how financial analysts would treat these items.

Management Applications

MA5-60. Managing Foreign Currency Risk   **LO4**

Fluctuations in foreign currency exchange rates can result in increased volatility of revenues, expenses, and profits. Companies generally attempt to reduce this volatility.

a. Identify two possible solutions to reduce the volatility effect of foreign exchange rate fluctuations.

b. What costs would arise if you implemented each of your solutions?

MA5-61. Ethics and Governance: Revenue Recognition   **LO1**

GAAP revenue recognition standards are based on broad principles rather than bright-line rules. This creates a certain amount of latitude in determining when revenue is earned. Assume a company that normally requires acceptance by its customers prior to recording revenue as earned delivers a product to a customer near the end of the quarter. The company believes customer acceptance is assured but cannot obtain it prior to quarter-end. Recording the revenue would assure "making its numbers" for the quarter. Although formal acceptance is not obtained, the salesperson records the sale, fully intending to obtain written acceptance as soon as possible.

a. What are the revenue recognition requirements in this case?

b. What are the ethical issues relating to this sale?

c. Assume you are on the board of directors of this company. What safeguards can you put in place to ensure the company's revenue recognition policy is followed?

Ongoing Project

(This ongoing project began in Module 1 and continues through most of the book; even if previous segments were not completed, the requirements are still applicable to any business analysis.) Analysis of financial statements commonly includes operating income and its components as explained in this module.

1. *Revenue Recognition*   Revenue is the largest item on the income statement, and we must assess it on a quantitative and qualitative basis.

   • Use horizontal analysis to identify any time trends.

   • Compare the horizontal analyses of the two companies.

   • Consider the current economic environment and the companies' competitive landscape. Given they operate in the same industry, you might expect similar revenue trends.

   • Read the management's discussion and analysis (MD&A) section of the 10-K to learn how the companies' senior managers explain revenue levels and changes.

   Our goal is to determine whether each company's revenue levels and changes seem appropriate and in line with external factors. *Additional analysis*: (a) If the company distinguishes among types of revenue on the income statement, use horizontal and vertical analyses to identify any changes in the product line mix or where sales are growing most quickly. Find the footnote on segment revenues and profits, and identify trends or significant changes. (b) Assess each company's revenue recognition policy by comparing it with the other and with those of some other close competitors. (c) Consider unearned revenue on the balance sheet. How big is it (common size), and is it fluctuating over time? (d) For companies that operate globally, determine the effect of foreign currency fluctuations on revenue. If these are substantial year after year, it might indicate that managers are not effectively hedging, and this would warrant additional investigation.

2. *Accounts Receivable*   The following provides some guidance for analyzing a company's accounts receivable.

   • Are sales primarily on credit, or is a typical sale transacted in cash? Consider the industry and the companies' business model.

   • What is the relative size of accounts receivable? How has this changed over the recent three-year period?

   • Determine the accounts receivable balance relative to gross accounts receivable.

   • What did the company record for bad debt expense? Compute the common size amount.

- Compute accounts receivable turnover and days sales outstanding for all three years reported on the income statement. One will need to obtain additional balance sheet information to be able to compute average balances for the denominator. Consider the current economic environment and the company's competitive landscape. Would one expect collection to have slowed down or sped up during the year?
- Does the company have any large customers that increase its credit risk?

For each point of analysis, compare across companies and over time. The goal is to determine whether each company's accounts receivable (levels and changes) seems appropriate and to gauge the quality of the receivables.

3. *Operating Expenses*   Review and analyze the income statement items.
   - Prepare a common-sized income statement by dividing each item on the income statement by total revenues, net.
   - Compare the common-sized values for the three years presented in the income statement. What changes are there, if any? Are material changes explained in the MD&A? Do the explanations seem reasonable given the current economic environment?
   - Does the company engage in research and development activities? Quantify the amount in dollar terms and common size. Do you observe any patterns? Is the level of R&D expense consistent with peers and industry?
   - Does the company have discontinued operations? If so, how will this impact future operations?

4. *Accounting Quality*   Evaluating accounting quality is more of an art than a science. The point is to form an overall opinion about the reliability of the numbers in the financial statements.
   - Does the company report non-GAAP earnings? What items do they exclude or include? Do the two companies report similar one-time items? Do the items seem reasonable, or do we detect some self-serving disclosures?
   - Consider the list in the Research Insight Box in the module, and use it to assess the quality of the two companies' reported numbers.
   - Use an online investment website to find key ratios for close competitors. Compare to our companies.
   - Find the consensus analysts' EPS forecast for the recent year-end. How did our companies fare? Were there any one-time items or unusual changes in any expenses that might have caused the company to just meet or beat the forecast? This could indicate earnings management.

Solutions to Review Problems

Review 5-1—Solution
Part I

1. Revenue is recognized for the amount the company expects to receive, which is sales price less anticipated returns.

2. The purchase price is apportioned between two components (performance obligations): the value of the copier and the value of the two-year service agreement. Revenue is immediately recognized on the first component. For the second component, revenue is deferred and recognized ratably over two years.

3. Revenue is recognized ratably over the year despite the fact that customers pay up front.

4. Revenue is recognized for the commission only, not the full sales price, because the company is acting as an agent for the other companies.

5. Product sales are recognized as revenue when the product is delivered to the franchisee. Accounting services are recognized as revenue on a monthly basis as the service is provided.

Part II

1. Revenue = $3,000,000 × ($500,000/$2,500,000) = $600,000.

   Gross profit = $600,000 − $500,000 = $100,000.

2. The cost of $500,000 exceeds the billing of $400,000, and the excess of $100,000 is reported as a current asset (such as construction in progress).

Review 5-2—Solution

1. "Charged to costs and expenses" represents the amount of returns allowances recorded during fiscal 2018 for sales during that year. This amount is included in Tiffany's income statement for the fiscal year.

2. "Deductions" is the dollar value of actual returns offset by the value of the merchandise returned (that reduces COGS by the same amount). The actual returns number is $10.1 million, which is close to the estimated amount charged to costs and expenses of $12.6 million. This indicates that Tiffany & Co is fairly accurate in its estimation process.

3. *a.*

$ millions	2019	2018	2017
Net sales.	$4,442.1	$4,169.8	$4,001.8
Charged to costs and expenses.	12.6	7.5	2.5
Gross sales.	$4,454.7	$4,177.3	$4,004.3
Allowance at year end	$17.5	$15	$9.6
Allowance/Gross sales.	0.39%	0.36%	0.24%

The sales return allowance is small at year end, compared to gross sales, likely because sales returns are made quickly after the purchase so the balance outstanding at any time is small. In fact, the amount outstanding is roughly equal to one day's sales ($4,442.1/365 days = $12.2).The amount has been increasing over time but is not of concern given its magnitude.

b.

$ millions	2019	2018	2017
Charged to costs and expenses.	$ 12.6	$ 7.5	$ 2.5
Gross sales.	$4,454.7	$4,177.3	$4,004.3
% returned merchandise	0.28%	0.18%	0.06%

The % of merchandise that Tiffany estimates will be returned has steadily increased over the three years, but the amount is so low as to be immaterial. There is no cause for concern here.

c. Tiffany's sales returns allowance seems a bit high considering the following ratio of actual to estimate.

$ millions	2019	2018	2017
Actual returns during the year	$12.6	$7.5	$2.5
Estimated returns for the year	$10.1	$2.1	$1.2
Adequacy.	125%	357%	208%

Review 5-3—Solution

The amount of cash received from the customers is the amount added to the liability.

Advanced Billings and Customer Deposits ($ millions)	
Balance at 1/1/2018 .	$26,656
+ Cash prepayments by customers during the year	??
– Revenue recognized during the year	(55,078)
= Balance at 12/31/2018 .	$32,720

Cash prepayments by customers during the year = $32,720 + $55,078 – $26,656 = $61,142

Review 5-4—Solution

1. In 2018, Google's EMEA revenues were 4 percentage points higher (24% versus 20% growth) as a result of the weakening $US vis-à-vis the other currencies in that region. As the $US weakened, foreign currency denominated income statements grew when translated into in $US. In 2017, the opposite was true, EMEA revenue growth would have been 2 percentage points higher (19% versus 21%) if not for the negative effect of the stronger $US.

2. All accounts in the income statement grow when the $US weakens: revenues, expenses, and profit. Because Alphabet is profitable (revenues are greater than expenses), the company will appear more profitable as a result of the weakening U.S. dollar.

3. Translation of the income statement does not affect cash flow. However, to the extent that Google transacts business in these foreign currencies, the amount of cash collected will likely be higher as the $US weakens.

Review 5-5—Solution

1. The estimate of total uncollectible accounts receivable as of December 31, 2018, for Coca-Cola is $490 million, calculated as follows. Coca-Cola will report Accounts receivable net of $3,395 million ($3,885 million − $490 million).

$ millions	Accounts Receivable	% Uncollectible	Estimated Allowance for Uncollectible Accounts (Receivable × % Uncollectible)
Current	$1,554	1.5%	$ 23
1–30 days past due	971	5.0%	49
31–60 days past due	544	14.0%	76
61–90 days past due	427	25.0%	107
91–120 days past due	272	54.0%	147
Over 120 days past due . . .	117	75.0%	88
Total	$3,885		$490

2. Coca-Cola must increase the allowance for uncollectible accounts balance by $30 million. The increase of $30 million in the allowance account is bad debt expense. Coca-Cola will record this amount in the 2018 income statement.

Allowance for Uncollectible Accounts	
Balance as of beginning of the year	$477
Plus: addition to the allowance for uncollectible accounts recognized as expense . . .	30
Less: write-offs of uncollectible accounts	(17)
Balance at end of year	$490

3. Coca-Cola's accounts receivable are of higher quality in 2017 because the allowance was proportionately smaller than in 2018.

	2018	2017
Accounts receivable, net	$3,395	$3,667
Allowance for doubtful accounts.	490	477
Accounts receivable, gross.	$3,885	$4,144
Allowance/AR gross	12.6%	11.5%

Review 5-6—Solution

1. The following would **not** be included in selling, general and administrative expense.
   - Utilities for the research laboratories—this would be included in the research and development expense because it relates to those activities.
   - Wages for manufacturing employees—these are costs to manufacture goods and would be included in cost of products sold.
   - License fees for software used to develop new products is part of the research and development process, so these costs would be included on that income statement line item.
   - Depreciation on machines that package and label finished goods—this is part of the cost to get the inventory ready for sale and would be included in cost of products sold.

2. Following is a summary of HPE's R&D expense for 2017 and 2018.

	2018	2017
R&D expense in $ millions	$1,663	$1,486
R&D expense as % of revenue	5.39%	5.15%

HPE has held R&D spending relatively constant over the two-year period. R&D costs include salaries and overhead for R&D employees including scientists, lab workers directly involved with R&D, as well as for personnel who indirectly assist and support R&D activities.

3. HPE discontinued (that is, sold off or closed) some operations during the 2018 fiscal year. The "Loss from discontinued operations" of $104 million included any profit or loss from those discontinued operations during the year. The loss also includes any gain or loss that HPE realized when it disposed of any assets of the discontinued operations.

Review 5-7—Solution

1. Companies, including Merck, publicly report non-GAAP information to communicate their view of the companies' ongoing, persistent earnings. Skeptics of such pro forma numbers suggest companies are simply trying to present their financial results in the best possible light.

2. First, Merck adjusts for one-time charges relating to acquisitions/divestitures and restructurings. In 2018, these include costs of $3,066 million and $658 million, respectively. Then, Merck adds back the cost of new joint ventures and collaborations including charges relating to the formation of oncology collaborations in 2018 (Eisai, $1,400 million) and 2017 (AstraZeneca, $2,350 million). Lastly, Merck adjusts for the tax effects of the adjustments and for the effects of the recent tax law changes. This latter charge was particularly large in 2017.

Module 6

Inventories, Accounts Payable, and Long-Term Assets

Inventories, Accounts Payable, and Long-Term Assets	
Inventories and Accounts Payable	**Property, Plant & Equipment**
▦ Inventory Costing Methods	▦ Depreciation and Book Value
▦ Footnote Disclosures	▦ Disposals, Impairments and Restructuring
▦ Effects of Inventory Costing	▦ Footnote Disclosures
▦ Inventory Disclosures	▦ Analysis Tools—Turnover, Useful Life, and
▦ Inventory Analysis	Percent Used Up
▦ Cash Conversion Cycle	
Review 6-1, 6-2, 6-3	Review 6-4, 6-5, 6-6

HD

We examine three balance sheet elements

- ■ Inventories
- ■ Accounts payable
- ■ Long-term assets
  (PPE assets and intangible assets)

We review the accounting mechanics followed by an analysis of these elements. **Home Depot** is the focus company and the dashboard below conveys income statement and balance sheet information for 2000 through 2018.

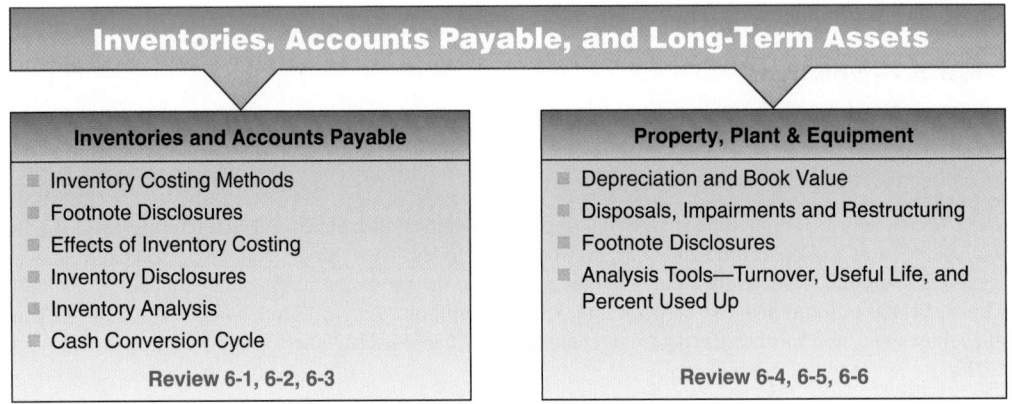

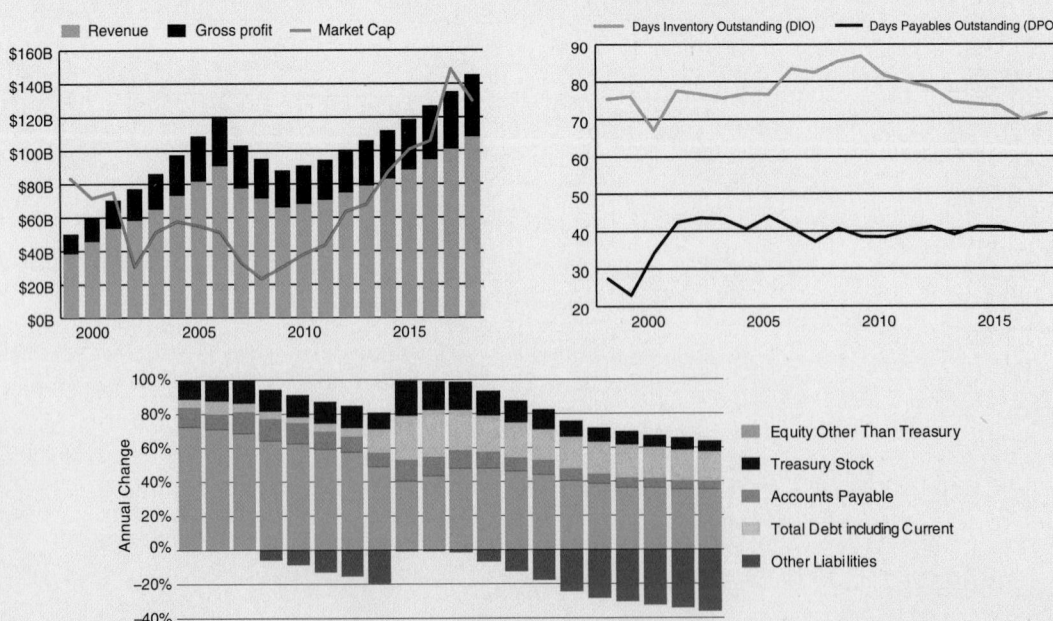

Road Map

LO	Learning Objective | Topics	Page	eLecture	Guided Example	Assignments
6-1	**Apply inventory costing methods.** Cost Flows :: FIFO :: LIFO :: Average Cost :: Financial Effects	6-3	e6–1	Review 6-1	1, 2, 3, 4, 13, 14, 23
6-2	**Examine inventory disclosures in financial statements.** LCM :: LIFO Liquidation :: LIFO Reserve and Adjustments	6-8	e6–2	Review 6-2	5, 11, 22, 24, 25, 26, 37
6-3	**Analyze inventories and the related accounts payable.** Gross Profit Margin :: Days Inventory Outstanding :: Inventory Turnover :: Days Payable Outstanding :: Cash Conversion Cycle	6-12	e6–3	Review 6-3	6, 10, 15, 19, 20, 22, 25, 27, 29, 32, 35, 36, 37, 41, 43
6-4	**Apply capitalization and depreciation of tangible assets.** Property :: Plant & Equipment :: Depreciation Methods :: R&D Facilities & Equipment	6-17	e6–4	Review 6-4	7, 8, 16, 17, 28, 33
6-5	**Evaluate asset sales, impairments, and restructuring activities.** Asset Sales :: Gains and Losses :: Asset Impairments	6-20	e6–5	Review 6-5	9, 12, 21, 28, 30, 33, 40, 42
6-6	**Analyze tangible assets and related activities.** PPE Turnover :: PPE Useful Life :: PPE Percent Used Up	6-25	e6–6	Review 6-6	18, 31, 32, 34, 38, 39, 42, 43

Inventory—Costing Methods

LO1
Apply
inventory
costing
methods.

For many companies, inventory is among the four largest assets on the balance sheet (along with receivables, property, plant & equipment (PPE), and intangible assets such as goodwill). On the income statement, cost of goods sold (which is directly related to inventory) is the largest expense for many companies and certainly for those in retailing and manufacturing. Companies can choose from among several methods to account for inventory costs and these accounting choices can greatly impact the balance sheet and income statement. Although rare, companies can and do change inventory costing methods if doing so enhances the quality of their financial reports and the company can justify the change. A company must disclose the change in financial statements.

In Module 2 we describe the following flow of costs.

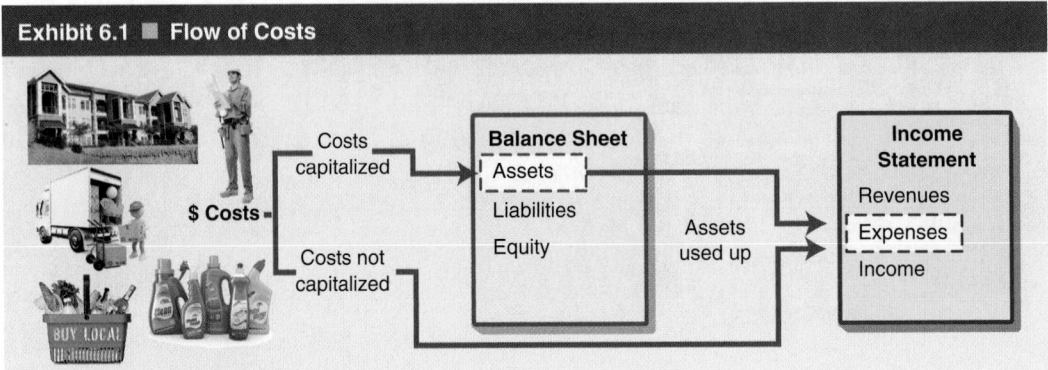

Exhibit 6.1 ■ Flow of Costs

Inventory expenditures follow the "Costs capitalized" line at the top of the graphic.

■ Cost of **inventory** is added to the balance sheet as an asset (capitalized) when it is purchased or manufactured.[1]

■ Inventory cost is transferred from the balance sheet to the income statement as **cost of goods sold** (COGS) when sold.[2] This COGS is deducted from sales to yield **gross profit**.

A typical income statement reports cost of goods sold as follows.

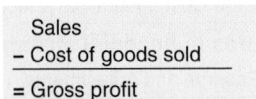

Sales
– Cost of goods sold
= Gross profit

As companies purchase or manufacture inventories, those costs are added to the balance sheet. Likewise, as companies sell inventories, they transfer the cost of those inventories to the income statement.

Measuring and analyzing the flow of inventory costs are important. If all inventory purchased or manufactured during the period is sold, then COGS is equal to the cost of the goods purchased or manufactured. However, when inventory remains at the end of a period (the usual case), companies must distinguish the cost of the inventories that are sold (reported as cost of goods sold in the income statement) from the cost of the inventories that remain as an asset on the balance sheet. The remaining inventory is available for sale in the next period. Exhibit 6.2 shows this cost flow graphically.

---

[1] **Manufacturing costs** consist of three components: cost of **direct (raw) materials** used in the product, cost of **direct labor** to manufacture the product, and **manufacturing overhead**. Direct materials cost is relatively easy to compute. Design specifications list the components of each product, and their purchase costs are readily determined. The direct labor cost per unit of inventory depends on how long each unit takes to construct and the wages and salaries paid for employees who work on that product. Overhead costs are also capitalized into inventory. These include all manufacturing costs other than direct materials and direct labor, such as utilities, supervisory personnel, repairs and depreciation on manufacturing PPE, and other related costs.

[2] Before issuing financial statements, companies compare the amount at which inventories are reported on the balance sheet with the current "market" value of the inventories. If the market value is less than the reported cost of the inventory, the company "writes down" the inventory to its market value. This process is called reporting inventories at the **lower of cost or market**, which we discuss later in the module.

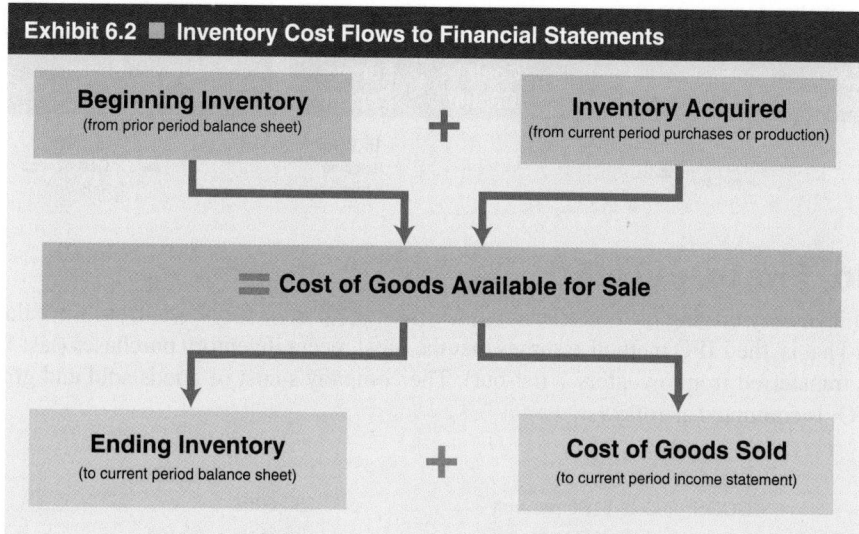

Exhibit 6.2 ■ Inventory Cost Flows to Financial Statements

Companies have a choice when it comes to determining the cost of goods sold and the cost of the inventory remaining on the balance sheet. To understand this, consider the example in Exhibit 6.3.

Exhibit 6.3 ■ Summary Inventory Records			
Inventory available on January 1	500 units	@ $100 per unit	$ 50,000
Inventory purchased during the period.	200 units	@ $150 per unit	30,000
Total cost of goods available for sale	700 units		$ 80,000
Inventory sold during the period.	450 units	@ $250 per unit	$112,500

This company began the period with 500 units of inventory that were purchased or manufactured for $50,000 ($100 each). During the period the company purchased and/or manufactured an additional 200 units costing $30,000. The total cost of goods available for sale for this period equals $80,000.

The company sold 450 units during the period for $250 per unit for total sales of $112,500. Accordingly, the company must remove the cost of the 450 units sold from the inventory account on the balance sheet and match this cost against the revenues generated from the sale. An important question is which costs should management remove from the balance sheet and report as cost of goods sold in the income statement? Three inventory costing methods (FIFO, LIFO, and average cost) are common and all are acceptable for U.S. GAAP.

First-In, First-Out (FIFO)

The FIFO inventory costing method transfers costs from inventory in the order that they were initially recorded. That is, FIFO assumes that the first costs recorded in inventory (first-in) are the first costs transferred from inventory (first-out). Applying FIFO to the data in Exhibit 6.3 means that the costs of the 450 units sold comes from *beginning* inventory, which consists of 500 units costing $100 each. The company's cost of goods sold and gross profit, using FIFO, is computed as follows.

Sales.	$112,500
COGS (450 @ $100 each).	45,000
Gross profit.	$ 67,500

The cost remaining in inventory and reported on the year-end balance sheet is $35,000 ($80,000 goods available for sale less $45,000 COGS). The following financial statement effects template captures the transaction.

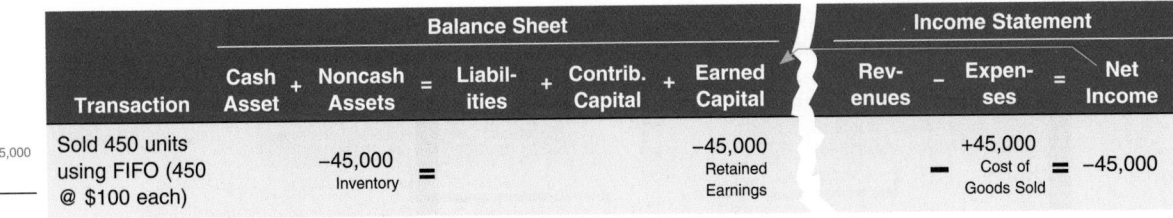

COGS . .45,000
INV 45,000

COGS
45,000 |
INV
| 45,000

Last-In, First-Out (LIFO)

The LIFO inventory costing method transfers the most recent inventory costs from the balance sheet to COGS. That is, the LIFO method assumes that the most recent inventory purchases (last-in) are the first costs transferred from inventory (first-out). The company's cost of goods sold and gross profit, using LIFO, is computed as follows.

Sales.		$112,500
COGS: 200 @ $150 per unit	$30,000	
250 @ $100 per unit	25,000	55,000
Gross profit.		$ 57,500

The cost remaining in inventory and reported on the year-end balance sheet is $25,000 (computed as $80,000 − $55,000). This is reflected in our financial statements effects template as follows.

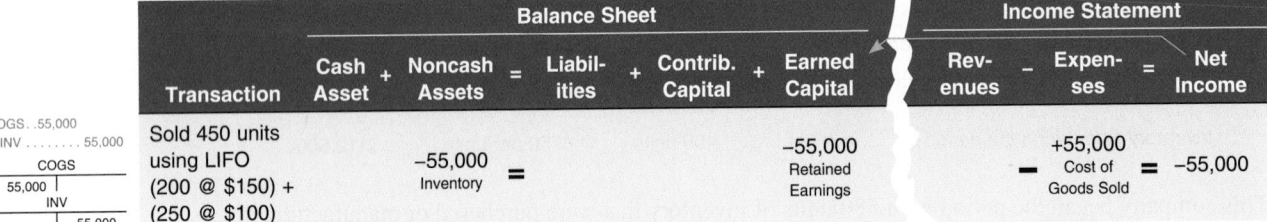

COGS . .55,000
INV 55,000

COGS
55,000 |
INV
| 55,000

Average Cost (AC)

The average cost method computes the cost of goods sold as an average of the cost to purchase or manufacture all of the inventories that were available for sale during the period. To calculate the average cost of $114.286 per unit, the company divides the total cost of goods available for sale by the number of units available for sale ($80,000/700 units). The company's sales, cost of sales, and gross profit follow.

Sales.	$112,500
COGS (450 @ $114.286 per unit)	51,429
Gross profit.	$ 61,071

The cost remaining in inventory and reported on the year-end balance sheet is $28,571 ($80,000 − $51,429). This is reflected in our financial statements effects template as follows.

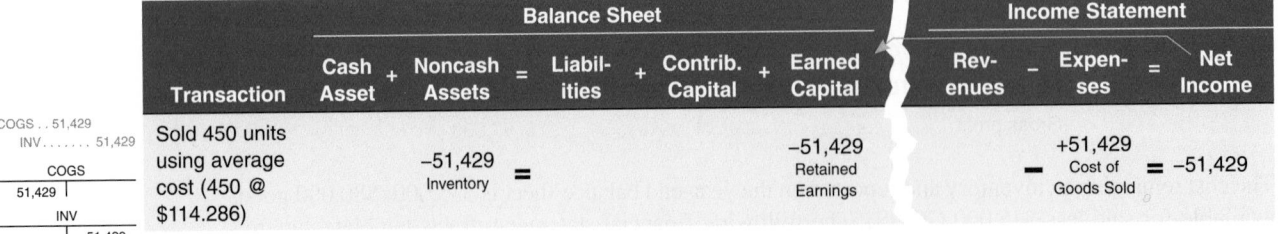

COGS . .51,429
INV 51,429

COGS
51,429 |
INV
| 51,429

The average cost method is commonly adopted when inventory purchases and sales are continuous during the year. This method is especially common for retail companies that stock (and constantly restock) nonseasonal items and for manufacturing companies that use commodities (or commoditized items) as raw materials. Technological advances such as bar codes, scanners, and RFIDs have enabled continuous inventory tracking, tracing, and counting. Enterprise resource planning (ERP) systems interface with these inventory management systems, and, together, these advances reduce the costs associated with inventory costing prompting more firms to adopt the average cost method. In its fiscal 2019 financial statements, **CVS Health Corporation** reports the following.

> Inventories are valued at the lower of cost or net realizable value using the weighted average cost method. Physical inventory counts are taken on a regular basis in each retail store and LTC pharmacy and a continuous cycle count process is the primary procedure used to validate the inventory balances on hand in each distribution center and mail facility to ensure that the amounts reflected in the accompanying consolidated financial statements are properly stated. During the interim period between physical inventory counts, CVS Health accrues for anticipated physical inventory losses on a location-by-location basis based on historical results and current trends.

It is important to understand that the inventory costing method a company chooses to prepare its income statement is independent of the actual flow of inventory. For example, the **Kroger** grocery store chain uses LIFO inventory but certainly does not sell the freshest products first.

Business Insight ■ Retail Method for Inventory Costing

Retailers such as Home Depot and Lowe's commonly estimate the cost of ending inventories using the *retail inventory method* (RIM). Retailers know the **cost** of the inventories purchased as well as their **retail** selling price. From this, the retailer computes the **cost-to-retail percentage** and applies that percentage to estimate the cost of the inventory still available at year-end (the ending inventory) as follows.

	Purchase Cost	Retail Selling Price
Beginning inventories	$100,000	$160,000
+ Purchases during the period	300,000	500,000
= Cost of goods available for sale	400,000	660,000
(Cost-to-retail percentage: $400,000/$660,000 = 60.6%)		
Sales		(420,000)
Estimated ending inventory at retail selling prices		$240,000
Estimated ending inventory at cost (60.6% × $240,000 retail)	(145,440)	
= Cost of goods sold	$254,560	

This retailer reports inventory of $145,440 on its balance sheet at year-end. The income statement reports sales of $420,000, cost of goods sold of $254,560, and gross profit of $165,440.

This method allows retailers to readily compute ending inventories at retail selling prices (Quantities available × Selling price). The company's inventory system tracks both the purchase cost and the retail selling price of inventories. These are inputs in the cost-to-retail percentage calculation. The cost-to-retail percentage is important and managers review the ratio regularly for reliability. **Home Depot** describes its inventory costing method as follows.

> The majority of the Company's Merchandise Inventories are stated at the lower of cost (first-in, first-out) or market, as determined by the *retail inventory method* . . . Independent physical inventory counts . . . are taken on a regular basis in each store and distribution center to ensure that amounts reflected in the accompanying Consolidated Financial Statements for Merchandise Inventories are properly stated.

Financial Statement Effects of Inventory Costing

This section describes the financial statement effects of different inventory costing methods.

Income Statement Effects

The three inventory costing methods yield differing levels of gross profit as Exhibit 6.4 shows.

Exhibit 6.4 ■ Income Effects from Inventory Costing Methods			
	Sales	**Cost of Goods Sold**	**Gross Profit**
FIFO..................	$112,500	$45,000	$67,500
LIFO..................	112,500	55,000	57,500
Average cost............	112,500	51,429	61,071

Recall that inventory costs *rose* during this period from $100 per unit to $150 per unit. The higher gross profit reported under FIFO arises because FIFO matches older, lower-cost inventory against current selling prices. To generalize: in an inflationary environment, FIFO yields higher gross profit than do LIFO or average cost methods.

In recent years, the gross profit impact from using the FIFO method has been minimal for companies due to lower rates of inflation and increased management focus on reducing inventory quantities through improved manufacturing processes and better inventory controls. The FIFO gross profit effect can still arise, however, with companies subject to high inflation and slow inventory turnover.

Balance Sheet Effects

In our illustration above, the ending inventory using LIFO is less than that reported using FIFO. In periods of rising costs, LIFO inventories are markedly lower than under FIFO. As a result, balance sheets using LIFO do not accurately represent the cost that a company would incur to replace its current investment in inventories. A second issue is that financial statement users cannot compare LIFO and FIFO inventory numbers across firms as the balance sheet and income statement numbers are not equivalent. Thus, U.S. GAAP requires that firms choosing LIFO also report (in their footnotes) the equivalent FIFO inventory amounts. The difference between FIFO and LIFO inventories is called the **LIFO reserve.** We discuss, below, how to use the LIFO reserve to better analyze inventories.

Caterpillar Inc. (CAT), for example, uses LIFO and reports inventories of $11,529 million on its 2018 balance sheet. CAT's inventory footnote (below) reports that under FIFO costing, inventories would have been $2,009 million greater, a 17% difference. This suggests that CAT's balance sheet omits over $2 billion in inventories.

> Inventories are stated at the lower of cost or net realizable value. Cost is principally determined using the last-in, first-out (LIFO) method. The value of inventories on the LIFO basis represented about 65 percent of total inventories at December 31, 2018 and 2017. If the FIFO (first-in, first-out) method had been in use, inventories would have been $2,009 million and $1,934 million higher than reported at December 31, 2018 and 2017, respectively.

Cash Flow Effects

When inventory costs rise, the LIFO method yields lower net income. Assuming that companies and investors prefer higher net income, one wonders why any company would use LIFO. The answer is taxes. Unlike most other accounting method choices, inventory costing methods affect taxable income. (U.S. IRS is the only taxing authority in the world to allow LIFO; LIFO is not permitted under IFRS. For background, see: https://www.researchgate.net/publication/268365773.) Using LIFO increases COGS, which reduces taxable income and taxes paid. The net result is a real cash savings. Companies weigh the cash flow effect against the financial reporting effect when selecting among LIFO, FIFO, and average cost.

Could companies strategically use FIFO for financial reporting (and present high net income to investors) and LIFO for tax purposes (and pay as little tax as possible)? The answer is NO. A "LIFO conformity rule" in the IRS tax code stipulates that if a company uses LIFO for its tax filing, it must also adopt LIFO for financial reporting. This rule limits companies' ability to cherry-pick among accounting methods. Further, the LIFO reserve quantifies the difference that LIFO creates.

Caterpillar's use of LIFO has created significant tax savings over the years. We compute this tax savings using CAT's footnote data.

	LIFO Reserve	Tax Rate	Tax Saving
LIFO reserve (cumulative through 2017)	$1,934 million	35%	$677 million
Change to the LIFO reserve in 2018	75 million	21%	16 million
LIFO reserve (cumulative through 2018)	$2,009 million		$693 million

Through 2017, CAT's cumulative taxable income was reduced by $1,934 million. (Cumulative here means the aggregate amount over the company's entire history.) With the 35% tax rate in effect during that period, the company saved $677 million in taxes ($1,934 × 35%), which increased after-tax cash flow by the same amount. In 2018, the LIFO reserve increased by another $75 million for a cumulative total of $2,009 million. In 2018, the tax laws changed and reduced the corporate tax rate to 21% (see discussions of the new tax act, in Modules 5 and 10). At 21%, the 2018 tax saving was $16 million. Through 2018, CAT's cumulative tax savings is $693 million. The upshot is that CAT's cumulative cash flows were higher by that amount because the company used LIFO for inventory costing.

While tax savings have traditionally motivated companies to choose LIFO, the drop in the corporate tax rate in 2017 has reduced potential tax savings. With smaller benefits associated with LIFO, we might see a decline in the number of companies using LIFO.

LO1 Review 6-1

At the beginning of the current period, assume that one of Home Depot's subsidiary companies holds 1,000 units of a certain product with a unit cost of $18. A summary of purchases during the current period follows. During the current period, the HD subsidiary sells 2,800 units.

		Units	Unit Cost	Cost
Beginning Inventory		1,000	$18.00	$18,000
Purchases:	#1	1,800	18.25	32,850
	#2	800	18.50	14,800
	#3	1,200	19.00	22,800
Cost of goods available for sale . . .		4,800		$88,450

Required
1. Assume that the HD subsidiary uses the first-in, first-out (FIFO) method for this product. Compute the product's cost of goods sold for the current period and the ending inventory balance.
2. Assume that the HD subsidiary uses the last-in, first-out (LIFO) method for this product. Compute the product's cost of goods sold for the current period and the ending inventory balance.
3. Assume that the HD subsidiary uses the average cost (AC) method for this product. Compute the product's cost of goods sold for the current period and the ending inventory balance.
4. As manager, which of these three inventory costing methods would you choose:
   a. To reflect what is probably the physical flow of goods? Explain.
   b. To minimize income taxes for the period? Explain.

Solution on p. 6-43.

Inventory—Reporting

Lower of Cost or Market (LCM)

Footnotes to financial statements describe the inventory accounting method a company uses. To illustrate, Home Depot reports $13,925 million in inventory on its balance sheet as a current asset for the year ended February 3, 2019. Following is an excerpt from Home Depot's footnote.

eLectures **LO2**
MBC Examine inventory disclosures in financial statements.

> The majority of our merchandise inventories are stated at the lower of cost (first-in, first-out) or market, as determined by the retail inventory method. As the inventory retail value is adjusted regularly to reflect market conditions, the inventory valued using the retail method approximates the lower of cost or market. We evaluate the inventory valued using a cost method at the end of each quarter to ensure that it is carried at the lower of cost or net realizable value.

Like many retailers, Home Depot uses FIFO to cost its inventory along with the retail inventory method that we explained above. Then, at the end of each accounting period, Home Depot compares the ending FIFO inventory balance with the market value of the inventory (its replacement cost). If the market value is less than the FIFO amount, Home Depot "writes down" the inventory to its market value. The result is that the inventory is carried on the balance sheet at whichever amount is lower: the cost of the inventory *or* its market value. This process is called reporting inventories at the **lower of cost or market** and creates the following financial statement effects.

■ Inventory book value is written down to current market value (replacement cost), reducing inventory and total assets.

■ Inventory write-down is reflected as an expense (part of cost of goods sold) on the income statement, reducing current period gross profit, income, and equity.

To illustrate, assume that a company has inventory on its balance sheet at a cost of $27,000. Management learns that the inventory's replacement cost is $23,000 and writes inventories down to a balance of $23,000. The following financial statement effects template shows the adjustment.

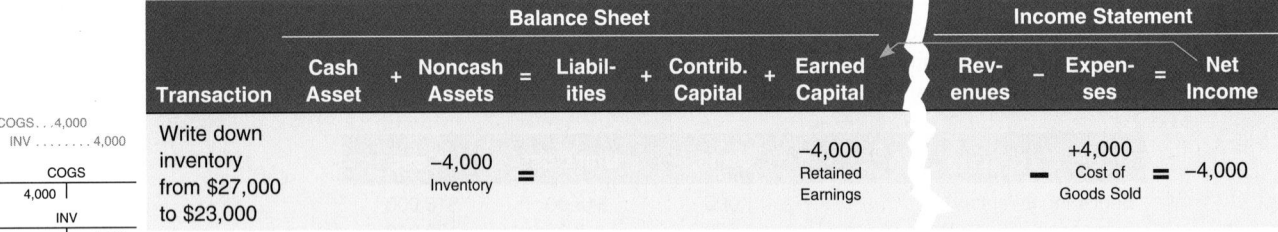

The inventory write-down (a noncash expense) is reflected in cost of goods sold and reduces gross profit by $4,000. Inventory write-downs are included in cost of goods sold. They are *not* reported in selling, general, and administrative expenses, which is common for other asset write-downs. A common occurrence of inventory write-downs is in connection with restructuring activities.

LIFO Reserve Adjustments to Financial Statements

CAT uses LIFO for most of its inventories. (Neither the IRS nor GAAP requires use of a single inventory costing method. That is, companies are allowed to, and frequently do, use different inventory costing methods for different types of inventory (such as spare parts versus finished goods) or inventory in different geographical locations.) We can use a LIFO reserve to adjust LIFO inventories on the balance sheet to their FIFO value using the following equation.

FIFO Inventory = LIFO Inventory + LIFO Reserve

We adjust CAT's inventory balances for 2017 and 2018 using balance sheet and footnote data as follows ($ in millions).

2018 FIFO inventory = $11,529 LIFO inventory + $2,009 LIFO reserve = $13,538

2017 FIFO inventory = $10,018 LIFO inventory + $1,934 LIFO reserve = $11,952

Comparing LIFO inventory balances across years for the same company can conceal any changes or trends, and thus, analysts typically adjust to FIFO numbers before calculating inventory ratios.

Disclosures for a LIFO Reserve Because companies can choose among the various inventory costing methods, their financial statements are often not comparable. The problem is most serious when companies hold large amounts of inventory and when prices markedly rise or fall. For example, consider comparing CAT to Kubota, a close competitor that uses the FIFO method to cost its inventory. The table below reports certain financial information for both companies for fiscal 2018.

Monetary amounts in millions	CAT LIFO as Reported	CAT FIFO as Adjusted	Kubota as Reported
Inventory.	$11,529	$13,538	¥ 370,698
LIFO reserve, 2018.	$ 2,009	—	—
LIFO reserve, 2017.	$ 1,934	—	—
Total assets	$78,509	$80,518	¥2,895,655
Inventory as a % of total assets	15%	17%	13%
Cost of goods sold	$36,997	$36,922	¥1,332,930
Revenue (equipment sales)	$51,822	$51,822	¥1,850,316
Cost of goods sold as a % of revenue . . .	71.39%	71.25%	72.04%

If we compare the information reported on each company's financial statements ('CAT LIFO as Reported' vs. 'Kubota as Reported') we would conclude that Caterpillar holds slightly more inventory than Kubota—15% of total assets for CAT vs. 13% for Kubota. But this is not an apples-to-apples comparison and such a conclusion is erroneous. Fortunately, companies that use LIFO must report their LIFO reserve, and we can use these disclosures to adjust the LIFO numbers to their FIFO equivalents. Once we convert CAT's inventory and its total assets to FIFO (by adding the LIFO reserve, as explained above), we find that the company holds 17% of total assets as inventory, a greater difference than first noted.

Balance Sheet Adjustments for a LIFO Reserve In general, to adjust for LIFO on the balance sheet, we must make three modifications and then recompute balance sheet totals and subtotals (current assets, total assets, and total equity).

▪ Increase inventories by the LIFO reserve.

▪ Increase tax liabilities by the tax rate applied to the LIFO reserve.

▪ Increase retained earnings for the difference.

As an example, to adjust CAT's 2018 balance sheet, we would:

▪ Increase inventories by $2,009 million.

▪ Increase tax liabilities by $693 million (see our computation above).

▪ Increase retained earnings by the difference of $1,316 million (computed as $2,009 million − $693 million).

Income Statement Adjustments for a LIFO Reserve To compare the income statements of companies that use LIFO, we must adjust cost of goods sold from LIFO to FIFO. Recall that: Cost of Goods Sold = Beginning Inventories + Purchases − Ending Inventories. To determine FIFO COGS, we must use the *change* in the LIFO reserve as follows.

> **FIFO COGS = LIFO COGS − Increase in LIFO Reserve (or + Decrease)**

During 2018, the change in CAT's LIFO reserve was $75 million ($2,009 million − $1,934 million). Had CAT *always used* FIFO, its 2018 COGS would have been $75 million lower (meaning gross profit and pretax income would be $75 million higher), and the company would have paid $16 million ($75 million × 21%) more in taxes. This does not make much difference either in dollar or percentage terms for CAT in 2018 because the LIFO reserve increased only slightly during the year. But in other years, and for other companies, the impact can be great.

LIFO Liquidations

When LIFO companies acquire inventory at different costs, they are required to account for each cost level as a separate inventory pool or layer (for example, there are the $100 and $150 units in our Exhibit 6.3 illustration). When companies reduce inventory levels, older inventory costs flow to the income statement. These older LIFO costs are often markedly lower than current inventory costs, assuming an inflationary environment. The net effect is that the LIFO cost of sales is lower than the equivalent FIFO cost of sales (the reverse of the typical situation). The liquidation boosts gross profit as older, lower costs are matched against current selling prices on the income statement.

The increase in gross profit resulting from a reduction of inventory quantities in the presence of rising costs is called **LIFO liquidation**. The effect of LIFO liquidation is evident in the following footnote from **Rite Aid**'s 10-K for the fiscal year ended March 2, 2019 (which Rite Aid labels fiscal 2019).

> **Inventory** (in $000s) At March 2, 2019 and March 3, 2018, inventories were $604,444 and $581,090, respectively, lower than the amounts that would have been reported using the first-in, first-out ("FIFO") cost flow assumption. . . During fiscal 2019, 2018 and 2017, a reduction in non-pharmacy inventories resulted in the liquidation of applicable LIFO inventory quantities carried at lower costs in prior years. This LIFO liquidation resulted in a $5,884, $2,707 and $2,375 cost of revenues decrease, with a corresponding reduction to the adjustment to LIFO for fiscal 2019, fiscal 2018 and fiscal 2017, respectively.

Rite Aid reports that reductions in inventory quantities in 2018 led to the sale (at current selling prices) of inventory that had a low balance sheet value—the inventory was valued using costs from prior years when those costs were much lower. As a result of these inventory reductions, COGS was lower, which increased income by $5,884 thousand in fiscal 2019. Fiscal years 2018 and 2017 were similarly affected.

IFRS Insight ■ Inventory Measurement under IFRS

Like GAAP, IFRS measures inventories at the lower of cost or market. The cost of inventory generally is determined using the FIFO (first-in, first-out) or average cost method; use of the LIFO (last-in, first-out) method is prohibited under IFRS.

Review 6-2 LO2

Refer to the information in Review 6-1. Consider each of the following as separate situations.

Required

1. Assume HD reports its inventories using the FIFO cost flow assumption as in #1 in Review 6-1 and that the market value (replacement cost) of the inventories on the financial statement date is $30,000. At what amount is inventories reported on the balance sheet?
2. Assume that the HD subsidiary utilizes the LIFO method and delays purchasing lot #3 until the next period. Compute cost of goods sold under this scenario and discuss how the LIFO liquidation affects profit.
3. Assume that the subsidiary uses LIFO for this product. In that case, the company would compute and report a LIFO reserve. What is the amount of LIFO reserve? How would that reserve affect the subsidiary's tax expense for the current period (as compared to FIFO) assuming a marginal tax rate of 21%?

Solution on p. 6-43.

Inventory—Analysis Tools

This section describes several useful tools for analysis of inventory and related accounts.

LO3
Analyze inventories and the related accounts payable.

Gross Profit Analysis

The **gross profit margin (GPM)** is gross profit divided by sales. This important ratio is closely monitored by management, analysts, and other external financial statement users. Exhibit 6.5 shows the gross profit margin on **Home Depot**'s sales for the past three years.

Exhibit 6.5 ■ Gross Profit Margin and Related Data for Home Depot

$ millions	Feb. 3, 2019 Fiscal 2018	Jan. 28, 2018 Fiscal 2017	Jan. 29, 2017 Fiscal 2016
Net sales.	$108,203	$100,904	$94,595
Cost of sales.	71,043	66,548	62,282
Gross profit.	$ 37,160	$ 34,356	$32,313
Gross profit margin.	34.3%	34.0%	34.2%
Inventories	$ 13,925	$ 12,748	
Accounts payable.	7,755	7,244	

The gross profit margin is commonly used instead of the dollar amount of gross profit as the GPM allows for comparisons across companies and over time. A decline in GPM is usually cause for concern since it indicates that the company has less ability to pass on increased product cost to customers or that the company is not effectively managing product costs. Home Depot's gross profit margin on product sales increased by 0.3 percentage points (from 34.0% to 34.3%) during the fiscal year ended February 3, 2019 (HD refers to this as fiscal 2018). Following is Home Depot's discussion of its gross profit from its Form 10-K.

> Gross profit increased $2.8 billion, or 8.2%, to $37.2 billion in fiscal 2018. Gross profit as a percent of net sales, or gross profit margin, was 34.3% in fiscal 2018 compared to 34.0% in fiscal 2017. The increase in gross profit margin for fiscal 2018 was primarily driven by a $598 million benefit from the adoption of ASU No. 2014-09 and a benefit from mix of products sold, partially offset by higher transportation and fuel costs in our supply chain and shrink. The additional week in fiscal 2018 contributed $615 million to gross profit.

The increase in Home Depot's gross profit margin in fiscal 2018 was partly due to factors outside Home Depot's control.

- It adopted the new revenue recognition standard (ASU No. 2014-09, see Module 5), which impacted the timing of revenue recognition. Footnote disclosures reveal that, due to the new standard: sales increased by $216 million, COGS decreased by $382 million, and gross profit increased by $598 million.

- The fiscal year that ended in February 2019 included a 53rd week. Home Depot, like most retailers, operates on a 52- or 53-week year. The company closes its fiscal year on the Sunday nearest to January 31st each year. That date was January 28 in 2018 (fiscal 2017) and February 3 in 2019 (fiscal 2018). This created a 53rd week for fiscal 2018. Home Depot 10-K revealed that the additional week contributed $615 million to gross profit. While this additional week adds to gross profit, it will have a negligible effect on gross profit margin because both cost of sales and sales will include the 53rd week.

It also reported that a portion of the change in gross profit resulted from operating factors within the company's control.

- It changed the mix of products sold and its gross margin increased. From this we can conclude that it sold higher-margin products, on average. However, it incurred higher transportation and fuel costs in the supply chain. Home Depot's use of the word *shrink* relates to the loss of inventory due to obsolescence, damage, theft, and a variety of other causes. The amount of this shrink is included in cost of goods sold.

It is important to distinguish between factors that Home Depot can control and those it cannot. These factors cause cash flow changes and, consequently, impact shareholder value.

Following is a brief list of factors that can adversely affect gross profit margins.

- Changes in product mix toward lower-margin products.
- New products introduced at low prices to gain market share.
- Increases in production costs.
- Decrease in production volume (lower production volume spreads out manufacturing overhead over a smaller number of units produced, thus increasing the cost per unit produced).
- Increases in supply-chain costs (such as procurement, transportation, technology, and insurance).
- More generous sales discounts or sales returns policies.
- Inventory obsolescence and/or overstocking.
- Warranty costs.
- General decline in economic activity.
- New competitors in the market.
- Regulation that inhibits sales or adds fees or taxes to products sold.

Competitive pressures mean that companies rarely have the opportunity to completely control gross profit with price increases. Improvements in gross profit on existing product lines typically arise from better management of supply chains, production processes, or distribution networks. Companies that succeed do so because of better performance on basic business processes.

Data Analytics Insight   ▪   Inventory Optimization

Companies have long used information technology including bar codes and RFIDs to manage inventory levels. The explosion of big data and powerful data analytics tools allow companies to better manage inventory quantity and quality and it enhances management of the supply chain. It is common to track inventory as it moves from manufacturer to distributor and to the final customer using scanning and GSP tracking technology. Expensive IT investments pay off when they help companies avoid upset customers, inventory carrying costs, and obsolescence write-downs. Predictive data analytics are especially common for retailers. AI-based tools can integrate internal sales and pricing data with macro-economic indicators, consumer demographics, social-media data, and weather forecasts, to fine-tune inventory items store by store and anticipate the timing of sales. Further, online shopping apps make "helpful suggestions" for additional purchases based on prior purchases and other data.

Days Inventory Outstanding and Inventory Turnover

A useful way to analyze inventory is to compare the income statement activity related to inventory (COGS) to inventory levels on the balance sheet. This helps us assess inventory management and provides insight into the company's efficiency in generating sales. We commonly calculate two inventory ratios.

Inventory turnover (IT) measures the number of times during the period that the company sells its inventory and is computed as follows.

$$\textbf{Inventory Turnover} = \textbf{Cost of Goods Sold}/\textbf{Average Inventory}$$

Average days inventory outstanding (DIO), also called *days inventory outstanding*, measures the days required to sell the average inventory available for sale and it is computed as follows.

$$\textbf{Average Days Inventory Outstanding} = 365/\textbf{Inventory Turnover} = \frac{365 \times \textbf{Average Inventory}}{\textbf{COGS}}$$

We use cost of goods sold in these ratios (instead of sales) because inventory is reported at cost whereas sales includes any gross profit on the inventory. We calculate average inventory as a simple average of the balance at the beginning and the balance at the end of the period.[3]

Recall that Home Depot's fiscal year that ends February 3, 2019, includes a 53rd week. We want to compare inventory turnover and DIO across years for Home Depot as well as to competitors. To do this, we begin with the data from Exhibit 6.3 and adjust the cost of goods sold for the 53rd week. The common approach is to multiply COGS by 52/53 under that assumption that Home Depot sold inventory evenly over all weeks in the fiscal year. (The inventory reported on the balance sheet is the amount at February 3, 2019, and does not require any adjustment.)

For Year Ended, $ millions	As Reported, February 3, 2019 (53 weeks)	As Adjusted, February 3, 2019 (52 weeks)
COGS......................	$71,043	$69,703 $71,043 × 52/53

Using the adjusted COGS, we calculate the two ratios for the year ended February 2019 ($ millions).

$$\text{Inventory Turnover} = \frac{\$69,703}{(\$13,925 + \$12,748)/2} = 5.23 \text{ times}$$

$$\text{Average Days Inventory Outstanding} = \frac{365}{5.23} = 69.8 \text{ days}$$

The results imply that Home Depot turned over (sold) its entire inventory 5.23 times during the year and that it took the company about 70 days, on average, to sell its average inventory. (Had we not adjusted for the 53rd week, the DIO would have been 68.5 days.)

The number of days required to turn over inventory varies widely by industry. At the high end, pharmaceutical and biotechnology companies have raw materials and finished goods inventory that include rare ingredients or patented molecules. At the low end are transportation and utility companies whose inventory line item on the balance sheet likely reflects fuel and other consumables primarily for internal use.

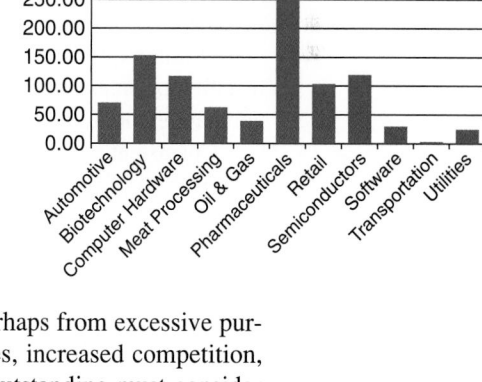

Overall, analysis of days inventory outstanding is important for at least two reasons.

1. *Inventory quality.* The ratios can be compared over time and across competitors. Fewer days is viewed favorably, because it implies that products are salable, preferably without undue discounting (we would compare profit margins to assess discounting). Conversely, more days implies that inventory is on the shelves for a longer period of time, perhaps from excessive purchases or production, missed fashion trends or technological advances, increased competition, and so forth. Our conclusions about higher or lower days inventory outstanding must consider alternative explanations including the following.

   • Product mix can include more (or less) higher margin inventories that sell more slowly. This can occur from business acquisitions that consolidate different types of inventory.

   • A company can change its promotion policies. Increased, effective advertising is likely to decrease days inventory outstanding. Advertising expense is in SG&A, not COGS. This means the additional advertising cost is in operating expenses, but the benefit is in gross profit and

---

[3] This formula uses average inventories. A variant of the ratio considers the number of days to sell the *ending* inventories (365 × Ending inventories/ COGS). For the year ended February 3, 2019, this ratio is as follows: $\text{Days Inventory Outstanding} = \frac{365}{(\$69,703/\$13,925)} = 72.9$. These two approaches address different issues: the "average days" tells us the number of days it took Home Depot to sell the inventory available for sale during the year. The second approach tells us the number of days it would take Home Depot to sell the current *ending* inventories. It is important that we first identify the issue under investigation and then choose the formula that best addresses that issue.

fewer days. If the promotion campaign is successful, the positive effects in margin and days should more than offset the promotion cost in SG&A.

- A company can realize improvements in manufacturing efficiency and lower investments in direct materials and work-in-process inventories. Such improvements reduce inventory and, consequently, decrease days inventory outstanding. Although a good sign, it does not yield any information about the desirability of a company's product line.

2. *Asset utilization.* Companies strive to optimize their inventory investment. Carrying too much inventory is expensive, and too little inventory risks stock-outs and lost sales (current and future). Companies can make the following operational changes to optimize inventory.

- Improved manufacturing processes can eliminate bottlenecks and the consequent buildup of work-in-process inventories.
- Just-in-time (JIT) deliveries from suppliers, which provide raw materials to the production line when needed, can reduce the level of raw materials and associated holding costs.
- Demand-pull production, in which raw materials are released into the production process when final goods are demanded by customers instead of producing for estimated demand, can reduce inventory levels. Harley-Davidson, for example, does not manufacture a motorcycle until it receives the customer's order; thus, Harley produces for actual, rather than estimated, demand.

Reducing inventories reduces inventory carrying costs, thus improving profitability and increasing cash flows. The reduction in inventory is reflected as an operating cash inflow in the statement of cash flows.

There is normal tension between the sales side of a company that argues for depth and breadth of inventory, and the finance side that monitors inventory carrying costs and seeks to maximize cash flow. Companies, therefore, seek to *optimize* inventory investment, not minimize it.

Days Payable Outstanding

Most companies purchase inventories on credit, meaning that suppliers allow companies to pay later. The supplier sets credit terms that specify when the invoice must be paid. Sometimes the supplier will offer a discount if the company pays more quickly. A typical invoice might include payment terms of 2/10, net 30, which means that the seller offers a 2% discount if the invoice is paid within 10 days and, if not, requires payment in full to be made in 30 days. Business-to-business (B2B) payables are usually non-interest bearing. This means accounts payable represent a low-cost financing source and companies should defer payment as long as allowed by the vendor.

Consistent with the ratios we calculated to analyze inventory, we can calculate **accounts payable turnover (APT)** that measures the number of payment cycles in the year.

$$\text{Accounts Payable Turnover} = \frac{\text{COGS}}{\text{Average Accounts Payable}}$$

The average length of time a company takes to pay its suppliers is reflected in the **days payable outstanding (DPO)** ratio.

$$\text{Days Payable Outstanding} = \frac{365}{\text{Accounts Payable Turnover}} = \frac{365 \times \text{Average Accounts Payable}}{\text{COGS}}$$

Similar to the inventory metrics above, we use COGS in the accounts payable ratios because payables relate to the purchase of inventories, which are reported at cost.[4] Again, we use the COGS adjusted for the 53rd week for Home Depot for the year ended February 2019; the two ratios are:

---

[4] Alternate versions of APT and DPO use inventory purchases instead of COGS (which are inventory sales). The rationale for this alternate definition is that the activity in accounts payable is directly related to purchases from and payments to suppliers. The link from COGS to payables is indirect, via the inventory account, which increases with inventory purchases and decreases with COGS. Nonetheless, it is more common to use COGS because they typically are a close approximation of purchases (and it's simpler).

$$\text{Accounts payable turnover} = \frac{\$69,703}{(\$7,755 + \$7,244)/2} = 9.29 \text{ times}$$

$$\text{Days payable outstanding} = \frac{365}{9.29} = 39.3 \text{ days}$$

This means Home Depot pays its suppliers in 39.3 days, on average. This is slightly longer than the typical supplier payment terms of 30 days. (Had we not adjusted for the 53rd week, the DPO would have been 38.5 days.)

Delaying payment to suppliers allows the purchasing company to increase its available cash (in other words, reduce its necessary level of cash). However, excessive delays (called "leaning on the trade") can damage supplier relationships. Remember, the purchaser's days payable outstanding is the seller's days sales outstanding in accounts receivable—this means as the purchaser gains cash from delaying payment, the seller loses an equal amount. As such, if delays become excessive, sellers might increase product cost or even choose to not sell to the purchaser. In managing the days accounts payable outstanding, companies must take care to maximize available cash while minimizing supply-chain disruption.

Cash Conversion Cycle

The cash conversion cycle is defined as:

	Days sales outstanding (accounts receivable)
+	Days inventory outstanding
−	Days payable outstanding
=	Cash conversion cycle

Each time a company completes one cash conversion cycle, it has purchased and sold inventory (realizing sales and gross profit), and paid accounts payable and collected accounts receivable. The cycle increases cash flow (unless the sales are unprofitable). The aim is to minimize the time to complete a cycle.

Home Depot's cash conversion cycle for the three-year period ending February 3, 2019, follows.

Amounts in Days	Feb. 3, 2019 (52 weeks adjusted)	Jan. 28, 2018	Jan. 29, 2017
Days sales outstanding (DSO)*	6.7	7.2	7.8
+ Days inventory outstanding (DIO) . .	69.8	69.4	73.5
− Days payable outstanding (DPO) . . .	(39.3)	(39.1)	(41.0)
= Cash conversion cycle	37.2	37.5	40.3

* We discuss DSO in Module 5.

Over the past three years, Home Depot has improved its cash conversion cycle from 40.3 days to 37.2 days. The biggest improvement was for inventory days, which dropped 3.7 days over the three-year period (73.5 days − 69.8 days = 3.7 days). Inventory management has been a strategic focus for Home Depot as explained in its February 2019 MD&A.

We centrally forecast and replenish over 98% of our store products through sophisticated inventory management systems and utilize a network of over 200 distribution centers to serve both our stores' and customers' needs. This network includes multiple distribution center platforms in the U.S., Canada, and Mexico tailored to meet the needs of our stores and customers based on the types of products, location, transportation, and delivery requirements. These platforms primarily include rapid deployment centers, stocking distribution centers, bulk distribution centers, and direct fulfillment centers. As part of our investment in One Home Depot Supply Chain, we will add a number of different fulfillment facilities designed to help us meet our goal of reaching 90% of the U.S. population with same or next day delivery for an extended home improvement product offering, including big and bulky goods. These facilities include more direct fulfillment centers and market delivery operations, or MDOs, which function as local hubs to consolidate freight for dispatch to customers for the final mile of delivery. In fiscal 2018, we began piloting these facilities.

Supply chain optimization is often cited as a key for effective inventory management. Inventories are recognized on the balance sheet when received at the distribution center and the days inventories outstanding clock starts ticking at that moment. Home Depot's challenge, then, is to minimize the time it takes to get the right amount of product from the distribution center to the store shelves. This involves accurate estimates of customer demand for products and an efficient logistics network.

As inventories decrease (all else equal), cash increases, and that increase can be large. For example, from 2017 to 2018, Home Depot reduced its DIO by 4.1 days from 73.5 to 69.4, which increased the company's cash balance by $747.5 million, computed as (Δ refers to 'change in'):

$$\Delta \text{ Cash} = \Delta \text{ Days Inventory Outstanding} \times (\text{COGS}/365)$$
$$= 4.1 \text{ days} \times (\$66{,}548 \text{ million}/365 \text{ days}) = \$747.5 \text{ million}$$

Managerial Decision   ■   You Are the Operations Manager

You are analyzing your inventory turnover report for the month and are concerned that the average days inventory outstanding is lengthening. What actions can you take to reduce average days inventory outstanding? [Answer, p. 6-28]

Review 6-3 LO3

Lowe's Companies Inc. is a competitor of Home Depot. It reports the following financial statement data for 2017, 2018 and 2019. Use these data to answer the requirements below.

$ millions	2017	2018	2019
Revenue	$65,017	$68,619	$71,309
Cost of goods sold	43,343	46,185	48,394
Gross profit.	21,674	22,434	22,915
Accounts receivable	0	0	0
Inventory.	10,458	11,393	12,561
Accounts payable	6,651	6,590	8,279

Required
1. Compute the gross profit margin for 2017, 2018, and 2019.
2. Compute the days inventory outstanding for 2018 and 2019.
3. Compute the days payable outstanding for 2018 and 2019.
4. Compute the cash conversion cycle for 2018 and 2019. By how many days did the cash conversion cycle improve during 2019?

Solution on p. 6-44.

5. Compute the cash effect in 2019 due to the 2019 change in the cash conversion cycle.

PPE Assets—Capitalization and Depreciation

LO4 Apply capitalization and depreciation of tangible assets.

Property, plant and equipment (PPE or PP&E, also called tangible or fixed assets) is the largest asset for most companies, and depreciation is often second in expenses to cost of goods sold on the income statement. Companies choose the method to compute depreciation, which can markedly impact the income statement and balance sheet. When companies dispose of PPE, a gain or loss often results. Understanding gains and losses on asset sales is important as we assess performance. Also, asset write-downs (and impairments) impact companies' current financial performance *and* future profitability. We must understand these accounting effects when we read and analyze and forecast financial statements.

When PPE is acquired, it is recorded at cost on the balance sheet. This is called *capitalization*, which explains why *expenditures* for PPE are called CAPEX. The amount capitalized on the balance sheet includes all costs to put the assets into service. This includes the cost of the PPE as well as transportation, duties, tax, and necessary costs to install and test the assets.

Instead of purchasing PPE outright, companies often enter into long-term equipment leases to increase operational flexibility or to take advantage of attractive financing terms. If the lease terms convey the "risks and rewards" of ownership, the equipment is capitalized just like other tangible assets. These lease assets are included in the company's PPE even though the company does not legally own the assets. The rationale is that the company operates the assets as if it did own them. (We discuss capital leases in detail in Module 10.)

Plant and Equipment

Once capitalized, the cost of plant and equipment is recognized as expense over the period of time that the assets produce revenues (directly or indirectly) in a process called depreciation. Depreciation recognizes *using up* of the asset over its useful life. Only assets that have a useful life are depreciated—**land, for example, does not have a determinable useful life and is therefore *not* depreciated**.

To determine depreciation expense, a company makes three estimates.

1. **Useful life**—period of time over which the asset is expected to generate measurable benefits.
2. **Salvage value**—amount expected for the asset when disposed of at the end of its useful life.
3. **Depreciation method**—estimate of how the asset is used up over its useful life.

With these three estimates, the company can determine a depreciation rate that approximates how the asset is used up over its life. The company uses that rate to systematically decrease the asset's balance sheet value (called the carrying value) such that, at the end of its useful life, the asset's carrying value equals its salvage value. When the asset is sold, the difference between the sales proceeds and its book value is recorded as a gain or loss on sale in the income statement.

Companies can use any reasonable method to depreciate assets. Straight-line depreciation is the most common method in the U.S. and around the world. Other methods include accelerated methods and the units of production method. Because these methods are infrequently used or are common to only certain industries, we discuss them only briefly.

Straight-Line Method

To illustrate, consider a machine with the following details: $100,000 cost, $10,000 salvage value, and a five-year useful life. Depreciation expense is recognized evenly over the estimated useful life of the asset as follows.

Depreciation Base	Depreciation Rate
Cost – Salvage value = $100,000 – $10,000 = $90,000	1/Estimated useful life = 1/5 years = 20%

Depreciation expense per year for this asset is $18,000, computed as $90,000 × 20%. For the asset's first full year of usage, $18,000 of depreciation expense is reported in the income statement. (If an asset is purchased midyear, it is typically depreciated only for the portion of the year it is used. For example, had the asset in this illustration been purchased on May 31, the company would report $10,500 of depreciation in the first year, computed as 7/12 × $18,000, assuming the company has a December 31 year-end.) This depreciation is reflected in the company's financial statements as follows.

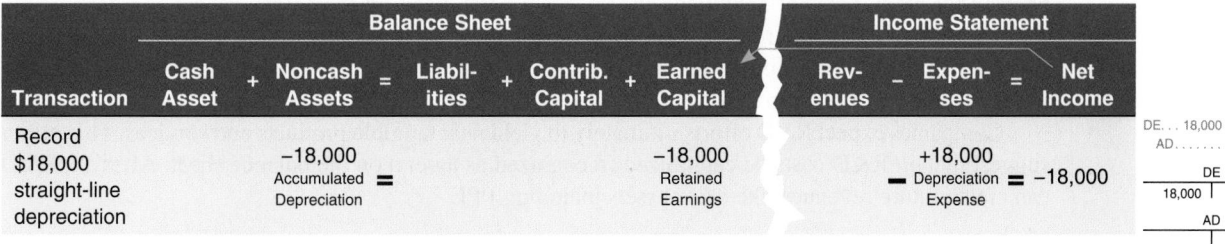

The accumulated depreciation (contra asset) account increases by $18,000, thus reducing net PPE by the same amount. Also, $18,000 of the asset cost is transferred from the balance sheet to the income statement as depreciation expense. At the end of the first year the asset is reported on the balance sheet as follows.

Machine, at cost	$100,000
Less accumulated depreciation	18,000
Machine, net (end of Year 1)	$ 82,000

Net book value ➤

Accumulated depreciation is the sum of all depreciation expense that has been recorded to date. The asset **net book value (NBV)**, or *carrying value*, is cost less accumulated depreciation. Although the word *value* is used here, it does not refer to market value. Depreciation is a cost allocation concept (transfer of costs from the balance sheet to the income statement), not a valuation concept.

In the second year of usage, another $18,000 of depreciation expense is recorded in the income statement and the net book value of the asset on the balance sheet follows.

Machine, at cost	$100,000
Less accumulated depreciation	36,000
Machine, net (end of Year 2)	$ 64,000

Net book value ➤

Accumulated depreciation of $36,000 now includes the sum of the first and second years' depreciation, and the net book value of the asset is now reduced to $64,000. After the fifth year, a total of $90,000 of accumulated depreciation will be recorded ($18,000 per year × 5 years), yielding a net book value for the machine of $10,000. The net book value at the end of the machine's useful life is exactly equal to the salvage value that management estimated when the asset was acquired.

Other Depreciation Methods

Accelerated depreciation methods record more depreciation in the early years of an asset's useful life (hence the term *accelerated*) and less depreciation in later years. At the end of the asset's useful life, the balance sheet will still report a net book value equal to the asset's salvage value. The difference between straight-line and accelerated depreciation methods is not in the total amount of depreciation, but in the rate at which costs are transferred from the balance sheet to the income statement.

Units-of-production method records depreciation according to asset use. Specifically, the depreciation base is cost less salvage value, and the depreciation rate is the units produced and sold during the year compared with the total expected units to be produced and sold. For example, if a truck is driven 10,000 miles out of a total expected 100,000 miles, 10% of its depreciable cost is reflected as depreciation expense. This method is common for extractive industries including oil and gas, timber, and coal.

Modified Accelerated Cost Recovery System (MACRS), an accelerated method, is required by the U.S. IRS to calculate taxable income. We discuss this in Module 10. It is important to note that regardless of the depreciation method a company chooses *for its published financial statements*, it has no impact on taxes paid.

Research and Development Facilities and Equipment

In a prior module, we introduce R&D expense and explain that it includes costs associated with property and buildings to be used as research facilities. Importantly, ***R&D facilities and equipment*** are not immediately expensed. If they are *general-use* in nature (such as a general research laboratory that can be used for many types of activities), the costs are capitalized on the balance sheet and depreciated over its useful life like other depreciable assets. Only those R&D facilities and equipment that are purchased specifically for a single R&D project, and have *no alternative use*, are expensed immediately in the income statement (an unusual situation).

Companies expect R&D efforts ultimately to yield new tangible products and services. This might suggest that *all* R&D costs be capitalized (recognized as assets) on the balance sheet. After all, R&D can create future revenues like other assets including PPE.

However, with the exception of facilities and equipment that have alternative uses, R&D costs are *not* capitalized. Instead, R&D costs are expensed in the income statement as they are incurred. The rationale for this accounting treatment is threefold.

- Whether any tangible projects or services will be developed is often uncertain while the R&D is ongoing. Indeed, many R&D efforts fail to produce any benefits whatsoever.
- Even for R&D programs that look promising, the timing of future products and services is uncertain.
- Salaries for R&D personnel are no different than for other personnel whose salaries and wages are expensed when incurred.

It is generally acknowledged that R&D costs, especially development costs associated with clearly defined products for which a workable prototype has been proven, do create future benefits and have the characteristics of assets. However, the measurement uncertainty argument prevails and R&D costs are not capitalized under GAAP and, with the exception of general-use R&D PPE assets, they are expensed when incurred.

LO4 Review 6-4

On January 2, assume that one of **Home Depot**'s subsidiary companies purchases equipment that fabricates a key product part. The equipment costs $95,000, and its estimated useful life is five years, after which it is expected to be sold for $10,000.

Required
1. Compute depreciation expense for each year of the equipment's useful life using the straight-line method of depreciation.
2. Show how the HD subsidiary reports the equipment on its balance sheet at the end of the third year assuming straight-line depreciation.

Solution on p. 6-44.

PPE Assets—Sales, Impairments, and Restructuring

This section discusses gains and losses from asset sales, restructurings, and the computation and disclosure of asset impairments.

LO5 Evaluate asset sales, impairments, and restructuring activities.

Asset Sales

The gain or loss on the sale (disposition) of a tangible asset is computed as follows.

> **Gain or Loss on Asset Sale = Proceeds from Sale – Net Book Value of Asset Sold**

An asset's net book value is its acquisition cost less accumulated depreciation. When an asset is sold, its acquisition cost and related accumulated depreciation are both removed from the balance sheet, and any gain or loss is reported in income from continuing operations.

Gains and losses on asset sales can be large, and analysts must be aware that these gains and losses are usually *transitory operating* income components. Financial statements do not typically report gains and losses from tangible asset sales because, if the gain or loss is small (immaterial), companies include the item in selling, general and administrative expenses. Footnotes can sometimes be informative. To illustrate, **Macy's Inc.** provides the following footnote disclosure relating to certain real estate sales.

> **Gains on Sale of Real Estate**   The Company recognized gains of $389 million in 2018 associated with sales of real estate, as compared to $544 million in 2017. 2018 included gains of $178 million related to the I. Magnin building in Union Square San Francisco. 2017 included gains of $234 million related to the Macy's Union Square location, $71 million related to the Macy's Brooklyn transaction, $47 million related to the downtown Minneapolis properties and $40 million related to the downtown Seattle Macy's location.

The various gains on sale that Macy's recognized reflect the difference between the sale proceeds and the amount at which the properties were reported on Macy's balance sheet on the date of sale, that is, their net book value (also called carrying value).

Asset Impairments

Tangible assets are reported at their net book values (original cost less accumulated depreciation). This is the case even if the market values of these assets increase subsequent to acquisition. As a result, there can be unrecognized gains hidden within the balance sheet.

On the other hand, if market values of PPE assets subsequently decrease—and the asset value is deemed to be permanently impaired—then, companies must write off the impaired cost and recognize losses on those assets. **Impairment** of PPE assets is determined by comparing the asset's net book value to the sum of the asset's *expected* future (undiscounted) cash flows. If the sum of expected cash flow is greater than net book value, there is no impairment. However, if the sum of the expected cash flow is less than net book value, the asset is deemed impaired and it is written down to its current fair value (generally, the present value of those expected cash flows). Exhibit 6.6 depicts this impairment analysis.

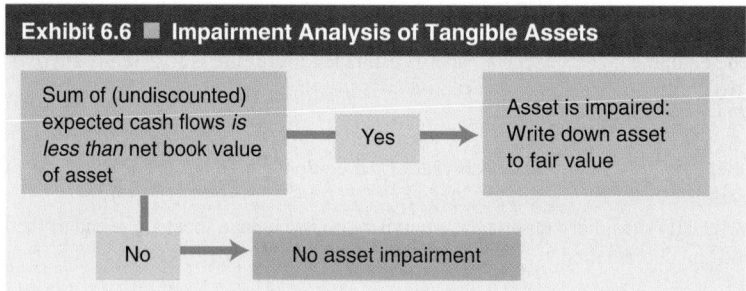

Exhibit 6.6 ■ Impairment Analysis of Tangible Assets

To record an impairment charge, the company reduces assets by the amount of the write-down and recognizes a loss in the income statement. To illustrate, a footnote to the 2018 Form 10-K of Dean Foods Company reports the following about asset impairments.

> **Asset Impairment Charges**   We evaluate our finite-lived intangible and long-lived assets for impairment when circumstances indicate that the carrying value may not be recoverable. Indicators of impairment could include, among other factors, significant changes in the business environment, the planned closure of a facility, or deteriorations in operating cash flows. . . The results of our 2018 impairment analysis indicated an impairment of our property, plant, and equipment at five of our production facilities, totaling $13.7 million. The impairments were the result of declines in operating cash flows at these production facilities on both a historical and forecasted basis. These impairment charges were recorded during the year ended December 31, 2018.

As operating cash flows declined in five of their production facilities, the management of Dean Foods concluded that it was unlikely that these locations would generate enough cash flow to absorb the cost of the PPE assets. Consequently, the facilities were deemed to be impaired and the assets were written down to their fair values, resulting in an impairment expense for 2018 of $13.7 million.

IFRS Insight   ■   PPE Valuation under IFRS

Like GAAP, companies reporting under IFRS must periodically assess long-lived assets for possible impairment. Unlike the two-step GAAP approach, IFRS uses a one-step approach: firms compare an asset's net book value to its current fair value (estimated as discounted expected future cash flows) to test for impairment and then reduce net book value to that fair value. Under IFRS, impairment losses can be reversed if the PPE subsequently regains its value. The PPE account is increased to the newly estimated recoverable amount, not to exceed the assets' initial cost adjusted for depreciation. GAAP prohibits such reversals.

Restructuring Costs

It is not uncommon for a company to face corporate challenges that are so great that the only way forward is to alter its organizational, operational, and financial structures. Such corporate "restructurings" are designed to turn a company around and are frequently initiated in response to poor performance, mounting debt, and shareholder pressure. A restructuring can involve eliminating business segments, selling major assets, downsizing the workforce, and reconfiguring debt. Ultimately, the goal of a restructuring is to positively impact a company's long-term financial performance. But in the short term, restructurings usually have large negative impacts on the company's income statement.

Disclosure of Restructuring Costs

Because of their magnitude, restructurings require enhanced disclosure either as a separate line item in the income statement or as a footnote. Restructuring costs typically include three components:

1. Employee severance or relocation costs.
2. Asset write-downs.
3. Other restructuring costs.

Reporting of employee severance or relocation costs. The first part, **employee severance or relocation costs**, represents accrued (estimated) costs to terminate or relocate employees as part of a restructuring program. To accrue those expenses, the company must:

- Estimate total costs of terminating or relocating selected employees; these costs might include severance pay (typically a number of weeks of pay based on the employee's tenure with the company), outplacement costs, and relocation or retraining costs for remaining employees.
- Report *total* estimated costs as an expense (and a liability) in the period the restructuring program is announced. Subsequent payments to employees reduce the restructuring accrual (the liability).

Reporting of asset write-downs. The second part of restructuring costs is **asset write-downs**, also called *write-offs* or *charge-offs*. Restructuring activities usually involve closure or relocation of manufacturing or administrative facilities. This can require the write-down of assets whose fair value is less than book value. For example, restructurings can necessitate the write-down of long-term assets (such as plant assets or goodwill) and of inventories. To determine the amount of the write-down, the company follows the approach in Exhibit 6.6. Remember that write-downs have no cash flow effects unless the write-down has tax consequences.

Reporting of other restructuring costs. The third part of restructuring costs is typically labeled "Other" and includes costs of vacating duplicative facilities, fees to terminate contracts (such as lease agreements and service contracts), and other exit costs (such as legal and asset-appraisal fees). Companies estimate and accrue these costs and reduce the restructuring liability as those costs are paid in cash.

For a company to use the term *restructuring* in the income statement and to accrue restructuring liabilities, the company is required to have a formal restructuring plan that is approved by its board of directors. Also, a company must identify the relevant employees and notify them of its plan. In each subsequent year, the company must disclose in its footnotes the original amount of the Restructuring liability (accrual), how much of that liability is settled in the current period (such as employee payments), how much of the original liability has been reversed because of original cost overestimation, any new accruals for unforeseen costs, and the current balance of the liability. This creates more transparent financial statements, which allow readers to see, in hindsight, if the initial restructuring accrual was overstated (requiring subsequent reversal) or understated (requiring subsequent additions to the restructuring accrual).

Business Insight ■ Pfizer's Restructuring

Pfizer explains its restructuring efforts as follows in its 2018 10-K.

> We incur significant costs in connection with acquiring, integrating and restructuring businesses and in connection with our global cost-reduction/productivity initiatives. For example:
>
> - In connection with acquisition activity, we typically incur costs associated with executing the transactions, integrating the acquired operations (which may include expenditures for consulting and the integration of systems and processes), and restructuring the combined company (which may include charges related to employees, assets and activities that will not continue in the combined company); and
>
> - In connection with our cost-reduction/productivity initiatives, we typically incur costs and charges associated with site closings and other facility rationalization actions, workforce reductions and the expansion of shared services, including the development of global systems.
>
> All of our businesses and functions may be impacted by these actions, including sales and marketing, manufacturing and R&D, as well as groups such as information technology, shared services and corporate operations. The following table provides the components of costs associated with acquisitions and cost-reduction/productivity initiatives:

$ millions	Employee Termination Costs	Asset Impairment Charges	Exit Costs	Accrual
Balance, January 1, 2017.	$1,547	$ —	$ 36	$1,583
Provision (Credit)	(181)	190	21	30
Utilization and other	(326)	(190)	9	(508)
Balance, December 31, 2017. . . .	1,039	—	66	1,105
Provision.	459	290	33	782
Utilization and other	(295)	(290)	(51)	(636)
Balance, December 31, 2018. . . .	$1,203	$ —	$ 49	$1,252

The table reflects Pfizer's restructuring transactions for 2017 and 2018. Companies are required to disclose the beginning-year balance of the restructuring liability. Pfizer reports this in the right-most "Accrual" column ($1,105 million for fiscal 2018). Companies must also report the changes in the restructuring liability for the year, which Pfizer reports separately for the three types of restructuring costs.

During 2018, Pfizer added a total of $782 million to the liability and recorded that amount as restructuring expense in its 2018 income statement. (On the income statement, Pfizer aggregated the $782 million with additional costs relating to other acquisitions, for a total of $1,044 million). During the year, the company reduced the liability by $636 million for the payment of employee termination costs ($295 million), asset impairment charges ($290 million), and exit costs ($51 million). The ending balance of $1,252 million is reported on Pfizer's 2018 balance sheet as a liability.

Analysis of Restructuring Costs

Restructuring costs are typically large and, as such, greatly affect reported profits. Our analysis must consider whether these costs are associated with the accounting period in which they are recognized. Following are some guidelines relating to the components of restructuring costs.

Analyzing employee severance or relocation costs and other costs. Companies are allowed to record costs relating to employee separation or relocation that are *incremental* and that do not benefit future periods. Similarly, other accrued costs must be related to the restructuring and not to expenses that would otherwise have been incurred in the future. Thus, accrual of these costs is treated like other liability accruals. We must, however, be aware of over- or understated costs and their effect on current and future profitability. Disclosure rules require a reconciliation of this restructuring accrual in future years (see the preceding Business Insight on Pfizer's restructuring). A reconciliation reveals either overstatements or understatements: overstatements are followed by a reversal of the restructuring liability, and understatements are followed by further accruals. Should a company develop a reputation for recurring reversals or understatements, its management loses credibility.

Research Insight ■ Restructuring Costs and Managerial Incentives

Research has investigated the circumstances and effects of restructuring costs. Some research finds that stock prices increase when a company announces a restructuring as if the market appreciates the company's candor. Research also finds that many companies that reduce income through restructuring costs later reverse a portion of those costs, resulting in a substantial income boost for the period of reversal. These reversals often occur when the company would have otherwise reported an earnings decline. Whether or not the market responds favorably to trimming the fat or simply disregards restructuring costs as transitory and, thus, as uninformative, managers have incentives to characterize such income-decreasing items as "one-time" on the income statement and routinely exclude such charges in non-GAAP, pro forma disclosures. These incentives often derive from contracts such as debt covenants and managerial bonus plans.

Analyzing asset write-downs. Asset write-downs accelerate (or catch up) the depreciation process to reflect asset impairment. Impairment implies the loss of cash-generating capability and, likely, occurs over several years. Thus, prior periods' profits were arguably not as high as reported, and the current period's profit is not as low. This measurement error is difficult to estimate and, thus, many analysts do not adjust balance sheets and income statements for write-downs. At a minimum, however, we must recognize the qualitative implications of restructuring costs for the profitability of recent prior periods and the current period.

Managerial Decision ■ You Are the Financial Analyst

You are analyzing the 10-K of a company that reports a large restructuring expense, involving employee severance and asset write-downs. How do you interpret and treat this cost in your analysis of the company's current and future profitability? [Answer, p. 6-29]

LO5 Review 6-5

Part 1. Refer to information in Review 6-4 and to its solution to answer the following requirements.

Required

a. Assume that the HD subsidiary uses the straight-line method of depreciation and estimates that, at the end of the third year, the equipment will generate $40,000 in cash flow over its remaining life and that it has a current fair value of $36,000. Is the equipment impaired? If so, what is the effect on the HD subsidiary financial statements?

b. Instead of the facts in part a, assume that, at the end of the third year, the HD subsidiary sells the equipment for $50,000 cash. What amount of gain or loss does the HD subsidiary report from this sale?

Part 2. The Coca-Cola Company reports the following reconciliation of its restructuring liability for 2018.

$ millions	Severance Pay and Benefits	Outside Services	Other Direct Costs	Total
Accrued balance as of December 31, 2017 . . .	$190	$ 1	$ 15	$206
2018				
Costs incurred	$164	$92	$252	$508
Payments	(209)	(83)	(211)	(503)
Noncash and exchange	(69)	—	(52)	(121)
Accrued balance as of December 31, 2018 . . .	$ 76	$10	$ 4	$ 90

Required

a. What amount of expense did Coca-Cola report in its income statement as restructuring expense in 2018?

b. What amount of restructuring liability did Coca-Cola report on its balance sheet for 2018?   **Solution on p. 6-44.**

PPE Assets—Analysis Tools

eLectures
MBC **LO6**
Analyze
tangible
assets and
related activities.

Home Depot reports $22,375 million of property and equipment, net of accumulated depreciation, on its balance sheet at February 3, 2019. Footnote disclosures reveal the following.

Net Property and Equipment The components of net property and equipment follow.

in millions	February 3, 2019	January 28, 2018
Land	$ 8,363	$ 8,352
Buildings.	18,199	18,073
Furniture, fixtures, and equipment	12,460	11,506
Leasehold improvements	1,705	1,637
Construction in process	820	538
Capital leases.	1,392	1,308
Property and equipment, at cost.	42,939	41,414
Less accumulated depreciation and capital lease amortization	20,564	19,339
Net property and equipment.	$22,375	$22,075

Depreciation and capital lease amortization expense, including depreciation expense included in cost of sales, follows.

For Fiscal Year Ended, in millions	Feb. 3, 2019 (Fiscal 2018)	Jan. 28, 2018 (Fiscal 2017)	Jan. 29, 2017 (Fiscal 2016)
Depreciation and capital lease amortization expense	$2,076	$1,983	$1,899

Property and Equipment, including Capitalized Lease Assets Building, furniture, fixtures, and equipment are recorded at cost and depreciated using the straight-line method over their estimated useful lives. Leaseholder improvements are amortized using the straight-line method over the original term of the lease or the useful life of the improvement, whichever is shorter. The estimated useful lives of our property and equipment follow.

	Life
Buildings.	5–45 years
Furniture, fixtures and equipment.	2–20 years
Leasehold improvements	5–45 years

We can use these data to compute key ratios to assess the productivity of Home Depot's PPE and its assets' relative age.

PPE Turnover

A crucial issue in analyzing PPE is determining their productivity (utilization). For example, what level of plant assets is necessary to generate a dollar of revenues? How capital intensive are the company and its competitors? To address these and similar questions, we use **PPE turnover**, defined as follows.

> **PPE Turnover (PPET) = Sales/Average PPE, net**

To calculate PPE turnover for Home Depot, we must adjust Sales for the 53rd week for the fiscal year ended February 3, 2019, as discussed earlier in the module: $108,203 × 52/53 = $106,161. Home Depot's PPE turnover is 4.8 ($106,161 million/[($22,375 million + $22,075 million)/2]).

Higher PPE turnover is preferable to lower. A higher PPE turnover implies a lower capital invest-ment for a given level of sales. Higher turnover, therefore, increases profitability because the company avoids asset carrying costs and because the freed-up assets can generate operating cash flow.

PPE turnover is lower for capital-intensive manufacturing companies than it is for companies in service or knowledge-based industries. To this point, consider the following chart of PPE turnover for selected industries. (The term *turnover* is a bit of a misnomer for PPE. Intuitively we can understand how accounts receivable, inventory, and accounts payable "turn over" as customers pay, and the com-pany sells inventory and pays suppliers. But for PPE, there is no equivalent concept and perhaps the ratio would be better named PPE productivity. Nonetheless, the label PPE turnover is widely used.)

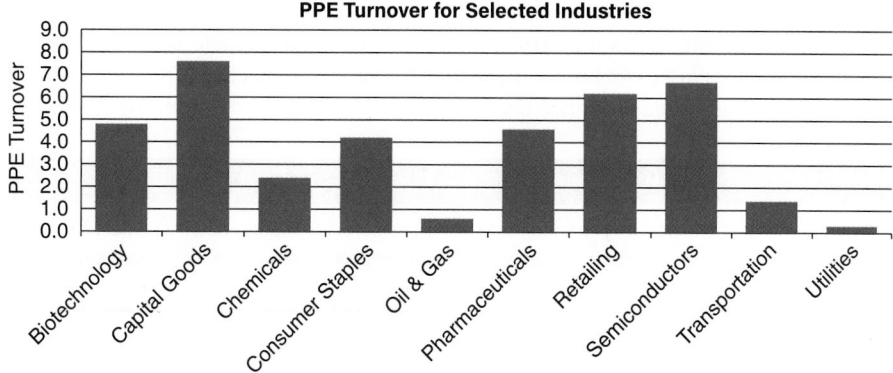

There is wide variability in PPE turnover rate across industries. Capital intensive industries such as utilities, transportation, and oil & gas report relatively low turnover rates, reflecting large levels of capital investment required to compete in those areas.

PPE Useful Life

Home Depot reports that the useful lives of its depreciable assets range from two years for furniture, fixtures and equipment to 45 years for buildings and leasehold improvements. The longer an asset's useful life, the lower the annual depreciation expense reported in the income statement and the higher the income each year. It might be of interest, therefore, to know whether a company's useful life esti-mates are more conservative or more aggressive than its competitors.

If we assume straight-line (SL) depreciation (which is consistent with the company's policy) and zero salvage value, we can estimate the average useful life for depreciable assets as follows.

> **Average useful life = Average depreciable asset cost / Depreciation expense**

We compute depreciable assets for 2018, by excluding two items from gross PPE of $42,939.

- Land of $8,363 million, which is never depreciated.

- Construction-in-progress of $820 million, which is not depreciated until the assets under construc-tion are completed and placed into service, which is when the company begins to use the assets.

Depreciable assets for 2018 are, therefore, $33,756 million ($42,939 million − $8,363 million − $820 million), and for 2017 are $32,524 million. The footnote disclosures reveal that the reported amount of $2,076 million of depreciation and amortization expense includes depreciation of the owned PPE assets and amortization of the leased PPE assets (capital lease assets), which are treated like purchased PPE assets for accounting purposes.

This means the average useful life for 2018 is

$$\text{Average useful life for 2018} = \frac{(\$33,756 + \$32,524)/2}{\$2,076} = 16 \text{ years}$$

PPE Percent Used Up

We can also estimate the proportion of a company's depreciable assets that have already been transferred to the income statement. This ratio reflects the percent of depreciable assets that are no longer productive and is computed as follows.

> **Percent used up = Accumulated depreciation / Average depreciable asset cost**

Home Depot's assets are 62% used up, computed as $20,564 million/([$33,756 million + $32,524 million)/2]). If a company replaced all of its assets evenly each year, the percent used up ratio would be 50%. Home Depot's depreciable assets are slightly older than this benchmark. Knowing the degree to which a company's assets are used up is of interest in forecasting future cash flows. If, for example, depreciable assets are 80% used up, we might anticipate a higher level of capital expenditures to replace aging assets in the near future. We also expect that older assets are less efficient and will incur higher maintenance costs.

Managerial Decision ■ You Are the Division Manager

You are the manager for a main operating division of your company. You are concerned that a declining PPE turnover is adversely affecting your division's return on net operating assets. What specific actions can you take to increase PPE turnover? [Answer, p. 6-29]

Review 6-6 LO6

Lowe's Companies Inc. reports the following selected financial data for 2019, 2018, and 2017.

$ millions	2019	2018	2017
Revenue.	$71,309	$68,619	$65,017
Depreciation and amortization	1,454	1,540	1,590
Gross property, plant, and equipment	35,863	36,940	36,918
Accumulated depreciation	(17,431)	(17,219)	(16,969)
Net property, plant and equipment	18,432	19,721	19,949
Footnote data			
Land	7,196	7,414	7,329
Buildings.	18,052	18,521	18,147
Machinery.	10,090	10,475	10,978
Construction in progress.	525	530	464

Required

Compute the following measures for 2019 and 2018. (For simplicity, assume that the entire amortization expense relates to property, plant and equipment assets.)
1. PPE turnover.
2. Average useful life.

Solution on p. 6-44.   3. Percent used up.

Global Accounting

Both GAAP and IFRS account similarly for operating assets. Although similarities in accounting dwarf any differences, we highlight some of the more notable differences.

Inventory There are two notable differences in accounting for inventory.
1. IFRS does not permit use of the LIFO method.
2. IFRS permits companies to reverse inventory write-downs; GAAP does not. This means that if markets recover and inventory previously "impaired" regains some or all of its value, it can be

revalued upwards. IFRS notes disclose this revaluation, if material, which permits us to recompute inventory and cost of sales amounts that are comparable to GAAP.

Property, plant, and equipment In accounting for tangible assets, four notable differences deserve mention.

1. GAAP requires the total cost of a tangible asset to be capitalized and depreciated over its useful life. Under IFRS, tangible assets are disaggregated into individual components and then each component is separately depreciated over its useful life. Thus, assets with components with vastly different useful lives can yield IFRS depreciation expense that is markedly different from that computed using GAAP.

2. Property, plant and equipment can be revalued upward to fair market value under IFRS. The latter will cause IFRS book values of PPE to be higher. Few companies have opted to revalue assets upwards but in some industries, such as real estate, the practice is common.

3. U.S. GAAP applies a two-step approach for determining impairments. Step 1: compare book value to *undiscounted* expected future cash flows; and Step 2: if book value is higher, measure impairment using *discounted* expected future cash flows. IFRS uses *discounted* expected future cash flows for both steps, which means IFRS uses one step. This results in more asset impairments under IFRS.

4. IFRS fair-value impairments for tangible assets can be reversed; that is, written back up after being written down. The notes to PPE articulate such reversals.

Research and Development All R&D costs are expensed under GAAP whereas IFRS allows development costs (but not research costs) to be capitalized as an intangible asset if all of the following six criteria are met.

- It is technically feasible to complete the asset.
- The company intends to complete the asset and use or sell it.
- The company is able to use or sell the asset.
- The company can use the asset to create economic benefits or there is a profitable market for the asset.
- The company has adequate resources to complete the asset.
- Costs related to the asset can be reliably measured.

For some companies and some industries these intangible assets are significant and the IFRS financial statements can be markedly different.

Restructuring There are two differences worth noting.

1. Under IFRS, restructuring expense is recognized when there is a plan for the restructuring and if the affected employees expect the plan to be implemented. Under GAAP, restructuring expense can be recognized earlier because the trigger is board approval of a plan.

2. Consistent with other IFRS accruals, a restructuring provision is recorded at its best estimate. This is usually the expected value or, in the case of a range of possible outcomes that are equally likely, the provision is recorded at the *midpoint* of the range. The GAAP estimate is at the most-likely outcome; and if there is a range of possible outcomes, the provision is recorded as the *minimum* amount of the range.

Guidance Answers

You Are the Operations Manager

Pg. 6-17 Companies need inventories to avoid lost sales opportunities; however, there are several ways to minimize inventory needs. (1) We can reduce product costs by improving product design to eliminate costly features that customers don't value. (2) We can use more cost-efficient suppliers; possibly producing in lower wage-rate parts of the world. (3) We can reduce raw material inventories with just-in-time delivery from suppliers. (4) We can eliminate production bottlenecks that increase work-in-process inventories. (5) We can manufacture for orders rather than for estimated demand to reduce finished goods inventories. (6) We can improve warehousing and distribution to reduce duplicate inventories. (7) We can monitor product sales and adjust product mix as demand changes to reduce finished goods inventories.

You Are the Financial Analyst

Pg. 6-24 Typically, restructuring charges have three components: severance costs, other restructuring-related expenses, and asset write-downs (including inventories, PPE, intangible assets, and goodwill). Write-downs occur when an asset's ability to generate cash flow declines and this decline reduces the asset's fair value below its book value (as reported on the balance sheet). Arguably, this decline in cash flow generating ability did not occur solely in the current year. Most likely the decline developed over several periods. It is not uncommon for companies to delay loss recognition, such as write-downs of assets. Thus, prior period income is, arguably, overstated and the current period income is understated. Turning to severance and other costs, GAAP permits restructuring expense to include only those costs that are *incremental* and will *not* benefit future periods. Like other accruals, restructuring might be over- or understated. In future periods, the company reports actual restructuring costs incurred, which will provide insight into the adequacy of the accrual in the earlier period.

You Are the Division Manager

Pg. 6-27 PPE is a difficult asset to reduce. Because companies need long-term operating assets, managers usually try to maximize throughput to reduce unit costs. Also, many companies form alliances to share administrative, production, logistics, customer service, IT, and other functions. These alliances take many forms (such as joint ventures) and are designed to spread ownership of assets among many users. The goal is to identify underutilized assets and to increase capacity utilization. Another solution might be to reconfigure the value chain from raw material to end user. Examples include the sharing of IT, or manufacturing facilities, outsourcing of production or administration such as customer service centers, and the use of special-purpose entities for asset securitization.

Questions

Q6-1. Why do relatively stable inventory costs across periods reduce the importance of management's choice of an inventory costing method?

Q6-2. Explain why using the FIFO inventory costing method will increase gross profit during periods of rising inventory costs.

Q6-3. If inventory costs are rising, which inventory costing method—first-in, first-out; last-in, first-out; or average cost—yields the (a) lowest ending inventory? (b) lowest net income? (c) largest ending inventory? (d) largest net income? (e) greatest cash flow, assuming the same method is used for tax purposes?

Q6-4. Even though it may not reflect their physical flow of goods, why might companies adopt last-in, first-out inventory costing in periods when costs are consistently rising?

Kaiser Aluminum
Corporation (KALU)

Q6-5. In a recent annual report, Kaiser Aluminum Corporation made the following statement in reference to its inventories: "The Company recorded pretax charges of approximately $19.4 million because of a reduction in the carrying values of its inventories caused principally by prevailing lower prices for alumina, primary aluminum, and fabricated products." What basic accounting principle caused Kaiser Aluminum to record this $19.4 million pretax charge? Briefly describe the rationale for this principle.

Q6-6. What does the cash conversion cycle measure?

Q6-7. How might a company affect its depreciation expense computation by selecting useful life and salvage value?

Q6-8. What is the benefit of accelerated depreciation for income tax purposes when the total depreciation taken over the asset's life is identical under any method of depreciation?

Q6-9. What factors determine the gain or loss on the sale of a PPE asset?

Q6-10 What three metrics comprise the cash conversion cycle? How could companies manage each of the three components to improve CCC?

Q6-11 Explain the concept of lower of cost or market. What benefit does the LCM rule create for financial statement users?

Q6-12. Identify the three typical categories of restructuring costs and their effects on the balance sheet and the income statement.

Assignments with the ⊛ logo in the margin are available in BusinessCourse.
See the Preface of the book for details.

Mini Exercises

M6-13. Computing Cost of Goods Sold and Ending Inventory Under FIFO, LIFO, and Average Cost   **LO1**
Assume that Madden Company reports the following initial balance and subsequent purchase of inventory.

Inventory balance at beginning of year.	1,300 units @ $150 each	$195,000
Inventory purchased during the year	1,700 units @ $180 each	306,000
Cost of goods available for sale during the year . . .	3,000 units	$501,000

Assume that 2,000 units are sold during the year. Compute the cost of goods sold for the year and the inventory on the year-end balance sheet under the following inventory costing methods.

a. FIFO
b. LIFO
c. Average Cost

M6-14. Computing Cost of Goods Sold and Ending Inventory Under FIFO, LIFO, and Average Cost   **LO1**
Wong Corporation reports the following beginning inventory and inventory purchases.

Inventory balance at beginning of year.	400 units @ $12 each	$ 4,800
Inventory purchased during the year	700 units @ $14 each	9,800
Cost of goods available for sale during the year . . .	1,100 units	$14,600

Wong sells 600 of its inventory units during the year. Compute the cost of goods sold for the year and the inventory on the year-end balance sheet under the following inventory costing methods.

a. FIFO
b. LIFO
c. Average Cost

M6-15. Computing and Evaluating Inventory Turnover for Two Companies   **LO3**
PriceSmart and Nordstrom report the following information in their respective January 2016 10-K reports relating to their two most recent fiscal years.   PriceSmart (PSMT)
JW Nordstrom (JWN)

	PriceSmart ($ thousands)			Nordstrom ($ millions)		
	Sales	Cost of Goods Sold	Inventories	Sales	Cost of Goods Sold	Inventories
2018	$3,053,754	$2,610,111	$321,025	$15,480	$10,155	$1,978
2017	2,910,062	2,487,146	310,946	15,137	9,890	2,027

a. Compute the 2018 inventory turnover for each of these two retailers.
b. Discuss any difference we observe in inventory turnover between these two companies. Does the difference confirm our expectations given their respective business models? Explain. (*Hint:* Nordstrom is a higher-end retailer and PriceSmart operates no-frills, warehouse stores.)
c. Describe ways that a retailer can improve its inventory turnover.

M6-16. Computing Depreciation   **LO4**
A delivery van costing $37,000 is expected to have a $2,900 salvage value at the end of its useful life of five years. Assume that the truck was purchased on January 1. Compute the depreciation expense for the first two calendar years under the straight-line depreciation method.

LO4

M6-17. Computing Depreciation for Partial Years

A company with a calendar year-end purchases a machine costing $129,000 on July 1, 2020. The machine is expected to be obsolete after five years (60 months) and, thereafter, no longer useful to the company. The estimated salvage value is $6,000. The company's depreciation policy is to record depreciation for the portion of the year that the asset is in service. Compute depreciation expense for both 2020 and 2021 under the straight-line depreciation method.

LO6

Texas Instruments
Inc. (TXN)

Intel Corporation
(INTC)

M6-18. Computing and Comparing PPE Turnover for Two Companies

Texas Instruments Inc. and Intel Corporation report the following information.

| $ millions | Intel Corporation | | Texas Instruments | |
	Sales	Plant, Property and Equipment, net	Sales	Plant, Property and Equipment, net
2018	$70,848	$48,976	$15,784	$3,183
2017	62,761	41,109	14,961	2,664

a. Compute the 2018 PPE turnover for both companies. Comment on any difference observed.

b. Discuss ways in which high-tech manufacturing companies like these can increase their PPE turnover.

LO3

Winnebago Industries
(WGO)

M6-19. Computing Cash Conversion Cycle for Two Years

Winnebago Industries has the following metrics for 2018 and 2017.

Amounts in days	2018	2017
Days sales outstanding	26.2	22.5
Days inventory outstanding	35.9	36.5
Days payable outstanding	17.0	17.0

Compute the cash conversion cycle for both years. What accounts for the change between the years?

LO3

M6-20. Using Inventory Analysis Tools

AutoZone and O'Reilly are two competitors in the retail automotive parts industry.

$ thousands	AutoZone	O'Reilly
Average 2018 Inventory	$ 3,912,878	$3,101,572
2018 Sales	11,221,077	9,536,428
2018 Cost of goods sold. . . .	5,247,331	4,496,462
Average 2017 Inventory	$ 3,757,001	$2,894,388
2017 Sales	10,888,676	8,977,726
2017 Cost of goods sold. . . .	5,149,056	4,257,043

a. Use the information above to compute the companies' gross profit margin and days inventory outstanding for both years.

b. Based on these two ratios, which company is more profitable selling its inventory? How has that changed from 2017 to 2018?

c. Based on these two ratios, which company is more efficient with its inventory? How has that changed from 2017 to 2018?

LO5

Winnebago Industries
(WGO)

M6-21. Asset Impairment

Winnebago Industries recorded an impairment loss of $462,000 on its corporate plane during a recent year. Assume that the plane originally cost the company $2,350,000 and had accumulated depreciation of $1,598,000 at the time of the impairment charge.

a. Why did the company record an impairment loss on the plane?

b. Explain how the company determined the amount of the impairment loss.

c. What was the plane's fair value at the end of the year?

E6-22.   Analyzing Inventory Levels and Write-downs

LO2, 3

Nvidia (NVDA)

Quarterly data for Nvidia Inc. for the most recent 10 quarters follows ($ millions).

Fiscal Year	Fiscal Quarter	Total Assets	Cost of Goods Sold	Inventories	Revenue
2016.......	4	$ 9,841	$ 824	$ 794	$2,173
2017.......	1	9,410	740	821	1,937
2017.......	2	9,402	879	855	2,230
2017.......	3	9,830	1,018	857	2,636
2017.......	4	11,241	1,056	796	2,911
2018.......	1	11,460	1,082	797	3,207
2018.......	2	12,882	1,089	1,090	3,123
2018.......	3	13,657	1,178	1,417	3,181
2018.......	4	13,292	899	1,575	2,205
2019.......	1	14,021	833	1,426	2,220

On November 16, 2018, after Nvidia's third quarter (Q3) 2018 earnings release, ExtremeTech reported:

- Nvidia stocks plummeted on Friday after the company released its earnings report. The company has, as of this writing, lost about 16 percent of its previous valuation. But what happens to a company after it reports earnings doesn't always make sense from a technical perspective.

- Nvidia's stock has taken a hammering today for basically having a weak Q3. Revenue in Nvidia's fiscal year Q3 2019 (Nvidia's calendar runs a year ahead of the actual physical date) was up significantly compared with the same time last year, but flat in Q3 compared with Q2. Nvidia's margin slipped a tiny bit but it's the company's inventory build that has analysts worried. Nvidia is currently holding $1.417B in product, up from $796M in January 2018 and $1.09B in Q2 2018. Nvidia blames this problem entirely on the decline of the cryptography market and has stated it will ship no new midrange cards to market through Q4 to give the channel time to work through the excess inventory build-up.   Source: **https://www.extremetech.com/gaming/280800-nvidia-stock-plummets-on-high-inventory-fears**

a. Calculate the inventory as a percent of total assets. Is the "inventory build" referred to by Extreme-Tech significant in common-size terms?

b. Determine the gross profit margin for each quarter. Did the margin slip a "tiny bit" in Q3 2018?

c. Have margins and inventory levels improved in the quarters subsequent to the ExtremeTech report?

E6-23.   Applying and Analyzing Inventory Costing Methods

LO1

At the beginning of the current period, Chen carried 1,000 units of its product with a unit cost of $32. A summary of purchases during the current period follows. Also, during the current period, Chen sold 2,800 units.

	Units	Unit Cost	Cost
Beginning Inventory	1,000	$32	$32,000
Purchases: #1.............	1,800	34	61,200
#2	800	38	30,400
#3	1,200	41	49,200

a. Assume that Chen uses the first-in, first-out method. Compute both cost of goods sold for the current period and the ending inventory balance. Use the financial statement effects template to record cost of goods sold for the period.

b. Assume that Chen uses the last-in, first-out method. Compute both cost of goods sold for the current period and the ending inventory balance.

c. Assume that Chen uses the average cost method. Compute both cost of goods sold for the current period and the ending inventory balance.

  d. Which of these three inventory costing methods would we choose to:
    1. Reflect what is probably the physical flow of goods? Explain.
    2. Minimize income taxes for the period? Explain.
    3. Report the largest amount of income for the period? Explain.

LO2   **E6-24.   Analyzing an Inventory Footnote Disclosure**

Illinois Tool Works
(ITW)

Illinois Tool Works reports the following footnote in its 10-K report. The company reports its inventories using the LIFO inventory costing method.

December 31 ($ millions)	2018	2017
Raw material..............................	$ 523	$ 465
Work-in-process...........................	161	141
Finished goods............................	731	703
LIFO reserve..............................	(97)	(89)
Total inventories	$1,318	$1,220

  a. What is the balance in inventories reported on the 2018 balance sheet?
  b. What would the 2018 balance sheet have reported for inventories had the company used FIFO inventory costing?
  c. What cumulative effect has the company's choice of LIFO over FIFO had on its pretax income as of year-end 2018? Explain.
  d. Assume the company has a 35% income tax rate for years prior to 2017 and a 21% rate thereafter. ITW's LIFO reserve was $86 million at December 31, 2016. As of the 2018 year-end, how much has the company saved in taxes by choosing the LIFO over FIFO method for costing inventory? Has the use of LIFO increased or decreased the company's cumulative taxes paid?
  e. What effect has the use of LIFO inventory costing had on the company's pretax income and tax expense for 2018 only (assume a 21% income tax rate)?

LO2, 3   **E6-25.   Quantifying the Effect of Inventory Write-offs on Ratios**

Under Armour, Inc
(UAA)

Under Armour reported the following in its 2018 Form 10-K. Under Armour's income statement reported 2018 cost of goods sold of $2,852,714 thousand. Its balance sheet reported inventories of $1,019,496 thousand in 2018 and $1,158,548 thousand in 2017.

> **Restructuring Plans** As previously announced, our Board of Directors approved restructuring plans designed to more closely align our financial resources with the critical priorities of our business and optimize operations. We recognized approximately $203.9 million of pre-tax charges in connection with our restructuring plan. The costs incurred during the year ended December 31, 2018, include the following:
>
> | Costs recorded in cost of goods sold ($ thousands) | 2018 |
> | --- | --- |
> | Inventory write-offs... | $20,801 |
> | Total cost recorded in cost of goods sold .... | $20,801 |

  a. Explain why Under Armour recorded an inventory write-off.
  b. What effect did the 2018 inventory write-off have on pretax income during 2018?
  c. Calculate inventory turnover and days inventory outstanding for 2018.
  d. If Under Armour had not written off inventory in 2018, what would it have reported for cost of goods sold in 2018? What would have been the inventory balances in 2018 and 2017?
  e. Use the adjusted cost of goods sold and inventory balances to recalculate inventory turnover and days inventory outstanding. Did the inventory write-off make a significant difference?

LO2   **E6-26.   Analyzing an Inventory Footnote Disclosure**

Deere & Co. (DE)

The inventory footnote from **Deere & Company**'s 2018 10-K follows.

> **Inventories**   A majority of inventory owned by Deere & Company and its U.S. equipment subsidiaries are valued at cost, on the "last-in, first-out" (LIFO) basis. Remaining inventories are

continued

continued from previous page

generally valued at the lower of cost, on the "first-in, first-out" (FIFO) basis, or net realizable value. The value of gross inventories on the LIFO basis at October 28, 2018, and October 29, 2017, represented 54 percent and 61 percent, respectively, of worldwide gross inventories at FIFO value. If all inventories had been valued on a FIFO basis, estimated inventories by major classification at October 28, 2018, and October 29, 2017, in millions of dollars would have been as follows:

$ millions	2018	2017
Raw materials and supplies	$2,233	$1,688
Work-in-process	776	495
Finished goods and parts	4,777	3,182
Total FIFO value	7,786	5,365
Less adjustment to LIFO value	1,637	1,461
Inventories	$6,149	$3,904

This footnote reveals that not all of Deere's inventories are reported using the same inventory costing method (companies can use different inventory costing methods for different inventory pools).

a. What amount does Deere report for inventories on its 2018 balance sheet?

b. What would Deere have reported as inventories on its 2018 balance sheet had the company used FIFO inventory costing for all of its inventories?

c. What cumulative effect has the use of LIFO inventory costing had, as of year-end 2018, on Deere's pretax income compared with the pretax income it would have reported had it used FIFO inventory costing for all of its inventories? Explain.

d. Assuming an average (cumulative) income tax rate of 30%, by what cumulative dollar amount has Deere's tax expense been affected by use of LIFO inventory costing as of year-end 2018? Has the use of LIFO inventory costing increased or decreased Deere's cumulative tax expense?

e. What effect has the use of LIFO inventory costing had on Deere's pretax income and tax expense for 2018 only (assume a 21% income tax rate)?

E6-27.   Analyzing Inventory from Data Visualization

The following data visualization depicts quarterly revenue, cost of goods sold, and gross profit margin for Amazon from Q2 2010 through Q1 2019.

LO3
Amazon Inc. (AMZN)

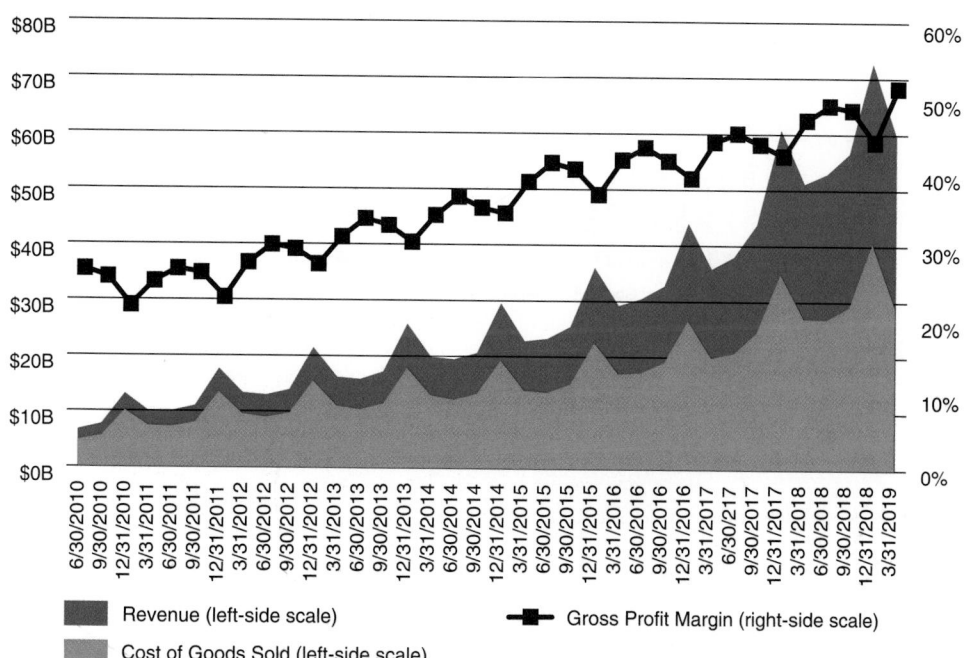

	Revenue (left-side scale)		Gross Profit Margin (right-side scale)
	Cost of Goods Sold (left-side scale)		

a. What trend do we observe in all three metrics from 2010 to 2019?
b. When does revenue spike each year? Why?
c. What pattern do we observe between revenue and gross margin? Explain.

LO4, 5   **E6-28.**   **Computing Depreciation, Net Book Value, and Gain or Loss on Asset Sale**

Zimmer Company owns an executive plane that originally cost $1,280,000. It has recorded straight-line depreciation on the plane for seven full years, calculated assuming a $160,000 expected salvage value at the end of its estimated 10-year useful life. Zimmer disposes of the plane at the end of the seventh year.

a. At the disposal date, what is the (1) cumulative depreciation expense and (2) net book value of the plane?
b. How much gain or loss is reported at disposal if the sales price is:
  1. A cash amount equal to the plane's net book value.
  2. $285,000 cash.
  3. $700,000 cash.

LO3   **E6-29.**   **Analyzing Inventory with Data Visualization**

Target (TGT)
Walmart (WMT)

Consider the following inventory graphics for Walmart and Target, two large US retailers who compete head to head. The graphs depict quarterly revenue, cost of goods sold, and gross profit margin from 2010 through 2019.

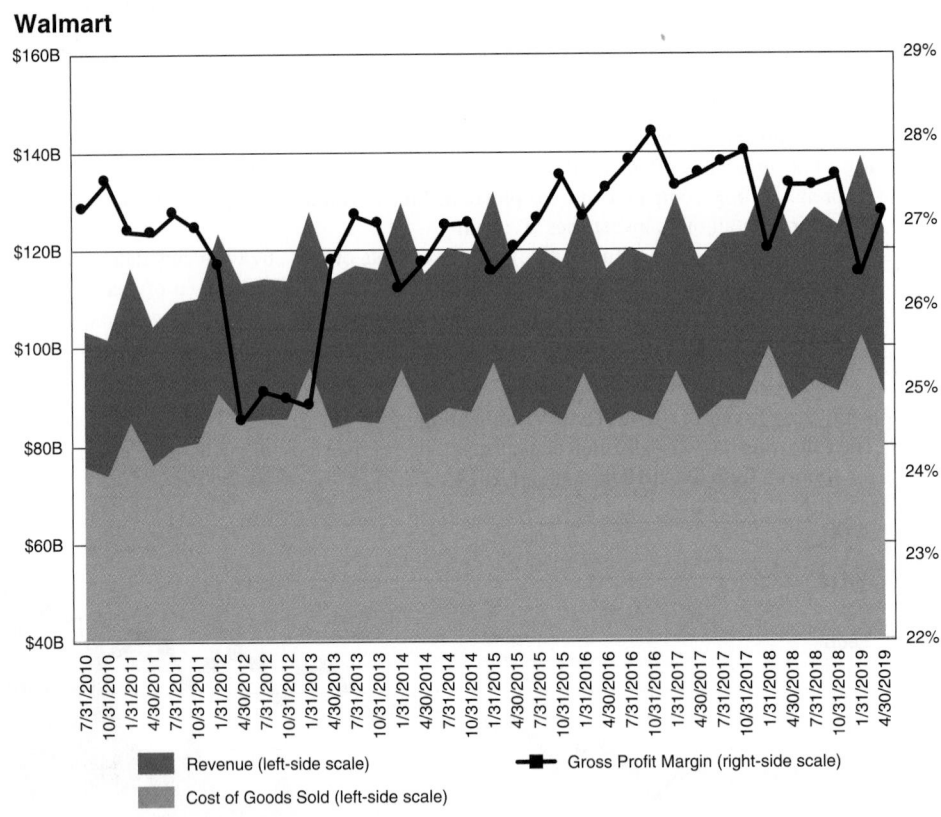

Walmart

Target

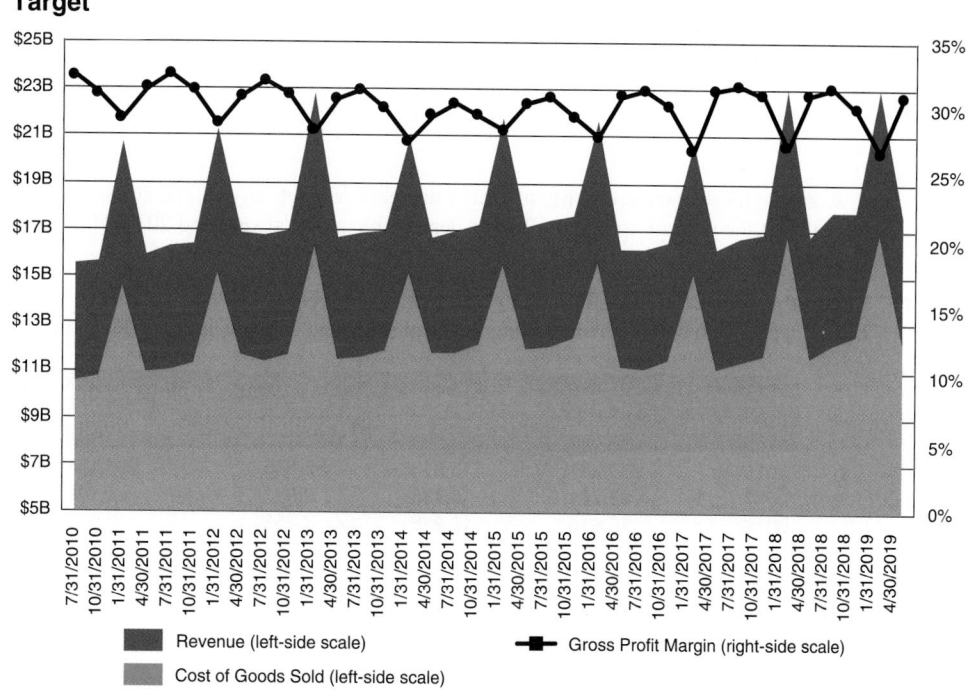

What similarities and differences do we see as compared to the Amazon graphic in E6-27?

E6-30.   **Computing Depreciation, Net Book Value, and Gain or Loss on Asset Sale**   **LO5**

Lynch Company owns and operates a delivery van that originally cost $46,400. Lynch has recorded straight-line depreciation on the van for four years, calculated assuming a $5,000 expected salvage value at the end of its estimated six-year useful life. Depreciation was last recorded at the end of the fourth year, at which time Lynch disposed of this van.

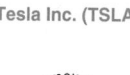

a. Compute the net book value of the van on the disposal date.

b. Compute the gain or loss on sale of the van if the disposal proceeds are:

     1. A cash amount equal to the van's net book value.

     2. $21,000 cash.

     3. $17,000 cash.

E6-31.   **Estimating Useful Life and Percent Used Up**   **LO6**

The property and equipment footnote from Tesla follows. Assume that 25% of the amount classified   Tesla Inc. (TSLA)
as "Land and buildings" pertains to the cost of the Land.

Property, Plant and Equipment   Our property, plant and equipment, net, consists of the following (in thousands):

December 31	2018	2017
Machinery, equipment, vehicles and office furniture.......	$ 6,328,966	$ 4,251,711
Tooling	1,397,514	1,255,952
Leaseholder improvements	960,971	789,751
Land and buildings.................................	4,047,006	2,517,247
Computer equipment, hardware and software	487,421	395,067
Construction in progress............................	807,297	2,541,588
	14,029,175	11,751,316
Less: Accumulated depreciation.....................	(2,699,098)	(1,723,794)
Total	$11,330,077	$10,027,522

continued

continued from previous page

> Depreciation expense during the years ended December 31, 2018, 2017, and 2016 was $1.11 billion, $769.3 million, and $477.3 million, respectively.

a. Compute the average useful life of Tesla's depreciable assets at year-end 2018.

b. Estimate the percent used up of Tesla's depreciable assets at year-end 2018. How do we interpret this figure?

LO3, 6

Intel Corp. (INTC)

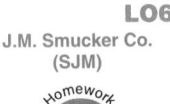

E6-32.   Computing and Evaluating Inventory and PPE Turnovers

Intel Corporation reports the following financial statement amounts in its 10-K reports.

$ millions	Sales	Cost of Goods Sold	Inventories	Plant, Property and Equipment, Net
2016	$59,387	$15,313	$5,553	$36,171
2017	62,761	15,685	6,983	41,109
2018	70,848	18,226	7,253	48,976

a. Compute the inventory and PPE turnover ratios for both 2017 and 2018.

b. What changes are evident in the turnover rates of Intel for these years? Discuss ways in which a company such as Intel can improve inventory and PPE turnover ratios.

LO4, 5

E6-33.   Computing and Assessing Plant Asset Impairment

On July 1, Arcola Company purchases equipment for $330,000. The equipment has an estimated useful life of 10 years and expected salvage value of $40,000. The company uses straight-line depreciation. Four years later, economic factors cause the fair value of the equipment to decline to $160,000. On this date, Arcola examines the equipment for impairment and estimates $185,000 in undiscounted expected cash inflows from this equipment.

a. Compute the annual depreciation expense relating to this equipment.

b. Compute the equipment's net book value at the end of the fourth year.

c. Apply the test of impairment to this equipment as of the end of the fourth year. Is the equipment impaired? Show supporting computations.

d. If the equipment is impaired at the end of the fourth year, compute the impairment loss.

LO6

J.M. Smucker Co. (SJM)

E6-34.   Computing Asset Related Ratios

J.M. Smucker included the following information in its April 2019 10-K.

$ millions	Apr. 30, 2019	Apr. 30, 2018
Sales.	$7,838.0	
Depreciation expense.	206.0	
Land	$ 122.1	$ 120.1
Buildings and fixtures	903.2	812.6
Machinery and equipment	2,185.0	2,111.5
Construction in progress.	321.8	212.1
Gross property, plant, and equipment	3,532.1	3,256.3
Accumulated depreciation	(1,619.7)	(1,527.2)
Total property, plant, and equipment	$1,912.4	$1,729.1

Required

a. Compute PPE turnover for fiscal year ended April 30, 2019.

b. Compute the average useful life of depreciable assets at April 30, 2019.

c. Compute the percentage used up of the PPE at April 30, 2019.

E6-35.   **Evaluating Grocery Stores Using Efficiency Ratios**

Below are data for three publicly traded grocery stores that range in size from local (Village Super Markets) to regional (Publix) to national (Kroger). Use the ratios below to answer the requirements. Assume that the companies sell roughly the same mix of products and face about the same inventory costs.

Fiscal 2018	Publix	Kroger	Village Super Market
Gross profit margin %...................	29.6%	21.7%	27.2%
Number of stores at year-end.............	1,211	2,764	30
Sales ($ per square foot)	$639	$677	$1,165
Sales per store ($ millions).............	$ 30	$ 44	$ 54
Average store size (thousand square feet)...	47	65	46
COGS (per square foot)	$450	$530	$ 848
Days inventory outstanding	26.5	25.7	12.6

Required

a. On average, which company has the freshest food?
b. Which company is least efficient with its space?
c. Which company has the lowest prices?
d. Which company is busiest?
e. Which company has the smallest stores?

LO3
Publix Super Markets
Inc. (PUSH)
Kroger Co. (KR)
Village Super Market
(VLGEA)

Problems

P6-36.   **Evaluating Turnover and Nontraditional Efficiency Ratios Across Industries**

The following information is taken from publicly traded retailers. The data come from the balance sheet, income statement, and Item 2 on the companies' Form 10-K filings. Use the information to answer the requirements.

$ millions	Revenue	COGS	Average Inventory	Retail SQ Footage (000s)	# of Stores
Autozone......	$ 11,221	$ 4,902	$ 3,913	41,066	6,202
Costco........	141,576	121,715	10,437	110,700	762
Home Depot ...	108,203	71,043	13,337	237,700	2,287
Lowe's........	71,309	48,396	11,977	209,000	2,015
O'Reilly	9,536	4,237	3,102	38,455	5,219
Walmart.......	511,729	374,623	44,026	1,129,000	11,361

Required

a. Compute the days inventory outstanding (DIO) for each company.
b. Compute the gross profit margin for each company.
c. Compare the DIO and gross profit margin for each of the three combinations of competitors. What do we observe? How are the two ratios related?
d. Compute the following two nontraditional efficiency metrics: Revenue per square foot and Revenue per store. What do we observe?

LO3

Autozone (AZO)
Costco (COST)
Home Depot (HD)
Lowe's (LOW)
O'Reilly (ORLY)
Walmart (WMT)

P6-37.   **Analyzing Inventories with Quarterly Data and LIFO Liquidation**

The inventory footnote from The Dow Chemical Company's first quarter 2019 SEC report follows. The company also reports cost of goods sold for Q1 of 2019 of $10,707 million.

Inventories, in millions	Mar. 31, 2019	Dec. 31, 2018
Finished goods........................	$5,703	$5,640
Work in process	2,239	2,214
Raw materials........................	940	941
Supplies	891	880
Total	$9,773	$9,675
Adjustment of inventories to a LIFO basis ...	(265)	(415)
Total inventories......................	$9,508	$9,260

LO2, 3
Dow Chemical Co.
(DOW)

Required

a. What inventory costing method does Dow Chemical use? As of Q1 of 2019, what is the effect on cumulative pretax income and cash flow of using this inventory costing method? (Assume a 30% average cumulative tax rate.) What is the effect on Q1 of 2019 pretax income and cash flow of using this inventory costing method, assuming a 21% tax rate?

b. Compute inventory turnover and average inventory days outstanding for Q1 of 2019. (*Hint:* How do we adjust the ratio for the number of days in a quarter instead of a year?) Comment on the level of these two ratios. Is the level what we expected?

c. Determine the FIFO values for inventories and cost of goods sold for Q1 of 2019. Recompute inventory turnover and DIO. Compare the ratios to those from part b. Which set of ratios would provide more useful analysis?

d. Explain why a reduction in the LIFO reserve increased income in Q1 of 2019.

LO6   **P6-38.**   **Estimating Useful Life and Percent Used Up**

lululemon athletica
(LULU)

The property and equipment section of the lululemon athletica 2018 balance sheet follows.

Property and Equipment (in thousands)	Feb. 3, 2019	Jan. 28, 2018
Land	$ 78,636	$ 83,048
Buildings.	38,030	39,278
Leasehold improvements	362,571	301,449
Furniture and fixtures	103,733	91,778
Computer hardware	69,542	61,734
Computer software.	230,689	173,997
Equipment and vehicles	15,009	14,806
Work in progress	74,271	51,260
Property and equipment, gross	972,481	817,350
Accumulated depreciation.	(405,244)	(343,708)
Property and equipment, net	$567,237	$473,642

Depreciation expense related to property and equipment was $122.4 million and $108.0 million for the years ended February 3, 2019, and January 28, 2018, respectively.

Required

a. Consider the level of the various PPE components. Does it seem likely that the company manufactures its own inventory? Why or why not?

b. What is meant by "work in progress"? Explain how this item will be accounted for in the coming months at lululemon.

c. Compute the estimated useful life of lululemon's depreciable assets.

d. Compute the estimated percent used up of lululemon's depreciable assets. How do we interpret this figure?

LO6   **P6-39.**   **Interpreting and Applying Disclosures on Property and Equipment**

Facebook Inc. (FB)

Following are selected disclosures from the 10-K report of Facebook Inc. Facebook reported 2018 sales of $55,838 million.

Property and Equipment, Net		
December 31, $ millions	2018	2017
Land	$ 899	$ 798
Buildings.	7,401	4,909
Leasehold improvements	1,841	959
Network equipment	13,017	7,998
Computer software, office equipment and other.	1,187	681
Construction in progress.	7,228	2,992
Total	31,573	18,337
Less: Accumulated depreciation.	(6,890)	(4,616)
Property and equipment, net	$24,683	$13,721

continued

continued from previous page

> Depreciation expense on property and equipment was $3.68 billion and $2.33 billion during 2018 and 2017, respectively.

Required

a. Compute the PPE turnover for 2018.

b. Estimate the useful life, on average, for its depreciable PPE assets.

c. By what percentage are Facebook's assets "used up" in 2018? What implication does the assets used up computation have for forecasting cash flows?

d. Consider the ratios in parts *a*, *b*, and *c*. Interpret them in light of the company's age and business model.

e. The list of PPE assets includes an asset labeled "Construction in progress." What is this asset and what types of costs are included on the balance sheet?

P6-40.   **Analyzing and Interpreting Restructuring Costs and Effects**

LO5

General Electric (GE) reports the following footnote disclosure (excerpted) in its 2018 10-K relating to its restructuring program.

General Electric (GE)

> **RESTRUCTURING**   Restructuring actions are an essential component of our cost improvement efforts to both existing operations and those recently acquired. Restructuring and other charges relate primarily to workforce reductions, facility exit costs associated with the consolidation of sales, service and manufacturing facilities, the integration of recent acquisitions, and other asset write-downs. We continue to closely monitor the economic environment and may undertake further restructuring actions to more closely align our cost structure with earnings and cost reduction goals.
>
> | Restructuring and Other Charges (In billions) | 2018 | 2017 | 2016 |
> | --- | --- | --- | --- |
> | Workforce reductions | $0.9 | $1.2 | $1.3 |
> | Plant closures & associated costs and other asset write-downs ... | 1.8 | 1.9 | 1.3 |
> | Acquisition/disposition net charges | 0.8 | 0.8 | 0.6 |
> | Other | 0.1 | 0.2 | 0.3 |
> | Total | $3.6 | $4.1 | $3.5 |
>
> For 2018, restructuring and other charges were $3.6 billion of which approximately $1.4 billion was reported in cost of products/services and $2.1 billion was reported in selling, general and administrative expenses (SG&A). These activities were primarily at Power, Corporate and Oil & Gas. Cash expenditures for restructuring and other charges were approximately $2.0 billion for the twelve months ended December 31, 2018.

Required

a. Briefly describe the company's 2018 restructuring program. Provide two examples of common noncash charges associated with corporate restructuring activities.

b. Using the financial statement effects template, show the effects on financial statements of the (1) 2018 restructuring charge of $3.6 billion, and (2) 2018 cash payment of $2.0 billion.

c. Assume that instead of accurately estimating the anticipated restructuring charge in 2018, the company overestimated them by $30 million. How would this overestimation affect financial statements in (1) 2018, and (2) 2019 when severance costs are paid in cash?

IFRS Applications

I6-41.   **Analyzing Inventory for Two Retail Grocery Companies**

LO3

Carrefour Group (headquartered in Boulogne-Billancourt, France) and Tesco PLC (headquartered in Welwyn Garden City, UK) compete head-to-head in the grocery space in the UK, Ireland, Central Europe, and North Africa. The following information comes from their 2018 annual reports.

Carrefour Group
Tesco PLC

	Carrefour Group in € millions		Tesco PLC in £ millions	
	2018	2017	2018	2017
Sales......................	€76,000	€78,315	£57,491	€55,917
Cost of sales...............	60,850	62,311	54,141	53,015
Gross profit.................	15,150	16,004	3,350	2,902
Inventory...................	6,135	6,690	2,263	2,301
Total assets	47,378	47,813	44,862	45,853

Required

a. Calculate gross profit margin for each year for both companies.

b. Determine the common-size inventory for each year for both companies.

c. Compute inventory turnover and days average inventory outstanding for 2018.

d. Based on the metrics in parts *a*, *b*, and *c*, how do we assess the two companies' inventory management?

LO5, 6   **I6-42.**   **Estimating Useful Life, Percent Used Up, and Gain or Loss on Disposal**

Husky Energy (HSE)

Husky Energy is one of Canada's largest integrated energy companies. Based in Calgary, Alberta, Husky is publicly traded on the Toronto Stock Exchange. The Company operates in Western and Atlantic Canada, the United States and the Asia Pacific Region with upstream and downstream business segments. The company uses IFRS to prepare its financial statements. During 2018, the company reported depreciation expense of $2,591 million. The property and equipment footnote follows.

Property, Plant and Equipment (in C$ millions)	Oil and Gas Properties	Processing, Transportation and Storage	Upgrading	Refining	Retail and Other	Total
Cost						
December 31, 2017	$ 41,815	$ 86	$ 2,599	$ 9,191	$ 2,930	$ 56,621
Additions......................................	2,465	12	62	744	151	3,434
Acquisitions....................................	64	—	—	3	—	67
Transfers from exploration and evaluation	79	—	—	—	—	79
Intersegment transfers	—	—	—	(5)	—	—
Changes in asset retirement obligations..............	43	2	(2)	(5)	7	45
Disposals and derecognition.......................	(632)	—	—	(10)	(1)	(643)
Exchange adjustments	362	1	—	773	3	1,139
December 31, 2018	$ 44,196	$101	$ 2,659	$10,691	$ 3,090	$ 60,742
Accumulated depletion, depreciation, amortization, and impairment						
December 31, 2017	$(26,016)	$ (47)	$(1,462)	$ (3,176)	$(1,842)	$(32,543)
Depletion, depreciation, amortization, and impairment. . . .	(1,811)	(2)	(123)	(503)	(152)	(2,591)
Disposals and derecognition.......................	586	—	—	10	—	596
Exchange adjustments	(138)	(1)	—	(264)	(1)	(404)
December 31, 2018	$(27,379)	$ (50)	$(1,585)	$ (3,933)	$(1,995)	$(34,942)
Net book value						
December 31, 2017	$15,799	$ 39	$ 1,137	$ 6,015	$ 1,088	$ 24,078
December 31, 2018	16,817	51	1,074	6,758	1,100	25,800

Required

a. Compute the average useful life of Husky Energy's depreciable assets in 2018. Assume that land is 10% of "Refining."

b. Estimate the percent used up of Husky Energy's depreciable assets in 2018. How do we interpret this figure?

c. Consider the disposals and derecognition during the year. This refers to assets that were sold and removed from the balance sheet during 2018. Calculate the net book value of the total PPE disposed during the year. Assume that Husky Energy received $4 million cash proceeds for the year. Determine the gain or loss on the disposal.

Management Applications

MA6-43. **Managing Operating Asset Reduction**   LO3, 6
Return on net operating assets (RNOA = NOPAT/Average NOA, see Module 4) is commonly used to evaluate financial performance. If managers cannot increase NOPAT, they can still increase this return by reducing the amount of net operating assets (NOA). List specific ways that managers could manage the following operating items.

    a. Inventories   *b.* Plant, property and equipment   *c.* Accounts payable

Ongoing Project

(This ongoing project began in Module 1 and continues through most of the book; even if previous segments were not completed, the requirements are still applicable to any business analysis.)

1. *Inventory*   The following provides some guidance for analysis of a company's inventory.
   - What is inventory for the company? Does the company manufacture inventory? What proportion of total inventory is raw materials? Work in process? Finished goods?
   - Compare the two companies' inventory costing methods. Adjust LIFO inventory and cost of goods sold if the company uses LIFO. Is the LIFO reserve significant? Estimate the tax savings associated with LIFO costing method. (Use the adjusted COGS and inventory figures for all calculations and ratios.)
   - What is the relative size of inventory? How has this changed over the recent three-year period?
   - Compute inventory turnover and days inventory outstanding and the cash conversion cycle for all three years reported on the income statement.
   - Compute gross profit margin in percentage terms. Consider the current economic environment and the companies' competitive landscape. Can we explain any changes in gross profit levels? Have costs for raw materials and labor increased during the year? Have sales volumes softened? What has happened to unit prices? Read the MD&A to determine senior management's take.
   - Does the company face any inventory-related risk? What has been done to mitigate this risk? Read the MD&A.

   For each point of analysis, compare across companies and over time.

2. *Tangible Assets*   The following provides some guidance to the companies' long-term (tangible) assets.
   - Are tangible assets significant for the companies? What proportion of total assets is held as tangible assets (PPE)? What exactly are the companies' tangible assets? That is, what is their nature?
   - Compare the two companies' depreciation policies. Do they differ markedly?
   - What is the relative size of tangible assets? How has this changed over the three-year period?
   - Did the company increase tangible assets during the year? Was the increase for outright asset purchases or did the company acquire assets via a merger or acquisition?
   - Compute PPE turnover.
   - Compute the average age of assets and percentage used up.
   - Are any assets impaired? Is the impairment charge significant? Is the impairment specific to the company or is the industry experiencing a downturn?

   For each point of analysis, compare across companies and over time.

3. *Restructuring Activities*   Have the companies restructured operations in the past three years?
   - Determine the amount of the expense on the income statement—look in the footnotes or the MD&A for additional information.
   - Are other close competitors also restructuring during this time period?
   - Read the footnotes and assess the company's restructuring plans. How many years will it take to fully execute the plan? What additional expenditures are required?
   - Find the restructuring liability on the balance sheet (again the notes will help). Does the liability seem reasonable over time? Compare it to total assets and total liabilities each year and look for any patterns.

Solutions to Review Problems

Review 6-1—Solution

Preliminary computation: Units in ending inventory = 4,800 available − 2,800 sold = 2,000 units

1. First-in, first-out (FIFO)

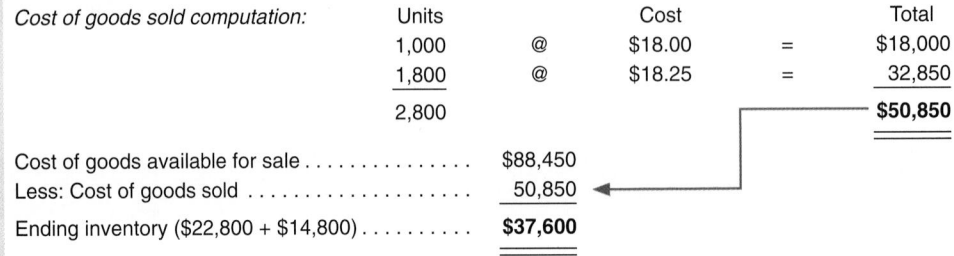

Cost of goods sold computation:	Units		Cost		Total
	1,000	@	$18.00	=	$18,000
	1,800	@	$18.25	=	32,850
	2,800				**$50,850**

Cost of goods available for sale	$88,450
Less: Cost of goods sold	50,850
Ending inventory ($22,800 + $14,800)	**$37,600**

2. Last-in, first-out (LIFO)

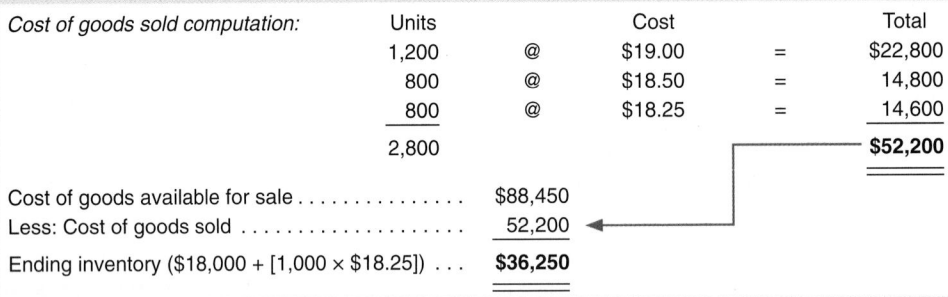

Cost of goods sold computation:	Units		Cost		Total
	1,200	@	$19.00	=	$22,800
	800	@	$18.50	=	14,800
	800	@	$18.25	=	14,600
	2,800				**$52,200**

Cost of goods available for sale	$88,450
Less: Cost of goods sold	52,200
Ending inventory ($18,000 + [1,000 × $18.25]) . . .	**$36,250**

3. Average cost (AC)

Average unit cost	= $88,450/4,800 units	= $18.427
Cost of goods sold	= 2,800 × $18.427	= $51,596
Ending inventory	= 2,000 × $18.427	= $36,854

4. *a.* FIFO is normally the method that most closely reflects physical flow. For example, FIFO would apply to the physical flow of perishable units and to situations where the earlier units acquired are moved out first because of risk of deterioration or obsolescence.

   b. LIFO results in the highest cost of goods sold during periods of rising costs (as in the HD subsidiary case); and, accordingly, LIFO yields the lowest net income and the lowest income taxes.

Review 6-2—Solution

1. Because the $30,000 market value of the inventories is less than the carrying value of the inventories under FIFO inventory costing, the inventories must be written down to their market value with the write-down reported in the income statement as an increase in COGS. The balance sheet will report the inventory at $30,000.

2. Last-in, first-out with LIFO liquidation

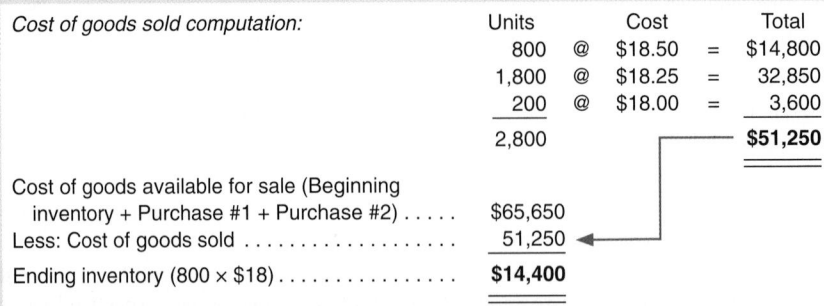

Cost of goods sold computation:	Units		Cost		Total
	800	@	$18.50	=	$14,800
	1,800	@	$18.25	=	32,850
	200	@	$18.00	=	3,600
	2,800				**$51,250**

Cost of goods available for sale (Beginning inventory + Purchase #1 + Purchase #2)	$65,650
Less: Cost of goods sold	51,250
Ending inventory (800 × $18)	**$14,400**

The company's LIFO gross profit has increased by $950 ($52,200 − $51,250) because of the LIFO liquidation. The reduction of inventory quantities matched older (lower) cost layers against current selling prices. The company has, in effect, dipped into lower-cost layers to boost current-period profit—all from a simple delay of inventory purchases.

3. The LIFO reserve is computed as the difference between the inventory cost at LIFO and FIFO. This is $37,600 − $36,250 = $1,350. Using LIFO for inventory costing for the subsidiary resulted in $284 of taxes being deferred in the current period, computed as $1,350 × 21%.

Review 6-3—Solution

$ millions	2019	2018	2017
1. Gross profit margin.	$\dfrac{\$22,915}{\$71,309} = 32.1\%$	$\dfrac{\$22,434}{\$68,619} = 32.7\%$	$\dfrac{\$21,674}{\$65,017} = 33.3\%$
2. Days inventory outstanding . .	$\dfrac{365}{\left[\dfrac{\$48,394}{\dfrac{\$12,561 + \$11,393}{2}}\right]} = 90.3$	$\dfrac{365}{\left[\dfrac{\$46,185}{\dfrac{\$11,393 + \$10,458}{2}}\right]} = 86.3$	
3. Days payable outstanding . . .	$\dfrac{365}{\left[\dfrac{\$48,394}{\dfrac{\$8,279 + \$6,590}{2}}\right]} = 56.1$	$\dfrac{365}{\left[\dfrac{\$46,185}{\dfrac{\$6,590 + \$6,651}{2}}\right]} = 52.3$	
4. Cash conversion cycle	0 + 90.3 − 56.1 = 34.2	0 + 86.3 − 52.3 = 34.0	

Analysis: The cash conversion cycle decreased by 0.2 days (34.2 − 34.0).

5. Δ Cash = Δ Cash Conversion Cycle Days × (COGS/365) = 0.2 days × ($48,394/365 days) = $26.5 million

Review 6-4—Solution

1. Straight-line depreciation expense = ($95,000 − $10,000)/5 years = $17,000 per year
2. The HD subsidiary reports equipment on its balance sheet at its net book value of $44,000.

Equipment, cost	$95,000
Less accumulated depreciation ($17,000 × 3)	51,000
Equipment, net (end of Year 3).	$44,000

Review 6-5—Solution

Part 1.

a. The equipment is impaired since the undiscounted expected cash flows of $40,000 are less than the $44,000 net book value of the equipment. The HD subsidiary must write down the equipment to its fair value of $36,000. The effect of this write-down is to reduce the net book value of the equipment by $8,000 ($44,000 − $36,000) and recognize a loss in the income statement.

b. The HD subsidiary must report a gain on this sale of $6,000, computed as proceeds of $50,000 less the net book value of the equipment of $44,000 (see Review 6-4, part 2).

Part 2.

a. Coca-Cola's restructuring expense for 2018 is the increase in the restructuring liability of $508 million.

b. Coca-Cola reports a restructuring liability of $90 million on its 2018 balance sheet.

Review 6-6—Solution

$ millions	2019	2018
PPE turnover	$\dfrac{\$71,309}{\left(\dfrac{\$18,432 + \$19,721}{2}\right)} = 3.7$	$\dfrac{\$68,619}{\left(\dfrac{\$19,721 + \$19,949}{2}\right)} = 3.5$
Average useful life	$\dfrac{\$18,052 + \$10,090}{\$1,454} = 19.4$	$\dfrac{\$18,521 + \$10,475}{\$1,540} = 18.8$
Percent used up	$\dfrac{\$17,431}{\$18,052 + \$10,090} = 62\%$	$\dfrac{\$17,219}{\$18,521 + \$10,475} = 59\%$

Module 7

Current and Long-Term Liabilities

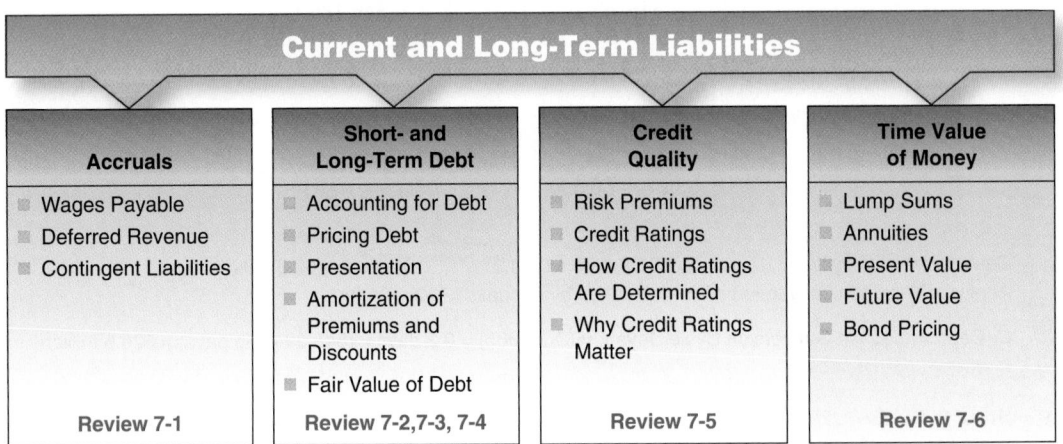

Current and Long-Term Liabilities			
Accruals	**Short- and Long-Term Debt**	**Credit Quality**	**Time Value of Money**
▨ Wages Payable ▨ Deferred Revenue ▨ Contingent Liabilities	▨ Accounting for Debt ▨ Pricing Debt ▨ Presentation ▨ Amortization of Premiums and Discounts ▨ Fair Value of Debt	▨ Risk Premiums ▨ Credit Ratings ▨ How Credit Ratings Are Determined ▨ Why Credit Ratings Matter	▨ Lump Sums ▨ Annuities ▨ Present Value ▨ Future Value ▨ Bond Pricing
Review 7-1	Review 7-2, 7-3, 7-4	Review 7-5	Review 7-6

We examine current and long-term liabilities

■ Current liabilities

  o Accrued liabilities, deferred revenue, and contingent liabilities (such as warranties)

  o Short-term debt and current maturities of long-term debt

■ Long-term liabilities

  o Bond pricing and the effective cost of debt

  o Footnote disclosures of long-term debt

  o Financial statement effects of bond repurchases

  o Fair-value disclosures

■ Bond credit ratings

  o Determinants of credit ratings

  o How credit ratings influence the effective cost of debt

  o Investment grade versus noninvestment grade credit ratings

  o Example of credit rating analysis for Verizon

  o Predictive ability of credit ratings for future rates

■ **Verizon Communications** is the focus company and the dashboard below conveys key financial information

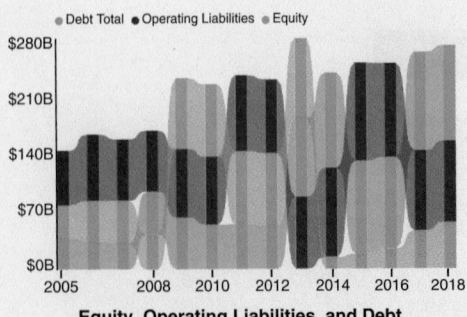

Equity, Operating Liabilities, and Debt

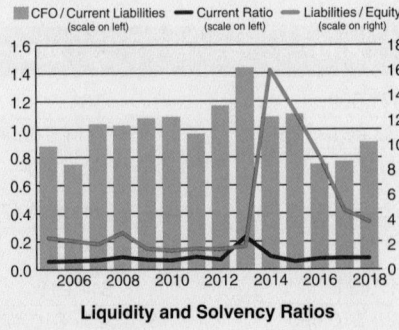

Liquidity and Solvency Ratios

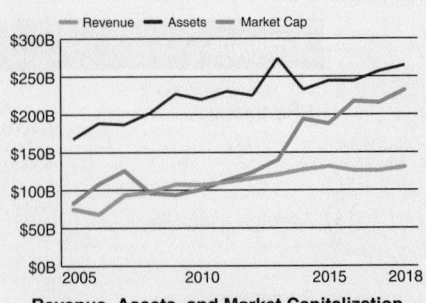

Revenue, Assets, and Market Capitalization

There's 5G.
Then there's Verizon 5G.

5G

Google

$399⁹⁹

$37⁵⁰

Road Map

LO	Learning Objective | Topics	Page	eLecture	Guided Example	Assignments
7–1	**Explain accounting for accrued liabilities.** Defined :: Contractual Liabilities :: Contingent Liabilities	7-3	e7–1	Review 7-1	1, 2, 7, 9, 13, 21, 27, 28, 29, 30, 50
7–2	**Analyze reporting for short-term debt.** Accounting for ST Debt :: Interest :: Maturities of LT Debt	7-7	e7–2	Review 7-2	8, 17, 46
7–3	**Determine the pricing of long-term debt.** Bond Details :: Par Bonds :: Discount Bonds :: Premium Bonds :: Cost of Debt	7-9	e7–3	Review 7-3	3, 10, 19, 20, 22, 31, 34, 35, 36, 37, 39, 45, 46, 47, 49, 51
7–4	**Analyze reporting for long-term debt.** Debt Disclosures :: Amortization :: Bond Repurchase :: Bond Fair Value	7-13	e7–4	Review 7-4	4, 6, 11, 12, 13, 14, 15, 16, 22, 26, 31, 32, 34, 35, 36, 37, 39, 46, 47, 48, 49
7–5	**Explain how quality of debt is determined.** Credit Ratings Defined :: Determinants of Ratings :: Importance of Ratings	7-16	e7–5	Review 7-5	5, 10, 18, 23, 33, 40, 41, 42, 46, 48, 52
7–6	**Apply time value of money concepts (Appendix 7A).** Present & Future Values :: Single Amounts and Annuities :: Using Excel or Calculator	7-25	e7–6	Review 7-6	19, 20, 22, 24, 25, 38, 43, 44

Accrued Liabilities

The current liabilities section of the balance sheet reports liabilities that will normally mature within one year from the balance sheet date. Following is the information that **Verizon Communications Inc.** provides in its 2018 annual report and footnotes.

Verizon Current Liabilities ($ millions)			
Reported on balance sheet		**Reported in footnotes**	
Current liabilities		Accounts payable and accrued liabilities	
Debt maturing within one year	$ 7,190	Accounts payable	$ 7,232
Accounts payable and accrued liabilities . .	22,501	Accrued expenses	5,948
Other current liabilities	8,239	Accrued vacation, salaries and wages . .	6,268
Total current liabilities	$37,930	Interest payable	1,570
		Taxes payable	1,483
			$22,501
		Other current liabilities	
		Dividends payable	$ 2,512
		Contract liability	4,207
		Other.	1,520
			$ 8,239

Verizon's current liabilities of $37,930 million includes the following usual categories.

■ **Debt maturing within one year and short-term debt.** This category typically includes loans from banks, commercial paper borrowings, and scheduled maturities of long-term bonds and notes. These are nonoperating liabilities.

■ **Accounts payable.** These are amounts owed to suppliers for the purchase of goods and services on account and are, therefore, operating liabilities. We discuss accounts payable with inventory in a prior module because accounts payable are typically related to inventory purchases.

■ **Accrued liabilities.** This category typically includes many different accruals. For Verizon, accrued liabilities includes unpaid salaries and wages, interest and taxes, customer deposits, and dividends payable to shareholders.

Accrued Liabilities Defined

eLectures
MBC **LO1** Explain accounting for accrued liabilities.

Accrued liabilities (or accruals) are adjustments that accountants make to the balance sheet after all transactions have been entered into the accounting records, and prior to the issuance of the financial statements, so that those statements fairly present the financial condition of the company. These adjustments recognize liabilities on the balance sheet (and the related expense on the income statement) that are not the result of external transactions (such as the purchase of goods or services on account that are recognized as accounts payable). Accrued liabilities are incurred in the current period and, therefore, must be recognized in the current period. Accrued liabilities fall into two broad categories.

1. **Accruals for routine contractual liabilities.** These accruals include items such as:
   ● Wages that the company is contractually obligated to pay to employees for work performed, but not yet paid for in the current period.
   ● Interest that is due in the current period on borrowed money, but has not yet been paid.
   ● Income taxes that are owed, but not yet paid, as a result of profit earned during the period.
   ● Other operating liabilities that have been incurred but not yet paid for in the current period (like rent, utilities, etc.).
2. **Accruals for contingent liabilities.** Contingent liabilities depend on the occurrence of a future uncertain event in order to determine whether a liability exists and, if so, in what amount. An example is litigation that has been brought against the company whose outcome and amount depends

upon adjudication. Another is warranty liabilities for products sold which depend upon the occurrence of product defects to require the company to repair or replace the product purchased.

Accruals for Contractual Liabilities—Wages Payable Example

Many companies pay employees bi-monthly. In the last two weeks of the month, then, employees have worked for the company, have earned wages, but have not yet been paid. If the liability for unpaid wages is not reflected on the month-end balance sheet, liabilities will be understated and wage expense will not be reflected in the income statement, thus overstating profit for the period. To correct for this, accountants make an entry to reflect the unpaid wage liability on the balance sheet and recognize wage expense in the income statement. When the wages are subsequently paid in the following month, cash decreases as does the wage liability.

The accrual entry and subsequent payment are reflected in our financial statement effects template.

	Balance Sheet						Income Statement			
Transaction	Cash Asset	+ Noncash Assets	= Liabil- ities	+ Contrib. Capital	+ Earned Capital		Rev- enues	– Expen- ses	= Net Income
Period 1: Accrued $75 for employee wages earned at period-end		=	+75 Wages Payable		–75 Retained Earnings			– +75 Wages Expense	= –75
Period 2: Paid $75 for wages earned in prior period	–75 Cash	=	–75 Wages Payable					–	=

WE 75
　　WP 75

　　　WE
　75 |
　　　WP
　　　　|　　75

WP 75
　　Cash 75

　　　WP
　75 |
　　　Cash
　　　　|　　75

The following financial statement effects result from this accrual and subsequent payment of employee wages.

- The effect of the accrual in period 1 is to increase wages payable on the balance sheet and to recognize wages expense on the income statement. Failure to recognize this liability and associated expense would understate liabilities on the balance sheet and overstate income in the current period.

- When the company pays employees in the following period, cash and wages payable both decrease. This payment does not result in expense because the expense was recognized in the prior period when the wages were earned by employees and the liability to pay those wages was incurred.

For example, Verizon reports accrued vacation, salaries, and wages of $6,268 million at the 2018 year-end. This represents the anticipated salaries and benefits earned by employees in 2018 that will be paid in 2019.

Other contractual accruals of this type are common and they relate to events that are certain. For example, companies can estimate fairly precisely unpaid rent and utilities, the amount of interest that is due in the current period on borrowed money, and income taxes that are owed as a result of profit earned during the period. All of these are included in accrued liabilities.

Accruals for Contractual Liabilities—Deferred Revenue Example

Deferred (or unearned) revenue represents deposits or other prepayments from customers that the company has not yet earned. Verizon collects cash in advance from customers who opt for prepaid phone plans, which are plans that enable customers to obtain wireless services without credit verification by paying for all services in advance. In some cases, Verizon collects deposits from commercial customers in advance of a major installation of communication equipment. Both of these types of prepayments are accrued liabilities until Verizon provides the related services; that is, until the prepaid plan is used or the installation is completed. At the end of fiscal 2018, Verizon's Other current liabilities account includes $4,207 million for Contract liabilities, which is deferred revenue that the company will earn in 2019. (We discuss deferred revenue more fully in a prior module.)

Accruals for Contingent Liabilities

Some accrued liabilities are less certain than others because the ultimate settlement of the liability is contingent on the outcome of some future event(s). Companies must record an accrual (a contingent liability) on the balance sheet, when two conditions are met.

1. It is "probable" that one or more future events will confirm that a liability existed at the financial statement date.

2. The amount required to settle the liability in the future can be reasonably determined at the financial statement date. The amount recorded should be the best estimate of the future expenditure required to settle the obligation. (If the best estimate of the expenditure is a range, and no amount in the range is a better estimate than any other, the company records the minimum amount in the range.)

Common examples of contingent liabilities include:

- Guarantees on the debt of another entity.
- Lawsuits (only for losses, never for lawsuits where the company stands to win).
- Product warranties and recalls.
- Environmental disasters and remediation.

Accruals for Contingent Liabilities—Warranties Example

Warranty liabilities are commitments that manufacturers make to their customers to repair or replace defective products within a specified period of time. If the obligation is *probable* and the amount *estimable* with reasonable certainty, GAAP requires manufacturers to record the expected cost of warranties as a liability and to record the related expected warranty expense in the income statement in the same period that the sales revenue is reported. And, for warranty liabilities, both the probability and the likely amount can be reasonably estimated based on past experience.

To illustrate, assume that a company estimates from past experience that defective units amount to 2% of sales and that each unit will cost $5 to replace. If sales during the period are $10,000, the estimated warranty expense is $1,000 ($10,000 × 2% × $5), and the entries to accrue this liability and to reflect its ultimate payment are shown in the template that follows.

Accruing warranty liabilities has the same effect on financial statements as accruing wages expense. That is, a liability is recorded on the balance sheet and an expense is reported in the income statement. When the defective product is later replaced (or repaired), the liability is reduced together with the cost of the inventory, cash paid for labor to repair the product, parts used in the repair, and any other costs that were necessary to satisfy the claim. (Only a portion of the products estimated to fail does so in the current period; we expect other product failures in future periods. Management monitors this estimate and adjusts it if failure is higher or lower than expected.) As in the accrual of wages, the expense and the liability are reported when incurred and not when paid.

	Balance Sheet						Income Statement		
Transaction	Cash Asset	+ Noncash Assets	= Liabil- ities	+ Contrib. Capital	+ Earned Capital		Rev- enues	− Expen- ses	= Net Income
WRE . . 1,000 **WRP . . . . 1,000** WRE 1,000 ⎮ WRP ⎮ 1,000 Accrued $1,000 of ex- pected warranty costs on units sold during the period			= +1,000 Warranty Payable		−1,000 Retained Earnings			− +1,000 Warranty Expense	= −1,000
WRP . . 1,000 **INV . . . . 1,000** WRP 1,000 ⎮ INV ⎮ 1,000 Delivered $1,000 in replacement products to settle warranty claims	−1,000 Inventory		= −1,000 Warranty Payable					−	=

Because the warranty liability and related expense are typically important items for manufacturing companies, information relating to this liability for the current and prior two periods is disclosed in the footnotes to the financial statements. Harley-Davidson's warranty footnote in its 2018 annual report is an example.

Product Warranty and Recall The Company currently provides a standard two-year limited warranty on all new motorcycles sold worldwide, except for Japan, where the Company provides a standard three-year limited warranty on all new motorcycles sold. In addition, the Company offers a one-year warranty for Parts & Accessories (P&A). The warranty coverage for the retail customer generally begins when the product is sold to a retail customer. The Company accrues for future warranty claims using an estimated cost based primarily on historical Company claim information. Additionally, the Company has from time-to-time initiated certain voluntary recall campaigns. The Company accrues for the estimated cost associated with voluntary recalls in the period that management approves and commits to the recall. Changes in the Company's warranty and recall liability were as follows (in thousands):

	2018	2017	2016
Balance, beginning of period	$ 94,200	$79,482	$74,217
Warranties issued during the period	53,367	57,834	60,215
Settlements made during the period	(79,300)	(82,554)	(99,298)
Recalls and changes to pre-existing warranty liabilities	63,473	39,438	44,348
Balance, end of period	$131,740	$94,200	$79,482

The liability associated with recalls was $73.3 million, $35.3 million, and $13.6 million at December 31, 2018, 2017, and 2016, respectively.

At the beginning of 2018, Harley-Davidson reported a reserve of $94,200 for estimated product warranty and safety recall costs (all $ in thousands for this discussion). During 2018, the company added $53,367 to the reserve relating to warranties on products sold in 2018. Then, the company added another $63,473 to update the estimates it made in prior periods—the actual costs to replace and repair recalled equipment came in significantly higher than anticipated and the company needed a catch-up accrual. As a result of these two accruals, Harley-Davidson recognized an expense of $116,840 ($53,367 + $63,473) in its 2018 income statement.

During 2018, the company paid out $79,300 to settle warranty claims. The settlements include cash paid to customers for refunds, wages paid to employees who repair the motorcycles, and the cost of parts used in repairs.

It is important to understand that only the increase in the liability impacts the income statement—the accrual ($116,840 in 2018) is recorded as warranty expense, which reduces pre-tax income. Payments made to settle warranty claims do not affect current-period income; they merely reduce the pre-existing liability.

GAAP requires that the warranty liability should reflect the estimated cost that the company expects to incur as a result of warranty claims. This is often a difficult estimate to make and is prone to error. Each period, the company examines the liability and updates the amount to reflect new, more accurate information, as we saw above, for Harley-Davidson. There is also the possibility that a company might intentionally underestimate its warranty liability to report higher current income, or overestimate it so as to depress current income and create an additional liability on the balance sheet (*cookie jar reserve*) that can be used to absorb future warranty costs and, thus, to reduce *future* expenses. The overestimation would shift income from the current period to one or more future periods. Warranty liabilities must, therefore, be examined closely and compared with sales levels. Any deviations from the historical relation of the warranty liability to sales, or from levels reported by competitors, should be scrutinized.

IFRS Insight ■ Provisions and Contingencies under IFRS

IFRS requires that a "provision" be recognized as a liability if a present obligation exists, if it is probable that an outflow of resources is required, and if the obligation can be reasonably estimated. These provisions are roughly equivalent to GAAP contingent liabilities that meet the bar for recognition on the balance sheet such as warranties and lawsuits that are probable and can be reasonably estimated. IFRS defines contingent liabilities as "possible but not probable" future obligations and, like under GAAP, are disclosed in footnotes, but not accrued.

Review 7-1 LO1

Consider the balance in the warranty and recall liability at Harley-Davidson for 2018 from the information above. Assume that in the next fiscal year, Harley-Davidson estimates a warranty liability of $70,000 on product sold and incurs a cost of $85,000 during the year to repair or replace defective products. (All $ in thousands for this review.)

Required
a. What amount of warranty expense will Harley-Davidson report in its income statement in 2019?
b. What will be the amount of warranty liability that Harley-Davidson reports on its 2019 balance sheet?
c. Assume that Harley-Davidson mistakenly accrues $90,000 for warranty liability in 2019 (instead of $70,000). What effect will this accrual mistake have on future income statements and balance sheets?

Solution on p. 7-48.

Short-Term Debt

LO2
Analyze reporting for short-term debt.

Companies generally seek to match the maturity of borrowings with the assets they are financing. While PPE assets are appropriately financed with long-term debt and/or equity, seasonal swings in working capital are often financed with a bank line of credit (short-term debt). In this case the bank commits to lend up to a maximum amount with the understanding that the amounts borrowed will be repaid in full sometime during the year. An interest-bearing note evidences any such borrowing.

When the company borrows these short-term funds, it reports the cash received on the balance sheet together with an increase in liabilities (notes payable). The note is reported as a current liability because the company expects to repay it within a year. Although this borrowing has no effect on income or equity, the borrower incurs (and the lender earns) *interest* on the note as time passes. GAAP requires the borrower to accrue the interest liability and the related interest expense each time financial statements are issued.

Accounting for Short-Term Debt

To illustrate, assume that Verizon borrows $1,000 cash on January 1. The note bears interest at a 12% annual rate, and the interest (3% per quarter) is payable on the first day of each subsequent quarter (April 1, July 1, October 1, January 1). Assuming that Verizon issues calendar-quarter financial statements, this borrowing results in the following financial statement effects for January 1 through April 1.

	Balance Sheet						Income Statement		
Transaction	Cash Asset	+ Noncash Assets	= Liabil- ities	+ Contrib. Capital	+ Earned Capital		Rev- enues	− Expen- ses	= Net Income
Jan 1: Borrow $1,000 cash and issue note payable	+1,000 Cash		= +1,000 Note Payable					−	=

Cash.. 1,000
NP........1,000

Cash
1,000 |

NP
| 1,000

continued

	Balance Sheet							Income Statement				
Transaction	Cash Asset	+	Noncash Assets	=	Liabil-ities	+	Contrib. Capital	+	Earned Capital		Rev-enues	−	Expen-ses	=	Net Income
Mar 31: Accrue quarterly inter-est on 12%, $1,000 note payable				=	+30 Interest Payable				−30 Retained Earnings			−	+30 Interest Expense	=	−30
Apr 1: Pay $30 cash for interest due	−30 Cash			=	−30 Interest Payable							−		=	

IE 30
  IP.............30

IE
30	

IP
	30

IP 30
  Cash 30

IP
30	

Cash
	30

The January 1 borrowing increases both cash and notes payable. On March 31, Verizon issues its quarterly financial statements. Although interest is not paid until April 1, the company has incurred three months' interest obligation as of March 31. Failure to recognize this liability and the expense incurred would not fairly present the financial condition of the company. Accordingly, the quarterly accrued interest payable is computed as follows.

$$\textbf{Interest Expense = Principal} \times \textbf{Annual Rate} \times \textbf{Portion of Year Outstanding}$$
$$\textbf{\$30} \quad = \quad \textbf{\$1,000} \quad \times \quad \textbf{12\%} \quad \times \quad \textbf{3/12}$$

The subsequent interest payment on April 1 reduces both cash and the interest payable that Verizon accrued on March 31. There is no expense reported on April 1, as it was recorded the previous day (March 31) when Verizon prepared its financial statements. (For fixed-maturity borrowings speci-fied in days, such as a 90-day note, we assume a 365-day year for interest accrual computations; see Review 7-2.)

Current Maturities of Long-Term Debt

Principal payments that must be made during the upcoming 12 months on long-term debt (such as for a mortgage or a maturing bond) are reported as current liabilities called *current maturities of long-term debt*. The current liabilities section of the Verizon 2018 balance sheet includes $7,190 million of "Debt maturing within one year." Some long-term debt, including mortgages, requires a periodic payment that is part principal and part interest. Note that the current maturity is the principal portion only of the payments that will be made in the upcoming year. Consider a five-year, 4% mortgage of $1 million that requires annual payments of $224,627. We can use a loan-amortization schedule such as the one below, to determine the principal amount outstanding at each reporting period.

Year	Interest at 4% on Principal Balance	Annual Payment	Principal Reduction (Ann Pymt— Int)	Principal Balance (Prior Bal.—Prin. Red.)
0				$1,000,000
1	$40,000	$224,627	$184,627	815,373
2	32,615	224,627	192,012	623,361
3	24,934	224,627	199,693	423,668
4	16,947	224,627	207,680	215,988
5	8,640	224,627	215,988	0

In the first year, the amount of interest accrued on the loan is $40,000 ($1 million × 4%). The remain-der of the annual payment of $224,627 is a reduction of the principal amount of the loan. On the day the mortgage was taken out, the balance sheet would show a current maturity of $184,627 with the remainder, $815,373, included in long-term debt. As the balance owed on the mortgage decreases, so too does the interest; the current portion increases each year.

Review 7-2 LO2

Assume that on January 15, Comcast borrowed $10,000 million on a 90-day, 6% note payable. The bank accrues interest daily based on a 365-day year. Comcast has a December 31 fiscal year-end.

Required
Use the financial statement effects template to show the following:
1. The interest accrual Comcast would make on March 31 when it prepares its first-quarter financial statements.
2. Comcast's payment of principal and interest when the note matures on April 14.

Solution on p. 7-49.

Long-Term Debt—Pricing

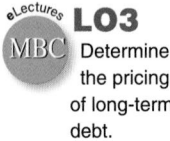

LO3

Determine the pricing of long-term debt.

Companies often include long-term nonoperating liabilities in their capital structure to fund long-term assets. Smaller amounts of long-term debt can be readily obtained from banks, private placements with insurance companies, and other credit sources. However, when a large amount of financing is required, the issuance of bonds (and notes) in capital markets is a cost-efficient way to raise funds. The following discussion uses bonds for illustration, but the concepts also apply to long-term notes.

Bonds are structured like any other borrowing. The borrower receives cash and agrees to pay it back with interest. Generally, the entire **face amount** (principal) of the bond is repaid at maturity (at the end of the bond's life) and interest payments are made in the interim (usually semiannually).

Companies that raise funds in the bond market normally work with an underwriter (like Goldman Sachs) to set the terms of the bond issue. The underwriter then sells individual bonds (usually in $1,000 denominations) from this general bond issue to its retail clients and professional portfolio managers (like The Vanguard Group), and receives a fee for underwriting the bond issue. These bonds are investments for individual investors, other companies, retirement plans and insurance companies.

After they are issued, the bonds can trade in the secondary market just like stocks. Market prices of bonds fluctuate daily despite the fact that the company's obligation for payment of principal and interest normally remains fixed throughout the life of the bond. Then, why do bond prices change? The answer is that the bond's fixed rate of interest can be higher or lower than the interest rates offered on other securities of similar risk. Because bonds compete with other possible investments, bond prices are set relative to the prices of other investments. In a competitive investment market, a particular bond will become more or less desirable depending on the general level of interest rates offered by competing securities. Just as for any item, competitive pressures will cause bond prices to rise and fall.

Before we discuss the mechanics of long-term debt pricing, we need to define two types of interest rates that we will use to price bonds.

- **Coupon (contract or stated) rate** The coupon rate of interest is stated in the bond contract; it is used to compute the dollar amount of interest payments that are paid (in cash) to bondholders during the life of the bond issue.

- **Market (yield or effective) rate** This is the interest rate that investors expect to earn on the investment in this debt security; this rate is used to price the bond.

The coupon (contract) rate is used to compute interest payments and the market (yield) rate is used to price the bond. The coupon rate and the market rate are nearly always different. This is because the coupon rate is fixed prior to issuance of the bond and normally remains fixed throughout its life. Market rates of interest, on the other hand, fluctuate continually with the supply and demand for bonds in the marketplace, general macroeconomic conditions, and the borrower's financial condition.

The bond price, both its initial sales price and the price it trades at in the secondary market subsequent to issuance, equals the present value of the expected cash flows to the bondholder. Specifically, bondholders normally expect to receive two different types of cash flows.

1. **Periodic interest payments** (usually semiannual) during the bond's life; these payments are called an *annuity* because they are equal in amount and made at regular intervals.

2. **Single payment** of the face (principal) amount of the bond at maturity; this is called a *lump-sum* because it occurs only once.

The bond price equals the present value of the periodic interest payments plus the present value of the single payment. If the present value of the two cash flows is equal to the bond's face value, the bond is sold at par. If the present value is less than or greater than the bond's face value, the bond sells at a discount or premium, respectively. We next illustrate the issuance of bonds at three different prices: at par, at a discount, and at a premium.

Pricing of Bonds Issued at Par

To illustrate a bond issued (sold) at par, assume that a bond with a face amount of $10 million has a 6% annual coupon rate payable semiannually (3% semiannual rate) and a maturity of 10 years. Semiannual interest payments are typical for bonds. This means that the issuer pays bondholders two interest payments per year. Each semiannual interest payment is equal to the bond's face value times the annual rate divided by two. Investors purchasing these bonds receive the following cash flows.

Cash Flows	Number of Payments	Dollars per Payment	Total Cash Flows
Semiannual interest payments......	10 years × 2 = 20	$10,000,000 × 3% = $300,000	$ 6,000,000
Principal payment at maturity.......	1	$10,000,000	10,000,000
			$16,000,000

Specifically, the bond agreement dictates that the borrower must make 20 semiannual payments of $300,000 each, computed as $10,000,000 × (6%/2). At maturity, the borrower must repay the $10,000,000 face amount. To price bonds, investors identify the *number* of interest payments and use that number when computing the present value of *both* the interest payments and the principal (face) payment at maturity.

The bond price is the present value of the periodic interest payments (the annuity) plus the present value of the principal payment (the lump sum). In our example, assuming that investors desire a 3% semiannual market rate (yield), the bond sells for $10,000,000, which is computed as follows.

	Payment	Present Value Factor[a]	Present Value
Interest................	$ 300,000	14.87747[b]	$ 4,463,200[d]
Principal...............	$10,000,000	0.55368[c]	5,536,800
			$10,000,000

[a] Mechanics of using tables to compute present values are explained in Appendix 7A; present value factors come from Appendix A near the end of the book.

[b] Present value of an ordinary annuity for 20 periods discounted at 3% per period.

[c] Present value of a single payment in 20 periods discounted at 3% per period.

[d] Rounded.

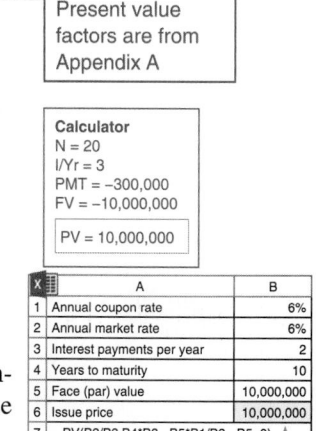

Present value factors are from Appendix A

Calculator
N = 20
I/Yr = 3
PMT = –300,000
FV = –10,000,000

PV = 10,000,000

X	A	B
1	Annual coupon rate	6%
2	Annual market rate	6%
3	Interest payments per year	2
4	Years to maturity	10
5	Face (par) value	10,000,000
6	Issue price	10,000,000
7	= PV(B2/B3,B4*B3,–B5*B1/B3,–B5, 0)	
8	= 10,000,000	

Because the bond contract pays investors a 3% semiannual rate when investors demand a 3% semiannual market rate, given the borrower's credit rating and the time to maturity, the investors purchase those bonds at the **par (face) value** of $10 million.

Pricing of Bonds Issued at a Discount

As a second illustration, assume investors demand a 4% semiannual return for the 3% semiannual coupon bond, while all other details remain the same. The bond now sells for $8,640,999, computed as follows.

```
Calculator
N = 20
I/Yr = 4
PMT = −300,000
FV = −10,000,000

PV = 8,640,967*

*rounding difference
```

X	A	B
1	Annual coupon rate	6%
2	Annual market rate	8%
3	Interest payments per year	2
4	Years to maturity	10
5	Face (par) value	10,000,000
6	Issue price	8,640,967
7	= PV(B2/B3,B4*B3,−B5*B1/B3,−B5, 0)	
8	= 8,640,967	

	Payment	Present Value Factor	Present Value
Interest	$ 300,000	13.59033[a]	$4,077,099
Principal	$10,000,000	0.45639[b]	4,563,900
			$8,640,999

[a] Present value of an ordinary annuity for 20 periods discounted at 4% per period.
[b] Present value of a single payment in 20 periods discounted at 4% per period.

Because the bond carries a coupon rate *lower* than what investors demand, the bond is less desirable and sells at a **discount**. More generally, bonds sell at a discount whenever the coupon rate is less than the market rate.

Pricing of Bonds Issued at a Premium

As a third illustration, assume that investors demand a 2% semiannual return for the 3% semiannual coupon bonds, while all other details remain the same. The bond now sells for $11,635,129, computed as follows.

```
Calculator
N = 20
I/Yr = 2
PMT = −300,000
FV = −10,000,000

PV = 11,635,143*

*rounding difference
```

X	A	B
1	Annual coupon rate	6%
2	Annual market rate	4%
3	Interest payments per year	2
4	Years to maturity	10
5	Face (par) value	10,000,000
6	Issue price	11,635,143
7	= PV(B2/B3,B4*B3,−B5*B1/B3,−B5, 0)	
8	= 11,635,143	

	Payment	Present Value Factor	Present Value
Interest	$ 300,000	16.35143[a]	$ 4,905,429
Principal	$10,000,000	0.67297[b]	6,729,700
			$11,635,129

[a] Present value of an ordinary annuity for 20 periods discounted at 2% per period.
[b] Present value of a single payment in 20 periods discounted at 2% per period.

Because the bond carries a coupon rate *higher* than what investors demand, the bond is more desirable and sells at a **premium**. More generally, bonds sell at a premium whenever the coupon rate is greater than the market rate.[1] Exhibit 7.1 summarizes this relation for bond pricing.

Exhibit 7.1 ■ Coupon Rate, Market Rate, and Bond Pricing

Coupon rate > market rate	→	Bond sells at a **premium** (above face amount)
Coupon rate = market rate	→	Bond sells at **par** (at face amount)
Coupon rate < market rate	→	Bond sells at a **discount** (below face amount)

Effective Cost of Debt

When a bond sells for par, the cost to the issuing company is the cash interest paid. In our first illustration above, the *effective cost* of the bond is the 6% interest paid by the issuer.

When a bond sells at a discount, the issuer must repay more (the face value when the bond matures) than the cash received at issuance (the discounted bond proceeds). This means that the effective cost of a discount bond is greater than if the bond had sold at par. A discount is a cost and, like any other cost, must eventually be transferred from the balance sheet to the income statement as an expense.

When a bond sells at a premium, the borrower received more cash at issuance than it must repay. The difference, the premium, is a benefit that must eventually find its way into the income statement as a *reduction* of interest expense. As a result of the premium, the effective cost of a premium bond is less than if the bond had sold at par.

Bonds are priced to yield the return (market rate) demanded by investors. Consequently, the effective rate of a bond *always* equals the yield (market) rate demanded by investors,

---

[1] Bond prices are often stated in percent form. For example, a bond sold at par is said to be sold at 100 (that is, 100% of par). The bond sold at $8,640,999 is said to be sold at 86.41 (86.41% of par, computed as $8,640,999/$10,000,000). The bond sold for a premium is said to be sold at 116.35 (116.35% of the bond's face value).

regardless of the coupon rate of the bond. This means that companies cannot influence the effective cost of debt by raising or lowering the coupon rate. Doing so will only result in a bond premium or discount. We discuss the factors affecting the yield demanded by investors later in the module.

The effective cost of debt is reflected in the amount of interest expense reported in the issuer's income statement. Because of bond discounts and premiums, interest expense is usually different from the cash interest paid.

Exhibit 7.2 demonstrates the difference between coupon rates and effective rates of interest. On April 2, 2019, **Verizon** issued €2,500 million and £500 million of debt including 0.875% notes with a face value of €1,250 million due April 8, 2027. The exhibit shows that the issue price of these notes was 99.631 (this is the percent of par value and indicates that the bonds were sold at a discount). Verizon's underwriters charged 0.3% in underwriting fees (€3,750,000) for underwriting and selling this debt issue, and thus, Verizon received proceeds of 99.331% of the face value, or €1,241,637,500. These notes paid interest annually on April 8. If we assume the notes were sold on April 8, 2019 (to simplify the calculations), we can determine that the effective rate on these notes was 0.9623%.

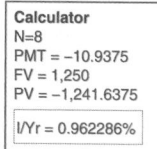

Calculator
N=8
PMT = −10.9375
FV = 1,250
PV = −1,241.6375

I/Yr = 0.962286%

	A	B
1	Annual coupon rate	0.8750%
2	Annual market rate	0.9623%
3	Interest payments per year	1
4	Years to maturity	8
5	Face (par) value	1,250,000,000
6	Issue price	1,241,637,500
7		
8	= RATE(B4*B3,−B5*B1/B3, B6,−B5, 0)	0.9623%
9	= 0.9623%	

Exhibit 7.2 ■ Announcement (Tombstone) of Debt Offering to Public

PROSPECTUS SUPPLEMENT
(To Prospectus Dated September 1, 2016)

Filed Pursuant to Rule 424(b)(2)
Registration No. 333-213439

€2,500,000,000
£500,000,000

verizon√

Verizon Communications Inc.

€1,250,000,000 0.875% Notes due 2027
€1,250,000,000 1.250% Notes due 2030
£500,000,000 2.500% Notes due 2031

We are offering €1,250,000,000 of our notes due 2027 (the "euro notes due 2027"), €1,250,000,000 of our notes due 2030 (the "euro notes due 2030" and, together with the euro notes due 2027, the "euro notes") and £500,000,000 of our notes due 2031 (the "sterling notes" and, together with the euro notes, the "notes"). The euro notes due 2027 will bear interest at the rate of 0.875% per year, the euro notes due 2030 will bear interest at the rate of 1.250% per year and the sterling notes will bear interest at the rate of 2.500% per year.

Interest on the euro notes due 2027 is payable in arrears on April 8 of each year, beginning on April 8, 2020. Interest on the euro notes due 2030 is payable in arrears on April 8 of each year, beginning on April 8, 2020. Interest on the sterling notes is payable in arrears on April 8 of each year, beginning on April 8, 2020.

The euro notes due 2027 will mature on April 8, 2027, the euro notes due 2030 will mature on April 8, 2030 and the sterling notes will mature on April 8, 2031.

We may redeem each series of notes, in whole or in part, at any time prior to maturity at the applicable redemption price to be determined using the procedure described in this prospectus supplement under "Description of the Notes—Redemption." In addition, each series of notes may be redeemed, at our option, in whole, but not in part, at any time prior to maturity at a price equal to 100% of the principal amount of such series of notes, plus accrued interest, in the event of certain developments affecting U.S. taxation as described under "Description of the Notes—Tax Redemption."

The notes will be our senior unsecured obligations and will rank equally with all of our unsecured and unsubordinated indebtedness. The euro notes will be issued in fully registered form and will be offered and sold in minimum denominations of €100,000 and integral multiples of €1,000 in excess of €100,000. The sterling notes will be issued in fully registered form and will be offered and sold in minimum denominations of £100,000 and integral multiples of £1,000 in excess of £100,000.

	euro notes due 2027	Total	euro notes due 2030	Total	sterling notes	Total
Public Offering Price(1)...	99.631%	€1,245,387,500	99.338%	€1,241,725,000	99.591%	£497,955,000
Underwriting Discount....	0.300%	€3,750,000	0.375%	€4,687,500	0.375%	£1,875,000
Proceeds to Verizon Communications Inc. (before expenses)	99.331%	€1,241,637,500	98.963%	€1,237,037,500	99.216%	£496,080,000

(1) Plus accrued interest, if any, from April 8, 2019, to the date of delivery.

We intend to apply to list the notes on the New York Stock Exchange ("NYSE"). We expect trading in the notes on the NYSE to begin within 30 days after the original issue, but the listing application is subject to review by the NYSE. Currently there is no public market for the notes. If such listing is obtained, we have no obligation to maintain such listing, and we may delist the notes at any time.

The underwriters are severally underwriting the notes being offered. The underwriters expect to deliver the notes in book-entry form only through the facilities of Clearstream Banking S.A. ("Clearstream") and Euroclear Bank S.A./N.V. ("Euroclear" and, together with Clearstream, the "clearing systems") against payment on or about April 8, 2019.

Joint Book-Running Managers

Barclays   **Deutsche Bank**   **J.P. Morgan**

Senior Co-Managers

RBC Capital Markets   **Santander**

Co-Managers

BNP PARIBAS   **Credit Suisse**   **Loop Capital Markets**   **Morgan Stanley**

Junior Co-Managers

CastleOak Securities, L.P.   **Drexel Hamilton**   **The Williams Capital Group, L.P.**

April 2, 2019

Source: Thomson Reuters WESTLAW

Review 7-3 LO3

On January 1, assume that Comcast issues $300,000 of 15-year, 10% bonds payable, yielding an effective semiannual interest rate of 4%. Interest is payable semiannually on June 30 and December 31.

Required

Solution on p. 7-49.

1. Calculate the issue price of this bond.
2. What would the bond issue price be if the semiannual effective interest rate is 6% instead of 4%?

Long-Term Debt—Reporting

LO4

Analyze reporting for long-term debt.

Balance Sheet Reporting

Companies typically have many debt issues outstanding and disclose the total amount owed as a long-term liability on the balance sheet. Footnotes provide details about each of the company's outstanding bonds and notes like the following for Verizon.

Long-Term Debt Outstanding long-term debt obligations as of December 31, 2018, are as follows.

At December 31,	Rates%	Maturities	2018	2017
Verizon Communications	1.38–4.00	2018–2042	$ 29,651	$ 31,370
	4.05–5.51	2020–2055	66,230	67,906
	5.82–6.90	2026–2054	5,658	5,835
	7.35–8.95	2029–2039	1,076	1,106
	Floating	2018–2025	4,657	6,684
VerizonWireless	6.80–7.88	2029–2032	234	234
Telephone subsidiaries—debentures	5.13–6.50	2028–2033	226	226
	7.38–7.88	2022–2032	341	341
	8.00–8.75	2022–2031	229	229
Other subsidiaries—notes payable, debentures and other	6.70–8.75	2018–2028	444	748
VerizonWireless and other subsidiaries—asset-backed debt	1.42–3.55	2021–2023	7,962	6,293
	Floating	2021–2023	2,139	2,620
Capital lease obligations (average rate of 4.1% and 3.6% in 2018 and 2017, respectively)			905	1,020
Unamortized discount, net of premium			(6,298)	(7,133)
Unamortized debt issuance costs			(541)	(534)
Total long-term debt, including current maturities			112,913	116,945
Less long-term debt maturing within one year			7,040	3,303
Total long-term debt			$105,873	$113,642

In general, companies report debt net of any discount (or including any premium) and also net of any debt issuance costs. Verizon subtracts Unamortized discount, net of premium, of $6,298 million and Unamortized debt issuance costs of $541 million to arrive at Total long-term debt, including current maturities, of $112,913 million in 2018. Then, Verizon subtracts $7,040 million, the amount of the debt that matures in the next year to arrive at the $105,873 million that is reported in the noncurrent liability section of the 2018 balance sheet.

Companies must provide a schedule of the maturities of their long-term debt in the footnotes to the financial statements. Following is the footnote disclosure of debt maturities in Verizon's 2018 annual report.

Maturities of long-term debt (secured and unsecured) outstanding, including current maturities, excluding unamortized debt issuance costs, at December 31, 2018.

continued

continued from previous page

Years	(dollars in millions)
2019	$ 7,058
2020	7,380
2021	6,999
2022	7,674
2023	5,903
Thereafter	78,439

The $7,058 million of long-term debt scheduled to mature in 2019 includes debt issuance costs of $18 million. The net amount $7,040 is reported as a current liability in the 2018 balance sheet (as reported in the debt footnote above). The remaining amounts through 2023 are scheduled maturities of long-term debt included in long-term debt on the balance sheet. In general, we look for significant amounts maturing in any one year as this raises the question whether the company will have the cash flow to make the required payment. We prefer to see a relatively level debt repayment schedule, like the one above, which allows for an orderly payment or refinancing. To assess whether these amounts are large, consider that Verizon's operating cash flow for 2018 is $34,339 million. So, while the amounts of maturing debt are not insignificant, they should be manageable for Verizon. The size of Verizon's total debt, however, is one reason why the company's credit rating is not high (we discuss credit ratings later in this module).

Income Statement Reporting

As discussed above, companies report long-term debt on the balance sheet net of the discount and debt issuance costs. When its bonds mature, however, the company must pay the face amount (the amount borrowed). This means that between the bond issuance and its maturity, the discount and debt issuance must decline to zero. This reduction of the discount and debt issuance over the life of the bond is called **amortization**, and the discount amortization results in additional interest expense in the income statement. This amortization causes the total interest expense to be greater than the cash interest payments. The opposite holds true for bonds and notes issued at a premium—the total interest expense is less than the cash interest paid. Consequently, the interest expense reported on the income statement each year represents the *effective cost* of debt, including both the cash interest paid plus a portion of the additional borrowing costs (or less a portion of the benefit of the premium). We discuss the amortization process in Appendix 7B.

Financial Statement Effects of Bond Repurchase

Companies report bonds payable at *historical (adjusted) cost.* Specifically, net bonds payable amounts follow from the amortization table, as do the related cash flows and income statement numbers. All financial statement relations are set when the bond is issued; they do not subsequently change.

Once issued, however, bonds trade in secondary markets. The yield rate used to compute bond prices for these subsequent transactions is the market interest rate prevailing at the time. These rates change daily based on the level of interest rates in the economy and the perceived creditworthiness of the bond issuer.

Companies can and sometimes do repurchase (or redeem or *retire*) their bonds prior to maturity. The bond indenture (contract agreement) can include provisions giving the company the right to repurchase its bonds directly from the bond holders. Or, the company can repurchase bonds in the open market. **Verizon** reports a "loss on the early extinguishment of debt" of $700 million in 2018 as described in the financial statement footnotes as follows.

During 2018 and 2017, we recorded losses on early debt redemptions of $0.7 billion and $2.0 billion, respectively. We recognize losses on early debt redemptions in Other income (expense), net, in our consolidated statements of income and within our Net cash used in financing activities in our consolidated statements of cash flows.

When a bond repurchase occurs, a gain or loss usually results, and is computed as follows.

> **Gain or Loss on Bond Repurchase = Net Bonds Payable – Repurchase Payment**

The net bonds payable, also referred to as the *book value,* is the net amount reported on the balance sheet. If the issuer pays more to retire the bonds than the amount carried on its balance sheet, it reports a loss on its income statement, usually called *loss on bond retirement.* The issuer reports a *gain on bond retirement* if the repurchase price is less than the net bonds payable.

How should we treat these gains and losses for analysis purposes? That is, do they carry economic effects? The answer is no—the gain or loss on repurchase is exactly offset by the present value of the future cash flow implications of the repurchase. (The Accounting Insight box that follows demonstrates this.) Further, the gain or loss on early retirement is a transitory item and, consequently, will not be repeated in future income statements.

Accounting Insight ■ Economics of Gains and Losses on Bond Repurchases

CVS repurchased its 6.25% Notes in 2014 and recorded a loss on the early extinguishment of debt. At the same time, CVS issued $850 million of 2.25% Notes. CVS used part of the proceeds to fund the repurchase of the 6.25% Notes. Because interest rates had dropped since the 6.25% Notes were issued, the market value of the 6.25% Notes had increased to $521 million in excess of their carrying amount. To repurchase the Notes, CVS had to pay the market price (and not the face value), which created a large "loss on the early extinguishment of debt."

Although CVS reported the $521 million loss in its income statement, there was no *economic* loss. We use a simple example to explain. Please refer to Exhibit 7B.1 relating to a $600,000 bond with a 3% coupon rate that was sold at a discount to yield 4%. At the end of period 2, the bond has a carrying amount on the balance sheet of $588,576.81.

Assume that at the end of period 2, the market rate of interest declines from 4% when the bond was issued, to 2% (1% semiannually). The drop in market rates will affect the market value of the bond. At the end of period 2, there are four interest payments of $9,000 remaining plus the $600,000 face amount of the bond at maturity. The present value of that stream of payments, discounted at the current market rate of 1% semiannual rate, is equal to $611,705.90 (the Excel formula is = PV(1%, 4, –9,000, –600,000)). To repurchase the bond, CVS would have to issue a new bond in the amount of $611,705.90 carrying a 1% coupon rate. Either way, CVS would report a loss on the early extinguishment of debt of $23,129.09 ($611,705.90 – $588,576.81).

Despite reporting an accounting loss on the early extinguishment of debt of $23,129.09, there is no economic loss. Why? Because the present value of the new debt is equal to $611,705.90 (the Excel formula is = PV(1%, 4, –6,117.06, –611,705.90), where 6,117.06 = $611,705.90 × 1%). The present value of the new debt is, therefore, equal to the present value of the remaining payments on the old debt, discounted at the new semiannual market rate of 1%. They are, therefore, equivalent and no economic loss has been sustained.

Fair Value Disclosures

An important analysis issue involves assessing the fair value of bonds and other long-term liabilities. This information is relevant for investors and creditors because it reveals unrealized gains and losses (similar to that reported for marketable securities). GAAP requires companies to provide information about current fair values of their long-term liabilities in footnotes as Verizon does in its 2018 10-K.

Fair Value of Short-Term and Long-Term Debt The fair value of our debt is determined using various methods, including quoted prices for identical terms and maturities, which is a Level 1 measurement, as well as quoted prices for similar terms and maturities in inactive markets and future cash flows discounted at current rates, which are Level 2 measurements. The fair value of our short-term and long-term debt, excluding capital leases, was as follows:

At December 31 (dollars in millions)	2018		2017	
	Carrying Amount	Fair Value	Carrying Amount	Fair Value
Short- and long-term debt, excluding capital leases	$112,159	$118,535	$116,075	$128,658

The increase in fair value is due to a decline in market rates of interest since the debt was initially issued (or to an increase in the credit rating of the company). These fair values are *not* reported on the balance sheet and changes in these fair values are not reflected in net income. The chief justification for not recognizing fair-value gain and losses is that such amounts can reverse with subsequent fluctuations in market rates of interest and the bonds are repaid at par at maturity.

LO4 Review 7-4

Assume that on January 1 Comcast issues $300,000 of 15-year, 10% bonds payable for $351,876, yielding an effective semiannual interest rate of 4%. Interest is payable semiannually on June 30 and December 31.

1. Show computations to confirm the issue price of $351,876.
2. Complete Comcast's financial statement effects template for
    a. bond issuance,
    b. semiannual interest payment and premium amortization on June 30 of the first year, and
    c. semiannual interest payment and premium amortization on December 31 of the first year.
3. Prepare an amortization table for the bonds for the first five years (See Exhibit 7B.2 for guidance).
4. Assume that at the end of year 5, Comcast repurchases the bonds on the open market. The effective semiannual interest rate has fallen to 2%. What will Comcast have to pay to repurchase these bonds? Determine any gain or loss on the repurchase transaction.

Solution on p. 7-49.

Quality of Debt

Credit Analysis

Credit analysis differs from the analysis of equity securities. While equity investors are focused on upside potential, lenders are primarily concerned with recouping the amount loaned (the "principal"), together with the interest earned on their loan. (We use the term **"lenders"** broadly to include traditional bank loans or bonds and notes that trade on the open market.) Their focus is on the company's ability to repay, which is largely determined by two factors.

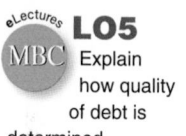

eLectures **LO5**
MBC Explain how quality of debt is determined.

1. **Level of indebtedness**—amount of principal and interest that must be repaid.
2. **Excess cash that the company is able to generate**—this provides the cash needed to repay the debt. The term "excess cash" means the cash the company is able to generate over and above what is needed for ongoing operating and investing activities, including bringing its products and/or services to market and maintaining and growing PPE infrastructure via capital expenditures (CAPEX).

The first factor is a *levels-based* focus and the second is a *flow-based* approach, and both are essential to a thorough investigation of a company's creditworthiness.

We discuss the credit analysis performed by Standard & Poor's in more detail below.[2] While each credit rating agency develops its own proprietary models, in general, the rating agencies take a *two-step approach* to evaluate the riskiness of a company's debt. The *first step* is to assess the likelihood of default (the nonpayment of amounts owed), relative to the likelihood of default for other companies. The relative likelihood of default can be gauged by an analysis of historical and forecasted levels of debt and the excess cash flow available to pay the indebtedness. The *second step* is to assess the potential loss that the lender will suffer in the event of default. The potential loss given default is generally a function of the structure of the debt. The following factors help to assess the collectibility of debt in the event of default.

■ How does the debt rank (senior or junior in order of payment) relative to other issuances by the same borrower?

---

[2] S&P Global Ratings (S&P) closest competitors are Moody's Investors Service and Fitch Ratings. Together, they are referred to as the Big Three credit rating agencies and they play a key role in global capital markets where they provide credit analysis for financial institutions, individual investors, and regulators.

- What collateral, if any, has been pledged to secure the debt in the event of nonpayment?
- What controls and restrictions have the lenders placed on the company to limit risk exposure?

Generally, lenders will require a higher interest rate as the creditworthiness of the borrower declines. This increase in interest rate is referred to as a *risk premium*. Earlier in the module we explained that the effective cost of debt to the issuing company is the market (yield) rate of interest used to price the bond, regardless of the bond coupon rate. The market rate of interest is usually defined as the yield on U.S. Government borrowings such as treasury bills, notes, and bonds, called the *risk-free rate,* plus a *risk premium* (also called a *spread*).

Yield Rate = Risk-Free Rate + Risk Premium

Both the treasury yield (the so-called risk-free rate) and the corporate yield vary over time as illustrated in the following graphic.

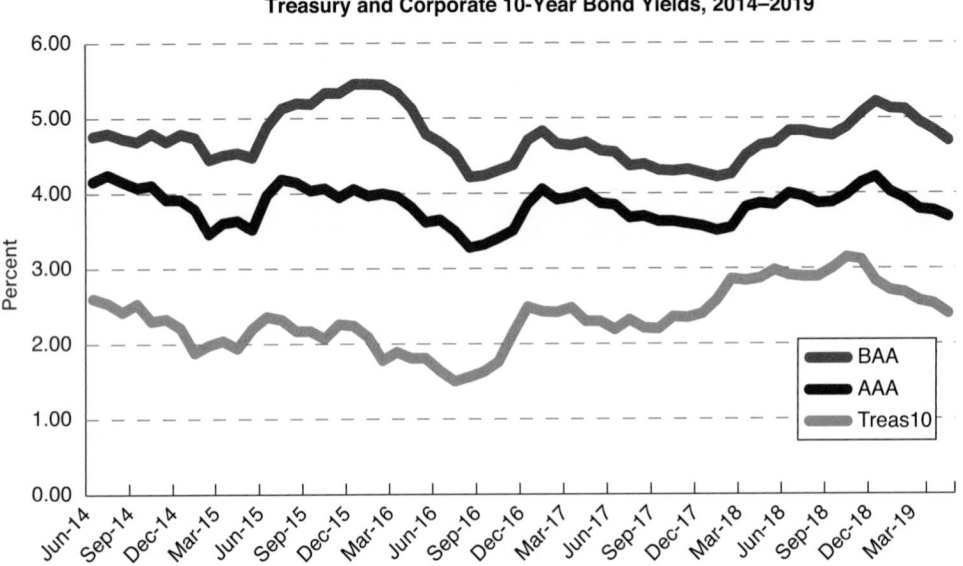

Treasury and Corporate 10-Year Bond Yields, 2014–2019

Source: Federal Reserve Bank of St. Louis.

The rate of interest that investors expect for a particular bond is a function of the risk-free rate and the risk premium, where the latter depends on the creditworthiness of the issuing entity.

The yield increases (shifts upward) as debt quality moves from Treasury securities (generally considered to be risk free), which is the highest-quality debt reflected in the lowest line in the graph, to the Aaa (highest) rated corporates and, finally, to the Baa (lower-rated) corporates shown in this graph. That is, higher credit-rated issuers warrant a lower rate than lower credit-rated issuers. This difference is substantial. For example, in May 2019, the average 10-year treasury bond yield was 2.40%, while the Aaa corporate bond yield was 3.69% and the average Baa (the lowest investment grade corporate bond) yield was 4.70%.

| Research Insight ■ Accounting Conservatism and Cost of Debt |

Research indicates that companies that use more conservative accounting policies incur a lower cost of debt. Research also suggests that while accounting conservatism can lead to lower-quality accounting income (because such income does not fully reflect economic reality), creditors are more confident in the numbers and view them as more credible. Evidence also implies that companies can lower the required return demanded by creditors (the risk premium) by issuing high-quality financial reports that include enhanced footnote disclosures and detailed supplemental reports.

What Are Credit Ratings?

A company's credit rating, also referred to as debt rating, credit quality, or creditworthiness, is related to default risk. **Default** refers to the nonpayment of interest and principal and/or the failure to adhere to the various terms and conditions (covenants) of the bond indenture. Companies that want to obtain bond financing from the capital markets normally first seek a rating on their proposed debt issuance from one of several rating agencies such as **S&P Global Ratings**, **Moody's Investors Service**, or **Fitch Ratings**. The aim of rating agencies is to rate debt so that its default risk is more accurately conveyed to, and priced by, the market. Each rating agency uses its own rating system, as Exhibit 7.3 shows. This exhibit includes the general description for each rating class—for example, AAA is assigned to debt of prime maximum safety (highest in creditworthiness). The dotted green line separates investment grade bonds from noninvestment grade or speculative bonds. Many investment managers are precluded from purchasing noninvestment grade bonds for their client portfolios, thus lessening the liquidity of the bonds.

Exhibit 7.3 ■ Corporate Debt Ratings and Descriptions			
S&P	**Moody's**	**Fitch**	**Description**
AAA	Aaa	AAA	Prime Maximum Safety
AA+	Aa1	AA+	High Grade, High Quality
AA	Aa2	AA	
AA–	Aa3	AA–	
A+	A1	A+	Upper-Medium Grade
A	A2	A	
A–	A3	A–	
BBB+	Baa1	BBB+	Lower-Medium Grade
BBB	Baa2	BBB	
BBB2	Baa3	BBB2	
BB+	Ba1	BB+	Noninvestment Grade
BB	Ba2	BB	Speculative
BB–	Ba3	BB–	
B+	B1	B+	Highly Speculative
B	B2	B	
B–	B3	B–	
CCC+	Caa1	CCC	Substantial Risk
CCC	Caa2		In Poor Standing
CCC–	Caa3		
CC	Ca		Extremely Speculative
C	C		May be in Default
		DDD	Default
		DD	
D		D	

What Determines Credit Ratings?

Verizon bonds are rated BBB+, Baa1, and A– by S&P Global Ratings, Moody's, and Fitch, respectively, as of 2018. In the text box, we provide excerpts from the S&P Global Ratings Credit Report for Verizon in 2019.

S&P Global Ratings determines its "anchor" credit rating from an analysis of the borrower's business risk and financial risk. It then adjusts the anchor credit rating by applying several modifiers: diversification of the borrower's revenue stream, capital structure, financial policy, liquidity and management/governance, and comparable ratings. This process is depicted in the following graphic.

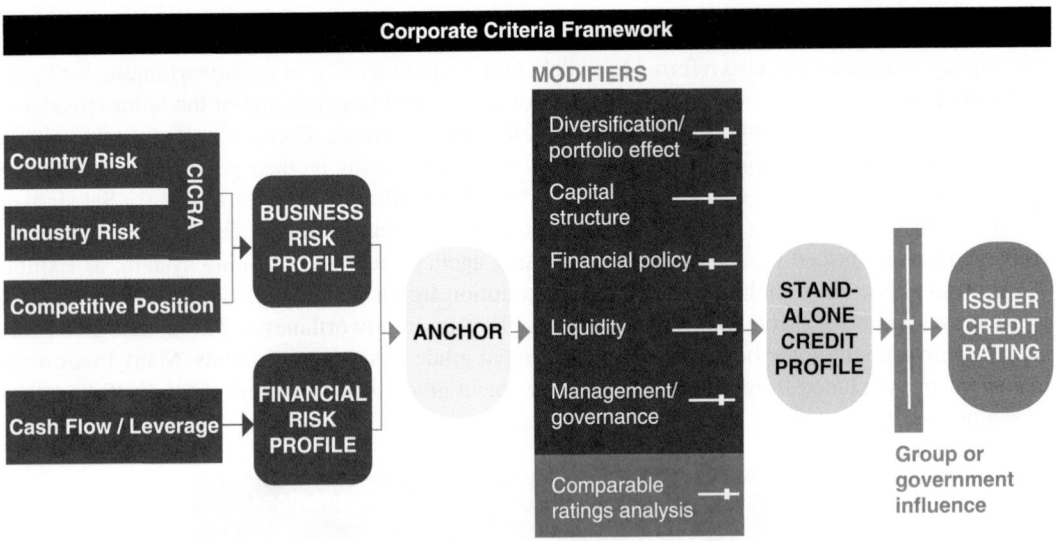

Corporate Criteria Framework

The objective of credit analysis is to assess the probability that the company will be able to make all required principal and interest payments when they come due. Large companies that are conservatively financed, dominant in their markets, and with large and predictable cash flows are more likely to meet debt obligations. Conversely, smaller companies facing intense competition in volatile markets carry more risk for lenders and will receive lower credit ratings.

Credit Ratings and Financial Ratios

Credit rating agencies use a variety of financial ratios to assess the level of debt relative to other balance sheet accounts and the required principal and interest payments relative to profitability and cash flow. Exhibit 7.4 provides a sample of these ratios. This table includes median values for each ratio across a range of credit ratings. As we move from the highest quality (Aaa) to speculative grade (Caaa-C) debt, the ratios weaken. For example, EBITA/Average assets is a variant of the Return on assets (ROA) metric that we discuss in Module 4. For the highest-rated companies, the median for this statistic in 2017 is 12.3%. The lowest-rated companies are one-third of that level. For operating margins (Operating profit / Sales) the range is even more striking with the highest-rated companies reporting a median operating margin of 24.8% and the lowest a median of 3.8%.

Similarly, the (Funds from operations (FFO) + Interest expense)/Interest expense is a variant of the times interest earned ratio that we discuss in the solvency section of Module 4. The highest-rated companies report a median value of 18.0 while the lowest report a level of 1.7, which means available funds barely cover interest payments. The FFO/Debt ratio, measuring the company's operating cash flow relative to the level of its debt, ranges from 40.4% to 5.7%.

Business Insight ■ Credit Rating Factors for Verizon Debt

S&P's credit analysis of Verizon's debt anchors on its **Business** risk and its **Financial** risk as of December 2018 year-end.

Business Risk: Strong

The business risk assessment reflects Verizon's strong position as the largest wireless provider in the U.S., with a leading brand and reputation for network quality. It also reflects the strength of its wireless EBITDA margins with substantial scale advantages and growth from Fios broadband services. Partial mitigating factors include a mature wireless market with limited near-term growth potential, as well as secular industry pressures and weak margins in its wireline business.

Financial Risk: Intermediate

We expect modest improvement in adjusted net leverage to around 2.6x to 2.7x in 2019 from 2.8x in 2018. We believe Verizon has good prospects to reduce leverage to the 2.5x area (our threshold for a higher rating) by 2020, although this depends on the amount and timing of spectrum license acquisitions. Additionally, the company's recently stated target for net unsecured debt to EBITDA of 1.75x–2.0x provides greater clarity on financial policy. We estimate that the upper end of this range translates into our adjusted leverage of 2.5x. We also expect FFO to total debt will be in the high-20% area, which is somewhat weak for our financial risk assessment.

Liquidity: Adequate

Our liquidity assessment is adequate and the short-term commercial paper (CP) rating is 'A-2'. We expect sources of liquidity to cover uses by about 1.3x for the next 12 months and for net sources to be positive even with a 15% decline in forecasted EBITDA. In addition, we believe Verizon has a high standing in the credit markets, evidenced by its track record of accessing both domestic and international debt markets, demonstrates prudent risk management, and has flexibility around the timing and amount of capital expenditures.

Verizon Communications Inc.

Ratings Score Snapshot

Issuer Credit Rating

BBB+/Positive/A-2

Business risk: Strong
- Country risk: Very low
- Industry risk: Intermediate
- Competitive position: Strong

Financial risk: Intermediate
- Cash flow/Leverage: Intermediate

Anchor: a–

Modifiers
- Diversification/Portfolio effect: Neutral (no impact)
- Capital structure: Neutral (no impact)
- Financial policy: Neutral (no impact)
- Liquidity: Adequate (no impact)
- Management and governance: Strong (no impact)
- Comparable rating analysis: Negative (–1 notch)

Stand-alone credit profile: bbb+
- Group credit profile: bbb+

The Business and Financial risk assessments combine to yield an overall rating of a–/bbb+ as shown in this matrix.

Business and Financial Risk Matrix						
	Financial Risk Profile					
Business Risk Profile	**Minimal**	**Modest**	**Intermediate**	**Significant**	**Aggressive**	**Highly Leveraged**
Excellent............	aaa/a+	aa	a+/a	a–	bbb	bbb–/bb+
Strong..............	aa/aa–	a+/a	a–/bbb+	bbb	bb+	bb
Satisfactory.........	a/a–	bbb+	bbb/bbb–	bbb–/bb+	bb	b+
Fair................	bbb/bbb–	bbb–	bb+	bb	bb–	b
Weak	bb+	bb+	bb	bb–	b+	b/b–
Vulnerable	bb–	bb–	bb–/b+	b+	b	b–

The **Liquidity** assessment as "adequate" reduces the anchor rating to the lower end of the range for bbb+.

Exhibit 7.4 ■ Ratio Values for Different Credit Ratings*

	EBITA/ Avg AT	EBITA/ Int Exp	EBITA Margin	Oper Margin	(FFO + Int Exp)/Int Exp	FFO/ Debt	RCF/Net Debt	Debt/ EBITDA	Debt/ Book Cap	CAPEX/ Dep Exp	Rev Vol
Aaa........	12.3%	12.0	30.6%	24.8%	18.0	40.4%	32.3%	1.9	42.8%	1.1	6.8
Aa.........	14.7%	20.7	24.9%	24.2%	20.0	45.9%	35.5%	1.7	41.5%	1.3	11.1
A..........	13.5%	11.4	19.0%	16.9%	11.9	35.7%	27.7%	2.2	46.7%	1.2	6.8
Baa........	10.4%	6.4	16.3%	15.0%	8.1	28.2%	27.5%	2.7	48.4%	1.2	10.7
Ba.........	8.8%	3.7	13.3%	11.2%	5.4	21.5%	22.1%	3.6	55.9%	1.1	14.4
B..........	6.6%	2.0	9.4%	7.6%	3.3	13.2%	13.5%	5.2	68.1%	1.0	18.7
Caa-C......	4.9%	0.7	6.5%	3.8%	1.7	5.7%	6.6%	7.2	94.4%	0.8	24.8

* Table reports 2017 median values by credit rating; from Moody's Financial Metrics™, Key Ratios by Rating and Industry for North American Non-Financial Corporates: December 2017 (reproduced with permission).

Ratio	Definition
EBITA/Average Assets	EBITA/Average of Current and Previous Year Assets
EBITA/Interest Expense	EBITA/Interest Expense
EBITA Margin	EBITA/Net Revenue
Operating Margin	Operating Profit/Net Revenue
(FFO + Interest Exp)/Interest Exp	(Funds From Operations + Interest Expense)/Interest Expense
FFO/Debt	Funds From Operations/(Short-Term Debt + Long-Term Debt)
RCF/Net Debt	(FFO − Preferred Dividends − Common Dividends − Minority Dividends)/(Short-Term Debt + Long-Term Debt − Cash & Cash Equivalents)
Debt/EBITDA	(Short-Term Debt + Long-Term Debt)/EBITDA
Debt/Book Capitalization	(Short-Term Debt + Long-Term Debt)/(Short-Term Debt + Long-Term Debt + Deferred Taxes + Minority Interest + Book Equity)
CAPEX/Depreciation Exp	Capital Expenditures/Depreciation Expense
Revenue Volatility	Standard Deviation of Trailing Five Years of Net Revenue Growth

where: EBITA = Earnings from continuing operations before interest, taxes, and amortization
      EBITDA = Earnings from continuing operations before interest, taxes, depreciation, and amortization
        FFO = Funds from Operations = Net income from continuing operations plus depreciation, amortization, deferred income taxes, and other noncash items

A review of these ratios indicates that Moody's considers the following factors, grouped by area of emphasis, as relevant in evaluating a company's ability to meet its debt service requirements.

1. Profitability ratios (first four metrics in footnote to Exhibit 7.4)
2. Cash flow ratios (metrics five, six, and seven in footnote to Exhibit 7.4)
3. Solvency ratios (metrics eight, nine, ten, and eleven in footnote to Exhibit 7.4)

A company's profitability, cash flow, and solvency are important factors in assessing the likelihood that it will successfully meet its debt obligations. In addition, credit rating agencies consider various aspects of the structure of the debt, including the following:

■ **Collateral** Companies can provide security for debt by pledging certain assets against the bond. This is like mortgages on assets. To the extent debt is secured, the debt holder is in a preferred position vis-à-vis other creditors.

■ **Covenants** Debt agreements (indentures) can restrict the behavior of the issuing company so as to protect debt holders. For example, covenants commonly prohibit excessive dividend payments, mergers and acquisitions, further borrowing, and commonly prescribe minimum levels for key liquidity and solvency ratios. These covenants provide debt holders an element of control over the issuer's operations because, unlike equity investors, debt holders have no voting rights.

■ **Options** Options are sometimes written into debt contracts. Examples are options to convert debt into stock and options allowing the issuing company to repurchase its debt before maturity (usually at a premium).

Verizon Credit Rating Example

In September 2013, Verizon entered into an agreement with Vodafone Group Plc to acquire Vodafone's 45% interest in Verizon Wireless, giving it sole ownership of the wireless carrier. The deal closed in 2014 with a purchase price of $130 billion, paid in a combination of cash and stock. During 2013 and 2014, Verizon's long-term debt increased from $48 billion to $116 billion. The increase in financial leverage resulted in a downgrade in Verizon's credit rating. As Moody's reported "the deal will cause leverage to spike and remain elevated for an extended time frame as higher interest expense and increased dividend payments offset the distributions that Verizon will retain as a result of acquiring 100% ownership of [Verizon Wireless], reducing the amount of cash available for debt reduction."

In the years following the acquisition, Verizon's creditworthiness has become important as bond buyers look to ascertain the company's ability to manage its debt load in addition to meeting significant competitive challenges from AT&T for wireless and Comcast on the cable side of its business. In this section, we discuss in depth the credit analysis on Verizon performed by S&P Global Ratings in 2019.

S&P Global Ratings provides the following summary of its credit analysis of Verizon.

Verizon Communications Inc.

Business Risk: STRONG

Vulnerable — Excellent

a-   bbb+   bbb+

Financial Risk: INTERMEDIATE

Highly leveraged — Minimal

Anchor   Modifiers   Group/Gov't

Issuer Credit Rating

BBB+ / Positive / A-2

Credit Highlights

Overview

Key Strengths	Key Risks
Strong market position as the largest wireless carrier in the U.S., with a leading brand reputation for network quality.	Modest wireless revenue growth due to mature industry conditions and significant competition.
Industry leader in wireless EBITDA margins with substantial scale advantages.	Secular industry declines for linear video and landline phone services.
Growth from Fios broadband services.	Weak wireline margins.
Consistent financial policy and commitment to leverage improvement.	Fifth generation (5G) wireless services will require substantial financial resources for spectrum license acquisitions and network deployment, with material revenue opportunities five to 10 years away.

Outlook: Positive

The positive outlook reflects our expectation for low-single-digit percent EBITDA growth, leverage approaching 2.5x, and funds from operations (FFO) to total debt in the high-20% area over the next couple of years. That said, potential debt-financed acquisitions, spectrum purchases, and higher levels of capital spending on network upgrades to support growth in data and video consumption could constrain near-term leverage improvement.

Downside scenario

We could revise the outlook to stable if the company allocates excess cash flow to share repurchases or makes a debt-financed acquisition. Given that 5G revenue opportunities are still uncertain and do not ramp until 2020–2021, at the earliest, we could revise the outlook back to stable if spectrum purchases are materially higher than our base case. While less likely, we could also revise the outlook to stable if wireless operations deteriorate, resulting in service revenue declines because of more aggressive competition.

Upside scenario

We could raise the rating if the company reaches and maintains S&P adjusted leverage of less than 2.5x. Given our expectation for very modest EBITDA growth over the next couple of years, we believe this could occur if Verizon commits to using excess cash flow for debt reduction. An upgrade would also need to be accompanied by growth in wireless revenue and a commitment to maintaining leverage below 2.5x longer term.

S&P Global Ratings cites Verizon's size, strong market position, greater profitability than its peers, and its consistent and transparent financial policy as contributory factors in its credit rating. Constraining the credit rating are the maturity of the industry (which limits growth potential), possible increases in competition, and uncertain costs of future licenses. S&P Global Ratings concludes with its expectation that Verizon will continue in its stated objective to reduce debt.

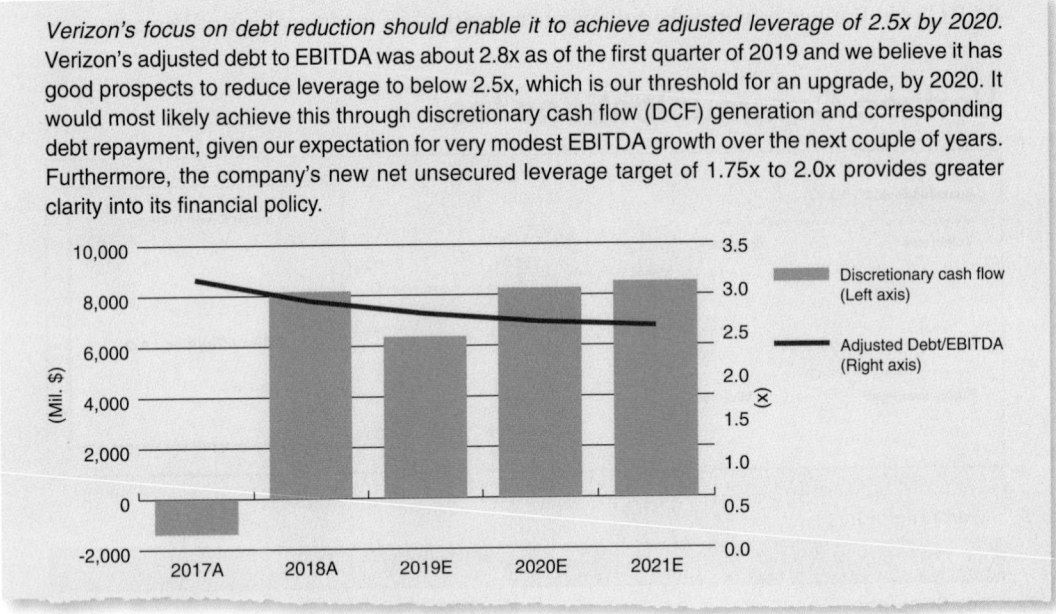

Verizon's focus on debt reduction should enable it to achieve adjusted leverage of 2.5x by 2020. Verizon's adjusted debt to EBITDA was about 2.8x as of the first quarter of 2019 and we believe it has good prospects to reduce leverage to below 2.5x, which is our threshold for an upgrade, by 2020. It would most likely achieve this through discretionary cash flow (DCF) generation and corresponding debt repayment, given our expectation for very modest EBITDA growth over the next couple of years. Furthermore, the company's new net unsecured leverage target of 1.75x to 2.0x provides greater clarity into its financial policy.

Why Credit Ratings Matter

Credit raters seek to estimate the relative probability that the company will default on its debt obligations (compared with companies in other credit ratings categories). As its credit ratings deteriorate, a company is more likely to be unable to make its debt payments and, consequently, it must pay a higher rate of interest on its borrowings to compensate investors for the risk of default.

So, how good are credit ratings at predicting defaults? Moody's provides the following graphic that illustrates the default rates for each ratings category five years into the future.

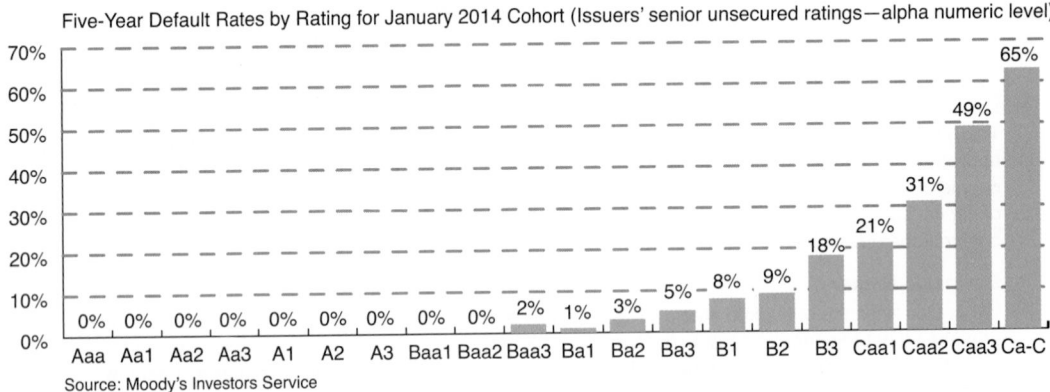

Five-Year Default Rates by Rating for January 2014 Cohort (Issuers' senior unsecured ratings—alpha numeric level)

Source: Moody's Investors Service

The forecast of default rates for 10 years after the initial rating is similar, and Moody's summarizes its findings as follows.

The five-year performance of Moody's January 2014 ratings was also strong. Five-year cumulative default rates through December 2018 by rating category increase moving down the rating scale, which shows that our ratings provided a strong rank-ordering of credit risk. Over the five-year period from January 2014 through December 2018, 291 issuers defaulted that had ratings outstanding at

continued

continued from previous page

the beginning of the period. Of these defaulters, 262 (90%) had a rating of B3 or lower one year prior to default, indicating that the ratings provided strong advance warning of default. None of the 291 defaulters had investment-grade ratings one year before default and only five had ratings higher than B1.

In Exhibit 7.3, we identify Baa as the lowest investment grade security, and the graphic above provides corroborating evidence. Below Baa2, the probability of a default begins to increase. On balance, the ratings methodologies used by S&P Global Ratings, Moody's, and Fitch are quite thorough and have a good track record of predicting default rates far into the future.

Managerial Decision ■ You Are the Vice President of Finance

Your company is currently rated B1/B+ by the Moody's and S&P Global Ratings credit rating agencies, respectively. You are considering restructuring to increase your company's credit rating. What types of restructurings might you consider? What benefits will your company receive from those restructurings? What costs will your company incur to implement such restructurings? [Answer, p. 7-32]

LO5 Review 7-5

Assume that Comcast's financial statements for the current period yield the following ratios.

Operating margin	14.2%	FFO/Debt	32.9%
Debt/EBITDA	2.1	EBITA/Interest Expense	3.9

Required

Using the four measures above for Comcast, infer a reasonable credit rating for Comcast.

Solution on p. 7-51.

Global Accounting

The FASB and the IASB have worked on a number of joint projects and the differences in accounting for liabilities are limited. We list here some differences that we encounter in studying IFRS financial statements and the implications for comparing GAAP and IFRS companies.

IFRS

■ Under U.S. GAAP, if a contingent liability is probable *and* if it can be reasonably estimated, it must be accrued. Under IFRS, companies can limit disclosure of contingent liabilities if doing so would severely prejudice the entity's competitive or legal position; for example, disclosing the amount of a potential loss on a lawsuit could sway the legal outcome. Accordingly, IFRS likely yields less disclosure of contingencies.

■ Accruals sometimes involve a range of estimates. If all amounts within the range are equally probable, U.S. GAAP requires the company to accrue the lowest number in the range whereas IFRS requires the company to accrue the expected amount. Also, contingencies are discounted under IFRS whereas U.S. GAAP records contingencies at their nominal value. For both of these reasons, contingent liabilities are likely smaller under U.S. GAAP.

■ IFRS offers more disclosure of liabilities and accruals. For each IFRS provision (the term used for accrued liabilities and expenses), the company must reconcile the opening and closing carrying amounts, describe any additional provision for the period, and explain any reversals for the period. Reconciliation is less prevalent under U.S. GAAP (required for example for allowance for doubtful accounts, warranty accruals, restructuring accruals). Recall that an over-accrual in one period shifts income to a subsequent period when the accrual is reversed. This increased transparency under IFRS might make it easier to spot earnings management.

Appendix 7A: Time Value of Money

LO6
Apply time value of money concepts.

This appendix explains the time value of money, which includes the concepts of present and future value. Time value of money concepts are important for pricing long-term bonds and notes, understanding the accounting for debt and other analysis purposes.

Present Value Concepts

Would you rather receive a dollar now or a dollar one year from now? Most people would answer a dollar now. Intuition tells us that a dollar received now is more valuable than the same amount received sometime in the future. Sound reasons exist for choosing the dollar now, the most obvious of which concerns risk. Because the future is uncertain, any number of events can prevent us from receiving the dollar a year from now. To avoid this risk, we choose the earlier date. Another reason is that the dollar received now could be invested. That is, one year from now, we would have the dollar and the interest earned on that dollar.

Present Value of a Single Amount

Risk and interest factors yield the following generalizations: (1) the right to receive an amount of money now, its **present value**, is worth more than the right to receive the same amount later, its **future value**; (2) the longer we must wait to receive an amount, the less attractive the receipt is; (3) the greater the interest rate the greater the amount we will receive in the future. (Putting 2 and 3 together we see that the difference between the present value of an amount and its future value is a function of both interest rate and time, that is, Principal × Interest Rate × Time); and (4) the more risk associated with any situation, the higher the interest rate.

To illustrate, let's compute the amount we would need to receive today (the present value) that would be equivalent to receiving $100 one year from now if money can be invested at 10%. We recognize intuitively that, with a 10% interest rate, the present value (the equivalent amount today) will be less than $100. The $100 received in the future must include 10% interest earned for the year. Thus, the $100 received in one year (the future value) must be 1.10 times the amount received today (the present value). Dividing $100/1.10, we obtain a present value of $90.91 (rounded). This means that we would do as well to accept $90.91 today as to wait one year and receive $100. To confirm the equality of the $90.91 receipt now to a $100 receipt one year later, we calculate the future value of $90.91 at 10% for one year as follows.

$$\$90.91 \times 1.10 \times 1 \text{ year} = \$100 \text{ (rounded)}$$

To generalize, we compute the present value of a future receipt by *discounting* the future receipt back to the present at an appropriate interest rate (also called the *discount rate*). We present this schematically below.

Present Value ← | Discounted for 1 year at 10% | ← Future Value
$90.91 $100

If either the time period or the interest rate were increased, the resulting present value would decrease. If more than one time period is involved, our future receipts include interest on interest. This is called *compounding*.

Time Value of Money Tables

Appendix A near the end of the book includes time value of money tables. Table 1 is a present value table that we can use to compute the present value of future amounts. A present value table provides present value factors (multipliers) for many combinations of time periods and interest rates that determine the present value of $1.

Present value tables are used as follows. First, determine the number of interest compounding periods involved (three years compounded annually are 3 periods, and three years compounded semiannually are 6 periods). The extreme left-hand column indicates the number of periods. It is important to distinguish between years and compounding periods. The table is for compounding periods (years × number of compounding periods per year).

Next, determine the interest rate per compounding period. Interest rates are usually quoted on a *per year* (annual) basis. The rate per compounding period is the annual rate divided by the number of compounding periods per year. For example, an interest rate of 10% *per year* would be 10% per period if compounded annually, and 5% *per period* if compounded semiannually.

Finally, locate the present value factor, which is at the intersection of the row of the appropriate number of compounding periods and the column of the appropriate interest rate per compounding period. Multiply this factor by the dollars that will be paid or received in the future.

All values in Table 1 are less than 1.0 because the present value of $1 received in the future is always smaller than $1. As the interest rate increases (moving from left to right in the table) or the number of periods increases (moving from top to bottom), the present value factors decline. This illustrates two important facts: (1) present values decline as interest rates increase, and (2) present values decline as the time lengthens. Consider the following three cases.

Case 1. Compute the present value of $100 to be received one year from today, discounted at 10% compounded semiannually.

Number of periods (one year, semiannually) = 2
Rate per period (10%/2) = 5%
Multiplier = 0.90703
Present value = $100.00 × 0.90703 = $90.70 (rounded)

Calculator
N = 2
I/Yr = 5
PMT = 0
FV = 100

PV = −90.70

	A	B
1	Discount Rate (rate)	5%
2	Number of Periods (nper)	2
3	Annuity (pmt)	0
4	Future value (fv)	100
5	Present value (pv)	(90.70)
6	= PV(B1,B2,B3,B4)	
7	= (90.70)	

Case 2. Compute the present value of $100 to be received two years from today, discounted at 10% compounded semiannually.

Number of periods (two years, semiannually) = 4
Rate per period (10%/2) = 5%
Multiplier = 0.82270
Present value = $100 × 0.82270 = $82.27 (rounded)

Calculator
N = 4
I/Yr = 5
PMT = 0
FV = 100

PV = −82.27

	A	B
1	Discount Rate (rate)	5%
2	Number of periods (nper)	4
3	Annuity (pmt)	0
4	Future value (fv)	100
5	Present value (pv)	(82.27)
6	= PV(B1,B2,B3,B4)	
7	= (82.27)	

Case 3. Compute the present value of $100 to be received two years from today, discounted at 12% compounded semiannually.

Number of periods (two years, semiannually) = 4
Rate per period (12%/2) = 6%
Multiplier = 0.79209
Present value = $100 = 0.79209 = $79.21 (rounded)

Calculator
N = 4
I/Yr = 6
PMT = 0
FV = 100

PV = −79.21

	A	B
1	Discount Rate (rate)	6%
2	Number of Periods (nper)	4
3	Annuity (pmt)	0
4	Future value (fv)	100
5	Present value (pv)	(79.21)
6	= PV(B1,B2,B3,B4)	
7	= (79.21)	

In Case 2, the present value of $82.27 is less than in Case 1 ($90.70) because the time increased from two to four compounding periods—the longer we must wait for money, the lower its value to us today. Then in Case 3, the present value of $79.21 was lower than in Case 2 because, while there were still four compounding periods, the interest rate per year was higher (12% annually instead of 10%)—the higher the interest rate the more interest that could have been earned on the money and therefore the lower the value today.

Present Value of an Annuity

In the examples above, we computed the present value of a single amount (also called a lump sum) made or received in the future. Often, future cash flows involve the same amount being paid or received each period. Examples include semiannual interest payments on bonds, quarterly dividend receipts, or monthly insurance premiums. If the payment or the receipt (the cash flow) is equally spaced over time and each cash flow is the same dollar amount, we have an *annuity*. One way to calculate the present value of the annuity would be to calculate the present value of each future cash flow separately. However, there is a more convenient method.

To illustrate, assume $100 is to be received at the end of each of the next three years as an annuity. When annuity amounts occur at the *end of each period*, the annuity is called an *ordinary annuity*. As shown below, the present value of this ordinary annuity can be computed from Table 1 by computing the present value of each of the three individual receipts and summing them (assume a 5% annual rate).

Future Receipts (ordinary annuity)			PV Multiplier (Table 1)		Present Value
Year 1	Year 2	Year 3			
$100			× 0.95238	=	$ 95.24
	$100		× 0.90703	=	90.70
		$100	× 0.86384	=	86.38
			2.72325		$272.32

Calculator
N = 3
I/Yr = 5
PMT = 100
FV = 0

PV = −272.32

	A	B
1	Discount Rate (rate)	5%
2	Number of Periods (nper)	3
3	Annuity (pmt)	100
4	Future value (fv)	0
5	Present value (pv)	(272.32)
6	= PV(B1,B2,B3,B4)	
7	= (272.32)	

Table 2 in Appendix A provides a single multiplier for computing the present value of an ordinary annuity. Referring to Table 2 in the row for three periods and the column for 5%, we see that the multiplier is 2.72325. When applied to the $100 annuity amount, the multiplier gives a present value of $272.33. As shown above, the same present value (with 1 cent rounding error) is derived by summing the three separate multipliers from Table 1. Considerable computations are avoided by using annuity tables.

Bond Valuation

Recall that a bond agreement specifies a pattern of future cash flows—usually a series of interest payments (cash outflow) and a single payment of the face amount at maturity (cash outflow), and bonds are priced using the prevailing market rate on the day the bond is sold (cash inflow). This is the case for the original bond issuance and for subsequent open-market sales. The market rate on the date of the sale is the rate we use to determine the bond's market value (its price). That rate is the bond's *yield*. The selling price of a bond is determined as follows.

1. Use Table 1 to compute the present value of the future principal payment at the prevailing market rate.
2. Use Table 2 to compute the present value of the future series of interest payments (the annuity) at the prevailing market rate.
3. Add the present values from steps 1 and 2.

We illustrate in Exhibit 7A.1 the price of $100,000, 8%, four-year bonds paying interest semiannually and sold when the prevailing market rate was (1) 8%, (2) 10%, or (3) 6%. Note that the price of 8% bonds sold to yield 8% is the face (or par) value of the bonds. A bond issue price of $93,537 (discount bond) yields 10%. A bond issue price of $107,020 (premium bond) yields 6%.

Calculator
N = 8
I/Yr = 4
PMT = −4,000
FV = −100,000

PV = 100,000

X	A	B
1	Annual coupon rate	8%
2	Annual market rate	8%
3	Interest payments per year	2
4	Years to maturity	4
5	Face (par) value	100,000
6	Issue price	100,000
7	= PV(B2/B3,B4*B3,−B5*B1/B3,−B5, 0)	
8	= 100,000	

Calculator
N = 8
I/Yr = 5
PMT = −4,000
FV = −100,000

PV = 93,537

X	A	B
1	Annual coupon rate	8%
2	Annual market rate	10%
3	Interest payments per year	2
4	Years to maturity	4
5	Face (par) value	100,000
6	Issue price	93,537
7	= PV(B2/B3,B4*B3,−B5*B1/B3,−B5, 0)	
8	= 93,537	

Calculator
N = 8
I/Yr = 3
PMT = −4,000
FV = −100,000

PV = 107,020

X	A	B
1	Annual coupon rate	8%
2	Annual market rate	6%
3	Interest payments per year	2
4	Years to maturity	4
5	Face (par) value	100,000
6	Issue price	107,020
7	= PV(B2/B3,B4*B3,−B5*B1/B3,−B5, 0)	
8	= 107,020	

Exhibit 7A.1 ■ Calculation of Bond Price Using Present Value Tables

Future Cash Flows	Multiplier (Table 1)	Multiplier (Table 2)	Present Values at 4% Semiannually
(1) $100,000 of 8%, 4-year bonds with interest payable semiannually priced to yield 8%.			
Principal payment, $100,000 (a single amount received after 8 semiannual periods)	0.73069		$ 73,069
Interest payments, $4,000 at end of each of 8 semiannual periods		6.73274	26,931
Present value (issue price) of bonds			$100,000

Future Cash Flows	Multiplier (Table 1)	Multiplier (Table 2)	Present Values at 5% Semiannually
(2) $100,000 of 8%, 4-year bonds with interest payable semiannually priced to yield 10%.			
Principal payment, $100,000 (a single amount received after 8 semiannual periods)	0.67684		$ 67,684
Interest payments, $4,000 at end of each of 8 semiannual periods		6.46321	25,853
Present value (issue price) of bonds			$ 93,537

Future Cash Flows	Multiplier (Table 1)	Multiplier (Table 2)	Present Values at 3% Semiannually
(3) $100,000 of 8%, 4-year bonds with interest payable semiannually priced to yield 6%.			
Principal repayment, $100,000 (a single amount received after 8 semiannual periods)	0.78941		$ 78,941
Interest payments, $4,000 at end of each of 8 semiannual periods		7.01969	28,079
Present value (issue price) of bonds			$107,020

Time Value of Money Computations Using a Calculator

We can use a financial calculator for time value of money computations. There are five important function keys for these calculations. If we know values for four of those five, the calculator will compute the fifth. Those function keys are:

N	Number of compounding (or discounting) periods
I/Yr	Interest (yield) rate per period—entered in % terms, for example, 12% is entered as 12 and not as 0.12. This key is labeled "interest per year" but it can handle any rate per different compounding periods; for example, if we have semiannual interest payments, our compounding periods are semiannual and the interest rate is the semiannual rate.
FV	Future value of the cash flows; this is a lump sum
PMT	Annuity (coupon) per discount period
PV	Present value of the cash flows; this is a lump sum

Calculator inputs follow for the three examples in Exhibit 7A.1. In these examples, the unknown value is the bond price, which is the present value (PV) of the bond's cash flows. (For additional instruction on entering inputs into a specific calculator, or how to do more complicated computations, review the calculator's user manual or review online calculator tutorials.)

A note about positive and negative signs for variables.   Financial calculators use a convention to capture the direction of cash flows. This can be understood by thinking about the direction of the cash flows from the company's perspective. Consider the examples in Exhibit 7A.1. The unknown value is the bond proceeds, the present value. From the perspective of the company, the interest payment is a cash outflow. We enter this in the calculator as a negative. Again, from the company's perspective, the cash paid to investors when the bond matures is a cash outflow (negative in the calculator). With both PMT and FV entered as negative numbers, the calculator returns a positive number—this can be understood as a cash inflow to the company. As long as we are consistent in the sign of our variables and we understand the calculator convention, we can interpret the result from the calculator. For example, if we enter PMT and FV as positive numbers, the PV returned is a negative number. (This would be considering cash flows from the investor's perspective.) Yet, be careful; if we enter PMT and FV with opposite signs, the result is nonsensical.

Example (1), Exhibit 7A.1: Bond priced to yield 8%.

N	=	8 (4 years × 2 periods per year = 8 semiannual periods)
I/Yr	=	4 (8% annual yield ÷ 2 periods per year = 4% semiannually)
FV	=	−100,000 (face value, which is the lump sum that must be repaid in the future, a cash outflow)
PMT	=	−4,000 ($100,000 × 4% semiannual coupon rate, a cash outflow)
PV	= 100,000	(output obtained from calculator)

Example (2), Exhibit 7A.1: Bond priced to yield 10%.

N = 8   I/Yr = 5   FV = −100,000   PMT = −4,000   PV = 93,537

Example (3), Exhibit 7A.1: Bond priced to yield 6%.

N = 8   I/Yr = 3   FV = −100,000   PMT = −4,000   PV = 107,020

Time Value of Money Computations Using Excel

We can use Excel or other spreadsheet software, to perform time value of money calculations. There are a number of functions for time value of money, but all of them involve the same six variables, which are:

rate	Interest (yield) rate per period, entered as either a percent (4%) or as a number 0.04. The variable is labeled rate and should be understood to mean per period; if we have semiannual interest payments, our compounding periods are semiannual and the interest rate is the semiannual rate

continued

continued from previous page

nper	Number of compounding or discounting periods
pmt	Annuity per discounting or compounding period; if there is no annuity, enter 0
pv	Present value of the cash flow; this is a lump sum
fv	Future value of the cash flow; this is a lump sum
type	Timing of the annuity payment, this is a 0 or 1 variable; if the annuity is paid at the end of each compounding period (as for interest payments), then type =0; if the annuity is paid at the beginning of each compounding period, then type =1 (type = 0 is the default value in Excel)

The Excel functions for present value and future value are as follows.

$$= \textbf{pv(rate,nper,pmt,fv,type)}$$

$$= \textbf{fv(rate,nper,pmt,pv,type)}$$

Unlike for a calculator, the variables must be entered in the correct order. Yet, once we open the bracket in the function, Excel prompts us for the variables in order. Similar to the calculator, Excel maintains the convention for positive and negative cash flows.

Example (1), Exhibit 7A.1: Bond priced to yield 8%.

rate	=	4% (8%/2 compounding periods = 4% semiannually)
nper	=	8 (4 years × 2 compounding periods = 8 semiannual periods)
pmt	=	−4,000 ($100,000 × 4% semiannual interest rate); this is a cash outflow so we enter a negative value
fv	=	−100,000 face value, which is the lump sum to be repaid in the future; this is a cash outflow so we enter a negative value
type	=	0 because interest is paid at the end of each semiannual period
	=	PV(rate,nper,pmt,fv,type)
	=	PV(4%, 8, −4000, −100000, 0) = 100,000

Example (2), Exhibit 7A.1: Bond priced to yield 10%.

= PV(5%, 8, −4000, −100000, 0) = 93,537

Example (3), Exhibit 7A.1: Bond priced to yield 6%.

= PV(3%, 8, −4000, −100000, 0) = 107,020

Excel is more powerful than a calculator because we can use cell addresses for the variables. For example, consider the three examples in Exhibit 7A.1 that could be defined as follows.

X	A	B
1	Annual coupon rate	8%
2	Annual market rate	8%
3	Interest payments per year	2
4	Years to maturity	4
5	Face (par) value	100,000
6	Annuity type	0
7	Issue price	100,000
8	= PV(B2/B3,B4*B3,−B5*B1/B3,−B5, B6)	
9	= 100,000	

The value in cell B7 is 100,000. By changing cell B2 to 10%, the present value in B7 immediately changes to $93,537 and then when B2 is set to 6%, cell B7 displays $107,020.

Future Value Concepts

Future Value of a Single Amount

The **future value** of a single sum is the amount that a specific investment is worth at a future date if invested at a given rate of compound interest. To illustrate, suppose that we decide to invest $6,000 in a savings account that pays 6% annual interest and we intend to leave the principal and interest in the account for five years. We assume that interest is credited to the account at the end of each year. The balance in the account at the end of five years is determined using Table 3 in Appendix A, which gives the future value of a dollar, as follows.

$$\text{Principal} \times \text{Factor} = \text{Future Value}$$
$$\$6,000 \times 1.33823 = \$8,029$$

Calculator
N = 5
I/Yr = 6
PMT = 0
PV = −6,000
FV = 8,029.35

X	A	B
1	Discount Rate (rate)	6%
2	Number of Periods (nper)	5
3	Annuity (pmt)	0
4	Present value (pv)	−6,000
5	Future value (fv)	8,029.35
6	= FV(B1,B2,B3,B4)	
7	= 8,029.35	

The factor 1.33823 is at the intersection of the row for five periods and the column for 6%.

Next, suppose that the interest is credited to the account semiannually rather than annually. In this situation, there are 10 compounding periods, and we use a 3% semiannual rate (one-half the annual rate because there are two compounding periods per year). The future value calculation follows.

$$\text{Principal} \times \text{Factor} = \text{Future Value}$$
$$\$6,000 \times 1.34392 = \$8,064$$

Calculator
N = 10
I/Yr = 3
PMT = 0
PV = −6,000
FV = 8,063.50

X	A	B
1	Discount Rate (rate)	3%
2	Number of Periods (nper)	10
3	Annuity (pmt)	0
4	Present value (pv)	−6,000
5	Future value (fv)	8,063.50
6	= FV(B1,B2,B3,B4)	
7	= 8,063.50	

Future Value of an Annuity

If, instead of investing a single amount, we invest a specified amount *each period,* then we have an annuity. To illustrate, assume that we decide to invest $2,000 at the end of each year for five years at an 8% annual rate of return. To determine the accumulated amount of principal and interest at the end of five years, we refer to Table 4 in Appendix A, which furnishes the future value of a dollar invested at the end of each period. The factor 5.86660 is in the row for five periods and the column for 8%, and the calculation is as follows.

$$\text{Periodic Payment} \times \text{Factor} = \text{Future Value}$$
$$\$2,000 \times 5.86660 = \$11,733$$

Calculator
N = 5
I/Yr = 8
PMT = −2,000
PV = 0
FV = 11,733.20

X	A	B
1	Discount Rate (rate)	8%
2	Number of Periods (nper)	5
3	Annuity (pmt)	−2,000
4	Present value (pv)	0
5	Future value (fv)	11,733.20
6	= FV(B1,B2,B3,B4)	
7	= 11,733.20	

If we decide to invest $1,000 at the end of each six months for five years at an 8% annual rate of return, we would use the factor for 10 periods at 4%, as follows.

$$\text{Periodic Payment} \times \text{Factor} = \text{Future Value}$$
$$\$1,000 \times 12.00611 = \$12,006$$

LO6 Review 7-6

For each of the separate cases *a*, *b*, and *c*, compute the sale price of a $5,000, five-year bond with a 6% coupon rate (annual rate with interest paid semiannually) sold to yield an annual rate of:

a.   4%

b.   6%

c.   8%

GuidedExamples
MBC

Solution on p. 7-51.

Appendix 7B: Amortization of Debt

As we saw in Exhibit 7.2, Verizon received €1,241,637,500 when it issued the €1,250,000,000 0.875% notes due in 2027. As detailed in the prospectus, the difference of €8,362,500 has two parts: the discount of €4,612,500 (€1,250,000,000 – €1,245,387,500) and the fees paid to bankers and underwriters to sell the notes of €3,750,000. The total difference of €8,462,500 is an additional borrowing cost for Verizon, a cost over and above the 0.875% interest the company will pay in cash each year. This additional borrowing cost is expensed on the income statement over the life of the notes (from 2019 to 2027) and reported with the 0.875% cash interest that Verizon pays to its lenders. Conversely, if Verizon had sold the notes at a premium, it would have received proceeds in excess of the €1,250 million face amount and that premium would subsequently be reported as a *reduction* of interest expense over the life of the notes. The process of recognizing the discount or premium as an adjustment to interest expense is called **amortization**.

Amortization of Discount

Companies amortize discounts and premiums using the effective interest method. To illustrate, assume that **Verizon** issues bonds with a face amount of $600,000, a 3% annual coupon rate payable semiannually (1.5% semiannual rate), a maturity of three years (six semiannual payment periods), and a market (yield) rate of 4% annual (2% semiannual). These facts yield a bond issue price of $583,195.71, which we round to $583,196 for the bond discount amortization table of Exhibit 7B.1.

The interest period is denoted in the left-most column. Period 0 is the point at which the bond is issued, and period 1 and following are successive six-month periods (recall, interest is paid semiannually). Column [A] is interest expense, which is reported in the income statement. Interest expense is computed as the bond's net balance sheet value (the carrying amount of the bond) at the beginning of the period (column [E]) multiplied by the 2% semiannual rate used to compute the bond issue price. Column [B] is cash interest paid, which is a constant $9,000 per the bond contract (face amount × coupon rate). Column [C] is discount amortization, which is the difference between interest expense and cash interest paid. Column [D] is the discount balance, which is the previous balance of the discount less the discount amortization in column [C]. Column [E] is the net bond payable, which is the $600,000 face amount less the unamortized discount from column [D].

Calculator
N = 6
I/Yr = 2
PMT = –9,000
FV = –600,000

PV = 583,195.71

	A	B
1	Annual coupon rate	3%
2	Annual market rate	4%
3	Interest payments per year	2
4	Years to maturity	3
5	Face (par) value	600,000
6	Issue price	583,195.71
7	= PV(B2/B3,B4*B3,–B5*B1/B3,–B5, 0)	
8	= 583,195.71	

Exhibit 7B.1 ■ Bond Discount Amortization Table

Period	[A] ([E] × market%) Interest Expense	[B] (Face × coupon%) Cash Interest Paid	[C] ([A] – [B]) Discount Amortization	[D] (Prior bal – [C]) Discount Balance	[E] (Face – [D]) Bond Payable, Net
0				$16,804	$583,196
1	$11,664	$ 9,000	$ 2,664	14,140	585,860
2	11,717	9,000	2,717	11,423	588,577
3	11,772	9,000	2,772	8,651	591,349
4	11,827	9,000	2,827	5,824	594,176
5	11,884	9,000	2,884	2,940	597,060
6	11,940	9,000	2,940	0	600,000
	$70,804	$54,000	$16,804		

Cash paid plus discount amortization equals interest expense

During the bond life, carrying value is adjusted to par and the discount to zero

The table shows amounts for the six interest payment periods. The amortization process continues until period 6, at which time the discount balance is 0 and the net bond payable is $600,000 (the maturity value). Each semiannual period, interest expense is recorded at 2%, the market rate of interest at the bond's issuance. This rate does not change over the life of the bond, even if the prevailing market interest rates change. An amortization table reveals the financial statement effects of the bond for its duration. Specifically, we see the income statement effects in column [A], the cash effects in column [B], and the balance sheet effects in columns [D] and [E].

Amortization of Premium

To illustrate amortization of a premium bond, we assume that Verizon issues bonds with a $600,000 face value, a 3% annual coupon rate payable semiannually (1.5% semiannual rate), a maturity of three years (six semiannual interest payments), and a 2% annual (1% semiannual) market interest rate. These facts yield a bond issue price of $617,386.43, which we round to $617,386. Exhibit 7B.2 shows the premium amortization table for this bond.

Interest expense is computed using the same process that we used for discount bonds. The difference is that the yield rate is 1% semiannual in the premium case. Cash interest paid follows from the bond contract (face amount × coupon rate), and the other columns' computations reflect the premium amortization. After period 6, the premium is fully amortized (equals zero) and the net bond payable balance is $600,000, the amount owed at maturity. Again, an amortization table reveals the financial statement effects of the bond—the income statement effects in column [A], the cash effects in column [B], and the balance sheet effects in columns [D] and [E].

Calculator
N = 6
I/Yr = 1
PMT = −9,000
FV = −600,000

PV = 617,386.43

	A	B
1	Annual coupon rate	3%
2	Annual market rate	2%
3	Interest payments per year	2
4	Years to maturity	3
5	Face (par) value	600,000
6	Issue price	617,386.43
7	= PV(B2/B3,B4*B3,−B5*B1/B3,−B5, 0)	
8	= 617,386.43	

Exhibit 7B.2 ■ Bond Premium Amortization Table

Period	[A] ([E] × market%) Interest Expense	[B] (Face × coupon%) Cash Interest Paid	[C] ([B] − [A]) Premium Amortization	[D] (Prior bal − [C]) Premium Balance	[E] (Face + [D]) Bond Payable, Net
0				$17,386	$617,386
1	$ 6,174	$ 9,000	$ 2,826	14,560	614,560
2	6,146	9,000	2,854	11,706	611,706
3	6,117	9,000	2,883	8,823	608,823
4	6,088	9,000	2,912	5,911	605,911
5	6,059	9,000	2,941	2,970	602,970
6	6,030	9,000	2,970	0	600,000
	$36,614	$54,000	$17,386		

During the bond life, carrying value is adjusted to par and the premium to zero

Cash paid less premium amortization equals interest expense

Guidance Answers

You Are the Vice President of Finance

Pg. 7-24 You might consider the types of restructuring that would strengthen financial ratios typically used to assess liquidity and solvency by the rating agencies. Such restructuring includes generating cash by reducing inventory, reallocating cash outflows from investing activities (PPE) to debt reduction, and issuing stock for cash and using the proceeds to reduce debt (an equity for debt recapitalization). These actions increase liquidity or reduce financial leverage and, thus, should improve debt rating. An improved debt rating will attract more investors because your current debt rating is below investment grade and is not a suitable investment for many professionally managed portfolios. An improved debt rating will also lower the interest rate on your debt. Offsetting these benefits are costs such as the following: (1) potential loss of sales from inventory stock-outs; (2) potential future cash flow reductions and loss of market power from reduced PPE investments; and (3) costs of equity issuances (equity costs more than debt because investors demand a higher return to compensate for added risk and, unlike interest payments, dividends are not tax deductible for the company), which can yield a net increase in the total cost of capital. All cost and benefits must be assessed before you pursue any restructuring.

Questions

Q7-1. What does the term *current liabilities* mean? What assets are usually used to settle current liabilities?

Q7-2. What is an accrual? How do accruals impact the balance sheet and the income statement?

Q7-3. What is the difference between a bond's coupon rate and its market interest rate (yield)?

Q7-4. Why do companies report a gain or loss when they repurchase their bonds? Is this a real economic gain or loss?

Q7-5. How do credit (debt) ratings affect the cost of borrowing for a company?

Q7-6. How would you interpret a company's reported gain or loss on the repurchase of its bonds?

Assignments with the ⬤ logo in the margin are available in ᵐʸBusinessCourse.
See the Preface of the book for details.

Mini Exercises

LO1
NCI Building Systems
(NCS)

M7-7. **Interpreting a Contingent Liability Footnote**

NCI Building Systems reports the following footnote to one of its recent 10-Ks related to its manufacturing of metal coil coatings and metal building components.

> We have discovered the existence of trichloroethylene in the ground water at our Southlake, Texas facility. Horizontal delineation concentrations in excess of applicable residential assessment levels have not been fully identified. We have filed an application with the Texas Commission of Environmental Quality ("TCEQ") for entry into the voluntary cleanup program. The cost of required remediation, if any, will vary depending on the nature and extent of the contamination. As of October 28, we have accrued $0.1 million to complete site analysis and testing. At this time, we cannot estimate a loss for any potential remediation costs, but we do not believe there will be a material adverse effect on our Consolidated Financial Statements.

a. How has NCI reported this potential liability on its balance sheet?

b. Does the $0.1 million accrual "to complete site analysis and testing" relate to a contingent liability? Explain.

LO2

M7-8. **Analyzing and Computing Financial Statement Effects of Interest**

Leahy Inc. signed a 90-day, 8% note payable for $13,800 on December 16. Use the financial statement effects template to illustrate the year-end December 31 accounting adjustment Leahy must make.

LO1

M7-9. **Analyzing and Determining Liability Amounts**

For each of the following situations, indicate the liability amount, if any, that is reported on the balance sheet of Bloomington Inc. at December 31, 2019.

a. Bloomington owes $220,000 at year-end 2019 for inventory purchases.

b. Bloomington agreed to purchase a $28,000 drill press in January 2020.

c. During November and December of 2019, Bloomington sold products to a customer and warranted them against product failure for 90 days. Estimated costs of honoring this 90-day warranty during 2020 are $3,100.

d. Bloomington provides a profit-sharing bonus for its executives equal to 5% of reported pretax annual income. The estimated pretax income for 2019 is $800,000. Bonuses are not paid until January of the following year.

LO3, 5
Citigroup Inc.
(C)

M7-10. **Interpreting Relations among Bond Price, Coupon, Yield, and Credit Rating**

The following appeared in **Markets Insider** (https://markets.businessinsider.com/bonds) regarding outstanding bonds issued by Citigroup Inc.

Price	Coupon (%)	Maturity	Yield to Maturity (%)	Moody's Ratings
166.43	6.80	2038	2.40	A3
122.70	5.15	2026	1.59	A3

a. Discuss the relation among the coupon rate, price, and yield for the bond maturing in 2038.

b. Compare the yields on the two bonds. Why are the yields different when the credit ratings are the same?

M7-11. Determining Gain or Loss on Bond Redemption

On April 30, one year before maturity, Middleton Company retired $200,000 of its 9% bonds payable at the current market price of 101 (101% of the bond face amount, or $200,000 × 1.01= $202,000). The bond book value on April 30 is $196,600, reflecting an unamortized discount of $3,400. Bond interest is currently fully paid and recorded up to the date of retirement. What is the gain or loss on retirement of these bonds? Is this gain or loss a real economic gain or loss? Explain.

LO4

M7-12. Interpreting Bond Footnote Disclosures

Marriott International reports the following long-term debt as part of its MD&A in its 2018 10-K.

LO4
Marriott International Inc. (MAR)

Maturity Date	Obligations Expiring by Period ($ millions)						
	Total	2019	2020	2021	2022	2023	Later Years
Long-term debt.	$9,347	$833	$912	$3,108	$1,114	$695	$2,685

a. What does this information indicate about Marriott's future payment obligations for 2019 through 2021?

b. What implications does this payment schedule have for our evaluation of Marriott's liquidity and solvency?

M7-13. Classifying Liability-Related Accounts as Balance Sheet or Income Statement Items

Indicate the proper financial statement classification (balance sheet or income statement) for each of the following liability-related accounts.

LO1, 4

a. Gain on Bond Retirement
b. Discount on Bonds Payable
c. Mortgage Notes Payable
d. Bonds Payable

e. Bond Interest Expense
f. Bond Interest Payable (due next period)
g. Premium on Bonds Payable
h. Loss on Bond Retirement

M7-14. Interpreting Bond Footnote Disclosures

Netflix reports the following information from the Management Discussion and Analysis section of its 2018 10-K.

LO4
Netflix Inc. (NFLX)

> The Notes include, among other terms and conditions, limitations on the Company's ability to create, incur or allow certain liens; enter into sale and lease-back transactions; create, assume, incur or guarantee additional indebtedness of certain of the Company's subsidiaries; and consolidate or merge with, or convey, transfer or lease all or substantially all of the Company's and its subsidiaries assets, to another person. As of December 31, 2018 and December 31, 2017, the Company was in compliance with all related covenants.

a. The operating and financing restrictions that Netflix reports are similar to those discussed in the section on credit ratings and the cost of debt. What effects might these covenants have on the degree of freedom that management has in running Netflix?

b. What pressures might management face if the company's ratios are near covenant limits?

M7-15. Analyzing Financial Statement Effects of Bond Redemption

Weiss Corporation issued $600,000 of 10%, 20-year bonds at 106 on January 1, 2015. Interest is payable semiannually on June 30 and December 31. Through January 1, 2020, Weiss amortized $10,000 of the bond premium. On January 1, 2020, Weiss retired the bonds at 103. Use the financial statement effects template to illustrate the bond retirement at January 1, 2020.

LO4

M7-16. Analyzing Financial Statement Effects of Bond Redemption

Camden Inc. issued $450,000 of 8%, 15-year bonds at 96 on July 1, 2015. Interest is payable semiannually on December 31 and June 30. Through June 30, 2020, Camden amortized $6,000 of the bond discount. On July 1, 2020, Camden retired the bonds at 101. Use the financial statement effects template to record the bond retirement.

LO4

LO2

M7-17. Analyzing and Computing Accrued Interest on Notes

During the current year, Penman Inc. issued three short-term notes payable with principal and interest due at the end of the term of the note. Compute interest accrued for each of the notes payable as of December 31 of the current year (assume a 365-day year).

Lender	Issuance Date	Principal	Interest Rate (%)	Term
Nissim......	11/21	$30,000	10%	120 days
Klein.......	12/13	22,000	8	90 days
Bildersee....	12/19	26,000	6	60 days

LO5

KLA-Tencor (KLAC)

M7-18. Interpreting Credit Ratings

KLA-Tencor reports the following information in the Management Discussion & Analysis section of its 2018 10-K report.

Our credit ratings as of June 30, 2018 are summarized below:

Credit Rating Agency	Rating
Fitch......................................	BBB+
Moody's...................................	Baa+
Standard & Poor's.........................	BBB

Factors that can affect our credit ratings include changes in our operating performance, the economic environment, conditions in the semiconductor and semiconductor equipment industries, business acquisitions, our financial position and changes in our business strategy.

a. Is KLA-Tencor above or below investment grade? *Hint:* See Exhibit 7.3.
b. KLA-Tencor has reduced the level of its financial leverage over the past several years. How does the reduction in financial leverage likely affect the company's credit ratings?
c. What effect will less financial leverage have on the company's borrowing costs? Explain.

LO3, 6

M7-19. Computing Bond Issue Price

Abbington Inc. issues $700,000 of 9% bonds that pay interest semiannually and mature in 10 years. Compute the bond issue price assuming that the prevailing market rate of interest is:

a. 8% per year compounded semiannually.
b. 10% per year compounded semiannually.

LO3, 6

M7-20. Computing Issue Price for Zero Coupon Bonds

Underwood Inc. issues $350,000 of zero coupon bonds that mature in 10 years. Compute the bond issue price assuming that the bonds' market rate is:

a. 8% per year compounded semiannually.
b. 10% per year compounded semiannually.

LO1

M7-21. Determining the Financial Statement Effects of Accounts Payable Transactions

Hobson Company had the following transactions relating to its accounts payable. Use the financial statement effects template to identify the effects (both amounts and accounts) for these transactions.

a. Purchases $1,260 of inventory on credit.
b. Sells inventory for $1,650 on credit.
c. Records $1,260 cost of sales for transaction *b*.
d. Receives $1,650 cash toward accounts receivable.
e. Pays $1,260 cash to settle accounts payable.

LO3, 4, 6

M7-22. Computing Bond Issue Price and Preparing an Amortization Table in Excel

On January 1, 2021, Springfield Inc. issues $400,000 of 8% bonds that pay interest semiannually and mature in 10 years (December 31, 2030).

a. Using the Excel PRICE function, compute the issue price assuming that the bonds' market rate is 7% per year compounded semiannually. (Use 100 for the redemption value to get a price as a percentage of the face amount, and use 1 for the basis.)
b. Prepare an amortization table in Excel to demonstrate the amortization of the book (carrying) value to the $400,000 maturity value at the end of the 20th semiannual period.

M7-23. **Determining Credit Ratings**

The chart below shows financial ratios for three companies. Use the data, along with Exhibit 7.4 to determine a bond rating for each of the three companies below.

	EBITA/ Average Assets	Operating Margin	EBITA Margin	EBITA/ Interest Expense	(FFO + Int Exp)/ Int Exp	Debt/ EBITDA	DEBT/ Book Capital- ization	FFO/ Debt	Retained Cash Flow/Net Debt	CAPEX/ Depre- ciation	Revenue Volatility
Company 1..	12.80%	16.30%	18.82%	15.0	13.4	1.6	38.12%	44.72%	37.64%	1.3	10.1
Company 2..	9.20%	11.40%	13.00%	2.8	5.1	3.3	48.60%	21.73%	21.92%	1.2	16.0
Company 3..	13.87%	18.62%	20.76%	22.2	20.5	1.3	39.87%	60.82%	32.79%	1.3	6.3

M7-24. **Applying Time Value of Money Concepts**

Complete the missing information in the table below. Assume that all bonds pay interest semiannually.

	Annual Yield	Years to Maturity	Coupon Rate	Face Value	Issue Proceeds
Firm 1 . . .	8.00%	15	7.00%	$ 300,000	?
Firm 2 . . .	3.00%	10	0.00%	?	$ 556,853
Firm 3 . . .	6.50%	?	5.00%	$ 500,000	$ 468,416
Firm 4 . . .	?	12	3.50%	$1,000,000	$1,147,822
Firm 5 . . .	0.80%	20	2.00%	$ 500,000	?

M7-25. **Applying Time Value of Money Concepts**

Ozona Minerals issued bonds that mature in 10 years. As is typical for bonds, Ozona Minerals must pay interest only on the $250 million face value. As part of the bond indenture, Ozona Minerals must make annual payments to a sinking fund, which is a pool of money set aside to help repay the bond issue. The sinking fund must be equal to 50% of the face value of the bonds in 10 years (at maturity). If Ozona Minerals can invest at 5%, what amount must the company add to the sinking fund each year to comply with the sinking fund requirement?

M7-26. **Calculating Gains and Losses on Early Retirement of Debt**

The data below pertain to bonds outstanding at 2020 year-end. For each of the following outstanding bonds, determine whether the company would record a gain or a loss if it decided to retire the bonds at the end of fiscal 2020. Calculate the amount of gain or loss.

	Face Value	Premium (Discount)	Fair Value
Firm 1	$ 450,000	$42,300	$502,189
Firm 2	1,000,000	(69,034)	947,482
Firm 3	250,000	—	244,893
Firm 4	500,000	2,033	498,574

Exercises

E7-27. **Analyzing and Computing Accrued Warranty Liability and Expense**

Canton Company sells a motor that carries a 60-day unconditional warranty against product failure. From prior years' experience, Canton estimates that 3% of units sold each period will require repair at an average cost of $160 per unit. During the current period, Canton sold 100,000 units and repaired 2,400 of those units.

a. How much warranty expense must Canton report in its current-period income statement?

b. What warranty liability related to current-period sales will Canton report on its current period-end balance sheet? Assume that actual repair costs are as estimated. (*Hint:* Remember that some units were repaired in the current period.)

c. What analysis issues must we consider with respect to reported warranty liabilities?

LO1   E7-28.   Analyzing Contingent and Other Liabilities

The following independent situations represent various types of liabilities. Analyze each situation and indicate which of the following is the proper accounting treatment for the company: (a) record a liability on the balance sheet, (b) disclose the liability in a financial statement footnote, or (c) neither record nor disclose any liability.

1. A stockholder has filed a lawsuit against Windsor Corporation. Clinch's attorneys have reviewed the facts of the case. Their review revealed that similar lawsuits have never resulted in a cash award and it is highly unlikely that this lawsuit will either.
2. Sterling Company signed a 60-day, 10% note when it purchased items from another company.
3. The Environmental Protection Agency notifies Stark Industries that a state where it has a plant is filing a lawsuit for groundwater pollution against Stark and another company that has a plant adjacent to Stark's plant. Test results have not identified the exact source of the pollution. Stark's manufacturing process often produces by-products that can pollute groundwater.
4. Franklin Company manufactured and sold products to a retailer that later sold the products to consumers. Franklin Company will replace the product if it is found to be defective within 90 days of the sale to the consumer. Historically, 1.2% of the products are returned for replacement.

LO1   E7-29.   Recording and Analyzing Warranty Accrual and Payment

Harley-Davidson Inc.
(HOG)

Refer to the discussion of and excerpt from the Harley-Davidson Inc. warranty reserve on page 7-6 to answer the following questions.

a. Using the financial statement effects template, record separately the 2018 warranty liability transactions relating to the (1) "Warranties issued during the period," (2) "Recalls and changes to preexisting warranty obligations," and (3) "Settlements made during the period."
b. Does the level of Harley-Davidson's warranty accrual appear to be reasonable?

LO1   E7-30.   Analyzing and Computing Accrued Wages Liability and Expense

Demski Company pays its employees on the 1st and 15th of each month. It is March 31 and the company is preparing financial statements for this quarter. Its employees have earned $96,000 since the 15th of March and have not yet been paid. How will Demski's balance sheet and income statement reflect the accrual of wages on March 31? What balance sheet and income statement accounts would be incorrectly reported if Demski failed to make this accrual (for each account indicate whether it would be overstated or understated)?

LO3, 4   E7-31.   Analyzing and Reporting Financial Statement Effects of Bond Transactions

On January 1, Remington Corp. issued $500,000 of 15-year, 10% bonds payable for $586,460 yielding an effective interest rate of 8%. Interest is payable semiannually on June 30 and December 31.

a. Show computations to confirm the issue price of $586,460.
b. Indicate the financial statement effects using the template for (1) bond issuance, (2) semiannual interest payment and premium amortization on June 30 of the first year, and (3) semiannual interest payment and premium amortization on December 31 of the first year.

LO4   E7-32.   Analyzing and Reporting Financial Statement Effects of Mortgages

On January 1, Patterson Inc. borrowed $1,000,000 on a 10%, 15-year mortgage note payable. The note is to be repaid in equal semiannual installments of $65,051 (payable on June 30 and December 31). Each mortgage payment includes principal and interest. Interest is computed using the effective interest method. Indicate the financial statement effects using the template for (a) issuance of the mortgage note payable, (b) payment of the first installment on June 30, and (c) payment of the second installment on December 31.

LO5   E7-33.   Assessing the Effects of Bond Credit Rating Changes

Ford Motor Co. (F)

Ford Motor Co. reports the following information from the Risk Factors and the Management Discussion and Analysis sections of its 2018 10-K report.

> **Credit Ratings**   Our short-term and long-term debt is rated by four credit rating agencies designated as nationally recognized statistical rating organizations ("NRSROs") by the U.S. Securities and Exchange Commission: DBRS, Fitch, Moody's, and S&P Global Ratings.
> In several markets , locally-recognized rating agencies also rate us. A credit rating reflects an assessment by the rating agency of the credit risk associated with a corporate entity or

continued

continued from previous page

particular securities issued by that entity. Rating agencies' ratings of us are based on information provided by us and other sources. Credit ratings are not recommendations to buy, sell, or hold securities , and are subject to revision or withdrawal at any time by the assigning rating agency. Each rating agency may have different criteria for evaluating company risk and, therefore, ratings should be evaluated independently for each rating agency.

There have been no rating actions taken by these NRSROs since the filing of our Quarterly Report on Form 10-Q for the quarter ended September 30, 2018.

The following chart summarizes certain of the credit ratings and outlook presently assigned by these four NRSROs :

	NRSRO RATINGS						
	Ford			Ford Credit			NRSROs
	Issuer Default Corporate/ Issuer Rating"	Long-Term Senior Unsecured	Outlook / Trend	Long-Term Senior Unsecured	Short-Term Unsecured	Outlook/ Trend	Minimum Long-Term Investment Grade Rating
DBRS	BBB	BBB	Stable	BBB	R-2M	Stable	BBB (low)
Fitch	BBB	BBB	Stable	BBB	F2	Stable	BBB–
Moody's . . .	N/A	Baa3	Negative	Baa3	P-3	Negative	Baa3
S&P	BBB	BBB	Negative	BBB	A-2	Negative	BBB–

a. What financial ratios do credit rating companies such as the four NRSROs listed above use to evaluate the relative riskiness of borrowers?

b. What economic consequences would there be if any of the four NRSROs upgraded Ford's credit rating? How would this affect the fair value of the company's bonds?

c. What type of actions can Ford take to improve its credit ratings?

E7-34. Analyzing and Reporting Financial Statement Effects of Bond Transactions
Winston Inc. reports financial statements each December 31. On May 1, of the current year, it issues $400,000 of 9%, 15-year bonds, with interest payable on October 31 and April 30. Assuming the bonds are sold at par on May 1, complete the financial statement effects template to reflect the following events: (a) bond issuance, (b) the first semiannual interest payment, and (c) retirement of $150,000 of the bonds at 102 on November 1 of the current year.

LO3, 4

E7-35. Analyzing and Reporting Financial Statement Effects of Bond Transactions
On January 1 of the current year, Banek Inc. issued $350,000 of 8%, nine-year bonds for $309,086, which implies a market (yield) rate of 10%. Semiannual interest is payable on June 30 and December 31 of each year.

a. Show computations to confirm the bond issue price.

b. Indicate the financial statement effects using the template for (1) bond issuance, (2) semiannual interest payment and discount amortization on June 30 of the current year, and (3) semiannual interest payment and discount amortization on December 31 of the current year.

LO3, 4

E7-36. Analyzing and Reporting Financial Statement Effects of Bond Transactions
On January 1 of the current year, Shields Inc. issued $1,000,000 of 9%, 20-year bonds for $1,098,964, yielding a market (yield) rate of 8%. Semiannual interest is payable on June 30 and December 31 of each year.

a. Show computations to confirm the bond issue price.

b. Indicate the financial statement effects using the template for (1) bond issuance, (2) semiannual interest payment and premium amortization on June 30 of the current year, and (3) semiannual interest payment and premium amortization on December 31 of the current year.

LO3, 4

E7-37. Determining Bond Prices, Interest Rates, and Financial Statement Effects
Deere & Company's 2018 10-K reports the following footnote relating to long-term debt for its equipment operations subsidiary. Deere's borrowings include $300 million, 7.125% notes, due in 2031 (highlighted below).

LO3, 4

Deere & Co (DE)

Long-term borrowings at October 28 consisted of the following in millions of dollars:

Notes and Debentures	2018	2017
4.375% notes due 2019		$ 750
8-1/2% debentures due 2022	$ 105	105
2.60% notes due 2022	1,000	1,000
6.55% debentures due 2028.	200	200
5.375% notes due 2029	500	500
8.10% debentures due 2030.	250	250
7.125% notes due 2031.	300	300
3.90% notes due 2042	1,250	1,250
Other notes	1,109	1,136
Total.	$4,714	$5,491

A recent price quote (from Markets Insider) on Deere's 7.125% notes follows.

Type	Issuer	Price	Coupon (%)	Maturity	Yield (%)	Moody's Rating	Callable
Corp	Deere & CO	131.03	7.125	2031	2.82%	A2	No

This price quote indicates that Deere's 7.125% notes have a market price of 131.03 (131.03% of face value), resulting in a yield of 2.82%.

a. Assuming that these notes were originally issued at par value, what does the market price reveal about interest rate changes since Deere issued its notes? (Assume that Deere's credit rating has remained the same.)

b. Does the change in interest rates since the issuance of these notes affect the amount of interest expense that Deere reports in its income statement? Explain.

c. How much cash would Deere have to pay to repurchase the 7.125% notes at the quoted market price of 131.03%? (Assume no interest is owed when Deere repurchases the notes.) How would the repurchase affect Deere's current income?

d. Assuming that the notes remain outstanding until their maturity, at what market price will the notes sell on their due date in 2031?

LO6

E7-38. **Computing Present Values of Single Amounts and Annuities**
Refer to Tables 1 and 2 in Appendix A near the end of the book to compute the present value for each of the following amounts.

a. $120,000 received 10 years hence if the annual interest rate is:
   1.   10% compounded annually.
   2.   10% compounded semiannually.

b. $2,000 received at the end of each year for the next eight years discounted at 8% compounded annually.

c. $800 received at the end of each six months for the next 15 years if the interest rate is 10% per year compounded semiannually.

d. $250,000 received 10 years hence discounted at 10% per year compounded annually.

LO3, 4

E7-39. **Analyzing and Reporting Financial Statement Effects of Bond Transactions**
On January 1 of the current year, Arbor Corporation issued $800,000 of 20-year, 11% bonds for $739,815, yielding a market (yield) rate of 12%. Interest is payable semiannually on June 30 and December 31.

a. Confirm the bond issue price.

b. Indicate the financial statement effects using the template for (1) bond issuance, (2) semiannual interest payment and discount amortization on June 30 of the current year, and (3) semiannual interest payment and discount amortization on December 31 of the current year.

E7-40. Interpreting Credit Rating Action

Moody's Investors Service issued the following press release (excerpts) on December 14, 2018, pertaining to a credit rating action for **Xerox Corporation**.

> New York, December 14, 2018—Moody's Investors Service downgraded Xerox Corporation's senior unsecured debt ratings to Ba1 from Baa3. The rating outlook is negative. As part of the rating actions, Moody's assigned Xerox a Ba1 Corporate Family Rating (CFR).
>
> **RATINGS RATIONALE** The downgrades reflect uncertainty about the company's ability to stabilize and grow its revenue base over the next few years given the secular decline in copier and printing demand as well as intense global competition. Xerox reported seven consecutive quarters of year over year revenue declines on a constant currency basis since the spin-off of the business process outsourcing segment despite major product launches in 2017.
>
> Moody's expects organic revenues to continue on a flat to declining trajectory over the next 12 to 18 months in the absence of an unlikely fundamental change in the company's revenue mix or market share.
>
> Xerox's Ba1 CFR is supported by the company's good market position in its core mid-range print and document outsourcing markets as well as solid leverage and free cash flow metrics. Roughly 78% of Xerox's revenue is derived from post-sale activities that include document outsourcing, managed print services, maintenance service, supplies (toner and paper), and finance income. These elements come with higher operating margins and provide some revenue predictability.
>
> The negative outlook reflects the persistent pressures on the company's core copier and printing business as well as execution challenges. The outlook could be changed to stable if the company demonstrates progress in stabilizing revenues and if Moody's expects the company will be able to maintain operating margins and free cash flow generation while keeping leverage in line with current levels.

a. What rating action did Moody's take on Xerox in December 2018?

b. Did the rating action change the investment grade of Moody's debt? (*Hint:* See Exhibit 7.3.) What is a likely economic outcome for Xerox?

c. What is the primary rationale for the downgrade?

d. Despite the downgrade, Moody's cites four reasons for the rating to be as high as it is. What are these four reasons?

E7-41. Calculating Ratios and Estimating Credit Rating

The following data are from **Amazon**'s 2018 10-K report ($ millions).

Revenue......................	$232,887		Net income	$ 10,073
Interest expense................	1,417		Capital expenditures (CAPEX).....	13,427
Tax expense....................	1,197		Total debt	23,495
Amortization expense...........	8,979		Average assets.................	146,979
Depreciation expense...........	6,362			

a. Use the data above to calculate the following ratios: EBITA/Average assets, EBITA Margin, EBITA/Interest expense, Debt/EBITDA, CAPEX/Depreciation Expense. Definitions for these ratios are in Exhibit 7.4.

b. Refer to Exhibit 7.4 and the ratios you calculated in part *a*. Estimate the credit rating that Moody's might assign to Amazon.

E7-42. Calculating Ratios and Estimating Credit Rating

The following data are from **Kellogg**'s 10-K report dated December 29, 2018 ($ millions).

Revenue...................	$13,547		Earnings from continuing operations ...	$ 1,344
Interest expense.............	287		Capital expenditures (CAPEX)........	578
Tax expense................	181		Total debt	8,893
Amortization expense.........	23		Average assets..................	17,066
Depreciation expense.........	493			

    a. Use the data above to calculate the following ratios: EBITA/Average assets, EBITA Margin, EBITA/ Interest expense, Debt/EBITDA, CAPEX/Depreciation Expense. Definitions for these ratios are in Exhibit 7.4.

    b. Refer to Exhibit 7.4 and the ratios you calculated in part *a.* Estimate the credit rating that Moody's might assign to Kellogg.

LO6   **E7-43.**   **Applying Time Value of Money Concepts**

Fulton Corporation purchases new manufacturing facilities and assumes a 10-year mortgage of $4 million. The annual interest rate on the mortgage is 5.5% and payments are due at the end of each year.

    a. Determine the mortgage payment that Fulton Corporation must make each year.

    b. Use Excel to prepare a mortgage amortization schedule for the 10 years.

    c. At the end of the first year, what amount will Fulton include as "current maturities of long-term debt" on its balance sheet?

LO6   **E7-44.**   **Applying Time Value of Money Concepts**

Manchester Corporation takes a 20-year mortgage of $15 million. The annual interest rate on the mortgage is 7% and payments are due at the end of each year.

    a. Determine the annual mortgage payment.

    b. Use the financial statement effects template to record the mortgage proceeds.

    c. Use the financial statement effects template to record the first two mortgage payments.

LO3   **E7-45.**   **Interpreting Graphical Bond Prices**

Boston Scientific
(BSX)

Consider the following price chart for Boston Scientific's 4.00% bond. The bond was issued at par in February 2018 and matures in March 2028. The following screen shot is from Markets Insider (August 9, 2019) and tracks the bond's daily price since issuance.

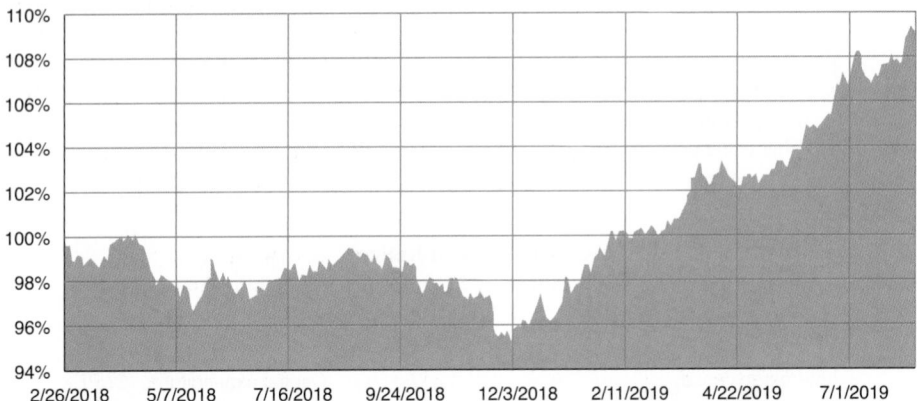

    a. At what approximate price is the bond trading on August 9, 2019?

    b. In late 2018, the bond was significantly below par. Explain how this could have happened.

    c. Consider the price movement during 2019. What is the relation of the bond's price to its yield during this period?

    d. Suggest three reasons for Boston Scientific's bond price to increase so significantly during the first half of 2019.

Problems

LO2, 3, 4, 5   **P7-46.**   **Interpreting and Analyzing Debt Footnotes**

PepsiCo Inc.
(PEP)

PepsiCo Inc. reports $32,248 million of long-term debt outstanding as of December 2018 in the following schedule to its 10-K report.

The following table summarizes the Company 's debt obligations:

Debt Obligations ($ millions)	2018	2017
Short-term debt obligations		
Current maturities of long-term debt................	$ 3,953	$ 4,020
Commercial paper (1.3%).........................	—	1,385
Other borrowings (6.0% and 4.7%)	73	80
	$ 4,026	$ 5,485
Long-term debt obligations		
Notes due 2018 (2.4%).........................	$ —	$ 4,016
Notes due 2019 (3.1% and 2.1%)	3,948	3,933
Notes due 2020 (3.9% and 3.1%)	3,784	3,792
Notes due 2021 (3.1% and 2.4%)	3,257	3,300
Notes due 2022 (2.8% and 2.6%)	3,802	3,853
Notes due 2023 (2.9% and 2.4%)	1,270	1,257
Notes due 2024–2047 (3.7% and 3.8 %)	16,161	17,634
Other, due 2018–2026 (1.3% and 1.3%)	26	31
	32,248	37,816
Less: current maturities of long-term debt obligations . . .	(3,953)	(4,020)
Total	$28,295	$33,796

In 2018, we completed a cash tender offer for certain notes issued by PepsiCo and predecessors to a PepsiCo subsidiary for $1.6 billion in cash to redeem the following amounts:

Interest Rate	Maturity Date	Amount Tendered
7.290%	September 2026	$ 11
7.440%	September 2026	$ 4
7.000%	March 2029	$357
5.500%	May 2035	$138
4.875%	November 2040	$410
5.500%	January 2040	$408

Our borrowing costs and access to capital and credit markets may be adversely affected by a downgrade or potential downgrade of our credit ratings.

Rating agencies routinely evaluate us, and their ratings of our long-term and short-term debt are based on a number of factors, including our cash generating capability, levels of indebtedness, policies with respect to shareholder distributions and our financial strength generally, as well as factors beyond our control, such as the then-current state of the economy and our industry generally. Any downgrade of our credit ratings by a credit rating agency, especially any downgrade to below investment grade, whether as a result of our actions or factors which are beyond our control, could increase our future borrowing costs, impair our ability to access capital and credit markets on terms commercially acceptable to us or at all, and result in a reduction in our liquidity.

Moody's Investors Service (www.moodys.com) reported the following regarding PepsiCo.

Rating Action: Moody's rates PepsiCo's new notes at A1; outlook stable
New York, July 25, 2019—Moody's today assigned an A1 rating to PepsiCo, Inc.'s senior unsecured notes being issued in 10 and 30 year tranches. All other ratings for the company remain unchanged. The outlook is stable. The proceeds will be used for general corporate purposes.

On August 9, 2019, **Markets Insider** reported the following details for notes due in 2022.

Type	Issuer	Price	Coupon(%)	Maturity	YTM(%)	Moody's Ratings
Corp	PEPSICO INC	102.27	2.75%	3/5/2022	1.87%	A1

Required

a. PepsiCo reports current maturities of long-term debt of $3,953 million as part of short-term debt. Why is this amount reported that way? Is this amount important to our analysis of PepsiCo? Explain.

b. The Markets Insider excerpt above reveals that the 2.75% notes due in 2022 are priced at 102.27, resulting in a yield to maturity of 1.87%. Assuming that the credit rating of PepsiCo has not changed, what does the pricing of this bond imply about interest rate changes since PepsiCo issued the bond?

c. During 2018, PepsiCo retired certain notes (early) with a cash tender offer. What was the total amount tendered? PepsiCo paid $1.6 billion cash for the tendered notes. Assume that the reported amounts tendered represent the net book value of the notes. What gain or loss did the company report on this early retirement of debt?

d. The Moody's rating action excerpt above reveals that the company issued new notes in 2019. From this ratings action, what can investors infer about PepsiCo's creditworthiness in 2019? How does this rating action affect the issue proceeds?

e. What type of actions can PepsiCo take to improve its credit ratings?

LO3, 4
Boston Scientific
Corporation (BSX)

P7-47.   Interpreting Debt Footnotes on Interest Rates and Interest Expense

Boston Scientific discloses the following as part of its long-term debt footnote in its December 31, 2018 10-K.

Borrowings and Credit Agreements

In millions, except interest rates	Issuance Date	Maturity Date	As of December 31, 2018	As of December 31, 2017	Semi-annual Coupon Rate
January 2020 Notes	December 2009	January 2020	$ 850	$ 850	6.000%
May 2020 Notes	May 2015	May 2020	600	600	2.850%
May 2022 Notes	May 2015	May 2022	500	500	3.375%
October 2023 Notes	August 2013	October 2023	450	450	4.125%
May 2025 Notes	May 2015	May 2025	750	750	3.850%
March 2028 Notes	February 2018	March 2028	1,000	—	4.000%
November 2035 Notes[1]	November 2005	November 2035	350	350	7.000%
January 2040 Notes	December 2009	January 2040	300	300	7.375%
Unamortized debt insurance discount and deferred financing cost		2020–2040	(29)	(24)	
Unamortized gain on fair value hedge		2020—2025	26	38	
Capital lease obligation		Various	6	1	
Long-term debt			$4,803	$3,815	

[1] Corporate credit rating improvements may result in a decrease in the adjusted interest rate on our November 2035 Notes to the extent that our lowest credit rating is above BBB– or Baa3. The interest rates on our November 2035 notes will be permanently reinstated to the issuance rate if the lowest credit ratings assigned to these senior notes is either A– or A3 or higher.

Boston Scientific discloses its required principal debt repayments due during each of the next five years and thereafter.

In millions	
2019	$2,248
2020	1,540
2021	0
2022	500
2023	450
Thereafter	2,400

Boston Scientific also discloses the following information.

Interest Expense The following table provides a summary of our *Interest expense* and average borrowing rate :

Year Ended December 31 (in millions)	2018	2017	2016
Interest expense	$(241)	$(229)	$(233)
Weighted average borrowing rate	3.6%	3.8%	4.0%
Cash paid for interest	$(262)	$(235)	$(233)

The price of the Boston Scientific's bonds in February 2019 follows.

Maturity date	Coupon	Current Price	Current Yield	Moody's Rating (02/21/2019)
2028	4.00%	109.35	2.80%	Baa2
2023	4.125%	101.57	2.41%	Baa2

Required

a. What amount of Boston Scientific's long-term debt is due in 2019?

b. What is the total amount of Boston Scientific's long-term debt at December 31, 2018, including the current maturities?

c. The company's balance sheet reports short-term debt including current maturities of $2,253 million and $1,801 million in 2018 and 2017, respectively. Compute the average effective interest rate on the company's total debt for fiscal 2018. Compare this to the average interest rate the company reports.

d. Explain how the amount of cash paid for interest can differ from the amount of interest expense recorded in the income statement.

e. The $1,000 million 4.00% note due in 2028 is priced at 109.35 (109.35% of face value, or $1,093.50 million) as of early 2019, resulting in a current yield of 2.8%. Assuming that the company's credit rating has not changed since the bond was issued, what does the pricing of this 4.00% bond imply about interest rate changes since Boston Scientific issued the bond?

f. Compare the bonds that mature in 2023 and 2028. Explain why the bond with the higher coupon rate (4.125%) has the lower yield (2.41%).

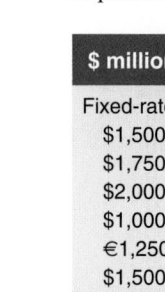

LO4, 5
Oracle Corp. (ORCL)

P7-48. Analyzing Debt Terms, Yields, Prices, and Credit Ratings
Reproduced below is the debt footnote from the May 31, 2019, 10-K report of Oracle Corporation.

$ millions	May 31, 2019	May 31, 2018
Fixed-rate senior notes:		
$1,500, 2.375%, due January 2019	—	$ 1,500
$1,750, 5.00%, due July 2019	$ 1,750	1,750
$2,000, 2.25%, due October 2019	2,000	2,000
$1,000, 3.875%, due July 2020	1,000	1,000
€1,250, 2.25%, due January 2021	1,393	1,446
$1,500, 2.80%, due July 2021	1,500	1,500
$4,250, 1.90%, due September 2021	4,250	4,250
$2,500, 2.50%, due May 2022	2,500	2,500
$2,500, 2.50%, due October 2022	2,500	2,500
$1,250, 2.625%, due February 2023	1,250	1,250
$1,000, 3.625%, due July 2023	1,000	1,000
$2,500, 2.40%, due September 2023	2,500	2,500
$2,000, 3.40%, due July 2024	2,000	2,000
$2,000, 2.95%, due November 2024	2,000	2,000
$2,500, 2.95%, due May 2025	2,500	2,500
€750, 3.125%, due July 2025	836	868
$3,000, 2.65%, due July 2026	3,000	3,000
$2,750, 3.25%, due November 2027	2,750	2,750
$500, 3.25%, due May 2030	500	500
$1,750, 4.30%, due July 2034	1,750	1,750
$1,250, 3.90%, due May 2035	1,250	1,250
$1,250, 3.85%, due July 2036	1,250	1,250
$1,750, 3.80%, due November 2037	1,750	1,750
$1,250, 6.50%, due April 2038	1,250	1,250
$1,250, 6.125%, due July 2039	1,250	1,250
$2,250, 5.375%, due July 2040	2,250	2,250
$1,000, 4.50%, due July 2044	1,000	1,000
$2,000, 4.125%, due May 2045	2,000	2,000
$3,000, 4.00%, due July 2046	3,000	3,000
$2,250, 4.00%, due November 2047	2,250	2,250
$1,250, 4.375%, due May 2055	1,250	1,250
Floating-rate senior notes:		
$500, three-month LIBOR plus 0.58%, due January 2019	—	500
$750, three-month LIBOR plus 0.51%, due October 2019	750	750
Revolving credit agreements and other borrowings:		
$2,500, LIBOR plus 0.50%, due June 2018	—	2,500
Other borrowings due August 2025	113	113
Total senior notes and other borrowings	56,342	60,927
Unamortized discount/issuance costs	(202)	(282)
Hedge accounting fair value adjustments(1)(4)	27	(26)
Total notes payable and other borrowings	56,167	60,619
Notes payable and other borrowings, current	4,494	4,491
Notes payable and other borrowings, noncurrent	$51,673	$56,128

Future principal payments (adjusted for the effects of the cross-currency swap agreements associated with the January 2021 Notes and July 2025 Notes) for all of our borrowings at May 31, 2019, were as follows:

$ millions	
Fiscal 2020	$ 4,500
Fiscal 2021	2,631
Fiscal 2022	8,250
Fiscal 2023	3,750
Fiscal 2024	3,500
Thereafter	33,984
Total	$56,615

Reproduced below is a summary of the market values as of August 10, 2019, of select Oracle bonds. Source: **Markets Insider** (https://markets.businessinsider.com/bonds).

Maturity Date	Amount $	Price	Coupon %	Yield to Maturity %
July 2020	$1,000	109.47	3.875%	2.613%
April 2038	$1,250	136.78	6.5%	3.36%
July 2039	$1,250	120.47	6.125%	3.45%

Required

a. What is the amount of debt reported on Oracle's May 31, 2019, balance sheet? What are the scheduled maturities for this indebtedness? Why is information relating to a company's scheduled maturities of debt useful in an analysis of its financial condition?

b. Oracle reported $2,082 million in interest expense in the notes to its 2019 income statement. In the note to its statement of cash flows, Oracle indicates that the cash portion of this expense is $2,059 million. What could account for the difference between interest expense and interest paid? Explain.

c. Oracle's long-term debt is rated A1 by Moody's, A+ by S&P Global Ratings, and A+ by Fitch. What factors would be important to consider in attempting to quantify the relative riskiness of Oracle compared with other borrowers? Explain.

d. Oracle's $1,250 million 6.5% notes traded at 136.78 as of August 10, 2019. What is the market value of these notes on that date? How is the difference between this market value and the $1,250 million face value reflected in Oracle's financial statements? What effect would the repurchase of this entire note issue have on Oracle's financial statements? What does the 136.78 price tell us about the general trend in interest rates since Oracle sold this bond issue? Explain.

e. Examine the yields to maturity of the three bonds in the table above. What relation do we observe between these yields and the maturities of the bonds? Also, explain why this relation applies in general.

IFRS Applications

I7-49. **Interpreting Bond Footnote Disclosures and Computing Effective Interest Rate**

In 2019, French grocery retailer **Carrefour** issued bonds as follows.

LO3, 4

Carrefour SA
(CRRFY)

Issue date	May 7, 2019
Issue amount (€M)	500
Annual coupon rate	1%
Maturity	May 17, 2027
Issue price	99.534

a. Determine the annual interest payments.

b. Determine the effective interest rate.

c. What amount of interest expense does the company report related to these bonds for the fiscal year ended December 31, 2019?

LO1

Bombardier Inc.
(BDRBF)

I7-50.   Analyzing Contingent Liabilities: Warranty Reserves

Headquartered in Montreal, Quebec, Canada, Bombardier Inc. is a multinational aerospace and transportation company, founded in 1941. The company manufactures regional aircraft, business jets, mass transportation equipment, and recreational equipment and is also a financial services provider. Bombardier is a Fortune Global 500 company and operates two segments: BA (Aerospace) and BT (Transportation). Bombardier's 2018 annual report is presented in U.S. dollars, and includes the following details about the company's provision for product warranties ($ millions).

Balance as at December 31 2017	$672
Additions	206
Utilization	(223)
Reversals	(106)
Accretion expense	2
Effect of changes in discount rates.	(1)
Disposal of CSALP business	(15)
Effect of foreign currency exchange rate changes	(20)
Balance as at December 31, 2018.	**$515**
Of which current	$403
Of which noncurrent	112
	$515

Required

a. In common language, explain what a provision for product warranties is. When do companies create such provisions?

b. What amount is included on the 2018 balance sheet for warranty provision?

c. What amount is included on the 2018 income statement related to warranties?

d. What is meant by "Utilization" in the table? What sort of costs does this entail?

Management Applications

LO3   **MA7-51.   Coupon Rate versus Effective Rate**

Assume that you are the CFO of a company that intends to issue bonds to finance a new manufacturing facility. A subordinate suggests lowering the coupon rate on the bond to lower interest expense and to increase the profitability of your company. Is the rationale for this suggestion a good one? Explain.

LO5   **MA7-52.   Ethics and Governance: Bond Covenants**

Because lenders do not have voting rights like shareholders do, they often reduce their risk by invoking various bond covenants that restrict the company's operating, financing, and investing activities. For example, debt covenants often restrict the amount of debt that the company can issue (in relation to its equity) and impose operating restrictions (such as the ability to acquire other companies or to pay dividends). Failure to abide by these restrictions can have serious consequences, including forcing the company into bankruptcy and potential liquidation. Assume that you are on the board of directors of a company that issues bonds with such restrictions. What safeguards can you identify to ensure compliance with those restrictions?

Ongoing Project

(This ongoing project began in Module 1 and continues through most of the book; even if previous segments were not completed, the requirements are still applicable to any business analysis.) Review liabilities that arise from operating and financing transactions, including the type and quantity of both categories. The goal is to consider how the companies are financed and whether they can repay their obligations as they come due in the short and longer term.

1. *Accrued liabilities.* Accrued liabilities arise from ordinary operations and provide interest-free financing.

   - Are operating liabilities large for the companies? Compare common-size amounts. What proportion of total liabilities are operating?
   - What are the companies' main operating liabilities?
   - Are there substantial contingencies? What gives rise to these? Read the footnote and determine whether the company has recorded a liability on its balance sheet for these contingencies.

2. *Short and Long-Term Debt.* Examine the debt footnote and consider the following questions.

   - What is the common-size debt and how does that compare to published industry averages?
   - What types of debt does the company have? Is it publicly traded? Are there bank loans? Other types of debt?
   - When does the debt mature? Determine if there is a large proportion due in the next year or two. If so, can the company refinance given its current level of debt?
   - What is the average interest rate on debt? Compare it to the coupon rates reported.
   - Read the footnote and the MD&A to see if there are any debt covenants and whether the company is in compliance.
   - If the company has publicly traded debt, determine its current price. Sharp drops in bond prices could indicate a deterioration in the company's credit quality.

3. *Credit Ratings.* Find the companies' credit ratings at two or three ratings agencies' websites.

   - What are the credit ratings and how do they compare across the agencies? Are the two companies similarly rated?
   - Have the ratings changed during the year? If so, why?
   - Are the companies on a credit watch or a downgrade list?
   - If possible, find a credit report online and read it to gain a better understanding of the companies' creditworthiness.
   - Calculate the ratios in Exhibit 7.4 for your firms. Compare the ratios to those for firms with similar credit ratings. Do the credit ratings for the firms seem reasonable?

Solutions to Review Problems

Review 7-1—Solution (in $000s)

a. $70,000, the amount of the additional warranty liability arising from current-year sales.

b. $131,740 (from the current year-end balance) + $70,000 − $85,000 = $116,740

c. The 2019 income statement understates profit by the additional mistaken accrual of $20,000. Thus, next year's balance sheet reports a warranty liability that is $20,000 too high. In a subsequent period, assuming that the actual warranty costs incurred are, indeed, $20,000 lower than originally estimated, the company will not need to accrue as much warranty liability. Consequently, future profit will be higher until the reported warranty liability is reduced (by recognition of costs incurred) to an accurate level. Profit has, therefore, been shifted from next year to a future period(s).

Review 7-2—Solution

IE 125
  IP. 125

	IE	
125		
	IP	
		125

NP . . .10,000
IP 125
IE 23
  Cash 10,148

	NP	
10,000		
	IP	
125		
	IE	
23		
	Cash	
		10,148

($ millions)	Balance Sheet						Income Statement		
Transaction	Cash Asset	+ Noncash Assets	= Liabil- ities	+ Contrib. Capital	+ Earned Capital		Rev- enues	− Expen- ses	= Net Income
Mar. 31: Ac- crue $125 interest expense*			= +125 Interest Payable		−125 Retained Earnings			− +125 Interest Expense	= −125
Apr 14: Pay principal and interest on note**	−10,148		= −125 Interest Payable −10,000 Note Payable		−23 Retained Earnings			− +23 Interest Expense	= −23

*Accrued interest = $10,000 × 0.06 × 76/365 = $125
** Interest expense = $10,000 × 0.06 × 14/365 = $23

Review 7-3—Solution

Calculator
N = 30
I/Yr = 4
PMT = −15,000
FV = −300,000

PV = 351,876

	A	B
1	Annual coupon rate	10%
2	Annual market rate	8%
3	Interest payments per year	2
4	Years to maturity	15
5	Face (par) value	300,000
6	Issue price	351,876
7	= PV(B2/B3,B4*B3,−B5*B1/B3,−B5, 0)	
8	= 351,876	

Issue price for $300,000, 15-year bonds that pay 10% interest discounted at 4% semiannually:

Present value of principal payment ($300,000 × 0.30832). . . . . $ 92,496
Present value of semiannual interest payments ($15,000 × 17.29203)   259,380

Issue price of bonds $351,876

Calculator
N = 30
I/Yr = 6
PMT = −15,000
FV = −300,000

PV = 258,706

	A	B
1	Annual coupon rate	10%
2	Annual market rate	12%
3	Interest payments per year	2
4	Years to maturity	15
5	Face (par) value	300,000
6	Issue price	258,706
7	= PV(B2/B3,B4*B3,−B5*B1/B3,−B5, 0)	
8	= 258,706	

Issue price for $300,000, 15-year bonds that pay 10% interest, discounted at 6% semiannually:

Present value of principal payment ($300,000 × 0.17411). . . . . $ 52,233
Present value of semiannual interest payments ($15,000 × 13.76483)   206,472

Issue price of bonds $258,705

Review 7-4—Solution

1.

Calculator
N = 30
I/Yr = 4
PMT = −15,000
FV = −300,000

PV = 351,876

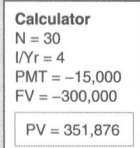

	A	B
1	Annual coupon rate	10%
2	Annual market rate	8%
3	Interest payments per year	2
4	Years to maturity	15
5	Face (par) value	300,000
6	Issue price	351,876
7	= PV(B2/B3,B4*B3,−B5*B1/B3,−B5, 0)	
8	= 351,876	

Issue price for $300,000, 15-year bonds that pay 10% interest, discounted at 4% semiannually:

Present value of principal payment ($300,000 × 0.30832). . . . . $ 92,496
Present value of semiannual interest payments ($15,000 × 17.29203)   259,380

Issue price of bonds $351,876

2.

Transaction	Cash Asset	+	Noncash Assets	=	Liabil-ities	+	Contrib. Capital	+	Earned Capital		Rev-enues	−	Expen-ses	=	Net Income
					Balance Sheet								**Income Statement**		
January 1: Issue 10% bonds	+351,876			=	+351,876 Long-Term Debt							**−**		**=**	
June 30: Pay interest and amortize bond premium[1]	−15,000			=	−925 Long-Term Debt				−14,075 Retained Earnings			**−**	+14,075 Interest Expense	**=**	−14,075
December 31: Pay interest and amortize bond premium[2]	−15,000			=	−962 Long-Term Debt				−14,038 Retained Earnings			**−**	+14,038 Interest Expense	**=**	−14,038

Cash 351,876
LTD 351,876

Cash	
351,876	

	LTD
	351,876

IE . . . 14,075
LTD . . 925
   Cash 15,000

IE	
14,075	

LTD	
925	

	Cash
	15,000

IE . . . 14,038
LTD . . 962
   Cash 15,000

IE	
14,038	

LTD	
962	

	Cash
	15,000

[1] $300,000 × 0.10 × 6/12 = $15,000 cash payment; 0.04 × $351,876 = $14,075 interest expense; the difference of $925 is the bond premium amortization, which reduces the net bond carrying amount.

[2] 0.04 × ($351,876 − $925) = $14,038 interest expense. The difference between this amount and the $15,000 cash payment ($962) is the premium amortization, which reduces the net bond carrying amount.

3.

Period	Interest Expense	Cash Interest Paid	Premium Amortization	Premium Balance	Bond Payable, Net
0				$51,876	$351,876
1	$14,075	$15,000	$ 925	50,951	350,951
2	14,038	15,000	962	49,989	349,989
3	14,000	15,000	1,000	48,989	348,989
4	13,960	15,000	1,040	47,949	347,949
5	13,918	15,000	1,082	46,867	346,867
6	13,875	15,000	1,125	45,742	345,742
7	13,830	15,000	1,170	44,572	344,572
8	13,783	15,000	1,217	43,355	343,355
9	13,734	15,000	1,266	42,089	342,089
10	13,684	15,000	1,316	40,773	340,773

4. Comcast would have to pay $447,163 to repurchase the bonds. This would yield a loss on debt repurchase of $106,390 computed as $447,163 − $340,773.

Calculator
N = 20
I/Yr = 2
PMT = −15,000
FV = −300,000

PV = 447,163

X	A	B
1	Annual coupon rate	10%
2	Annual market rate	4%
3	Interest payments per year	2
4	Years to maturity	10
5	Face (par) value	300,000
6	Issue price	447,163
7	= PV(B2/B3,B4*B3,−B5*B1/B3,−B5, 0)	
8	= 447,163	

Review 7-5—Solution

Ratio	Result	Rating
Operating margin	14.2%	Baa
Debt/EBITDA	2.1	A
FFO/Debt	32.9%	Baa
EBITA/Interest Expense	3.9	Ba
Overall composite		**Baa**

Review 7-6—Solution

Using the Excel formula PV(rate,nper, pmt,[fv],[type])

a. $5,449.13

b. $5,000.00

c. $4,594.46

Module 8

Stock Transactions, Dividends, and EPS

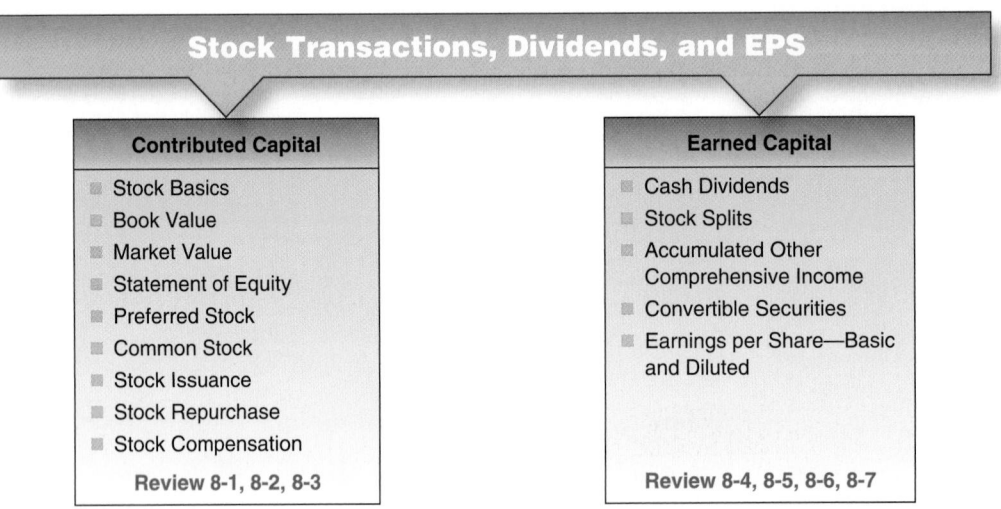

Stock Transactions, Dividends, and EPS	
Contributed Capital	**Earned Capital**
■ Stock Basics	■ Cash Dividends
■ Book Value	■ Stock Splits
■ Market Value	■ Accumulated Other Comprehensive Income
■ Statement of Equity	■ Convertible Securities
■ Preferred Stock	■ Earnings per Share—Basic and Diluted
■ Common Stock	
■ Stock Issuance	
■ Stock Repurchase	
■ Stock Compensation	
Review 8-1, 8-2, 8-3	Review 8-4, 8-5, 8-6, 8-7

PREVIEW   JNJ

■ We examine topics related to stockholders' equity, including:

- o Issuance and repurchase of common stock
- o Payment of dividends
- o Stock splits
- o Convertible securities
- o Stock-based compensation
- o Earnings per share and book value per share
- o Accumulated other comprehensive income

■ **Johnson & Johnson** is the focus company and the dashboard below conveys key financial information.

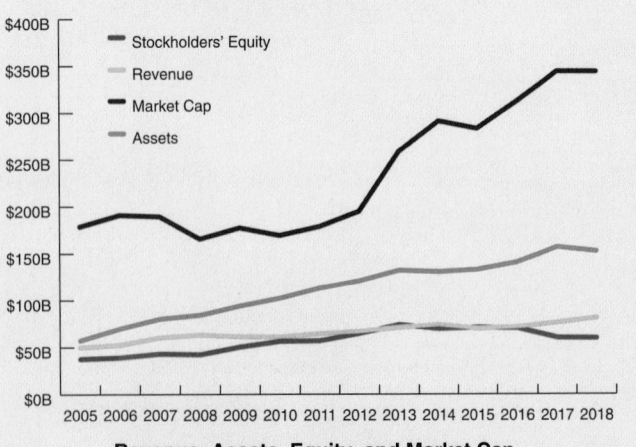

Revenue, Assets, Equity, and Market Cap

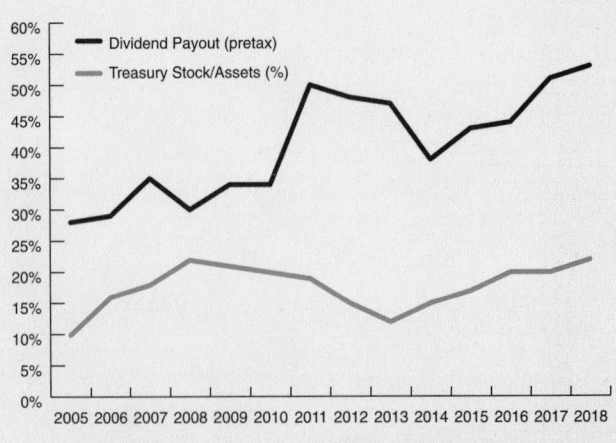

Dividend Payout (Pretax) and Treasury Stock/Assets

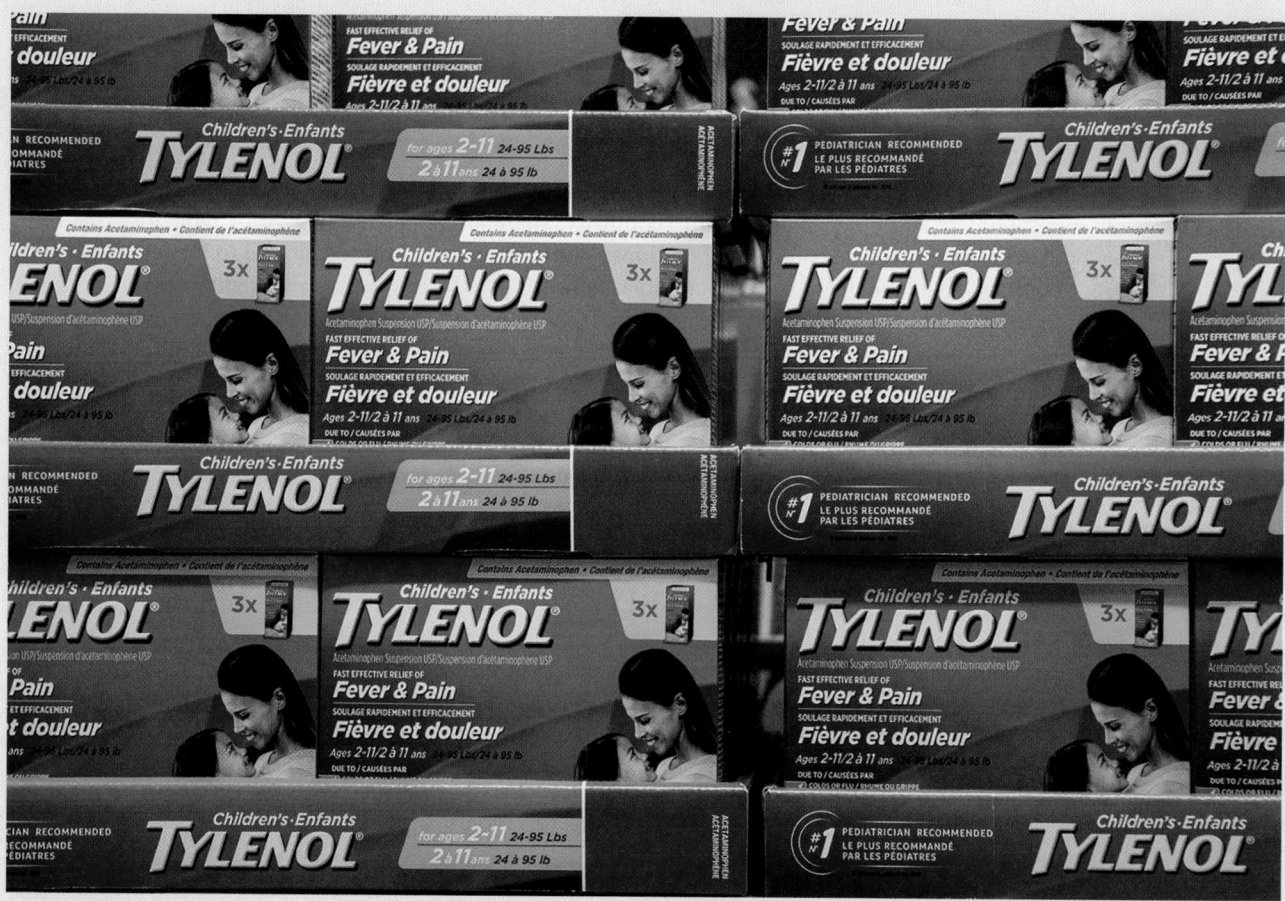

Road Map

LO	Learning Objective | Topics	Page	eLecture	Guided Example	Assignments
8–1	**Examine stock as a financing source and explain its various features.** Equity Terms :: Stockholders' Equity :: Preferred Stock :: Common Stock :: Market Capitalization	8-3	e8–1	Review 8-1	1, 2, 3, 6, 7, 11, 12, 13, 15, 21, 24, 37, 40, 45, 46, 48, 49, 52, 53, 54, 55, 62, 63
8–2	**Analyze stock issuances and repurchases.** Stock Issuance :: Stock Repurchase :: Retirement of Repurchases	8-9	e8–2	Review 8-2	5, 7, 9, 10, 19, 22, 35, 36, 37, 40, 42, 45, 46, 49, 50, 52, 53, 54, 55, 62, 63
8–3	**Interpret stock-based compensation, including restricted stock and options.** Compensation Types :: Compensation Accounting :: Disclosures	8-13	e8–3	Review 8-3	17, 26, 37, 38, 51, 54, 55, 58, 59, 61, 63
8–4	**Analyze cash dividends and stock splits.** Dividend Payout :: Dividend Yield :: Financial Effects :: Stock Splits	8-16	e8–4	Review 8-4	4, 8, 23, 25, 27, 28, 29, 31, 32, 39, 41, 42, 43, 44, 45, 53, 54, 62, 63
8–5	**Interpret accumulated other comprehensive income and its components.** AOCI Disclosure and Interpretation :: Other Comprehensive Income	8-19	e8–5	Review 8-5	16, 33, 50, 54, 55, 62, 63
8–6	**Analyze convertible securities and their financial effects.** Disclosures and Interpretation :: Financial Effects	8-22	e8–6	Review 8-6	18, 34, 47, 50, 56, 57
8–7	**Interpret earnings per share.** Basic EPS :: Diluted EPS	8-23	e8–7	Review 8-7	14, 20, 30, 47, 56, 60

Stockholders' Equity and Classes of Stock

LO1
Examine stock as a financing source and explain its various features.

Companies raise funds by selling shares of stock to investors in addition to borrowing. But, unlike debtholders and other lenders to the company, shareholders elect a Board of Directors that hires executives to oversee company operations. While interest and principal paid to lenders is fixed by contract, shareholders have no contractual return. There is, however, the potential for shareholders to receive dividends and derive large value from future price appreciation of company stock.

The stockholders' equity section of the balance sheet reports the book value of the stockholders' investment, as determined under accounting rules (GAAP). This measurement of book value differs from the market value of stockholders' investment, which is computed as share price multiplied by the number of shares outstanding. Market value is determined by supply and demand for the company's outstanding shares in the marketplace as shares are actively traded among investors.

There are two types of stockholders' equity accounts: contributed capital and earned capital. **Contributed capital** is the net funding a company receives from issuing and reacquiring its shares; that is, the funds received from issuing shares less any funds paid to repurchase such shares. **Earned capital** includes two accounts: retained earnings and accumulated other comprehensive income (AOCI). Retained earnings is the cumulative net income (loss) that the company has earned but not paid out to stockholders as dividends. (Retained earnings can include the effects of retiring common stock as we discuss in the Business Insight box later in the module.) AOCI is the cumulative net *unrealized* (holding) gains or losses related to key balance sheet accounts (primarily pensions, investment securities, derivatives, and foreign currencies). These holding gains and losses will flow to the income statement, and be included in retained earnings, when they are *realized*.

We explain the components of stockholders' equity section of the balance sheet, the different classes of stock, how we account for share issuances (sales) and repurchases (Treasury stock), and the reporting for dividends to shareholders, stock splits, and convertible securities. We also describe the concept of other comprehensive income and two measures of earnings per share (EPS) that are regularly discussed in the financial press.

Stockholders' Equity Accounts

When the company is incorporated, shareholders of the company authorize management to issue (sell) shares of stock. After that, the company's management is free to manage the company, consistent with its policies and under the watchful eye of the Board of Directors (representatives of the shareholders who are elected by them and look out for their interests). Over time, stockholders expect their equity to increase and the stockholders' equity section of the balance sheet represents a score card, in a sense, that records how well management has performed with the capital entrusted to them by the shareholders.

The stockholders' equity section of Johnson & Johnson's (JNJ) balance sheet, shown in Exhibit 8.1, includes the following accounts (see the Business Insight box for definitions).

Contributed Capital

- **Preferred stock.** Johnson & Johnson is authorized to issue up to 2,000,000 preferred shares, but to date has not issued any—the balance is $0.
- **Common stock.** The balance sheet reveals a number of details about the Johnson & Johnson common stock:
  - **Par value.** The par value of its common stock (as stated in its charter) is $1 per share.
  - **Authorized shares.** It can issue up to 4,320,000,000 shares without further approval from shareholders.
  - **Issued shares.** To date, it has sold (issued) 3,119,843,000 shares at the $1 par value and thus, the common stock account has a balance of $3,120 million. It does not report any additional

paid-in capital. We can infer that no shares were sold for more than the $1 par value. (See the Coca-Cola illustration on page 8-9 for an example of additional paid-in capital, which Coca-Cola labels "capital surplus.")

Earned Capital

- **Treasury stock.** The company routinely repurchases its own shares on the open market. As of the 2018 year-end, the company held 457,519,000 treasury shares for which it paid $34,362 million. Like all balance sheet accounts, the treasury stock balance is a cumulative amount that reflects open-market repurchases and subsequent resale of its shares. The account has increased during the year, which implies that Johnson & Johnson purchased additional shares during the current year, net of any shares sold back to the market or granted to employees.

- **Accumulated Other Comprehensive Income (AOCI).** This account reflects the cumulative total of changes to stockholders' equity other than from transactions with owners and transactions reflected in net income. This account can be a positive or negative amount.

- **Retained earnings.** Defined as the cumulative net income recorded since the company's inception less all of the dividends the company has ever paid out to shareholders, which nets to $106,216 million. Retained earnings increased in 2018 primarily because during that year net income exceeded the amount of dividends paid out.

Exhibit 8.1 ■ Stockholders' Equity Section from Johnson & Johnson's Balance Sheet

Shareholders' equity ($ millions, except par value per share)	2018	2017
Preferred stock — without par value (authorized and unissued 2,000,000 shares) . . .	$ —	$ —
Common stock — par value $1.00 per share		
(authorized 4,320,000,000 shares; issued 3,119,843,000 shares)	3,120	3,120
Accumulated other comprehensive income (loss)	(15,222)	(13,199)
Retained earnings	106,216	101,793
	94,114	91,714
Less: common stock held in treasury, at cost		
(457,519,000 shares and 437,318,000 shares)	34,362	31,554
Total shareholders' equity.	$ 59,752	$ 60,160

Book Value per Share A measure commonly used by analysts and the financial press is *book value per share*. This is the equity (net book value) of the company that is available to common shareholders and is defined as:

$$\text{Book value per share} = \left(\text{Stockholders' equity} - \text{Preferred stock} \right) \Big/ \text{Number of common shares outstanding}$$

Johnson & Johnson's book value per share at the end of 2018 follows:

$$\text{JNJ book value per share} = \frac{\$59,752 \text{ million}}{\left(3,119,843 \text{ thousand shares} - 457,519 \text{ thousand shares} \right)} = \$22.44 \text{ per share}$$

Market-to-Book In comparison, JNJ's market price per share was $129.05 on December 31, 2018 (the last trading day before JNJ's fiscal year-end). The ratio of market price per share to book value per share is the **market-to-book ratio**. For JNJ, at year-end 2018, market-to-book was 5.75. The median market-to-book for the S&P 500 companies at the end of 2018 was 2.91. So, the market values JNJ higher (relative to the book value of its equity) than the median S&P 500 company.

Business Insight	■	Stockholders' Equity Terms and Phrases

Following are common terms and phrases relating to stockholders' equity that we encounter in the financial press.

- **Board of directors.** Shareholders' elected representatives who hire the CEO and oversee company operations.
- **Preferred stock.** Generally non-voting shares that convey, 1) a dividend preference—preferred stockholders receive dividends on their shares before common stockholders, and 2) a liquidation preference—if a company fails and is liquidated, the assets are sold and liabilities paid; then any remaining cash is paid first to preferred shareholders before payment is made to common shareholders.
- **Common stock.** Shares that allow the holder to elect the company's board of directors and vote on important company issues such as whether to adopt employee benefit plans, acquire other companies, divest current companies, and reorganize or liquidate the company. Common shares receive dividends after preferred shareholders have been paid their required dividends.
- **Dividends.** Company profit that is distributed to shareholders. Profit not distributed as dividends is reinvested in the business and shown on the balance sheet as retained earnings.
- **Declaration date.** The date the board of directors authorizes the payment of the dividend (declares the dividend).
- **Date of record.** The date the company prepares the list of current stockholders to which the dividend will be paid.
- **Date of payment.** The date the dividend is paid to stockholders (who held the stock on the date of record).
- **Residual claim.** When a company voluntarily ceases operations or fails and is liquidated, all assets are sold and liabilities paid. Each shareholder is entitled to their proportional share of the residual cash, if any. Shareholders are called residual claimants.
- **Authorized shares.** The maximum number of shares that a company can sell (issue) without approval from the shareholders.
- **Issued shares.** The number of shares that have been sold (issued) to date. This is a cumulative number.
- **Outstanding shares.** The number of shares that are outstanding in the market, determined as the number of issued shares less the number of shares that have been repurchased by the company.
- **Treasury shares.** The number of shares that the company has repurchased and holds for resale or for employee compensation plans.
- **Initial public offering (IPO).** An initial sale of stock to the public.
- **Par value** and **Additional paid-in capital.** The per share amount (stated in a company's charter) that will be recorded in the common stock account when stock is sold (issued). Par value is unrelated to the stock's market value. The excess of the issue price over the par value is added to the Additional paid-in capital account (also called capital surplus, or capital in excess of par).
- **Paid-in capital.** The *total* amount of cash and other assets paid in to the company by stockholders in exchange for capital stock.
- **Market price.** The published price at which a share of stock can be purchased ("ask") or sold ("bid").
- **Market capitalization.** The market value of all outstanding shares; also called *market cap*.
- **Stock split.** Proportional issuance of shares to stockholders (and a consequent proportional reduction in par value) with no exchange of cash. A stock split does not affect the value of the company. Because the number of outstanding shares increases, while the value of the company remains unchanged, the share price declines proportionally. One goal of a stock split is to reduce the share price to make the stock more marketable.

Statement of Stockholders' Equity

The statement of stockholders' equity reconciles the beginning and ending balances of the contributed and earned stockholders' equity accounts. It highlights the following.

- How net income and dividends impact retained earnings.
- Cash raised from new shares issued.
- Cash used to repurchase shares in the open market.
- Changes in key balance sheet accounts not recorded in net income or not arising from transactions with shareholders. Each year, these changes are included in an account called **Other Comprehensive Income** (OCI), and the *cumulative* sum of that account is reflected in an equity account called **Accumulated Other Comprehensive Income** (AOCI).

Johnson & Johnson's statement of stockholders' equity, shown in Exhibit 8.2, reveals the following key activities from 2018.

❶ Net income is added to retained earnings, increasing it by $15,297 million.

❷ Cash dividends paid to stockholders reduce retained earnings by $9,494 million.

❸ JNJ's policy is to use treasury shares for employee stock-based compensation plans—see discussion of stock-based compensation later in the module. Treasury stock always has a negative balance because stock buybacks are the opposite of a stock sale. In the statement of stockholders' equity, the positive $3,060 indicates that treasury stock is *reduced* by $3,060 million, which is the *original cost* of the treasury shares used for compensation during the year. In exchange for the shares, employees paid cash of $1,949 million only because Johnson & Johnson awarded the stock-based compensation grants when the stock price was lower. The $1,111 million difference reduced retained earnings.

❹ JNJ purchased additional stock on the open market during the year at a cost of $5,868 million, which is shown as a negative number, increasing the treasury stock account. A portion of the stock repurchase was related to a general share buy-back program. Another portion was to forestall a potential drop in stock price from a dilution related to the stock-based compensation plans.

❺ JNJ reported other comprehensive loss of $1,791 million—we explain this in the accumulated other comprehensive income section of this module. Changes in AOCI can be positive or negative.

In 2018, certain accounting rules changed, including those for revenue recognition and income taxes (see Module 5 for a detailed discussion). In adopting the new rules, companies had to make retrospective "catch-up" adjustments to certain equity accounts. JNJ reported a total cumulative adjustment of $(486) million, split between retained earnings $(254 million) and AOCI $(232 million)—see the first row following the beginning balance in Exhibit 8.2.

Exhibit 8.2 ■ Johnson & Johnson's Statement of Stockholders' Equity

$ millions	Total	Retained Earnings	Accumulated Other Comprehensive Income	Common Stock Issued	Treasury Stock
Balance, December 31, 2017....	$60,160	$101,793	$(13,199)	$3,120	$(31,554)
Cumulative adjustment.........	(486)	(254)	(232)		
❶ Net earnings................	15,297	15,297			
❷ Cash dividends paid..........	(9,494)	(9,494)			
❸ Employee compensation and stock option plans...........	1,949	(1,111)			3,060
❹ Repurchase of common stock ...	(5,868)				(5,868)
Other......................	(15)	(15)			
❺ Other comprehensive income (loss), net of tax	(1,791)		(1,791)		
Balance, December 30, 2018....	$59,752	$106,216	$(15,222)	$3,120	$(34,362)

Preferred Stock

Preferred stock is a multi-use security with a number of desirable features. In addition to usual dividend and liquidation preferences, preferred stock has two other common features.

■ **Yield.** Preferred stock can be structured to provide investors with a dividend yield that is similar to an interest rate on a bond. Dividends, unlike interest expense, are not deductible for tax purposes. Therefore, the after-tax cost to the company for preferred dividends is higher than the after-tax effective interest rate on a bond.

■ **Conversion privileges.** Preferred stock can contain an option that allows investors to convert their preferred shares into common shares at a predetermined number of common shares per preferred share.

Both of these features are illustrated in the Corning Inc. convertible preferred stock as reported on its balance sheet and related footnote.

At December 31 (In millions, except share amounts)	2018	2017
Shareholders' Equity		
Convertible preferred stock, Series A—Par value 100 per share; shares authorized 3,100; shares issued: 2,300	$2,300	$2,300

Fixed Rate Cumulative Convertible Preferred Stock, Series A. On January 15, 2014, Corning designated a new series of its preferred stock as Fixed Rate Cumulative Convertible Preferred Stock, Series A, par value $100 per share, and issued 1,900 shares of preferred stock at an issue price of $1 million per share, for an aggregate issue price of $1.9 billion, to Samsung Display with the acquisition of its equity interest in Samsung Corning Precision Materials. Corning also issued to Samsung Display an additional amount of preferred stock at closing, for an aggregate issue price of $400 million in cash.

Dividends on the preferred stock are cumulative and accrue at the annual rate of 4.25% on the per share issue price of $1 million...The preferred stock is convertible at the option of the holder and the Company upon certain events, at a conversion rate of 50,000 shares of Corning's common stock per one share of preferred stock... The Company has the right, at its option, to cause some or all the shares of preferred stock to be converted into common stock, if, for 25 trading days (whether or not consecutive) within any period of 40 consecutive trading days, the closing price of common stock exceeds $35 per share.

Corning's convertible preferred stock pays a dividend of 4.25% of par value, meaning that the preferred shareholder, Samsung Display, receives an annual dividend of $97.75 million ($2,300 million × 4.25%). Interestingly, this yield is higher than the effective rate on the company's debt securities.

The conversion would have a number of effects creating some pros and cons to the conversion. The preferred shareholder would convert each preferred share into 50,000 common shares. Each preferred share was issued for $1 million, which would convert to $1.5105 million of common stock (2018 year-end stock price of $30.21 × 50,000 shares). And Samsung Display would benefit from any future price appreciation in Corning's common stock. This seems like a good trade. However, there is a downside—the preferred dividend per share is $42,500 whereas the dividends on 50,000 common shares in 2018 were only $9,000 ($0.18 per share). Thus, under the conversion the preferred shareholder would receive a much lower yield. They would also relinquish their liquidation preference—senior position in bankruptcy—although this is only an issue if Corning is in financial difficulty. The conversion decision depends upon a careful evaluation of Corning's future prospects and consequent stock-price increase.

Common Stock

Johnson & Johnson has one class of common stock that has the following attributes (see Exhibit 8.1).

- A par value of $1.00 per share. **Par value** is an arbitrary amount set when the company was formed and has no relation to, or impact on, the stock's market value. Generally, par value is irrelevant from an analysis perspective. It is only used to allocate proceeds from stock issuances between the two contributed capital accounts on the balance sheet: common stock and additional paid-in capital.

- 4,320,000,000 shares of stock have been **authorized** for issuance. The company cannot issue (sell) more shares than have been authorized. If more shares are needed, say for an acquisition, the stockholders must vote to authorize more shares.

- To date, JNJ has **issued** (sold) 3,119,843,000 shares of common stock. The number of issued shares is a cumulative amount. Year-over-year changes in the number of issued shares represent the number of shares of stock issued in the current year.

■ To date, JNJ has repurchased 457,519,000 shares from its stockholders at a cumulative cost of $34,362 million. These shares are currently held in the company's treasury, hence the name **treasury stock**. These shares neither have voting rights nor do they receive dividends.

■ Number of **outstanding shares** is equal to the issued shares less treasury shares. There were 2,662,324,000 (3,119,843,000 − 457,519,000) shares outstanding at the end of 2018.

■ Number of outstanding common shares multiplied by the market price per share yields the **market capitalization** (or *market cap*) for the company. As of December 31, 2018, JNJ's market capitalization was $343.6 billion (2,662,324,000 shares outstanding × $129.05 per share).

Business Insight ■ Noncontrolling Interests

Many companies report an additional equity account called **noncontrolling interest**. This account arises when the company controls a subsidiary but does not own all of the subsidiary's stock. That is, the company has control of the subsidiary but does not own 100% of its stock. The noncontrolling interest is the portion of the subsidiary's stock NOT owned by the company. The noncontrolling interest account increases with any additional investment made by the noncontrolling shareholders and by their share of the subsidiary's net income whose common stock they own. The account decreases by any dividends paid to the noncontrolling shareholders and by their share of any net losses of the subsidiary. For most companies, the dollar amount of noncontrolling interest is small as illustrated in the following excerpt from the equity section of **PepsiCo**'s 2018 balance sheet.

In millions, except per share amounts	2018	2017
Preferred stock, no par value	$ —	$ 41
Repurchased preferred stock	—	(197)
PepsiCo Common Shareholders' Equity		
Common stock, par value 1 2/3¢ per share (authorized 3,600 shares; issued, net of repurchased common stock at par value: 1,409 and 1,420 shares, respectively)	$ 23	$ 24
Capital in excess of par value	3,953	3,996
Retained earnings	59,947	52,839
Accumulated other comprehensive loss	(15,119)	(13,057)
Repurchased common stock, in excess of par value (458 and 446 shares, respectively)	(34,286)	(32,757)
Total PepsiCo Common Shareholders' Equity	14,518	11,045
Noncontrolling interests	84	92
Total Equity	$14,602	$10,981

The relative magnitude of noncontrolling interest that PepsiCo reports ($84 million compared with $14,602 million of total equity) is typical. For comparison, the median noncontrolling interest as a percent of total liabilities and equity for the S&P 500 companies in 2018 was 0.04% (only 50 companies in the S&P 500 report noncontrolling interest as a percent of total liabilities and equity of greater than 10%). We further explain noncontrolling interest in a later module.

LO1 Review 8-1

Stockholders' equity reflects owner financing of an enterprise.

Required

For each of the following, (1) indicate whether the statement is true or false regarding stockholders' equity, and (2) for any identified false statement, indicate how to correct that statement.

___ a. Stockholders' equity represents the market value of the company.

___ b. Stockholders do not manage the company directly, but oversee its operations through its Board of Directors.

___ c. Issued shares represents the number of shares that have been sold to investors.

___ d. Outstanding shares represents the number of shares issued less the number of shares repurchased by the company.

___ e. Preferred stock is entitled to the same per share dividends as common stock.

___ f. Treasury stock represents the cumulative total cost of shares that the company has repurchased, net of any subsequent sales of the treasury shares. Assume no repurchased shares are retired.

Solution on p. 8-51.

Stock Transactions

LO2

Analyze stock issuances and repurchases.

Stock Issuance

Companies issue stock to obtain cash and other assets for use in their business. Stock issuances increase assets (cash) by the issue proceeds: the number of shares sold multiplied by the price of the stock on the issue date. Equity increases by the same amount, which is reflected in contributed capital accounts. If the stock has a par value, the common stock account increases by the number of shares sold multiplied by its par value. The additional paid-in capital account increases by the remainder. Stock can also be issued as "no-par" or as "no-par with a stated value." For no-par stock, the common stock account is increased by the entire proceeds of the sale and no amount is assigned to additional paid-in capital. For no-par stock with a stated value, the stated value is treated just like par value; that is, common stock is increased by the number of shares multiplied by the stated value, and the remainder is assigned to the additional paid-in capital account.

Stock Issuance Financial Effects   To illustrate, assume that JNJ issues 1,000 shares with a $1.00 par value common stock at a market price of $100 cash per share. This stock issuance has the following financial statement effects.

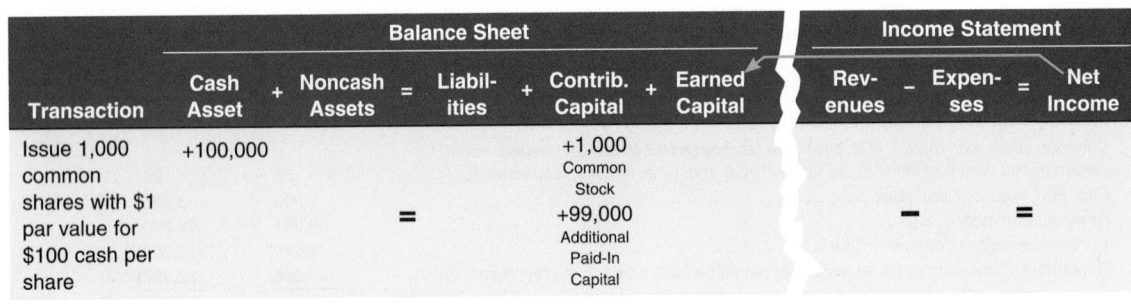

Specifically, the stock issuance affects the financial statements as follows.

1. Cash increases by $100,000 (1,000 shares × $100 per share).
2. Common stock increases by the par value of shares sold: 1,000 shares × $1 par value = $1,000.
3. Additional paid-in capital increases by the $99,000 difference between the issue proceeds and par value ($100,000 − $1,000).

Once shares are issued, they are traded in the open market among investors. The proceeds of those sales and their associated gains and losses, as well as fluctuations in the company's stock price subsequent to issuance, do not affect the issuing company and are not recorded in its accounting records.

Stock Disclosures and Interpretation   Using our stock issuance illustration above, we can interpret the common stock and additional paid-in capital (capital surplus) disclosures on Coca-Cola's balance sheet.

December 31 (In millions, except par value)	2018	2017
The Coca-Cola Company Shareowners' Equity		
Common stock, $0.25 par value; Authorized—11,200 shares;		
Issued—7,040 and 7,040 shares, respectively	$ 1,760	$ 1,760
Capital surplus	16,520	15,864
Reinvested earnings	63,234	60,430
Accumulated other comprehensive income (loss)	(12,814)	(10,305)
Treasury stock, at cost — 2,772 and 2,781 shares, respectively	(51,719)	(50,677)
Equity attributable to shareowners of the Coca-Cola Company	$16,981	$17,072

As of December 31, 2018, Coca-Cola has issued 7,040 million shares of common stock for total proceeds of $18,280 million ($1,760 million + $16,520 million). The $1,760 million in common stock is the total par value for the 7,040 million shares ($0.25 × 7,040 million). The $16,520 million capital surplus account (another title for additional paid-in capital) is the difference between the $18,280 million total issue proceeds and the $1,760 million par value. The average price at which Coke issued the 7,040 million shares is $2.60 ($18,280 million/7,040 million shares issued).

> **IFRS Alert**
> Stock terminology can differ between IFRS and GAAP. Under IFRS, common stock is called *share capital* and additional paid-in capital (APIC) is called *share premium*. Despite different terminology, the accounting is similar.

> **Research Insight** ◼ Stock Issuance and Stock Returns
>
> Research shows that, historically, companies issuing equity securities experience unusually low stock returns for several years following those offerings. Evidence suggests that this poor performance is partly due to overly optimistic estimates of long-term growth by equity analysts. That optimism causes offering prices to be too high. This over-optimism is most pronounced when the analyst is employed by the brokerage firm that underwrites the stock issue. There is also evidence that companies manage earnings upward prior to an equity offering. This means the observed decrease in returns following an issuance likely reflects the market's negative reaction, on average, to lower earnings, especially if the company fails to meet analysts' forecasts.

Stock Repurchase (Treasury Stock)

JNJ has repurchased 457,519,000 shares of its common stock for a cumulative cost of $34,362 million as of December 31, 2018 (see Exhibit 8.1). One reason a company repurchases shares is because it believes that the market undervalues them. The logic is that the repurchase sends a favorable signal to the market about the company's financial condition, which positively impacts its share price and, thus, allows it to resell those shares for a "gain." Any such gain on resale, however, is *never* reflected in the income statement. Instead, any excess of the resale price over the repurchase price is added to additional paid-in capital. GAAP prohibits companies from reporting gains and losses from stock transactions with their own stockholders.

Another reason companies repurchase shares is to offset the dilutive effects of share-based compensation plans including an employee stock option program. When an employee exercises stock options, the number of shares outstanding increases. Because net income is unchanged, these additional shares reduce earnings per share and are, therefore, *dilutive*. In response, many companies repurchase an equivalent number of shares in the open market to keep outstanding shares constant.

A stock repurchase reduces the size of the company (cash declines and, thus, total assets decline). A repurchase has the opposite financial statement effects from a stock issuance. That is, cash decreases by the price of the shares repurchased (number of shares repurchased multiplied by the purchase price per share), and stockholders' equity decreases by the same amount. The decrease in equity is recorded in a contra equity account called treasury stock. Treasury stock (the contra equity account) has a negative balance, which reduces stockholders' equity. Thus, when the treasury stock contra equity account increases, total stockholders' equity decreases.

When the company subsequently resells treasury stock, there is no accounting gain or loss. Instead, the difference between the proceeds received and the original purchase price of the treasury stock is reflected as an increase or decrease to additional paid-in capital.

Stock Repurchase Financial Effects To illustrate, assume that 200 common shares of JNJ previously issued for $100 are repurchased for $90 cash per share. This repurchase has the following financial statement effects.

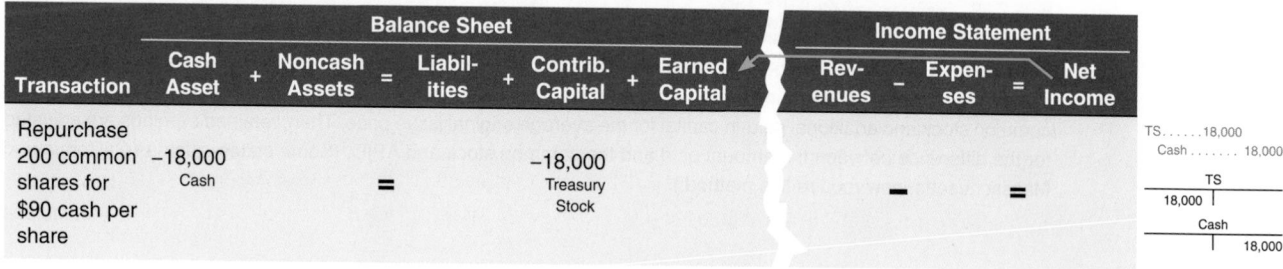

	Balance Sheet							Income Statement					
Transaction	Cash Asset	+	Noncash Assets	=	Liabilities	+	Contrib. Capital	+	Earned Capital		Revenues	−	Expenses	=	Net Income
Repurchase 200 common shares for $90 cash per share	−18,000 Cash			=			−18,000 Treasury Stock					−		=	

TS......18,000
 Cash.......18,000

TS
18,000 |

 Cash
  | 18,000

Assets (cash) and stockholders' equity both decrease. Treasury stock (a contra equity account) increases by $18,000, which reduces stockholders' equity by that amount.

Reselling Treasury Stock   Assume that these 200 shares of treasury stock are subsequently resold for $95 cash per share. This resale of treasury stock has the following financial statement effects.

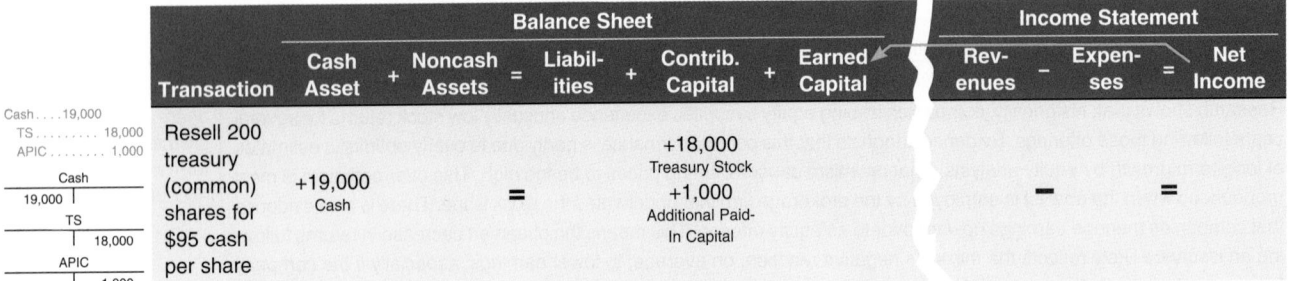

Cash assets increase by $19,000 (200 shares × $95 per share), the treasury stock account is reduced by the $18,000 cost of the treasury shares issued (thus increasing contributed capital), and the $1,000 excess (200 shares × $5 per share) is reported as an increase in additional paid-in capital. (If the resale price is below the repurchase price, then additional paid-in capital is reduced until it reaches a zero balance, after which retained earnings is reduced.) Again, there is no effect on the income statement as companies are prohibited from reporting gains and losses from repurchases and reissuances of their own stock.

Treasury Stock Disclosures and Interpretation   The treasury stock section of JNJ's balance sheet is reproduced below.

In millions, except for share amounts	2018	2017
Common stock held in treasury, at cost (457,519,000 shares and 437,318,000 shares)	34,362	31,554

JNJ repurchased a cumulative total of 457,519,000 shares of common stock for $34,362 million, an average repurchase price of $75.10 per share. These shares, while legally owned by JNJ, have no voting rights and receive no dividends. Treasury shares can be resold should JNJ need to raise capital or acquire another entity. Treasury shares can also be used to compensate employees and executives. Sometimes, companies "retire" treasury stock. In that event, the treasury stock account is reduced by the cost of the treasury shares retired (thus increasing stockholders' equity) and the common stock and APIC accounts are likewise reduced (thus reducing stockholders' equity by the same amount). When treasury shares are retired, total stockholders' equity remains unchanged.

> **IFRS Alert**
> Accounting for stock repurchases under IFRS is similar to GAAP except that IFRS provides little guidance on how to allocate the treasury stock to equity accounts. Thus, repurchases can be recorded as an increase to treasury stock, or as a decrease to common stock and APIC (share capital and premium), retained earnings (reserves), or some combination.

Managerial Decision ■ You Are the Chief Financial Officer

As CFO, you believe that your company's stock price is lower than its real value. You are considering various alternatives to increase that price, including the repurchase of company stock in the market. What are some factors you should consider before making your decision? [Answer, p. 8-29]

Business Insight ■ Companies Increasingly Choose Retirement for Treasury Stock

In recent years, a large number of companies have not applied the *Treasury Stock* method as described in this section, but instead applied the *Retirement* method. Under the retirement method, stock repurchases reduce both common stock and additional paid-in capital for the average original issue price. Then, retained earnings are adjusted for the difference between the amount paid and the common stock and APIC. (Some states, such as California and Massachusetts, now require this method.)

continued

continued from previous page

The following stockholders' equity statement from Microsoft demonstrates the retirement method. We see that the repurchase reduces common stock (and APIC) by $3,033 million and retained earnings by $7,699 million for a total cost of $10,732 million. Interestingly, this helps explain why Microsoft reports such a low balance for retained earnings.

Microsoft's Statement of Stockholders' Equity

Year Ended June 30 (In millions)	2018
Common stock and paid-in capital	
Balance, beginning of period	$69,315
Common stock issued	1,002
Common stock repurchased	(3,033)
Stock-based compensation expense	3,940
Other, net	(1)
Balance, end of period	71,223
Retained earnings	
Balance, beginning of period	17,769
Net income	16,571
Common stock cash dividends	(12,917)
Common stock repurchased	(7,699)
Cumulative effect of accounting change	(42)
Balance, end of period	13,682
Accumulated other comprehensive income	
Balance, beginning of period	627
Other comprehensive income (loss)	(2,856)
Cumulative effect of accounting change	42
Balance, end of period	(2,187)
Total stockholders' equity	$82,718

LO2 Review 8-2

Following is the equity section of Coca-Cola Company balance sheet for December 31, 2018 and 2017.

COCA-COLA COMPANY SHAREOWNERS' EQUITY (In millions, except par value)	Dec. 31, 2018	Dec. 31, 2017
Common stock, $0.25 par value; Authorized—11,200 shares; Issued—7,040 and 7,040 shares, respectively	$ 1,760	$ 1,760
Capital surplus	16,520	15,864
Reinvested earnings	63,234	60,430
Accumulated other comprehensive income (loss)	(12,814)	(10,305)
Treasury stock, at cost — 2,772 and 2,781 shares, respectively	(51,719)	(50,677)
Equity attributable to shareowners of the Coca-Cola Company	16,981	17,072
Equity attributable to noncontrolling interests	2,077	1,905
Total equity	$19,058	$18,977

Required

a. How much additional common stock did Coca-Cola issue during the first quarter of 2018? Explain.

b. Assume that Coca-Cola issued 400,000 shares during the first quarter at $45 per share. Use the financial statement effects template to record this transaction.

c. Assume that during the first quarter, Coca-Cola purchased approximately 22 million shares on the open market at an average price of $43.45 per share. Use the financial statement effects template to record this transaction. Round numbers to millions.

d. Assume the company sold 30 million shares of treasury stock for $964 million. The treasury shares had an original cost of $15.77 per share. Determine the effect of this transaction on the treasury stock and capital surplus accounts. Round numbers to millions.

Solution on p. 8-51.

Stock-Based Compensation

LO3 Interpret stock-based compensation, including restricted stock and options.

Common stock has been an important component of executive compensation for decades. The general idea follows: If the company executives own stock, they will have an incentive to increase its value. This aligns the executives' interests with those of other stockholders. Although the strength of this alignment is the subject of much debate, its logic compels boards of directors of most American companies to use stock-based compensation.

Characteristics of Stock-Based Compensation Plans

Companies use a range of stock-based compensation plans. The Business Insight box below provides details of the types of plans, but they share the following features.

- **Create incentives for employees to think and act like shareholders.** The amount of the stock award is often tied to corporate performance targets including sales, income, and stock price. Stock-based compensation plans motivate employees to work hard and make decisions that improve company performance.

- **Encourage employee retention and longevity.** With most plans, employees earn the right to own or purchase shares over time. The period of time over which ownership rights are earned is called the *vesting* period (usually a few years). During this vesting period, employees have greater incentive to stay with the company.

Johnson & Johnson's compensation plans include stock options, restricted stock units (RSUs), and performance share units (these are RSUs that will only be awarded if certain performance targets are met, which creates additional incentives for employees).

Business Insight ■ Types of Stock-Based Compensation Plans

The following stock-based compensation plans are widely in use today and we often see companies maintain more than one of these plans at the same time.

- **Restricted stock.** Shares are issued to the employee but the employee is *not* free to sell the shares during a restriction period. This creates an incentive for the employee to remain with the company. During the restriction period, the employee has the rights of a shareholder, other than the ability to sell the shares.
- **Restricted stock units (RSUs).** Employee is awarded the right to receive a specified number of shares (or cash equivalent) after a vesting period. Unlike restricted stock, shares are not issued to the employee until after the restriction period, at which time the employee has all of the rights of a shareholder (but not during the vesting period).
- **Employee stock options.** Employees are given the right to purchase shares at a fixed (strike) price for a specified period of time. Similar to restricted stock, there is a waiting period (called a vesting period) before the employee can purchase the shares.
- **Stock appreciation rights (SARs).** Employees are paid in cash or stock for the increase in share price, but do not purchase shares of stock. This is similar to a stock option but with no share purchase required.
- **Employee share purchase plans.** Employees are permitted to purchase shares directly from the company at a discounted price, typically a set percentage (such as 85%) of the prevailing market price.

Most stock-based compensation plans contain forfeiture provisions—if the employee is terminated for cause or leaves the company before the rights to receive shares are vested, the award is forfeited.

Analysis of Stock-Based Compensation Plans

There are two analysis issues relating to stock-based compensation plans: recognition of the *expense* and potential *dilution*.

Expense Recognition The expense side is straightforward. When shares or options are awarded to employees, companies estimate the fair value of the award and recognize the fair value as compensation expense in the income statement over the period in which the employee provides service.

Potential Dilution Dilution relates to the number of common shares outstanding that have a claim against the company's earnings or net assets. For example, if a company earns $1 million and there are 1,000,000 shares outstanding, the earnings per share (EPS) available to pay dividends is $1. But, if there are 2,000,000 shares outstanding, the EPS available to pay dividends is only $0.50. The drop in EPS due to the increase in the number of outstanding shares is called *dilution* and companies are required to report diluted EPS in their annual reports—we discuss EPS later in this module. In the same way, dilution affects the value of each share of stock. If a company is worth $10 million, the per share price of the company's stock will be half as much if there are 2,000,000 shares outstanding than if there are only 1,000,000.

Mindful of shareholder concerns about the potential dilution of their stock holdings, companies often repurchase shares in an effort to counter the dilutive effects of share issuances under stock-based compensation plans. Johnson & Johnson describes this in its footnotes.

> The Company settles employee benefit equity issuances with treasury shares. Treasury shares are replenished throughout the year for the number of shares used to settle employee benefit equity issuances.

To work through the analysis issues relating to employee stock compensation plans, it is important for us to understand:

- How stock-based compensation expense is measured and recorded in the income statement.
- Dilutive effects of stock-based compensation and the cash cost incurred to offset that dilution.
- Dilutive effects of stock-based compensation on earnings per share (EPS).

Accounting for Stock-Based Compensation

Regardless of the type of stock-based compensation plan, there are common accounting steps.

- When the award is granted to employees, the company estimates the fair value of the award.
- The fair value of the award is recorded as an expense in the income statement, ratably over the vesting period, and APIC is increased by the same amount.
- When the shares are issued, common stock and additional paid-in capital increase in the same manner as for cash-based stock issuances, as described above.

Stock-based compensation expense is included on the income statement but rarely reported as a separate line item. Like other forms of compensation, the expense is included in cost of goods sold (for employees in R&D and manufacturing) or selling general and administrative expense (for employees in selling and administration and executive roles). However, we can determine the amount of the expense from the statement of cash flows. Because stock-based compensation expense is a noncash expense, companies add back this expense in the statement of cash flow as in the following excerpt from the JNJ statement from 2018.

JOHNSON & JOHNSON AND SUBSIDIARIES Consolidated Statements of Cash Flows			
$ millions	2018	2017	2016
Cash flows from operating activities			
Net earnings.	$15,297	$1,300	$16,540
Adjustments to reconcile net earnings to cash flows from operating activities:			
Depreciation and amortization of property and intangibles.	6,929	5,642	3,754
Stock-based compensation	**978**	**962**	**878**

JNJ adds back the $978 million of stock-based compensation expense, which is included in net income on the income statement, to arrive at cash from operations. (This is similar to the $6,929 million add-back for depreciation expense.)

Interpretation of Stock-Based Compensation The stock-based compensation add-back might lead some to conclude that this form of compensation is cash free. But this is erroneous—a real cash cost occurs when the company buys new treasury shares in the open market to offset the dilution created by the share award to the employees. Consider also that the company used stock-based compensation instead of paying higher salaries or bonuses in cash. The employees bartered for stock. So while companies and analysts often add stock-based compensation expense back when computing and reporting non-GAAP measures such as EBIT and EBITDA, that treatment is not correct. *Stock-based compensation expense* is a real cash cost. To accurately evaluate and forecast operating cash flow, analysts must either include stock-based compensation expense or recognize the related treasury-stock purchase as an operating cash outflow.

In addition to the cash cost that JNJ will incur to offset the potential dilution relating to shares that will be issued to employees, JNJ's earnings per share will be affected. Fortunately, the effect of this potential dilution is a required disclosure in a statistic called diluted earnings per share that is reported on the income statement with details provided in a related footnote disclosure. We discuss diluted earnings per share later in this module.

Footnote Disclosures for Stock-Based Compensation

Footnotes to the 10-K contain extensive descriptions of stock-based compensation plans that describe two facets of a company's stock-based compensation: plan activity and fair value.

Plan Activity Disclosure for plan activity includes:

- Number of shares granted to employees during the year (to illustrate potential dilution to existing shareholders).
- Number of shares issued during the year to satisfy awards that vested.
- Any shares forfeited—when employees leave the company or fail to exercise options within the specified time period.

For example, Johnson & Johnson provides the following information related to activity for its three types of compensation plans.

Shares in thousands	Outstanding Stock Options	Outstanding Restricted Share Units	Outstanding Performance Share Units
Shares at December 31, 2017	111,306	20,161	2,625
Granted.	17,115	6,074	1,142
Issued.		(6,684)	(1,151)
Options exercised.	(16,228)		
Canceled or forfeited or adjusted	(2,541)	(1,091)	(122)
Shares at December 30, 2018	109,652	18,460	2,494

Fair Value and Expense Disclosure for fair value and expense includes:

- Fair value of the stock-based compensation awards.
- How fair value is determined. Restricted stock awards are valued using the share price on the date of the award. Stock option plans are valued using option pricing models. The two most common models are the Black-Scholes model and the bilateral model (also called lattice method).
- The expense on the income statement.
- Value of the shares issued to employees over and above the price the employee paid for shares. This difference is called the intrinsic value.

For example, JNJ provides fair value details for its stock option plan in its 2018 10-K. Similar schedules are usually provided for each type of stock-based compensation plan.

	2018	2017	2016
Risk-free rate	2.77%	2.25%	1.51%
Expected volatility.	15.77%	15.30%	15.76%
Expected life (in years).	7.0	7.0	7.0
Expected dividend yield	2.70%	2.90%	3.10%

JNJ disclosed the following per share fair values for stock-based awards during the year.

Stock options	$17.98
Restricted share units	119.67
Performance share units	120.64

Interpretation of Fair Values for Different Stock-Based Awards For JNJ, the fair value of RSUs is much higher than the fair value of the options because the two compensation arrangements differ greatly. If stock price drops between the grant date and the time the shares are issued, the employee with the RSU will still receive something of value (the share). The employee with an option could buy the stock at the predetermined (higher) price. Because it makes no economic sense to pay more for the stock than its market value, the option is worthless and the employee is left empty handed.

The appendix to this module discusses additional accounting and analysis issues for share-based compensation.

LO3 Review 8-3

Coca-Cola Company has a number of stock-based compensation plans including stock options, RSUs, and employee stock purchase plans. The company reports the following activity for its stock options.

In millions	Shares
Outstanding on January 1, 2018	173
Granted	8
Exercised	(47)
Forfeited/expired	(1)
Outstanding on December 31, 2018	133

The company also reports the following information in its footnotes.
- Total stock-based compensation expense of $225 million for 2018.
- Fair value of stock options granted during 2018 of $10.58 and the options' strike price averaged $36.74.
- Granted 2,183 thousand performance share units during 2018 with a fair value of $38.45 per share.

Required
a. How did Coca-Cola's stock-based compensation expense affect net income for the year?
b. How did the stock-based compensation expense affect cash from operations? Can we infer from this that the expense involves no cash outflow for Coca-Cola?
c. Consider the fair value of the stock options granted during the year. If these options vest over four years, determine the related compensation expense for 2018.
d. Consider the fair value of the performance share units granted during the year. If the average restriction period is two years, determine the related compensation expense for 2018.
e. Explain why the fair value per share of the performance share units is so much larger than the stock option fair value.

Solution on p. 8-52.

Dividends and Stock Splits

In this section, we discuss the following topics related to earned capital accounts.

LO4
Analyze cash dividends and stock splits.

- ◼ Dividends, which can be paid in cash, in land, in other property, or in additional shares of stock (stock dividends).

- ◼ Stock splits, where the company distributes additional shares of stock to existing shareholders.

Cash Dividend Disclosures

Johnson & Johnson reports retained earnings of $106,216 million, which is higher than the prior year. Many companies, but not all, pay dividends and reasons for dividend payments vary. JNJ reports that it "increased its dividend in 2018 for the 56th consecutive year," paying $3.54 per share in 2018. Companies typically pay dividends on a quarterly basis.

Investors and financial analysts closely monitor dividend payments. It is generally perceived that the level of dividend payments is related to the company's expected long-term recurring income. Accordingly, dividend increases are usually viewed as positive signals about future performance and are accompanied by stock price increases. By that logic, companies rarely reduce their dividends unless absolutely necessary because dividend reductions are often met with substantial stock price declines.

Dividend Payout and Yield

IFRS Alert
The dividend payout ratio is called "dividend cover" in some IFRS countries.

Two common metrics that analysts use to assess a company's dividends are dividend payout and dividend yield. These ratios are computed for common stock dividends and not for preferred stock because, as we explain below, most preferred stock has a stated dividend rate such that a "payout" ratio is not meaningful.

Dividend Payout The dividend payout ratio measures the proportion of the company's earnings that is paid out as dividend—it is defined as:

$$\text{Dividend payout} = \frac{\text{Common stock dividends per share}}{\text{Basic earnings per share (EPS)}}$$

During 2018, JNJ reported dividends per share of $3.54 and basic earnings per share of $5.70. The dividend payout ratio is 62% ($3.54/$5.70). By comparison, the median dividend payout ratio for S&P 500 companies in 2018 is 30%, with 17% of those companies not paying any dividends at all. More mature, profitable companies, such as JNJ, tend to have a higher payout ratio because they have fewer investment opportunities that require cash.

Dividend Yield Dividend yield is tied to the current market value of the company's stock and is defined as:

$$\text{Dividend yield} = \frac{\text{Common stock dividends per share}}{\text{Current share price}}$$

The ratio measures the cash return to stockholders given the cash investment. Of course, the other way to earn a return is via stock price appreciation, but dividend yield reflects only the one-year cash return. Given JNJ's dividends per share in 2018 of $3.54 and its closing share price on December 31, 2018, of $129.05, the dividend yield is 2.7% ($3.54/$129.05).

Cash Dividends Financial Effects

Cash dividends reduce both cash and retained earnings by the amount of the cash dividends paid. To illustrate, assume that JNJ declares and pays cash dividends in the amount of $10 million. The financial statement effects of this cash dividend payment are as follows.

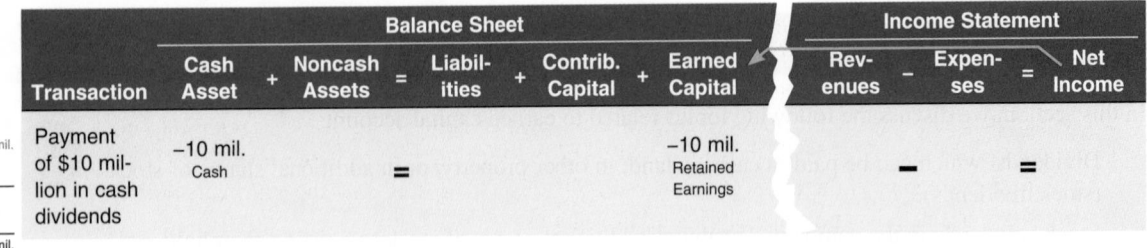

Dividend payments *do not* affect net income. They directly reduce retained earnings and bypass the income statement.

Cumulative Dividends in Arrears   Dividends on preferred stock have priority over those on common stock, including unpaid prior years' preferred dividends (called *dividends in arrears*) when preferred stock is cumulative. To illustrate, assume that a company has 15,000 shares of $50 par value, 8% preferred stock outstanding; assume that the preferred stock is cumulative, which means that any unpaid dividends accumulate and must be paid before common dividends. The company also has 50,000 shares of $5 par value common stock outstanding. During its first three years in business, assume that the company declares $20,000 dividends in the first year, $260,000 of dividends in the second year, and $60,000 of dividends in the third year. Cash dividends paid to each class of stock in each of the three years follows.

	Preferred Stock	Common Stock
Year 1—$20,000 cash dividends paid		
Current-year dividend (15,000 shares × $50 par × 8%; but only $20,000 paid, leaving $40,000 in arrears)	$20,000	
Balance to common		$ 0
Year 2—$260,000 cash dividends paid		
Dividends in arrears from Year 1 ([15,000 shares × $50 par × 8%] – $20,000)	40,000	
Current-year dividend (15,000 shares × $50 par × 8%)	60,000	
Balance to common		160,000
Year 3—$60,000 cash dividends paid		
Current-year dividend (15,000 shares × $50 par × 8%)	60,000	
Balance to common		0

Dividends need not be paid in cash. Many companies pay dividends in the form of additional shares of stock. Companies can also distribute additional shares to their shareholders via a stock split. We cover both of these distributions in this section.

Stock Split

A **stock split** happens when a company issues additional common shares to its existing stockholders. Stock splits are usually prompted by the company's desire to reduce its stock price in order to improve marketability of the shares. There seems to be a psychological hurdle for investors when the price of a share exceeds $100. A typical stock split is 2-for-1, which means that the company distributes one additional share for each share owned by shareholders. Because there is no cash flow effect from a stock split, the company's market cap is unaffected by the split. Following the distribution each investor owns twice as many shares that are each worth approximately half as much. So the total market value of their investment is unchanged. Although the split itself has little effect on shareholders, the price per share is reduced, thus increasing the marketability of the shares.

A stock split is not a monetary transaction and, as such, there are no financial statement effects. However, companies must disclose the number of shares outstanding for all periods presented in the financial statements. Additionally, companies must reduce the par value of the stock proportionally (to ½ of the previous par value for a 2:1 stock split) and historical financial statements presented in the current 10-K must be adjusted likewise.

Stock Split in Form of Dividend   One common way to perform a stock split is to declare a dividend *payable in company stock*. The company adds the par value of the stock distributed to the common stock account and subtracts the same amount from retained earnings (similar to a cash dividend). Thus, there is no net effect on total stockholders' equity. For example, TJX Companies Inc. announced a two-for-one stock split in the form of a stock dividend, paid on November 6, 2018, to the shareholders of record at the close of business on October 30, 2018. After the split, outstanding common shares doubled to approximately 1.3 million shares.

Review 8-4 LO4

Wells Fargo (WFC) reports the following information in its 2018 financial statements.

For 12 Months Ended	2018	2017
Preferred stock: Cash dividends paid ($ millions)	$(1,622)	$(1,629)
Common stock: Cash dividends paid ($ millions).	$(7,692)	$(7,480)
Earnings per common share ($ per share).	$4.31	$4.14
Dividends declared per common share ($ per share)	$1.64	$1.54

Required

a. Use the financial statement effects template to record the preferred and common stock dividends for 2018.

b. If Wells Fargo had paid $100 million more in common stock dividends in 2018, what would have been the after-tax effect on net income for that year?

c. Compute the dividend payout ratio for 2017 and 2018.

d. Given Wells Fargo's closing stock price of $46.08 on December 31, 2018, compute the dividend yield ratio for 2018.

Solution on p. 8-52.

Accumulated Other Comprehensive Income

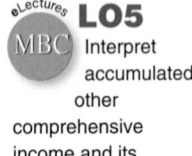

LO5
Interpret accumulated other comprehensive income and its components.

Unrealized gains and losses arise when the fair value of an asset or liability on the balance sheet differs from its cost. For most assets and liabilities (see below), unrealized gains and losses are not reflected in net income nor in retained earnings because the company has had no transaction to create a realized gain or loss.

There are selected items recorded on the balance sheet at fair value—see list below. For the accounts listed below, any unrealized gains or losses are captured in the asset or liability section of the balance sheet. However, because unrealized gains or losses are not reported in net income or retained earnings, the balance sheet does not balance. To solve this issue, unrealized gains and losses are added to **accumulated other comprehensive income (AOCI)**, a stockholders' equity account that captures unrealized gains and losses on certain assets and liabilities. Unrealized gains and losses are "held" in AOCI until the related asset is sold (or liability settled) and any gain or loss is realized.

AOCI Components

Following are common items in AOCI—we further describe these items in later modules.

- **Foreign currency translation adjustments.** Foreign subsidiaries often maintain their financial statements in foreign currencies and these statements are translated into $US before the subsidiaries' financial statements are included in the company's 10-K. The strengthening and weakening of the $US vis-à-vis foreign currencies results in decreases and increases in the $US-value of subsidiaries' assets and liabilities. Because subsidiaries normally have positive equity (assets exceed liabilities), a weaker $US creates an unrealized foreign currency gain. Conversely, a stronger $US creates an unrealized loss. These unrealized gains or losses in the $US value of foreign subsidiaries' assets and liabilities are included in AOCI.

- **Gains and losses on available-for-sale investments in debt securities.** Investments in certain types of marketable debt securities are reported at fair value on the asset side of a company's balance sheet. If the fair value differs from the securities' cost, there are unrealized gains and losses on these securities included in AOCI. Beginning in 2018, gains and losses on available-for-sale *equity* securities are no longer deferred in AOCI until the securities are sold. New standards require firms measure these equity securities at fair value with changes in the fair value flowing to the income statement.

- **Employee benefit plans.** Unrealized gains and losses on some pension investments and pension liabilities are reported in AOCI.

- **Gains and losses on derivatives and hedges.** Unrealized gains and losses on certain financial securities (derivatives) that companies purchase to hedge exposures to interest rate, foreign exchange rate, and commodity price risks are included in AOCI.

AOCI Disclosures and Interpretation

Following is the reconciliation of beginning and ending balances in AOCI for Johnson & Johnson.

$ millions	Foreign Currency Translation	Gain/ (Loss) On Securities	Employee Benefit Plans	Gain/ (Loss) On Derivatives and Hedges	Total Accumulated Other Comprehensive Income (Loss)
January 3, 2016	$(8,435)	$604	$(5,298)	$ (36)	$(13,165)
Net 2016 changes	(612)	(193)	(682)	(249)	(1,736)
January 1, 2017	(9,047)	411	(5,980)	(285)	(14,901)
Net 2017 changes	1,696	(179)	(170)	355	1,702
December 31, 2017	(7,351)	232	(6,150)	70	(13,199)
Cumulative adjustment to retained earnings		(232)			(232)
Net 2018 changes	(1,518)	—	(8)	(265)	(1,791)
December 30, 2018	$(8,869)	$ —	$(6,158)	$(195)	$(15,222)

As is typical of many companies, JNJ's accumulated other comprehensive income account has become more negative over the past few years for two main reasons.

1. **Foreign currency translation.** JNJ's foreign subsidiaries maintain financial statements in their domestic currencies. To consolidate (combine) those income statements and balance sheets, JNJ first translates all the foreign currency numbers into $US using the rates that prevail on the balance sheet date. As the $US weakens or strengthens vis-à-vis foreign currencies, JNJ's foreign subsidiaries' assets and liabilities are translated into higher or lower amounts, respectively. This creates foreign currency translation gains or losses, which are aggregated each period in AOCI. A stronger US dollar in 2018 created additional unrealized losses of $1,518 million and AOCI became more negative. We discuss the effects of foreign currency translation in Module 9.

2. **Employee benefit plans.** Certain gains and losses on pension and other post-retirement benefit plans are not included in net income but are instead deferred and held in AOCI until recognized on the income statement in future years. We discuss the accounting for pension and other post-retirement benefit plans in Module 10.

Gains and losses on securities and on derivatives are less significant for JNJ (and for most other companies) because these activities are much smaller than foreign subsidiaries and pension plans. Gains and losses on securities have a $0 balance for JNJ in 2018 owing to the new accounting rules for marketable securities. JNJ, like many other companies, made a cumulative adjustment to the opening balance of AOCI (and to retained earnings) in 2018 when the company adopted the new marketable-securities standard. We discuss the accounting for investments in marketable securities in Module 9 and investments in derivative securities in Module 10.

Comprehensive Income During the year, market values on the AOCI items inevitably change and so do the unrealized gains and losses in AOCI. Remember, changes in unrealized gains and losses do not flow to the income statement as they are not part of net income. Instead, those changes are aggregated and labeled **other comprehensive income (OCI)**. The following graphic depicts the relation between net income and retained earnings and between comprehensive income and AOCI.

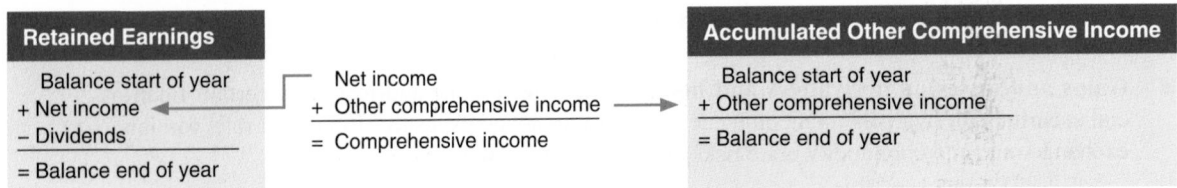

Following is JNJ's statement of comprehensive income for the year.

Consolidated Statements of Comprehensive Income ($ millions)	12 Months Ended		
	2018	2107	2016
Net earnings.	$15,297	$1,300	$16,540
Other comprehensive income (loss), net of tax			
Foreign currency translation	(1,518)	1,696	(612)
Securities:			
Unrealized holding gain (loss) arising during period . . .	(1)	159	(52)
Reclassifications to earnings.	1	(338)	(141)
Net change	—	(179)	(193)
Employee benefit plans:			
Prior service credit (cost), net of amortization.	(44)	2	21
Gain (loss), net of amortization	(56)	29	(862)
Effect of exchange rates	92	(201)	159
Net change	(8)	(170)	(682)
Derivatives & hedges:			
Unrealized gain (loss) arising during period	(73)	(4)	(359)
Reclassifications to earnings.	(192)	359	110
Net change	(265)	355	(249)
Other comprehensive income (loss).	(1,791)	1,702	(1,736)
Comprehensive income	$13,506	$3,002	$14,804

During 2018, JNJ reported other comprehensive loss of $1,791 million. This represents the amount by which AOCI changed during the year, primarily due to the foreign currency translation loss of $1,518 million owing to a stronger US dollar. (See that the components of other comprehensive income are the same components as shown in the "Net 2018 changes" row of Johnson & Johnson's AOCI reconciliation. There is no cash effect from unrealized gains and losses or from any changes in unrealized gains and losses over time.)

For analysis purposes, recall that unrealized gains or losses do not affect net income until the assets are sold or the liabilities settled. If the company anticipates selling the assets or settling the liabilities in the short run (say, within the next quarter), those unrealized gains or losses would flow to net income and this could affect our assessment of company profitability and cash flow. But over the long run, unrealized gains and losses might change substantially (as market prices move) and thus, there is no reliable way to include unrealized gains and losses in our analysis.

Review 8-5 LO5

The annual report of The Coca-Cola Company discloses the following related to accumulated other comprehensive income (AOCI).

Year Ended December 31	2018	2017	2016
Net foreign currency translation adjustments.	$(2,035)	$861	$ (626)
Net gains (losses) on derivatives	(7)	(433)	(382)
Net unrealized gains (losses) on available-for-sale securities	(34)	188	17
Net change in pension and other benefit liabilities	29	322	(53)
Accumulated other comprehensive income (loss)	$(2,047)	$938	$(1,044)

continued

continued from previous page

Required

a. On average, during 2018, did the $US strengthen or weaken vis-à-vis currencies of countries where Coca-Cola has subsidiaries? How do we know?

b. Consider unrealized losses on the available-for-sale securities of $34 million at year-end. What would have been the effect on pretax income if Coca-Cola had sold all of these securities on December 31, 2018?

c. Consider an unrealized loss on the derivatives of $7 million at year-end. Is it accurate to conclude that the market value of these derivatives decreased during the year? Explain.

Solution on p. 8-52.

Convertible Securities

eLectures **LO6**

MBC Analyze convertible securities and their financial effects.

When common stock is issued, the company receives proceeds equal to the market price of the stock multiplied by the number of shares sold. So, the higher the stock price, the greater the proceeds. Preferred stock and long-term bonds are sold in much the same way, and their market price on the date of sale determines the cash proceeds to the company.

Companies can increase the cash proceeds by including provisions in the preferred stock and bonds agreements that make the securities more desirable. One such provision is a **conversion option** that allows the holder of those securities to convert them into common stock at a preset price. While investors own the preferred stock or long-term bond, they receive dividend or interest payments and will have a senior position to common shareholders in the event that the company fails and is liquidated (meaning the preferred stock or bond investors are paid before the common shareholders).

On the other hand, if the company performs well and its prospects are good, the preferred stock or bond investors can exchange their securities for common stock at a pre-agreed exchange ratio. They have the option to become common shareholders. In that case, they can benefit from the company's upside potential and the value of their common shares will increase as the market value of the company increases. This conversion option is valuable to investors and they are willing to pay a higher price for convertible preferred stock or convertible bonds when they are issued. For the company, the issue proceeds are higher.

Convertible Securities Disclosures and Interpretation Earlier in this module we described a 4.25% convertible preferred stock at Corning Inc. that is convertible (at the shareholder's option) into 50,000 common shares for each preferred share. This is an attractive feature for investors and it allowed Corning to realize a higher market price for its preferred stock.

Bonds can have a similar conversion option. Until bonds are converted, bondholders enjoy interest income and a senior position in liquidation. But, if the company performs well, bondholders can convert their bonds into common stock and enjoy all of the benefits of a common shareholder.

For many years, Tesla has used convertible bonds to finance its growth. As of 2018, Tesla had outstanding convertible bonds amounting to $5.7 billion, over half of its total long-term debt of $11 billion. By way of example, consider the following disclosure in Tesla's 10-K.

> In March 2017, we issued $977.5 million in aggregate principal amount of 2.375% Convertible Senior Notes due in March 2022 in a public offering. The net proceeds from the issuance, after deducting transaction costs, were $965.9 million. Each $1,000 of principal of the 2022 Notes is initially convertible into 3.0534 shares of our common stock, which is equivalent to an initial conversion price of $327.50 per share. Holders of the 2022 Notes may convert, at their option, on or after December 15, 2021.

After December 15, 2021, bondholders can exchange each $1,000 bond for 3.0534 shares of Tesla common stock. Until then, the bondholders earn 2.375% interest. Conversion of these bonds is advantageous to the bondholder if Tesla's stock rises above the $327.50 conversion price (computed as $1,000/3.0534). On December 31, 2018, Tesla common stock was valued at $332.80, making conversion attractive, but that option was not available because the conversion feature kicks in on December 15, 2021.

Convertible Securities Financial Effects To see the effects that conversion would have on Tesla's financial statements, assume that on December 31, 2021, bondholders convert $600 million (of the total $977.5 million bond issue) into 1,832,040 common shares of common stock with a par value of $0.001 per share ([$600 million/$1,000] × 3.0534 shares). The financial statement effects of the conversion are as follows (Tesla reports its balance sheet in $000s).

L-T Debt . . 600,000
CS 1.83
APIC 599,998.17

LTD
600,000

CS
1.83

APIC
599,998.17

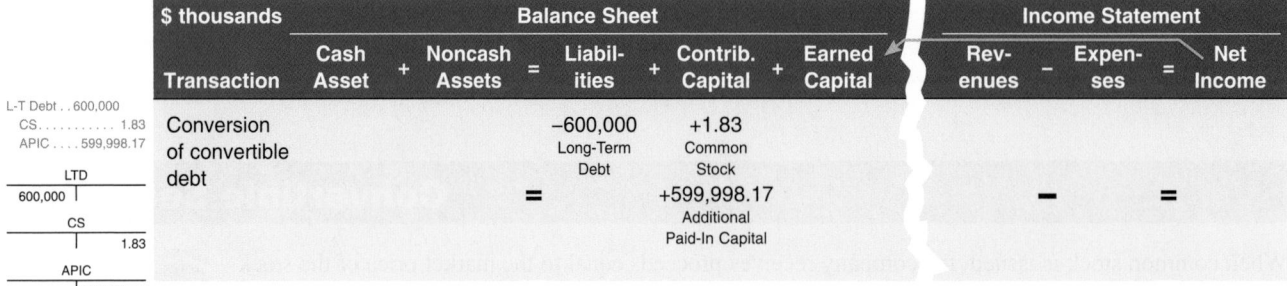

$ thousands	Balance Sheet						Income Statement				
Transaction	Cash Asset	+	Noncash Assets	=	Liabil-ities	+	Contrib. Capital	+	Earned Capital		Rev-enues	−	Expen-ses	=	Net Income
Conversion of convertible debt					−600,000 Long-Term Debt =		+1.83 Common Stock +599,998.17 Additional Paid-In Capital				−		=

Upon conversion, the debt is removed from the balance sheet at its book value ($600 million assumed in this case) and the common stock is issued for that amount, resulting in an increase in the Common Stock account of $1,832 (1,832,040 shares at par value of $0.001 per share). Additional paid-in capital is increased for the remaining amount. No gain or loss (or cash inflow or outflow) is recognized as a result of the conversion.

IFRS Insight   Convertible Securities under IFRS

Unlike GAAP, convertible securities (called *compound financial instruments* under IFRS) are split into separate debt and equity components. The idea is that the conversion premium is akin to a call option on the company's stock. This embedded option has a value of its own even if it is not legally detachable. Thus, under IFRS, the proceeds from the issuance are allocated between the liability component (at fair value) and an equity component (the residual amount).

Review 8-6 LO6

MBC

Assume that Express Scripts Inc. has issued the following convertible debentures: each $1,000 bond is convertible into 200 shares of $1 par common. Assume that the bonds were sold at a discount, and that each bond has a current unamortized discount equal to $150.

Required

Solution on p. 8-53.   Use the financial statements effect template to record the conversion of one of these convertible debentures.

Earnings per Share (EPS)

LO7
MBC Interpret earnings per share.

A common metric reported in the financial press is earnings per share (EPS). EPS is the only ratio defined by GAAP, a testimony to this ratio's perceived importance for users. During the "earnings season"—the time each quarter when public companies release their quarterly earnings reports—EPS disclosures are followed obsessively by Wall Street analysts and investors.

We must be careful in using EPS when comparing companies' operating results, as the number of shares outstanding is not necessarily proportional to the income level—that is, a company with twice the level of net income does not necessarily have double the number of common shares outstanding. Management controls the number of common shares outstanding and there is no relation between firm size and number of shares outstanding. For example, consider that JNJ reports Basic EPS of $5.70 for 2018, while in the same year, Berkshire Hathaway reports Basic EPS of $2,446! This is because Berkshire Hathaway has so few common shares outstanding, not necessarily because it has stellar profits.

Potential ownership dilution is another concern. As we described earlier, stock options awarded to employees under stock-based compensation plans and convertible securities, such as Dow's convertible preferred stock and Xilinx's convertible notes, all have the potential to increase the number of common shares outstanding. Existing shareholders usually take a dim view of this because more common stock outstanding dilutes the ownership of existing shareholders. This is because there are more shareholders laying claim to the available dividends *and* the new shareholders will share equally in the proceeds of liquidation if the company fails. Current shareholders are, therefore, concerned about potential dilution.

To communicate the potential impact of dilution in earnings available for the payment of dividends to shareholders, accounting regulation requires companies to report two EPS statistics.

■ **Basic EPS.** Basic EPS is computed as:

$$\text{Basic EPS} = \frac{\text{Net income} - \text{Dividends on preferred stock}}{\text{Weighted average number of common shares outstanding during the year}}$$

Subtracting preferred stock dividends, in the numerator, yields the income available for dividend payments to common shareholders. The denominator is the average number of common shares outstanding during the year.

■ **Diluted EPS.** Diluted EPS reflects the impact of additional shares that would be issued if all stock options and convertible securities are converted into common shares at the beginning of the year. Diluted EPS never exceeds basic EPS.

Exhibit 8.3 highlights the difference between the two ratios.

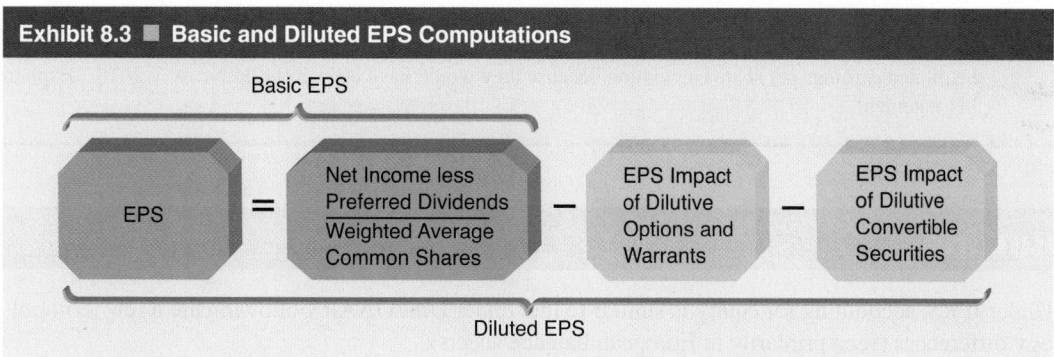

Exhibit 8.3 ■ Basic and Diluted EPS Computations

EPS Disclosures JNJ reports the following table of basic and diluted EPS for 2018.

In millions, except per share amounts[†]	2018	2017	2016
Basic net earnings per share	$5.70	$0.48	$6.04
Average shares outstanding—basic	2,681.5	2,692.0	2,737.3
Potential shares exercisable under stock option plans	139.0	139.7	142.4
Less: shares repurchased under treasury stock method	(92.5)	(87.3)	(92.1)
Convertible debt shares	0.7	0.9	1.3
Adjusted average shares outstanding—diluted	2,728.7	2,745.3	2,788.9
Diluted net earnings per share	$5.61	$0.47	$5.93

[†] The diluted net earnings per share calculation included the dilutive effect of convertible debt that is offset by the related reduction in interest expense of $1 million after-tax for 2018 and 2017, and $2 million for 2016. The diluted net earnings per share calculation for 2018, 2017, and 2016 included all shares related to stock options, as the exercise price of all options was less than the average market value of the Company's stock .

The denominator in diluted earnings per share calculation presumes the most-extreme case: at the beginning of the year, all employees exercise their right to purchase common shares and all convertible debt holders convert their notes to common shares.

JNJ uses the treasury-stock method to determine the dilutive effect of stock options. The method assumes that all options are exercised (139.0 million shares) and that the company uses the proceeds to repurchase shares on the open market at the current stock price (92.5 million shares). The 46.5 million share increase is the net of the shares issued to option holders less the new treasury shares (139.0 million – 92.5 million).

The combined effect is to increase the number of shares in the denominator from 2,681.5 million shares used for the basic EPS calculation to 2,728.7 shares used for the diluted EPS calculation.[1] The increase in the number of shares in the denominator reduces $5.70 for basic EPS to $5.61 for diluted EPS. Diluted EPS is never greater than basic EPS.

Review 8-7 LO7

Autozone reports the following reconciliation of basic net earnings per share to diluted net earnings per share for 2018.

In thousands	2018
Net income (basic and diluted).....................	$1,337,536
Weighted average shares outstanding—basic..........	26,970
Effect of dilutive stock equivalents	454

Required

a. Compute basic EPS for 2018.

b. Compute diluted EPS 2018.

c. Autozone's footnotes contain the following statement: "There were 847,279 stock options excluded from the diluted earnings per share calculation because they would have been anti-dilutive as of 2018." Explain this statement.

Solution on p. 8-53.

Global Accounting

IFRS

Under IFRS, accounting for equity is similar to that under U.S. GAAP. Following are a few terminology differences (seen primarily in European balance sheets).

U.S. GAAP	IFRS
Common stock	Share capital or Ordinary shares
Preferred shares	Preference shares
Additional paid-in capital	Share premium
Retained earnings	Reserves
Accumulated other comprehensive income	Other equity or Other components of equity
—	Revaluation surplus or Revaluation reserve*
Treasury stock	Own shares

* Certain assets including fixed assets and intangible assets may be revalued upwards (and later, revalued downwards) under IFRS. These revaluations do not affect net income or retained earnings but, instead, are reported in a separate equity account. For comparative purposes our analysis might exclude revaluations from both equity and the asset accounts to which they relate.

U.S. GAAP has a more narrow definition of liabilities than IFRS. Therefore, more items are classified as liabilities under IFRS. For example, some preferred shares are deemed liabilities under IFRS and equity under GAAP. (Both systems classify preferred shares that are mandatorily redeemable or

---

[1] JNJ notes that diluted EPS includes the dilutive effect of the exercise of all outstanding stock options. The effects of dilutive securities are only included if they actually reduce the EPS number. **Antidilutive** securities *increase* EPS, and are, thus, excluded from the computation. An example of an antidilutive security is employee stock options with an exercise price greater than the stock's current market price. The company could repurchase more shares than would be issued to option holders. This would decrease the number of shares outstanding. These underwater (or out-of-the-money) options are antidilutive and are, therefore, excluded from the EPS computation.

redeemable at the option of the shareholder, as liabilities.) For comparative purposes, we look at classification of preferred shares that are not mandatorily redeemable and make the numbers consistent. To do this we add preference shares classified as liabilities under IFRS to equity.

Treasury stock transactions are sometimes difficult to identify under IFRS because companies are not required to report a separate line item for treasury shares on the balance sheet. Instead treasury share transactions reduce share capital and share premium. We must review the statement of shareholders' equity to assess stock repurchases for IFRS companies.

For example, at March 31, 2018, **BT Group plc** reports the following in the equity section of its IFRS balance sheet (in £ millions).

Ordinary shares	£ 499
Share premium	1,051
Own shares	(186)
Merger reserve	6,647
Other reserves	534
Retained profit (loss)	1,759
Total equity	**£10,304**

Its balance sheet reports no treasury stock line item, but footnotes disclose that BT Group's "own shares" of £(186) million changed as follows over the prior year.

£ millions	Own Shares
At 1 April 2017	£ (96)
Net buyback of own shares	(90)
At 31 March 2018	**£(186)**

Appendix 8A: Stock-Based Compensation: Reporting and Analyzing

There are four broad types of share-based compensation plans.

1. Employee stock purchase plans
2. Stock awards (unrestricted and restricted)
3. Stock options
4. Stock appreciation rights

Whichever type of plan is used, the accounting objective is the same: *to record the fair value of compensation as expense over the periods in which employees perform services* (the vesting period).

This requires determining the fair value of the compensation and the vesting period. The fair value for each of the types is discussed below along with some important features of each.

Employee Stock Purchase Plans (ESPP)

Compensation expense is the amount of any discount the employee receives when stock is purchased. Common features are:

- Employees can purchase the company's stock at a discount, commonly ~15%.

- Employees can purchase stock up to a maximum that can be a flat amount (such as $25,000) or based on the employee's salary (such as 15% of gross salary).

- Payroll deductions are made monthly and employees can choose when to purchase the stock (such as purchasing when price is low).

Stock Awards

Compensation expense is market price of the stock at the grant date. Common feature is:

- Employee granted shares with no restrictions. Not a strong incentive because employee can sell stock or leave the company.

Stock Awards—Restricted Stock Awards
Compensation expense is the market price of the stock at the grant date. Common features are:

- Employee granted shares (and legally owns them) but is "restricted" from selling shares until the vesting date (to encourage employee retention).
- Shares are forfeited if employee quits before vesting date.
- Often shares are forfeited if performance targets are not met.
- Employee may or may not receive dividends between the grant date and the vesting date, depending on the plan details. But, restricted stock holds no vote.

Stock Awards—Restricted Stock Units (RSU)
Compensation expense is market price of the stock at the grant date. Common features are:

- Employee receives a stock "unit" but no actual stock, the employee does not legally own any stock. A stock unit is typically equivalent to one share.
- Employer delivers stock (or cash) to the employee based on a vesting schedule.
- Employee cannot receive dividends during restriction period as employee does not own any stock.
- Often RSUs are forfeited if performance targets are not met.
- Unlike restricted stock, RSUs do not dilute EPS because no shares are issued.

Stock Options

Compensation expense is the estimated fair value of the options at the grant date. Fair value is measured with a model that requires assumptions. Common features are:

- Employee has right to buy shares in the future, at a price specified at the grant date.
- The employee cannot buy shares before the vesting date.
- Options are forfeited if employee quits before vesting period.
- The employee cannot sell the options.

For stock options, understanding some of the vocabulary is helpful:

- *Employee stock option:* Security that gives employee the right, but not obligation, to purchase stock at a predetermined price.
- *Grant date:* Date the option is awarded to the employee.
- *Exercise:* Purchase of stock pursuant to an option.
- *Exercise price:* Predetermined price at which the stock can be purchased. This is also called the strike price or grant price. In most plans, the exercise price is the stock price on the grant date.
- *Option term:* Length of time employee can hold the option before it expires. Typically 7–10 years.
- *Vesting:* Requirement(s) that must be met for employee to have right to exercise the option. Usually options vest with continuation of employment for a specific period of time (such as 4 years) or the meeting of a performance goal (such as revenue growth).
- *Expiry date:* Date after which the option can no longer be exercised. Once vested, the employee can exercise the option at the grant price at any time over the option term up to the expiration date.
- *Intrinsic value:* Difference between the current stock price and the exercise price. As the stock price rises so does intrinsic value.

At-the-money option	Intrinsic value = 0	Current stock price = Exercise price
In-the-money option	Intrinsic value > 0	Current stock price > Exercise price
Out-of-the-money option.	Intrinsic value < 0	Current stock price < Exercise price

- *Option fair value:* Value of the option that considers the intrinsic value and the time value of the option. Determined with a valuation model, most frequently Black-Scholes or lattice model.

Stock Appreciation Rights (SAR)

Compensation expense is the estimated fair value of the SARs at the grant date. Fair value is measured with a model that requires assumptions. Fair value is usually the same as an option with similar terms. Common features are:

- Employee benefits by the amount of any stock price increase but without having to buy shares.
- Settlement date is determined at the grant date (similar to vesting period).
- "Stock appreciation" is the increase in the market price since the grant date; SAR has no value if stock price falls.
- SARs can be settled in stock or cash, depending on plan details.
- Similar to stock option but with no exercise price.

Some plans allow for RSUs and SARs to settle in either stock or cash. If they settle in cash (or if the employee has a cash option), the RSU or SAR is considered a liability. The amount of compensation (and related liability) is estimated each period and adjusted quarterly to reflect changes in the fair value of the RSUs or SARs until the settlement date.

Summary of Share-Based Compensation

The following chart summarizes the accounting for various types of stock-based compensation plans.

	Cash	Liability	Common Stock	APIC	Deferred Comp	Treasury Stock	Retained Earnings	Comp Expense
Employee stock purchase plan								
At purchase: Compensation expense	+		+	+			−	+
Stock grants (awards)								
Grant: Fair value of stock			+	+			−	+
Restricted stock								
Grant: Fair value of restricted stock				+	−			
Vesting: Proportion of restricted stock that vests					+		−	+
Restricted stock units or Stock appreciation rights settled in cash								
Grant: Fair value of restricted stock unit		+					−	+
Settlement: Cash to employee	−	−						
Stock options								
Grant: Fair value of options				+			−	+
Exercise: New shares issued	+		+	+				
Exercise: Treasury shares issued	+					+		

The chart shows that some plans have cash effects while others do not. Some plans affect common stock and APIC when shares are issued; other plans have no such effect because stock is not issued at all.

Analysis Implications

There are several analysis implications for share-based compensation.

- **Magnitude of Awards**—We consider both the absolute and relative size of compensation expense each period. Large increases or decreases are examined to determine the cause. Footnotes and the MD&A section provide details. For JNJ, stock compensation is increasing in dollar terms, but fairly constant relative to total sales, over the past five years. The proportion of stock-based compensation to sales varies greatly by industry (see graphic), which highlights the need to evaluate any metric against competitors and industry benchmarks.

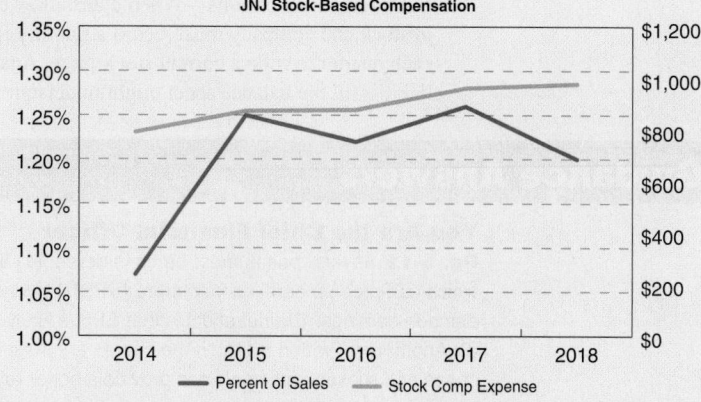

- **Dilution potential**—Large compensation plans can create large dilution that is not fully captured in diluted EPS. The dilution calculation for EPS includes all vested shares but none of the unvested shares.

For example, JNJ's diluted EPS included 38.2 million dilutive shares, net (2,795.4 million – 2,757.2 million). But the footnotes reveal that an additional 486 million shares are yet to be granted and, as such, are not included in diluted EPS. One way to quantify this missing dilution is to recompute EPS with a denominator that includes unvested shares. This will be a worst-case scenario because not all unvested shares are ultimately issued, but the adjusted EPS measure could be informative.

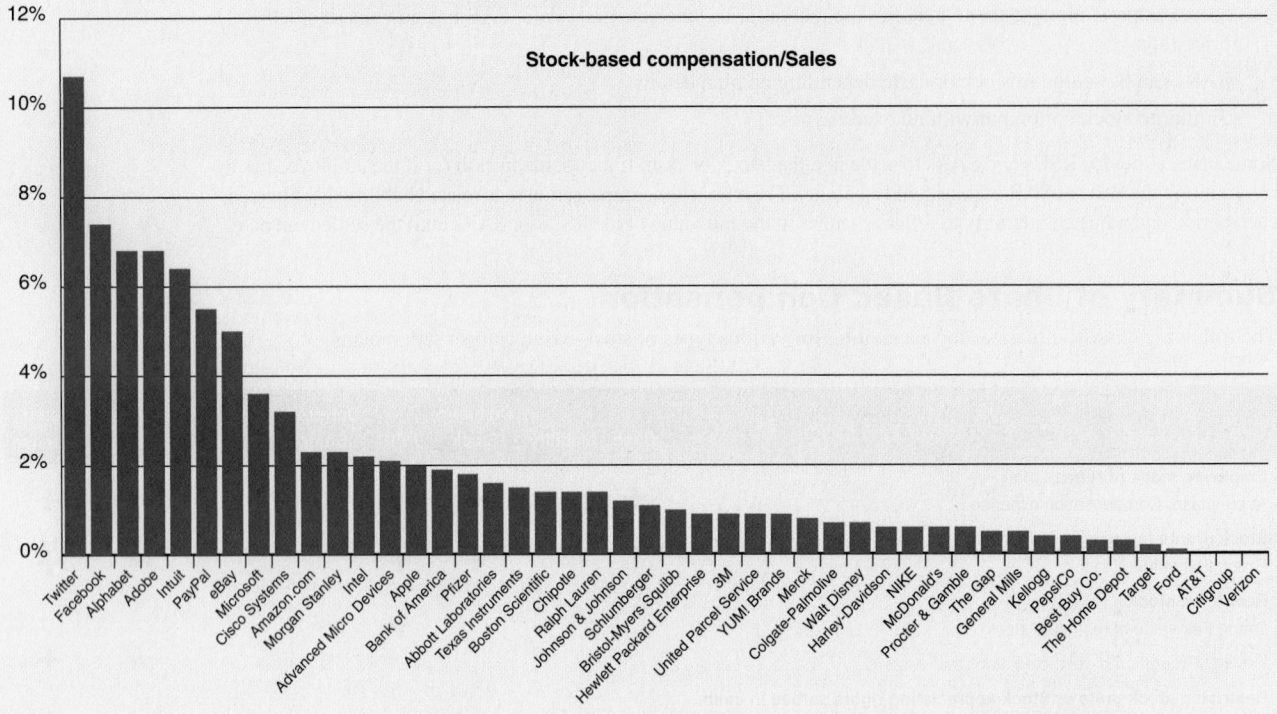

- **Tax benefit**—Companies cannot deduct GAAP share-based compensation expense for tax purposes. The tax laws do permit companies to deduct the *intrinsic* value of shares issued. This can be much larger than the GAAP expense and can create large tax savings. To assess this, analysts look at footnotes to determine the size of the tax benefit in the current period as well as the *intrinsic* value of outstanding shares and options. For example, JNJ reports the total intrinsic value of options exercised was $1,028 million, which gave rise to a tax benefit of $192 million. The intrinsic value of outstanding options is $3,214 million, a considerable amount of potential future cash flow. Footnotes to the financial statements include these details.

- **Model assumptions**—Companies select assumptions used in the models that they use to estimate fair value. Analysts examine the assumptions, compare them to prior years and to assumptions used by competitors.

- **Cash flow implications**—When plans allow employees the choice to settle the award in cash instead of in stock, the company must record a liability for the potential cash outflow. This liability must be adjusted each quarter to reflect current stock price. Analysts must consider that for "hot" stocks, this means the liability on the balance sheet might understate the eventual cash outflow.

Guidance Answers

You Are the Chief Financial Officer

Pg. 8-11 Several points must be considered. (1) Buying stock back reduces the number of shares outstanding, which can prop up earnings per share (EPS). However, foregone earnings from the cash used for repurchases can dampen earnings. The net effect is that EPS is likely to increase because of the reduced shares in the denominator. (2) Another motivation is that, if the shares are sufficiently undervalued (in management's opinion), the stock repurchase and subsequent resale can provide a better return than alternative investments. (3) Stock repurchases send a strong signal to the market that management feels its stock is undervalued. This is more credible than merely making that argument with analysts. On the other hand, company cash is diverted from other investments. This is bothersome if such investments are mutually exclusive either now or in the future.

Superscript ^A denotes assignments based on Appendix 8A.

Q8-1. Define *par value stock*. What is the significance of a stock's par value from an accounting and analysis perspective?

Q8-2. What are the basic differences between preferred stock and common stock? That is, what are the typical features of preferred stock?

Q8-3. What features make preferred stock similar to debt? Similar to common stock?

Q8-4. What is meant by preferred dividends in arrears? If dividends are two years in arrears on $500,000 of 6% preferred stock, and dividends are declared at the end of this year, what amount of total dividends must the company pay to preferred stockholders before paying any dividends to common stockholders?

Q8-5. Distinguish between authorized shares and issued shares. Why might the number of shares issued be more than the number of shares outstanding?

Q8-6. Describe the difference between contributed capital and earned capital. Specifically, how can earned capital be considered as an investment by the company's stockholders?

Q8-7. How does the account "additional paid-in capital" (APIC) arise? Does the amount of APIC reported on the balance sheet relative to the common stock amount provide any information about the financial condition of the company?

Q8-8. Define *stock split*. What are the major reasons for a stock split?

Q8-9. Define *treasury stock*. Why might a corporation acquire treasury stock? How is treasury stock reported in the balance sheet?

Q8-10. If a corporation purchases 10,000 shares of its own common stock at $10 per share and resells them at $14 per share, where would the $40,000 increase in capital be reported in the financial statements? Why is no gain reported?

Q8-11. A corporation has total stockholders' equity of $18,995,250 and one class of $2 par value common stock. The corporation has 500,000 shares authorized; 300,000 shares issued; and 15,000 shares as treasury stock. What is its book value per share?

Q8-12. What is meant by the *market cap* of a company and how is it determined?

Q8-13. When a company reports negative retained earnings on the balance sheet (a deficit), can we conclude that the company has reported significant net losses on the income statement?

Q8-14. Employee stock options potentially dilute earnings per share (EPS). What can companies do to offset these dilutive effects and how might this action affect the balance sheet?

Q8-15. What information is reported in a statement of stockholders' equity?

Q8-16. What items are typically reported under the stockholders' equity category of accumulated other comprehensive income (AOCI)?

Q8-17. What are three common forms of stock-based compensation and why do companies use such forms of compensation?

Q8-18. Describe the accounting for a convertible bond. Can the conversion ever result in the recognition of a gain in the income statement?

Assignments with the ⬤ logo in the margin are available in BusinessCourse.
See the Preface of the book for details.

Mini Exercises

LO2

M8-19. Analyzing and Identifying Financial Statement Effects of Stock Issuances

During the current year, Austin Company, (*a*) issues 8,000 shares of $50 par value preferred stock at $84 cash per share and (*b*) issues 19,000 shares of $1 par value common stock at $10 cash per share. Indicate the financial statement effects of these two issuances using the financial statement effects template.

LO7

Bank of America
Corp. (BAC)

M8-20. Understanding EPS Calculations

On its Form 10-K for the year ended December 31, 2018, Bank of America Corp. reported information related to basic earnings per share. Fill in the missing information.

$ millions, except per share amounts	2018	2017	2016
Net income	$28,147	$18,232	*d*
Preferred stock dividends	1,451	*b*	$ 1,682
Net income applicable to common shareholders	26,696	*c*	$16,140
Average common shares outstanding	10,096.5	10,195.6	*e*
Basic earnings per share	*a*	$1.63	$1.57

LO1

Cisco Systems Inc.
(CSCO)

M8-21. Distinguishing Between Common Stock and Additional Paid-in Capital

Following is the stockholders' equity section from the Cisco Systems Inc. balance sheet for the third quarter of fiscal 2019.

Shareholders' Equity (in millions, except par value)	April 27, 2019
Preferred stock, no par value: 5 shares authorized; none issued and outstanding	$ —
Common stock and additional paid-in capital, $0.001 par value: 20,000 shares authorized; 4,313 shares issued and outstanding	40,577
Retained earnings (Accumulated deficit)	(2,877)
Accumulated other comprehensive income (loss)	(896)
Total equity	$36,804

a. For the $40,577 million reported as "common stock and additional paid-in capital," what portion is common stock and what portion is additional paid-in capital?
b. Explain why Cisco does not report the two components described in part *a* separately.
c. Cisco's stock price was $55.88 on April 26, 2019 (the closest trading day to fiscal year-end). Determine Cisco's market capitalization that day.

LO2

M8-22. Identifying Financial Statement Effects of Stock Issuance and Repurchase

On January 1, Centaur Inc. issues 7,000 shares of $100 par value preferred stock at $300 cash per share. On March 1, the company repurchases 7,000 shares of previously issued $1 par value common stock at $156 cash per share. Use the financial statement effects template to record these two transactions.

LO4

Aflac Inc. (AFL)

M8-23. Assessing the Financial Statement Effects of a Stock Split

The following is taken from a Motley Fool article dated June 15, 2018, concerning Aflac Inc.

> **Quacking about a split.** Supplemental-insurance giant Aflac is best known for the white duck it has as its spokesperson, but the insurance products it provides to workers in the U.S. and Japan help millions get the coverage they need in areas that few insurance companies cover. That's been a successful model, and the insurer has seen its share price rise substantially over the years. In February, Aflac announced that it would do a 2-for-1 split effective March 16, putting it in the form of a 100% stock dividend. CEO Daniel Amos celebrated the announcement, noting that "this is the ninth split of the company's common stock since listing on the NYSE in 1974 and the first in 17 years." Aflac pointed to improving liquidity as a key reason for the move.

a. Aflac's common stock has a par value of $0.10. What adjustments will it make to its balance sheet as a result of the stock split?

b. Why is Aflac splitting its stock?

M8-24. Reconciling Common Stock and Treasury Stock Balances

Following is the stockholders' equity section from the The Walt Disney Company balance sheet.

Stockholders' equity, $ millions	Sep. 29, 2018	Sep. 30, 2017
Preferred stock	$ 0	$ 0
Common stock, $0.01 par value, Authorized—4.6 billion shares, Issued—2.9 billion shares	36,779	36,248
Retained earnings	82,679	72,606
Accumulated other comprehensive loss	(3,097)	(3,528)
Stockholders' Equity subtotal before Treasury Stock, Total	116,361	105,326
Treasury stock, at cost, 1.4 billion shares	(67,588)	(64,011)
Total Disney Shareholders' equity	48,773	41,315
Noncontrolling interests	4,059	3,689
Total equity	$ 52,832	$ 45,004

a. How many shares are issued at September 29, 2018? The par value of these shares is $0.01 per share. Where is this information reported on the balance sheet?

b. How many shares are outstanding at 2018 fiscal year-end?

c. Determine the average price at which Disney issued its common stock.

d. Use the treasury stock account to determine the average price Disney paid when it repurchased its common shares.

M8-25. Identifying and Analyzing Financial Statement Effects of Cash Dividends

On March 15, 2018, Bank of America issued 94,000 shares of 5.875% Fixed-to-Floating Rate Non-Cumulative Preferred Stock, Series FF for $2.35 billion. Dividends are payable semiannually on or about March 15 and September 15.

a. Assume the stock was issued at face value. What is the face value of each Series FF share?

b. What will be the total dividend for the year ended December 31, 2018, assuming that the number of shares remains unchanged?

M8-26.[A] Estimating Stock-Based Compensation Expense

Pedernales Corp. has several types of stock-based compensation plans including a stock purchase plan that allows employees to buy shares at a 15% discount. During the current year, employees purchased 25,000 shares under this plan. Also, the company granted 20,000 stock options with estimated fair value of $10.10 per option. The options vest ratably over three years. Pedernales's average stock price during this year was $78.94. Determine Pedernales's stock-based compensation expense for the current year.

M8-27. Identifying, Analyzing, and Explaining the Effects of a Stock Split

On September 1, Apstein Company has 300,000 shares of $9 par value ($148 market value) common stock that are issued and outstanding. Its balance sheet on that date shows the following account balances relating to its common stock.

Common stock	$2,700,000
Paid-in capital in excess of par value	1,680,000

On September 2, Apstein splits its stock 3-for-2 and reduces the par value to $6 per share.

a. How many shares of common stock are issued and outstanding immediately after the stock split?

b. What is the dollar balance of the common stock account immediately after the stock split?

c. What is the likely reason that Apstein Company split its stock?

M8-28. Determining Cash Dividends to Preferred and Common Shareholders

Sinclair Company has outstanding 40,000 shares of $50 par value, 6% cumulative preferred stock and 100,000 shares of $10 par value common stock. The company declares and pays cash dividends amounting to $280,000.

a. If there are no preferred dividends in arrears, how much in total dividends, and in dividends per share, does Sinclair pay to each class of stock?

b. If there are one year's dividends in arrears on the preferred stock, how much in total dividends, and in dividends per share, does Sinclair pay to each class of stock?

LO4 **M8-29. Reconciling Retained Earnings**

Use the following data to reconcile the 2019 retained earnings for Springwerth Company (that is, explain the change in retained earnings during the year).

Total retained earnings, December 31, 2018	$537,000
Stock dividends declared and paid in 2019	46,000
Cash dividends declared and paid in 2019.	55,000
Net income for 2019.	203,000

LO7 **M8-30. Calculating and Interpreting EPS Information**

Wells Fargo (WFC) Wells Fargo reports the following information in its Form 10-K.

In millions	2018	2017
Wells Fargo net income	$22,393	$22,183
Preferred stock dividends.	$ 1,556	$ 1,629
Common stock dividends	$ 7,955	$ 7,708
Average common shares outstanding	4,799.7	4,964.6
Diluted average common shares outstanding	4,838.4	5,017.3

a. Determine Wells Fargo's basic EPS for fiscal 2018 and for fiscal 2017.

b. Compare the number of common shares outstanding used for the 2018 Basic and Diluted EPS ratios. Provide three examples that explain why the two numbers differ.

LO4 **M8-31. Calculating and Recording Cash Dividends**

McDonald's (MCD) On May 23, 2019, McDonald's Board of Directors declared a quarterly cash dividend of $1.16 per share of common stock payable on June 17, 2019, to shareholders of record at the close of business on June 3, 2019. Assume that there were 785.2 million shares outstanding during this time period.

Use the financial statement effects template to record the transactions for the following dates:

a. May 23, 2019

b. June 3, 2019

c. June 17, 2019

LO4 **M8-32. Determining Effects of Stock Splits**

Apple Inc. (AAPL) Apple Inc. has had the following stock splits since its inception.

Effective Date	Split Amount
June 9, 2014.	7 for 1
February 28, 2005	2 for 1
June 21, 2000.	2 for 1
June 16, 1987.	2 for 1

a. If the par value of Apple shares was originally $1, what would Apple report as par value per share on its 2018 balance sheet?

b. On August 23, 2019, Apple's stock traded for about $206.50. All things equal, if Apple had never had a stock split, what would a share of Apple have traded for that same day?

LO5 **M8-33. Interpreting Comprehensive Income and AOCI**

Indicate whether each of the following statements is true or false. If false, indicate how to correct the statement.

a. The amount reported for accumulated other comprehensive income (AOCI) on the balance sheet must be a positive amount consistent with all other stockholders' equity accounts.

b. Changes in AOCI are reflected in other comprehensive income, which is different from net income.

c. Other comprehensive income does not imply a change in cash.

M8-34. Analyzing Financial Statement Effects of Convertible Securities

CenterPoint Energy reports the following footnote to its 2018 10-K. *Note:* A **depositary share** is a U.S. dollar-denominated equity *share* of a foreign-based company available for purchase on an American stock exchange.

LO6
CenterPoint Energy
(CNP)

> **Series B Preferred Stock**   On October 1, 2018, CenterPoint Energy completed the issuance of 19,550,000 depositary shares, each representing a 1/20th interest in a share of its Series B Preferred Stock, at a price of $50 per depositary share. The Series B Preferred Stock has a per share value of $1,000. A holder of the Series B Preferred Stock may, at any time prior to September 1, 2021, elect to convert shares of the Series B Preferred Stock at the conversion rate of 30.5820 shares of Common Stock per share of the Series B Preferred Stock.

a. How many Series B Preferred share equivalents did CenterPoint issue on October 1, 2018?
b. Describe the effects on CenterPoint's balance sheet if the preferred stock are all converted prior to September 1, 2021.
c. Would the conversion affect earnings? Explain.

Exercises

E8-35. Identifying and Analyzing Financial Statement Effects of Stock Transactions

Melo Company reports the following transactions relating to its stock accounts in the current year. Use the financial statement effects template to indicate the effects from each of these transactions.

LO2

Mar. 2	Issued 10,000 shares of $1 par value common stock at $30 cash per share.
Apr. 14	Issued 15,000 shares of $100 par value, 8% preferred stock at $250 cash per share.
June 30	Purchased 3,000 shares of its own common stock at $22 cash per share.
Sep. 25	Sold 1,500 shares of its treasury stock at $26 cash per share.

E8-36. Identifying and Analyzing Financial Statement Effects of Stock Transactions

Pyle Corp. reports the following transactions relating to its stock accounts in the current year. Use the financial statement effects template to indicate the effects from each of these transactions.

LO2

Feb. 3	Issued 40,000 shares of $5 par value common stock at $27 cash per share.
Feb. 27	Issued 9,000 shares of $50 par value, 8% preferred stock at $88 cash per share.
Mar. 31	Purchased 5,000 shares of its own common stock at $30 cash per share.
June 25	Sold 3,000 shares of its treasury stock at $38 cash per share.
July 15	Sold the remaining 2,000 shares of treasury stock at $29 cash per share.

E8-37. Analyzing and Computing Average Issue Price and Treasury Stock Cost

Following is the stockholders' equity section from the Campbell Soup Company balance sheet. *Note:* Campbell's uses *shareowners' equity* in lieu of the more common title of stockholders' equity.

LO1, 2, 3

Campbell Soup Co.
(CPB)

Shareowners' Equity (millions, except per share amounts)	July 29, 2018	July 30, 2017
Preferred stock: authorized 40 shares; none issued	$ —	$ —
Capital stock, $.0375 par value; authorized 560 shares; issued 323 shares.	12	12
Additional paid-in capital.	349	359
Earnings retained in the business	2,224	2,385
Capital stock in treasury, at cost.	(1,103)	(1,066)
Accumulated other comprehensive loss.	(118)	(53)
Total Campbell Soup Company shareowners' equity.	1,364	1,637
Noncontrolling interests	9	8
Total equity	$1,373	$1,645

Campbell Soup Company also reports the following statement of stockholders' equity.

(millions, except per share amounts)	Capital Stock				Additional Paid-in Capital	Earnings Retained in the Business	Accumulated Other Comprehensive Income (Loss)	Noncontrolling Interests	Total Equity
	Issued		In Treasury						
	Shares	Amount	Shares	Amount					
Balance at July 30, 2017	323	$12	(22)	$(1,066)	$359	$2,385	$(53)	$8	$1,645
Net earnings.						261			261
Other comprehensive income (loss).							(65)	1	(64)
Dividends ($1.40 per share)						(422)			(422)
Treasury stock purchased			(2)	(86)					(86)
Treasury stock issued under management incentive and stock option plans.			2	49	(10)				39
Balance at July 29, 2018	323	$12	(22)	$(1,103)	$349	$2,224	$(118)	$9	$1,373

a. Show the computation, using par value and share numbers, to arrive at the $12 million in the capital (common) stock account.

b. At what average price were the Campbell Soup shares issued?

c. Reconcile the beginning and ending balances of retained earnings.

d. Campbell Soup reports an increase in shareowners' equity relating to the exercise of stock options (titled "Treasury stock issued under management incentive and stock option plans"). This transaction involves the purchase of common stock by employees at a preset price. Describe how this set of transactions affects stockholders' equity.

e. Describe the transaction relating to the "Treasury stock purchased" line in the statement of shareowners' equity.

f. Campbell Soup's stock price was $32.99 on July 29, 2018. Determine the company's market capitalization that day.

g. Calculate and interpret the company's market-to-book ratio at July 29, 2018.

LO3   **E8-38.**[A]   **Analyzing Stock-Based Compensation**
Hearne Inc. began business on March 1, 2020. At that time, it granted 250,000 options, with a strike price of $5, to computer engineers in lieu of signing bonuses. The fair value of each option was estimated at $1 and the options vest over four years.

a. What benefits did Hearne create by granting options to the engineers instead of cash signing bonuses?

b. What is the total expense that the company will record associated with the options granted in 2020?

c. What will Hearne record in 2020 for stock-option compensation expense?

d. How will the exercise of the options impact the balance sheet, income statement, and statement of cash flows?

LO4   **E8-39.**   **Analyzing Cash Dividends on Preferred and Common Stock**
Haas Enterprise Inc. has outstanding 30,000 shares of $50 par value, 6% preferred stock and 70,000 shares of $1 par value common stock. During its first three years in business, it declared and paid no cash dividends in the first year, $310,000 in the second year, and $90,000 in the third year.

a. If the preferred stock is cumulative, determine the total amount of cash dividends paid to each class of stock in each of the three years.

b. If the preferred stock is noncumulative, determine the total amount of cash dividends paid to each class of stock in each of the three years.

E8-40.　**Analyzing and Computing Issue Price and Shares Outstanding**

Following is the stockholders' equity section from Public Storage's 2018 balance sheet.

LO1, 2

Public Storage Corp. (PSA)

(in thousands, except share data)	December 31, 2018
Preferred Shares, $0.01 par value, 100,000,000 shares authorized, 161,000 shares issued and outstanding............................	$4,025,000
Common Shares, $0.10 par value, 650,000,000 shares authorized, 174,130,881 shares issued and outstanding	17,413
Paid-in capital..	5,718,485
Accumulated deficit	(577,360)
Accumulated other comprehensive loss...................	(64,060)
Total Public Storage shareholders' equity	9,119,478
Noncontrolling interests	25,250
Total equity..	$9,144,728

a. Show the computation to derive the $17,413 thousand for common stock.

b. At what average price has Public Storage issued its common stock?

c. At what average price has the company issued its preferred shares?

d. The company reports Accumulated deficit of $(577,360). What would this account be called if the balance was positive rather than negative?

e. Public Storage has reported more than $1 billion in net income in each of the past five years. Given this, what are two plausible reasons for the accumulated deficit?

f. What does the Noncontrolling interests account of $25,250 thousand represent?

E8-41.　**Analyzing Cash Dividends on Preferred and Common Stock**

Torres Company began business on June 30, 2018. At that time, it issued 25,000 shares of $40 par value, 8% cumulative preferred stock and 100,000 shares of $5 par value common stock. Through the end of 2020, there has been no change in the number of preferred and common shares outstanding.

LO4

a. Assume the company declared and paid cash dividends of $103,000 in 2018, $0 in 2019, and $461,000 in 2020. Compute the total cash dividends and the dividends per share paid to each class of stock in 2018, 2019, and 2020.

b. Assume the company declared and paid cash dividends of $0 in 2018, $160,000 in 2019, and $278,000 in 2020. Compute the total cash dividends and the dividends per share paid to each class of stock in 2018, 2019, and 2020.

E8-42.　**Identifying and Analyzing Financial Statement Effects of Stock Repurchase and Dividends**

Quinn Company has outstanding 25,000 shares of $10 par value common stock that was issued for an average of $24 per share. It also has $514,000 of retained earnings. The company repurchases and retires 2,000 shares at $32 per share. Near the current year-end, the company declares and pays a cash dividend of $1.80 per share. Use the financial statement effects template to record the share repurchase and dividend transactions.

LO2, 4

E8-43.　**Identifying and Analyzing Financial Statement Effects of Dividends**

The statement of shareholders' equity of Public Storage Corporation for the year ended December 31, 2018, reports the following dividends paid to shareholders ($ thousands).

LO4

Public Storage Corp. (PSA)

Distributions to equity holders	
Preferred shares...	$ 216,316
Common shares...	$1,396,364

The 2018 balance sheet includes the following ($ thousands).

Preferred Shares, $0.01 par value, 100,000,000 shares authorized, 161,000 shares issued and outstanding..	$4,025,000
Common Shares, $0.10 par value, 650,000,000 shares authorized, 174,130,881 shares issued and outstanding..	$ 17,413

a. Use the financial statement effects template to indicate the effects of the dividend payments.

b. Determine the dividends per share for both classes of stock.

LO4   **E8-44.   Analyzing Financial Statement Effects of Dividends**

The stockholders' equity of DiFrancesco Company at March 31, 2019, is shown below.

4% preferred stock, $1,000 par value, 25,000 shares authorized, 10,000 shares issued and outstanding.	$10,000,000
Common stock, $1 par value, 3,000,000 shares authorized, 700,000 shares issued . . .	700,000
Additional paid-in capital—preferred stock.	60,000
Additional paid-in capital—common stock	17,150,000
Retained earnings	49,005,689
Total stockholders' equity	$76,915,689

The following transactions, among others, occurred during the fiscal year ended March 31, 2020.

April 15, 2019	Declare and pay preferred dividends of $400,000
April 15, 2019	Declare and pay common dividends of $1.30 per share
October 1, 2019	Execute a 3-for-1 stock split of the common stock when the stock price was $140 per share
March 1, 2020	Declare and pay common dividends of $0.50 per share

a. Use the financial statement effects template to indicate the effects of these transactions.
b. At March 31, 2020, the company reported net income for the year of $8,900,610. Compute retained earnings as of March 31, 2020.

LO1, 2, 4   **E8-45.   Analyzing Shareholders' Equity Transactions Using Graphical Data**

The following dashboard was developed using **PowerBI** with data collected from 10-K filings for the S&P 500 for fiscal 2010 through 2018. Access the dashboard at the myBusinessCourse website to answer the requirements.

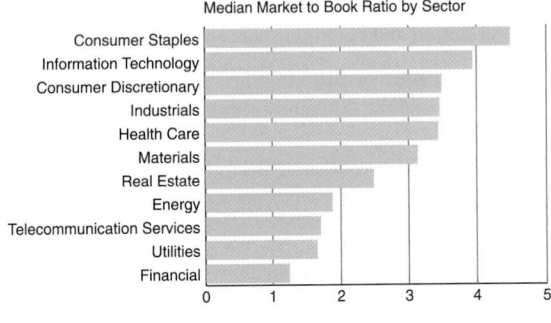

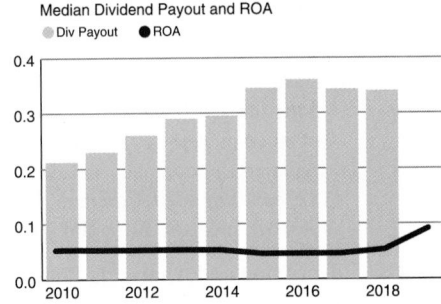

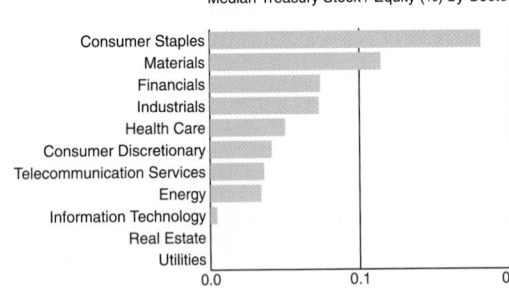

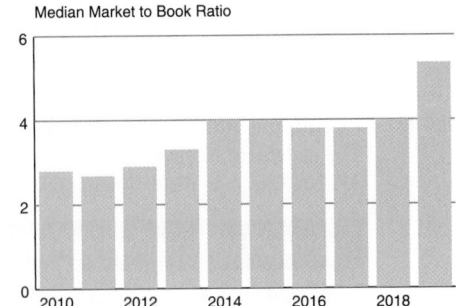

a. Which industry sector exhibits the highest market-to-book ratios, on average? Does the proportion of treasury shares held by firms in this sector explain the high market-to-book ratio?
b. What industry sectors exhibit the lowest market-to-book ratios? What might explain low ratios in these sectors?
c. What pattern do we observe in market-to-book ratios over time?
d. From the graphic of dividend payout ratio and return on assets, we might conclude that there is no relation between the two metrics. From the online dashboard, display the graphic for the Energy sector. What relation do we observe and what might explain this. *Hint:* Is this relation mechanical in any way?

E8-46. Analyzing and Computing Issue Price, Treasury Stock Cost, and Shares Outstanding

Following is the stockholders' equity section of the December 31, 2018, Caterpillar Inc. balance sheet.

LO1, 2
Caterpillar Inc.
(CAT)

Stockholders' Equity ($ millions)	2018
Common stock of $1.00 par; Authorized shares: 2,000,000,000;	
Issued 814,894,624 shares at paid-in amount	$ 5,827
Treasury stock 239,351,886 shares, at cost.	(20,531)
Profit employed in the business	30,427
Accumulated other comprehensive income (loss)	(1,684)
Noncontrolling interests	41
Total stockholders' equity	$14,080

   a. How many shares of Caterpillar common stock are outstanding at year-end 2018?

   b. What does the phrase "at paid-in amount" in the common stock account mean?

   c. At what average cost has Caterpillar repurchased its stock as of year-end 2018?

   d. Why would a company such as Caterpillar want to repurchase its common stock?

   e. What is meant by "Profit employed in the business"? The account balance was $26,301 million at the start of the year and the company reported net income of $6,147 million for the year. What amount did the company record as dividends in 2018?

E8-47. Analyzing Convertible Preferred Stock

Xerox Corp. reports the following stockholders' equity information in its 10-K report.

LO6, 7
Xerox Corporation
(XRX)

Shareholders' Equity (in millions, except par value)	December 31	
	2018	2017
Series A convertible preferred stock	$ 214	$ 214
Common stock, $1 par value	232	255
Additional paid-in capital	3,321	3,893
Treasury stock, at cost	(55)	0
Retained earnings	5,072	4,856
Accumulated other comprehensive loss	(3,565)	(3,748)
Xerox shareholders' equity	$5,005	$5,256

Preferred Stock   As of December 31, 2018 , we had one class of preferred stock outstanding. We have issued 180,000 shares of Series B Convertible Perpetual Preferred Stock that have an aggregate liquidation value of $180 and a carrying value of $214. The Series B Convertible Preferred Stock pays quarterly cash dividends at a rate of 8% per year. Each share of Preferred Stock is convertible at any time, at the option of the holder, into 37.4532 shares of common stock for a total of 6,742 thousand shares (reflecting an initial conversion price of approximately $26.70 per share of common stock), subject to customary anti-dilution adjustments.

Required

   a. At December 31, 2018, Xerox reports $214 million of 8% Series B Convertible Preferred stock. What is the dollar amount of dividends that Xerox must pay on this stock (assume a par value of $1,000 per share)?

   b. Describe the effects that will occur to Xerox's balance sheet and its income statement when the Convertible Preferred stock is converted.

   c. What is the benefit, if any, of issuing equity securities with a conversion feature? How are these securities treated in the computation of earnings per share (EPS)?

LO1
Merck & Co. Inc.
(MRK)

E8-48. **Analyzing and Computing Issue Price, Treasury Stock Cost, and Shares Outstanding**
Following is the stockholders' equity section of the 2018 Merck & Co. Inc. balance sheet.

Stockholders' Equity ($ millions)	2018
Common stock, $0.50 par value; Authorized—6,500,000,000 shares;	
Issued—3,577,103,522 shares....................................	$ 1,788
Other paid-in capital..	38,808
Retained earnings	42,579
Accumulated other comprehensive loss............................	(5,545)
Stockholders' equity before deduction for treasury stock..............	77,630
Less treasury stock, at cost: 984,543,979 shares	50,929
Total Merck & Co. Inc. stockholders' equity	$26,701

a. Show the computation of the $1,788 million in the common stock account.
b. At what average price were the Merck common shares issued?
c. At what average cost was the Merck treasury stock purchased?
d. How many common shares are outstanding as of December 31, 2018?
e. Use an online investment site to determine Merck's closing stock price on December 31, 2018. Use that amount to calculate the company's market cap for that day.

Problems

LO1, 2

P8-49. **Identifying and Analyzing Financial Statement Effects of Stock Transactions**
The stockholders' equity section of XPress Media Company for the current year follows.

8% preferred stock, $25 par value, 50,000 shares authorized;	
8,400 shares issued and outstanding.........................	$210,000
Common stock, $10 par value, 200,000 shares authorized;	
50,000 shares issued and outstanding........................	500,000
Paid-in capital in excess of par value—preferred stock	85,000
Paid-in capital in excess of par value—common stock	300,000
Retained earnings	370,000

During the year, the following transactions occurred.

Jan.	10	Issued 28,000 shares of common stock for $18 cash per share.
Jan.	23	Repurchased 8,000 shares of common stock at $20 cash per share.
Mar.	14	Sold one-half of the treasury shares acquired January 23 for $22 cash per share.
July	15	Issued 2,600 shares of preferred stock for $128,000 cash.
Nov.	15	Sold 1,000 of the treasury shares acquired January 23 for $26 cash per share.

Required
a. Use the financial statement effects template to indicate the effects from each of these transactions.
b. Prepare the stockholders' equity section of the balance sheet assuming the company reports net income of $121,000 for the current year.

LO2, 5, 6
Under Armour Inc.
(UA)

P8-50. **Analyzing Stockholders' Equity Including AOCI and Convertible Securities**
Under Armour reported the following stockholders' equity section of the balance sheet for the fiscal year ended December 31, 2018.

Stockholders' Equity ($ 000s)	2018	2017
Class A Common Stock, $0.0003 1/3 par value; 400,000,000 shares authorized as of December 31, 2018 and 2017; 187,710,319 shares issued and outstanding as of December 31, 2018 and 185,257,423 shares issued and outstanding as of December 31, 2017..........................	$ 62	$ 61
Class B Convertible Common Stock, $0.0003 1/3 par value; 34,450,000 shares authorized, issued and outstanding as of December 31, 2018 and 2017	11	11
Class C Common Stock, $0.0003 1/3 par value; 400,000,000 shares authorized as of December 31, 2018 and 2017; 226,421,963 shares issued and outstanding as of December 31, 2018, and 222,375,079 shares issued and outstanding as of December 31, 2017.......................	75	74
Additional paid-in capital..	916,628	872,266
Retained earnings	1,139,082	1,184,441
Accumulated other comprehensive loss	(38,987)	(38,211)
Total stockholders' equity...	$2,016,871	$2,018,642

Under Armour reports additional information related to the three classes of stock in its 10-K.

> Under Armour's Class A Common Stock and Class C Common Stock are traded on the New York Stock Exchange under the symbols "UAA" and "UA", respectively. As of January 31, 2019, there were 1,628 record holders of our Class A Common Stock, 6 record holders of Class B Convertible Common Stock which are beneficially owned by our Chief Executive Officer and Chairman of the Board Kevin A. Plank, and 1,216 record holders of our Class C Common Stock. Our Class A common stock has one vote per share, our Class B common stock has 10 votes per share and our Class C common stock has no voting rights (except in limited circumstances).

Required

a. Complete the following table to determine the % ownership and voting power for each class of stock.

	Class A	Class B	Class C	Total
Shares authorized	_____	_____	_____	_____
Shares issued and outstanding	_____	_____	_____	_____
Proportion of ownership of Under Armour ...	_____	_____	_____	100%
Shareholders of record...................	_____	_____	_____	NA
Votes per share	_____	_____	_____	NA
Total votes	_____	_____	_____	_____
Proportion of voting rights...............	_____	_____	_____	100%

b. Class B Convertible Common Stock can be converted on a 1-for-1 basis into Class A stock. Explain the balance sheet effect if all outstanding shares were converted. What repercussions would this have for the CEO, Kevin Plank?

c. In June 2015, the company created nonvoting Class C common stock and issued Class C shares primarily for employee share-based compensation plans. Explain the incentives such compensation plans create. Why would Under Armour create another class of stock for this purpose?

d. During the year, foreign currency translation losses increased by $23,576 and unrealized losses on cash flow hedges (derivatives) decreased by $22,800. Use this information to reconcile the accumulated other comprehensive loss account. What can you conclude about changes in $US against currencies of countries where Under Armour has subsidiaries?

LO3   **P8-51.**   **Identifying and Analyzing Financial Statement Effects of Stock-Based Compensation**

The stockholders' equity of Aspen Corporation at December 31, 2019, follows.

7% Preferred stock, $100 par value, 20,000 shares authorized;	
4,000 shares issued and outstanding.	$ 400,000
Common stock, $15 par value, 300,000 shares authorized;	
30,000 shares issued and outstanding.	450,000
Paid-in capital in excess of par value—preferred stock	36,000
Paid-in capital in excess of par value—common stock	360,000
Retained earnings	325,000
Total stockholders' equity.	$1,571,000

The following transactions, among others, occurred during the following year.
- Employees exercised 12,000 stock options that were granted in 2015 and had a three-year vesting period. These options had an estimated fair value of $2 at the grant date, and an exercise price of $16. There were no other vested or unvested options after this exercise.
- Awarded 1,000 shares of stock to new executives, when the stock price was $36.
- Sold 10,000 shares to employees under the company-wide stock purchase plan. Under the plan, employees purchased the shares at a 10% discount when the stock price was $33 per share.
- Granted 40,000 new stock options, with a strike price of $34 and an estimated fair value of $6. The options vest over three years.

Required
Prepare the December 31, 2019, statement of stockholders' equity assuming that the company reports 2019 pretax income of $483,000 before the effects of stock-based compensation. Assume the company has a 35% tax rate.

LO1, 2   **P8-52.**   **Identifying and Analyzing Financial Statement Effects of Stock Transactions**

The stockholders' equity of Gaulin Company at the start of the current year follows.

Common stock, $5 par value, 500,000 shares authorized;	
350,000 shares issued and outstanding.	$1,750,000
Paid-in capital in excess of par value.	800,000
Retained earnings	634,000

During the current year, the following transactions occurred.

Jan.	5	Issued 10,000 shares of common stock for $13 cash per share.
Jan.	18	Repurchased 4,000 shares of common stock at $16 cash per share.
Mar.	12	Sold one-fourth of the treasury shares acquired January 18 for $19 cash per share.
July	17	Sold 500 shares of treasury stock for $14 cash per share.
Oct.	1	Issued 5,000 shares of 8%, $25 par value preferred stock for $36 cash per share. This is the first issuance of preferred shares from the 50,000 authorized preferred shares.

Required
a. Use the financial statement effects template to indicate the effects of each transaction.
b. Prepare the current year, stockholders' equity section of the balance sheet assuming that the company reports net income of $76,900 for the year.

LO1, 2, 4   **P8-53.**   **Identifying and Analyzing Financial Statement Effects of Stock Transactions**

Following is the stockholders' equity of Sharp Corporation at the start of the current year.

8% preferred stock, $50 par value, 10,000 shares authorized;	
8,000 shares issued and outstanding.	$ 400,000
Common stock, $20 par value, 50,000 shares authorized;	
25,000 shares issued and outstanding.	500,000
Paid-in capital in excess of par value—preferred stock	70,000
Paid-in capital in excess of par value—common stock	385,000
Retained earnings	238,000
Total stockholders' equity.	$1,593,000

The following transactions, among others, occurred during the current year.

Jan. 15   Issued 1,000 shares of preferred stock for $60 cash per share.

Jan. 20   Issued 4,000 shares of common stock at $34 cash per share.

May 18   Announced a 2-for-1 common stock split, reducing the par value of the common stock to $10 per share. The number of shares authorized was increased to 100,000 shares.

June 1   Issued 2,000 shares of common stock for $56,000 cash.

Sep. 1   Repurchased 2,500 shares of common stock at $16 cash per share.

Oct. 12   Sold 900 treasury shares at $19 cash per share.

Dec. 22   Issued 500 shares of preferred stock for $57 cash per share.

Required

Use the financial statement effects template to indicate the effects of each transaction.

P8-54. Analyzing and Interpreting Equity Accounts and Comprehensive Income

Following is the statement of shareholders' equity from the 2019 10-K for Procter & Gamble Company.

LO1, 2, 3, 4, 5

The Procter & Gamble Company (PG)

Consolidated Statement of Shareholders' Equity										
Dollars in millions; Shares in thousands	**Common Shares Outstanding**	**Common Stock**	**Preferred Stock**	**Additional Paid-in Capital**	**Reserve for ESOP Debt Retirement**	**Accumulated Other Comprehensive Income (Loss)**	**Treasury Stock**	**Retained Earnings**	**Non-controlling Interest**	**Total**
Balance, June 30, 2018	2,498,093	$4,009	$ 967	$63,846	$(1,204)	$(14,749)	$ (99,217)	$98,641	$590	$52,883
Impact of adoption of new accounting standards					(326)			(200)	(27)	(553)
Net earnings.								3,897	69	3,966
Other comprehensive income (loss).						139			1	140
Dividends and dividend equivalents ($2.8975 per share)										
Common.								(7,256)		(7,256)
Preferred, net of tax benefits								(263)		(263)
Treasury stock purchases.	(53,714)						(5,003)			(5,003)
Employee stock plans.	55,734			93			3,781			3,874
Preferred stock conversions.	4,638		(39)	6			33			—
ESOP debt impacts					58			99		157
Noncontrolling interest, net.				(118)					(248)	(366)
Balance, June 30, 2019	2,504,751	$4,009	$ 928	$63,827	$(1,146)	$(14,936)	$(100,406)	$94,918	$385	$47,579

Required

Homework MBC

a. How many shares of common stock did Procter & Gamble issue when convertible Class A preferred stock was converted during fiscal year ended June 30, 2019? At what average price were the preferred shares converted? Did the company issue new (previously unissued) shares for the preferred share conversion?

b. How many shares did the company issue for employee stock plans during the year? At what average price were the common shares issued to employees? Did the company issue new shares for the employee stock plans awards?

c. The company reported basic EPS of $1.40 for the year. The company's stock price on June 28, 2019 (the closest day before the fiscal year-end) was $109.65. Calculate the dividend payout and dividend yield ratios.

d. How many shares of stock did PG repurchase during the year? At what average price per share? Why does PG repurchase its own stock?

e. Compute the company's market cap at June 28, 2019. What is the market-to-book ratio on that day?

LO1, 2, 3, 5
Alphabet Inc. (GOOG)

P8-55.   **Analyzing and Interpreting Equity Accounts and Accumulated Other Comprehensive Income**
Following is the stockholders' equity section of Alphabet Inc. along with its components of AOCI and related footnote disclosures.

| Alphabet Inc.
CONSOLIDATED STATEMENTS OF STOCKHOLDERS ' EQUITY
(In millions, except share amounts which are reflected in thousands) | | | | | |
| | Class A and Class B
Common Stock, Class C Capital
Stock and Additional Paid-In Capital | | Accumulated
Other
Comprehensive
Income (Loss) | Retained
Earnings | Total
Stockholders'
Equity |
	Shares	Amount			
Balance as of December 31, 2017..............	694,783	$40,247	$(992)	$113,247	$152,502
Cumulative effect of accounting change	0	0	(98)	(599)	(697)
Common and capital stock issued	8,975	148	0	0	148
Stock-based compensation expense	0	9,353	0	0	9,353
Tax withholding related to vesting of restricted stock units and other.....................	0	(4,782)	0	0	(4,782)
Repurchases of capital stock	(8,202)	(576)	0	(8,499)	(9,075)
Sale of subsidiary shares	0	659	0	0	659
Net income	0	0	0	30,736	30,736
Other comprehensive loss	0	0	(1,216)	0	(1,216)
Balance as of December 31, 2018	695,556	$45,049	$(2,306)	$134,885	$177,628

The components of AOCI, net of tax, were as follows (in millions).

	Foreign Currency Translation Adjustments	Unrealized Gains (Losses) on Available- for-Sale Investments	Unrealized Gains (Losses) on Cash Flow Hedges	Total
Balance as of December 31, 2017.....................	$(1,103)	$ 233	$(122)	$ (992)
Other comprehensive income (loss) before reclassifications...	(781)	(10)	264	(527)
Amounts excluded from the assessment of hedge effectiveness recorded in AOCI	0	0	26	26
Amounts reclassified from AOCI......................	0	(911)	98	(813)
Other comprehensive income (loss).....................	(781)	(921)	388	(1,314)
Balance as of December 31, 2018.....................	$(1,884)	$(688)	$ 266	$(2,306)

Class A and Class B Common Stock and Class C Capital Stock   Our board of directors has authorized three classes of stock, Class A and Class B common stock, and Class C capital stock. The rights of the holders of each class of our common and capital stock are identical, except with respect to voting. Each share of Class A common stock is entitled to one vote per share. Each share of Class B common stock is entitled to 10 votes per share. Class C capital stock has no voting rights, except as required by applicable law. Shares of Class B common stock may be converted at any time at the option of the stockholder and automatically convert upon sale or transfer to Class A common stock.

Share Repurchases   In October 2016, the board of directors of Alphabet authorized the company to repurchase up to $7.0 billion of its Class C capital stock, which was completed during 2018. In January 2018, the board of directors of Alphabet authorized the company to repurchase up to $8.6 billion of its Class C capital stock. The repurchases are being executed from time to time, subject to general business and market conditions and other investment opportunities. The repurchase program does not have an expiration date.

Required

a. What amount of dividends did Alphabet pay in 2018 for all three classes of common stock combined?

b. Alphabet uses stock-based compensation for broad classes of employees. What amount did the company record for this expense in 2018? What was the total cash effect of this expense in 2018?

c. During 2018, Alphabet issued common stock, primarily for share-based compensation awards. How many shares did the company issue? At what average price were these shares issued?

d. During 2018, the company repurchased Class C capital stock for cash. How many shares did the company repurchase and retire? What was the total amount of cash used for the transaction? What was the average price paid for the shares? At what average price were these shares originally issued? (*Hint:* See Additional paid-in capital account on the statement of shareholders' equity.)

e. What items affect Alphabet's accumulated other comprehensive income? Consider the foreign currency translation adjustment of $781 million. Explain how this loss arose during 2018.

P8-56. **Interpreting Disclosure on Convertible Debentures**

On March 2, 2017, Snapchat undertook its initial public offering (IPO). Following is Snapchat's balance sheet for its first two fiscal years as a public company.

LO6, 7
Snapchat (SNAP)

Consolidated Balance Sheets		
December 31 (in thousands, except par value)	2017	2018
Assets		
Current assets		
Cash and cash equivalents	$ 334,063	$ 387,149
Marketable securities	1,708,976	891,914
Accounts receivable, net of allowance	279,473	354,965
Prepaid expenses and other current assets	44,282	41,900
Total current assets	2,366,794	1,675,928
Property and equipment, net	166,762	212,560
Intangible assets, net	166,473	126,054
Goodwill	639,882	632,370
Other assets	81,655	67,194
Total assets	$3,421,566	$2,714,106
Liabilities and Stockholders' Equity		
Current liabilities		
Accounts payable	$ 71,194	$ 30,876
Accrued expenses and other current liabilities	275,062	261,815
Total current liabilities	346,256	292,691
Other liabilities	82,983	110,416
Total liabilities	429,239	403,107
Commitments and contingencies		
Stockholders' equity		
Class A nonvoting common stock, $0.00001 par value. 3,000,000 shares authorized, 883,022 shares issued and outstanding at December 31, 2017, and 3,000,000 shares authorized, 999,304 shares issued and outstanding at December 31, 2018.	9	10
Class B voting common stock, $0.0000 par value. 700,000 shares authorized, 122,564 shares issued and outstanding at December 31, 2017, and 700,000 shares authorized, 93,845 shares issued and outstanding at December 31, 2018.	1	1
Class C voting common stock, $0.0000 1 par value. 260,888 shares authorized, 216,616 shares issued and outstanding at December 31, 2017, and 260,888 shares authorized, 224,611 shares issued and outstanding at December 31, 2018.	2	2
Additional paid-in capital	7,634,825	8,220,417
Accumulated other comprehensive income	14,157	3,147
Accumulated deficit	(4,656,667)	(5,912,578)
Total stockholders' equity	2,992,327	2,310,999
Total liabilities and stockholders' equity	$3,421,566	$2,714,106

Snapchat reported the following in a Form 8-K dated August 9, 2019.

> **Purchase Agreement** On August 6, 2019, we entered into a purchase agreement with Goldman Sachs, Morgan Stanley, and J.P. Morgan relating to the sale by us of an aggregate of $1.265 billion principal amount of our 0.75% Convertible Senior Notes due 2026 in a private offering. The Notes are convertible into cash, shares of our Class A common stock, or a combination thereof, at our election, at an initial conversion rate of 43.8481 shares of Class A common stock per $1,000 principal amount of the Notes, which is equivalent to an initial conversion price of approximately $22.81 per share of Class A common stock. Holders of the Notes may convert all or a portion of their Notes at their option prior to May 1, 2026, in multiples of $1,000 principal amount, only under the following circumstances:
>
> - during any calendar quarter commencing after December 31, 2019, if the last reported sale price of Class A common stock for at least 20 trading days (whether or not consecutive) during the period of 30 consecutive trading days . . . is greater than or equal to 130% of the applicable conversion price of the Notes on each such trading day;

Required:

a. Why did Snapchat wait two years to issue debt? Why did the company not do so during the time of the IPO?

b. What will be the balance sheet effect of the sale of the convertible senior notes? How will this affect the company's leverage?

c. Confirm the initial conversion price of $22.81 per share. At what price did SNAP stock close on August 9, 2019 (use on online investment site to determine the closing price that day)? Compare the two prices and explain why the three investment banks might enter into the purchase agreement described above.

d. After December 31, 2019, what minimum stock price is required to permit note holders to convert to Class A common stock?

e. What will Snapchat record as interest expense on the convertible senior notes in fiscal 2019?

f. How will the convertible senior notes impact the computation of basic and diluted earnings per share (EPS)?

g. Assume that on January 2020, SNAP has traded at around $30 for a month and that bondholders convert $400 million notes. Explain how the conversion will affect debt and equity. Which accounts and by how much?

LO6

Gladiator Investment
Corporation (GAIN)

P8-57. **Interpreting Disclosure on Convertible Preferred Securities**

Gladiator Investment Corporation includes the following in its 10-K for the fiscal year ended March 31, 2019.

Mandatorily Redeemable Senior Securities ($ thousands)	
Class and Year	**Amount Outstanding**
7.125% Series A Cumulative Term Preferred Stock	
March 31, 2019.	—
March 31, 2018.	—
6.75% Series B Cumulative Term Preferred Stock	
March 31, 2019.	—
March 31, 2018.	41,400
6.50% Series C Cumulative Term Preferred Stock due 2022	
March 31, 2019.	—
March 31, 2018.	40,250
6.25% Series D Cumulative Term Preferred Stock due 2023	
March 31, 2019.	57,500
March 31, 2018.	57,500
6.375% Series E Cumulative Term Preferred Stock due 2025	
March 31, 2019.	74,750
March 31, 2018.	—

Required

a. Explain what is meant by "mandatorily redeemable preferred stock."

b. Assume that the company issued new stock on the first day of the fiscal year. What total amount of preferred stock dividends must Gladiator Investment pay during the year ended March 31, 2018?

c. What total amount of preferred stock dividends must Gladiator Investment pay during the year ended March 31, 2019?

d. During the fiscal year ended March 31, 2018, the company issued Series E preferred stock and used the proceeds to redeem all of the Series B and Series C stock at face value. Use the financial statement effects template to record these transactions.

P8-58.   Identifying and Analyzing Financial Statement Effects of Share-Based Compensation   LO3

Weaver Industries implements a new share-based compensation plan in 2017. Under the plan, the company's CEO and CFO each will receive nonqualified stock options to purchase 100,000, no par shares. The options vest ratably (1/3 of the options each year) over three years, expire in 10 years, and have an exercise (strike) price of $27 per share. Weaver uses the Black-Scholes model to estimate a fair value per option of $18.

Required

a. Use the financial statement effects template to record the compensation expense related to these options for each year 2017 through 2019.

b. In 2020, the company's stock price is $24. If you were the Weaver Industries CEO, would you exercise your options? Explain.

c. In 2022, the company's stock price is $46 and the CEO exercises all of her options. Use the financial statement effects template to record the exercise.

P8-59.   Interpreting Disclosure on Employee Stock Options   LO3

Intel Corporation reported the following in its 2018 10-K report.

Intel Corporation
(INTC)

> **Share-Based Compensation** Share-based compensation recognized in 2018 was $1.5 billion ($1.4 billion in 2017 and $1.4 billion in 2016). During 2018, the tax benefit that we realized for the tax deduction from share-based awards totaled $399 million ($520 million in 2017 and $616 million in 2016). We grant RSUs with a service condition, as well as RSUs with both a market condition and a service condition, which we call outperformance stock units (OSUs). We estimate the fair value of Restricted Stock Units (RSUs) with a service condition using the value of our common stock on the date of grant, reduced by the present value of dividends expected to be paid on our shares of common stock prior to vesting. We estimate the fair value of OSUs using a Monte Carlo simulation model on the date of grant. We base expected volatility for OSUs on historical volatility. We based the weighted average estimated value of RSU and OSU grants on the weighted average assumptions for each period as follows.

RSUs and OSUs	Dec 29, 2018	Dec 30, 2017	Dec 31, 2016
Estimated values	$48.95	$35.30	$29.76
Risk-free interest rate	2.4%	1.4%	0.9%
Dividend yield	2.4%	2.9%	3.3%
Volatility	22%	23%	23%

> Additional information with respect to RSU activity is as follows.

> **Restricted Stock Unit Awards**   RSU activity in 2018 was as follows.

	Number of RSUs (in millions)	Weighted Average Grant-Date Fair Value
December 30, 2017	100.4	$32.36
Granted	36.4	48.95
Vested	(39.5)	31.64
Forfeited	(7.4)	36.23
December 29, 2018	89.9	$39.07

Required

a. What is the main difference between Intel's RSUs and OSUs?

b. What amount did Intel record in 2018 for share-based compensation expense?

c. What is the total fair value of RSUs granted in 2018? Why is this amount not equal to the 2018 share-based compensation expense?

d. Imagine that during 2018, all employees immediately sold their shares when their RSUs vested. What profit would the employees have made (before tax)? *Hint:* Use the RSU average grant-date fair value to approximate Intel's average stock price in 2018.

e. Provide two reasons why an employee would forfeit their RSUs.

LO7   **P8-60.**   **Analyzing Stockholders' Equity and EPS**

The following dashboard depicts equity related information for firms in four industries: Pharmaceuticals, Financial services, Retail, and Heavy equipment manufacturers. Access the dashboard at the myBusinessCourse website to answer the requirements.

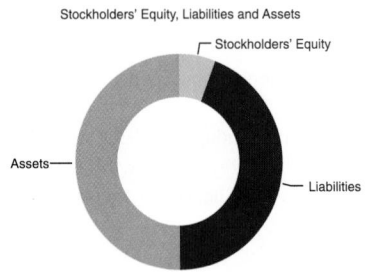

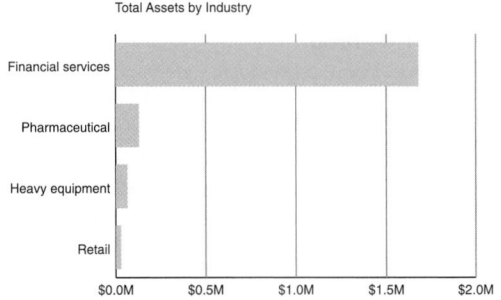

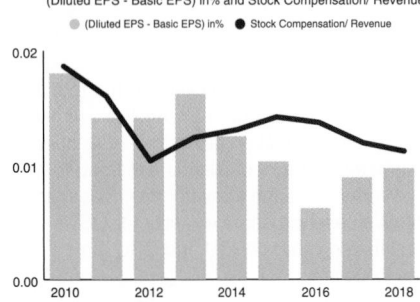

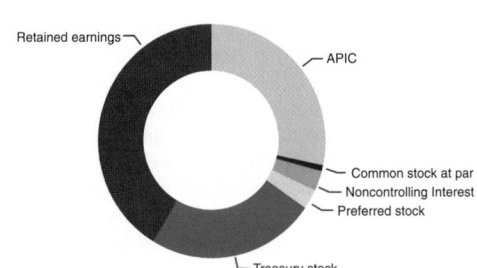

Required

a. Which industry has the smallest proportion of assets financed by owners? Why might that be?

b. Which industry has the largest proportion of treasury stock in their capital structure?

c. Across all four industries, what pattern do we observe in diluted versus basic EPS over time? Is this pattern different for any of the four industries?

P8-61.   **Interpreting Disclosure on Share-Based Compensation**

> lululemon athletica reported the following information for the fiscal year ended February 3, 2019.

LO3
lululemon athletica
(LULU)

A summary of the balances of the Company's stock-based compensation plans as of February 3, 2019, January 28, 2018, and January during the fiscal years then ended is presented below:

(In thousands, except per share amounts)	Stock Options		Performance-Based Restricted Stock Units		Restricted Shares		Restricted Stock Units	
	Number	Weighted-Average Exercise Price	Number	Weighted-Average Grant Date Fair Value	Number	Weighted-Average Grant Date Fair Value	Number	Weighted-Average Grant Date Fair Value
Balance at								
January 31, 2016 ..	867	$49.54	395	$ 58.58	31	$ 57.67	333	$55.91
Granted.	428	68.63	164	68.64	17	69.94	216	68.15
Exercised/vested	191	36.76	7	64.36	34	58.39	91	56.87
Forfeited/expired.	186	58.87	162	62.54	—	—	98	55.95
Balance at								
January 29, 2017 ..	918	$59.20	390	$ 61.05	14	$ 70.54	360	$62.99
Granted.	619	52.34	192	52.38	24	52.38	336	52.83
Exercised/vested	109	51.62	—	—	14	70.29	135	60.64
Forfeited/expired.	311	58.09	253	55.30	3	51.72	134	57.28
Balance at								
January 28, 2018 ..	1,117	$56.44	329	$ 60.42	21	$ 52.45	427	$57.54
Granted.	388	96.96	123	102.49	6	124.19	257	88.75
Exercised/vested	316	56.29	39	63.04	21	52.45	174	58.94
Forfeited/expired.	319	59.76	133	61.71	—	—	70	66.90
Balance at								
February 3, 2019. . .	870	$73.34	280	$ 78.01	6	$124.19	440	$73.73

Stock-based compensation expense charged to income for the plans was $29 .6 million, $17 .6 million , and $16.8 million for the years ended February 3, 2019, January 28, 2018, and January 29, 2017, respectively.

Required

a. How do stock options and restricted shares differ? In what respects are they the same?

b. Why do companies impose vesting periods on restricted stock grants?

c. Consider the stock option activity. Compare the weighted average exercise price of the granted stock options and exercised options each year. What explains the difference in the two amounts each year?

d. Use the financial statement effects template to record the restricted shares granted during 2018. The common stock has a $0.005 par value per share.

e. Use the financial statement effects template to record the total 2018 compensation expense related to Lululemon's share-based compensation activity. Include the tax effects of the compensation expense. Assume a tax rate of 21%.

IFRS Applications

I8-62.   **Analyzing and Interpreting Equity Accounts and Comprehensive Income**

> Henkel AG & Co. is an international, fast-moving consumer goods (FMCG) company headquartered in Düsseldorf, Germany. Following is its shareholders' equity statement, prepared using IFRS, from its 2018 annual report.

LO1, 2, 4, 5
Henkel AG & Co.

In millions euro	Ordinary Shares	Pre-ferred Shares	Capital Reserve	Treasury Shares	Retained Earnings	Currency Transla-tion	Hedge Reserve	Reserve for Equity & Debt Instru-ments	Shareholders of Henkel AG & Co. KGaA	Non-Controlling Interests	Total
Issued Capital						**Other Components of Equity**					
At January 1, 2018 (adjusted)	€260	€178	€652	€(91)	€16,042	€(1,332)	€(198)	€3	€15,514	€ 74	€15,588
Net income	—	—	—	—	2,311	—	—	—	2,311	19	2,330
Other comprehensive income	—	—	—	—	(134)	146	(1)	—	11	—	11
Total comprehensive income for the period	—	—	—	—	2,177	146	(1)	—	2,322	19	2,341
Dividends	—	—	—	—	(772)	—	—	—	(772)	(16)	(788)
Sale of treasury shares	—	—	—	—	—	—	—	—	—	—	—
Changes in ownership interest with no change in control	—	—	—	—	—	—	—	—	—	—	—
Other changes in equity	—	—	—	—	(48)	—	—	—	(48)	—	(48)
At December 31, 2018	€260	€178	€652	€(91)	€17,399	€(1,186)	€(199)	€3	€17,016	€ 77	€17,093

Required

a. Did Henkel issue any additional ordinary or preferred shares during 2018?

b. How much did Henkel pay in dividends during 2018? To whom were these dividends paid?

c. Did the company repurchase any stock during 2018?

d. Did Henkel sell any treasury shares?

e. Consider the currency translation account. Explain how the change of €146 arose during the year.

f. Henkel reports noncontrolling interest of €77. Why did this account increase during the year?

g. Compute return on equity for 2018. (*Hint:* Use the net income attributable to controlling interest [shareholders of Henkel] and equity attributable to controlling interest.)

LO1, 2, 3, 4, 5 **I8-63.** **Analyzing Stockholders' Equity Accounts and Transactions**

Nutrien Ltd. (NTR)

Nutrien Ltd.—the world's largest potash producer—is a Canadian corporation based in Saskatoon, Saskatchewan. The following is information taken from its financial statements reported in $US but prepared in accordance with IFRS.

(In millions of dollars)	Share Capital	Contributed Surplus	Net Fair Value Loss on Investments	Net Actuarial Gain on Defined Benefit Plans	Loss on Currency Translation of Foreign Operations	Other	Total Accumulated Other Comprehensive Income	Retained Earnings	Total Equity
Accumulated Other Comprehensive (Loss) Income ("AOCI")									
Balance—December 31, 2017	$ 1,806	$230	$73	$—	$(2)	$(46)	$25	$6,242	$ 8,303
Merger impact (Notes 3 and 11)	15,898	7	—	—	—	—	—	(1)	15,904
Net earnings	—	—	—	—	—	—	—	3,573	3,573
Other comprehensive (loss) income	—	—	(99)	54	(249)	(8)	(302)	—	(302)
Share repurchased (Note 24)	(998)	(23)	—	—	—	—	—	(831)	(1,852)
Dividends declared	—	—	—	—	—	—	—	(1,273)	(1,273)
Effect of share-based compensation including issuance of common shares	34	17	—	—	—	—	—	—	51
Transfer of net actuarial gain on defined benefit plans	—	—	—	(54)	—	—	(54)	54	—
Transfer of net loss on sale of investment	—	—	19	—	—	—	19	(19)	—
Transfer of net loss on cash flow hedges	—	—	—	—	—	21	21	—	21
Balance—December 31 , 2018	$16,740	$231	$(7)	$—	$(251)	$(33)	$(291)	$7,745	$24,425

continued

continued from previous page

Authorized The company is authorized to issue an unlimited number of common shares without par value and an unlimited number of preferred shares. The common shares are not redeemable or convertible. The preferred shares may be issued in one or more series with rights and conditions to be determined by the Board of Directors. No first preferred shares have been issued.

Issued	Number of Common Shares
Balance, December 31, 2017.	644,197,473
Issued under option plans	670,201
Repurchased	(36,332,197)
Balance, December 31, 2018.	608,535,477

a. How many shares are authorized at December 31, 2018?

b. How many shares are issued at December 31, 2018? At what average price were these shares issued as of December 31, 2018?

c. How many shares are issued under option plans at December 31, 2018? At what average price were these shares issued?

d. Does the company have any treasury stock? How do we know?

e. On December 14, 2018, the company's Board of Directors declared a quarterly dividend of $0.43 per share, payable to all shareholders of record on March 29, 2019. Assuming that the number of shares outstanding on March 29, 2019, is the same as on December 31, 2018, what dividends will the company pay?

f. Comprehensive income includes net income plus other comprehensive income. What was the company's comprehensive income for 2018? Why does it differ from net income for 2018?

Ongoing Project

(This ongoing project began in Module 1 and continues through most of the book; even if previous segments were not completed, the requirements are still applicable to any business analysis.) Company analysis should consider how the companies are financed and what transactions were executed with stockholders during the recent year.

1. *Contributed Capital.* Use the balance sheet and the statement of stockholders' equity to determine how the company has structured its equity.

   • What proportion of assets are financed with equity?

   • What classes of equity does the company have? What transactions occurred during the year?

   • Does the company have treasury stock? Read the MD&A and the footnotes to determine the main reason for holding treasury stock. Assess the treasury stock transactions during the year. How much was spent and/or received? What did the company do with the proceeds? Compare the average price paid for treasury shares to the current stock price.

   • Does the company use share-based compensation? What types of plans are used? What was the magnitude of the compensation? What is the magnitude of the outstanding (unvested) options and/or shares? Compare the level of treasury shares to outstanding (unvested) options and/or shares.

   • Compute the market capitalization of the firms and compare to the book value of equity. Find an online source for the average market-to-book ratio for the industry and see where the firms fit. Follow up on anything unusual.

2. *Earned Capital.* Recall that the least costly form of financing is internal—that is, plowing earned profits (and cash) into new investments is a low-cost means to grow the company and return even more to stockholders.

   • How profitable were the companies? Compare return on equity for the three-year period and determine causes for major differences over time and between companies.

   • Review accumulated other comprehensive income and determine the main components of that account. How did AOCI change during the year?

- Did the companies pay dividends? Compute the dividend payout and the dividend yield for all three years and compare them.
- Did the company have any stock splits?

3. *Convertible Securities.*   Read the debt footnote to determine if the company has any convertible securities.

- What types of convertible securities are outstanding?
- Are these securities substantive? To assess this, consider their common size and their effect on diluted earnings per share.
- Did the company have any convertible transactions during the year? If yes, determine the effect on the balance sheet and income statement.

Solutions to Review Problems

Review 8-1—Solution

a. False. Stockholders' equity is the book value (determined in accordance with GAAP) of the company. It represents the claim that shareholders have against the net assets (assets less liabilities) of the company.

b. True. The Board of Directors is the elected representatives of the shareholders who hire the company's CEO and oversee its operations.

c. True. Issued shares represents the cumulative number of shares that have been sold (issued) to date.

d. True. Outstanding shares is equal to the cumulative number of shares that have been issued less the cumulative number of shares that have been subsequently repurchased by the company.

e. False. The amount of annual dividends per share for preferred stock is usually fixed. Common stock receives any remaining dividends after preferred shareholders have been paid and there is no limit to the amount of dividends that common shareholders can receive.

f. True. Treasury stock represents the cumulative dollar amount of all share repurchases and subsequent resales on the open market.

Review 8-2—Solution

a. The common stock account did not change during this period, either in the number of shares issued (7,040 million) or in dollars ($1,760 million). Thus, we conclude that the company issued no new stock during the year.

b. (in millions)

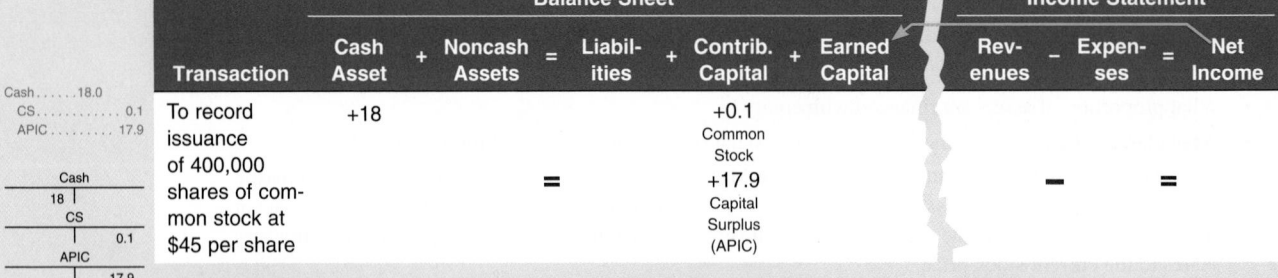

c. (in millions)

d. The company will decrease the treasury stock account by $473 million, the original cost of the shares (30 million shares × $15.77 per share). The difference between the market value of the treasury shares ($964 million) and the cost ($473 million) is added to the Capital Surplus account, increasing it by $491 million.

Review 8-3—Solution

a. Coca-Cola's income before tax was reduced by $225 million for the stock-based compensation expense. This was included in "other" line items on the income statement rather than disclosed separately.

b. Stock-based compensation does not affect cash flow; it is a noncash expense. There is a real cash outflow associated with the compensation—the company buys treasury shares to use for compensation instead of issuing new stock. The cost of the treasury shares is a real cash cost.

c. The fair value of the total stock option grant is $84.64 million computed as $10.58 fair value per share × 8 million shares. With a vesting period of four years, the amount of stock option compensation expense on the 2018 income statement is $21.16 million.

d. The fair value of the total performance share units grant is $83.9 million computed as $38.45 fair value per share × 2,183 thousand shares. With a restriction period of two years, the amount of stock option compensation expense on the 2018 income statement is $41.95 million.

e. There is a chance that the options will not be exercised. If the stock price falls below the option strike price of $36.74 by the time the options expire, the option will have no value to the employee. But even if the stock price falls, the performance share units will have value, albeit less than at the grant date. The other issue is that the restriction period for the performance share units is only two years, whereas the vesting period for the options is four years.

Review 8-4—Solution

a. (in millions)

Transaction	Balance Sheet					Income Statement		
	Cash Asset	+ Noncash Assets	= Liabilities	+ Contrib. Capital	+ Earned Capital	Revenues	− Expenses	= Net Income
To record preferred and common stock dividend	−9,314		=		−9,314 Retained Earnings		−	=

RE 9,314
    Cash 9,314

RE	
9,314	

Cash	
	9,314

b. If Wells Fargo had paid $100 million more in common stock dividends in 2018, net income would not have been affected. Dividends are not included when we determine net income; they are a return of the net income to shareholders.

c.

	2018	2017
Dividends declared per common share ($ per share)	$1.64	$1.54
Earnings per common share ($ per share).	$4.31	$4.14
Dividend payout ratio	38.1%	37.2%

d. The WFC closing stock price on December 31, 2018, was $46.08. The dividend yield ratio for 2018 is 3.56% ($1.64/$46.08).

Review 8-5—Solution

a. The unrealized loss increased during the year. On average, the U.S. dollar strengthened in 2018 vis-à-vis currencies of countries where Coca-Cola has subsidiaries. This means that the assets and liabilities of foreign subsidiaries, when translated to U.S. dollars, lost value. If the subsidiary is solvent (assets > liabilities), then equity declines and that is reflected in negative other comprehensive income.

b. If the securities had been sold, the unrealized loss of $34 million would be realized in the income statement as a reduction in "other income" before tax.

c. Yes, the unrealized "loss" of $7 million arises because the fair value of the derivative investments has declined during the year.

Review 8-6—Solution

LTD....... 850
CS.......... 200
APIC........ 650

LTD	
850	

CS	
	200

APIC	
	650

		Balance Sheet					Income Statement		
Transaction	Cash Asset	+ Noncash Assets	= Liabil-ities	+ Contrib. Capital	+ Earned Capital	Rev-enues	– Expen-ses	= Net Income
Convert a bond with $850 book value into 200 common shares with $1 par value		=	−850 Long-Term Debt	+200 Common Stock +650 Additional Paid-In Capital		–	=

Review 8-7—Solution

a. $\text{Basic EPS} = \dfrac{\$1,337,536,000}{26,970,000} = \$49.59$

b. $\text{Diluted EPS} = \dfrac{\$1,337,536,000}{(26,970,000 + 454,000)} = \$48.77$

c. Anti-dilutive means that including the stock-option effects would increase EPS (as opposed to diluting the EPS) because the options' exercise price is greater than the stock's current market price. These underwater (or out-of-the-money) options are anti-dilutive and are, therefore, excluded from the diluted EPS computation.

Intercorporate Investments

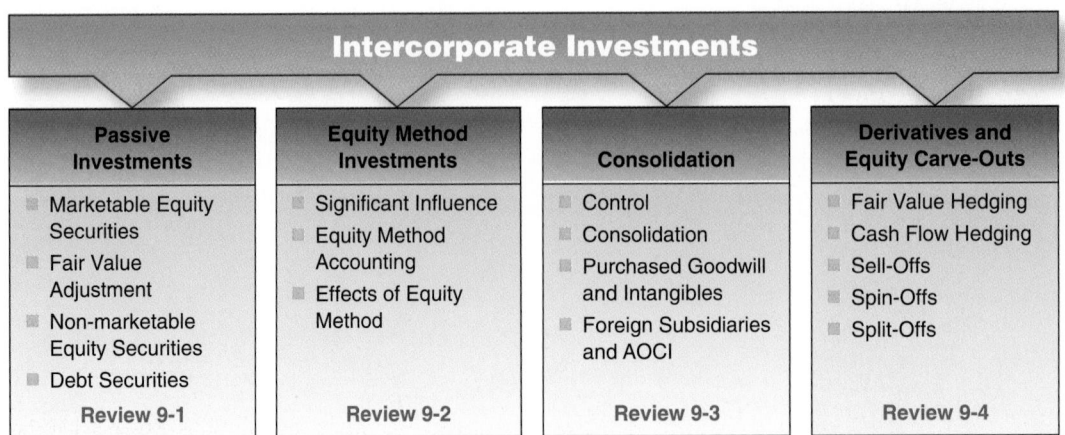

Intercorporate Investments			
Passive Investments	**Equity Method Investments**	**Consolidation**	**Derivatives and Equity Carve-Outs**
▪ Marketable Equity Securities ▪ Fair Value Adjustment ▪ Non-marketable Equity Securities ▪ Debt Securities	▪ Significant Influence ▪ Equity Method Accounting ▪ Effects of Equity Method	▪ Control ▪ Consolidation ▪ Purchased Goodwill and Intangibles ▪ Foreign Subsidiaries and AOCI	▪ Fair Value Hedging ▪ Cash Flow Hedging ▪ Sell-Offs ▪ Spin-Offs ▪ Split-Offs
Review 9-1	Review 9-2	Review 9-3	Review 9-4

PREVIEW   GOOG

We examine topics related to investments, including the following.

■ Investments of excess cash in marketable equity and debt securities.

■ Strategic investments in equity securities in which the investor company has significant influence.

■ Investments in equity securities of privately held companies prior to an initial public offering.

■ Consolidation of subsidiaries that the investor company (the parent) controls.

■ Recognition of intangibles, including goodwill.

■ Hedging of risks using derivatives (Appendix A).

■ Unlocking business value using equity carve outs (Appendix B).

■ Alphabet Inc. is the focus company and the dashboard below conveys key financial information.

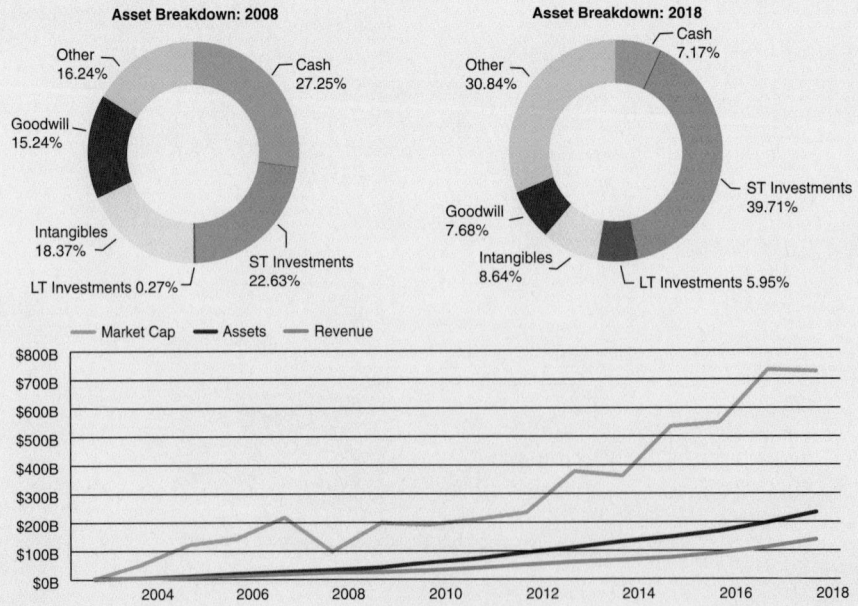

Road Map

LO	Learning Objective | Topics	Page	eLecture	Guided Example	Assignments
9–1	**Examine and interpret marketable securities reporting.** Passive Investments :: Marketable Equity Securities :: Fair Value Adjustment :: Non-Marketable Equity Securities :: Debt Securities	9-3	e9–1	Review 9-1	1, 2, 3, 13, 14, 19, 27, 28, 29, 30, 31, 34, 47, 52
9–2	**Analyze and interpret equity method investments.** Significant Influence :: Equity Method Accounting :: Effects of Equity Method	9-12	e9–2	Review 9-2	4, 5, 17, 18, 20, 32, 34, 35, 36, 37, 48, 51, 52
9–3	**Explain consolidation and interpret consolidated reports.** Control :: Consolidation for Investments with Control :: Purchased Goodwill and Intangibles :: Foreign Subsidiaries and AOCI :: Limitations of Consolidated Reporting	9-17	e9–3	Review 9-3	6, 7, 10, 11, 21, 22, 23, 30, 33, 38, 39, 41, 42, 43, 44, 49, 50, 52
9–4	**Describe and interpret derivative disclosures (Appendix 9A).** Fair Value Hedging :: Cash Flow Hedging :: Analysis of Derivatives	9-29	e9–4	Review 9-4	8, 9, 15, 16, 44, 45, 46
9–5	**Explain equity carve-outs and their financial statement impact (Appendix 9B).** Sell-offs :: Split-offs :: Spin-offs :: Analysis of Equity Carve-outs	9-32			12, 24, 25, 26, 40, 53

Intercorporate Investments

LO1 Examine and interpret marketable securities reporting.

It is common for one company to purchase the voting stock of another. These purchases, called *intercorporate equity investments*, typically have one or more of the following strategic aims.

■ **Short-term investment of excess cash.**   Companies might invest excess cash during slow times of the year (after receivables are collected and before seasonal production begins), or to maintain liquidity in order to counter strategic moves by competitors, or to quickly respond to acquisition opportunities.

■ **Strategic alliances.**   Companies use intercorporate investments to gain access to needed resources or expertise such as research and development activities, an established supply chain or distribution market, or production and marketing expertise.

■ **Targeted projects.**   Companies might invest in a partnership or joint venture (with equity ownership) to accomplish specific short- to medium-term outcomes such as construction projects or research endeavors. Partnerships and joint ventures can increase the return to the venture partners' investments and reduce risks associated with going it alone.

■ **Market penetration or expansion.**   Companies might acquire control of other companies to integrate vertically (by buying a supplier or a customer) or horizontally (by buying a competitor). These investments can help the company expand in existing product or geographic markets or penetrate new markets.

The level of ownership interest the investor (the purchaser) acquires directly affects the level of influence or control the investor has over the investee company (the company whose securities are purchased), as shown in Exhibit 9.1.

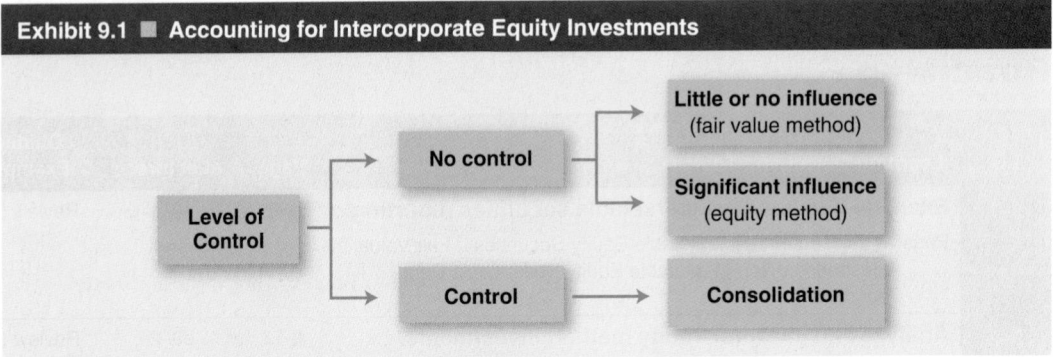

Exhibit 9.1 ■ Accounting for Intercorporate Equity Investments

There are three levels of influence or control.

■ **Little or no influence (passive investments).**   The investor has a relatively small investment and cannot exert influence over the investee. The investor's goal is to realize dividend income and capital gains. Generally, the investor is deemed to have little to no influence if it owns less than 20% of the investee's outstanding voting stock.

■ **Significant influence.**   The investor can exert "significant influence" over the investee by virtue of the percentage of the outstanding voting stock it owns or owing to legal agreements between the investor and investee, such as a license to use technology. Absent evidence to the contrary, significant influence is presumed when the investor owns between 20% and 50% of the outstanding voting shares.

■ **Control.**   When a company has control over an investee, it has the ability to elect a majority of the board of directors and, as a result, the ability to affect the investee's strategic direction and the hiring of executive management. Control is generally presumed if the investor company owns more than 50% of the outstanding voting stock of the investee company but can sometimes occur at less than 50% stock ownership by virtue of legal agreements, technology licensing, or other contractual means. The determining factor is the ability to control strategic decisions.

The level of influence/control determines the specific accounting method applied and its financial statement implications as outlined in Exhibit 9.2.

Exhibit 9.2 ■ Investment Type, Accounting Treatment, and Financial Statement Effects				
	Accounting	Balance Sheet Effects	Income Statement Effects	Cash Flow Effects
Little or no influence (passive investment)	Fair value method	• Investment account is reported at fair value	• Dividends and capital gains and losses included in income • Interim changes in fair value affect income	• Dividends are operating cash inflows • Sale proceeds are investing cash inflows • Purchases are cash outflows from investing activities
Significant influence	Equity method	• Investment account equals percent owned of investee company's equity since acquired*	• Dividends reduce investment account • Investor reports income equal to percent owned of investee income • Sale of investment yields capital gain or loss	• Dividends are operating cash inflows • Sale proceeds are investing cash inflows • Purchases are cash outflows from investing activities
Control	Consolidation	• Balance sheets of investor and investee are combined	• Income statements of investor and investee are combined • Sale of investee yields capital gain or loss	• Cash flows of investor and investee are combined and retain original classification (operating, investing, or financing) • Sale and purchase of investee are investing cash flows

*Investments are often acquired at purchase prices in excess of book value (the median market price of S&P 500 companies was 2.7 times their book value as of August 2019). In this case, the investment account exceeds the proportionate ownership of the investee's equity.

As Exhibit 9.2 shows, there are three basic reporting issues to consider: (1) how investment income and capital gains are recognized in the income statement, (2) at what amount the investment is reported on the balance sheet, and (3) how the cash flow statement classifies cash received and used for the investment. Next we discuss these issues for the three investment types.

Passive Investments in Equity Securities

There are many types of equity securities and many reasons for investing in them. Most often, companies buy marketable equity securities as a passive investment because they provide a short-term return. Marketable equity securities are financial instruments that can be bought and sold on a public exchange whereas non-marketable equity securities are shares of stock of private companies. In this section we examine the accounting for both marketable and non-marketable equity securities. Accounting differs for equity versus debt and, in a later section, we discuss debt investments.

Acquisition and Sale

When a company makes a passive investment in marketable or non-marketable equity securities, it records the shares acquired on the balance sheet at fair value; that is, the purchase price. This is the same as accounting for the acquisition of other assets, such as inventories or PPE. Subsequent to acquisition, these investments are classified on the balance sheet as current or long-term assets, depending on management's expectations about their ultimate holding period.

When investments are sold, any recognized gain or loss on sale is equal to the difference between the proceeds received and the book (carrying) value of the investment on the balance sheet as follows.

Gain or Loss on Sale = Proceeds from Sale – Book Value of Investment Sold

To illustrate the acquisition and sale of a passive investment in equity securities, assume Alphabet purchases 1,000 shares of Juniper Networks for $20 cash per share (this includes transaction costs such as brokerage fees). Alphabet subsequently sells 400 of the 1,000 shares for $23 cash per share (assume no change in the investment book value). The following financial statement effects template shows how these transactions affect Alphabet.

	Balance Sheet					Income Statement		
Transaction	Cash Asset	+ Noncash Assets	= Liabil- ities	+ Contrib. Capital	+ Earned Capital	Rev- enues	− Expen- ses	= Net Income
1. Purchase 1,000 shares of Juniper common stock for $20 cash per share	−20,000 Cash	+20,000 Marketable Securities =				−	=	
2. Sell 400 shares of Ju- niper common stock for $23 cash per share	+9,200 Cash	−8,000 Marketable Securities =			+1,200 Retained Earnings	+1,200 Gain on Sale	−	= +1,200

MS 20,000
  Cash 20,000

MS	
20,000	

Cash	
	20,000

Cash.....9,200
  MS......... 8,000
  GN......... 1,200

Cash	
9,200	

MS	
	8,000

GN	
	1,200

Income statements include the gain or loss on sale of marketable securities as a component of *other income*, which is typically reported separately from operating income and often aggregated with interest and dividend income.

Fair-Value Method for Investments in Equity Security

On the balance sheet, companies must report all passive investments in equity securities at fair value. Moreover, changes in the fair value of equity securities during the current period flow to current period net income. As the market value of equity securities fluctuates so do the balance sheet and the income statement. This is known as fair-value method of accounting.

What is fair value? Accounting rules lay out three specific ways to determine fair value and all three are acceptable (in order of preferred usage).

■ **Level 1** Quoted market prices if the security is traded in active markets.

■ **Level 2** Quoted market prices in active markets for similar securities and model-based valuation techniques if all significant inputs are observable in the market or can be derived from observable market data.

■ **Level 3** Unobservable inputs that are supported by little or no market activities.

When we think of investments in equity securities, we generally think of investments in marketable securities that are traded on organized exchanges (such as NYSE and NASDAQ). These securities are reported at fair value at each reporting date using their quoted market prices (Level 1) or quoted market prices for similar securities (Level 2). For non-marketable securities, companies use Level 3 inputs to determine the fair value, as we explain below.

Fair Value Adjustments To illustrate the accounting for changes in fair value subsequent to purchase (and before sale), assume Alphabet's investment in Juniper Networks (600 remaining shares purchased for $20 per share) increases in value to $25 per share at year-end. The investment account must be adjusted to fair value to reflect the $3,000 unrealized gain ($5-per-share increase for 600 shares) as follows.

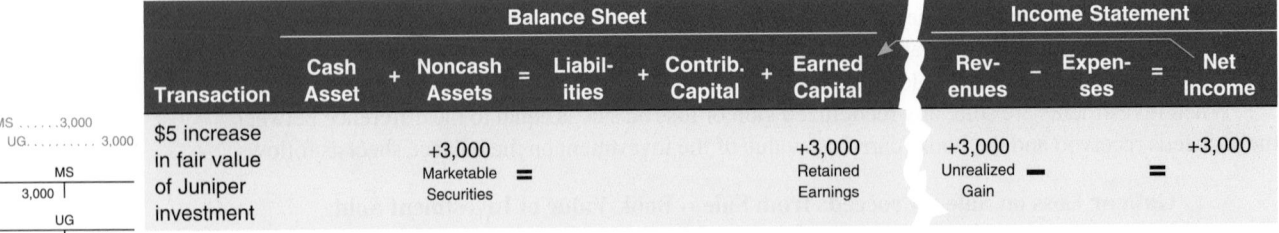

	Balance Sheet					Income Statement		
Transaction	Cash Asset	+ Noncash Assets	= Liabil- ities	+ Contrib. Capital	+ Earned Capital	Rev- enues	− Expen- ses	= Net Income
$5 increase in fair value of Juniper investment		+3,000 Marketable Securities =			+3,000 Retained Earnings	+3,000 Unrealized Gain	−	= +3,000

MS 3,000
  UG.......... 3,000

MS	
3,000	

UG	
	3,000

The investment account increases by $3,000 to reflect the increase in the stock's fair value, and the unrealized gain is recorded as income, thus increasing both reported income and retained earnings for the period. (Our illustration uses a portfolio with only one security for simplicity. Portfolios usually consist of multiple securities, and the unrealized gain or loss is computed based on the total cost and total market value of the entire portfolio.)

Marketable Equity Securities

Alphabet has investments in marketable equity securities of $1,222 million at December 31, 2018. In a footnote, the company reports the following ($ millions).

From time to time, we may hold marketable equity securities obtained through acquisitions or strategic investments in private companies that subsequently go public.

As of December 31, 2018	Cash and Cash Equivalents	Marketable Securities
Level 1:		
Money market funds.	$3,493	$ 0
Marketable equity securities.	0	994
	3,493	994
Level 2:		
Mutual funds.	0	228
Total	$3,493	$1,222

Some of Alphabet's marketable equity securities trade frequently and prices are easily observable, and for those securities, Alphabet reported Level 1 fair value of $994 million. The mutual funds are apparently infrequently traded and Alphabet reported Level 2 fair value of $228 million. The total of $1,222 million is not reported as a separate balance sheet line item, but instead, reported along with marketable debt securities.

Non-Marketable Equity Securities

In addition to its marketable equity securities, Alphabet invests in non-marketable equity securities—the stock of privately held companies with no publicly available stock price. These investments allow Alphabet early access to new technologies or the opportunity to invest prior to an initial public offering.

Because, by definition, investments in non-marketable securities lack readily determined market values, we might think that they would be exempt from fair-value adjustment. However, this is not so. Accounting rules require that such securities must also be reported at fair value on the balance sheet with fair-value changes recognized in current income.

Companies use Level 3 inputs to value these non-marketable securities and valuation techniques commonly include the use of market multiples, discounted cash flow approaches, and a variety of other methods that utilize forecasts and other inputs in a valuation model to estimate the fair value of the security.

At year-end 2018, Alphabet's non-marketable equity security portfolio had a fair value of $12.3 billion. Alphabet discusses the inherent difficulty of valuing these securities in this excerpt from its 2018 10-K.

Our non-marketable equity securities not accounted for under the equity method are adjusted to fair value for observable transactions for identical or similar investments of the same issuer or impairment (referred to as the measurement alternative). . . These investments, especially those that are in the early stages, are inherently risky because the technologies or products these companies have under development are typically in the early phases and may never materialize and they may experience a decline in financial condition, which could result in a loss of a substantial part of our investment in these companies. The success of our investment in any private company is also typically dependent on the likelihood of our ability to realize value in our investments through liquidity events such as public offerings, acquisitions, private sales or other favorable market events reflecting appreciation to the cost of our initial investment. As of December 31, 2018, the carrying value of our non-marketable equity securities, which were accounted for under the measurement (i.e. fair-value) alternative, was $12.3 billion. Valuations of our equity investments in private companies are inherently more complex due to the lack of readily available market data. Volatility in the global economic climate and financial markets could result in a significant impairment charge on our non-marketable equity securities.

Initial Adoption of New Accounting Rules

Prior to January 1, 2018, companies accounted for non-marketable equity securities at cost (original purchase cost), recognizing as income any dividends received and any gains and losses realized on sale of securities. This meant unrealized gains and losses were omitted from both the balance sheet and the income statement. As an example, immediately prior to adopting the new accounting standard, Alphabet reported non-marketable securities on the balance sheet at a cost of $4.5 billion when those same securities had a fair value of $8.8 billion. This meant the previous accounting rules omitted $4.3 billion of unrealized gains for Alphabet. This was indicative of a larger issue among U.S. companies.

Many companies, including Alphabet, adopted the new accounting standard *prospectively*, meaning that the company did *not* go back and restate prior financial statements; instead, they recognized any gains or losses in the adoption year. Following is Alphabet's description of its adoption of the new accounting standard in 2018.

Our non-marketable equity securities are investments in privately held companies without readily determinable market values. Because we adopted ASU 2016-01 prospectively, we recognize unrealized gains that occurred in prior periods in the first period after January 1, 2018 when there is an observable transaction for our securities. The following is a summary of unrealized gains and losses recorded in other income (expense), net, and included as adjustments to the carrying value of non-marketable equity securities held as of December 31, 2018 (in millions):

Twelve Months Ended	December 31, 2018
Upward adjustments.	$4,285
Downward adjustments (including impairment)	(178)
Total unrealized gain (loss) for non-marketable equity securities.	$4,107

The newly adopted fair-value method caused an upward adjustment of $4,107 million to Alphabet's investments account on the balance sheet. Alphabet also included that upward adjustment in its 2018 income statement on the "Other income" line (highlighted in following table). The following excerpt comes from Alphabet's 2018 income statement, where the total $8,592 million includes the $4,107 million of unrealized gains along with $4,487 million of interest income, realized gains on sales of securities, and other items).

Year Ended December 31, in millions	2016	2017	2018
Income from operations	$23,716	$26,146	$26,321
Other income (expense), net	434	1,047	8,592
Income before income taxes	24,150	27,193	34,913
Provision for income taxes	4,672	14,531	4,177
Net income	$19,478	$12,662	$30,736

This one-time (transitory) income item helps explain the significant increase in Alphabet's profitability in 2018 compared with the prior year. (Another factor is income tax expense that increased significantly in 2017 as a result of tax legislation passed that year; see our discussion of income taxes in Modules 5 and 10.)

Investments in Debt Securities

Companies often purchase debt securities, including bonds issued by other companies or by the U.S. government. For example, Alphabet reports investments in time deposits, corporate bonds, U.S. government agency bonds, and municipal securities. Companies can choose to classify investments in debt securities as either:

- **Held-to-maturity securities (HTM).**   Debt securities that the investor has the intent and ability to hold to their maturity.
- **Available-for-sale securities (AFS).**   Debt securities that may be sold prior to their scheduled maturities to meet liquidity needs or risk management objectives.
- **Trading securities.**   Debt securities that are held for a short period of time and are intended to be actively traded. These securities are accounted for like equity securities (reported at fair value on the balance sheet with changes in fair value recognized in current income).

Held-to-Maturity (HTM) Debt Securities

Many debt securities have maturity dates—dates when the security must be repaid by the borrower. If a company buys debt securities, and *management intends to hold the securities to maturity* (as opposed to selling them early), the securities are classified as **held-to-maturity** (HTM). Exhibit 9.3 identifies the reporting of these securities.

Changes in fair value of held-to-maturity securities do not affect either the balance sheet or the income statement. The presumption is that these investments will indeed be held to maturity, at which time their market value will be exactly equal to their face value. Fluctuations in fair value, as a result, are less relevant. Any interest earned is recorded in current income. (GAAP gives companies an option to report held-to-maturity investments at fair value; if this fair value option is elected, the accounting for held-to-maturity securities is like that for marketable equity securities, discussed above.)

Exhibit 9.3 ■ Accounting Treatment for Held-to-Maturity Debt Investments		
Investment Classification	**Reporting of Fair Value Changes**	**Reporting Interest Received and the Gains and Losses on Sale**
Held-to-Maturity (HTM)	Fair value changes are *not* reported in either the balance sheet or income statement (HTM is reported at *amortized cost*)	Interest reported as *other income* in income statement If sold before maturity (the exception), any gain or loss on sale is reported in income statement

Because the value of debt securities fluctuates with the prevailing rate of interest, the market value of the security will be greater than its face value if current market interest rates are lower than what the security pays for interest. In that case, the acquirer will pay a premium for the security. Conversely, if current market interest rates exceed what the security pays in interest, the acquirer will purchase the security at a discount. (We cover premiums and discounts on debt securities in more detail in more detail in Module 7.) Either way, the company records the investment at its acquisition cost (like any other asset) and amortizes any discount or premium over the remaining life of the held-to-maturity investment. At any point in time, the acquirer's balance sheet carries the investment at "amortized cost," which is never adjusted for subsequent market value changes.

Available-for-Sale Debt Securities

Like marketable equity securities, available-for-sale (AFS) debt securities are reported at fair value on the balance sheet. However, changes in fair value for AFS debt securities do **not** flow to the income statement. Instead, these unrealized gains and losses are transferred to the equity section of the balance sheet to an account called "accumulated other comprehensive income" (AOCI).

Fair Value and Unrealized Gains To illustrate, assume that the fair value of a company's AFS debt securities increased by $3,000 during the year they were acquired. The company increases the fair value on the balance sheet by $3,000 and the unrecognized gain is reported in accumulated other comprehensive income (AOCI). The financial statement effects template below shows this accounting.

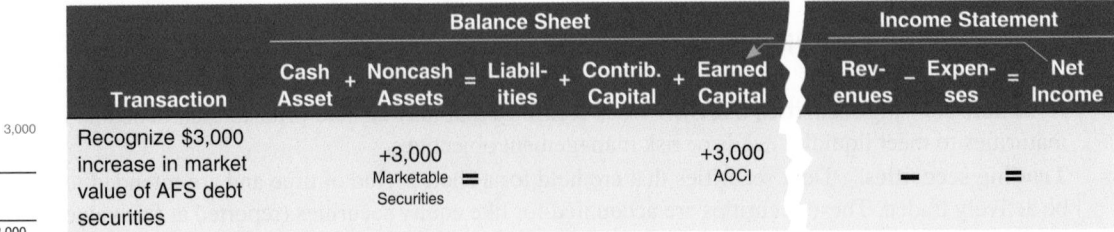

MS 3,000
  AOCI 3,000

        MS
  3,000 |

        AOCI
        | 3,000

	Balance Sheet						Income Statement		
Transaction	Cash Asset	+ Noncash Assets	= Liabil- ities	+ Contrib. Capital	+ Earned Capital		Rev- enues	− Expen- ses	= Net Income
Recognize $3,000 increase in market value of AFS debt securities		+3,000 Marketable Securities	=		+3,000 AOCI		−	=	

Alphabet describes its investment in AFS debt securities (which totals over $91 billion) as follows.

> We have classified and accounted for our marketable debt securities as available-for-sale. After consideration of our risk versus reward objectives, as well as our liquidity requirements, we may sell these debt securities prior to their stated maturities. As we view these securities as available to support current operations, we classify highly liquid securities with maturities beyond 12 months as current assets under the caption marketable securities on the Consolidated Balance Sheets. We carry these securities at fair value, and report the unrealized gains and losses, net of taxes, as a component of stockholders' equity, except for unrealized losses determined to be other-than-temporary, which we record within other income (expense), net. We determine any realized gains or losses on the sale of marketable debt securities on a specific identification method, and we record such gains and losses as a component of other income (expense), net.

The following table provides details of Alphabet's debt securities portfolio ($ millions).

As of December 31, 2018	Adjusted Cost	Gross Unrealized Gains	Gross Unrealized Losses	Fair Value	Cash and Cash Equivalents	Marketable Securities	Non- Marketable Securities
Level 2:							
Time deposits.....................	$ 2,202	$ 0	$ 0	$ 2,202	$2,202	$ 0	$ 0
Government bonds.................	53,634	71	(414)	53,291	3,717	49,574	0
Corporate debt securities............	25,383	15	(316)	25,082	44	25,038	0
Mortgage-backed and asset-backed securities......................	16,918	11	(324)	16,605	0	16,605	0
	98,137	97	(1,054)	97,180	5,963	91,217	0
Level 3:							
Non-marketable debt securities	147	116	0	263	0	0	263
Total	$98,284	$213	$(1,054)	$97,443	$5,963	$91,217	$263

This footnote discloses adjusted cost of $98,284 million and fair value of $97,443 million. Alphabet reports the total fair value of these securities in three line items on the balance sheet: cash and cash equivalents of $5,963 million, marketable securities of $91,217 million, and non-marketable debt securities of $263 million. As the table reveals, the company values most of these debt securities using Level 2 inputs.

Realized Gains When the company ultimately sells the securities, it transfers any related gains or losses from AOCI into current-period income. That is, the previously unrealized gain or loss is now realized because of the sale and therefore recognized on the income statement. During 2018, Alphabet "reclassified" a previously deferred gain of $911 million relating to the sale of its AFS debt securities as reported in the following table.

Alphabet Inc. CONSOLIDATED STATEMENTS OF COMPREHENSIVE INCOME Year Ended December 31 (In millions)	2016	2017	2018
Net income	$19,478	$12,662	$30,736
Other comprehensive income (loss):			
Change in foreign currency translation adjustment	(599)	1,543	(781)
Available-for-sale investments:			
Change in net unrealized gains (losses)	(314)	307	88
Less: reclassification adjustment for net (gains) losses included in net income. . .	221	105	(911)
Net change (net of tax effect of $0, $0, and $156)	(93)	412	(823)
Cash flow hedges:			
Change in net unrealized gains (losses)	515	(638)	290
Less: reclassification adjustment for net (gains) losses included in net income. . .	(351)	93	98
Net change (net of tax effect of $64, $247, and $103)	164	(545)	388
Other comprehensive income (loss)	(528)	1,410	(1,216)
Comprehensive income	$18,950	$14,072	$29,520

Financial Statement Disclosures

Companies are required to disclose cost and fair values of their passive investment portfolios in footnotes to financial statements. Alphabet reports the accounting policies for its investments in the following footnote to its 2018 10-K report.

> **Cash, Cash Equivalents, and Marketable Securities** We invest all excess cash primarily in government bonds, corporate debt securities, mortgage-backed and asset-backed securities, time deposits, and money market funds. We classify all investments that are readily convertible to known amounts of cash and have stated maturities of three months or less from the date of purchase as cash equivalents and those with stated maturities of greater than three months as marketable securities.

Following is the asset section of Alphabet's 2018 balance sheet (in millions).

December 31	2017	2018
Assets		
Current assets		
Cash and cash equivalents	$ 10,715	$ 16,701
Marketable securities	91,156	92,439
Total cash, cash equivalents, and marketable securities . . .	101,871	109,140
Accounts receivable, net of allowance of $674 and $729	18,336	20,838
Income taxes receivable, net	369	355
Inventory	749	1,107
Other current assets	2,983	4,236
Total current assets	124,308	135,676
Non-marketable investments	7,813	13,859
Deferred income taxes	680	737
Property and equipment, net	42,383	59,719
Intangible assets, net	2,692	2,220
Goodwill	16,747	17,888
Other noncurrent assets	2,672	2,693
Total assets	$197,295	$232,792

Alphabet's investments are reported in the three highlighted line items: cash and cash equivalents (marketable securities that mature within 90 days of the balance sheet date are essentially equivalent to cash and are therefore included in cash and cash equivalents), marketable securities, and non-marketable investments.

The following table reconciles these three balance sheet line items to the various investments discussed above.

December 31, 2018 ($ millions)	Cash and Cash Equivalents	Marketable Securities	Non-marketable Investments
Cash..........................	$ 7,245		
Marketable equity securities.......	3,493	$ 1,222	
Non-marketable equity securities...			$12,275
Equity-method investments........			1,321
Debt securities	5,963	91,217	263
Balance sheet total.............	$16,701	$92,439	$13,859

Review 9-1 LO1

Assume **Microsoft** had the following four transactions involving investments in marketable securities. Use this information to answer requirement *a*.

1. Purchased 1,000 shares of **Juniper Networks** common stock for $22 cash per share.
2. Received cash dividend of $2.50 per share on Juniper Networks common stock.
3. Year-end market price of Juniper Networks common stock is $27 per share.
4. Sold all 1,000 shares of Juniper Networks common stock for $27,000 cash in the next period.

Microsoft reports the following table in the footnotes to its 2018 10-K. Use this information to answer requirements *b* through *d*.

In millions	Cost Basis	Unrealized Gains	Unrealized Losses	Recorded Basis	Cash and Cash Equivalents	Short-Term Investments	Equity and Other Investments
June 30, 2018							
Cash.....................	$ 3,942	$ 0	$ 0	$ 3,942	$ 3,942	$ 0	$ 0
Mutual funds...............	246	0	0	246	246	0	0
Commercial paper	2,513	0	0	2,513	2,215	298	0
Certificates of deposit........	2,058	0	0	2,058	1,865	193	0
U.S. government and agency securities...............	109,862	62	(1,167)	108,757	3,678	105,079	0
Foreign government bonds.....	5,182	1	(10)	5,173	0	5,173	0
Mortgage- and asset-backed securities................	3,868	4	(13)	3,859	0	3,859	0
Corporate notes and bonds	6,947	21	(56)	6,912	0	6,912	0
Municipal securities	271	37	(1)	307	0	307	0
Common and preferred stock...	1,220	95	(10)	1,305	0	0	1,305
Other investments	558	0	0	558	0	1	557
Total	$136,667	$220	$(1,257)	$135,630	$11,946	$121,822	$1,862

Required

a. Use the financial statement effects template to record the four transactions.

b. What amount does Microsoft report as investments on its balance sheet? What does this balance represent?

c. What proportion of the total portfolio is equity securities?

Solution on p. 9-55.   *d.* Compare the cost and fair value of the portfolio. What accounts for the difference in value?

Equity Investments with Significant Influence

Many companies make equity investments that yield them significant influence over the investee companies. These intercorporate investments are usually made for strategic reasons such as the following.

LO2

Analyze and interpret equity method investments.

■ **Prelude to acquisition.** Significant ownership can allow the investor company to gain a seat on the board of directors, from which it can learn much about the investee company, its products, and its industry.

■ **Strategic alliance.** Strategic alliances permit the investor to gain trade secrets, technical know-how, or access to restricted markets. For example, a company might buy an equity interest in a company that provides inputs for the investor's production process. This relationship is closer than the usual supplier–buyer relationship and will convey benefits to the investor company.

■ **Pursuit of research and development.** Many research activities in the pharmaceutical, software, and oil and gas industries are conducted jointly. The common motivation is to reduce the investor's risk or the amount of capital investment. The investment often carries an option to purchase additional shares, which the investor can exercise if the research activities are fruitful.

The investment can take a number of forms, including marketable securities, as well as other ownership arrangements, such as partnerships, joint ventures, and limited liability companies. A crucial feature in each of these investments is that the investor company has a level of ownership that is sufficient for it to exert *significant influence* over the investee company. GAAP requires that such investments be accounted for using the *equity method*.

Significant influence is the ability of the investor to affect the financing, investing, and operating policies of the investee. Ownership levels of 20% to 50% of the outstanding common stock of the investee typically convey significant influence. Significant influence can also exist when ownership is less than 20%. Evidence of such influence can be that the investor company is able to gain a seat on the board of directors of the investee, or the investor controls technical know-how or patents that are used by the investee, or the investor is able to exert significant influence by virtue of legal contracts with the investee. (There is growing pressure from regulators for determining significant influence by the facts and circumstances of the investment instead of a strict ownership percentage rule.)

Accounting for Investments with Significant Influence

Companies must use the **equity method** when significant influence exists. The equity method reports the investment on the balance sheet at an amount equal to the percentage of the investee's equity owned by the investor; hence, the name equity method. (This assumes acquisition at book value; acquisition at an amount greater than book value is covered later in this section.) Unlike passive investments, whose carrying amounts increase or decrease with the *market value* of the investee's stock, equity method investments increase (decrease) with increases (decreases) in the investee's *stockholders' equity*.

Equity method accounting is summarized as follows.

■ Investments are recorded at their purchase cost.

■ Dividends received are treated as a recovery of the investment and, thus, reduce the investment balance (dividends are not reported as income).

■ The investor reports income equal to its percentage share of the investee's reported net income; the investment account is increased by the percentage share of the investee's income or decreased by the percentage share of any loss.

■ Changes in fair value do not affect the investment's carrying value. (GAAP gives companies an option to report equity method investments at fair value unless those investments relate to consolidated subsidiaries; we discuss consolidation later in the module.)

To illustrate the equity method, consider the following scenario: Assume Google (an Alphabet subsidiary) acquires a 30% interest in Mitel Networks, a company seeking to develop a new technology. This investment is a strategic alliance for Google. At the acquisition date, Mitel's balance sheet reports $1,000 of stockholders' equity, and Google purchases a 30% stake for $300, giving it the ability to exert significant influence over Mitel. At the first year-end, Mitel reports profits of $100 and pays $20 in cash dividends to its shareholders ($6 to Google). Following are the financial statement effects for Google from this investment using the equity method.

	Balance Sheet					Income Statement		
Transaction	**Cash Asset** +	**Noncash Assets** =	**Liabil-ities** +	**Contrib. Capital** +	**Earned Capital**	**Rev-enues** −	**Expen-ses** =	**Net Income**
1. Purchase 30% investment in Mitel for $300 cash	−300 Cash	+300 Investment in Mitel =				−	=	
2. Mitel reports $100 income; Google's share is $30		+30 Investment in Mitel =			+30 Retained Earnings	+30 Equity Income −	=	+30
3. Mitel pays $20 cash dividends; $6 to Google	+6 Cash	−6 Investment in Mitel =				−	=	
Ending balance of Google's investment account		324						

EMI 300
　Cash 300

EMI	
300	
Cash	
	300

EMI 30
　EI 30

EMI	
30	
EI	
	30

Cash 6
　EMI 6

Cash	
6	
EMI	
	6

The investment is initially reported on Google's balance sheet at its purchase price of $300, representing a 30% interest in Mitel's total stockholders' equity of $1,000. During the year, Mitel's equity increases to $1,080 ($1,000 plus $100 income and less $20 dividends). Likewise, Google's investment increases by $30 to reflect its 30% share of Mitel's $100 income, and decreases by $6, relating to its share of Mitel's dividends. After these transactions, Google's investment in Mitel is reported on Google's balance sheet at 30% of $1,080, or $324.

Google's investment in Mitel is an asset just like any other asset. As such, it must be tested annually for impairment. If the investment is found to be permanently impaired, Google must reduce the investment amount on the balance sheet and report a loss on the write-down of the investment in its income statement (unlike investments accounted for using the market method, equity method investments are not written up if fair values increase). If and when Google sells Mitel, any gain or loss on the sale is reported in Google's income statement. The gain or loss is computed as the difference between the sales proceeds and the investment's carrying value on the balance sheet. For example, if Google sold Mitel for $500, Google would report a gain on sale of $176 ($500 proceeds − $324 balance sheet value).

Companies often pay more than book value when they make equity investments. For example, if Google paid $400 for its 30% stake in Mitel, Google would initially report its investment at its $400 purchase price. The $400 investment consists of two parts: the $300 equity investment described above and the $100 additional investment. Google is willing to pay the higher purchase price because it believes Mitel's reported equity is below its current market value. Perhaps some of Mitel's assets are reported at costs that are below market values or Mitel has intangible assets such as a patent or internally generated goodwill that are missing from its balance sheet. The $300 portion of the investment is accounted for as described above. Google's management must decide how to allocate the excess of the amount paid over the book value of the investee company's equity and account for the excess accordingly. For example, if management decides the $100 relates to unrecognized depreciable assets, the $100 is depreciated over the assets' estimated useful lives. Or, if it relates to identifiable intangible assets that have a determinable useful life (such as patents), it is amortized over the useful lives of the intangible assets (however, if it relates to goodwill, it is not amortized).

Two final points about equity method accounting: First, there can be a substantial difference between the book value of an equity method investment and its fair value. An increase in value is not recognized until the investment is sold. If the fair value of the investment has permanently declined, however, the investment is deemed impaired and written down to that lower fair value. Second, if the investee company reports income, the investor company reports its share. Recognition of equity income by the investor, however, does not mean it has received that income in cash. Cash is only received if the investee pays a dividend. To highlight this, the operating section of the investor's statement of cash flows (prepared using the indirect method) will include a reconciling item (a deduction from net income in computing operating cash flow) for its percentage share of the investee's net income in excess of cash dividends received.

Research Insight ■ Equity Income and Stock Prices

Under the equity method of accounting, the investor does not recognize as income any dividends received from the investee, nor any changes in the investee's fair value, until the investment is sold. However, research has found a positive relation between investors' and investees' stock prices at the time of investees' earnings and dividend announcements. This suggests the market includes information regarding investees' earnings and dividends when assessing the stock prices of investor companies and implies the market looks beyond the book value of the investment account in determining stock prices of investor companies.

Equity Method Accounting and ROE Effects

The investor company reports equity method investments on the balance sheet at an amount equal to the percentage owned of the investee company's equity when that investment is acquired at book value. To illustrate, consider the case of the **Altria Group Inc.**'s equity investment in **AB InBev/ SABMiller**. Altria owns approximately 10.1% economic and voting interest of AB InBev and provides the following disclosure in its 2018 10-K.

Investment in AB InBev/SABMiller At December 31, 2018, Altria had an approximate 10.1% ownership of AB InBev, consisting of approximately 185 million restricted shares of AB InBev (the "Restricted Shares") and approximately 12 million ordinary shares of AB InBev. Altria accounts for its investment in AB InBev under the equity method of accounting because Altria has the ability to exercise significant influence over the operating and financial policies of AB InBev, including having active representation on AB InBev's Board of Directors ("AB InBev Board") and certain AB InBev Board Committees. Through this representation, Altria participates in AB InBev policy making processes. Summary financial data of AB InBev is as follows:

For the Years Ended December 31 ($ millions)	2018[1]	2017[1]
Net revenues	$55,500	$56,004
Gross profit	34,986	34,376
Earnings from continuing operations	9,020	6,769
Net earnings	9,020	6,845
Net earnings attributable to AB InBev	7,641	5,473

At December 31 ($ millions)	2018[1]	2017[1]
Current assets	$ 20,289	$ 30,920
Long-term assets	207,921	213,696
Current liabilities	32,019	37,765
Long-term liabilities	130,812	134,236
Noncontrolling interests	7,251	10,639

[1] Reflects one-quarter lag.

At December 31, 2018, Altria's carrying amount of its equity investment in AB InBev exceeded its share of AB InBev's net assets attributable to equity holders of AB InBev by approximately $11.8 billion. Substantially all of this difference is comprised of goodwill and other indefinite-lived intangible assets (consisting primarily of trademarks). . . The fair value of Altria's equity investment in AB

continued

continued from previous page

InBev at December 31, 2018 and 2017 was $13.1 billion and $22.1 billion, respectively, compared with its carrying value of $17.7 billion and $18.0 billion, respectively. Based on Altria's evaluation of the duration and magnitude of the fair value decline, AB InBev's financial condition and near-term prospects, and Altria's intent and ability to hold its investment in AB InBev until recovery, Altria concluded that the decline in fair value of its investment in AB InBev below its carrying value is temporary and, therefore, no impairment was recorded.

From the table above, we can derive AB InBev's 2018 balance sheet as follows.

$ millions	
Current assets	$ 20,289
Long-term assets	207,921
Total assets	$228,210
Current liabilities	$ 32,019
Long-term liabilities	130,812
Total liabilities	162,831
AB InBev equity	58,128
Noncontrolling interests	7,251
Total equity	65,379
Total liabilities and equity	$228,210

Altria's share of AB InBev's equity is $5.9 billion (calculated $10.1\% \times \$58,128$ million). But Altria's footnote discloses that the carrying value of the AB InBev investment is $17.7 billion. The excess of $11.8 billion ($17.7 billion − $5.9 billion) relates to "goodwill and other indefinite-lived intangible assets." Because these intangible assets are viewed as "indefinite-lived," Altria is not required to amortize them, thereby avoiding additional amortization expense in Altria's income statement.

Altria avoided another expense related to the AB InBev investment. As of 2018, the $17.7 billion carrying value exceeded the investment's $13.1 billion fair value. Had Altria deemed the decline to be "other than temporary," the company would have had to write down the investment to fair value. This would have created an impairment loss of $4.6 billion on Altria's 2018 income statement. Altria concluded, however, that the investment's decline in fair value is temporary, thereby avoiding a significant income-statement impact.

Underlying Financial Statement Components It is helpful to visualize the equity investment in relation to the underlying assets and liabilities. Following is a summary of the Altria 2018 balance sheet ($ millions).

Altria	
Cash	$ 1,333
Noncash assets	36,605
Investment in SABMiller	17,700
Total assets	$55,638

AB InBev	
Total assets	$228,210
Liabilities	$162,831
Stockholders' equity	65,379
Liabilities and equity	$228,210

The $17,700 million equity investment on Altria's balance sheet represents a 10.1% investment in a very large company with assets of over $228 billion and liabilities of nearly $163 billion. Although unreported liabilities are not a serious concern for beer manufacturers, we might want to know more about the investee company if the investment were in a pharmaceutical company with significant potential liabilities or in a venture with highly variable cash flows. The investor company may have no direct legal obligation for the investee's liabilities, but it might need to fund the investee company, via additional investment or advances to maintain the investee's viability, if the company is important to the investor's strategic plan. Further, companies that routinely fund research and development activities through equity investments in other companies, a common practice in the pharmaceutical and software industries, can find themselves supporting underperforming equity-method investments to ensure continued external funding. One cannot always assume, therefore, the investee's liabilities and business fortunes will not adversely affect the investor.

Unreported liabilities are of particular concern when the investee company reports losses that are substantial. In extreme cases, the investee company can become insolvent (when equity is negative) as the growing negative balance in retained earnings more than offsets contributed capital. Once the equity of the investee company reaches zero, the investor must discontinue accounting for the investment by the equity method. Instead, it accounts for the investment at cost with a zero balance and no further recognition of its proportionate share of investee company losses (until the investee company's equity becomes positive again). In this case, the investor's income statement no longer includes the losses of the investee company and its balance sheet no longer reports the troubled investee company. Unreported liabilities can be especially problematic in this case.

To summarize, under equity method accounting, only the investor's proportion of the investee's equity is reported on the balance sheet (not the underlying assets and liabilities), and only the investor's proportion of the investee's earnings is reported in the income statement (not the underlying sales and expenses). This is illustrated as follows using Google's 30% investment in Mitel. The investee's income statement and balance sheet at the end of the first year is as follows.

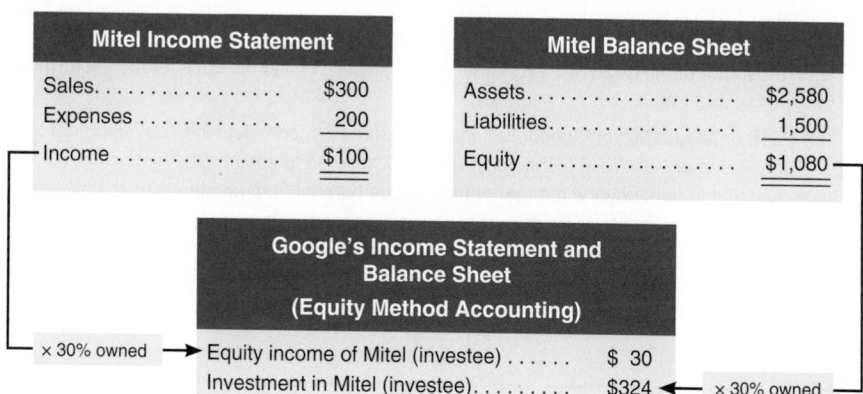

Analysis Implications From an analysis standpoint, because the assets and liabilities are left off the Google balance sheet, and because the sales and expenses are omitted from the Google income statement, the *components* of ROE are markedly affected as follows.

- **Net operating profit margin (NOPM = NOPAT/Sales).** Most analysts include equity income (sales less expenses) in NOPAT because it relates to operating investments. However, investee's sales are not included in the NOPM denominator. The reported NOPM is, thus, overstated.

- **Net operating asset turnover (NOAT = Sales/Average NOA).** Investee's sales are excluded from the NOAT numerator, and net operating assets in excess of the investment balance are excluded from the denominator. This means the impact on NOAT is *indeterminate*.

- **Financial leverage (FLEV = Net nonoperating obligations/Average equity).** Financial leverage is understated due to the absence of investee liabilities in the numerator.

Although ROE components are affected, ROE is unaffected by equity method accounting because the correct amount of investee net income and equity *is* included in the ROE numerator and denominator, respectively. Still, the evaluation of the quality of ROE is affected. Analysis using reported equity method accounting numbers would use an overstated NOPM and an understated FLEV because the numbers are based on net balance sheet and net income statement numbers. As we discuss in a later module, analysts should adjust reported financial statements for these types of items before conducting analysis. One such adjustment might be to consolidate (for analysis purposes) the equity method investee with the investor company.

Managerial Decision ■ **You Are the Chief Financial Officer**

You are receiving capital expenditure requests for long-term operating asset purchases from various managers. What potential courses of action can you consider? Explain. [Answer, p. 9-36]

Review 9-2 LO2

Consider the following items related to equity method investments at Intel for fiscal 2018.

a. Record the following five hypothetical transactions at Intel, using a financial statement effects template.
1. Purchased 5,000 shares of LookSmart common stock at $10 cash per share; these shares reflect 30% ownership of LookSmart.
2. Received a $2-per-share cash dividend on LookSmart common stock.
3. Recorded an accounting adjustment to reflect $100,000 income reported by LookSmart.
4. Year-end market price of LookSmart has increased to $12 per common share.
5. Sold all 5,000 shares of LookSmart common stock for $90,000 cash in 2019.

b. Intel reports a 49% equity investment in IM Flash Technologies LLC (IMFT), which is a joint venture with Micron Technology Inc. Assume that on its 2018 financial statements, IMFT reports net income of $750 million and stockholders' equity of $4,000 million. What will Intel report in 2018 as equity-method income related to IMFT? What will be the carrying value of the IMFT equity investment on Intel's 2018 balance sheet (assume the investment was purchased at book value)?

c. Intel reported the following in its 2018 10-K. Describe the reason for and the effect of the impairment charge.

> "In July 2018, Intel and Micron announced that they agreed to complete joint development for the second generation of 3D XPoint technology, which is expected to occur in the first half of 2019 and technology development beyond that generation will be pursued independently by the two companies to optimize the technology for their respective product and business needs. We recognized an impairment charge of $290 million during the third quarter of 2018. This reduced the carrying value of our equity method investment in IMFT to $1.6 billion in line with our expectation of future cash flows."

Solution on p. 9-55.

Equity Investments with Control

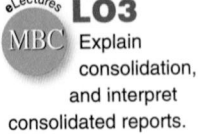

LO3
Explain consolidation, and interpret consolidated reports.

This section discusses accounting for investments where the investor company "controls" the investee company. For example, in its footnote describing its accounting policies, Alphabet reports the following.

> **Basis of Consolidation** The consolidated financial statements of Alphabet include the accounts of Alphabet and entities consolidated under the variable interest and voting models. Noncontrolling interests are not presented separately as the amounts are not material. All intercompany balances and transactions have been eliminated.

This means Alphabet financial statements are an aggregation (an adding up) of those of the parent company, Alphabet, and all its subsidiary companies less any intercompany activities such as inter-company sales or receivables.

Accounting for Investments with Control

Accounting for business combinations (acquiring a controlling interest) goes one step beyond equity method accounting. Under the equity method, the investor's investment balance represents the pro-portion of the investee's equity owned by the investor, and the investor company's income statement includes its proportionate share of the investee's income. Once control over the investee company is achieved, GAAP requires consolidation for financial statements issued to the public (but not for the internal financial records of the separate companies).

What is control? The big picture is that control is exercised through economic power. Determin-ing economic power can be complicated, but the following items are consistent with economic power.

- The investor has the ability to influence the investee's decision-making.
- The investor can influence the investee's financial results through contractual rights and obligations.
- The investor is exposed to variable returns; that is, the investor will absorb any losses as well as benefit from any gains.
- The investor has the right to receive residual returns.

If these items are in play, the investment is a **variable interest entity (VIE)** where the investor is the primary beneficiary. All VIEs must be consolidated.

If the VIE test is *not* met, there is a second test: the voting interest test. This test is much more straightforward. If the investor holds more than 50% of the voting stock of the investee, then economic control is in evidence and the investment must be consolidated. We see from Alphabet's footnote above that it consolidates VIEs and all wholly-owned entities (as Alphabet owns 100% of the voting stock).

Consolidation accounting includes 100% of the investee's assets and liabilities on the investor's balance sheet and 100% of the investee's sales and expenses on the investor's income statement. Specifically, the consolidated balance sheet includes the gross assets and liabilities of the investee company, and the income statement includes the investee's gross sales and expenses rather than just the investor's share of the investee company's net assets or income. All intercompany sales and expenses, and receivables and payables, are eliminated in the consolidation process to avoid double-counting when, for example, goods are sold from the investee (called a subsidiary) to the investor (called the parent company) for resale to the parent's ultimate customers.

> **IFRS Alert**
> Consolidation accounting is generally similar to IFRS; differences exist in technical details, but not with presentation of consolidated financial statements.

Investments Purchased at Book Value: Subsidiary Wholly-Owned To illustrate, consider the following scenario. Penman Company acquires 100% of the common stock of Nissim Company and issues its own stock to Nissim shareholders. The purchase price of $3,000 (in Penman stock) is equal to the book value of Nissim's stockholders' equity ($2,000 contributed capital plus $1,000 retained earnings). During the next year, Nissim earned $400, bringing its retained earnings to $1,400. On its balance sheet, Penman accounts for the investment in Nissim using the equity method. This is important. Even if the investor (the parent) owns 100% of the investee (the subsidiary), the inves-tor may still record the investment on its (parent-company) balance sheet using the equity method described in the previous section. That is, Penman records an initial balance in the equity investment account in the amount of the purchase price, which is equal to Nissim's stockholders' equity. Thereaf-ter, the equity investment account on Penman's balance sheet will increase and decrease with Nissim's stockholders' equity, reflecting profits earned, losses incurred, and dividends paid.

Because Penman Company owns 100% of the stock of its subsidiary (and, therefore, controls the activities of Nissim), GAAP requires consolidation. That process, shown in Exhibit 9.4, involves summing each balance sheet and income statement account for the two companies *after eliminating any intercompany transactions* (such as the investment Penman has in Nissim Company, together with any intercompany sales/purchases and receivables/payables).

Exhibit 9.4 shows the balance sheets of Penman and Nissim in the first two columns, the consolidating adjustments in the next column, and the consolidated balance sheet in the far right column. The consolidated balance sheet reports total assets of $21,400, total liabilities of $7,000, and equity of $14,400. Because Penman owns 100% of the stock of Nissim and the purchase was made at book value, the equity investment account on Penman's balance sheet equals Nissim's stockholders' equity to which it relates. Both amounts are removed in the consolidation process and each row in the balance sheet is then summed to arrive at the consolidated totals. The result of this process is to remove both the equity investment account and Nissim's stockholders' equity from the consolidated balance sheet and to replace the equity investment with the assets and liabilities of Nissim to which it relates. *The consolidated stockholders' equity equals the equity of the parent company—this is always the case when the subsidiary is wholly owned.*

The consolidated income statement is shown in Exhibit 9.4. Penman reports equity income in its income statement equal to the net income reported by Nissim Company. The effect of the consolidation process is to remove the equity income account in Penman's income statement and replace it with the sales and expenses of Nissim Company to which it relates. This is accomplished by summing the rows in the income statement and eliminating the equity income account to yield the consolidated income statement. *The consolidated net income equals the net income of the parent company—this is always the case* (because the equity income the parent reports equals the net income of the subsidiary when the subsidiary is wholly owned).

Exhibit 9.4 ■ **Mechanics of Consolidation Accounting (Wholly-Owned Subsidiary, Purchased at Book Value)**

	Penman Company	Nissim Company	Consolidating Adjustments	Consolidated
Balance Sheet				
Current assets	$ 6,000	$ 1,400		$ 7,400
Investment in Nissim	3,400	0	(3,400)	0
PPE, net	10,000	4,000		14,000
Total assets	$19,400	$ 5,400		$21,400
Liabilities.	$ 5,000	$ 2,000		$ 7,000
Contributed capital	10,000	2,000	(2,000)	10,000
Retained earnings	4,400	1,400	(1,400)	4,400
Total liabilities and equity	$19,400	$ 5,400		$21,400
Income statement				
Sales.	$25,000	$10,000		$35,000
Cost of goods sold	(20,000)	(7,000)		(27,000)
Gross profit.	5,000	3,000		8,000
Operating expenses	(3,600)	(2,600)		(6,200)
Equity income from investment . . .	400	—	(400)	0
Net income	$ 1,800	$ 400		$ 1,800

Investments Purchased at Book Value: Subsidiary <u>Not</u> Wholly-Owned When a subsidiary is not wholly-owned, we account for the equity interest of noncontrolling shareholders in addition to that of the parent's stockholders. This will affect both the balance sheet and the income statement. To illustrate, assume Penman acquires 80% of Nissim instead of 100%, as in our previous example. Now, the equity investment account on Penman's balance sheet will reflect only 80% of Nissim's equity, and the equity income it reports in its income statement will only reflect 80% of Nissim's net income. The remaining 20% of the net assets of the subsidiary and its net income are owned by noncontrolling shareholders. Their share in the net assets of Nissim is reflected on the consolidated balance sheet in a new account titled **noncontrolling interest**. In addition, we apportion Nissim's net income into the 80%, or $320, attributed to Penman's shareholders and the 20%, or $80, attributed to noncontrolling shareholders.

We demonstrate the accounting for noncontrolling interests in Exhibit 9.5. Again, the balance sheets of Penman and Nissim are shown in the first two columns. The consolidating adjustments are shown in the third column and the consolidated balance sheet and income statement in the last column. The claim of noncontrolling shareholders on Nissim's net assets is recognized in consolidated equity in an account called noncontrolling interest. The $680 noncontrolling interest on the consolidated balance sheet represents the 20% share of the net assets at acquisition ($3,000 × 20% = $600) plus the 20% share of Nissim's net income ($400 × 20% = $80). The $2,720 equity investment account on Penman's balance sheet reflects its 80% interest in Nissim's equity ([$2,000 + $1,400] × 80%). That equity investment account is eliminated in the consolidation process.

Business Insight ■ Accounting for Noncontrolling Interests

When a company acquires less than 100% of a subsidiary, it must account for the interests of the noncontrolling share-holders separately from those of its own shareholders. This has two implications for consolidated financial statements.

1. Consolidated net income is first computed for the company as a whole as revenues less expenses. Then, it is allocated to the portion attributable to the parent's shareholders and the noncontrolling shareholders in proportion to their respective ownership interests.
2. The cumulative balance of the noncontrolling interests is reported on the balance sheet in the stockholders' equity section. It is increased each year by the net income allocated to noncontrolling interests and is decreased by any dividends paid to those noncontrolling shareholders.

The consolidated income statement shows the consolidated revenues, consolidated expenses, and consolidated net income. The $320 equity income account in Penman's income statement reflects 80% of Nissim's net income that it owns ($400 × 80%). This equity income account is eliminated in the consolidation process just like the equity investment account on the balance sheet. When less than 100% of the subsidiary is owned by the parent, the consolidated income statement allocates net income into that portion *attributable to the parent (controlling) shareholders* (80% here) and that portion *attributable to the noncontrolling shareholders* (20% here).

Exhibit 9.5 ■ **Mechanics of Consolidation Accounting**
(Subsidiary Not Wholly-Owned, Purchased at Book Value)

	Penman Company	Nissim Company	Consolidating Adjustments	Consolidated
Balance Sheet				
Current assets	$ 6,000	$1,400		$ 7,400
Investment in Nissim	2,720	0	2,720	0
PPE, net	10,000	4,000		14,000
Total assets	$18,720	$5,400		$21,400
Liabilities.	$ 5,000	$2,000		$ 7,000
Contributed capital	9,400	2,000	(2,000)	9,400
Retained earnings	4,320	1,400	(1,400)	4,320
Noncontrolling interest			680	680
Total liabilities and equity	$18,720	$5,400		$21,400
Income statement				
Sales.	$25,000	$10,000		$35,000
Cost of goods sold	(20,000)	(7,000)		(27,000)
Gross profit.	5,000	3,000		8,000
Operating expenses	(3,600)	(2,600)		(6,200)
Equity income from investment	320	—	(320)	0
Net income	$ 1,720	$ 400		$ 1,800
Net income attributable to noncontrolling interest . . .				80
Net income attributable to Penman shareholders . . .				$ 1,720

Investments Purchased <u>above</u> Book Value The illustrations above assume the purchase price of the acquisition equals the book value of the investee company. It is more often the case, however, that the purchase price exceeds the book value. This might arise, for example, if an investor company believes it is acquiring something of value that is not reported on the investee's balance sheet—such as tangible assets whose market values have risen above book value or unrecorded intangible assets, such as patents or corporate synergies. When the acquisition price exceeds book value, all net assets acquired (both tangible and intangible) must be recognized on the consolidated balance sheet.

To illustrate, let's return to the example of Exhibit 9.4 in which Penman acquires 100% interest in Nissim. Let's now assume Penman paid a premium to Nissim of $1,000 more than the book value of Nissim's stockholders' equity on the acquisition date (see the increase in Penman's contributed capital to $11,000 reflecting the additional $1,000 of stock issued to Nissim's shareholders). Assume Penman paid the additional $1,000 because Penman expects to realize $1,000 in additional value from corporate synergies, such as increased market presence, ability to consolidate offices, and increased buying power. General synergies such as this are recognized on the balance sheet as an intangible asset with an indefinite useful life, called **goodwill**. The $4,000 investment account now reflects two components: the book value acquired of $3,000 (as before) and an additional $1,000 of newly acquired assets (goodwill asset). Exhibit 9.6 shows the balance sheets of the two companies along with the consolidating adjustments and the consolidated balance sheet, on the date of acquisition. (Note that this example is at the acquisition date and does not include the $400 earned by Nissim during the ensuing year.)

Exhibit 9.6 ■ Mechanics of Consolidation Accounting (Purchase Price above Book Value)				
	Penman Company	Nissim Company	Consolidating Adjustments	Consolidated
Current assets	$ 6,000	$1,000		$ 7,000
Investment in Nissim	4,000	0	(4,000)	0
PPE, net.	10,000	4,000		14,000
Goodwill			1,000	1,000
Total assets	$20,000	$5,000		$22,000
Liabilities.	$ 5,000	$2,000		$ 7,000
Contributed capital	11,000	2,000	(2,000)	11,000
Retained earnings	4,000	1,000	(1,000)	4,000
Total liabilities and equity	$20,000	$5,000		$22,000

The consolidated current assets and liabilities are the sum of those accounts on each company's balance sheet. The investment account, however, includes $1,000 of the newly acquired goodwill asset that must now be reported on the consolidated balance sheet. The consolidation process in this case has two steps. First, the $3,000 equity of Nissim Company is eliminated against the equity investment account as before. Then, the remaining $1,000 of the investment account is eliminated and the newly acquired asset ($1,000 of goodwill, which is not reported on Nissim's balance sheet) is added to the consolidated balance sheet. The goodwill asset is now recognized on the consolidated balance sheet as a separate asset that has an indefinite life. This means goodwill is not routinely amortized. But, like all other assets, goodwill must be tested annually for impairment and written down (or written off entirely) if found to be impaired.

In our example here, we recognized just one intangible asset: goodwill. Often, the excess purchase price is assigned to several intangible assets that have a useful life (such as the value of brands, patents, licensing agreements, and customer relationships; see the text box below for more details). If recognized, the costs of such intangible assets (other than goodwill) are amortized over their useful lives in the same manner we depreciate a tangible asset. Consolidated net income is reduced by the amortization of those intangible assets. As with goodwill, the other intangible assets are tested periodically for impairment and adjusted as needed with any write-off reflected as a reduction of equity income.

Under current accounting standards, companies are required to assess the possible impairment of goodwill on an annual basis or more often if circumstances indicate that impairment is likely.

That assessment compares the fair value of the investment in the subsidiary with the amount at which the subsidiary is reported on the parent's balance sheet (the book value of the equity investment). If the fair value is less, the parent company must write down the equity investment to its fair value and record the impairment loss in its income statement.

The **Kraft Heinz Company** provides an example. In 2018, the company reported an impairment loss of $15.5 billion as described in its footnote disclosures.

> For the fourth quarter of 2018, in connection with the preparation of our year-end financial statements, we assessed the changes in circumstances that occurred during the quarter to determine if it was more likely than not that the fair values of any reporting units or brands were below their carrying amounts. Although our annual impairment test is performed during the second quarter, we perform this qualitative assessment each interim reporting period.
>
> While there was no single determinative event or factor, the consideration in totality of several factors that developed during the fourth quarter of 2018 led us to conclude that it was more likely than not that the fair values of certain reporting units and brands were below their carrying amounts. These factors included: (i) a sustained decrease in our share price in November and December of 2018 . . . (ii) the completion of our fourth quarter results, which were below management's expectations . . . (iii) the development and approval of our 2019 annual operating plan in December 2018, which provided additional insights into expectations and priorities for the coming years, such as lower growth and margin expectations; (iv) the announcement in November 2018 to sell certain assets in our natural cheese portfolio in Canada . . . (v) fluctuations in foreign exchange rates in certain countries; (vi) increased interest rates in certain locations, including an increase in the United States in December 2018; and (vii) increased and prolonged economic and regulatory uncertainty in the United States and global economies as of the end of December 2018.
>
> As we determined that it was more likely than not that the fair values of certain reporting units or brands were below their carrying amounts, we performed an interim impairment test as of December 29, 2018. As a result of our interim impairment test, we recognized goodwill impairment losses of $6.9 billion and indefinite-lived intangible asset impairment losses of $8.6 billion in the fourth quarter of 2018.

The combined impairment charges of $15.5 billion resulted in a net loss of $10.2 billion on Kraft Heinz's 2018 income statement. Although the write-off is a noncash charge, it sent investors a message about management's expectations for its brands. Shares of Kraft Heinz dropped 27% following the announcement.

Accounting Insight ▪ Accounting for Acquired Intangible Assets

The market value of a company's equity can differ substantially from its book value because of unrecorded assets. These unrecorded assets typically relate to intangible assets such as market position, brand equity, managerial talent, and internally developed technology. When companies are acquired, however, such unrecorded assets are recognized on the acquirer's balance sheet. The purchase price is allocated to the assets acquired and the liabilities assumed. First tangible assets, such as PPE and inventory, are identified and valued. Then, intangible assets are identified and valued. All these assets are recorded on the acquirer's consolidated balance sheet at fair market value just like any other purchased asset. Finally, any excess purchase price is allocated to Goodwill. Common types of intangible assets recognized during acquisitions follow.

- Marketing-related assets such as trademarks and Internet domain names
- Customer-related assets such as customer lists and customer contracts
- Artistic-related assets such as plays, books, and videos
- Contract-based assets such as licensing, lease contracts, and franchise and royalty agreements
- Technology-based assets such as patents, in-process research and development, software, databases, and trade secrets

For example, in 2015, when **Heinz** acquired **Kraft** for $52,637 million, the purchase price was allocated to the acquired assets and liabilities as follows ($ millions).

continued

continued from previous page

Cash	$ 314
Other current assets	3,423
Property, plant and equipment	4,193
Identifiable intangible assets	49,749
Other noncurrent assets	214
Trade and other payables	(3,026)
Long-term debt	(9,286)
Net postemployment benefits and other noncurrent liabilities	(4,734)
Deferred income tax liabilities	(17,239)
Net assets acquired	23,608
Goodwill on acquisition	29,029
Total consideration	$52,637

Heinz allocated $49,749 million of the purchase price to identifiable intangible assets, which consisted of the following.

	Preliminary Fair Value ($ millions)	Weighted Average Life (in years)
Indefinite-lived trademarks	$45,082	—
Definite-lived trademarks	1,690	24
Customer relationships	2,977	29
Total identifiable intangible assets	$49,749	

Once recognized, intangible assets with definite useful lives are amortized over their remaining lives. For example, Heinz will amortize the customer relationships over 29 years. Other intangible assets that are considered to be indefinite-lived assets (such as the indefinite-lived trademarks) remain on the balance sheet at their initial value. Annually, Heinz tested the fair value of the acquired intangible assets, and as we saw above, deemed them impaired in 2018. The company recorded a $15.5 billion impairment charge, reducing the balance sheet value of the assets by 20% only three years after their acquisition.

Consolidation of Foreign Subsidiaries (Cumulative Translation Adjustment)

Foreign subsidiaries that are headquartered outside of the U.S. typically conduct business and maintain their accounting records in their own domestic currencies rather than in U.S. dollars. Before the U.S. parent company can consolidate the foreign subsidiary, the foreign currency denominated financial statements must be translated into $US. From day to day, the exchange rate between the $US and the foreign currency changes. So while the value of any of the subsidiary's transactions is known with certainty, its $US equivalent will change depending on the prevailing exchange rate the day the financials are translated.

Consider the example below where a European subsidiary has no changes in its balance sheet during the year (including no net income). Assume the $US strengthens during the year vis-à-vis the euro, such that each euro purchases fewer $US ($1.25 dropping to $1.10).

	December 31, 2017		December 31, 2018	
Balance Sheet	€	$	€	$
Assets	$2,000	$2,500	$2,000	$2,200
Liabilities	500	625	500	550
Net assets	1,500	**1,875**	1,500	**1,650**
Exchange Rates				
$US/Euro	1.25		1.100	

The euro-denominated balance sheet does not change year over year, but the translated and consolidated values vary greatly. The upshot is the foreign currency-denominated balance sheet shrinks when the $US strengthens.[1]

At consolidation, the foreign subsidiary's assets and liabilities are reported on the parent's balance sheet at their $US value translated at the rate prevailing on the balance sheet date. Recall that during consolidation, the subsidiary's equity is *not* added to the parent's balance sheet. From the example above, we see that adding the assets and liabilities causes the balance sheet to be out of balance in $US. To balance, we adjust stockholders' equity for the difference. We add the change in net assets arising from the change exchange rate to an account called the **cumulative translation adjustment**. In the example above, the net assets of €1,500 translates to **$1,875** at the start of the year (December 31, 2017) and **$1,650** at the end (December 31, 2018), a decrease of $225. To balance, we adjust equity downward by $225. Thus, the cumulative translation adjustment account has a negative balance. This balance is reported in AOCI. The parent's consolidated balance sheet will include the following amounts.

December 31, 2018	€	$
Assets.	$2,000	$2,200
Liabilities.	500	550
Cumulative translation adjustment		(225)

To sum up, when the $US strengthens, the cumulative translation adjustment is negative. Conversely, when the $US weakens, the foreign subsidiary's assets and liabilities increase, as does stockholders' equity, and that increase is evidenced by a positive cumulative translation adjustment on the parent's balance sheet. The cumulative translation adjustment account remains on the balance sheet as long as the company owns the foreign subsidiary. The account balance typically fluctuates between negative and positive values as the $US strengthens and weakens vis-à-vis foreign currencies over time. If the subsidiary is sold, however, the related cumulative translation adjustment amount is transferred from AOCI into current income. The following footnote disclosure from The Hershey Company in 2018 is illustrative (in $000s).

	Pre-Tax Amount	Tax (Expense) Benefit	After-Tax Amount
Net income including noncontrolling interest			$1,171,051
Foreign currency translation adjustments			
Foreign currency translation gains (losses) during period	$(31,143)	$—	(31,143)
Reclassification to earnings due to the sale of businesses	25,131	—	25,131
	⋮	⋮	⋮

During 2018, the $US strengthened and The Hershey Company recorded other comprehensive loss of $31,143 thousand. Also during 2018, the company sold a subsidiary and reclassified a related foreign currency translation gain of $25,131 thousand into current income. The sale of the subsidiary converted the previously unrealized currency translation gain to a realized gain and this increased the total gain on the sale of the subsidiary in 2018.

Most companies aggregate the cumulative translation adjustment with similar adjustments in AOCI.[2] Alphabet reports AOCI as part of its stockholders' equity accounts, as follows.

---

[1] We discuss this same effect on the income statement in Module 5. In short, when the foreign currency-denominated income statement is translated to $US, a stronger $US means lower sales, expenses, and profit.

[2] Other adjustments that are included in AOCI relate to available-for-sale debt securities and derivative securities, as discussed in this module, and pension adjustments, discussed in a later module. The common feature of all of these adjustments is that they represent unrealized gains and losses on various assets and liabilities. The unrealized gains and losses are recognized in income (realized) *only when* the asset or liability is removed from the balance sheet (sold, settled, or disposed of).

Stockholders' Equity as of December 31 ($ millions)	2017	2018
Convertible preferred stock, $0.001 par value per share, 100,000 shares authorized; no shares issued and outstanding	$ 0	$ 0
Class A and Class B common stock, and Class C capital stock and additional paid-in capital, $0.001 par value per share: 15,000,000 shares authorized (Class A 9,000,000, Class B 3,000,000, Class C 3,000,000); 694,783 (Class A 298,470, Class B 46,972, Class C 349,341) and 695,556 (Class A 299,242, Class B 46,636, Class C 349,678) shares issued and outstanding	40,247	45,049
Accumulated other comprehensive income (loss)	(992)	(2,306)
Retained earnings	113,247	134,885
Total stockholders' equity	$152,502	$177,628

For Alphabet, AOCI decreases by $1,314 million in 2018. The change includes other comprehensive loss of $1,216 million (as detailed below) and an adjustment of $(98) million to the AOCI beginning balance for catch-up charges related to various accounting rule changes during the year.

The year-over-year change in AOCI is formally called **other comprehensive income (or loss)**. The financial statements for all companies include a statement of comprehensive income that explains the changes in the AOCI account. The statement of comprehensive income is either presented at the bottom of the income statement or on its own immediately after the income statement. Alphabet, for example, chose the latter. (As explained in more detail in a prior module, Comprehensive income = Net income + Other comprehensive income. For Alphabet in 2018, Comprehensive income = $29,520 million, the sum of Net income ($30,736 million) and Other comprehensive loss ($1,216 million).)

ALPHABET INC. Consolidated Statements of Comprehensive Income Year Ended December 31 ($ millions)	2016	2017	2018
Net income	$19,478	$12,662	$30,736
Other comprehensive income (loss):			
Change in foreign currency translation adjustment	(599)	1,543	(781)
Available-for-sale investments:			
Change in net unrealized gains (losses)	(314)	307	88
Less: reclassification adjustment for net (gains) losses included in net income	221	105	(911)
Net change (net of tax effect of $0, $0, and $156)	(93)	412	(823)
Cash flow hedges:			
Change in net unrealized gains (losses)	515	(638)	290
Less: reclassification adjustment for net (gains) losses included in net income	(351)	93	98
Net change (net of tax effect of $64, $247, and $103)	164	(545)	388
Other comprehensive income (loss)	(528)	1,410	(1,216)
Comprehensive income	$18,950	$14,072	$29,520

To conclude, the strengthening or weakening of the $US that causes fluctuations in assets and liabilities, and the cumulative translation adjustment has no effect on cash flow. Changes in the cumulative translation adjustment account are not reflected in net income; the fluctuations are included in AOCI and remain in stockholders' equity as long as the parent owns the foreign subsidiary. If and when a foreign subsidiary is sold, any remaining amount in AOCI that relates to the foreign subsidiary is removed from stockholders' equity and reported in net income.

Consolidation Disclosures To illustrate consolidation mechanics, we consider Caterpillar. The company's Form 10-K reports consolidated financial statements: the parent company financial statements (Machinery and Power Systems) are combined with those of the subsidiary (Financial Products). Exhibit 9.7 (taken from Caterpillar's 10-K) reports the parent and the subsidiary balance sheets separately as well as the adjustments that yield the consolidated financial statements.

Exhibit 9.7 ■ Caterpillar Consolidated Balance Sheet

December 31, 2018 ($ millions)	Machinery & Power Systems	Financial Products	Consolidating Adjustments	Consolidated
Balance sheet				
Current assets	$24,401	$15,862	❹ $(1,660)	$38,603
Noncurrent assets	20,402	20,206	❹ (702)	39,906
Investment in Financial Products subsidiaries	❶ 3,672		❸ (3,672)	—
Total assets	$48,475	$36,068	$(6,034)	$78,509
Current liabilities	$15,814	$14,065	❹ $(1,661)	$28,218
Long-term liabilities	18,581	18,331	❹ (701)	36,211
Stockholders' Equity:				
Common stock	5,827	919	(919)	5,827
Treasury stock	(20,531)	0		(20,531)
Retained earnings	30,427	3,543	(3,543)	30,427
Accumulated other comprehensive income	(1,684)	(943)	943	(1,684)
Noncontrolling interests	41	153	(153)	41
Total stockholders' equity	14,080	❷ 3,672	❸ (3,672)	14,080
Total liabilities and equity	$48,475	$36,068	$(6,034)	$78,509
Income statement				
Revenues	$51,822	$ 3,362	❹ $ (462)	$54,722
Operating costs	(43,667)	(2,840)	❹ 78	(46,429)
Operating profit	8,155	522	(384)	8,293
Other income (expense)	(815)	(16)	❹ 384	(447)
Profit before taxes	7,340	506	0	7,846
Provision for income taxes	(1,574)	(124)	—	(1,698)
Equity in profit of Financial Products subsidiaries	❺ 362		❺ (362)	—
Profit of consolidated companies	6,128	382	(362)	6,148
Less: profit (loss) attributable to noncontrolling interests	(19)	20		1
Profit attributable to Caterpillar shareholders	$ 6,147	$ 362	$ (362)	$ 6,147

Following are a few observations relating to Exhibit 9.7.

❶ The parent company (Machinery and Power Systems) reports an investment on its balance sheet called "Investment in Financial Products subsidiaries" with a balance of $3,672 million in 2018. This investment represents the parent's investment in its wholly-owned subsidiaries, and it is accounted for using the equity method. On the parent's books, this investment account represents net assets (total assets less total liabilities) of the Financial Products subsidiaries in the same way **Altria**'s balance sheet represents the percentage it owns of the net assets of AB InBev. The parent maintains its separate parent company financial records for taxation and other internal decision-making purposes. But for external reporting purposes, Caterpillar must present consolidated financial statements. (Caterpillar controls its Financial Products subsidiaries. Altria does not control AB InBev. That is why Caterpillar must consolidate its Financial Products subsidiaries while Altria reports AB InBev as an equity investment.)

❷ The subsidiary balance sheet reports total stockholders' equity in the amount of $3,672 million, the same amount as the equity investment on the parent's balance sheet. That is not a coincidence. As we discuss earlier in this module, if the investment is acquired at book value and the investee company is wholly-owned, the investment account on the parent's balance sheet will always be equal to the stockholders' equity of the subsidiary (investee) company. In this case, Caterpillar formed (not acquired) its financial products subsidiary, which is why the equity investment balance equals the equity of the financial products subsidiary and there are no recorded intangible assets.

❸ The consolidation process eliminates all intercompany investments, including intercompany sales and receivables, which we discuss below. Then, the rows are summed to yield the consolidated totals reported. This first group of eliminations removes the equity investment of $3,672 million from total assets and the subsidiary's stockholders' equity. Notice that the equity investment shows a zero balance (and is, therefore, not reported) on the consolidated balance sheet. Notice also that consolidated stockholders' equity is equal to parent company stockholders' equity (that will always be the case if the parent uses the equity method to account for its investment in the subsidiary).

❹ All intercompany transactions are eliminated in both the income statement and the balance sheet to avoid double counting. These include intercompany sales (and offsetting purchases) and intercompany receivables (and offsetting payables).

❺ Finally, because the subsidiaries are wholly-owned, the parent company reports equity income equal to the net income of its subsidiaries ($362 million). This income statement line is eliminated during the consolidation process and replaced by the revenues and expenses to which it relates. Net income remains unchanged, but the consolidated income statement reports the sales and expenses of its Financial Products subsidiaries rather than just the net income.

Following the eliminations of *all intercompany transactions*, the adjusted balance sheets and income statement line items are summed to yield the financial statements reported in Caterpillar's 10-K. In the case that a subsidiary is controlled but not wholly-owned, the consolidated financial statements will also reflect the *noncontrolling interest*, which we discuss above.

Limitations of Consolidation Reporting

Consolidation of financial statements is meant to present a financial picture of the entire set of companies under the control of the parent. Because investors typically purchase stock in the parent company and not in the subsidiaries, a consolidated view is more relevant than the parent company reporting subsidiaries as equity investments in its balance sheet. Still, we must be aware of certain limitations of consolidation.

1. Consolidated income does not imply the parent company has received any or all of the subsidiaries' net income as cash. The parent can only receive cash from subsidiaries via dividend payments. Conversely, the consolidated cash is not automatically available to the individual subsidiaries. It is quite possible, therefore, for an individual subsidiary to experience cash flow problems even though the consolidated group has strong cash flows. Likewise, unguaranteed debts of a subsidiary are not obligations of the consolidated group. Thus, even if the consolidated balance sheet is strong, creditors of a failing subsidiary are often unable to sue the parent or other subsidiaries to recoup losses.

2. Consolidated balance sheets and income statements are a mix of the various subsidiaries, often from different industries. Comparisons across companies, even if in similar industries, are often complicated by the different mix of subsidiary companies.

3. Consolidated disclosures are highly aggregated, which can preclude effective analysis. Consolidated numbers can mask poorly performing subsidiaries whose losses are offset by the positive performance of others.

Review 9-3 LO3

On January 1, assume Intel purchased all of the common shares of EarthLink for $600,000 cash—this is $200,000 more than the book value of EarthLink's stockholders' equity. Balance sheets of the two companies immediately after the acquisition follow.

continued

continued from previous page

	Intel (Parent)	EarthLink (Subsidiary)	Consolidating Adjustments	Consolidated
Current assets	$1,000,000	$100,000		
Investment in EarthLink	600,000	—		
PPE, net	3,000,000	400,000		
Total assets	$4,600,000	$500,000		
Liabilities.	$1,000,000	$100,000		
Contributed capital	2,000,000	200,000		
Retained earnings	1,600,000	200,000		
Total liabilities and equity	$4,600,000	$500,000		

During purchase negotiations, EarthLink's PPE was appraised at $500,000, and Earthlink had unrecorded patents with a fair value of $25,000. All of EarthLink's remaining assets and liabilities were appraised at values approximating their book values. Also, Intel concluded that payment of an additional $75,000 was warranted because of anticipated corporate synergies. Prepare the consolidating adjustments and the consolidated balance sheet at acquisition.

Solution on p. 9-56.

Global Accounting

Both U.S. GAAP and IFRS account similarly for investments by companies in the debt and equity securities of other companies. However, differences exist, and we highlight the notable ones here.

IFRS

Passive Investments

- Under IFRS, the definition of financial instrument is much broader, including, for example, accounts receivable and loans to customers or associates. For analysis, such instruments are disclosed in the notes, which will aid our reclassification for comparison purposes.

- Under IFRS, all equity instruments are measured at fair value through profit or loss (FVTPL). Companies can make an irrevocable choice to measure equity instruments at fair value through other comprehensive income (FVOCI) with no subsequent reclassification to profit or loss.

- Under IFRS, there are three classifications of investments in debt instruments: (1) amortized cost, (2) FVOCI (with subsequent reclassification to profit or loss), or (3) FVTPL, depending on the company's reasons for holding the instruments.

Equity Method Investment

- U.S. GAAP permits companies to elect to report equity method investments at fair value with changes in fair value to net income. IFRS only permits this option for mutual funds, insurance companies, and similar entities.

- IFRS distinguishes between joint ventures (where the parties have claims on the net assets of the venture) and joint operations (where parties have direct rights to the assets and obligations of the venture). IFRS companies account for joint ventures like GAAP companies, where they use equity method of accounting. However, for joint operations, companies include their share of assets, liabilities, income and expenses.

Consolidation GAAP sets out two ways to determine whether or not consolidation is required—the VIE model and the voting interest model, as discussed above. Under IFRS, consolidation is required when the investor controls the investee; that is, when the investor has power over the investee, is exposed to variable returns from the investee, or can exercise power to affect the amount of return from the investee.

- Under IFRS, companies can measure noncontrolling interests either at fair value (full goodwill approach) or at the proportionate share of the identifiable net assets acquired (purchased goodwill approach). U.S. GAAP permits fair value only. This IFRS-GAAP difference affects ratios based on operating assets, such as return on net operating assets (RNOA). Because goodwill is not routinely amortized, the difference will have no income statement impact (recall that we exclude noncontrolling interest from our calculation of return on equity).

■ Under U.S. GAAP, parent and subsidiary accounting policies do not need to conform. Under IFRS, parent and subsidiary accounting policies must conform.

■ IFRS fair value impairments for intangible assets, excluding goodwill, can be later reversed (that is, written back up after being written down). Companies must have reliable evidence that the value of the intangible has been restored, and the reversal cannot exceed the original impairment.

Appendix 9A: Accounting for Derivatives

LO4
Describe and interpret derivative disclosures.

Companies routinely face many market-related risks in addition to the risks they face in the ordinary course of business. These risks derive from changes in:

■ Interest rates   ■ Foreign exchange rates
■ Commodity prices   ■ Marketable security prices

Generally, these risks are beyond the company's control and can cause earnings and cash flow volatility that is difficult to manage. Fortunately, companies can mitigate these types of risk exposures by purchasing a financial security whose value is negatively correlated with the specific risk the company faces or by entering into a contract that locks in a future value. This transfer of risk is called hedging and it works best when the hedging instrument (including futures and forward contracts, swap agreements, and options) generates earnings and cash flows that exactly offset the adverse effects of the hedged item (debt, commodities, foreign currency or marketable securities). Collectively, these contracts and securities are called **derivatives** because their value derives from the value of some underlying asset. Derivatives, therefore, act like an insurance policy. However, while the company may protect itself from loss by using a derivative, it also gives up the prospect of gains. That is, if the hedged item increases in value, the gain will be offset by a loss on the derivative. The core idea of hedging is to insulate against potential losses and not to speculate on potential gains.

The following excerpts from the 10-K footnotes provide good examples.

■ **Tiffany & Co.** "The Company periodically hedges a portion of its forecasted purchases of precious metals for use in its internal manufacturing operations in order to manage the effect of volatility in precious metal prices."

■ **Michael Kors Holdings LTD.** "The Company in its normal course of business enters into transactions with foreign suppliers and seeks to minimize risks related to certain forecasted inventory purchases."

■ **Harley-Davidson Inc.** "The Company utilizes commodity contracts to hedge portions of the cost of certain commodities consumed in the Company's motorcycle production and distribution operations."

■ **Southwest Airlines Inc.** "The Company purchases jet fuel at prevailing market prices, but seeks to manage market risk through execution of a documented hedging strategy. The Company utilizes financial derivative instruments, on both a short-term and a long-term basis, as a form of insurance against the potential for significant increases in fuel prices."

■ **Cisco Systems Inc.** "Our equity portfolio consists of securities with characteristics that most closely match the Standard & Poor's 500 Index or Nasdaq Composite Index . . . To manage our exposure to changes in the fair value of certain equity securities, we may enter into equity derivatives designated as hedging instruments."

■ **Verizon** "We enter into interest rate swaps to achieve a targeted mix of fixed and variable rate debt. We principally receive fixed rates and pay variable rates based on the LIBOR, resulting in a net increase or decrease to Interest expense."

Hedge accounting is complex and derivative footnotes are among the most difficult to interpret. In general, hedging transactions fall into two groups.

1. **Hedging the fair value of a recognized asset or liability.** Cisco reports marketable securities on its balance sheet that are subject to price fluctuations. To protect against price declines, Cisco can purchase put options to lock in the sale price of the securities. Verizon has fixed-rate debt, the fair value of which

changes inversely with interest rates. Verizon can use a fixed-to-floating interest rate swap to hedge the value of the debt. The hedging of reported assets and liabilities is called a **fair value hedge**.

2. **Hedging future cash flows from forecasted transactions.** Tiffany, Michael Kors, Harley-Davidson and Southwest Airlines all face risks that purchase costs may increase, thus lessening profit as higher costs are matched against sales. To protect against adverse price increases, these companies can execute forward contracts or other securities that lock in the future cost. The hedging of forecasted transactions is called a **cash flow hedge**.

Like other marketable securities that we discussed earlier, derivatives are subject to fair value accounting.

- **Fair value hedges**. Both the derivative and the recognized asset or liability (the hedged item) are reported at fair value on the balance sheet. Changes in fair value for both are recognized in current earnings. If the hedge is effective, changes in the fair value of the hedged asset or liability will be offset by opposite changes in the fair value of the derivative, leaving income relatively unaffected.

- **Cash flow hedges**. The derivative is reported at fair value on the balance sheet. Recall, there is no hedged item with a cash flow hedge. Because cash flow hedges relate to *forecasted* transactions, changes in the fair value of the derivative are deferred until the related transaction occurs. The unrealized gain or loss is included in other comprehensive income and recognized in stockholders' equity as accumulated other comprehensive income. Then, when the hedged transaction occurs, the deferred gain or loss is transferred ("reclassified") from AOCI into current earnings in the same income statement line item that includes the hedged transaction.

The bottom line is that all changes in the fair value of the derivative securities are recognized in income, just like for any other marketable security. The only difference between the two types of derivative transactions is one of timing, where fair value hedges are recognized immediately and cash flow hedges are deferred until the hedged transaction occurs.

Business Insight ■ Counterparty Risk

The purpose of derivatives is to transfer risk from one company to another. For example, a company might be concerned about the possible decline in the $US value of an account receivable denominated in euros. In order to hedge that risk, the company might execute a forward contract to sell euros and receive $US. That forward contract only has value, however, if the party on the other side of the transaction (the counterparty) ultimately buys euros from the company when the contract matures. If the counterparty fails to honor its part of the agreement, the forward contract is of no value. The risk that the other party might not live up to its part of the bargain is known as *counterparty risk*. Counterparty risk is very real. Many companies require counterparties to back up their agreement with cash collateral or other acceptable forms of guarantees (e.g., a bank letter of credit). As a result, there is a hidden risk in companies' use of derivatives that is difficult to quantify.

Analysis of Derivatives

The footnote disclosures relating to financial derivatives provide details about the amounts and types of derivatives used by the company and the purposes for which they are used. Tables report:

- Notional (contact) amounts of derivatives in force.
- Fair values.
- Balance sheet location of where these derivative assets and liabilities are reported.

Companies also typically disclose that they do not use derivatives for speculative purposes. The implication is that there is some asset or liability or anticipated transaction offsetting the effect of the derivative so that the gains or losses are not one-sided.

One of the key analysis questions relates to the impact of derivatives on profitability and cash flow.

- For **fair value hedges**, as the fair value of the hedged item (asset or liability) changes, so does the fair value of the hedge (derivative security). Both changes are included in current earnings and their offsetting effects leaving net income relatively unaffected. So, the effect of fair value hedges on reported profit is usually not significant.

- For **cash flow hedges**, it is different. Hedges are purchased in advance of an anticipated or forecasted transaction, sometimes with a long lead time. The forecasted amount and timing of the transaction might not perfectly coincide with the actual transaction. As a result, the gain or loss on the derivative may not match the amount of the loss or gain on the transaction, leaving net income exposed to volatility—albeit by less volatility than if the forecasted transaction had not been hedged. The most significant disclosure relates to the dollar amount of deferred gain or loss that is transferred into current earnings from AOCI during the year. This is the amount by which current profit has been affected by the company's use of derivatives to hedge market risk.

Although footnote disclosures (which are extensive) provide information about the magnitude of the company's use of derivatives to mitigate risk and the impact on current earnings of the reclassification of deferred gains and losses on cash flow hedged, they do not provide us with a clear picture of the degree of risk the company faces or the extent to which that risk has been mitigated. That has been an ongoing objection to the derivative disclosures and, in 2013 the CFA Institute, a global association of investment professionals, published a report titled "User Perspectives on Financial Instrument Risk Disclosures Under International Financial Reporting Standards Derivatives and Hedging Activities Disclosures (Volume 2)" that compiled feedback from investment managers relating to the quality of derivatives disclosures. The study focused on disclosures mandated by IFRS, but the findings are relevant for U.S. GAAP as well in that the derivative accounting standards are similar under both standards.

The 2013 CFA Institute study reported low user satisfaction with the quality of derivative disclosures. The report summarized its finding as follows.

> Respondents indicated that hedge accounting and disclosure requirements are complex and confusing for users and they do not readily communicate key economic information (e.g. nature of hedging strategies, hedged versus unhedged exposures and hedge effectiveness). The highly complex and arcane nature of hedge accounting rules, along with the partial information regarding hedging activities addressed by hedge accounting disclosures, does not help users to discern the entirety of risk management practices of reporting companies. This explains the ratings of moderate importance of, and low satisfaction with, hedge accounting disclosures.

In sum, footnote disclosures relating to derivatives are very complex, often quite lengthy, and difficult to decipher. While we do obtain some important information about how changes in derivatives' fair values affect reported profit, on balance, the disclosures do not inform us about the company's overall risk exposure and the degree to which management has hedged the company's exposure.

Review 9-4 LO4

PepsiCo Inc. reports the following table in its footnote relating to derivatives.

Losses/(gains) on our hedging instruments are categorized as follows:

	Fair Value/Non-designated Hedges Losses/(Gains) Recognized in Income Statement[a]		Cash Flow and Net Investment Hedges			
			Losses/(Gains) Recognized in Accumulated Other Comprehensive Loss		Losses/(Gains) Reclassified from Accumulated Other Comprehensive Loss into Income Statement[b]	
	2018	2017	2018	2017	2018	2017
Foreign exchange. . .	$ 9	$(15)	$(52)	$ 62	$ (8)	$ 10
Interest rate	53	101	110	(195)	119	(184)
Commodity	117	(48)	3	3	—	3
Net investment	—	—	(77)	157	—	—
Total	$179	$ 38	$(16)	$ 27	$111	$(171)

[a] Foreign exchange derivative losses/gains are primarily included in selling, general, and administrative expenses. Interest rate derivative losses/gains are primarily from fair value hedges and are included in interest expense. These losses/gains are substantially offset by decreases/increases in the value of the underlying debt, which are also included in interest expense. Commodity derivative losses/gains are included in either cost of sales or selling, general and administrative expenses, depending on the underlying commodity.

[b] Foreign exchange derivative losses/gains are primarily included in cost of sales. Interest rate derivative losses/gains are included in interest expense. Commodity derivative losses/gains are included in either cost of sales or selling, general and administrative expenses, depending on the underlying commodity.

Required

1. What types of risks did PepsiCo hedge with its derivatives in 2018?
2. Did PepsiCo classify these derivatives as fair or cash flow hedges? How do we know?
3. What types of commodities might PepsiCo hedge? What income statement account would include gains and losses on these commodity hedges?

Solution on p. 9-56.

Appendix 9B: Equity Carve-Outs

Companies divest their subsidiaries, in whole or in part, for a variety of reasons, including the following.

eLectures **LO5**
MBC Explain equity carve-outs and their financial statement impact.

- As strategies evolve, some businesses in the consolidated entity might no longer be consistent with the current strategy and divestment allows management to focus on "core" operating activities.
- Divestiture can help capture some of the value created by high-performing subsidiaries whose performance is obscured by highly aggregated consolidated financial statements and related disclosures.
- Divestitures may present an effective means to raise cash for expansion, to bolster liquidity, or to reduce debt.
- Regulatory authorities might insist a company divest of certain business lines to increase competition as a precondition for approval of an acquisition.

These divestitures, or **equity carve-outs**, take many forms including the following.
① **Sell-offs.** The parent company sells its shares of the subsidiary company to an unrelated party.
② **IPOs.** The subsidiary company sells unissued shares to the public making the event an initial public offering. The parent company's ownership will be diluted but control can be retained (or not). If the parent retains control, the larger subsidiary company has new noncontrolling shareholders.
③ **Spin-offs.** The parent company declares a dividend, and instead of using cash, distributes all of the shares in the subsidiary company. The former subsidiary can have new leadership, free of the former parent company, and the subsidiary's shares can be publicly traded on an organized exchange.
④ **Split-offs.** The parent company repurchases its own shares. But rather than using cash for the buyback, the parent uses shares of the subsidiary company. As with a spin-off, the former subsidiary can be publicly traded. The chief difference between a spin-off and a split-off is the voluntary nature of a split-off; each shareholder decides whether or not to exchange their shares.

We illustrate the accounting for each of these transactions in Exhibit 9B.1.

Exhibit 9B.1 ▪

			Balance Sheet					Income Statement		
	Transaction	Cash Asset	+ Noncash Assets	= Liabil- ities	+ Contrib. Capital	+ Earned Capital		Rev- enues	− Expen- ses	= Net Income
① Sell-off	Sell shares of wholly-owned subsidiary with a carrying value of $800, for $1,000 in cash.	1,000	−800 Investment in subsidiary	=		200 Retained Earnings		200 Gain on sale	=	200
② IPO	Sell new shares of wholly-owned subsidiary with a carrying value of $800, for $300 cash.	300		=	300 APIC/NCI				=	
③ Spin-off	Distribute shares of wholly-owned subsidiary with a carrying value of $800, as a dividend.		−800 Investment in subsidiary	=		−800 Retained Earnings			=	
④ Split-off	Buyback own shares using shares of wholly-owned subsidiary with a carrying value of $800.		−800 Investment in subsidiary		−800 Treasury stock				=	

① **Sell-offs.** The simplest form of divestiture is a sell-off, the outright sale of a business unit. In this case, the company sells its equity interest to an unrelated party. The sale is accounted for just like the sale of any other asset. Specifically, any excess (deficit) of cash received over the book value of the business unit sold is recorded as a gain (loss) on the sale. To illustrate, in 2018, International Paper Company sold its North American Consumer Packaging business as disclosed in the following 10-K excerpt ($ millions).

On January 1, 2018, the Company completed the transfer of its North American Consumer Packaging business. . . to Graphic Packaging International Partners, LLC. International Paper is accounting for its ownership interest in the combined business under the equity method. The Company determined the fair value of its investment in the combined business to be $1.1 billion and recorded a pre-tax gain of $488 million ($364 million, net of tax) in 2018. The fair value was calculated using a market approach using inputs classified as Level 2 and Level 3 within the fair value hierarchy.

The financial statement effects of this transaction follow.

- International Paper received consideration of $1.1 billion.
- International Paper reported a gain on sale of $488 million, implying that the carrying value of the investment in the North American Consumer Packaging business was $612 million ($1.1 billion − $488 million).
- On the statement of cash flows, International Paper subtracts the $488 million noncash gain on sale to reconcile net income and cash from operating activities. The $1.1 billion cash proceeds are reported as a cash inflow in the investing section.

Because selling off the North American Consumer Packaging business represented a strategic business shift having a major effect on International Paper's operations and financial results, the company reported the North American Consumer Packaging business as a discontinued operation.

② **IPOs.** An initial public offering (IPO) by a subsidiary involves the sale of previously unissued shares to the public. To record the stock sale, the subsidiary increases both cash and paid-in capital as we discuss in Module 8 (see *Stock issuance*). The parent company reports the subsidiary as an equity-method investment on its balance sheet as we discuss earlier in this module. To reflect the change in percentage ownership of the subsidiary, the parent adjusts the carrying value of the equity-method investment and balances the transaction by adjusting its own additional paid-in capital. At consolidation, the parent reports a new noncontrolling interest to reflect the IPO shares. We illustrate these steps with the following example.

- Assume a wholly-owned subsidiary has a book value of stockholders' equity of $800,000, with 800,000 shares outstanding.
- The parent's balance sheet reports the subsidiary as an equity-method investment of $800,000 (that is, the parent acquired the subsidiary at book value).
- The subsidiary sells 200,000 no-par shares to unrelated parties for $300,000, bringing the outstanding shares increase to 1,000,000. The parent's ownership interest falls to 80%.
- The subsidiary's stockholders' equity increases to $1,100,000 ($800,000 before the stock issuance + $300,000 proceeds from the stock issuance). The parent now owns an 80% interest in a subsidiary that has stockholders' equity of $1,100,000.
- The parent makes the following accounting adjustments:
  - Increases the equity-method investment by $80,000 ($1,100,000 × 80% − $800,000) bringing the carrying value to $880,000.
  - Increases APIC by $80,000.
- In the consolidation process, the parent eliminates the equity-method investment together with the stockholders' equity of the subsidiary. The parent records noncontrolling interest of $220,000 ($1,100,000 × 20%).

Each of these steps is illustrated in the following table (in thousands).

		Balance Sheet							Income Statement		
	Transaction	Cash Asset	+ Noncash Assets	= Liabil- ities	+ Contrib. Capital	+ Earned Capital			Rev- enues	− Expen- ses	= Net Income
② IPO	Step 1: subsidiary records the sale of stock	+300		=	+300 APIC				**–**		=
	Step 2: parent increases equity investment to recognize the stock sale by the subsidiary		+80 Equity investment	=	+80 APIC				**–**		=

continued

continued from previous page

		Balance Sheet								Income Statement				
Transaction		Cash Asset	+	Noncash Assets	=	Liabil- ities	+	Contrib. Capital	+	Earned Capital		Rev- enues	− Expen- ses	= Net Income
② IPO	Step 3: consolidation elimination entries	−880 Equity investment	=					−1,100 Subsidiary's equity +220 Noncontrolling interest					**–**	**=**
	Net effect of steps 1–3	+300						+80 – APIC +220 Noncontrolling interest						

③ **Spin-offs.** In a spin-off, the parent company distributes to its stockholders the shares of the subsidiary company as a dividend, giving its stockholders direct ownership of the subsidiary rather than through the parent company. In recording this dividend, the parent company reduces retained earnings by the book value of the equity method investment, thereby removing the investment in the subsidiary from the parent's balance sheet. The accounting is similar to a cash dividend in that retained earnings is reduced by the dollar amount of the dividend. The difference is that the dividend is paid in shares of stock (a property dividend) rather than in cash.

> Netgear Inc. combined an IPO of its subsidiary with a subsequent spin-off of that subsidiary.

On February 6, 2018, the Company announced that its Board of Directors had unanimously approved the pursuit of a separation of its smart camera business "Arlo" from NETGEAR (the "Separation") to be effected by way of initial public offering ("IPO") and spin-off. On August 2, 2018, Arlo and NETGEAR announced the pricing of Arlo's IPO and subsequently listed on the New York Stock Exchange on August 3, 2018 under the symbol "ARLO". On August 7, 2018, we completed the IPO of 11,747,250 shares of common stock . . . (and) the Company held 62,500,000 shares of Arlo common stock, representing approximately 84.2% of the outstanding shares. On December 31, 2018, the Company completed the distribution of these 62,500,000 shares to its stockholders (the "Distribution") and no longer owns any shares of Arlo common stock. Upon completion of the Distribution, the Company ceased to own a controlling financial interest in Arlo and Arlo's historical financial results for periods presented are reflected in our consolidated financial statements as discontinued operations.

NETGEAR, INC.
CONSOLIDATED STATEMENTS OF STOCKHOLDERS' EQUITY

(In thousands)	Common Stock		Additional Paid-In Capital	Accumulated Other Comprehensive Income (Loss)	Retained Earnings (Losses)	Non-controlling Interest	Total
	Shares	Amount					
Balance as of December 31, 2017	31,320	$31	$603,137	$(851)	$ 128,168	$ —	$730,485
Adoption of ASU 2014-09 (ASC 606 Rev Rec), ASU2016-16, and ASU 2018-02, net of tax . . .	—	—	—	—	8,593	—	8,593
Change in unrealized gains and losses on available-for-sale securities, net of tax	—	—	—	78	—	—	78
Change in unrealized gains and losses on derivatives,net of tax	—	—	—	758	—	—	758
Net loss attributable to NETGEAR, Inc.	—	—	—	—	(9,162)	—	(9,162)
Net loss attributable to noncontrolling interest	—	—	—	—	—	(9,167)	(9,167)
Stock-based compensation expense	—	—	31,966	—	—	—	31,966
Stock-based compensation expense for Arlo's shares	—	—	—	—	—	942	942
A Sale of Arlo's common stock	—	—	146,088	—	—	24,158	170,246
Repurchases of common stock	(473)	—	—	—	(30,000)	—	(30,000)
Restricted stock unit withholdings	(138)	—	—	—	(8,065)	—	(8,065)
Issuance of common stock under stock-based compensation plans	853	1	12,394	—	—	—	12,395
B Distribution of Arlo	—	—	—	—	(255,584)	(15,933)	(271,517)
December 31, 2018	31,562	$32	$793,585	$ (15)	$(166,050)	$ —	$627,552

To recap the transactions: Netgear owned 62,500,000 shares (100% ownership) of Arlo Technologies. In August 2018, Arlo sold 11,747,250 shares of stock to the public (on the NYSE) bringing the total shares outstanding to 74,247,250 and dropping Netgear's ownership to 84.2%. This transaction (highlighted and marked A, in the table above) shows the IPO increased APIC by $146,088 thousand and noncontrolling interest by $24,128 thousand. Then, on December 31, 2018, Netgear distributed all of its 62,500,000 shares of Arlo to Netgear shareholders. This "dividend" (highlighted and marked B, in the table above) decreases retained earnings by $255,584 thousand and decreases noncontrolling interest by $15,933 thousand.

Accounting Insight ■ Deconsolidation of a Subsidiary

When a subsidiary issues stock in an IPO, the parent's percentage of ownership decreases. In the examples in this section, the parent retains control over the subsidiary. However, an IPO could conceivably reduce the parent's ownership to the point at which it no longer controls the subsidiary. In that case, the parent must deconsolidate the subsidiary— the equity-method investment is increased (or decreased) to its fair value and a gain (or loss) on the revaluation is recognized in current earnings. Subsequently, the former parent company will account for the investment using the methods appropriate given the level of ownership and the marketability of the former subsidiary's stock (equity method, fair value, or non-marketable securities). **Nextera Energy Inc.** (NEE) deconsolidated one of its subsidiary companies (NEP) in 2018 as disclosed in this excerpt from its 10-K filing.

> NextEra Energy Partners, LP - NEP owns or has an interest in a portfolio of wind and solar projects and a portfolio of seven long-term contracted natural gas pipeline assets located in Texas. NEP was deconsolidated from NEE for financial reporting purposes in January 2018 . . . Subsequent to deconsolidation, NEE owns a noncontrolling interest in NEP and began reflecting its ownership interest in NEP as an equity method investment with its earnings from NEP as equity in earnings of equity method investees . . . In connection with the deconsolidation, NEE recorded an initial investment in NEP of approximately $4.4 billion based on the fair value of NEP common units. The fair value was based on the market price of NEP common units as of January 1, 2018, which resulted in NEE recording a gain of approximately $3.9 billion ($3.0 billion after tax) for the year ended December 31, 2018. Total assets of approximately $7.8 billion, primarily property, plant and equipment, total liabilities of approximately $4.8 billion, primarily long-term debt, and total noncontrolling interests of approximately $2.7 billion were removed from NEE's balance sheet as part of the deconsolidation. [emphasis added]

Once Nextera no longer controlled NEP, it deconsolidated the subsidiary. On its balance sheet, Nextera increased the fair value of NEE to $4.4 billion and recognized a gain of $3.9 billion, which represented more than half of Nextera's 2018 pre-tax profit of $7.4 billion.

④ **Split-offs.** The split-off is a fourth form of equity carve-out, where the parent company buys back its own stock using the shares of the subsidiary company instead of cash. After completing this transaction, the subsidiary is an independent, publicly traded company. The parent treats the split-off like any other purchase of treasury stock. As such, the parent increases its treasury stock account and decreases the equity method investment account, reflecting the distribution of that asset. **CBS Corporation** provides an example in this excerpt from its 2018 10-K.

> On November 16, 2017, the Company completed the split-off of CBS Radio through an exchange offer, in which the Company accepted 17.9 million shares of CBS Corp Class B Common Stock from its stockholders in exchange for the 101.4 million shares of CBS Radio common stock that it owned... CBS Radio has been presented as a discontinued operation in the consolidated financial statements for all periods presented.

CBS CORPORATION AND SUBSIDIARIES CONSOLIDATED STATEMENTS OF STOCKHOLDERS' EQUITY						
	2018		2017		2016	
Year Ended December 31 (In millions)	Shares	Amount	Shares	Amount	Shares	Amount
Treasury Stock, at cost:						
Balance beginning of year	489	(22,258)	455	(20,201)	401	(17,205)
Class B Common Stock purchased	11	(600)	16	(1,050)	54	(2,997)
CBS Radio Split-Off	—	—	18	(1,007)	—	—
Shares paid for tax withholding for stock-based compensation . . .	1	(59)	1	(89)	1	(58)
Issuance of stock for deferred compensation	—	—	—	—	—	1
Retirement of treasury stock	(1)	59	(1)	89	(1)	58
Balance, end of year	500	(22,858)	489	(22,258)	455	(20,201)

continued from previous page

As the highlighted transaction in the table above shows, CBS Corp recorded a treasury stock transaction where shares of stock were distributed rather than cash. The treasury stock account decreased by $1,007 million as did the carrying value of CBS Corp's equity method investment in CBS Radio.

Analysis of Equity Carve-Outs

We see that the only type of equity carve-out that affects the income statement is a sell-off, which is the outright sale of the subsidiary. After an equity carve-out, the consolidated entity will no longer report the profits and cash flow (positive or negative) of the divested business unit. As such, the divestiture should be treated like any other nonoperating transaction as the consolidated entity will no longer include the operations of the divested subsidiary. And, although many equity carve-out transactions relate to discontinued operations, they may not be reported as such because the rules for reporting discontinued operations require a strategic change for the company and a significant financial effect. Footnotes will reveal the details of the transaction and whether it is reported as a discontinued operation or comingled with other operating activities.

Business Insight ■ Bloomberg U.S. Spin-Off Index

Equity carve-outs can unlock significant value for shareholders. When no longer operated as a subsidiary of a large conglomerate, a company can often be more nimble and responsive to a fast-changing business environment. In short, the operations are worth more as a standalone than as a subsidiary. A number of studies show that equity carve-outs historically have generated far better returns than the overall stock market. The Bloomberg U.S. Spin-Off Index tracks the stock price performance of companies spun off from larger companies within the past three years. In 2018, the index included 35 equities each with a value over $1 billion and the index as a whole outperformed the broader market by nine percentage points.

Guidance Answers

You Are the Chief Financial Officer

Pg. 9-17 Capacity utilization is important. If long-term operating assets are used inefficiently, cost per unit produced is too high. Cost per unit does not relate solely to manufacturing products. It also applies to the cost of providing services and many other operating activities. However, if we purchase assets with little productive slack, our costs of production at peak levels can be excessive. Further, the company may be unable to service peak demand and risks losing customers. In response, the company might explore strategic alliances. These take many forms. Some require a simple contract to use another company's manufacturing, service, or administrative capability for a fee (*Note:* These executory contracts are not recorded under GAAP). Another type of alliance is a joint venture to share ownership of manufacturing or IT facilities. In this case, if demand can be coordinated with that of a partner, perhaps operating assets can be more effectively used. As chief financial officer, what thoughts do you have?

Superscript ^A(B) denotes assignments based on Appendix 9A(9B).

Questions

Q9-1. What is a passive investment? Why do companies have passive investments?

Q9-2. What is an unrealized gain (loss)? Explain.

Q9-3. Where are unrealized gains and losses related to marketable equity securities reported in the financial statements?

Q9-4. What does significant influence imply regarding intercorporate investments? Describe the accounting procedures used for such investments.

Q9-5. On January 1 of the current year, Tse Company purchases 30% of the common stock of Green Company for $1,300,000 cash. This ownership allows Tse to exert significant influence over Green. During the year, Green reports $220,000 of net income and pays $42,000 in cash dividends. At year-end, what amount should appear in Tse's balance sheet for its investment in Green?

Q9-6.   What accounting method is used when a stock investment represents more than 50% of the investee company's voting stock and allows the investor company to "control" the investee company? Explain.

Q9-7.   What is the underlying objective of consolidated financial statements?

Q9-8.[A]   What is a derivative? How do companies use them to hedge risk?

Q9-9.[A]   For accounting purposes, what are the two types of hedges? How are unrealized derivative gains and losses treated under each accounting method?

Q9-10.   What are some limitations of consolidated financial statements?

Q9-11.   How does a weakening $US affect the consolidated balance sheet of a company with foreign subsidiaries?

Q9-12.[B]   What is the difference between a spin-off and a split-off?

Assignments with the 🌐 logo in the margin are available in BusinessCourse.
See the Preface of the book for details.

Mini Exercises

LO1

M9-13.   Accounting for Marketable Equity Securities
Assume that Bava Company purchases 23,000 common shares of Jones Company for $12 cash per share. During the year, Bava receives a cash dividend of $1.30 per common share from Jones, and the year-end market price of Jones common stock is $13 per share. How much income does Bava report relating to this investment for the year?

LO1
Amgen Inc. (AMGN)

M9-14.   Interpreting Disclosures of Investment Securities
Amgen Inc. reports the following disclosure relating to its accumulated other comprehensive income.

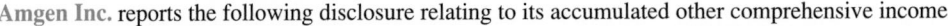

$ millions	Foreign Currency Translation	Cash Flow Hedges	Available-for-Sale Securities	Other	AOCI
Balance as of December 31, 2017	$(529)	$(6)	$ (144)	$—	$(679)
Cumulative effect of change in accounting principle, net of tax	—	—	(9)	—	(9)
Foreign currency translation adjustments.	(141)	—	—	—	(141)
Unrealized (losses) gains.	—	61	(556)	—	(495)
Reclassification adjustments to income	—	262	365	—	627
Other.	—	—	—	(2)	(2)
Income taxes	—	(76)	6	—	(70)
Balance as of December 31, 2018	$(670)	$241	$(338)	$ (2)	$(769)

a. Amgen reports unrealized gains and losses on available-for-sale securities as part of AOCI. Which of the following types of investments could be included in this account? Select all that apply.
   i.   Bonds issued by US corporations.
   ii. Common stock traded on US stock exchange.
   iii. Common stock traded on foreign stock exchange.
   iv. Debt securities issued by a foreign government.
   v.   Municipal bonds.
   vi. U.S. Treasury bills.

b. Consider the securities held in the available-for-sale portfolio at December 31, 2018. Which of the following is true?
   i.   At December 31, 2018, the fair value of the securities was $338 million less than their amortized cost.
   ii. At December 31, 2018, the fair value of the securities was $338 million greater than their amortized cost.
   iii. At December 31, 2018, the fair value of the securities was $338 million lower than their value at December 31, 2017.

    iv. At December 31, 2018, the fair value of the securities was $194 million lower than their value at December 31, 2017

  c. Consider the securities held in the available-for-sale portfolio at December 31, 2018. During the year, by how much did the market value of those securities increase or decrease?

    i. Decreased by $338 million.

    ii. Decreased by $556 million.

    iii. Increased by $556 million.

    iv. Decreased by $191 million.

  d. Amgen increased AOCI by $365 million for reclassification adjustments to income. Which of the following best describes what this line item means.

    i. During 2018, Amgen sold available-for-sale securities and realized a loss of $365 million.

    ii. During 2018, Amgen sold available-for-sale securities and realized a gain of $365 million.

    iii. During 2018, Amgen sold available-for-sale securities that had unrealized gains of $365 million at December 31, 2017.

    iv. During 2018, Amgen sold available-for-sale securities that had unrealized losses of $365 million at December 31, 2017.

M9-15. Analyzing Derivatives and Hedging

Refer to the information for Amgen in M9-14. This information reports activity related to Amgen's cash flow hedges.

  a. Explain how this type of hedging works. Provide an example of how Amgen might use this type of hedging strategy.

  b. How did the hedges affect net income for 2018?

  c. If these same hedges had instead been fair value hedges, what amount would have been added to AOCI for the year?

LO4
Amgen Inc. (AMGN)

M9-16. Analyzing Derivatives and Hedging

For each of the following, indicate whether the hedge would be classified as a fair value hedge or a cash flow hedge.

  a. Morningstar locks in a price on a forward contract to buy soybeans over the next 12 months.

  b. General Motors enters into a foreign currency futures contract on Canadian dollars to hedge its C$200 million bond issuance.

  c. American Airlines takes delivery of 10 new Airbus jets. The contract was denominated in euros instead of $US. American Airlines will settle the accounts payable in six months. To hedge its exposure, American Airlines buys € denominated futures contracts.

  d. Apple Inc. has foreign currency options to buy Chinese Yuan to hedge payments to FoxConn, the Chinese company that manufactures Apple products.

  e. Poole Construction signs a contract to build a soccer stadium in Mexico. The contract is denominated in Mexican pesos. Poole buys foreign currency options to sell Mexican pesos.

LO4
Morningstar (MORN)
General Motors (GM)
American Airlines (AAL)
Apple Inc. (AAPL)
Poole Construction

Homework
MBC

M9-17. Analyzing and Interpreting Equity Method Investments

Concord Company purchases an investment in Bloomingdale Company at a purchase price of $2 million cash, representing 30% of the book value of Bloomingdale. During the year, Bloomingdale reports net income of $300,000 and pays cash dividends of $90,000. At the end of the year, the fair value of Concord's investment is $2.4 million.

  a. What amount does Concord report on its balance sheet for its investment in Bloomingdale at year-end?

  b. What amount of income from investments does Concord report for the year? Explain.

  c. The fair value of Bloomingdale increased during the year creating an unrealized gain for Concord. This unrealized gain in the fair value of the Bloomingdale investment (choose one and explain):

    (1) Is not reflected on either its income statement or balance sheet.

    (2) Is reported in its current income.

    (3) Is reported on its balance sheet only.

    (4) Is reported in its accumulated other comprehensive income.

LO2

Homework
MBC

M9-18. Computing Income for Equity Method Investments

Kross Company purchases an equity investment in Penno Company at a purchase price of $2.5 million, representing 40% of the book value of Penno. During the current year, Penno reports net income of $300,000 and pays cash dividends of $100,000. At the end of the year, the fair value of Kross's investment is $2.65 million. What amount of income does Kross report relating to this investment in Penno for the year? Explain.

LO2

Homework
MBC

LO1   **M9-19. Marketable Debt Securities**

Facebook Inc (FACE)

Facebook reports the following in its 2018 10-K.

The following table summarizes, for assets or liabilities measured at fair value, the respective fair value and the classification by level of input within the fair value hierarchy (in millions):

Description	December 31, 2018	Fair Value Measurement at Reporting Date Using		
		Quoted Prices in Active Markets for Identical Assets (Level 1)	Significant Other Observable Inputs (Level 2)	Significant Unobservable Inputs (Level 3)
Cash equivalents:				
Money market funds	$ 6,792	$ 6,792	$ —	$—
U.S. government securities	90	90	—	—
U.S. government agency securities	54	54	—	—
Certificate of deposits and time deposits . . .	369	—	369	—
Corporate debt securities.	1	—	1	—
Marketable securities:				
U.S. government securities	13,836	13,836	—	—
U.S. government agency securities	8,333	8,333	—	—
Corporate debt securities.	8,926	—	8,926	—
Total cash equivalents and marketable securities.	$38,401	$29,105	$9,296	$—

The gross unrealized losses on our marketable securities were $357 million and $289 million as of December 31, 2018 and 2017, respectively. The gross unrealized gains for both periods were not significant.

a. What does Facebook report as Cash equivalents at December 31, 2018? As Marketable securities?

b. What is the chief difference between Cash equivalents and Marketable securities?

c. What is the cost of its marketable securities? *Hint:* Consider that its marketable securities are in a loss position.

LO2   **M9-20. Interpreting Disclosures on Investments in Affiliates**

Pfizer, Inc. (PFE)

Pfizer's 10-K report includes the following footnote disclosure.

On December 19, 2018, we announced that we entered into a definitive agreement with GSK under which we . . . will combine our respective consumer healthcare businesses into a new consumer healthcare joint venture that will operate globally under the GSK Consumer Healthcare name. In exchange for contributing our Consumer Healthcare business, we will receive a 32% equity stake in the company and GSK will own the remaining 68%.

a. How will Pfizer account for its 32% equity stake in GSK Consumer Healthcare?

b. If the joint venture distributes cash of $350 million in 2019 what will be the effect on Pfizer's 2019 balance sheet and income statement?

c. Assume that the joint venture generated profit of $1,400 million in 2019. How will this affect Pfizer's 2019 income statement?

LO3   **M9-21. Computing Consolidating Adjustments and Noncontrolling Interest**

Patterson Company purchases 80% of Kensington Company's common stock for $400,000 cash when Kensington Company has $200,000 of common stock and $300,000 of retained earnings. If a consolidated balance sheet is prepared immediately after the acquisition, what amounts are eliminated when preparing that statement? What amount of noncontrolling interest appears in the consolidated balance sheet?

LO3   **M9-22. Computing Consolidated Net Income**

Bedford Company purchased a 90% interest in Midway Company on January 1 of the current year, and the purchase price reflected 90% of Midway's book value of equity. Bedford Company had $400,000

net income for the current year *before* recognizing its share of Midway Company's net income. If Midway Company had net income of $90,000 for the year, what is the consolidated net income attributable to Bedford shareholders for the year?

M9-23. **Assigning Purchase Price in Acquisitions**

LO3

Jasper Company acquired 80% of Fey Company at the beginning of the current year. Jasper paid $150,000 more than the book value of Fey's stockholders' equity and determined that this excess purchase price related to intangible assets. How does the $150,000 appear on the consolidated Jasper Company balance sheet if the intangible assets acquired related to (*a*) patents or, alternatively, (*b*) goodwill? How would each scenario affect the consolidated income statement?

M9-24. **Interpreting a Divestiture Disclosure**

LO5
Jack in the Box
(JACK)

In early 2018, Jack in the Box completed its divestiture of wholly-owned subsidiary Qdoba, to private investors for $305 million. CNBC.com reported the following statement attributed to Lenny Comma, CEO and chairman of Jack in the Box.

> For the past several months, we have worked closely with our financial advisors and evaluated various strategic alternatives with respect to Qdoba, including a sale or spin-off, as well as opportunities to refranchise company restaurants. Following the completion of this robust process, our Board of Directors has determined that the sale of Qdoba is the best alternative for enhancing shareholder value and is consistent with the Company's desire to transition to a less capital-intensive business model."

a. From the facts provided, what sort of equity carve-out does this seem to be?

b. Explain how the deal could "enhance value" for Jack in the Box shareholders.

c. What effects will the Qdoba carve-out have on Jack in the Box's balance sheet and income statement.

M9-25. **Interpreting a Proposed Split-Off Disclosure**

LO5
General Electric (GE)

On October 19, 2015, the following was reported in an article at StreetInsider.com.

> General Electric commenced an offer to exchange GE common stock for common stock of Synchrony Financial presently owned by GE. This exchange offer is in connection with the previously announced separation of Synchrony, the largest provider of private label credit cards in the United States, from GE. The exchange offer is expected to conclude the week of November 16, 2015. The exchange offer is designed to provide GE shareholders an opportunity to exchange their shares of GE common stock for shares of Synchrony common stock at a 7% discount, subject to an upper limit of 1.1308 shares of Synchrony common stock per share of GE common stock.

a. This transaction is a split-off. How do we know?

b. How will the proposed split-off affect the number of GE shares outstanding?

c. Given the details revealed in the news article, does the split-off appear to be pro-rata or non pro-rata?

M9-26. **Interpreting Disclosure Related to IPO Carve-Out**

LO5
Gap Inc. (GPS)

The Gap reports the following in its Form 8-K dated February 28, 2019.

> GAP Inc. today announced plans to create two independent publicly traded companies: Old Navy, a category-leader in family apparel, and a yet-to-be-named company ("NewCo"), which will consist of the iconic Gap brand, Athleta, Banana Republic, Intermix and Hill City. Gap Inc. expects to effect the separation through a spin-off that is intended to generally be tax-free to Gap Inc.'s shareholders for U.S. federal income tax purposes. Upon separation, Gap Inc. shareholders are expected to receive a pro-rata stock distribution and as a result own shares in both NewCo and Old Navy in equal proportion. The transaction is currently targeted to be completed in 2020.

a. Describe the accounting for the spin-off component of this transaction.

b. What effects did this transaction have on The Gap balance sheet and income statement?

Exercises

LO1   E9-27.   Assessing Financial Statement Effects of Marketable Equity Securities

Use the financial statement effects template to record the following four transactions involving investments in marketable equity securities.

a. Purchased 18,000 common shares of Baez Inc. for $12 cash per share.
b. Received a cash dividend of $1.20 per common share from Baez.
c. Year-end market price of Baez common stock was $11.25 per share.
d. Sold all 18,000 common shares of Baez for $213,600.

LO1   E9-28.   Assessing Financial Statement Effects of Marketable Equity Securities

Use the financial statement effects template to record the accounts and amounts for the following four transactions involving investments in marketable equity securities.

a. Purchased 20,000 common shares of Heller Co. at $16 cash per share.
b. Received a cash dividend of $1.25 per common share from Heller.
c. Year-end market price of Heller common stock is $17.50 per share.
d. Sold all 20,000 common shares of Heller for $315,600 cash.

LO1   E9-29.   Marketable Debt Securities

Use the financial statement effects template to record the accounts and amounts for the following four transactions involving investments in marketable debt securities classified as available-for-sale securities.

a. Purchased 5,000 bonds with a face value of $1,000 per bond. The bonds are purchased at par for cash and pay interest at an annual rate of 4%.
b. Received semi-annual cash interest of $100,000.
c. Year-end fair value of the bonds is $978 per bond.
d. Shortly after year-end, Loudder sold all 5,000 bonds for $970 per bond.

LO1, 3   E9-30.   Interpreting Footnotes on Security Investments

Snapchat Inc. (SNAP)

Snapchat reports the following information in its 2018 10-K report.

The table below presents the changes in accumulated other comprehensive income (loss) ("AOCI") by component and the reclassifications out of AOCI:

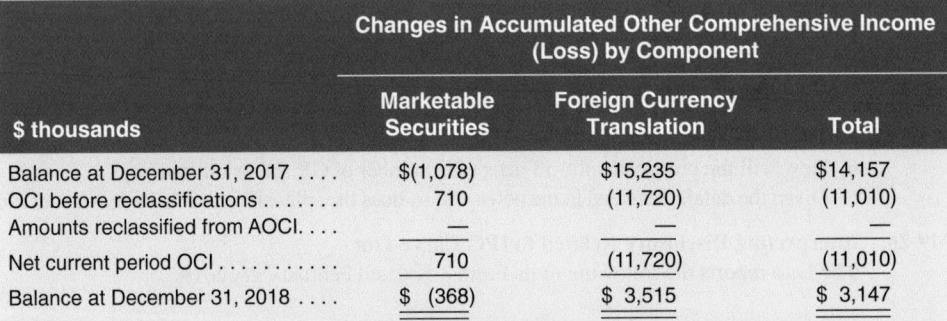

$ thousands	Marketable Securities	Foreign Currency Translation	Total
Balance at December 31, 2017	$(1,078)	$15,235	$14,157
OCI before reclassifications	710	(11,720)	(11,010)
Amounts reclassified from AOCI. ...	—	—	—
Net current period OCI	710	(11,720)	(11,010)
Balance at December 31, 2018	$ (368)	$ 3,515	$ 3,147

Changes in Accumulated Other Comprehensive Income (Loss) by Component

Footnotes report the following information on Snapchat's marketable debt securities.

$ thousands	Cost or Amortized Cost	Gross Unrealized Gains	Gross Unrealized Losses	Total Estimated Fair Value
Cash............................	$ 279,950	$—	$ —	$ 279,950
Level 1 securities:				
U.S. government securities	735,988	12	(175)	735,825
U.S. government agency securities ...	181,032	4	(36)	181,000
Level 2 securities:				
Corporate debt securities...........	35,819	1	(18)	35,802
Commercial paper	33,193	—	—	33,193
Certificates of deposit	13,293	—	—	13,293
Total	$1,279,275	$17	$(229)	$1,279,063

a. Snapchat's AOCI account includes unrealized gains and losses from two sources. What are those sources?

b. Snapchat reported net loss for the year of $1,255,911 thousand. Determine comprehensive income for the year.

c. During 2018, did the currencies in the countries where Cisco's subsidiaries were headquartered weaken or strengthen?

d. Snapchat uses Level 1 and Level 2 inputs to determine fair value for its marketable debt investments. Explain the difference between these two inputs.

e. Consider the Level 1 securities, which relate to investments in U.S. government debt securities. On average, has the market rate of interest for these securities increased or decreased since Snapchat bought these securities?

E9-31. **Interpreting Footnote Disclosures for Investments**

LO1

CNA Financial Corporation provides the following footnote to its 2018 10-K report.

CNA Financial
Corporation (CNA)

> **Investments** The company classifies its fixed maturity securities as either available-for-sale or trading, and as such, they are carried at fair value. Changes in fair value of trading securities are reported within Net investment income on the Consolidated Statements of Operations. Changes in fair value related to available-for-sale securities are reported as a component of Other comprehensive income.

The following table provides a summary of fixed maturity and equity securities.

December 31, 2018 ($ millions)	Cost or Amortized Cost	Gross Unrealized Gains	Gross Unrealized Losses	Estimated Fair Value
Fixed maturity securities available-for-sale				
Corporate and other bonds	$18,764	$791	$395	$19,160
States, municipalities and political subdivisions	9,681	1,076	9	10,748
Asset-backed:				
Residential mortgage-backed	4,815	68	57	4,826
Commercial mortgage-backed	2,200	28	32	2,196
Other asset-backed	1,975	11	24	1,962
Total asset-backed	8,990	107	113	8,984
U.S. Treasury and obligations of government sponsored enterprises	156	3	—	159
Foreign government	480	5	4	481
Redeemable preferred stock	10	—	—	10
Total fixed maturity securities available-for-sale	38,081	1,982	521	39,542
Total fixed maturity securities trading	4	—	—	4
Total fixed maturity securities	$38,085	$1,982	$521	$39,546

a. At what amount does CNA report its investment in marketable debt securities on its balance sheet? In your answer, identify the portfolio's fair value, cost, and any unrealized gains and losses.

b. Compute the net unrealized gain or loss on CNA's investment portfolio. How do CNA's balance sheet and income statement reflect this net unrealized gain or loss?

c. How do CNA's balance sheet and income statement reflect gains and losses realized from the sale of available-for-sale securities?

E9-32. **Assessing Financial Statement Effects of Equity Method Securities**

LO2

Use the financial statement effects template (with amounts and accounts) to record the following transactions involving investments in marketable securities accounted for using the equity method.

a. Purchased 12,000 common shares of Bakersfield Co. at $9 per share; the shares represent 30% ownership in Bakersfield.

b. Received a cash dividend of $1.25 per common share from Bakersfield.

c. Bakersfield reported annual net income of $60,000.

d. Sold all 12,000 common shares of Bakersfield for $114,500.

LO3

Salesforce (CRM)

E9-33.   Assessing Acquisition Announcement

Salesforce Inc. included the following note with its 10-Q dated July 31, 2019.

> **Subsequent event** On August 1, 2019, pursuant to an Agreement and Plan of Merger dated June 9, 2019, the Company acquired all of the outstanding capital stock of Tableau, which provides a self-service analytics platform that enables users to easily access, prepare, analyze, and present findings in their data. The preliminary acquisition date fair value of the consideration transferred for Tableau is estimated to be approximately $14.9 billion comprised of $14.6 billion in common stock issued, or approximately 96 million shares, and $0.3 billion related to the fair value of stock options and restricted stock awards assumed. The Company will include the financial results of Tableau in the condensed consolidated financial statements from the date of the acquisition on August 1, 2019.

a. How will the investment in Tableau appear on the Salesforce parent-only balance sheet?

b. In its SEC filings, how will Salesforce Inc. account for the investment in Tableau?

c. In its June 30, 2019, 10-Q report, Tableau reported net assets of just over $1 billion. What is an approximation of the intangible assets and goodwill that Salesforce will report on its consolidated balance sheet?

LO1, 2

Homework
MBC

E9-34.   Assessing Financial Statement Effects Investments

On January 1, 2018, Ball Corporation purchased shares of Leftwich Company common stock.

a. Assume that the stock acquired by Ball represents 15% of Leftwich's voting stock and that Ball has no influence over Leftwich's business decisions. Use the financial statement effects template (with amounts and accounts) to record the following transactions.

   1. Ball purchased 5,000 common shares of Leftwich at $15 cash per share.

   2. Leftwich reported annual net income of $40,000.

   3. Ball received a cash dividend of $1.10 per common share from Leftwich.

   4. Year-end market price of Leftwich common stock is $19 per share.

b. Assume that the stock acquired by Ball represents 30% of Leftwich's voting stock and that Ball accounts for this investment using the equity method because it is able to exert significant influence. Use the financial statement effects template (with amounts and accounts) to record the following transactions.

   1. Ball purchased 5,000 common shares of Leftwich at $15 cash per share.

   2. Leftwich reported annual net income of $40,000.

   3. Ball received a cash dividend of $1.10 per common share from Leftwich.

   4. Year-end market price of Leftwich common stock is $19 per share.

LO2

Ford Motor Company
(F)

E9-35.   Interpreting Equity Method Investment Footnotes

Ford Motor Company includes the following table in its 2018 Form 10-K. The table reports the ownership percentages and carrying value of equity method investments (in millions, except percentages).

	Investment Balance		Ownership Percentage
Automotive Sector	**2017**	**2018**	**December 31, 2018**
Changan Ford Automobile Corporation, Limited	$1,144	$ 950	50.0%
Jiangling Motors Corporation, Limited	675	543	32.0
AutoAlliance (Thailand) Co., Ltd.	439	431	50.0
Ford Otomotiv Sanayi Anonim Sirketi.	329	247	41.0
Getrag Ford Transmissions GmbH.	222	236	50.0
FFS Finance South Africa (Pty) Limited	71	81	50.0
Changan Ford Mazda Engine Company, Ltd.	84	71	25.0
Ionity Holding GmbH & Co. KG	12	42	25.0
DealerDirect LLC	33	33	97.7
RouteOne LLC	24	31	30.0
Thirdware Solutions Limited	12	12	20.0
Percepta, LLC.	8	10	45.0
Chongqing ANTE Trading Co., Ltd.	5	6	10.0
U.S. Council for Automotive Research LLC	5	6	33.3
Crash Avoidance Metrics Partnership LLC.........	3	4	50.0
Blue Diamond Parts, LLC.	3	3	25.0
CNF-Administradora de Consorcio Nacional Ltda....	6	3	33.3
Automotive Fuel Cell Cooperation Corporation	10	—	49.9
Total Automotive sector	$3,085	$2,709	

a. What does Ford report on its balance sheet at December 31, 2018, for its investment in equity method affiliates? Does this reflect the adjusted cost or fair value of Ford's interest in these companies?

b. Approximate the total stockholders' equity of the Changan Ford Mazda Engine Company at the end of 2018. Explain.

c. Ford owns 97.7% of DealerDirect LLC yet this investment was not consolidated. Speculate on why this might be the case.

d. Assume Getrag Ford Transmission GmbH paid no dividends in 2018. Determine Getrag's net income for the year.

e. Explain why Ford has so many equity-method investments.

f. Ford's 2018 income statement included income from equity method investments of $1,780 million. Approximate the dividends and distributions that Ford received from the equity method affiliates during 2018.

E9-36. Analyzing and Interpreting Disclosures on Equity Method Investments

LO2

Cummins Inc. (CMI)

Cummins Inc. reports investments in affiliated companies, consisting mainly of investments in six manufacturing joint ventures. Cummins provides the following financial information on its investee companies in a footnote to its 10-K report.

Equity Investee Financial Summary, $ millions	For years ended December 31		
	2018	2017	2016
Net sales.	$7,352	$7,050	$5,654
Gross margin	1,373	1,422	1,182
Net income	647	680	499
Cummins' share of net income	$ 336	$ 308	$ 260
Royalty and interest income	58	49	41
Total equity, royalty and interest from investees	$ 394	$ 357	$ 301
Current assets	$3,401	$3,416	
Noncurrent assets	1,449	1,379	
Current liabilities	(2,669)	(2,567)	
Noncurrent liabilities	(218)	(237)	
Net assets	$1,963	$1,991	
Cummins' share of net assets	$1,144	$1,116	

a. What assets and liabilities of unconsolidated affiliates are omitted from Cummins' balance sheet as a result of the equity method of accounting for those investments?

b. Do the liabilities of the unconsolidated affiliates affect Cummins directly? Explain.

c. How does the equity method impact Cummins' ROE and its RNOA components (net operating asset turnover and net operating profit margin)?

E9-37. Interpreting Equity Method Investment Footnotes

LO2

AT&T Inc. (T)

AT&T reports the following footnote to its 2018 10-K report.

Equity Method Investments Investments in partnerships, joint ventures and less than majority-owned subsidiaries in which we have significant influence are accounted for under the equity method . . . The following table is a reconciliation of our investments in equity affiliates as presented on our consolidated balance sheets.

$ millions	2018	2017
Beginning of year	$1,560	$1,674
Additional investments	237	51
Time Warner investments acquired	4,912	—
Acquisition of remaining interest in Otter Media	(166)	—
Equity in net income of affiliates	(48)	(128)
Dividends and distributions received	(243)	(46)
Sale of América Móvil shares	(14)	22
Other adjustments	7	(13)
End of year	$6,245	$1,560

Undistributed earnings from equity affiliates were $292 and $174 at December 31, 2018 and 2017, respectively.

a. At what amount is the equity investment in affiliates reported on AT&T's balance sheet?
b. Did affiliates pay dividends in 2018? How do you know?
c. How much income did AT&T report in 2018 relating to this investment in affiliates?
d. Interpret the AT&T statement that "undistributed earnings from equity affiliates were $292 and $174 at December 31, 2018 and 2017, respectively."
e. How does use of the equity method impact AT&T's ROE and its RNOA components (net operating asset turnover and net operating profit margin)?
f. AT&T accounts for its investment in affiliates under the equity method. Why?

LO3   **E9-38.**   **Constructing the Consolidated Balance Sheet at Acquisition**

On January 1 of the current year, Liu Company purchased all of the common shares of Reed Company for $380,000 cash. Balance sheets of the two firms immediately after the acquisition follow.

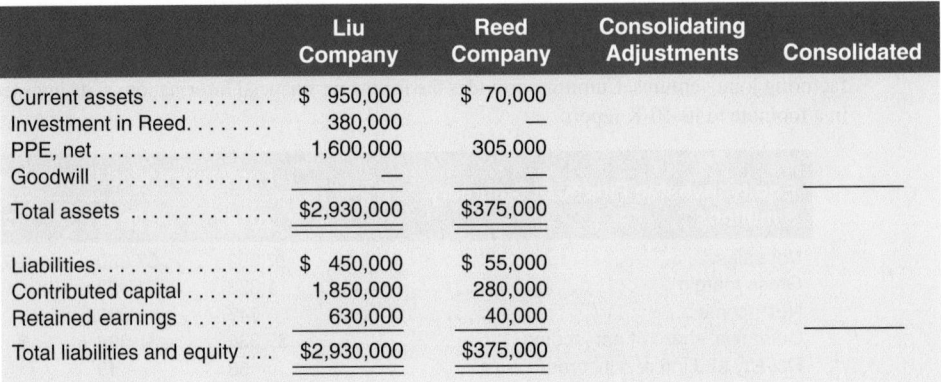

	Liu Company	Reed Company	Consolidating Adjustments	Consolidated
Current assets	$ 950,000	$ 70,000		
Investment in Reed.	380,000	—		
PPE, net	1,600,000	305,000		
Goodwill	—	—		
Total assets	$2,930,000	$375,000		
Liabilities.	$ 450,000	$ 55,000		
Contributed capital	1,850,000	280,000		
Retained earnings	630,000	40,000		
Total liabilities and equity . . .	$2,930,000	$375,000		

During purchase negotiations, Reed's PPE was appraised at $332,000, and all of its remaining assets and liabilities were appraised at values approximating their book values. Liu also concluded that an additional $33,000 (for goodwill) demanded by Reed's shareholders was warranted because Reed's earning power was better than the industry average. Prepare the consolidating adjustments and the consolidated balance sheet at acquisition.

LO3   **E9-39.**   **Constructing the Consolidated Balance Sheet at Acquisition**

Winston Company purchased all of Marcus Company's common stock for $600,000 cash on January 1, at which time the separate balance sheets of the two corporations appeared as follows.

	Winston Company	Marcus Company	Consolidating Adjustments	Consolidated
Investment in Marcus	$ 600,000	$ —		
Other assets	2,300,000	700,000		
Goodwill	—	—		
Total assets	$2,900,000	$700,000		
Liabilities.	$ 900,000	$160,000		
Contributed capital	1,400,000	300,000		
Retained earnings	600,000	240,000		
Total liabilities and equity . . .	$2,900,000	$700,000		

During purchase negotiations, Winston determined the appraised value of Marcus's Other Assets was $720,000, and all of its remaining assets and liabilities were appraised at values approximating their book values. The balance of the purchase price was ascribed to goodwill. Prepare the consolidating adjustments and the consolidated balance sheet at acquisition.

LO5   **E9-40.**   **Assessing Financial Statement Effects from a Subsidiary Stock Issuance**

Sykora Company owns 80% of Walton Company. Information reported by Sykora and Walton as of the current year-end follows.

Sykora Company		**Walton Company**	
Shares owned of Walton	80,000	Shares outstanding	100,000
Book value of investment in Walton . . .	$720,000	Book value of equity	$900,000
		Book value per share	$9

Assume Walton issues 60,000 additional shares of previously authorized but unissued common stock solely to outside investors (none to Sykora) for $14 cash per share. Indicate the financial statement effects of this stock issuance on Sykora using the financial statement effects template.

E9-41. Estimating Goodwill Impairment

On January 1 of the current year, Engel Company purchases 100% of Ball Company for $8.4 million. At the time of acquisition, the fair value of Ball's tangible net assets (excluding goodwill) is $8.1 million. Engel ascribes the excess of $300,000 to goodwill. Assume the fair value of Ball declines to $6.25 million and the fair value of Ball's tangible net assets is estimated at $6.15 million as of December 31.

LO3

a. Determine if the goodwill has become impaired and, if so, the amount of the impairment.
b. What impact does the impairment of goodwill have on Engel's financial statements?

E9-42. Allocating Purchase Price

Capri Holdings, the parent company of Michael Kors and Jimmy Choo, reports the following footnote to its 10-K report dated March 31, 2019.

LO3

Capri Holdings (CPRI)

On December 31, 2018, the Company completed the acquisition of Versace for a total enterprise value of approximately €1.753 billion (or approximately $2.005 billion). The following table summarizes the preliminary purchase price allocation of fair values of the assets acquired and liabilities assumed at the date of acquisition (in millions).

	December 31, 2018
Cash and cash equivalents	$ 41
Accounts receivable	82
Inventory	197
Other current assets	39
Current assets	359
Property and equipment	89
Goodwill	878
Brand	948
Customer relationships	203
Favorable lease	16
Deferred tax assets	24
Other assets	135
Total assets acquired	$2,652
Accounts payable	$ 144
Short-term debt	57
Other current liabilities	99
Current liabilities	300
Deferred tax liabilities	289
Other liabilities	54
Total liabilities assumed	$ 643
Less: Noncontrolling interest in joint ventures	$ 4
Fair value of net assets acquired	$2,005
Fair value of acquisition consideration	$2,005

a. Of the total assets acquired, what portion is allocated to net intangible assets? What amount was allocated to tangible assets such as inventory and PPE?
b. Are Versace's assets and liabilities reported on the Capri Holdings consolidated balance sheet at the book value or at the fair value on the date of the acquisition? Explain.
c. How are each of the intangible assets accounted for subsequent to the acquisition?
d. Describe the accounting for goodwill. Why is an impairment test difficult to apply?

E9-43. Constructing the Consolidated Balance Sheet at Acquisition

Easton Company acquires 100 percent of the outstanding voting shares of Harris Company. To obtain these shares, Easton pays $420,000 in cash and issues 5,000 of its $10 par value common stock. On this

LO3

date, Easton's stock has a fair value of $72 per share, and Harris's book value of stockholders' equity is $560,000. Easton is willing to pay $780,000 for a company with a book value of $560,000 because it believes that (1) Harris's buildings are undervalued by $80,000 and (2) Harris has an unrecorded patent that Easton values at $60,000. Easton considers the remaining balance sheet items to be fairly valued (no book-to-market difference). The remaining $80,000 of the purchase price is ascribed to corporate synergies and other general unidentifiable intangible assets (goodwill). The balance sheets at the acquisition date follow.

	Easton Company	Harris Company	Consolidating Adjustments	Consolidated
Cash.................	$ 168,000	$ 80,000		
Receivables	320,000	180,000		
Inventory..............	440,000	260,000		
Investment in Harris	780,000	—		
Land.................	200,000	120,000		
Buildings, net	800,000	220,000		
Equipment, net..........	240,000	100,000		_____
Total assets	$2,948,000	$960,000		========
Accounts payable........	$ 320,000	$ 60,000		
Long-term liabilities.......	760,000	340,000		
Common stock..........	1,000,000	80,000		
Additional paid-in capital. . .	148,000	—		
Retained earnings	720,000	480,000		_____
Total liabilities & equity....	$2,948,000	$960,000		========

a. Show the breakdown of the investment into the book value acquired, the excess of fair value over book value, and the portion of the investment representing goodwill.

b. Prepare the consolidating adjustments and the consolidated balance sheet on the date of acquisition.

c. How will the excess of the purchase price over book value acquired be treated in years subsequent to the acquisition?

LO3, 4   **E9-44.**   **Foreign Currency Translation Adjustment and Derivatives**

General Mills Inc.
(GIS)

General Mills reported the following statement of comprehensive income in its fiscal 2019 Form 10-K.

For 12 Months Ended ($ millions)	May 26, 2019	May 27, 2018	May 28, 2017
Net earnings, including earnings attributable to redeemable and noncontrolling interests	$1,786.2	$2,163.0	$1,701.1
Other comprehensive income (loss), net of tax:			
Foreign currency translation.......................	(82.8)	(37.0)	6.3
Net actuarial (loss) income.......................	(253.4)	140.1	197.9
Other fair value changes:			
Securities......................................	—	1.2	0.8
Hedge derivatives	12.1	(50.8)	53.3
Reclassification to earnings:			
Securities....................................	(2.0)	(5.1)	—
Hedge derivatives	0.9	17.4	(25.7)
Amortization of losses and prior service costs	84.6	117.6	122.5
Other comprehensive (loss) income, net of tax	(240.6)	183.4	355.1
Total comprehensive income	1,545.6	2,346.4	2,056.2
Comprehensive(loss) income attributable to redeemable and noncontrolling interests	(10.7)	70.5	31.0
Comprehensive income attributable to General Mills....	$1,556.3	$2,275.9	$2,025.2

Required

a. Comprehensive income for fiscal year ended May 26, 2019, includes a loss of $82.8 million related to foreign currency translation. Explain what this loss means.

b. On average, did the $US weaken or strengthen vis-à-vis the currencies of the companies' foreign subsidiaries?

    c. What was the cash portion of the foreign currency translation loss in fiscal year 2019?

    d. Comprehensive income for fiscal year ended May 26, 2019, includes a gain of $12.1 million related to hedge derivatives. Is this a fair value or a cash flow hedge?

    e. Provide four examples of hedging transactions General Mills might engage in.

    f. How did the cash flow hedges affect net income during the fiscal year ended May 26, 2019?

E9-45. **Hedging and Use of Derivatives**

    Intel reports the following in its Form 10-K for fiscal 2018.

LO4

Intel Corporation
(INTC)

Homework
MBC

> We are exposed to currency exchange risks of non-U.S.-dollar-denominated investments in debt instruments and loans receivable, and may economically hedge this risk with foreign currency contracts, such as currency forward contracts or currency interest rate swaps. Gains or losses on these non-U.S.-currency investments are generally offset by corresponding losses or gains on the related hedging instruments. We are exposed to currency exchange risks from our non-U.S.-dollar-denominated debt indebtedness and may use foreign currency contracts designated as cash flow hedges to manage this risk.
>
>   Substantially all of our revenue is transacted in U.S. dollars. However, a significant portion of our operating expenditures and capital purchases are incurred in other currencies, primarily the euro, the Japanese yen, the Israeli shekel, and the Chinese yuan. We have established currency risk management programs to protect against currency exchange rate risks associated with non-U.S. dollar forecasted future cash flows and existing non-U.S. dollar monetary assets and liabilities. We may also hedge currency risk arising from funding of foreign currency-denominated future investments. We may utilize foreign currency contracts, such as currency forwards or option contracts in these hedging programs.

Required

    a. Consider the first paragraph in Intel's footnote. Explain whether this describes fair value or cash flow hedges.

    b. Suppose, at year-end, there was an unrealized loss on Intel's currency forward contracts described in the first paragraph. How would Intel report the derivative on the balance sheet? How would the income statement be affected?

    c. Consider the second paragraph in Intel's footnote. Explain whether this describes fair value or cash flow hedges.

    d. Suppose, at year-end, there was an unrealized loss on Intel's currency forward contracts that hedge forecasted future cash flows as described in the second paragraph. How would Intel report the derivative on the balance sheet? How would the income statement be affected?

    e. What is hedge ineffectiveness and how does it affect Intel's income statement?

E9-46. **Hedging and Use of Derivatives**

    Ford Motor Company reports the following in its Form 10-K for fiscal 2018.

LO4

Ford Motor Company
(F)

> Commodity price risk is the possibility that our financial results could be worse than planned because of changes in the prices of commodities used in the production of motor vehicles, such as base metals (e.g., steel, copper, and aluminum), precious metals (e.g., palladium), energy (e.g., natural gas and electricity), and plastics/resins (e.g., polypropylene). Accordingly, our normal practice is to use derivative instruments, when available, to hedge the price risk with respect to forecasted purchases of certain commodities that we can economically hedge (primarily base metals and precious metals). In our hedging actions, we use derivative instruments commonly used by corporations to reduce commodity price risk (e.g., financially settled forward contracts).

Ford's statement of comprehensive income for 2018 follows.

$ millions	2016	2017	2018
Net income	$4,600	$7,757	$3,695
Other comprehensive income (loss), net of tax			
Foreign currency translation.	(1,024)	314	(523)
Marketable securities	(8)	(34)	(11)
Derivative instruments	219	(265)	183
Pension and other postretirement benefits.	56	37	(56)
Total other comprehensive income (loss), net of tax	(757)	52	(407)
Comprehensive income.	3,843	7,809	3,288
Less: Comprehensive income (loss) attributable to noncontrolling interests . . .	10	24	18
Comprehensive income attributable to Ford Motor Company.	$3,833	$7,785	$3,270

Required

a. What sort of risks does Ford hedge?

b. Ford describes its hedging strategy. What sort of hedges are these, cash flow or fair value? Explain.

c. The statement of comprehensive income discloses a line item labeled "Derivative instruments." What does this line item represent?

d. The comprehensive income (loss) from derivatives instruments is $219 million for 2016, $(265) million for 2017, and $183 million for 2018. What can we conclude about the fair value of the derivatives for each of these years?

LO1   **E9-47.**   **Interpreting Graphical Data to Assess Investments**

The graphics below include data for all S&P 500 information-technology companies with positive equity for 2008 to 2018. Access the dashboard at the **myBusinessCourse** website to answer the requirements.

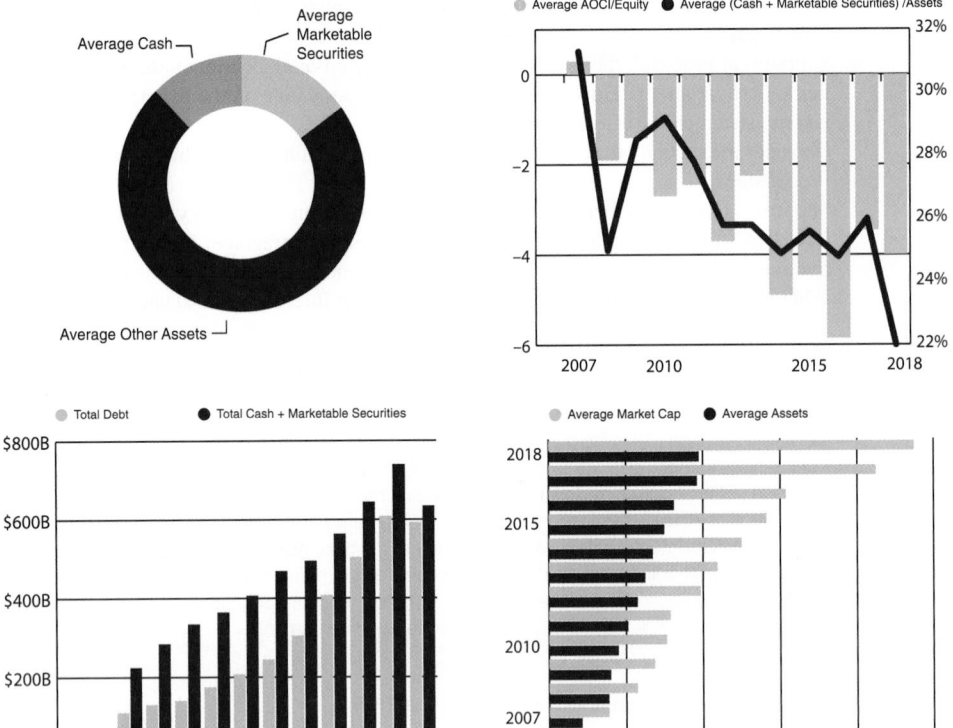

Required

a. Consider the pie chart. Explain what the graph depicts. What is included in the black portion of the graphic? In what year is the proportion of Cash the smallest? *Hint*: Interact with data in the dashboard to answer this question.

b. The bar-line graphic (top right panel) reports the average AOCI as a proportion of equity, by year. What do we observe about the magnitude of AOCI across the 11 years? Does the average firm have unrealized gains or losses? What does the line in this graphic measure? Does it reveal any deeper understanding about the magnitude of AOCI?

c. Consider the vertical bar chart that depicts total debt and total liquid assets (the aggregate for all the companies in the data set) (bottom left panel). In what year was the total debt outstanding at its peak? What amount of debt was outstanding?

d. Consider the vertical bar chart (bottom left panel) and compare the aggregate total debt and total liquid assets. Interpret the trend. What two or three conclusions can we make from this graphic? Does the relation between the two measures hold true for all firms in the dataset?

e. The horizontal bar graph (bottom right panel) plots total assets and market cap over time. What trend do we observe over time? What is the relation between the two metrics over time? Provide two or three explanations for what we observe.

Problems

P9-48. **Analyzing and Interpreting Disclosures on Equity Method Investments**

General Mills Inc. invests in a number of joint ventures to manufacture and distribute its food products, as discussed in the following footnote to its 10-K report for the fiscal year ended May 26, 2019.

LO2
General Mills Inc. (GIS)

INVESTMENTS IN UNCONSOLIDATED JOINT VENTURES

We have a 50 percent equity interest in Cereal Partners Worldwide (CPW), which manufactures and markets ready-to-eat cereal products in more than 130 countries outside the United States and Canada. CPW also markets cereal bars in several European countries and manufactures private label cereals for customers in the United Kingdom. We have guaranteed a portion of CPW's debt and its pension obligation in the United Kingdom.

We also have a 50 percent equity interest in Häagen-Dazs Japan, Inc. (HDJ). This joint venture manufactures and markets Häagen-Dazs ice cream products and frozen novelties.

Results from our CPW and HDJ joint ventures are reported for the 12 months ended March 31. Joint venture related balance sheet activity follows:

$ millions	May 26, 2019	May 27, 2018
Cumulative investments	$452.9	$499.6
Goodwill and other intangibles	472.1	488.7
Aggregate advances included in cumulative investments . . .	249.0	295.3

Joint venture earnings and cash flow activity follows:

Fiscal Year ($ millions)	2019	2018	2017
Sales to joint ventures	$ 4.2	$ 7.4	$ 7.0
Net advances (repayments)	(0.1)	17.3	(3.3)
Dividends received	86.7	113.2	75.6

Summary combined financial information for the joint ventures on a 100 percent basis follows:

Fiscal Year ($ millions)	2019	2018	2017
Net sales			
CPW.	$1,674.7	$1,734.0	$1.648.4
HDJ.	396.2	430.4	435.1
Total net sales	2,043.9	2,164.4	2,083.5
Gross margin	744.4	853.6	865.9
Earnings before income taxes	155.4	216.2	243.3
Earnings after income taxes.	111.9	176.7	190.3

$ millions	May 26, 2019	May 27, 2018
Current assets	$ 895.6	$ 938.5
Noncurrent assets	839.2	902.5
Current liabilities.	1,517.3	1,579.3
Noncurrent liabilities.	77.1	72.6

Required

a. How does General Mills account for its investments in joint ventures? How are these investments reflected on General Mills' balance sheet, and how, generally, is income recognized on these investments? Estimate the amount of income that General Mills included in its 2019 income statement as Equity method income.

b. Does the $117.5 million investment reported on General Mills' balance sheet sufficiently reflect the assets and liabilities required to conduct these operations? Explain. *Note:* The $452.9 million disclosed includes cash advances to the joint venture partners of $335.4 million. The net $117.5 million represents the equity method investment.

c. Do you believe the liabilities of these joint venture entities represent actual obligations of General Mills? Explain.

d. What potential problem(s) does equity method accounting present for analysis purposes?

LO3   **P9-49.**   **Analyzing and Interpreting Disclosures on Consolidations**

Snap-on Incorporated
(SNA)

Snap-on Incorporated consists of two business units: the manufacturing company (parent corporation) and a wholly-owned finance subsidiary. These two units are consolidated in Snap-on's 10-K report. Following is a supplemental disclosure Snap-on includes in its 10-K report that shows the separate balance sheets of the parent and the subsidiary. This supplemental disclosure is not mandated under GAAP but is voluntarily reported by Snap-on as useful information for investors and creditors. Using this disclosure, answer the following questions.

Required

a. Do the parent and subsidiary companies each maintain their own financial statements? Explain. Why does GAAP require consolidation instead of separate financial statements of individual companies?

b. What is the balance of Investments in Financial Services as of December 31, 2018, on the parent's balance sheet? What is the equity balance of the financial services subsidiary to which this relates as of December 31, 2018? Do you see a relation? Will this relation always exist?

c. Refer to your answer for part *a*. How does the equity method of accounting for the investment in the subsidiary obscure the actual financial condition of the parent company as compared with the consolidated financial statements?

d. Recall that the parent company uses the equity method of accounting for its investment in the subsidiary and that this account is eliminated in the consolidation process. What is the relation between consolidated net income and the net income of the parent company? Explain.

e. What is the implication for the consolidated balance sheet if the fair value of the financial services subsidiary (subsequent to acquisition) is greater than the book value of its stockholders' equity?

$ millions	Operations* 2018	Operations* 2017	Financial Services 2018	Financial Services 2017
Assets				
Current assets				
Cash and cash equivalents	$ 140.5	$ 91.8	$ 0.4	$ 0.2
Intersegment receivables	15.1	17.1	—	—
Trade and other accounts receivable—net	692.1	674.9	0.5	0.7
Finance receivables—net	—	—	518.5	505.4
Contract receivables—net	6.6	9.4	91.7	87.4
Inventories—net	673.8	638.8	—	—
Prepaid expenses and other assets	100.2	117.6	0.5	0.7
Total current assets	1,628.3	1,549.6	611.6	594.4
Property and equipment—net	493.5	482.4	1.6	2.0
Investment in Financial Services	329.5	317.4	—	—
Deferred income tax assets	45.8	25.2	18.9	26.8
Intersegment long-term notes receivable	701.3	583.7	—	—
Long-term finance receivables—net	—	—	1,074.4	1,039.2
Long-term contract receivables—net	11.9	13.2	333.0	309.4
Goodwill	902.2	924.1	—	—
Other intangibles—net	232.9	253.7	—	—
Other assets	51.9	63.1	0.1	—
Total assets	$4,397.3	$4,212.4	$2,039.6	$1,971.8

continued

continued from previous page

$ millions	Operations* 2018	Operations* 2017	Financial Services 2018	Financial Services 2017
Liabilities and Equity				
Current liabilities				
Notes payable and current maturities of long-term debt....	$ 186.3	$ 183.2	$ —	$ 250.0
Accounts payable	199.6	177.1	1.5	1.1
Intersegment payables	—	—	15.1	17.1
Accrued benefits	52.0	55.8	—	—
Accrued compensation	66.8	67.8	4.7	3.7
Franchisee deposits	67.5	66.5	—	—
Other accrued liabilities.................................	355.4	366.0	26.1	29.7
Total current liabilities	927.6	916.4	47.4	301.6
Long-term debt and intersegment long-term debt.........	—	—	1,647.3	1,337.3
Deferred income tax liabilities........................	41.4	28.4	—	—
Retiree health care benefits	31.8	36.0	—	—
Pension liabilities	171.3	158.9	—	—
Other long-term liabilities	106.6	100.4	15.4	15.5
Total liabilities	1,278.7	1,240.1	1,710.1	1,654.4
Total shareholders' equity attributable to Snap-on Inc....	3,098.8	2,953.9	329.5	317.4
Noncontrolling interests	19.8	18.4	—	—
Total equity	3,118.6	2,972.3	329.5	317.4
Total liabilities and equity	$4,397.3	$4,212.4	$2,039.6	$1,971.8

*Snap-on Operations include Financial Services using the equity method.

IFRS Applications

I9-50. **Allocating Purchase Price Including Intangibles**

LO3
Deutsche Telekom AG

Deutsche Telekom AG, headquartered in Bonn, Germany, is the largest telecommunications company in Europe. The company uses IFRS to prepare its financial statements. Assume that during 2019, Deutsche Telekom acquired a controlling interest in **Hellenic Telecommunications Organization S.A.** (Hellenic). The table below shows the pre- and post-acquisition values of Hellenic's assets.

€ millions	Fair Value at Acquisition Date	Carrying Amounts Immediately Prior to Acquisition
Cash and cash equivalents	€ 1,558	€ 1,558
Noncurrent assets	195	158
Other assets.................	1,716	1,716
Current assets..............	3,469	3,432
Intangible assets.............	5,348	4,734
Goodwill	2,500	3,835
Property, plant, and equipment...	6,965	5,581
Other assets.................	823	782
Noncurrent assets...........	15,636	14,932
Assets....................	€19,105	€18,364

Required

a. At the acquisition, which measurement does the company use, fair value or carrying value, to record the acquired tangible and intangible assets on its consolidated balance sheet?

b. At the acquisition date, why is fair value of goodwill less than its carrying value?

c. What are some possible reasons why intangible assets increased in value at the acquisition date?

d. Describe accounting for goodwill. Why is an impairment test challenging?

LO2
BHP Billiton Limited
(BHP)

I9-51.   Interpreting Equity Method Investment Footnotes

BHP Billiton Limited discovers, acquires, develops, and markets natural resources worldwide. Head-quartered in Melbourne Australia, the company explores for, develops, produces, and markets oil and gas in the Gulf of Mexico, Western Australia, and Trinidad and Tobago. It also explores for copper, silver, lead, zinc, molybdenum, uranium, gold, iron ore, and metallurgical and thermal coal. The company's 2018 annual report included the following disclosure related to its many equity-method investments.

The movement for the year in the Group's investments accounted for using the equity method is as follows:

Year ended 30 June 2018 (US$M)	Investment in Associates
At the beginning of the financial year	$2,448
Share of operating profit of equity accounted investments. . . .	656
Investment in equity accounted investments	62
Dividends received from equity accounted investments.	(693)
At the end of the financial year.	$2,473

BHP reports additional information for its equity method investments including the following information pertaining to two specific equity method investments. During the year, these two associates, Cerrejon and Antamina, reported net profit of $576 million and $1,613 million, respectively.

Shareholdings in Associates	Country of Incorporation/ Principal Place of Business	Principal Activity	Reporting Date	Ownership Interest 2018%
Carbones del Cerrejón LLC (Cerrejón)	Anguilla/ Colombia	Coal mining in Colombia	31 December	33.33
Compañía Minera Antamina S.A. (Antamina)	Peru	Copper and zinc mining	31 December	33.75

Required

a. The company uses the equity method to account for its investment in associates and joint ventures. Why is this the appropriate method for the two investments disclosed in the footnotes?

b. What total amount of equity method income did BHP include in its 2018 income statement? What amount did BHP include from the two specific associates, Cerrejon and Antamina?

c. Explain why dividends received of $693 million are shown as a decrease to the equity method investment account.

d. How does the use of the equity method impact Billiton's ROE and its RNOA components (net operating asset turnover and net operating profit margin) as compared to the case of consolidation?

Management Applications

LO1, 2, 3   **MA9-52.   Determining the Reporting of an Investment**

Assume your company acquires 20% of the outstanding common stock of APEX Software as an investment. You also have an option to purchase the remaining 80%. APEX is developing software (its only activity) it hopes to eventually package and sell to customers. You do not intend to exercise your option unless its software product reaches commercial feasibility. APEX has employed your software engineers to assist in the development efforts, and you are integrally involved in its software design. Your ownership interest is significant enough to give you influence over APEX's software design specifications.

Required

a. Describe the financial statement effects of the three possible methods to accounting for this investment (fair value, equity, and consolidation).

    b. What method of accounting is appropriate for this investment (fair value, equity, or consolidation)? Explain.

Ongoing Project

(This ongoing project began in Module 1 and continues through most of the book; even if previous segments were not completed, the requirements are still applicable to any business analysis.) Company analysis should include an assessment of the companies' various investments, transactions during the year, the effect on net income, and the balance sheet results at year-end.

1. *Investments in Marketable Securities.* To analyze nonoperating investments in marketable debt and equity securities, consider the following questions that will help us understand both companies' level of excess cash and how they invest it:

   - What is the magnitude of the investments in common-size terms? Has this changed over time? What proportion is short-term versus long-term?
   - What types of investments does the company hold—debt, equity, private-company equity?
   - What explanation do the companies provide for their level of investments? Does the MD&A section of the Form 10-K discuss plans for expansion or other strategic initiatives that would require cash?

2. *Investments with Significant Influence.* Our goal is to assess how the companies structure their operations to better understand their strategies.

   - What types of investments does the company have: associates, joint ventures, or other?
   - Why does the company engage in equity-method investments; what is their intent? Read the MD&A section of the Form 10-K and the financial statement footnotes.
   - What are the main equity-method investments? (IFRS: Does the company have any proportionate consolidation?) How large are these in common-size terms?
   - Have there been changes during the year in terms of new investments or disposals? The MD&A and footnotes will be instructive.
   - Are the equity method investments profitable? Do they provide cash dividends?

3. *Investments with Control (Consolidations).* Most multinational corporations are consolidated entities that structure their operations to meet many goals, including legal requirements, tax planning, and foreign ownership restrictions. Financial statements will not report information to completely comprehend all these intricacies; the goal here is to understand the companies' structure at a very high level.

   - What types of companies does the company control? What are the main subsidiaries?
   - What strategic advantages do these subsidiaries afford? Foreign? Domestic? Supplier or distributors? Read the MD&A section of the Form 10-K and the financial statement footnotes to learn about strategic investment and plans for the future.
   - Have there been new investments during the year? How were these acquisitions financed (debt, equity)? Did these yield intangible assets including goodwill? What proportion of the acquisition price was allocated to intangibles?
   - Were there disposals during the year? Why were these made? Did the transaction cause a gain or loss?
   - Gauge the significance of previously acquired intangibles in common-size terms. Have any been impaired during the year?
   - If the company reports subsidiary-level profit, which are the most profitable? The least?

Solutions to Review Problems

Review 9-1—Solution

a.

MS 22,000
  Cash 22,000

MS
22,000	

Cash
	22,000

Cash 2,500
  DI 2,500

Cash
2,500	

DI
	2,500

MS 5,000
  UG 5,000

MS
5,000	

UG
	5,000

Cash 27,000
  MS 27,000

Cash
27,000	

MS
	27,000

	Balance Sheet							Income Statement		
Transaction	Cash Asset	+	Noncash Assets	=	Liabil- ities	+	Contrib. Capital	+	Earned Capital	Rev- enues	−	Expen- ses	=	Net Income
1. Purchased 1,000 shares of Juniper common stock for $22 cash per share	−22,000 Cash		+22,000 Marketable Securities	=							−		=	
2. Received cash dividend of $2.50 per share on Juniper common stock	+2,500 Cash			=					+2,500 Retained Earnings	+2,500 Dividend Income	−		=	+2,500
3. Year-end market price of Juniper common stock is $27 per share			+5,000 Marketable Securities	=					+5,000 Retained Earnings	+5,000 Unrealized Gain	−		=	+5,000
4. Sold 1,000 shares of Juniper common stock for $27,000 cash	+27,000 Cash		−27,000 Marketable Securities	=							−		=	

b. Microsoft's investment portfolio includes both debt and equity securities. The balance sheet reports the investments at fair value totaling $135,630 million (which Microsoft calls "Recorded Basis" in the footnote).

c. Less than 1% of the total portfolio is equity securities ($1,305 million/$135,630 million).

d. Microsoft's investment portfolio has a cost of $136,667 million and a fair value of $135,630 million. Most of the unrealized loss related to U.S. government bonds whose market values have declined as interest rates have risen. These unrealized losses are unlikely to be realized, however, if the bonds are held to maturity as they will mature at par value.

Review 9-2—Solution

a.

EMI 50,000
  Cash 50,000

EMI
50,000	

Cash
	50,000

Cash 10,000
  EMI 10,000

Cash
10,000	

EMI
	10,000

EMI 30,000
  EI 30,000

EMI
30,000	

EI
	30,000

	Balance Sheet							Income Statement		
Transaction	Cash Asset	+	Noncash Assets	=	Liabil- ities	+	Contrib. Capital	+	Earned Capital	Rev- enues	−	Expen- ses	=	Net Income
1. Purchased 5,000 shares of LookSmart common stock at $10 cash per share; these shares reflect 30% ownership	−50,000 Cash		+50,000 Investment in LookSmart	=							−		=	
2. Received a $2 per share cash dividend on LookSmart stock	+10,000 Cash		−10,000 Investment in LookSmart	=							−		=	
3. Record 30% share of the $100,000 income reported by LookSmart			+30,000 Investment in LookSmart	=					+30,000 Retained Earnings	+30,000 Equity Income	−		=	+30,000

continued

continued from previous page

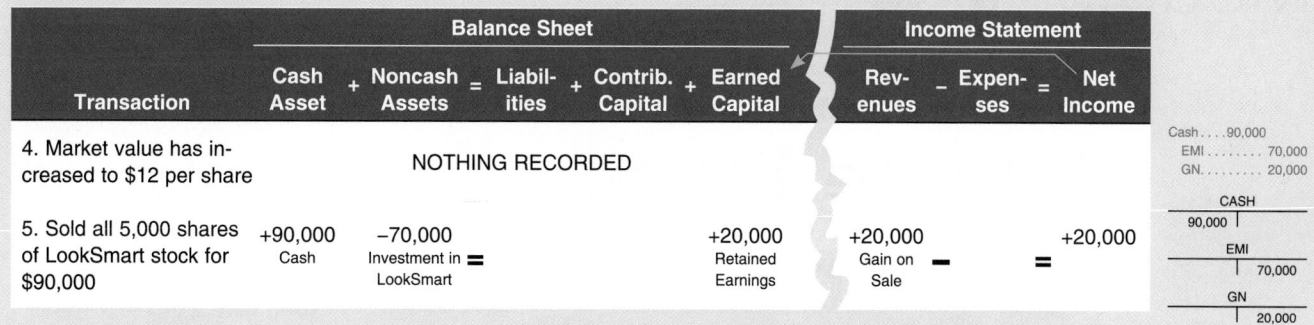

Transaction	Balance Sheet					Income Statement		
	Cash Asset	+ Noncash Assets	= Liabil- ities	+ Contrib. Capital	+ Earned Capital	Rev- enues	– Expen- ses	= Net Income
4. Market value has increased to $12 per share	NOTHING RECORDED							
5. Sold all 5,000 shares of LookSmart stock for $90,000	+90,000 Cash	–70,000 Investment in LookSmart =			+20,000 Retained Earnings	+20,000 Gain on Sale –		= +20,000

Cash....90,000
EMI........ 70,000
GN......... 20,000

CASH
90,000 |

EMI
| 70,000

GN
| 20,000

b. Intel owns 49% of IMFT. It will, therefore, report $367.5 million of equity income and its equity investment will be carried at $1,960 million on its balance sheet (assuming the investment was purchased at book value).

c. The investment must be written down to fair value if the decline in value is deemed to be other than temporary. In this case, Intel determined that the expected cash flows for IMFT had declined and are expected to remain at lower levels indefinitely. Consequently, it reduced the carrying amount of its equity investment and recorded an impairment charge for the write-down, which affected net income for the year of the write-down.

Review 9-3—Solution

	Intel (Parent)	EarthLink (Subsidiary)	Consolidating Adjustments	Consolidated
Current assets	$1,000,000	$100,000		$1,100,000
Investment in EarthLink	600,000	—	(600,000)	
PPE, net	3,000,000	400,000	100,000	3,500,000
Intangible assets (patents)	—	—	25,000	25,000
Goodwill	—	—	75,000	75,000
Total assets	$4,600,000	$500,000		$4,700,000
Liabilities.	$1,000,000	$100,000		$1,100,000
Contributed capital	2,000,000	200,000	(200,000)	2,000,000
Retained earnings	1,600,000	200,000	(200,000)	1,600,000
Total liabilities and equity	$4,600,000	$500,000		$4,700,000

Explanation: The $600,000 investment account is eliminated together with the $400,000 book value of Earth-Link's equity to which Intel's investment relates. The remaining $200,000 consists of the additional $100,000 in PPE assets, $25,000 in unrecorded intangibles, and $75,000 in goodwill from expected corporate synergies. Following these adjustments, the balance sheet items are summed to yield the consolidated balance sheet.

Review 9-4—Solution

1. PepsiCo used derivatives to hedge foreign currency risk, interest rate risk, and price risk in the commodities it uses to produce its products.

2. PepsiCo employs both fair value and cash flow hedges. We see this by looking at the column headings in the table, both fair value and cash flow hedges are tabulated.

3. PepsiCo would likely hedge sugar (for sodas), corn and wheat (for snack products), and aluminum (for cans), among other types of commodities. Gains and losses on these derivatives would be included in cost of goods sold. The footnote corroborates that conclusion.

Module 10

Leases, Pensions, and Income Taxes

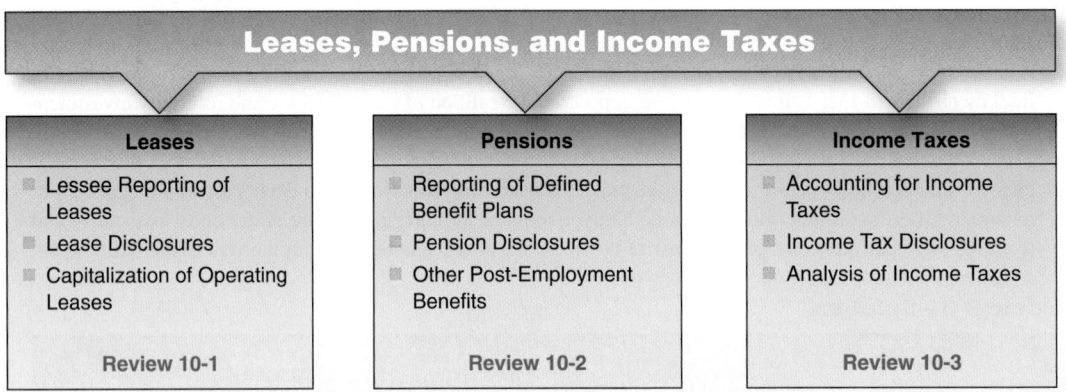

Leases, Pensions, and Income Taxes

Leases	Pensions	Income Taxes
▪ Lessee Reporting of Leases	▪ Reporting of Defined Benefit Plans	▪ Accounting for Income Taxes
▪ Lease Disclosures	▪ Pension Disclosures	▪ Income Tax Disclosures
▪ Capitalization of Operating Leases	▪ Other Post-Employment Benefits	▪ Analysis of Income Taxes
Review 10-1	Review 10-2	Review 10-3

We analyze three important items that affect financial statements.

▪ Leases
  ○ New lease accounting standard that requires firms to recognize on the balance sheet most leases.
  ○ Lease accounting disclosures.
▪ Pensions and other post-employment benefit plans
  ○ Recognition of pension assets and obligations on the balance sheet and income statement.
  ○ How companies use current pension accounting standards to smooth effects of pension expense.
  ○ Sufficiency of pension plan assets to cover promised pension payments to retirees.
  ○ Effects of changing estimates used to compute pension liability and expense.

  ○ Mark-to-market pension accounting and pension settlements.
▪ Income taxes
  ○ Balance sheet and income statement differences between U.S. GAAP and tax regulations.
  ○ Deferred tax assets and liabilities.
  ○ How changes in the valuation allowance for deferred tax assets affect net income.
  ○ Income tax footnote disclosures.
  ○ Financial reporting consequences of the U.S. Tax Cuts and Jobs Act of 2017.
▪ The dashboard below conveys financial information for Module 10 focus companies: **Microsoft**, **Deere** and **HP**.

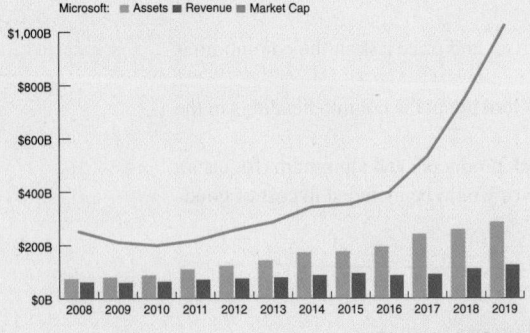

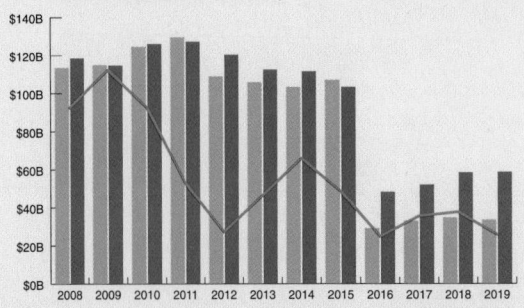

Road Map

LO	Learning Objective | Topics	Page	eLecture	Guided Example	Assignments
10–1	**Analyze and interpret lease disclosures.** Lessee Reporting :: New Lease Rules :: Footnote Disclosure :: Capitalization	10-3	e10–1	Review 10-1	1, 2, 3, 14, 15, 20, 28, 29, 30, 36, 38, 39, 40
10–2	**Analyze and interpret pension disclosures.** Reporting of Defined Benefit Pensions :: Balance Sheet :: Income Statement :: Fair Value Accounting :: Footnote Disclosure—Pension Plan Assets and PBO :: Future Cash Flows :: Profit and Analysis Implications :: Other Post-Employment Benefits	10-11	e10–2	Review 10-2	4, 5, 6, 7, 12, 16, 17, 18, 19, 21, 26, 27, 31, 32, 33, 37, 41, 42, 46
10–3	**Analyze and interpret income tax reporting.** Timing Differences :: Deferred Tax Assets and Liabilities :: Disclosures for Income Taxes :: Analysis of Income Taxes	10-24	e10–3	Review 10-3	8, 9, 10, 11, 13, 22, 23, 24, 25, 34, 35, 43, 44, 45, 47

Leases

eLectures **LO1**
MBC Analyze and interpret lease disclosures.

A lease is a contract between the owner of an asset (the **lessor**) and the party desiring to use that asset (the **lessee**). Since this is a private arrangement between two willing parties, it is governed only by applicable commercial law and can include whatever provisions the parties negotiate. Leases generally include the following terms.

- Lessor grants the lessee the unrestricted right to use the asset during the lease term.
- Lessee agrees to maintain the asset and make periodic payments to the lessor. Lease payments are set at an amount that yields an acceptable return on the lessor's investment in the leased asset, commensurate with the lessee's credit rating.
- Title to the asset remains with the lessor, who usually takes physical possession of the asset at lease-end unless the lessee negotiates the right to purchase the asset at its market value or other predetermined price.

Leases serve as a financing vehicle similar to a secured bank loan. However, leasing has a few advantages compared to bank financing.

- Leases often require less equity investment by the lessee (borrower). Leases usually require the first lease payment be made at the inception of the lease. For a 60-month lease, this amounts to a 1/60 (1.7%) investment by the lessee, compared with a bank loan typically requiring 20%–30% equity investment by the borrower.
- Because leases are contracts between two parties, their terms can be structured to meet both parties' needs. For example, a lease can allow variable payments to match the lessee's seasonal cash inflows or have graduated payments for start-up companies.
- Leasing can be utilized to finance the acquisition of any asset, including vehicles, equipment, and real estate.

The ability to finance a greater proportion of the asset's cost, coupled with the flexibility that the leasing contract provides, has made this a popular form of financing, amounting to over $1 trillion in equipment financing alone (Source: Equipment Leasing & Finance Foundation, 2017).

New Lease Reporting Standard

The FASB issued a new lease accounting standard effective for all U.S. companies in 2019. Under the pre-2019 accounting standard, companies' balance sheets did not include the lease assets and lease liabilities if the company classified the lease as an "operating" lease (see the Practice Insight box "Delta Airlines Prospective Adoption of 2019 Lease Accounting Standard"). Under current GAAP, these operating lease assets and liabilities are now included on companies' balance sheets.

The new standard requires companies classify all leases as either a finance lease or an operating lease.

- **Finance leases** transfer **control of the lease asset** to the lessee. Finance leases are effectively like purchasing the asset and financing the purchase with a collateralized loan.
- **Operating leases** transfer **control of the use of the lease asset**, but not the asset itself. Any lease of 12 months or more not classified as a finance lease is classified as an operating lease.

As they adopt the new standard, companies must choose between two transition options.

1. **Retroactive adoption:** implement the new standard in the current year and restate all prior periods presented in the financial statements. This means that the current-year financial statements and the comparative financial statements (the prior year balance sheet and the two prior years' income statements) all conform to the new standard.
2. **Prospective adoption:** implement the new standard without restatement of the prior periods. This means that the company reports current-period leasing activities under the *new* accounting standard and leasing activities in the prior periods under the *old* standard.

Microsoft chose the first (retroactive) approach and restated its prior year's financial statements in the year of adoption. Consequently, Microsoft's current balance sheet reports both operating and finance leases under the current lease accounting standard for both years. Thus, we can directly compare the financial statements in the current 10-K, across the years presented.

Delta Airlines chose the second (prospective) approach. (See the Practice Insight box "Delta Airlines Prospective Adoption of the 2019 Lease Accounting Standard"). As a result of its prospective adoption of the new standard, Delta's fiscal 2019 financial statements include both the new lease-accounting standard (2019 numbers) and the old standard (2018 and 2017 numbers). Unlike for Microsoft, we cannot directly compare the financial statement in Delta's current 10-K, across the years.

Because companies were free to decide whether they would use the retroactive approach or the prospective approach, financial statements will reflect a mix of old and new standards for the next few years. Consequently, it's important for us to understand both lease standards and this module addresses both.

We begin with a general discussion of lease accounting and then use Microsoft Corporation to illustrate the accounting mechanics.

Lessee Reporting Example—Microsoft Corporation

Companies report all leases on the balance sheet as both lease assets and lease liabilities. As companies describe their leases in footnotes, they distinguish between operating and finance leases. Microsoft provides the following lease disclosure in its 2019 10-K.

Leases We have operating and finance leases for datacenters, corporate offices, research and development facilities, retail stores, and certain equipment. Our leases have remaining lease terms of 1 year to 20 years, some of which include options to extend the leases for up to 5 years, and some of which include options to terminate the leases within 1 year... We determine if an arrangement is a lease at inception. Operating leases are included in operating lease right-of-use ("ROU") assets, other current liabilities, and operating lease liabilities in our consolidated balance sheets. Finance leases are included in property and equipment, other current liabilities, and other long-term liabilities in our consolidated balance sheets. ROU assets represent our right to use an underlying asset for the lease term and lease liabilities represent our obligation to make lease payments arising from the lease. Operating lease ROU assets and liabilities are recognized at commencement date based on the present value of lease payments over the lease term. As most of our leases do not provide an implicit rate, we generally use our incremental borrowing rate based on the estimated rate of interest for collateralized borrowing over a similar term of the lease payments at commencement date. The operating lease ROU asset also includes any lease payments made and excludes lease incentives. Our lease terms may include options to extend or terminate the lease when it is reasonably certain that we will exercise that option. Lease expense for lease payments is recognized on a straight-line basis over the lease term.

On its balance sheet, Microsoft reports assets relating to both operating and finance leases.

June 30 ($ in millions)	2019	2018
Assets		
Current assets		
Cash and cash equivalents	$ 11,356	$ 11,946
Short-term investments	122,463	121,822
Total cash, cash equivalents, and short-term investments.	133,819	133,768
Accounts receivable, net of allowance for doubtful accounts of $411 and $377	29,524	26,481
Inventories	2,063	2,662
Other	10,146	6,751
Total current assets	175,552	169,662
Property and equipment, net of accumulated depreciation of $35,330 and $29,223	36,477	29,460
Operating lease right-of-use assets	7,379	6,686
Equity investments	2,649	1,862
Goodwill	42,026	35,683
Intangible assets, net	7,750	8,053
Other long-term assets.	14,723	7,442
Total assets.	$286,556	$258,848

Finance leases

Operating leases

Microsoft includes the finance lease assets in PPE and reports the operating lease right-of-use assets (highlighted) on a separate line item. Microsoft reports the lease liabilities on its 2019 balance sheet.

June 30 ($ in millions)	2019	2018
Liabilities and stockholders' equity		
Current liabilities		
Accounts payable.	$ 9,382	$ 8,617
Current portion of long-term debt.	5,516	3,998
Accrued compensation	6,830	6,103
Short-term income taxes	5,665	2,121
Short-term unearned revenue	32,676	28,905
Other	9,351	8,744
Total current liabilities.	69,420	58,488
Long-term debt.	66,662	72,242
Long-term income taxes.	29,612	30,265
Long-term unearned revenue.	4,530	3,815
Deferred income taxes	233	541
Operating lease liabilities	6,188	5,568
Other long-term liabilities	7,581	5,211
Total liabilities.	184,226	176,130
Stockholders' equity		
Common stock and paid-in capital – shares authorized 24,000;		
outstanding 7,643 and 7,677	78,520	71,223
Retained earnings	24,150	13,682
Accumulated other comprehensive loss	(340)	(2,187)
Total stockholders' equity.	102,330	82,718
Total liabilities and stockholders' equity	$286,556	$258,848

(Balance sheet annotations: "Operating and Finance leases" → Current portion of long-term debt; "Finance leases" → Long-term debt; "Operating leases" → Operating lease liabilities.)

Under the pre-2019 accounting standard, operating leases were *omitted* from the balance sheet. With over $7 billion in operating leases, Microsoft's balance sheet demonstrates that these omissions can be large. Under the old standard, assets and liabilities were both understated, which markedly affected profitability, asset use, and especially leverage ratios. The analyst community lobbied FASB for many years to correct this accounting issue, and it was finally resolved by the passage of the new standard.

We now turn to lease accounting: how operating and financing leases are reported on the balance sheet, the ways lease costs are reflected as expenses in the income statement, and how these lease costs affect the statement of cash flows.

Lease Accounting

The first step in lease accounting is to determine whether a lease is operating or financing. If the lease is economically similar to the purchase of an asset, the company must classify the lease as financing. In particular, finance leases meet one or more of the following criteria.

- **Transfer of ownership.** The lease transfers ownership of the underlying asset to the lessee by the end of the lease term.
- **Purchase option.** The lease grants the lessee an option to purchase the underlying asset that the lessee is reasonably certain to exercise.
- **Lease term.** The lease term is for a major part of the remaining economic life of the underlying asset.
- **Present value.** The present value of the sum of the lease payments and any residual value guaranteed by the lessee that is not already included in the lease payments equals or exceeds substantially all of the fair value of the underlying asset.
- **Specialized asset.** The underlying asset is of such a specialized nature that it is expected to have no alternative use to the lessor at the end of the lease term.

Any lease of 12 months or more not classified as a finance lease is classified as an operating lease.

Lease Accounting and the Balance Sheet

Both operating and finance leases are recognized on the balance sheet.

■ A **lease liability** is recognized at the present value of the remaining lease payments (see below).

■ A **right-of-use asset** is recognized at an amount calculated as follows.

> Amount of the lease obligation
> + Lease payments made to the lessor at or before the lease commencement date
> − Lease incentives received from the lessor
> + Initial direct costs of right-of-use asset incurred by the lessee.
> _____
> = Right-of-use asset

This means the right-of-use asset will often be greater than the related lease liability at inception of the lease. (The difference is the net cash paid for the upfront costs.) The year the company adopts the new accounting standard is considered to be the year of inception for preexisting operating leases.

The balance sheet presents lease liabilities and right-of-use assets separately (not the net amount). Finance lease assets are typically included in PPE, and lease liabilities are included with debt. Operating lease assets and liabilities are each reported in a separate line item if material.

The amount reported on the balance sheet for the lease obligation and right-of-use lease asset relates to the payments that the company will make under the lease terms. Footnotes also disclose a schedule of such lease payments for both operating and finance leases. For example, Microsoft discloses the following in its 2019 10-K.

Maturities of lease liabilities were as follows:

Year Ending June 30 (In millions)	Operating Leases	Finance Leases
2020	$1,678	$ 591
2021	1,438	616
2022	1,235	626
2023	1,036	631
2024	839	641
Thereafter	2,438	5,671
Total lease payments	8,664	8,776
Less imputed interest	(961)	(2,202)
Total	$7,703	$6,574

Total forecasted lease payments for operating leases are $8,664 million in FY2019. However, Microsoft's balance sheet includes liabilities of $7,703 million (current liability of $1,515 million relating to payments to be made in the upcoming year and long-term liability of $6,188 million), which is the present value of the forecasted lease payments discounted at 3.15%. Exhibit 10.1 illustrates the present value calculation. The Business Insight box below explains the discount rate. (The 3.15% discount rate used in this example is consistent with the assumed payment stream, an approach commonly used in practice. Microsoft's actual discount rate is 3%, as disclosed in its 2019 10-K.)

Exhibit 10.1 ■ Present Value of Operating Lease Payments ($ millions)				
	A	B	C	D	E
1	Year	Operating Lease Payment	Discount Factor ($i = 0.0315$)	Present Value	Cell Formula
2	1	$1,678	0.96946	$1,627	=PV(B10,A2,0,−B2)
3	2	1,438	0.93986	1,352	=PV(B10,A3,0,−B3)
4	3	1,235	0.91116	1,125	=PV(B10,A4,0,−B4)
5	4	1,036	0.88333	915	=PV(B10,A5,0,−B5)
6	5	839	0.85636	718	=PV(B10,A6,0,−B6)
7	>5	$2,438 ($839 × 2.906 years)	2.73602 × 0.85636	1,966	=PV(B10,B9,−B6,0,0)*PV(B10,A6,0,−1)
8	Total payments	$8,664		$7,703	=SUM(D2:D7)
9	Remaining life	2.906			=B7/B6
10	Discount rate	3.15%			

The total *operating* lease liability of $7,703 million consists of a portion maturing in the next year, which is reported as a current liability and the remainder, reported as a long-term liability, as highlighted in Microsoft's balance sheet above. The table above shows a current portion of $1,627 million, slightly higher than the $1,515 million Microsoft reports in its footnotes. The difference arises because Microsoft uses a specific discount rate for each lease, whereas we use an average of 3.15% for all leases.

Microsoft uses the same approach to compute the present value of its forecasted *finance* lease payments and reports $6,574 million on the balance sheet. (See "Maturities of lease liabilities" table above.) Of the total finance lease liability, Microsoft includes $317 million in the Current portion of long-term debt and $6,257 million in Long-term debt (disclosed in footnotes). In subsequent years, these leases will be reported at the present value of the remaining lease payments, and are included with any new leases on the balance sheet.

Business Insight ■ **Imputed Discount Rate Computation for Leases**

Microsoft reports total undiscounted minimum operating lease payments of $8,664 million and a discounted value for those lease payments of $7,703 million. Using Excel, we can use the IRR function to estimate the *implicit* discount rate that Microsoft used for its capital lease computations. The following spreadsheet lays out the calculations.

Amounts in cells B2 through G2 are from Microsoft's lease footnote shown earlier in this section. Cells H2 through J2 sum to $2,438 million, the total lease payments due after 2023 (year 5). We assume that Microsoft continues to pay $839 million per year (the same as in 2023) with a final payment of $760 million, until the $2,438 million is used up. The IRR functions estimates that Microsoft used a discount rate of 3.15% to capitalize its operating leases in its FY2019 balance sheet.

In this method we make assumptions about the remaining useful life of the lease assets (total remaining payments divided by the payment in year 5). Many firms disclose the weighted average discount rate and the weighted average remaining lease term used to determine the present value of future lease payments. If provided, these assumptions are a more exact way to corroborate the disclosed present value or implicit interest rates.

B3	▼	⋮ × ✓	*fx*	=IRR(B2:J2,0.1)					
◢	A	B	C	D	E	F	G	H	I	J
1	N	0	1	2	3	4	5	6	7	8
2	Amount	(7,703)	1,678	1,438	1,235	1,036	839	839	839	760
3	IRR*	3.15%								
4									=2,438	
5		*Formula for cell B3 is =IRR(B2:J2,0.1), as shown in the formula bar at the top of the sheet								

Lease Accounting and the Income Statement

Total expense over the lifetime of the lease is recognized in the income statement in an amount equal to the total remaining lease payments plus total amortization of any up-front costs. Assume, for example, a company executes a five-year lease requiring annual payments of $22,463 and pays $5,000 of initial direct costs prior to commencing the lease. The present value of the lease payments at 4% is $100,000 and the company recognizes a lease liability for that amount. The company also recognizes a right-of-use asset of $105,000 (the $100,000 present value of the lease payments plus the $5,000 up-front direct costs).

The total lease cost under both operating and finance leases over the five-year life of the lease is: $22,463 lease payments × 5 years + $5,000 upfront costs = $117,314. The income statement will reflect this amount differently, however, for operating and finance leases.

■ **Operating lease.** Lease expense of $23,463 ($117,314/5 years) is recognized each period as rent expense in arriving at income from operating activities.

■ **Finance lease.** Lease expense includes interest on the lease liability plus straight-line amortization of the right-of-use asset. For the first year, lease expense is equal to $100,000 × 4% + $105,000/5 = $25,000. Also:

  ● Amortization of the right-of-use asset will be included in income from operations (similar to depreciation expense relating to PPE assets).

  ● Interest expense will be reported after operating income.

  ● Operating profit will be higher than by the amount of interest expense recognized as nonoperating.

Appendix 10A provides a detailed example of the accounting for operating and finance leases.

Statement of Cash Flows

The statement of cash flows will be impacted by the classification of leases in a similar manner to the income statement.

■ **Operating lease.** Cash flow from operating activities includes the entire lease payment.

■ **Finance lease.** The lease payments include payment of accrued interest and reduction of the principal balance of the lease liability. The interest portion is included in net income and, therefore, in net cash flows from operating activities. The portion representing the payment of the principal balance of the lease liability is considered a financing activity. Net cash flows from operating activities will therefore be higher for finance leases by the amount of the payment allocated to reduction of the lease liability.

Practice Insight ■ Delta Airlines Prospective Adoption of 2019 Lease Accounting Standard

Delta Airlines adopted the new lease accounting standard as disclosed in notes to its 2019 10-K.

> **Leases** During the December 2018 quarter, we adopted ASU No. 2016-02, "Leases (Topic 842)," which requires leases with durations greater than twelve months to be recognized on the balance sheet. We adopted the standard using the modified retrospective approach with an effective date as of the beginning of our fiscal year, January 1, 2018. Prior year financial statements were not recast under the new standard and, therefore, those amounts are not presented below.

Contrary to Microsoft's retroactive adoption of the standard, Delta did not restate its 2017 balance sheet. Consequently, operating leases are recognized on the balance sheet for 2018 (the year of adoption) and not for 2017 (under the previous accounting standard—see the following Accounting Insight box). Delta's noncurrent assets increased in 2018 by $5,994 million as seen in this excerpt from its balance sheet.

December 31 (in millions)	2018	2017
Noncurrent Assets		
Property and equipment, net of accumulated depreciation and amortization of $15,823 and $14,097 at December 31, 2018 and 2017, respectively	$28,335	$26,563
Operating lease right-of-use assets	5,994	0
Goodwill	9,781	9,794
Identifiable intangibles, net of accumulated amortization of $862 and $845 at December 31, 2018 and 2017, respectively	4,830	4,847
Cash restricted for airport construction	1,136	0
Deferred income taxes, net	242	1,354
Other noncurrent assets	3,608	3,309
Total noncurrent assets	$53,926	$45,867

Likewise, Delta's liabilities increased by $6,756 million; and $5,801 million of this is reported separately as a noncurrent liability (the remainder is included in current liabilities).

December 31 (in millions)	2018	2017
Noncurrent Liabilities		
Long-term debt and finance leases	$ 8,253	$ 6,592
Pension, postretirement and related benefits	9,163	9,810
Loyalty program deferred revenue	3,652	3,559
Noncurrent operating leases	5,801	—
Other noncurrent liabilities	1,132	2,221
Total noncurrent liabilities	$28,001	$22,182

Because it chose not to adopt the new leasing standard retrospectively, Delta's 2017 balance sheet is prepared under the former lease standard, impairing the comparability between the two years. Analysts must, therefore, adjust Delta's prior year balance sheet as we discuss in our "Analysis Issues" section of the text.

Accounting Insight   ■   Pre-2019 Lease Accounting Standard

Under the pre-2019 lease accounting standard, GAAP identified two different approaches for the reporting of leases by the lessee. These are summarized in Exhibit 10.2.

Exhibit 10.2 ■ Financial Statement Effects of Lease Type for the Lessee				
Lease Type	**Assets**	**Liabilities**	**Expenses**	**Cash Flows**
Capital	Lease asset reported	Lease liability reported	Depreciation and interest expense	Payments per lease contract
Operating. . . .	Lease asset **not** reported	Lease liability **not** reported	Rent expense	Payments per lease contract

Under the **operating lease method**, lease assets and lease liabilities were not recorded on the balance sheet. The company merely disclosed key details of the transaction in the lease footnote. The income statement reported the lease payment as rent expense. The cash outflows (payments to lessor) per the lease contract were included in the operating section of the statement of cash flows. (This is still the case with the post-2019 accounting standards.)

For **capital leases**, both the lease asset and lease liability were reported on the balance sheet. In the income statement, depreciation of the lease asset and interest expense on the lease liability were reported instead of rent expense. Further, although the cash payments to the lessor are identical whether or not the lease is capitalized on the balance sheet, the cash flows were classified differently for capital leases—that is, each payment was part interest (operating cash flow) and part principal (financing cash flow). Consequently, operating cash flows were greater when a lease was classified as a capital lease. (This is still the case with the post-2019 accounting standards.)

The benefits of applying the operating method for leases were obvious to managers (including healthier Du Pont ratios). Thus, some managers actively avoided capital lease treatment. Moreover, the pre-2019 rigid capitalization rules created an unintended negative consequence: managers seeking off-balance-sheet financing could, and routinely did, deliberately structure their leases around GAAP rules so as to avoid capital lease treatment. Analysts and other financial statement users objected to the pre-2019 rules that skewed ratios and created hidden leverage.

Summary of Lease Accounting and Reporting

A summary of the effects of the new standard on the balance sheet, the income statement, and the statement of cash flows follows.

	Operating Lease	**Finance Lease**
Balance Sheet (same for both operating and finance leases)	• All leases are recognized on the balance sheet (except leases with a term of less than 12 months). • Lease asset is reported as either PPE or a "right-of-use" asset that is amortized over the lease life. • Lease liability is reduced by principal payments each period, like a mortgage. • Accounting treatment is similar to recording a PPE asset that is purchased and financed with borrowed money (both the asset and liability are reported on the balance sheet).	
Income Statement	• Rent expense is recognized for the straight-line amortization of the total lease payments plus up-front costs.	• Straight-line amortization expense of the right-of-use asset, *plus* • Interest expense is recognized on the lease liability.
Statement of Cash Flows	• Lease payments are classified as operating cash flow.	• Interest portion of lease payments is classified as operating cash flow. • Principal portion of lease payments is classified as financing cash flow.

For both operating and financing leases, the balance sheet treatment is identical. However, the income statement and statement of cash flows presentation depend on the lease classification (operating versus financing).

■   Income statement
  ● Operating leases: Level rent expense recorded each period (an operating item).

- Finance leases: Amortization expense recorded each period (an operating item) and interest expense accrued on the lease liability (a nonoperating item). The expense decreases each year because the total expense includes a level asset amortization expense plus a decreasing interest expense (lower in later years because the interest accrual is calculated on a decreasing lease liability).
- Statement of cash flows
  - Operating leases: Rent expense is reported in net income and, thus, is included in net cash from operating activities. The amortization of direct costs (non-cash portion of rent expense) is added back as a reconciling item.
  - Finance leases: Amortization expense is an add-back in net cash from operating activities. Interest expense is reported in net income and, thus, is included in net cash from operating activities. Repayment of the lease obligation is classified as a financing activity.

Analysis Issues Relating to Leases

There are two significant analysis issues relating to leases.

1. Treatment of operating leases prior to adoption of the 2019 accounting standard.
2. Different accounting treatments for operating and finance leases.

Delta Airlines provides an example of the first analysis issue (see the Practice Insight box above). In 2018, Delta adopted the new lease accounting standard prospectively and recognized right-of-use assets and lease liabilities for operating leases for 2018 only. Delta did not restate the prior year balance sheet and income statement, thereby impairing comparability. This is evident from Delta Airlines balance sheet that reports $5,994 million in right-of-use assets and $5,801 million in noncurrent operating lease liabilities for 2018, with $0 reported as a comparable number in 2017. Although comparability will increase over time as previous lease accounting standards are no longer reported alongside the new standard, the lack of comparability will continue to plague analysis of older financial statements. Thus, we need an approach to restore comparability of the financial statements across time.

The second issue relates to the differing accounting treatment for operating and finance leases. This clouds analysis for companies that have both types of leases. It also impairs cross-firm comparisons when companies have differing proportions of operating and finance leases.

Credit rating companies consider the following issues and they adjust for lease reporting issues.

1. **Postadoption reporting of leases—balance sheet.** Generally, credit raters accept the dollar amounts reported by companies for right-of-use assets and lease obligations.
2. **Postadoption reporting of leases—income statement.** Postadoption balance sheets reflect operating and finance leases equally and therefore credit raters simply compare balance sheets across firms. However, income statements and statements of cash flow are not comparable, as we discussed above. Therefore, credit rating companies must adjust for these differences before comparing one company to another.
3. **Prospective adoption of the lease standard.** For companies that adopt the new lease accounting standard on a prospective basis, current and prior years are not comparable (see our Practice Insight box "Delta Airlines Prospective Adoption of 2019 Lease Accounting Standard"). Credit raters' adjustment follows the same method discussed above to capitalize the operating leases using footnote disclosures of future operating lease payments.

The credit rating companies' objective is to recognize all lease assets and lease obligations on the balance sheet and to present lease expense uniformly.

IFRS Insight   ■   Lease Accounting under IFRS

Post 2019, there are few differences between U.S. GAAP and IFRS lease accounting standards. One distinction is that IFRS has a single model of lease classification: all leases are accounted for similar to a finance lease under U.S. GAAP.

Review 10-1 LO1

Following is the leasing footnote disclosure from Delta Airlines's 2018 10-K report.

We lease property and equipment under finance and operating leases. For leases with terms greater than 12 months, we record the related asset and obligation at the present value of lease payments over the term.

The table below reconciles the undiscounted cash flows for each of the first five years and total of the remaining years to the finance lease liabilities and operating lease liabilities recorded on the balance sheet.

(in millions)	Operating Leases	Finance Leases
2019	$ 1,172	$ 127
2020	1,000	89
2021	819	75
2022	692	33
2023	654	27
Thereafter	4,200	111
Total minimum lease payments	8,537	462
Less: amount of lease payments representing interest	(1,781)	(59)
Present value of future minimum lease payments	6,756	403
Less: current obligations under leases	(955)	(109)
Long-term lease obligations	$ 5,801	$ 294

Required

1. Using Excel and a discount rate of 4.42%, confirm the present value of the future minimum lease payments for operating leases of $6,756 million.

Solution on p. 10-67.

2. Describe how the $6,756 million will appear on Delta Airlines's balance sheet for 2018.

Pensions

LO2
Analyze and interpret pension disclosures.

Companies frequently offer postretirement benefit plans for their employees. There are two general types of plans.

1. **Defined contribution plan.**   This plan requires the company to make periodic contributions to an employee's account (usually with a third-party trustee like a bank), and many plans require an employee matching contribution. Following retirement, the employee makes periodic withdrawals from that account. A tax-advantaged 401(k) account is a typical example. Under a 401(k) plan, the employee makes contributions that are exempt from federal taxes until they are withdrawn by the employee after retirement.

2. **Defined benefit plan.**   This plan also requires the company make periodic payments to a third party, which then makes payments to an employee after retirement. Payments are usually based on years of service and the employee's salary. The company may *or may not* set aside sufficient funds to cover these obligations (federal law does set minimum funding requirements). As a result, defined benefit plans can be overfunded or underfunded. All pension investments are retained by the third party until paid to the employee. In the event of bankruptcy, employees have the standing of a general creditor, but usually have additional protection in the form of government pension benefit insurance.

The financial statement implications and the accounting for defined contribution plans is similar to a simple accrual of wages payable. When the company becomes liable to make its contribution, it accrues the liability and related expense. Later, when the company makes the payment, its cash and the liability are reduced. The amount of the liability is certain and the company's obligation is fully satisfied once payment has been made.

A defined benefit plan is not so simple. For that type of plan, the company has made a promise to make annual payments to retirees based on a formula that typically includes the employee's final salary level and years of service, both of which are not determined for maybe 30–40 years in the future. Estimating the amount of the liability is difficult and prone to error. While companies typically set aside some cash to fund promised future payments, usually they make only the minimum contribution required by law. This makes it uncertain whether there will be sufficient funds available to make required payments to retirees.

The accounting for defined benefit plans is subjective, amounts are uncertain, and companies frequently revise their estimates. Footnote disclosures are often lengthy and difficult to decipher. Nonetheless, it is possible to use the disclosures to assess how a defined benefit plan impacts company performance and financial condition.

Defined Benefit Pension Plans on the Balance Sheet

The amount reported on the balance sheet for pension and other post-employment obligations is actually a net amount (Projected benefit obligation – Pension plan assets). This amount is called the *funded status* and is most often a net liability because companies' pension obligations are typically greater than the pension plan assets set aside to pay those liabilities. Funded status is reported on the balance sheet as follows.

Assets	Liabilities and Equity
Cash	Accounts payable
Accounts receivable	Accrued liabilities
⋮	⋮
	Long-term debt
PPE, net	Pension and Postretirement Benefit Obligations
Intangible assets	⋮
⋮	Stockholders' equity
Total Assets	Total Liabilities and Equity

Here we label the funded status as Pension and Postretirement Benefit Obligations, but companies use many other account titles. Funded status is the net balance of two accounts.

- **Pension plan assets.** Think of this account as an investment portfolio with a variety of marketable debt and equity securities. The portfolio provides a return that will fund future payments to retirees. Each period the investment account increases with investment income (interest, dividends, and gains) and as the company contributes additional cash to the portfolio. The investment account decreases with investment losses and as cash is paid to retirees.

- **Projected benefit obligation (PBO).** This liability represents the present value of the company's estimated future payments to retirees. It is similar in concept to the present value of the lease liability that we computed earlier. A company must estimate its future payments that will be required. The following factors make it difficult to project future payments (and companies typically hire actuarial advisors to do this job).
  - Payments often do not occur for many decades into the future.
  - Number of eligible employees is uncertain.
  - Employees' longevity with the company is unknown.
  - Payments depend on employees' final salary levels, which must be estimated.

  A company must then compute the present value of the future cash outflows to determine the projected benefit obligation. This liability decreases when the company pays benefits to its retirees.

- **Funded status.** The balance sheet reports the funded status, calculated as the difference between the projected benefit obligation and the market value of the plan assets. If the plan assets exceed the projected benefit obligation, the pension plan is said to be *overfunded* and a net asset is reported on the balance sheet. However, as is more often the case, the funded status is a net liability. In this case, the pension plan is said to be *underfunded* and a liability for the unfunded amount is reported on the balance sheet.

For S&P 500 firms from 2009–2018, pension assets have averaged about 80% of projected benefit obligations, indicating that underfunding is common. As the stock market increased in value during the 2016–2018 period, plan assets as a percentage of pension obligations increased to nearly 87%.

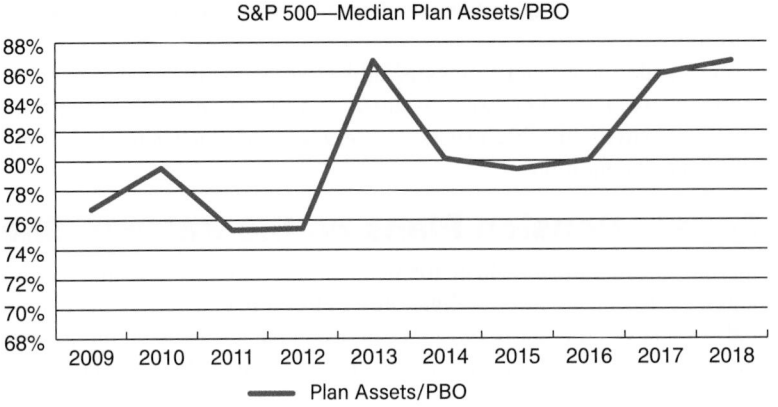

Analysis Issue—Sufficiency of Plan Assets to Pay Pension Obligations

An analysis issue arises when the plan assets are insufficient to cover the PBO. For example, FedEx reported the following fiscal year 2019 balances for its projected benefit obligations (PBO), pension plan assets, and funded status.

$ millions	U.S. Pension Plans		International Pension Plans		Postretirement Healthcare Plans	
	2019	2018	2019	2018	2019	2018
PBO/APBO at the end of year	$26,554	$22,653	$2,301	$2,167	$ 1,221	$ 955
Change in plan assets						
Fair value of plan assets at the beginning of year	$22,057	$24,933	$1,509	$1,379	$ —	$ —
Actual return on plan assets	984	1,609	94	49	—	—
Company contributions	1,034	2,547	91	84	73	42
Benefits paid	(755)	(854)	(38)	(46)	(123)	(80)
Settlements	—	(6,178)	(13)	(5)	—	—
Other	—	—	(65)	48	50	38
Fair value of plan assets at the end of year	$23,320	$22,057	$1,578	$1,509	$ —	$ —
Funded status of the plans	$ (3,234)	$ (596)	$ (723)	$ (658)	$(1,221)	$(955)

For 2019, FedEx reported domestic and international pension plans along with postretirement health-care plans with a combined negative funded status of $5,178 million ($3,234 million + $723 million + $1,221 million). This represents significantly underfunded plans. Employees and analysts are keenly interested in the likelihood that the company will be able to pay its pension obligations to retirees. This negative funded status is, therefore, cause for some concern.

However, funded status is not the only measure we can use to assess the company's ability to pay its pension obligations. While comparing the pension assets and liabilities is important, it is more important to consider cash flow in the coming years. Companies are required to provide a schedule of the expected benefit payments to retirees for the next five years and for the five-year period thereafter (this is a similar schedule to the projected lease payments that we illustrated earlier in this module). FedEx provides the following schedule in its 2019 10-K.

Benefit payments, which reflect expected future service, are expected to be paid as follows for the years ending May 31 (in millions):

	U.S. Pension Plans	International Pension Plans	Postretirement Healthcare Plans
2020	$1,027	$ 45	$ 87
2021	971	46	98
2022	1,051	47	109
2023	1,138	55	117
2024	1,230	61	121
2025–2029	7,515	396	473

For fiscal 2020, FedEx forecasts payments of $1,159 million for its combined plans ($1,027 million + $45 million + $87 million) and expects payments to retirees to increase slightly over the ensuing years. The analysis question is whether the pension plan assets will generate investment returns sufficient to cover the required pension payments to retirees.

In 2019, FedEx generated Pension plan (domestic and international) asset returns of $1,078 million ($984 million + $94 million), exceeding the $793 million of benefit payments required that year ($755 million + $38 million). The graph below reports plan asset returns and benefit payments for the past 10 years for FedEx.

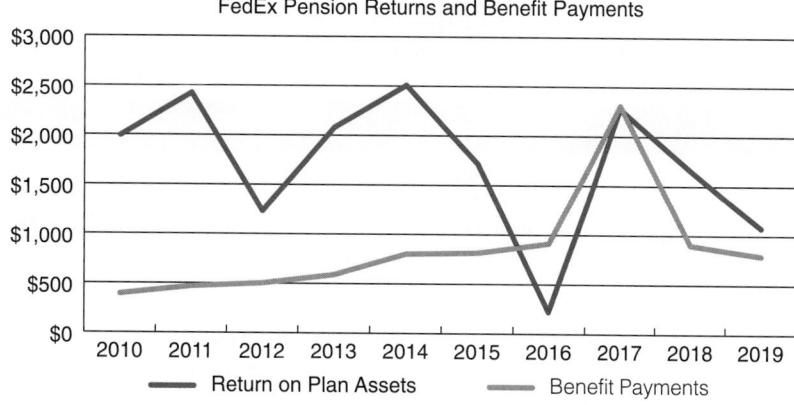

Over the past 10 years, FedEx has generated $17.2 billion of investment returns and paid $8.5 billion of benefits to retirees. Although the Pension and Healthcare plans report a negative funded status, the plans are generating sufficient returns to cover benefit payments. (Benefit payments were higher in 2017 because FedEx's U.S. Pension Plans were amended to permit former employees with a vested traditional pension benefit to make a one-time, irrevocable election to receive their benefits in a lump-sum distribution. Approximately 18,300 former employees elected to receive this lump-sum distribution and FedEx paid a total of $1.3 billion in May 2017.)

The bottom line is that the cash for benefit payments must come from the pension plan assets. Either the plan assets must generate sufficient returns to fund benefit payments (which they did for FedEx), or the company must make additional contributions to the pension plan assets. Severely underfunded plans might not have sufficient assets to cover the projected payments to retirees. In this case, the company might need to use operating cash flow, or worse, borrow to cover its pension benefit obligations. The decline in the financial condition and ultimate bankruptcy of General Motors was due in large part to its inability to pay its pension and healthcare obligations from pension assets. The company was forced to divert much needed operating cash flow and to borrow funds to meet its pension payment obligations.

To summarize, the PBO is the present value of the expected benefit payments, and the plan assets is the fair value of the investment portfolio on the statement date. Companies net these two amounts and report the funded status on the balance sheet. Computing the PBO presents a big challenge for the reasons listed above. Given these difficulties, we must remember that the PBO is an *informed* estimate full of uncertainty.

IFRS Insight ■ Reporting of Pension Funded Status under IFRS

Like U.S. GAAP, IFRS requires companies to report the funded status of their defined benefit pension plans on the balance sheet. The IFRS calculation of the unfunded status is slightly different than under GAAP. The IFRS unfunded status is calculated as projected benefit obligation minus the fair value of plan assets; but, unlike GAAP, any actuarial gains are added (losses are subtracted). There are other differences in detailed computations, which means that for pension assets and liabilities it is difficult to reliably compare GAAP and IFRS reports.

Defined Benefit Pension Plans on the Income Statement

A useful way to think about pensions and healthcare expense in the income statement is to recall the accounting equation and how it applies to the funded status liability.

$$\text{Assets} = \text{Liabilities} + \text{Equity}$$

As liabilities increase, holding assets constant, equity must decrease (an expense). And, as liabilities fall, equity must increase (income). Recall that companies report the funded status of their pension plan (PBO − Plan assets) and that the funded status is frequently a net liability. Looking at a funded status liability, then, we are talking about increases and decreases to the liability, other than from company cash contributions and cash payment of benefits to retirees (those cash payments are not expenses).

Apart from the cash contributions and payments, there are several items that cause the funded status liability to increase or decrease. These items create pension expense in the income statement.

Item	Effect on Funded Status Liability	Effect on Income Statement
Service cost	Increase	Expense
Interest cost	Increase	Expense
Returns on plan assets. . .	Increase (Decrease)	Income (Expense)
Actuarial adjustments	Increase (Decrease)	(Expense) Income

- **Service cost.** Pension benefits are usually based on years of service and salary levels at retirement. As employees work another year for the company, their cumulative years of service increase as does their salary level. This increases the benefits due to them at retirement. The increase in the funded status liability results in pension expense, and this expense is called *service cost* since it relates to the service provided to the company by employees that year.
- **Interest cost.** The PBO is computed as the present value of the expected benefit payments. Each year, the liability increases by the interest accrued on the PBO liability, computed using the discount rate. This expense is called *interest cost*.
- **Investment returns.** If a pension investment portfolio generates a positive investment return, plan assets increase and the funded status liability decreases. This creates income (a reduction of pension expense). However, if the pension investment portfolio reports a loss, plan assets decrease and the funded status liability increases, resulting in additional pension expense.
- **Actuarial adjustments.** The computation of the PBO requires a number of estimates about future payments, pension investment portfolio returns, and discount rates. Companies can, and often do, change these estimates, which affects the amount of the PBO and the funded status liability.
  - *Wage inflation.* If a company increases its assumption about the level of wage inflation, estimated salary levels at retirement will be higher and the pension liability increases, resulting in expense in the income statement.
  - *Years of benefit payments.* If the company assumes a longer period of time for the payment of benefits to retirees, the pension liability increases, resulting in expense in the income statement.
  - *Discount rate.* While a higher discount rate reduces the present value of the PBO, the ensuing annual interest cost is at a higher rate but accrued on a lower PBO. The net effect on

the pension liability is, therefore, indeterminate. An increase in the discount rate may or may not create additional pension expense.

● *Investment returns.* Investment returns on plan assets offset pension expense. So as investment returns increase, pension expense decreases (we discuss below the different ways in which investment returns are recognized in the income statement).

As the company changes estimates, pension expense reported in the income statement changes as well. Fortunately, companies are required to report the levels of these estimates in footnote disclosures, and these disclosures help analysts to better understand the effects on reported profits. We will discuss the analysis of these footnote disclosures later. Before that, we need to better understand the different ways in which pension expense is recognized in the income statement.

Pension Expense Smoothing

Reporting the funded status net liability, rather than reporting pension assets and the pension benefit obligation (PBO) separately, was a concession by the FASB to gain support for passage of the pension accounting standard. During deliberation of the pension standard, companies expressed concern over recognizing the full PBO as a liability on the balance sheet and found the recognition of a net (smaller) liability more palatable.

The FASB also made another significant concession. Companies were concerned about the increase in volatility of reported earnings that would result if changes in plan assets and the PBO were reflected in current earnings. For example, as pension asset returns increased in bull markets and decreased in bear markets, so would reported earnings. And if, for example, companies lowered the estimated discount rate, the PBO would increase and that increase would hit current earnings as an expense.

To allay these concerns, the FASB agreed to a mechanism that would *smooth* pension expense: companies could hold certain gains and losses in accumulated other comprehensive income (AOCI) in the equity section of the balance sheet and transfer them to the income statement over time. In particular, the income effects relating to the following two items would be included in other comprehensive income (rather than in net income) and carried in AOCI (rather than in retained earnings):

1. Large investment gains and losses on pension assets.
2. Changes in the PBO that arise from changes in estimates in actuarial assumptions.

This AOCI mechanism essentially defers gains and losses arising from these two sources. These deferred amounts remain in AOCI unless they became very large, at which point, they are reclassified from AOCI into the current period income statement as either income or expense. (To avoid reclassification, the deferred amounts must be less than 10% of the PBO or pension plan asset investments, whichever is greater. The excess, if any, is amortized to the income statement until no further excess remains. When the excess is eliminated, for example, by investment returns or company contributions, the amortization ceases.) The bottom line is that as long as the total deferred gains or losses are not excessive, they remain on the balance sheet in AOCI and are, therefore, not included in the income statement.

Details of how the deferral mechanism works follow.

1. Instead of recognizing actual returns on pension assets in the income statement, companies recognize an **expected return** that represents the long-term rate of return that the company expects to earn on pension investments given the expected composition of the investment portfolio.
2. Only the amortization of *excess* deferred gains or losses is recognized in current income.

For most companies, pension expense is computed as follows.

Net Pension Expense	
	Service cost
+	Interest cost
−	*Expected* return on pension plan assets
±	Amortization of deferred amounts, if any
=	Net pension expense

With this background, we can now better understand how the pension plan assets and pension benefit obligation (PBO) are updated each year.

Pension Plan Assets
Pension plan assets, beginning balance
+ Actual returns on investments (interest, dividends, gains and losses)
+ Company contributions to pension plan
− Benefits paid to retirees
= Pension plan assets, ending balance

Projected Benefit Obligation
Projected benefit obligation, beginning balance
+ Service cost
+ Interest cost
+/− Actuarial losses (gains)
− Benefits paid to retirees
= Projected benefit obligation, ending balance

- **Pension plan assets** increase by actual investment returns or decrease by investment losses and by additional contributions by the company. The plan assets decrease by any benefits paid to retirees.
- **Projected benefit obligation (PBO)** increases to recognize additional service provided by employees (service cost) and by interest accrued on the PBO liability. It also increases (decreases) as deferred losses (gains) are recognized in income, and it decreases by any benefit payments paid to retirees.

We see that benefits are paid from the pension plan assets, and the payments reduce both the plan assets and the PBO liability when paid.

Pension footnotes disclose details about plan assets and the PBO as well as the components of pension expense. We use Deere & Company as an example and focus only on its U.S. Pension Benefit plan to simplify our exposition. The Deere footnotes provide a good illustration of how pension expense is smoothed for the vast majority of companies. The following disclosures come from Deere's 2018 10-K.

Pension Plan ($ millions)	2018	2017
Change in benefit obligations		
Beginning of year balance	$(13,166)	$(13,086)
❶ Service cost	(293)	(274)
❷ Interest cost	(390)	(361)
❹ Actuarial gain (loss)	1,012	(35)
❺ Benefits paid	711	704
Settlements/curtailments		2
Acquisition*	(29)	
Foreign exchange and other	47	(116)
End of year balance	(12,108)	(13,166)
Change in plan assets (fair value)		
Beginning of year balance	12,093	11,137
❸ Actual return on plan assets	316	1,517
❻ Employer contribution	938	62
❺ Benefits paid	(711)	(704)
Settlements		(2)
Foreign exchange and other	(34)	83
End of year balance	12,602	12,093
❼ Funded status	$ 494	$ (1,073)
Weighted-average assumptions		
Discount rates	4.1%	3.6%
Rate of compensation increase	3.8%	3.8%

Net Periodic Pension Cost ($ millions)	2018	2017
Pensions		
❶ Service cost	$293	$274
❷ Interest cost	390	361
❸ Expected return on plan assets	(775)	(790)
❹ Amortization of actuarial loss	226	247
Amortization of prior service cost	12	12
Settlements/curtailments	8	2
Net cost	$154	$106
Weighted-average assumptions		
Discount rates—service cost	3.5%	3.5%
Discount rates—interest cost	3.2%	3.0%
Rate of compensation increase	3.8%	3.8%
Expected long-term rates of return	6.9%	7.3%

Deere discloses the funded status (the net of the PBO liability and pension plan assets) on the left-hand side of the table. We see that the funded status is positive in 2018 (a net asset) and negative in 2017 (a net liability). Deere discloses the pension expense components on the right-hand side of the table. Items that increase (decrease) the funded status are recognized as expense (income). Remember that pension expense or income is only recognized from accruals, not from cash contributions by the company or cash payments to retirees.

Service and interest cost

❶ Service cost. Deere employees provided another year of service to the company, which increases future benefits and the PBO by $293 million (liabilities are reported as a negative amount in this table). We see that the service cost increase in PBO is also reflected as an increase in pension cost. Under current GAAP, only the service cost is reported in operating income. The other components of pension cost are reported as other income (expense) below income from operations.

❷ Interest cost. PBO is the present value of forecasted pension obligations and is initially recognized as its present value. Each year the company accrues interest on the PBO using the discount rate. In 2018, this increased the PBO by $390 million. The interest cost component of pension expense increased by the same amount.

Investment returns

❸ Actual returns on pension investments for 2018 were $316 million and these increased the plan assets. Returns include gains (losses) on sales of investments along with interest and dividend income. In both 2017 and 2018, investment returns were positive, but returns can also be negative (for example, in a bear market).

Actual returns are not a component of pension expense. Rather *expected* return is recognized as income, which reduces pension cost. In 2018, expected return was $775 million. Deere estimates the expected return using an expected long-term rate of return on plan assets, which was 6.9% in 2018. Comparing the expected returns in the pension expense table to actual returns in the plan assets table, we see that the latter are relatively more volatile over time. As a result, pension expense is smoother by the use of expected returns rather than actual returns. This was the intended stabilizing effect of the pension accounting standard.

Actuarial gains (losses)

❹ Actuarial gain (loss). Deere invokes a number of actuarial assumptions in estimating PBO. Deere can change these assumptions to reflect changing macroeconomic conditions. The increases (decreases) in PBO that result from changes in actuarial assumptions are called actuarial gains (losses). In 2018, Deere increased the discount rate from 3.6% to 4.1% (see the 'Weighted-average assumptions' at the bottom of the table). The increase in discount rate lowered the PBO liability, which was reflected as a $1,012 million *gain* in Deere's PBO table.

The vast majority of companies do not reflect current period actuarial gains and losses in pension expense. Instead, companies carry the gains and losses in AOCI and gradually amortize them to pension expense. Deere amortizes $226 million of deferred actuarial losses during 2018. We see that the amortization is of a deferred loss (because it increases pension expense in 2018), but Deere recognized an actuarial *gain* of $1,012 million in the PBO in 2018. These two amounts will often be quite different because the PBO reflects the current period actuarial gains or losses and the pension expense represents the amortization of the cumulative actuarial gains or losses. The bottom line is that only a small proportion of the gains (losses) recognized in the PBO will ever be reflected in pension expense. That is the smoothing effect of the pension accounting standard. (See the text box on Amortization of Deferred Amounts).

Cash transactions

❺ Benefits paid. During 2018, benefits of $711 million were paid to retirees and Deere decreased the PBO by that amount. The payments came from the investment portfolio (pension plan assets) and so Deere also decreased that account by $711 million. Remember that payments to retirees do not affect pension expense for the year.

❻ Employer contributions. Deere's 2018 cash contributions of $938 million are reflected as an increase in the pension plan assets (and not reflected in income).

Funded status

❼ Funded status. Deere ended the year with a PBO balance of $12,108 million, pension plan assets of $12,602 million, and a positive funded status of $494 million (a net asset). This means that the pension plan was over-funded at the end of the year. In the previous year, Deere reported a funded status liability of $(1,073) million, indicating an under-funded plan.

Accounting Insight ■ Amortization of Deferred Amounts

Pension expense includes amortization of previously deferred amounts that arise from two sources: unexpected return on pension assets and changes in actuarial assumptions.

Unexpected returns on pension plan assets. Pension expense includes the *expected* rate of return on pension assets rather than the *actual* rate of return. Pension assets increase with positive returns and decrease with negative returns, and those increases and decreases result in increases and decreases in equity, just like the effects of changes in the PBO. Using *actual* returns on pension assets would make pension expense and net income more volatile. To win approval for the pension standard from corporations, the FASB offered the use of a more stable long-term *expected* rate of return in the computation of pension expense. Actual returns usually differ from expected returns, and that *unexpected* return is included in OCI (and carried in AOCI) just like the deferred actuarial gains and losses relating to the PBO.

AOCI includes both deferred actuarial gains and losses on the PBO and deferred unexpected gains and losses on pension assets. The AOCI balance, therefore, fluctuates over time, becoming positive in some years and negative in others. As long as it doesn't become too large, these deferred gains and losses remain on the balance sheet, not in the income statement.

Changes in actuarial assumptions. To estimate the projected benefit obligation (PBO), companies must make assumptions about the following:

- Proportion of current workers that will ultimately retire from the company and will become eligible for pension payments.
- Expected rate of wage inflation that will, together with length of service, determine employees' benefits.
- Number of years that employees will live (will receive annual pension payments) after retirement.
- Discount rate to use in computing the present value of the estimated payments upon retirement.

Each of these estimates is called an actuarial assumption and companies frequently change these assumptions as inflation rates and interest rates change and as new information about the employee population becomes available.

A change in any of these actuarial assumptions changes the PBO liability. From the accounting equation (Assets = Liabilities + Equity), we know that if liabilities increase, equity must decrease, and if liabilities decrease, equity must increase. The vast majority of companies treat the change in equity arising from a change in estimates as a deferred gain (if the PBO decreases) or a deferred loss (if the PBO increases), recognizing the deferred gain or loss in other comprehensive income in the current year and, ultimately, in accumulated other comprehensive income (AOCI), a component of equity on the balance sheet. Those deferred gains and losses continue to be recognized in AOCI until they become large, at which point, they are reclassified from AOCI into the current period income statement as either income or expense.[1] As long as the total deferred gains or losses are not excessive, they can remain on the balance sheet in AOCI for a very long time. The deferral of actuarial gains and losses was a concession by the FASB to pave the way for passage of the pension accounting standard.

Fair Value Accounting for Pensions

The use of expected returns and the deferral and future amortization of actuarial gains and losses serves to smooth reported pension expense and, thereby, dampens earnings volatility. While the majority of companies continue to defer unexpected returns and actuarial gains and losses, recognizing them only if they exceed certain size limits, a number of large public companies have started to recognize those gains and losses in current earnings. AT&T, for example, adopted fair-value accounting for pensions in 2010 and now recognizes in current income the actual returns on pension assets (rather than expected returns) and gains (losses) arising from changes in actuarial assumptions. Following is an excerpt from the AT&T 2018 Form 10-K ($ millions).

---

[1] To avoid amortization, the deferred amounts must be less than 10% of the PBO or pension investments, whichever is greater. The excess, if any, is amortized until no further excess remains. When the excess is eliminated (by investment returns or company contributions, for example), the amortization ceases.

> We recognize gains and losses on pension and postretirement plan assets and obligations immediately in our operating results. . . Our combined net pension and postretirement cost (credit) recognized in our consolidated statements of income was $(4,251), $155 and $303 for the years ended December 31, 2018, 2017 and 2016.

AT&T's actuarial gain arose from a higher discount rate used to compute the PBO, which reduced the PBO and created a gain. The gain was offset, in part, by the fact that the actual return on pension assets was less than the expected return. The net actuarial (non-cash) gain increased AT&T's earnings by $4,117 million in 2018, or 16.5% of pretax earnings. Had AT&T accounted for its pension and other postretirement plans (OPEB) using the conventional approach, the gains would have flowed through other comprehensive income and earnings would have been unaffected.

AT&T's fair-value approach greatly increases earnings volatility as illustrated in the following graph that shows AT&T's actuarial gains and losses over the past six years.

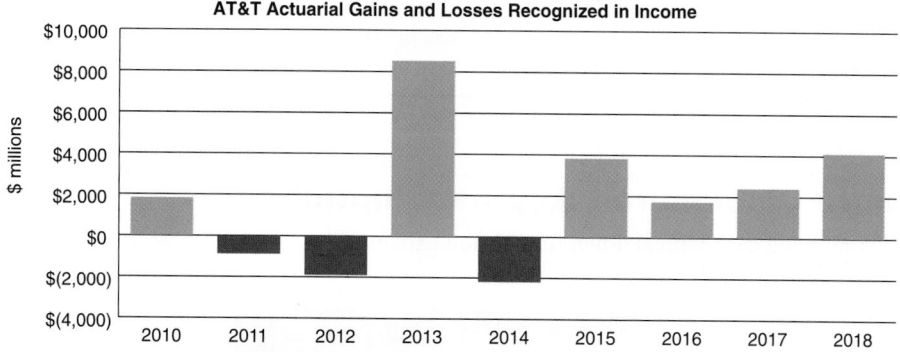

Other companies that have adopted fair value accounting for pensions and OPEB include Verizon, IBM, Honeywell, FedEx and UPS.

Although U.S. GAAP allows companies to recognize actuarial gains either immediately in current income or deferred in accumulated other comprehensive income (AOCI) and, subsequently amortized to income if they exceed certain limits, International Financial Reporting Standards (IFRS) does not allow an option to recognize actuarial gains and losses in income at all. Instead, IFRS requires actuarial gains and losses be deferred in accumulated other comprehensive income with no subsequent amortization. As a result, these gains are deferred indefinitely.

Research Insight ■ Valuation Implications of Pension Footnote Disclosures

The FASB requires footnote disclosure of the major components of pension cost presumably because it is useful for investors. Pension-related research has examined whether investors assign different valuation multiples to the components of pension cost when assessing company market value. Research finds that the market does, indeed, attach different interpretations to pension components, reflecting differences in information about perceived permanence in earnings.

Business Insight ■ Accounting for Pension Plan Settlements

Companies have long been moving away from traditional pensions and replacing them with Defined Contribution Plans (such as 401k plans), stock-based plans, and other forms of compensation. Under U.S. GAAP, pension obligations are deemed "settled" if the company makes an irrevocable action that relieves the company of its responsibility for pension benefit payments in the future.

Often companies settle their pension obligations by making lump-sum cash payments to plan participants. Another means to settle the obligation is to purchase nonparticipating annuity contracts from insurance companies

continued

continued from previous page

to cover vested benefits (buy-out contracts). The contracts off-load the responsibility for pension benefit payments to the insurance company. **FedEx** is an example of this sort of arrangement. In 2018, FedEx entered into an agreement with **Metropolitan Life Insurance Co.** to purchase a group annuity contract that transfers responsibility of pension benefits for 41,000 FedEx retirees and beneficiaries. FedEx described the transaction in a May 2018 press release.

> MEMPHIS, Tenn., May 8, 2018—FedEx Corp. (NYSE: FDX) announced today it has entered into an agreement with Metropolitan Life Insurance Company ("Metropolitan Life") to purchase a group annuity contract and transfer approximately $6 billion of the company's U.S. pension plan obligations. . . As a result of the transaction, FedEx expects to recognize a one-time non-cash pension settlement charge, which will be included in the fiscal 2018 year-end mark-to-market pension accounting adjustments that will be reported in the company's fiscal 2018 fourth quarter earnings release.

Settlement of the pension obligations triggers a settlement gain or loss that generally equals the net gain or loss remaining in AOCI, including any new actuarial gain or loss resulting from the measurement of the PBO and the plan assets on the settlement date. FedEx recognized a $210 million settlement loss in its 2018 income statement.

Footnote Disclosure—Key Assumptions

Recall the following earlier breakdown for pension expense.

Net Pension Expense
Service cost
+ Interest cost
− *Expected* return on pension plan assets
± Amortization of deferred amounts, if any
= Net pension expense

Interest cost is the product of the PBO and the discount rate. This discount rate is set by the company. The expected dollar return on pension assets is the product of the pension plan asset balance and the expected long-run rate of return on the investment portfolio. This rate is also set by the company. Further, PBO is affected by the expected rate of wage inflation, termination and mortality rates, all of which are estimated by the company.

Under U.S. GAAP, companies must disclose the rates and assumptions used to estimate PBO and pension expense. (Pension plan assets do not rely on rate assumptions because the returns and asset fair values are directly measurable.) Deere reported the rates it used immediately beneath the tables in its pension footnote. Other companies report these assumptions separately in other footnotes. During 2018, Deere increased the discount rate used to compute the present value of its PBO, from 3.6% to 4.1%, while leaving unchanged its estimate of the rate of compensation increase. The increase in the discount rate reduced the PBO present value by $1,012 million, resulting in an actuarial gain of that amount. On the expense side, Deere increased the interest rate used to compute the interest component of pension expense from 3.0% to 3.2% and reduced the expected long-term rate of return on pension investments from 7.3% to 6.9%. Respectively, these changes resulted in increased interest cost and reduced investment returns, both of which increased pension expense for the year.

Changes in assumptions have the following general effects on pension expense and, thus, profitability. This table summarizes the effects of increases in the various rates. Decreases have the exact opposite effects.

Assumption Change	Probable Effect on Pension Expense	Reason for Effect
Discount (interest) rate ↑...	↑ or ↓	While the higher discount rate reduces the PBO, the lower PBO is multiplied by a higher rate when the company computes the interest component of pension expense. The net effect is, therefore, indeterminate.
Investment return ↑.......	↓	The dollar amount of expected return on plan assets is the product of the plan assets balance and the expected long-term rate of return. Increasing the return increases the expected return on plan assets, thus reducing pension expense.
Wage inflation ↑	↑	The expected rate of wage inflation affects future wage levels that determine expected pension payments. An increase, thus, increases PBO, which increases both the service and interest cost components of pension expense.

Analysis Implications

There are three important analysis issues relating to pensions.

1. To what extent will the company's pension plans compete with investing and financing needs for the available cash flows?

2. In what ways has the company's choice of estimates affected its profitability?

3. Should pension costs and funded status be treated as operating or nonoperating?

Regarding the first issue, pension plan assets are the source of funds to pay benefits to retirees, and federal law (Employee Retirement Income Security Act) sets minimum standards for pension contributions. Consequently, if investment returns are insufficient, companies must make up the shortfall with additional contributions. Any such additional contributions compete for available operating cash flows with other investing and financing activities. This can be especially severe in a business downturn when operating cash flows are depressed. As pension payments are contractual, companies can be forced to postpone needed capital investment to make the contributions necessary to ensure funding of their pension plans as required by law or labor agreements. Analysts must be aware of funding requirements when projecting future cash flows.

Regarding the second issue, accounting for pensions requires several assumptions, including the expected return on pension investments, the expected rate of wage inflation, the discount rate used to compute the PBO, and other actuarial assumptions that are not reported in footnotes (mortality rates, for example). Each of these assumptions affects reported profit, and analysts must be aware of changes in these assumptions and their effects on profitability. An increase in reported profit that is due to an increase in the expected return on pension investments, for example, is not related to core operating activities and, further, might not be sustainable. Such changes in estimates must be considered in our evaluation of reported profitability.

The third analysis issue relates to the operating vs. nonoperating treatment of pension expense and funded status. Pension expense includes service cost, interest costs, and actuarial cost components (and gains and losses for companies that opt for fair-value accounting). Service cost is, arguably, more related to operating activities than the other components, because service cost arises from the increase in pension benefits earned by employees as they continue to work for the company. Consequently, many analysts argue for operating treatment of service costs. In 2017, the FASB issued new accounting standards relating to the recognition of pension cost. Under current GAAP, companies are required to report the service cost component of pension cost in the same line item or items as other compensation costs. The other components of pension expense are to be presented in the income statement separately from the service cost component and outside of income from operations.

The operating vs. nonoperating analysis of the funded status on the balance sheet is more difficult. The pension obligation represents a form of compensation and, in that sense, it is operating in nature. However, U.S. GAAP defines the PBO as the "actuarial *present value* . . . of all benefits attributed by the pension benefit formula to employee service rendered before that date" [emphasis ours]. It is the present-value requirement that results in the need to accrue interest expense as a component of pension expense, leading to the argument that a portion of the PBO might be considered as nonoperating. In our view, the GAAP requirement to discount future pension obligations does not change the character of the obligation and, for that reason, we treat the funded status liability as operating. (Very few companies report a net pension *asset*. But, if they do, we consider the PBO to be equal to zero and treat the excess pension assets as nonoperating as they comprise marketable securities, which we generally treat as nonoperating.)

Other Post-Employment Benefits (OPEB)

In addition to pension benefits, many companies provide healthcare and insurance benefits to retired employees. These benefits are referred to as **other post-employment benefits (OPEB)**. These benefits present reporting challenges similar to pension accounting. However, companies most often provide these benefits on a "pay-as-you-go" basis and it is rare for companies to make contributions in advance for OPEB. As a result, this liability, known as the **accumulated post-employment benefit obligation (APBO)**, is largely, if not totally, unfunded. GAAP requires that the unfunded APBO liability, net of any unrecognized amounts, be reported in the balance sheet and the annual service costs and interest costs be accrued as expenses each year. This requirement is controversial for two reasons. First, future healthcare costs are especially difficult to estimate, so the value of the resulting APBO (the present value of the future benefits) is fraught with error. Second, these benefits are provided at the discretion of the employer and can be altered or terminated at any time. Consequently, employers argue that without a legal obligation to pay these benefits, the liability should not be reported in the balance sheet. (For a more complete discussion of OPEB issues, see: **https://www.pwc.com/us/en/corporate-governance/assets/pension-paper.pdf**.)

These other post-employment benefits can produce large liabilities. For example, Deere's footnotes report a funded status for the company's healthcare obligation of $(4,753) million in 2018, consisting of an APBO liability of $5,472 million and OPEB plan assets of $719 million. Our analysis of cash flows related to pension obligations can be extended to other post-employment benefit obligations. For example, in addition to its pension payments, Deere discloses that it is obligated to make healthcare payments to retirees totaling about $320 million to $345 million per year. Because healthcare obligations are rarely funded until payment is required (federal minimum funding standards do not apply to OPEB and there is no tax benefit to pre-funding), there are no investment returns to fund the payments. Our analysis of projected cash flows must consider this potential cash outflow in addition to that relating to pension obligations.

Research Insight   ■   Valuation of Nonpension Post-Employment Benefits

The FASB requires employers to accrue the costs of all nonpension post-employment benefits, known as *accumulated post-employment benefit obligation* (APBO). These benefits consist primarily of healthcare and insurance. This requirement is controversial due to concerns about the reliability of the liability estimate. Research finds that the APBO (alone) is associated with company value. However, when other pension-related variables are included in the research, the APBO liability is no longer useful in explaining company value. Research concludes that the pension-related variables do a better job at conveying value-relevant information than the APBO number alone, which implies that the APBO number is less reliable.

Review 10-2 LO2

Following is the pension disclosure footnote from American Airlines' 10-K report (in millions).

Pension Benefits	2018	2017
Benefit obligation at beginning of period	$18,275	$17,238
Service cost	3	2
Interest cost	674	721
Actuarial (gain) loss	(1,910)	1,016
Settlements	(4)	(4)
Benefit payments	(662)	(726)
Other	2	28
Obligation at December 31	$16,378	$18,275

continued

continued from previous page

Pension Benefits	2018	2017
Fair value of plan assets at beginning of period.	$11,395	$10,017
Actual return on plan assets	(1,151)	1,797
Employer contributions	475	286
Settlements.	(4)	(4)
Benefit payments	(662)	(726)
Other.	—	25
Fair value of plan assets at end of period.	$10,053	$11,395
Funded status at end of period.	$ (6,325)	$ (6,880)

Following is American Airlines' footnote for its pension cost as reported in its income statement (in millions).

Pension Benefits	2018	2017
Defined benefit plans:		
Service cost	$ 3	$ 2
Interest cost	674	721
Expected return on assets	(905)	(790)
Settlements.	—	1
Amortization of:		
Prior service cost (benefit).	28	28
Unrecognized net loss (gain).	141	144
Net periodic benefit cost (income)	$ (59)	$106

Required

1. What factors impact American Airlines' pension benefit obligation during 2018?
2. What factors impact American Airlines' pension plan assets during 2018?
3. What amount is reported on the balance sheet relating to American Airlines defined benefit pension plan?
4. How does the expected return on plan assets affect pension expense?
5. How does American Airlines' expected return on plan assets compare with its actual return (in $ millions) for 2018?
6. How much net pension expense is reflected in American Airlines' 2018 income statement?
7. Assess American Airlines' ability to meet payment obligations to retirees.

Solution on p. 10-68.

Income Taxes

When preparing financial statements for stockholders and other external constituents, companies use GAAP. But when companies prepare their income tax returns, they prepare financial statements using the *Internal Revenue Code (IRC)*. These two sets of accounting rules recognize revenues and expenses differently in many cases and, as a result, can yield markedly different levels of income. In general, companies desire to report lower income to taxing authorities than they do to their stockholders so that they can reduce their tax liability and increase after-tax cash flow. This practice is acceptable so long as the financial statements are prepared in conformity with GAAP and tax returns are filed in accordance with the IRC.

eLectures **LO3**
MBC Analyze and interpret income tax reporting.

Timing Differences Create Deferred Tax Assets and Liabilities

As an example, consider the depreciation of long-term assets. For financial reports, companies typically depreciate long-term assets using straight-line depreciation (meaning the same amount of depreciation expense is reported each year over the useful life of the asset). However, for tax returns, companies use an *accelerated* method of depreciation (meaning more depreciation is taken in the early years of the asset's life and less depreciation in later years). When a company depreciates assets at an accelerated rate for tax purposes, the depreciation deduction for tax purposes is higher and taxable income is lower in the early years of the assets' lives. As a result, taxable income and tax payments are reduced and after-tax cash flow is increased. That excess cash can then be reinvested in the business to increase its returns to stockholders.

To illustrate, assume that Southwest Airlines purchases an asset with a five-year life. It depreciates that asset using the straight-line method (equal expense per year) when reporting to stockholders and depreciates the asset at a faster rate (accelerated depreciation) for tax purposes. Annual (full year) depreciation expense under these two methods is depicted in Exhibit 10.3.

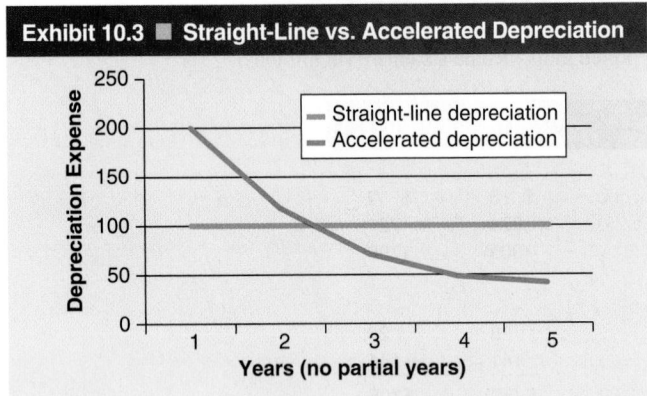

Exhibit 10.3 ■ **Straight-Line vs. Accelerated Depreciation**

During the first 2.5 years in this example, depreciation is higher in the company's tax returns than it is in its GAAP financial statements. In the last 2.5 years, this is reversed, with lower depreciation expense for tax purposes. Taxable income and tax payments are, therefore, higher during the last 2.5 years. The same total amount of depreciation is recognized under both methods over the five-year life of the asset. Only the timing of the recognition of the expense differs.[2]

Illustration of Deferred Tax Liabilities We use this timing concept to illustrate the accounting for a **deferred tax liability**. Assume that a company purchases a depreciable asset with a cost of $100 and a two-year useful life. For financial reporting purposes (for GAAP-based reports), it depreciates the asset using the straight-line method, which yields depreciation expense of $50 per year. For tax reporting (when filing income tax returns), it depreciates the asset on an accelerated basis, which yields depreciation deduction of $75 in the first year and $25 in the second year (the same total amount of depreciation is reported under the two depreciation methods; only the amount of depreciation reported per year differs). Assume that this company reports income before depreciation and taxes of $200 and that its tax rate is 40%. Its income statements, for both financial reporting and tax reporting, for the asset's first year are in Exhibit 10.4A.

Exhibit 10.4A ■ **Year 1 Income Statements: Financial Reporting vs. Tax Reporting**

Year 1	Financial Reporting	Tax Reporting
Income before depreciation	$200	$200
Depreciation	50	75
Income before tax.	150	125
Income tax (40%)	60 [expense]	50 [cash paid]
Net income	$ 90	$ 75

This company records income tax expense and a related deferred tax liability for the first year as reflected in the following financial statement effects template:

---

[2] The Modified Accelerated Cost Recovery System (MACRS) is the current method of accelerated asset depreciation required by the United States income tax code. Under MACRS, all assets are divided into classes that dictate the number of years over which an asset's cost is "recovered" and the percentage of the asset cost that can be depreciated per year is fixed by regulation. For a five-year asset, such as in our example, the MACRS depreciation percentages per year are 20%, 32%, 19.2%, 11.52%, 11.52%, and 5.76%. MACRS assumes that assets are acquired in the middle of the year, hence a half-year depreciation in Year 1 and a half-year depreciation in Year 6. The point after which straight-line depreciation exceeds MACRS depreciation is after about 2.5 years as assumed in the example.

Year 1	Balance Sheet					Income Statement		
Transaction	Cash Asset	+ Noncash Assets	= Liabil- ities	+ Contrib. Capital	+ Earned Capital	Rev- enues	− Expen- ses	= Net Income
Record tax expense: expense exceeds cash because of deferral of tax	−50 Cash		+10 Deferred Tax Liability		−60 Retained Earnings		+60 Tax Expense	−60

```
TE......... 60
  DTL........... 10
  Cash.......... 50
        TE
 60 |
       DTL
          | 10
      Cash
          | 50
```

The reduction in cash reflects the payment of taxes owed to the taxing authority. The increase in deferred tax liability represents an estimate of additional tax that will be payable in the second year (which is the tax liability deferred in the first year). This liability for a future tax payment arises because second-year depreciation expense for tax purposes will be only $25, resulting in taxes payable of $70, which is $10 more than the income tax expense the company reports in its income statement to shareholders in Year 2 as we illustrate in Exhibit 10.4B.

Exhibit 10.4B ■ Year 2 Income Statements: Financial Reporting vs. Tax Reporting

Year 2	Financial Reporting	Tax Reporting
Income before depreciation	$200	$200
Depreciation	50	25
Income before tax.	150	175
Income tax (40%)	60 [expense]	70 [cash paid]
Net income	$ 90	$105

At the end of Year 1, the company knows that this additional tax must be paid in Year 2 because the financial reporting and tax reporting depreciation schedules are set when the asset is placed in service. Given these known amounts, the company accrues the deferred tax liability in Year 1 in the same manner as it would accrue any estimated future liability, say for wages payable, by recognizing a liability and the related expense.

At the end of Year 2, the additional income tax is paid and the company's deferred tax liability is now satisfied. Financial statement effects related to the tax payment and expense in Year 2 are reflected in the following template:

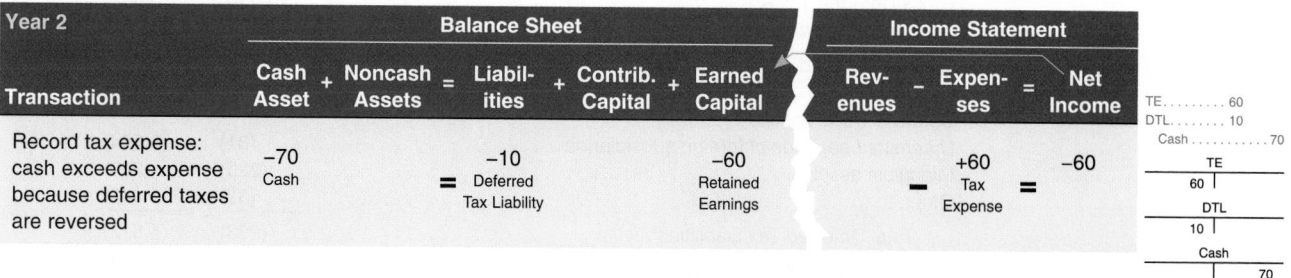

Year 2	Balance Sheet					Income Statement		
Transaction	Cash Asset	+ Noncash Assets	= Liabil- ities	+ Contrib. Capital	+ Earned Capital	Rev- enues	− Expen- ses	= Net Income
Record tax expense: cash exceeds expense because deferred taxes are reversed	−70 Cash		−10 Deferred Tax Liability		−60 Retained Earnings		+60 Tax Expense	−60

```
TE......... 60
DTL........ 10
  Cash.......... 70
        TE
 60 |
       DTL
 10 |
      Cash
          | 70
```

The income tax expense for financial reporting purposes is $60 each year. However, the cash payment for taxes is $70 in Year 2; the $10 excess reduces the deferred tax liability accrued in Year 1.

Illustration of Deferred Tax Assets   Deferred tax assets arise when the tax payment is *greater* than the tax expense for financial reporting purposes (opposite of the illustration above).

For example, restructuring accruals give rise to deferred tax assets. In the year in which a company approves a reorganization plan, it will accrue a restructuring liability for estimated employee severance payments and other costs and it will write down assets to their market values (this reduces the net book value of those assets on the balance sheet). However, for tax purposes, restructuring costs are not deductible until paid in the future, and asset write-downs are not deductible until the loss is realized when the asset is sold. As a result, the restructuring accrual is not a liability for tax reporting until the company makes the payment, and the write-down of assets is not a deductible expense for tax purposes until the assets are sold. Both of these differences (the liability and the assets) give rise to a deferred tax asset. The deferred tax asset will be transferred to the income statement in the future as an expense when the company pays the restructuring costs and sells the impaired assets for a loss.

Another common deferred tax asset relates to **tax loss carryforwards**. Specifically, when a company reports a loss for tax purposes, it can carry the loss forward indefinitely to reduce future taxable income. (Prior to the 2017 tax law changes, losses could be carried back two years and forward for 20 years. See the Analysis Insight box on page 10-30.) This creates a benefit (an "asset") for tax reporting for which there is no corresponding financial reporting asset. Thus, the company records a deferred tax asset but only if the company is "more likely than not" to be able to use the loss to reduce future taxes. This depends on the company's assessment of whether it will have sufficient profits in the future. (We return to this issue later in the module.)

Reporting Deferred Tax Assets and Liabilities

In financial statement footnotes, companies must disclose the components of deferred tax liabilities and assets. **HP Inc.**'s deferred tax footnote (shown in Exhibit 10.5) reports net deferred tax assets of $2,624 million and total deferred tax liabilities of $293 million at the end of fiscal 2018. HP's deferred tax assets primarily relate to loss carryforwards. Its deferred tax liabilities relate to estimated tax on unremitted earnings for foreign subsidiaries (see the text box below). Other companies with significant investments in PPE assets report deferred tax liabilities relating to accelerated depreciation, as illustrated at the start of this section.

Exhibit 10.5 ■ Deferred Taxes Footnote for HP Inc.		
As of October 31 (in millions)	**2018**	**2017**
Deferred Tax Assets		
Loss and credit carryforwards	$ 8,204	$ 9,914
Intercompany transactions—excluding inventory	994	1,901
Fixed assets	151	256
Warranty	194	219
Employee and retiree benefits	401	519
Deferred Revenue	164	231
Other	422	511
Gross Deferred Tax Assets	10,530	13,551
Valuation allowances	(7,906)	(8,807)
Net Deferred Tax Assets	2,624	4,744
Deferred Tax Liabilities		
Unremitted earnings of foreign subsidiaries	(31)	(5,554)
Intangible assets	(229)	(209)
Other	(33)	(49)
Total Deferred Tax Liabilities	(293)	(5,812)
Net Deferred Tax Assets (Liabilities)	$ 2,331	$ (1,068)

Under U.S. GAAP, companies compute deferred tax assets and liabilities as follows.

- **Deferred tax asset** Future estimated tax deductible expense or loss × Estimated tax rate
- **Deferred tax liability** Future estimated taxable income × Estimated tax rate

Deferred tax assets. HP reports tax loss carryforwards that can be applied to reduce future taxable income and decrease HP's income tax bill that year. The $8,204 million deferred tax asset represents the cash benefit HP will receive when loss carryforwards are applied to reduce future taxable income. This means that HP expects to save $8,204 million in future taxes. HP computes the reported amount as: Estimated tax deductible *loss* that will be applied to future tax returns × Estimated tax rate.

Deferred tax liabilities. The $31 million that HP reports for estimated future taxes on unremitted earnings of foreign subsidiaries represents the cash HP will pay in tax when the foreign subsidiary profits become taxable. The $31 million reported amount is computed as: Estimated future taxable *income* × Estimated tax rate.

Both deferred tax assets and deferred tax liabilities are computed using the tax rates in effect when the financial statements are prepared. If the tax rates change, so do the reported deferred tax assets and liabilities. The text box below discusses the effects of the U.S. Tax Cuts and Jobs Act of 2017 (TCJA).

Valuation Allowance for Deferred Tax Assets

Companies must establish a valuation allowance for deferred tax assets if the future realization of the tax benefits is uncertain. (HP provides an allowance of $7,906 million in Exhibit 10.5 above) The allowance reduces reported assets and increases tax expense, which reduces equity. (This allowance is similar to accounting for the write-down of any asset.) Once the deferred tax asset valuation allowance is established, it can be reduced (reversed) by one of two events.

- **The company writes off a deferred tax asset.** In this case, the asset is reduced to zero and the amount written off is subtracted from the deferred tax valuation allowance. There is no effect on income from this write-off. (This is similar to the accounting for a write-off of an uncollectible account receivable against the allowance for uncollectible accounts, which has no effect on income.) A typical example of a deferred tax asset write-off occurs when net operating loss carryforwards (NOLs) expire before they can be used to offset other profits.
- **The company determines that the deferred tax assets *will* be realized.** If the company decides that the realization of the deferred tax assets is more likely than not, it can reverse the deferred tax asset valuation allowance. In that case, the deferred tax asset valuation allowance is reduced and tax expense is reduced by the same amount, thus *increasing* net income.

We see that HP's deferred tax footnote in Exhibit 10.5, includes a valuation allowance in both 2017 and 2018 and that the allowance decreased in 2018. The footnote below explains that in 2018 the company adjusted the valuation allowance because certain foreign tax rules changed during the year, thereby increasing the value of the future benefit.

Taxes on Earnings

HP recognizes deferred tax assets and liabilities for the expected tax consequences of temporary differences between the tax bases of assets and liabilities and their reported amounts using enacted tax rates in effect for the year the differences are expected to reverse. HP records a valuation allowance to reduce the deferred tax assets to the amount that is more likely than not to be realized.

Deferred Tax Asset Valuation Allowance

The deferred tax asset valuation allowance and changes were as follows:

As of October 31 (in millions)	2018	2017	2016
Balance at beginning of year	$8,807	$8,520	$7,114
Income tax (benefit) expense	(897)	297	1,421
Other comprehensive income, currency translation and charges to other accounts	(4)	(10)	(15)
Balance at end of year	$7,906	$8,807	$8,520

Gross deferred tax assets as of October 31, 2018, 2017 and 2016, were reduced by valuation allowances of $7.9 billion, $8.8 billion and $8.5 billion, respectively. The total valuation allowance decreased by $901 million in fiscal year 2018, associated primarily with foreign net operating losses and U.S. deferred tax assets that are anticipated to be realized at a lower effective rate than the federal statutory tax rate due to certain future U.S. international tax reform implications.

The decrease in the valuation allowance had the following effects: HP's deferred tax assets and net income both increased by $901 million in 2018 ($897 million + $4 million).

Disclosures for Income Taxes

Following is an excerpt from HP's 2018 income statement (highlight ours).

For Fiscal Years Ended October 31 ($ millions)	2018	2017	2016
Earnings from continuing operations before taxes........	$3,013	$3,276	$3,761
Benefit from (provision for) taxes.....................	2,314	(750)	(1,095)
Net earnings from continuing operations	5,327	2,526	2,666
Net loss from discontinued operations	—	—	(170)
Net earnings.....................................	$5,327	$2,526	$2,496

The tax expense reported on the income statement relates to taxes that will be paid to federal, state, and municipal taxing authorities as well as income taxes levied by foreign governments. We see that HP reported a tax benefit in FY2018 that resulted from the U.S. Tax Cuts and Jobs Act of 2017 (TCJA) (see text box below). That tax benefit increased HP's net income by $2,314 million in 2018.

Companies are required to disclose in their footnotes the portion of income tax expense that is currently payable and the amount that relates to deferred taxes. HP's disclosure for fiscal 2018 follows.

For Fiscal Years Ended October 31 ($ millions)	2018	2017	2016
U.S. federal taxes:			
Current	$ 751	$189	$ 439
Deferred	(3,132)	197	470
Non-U.S. taxes:			
Current	528	302	288
Deferred	(563)	4	(123)
State taxes:			
Current	61	20	(35)
Deferred	41	38	56
	$(2,314)	$750	$1,095

- **Current tax expense.** Current tax expense is determined from the company's tax returns; it is the amount that must be paid (in cash) to tax authorities for current year operations. Some of these taxes are paid during the year as the company makes installments. The remaining balance is included as a current liability. For fiscal 2018, HP's current tax expense was $1,340 million (= $751 million + $528 million + $61 million).
- **Deferred tax expense.** Deferred tax expense is the effect on tax expense from changes in deferred tax liabilities and deferred tax assets. For fiscal 2018, this was a net tax benefit of $3,654 million, reducing tax expense and increasing deferred tax assets.

Companies are also required to reconcile the difference between the U.S. corporate tax rate and the company's **effective tax rate** (computed as Tax expense/Pretax income). HP's tax reconciliation table follows.

For Fiscal Years Ended October 31 ($ millions)	2018	2017	2016
U.S. federal statutory income tax rate from continuing operations..........	23.3%	35.0%	35.0%
State income taxes from continuing operations, net of federal tax benefit....	0.5%	1.4%	1.1%
Lower rates in other jurisdictions, net................................	(10.9)%	(13.2)%	(9.3)%
U.S. tax reform impacts	(35.8)%	—%	—%
Research and development ("R&D") credit	(0.7)%	(0.5)%	(2.4)%
Valuation allowances	(9.3)%	(1.9)%	(1.2)%
Uncertain tax positions and audit settlements	(50.3)%	0.4%	11.7%
Indemnification related items	5.2%	(0.3)%	(4.1)%
Other, net	1.2%	2.0%	(1.7)%
	(76.8)%	22.9%	29.1%

The effective tax rate reconciliation table not only provides insight into the company's effective tax rate, it also provides valuable information about transitory items that have affected income taxes and, therefore, net income. In 2018, for example, HP reported reductions to the effective tax rate of 35.8% from U.S. Tax Reform impacts and 50.3% from "Uncertain tax positions and audit settlements." Tax reductions like these are not likely to recur in the foreseeable future. Accordingly, we would likely not want to use this negative 2018 tax rate to forecast future tax rates.

Analysis of Income Tax Disclosures

Analysis of deferred taxes can yield useful insights. Some revenue accruals (such as accounts receivable for longer-term contracts) increase deferred tax liabilities as GAAP income exceeds taxable income (similar to the effect of using straight-line depreciation for financial reporting purposes and accelerated depreciation for tax returns).

An increase in deferred tax liabilities indicates that a company is reporting higher GAAP income relative to taxable income and can indicate the company is managing earnings upwards. Although an increase in deferred tax liabilities can legitimately result, for example, from an increase in depreciable assets and the use of accelerated depreciation for tax purposes, we must be aware of the possibility that the company might be improperly reporting revenues.

The income tax footnote also reveals any changes in the deferred tax asset valuation account. A decrease in the valuation allowance is often triggered by the write-off of deferred tax assets, typically relating to net operating loss carryforwards (NOLs). These carryforwards allow companies to offset current losses against future income indefinitely, but they are capped to 80% of taxable income. NOL carryforwards cannot be used to offset profits across subsidiary companies. (Prior to the TCJA, firms could carry NOLs back two years and forward 20 years. The TCJA eliminated the carryback and extended carry forwards indefinitely. These new rules changed the likelihood that NOLs would be used for many firms, which increased the deferred tax asset, or reduced the related valuation allowances.)

As we illustrate with HP, Inc. above, companies can (and do) increase their estimate on the recoverability of deferred tax assets. When they do, the valuation allowance is reduced, thereby increasing deferred tax assets and increasing net income dollar-for-dollar by a reduction of income tax expense. The income tax footnote will reveal any such changes in the deferred tax valuation allowance and also the impact on net income.

The reconciliation of statutory and effective tax rates can reveal important transitory items that might impact our forecast of future tax rates. Income tax expense is a large expense item for most companies and the rate we use in our forecasts can greatly affect our expectations of future net income.

Analysis Insight ▪ U.S. Tax Cuts and Jobs Act of 2017

HP reported a tax *benefit* of $2,314 million in 2018, compared with a tax *expense* of $750 million in the prior year on comparable levels of reported pretax profit. This unusual tax situation for HP and a myriad of other companies arose from the U.S. Tax Cuts and Jobs Act of 2017. This new tax law significantly changed the income tax structure for U.S. corporations in key ways.

- It reduced the corporate tax rate from 35% to 21%.
- It taxed income earned outside the U.S. even if the cash profit remained abroad.

As a result of this legislation, some companies reported significant tax expense increases in 2017 and 2018 and others, like HP, reported tax decreases that significantly increased reported profits. The effects of this tax legislation are great for many companies, and will confound any historical analysis of the income statement. HP discusses the significant effects of the TCJA in the following excerpt from its income tax footnote.

> In fiscal year 2018, HP recorded $2.8 billion of net income tax benefits related to discrete items in the provision for taxes which include impacts of the TCJA . . . [A]s of October 31, 2018, HP recorded a . . . $5.6 billion net benefit for the decrease in its deferred tax liability on unremitted foreign earnings, partially offset by $3.3 billion net expense for the deemed repatriation tax payable in installments over eight years, a $1.2 billion net expense for the remeasurement of its deferred assets and liabilities to the new U.S. statutory tax rate and a $317 million valuation allowance on net expense related to deferred tax assets that are expected to be realized at a lower rate.

continued

continued from previous page

There were two main tax effects of the TCJA on income tax expense for U.S. companies.

1. **Tax on unremitted profit on foreign subsidiaries.** Under prior tax laws, profits earned by foreign subsidiaries were not taxed in the U.S. until the cash was repatriated via a dividend to the U.S. parent company. U.S. GAAP allowed companies to postpone recording the related tax expense, provided that the company asserted the foreign profits were "indefinitely invested abroad." These incentives to keep foreign profits outside the U.S. led to nearly $3 trillion cumulative unrepatriated foreign earnings of U.S. companies in 2017. The TCJA moved the U.S. to a territorial system, meaning that companies could repatriate foreign profits earned after 2017, without triggering any U.S. tax. The TCJA also mandated that *previously earned* foreign profits would be taxed in 2018, whether foreign earnings were ever repatriated. While companies can elect to pay the "mandatory transition tax" over eight years, under U.S. GAAP, companies must recognize the entire transition tax liability and related income tax expense in 2018.

2. **Reduction of deferred tax assets (liabilities).** Under U.S. GAAP, deferred tax assets and liabilities are computed as the product of future taxable loss (income) and the estimated tax rate, which was 35% prior to the TCJA. With the passage of the TCJA, the corporate tax rate fell to 21%. This had the effect of reducing all deferred taxes, both assets and liabilities. A decrease to the deferred tax asset account resulted in additional tax expense and lower net income. A reduction in deferred tax liabilities had the opposite effect, a tax benefit (a negative tax expense) increased net income. The TCJA created winners and losers: companies with significant deferred tax assets reported lower net income while companies with significant deferred tax liabilities saw tax expenses plummet. Many companies reported large tax benefits and inflated net income in 2017 (or in 2018 for non-calendar-year companies like HP).

The "catch-up" tax on income previously earned by foreign subsidiaries and the revaluation of deferred tax assets and liabilities using the lower corporate tax rates *are both transitory items* that affected the income statements of U.S. companies in 2017 or 2018. These tax impacts were substantial for many companies, resulting in a lack of comparability with prior years and complicating the choice of the appropriate tax rate to use to analyze performance analysis and to forecast future income statements (see Module 12).

Expanded Explanation of Deferred Taxes

The earlier example showed that total depreciation over the life of the asset is the same under both tax and financial reporting, and that the only difference is the timing of the expense or tax deduction. Because depreciation differs each year, the amount at which the equipment is reported will differ as well for book and tax purposes (cost less accumulated depreciation is called *net book value* for financial reporting purposes and *tax basis* for tax purposes). These book vs. tax differences are eliminated at the end of the asset's useful life.

Expanded Example of a Deferred Tax Liability: PPE

To understand this concept more completely, we modify the example from the module to include a third year. Assume that the company purchases PPE assets at the start of Year 1 for $120. For financial reporting purposes, the company uses straight-line depreciation and records depreciation of $40 each year (with zero salvage). For tax purposes, assume that the company takes tax depreciation deductions of $60, $50, and $10. Exhibit 10.6 reports the annual depreciation along with the asset's net book value and its tax basis, for each year-end.

The third column in Exhibit 10.6 shows the "book-tax" difference, which is the difference between GAAP net book value and the tax basis at the end of each year. The fourth column shows the deferred tax liability at the end of each period, computed as the book-tax difference times the tax rate. We see from the fourth column that when the financial reporting net book value is greater than the tax basis, the company has a deferred tax liability on its balance sheet (as in Years 1 and 2). Companies' footnotes provide information about deferred taxes. For example, Southwest Airlines' footnote reports a deferred tax liability of $4,429 million for its accelerated depreciation on its property, plant and equipment, which indicates the tax basis for PPE is less than GAAP net book value, on average, for Southwest's PPE.

Accounting standards require a company to first compute the taxes it owes (per its tax return), then to compute any changes in deferred tax liabilities and assets, and finally to compute tax expense

Exhibit 10.6 ■ Book and Tax Depreciation and Carrying Value

	Financial Reporting (Net Book Value)	Tax Reporting (Tax Basis)	Book vs. Tax Difference	Deferred Tax Liability (Book vs. Tax Difference × Tax Rate)	Deferred Tax Expense (Increase or Decrease in Deferred Tax Liability)
At purchase: PPE carrying value	$120	$120	$ 0	$ 0	
Year 1: Depreciation	(40)	(60)			
End of Year 1: PPE carrying value	80	60	$20 ($80 – $60)	$ 8 ($20 × 40%)	$ 8 ($8 – $0)
Year 2: Depreciation	(40)	(50)			
End of Year 2: PPE carrying value	40	10	$30 ($40 – $10)	$12 ($30 × 40%)	$ 4 ($12 – $8)
Year 3: Depreciation	(40)	(10)			
End of Year 3: PPE carrying value	0	0	$ 0 ($0 – $0)	$ 0	$(12) ($0 – $12)

reported in the income statement (as a residual amount). Thus, tax expense is not computed as pretax income multiplied by the company's tax rate as we might initially expect. Instead, tax expense is computed as follows.

Tax Expense = Taxes Paid – Increase (or + Decrease) in Deferred Tax Assets + Increase (or – Decrease) in Deferred Tax Liabilities

The far-right column in Exhibit 10.6 shows the deferred tax expense per year, which is the amount added to, or subtracted from, taxes paid, to arrive at the tax expense. If we assume this company had $100 of pre-depreciation income, its taxable income and tax expense (assuming a 40% rate) follow.

	Taxes Paid	Deferred Tax Expense	Total Tax Expense
Year 1	$16 ($100 – $60) × 40%	$ 8	$24
Year 2	$20 ($100 – $50) × 40%	$ 4	$24
Year 3	$36 ($100 – $10) × 40%	$(12)	$24

In this example, the timing difference between the financial reporting and tax reporting derives from PPE and creates a deferred tax liability. Other differences between the two sets of books create other types of deferred tax accounts.

Rules for Deferred Tax Assets and Liabilities from Timing Differences Between GAAP and Tax

Exhibit 10.7 shows the relation between the financial reporting and tax reporting net book values, and the resulting deferred taxes (liability or asset) on the balance sheet.

Exhibit 10.7 ■ Sources of Deferred Tax Assets and Liabilities

For Assets...

Financial reporting net book value	> Tax reporting net book value	→ Deferred tax liability on balance sheet
Financial reporting net book value	< Tax reporting net book value	→ Deferred tax asset on balance sheet

For Liabilities...

Financial reporting net book value	< Tax reporting net book value	→ Deferred tax liability on balance sheet
Financial reporting net book value	> Tax reporting net book value	→ Deferred tax asset on balance sheet

Expanded Example of a Deferred Tax Asset: Restructuring Costs

A common deferred tax asset relates to accrued restructuring costs (a liability for financial reporting purposes). Restructuring costs are not deductible for tax purposes until paid in the future and, thus, there is no accrual restructuring liability for tax reporting, which means it has a tax basis of $0. To explain how this timing difference affects tax expense, assume that a company accrues $300 of restructuring costs in Year 1 and settles the liability in Year 2 as follows.

	Financial Reporting (Net Book Value)	Tax Reporting (Tax Basis)	Book vs. Tax Difference	Deferred Tax Asset (Book vs. Tax Difference × Tax Rate)	Deferred Tax Expense (Change in Deferred Tax Asset)
Year 1: Accrue restructuring costs . . .	$(300)	$ 0			
End of Year 1: Liability book value . . .	$ 300	$ 0	$300	$120	$(120)
			($300 – $0)	($300 × 40%)	($120 – $0)
Year 2: Pay restructuring costs.		$(300)			
End of Year 2: Liability book value . . .	$ 0	0	$ 0	$ 0	$120
			($0 – $0)	($0 × 40%)	($120 – $0)

Timing differences created by the restructuring liability yield a deferred tax asset in Year 1. Timing differences disappear in Year 2 when the company pays cash for restructuring costs. To see how tax expense is determined, assume that this company has $500 of pre-restructuring income each year; computations follow.

	Taxes Paid	Deferred Tax Expense	Total Tax Expense
Year 1.	$200	$(120)	$ 80
	($500 – $0) × 40%		
Year 2.	$ 80	$ 120	$200
	($500 – $300) × 40%		

Deferred tax accounts derive from timing differences between GAAP expenses and tax deductions. This creates differences between the net book value and the tax basis for many assets and liabilities. HP's deferred tax footnote (see Exhibit 10.5) reports several deferred tax assets and liabilities that explain its book-tax difference and the tax basis.

Review 10-3 LO3

Part 1

Refer to the following information from footnotes to FedEx's 2018 Form 10-K.

The components of the provision for income taxes for the years ended May 31 were as follows ($ millions):

	2018	2017	2016
Current provision (benefit)			
Domestic			
Federal	$(540)	$ 269	$513
State and local.	43	88	72
Foreign	461	285	200
	(36)	642	785
Deferred provision (benefit)			
Domestic			
Federal	271	989	155
State and local.	125	59	(18)
Foreign	(579)	(108)	(2)
	(183)	940	135
Provision for income taxes	$(219)	$1,582	$920

continued

continued from previous page

A reconciliation of total income tax expense and the amount computed by applying the statutory federal income tax rate (29.2% in 2018 and 35% in 2017 and 2016) to income before taxes for the years ended May 31 is as follows (in millions):

	2018	2017	2016
Taxes computed at federal statutory rate	$ 1,271	$1,603	$959
Increases (decreases) in income tax from:			
Goodwill impairment charge	109	—	—
State and local income taxes, net of federal benefit	119	99	33
Foreign operations	43	(19)	(50)
Corporate structuring transactions	(255)	(68)	(76)
Tax Cuts and Jobs Act	(1,357)	—	—
Foreign tax credits from distributions	(225)	—	—
Uncertain tax positions	86	—	—
TNT Express integration and acquisition costs.	20	25	40
Other, net	(30)	(58)	14
	$ (219)	$1,582	$920
Effective Tax Rate	(5.0)%	34.6%	33.6%

Required

1. What is the total income tax expense that FedEx reports in its 2018 income statement?
2. What amount of its total tax expense did (or will) FedEx pay in cash (that is, what amount is currently payable)?
3. Explain how FedEx calculates its income tax expense.
4. What was the effective tax rate for FedEx for 2018? Why is FedEx reporting a negative effective tax rate for 2018?

Part 2

Refer to the footnote disclosures from FedEx above along with the following additional disclosures.

	2018		2017	
$ millions	Deferred Tax Assets	Deferred Tax Liabilities	Deferred Tax Assets	Deferred Tax Liabilities
Property equipment, leases and intangibles.	$ 752	$3,663	$ 124	$4,993
Employee benefits	595	31	1,951	—
Self-insurance accruals	494	—	745	—
Other.	416	602	692	660
Net operating loss/credit carryforwards	1,146	—	1,069	—
Valuation allowances	(711)	—	(738)	—
	$2,692	$4,296	$3,843	$5,653

Our 2018 tax rate was favorably impacted by the enactment of the TCJA during the third quarter. In accordance with SAB 118, we have recorded a provisional benefit of $1.15 billion related to the remeasurement of our net U.S. deferred tax liability.

Required

1. To what does the property, equipment, leases and intangibles deferred tax liability of $3,663 million relate?
2. To what does the employee benefits deferred tax asset of $595 million relate?
3. Describe the way in which the property, equipment, leases and intangibles deferred tax liability is computed. Why did FedEx report a $1.15 billion income tax benefit as a result of the TCJA

Solution on p. 10-68.

Global Accounting

IFRS

We discussed three major areas of reporting in this module: leases, pensions, and taxes. There are several differences between U.S. GAAP and IFRS on these items, which we highlight below.

Leases The new lease accounting rules narrowed the difference between U.S. GAAP and IFRS. Under both standards, companies must recognize a right-of-use (ROU) asset and a lease liability on the balance sheet. This means the balance sheets of U.S. and international companies will be comparable. However, the income statement treatment and cash flow presentation differ. IFRS does not allow for operating leases; all leases under IFRS must be classified as finance leases with interest expense and ROU amortization on the income statement. Investors can overcome analytical challenges with the adjustments laid out earlier in this module.

Pensions For pension accounting, there are several disclosure differences and one notable accounting difference. The accounting difference pertains to actuarial gains and losses. U.S. GAAP permits deferral of actuarial gains and losses and then amortizes them to net income over time. A notable difference is that IFRS companies can recognize all actuarial gains and losses in comprehensive income in the year they occur, and they are *never* reported on the IFRS income statement. Many IFRS companies select this option. Turning to disclosure, one difference is that pension expense is not reported as a single item under IFRS; various components can be aggregated with other expenses. For example, interest cost can be included with other interest expenses and reported as finance expense under IFRS. A second disclosure difference is that IFRS companies do not disclose the full funded status of their pension plan on the balance sheet as U.S. GAAP requires. However, they must do so in the footnotes.

Income Taxes The two accounting standards are largely the same when it comes to accounting for deferred taxes. One difference of note, pertains to the valuation allowance. Under GAAP, deferred tax assets are recognized in full, and then reduced by a valuation allowance if it is considered more likely than not that some portion of the deferred taxes will not be realized. With IFRS, deferred tax assets are recognized net, that is, if it is more likely than not that future taxable profits will be high enough for the company to use the deferred tax assets. The end result is the same but without the initial recognition of a valuation allowance and any subsequent reversal.

Appendix 10A: Lease Accounting Example— Finance and Operating Leases

We illustrate the accounting for finance leases and operating leases under the 2019 accounting standard. Assume a company leases equipment with the following lease terms.

- Term: 5 years.
- Annual Payments: $22,463 at year-end.
- Initial direct costs paid by lessee: $5,000.
- Present value of lease payments, discounted at 4%: $100,000.

The table below shows the accounting treatment for both a finance lease and an operating lease.

		Lease Liability				Finance Lease				Operating Lease	
Year	Payments	Interest Portion	Decrease in Lease Liability	Lease Liability Balance	ROU Asset Amortization Expense	ROU Asset Balance	Interest Expense + Amortization Expense		Rent Expense	ROU Asset Amortization	ROU Asset Balance
0				❶ $100,000		❺ $105,000					❼ $105,000
1	$ 22,463	❷ $ 4,000	❸ $18,463	❹ $ 81,537	❻ $ 21,000	84,000	$25,000		❽ $ 23,463	❾ $ 19,463	85,537
2	22,463	3,261	19,201	62,336	21,000	63,000	24,261		23,463	20,201	65,336
3	22,463	2,493	19,969	42,367	21,000	42,000	23,493		23,463	20,969	44,367
4	22,463	1,695	20,768	21,599	21,000	21,000	22,695		23,463	21,768	22,599
5	22,463	864	21,599	0	21,000	0	21,864		23,463	22,599	—
Total	$112,314	$12,314			$105,000		$117,314		$117,314	$105,000	

❶ The lease liability, for both the finance lease and operating lease, is recognized at $100,000, which is the present value of the remaining lease payments discounted at 4%.

❷ The interest portion is the beginning balance of the lease liability × discount rate: $4,000 = $100,000 × 4% for Year 1.

❸ The lease liability is reduced by the difference between the lease payment and the interest portion: $18,463 = $22,463 − $4,000 for Year 1.

❹ The lease liability ending balance is equal to the beginning balance less the liability reduction during the year: $81,537 = $100,000 − $18,463 for Year 1.

❺ Right-of-use (ROU) asset is recognized at the initial balance of the lease liability plus any lease payments made to the lessor at or before the commencement date (and less any lease incentives received) and plus any initial direct costs incurred by the lessee: $105,000 = $100,000 + $5,000.

❻ ROU amortization for the finance lease is straight-line over the lease term: $21,000 = $105,000 / 5 years.

❼ ROU recognized for the operating lease is the same as for the finance lease at the inception of the lease. Over time, the two amounts deviate because the asset is amortized straight-line for finance leases but not for operating leases. (See #9, below).

❽ Rent expense recognized in the income statement for an operating lease is equal to the lease payment plus the straight-line amortization of any initial direct costs incurred by the lessee: $23,463 = $22,463 + $5,000/5 years.

❾ ROU amortization for an operating lease is not straight-line. It is equal to the rent expense for the operating lease less the interest amount for the year: $19,463 = $22,463 − $4,000 for Year 1. Interest is *not* recorded as an expense for an operating lease, but the amount is relevant because it is used to compute ROU amortization.

We see that lease expense for a finance lease exceeds that for an operating lease in the early years and is less in later years.

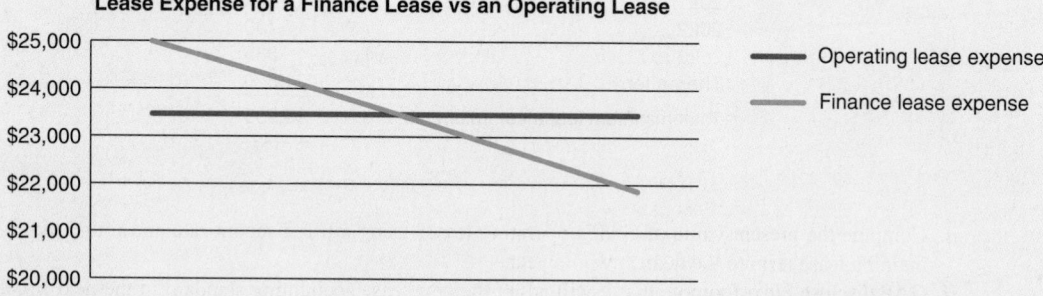

Lease Expense for a Finance Lease vs an Operating Lease

— Operating lease expense
— Finance lease expense

For companies with leases at approximately their mid-point in duration, the expense will be about the same for the two different lease types. However, income statement classification of total lease expense differs across the two lease types as follows.

- Expense for a finance lease consists of interest (nonoperating) and amortization of the right-of-use asset (operating).
- Expense for an operating lease is rent expense (operating).

Questions

Q10-1. Under the lease standards effective for 2019, how are leases treated on the balance sheet?

Q10-2. What are the four criteria that distinguish a finance lease from an operating lease?

Q10-3. Is the expense of a lease over its entire life the same for operating and finance leases? Explain.

Q10-4. What are the economic and accounting differences between a defined contribution plan and a defined benefit plan?

Q10-5. Under what circumstances will a company report a net pension asset? A net pension liability?

Q10-6. What are the components of pension expense that are reported in the income statement?

Q10-7. What effect does the use of expected returns on pension investments and the deferral of unexpected gains and losses on those investments have on income?

Q10-8. What are the two components of income tax expense?

Q10-9. Why do deferred taxes arise?

Q10-10. What is a valuation allowance for deferred tax assets?

Q10-11. Describe the income statement effect if a company reduced a deferred tax asset valuation allowance by $10 million.

Q10-12. What is a tax loss carryforward and how does it create an economic benefit for a company?

Q10-13. How do companies compute income tax expense for financial reporting purposes?

Assignments with the ⬤ logo in the margin are available in BusinessCourse.
See the Preface of the book for details.

Mini Exercises

M10-14. Analyzing and Interpreting Lease Footnote Disclosures

The **GAP Inc.** discloses the following schedule to its fiscal 2018 (ended February 2, 2019) 10-K report relating to its operating leasing activities.

> The aggregate minimum noncancelable annual lease payments under leases in effect on February 2, 2019, are as follows:
>
> | Fiscal Year ($ millions) | |
> |---|---:|
> | 2019 | $1,156 |
> | 2020 | 1,098 |
> | 2021 | 892 |
> | 2022 | 730 |
> | 2023 | 539 |
> | Thereafter | 1,520 |
> | Total minimum lease commitments | $5,935 |

a. Compute the present value of GAP's operating leases using a 6% discount rate and round the remaining lease term to the nearest whole year.

b. GAP disclosed in a footnote that it will adopt the new lease accounting standard in the next fiscal year. Had the company adopted the standard for the year ended February 2, 2019, and classified its leases as operating leases, what would have been the balance sheet impact from the leases disclosed above?

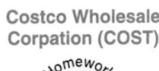

M10-15. Analyzing and Capitalizing Operating Lease Payments Disclosed in Footnotes

Costco Wholesale Corporation discloses the following in footnotes to its 10-K report relating to its leasing activities.

> At September 2, 2018, we operated 762 membership warehouses.
>
> | | Own Land and Building | Lease Land and/or Building | Total |
> |---|---:|---:|---:|
> | United States and Puerto Rico.... | 426 | 101 | 527 |
> | Canada. | 86 | 14 | 100 |
> | Mexico | 38 | 1 | 39 |
> | United Kingdom | 22 | 6 | 28 |
> | Japan | 12 | 14 | 26 |
> | Korea | 11 | 4 | 15 |
> | Taiwan | — | 13 | 13 |
> | Australia | 7 | 3 | 10 |
> | Spain | 2 | — | 2 |
> | Iceland | — | 1 | 1 |
> | France | 1 | — | 1 |
> | Total | 605 | 157 | 762 |

continued

continued from previous page

At September 2, 2018, our commitments to make future payments under contractual obligations were as follows:

Contractual obligations	Payments Due by Fiscal Year				
	2019	2020 to 2021	2022 to 2023	2024 and thereafter	Total
Operating leases	$227	$407	$358	$2,215	$3,207
Capital lease obligations.	34	71	72	647	824

a. From these disclosures it appears that Costco has not yet adopted the new leasing standard. How do we know this?

b. How would Costco determine if each of the lease contracts listed under Lease Land and/or Building would be a finance lease or an operating lease?

c. From the disclosure details, do you think the Lease Land and/or Building leases are operating or finance leases?

M10-16. Analyzing and Interpreting Pension Disclosures—Expenses and Returns

Stanley Black & Decker Inc. discloses the following pension footnote for 2018 in its 10-K report.

LO2

Stanley Black & Decker Inc. (SWK)

$ millions	U.S. Plans	Non-U.S. Plans	Total
Service cost	$ 7.5	$15.2	$ 22.7
Interest cost	42.8	28.6	71.4
Expected return on plan assets	(68.7)	(46.5)	(115.2)
Amortization of prior service cost (credit) . . .	1.1	(1.3)	(0.2)
Actuarial loss amortization	7.8	8.5	16.3
Settlement/curtailment loss	—	0.7	0.7
Net periodic pension (benefit) expense	$ (9.5)	$ 5.2	$ (4.3)

a. How much pension expense does Stanley Black & Decker report in its 2018 income statement?

b. Explain, in general, how expected return on plan assets affects reported pension expense. How did expected return affect Stanley Black & Decker's 2018 pension expense?

c. Explain use of the word "expected" as it relates to pension plan assets.

M10-17. Analyzing and Interpreting Pension Disclosures—PBO and Funded Status

YUM! Brands Inc. discloses the following pension footnote in its 10-K report.

LO2

YUM! Brands Inc. (YUM)

Pension Benefit Obligation ($ millions)	2018
Change in benefit obligation	
Benefit obligation at beginning of year	$1,007
Service cost	8
Interest cost	38
Plan amendments.	1
Special termination benefits	1
Benefits paid.	(73)
Actuarial (gain) loss	(109)
Benefit obligation at end of year.	$ 873

a. Explain the terms "service cost" and "interest cost."

b. How do actuarial losses arise?

c. The fair value of YUM!'s pension assets is $755 million as of 2018. What is the funded status of the plan, and how will this be reflected on YUM!'s balance sheet?

M10-18. Analyzing and Interpreting Pension Disclosures—Plan Assets and Cash Flow

YUM! Brands Inc. discloses the following pension footnote in its 10-K report.

Pension Plan Assets ($ millions)	2018
Fair value of plan assets at beginning of year	$864
Actual return on plan assets	(49)
Employer contributions	13
Benefits paid	(73)
Fair value of plan assets at end of year	$755

  a. How does the "actual return on plan assets" of $(49) million affect YUM!'s reported profits for 2018?

  b. YUM! Brands contributed $13 million cash to the pension plan investment account (asset) during the year. Which of the following is true?

   i. YUM! recognized the $13 million cash payment as a pension expense in 2018.

   ii. YUM! did not recognize the $13 million cash payment as a pension expense in 2018 because it is not tax deductible.

   iii. YUM! did not recognize the 13 million cash payment as a pension expense in 2018 because it relates to employees' service in prior periods.

   iv. YUM! did not recognize the $13 million cash payment as a pension expense in 2018 because benefits of $73 million were paid to employees and that amount represents the pension expense.

   v. None of the above.

  c. YUM!'s pension plan paid out $73 million in benefits during 2018. How is this payment reported?

M10-19. Analyzing and Interpreting Retirement Benefit Footnote

lululemon athletica discloses the following footnote relating to its retirement plans in its 10-K report for the year ended February 3, 2019.

> During fiscal 2016, the Company began offering pension plans to its eligible employees in Canada and the United States. Participating employees may elect to defer and contribute a portion of their eligible compensation to a plan up to limits stated in the plan documents, not to exceed the dollar amounts set by applicable laws. The Company matches 50% to 75% of the contribution depending on the participant's length of service, and the contribution is subject to a two year vesting period. The Company's net expense for the plans was $6.4 million, $5.2 million, and $3.2 million for the years ended February 3, 2019, January 28, 2018, and January 29, 2017, respectively.

  a. Does lululemon athletica have a defined contribution or defined benefit pension plan? Explain.

  b. How does lululemon athletica account for its contributions to its retirement plan?

  c. How does lululemon athletica report its obligation for its retirement plan on the balance sheet?

M10-20. Analyzing Adoption of New Lease Standard

AT&T Inc. provided the following footnote in its 10-Q report for the first quarter of fiscal 2019.

> As of January 1, 2019, we adopted, with modified retrospective application, Accounting Standards Update (ASU) No. 2016-02, Leases (Topic 842) as modified (ASC 842), which replaces existing leasing rules with a comprehensive lease measurement and recognition standard and expanded disclosure requirements.
>
>   Using the modified retrospective transition method of adoption, we did not adjust the balance sheet for comparative periods but recorded a cumulative effect adjustment to retained earnings on January 1, 2019. We elected the package of practical expedients permitted under the transition guidance within the new standard. Our accounting for finance leases did not change from our prior accounting for capital leases.
>
>   The adoption of ASC 842 resulted in the recognition of an operating lease liability of $22,121 and an operating right-of-use asset of the same amount. Existing prepaid and deferred rent accruals were recorded as an offset to the right-of-use asset, resulting in a net asset of $20,960. The cumulative effect of the adoption to retained earnings was an increase of $316 reflecting the reclassification of deferred gains related to sale/leaseback transactions. The standard will have no impact on our debt-covenant compliance under our current agreements.

On January 1, 2019, after adopting the new standard, AT&T's balance sheet reported the following amounts ($ millions).

Total assets ..... $531,864   Total liabilities.... $445,290   Total equity...... $86,574

Required

a. When AT&T adopted the new standard, what were the dollar effects on total assets and on total liabilities?

b. AT&T used the modified retrospective transition method of adoption. Explain what this means and describe the dollar impact on retained earnings.

c. Quantify in percentage terms, the size of the dollar effect of the adoption of the new standard on AT&T's assets, liabilities, and equity.

M10-21. Analyzing and Interpreting Pension Plan Benefit Footnotes

Lockheed Martin Corporation discloses the following funded status for its defined benefit pension plans in its 10-K report.

LO2

Lockheed Martin
Corporation (LMT)

Defined Benefit Pension Plans ($ millions)	2018
Unfunded status of the plans	$(11,303)

Lockheed contributed $5,000 million to its pension plan assets in 2018, up drastically from $46 million in the prior year. The company also reports that it is obligated for the following expected payments to retirees in the next five years.

$ millions	Qualified Pension Benefits
2019	$ 2,350
2020	2,390
2021	2,470
2022	2,550
2023	2,610
Years 2024–2028	13,670

a. How is this funded status reported in Lockheed's balance sheet under current GAAP?

b. How should we interpret this funded status in our analysis of the company?

c. What likely effect did the bull market from 2015 through 2019 have on Lockheed's contribution to its pension plans? Explain.

M10-22. Analyzing and Interpreting Income Tax Disclosures

Apple Inc. reports the following footnote disclosure to its 2018 10-K report ($ millions).

LO3

Apple Inc. (AAPL)

The provision for income taxes consisted of the following:

Fiscal Year Ended	September 29, 2018
Federal	
Current	$41,425
Deferred	(33,819)
	7,606
State	
Current	551
Deferred	48
	599
Foreign	
Current	3,986
Deferred	1,181
	5,167
Total	$13,372

a. What amount of income tax expense does Apple report in its income statement for 2018?
b. How much of Apple's income tax expense is current (as opposed to deferred)?
c. Why do deferred tax assets and liabilities arise? How do they impact the tax expense that Apple reports in its 2018 income statement?

LO3
Walmart (WMT)

M10-23. Analyzing and Interpreting Income Tax Footnote
The following is an excerpt from Walmart's Form 10-K for the fiscal year ended January 31, 2019.

A summary of the provision for income taxes is as follows ($ millions):

Current:	
U.S. federal.	$2,763
U.S. state and local.	493
International	1,495
Total current tax provision	4,751
Deferred:	
U.S. federal.	(361)
U.S. state and local.	(16)
International	(93)
Total deferred tax expense (benefit).	$ (470)

Required
a. What amount of income tax expense does Walmart report in its income statement for the fiscal year ended January 31, 2019?
b. How much of Walmart's income tax expense was determined from the company's tax returns?
c. How did deferred taxes affect Walmart's tax expense for the year?

LO3
Walmart (WMT)

M10-24. Analyzing Tax Expense
Refer to the excerpt from Walmart's Form 10-K in M10-23. Consider the deferred portion of Walmart's tax provision. Which of the following is plausible? (*Hint*: Consider the tax expense equation.)
a. Walmart's deferred tax assets increased during the year.
b. Walmart's deferred tax liabilities decreased during the year.
c. Both *a* and *b* are plausible.
d. Neither *a* nor *b* is plausible.

LO3

M10-25. Analyzing Tax Expense
Crestview Holdings reported the following in its 2020 financial statements.

$ millions	2020	2019
Total deferred tax assets	$ 821	$ 764
Total deferred tax liabilities.	4,089	3,126
Current provision for income taxes.	1,372	134

Required
Compute the deferred tax expense for the company for 2020.

LO2
Bristol Myers Squibb (BMY)

M10-26. Analyzing Footnote Disclosure of Pension Buy-out
In a press release dated December 3, 2018, Bristol Myers Squibb disclosed the following with respect to its pension plans (excerpted).

NEW YORK (BUSINESS WIRE) Bristol-Myers Squibb Company (NYSE: BMY) today announced it will transfer $3.8 billion of U.S. pension obligations through a full termination of its U.S. Retirement Income Plan. The obligations will be distributed through a combination of lump sums to Plan participants who elect such payments, and the purchase of a group annuity contract from Athene Annuity and Life Company, for all remaining liabilities.

continued

continued from previous page

> The Plan includes approximately 4,800 active employees, 1,400 retirees and their beneficiaries receiving benefits, and 18,000 prior Bristol-Myers Squibb employees who have not yet initiated their benefits. Current Plan provisions, benefit payment options and in-pay benefits will remain available for all participants.
>
> Upon closing of this transaction in the third quarter of 2019, the Company expects a non-cash pre-tax pension settlement charge of approximately $1.5 billion–$2 billion.

Required

a. In plain language, explain this transaction. Why would the company engage in such a transaction?

b. What are the two payout options available to the company's employees, retirees, and prior employees?

c. At December 31, 2018, Bristol Myers Squibb reported a funded status of $163 million on its balance sheet. What will be the net funded status at December 31, 2019? For this question, assume the $163 million relate solely to the U.S. Retirement Income Plan.

M10-27. **Analyzing Footnote Disclosure of Pension Income**

In its 2018 10-K, Norfolk Southern Railroad reported the following in a footnote labeled "Other income, net."

LO2
Norfolk Southern
Railroad (NSC)

($ in millions)	2018	2017	2016
Net pension and other postretirement benefit cost.	$61	$ 64	$ 65
Rental income.	5	87	93
External advisor costs	—	—	(20)
Other.	1	5	(2)
Total	$67	$156	$136

Required

a. Explain how Norfolk Southern could report "income" of $61 million related to its pension and other postretirement plans as opposed to an expense.

b. For purposes of analysis, would we classify this 'Other income, net' as operating or nonoperating?

Exercises

E10-28. **Analyzing and Interpreting Leasing Footnote**

Lowe's Companies reports the following footnote relating to its leased facilities in its first quarter report dated May 3, 2019

LO1
Lowe's Companies
Inc. (LOW)

> During the first quarter of fiscal 2019, the Company adopted ASU 2016-02, Leases (Topic 842), which requires leases to be recognized on the balance sheet. The Company leases certain retail stores, warehouses, distribution centers, office space, land and equipment under finance and operating leases.
>
> The table below presents the Company's operating lease-related assets and liabilities recorded on the balance sheet.

(in millions)	Classification	May 3, 2019
Assets		
Operating lease assets	Operating lease right-of-use assets	$3,926
Liabilities		
Current.	Current operating lease liabilities	500
Noncurrent.	Noncurrent operating lease liabilities	4,064

continued

continued from prior page

Maturity of Lease Liabilities (In millions)	Operating Leases
2019	$ 463
2020	664
2021	636
2022	642
2023	554
After 2023..............................	2,934
Total lease payments	5,893
Less: interest	(1,329)
Present value of lease liabilities	$4,564

a. Use Excel to confirm that Lowe's capitalized its operating leases using a rate of about 4%. *Note:* The company discloses the remaining maturity of its operating leases is 10.68 years (after 2023), which can be used to determine the annual payment in years after 2023.
b. What effect did the initial capitalization of the operating leases have on Lowe's assets and liabilities?
c. How will Lowe's treat the operating right-of-use asset on its balance sheet over the life of the lease?
d. How will Lowe's treat the operating lease liability on its balance sheet over the life of the lease?

LO1

Verizon
Communications Inc.
(VZ)

E10-29. Analyzing and Interpreting Footnote on Operating and Capital Leases

Verizon Communications Inc. provides the following footnote relating to adoption of the new lease accounting standards (Topic 842) in its 10-Q report for the quarter ended March 31, 2019.

The cumulative after-tax effect of the changes made to our condensed consolidated balance sheet for the adoption of Topic 842 were as follows:

($ millions)	At December 31, 2018	Adjustments due to Topic 842	At January 1, 2019
Prepaid expenses and other.............	$ 5,453	$ (329)	$5,124
Operating lease right-of-use assets	—	23,241	23,241
Other assets.........................	11,717	(2,048)	9,669
Accounts payable and accrued liabilities ...	22,501	(3)	22,498
Other current liabilities	8,239	(2)	8,237
Current operating lease liabilities	—	2,931	2,931
Deferred income taxes	33,795	139	33,934
Noncurrent operating lease liabilities	—	19,203	19,203
Other liabilities	13,922	(1,815)	12,107
Retained earnings	43,542	410	43,952
Noncontrolling interests	1,565	1	1,566

Rent expense for operating leases is recognized on a straight-line basis over the term of the lease and is included in either Cost of services or Selling, general and administrative expense in our condensed consolidated statements of income, based on the use of the facility on which rent is being paid.

a. What is the amount of the right-of-use asset the company added to its balance sheet upon adoption of the new standard?
b. How will Verizon treat the right-of-use asset on the balance sheet during the life of the lease?
c. Assume the right-of-use assets had a weighted average lease term of 12 years. Approximate the effect the operating leases had on Verizon's income statement in Q1 2019.
d. What is the amount of the total operating lease liabilities the company added to its balance sheet upon adoption of the new standard? Explain what this amount represents.
e. The company decided to adopt the standard with a modified retrospective method and did not adjust numbers on the comparative balance sheet. What analysis challenges does this create?

E10-30. Analyzing, Interpreting, and Capitalizing Operating Leases

TJX Companies Inc. reports the following balance sheet in its 2019 first-quarter report (10-Q).

LO1

TJX Companies Inc.
(TJX)

$ thousands	May 4, 2019	February 2, 2019
Assets		
Current assets		
Cash and cash equivalents	$ 2,235,056	$ 3,030,229
Accounts receivable, net	393,276	346,298
Merchandise inventories	5,057,202	4,579,033
Prepaid expenses and other current assets	381,678	513,662
Total current assets	8,067,212	8,469,222
Net property at cost	5,018,598	5,255,208
Noncurrent deferred income taxes, net	5,801	6,467
Operating lease right-of-use assets	8,810,367	—
Goodwill	96,685	97,552
Other assets	490,401	497,580
Total Assets	$22,489,064	$14,326,029
Liabilities		
Current liabilities		
Accounts payable	$ 2,578,370	$ 2,644,143
Accrued expenses and other current liabilities	2,468,588	2,733,076
Current portion of operating lease liabilities	1,343,243	—
Federal, state and foreign income taxes payable	190,818	154,155
Total current liabilities	6,581,019	5,531,374
Other long-term liabilities	752,968	1,354,242
Noncurrent deferred income taxes, net	167,283	158,191
Long-term operating lease liabilities	7,621,531	—
Long-term debt	2,234,368	2,233,616
Shareholders' Equity		
Preferred stock, authorized 5,000,000 shares, par value $1, no shares issued	—	—
Common stock, authorized 1,800,000,000 shares, par value $1, issued and outstanding 1,212,667,546; 1,217,182,508 and 1,250,405,376 respectively	1,212,668	1,217,183
Additional paid-in capital	—	—
Accumulated other comprehensive loss	(633,282)	(630,321)
Retained earnings	4,552,509	4,461,744
Total shareholders' equity	5,131,895	5,048,606
Total Liabilities and Shareholders' Equity	$22,489,064	$14,326,029

TJX reported the following in its 10-K report for the year ended February 2, 2019.

The following is a schedule of future minimum lease payments for continuing operations as of February 2, 2019:

In thousands	Operating Leases
Fiscal year 2020	$1,676,700
2021	1,603,378
2022	1,441,444
2023	1,253,420
2024	1,042,184
Later years	2,774,845
Total future minimum lease payments	$9,791,971

Required

a. The company adopted the new lease standard using the modified retrospective method which does not require restatement of comparative numbers on the balance sheet. What analysis challenge does this present if we want to analyze TJX at May 4, 2019?

b. Assume a discount rate of 3.75% to determine the present value of the operating lease payments at fiscal-year-end February 2, 2019. Use Excel and do not round any of your numbers or subtotals.

c. What adjustments might we make to the fiscal-year-end numbers to increase comparability of the TJX balance sheet numbers?

d. Did the new lease standard have a material effect on the TJX balance sheet? Explain.

LO2   **E10-31. Analyzing and Interpreting Pension Disclosures**

General Mills Inc.
(GIS)

General Mills Inc. reports the following pension footnote in its 10-K report.

Defined Benefit Pension Plans ($ millions)	Fiscal Year 2019
Change in Plan Assets	
Fair value at beginning of year	$6,177.4
Actual return on assets	391.9
Employer contributions	30.4
Plan participant contributions	3.9
Benefits payments	(305.2)
Foreign currency	(6.8)
Fair value at end of year	$6,291.6
Change in Projected Benefit Obligation	
Benefit obligation at beginning of year	$6,416.0
Service cost	94.6
Interest cost	248.0
Curtailment/other	(0.7)
Plan participant contributions	3.9
Actuarial loss	301.8
Benefits payments	(305.8)
Foreign currency	(7.1)
Projected benefit obligation at end of year	$6,750.7

Estimated benefit payments . . . are expected to be paid from fiscal 2020–2029 as follows:

$ millions	Defined Benefit Pension Plans
2020	$ 319.0
2021	324.9
2022	331.8
2023	338.8
2024	346.3
2025–2029	1,856.4

a. Describe what is meant by *service cost* and *interest cost*.

b. What is the total amount paid to retirees during fiscal 2019? What is the source of funds to make these payments to retirees?

c. Compute the 2019 funded status for the company's pension plan.

d. What are actuarial gains and losses? What are the plan amendment adjustments, and how do they differ from the actuarial gains and losses?

e. General Mills projects payments to retirees of between $320 and $350 million per year. How is the company able to contribute only $30.4 million to its pension plan?

f. What effect would a substantial decline in the financial markets have on General Mills' contribution to its pension plans?

E10-32. **Analyzing and Interpreting Pension and Healthcare Footnote**

Norfolk Southern Railroad reports the following pension and other postretirement benefits footnote as part of its 10-K report.

December 31, 2018 ($ millions)	Pension Benefits	Other Post-Retirement Benefits
Change in Benefit Obligation		
Benefit obligation at beginning of year	$2,541	$510
Service cost	39	7
Interest cost	83	15
Actuarial losses (gains)	(149)	(24)
Benefits paid/settlements	(143)	(42)
Benefit obligation at end of year	$2,371	$466
Change in plan assets		
Fair value of plan assets at beginning of year	$2,373	$201
Actual return on plan assets	(143)	(19)
Employer contribution	18	18
Benefits paid	(143)	(42)
Fair value of plan assets at end of year	$2,105	$158
Net cost benefit		
Service cost	$ 39	$ 7
Interest cost	83	15
Expected return on plan assets	(177)	(15)
Amortization of net losses	57	—
Amortization of prior service cost (benefit)	—	(24)
Net cost (benefit)	$ 2	$ (17)

a. Describe what is meant by *service cost* and *interest cost* (the service and interest costs appear both in the reconciliation of the PBO and in the computation of pension expense).

b. What is the actual return on the pension and other postretirement benefits plan investments in 2018? Was Norfolk Southern's profitability impacted by this amount?

c. Provide an example under which an "actuarial gain," such as the 2018 gain of $149 million that Norfolk Southern reports, might arise.

d. What is the source of funds to make payments to retirees?

e. How much did Norfolk Southern contribute to its pension and other postretirement benefits plans in 2018?

f. How much cash did retirees receive from the pension plan and the other post-retirement benefits plans in 2018? How much cash did Norfolk Southern pay these retirees?

g. Show the computation of the funded status for the pension and other postretirement benefits plans in 2018.

E10-33. **Analyzing and Interpreting Pension and Healthcare Disclosures**

Verizon Communications Inc. reports the following pension footnote as part of its 10-K report.

December 31, 2018 ($ millions)	Pension
Change in Benefit Obligations	
Beginning of year	$21,531
Service cost	284
Interest cost	690
Plan amendments	230
Actuarial (gain) loss, net	(1,418)
Benefits paid	(1,475)
Curtailment and termination benefits	181
Settlements paid	(456)
End of year	$19,567

continued

continued from prior page

December 31, 2018 ($ millions)	Pension
Change in Plan Assets	
Beginning of year	$19,175
Actual return on plan assets	(494)
Company contributions	1,066
Benefits paid	(1,475)
Settlements paid	(456)
End of year	$17,816

The following table summarizes the components of net periodic benefit cost related to our pension plans.

Years Ended December 31, 2018 ($ millions)	Pension
Service cost—cost of services	$ 230
Service cost—selling, general and administrative expense	54
Service cost	284
Amortization of prior service cost (credit)	48
Expected return on plan assets	(1,293)
Interest cost	690
Remeasurement loss (gain), net	369
Curtailment and termination benefits	181
Total	$ 279

Verizon discloses the following assumptions related to its pension plans.

At December 31	2018	2017
Discount rate used in determining benefit obligations	4.4%	3.7%
Expected return on plan assets	7.0%	7.7%

a. Describe what is meant by *service cost* and *interest cost.*

b. What payments did retirees receive during fiscal 2018 from the pension plans? What is the source of funds to make payments to retirees?

c. Show the computation of Verizon's 2018 funded status for the pension plans.

d. What expense does Verizon's income statement report for its pension plans?

e. Why does Verizon distinguish between the Service cost for Cost of services and for Selling, general and administrative expense?

f. Consider the two pension-related assumptions above. Indicate whether the 2018 assumptions will increase, decrease, or have no effect on each of the following three pension plan elements *relative to the assumption in 2017*: PBO; Pension Plan Assets; and 2018 Pension Expense.

LO3   **E10-34.   Analyzing and Interpreting Income Tax Disclosures**

The Boeing Company (BA)

Homework
MBC

The income tax footnote to the 2018 financial statements for Boeing follows.

The components of income before tax were:

Years ended December 31 ($ millions)	2018	2017	2016
U.S.	$11,166	$9,660	$5,386
Non-U.S.	438	447	397
Total	$11,604	$10,107	$5,783

continued

continued from previous page

Income tax expense/(benefit) consisted of the following:

Years ended December 31 ($ millions)	2018	2017	2016
Current tax expense			
U.S. federal	$1,873	$1,276	$1,193
Non-U.S.	169	149	133
U.S. state	97	23	15
Total current	$2,139	$1,448	$1,341
Deferred tax expense			
U.S. federal	$ (996)	$ 204	$ (544)
Non-U.S.	(4)	3	(4)
U.S. state	5	(6)	(44)
Total deferred	$ (995)	$ 201	$ (592)

a. What is the amount of income tax expense reported by Boeing each year?
b. What percentage of total tax expense is currently payable for each year?
c. What is Boeing's effective (average) tax rate for each year?
d. Use the pretax information to determine the effective tax rate for U.S. and Non-U.S. operations for each year. What do we observe?
e. Determine the cash tax rate for U.S. operations for each year. *Hint:* Current tax expense is paid in cash; compare the rates calculated to the U.S. statutory rates each year: 2017 and 2018: 21%, and 2016: 35%.

E10-35. Analyzing and Interpreting Income Tax Disclosures

Colgate-Palmolive reports the following income tax footnote disclosure in its 10-K report.

LO3
Colgate-Palmolive
(CL)

Deferred Tax Balances at December 31 ($ millions)	2018	2017
Deferred tax liabilities		
Goodwill and intangible assets	$(344)	$(311)
Property, plant and equipment	(311)	(306)
Deferred withholding tax	(181)	(119)
Other	(75)	(63)
Total deferred tax liabilities	(911)	(799)
Deferred tax assets		
Pension and other retiree benefits	354	375
Tax credits and tax loss carryforwards	89	48
Accrued liabilities	180	197
Stock-based compensation	95	90
Other	164	82
Total deferred tax assets	882	792
Valuation allowance	(54)	(9)
Net deferred tax assets	828	783
Net deferred income taxes	$ (83)	$ (16)
Deferred taxes included within		
Assets		
Deferred income taxes	152	188
Liabilities		
Deferred income taxes	(235)	(204)
Net deferred income taxes	$ (83)	$ (16)

a. Colgate reports $311 million of deferred tax liabilities in 2018 relating to "Property." Explain how such liabilities arise.

b. Describe how a deferred tax asset can arise from pension and other retiree benefits.

c. Colgate reports $89 million in deferred tax assets for 2018 relating to tax loss and tax credit carryforwards. Describe how tax loss carryforwards arise and under what conditions the resulting deferred tax assets will be realized.

d. Colgate's income statement reports income tax expense of $906 million in 2018. Assume that cash paid for income tax is $847 million and that taxes payable decreased by $8 million. Use the financial statement effects template to record tax expense for 2018. (*Hint:* Show the effects of changes in deferred taxes.)

LO1 **E10-36. Using Graphical Data to Interpret Operating Lease Footnotes**

The following graphics relate to operating leases for S&P 500 firms from 2010 through 2018. The data come from the period before the new lease standards because most firms adopted the standard in fiscal 2019 (the first mandated year). Present values are calculated with a 5% discount rate. Access the dashboard at myBusinessCourse to answer the requirements.

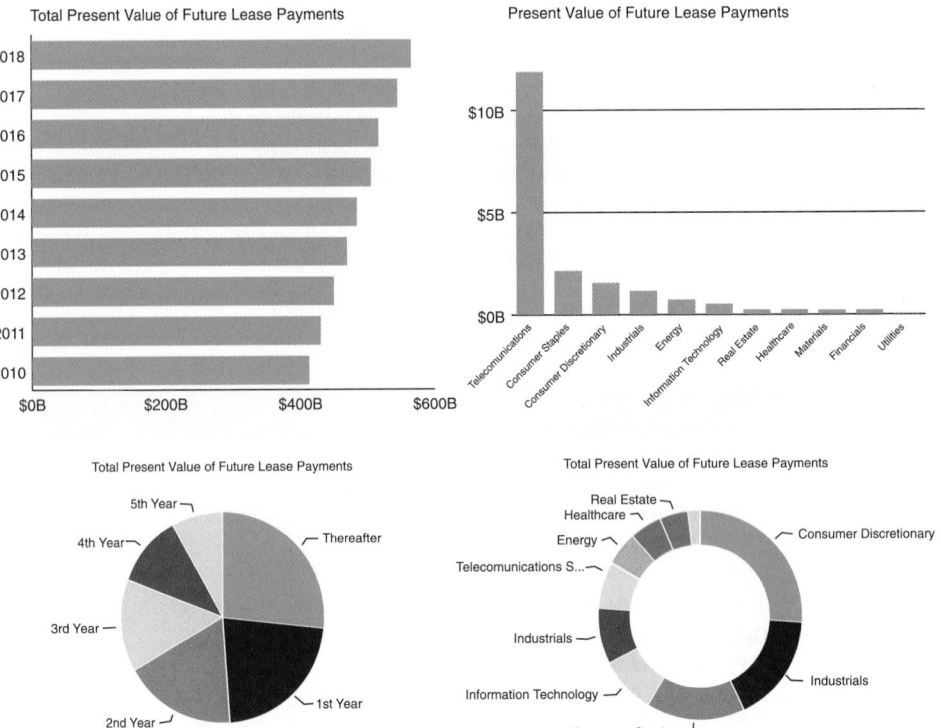

Required

a. Consider the top left panel. What pattern do we observe for the overall level of operating leases over time? How does this affect our analysis of a company's leverage?

b. Consider the bottom right panel. Which industrial sector has the most operating leases? What types of companies are in that sector? What sort of assets are typically leased in this sector?

c. Consider the top right panel. Which industrial sector has the largest average operating leases? What types of companies are in that sector? What sorts of assets are typically leased in this sector?

d. Consider the pie chart that shows lease payments by year (bottom left panel). How could we use this graphic to determine which sector has the longest lease terms?

LO2 **E10-37. Using Graphical Data to Interpret Pension Footnotes**

The following graphics relate to pensions for S&P 500 firms from 2010 through 2018. Access the dashboard at myBusinessCourse to answer the requirements.

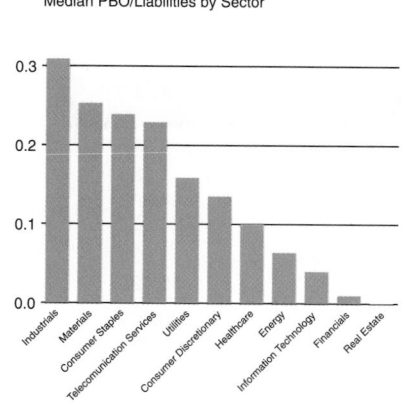

Median PBO/Liabilities by Sector

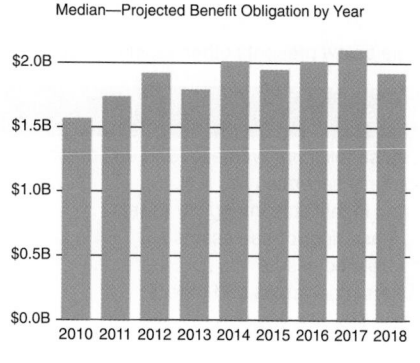

Median—Projected Benefit Obligation by Year

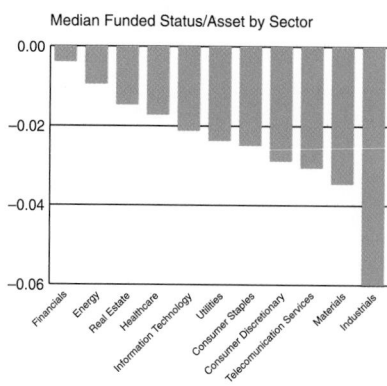

Median Funded Status/Asset by Sector

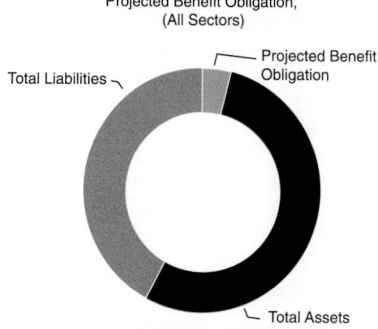

Projected Benefit Obligation, (All Sectors)

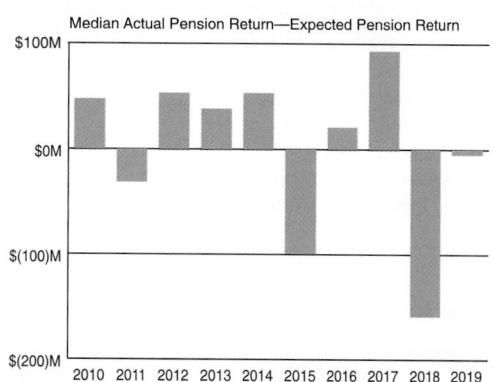

Median Actual Pension Return—Expected Pension Return

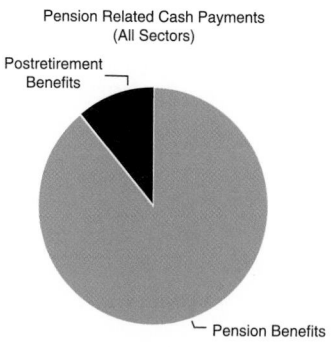

Pension Related Cash Payments (All Sectors)

Required

a. Which sector has the largest PBO? What types of companies are in that sector?

b. Do we observe a pattern for PBO over time? Looking across all sectors, which year had the highest median PBO? Does that hold for all sectors?

c. Compare the size of the PBO by sector to the funded status by sector (top left graphic compared to top right graphic). What pattern do we observe?

d. Consider the graphic in the lower middle. This displays the actual return on pension assets minus the expected returns (in $ millions). Explain how actual returns could differ from expected returns. What does it mean for bars above versus below the $0 line in this graphic?

e. Consider the pie chart that displays the cash payments for pension and healthcare benefits. Looking across all sectors, what is the relative magnitude of the two cash outflows? In which sector are postretirement benefits the largest compared to pension benefits paid?

Problems

P10-38. **Analyzing, Interpreting, and Capitalizing Operating Leases**

Goldman Sachs' SEC filing for the quarter ended March 31, 2019, report contains the following lease footnote.

LO1

The Goldman Sachs Group Inc.

(GS)

> **Leases (ASC 842).** In February 2016, the FASB issued ASU No. 2016-02, Leases (Topic 842). This ASU requires that, for leases longer than one year, a lessee recognize in the statements of financial condition a right-of-use asset and a lease liability. It also requires that for finance leases, a lessee recognize interest expense on the lease liability, separately from the amortization of the right-of-use asset in the statements of earnings, while for operating leases, such amounts should be recognized as a combined expense. The firm adopted this ASU in January 2019 under a modified retrospective approach.

continued

continued from previous page

The table below presents other assets by type.

$ in millions	March 2019	December 2018
Property, leasehold improvements and equipment ...	$19,277	$18,317
Held-to-maturity securities	5,841	1,288
Goodwill and identifiable intangible assets..........	4,092	4,082
Operating lease right-of-use assets	2,386	—
Income tax-related assets	1,729	1,529
Miscellaneous receivables and other	4,358	5,424
Total	$37,683	$30,640

The table below presents other liabilities by type.

$ in millions	March 2019	December 2018
Compensation and benefits	$ 3,110	$ 6,834
Income tax-related liabilities	3,080	2,864
Operating lease liabilities	2,413	—
Noncontrolling interests	1,565	1,568
Employee interests in consolidated funds	122	122
Accrued expenses and other	5,884	6,219
Total	$16,174	$17,607

The table below presents information about future operating lease payments.

$ in millions	March 2019
Remainder of 2019.......................................	$ 318
2020	341
2021	262
2022	235
2023	204
2024	193
2025–thereafter	2,494
Total undiscounted lease payments	4,047
Imputed interest	(1,634)
Total operating lease liabilities	$ 2,413
Weighted average remaining lease term	18 years
Weighted average discount rate............................	4.85%

Goldman Sachs's 10-K report for the year ended December 31, 2018, included the following table about future cash payments required under operating leases.

The table below presents future minimum rental payments, net of minimum sublease rentals.

$ in millions	December 2018
2019	$ 281
2020	271
2021	218
2022	177
2023	142
2024 – thereafter	1,310
Total	$2,399

Required

a. Explain in plain language what "right-to-use assets" are; that is, how do they convey an economic benefit to the company?

b. What operating lease liability did Goldman Sachs report for the quarter ended March 31, 2019?

c. How does Goldman Sachs determine the amount of operating lease liabilities to add to its balance sheet?

d. Use an Excel spreadsheet and the information on future operating lease payments to verify the total liabilities of $2,413 million on the 2019 Form 10-Q. *Hint*: The amount might not be exactly $2,413.

e. What right-of-use assets did Goldman Sachs report for the quarter ended March 31, 2019? Given Goldman Sachs' business, what does the company lease under its operating leases?

f. Why might the right-of-use asset amount that Goldman Sachs added to the January 2019 balance sheet differ from the related operating lease liabilities?

g. Use the information on rental payments from the December 2018 Form 10-K, to calculate the present value of future payments at year-end. Use the same average weighted lease term and discount rate Goldman Sachs discloses in the 2019 Form 10-Q.

h. How would we adjust the December 2018 balance sheet to enhance comparability?

P10-39. Applying New Lease Accounting Standards for Operating Leases

On January 1 of the current year, CCH Corporation entered into the following lease contract. Based on the facts, CCH Corporation classifies the lease as an operating lease. The company has a 5% cost of debt capital.

LO1

Leased asset: Office space.   Annual lease payment: $115,487 due at each year-end.
Lease term: 5 years.   Upfront fees: $10,000 paid in cash.

Required

a. Explain how the facts support the classification of the lease as an operating lease.

b. Determine the amount of the lease liability that CCH will add to its balance sheet at the inception of the lease.

c. What amount will be added to the balance sheet as an asset? What will CCH Corporation call the asset on the balance sheet?

d. Prepare a lease amortization schedule that shows the interest and principal portions of each lease payment.

e. Use the financial statement effects template to record the lease inception and lease payments for the first two years of the lease term. Also show the asset and lease amortization for those same two years.

f. At the end of the current year, what additional disclosure would CCH make in its footnotes pertaining to the four remaining lease payments?

g. CCH Corporation also has finance leases. To enhance comparability, what adjustments would we make to the CCH income statement in the current year?

P10-40. Analyzing, Interpreting, and Capitalizing Operating Leases

On January 1, 2020, Alexander Mack Adventures Inc. entered into land leases that grant unrestricted access to property in Texas where the company plans to build an RV resort. Lease details follow.

LO1

- Lease term: 15 years.
- Upfront fees: $450,000 paid in cash.
- Annual lease payment: $500,000 due at each year-end.
- Lessee responsible for property tax and insurance.

The company also leased computer equipment with the following details.

- Lease term: 4 years.
- Upfront fees: $5,000.
- Annual lease payments: $24,694.
- Lessee has option to purchase equipment for $1 at end of lease.

Required

a. Given the lease contract facts, determine the classification for each of the two leases (operating or finance).

b. Determine the amount of the lease liability that Alexander Mack will add to its balance sheet at the inception of each lease. The company has a 9% cost of debt capital.

c. What asset will the company add to its balance sheet for each lease?

d. For each lease, prepare an amortization schedule that shows the interest and principal portions of each lease payment.

e. What will be the income statement effect of the land lease in 2020?

    f. What will be the income statement effect of the equipment lease in 2020?

    g. For fiscal 2020, what additional disclosure would Alexander Mack make in its footnotes pertaining to the remaining land lease payments?

    h. On December 31, 2021, what amount will be on the balance sheet (asset and liability) for each of the leases?

    i. To enhance comparability, what adjustments would we make to the Alexander Mack income statement in 2020?

LO2

P10-41. **Analyzing and Interpreting Pension Disclosures**

DowDuPont Inc. (DD)

DowDuPont's 10-K report has the following disclosures related to its retirement plans ($ millions).

Obligations and Funded Status ($ millions)	December 31, 2018
Change in projected benefit obligations	
Benefit obligations at beginning of year	$ 57,401
Service cost	651
Interest cost	1,638
Plan participants' contributions	29
Actuarial changes in assumptions and experience	(2,832)
Benefits paid	(3,223)
Plan amendments	34
Acquisitions/divestitures/other	(57)
Effect of foreign exchange rates	(627)
Benefit obligation at end of year	$53,014
Change in plan assets	
Fair value of plan assets at beginning of year	$ 43,685
Actual return on plan assets	(1,524)
Employer contributions	2,964
Plan participants' contributions	29
Benefits paid	(3,223)
Acquisitions/divestitures/other	(7)
Effect of foreign exchange rates	(462)
Fair value of plan assets at end of year	$ 41,462
Funded status	
U.S. plan with plan assets	$ (6,956)
Non-U.S. plans with plan assets	(2,751)
All other plans	(1,845)
Funded status at end of year	$(11,552)

Components of Net Periodic Benefit Cost ($ millions)	December 31, 2018
Net periodic benefit cost	
Service cost	$ 651
Interest cost	1,638
Expected return on plan assets	(2,846)
Amortization of prior service credit	(24)
Amortization of unrecognized (gain) loss	649
Curtailment/settlement/other	(10)
Net periodic benefit costs—Total	$ 58

Weighted-Average Assumptions used to Determine Net Periodic Benefit Cost for Years Ended December 31	2018	2017
Discount rate	3.80%	3.26%
Expected return on plan assets	6.68%	6.94%
Rate of compensation increase	3.95%	3.88%

The following benefit payments, which reflect future service, as appropriate, are expected to be paid:

$ millions	Pension Benefits
2019	$ 3,197
2020	3,172
2021	3,182
2022	3,198
2023	3,219
2024–2028	16,078
Total	$32,046

Required

a. How much pension expense does DowDuPont report in its 2018 income statement? Would 2018 pension expense have been higher or lower if DowDuPont had not changed the "Rate of compensation increase" from 2017 to 2018?

b. DowDuPont reports a $2,846 million expected return on pension plan assets as an offset to 2018 pension expense. Estimate what the expected return would have been had DowDupont not changed the assumption on the expected return in 2018. What is DowDuPont's actual gain or loss realized on its 2018 pension plan assets? What is the purpose of using this expected return instead of the actual gain or loss (return)?

c. What main factors (and dollar amounts) affected DowDuPont's pension liability during 2018? What main factors (and dollar amounts) affected its pension plan assets during 2018?

d. What does the term *funded status* mean? What is the funded status of the 2018 DowDuPont pension plans?

e. DowDuPont increased its discount rate during 2018. What effect(s) does this have on its balance sheet and its income statement?

f. How did DowDuPont's pension plan affect the company's cash flow in 2018? (Identify any inflows and outflows, including amounts.)

g. Explain how the returns on pension assets affect the amount of cash that DowDuPont must contribute to fund the pension plan.

P10-42. Analyzing and Interpreting Pension Disclosures

Johnson & Johnson provides the following footnote disclosures in its 10-K report relating to its defined benefit pension plans and its other postretirement benefits.

LO2
Johnson & Johnson
(JNJ)

December 31, 2018 ($ millions)	Retirement Plans	Other Benefit Plans
Change in Benefit Obligation		
Projected benefit obligation—beginning of year	$33,221	$4,582
Service cost	1,283	269
Interest cost	996	148
Plan participant contributions	66	—
Amendments	26	—
Actuarial (gains) losses	(2,326)	(119)
Divestitures & acquisitions	(29)	—
Curtailments & settlements & restructuring	(21)	—
Benefits paid from plan.	(1,018)	(383)
Effect of exchange rates.	(528)	(17)
Projected benefit obligation—end of year.	$31,670	$ 4,480

continued

continued from previous page

December 31, 2018 ($ millions)	Retirement Plans	Other Benefit Plans
Change in Plan Assets		
Plan assets at fair value—beginning of year	$28,404	$ 281
Actual return (loss) on plan assets	(1,269)	—
Company contributions.	1,140	282
Plan participant contributions	66	—
Settlements.	(13)	—
Divestitures & acquisitions	(17)	—
Benefits paid from plan assets	(1,018)	(383)
Effect of exchange rates.	(475)	—
Plan assets at fair value—end of year	$26,818	$ 180
Funded status—end of year	$ (4,852)	$(4,300)

December 31, 2018 ($ millions)	Retirement Plans	Other Benefit Plans
Service cost	$1,283	$269
Interest cost	996	148
Expected return on plan assets	(2,212)	(7)
Amortization of prior service cost (credit)	3	(31)
Recognized actuarial losses.	852	123
Curtailments and settlements.	1	—
Net periodic benefit cost.	$ 923	$502

	Retirement Plans		Other Benefit Plans	
Worldwide Benefit Plans	2018	2017	2018	2017
Discount rate	3.60%	3.98%	3.62%	3.94%
Expected long-term rate of return on plan assets.	8.46	8.43	—	—
Rate of increase in compensation levels	3.98	4.01	4.29	4.31

Required

a. How much pension and other benefit expense does Johnson & Johnson report in its 2018 income statement?

b. The company reports a $2,212 million expected return on pension plan assets as an offset to 2018 pension expense. Approximately, how is this amount computed? What is the actual gain or loss realized on its 2018 pension plan assets? What is the purpose of using this expected return instead of the actual gain or loss?

c. What factors affected the company's pension liability during 2018? What factors affected the pension plan assets during 2018?

d. What does the term *funded status* mean? What is the funded status of the 2018 pension plans and postretirement benefit plans?

e. The company decreased its discount rate on retirement plans from 3.98% to 3.60%. What effect(s) does this decrease have on its balance sheet and its income statement?

f. How did Johnson & Johnson's pension plan affect the company's cash flow in 2018?

g. Why are the plan assets so small for Other benefit plans compared to the Pension plans?

h. The company reports an actuarial gain of $2,326, which is subtracted from the PBO. Explain what this is and how this item affected net income in 2018.

LO3 **P10-43. Analyzing and Interpreting Tax Footnote (Financial Statement Effects Template)**

Snapchat Inc. (SNAP)

Snapchat Inc. reports total tax expense of $2,547 thousand on its income statement for year ended December 31, 2018, and paid cash of $3,958 thousand for taxes and decreased taxes payable by $755

thousand. The tax footnote in the company's 10-K filing reports the following deferred tax assets and liabilities information.

The domestic and foreign components of pre-tax loss were as follows:

Year Ended December 31 (in thousands)	2017	2018
Domestic	$ (969,922)	$(3,027,580)
Foreign	(283,442)	(435,828)
Loss before income taxes	$(1,253,364)	$(3,463,408)

The significant components of net deferred tax balances were as follows:

December 31 (in thousands)	2017	2018
Deferred tax assets		
Accrued expenses	$ 10,534	$ 21,056
Deferred revenue	2,142	976
Intangible assets	140,771	140,494
Stock-based compensation	396,604	254,255
Net operating losses	473,110	849,224
Tax credit carryforwards	124,078	235,300
Property and equipment	—	203
Other	2,015	322
Total deferred tax assets	$ 1,149,254	$ 1,501,830
Deferred tax liability		
Property and equipment	$ (5,883)	$ —
Total deferred tax liabilities	(5,883)	—
Total net deferred tax assets before valuation allowance	1,143,371	1,501,830
Valuation allowance	(1,144,543)	(1,502,346)
Net deferred taxes	$ (1,172)	$ (516)

Required

a. Snapchat's gross deferred tax assets increased during 2018. What two items explain the majority of the increase?

b. In 2017, Snapchat reported deferred tax liabilities. Explain how this liability arose.

c. Why does the company record a valuation allowance? Given the size of the 2018 allowance, what is the company's expectation of future pretax income?

d. Explain how the valuation allowance affected 2018 net income.

e. Use the financial statement effects template to record income tax expense for fiscal year 2018 along with the changes in both deferred tax assets and liabilities and the valuation allowance.

P10-44. Analyzing and Interpreting Income Tax Footnote

Consider the following income tax footnote information for Oracle for the fiscal year ended May 31, 2019 (fiscal year 2019).

LO3

Oracle Corporation (ORCL)

The following is a geographical breakdown of income before the provision for income taxes:

Year Ended May 31 (in millions)	2019	2018	2017
Domestic	$ 3,774	$ 3,366	$ 3,674
Foreign	8,494	9,058	8,006
Income before provision for income taxes	$12,268	$12,424	$11,680

continued

continued from previous page

The provision for income taxes consisted of the following:

Year Ended May 31 ($ in millions)	2019	2018	2017
Current provision:			
Federal.	$ 979	$8,320	$ 936
State.	300	264	257
Foreign.	1,097	1,100	1,475
Total current provision	$2,376	$9,684	$2,668
Deferred benefit:			
Federal.	$ 483	$ (827)	$ (158)
State.	(28)	(26)	(29)
Foreign.	(1,646)	6	(253)
Total deferred benefit	$(1,191)	$ (847)	$ (440)
Total provision for income taxes.	$ 1,185	$8,837	$2,228

The provision for income taxes differed from the amount computed by applying the federal statutory rate to our income before provision for income taxes as follows:

Year Ended May 31 ($ in millions)	2019	2018	2017
U.S. federal statutory tax rate.	21.0%	29.2%	35.0%
Tax provision at statutory rate	$2,576	$3,629	$4,088
Impact of the Tax Act of 2017:			
One-time transition tax.	(529)	7,781	—
Deferred tax effects	140	(911)	—
Foreign earnings at other than United States rates	(789)	(995)	(1,312)
State tax expense, net of federal benefit	197	142	150
Settlements and releases from judicial decisions and			
statute expirations, net	(132)	(252)	(189)
Domestic production activity deduction	—	(87)	(119)
Federal research and development credit	(158)	(174)	(127)
Stock-based compensation	(201)	(302)	(149)
Other, net	81	6	(114)
Total provision for income taxes.	$1,185	$8,837	$2,228

The components of our deferred tax assets and liabilities were as follows:

May 31 (in millions)	2019	2018
Deferred tax assets:		
Accruals and allowances	$ 541	$ 567
Employee compensation and benefits.	646	664
Differences in timing of revenue recognition	322	338
Basis of property, plant and equipment and intangible assets.	1,238	—
Tax credit and net operating loss carryforwards	3,717	2,614
Total deferred tax assets	6,464	4,183
Valuation allowance.	(1,266)	(1,308)
Total deferred tax assets, net.	5,198	2,875
Deferred tax liabilities:		
Unrealized gain on stock	(78)	(78)
Acquired intangible assets.	(973)	(1,254)
GILTI deferred	(1,515)	—
Basis of property, plant and equipment and intangible assets.	—	(158)
Other	(200)	(48)
Total deferred tax liabilities.	(2,766)	(1,538)
Net deferred tax assets	$2,432	$1,337

Required

a. What is the total amount of income tax expense that Oracle reports in its fiscal 2019 income statement? What portion of this expense did Oracle pay during 2019 or expect to pay in 2020?

b. Explain how the deferred tax liability called "Acquired intangible assets" arises. Under what circumstances will the company settle this liability? Under what circumstances might this liability be deferred indefinitely?

c. Explain how the deferred tax asset called "Employee compensation and benefits" arises. Why is it recognized as an asset?

d. Explain how the deferred tax asset called "Tax credit and net operating loss carryforwards" arises. Under what circumstances will Oracle realize the benefits of this asset?

e. Oracle reports a 2019 valuation allowance of $1,266 million. How does this valuation allowance arise? How did the change in valuation allowance for 2019 affect net income? Valuation allowances typically relate to questions about the realizability of tax loss carryforwards. Under what circumstances might Oracle not realize the benefits of its tax loss carryforwards?

f. Calculate Oracle's effective (average) tax rate for each year.

g. Oracle reconciles the difference between its total provision for income tax and the statutory rate. What item explains most of the difference in fiscal 2017 compared to fiscal 2018?

h. If not for the effects of the Tax Cuts and Jobs Act of 2017, what would have been Oracle's effective tax rate each year?

P10-45. Analyzing and Interpreting Effects of TCJA Tax Law Changes

Pfizer Inc. reports the following footnote disclosure in its 2018 Form 10-K.

The following table provides the components of *Income from continuing operations before provision (benefit) for taxes on income*:

LO3

Pfizer Inc. (PFE)

Homework
MBC

Year Ended December 31, $ millions	2018	2017	2016
United States	$ (4,403)	$ (6,879)	$(8,534)
International	16,288	19,184	16,886
Income from continuing operations before provision for taxes	$11,885	$12,305	$ 8,351

The following table provides the components of *Provision (benefit) for taxes on income* based on the location of the taxing authorities:

$ millions	2018	2017	2016
United States			
Current income taxes:			
Federal	$ 668	$ 1,267	$ 342
State and local	9	45	(52)
Deferred income taxes:			
Federal	$(1,663)	$ (2,064)	$ (419)
State and local	16	(304)	(106)
Total U.S. tax provision	$ (970)	$ (1,055)	$ (235)
TCJA[a]			
Current income taxes	$(3,035)	$ 13,135	—
Deferred income taxes	2,439	(23,795)	—
Total TCJA tax provision	$ (596)	$(10,660)	—
International			
Current income taxes	$ 2,831	$ 2,709	$1,532
Deferred income taxes	(558)	(42)	(175)
Total international tax provision	$ 2,273	$ 2,667	$1,358

(a) In the fourth quarter of 2017, we recorded an estimate of certain tax effects of the TCJA, including (i) the impact on deferred tax assets and liabilities from the reduction in the U.S. Federal corporate tax rate from 35% to 21%, (ii) the impact on valuation allowances and other state income tax considerations, (iii) the $15.2 billion repatriation tax liability on accumulated post-1986 foreign earnings for which we plan to elect, with the filing of our 2018 U.S. Federal Consolidated Income Tax Return, payment over eight years through 2026 that is reported in Other taxes payable in our consolidated balance sheet as of December 31, 2017 and (iv) deferred taxes on basis differences expected to give rise to future taxes on global intangible low-taxed income. As a result of the TCJA, in the fourth quarter of 2017, we reversed an estimate of the deferred taxes that are no longer expected to be needed due to the change to the territorial tax system.

Required

a. What is the amount of income tax expense reported by Pfizer for each year? What amount is current versus deferred?

b. What is Pfizer's effective (average) tax rate for each year?

c. Use the pretax information to determine the effective tax rate for U.S. operations for each year.

d. The footnote includes amounts related to the TCJA of 2017. What was the effect on the company's tax expense in 2017 and 2018 due to the TCJA?

e. Pfizer lists four TCJA items that impacted their 2017 tax provision. Explain how each of the four items might have affected Pfizer's 2017 tax expense.

IFRS Applications

LO2
Nutrien Ltd. (NTR)

I10-46. Analyzing and Interpreting Pension Disclosures

Nutrien, the world's largest potash producer, is a multinational corporation based in Saskatoon, Saskatchewan. The company produces nitrogen and phosphate used to produce fertilizer. At the end of 2018, the company controlled 34% of the world's potash production capacity. Below is Nutrien's pension footnote for 2018.

$ millions	Obligation	Plan Assets	Net
Balance—December 31, 2017	$(1,831)	$1,380	$(451)
Merger impact[1]	(347)	205	(142)
Components of defined benefit expense recognized in earnings			
Current service cost for benefits earned during the year	(67)	—	(67)
Interest (expense) income	(77)	62	(15)
Past service cost, including curtailment gains and settlements	157	—	157
Foreign exchange rate changes and other	39	(27)	12
Subtotal of components of defined benefit expense recognized in earnings	52	35	87
Remeasurements of the net defined benefit liability recognized in OCI during the year			
Actuarial gain arising from:			
Changes in financial assumptions	210	—	210
Changes in demographic assumptions	11	—	11
Loss on plan assets (excluding amounts included in net interest)	—	(149)	(149)
Subtotal of remeasurements	221	(149)	72
Cash flows			
Contributions by plan participants	(6)	6	—
Employer contributions	—	53	53
Benefits paid	114	(114)	—
Subtotal of cash flows	108	(55)	53
Balance—December 31, 2018	$(1,797)	$1,416	$(381)

[1]The Company acquired Agrium's pension and other postretirement benefit obligations, representing the fair values at the acquisition date as described in Note 3.

Required

a. How much pension expense does the company report in its 2018 income statement?

b. What factors affected the company's pension liability during 2018? What factors affected the pension plan assets during 2018?

c. What does the term *funded status* mean? What is the funded status of the 2018 pension plans and postretirement benefit plans?

d. The company increased its discount rate on the pension obligation from 3.65% to 4.22% in 2018. What effect(s) does this increase have on the company's balance sheet and income statement?

e. How did Nutrien's pension plan affect the company's cash flow in 2018?

LO3
BMW Group (BMW)

I10-47. Analyzing and Interpreting Income Tax Footnote

Bayerische Motoren Werke AG, commonly referred to as BMW, is a German multinational company that produces automobiles and motorcycles. The company was founded in 1916 as a manufacturer of aircraft engines, which it produced from 1917 until 1918 and again from 1933 to 1945. BMW includes the following footnotes in its 2018 annual report.

Taxes on income of the BMW Group comprise the following:

in € million	2018	2017*
Current tax expense	€2,220	€2,558
Deferred tax expense (+)/deferred tax income (–)	355	–558
thereof relating to temporary differences	641	–502
thereof relating to tax loss carryforwards and tax credits	–286	–56
Income taxes	€2,575	€2,000

The difference between the expected tax expense based on the underlying tax rate for Germany and actual tax expense is explained in the following reconciliation:

in € million	2018	2017*
Profit before tax	€9,815	€10,675
Tax rate applicable in Germany	30.8%	30.7%
Expected tax expense	3,023	3,277
Variances due to different tax rates	–359	–1,026
Tax increases (+)/tax reductions (–) as a result of nondeductible expenses and tax-exempt income	141	58
Tax expense (+)/benefits (–) for prior years	–16	–104
Other variances	–214	– 205
Actual tax expense	2,575	€ 2,000

The allocation of deferred tax assets and liabilities to balance sheet line items at 31 December is shown in the following table:

in € million	Deferred Tax Assets 2018	Deferred Tax Liabilities 2018
Intangible assets	€ 22	€ 3,077
Property, plant and equipment	171	359
Leased products	487	5,210
Other investments	3	20
Sundry other assets	1,185	3,254
Tax loss carryforwards and capital losses	891	—
Provisions	5,323	29
Liabilities	2,570	620
Eliminations	3,180	981
	13,832	13,550
Valuation allowances on tax loss carryforwards and capital losses	–498	—
Netting within tax jurisdictions	–11,744	–11,744
Deferred taxes	1,590	1,806
	€ —	€ 216

Required

a. What income tax expense does BMW report in its 2018 income statement? How much of this expense was paid during the year or is currently payable?

b. Determine the company's effective tax rate.

c. What is the company's marginal (statutory) tax rate?

d. Does BMW report a net deferred tax asset or liability on its balance sheet?

e. BMW reports a deferred tax asset and a deferred tax liability related to "Property, plant and equipment." Explain how both an asset and a liability can arise from this item.

f. BMW includes a valuation allowance of €498 million related to tax loss carryforwards. Explain how this valuation allowance arises.

Ongoing Project

(This ongoing project began in Module 1 and continues through most of the book; even if previous segments were not completed, the requirements are still applicable to any business analysis.)   Your project should include a discussion of leases (capital and operating), defined benefit obligations, as well as deferred tax assets and liabilities. The objective is to gain a deeper understanding of all of the obligations the company faces and how they affect key performance and leverage ratios.

1. *Financing and Operating Leases.*   Read the debt and lease footnotes to determine whether the company uses leases.

   • Does the company use leases? What types of assets are leased?

   • What proportion of leases are finance versus operating?

   • Are leases a substantial component of overall financing?

   • Determine the discount rate implicit in the company's leases.

   • Has the company adopted the new standard for leases? What was the balance sheet impact of the adoption?

2. *Pensions.*   Read the pension footnote to determine whether the company has defined benefit obligations.

   • What is the funded status of the pension and other benefits plans? Is the underfunded or overfunded obligation substantial? Compare between the companies.

   • Are the plans substantial to the company?

   • How much pension expense does each company report in its income statement? Is this a substantial amount?

   • Compare the cash paid into the plan assets to the amounts paid to retirees. Assess the cash flow implications of the company's future payment obligations. The point is to determine whether the company will be able to meet its obligations as they come due.

3. *Income Tax Disclosures and Strategies.* Examine the income tax expense and deferred tax assets and liabilities.

   • Analyze the footnotes and assess the company's effective tax rate. Is it a consistent rate? If not, do the fluctuations seem reasonable?

   • What was the effect of the 2017 TCJA on the provision for income taxes? How did the new law change the company's effective tax rate?

   • Do the deferred tax assets and liabilities seem appropriate given the company's industry?

   • Is there a valuation allowance? If so, how big is it relative to total deferred tax assets? Has the valuation allowance changed markedly during the year? This might indicate income shifting.

Solutions to Review Problems

Review 10-1—Solution

1. Using Excel, the present value of $6,756 million for operating leases, discounted at 4.42%, is computed as follows ($2 rounding difference).

Year ($ millions)	Operating Lease Payment	Discount Factor 4.42%	Present Value
1	$1,172	0.95767	$1,122
2	1,000	0.91713	$917
3	819	0.87831	$719
4	692	0.84113	$582
5	654	0.80553	$527
>5	4,200	5.48688 × 0.80553	$2,891
Remaining life.	6.422*		$6,758
Total payments	$8,537		

* $4,200/$654 = 6.422 years

2. Delta Airlines' balance sheet will recognize a lease liability of $6,758 million together with a lease asset (titled as "Operating lease right-of-use assets") of about the same amount.

Review 10-2—Solution

1. American Airlines' pension benefit obligation increases by service cost and interest cost, and decreases with actuarial gains (which are decreases in the pension liability as a result of changes in actuarial assumptions). It is decreased by the payment of benefits to retirees.
2. American Airlines' pension assets decrease by negative investment returns for the period and increase by cash contributions made by the company. Assets decrease by benefits paid to retirees.
3. American Airlines' funded status is $(6,325) million ($16,378 million PBO – $10,053 million pension assets) as of 2018. The negative amount indicates that the plan is underfunded. Consequently, this amount is reflected as a liability on American's balance sheet.
4. Expected return on plan assets acts as an offset to service cost and interest cost in computing net pension cost. As the expected return increases, net pension expense decreases.
5. American Airlines' expected loss of $905 million is less than its actual loss of $1,151 million in 2018.
6. American Airlines reports a net pension *income* of $59 million in its 2018 income statement.
7. American Airlines' funded status is negative, indicating an underfunded plan. In 2018, the company contributed $475 million to the pension plan, up from $286 million in the prior year. If returns on pension plan assets continue to decline, the company will be forced to increase its cash contribution.

Review 10-3—Solution

Part 1

1. Total income tax benefit was $219 million in 2018, compared with tax expense of $1,582 million in the prior year.
2. The current portion of FedEx's tax provision was $(36) million.
3. Income tax expense is the sum of current taxes (that is, currently payable as determined from the company's federal, state, and foreign tax returns) plus the change in deferred tax assets and liabilities. It is a calculated figure, not a percentage that is applied to pretax income. For 2018, FedEx tax expense was decreased by the deferred provision (an asset) of $183 million.
4. FedEx's effective tax rate for fiscal 2018 is (5.0)%. FedEx's tax reconciliation indicates that it received a tax benefit of $1,357 from the Tax Cuts and Jobs Act of 2017. Benefits such as these typically result from the reduction of deferred tax liabilities that are now computed using a lower tax rate than the one in effect when the liabilities were initially recognized.

Part 2

1. FedEx is depreciating its long-term PPE and lease assets more quickly for tax purposes than it does for financial reporting purposes. Consequently, FedEx' taxable income will be higher in future years as less depreciation expense is recognized, resulting in additional income tax liability that is recognized as a deferred tax lability on its balance sheet.
2. FedEx is recognizing accrued employee benefit expense in its income statement that will not be deductible for tax purposes until paid in the future. These future payments will reduce taxable income and the income tax liability, and that future reduction of tax liability is a future benefit that is recognized on the balance sheet as a deferred tax asset.
3. The total expected increase in taxable income (from lower expected tax depreciation expense) is multiplied by the expected tax rate to yield the dollar amount of deferred tax assets and liabilities that are reported on the balance sheet. Prior to the passage of the TCJA, this future taxable income was multiplied by the 35% corporate tax rate. After passage of the TCJA, this future income was multiplied by the new 21% corporate tax rate, resulting in lower deferred tax liability. The reduction of the deferred tax liability is recognized in the income statement as a reduction of income tax expense, thus increasing net income dollar-for-dollar.

Module 11
Cash Flows

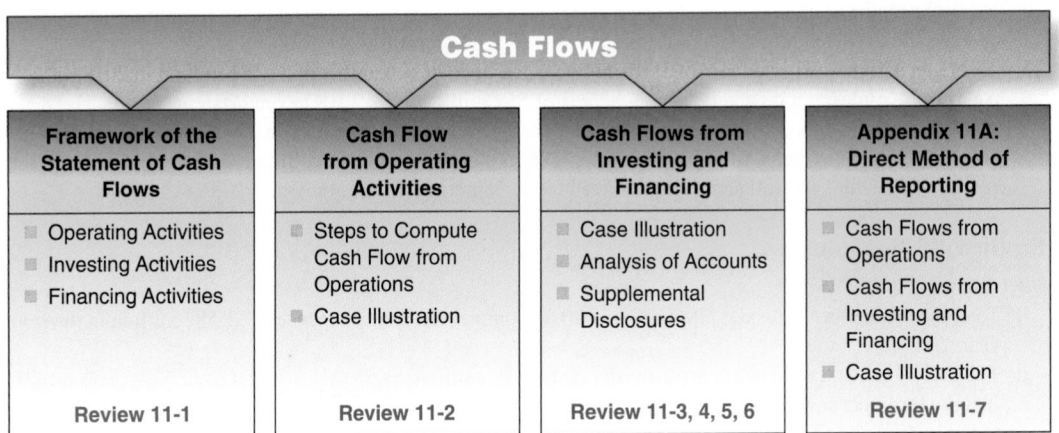

Cash Flows			
Framework of the Statement of Cash Flows	**Cash Flow from Operating Activities**	**Cash Flows from Investing and Financing**	**Appendix 11A: Direct Method of Reporting**
▪ Operating Activities ▪ Investing Activities ▪ Financing Activities	▪ Steps to Compute Cash Flow from Operations ▪ Case Illustration	▪ Case Illustration ▪ Analysis of Accounts ▪ Supplemental Disclosures	▪ Cash Flows from Operations ▪ Cash Flows from Investing and Financing ▪ Case Illustration
Review 11-1	Review 11-2	Review 11-3, 4, 5, 6	Review 11-7

PREVIEW   SBUX

We examine the statement of cash flows, including

▪ Preparing the statement of cash flows, including how to determine net cash flows from

  ○ **Operating activities**   ○ **Investing activities**   ○ **Financing activities**

▪ Analyzing and interpreting the statement of cash flows.

▪ Drawing insights from cash flows that are not apparent from the income statement and balance sheet.

▪ Preparing a direct-method statement of cash flows.

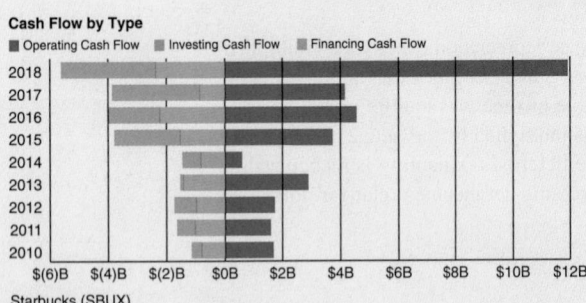

Starbucks (SBUX)

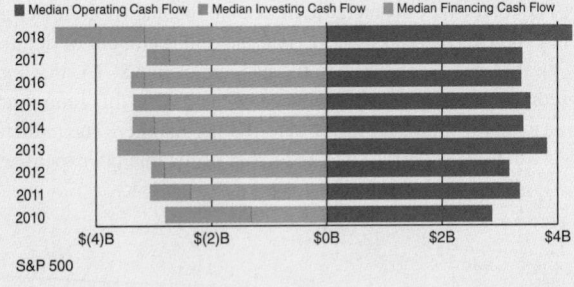

S&P 500

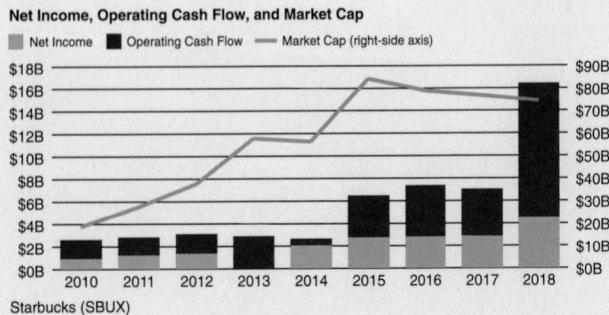

Starbucks (SBUX)

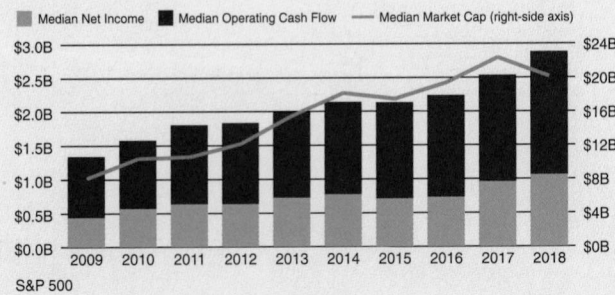

S&P 500

Road Map

LO	Learning Objective	Topics	Page	eLecture	Guided Example	Assignments
11–1	**Describe the framework for the statement of cash flows.** Relations Among Financial Statements :: Statement of Cash Flows Structure :: Operating Activities Preview :: Investing Activities Preview :: Financing Activities Preview	11-3	e11–1	Review 11-1	1, 2, 3, 4, 22, 23, 30, 49, 50, 51, 56, 57, 58
11–2	**Determine and analyze net cash flows from operating activities.** Steps to Compute Net Cash Flows from Operating Activities	11-9	e11–2	Review 11-2	9, 10, 11, 13, 24, 25, 31, 32, 33, 34, 43, 44, 45, 46, 47, 48, 49, 50, 51
11–3	**Determine and analyze net cash flows from investing activities.** Analyze Remaining Noncash Assets	11-16	e11–3	Review 11-3	5, 10, 12, 32, 36, 38, 43, 44, 45, 46, 47, 48, 49, 50, 52, 53, 54, 55
11–4	**Determine and analyze net cash flows from financing activities.** Analyze Liabilities and Equity :: Balance Sheet Accounts and Cash Flow Effects :: Supplemental Disclosures for Indirect Method	11-18	e11–4	Review 11-4	5, 6, 12, 32, 36, 38, 43, 44, 45, 46, 47, 48, 49, 50, 52, 53, 54, 55
11–5	**Examine and interpret cash flow information.** Cash Flow Components :: Cash Flow Patterns :: Usefulness of Statement of Cash Flows	11-21	e11–5	Review 11-5	7, 21, 28, 39, 40, 42, 49, 50, 51, 56, 57, 58
11–6	**Compute and interpret ratios based on operating cash flows.** Ratio Analyses of Cash Flows :: Free Cash Flow	11-27	e11–6	Review 11-6	19, 20, 29, 41, 42, 56, 57
11–7	**Explain and construct a direct method statement of cash flows (Appendix 11A).** Cash Flows from Operating Activities :: Cash Flows from Investing and Financing	11-29	e11–7	Review 11-7	8, 14, 15, 16, 17, 18, 26, 27, 35, 36, 37, 52, 53, 54, 55

Framework for Statement of Cash Flows

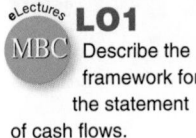

LO1
Describe the framework for the statement of cash flows.

The **statement of cash flows** is a financial statement that summarizes information about the flow of cash into and out of a company.[1] Information provided in a statement of cash flows helps managers, investors, and creditors assess the company's ability to generate positive future net cash flows and to meet its debt obligations, its need for external financing, and its ability to pay its dividends. The balance sheet reports the company's financial position at a point in time (the end of each period), whereas the statement of cash flows explains the change in one of its components—cash—from one balance sheet date to the next. The income statement reveals the results of the company's operating activities for the period, and these operating activities are a major contributor to the change in cash as reported in the statement of cash flows.

Relation Among Financial Statements

Each financial statement reveals a different view of the company, and a thorough financial analysis requires us to scrutinize the information contained in each.

Income Statement Insights The income statement informs us about the degree to which consumers value the products and/or services offered by the company. How much does it cost to produce them, and can the company set prices that pass on these production costs to its customers? Is the company able to control labor costs, both for salaries and wages and for benefits offered to employees? Can the company effectively manage its overhead costs? How well is it insulated against fluctuations in interest rates, commodity prices, or foreign exchange rates? How well can it control its income tax obligations? These are but a few of the important questions that can be answered by our analysis of the income statement.

Balance Sheet Insights The balance sheet informs us about the resources available to the company and the claims against those resources by creditors and owners. From the balance sheet, we learn about the magnitude of investment in net working capital and PPE assets required for the company to conduct business. This is impacted by the company's business model and the norms of the industries in which the company operates. We are able to estimate the extent to which the company relies upon borrowed funds, the structure of that indebtedness, and the degree to which the company has (or can generate) the liquidity required to meet its debt obligations. We also learn about the company's equity investors and the claims they have on the net assets and income of the company. Whereas the income statement provides us with insight into the economics of the company's operations, the balance sheet informs us about the resources the company uses in its operations and the claims against those resources.

Statement of Cash Flows Insights As we will learn in this module, the statement of cash flows is prepared from the company's income statement and comparative balance sheets. At first glance, it might appear that the information contained in the statement of cash flows is redundant. However, to treat the statement of cash flows as a secondary statement would ignore potential information that can assist us in our analysis of the company. In particular, the statement of cash flows offers information along the following four dimensions.

- **Activity type** The statement of cash flows is structured to highlight three primary activities of the company: **operating activities, investing activities,** and **financing activities.** Neither the income statement nor the balance sheet presents that perspective.

- **Liquidity** The statement of cash flows emphasizes the role cash plays in the company's day-to-day operations; it is cash that pays employees, cash that pays debt, and cash that provides a return to equity holders in the form of dividends. Finance professionals often focus on free cash flow, and for good reason. Companies that fail typically do so because they lack the cash flow necessary to conduct their business. A focus solely on GAAP profit can obscure a deterioration of liquidity that can lead to company failure.

---

[1] The statement of cash flows explains the change in a firm's cash *and* cash equivalents. **Cash equivalents** are short-term, highly liquid investments that are (1) easily convertible into a known cash amount and (2) close enough to maturity so that their market value is not sensitive to interest rate changes (generally, investments with initial maturities of three months or less). Treasury bills, commercial paper (short-term notes issued by corporations), and money market funds are typical examples of cash equivalents.

■ **Additional detail** As an added benefit, the statement of cash flows highlights important operating items that are often not reported as separate line items in the income statement, such as depreciation on building and equipment assets, impairments of tangible and intangible assets, the cost of stock-based compensation, the excess of reported equity income over dividends received from investee companies, the cash portion of interest expense and income tax expense, and the gain or loss on the sales of assets. In addition, the statement of cash flows highlights items that are *not* reflected in the income statement, such as capital expenditures (CAPEX), dividend payments, and the repayment of the principal portion of company debt.

■ **Earnings quality** The statement of cash flows provides insight into the "quality" of company earnings. All profit must eventually be received in cash. So, when profit and operating cash flow diverge, we must investigate the reasons for the divergence because cash flow ultimately drives company value. If net income grows at a faster pace than operating cash flows, our analysis attempts to understand whether cash flow will increase in the future or whether income has been improperly recognized, only to be reversed in the future. Our assessment of the quality of company earnings is a difficult challenge but one that is aided considerably by a thorough understanding of the statement of cash flows.

Statement of Cash Flows Structure

The statement of cash flows classifies cash receipts and cash payments into one of three categories.

■ **Operating activities** Operating activities measure the net cash inflows and outflows as a result of the company's transactions with its customers. We generally prefer operating cash flows to be positive, although companies can report net cash outflows for operating activities in the short run during periods of growth (as the company builds up inventory and hires staff to grow operations in anticipation of future sales and cash inflows).

■ **Investing activities** Investing activities relate to investments, joint ventures, and capital expenditures for PPE. Outflows occur when a company purchases these assets, and inflows occur when they are sold.

■ **Financing activities** Financing activities relate to long-term debt and stockholders' equity. Cash inflows result from borrowing money and issuing stock to investors. Outflows occur when a company repays debt, repurchases stock, or pays dividends to shareholders.

The combined effects on cash of all three categories explain the net change in cash for that period:

	Beginning cash balance (the ending cash balance from prior year's balance sheet)
+	Change in cash during the period
=	Ending cash balance for current year (reported on current year's balance sheet)

Statement of Cash Flows Preparation Overview The statement of cash flows is prepared using data from the income statement and the balance sheet.

■ **Income statement** For the *indirect* method of preparing the operating section, we begin with net income as a source of cash and adjust net income for noncash items that are included in the computation of net income.[2]

■ **Balance sheet** We consider the change in each balance sheet account and determine the cash generated or used by the change in the account balance. The graphic below shows how balance sheet categories relate to the three sections of the statement of cash flows.

---

[2] Firms can choose to present operating cash flows either directly, by reporting operating cash receipts from customers and cash payments to suppliers and employees, or indirectly, by reconciling net income and cash flow from operating activities. While firms are encouraged to use the simpler direct method, most U.S. companies continue to use the indirect method. Our discussion here addresses the indirect method, and we return to the direct method at the end of the module.

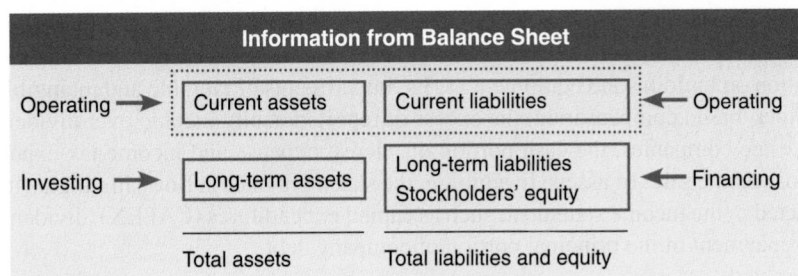

Information from Balance Sheet

Operating →	Current assets	Current liabilities	← Operating
Investing →	Long-term assets	Long-term liabilities / Stockholders' equity	← Financing
	Total assets	Total liabilities and equity

There are two exceptions to the balance sheet classification in the graphic above; both involve the current section of the balance sheet where items are not classified as operating activities.

■ **Current (Nonoperating) assets** classified as investing activities such as marketable securities.

■ **Current (Nonoperating) liabilities** classified as financing activities such as the principal balance of short-term debt and current maturities of long-term debt.

Statement of Cash Flows for Starbucks Exhibit 11.1 reproduces Starbucks' statement of cash flows. Starbucks reports $11,937.8 million in net cash inflows from operating activities in 2018. This is much greater than its net income of $4,518.0 million, which highlights that net income and operating cash flow are different measures. (Later in this module, we explain all the items included in the operating section of Starbucks' statement of cash flows). The company used $2,361.5 million of cash for investing activities, primarily for purchases of PPE (called capital expenditures or CAPEX), and also used $3,242.8 million of cash for financing activities to pay dividends and repurchase common stock. In sum, Starbucks increased its cash by $6,294 million (after considering foreign exchange effects), from $2,462.3 million at the beginning of fiscal 2018 to $8,756.3 million at the end of fiscal 2018.

Overall, Starbucks' cash flow picture is strong for three reasons.

■ The company is generating positive cash from operating activities, its core business.

■ The company is investing in the maintenance and growth of its infrastructure with capital expenditures (CAPEX).

■ The company is returning cash to shareholders through dividends and share repurchases.

In analyzing the statement of cash flows, we should not necessarily conclude the company is better off if the ending balance of cash increases and worse off if cash decreases. It is not the *change* in cash that is most important but the reasons behind the change. For example, what are the sources of cash inflows? Are these sources of cash transitory, or can we expect the cash flows to continue? Are these sources mainly from operating activities, or did sales of investments or PPE generate cash flow? To what uses have cash inflows been put? Such questions and answers are key to properly using the statement of cash flows.

Operating Activities Preview

The focus of **operating activities** of companies is to generate cash from selling goods or services at a profit. Following are examples of cash inflows and outflows relating to operating activities.

Operating Activities

Cash Inflows ⬆	**Cash Outflows**
■ Receipts from customers for sales made or services rendered.	■ Payments to employees or suppliers.
	■ Payments to purchase inventories.
■ Receipts of interest and dividends.	■ Payments of interest to creditors.
■ Other receipts that are not related to investing or financing activities, such as lawsuit settlements and refunds received from suppliers.	■ Payments of taxes to government.
	■ Other payments that are not related to investing or financing activities, such as contributions to charity.

Exhibit 11.1 ■ Statement of Cash Flows for Starbucks Corporation			
Fiscal Year Ended ($ millions)	**Sept. 30, 2018**	**Oct. 1, 2017**	**Oct. 2, 2016**
Operating Activities			
Net earnings including noncontrolling interests	$4,518.0	$2,884.9	$2,818.9
Adjustments to reconcile net earnings to net cash provided by operating activities:			
Depreciation and amortization	1,305.9	1,067.1	1,030.1
Deferred income taxes, net	714.9	95.1	265.7
Income earned from equity method investees	(242.8)	(310.2)	(250.2)
Distributions received from equity method investees	226.8	186.6	223.3
Gain resulting from acquisition of joint venture	(1,376.4)	—	—
Net gain resulting from divestiture of certain retail operations	(499.2)	(93.5)	(6.1)
Stock-based compensation	250.3	176.0	218.1
Goodwill impairments	37.6	87.2	—
Other	89.0	68.9	45.1
Cash provided by changes in operating assets and liabilities:			
Accounts receivable	131.0	(96.8)	(55.6)
Inventories	(41.2)	14.0	(67.5)
Accounts payable	391.6	46.4	46.9
Deferred revenue	7,109.4	130.8	180.4
Other operating assets and liabilities	(677.1)	(4.7)	248.8
Net cash provided by operating activities	11,937.8	4,251.8	4,697.9
Investing Activities			
Purchase of investments	(191.9)	(674.4)	(1,585.7)
Sales of investments	459.0	1,054.5	680.7
Maturities and calls of investments	45.3	149.6	27.9
Acquisitions, net of cash acquired	(1,311.3)	—	—
Additions to property, plant and equipment	(1,976.4)	(1,519.4)	(1,440.3)
Net proceeds from the divestiture of certain operations	608.2	85.4	69.6
Other	5.6	54.3	24.9
Net cash used by investing activities	(2,361.5)	(850.0)	(2,222.9)
Financing Activities			
Proceeds from issuance of long-term debt	5,584.1	750.2	1,254.5
Repayments of long-term debt	—	(400.0)	—
Proceeds from issuance of common stock	153.9	150.8	160.7
Cash dividends paid	(1,743.4)	(1,450.4)	(1,178.0)
Repurchase of common stock	(7,133.5)	(2,042.5)	(1,995.6)
Minimum tax withholdings on share-based awards	(62.7)	(82.8)	(106.0)
Other	(41.2)	(4.4)	(8.4)
Net cash used by financing activities	(3,242.8)	(3,079.1)	(1,872.8)
Effect of exchange rate changes on cash and cash equivalents	(39.5)	10.8	(3.5)
Net increase in cash and cash equivalents	6,294.0	333.5	598.7
Cash and Cash Equivalents:			
Beginning of period	2,462.3	2,128.8	1,530.1
End of period	$8,756.3	$2,462.3	$2,128.8

These cash inflows and outflows affect net income. Accordingly, net income is the first line of the operating cash flow section of the statement of cash flows. This reflects the idea that the company generates cash from selling its goods or services to its customers.

Net income commonly includes items that do not involve the receipt or payment of cash. Depreciation expense is an example. Cash is spent when the depreciable asset (such as equipment or a building) is purchased. Depreciation expense is an accounting process that allocates the cash cost over the useful life of the asset. Although there is no cash outflow with annual depreciation expense, it is reported as an expense in computing net income. Because the focus of the statement of cash flows is on cash, we need to "undo" the effect of depreciation and other noncash expenses. We do that by *adding it back* to offset the expense (i.e., undo the negative effect) in the income statement.

Let's consider further adjustments to get operating cash flow. During the year, the company might decide whether to use cash to grow the firm. For example, the company might purchase additional inventories to have goods available for future sales. This use of cash increases inventory but has no effect on net income. As another example, the company can extend credit to its customers as a strategic move to generate additional sales. This action increases sales, but instead of receiving cash, the company's accounts receivable increases. The statement of cash flows shows an increase in inventories and an increase in accounts receivable as negative amounts to indicate the company has invested cash in the growth of assets (inventory and accounts receivable). Conversely, cash is freed up when the company reduces its receivables or inventory levels, and the statement of cash flows shows such decreases as positive amounts.

On the liability side, companies can conserve cash by borrowing from their suppliers or other operating creditors. An increase in liabilities signals an increase in borrowing, an inflow of cash, which is reported as a positive amount in the statement of cash flows. As the company uses cash to repay borrowed amounts, the statement of cash flows shows the reduction of the liability as a negative amount, indicating a cash outflow.

Companies prepare the statement of cash flows using their income statement and balance sheets (to calculate changes in accounts between the current and prior years). The preparation is mainly a mechanical process with limited discretion. A simple but common computation of operating cash flow follows.

	Net income (– if a net loss)
+	Depreciation expense
–	Increases in current assets
+	Decreases in current assets
+	Increases in current liabilities
–	Decreases in current liabilities
=	Cash from operating activities

Understanding how increases and decreases in assets and liabilities affect cash flow is key to understanding the information contained in the statement of cash flows. To help, keep the following decision rules in mind.

Balance Sheet Account	Increase in Account	Decrease in Account
Assets (noncash)	Cash Outflow	Cash Inflow
Liabilities and equity	Cash Inflow	Cash Outflow

This table applies to all sections of the statement of cash flows. (When we examine a statement of cash flows such as Starbucks', see Exhibit 11.1, the cash flow effect of an item does not always agree with the change in the balance sheet account. This can be due to several factors. One factor is when a company uses its own stock to acquire another entity. There is no cash effect from a stock acquisition and, hence, it is not reported in the statement of cash flows. Yet, the company does increase its assets and liabilities when it adds the acquired company's assets and liabilities to its balance sheet.)

Knowledge of how companies record cash inflows and outflows not only sheds light on the information contained in the statement of cash flows, it also helps managers with business decisions. For instance, managers can increase cash by decreasing the levels of receivables and inventories, perhaps by better managing the quantities and types of inventories to reduce slow-moving items or by being smarter about which customers to extend credit to, and in what amounts, to minimize slow-paying customers. Similarly, managers can increase cash by increasing the levels of accounts payable and accrued liabilities. (This must be done with care, however, as one company's payables are another company's receivables and slowing down payment could jeopardize future transactions with the vendor or supplier.) Managing cash balances by managing current asset and current liability accounts is called *working capital management*, an important activity for all companies.

Investing Activities Preview

A firm's transactions involving (1) the acquisition and disposal of PPE assets and intangible assets, (2) the purchase and sale of stocks, bonds, and other securities (that are not cash equivalents), and (3) the lending and subsequent collection of money constitute the basic components of its **investing activities**. The related cash receipts and payments appear in the investing activities section of the statement of cash flows. Examples of these cash flows follow.

Investing Activities	
Cash Inflows 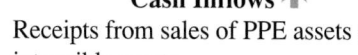	**Cash Outflows**
▪ Receipts from sales of PPE assets and intangible assets.	▪ Payments to purchase PPE assets and intangible assets.
▪ Receipts from sales of investments in stocks, bonds, and other securities (other than cash equivalents).	▪ Payments to purchase stocks, bonds, and other securities (other than cash equivalents).
▪ Receipts from repayments of loans by borrowers.	▪ Payments made to lend money to borrowers.

Financing Activities Preview

A firm engages in **financing activities** when it obtains resources from owners, returns resources to owners, borrows resources from creditors, and repays amounts borrowed. Cash flows related to these transactions are reported in the financing activities section of the statement of cash flows. Examples of these cash flows follow.

Financing Activities	
Cash Inflows	**Cash Outflows**
▪ Receipts from issuances of common stock and preferred stock and from sales of treasury stock.	▪ Payments to acquire treasury stock.
▪ Receipts from issuances of bonds payable, mortgage notes payable, and other notes payable.	▪ Payments of dividends.
	▪ Payments to settle outstanding bonds payable, mortgage notes payable, and other notes payable.

LO1 Review 11-1

Identify each transaction as one of the following activities: operating (O), investing (I), or financing (F).

Transaction	Classification
1. Payments of dividends	_____
2. Payments to purchase PPE assets and intangible assets	_____
3. Payments to employees or suppliers	_____
4. Payments to purchase inventories	_____
5. Receipts from issuances of bonds payable, mortgage notes payable, and other notes payable.	_____
6. Receipts from sales of investments in stocks, bonds, and other securities (other than cash equivalents)	_____

continued

continued from previous page

Transaction	Classification
7. Payments of interest to creditors	_____
8. Receipts from issuances of common stock and preferred stock and from sales of treasury stock	_____
9. Receipts of interest and dividends	_____
10. Payments to purchase stocks, bonds, and other securities (other than cash equivalents)	_____
11. Receipts from customers for sales made or services rendered.	_____
12. Payments to acquire treasury stock	_____
13. Other receipts such as lawsuit settlements and refunds received from suppliers . . .	_____
14. Payments of taxes to government	_____
15. Payments to settle outstanding bonds payable, mortgage notes payable, and other notes payable	_____
16. Receipts from sales of PPE assets and intangible assets	_____
17. Other payments such as contributions to charity	_____
18. Receipts from repayments of loans by borrowers	_____
19. Payments made to lend money to borrowers	_____

Solution on p. 11-56.

Cash Flow from Operating Activities

LO2

MBC Determine and analyze net cash flows from operating activities.

The first section of a statement of cash flows presents a firm's net cash flow from operating activities. Two alternative formats are used to report the net cash flow from operating activities: the *indirect method* and the *direct method. Both methods report the same amount of net cash flow from operating activities.* (Net cash flows from investing and financing activities are prepared in the same manner under both the indirect and direct methods; only the format for cash flows from operating activities differs.)

The **indirect method** starts with net income and applies a series of adjustments to net income to convert it to net cash flow from operating activities. *More than 98% of companies preparing the statement of cash flows use the indirect method.* The indirect method is popular because it is easier and less expensive to prepare than the direct method and the direct method requires a supplemental disclosure showing the indirect method (thus, essentially reporting both methods).

The remainder of this module discusses the preparation of the statement of cash flows. The indirect method is presented in this section, and the direct method is presented in the Appendix. (These discussions are independent of each other; both provide complete coverage of the preparation of the statement of cash flows.)

To prepare a statement of cash flows, we need a firm's income statement, comparative balance sheets, and some additional data taken from the accounting records. Exhibit 11.2 presents this information for Java House. We use these data to prepare Java House's 2020 statement of cash flows using the indirect method. Java House's statement of cash flows explains the $25,000 increase in cash (from $10,000 to $35,000) that occurred during 2020 by classifying the firm's cash flows into operating, investing, and financing categories.

Exhibit 11.2 ■ Financial Data of Java House

JAVA HOUSE Income Statement For Year Ended December 31, 2020		
Sales.		$250,000
Cost of goods sold	$148,000	
Wages expense	52,000	
Insurance expense.	5,000	
Depreciation expense.	10,000	
Income tax expense	11,000	
Gain on sale of land	(8,000)	218,000
Net income		$ 32,000

JAVA HOUSE Balance Sheet	Dec. 31, 2020	Dec. 31, 2019
Assets		
Cash.	$ 35,000	$ 10,000
Accounts receivable	39,000	34,000
Inventory.	54,000	60,000
Prepaid insurance.	17,000	4,000
Long-term investments	15,000	—
PPE	180,000	200,000
Accumulated depreciation . . .	(50,000)	(40,000)
Patent.	60,000	—
Total assets	$350,000	$268,000
Liabilities and Equity		
Accounts payable.	$ 10,000	$ 19,000
Income tax payable	5,000	3,000
Common stock	260,000	190,000
Retained earnings	75,000	56,000
Total liabilities and equity	$350,000	$268,000

Additional Data for 2020

1. Purchased all of the long-term investments for cash at year-end.
2. Sold land costing $20,000 for $28,000 cash.
3. Acquired a $60,000 patent at year-end by issuing common stock.
4. All accounts payable relate to merchandise purchases.
5. Issued common stock for $10,000 cash.
6. Declared and paid cash dividends of $13,000.

Steps to Compute Net Cash Flow from Operating Activities

The following four steps are applied to construct the operating activities section of the statement of cash flows.

① **Begin with net income** The first line of the operating activities section of the statement of cash flows is net income, which is the bottom line from the income statement. This amount is recorded as a positive amount for net income and as a negative amount for a net loss.

② **Adjust net income (loss) for *noncash* revenues, expenses, gains, and losses**

   a. **Noncash revenues and expenses** The income statement often includes noncash expenses, such as depreciation and amortization. These expenses are allocations of asset costs over their useful lives to match the revenues generated from those assets. The cash outflow normally occurs when the asset is acquired, which is reported in the *investing* section. Depreciation and amortization expenses do not entail cash outflows. Hence, we must eliminate them from the statement of cash flows by adding them back (to "zero them out" because they are negative amounts in the net income computation).

   b. **Gains and losses** Gains and losses on sales of assets are part of investing activities, not operating activities (unless the company is in the business of buying and selling assets). Thus, we must remove them from the operating section and record the net cash inflows or outflows in the investing section; namely, gains on sales are subtracted from income and losses on sales are added to income.

③ **Adjust net income (loss) for changes in current assets and current liabilities** Net income must be adjusted for changes in current assets and current liabilities (the operating section of the balance sheet). A decrease (from prior year to current year) in a noncash current asset is identified as a cash inflow, and an increase is identified as a cash outflow. Conversely, an increase in a current liability is identified as a cash inflow and a decrease as a cash outflow. To make this computation, we use the following guide.

Balance Sheet Account	Increase in Account	Decrease in Account
Current assets (excluding cash).......	**Cash Outflow**	**Cash Inflow**
Current liabilities...................	**Cash Inflow**	**Cash Outflow**

④ **Sum the amounts from Steps 1, 2, and 3 to get net cash flows from operating activities**

Exhibit 11.3 summarizes the adjustments to net income in determining operating cash flows. These are adjustments applied under the indirect method of computing cash flow from operations.

Exhibit 11.3 ■ Converting Net Income to Net Cash Flow from Operating Activities	Add (+) or Subtract (−) from Net Income
Net income..	$ #
Add depreciation and amortization...........................	+
Add (subtract) losses (gains) on asset and liability dispositions....	+ or −
Adjust for changes in noncash current assets	
Subtract increases in noncash current assets.................	−
Add decreases in noncash current assets...................	+
Adjust for changes in current liabilities	
Add increases in current liabilities.........................	+
Subtract decreases in current liabilities.....................	−
Net cash flow from operating activities........................	$ #

Adjustments for noncash revenues, expenses, gains, and losses — applies to rows: Add depreciation and amortization; Add (subtract) losses (gains) on asset and liability dispositions.

Adjustments for changes in noncash current assets and current liabilities — applies to rows: Adjust for changes in noncash current assets through Subtract decreases in current liabilities.

To better understand the adjustments for current assets and current liabilities, the following table provides brief explanations of adjustments for receivables, inventories, and payables and other accruals.

	Change in Account Balance	Inference Drawn	Adjustment to Net Income to Operating Cash Flow
Receivables	Increase	Sales and net income increase, but cash is not yet received	Deduct increase in receivables from net income
	Decrease	More cash is received than is reported in sales and net income	Add decrease in receivables to net income
Inventories	Increase	Cash is paid for inventories that are not yet reflected in cost of goods sold	Deduct increase in inventories from net income
	Decrease	Cost of goods sold includes inventory costs that were paid for in a prior period	Add decrease in inventories to net income
Payables and Accruals	Increase	More goods and services are acquired on credit, delaying cash payment	Add increase in payables and accruals to net income
	Decrease	More cash is paid than that reflected in cost of goods sold or operating expenses	Deduct decrease in payables and accruals from net income

Java House Case Illustration

We next explain and illustrate these adjustments with Java House's data from Exhibit 11.2.

Revenues and Expenses with No Cash Flow Effects

Depreciation and amortization expenses represent write-offs of previously recorded assets, so-called noncash expenses. Because depreciation and amortization expenses are subtracted in computing net income, we add these expenses to net income as we convert it to a related net operating cash flow. Adding these expenses to net income eliminates them from the income statement and is a necessary adjustment to obtain cash income. Java House had $10,000 of 2020 depreciation expense, so this amount is added to Java House's net income of $32,000.

Net income	$32,000
Add depreciation	**10,000**

Gains and Losses with No Cash Flow Effects

The income statement can contain gains and losses that relate to investing or financing activities. Gains and losses from the sale of investments, PPE assets, or intangible assets illustrate gains and losses from investing (not operating) activities. A gain or loss from the retirement of bonds payable is an example of a financing gain or loss. The full cash flow effect from these types of events is reported in the investing or financing sections of the statement of cash flows. Therefore, the related gains or losses must be eliminated as we convert net income to net cash flow from operating activities. To eliminate their impact on net income, gains are subtracted and losses are added to net income. Java House had an $8,000 gain from the sale of land. This gain relates to an investing activity, so it is subtracted from Java House's net income.

Net income	$32,000
Add depreciation.	10,000
Subtract gain on sale of land	**(8,000)**

Change in Current Operating Assets—Accounts Receivable

Credit sales increase accounts receivable; cash collections on account decrease accounts receivable. If, overall, accounts receivable decrease during a year, then cash collections from customers exceed credit sales revenue by the amount of the decrease. Because sales are added in computing net income, the decrease in accounts receivable is added to net income. In essence, this adjustment replaces the sales amount with the larger amount of cash collections from customers. If accounts receivable increase during a year, then sales revenue exceeds the cash collections from customers by the amount of the increase. Because sales are added in computing net income, the increase in accounts receivable is subtracted from net income as we convert it to a net cash flow from operating activities. In essence, this adjustment replaces the sales amount with the smaller amount of cash collections from customers. Java House's accounts receivable increased $5,000, so this increase is subtracted from net income under the indirect method.

Net income	$32,000
Add depreciation.	10,000
Subtract gain on sale of land	(8,000)
Subtract accounts receivable increase	**(5,000)**

Change in Current Operating Assets—Inventory

The adjustment for an inventory change is one of two adjustments to net income that together cause the cost of goods sold expense to be replaced by an amount representing the cash paid during the period for merchandise purchased. The second adjustment, which we examine shortly, is for the change in accounts payable. The effect of the inventory adjustment alone is to adjust net income for the difference between the cost of goods sold and the cost of merchandise purchased during the period. The cost of merchandise purchased increases inventory; the cost of goods sold decreases inventory. An overall decrease in inventory during a period must mean, therefore, that the cost of merchandise purchased was less than the cost of goods sold, by the amount of the decrease. Because cost of goods sold was subtracted in computing net income, the inventory decrease is added to net income. After this adjustment, the effect of the cost of goods sold on net income has been replaced by the smaller cost of merchandise purchased. Similarly, if inventory increased during a period, the cost of merchandise purchased is larger than the cost of goods sold by the amount of the increase. To replace the cost of goods sold with the cost of merchandise purchased, the inventory increase is subtracted from net income. Java House's inventory decreased $6,000, so this decrease is added to net income.

Net income	$32,000
Add depreciation.	10,000
Subtract gain on sale of land	(8,000)
Subtract accounts receivable increase.	(5,000)
Add inventory decrease	**6,000**

Change in Current Operating Assets—Prepaid Expenses

Cash prepayments of various expenses increase a firm's prepaid expenses. When the related expenses for the period are subsequently recorded, the prepaid expenses decrease. An overall decrease in prepaid expenses for a period means the cash prepayments were less than the related expenses. Because the expenses were subtracted in determining net income, the indirect method adds the decrease in prepaid expenses to net income as it is converted to a cash flow amount. The effect of the addition is to replace the expense amount with the smaller cash payment amount. Similarly, an increase in prepaid expenses is subtracted from net income because an increase means the cash prepayments during the year were more than the related expenses. Java House's prepaid insurance increased $13,000, so this increase is deducted from net income.

Net income	$32,000
Add depreciation.	10,000
Subtract gain on sale of land	(8,000)
Subtract accounts receivable increase.	(5,000)
Add inventory decrease	6,000
Subtract prepaid insurance increase	**(13,000)**

Change in Current Operating Liabilities—Accounts Payable

When merchandise is purchased on account, accounts payable increase by the cost of the goods purchased. Accounts payable decrease when cash payments are made to settle the accounts. An overall decrease in accounts payable during a year means cash payments for purchases were more than the cost of the purchases. An accounts payable decrease, therefore, is subtracted from net income under the indirect method. The deduction, in effect, replaces the cost of merchandise purchased with the larger cash payments for merchandise purchased. (Recall that the earlier inventory adjustment replaced the cost of goods sold with the cost of merchandise purchased.) In contrast, an increase in accounts payable means cash payments for purchases were less than the cost of purchases for the period. Thus, an accounts payable increase is added to net income as it is converted to a cash flow amount. Java House shows a $9,000 decrease in accounts payable. This decrease is subtracted from net income.

Net income	$32,000
Add depreciation.	10,000
Subtract gain on sale of land	(8,000)
Subtract accounts receivable increase.	(5,000)
Add inventory decrease	6,000
Subtract prepaid insurance increase	(13,000)
Subtract accounts payable decrease	**(9,000)**

Change in Current Operating Liabilities—Accrued Liabilities

Changes in accrued liabilities are interpreted the same way as changes in accounts payable. A decrease means cash payments exceeded the related expense amounts; an increase means cash payments were less than the related expenses. Decreases are subtracted from net income; increases are added to net income. Java has one accrued liability, income tax payable, and it increased by $2,000. The $2,000 increase is added to net income.

Net income	$32,000
Add depreciation.	10,000
Subtract gain on sale of land	(8,000)
Subtract accounts receivable increase.	(5,000)
Add inventory decrease	6,000
Subtract prepaid insurance increase	(13,000)
Subtract accounts payable decrease	(9,000)
Add income tax payable increase.	**2,000**

Net Cash from Operating Activities

We have identified all of the adjustments to convert Java House's net income to its net cash flow from operating activities. The operating activities section of the statement of cash flows appears as follows under the indirect method.

Net income	$32,000
Add (deduct) items to convert net income to cash basis:	
Depreciation	10,000
Gain on sale of land	(8,000)
Accounts receivable increase	(5,000)
Inventory decrease	6,000
Prepaid insurance increase	(13,000)
Accounts payable decrease	(9,000)
Income tax payable increase	2,000
Net cash provided by operating activities	**$15,000**

To summarize, net cash from operating activities begins with net income (loss) and eliminates noncash expenses (such as depreciation) and noncash revenues, and any noncash gains and losses that are properly reported in the investing and financing sections. Next, cash inflows (outflows) relating to changes in the level of current operating assets and liabilities are added (subtracted) to yield net cash flows from operating activities. During the period, Java House earned cash operating profits of $34,000 ($32,000 + $10,000 − $8,000) and used $19,000 of cash (−$5,000 + $6,000 − $13,000 − $9,000 + $2,000) to increase net working capital. Cash outflows relating to the increase in net working capital are a common occurrence for growing companies, and this net asset increase must be financed just like the increase in PPE assets.

Business Insight ■ Starbucks' Adjustments for Operating Cash Flow

Starbucks reports $4,518.0 million for 2018 net earnings, including noncontrolling interests, along with $11,937.8 million of operating cash inflows (see Exhibit 11.1). Differences between net income and operating cash flow are due to:

- Depreciation and amortization expense of $1,305.9 million (similar to the addback for Java House).
- Loss from equity method investees of $242.8 million that is included in net income. This is followed by the addition of $226.8 million from dividends received from those equity method investees. Equity income is not received in cash until the investee pays dividends to the investors (including Starbucks).

continued

continued from previous page

- Gains of $1,376.4 million on the acquisition of a joint venture and of $499.2 million on the divestiture of certain retail operations are subtracted to remove the noncash gains. The statement of cash flows shows the cash received as an investing inflow. (This is similar to the gain on sale of land for Java House.)
- Stock-based compensation expense of $250.3 million, which is noncash compensation expense paid in the form of shares of stock.

All of these noncash items are removed from reported net income to yield net cash flow from operating activities. Starbucks' operating cash flow also includes the cash generated by or used for working capital accounts as discussed above for Java House. This includes

- Decrease in accounts receivable, $131.0 million
- Increase in inventories, $41.2 million
- Increase in accounts payable, $391.6 million
- Increase in deferred revenue, $7,109.4 (from the new revenue recognition standard) representing cash received from customers but not included in net income because performance obligations had not yet been earned by year-end

---

Managerial Decision   ■   You Are the Securities Analyst

You are analyzing a company's statement of cash flows. The company has two items relating to its accounts receivable. First, the company finances the sale of its products to some customers; the increase to notes receivable is classified as an investing activity. Second, the company sells its accounts receivable to a separate entity, such as a trust. As a result, sale of receivables is reported as an asset sale; this reduces receivables and yields a gain or loss on the sale (in this case, the company is not required to consolidate the trust). This action increases the company's operating cash flows. How should you interpret this cash flow increase? [Answer, p. 11-32]

Review 11-2 LO2

Expresso Royale's income statement and comparative balance sheets follow.

EXPRESSO ROYALE Income Statement For Year Ended December 31, 2020		
Sales.		$385,000
Dividend income.		5,000
		390,000
Cost of goods sold	$233,000	
Wages expense	82,000	
Advertising expense.	10,000	
Depreciation expense.	11,000	
Income tax expense	17,000	
Loss on sale of investments	2,000	355,000
Net income		$ 35,000

continued

continued from previous page

EXPRESSO ROYALE Balance Sheets		
	Dec. 31, 2020	**Dec. 31, 2019**
Assets.		
Cash.	$ 8,000	$ 12,000
Accounts receivable	22,000	28,000
Inventory.	94,000	66,000
Prepaid advertising.	12,000	9,000
Available-for-sale investments	30,000	41,000
Fair value adjustment to investments.	—	(1,000)
Property, plant & equipment (PPE).	178,000	130,000
Accumulated depreciation	(72,000)	(61,000)
Total assets	$272,000	$224,000
Liabilities and Equity.		
Accounts payable.	$ 27,000	$ 14,000
Wages payable.	6,000	2,500
Income tax payable	3,000	4,500
Common stock	139,000	125,000
Retained earnings	97,000	79,000
Unrealized loss on available-for-sale investments (AOCI) . . .	—	(1,000)
Total liabilities and equity	$272,000	$224,000

Cash dividends of $17,000 were declared and paid during 2020. PPE was purchased for cash in 2020, and, later in the year, additional common stock was issued for cash. Investments costing $11,000 and carried at $10,000 were sold for cash at a $2,000 realized loss in 2020; an unrealized loss of $1,000 on these investments had been recorded in 2019 (at December 31, 2020, the cost and fair value of unsold investments are equal).

Required
Compute Expresso Royale's operating cash flow for 2020 using the indirect method.

Solution on p. 11-56.

Computing Cash Flows from Investing Activities

Analyze Remaining Noncash Assets

Investing activities cause changes in asset accounts. Usually, the accounts affected (other than cash) are noncurrent asset accounts, such as PPE assets and long-term investments, although short-term investment accounts can also be affected. To determine the cash flows from investing activities, *we analyze changes in all noncash asset accounts not used in computing net cash flow from operating activities.* Our objective is to identify any investing cash flows related to these changes.

We can draw on our following decision rule to see how changes in assets such as investments and PPE affect cash flow.

eLectures
MBC **LO3** Determine and analyze net cash flows from investing activities.

Balance Sheet Account	Increase in Account	Decrease in Account
Assets (noncash)	Cash Outflow	Cash Inflow

Java House Case Illustration
Analyze Change in Investments

Java House's comparative balance sheets (see Exhibit 11.2) show available-for-sale investments increased $15,000 during the year. The increase means investments must have been purchased, and the additional data reported indicates cash was spent to purchase investments. Purchasing investments is an investing activity. Thus, a $15,000 purchase of investments is reported as a cash outflow from investing activities in the statement of cash flows.

Cash flows from investing activities	
Purchase of investments	$(15,000)

Analyze Change in PPE

Java House's PPE decreased $20,000 during the year. PPE decreases as the result of disposals, and the additional data for Java House indicate land was sold for cash. Selling land is an investing activity. Thus, the sale of land for $28,000 is reported as a cash inflow from investing activities in the statement of cash flows. (Recall that the $8,000 gain on sale of land was deducted as a reconciling item in the operating section; see above.)

Cash flows from investing activities	
Purchase of stock investments.	$(15,000)
Sale of land.	28,000

Analyze Change in Accumulated Depreciation

Java House's accumulated depreciation increased $10,000 during the year. Accumulated depreciation increases when depreciation expense is recorded. Java House's depreciation expense was $10,000, so the total change in accumulated depreciation is the result of the recording of depreciation expense. As previously discussed, there is no cash flow related to the recording of depreciation expense, and we previously adjusted for this expense in our computation of net cash flows from operating activities.

Analyze Change in Patent

We see from the comparative balance sheets that Java House had an increase of $60,000 for a patent. The increase means a patent was acquired, and the additional data indicate common stock was issued to obtain a patent. This event is a noncash investing (acquiring a patent) and financing (issuing common stock) transaction that must be disclosed as supplementary information to the statement of cash flows.

Net Cash from Investing Activities

The investing activities section of the statement of cash flows appears as follows.

Cash flows from investing activities	
Purchase of stock investments.	$(15,000)
Sale of land.	28,000
Net cash provided by investing activities	$ 13,000

Business Insight ■ Starbucks' Investing Activities

Starbucks used $2,361.5 million cash for investing activities in 2018. Three line items on the statement of cash flows relate to investments: the buying, selling, and maturing of marketable securities throughout the year as Starbucks invests its excess cash to generate interest, dividends, and capital gains. The company used cash of $191.9 million to purchase new securities and received cash of $459.0 million and $45.3 million from security sales and maturities, respectively. Starbucks also spent $1,311.3 million cash to acquire other companies. Note that this is the cash portion of the acquisitions. The company might also have issued debt and stock to finance its acquisition, which would be excluded from the investing section of the statement of cash flows but would be specifically listed as a noncash investing activity in a footnote. The company received $608.2 million cash as proceeds from selling certain operations. This relates to the gain on sale of $499.2 million reported in the operating section of the statement of cash flows. Starbucks invested $1,976.4 million in PPE. These expenditures might have been for company-owned property or for leasehold improvements on leased property.

LO3 Review 11-3

Refer to the data in Review 11-2, to answer the requirement below.

Required

Prepare Expresso Royale's cash flows from investing activities for 2020.

Solution on p. 11-57.

Cash Flows from Financing Activities

Analyze Remaining Liabilities and Equity

LO4
Determine and analyze net cash flows from financing activities.

Financing activities cause changes in liability and stockholders' equity accounts. Usually, the accounts affected are noncurrent accounts, such as bonds payable and common stock, although a current liability such as short-term notes payable can also be affected. To determine the cash flows from financing activities, *we analyze changes in all liability and stockholders' equity accounts that were not used in computing net cash flow from operating activities.* Our objective is to identify any financing cash flows related to these changes.

We can draw on our following decision rule to see how changes in liabilities, such as short- and long-term debt, and equity accounts, such as common stock and treasury stock, affect cash flow.

Balance Sheet Account	Increase in Account	Decrease in Account
Liabilities and equity	Cash Inflow	Cash Outflow

Java House Case Illustration

Analyze Change in Common Stock

Java House's common stock increased $70,000 during the year (see Exhibit 11.2). Common stock increases when shares of stock are issued. As noted in discussing the patent increase, common stock with a $60,000 par value was issued in exchange for a patent. This event is disclosed as a noncash investing and financing transaction. The other $10,000 increase in common stock, as noted in the additional data, resulted from an issuance of stock for cash. Issuing common stock is a financing activity, so a $10,000 cash inflow from a stock issuance appears as a financing activity in the statement of cash flows.

Cash flows from financing activities	
Issuance of common stock.	$10,000

Analyze Change in Retained Earnings

Retained earnings grew from $56,000 to $75,000 during the year—a $19,000 increase. This increase is the net result of Java House's $32,000 of net income (which increased retained earnings) and a $13,000 cash dividend (which decreased retained earnings). Because every item in Java House's income statement was considered in computing the net cash provided by operating activities, only the cash dividend remains to be considered. Paying a cash dividend is a financing activity. Thus, a $13,000 cash dividend appears as a cash outflow from financing activities in the statement of cash flows.

Cash flows from financing activities	
Issuance of common stock.	$10,000
Payment of dividends	(13,000)

Net Cash from Financing Activities

The financing activities section of the statement of cash flows appears as follows.

Cash flows from financing activities	
Issuance of common stock................................	$10,000
Payment of dividends......................................	(13,000)
Net cash used by financing activities	$ (3,000)

We have now completed the analysis of all of Java House's noncash balance sheet accounts and can prepare the 2020 statement of cash flows. Exhibit 11.4 shows this statement.

If there are cash inflows and outflows from similar types of investing and financing activities, the inflows and outflows are reported separately (rather than reporting only the net difference). For example, proceeds from the sale of PPE are reported separately from outlays made to acquire PPE. Similarly, funds borrowed are reported separately from debt repayments, and proceeds from issuing stock are reported separately from outlays to acquire treasury stock.

Business Insight ■ Starbucks' Financing Activities

Highlights of Starbucks' 2018 financing activities include the receipt of $153.9 million cash from stock issuances. Only stock issued for cash is reflected in the statement of cash flows. Stock issued in connection with acquisitions is not reflected because it does not involve cash. Issuance of stock is often related to the exercise of employee stock options, and companies frequently repurchase stock to offset the dilutive effect of granting the options and to have stock to sell to employees who exercise their options. Starbucks reports a cash inflow of $5,584.1 million from borrowings, and no debt repayments during the year. Starbucks returned $8,876.9 million ($1,743.4 million + $7,133.5 million) to shareholders during the year in the form of dividend payments and share repurchases. The net effect is a decrease in cash of $3,242.8 million from all financing activities, including a $39.5 million reduction of cash labeled "Effect of exchange rate changes on cash and cash equivalents," which relates to the decrease in the U.S. dollar ($US) equivalent value of cash held by foreign subsidiaries as a result of a stronger $US.

Review 11-4A LO4

Solution on p. 11-57.

Refer to the data in Review 11-2, to answer the requirement below.

Required
Prepare Expresso Royale's cash flows from financing activities for 2020.

Computing Cash Flows from Balance Sheet Accounts

Drawing on the Java House illustration, we can summarize the cash flow effects of the income statement and balance sheet information and categorize them into the operating, investing, and financing classifications in the following table.

The current year's cash balance increases by $25,000, from $10,000 to $35,000. Formal preparation of the statement of cash flows can proceed once we have addressed one final issue: required supplemental disclosures. We discuss that topic in the next section.

Account	Change	Source or Use of Cash	Cash Flow Effect	Classification on SCF
Current assets				
Accounts receivable..........	+5,000	Use	−5,000	Operating
Inventories.................	−6,000	Source	+6,000	Operating
Prepaid insurance............	+13,000	Use	−13,000	Operating
Noncurrent assets				
PPE related				Investing
Accumulated depreciation ...	+10,000	Neither	+10,000	Operating
Sale of land				
Proceeds...............	+28,000	Source	+28,000	Investing
Gain...................	−8,000	Neither	−8,000	Operating
Investments.................	+15,000	Use	−15,000	Investing
Current liabilities				
Accounts payable............	−9,000	Use	−9,000	Operating
Income tax payable...........	+2,000	Source	+2,000	Operating
Long-term liabilities				Financing
Stockholders' equity				
Common stock	+10,000	Source	+10,000	Financing
Retained earnings				
Net income................	+32,000	Source	+32,000	Operating
Dividends.................	+13,000	Use	−13,000	Financing
Total (net cash flow)			+25,000	

Supplemental Disclosures for the Indirect Method

When the indirect method is used in the statement of cash flows, separate disclosures are required for: (1) cash paid for interest and cash paid for income taxes, (2) a schedule or description of all noncash investing and financing transactions, and (3) the firm's policy for determining which highly liquid, short-term investments are treated as cash equivalents. Noncash investing and financing activities include the issuance of stocks, bonds, or leases in exchange for PPE assets or intangible assets; the exchange of long-term assets for other long-term assets; and the conversion of long-term debt into common stock.

Java House Case Illustration for Supplemental Disclosures

Cash Paid for Interest Java House incurred no interest cost during the year.

Cash Paid for Income Taxes Java House did pay income taxes. Our discussion of the $2,000 change in income tax payable during the year revealed that the increase meant cash tax payments were less than income tax expense by the amount of the increase. Income tax expense was $11,000, so the cash paid for income taxes was $2,000 less than $11,000, or $9,000.

Noncash Investing and Financing Activities Java House had one noncash investing and financing event: the issuance of common stock to acquire a patent. This event, as well as the cash paid for income taxes, is disclosed as supplemental information to the statement of cash flows in Exhibit 11.4.

Exhibit 11.4 ■ Statement of Cash Flows for Indirect Method with Supplemental Disclosures

JAVA HOUSE
Statement of Cash Flows
For Year Ended December 31, 2020

Net cash flow from operating activities

Net income	$32,000	
Add (deduct) items to convert net income to cash basis:		
Depreciation	10,000	
Gain on sale of land	(8,000)	
Accounts receivable increase	(5,000)	
Inventory decrease	6,000	
Prepaid insurance increase	(13,000)	
Accounts payable decrease	(9,000)	
Income tax payable increase	2,000	
Net cash provided by operating activities		$15,000
Cash flows from investing activities		
Purchase of investments	(15,000)	
Sale of land	28,000	
Net cash provided by investing activities		13,000
Cash flows from financing activities		
Issuance of common stock	10,000	
Payment of dividends	(13,000)	
Net cash used by financing activities		(3,000)
Net increase in cash		25,000
Cash at beginning of year		10,000
Cash at end of year		$35,000

Supplemental cash flow disclosures		
Cash paid for income taxes		$ 9,000
Schedule of noncash investing and financing activities		
Issuance of common stock to acquire patent		$60,000

Review 11-4B LO4

Refer to the balance sheet for Expresso Royale, and to the solutions for Reviews 11-2, 11-3, and 11-4A, to answer the requirements below.

Required

Solution on p. 11-57.

a.   Compute the change in cash by considering cash flow from operating, investing, and financing activities.

b.   Use the change in cash computed in part *a* to reconcile the beginning and ending cash balances for 2020.

Analysis of Cash Flow Information

Cash Flow Components

LO5
Examine and interpret cash flow information.

Typically, established companies have positive cash flow from operating activities. This cash flow provides most (if not all) of the total cash required to grow the business while maintaining appropriate levels of net working capital. On average, net cash flow from investing activities is negative as companies grow the PPE infrastructure needed to support the business. (Any excess cash invested in marketable securities typically generates cash flow, but this is small relative to the larger cash outflow for PPE and acquisitions.) Financing activities make up the difference between cash generated by operating activities and cash used by investing activities. Companies that generate more cash from operating activities than is required to support investing activities use that excess cash to pay down indebtedness, repurchase stock, or pay additional dividends. Companies that need cash for investing activities typically generate it from financing activities.

Exhibit 11.5 presents various cash flow items as a percentage of total revenues for the S&P 500 companies in fiscal 2018. The median operating cash flow is 19.7% of total revenues, of which net income explains 11.4 percentage points, and the add-backs for depreciation and stock-based compensation explain 3.1 and 0.7 percentage points, respectively. The remaining 4.5 percentage points relate to cash inflows and outflows from net working capital accounts.

Investing activities typically represent an outflow of cash equal to 8.0% of revenues, with CAPEX comprising 45% of the total (3.6 percentage points out of 8.0). Other investing activities generally relate to investment of excess cash in marketable securities. The median S&P company generates more operating cash flow than is required for investing activities and reports negative cash flow of 8.2% of revenues for financing activities. These activities generally include the payment of dividends, the repayment of debt, and the repurchase of common stock.

Exhibit 11.5 ■ Statement of Cash Flow Items as a Percentage of Total Revenues—SP500 in 2018						
	Net Income	Depreciation and Amortization	Stock-Based Compensation	Cash from Operations	Cash from Investing	Capital Expenditure	Cash from Financing
2018 Median. . . .	11.4%	3.1%	0.7%	19.7%	(8.0)%	(3.6)%	(8.2)%

During 2018, S&P companies were profitable (only 10 of the 500 companies report a net loss greater than 5% of revenues) and generated sizeable operating cash flows. It is common for large companies to generate more operating cash flow than is required for investing activities, thus permitting the payment of dividends, the retirement of debt, and the repurchase of common stock. We expect this profile for a healthy, mature company.

Research Insight ■ Net Income Versus Cash Flows

By definition, GAAP net income consists of two components: cash and noncash items. Accountants call the noncash items "accruals" (defined as the difference between net income and cash from operations). Finance and accounting research investigates whether, and how, net earnings, operating cash flows, and accruals each predict (1) future earnings or future cash flows (this line of research is called predictability research), and (2) stock price (this line of research is called value-relevance research).

Although the statement of cash flows is very useful in a number of analysis situations, predictability research shows it is net income and not current operating cash flow that better predicts future net income. Predictability research by Richard Sloan (*The Accounting Review*, 1996) found that the two components of net income (accruals and cash flows) have different impacts on future earnings; specifically, cash flows are more persistent, meaning they have longer-term implications for future earnings than accruals do. Later, work by Tuomo Vuolteenaho (*Journal of Finance*, 2002) found that, in addition to information about future earnings, the accruals and cash flows explain the riskiness of the firm. The interpretation is that, because accruals are less persistent and they fluctuate more, they signal additional risk. One way to use this finding in our analysis is to compute the ratio of operating cash flow to net income: the higher that number, the lower the firm's operating risk.

Early value-relevance research from the late 1960s found that when firms announced that their earnings were higher (lower) than the prior year's earnings, stock price increased (decreased). This sparked much research into the relevance of accounting earnings for stock prices. With growth in the sources and speed of information, our current understanding is that, although earnings are important for stock prices, most of the information conveyed by earnings is factored into stock price long before the company announces its official numbers. For example, Ray Ball and Lakshmanan Shivakumar (*Journal of Accounting Research*, 2008) find that earnings announcement events only account for 1% to 2% of the stock price movement each year. Later, value-relevance research investigated whether the stock market reacts differently to cash flow versus the accruals components of earnings. For example, Sloan's (1996) finding came to be known as the *accrual anomaly*—the fact that stock prices do not differentiate between accruals and cash flows—which causes mispricing because accruals fluctuate more wildly than cash flows. However, markets learn quickly from their mistakes, and evidence of the accrual anomaly has decreased steadily since 1996. In sum, both of these research streams are ongoing and active areas as academics and analysts seek to understand how the various earnings components are related to future firm profitability as well as how the income statement, balance sheet, and statement of cash flows separately and collectively inform investors about firm value and riskiness.

Cash Flow Patterns

A product life-cycle framework can be helpful in interpreting cash flow patterns. This framework proposes four stages for products or services: (1) introduction, (2) growth, (3) maturity, and (4) decline. The following figure plots the usual patterns for revenues, income, and cash flows at each of these four stages. For revenues, the top line number, we see the common pattern of growth over the first two stages, then a leveling out at maturity, then finally a decline. The length of time between introduction and decline depends on many of the factors considered by Porter's forces or a SWOT analysis. For example, products with short lives and those subject to fashion trends, technical innovation, or obsolescence will have a shorter life cycle, and revenue will be at greater risk of fluctuation. Knowledge of product life cycles can help us assess the transitory or persistent nature of revenues.

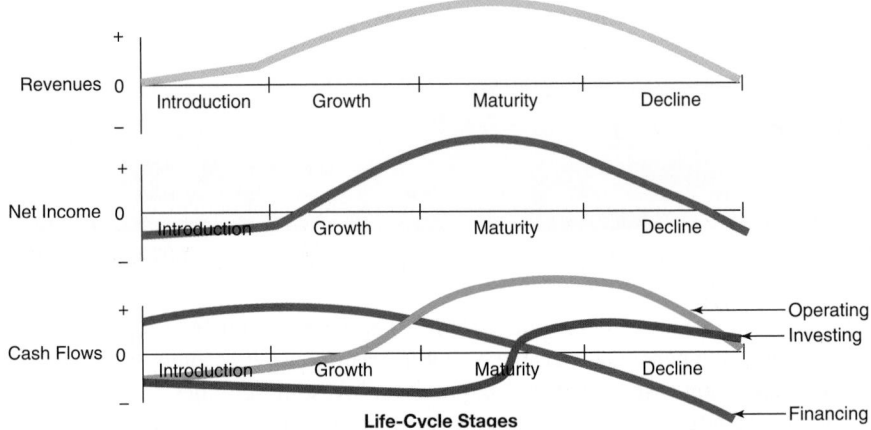

The second graph in the figure shows net income behavior over the four life-cycle stages. We commonly see losses in the introductory stage as companies struggle to recover startup costs and establish revenue streams. Net income commonly peaks during the maturity stage before a gradual decrease in the decline stage. The third graph highlights cash flows from operating, investing, and financing over the product life cycle. Although we see variations due to product success, strategic planning, and cost controls, these trends for each cash flow are fairly descriptive.

In general, during the introductory stage, revenues are limited, which results in low income and operating cash flows. The introductory stage also sees cash outflows for investing and cash inflows for financing. During the growth stage, revenues, income, and operating cash flows all increase, whereas both investing and financing cash flows increase or level out (each depending on predictions of future growth). The maturity stage sees peaks, and maybe some eventual decline, for revenues, income, and operating cash flows. This occurs as investing cash flows drop off, rendering additional financing cash inflows unnecessary. The decline stage brings large decreases in revenues, income, and operating cash flows. In decline, companies distribute cash flows for financing sources (repay debt, buy back stock, pay dividends) and realize some incoming investing cash flows as assets are gradually sold off. In summary, knowledge of product life cycles can help us understand the underlying economics, which will inform our business analysis. It can also help us interpret and possibly predict future streams of revenues, income, and cash flows.

Lowe's Companies is a solid, healthy company whose cash flow pattern (shown in Exhibit 11.6) is consistent with the pattern for mature-stage companies. Lowe's operating cash flow has grown throughout this period and provides sufficient cash to support the growth of net working capital and to partially finance the investment in PPE. Financing activities provide the remaining cash needed for investing activities. Notice how the investing and financing cash flows move in opposite directions, indicating greater financing inflows when cash outflows for investing activities increase, and vice versa. Most mature, healthy companies exhibit a similar cash flow profile.

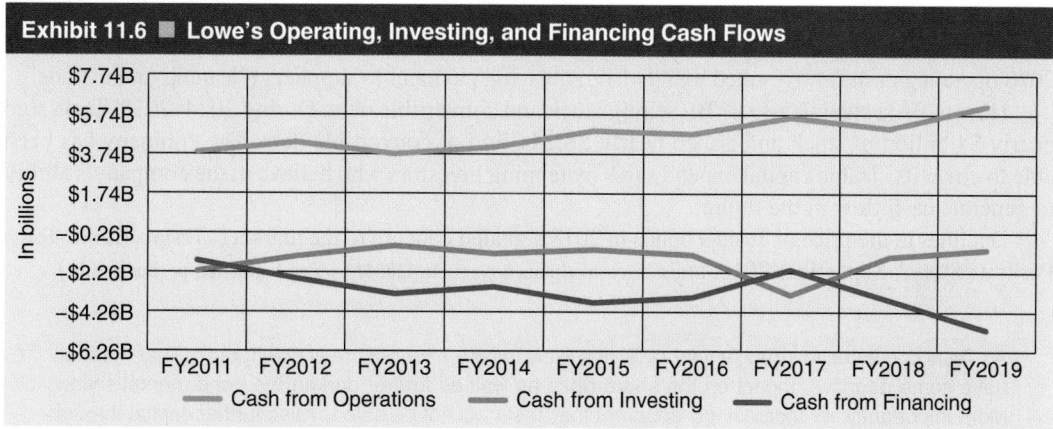

Exhibit 11.6 ■ Lowe's Operating, Investing, and Financing Cash Flows

Southwest Airlines also provides a strong cash flow picture—shown in Exhibit 11.7. As its operating cash flows have soared, Southwest has been able to both invest in PPE and to return cash to investors via stock repurchases and dividends.

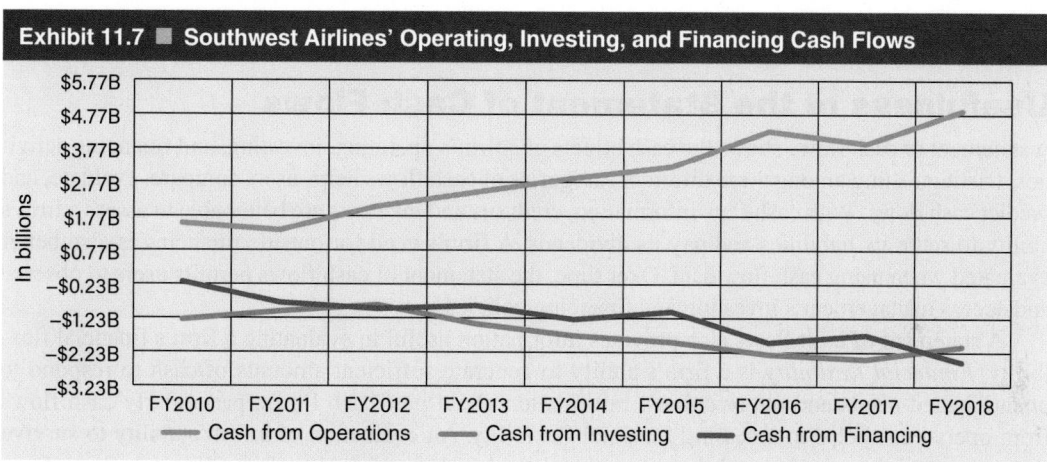

Exhibit 11.7 ■ Southwest Airlines' Operating, Investing, and Financing Cash Flows

During 2014–2018, **Tesla Inc.** reported losses totaling nearly $5 billion and it spent nearly $10.3 billion on CAPEX—shown in Exhibit 11.8.

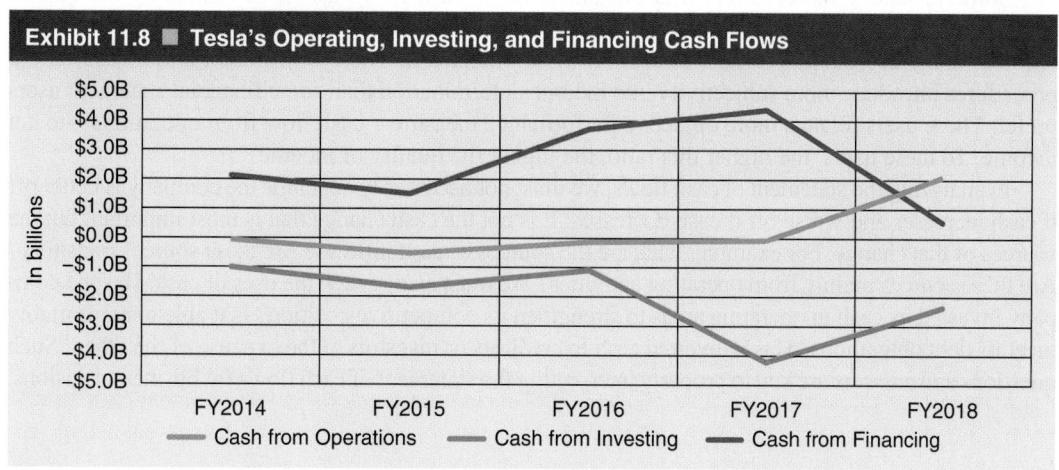

Exhibit 11.8 ■ Tesla's Operating, Investing, and Financing Cash Flows

At first glance, in the face of significant net losses in its income statement, Tesla's positive operating cash flow in 2018 seems to indicate that the company has turned the corner. Upon closer inspection, the 2018 operating cash flow resulted mainly from delaying payment to suppliers ("leaning on the trade").

How is Tesla staying afloat? By selling stock and convertible debt. During 2014–2018, Tesla sold nearly $4 billion of stock and issued nearly $8.2 billion of convertible debt. The company has been able to cover its sizable capital expenditures by tapping investors who believe in the company's ability to generate cash flow in the future.

Declines in the price of Tesla's bonds in 2018 signaled concern to the market ("Tesla's Bonds Tell a Perilous Story," September 2018, **https://seekingalpha.com/article/4205414-teslas-bonds-tell-perilous-story**).

> As Tesla continues to struggle financially, it's likely to face a further credit downgrade. That will likely have some negative impact on the share price as well as further darken the bond market's view. More importantly, it's increasingly apparent that Tesla will not be able to raise further capital through the debt market without accepting far harsher terms than it has enjoyed to date. Last year, the bond market believed in Elon's promises. Now, it only believes in what he can deliver.

We can gain insight into Tesla's financial condition by analyzing its statement of cash flows as explained next.

Usefulness of the Statement of Cash Flows

A statement of cash flows shows the cash effects of a firm's operating, investing, and financing activities. Distinguishing among these different categories of cash flows helps users compare, evaluate, and predict cash flows. With cash flow information, creditors and investors are better able to assess a firm's ability to settle its liabilities and pay its dividends. A firm's need for outside financing is also better evaluated when using cash flow data. Over time, the statement of cash flows permits users to observe and access management's investing and financing policies.

A statement of cash flows also provides information useful in evaluating a firm's financial flexibility. *Financial flexibility* is a firm's ability to generate sufficient amounts of cash to respond to unanticipated needs and opportunities. Information about past cash flows, particularly cash flows from operations, helps in assessing financial flexibility. An evaluation of a firm's ability to survive an unexpected drop in demand, for example, should include a review of its past cash flows from operations. The larger these cash flows, the greater is the firm's ability to withstand adverse changes in economic conditions. Other financial statements, particularly the balance sheet and its notes, also contain information useful for judging financial flexibility.

Some investors and creditors find the statement of cash flows useful in evaluating the quality of a firm's income. As we know, determining income under accrual accounting procedures (GAAP) requires many accruals, deferrals, allocations, and valuations. These adjustment and measurement procedures introduce more subjectivity into income determination than some financial statement users prefer. These users relate a more objective performance measure—cash flow from operations—to net income. To these users, the higher this ratio, the higher the quality of income.

In analyzing the statement of cash flows, we must not necessarily conclude the company is better off if cash increases and worse off if cash decreases. It is not the cash change that is most important but the sources of that change. For example, what are the sources of cash inflows? Are these sources transitory? Are these sources mainly from operating activities? We must also review the uses of cash. Has the company invested its cash in operating areas to strengthen its competitive position? Is it able to comfortably meet its debt obligations? Has it diverted cash to creditors or investors at the expense of the other? Such questions and answers are key to properly interpreting the statement of cash flows for business decisions.

Research Insight ■ Cash Flow Patterns as an Indicator of Firm Life Cycle

A company can operate in several industries simultaneously and produce multiple products within each industry. This can make it difficult to identify the life-cycle stage because the company is a composite of many overlapping but distinct product life-cycle stages. Understanding a firm's life-cycle stage is important because life cycle affects the firm's production behavior, its investing activities, its market share, and many other pieces of information useful to analysis. Research shows cash flow patterns (net inflow or outflow) provide a reliable way to assess the overall life-cycle stage of the company, as follows.

	Introduction	Growth	Maturity	Decline
Operating	−	+	+	−
Investing	−	−	+/−	+
Financing	+	+	−	+/−

Using cash flow patterns to identify firm life-cycle stage, current research finds profitability ratios are consistent with expected economic behavior at each life-cycle stage. As demonstrated in the following graph, net operating profit margin (NOPM) is maximized in the growth stage when companies are able to differentiate their brands.

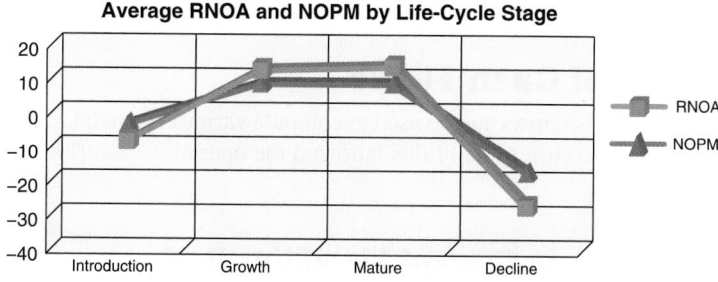

By comparison, return on net operating assets (RNOA) and net operating asset turnover (NOAT) are maximized in the maturity stage as market saturation is reached, but operating efficiencies allow the firm to maintain (or increase) profitability.

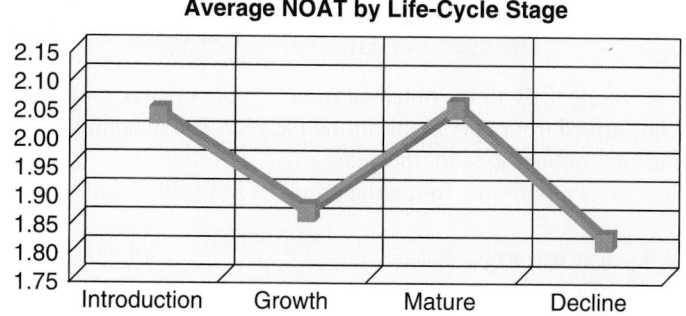

In addition, life-cycle stage as measured by cash flow patterns explains stock market valuation and stock returns. On average, mature-stage companies have abnormally high stock returns (as compared with the expected return for similar companies). One explanation is that investors underestimate the persistence of the mature company's profitability because they do not know the company's life-cycle stage and expect profits (and stock prices) to quickly revert to "normal" levels. (Source: Victoria Dickinson, "Cash Flow Patterns as a Proxy for Firm Life Cycle," *The Accounting Review*, November 2011, 86(6): 1969–1994.)

Review 11-5 LO5

The following information is taken from the Form 10-K for Starbucks and Farmer Brothers. The latter company is a small, publically traded coffee roaster.

	Revenue	Net Income	Depreciation	Stock-Based Compensation	Cash from Operations	Cash from Investing	CAPEX	Cash from Financing
Starbucks ($ millions)...	$24,719.5	$4,518.3	$1,304.9	$250.3	$11,937.8	$(2,361.5)	$(1,976.4)	$(3,242.8)
Farmer Brothers ($ 000s).....	$595,942	$(73,595)	$31,065	$3,674	$35,450	$(32,361)	$(34,760)	$1,456

Required
Consider the cash flow patterns for both companies in answering the following questions.

a. Compute the cash flow percentages shown in Exhibit 11.5 for both companies. How does each company's percentages compare with the medians for the S&P reported in that exhibit?

Solution on p. 11-57.   b. At what stage in its life cycle is each company? Explain.

Ratio Analyses of Cash Flows

LO6
MBC Compute and interpret ratios based on operating cash flows.

Data from the statement of cash flows can be used to compute various financial ratios. Two such ratios are the operating cash flow to current liabilities ratio and the operating cash flow to capital expenditures ratio.

Operating Cash Flow to Current Liabilities Ratio

Two liquidity measures previously introduced—the current ratio and the quick ratio—emphasize the relation of current assets to current liabilities in an attempt to measure the ability of the firm to pay current liabilities when they become due. The **operating cash flow to current liabilities ratio** is another liquidity measure of the company's ability to liquidate current liabilities and is calculated as follows.

$$\text{Operating Cash Flow to Current Liabilities} = \frac{\text{Cash Flow from Operating Activities}}{\text{Average Current Liabilities}}$$

Net cash flow from operating activities is obtained from the statement of cash flows; it represents the excess amount of cash derived from operations during the year. The denominator is the average of the beginning and ending current liabilities for the year.

To illustrate, Starbucks reports the following amounts in its 2018 financial statements.

Cash flow from operating activities...................	$11,937.8 million
Current liabilities at beginning of the year	5,684.2 million
Current liabilities at end of the year	4,220.7 million

Starbucks' operating cash flow to current liabilities ratio of 2.41 is computed as follows.

$11,937.8 million/[($5,684.2 million + $4,220.7 million)/2] = 2.41

The higher this ratio, the stronger is a firm's ability to settle current liabilities as they come due. Our analysis would compare this ratio over time and against peer companies. In 2018, the average for large public companies was 0.5.

Operating Cash Flow to Capital Expenditures Ratio

To remain competitive, an entity must be able to replace and expand, when appropriate, its PPE assets. A ratio that helps assess a firm's ability to do this from internally generated cash flow is the **operating cash flow to capital expenditures ratio**, which is computed as follows.

$$\text{Operating Cash Flow to Capital Expenditures} = \frac{\text{Cash Flow from Operating Activities}}{\text{Capital Expenditures}}$$

The numerator in this ratio comes directly from the operating section of the statement of cash flows. Information for the denominator comes directly from the investing section of the statement of cash flows. Additional information about capital expenditures can be found in a number of related disclosures. Data on capital expenditures are part of the required industry segment disclosures in notes to the financial statements. Also, capital expenditures often appear in the comparative selected financial data presented as supplementary information to the financial statements. Finally, management's discussion and analysis of the statements commonly identify the annual capital expenditures.

A ratio in excess of 1.0 means the firm's current operating activities are providing cash in excess of the amount needed to provide the desired level of plant capacity and would normally be considered a sign of financial strength. This ratio is also viewed as an indicator of long-term solvency—a ratio exceeding 1.0 means there is operating cash flow in excess of capital needs that can then be used to repay outstanding long-term debt.

The interpretation of this ratio for a firm is influenced by its trend in recent years, the ratios for other firms in the same industry, and the stage of the firm's life cycle. A firm in the early stages of its life cycle, during rapid expansion, is expected to experience a lower ratio than a firm in the mature stage of its life cycle, when maintenance of plant capacity is more likely than expansion of capacity.

To illustrate the ratio's computation, Starbucks reported capital expenditures in 2018 of $1,976.4 million. Starbucks' operating cash flow to capital expenditures ratio for that same year is 6.04 ($11,937.8 million/$1,976.4 million). As before, our analysis would compare this ratio against Starbucks over time and against peer companies.

Free Cash Flow

Free cash flow is a common financial metric we encounter in the financial press. It is also common to see firm value estimated by discounting a company's future free cash flows (this is the DCF valuation model, which we discuss in a later module). A common definition of free cash flow (seen in finance textbooks and in use by business writers) is operating cash flows less capital expenditures (CAPEX). In this definition, "operating cash flows" is not equal to net cash flows from operating activities reported in the statement of cash flows because the latter includes items such as the effects from interest (both expense and revenue). The following table shows the definition of free cash flow commonly found in finance textbooks. The table also shows that this definition is approximately equivalent to: Free cash flow = Net operating profit after tax (NOPAT) − Increase in net operating assets (NOA). (We explain NOPAT and NOA in Module 4.)

Traditional Finance Definition	As Defined in This Text
Earnings before interest and taxes, adjusted for noncash revenues and expenses − Taxes (in the absence of interest revenue and interest expense)	Net operating profit after tax (NOPAT)
− Investments in working capital − Capital expenditures (CAPEX)	− Increase in net operating assets (NOA)
= Free cash flow	= Free cash flow

The value of a firm is related to its expected free cash flow. By expressing free cash flows in terms of NOPAT and the increase in NOA, we see two specific means to increase firm value:

- Increase NOPAT
- Control NOA growth

To increase free cash flow, companies aim to achieve both of these objectives without adversely affecting the other. For example, it is not enough to increase NOPAT by increasing revenues and operating profits if these actions increase NOA to the point that the beneficial profit effects are offset by the negative effects of higher NOA. Conversely, it is not enough to reduce NOA if doing so reduces sales and operating profit to a greater extent. The challenge to managers is to find a set of actions that optimizes net operating profit and the required level of net operating assets. This is the art of management. (We discuss this further in our valuation module.)

Review 11-6 LO6

Following is financial statement data for McDonald's Corporation for 2018 ($ millions).

Cash flow provided by operations	$6,966.7
Current liabilities at beginning of the year	2,890.6
Current liabilities at end of the year	2,973.5
Capital expenditures	2,741.7

Required

1. Compute the operating cash flow to current liabilities ratio.
2. Compute the operating cash flow to capital expenditures ratio.

Solution on p. 11-58.

3. From the two ratios you computed, does it appear that McDonald's is liquid and solvent? Explain.

Appendix 11A: Direct Method Reporting for Statement of Cash Flows

eLectures LO7

MBC Explain and construct a direct method statement of cash flows.

To prepare a statement of cash flows, we need a firm's income statement, comparative balance sheets, and some additional data taken from the accounting records. Exhibit 11.2 presents this information for Java House. We use these data to prepare Java House's 2020 statement of cash flows using the direct method. Java House's statement of cash flows explains the $25,000 increase in cash (from $10,000 to $35,000) that occurred during the year by classifying the firm's cash flows into operating, investing, and financing categories. To get the information to construct the statement, we do the following.

1. **Use the direct method to determine individual cash flows from operating activities.** We use changes that occurred during the year in various current asset and current liability accounts.
2. **Determine cash flows from investing activities.** We do this by analyzing changes in noncurrent asset accounts.
3. **Determine cash flows from financing activities.** We do this by analyzing changes in liability and stockholders' equity accounts.

The net cash flows from investing and financing are identical to those prepared using the indirect method. Only the format of the net cash flows from operating activities differs between the two methods, not the total amount of cash generated from operating activities.

Cash Flows from Operating Activities

The **direct method** presents net cash flow from operating activities by showing the major categories of operating cash receipts and payments. The operating cash receipts and payments are usually determined by converting the accrual revenues and expenses to corresponding cash amounts. It is efficient to do it this way because the accrual revenues and expenses are readily available in the income statement.

Converting Revenues and Expenses to Cash Flows

Exhibit 11.9 summarizes the procedures for converting individual income statement items to corresponding cash flows from operating activities.

Java House Case Illustration

We next explain and illustrate the process of converting Java House's revenues and expenses to corresponding cash flows from operating activities under the direct method.

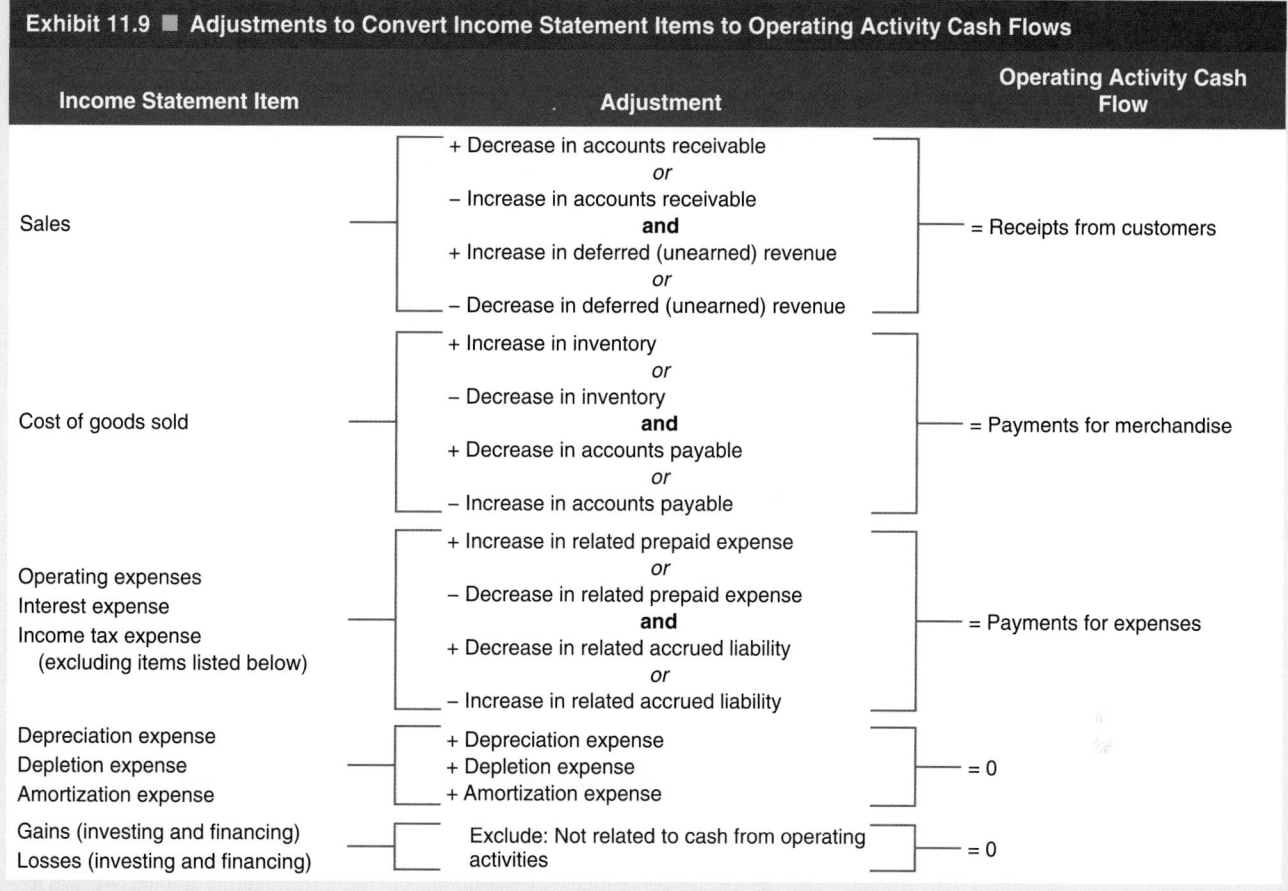

Exhibit 11.9 ■ Adjustments to Convert Income Statement Items to Operating Activity Cash Flows

Income Statement Item	Adjustment	Operating Activity Cash Flow
Sales	+ Decrease in accounts receivable *or* – Increase in accounts receivable **and** + Increase in deferred (unearned) revenue *or* – Decrease in deferred (unearned) revenue	= Receipts from customers
Cost of goods sold	+ Increase in inventory *or* – Decrease in inventory **and** + Decrease in accounts payable *or* – Increase in accounts payable	= Payments for merchandise
Operating expenses Interest expense Income tax expense (excluding items listed below)	+ Increase in related prepaid expense *or* – Decrease in related prepaid expense **and** + Decrease in related accrued liability *or* – Increase in related accrued liability	= Payments for expenses
Depreciation expense Depletion expense Amortization expense	+ Depreciation expense + Depletion expense + Amortization expense	= 0
Gains (investing and financing) Losses (investing and financing)	Exclude: Not related to cash from operating activities	= 0

Convert Sales to Cash Received from Customers

During the year, accounts receivable increased $5,000. This increase means that cash collections on account (which decrease accounts receivable) were less than credit sales (which increase accounts receivable). We compute cash received from customers as follows:

	Sales	$250,000
–	Increase in accounts receivable	(5,000)
=	Cash received from customers	$245,000

Convert Cost of Goods Sold to Cash Paid for Merchandise Purchased

The conversion of cost of goods sold to cash paid for merchandise purchased is a two-step process. First, cost of goods sold is adjusted for the change in inventory to determine the amount of purchases during the year. Second, the purchases amount is adjusted for the change in accounts payable to derive the cash paid for merchandise purchased. Inventory decreased from $60,000 to $54,000. This $6,000 decrease indicates the cost of goods sold exceeded the cost of goods purchased during the year. The year's purchases amount is computed as follows:

	Cost of goods sold	$148,000
–	Decrease in inventory	(6,000)
=	Purchases	$142,000

During the year, accounts payable decreased $9,000. This decrease reflects the fact that cash payments for merchandise purchased on account (which decrease accounts payable) exceeded purchases on account (which increase accounts payable). The cash paid for merchandise purchased, therefore, is computed as follows:

Purchases	$142,000
+ Decrease in accounts payable	9,000
= Cash paid for merchandise purchased	$151,000

Convert Wages Expense to Cash Paid to Employees

No adjustment to wages expense is needed. The absence of any beginning or ending accrued liability for wages payable means wages expense and cash paid to employees as wages are the same amount: $52,000.

Convert Insurance Expense to Cash Paid for Insurance

Prepaid insurance increased $13,000. The $13,000 increase reflects the excess of cash paid for insurance during the year (which increases prepaid insurance) over the year's insurance expense (which decreases prepaid insurance). Starting with the insurance expense, the cash paid for insurance is computed as follows:

Insurance expense	$ 5,000
+ Increase in prepaid insurance	13,000
= Cash paid for insurance.	$18,000

Eliminate Depreciation Expense and Other Noncash Operating Expenses

Depreciation expense is a noncash expense. Because it does not represent a cash payment, depreciation expense is eliminated (by adding it back) as we convert accrual expense amounts to the corresponding amounts of cash payments. If Java House had any amortization expense or depletion expense, the company would eliminate it for the same reason. The amortization of an intangible asset and the depletion of a natural resource are noncash expenses.

Convert Income Tax Expense to Cash Paid for Income Taxes

The increase in income tax payable from $3,000 at December 31, 2019, to $5,000 at December 31, 2020, means 2020's income tax expense (which increases income tax payable) was $2,000 more than 2020's tax payments (which decrease income tax payable). Starting with income tax expense, we calculate cash paid for income taxes as follows:

Income tax expense	$11,000
− Increase in income tax payable	(2,000)
= Cash paid for income taxes.	$ 9,000

Omit Gains and Losses Related to Investing and Financing Activities

The income statement may contain gains and losses related to investing or financing activities. Examples include gains and losses from the sale of PPE and gains and losses from the retirement of bonds payable. Because these gains and losses are not related to operating activities, we omit them as we convert income statement items to various cash flows from operating activities. The cash flows relating to these gains and losses are reported in the investing activities or financing activities sections of the statement of cash flows. Java House had an $8,000 gain from the sale of land this year. This gain is excluded; no related cash flow appears within the operating activities category.

We have now applied the adjustments to convert each accrual revenue and expense to the corresponding operating cash flow. We use these individual cash flows to prepare the operating activities section of the statement of cash flows, which we can see in Exhibit 11.10.

Exhibit 11.10 ■ Direct Method Operating Section of Statement of Cash Flows

Cash received from customers.		$245,000
Cash paid for merchandise purchased.	$151,000	
Cash paid to employees.	52,000	
Cash paid for insurance	18,000	
Cash paid for income taxes	9,000	230,000
Net cash provided by operating activities.		$ 15,000

Cash Flows from Investing and Financing

The reporting of investing and financing activities in the statement of cash flows is identical under the indirect and direct methods. Thus, we simply refer to the previous sections in this appendix for explanations.

Supplemental Disclosures

When the direct method is used for the statement of cash flows, three separate disclosures are required: (1) a reconciliation of net income to the net cash flow from operating activities, (2) a schedule or description of all noncash investing and financing transactions, and (3) the firm's policy for determining which highly liquid, short-term investments are treated as cash equivalents. The firm's policy regarding cash equivalents is placed in the financial statement notes. The other two separate disclosures are reported either in the notes or at the bottom of the statement of cash flows.

The required reconciliation is essentially the indirect method of computing cash flow from operating activities. *Thus, when the direct method is used in the statement of cash flows, the indirect method is a required separate disclosure.* We discussed the indirect method earlier in this module.

Java House did have one noncash investing and financing event during the year: the issuance of common stock to acquire a patent. This event is disclosed as supplemental information to the statement of cash flows in Exhibit 11.4.

LO7 Review 11-7

Refer to the data in Review 11-2 to answer the requirement below.

Required

Compute Expresso Royale's net cash flow from operating activities using the direct method.

Solution on p. 11-58.

Guidance Answers

You Are the Securities Analyst

Pg. 11-15 Many companies, but not all, treat customers' notes receivable as an investing activity. In 2005, the Securities and Exchange Commission (SEC) became concerned with this practice and issued letters to a number of companies objecting to this accounting classification. "Presenting cash receipts from receivables generated by the sale of inventory as investing activities in the company's consolidated statements of cash flows is not in accordance with GAAP," wrote the chief accountant for the SEC's division of corporation finance in her letter to the companies ("Little Campus Lab Shakes Big Firms—Georgia Tech Crew's Report Spurs Change in Accounting for Operating Cash Flow," March 1, 2005, *Wall Street Journal*). The SEC's position is that these notes receivable are an operating activity and analysts are certainly justified in treating them likewise. Concerning the sale of receivables, so long as the separate entity (a trust in this case) is properly structured, the transaction can be treated as a sale (rather than require consolidation) with a consequent reduction in receivables and a gain or loss on the sale recorded in the income statement. Many analysts treat this as a financing activity and argue that the cash inflow should not be regarded as an increase in operating cash flows. Bottom line: Many argue that operating cash flows do not increase as a result of these two transactions and analysts should adjust the statement of cash flows to properly classify the financing of receivables as an operating activity and the sale of receivables as a financing activity.

Superscript ^A^ denotes assignments based on Appendix 11A.

Questions

Q11-1.   What is the definition of cash equivalents? Give three examples of cash equivalents.

Q11-2.   Why are cash equivalents included with cash in a statement of cash flows?

Q11-3.   What are the three major types of activities classified on a statement of cash flows? Give an example of a cash inflow and a cash outflow in each classification.

Q11-4.   In which of the three activity categories of a statement of cash flows would each of the following items appear? Indicate whether each item represents a cash inflow or a cash outflow.

    a.   Cash purchase of equipment.   *e.*   Cash proceeds from issuing stock.

    b.   Cash collection on loans receivable.   *f.*   Cash receipts from customers.

    c.   Cash dividends paid.   *g.*   Cash interest paid.

    d.   Cash dividends received.   *h.*   Cash interest received.

Q11-5.   Traverse Company acquired a $3,000,000 building by issuing $3,000,000 worth of bonds payable. In terms of cash flow reporting, what type of transaction is this? What special disclosure requirements apply to a transaction of this type?

Q11-6.   Why are noncash investing and financing transactions disclosed as supplemental information to a statement of cash flows?

Q11-7.   Why is a statement of cash flows a useful financial statement?

Q11-8.^A^   What is the difference between the direct method and the indirect method of presenting net cash flow from operating activities?

Q11-9.   In determining net cash flow from operating activities using the indirect method, why must we add depreciation back to net income? Give an example of another item that is added back to net income under the indirect method.

Q11-10.   Vista Company sold for $98,000 cash land originally costing $70,000. The company recorded a gain on the sale of $28,000. How is this event reported in a statement of cash flows using the indirect method?

Q11-11.   A firm uses the indirect method. Using the following information, what is its net cash flow from operating activities?

Net income	$99,000
Accounts receivable decrease	13,000
Inventory increase	9,000
Accounts payable decrease	3,500
Income tax payable increase	1,500
Depreciation expense.	12,000

Q11-12.   What separate disclosures are required for a company that reports a statement of cash flows using the indirect method?

Q11-13.   If a business had a net loss for the year, under what circumstances would the statement of cash flows show a positive net cash flow from operating activities?

Q11-14.^A^   A firm is converting its accrual revenues to corresponding cash amounts using the direct method. Sales on the income statement are $925,000. Beginning and ending accounts receivable on the balance sheet are $58,000 and $44,000, respectively. What is the amount of cash received from customers?

Q11-15.^A^   A firm reports $86,000 wages expense in its income statement. If beginning and ending wages payable are $3,900 and $2,800, respectively, what is the amount of cash paid to employees?

Q11-16.^A^   A firm reports $43,000 advertising expense in its income statement. If beginning and ending prepaid advertising are $6,000 and $7,600, respectively, what is the amount of cash paid for advertising?

Q11-17.[A] Rusk Company sold equipment for $5,100 cash that had cost $35,000 and had $29,000 of accumulated depreciation. How is this event reported in a statement of cash flows using the direct method?

Q11-18.[A] What separate disclosures are required for a company that reports a statement of cash flows using the direct method?

Q11-19. How is the operating cash flow to current liabilities ratio calculated? Explain its use.

Q11-20. How is the operating cash flow to capital expenditures ratio calculated? Explain its use.

Q11-21. For each of the following cash flow patterns, identify whether the company is in the introduction, growth, maturity, or decline stage of its life cycle.

Life-Cycle Stage	Operating Cash Flow	Investing Cash Flow	Financing Cash Flow
a.	+	−	+
b.	+	−	−
c.	−	−	+
d.	−	+	−

Assignments with the ⓂⒷⒸ logo in the margin are available in BusinessCourse.
See the Preface of the book for details.

Mini Exercises

M11-22. **Classification of Cash Flows**   **LO1**

For each of the following items, indicate whether the cash flow relates to an operating activity, an investing activity, or a financing activity. Also indicate whether the item is a cash inflow or outflow.

a. Cash received from customers for services rendered . . . . _____ _____

b. Sale of long-term investments for cash . . . . _____ _____

c. Acquisition of PPE for cash . . . . _____ _____

d. Payment of income taxes . . . . _____ _____

e. Bonds payable issued for cash . . . . _____ _____

f. Payment of cash dividends declared in previous year . . . . _____ _____

g. Purchase of short-term investments (not cash equivalents) for cash . . . _____ _____

h. Purchases of inventory for cash . . . . _____ _____

M11-23. **Classification of Cash Flows**   **LO1**

Fitbit Inc. reports the following items in its 2018 statement of cash flows. For each item, indicate whether it would appear in the operating, investing, or financing section of the statement of cash flows (in $ thousands).

Fitbit Inc. (FIT)

a. Change in accounts payable	$ 35,207
b. Repayment of debt	747
c. Stock-based compensation	97,009
d. Proceeds from issuance of common stock	21,470
e. Change in inventories.	(12,860)
f. Purchase of property and equipment	(52,880)
g. Acquisitions, net of cash acquired	(19,253)
h. Net loss.	(185,829)
i. Depreciation	48,889
j. Purchase of marketable securities.	(353,948)

LO2   **M11-24.**   **Net Cash Flow from Operating Activities (Indirect Method)**
The following information was obtained from Galena Company's comparative balance sheets. Assume Galena Company's 2020 income statement showed depreciation expense of $9,000, a gain on sale of investments of $11,000, and a net income of $40,000. Calculate the net cash flow from operating activities using the indirect method.

	May 31, 2020	May 31, 2019
Cash..............................	$ 19,000	$ 10,000
Accounts receivable.................	45,000	35,000
Inventory..........................	55,000	49,000
Prepaid rent	6,000	7,000
Long-term investments...............	20,000	34,000
PPE	150,000	106,000
Accumulated depreciation	42,000	33,000
Accounts payable....................	25,000	20,000
Income tax payable	4,000	6,000
Common stock	121,000	92,000
Retained earnings	106,000	91,000

LO2   **M11-25.**   **Interpreting Changes in Operating Assets and Liabilities**
Amgen Inc. (AMGN)

Amgen Inc. reports the following adjustments to net income in its 2018 statement of cash flows. Use the sign of each amount to indicate whether each current operating asset or liability increased or decreased during the year.

Change in Current Operating Asset or Liability	
Trade receivables, net	$ (378)
Inventories	(3)
Other assets....................................	35
Accounts payable................................	(143)
Accrued income taxes, net........................	(361)
Long-term tax liabilities...........................	258
Other liabilities	1,214

LO7   **M11-26.**   **Operating Cash Flows (Direct Method)**
Calculate the cash flow for each of the following cases.

a.   Cash paid for rent:

Rent expense	$65,000
Prepaid rent, beginning year	11,000
Prepaid rent, end of year	8,000

b.   Cash received as interest:

Interest income...................	$15,500
Interest receivable, beginning year....	3,000
Interest receivable, end of year	3,800

c.   Cash paid for merchandise purchased:

Cost of goods sold	$87,000
Inventory, beginning year	19,000
Inventory, end of year..............	23,000
Accounts payable, beginning year	11,000
Accounts payable, end of year.......	8,000

M11-27.   **Operating Cash Flows (Direct Method)**

LO7

Howell Company's current-year income statement reports the following.

Sales.	$785,000
Cost of goods sold	450,000
Gross profit.	$335,000

Comparative balance sheets show the following (accounts payable relate to merchandise purchases).

	End of Year	Beginning of Year
Accounts receivable	$ 68,000	$60,000
Inventory.	109,000	99,000
Prepaid expenses.	2,000	8,000
Accounts payable	31,000	36,000

Compute current-year cash received from customers and cash paid for merchandise purchased.

M11-28.   **Using Statement of Cash Flow Information to Assess Company Life-Cycle Stage**

LO5

For each of the following cash flow amounts ($ millions), identify whether the company is in the introduction, growth, maturity, or decline stage of its life cycle.

Company	Operating Cash Flow	Investing Cash Flow	Financing Cash Flow
a	$2,281	$(3,451)	$1,907
b	6,334	3,220	(2,008)
c	(405)	(1,728)	3,518
d	3,702	(2,440)	1,330
e	70	2,005	815
f	5	(530)	876
g	(2,580)	(4,200)	7,459
h	(409)	5,581	(2,406)

M11-29.   **Compute and Interpret Cash Flow Ratios**

LO6

Use the following information to compute and interpret cash flow ratios.

Company	Operating Cash Flow	Average Current Liabilities	CAPEX
a	$2,106	$6,581	$2,425
b	5,668	2,181	1,007
c	3,702	3,365	1,220
d	2,700	5,192	1,984

Required

a. Compute the operating cash flow to current liabilities ratio for each company. Compared to the average of 0.5 for large public companies, assess each company's liquidity as low, medium, or high (i.e., its ability to settle liabilities as they come due).

b. Compute the operating cash flow to CAPEX ratio for each company. Compared to the rule of thumb of 1.0, assess the company's solvency as either low, medium, or high.

M11-30.   **Computing and Comparing Income and Cash Flow Measures**

LO1

Penno Corporation recorded service revenues of $200,000 during the current year, of which $170,000 were on credit and $30,000 were for cash. Moreover, of the $170,000 credit sales, Penno collected $20,000 cash on those receivables before year-end. The company also paid $25,000 cash for wages during the year. Its employees also earned another $15,000 in wages during the last few weeks of the year, which were not yet paid at year-end.

Required

a. Compute the company's net income for the year.

b. How much net cash inflow or outflow did the company generate during the year? Explain why Penno's net income and net cash flow differ.

Exercises

LO2   **E11-31.**   **Net Cash Flow from Operating Activities (Indirect Method)**

Lincoln Company owns no PPE and reported the following income statement for the current year.

Sales.		$700,000
Cost of goods sold	$425,000	
Wages expense	110,000	
Rent expense	38,000	
Insurance expense	15,000	588,000
Net income		$112,000

Additional balance sheet information about the company follows:

	End of Year	Beginning of Year
Accounts receivable	$56,000	$48,000
Inventory.	60,000	66,000
Prepaid insurance.	7,000	5,000
Accounts payable.	22,000	18,000
Wages payable.	11,000	15,000

Use the information to calculate the net cash flow from operating activities under the indirect method.

LO2, 3, 4   **E11-32.**   **Statement of Cash Flows (Indirect Method)**

Use the following information about Lund Corporation for the month of August to prepare a statement of cash flows for August under the indirect method.

Accounts payable increase.	$ 9,000
Accounts receivable increase.	4,000
Accrued liabilities decrease	3,000
Amortization expense.	6,000
Cash balance, beginning of August	22,000
Cash balance, end of August	15,000
Cash paid as dividends	29,000
Cash paid to purchase land	90,000
Cash paid to retire bonds payable at par	60,000
Cash received from issuance of common stock.	35,000
Cash received from sale of equipment.	17,000
Depreciation expense.	29,000
Gain on sale of equipment	4,000
Inventory decrease.	13,000
Net income	76,000
Prepaid expenses increase	2,000

LO2   **E11-33.**   **Operating Section of Statement of Cash Flows (Indirect Method)**

Nike Inc. (NKE)

Following are the income statement and balance sheet for Nike Inc. for the year ended May 31, 2019, and a forecasted income statement and balance sheet for 2020.

NIKE INC. Income Statement For Year Ended May 31		
$ millions	May 31, 2019 Actual	May 31, 2020 Est.
Revenues	$39,117	$42,246
Cost of sales.	21,643	23,362
Gross profit.	17,474	18,884
Demand creation expense	3,753	4,056
Operating overhead expense.	8,949	9,674
Total selling and administrative expense	12,702	13,730
Interest expense (income), net.	49	49
Other (income) expense, net	(78)	(78)
Income before income taxes	4,801	5,183
Income tax expense	772	1,037
Net income	$ 4,029	$ 4,146

NIKE INC. Balance Sheet May 31		
$ millions	May 31, 2019 Actual	May 31, 2020 Est.
Current assets		
Cash and equivalents	$ 4,466	$ 6,881
Short-term investments.	197	197
Accounts receivable, net.	4,272	4,605
Inventories	5,622	6,083
Prepaid expenses and other current assets	1,968	2,112
Total current assets.	16,525	19,878
Property, plant and equipment, net.	4,744	5,259
Identifiable intangible assets, net	283	281
Goodwill	154	154
Deferred income taxes and other assets	2,011	2,155
Total assets	$23,717	$ 27,727
Current liabilities		
Current portion of long-term debt	$ 6	$ 3
Notes payable.	9	0
Accounts payable	2,612	2,830
Accrued liabilities	5,010	5,407
Income taxes payable.	229	253
Total current liabilities	7,866	8,493
Long-term debt.	3,464	3,461
Deferred income taxes and other liabilities.	3,347	3,633
Total liabilities	14,677	15,587
Shareholders' equity		
Common stock at stated value	3	3
Capital in excess of stated value	7,163	7,488
Accumulated other comprehensive income	231	231
Retained earnings	1,643	4,418
Total shareholders' equity.	9,040	12,140
Total liabilities and shareholders' equity	$23,717	$27,727

Prepare the operating activities section of a forecasted statement of cash flows for 2020 using the indirect method. Treat deferred tax assets and liabilities as operating. Operating expenses (cost of sales) for 2020 include estimated depreciation expense of $751 million, amortization expense of $2 million, and stock-based compensation of $325 million. (*Hint*: Stock-based compensation is a noncash expense like depreciation and must be added back in the operating section. The amount expensed is also added to Nike's "Capital in excess of stated value" account in the balance sheet.)

LO2   **E11-34.**   **Operating Section of Statement of Cash Flows (Indirect Method)**

Medtronic PLC
(MDT)

Following are the income statement and balance sheet for Medtronic PLC for the year ended April 29, 2019, and a forecasted income statement and balance sheet for 2020.

MEDTRONIC PLC Income Statement For Fiscal Year Ended		
$ millions	April 2019 Actual	April 2020 Est.
Net sales.	$ 30,557	$33,002
Costs and expenses		
Cost of products sold	9,155	9,901
Research and development expense.	2,330	2,508
Selling, general, and administrative expense.	10,418	11,254
Amortization of intangible assets	1,764	1,914
Restructuring charges, net.	198	149
Certain litigation charges, net.	166	150
Other operating expense, net.	258	258
Operating profit (loss).	6,268	6,868
Other nonoperating income, net.	(373)	(373)
Interest expense.	1,444	1,444
Income (loss) before income taxes.	5,197	5,797
Income tax provision.	547	870
Net income (loss)	4,650	4,927
Net (income) loss attributable to noncontrolling interests.	(19)	(19)
Net income (loss) attributable to Medtronic	$ 4,631	$ 4,908

MEDTRONIC PLC Balance Sheet At Fiscal Year-End		
$ millions	Apr. 29, 2019 Actual	Apr. 30, 2020 Est.
Current assets		
Cash and cash equivalents.	$ 4,393	$ 7,098
Investments.	5,455	5,455
Accounts receivable, net.	6,222	6,732
Inventories, net	3,753	4,059
Other current assets	2,144	2,310
Total current assets.	21,967	25,654
Property, plant, and equipment, net	4,675	4,988
Goodwill	39,959	39,959
Other intangible assets, net	20,560	18,646
Tax assets	1,519	1,650
Other assets.	1,014	1,089
Total assets	$ 89,694	$91,986

continued

continued from previous page

$ millions	Apr. 29, 2019 Actual	Apr. 30, 2020 Est.
Current liabilities		
Current debt obligations	$ 838	$ 2,058
Accounts payable	1,953	2,112
Accrued compensation	2,189	2,376
Accrued income taxes.	567	627
Other accrued expenses.	2,925	3,168
Total current liabilities	8,472	10,341
Long-term debt.	24,486	22,428
Accrued compensation and retirement benefits.	1,651	1,651
Accrued income taxes	2,838	3,069
Deferred tax liabilities.	1,278	1,386
Other liabilities	757	825
Total liabilities.	39,482	39,700
Shareholders' equity		
Ordinary shares— par value $0.0001, 2.6 billion shares authorized,		
1,340,697,595 shares issued and outstanding.	—	—
Additional paid-in capital.	26,532	26,532
Retained earnings	26,270	28,325
Accumulated other comprehensive loss.	(2,711)	(2,711)
Total shareholders' equity.	50,091	52,146
Noncontrolling interests	121	140
Total equity	50,212	52,286
Total liabilities and equity	$89,694	$91,986

Begin with forecasted Net income of $4,927 million and prepare the operating activities section of a forecasted statement of cash flows for April 30, 2020, using the indirect method. Operating expenses (such as cost of sales and selling, general, and administrative expenses) for 2020 include estimated depreciation expense of $953 million. Estimated 2020 retained earnings reflects dividends of $2,853 million.

E11-35. **Operating Cash Flows (Direct Method)**

LO7

Calculate the cash flow for each of the following cases.

a. Cash paid for advertising:

Advertising expense.	$62,000
Prepaid advertising, beginning of year.	11,000
Prepaid advertising, end of year.	15,000

b. Cash paid for income taxes:

Income tax expense.	$29,000
Income tax payable, beginning of year.	7,100
Income tax payable, end of year	4,900

c. Cash paid for merchandise purchased:

Cost of goods sold	$180,000
Inventory, beginning of year	30,000
Inventory, end of year.	25,000
Accounts payable, beginning of year	10,000
Accounts payable, end of year.	12,000

LO3, 4, 7   **E11-36.**   **Statement of Cash Flows (Direct Method)**

Use the following information about the 2020 cash flows of Mason Corporation to prepare a statement of cash flows under the direct method.

Cash balance, end of 2020.	$ 12,000
Cash paid to employees and suppliers.	148,000
Cash received from sale of land.	40,000
Cash paid to acquire treasury stock.	10,000
Cash balance, beginning of 2020.	16,000
Cash received as interest.	6,000
Cash paid as income taxes	11,000
Cash paid to purchase equipment	89,000
Cash received from customers.	194,000
Cash received from issuing bonds payable . .	30,000
Cash paid as dividends	16,000

LO7   **E11-37.**   **Operating Cash Flows (Direct Method)**

Refer to the information in Exercise E11-31. Prepare the operating activities section of the statement of cash flows using the direct method.

LO3, 4   **E11-38.**   **Investing and Financing Cash Flows**

During the current year, Paxon Corporation's intangible assets account (at cost) increased $15,000, which was the net result of purchasing new intangible assets costing $80,000 and selling other intangible assets costing $65,000 at a $6,000 loss. Also, its bonds payable account decreased $40,000, the net result of issuing $100,000 of bonds at $103,000 and retiring bonds with a face value (and book value) of $140,000 at a $9,000 gain. What items and amounts appear in the (a) cash flows from investing activities and (b) cash flows from financing activities sections of its statement of cash flows?

LO5   **E11-39.**   **Using Graphical Statement of Cash Flow Information to Assess Company Life-Cycle Stage**

Facebook (FB)

Consider the following statement of cash flows information for Facebook. Does the company's cash flows conform with the typical life-cycle patterns?

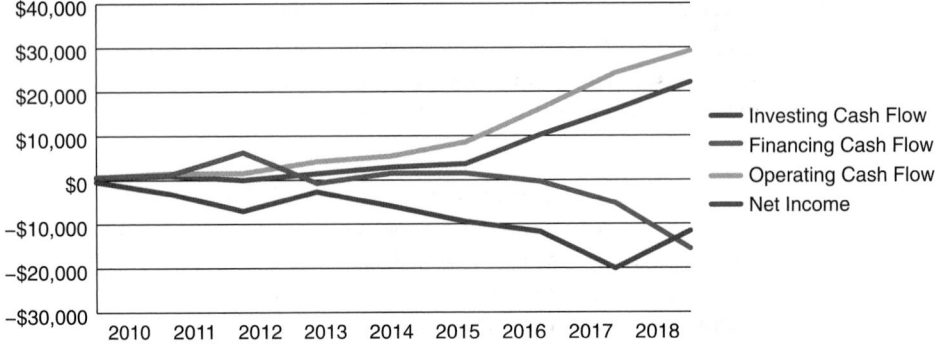

LO5   **E11-40.**   **Using Statement of Cash Flow Information to Assess Company Life-Cycle Stage**

Arconic Inc (ARNC)
Carmax Inc (KMX)
Flowserve Corp (FLS)
Fluor Corp (FLR)

Use the following information, taken from the 2018 statement of cash flows from each of the respective companies, to complete the requirements.

$ millions	Net Income	Cash from Operations	Cash from Investing	Cash from Financing
Arconic Inc	$642	$217	$565	$(649)
Carmax Inc	842	163	(309)	186
Flowserve Corp.	120	191	(81)	(173)
Fluor Corp.	225	162	1	(140)

Required

a. Identify each company's life-cycle stage (introduction, growth, maturity, or decline).

b. Rank-order each company from least to most mature. (*Hint:* All four companies have cash from operations of about $200 million. Graph the cash from investing and from financing, and then use the graphic [showing revenue, income, and cash flow by life cycle] to evaluate the relative size of the three types of cash flow.)

E11-41. **Compute Ratios from Statement of Cash Flow Information**

Use the following information, taken from each of the company's 2018 financial statements, to complete the requirements.

LO6

Arconic Inc (ARNC)

Carmax Inc (KMX)

Flowserve Corp (FLS)

Fluor Corp (FLR)

Company ($ millions)	Cash from Operations	Current Liabilities	CAPEX
Arconic Inc	$217	$3,520	$768
Carmax Inc	163	1,312	305
Flowserve Corp.	191	1,081	84
Fluor Corp	162	3,553	211

Required

a. Compute the operating cash flow to current liabilities ratio for each company.

b. Rank-order each company from low to high liquidity (ability to pay liabilities as they come due). Do any of the companies have liquidity difficulties?

c. Compute the operating cash flow to CAPEX ratio for each company. Compared with the rule of thumb of 1.0, assess each company's solvency as either low, medium, or high.

d. Rank-order each company from low to high solvency. Do any of the companies have solvency difficulties?

E11-42. **Interpret Cash Flow Patterns and Ratios**

The following information is taken from the 2018 Form 10-K for each of the following technology companies.

LO5, 6

Cisco Systems Inc. (CSCO)

Oracle Corporation (ORCL)

Seagate Technology plc (STX)

Company ($ millions)	Operating Cash Flow	Investing Cash Flow	Financing Cash Flow	Average Current Liabilities	CAPEX
Cisco Systems Inc.	$13,666	$15,324	$(31,764)	$27,035	$ 834
Oracle Corporation	14,551	26,557	(42,056)	18,630	1,660
Seagate Technology plc	2,113	(1,588)	(1,211)	3,190	366

Required

a. Compute the operating cash flow to current liabilities ratio for each company. Compared to the average of 0.5, assess as low, medium, or high, each company's ability to settle liabilities as they come due.

b. Compute the operating cash flow to CAPEX ratio for each company. Compared to the rule of thumb of 1.0, assess each company's solvency as either low, medium, or high.

c. Each of the three companies is in the mature stage of its life cycle. Consider the graphic shown earlier in the module that graphs the cash flow patterns. Use the graphic to rank the companies from least mature to most mature.

Problems

LO2, 3, 4   **P11-43.**   **Statement of Cash Flows (Indirect Method)**

Wolff Company's income statement and comparative balance sheets follow.

WOLFF COMPANY Income Statement For Year Ended December 31, 2019		
Sales.		$635,000
Cost of goods sold	$430,000	
Wages expense	86,000	
Insurance expense.	8,000	
Depreciation expense.	17,000	
Interest expense.	9,000	
Income tax expense	29,000	579,000
Net income		$ 56,000

WOLFF COMPANY Balance Sheet	Dec. 31, 2019	Dec. 31, 2018
Assets		
Cash.	$ 11,000	$ 5,000
Accounts receivable	41,000	32,000
Inventory.	90,000	60,000
Prepaid insurance.	5,000	7,000
PPE	250,000	195,000
Accumulated depreciation	(68,000)	(51,000)
Total assets	$329,000	$248,000
Liabilities and Stockholders' Equity		
Accounts payable.	$ 7,000	$ 10,000
Wages payable.	9,000	6,000
Income tax payable	7,000	8,000
Bonds payable	130,000	75,000
Common stock	90,000	90,000
Retained earnings	86,000	59,000
Total liabilities and equity	$329,000	$248,000

Cash dividends of $29,000 were declared and paid during 2019. Also in 2019, PPE was purchased for cash, and bonds payable were issued for cash. Bond interest is paid semiannually on June 30 and December 31. Accounts payable relate to merchandise purchases.

Required

a. Compute the change in cash that occurred during 2019.

b. Prepare a 2019 statement of cash flows using the indirect method.

LO2, 3, 4   **P11-44.**   **Statement of Cash Flows (Indirect Method)**

Seagate Technology
(STX)

Following are the income statement and balance sheet for Seagate Technology for the year ended June 28, 2019, and a forecasted income statement and balance sheet for 2020.

SEAGATE TECHNOLOGY PLC Consolidated Statements of Income		
For Years Ended ($ millions)	June 2019 Actual	June 2020 Est.
Revenue...............................	$10,390	$10,910
Cost of revenue	7,458	7,833
Product development	991	1,036
Marketing and administrative	453	480
Amortization of intangibles	23	23
Restructuring and other, net...........	(22)	—
Total operating expenses	8,903	9,372
Income from operations	1,487	1,538
Interest income.......................	84	84
Interest expense......................	(224)	(224)
Other, net	25	25
Other expense, net....................	(115)	(115)
Income before income taxes	1,372	1,423
(Benefit) provision for income taxes...	(640)	299
Net income...........................	$ 2,012	$ 1,124

SEAGATE TECHNOLOGY PLC Consolidated Balance Sheet		
$ millions	June 2019 Actual	June 2020 Est.
Current assets		
Cash and cash equivalents................	$2,220	$2,583
Accounts receivable, net.................	989	1,036
Inventories	970	1,015
Other current assets	184	196
Total current assets....................	4,363	4,830
Property, equipment and leasehold improvements, net ...	1,869	1,971
Goodwill	1,237	1,237
Other intangible assets, net	111	88
Deferred income taxes	1,114	1,167
Other assets, net	191	196
Total Assets	$8,885	$9,489
Current liabilities		
Accounts payable	$1,420	$1,495
Accrued employee compensation..........	169	175
Accrued warranty	91	98
Accrued expenses	552	578
Total current liabilities	2,232	2,346
Long-term accrued warranty.............	104	109
Long-term accrued income taxes.........	4	4
Other noncurrent liabilities	130	142
Long-term debt, less current portion....	4,253	4,253
Total Liabilities	6,723	6,854
Shareholders' equity		
Ordinary shares—par value $0.0001, 2.6 billion shares authorized.....................	—	—
Additional paid-in capital...............	6,545	6,644
Accumulated other comprehensive loss..............	(34)	(34)
Accumulated deficit	(4,349)	(3,975)
Total shareholders' equity..............	2,162	2,635
Total liabilities and shareholders' equity	$8,885	$9,489

The following additional information pertains to the balance sheet and income statement for the year ended June 30, 2020 ($ millions).

Depreciation expense (included in operating expenses) . . .	$531
Stock-based compensation	99
Amortization expense.	23
Capital expenditures.	633
Dividends	750

Required
Prepare a forecasted statement of cash flows for June 2020 using the indirect method. (*Hint:* Stock-based compensation is a noncash expense like depreciation and must be added back in the operating section. The amount expensed is also added to the company's "Additional paid-in capital" account in the balance sheet.)

LO2, 3, 4   **P11-45.**   **Statement of Cash Flows (Indirect Method)**

Arctic Company's income statement and comparative balance sheets follow.

ARCTIC COMPANY Income Statement For Year Ended December 31, 2019		
Sales.		$728,000
Cost of goods sold	$534,000	
Wages expense	190,000	
Advertising expense.	31,000	
Depreciation expense.	22,000	
Interest expense.	18,000	
Gain on sale of land	(25,000)	770,000
Net loss.		$ (42,000)

ARCTIC COMPANY Balance Sheet	Dec. 31, 2019	Dec. 31, 2018
Assets		
Cash.	$ 49,000	$ 28,000
Accounts receivable	42,000	50,000
Inventory.	107,000	113,000
Prepaid advertising.	10,000	13,000
PPE	360,000	222,000
Accumulated depreciation	(78,000)	(56,000)
Total assets	$490,000	$370,000
Liabilities and Stockholders' Equity		
Accounts payable.	$ 17,000	$ 31,000
Interest payable	6,000	—
Bonds payable	200,000	—
Common stock	245,000	245,000
Retained earnings	52,000	94,000
Treasury stock	(30,000)	—
Total liabilities and equity	$490,000	$370,000

During 2019, Arctic sold land for $70,000 cash that had originally cost $45,000. Arctic also purchased equipment for cash, acquired treasury stock for cash, and issued bonds payable for cash in 2019. Accounts payable relate to merchandise purchases.

Required

a. Compute the change in cash that occurred during 2019.

b. Prepare a 2019 statement of cash flows using the indirect method.

P11-46. **Statement of Cash Flows (Indirect Method)**

LO2, 3, 4

Dair Company's income statement and comparative balance sheets follow.

DAIR COMPANY Income Statement For Year Ended December 31, 2019		
Sales.		$700,000
Cost of goods sold	$440,000	
Wages and other operating expenses	95,000	
Depreciation expense.	22,000	
Amortization expense.	7,000	
Interest expense.	10,000	
Income tax expense	36,000	
Loss on bond retirement.	5,000	615,000
Net income		$ 85,000

DAIR COMPANY Balance Sheet		
	Dec. 31, 2019	Dec. 31, 2018
Assets		
Cash	$ 27,000	$ 18,000
Accounts receivable	53,000	48,000
Inventory.	103,000	109,000
Prepaid expenses.	12,000	10,000
PPE	360,000	336,000
Accumulated depreciation	(87,000)	(84,000)
Intangible assets.	43,000	50,000
Total assets	$511,000	$487,000
Liabilities and Stockholders' Equity		
Accounts payable	$ 32,000	$ 26,000
Interest payable	4,000	7,000
Income tax payable	6,000	8,000
Bonds payable	60,000	120,000
Common stock	252,000	228,000
Retained earnings	157,000	98,000
Total liabilities and equity	$511,000	$487,000

During 2019, the company sold for $17,000 cash old equipment that had cost $36,000 and had $19,000 accumulated depreciation. Also in 2019, new equipment worth $60,000 was acquired in exchange for $60,000 of bonds payable, and bonds payable of $120,000 were retired for cash at a loss. A $26,000 cash dividend was declared and paid in 2019. Any stock issuances were for cash.

Required

a. Compute the change in cash that occurred in 2019.

b. Prepare a 2019 statement of cash flows using the indirect method.

c. Prepare separate schedules showing (1) cash paid for interest and for income taxes and (2) noncash investing and financing transactions.

LO2, 3, 4
Automatic Data
Processing, Inc. (ADP)

P11-47.   **Statement of Cash Flows (Indirect Method)**

Following are the income statement and balance sheet for **ADP Inc.**, for the year ended June 30, 2019, and a forecasted income statement and balance sheet for 2020.

AUTOMATIC DATA PROCESSING INC. Consolidated Balance Sheets		
$ millions	June 30, 2019 Actual	June 30, 2020 Est.
Current assets		
Cash and cash equivalents.	$ 1,949.2	$ 2,077.6
Accounts receivable, net.	2,439.3	2,755.1
Other current assets	519.6	592.7
Total current assets before funds held for clients	4,908.1	5,425.4
Funds held for clients	29,434.2	33,253.4
Total current assets.	34,342.3	38,678.8
Long-term receivables, net.	23.8	32.0
Property, plant and equipment, net.	764.2	762.9
Capitalized contract cost, net	2,428.5	2,739.1
Other assets	934.4	1,057.2
Goodwill	2,323.0	2,323.0
Intangible assets, net	1,071.5	1,252.5
Total assets	$41,887.7	$46,845.5
Current liabilities		
Accounts payable	$ 125.5	$ 144.2
Accrued expenses and other current liabilities	1,759.0	1,986.2
Accrued payroll and payroll-related expenses	721.1	816.9
Dividends payable.	340.1	365.4
Short-term deferred revenues.	220.7	256.3
Obligations under reverse repurchase agreements	262.0	288.3
Income taxes payable.	54.8	63.2
Total current liabilities before client funds obligations.	3,483.2	3,920.5
Client funds obligations.	29,144.5	32,933.0
Total current liabilities	32,627.7	36,853.5
Long-term debt.	2,002.2	2,002.2
Other liabilities	798.7	897.0
Deferred income taxes	659.9	752.8
Long-term deferred revenues.	399.3	448.5
Total liabilities	36,487.8	40,954.0
Shareholders' equity		
Preferred stock, $1.00 par value: Authorized, 0.3 shares; issued, none . . .	—	—
Common stock, $0.10 par value: authorized, 1,000.0 shares;		
issued, 638.7 shares; outstanding 434.2 shares	63.9	63.9
Capital in excess of par value.	1,183.2	1,350.5
Retained earnings	17,500.6	18,574.9
Treasury stock - at cost: 204.5 shares	(13,090.5)	(13,840.5)
Accumulated other comprehensive loss.	(257.3)	(257.3)
Total stockholders' equity	5,399.9	5,891.5
Total liabilities and stockholders' equity	$41,887.7	$46,845.5

AUTOMATIC DATA PROCESSING INC. Statements of Consolidated Earnings		
For Years Ended ($ millions)	Jun. 30, 2019 Actual	June 30, 2020 Est.
Revenues, other than interest on funds held for clients and PEO revenues . . .	$ 9,375.8	$10,594.7
Interest on funds held for clients.	561.9	634.9
PEO revenues	4,237.5	4,788.4
Total revenues	14,175.2	16,018.0
Expenses		
Operating expenses.	7,145.9	8,073.1
Systems development and programming costs	636.3	720.8
Depreciation and Amortization	304.4	460.5
Total cost of revenues	8,086.6	9,254.4
Selling, general, and administrative expenses.	3,064.2	3,459.9
Interest expense.	129.9	129.9
Total expenses	11,280.7	12,844.2
Other (income) expense, net	(111.1)	(111.1)
Earnings before income taxes	3,005.6	3,284.9
Provision for income taxes	712.8	821.2
Net earnings.	$ 2,292.8	$ 2,463.7

Additional information and assumptions related to the estimated 2020 income statement and balance sheet are as follows ($ millions):

Depreciation expense.	$ 184.4
Amortization expense.	276.1
Stock-based compensation expense . . .	167.3
CAPEX	183.1
Newly acquired intangibles.	457.1
Stock repurchases	750.0
Dividends declared.	1,389.4

Required

Prepare a forecasted statement of cash flows for 2020 using the indirect method. (*Hint*: Stock-based compensation is a noncash expense like depreciation and must be added back in the operating section. The amount expensed is also added to Nike's "Capital in excess of par value" account on the balance sheet.)

P11-48. **Statement of Cash Flows (Indirect Method)**

LO2, 3, 4

Rainbow Company's income statement and comparative balance sheets follow.

RAINBOW COMPANY Income Statement For Year Ended December 31, 2019		
Sales.		$750,000
Dividend income.		15,000
		765,000
Cost of goods sold	$440,000	
Wages and other operating expenses	130,000	
Depreciation expense.	39,000	
Patent amortization expense	7,000	
Interest expense.	13,000	
Income tax expense	44,000	
Loss on sale of equipment	5,000	
Gain on sale of investments.	(10,000)	668,000
Net income		$ 97,000

RAINBOW COMPANY Balance Sheet		
	Dec. 31, 2019	Dec. 31, 2018
Assets		
Cash and cash equivalents	$ 19,000	$ 25,000
Accounts receivable	40,000	30,000
Inventory.	103,000	77,000
Prepaid expenses.	10,000	6,000
Investments—Available-for-sale.	—	57,000
Land	190,000	100,000
Buildings.	445,000	350,000
Accumulated depreciation—Buildings	(91,000)	(75,000)
Equipment	179,000	225,000
Accumulated depreciation—Equipment	(42,000)	(46,000)
Patents	50,000	32,000
Total assets	$903,000	$781,000
Liabilities and Stockholders' Equity		
Accounts payable	$ 20,000	$ 16,000
Interest payable	6,000	5,000
Income tax payable	8,000	10,000
Bonds payable	155,000	125,000
Preferred stock ($100 par value)	100,000	75,000
Common stock ($5 par value)	379,000	364,000
Paid-in capital in excess of par value—Common. . .	133,000	124,000
Retained earnings	102,000	55,000
AOCI (unrealized gain on investments)	—	7,000
Total liabilities and equity	$903,000	$781,000

During 2019, the following transactions and events occurred in addition to the company's usual business activities.

1. Sold AFS investments costing $50,000 for $60,000 cash. Unrealized gains totaling $7,000 related to these investments had been recorded in earlier years.
2. Purchased land for cash.
3. Capitalized an expenditure made to improve the building.
4. Sold equipment for $14,000 cash that originally cost $46,000 and had $27,000 accumulated depreciation.
5. Issued bonds payable at face value for cash.
6. Acquired a patent with a fair value of $25,000 by issuing 250 shares of preferred stock at par value.
7. Declared and paid a $50,000 cash dividend.
8. Issued 3,000 shares of common stock for cash at $8 per share.
9. Recorded depreciation of $16,000 on buildings and $23,000 on equipment.

Required

a. Compute the change in cash and cash equivalents that occurred during 2019.
b. Prepare a 2019 statement of cash flows using the indirect method.
c. Prepare separate schedules showing (1) cash paid for interest and for income taxes and (2) noncash investing and financing transactions.

P11-49. **Interpreting the Statement of Cash Flows**

Following is the statement of cash flows for Stryker Corp.

STRYKER CORPORATION Consolidated Statements of Cash Flows For Year Ended December 31, 2018 ($ millions)	
Operating activities	
Net earnings (loss)	$3,553
Adjustments to reconcile net earnings to net cash provided by operating activities:	
Depreciation	306
Amortization of intangible assets	417
Share-based compensation	119
Recall charges, net of insurance proceeds	23
Sale of inventory stepped up to fair value at acquisition	16
Deferred income tax benefit (expense)	(1,582)
Changes in operating assets and liabilities	
Accounts receivable	(60)
Inventories	(385)
Accounts payable	116
Accrued expenses and other liabilities	289
Recall-related payments	(90)
Income taxes	(156)
Other, net	44
Net cash provided by operating activities	2,610
Investing activities	
Acquisitions, net of cash acquired	(2,451)
Purchases of marketable securities	(226)
Proceeds from sales of marketable securities	394
Purchases of property, plant and equipment	(572)
Other investing, net	(2)
Net cash used in investing activities	(2,857)
Financing activities	
Proceeds and payments on short-term borrowings, net	(1)
Proceeds from issuance of long-term debt	3,126
Payments on long-term debt	(669)
Dividends paid	(703)
Repurchase of common stock	(300)
Cash paid for taxes from withheld shares	(120)
Payments to purchase noncontrolling interest	(14)
Other financing, net	10
Net cash provided by (used in) financing activities	1,329
Effect of exchange rate changes on cash and cash equivalents	(8)
Change in cash and cash equivalents	1,074
Cash and cash equivalents at beginning of year	2,542
Cash and cash equivalents at end of year	$3,616

Required

a. Why does the company add back depreciation to compute net cash flows from operating activities?

b. Explain why the change in accounts receivable and inventories are reported as adjustments to net earnings. Did the accounts receivable and inventories balances increase or decrease during the year?

c. Stryker reports that it invested $572 million in property, plant and equipment. Is this an appropriate type of expenditure for the company to make? What relation should expenditures for PPE have with depreciation expense?

d. Stryker paid $300 million to repurchase its common stock in fiscal 2018 and, in addition, paid dividends of $703 million. Thus, it paid $1,003 million of cash to its stockholders during the year. How do we evaluate that use of cash relative to other possible uses for the company's cash?

e. Provide an overall assessment of the company's cash flows for fiscal 2018. In the analysis, consider the sources and uses of cash.

LO1, 2, 3, 4, 5
Verizon
Communications Inc.
(VZ)

P11-50.   **Interpreting the Statement of Cash Flows**

Following is the statement of cash flows for Verizon Communications Inc.

VERIZON COMMUNICATIONS INC. Statement of Cash Flows For Year Ended December 31, 2018 ($ millions)	
Cash Flows from Operating Activities	
Net Income	$16,039
Adjustments to reconcile net income to net cash provided by operating activities:	
Depreciation and amortization expense	17,403
Employee retirement benefits	(2,657)
Deferred income taxes	389
Provision for uncollectible accounts	980
Equity in losses of unconsolidated businesses, net of dividends received	231
Oath goodwill impairment	4,591
Changes in current assets and liabilities, net of effects from acquisition/disposition of businesses:	
Accounts receivable	(2,667)
Inventories	(324)
Prepaid expenses and other	37
Accounts payable and accrued liabilities and other current liabilities	1,777
Discretionary employee benefits contributions	(1,679)
Other, net	219
Net cash provided by operating activities	34,339
Cash Flows from Investing Activities	
Capital expenditures (including capitalized software)	(16,658)
Acquisitions of businesses, net of cash acquired	(230)
Acquisitions of wireless licenses	(1,429)
Other, net	383
Net cash used in investing activities	(17,934)
Cash Flows from Financing Activities	
Proceeds from long-term borrowings	5,967
Proceeds from asset-backed long-term borrowings	4,810
Repayments of long-term borrowings and capital lease obligations	(10,923)
Repayments of asset-backed long-term borrowings	(3,635)
Dividends paid	(9,772)
Other, net	(1,824)
Net cash used in financing activities	(15,377)
Increase (decrease) in cash, cash equivalents and restricted cash	1,028
Cash, cash equivalents and restricted cash, beginning of period	2,888
Cash, cash equivalents and restricted cash, end of period (Note 1)	$ 3,916

Required

a. Why does Verizon add back depreciation to compute net cash flows from operating activities? What does the size of the depreciation add-back indicate about the relative capital intensity of this industry?

b. Verizon reports that it invested $16,658 million in property and equipment. These expenditures are necessitated by market pressures as the company faces stiff competition from other communications companies, such as Comcast. Where in the 10-K might we find additional information about these capital expenditures to ascertain whether Verizon is addressing the company's most pressing needs? What relation might we expect between the size of these capital expenditures and the amount of depreciation expense reported?

c. Determine the net cash flow associated with debt in 2018. Verizon's balance sheet reveals that the company has $113,063 million of debt at 2018 year-end. What problem does Verizon's high debt load pose for its ability to maintain the level of capital expenditures necessary to remain competitive in its industry?

d. During the year, Verizon paid dividends of $9,772 million but did not repay a sizable portion of its debt. How do dividend payments differ from debt payments? Why would Verizon continue to pay dividends in light of cash demands for needed capital expenditures and debt repayments?

e. Provide an overall assessment of Verizon's cash flows for 2018. In the analysis, consider the sources and uses of cash.

P11-51. **Reconciling and Computing Operating Cash Flows from Net Income**

LO1, 2, 5

Petroni Company reports the following selected results for its current calendar year.

Net income	$130,000
Depreciation expense	28,000
Accounts receivable increase	10,000
Accounts payable increase	6,000
Prepaid expenses decrease	3,000
Wages payable decrease	4,000

Required

a. Prepare the operating section only of Petroni Company's statement of cash flows for the year.

b. Does the positive sign on depreciation expense indicate the company is generating cash by recording depreciation? Explain.

c. Explain why the increase in accounts receivable is a use of cash in the statement of cash flows.

d. Explain why the decrease in prepaid expense is a source of cash in the statement of cash flows.

P11-52. **Statement of Cash Flows (Direct Method)**

LO3, 4, 7

Refer to the data for Wolff Company in Problem P11-43.

Required

a. Compute the change in cash that occurred during 2019.

b. Prepare a 2019 statement of cash flows using the direct method.

P11-53. **Statement of Cash Flows (Direct Method)**

LO3, 4, 7

Refer to the data for Arctic Company in Problem P11-45.

Required

a. Compute the change in cash that occurred during 2019.

b. Prepare a 2019 statement of cash flows using the direct method.

P11-54. **Statement of Cash Flows (Direct Method)**

LO3, 4, 7

Refer to the data for Dair Company in Problem P11-46.

Required

a. Compute the change in cash that occurred in 2019.

b. Prepare a 2019 statement of cash flows using the direct method. Use one cash outflow for "cash paid for wages and other operating expenses." Accounts payable relate to inventory purchases only.

c. Prepare separate schedules showing (1) a reconciliation of net income to net cash flow from operating activities (see Exhibit 11.3) and (2) noncash investing and financing transactions.

P11-55. **Statement of Cash Flows (Direct Method)**

LO3, 4, 7

Refer to the data for Rainbow Company in Problem P11-48.

Required

a. Compute the change in cash that occurred in 2019.

b. Prepare a 2019 statement of cash flows using the direct method. Use one cash outflow for "cash paid for wages and other operating expenses." Accounts payable relate to inventory purchases only.

c. Prepare separate schedules showing (1) a reconciliation of net income to net cash flow from operating activities (see Exhibit 11.3) and (2) noncash investing and financing transactions.

LO1, 5, 6
Amgen Inc. (AMGN)

P11-56. **Interpreting the Statement of Cash Flows**

Following is the statement of cash flows of Amgen Inc.

AMGEN INC. CONSOLIDATED STATEMENTS OF CASH FLOWS			
For Years Ended December 31, $ millions	2018	2017	2016
Cash flows from operating activities			
Net income	$ 8,394	$ 1,979	$ 7,722
Depreciation and amortization	1,946	1,955	2,105
Stock-based compensation expense	311	329	311
Deferred income taxes	(363)	(1,330)	183
Other items, net	386	334	32
Changes in operating assets and liabilities, net of acquisitions:			
Trade receivables, net.	(378)	(58)	(214)
Inventories	(3)	133	(80)
Other assets	35	(24)	(128)
Accounts payable	(143)	424	(44)
Accrued income taxes, net	(361)	523	(301)
Long-term tax liabilities	258	6,681	445
Other liabilities	1,214	231	323
Net cash provided by operating activities	11,296	11,177	10,354
Cash flows from investing activities			
Purchases of marketable securities	(18,741)	(33,607)	(28,094)
Proceeds from sales of marketable securities	28,356	24,240	17,958
Proceeds from maturities of marketable securities.	5,412	6,174	2,459
Purchases of property, plant and equipment	(738)	(664)	(738)
Cash acquired in acquisition, net of cash paid	195	(19)	—
Other.	(145)	(148)	(243)
Net cash used in investing activities	14,339	(4,024)	(8,658)
Cash flows from financing activities			
Net proceeds from issuance of debt.	—	4,476	7,318
Repayment of debt	(1,121)	(4,405)	(3,725)
Repurchases of common stock.	(17,794)	(3,160)	(2,965)
Dividends paid	(3,507)	(3,365)	(2,998)
Withholding taxes arising from shares withheld for share-based payments. . .	(126)	(191)	(260)
Other.	58	51	31
Net cash used in financing activities	(22,490)	(6,594)	(2,599)
Increase (decrease) in cash and cash equivalents	3,145	559	(903)
Cash and cash equivalents at beginning of period.	3,800	3,241	4,144
Cash and cash equivalents at end of period	$ 6,945	$ 3,800	$ 3,241

Required

a. What does Amgen report as net cash from operating activities in 2018? What is net income for the year? Much of this difference is the result of depreciation. Why is Amgen adding depreciation to net income in the computation of operating cash flows?

b. In determining cash provided by operating activities, Amgen adds $311 million relating to stock-based compensation expense in 2018. What is the purpose of this addition?

c. Amgen reports $(378) million relating to trade receivables. What does the negative sign on this amount signify about the change in receivables during the year compared with the negative sign on accounts payable in 2018?

d. Calculate and compare operating cash flow with current liabilities and operating cash flow with capital expenditures for 2018 and 2017. Current liabilities were $13,488 million, $9,020 million, and $11,204 million at the end of 2018, 2017, and 2016, respectively.

e. Does the composition of Amgen's cash flow present a "healthy" picture for 2018? Explain.

P11-57. **Interpreting the Statement of Cash Flows**

Following is the statement of cash flows of Thermo Fisher Scientific.

THERMO FISHER SCIENTIFIC INC. Consolidated Statement of Cash Flows	
For Year Ended December 31, $ millions	**2018**
Operating Activities	
Net Income.	$2,938
Adjustments to reconcile net income to net cash provided by operating activities:	
Depreciation and amortization	2,267
Change in deferred income taxes.	(379)
Noncash stock-based compensation	181
Other noncash expenses, net.	106
Changes in assets and liabilities, excluding the effects of acquisitions:	
Accounts receivable	(366)
Inventories	(324)
Other assets	54
Accounts payable	201
Other liabilities	(42)
Contributions to retirement plans	(93)
Net cash provided by operating activities.	4,543
Investing Activities	
Acquisitions, net of cash acquired	(536)
Purchase of property, plant and equipment	(758)
Proceeds from sale of property, plant and equipment	50
Other investing activities, net	(9)
Net cash used in investing activities.	(1,253)
Financing Activities	
Net proceeds from issuance of debt.	690
Repayment of debt.	(2,052)
Proceeds from issuance of commercial paper	5,060
Repayments of commercial paper	(5,254)
Purchases of company common stock.	(500)
Dividends paid	(266)
Net proceeds from issuance of company common stock under employee stock plans . . .	136
Other financing activities	(51)
Net cash (used in) provided by financing activities.	(2,237)
Exchange Rate Effect on Cash	(297)
Increase in Cash, Cash Equivalents and Restricted Cash.	756
Cash, Cash Equivalents and Restricted Cash at Beginning of Period.	1,361
Cash, Cash Equivalents and Restricted Cash at End of Period.	$2,117

Required

a. What amounts does the company report for net income and cash from operating activities? What one item explains most of this difference? Why does the company add these amounts in the computation of operating cash flows?

b. Thermo Fisher Scientific reports a positive amount of $181 million relating to noncash stock-based compensation. What does this positive amount signify?

c. Thermo Fisher Scientific reports a cash outflow of $758 million relating to the acquisition of PPE. Is this cash outflow a cause for concern? Explain. Did the company dispose of any PPE during 2018? How do we know?

d. Thermo Fisher Scientific's net cash flows from financing activities is $(2,237) million. For what purposes is Thermo Fisher Scientific using this cash?

e. Calculate the operating cash flow to current liabilities ratio and the operating cash flow to capital expenditures ratio. Current liabilities were $6,147 million in 2018 and $7,048 million in 2017. What do these ratios measure?

f. The cash balance increased by $756 million during the year. Does Thermo Fisher Scientific present a "healthy" cash flow picture for the year? Explain.

IFRS Applications

LO1, 5   **I11-58.**   **Interpreting Graphical Cash Flow Data**
Nutrien Ltd. (NTR)   Nutrien Ltd., a Canadian agri-business company, reported the following in its 2018 annual report.

The graph below represents the significant changes in Nutrien's cash flows in 2018.

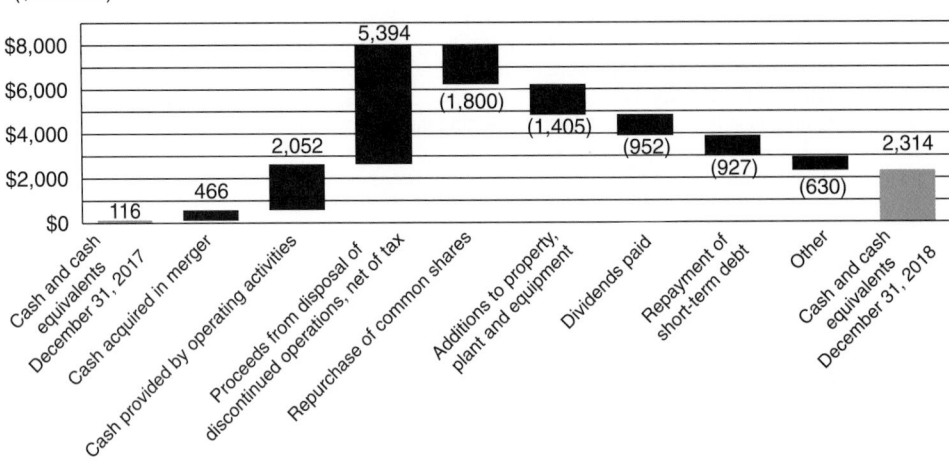

Required
a. Determine the change in cash and cash equivalents for Nutrien for 2018.
b. Classify each of the black bars in the graphic as operating, investing, or financing cash flows. Assume that "Other" relates entirely to investing cash flows.
c. Use the data to complete the following abbreviated statement of cash flows.

$ millions	2018
Cash from operating activities	_____
Cash from investing activities	_____
Cash from financing activities	_____
Cash flow for the year	_____
Cash and cash equivalents, start of year	_____
Cash and cash equivalents, end of year	_____

Solutions to Review Problems

Review 11-1—Solution

Transaction	Classification
1. Payments of dividends.	F
2. Payments to purchase PPE assets and intangible assets.	I
3. Payments to employees or suppliers.	O
4. Payments to purchase inventories.	O
5. Receipts from issuances of bonds payable, mortgage notes payable, and other notes payable.	F
6. Receipts from sales of investments in stocks, bonds, and other securities (other than cash equivalents).	I
7. Payments of interest to creditors.	O
8. Receipts from issuances of common stock and preferred stock and from sales of treasury stock.	F
9. Receipts of interest and dividends.	O
10. Payments to purchase stocks, bonds, and other securities (other than cash equivalents).	I
11. Receipts from customers for sales made or services rendered.	O
12. Payments to acquire treasury stock.	F
13. Other receipts such as lawsuit settlements and refunds received from suppliers.	O
14. Payments of taxes to government.	O
15. Payments to settle outstanding bonds payable, mortgage notes payable, and other notes payable.	F
16. Receipts from sales of PPE assets and intangible assets.	I
17. Other payments such as contributions to charity.	O
18. Receipts from repayments of loans by borrowers.	I
19. Payments made to lend money to borrowers.	I

Review 11-2—Solution

Net cash flow from operating activities	
Net income	$35,000
Add (deduct) items to convert net income to cash basis	
Depreciation	11,000
Loss on sale of investments	2,000
Accounts receivable decrease	6,000
Inventory increase	(28,000)
Prepaid advertising increase	(3,000)
Accounts payable increase	13,000
Wages payable increase	3,500
Income tax payable decrease	(1,500)
Net cash provided by operating activities	$38,000

Review 11-3—Solution

Cash Flows from Investing Activities	
Sale of investments.	$ 9,000
Purchase of PPE.	(48,000)
Net cash used by investing activities	$(39,000)

Review 11-4A—Solution

Cash Flows from Financing Activities	
Issuance of common stocks	$ 14,000
Payment of dividends	(17,000)
Net cash used by financing activities	$(3,000)

Review 11-4B—Solution

a. The change in cash = $38,000 + $(39,000) + $(3,000) = $(4,000).

b.		
	Net decrease in cash	$ (4,000)
	Cash at beginning of year.	12,000
	Cash at end of year	$ 8,000

Review 11-5—Solution

a.

	Net Income	Depreciation	Stock-Based Compensation	Cash from Operations	Cash from Investing	CAPEX	Cash from Financing
Starbucks	18.3%	5.3%	1.0%	48.3%	(9.6%)	(8.0%)	(13.1%)
Farmer Brothers . . .	(12.3%)	5.2%	0.6%	5.9%	(5.4%)	(5.8%)	0.2%
Exhibit 11.5	11.4%	3.1%	0.7%	19.7%	(8.0%)	(3.6%)	(8.2%)

Starbucks' percentages are larger than for the median S&P 500 firm. In contrast, Farmer Brothers reports percentages that are markedly weaker. Also, Farmer Brothers' cash generated from each of its three business activities is low as compared with Starbucks and the S&P firms.

b. Both companies' cash flow patterns are roughly the same (+ − −), which reflects that both are relatively mature companies.

Review 11-6—Solution

1. $\dfrac{\$6,966.7}{(\$2,890.6+\$2,973.5)\,/\,2}=2.38$

2. $\dfrac{\$6,966.7}{\$2,741.7}=2.54$

3. Yes, both ratios are strong. The operating cash flow to current liabilities ratio is much higher than the benchmark of 0.5, and the operating cash flow to capital expenditures ratio is much higher than 1.0

Review 11-7—Solution

Cash received from customers.	$391,000	$385,000 sales + $6,000 accounts receivable decrease
Cash received as dividends	5,000	$5,000 dividend income
Cash paid for merchandise purchased.	(248,000)	$233,000 cost of goods sold + $28,000 inventory increase − $13,000 accounts payable increase
Cash paid to employees.	(78,500)	$82,000 wages expense − $3,500 wages payable increase
Cash paid for advertising	(13,000)	$10,000 advertising expense + $3,000 prepaid advertising increase
Cash paid for income taxes	(18,500)	$17,000 income tax expense + $1,500 income tax payable decrease
Net cash provided by operating activities.	$ 38,000	

Module 12

Financial Statement Forecasting

Financial Statement Forecasting

Forecasting Process	Forecasting the Income Statement	Forecasting the Balance Sheet	Forecasting the Statement of Cash Flows	Additional Forecasting Issues
▪ Adjusted Financial Statements ▪ Forecasting Order ▪ Morgan Stanley Method ▪ Mechanics	▪ Revenue Growth ▪ Operating Expenses ▪ Nonoperating Expenses ▪ Income taxes	▪ Operating and Nonoperating Assets and Liabilities ▪ Equity ▪ Using Segment Data	▪ Operating Activities ▪ Investing Activities ▪ Financing Activities	▪ Multiyear Forecasting—Appendix 12B ▪ Parsimonious method—Appendix 12C
Review 12-1	Review 12-2	Review 12-3, 12-4	Review 12-5	Review 12-6, 12-7

PREVIEW

PG

We describe the process for forecasting financial statements, including:

- Forecasting the income statement, including the use of company guidance.
- Forecasting the balance sheet.
- Forecasting cash as a plug figure to balance the balance sheet, and interpreting the forecasted cash balance.
- Building forecasts from the bottom up by using segment disclosures.
- Multiyear forecasting, including achieving targeted cash balances by adjusting debt levels.
- Forecasting the statement of cash flows.
- Parsimonious method of forecasting NOPAT, NOA, and RNOA.

We show excerpts from Morgan Stanley analysts' spreadsheets to illustrate the forecasting process. Appendix 12D includes excerpts of the Morgan Stanley analyst research report on Procter & Gamble, this module's focus company. The dashboard below conveys key financial information for P&G.

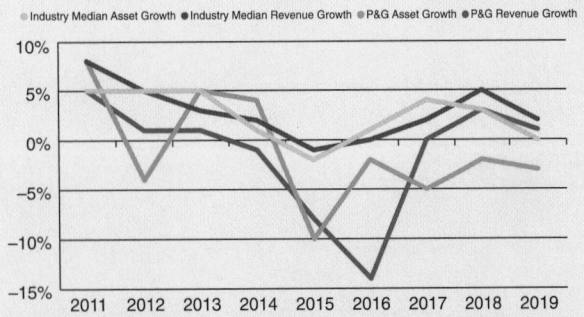

Consumer Discretionary Industry Asset and Revenue Growth

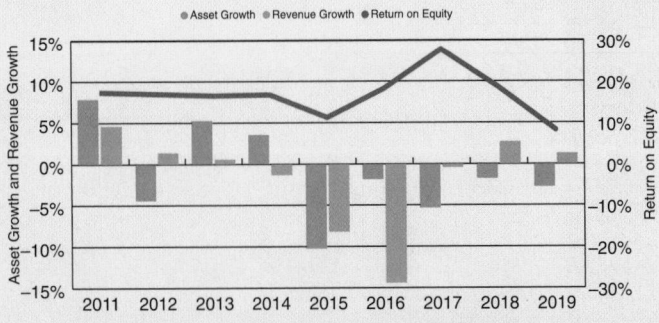

P&G Asset and Revenue Growth and Return on Equity

Road Map

LO	Learning Objective | Topics	Page	eLecture	Guided Example	Assignments
12–1	**Explain the process of forecasting financial statements.** Adjusted Financial Statements :: Forecasting Order :: Morgan Stanley :: Mechanics :: Consistency and Precision :: Sensitivity	12-3	e12–1	Review 12-1	1, 2, 3, 4, 9, 35
12–2	**Forecast revenues and the income statement.** Overview :: Sales Driver :: COGS :: SGA :: Income Taxes	12-8	e12–2	Review 12-2	7, 11, 12, 13, 17, 20, 21, 23, 25, 28, 32, 33, 35
12–3	**Forecast the balance sheet.** Overview :: PPE :: Intangibles :: LTD :: Retained Earnings :: Treasury Stock :: Cash Plug :: Normal Cash :: Deviation from Norm :: Capital Structure	12-12	e12–3	Review 12-3	6, 8, 10, 14, 15, 16, 18, 19, 21, 23, 25, 27, 32, 33
12–4	**Prepare forecasts using segment data.** Segment Data	12-16	e12–4	Review 12-4	28, 29, 32
12–5	**Forecast the statement of cash flows (Appendix 12A).** Operating :: Investing :: Financing	12-19	e12–5	Review 12-5	22, 24, 26, 32, 33
12–6	**Prepare multiyear forecasts of financial statements (Appendix 12B).** Motivation :: Long-Term Assumptions :: Check for Reasonableness	12-20	e12–6	Review 12-6	5, 34
12–7	**Apply a parsimonious method for forecasting net operating profit and net operating assets (Appendix 12C).**	12-22	e12–7	Review 12-7	30, 31

Forecasting Process

LO1
Explain the process of forecasting financial statements.

Forecasting financial performance is integral to a variety of business decisions. In addition to using financial forecasts to value stocks and inform investment decisions, investors and analysts might be interested in evaluating the creditworthiness of a prospective borrower. In that case, they forecast the borrower's cash flows to estimate its ability to repay its obligations, and bond ratings are influenced by those forecasts. Company managers also frequently forecast future cash flows to evaluate alternative strategic investment decisions as well as to evaluate the shareholder value that strategic investment alternatives will create. All of these decisions require accurate financial forecasts. In this module, we illustrate the most common method to forecast the income statement, balance sheet, and statement of cash flows.

Adjusted Financial Statements The forecasting process begins with a retrospective analysis. That is, we analyze current and prior years' statements to be sure that they accurately reflect the company's financial condition and performance. If we believe that they do not, we adjust those statements to reflect the company's net operating assets and liabilities and operating income that we expect to persist.

Why do we adjust historical results? The answer is that income statements can contain one-time (transitory and/or nonoperating) income or expense items that affect reported profit. Because our objective is to forecast *future* income and cash flow, we must first identify and eliminate transitory items because, by definition, they will not recur.

This adjusting process, also referred to as recasting, reformulating, or scrubbing the numbers, involves estimates. This estimation process requires judgment and varies by firm. Following are items frequently encountered.

- *Restructuring expenses* (Module 5). If the restructuring activity is unusual and management discussion indicates that it is unlikely to recur, we eliminate the expense in our forecast. If the restructuring activity is recurring, we don't eliminate but normalize the amount over the past years impacted.

- *Litigation expenses* (Module 5). Significant litigation expenses can skew results. We eliminate them from our forecast if they are transitory, or normalize the amount if litigation is a routine occurrence but the amount varies year over year.

- *Discontinued operations* (Module 5). Discontinued operations are one-time events that we eliminate because they will not affect future operations.

- *Gains and losses on asset dispositions and impairments* (Module 6). These gains and losses are one-time occurrences that we always eliminate and normalize their amounts over the periods impacted before we begin forecasting.

- *Unusual income tax expense or benefit* (Module 10). Changes in tax laws can significantly affect the effective tax rate. We need to identify unusual, one-time tax expenses and benefits to better isolate the effective tax rate that will persist.

- *Acquisitions and divestitures* (Modules 9 and 12). Acquisitions and divestitures affect the income statement from the date of the transaction. Footnote disclosures typically provide comparable historical data we can use to develop better forecast assumptions.

Forecasting Order of Financial Statements The forecasting process estimates future income statements, balance sheets, and statements of cash flows, in that order. The reason for this ordering is that each statement uses information from the preceding statement(s). For example, we update retained earnings on the balance sheet to reflect our forecast of the company's net income. And the forecasted income statement and balance sheets are used in preparing forecasts for the statement of cash flows, which follows the same process we illustrate in the module on preparing the historical statement of cash flows.

To illustrate the forecasting process, we start with the P&G financial statements for the fiscal year (FY) ended June 30, 2019 (FY2019), and use them to forecast the company's financial statements for FY2020. (See Appendix 12B for P&G financial statements for FY2019 and the FY2020 forecast.)

In Appendix 12B, we illustrate the process to extend the forecasts to FY2021 and future years. We explain interpretation of the forecasted balance for cash and the adjustments that we can make to our forecasted balance sheet and income statement to achieve a desired level of cash.

Morgan Stanley Forecasting Process Later in this module we provide excerpts from the Morgan Stanley research report on P&G and the spreadsheet Morgan Stanley analysts used in their forecasting process. Appendix 12D to this module includes excerpts from the published Morgan Stanley report. We have benefitted from conversations with Morgan Stanley analysts and are grateful for the background information that they provided us that informs the forecasting process in this module.[1]

Forecasting Mechanics The revenues (sales) forecast is, arguably, the most crucial and difficult estimate in the forecasting process. It is a crucial estimate because other income-statement and balance-sheet accounts derive, either directly or indirectly, from the revenues forecast. As a result, both the income statement and balance sheet grow with increases in revenues. The income statement reflects this growth concurrently. However, different balance sheet accounts reflect revenue growth in different ways. Some balance sheet accounts anticipate (or lead) revenue growth (inventories are one example). Some accounts reflect this growth concurrently (accounts receivable). And some accounts reflect revenue growth with a lag (for example, companies usually expand property, plant, and equipment (PPE) only after growth is deemed sustainable). Conversely, when revenues decline, so do the income statement and balance sheet, as the company shrinks to cope with adversity. Such actions include reduction of overhead costs and divestiture of excess assets. Exhibit 12.1 highlights crucial income statement and balance sheet relations that are impacted by the revenues forecast.

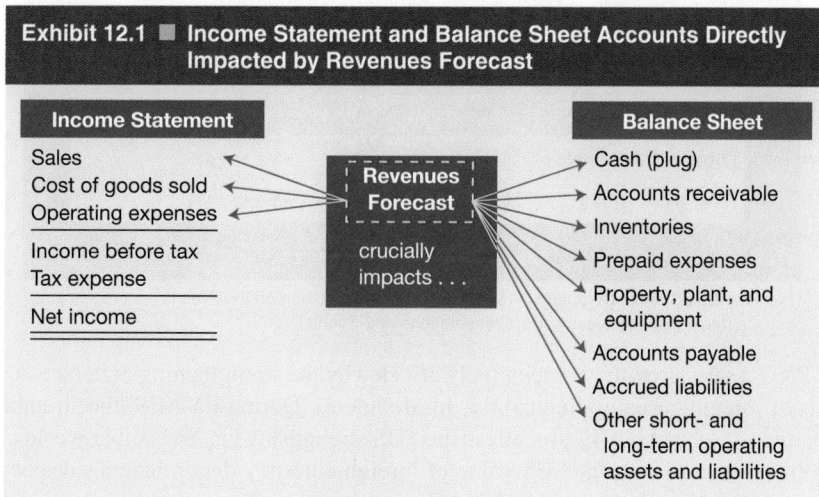

Exhibit 12.1 ■ Income Statement and Balance Sheet Accounts Directly Impacted by Revenues Forecast

Forecasting Consistency and Precision It is important to keep two points in mind.

- **Internal consistency.** The forecasted income statement, balance sheet, and statement of cash flows are linked in the same way historical financial statements are. That is, they must articulate (link together within and across time), as we explain Module 2. Preparing a forecasted statement of cash flows, although tedious, is often a useful way to uncover forecasting assumptions that are inconsistently applied across financial statements (such as capital expenditures, depreciation, debt payments, and dividends). If the forecasted cash balance on the balance sheet agrees with that on the statement of cash flows, it is likely that our income statement and balance sheet articulate. We also must ensure that our forecast assumptions are internally consistent. For example, it is

---

[1] Please note that materials that are referenced herein comprise excerpts from Morgan Stanley research reports. MS has provided their materials here as a courtesy. Therefore, MS and Cambridge do not undertake to advise you of changes in the opinions or information set forth in these materials. These materials should not be relied on as investment advice. These materials are only as current as the publication date of the underlying Morgan Stanley research. For important disclosures, stock price charts, and equity rating histories regarding companies that are the subject of the underlying Morgan Stanley research, see www.morganstanley.com/researchdisclosures.

unadvisable to forecast an increased gross profit margin during an economic recession unless we can make compelling arguments based on known business facts about the company.

- **Level of precision.** Computing forecasts to the "nth decimal place" is easy using spreadsheets. This increased precision makes the resulting forecasts appear more precise, but they are not necessarily more accurate. As we discuss in this module, our financial statement forecasts are highly dependent on our revenues forecast. Whether revenues are expected to grow by 2% or 3% can markedly impact profitability and other forecasts. Estimating cost of goods sold (COGS) and other items to the nth decimal place is meaningless if we have imprecise revenue forecasts. Consequently, borderline decisions that depend on a high level of forecasting precision are ill-advised.

Company Guidance

Companies frequently provide guidance to analysts and other users of financial reports for forecasting purposes. P&G provided the following guidance for FY2020 when it presented its FY2019 financial results. We can use this guidance to inform our forecast assumptions.

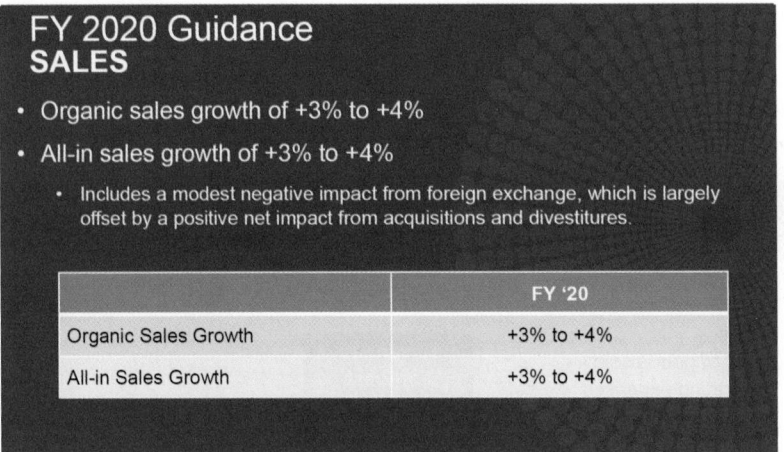

The Procter & Gamble Company Q4 2019 Earnings Presentation on the P&G Investor Relations website (http://www.pginvestor.com/Presentations-and-Events)

In FY2019, P&G's sales growth was negatively affected by the strengthening $US (see our discussion of the effects of foreign currency fluctuations in Module 5). During FY2019, the strengthening $US reduced reported sales by about 4%; recall, as the $US strengthens vis-à-vis other world currencies in which P&G transacts business, the $US value of foreign-currency-denominated sales decreases. For FY2019, in the MD&A section of its 10-K, P&G provides the following table.

Total Company	Net Sales Growth	Foreign Exchange Impact	Acquisition & Divestiture Impact/Other	Organic Sales Growth
FY2019.........	1%	4%	—%	5%

Total sales increased by 1% in FY2019, from $66,832 million to $67,684 million. Absent foreign currency effects and the effects of acquisitions and divestitures, P&G's organic sales would have increased by 5% (overall 1% net sales increase plus 4% negative foreign-currency effect). P&G does not anticipate a significant foreign currency exchange rate effect in FY2020. Consequently, P&G's All-in sales growth estimate of 3% to 4% is equal to its estimate of Organic sales growth. We use 3.5% growth, the midpoint of the range, in our forecasting process.

P&G provides guidance for its effective tax rate. For FY2020, P&G forecasts an effective tax rate of 17% to 18% (which results in the 17.5% we use in our forecasts).

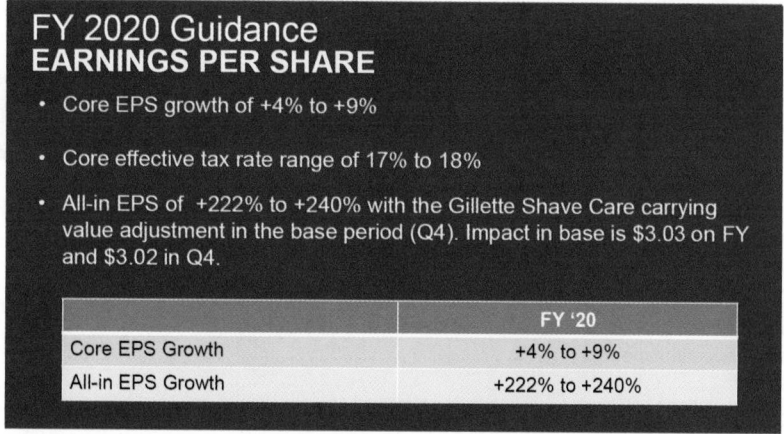

FY 2020 Guidance
EARNINGS PER SHARE

- Core EPS growth of +4% to +9%

- Core effective tax rate range of 17% to 18%

- All-in EPS of +222% to +240% with the Gillette Shave Care carrying value adjustment in the base period (Q4). Impact in base is $3.03 on FY and $3.02 in Q4.

	FY '20
Core EPS Growth	+4% to +9%
All-in EPS Growth	+222% to +240%

The Procter & Gamble Company Q4 2019 Earnings Presentation on the P&G Investor Relations website (http://www.pginvestor.com/Presentations-and-Events)

P&G provides guidance regarding anticipated capital spending (CAPEX), dividends, and share repurchases.

FY 2020 Guidance
CASH GENERATION AND USAGE

- Free Cash Flow Productivity: 90%

- Capital Spending, % Sales: 4.5% to 5.0%

- Dividends: Over $7.5B

- Direct Share Repurchase: $6 to $8B

The Procter & Gamble Company Q4 2019 Earnings Presentation on the P&G Investor Relations website (http://www.P&Ginvestor.com/Presentations-and-Events)

We use this guidance to produce the following forecasts.

- CAPEX as 4.75% of sales, the midpoint of the guidance for capital spending.
- Dividends of $7.5 billion.
- Share repurchases (treasury stock purchases) of $7 billion, the midpoint of the guidance.

LO1 Review 12-1

The FY2019 income statement and balance sheet for General Mills, a competitor of P&G, follow. Use them to answer the required questions.

Required

a. Which two nonrecurring items on the 2019 income statement would we consider eliminating before beginning the forecasting process?
b. In what order do we forecast the financial statements? Explain why this order is important.
c. What income statement amount do we forecast first?
d. Identify at least three forecasted expenses that are directly or indirectly related to revenue.
e. Identify at least three forecasted balance sheet accounts that are directly or indirectly related to forecasted revenue.

continued

continued from previous page

GENERAL MILLS INC.
Consolidated Statements of Earnings

12 Months Ended, $ millions	May 26, 2019
Net sales.	$16,865.2
Cost of sales.	11,108.4
Selling, general, and administrative expenses	2,935.8
Divestitures (loss)	30.0
Restructuring, impairment, and other exit costs	275.1
Operating profit.	2,515.9
Benefit plan nonservice income	(87.9)
Interest, net.	521.8
Earnings before income taxes and after-tax earnings from joint ventures	2,082.0
Income taxes	367.8
After-tax earnings from joint ventures.	(72.0)
Net earnings, including earnings attributable to redeemable and noncontrolling interests	1,786.2
Net earnings attributable to redeemable and noncontrolling interests	33.5
Net earnings attributable to General Mills	$ 1,752.7

GENERAL MILLS INC.
Consolidated Balance Sheet

$ millions, except par value	May 26, 2019
Current assets	
Cash and cash equivalents.	$ 450.0
Receivables	1,679.7
Inventories	1,559.3
Prepaid expenses and other current assets	497.5
Total current assets.	4,186.5
Land, buildings, and equipment	3,787.2
Goodwill	13,995.8
Other intangible assets.	7,166.8
Other assets.	974.9
Total assets	$30,111.2
Current liabilities	
Accounts payable	$ 2,854.1
Current portion of long-term debt	1,396.5
Notes payable.	1,468.7
Other current liabilities	1,367.8
Total current liabilities	7,087.1
Long-term debt.	11,624.8
Deferred income taxes	2,031.0
Other liabilities	1,448.9
Total liabilities.	22,191.8
Redeemable interest value.	551.7
Stockholders' equity	
Common stock, 754.6 shares issued, $0.10 par value.	75.5
Additional paid-in capital.	1,386.7
Retained earnings	14,996.7
Common stock in treasury, at cost	(6,779.0)
Accumulated other comprehensive loss.	(2,625.4)
Total stockholders' equity	7,054.5
Noncontrolling interests	313.2
Total equity	7,367.7
Total liabilities and equity	$30,111.2

Solution on p. 12-51.

Forecasting the Income Statement

Exhibit 12.2 presents the FY2019 income statement for Procter & Gamble together with our forecast of the statements for FY2020.

LO2
Forecast revenues and the income statement

Overview Here is a high-level overview—computational details follow.

- **Sales estimate.** The forecasting process begins with an estimate of the sales growth rate. For our illustration, we assume a 3.5% growth rate, informed by P&G's guidance. Given the assumed 3.5% growth in sales, forecasted 2020 sales are $70,053 million ($67,684 million × 1.035).

- **Expense estimates.** To estimate operating expenses (cost of goods sold and selling, general, and administrative [SG&A] expenses) we apply a percentage of sales ratio to forecasted sales. For nonoperating expenses (such as interest expense and interest revenue), we initially assume they will not change ("no change") unless we believe interest rates are likely to shift greatly during the forecast period. (In Appendix 12B, we relax the "no change" assumption because we add debt to achieve a desired level of cash. Additional debt causes interest expense to increase. We discuss these additional steps in Appendix 12B.)

- **One-time item estimates.** One-time items such as asset impairments and discontinued operations, are, by definition, not expected to recur. We forecast these items to be $0.

- **Tax estimate.** Income tax expense is forecasted based on PG's guidance of 17.5% of pretax income.

- **Noncontrolling interest estimate.** A common assumption is no change in the ratio of noncontrolling interest to consolidated net income. For our P&G illustration, we adopt that assumption.

For each line item in the income statement, we summarize our forecasting assumptions in the rightmost column of Exhibit 12.2, and we discuss those assumptions in depth in the following sections.

Exhibit 12.2 ■ Forecast of P&G's FY2020 Income Statement

$ millions	Actual FY2019	% of Net Sales	Computations	FY2020 Est.	% of Net Sales	Explanation
Net sales..............................	$67,684	100.0%	$67,684 × 1.035	**$70,053**	100.0%	Use P&G's guidance that sales will increase about 3.5%. Sales forecast equals current sales × (1 + growth rate %).
Cost of products sold....................	34,768	51.4%	$70,053 × 51.4%	**36,007**	51.4%	Assume COGS as % of sales will remain unchanged from FY2019.
Selling, general, and administrative expense...	19,084	28.2%	$70,053 × 28.2%	**19,755**	28.2%	Assume SGA as % of sales will remain unchanged from FY2019.
Goodwill & indefinite lived intangibles impairment charges..................	8,345	12.3%	none	**0**		The Goodwill impairment charge is a transitory item and we eliminate that expense in FY2020.
Operating income.......................	5,487	8.1%	subtotal	**14,291**	20.4%	
Interest expense........................	509	0.8%	computed	**483**	0.7%	Interest expense is discussed below.
Interest income........................	220	0.3%	no change	**220**	0.3%	Assume no change in interest revenue.
Other nonoperating income, net............	871	1.3%	none	**0**	0.0%	FY2019 nonoperating income relates to the dissolution of a partnership and early extinguishment of debt, and we assume none for FY2020 given no evidence of planned divestitures or debt retirement.
Earnings from continuing operations before income taxes.......................	6,069	9.0%	subtotal	**14,028**	20.0%	
Income taxes on continuing operations.......	2,103	3.1%	$14,014 × 17.5%	**2,455**	3.5%	Assume effective tax rate of 17.5% per P&G guidance.
Net earnings...........................	3,966	5.9%	subtotal	**11,573**	16.5%	
Less: Net earnings attributable to noncontrolling interests.................	69	0.1%	$11,562 × 1.7%	**197**	0.3%	Assume noncontrolling interests as % of net earnings (1.7%) continues.
Net earnings attributable to P&G...........	$ 3,897	5.8%	subtotal	**$11,376**	16.2%	

Sales as the Income Statement Forecast Driver   We forecast most income statement line items in Exhibit 12.2 as a percent of sales. (One exception is tax expense, which is commonly set as a percent of pretax profit.) Unless we are aware of transitory items that affect the current year's income statement, we use the current year percentage of sales in our forecast.

Cost of Goods Sold (COGS)   Companies often discuss COGS in the Management Discussion & Analysis (MD&A) section of their 10-K report. This discussion typically provides insight into recent trends as well as anticipated effects of planned restructuring or other process improvement activities. P&G discusses its gross margin in the following excerpt from its FY2019 10-K.

> Gross margin increased 10 basis points to 48.6% of net sales in 2019. Gross margin benefited 160 basis points from total manufacturing cost savings (130 basis points net of product and packaging reinvestments), 60 basis points of positive pricing impacts and 50 basis points from lower restructuring costs. These were offset by:
> - a 100 basis-point decline from unfavorable product mix and other impacts (primarily mix within segments due to the growth of lower margin product forms and the club channel in certain categories and due to the disproportionate growth of the Fabric Care category, which is one of our largest categories and has lower than company-average gross margins),
> - an 80 basis-point negative impact due to higher commodity costs and
> - a 50 basis-point negative impact from unfavorable foreign exchange.

Gross margins did not change significantly in FY2019 as price increases and favorable manufacturing cost savings from P&G's productivity initiatives were largely offset by unfavorable product mix changes to lower gross profit products, higher commodity costs, and unfavorable foreign exchange fluctuations (exchange rate effects affect expenses in the same way they affect sales). Therefore, we use the FY2019 percent COGS to sales (51.4%).

SGA Expense   To forecast SG&A for FY2020, we use the FY2019 percent SG&A to sales (28.2%) because the company does not disclose any significant operational changes to SG&A in the following excerpt from its FY2019 10-K.

> Total SG&A was relatively unchanged at $19.1 billion, as a decrease in marketing spending was offset by an increase in overhead costs and in other net operating expenses. SG&A as a percentage of net sales decreased 30 basis points to 28.2%. Reductions in marketing spending as a percentage of net sales were partially offset by an increase in overhead costs and other net operating expenses as a percentage of sales.
> - Marketing spending as a percentage of net sales decreased 80 basis points due to the positive scale impacts of the organic net sales increase, reductions in agency compensation and the impact of adopting the new standard on "Revenue from Contracts with Customers" which prospectively reclassified certain customer spending from marketing (SG&A) expense to a reduction of net sales.
> - Overhead costs as a percentage of net sales increased 30 basis points, as productivity savings and fixed cost leverage from the increased organic net sales, were more than offset by the impact of inflation, higher incentive compensation costs and other cost increases, including the ongoing and integration-related overhead costs of the Merck OTC acquisition.
> - Other net operating expenses as a percentage of net sales increased 20 basis points primarily due to an increase in foreign exchange transactional charges and the net impact of changes in indirect tax reserves, partially offset by the gain on sale of real estate in the current year.

We forecast SG&A expense as Sales × Current year SGA percentage of sales, which yields $19,755 million ($70,053 million × 28.2%).

Interest Expense   We forecast interest expense as Average debt balance during the year × Estimated % interest rate. For FY2019, P&G reported $509 million of interest expense and an average debt balance of $30,689 million, yielding an average interest rate of 1.7% ($509 million/$30,689 million).

P&G begins the FY2020 year with $30,092 million ($9,697 million + $20,395 million) of short-term and long-term debt and predicts contractual payments of $3,388 for FY2020, yielding an anticipated debt balance of $28,320 for FY2020 ($30,092 − $3,388). For the initial forecast, we assume no additional borrowing during the year (we relax that assumption in Appendix 12B when we perform a multiyear forecast). Our forecast for FY2020 interest expense is $483 million calculated as 1.7% × ($30,092 + $26,704)/2.

Income Tax Expense Income tax expense (labeled "Income taxes on continuing operations" by P&G) is often a large expense item. We estimate tax expense by applying an estimated tax rate to pretax income. For FY2020, we use an effective tax rate of 17.5% as provided in PG's guidance. In the absence of company guidance, we can use disclosures in the income tax footnote to get a tax rate estimate. Following is the effective tax rate disclosure in P&G's FY2019 10-K.

Years Ended June 30 ($ millions)	2019	2018	2017
U.S. federal statutory income tax rate	21.0%	28.1%	35.0%
Country mix impacts of foreign operations	(0.5)%	(4.7)%	(6.8)%
Changes in uncertain tax positions	(0.3)%	(0.3)%	(2.0)%
Excess tax benefits from the exercise of stock options	(3.8)%	(0.4)%	(1.3)%
Goodwill impairment	22.8%	—%	—%
Net transitional impact U.S. Tax Act	—%	4.5%	—%
Other	(4.5)%	(1.2)%	(1.8)%
Effective income tax rate	34.7%	26.0%	23.1%

The aim of reviewing the tax table in the footnotes is to determine the tax rate to use for our forecasts. We look for any transitory items that affect the company's tax rate and we exclude such items in our forecast. In FY2019, for example, P&G's effective tax rate increased by 22.8 percentage points due to the Goodwill impairment that reduced pre-tax profit without a consequent reduction of income tax expense (Goodwill write-offs are generally not a tax-deductible expense). Given that the Goodwill impairment is a one-time occurrence, we would forecast a tax rate of 11.9% (34.7% effective tax rate less 22.8%). In addition, the line item labeled as "Other" increased by 2 to 3 percentage points over the previous two years. Adding that amount, then, results in an estimate of the effective tax rate that is close to the 17.5% rate in P&G's guidance.

Impact of Acquisitions When one company acquires another, the revenues and expenses of the acquired company are consolidated, but only from the date of acquisition onward (we discuss the consolidation process in an earlier module). Acquisitions can greatly impact the acquirer's income statement, especially if the acquisition occurs toward the beginning of the acquirer's fiscal year. In FY2019 P&G did not have any material acquisitions. Therefore, we use P&G's acquisition of **Gillette** in October 2005 as an example. In its June 30, 2006, fiscal year-end income statement (ending eight months following the acquisition), P&G reported the following for sales.

Years Ended June 30 ($ millions)	2006	2005	2004
Net sales	$68,222	$56,741	$51,407

These net sales amounts include Gillette product sales from October 2005 onward (for fiscal 2006), and none of Gillette's sales is reported in fiscal 2005 or fiscal 2004. P&G's 2006 sales growth of 20.2% ([$68,222 million/$56,741 million] − 1) was, therefore, not P&G's organic growth, and we would have been remiss in forecasting a 20.2% increase for fiscal 2007.

Importantly, until all three annual income statements in the 10-K include the acquired company, the acquirer is required to disclose what revenue and net income would have been had the acquired company been consolidated for all three years reported in the current annual report. This "what if" disclosure is called *pro forma* disclosure. Procter & Gamble's pro forma disclosure in the footnotes to its 2006 10-K includes the following discussion and table.

The following table provides pro forma results of operations for the years ended June 30, 2006, 2005, and 2004, as if Gillette had been acquired as of the beginning of each fiscal year presented.

Pro Forma Results; Years Ended June 30,	2006	2005	2004
Net sales ($ millions)	$71,005	$67,920	$61,112
Net earnings ($ millions)	8,871	8,522	7,504
Diluted net earnings per common share	2.51	2.29	1.98

Using this disclosure, we would have been able to compute the growth rate in sales for 2006 as 4.5% ([$71,005 million/$67,920 million] − 1), and we would have used the pro forma net sales for 2006 as our forecasting base. That is, assuming a continuation of this 4.5% growth rate, we would have forecasted 2007 net sales as $74,200 million (calculated as $71,005 million × 1.045). P&G was careful to point out, however, that the pro forma earnings estimate must be viewed with caution.

Pro forma results do not include any anticipated cost savings or other effects of the planned integration of Gillette. Accordingly, such amounts are not necessarily indicative of the results if the acquisition had occurred on the dates indicated or that may result in the future.

Impact of Divestitures When companies divest of discontinued operations, they are required to:

- Exclude sales and expenses of discontinued operations from the continuing operations portion of their income statements.

- Report net income and gain (loss) on sale of the divested entity, net of tax, below income from continuing operations.

- Segregate the assets and liabilities of discontinued operations and report them on separate line items—these are labeled "assets held for sale" or "liabilities held of sale" on the balance sheet.

In FY2019 P&G did not have any major brand divestitures. Therefore, we use FY2016 to illustrate the related forecasting issues. P&G reports assets and liabilities held for sale on its FY2016 balance sheet at $7,185 million and $2,343 million, respectively. In our FY2017 forecasts, we assume these discontinued operations will be sold in FY2017 at book value and, consequently, report both the assets and liabilities of discontinued operations at a zero balance in our FY2017 forecast.

Reassessing Financial Statement Forecasts After preparing the forecasted financial statements, it is useful to reassess whether they are reasonable in light of current economic and company conditions. This task is subjective and benefits from the forecaster's knowledge of company, industry, and economic factors. Many analysts and managers prepare "what-if" forecasted financial statements. Specifically, they change key assumptions, such as the forecasted sales growth or key cost ratios, and then recompute the forecasted financial statements. These alternative forecasting scenarios indicate the sensitivity of a set of predicted outcomes to different assumptions about future economic conditions. Such sensitivity estimates can be useful for setting contingency plans and in identifying areas of vulnerability for company performance and condition.

Review 12-2 LO2

Refer to the FY2019 income statement and balance sheet for General Mills in Review 12-1.

Required
Use the following assumptions to forecast the General Mills income statement for FY2020.
- Net sales will increase by 1.5% (150 basis points) in FY2020.
- Cost of sales: 65.9% of forecasted sales.
- SGA expenses: 17.4% of forecasted sales.
- No announced divestitures for FY2020.

continued

continued from previous page

- Restructuring, impairment, and other exit costs: 1.6% of forecasted sales.
- Tax expense as a percentage of pretax income: 17.7%
- Benefit plan nonservice income is assumed to be zero.
- The following line items remain unchanged in dollar terms:
  ○ Interest, net.
  ○ After-tax earnings from joint ventures.
  ○ Net earnings attributable to redeemable and noncontrolling interests.

Solution on p. 12-52.

Forecasting the Balance Sheet

Our forecast of the balance sheet in Exhibit 12.3 begins with estimates for all assets *other than cash* (which is the **plug** amount as we explain below), all liabilities, and all equity accounts.

eLectures **LO3**
MBC Forecast the balance sheet.

Overview Here is a high-level overview of balance sheet forecasting—details follow.

- **Working capital accounts.** We use an assumed percentage of forecasted sales to estimated accounts receivable, inventories, accounts payable, and accrued liabilities.

- **PPE and intangible assets.** To forecast PPE, we increase the prior year's balance by estimated CAPEX and reduce the estimate by forecasted depreciation expense (we discuss the forecasting of PPE assets below). We forecast intangible assets by subtracting forecasted amortization expense.

- **Current and long-term debt.** We assume P&G will make all contractual payments of long-term debt. We reduce the prior year's long-term debt balance by the current maturities of long-term debt reported in the footnotes. We assume current and long-term debt remains unchanged. (We discuss refining this assumption later.)

- **Stockholders' equity.** We assume paid-in capital accounts remain at prior years' levels, except for planned repurchases of treasury stock, as reported by P&G in its FY2019 earnings release. Retained earnings is increased by forecasted net income and reduced by estimated dividends. (We discuss the forecasting of dividends below.)

The last step in the forecasting process is to balance the balance sheet. To do this, we determine the amount needed in the Cash account to balance the balance sheet, computed as total assets (equal to total liabilities and equity) less all other asset balances. This balancing figure is referred to as the *plug* amount.

Working Capital Accounts Working capital accounts that are operating in nature are forecasted using the historical relation of each working capital account divided by sales, then multiplied by the forecasted sales. Items that are nonoperating are usually assumed to have no change, or are predicted using company guidance such as with debt due within one year.

PPE (Property, Plant and Equipment) Assets

Capital Expenditures (CAPEX). P&G provides guidance about anticipated purchases of PPE assets (called capital expenditures or CAPEX). The company reports that FY2020 CAPEX is expected to be 4.5% to 5% of sales. We use the midpoint of 4.75% of sales and forecast FY2020 CAPEX of $3,328 million ($70,053 million of forecasted sales × 4.75%).

In the absence of company guidance (or as a check on its accuracy), we can estimate CAPEX as a percentage of forecasted sales. To compute the percentage, we use CAPEX as reported in the current period statement of cash flows along with current period sales, as follows.

$$\text{Forecasted CAPEX} = \frac{\text{Current year CAPEX}}{\text{Current year Sales}} \times \text{Forecasted Sales}$$

P&G's 2019 statement of cash flows reports CAPEX of $3,347 million, which yields an historical rate of 4.9% of sales ($3,347 million/$67,684 million). This is consistent with the 4.5% to 5% range provided in P&G's guidance.

Exhibit 12.3 ■ Forecast of P&G's FY2020 Balance Sheet

$ millions, except per share amounts	2019 Actual	% of Sales	Computations	2020 Est.	% of Sales	Explanation
Current assets						
Cash and cash equivalents	$ 4,239	6.3%	Plug	$ (1,550)	0.1%	Plug to balance the balance sheet.*
Available-for-sale investment securities	6,048	8.9%	no change	6,048	8.6%	Assume no change.
Accounts receivable	4,951	7.3%	$70,053 × 7.3%	5,114	7.3%	Forecast working capital accounts
Inventories	5,017	7.4%	$70,053 × 7.4%	5,184	7.4%	as a % of sales using prior year's
Prepaid expenses and other current assets . . .	2,218	3.3%	$70,053 × 3.3%	2,312	3.3%	% unless information suggests otherwise.**
Total current assets	22,473	33.2%	subtotal	17,108	26.7%	
Property, plant, and equipment, net	21,271	31.4%	$3,328 – $2,604	21,995	31.4%	CAPEX estimates are from P&G guidance, and depreciation expense is computed as a % of prior year PPE, gross.
Goodwill	40,273	59.5%	no change	40,273	57.5%	Assume no changes because goodwill is not amortized.
Trademarks and other intangible assets, net . . .	24,215	35.8%	($359)	23,856	34.1%	Apply estimated amortization expense from footnotes of P&G.
Other noncurrent assets	6,863	10.1%	no change	6,863	9.8%	Assume no change.
Total assets	$115,095	170.0%	subtotal	$110,095	159.5%	
Current liabilities						
Accounts payable	$ 11,260	16.6%	$70,053 × 16.6%	$ 11,629	16.6%	Forecast working capital accounts
Accrued and other liabilities	9,054	13.4%	$70,053 × 13.4%	9,387	13.4%	as % of sales unless information suggests otherwise.
Debt due within one year	9,697	14.3%	($3,388) + $2,009	8,318	16.1%	Use footnotes to get current maturities of long-term debt. Assume other debt remains unchanged.
Total current liabilities	30,011	44.3%	subtotal	29,334	46.1%	
Long-term debt	20,395	30.1%	($2,009)	18,386	24.3%	Use footnotes to get current maturities of long-term debt to be repaid.
Deferred income taxes	6,899	10.2%	$70,053 × 10.2%	7,145	10.2%	Assume no change as a % of sales.
Other noncurrent liabilities	10,211	15.1%	$70,053 × 15.1%	10,578	15.1%	Assume no change as a % of sales.
Total liabilities	67,516	99.8%	subtotal	65,443	95.7%	
Shareholders' equity						
Convertible Class A preferred stock	928	1.4%	no change	928	1.3%	
Nonvoting Class B preferred stock	0	0.0%	no change	0	0.0%	Assume no change in paid-in capital
Common stock, stated value $1 per share	4,009	5.9%	no change	4,009	5.7%	accounts.
Additional paid-in capital	63,827	94.3%	no change	63,827	91.1%	
Reserve for ESOP debt retirement	(1,146)	(1.7)%	no change	(1,146)	(1.6)%	Assume no change.
Accumulated other comprehensive income (loss)	(14,936)	(22.1)%	no change	(14,936)	(21.3)%	Assume no change.
Treasury stock	(100,406)	(148.3)%	($7,000)	(107,406)	(153.3)%	Use P&G guidance.
Retained earnings	94,918	140.2%	$11,573 – $7,500	98,794	141.0%	Increased by forecasted net income less forecasted dividends.
Noncontrolling interest	385	0.6%	+ $197	582	0.8%	Increased by net income allocated to noncontrolling interests.
Total shareholders' equity	47,579	70.3%	subtotal	44,652	63.7%	
Total liabilities and shareholders' equity	$115,095	170.0%	subtotal	$110,095	159.5%	

* $(1,561) = $110,084 – $6,048 – $5,114 – $5,184 – $2,312 – $21,995 – $40,273 – $23,856 – $6,863.

** To simplify, we forecast accounts as a percent of sales, including inventories and accounts payable. Analysts sometimes use a percent of COGS for inventory and for accounts payable estimates because both are expressed in input (not output) costs. Either approach is reasonable if used consistently. One could also forecast working capital accounts using turnover rates or days as follows:

Forecasted account balance = Forecasted revenues (or COGS)/Turnover rate, or = Forecasted days outstanding × [Forecasted revenues (or COGS)/365]

Depreciation Expense. Depreciation expense is usually reported in the statement of cash flows (or in the notes). (*Note:* If depreciation expense is combined with amortization expense, we can isolate the depreciation component by subtracting amortization expense, which is frequently reported separately in footnotes—or, if not separately reported, we may use the change in accumulated amortization.) It is common to estimate depreciation as:

$$\text{Forecasted depreciation expense} = \frac{\text{Current year depreciation expense}}{\text{Prior year PPE, gross}} \times \text{Current year PPE, gross}$$

P&G's 2019 statement of cash flows reports depreciation and amortization expense of $2,824 million. Footnotes report amortization expense in 2019 of $349 million. Thus, we calculate 2019 depreciation expense as $2,475 million ($2,824 million − $349 million). The PPE footnote reports 2018 PPE, gross of $41,487 million, and 2019 PPE, gross of $43,393 million. We calculate a depreciation expense forecast assumption of 6.0% ($2,475 million expense/$41,487 million PPE, gross) and an estimated 2020 depreciation expense of $2,604 million (6.0% × $43,393 million).

PPE, net. Drawing on the forecasted CAPEX and forecasted depreciation above, the PPE, net is forecasted as:

$$\text{Forecasted PPE, net} = \text{Current PPE, net} + \text{Forecasted CAPEX} - \text{Forecasted depreciation expense}$$

Forecasted 2020 PPE, net is $21,995 million, computed as $21,271 million + $3,328 million − $2,604 million.

Intangible Assets Intangible assets, other than goodwill, are typically forecasted to decrease during the year by the amount of amortization (it is common to assume no change in amortization expense).

$$\text{Forecasted intangible assets} = \text{Current year intangible assets} - \text{Forecasted amortization expense}$$

Alternatively, the company might provide guidance. Footnotes to the P&G's FY2019 Form 10-K provide the following schedule of expected amortization expense that we use for its FY2020 forecast. We forecast that intangible assets will decrease by $359 million in FY2020.

Years Ending June 30 ($ millions)	2020	2021	2022	2023	2024
Estimated amortization expense	**$359**	$309	$290	$278	$267

Long-Term Debt (LTD) Companies report maturities of long-term debt for the next five years in the long-term debt footnote. We use this disclosure to forecast long-term debt:

Forecasted LTD = Current year LTD − Current maturities of LTD

Footnotes to P&G's FY2019 Form 10-K provide the following schedule of maturities of LTD that we use in our forecasts.

Years Ending June 30 ($ millions)	2020	2021	2022	2023	2024
Debt maturities	**$3,388**	**$2,009**	$2,840	$2,465	$2,461

P&G's balance sheet does not separately report current maturities of long-term debt. Instead, the current maturities amount is aggregated with other short-term debt and reported as "Debt due within one year." To forecast current maturities, we subtract $3,388 million from debt due within one year to reflect the amount that matures and will be paid in FY2020. We then add $2,009 million, the amount that comes due in FY2021. We subtract $2,009 million from long-term debt to reflect the reclassification from long-term to current.

Retained Earnings We forecast retained earnings as follows.

= Current year retained earnings + Forecasted net income − Forecasted dividends

Dividends. Companies frequently provide guidance as to expected dividends. If not, a common approach is to estimate dividends using the dividend payout ratio.

$$\text{Forecasted dividends} = \frac{\text{Current year dividends}}{\text{Current year net income}} \times \text{Forecasted net income}$$

This method will be less exact if a company reports significant one-time items. In that case, we exclude the one-time item in the payout ratio calculation. P&G's dividend payout ratio for FY2019, computed on earnings before the intangibles impairment expense, is 60.9% ($7,498 million dividends paid in FY2019 divided by $12,311 million in FY2019 net income before intangibles impairment expense). We estimate FY2020 dividends by applying the FY2019 payout ratio to forecasted net income ($11,365 million × 60.9% = $6,921 million). P&G's guidance is for dividends of "$7.5B+" (see the Company Guidance section). The forecasted dividends of $6,921 million are just slightly below that guidance. We include the guidance in our forecast because it is more precise.

Treasury Stock Many companies have multiyear stock repurchase programs, which are disclosed in footnotes or in the MD&A section of the 10-K. Often, in the year-end press release, companies provide guidance and/or disclosures about their planned treasury stock activity. Absent explicit disclosures or guidance, we can forecast future repurchases using historic data, either from the most recent year or by looking for a trend over the past two or three years. For P&G, we use the midpoint of guidance provided by managers and forecast $7B of additional repurchases in FY2020.

The forecasting process estimates the balances of all assets *other than cash*, all liabilities, and all equity accounts. The last step is to compute the amount of cash needed to balance the balance sheet (the *plug*).

Cash Plug (the *plug*) The **plug** is computed as total assets (equal to total liabilities and equity) less all other asset balances. We assess the forecasted cash balance and determine if it deviates from its historical norm. We use the current year cash-to-sales percentage as a *normal* level of cash. This assumes the amount reported in the current balance sheet represents an appropriate level of cash the company needs to conduct its operations.

Estimating the Normal Cash Level P&G's cash balance in 2019 is $4,239 million or 6.3% of 2019 sales. Applying that percentage to our forecasted sales of $70,053 million yields a normal level of cash of $4,413 million ($70,053 million × 6.3%). Our forecasted cash balance of $(1,550) million in Exhibit 12.3 is, therefore, too low.

When Cash Plug Deviates from Norm When the forecasted cash level deviates from the target cash balance, we can consider adjusting the forecasted cash balance in two ways.

- **Cash balance much HIGHER than normal** This indicates the company is generating more cash than expected, most typically from operations. Our forecasts might assume that such excess liquidity can be invested in marketable securities, used to pay down debt, repurchase stock, increase dividend payments, or any combination of these actions.

- **Cash balance much LOWER than normal** This indicates the company is not generating sufficient cash, usually as a result of net losses, significant dividend payments, stock repurchases, and/or operating assets increasing more than operating liabilities; remember, we are assuming no changes in debt and equity levels for our initial forecast. To return cash to normal levels, we might expect the company would borrow money, sell stock, and/or liquidate marketable securities. Under those assumptions, we would adjust the forecasted balance sheet by increasing cash to a normal level and adjust debt or equity to reflect the means by which additional cash was raised. Alternatively, we might expect the company would reduce dividends, cut capital expenditures, slash inventory and/or take other operating action. Raising cash in this way likely has serious costs and, for that reason, we rarely make assumptions of this sort. It is more likely the company would raise cash through investing and financing activities.

In Appendix 12B, we illustrate a method to achieve a target level of cash in our multiyear forecasts. The method involves adding debt to the balance sheet and adjusting interest expense on the income statement as needed.

Maintaining the Capital Structure When we adjust cash by forecasting an increase or decrease in debt and/or stock, we might inadvertently impact the company's capital structure—namely, the proportion of debt and equity. If we assume the company's current capital structure is appropriate, we should attempt to maintain that historic debt-to-equity ratio when we forecast additional borrowing, debt repayment, stock sales, or stock repurchases.

LO3 Review 12-3

Refer to the FY2019 income statement and balance sheet for General Mills along with the forecasted FY2020 income statement in Reviews 12-1 and 12-2.

Required
1. Use that information and the following assumptions to forecast General Mills balance sheet for FY2020.
- Unless noted in other assumptions, all assets and liabilities as a percentage of FY2019 sales remain unchanged.
- Depreciation expense for FY2020 is $580.1 million.
- Forecast FY2020 CAPEX as 3.19% of sales.
- Goodwill remains unchanged.
- Form 10-K reports that amortization expense for each of the next five fiscal years will be $40 million.
- Notes payable remain unchanged.
- Long-term debt footnotes reveal that principal payments due on long-term debt in the next five years follow ($ millions).

Year Ending May	2020	2021	2022	2023	2024
Debt maturities	$1,396.5	$2,114.4	$1,224.1	$1,060.2	$1,750.0

- There will be no stock repurchases in FY2020.
- Dividends in FY2020 are forecasted as 67.4% of net income attributable to General Mills' shareholders.
- Noncontrolling interest will increase by $33.5 million, the amount forecast as noncontrolling interest on the income statement (from Review 12-2).

2. What conclusion do we draw from the forecasted cash balance?

Solution on p. 12-52.

Building Forecasts from the Bottom Up

The sales forecast that we illustrate above relies on company guidance to form assumptions and estimates. An alternative approach that financial analysts typically use relies on information from conference calls with company management and other proprietary data sources. Analysts often prepare separate sales forecasts for the company's business segments and then sum up the segment sales to arrive at the overall sales estimate.

eLectures LO4
Prepare forecasts using segment data.

Segment Data

Companies are required to report financial data for each operating segment and to reconcile the segment totals to the reported amounts in the income statement and balance sheet for the company as a whole. Financial analysts frequently develop the sales forecasts as the sum of forecasts for the company's operating segments.[2] P&G's 10-K segment disclosure includes the following table of current and historical data for each of its five operating segments.

---

[2] GAAP defines an **operating segment** as "a component of a public entity that has all of the following characteristics. (1) It engages in business activities from which it may earn revenues and incur expenses (including revenues and expenses relating to transactions with other components of the same public entity). (2) Its operating results are regularly reviewed by the public entity's chief operating decision maker to make decisions about resources to be allocated to the segment and assess its performance. (3) Its discrete financial information is available."

Global Segment Results ($ millions)		Net Sales	Earnings (Loss) from Continuing Operations Before Income Taxes	Net Earnings (Loss) from Continuing Operations	Depreciation and Amortization	Total Assets	Capital Expenditures
Beauty	2019	$12,897	$ 3,282	$ 2,637	$ 272	$ 5,362	$ 634
	2018	12,406	3,042	2,320	236	4,709	766
	2017	11,429	2,546	1,914	220	4,184	599
Grooming	2019	6,199	1,777	1,529	429	20,882	367
	2018	6,551	1,801	1,432	447	22,609	364
	2017	6,642	1,985	1,537	433	22,759	341
Health Care	2019	8,218	1,984	1,519	294	7,708	363
	2018	7,857	1,922	1,283	230	5,254	330
	2017	7,513	1,898	1,280	209	5,194	283
Fabric & Home Care	2019	22,080	4,601	3,518	557	7,620	984
	2018	21,441	4,191	2,708	534	7,295	1,020
	2017	20,717	4,249	2,713	513	6,886	797
Baby, Feminine & Family Care	2019	17,806	3,593	2,734	861	9,271	819
	2018	18,080	3,527	2,251	899	9,682	1,016
	2017	18,252	3,868	2,503	874	9,920	1,197
Corporate	2019	484	(9,168)	(7,971)	411	64,252	180
	2018	497	(1,157)	(133)	488	68,761	221
	2017	505	(1,289)	247	571	71,463	167
Total company	2019	$67,684	$ 6,069	$ 3,966	$2,824	$115,095	$3,347
	2018	66,832	13,326	9,861	2,834	118,310	3,717
	2017	65,058	13,257	10,194	2,820	120,406	3,384

Instead of using only trends in the top line of the income statement, sales growth forecasts are more accurate when they incorporate *all* available data. In P&G's case, its product lines segment disclosures provide a wealth of information that can be used to forecast sales for each operating segment; and then summing the segment forecasts yields top line sales forecasts.

To illustrate, Morgan Stanley analysts use both published data (such as the segment disclosures) and proprietary databases to forecast sales growth *by product segment* and *by quarter*. Following is an excerpt from its forecasting spreadsheet for P&G's Beauty segment.

	A	B	BO	BT	BY	CD	CI	CN	CO	CP	CQ	CR	CS
1	Procter & Gamble Co. (PG)												
5	Segment Breakdown		FY2014	FY2015	FY2016	FY2017	FY2018	FY2019	Sep-19E	Dec-19E	Mar-20E	Jun-20E	FY2020E
15	Beauty Care		13,398.0	12,608.0	11,477.0	11,429.0	12,406.0	12,897.0	3,463.2	3,529.0	3,181.4	3,325.8	13,499.5
16	Organic Sales Growth		0.0 %	−1.2 %	0.2 %	3.0 %	6.5 %	8.0 %	5.0 %	4.5 %	4.0 %	4.0 %	4.4 %
17	Volume (Organic)		0.3 %	−2.9 %	−1.9 %	1.3 %	1.5 %	1.7 %	2.0 %	2.0 %	2.0 %	2.0 %	2.0 %
18	Pricing		0.2 %	2.2 %	2.0 %	0.7 %	0.0 %	2.0 %	2.0 %	1.5 %	1.0 %	1.0 %	1.4 %
19	Mix		−0.5 %	−0.5 %	0.3 %	1.3 %	5.0 %	4.3 %	1.0 %	1.0 %	1.0 %	1.0 %	1.0 %
20	FX Impact		−2.2 %	−5.1 %	−5.6 %	−1.8 %	2.2 %	−4.2 %	0.3 %	0.6 %	−0.1 %	0.3 %	0.3 %
21	Acq/Div		0.0 %	−0.3 %	−3.7 %	−2.0 %	0.0 %	0.3 %	0.0 %	0.0 %	0.0 %	0.0 %	0.0 %
22	% Sales Growth		−32.9 %	−5.9 %	−9.0 %	−0.4 %	8.5 %	4.0 %	5.3 %	5.1 %	3.9 %	4.3 %	4.7 %

We see that Morgan Stanley analysts forecast organic sales growth, including the effects of changes in *unit volume*, the effects of expected *price increases,* and the effects, if any, of expected changes in *product mix*. Their forecast includes an expected foreign-currency increase of 0.3% and no acquisition effects for that segment. In sum, Morgan Stanley analysts forecast an increase in net sales of 4.7% for the Beauty segment from $12,897 million to $13,500 million—consisting of the following components.

Organic sales growth	4.4%
Volume (organic)	2.0%
Pricing	1.4%
Mix	1.0%
Foreign exchange impact	0.3%
Acquisitions and divestitures	0.0%
Sales growth	4.7%

Similar estimates are made for the other four operating segments. Top line sales growth estimates then are the sum of sales estimates for the five operating segments along with the corporate entity.

	A	B	BO	BT	BY	CD	CI	CN	CO	CP	CQ	CR	CS
1	Procter & Gamble Co. (PG)												
3													
5	**Segment Breakdown**		FY2014	FY2015	FY2016	FY2017	FY2018	FY2019	Sep-19E	Dec-19E	Mar-20E	Jun-20E	FY2020E
6	**Total Sales**		74,401.0	70,752.0	65,299.0	65,058.0	66,832.0	67,684.0	17,718.8	18,519.8	16,987.5	17,682.9	70,909.0
7	Organic Sales Growth		2.6 %	1.6 %	0.8 %	2.2 %	1.3 %	5.2 %	4.0 %	3.9 %	3.3 %	3.2 %	3.6 %
8	Volume (Organic)		2.4 %	−1.0 %	−1.2 %	2.4 %	1.6 %	2.3 %	2.0 %	2.0 %	2.1 %	2.0 %	2.0 %
9	Pricing		0.7 %	1.7 %	1.5 %	−0.3 %	−1.1 %	1.5 %	1.6 %	1.5 %	0.8 %	0.8 %	1.2 %
10	Mix		−0.5 %	0.9 %	0.2 %	0.1 %	0.7 %	1.3 %	0.4 %	0.4 %	0.3 %	0.4 %	0.4 %
11	FX Impact		−2.5 %	−5.9 %	−6.2 %	−1.9 %	1.9 %	−3.7 %	0.3 %	0.6 %	−0.1 %	0.3 %	0.3 %
12	Acq/Div		−0.2 %	−0.2 %	−1.9 %	−0.7 %	−0.4 %	−0.1 %	1.9 %	1.7 %	0.0 %	0.0 %	0.9 %
13	% Sales Growth		−9.9 %	−4.9 %	−7.7 %	−0.4 %	2.7 %	1.3 %	6.2 %	6.2 %	3.2 %	3.4 %	4.8 %

For FY2020, Morgan Stanley analysts forecast total sales growth of 4.8%. This estimate is about 1 percentage point higher than the assumption we used in our forecast, by using the midpoint of company guidance. The Morgan Stanley assumption (4.8%) includes an estimate for foreign currency effects and acquisitions that the company guidance does not include.

LO4 Review 12-4

Refer to the following information for **General Mills** to answer the requirements. The segment information footnote to General Mills' 2019 10-K reports the following sales for operating units within the company's North America retail segment.

In millions	2019	2018
U.S. Meals & Baking	$3,839.8	$ 3,865.7
U.S. Cereal	2,255.4	2,251.8
U.S. Snacks	2,060.9	2,140.5
U.S. Yogurt and other	906.7	927.4
Canada	862.4	930.0
Total	$9,925.2	$10,115.4

We assume the following estimates for growth in units for each segment.

U.S. Meals & Baking	1.5%
U.S. Cereal	2.0%
U.S. Snacks	(0.5)%
U.S. Yogurt and other	1.0%
Canada	(1.0)%

Required

a. Forecast FY2020 sales for each of the five segments. What will FY2020 sales be for the total U.S. retail segment?

b. What is the overall forecasted growth rate for the total U.S. retail segment?

Solution on p. 12-53.

Appendix 12A: Forecasting the Statement of Cash Flows

eLectures
MBC **LO5**
Forecast the
statement of
cash flows.

Forecasting the statement of cash flows is useful for a number of planning and control activities, including cash management, operating budgets, and capital budgeting decisions (CAPEX). To prepare the forecasted statement of cash flows, we use our forecasts of the income statement and balance sheet and then follow the preparation procedures explained in the statement of cash flow module. That process begins with net income, adds back or deducts any noncash expenses or revenues, and then recognizes the cash flow effect of changes in working capital followed by changes in the remaining asset, liability, and equity items. A common method is to compute changes in each of the line items on the forecasted balance sheet and then classify those changes to either the operating, investing, or financing sections of the forecasted statement of cash flows.

Exhibit 12A.1 shows the forecasted statement of cash flows for Procter & Gamble. It reveals operating cash flows of $15,427 million, investing cash outflows of $3,328 million, and a large financing cash outflow of $17,888 million.

Exhibit 12A.1 ■ One-Year Forecast of P&G's Statement of Cash Flows

Statement of Cash Flows
For Fiscal Year Ended 2020

$ millions	Computations	2020 Est.
Cash flow from operating activities		
Net income		$11,573
Add: Depreciation.		2,604
Add: Amortization		359
Change in accounts receivable	$4,951 − $5,114	(163)
Change in inventories.	$5,017 − $5,184	(167)
Change in prepaid expenses and other current	$2,218 − $2,312	(94)
Change in accounts payable	$11,629 − $11,260	369
Change in accrued other liabilities	$9,387 − $9,054	333
Change in deferred income taxes.	$7,145 − $6,899	246
Change in other noncurrent liabilities	$10,578 − $10,211	367
Net cash from operating activities		15,427
Capital expenditures.	$70,053 × 4.75%	(3,328)
Change in available-for-sale securities.	no change	0
Net cash from investing activities		(3,328)
Dividends		(7,500)
Increase in short-term debt.		(1,379)
Decrease in long-term debt		(2,009)
Purchase of treasury shares.		(7,000)
Net cash from financing activities.		(17,888)
Net change in cash.		(5,789)
Beginning cash.		4,239
Ending cash		$ (1,550)

The forecasted statement of cash flows highlights financing cash outflows as the main cause for the forecasted decline in cash. While operating cash flows continue to be strong, P&G's guidance includes plans to continue to repurchase common stock (approximately $7,000 million), pay dividends (approximately $7,500 million), and purchase CAPEX (approximately $3,328 million). In this first forecasting iteration, we forecast a decrease in cash of $(5,789) million, which reduces P&G's cash balance from $4,239 million to $(1,550) million. The drop in cash arises due to the planned outflows for CAPEX, the payment of dividends, and the repurchase of stock with no borrowings forecasted at this point. Such a low cash balance is not plausible. In Appendix 12B, we discuss how to modify the forecasts to derive an appropriate cash balance.

Business Insight ■ Do Currency Fluctuations Affect Cash Flow?

A stronger $US vis-à-vis other world currencies results in less income as foreign currency-denominated revenues are translated into fewer $US. As sales decline, so do profits. Because net income is the first line in the statement of cash flows, it is reasonable to ask whether the profit decline resulting from a strengthening $US implies P&G's cash flows will also decline. If so, we would expect such a decline to affect P&G's stock price. The short answer is that it is unlikely that P&G's cash flows will be greatly affected.

Before companies can consolidate their foreign subsidiaries, the foreign-currency denominated subsidiary income statements, balance sheets, and statements of cash flows must first be translated to $US equivalents. To accomplish this, each financial statement item is multiplied by an exchange rate to yield the $US equivalent. We can think of the translation process as a spreadsheet with the foreign currency-denominated subsidiary financial statements in the first column, the exchange rate in the second, and the $US equivalent financial statements in the third, as the product of the first two columns. There are no transactions involved in this process, so it is reasonable to expect there to be no effect on cash flow from the translation process.

So, why does the forecasted decline in profit not result in a decline in cash flow? P&G's balance sheet also shrinks with the strengthening $US, and the reduction in net assets (recorded as a cash *inflow* in the statement of cash flows) exactly offsets the reduction in profit (recorded as a cash *outflow*), leaving net cash unaffected, just as we would expect given there are no transactions in the translation process.

LO5 Review 12-5

Refer to the FY2019 income statement and balance sheet for General Mills along with its forecasted FY2020 income statement and balance sheet in Reviews 12-1, 12-2, and 12-3.

Required
Use that information to prepare the General Mills' forecasted statement of cash flows for FY2020.

Solution on p. 12-54.

Appendix 12B: Multiyear Forecasting with Target Cash and New Debt Financing

Exhibit 12B.1 shows the mechanics to forecast financial statements for more than one year ahead. Forecasting for multiple years proceeds in the same way as for one-year forecasting, illustrated above. Analysts typically need multiyear forecasts to value a firm's equity valuation, assess its ability to repay its debt, and to assign a credit rating. Managers also typically use multiyear forecasts in the planning process, including cash flow budgeting, capital expenditure plans, divestiture decisions, and mergers and acquisitions.

LO6 Prepare multiyear forecasts.

Consistent with the one-year-ahead forecasts, we balance the balance sheet with a "plug" to the cash account. We extend this example to illustrate the process to adjust the cash balance to a "normal" level, in this case by adding debt.

How much cash is "normal"? We assume that the cash-to-sales ratio in the current financial statements represents the company's "target" cash level. That is, we assume the company has made appropriate financing decisions to achieve the optimal level of cash in the current year. For FY2019, the reported cash balance of $4,239 million is 6.3% of reported sales of $67,684. If the company maintains the same level of cash as a percentage of forecasted sales, the target level of cash will be $4,413 (forecasted FY2020 sales of $70,053 × 6.3%). In Exhibit 12.3, our forecasted cash balance is $(1,550) million. Consequently, we assume additional borrowing of $6,000 million (rounded up). This additional borrowing is necessary to achieve the target cash-to-sales percentage of 6.3% because P&G will not generate sufficient cash from operating activities to cover forecasted CAPEX, debt payments, dividend payments, and anticipated repurchases of stock. With additional debt, forecasted interest expense will increase by $51 million ($6,000 million × 1.7%/2), assuming an average interest rate of 1.7% and borrowing evenly over the year. With the additional debt and after tax interest, the forecasted cash balance is $4,408 million, 6.3% of forecasted sales.

To forecast FY2021, we use the same methodology that we use for our one-year forecast. We start by forecasting sales for FY2021, assuming growth will continue to be 3.5%. We assume that expenses increase proportionately, that CAPEX will remain at the same percentage of sales, that dividends will be $7,500 million, and that the company will repurchase $7,000 million of stock. With a target cash-to-sales of 6.3%, we forecast additional borrowings of $4,150 million.

Exhibit 12B.1 ■ Forecast of P&G's FY2020 and FY2021 Income Statements and Balance Sheets

Income Statements ($ millions)	2019 Act.	% of Sales	Computations	2020 Est.	% of Sales	Computations	2021 Est.	% of Sales
Net sales	$67,684	100.0%	$67,684 × 1.035	$70,053	100.0%	$70,053 × 1.035	$72,505	100.0%
Cost of products sold	34,768	51.4%	$70,053 × 51.4%	36,007	51.4%	$72,505 × 51.4%	37,268	51.4%
Selling, general, and administrative expense	19,084	28.2%	$70,053 × 28.2%	19,755	28.2%	$72,505 × 28.2%	20,446	28.2%
Goodwill & indefinite lived intangibles impairment charges	8,345	12.3%	none	0		none	0	0.0%
Operating income	5,487	8.1%	subtotal	14,291	20.4%	subtotal	14,791	20.4%
Interest expense	509	0.8%	computed	534	0.8%	computed	574	0.8%
Interest income	220	0.3%	no change	220	0.3%	no change	220	0.3%
Other nonoperating income, net	871	1.3%	none	0	0.0%	none	0	0.0%
Earnings from continuing operations before income taxes	6,069	9.0%	subtotal	13,977	20.0%	subtotal	14,437	19.9%
Income taxes on continuing operations	2,103	3.1%	$13,977 × 17.5%	2,446	3.5%	$14,437 × 17.5%	2,526	3.5%
Net earnings	3,966	5.9%	subtotal	11,531	16.4%	subtotal	11,911	16.4%
Less: net earnings attributable to noncontrolling interests	69	0.1%	$11,531 × 1.7%	196	0.3%	$11,911 × 1.7%	202	0.3%
Net earnings attributable to Procter & Gamble	$ 3,897	5.8%	subtotal	$11,335	16.2%	subtotal	$11,709	16.1%

Balance Sheets ($ millions)	2019 Act.	% of Sales	Computations	2020 Est.	% of Sales	Computations	2021 Est.	% of Sales
Current assets								
Cash and cash equivalents	$ 4,239	6.3%	Plug	$ 4,408	6.3%	Plug	$ 4,544	6.3%
Available-for-sale investment securities	6,048	8.9%	no change	6,048	8.6%	no change	6,048	8.3%
Accounts receivable	4,951	7.3%	$70,053 × 7.3%	5,114	7.3%	$72,505 × 7.3%	5,293	7.3%
Inventories	5,017	7.4%	$70,053 × 7.4%	5,184	7.4%	$72,505 × 7.4%	5,365	7.4%
Prepaid expenses and other current assets	2,218	3.3%	$70,053 × 3.3%	2,312	3.3%	$72,505 × 3.3%	2,393	3.3%
Total current assets	22,473	33.2%		23,066	32.9%		23,643	32.6%
Property, plant, and equipment, net	21,271	31.4%	$3,328 – $2,604	21,995	31.4%	$3,444 – $2,803	22,636	31.2%
Goodwill	40,273	59.5%	no change	40,273	57.5%	no change	40,273	55.5%
Trademarks and other intangible assets, net	24,215	35.8%	($359)	23,856	34.1%	($309)	23,547	32.5%
Other noncurrent assets	6,863	10.1%	no change	6,863	9.8%	no change	6,863	9.5%
Total assets	$115,095	170.0%	total	$116,053	165.7%	total	$116,962	161.3%
Current liabilities								
Accounts payable	11,260	16.6%	$70,053 × 16.6%	$ 11,629	16.6%	$72,505 × 16.6%	$ 12,036	16.6%
Accrued and other liabilities	9,054	13.4%	$70,053 × 13.4%	9,387	13.4%	$72,505 × 13.4%	9,716	13.4%
Debt due within one year	9,697	14.3%	($3,388) + $2,009	8,318	11.9%	($2,009) + $2,840	9,149	12.6%
Total current liabilities	30,011	44.3%		29,334	41.9%		30,901	42.6%
Long-term debt	20,395	30.1%	$6,000 – $2,009	24,386	34.8%	$4,150 – $2,840	25,696	35.4%
Deferred income taxes	6,899	10.2%	$70,053 × 10.2%	7,145	10.2%	$72,505 × 10.2%	7,396	10.2%
Other noncurrent liabilities	10,211	15.1%	$70,053 × 15.1%	10,578	15.1%	$72,505 × 15.1%	10,948	15.1%
Total liabilities	67,516	99.8%	subtotal	71,443	102.0%	subtotal	74,941	103.4%
Shareholders' equity								
Convertible Class A preferred stock	928	1.4%	no change	928		no change	928	1.5%
Nonvoting Class B preferred stock								
Common stock, stated value $1 per share	4,009	5.9%	no change	4,009	5.7%	no change	4,009	5.5%
Additional paid-in capital	63,827	94.3%	no change	63,827	91.1%	no change	63,827	88.0%
Reserve for ESOP debt retirement	(1,146)	(1.7)%	no change	(1,146)	(1.6)%	no change	(1,146)	(1.6)%
Accumulated other comprehensive income (loss)	(14,936)	(22.1)%	no change	(14,936)	(21.3)%	no change	(14,936)	(20.6)%
Treasury stock, at cost	(100,406)	(148.3)%	($7,000)	(107,406)	(153.3)%	($7,000)	(114,406)	(157.8)%
Retained earnings	94,918	140.2%	$11,335 – $7,500	98,753	141.0%	$11,709 – $7,500	102,962	142.0%
Noncontrolling interest	385	0.6%	+ $196	581	0.8%	+ $202	783	1.1%
Total shareholders' equity	47,579	70.3%	subtotal	44,610	63.7%	subtotal	42,021	58.0%
Total liabilities and shareholders' equity	$115,095	170.0%	total	$116,053	165.7%	total	$116,962	161.3%

Forecasting Sensitivity Analysis Analysts commonly perform a sensitivity analysis of their forecasts. Typically, analysts prepare additional forecasts (characterized as Bull and Bear scenarios) and present these together with their "most likely" scenario forecasts. The forecasted cash flow and resulting stock price estimates are, then, recomputed under these additional assumptions to develop a possible range of stock prices that are included in the analyst's report. We provide an example of this sensitivity analysis in Appendix 12D that provides excerpts from the Morgan Stanley analysis report on P&G following its FY2019 year-end.

LO4 Review 12-6

Refer to the FY2019 income statement and balance sheet for General Mills along with the forecasted FY2020 income statement and balance sheet, in Reviews 12-1, 12-2, and 12-3.

Required

a. Adjust the 2020 forecasted financial statements to:
- Increase the current portion of long-term debt by $700 million so the ending cash balance is at the prior year cash-to-sales target of 2.7%.
- Increase interest expense due to the new debt, calculated as $700 million × (3.4%/2), which is the average new borrowing multiplied by the prior year average interest rate.

b. Forecast the 2021 balance sheet and income statement using the following assumptions:
- Sales will increase by 1.5% in FY2021.
- Operating expenses as a percentage of sales will remain unchanged from FY2020 levels.
- Restructuring, impairment, and other exit costs are expected to be 1.6% of forecasted sales.
- Add $2,100 million of additional short-term debt to achieve the targeted cash balance of approximately 2.7% of sales. Adjust interest by adding a half-year interest on the additional short-term debt using 3.4% with the same adjustment to interest expense that we used for 2020.
- Dividend payments will be 67.4% of forecasted net income attributable to General Mills' shareholders.
- CAPEX will be 3.19% of forecasted sales and depreciation expense will be $588.8 million.
- Current maturities of LTD are $1,224.1 million for 2021.

Solution on p. 12-54.

Appendix 12C: Parsimonious Method for Forecasting NOPAT and NOA

This appendix explains a parsimonious method to obtain forecasts for net operating profit after tax (NOPAT) and for net operating assets (NOA). This method requires three crucial inputs.

eLectures **LO7**
MBC Apply a parsimonious method for forecasting net operating profit and net operating assets.

1. Sales growth.
2. Net operating profit margin (NOPM); defined in Module 4 as NOPAT divided by sales.
3. Net operating asset turnover (NOAT); defined in Module 4 as sales divided by average NOA. (For forecasting purposes, we define NOAT as sales divided by *year-end* NOA instead of average NOA because we want to forecast year-end values.)

Multiyear Forecasting with Parsimonious Method

We use Procter & Gamble's 2019 income statement from Exhibit 12.2, and its 2019 balance sheet from Exhibit 12.3, to determine the following measures. P&G's 2019 income statement includes a pretax goodwill impairment of $8,345 million, which is a nonrecurring item. The Form 10-K reports that the impairment is $8,000 million after-tax; we add this back to calculate a measure of persistent NOPAT. We assume that P&G's statutory tax rate is 22% on nonoperating revenues and expenses.

$ millions	2019
Sales.	$67,684
NOPAT ($5,487 + $8,000 − [$2,103 + ($509 − $220 − $871) × 22%]).	$11,512
NOA ($115,095 − $4,239 − $6,048 − $11,260 − $9,054 − $6,899 − $10,211)*.	$67,384
NOPM ($11,512/$67,384).	17%
NOAT ($67,684/$67,384)*.	1.00

*We use ending balance sheet amounts, rather than average amounts, because we forecast *ending* balance sheet amounts.

Each year's forecasted sales is the prior year sales multiplied successively by (1 + growth rate) and then rounded to whole digits. Consistent with our prior revenue growth rate assumptions for P&G, we define "1 + growth rate" as 1.035 for 2020 onward. NOPAT is computed using forecasted (and rounded) sales each year times the 2019 NOPM of 17%; and NOA is computed using forecasted (and rounded) sales divided by the 2019 NOAT of 1.00. Forecasted numbers for 2020–2023 are in Exhibit 12C.1; supporting computations are in parentheses.

This forecasting process can be continued for any desired forecast horizon. Also, the forecast assumptions such as sales growth, NOPM, and NOAT can be varied by year, if desired. This parsimonious method is simpler than the method illustrated in this module. However, its simplicity forgoes information that can improve forecast accuracy.

Exhibit 12C.1 ■ P&G Parsimonious Method Forecasts of Sales, NOPAT, and NOA

$ millions	Current 2019	Horizon Period			
		2020 Est.	2021 Est.	2022 Est.	2023 Est.
Net sales growth.......		3.5%	3.5%	3.5%	3.5%
Sales (unrounded)	$67,684	**$70,052.94**	**$72,504.79**	**$75,042.46**	**$77,668.95**
		($67,684 × 1.035)	($70,052.94 × 1.035)	($72,504.79 ×1.035)	($75,042.46 × 1.035)
Sales (rounded)	$67,684	**$70,053**	**$72,505**	**$75,042**	**$77,669**
NOPAT[1]	$11,512	**$11,909**	**$12,326**	**$12,757**	**$13,204**
		($70,053 × 17%)	($72,505 × 17%)	($75,042 × 17%)	($77,669 × 17%)
NOA[2]	$67,384	**$70,053**	**$72,505**	**$75,042**	**$77,669**
		($70,053/1.0)	($72,505/1.0)	($75,042/1.0)	($77,669/1.0)

[1] Forecasted NOPAT = Forecasted net sales (rounded) × 2019 NOPM of 17%

[2] Forecasted NOA = Forecasted net sales (rounded) ÷ 2019 NOAT of 1.0

Review 12-7 LO6

Refer to Review 12-1 and the fiscal 2019 income statement and balance sheet for General Mills (GIS).

a. The 2019 income statement includes two nonpersistent items: Diverstiture loss and Restructuring. Assume that these are not expected to recur and that the after-tax amounts for these items are $24.4 million and $224.0 million respectively. Adjust net income (after-tax) to eliminate these two one-time items. Use the adjusted net income to calculate NOPAT and NOPM. Assume a marginal tax rate of 23%.

b. Assume a sales growth rate of 1.5% and NOAT of 0.77. Use the parsimonious forecast model to project General Mill's sales, NOPAT, and NOA for 2020 through 2023.

Solution on p. 12-55.

Appendix 12D: Morgan Stanley's Forecast Report on Procter & Gamble

Following is the Morgan Stanley analysts' report on Procter & Gamble that the firm issued on July 31, 2018 (pages 9–13 of the report consist of the customary disclosure information typical of analyst reports). *Please note that materials that are referenced herein comprise excerpts from Morgan Stanley research reports. MS has provided their materials here as a courtesy. Therefore, MS and Cambridge do not undertake to advise you of changes in the opinions or information set forth in these materials. These materials should not be relied on as investment advice. These materials are only as current as the publication date of the underlying Morgan Stanley research. For important disclosures, stock price charts, and equity rating histories regarding companies that are the subject of the underlying Morgan Stanley research, see www.morganstanley.com/researchdisclosures.*

Morgan Stanley | RESEARCH

July 31, 2019 10:00 AM GMT

Procter & Gamble Co. | North America

Reiterate OW; PG Results are Head and Shoulders Above Peers

MORGAN STANLEY & CO. LLC

Dara Mohsenian, CFA
EQUITY ANALYST
Dara.Mohsenian@morganstanley.com   +1 212 761-6575

Filippo Falorni, CFA
RESEARCH ASSOCIATE
Filippo.Falorni@morganstanley.com   +1 212 296-4965

Scott Rotondi
RESEARCH ASSOCIATE
Scott.Rotondi@morganstanley.com   +1 212 761-9196

Sydney A Adams
RESEARCH ASSOCIATE
Sydney.Adams@morganstanley.com   +1-212-761-1727

⬈ Stock Rating	◉ Industry View	◉ Price Target
Overweight	Cautious	$129.00

Robust 4Q topline results support our view that PG's organic sales growth trajectory has sustainably improved, which when combined with inflecting gross margins, should drive above peer EPS growth. Relative valuation vs. HPC peers remains compelling despite stock outperformance. Reiterate OW.

WHAT'S CHANGED	Procter & Gamble Co. (PG.N)	From	To
	Price Target	$120.00	**$129.00**

Strong, High Quality Quarter: Following a substantial topline and EPS beat vs. fiscal Q4 consensus, PG's stock rose 4% (vs. the S&P 500 -0.3%), with very strong +7.0% (7.5% un-rounded) organic sales growth in 4Q (vs. +5% market expectations) and a gross margin inflection (+120 bps yoy and 65 bps above consensus) offset by greater than expected reinvestment on the profit line, while EPS was bolstered by below the profit line items, including a lower tax rate. Topline strength was driven by above-consensus sales in nearly every division and was PG's best organic sales growth in 13 years. PG's gross margin increase of +120 bps y-o-y was also the best result so far in US CPG this EPS season (above +110 bps at KMB and +30 bps at CL). Growth was led by Health Care (10%), Fabric and Home Care (10%), and Beauty (8%) but was broad-based with 8 of PG's 10 global categories gaining or holding share and a weighted avg market share gain of +21 bps y-o-y vs 5 bps last quarter and a 7 bp four quarter trailing average. Untracked channel growth was particularly strong with 25% organic sales growth, with e-commerce now 8% of sales mix, and strong club channel trends. Along with broad based strength across PG's portfolio and a confident tone on the growth outlook, PG was constructive on the HPC industry environment given: (a) healthy market topline growth, (b) price realization is improving, evident in PG's results and the HPC industry more broadly, and (c) promotional intensity is down on a y-o-y basis, particularly in the US, where category levels have indexed at 94 vs the prior year (and PG at 92). While pricing will likely dissipate from here as PG cycles increases and as promotion picks up with lower commodities, it sounds like the pricing environment has remained very rational so far. Net, 4Q results give us greater conviction in our call that PG organic topline growth has sustainably rebounded and GM's are inflecting, the

Procter & Gamble Co. (PG.N, PG US)

Household & Personal Care / United States of America

Stock Rating	Overweight
Industry View	Cautious
Price target	$129.00
Shr price, close (Jul 30, 2019)	$120.41
Mkt cap, curr (mm)	$319,251
52-Week Range	$121.75-78.49

Fiscal Year Ending	06/19	06/20e	06/21e	06/22e
ModelWare EPS ($)	4.52	4.86	5.07	5.33
P/E	24.3	24.8	23.7	22.6
EPS ($)§	4.47	4.74	5.05	5.51
Div yld (%)	2.5	2.4	2.5	2.6

Unless otherwise noted, all metrics are based on Morgan Stanley ModelWare framework
§ = Consensus data is provided by Thomson Reuters Estimates
e = Morgan Stanley Research estimates

QUARTERLY MODELWARE EPS ($)

Quarter	2019	2020e Prior	2020e Current	2021e Prior	2021e Current
Q1	1.12	1.21	1.26	1.29	1.32
Q2	1.25	1.34	1.37	1.42	1.43
Q3	1.06	1.09	1.11	1.16	1.16
Q4	1.10	1.08	1.12	1.15	1.17

e = Morgan Stanley Research estimates

Morgan Stanley | RESEARCH

key drivers of our OW thesis. We see PG's stock as still compelling here, at a discounted P/E to CL and CLX despite clearly superior LT topline/EPS growth in our minds.

Raising EPS Estimates: Post initial FY20 guidance and strong Q4 results, we are raising FY20 EPS by 3% to $4.86, in the upper half of PG's $4.70-$4.92 range. Our PT increases $9 to $129 due to higher EPS and an increased multiple (26x CY20e) given greater confidence in higher PG growth than peers.

Q4 Details: PG Q4 core EPS of $1.10 was above the $1.05 consensus ($1.06 MSe) and very high quality as large topline upside, on robust +7.5% unrounded (7% rounded) organic sales growth, and a 65 bp GM beat, was mostly offset by greater than expected SG&A, driving an in-line (+0.3%) profit beat vs. consensus. EPS upside was driven by below the profit line items including a lower tax rate that flattered EPS by 3 cents vs our model. Organic sales growth of +7% (or ~7.5% un-rounded) came in far ahead of consensus of +4.3% (and 5% street expectations), while +4.25% two-year average growth also accelerated vs. +2.8% in the first three quarters of 2019. Topline growth was balanced with 3% price, 3% volume, and 2% mix. Pricing improved sequentially, up +3% vs. +2% in 3Q19, +1% in 2Q19, flat in 1Q19 and a -2% y-o-y decline in 2H18. A reported +1.4% topline beat was boosted by better than expected gross margins, which expanded a large +120 bps yoy, including -40 bps of FX, +200 bps from productivity, +160 bps from pricing, -60 bps from commodities, -120 bps of unfavorable product mix and other, and -20 bps of innovation reinvestment. Core SG&A as a % of sales decreased -20 bps yoy (worse than the -100 bps consensus, largely driven by reinvestment), including +30 bps of unfavorable FX, with -190 bps from sales leverage, -140 bps of marketing expense and overhead savings, -100 bps from the gain on Boston real estate, +170 bps from marketing reinvestment, +180 bps from capability investment in sales, R&D, and higher compensation costs, and +30 bps from Merck OTC costs. Net, operating profit beat consensus by ~0.3%, with OM's +132 bps y-o-y, as PG clearly reinvested gross profit upside.

Strong Segment Results: PG results were strong across all segments, with upside vs. consensus in each segment. Beauty was up a strong +8% (volume +1%, price +2%, mix +5%), vs. consensus of +6.8%, with Skin and Personal Care organic sales up +mid-teens driven by growth of the super-premium SK-II brand and Olay Skin Care and increased pricing, while Hair Care organic sales increased +LSD%. Health Care was +10% (volume +3%, price +3%, mix +4%), vs. consensus of +4.6%, with Personal Health Care up mid-teens due to innovation, a late season increase in cough and cold incidents and favorable mix due to higher growth in developed regions and Oral Care up +HSD% on premium innovation and positive mix. Fabric & Home Care was up +10% (volume +5%, price +4%, mix +1%), vs. consensus of +6.0%, with +DD% growth in both Fabric Care and Home Care. Baby, Feminine & Family Care organic sales were up +5% (volume +1%, price +3%, mix +1%) vs. consensus of +1.8%. Baby Care increased +LSD% due to devaluation-related price increases and positive mix from growth of premium products, partially offset by reduced volumes due to increased pricing, competitive activity and category contraction in certain markets, Feminine Care organic sales increased +HSD%, and Family Care organic sales increased +MSD%. Grooming was up +4% (volume -1%, price +3%, mix +1%), vs. consensus of +1.0%.

Initial FY20 Guidance: PG provided initial organic sales growth guidance of +3-4% for FY20, with all-in sales growth of +3-4%, including a modest negative

Morgan Stanley | RESEARCH

UPDATE

impact from FX which is largely offset by a positive impact from acquisitions and divestitures. The company expects +4-9% core EPS growth (wider than the usual range) on a base of $4.52 (implies $4.70-$4.93), which at its midpoint of ~$4.82 is ~1.7% above the prior consensus of $4.74 (MSe $4.72), or at a seemingly more realistic high-end 4% above consensus. PG's earnings guidance incorporates a modest net benefit from commodities, foreign exchange, transportation, and tariffs. PG expects the core effective tax rate for FY20 to be in the range of 17-18%. adjusted free cash flow productivity of 90% or better for FY20, $7.5 billion in dividend, repurchases of $6-8 billion of common shares, and capital spending ar 4.5-5% of sales.

Gillette Impairment: PG took an $8B after-tax non-cash impairment charge to adjust the carrying values of goodwill and trade name intangible assets in the Gillette Shave Care business primarily due to significant currency devaluations that have occurred since the 2005 deal close, as well as negative impacts from market contraction of blades and razors in developed markets due to lower shaving frequency and competitive activity. PG indicated the Shave Care business continues to be a strategic business.

Exhibit 1: PG Organic Sales Growth Accelerated in 4Q19...

P&G Organic Sales Growth

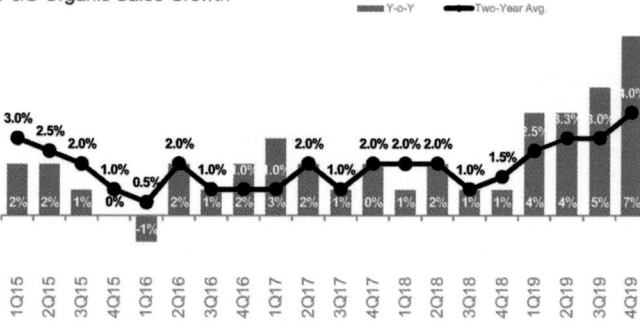

Source: Company data, Morgan Stanley Research

Exhibit 2: ...Led By Improving Category Growth and More Moderate Market Share Gains

PG Wtd. Average Total Value Share YoY (bps) Change

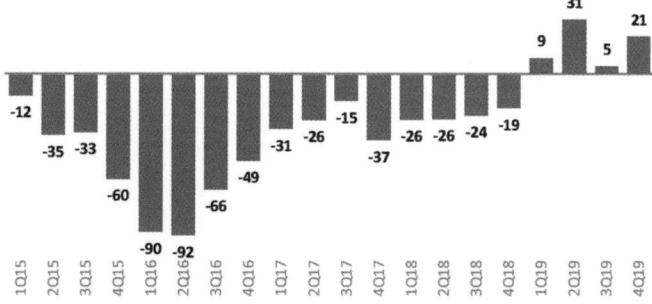

Source: Company data, Morgan Stanley Research

Morgan Stanley | RESEARCH

Risk-Reward: Procter & Gamble (PG)
Risk-Reward Remains Favorable

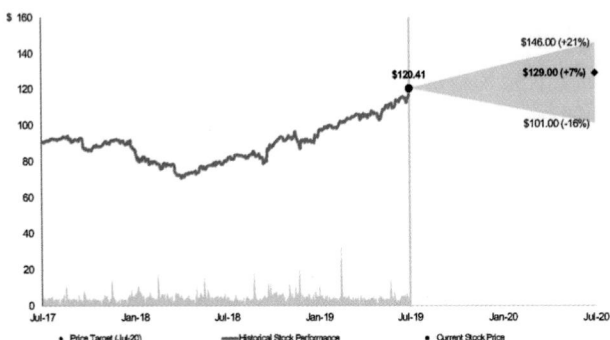

Source: Thomson Reuters, Morgan Stanley Research

Price Target	$129

Derived from base case scenario

Bull $146

28x Bull Case CY20e EPS

Topline rebounds to >4.0% organic sales growth. Revenue upside (~125 bps int'l upside and ~100 bps US upside) as PG's marketing/innovation focus drives market share improvement. Cost cutting above our forecast and better than expected price realization drive margin upside, and in turn ~10% EPS growth. Valuation expands to 28x CY20e EPS.

Base $129

26x Base Case CY20e EPS

Improving sales growth + margin expansion. We forecast organic sales growth of ~3.5-4.0% going forward (above HPC peers) led by improving US results on building market share momentum. Better price realization and continued cost savings support ~70 bps of OM expansion/yr, driving HSD% EPS growth. We apply a multiple of 26x to CY20e EPS, a slight premium to PG's 3-yr avg given accelerating fundamentals.

Bear $101

21.5x Bear Case CY20e EPS

US led topline/margin downside. Our US bear case scenario plays out: -80/-50 bps pricing/volume downside along with ~20 bps of margin downside on greater reinvestment. Outside the US, ~125 bps of topline downside and ~50 bps of margin downside drive muted LSD% EPS growth. Valuation contracts to 21.5x CY20e EPS.

Investment Thesis

■ **Topline Momentum Looks Sustainable:** We believe strategy tweaks put in place in recent years are bearing fruit and can accelerate PG topline growth back to the ~3.5-4% range. In the US, improving breadth of performance and reduced promotional intensity give us confidence that market share momentum is sustainable, which, combined with an improving price outlook and greater agility as organizational changes are implemented, supports topline growth above HPC peers.

■ **Improving Margin Outlook:** Following 2 years of FY gross margin declines, we see a FY GM inflection led by improving price realization and a less onerous commodity headwind. When combined with a sizable cost savings program (worth ~15% to annual profit), we see scope for ~100 bps of annual margin expansion in FY20, and in turn HSD% EPS growth delivery over the next several years.

■ **Valuation Looks Compelling on a Relative Basis:** With PG trading at ~25x CY20e EPS, a discount to HPC peers CL and CLX, relative valuation looks compelling considering our call for PG fundamentals to positively inflect after years of underperformance vs. more expensive HPC peers.

Risks to Achieving Price Target

■ Risks include macro pressures, pricing fluctuations, cost-cutting, execution issues, market share vacillations, and currency & commodity volatility.

Exhibit 3: Bear to Bull: Topline Trends Should Be the Key Stock Driver

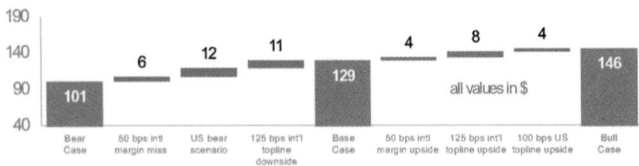

Source: Company data, Morgan Stanley Research estimates

UPDATE

Morgan Stanley | RESEARCH

Exhibit 4: PG Income Statement

Income Statement	FY2013	FY2014	FY2015	FY2016	FY2017	FY2018	Sep-18	Dec-18	Mar-19	Jun-19	FY2019	Sep-19 E	Dec-19 E	Mar-20 E	Jun-20 E	FY2020E	FY2021E	FY2022E
Sales	**82,581.0**	**74,401.0**	**70,749.0**	**65,299.0**	**65,058.0**	**66,832.0**	**16,690.0**	**17,438.0**	**16,462.0**	**17,094.0**	**67,684.0**	**17,718.8**	**18,519.8**	**16,987.5**	**17,682.9**	**70,909.0**	**73,134.5**	**75,458.8**
% Growth	-1.3%	-9.9%	-4.9%	-7.7%	-0.4%	2.7%	0.2%	0.2%	1.1%	3.6%	1.3%	6.2%	6.2%	3.2%	3.4%	4.8%	3.1%	3.2%
% Organic Growth	2.8%	2.6%	1.6%	0.8%	2.2%	1.3%	4.0%	4.0%	5.0%	7.0%	5.2%	4.0%	3.9%	3.3%	3.2%	3.6%	3.2%	3.2%
Cost of Sales	-39,743.0	-38,729.0	-36,537	-32,285	-32,140	-33,707	-8,438.0	-8,796.0	-8,362.0	-8,746.0	-34,342	-8,780.9	-9,156.5	-8,459.1	-8,872.7	-35,269.3	-36,193.4	-37,230.4
% of Sales	48.1%	52.1%	51.6%	49.4%	49.4%	50.4%	50.6%	50.4%	50.8%	51.2%	50.7%	49.6%	49.4%	49.8%	50.2%	49.7%	49.5%	49.3%
% of Sales Bps Change	-245	393	-41	-220	-4	103	150	86	-2	-120	30	-100	-100	-100	-99	-100	-25	-15
Gross Profit	**40,373.0**	**35,672.0**	**34,212.0**	**33,014.0**	**32,918.0**	**33,125.0**	**8,252.0**	**8,642.0**	**8,100.0**	**8,348.0**	**33,342.0**	**8,937.9**	**9,363.3**	**8,528.5**	**8,810.1**	**35,639.8**	**36,941.2**	**38,228.4**
Gross Margin %	48.9%	47.9%	48.4%	50.6%	50.6%	49.6%	49.4%	49.6%	49.2%	48.8%	49.26%	50.4%	50.6%	50.2%	49.8%	50.3%	50.5%	50.7%
Gross Margin Bps Change	-54	-94	41	220	4	-103	-150	-86	2	120	-30	100	100	100	99	100	25	15
SG&A Expense (ex Incremental Restructuring)	**-25,166.0**	**-21,012.0**	**-20,348**	**-18,967**	**-18,761**	**-19,037**	**-4,625.0**	**-4,660.0**	**-4,823.0**	**-4,998.0**	**-19,106**	**-4,925.3**	**-5,004.3**	**-5,002.7**	**-5,266.9**	**-20,199.2**	**-20,550.4**	**-20,996.0**
% of Sales	30.5%	28.2%	28.8%	29.0%	28.8%	28.5%	27.7%	26.7%	29.3%	29.2%	28.2%	27.8%	27.0%	29.4%	29.8%	28.5%	28.1%	27.8%
% Growth	-1.9%	-16.5%	-3.2%	-6.8%	-1.1%	1.5%	-2.5%	-2.6%	3.4%	3.2%	0.4%	6.5%	7.4%	3.7%	5.4%	5.7%	1.7%	2.2%
% of Sales Bps Change	-18	-223	52	29	-21	-35	-77	-78	65	-12	-26	9	30	15	55	26	-39	-27
Operating Income (ex Incremental Restructuring)	**15,207.0**	**14,660.0**	**13,864.0**	**14,047.0**	**14,157.0**	**14,088.0**	**3,627.0**	**3,982.0**	**3,277.0**	**3,350.0**	**14,236.0**	**4,012.6**	**4,359.1**	**3,525.7**	**3,543.2**	**15,440.6**	**16,390.8**	**17,232.4**
Operating Margin	18.4%	19.7%	19.6%	21.5%	21.8%	21.1%	21.7%	22.8%	19.9%	19.6%	21.0%	22.6%	23.5%	20.8%	20.0%	21.8%	22.4%	22.8%
% Growth	-3.2%	-3.6%	-5.4%	1.3%	0.8%	-0.5%	-3.0%	-0.1%	-2.0%	11.0%	1.1%	10.6%	9.5%	7.6%	5.8%	8.5%	6.2%	5.1%
Operating Margin Bps Change	-36	129	-11	192	25	-68	-73	-8	-63	132	-5	91	70	85	44	74	64	42
Interest Expense	-667.0	-710.0	-626.0	-579.0	-465.0	-506.0	-129.0	-138.0	-131.0	-111.0	-509.0	-114.2	-117.1	-116.8	-115.2	-463.3	-499.8	-495.7
Other Non-Operating Income, Net	391.9	308.0	589.0	506.0	506.0	828.0	163.0	162.0	183.5	154.9	663.4	163.0	162.0	183.5	154.9	663.4	663.4	663.4
Pretax Income	**14,931.9**	**14,258.0**	**13,827.0**	**13,974.0**	**14,198.0**	**14,410.0**	**3,661.0**	**4,006.0**	**3,329.5**	**3,393.9**	**14,390.4**	**4,061.4**	**4,403.9**	**3,592.4**	**3,582.9**	**15,640.7**	**16,554.4**	**17,400.1**
Taxes	-3,440.8	-2,949.0	-2,879	-3,437	-3,381	-3,095	-734.0	-712.0	-509.5	-488.9	-2,444	-710.8	-770.7	-628.7	-627.0	-2,737.1	-3,145.3	-3,393.0
Tax Rate	23.0%	20.7%	20.8%	24.6%	23.8%	21.5%	20.0%	17.8%	15.3%	14.4%	17.0%	17.5%	17.5%	17.5%	17.5%	17.5%	19.0%	19.5%
Minority Interests	-90.0	-141.5	-103.0	-96.0	-85.0	-111.0	-12.0	-22.0	-31.0	-4.0	-69.0	-12.0	-22.0	-31.0	-4.0	-69.0	-72.5	-76.1
Net Income	**11,401.1**	**11,167.5**	**10,845.0**	**10,441.0**	**10,732**	**11,204.0**	**2,915.0**	**3,272.0**	**2,789.0**	**2,901.0**	**11,877.0**	**3,338.7**	**3,611.2**	**2,932.7**	**2,951.9**	**12,834.6**	**13,336.6**	**13,931.0**
EPS Diluted (Core)	**$3.89**	**$3.85**	**$3.76**	**$3.67**	**$3.92**	**$4.22**	**$1.12**	**$1.25**	**$1.06**	**$1.10**	**$4.52**	**$1.26**	**$1.37**	**$1.11**	**$1.12**	**$4.86**	**$5.07**	**$5.33**
EPS % Growth	0.9%	-1.2%	-2.2%	-2.4%	6.7%	7.7%	2.5%	4.9%	5.6%	17.1%	7.1%	13.0%	9.6%	5.1%	2.1%	7.6%	4.4%	5.0%
Basic Shares	2,739.7	2,709.8	2,688.7	2,693.7	2,594.8	2,524.6	2491.4	2499.7	2508.3	2498.1	2,499.4	2516.4	2510.7	2508.4	2507.3	2,510.7	2,498.3	2,484.6
Diluted Shares	2,930.6	2,904.4	2,883.6	2,844.5	2,740.4	2,656.7	2612.1	2623.0	2637.7	2945.9	2,629.7	2646.4	2640.7	2638.4	2637.3	2,640.7	2,628.3	2,614.6

Source: Company data, Morgan Stanley Research estimates

Morgan Stanley | RESEARCH

UPDATE

Exhibit 5: PG Balance Sheet

Balance Sheet	FY2013	FY2014	FY2015	FY2016	FY2017	FY2018	Sep-18	Dec-18	Mar-19	Jun-19	FY2019	Sep-19 E	Dec-19 E	Mar-20 E	Jun-20 E	FY2020 E	FY2021E	FY2022E
Assets																		
Surplus Cash	0.0	0.0	0.0	0.0	0.0	0.0	0.0	0.0	0.0	0.0	0.0	0.0	0.0	0.0	0.0	0.0	0.0	0.0
Cash & Equivalents	5,947.0	8,558.0	6,836.0	7,102.0	5,569.0	2,569.0	2,545.0	3,696.0	2,738.0	4,239.0	4,239.0	4,239.0	4,239.0	4,239.0	4,239.0	4,239.0	4,239.0	4,239.0
Investment Securities	6,508.0	2,128.0	2,128.0	6,246.0	9,568.0	9,281.0	8,708.0	8,421.0	7,085.0	6,048.0	6,048.0	6,048.0	6,048.0	6,048.0	6,048.0	6,048.0	6,048.0	6,048.0
Receivables, Net	6,909.0	6,386.0	6,759.0	4,373.0	4,594.0	4,686.0	5,035.0	5,055.0	5,198.0	4,951.0	4,951.0	5,699.7	5,739.0	5,703.7	5,475.2	5,475.2	5,996.3	6,544.5
Inventories	4,979.0	4,568.0	4,979.0	4,716.0	4,624.0	4,738.0	5,182.0	5,281.0	5,358.0	5,017.0	5,017.0	5,392.6	5,497.4	5,420.2	5,089.7	5,089.7	5,391.7	5,718.0
Deferred Income Taxes	846.1	1,356.0	1,507.0	00.0	00.0	00.0	00.0	00.0	00.0	00.0	00.0	00.0	00.0	00.0	00.0	00.0	00.0	00.0
Prepaid Expenses and Other Current Assets	3,678.0	6,939.9	7,140.0	1,838.0	2,139.0	2,046.0	1,876.0	1,978.0	1,933.0	2,218.0	2,218.0	1,876.0	1,978.0	1,933.0	2,218.0	2,218.0	2,218.0	2,218.0
Total Current Assets	23,990.0	31,617.0	29,646.0	33,782.0	26,494.0	23,320.0	23,346.0	24,431.0	22,312.0	22,473.0	22,473.0	23,255.4	23,501.4	23,343.9	23,069.9	23,069.9	23,892.9	24,767.6
PP&E, Net	21,666.0	22,304.0	20,268.0	19,385.0	19,893.0	20,600.0	20,590.0	20,822.0	20,993.0	21,271.0	21,271.0	21,713.8	21,731.4	21,726.3	21,679.6	21,679.6	21,910.4	21,979.5
Goodwill, Net	55,188.0	52,832.0	42,430.0	44,350.0	44,699.0	45,175.0	45,225.0	46,932.0	46,753.0	40,273.0	40,273.0	40,273.0	40,273.0	40,273.0	40,273.0	40,273.0	40,273.0	40,273.0
Other Intangible Assets, Net	31,572.0	31,715.0	31,715.0	24,527.0	24,187.0	23,902.0	23,919.0	25,947.0	25,836.0	24,215.0	24,215.0	24,215.0	24,215.0	24,215.0	24,215.0	24,215.0	24,215.0	24,215.0
Other Assets	6,847.0	5,798.0	5,436.0	5,092.0	5,133.0	5,313.0	5,360.0	5,555.0	5,779.0	6,863.0	6,863.0	6,863.0	6,863.0	6,863.0	6,863.0	6,863.0	6,863.0	6,863.0
Total Assets	139,263.0	144,266.0	129,495.0	127,136.0	120,406.0	118,310.0	118,440.0	123,687.0	121,673.0	115,095.0	115,095.0	116,320.1	116,583.8	116,421.2	116,100.5	116,100.5	117,154.4	118,098.1
Liabilities																		
Short-Term Debt	0.0	00.0	00.0	00.0	00.0	00.0	0.0	0.0	0.0	0.0	0.0	1,893.2	1,618.3	1,722.0	743.2	743.2	596.0	203.0
Notes and Loan Payable	12,432.0	15,606.0	12,021.0	11,653.0	13,554.0	10,423.0	10,508.0	12,113.0	8,911.0	9,697.0	9,697.0	9,697.0	9,697.0	9,697.0	9,697.0	9,697.0	9,697.0	9,697.0
Current Portion of Long-Term Debt	8,777.0	8,461.0	8,257.0	9,325.0	9,632.0	10,344.0	10,243.0	10,266.0	10,207.0	11,260.0	11,260.0	10,659.3	10,686.7	10,325.5	11,423.2	11,423.2	11,663.2	11,996.8
Accounts Payable	8,828.0	8,659.0	9,512.0	9,792.0	7,024.0	7,470.0	8,469.0	8,861.0	9,252.0	9,054.0	9,054.0	8,849.3	9,270.0	9,411.5	9,224.4	9,224.4	9,411.0	9,465.1
Accrued and Other Liabilities	30,037.0	33,726.0	29,790.0	30,770.0	30,210.0	28,237.0	29,220.0	31,247.0	28,370.0	30,011.0	30,011.0	31,098.8	31,272.0	31,155.9	31,087.8	31,087.8	31,320.1	31,361.9
Total Current Liabilities	30,037.0	33,726.0	29,790.0	30,770.0	30,210.0	28,237.0	29,220.0	31,247.0	28,370.0	30,011.0	30,011.0	31,098.8	31,272.0	31,155.9	31,087.8	31,087.8	31,320.1	31,361.9
Long-Term Debt	19,111.0	19,811.0	18,329.0	18,945.0	18,038.0	20,863.0	20,779.0	21,514.0	21,359.0	20,395.0	20,395.0	20,395.0	20,395.0	20,395.0	20,395.0	20,395.0	20,395.0	20,395.0
Deferred Income Taxes	10,827.0	11,537.0	18,326.0	9,113.0	8,126.0	6,163.0	6,179.0	6,872.0	6,951.0	6,899.0	6,899.0	6,899.0	6,899.0	6,899.0	6,899.0	6,899.0	6,899.0	6,899.0
Other Liabilities	10,579.0	8,487.0	00.0	10,325.0	8,254.0	10,164.0	9,758.0	9,611.0	9,441.0	10,211.0	10,211.0	10,211.0	10,211.0	10,211.0	10,211.0	10,211.0	10,211.0	10,211.0
Total Liabilities	70,554.0	73,561.0	66,445.0	69,153.0	64,628.0	65,427.0	65,936.0	69,244.0	66,121.0	67,516.0	67,516.0	68,603.8	68,777.0	68,660.9	68,592.8	68,592.8	68,825.1	68,866.9
Shareholders' Equity																		
Preferred Stock	1,137.0	1,128.0	1,128.0	1,043.0	1,010.0	1,010.0	1,010.0	1,010.0	1,010.0	1,010.0	1,010.0	1,010.0	1,010.0	1,010.0	1,010.0	1,010.0	1,010.0	1,010.0
Common Stock	4,009.0	4,009.0	4,009.0	4,009.0	4,009.0	4,009.0	4,009.0	4,009.0	4,009.0	4,009.0	4,009.0	4,009.0	4,009.0	4,009.0	4,009.0	4,009.0	4,009.0	4,009.0
Additional Paid-In Capital	63,538.0	63,638.0	63,638.0	63,617.0	63,513.0	63,513.0	63,513.0	63,513.0	63,513.0	63,513.0	63,513.0	63,513.0	63,513.0	63,513.0	63,513.0	63,513.0	63,513.0	63,513.0
Retained Earnings	80,197.0	84,656.0	88,214.0	88,167.0	96,189.0	100,083.0	101,145.0	102,567.0	103,498.0	104,462.0	104,462.0	105,895.2	107,605.2	108,638.3	109,615.4	109,615.4	115,001.2	120,706.5
Accumulated Other Comprehensive Income (Loss)	-7,499.0	-11,070.0	-11,070.0	-15,330.0	-14,478.0	-14,263.0	-14,452.0	-13,184.0	-11,756.0	-18,943.0	-18,943.0	-18,239.0	-17,438.0	-17,438.0	-16,917.7	-16,917.7	-13,991.9	-11,035.4
Reserve for ESOP Debt Retirement	-1,352.0	-1,346.0	-1,346.0	-1,299.0	-1,248.0	-1,248.0	-1,248.0	-1,248.0	-1,248.0	-1,248.0	-1,248.0	-1,248.0	-1,248.0	-1,248.0	-1,248.0	-1,248.0	-1,248.0	-1,248.0
Treasury Stock	-71,966.0	-77,648.0	-82,252.0	-82,900.0	-93,925.0	-100,929.0	-102,181.0	-102,932.0	-104,182.0	-105,932.0	-105,932.0	-107,932.0	-109,932.0	-111,432.0	-113,182.0	-113,182.0	-120,682.0	-128,432.0
Minority Interests	645.0	729.0	729.0	666.0	708.0	708.0	708.0	708.0	708.0	708.0	708.0	708.0	708.0	708.0	708.0	708.0	708.0	708.0
Total Shareholders' Equity	68,709.0	70,705.0	63,050.0	57,983.0	55,778.0	52,883.0	52,504.0	54,443.0	55,552.0	47,579.0	47,579.0	47,716.3	47,806.8	47,760.3	47,507.7	47,507.7	48,329.3	49,231.2
Total Liabilities & SE	139,263.0	144,266.0	129,495.0	127,136.0	120,406.0	118,310.0	118,440.0	123,687.0	121,673.0	115,095.0	115,095.0	116,320.1	116,583.8	116,421.2	116,100.5	116,100.5	117,154.4	118,098.1

Source: Company data, Morgan Stanley Research estimates

7

Morgan Stanley | RESEARCH

UPDATE

Exhibit 6: PG Cash Flow Statement

Cash Flow	FY2013	FY2014	FY2015	FY2016	FY2017	FY2018	Sep-18	Dec-18	Mar-19	Jun-19	FY2019	Sep-19 E	Dec-19 E	Mar-20 E	Jun-20 E	FY2020E	FY2021E	FY2022E
Net Income	11,401.1	11,167.5	10,845.0	10,441.0	10,732.0	11,204.0	2,915.0	3,272.0	2,789.0	2,901.0	11,877.0	3,338.7	3,611.2	2,932.7	2,951.9	12,834.6	13,336.6	13,931.0
Adjustments:																		
Depreciation and Amortization	2982.0	3141.0	3134.0	3078.0	2820.0	2834.0	643.0	650.0	711.0	820.0	2824.0	677.2	699.0	755.6	862.2	2994.1	3096.4	3175.7
Stock-Based Compensation Expense	346.0	360.0	337.0	335.0	351.0	395.0	102.0	79.0	118.0	216.0	515.0	104.0	80.6	120.4	220.3	525.3	535.8	546.5
Deferred Income Taxes	-307.0	-44.0	-803.0	-815.0	-601.0	-1844.0	34.0	3.0	-61.0	-387.0	-411.0	0.0	0.0	0.0	0.0	0.0	0.0	0.0
Other	-607.1	463.5	-265.0	572.0	-268.0	-1173.0	-65.0	-65.0	-13.0	-101.0	-244.0	342.0	-102.0	45.0	-285.0	0.0	0.0	0.0
Changes in A/L:																		
Receivables	-415.0	87.0	349.0	35.0	-322.0	-177.0	-475.0	77.0	-151.0	273.0	-276.0	-748.7	-39.2	35.3	228.5	-524.2	-521.1	-548.3
Inventories	-225.0	8.0	313.0	116.0	71.0	-188.0	-494.0	-37.0	-70.0	362.0	-239.0	-375.6	-104.8	77.2	330.5	-72.7	-302.0	-326.3
A/P, Accrued and Other Liabilities	1253.0	1.0	928.0	1286.0	-149.0	1385.0	933.0	208.0	300.0	415.0	1856.0	-805.4	448.1	-219.7	910.7	333.6	389.4	424.8
Other Operating Assets and Liabilities	445.0	-1226.0	-230.0	308.0	119.0	2431.0	-26.0	-180.0	-106.0	-348.0	-660.0	0.0	0.0	0.0	0.0	0.0	0.0	0.0
Cash Provided by Operations	14,873.0	13,958.0	14,608.0	15,435.0	12,753.0	14,867.0	3,567.0	4,007.0	3,517.0	4,151.0	15,242.0	2,532.2	4,592.9	3,746.5	5,219.1	16,090.7	16,535.2	17,203.5
Cash Flows from Investing Activities:																		
Capital Expenditures	-4,008.0	-3,848.0	-3,736.0	-3,314.0	-3,384.0	-3,717.0	-1086.0	-701.0	-752.0	-814.0	-3,347.0	-1,120.0	-716.7	-750.5	-815.5	-3,402.7	-3,327.2	-3,244.8
Proceeds from Asset Sales	584.0	570.0	498.0	432.0	571.0	269.0	9.0	9.0	4.0	372.0	394.0	0.0	0.0	0.0	0.0	0.0	0.0	0.0
Payment for Acquisitions	-1145.0	-24.0	-3784.0	-186.0	-16.0	-109.0	-237.0	-3611.0	-95.0	-2.0	-3945.0							
Other	-1,726.0	-805.0	132.0	-2,507.0	-2,890.0	-46.0	443.0	458.0	1,416.0	1,091.0	3,408.0							
Cash Used for Investing Activities	-6,295.0	-4,107.0	-2,890.0	-5,575.0	-5,689.0	-3,511.0	-865.0	-3845.0	573.0	647.0	-3,490.0	-1120.0	-716.7	-750.5	-815.5	-3,402.7	-3,327.2	-3,244.8
Cash Flows from Financing Activities:																		
Change in Short-Term Debt	3,406.0	3304.0	-2580.0	-418.0	2727.0	-3437.0	24.0	1182.0	-3038.0	-383.0	-2215.0	1863.2	-274.9	103.6	-978.7	743.2	-157.2	-383.0
Change in Long-Term Debt	-1,421.0	239.0	-1374.0	1703.0	-1328.0	2199.0	0.0	1390.0	-24.0	32.0	1398.0	0.0	0.0	0.0	0.0	0.0	0.0	0.0
Dividends Paid	-6,519.0	-6,911.0	-7,287.0	-7,436.0	-7,236.0	-7,310.0	-1863.0	-1800.0	-1858.0	-1937.0	-7,498.0	-1905.4	-1901.3	-1889.6	-1974.8	-7,681.2	-7,950.9	-8,225.7
Purchase of Treasury Shares	-5,986.0	-6,005.0	-4,604.0	-5,734.0	-5,204.0	-7,004.0	-1252.0	-751.0	-1250.0	-1750.0	-5,003.0	-2000.0	-2000.0	-1500.0	-1750.0	-7,250.0	-7,500.0	-7,750.0
Proceeds From Stock Options, Other	3,449.0	2,094.0	2,816.0	2,672.0	2,473.0	1,177.0	425.0	1,061.0	1,104.0	734.0	3,324.0	600.0	300.0	300.0	300.0	1,500.0	2,400.0	2,400.0
Cash Used for Financing Activities	-7,071.0	-7,279.0	-13,029.0	-9,213.0	-8,568.0	-14,375.0	-2,666.0	1,032.0	-5,066.0	-3,304.0	-9,994.0	-1,412.2	-3,876.2	-2,996.0	-4,403.6	-12,688.0	-13,208.1	-13,958.7
Cash Provided by Discontinued Operations	0.0	0.0	0.0	0.0	0.0	0.0	0.0	0.0	0.0	0.0	0.0	0.0	0.0	0.0	0.0	0.0	0.0	0.0
Exchange Rate Effect on Cash / Other	4.0	39.0	-411.0	-381.0	-29.0	19.0	-70.0	-43.0	18.0	7.0	-88.0	0.0	0.0	0.0	0.0	0.0	0.0	0.0
Net Increase (Decrease) in Cash and Cash Equivs	1511.0	2611.0	-1722.0	266.0	-1533.0	-3000.0	-24.0	1151.0	-958.0	1501.0	1670.0	0.0	0.0	0.0	0.0	0.0	0.0	0.0
Cash and Cash Equivs, Beg	4,436.0	5,947.0	8,558.0	6,836.0	7,102.0	5,569.0	2,599.0	2,545.0	3,696.0	2,738.0	2,569.0	4,239.0	4,239.0	4,239.0	4,239.0	4,239.0	4,239.0	4,239.0
Cash and Cash Equivs, End	5,947.0	8,558.0	6,836.0	7,102.0	5,569.0	2,569.0	2,545.0	3,696.0	2,738.0	4,239.0	4,239.0	4,239.0	4,239.0	4,239.0	4,239.0	4,239.0	4,239.0	4,239.0

Source: Company data, Morgan Stanley Research estimates

Questions

Q12-1. Identify at least two applications that use forecasted financial statements.

Q12-2. In what order do we normally forecast the financial statements? Explain the logic of this order.

Q12-3. Why do we begin the forecasting process by adjusting the financial statements?

Q12-4. What does the concept of financial statement articulation mean in the forecasting process?

Q12-5. Analysts commonly perform a sensitivity analysis following preparation of financial forecasts. What is meant by sensitivity analysis, and why is it important?

Q12-6. Cash is forecast as the last item on the balance sheet. Why is this the case?

Q12-7. In addition to recent revenues trends, what other types and sources of information can we use to help us forecast revenues?

Q12-8. Why do we refine the forecasted cash balance? How might we deal with a cash balance that is much too low compared with the company's normal cash level?

Q12-9. Identify at least three sources of additional information we could use to refine our forecast assumptions.

Q12-10. Capital expenditures are usually an important cash outflow for a company, and they figure prominently into forecasts of net operating assets. What sources of information about capital expenditures can we draw upon?

Assignments with the ⬤ logo in the margin are available in ᵐʸBusinessCourse.
See the Preface of the book for details.

Mini Exercises

LO2   **M12-11. Forecast an Income Statement**

Automatic Data
Procession (ADP)

ADP reports the following income statement.

AUTOMATIC DATA PROCESSING INC. Statement of Consolidated Earnings For Year Ended June 30, 2019, $ millions	
Total revenues	$14,175.2
Operating expenses	7,145.9
Systems development and programming costs	636.3
Depreciation and amortization	304.4
Total cost of revenues	8,086.6
Selling, general, and administrative expenses	3,064.2
Interest expense	129.9
Total expenses	11,280.7
Other (income) expense, net	(111.1)
Earnings before income taxes	3,005.6
Provision for income taxes	712.8
Net earnings	$ 2,292.8

Forecast ADP's 2020 income statement assuming the following income statement relations. All percentages (other than total revenue growth and provision for income taxes) are based on historic percent of total revenues.

Total revenues growth	13%
Depreciation and amortization	$460.5 million
Interest expense	No change
Other (income) expense, net	No change
Income tax rate	25%

M12-12. Forecast an Income Statement

Seagate Technology reports the following income statement for fiscal 2019.

LO2
Seagate Technology
PLC (STX)

Homework
MBC

SEAGATE TECHNOLOGY PLC Consolidated Statement of Income For Year Ended June 28, 2019, $ millions	
Revenue	$10,390
Cost of revenue	7,458
Product development	991
Marketing and administrative	453
Amortization of intangibles	23
Restructuring and other, net	(22)
Total operating expenses	8,903
Income from operations	1,487
Interest income	84
Interest expense	(224)
Other, net	25
Other expense, net	(115)
Income before income taxes	1,372
(Benefit) provision for income taxes	(640)
Net income	$ 2,012

Forecast Seagate's 2020 income statement assuming the following income statement relations ($ millions).

Revenue growth	5%
Cost of revenue	71.8% of revenue
Product development	9.5% of revenue
Marketing and administrative	4.4% of revenue
Amortization of intangibles	No change
Restructuring and other, net	$0
Interest income	No change
Interest expense	No change
Other, net	No change
Income tax rate	21%

M12-13. Forecast an Income Statement

Following is the income statement for Medtronic PLC.

LO2
Medtronic PLC (MDT)

Homework
MBC

Consolidated Statement of Income ($ millions) For Fiscal Year Ended	April 26, 2019
Net sales	$30,557
Costs and expenses	
Cost of products sold	9,155
Research and development expense	2,330
Selling, general, and administrative expense	10,418
Amortization of intangible assets	1,764
Restructuring charges, net	198
Certain litigation charges	166
Other operating expense, net	258
Operating profit (loss)	6,268
Other nonoperating income, net	(373)
Interest expense	1,444
Income (loss) before income taxes	5,197
Income tax provision	547
Net income (loss)	4,650
Net (income) loss attributable to noncontrolling interests	(19)
Net income (loss) attributable to Medtronic	$ 4,631

Use the following assumptions to prepare a forecast of the company's income statement for FY2020.

Net sales increase	8%
Cost of products sold	30.8% of net sales
Research and development expense.	7.6% of net sales
Selling, general, and administrative expense.	34.1% of net sales
Amortization of intangible assets	5.8% of net sales
Restructuring charges, net.	75% of 2019 restructuring expense
Certain litigation charges	$150 million
Other operating expense, net.	No change in $ amount
Interest expense.	No change in $ amount
Income tax provision.	15% of pretax income
Income attributable to noncontrolling interests.	No change

LO3 **M12-14. Adjust the Cash Balance**

The forecast of the income statement and balance sheet for Next Generation yields the following.

$ millions	2019 Actual	2020 Est.
Cash and cash equivalents	$ 4,558	$ 6,127
Net sales.	42,668	43,552
Marketable securities	5,980	5,980
Long-term debt.	21,930	21,485
Treasury stock	(4,561)	(4,811)

Required

a. Does forecasted cash deviate from the normal level for this company?
b. Is the deviation in part a large enough to require adjustment? Explain.
c. Suggest three ways to adjust the forecasted cash balance.
d. If we used marketable securities to adjust the cash balance, what would be the adjusted forecast for marketable securities?
e. If we used treasury stock to adjust the cash balance, what would be the adjusted forecast for treasury stock?

LO3 **M12-15. Adjust the Cash Balance**

We obtain the following 2020 forecasts of selected financial statement line items for Journey Company.

$ millions	2019 Actual	2020 Est.
Net sales.	$708,554	$740,439
Marketable securities	67,096	62,096
Long-term debt.	346,558	308,437
Treasury stock (deducted from equity).	51,174	51,174
Cash generated by operations		57,696
Cash used for investing		(14,908)
Cash used for financing		(54,660)
Total net change in cash.		(11,872)
Cash at beginning of period		51,141
Cash at end of period.		$ 39,269

Required

a. Does forecasted cash deviate from the normal level for this company?
b. Is the deviation in part a large enough to require adjustment? Explain.
c. Identify three ways to adjust the forecasted cash balance.
d. Complete the following statement of cash flows *assuming long-term debt is used* to adjust the forecasted cash balance.

Cash generated by operations	
Cash used for investing	
Cash used for financing	_____
Total change in cash.	
Cash at beginning of period	_____
Cash at end of period.	_____

e. Complete the following statement of cash flows *assuming marketable securities are used* to adjust the forecasted cash balance.

Cash generated by operations	
Cash used for investing	
Cash used for financing	_____
Total change in cash.	
Cash at beginning of period	_____
Cash at end of period.	══════

M12-16. Forecast the Balance Sheet

Following is the balance sheet for **Medtronic PLC** for FY2019 ended April 26, 2019.

Consolidated Balance Sheet ($ millions)	April 26, 2019
Current assets	
Cash and cash equivalents.	$ 4,393
Investments.	5,455
Accounts receivable, less allowances of $190	6,222
Inventories, net	3,753
Other current assets	2,144
Total current assets.	21,967
Property, plant, and equipment, net	4,675
Goodwill	39,959
Other intangible assets, net	20,560
Tax assets	1,519
Other assets	1,014
Total assets	$89,694
Current liabilities	
Current debt obligations	$ 838
Accounts payable	1,953
Accrued compensation	2,189
Accrued income taxes.	567
Other accrued expenses.	2,925
Total current liabilities	8,472
Long-term debt	24,486
Accrued compensation and retirement benefits	1,651
Accrued income taxes	2,838
Deferred tax liabilities	1,278
Other liabilities	757
Total liabilities	39,482
Shareholders' equity	
Ordinary shares	0
Additional paid-in capital.	26,532
Retained earnings	26,270
Accumulated other comprehensive loss.	(2,711)
Total shareholders' equity.	50,091
Noncontrolling interests	121
Total equity	50,212
Total liabilities and equity	$89,694

Required

Use the following assumptions to forecast the company's balance sheet for FY2020.

Forecasted FY2020 net income including noncontrolling interest	$4,927 million
Forecasted FY2020 net sales.	$33,002 million
Accounts receivable, less allowance	20.4% of net sales
Inventories, net.	12.3% of net sales
Other current assets.	7% of net sales
Goodwill	No change
Tax assets	5% of net sales
Other assets.	3.3% of net sales
Accounts payable.	6.4% of net sales
Accrued compensation (current liability).	7.2% of net sales
Accrued compensation and retirement benefits (noncurrent liability). . .	No change
Accrued income taxes (current liability)	1.9% of net sales
Other accrued expenses	9.6% of net sales
Accrued income taxes (noncurrent liability)	9.3% of net sales
Deferred tax liabilities.	4.2% of net sales
Other liabilities	2.5% of net sales
Ordinary shares	No change
Accumulated other comprehensive loss.	No change
Net income attributable to noncontrolling interest	$19 million
Dividends in FY2020	$2,853 million
CAPEX in FY2019 (to be forecast as % of net sales)	$1,134 million
Depreciation expense in FY2020	$950 million
Amortization expense in FY2020	$1,914 million
Debt due in FY2020	$838 million
Debt due in FY2021.	$2,058 million

LO2

Honeywell
International Inc.
(HON)

M12-17. Adjust the Income Statement

Following is information from the tax footnote from the 2018 10-K for Honeywell International.

Years Ended December 31	2018	2017	2016
The U.S. federal statutory income tax rate is reconciled to our effective income tax rate as follows:			
U.S. federal statutory income tax rate.	21.0%	35.0%	35.0%
Taxes on non-U.S. earnings	0.2	(12.8)	(8.0)
U.S. state income taxes	1.6	1.4	1.1
Reserves for tax contingencies.	0.3	1.6	1.2
Employee share-based payments.	(0.7)	(2.9)	(2.0)
U.S. tax reform	(5.8)	56.0	—
Reduction on taxes on unremitted earnings	(14.2)	—	—
Separation tax costs	5.5		
All other items—net.	0.9	(1.1)	(2.5)
	8.8%	77.2%	24.8%

The **effective tax rate for 2018** was lower than the U.S. federal statutory rate of 21% primarily attributable to internal restructuring initiatives that resulted in a reduction of accrued withholding taxes of approximately $1.1 billion related to unremitted foreign earnings. In addition, we recorded a tax benefit of approximately $440 million as a reduction to our 2017 provisional estimate of impacts from what is commonly referred to as the U.S. Tax Cuts and Jobs Act.

The effective tax rate for 2017 was higher than the U.S. federal statutory rate of 35% primarily from the estimated impacts of U.S. Tax Reform of approximately $3.8 billion, partially offset by lower tax rates on non-U.S. earnings.

a. What adjustments, if any, should we consider before forecasting Honeywell's 2020 income?

b. Adjust Honeywell's effective tax rate for each of the three years to reflect persistent factors.

M12-18. Refine Assumptions for PPE Forecast

Refer to the Medtronic PLC financial information in E12-25 (pertaining to 2019 fiscal year ended April 26, 2019).

Required

a. Use the financial statements along with the additional information below to forecast property, plant and equipment, net for fiscal year ended April 2020.

$ millions	April 27, 2018 Actual	April 26, 2019 Actual	April 2020 Forecast
Net sales.	$29,953	$30,557	$33,002
CAPEX	1,068	1,134	
Depreciation expense.	821	895	
Property, plant, and equipment, gross	10,259	10,920	

b. Suppose the company discloses in a press release that accompanies its year-end SEC filing that anticipated CAPEX for fiscal year ended April 2020 is $1.5 billion. Use this guidance to refine your forecast of property, plant and equipment, net for fiscal year ended April 2020.

M12-19. Refine Assumptions for Dividend and Retained Earnings Forecast

Refer to the Medtronic PLC financial information in E12-25 for the fiscal year ended April 26, 2019.

Required

a. Use the financial statements along with the additional information below to forecast retained earnings for the fiscal year ended April 2020.

Forecasted net income to Medtronic shareholders for fiscal 2020	$4,908 million
Dividends to Medtronic shareholders in fiscal 2019	2,693 million

b. Suppose the MD&A section of the Form 10-K and additional guidance from the company reveals the following additional information. "Ordinary cash dividends declared and paid totaled 50.0 cents per share for each quarter of fiscal year 2019."

At year end April 26, 2019, the company had 1,340,697,595 shares issued and outstanding. Use this information to refine your forecast of retained earnings for the fiscal year ended April 2020. Why might the two forecasted amounts differ? Which is more accurate?

M12-20. Use Segment Information to Refine Sales Forecast

To forecast sales growth for Best Buy for the fiscal year ended February 2, 2019, we begin with the following historical sales information.

$ millions	2015	2016	2017	2018	2019
Net sales.	$40,339	$39,528	$39,403	$42,151	$42,879

Required

a. Determine the sales-growth rate (in percentage) for each of the years 2016 to 2019.
b. If we were to use the 2019 growth to forecast 2020 sales, what rate would we use?
c. The annual report reveals the fiscal year ended February 2018 included a 53rd week (as is common for retailers, every four years). Use this information to refine the sales-growth rates for 2018 and 2019. (*Hint:* Consider multiplying sales for a 53-week year by 52/53 to get an apples-to-apples comparison with numbers from 52-week years.)

Exercises

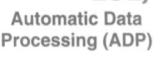

E12-21. **Analyze, Forecast, and Interpret Income Statement and Balance Sheet**

Following are the income statement and balance sheet of **ADP Inc.**

AUTOMATIC DATA PROCESSING INC. Statement of Consolidated Earnings For Year Ended June 30, 2019, $ millions	
Total revenues	$14,175.2
Operating expenses	7,145.9
Systems development and programming costs	636.3
Depreciation and amortization	304.4
Total cost of revenues	8,086.6
Selling, general, and administrative expenses	3,064.2
Interest expense	129.9
Total expenses	11,280.7
Other (income) expense, net	(111.1)
Earnings before income taxes	3,005.6
Provision for income taxes	712.8
Net earnings	$ 2,292.8

AUTOMATIC DATA PROCESSING INC. Balance Sheet	
$ millions	**June 30, 2019**
Current assets	
Cash and cash equivalents	$ 1,949.2
Accounts receivable, net	2,439.3
Other current assets	519.6
Total current assets before funds held for clients	4,908.1
Funds held for clients	29,434.2
Total current assets	34,342.3
Long-term receivables, net	23.8
Property, plant and equipment, net	764.2
Capitalized contract cost, net	2,428.5
Other assets	934.4
Goodwill	2,323.0
Intangible assets, net	1,071.5
Total assets	$41,887.7
Current liabilities	
Accounts payable	$ 125.5
Accrued expenses and other current liabilities	1,759.0
Accrued payroll and payroll-related expenses	721.1
Dividends payable	340.1
Short-term deferred revenues	220.7
Obligations under reverse repurchase agreements	262.0
Income taxes payable	54.8
Total current liabilities before client funds obligations	3,483.2
Client funds obligations	29,144.5
Total current liabilities	32,627.7
Long-term debt	2,002.2
Other liabilities	798.7
Deferred income taxes	659.9
Long-term deferred revenues	399.3
Total liabilities	36,487.8

continued

continued from previous page

AUTOMATIC DATA PROCESSING INC.	
Balance Sheet	
$ millions	**June 30, 2019**
Shareholders' equity	
Preferred stock, $1.00 par value: Authorized, 0.3 shares; issued, none	
Common stock, $0.10 par value: Authorized, 1,000.0 shares;	
issued, 638.7 shares; outstanding 434.2 shares	63.9
Capital in excess of par value.	1,183.2
Retained earnings	17,500.6
Treasury stock, at cost: 204.5 shares.	(13,090.5)
Accumulated other comprehensive loss.	(257.3)
Total stockholders' equity	5,399.9
Total liabilities and stockholders' equity	$41,887.7

a. Forecast ADP's 2020 income statement and balance sheet using the following relations ($ millions). Assume total revenues grow by 13% in 2020. All other percentages (other than sales growth and provision for income taxes) are based on historic percent of total revenues.
   - CAPEX for 2020 will be 1.1% of total revenue, and depreciation will be $184.4 million.
   - Goodwill, long-term debt, preferred stock, common stock, and Accumulated other comprehensive loss will not change for the year.
   - The company will acquire intangibles equal to 2.9% of total revenues and will record amortization expense of $276.1 million.
   - Income taxes will be 25% of pretax income and income taxes payable will be 7.7% of 2020 tax expense.
   - The company will award $167.3 million of stock-based compensation, which increases Capital in excess of par value by the same amount. Assume that the company routinely includes this form of compensation in operating expenses each year.
   - The company will continue its stock repurchases. ADP will repurchase $750 million of treasury stock.
   - Dividends will be $1,389.4 in 2020, and dividends payable will be 26.3% of dividends.

b. What does the forecasted adjustment to balance the accounting equation from part *a* reveal to us about the forecasted cash balance and related financing needs of the company? Explain.

E12-22. Forecast the Statement of Cash Flows

Refer to the ADP Inc. financial information in E12-21. Prepare a forecast of FY2020 statement of cash flows.

LO5

Automatic Data
Processing (ADP)

MBC

E12-23. Analyze, Forecast, and Interpret Both Income Statement and Balance Sheet

Following are the income statement and balance sheet of Seagate Technology for fiscal 2019.

LO2, 3

Seagate Technology
PLC (STX)

MBC

SEAGATE TECHNOLOGY PLC	
Consolidated Statement of Income	
For Year Ended June 28, 2019 ($ millions)	
Revenue.	$10,390
Cost of revenue	7,458
Product development	991
Marketing and administrative	453
Amortization of intangibles	23
Restructuring and other, net.	(22)
Total operating expenses	8,903
Income from operations	1,487
Interest income.	84
Interest expense.	(224)
Other, net	25
Other expense, net.	(115)
Income before income taxes	1,372
(Benefit) provision for income taxes.	(640)
Net income.	$ 2,012

SEAGATE TECHNOLOGY PLC
Consolidated Balance Sheet
June 28, 2019 ($ millions)

Current assets
Cash and cash equivalents	$2,220
Accounts receivable, net	989
Inventories	970
Other current assets	184
Total current assets	4,363
Property, equipment and leasehold improvements, net	1,869
Goodwill	1,237
Other intangible assets, net	111
Deferred income taxes	1,114
Other assets, net	191
Total assets	$8,885

Current liabilities
Accounts payable	$1,420
Accrued employee compensation	169
Accrued warranty	91
Accrued expenses	552
Total current liabilities	2,232
Long-term accrued warranty	104
Long-term accrued income taxes	4
Other noncurrent liabilities	130
Long-term debt, less current portion	4,253
Total liabilities	6,723

Shareholders' equity
Ordinary shares— par value $0.0001, 2.6 billion shares authorized, 1,340,697,595 and 1,354,218,154 shares issued and outstanding, respectively	—
Additional paid-in capital	6,545
Accumulated other comprehensive loss	(34)
Accumulated deficit	(4,349)
Total shareholders' equity	2,162
Total liabilities and shareholders' equity	$8,885

a. Forecast Seagate Technology's 2020 income statement and balance sheet using the forecast assumptions, which are expressed as a percentage of revenue unless otherwise indicated.

Accounts receivable, net	9.5%
Inventories	9.3%
Other current assets	1.8%
Deferred income taxes	10.7%
Other assets, net	1.8%
Accounts payable	13.7%
Accrued employee compensation	1.6%
Accrued warranty	0.9%
Accrued expenses	5.3%
Long-term accrued warranty	1.0%
Other noncurrent liabilities	1.3%

- Assume that revenue will grow by 5%, and the tax rate will be 21%.
- Forecast no change in the following income statement accounts: Amortization of intangibles, Interest income, Interest expense, and Other, net.
- Forecast no change in the following balance sheet accounts: Goodwill, Long-term accrued income taxes, Long-term debt, less current portion, Ordinary shares, and Accumulated other comprehensive loss.
- Assume that in 2020, CAPEX will be 5.8% of revenue, and depreciation expense will be 5.4% of Property, equipment and leasehold improvements, gross at the start of the year, which was $9,835 million.

- Assume that in 2020, the company awards $99 million of stock-based compensation which increases Additional paid-in capital by the same amount. Assume that the company routinely includes this form of compensation in operating expenses each year.
- The company has a dividend payout ratio of 35.4% of net income.

b. What does the forecasted adjustment to balance the accounting equation from part *a* reveal to us about the forecasted cash balance and related financing needs of the company? Explain.

E12-24. Forecast the Statement of Cash Flows

Refer to the Seagate Technology (STX) financial information from E12-23. Prepare a forecast of its FY2020 statement of cash flows.

LO5
Seagate Technology
PLC (STX)
Homework

MBC

E12-25. Forecast Income Statement and Balance Sheet

Following are the income statement and balance sheet for Medtronic PLC.

LO2, 3
Medtronic PLC (MDT)
Homework

MBC

Consolidated Statement of Income ($ millions) For Fiscal Year Ended	April 26, 2019
Net sales.	$30,557
Costs and expenses	
Cost of products sold	9,155
Research and development expense.	2,330
Selling, general, and administrative expense.	10,418
Amortization of intangible assets	1,764
Restructuring charges, net.	198
Certain litigation charges	166
Other operating expense, net.	258
Operating profit (loss).	6,268
Other nonoperating income, net.	(373)
Interest expense.	1,444
Income (loss) before income taxes.	5,197
Income tax provision.	547
Net income (loss)	4,650
Net (income) loss attributable to noncontrolling interests.	(19)
Net income (loss) attributable to Medtronic	$ 4,631

Consolidated Balance Sheet ($ millions)	April 26, 2019
Current assets	
Cash and cash equivalents.	$ 4,393
Investments.	5,455
Accounts receivable, less allowances of $190	6,222
Inventories, net.	3,753
Other current assets.	2,144
Total current assets.	21,967
Property, plant, and equipment, net.	4,675
Goodwill.	39,959
Other intangible assets, net.	20,560
Tax assets	1,519
Other assets.	1,014
Total assets	$89,694
Current liabilities	
Current debt obligations	$838
Accounts payable	1,953
Accrued compensation	2,189
Accrued income taxes.	567
Other accrued expenses.	2,925
Total current liabilities	8,472

continued

continued from previous page

Consolidated Balance Sheet ($ millions)—continued	April 26, 2019
Long-term debt.	24,486
Accrued compensation and retirement benefits.	1,651
Accrued income taxes	2,838
Deferred tax liabilities.	1,278
Other liabilities	757
Total liabilities.	39,482
Shareholders' equity	
Ordinary shares	0
Additional paid-in capital.	26,532
Retained earnings	26,270
Accumulated other comprehensive loss.	(2,711)
Total shareholders' equity.	50,091
Noncontrolling interests	121
Total equity.	50,212
Total liabilities and equity	$89,694

Required

a. Use the following assumptions to prepare a forecast of the company's income statement and balance sheet for fiscal year 2020, ended in April 2020.

Income Statement assumptions	
Net sales increase	8%
Cost of product sold	30.0% of net sales
Research and development expense.	7.6% of net sales
Selling, general, and administrative expense.	34.1% of net sales
Amortization of intangible assets	5.8% of net sales
Restructuring charges, net	75% of 2019 expense
Certain litigation charges	$150 million
Other operating expense, net.	No change
Interest expense.	No change
Income tax provision.	15% of pre-tax income
Income to noncontrolling interests	No change
Balance sheet assumptions	
Accounts receivable, less allowances	20.4% of net sales
Inventories, net.	12.3% of net sales
Other current assets.	7% of net sales
Goodwill	No change
Tax assets	5% of net sales
Other assets.	3.3% of net sales
Accounts payable.	6.4% of net sales
Accrued compensation (current liability).	7.2% of net sales
Accrued income taxes (current liability)	1.9% of net sales
Accrued income taxes (noncurrent liability)	9.3% of net sales
Other accrued expenses	9.6% of net sales
Accrued compensation and retirement benefits (noncurrent liability). . .	No change
Deferred tax liabilities.	4.2% of net sales
Other liabilities	2.5% of net sales
Ordinary shares	No change
Accumulated other comprehensive loss.	No change
Net income attributable to noncontrolling interest	$19 million
Dividends in FY2020	$2,853 million
CAPEX in FY2019, forecast CAPEX at historic % of net sales	$1,134 million
Depreciation expense in FY2020.	$950 million
Amortization expense in FY2020	$1,914 million
Debt due in FY2020	$838 million
Debt due in FY2021	$2,058 million

b. What does the forecasted adjustment to balance the accounting equation from part *a* reveal to us about the forecasted financing needs of the company? Explain.

E12-26. Forecast the Statement of Cash Flows

LO5
Medtronic PLC (MDT)

Refer to the Medtronic PLC financial information in E12-25.

Required

Use the information to forecast Medtronic's statement of cash flows for the fiscal year ended April 2020.

E12-27. Refine Cash Balance and Consider Capital Structure

LO3

Consider the following actual 2019 data along with forecasted 2020 data for selected balance sheet and income statement numbers.

$ millions	FY2019 Actual	FY2020 Est.
Net sales.	$29,009	$32,102
Total assets	14,592	16,051
Total liabilities	8,755	9,923
Total equity	5,837	6,128
Cash	2,918	4,378
Marketable securities	730	730
Treasury stock	(2,189)	(2,627)

Required

a. Calculate the company's normal cash level as a percentage of net sales.
b. Determine the amount of adjustment needed to return cash to a normal level. Is an adjustment warranted? Explain.
c. Compute the liabilities-to-equity ratio for both years. What do we observe?
d. Adjust marketable securities so the forecasted cash balance is at its normal level. What affect does this have on the forecasted liabilities-to-equity ratio?
e. Adjust long-term debt so the forecasted cash balance is at its normal level. What effect does this have on the forecasted liabilities-to-equity ratio?
f. Adjust treasury stock so the forecasted cash balance is at its normal level. What effect does this have on the forecasted liabilities-to-equity ratio?
g. Adjust both long-term debt and marketable securities so as to adjust the forecasted cash balance. In so doing, make sure we preserve the company's liabilities-to-equity ratio. (*Hint:* Use "Goal Seek" under the "What-If Analysis" in Excel to determine the proportion of long-term debt versus treasury stock needed to ensure the forecasted liabilities-to-equity ratio remains at its historical level.)
h. Adjust both long-term debt and treasury stock so as to adjust the forecasted cash balance. In so doing, make sure we preserve the company's liabilities-to-equity ratio. (*Hint:* Use "Goal Seek" under the "What-If Analysis" in Excel to determine the proportion of long-term debt versus treasury stock needed to ensure the forecasted liabilities-to-equity ratio remains at its historical level.)

E12-28. Use Segment Disclosures to Forecast Income Statement

LO2, 4

Thermo Fisher
Scientific (TMO)

Following are revenue and cost of revenue numbers for Thermo Fisher Scientific.

THERMO FISHER SCIENTIFIC INC. Consolidated Statement of Income		
For Year Ended December 31 ($ millions)	2018	2017
Revenues		
Product revenues	$18,868	$17,374
Service revenues	5,490	3,544
Total revenues	24,358	20,918

continued

continued from previous page

THERMO FISHER SCIENTIFIC INC. Consolidated Statement of Income		
For Year Ended December 31 ($ millions)	2018	2017
Costs and operating expenses		
Product cost of revenues	9,682	8,975
Service cost of revenues.	3,819	2,495
Total cost of revenues............................	13,501	11,470
Selling, general and administrative expenses.	6,057	5,504
Research and development expenses	967	887
Restructuring and other costs, net	50	97
Total costs and operating expenses	20,575	17,958
Operating income.	3,783	2,960
Other expense, net.	(521)	(531)
Income from continuing operations before income taxes...	3,262	2,429
Income tax expense	324	201
Income from continuing operations	2,938	2,228
Loss from discontinued operations.	—	(3)
Net income	$ 2,938	$ 2,225

Required

a. Use the historic growth in total revenues (from 2017 to 2018) rounded to three decimal places, to forecast *total* revenue for 2019. Use the historic rate of total cost of revenues to total revenues to forecast *total* cost of revenues. Other forecast assumptions follow:

Selling, general and administrative expenses	24.9% of total revenues
Research and development expenses	4.0% of total revenues
Restructuring and other costs, net	$0
Other expense, net	No change
Income tax expense	23% of pretax income

b. Refine your forecast by using the separate historic growth in product revenues and service revenues (from 2017 to 2018) rounded to three decimal places, to estimate 2019 product and service revenues respectively for 2019. Also, use the historic growth in cost of revenues for each segment to forecast separate segment cost of revenues. Assume other forecast assumptions are as in part *a*.

c. Do the two forecasts differ significantly between part *a* and *b*? Which forecasted income statement do we believe is more accurate?

LO4

Honeywell
International Inc.
(HON)

E12-29.   Use Segment Disclosures to Forecast Revenue

Following are 2017 and 2018 revenue data for Honeywell International's four segments. Use these data to forecast its 2019 revenue.

Honeywell International Segment Sales and Business-Unit Sales by Segment		
$ millions	2018	2017
Aerospace sales		
Commercial aviation original equipment.....................	$ 2,833	$ 2,475
Commercial aviation aftermarket	5,373	5,103
Defense and space......................................	4,665	4,053
Transportation systems..................................	2,622	3,148
Total aerospace sales....................................	$15,493	$14,779
Honeywell building technologies sales		
Homes..	$ 3,928	$ 4,482
Buildings..	5,370	5,295
Total Honeywell building technologies sales.................	$ 9,298	$ 9,777

continued

continued from previous page

Honeywell International Segment Sales and Business-Unit Sales by Segment		
$ millions	**2018**	**2017**
Performance materials and technologies sales		
UOP Russell LLP	$ 2,845	$ 2,753
Process solutions	4,981	4,795
Advanced materials	2,848	2,791
Total performance materials and technologies sales	$10,674	$10,339
Safety and productivity solutions sales		
Safety	$ 2,278	$ 2,169
Productivity solutions	4,059	3,470
Total safety and productivity solutions sales.	$ 6,337	$ 5,639
Total consolidated sales	$41,802	$40,534

    a. Calculate historic (year-on-year) sales growth for each business unit, segment, and total consolidated sales. Calculate the rate to 4 decimal places (e.g. 2.15%).

    b. Use the historic growth in Total consolidated sales (from 2017 to 2018) to estimate total consolidated sales for 2019.

    c. Refine the sales forecast by using the sales growth rates for each of the four segments (from 2017 to 2018) to estimate 2019 sales for each segment. Determine a forecast for total consolidated sales for 2019.

    d. Refine the sales forecast further by using the sales growth rates for each of the business units within each of the four segments. This means we use the separate historic growth for each line item in the table to estimate 2019 total consolidated sales.

    e. Which approach do we believe is more accurate in forecasting total consolidated sales?

E12-30. Projecting NOPAT and NOA Using Parsimonious Forecasting Method

Following are **Target**'s sales, net operating profit after tax (NOPAT), and net operating assets (NOA) for its year ended February 2, 2019 ($ millions).

Sales.	$75,356
Net operating profit after tax (NOPAT)	3,264
Net operating assets (NOA)	21,016

Use the parsimonious method to forecast Target's sales, NOPAT, and NOA for years ended February 2020 through 2023 using the following assumptions.

Sales growth per year.	3.6%
Net operating profit margin (NOPM).	4.3%
Net operating asset turnover (NOAT), based on NOA at February 2, 2019 . . .	3.59

LO7

Target Corporation (TGT)

E12-31. Projecting NOPAT and NOA Using Parsimonious Forecasting Method

Following are **Logitech**'s sales, net operating profit after tax (NOPAT), and net operating assets (NOA) for its fiscal year ended March 31, 2019 ($ thousands).

Net sales.	$2,788,322
Net operating profit after tax (NOPAT)	211,362
Net operating assets (NOA)	571,823

Use the parsimonious method to forecast Logitech's sales, NOPAT, and NOA for fiscal years ended March 31, 2020 through 2023 using the following assumptions.

Net sales growth per year.	7.00%
Net operating profit margin (NOPM).	7.58%
Net operating asset turnover (NOAT), based on NOA at fiscal year-end	4.88

LO7

Logitech Inc. (LOGI)

Problems

LO2, 3, 4, 5
Costco Wholesale
Corporation (COST)

P12-32.   Forecast the Income Statement, Balance Sheet, and Statement of Cash Flows
Following are fiscal year financial statements of Costco.

COSTO WHOLESALE CORP Consolidated Statements of Income		
For Year Ended ($ millions)	Sep. 1, 2019	Sep. 2, 2018
Net sales.	$149,351	$138,434
Membership fees	3,352	3,142
Total revenue	152,703	141,576
Merchandise costs	132,886	123,152
Selling, general and administrative.	14,994	13,876
Preopening expenses.	86	68
Operating income.	4,737	4,480
Interest expense.	(150)	(159)
Interest income and other, net	178	121
Income before income taxes	4,765	4,442
Provision for income taxes	1,061	1,263
Net income including noncontrolling interests	3,704	3,179
Net income attributable to noncontrolling interests.	(45)	(45)
Net income attributable to Costco	$ 3,659	$ 3,134

COSTO WHOLESALE CORP Consolidated Balance Sheets		
In millions, except par value	Sep. 1, 2019	Sep. 2, 2018
Current Assets		
Cash and cash equivalents.	$ 8,384	$ 6,055
Short-term investments.	1,060	1,204
Receivables, net.	1,535	1,669
Merchandise inventories.	11,395	11,040
Other current assets	1,111	321
Total current assets.	23,485	20,289
Property and Equipment		
Land.	6,417	6,193
Buildings and improvements	17,136	16,107
Equipment and fixtures.	7,801	7,274
Construction in progress.	1,272	1,140
Gross property and equipment.	32,626	30,714
Less accumulated depreciation and amortization	(11,736)	(11,033)
Net property and equipment.	20,890	19,681
Other assets.	1,025	860
Total assets	$45,400	$40,830

continued

continued from previous page

COSTO WHOLESALE CORP Consolidated Balance Sheets		
In millions, except par value	**Sep. 1, 2019**	**Sep. 2, 2018**
Current Liabilities		
Accounts payable	$11,679	$11,237
Accrued salaries and benefits.	3,176	2,994
Accrued member rewards.	1,180	1,057
Deferred membership fees	1,711	1,624
Current portion of long-term debt	1,699	90
Other current liabilities	3,792	2,924
Total current liabilities	23,237	19,926
Long-term debt, excluding current portion	5,124	6,487
Other liabilities	1,455	1,314
Total liabilities	29,816	27,727
Equity		
Preferred stock $.01 par value; 100,000,000 shares authorized; no shares issued and outstanding	—	—
Common stock $0.01 par value; 900,000,000 shares authorized; 439,625,000 and 438,189,000 shares issued and outstanding	4	4
Additional paid-in capital.	6,417	6,107
Accumulated other comprehensive loss.	(1,436)	(1,199)
Retained earnings	10,258	7,887
Total Costco stockholders' equity.	15,243	12,799
Noncontrolling interests	341	304
Total equity	15,584	13,103
Total liabilities and equity	$45,400	$40,830

Required

Forecast Costco's income statement, balance sheet, and statement of cash flows for the year ended September 1, 2020. Combine all property and equipment accounts into Net property and equipment. What do the forecasts imply about Costco's financing needs in 2020?

Forecasts assumptions

Forecast Net sales *and* Membership fees using their respective historical growth rates (2018 to 2019). Forecast the following as a percentage of Net sales:

- Merchandise costs
- Merchandise inventories
- Accrued member rewards
- Receivables, net
- Accounts payable
- Forecast income tax as 23% of pretax income

Forecast Deferred membership fees as a percentage of Membership fees.

Assume no change in the balance of the following:

- Preopening expenses
- Interest expense
- Interest income
- Net income attributable to noncontrolling interest
- Short-term investments
- Preferred stock
- Common stock
- Accumulated other comprehensive loss

Debt maturing in fiscal 2020 and 2021 is $1,699 million and $1,094 million, respectively.
The company anticipates repurchasing $250 million in common stock in fiscal 2020.
The 2019 statement of cash flows reports the following:

- Depreciation expense of $1,492 million
- Dividends of $1,038 million (to forecast 2020 dividends, use the 2019 dividend payout ratio as a percentage of net income attributable to Costco shareholders)
- Stock-based compensation (a noncash expense that is included in SG&A expense and is added to Additional paid-in capital) of $595 million
- CAPEX of $2,998 million

Forecast all other items as a percentage of total revenues.
Note: Round historical rates to three decimal places. For example, round 0.04556 to 4.6%.

LO2, 3, 5   **P12-33.**   **Forecast the Income Statement, Balance Sheet, and Statement of Cash Flows**

Following are the financial statements of Victoria Inc.

VICTORIA INC. Consolidated Income Statements		
For Year Ended December 31 ($ millions)	2019	2018
Revenues.	$32,376	$30,601
Cost of sales.	17,405	16,534
Gross profit.	14,971	14,067
Research and development expense.	3,278	3,213
Operating overhead expense.	7,191	6,679
Total selling and administrative expense	10,469	9,892
Interest expense, net	19	28
Other (income) expense, net	(140)	(58)
Income before income taxes	4,623	4,205
Income tax expense	863	932
Net income.	$ 3,760	$ 3,273

VICTORIA INC. Consolidated Balance Sheets		
December 31 ($ millions)	2019	2018
Current assets		
Cash and equivalents	$ 3,138	$ 3,852
Short-term investments.	2,319	2,072
Accounts receivable, net.	3,241	3,358
Inventories	4,838	4,337
Prepaid expenses and other current assets	1,489	1,968
Total current assets.	15,025	15,587
Property, plant and equipment, net.	3,520	3,011
Identifiable intangible assets, net	281	281
Goodwill	131	131
Deferred income taxes and other assets	2,439	2,587
Total assets	$21,396	$21,597
Current liabilities		
Current portion of long-term debt	$ 44	$ 107
Notes payable.	1	74
Accounts payable	2,191	2,131
Accrued liabilities	3,037	3,949
Income taxes payable.	85	71
Total current liabilities	5,358	6,332
Long-term debt.	2,010	1,079
Deferred income taxes and other liabilities.	1,770	1,479
Total liabilities	9,138	8,890
Shareholders' equity		
Class A convertible common stock.	0	0
Class B common stock.	3	3
Capital in excess of stated value	7,786	6,773
Accumulated other comprehensive income	318	1,246
Retained earnings	4,151	4,685
Total shareholders' equity.	12,258	12,707
Total liabilities and shareholders' equity	$21,396	$21,597

Required

Forecast Victoria's 2020 income statement, balance sheet, and statement of cash flows.

- Round the revenue growth rate to the nearest whole percent.
- Round forecasts to $ millions.
- Assume no change for interest expense, net, other (income) expense, net, short-term investments, goodwill, notes payable, all classes of common stock, capital in excess of stated value, and accumulated other comprehensive income.
- For 2019, capital expenditures are $1,143 million, depreciation expense is $649 million, amortization expense is $13 million, and dividends are $1,022 million. Forecast CAPEX as a percentage of revenue. Forecast depreciation and amortization as a percentage of beginning-year PPE, net and beginning-year intangibles, respectively. Forecast dividends as a percentage of net income.
- Footnotes reveal that the current portion of long-term debt due in 2021 is $6 million.
- Estimate forecast assumptions for all other balance sheet and income statement items as a percentage of Revenues, rounded to three decimal places (for example, Inventories/Revenues is 0.14943 or 14.9%).
- Assume tax expense is 18.7% of pretax income.

What do the forecasts imply about the company's cash balance and related financing needs for the upcoming year?

P12-34. Two-Year-Ahead Forecast of Financial Statements

Following are the financial statements of Target Corporation from its fiscal year ended February 2, 2019.

LO6

Target Corporation
(TGT)

TARGET CORPORATION Consolidated Statements of Financial Position		
For Fiscal Years Ended ($ millions)	**Feb. 2, 2019**	**Feb. 3, 2018**
Assets		
Cash and cash equivalents	$1,556	$2,643
Inventory	9,497	8,597
Other current assets	1,466	1,300
Total current assets	12,519	12,540
Property and equipment		
Land	6,064	6,095
Buildings and improvements	29,240	28,131
Fixtures and equipment	5,912	5,623
Computer hardware and software	2,544	2,645
Construction-in-progress	460	440
Accumulated depreciation	(18,687)	(18,398)
Property and equipment, net	25,533	24,536
Operating lease assets	1,965	1,884
Other noncurrent assets	1,273	1,343
Total assets	$41,290	$40,303
Liabilities and shareholders' investment		
Accounts payable	$9,761	$8,677
Accrued and other current liabilities	4,201	4,094
Current portion of long-term debt and other borrowings	1,052	281
Total current liabilities	15,014	13,052
Long-term debt and other borrowings	10,223	11,117
Noncurrent operating lease liabilities	2,004	1,924
Deferred income taxes	972	693
Other noncurrent liabilities	1,780	1,866
Total noncurrent liabilities	14,979	15,600
Shareholders' investment		
Common stock	43	45
Additional paid-in capital	6,042	5,858
Retained earnings	6,017	6,495
Accumulated other comprehensive loss	(805)	(747)
Total shareholders' investment	11,297	11,651
Total liabilities and shareholders' investment	$41,290	$40,303

TARGET CORPORATION Consolidated Statements of Operations			
12 Months Ended ($ millions)	**Feb. 2, 2019**	**Feb. 3, 2018**	**Jan. 28, 2017**
Total revenue	$75,356	$72,714	$70,271
Cost of sales.	53,299	51,125	49,145
Selling, general and administrative expenses	15,723	15,140	14,217
Depreciation and amortization (exclusive of depreciation			
included in cost of sales).	2,224	2,225	2,045
Operating income.	4,110	4,224	4,864
Net interest expense.	461	653	991
Net other (income) expense	(27)	(59)	(88)
Earnings from continuing operations before income taxes. . . .	3,676	3,630	3,961
Provision for income taxes	746	722	1,295
Net earnings from continuing operations	2,930	2,908	2,666
Discontinued operations, net of tax	7	6	68
Net earnings.	$ 2,937	$ 2,914	$ 2,734

Required

Forecast Target's income statements and balance sheets for the fiscal years ended February 2020 and 2021. Combine the forecasted property and equipment accounts into one account, titled Property and equipment, net. For cost of goods sold and for selling, general and administrative expenses, use the historic percent of revenue for forecasts. Use the following assumptions and data.

Assumptions ($ millions)	
Inventory as % Total revenue.	12.6%
Other current assets as % Total revenue	1.9%
Operating lease assets as % Total revenue.	2.6%
Other noncurrent assets as % Total revenue	1.7%
Accounts payable as % Total revenue	13.0%
Accrued and other current liabilities as % Total revenue	5.6%
Noncurrent operating lease liabilities	No change
Deferred income taxes as % Total revenue	1.3%
Other noncurrent liabilities as % Total revenue	2.4%
Common stock	No change
Additional paid-in capital.	No change
Accumulated other comprehensive loss.	No change
CAPEX/Current period total revenue	4.70%
Dividends for year ended February 2019.	$1,335
Dividend payout	45.5%
Forecasted depreciation expense for year ended February 2020	$2,565
Forecasted depreciation expense for year ended February 2021	$2,778
Amortization expense.	$0
Net interest expense.	No change
Net other (income) expense	No change
Stock buybacks per year	$0
Tax rate (as % pretax income)	20%
Long term debt, current portion at February 2019	$1,052
Long term debt, current portion at February 2020	$1,002
Long-term debt, current portion at February 2021	$1,094

P12-35. **Sensitivity Analysis of Forecasted Income Statement**   LO1, 2

Following is the income statement for Sun Savers Inc. for the year ended December 31, 2019.

Consolidated Statements of Operations			
For Year Ended December 31 ($ thousands)	2019	2018	2017
Net sales.	$3,578,995	$3,391,187	$3,309,616
Cost of sales.	2,659,728	2,566,246	2,444,984
Gross profit.	919,267	824,941	864,632
Operating expenses			
Research and development	130,593	143,969	134,300
Selling, general, and administrative	255,192	253,827	270,261
Production startup	16,818	5,146	2,768
Restructuring and asset impairments	—	—	86,896
Total operating expenses	402,603	402,942	494,225
Operating income.	516,664	421,999	370,407
Foreign currency (loss) gain, net	(6,868)	(1,461)	893
Interest income.	22,516	18,030	16,752
Interest expense, net	(6,975)	(1,982)	(1,884)
Other expense, net.	(5,502)	(4,485)	(5,189)
Income before taxes and equity in earnings of unconsolidated affiliates . . .	519,835	432,101	380,979
Income tax benefit (expense).	6,156	(31,188)	(30,098)
Equity in earnings (loss) of unconsolidated affiliates, net of tax.	20,430	(4,949)	(163)
Net income .	$ 546,421	$ 395,964	$ 350,718

Required

a. Compute the effective tax rate for Sun Savers for each of the three years presented (to four decimal places such as 0.1234 or 12.34%). What do we observe? What might explain this rate?

b. Use the following assumptions to forecast the 2020 income statement.

Net sales growth.	6%
Cost of sales.	74.0% of net sales
Research and development	3.6% of net sales
Selling, general, and administrative	7.1% of net sales
Production startup	0.5% of net sales
Restructuring and asset impairments.	$0
Foreign currency (loss) gain, net	$0
Interest income, Interest expense, net, and Other expense, net . . .	No change in $
Income tax benefit (expense).	Effective rate for 2019
Equity in earnings (loss) of unconsolidated affiliates, net of tax.	Increase by 10% over FY2019

c. Compute the percent change in net income from actual 2019 to the 2020 forecasted net income.

d. Perform a sensitivity analysis by changing the effective tax rate and seeing the change in net income. Instead of using the 2019 effective tax rate, use the average effective tax rate that prevailed over the 2017 and 2018 period. Again, compute the tax rate to four decimal places. Compute the percent change in net income from actual 2019 to the 2020 forecasted net income. How sensitive is net income to the change in tax rate?

e. Perform a sensitivity analysis by changing the growth rate for net sales. Forecast the income statement for a range of growth rates, from 5% to 7% in 50-basis-point increments (i.e., 5%, 5.5%, 6%, 6.5%, and 7%). For this part, use an effective tax rate of 7.56%.

f. Perform a sensitivity analysis by changing the cost of sales percent to determine the effect on net income (not the entire income statement, only net income). Vary the cost of sales percent up and down by 50 basis points from 74%. For this part, use an effective tax rate of 7.56% and include the entire range of sales growth rates from 5% to 7%. That is, generate a table that shows net income for three cost-of-sales percentages and five sales-growth rates. For each cell, compute the percent change in net income from actual 2019 to the 2020 forecasted net income.

Ongoing Project

(This ongoing project began in Module 1 and continues through most of the book; even if previous segments were not completed, the requirements are still applicable to any business analysis.) This module describes methods commonly used to forecast financial statements. The module shows how to forecast a complete set of financial statements (for one or more years). The module concludes with a parsimonious forecast of select balance sheet and income statement metrics. A project can include both types of forecasts. We can use the full set of financial statements to analyze the company's near-term future performance and position. We can then use the parsimonious forecast for longer-term forecasts as inputs for valuation models that estimate the company's stock price. Importantly, use a spreadsheet for the forecasting process. The SEC website has "interactive data" for annual reports—these are spreadsheet-like arrays that can be copied into a spreadsheet. Also, many companies include on their investor relations page an Excel version of their financial statements. Define as many cells as possible with formulas, and reference income statement totals to the related balance sheet accounts. To balance the balance sheet, define the cash account to be equal to the difference between forecasted assets and liabilities plus stockholders' equity.

1. *Forecasting Preliminaries*   Begin with the adjusted set of financial statements that reflect the company's net operating assets and its operating income that we expect to persist into the future. This requires that we exclude one-time items and adjust other items to reflect anticipated levels of ongoing activities.

2. *Model Assumptions and Inputs*   The assumptions we use critically impact forecasted numbers. Be as thorough as possible in research and analysis in determining model inputs. The most critical assumption is sales growth. Before we begin, adjust any fiscal years to take care of the "13th week" (or 53rd week) problem. Then, use all the reported years' sales numbers to compute historical growth numbers. Observe any trends. If the company reports segment sales, compute growth of each segment and compare it with total sales growth. We should forecast each segment separately if growth differs by segment. Read the company's MD&A, the footnotes, and any guidance the company voluntarily provides. Obtain an industry report and, determine a consensus about sales expectations and the cost environment. As discussed in the module, we assume most costs (including COGS and SGA) will not deviate from their historical percentages unless there is evidence to suggest otherwise. Again, scour the footnotes. In the end, use sound judgment and remember that forecasted numbers are subjective.

3. *Forecast the Income Statement*   Use the sales growth assumption to forecast sales for the next fiscal year. Use cost-level assumptions to forecast all the operating expenses. At this first stage, we typically leave nonoperating expenses and revenues unchanged from prior-year dollar levels. We return to fine-tune these after we forecast the balance sheet. Forecast a preliminary tax expense and net income. We need those numbers to complete the balance sheet.

4. *Forecast the Balance Sheet*   Use the percentage of sales approach to forecast each operating asset and liability, and follow the method described in the module to forecast PPE and intangible assets. Certain operating assets and liabilities will be forecasted to remain unchanged year over year unless we learn otherwise from the financial statements. Forecast debt using the information about scheduled debt maturities. Pay careful attention to forecasting dividends and any stock repurchases or issuances.

5. *Forecast the Statement of Cash Flows*   We construct a statement of cash flows from the company's current balance sheet (from the Form 10-K or annual report) and the forecasted balance sheet. The net income number forecasted will also tie in. Remember that this statement is a mechanical operation, requiring no assumptions or new calculations.

Solutions to Review Problems

Review 12-1—Solution

a. The income statement has two potential "one-time" items that we would consider eliminating:
Divestitures loss and Restructuring, impairment, and other exit costs. While restructuring has appeared on the income statement over the past three years, the amounts differ; we could also consider normalizing the adjustment to the three-year average.

b. We forecast financial statements in the following order: income statement, balance sheet, statement of cash flows. This order is important because income statement activity determines many balance sheet account balances, including retained earnings. Cash flows cannot be determined without net income (which determines cash from operating activities) and balance sheet accounts (which affect all three types of cash flows).

c. The first, and most crucial, income statement amount forecasted is revenue.

d. The following forecasted expenses are related to forecasted revenue.
   - Cost of goods sold—directly.
   - Selling, general, and administrative expense—directly.
   - Depreciation—indirectly to the extent that revenue drives new PPE purchases.
   - Income tax—indirectly via pretax income, which increases with revenue.

e. The following forecasted balance sheet accounts are related to forecasted revenue.
   - Receivables.
   - Inventories.
   - Prepaid expenses.
   - Land, buildings, and equipment—to the extent that revenue drives new PPE purchases.
   - Accounts payable—related to cost of sales, which is determined by revenue.
   - Other current liabilities—those liabilities that are related to accrued operating expenses are directly determined by revenue.

Review 12-2—Solution

Income Statement ($ millions)	FY2019 Actual	% of Sales	Computations	FY2020 Est.
Net sales.	$16,865.2	100.0%	$16,865.2 × 1.015	$17,118.2
Cost of sales.	11,108.4	65.9%	$17,118.2 × 65.9%	11,280.9
Selling, general, and administrative expenses	2,935.8	17.4%	$17,118.2 × 17.4%	2,978.6
Divestitures loss	30.0	0.2%	Assumed $0	—
Restructuring, impairment, and other exit costs . . .	275.1	1.6%	$17,118.2 × 1.6%	273.9
Operating profit.	2,515.9	14.9%		2,584.8
Benefit plan nonservice income	(87.9)	0.5%	Assumed $0	—
Interest, net.	521.8	3.1%	no change	521.8
Earnings before income taxes and after-tax earnings from joint ventures	2,082.0	12.3%	subtotal	2,063.0
Income taxes	367.8	2.2%	$2,063 × 17.7%	365.2
After-tax earnings from joint ventures.	(72.0)	0.0%	no change	(72.0)
Net earnings, including earnings attributable to redeemable and noncontrolling interests	1,786.2	10.6%	subtotal	1,769.8
Net earnings attributable to redeemable and noncontrolling interests.	33.5	0.2%	no change	33.5
Net earnings attributable to General Mills	$ 1,752.7	10.4%	total	$ 1,736.3

Review 12-3—Solution

1.

Balance Sheet ($ millions)	FY2019	% of Sales	Computations	FY2020
Current assets				
Cash and cash equivalents.	$ 450.0	2.7%	Plug	$ (233.4)
Receivables	1,679.7	10.0%	$17,118.2 × 10.0%	1,711.8
Inventories	1,559.3	9.2%	$17,118.2 × 9.2%	1,574.9
Prepaid expenses and other current assets . .	497.5	2.9%	$17,118.2 × 2.9%	496.4
Total current assets.	4,186.5	24.8%	subtotal	3,549.7
Land, buildings, and equipment	3,787.2	22.5%	$546.1 CAPEX – $580.1 depreciation	3,753.2
Goodwill	13,995.8	83.0%	no change	13,995.8
Other intangible assets.	7,166.8	42.5%	Minus $40 amortization	7,126.8
Other assets	974.9	5.8%	$17,118.2 × 5.8%	992.9
Total assets	$30,111.2	178.5%	total	$29,418.4

continued

continued from prior page

Balance Sheets ($ millions)	FY2019	% of Sales	Computations	FY2020
Current liabilities				
Accounts payable	$ 2,854.1	16.9%	$17,118.2 × 16.9%	$ 2,893.0
Current portion of long-term debt	1,396.5	8.3%	($1,396.5) + $2,114.4	2,114.4
Notes payable	1,468.7	8.7%	no change	1,468.7
Other current liabilities	1,367.8	8.1%	$17,118.2 × 8.1%	1,386.6
Total current liabilities	7,087.1	42.0%	subtotal	7,862.7
Long-term debt	11,624.8	68.9%	$11,624.8 − $2,114.4	9,510.4
Deferred income taxes	2,031.0	12.0%	$17,118.2 × 12.0%	2,054.2
Other liabilities	1,448.9	8.6%	$17,118.2 × 8.6%	1,472.2
Total liabilities	22,191.8	131.6%	subtotal	20,899.5
Redeemable interest value	551.7	3.3%	no change	551.7
Stockholders' equity				
Common stock	75.5	0.4%	no change	75.5
Additional paid-in capital	1,386.7	8.2%	no change	1,386.7
Retained earnings	14,996.7	88.9%	$1,736.3 income − $1,170.3 dividends	15,562.7
Common stock in treasury, at cost	(6,779.0)	(40.2)%	no change	(6,779.0)
Accumulated other comprehensive loss	(2,625.4)	(15.6)%	no change	(2,625.4)
Total stockholders' equity	7,054.5	41.8%	subtotal	7,620.5
Noncontrolling interests	313.2	1.9%	+ $33.5 from forecasted income statement	346.7
Total equity	7,367.7	43.7%	subtotal	7,967.2
Total liabilities and equity	$30,111.2	178.5%	total	$29,418.4

2. The negative balance for cash indicates that the company will not generate sufficient cash from operations to cover its CAPEX, debt service requirements and expected dividend payments.

Review 12-4—Solution

a.

$ millions	FY2019 Actual Sales	Estimated Growth Rate	FY2020 Est. Sales
U.S. Meals & Baking	$3,839.8	1.50%	$ 3,897.4
U.S. Cereal	2,255.4	2.00%	2,300.5
U.S. Snacks	2,060.9	(0.50)%	2,050.6
U.S. Yogurt and Other	906.7	1.00%	915.8
Canada	862.4	(1.00)%	853.8
	$9,925.2		$10,018.0

b. The overall growth rate for the total U.S. retail segment is 0.93%, which is computed as ($10,018/$9,925.2) − 1. This growth rate implies that sales are expected to increase by about 1% in FY2020.

Review 12-5—Solution

Statement of Cash Flows		
For Fiscal Year Ended 2020 ($ millions)	Computations	2020 Est.
Net earnings, including earnings attributable to redeemable and noncontrolling interests ...		$1,769.8
Add: depreciation		580.1
Add: amortization		40.0
Change in receivables	$1,679.7 – $1,711.8	(32.1)
Change in inventories	$1,559.3 – $1,574.9	(15.6)
Change in prepaid expenses and other current assets	$497.5 – $496.4	1.1
Change in other assets	$974.9 – $992.9	(18.0)
Change in accounts payable	$2,893.0 – $2,854.1	38.9
Change in other current liabilities	$1,386.6 – $1,367.8	18.8
Change in deferred income taxes	$2,054.2 – $2,031.0	23.2
Change in other long-term liabilities	$1,472.2 – $1,448.9	23.3
Net cash from operating activities		2,429.5
Capital expenditures	$17,118 × 3.19%	(546.1)
Net cash from investing activities		(546.1)
Dividends		(1,170.3)
Change in current maturities of long-term debt	$2,114.4 – $1,396.5	717.9
Change in long-term debt	$9,510.4 – $11,624.8	(2,114.4)
Purchase of treasury shares	none	—
Net cash from financing activities		(2,566.8)
Net change in cash		(683.4)
Beginning cash		450.0
Ending cash		$ (233.4)

Review 12-6—Solution

Income Statement ($ millions)	FY2019 Actual	% of Sales	Computations	FY2020 Forecast	% of Sales	Computations	FY2021 Forecast	% of Sales
Net sales	$16,865.2	100.0%	$16,865.2 × 1.015	$17,118.2	100.0%	$17,118.2 × 1.015	$17,375.0	100.0%
Cost of sales	11,108.4	65.9%	$17,118.2 × 65.9%	11,280.9	65.9%	$17,375.0 × 65.9%	11,450.1	65.9%
Selling, general, and administrative expenses	2,935.8	17.4%	$17,118.2 × 17.4%	2,978.6	17.4%	$17,375.0 × 17.4%	3,023.3	17.4%
Divestitures loss	30.0	0.2%	Assumed $0	—	0.0%	Assumed $0	—	0.0%
Restructuring, impairment, and other exit costs	275.1	1.6%	$17,118.2 × 1.6%	273.9	1.6%	$17,375.0 × 1.6%	278.0	1.6%
Operating profit	2,515.9	14.9%	subtotal	2,584.8	15.1%	subtotal	2,623.6	15.1%
Benefit plan nonservice income	(87.9)	(0.5)%	Assumed $0	—	—	Assumed $0	—	—
Interest, net	521.8	3.1%	$700 × (3.4%/2)	533.7	3.1%	$2,100 × (3.4%/2)	569.4	3.3%
Earnings before income taxes and after-tax earnings from joint ventures	2,082.0	12.3%	subtotal	2,051.1	12.0%	subtotal	2,054.2	11.8%
Income taxes	367.8	2.2%	$2,051.1 × 17.7%	363.0	2.1%	$2,054.2 × 17.7%	363.6	2.1%
After-tax earnings from joint ventures	72.0	0.0%	no change	72.0	0.4%	no change	72.0	0.4%
Net earnings, including earnings attributable to redeemable and noncontrolling interests	1,786.2	10.6%	subtotal	1,760.1	10.3%	subtotal	1,762.6	10.1%
Net earnings attributable to redeemable and noncontrolling interests	33.5	0.2%	Add amount from forecasted income statement	33.5	0.2%	Add amount from forecasted income statement	33.5	0.2%
Net earnings attributable to General Mills	$ 1,752.7	10.4%	total	$1,726.6	10.1%	total	$ 1,729.1	9.9%

continued

continued from prior page

Balance Sheets ($ millions)	FY2019 Actual	% of Sales	Computations	FY2020 Forecast	% of Sales	Computations	FY2021 Forecast	% of Sales
Current assets								
Cash and cash equivalents	$ 450.0	2.7%	Plug	$ 463.5	2.7%	Plug	$ 466.2	2.7%
Receivables	1,679.7	10.0%	$17,118.2 × 10.0%	1,711.8	10.0%	$17,375.0 × 10.0%	1,737.5	10.0%
Inventories	1,559.3	9.2%	$17,118.2 × 9.2%	1,574.9	9.2%	$17,375.0 × 9.2%	1,598.5	9.2%
Prepaid expenses and other current assets...	497.5	2.9%	$17,118.2 × 2.9%	496.4	2.9%	$17,375.0 × 2.9%	503.9	2.9%
Total current assets	4,186.5	24.8%	subtotal	4,246.6	24.8%	subtotal	4,306.1	24.8%
Land, buildings, and equipment	3,787.2	22.5%	$546.1 – $580.1	3,753.2	21.9%	$554.3 – $588.8	3,718.7	21.4%
Goodwill	13,995.8	83.0%	no change	13,995.8	81.8%	no change	13,995.8	80.6%
Other intangible assets	7,166.8	42.5%	Minus $40 amortization	7,126.8	41.6%	Minus $40 amortization	7,086.8	40.8%
Other assets	974.9	5.8%	$17,118.2 × 5.8%	992.9	5.8%	$17,375.0 × 5.8%	1,007.8	5.8%
Total assets	$30,111.2	178.5%	total	$30,115.3	175.9%	total	$30,115.2	173.3%
Current liabilities								
Accounts payable	$ 2,854.1	16.9%	$17,118.2 × 16.9%	$ 2,893.0	16.9%	$17,375.0 × 16.9%	$ 2,936.4	16.9%
Current portion of long-term debt	1,396.5	8.3%	($1,396.5) + $2,114.4 + $700	2,814.4	16.4%	($2,814.4) + $1,224.1 + $2,100	3,324.1	19.1%
Notes payable	1,468.7	8.7%	no change	1,468.7	8.6%	no change	1,468.7	8.5%
Other current liabilities	1,367.8	8.1%	$17,118.2 × 8.1%	1,386.6	8.1%	$17,375.0 × 8.1%	1,407.4	8.1%
Total current liabilities	7,087.1	42.0%	subtotal	8,562.7	50.0%	subtotal	9,136.6	52.6%
Long-term debt	11,624.8	68.9%	$11,624.8 – $2,114.4	9,510.4	55.6%	$9,510.4 – $1,224.1	8,286.3	47.7%
Deferred income taxes	2,031.0	12.0%	$17,118.2 × 12.0%	2,054.2	12.0%	$17,375.0 × 12.0%	2,085.0	12.0%
Other liabilities	1,448.9	8.6%	$17,118.2 × 8.6%	1,472.2	8.6%	$17,375.0 × 8.6%	1,494.3	8.6%
Total liabilities	22,191.8	131.6%	subtotal	21,599.5	126.2%	subtotal	21,002.2	120.9%
Redeemable interest value	551.7	3.3%	no change	551.7	3.2%	no change	551.7	3.2%
Stockholders' equity								
Common stock, 754.6 shares issued, $0.10 par value	75.5	0.4%	no change	75.5	0.4%	no change	75.5	0.4%
Additional paid-in capital	1,386.7	8.2%	no change	1,386.7	8.1%	no change	1,386.7	8.0%
Retained earnings	14,996.7	88.9%	$1,726.6 – $1,163.7	15,559.6	90.9%	$1,729.1 – $1,165.4	16,123.3	92.8%
Common stock in treasury, at cost	(6,779.0)	(40.2)%	no change	(6,779.0)	(39.6)%	no change	(6,779.0)	(39.0)%
Accumulated other comprehensive loss	(2,625.4)	(15.6)%	no change	(2,625.4)	(15.3)%	no change	(2,625.4)	(15.1)%
Total stockholders' equity	7,054.5	41.8%	subtotal	7,617.4	44.5%	subtotal	8,181.1	47.1%
Noncontrolling interests	313.2	1.9%	$33.5 from income statement	346.7	1.8%	$33.5 from income statement	380.2	2.2%
Total equity	7,367.7	43.7%	subtotal	7,964.1	46.5%	subtotal	8,561.3	49.3%
Total liabilities and equity	$30,111.2	178.5%	total	$31,115.3	175.9%	total	$30,115.2	173.3%

Review 12-7—Solution

a. We adjust net income by adding back the effects of the two one-time items, as follows.

Net income, as reported	$1,786.2
Add back: Divestitures loss, after tax	24.4
Add back: Restructuring, impairment, and other exit costs, after tax	224.0
Net income, as restated	$2,034.6

$$\text{NOPAT} = \text{Net income} + \text{NNE} = \$2,034.6 + [(1\text{-}23\%) \times (\$521.8 - \$87.9] = \$2,368.7$$
$$\text{NOPM} = \$2,368.7/\$16,865.2 = 14.0\%$$

b.

$ millions	Current 2019	2020	2021	2022	2023
Net sales growth	1.5%	1.5%	1.5%	1.5%	1.5%
Net sales unrounded	$16,865.2	**$17,118.18** ($16,865.20 × 1.015)	**$17,374.95** ($17,118.18 × 1.015)	**$17,635.57** ($17,374.95 × 1.015)	**$17,900.11** ($17,635.57 × 1.015)
Net sales rounded		**$17,118.2**	**$17,375.0**	**$17,635.6**	**$17,900.1**
NOPM	14.0%	14.0%	14.0%	14.0%	14.0%
NOPAT	$ 2,368.7	**$2,396.5** ($17,118.2 × 14.0%)	**$2,432.5** ($17,375.0 × 14.0%)	**$2,469.0** ($17,635.6 × 14.0%)	**$2,506.0** ($17,900.1 × 14.0%)
NOAT	0.77	0.77	0.77	0.77	0.77
NOA	$21,959.4	**$22,231.4** ($17,118.2/0.77)	**$22,564.9** ($17,375.0/0.77)	**$22,903.4** ($17,635.6/0.77)	**$23,246.9** ($17,900.1/0.77)

Module 13

Using Financial Statements for Valuation

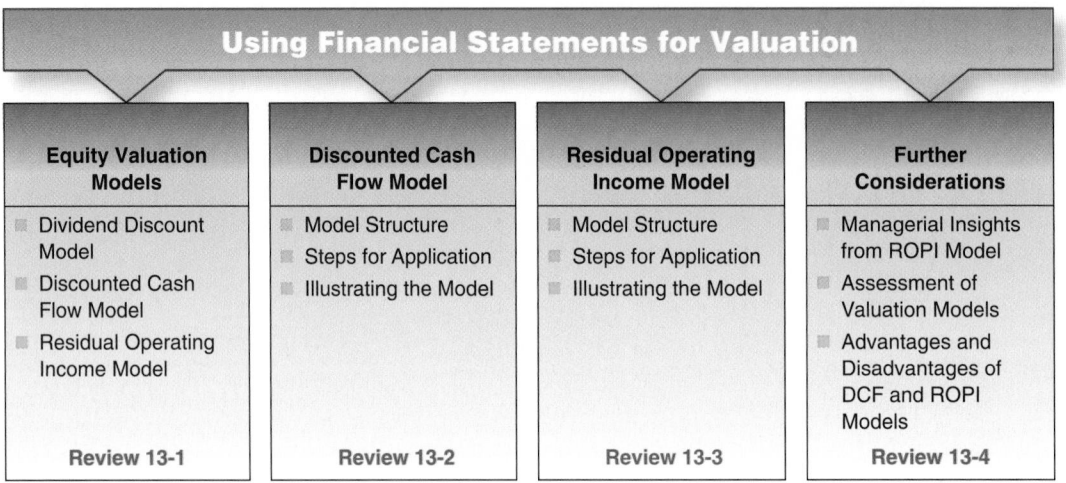

Using Financial Statements for Valuation			
Equity Valuation Models	**Discounted Cash Flow Model**	**Residual Operating Income Model**	**Further Considerations**
▪ Dividend Discount Model ▪ Discounted Cash Flow Model ▪ Residual Operating Income Model	▪ Model Structure ▪ Steps for Application ▪ Illustrating the Model	▪ Model Structure ▪ Steps for Application ▪ Illustrating the Model	▪ Managerial Insights from ROPI Model ▪ Assessment of Valuation Models ▪ Advantages and Disadvantages of DCF and ROPI Models
Review 13-1	**Review 13-2**	**Review 13-3**	**Review 13-4**

PREVIEW

We explain use of financial statement information to estimate the value of a company, including use of

■ Forecasts of a company's sales, profit, and cash flow.

■ Discounted Cash Flow (DCF) method of valuation and illustration of its application.

■ Residual operating income (ROPI) method of valuation and illustration of its application.

We also discuss managerial insights we gain from an understanding of valuation models and illustrate the types of actions managers can take to increase company value. An appendix to this module shows an example analyst report and valuation of Procter & Gamble by Deutsche Bank.

■ **Procter & Gamble** is the focus company and the dashboard below conveys key financial information.

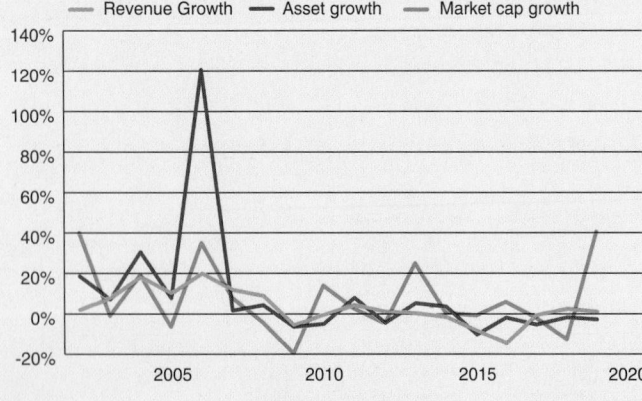

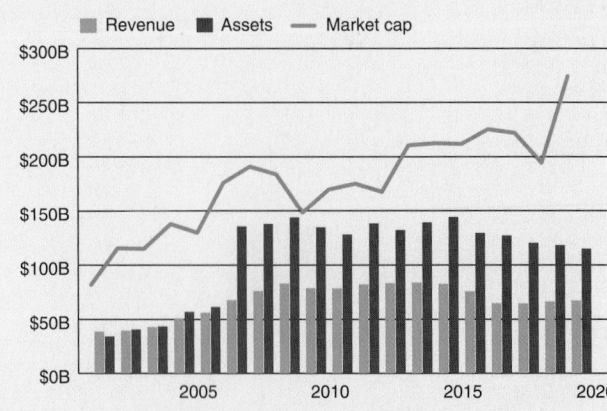

Road Map

LO	Learning Objective | Topics	Page	eLecture	Guided Example	Assignments
13-1	**Identify equity valuation models and explain the information required to value equity securities.** Dividend Discount Model :: Discounted Cash Flow Model :: Residual Operating Income Model :: Valuation Model Inputs	13-3	e13–1	Review 13-1	1, 2, 9, 20, 23, 26, 27, 30, 31
13-2	**Describe and apply the discounted free cash flow model to value equity securities.** DCF Model Structure :: Steps in Applying the DCF Model :: Illustrating the DCF Model	13-5	e13–2	Review 13-2	3, 4, 11, 13, 16, 18, 20, 21, 23, 26, 28, 30, 32
13-3	**Describe and apply the residual operating income model to value equity securities.** ROPI Model Structure :: Steps in Applying the ROPI Model :: Illustrating the ROPI Model	13-9	e13–3	Review 13-3	5, 6, 7, 10, 12, 14, 17, 19, 22, 23, 25, 27, 29, 31, 33
13-4	**Explain how equity valuation models can inform managerial decisions.** Managerial Insights :: Assessment of Valuation Models	13-11	e13–4	Review 13-4	8, 15, 24, 25, 34

Equity Valuation Models

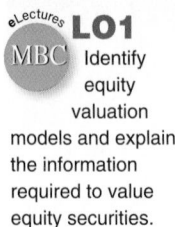

LO1 Identify equity valuation models and explain the information required to value equity securities.

Investors, analysts, and managers use accounting information to value a company. This module describes several approaches to equity valuation. We know that the value of a debt security is the present value of the interest and principal payments that the investor *expects* to receive in the future. The valuation of equity securities is similar in that it is also based on expectations. The difference lies in the increased uncertainty surrounding the timing and amount of payments from equity securities. There are many types of equity valuation models in use today, but they share at least three common features. All equity valuation models:

- Assume that a particular fundamental variable determines equity value—we discuss three fundamental variables: dividends, free cash flows, and residual operating income.

- Forecast the fundamental variable for the remainder of the company's life. Generating an infinite stream of forecasts is not realistic; consequently, we typically estimate the fundamental variable over a horizon period, often 4 to 10 years. Then, we make simplifying assumptions about the terminal period, which encompasses the years subsequent to the horizon period. A key assumption is that the fundamental variables as forecasted for the terminal period continue into perpetuity.

- Use time value of money techniques to determine the present value of the future estimated amounts. The discount factor depends on the fundamental variable in the model. We must estimate the discount factor, which requires data from external sources and additional assumptions.

Dividend Discount Model

The basis of equity valuation is the premise that the value of an equity security is determined by the payments that the investor can expect to receive. Equity investments involve two types of payoffs: (1) dividends received while the security is owned and (2) capital gains when the security is sold. The future stock price is, itself, also assumed to be related to the expected dividends that the new investor expects to receive; as a result, the expected receipt of dividends is the sole driver of stock price under this type of valuation model. The value of an equity security is, then, based on the present value of expected dividends plus the present value of the security at the end of the forecasted holding period. The present value is determined using the firm's cost of equity capital as the discount rate. This **dividend discount model** is appealing in its simplicity and its intuitive focus on dividend distribution. As a practical matter, however, the model is not always useful because many companies that have a positive stock price have never paid a dividend, and are not expected to pay a dividend in the foreseeable future.

Discounted Cash Flow Model

The most widely used model to estimate the value of common stock is the **discounted cash flow (DCF) model**. This model focuses on the company's operating and investing activities; that is, on its ability to *generate cash*. This makes the DCF model more practical than the dividend discount model. The DCF model first estimates the value of the company (the *enterprise value*) and, then, determines the shareholders' portion, or the equity value as the enterprise value less the value of the company's debt. The DCF model takes as its fundamental input variable, the expected *free cash flows to the firm*, which are defined as operating cash flows net of the expected new investments in net operating assets (such as property, plant and equipment) that are required to support the business. The DCF model uses the weighted average cost of capital (WACC) to discount the expected future free cash flows.

Residual Operating Income Model

Another approach to equity valuation also focuses on operating and investing activities. It is known as the **residual operating income (ROPI) model**. This model uses both net operating profits after tax (NOPAT) and the net operating assets (NOA) to determine equity value (see Module 4 for complete descriptions of the NOPAT and NOA measures). This approach highlights the importance of return on net operating assets (RNOA), and the disaggregation of RNOA into net operating profit margin and NOA turnover. We discuss the implications of this insight for managers later in this module.

Valuation Model Inputs

To illustrate the valuation models, we use Procter & Gamble (P&G). Exhibit 13.1 provides model inputs used to estimate the models including sales, net operating profit after tax (NOPAT) and net operating assets (NOA). We obtain the model inputs for FY2019 from P&G's actual 2019 financial statements (from Exhibit 12.2). Before calculating NOPAT, we adjust for certain nonrecurring items (including a goodwill impairment of $8,000 million after-tax in 2019). The forecasted variables for FY2020 and FY2021 come from the forecasted income statements and balance sheets developed in the forecasting module and shown in Exhibits 12.2 and 12.3.[1] Forecasted financial statements (not included here) are also used to get forecasts for FY2022 and FY2023. For the terminal period, we assume a terminal growth rate of 2%. These forecasted numbers are generated using the approach we describe in our forecasting module that utilizes all of the information in the 10-K and its notes. We describe an alternate approach in our Analysis Insight Box on *Parsimonious Model Forecasts* below.

Exhibit 13.1 ■ Forecasts for Procter & Gamble

		Forecast Horizon Period				
$ millions	Reported 2019	2020	2021	2022	2023	Terminal Period
Sales................................	$67,684	$70,053	$72,505	$75,042	$77,669	$79,222
Sales growth.......................		3.5%	3.5%	3.5%	3.5%	2.0%
Net operating profit after tax (NOPAT)	$11,512	$11,776	$12,187	$12,607	$13,048	$13,309
Net operating assets (NOA)	$67,384	$66,858	$66,274	$68,846	$71,256	$72,681

To estimate the valuation models, we use a short four-year horizon period to simplify the exposition and to reduce the computational burden. In practice, investors and analysts use spreadsheets to forecast future cash flows and value the equity security, and typically have a forecast horizon of 7–10 periods. We assume a terminal period growth rate of 2% for sales, NOPAT and NOA for years 2024 and beyond.

Analysis Insight ■ Parsimonious Model Forecasts

One alternative to using detailed forecasts of the income statement and balance sheet is to use the parsimonious forecasting method that we describe in Appendix 12C. That method uses sales growth and ratios of NOPM and NOAT, computed from current (or recent) financial statements, to forecast future sales, NOPAT, and NOA. In its simple form, that method assumes that NOPM and NOAT remain unchanged during the forecast horizon and terminal period. Exhibit 13.2 shows the parsimonious forecasts for P&G (derived in Module 12) using a sales growth of 3.5% for the forecast horizon and 2% for the terminal period, along with NOPM of 17.0% (the 2019 NOPM) and NOAT of 1.00 (the 2019 NOAT). As expected, the numbers differ slightly from the full forecasted financials in Exhibit 13.1 because this parsimonious model has different assumptions.

Exhibit 13.2 ■ Valuation Model Inputs from Parsimonious Forecast Method

		Forecast Horizon Period				
Procter & Gamble	Reported 2019	2020	2021	2022	2023	Terminal Period
Sales growth..............		3.5%	3.5%	3.5%	3.5%	2.0%
Sales (unrounded)	$67,684	$70,052.94	$72,504.79	$75,042.46	$77,668.95	$79,222.33
		($67,684 × 1.035)	($70,052.94 × 1.035)	($72,504.79 × 1.035)	($75,042.46 × 1.035)	($77,668.95 × 1.02)
Sales (rounded)..............		$70,053	$72,505	$75,042	$77,669	$79,222
NOPAT (Sales rounded × 17%) ...	11,512	$11,909	$12,326	$12,757	$13,204	$13,468
NOPM assumed to be 17.0%.....		($70,053 × 17.0%)	($72,505 × 17.0%)	($75,042 × 17.0%)	($77,669 × 17.0%)	($79,222 × 17.0%)
NOA	67,384	70,053	72,505	75,042	77,669	79,222
NOAT assumed to be 1.00.......		($70,053/1.0)	($72,505/1.0)	($75,042/1.0)	($77,669/1.0)	($79,222/1.0)

---

[1] **NOPAT** equals revenues less operating expenses such as cost of goods sold, selling, general, and administrative expenses, and taxes. NOPAT excludes any interest revenue and interest expense and any gains or losses from financial investments. NOPAT reflects the operating side of the firm as opposed to nonoperating activities such as borrowing and security investment activities. **NOA** equals operating assets less operating liabilities. (See Module 4.)

Review 13-1 LO1

We discussed three types of valuation models: dividend discount model, discounted cash flow model, and residual operating income model.

Required

For each of the following statements *a* through *j*, identify whether it is True or False for each of the three valuation models.

	Dividend Discount	Discounted Cash Flow	Residual Operating Income
a. Uses net present value concepts	_____	_____	_____
b. Operating cash flows affect value.	_____	_____	_____
c. Estimates a company's enterprise value	_____	_____	_____
d. Dividends to shareholders is a model input	_____	_____	_____
e. Free cash flow is a model input	_____	_____	_____
f. Estimates equity value of the firm.	_____	_____	_____
g. Capital expenditures affect estimated value.	_____	_____	_____
h. Requires forecasts of future amounts.	_____	_____	_____
i. Operating profit affects value	_____	_____	_____
j. Yields insight into value drivers	_____	_____	_____

Solution on p. 13-38.

Discounted Cash Flow (DCF) Model

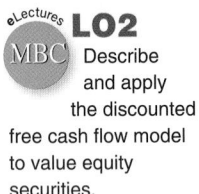

LO2 Describe and apply the discounted free cash flow model to value equity securities.

The discounted cash flow (DCF) model defines firm value as follows.

> **Firm Value = Present Value of Expected Free Cash Flows to Firm**

The expected free cash flows to the firm include cash flows arising from the operating side of the business; that is, cash generated from the firm's operating activities (not from nonoperating activities such as interest paid on debt or dividends received on investments). Importantly, free cash flows to the firm do not include the cash flows from financing activities.

DCF Model Structure

Free cash flows to the firm (FCFF) equal net operating profit after tax that is not used to grow net operating assets. Using the terminology of Module 4 we can define FCFF as follows (see Business Insight box below for a more traditional definition).

> **FCFF = NOPAT – Increase in NOA**

where

> **NOPAT = Net operating profit after tax**
>
> **NOA = Net operating assets**

Net operating profit after tax is normally positive and net operating assets normally increase each year. The difference between the two (positive or negative) represents the net cash flows available to creditors and shareholders. Positive FCFF imply that there are funds available for distribution to creditors and shareholders, either in the form of debt repayments, dividends, or stock repurchases (treasury stock). Negative FCFF imply that the firm requires additional funds from creditors and/or shareholders, in the form of new loans or equity investments, to support its business activities.

Business Insight ■ Definitions of Free Cash Flow

We often see free cash flows to the firm (unlevered free cash flow) defined as follows.

FCFF = Net cash flow from operating activities – Capital expenditures

Although similar to the definition in this book, NOPAT – Increase in NOA, there are important differences.

- Net cash flow from operating activities uses net income as the starting point; net income, of course, comingles both operating and nonoperating components (such as selling expense and interest expense). Analysts sometimes correct for this by adding back items such as after-tax net interest expense. That is, the FCFF measure can be refined by beginning with earnings before interest and taxes (EBIT) and subtracting taxes.

- Income tax expense (in net income) includes the effect of the interest tax shield (see Module 4); the usual NOPAT definition includes only the tax on operating income.

- Net cash flow from operating activities also includes nonoperating items in working capital, such as changes in interest payable. NOA focuses only on operating activities.

- Capital expenditures include direct purchases of PPE assets but exclude long-term assets acquired with stock (instead of cash), say in the acquisition of a company. Changes in NOA is a more comprehensive measure of asset growth.

We must be attentive to differences in definitions for free cash flow so that we understand the analytical choices we make and their implications for equity valuation. Knowing that there is not one "universal" way to define FCFF helps us interpret analyst research reports that apply different definitions of free cash flow.

Steps in Applying the DCF Model

Application of the DCF model to equity valuation involves five steps:

1. Forecast and discount FCFF for the **horizon period**.[2]

2. Forecast and discount FCFF for the post-horizon period, called **terminal period**.[3]

3. Sum the present values of the horizon and terminal periods to yield firm (enterprise) value.

4. Subtract net nonoperating obligations (NNO), along with any noncontrolling interest (NCI), from firm value to yield equity value. If NNO is positive, the usual case, we subtract it in step 4; if NNO is negative, we add it. (For many, but not all, companies, NNO is positive because nonoperating liabilities exceed nonoperating assets.)

5. Divide firm equity value by the number of shares outstanding to yield stock value per share.

Illustrating the DCF Model

To illustrate the DCF model for Procter & Gamble, we start with the forecasted model inputs from Exhibit 13.1 and use these to compute FCFF.

---

[2] When discounting FCFF, the appropriate discount rate (r_w) is the **weighted average cost of capital** (**WACC**), where the weights are the relative percentages of debt (d) and equity (e) in the capital structure applied to the expected returns on debt (r_d) and equity (r_e), respectively. P&G has two types of equity, common and preferred. Therefore, the company's weighted average cost of capital has three components: WACC = r_w = (r_d × % of debt) + (r_e × % of equity) + (r_{ps} × % of preferred stock).

[3] For an assumed growth, g, the terminal period (T) present value of FCFF in perpetuity (beyond the horizon period) is given by, $\frac{FCFF_T}{r_w - g}$, where $FCFF_T$ is the free cash flow to the firm for the terminal period, r_w is WACC, and g is the assumed long-term growth rate of those cash flows. The resulting amount is then discounted back to the present using the horizon-end-period discount factor.

Exhibit 13.3 ■ Application of Discounted Cash Flow Model

P&G—DCF ($ millions, except per share value and discount factors)	Reported 2019	Forecast Horizon Period				Terminal Period
		2020	2021	2022	2023	
Sales..........................		$ 70,053	$72,505	$75,042	$77,669	$79,222
NOPAT.........................		11,776	12,187	12,607	13,048	13,309
NOA...........................		66,858	66,274	68,846	71,256	72,681
Increase in NOA.................		(526)	(584)	2,572	2,410	1,425
FCFF (NOPAT – Increase in NOA)......		12,302	12,771	10,035	10,638	11,884
Discount factor $[1/(1 + r_w)]^t$*...........		0.94491	0.89286	0.84367	0.79720	
Present value of horizon FCFF........		11,624	11,403	8,466	8,481	
Cum present value of horizon FCFF	$ 39,974					
Present value of terminal FCFF........	247,361					
Total firm value....................	287,335					
Less (plus) NNO**.................	19,805					
Less noncontrolling interest..........	385					
Firm equity value.................	$267,145					
Shares outstanding................	2,504.7					
Stock value per share..............	$ 106.66					r_w = 0.0583 g = 0.020

* To simplify present value computations, the discount factors are rounded to five decimal places.

** Net nonoperating obligations (NNO) is computed as nonoperating obligations minus nonoperating assets: ($9,697 + $20,395 – $4,239 – $6,048 = $19,805). Data from 2019 financial statements, see Module 12, pages 12-8 and 12-13.

Exhibit 13.3 concludes with the estimated P&G equity value of $267,145 million, and a stock price of $106.66 per share (computed as $267,145 million/2,504.7 million shares). To determine present value, we used a weighted average cost of capital WACC(r_w) of 5.83% as the discount rate.[4] Specifically, we valued P&G's stock as follows.

1. **Compute present value of horizon period FCFF.** We compute the forecasted 2020 FCFF of $12,302 million from the forecasted 2020 NOPAT less the forecasted change in NOA in 2020. The present value of $12,302 million as of 2020 is $11,624 million, computed as $12,302 million × 0.94491 (the present value factor for one year at 5.83%). Similarly, the present value of forecasted 2021 FCFF (two years from the current date) is $11,403 million, computed as $12,771 million × 0.89286, and so on through 2023. The sum of these present values (cumulative present value) is $39,974 million.

2. **Compute present value of terminal period FCFF.** The present value of the terminal period FCFF is $247,361 million, computed as [$11,884 million/(0.0583 – 0.02)]/1.0583^4.

3. **Compute firm equity value.** We sum the present value of the horizon period FCFF and terminal period FCFF to get firm (enterprise) value of $287,335 million. We subtract the value of P&G's net nonoperating obligations of $19,805 million and the book value of its noncontrolling interest of $385 million to yield P&G's equity value of $267,145 million. We divide P&G's equity value by the 2,504.7 million shares outstanding to obtain the estimated per share value (the stock price) of $106.66.

We perform this valuation as of June 30, 2019, P&G's year-end. P&G's stock closed at $110.49 on June 30, 2019. Our valuation estimate of $106.66 indicates that the stock is slightly overvalued as of that date.

Managerial Decision ■ You Are the Chief Financial Officer

Assume that you are the CFO of a company that has a large investment in plant assets and sells its products on credit. Identify steps you can take to increase cash flow and, hence, your company's firm value. [Answer p. 13-25]

---

[4] We compute P&G's WACC as described in the text box below. To learn more about weighted average cost of capital (WACC) and how it is computed, see finance-oriented books such as *Corporate Valuation: Theory, Evidence and Practice* by Holthausen and Zmijewski, 2020, Cambridge Business Publishers.

Practice Insight ■ Procter & Gamble's WACC

P&G's WACC is computed as the cost of debt, common equity, and preferred stock, weighted by their proportion in the company's capital structure as follows.

	Cost	Weight
R_d (cost of debt, after tax)	1.56%	11.2%
R_e (cost of equity)	6.29%	88.5%
R_{ps} (cost of preferred stock)	28.34%	0.3%
WACC (Σ cost × weight)	5.83%	

Specifically, the components of WACC are computed as follows.

- **R_d (cost of debt)**—P&G provides the effective cost of short- and long-term debt in its debt footnotes.

	%	Rate	Weighted Rate
Short-term debt	21.0%	0.5%	0.105%
Long-term debt	79.0%	2.4%	1.896%
			2.001%

  To arrive at the overall cost of debt, we weight the short-term and long-term average interest rates by the relative proportion of the ST and LT debt. The result is a 2% average pretax cost of debt. We then multiply this pretax cost of debt by 1 – 22% (the federal and state combined statutory tax rate) to yield the 1.56% after-tax debt cost.

- **R_e (cost of equity)**—the cost of equity is given by the capital asset pricing model (CAPM) using the 10-year government bond rate of 2.03%, the P&G beta from Bloomberg of 0.71, both as of P&G's year-end of 6/30/19, and an assumed market premium of 6%.

$$R_e = 2.03\% + (0.71 \times 6\%) = 6.29\%$$

- **R_{ps} (cost of preferred stock)**—the cost of preferred stock is computed by dividing the dividends to preferred stockholders by the book value of the preferred stock.

$$R_{ps} = \$263 \text{ million}/\$928 \text{ million} = 28.34\%$$

LO2 Review 13-2

Following are financial data and forecast assumptions for General Mills (GIS) for its fiscal-year-end May 26, 2019.

	Reported 2019	Forecast Horizon Period				Terminal Period
General Mills ($ millions)		2020	2021	2022	2023	
Sales		$17,118.2	$17,375.0	$17,635.6	$17,900.1	$18,168.6
Sales growth		1.5%	1.5%	1.5%	1.5%	1.5%
Net operating profit after tax (NOPAT)	$ 2,368.7	$ 2,396.5	$ 2,432.5	$ 2,469.0	$ 2,506.0	$ 2,543.6
Net operating assets (NOA)	$21,959.4	$22,231.4	$22,564.9	$22,903.4	$23,246.9	$23,595.6

Equity Valuation Model Assumptions ($ and shares in millions)	
Weighted average cost of capital	5.89%
Net nonoperating obligations (NNO)	$14,591.7
Noncontrolling interest	$ 313.2
Number of common shares outstanding	601.9

Required

a. Apply the discounted cash flow (DCF) model to obtain General Mills's stock price estimate as of its fiscal-year-end May 26, 2019.

b. Compare the stock price estimate from part *a* to the actual stock price at May 28, 2019. (*Note:* May 26, 2019, was not a trading day, so use the closest prior trading day as the actual stock price.) What does our valuation estimate imply about the stock's value?

Solution on p. 13-38.

Residual Operating Income (ROPI) Model

eLectures **LO3**
MBC Describe
and apply
the residual
operating income
model to value equity
securities.

The residual operating income (ROPI) model focuses on net operating profit after tax (NOPAT) and net operating assets (NOA). This means it uses key measures from both the income statement and balance sheet in determining firm value.

ROPI Model Structure

The ROPI model defines firm value as the sum of two components.

> **Firm Value = NOA + Present Value of Expected ROPI**

where

> **NOA = Net operating assets**

> **ROPI = Residual operating income**

Net operating assets (NOA) are the foundation of firm value under the ROPI model. The ROPI model adds an adjustment in the second term that corrects for any possible undervaluation or overvaluation of NOA. This adjustment is the present value of expected residual operating income, and is defined as follows.

$$\textbf{ROPI} = \underbrace{\textbf{NOPAT} - (\textbf{NOA}_{\textbf{Beg}} \times \textbf{\textit{r}}_{\textbf{\textit{w}}})}_{\textbf{Expected NOPAT}}$$

where

> $\textbf{NOA}_{\textbf{Beg}}$ = Net operating assets at beginning (Beg) of period

> $\textbf{\textit{r}}_{\textbf{\textit{w}}}$ = Weighted average cost of capital (WACC)

Residual operating income (ROPI) is the net operating profit a firm earns over and above the return that the operating assets are expected to earn given the firm's WACC.[5] Shareholders expect the company to use NOA to generate, at least, a "hurdle" profit to cover the cost of capital (WACC). Companies that earn profits over and above that hurdle create value for shareholders. This is the concept of residual income: that is, income earned over and above the minimum amount of return required by investors.

Understanding the ROPI model helps us reap the benefits from the disaggregation of return on net operating assets (RNOA) in Module 4. In addition, the ROPI model is the foundation for many internal and external performance evaluation and compensation systems marketed by management consulting and accounting services firms.[6]

Steps in Applying the ROPI Model

Application of the ROPI model to equity valuation involves five steps.

1. Forecast and discount ROPI for the horizon period.[7]
2. Forecast and discount ROPI for the terminal period.[8]

---

[5] If the assets earn more than expected, it could be because NOA does not capture all of the firms' assets. For example, R&D and advertising are not fully and contemporaneously reflected on the balance sheet as assets though they likely produce future cash inflows. Likewise, internally generated goodwill is not fully reflected on the balance sheet as an asset. Similarly, assets are generally not written up to reflect unrealized gains. Conversely, sometimes the balance sheet overstates the true value of NOA. For example, companies can delay the write-down of impaired assets and, thus, overstate their book values. These examples, and a host of others, can yield reported values of NOA that differ from the fair value of operating assets.

[6] Examples are economic value added (EVA™) from Stern Stewart & Company, the economic profit model from McKinsey & Co., the cash flow return on investment (CFROI™) from Holt Value Associates, the economic value management from KPMG, and the value builder from PricewaterhouseCoopers (PwC).

[7] The present value of expected ROPI uses the weighted average cost of capital (WACC) as its discount rate; same as with the DCF model.

[8] For an assumed growth, g, the present value of the perpetuity of ROPI beyond the horizon period, is given by $\frac{\text{ROPI}_T}{r_w - g}$, where ROPI_T is the residual operating income for the terminal period, r_w is WACC for the firm, and g is the assumed growth rate of ROPI_T following the horizon period. The resulting amount is then discounted back to the present using the WACC, computed over the length of the horizon period.

3. Sum the present values from both the horizon and terminal periods; then add this sum to current NOA to get firm (enterprise) value.

4. Subtract net nonoperating obligations (NNO), along with any noncontrolling interest, from firm value to yield firm equity value.

5. Divide firm equity value by the number of shares outstanding to yield stock value per share.

Illustrating the ROPI Model

To illustrate the ROPI model, we return to Procter & Gamble. Forecasted financials for P&G (forecast horizon of FY2020 through FY2023 and terminal period of FY2024) are in Exhibit 13.4. The forecasts (in bold) are for sales, NOPAT, and NOA (the same forecasts we use to illustrate the DCF model).

Exhibit 13.4 ■ Application of Residual Operating Income Model

P&G—ROPI ($ millions, except per share value and discount factors)	Reported 2019	Forecast Horizon Period				Terminal Period
		2020	2021	2022	2023	
Sales.		$70,053	$72,505	$75,042	$77,669	$79,222
NOPAT		11,776	12,187	12,607	13,048	13,309
NOA	$ 67,384	66,858	66,274	68,846	71,256	72,681
ROPI (NOPAT − [NOA$_{Beg}$ × r_w])		7,848	8,289	8,743	9,034	9,155
Discount factor [1/(1 + r_w)^t]*		0.94491	0.89286	0.84367	0.79720	
Present value of horizon ROPI.		7,416	7,401	7,376	7,202	
Cum present value of horizon ROPI.	29,395					
Present value of terminal ROPI	190,558					
NOA	67,384					
Total firm value	287,337					
Less (plus): NNO**	19,805					
Less: NCI	345					
Firm equity value	$267,147					
Shares outstanding.	2,504.7					
Stock value per share.	$ 106.66				r_w = 0.0583	
					g = 0.020	

* To simplify present value computations, the discount factors are rounded to five decimal places.

** Net nonoperating obligations (NNO) is computed as nonoperating obligations minus nonoperating assets:
$9,697 + $20,395 − $4,239 − $6,048 = $19,805.

The bottom line of the ROPI valuation is the estimated P&G stock price of $106.66 per share, which is the same per share value we estimate in Exhibit 13.3 using the DCF valuation model. The present value computations use a 5.83% WACC as the discount rate. Specifically, we obtain the ROPI stock valuation as follows.

1. **Compute present value of horizon period ROPI.** The forecasted 2020 ROPI of $7,848 million is computed from the forecasted 2020 NOPAT ($11,776 million) less the product of beginning period NOA ($67,384 million) and WACC (0.0583). The present value of this ROPI as of 2020 is $7,416 million, computed as $7,848 million × 0.94491 (the present value factor for one year at 5.83%). Similarly, the present value of 2021 ROPI (two years hence) is $7,401 million, computed as $8,289 million × 0.89286, and so on through 2023. The sum of these present values (cumulative present value) is $29,395 million.

2. **Compute present value of terminal period ROPI.** The present value of the terminal period ROPI is $190,558 million, computed as [$9,155 million/(0.0583 − 0.02)]1.0583^4.

3. **Compute firm equity value.** We sum the present values from the horizon period ($29,395 million) and terminal period ($190,558 million), plus FY2019 NOA ($67,384 million), to obtain P&G's total firm (enterprise) value of $287,337 million. We then subtract the value of net nonoperating obligations of $19,805 million and noncontrolling interests of $385 million to yield firm equity value of $267,147 million. Dividing firm equity value by the 2,504.7 million shares outstanding yields the estimated per share value of $106.66.

We perform this valuation using data from the financial statements dated June 30, 2019, P&G's fiscal-year-end. P&G's stock closed at $110.49 on that date. As with the DCF model valuation, our valuation estimate of $106.66 suggests that P&G's stock is slightly overvalued as of this date.

The ROPI model and the DCF models yield identical per share estimates. This is the case so long as the firm is in a steady state, that is, when both NOPAT and NOA are growing at the same rate such that RNOA is the same each year. When this steady-state condition is not met, the two models yield different valuations. This could happen, for example, when we predict different terminal period growth rates or when profit margins are predicted to change. In practice, we often compute estimated stock values from several models and use qualitative analysis to determine an overall price estimate.

Review 13-3 LO3

Refer to the financial data and forecast assumptions for General Mills in Review 13-2.

Required
a. Apply the residual operating income (ROPI) model to obtain GIS's stock price estimate as of its fiscal-year-end May 26, 2019.
b. Compare the stock price estimate from part *a* to the actual stock price at May 28, 2019. (*Note*: May 26, 2019, was not a trading day, so use the closest prior trading day as the actual stock price.) What does our valuation estimate imply about the stock's value?

Solution on p. 13-39.

Further Considerations Involving Valuation Models

LO4

MBC Explain how equity valuation models can inform managerial decisions.

Managerial Insights from the ROPI Model

The ROPI model defines firm value as the sum of NOA and the present value of expected residual operating income as follows.

$$\text{Firm Value} = \text{NOA} + \text{Present Value of } [\text{NOPAT} - (\text{NOA}_{\text{Beg}} \times r_w)]$$

ROPI

Increasing ROPI, therefore, increases firm value. Managers can increase ROPI in two ways.

1. Decrease the NOA required to generate a given level of NOPAT (improve efficiency).
2. Increase NOPAT with the same level of NOA investment (improve profitability).

These are two very important observations. It means that achieving better performance requires effective management of *both* the balance sheet and the income statement. Most operating managers are accustomed to working with income statements. Further, they are often evaluated on profitability outcomes, such as achieving desired levels of sales and gross profit or efficiently managing operating expenses. The ROPI model focuses management attention on the balance sheet as well.

The two points above highlight two paths to increase ROPI and, accordingly, firm value.

Reduce NOA and maintain NOPAT First, let's consider how management can reduce the level of NOA while maintaining a given level of NOPAT. Many managers begin by implementing procedures that reduce net operating working capital, such as the following.

■ Reducing receivables through
  ● Better assessment of customers' credit quality
  ● Better controls to identify delinquencies and automated payment notices
  ● More accurate and timely invoicing
■ Reducing inventories through
  ● Use of less costly components (of equal quality) and production with lower wage rates
  ● Elimination of product features not valued by customers

- Outsourcing to reduce product cost
- Just-in-time deliveries of raw materials
- Elimination of manufacturing bottlenecks to reduce work-in-process inventories
- Producing to order rather than to estimated demand
- Increasing payables through
  - Extending the payment of low or no-cost payables (so long as supplier relationships are unharmed)

Management would next look at its long-term operating assets for opportunities to reduce unnecessary operating assets, such as the following.

- Sale of unnecessary property, plant or equipment
- Acquisition of production and administrative assets in partnership with other entities for greater throughput
- Acquisition of finished or semifinished goods from suppliers to reduce manufacturing assets

Increase NOPAT for same NOA The second path to increase ROPI and, accordingly, firm value is to increase NOPAT with the same level of NOA investment. Management would look to strategies that maximize NOPAT, such as the following.

- Increasing gross profit dollars through
  - Better pricing and mix of products sold
  - Reduction of raw material and labor cost without sacrificing product quality, perhaps by outsourcing, better design, or more efficient manufacturing
  - Increase of throughput to minimize overhead costs per unit (provided inventory does not build up)
- Reducing selling, general, and administrative expenses through
  - Better management of personnel
  - Reduction of overhead
  - Use of derivatives to hedge commodity and interest costs
  - Minimization of tax expense

Before undertaking any of these actions, managers must consider both short- and long-run implications for the company. The ROPI model helps managers assess company performance (income statement) relative to the net operating assets committed (balance sheet).

Managerial Decision ■ You Are the Chief Financial Officer

The residual operating income (ROPI) model highlights the importance of increasing NOPAT and reducing net operating assets, which are the two major components of the return on net operating assets (RNOA). What specific steps can you take to improve RNOA through improvement of its components: net operating profit margin and net operating asset turnover? [Answer, p. 13-25]

Assessment of Valuation Models

Exhibit 13.5 provides a brief summary of the advantages and disadvantages of the DCF and ROPI models. Neither model dominates the other, and both are theoretically equivalent. Instead, professionals must choose the model that performs best under practical circumstances.

There are numerous other equity valuation models in practice. Many require forecasting, but several others do not. A quick review of selected models follows.

The **method of comparables model** (often called *multiples model*) predicts equity valuation or stock value using price multiples. Price multiples are defined as stock price divided by some key financial statement number. That financial number varies across investors but is usually one of the following: net income, net sales, book value of equity, total assets, or cash flow. The method then compares companies' multiples to those of their competitors to assign value.

The **net asset valuation model** draws on the financial reporting system to assign value. That is, equity is valued as reported assets less reported liabilities. Some investors adjust reported assets and liabilities for several perceived shortcomings in GAAP prior to computing net asset value. This method is commonly applied when valuing privately held companies.

There are additional models applied in practice that involve dividends, cash flows, research and development outlays, accounting rates of return, cash recovery rates, and real option models. Further, some practitioners, called *chartists* and *technicians,* chart price behavior over time and use it to predict equity value.

Exhibit 13.5 ■ Advantages and Disadvantages of DCF and ROPI Valuation Models

Model	Advantages	Disadvantages	Performs Best

DCF	• Popular and widely accepted model
	• Cash flows are unaffected by accrual accounting
	• FCFF is intuitive
		• Cash investments in PPE assets are treated as cash outflows, even though they create shareholder value
		• Value not recognized unless evidenced by cash flows
		• Computing FCFF can be difficult as operating cash flows are affected by
		  – Cutbacks on investments (receivables, inventories, plant assets); can yield short-run benefits at long-run cost
		  – Securitization, which GAAP treats as an operating cash flow when many view it as a financing activity
			• When the firm reports positive FCFF
			• When FCFF grows at a relatively constant rate

ROPI	• Focuses on value drivers such as profit margins and asset turnovers • Uses both balance sheet and income statement, including accrual accounting information • Reduces weight placed on terminal period value	• Financial statements do not reflect all company assets, especially for knowledge-based industries (for example, R&D assets and goodwill) • Requires knowledge of accrual accounting	• When financial statements reflect more of the assets and liabilities; including those items often reported off-balance-sheet

Research Insight ■ Using Models to Identify Mispriced Stocks

Implementation of the ROPI model can include parameters to capture differences in growth opportunities, persistence of ROPI, and the conservatism in accounting measures. Research finds differences in how such factors, across firms and over time, affect ROPI and changes in NOA. This research also hints that investors do not entirely understand the properties underlying these factors and, consequently, individual stocks can be mispriced for short periods of time. Other research contends that the apparent mispricing is due to an omitted valuation variable related to riskiness of the firm.

Review 13-4 LO4

Consider the following operating activities *a* through *d* that General Mills managers could pursue.

Required
For each action: (i) explain the likely effect on ROPI by considering how net operating profit after tax (NOPAT) and net operating assets (NOA) would be affected, and (ii) identify any potential negative consequences for such an action.

a. Delay payment on vendor invoices by two days.
b. Offer new discounts to avoid inventory spoilage by tracking shelf life more closely to identify those products for special discounts whose "sell by" date is nearing.
c. Replace certain traditional marketing media like print ads, mailers, and coupons with social media channels for in-store promotions.
d. Lease transportation equipment for peak periods instead of purchasing PPE to cover peak periods.

Solution on p. 13-39.

Global Accounting

There are no differences in the method or technique of valuing equity securities using IFRS financial statements. We can use the DCF or the ROPI method with IFRS data as inputs and determine intrinsic values. Regarding other inputs, it is important to note that WACC varies across countries. This is readily apparent when we recognize that the risk-free rate used to compute WACC is country specific; for example, the following table shows the yield on 10-year government debt for several countries as of November 2019 (www.bloomberg.com/markets/rates-bonds). In comparison to countries such as Japan and Germany, countries such as Greece and Brazil are riskier because of their debt levels and economic troubles. The higher the country risk, the higher the yield demanded on that country's debt.

Country	Yield to Maturity
Japan	(0.10)%
Germany	(0.36)%
United States	1.77%
United Kingdom	0.70%
Australia	1.10%
Brazil	6.85%
Greece	4.89%

Appendix 13A: Derivation of Free Cash Flow Formula

Derivation of the free cash flow formula follows; our thanks to Professor Jim Boatsman for this exposition.

$$\text{Assets} = \text{Liabilities} + \text{Stockholders' Equity (SE)}$$
$$\text{NOA} = \text{NNO} + \text{SE}$$
$$\Delta\text{NOA} = \Delta\text{NNO} + \Delta\text{SE} \quad \text{[in change form, where } \Delta \text{ refers to change]}$$
$$\Delta\text{NOA} = \Delta\text{NNO} + \Delta\text{Contributed Capital (CC)} + \text{Net Income} - \text{Dividends (DIV)} \quad \text{[substituting for SE]}$$
$$\Delta\text{NOA} = \Delta\text{NNO} + \Delta\text{CC} + (\text{NOPAT} - \text{NNE}) - \text{DIV} \quad \text{[substituting for NI]}$$
$$-\text{NOPAT} + \Delta\text{NOA} = \Delta\text{NNO} + \Delta\text{CC} - \text{NNE} - \text{DIV} \quad \text{[rearranging terms]}$$
$$\text{NOPAT} - \Delta\text{NOA} = \text{NNE} - \Delta\text{NNO} - \Delta\text{CC} + \text{DIV} \quad \text{[multiplying by } -1]$$

Free cash flows to the firm (FCFF)

Net payments to holders of net nonoperating obligations and of stock

Appendix 13B: Deutsche Bank Valuation of Procter & Gamble

We explain the forecasting process in Module 12 and reproduce an analyst report on forecasted financial statements for Procter & Gamble in Appendix 12C. In this appendix we extend that analysis and reproduce an analyst forecasted stock price for P&G. We include below an excerpt from the Deutsche Bank valuation report.

Qualitative and Quantitative Summary

This excerpt provides a qualitative and quantitative summary from Deutsche Bank's report as of July 30, 2019 (*reproduced with permission*).

Deutsche Bank
Research

Rating	Company	Date
Hold	**Procter & Gamble**	30 July 2019
		Forecast Change

North America
United States

Consumer
**Cosmetics, Household
& Personal Care**

	Reuters	Bloomberg	Exchange	Ticker
	PG.N	PG US	NYS	PG

Price at 30 Jul 2019 (USD)	120.41
Price target	124.00
52-week range	116.00 - 78.87

The Profit & Growth Company

Valuation & Risks

Steve Powers
Research Analyst
+1-212-250-5480

Faiza Alwy
Research Analyst
+1-212-250-7611

Christopher Barnes
Research Associate
+1-212-454-0778

Katy Ansel
Research Associate
+1-212-250-1027

Key takeaways from PG's 4Q19 results (Hint: Everything is pretty awesome)
When it's working, it's working… Earlier this morning, PG delivered well-balanced results highlighted by roughly +7.5% organic growth, broad-based across all categories/regions. Investors deservingly rewarded PG today, with the stock outperforming the market by about +4 pts. From our point of view, PG is firing on all cylinders and doing a lot of things right—from innovation, to marketing, to in-store/on-shelf execution—amidst a favorably trending macro, consumer, and retailer environment, as well as a broadly rational competitive environment. However, with interest rates near lows and a defensive market posture near highs, the market is rewarding this performance with a near-25x forward multiple (a 15-year high), implicitly discounting (to us) that the good times roll on with minimal interruption for (at least) some time longer.

Possible? Yes – the momentum is impressive. However, while we remain generally constructive/optimistic on PG's earnings power (our FY20 estimates assume the high-end of the company's guidance range: +4% organic growth, EPS $4.91), we see limited room for further multiple expansion, and see anticipated earnings growth subject to potential downside risk from heightened competition, macro deceleration, elevated retail pressure, a simple inability to cycle year-over-year comparisons as adeptly as expected, or periods/places of misexecution (even if we concur with, and have been broadly impressed by, the evolution of PG's superiority strategy). While we admire PG's current focus on expanding categories and improving overall market growth, the reality is that is likely easier done (although not to imply "easy") when consumers, retailers, and competitors appear accommodating—conditions that to us risk becoming less "awesome" over time.

Key changes			
TP	116.00 to 124.00	↑	6.9%
EPS (USD)	4.87 to 4.91	↑	0.8%
Revenue (USDm)	70,216.1 to 70,647.4	↑	0.6%

Source: Deutsche Bank

We commend PG and raise our PT to $124, yet maintain our Hold rating.

Estimate changes and Valuation
We have modestly raised our FY20 EPS estimate to $4.91 (from $4.87) effectively flowing through the FY19 beat. Our EPS growth rate remains broadly unchanged at +8.5%. We have also raised our FY20 organic growth estimate to +4.0% from 3.5%, following continued strong and accelerating organic trends through FY19.

Our $124 price target is DCF-based (10-years), assuming +3.5% normalized top-line growth, +5% normalized EBIT growth, implying a ~23.5x multiple on 13-24

30 July 2019
Cosmetics, Household & Personal Care
Procter & Gamble

month EPS. We assume a WACC of 6.5% and a 1.5% terminal growth rate (in-line with expected long-term category growth). Upside risks: better-than-expected top-line growth, further improvement in macro/consumer trends, higher than expected productivity savings, commodity deflation, weaker USD, and value-accretive capital deployment. Downside risks: rotation out of staples, volatility in input costs and short supplies of raw materials, stronger dollar, more challenged competitive environment, unfavorable macro and consumption environment, and greater than anticipated cost of growth.

Figure 1: Discounted Cash Flow Analysis

Terminal Value Growth Rate	1.5%
WACC	6.5%

Period	4Q19 TTM	4QE20 TTM	4QE21 TTM	4QE22 TTM	4QE23 TTM	4QE24 TTM	4QE25 TTM	4QE26 TTM	4QE27 TTM	4QE28 TTM	4QE28 TTM
Revenue	$67,684	$70,647	$73,200	$75,630	$78,147	$80,755	$83,457	$86,256	$89,156	$92,162	$95,276
Revenue Growth		4.4%	3.6%	3.3%	3.3%	3.3%	3.3%	3.4%	3.4%	3.4%	3.4%
Operating Margin	21.0%	21.9%	22.3%	22.6%	22.9%	23.2%	23.5%	23.8%	24.1%	24.4%	24.8%
EBIT	14,236	15,492	16,345	17,100	17,898	18,736	19,616	20,540	21,511	22,532	23,604
Tax Rate	17.5%	17.5%	17.5%	17.5%	17.5%	17.5%	17.5%	17.5%	17.5%	17.5%	17.5%
After-tax EBIT	11,745	12,781	13,484	14,108	14,766	15,457	16,183	16,945	17,747	18,589	19,474
+: D&A	2,824	3,038	3,221	3,403	3,517	3,634	3,756	3,882	4,012	4,147	4,287
+: Capital Expenditures	(3,347)	(3,364)	(3,587)	(3,706)	(3,829)	(3,957)	(4,089)	(4,227)	(4,369)	(4,516)	(4,669)
+/- : Changes in Working Capital	681	220	373	362	376	391	406	422	439	456	474
Unlevered Free Cash Flow	11,903	12,675	13,491	14,167	14,830	15,525	16,255	17,023	17,829	18,676	19,566
Terminal Value											397,192
Discounted Cash Flow		12,675	12,668	12,491	12,277	12,068	11,865	11,666	11,473	11,285	236,449

Discounted Cash Flow	344,915				EBITDA Exit	14.2x
-: Net Debt	22,254				Sales CAGR	3.4%
Implied Equity Value	322,661		13-24 mth EPS	$5.25	EBIT CAGR	4.8%
Shares Outstanding	2,611		Implied 13-24 mth P/E	23.5x	Margin growth	0.3%
Implied 12-month Target Price	$124		13-24 mth EV/EBITDA	17.6x		

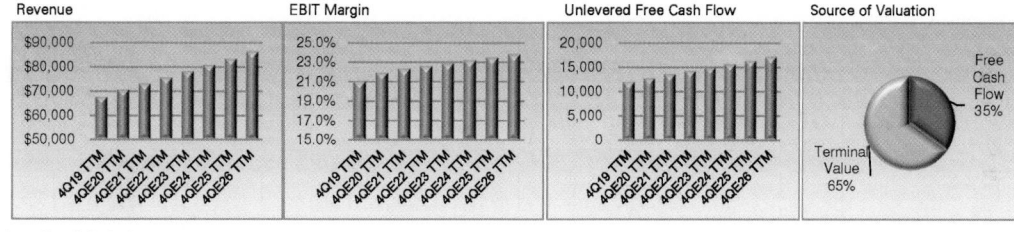

Source : Deutsche Bank estimates

30 July 2019
Cosmetics, Household & Personal Care
Procter & Gamble

Financial Model

Figure 2: PG quarterly income statement

(fy ending June, $ in millions, except per share amounts)

| | | 2019 | | | | | 2020E | | | | | 2021E | | | | |
INCOME STATEMENT	FY18	1Q Sep	2Q Dec	3Q Mar	4Q Jun	FY19	1QE Sep	2QE Dec	3QE Mar	4QE Jun	FY20E	1QE Sep	2QE Dec	3QE Mar	4QE Jun	FY21E
Net Sales	66,832	16,690	17,438	16,462	17,094	67,684	17,612	18,579	16,953	17,503	70,647	18,251	19,251	17,565	18,133	73,200
Cost of Goods Sold	33,707	8,438	8,796	8,362	8,746	34,342	8,728	9,195	8,544	8,798	35,265	8,990	9,470	8,799	9,060	36,319
Gross Profit	33,125	8,252	8,642	8,100	8,348	33,342	8,884	9,384	8,410	8,705	35,383	9,261	9,781	8,765	9,073	36,881
Gross margin	49.6%	49.4%	49.6%	49.2%	48.8%	49.3%	50.4%	50.5%	49.6%	49.7%	50.1%	50.7%	50.8%	49.9%	50.0%	50.4%
GM chg. in bps	-1323 bps	-150 bps	-86 bps	2 bps	120 bps	-30 bps	100 bps	95 bps	40 bps	90 bps	82 bps	30 bps	30 bps	30 bps	30 bps	30 bps
SG&A expenses	19,037	4,625	4,660	4,823	4,998	19,106	4,854	4,881	4,941	5,214	19,891	5,012	5,039	5,102	5,383	20,536
SG&A as % of sales	28.5%	27.7%	26.7%	29.3%	29.2%	28.2%	27.6%	26.3%	29.1%	29.8%	28.2%	27.5%	26.2%	29.0%	29.7%	28.1%
SG&A ratio chg. in bps	-21 bps	-77 bps	-78 bps	65 bps	-12 bps	-26 bps	-15 bps	-45 bps	-15 bps	55 bps	-7 bps	-10 bps	-10 bps	-10 bps	-10 bps	-10 bps
Adjusted Operating Profit	14,088	3,627	3,982	3,277	3,350	14,236	4,030	4,503	3,468	3,491	15,492	4,249	4,743	3,663	3,690	16,345
Operating Margin	21.1%	21.7%	22.8%	19.9%	19.6%	21.0%	22.9%	24.2%	20.5%	19.9%	21.9%	23.3%	24.6%	20.9%	20.3%	22.3%
OM chg. in bps	-1302 bps	-73 bps	-8 bps	-63 bps	132 bps	-5 bps	115 bps	140 bps	55 bps	35 bps	90 bps	40 bps	40 bps	40 bps	40 bps	40 bps
Interest expense	259	76	75	79	59	289	69	69	72	72	283	69	69	72	72	283
Ann. interest rate on Total Debt	1.2%	1.3%	1.2%	1.4%	1.0%	1.2%	1.2%	1.2%	1.2%	1.2%	1.2%	1.2%	1.2%	1.2%	1.2%	1.2%
Other expense/(income)	(584)	(110)	(100)	(131)	(192)	(533)	(123)	(130)	(119)	(123)	(495)	(128)	(135)	(123)	(127)	(512)
Other expense/(income) as % of s	-0.9%	-0.7%	-0.6%	-0.8%	-1.1%	-0.8%	-0.7%	-0.7%	-0.7%	-0.7%	-0.7%	-0.7%	-0.7%	-0.7%	-0.7%	-0.7%
Adjusted Pretax income	14,413	3,661	4,007	3,329	3,483	14,480	4,084	4,564	3,515	3,542	15,704	4,308	4,808	3,714	3,744	16,575
Adj. Pretax Margin	21.6%	21.9%	23.0%	20.2%	20.4%	21.4%	23.2%	24.6%	20.7%	20.2%	22.2%	23.6%	25.0%	21.1%	20.6%	22.6%
Adjusted taxes	3,095	734	713	509	578	2,534	715	799	615	620	2,748	754	841	650	655	2,901
Adj. effective tax rate	21.5%	20.0%	17.8%	15.3%	16.6%	17.5%	17.5%	17.5%	17.5%	17.5%	17.5%	17.5%	17.5%	17.5%	17.5%	17.5%
Noncontrolling Interest	114	12	22	31	4	69	12	22	31	4	69	12	22	31	4	69
Adjusted Net Income	11,204	2,915	3,272	2,789	2,901	11,877	3,357	3,743	2,869	2,918	12,887	3,542	3,945	3,033	3,085	13,605
Net Margin	16.8%	17.5%	18.8%	16.9%	17.0%	17.5%	19.1%	20.1%	16.9%	16.7%	18.2%	19.4%	20.5%	17.3%	17.0%	18.6%
Convert. Preferred Dividends	265	66	65	64	64	259	69	68	67	67	269	71	70	69	70	281
Net Income After Preferred	10,939	2,849	3,207	2,725	2,837	11,618	3,289	3,675	2,802	2,851	12,617	3,471	3,874	2,964	3,015	13,324
CORE EPS																
Diluted shares	2,657	2,612	2,623	2,638	2,646	2,630	2,642	2,632	2,621	2,611	2,627	2,602	2,594	2,586	2,578	2,590
CORE EPS - adjusted	$4.22	$1.12	$1.25	$1.06	$1.10	$4.52	$1.27	$1.42	$1.09	$1.12	$4.91	$1.36	$1.52	$1.17	$1.20	$5.25
Dividends	$2.79	$0.72	$0.72	$0.72	$0.75	$2.90	$0.75	$0.75	$0.75	$0.78	$3.01	$0.78	$0.78	$0.78	$0.81	$3.14
AS REPORTED																
GAAP Diluted EPS	$3.67	$1.22	$1.22	$1.04	($2.12)	$1.48	$1.27	$1.42	$1.09	$1.12	$4.91	$1.36	$1.52	$1.17	$1.20	$5.25
EBITDA																
EBIT	14,088	3,627	3,982	3,277	3,350	14,236	4,030	4,503	3,468	3,491	15,492	4,249	4,743	3,663	3,690	16,345
+: D&A	2,834	643	650	711	820	2,824	757	799	729	753	3,038	803	847	773	798	3,221
ADJUSTED EBITDA	16,922	4,270	4,632	3,988	4,170	17,060	4,787	5,302	4,197	4,244	18,530	5,052	5,590	4,436	4,487	19,565
% Growth																
Total Net Sales	2.7%	0.2%	0.2%	1.1%	3.6%	1.3%	5.5%	6.5%	3.0%	2.4%	4.4%	3.6%	3.6%	3.6%	3.6%	3.6%
Gross profit	-18.9%	-2.7%	-1.5%	1.1%	6.2%	0.7%	7.7%	8.6%	3.8%	4.3%	6.1%	4.2%	4.2%	4.2%	4.2%	4.2%
SG&A	2.0%	-2.5%	-2.6%	3.4%	3.2%	0.4%	5.0%	4.8%	2.5%	4.3%	4.1%	3.3%	3.2%	3.3%	3.3%	3.2%
Adjusted Operating profit	-36.5%	-3.0%	-0.1%	-2.0%	11.0%	1.1%	11.1%	13.1%	5.8%	4.2%	8.8%	5.4%	5.3%	5.6%	5.7%	5.5%
Adjusted Pretax income	-34.6%	-4.8%	-2.4%	-1.9%	13.5%	0.5%	11.6%	13.9%	5.6%	1.7%	8.5%	5.5%	5.4%	5.7%	5.7%	5.5%
Net income	-39.6%	-0.4%	3.1%	5.3%	18.3%	6.0%	15.2%	14.4%	2.9%	0.6%	8.5%	5.5%	5.4%	5.7%	5.7%	5.6%
Diluted EPS	-43.9%	15.5%	30.3%	9.6%	-393.8%	-59.6%	3.7%	16.8%	5.2%	-152.7%	231.1%	7.1%	6.9%	7.2%	7.1%	7.1%
Core EPS	-37.7%	2.5%	4.9%	5.6%	17.1%	7.1%	13.9%	14.0%	3.5%	1.9%	8.6%	7.1%	6.9%	7.2%	7.1%	7.1%
Dividends	3.3%	4.0%	4.0%	4.0%	4.0%	4.0%	4.0%	4.0%	4.0%	4.0%	4.0%	4.0%	4.0%	4.0%	5.0%	4.3%
Diluted EPS (GAAP)	-43.9%	15.5%	30.3%	9.6%	-393.8%	-59.6%	3.7%	16.8%	5.2%	-152.7%	231.1%	7.1%	6.9%	7.2%	7.1%	7.1%
Core EPS - 2 yr. stacked	-92.5%	-68.8%	15.0%	10.1%	27.9%	-30.6%	16.4%	18.9%	9.1%	19.1%	15.7%	21.0%	20.9%	10.7%	9.0%	15.7%

Source : Deutsche Bank estimates and analysis, Company filings

30 July 2019
Cosmetics, Household & Personal Care
Procter & Gamble

Appendix 1

Important Disclosures

*Other information available upon request

Disclosure checklist			
Company	Ticker	Recent price*	Disclosure
Procter Gamble	PG.N	116.0 (USD) 29 Jul 2019	1, 7, 8, 14, 15

*Prices are current as of the end of the previous trading session unless otherwise indicated and are sourced from local exchanges via Reuters, Bloomberg and other vendors . Other information is sourced from Deutsche Bank, subject companies, and other sources. For disclosures pertaining to recommendations or estimates made on securities other than the primary subject of this research, please see the most recently published company report or visit our global disclosure look-up page on our website at https://research.db.com/Research/Disclosures/CompanySearch. Aside from within this report, important risk and conflict disclosures can also be found at https://research.db.com/Research/Topics/Equities?topicId=RB0002. Investors are strongly encouraged to review this information before investing.

Important Disclosures Required by U.S. Regulators

Disclosures marked with an asterisk may also be required by at least one jurisdiction in addition to the United States.See Important Disclosures Required by Non-US Regulators and Explanatory Notes.

1. Within the past year, Deutsche Bank and/or its affiliate(s) has managed or co-managed a public or private offering for this company, for which it received fees.

7. Deutsche Bank and/or its affiliate(s) has received compensation from this company for the provision of investment banking or financial advisory services within the past year.

8. Deutsche Bank and/or its affiliate(s) expects to receive, or intends to seek, compensation for investment banking services from this company in the next three months.

14. Deutsche Bank and/or its affiliate(s) has received non-investment banking related compensation from this company within the past year.

15. This company has been a client of Deutsche Bank Securities Inc. within the past year, during which time it received non-investment banking securities-related services.

Important Disclosures Required by Non-U.S. Regulators

Disclosures marked with an asterisk may also be required by at least one jurisdiction in addition to the United States.See Important Disclosures Required by Non-US Regulators and Explanatory Notes.

1. Within the past year, Deutsche Bank and/or its affiliate(s) has managed or co-managed a public or private offering for this company, for which it received fees.

7. Deutsche Bank and/or its affiliate(s) has received compensation from this company for the provision of investment banking or financial advisory services within the past year.

For disclosures pertaining to recommendations or estimates made on securities other than the primary subject of this research, please see the most recently published company report or visit our global disclosure look-up page on our website at https://research.db.com/Research/Disclosures/CompanySearch

Analyst Certification

The views expressed in this report accurately reflect the personal views of the undersigned lead analyst(s) about the subject issuer and the securities of the issuer. In addition, the undersigned lead analyst(s) has not and will not receive any compensation for providing a specific recommendation or view in this report. Steve Powers.

30 July 2019
Cosmetics, Household & Personal Care
Procter & Gamble

Historical recommendations and target price: Procter Gamble (PG.N)
(as of 07/29/2019)

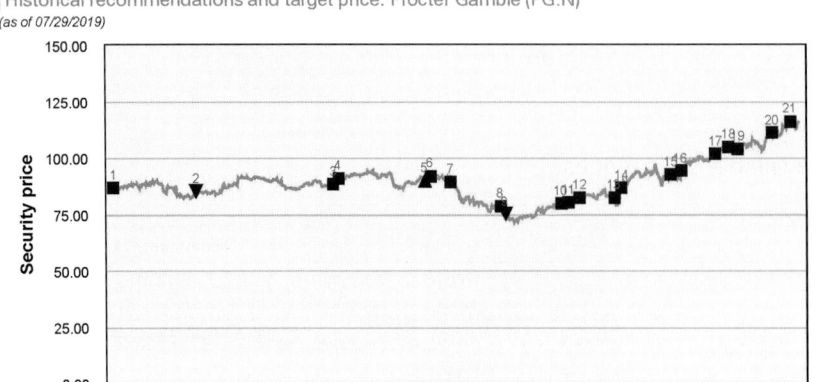

Current Recommendations

Buy
Hold
Sell
Not Rated
Suspended Rating

** Analyst is no longer at
Deutsche Bank

1.	08/03/2016	Buy, Target Price Change USD 95.00 William Schmitz**
2.	12/13/2016	Downgraded to Hold, Target Price Change USD 90.00 William Schmitz**
3.	07/20/2017	Hold, Target Price Change USD 92.00 Faiza Alwy
4.	07/28/2017	Hold, Target Price Change USD 94.00 Faiza Alwy
5.	12/13/2017	Upgraded to Buy, Target Price Change USD 101.00 Stephen Powers
6.	12/22/2017	Buy, Target Price Change USD 102.00 Stephen Powers
7.	01/24/2018	Buy, Target Price Change USD 100.00 Stephen Powers
8.	04/13/2018	Buy, Target Price Change USD 88.00 Stephen Powers
9.	04/20/2018	Downgraded to Hold, Target Price Change USD 80.00 Stephen Powers
10.	07/19/2018	Hold, Target Price Change USD 81.00 Stephen Powers
11.	07/31/2018	Hold, Target Price Change USD 84.00 Stephen Powers
12.	08/16/2018	Hold, Target Price Change USD 85.00 Stephen Powers
13.	10/10/2018	Hold, Target Price Change USD 82.00 Stephen Powers
14.	10/22/2018	Hold, Target Price Change USD 83.00 Stephen Powers
15.	01/08/2019	Hold, Target Price Change USD 87.00 Stephen Powers
16.	01/24/2019	Hold, Target Price Change USD 90.00 Stephen Powers
17.	03/20/2019	Hold, Target Price Change USD 99.00 Stephen Powers
18.	04/10/2019	Hold, Target Price Change USD 100.00 Stephen Powers
19.	04/24/2019	Hold, Target Price Change USD 106.00 Stephen Powers
20.	06/17/2019	Hold, Target Price Change USD 109.00 Stephen Powers
21.	07/16/2019	Hold, Target Price Change USD 116.00 Stephen Powers

---

Equity Rating Key

Buy: Based on a current 12- month view of total share-holder return (TSR = percentage change in share price from current price to projected target price plus pro-jected dividend yield) , we recommend that investors buy the stock.

Sell: Based on a current 12-month view of total share-holder return, we recommend that investors sell the stock.

Hold: We take a neutral view on the stock 12-months out and, based on this time horizon, do not recommend either a Buy or Sell.

Newly issued research recommendations and target prices supersede previously published research.

Equity rating dispersion and banking relationships

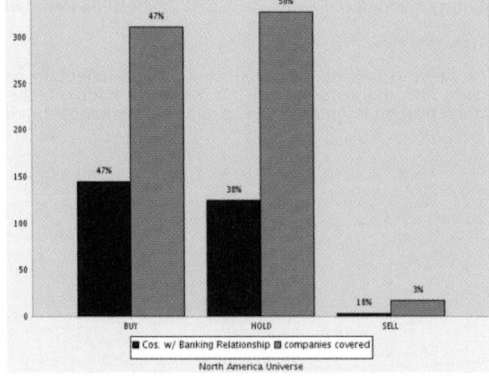

30 July 2019
Cosmetics, Household & Personal Care
Procter & Gamble

Additional Information

The information and opinions in this report were prepared by Deutsche Bank AG or one of its affiliates (collectively 'Deutsche Bank'). Though the information herein is believed to be reliable and has been obtained from public sources believed to be reliable, Deutsche Bank makes no representation as to its accuracy or completeness. Hyperlinks to third-party websites in this report are provided for reader convenience only. Deutsche Bank neither endorses the content nor is responsible for the accuracy or security controls of those websites.

If you use the services of Deutsche Bank in connection with a purchase or sale of a security that is discussed in this report, or is included or discussed in another communication (oral or written) from a Deutsche Bank analyst, Deutsche Bank may act as principal for its own account or as agent for another person.

Deutsche Bank may consider this report in deciding to trade as principal. It may also engage in transactions, for its own account or with customers, in a manner inconsistent with the views taken in this research report. Others within Deutsche Bank, including strategists, sales staff and other analysts, may take views that are inconsistent with those taken in this research report. Deutsche Bank issues a variety of research products, including fundamental analysis, equity-linked analysis, quantitative analysis and trade ideas. Recommendations contained in one type of communication may differ from recommendations contained in others, whether as a result of differing time horizons, methodologies, perspectives or otherwise. Deutsche Bank and/or its affiliates may also be holding debt or equity securities of the issuers it writes on. Analysts are paid in part based on the profitability of Deutsche Bank AG and its affiliates, which includes investment banking, trading and principal trading revenues.

Opinions, estimates and projections constitute the current judgment of the author as of the date of this report. They do not necessarily reflect the opinions of Deutsche Bank and are subject to change without notice. Deutsche Bank provides liquidity for buyers and sellers of securities issued by the companies it covers. Deutsche Bank research analysts sometimes have shorter-term trade ideas that may be inconsistent with Deutsche Bank's existing longer-term ratings. Some trade ideas for equities are listed as Catalyst Calls on the Research Website (https://research.db.com/Research/) , and can be found on the general coverage list and also on the covered company's page. A Catalyst Call represents a high-conviction belief by an analyst that a stock will outperform or underperform the market and/or a specified sector over a time frame of no less than two weeks and no more than three months. In addition to Catalyst Calls, analysts may occasionally discuss with our clients, and with Deutsche Bank salespersons and traders, trading strategies or ideas that reference catalysts or events that may have a near-term or medium-term impact on the market price of the securities discussed in this report, which impact may be directionally counter to the analysts' current 12-month view of total return or investment return as described herein. Deutsche Bank has no obligation to update, modify or amend this report or to otherwise notify a recipient thereof if an opinion, forecast or estimate changes or becomes inaccurate. Coverage and the frequency of changes in market conditions and in both general and company-specific economic prospects make it difficult to update research at defined intervals. Updates are at the sole discretion of the coverage analyst or of the Research Department Management, and the majority of reports are published at irregular intervals. This report is provided for informational purposes only and does not take into account the particular investment objectives, financial situations, or needs of individual clients. It is not an offer or a solicitation of an offer to buy or sell any financial instruments or to participate in any particular trading strategy. Target prices are inherently imprecise and a product of the analyst's judgment. The financial instruments discussed in this report may not be suitable for all investors, and investors must make their own informed investment decisions. Prices and availability of financial instruments are subject to change without notice, and investment transactions can lead to losses as a result of price fluctuations and other factors. If a financial instrument is denominated in a currency other than an investor's currency, a change in exchange rates may adversely affect the investment. Past performance is not necessarily indicative of future results. Performance calculations exclude transaction costs, unless otherwise indicated. Unless otherwise indicated, prices are current as of the end of the previous trading session and are sourced from local exchanges via Reuters, Bloomberg and other vendors. Data is also sourced from Deutsche Bank, subject companies, and other parties.

The Deutsche Bank Research Department is independent of other business divisions of the Bank. Details regarding our organizational arrangements and information barriers we have to prevent and avoid conflicts of interest with respect to our research are available on our website (https://research.db.com/Research/) under Disclaimer.

Macroeconomic fluctuations often account for most of the risks associated with exposures to instruments that promise to pay fixed or variable interest rates. For an investor who is long fixed-rate instruments (thus receiving these cash flows), increases in interest rates naturally lift the discount factors applied to the expected cash flows and thus cause a loss. The longer the maturity of a certain cash flow and the higher the move in the discount factor, the higher will be the loss. Upside surprises in inflation, fiscal funding needs, and FX depreciation rates are among the most common adverse macroeconomic shocks to receivers. But counterparty exposure, issuer creditworthiness, client segmentation, regulation (including changes in assets holding limits for different types of investors), changes in tax policies, currency convertibility (which may constrain currency conversion, repatriation of profits and/or liquidation of positions), and settlement issues related to local clearing houses are also important risk factors. The sensitivity of fixed-income instruments to macroeconomic shocks may be mitigated by indexing the contracted cash flows to inflation, to FX depreciation, or to specified interest rates – these are common in emerging markets. The index fixings may – by construction – lag or mis-measure the actual move in the underlying variables they are intended to track. The choice of the proper fixing (or metric) is particularly important in swaps markets, where floating coupon rates (i.e., coupons indexed to a typically short-dated interest rate reference index) are exchanged for fixed coupons. Funding in a currency that differs from the currency in which coupons are denominated carries FX risk. Options on swaps (swaptions) the risks typical to options in addition to the risks related to rates movements.

Derivative transactions involve numerous risks including market, counterparty default and illiquidity risk. The appropriateness

30 July 2019
Cosmetics, Household & Personal Care
Procter & Gamble

of these products for use by investors depends on the investors' own circumstances, including their tax position, their regulatory environment and the nature of their other assets and liabilities; as such, investors should take expert legal and financial advice before entering into any transaction similar to or inspired by the contents of this publication. The risk of loss in futures trading and options, foreign or domestic, can be substantial. As a result of the high degree of leverage obtainable in futures and options trading, losses may be incurred that are greater than the amount of funds initially deposited – up to theoretically unlimited losses. Trading in options involves risk and is not suitable for all investors. Prior to buying or selling an option, investors must review the 'Characteristics and Risks of Standardized Options", at http://www.optionsclearing.com/about/publications/character-risks.jsp. If you are unable to access the website, please contact your Deutsche Bank representative for a copy of this important document.

Participants in foreign exchange transactions may incur risks arising from several factors, including the following: (i) exchange rates can be volatile and are subject to large fluctuations; (ii) the value of currencies may be affected by numerous market factors, including world and national economic, political and regulatory events, events in equity and debt markets and changes in interest rates; and (iii) currencies may be subject to devaluation or government-imposed exchange controls, which could affect the value of the currency. Investors in securities such as ADRs, whose values are affected by the currency of an underlying security, effectively assume currency risk.

Unless governing law provides otherwise, all transactions should be executed through the Deutsche Bank entity in the investor's home jurisdiction. Aside from within this report, important conflict disclosures can also be found at https://research.db.com/Research/ on each company's research page. Investors are strongly encouraged to review this information before investing.

Deutsche Bank (which includes Deutsche Bank AG, its branches and affiliated companies) is not acting as a financial adviser, consultant or fiduciary to you or any of your agents (collectively, "You" or "Your") with respect to any information provided in this report. Deutsche Bank does not provide investment, legal, tax or accounting advice, Deutsche Bank is not acting as your impartial adviser, and does not express any opinion or recommendation whatsoever as to any strategies, products or any other information presented in the materials. Information contained herein is being provided solely on the basis that the recipient will make an independent assessment of the merits of any investment decision, and it does not constitute a recommendation of, or express an opinion on, any product or service or any trading strategy.

The information presented is general in nature and is not directed to retirement accounts or any specific person or account type, and is therefore provided to You on the express basis that it is not advice, and You may not rely upon it in making Your decision. The information we provide is being directed only to persons we believe to be financially sophisticated, who are capable of evaluating investment risks independently, both in general and with regard to particular transactions and investment strategies, and who understand that Deutsche Bank has financial interests in the offering of its products and services. If this is not the case, or if You are an IRA or other retail investor receiving this directly from us, we ask that you inform us immediately.

In July 2018, Deutsche Bank revised its rating system for short term ideas whereby the branding has been changed to Catalyst Calls ("CC") from SOLAR ideas; the rating categories for Catalyst Calls originated in the Americas region have been made consistent with the categories used by Analysts globally; and the effective time period for CCs has been reduced from a maximum of 180 days to 90 days.

United States: Approved and/or distributed by Deutsche Bank Securities Incorporated, a member of FINRA, NFA and SIPC. Analysts located outside of the United States are employed by non-US affiliates that are not subject to FINRA regulations.

Germany: Approved and/or distributed by Deutsche Bank AG, a joint stock corporation with limited liability incorporated in the Federal Republic of Germany with its principal office in Frankfurt am Main. Deutsche Bank AG is authorized under German Banking Law and is subject to supervision by the European Central Bank and by BaFin, Germany's Federal Financial Supervisory Authority.

United Kingdom: Approved and/or distributed by Deutsche Bank AG acting through its London Branch at Winchester House, 1 Great Winchester Street, London EC2N 2DB. Deutsche Bank AG in the United Kingdom is authorised by the Prudential Regulation Authority and is subject to limited regulation by the Prudential Regulation Authority and Financial Conduct Authority. Details about the extent of our authorisation and regulation are available on request.

Hong Kong: Distributed by Deutsche Bank AG, Hong Kong Branch or Deutsche Securities Asia Limited (save that any research relating to futures contracts within the meaning of the Hong Kong Securities and Futures Ordinance Cap. 571 shall be distributed solely by Deutsche Securities Asia Limited). The provisions set out above in the 'Additional Information' section shall apply to the fullest extent permissible by local laws and regulations, including without limitation the Code of Conduct for Persons Licensed or Registered with the Securities and Futures Commission.

India: Prepared by Deutsche Equities India Private Limited (DEIPL) having CIN: U65990MH2002PTC137431 and registered office at 14th Floor, The Capital, C-70, G Block, Bandra Kurla Complex Mumbai (India) 400051. Tel: + 91 22 7180 4444. It is registered by the Securities and Exchange Board of India (SEBI) as a Stock broker bearing registration no.: INZ000252437; Merchant Banker bearing SEBI Registration no.: INM000010833 and Research Analyst bearing SEBI Registration no.: INH000001741. DEIPL may have received administrative warnings from the SEBI for breaches of Indian regulations. Deutsche Bank and/or its affiliate(s) may have debt holdings or positions in the subject company. With regard to information on associates, please refer to the "Shareholdings" section in the Annual Report at: https://www.db.com/ir/en/annual-reports.htm.

30 July 2019
Cosmetics, Household & Personal Care
Procter & Gamble

Japan: Approved and/or distributed by Deutsche Securities Inc.(DSI). Registration number - Registered as a financial instruments dealer by the Head of the Kanto Local Finance Bureau (Kinsho) No. 117. Member of associations: JSDA, Type II Financial Instruments Firms Association and The Financial Futures Association of Japan. Commissions and risks involved in stock transactions - for stock transactions, we charge stock commissions and consumption tax by multiplying the transaction amount by the commission rate agreed with each customer. Stock transactions can lead to losses as a result of share price fluctuations and other factors. Transactions in foreign stocks can lead to additional losses stemming from foreign exchange fluctuations. We may also charge commissions and fees for certain categories of investment advice, products and services. Recommended investment strategies, products and services carry the risk of losses to principal and other losses as a result of changes in market and/or economic trends, and/or fluctuations in market value. Before deciding on the purchase of financial products and/or services, customers should carefully read the relevant disclosures, prospectuses and other documentation. 'Moody's', 'Standard Poor's', and 'Fitch' mentioned in this report are not registered credit rating agencies in Japan unless Japan or 'Nippon' is specifically designated in the name of the entity. Reports on Japanese listed companies not written by analysts of DSI are written by Deutsche Bank Group's analysts with the coverage companies specified by DSI. Some of the foreign securities stated on this report are not disclosed according to the Financial Instruments and Exchange Law of Japan. Target prices set by Deutsche Bank's equity analysts are based on a 12-month forecast period.

Korea: Distributed by Deutsche Securities Korea Co.

South Africa: Deutsche Bank AG Johannesburg is incorporated in the Federal Republic of Germany (Branch Register Number in South Africa: 1998/003298/10).

Singapore: This report is issued by Deutsche Bank AG, Singapore Branch or Deutsche Securities Asia Limited, Singapore Branch (One Raffles Quay #18-00 South Tower Singapore 048583, +65 6423 8001), which may be contacted in respect of any matters arising from, or in connection with, this report. Where this report is issued or promulgated by Deutsche Bank in Singapore to a person who is not an accredited investor, expert investor or institutional investor (as defined in the applicable Singapore laws and regulations), they accept legal responsibility to such person for its contents.

Taiwan: Information on securities/investments that trade in Taiwan is for your reference only. Readers should independently evaluate investment risks and are solely responsible for their investment decisions. Deutsche Bank research may not be distributed to the Taiwan public media or quoted or used by the Taiwan public media without written consent. Information on securities/instruments that do not trade in Taiwan is for informational purposes only and is not to be construed as a recommendation to trade in such securities/instruments. Deutsche Securities Asia Limited, Taipei Branch may not execute transactions for clients in these securities/instruments.

Qatar: Deutsche Bank AG in the Qatar Financial Centre (registered no. 00032) is regulated by the Qatar Financial Centre Regulatory Authority. Deutsche Bank AG - QFC Branch may undertake only the financial services activities that fall within the scope of its existing QFCRA license. Its principal place of business in the QFC: Qatar Financial Centre, Tower, West Bay, Level 5, PO Box 14928, Doha, Qatar. This information has been distributed by Deutsche Bank AG. Related financial products or services are only available only to Business Customers, as defined by the Qatar Financial Centre Regulatory Authority.

Russia: The information, interpretation and opinions submitted herein are not in the context of, and do not constitute, any appraisal or evaluation activity requiring a license in the Russian Federation.

Kingdom of Saudi Arabia: Deutsche Securities Saudi Arabia LLC Company (registered no. 07073-37) is regulated by the Capital Market Authority. Deutsche Securities Saudi Arabia may undertake only the financial services activities that fall within the scope of its existing CMA license. Its principal place of business in Saudi Arabia: King Fahad Road, Al Olaya District, P.O. Box 301809, Faisaliah Tower - 17th Floor, 11372 Riyadh, Saudi Arabia.

United Arab Emirates: Deutsche Bank AG in the Dubai International Financial Centre (registered no. 00045) is regulated by the Dubai Financial Services Authority. Deutsche Bank AG - DIFC Branch may only undertake the financial services activities that fall within the scope of its existing DFSA license. Principal place of business in the DIFC: Dubai International Financial Centre, The Gate Village, Building 5, PO Box 504902, Dubai, U.A.E. This information has been distributed by Deutsche Bank AG. Related financial products or services are available only to Professional Clients, as defined by the Dubai Financial Services Authority.

Australia and New Zealand: This research is intended only for 'wholesale clients' within the meaning of the Australian Corporations Act and New Zealand Financial Advisors Act, respectively. Please refer to Australia-specific research disclosures and related information at https://australia.db.com/australia/content/research-information.html Where research refers to any particular financial product recipients of the research should consider any product disclosure statement, prospectus or other applicable disclosure document before making any decision about whether to acquire the product. In preparing this report, the primary analyst or an individual who assisted in the preparation of this report has likely been in contact with the company that is the subject of this research for confirmation/clarification of data, facts, statements, permission to use company-sourced material in the report, and/or site-visit attendance. Without prior approval from Research Management, analysts may not accept from current or potential Banking clients the costs of travel, accommodations, or other expenses incurred by analysts attending site visits, conferences, social events, and the like. Similarly, without prior approval from Research Management and Anti-Bribery and Corruption ("ABC") team, analysts may not accept perks or other items of value for their personal use from issuers they cover.

Additional information relative to securities, other financial products or issuers discussed in this report is available upon

30 July 2019
Cosmetics, Household & Personal Care
Procter & Gamble

.

David Folkerts-Landau
Group Chief Economist and Global Head of Research

Pam Finelli	Michael Spencer	Steve Pollard
Global Chief Operating Officer Research	Head of APAC Research	Head of Americas Research Global Head of Equity Research

Anthony Klarman	Kinner Lakhani	Joe Liew
Global Head of Debt Research	Head of EMEA Equity Research	Head of APAC Equity Research

Jim Reid	Francis Yared	George Saravelos	Peter Hooper
Global Head of Thematic Research	Global Head of Rates Research	Head of FX Research	Global Head of Economic Research

Andreas Neubauer
Head of Germany Research

Spyros Mesomeris
Global Head of Quantitative and QIS Research

International Production Locations

Deutsche Bank AG	**Deutsche Bank AG**	**Deutsche Bank AG**	**Deutsche Securities Inc.**
Deutsche Bank Place	Equity Research	Filiale Hongkong	2-11-1 Nagatacho
Level 16	Mainzer Landstrasse 11-17	International Commerce Centre,	Sanno Park Tower
Corner of Hunter & Phillip Streets	60329 Frankfurt am Main	1 Austin Road West, Kowloon,	Chiyoda-ku, Tokyo 100-6171
Sydney, NSW 2000	Germany	Hong Kong	Japan
Australia	Tel: (49) 69 910 00	Tel: (852) 2203 8888	Tel: (81) 3 5156 6770
Tel: (61) 2 8258 1234			

Deutsche Bank AG London	**Deutsche Bank Securities Inc.**
1 Great Winchester Street	60 Wall Street
London EC2N 2EQ	New York, NY 10005
United Kingdom	United States of America
Tel: (44) 20 7545 8000	Tel: (1) 212 250 2500

Concluding Observations of Analyst Report

We make four observations on the Deutsche Bank analyst report regarding P&G's target stock price.

1. The analyst report defines free cash flow to the firm as follows:

	Earnings before interest and taxes (EBIT)
−	Taxes (EBIT × assumed tax rate)
+	Depreciation and amortization
−	Capital expenditures
−	Increase in working capital
=	Free cash flow to the firm

2. This analyst report uses the same DCF computation we describe in this module. Free cash flow estimates for the nine-year forecast horizon (4QE20-4QE28) and the terminal year (also labeled 4QE28) are discounted at the weighted average cost of capital, resulting in a total firm value of $344,915 million. The analyst, then, subtracts P&G's debt of $22,254 million, to yield the implied equity value of $322,661, or $124 per share, based on 2,611 million shares outstanding.

3. The cost of equity capital is estimated using the capital asset pricing model (CAPM) as we describe in the module. The analyst's estimated WACC of 6.5% is higher than the 5.83% WACC that we assume in the module. It is not uncommon that model assumptions differ among analysts.

4. Bottom line: We see that this analyst's $124 stock price target is higher than the $110.49 stock price estimate that we independently determined in this module. There are a number of differences between our forecast and that of the Deutsche Bank analyst, including growth rates, margins, and WACC.

Guidance Answers

You Are the Chief Financial Officer

Pg. 13-6 Cash flow can be increased by reducing assets. For example, receivables can be reduced by the following.

- Encouraging up-front payments or progress billings on long-term contracts
- Increasing credit standards to avoid slow-paying accounts before sales are made
- Monitoring account age and sending reminders to past-due customers
- Selling accounts receivable to a financial institution or special-purpose entity

As another example of asset reduction, plant assets can be reduced by the following.

- Selling unused or excess plant assets
- Forming alliances with other companies to share specialized plant assets
- Owning assets in a special-purpose entity with other companies
- Selling production facilities to a contract manufacturer and purchasing the output

You Are the Chief Financial Officer

Pg. 13-12 RNOA can be disaggregated into its two key drivers: net operating profit margin and net operating asset turnover. Net operating profit margin can be increased by improving gross profit margins (better product pricing, lower-cost manufacturing, etc.) and closely monitoring and controlling operating expenses. Net operating asset turnover can be increased by reducing net operating working capital (better monitoring of receivables, better management of inventories, carefully extending payables, etc.) and making more effective use of plant assets (disposing of unused assets, forming corporate alliances to increase plant asset capacity, selling productive assets to contract producers and purchasing the output, etc.). The ROPI model effectively focuses managers on the balance sheet *and* income statement.

Questions

Q13-1.   Explain how information contained in financial statements is useful in pricing securities. Are there some components of earnings that are more useful than others in this regard? What nonfinancial information might also be useful?

Q13-2. In general, what role do expectations play in pricing equity securities? What is the relation between security prices and expected returns (the discount rate, or WACC, in this case)?

Q13-3. What are free cash flows to the firm (FCFF) and how are they used in the pricing of equity securities?

Q13-4. Define the weighted average cost of capital (WACC).

Q13-5. Define net operating profit after tax (NOPAT).

Q13-6. Define net operating assets (NOA).

Q13-7. Define the concept of residual operating income (ROPI). How is residual operating income used in pricing equity securities?

Q13-8. What insight does disaggregation of RNOA into net operating profit margin and net operating asset turnover provide for managing a company?

Assignments with the 🅜 logo in the margin are available in BusinessCourse.
See the Preface of the book for details.

Mini Exercises

M13-9. Interpreting Earnings Announcement Effects on Stock Prices

On November 2, 2016, Facebook Inc. announced its 2016 third quarter results. Revenues were up nearly 50% from 2015 and earnings were up a whopping 180% ($5,944 million compared to $2,127 million.) Yet, in the ensuing days, Facebook's stock value fell 7% according to CNBC. Why do you believe that the company's stock price fell despite the good news?

LO1
Facebook Inc. (FB)

M13-10. Computing Residual Operating Income (ROPI)

Home Depot reports net operating profit after tax (NOPAT) of $12,073 million for the fiscal year ended February 3, 2019. Its net operating assets at the beginning of the fiscal year are $24,887 million. Assuming a 7.85% weighted average cost of capital (WACC), what is Home Depot's residual operating income for the fiscal year ended February 3, 2019? Show computations.

LO3
Home Depot Inc. (HD)

M13-11. Computing Free Cash Flows to the Firm (FCFF)

Home Depot reports net operating profit after tax (NOPAT) of $12,073 million for the fiscal year ended February 3, 2019. Its net operating assets at the beginning of and end of the fiscal year ended February 3, 2019, are $24,887 million and $25,546 million, respectively. What are Home Depot's free cash flows to the firm (FCFF) for the year ended February 3, 2019? Show computations.

LO2
Home Depot Inc. (HD)

M13-12. Computing, Analyzing, and Interpreting Residual Operating Income (ROPI)

In its annual report for the fiscal year ended July 27, 2019, Cisco Systems reports net operating income after tax (NOPAT) of $11,346 million. As of the beginning of the fiscal year it reports net operating assets of $22,225 million.

a. Did Cisco earn positive residual operating income (ROPI) if its weighted average cost of capital (WACC) is 7.6%? Explain.

b. At what level of WACC would Cisco not report positive residual operating income for the year? Explain.

LO3
Cisco Systems (CSCO)

M13-13. Estimating Share Value Using the DCF Model

Following are forecasts of Target Corporation's sales, net operating profit after tax (NOPAT), and net operating assets (NOA) as of February 2, 2019, which we label fiscal year 2018.

LO1, 2
Target Corporation (TGT)

$ millions	Reported 2018	Forecast Horizon Period				Terminal Period
		2019	2020	2021	2022	
Sales.	$75,356	$79,124	$83,080	$87,234	$91,596	$93,428
NOPAT	3,269	3,402	3,572	3,751	3,939	4,017
NOA	23,020	24,197	25,407	26,677	28,011	28,571

Answer the following requirements assuming a terminal period growth rate of 2%, a discount rate (WACC) of 7.63%, common shares outstanding of 517.8 million, and net nonoperating obligations (NNO) of $11,723 million.

a. Estimate the value of a share of Target common stock using the discounted cash flow (DCF) model as of February 2, 2019.
b. Target Corporation (TGT) stock closed at $77.12 on March 13, 2019, the date the 10-K was filed with the SEC. How does your valuation estimate compare with this closing price? What do you believe are some reasons for the difference?

LO3

Target Corporation
(TGT)

M13-14. Estimating Share Value Using the ROPI Model

Refer to the information for Target Corporation in M13-13 to answer the following requirements.

a. Estimate the value of a share of Target common stock using the residual operating income (ROPI) model as of February 2, 2019.
b. Target Corporation (TGT) stock closed at $77.12 on March 13, 2019, the date the 10-K was filed with the SEC. How does your valuation estimate compare with this closing price? What do you believe are some reasons for the difference?

LO4

Alcoa Corp. (AA)

M13-15. Assess the Effects of Managerial Actions on ROPI and Components

Alcoa's Form 10-Q for the third quarter ended September 30, 2019, included the following disclosure.

> In September 2019, Alcoa Corporation announced the implementation of a new operating model that will result in a leaner, more integrated, operator-centric organization. Effective November 1, 2019, the new operating model eliminates the business unit structure, consolidates sales, procurement and other commercial capabilities at an enterprise level, and streamlines the Executive Team from 12 to seven direct reports to the Chief Executive Officer. The new structure will reduce overhead with the intention of promoting operational and commercial excellence, and increasing connectivity between the Company's plants and leadership.

By undertaking these actions, the company hopes to improve its ROPI. Identify at least four specific ways that these actions can happen *and* the direction of the effects from each on NOPAT and NOA.

Exercises

LO2

Illinois Tool Works
Inc. (ITW)

E13-16. Estimating Share Value Using the DCF Model

Following are forecasts of Illinois Tool Works Inc. sales, net operating profit after tax (NOPAT), and net operating assets (NOA) as of December 31, 2018.

$ millions	Reported 2018	Forecast Horizon Period					Terminal Period
		2019	2020	2021	2022		
Sales.	$14,768	$15,654	$16,593	$17,589	$18,644		$19,017
NOPAT	2,711	2,880	3,053	3,236	3,430		3,499
NOA	9,462	10,028	10,630	11,268	11,944		12,183

Answer the following requirements assuming a discount rate (WACC) of 7.35%, a terminal period growth rate of 2%, common shares outstanding of 328.1 million, and net nonoperating obligations (NNO) of $6,204 million.

a. Estimate the value of a share of ITW's common stock using the discounted cash flow (DCF) model as of December 31, 2018.
b. Illinois Tool Works Inc. closed at $144.21 on February 15, 2019, the date the 10-K was filed with the SEC. How does your valuation estimate compare with this closing price? What do you believe are some reasons for the difference?

E13-17. Estimating Share Value Using the ROPI Model

Refer to the information for Illinois Tool Works Inc. in E13-16 to answer the following requirements.

a. Estimate the value of a share of Illinois Tool Works Inc. common stock using the residual operating income (ROPI) model as of December 31, 2018.

b. Illinois Tool Works stock closed at $144.21 on February 15, 2019, the date the 10-K was filed with the SEC. How does your valuation estimate compare with this closing price? What do you believe are some reasons for the difference?

LO3

Illinois Tool Works
Inc. (ITW)

Homework

MBC

E13-18. Estimating Share Value Using the DCF Model

Following are forecasts of sales, net operating profit after tax (NOPAT), and net operating assets (NOA) as of December 31, 2018, for Humana.

LO1, 2

Humana (HUM)

Homework

MBC

	Reported	Forecast Horizon Period				Terminal
$ millions	2018	2019	2020	2021	2022	Period
Sales.	$56,912	$57,766	$58,632	$59,512	$60,404	$61,008
NOPAT.	2,492	2,542	2,580	2,619	2,658	2,684
NOA	4,032	4,097	4,158	4,221	4,284	4,327

Answer the following requirements assuming a discount rate (WACC) of 7.8%, a terminal period growth rate of 1%, common shares outstanding of 135.6 million, net nonoperating obligations (NNO) of $(6,129) million, which is negative because Humana's nonoperating assets exceed its nonoperating liabilities, and no noncontrolling interest (NCI) on the balance sheet.

a. Estimate the value of a share of Humana's common stock using the discounted cash flow (DCF) model as of December 31, 2018.

b. Humana (HUM) stock closed at $307.56 on February 21, 2019, the date the 10-K was filed with the SEC. How does your valuation estimate compare with this closing price? What do you believe are some reasons for the difference?

E13-19. Estimating Share Value Using the ROPI Model

Refer to the information for Humana in E13-18 to answer the following requirements.

a. Estimate the value of a share of common stock using the residual operating income (ROPI) model as of December 31, 2018.

b. Humana (HUM) stock closed at $307.56 on February 21, 2019, the date the 10-K was filed with the SEC. How does your valuation estimate compare with this closing price? What do you believe are some reasons for the difference?

LO3

Humana (HUM)

Homework

MBC

E13-20. Identifying and Computing Net Operating Assets (NOA) and Net Nonoperating Obligations (NNO)

Following are the balance sheets and statement of earnings for Home Depot Inc. for fiscal year ended February 3, 2019, which the company labels fiscal year 2018.

LO1, 2

Home Depot Inc. (HD)

Homework

MBC

THE HOME DEPOT INC. Consolidated Balance Sheets		
$ millions, except par value	February 3, 2019	January 28, 2018
Assets		
Current assets		
Cash and cash equivalents.	$ 1,778	$ 3,595
Receivables, net	1,936	1,952
Merchandise inventories.	13,925	12,748
Other current assets	890	638
Total current assets.	18,529	18,933
Net property and equipment.	22,375	22,075
Goodwill	2,252	2,275
Other assets.	847	1,246
Total assets.	$44,003	$44,529

continued

continued from previous page

THE HOME DEPOT INC. Consolidated Balance Sheets		
$ millions, except par value	February 3, 2019	January 28, 2018
Liabilities and Stockholders' Equity		
Current liabilities		
Short-term debt	$ 1,339	$ 1,559
Accounts payable	7,755	7,244
Accrued salaries and related expenses	1,506	1,640
Sales taxes payable	656	520
Deferred revenue	1,782	1,805
Income taxes payable	11	54
Current installments of long-term debt	1,056	1,202
Other accrued expenses	2,611	2,170
Total current liabilities	16,716	16,194
Long-term debt, excluding current installments	26,807	24,267
Deferred income taxes	491	440
Other long-term liabilities	1,867	2,174
Total liabilities	45,881	43,075
Common stock, par value $0.05; authorized: 10,000 shares; issued: 1,782 at February 3, 2019 and 1,780 shares at January 28, 2018; outstanding: 1,105 shares at February 3, 2019 and 1,158 shares at January 28, 2018	89	89
Paid-in capital	10,578	10,192
Retained earnings	46,423	39,935
Accumulated other comprehensive loss	(772)	(566)
Treasury stock, at cost, 677 shares at February 3, 2019 and 622 shares at January 28, 2018	(58,196)	(48,196)
Total stockholders' (deficit) equity	(1,878)	1,454
Total liabilities and stockholders' equity	$44,003	$44,529

THE HOME DEPOT INC. Consolidated Statements of Earnings		
For Fiscal Year Ended ($ millions)	February 3, 2019	January 28, 2018
Net Sales	$108,203	$100,904
Cost of sales	71,043	66,548
Gross profit	37,160	34,356
Operating expenses		
Selling, general and administrative	19,513	17,864
Depreciation and amortization	1,870	1,811
Impairment loss	247	0
Total operating expenses	21,630	19,675
Operating income	15,530	14,681
Interest and other (income) expense:		
Interest and investment income	(93)	(74)
Interest expense	1,051	1,057
Other	16	0
Interest and other, net	974	983
Earnings before provision for income taxes	14,556	13,698
Provision for income taxes	3,435	5,068
Net earnings	$ 11,121	$ 8,630

a. Compute net operating assets (NOA) and net nonoperating obligations (NNO) for the fiscal year ended February 3, 2019.
b. For the fiscal year ended February 3, 2019, show that: NOA = NNO + Stockholders' equity.
c. Compute net operating profit after tax (NOPAT) for the year ended February 3, 2019. Assume a federal and state combined statutory tax rate of 22%. Also, consider the Impairment loss of $247 million before tax ($193 million after tax) to be a nonpersistent item. Exclude the after-tax amount from your NOPAT calculation.

E13-21. Estimating Share Value Using the DCF Model

Following are forecasts of Home Depot's sales, net operating profit after tax (NOPAT), and net operating assets (NOA) as of February 3, 2019, which the company labels fiscal 2018.

LO1, 2
Home Depot Inc. (HD)

| | Reported | Forecast Horizon Period | | | | Terminal |
$ millions	2018	2019	2020	2021	2022	Period
Sales............	$108,203	$115,777	$123,882	$132,553	$141,832	$144,669
NOPAT..........	12,073	12,967	13,875	14,846	15,885	16,203
NOA............	25,546	27,332	29,245	31,292	33,483	34,152

Answer the following requirements assuming a discount rate (WACC) of 7.85%, a terminal period growth rate of 2%, common shares outstanding of 1,105 million, net nonoperating obligations (NNO) of $27,424 million.

a. Estimate the value of a share of Home Depot's common stock using the discounted cash flow (DCF) model as of February 3, 2019.
b. Home Depot stock closed at $190.06 on March 28, 2019, the date the Form 10-K was filed with the SEC. How does your valuation estimate compare with this closing price? What do you believe are some reasons for the difference?

E13-22. Estimating Share Value Using the ROPI Model

Refer to the information for Home Depot Inc. in E13-21 to answer the following requirements.

LO3
Home Depot Inc. (HD)

a. Estimate the value of a share of Home Depot common stock using the residual operating income (ROPI) model as of February 3, 2019.
b. Home Depot stock closed at $190.06 on March 28, 2019, the date the Form 10-K was filed with the SEC. How does your valuation estimate compare with this closing price? What do you believe are some reasons for the difference?

E13-23. Explaining the Equivalence of Valuation Models and the Relevance of Earnings

This module focused on two different valuation models: the discounted cash flow (DCF) model and the residual operating income (ROPI) model. The models focus on free cash flows to the firm and on residual operating income, respectively. We stressed that these two models are theoretically equivalent.

LO1, 2, 3

a. What is the *intuition* for why these models are equivalent?
b. Some analysts focus on cash flows as they believe that companies manage earnings, which presumably makes earnings less relevant. Are earnings relevant? Explain.

E13-24. Applying and Interpreting Value Driver Components of RNOA

The net operating profit margin and the net operating asset turnover components of return on net operating assets are often termed *value drivers,* which refers to their positive influence on stock value by virtue of their role as components of return on net operating assets (RNOA).

LO4

a. How do profit margins and asset turnover ratios influence stock values?
b. Assuming that profit margins and asset turnover ratios are value drivers, what insight does this give us about managing companies if the goal is to create shareholder value?

E13-25. Quantify the Effects of Managerial Actions on ROPI and Components

Rincon Farms Inc. reports the following financial data just prior to its fiscal year ended December 31, 2019 ($ millions).

LO4

RINCON FARMS INC. Balance Sheet			
Cash.........................	$ 100	Accounts payable...............	$ 300
Accounts receivable.............	300	Long-term debt.................	600
Inventory.....................	500		
Property, plant & equipment.......	1,000	Equity	1,000
Total assets	$1,900	Total liabilities and equity	$1,900

	Actual Dec. 2019	Forecasted Dec. 2020
Sales.....................	$1,200	$1,310
NOPAT	$ 210	$ 216
NOA	$1,500	$1,545
WACC....................	7%	

Required

a. Compute ROPI for 2019 and 2020. Net operating assets (NOA) at the beginning of 2019 were $1,350.

b. The company is contemplating taking the following actions before the end of 2019. (These actions are not reflected in any of the financial data reported above.) For each of the actions, determine the effect on residual operating income for the fiscal year ended December 31, 2020.

   1. Reduce inventory by 10%, which reduces accounts payable by 5%.
   2. Decrease property, plant and equipment (PPE) by 20% with no consequent impact on NOPAT.
   3. Engage in a sale leaseback of a major building. The company will sell 50% of its PPE at book value and increase rental costs by $30 after tax, per year.
   4. Increase debt $300, which increases interest expense by $15.

Problems

LO1, 2 **P13-26.** **Forecasting with the Parsimonious Method and Estimating Share Value Using the DCF Model**
Cisco Systems (CSCO)

Homework
MBC

Following are income statements and balance sheets for Cisco Systems.

CISCO SYSTEMS Consolidated Statements of Operations		
Year Ended ($ millions)	July 27, 2019	July 28, 2018
Revenue		
Product	$39,005	$36,709
Service	12,899	12,621
Total revenue.......................................	51,904	49,330
Cost of sales		
Product	14,863	14,427
Service	4,375	4,297
Total cost of sales	19,238	18,724
Gross margin	32,666	30,606
Operating expenses		
Research and development	6,577	6,332
Sales and marketing................................	9,571	9,242
General and administrative.........................	1,827	2,144
Amortization of purchased intangible assets.......	150	221
Restructuring and other charges...................	322	358
Total operating expenses	18,447	18,297

continued

continued from previous page

CISCO SYSTEMS Consolidated Statements of Operations Year Ended ($ millions)	July 27, 2019	July 28, 2018
Operating income	14,219	12,309
Interest income	1,308	1,508
Interest expense	(859)	(943)
Other income (loss), net	(97)	165
Interest and other income (loss), net	352	730
Income before provision for income taxes	14,571	13,039
Provision for income taxes	2,950	12,929
Net income	$11,621	$ 110

CISCO SYSTEMS INC. Consolidated Balance Sheets $ millions, except par value	July 27, 2019	July 28, 2018
Assets		
Current assets		
Cash and cash equivalents	$11,750	$ 8,934
Investments	21,663	37,614
Accounts receivable, net of allowance for doubtful accounts of		
$136 at July 27, 2019 and $129 at July 28, 2018	5,491	5,554
Inventories	1,383	1,846
Financing receivables, net	5,095	4,949
Other current assets	2,373	2,940
Total current assets	47,755	61,837
Property and equipment, net	2,789	3,006
Financing receivables, net	4,958	4,882
Goodwill	33,529	31,706
Purchased intangible assets, net	2,201	2,552
Deferred tax assets	4,065	3,219
Other assets	2,496	1,582
Total assets	$97,793	$108,784
Liabilities and equity		
Current liabilities		
Short-term debt	$10,191	$ 5,238
Accounts payable	2,059	1,904
Income taxes payable	1,149	1,004
Accrued compensation	3,221	2,986
Deferred revenue	10,668	11,490
Other current liabilities	4,424	4,413
Total current liabilities	31,712	27,035
Long-term debt	14,475	20,331
Income taxes payable	8,927	8,585
Deferred revenue	7,799	8,195
Other long-term liabilities	1,309	1,434
Total liabilities	64,222	65,580

continued

continued from previous page

CISCO SYSTEMS INC. Consolidated Balance Sheets		
$ millions, except par value	July 27, 2019	July 28, 2018
Equity:		
Cisco shareholders' equity		
Preferred stock, no par value: 5 shares authorized; none issued and outstanding.	—	—
Common stock and additional paid-in capital, $0.001 par value: 20,000 shares authorized; 4,250 and 4,614 shares issued and outstanding at July 27, 2019, and July 28, 2018, respectively	40,266	42,820
(Accumulated deficit) Retained earnings	(5,903)	1,233
Accumulated other comprehensive income (loss)	(792)	(849)
Total Cisco shareholders' equity	33,571	43,204
Total equity	33,571	43,204
Total liabilities and equity	$97,793	$108,784

Required

a. Compute net operating assets (NOA) for 2019.

b. Compute net operating profit after tax (NOPAT) for 2019, assuming a federal and state statutory tax rate of 22%. Assume that all items on the 2019 income statement will persist.

c. Use the parsimonious forecast method, as shown in Analysis Insight box on page 13-4, to forecast Cisco's sales, NOPAT, and NOA for 2020 through 2023 *and* the terminal period using the following assumptions.

Sales growth 2020–2023	5%
Terminal growth	1%
Net operating profit margin.	2019 rate rounded to three decimal places
Net operating asset turnover	2019 rate rounded to three decimal places

d. Estimate the value of a share of Cisco common stock using the discounted cash flow (DCF) model as of July 27, 2019; assume a discount rate (WACC) of 7.6%, common shares outstanding of 5,029 million, and net nonoperating obligations (NNO) of $(8,747) million (NNO is negative, which means that Cisco has net nonoperating investments).

e. Cisco stock closed at $48.42 on September 5, 2019, the date the Form 10-K was filed with the SEC. How does your valuation estimate compare with this closing price? What do you believe are some reasons for the difference? What investment decision is suggested from your results?

LO1, 3   **P13-27.** **Forecasting with Parsimonious Method and Estimating Share Value Using the ROPI Model**

Cisco Systems
(CSCO)

Refer to the information for Cisco Systems in P13-26 to answer the following requirements.

Required

a. Estimate the value of a share of Cisco common stock using the residual operating income (ROPI) model as of July 27, 2019.

b. Cisco stock closed at $48.42 on September 5, 2019, the date the Form 10-K was filed with the SEC. How does your valuation estimate compare with this closing price? What do you believe are some reasons for the difference? What investment decision is suggested from your results?

LO2   **P13-28.** **Estimating Share Value Using the DCF Model**

AT&T Inc. (T)

Following are forecasted sales, NOPAT, and NOA for AT&T for 2019 through 2022.

	Reported	Forecast Horizon Period			
$ millions	2018	2019	2020	2021	2022
Sales.	$170,756	$181,001	$191,861	$203,373	$215,576
NOPAT	20,895	22,082	23,407	24,812	26,300
NOA	369,039	390,931	414,387	439,251	465,607

Required

a. Forecast the terminal period values assuming a 2% terminal period growth rate.

b. Estimate the value of a share of AT&T common stock using the discounted cash flow (DCF) model as of December 31, 2018; assume a discount rate (WACC) of 5.7%, common shares outstanding of 7,281.6 million, net nonoperating obligations (NNO) of $175,155 million, and noncontrolling interest (NCI) from the balance sheet of $9,795 million.

c. AT&T closed at $30.85 on February 20, 2019, the date the Form 10-K was filed with the SEC. How does your valuation estimate compare with this closing price?

d. If WACC has been 6.2%, what would the valuation estimate have been? What about if WACC has been 5.2%?

P13-29. Estimating Share Value Using the ROPI Model

Refer to the information for **AT&T** in P13-28 to answer the following requirements.

LO3

AT&T Inc. (T)

Required

a. Estimate the value of a share of AT&T common stock using the residual operating income (ROPI) model as of December 31, 2018.

b. AT&T stock price was $30.85 on February 20, 2019, the date the Form 10-K was filed with the SEC. How does your valuation estimate compare with this closing price? What do you believe are some reasons for the difference? What investment decision is suggested from your results?

P13-30. Forecasting with Parsimonious Method and Estimating Share Value Using the DCF Model

Following are income statements and balance sheets for **Nike Inc.**

LO1, 2

Nike Inc. (NKE)

NIKE INC. Consolidated Income Statements		
For Year Ended ($ millions)	May 31, 2019	May 31, 2018
Revenues	$39,117	$36,397
Cost of sales	21,643	20,441
Gross profit	17,474	15,956
Demand creation expense	3,753	3,577
Operating overhead expense	8,949	7,934
Total selling and administrative expense	12,702	11,511
Interest expense (income), net	49	54
Other (income) expense, net	(78)	66
Income before income taxes	4,801	4,325
Income tax expense	772	2,392
Net income	$ 4,029	$ 1,933

NIKE INC. Consolidated Balance Sheets		
$ millions	May 31, 2019	May 31, 2018
Current assets		
Cash and equivalents	$ 4,466	$ 4,249
Short-term investments	197	996
Accounts receivable, net	4,272	3,498
Inventories	5,622	5,261
Prepaid expenses and other current assets	1,968	1,130
Total current assets	16,525	15,134
Property, plant and equipment, net	4,744	4,454
Identifiable intangible assets, net	283	285
Goodwill	154	154
Deferred income taxes and other assets	2,011	2,509
Total assets	$23,717	$22,536

continued

continued from previous page

NIKE INC. Consolidated Balance Sheets $ millions	May 31, 2019	May 31, 2018
Current liabilities		
Current portion of long-term debt	$ 6	$ 6
Notes payable.	9	336
Accounts payable	2,612	2,279
Accrued liabilities	5,010	3,269
Income taxes payable.	229	150
Total current liabilities.	7,866	6,040
Long-term debt	3,464	3,468
Deferred income taxes and other liabilities.	3,347	3,216
Commitments and contingencies (Note 18)		
Shareholders' equity		
Common stock at stated value:		
Class A convertible—315 and 329 shares outstanding.	—	—
Class B—1,253 and 1,272 shares outstanding.	3	3
Capital in excess of stated value	7,163	6,384
Accumulated other comprehensive income (loss)	231	(92)
Retained earnings.	1,643	3,517
Total shareholders' equity.	9,040	9,812
Total liabilities and shareholders' equity.	$23,717	$22,536

Required

a. Compute net operating assets (NOA) and net nonoperating obligations (NNO) for 2019. The company's NNO is negative because cash exceeds debt.

b. Compute net operating profit after tax (NOPAT) for 2019 assuming a federal and state statutory tax rate of 22%.

c. Use the parsimonious forecast method, as shown in the Analysis Insight box on page 13-4, to forecast sales, NOPAT, and NOA for 2020 through 2023 using the following assumptions.

Sales growth.	8%
Net operating profit margin (NOPM).	2019 ratios rounded to three decimal places
Net operating asset turnover (NOAT), year-end. . .	2019 ratios rounded to three decimal places

Forecast the terminal period value assuming a 2% terminal period growth and using the NOPM and NOAT assumptions above.

d. Estimate the value of a share of Nike's common stock using the discounted cash flow (DCF) model as of May 31, 2019; assume a discount rate (WACC) of 6.8% and common shares outstanding of 1,682 million.

e. Nike's stock closed at $86.70 on July 23, 2019, the date the Form 10-K was filed with the SEC. How does your valuation estimate compare with this closing price? What do you believe are some reasons for the difference? What investment decision is suggested from your results?

LO1, 3   **P13-31.** **Forecasting with the Parsimonious Method and Estimating Share Value Using the ROPI Model**

Nike Inc. (NKE)   Refer to the information for Nike Inc. in P13-30 to answer the following requirements.

Required

a. Estimate the value of a share of Nike common stock using the residual operating income (ROPI) model as of May 31, 2019. For simplicity, prepare your forecasts in $ millions.

b. Nike's stock closed at $86.70 on July 23, 2019, the date the Form 10-K was filed with the SEC. How does your valuation estimate compare with this closing price? What do you believe are some reasons for the difference? What investment decision is suggested from your results?

P13-32. Estimating Share Value Using the DCF Model

LO2
Colgate-Palmolive
Company (CL)

Following are forecasted sales, NOPAT, and NOA for Colgate-Palmolive Company for 2019 through 2022.

Colgate Palmolive (CL) $ millions	Reported 2018	Forecast Horizon Period			
		2019	2020	2021	2022
Sales.	$15,544	$16,010	$16,491	$16,985	$17,495
NOPAT	2,737	2,818	2,902	2,989	3,079
NOA	5,837	6,012	6,193	6,378	6,570

Required

a. Forecast the terminal period values assuming a 1% terminal period growth for all three model inputs, that is Sales, NOPAT, and NOA.

b. Estimate the value of a share of Colgate-Palmolive common stock using the discounted cash flow (DCF) model; assume a discount rate (WACC) of 5.7%, common shares outstanding of 862.9 million, net nonoperating obligations (NNO) of $5,640 million, and noncontrolling interest (NCI) from the balance sheet of $299 million.

c. Colgate-Palmolive's stock closed at $66.70 on February 21, 2019, the date the Form 10-K was filed with the SEC. How does your valuation estimate compare with this closing price? What do you believe are some reasons for the difference?

d. The forecasts you completed assumed a terminal growth rate of 1%. What if the terminal rate had been 2%. What would your estimated stock price have been?

e. What would WACC have to be to warrant the actual stock price on February 21, 2019?

P13-33. Estimating Share Value Using the ROPI Model

LO3

Colgate-Palmolive
Company (CL)

Refer to the information for Colgate-Palmolive in P13-32 to answer the following requirements.

Required

a. Estimate the value of a share of Colgate-Palmolive common stock using the residual operating income (ROPI) model.

b. Colgate-Palmolive stock closed at $66.70 on February 21, 2019, the date the Form 10-K was filed with the SEC. How does your valuation estimate compare with this closing price? What do you believe are some reasons for the difference? What investment decision is suggested from your results?

Management Applications

MA13-34. Management Application: Operating Improvement versus Financial Engineering

LO4

Assume that you are the CEO of a small publicly traded company. The operating performance of your company has fallen below market expectations, which is reflected in a depressed stock price. At your direction, your CFO provides you with the following recommendations that are designed to increase your company's return on net operating assets (RNOA) and your operating cash flows, both of which will, presumably, result in improved financial performance and an increased stock price.

1. To improve net cash flow from operating activities, the CFO recommends that your company reduce inventories (raw material, work-in-progress, and finished goods) and receivables (through selective credit granting and increased emphasis on collection of past due accounts).

2. The CFO recommends that your company lengthen the time taken to pay accounts payable (lean on the trade) to increase net cash flows from operating activities.

3. Because your company's operating performance is already depressed, the CFO recommends that you take a "big bath;" that is, write off all assets deemed to be impaired and accrue excessive liabilities for future contingencies. The higher current period expense will, then, result in higher future period income as the assets written off will not be depreciated and your company will have a liability account available to absorb future cash payments rather than recording them as expenses.

4. The CFO recommends that your company increase its estimate of expected return on pension investments. This will reduce pension expense and increase operating profit, a component of net operating profit after tax (NOPAT) and, thus, of RNOA.

5. The CFO recommends that your company share ownership of its outbound logistics (trucking division) with another company in a joint venture. This would have the effect of increasing throughput, thus spreading overhead over a larger volume base, and would remove the assets from your company's balance sheet since the joint venture would be accounted for as an equity method investment.

Evaluate each of the CFO's recommendations. In your evaluation, consider whether each recommendation will positively impact the operating performance of your company or whether it is cosmetic in nature.

Ongoing Project

(This ongoing project began in Module 1 and continues through most of the book; even if previous segments were not completed, the requirements are still applicable to any business analysis.) Two common models used to estimate the value of company's equity are the discounted cash flow (DCF) model and the residual operating income (ROPI) model. Estimate the value of equity and a stock price for the company(ies) under analysis. The aim is to determine an independent measure of value and assess whether the stock appears to be over- or under-valued. Begin with a forecast of the company's balance sheet and income statement. See Module 12 and follow the forecasting steps outlined there.

1. *Model Assumptions and Inputs.* In addition to the assumptions used for the forecasts, we require several additional inputs.

   - Weighted average cost of capital (WACC) is required to discount future amounts to derive present values. We can find estimates at a number of websites. Find the latest WACC at three or more sites and explore why they differ. One approach would be to use an average in the calculation and then perform sensitivity analysis for the high and the low in the range.

   - Net nonoperating obligations (NNO) is needed to determine the value of equity from total enterprise value.

   - Number of shares outstanding. Recall that shares outstanding is equal to shares issued less treasury shares. The balance sheet typically reports both numbers but if not, we can find the amounts in the statement of shareholders' equity or in a footnote.

2. *Model Estimation.* Use a spreadsheet and estimate the DCF and the ROPI models respectively. Here are some tips.

   - Pay close attention to the rounding conventions described in the footnotes in Exhibits 13.3 and 13.4. Use the spreadsheet rounding functions. *Note:* Setting the format of a cell to "no decimals" is not the same as rounding the number; with the former, the decimals are still there, but they are not displayed.

   - Make sure that NNO is subtracted from total enterprise value. In some cases, NNO is a negative number; this occurs when nonoperating assets such as cash and marketable securities exceed nonoperating liabilities. By subtracting this negative NNO, the value of equity will be greater than the enterprise value of the firm.

   - The stock prices obtained are point estimates derived from a specific set of assumptions. To understand the impact of each assumption, compute alternative stock prices by varying the assumptions. The point is to determine a range of stock prices that derive from a reasonable set of assumptions. One approach is to increase and decrease each of the model assumptions by a reasonable amount such as +/− 10%. Use the spreadsheet functions to perform this sensitivity analysis. Identify which assumptions are most important or impactful.

   - Determine the company's actual stock price. Compare the per share estimate to the actual stock price and form an opinion about the relative value. Is the stock over- or under-valued according to the model?

3. *Interpretation.* The final step in the project is to evaluate the companies based on all the analysis performed in the ongoing project.

   - Revisit the conclusions made about the companies' performance (profit and margin analysis), asset efficiency, solvency, liquidity, off-balance-sheet financing, and future opportunities based on analysis of strengths, weaknesses, opportunities, and threats. Our goal is to assimilate the various components of analysis and to synthesize what we discovered and learned.

- Access one or more analyst reports for each company. How do the other professionals see the firms? How does their view differ from ours?

- Our analysis was based primarily on historical data from financial statements. What additional information would we like to have to refine our opinion? Is this missing information critical to our opinion?

- Based on our analysis, would we consider investing in the company? Explain.

Solutions to Review Problems

Review 13-1—Solution

	Dividend Discount	Discounted Cash Flow	Residual Operating Income
a. Uses net present value concepts.	True	True	True
b. Operating cash flows affect value	False	True	False
c. Estimates a company's enterprise value	False	True	True
d. Dividends to shareholders is a model input	True	False	False
e. Free cash flow is a model input	False	True	False
f. Estimates equity value of the firm	True	True	True
g. Capital expenditures affect estimated value	False	True	True*
h. Requires forecasts of future amounts	True	True	True
i. Operating profit affects value.	False	False	True
j. Yields insight into value drivers	False	False	True

*Net operating assets change during the year due, in part, to CAPEX. So while CAPEX is not the only model input, expenditures for PPE do affect the ROPI model inputs.

Review 13-2—Solution

a.

GIS—DCF ($ millions, except per share value and discount factors)	Reported 2019	Forecast Horizon Period				Terminal Period
		2020	2021	2022	2023	
Sales.		$17,118.2	$17,375.0	$17,635.6	$17,900.1	$18,168.6
NOPAT		2,396.5	2,432.5	2,469.0	2,506.0	2,543.6
NOA		22,231.4	22,564.9	22,903.4	23,246.9	23,595.6
Increase in NOA.		272.0	333.5	338.5	343.5	348.7
FCFF (NOPAT − Increase in NOA).		2,124.5	2,099.0	2,130.5	2,162.5	2,194.9
Discount factor [$1/(1 + r_w)^t$]		0.94438	0.89185	0.84224	0.79539	
Present value of horizon FCFF.		2,006.3	1,872.0	1,794.4	1,720.0	
Cum present value of horizon FCFF	$ 7,392.7					
Present value of terminal FCFF	39,768.0					
Total firm value	47,160.7					
Less: NNO	14,591.7					
Less: NCI	313.2					
Firm equity value	$32,255.8					
Shares outstanding.	601.9					
Stock value per share.	$ 53.59					

$r_w = 0.0589$

$g = 0.015$

b. The stock price on May 28, 2019 (the closest trading day prior to the fiscal-year-end) was $52.81 per share. The part *a* valuation of $53.59 per share implies that the stock is slightly undervalued on that date.

Review 13-3—Solution

a.

GIS—ROPI (In millions, except per share value and discount factors)	Reported 2019	Forecast Horizon Period				Terminal Period
		2020	2021	2022	2023	
Sales.		$17,118.2	$17,375.0	$17,635.6	$17,900.1	$18,168.6
NOPAT		2,396.5	2,432.5	2,469.0	2,506.0	2,543.6
NOA	$21,959.4	22,231.4	22,564.9	22,903.4	23,246.9	23,595.6
ROPI (NOPAT − [NOA$_{Beg}$ × r_w])		1,103.1	1,123.1	1,139.9	1,157.0	1,174.4
Discount factor [1/(1 + r_w)^t]		0.94438	0.89185	0.84224	0.79539	
Present value of horizon ROPI.		1,041.7	1,001.6	960.1	920.3	
Cum present value of horizon ROPI.	3,923.7					
Present value of terminal ROPI	21,278.0					
NOA	21,959.4					
Total firm value	47,161.1					
Less: NNO	14,591.7					
Less: NCI	313.2					
Firm equity value	$32,256.2					
Shares outstanding.	601.9					
Stock value per share.	$ 53.59				r_w = 0.0589	
					g = 0.015	

b. The stock price on May 28, 2019 (the closest trading day prior to the fiscal-year-end) was $52.81 per share. The part *a* valuation of $53.59 per share implies that the stock is slightly undervalued on that date.

Review 13-4—Solution

a. (i) Delaying payment would improve ROPI because accounts payable balance would increase, which would decrease NOA.

(ii) A potential negative consequence would be if suppliers increase their prices to counter delayed payment. In that case, ROPI could be worsened because cost of goods sold would increase.

b. (i) Reducing inventory spoilage would reduce COGS, which would improve NOPAT.

(ii) Selling at a discount may cause customers to expect the discount on other products, which could create pressure on margins.

c. (i) Using social media could cut down on advertising expenses.

(ii) The impact of the new marketing on sales is a crucial factor. If the traditional marketing media were highly effective, moving away from them could actually harm sales. The cost savings and sales outcomes need to be determined to assess the impact on ROPI.

d. (i) If the lease costs are lower than the cash outlay needed for CAPEX, this could increase ROPI by increasing NOPAT and decreasing NOA.

(ii) The availability of leased equipment might be questionable, which could lead to lost sales.

Module 14

Managerial Accounting for MBAs

Managerial Accounting for MBAs				
Uses of Accounting Information	**Organizations: Missions, Goals, and Strategies**	**Changing Environment of Business**	**Ethics in Managerial Accounting**	**Cost Drivers**
▨ Financial Accounting ▨ Managerial Accounting ▨ Strategic Cost Management	▨ Strategic Position Analysis ▨ Managerial Accounting and Goal Attainment ▨ Planning, Organizing, and Controlling	▨ Global Competition and Its Key Dimensions ▨ Big Data and Analysis ▨ Robotics and Cognitive Technologies ▨ Enterprise Risk Management (ERM)	▨ Codes of Ethics ▨ Corporate Governance ▨ Sustainability Accounting and Corporate Social Responsibility	▨ Structural Cost Drivers ▨ Organizational Cost Drivers ▨ Activity Cost Drivers
Review 14-1, 14-2	Review 14-3	Review 14-4	Review 14-5	Review 14-6

PREVIEW

ABF

In the last ten years, the percentage of sales made through e-commerce has more than doubled. In the first half of 2019 alone, retailers announced closures of 7,037 brick-and-mortar stores up from 5,864 closures in all of 2018.[1]

So who was the fastest growing retailer in the U.S. in 2018 according to *Business Insider*?[2] Primark, a subsidiary of Associated British Foods, is a European clothing chain that only sells its merchandise in brick-and-mortar stores. You can view Primark products online, but you have to physically go to a store to buy them.

Primark's remarkable growth (up 103% from 2017) is attributed to low retail prices, which average over 200% lower than other retailers in the United States.[3] The company keeps it costs down by buying in bulk and limiting its advertising costs.

Information provided by managerial accounting systems is critical in companies, like Primark, that operate on low gross profit margins. For example, Primark relied on information provided by the company's management accounting system in making the decision not to sell online. An analysis of the shipping and high return costs associated with e-commerce indicated that expanding into that market would simply drive sales prices too high for their customer base.

Primark also uses management accounting information to focus and evaluate its product line. Primark sells a large range of licensed products (Disney, Game of Thrones, Rolling Stones). The company has found that creating themed, in-store departments turns Primark into a "shopping destination," which results in higher revenues. Throughout this book, we will learn how management accounting provides useful information for making informed business decisions.

Road Map

LO	Learning Objective | Topics	Page	eLecture	Guided Example	Assignments
LO1	**Contrast the different uses of financial and managerial accounting information.** Financial Accounting :: Managerial Accounting :: Institute of Management Accountants	14-3	e14–1	Review 14-1	12, 13, 14, 21
LO2	**Describe the three themes of strategic cost management and illustrate how strategic cost management can be used to create a long-term competitive advantage.** Strategic Cost Management :: Strategic Position Analysis :: Cost Driver Analysis :: Value Chain Analysis	14-5	e14–2	Review 14-2	12
LO3	**Examine how an organization's mission, goals, and strategies affect managerial accounting.** Missions and Goals :: Strategic Position Analysis :: Cost Leadership :: Product or Service Differentiation :: Market Niche :: Goal Attainment :: Planning, Organizing and Controlling	14-6	e14–3	Review 14-3	12, 15, 16, 17, 22, 23, 24, 25, 27, 28, 34
LO4	**Analyze how trends in the business environment impact the role of management accounting.** Global Competition :: Big Data Analysis :: Robotics and Cognitive Technologies :: Enterprise Risk Management	14-12	e14–4	Review 14-4	18
LO5	**Assess the nature of the ethical dilemmas managers and accountants confront.** Ethical Dilemmas :: Codes of Ethics :: Corporate Governance and SOX :: Sustainability Accounting :: Corporate Social Responsibility	14-13	e14–5	Review 14-5	12, 29, 30, 31, 32
LO6	**Demonstrate the use of structural, organizational, and activity cost drivers.** Business Activities :: Structural, Organizational, and Activity Cost Drivers	14-17	e14–6	Review 14-6	12, 19, 20, 26, 33

Managers of organizations such as Primark are required to make strategic decisions every day in order to remain competitive in the marketplace. These decisions might involve answering questions such as: What is our target market? How do we create awareness within our target market? What products should we offer and at what price? How many employees should we hire? How much should we pay our employees? Which suppliers should we use to fulfill our orders? And, how much money should we invest in capital resources? In order to make these decisions, and to achieve their organizations' goals, managers must have an understanding of, and access to, timely and reliable information.

Managerial accounting is defined as the activities carried out to provide managers and other employees with financial reporting information and control to assist management in the formulation and implementation of an organization's strategy. We begin our exploration of managerial accounting by discussing the differences between managerial and financial accounting and by investigating how competitive strategy affects the way organizations use managerial accounting information. Next, we explore how the emergence of global competition and changes in technology have increased the need to understand managerial accounting concepts. We also examine the interrelationships among measurement, management, and ethics. Finally, we provide an overview of factors that influence costs in an organization and how these factors have changed in recent years.

Uses of Accounting Information

eLectures
MBC **LO1** Contrast the different uses of financial and managerial accounting information.

Accounting information attempts to satisfy the needs of a variety of individuals and agencies that make decisions about and for organizations. These decision makers can be classified by their relation to a business as either external users or internal users. **Financial accounting** is designed primarily for decision makers outside of the company, whereas managerial accounting is designed primarily for decision makers within the company.

Financial Accounting

Financial accounting, as discussed in the first half of this book, is an information-processing system that generates general-purpose reports of financial operations (income statement and statement of cash flows) and financial position (balance sheet) for an organization. Although financial accounting is used by decision makers inside and outside the firm, financial accounting typically emphasizes external users, such as security investors, analysts, and lenders. Adding to this external orientation are external financial reporting requirements determined by law and generally accepted accounting principles.

Financial accounting is also concerned with keeping records of the organization's assets, obligations, and the collection and payment of cash. An organization cannot survive without converting sales into cash, paying for purchases, meeting payroll, and keeping track of its assets.

Managers often use income statements and balance sheets as a starting point in evaluating and planning the firm's overall activities. Managers learn a great deal by performing a comparative analysis of their firm and competing firms. Corporate goals are often stated using financial accounting numbers such as net income, or ratios such as return on investment and earnings per common share. However, internal decision makers often find the information provided in financial statements of limited value in managing day-to-day operating activities. They often complain that financial accounting information is too aggregated, prepared too late, based on irrelevant past costs, and not action oriented. For example, the costs of all items produced and sold or all services rendered are summarized in a single line in most financial statements, making it impossible to determine the costs of individual products or services. Financial accounting procedures, acceptable for costing inventories as a whole, often produce misleading information when applied to individual products. Even when they are accurately determined, the costs of individual products or services are rarely detailed enough in overall financial statements to provide the information needed for decisions concerning the factors that influence costs. Financial accounting reports, seldom prepared more than once a month, are not timely enough for use in the management of day-to-day activities that cause excess costs. Finally, financial accounting reports, to a great extent, are based on historical costs rather than on current or future costs. Managers are more interested in future costs than in historical costs such as last year's depreciation.

While financial accounting information is useful in making some management decisions, its primary emphasis is not on internal decision making.

Managerial Accounting

As emphasized in our Primark example, managers are constantly faced with the need to understand and control costs, make important product decisions, coordinate resources, and guide and motivate employees. Managerial accounting provides an information framework to organize, evaluate, and report proprietary data in light of an organization's goals. This information is directed to managers and other employees within the organization. Managerial accounting reports can be designed to meet the information needs of internal decision makers. Top management may need only summary information prepared once a month for each business unit. An engineer responsible for hourly production scheduling may need continuously updated and detailed information concerning the cost of alternative ways of producing a product.

Because of the intensity of competition and the shorter life cycles of new products and services, managerial accounting is crucial to an organization's success. All managers must understand the financial implications of their decisions. While accountants are available to assist in obtaining and evaluating relevant information, individual managers are responsible for requesting information, analyzing it, and making the final decisions.

Business Insight ■ Strategic Thinking Requires a Company to Think Inside the Consumer's Sphere

Selling a used car can be difficult in any country, but prior to 2014 it was even more difficult in Russia where there were very few used car dealers located outside of major cities. CarPrice founders offered consumers a digital alternative when they opened the first Russian online, real-time auction for used cars in June 2014.

With CarPrice, sellers complete an online form and then take their car to a CarPrice location where it is inspected and rated. Once the paperwork is checked, CarPrice conducts a 30-minute online auction reaching over 30,000 dealers. If the seller accepts the winning bid, they immediately receive the agreed-upon payment. If the seller isn't satisfied with the price, they are free to leave with their car. There are no fees to the seller in either case. CarPrice boasts that the entire process can be completed in 1.5–2 hours.

Managerial accounting helps guide companies like CarPrice through the myriad of growth opportunities available to them, while providing information about their costs and profits.

Sources: The Boston Consulting Group, "The 2018 BCG Local Dynamos: Emerging-Market Companies Up Their Game," October 2018; and carprice.ru.

Managerial accounting information exists to serve the needs of management. Hence, it is subject to a cost-benefit analysis and should be developed only if the perceived benefits exceed the costs of development and use. Also, while financial measures are often used in managerial accounting, they are not used to the exclusion of other measures. Money is simply a convenient way of expressing events in a form suitable to summary analysis. When this is not possible or appropriate, nonfinancial measures are used. Time, for example, is often an important element of quality or service. Hence, many performance measures focus on time, for example:

■ Internet vendors such as UPS and Amazon.com track delivery time.

■ Fire departments and police departments measure the response time to emergency calls.

■ Airlines, such as Delta Airlines as well as the Federal Aviation Administration, monitor the number of on-time departures and arrivals.

About IMA® (Institute of Management Accountants)

No external standards (such as requirements of the Securities and Exchange Commission) are imposed on information provided to internal users. However the IMA®—the association of accountants and financial professionals in business—acts as a guide for defining the role and best practices of managerial accounting. Globally, IMA supports the profession through research, the CMA® (Certified Management Accountant) program, continuing education, networking, and advocacy of the highest ethical business practices. In 2019, the IMA updated its Management Accounting Competency Framework. The

framework emphasizes the need for management accountants to partner in planning and decision making, to create performance management systems, and to provide expertise in financial reporting and control.[4]

The IMA's CMA program focuses specifically on the competencies required by organizations and CFOs to protect investors and drive business value. The CMA tests professional competency in financial planning and analysis, risk management and internal controls, strategic costing, decision support, performance management, corporate finance, ethics, and more. CMA-certified professionals work within organizations of all sizes, industries, and types, including manufacturing and services, public and private enterprises, not-for-profit organizations, academic institutions, government entities, and multinational corporations. To become certified, a qualified professional must be a member of IMA, pass a two-part exam, stay current through continuing education, and abide by IMA's *Statement of Ethical Professional Practice*. Based on a study cited by the CMA,[5] CMAs have a 55% salary advantage globally. That advantage increases to 70% for CMAs ages 20–29. For more information about IMA, please visit www.imanet.org.

The significant differences between financial and managerial accounting are summarized in Exhibit 14.1.

EXHIBIT 14.1 ■ Differences Between Financial and Managerial Accounting	
Financial Accounting	**Managerial Accounting**
Information for internal *and* external users	Information for internal users
General-purpose financial statements	Special-purpose information and reports
Statements are highly aggregated	Information is aggregated or detailed, depending on need
Relatively long reporting periods	Reporting periods are long or short, depending on need
Report on past decisions	Oriented toward current and future decisions
Follows generally accepted accounting principles	Not constrained by generally accepted accounting principles
Must conform to external standards	No external standards
Emphasizes objective data	Encourages subjective data, if relevant

Review 14-1 LO1

The previous discussion has focused on understanding the difference between financial and managerial accounting and the broader context of managerial accounting within a company.

Required

Identify the statements and phrases from the following list that are primarily relevant to managerial accounting, as opposed to financial accounting:

1. Preparing periodic financial statements
2. A company's strategic position
3. Calculates earnings per share for stockholders
4. Summarizes information about past events
5. Is not based on generally accepted accounting principles
6. Must conform to external standards
7. Helping managers make decisions is its primary purpose
8. Encourages use of selective data, if relevant
9. Is tailored to the needs of the company and its managers

Solution on p. 14-26. 10. Receives guidance from the IMA as to its role in helping an organization achieve its goals

eLectures

LO2 Describe the three themes of strategic cost management and illustrate how strategic cost management can be used to create a long-term competitive advantage.

Strategic Cost Management

Most businesses are under constant pressure to reduce costs to remain competitive. A 2019 study by the accounting firm Deloitte reported that intensified competition within peer groups and the need for investment in growth areas were the primary drivers of cost management measures.[6]

During recent years, the rapid introduction of improved and new products and services has shortened the market lives of products and services. Some products, such as personal computers, can be

---

[4] http://www.imanet.org/career-resources/management-accounting-competencies
[5] Gregory L. Krippel PhD, and Sheila Mitchell CPA, "The CMA Advantage: An Update," *Strategic Finance*, September 2017, pp. 39-45.
[6] "Save-to-Transform as a Catalyst for Embracing Digital Disruption," Deloitte's second biennial global cost survey, 2019.

obsolete within two or three years after introduction. At the same time, the increased use of complex automated equipment makes it difficult to change production procedures after production begins. Combining short product life cycles with automated production results in an environment where most costs are determined by decisions made before production begins (decisions concerning product design and production procedures).

In response to these trends, a strategic approach to managerial accounting, referred to as *strategic cost management* has emerged. Strategic cost management is a blending of three themes:

1. **Strategic position analysis**—an examination of an organization's basic way of competing to sell products or services.
2. **Cost driver analysis**—the study of factors that cause or influence costs.
3. **Value chain analysis**—the study of value-producing activities, stretching from basic raw materials to the final consumer of a product or service.[7]

We define **strategic cost management** as making decisions concerning specific cost drivers within the context of an organization's business strategy, internal value chain, and position in a larger value chain stretching from the development and use of resources to final consumers. Strategic position analysis is considered in this module as part of an organization's strategy. Cost driver analysis is also introduced in this module and examined further in Module 15. Value chain analysis is discussed in Module 21.

LO2 Review 14-2

Discuss the three themes that are blended to form the idea of strategic cost management. Do some research online in newspapers and identify a business that seems to demonstrate the use of each of the strategies.

Solution on p. 14-27.

Missions, Goals, and Strategies

An Organization's Mission and Goals

An organization's **mission** is the basic purpose toward which its activities are directed. Although there is no published mission statement for **Primark**, one of the company's slogans, "Amazing Fashions, Amazing Prices," makes it clear that providing customers with inexpensive, high-quality clothing is the mission. **TED** is a nonprofit devoted to spreading ideas, usually in the form of short, powerful talks (18 minutes or less). TED's mission statement is simply two words: "Spread ideas."[8] Organizations vary widely in their missions. One benefit of a mission statement is to help focus all the activities of an organization. For instance, the former chairman and CEO of Coca-Cola stated that the mission of **The Coca-Cola Company** is "to create value over time for the owners of our business." He went on to say:

LO3 Examine how an organization's mission, goals, and strategies affect managerial accounting.

> Our society is based on democratic capitalism. In such a society, people create specific institutions to help meet specific needs. Governments are created to help meet social needs. . . Businesses such as ours are created to meet economic needs. The common thread between these institutions is that they can flourish only when they stay focused on the specific need they were created to fulfill. When institutions try to broaden their scope beyond their natural realms, when for example they try to become all things to all people, they fail.[9]

The CEO of Coca-Cola believed that Coca-Cola best contributes to society and helps government and other organizations fulfill their missions by staying focused on shareholder value. He believed

---

[7] John K. Shank, "Strategic Cost Management: New Wine, or Just New Bottles?" *Journal of Management Accounting Research,* Fall 1989, p. 50.
[8] https://www.ted.com/about/our-organization
[9] Roberto Goizueta, "Why Shareholder Value?" *CEO Series Issue No. 13,* February 1997, Center for the Study of American Business, Washington University in St. Louis, p. 2.

focusing on economics keeps a company financially healthy, and a healthy company fulfills its responsibilities. Conversely, a bankrupt company is incapable of paying taxes, employing people, serving customers, supporting charitable institutions, or making other contributions to society. Coca-Cola's current mission statement, "To refresh the world. To inspire moments of optimism and happiness. And to create value and make a difference," still emphasizes the creation of shareholder value.

We frequently distinguish between organizations on the basis of profit motive. **For-profit organizations** have profit as a primary objective, whereas **not-for-profit organizations** do not have profit as a primary objective. Clearly, the Coca-Cola Company is a for-profit organization, whereas TED and United Way are not-for-profit organizations. (The term *nonprofit* is frequently used to refer to what we have identified as not-for-profit organizations.) Regardless of whether a profit motive exists, organizations must use resources wisely. Every dollar United Way spends for administrative salaries is a dollar that cannot be used to support charitable activities. Not-for-profit organizations, including governments, can go bankrupt if they are unable to meet their financial obligations. All organizations, for-profit and not-for-profit, should use managerial accounting concepts to ensure that resources are used wisely.

A **goal** is a definable, measurable objective. Based on the organization's mission, management sets a number of goals. For-profit organizations have some measure of profitability or shareholder value as one of their stated or implicit goals. The mission of a paper mill located in a small town is to provide quality paper products in order to earn a profit for its owners. The paper mill's goals might include earning an annual profit equal to 10% of average total assets, maintaining annual dividends of $2 per share of common stock, developing a customer reputation for above-average quality and service, providing steady employment for area residents, and meeting or exceeding environmental standards.

A clear statement of mission and well-defined goals provides an organization with an identity and unifying purpose, thereby ensuring that all employees are heading in the same direction. Having developed a mission and a set of goals, employees are more apt to make decisions that move the organization toward its defined purpose.

A **strategy** is a course of action that will assist in achieving one or more goals. Much of this text will focus on the financial aspects of selecting strategies to achieve goals. For example, if an organization's goal is to improve product quality, possible strategies for achieving this goal include investing in new equipment, implementing additional quality inspections, prescreening suppliers, reducing batch size, redesigning products, training employees, and rearranging the shop floor. Managerial accounting information will assist in determining which of the many alternative strategies for achieving the goal of quality improvement are cost effective. The distinction between mission, goals, and strategies is illustrated in Exhibit 14.2.

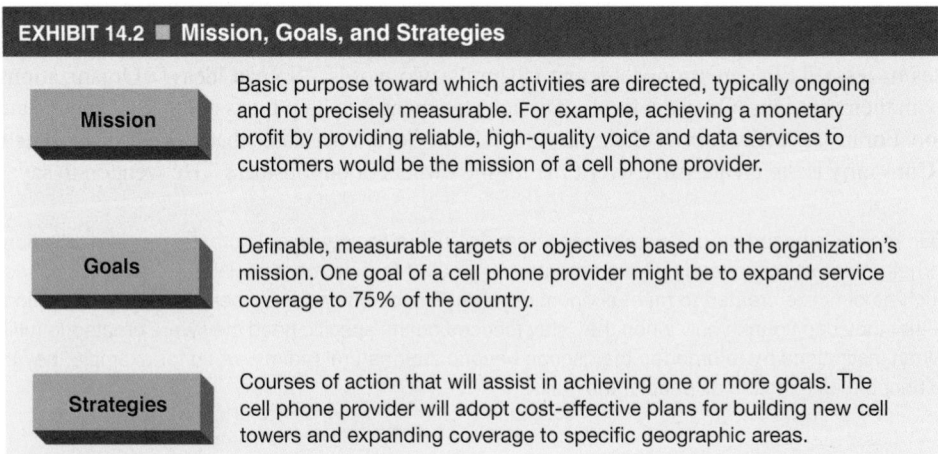

EXHIBIT 14.2 ■ Mission, Goals, and Strategies

Mission — Basic purpose toward which activities are directed, typically ongoing and not precisely measurable. For example, achieving a monetary profit by providing reliable, high-quality voice and data services to customers would be the mission of a cell phone provider.

Goals — Definable, measurable targets or objectives based on the organization's mission. One goal of a cell phone provider might be to expand service coverage to 75% of the country.

Strategies — Courses of action that will assist in achieving one or more goals. The cell phone provider will adopt cost-effective plans for building new cell towers and expanding coverage to specific geographic areas.

Strategic Position Analysis

In competitive environments, managers must make a fundamental decision concerning their organization's goal for positioning itself in comparison to competitors. This goal is referred to as the organization's **strategic position**. Much of the organization's strategy depends on this strategic positioning goal. Michael Porter, a highly regarded expert on business strategy, has identified three possible strategic positions that lead to business success.[10]

1. Cost leadership
2. Product or service differentiation
3. Market niche

According to Porter, cost leadership

> requires aggressive construction of efficient-scale facilities, vigorous pursuit of cost reductions from experience, tight cost and overhead control, avoidance of marginal customer accounts, and cost minimization in areas like R&D [research and development], service, sales force, advertising, and so on. A great deal of managerial attention to cost control is necessary to achieve these aims. Low cost relative to competitors becomes the theme running through the entire strategy, though quality, service, and other areas cannot be ignored.[11]

Achieving cost leadership allows an organization to achieve higher profits selling at the same price as competitors or by allowing the firm to aggressively compete on the basis of price while remaining profitable. One of the first companies to successfully use a cost leadership strategy was **Carnegie Steel Company**.

> Carnegie's operating strategy was to push his own direct costs below his competitors so that he could charge prices that would always ensure enough demand to keep his plants running at full capacity. This strategy prompted him to require frequent information showing his direct costs in relation to those of his competitors. Possessing that information and secure in the knowledge that his costs were the lowest in the industry, Carnegie then mercilessly cut prices during economic recessions. While competing firms went under, he still made profits. In periods of prosperity, when customers' demands exceeded the industry's capacity to produce, Carnegie joined others in raising prices.[12]

Primark and **Southwest Airlines** are current examples of successful businesses competing with a strategy of cost leadership. Although **Amazon.com** uses the Internet to differentiate itself from traditional booksellers, its primary strategic position is cost leadership.

Business Insight ■ McDonald's Adds a Service Differentiation Strategy to the Mix

Three weeks before Steve Easterbrook took over as Chief Executive Officer in early 2015, **McDonald's** announced its worst year in decades. Consumer preferences were changing, and fast-food competitors were responding to consumer demands. **Chipotle** and **Chick-fil-A** were attracting new customers with new menu items. **Burger King** had already experimented with order delivery.

Focusing on cost leadership, **McDonald's** primary business strategy, was not enough to maintain the growth and profits that its investors and franchise owners expected. In 2017, **McDonald's** introduced its Velocity Growth Plan. Three growth accelerators were identified in that plan: Digital, Delivery, and Experience of the Future. All three focused on improved service for the customer. **McDonald's** entered into a partnership with **Uber** (and later with **Door Dash**) for delivery services, added mobile app ordering with curbside pickup, and installed touchscreen kiosks in upgraded restaurants for order customization. In 2019, **McDonald's** acquired two technology companies focused on making drive-through ordering faster and more accurate.

McDonald's adoption of service differentiation as a secondary strategy has proved to be worthwhile. Profit margin ratios increased from 19% in 2016 to 28.2% in 2018.

Sources: Thomas Buckely and Leslie Patton, "McDonald's CEO Wants Big Macs to Keep Up with Big Tech," *Bloomberg Business Week*, September 25, 2019.

---

[10] Michael E. Porter, *Competitive Strategy* (New York: The Free Press, 1980), p. 35.

[11] Porter, p. 35.

[12] H. Thomas Johnson and Robert S. Kaplan, *Relevance Lost: The Rise and Fall of Management Accounting* (Boston: Harvard Business School Press, 1987), pp. 33–34.

Conversely, while an organization might compete primarily on the basis of price, management must take care to ensure their product or service remains attuned to changing customer needs and preferences. In the early twentieth century, General Motors employed a differentiation strategy, focusing on the rapid introduction of technological change in new automobile designs to overcome the market dominance of the Model T produced by Ford Motor Company. While successfully following a cost leadership strategy for years, Ford made the mistake of excluding other considerations such as vehicle performance and customer desires for different colors.

The third possible strategic position, according to Porter, focuses on a specific market niche such as a buyer group, segment of the product line, or geographic market and

rests on the premise that the firm is thus able to serve its narrow strategic target more effectively or efficiently than competitors who are competing more broadly. As a result, the firm achieves either differentiation from better meeting the needs of the particular target, or lower costs in serving the target, or both. Even though the focus strategy does not achieve low costs or differentiation for the market as a whole, it does achieve one or both of these positions vis-à-vis its narrow market target.[13]

Business Insight ■ Managerial Accounting Is Key to Creating New Business Models

YY, one of the largest live-streaming companies in the world, has adopted a unique business model in the entertainment market. Instead of generating revenue from advertisers, the Chinese company collects fees from users who are allowed to buy gifts for their favorite performers (amateur singers, dancers, and comedians) and purchase virtual goods for use in online games. Users can also pay a monthly subscription fee, which gives them priority entrance to live-streamed performances and access to other enhanced features. To appeal to younger audiences, the company introduced participant-focused live streaming in 2017, where users can interact directly with the performers.

On average, over 90 million users per month were engaged with YY in the fourth quarter of 2018. Revenues for 2018 exceeded $2.2 billion.

Managerial accounting helps companies like YY understand the cost of delivering their services, and the costs of adapting their business model to access new markets.

Sources: The Boston Consulting Group, "The 2018 BCG Local Dynamos: Emerging-Market Companies Up Their Game," October 2018; and YY Inc. Form 20-F: *Annual Report Pursuant to Section 13 or 15(D) of the Securities Exchange Act of 1934* for the fiscal year ended December 31, 2018.

YY, highlighted in the Business Insight box above, is following a market niche strategy. It identified behaviors of its target market, and using management accounting information, is adapting its model to better fit its market's needs.

Managerial Accounting and Goal Attainment

A major purpose of managerial accounting is to support the achievement of goals. Hence, determining an organization's strategic position goal has implications for the operation of an organization's managerial accounting system.

Careful budgeting and cost control with frequent and detailed performance reports are critical with a goal of cost leadership. When the product is difficult to distinguish from that of competitors', price is the primary basis of competition. Under these circumstances, everyone in the organization should continuously apply managerial accounting concepts to achieve and maintain cost leadership. The managerial accounting system should constantly compare actual costs with budgeted costs and signal the existence of significant differences. A simplified version of a *performance report* for costs during a budget period is as follows:

Budgeted (planned) Costs	Actual Costs	Deviation from Budget	Percent Deviation
$560,000	$595,000	$35,000 unfavorable	6.25%

[13] Porter, pp. 38–39.

Frequent and detailed comparisons of actual and budgeted costs are less important when a differentiation strategy is followed. This is especially true when products have short life cycles or production is highly automated. In these situations, most costs are determined before production begins and there is little opportunity to undertake cost reduction activities thereafter.

With short product lives or automated manufacturing, exceptional care must go into the initial design of a product or service and the determination of how it will be produced or delivered. Here, detailed cost information assists in design and scheduling decisions. A simplified version of the predicted costs of producing one batch of a specialty product is as follows:

Engineering and scheduling (12 hours @ $70)	$ 840
Materials (detail omitted)	3,500
Equipment setup (2.5 hours @ $100).	250
Machine operation (9.5 hours @ $90)	855
Materials movement.	150
Packing and shipping	675
Total	$6,270

When a differentiation strategy is followed, it often pays to work closely with customers to find ways to enhance the perceived value of a product or service. This leads to an analysis of costs from the customer's viewpoint. The customer may not want a costly feature. Alternatively, the customer may be willing to pay more for an additional feature that will reduce subsequent operating costs.

Planning, Organizing, and Controlling

The process of selecting goals and strategies to achieve these goals is often referred to as **planning**. The implementation of plans requires the development of subgoals and the assignment of responsibility to achieve subgoals to specific individuals or groups within an organization. This process of making the organization into a well-ordered whole is called **organizing**. In organizing, the authority to take action to implement plans is delegated to other managers and employees.

Developing an **organization chart** illustrating the formal relationships that exist between the elements of an organization is an important part of organizing. An organization chart for Crown Department Stores is illustrated in Exhibit 14.3. The blocks represent organizational units, and the lines represent relationships between the units. Authority flows down through the organization. Top management delegates authority to use resources for limited purposes to subordinate managers who, in turn, delegate to their subordinates more limited authority for accomplishing more structured tasks. Responsibility flows up through the organization. People at the bottom are responsible for specific tasks, but the president is responsible for the operation of the entire organization.

A distinction is often made between line and staff departments. *Line departments* engage in activities that create and distribute goods and services to customers. *Staff departments* exist to facilitate the activities of line departments. In Exhibit 14.3, we see that Crown Department Stores has two levels of staff organizations—corporate and store. The corporate staff departments are Purchasing, Advertising, Operations, Treasurer, and Controller. Staff departments at the store level are Personnel, Accounting, and Maintenance. All other units are line departments. A change in plans can necessitate a change in the organization. For example, Crown's plan to discontinue the sale of hardware and add an art department during the coming year will necessitate an organizational change.

Controlling is the process of ensuring that results agree with plans. A brief example of a performance report for costs is presented above. In the process of controlling operations, actual performance is compared with plans.

With a cost leadership strategy and long-lived products, if actual results deviate significantly from plans, an attempt is made to bring operations into line with plans, or the plans are adjusted. The original plan is adjusted if it is deemed no longer appropriate because of changed circumstances.

With a differentiation strategy and short-lived products, design and scheduling personnel will consider previous errors in predicting costs as they plan new products and services. Hence, the process of controlling feeds forward into the process of planning to form a continuous cycle coordinated through the management accounting system. This cycle is illustrated in Exhibit 14.4.

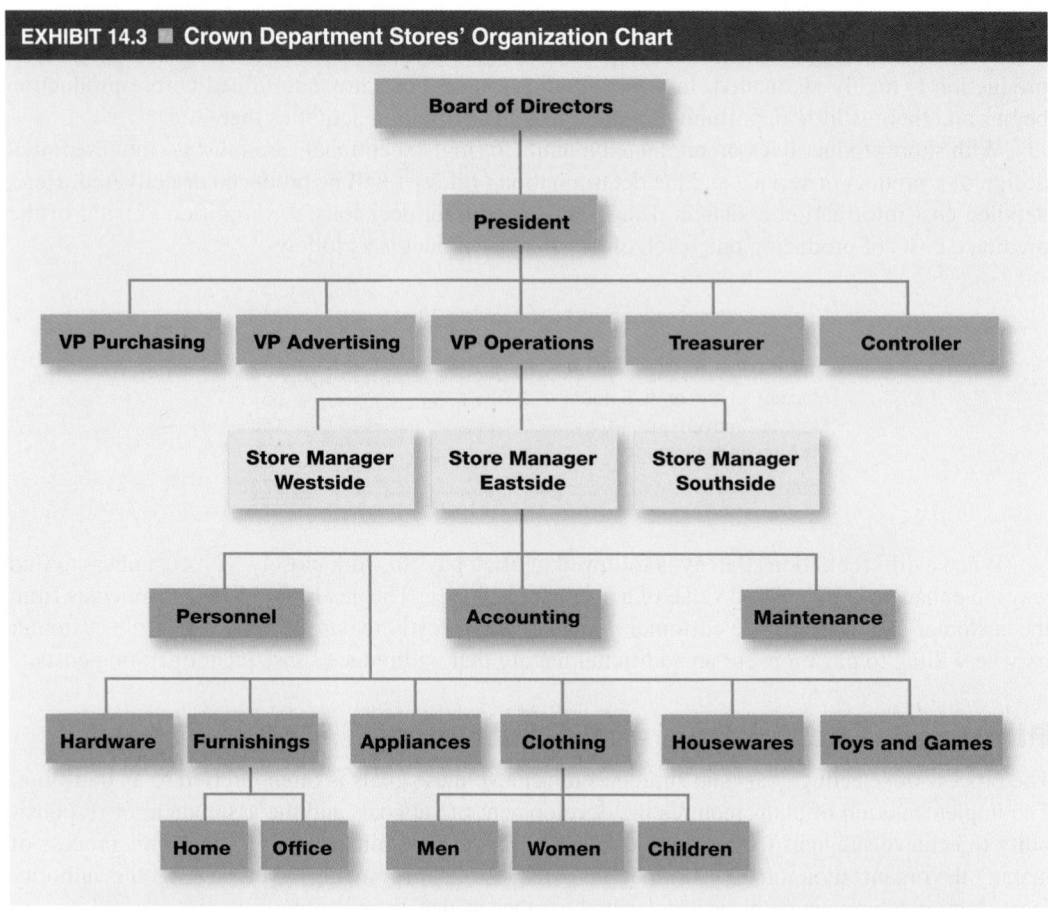

EXHIBIT 14.3 ■ Crown Department Stores' Organization Chart

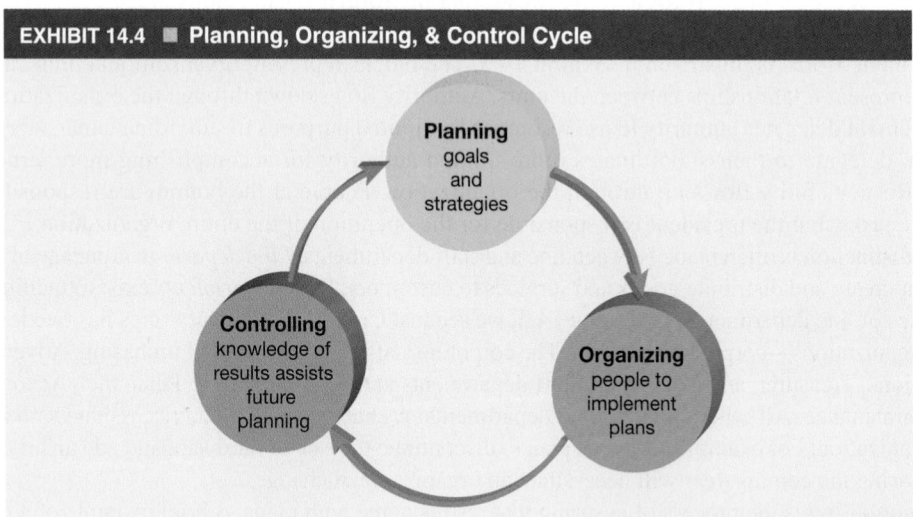

EXHIBIT 14.4 ■ Planning, Organizing, & Control Cycle

Review 14-3 LO3

A major purpose of managerial accounting is to support the achievement of goals. Discuss a few ways that managerial accountants can help support the achievement of goals, specifically those of cost leadership and differentiation.

Solution on p. 14-27.

Changing Environment of Business

The changing environment of business includes trends such as the global economic system, big data and predictive analytics, robotics and cognitive technologies, and enterprise risk management (ERM). Additional items such as lean manufacturing and just-in-time inventory will be discussed later in Module 20.

LO4 Analyze how trends in the business environment impact the role of management accounting.

Global Competition and Its Key Dimensions

The move away from isolated national economic systems toward an interdependent global economic system has become increasingly pronounced. International treaties, such as the North American Free Trade Agreement and the General Agreement on Tariffs and Trade, merely recognize an already existing and inevitable condition made possible by advances in telecommunications (to move data), computers (to process data into information), and transportation (to move products and people).

The labels of origins on goods (Japan, Germany, Canada, Taiwan, China, and so forth) only scratch the surface of existing global relationships. Behind labels designating a product's final assembly point are components from all over the world.

The move toward a global economy has heightened competition and reduced selling prices to such an extent that there is little or no room for error in managing costs or pricing products. Moreover, customers are not just looking for the best price. Well-informed buyers routinely search the world for the product or service that best fits their needs on the three interrelated dimensions of price/cost, quality, and service; hence, these are the three key dimensions of competition.

To customers, *price/cost* includes not only the initial purchase price but also subsequent operating and maintenance costs. To compete on the basis of price, the seller must carefully manage costs. Otherwise, reduced prices might squeeze product margins to such an extent that a sale becomes unprofitable. Hence, price competition implies cost competition.

Quality refers to the degree to which products or services meet the customer's needs. *Service* includes things such as timely delivery, helpfulness of sales personnel, and subsequent support.

Managers of successful companies know they compete in a global market with instant communications. Because the competition is hungry and always striving to gain a competitive advantage, world-class companies must continuously struggle to improve performance on these three interrelated dimensions: price/cost, quality, and service. Throughout this text, we examine how firms successfully compete on these three dimensions.

Big Data and Analysis

Given recent advancements in technology, there is a vast amount of data available to organizations. However, it can be difficult to turn this data into useful and predictive information. Big data is unique in that it is so large or complex, traditional analysis methods are often inadequate. In 2016, IMA and Robert Half worked together to publish a report, *Building a Team to Capitalize in Big Data*. Based on their research, there is a shortage of finance and accounting professionals who have the skills to effectively analyze **big data**. "Finance leaders face significant shortages of accounting and finance professionals who possess the technical and nontechnical skills required for data analytics initiatives." Organizations are in need of employees who have the abilities to: identify key data trends, perform data mining and extraction, conduct operational and decision analysis, recommend process improvement, and conduct strategic thinking and execution.

Robotics and Cognitive Technologies

Robotic process automation (RPA) "is an application of technology, governed by business logic and structured inputs, aimed at automating business processes."[14] More than 420,000 robots, generating $16.5 billion in revenue worldwide, were installed in 2018.[15]

---

[14] Clint Boulton, "What Is RPA? A Revolution in Business Process Automation," *CIO*, September 2018, https://www.cio.com/article/3236451/what-is-rpa-robotic-process-automation-explained.html

[15] Alexandre Tanzi, "Annual Investments in Robotics Rose to World Record $16.5 Billion," *Bloomberg*, September 2019.

Artificial intelligence (AI) can be defined as technologies that "perform tasks that previously required human intelligence, such as extracting meaning from images, text or speech, detecting patterns and anomalies, and making recommendations, predictions, or decisions."[16]

Cognitive technologies (or intelligent automation) combine RPA with AI. Examples include machine learning applications that use algorithms to predict what a particular customer is likely to buy and natural language processing chatbots that provide customer support. A specific use in accounting might involve using machine learning applications to predict, based on past performance and current cash flows, when a loan covenant might be breached.[17]

In May 2019, Deloitte surveyed over 500 executives in 26 different countries. Fifty-eight percent of the executives reported that they had either already incorporated or were in the process of incorporating cognitive technologies into their business operations. Increased productivity and cost reduction, greater accuracy, and an improved customer experience were seen as the greatest benefits of the new technologies. Those organizations that had successfully incorporated cognitive technologies reported a 27% reduction in costs with an average payback of nine months.

Incorporating new technologies doesn't come without challenges. Accountants will need to develop new skills to meet those challenges.

Enterprise Risk Management (ERM)

Organizations are constantly faced with uncertainty from the environment, competitors, and other factors that could result in significant risk or loss. The Committee of Sponsoring Organizations (COSO) defines **enterprise risk management (ERM)** as "the culture, capabilities and practices, integrated with strategy-setting and performance, that organizations rely on to manage risk in creating, preserving, and realizing value."[18] By better understanding the types and potential costs of these risks, management accountants can help their organizations devise strategies to better predict and minimize their exposures to risk. In Module 9 we will discuss how an organization's budgeting model is used to evaluate the financial impact of a risk and to determine, from a financial perspective, the best response to risk.

Review 14-4 LO4

MBC

Big data analysis and ERM are of growing interest to leaders of organizations. Discuss briefly how the influence of each might affect the role of management accountants.

Solution on p. 14-27.

Ethics in Managerial Accounting

eLectures **LO5**
MBC Assess the
nature of
the ethical
dilemmas managers
and accountants
confront.

Ethics deals with the moral quality, fitness, or propriety of a course of action that can injure or benefit people. Ethics goes beyond legality, which refers to what is permitted under the law, to consider the moral quality of an action. Because situations involving ethics are not guided by well-defined rules, they are often subjective.

Although some actions are clearly ethical (working a full day in exchange for a full day's pay) and others are clearly unethical (pumping contaminants into an underground aquifer used as a source of drinking water), managers are often faced with situations that do not fall clearly into either category such as the following:

---

[16] Deloitte Insights, "Automation with Intelligence: Reimagining the Organization in the 'Age of With,'" 2019.

[17] Katie Canell, "Accountancy and Technology: The Journey to Cognitive Intelligence," *AccountancyAge*, October 18, 2018.

[18] *Enterprise Risk Management—Integrating with Strategy and Performance,* Committee of Sponsoring Organizations of the Treadway Commission, June 2017.

- Accelerating or decelerating shipments at the end of the quarter to meet current earnings forecasts.
- Keeping inventory that is unlikely to be used so as to avoid recording a loss.
- Purchasing supplies from a relative or friend rather than seeking bids.
- Basing a budget on an overly optimistic sales forecast.
- Assigning some costs of Contract A to Contract B to avoid an unfavorable performance report on Contract A.

Many ethical dilemmas involve actions that are perceived to have desirable short-run consequences and highly probable undesirable long-run consequences. The ethical action is to face an undesirable situation now to avoid a worse situation later, yet the decision maker prefers to believe that things will work out in the long run, is not overly concerned with the consequences of not doing well in the short run, or simply does not care about the future because the problem will then belong to someone else. In a situation that is clearly unethical, the future consequences are known to be avoidable and undesirable. In situations involving questionable ethics, there is some hope that things will work out:

- Next year's sales will more than make up for the accelerated shipments.
- The obsolete inventory can be used in a new nostalgia line of products.
- The relative or friend may charge more but provides excellent service.
- Sales staff will be motivated by corporate optimism.
- Employees will make up for the cost shift by working extra hard and more efficiently with the remaining work on Contract B.

When forced to think about the situation, most employees want to act in an ethical manner. The problem faced by personnel involved in measurement and reporting is that while they may question the propriety of a proposed action, and the arguments may be plausible, they want to be team players, and their careers can be affected by "whistle-blowing." Of course, careers are also affected when individuals are identified as being involved in unethical behavior.

Major ethical dilemmas often evolve from a series of small compromises, none of which appears serious enough to warrant taking a stand on ethical grounds. WorldCom is such a case, in which managers deferred expenses inappropriately over several periods to meet profit forecasts, expecting to recognize them at a later time when sales improved. Unfortunately, these small compromises establish

---

Business Insight ■ Violations of Ethical Standards for Management Accountants at Toshiba

Toshiba is a 140-year-old company that started making telegraph equipment in 1875 and has since expanded into a diverse line of products. In 2015, Toshiba had over 200,000 employees worldwide and ranked as 356 in the list of the world's largest public companies.

At the end of 2015, Japanese regulators fined Toshiba Corporation with a record fine of ¥7.37 billion ($60 million). This fine was in response to accounting violations between 2008 and 2014 that inflated profits by $1.2 billion to meet unrealistic profit targets. Toshiba's accountants, under pressure from executives, delayed the recognition of losses.

The Institute of Management Accountants (IMA) has developed four standards of ethical conduct for management accountants and financial managers.

1. Competence: Perform their professional duties in accordance with relevant laws, regulations, and technical standards.
2. Confidentiality: Refrain from disclosing confidential information acquired in the course of their work except when authorized, unless legally obligated to do so.
3. Integrity: Refrain from engaging in or supporting any activity that would discredit the profession.
4. Credibility: Communicate information fairly and objectively.

Toshiba and its auditors violated all or part of each of these standards.

Sources: Pavel Alpeyev and Takashi Amano, "Toshiba Said to Face Biggest Fine by Japan's Financial Regulator," *Bloomberg Technology*, December 6, 2015.
Pavel Alpeyev and Takashi Amano, "Toshiba to Restate at Least 152 Billion Yen of Past Profits," *Bloomberg Technology*, July 20, 2015.
"Standards of Ethical Conduct for Management Accountants," *Accountingverse*, accessed July 19, 2016.

a pattern of behavior that is increasingly difficult to reverse. The key to avoiding these situations is recognizing the early warning signs of situations that involve questionable ethical behavior and taking whatever action is appropriate.

Codes of Ethics

Codes of ethics are often developed by professional organizations to increase members' awareness of the importance of ethical behavior and to provide a reference point for resisting pressures to engage in actions of questionable ethics. These professional organizations include the American Bar Association, the American Institute of Certified Public Accountants, the American Medical Association, and the Institute of Management Accountants (IMA).

Many corporations have established codes of ethics. Hershey's has a 31-page published document "In Good Company," which lists and explains Hershey's code of conduct. One of the important goals of corporate codes of ethics is to provide employees with a common foundation for addressing ethical issues. These codes provide a summary of a company's policies that define ethical standards of employee conduct, and they often include broad philosophical statements about behavior. Hershey's code states, "Every day provides new opportunities to do the right thing. Let this Code and your good judgment be your guide."[19]

Corporate Governance

Corporate governance refers to the system of policies, processes, laws, and regulations that affect the way a company is directed and controlled. At the highest level, the system of corporate governance for a company is the responsibility of the board of directors, but it affects all stakeholders, including employees, creditors, customers, vendors, and the community at large. The large number of corporate failures of the last decade brought the topic of corporate governance to the forefront.

The collapse of Enron, along with its independent auditor, Arthur Andersen, prompted the U.S. Congress to pass the Sarbanes-Oxley Act of 2002 (or SOX), which was intended to address weaknesses affecting U.S. capital markets. Although SOX deals primarily with issues pertaining to the relationship between publicly traded companies and the capital markets, some of its requirements have become a standard for corporate responsibility and governance affecting both public and private companies, as well as not-for-profit organizations.

SOX consists of 66 sections, including such topics as external auditing standards, auditor conflicts of interest, codes of ethics for financial officers, review of internal controls, and criminal penalties for fraud. Probably the most important provisions of SOX, from a managerial accounting standpoint, are those related to internal control systems. **Internal control systems** generally are made up of the policies and procedures that exist to ensure that company objectives are achieved with regard to (a) effectiveness and efficiency of operations, (b) reliability of financial reporting, and (c) compliance with laws and regulations.

SOX imposes the requirement that CEOs and CFOs annually review and assess the effectiveness of their company's internal controls over financial reporting, and issue a report of their assessment. Although many CEOs and CFOs have argued that the cost of SOX compliance is unjustified by the benefits to investors, the following Research Insight provides evidence that SOX is improving the quality of financial reporting. Even though SOX limits the internal control review to aspects of the system related to financial reporting, in practice there is very little that takes place in any organization that does not impact the financial statements. Therefore, if SOX is resulting in improvements in data that goes into financial reports, it is likely that data supporting managerial accounting is also enhanced by a more reliable internal control system.

Many of the models and processes that we discuss in this text have either a direct or indirect impact on a company's financial statements; hence, they are likely subject to the SOX internal control review. An overlap often exists between the systems that produce the data for the external financial statements and those that produce data for internal decision making. For example, cost data produced by the product costing system is often used for both financial reporting and managerial decision-making

---

[19] https://www.thehersheycompany.com/content/dam/corporate-us/documents/investors/business-code-of-conduct.pdf

purposes. A more detailed discussion of SOX and internal control systems can typically be found in financial accounting and auditing textbooks.

Research Insight   ■   SOX Gives Important Internal Control Information to Financial Markets

An important question that accounting researchers ask about any disclosure is whether the disclosure is useful to the financial markets. A team of researchers from Shanghai and Hong Kong have shown that information provided by SOX about internal controls directly influences the pricing of Credit Default Swaps (CDS), a transaction that allows lenders to hedge the risk of their loans. CDS provide the firm's owners with insurance if the firm goes bankrupt, so the connection between information about internal control and the price of this type of insurance suggests that SOX is releasing important information about the way the firm is run.

The impact of good internal control on annual debt interest expense is meaningful. Firms with good controls book, on average, $35.7 million less in annual debt interest expense than firms with material weaknesses in their internal controls. This study shows that the relationship between CDS pricing and internal control holds, not only for the material weakness disclosures, but also as internal controls deteriorate over time, leading up to the material weakness. To the extent that the firm is concerned about the cost of debt, SOX-mandated disclosures provide pressure for good internal controls. This may improve the information that is provided to management accounting systems.

Source: Dragon Yongjun Tang, Feng Tian, and Hong Yan, "Internal Control Quality and Credit Default Swap Spreads," *Accounting Horizons*, September 2015, Vol. 29, No. 3, pp. 603–629.

Sustainability Accounting and Corporate Social Responsibility

Sustainability accounting and corporate social responsibility are increasingly important to managers. "Since the 1960s environmentalists have been concerned with the impact of economic growth and the increasingly rapid use of the world's resources. In recent years, these concerns have increased because of the impact of greenhouse gases, caused by the burning of fossil fuels, on global warming."[20] John Elkington introduced the concept of the Triple Bottom Line (TBL), which incorporates traditional financial performance and accountability to shareholders, as well as broader accountability through both environmental and social impacts.[21]

These concepts entail balancing the objective of profitability with the objective of giving proper attention to issues such as environmental sustainability and energy conservation, and avoiding actions that would lower the quality of life in the communities in which a company operates and sells its products or services. In earlier generations it would have meant giving a day's wage for a day's labor, not hiring underage children, or not dumping untreated waste into the local river.

Managerial accounting includes a variety of models that help managers determine the cost of a particular activity or product, or the benefits and costs of various decision alternatives. Although such models in their current state of development may not take into account all external social costs, accountants are more aware today than in the past of the need to consider such costs. For example, when calculating the cost of building a new capital asset that is going to last for 25 years, it is necessary to include in that calculation the present value of the cost of the ultimate disposal of the asset, including any environmental cleanup.

Being a socially responsible company does not mean abandoning the profit motive or the goal of providing an attractive return to investors. It means that while pursuing these essential objectives, a for-profit company attempts to measure the total benefits and costs of its actions and accepts the responsibility for those actions. Also, being a good competitor should not be confused with social responsibility. For example, many companies offer certain fringe benefits, such as on-site childcare, because it attracts better employees, not because they feel they have a social responsibility to provide such services. Obviously, the line between being a good competitor and being socially responsible is sometimes blurred.

---

[20] *The Evolution of Accountability Sustainability Reporting for Accountants*, IMA 2014.
[21] John Elkington, founder of "SustainAbility," 1987.

Review 14-5 LO5

How can managerial accounting help support corporate social responsibility?

Solution on p. 14-27.

Cost Drivers

LO6 Demonstrate the use of structural, organizational, and activity cost drivers.

The foundation for the managerial accounting concepts covered in this text is the ability to identify and measure the activities of an organization. In this module, we introduce the idea of business activities and what drives the costs related to those activities.

An **activity** is a unit of work. To serve a customer at a restaurant such as **Fleming's Prime Steakhouse**, a server might perform the following units of work:

■ Seat customer and offer menu

■ Take customer order

■ Send order to kitchen

■ Bring food to customer

■ Serve and replenish beverages

■ Determine and bring bill to customer

■ Accept and process payment

■ Clear and reset table

Each of these is an activity, and the performance of each activity consumes resources that cost money. To manage activities and their costs, it is necessary to understand how costs respond to **cost drivers**, which are the factors that cause or influence costs.

The most basic cost driver is customer demand. Without customer demand for products or services, the organization cannot exist. To serve customers, managers and employees make a variety of decisions and take numerous actions. These decisions and actions, undertaken to satisfy customer demand, drive costs. While these cost drivers may be classified in a variety of ways, we believe that dividing them into the three categories of structural, organizational, and activity cost drivers, as summarized in Exhibit 14.5, provides a useful foundation for the study of managerial accounting.

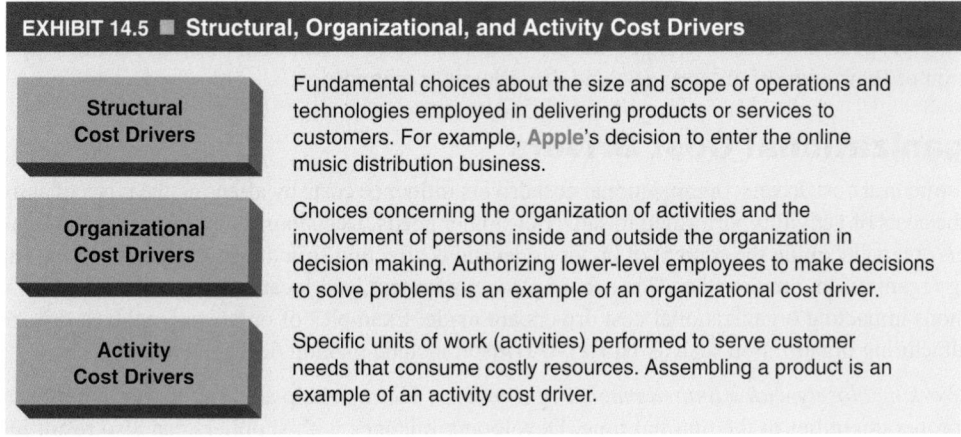

EXHIBIT 14.5 ■ Structural, Organizational, and Activity Cost Drivers

Structural Cost Drivers	Fundamental choices about the size and scope of operations and technologies employed in delivering products or services to customers. For example, Apple's decision to enter the online music distribution business.
Organizational Cost Drivers	Choices concerning the organization of activities and the involvement of persons inside and outside the organization in decision making. Authorizing lower-level employees to make decisions to solve problems is an example of an organizational cost driver.
Activity Cost Drivers	Specific units of work (activities) performed to serve customer needs that consume costly resources. Assembling a product is an example of an activity cost driver.

Structural Cost Drivers

The types of activities and the costs of activities performed to satisfy customer needs are influenced by an organization's size, its location, the scope of its operations, and the technologies used. Decisions affecting structural cost drivers are made infrequently, and once made, the organization is committed to a course of action that will be difficult to change. For a chain of retail stores such as Target, possible structural cost drivers include:

- *Determining the size of stores.* This affects the variety of merchandise that can be carried and operating costs.
- *Determining the type of construction.* While a lean warehouse type of construction is less expensive, it is not an appropriate setting for selling high-fashion clothing.
- *Determining the location of stores.* Locating in a shopping mall can cost more and subject the store to mall regulations but provides for more customer traffic and shared advertising.
- *Determining types of technology to employ in stores.* A computerized system for maintaining all inventory and sales data requires a large initial investment and fixed annual operating costs while providing more current information. However, the computerized inventory and sales systems can be less expensive at high sales volumes than a less costly system relying more on clerks taking physical inventory.

An important structural cost driver for many companies is the decision to redefine their company's product offering. The following Business Insight illustrates how the auto industry is rethinking what

---

Business Insight ■ Auto Manufacturer Begins Structural Shift to Match Changing Car Culture

In November 2018, Mary Barra, chief executive officer of General Motors Co. (GM), announced the biggest layoff of employees since the company's bankruptcy in 2009. This layoff wasn't about declining sales or profits, though. GM had reported operating profits in all but one year since 2010. This layoff was part of GM's planned transition from the sales of sedans and small cars to the sale of electric vehicles and self-driving cars. In an interview, Barra said, "Once you start to believe in the science of global warming and look at the regulatory environment around the world, it becomes pretty clear that to win in the future, you've got to win" with electric and driverless vehicles.

The company had already invested $500 million in Lyft Inc. in 2016 with the intention of "marrying GM's self-drive technology with the ride-hailing brand." And in 2017, GM acquired Cruise Automation, a self-driving vehicle startup, to work on technical difficulties slowing down development of GM's own autonomous vehicles. GM management believes that it is the only company with the cash, the facilities, and the engineering talent to claim the lead position in a ride-sharing industry that is expected to generate $1.3 billion in revenue globally by 2030.

For now, sales of GM's electric car, the Chevrolet Bolt, generate losses of about $9,000 each and the expected 2019 rollout of its self-driving car, Cruise, has been postponed. This means Barra has to depend on sales in its traditional businesses to keep money flowing. Information from GM's management accounting system is critical as the company transitions to a new business model.

Sources: David Welch and Bryan Gruley, "GM's Mary Barra Bets Big on an Electric, Self-Driving Future," *Bloomberg Businessweek*, September 19, 2019.

"product" they bring to market. Traditionally their product was manufacturing cars. Now they are thinking broader in terms of transportation. This has led to investments in ride hailing apps, the creation of their own driver services, and driverless car technology.

Organizational Cost Drivers

Like structural cost drivers, organizational cost drivers influence costs by affecting the types of activities and the costs of activities performed to satisfy customer needs. Decisions that affect organizational cost drivers are made within the context of previous decisions affecting structural cost drivers. In a manufacturing organization, previous decisions about plant, equipment, and location are taken as a given when decisions impacting organizational cost drivers are made. Examples of organizational cost drivers at a manufacturing organization such as Harley-Davidson include making decisions regarding

- *Working closely with a limited number of suppliers.* This can help achieve proper materials in the proper quantities at the optimal time. Developing linkages with suppliers can also result in suppliers' initiatives that improve the profitability of both organizations.

- *Providing employees with cost information and authorizing them to make decisions.* This helps improve decision speed and reduce costs while making employees more customer oriented. Production employees may, for example, offer product design suggestions that reduce manufacturing costs or reduce defects.

- *Reorganizing the existing equipment in the plant so that sequential operations are closer.* This more efficient layout reduces the cost of moving inventory between workstations.

- *Designing components of a product so they can fit together only in the correct manner.* This can reduce defects as well as assembly time and cost.

- *Manufacturing a low-volume product on low-speed, general-purpose equipment rather than high-speed, special-purpose equipment.* Assuming the special-purpose equipment is more difficult and costly to set up for a new job, this decision can increase operating time and operating cost while reducing setup time and setup cost.

The following Business Insight illustrates how an innovative software startup managed a key organizational cost driver to keep down costs and achieve profitability.

Business Insight ■ Software Company Increases Sales at a Lower Cost Without Sales Department

Atlassian, a company without a commissioned direct salesforce, had revenues of $1,210 million in Fiscal 2019. The company, known for its team collaboration software, is valued at $26.6 billion and is competing with industry giants such as IBM, Microsoft, and Google. While unconventional, the benefit to Atlassian's approach shows up in its 19% revenue-to-sales/marketing cost ratio, where Atlassian beats its peers by 30% or more.

The decision to develop the business without a traditional sales department was an organic one. Launched while the founders Scott Farquhar and Mike Cannon-Brooks were in school, at first they simply lacked the time and resources for a formal sales department. Effort was focused on developing and delivering the product, not on selling it. Now customers are guided through the purchase process online, and requests for a sales rep visit are politely declined. As the company has matured, it has learned that this strategy has increased sales at a low cost.

As young firms develop, management accountants can help decision makers think carefully about the future organizational costs associated with structural decisions like those Cannon-Brooks and Farquhar faced as students.

Sources: Dina Bass, "This $5 Billion Software Company Has No Sales Staff," *Bloomberg Businessweek*, May 19, 2016; and Peter High, "Atlassian President Drives the Company North of $1 Billion in Revenue" *Forbes*, June 10, 2019.

Activity Cost Drivers

Activity cost drivers are specific units of work (activities) performed to serve customer needs that consume costly resources. Several examples of activities in a restaurant were mentioned previously. The customer may be outside the organization, such as a client of an advertising firm, or inside the organization, such as an accounting office that receives maintenance services. Because the performance of activities consumes resources and resources cost money, the performance of activities drives costs.

The basic decisions concerning which available activities will be used to respond to customer requests precede the actual performance of activities. At the activity level, execution of previous plans and following prescribed activities are important. All of the examples of structural and organizational cost drivers involved making decisions. In the following list of activity cost drivers for a manufacturing organization, note the absence of the decision-oriented words:

- Placing a purchase order for raw materials
- Inspecting incoming raw materials
- Moving items being manufactured between workstations
- Setting up a machine to work on a product
- Spending machine time working on a product
- Spending labor time working on a product
- Hiring and training a new employee
- Packing an order for shipment
- Processing a sales order
- Shipping a product

In managing costs, management makes choices concerning structural and organizational cost drivers. These decisions affect the types of activities required to satisfy customer needs. Because different types of activities have different costs, management's decisions concerning structural and organizational cost drivers ultimately affect activity costs and profitability. Good decision making at the level of structural and organizational cost drivers requires an understanding of the linkages among the types of cost drivers and the costs of different activities.

Managerial Decision ■ You Are the CEO

How can you use information about structural, organizational, and activity cost drivers to help you in implementing the organization's strategy? [Answer, p. 14-20]

LO6 Review 14-6

Classify each of the following as a structural, organizational, or activity cost driver.

a. Meals served to airplane passengers aboard Delta Airlines.
b. GM's decision to manufacture the Bolt, an all-electric automobile.
c. Zenith's decision to sell its computer operations and focus on the core television business.
d. Number of tax returns filed electronically by H&R Block.
e. Number of passenger cars in an Amtrak train.
f. Coors' decision to expand its market area east from the Rocky Mountains.
g. Boeing's decision to invite airlines to assist in designing the model 777 airplane.
h. Daimler Benz's decision to use cross-disciplinary teams to design a new automobile.
i. St. Jude Hospital's decision to establish review committees on the appropriateness and effectiveness of medical procedures for improving patient care.
j. Harley-Davidson's efforts to restructure production procedures to reduce inventories and machine setup times.

Solution on p. 14-28.

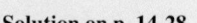

Guidance Answers

You Are the CEO
Pg. 14-20 It is important that an organization's cost structure be aligned with its strategy. If your goal is to be a cost leader (such as Wal-Mart or Costco), you will want to make sure that the structural cost drivers, such as the type of buildings acquired and the displays used, are consistent with this strategy. As the CEO of Wal-Mart, you would not permit many of the costs that would be incurred in an organization such as Tiffany or Nordstrom.

Questions

Q14-1. Contrast financial and managerial accounting on the basis of user orientation, purpose of information, level of aggregation, length of time period, orientation toward past or future, conformance to external standards, and emphasis on objective data.

Q14-2. What three themes are a part of strategic cost management?

Q14-3. Distinguish between a mission and a goal.

Q14-4. Describe the three strategic positions that Porter views as leading to business success.

Q14-5. Distinguish between how managerial accounting would support the strategy of cost leadership and the strategy of product differentiation.

Q14-6. Why are the phases of planning, organizing, and controlling referred to as a continuous cycle?

Q14-7. Identify three advances that have fostered the move away from isolated national economic systems toward an interdependent global economy.

Q14-8. What are the three interrelated dimensions of today's competition?

Q14-9. How can top management establish an ethical tone in an organization?

Q14-10. Describe how pressures to have desirable short-run outcomes can lead to ethical dilemmas.

Q14-11. Differentiate among structural, organizational, and activity cost drivers.

Assignments with the ⓦ logo in the margin are available in BusinessCourse.
See the Preface of the book for details.

Mini Exercises

LO1, 2, 3, 5, 6

M14-12. Management Accounting Terminology

Match the following terms with the best descriptions. Each description is used only once.

Terms

1. Ethics
2. Mission
3. Controlling
4. Goal
5. Cost drivers
6. Quality
7. Balance sheet
8. Income statement
9. Strategic cost management
10. Financial accounting
11. Activity cost driver
12. Structural cost driver
13. Managerial accounting
14. Resources
15. Product differentiation

Description

a. Making decisions concerning specific cost drivers
b. Factors that influence costs
c. Reports a company's financial position
d. Accounting for external users
e. Increase year 2020 sales by 10% over year 2019 sales
f. Shows the results of operations for a period of time
g. Packing an order for shipment
h. Deciding to limit market focus to a region rather than the entire nation
i. The degree to which a new e-book reader meets a buyer's expectations
j. Used internally to make decisions
k. Consumed by activities
l. The propriety of taking some action
m. Reduces customer price sensitivity
n. Basic purpose toward which activities are directed
o. Comparing the budget with the actual results

LO1

M14-13. Financial and Managerial Accounting

Indicate whether each phrase is more descriptive of financial accounting or managerial accounting.

    a. May be subjective
    b. Often used to obtain financing
    c. Typically prepared quarterly or annually
    d. May measure time or customer satisfaction
    e. Future oriented
    f. Has a greater emphasis on cost-benefit analysis
    g. Keeps records of assets and liabilities
    h. Highly aggregated statements
    i. Must conform to external standards
    j. Special-purpose reports
    k. Decision-making tool
    l. Income statement, balance sheet, and statement of cash flows

M14-14. Institute of Managerial Accountants **LO1**
What is the role of managerial accounting according to the IMA, and how does the IMA try to influence the best practices of managerial accountants?

M14-15. Missions, Goals, and Strategies **LO3**
Identify each of the following as a mission, goal, or strategy.

    a. Budget time for study, sleep, and relaxation
    b. Provide shelter for the homeless
    c. Provide an above-average return to investors
    d. Protect the public
    e. Locate fire stations so that the average response time is less than five minutes
    f. Overlap police patrols so that there are always police cars on major thoroughfares
    g. Achieve a 12% market share
    h. Lower prices and costs
    i. Select the most scenic route to drive between Las Vegas and Denver
    j. Graduate from college

M14-16. Line and Staff Organization **LO3**
Presented are the names of several departments often found in a merchandising organization such as Target.

a. Maintenance	*d.* Payroll
b. Home Furnishings	*e.* Human Resources
c. Store Manager	*f.* Advertising

Target (TGT)

Required
Identify each as a line or a staff department.

M14-17. Line and Staff Organization **LO3**
Presented are the names of several departments often found in a manufacturing organization such as KraftHeinz.

a. Manager, Plant 2	*d.* Controller
b. Design Engineering	*e.* Property Accounting
c. President	*f.* Sales Manager, District 1

KraftHeinz (KHC)

Required
Identify each as a line or a staff department.

M14-18. Changing Business Environment **LO4**
Identify some trends that should be considered when developing the role and processes of an organization's managerial accounting strategy.

M14-19. Classifying Cost Drivers **LO6**
Classify each of the following as structural, organizational, or activity cost drivers.

Apple Inc. (AAPL)
IBM (IBM)
Canon (CA)

    a. Apple Inc. reorganizes production facilities from a layout in which all similar types of machines are grouped together to a layout in which a set of machines is designated for the production of a particular product and that set of machines is grouped together.
    b. A cable television company decides to start offering telephone service.
    c. IBM decides to stop making personal computers.

d. Canon decides to start making high-volume photocopy equipment to compete head-to-head with Xerox.

e. The number of meals a cafeteria serves.

f. The number of miles a taxi is driven.

g. A company eliminates the position of supervisor and has each work group elect a team leader.

h. Tesla empowers employees to halt production if a quality problem is identified.

i. The number of tons of grain a ship loads.

j. Northbrook Mall decides to build space for 80 additional stores.

Tesla Motors Inc. (TSLA)

LO6 **M14-20. Classifying Cost Drivers**

Henderson Construction managers provide design and construction management services for various commercial construction projects. Senior managers are trying to apply cost driver concepts to their firm to better understand Henderson's costs.

Required

Classify each of the following actions or decisions as structural, organizational, or activity cost drivers.

a. The decision to be a regional leader in computer-assisted design services.

b. The decision to allow staff architects to follow a specific project through to completion.

c. The daily process of inspecting the progress on various construction projects.

d. The process of conducting extensive client interviews to assess the exact needs for Henderson services.

e. The decision to expand the market area by establishing an office in another state.

f. The decision to use only Henderson staff rather than relying on subcontractors.

g. The process of receiving approval from government authorities along with appropriate permits for each project.

h. The decision to organize the workforce into project teams.

i. The decision to build a new headquarters facility with areas for design and administration as well as storage and maintenance of construction equipment.

j. The process of grading building sites and preparing forms for foundations.

Exercises

LO1 **E14-21. Financial and Managerial Accounting**

KraftHeinz (KHC)

Assume Katie Milling has just been promoted to product manager at KraftHeinz. Although she is an accomplished sales representative and well versed in market research, her accounting background is limited to reviewing her paycheck, balancing her checkbook, filing income tax returns, and reviewing the company's annual income statement and balance sheet. She commented that while the financial statements are no doubt useful to investors, she just doesn't see how accounting can help her be a good product manager.

Required

Based on her remarks, it is apparent that Katie's view of accounting is limited to financial accounting. Explain some of the important differences between financial and managerial accounting and suggest some ways managerial accounting can help Katie be a better product manager.

LO3 **E14-22. Developing an Organization Chart**

Develop an organization chart for a three-outlet bakery chain with a central baking operation and deliveries every few hours. Assume the business is incorporated and that the president has a single staff assistant. Also assume that the delivery truck driver reports to the bakery manager.

LO3 **E14-23. Identifying Monetary and Nonmonetary Performance Measures**

Stanford University
Good Samaritan Hospital
Walgreen Boots Alliance (WBA)
Starwood Hotels and Resorts (HOT)
United Parcel Service (UPS)

Identify possible monetary and nonmonetary performance measures for each of the following situations. One nonmonetary measure should relate to quality, and one should relate to time.

a. Stanford University wishes to evaluate the success of last year's graduating class.

b. Good Samaritan Hospital wishes to evaluate the performance of its emergency room.

c. Walgreen Boots Alliance wishes to evaluate the performance of its online order–filling operations.

d. Starwood Hotels wishes to evaluate the performance of registration activities at one of its hotels.

e. United Parcel Service wishes to evaluate the success of its operations in Knoxville.

E14-24. Identifying Monetary and Nonmonetary Performance Measures LO3

Identify possible monetary and nonmonetary performance measures for each of the following situations. One nonmonetary measure should relate to quality, and one should relate to time.

EarthLink (ELNK)
Comcast (CMCSA)
Asustek Computer Inc.

a. EarthLink's evaluation of the performance of its Internet service in Chicago.
b. Comcast Cable's evaluation of the performance of new customer cable installations in Springfield.
c. Asustek Computer's evaluation of the performance of its logistical arrangements for delivering computers to its U.S. customers.
d. Target's evaluation of the performance of its website.
e. Emory University's evaluation of the success of its freshman admissions activities.

Target Corporation (TGT)
Emory University

E14-25. Identifying Information Needs of Different Managers LO3

Matt Parker operates a number of auto dealerships for Toyota and General Motors. Identify possible monetary and nonmonetary performance measures for each of the following situations. One nonmonetary measure should relate to quality, and one should relate to time.

Toyota (TM)
General Motors (GM)

a. An individual sales associate.
b. The sales manager of a single dealership.
c. The general manager of a particular dealership.
d. The corporate chief financial officer.
e. The president of the corporation.

E14-26. Activities and Cost Drivers LO6

For each of the following activities, select the most appropriate cost driver. Each cost driver may be used only once.

Activity	Cost Driver
1. Pay vendors	a. Number of different raw material items
2. Receive material deliveries	b. Number of classes offered
3. Inspect raw materials	c. Number of machine hours
4. Plan for purchases of raw materials	d. Number of employees
5. Packaging	e. Number of maintenance hours
6. Supervision	f. Number of units of raw materials received
7. Employee training	g. Number of new customers
8. Operating machines	h. Number of deliveries
9. Machine maintenance	i. Number of checks issued
10. Opening accounts at a bank	j. Number of customer orders

Management Applications

MA14-27. Goals and Strategies LO3

a. What is your instructor's goal for students in this course? What strategies has he or she developed to achieve this goal?
b. What is your goal in this course? What strategies will help you achieve this goal?
c. What is your goal for this semester or term? What strategies will help you achieve this goal?
d. What is your next career goal? What strategies will help you achieve this goal?

MA14-28. Product Differentiation LO3

You are the owner of Lobster's Unlimited. You have no trouble catching lobsters, but you have difficulty in selling all that you catch. The problem is that all lobsters from all vendors look the same. You do catch high-quality lobsters, but you need to be able to tell your customers that your lobsters are better than those sold by other vendors.

Required

a. What are some possible ways of distinguishing your lobsters from those of other vendors?
b. Explain the possible results of this differentiation.

MA14-29. Ethics and Short-Term Borrowing LO5

Rory, an administrative assistant, is in charge of petty cash for a local law firm. Normally, about $300 is kept in the petty cash box. When Rory is short on cash and needs some for lunch or to pay her babysitter, she sometimes takes a few dollars from the box. Because she is in charge of the box, nobody knows that she takes the money, and she always replaces it within a few days.

Required

a. Is Rory's behavior ethical?

b. Assume that Rory has recently had major problems meeting her bills. She also is in charge of purchasing supplies for the office from petty cash. Last week when she needed $50 for the babysitter, she falsified a voucher for the amount of $50. Is this behavior ethical?

LO5   MA14-30. Ethics and Travel Reimbursement

Jake takes many business trips throughout the year. All of his expenses are paid by his company. Last week he traveled to Rio De Janeiro, Brazil, and stayed there on business for five days. He is allowed a maximum of $50 per day for food and $150 per day for lodging. To his surprise, the food and accommodations in Brazil were much less than he expected. Being upset about traveling last week and having to sacrifice tickets he'd purchased to a Cubs baseball game, he decided to inflate his expenses a bit. He increased his lodging expense from $80 per day to $100 per day and his food purchased from $30 per day to $40 per day. Therefore, for the five-day trip, he overstated his expenses by $150 total. After all, the allowance was higher than the amount he spent.

Required

Assume that the company would never find out that he had actually spent less. Are Jake's actions ethical? Are they acceptable?

LO5   MA14-31. Ethical Issues with Supplier-Buyer Partnerships

Tom Wopat was excited to learn of his appointment as Circuit Electronics Corporation's sales representative to Household Appliance Inc. For the past four years, Circuit Electronics has supplied all of the electric switches used in Household's washers and dryers. As Circuit Electronics' sales representative, Tom's job involves the following tasks.

1. Working with Household engineers to design electric switches that can be manufactured to meet Household's cost and quality requirements.
2. Assisting Household in resolving any problems related to electric switches.
3. Monitoring the inventory levels of electric switches at Household and placing orders for additional switches when appropriate.

This appointment will require Tom to move to Stuttgart, Germany, for two years. Although Tom has mixed feelings about the move, he is familiar with the success of the program in improving Circuit Electronics' financial performance. He is also very much aware of the fact that the two previous sales representatives received promotions at the end of their appointments.

As Tom toured the Household factory in Stuttgart with his predecessor, Catherine Bach, his excitement turned to concern. It became apparent that Circuit Electronics had not been supplying Household with the best available switches at the lowest possible costs. Although the switches were adequate, they were more likely to wear out after five or six years of use than would switches currently on the market (and being used by Household's competitors). Furthermore, taking into account the current number of switches in transit by ship from North America to Europe, it also appeared that the inventory level of electric switches would soon be more than enough to satisfy Household's needs for the next four months.

Required

If you were Tom, what would you do?

LO5   MA14-32. Expected Values of Questionable Decisions

Exxon Mobil (XOM)

The members of the jury had to make a decision in a lawsuit brought by the State of Alabama against Exxon Mobil. The suit revolved around natural-gas wells that Exxon drilled in state-owned waters. After signing several leases obligating Exxon to share revenues with Alabama, company officials started questioning the terms of the agreement that prohibited deducting several types of processing costs before paying the state royalties.

Royal Dutch Shell (RDSB)

During the course of the trial, a memo by an in-house attorney of Exxon Mobil came to light. The memo noted that Royal Dutch Shell, which had signed a similar lease, interpreted it "in the same manner as the state." The memo then presented arguments the company might use to claim the deduction, estimated the probability of the arguments being successful (less than 50%), and proceeded to consider whether Exxon should obey the law using a cost-benefit analysis. According to the memo, "If we adopt anything beyond a 'safe' approach, we should anticipate a quick audit and subsequent litigation." The memo also observed that "our exposure is 12 percent interest on underpayments calculated from the due date, and the cost of litigation." Deducting the questionable costs did, indeed, result in an audit and a lawsuit.[22]

Required

If you were a member of the jury, what would you do? Why?

MA14-33. Management Decisions Affecting Cost Drivers   LO6

An avid bicycle rider, you have decided to use an inheritance to start a new business to sell and repair bicycles. Two college friends have already accepted offers to work for you.

Required

a. What is the mission of your new business?
b. Suggest a strategic positioning goal you might strive for to compete with area hardware and discount stores that sell bicycles.
c. Identify two items that might be long-range goals.
d. Identify two items that might be goals for the coming year.
e. Mention two decisions that will be structural cost drivers.
f. Mention two decisions that will be organizational cost drivers.
g. Identify two activity cost drivers.

MA14-34. Success Factors and Performance Measurement   LO3

Three years ago, Vincent Chow completed his college degree. The economy was in a depressed state at the time, and Vincent managed to get an offer of only $25,000 per year as a bookkeeper. In addition to its relatively low pay, this job had limited advancement potential. Since Vincent was an enterprising and ambitious young man, he instead started a business of his own. He was convinced that because of changing lifestyles, a drive-through coffee establishment would be profitable. He was able to obtain backing from his parents to open such an establishment close to the industrial park area in town. Vincent named his business The Cappuccino Express and decided to sell only two types of coffee: cappuccino and decaffeinated.

As Vincent had expected, The Cappuccino Express was very well received. Within three years, Vincent had added another outlet north of town. He left the day-to-day management of each site to a manager and turned his attention toward overseeing the entire enterprise. He also hired an assistant to do the record keeping and other selected chores.[23]

Required

a. Develop an organization chart for The Cappuccino Express.
b. What factors can be expected to have a major impact on the success of The Cappuccino Express?
c. What major tasks must Vincent undertake in managing The Cappuccino Express?
d. What are the major costs of operating The Cappuccino Express?
e. Vincent would like to monitor the performance of each site manager. What measure(s) of performance should he use?
f. If you suggested more than one measure, which of these should Vincent select if he could use only one?
g. Suppose that last year, the original site had yielded total revenues of $146,000, total costs of $122,000, and hence, a profit of $24,000. Vincent had judged this profit performance to be satisfactory. For the coming year, Vincent expects that due to factors such as increased name recognition and demographic changes, the total revenues will increase by 20% to $175,200. What amount of profit should he expect from the site? Discuss the issues involved in developing an estimate of profit.

Solutions to Review Problems

Review 14-1—Solution

2, 5, 7, 8, 9, and 10

[22] Mike France, "When Big Oil Gets Too Slick," *Business Week,* April 9, 2001, p. 70.
[23] Based on Chee W. Chow, "Instructional Case: Vincent's Cappuccino Express—A Teaching Case to Help Students Master Basic Cost Terms and Concepts Through Interactive Learning," *Issues in Accounting Education,* Spring 1995, pp. 173–190.

Review 14-2—Solution

Below are the three themes involved in strategic position analysis and a possible example of each.

1. **Strategic position analysis is an examination of an organization's basic way of competing to sell products or services.** This might be relevant for a company like Uber. Uber originally started as a luxury brand, using high-end "black" cars. Its position was "everyone's private driver." As the first to market this concept, it has been very successful and has caused a number of changes in the industry. Uber's strategic positioning is very different from Lyft's, which according to its CMO, is more environmental. Lyft wants to focus on having fewer cars on the road and filling empty seats.[24]
2. **Cost driver analysis is the study of factors that cause or influence costs.** IKEA is a Swedish furniture retailer that changed the industry with its low-cost leadership. It offers inexpensive but stylish furniture and keeps prices low by controlling its costs. It offers a basic level of service and does not assemble or deliver furniture. It also produces its products in low-wage countries.[25]
3. **Value chain analysis is the study of value-producing activities, stretching from basic raw materials to the final consumer of a product or service.** Starbucks is a well-known example of value chain analysis. It focuses on selecting the highest quality beans, operates in 65 countries, and has few if any intermediaries involved in the selling of its products; it has a high level of customer service with a related commitment to human resources management.[26]

Review 14-3—Solution

When an organization's goal is cost leadership, managerial accountants can partner with management to develop budgets and to prepare frequent and detailed performance reports against those budgets. This allows managers and employees to analyze areas in which the company's activities cost more than expected and to work together to find ways to further reduce those costs. When an organization's goal is differentiation, managerial accountants can partner with customers, marketing, and sales to help identify ways to increase the perceived value of the products or services. This might be done through an analysis of costs from a customer's point of view, enabling the organization to better understand what features the customer is willing to pay for.

Review 14-4—Solution

Big Data and Analysis—Given recent advancements in technology, there is a vast amount of data available to organizations. However, it can be difficult to turn this data into useful and predictive information. Organizations are in need of employees who have the abilities to: identify key data trends, perform data mining and extraction, conduct operational and decision analysis, recommend process improvement, and conduct strategic thinking and execution.

ERM—Organizations are constantly faced with uncertainty from the environment, competitors, and other factors that could result in significant risk or loss. By better understanding the types and potential costs of these risks, management accountants can help their organizations devise strategies to better predict and minimize exposure to risk.

Review 14-5—Solution

Managerial accounting includes a variety of models that help managers determine the cost of a particular activity or product or the benefits and costs of various decision alternatives. Although such models in their current state of development may not take into account all external social costs, accountants are more aware today than in the past of the need to consider such costs. Being a socially responsible company does not mean abandoning the profit motive or the goal of providing an attractive return to investors. It means that while pursuing these essential objectives, a for-profit company attempts to measure the total benefits and costs of its actions and accepts the responsibility for those actions.

---

[24] Dean Millson, "Uber vs. Lyft–Brand Positioning, Customer Expectation and Internal Culture," *Brand & Strategy*, February 18, 2016, http://brandingandstrategyblog.com/brand-strategy/uber-vs-lyft-brands-effect-customer-expectation-internal-culture/

[25] http://smallbusiness.chron.com

[26] Prableen Bajpai, "Starbucks as an Example of the Value Chain Model," *Investopedia*, October 31, 2014.

Review 14-6—Solution

a. Activity cost driver
b. Structural cost driver
c. Structural cost driver
d. Activity cost driver
e. Activity cost driver
f. Structural cost driver
g. Organizational cost driver
h. Organizational cost driver
i. Organizational cost driver
j. Organizational cost driver

Module 15

Cost Behavior, Activity Analysis, and Cost Estimation

Cost Behavior, Activity Analysis, and Cost Estimation			
Cost Behavior Analysis	**Cost Estimation**	**Additional Issues in Cost Estimation**	**Alternative Cost Driver Classifications**
▪ Four Basic Cost Behavior Patterns ▪ Factors Affecting Cost Behavior Patterns ▪ Total Cost Function for an Organization or Segment ▪ Relevant Range ▪ Additional Cost Behavior Patterns ▪ Committed and Discretionary Fixed Costs	▪ High-Low Cost Estimation ▪ Scatter Diagrams ▪ Least-Squares Regression	▪ Changes in Technology and Prices ▪ Matching Activity and Costs ▪ Identifying Activity Cost Drivers	▪ Manufacturing Cost Hierarchy ▪ Customer Cost Hierarchy
Review 15-1, 15-2	**Review 15-3**	**Review 15-4**	**Review 15-5**

PREVIEW

SQ

The creator of Twitter, Jack Dorsey, founded Square, Inc. in 2009 to address a void in payment processing services for small, portable businesses. Square makes a postage stamp-sized plastic card reader that attaches to smartphones, which gives businesses such as food trucks, kiosk boutiques, taxi drivers, and the like the ability to accept credit card payments. Square also has an online payment app, and in 2016, Square introduced Virtual Terminal, which enables sellers to accept payments from their computers through the Square Dashboard.

The San Francisco–based company has been so successful that it now processes over $90 billion in transactions each year. Square provides the card readers, the Dashboard App, and the Virtual Terminal to businesses free of charge but collects a per transaction fee to compensate for its services.

The cost of making the card readers is directly related to the number of new businesses adopting the technology. In other words, the hardware cost is driven by the number of new merchants in any given period. But the number of new adoptions is difficult to estimate in advance. The costs associated with processing payments are even more difficult to predict. Consider that the company remits most of the payments received from customers' credit card companies to the merchant, minus Square's fee. However, what is Square's cost of processing each payment? Does the cost of processing a payment differ based on volume or seasonality?

To predict processing costs, we must be able to predict merchant sales volume or number of transactions. If the processing costs vary proportionately with this activity, the processing costs are referred to as variable costs. What about the costs that do not vary with the number or type of transactions processed? Many of Square's employees are salaried engineers and software developers. These costs are likely to be unrelated to the number of card readers issued or payments processed. We call costs that do not vary with activity fixed costs. As we'll see throughout the module, many costs are neither variable nor fixed, but a mixture of the two. Mixed costs present a challenge to a company in estimating future costs. Square needs the ability to accurately predict its future costs if it is to maintain the financial flexibility necessary to remain competitive.

Road Map

LO	Learning Objective	Topics	Page	eLecture	Guided Example	Assignments
LO1	**Identify basic patterns of how costs respond to changes in activity cost drivers.** Cost Behavior Patterns :: Variable Costs :: Fixed Costs :: Mixed Costs :: Step Costs :: Factors Affecting Cost Behavior	15-3	e15–1	Review 15-1	11, 12, 13, 14, 21, 22
LO2	**Determine a linear total cost-estimating equation.** Total Cost Function :: Relevant Range :: Economic vs Accounting Cost Structures :: Additional Cost Behavior Patterns :: Committed and Discretionary Fixed Costs	15-6	e15–2	Review 15-2	13, 14, 15, 16, 17, 21, 22, 23, 24, 25
LO3	**Calculate and compare three different approaches to cost estimation.** High-Low Cost Estimation :: Scatter Diagrams :: Least Squares Regression	15-11	e15–3	Review 15-3	13, 14, 18, 19, 20, 21, 23, 24, 25, 29, 30, 33, 34, 35
LO4	**Identify and discuss problems encountered in cost estimation.** Additional Issues :: Changes in Technology and Prices :: Matching Activity and Costs :: Identifying Activity Cost Drivers	15-17	e15–4	Review 15-4	19, 20, 25, 31, 34
LO5	**Describe and develop alternative classifications for activity cost drivers.** Alternative Classifications :: Manufacturing Cost Hierarchy :: Customer Cost Hierarchy	15-18	e15–5	Review 15-5	26, 27, 28, 32

Cost Behavior Analysis

eLectures **LO1**
MBC Identify basic patterns of how costs respond to changes in activity cost drivers.

This module introduces **cost behavior**, which refers to the relationship between a given cost item and the quantity of its related cost driver. Cost behavior, therefore, explains how the total amount for various costs responds to changes in activity volume. Understanding cost behavior is essential for estimating future costs. In this module we examine several typical cost behavior patterns and methods for developing cost equations that are useful for predicting future costs.

Four Basic Cost Behavior Patterns

Although there are an unlimited number of ways that costs can respond to changes in activity cost drivers, as a starting point it is useful to classify cost behavior into four categories: **variable costs**, **fixed costs**, **mixed costs**, and **step costs**. Graphs of each are presented in Exhibit 15.1. Observe that total cost (the dependent variable) is measured on the vertical axis, and total activity (the independent variable) is measured on the horizontal axis. Consider pizza franchise Domino's. Domino's specializes in quick delivery and online order tracking. Customers can pick from signature pies like ExtravaganZZa, or they can create their own and choose the type of dough, sauce, and toppings. Domino's has been the global pizza chain leader in revenue since 2017. To manage its growth, the company must understand the behavior underlying its cost structure.

1. Variable costs change in total in direct proportion to changes in activity. Their total amount increases as activity increases, equaling zero dollars when activity is zero and increasing at a constant amount per unit of activity. The higher the variable cost per unit of activity, the steeper the slope (incline) of the line representing total cost. With the number of pizzas served as the activity cost driver for Domino's locations, the cost of cheese is an example of a variable cost.

2. **Fixed costs** do not change in response to a change in activity volume. Hence, a line representing total fixed costs is flat with a slope of zero. With the number of Domino's pizzas sold as the activity cost driver, annual depreciation, property taxes, and property insurance are examples of fixed costs. While fixed costs may respond to structural and organizational cost drivers over time, they do not respond to short-run changes in activity cost drivers.

3. Mixed costs (sometimes called **semivariable costs**) contain a fixed and a variable cost element. Total mixed costs are positive (like fixed costs) when activity is zero, and they increase in a linear fashion (like total variable costs) as activity increases. With the number of pizzas sold as the cost driver, the cost of electric power is an example of a mixed cost. Some electricity is required to provide basic lighting (fixed cost), while an increasing amount of electricity is required to prepare food as the number of pizzas served increases (variable cost).

4. **Step costs** are constant within a narrow range of activity but shift to a higher level when activity exceeds the range. Total step costs increase in a steplike fashion as activity increases. With the number of pizzas served as the cost driver, employee wages is an example of a step cost. Up to a certain number of pizzas, only a small staff needs to be on duty. Beyond that number, additional employees are needed for quality service and so forth.

The relationship between total cost (Y axis) and total activity (X axis) for the four cost behavior patterns is mathematically expressed as follows:

$$\text{Variable cost: } Y = bX$$

where

b = the variable cost per unit, sometimes referred to as the slope of the cost function.

$$\text{Fixed cost: } Y = a$$

where

a = total fixed costs. The slope of the fixed cost function is zero because fixed costs do not change with activity.

Exhibit 15.1 ■ Cost Behavior Patterns

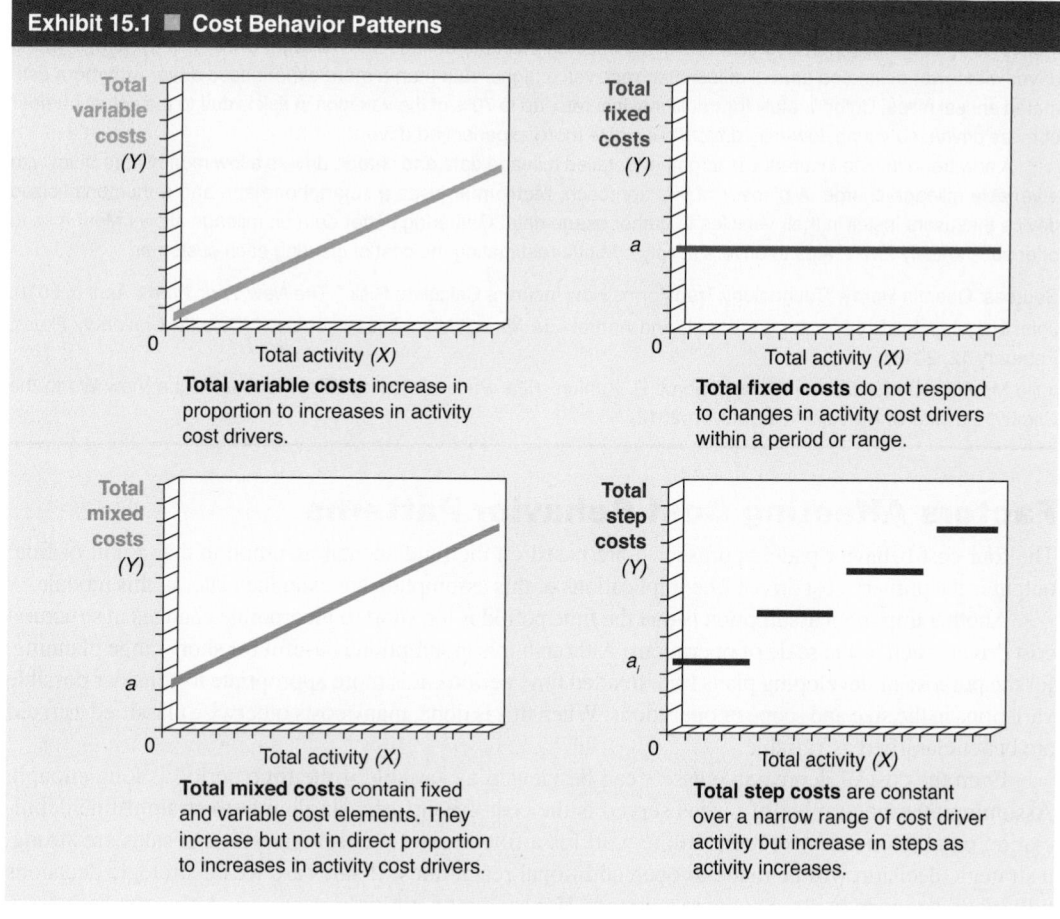

Total variable costs increase in proportion to increases in activity cost drivers.

Total fixed costs do not respond to changes in activity cost drivers within a period or range.

Total mixed costs contain fixed and variable cost elements. They increase but not in direct proportion to increases in activity cost drivers.

Total step costs are constant over a narrow range of cost driver activity but increase in steps as activity increases.

$$\text{Mixed cost: } Y = a + bX$$

where

a = total fixed cost element

b = variable cost element per unit of activity.

$$\text{Step cost: } Y = a_i$$

where

a_i = the step cost within a specific range of activity, identified by the subscript i.

The total cost function of most organizations has shifted in recent years toward more fixed costs and fewer variable costs, making it increasingly important for organizations to manage their fixed costs. Some organizations have reversed this trend by outsourcing activities rather than performing the activities internally. This eliminates some fixed costs in exchange for additional variable costs per unit of outsourced activity. The Business Insight box below provides a few examples of how understanding costs can lead to better pricing decisions.

Business Insight ■ Understanding Costs Is Key to Pricing

Pricing affects firm performance, and understanding the cost of servicing a customer is the key to effective pricing. Analysts from the Strategy and Operations practice of Deloitte Consulting recommend using rich datasets to segment customers based on needs and behavior. Careful segmenting allows the firm to find the most profitable match of customers with services and prices.

    The auto insurance industry is an interesting case. The cost of service is driven by the risk of a claim. Traditionally, auto insurers collect a list of risk factors when calculating the cost of insuring a particular driver. This list includes

continued

continued from previous page

factors such as age, gender, address, and sometimes an estimate of expected mileage. Under this system, a young driver with fewer estimated annual miles often receives a higher rate than a more experienced driver with more estimated annual miles. Unfortunately for traditional insurers, up to 70% of the variation in risk is due to the actual number of miles driven; so young, low-mile drivers subsidize more experienced drivers.

A new trend in auto insurance is to gather detailed mileage data and charge drivers a low monthly premium with a variable mileage charge. A pioneer of this approach, Metromile, uses a smartphone app and a thumbnail-sized device that users install in their vehicles to gather usage data. Gathering better data on mileage allows Metromile to offer substantially lower rates to drivers simply by better estimating the cost of insuring each customer.

Sources: Quentin Hardy, "Technology Transforms How Insurers Calculate Risk," *The New York Times*, April 6, 2016. John Hagel, John Brown, Maggie Wooll, and Andrew de Maar, "Align Price with Use," *Deloitte University Press*, February 12, 2016. Julie Meehan, Chuck Davenport, and Shruti R. Kahlon, "The Price of Pricing Effectiveness: Is the View Worth the Climb?" *Deloitte University Press*, July 1, 2012.

Factors Affecting Cost Behavior Patterns

The four cost behavior patterns presented are based on the fundamental assumption that a unit of final output is the primary cost driver. The implications of this assumption are examined later in this module.

Another important assumption is that the time period is too short to incorporate changes in structural cost drivers such as the scale of operations. Although this assumption is useful for short-range planning, for the purpose of developing plans for extended time periods, it is more appropriate to consider possible variations in the size and scope of operations. When this is done, many costs otherwise classified as fixed are better classified as variable.

Even the cost of depreciable assets can be viewed as variable if the time period is long enough. Assuming that the number of pizzas served is the cost driver, for a single month straight-line depreciation on all Domino's locations in the world is a fixed cost. Over several years, if sales are strong, a strategic decision will be made to open additional restaurants; if sales are weak, strategic decisions will likely be made to close some restaurants. Hence, over a multiple-year period, the number of restaurants varies with sales volume, making depreciation appear as a variable cost with sales revenue as the cost driver.

Fixed costs are easily identified. They are the same at each activity level. Variable and mixed costs can be determined by dividing total costs by monthly sales at two activity levels. The quotients of variable costs will be the same at both levels. The quotients of mixed costs will be lower at the higher activity level. This is because the fixed costs are spread over a larger number of units.

Review 15-1 LO1

Assume a local Subway reported the following results for April and May:

	April	May
Sandwiches sold.	2,100	2,700
Cost of food sold.	$1,575	$2,025
Wages and salaries	1,525	1,675
Rent on building	1,500	1,500
Depreciation on equipment.	200	200
Utilities	710	770
Supplies	225	255
Miscellaneous.	113	131
Total	$5,848	$6,556

Required

Solution on p. 15-32.   Identify each cost as being fixed, variable, or mixed.

Total Cost Function for an Organization or Segment

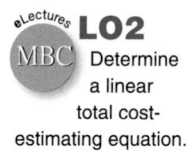

To obtain a general understanding of an organization, to compare the cost structures of different organizations, or to perform preliminary planning activities, managers are often interested in how total costs respond to a single measure of overall activity such as units sold or sales revenue. This overview can be useful, but presenting all costs as a function of a single cost driver is seldom accurate enough to support decisions concerning products, services, or activities. Doing so implies that all of an organization's costs can be manipulated by changing a single cost driver. This is seldom true.

In developing a total cost function, the independent variable usually represents some measure of the goods or services provided customers, such as total student credit hours in a university, total sales revenue in a store, total guest-days in a hotel, or total units manufactured in a factory. The resulting cost function is illustrated in Exhibit 15.2.

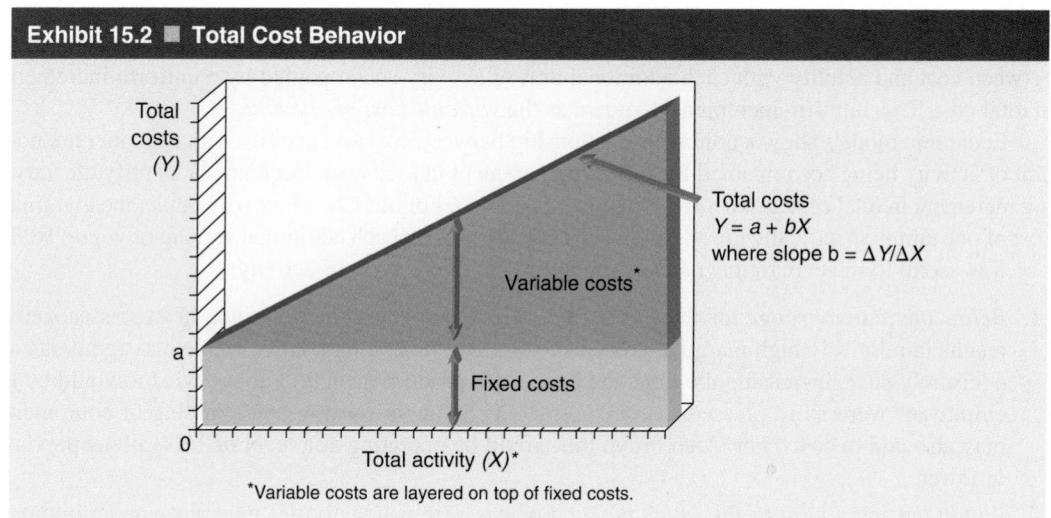

Exhibit 15.2 ■ Total Cost Behavior

The equation for total costs is:

$$Y = a + bX$$

where

> **Y = total costs**
> **a = vertical axis intercept (an approximation of fixed costs)**
> **b = slope (an approximation of variable costs per unit of X)**
> **X = value of independent variable (activity level)**

In situations where the variable, fixed, and mixed costs, and the related cost functions, can be determined, a total cost equation can be useful in predicting future costs for various activity levels. For example, assume that Coco Froyo frozen yogurt shop's only fixed cost is the depreciation on its frozen yogurt making machines. Coco Froyo's monthly depreciation is $1,200. Also assume that the variable cost per frozen yogurt served is $3.25. Therefore, the total cost equation for Coco Froyo is:

Y = $1,200 + $3.25 (number of yogurts served)

If the shop expects to serve 1,600 frozen yogurts in July, it can then estimate its total July costs to be:

$6,400 = $1,200 + $3.25 (1,600)

Relevant Range

Generally, a total cost equation is useful for predicting costs in only a limited range of activity. The **relevant range** of a total cost equation is that portion of the range associated with the fixed cost of the current or expected capacity. In our Coco Froyo example, it is able to produce a maximum of 50 gallons of frozen yogurt per day with a single machine. If it has four machines in operation, and if it can readily adjust its fixed capacity cost by increasing or decreasing the number of machines, the relevant range of activity for the shop's current total cost equation is 151 to 200 gallons. (The maximum number of gallons that can be produced with four machines producing 50 gallons per machine is 200 gallons. The minimum number of gallons of yogurt produced before one of the machines could be discontinued is 151 gallons.) In the future, if the shop expects to operate at more than 200 gallons per day, the current total cost equation would not predict total cost accurately, because fixed costs would have to be increased for additional machines. Conversely, if it expects to operate at 150 gallons or fewer, it may reduce the number of machines in the shop, thereby reducing total fixed costs.

The use of straight lines in accounting models of cost behavior assumes a linear relationship between cost and activity with each additional unit of activity accompanied by a uniform increment in total cost. This uniform increment is known as the *variable cost of one unit.*

Economic models show a nonlinear relationship between cost and activity with each incremental unit of activity being accompanied by a varying increment in total cost. Economists identify the varying increment in total cost as the **marginal cost** *of one unit.* For our Coco Froyo example, the marginal cost of one unit is specifically the additional costs incurred with each additional serving of yogurt sold.

It is useful to relate marginal costs to the following three levels of activity:

1. *Below the activity range for which the facility was designed,* the existence of excess capacity results in relatively high marginal costs. Having extra time, employees complete assignments at a leisurely pace, increasing the time and the cost to produce each unit above what it would be if employees were more pressed to complete work. Frequent starting and stopping of equipment may also add to costs. For Coco Froyo this would be operating at a level of 150 gallons per day or fewer.

2. *Within the activity range for which the facility was designed,* activities take place under optimal circumstances and marginal costs are relatively low. For Coco Froyo this would be operating within a range of 151 to 200 gallons per day.

3. *Above the activity range for which the facility was designed,* the existence of capacity constraints again results in relatively high marginal costs. Near capacity, employees may be paid overtime wages, less-experienced employees may be used, regular equipment may operate less efficiently, and old equipment with high energy requirements may be placed in service. For Coco Froyo this would be operating at a level of more than 200 gallons per day.

Based on marginal cost concepts, the economists' short-run total cost function is illustrated in the first graph in Exhibit 15.3. To clarify the concept, we use the capacity information for Coco Froyo.

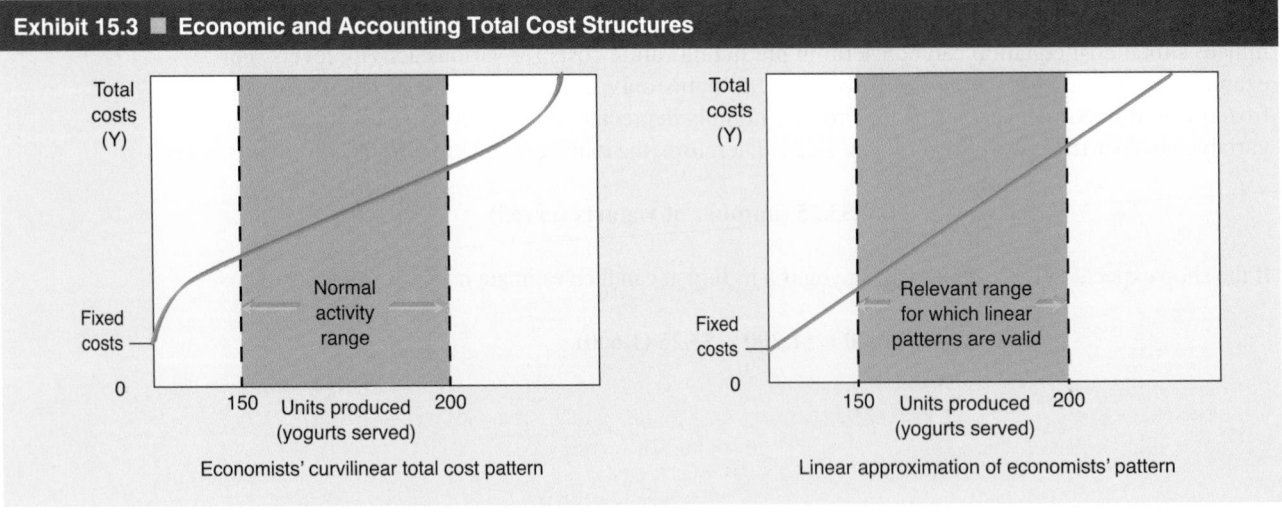

Exhibit 15.3 ■ Economic and Accounting Total Cost Structures

Economists' curvilinear total cost pattern

Linear approximation of economists' pattern

The vertical axis intercept represents capacity costs. In this simple example, our only capacity, or fixed cost, is depreciation. Corresponding to the high marginal costs at low levels of activity, the initial slope is quite steep. In the normal activity range, where marginal costs are relatively low, the slope becomes less steep. Then, corresponding to high marginal costs above the normal activity range, the slope of the economists' total cost function increases again.

Business Insight ■ Firm Makes Warehouse Costs Variable

A warehouse is an essential but risky investment for many businesses. The risk is that actual activity will be above or below the level for which the facility was designed. The Raj India Trading Co., a Seattle-area importer, found itself in just this situation when changes to its product lines left it with a vastly underused warehouse. Rather than find a new, smaller warehouse, owner Jeff Lykins used the services of Flexe Inc. to rent out the unused space on a month-to-month basis.

While industrial real estate vacancy was low in 2015 (around 5% in key areas such as Seattle and Southern California), experts agreed that there was a surplus of warehouse space. Flexe Inc. carved out a niche by connecting companies in need of warehouse space and companies with unused space. Flexe let those who needed more space rent it by the pallet and helped those with too much space integrate the new pallets into their existing workflow. Flexe helped companies with fixed warehouse costs maintain usage and consume excess capacity.

Sources: David Morris, "This Startup Could Change the Game for Same-day Shipping," *Fortune*, October 9, 2015. Erica E. Phillips, "Collaborative Logistics Comes to the Warehouse," *Wall Street Journal*, June 12, 2015.

If the economists' total cost curve is valid, how can we reasonably approximate it with a straight line? The answer to this question is in the notion of a *relevant range*. A linear pattern may be a poor approximation of the economists' curvilinear pattern over the entire range of possible activity, but a linear pattern as illustrated in the right-hand graph in Exhibit 15.3 is often sufficiently accurate within the range of probable operations. The range of activity within which a linear cost function is valid is called the relevant range. Linear estimates of cost behavior are valid only within the relevant range. Extreme care must be exercised when making comments about cost behavior outside the relevant range.

Additional Cost Behavior Patterns

Although we have considered the most frequently used cost behavior patterns, remember that there are numerous ways that costs can respond to changes in activity. Avoid the temptation to automatically assume that the cost in question conforms to one of the patterns discussed in this module. As illustrated by the preceding Business Insight box, it is important to think through each situation and then select a behavior pattern that seems logical and fits the known facts.

Particular care needs to be taken with the vertical axis. So far, all graphs have placed *total* costs on the vertical axis. Miscommunication is likely if one party is thinking in terms of *total* costs while the other is thinking in terms of *variable* or *average* costs. FIXthat4U is a smartphone and tablet repair store. FIXthat4U's monthly fixed costs include rent and depreciation on tools and furniture. Its variable costs include direct labor and any materials used up in the repair such as new screens. Consider FIXthat4U's following cost function:

$$\text{Total costs} = \$3,000 + \$5X$$

where

$$X = \text{customer repairs}$$

The total, variable cost per unit, and average cost per unit at various levels of activity are computed here and graphed in Exhibit 15.4 on the following page. As the number of customer repairs increases, total costs increase, the variable costs of each repair remain constant, and the average cost decreases because fixed costs are spread over a larger number of repairs.

Customer Repairs	Total Costs	Average Cost*	Variable Costs per Repair
100	$3,500	$35.00	$5.00
200	4,000	20.00	5.00
300	4,500	15.00	5.00
400	5,000	12.50	5.00
500	5,500	11.00	5.00

* Total costs/customer repairs

To predict total costs for the coming period, FIXthat4U's management will use the first graph in Exhibit 15.4. To determine the minimum price required to avoid a loss on each additional repair, management is interested in the variable costs per customer repair, yet if a manager inquired as to the cost of each customer repair, a financial accountant would probably provide average cost information, as illustrated in the third graph in Exhibit 15.4. The specific average cost would likely be a function of the number of customer repairs during the most recent accounting period.

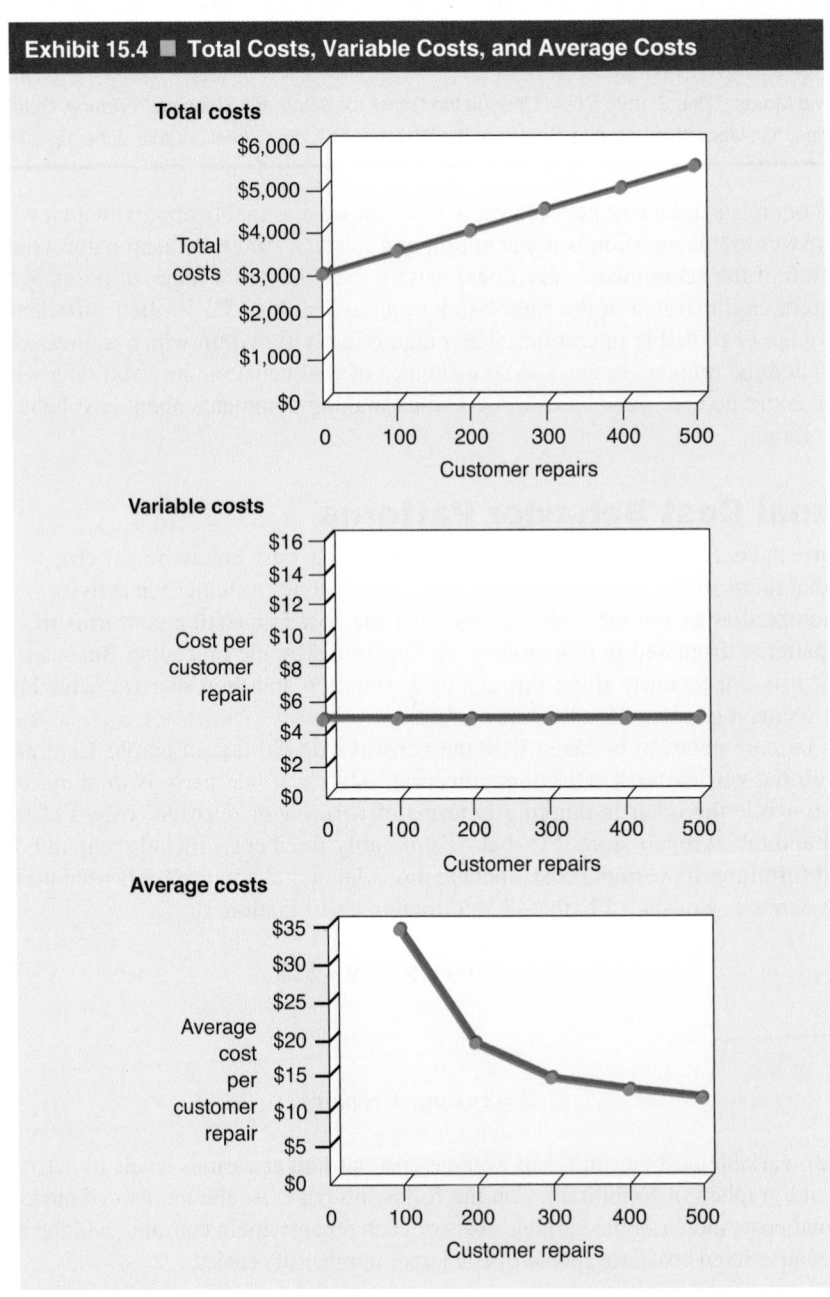

Exhibit 15.4 ■ Total Costs, Variable Costs, and Average Costs

Errors can occur if last period's average costs, perhaps based on a volume of 500 repairs, were used to predict total costs for a future period when the anticipated volume was some other amount, say 300 repairs. Using average costs, based on the 500 repairs, the predicted total costs of 300 repairs are $3,300 ($11 × 300). In fact, using the proper total cost function, a more accurate prediction of total costs is $4,500 [$3,000 + ($5 × 300)]. The prediction error could cause a number of problems. If management budgeted $3,300 to pay bills and the bills actually totaled $4,500, the company might have to curtail activities or borrow under unfavorable terms to avoid running out of cash.

Because variable costs per unit remain constant within the relevant range, the average cost per unit will increase or decrease based on the change in the fixed cost per unit. To determine the number of customer repairs needed to lower the average cost to $9, the average fixed cost must be $4 ($9 − $5 variable cost per unit). That would occur when volume was 750 repairs ($3,000/$4).

Research Insight ■ Managers Use Procurement to Control Risk

In a recent study of cost data from California Hospitals, researchers analyzed the way that firms adjust committed costs in response to external risk. The study shows that managers seek to mitigate the effects of both demand uncertainty and financial risk through procurement decisions. The study considers three procurement choices that affect committed costs:

1. Deliver new services through outsourcing or onsite.
2. Rent or purchase new equipment.
3. Structure labor costs to be more flexible versus fixed.

The researchers found that hospitals facing greater uncertainty limited committed costs, for example, limiting capital expenditures on equipment. This study highlights that managers can make cost-structure decisions that protect their organizations from the risk of demand uncertainty.

Source: Martin Holzhacker, Ranjani Krishnan, and Matthias D. Mahlendorf, "Unraveling the Black Box of Cost Behavior: An Empirical Investigation of Risk Drivers, Managerial Resource Procurement, and Cost Elasticity," *The Accounting Review* 90, no. 6 (2015): 2305-2335.

Committed and Discretionary Fixed Costs

Fixed costs are often classified as *committed* or *discretionary,* depending on their immediate impact on the organization if management attempts to change them. **Committed fixed costs**, sometimes referred to as **capacity costs**, are the fixed costs required to maintain the current service or production capacity or to fill previous legal commitments. Examples of committed fixed costs include depreciation, property taxes, rent, and interest on bonds.

Committed fixed costs are often the result of structural decisions about the size and nature of an organization. For example, years ago the management of Santa Fe Railroad made decisions concerning what communities the railroad would serve. Track was laid on the basis of those decisions and BNSF Railway, the company that acquired Santa Fe Railroad, now pays property taxes each year on the railroad's miles of track. These property taxes could be reduced by disposing of track. However, reducing track would also diminish the Santa Fe's capacity to serve.

Discretionary fixed costs, sometimes called **managed fixed costs**, are set at a fixed amount each period at the discretion of management. It is possible to reduce discretionary fixed costs without reducing production or service capacity in the short term. Typical discretionary fixed costs include advertising, maintenance, charitable contributions, employee training, and research and development.

Maintenance expenditures for discretionary fixed costs are frequently regarded as investments in the future. Research and development, for example, is undertaken to develop new or improved products that can be profitably produced and sold in future periods. During periods of financial well-being, organizations may make large expenditures on discretionary cost items. Conversely, during periods of financial stress, organizations likely reduce discretionary expenditures before reducing capacity costs. Unfortunately, fluctuations in the funding of discretionary fixed costs may reduce the effectiveness of long-range programs. A high-quality research staff may be difficult to reassemble if key personnel are laid off. Even the contemplation of layoffs may reduce the staff's effectiveness. In all periods, discretionary costs are subject to debate and are likely to be changed in the budgeting process.

Review 15-2 LO2

Identify each of the following cost behavior patterns as variable, committed fixed, discretionary fixed, mixed, or step.

a. Total cost of bakery products used at a McDonald's restaurant when the number of meals served is the activity cost driver.

b. Total cost of operating the Mayo Clinic when the number of patients served is the cost driver.

c. Total property taxes for a Midas auto repair shop when the number of vehicles serviced is the cost driver.

d. Total cost of motherboards used by Apple when the number of computers manufactured and shipped is the cost driver.

e. Total cost of secretarial services at Indiana University with each secretary handling the needs of ten faculty members and where part-time secretarial help is not available. The number of faculty is the cost driver.

f. Total advertising costs for International Business Machines (IBM).

g. Automobile rental costs incurred at Alamo in Orlando, Florida, when there is no mileage charge. The cost driver is the number of miles driven.

h. Automobile rental cost incurred at Hertz in Dallas, Texas, which has a base charge plus a mileage charge. The cost driver is the number of miles driven.

i. Salaries paid to personnel while conducting on-campus employment interviews for Champion International. Number of on-campus interviews is the cost driver.

Solution on p. 15-32. j. The cost of contributions to educational institutions by Microsoft Corporation.

Cost Estimation

LO3

Calculate and compare three different approaches to cost estimation.

Cost estimation, the determination of the relationship between activity and cost, is an important part of cost management. In this section, we develop equations for the relationship between total costs and total activity.

To properly estimate the relationship between activity and cost, we must be familiar with basic cost behavior patterns and cost-estimating techniques. Costs known to have a variable or a fixed pattern are readily estimated by interviews or by analyzing available records. Sales commission per sales dollar, a variable cost, might be determined to be 15% of sales. In a similar manner, annual property taxes might be determined by consulting tax documents.

Mixed (semivariable) costs, which contain fixed and variable cost elements, are more difficult to estimate. According to a basic rule of algebra, two equations are needed to determine two unknowns. Following this rule, at least two observations are needed to determine the variable and fixed elements of a mixed cost.

High-Low Cost Estimation

The most straightforward approach to determining the variable and fixed elements of mixed costs is to use the **high-low method of cost estimation**. This method utilizes data from two time periods, a *representative* high-activity period and a *representative* low-activity period, to estimate fixed and variable costs. Assuming identical fixed costs in both periods, any difference in total costs between these two periods is due entirely to variable costs. The variable costs per unit are found by dividing the difference in total costs by the difference in total activity:

$$\text{Variable costs per unit} = \frac{\text{Difference in total costs}}{\text{Difference in activity}}$$

Once variable costs are determined, fixed costs, which are identical in both periods, are computed by subtracting the total variable costs of either the high or the low activity period from the corresponding total costs.

Fixed costs = Total costs – Variable costs

Assume a retailer such as Pottery Barn wants to develop a monthly cost function for its packaging department and that the number of shipments is believed to be the primary cost driver. The following observations are available for the first four months of the year.

		Number of Shipments	Packaging Costs
(Low-activity period)	January.....................	6,000	$17,000
	February.....................	9,000	26,000
(High-activity period)	March	12,000	32,000
	April	10,000	20,000

Equations for total costs for the packaging department in January and March (the periods of lowest and highest activity) follow:

$$\textbf{January: \$17,000 = a + b (6,000 shipments)}$$
$$\textbf{March: \$32,000 = a + b (12,000 shipments)}$$

where

$$\textbf{a = fixed costs per month}$$
$$\textbf{b = variable costs per shipment}$$

Solving for the estimated variable costs per shipment:

$$\textbf{b} = \frac{\textbf{Difference in total costs}}{\textbf{Difference in activity}}$$
$$\textbf{b} = \frac{\textbf{\$32,000 – \$17,000}}{\textbf{12,000 – 6,000}}$$
$$= \textbf{\$2.50}$$

Next, the estimated monthly fixed costs are determined by subtracting variable costs from total costs of *either* the January or March equation:

$$\textbf{a = Total costs – Variable costs}$$
$$\textbf{January : a = \$17,000 – (\$2.50 per shipment} \times \textbf{6,000 shipments)}$$
$$= \textbf{\$2,000}$$

or

$$\textbf{March : a = \$32,000 – (\$2.50 per shipment} \times \textbf{12,000 shipments)}$$
$$= \textbf{\$2,000}$$

The cost-estimating equation for total packaging department costs is:

$$\textbf{Y = \$2,000 + \$2.50X}$$

where

$$\textbf{X = number of shipments}$$
$$\textbf{Y = total costs for the packaging department}$$

The concepts underlying the high-low method of cost estimation are illustrated in Exhibit 15.5.

Cost prediction, the forecasting of future costs, is a common purpose of cost estimation. Previously developed estimates of cost behavior are often the starting point in predicting future costs. Continuing the Pottery Barn example, if 5,000 shipments are budgeted for June, the predicted June packaging department costs are $14,500 [$2,000 + ($2.50 per shipment × 5,000 shipments)].

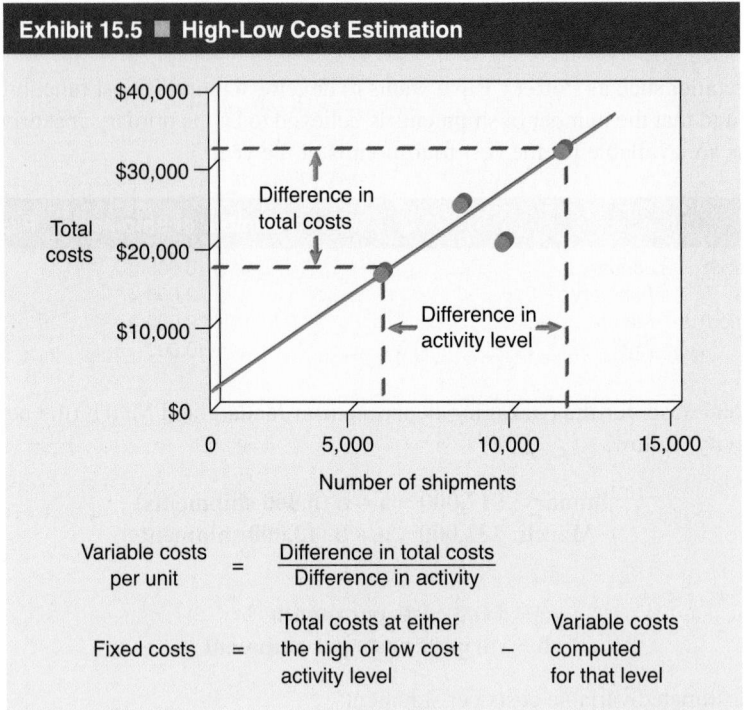

Exhibit 15.5 ■ High-Low Cost Estimation

$$\text{Variable costs per unit} = \frac{\text{Difference in total costs}}{\text{Difference in activity}}$$

Fixed costs = Total costs at either the high or low cost activity level − Variable costs computed for that level

Scatter Diagrams

A **scatter diagram** is a graph of past activity and cost data, with individual observations represented by dots. Plotting historical cost data on a scatter diagram is a useful approach to cost estimation, especially when used in conjunction with other cost-estimating techniques. As illustrated in Exhibit 15.6, a scatter diagram helps in selecting high and low activity levels representative of normal operating conditions. The periods of highest or lowest activity may not be representative because of the cost of overtime, the use of less efficient equipment, strikes, and so forth. If the goal is to develop an equation to predict costs under normal operating conditions, then the equation should be based on observations of normal operating conditions. A scatter diagram is also useful in determining whether costs can be reasonably approximated by a straight line.

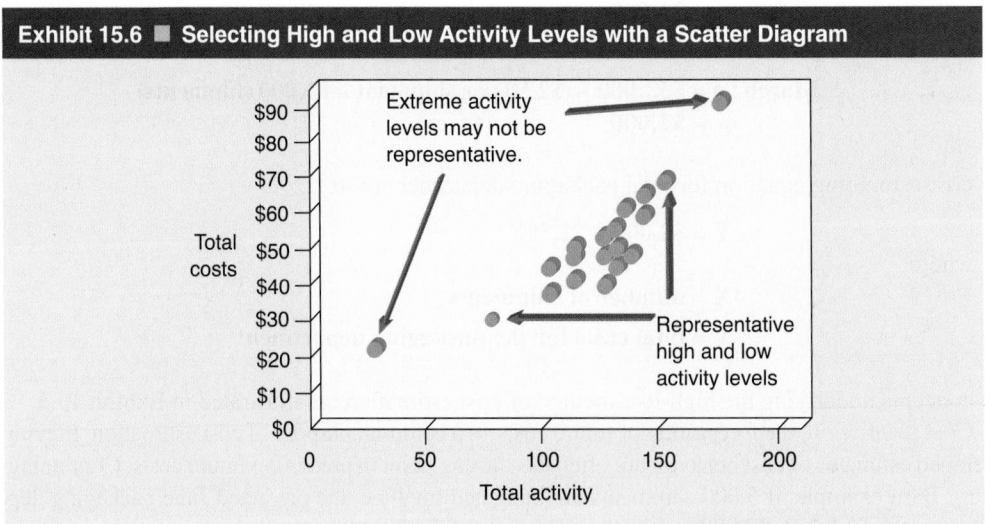

Exhibit 15.6 ■ Selecting High and Low Activity Levels with a Scatter Diagram

Scatter diagrams are sometimes used alone as a basis of cost estimation. This requires the use of professional judgment to draw a representative straight line through the plot of historical data. Typically, the analyst tries to ensure that an equal number of observations are on either side of the line while minimizing the total vertical differences between the line and actual cost observations at each value of the independent variable. Once a line is drawn, cost estimates at any representative volume are made by studying the line. Where the line crosses the Y axis represents total fixed costs. Variable cost per unit is calculated by solving the cost-estimating equation using total cost and activity from one of the points closest to the line. Alternatively, an equation for the line may be developed by applying the high-low method to any two points on the line.

Least-Squares Regression

Least-squares regression analysis uses a mathematical technique to fit a cost-estimating equation to the observed data. The technique mathematically accomplishes what the analyst does visually with a scatter diagram. The least-squares technique creates an equation that minimizes the sum of the vertical squared differences between the estimated and the actual costs at each observation. Each of these differences is an estimating error. Using the packaging department example, the least-squares criterion is illustrated in Exhibit 15.7. Estimated values of total monthly packaging costs are represented by the straight line, and the actual values of total monthly packaging costs are represented by the dots. For each dot, such as the one at a volume of 10,000 shipments, the line is fit to minimize the vertical squared differences.

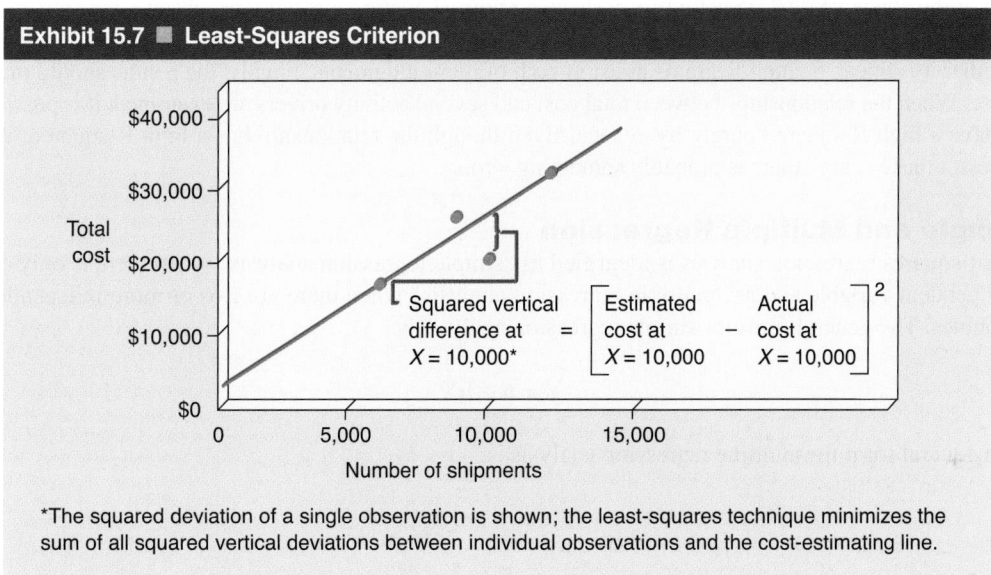

Exhibit 15.7 ■ Least-Squares Criterion

$$\text{Squared vertical difference at } X = 10{,}000^* = \left[\text{Estimated cost at } X = 10{,}000 - \text{Actual cost at } X = 10{,}000\right]^2$$

*The squared deviation of a single observation is shown; the least-squares technique minimizes the sum of all squared vertical deviations between individual observations and the cost-estimating line.

Values of *a* and *b* can be manually calculated using a set of equations developed by mathematicians or by using spreadsheet software packages such as **Microsoft** Excel®. Many calculators also have built-in functions to compute these coefficients. The least-squares equation for monthly packaging costs is:

$$Y = \$3{,}400 + \$2.20X$$

Using the least-squares equation, the predicted June packaging department costs with 5,000 budgeted shipments are $14,400 [$3,400 + ($2.20 per shipment × 5,000 shipments)]. Recall that the high-low method predicted June costs of $14,500. Although this difference is small, we should consider which prediction is more reliable.

Advantage of Least-Squares Regression

Mathematicians regard least-squares regression analysis as superior to both the high-low and the scatter diagram methods. It uses all available data, rather than just two observations, and does not rely on subjective judgment in drawing a line. Statistical measures are also available to determine how well a least-squares equation fits the historical data. These measures are often contained in the output of spreadsheet software packages.

In addition to the vertical axis intercept and the slope, least-squares regression calculates the coefficient of determination. The **coefficient of determination** is a measure of the percent of variation in the dependent variable (such as total packaging department costs) that is explained by variations in the independent variable (such as total shipments). Statisticians often refer to the coefficient of determination as R-squared and represent it as R^2.

The coefficient of determination can have values between zero and one, with values close to zero suggesting that the equation is not very useful and values close to one indicating that the equation explains most of the variation in the dependent variable. When choosing between two cost-estimating equations, the one with the higher coefficient of determination is generally preferred. The coefficient of determination for the packaging department cost-estimating equation, determined using least-squares regression analysis, is 0.68. This means that 68% of the variation in packaging department costs is explained by the number of shipments.

Managers, Not Models, Are Responsible

Although computers make least-squares regression easy to use, the generated output should not automatically be accepted as correct. Statistics and other mathematical techniques are tools to help managers make decisions. Managers, not mathematical models, are responsible for decisions. Judgment should always be exercised when considering the validity of the least-squares approach, the solution, and the data. If the objective is to predict future costs under normal operating conditions, observations reflecting abnormal operating conditions should be deleted. Also examine the cost behavior pattern to determine whether it is linear. Scatter diagrams assist in both of these judgments. Finally, the results should make sense. When the relationships between total cost and several activity drivers are examined, it is possible to have a high R-squared purely by chance. Even though the relationship has a high R-squared, if it "doesn't make sense" there is probably something wrong.

Simple and Multiple Regression

Least-squares regression analysis is identified as "simple regression analysis" when there is only one independent variable and as "multiple regression analysis" when there are two or more independent variables. The general form for simple regression analysis is:

$$Y = a + bX$$

The general form for multiple regression analysis is:

$$Y = a + \Sigma b_i X_i$$

In this case, the subscript i is a general representation of each independent variable. When there are several independent variables, i is set equal to 1 for the first, 2 for the second, and so forth. The total variable costs of each independent variable are computed as $b_i X_i$, with b_i representing the variable cost per unit of independent variable X_i. The Greek symbol sigma, Σ, indicates that the costs of all independent variables are summed in determining total variable costs.

As an illustration, assume that Staples' costs are expressed as a function of the unit sales of its two products: executive desks and task desks. Assume fixed costs are $18,000 per month and the variable costs are $250 per executive desk and $120 per task desk. The mathematical representation of monthly costs with two variables is:

$$Y = a + b_1 X_1 + b_2 X_2$$

where

$$a = \$18,000$$
$$b_1 = \$250 \text{ per executive desk}$$
$$b_2 = \$120 \text{ per task desk}$$
$$X_1 = \text{unit sales of executive desks}$$
$$X_2 = \text{unit sales of task desks}$$

During a month if 105 executive desks and 200 task desks are sold, Staples' estimated total costs are:

$$Y = \$18,000 + \$250(105) + \$120(200)$$
$$= \$68,250$$

In addition to estimating costs, multiple regression analysis can be used to determine the effect of individual product features on the market value of a product or service. Multiple regression can be done in Excel or in data analysis applications like Tableau or Python. The following Research Insight reports on insurance companies that use lifestyle and health behaviors to predict future health issues using a model similar to multiple regression analysis. These predictions are used to motivate changes in behavior that will ultimately improve employee health and reduce costs.

Research Insight ■ Regression Modeling and Data Analytics

Regression analysis is one of the primary tools used in predictive analytics. Predictive analytics is the use of current and historical data to predict future outcomes and trends. The extensive amount of data that companies are now able to collect increases the use and value of predictive analytic models.

How can companies use data analytics to reduce costs? To lower costs of employee turnover, companies have used data analytics to analyze the potential fit of applicants for open positions and to monitor employee frustration levels. Chime Bank used data analytics to cut the cost of testing new website content.

Kaiser Permanente, a hospital and health-insurance company, has reduced readmission costs by using data to better monitor and assess patients recovering from a cardiac event (heart attacks, bypass surgery, and heart failure). Patients are given smartwatches to use over an eight-week rehab program. The smartwatch collects data such as steps taken and pulse levels. Patients send Kaiser details of exercise sessions and symptoms through a mobile app accessible through their watch. In return, reminders are sent to patients about medication and exercise. If the patient isn't meeting program goals, health-providers can follow up with phone calls. Kaiser is also able to use the data collected to determine the most effective program plans. In the first year, readmission rates for participating patients were less than 2%, compared to 10% to 15%, on average, for patients in clinic rehab programs.

Source: Kayla Matthews, "6 Ways Companies Are Using Data Analytics to Reduce Expenses," *InsideBIGDATA*, February 24, 2019. Agam Shah, "Kaiser Permanente Bets on Smartwatches to Lower Costs," *Wall Street Journal*, January 15, 2020.

Managerial Decision ■ You Are the Purchasing Manager

Your department has been experiencing increased activity in recent periods as the company has grown, and you have observed that the average cost per purchase order processed has been declining, but not at a constant rate. You have been given an estimate by the production manager of the number of purchase orders that will be processed next period and have been asked by the accounting department to provide within one hour an estimate of the cost to process those orders. How can the scatter diagram method help you to meet this deadline? [Answer, p. 15-21]

LO3 Review 15-3

Assume a local Subway reported the following results for April and May:

	April	May
Sandwiches sold.	2,100	2,700
Cost of food sold.	$1,575	$2,025
Wages and salaries	1,525	1,675
Rent on building	1,500	1,500
Depreciation on equipment.	200	200
Utilities	710	770
Supplies	225	255
Miscellaneous.	113	131
Total	$5,848	$6,556

continued

continued from previous page

Required

a. Using the high-low method, create an equation for each of the following costs in April: cost of food, wages and salaries, rent on building, and total monthly costs.

b. Predict total costs for monthly volumes of 1,000 and 2,000 sandwiches.

c. Predict the average cost per unit at monthly volumes of 1,000 and 2,000 sandwiches. Explain why the average costs differ at these two volumes.

Solution on p. 15-33.

Additional Issues in Cost Estimation

LO4
eLectures MBC

Identify and discuss problems encountered in cost estimation.

We have mentioned several items to be wary of when developing cost-estimating equations:

- Data that are not based on normal operating conditions.
- Nonlinear relationships between total costs and activity.
- Obtaining a high R-squared purely by chance.

Additional items of concern include

- Changes in technology or prices.
- Matching activity and cost within each observation.
- Identifying activity cost drivers.

Changes in Technology and Prices

Changes in technology and prices make cost estimation and prediction difficult. When telecommunications companies changed from using landlines to voice over internet protocol (VOIP) to place long-distance telephone calls, cost estimates based on the use of fiber optic cables were of little or no value in predicting future costs. Care must be taken to make sure that data used in developing cost estimates are based on the existing technology. When this is not possible, professional judgment is required to make appropriate adjustments.

Only data reflecting a single price level should be used in cost estimation and prediction. If prices have remained stable in the past but then uniformly increase by 20%, cost-estimating equations based on data from previous periods will not accurately predict future costs. In this case, all that is required is a 20% increase in the prediction. Unfortunately, adjustments for price changes are seldom this simple. The prices of various cost elements are likely to change at different rates and at different times. Furthermore, there are probably several different price levels included in the past data used to develop cost-estimating equations. If data from different price levels are used, an attempt should be made to restate them to a single price level.

Matching Activity and Costs

The development of accurate cost-estimating equations requires the matching of the activity to related costs within each observation. This accuracy is often difficult to achieve because of the time lag between an activity and the recording of the cost of resources consumed by the activity. Current activities usually consume electricity, but the electric bill won't be received and recorded until next month. Driving an automobile requires routine maintenance for items such as lubrication and oil, but the auto can be driven several weeks or even months before the maintenance is required. Consequently, daily, weekly, and perhaps even monthly observations of miles driven and maintenance costs are unlikely to match the costs of oil and lubrication with the cost-driving activity, miles driven.

In general, the shorter the time period, the higher the probability of error in matching costs and activity. The cost analyst must carefully review the database to verify that activity and cost are matched within each observation. If matching problems are found, it may be possible to adjust the data (perhaps by moving the cost of electricity from one observation to another). Under other circumstances, it may be necessary to use longer periods to match costs and activity.

Identifying Activity Cost Drivers

Identifying the appropriate activity cost driver for a particular cost requires judgment and professional experience. In general, the cost driver should have a logical, causal relationship with costs. In many cases, the identity of the most appropriate activity cost driver, such as miles driven for the cost of automobile gasoline, is apparent. In other situations, where different activity cost drivers might be used, scatter diagrams and statistical measures, such as the coefficient of determination, are helpful in selecting the activity cost driver that best explains past variations in cost. When scatter diagrams are used, the analyst can study the dispersion of observations around the cost-estimating line. In general, a small dispersion is preferred. If regression analysis is used, the analyst considers the coefficient of determination. In general, a higher coefficient of determination is preferred. The relationship between the activity cost driver and the cost must seem logical, and the activity data must be available.

LO4 Review 15-4

Identify some common activity drivers that might be used to state a volume of activity in a manufacturing operation. What general criterion might be used in choosing a driver?

Solution on p. 15-33.

Alternative Cost Driver Classifications

So far we have examined cost behavior and cost estimation using only a unit-level approach, which assumes changes in costs are best explained by changes in the number of units of product or service provided customers. This approach may have worked for **Carnegie Steel Company**, but it is inappropriate for multidimensional organizations, such as **Square**. The unit-level approach becomes increasingly inaccurate for analyzing cost behavior when organizations experience the following types of changes:

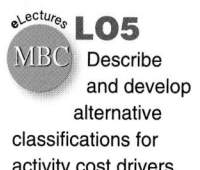

LO5
Describe and develop alternative classifications for activity cost drivers.

- From face-to-face customer interactions to web-based interface,

- From stand-alone products to products with multiple layers of customer interface, such as Square's hardware versus the processing of payments executed by Square for its customers, and

- From internet-based operations to mobile platforms, thus engaging a more geographically diverse set of customers.

Exhibit 15.8 illustrates the composition of total manufacturing costs for the past century, illustrating changes in the percentage of manufacturing costs for three major cost categories.

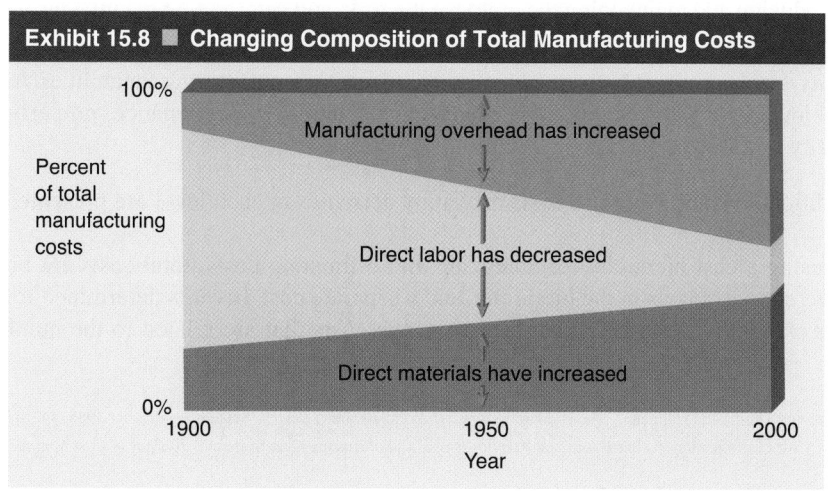

Exhibit 15.8 ■ Changing Composition of Total Manufacturing Costs

1. **Direct materials**, the cost of primary raw materials converted into finished goods, have increased slightly as organizations purchase components they formerly fabricated. The word "direct" is used to indicate costs that are easily or directly traced to a finished product or service.

2. **Direct labor**, the wages earned by production employees for the time they spend converting raw materials into finished products, has decreased significantly as employees spend less time physically working on products and more time supporting automated production activities.

3. **Manufacturing overhead**, which includes all manufacturing costs other than direct materials and direct labor, has increased significantly due to automation, product diversity, and product complexity.

Changes in the composition of manufacturing costs have implications for the behavior of total costs and the responsiveness of costs to changes in cost drivers. Because direct materials and direct labor vary directly with the number of units, they are easy to measure. In the past, when manufacturing overhead was relatively small, it was possible to assume units of product or service was the primary cost driver. This is no longer true. Units of final product is no longer an adequate explanation of changes in manufacturing overhead for many organizations.

The past tendency to ignore overhead, while focusing on direct materials and direct labor, led one researcher to describe overhead-causing activities as "the hidden factory."[1] To better understand the hidden factory, several researchers have developed frameworks for categorizing cost-driving activities. The crucial feature of these frameworks is the inclusion of nonunit cost drivers. Depending on the characteristics of a particular organization, as well as management's information needs, there are an almost unlimited number of cost driver classification schemes. We consider two frequently applied cost driver classification schemes: one based on a manufacturing cost hierarchy and a second based on a customer cost hierarchy. We also illustrate variations of each.

Manufacturing Cost Hierarchy

The most well-known framework, developed by Cooper[2] and Cooper and Kaplan[3] for manufacturing situations, classifies activities into the following four categories.

1. A **unit-level activity** is performed *for each unit* of product produced. Christofle is a French manufacturer of high-end silver flatware. In the production of forks, the stamping of each fork into the prescribed shape is an example of a unit-level cost driver.

2. A **batch-level activity** is performed *for each batch* of product produced. At Christofle, a batch is a number of identical units (such as a fork of a specific design) produced at the same time. Batch-level activities include setting up the machines to stamp each fork in an identical manner, moving the entire batch between workstations (i.e., molding, stamping, and finishing), and inspecting the first unit in the batch to verify that the machines are set up correctly.

3. A **product-level activity** is performed *to support* the production of *each different type of product*. At Christofle, product-level activities for a specific pattern of fork include initially designing the fork, producing and maintaining the mold for the fork, and determining manufacturing operations for the fork.

4. A **facility-level activity** is performed *to maintain* general manufacturing capabilities. At Christofle, facility-level activities include plant management, building maintenance, property taxes, and electricity required to sustain the building.

Several additional examples of the costs driven by activities at each level are presented in Exhibit 15.9.

When using a cost hierarchy for analyzing and estimating costs, total costs are broken down into the different cost levels in the hierarchy, and a separate cost driver is determined for each level of cost. For example, using the above hierarchy, the costs that are related to the number of units

---

[1] Jeffrey G. Miller and Thomas E. Vollmann, "The Hidden Factory," *Harvard Business Review,* September-October 1985, pp. 1415–150.

[2] Robin Cooper, "Cost Classification in Unit-Based and Activity-Based Manufacturing Cost Systems," *Journal of Cost Management,* Fall 1990, pp. 4–14.

[3] Robin Cooper and Robert S. Kaplan, "Profit Priorities from Activity-Based Costing," *Harvard Business Review,* May-June 1991, pp. 130–135.

produced (such as direct materials or direct labor) may have direct labor hours or machine hours as the cost driver; whereas batch costs may be driven by the number of setups of production machines or the number of times materials are moved from one machine to another. Other costs may be driven by the number of different products produced. Facility-level costs are generally regarded as fixed costs and do not vary unless capacity is increased or decreased.

Exhibit 15.9 ■ Hierarchy of Activity Costs		
Activity Level	**Reason for Activity**	**Examples of Activity Cost**
1. Unit level	Performed for each unit of product produced or sold	• Cost of raw materials • Cost of inserting a component • Utilities cost of operating equipment • Some costs of packaging • Sales commissions
2. Batch level	Performed for each batch of product produced or sold	• Cost of processing sales order • Cost of issuing and tracking work order • Cost of equipment setup • Cost of moving batch between workstations • Cost of inspection (assuming same number of units inspected in each batch)
3. Product level	Performed to support each different product that can be produced	• Cost of product development • Cost of product marketing such as advertising • Cost of specialized equipment • Cost of maintaining specialized equipment
4. Facility level	Performed to maintain general manufacturing capabilities	• Cost of maintaining general facilities such as buildings and grounds • Cost of nonspecialized equipment • Cost of maintaining nonspecialized equipment • Cost of real property taxes • Cost of general advertising • Cost of general administration such as the plant manager's salary

Customer Cost Hierarchy

The manufacturing hierarchy presented is but one of many possible ways of classifying activities and their costs. Classification schemes should be designed to fit the organization and meet user needs. A merchandising organization or the sales division of a manufacturing organization might use the following hierarchy.

1. **Unit-level activity**: performed for each unit sold.
2. **Order-level activity**: performed for each sales order.
3. **Customer-level activity:** performed to obtain or maintain each customer.
4. **Facility-level activity:** performed to maintain the general sales or store function.

This classification scheme assists in answering questions concerning the cost of individual orders or individual customers.

If an organization sells to distinct market segments (for profit, not for profit, and government), the cost hierarchy can be modified as follows:

1. Unit-level activity
2. Order-level activity
3. Customer-level activity
4. **Market-segment-level activity:** performed to obtain or maintain operations in a segment.
5. Facility-level activity

The market-segment-level activities and their related costs differ with each market segment. This classification scheme assists in answering questions concerning the profitability of each segment.

Finally, an organization that completes unique projects for different market segments (such as buildings for **IBM** and the **U.S. Department of Defense**) can use the following hierarchy to determine the profitability of each segment:

1. **Project-level activity:** performed to support the completion of each project.
2. Market-segment-level activity
3. Facility-level activity

The possibilities are endless. The important point is that both the cost hierarchy and the costs included in the hierarchy be tailored to meet the specific circumstances of an organization and the interests of management.

Review 15-5 **LO5**

Customer Cost Hierarchy Consider the pizza chain Blaze Pizza. It custom builds and cooks each pizza to order. Items 1–6 represent cost activities a particular store might incur.

1. Pepperoni on the pizza
2. Wood to fuel the fire used to cook the pizzas
3. Insurance on the building
4. The labor hours worked by the employee building and cooking each pizza
5. The sales calls made to local organizations to promote the pizzas for catering special events
6. The number of pizza orders received

Required
Classify each cost activity above, in the most appropriate level of the proposed customer cost hierarchy. Each cost activity may be used more than once.

_____   *a.* Unit-level—performed for each unit sold
_____   *b.* Order-level—performed for each sales level
_____   *c.* Customer-level—performed to obtain or maintain each customer
Solution on p. 15-33.   _____   *d.* Store(facility)-level—performed to maintain the general store functions

Guidance Answers

You Are the Purchasing Manager
Pg. 15-16 One of the quickest methods for gaining a general understanding of the relationship between a given cost and its cost driver is to graph the relationship using data from several recent periods. As purchasing manager you could probably quickly obtain information about the amount of the total purchasing department costs and number of purchase orders processed for each of the most recent eight or ten periods. By graphing these data with costs on the vertical axis and number of purchase orders on the horizontal axis, you should be able to visually determine if there is an obvious behavioral pattern (variable, fixed, or mixed). Since costs have been declining as volume has increased, this would suggest that there are some fixed costs, and that they have been declining on a per unit basis as they are spread over an increasing number of purchase orders. Using two representative data points in the scatter diagram, you can plot a cost curve on the graph, and then use the data for those two points to calculate the estimated fixed and variable costs using the high-low cost estimation method. Using these cost estimates, you can predict the total cost for next period. This method may not give you a precise estimate of the cost, but coupled with your subjective estimate of cost based on your experience as manager of the department, it should give you more confidence than merely making a best guess. Hopefully, you will have an opportunity before presenting your budget for the next period to conduct additional analyses using more advanced methods.

Q15-1. Briefly describe variable, fixed, mixed, and step costs and indicate how the total cost function of each changes as activity increases within a time period.

Q15-2. Why is presenting all costs of an organization as a function of a single independent variable, although useful in obtaining a general understanding of cost behavior, often not accurate enough to make specific decisions concerning products, services, or activities?

Q15-3. Explain the term "relevant range" and why it is important in estimating total costs.

Q15-4. How are variable and fixed costs determined using the high-low method of cost estimation?

Q15-5. Distinguish between cost estimation and cost prediction.

Q15-6. Why is a scatter diagram helpful when used in conjunction with other methods of cost estimation?

Q15-7. Identify two advantages of least-squares regression analysis as a cost-estimating technique.

Q15-8. Why is it important to match activity and costs within each observation? When is this matching problem most likely to exist?

Q15-9. During the past century, how have direct materials, direct labor, and manufacturing overhead changed as a portion of total manufacturing costs? What is the implication of the change in manufacturing overhead for cost estimation?

Q15-10. Distinguish between the unit-, batch-, product-, and facility-level activities of a manufacturing organization.

Assignments with the ⓜ logo in the margin are available in 𝐁usinessCourse.
See the Preface of the book for details.

Mini Exercises

M15-11. Classifying Cost Behavior   **LO1**
Classify the total costs of each of the following as variable, fixed, mixed, or step. Sales volume is the
cost driver.

    a. Salary of the department manager
    b. Memory chips in a computer assembly plant
    c. Real estate taxes
    d. Salaries of quality inspectors when each inspector can evaluate a maximum of 1,000 units per day
    e. Wages paid to production employees for the time spent working on products
    f. Electric power in a factory
    g. Raw materials used in production
    h. Automobiles rented on the basis of a fixed charge per day plus an additional charge per mile driven
    i. Sales commissions
    j. Straight-line depreciation on office equipment

M15-12. Classifying Cost Behavior   **LO1**
Classify the total costs of each of the following as variable, fixed, mixed, or step.

    a. Straight-line depreciation on a building
    b. Maintenance costs at a hospital
    c. Rent on a photocopy machine charged as a fixed amount per month plus an additional charge per copy
    d. Cost of goods sold in a bookstore
    e. Salaries paid to temporary instructors in a college as the number of course sessions varies
    f. Lumber used by a house construction company
    g. The costs of operating a research department
    h. The cost of hiring a dance band for three hours
    i. Laser printer paper for a department printer
    j. Electric power in a restaurant

LO1, 2, 3   M15-13. Classifying Cost Behavior

For each of the following situations, select the most appropriate cost behavior pattern (as shown in the illustrations following this problem) where the lines represent the cost behavior pattern, the vertical axis represents costs, the horizontal axis represents total volume, and the dots represent actual costs. Each pattern may be used more than once.

Graphs for Mini Exercise 15-13

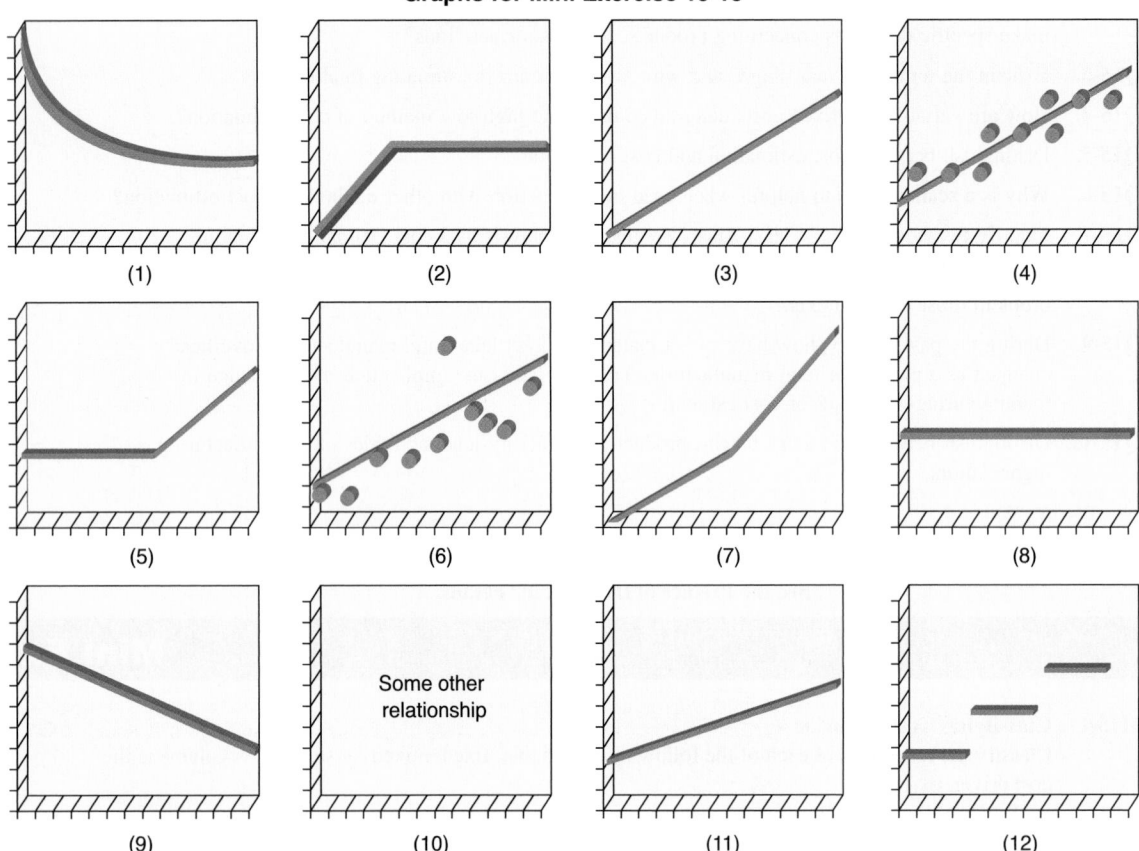

a. Variable costs per unit
b. Total fixed costs
c. Total mixed costs
d. Average fixed costs per unit
e. Total current manufacturing costs
f. Average variable costs
g. Total costs when employees are paid $15 per hour for the first 40 hours worked each week and $20 for each additional hour
h. Total costs when employees are paid $15 per hour and guaranteed a minimum weekly wage of $300
i. Total costs per day when a consultant is paid $200 per hour with a maximum daily fee of $1,000
j. Total variable costs
k. Total costs for salaries of social workers where each social worker can handle a maximum of 25 cases
l. A water bill where a flat fee of $800 is charged for the first 100,000 gallons and additional water costs $0.005 per gallon
m. Total variable costs properly used to estimate step costs
n. Total materials costs
o. Rent on exhibit space at a convention

LO1, 2, 3   M15-14. Classifying Cost Behavior

For each of the graphs displayed following this problem, select the most appropriate cost behavior pattern where the lines represent the cost behavior pattern, the vertical axis represents total costs, the horizontal axis represents total volume, and the dots represent actual costs. Each pattern may be used more than once.

Graphs for Mini Exercise 15-14

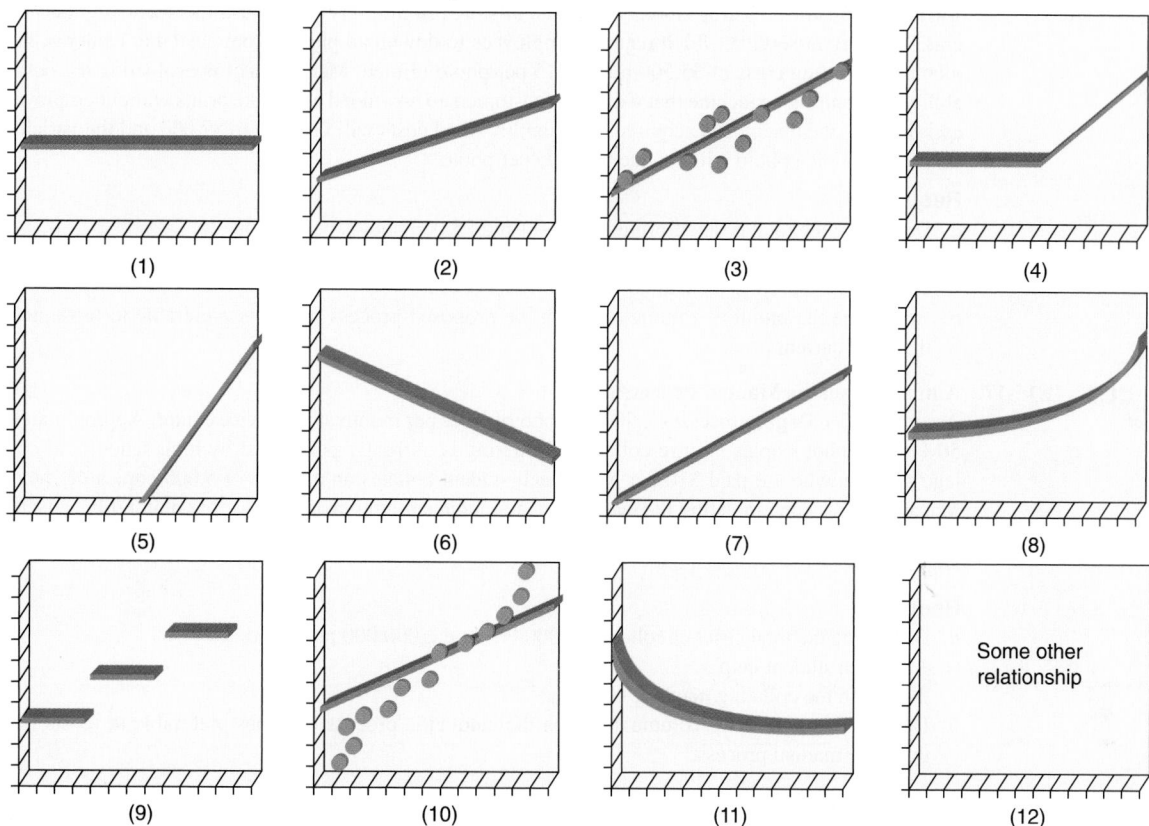

a. A cellular telephone bill when a flat fee is charged for the first 500 minutes of use per month and additional use costs $0.25 per minute
b. Total selling and administrative costs
c. Total labor costs when employees are paid per unit produced
d. Total overtime premium paid production employees
e. Average total cost per unit
f. Salaries of supervisors when each one can supervise a maximum of 10 employees
g. Total idle time costs when employees are paid for a minimum 40-hour week
h. Materials costs per unit
i. Total sales commissions
j. Electric power consumption in a restaurant
k. Total costs when high volumes of production require the use of overtime and obsolete equipment
l. A good linear approximation of actual costs
m. A linear cost estimation valid only within the relevant range

Exercises

E15-15. Computing Average Unit Costs

Assume the total monthly operating costs of a **McDonald's** restaurant are:

$$\$40,000 + \$0.75X$$

where

$$X = \text{Number of salad orders}$$

Required
a. Determine the average cost per salad at each of the following monthly volumes: 1,000; 10,000; 50,000; 100,000.
b. Determine the monthly volume at which the average cost per serving is $2.35.

LO2
McDonald's
(MCD)

Homework
MBC

LO2

Bartell's

E15-16. Automatic versus Manual Processing

Bartell's, a Seattle area drug store, operates an in-store printing service for customers with digital cameras. The current service, which requires employees to download photos from customer cameras, has monthly operating costs of $5,500 plus $0.15 per photo printed. Management is evaluating the desirability of acquiring a machine that will allow customers to download and make prints without employee assistance. If the machine is acquired, the monthly fixed costs will increase to $7,000 and the variable costs of printing a photo will decline to $0.05 per photo.

Required

a. Determine the total costs of printing 10,000 and 25,000 photos per month:
  1. With the current employee-assisted process.
  2. With the proposed customer self-service process.
b. Determine the monthly volume at which the proposed process becomes preferable to (costs less than) the current process.

LO2

Office Depot
(ODP)

E15-17. Automatic versus Manual Processing

Assume Office Depot processes 2,500,000 photocopies per month at its service center. Approximately 50% of the photocopies require collating. Collating is currently performed by high school and college students who are paid $10 per hour. Each student collates an average of 5,000 copies per hour. Management is contemplating the lease of an automatic collating machine that has a monthly capacity of 6,000,000 photocopies, with lease and operating costs totaling $3,000, plus $0.05 per 1,000 units collated.

Required

a. Determine the total costs of collating 1,000,000 and 2,000,000 per month:
  1. With student help.
  2. With the collating machine.
b. Determine the monthly volume at which the automatic process becomes preferable to (costs less than) the manual process.

LO3

YRC Worldwide
(YRCW)

E15-18. High-Low Cost Estimation

Assume the local YRC Worldwide delivery service hub has the following information available about fleet miles and operating costs:

Year	Miles	Operating Costs
Year 1	695,000	$219,500
Year 2	855,000	267,500

Required

Use the high-low method to develop a cost-estimating equation for total annual operating costs.

LO3, 4

Pearle Vision (LUX)

E15-19. Scatter Diagrams and High-Low Cost Estimation

Assume the local Pearle Vision has the following information on the number of sales orders received and order-processing costs.

Month	Sales Orders	Order-Processing Costs
1	3,300	$ 90,970
2	1,650	55,412
3	4,840	132,770
4	3,080	90,090
5	2,530	76,752
6	1,320	47,410
7	2,200	68,750

Required

a. Use information from the high- and low-volume months to develop a cost-estimating equation for monthly order-processing costs.
b. Plot the data on a scatter diagram. Using the information from representative high- and low-volume months, develop a cost-estimating equation for monthly production costs.
c. What factors might have caused the difference in the equations developed for requirements (a) and (b)?

E15-20. Scatter Diagrams and High-Low Cost Estimation

From April 1 through October 31, Coles County Highway Department hires temporary employees to mow and clean the right-of-way along county roads. The County Road Commissioner has asked you to help her in determining the variable labor cost of mowing and cleaning a mile of road. The following information is available regarding current-year operations:

Month	Miles Mowed and Cleaned	Labor Costs
April	240	$6,800
May	305	7,680
June	325	8,310
July	275	7,200
August	220	6,550
September	200	5,760
October	75	4,960

Required

a. Use the information from the high- and low-volume months to develop a cost-estimating equation for monthly labor costs.

b. Plot the data on a scatter diagram. Using the information from representative high- and low-volume months, use the high-low method to develop a cost-estimating equation for monthly labor costs.

c. What factors might have caused the difference in the equations developed for requirements (a) and (b)?

d. Adjust the equation developed in requirement (b) to incorporate the effect of an anticipated 5% increase in wages.

E15-21. Cost Behavior Analysis in a Restaurant: High-Low Cost Estimation

Assume a Potbelly's restaurant has the following information available regarding costs at representative levels of monthly sales (meals served):

	Monthly Sales in Units		
	5,000	7,000	10,000
Cost of food sold	$ 7,500	$10,500	$15,000
Wages and fringe benefits	5,900	5,940	6,000
Fees paid delivery help	6,000	8,400	12,000
Rent on building	3,500	3,500	3,500
Depreciation on equipment	850	850	850
Utilities	600	640	700
Supplies (soap, floor wax, etc.)	400	480	600
Administrative costs	1,200	1,200	1,200
Total	$25,950	$31,510	$39,850

Required

a. Identify each cost as being variable, fixed, or mixed.

b. Use the high-low method to develop a schedule identifying the amount of each cost that is mixed or variable per unit. Total the amounts under each category to develop an equation for total monthly costs.

c. Predict total costs for a monthly sales volume of 8,500 units.

E15-22. Developing an Equation from Average Costs

Tucker Pup's Pet Resort offers dog boarding services in Chicago. Assume that in March, when dog-days occupancy was at an annual low of 150 days, the average cost per dog-day was $65. In July, when dog-days were at a capacity level of 600, the average cost per dog-day was $20.

Required

a. Develop an equation for monthly operating costs.

b. Determine the average boarding cost per dog-day at an annual volume of 4,500 dog-days.

LO2, 3
Brenthaven

E15-23. Selecting an Independent Variable: Scatter Diagrams

Brenthaven produces protective cases for mobile technology. The cases are sold internationally, online, and through retail partners. Presented is information on production costs and inventory changes for five recent months:

	January	February	March	April	May
Finished goods inventory in units:					
Beginning	20,000	30,000	20,000	5,000	35,000
Manufactured	35,000	45,000	40,000	50,000	60,000
Available.	55,000	75,000	60,000	55,000	95,000
Sold	(25,000)	(55,000)	(55,000)	(20,000)	(65,000)
Ending	30,000	20,000	5,000	35,000	30,000
Manufacturing costs	$525,000	$615,000	$550,000	$745,000	$800,000

Required

a. With the aid of scatter diagrams, determine whether units sold or units manufactured is a better predictor of manufacturing costs.

b. Prepare an explanation for your answer to requirement (a).

c. Which independent variable, units sold or units manufactured, should be a better predictor of selling costs? Why?

LO2, 3
Cambridge
SoundWorks

Homework
MBC

E15-24. Selecting a Basis for Predicting Shipping Expenses (Requires Computer Spreadsheet[*])

Cambridge SoundWorks sell portable speakers systems and bluetooth headphones. In an effort to improve the planning and control of shipping expenses, management is trying to determine which of three variables—units shipped, weight shipped, or sales value of units shipped—has the closest relationship with shipping expenses. The following information is available:

Month	Units Shipped	Weight Shipped (lbs.)	Sales Value of Units Shipped	Shipping Expenses
May.	10,000	7,500	$350,000	$38,000
June	12,000	8,760	432,000	42,000
July	15,000	9,200	420,000	50,100
August	20,000	10,500	400,000	72,500
September	12,000	7,600	300,000	41,000
October.	8,000	6,000	320,000	35,600

Required

a. With the aid of a spreadsheet program, determine whether units shipped, weight shipped, or sales value of units shipped has the closest relationship with shipping expenses.

b. Using the independent variable that appears to have the closest relationship to shipping expenses, develop a cost-estimating equation for total monthly shipping expenses.

c. Use the equation developed in requirement (b) to predict total shipping expenses in a month when 14,000 units, weighing 9,380 lbs., with a total sales value of $420,000 are shipped.

Problems

LO2, 3, 4
Midnight Cookie
Company

P15-25. High-Low and Scatter Diagrams with Implications for Regression

Midnight Cookie Company produces and delivers gourmet cookies and ice cream until 1:30 a.m. from its three Seattle area locations. Presented is monthly cost and sales information for cookies at one of Midnight's locations.

---

[*] This assignment requires the use of a computer spreadsheet such as Excel® to solve. This assignment assumes previous knowledge of computer spreadsheets.

Month	Sales (Dozens)	Total Costs
January.	6,800	$30,650
February	7,800	35,336
March	5,500	29,700
April	1,000	25,000
May.	6,100	30,600
June	4,500	28,670

Required

a. Using the high-low method, develop a cost-estimating equation for total monthly costs.

b. 1. Plot the equation developed in requirement (a).

    2. Using the same graph, develop a scatter diagram of all observations for the cookie shop. Select representative high and low values and draw a second cost-estimating equation.

c. Which is a better predictor of future costs? Why?

d. If you decided to develop a cost-estimating equation using least-squares regression analysis, should you include all the observations? Why or why not?

e. Mention two reasons that the least-squares regression is superior to the high-low and scatter diagram methods of cost estimation.

P15-26. **Multiple Cost Drivers**

Newman's Own manufactures a variety of specialty salad dressings. Production runs are both high-volume and low-volume activities, depending on customer orders. Assume the following represents general manufacturing costs (manufacturing overhead) and each cost's related activity cost driver for Newman's Own.

Level	Total Cost	Units of Cost Driver
Unit.	$600,000	20,000 machine hours
Batch	40,000	400 customer orders
Product.	84,000	15 products

The lime vinaigrette dressing required 1,000 machine hours to fill 60 customer orders for a total of 4,000 cases.

Required

a. Assuming all manufacturing overhead is estimated and predicted on the basis of machine hours, determine the predicted total overhead costs to produce the 4,000 cases of lime vinaigrette.

b. Assuming manufacturing overhead is estimated and predicted using separate rates for machine hours, customer orders, and products (a multiple-level cost hierarchy), determine the predicted total overhead costs to produce the 4,000 cases of lime vinaigrette.

c. Calculate the error in predicting manufacturing overhead using machine hours versus using multiple cost drivers. Indicate whether the use of only machine hours results in overpredicting or underpredicting the costs to produce 4,000 cases of lime vinaigrette.

d. Looking just at batch level costs, calculate the error in predicting those costs using machine hours versus using customer orders. Indicate whether the use of only machine hours results in overpredicting or underpredicting the batch-level costs to produce 4,000 cases of lime vinaigrette.

e. Looking just at product-level costs, calculate the error in predicting those costs using machine hours versus using number of products. Indicate whether the use of only machine hours results in overpredicting or underpredicting the product-level costs to produce 4,000 cases of lime vinaigrette.

P15-27. **Unit- and Batch-Level Cost Drivers**

Kentucky Fried Chicken (a reportable operating segment of Yum Brands Inc.), a fast-food restaurant, serves fried chicken. The managers are considering an "all you can eat" promotion and want to know the costs before setting a price. Each batch must be 50 pieces. The chicken is precut by the chain headquarters and sent to the stores in 10-piece bags. Each bag costs $5. Preparing a batch of 50 pieces of chicken with KFC's special coating takes one employee two hours. The current wage rate is $10 per hour. Another cost driver is the cost of putting fresh oil into the fryers. New oil, costing $9, is used for each batch.

Required

a. Determine the cost of preparing one batch of 50 pieces.
b. If management projects that it will sell 150 pieces of fried chicken, determine the total cost and the cost per piece.
c. If management estimates the sales to be 350 pieces, determine the total costs.
d. How much will the batch costs increase if the government raises the minimum wage to $12 per hour?
e. If management decided to increase the number of pieces in a batch to 100, determine the cost of preparing 350 pieces. Assume that the batch would take twice as long to prepare, pay rate stays at $10 per hour, and management wants to replace the oil after 100 pieces are cooked. Assume no change in expected sales volume. Note that only full batches can be prepared.

LO5   **P15-28.   Optimal Batch Size**
This is a continuation of parts c and e of P15-27.

Required

Should management increase the batch size to 100? Why or why not?

Management Applications

LO3   **MA15-29.   Significance of High R-Squared**
Drew Conner had always been suspicious of "newfangled mathematical stuff," and the most recent suggestion of his new assistant merely confirmed his belief that schools are putting a lot of useless junk in students' heads. It seems that after an extensive analysis of historical data, the assistant suggested that the number of pounds of scrap was the best basis for predicting manufacturing overhead. In response to Mr. Conner's rage, the slightly intimidated assistant indicated that of the 35 equations he tried, pounds of scrap had the highest coefficient of determination with manufacturing overhead.

Required

Comment on Conner's reaction. Is it justified? Is it likely that the number of pounds of scrap is a good basis for predicting manufacturing overhead? Is it a feasible basis for predicting manufacturing overhead?

LO3   **MA15-30.   Estimating Machine Repair Costs**
In an attempt to determine the best basis for predicting machine repair costs, the production supervisor accumulated daily information on these costs and production over a one-month period. Applying simple regression analysis to the data, she obtained the following estimating equation:

$$Y = \$800 - \$2.60X$$

where

$$Y = \text{total daily machine repair costs}$$
$$X = \text{daily production in units}$$

Because of the negative relationship between repair costs and production, she was somewhat skeptical of the results, even though the R-squared was a respectable 0.765.

Required

a. What is the most likely explanation of the negative variable costs?
b. Suggest an alternative procedure for estimating machine repair costs that might prove more useful.

LO4   **MA15-31.   Ethical Problem Uncovered by Cost Estimation**
Westfield owns and provides management services for several shopping centers. After five years with the company, James Heller was recently promoted to the position of manager of one of Westfield's smaller malls on the outskirts of a downtown area. When he accepted the assignment, James was told that he would hold the position for only a couple of years because that mall would likely be torn down to make way for a new sports stadium. James was also told that if he did well in this assignment, he would be in line for heading one of the company's new 200-store operations that were currently in the planning stage.

While reviewing the mall's financial records for the past few years, James observed that last year's oil consumption was up by 8%, even though the number of heating degree days was down by 4%. Somewhat curious, James uncovered the following information:

- The mall is heated by forced-air oil heat. The furnace is five years old and has been well maintained.

- Fuel oil is kept in four 5,000-gallon underground oil tanks. The oil tanks were installed 25 years ago.
- Replacing the tanks would cost $80,000. If pollution was found, cleanup costs could go as high as $2,000,000, depending on how much oil had leaked into the ground and how far it had spread.
- Replacing the tanks would add more congestion to the mall's parking situation.

Required
What should James do? Explain.

MA15-32. Activity Cost Drivers and Cost Estimation   **LO5**

Market Street Soup Company produces ten varieties of soup in large vats, several thousand gallons at a time. The soup is distributed to several categories of customers. Some soup is packaged in large containers and sold to college and university food services. Some is packaged in half-gallon or small containers and sold through wholesale distributors to grocery stores. Finally, some is packaged in a variety of individual servings and sold directly to the public from trucks owned and operated by Market Street Soup Company. Management has always assumed that costs fluctuated with the volume of soup, and cost-estimating equations have been based on the following cost function:

$$\text{Estimated costs} = \text{Fixed costs} + \text{Variable costs per gallon} \times \text{Production in gallons}$$

Lately, however, this equation has not been a very accurate predictor of total costs. At the same time, management has noticed that the volumes and varieties of soup sold through the three distinct distribution channels have fluctuated from month to month.

Required
a. What *relevant* major assumption is inherent in the cost-estimating equation currently used by Market Street Soup Company?
b. Why might Market Street Soup Company wish to develop a cost-estimating equation that recognizes the hierarchy of activity costs? Explain.
c. Develop the general form of a more accurate cost-estimating equation for Market Street Soup Company. Clearly label and explain all elements of the equation, and provide specific examples of costs for each element.

MA15-33. Multiple Regression Analysis for a Special Decision (Requires Computer Spreadsheet[*])   **LO3**

For billing purposes, assume Phoenix Family Medical Clinic classifies its services into one of four major procedures, X1 through X4. A local business has proposed that Phoenix provide health services to its employees and their families at the following set rates per procedure:

Phoenix Family
Medical Clinic

X1	$100
X2	200
X3	60
X4	300

Because these rates are significantly below the current rates charged for these services, management has asked for detailed cost information on each procedure. The following information is available for the most recent 12 months.

Month	Total Cost	Number of Procedures			
		X1	X2	X3	X4
1	$17,250	30	25	155	19
2	18,750	38	30	135	23
3	20,250	50	20	105	38
4	14,250	20	25	90	25
5	15,000	68	15	120	20
6	20,250	90	19	158	14
7	19,125	20	30	143	28
8	16,125	16	30	132	20
9	19,500	60	21	93	35
10	16,500	20	22	75	35
11	17,100	20	18	113	33
12	19,875	72	15	150	30

---

[*]This assignment requires the use of a computer spreadsheet such as Excel® to solve. This assignment assumes previous knowledge of computer spreadsheets.

Required

a. Use multiple regression analysis to determine the unit cost of each procedure. How much variation in monthly cost is explained by your cost-estimating equation?

b. Evaluate the rates proposed by the local business. Assuming Phoenix has excess capacity and no employees of the local business currently patronize the clinic, what are your recommendations regarding the proposal?

c. Evaluate the rates proposed by the local business. Assuming Phoenix is operating at capacity and would have to turn current customers away if it agrees to provide health services to the local business, what are your recommendations regarding the proposal?

LO3, 4

Kendrick Anderson
Furniture Maker, LLC

MA15-34. Cost Estimation, Interpretation, and Analysis (Requires Computer Spreadsheet[*])

Kendrick Anderson Furniture Maker, LLC creates custom tables in Atlanta. Assume that the following represents monthly information on production volume and manufacturing costs since the company started operations.

	Total Manufacturing Costs	Total Tables Produced	Living Room Tables Produced	Dining Room Tables Produced
June Year 1	$71,000	110	25	85
July	57,500	90	45	45
August	79,724	130	15	115
September	64,250	95	36	59
October.	57,300	76	24	52
November.	60,900	92	48	44
December.	62,700	105	24	81
January Year 2	70,130	110	50	60
February.	68,400	102	20	82
March	57,400	81	25	56
April	105,790	142	102	40
May.	74,750	125	22	103
June	74,290	115	15	100
July	66,500	106	18	88
August	49,888	85	28	57
September	72,668	116	55	61
October.	71,700	120	81	39
November.	74,200	120	30	90
December.	54,900	72	18	54

Required

a. Use the high-low method to develop a cost-estimating equation for total manufacturing costs. Interpret the meaning of the "fixed" costs and comment on the results.

b. Use the chart feature of a spreadsheet to develop a scatter graph of total manufacturing costs and total units produced. Use the graph to identify any unusual observations.

c. Excluding any unusual observations, use the high-low method to develop a cost-estimating equation for total manufacturing costs. Comment on the results, comparing them with the results in requirement (a).

d. Use simple regression analysis to develop a cost-estimating equation for total manufacturing costs. What advantages does simple regression analysis have in comparison with the high-low method of cost estimation? Why must analysts carefully evaluate the data used in simple regression analysis?

e. A customer has offered to purchase 50 dining room tables for $452 per table. Management has asked your advice regarding the desirability of accepting the offer. What advice do you have for management? Additional analysis is required.

LO3

MA15-35. Simple and Multiple Regression (Requires Computer Spreadsheet[*])

Dan Mullen is employed by a mail-order distributor and reconditions used desktop computers, broadband routers, and laser printers. Dan is paid $12 per hour, plus an extra $6 per hour for work in excess of 40 hours per week. The distributor just announced plans to outsource all reconditioning work so Dan will need to start looking for a new job. Because the distributor is pleased with the quality of Dan's work, he

---

[*]This exercise requires the use of a computer spreadsheet such as Excel® to solve. This assignment assumes previous knowledge of computer spreadsheets.

has been asked to enter into a long-term contract to recondition used desktop computers at a rate of $50 per computer, plus all parts. The distributor also offered to rent all necessary equipment to Dan at a rate of $300 per month. Dan has been informed that he should plan on reconditioning as many computers as he can handle, up to a maximum of 20 per week.

Dan has room in his basement to set up a work area, but he is unsure of the economics of accepting the contract, as opposed to working for a local computer repair shop at $14 per hour. Data related to the time spent and the number of units of each type of electronic equipment Dan has reconditioned in recent weeks is as follows:

Week	Laser Printers	Broadband Routers	Desktop Computers	Total Units	Total Hours
1	3	6	6	15	42
2	0	8	7	15	40
3	3	3	8	14	41
4	1	3	13	17	46
5	10	7	5	22	50
6	4	9	4	17	43
7	4	9	4	17	43
8	4	5	6	15	44
9	1	5	11	17	48
10	7	5	6	18	44
Total				167	441

Required

Assuming he wants to work an average of 40 hours per week, what should Dan do?

Solutions to Review Problems

Review 15-1—Solution

Fixed costs are easily identified. They are the same at each activity level. Variable and mixed costs are determined by dividing the total costs for an item at two activity levels by the corresponding units of activity. The quotients of the variable cost items will be identical at both activity levels. The quotients of the mixed costs will differ, being lower at the higher activity level because the fixed costs are being spread over a larger number of units.

Cost	April	May	Behavior
Cost of food sold.	$1,575/2,100 = 0.750	$2,025/2,700 = 0.750	Variable
Wages and salaries	$1,525/2,100 = 0.726	$1,675/2,700 = 0.620	Mixed
Rent on building	NA	NA	Fixed
Depreciation on equipment.	NA	NA	Fixed
Utilities	$710/2,100 = 0.338	$770/2,700 = 0.285	Mixed
Supplies	$225/2,100 = 0.107	$255/2,700 = 0.094	Mixed
Miscellaneous.	$113/2,100 = 0.054	$131/2,700 = 0.049	Mixed

Review 15-2—Solution

a. Variable cost
b. Mixed cost
c. Committed fixed cost
d. Variable cost
e. Variable cost
f. Discretionary fixed cost
g. Fixed cost (Without knowing the purpose of renting the car, the cost cannot be classified as committed or discretionary.)
h. Mixed cost
i. Variable cost
j. Discretionary fixed cost

Review 15-3—Solution

a. The cost of food sold was classified as a variable cost. Hence, the cost of food may be determined by dividing the total cost of food sold at either observation by the corresponding number of sandwiches.

$$b = \frac{\$1,575 \text{ total variable costs}}{2,100 \text{ units}}$$

$$= \$0.75X$$

Wages and salaries were previously classified as a mixed cost. Hence, the cost of wages and salaries is determined using the high-low method.

(variable cost) $$b = \frac{\$1,675 - \$1,525}{2,700 - 2,100}$$

$$= 0.25X$$

(fixed cost) $$a = \$1,525 \text{ total cost} - (\$0.25 \times 2,100) \text{ variable cost}$$

$$= \$1,000$$

Rent on building was classified as a fixed cost.

$$a = \$1,500$$

Total monthly costs most likely follow a mixed cost behavior pattern. Hence, they can be determined using the high-low method.

$$b = \frac{\$6,556 - \$5,848}{2,700 - 2,100}$$

$$= \$1.18X$$

$$a = \$5,848 - (\$1.18 \times 2,100)$$

$$= \$3,370$$

$$\text{Total costs} = \$3,370 + \$1.18X$$

where

$$X = \text{unit sales}$$

b. and *c.*

Volume	Total Costs	Average Cost per Sandwich
1,000.	$3,370 + ($1.18 × 1,000) = $4,550	$\frac{\$4,550}{\$1,000} = \$4.550$
2,000.	$3,370 + ($1.18 × 2,000) = $5,730	$\frac{\$5,730}{\$2,000} = \$2.865$

The average costs differ at 1,000 and 2,000 units because the fixed costs are being spread over a different number of units. The larger the number of units, the smaller the average fixed cost per unit.

Review 15-4—Solution

Some common activity drivers for stating volume of activity in a manufacturing operation might include direct labor hours, machine hours, units of material produced, and units of finished product. The selection of the most appropriate basis requires judgment and professional experience. The relationship between the activity cost driver and the cost must seem logical and the activity data must be available.

Review 15-5—Solution

1. Unit-level
2. Store-level
3. Store-level
4. Unit-level
5. Customer-level
6. Order-level

Module 16

Cost-Volume-Profit Analysis and Planning

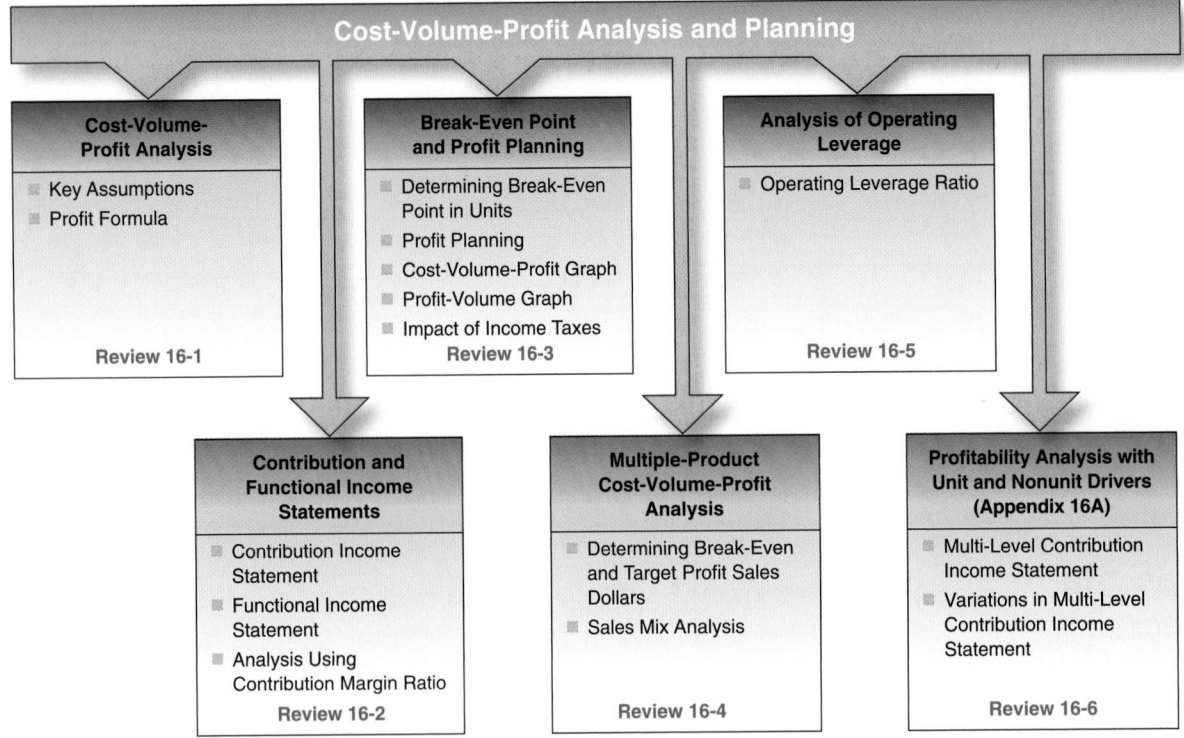

Based in Cerritos, California, Razor USA, LLC designs and manufactures an array of rideable devices ranging from kick scooters to self-balancing hoverboards. Razor, as it is commonly known, was founded in 2000 and has experienced tremendous growth. Razor's first product, the model A kick scooter, sold over 5 million units within six months of its introduction and won the 2000 Toy of The Year award. By 2010, Razor had sold over 35 million scooters. Razor built on its kick scooter success and expanded its product line to include electric scooters, a modern version of the Scream Machine™, go-karts, electric motor bikes, and self-balancing hoverboards.

Razor is redefining the "ride on" category of toys and is well positioned for continued success, but how much should it charge for its products? How many units does Razor need to sell to break even? How many units does it need to sell to reach its target profit? These are questions that managers within Razor must answer.

Profitability analysis involves examining the relations between revenues, costs, and profits. Performing profitability analysis requires an understanding of selling prices and the behavior of activity cost drivers. Profitability analysis is widely used to make better decisions regarding existing or proposed products or services. Typically, it is performed before decisions are finalized in the operating budget for a future period.

If Razor is to accomplish its goals, it must generate profits, meaning that its revenues must exceed its costs. Razor's manufacturing processes consume energy and raw materials. The price of these inputs changes over time. By decomposing Razor's costs into its variable and fixed components, the company can perform profitability analyses to determine where to direct its future efforts. In fact, Razor can utilize the tools presented in this module to determine how much revenue it has to generate to achieve a desired profit.

Road Map

LO	Learning Objective | Topics	Page	eLecture	Guided Example	Assign-ments
LO1	**Describe the uses and limitations of traditional cost-volume-profit analysis.** CVP Analysis :: Key Assumptions :: Profit Formula	16-3	e16–1	Review 16-1	39
LO2	**Prepare and contrast contribution and functional income statements.** Contribution Income Statement :: Contribution Margin :: Unit Contribution :: Contribution Margin Ratio	16-7	e16–2	Review 16-2	17, 29, 41
LO3	**Apply cost-volume-profit analysis to find a break-even point and for preliminary profit planning.** Break-Even :: Profit Planning :: Cost-Volume-Profit Graph :: Profit-Volume Graph :: Impact of Taxes	16-9	e16–3	Review 16-3	11, 12, 13, 14, 15, 17, 18, 19, 20, 21, 22, 24, 25, 28, 29, 30, 31, 32, 33, 34, 36, 37, 40, 41
LO4	**Analyze the profitability and sales mix of a multiple-product firm.** Break-Even and Target Profit Sales Dollars :: Sales Mix Analysis	16-15	e16–4	Review 16-4	16, 23, 34, 35, 37, 38
LO5	**Apply operating leverage ratio to assess opportunities for profit and the risks of loss.** Operating Leverage :: Operating Leverage Ratio	16-18	e16–5	Review 16-5	21, 22, 40
LO6	**Perform profitability analysis with unit and nonunit cost drivers (Appendix 16A).** Multi-Level Contribution Income Statement :: Cost Hierarchy and Contribution Income Statement	16-21	e16–6	Review 16-6	26, 27

What fee should we charge for a subscription to our services? How many units do we need to sell to break even? How many units do we need to sell to reach our target profit?

Profitability analysis involves examining the relationships among revenues, costs, and profits. Performing profitability analysis requires an understanding of selling prices and the behavior of activity cost drivers. Profitability analysis is widely used to make better decisions regarding existing or proposed products or services. Typically, it is performed before decisions are finalized in the operating budget for a future period.

This module introduces basic approaches to profitability analysis and planning. We consider single-product, multiple-product, and service organizations; income taxes; sales mix; and the effects of cost structure on the relation between profit potential and the risk of loss.

Cost-Volume-Profit Analysis

LO1
Describe the uses and limitations of traditional cost-volume-profit analysis.

Cost-volume-profit (CVP) analysis is a technique used to examine the relationships among the total volume of an independent variable, total costs, total revenues, and profits for a time period (typically a quarter or year). With CVP analysis, volume refers to a single activity cost driver, such as unit sales, that is assumed to correlate with changes in revenues, costs, and profits.

Cost-volume-profit analysis is useful in the early stages of planning because it provides an easily understood framework for discussing planning issues and organizing relevant data. CVP analysis is widely used by for-profit as well as not-for-profit organizations. It is equally applicable to service, merchandising, and manufacturing firms.

In for-profit organizations, CVP analysis is used to answer such questions as these: How many photocopies must the local **Staples** store produce to earn a profit of $80,000? At what dollar sales volume will **Whole Foods**' total revenues and total costs be equal? What profit will **Target** earn at an annual sales volume of $75 billion? What will happen to the profit of **Panera Bread** if there is a 20% increase in the cost of food and a 10% increase in the selling price of meals? The Research Insight box on the following page indicates how the role of managerial accounting is expanding. With greater availability of data, managers can efficiently perform more analyses to help guide CVP decisions.

In not-for-profit organizations, CVP analysis is used to establish service levels, plan fund-raising activities, and determine funding requirements. How many meals can the downtown **Salvation Army** serve with an annual budget of $600,000? How many tickets must be sold for the benefit concert to raise $20,000? Given the current cost structure, current tuition rates, and projected enrollments, how much money must **DePaul University** raise from other sources?

Key Assumptions

CVP analysis is subject to a number of assumptions. Although these assumptions do not negate the usefulness of CVP models, especially for a single product or service, they do suggest the need for further analysis before plans are finalized. Among the more important assumptions are

1. *All costs are classified as fixed or variable.* This assumption is most reasonable when analyzing the profitability of a specific event (such as a concert) or the profitability of an organization that produces a single product or service on a continuous basis.

2. *The total cost function is linear within the relevant range.* This assumption is often valid within a relevant range of normal operations, but over the entire range of possible activity, changes in efficiency are likely to result in a nonlinear cost function.

3. *The total revenue function is linear within the relevant range.* Unit selling prices are assumed constant over the range of possible volumes. This implies a purely competitive market for final products or services. In some economic models in which demand responds to price changes, the revenue function is nonlinear. In these situations, the linear approximation is accurate only within a limited range of activity.

4. *The analysis is for a single product, or the sales mix of multiple products is constant.* The **sales mix** refers to the relative portion of unit or dollar sales derived from each product or service. If products have different selling prices and costs, changes in the mix affect CVP model results.

5. *There is only one cost driver: unit or sales dollar volume.* In a complex organization it is seldom possible to represent the multitude of factors that drive cost with a single cost driver.

Research Insight ■ Data-Driven Planning Central to Management Accounting

The role of management accounting is expanding to include planning driven by data science. This work is often called financial planning and analysis (FP&A) and is used widely enough that a professional accrediting program has been launched by the **Association for Financial Professionals (AFP)**.

The central function of the FP&A group within a company is to inform decisions with data. **GoDaddy Inc.** called on its FP&A group to help guide the domain-name seller's international expansion. The team developed purpose-built growth metrics to help executives allocate marketing dollars across the 40 countries where GoDaddy does business. By finding the correct metric to drive resource decisions, GoDaddy was able to increase the share of sales from foreign markets to 26% of total sales. Its CFO claims that the FP&A group's contribution tripled foreign growth.

At **Dunkin Brands Group Inc.**, the FP&A group has influence in every department, helping managers and employees across the organization find ways to improve processes and practices. Dunkin's 36-member FP&A team took on the key job of mining loyalty data to find ways to get customers back into the store throughout the day and increasing the amount that the customers spent. This effort led to a 2.2% growth in same-store sales over nine months.

While Dunkin is deeply committed to FP&A (its CFO was the VP of FP&A), other firms are adopting this approach more slowly. The consulting firm CEB notes that 61% of FP&A directors do not feel that top managers take their contributions seriously. As this perception changes, accountants trained in management accounting principles will have the chance to influence companies with their analyses.

Source: Alix Stuart, "Metrics Sell Doughnuts and More," *Wall Street Journal*, December 21, 2015.

Business Insight ■ Amazon Explores New Customer Experience for In Store Shopping

Amazon owns **Whole Foods** and is now exploring checkout-free convenience stores. Customers can go to an Amazon Go store and make in-store purchases. This shopping experience is truly unique in that shoppers do not "check out." They merely walk in, pick out what they want, and walk out. Amazon uses technology that can detect when products are moved between the shelf and the cart; and when you leave the store, your Amazon account is charged and you are sent a receipt.

The grocery store industry is already a low margin industry. How much will this cost? Although some overhead costs will go down such as in-store employees, the cost of creating and maintaining the complex technology required for this to work well is not cheap, and the overall costs will likely be higher than those of a traditional bricks-and-mortar store. Will customers pay higher prices for the convenience of not having to wait in lines and not having to go through a checkout process?

Much is still to be determined, and in order for this to be a successful endeavor, Amazon must closely analyze its cost, volume, and profit implications. Regardless, this will be a significant learning experiment for the company.

Sources: Rob Lenihan, "Amazon Is Said to Plan Cashierless Go Supermarkets, Pop-Ups as Soon as Q1," https://www.thestreet.com/investing/stocks/amazon-looking-to-open-cashier-free-go-supermarkets-pop-up-stores-15174680?puc=yahoo&cm_ven=YAHOO&yptr=yahoo, November 20, 2019.
Rich Hardy, "Is Amazon Go's Checkout-Free Store the Future of Retail, or just an Expensive Gimmick?" https://newatlas.com/amazon-go-future-retail-publicity-stunt/53077/, January 23, 2018.

When applied to a single product (such as pounds of potato chips), service (such as the number of pages printed), or event (such as the number of tickets sold to a banquet), it is reasonable to assume the single independent variable is the cost driver. The total costs associated with the single product, service, or event during a specific time period are often determined by this single activity cost driver.

Although cost-volume-profit analysis is often used to understand the overall operations of an organization or business segment, accuracy decreases as the scope of operations being analyzed increases.

Profit Formula

The profit associated with a product, service, or event is equal to the difference between total revenues and total costs as follows:

$$\pi = R - Y$$

where

$$\pi = \textbf{Profit}$$
$$R = \textbf{Total revenues}$$
$$Y = \textbf{Total costs}$$

The revenues are a function of the unit sales volume and the unit selling price, while total costs for a time period are a function of the fixed costs per period and the unit variable costs as follows:

$$R = pX$$
$$Y = a + bX$$

where

$$p = \textbf{Unit selling price}$$
$$a = \textbf{Fixed costs}$$
$$b = \textbf{Unit variable costs}$$
$$X = \textbf{Unit sales}$$

The equation for profit can then be expanded to include the above details of the total revenue and total cost equations as follows:

$$\pi = pX - (a + bX)$$

Using information on the selling price, fixed costs per period, and variable costs per unit, this formula is used to predict profit at any specified activity level.

To illustrate, assume that **Razor**'s only product is a standard kick scooter that it manufactures and sells to merchandisers at $60 per completed scooter. Applying inventory minimization techniques, Razor does not maintain inventories of raw materials or finished goods. Instead, newly purchased raw materials are delivered directly to the factory, and finished goods are loaded directly onto trucks for shipment. Razor's variable and fixed costs follow.

1. **Direct materials** refer to the cost of the primary raw materials converted into finished goods. Because the consumption of raw materials increases as the quantity of goods produced increases, *direct materials represents a variable cost*. Razor's raw materials consist primarily of nuts and bolts, rubber wheels, bearings, steel frames, and packaging materials. Razor also treats the costs of purchasing, receiving, and inspecting these materials as part of the cost of direct materials. Assume that all together, these costs are $20 per completed scooter.

2. **Direct labor** refers to wages earned by production employees for the time they spend working on the conversion of raw materials into finished goods. Based on Razor's manufacturing procedures, *direct labor represents a variable cost*. Further assume these costs are $10 per completed scooter.

3. **Variable manufacturing overhead** includes all other variable costs associated with converting raw materials into finished goods. Assume Razor's variable manufacturing overhead costs include the costs of lubricants for cutting and packaging machines, electricity to operate these machines, and the cost to move materials between receiving and shipping. These costs are $3 per completed scooter.

4. **Variable selling and administrative costs** include all variable costs other than those directly associated with converting raw materials into finished goods. Assume at Razor, these costs include sales commissions and transportation of finished goods to merchandisers. These costs are $5 per completed scooter.

5. **Fixed manufacturing overhead** includes all fixed costs associated with converting raw materials into finished goods. Suppose Razor's fixed manufacturing costs include the depreciation, property taxes, and insurance on buildings and machines used for manufacturing, the salaries of manufacturing supervisors, and the fixed portion of electricity used to light the factory. Further assume these costs are $35,000 per month.

6. **Fixed selling and administrative costs** include all fixed costs other than those directly associated with converting raw materials into finished goods. These costs include the salaries of Razor's divisional manager and many other staff personnel such as accounting and marketing. Also included are depreciation, property taxes, insurance on facilities used for administrative purposes, and any related utilities costs. Assume these costs are $15,000 per month.

Razor's hypothetical variable and fixed costs are summarized here.

Variable Costs per Scooter			Fixed Costs per Month	
Manufacturing...............			Manufacturing overhead..........	$35,000
Direct materials..............	$20		Selling and administrative.........	15,000
Direct labor.................	10		Total	$50,000
Manufacturing overhead........	3	$33		
Selling and administrative.........		5		
Total		$38		

The cost estimation techniques discussed in Module 15 can be used to determine many detailed costs. Least-squares regression, for example, might be used to determine the variable and monthly fixed amount of electricity used in manufacturing. Assume Razor manufactures and sells a single product on a continuous basis with all sales to merchandisers under standing contracts. Therefore, it is reasonable to assume that in the short run, Razor's total monthly costs respond to a single cost driver, scooters sold. Combining all this information, Razor's profit equation is assumed to be

$$\text{Profit} = \$60X - (\$50,000 + \$38X)$$

where

$$X = \text{scooters sold}$$

Using this equation, Razor's profit at a volume of 5,400 units is $68,800, computed as ($60 × 5,400) − [$50,000 + ($38 × 5,400)].

LO1 Review 16-1

Benchmark Paper Company's only product is high-quality photocopy paper that it manufactures and sells to wholesale distributors at $14 per carton. Applying inventory minimization techniques, Benchmark does not maintain inventories of raw materials or finished goods. Newly purchased raw materials are delivered directly to the factory, and finished goods are loaded directly onto trucks for shipment. Benchmark's variable and fixed costs follow:

Variable Costs per Carton			Fixed Costs per Month	
Manufacturing			Manufacturing overhead...........	$ 2,000
Direct materials..............	$1.25		Selling and administrative..........	8,000
Direct labor................	0.50		Total	$10,000
Manufacturing overhead.......	2.50	$4.25		
Selling and administrative.......		1.00		
Total		$5.25		

Required

a. Determine Benchmark's profit equation.

b. Using your equation, calculate Benchmark's profit at a volume of 6,200 cartons.

Solution on p. 16-36.

Contribution and Functional Income Statements

Contribution Income Statement

LO2 Prepare and contrast contribution and functional income statements.

To provide more detailed information on anticipated or actual financial results at a particular sales volume, a contribution income statement is often prepared. Razor's hypothetical contribution income statement for a volume of 5,400 units is in Exhibit 16.1. In a **contribution income statement**, costs are classified according to behavior as variable or fixed, and the **contribution margin** (the difference between total revenues and total variable costs) that goes toward covering fixed costs and providing a profit is emphasized.

Exhibit 16.1 ■ Contribution Income Statement

RAZOR COMPANY Contribution Income Statement For a Monthly Volume of 5,400 Scooters		
Sales (5,400 × $60)		$324,000
Less variable costs		
Direct materials (5,400 × $20)	$108,000	
Direct labor (5,400 × $10)	54,000	
Manufacturing overhead (5,400 × $3)	16,200	
Selling and administrative (5,400 × $5)	27,000	(205,200)
Contribution margin		118,800
Less fixed costs		
Manufacturing overhead	35,000	
Selling and administrative	15,000	(50,000)
Profit		$ 68,800

Functional Income Statement

Contrast the contribution income statement in Exhibit 16.1 with Razor's hypothetical income statement in Exhibit 16.2. This statement is called a **functional income statement** because costs are classified according to function (rather than behavior), such as manufacturing, selling, and administrative. This is the type of income statement typically included in corporate annual reports.

A problem with a functional income statement is the difficulty of relating it to the profit formula in which costs are classified according to behavior rather than function. The relationship between sales volume, costs, and profits is not readily apparent in a functional income statement. Consequently, we emphasize contribution income statements because they provide better information to internal decision makers.

Exhibit 16.2 ■ Functional Income Statement

RAZOR COMPANY Functional Income Statement For a Monthly Volume of 5,400 Cartons		
Sales (5,400 × $60)		$324,000
Less cost of goods sold		
Direct materials (5,400 × $20)	$108,000	
Direct labor (5,400 × $10)	54,000	
Variable manufacturing overhead (5,400 × $3)	16,200	
Fixed manufacturing overhead	35,000	(213,200)
Gross margin		110,800
Less other expenses		
Variable selling and administrative (5,400 × $5)	27,000	
Fixed selling and administrative	15,000	(42,000)
Profit		$ 68,800

Analysis Using Contribution Margin Ratio

While the contribution income statement (shown in Exhibit 16.1) presents information on total sales revenue, total variable costs, and so forth, it is sometimes useful to present information on a per-unit or portion of sales basis.

	Total	Per Unit	Ratio to Sales
Sales (5,400 units)	$324,000	$60	1.0000
Variable costs.	(205,200)	38	0.6333*
Contribution margin	118,800	$22	0.3667
Fixed costs	(50,000)		
Profit.	$ 68,800		

* Rounded

The per-unit information assists in short-range planning. The **unit contribution margin** is the difference between the unit selling price and the unit variable costs. It is the amount, $22 in this case, that each unit contributes toward covering fixed costs and earning a profit.

The contribution margin is widely used in **sensitivity analysis** (the study of the responsiveness of a model to changes in one or more of its independent variables). Razor's income statement is an economic model of the firm, and the unit contribution margin indicates how sensitive Razor's income model is to changes in unit sales. If, for example, sales increase by 100 scooters per month, the increase in profit is readily determined by multiplying the 100-scooter increase in sales by the $22 unit contribution margin as follows:

100 (scooter sales increase) × $22 (unit contribution margin) = $2,200 (profit increase)

There is no increase in fixed costs, so the new profit level becomes $71,000 ($68,800 + $2,200) per month.

When expressed as a ratio to sales, the sales margin is identified as the **contribution margin ratio**. It is the portion of each dollar of sales revenue contributed toward covering fixed costs and earning a profit. In the abbreviated income statement above, the portion of each dollar of sales revenue contributed toward covering fixed costs and earning a profit is $0.3667 ($118,800 ÷ $324,000). This is Razor's assumed contribution margin ratio. If sales revenue increases by $6,000 per month, the increase in profits is computed as follows:

$6,000 (sales increase) × 0.3667 (contribution margin ratio) = $2,200 (profit increase)

The contribution margin ratio is especially useful in situations involving several products or when unit sales information is not available.

Review 16-2 LO2

Assume Solo Cup Company produces 16-ounce beverage containers. Further assume Solo sells the cups for $40 per box of 50 containers. Variable and fixed costs follow:

Variable Costs per Box			Fixed Costs per Month	
Manufacturing			Manufacturing overhead.	$15,000
Direct materials.	$15		Selling and administrative.	10,000
Direct labor	3		Total	$25,000
Manufacturing overhead.	10	$28		
Selling and administrative.		2		
Total		$30		

Suppose in September, Solo produced and sold 3,000 boxes of beverage containers.

continued

continued from previous page

Required
a. Prepare a contribution income statement for September.

Solution on p. 16-36.   b. Determine Solo's unit contribution margin and contribution margin ratio.

Break-Even Point and Profit Planning

LO3
Apply cost-volume-profit analysis to find a break-even point and for preliminary profit planning.

The **break-even point** occurs at the unit or dollar sales volume when total revenues equal total costs. The break-even point is of great interest to management. Until break-even sales are reached, the product, service, event, or business segment of interest operates at a loss. Beyond this point, increasing levels of profits are achieved. Also, management often wants to know the **margin of safety**, the amount by which actual or planned sales exceed the break-even point. Other questions of interest include the probability of exceeding the break-even sales volume and the effect of some proposed change on the break-even point.

Determining Break-Even Point in Units

In determining the break-even point, the equation for total revenues is set equal to the equation for total costs and then solved for the break-even unit sales volume. Using the general equations for total revenues and total costs, the following results are obtained. Setting total revenues equal to total costs:

$$\text{Total revenues} = \text{Total costs}$$
$$pX = a + bX$$

Solving for the break-even unit sales volume:

$$pX - bX = a$$
$$(p - b)X = a$$
$$X = a/(p - b)$$

In words:

$$\text{Break-even unit sales volume} = \frac{\text{Fixed costs}}{\text{Selling price per unit} - \text{Variable costs per unit}}$$

Because the denominator is the unit contribution margin, the break-even point is also computed by dividing fixed costs by the unit contribution margin:

$$\text{Break-even unit sales volume} = \frac{\text{Fixed costs}}{\text{Unit contribution margin}}$$

With an assumed $22 unit contribution margin and fixed costs of $50,000 per month, Razor's break-even point is 2,273[*] units per month ($50,000 ÷ $22). Stated another way, at a $22 per-unit contribution margin, 2,273 units of sales are required to cover $50,000 of fixed costs. With a break-even point of 2,273 units, the monthly margin of safety for a sales volume of 5,400 units is 3,127 units (5,400 expected unit sales − 2,273 break-even unit sales). The expected profit at a sales volume of 5,400 units is $68,794 (3,127 unit margin of safety × $22 unit contribution margin). (The difference between the calculated $68,794 and the profit of $68,800 in Exhibit 16.1 and 3.2 is due to rounding.)

[*] Rounded UP to the nearest whole unit

The break-even point concept is applicable to a wide variety of business and personal planning situations. The following Research Insight box illustrates how a personal financial planner might use break-even point concepts to assist a client making a retirement decision.

Research Insight   ■   Determining the Cash Break-Even Point for Delaying Retirement

Social Security retirement benefits are a function of years worked, contributions to the Social Security System, and the age at which the recipient files for Social Security retirement benefits. Currently, persons retiring at age 67 are entitled to "full" retirement benefits, while those retiring at age 62 are eligible for only 70% of "full" benefits. A person contemplating retirement at age 62 might ask: (1) how large is the reduction in benefits and (2) what is the break-even age at which the benefits from delaying retirement until age 67 equals the cumulative benefits from retiring at age 62?

An individual with the analytic skills obtained from a managerial accounting course can readily determine the answers to these questions after consulting the Social Security website www.ssa.gov. Others might consult a personal financial planner.

(1)   Assume the individual's full Social Security retirement benefits at age 67 are $2,265 per month. If that person started receiving benefits at age 62, the monthly benefits are reduced by 30% or $679.50 ($2,265 × 0.30) to $1,585.50.

(2)   With retirement at age 62, the early retiree would receive total benefits of $95,130 ($1,585.50 × 12 months × 5 years) by age 67, the normal "full" age. Treating this as a fixed amount to be recovered by the subsequent incremental monthly benefits of $679.50 from delaying the receipt of monthly benefits to age 67, the break-even age is computed as follows:

Months beyond age 67 = $95,130/$679.50 = 140 months or 11.67 years.
Hence, the break-even age is 78.67 years (67 + 11.67).

The analysis suggests that life expectancy is an important consideration in deciding when to start taking Social Security benefits.

Note that this analysis does not consider any return on the $95,130 that might be earned by investing the benefits received during early retirement. Such returns would increase the break-even age. Nor does it consider the lost wages that could have been earned between age 62 and age 67.

Source: www.ssa.gov

Profit Planning

Establishing profit objectives is an important part of planning in for-profit organizations. Profit objectives are stated in many ways. They can be set as a percentage of last year's profits, as a percentage of total assets at the start of the current year, or as a percentage of owners' equity. They might be based on a profit trend, or they might be expressed as a percentage of sales. The economic outlook for the firm's products as well as anticipated changes in products, costs, and technology are also considered in establishing profit objectives.

Before incorporating profit plans into a detailed budget, it is useful to obtain some preliminary information on the feasibility of those plans. Cost-volume-profit analysis is one way of doing this. By manipulating cost-volume-profit relationships, management can determine the sales volume corresponding to a desired profit. Management might then evaluate the feasibility of this sales volume. If the profit plans are feasible, a complete budget might be developed for this activity level. The required sales volume might be infeasible because of market conditions or because the required volume exceeds production or service capacity, in which case management must lower its profit objective or consider other ways of achieving it. Alternatively, the required sales volume might be less than management believes the firm is capable of selling, in which case management might raise its profit objective.

Assume that Razor's management desires to know the unit sales volume required to achieve a monthly profit of $75,000. Using the profit formula, the required unit sales volume is determined by setting profits equal to $75,000 and solving for X, the unit sales volume.

$$\text{Profit = Total revenues – Total costs}$$
$$\$75,000 = \$60X - (\$50,000 + \$38X)$$

Solving for X

$$\$60X - \$38X = \$50,000 + \$75,000$$
$$X = (\$50,000 + \$75,000) \div \$22$$
$$= 5,682 \text{ units (rounded UP to the nearest whole unit)}$$

The total contribution must cover the desired profit as well as the fixed costs. Hence, the target sales volume required to achieve a desired profit is computed as the fixed costs plus the desired profit, all divided by the unit contribution margin.

$$\text{Target unit sales volume} = \frac{\text{Fixed costs} + \text{Desired profit}}{\text{Unit contribution margin}}$$

The Business Insight box below discusses how Enjoy Technology plans to turn a profit through increased sales volume.

Business Insight ■   White-Glove, Same-Day Delivery

Ron Johnson definitely understands what attracts consumers. He helped Target create its "cheap-chic" identity and develop its popular product partnerships with designers and then moved to Apple where he pioneered the successful Genius Bars and free classes available at company retail stores.

He's now applying his knowledge of consumer preferences, combining the convenience of online shopping with the personal attention received at brick-and-mortar stores. Currently, Enjoy Technology, a company he co-founded in 2015, works with major telecom carriers [AT&T (US), British Telcom (UK), and Rogers (Canada)] to offer free same-day delivery and setup of phones and other products to consumers in their homes or another location of their choice.

In an interview, Johnson said: "I've been watching e-commerce grow for 20 years. Every product has the same last mile. Apple creates a premium last-mile store. How should a premium brand go to market for customers buying online? We extend that online-purchasing experience and bring everything you do in the store to the home. It's smart last mile."

Enjoy employees visit on average seven to eight AT&T customers a day and in over 50% of those visits, customers have purchased additional products, services, or warranty plans. Enjoy gets paid a percentage of the additional profit created by Enjoy employees.

Johnson expects to turn a profit in 2020 when sales volume is expected to exceed the break-even point.

Source: Andria Cheng, "Ron Johnson Made Apple Stores the Envy of Retail and Target Hip, But This Startup May Be His Crowning Achievement," *Forbes*, January 17, 2020.

Cost-Volume-Profit Graph

A **cost-volume-profit graph** illustrates the relationships among activity volume, total revenues, total costs, and profits. Its usefulness comes from highlighting the break-even point and depicting revenue, cost, and profit relationships over a range of activity. This representation allows management to view the relative amount of important variables at any graphed volume. Razor's hypothetical monthly CVP graph is in Exhibit 16.3. Total revenues and total costs are measured on the vertical axis, with unit sales measured on the horizontal axis. Separate lines are drawn for total variable costs, total costs, and total revenues. The vertical distance between the total revenue and the total cost lines depicts the amount of profit or loss at a given volume. Losses occur when total revenues are less than total costs; profits occur when total revenues exceed total costs.

The total contribution margin is shown by the difference between the total revenue and the total variable cost lines. Observe that as unit sales increase, the contribution margin first goes to cover the fixed costs. Beyond the break-even point, any additional contribution margin provides a profit.

Profit-Volume Graph

In cost-volume-profit graphs, profits are represented by the difference between total revenues and total costs. When management is primarily interested in the impact of changes in sales volume on profits and less interested in the related revenues and costs, a **profit-volume graph** is sometimes used. A profit-volume graph illustrates the relationship between volume and profits; it does not show revenues and costs. Profits are read directly from a profit-volume graph, rather than being computed as the difference between total revenues and total costs. Profit-volume graphs are developed by plotting either unit sales or total revenues on the horizontal axis.

The Business Insight box below discusses that GlaxoSmithKline expects a future reduction in its process costs. This would lead to a reduction in its required sales to breakeven.

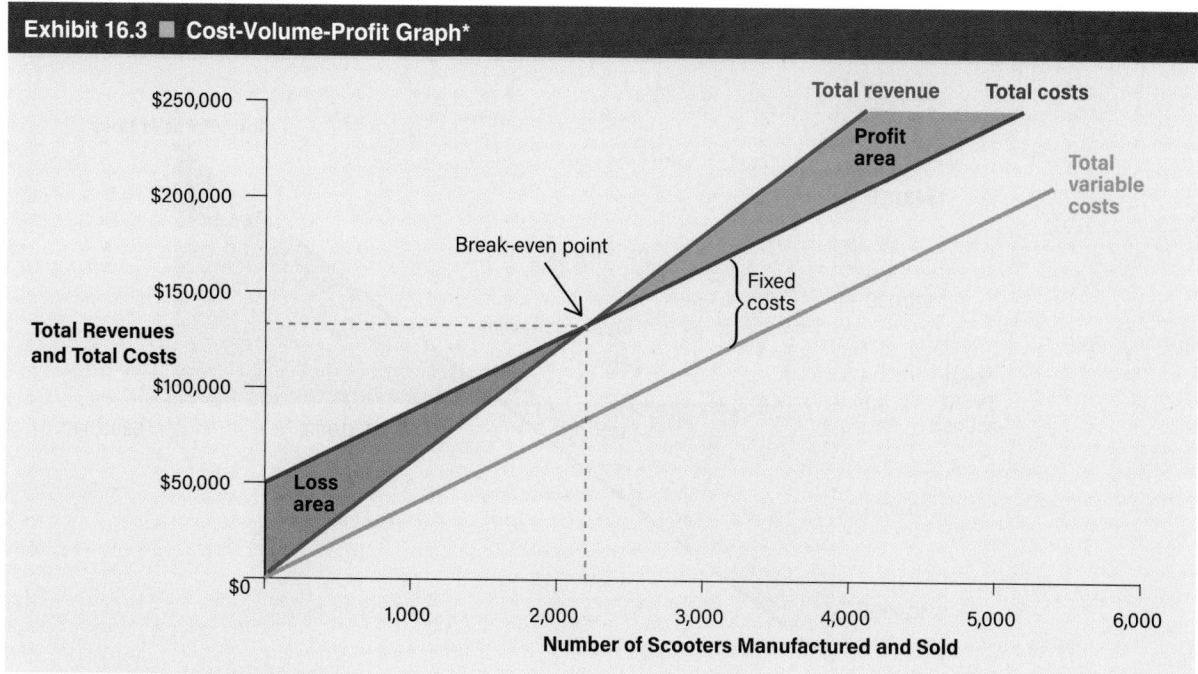

Exhibit 16.3 ■ Cost-Volume-Profit Graph*

* The three lines are developed as follows:

1. **Total variable costs** line is drawn between the origin and total variable costs at an arbitrary sales volume. At 3,000 units, total variable costs are $114,000 (3,000 × $38).

2. **Total revenues** line is drawn through the origin and a point representing total revenues at some arbitrary sales volume. At 3,000 units, Razor's hypothetical total revenues are $180,000 (3,000 × $60).

3. **Total costs** line is computed by layering fixed costs, $50,000 in this case, on top of total variable costs. This gives a vertical axis intercept of $50,000 and total costs of $164,000 at 3,000 units.

Razor's assumed monthly profit-volume graph is presented in Exhibit 16.4. Profit or loss is measured on the vertical axis, and volume (total revenues) is measured on the horizontal axis, which intersects the vertical axis at zero profit. A single line, representing total profit, is drawn intersecting the vertical axis at zero sales volume with a loss equal to the fixed costs. The profit line crosses the horizontal axis at the break-even sales volume. The profit or loss at any volume is depicted by the vertical difference between the profit line and the horizontal axis. The slope of the profit line is determined by the contribution margin. The greater the contribution margin ratio or the unit contribution margin, the steeper the slope of the profit line.

Business Insight ■ Drugmaker Looks to Bioelectronics to Change Cost Structure

At **Galvani Bioelectronics** (a partnership between **GlaxoSmithKline (GSK)** and **Verily Life Sciences** (a subsidiary of **Alphabet, Inc.**), treatments are not pills or serums delivering doses of chemicals to the entire body but rice-sized devices attached to nerve bundles. The innovation here is treating illness as a programming problem rather than as a chemical problem. The nervous system can be viewed as a communication system carrying messages about the body's operations. To the extent that problematic messages can be edited, many health problems can be solved by implanting and programming these devices. In addition to finding new solutions to old pathologies, GSK hopes to eventually change the cost structure of drug companies. GSK has started a venture capital effort worth $50 million that funds 100 independent researchers and 30 employees.

Development costs are exploding for conventional molecular drug therapies. The average drug takes 10 years and $2.6 billion to bring to market. GSK is betting that basic engineering innovations in bioelectronics will allow new therapies to be tested and implemented more quickly and at lower cost. This could potentially change some therapies into software problems rather than manufacturing problems, eliminating many of the process costs involved in manufacturing drugs under the current model. These investments remain risky, but GSK is hoping that its investment in this technology changes the cost structure of the drug business.

Source: Matthew Campbell, "Only One Big Drugmaker Is Working on a Nanobot Cure," *Bloomberg Businessweek*, June 9, 2016.

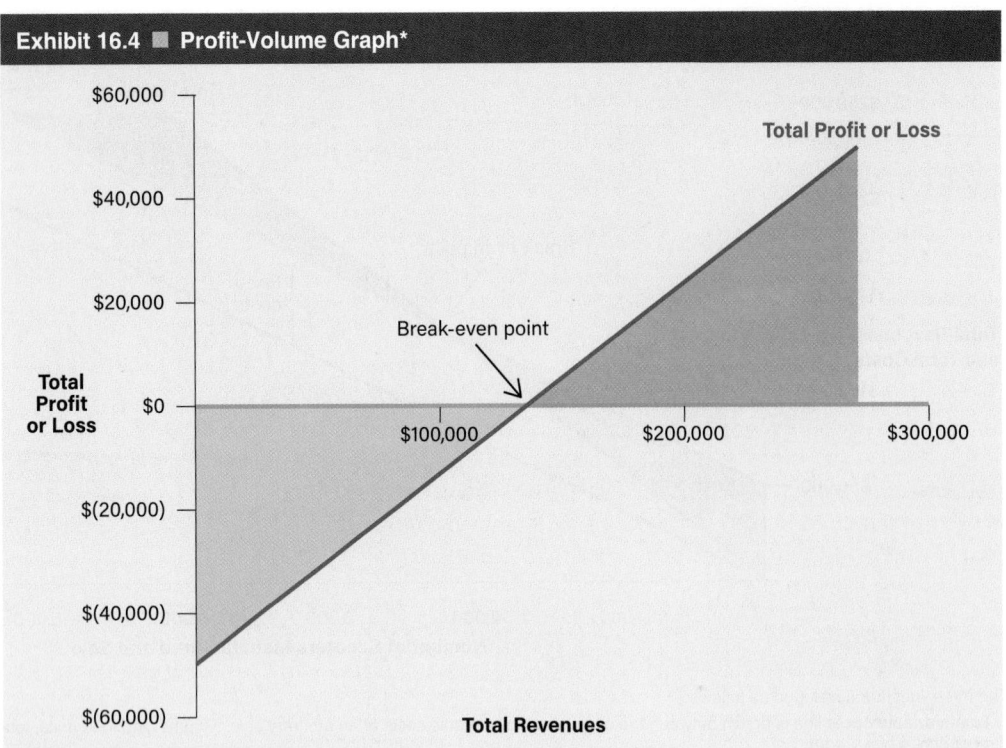

Exhibit 16.4 ■ Profit-Volume Graph*

* The profit line is drawn by determining and plotting profit or loss at two different volumes and then drawing a straight line through the plotted values. Perhaps the easiest values to select are the loss at a volume of zero (with a loss equal to the fixed costs) and the volume at which the profit line crosses the horizontal axis (this is the break-even volume).

Impact of Income Taxes

Income taxes are imposed on individuals and for-profit organizations by government agencies. The amount of an individual's or organization's income tax is determined by laws that specify the calculation of taxable income (the income subject to tax) and the calculation of the amount of tax on taxable income. Income taxes are computed as a percentage of taxable income, with increases in taxable income usually subject to progressively higher tax rates. The laws governing the computation of taxable income differ in many ways from the accounting principles that guide the computation of accounting income. Consequently, taxable income and accounting income are seldom the same.

In the early stages of profit planning, income taxes are sometimes incorporated in CVP models by assuming that taxable income and accounting income are identical and that the tax rate is constant. Although these assumptions are seldom true, they are useful for assisting management in developing an early prediction of the sales volume required to earn a desired after-tax profit. Once management has developed a general plan, this early prediction should be refined with the advice of tax experts.

Assuming taxes are imposed at a constant rate per dollar of before-tax profit, income taxes are computed as before-tax profit multiplied by the tax rate. After-tax profit is equal to before-tax profit minus income taxes.

$$\textbf{After-tax profit} = \textbf{Before-tax profit} - (\textbf{Before-tax profit} \times \textbf{Tax rate})$$

After-tax profit can also be expressed as before-tax profit times 1 minus the tax rate.

$$\textbf{After-tax profit} = \textbf{Before-tax profit} \times (\textbf{1} - \textbf{Tax rate})$$

This formula can be rearranged to isolate before-tax profit as follows:

$$\textbf{Before-tax profit} = \frac{\textbf{After-tax profit}}{(\textbf{1} - \textbf{Tax rate})}$$

Since all costs and revenues in the profit formula are expressed on a before-tax basis, the most straightforward way of determining the unit sales volume required to earn a desired after-tax profit is to

1. Determine the required before-tax profit.
2. Substitute the required before-tax profit into the profit formula.
3. Solve for the required unit sales volume.

To illustrate, assume that Razor is subject to a 40% tax rate and that management desires to earn an after-tax profit of $75,000 for November. The required before-tax profit is $125,000 [$75,000 ÷ (1 − 0.40)], and the unit sales volume required to earn this profit is 7,955 units [($50,000 + $125,000) ÷ $22]. Rounded to the nearest whole unit.

Income taxes increase the sales volume required to earn a desired after-tax profit. A 40% tax rate increased the sales volume required for Razor to earn an after-tax profit of $75,000 from 5,682 to 7,955 units. These amounts are verified in Exhibit 16.5.

Another way to remember the computation of before-tax profit is shown on the right side of Exhibit 16.5. The before-tax profit represents 100% of the pie, with 40% going to income taxes and 60% remaining after taxes. Working back from the remaining 60% ($75,000), we can determine the 100% (before-tax profit) by dividing after-tax profit by 0.60.

Exhibit 16.5 ■ Contribution Income Statement with Income Taxes

RAZOR COMPANY Contribution Income Statement Planned for the Month of November			
Sales (7,955 × $60)		$477,300	
Less variable costs			
Direct materials (7,955 × $20)	$159,100		
Direct labor (7,955 × $10)	79,550		
Manufacturing overhead (7,955 × $3)	23,865		
Selling and administrative (7,955 × $5)	39,775	(302,290)	
Contribution margin		175,010	
Less fixed costs			
Manufacturing overhead	35,000		
Selling and administrative	15,000	50,000	
Before-tax profit		125,000*	100%
Income taxes ($125,000 × 0.40)		(50,000)	(40)%
After-tax profit		$ 75,000	60%

*Calculated total is $125,010. Difference is due to rounding.

LO3 Review 16-3

Assume Solo Cup Company produces 16-ounce beverage containers. Further assume Solo sells the cups for $40 per box of 50 containers. Variable and fixed costs follow:

Variable Costs per Box			Fixed Costs per Month		
Manufacturing			Manufacturing overhead	$15,000	
Direct materials	$15		Selling and administrative	10,000	
Direct labor	3		Total	$25,000	
Manufacturing overhead	10	$28			
Selling and administrative		2			
Total		$30			

continued

continued from previous page

Suppose in September, Solo produced and sold 3,000 boxes of beverage containers.

Required

a. Prepare a cost-volume-profit graph with unit sales as the independent variable. Label the revenue line, total costs line, fixed costs line, loss area, profit area, and break-even point. The recommended scale for the horizontal axis is 0 to 5,000 units, and the recommended scale for the vertical axis is $0 to $200,000.

b. Determine Solo's monthly break-even point in units.

c. Determine the monthly dollar sales required for a monthly profit of $5,000 (ignoring taxes).

d. Assuming Solo is subject to a 40% income tax, determine the monthly unit sales required to produce a monthly after-tax profit of $4,500.

Solution on p. 16-37.

Multiple-Product Cost-Volume-Profit Analysis

Determining Break-Even and Target Profit Sales Dollars

eLectures
MBC **LO4**
Analyze the profitability and sales mix of a multiple-product firm.

Unit cost information is not always available or appropriate when analyzing cost-volume-profit relationships of multiple-product firms. Assuming the sales mix is constant, the contribution margin ratio (the portion of each sales dollar contributed toward covering fixed costs and earning a profit) can be used to determine the break-even dollar sales volume or the dollar sales volume required to achieve a desired profit. Treating a dollar of sales revenue as a unit, the break-even point in dollars is computed as fixed costs divided by the contribution margin ratio (the number of cents from each dollar of revenue contributed to covering fixed costs and providing a profit).

$$\text{Dollar break-even point} = \frac{\text{Fixed costs}}{\text{Contribution margin ratio}}$$

If unit selling price and cost information were not available, Razor's dollar break-even point could be computed as $136,351 ($50,000 ÷ 0.3667). Rounded to the nearest whole unit.

Corresponding computations can be made to find the dollar sales volume required to achieve a desired profit as follows.

$$\text{Target dollar sales volume} = \frac{\text{Fixed costs} + \text{Desired profit}}{\text{Contribution margin ratio}}$$

To achieve a desired profit of $82,000, Razor needs sales of $359,967 [($50,000 + $82,000) ÷ 0.3667]. Rounded to the nearest whole unit.

These relationships can be graphed by placing sales dollars, rather than unit sales, on the horizontal axis. The slope of the variable and total cost lines, identified as the **variable cost ratio**, presents variable costs as a portion of sales revenue. It indicates the number of cents from each sales dollar required to pay variable costs. The Business Insight box below demonstrates how CVP information can be developed from the published financial statements of a multiple-product firm.

Sales Mix Analysis

Sales mix refers to the relative portion of unit or dollar sales that are derived from each product. One of the limiting assumptions of the basic cost-volume-profit model is that the analysis is for a single product or the sales mix is constant. When the sales mix is constant, managers of multiple-product organizations can use the average unit contribution margin, or the average contribution margin ratio, to determine the break-even point or the sales volume required for a desired profit. Often, however, management is interested in the effect of a change in the sales mix rather than a change in the sales volume at a constant mix. In this situation, it is necessary to determine either the average unit contribution margin or the average contribution margin ratio for each alternative mix.

Business Insight	■	Using CVP for Financial Analysis and Prediction

Microsoft Corporation is a technology company that develops and supports software, services, devices, and solutions. We can use historical data to predict future costs through the cost-volume-profit method. We used data from the condensed 2018 and 2017 income statements (in millions) to predict 2019 costs:

	For the Year Ending	
	June 30, 2018	June 30, 2017
Sales.	$110,360	$ 96,571
Cost of sales and operating expenses	(75,302)	(67,546)
Operating profit.	$ 35,058	$ 29,025

We can use the high-low method to understand Microsoft's cost-volume-profit relationships and forecast profits based on expected sales. The first step is to calculate variable costs as a percentage of sales:

$$\text{Variable cost ratio} = \frac{\$75,302 - \$67,546}{\$110,360 - \$96,571} = 0.5625$$

Next, use this ratio to estimate Microsoft's fixed costs by subtracting variable costs from total costs for either period. Based on 2018 revenues and variable costs, we can calculate fixed costs as:

Annual fixed costs = $75,302 – ($110,360 × 0.5625) = $13,225 million

Our estimate of Microsoft's cost function is:

Total annual costs = $13,225 million + (0.5625 × Sales)

Microsoft's break-even sales can be calculated using fixed cost and contribution margin (1 minus the variable cost ratio).

Break-even point = $13,225 million/(1 – 0.5625) = $30,229 million

In 2019 sales were $125,843 million and operating income was $42,959 million. Based on the CVP relationships developed above and 2019 sales, the predicted level of operating income is:

Predicted operating income = $125,843 – [($125,843 × 0.5625) + $13,225] = $41,831

The difference between the estimated operating income and actual results suggests that Microsoft's cost structure has changed slightly over the past three years.

Unit Sales Analysis

Assume that **Hallmark Cards** sells two kinds of greeting cards, regular and deluxe. At a 1:1 (one-to-one) unit sales mix in which Hallmark sells one box of regular cards for every box of deluxe cards, assume the following revenue and cost information is available:

	Regular Box	Deluxe Box	Average Box*
Unit selling price.	$4	$12	$8
Unit variable costs	(3)	(3)	(3)
Unit contribution margin	$1	$ 9	$5
Fixed costs per month			$15,000

* At a 1:1 sales mix, the average unit contribution margin is $5[{($1 × 1 unit) + ($9 × 1 unit)} ÷ 2 units].

At a 1:1 mix, Hallmark's assumed monthly break-even sales volume is 3,000 units ($15,000 ÷ $5), consisting of 1,500 boxes of regular cards and 1,500 boxes of deluxe cards. The top line in Exhibit 16.6 represents the current sales mix. Suppose management wants to know the break-even sales volume if the unit sales mix became 3:1; that is, on average, a sale of 4 units contains 3 regular units and 1 deluxe unit. With no changes in the selling prices or variable costs of individual products, the average contribution margin becomes $3[{($1 × 3 units) + ($9 × 1 unit)} ÷ 4 units], and the revised break-even sales volume is 5,000 units ($15,000 ÷ $3). The revised break-even sales volume includes 3,750 boxes of regular cards [5,000 × $\frac{3}{4}$] and 1,250 boxes of deluxe cards [5,000 × $\frac{1}{4}$].

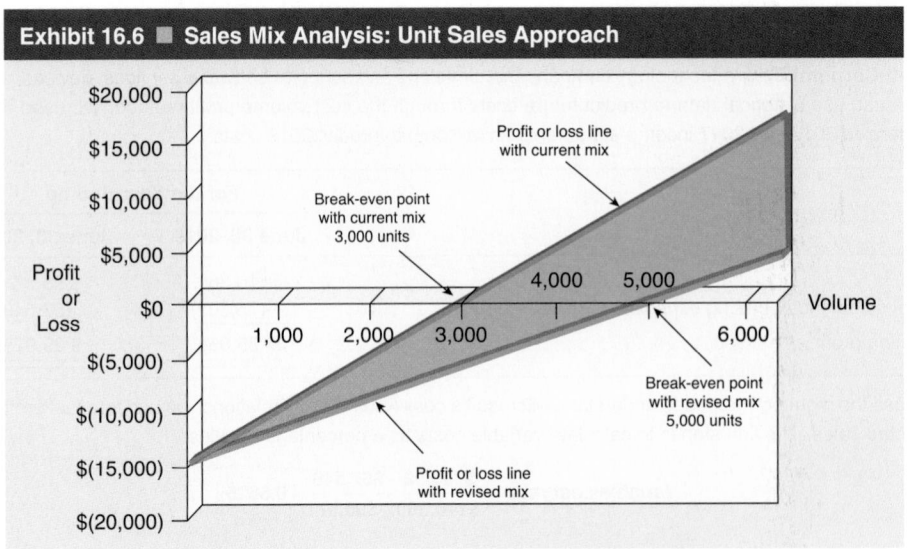

Exhibit 16.6 ■ Sales Mix Analysis: Unit Sales Approach

The bottom line in Exhibit 16.6 represents the revised sales mix. Because a greater portion of the revised mix consists of lower contribution margin regular cards, the shift in the mix increases the break-even point.

Sales Dollar Analysis

The preceding analysis focused on units and the unit contribution margin. An alternative approach focuses on sales dollars and the contribution margin ratio. Following this approach, the sales mix is expressed in terms of sales dollars.

Assume Hallmark's current sales dollars are 25% from regular cards and 75% from deluxe cards. The following display indicates the contribution margin ratios at the current sales mix and monthly volume of 5,400 units.

	Regular	Deluxe	Total
Unit sales	2,700	2,700	
Selling price	$4.00	$12.00	
Sales	$10,800	$32,400	$43,200
Variable costs	8,100	8,100	16,200
Contribution margin	$ 2,700	$24,300	$27,000
Contribution margin ratio	0.25	0.75	0.625

If monthly fixed costs are $15,000, Hallmark's current break-even sales revenue is $24,000 ($15,000 ÷ 0.625), consisting of $6,000 from regular cards ($24,000 × 0.25) and $18,000 from deluxe cards ($24,000 × 0.75). The top line in Exhibit 16.7 illustrates the current sales mix.

Now suppose management wants to know the break-even sales volume if the dollar sales mix became 70% regular and 30% deluxe. With no changes in the selling prices or variable costs of individual products, the total contribution margin ratio becomes 0.40 [(0.25 × 0.70) + (0.75 × 0.30)], and the revised break-even sales volume is $37,500 ($15,000 ÷ 0.40). The revised break-even sales volume includes $26,250 from regular cards ($37,500 × 0.70) and $11,250 from deluxe cards (37,500 × 0.30).

The bottom line in Exhibit 16.7 represents the revised sales mix. Because a greater portion of the revised mix consists of lower contribution ratio regular cards, the shift in the mix increases the break-even point.

Sales mix analysis is important in multiple-product or service organizations. Management is just as concerned with the mix of products as with the total unit or dollar sales volume. A shift in the sales mix can have a significant impact on the bottom line. Profits may decline, even when sales increase, if the mix shifts toward products or services with lower unit margins. Conversely, profits may increase, even when sales decline, if the mix shifts toward products or services with higher unit margins. Other things being equal, managers of for-profit organizations strive to increase sales of high-margin products or services.

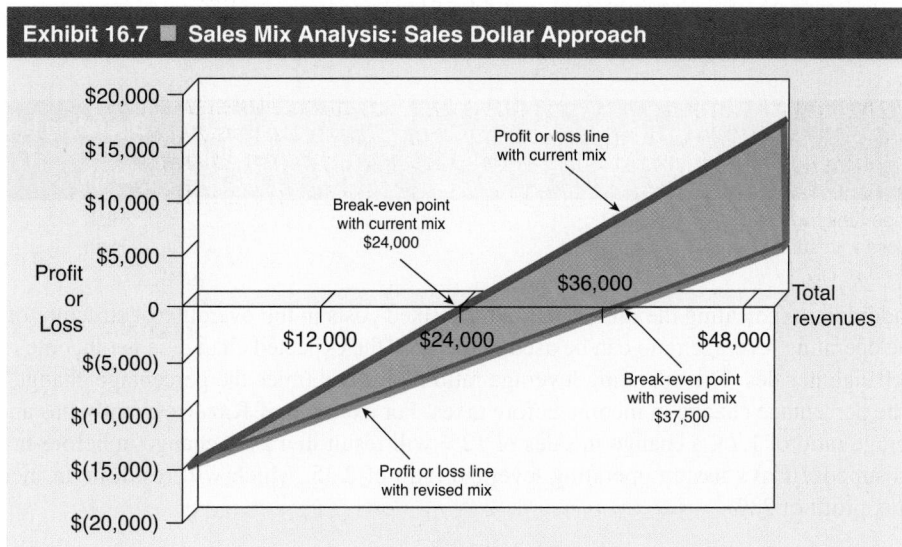

Exhibit 16.7 ■ **Sales Mix Analysis: Sales Dollar Approach**

LO4 Review 16-4

Suppose the Coffee Bean has a new shop in a Cambridge village shopping center that sells high-end teas and coffees. Further, suppose it has added smoothie drinks to its product line. Below are the assumed sales and cost data for the company:

	Coffee	Tea	Smoothie
Sales price per (12 oz.) serving	$1.35	$1.25	$1.95
Variable cost per serving	0.60	0.45	0.75
Fixed costs per month $8,000			

Suppose the company sells each month an average of 6,000 servings of coffee, 3,750 servings of tea, and 2,250 servings of smoothies.

Required
a. Calculate the current before-tax profit, contribution margin ratio, and sales mix based on sales dollars.
b. Using a sales dollar analysis, calculate the monthly break-even point assuming the sales mix does not change.

Solution on p. 16-37.

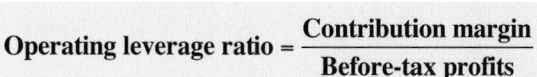

Analysis of Operating Leverage

Operating leverage refers to the extent that an organization's costs are fixed. The **operating leverage ratio** is computed as the contribution margin divided by before-tax profit as follows.

eLectures **LO5**
MBC Apply operating leverage ratio to assess opportunities for profit and the risks of loss.

$$\text{Operating leverage ratio} = \frac{\text{Contribution margin}}{\text{Before-tax profits}}$$

The rationale underlying this computation is that as fixed costs are substituted for variable costs, the contribution margin as a percentage of income before taxes increases. Hence, a high degree of operating leverage signals the existence of a high portion of fixed costs. As noted in Module 14, the shift from labor-based to automated activities has resulted in a decrease in variable costs and an increase in fixed costs, producing an increase in operating leverage.

Operating leverage is a measure of risk and opportunity. Other things being equal, the higher the degree of operating leverage, the greater the opportunity for profit with increases in sales. Conversely, a higher degree of operating leverage also magnifies the risk of large losses with a decrease in sales.

	Operating Leverage	
	High	**Low**
Profit opportunity with sales increase.	High	Low
Risk of loss with sales decrease.	High	Low

In addition to indicating the relative amount of fixed costs in the overall cost structure of a company, the operating leverage ratio can be used to measure the expected change in net income resulting from a change in sales. The operating leverage ratio multiplied times the percentage change in sales equals the percentage change in income before taxes. For example, if Razor currently has an operating leverage ratio of 1.73, a change in sales of 12% will result in a 21% change in before-tax profit; whereas suppose Envy has an operating leverage ratio of 2.35, which will result in an increase in before-tax profit of 28%.

	Current		Projected	
	Razor	**Envy**	**Razor**	**Envy**
Unit selling price.	$ 60	$ 60	$ 60	$ 60
Unit variable costs	(38)	(30)	(38)	(30)
Unit contribution margin	$ 22	$ 30	$ 22	$ 30
Unit sales	× 5,400	× 5,400	× 6,048	× 6,048
Contribution margin	$118,800	$162,000	$133,056	$181,440
Fixed costs	(50,000)	(93,200)	(50,000)	(93,200)
Before-tax profit	$ 68,800	$ 68,800	$ 83,056	$ 88,240
Contribution margin	$118,800	$162,000		
Before-tax profit	÷ 68,800	÷ 68,800		
Operating leverage ratio.	1.73*	2.35*		
Percent increase in sales			12%	12%
Percent increase in income before taxes			21%*	28%*

* Rounded

Although both companies have identical before-tax profits at a sales volume of 5,400 units, assume Envy has a higher degree of operating leverage and its profits vary more with changes in sales volume.

If sales are projected to increase by 12%, from 5,400 to 6,048 units, the percentage of increase in each firm's profits is computed as the percent change in sales multiplied by the degree of operating leverage.

	Razor	Envy
Increase in sales.	12%	12%
Degree of operating leverage.	× 1.73	× 2.35
Increase in profits.	21%*	28%*

* Rounded

As noted in the following Business Insight box, operating leverage is an important consideration when changes in demand, and consequently sales, occur.

Business Insight ■   Mining Companies Fight for Financial Flexibility When Prices Fall

While larger mining companies like BHP and Rio Tinto have the flexibility to maintain output when ore prices fall, smaller miners like the Australian Fortescue Metals Group struggle to deal with low prices. Cost cutting can only help so much when debt is nearly four times earnings. This makes Fortescue's profit exceptionally sensitive to sale price and volume; hence, China's slowdown in economic growth has corresponded to a 90% drop in profit for the company. As a result, Fortescue and other mid-sized mining firms are rushing to restructure their debt.

     In response to the same pressures, other mining companies, like AngloAmerican, are selling assets to reduce operational leverage. In contrast, South32, a BHP spin-off, is less sensitive to demand fluctuations because its net debt is less than a quarter of pretax earnings. South32's more nimble financial structure makes it much easier for the company to deal with fluctuations in price and demand. Financial flexibility is an important consideration in industries such as mining, where fixed costs are high and demand is sensitive to macroeconomic fluctuations.

Source: "Miners: In Search of Flexibility," *Financial Times*, August 25, 2015, London edition, 14.

     Management is interested in measures of operating leverage to determine how sensitive profits are to changes in sales. Risk-averse managers strive to maintain a lower operating leverage, even if this results in some loss of profits. One way to reduce operating leverage is to use more direct labor and less automated equipment. Another way is to contract outside organizations to perform tasks that could be done internally. While operating leverage is a useful analytic tool, long-run success comes from keeping the overall level of costs down, while providing customers with the products or services they want at competitive prices.

Managerial Decision ■   You Are the Division Manager

As manager of a division responsible for both production and sales of products and, hence, division profits, you are looking for ways to leverage the profits of your division to a higher level. You are considering changing your cost structure to include more fixed costs and less variable costs by automating some of the production activities currently performed by people. What are some of the considerations that you should keep in mind as you ponder this decision? [Answer, p. 16-24]

LO5 Review 16-5

Suppose the Coffee Bean has a new shop in a Cambridge village shopping center that sells high-end teas and coffees. Further, suppose it has added smoothie drinks to its product line. Below are the assumed sales and cost data for the company:

	Coffee	Tea	Smoothie
Sales price per (12 oz.) serving	$1.35	$1.25	$1.95
Variable cost per serving	0.60	0.45	0.75
Fixed costs per month $8,000			

Suppose the company sells each month an average of 6,000 servings of coffee, 3,750 servings of tea, and 2,250 servings of smoothies.

Required
Calculate Coffee Bean's operating leverage ratio. If sales increase by 20%, by how much will before-tax income be expected to change? If sales decrease by 20%, by how much will before-tax income be expected to change? **Solution on p. 16-38.**

Appendix 16A: Profitability Analysis with Unit and Nonunit Cost Drivers

LO6
Perform profitability analysis with unit and nonunit cost drivers.

A major limitation of cost-volume-profit analysis and the related contribution income statement is the exclusive use of unit-level activity cost drivers. Even when multiple products are considered, the CVP approach either restates volume in terms of an average unit or in terms of a dollar of sales volume. Additionally, CVP analysis does not consider other categories of cost drivers.

We now expand profitability analysis to incorporate nonunit cost drivers. While the addition of multiple levels of cost drivers makes it difficult to develop graphical relationships (illustrating the impact of cost driver changes on revenues, costs, and profits), it is possible to modify the traditional contribution income statement to incorporate a hierarchy of cost drivers. The expanded framework is not only more accurate, but it encourages management to ask important questions concerning costs and profitability.

Multi-Level Contribution Income Statement

To illustrate the use of profitability analysis with unit and nonunit cost drivers, assume Anthropologie, a multiple-product merchandising organization, has the following cost hierarchy:

Unit-level activities	
Cost of goods sold	$0.80 per sales dollar
Order-level activities	
Cost of processing order.	$20 per order
Customer-level activities	
Mail, phone, sales visits, recordkeeping, etc.	$200 per customer per year
Facility-level costs	
Depreciation, manager salaries, insurance, etc.	$120,000 per year

Assume that Anthropologie is subject to a 40% income tax rate and has the following plans for next year:

Sales.	$3,000,000
Number of sales orders	3,200
Number of customers	400

While Anthropologie's plans could be summarized in a functional income statement, we have previously considered the limitations of such statements for management. Contribution income statements are preferred because they correspond to the cost classification scheme used in CVP analysis. In this case, Anthropologie's cost structure (unit level, order level, customer level, and facility level) does not correspond to the classification scheme used in traditional contribution income statements (variable and fixed). The problem occurs because traditional contribution income statements consider only unit-level cost drivers. When a larger set of unit and nonunit cost drivers is used for cost analysis, an expanded contribution income statement should be used for profitability analysis.

A hypothetical multi-level contribution income statement for Anthropologie is presented in Exhibit 16A.1. Costs are separated using a cost hierarchy and there are several contribution margins, one for each level of costs that responds to a short-run change in activity. Suppose that in the case of Anthropologie, the contribution margins are at the unit level, order level, and customer level. Because the facility-level costs do not vary with short-run variations in activity, the final customer-level contribution goes to cover facility-level costs and to provide for a profit. If a company had a different activity cost hierarchy, it would use a different set of contribution margins.

Exhibit 16A.1 ■ Multi-Level Contribution Income Statement with Taxes

ANTHROPOLOGIE
Multi-Level Contribution Income Statement
For Next Year

Sales.	$3,000,000
Less unit-level costs	
Cost of goods sold ($3,000,000 × 0.80)	(2,400,000)
Unit-level contribution margin.	600,000
Less order-level costs	
Cost of processing order (3,200 orders × $20)	(64,000)
Order-level contribution margin	536,000
Less customer-level costs	
Mail, phone, sales visits, recordkeeping, etc. (400 customers × $200)	(80,000)
Customer-level contribution margin	456,000
Less facility-level costs	
Depreciation, manager salaries, insurance, etc..	(120,000)
Before-tax profit	336,000
Income taxes ($336,000 × 0.40).	(134,400)
After-tax profit.	$ 201,600

A number of additional questions of interest to management can be formulated and answered using the multi-level hierarchy. Consider the following examples:

■ Holding the number of sales orders and customers constant, what is the break-even dollar sales volume? The answer is found by treating all other costs as fixed and dividing the total nonunit-level costs by the contribution margin ratio. Here the contribution margin ratio indicates how many cents of each sales dollar is available for profits and costs above the unit level.

Unit-Level Break-Even Point in Dollars with No Changes in Other Costs	=	Current Order-Level Costs	+	Current Customer-Level Costs	+	Facility-Level Costs
		Contribution Margin Ratio				

$$= (\$64,000 + \$80,000 + \$120,000) \div (1 - 0.80)$$
$$= \$1,320,000$$

■ What order size is required to break even on an individual order? Answering this question might help management to evaluate the desirability of establishing a minimum order size. To break even, each order must have a unit-level contribution equal to the order-level costs. Any additional contribution is used to cover customer- and facility-level costs and provide for a profit.

$$\textbf{Break-even order size} = \$20 \div (1 - 0.80)$$
$$= \$100$$

■ What sales volume is required to break even on an average customer? Answering this question might help management to evaluate the desirability of retaining certain customers. Based on the preceding information, an average customer places 8 orders per year (3,200 orders ÷ 400 customers). With costs of $20 per order and $200 per customer, the sales to an average customer must generate an annual contribution of $360 [($20 × 8) + $200]. Hence, the break-even level for an average customer is $1,800 [$360 ÷ (1 − 0.80)]. Management might consider discontinuing relations with customers with annual purchases of less than this amount. Alternatively, they might inquire as to whether such customers could be served in a less costly manner.

The concepts of multi-level break-even analysis and profitability analysis are finding increasing use as companies such as FedEx, Best Buy, and Bank of America strive to identify profitable and unprofitable customers. At FedEx, customers are sometimes rated as "the good, the bad, and the ugly." FedEx strives to retain the "good" profitable customers, turn the "bad" into profitable customers, and ignore the "ugly" who seem unlikely to become profitable.

Variations in Multi-Level Contribution Income Statement

Classification schemes should be designed to fit the organization and user needs. In Module 15, when analyzing the costs of a manufacturing company, we used a manufacturing cost hierarchy. While formatting issues can seem mundane and routine, format is important because the way information is presented encourages certain types of questions while discouraging others. Hence, management accountants must inquire as to user needs before developing management accounting reports, just as users of management accounting information should be knowledgeable enough to request appropriate information and know whether the information they are receiving is the information they need. With computers to reduce computational drudgery and to provide a wealth of available data, the most important issues involve identifying the important questions and presenting information to address those questions.

In the case of Anthropologie, we used a customer cost hierarchy with information presented in a single column. A multiple-column format is also useful for presenting and analyzing information. Assume that Anthropologie's managment believes that the differences between the in-store and internet-based markets are such that these markets could be better served with separate marketing activities. They would have two market segments, one for the in-store customers and one for internet-based customers, giving the following cost hierarchy:

1. Unit-level activities
2. Order-level activities
3. Customer-level activities
4. Market segment activities
5. Facility-level activities

One possible way of presenting Anthropologie's hypothetical multi-level income statement with two market segments is shown in Exhibit 16A.2. The details underlying the development of this statement are not presented. In developing the statement, we assume the mix of units sold, their cost structure, and the costs of processing an order are unchanged. Finally, we present new market segment costs and assume that the addition of the segments allows for some reduction in previous facility-level costs.

The information in the total column is all that is required for a multi-level contribution income statement. The information in the two detailed columns for the government and private segments can, however, prove useful in analyzing the profitability of each. Observe that the facility-level costs, incurred for the benefit of both segments, are not assigned to specific segments. Depending on the nature of the goods sold, it may be possible to further analyze the profitability of each product (or type of product) sold in each market segment. The profitability analysis of business segments is more closely examined in Module 24.

Exhibit 16A.2 ■ Multi-Level Contribution Income Statement with Segments and Taxes

ANTHROPOLOGIE
Multi-Level Contribution Income Statement
For Next Year

	In-Store Segment	Internet Segment	Total
Sales.	$1,500,000	$2,000,000	$3,500,000
Less unit-level costs			
Cost of goods sold (0.80)	(1,200,000)	(1,600,000)	(2,800,000)
Unit-level contribution margin.	300,000	400,000	700,000
Less order-level costs			
Cost of processing order			
(1,000 × $20; 3,000 × $20)	(20,000)	(60,000)	(80,000)
Order-level contribution margin	280,000	340,000	620,000
Less customer-level costs			
Mail, phone, sales visits, recordkeeping, etc.			
(150 × $200, 300 × $200)	(30,000)	(60,000)	(90,000)
Customer-level contribution margin	250,000	280,000	530,000
Less market segment-level costs	(80,000)	(20,000)	(100,000)
Market segment-level contribution	$ 170,000	$ 260,000	430,000
Less facility-level costs			
Depreciation, manager salaries, insurance, etc.			(90,000)
Before-tax profit			340,000
Income taxes ($340,000 × 0.40).			(136,000)
After-tax profit.			$ 204,000

LO6 Review 16-6

7-Eleven operates a number of convenience stores worldwide. Assume that an analysis of operating costs, customer sales, and customer patronage reveals the following:

Fixed costs per store	$80,000/year
Variable cost ratio.	0.80
Average sale per customer visit	$17.00
Average customer visits per week	1.50
Customers as portion of city population	0.05

Required
Determine the city population required for a single 7-Eleven to earn an annual profit of $40,000.   Solution on p. 16-38.

Guidance Answers

You Are the Division Manager
Pg. 16-20 Fixed costs represent a two-edged sword. When a company is growing its sales, fixed costs cause profits to grow faster than sales; however, if a company should experience declining sales, the rate of reduction in profits is greater than the rate of reduction in sales. When sales decline, variable costs decline proportionately, while fixed costs continue. For this reason, when a company faces serious declines that are expected to continue, one of the first steps its top management should consider is reducing capacity in order to reduce fixed costs. The automobile companies in the U.S. have been employing this technique in recent years to try to offset the effect of sales lost to importers.

Questions

Q16-1. What is cost-volume-profit analysis and when is it particularly useful?

Q16-2. Identify the important assumptions that underlie cost-volume-profit analysis.

Q16-3. When is it most reasonable to use a single independent variable in cost-volume-profit analysis?

Q16-4. Distinguish between a contribution and a functional income statement.

Q16-5. What is the unit contribution margin? How is it used in computing the unit break-even point?

Q16-6. What is the contribution margin ratio and when is it most useful?

Q16-7. How is the break-even equation modified to take into account the sales required to earn a desired profit?

Q16-8. How does a profit-volume graph differ from a cost-volume-profit graph? When is a profit-volume graph most likely to be used?

Q16-9. What impact do income taxes have on the sales volume required to earn a desired after-tax profit?

Q16-10. How are profit opportunities and the risk of losses affected by operating leverage?

Assignments with the ⓜ logo in the margin are available in Business Course.
See the Preface of the book for details.

Mini Exercises

M16-11. Profitability Analysis

     Assume Strands Salon, a San Diego hair salon, provides cuts, perms, and hairstyling services. Annual fixed costs are $225,000, and variable costs are 45% of sales revenue. Last year's revenues totaled $450,000.

LO3
Strands Salon

     Required
     a. Determine its break-even point in sales dollars.
     b. Determine last year's margin of safety in sales dollars.
     c. Determine the sales dollar required for an annual pretax profit of $200,000.

LO3   **M16-12. Cost-Volume-Profit Graph: Identification and Sensitivity Analysis**
A typical cost-volume-profit graph is presented below.

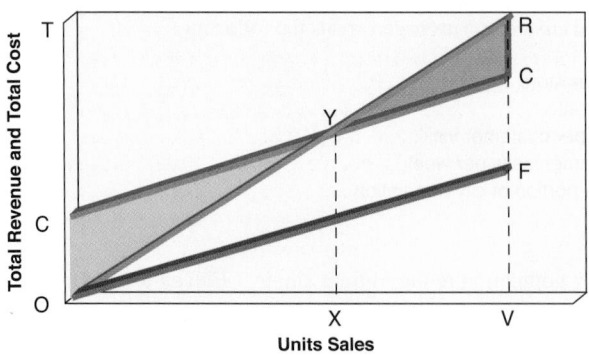

Required
a. Identify each of the following:
1. Line OF
2. Line OR
3. Line CC
4. The difference between lines OF and OV at any given number of unit sales
5. The difference between lines CC and OF at any given number of unit sales
6. The difference between lines CC and OV at any given number of unit sales
7. The difference between lines OR and OF at any given number of unit sales
8. Point X
9. Area CYO
10. Area RCY
b. Indicate the effect of each of the following independent events on lines CC, OR, and the break-even point:
1. A decrease in fixed costs
2. An increase in unit selling price
3. An increase in the variable costs per unit
4. An increase in fixed costs and a decrease in the unit selling price
5. A decrease in fixed costs and a decrease in the unit variable costs

LO3   **M16-13. Profit-Volume Graph: Identification and Sensitivity Analysis**
A typical profit-volume graph follows.

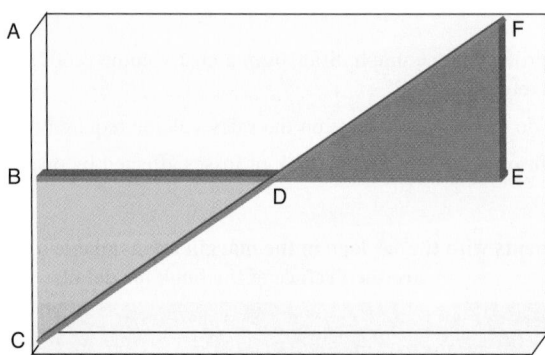

Required
a. Identify each of the following:
1. Area BDC
2. Area DEF
3. Point D
4. Line AC
5. Line BC
6. Line EF

  b. Indicate the effect of each of the following on line CF and the break-even point:
1. An increase in the unit selling price
2. An increase in the variable costs per unit
3. A decrease in fixed costs
4. An increase in fixed costs and a decrease in the unit selling price
5. A decrease in fixed costs and an increase in the variable costs per unit

M16-14. Preparing Cost-Volume-Profit and Profit-Volume Graphs

LO3

Connie's Pizza

Assume a **Connie's Pizza** shop has the following monthly revenue and cost functions:

$$\text{Total revenues} = \$20.00X$$

$$\text{Total costs} = \$35{,}000 + \$6.00X$$

Required

a. Prepare a graph (similar to that in Exhibit 16.3) illustrating Connie's cost-volume-profit relationships. The vertical axis should range from $0 to $120,000, in increments of $20,000. The horizontal axis should range from 0 units to 6,000 units, in increments of 2,000 units.

b. Prepare a graph (similar to that in Exhibit 16.4) illustrating Connie's profit-volume relationships. The horizontal axis should range from 0 units to 6,000 units, in increments of 2,000 units.

c. When is it most appropriate to use a profit-volume graph?

M16-15. Preparing Cost-Volume-Profit and Profit-Volume Graphs

LO3

Manu's Tacos

Manu's Tacos sells seven different burritos at a fixed price of $9. Assume variable costs are $6 per burrito and fixed operating costs are $120,000 per year.

Required

a. Determine the annual break-even point in tacos.

b. Prepare a cost-volume-profit graph for the company. Use a format that emphasizes the contribution margin. The vertical axis should vary between $0 and $800,000 in increments of $100,000. The horizontal axis should vary between 0 tacos and 80,000 tacos, in increments of 10,000 tacos. Label the graph in thousands.

c. Prepare a profit-volume graph for the company. The vertical axis should vary between $(150,000) and $150,000 in increments of $50,000. The horizontal axis should vary as described in requirement (*b*). Label the graph in thousands.

d. Evaluate the profit-volume graph. In what ways is it superior and in what ways is it inferior to the traditional cost-volume-profit graph?

M16-16. Multiple Product Break-Even Analysis

LO4

Dick's Sporting Goods (DKS)

Bauer

Warrior

CCM

Assume **Dick's Sporting Goods** sells three types of youth hockey sticks: **Bauer**, **Warrior**, and **CCM**. Presented is information for Dick's three products.

	Bauer	Warrior	CCM
Unit selling price	$180	$120	$100
Unit variable costs	120	75	60
Unit contribution margin	$ 60	$ 45	$ 40

With monthly fixed costs of $150,000, the company sells two Bauer sticks for each Warrior, and three Warrior for each CCM.

Required

Determine the number of Warrior sticks sold at the monthly break-even point.

E16-17. Contribution Income Statement and Cost-Volume-Profit Graph

LO2, 3

Picnic Time

Picnic Time produces a picnic basket that is sold for $100 per unit. Assume the company produced and sold 4,000 baskets during July. There were no beginning or ending inventories. Variable and fixed costs follow.

Variable Costs per Unit			Fixed Costs per Month	
Manufacturing:			Manufacturing overhead.........	$ 36,000
Direct materials...............	$25		Selling and administrative........	68,000
Direct labor..................	15		Total	$104,000
Manufacturing overhead........	5	$45		
Selling and administrative.........		4		
Total		$49		

Required

a. Prepare a contribution income statement for July.

b. Prepare a cost-volume-profit graph. Label the horizontal axis in units with a maximum value of 8,000. Label the vertical axis in dollars with a maximum value of $1,000,000. Draw a vertical line on the graph for the current (4,000) unit sales level, and label total variable costs, total fixed costs, and total profits at 4,000 units.

LO3

DiPinto Electric
Guitars & Basses

E16-18. Contribution Margin Concepts

DiPinto Electric Guitars & Basses sells musical instruments in Philadelphia. Assume the following information comes from the company's prior year records.

	Fixed	Variable	Total
Sales.......................................			$800,000
Costs			
Goods sold		$346,000	
Labor.....................................	$180,000	40,000	
Supplies	10,000	4,000	
Utilities	9,000	5,000	
Rent	48,000	—	
Advertising	10,000	—	
Miscellaneous.............................	10,000	5,000	
Total costs................................	$267,000	$400,000	(667,000)
Net income			$133,000

Required

a. Determine the annual break-even dollar sales volume.

b. Determine the current margin of safety in dollars.

c. Prepare a cost-volume-profit graph for the guitar shop. Label both axes in dollars with maximum values of $1,000,000. Draw a vertical line on the graph for the current ($800,000) sales level, and label total variable costs, total fixed costs, and total profits at $800,000 sales.

d. What is the annual break-even dollar sales volume if management makes a decision that increases fixed costs by $50,000?

LO3

Cliff Consulting

E16-19. Product Planning with Taxes

Assume that last year, **Cliff Consulting**, a firm in Berkeley, CA, had the following contribution income statement:

CLIFF CONSULTING Contribution Income Statement For the Year Ended September 30		
Sales revenue..		$1,200,000
Variable costs		
Cost of services	$480,000	
Selling and administrative...............................	60,000	540,000
Contribution margin		660,000
Fixed costs—selling and administrative		440,000
Before-tax profit		220,000
Income taxes 21%		46,200
After-tax profit..		$ 173,800

Required

a. Determine the annual break-even point in sales revenue.

b. Determine the annual margin of safety in sales revenue.

c. What is the break-even point in sales revenue if management makes a decision that increases fixed costs by $80,000?

d. With the current cost structure, including fixed costs of $440,000, what dollar sales revenue is required to provide an after-tax net income of $250,000?

e. Prepare an abbreviated contribution income statement to verify that the solution to requirement (d) will provide the desired after-tax income.

E16-20. Not-for-Profit Applications

Determine the solution to each of the following independent cases:

a. Collings College has annual fixed operating costs of $20,000,000 and variable operating costs of $2,400 per student. Tuition is $12,000 per student for the coming academic year, with a projected enrollment of 2,000 students. Expected revenues from endowments and federal and state grants total $400,000. Determine the amount the college must obtain from other sources.

b. The Collings College Student Association is planning a fall concert. Expected costs (renting a hall, hiring a band, etc.) are $15,000. Assuming 2,000 people attend the concert, determine the break-even price per ticket. How much will the association lose if this price is charged and only 1,500 tickets are sold?

c. City Hospital has a contract with the city to provide indigent health care on an outpatient basis for $125 per visit. The patient will pay $10 of this amount, with the city paying the balance ($115). Determine the amount the city will pay if the hospital has 5,000 patient visits.

d. A civic organization is engaged in a fund-raising program. On Civic Sunday, it will sell newspapers at $2.50 each. The organization will pay $1.75 for each newspaper. Costs of the necessary permits, signs, and so forth are $750. Determine the amount the organization will raise if it sells 3,000 newspapers.

e. Christmas for the Needy is a civic organization that provides Christmas presents to disadvantaged children. The annual costs of this activity are $10,000, plus $20 per present. Determine the number of presents the organization can provide with $30,000.

LO3

E16-21. Alternative Production Procedures and Operating Leverage

Assume Sharpie, a brand of Newell Brands, is planning to introduce a new executive pen that can be manufactured using either a capital-intensive method or a labor-intensive method. The predicted manufacturing costs for each method are as follows:

LO3, 5
Newell Brands (NWL)

	Capital Intensive	Labor Intensive
Direct materials per unit	$10.00	$12.00
Direct labor per unit	$ 4.00	$12.00
Variable manufacturing overhead per unit	$ 5.00	$ 2.00
Fixed manufacturing overhead per year.	$1,800,000	$500,000

Sharpie's market research department has recommended an introductory unit sales price of $100. Selling costs under either method are predicted to be $250,000 per year, plus $4 per unit sold.

Required

a. Determine the annual break-even point in units if Sharpie uses the
   1. Capital-intensive manufacturing method.
   2. Labor-intensive manufacturing method.

b. Determine the annual unit volume at which Sharpie is indifferent between the two manufacturing methods.

c. Management wants to know more about the effect of each alternative on operating leverage.
   1. Explain operating leverage and the relationship between operating leverage and the volatility of earnings.
   2. Compute operating leverage for each alternative at a volume of 100,000 units.
   3. Which alternative has the higher operating leverage? Why?

LO3, 5
Willamette Valley Fruit
Company

E16-22. Contribution Income Statement and Operating Leverage

Willamette Valley Fruit Company started as a small cannery-style operation in 1999. The company now processes, on average, 20 million pounds of berries each year. Flash-frozen berries are sold in 30 pound packs to retailers. Assume 650,000 packs were sold for $75 each last year. Variable costs were $42 per pack and fixed costs totaled $14,250,000.

Required

a. Prepare a contribution income statement for last year.
b. Determine last year's operating leverage.
c. Calculate the percentage change in profits if sales decrease by 10%.
d. Management is considering the purchase of several new pieces of packaging equipment. This will increase annual fixed costs to $15,500,000 and reduce variable costs to $40 per crate. Calculate the effect of this acquisition on operating leverage and explain any change.

LO4
TPG Tax &
Accounting

E16-23. Multiple Product Break-Even Analysis

TPG Tax & Accounting is a full-service CPA firm located in Apache Junction, Arizona. Assume that tax return services are classified into one of three categories: standard, complex, and full-service (includes end-of-year bookkeeping with tax return preparation). Assume that TPG's fixed costs (rent, utilities, wages, and so forth) totaled $180,000 last year. Additional information from the prior year follows.

	Standard	Complex	Full-Service
Billing rate.	$125.00	$250.00	$150.00
Average variable costs	(45.00)	(65.00)	(50.00)
Average contribution margin.	$ 80.00	$185.00	$100.00
Number of returns prepared	1,000	200	800

Required

a. Using sales dollar analysis, determine TPG's break-even dollar sales volume.
b. Determine TPG's margin of safety in sales dollars. *Hint:* Use the weighted average billing rate.
c. Prepare a profit-volume graph for Joe's Tax Service.

LO3

E16-24. Cost-Volume-Profit Relations: Missing Data

Following are data from four separate companies.

	Case A	Case B	Case C	Case D
Unit sales	2,500	1,600	?	?
Sales revenue.	$80,000	?	?	$240,000
Variable cost per unit	$20	$2	$24	?
Contribution margin	?	$1,600	?	?
Fixed costs	$14,000	?	$164,000	?
Net income	?	$900	?	?
Unit contribution margin	?	?	?	$30
Break-even point (units)	?	?	8,000	4,000
Margin of safety (units)	?	?	600	2,000

Required

Supply the missing data in each independent case.

LO3

E16-25. Cost-Volume-Profit Relations: Missing Data

Following are data from four separate companies.

	Case 1	Case 2	Case 3	Case 4
Sales revenue.	$90,000	$150,000	?	?
Contribution margin	$45,000	?	$40,000	?
Fixed costs	$30,000	?	?	?
Net income	?	$15,000	$24,000	?
Variable cost ratio.	?	0.40	?	0.60
Contribution margin ratio	?	?	0.25	?
Break-even point (dollars)	?	?	?	$150,000
Margin of safety (dollars)	?	?	?	$125,000

Required

Supply the missing data in each independent case.

E16-26. Customer-Level Planning

Circle K, a company of **Alimentation Couche-Tard**, operates a number of convenience stores world-wide. Assume that an analysis of operating costs, customer sales, and customer patronage reveals the following:

Fixed costs per store	$125,000
Variable cost ratio	0.60
Average sale per customer visit	$10.00
Average customer visits per week	2.00
Customers as portion of city population	.05

LO6

Circle K
Alimentation
Couche-Tard (AID)

Homework
MBC

Required

Determine the city population required for a single Circle K to earn an annual profit of $75,000.

E16-27. Multiple-Level Break-Even Analysis

Kucera Associates provides marketing services for a number of small manufacturing firms. Kucera receives a commission of 10% of sales. Operating costs are as follows:

LO6

Homework
MBC

Unit-level costs	$0.05 per sales dollar
Sales-level costs	$400 per sales order
Customer-level costs	$1,000 per customer per year
Facility-level costs	$75,000 per year

Required

a. Determine the minimum order size in sales dollars for Kucera to break even on an order.
b. Assuming an average customer places five orders per year, determine the minimum annual sales required to break even on a customer.
c. What is the average order size in (*b*)?
d. Assuming Kucera currently serves 100 customers, with each placing an average of five orders per year, determine the minimum annual sales required to break even.
e. What is the average order size in (*d*)?
f. Explain the differences in the answers to (*a*), (*c*), and (*e*).

Problems

P16-28. Profit Planning with Taxes

Carron Net Company manufactures sports nets for virtually every outdoor sport. Assume Carron sells nets for $50, on average, per unit. Last year, the company manufactured and sold 30,000 nets to obtain an after-tax profit of $275,000. Variable and fixed costs follow.

LO3

Carron Net Company

Variable Costs per Unit		Fixed Costs per Year	
Manufacturing	$20	Manufacturing	$232,250
Selling and administrative	4	Selling and administrative	204,000
Total	$24	Total	$436,250

Required

a. Determine the tax rate the company paid last year.
b. What unit sales volume is required to provide an after-tax profit of $400,000?
c. If the company reduces the unit variable cost by $4 and increases fixed manufacturing costs by $53,000, what unit sales volume is required to provide an after-tax profit of $400,000?
d. What assumptions are made about taxable income and tax rates in requirements (*a*) through (*c*)?

P16-29. Contribution Income Statement, Cost-Volume-Profit Graph, and Taxes

Jail and Sail: Alcatraz Tour and Cruise provides sunset sightseeing tours of Alcatraz and the San Francisco Bay. Tickets cost $140 each. Assume 2,200 customers were served in July.

LO2, 3

Jail and Sail: Alcatraz
Tour and Cruise

Variable Costs per Customer		Fixed Costs per Month	
Admission fees.	$60	Operations	$50,000
Overhead	25	Selling and administration	12,500
Hors d'oeuvres	15		
Selling and administrative.	2		
Total	$102	Total	$62,500

Jail and Sail is subject to an income tax rate of 21%.

Required

a. Prepare a contribution income statement for July.

b. Determine Jail and Sail's monthly break-even point in units.

c. Determine Jail and Sail's margin of safety in units for July.

d. Determine the unit sales required for a monthly after-tax profit of $20,000.

e. Prepare a cost-volume-profit graph. Label the horizontal axis in units with a maximum value of 4,000. Label the vertical in dollars with a maximum value of $600,000. Draw a vertical line on the graph for the current (2,200) unit level and label total variable costs, total fixed costs, and total before-tax profits at 2,200 units.

LO3 **P16-30.** **High-Low Cost Estimation and Profit Planning**

Comparative income statements for Bismark Products Inc. follow:

BISMARK PRODUCTS INC. Comparative Income Statements For Years Ending December 31		
	Year 1	**Year 2**
Unit sales	6,250	9,375
Sales revenue.	$100,000	$150,000
Expenses	(85,000)	(105,000)
Pretax profit (loss)	$ 15,000	$ 45,000

Required

a. Determine the break-even point in units.

b. Determine the unit sales volume required to earn a pretax profit of $25,000.

LO3 **P16-31.** **CVP Analysis and Special Decisions**

Smoothie Company

Smoothie Company produces fruit purees which it sells to smoothie bars and health clubs. Assume the most recent year's sales revenue was $5,800,000. Variable costs were 55% of sales and fixed costs totaled $1,560,000. Smoothie is evaluating two alternatives designed to enhance profitability.

- One staff member has proposed that Smoothie purchase more automated processing equipment. This strategy would increase fixed costs by $250,000 but decrease variable costs to 50% of sales.
- Another staff member has suggested that Smoothie rely more on outsourcing for fruit processing. This would reduce fixed costs by $250,000 but increase variable costs to 60% of sales.

Required

a. What is the current break-even point in sales dollars?

b. Assuming an income tax rate of 20%, what dollar sales volume is currently required to obtain an after-tax profit of $1,000,000?

c. In the absence of income taxes, at what sales volume will both alternatives (automation and outsourcing) provide the same profit?

d. Briefly describe one strength and one weakness of both the automation and the outsourcing alternatives.

LO3 **P16-32.** **Break-Even Analysis in a Not-for-Profit Organization**

Melford Hospital operates a general hospital but rents space to separately owned entities rendering specialized services such as pediatrics and psychiatry. Melford charges each separate entity for patients' services (meals and laundry) and for administrative services (billings and collections). Space and bed rentals are fixed charges for the year, based on bed capacity rented to each entity. Melford charged the following costs to Pediatrics this year:

	Patient Services (Variable)	Bed Capacity (Fixed)
Dietary	$ 800,000	
Janitorial		$ 95,000
Laundry	375,000	
Laboratory	600,000	
Pharmacy	460,000	
Repairs and maintenance		40,000
General and administrative		1,750,000
Rent		2,000,000
Billings and collections	400,000	
Total	$2,635,000	$3,885,000

In addition to these charges from Melford Hospital, Pediatrics incurred the following personnel costs:

	Annual Salaries*
Supervising nurses	$135,000
Nurses	270,000
Assistants	240,000
Total	$645,000

* These salaries are fixed within the ranges of annual patient-days considered in this problem.

During the year, Pediatrics charged each patient $400 per day, had a capacity of 80 beds, and had revenues of $8,000,000 for 365 days. Pediatrics operated at 100% capacity on 90 days during this period. It is estimated that during these 90 days, the demand exceeded 100 beds.

Melford will have 20 additional beds available for rent next year. If Pediatrics rents the beds from Melford, the additional rental would proportionately increase Pediatrics' annual fixed charges that are based on bed capacity.

Required

a. Calculate the minimum number of patient-days required for Pediatrics to break even next year, if the additional beds are not rented. Patient demand is unknown, but assume that revenue per patient-day, cost per patient-day, cost per bed, and salary rates next year will be consistent with the current year.

b. Assume Pediatrics rents the extra 20-bed capacity from Melford during the busy 90-day period. Determine the net increase or decrease in earnings by preparing a schedule of increases in revenues and costs for next year. Assume that patient demand, revenue per patient-day, cost per patient-day, cost per bed, and salary rates remain the same as the current year.

(CPA adapted)

P16-33. CVP Analysis of Alternative Products

Assume Converse, a Nike company, plans to expand its manufacturing capacity to allow up to 30,000 pairs of a new shoe product each year. Because only one product can be produced, management is deciding between the production of the Roadrunner for backpacking and the Trail Runner for exercising. A marketing analysis indicates Converse could sell between 12,000 and 20,000 pairs of either product.

The accounting department has developed the following price and cost information:

	Product	
	Roadrunner	Trail Runner
Selling price per pair	$140	$125
Variable costs per pair	80	75
Fixed production costs	$150,000	$100,000

Additional annual facility costs, regardless of product, are estimated at $100,000. Assume Converse is subject to a 20% income tax rate.

Required

a. Determine the number of pairs of each product that Converse must sell to obtain an after-tax profit of $50,000.

b. Determine the number of pairs of each product Converse must sell to obtain identical before-tax profit.

c. For the solution to requirement (b), calculate Converse's after-tax profit or loss.

d. Which product should Converse produce if both products were guaranteed to sell at least 18,000 pairs? Verify your solution with calculations.

e. How much would the variable costs per pair of the product *not* selected in requirement (d) have to fall before both products provide the same profit at sales of 18,000 pairs? Verify your solution with calculations.

LO3, 4

Microsoft (MSFT)

P16-34. CVP Analysis Using Published Financial Statements

Condensed data in millions of dollars from Microsoft's 2019 and 2018 income statements follow:

	2019	2018
Revenues	$125,843	$110,360
Total cost of revenues and operating expenses	82,884	75,302
Operating income	$ 42,959	$ 35,058

Required

a. Develop a cost-estimation equation for Microsoft's annual cost of revenues and operating expenses using revenues as the activity.

b. Determine Microsoft's annual break-even point.

c. Predict operating profit for 2020, assuming 2020 sales of $150,000 million.

d. Identify the assumptions required to use the equations and amounts computed above.

LO4

UCLA Store

P16-35. Multiple-Product Profitability Analysis, Multiple-Level Profitability Analysis

Assume UCLA Store sells new college textbooks at the publishers' suggested retail prices and pays the publishers an amount equal to 70% of the suggested retail price. The store's other variable costs average 5% of sales revenue and annual fixed costs amount to $420,000.

Required

a. Determine the bookstore's annual break-even point in sales dollars.

b. Assuming an average textbook has a suggested retail price of $125, determine the bookstore's annual break-even point in units.

c. UCLA Store is planning to add used book sales to its operations. A typical used book costs the store 25% of the suggested retail price of a new book. The bookstore plans to sell used books for 75% of the suggested retail price of a new book. Assuming unit sales are unchanged, describe the effect on bookstore profitability of shifting sales toward more used and fewer new textbooks.

d. Chicago Publishers produces and sells new textbooks to college and university bookstores. Assume typical project-level costs total $285,000 for a new textbook. Production and distribution costs amount to 20% of the net amount the publisher receives from the bookstores. Textbook authors are paid a royalty of 15% of the net amount received from the bookstores. Determine the dollar sales volume required for Chicago to break even on a new textbook. This is the amount the bookstore pays the publisher, not the bookstore's sales revenue.

e. For a project with predicted sales of 10,000 new books at $125 each, determine
   1. The bookstores' unit-level contribution.
   2. The publisher's project-level contribution.
   3. The author's royalties.

LO3

Spalding

P16-36. Multiple-Product Profitability Analysis

Spalding produces acrylic and polycarbonate basketball backboard and rim sets. Assume the following represents sales information for last year.

	Acrylic	Polycarbonate	Total
Units manufactured and sold	2,000	3,500	5,500
Sales revenue.	$600,000	$735,000	$1,335,000
Variable costs.	346,750	454,250	801,000
Contribution margin	$253,250	$280,750	$ 534,000
Fixed costs			(425,630)
Before-tax profit			108,370
Income taxes (20%)			(21,674)
After-tax profit.			$ 86,696

Required

a. Determine the current break-even point in sales dollars.

b. With the current product mix and break-even point, determine the average unit contribution margin and unit sales.

c. Sales representatives believe that the total sales will increase to 5,750 units, with the sales mix likely shifting to 80% polycarbonate and 20% acrylic over the next few years. Evaluate the desirability of this projection.

P16-37. Multiple-Product Break-Even Analysis   LO3, 4

Currently, Corner Lunch Counter sells only Super Burgers for $5.50 each. During a typical month, the Counter reports a profit of $12,125 with sales of $68,750 and fixed costs of $36,000. Management is considering the introduction of a new Super Chicken Sandwich that will sell for $7.00 and have variable costs of $2.50. The addition of the Super Chicken Sandwich will require hiring additional personnel and renting additional equipment. These actions will increase monthly fixed costs by $5,400.

In the short run, management predicts that Super Chicken sales will average 7,500 sandwiches per month. However, almost all short-run sales of Super Chickens will come from regular customers who switch from Super Burgers to Super Chickens. Consequently, management predicts monthly sales revenue from Super Burgers will decline $27,500 (5,000 units). In the long run, management predicts that Super Chicken sales will increase to 9,000 sandwiches per month and that Super Burger sales will increase to 16,000 burgers per month.

Required

a. Determine each of the following:

1. The current monthly break-even point in sales dollars.
2. The short-run monthly profit and break-even point in sales dollars subsequent to the introduction of Super Chickens.
3. The long-run monthly profit and break-even point in sales dollars subsequent to the introduction of Super Chickens.

b. Based on your analysis, what are your recommendations?

P16-38. Multi-Level Profitability Analysis   LO4

AccuMeter manufactures and sells its only product (Z1) in lot sizes of 1,000 units. Because of this approach, lot (batch)-level costs are regarded as variable for CVP analysis. Presented is sales and cost information for the year:

Sales revenue (75,000 units at $65).	$4,875,000
Direct materials (75,000 units at $20).	1,500,000
Processing (75,000 units at $15)	1,125,000
Setup (150 lots at $2,500)	375,000
Batch movement (150 lots at $500)	75,000
Order filling (150 lots at $250)	37,500
Fixed manufacturing overhead.	1,000,000
Fixed selling and administrative	450,000

Required

a. Prepare a traditional contribution income statement in good form.

b. Prepare a multi-level contribution income statement in good form. (*Hint:* First determine the appropriate cost hierarchy.)

    c. What is the current contribution per lot (batch) of 1,000 units?

    d. Management is contemplating introducing a limited number of specialty products. One product would sell for $80 per unit and have direct materials costs of $35 per unit. All other costs and all production and sales procedures will remain unchanged. What lot (batch) size is required for a contribution of $800 per lot?

Management Applications

LO1   **MA16-39. Ethics and Pressure to Improve Profit Plans**

Art Conroy is the assistant controller of New City Muffler, Inc., a subsidiary of New City Automotive, which manufactures tailpipes, mufflers, and catalytic converters at several plants throughout North America. Because of pressure for lower selling prices, New City Muffler has had disappointing financial performance in recent years. Indeed, Conroy is aware of rumblings from corporate headquarters threatening to close the plant.

One of Conroy's responsibilities is to present the plant's financial plans for the coming year to the corporate officers and board of directors. In preparing for the presentation, Conroy was intrigued to note that the focal point of the budget presentation was a profit-volume graph projecting an increase in profits and a reduction in the break-even point.

Curious as to how the improvement would be accomplished, Conroy ultimately spoke with Paula Mitchell, the plant manager. Mitchell indicated that a planned increase in productivity would reduce variable costs and increase the contribution margin ratio.

When asked how the productivity increase would be accomplished, Mitchell made a vague reference to increasing the speed of the assembly line. Conroy commented that speeding up the assembly line could lead to labor problems because the speed of the line was set by union contract. Mitchell responded that she was afraid that if the speedup were opened to negotiation, the union would make a big "stink" that could result in the plant being closed. She indicated that the speedup was the "only way to save the plant, our jobs, and the jobs of all plant employees." Besides, she did not believe employees would notice a 2% or 3% increase in speed. Mitchell concluded the meeting observing, "You need to emphasize the results we will accomplish next year, not the details of how we will accomplish those results. Top management does not want to be bored with details. If we accomplish what we propose in the budget, we will be in for a big bonus."

Required

What advice do you have for Art Conroy?

LO3, 5   **MA16-40. CVP Analysis with Changing Cost Structure**

Cincinnati Bell (CBB)

Cincinnati Bell was formed in the 1870s as a telegraph provider. In the 1890s it expanded, bringing telephone services to Cincinnati and surrounding areas. The early equipment was quite primitive by today's standards. All calls were handled manually by operators, and all customers were on party lines. By the 1970s, however, all customers were on private lines, and mechanical switching devices handled routine local and long distance calls. Operators remained available for directory assistance, credit card calls, and emergencies. In the 1990s Cincinnati Bell added local Internet connections as an optional service to its regular customers.

Required

    a. Using a unit-level analysis, develop a graph with two lines, representing Cincinnati Bell's cost structure (1) in the 1970s and (2) in the late 1990s. Be sure to label the axes and lines.

    b. With sales revenue as the independent variable, what is the likely impact of the changed cost structure on Cincinnati Bell's (1) contribution margin percent and (2) break-even point?

    c. Discuss how the change in cost structure affected Cincinnati Bell's operating leverage and how this affects profitability under rising or falling sales scenarios.

MA16-41. Cost Estimation and CVP Analysis   LO2, 3

Presented are the functional income statements of Regional Distribution Inc. for two recent years:

REGIONAL DISTRIBUTION INC. Functional Income Statements For Years Ending December 31, Year 1 and Year 2				
		Year 1		Year 2
Sales.		$1,800,000		$1,585,000
Expenses				
Cost of goods sold	$1,350,000		$1,188,750	
Shipping	68,500		65,250	
Sales order processing	20,650		19,850	
Customer relations	55,000		48,800	
Depreciation	30,000		30,000	
Administrative	90,500	(1,614,650)	90,000	(1,442,650)
Before-tax profit		185,350		142,350
Income taxes (20%)		(37,070)		(28,470)
After-tax profit.		$ 148,280		$ 113,880

Required

a. Determine Regional Distribution's break-even point in sales dollars.
b. What dollar sales volume is required to earn an after-tax profit of $250,000?
c. Assuming sales of $4,000,000 next year, prepare a budgeted contribution income statement.
d. Discuss the reliability of the calculations in requirements (a–c), including the limitations of the CVP model and how they affect the reliability of the model.

Solutions to Review Problems

Review 16-1—Solution

a. Profit = $14X − ($10,000 + 5.25X)
b. At a volume of 6,200 cartons, Benchmark's profit is $44,250.
   Computed as ($14 × 6,200) − [$10,000 + ($5.25 × 6,200)]
   $86,800 − $42,550 = $44,250

Review 16-2—Solution

a.

SOLO CUP COMPANY Contribution Income Statement For the Month of September		
Sales (3,000 × $40)		$120,000
Less variable costs		
Direct materials (3,000 × $15)	$45,000	
Direct labor (3,000 × $3)	9,000	
Manufacturing overhead (3,000 × $10).	30,000	
Selling and administrative (3,000 × $2)	6,000	(90,000)
Contribution margin		30,000
Less fixed costs		
Manufacturing overhead.	15,000	
Selling and administrative.	10,000	(25,000)
Profit.		$ 5,000

b.

Selling price	$40 per unit
Variable costs	(30) per unit
Contribution margin	$10 per unit

$$\text{Contribution margin ratio} = \frac{\text{Unit contribution margin}}{\text{Unit selling price}}$$
$$= \$10 \div \$40$$
$$= 0.25$$

Review 16-3—Solution

a.

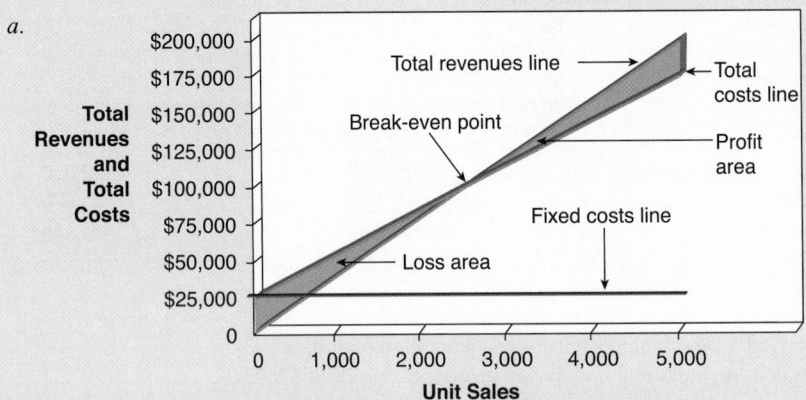

b.

$$\text{Break-even point} = \frac{\text{Fixed costs}}{\text{Unit contribution margin}}$$
$$= \$25,000 \div \$10$$
$$= 2,500 \text{ units}$$

c.

$$\text{Required dollar sales} = \frac{\text{Fixed costs} + \text{Desired profit}}{\text{Contribution margin ratio}}$$
$$= (\$25,000 + \$5,000) \div 0.25$$
$$= \$120,000$$

d.

$$\text{Required unit sales} = \frac{\text{Fixed costs} + \text{Desired before-tax profit}}{\text{Unit contribution margin}}$$

$$\text{Desired before-tax profit} = \$4,500 \div (1 - 0.40) = \$7,500$$
$$\text{Required unit sales} = (\$25,000 + \$7,500) \div \$10$$
$$= 3,250 \text{ units}$$

Review 16-4—Solution

a.

	Coffee	Tea	Smoothies	Total
Monthly unit sales.	6,000	3,750	2,250	
Selling price	$1.35	$1.25	$1.95	
Sales.	$8,100.00	$4,687.50	$4,387.50	$17,175.00
Variable costs	3,600.00	1,687.50	1,687.50	6,975.00
Contribution margin	$4,500.00	$3,000.00	$2,700.00	10,200.00
Fixed costs				8,000.00
Before-tax profit				$ 2,200.00
Contribution margin (CM) ratio	0.5556	0.6400	0.6154	0.5939
Current sales mix (based on sales dollars)	47.16%	27.29%	25.55%	

b.

$$\text{Break-even} = \frac{\text{Fixed costs}}{\text{Total contribution margin ratio}}$$

$$= \frac{\$8,000}{0.5939}$$

$$= \$13,470$$

Proof:			Sales		C/M Ratio	
Coffee:	$13,470 × 47.16%	=	$ 6,352.45	× 0.5556 =	$3,529.42	
Tea:	$13,470 × 27.29%	=	3,675.96	× 0.6400 =	2,352.62*	
Smoothies:	$13,470 × 25.55%	=	3,441.59	× 0.6154 =	2,117.96*	
			$13,470.00			
Total contribution margin					8,000.00	
Fixed costs					8,000.00	
Before-tax profit					–0–	

* Amounts adjusted to correct for minor rounding error.

Review 16-5—Solution

The Coffee Bean has an operating leverage of 4.636, calculated as a contribution margin of $10,200 divided by before-tax profit of $2,200. Therefore, if sales dollars increase by 20% to $20,610, before-tax profit should increase by 4.636 times 20%, or 92.73%, to $4,240. Because of the leverage caused by fixed costs, a 20% increase in sales results in a 92.73% increase in before-tax profit. Conversely, a 20% decrease in sales would result in a 92.73% decrease in before-tax profits to $160.

Proof:	20% Sales Increase	20% Sales Decrease
Sales..	$20,610	$13,740
CM %	× 0.5939	× 0.5939
Total CM	12,240	8,160
Fixed costs	8,000	8,000
Before-tax profit	$ 4,240	$ 160

Current before-tax profit of $2,200 × (1 + 0.9273) = $4,240
Current before-tax profit of $2,200 × (1 − 0.9273) = $160

Review 16-6—Solution

Weekly contribution per average customer:

$17 sales per visit × (1 − 0.80) contribution ratio × 1.50 visits = $5.10

Annual contribution per customer = $5.10 × 52 weeks = $265.20

Customers required for desired profit = ($80,000 + $40,000)/$265.20 = 453 (rounded up to the next whole number)

Required population = 453 customers/0.05 customers in population = 9,060

Module 17

Relevant Costs and Benefits for Decision Making

Relevant Costs and Benefits for Decision Making			
Identifying Relevant Costs	**Differential Analysis of Relevant Costs**	**Applying Differential Analysis**	**Use of Limited Resources**
▪ Relevance of Future Revenues ▪ Relevance of Outlay Costs ▪ Irrelevance of Sunk Costs ▪ Sunk Costs Can Cause Ethical Dilemmas ▪ Relevance of Disposal and Salvage Values ▪ Relevance of Opportunity Costs	▪ Differential Cost Analysis	▪ Multiple Changes in Profit Plans ▪ Special Orders ▪ Outsourcing Decisions ▪ Sell or Process Further	▪ Single Constraint ▪ Multiple Constraints ▪ Theory of Constraints ▪ Limitations of Decision Analysis Models
Review 17-1	Review 17-2	Review 17-3, 17-4, 17-5, 17-6	Review 17-7

Every day companies, both large and small, are faced with making critical decisions that can drastically alter their likelihood of success. Some of these decisions are long term in nature, such as where a company should invest in property, plant, and equipment. Others are short-run decisions, such as whether or not to sell a product or service to a new customer at a price that is below the normal market price.

San Francisco startup company Uber got its start from pondering a common dilemma: how to get home from the club late at night. Founder Travis Kalanick explains that he and a friend joked, ". . . let's go buy 10 Mercedes S-Classes, let's go hire 20 drivers, let's get parking garages and let's make it so we could push a button and an S-Class would roll up, for only us, in the city of San Francisco, where you cannot get a ride." Shortly thereafter, an iPhone application called Uber was launched in 2010. Uber has now expanded to over 700 cities in 63 countries.

Uber's intent was to act as a broker by matching riders to available drivers with a summons via smartphones. But the company first had to decide whether it should purchase cars and pay for insurance, storage, and other associated costs or whether to contract with existing drivers, either limousine companies or individual drivers. In the end, Uber decided to contract with partners (limo companies or individuals) who had their own vehicles. These partners take responsibility for licensing, vehicle cost and maintenance, gas, auto insurance, and storage. In return, Uber trains the drivers on the software platform and pays them a percentage of the fare.

By acting as a broker instead of owning its own vehicles, Uber was able to minimize its fixed costs. This "operating leverage" results in a greater benefit from increases in customers, because the fixed costs don't need to increase to handle the higher capacity. However, the company's capacity is limited by how many drivers it has on contract. This limited resource can be maximized by minimizing the downtime of its drivers. Uber invested in engineers to build algorithms to manage its supply of drivers and demand of riders. The efficient management of this limited resource benefits both drivers (who are more likely to be engaged in fare-generating activity) and riders, who can use the software's tracking feature to see their car's progress toward the predetermined pickup destination.

Uber has successfully changed the way people think about transportation. It reported $11.3 billion in net revenue in 2018. However it also spent approximately $1.16 for every $1.00 of revenue it earned, with 2018 operating losses of $1.8 billion.

As Uber emphasizes growth over pofits, the company is betting that investing in areas such as mapping technology, food delivery, and autonomous vehicles will reduce the real cost of transportation.

In this module, we will learn how to incorporate the relevant revenues and costs to simplify decision making, even when operating in a complex, changing environment.

Road Map

LO	Learning Objective | Topics	Page	eLecture	Guided Example	Assignments
17-1	**Distinguish between relevant and irrelevant revenues and costs.** Future Revenues :: Outlay Costs :: Sunk Costs :: Disposal and Salvage Values :: Opportunity Costs	17-3	e17-1	Review 17-1	11, 12, 13, 14, 15, 16, 17, 18, 19, 20, 21, 22, 23, 24, 28, 29, 30, 31, 32, 33, 34, 35, 36
17-2	**Analyze relevant costs and indicate how they differ under alternative decision scenarios.** Differential Costs	17-7	e17-2	Review 17-2	13, 15, 16, 17, 18, 19, 20, 21, 22, 23, 24, 28, 29, 30, 31, 32, 33, 34, 35, 36
17-3	**Apply differential analysis to evaluate changes in profit plans.** Multiple Changes in Profit Plans	17-8	e17-3	Review 17-3	28, 29, 33, 34, 36
17-4	**Apply differential analysis to evaluate whether to accept a special order.** Special Orders :: Time Span and Opportunity Costs :: Qualitative Considerations	17-10	e17-4	Review 17-4	16, 18, 19, 20, 31, 32, 33, 34
17-5	**Apply differential analysis to evaluate outsourcing decisions.** Make or Buy :: Opportunity Costs :: Qualitative Risk Factors	17-13	e17-5	Review 17-5	21, 22, 23, 33, 34
17-6	**Apply differential analysis to evaluate whether to sell or further process a product.** Single Product Decisions :: Joint Product Decisions	17-16	e17-6	Review 17-6	17, 24, 27
17-7	**Allocate limited resources for purposes of maximizing short-run profit.** Single Constraint :: Multiple Constraints :: Theory of Constraints :: Limitations of Decision Analysis Models	17-18	e17-7	Review 17-7	25, 26

The purpose of this module is to examine approaches to identifying and analyzing revenue and cost information for specific decisions, such as the decision to outsource. Our emphasis is on identifying **relevant costs** (future costs that differ among competing decision alternatives) and distinguishing relevant costs from **irrelevant costs** that do not differ among competing decision alternatives. We consider a number of frequently encountered decisions: to make multiple changes in profit plans, to accept or reject a special order, to acquire a component or service internally or externally, to sell a product or process it further, and how to best use limited capacity. These decision situations are not exhaustive; they only illustrate relevant cost concepts. Once we understand these concepts, we can apply them to a variety of decision scenarios.

Although our focus in this module is on profit maximization, decisions should not be based solely on this criterion, especially maximizing profit in the short run. Managers must consider the implications decision alternatives have on long-run profit, as well as legal, ethical, social, and other nonquantitative factors. These factors can lead management to select a course of action other than that selected by financial information alone.

Identifying Relevant Costs

eLectures **LO1**
MBC Distinguish
between
relevant and
irrelevant revenues
and costs.

For a specific decision, the key to relevent cost analysis is first to identify the relevant costs (and revenues) and then to organize them in a manner that clearly indicates how they differ under each alternative. Consider the following equipment replacement decision.

Beats by Dr. Dre (Beats), a subsidiary of **Apple Inc.**, produces headphones and supplies high-quality components and equalizer software to HP for its line of personal computers. Assume that one of its components used in wireless headsets is forecasted to sell 10,000 units during the coming year at a price of $20 per unit. Further assume that each of Beats' components is manufactured with separate machines in a shared plant.

The machine used in the manufacture of headset components is two years old and has a remaining useful life of four years. Its purchase price was $90,000 (new), and it has an estimated salvage value of zero dollars at the end of its useful life. Its current book value (original cost less accumulated depreciation) is $60,000, but it could be sold today for only $35,000.

Headset component costs	
Direct materials	$3.00 per unit
Conversion	5.00 per unit
Selling and distribution	1.00 per unit
Inspection and adjustment	$500 per batch
	(1,000 units)
Depreciation on machines	$15,000 per year
Machine maintenance	$ 200 per month
Advertising	$ 5,000 per year
Common costs	
Administrative salaries	$65,000 per year
Building operations	23,000 per year
Building rent	24,000 per year

Management is evaluating the desirability of replacing the machine with a new machine. The new machine costs $80,000, has a useful life of four years, and a predicted salvage value of zero dollars at the end of its useful life. Although the new machine has the same production capacity as the old machine, its predicted operating costs are lower because it consumes less electricity. Further, because of a computer control system, the new machine allows production of twice as many units between inspections and adjustments, and the cost of inspections and adjustments is lower. The new machine requires only annual, rather than monthly, overhauls. Hence, machine maintenance costs are lower. Costs for the new machine are predicted as follows:

Conversion costs	$4.00 per unit
Inspection and adjustment	$ 300 per batch (2,000 units)
Machine maintenance	$ 200 per year

All other costs and all revenues remain unchanged.

The decision alternatives are to keep the old machine or to replace it with a new machine. An analysis of how costs and revenues differ under each alternative assists management in making the best choice. The first objective of this module is to study the distinction between relevant and irrelevant items. After evaluating the relevance of each item, we develop an analysis of relevant costs.

Relevance of Future Revenues

Revenues, which are inflows of resources from the sale of goods and services, are relevant to a decision only if they differ between alternatives. In this example, revenues are not relevant because they are identical under each alternative. They would be relevant if the new machine had greater capacity or if management intended to change the selling price should it acquire the new machine. (The $35,000 disposal value of the old machine is an inflow. However, *revenues* refer to resources from the sale of goods and services to customers in the normal course of business. We include the sale of the old machine under disposal and salvage values.)

The hypothetical keep-or-replace decision facing Beats' management might be called a **cost reduction proposal** because it is based on the assumption that the organization is committed to an activity and that management desires to minimize the cost of activities. Here, the two alternatives are either to continue operating with the old machine or to replace it with a new machine.

Although this approach is appropriate for many activities, managers should remember that they have another alternative—discontinue operations. To simplify the analysis, managers normally do not consider the alternative to discontinue when operations appear to be profitable. However, if there is any doubt about an operation's profitability, this alternative should be considered. Because revenues change if an operation is discontinued, revenues are relevant whenever this alternative is considered.

Relevance of Outlay Costs

Outlay costs are costs that require future expenditures of cash or other resources. Outlay costs that differ under the decision alternatives are relevant; outlay costs that do not differ are irrelevant. Assume Beats' relevant and irrelevant outlay costs for the equipment replacement decision follow.

Relevant Outlay Costs	Irrelevant Outlay Costs
Conversion Costs	Direct Materials
Inspection and Adjustment Costs	Selling and Distributon
Cost of New Machine	Advertising
Machine Maintenance	Common Outlay Costs

Irrelevance of Sunk Costs

Sunk costs result from past decisions that cannot be changed. Suppose we purchased a car for $30,000 five years ago. Today we must decide whether to purchase another car or have major maintenance performed on our current car. In making this decision, the purchase price of our current car is a sunk cost.

Although the relevance of outlay costs is determined by the decision scenario, sunk costs are never relevant. The cost of the old machine is a sunk cost, not a future cost. This cost and the related depreciation result from the past decision to acquire the old machine. Even though all the outlay costs discussed earlier would be relevant to a decision to continue or discontinue operations, the sunk cost of the old machine is not relevant even to this decision.

If management elects to keep the old machine, its book value will be depreciated over its remaining useful life of four years. However, if management elects to replace the old machine, its book value is written off when it is replaced. Even if management elects to discontinue operations, the book value of the old machine must be written off.

Sunk Costs Can Cause Ethical Dilemmas

Although the book value of the old machine has no economic significance, the accounting treatment of past costs may make it psychologically difficult for managers to regard them as irrelevant. If management replaces the old machine, a $25,000 accounting loss is recorded in the year of replacement:

Book value	$60,000
Disposal value	(35,000)
Loss on disposal.	$25,000

The possibility of recording an accounting loss can create an ethical dilemma for managers. Although an action may be desirable from the long-run viewpoint of the organization, in the short run, choosing the action may result in an accounting loss. Fearing the loss will lead superiors to question her judgment, a manager might prefer to use the old machine (with lower total profits over the four-year period) as opposed to replacing it and being forced to record a loss on disposal. Although this action may avoid raising troublesome questions in the near term, the cumulative effect of many decisions of this nature is harmful to the organization's long-run economic health.

From an economic viewpoint, the analysis should focus on future costs and revenues that differ. The decision should not be influenced by sunk costs. Although there is no easy solution to this behavioral and ethical problem, managers and management accountants should be aware of its potential impact.

Managerial Decision ■ You Are the Vice President of Manufacturing

You recently made the decision to purchase a very expensive machine for your manufacturing plant that used technology that was well established over several years. The purchase of this machine was a major decision supported by the chief financial officer, based solely on your recommendation. Shortly after making the purchase, you were attending a trade convention where you learned of new technology that is now available that essentially renders obsolete the machine you recently purchased. You feel that it may be best for the company to acquire the new technology since most of your competitors will be using it soon; however, you feel that this cannot be done now that you have recently purchased the new machine. What should you do? [Answer, p. 17-21]

Relevance of Disposal and Salvage Values

Beats' assumed revenues (inflows of resources from operations) from the sale of headset components were discussed earlier. The sale of fixed assets is also a source of resources. Because the sale of fixed assets is a nonoperating item, cash inflows obtained from these sales are discussed separately.

The disposal value of the old machine is a relevant cash inflow. It is obtained only if the replacement alternative is selected. Any salvage value available at the end of the useful life of either machine is also relevant. A loss on disposal can have a favorable tax impact if the loss can be offset against taxable gains or taxable income. To simplify the analysis, we ignore any tax implications at this point. The tax effects related to capital asset transactions are discussed in Module 25.

Relevance of Opportunity Costs

When making a decision between alternative courses of action, accepting one alternative results in rejecting the other alternative(s). Any benefit foregone as a result of rejecting one opportunity in favor of another opportunity is described as an **opportunity cost** of the accepted alternative.

For example, if you are employed at a salary of $40,000 per year and you have the opportunity to continue to work or the opportunity to go back to school full-time for two years to earn a graduate degree, the cost of getting the degree includes not only all the outlay costs for tuition, books, and so forth, it also includes the salary foregone (or opportunity cost) of $40,000 per year. So, if your tuition and other outlay costs are going to be $25,000 per year for two years, the cost of earning the degree will be $50,000 of outlay costs and $80,000 of opportunity costs, for a total cost of earning the degree of $130,000. Opportunity costs are always relevant in making decisions among competing alternatives.

The following is a summary of all the relevant and irrelevant costs discussed in this section.

Relevant Costs		Irrelevant Costs	
Future costs that differ among competing alternatives		Future costs that do not differ among competing alternatives	
Opportunity Costs	**Relevant Outlay Costs**	**Irrelevant Outlay Costs**	**Sunk Costs**
Net benefits foregone of rejected alternatives	Future costs requiring future expenditures that differ	Future costs requiring future expenditures that do not differ	Historical costs resulting from past decisions

---

Research Insight ■ Why Don't Managers Always Ignore Sunk Costs?

For decades, business school students have learned that sunk costs are irrelevant to decision making; however, managers still find these costs difficult to ignore. Researchers have shown that, far from ignoring sunk costs, many managers increase commitment to a project as sunk costs increase. Recent experimental research from a team at the University of Melbourne in Australia sheds more light on the precise motivations of managers who choose not to ignore sunk costs. The researchers found that the managers' personal motivations interact with the context of the specific project and the related sunk costs. Their study found that individuals who are focused on promotion become increasingly fixated on completion as the end of the project nears. While other managers are able to ignore fixed costs more consistently throughout the project life cycle, those who are focused on promotion are most likely to continue to invest in a project that should be abandoned when the project is close to completion. As managerial accountants advise executive teams, this type of bias should be kept in mind.

Source: Adam P. Barsky and Michael J. Zyphur, "Disentangling Sunk-Costs and Completion Proximity: The Role of Regulatory Focus," *Journal of Experimental Social Psychology* 65 (2016): 105-108.

LO1 Review 17-1

TaylorMade-Adidas Golf Company, a subsidiary of Adidas, manufactures golf clubs using "adjustable weight technology" or AWT. Suppose a European machine company has proposed to sell TaylorMade a new highly automated machine that would reduce significantly the labor cost of producing its golf clubs. The cost of the machine is $1,000,000, and would have an expected life of five years, at the end of which it would have a residual value of $100,000. It has an estimated operating cost of $10,000 per month. The direct labor cost savings per club from using the machine is estimated to be $5 per club. In addition, one monthly salaried manufacturing manager, whose salary is $6,000 per month would no longer be needed. Assume the Vice President of Manufacturing earns $10,000 per month. Also, the new machine would free up about 5,000 square feet of space from the displaced workers. Assume TaylorMade's building is held under a 10-year lease that has eight years remaining. The current lease cost is $1 per square foot per month. TaylorMade may be able to use the space for other purposes, and it has received an offer to rent it to a nearby related company for $3,500 per month.

Required
Identify all of the costs described above as either "relevant" or "irrelevant" to the decision to acquire the new machine.

Solution on p. 17-36.

Differential Analysis of Relevant Costs

eLectures **LO2**
MBC Analyze
relevant
costs and
indicate how
they differ under
alternative decision
scenarios.

Differential cost analysis is an approach to the analysis of relevant costs that focuses on the costs that differ under alternative actions. A differential analysis of relevant costs for Beats' equipment replacement decision is in Exhibit 17.1. Replacement provides a net advantage of $17,800 over the life of both machines versus keeping the old machine.

An alternative analysis to that presented in Exhibit 17.1 is to present all revenues and costs (relevant and irrelevant) for each alternative in separate columns, such that the bottom line of the analysis is the total profit or loss for each alternative. This method is preferred if the goal is to determine the total profitability of each alternative. If the goal is to determine which of the two alternatives is most profitable, then a differential analysis is preferred.

Exhibit 17.1 ■ Differential Analysis for Beats' Equipment Replacement

	Four-Year Totals		
	Replace with New Machine	**Keep Old Machine**	**Difference (effect of replacement on income)**
Conversion			
Old machine (10,000 units × $5 × 4 years).............		$200,000	
New machine (10,000 units × $4 × 4 years)............	$160,000		($40,000)
Inspection and adjustment			
Old machine (10* setups × $500 × 4 years).............		20,000	
New machine (5** setups × $300 × 4 years)	6,000		(14,000)
Machine maintenance			
Old machine ($200 per month × 12 months × 4 years) ...		9,600	
New machine ($200 per year × 4 years)...............	800		(8,800)
Disposal of old machine.............................	(35,000)		(35,000)
Cost of new machine	80,000		80,000
Totals	$211,800	$229,600	($17,800)
Advantage of replacement...........................		$17,800	

* Old machine: 10,000 units ÷ 1,000 units per batch
** New machine: 10,000 units ÷ 2,000 units per batch

Assuming the organization is committed to providing a particular product or service, a differential analysis of relevant costs (as shown in Exhibit 17.1) is preferred to a complete analysis of all costs and revenues for a number of reasons:

■ A differential analysis focuses on only those items that differ, providing a clearer picture of the impact of the decision. Management is less apt to be confused by this analysis than by one that combines relevant and irrelevant items.

■ A differential analysis contains fewer items, making it easier and quicker to prepare.

■ A differential analysis can help to simplify complex situations (such as those encountered by multiple-product or multiple-plant firms), when it is difficult to develop complete firmwide statements to analyze all decision alternatives.

Before preparing a differential analysis, it is always desirable to reassess the organization's commitment to a product or service. This helps avoid "throwing good money after bad." If Beats currently had large annual losses, acquiring the new machine would merely reduce total losses over the next four years by $17,800. In this case, discontinuing operations (a third alternative) should also be considered.

TaylorMade-Adidas Golf Company, a subsidiary of Adidas, manufactures golf clubs using "adjustable weight technology" or AWT. Suppose a European machine company has proposed to sell TaylorMade a new highly automated machine that would reduce significantly the labor cost of producing its golf clubs. The cost of the machine is $1,000,000, and would have an expected life of five years, at the end of which it would have a residual value of $100,000. It has an estimated operating cost of $10,000 per month. The direct labor cost savings per club from using the machine is estimated to be $5 per club. In addition, one monthly salaried manufacturing manager, whose salary is $6,000 per month would no longer be needed. Assume the Vice President of Manufacturing earns $10,000 per month. Also, the new machine would free up about 5,000 square feet of space from the displaced workers. Assume TaylorMade's building is held under a 10-year lease that has eight years remaining. The current lease cost is $1 per square foot per month. TaylorMade may be able to use the space for other purposes, and it has received an offer to rent it to a nearby related company for $3,500 per month.

Required

a. Assuming the new machine would be used to produce an average of 5,000 clubs per month, prepare a differential analysis of the relevant costs of buying the machine and using it for the next five years, versus continuing to use hand labor.

b. In addition to the quantitative analysis in requirement *a*, what qualitative considerations are important for making the right decision?

Solution on p. 17-36.

Applying Differential Analysis

Differential analysis is used to provide information for a variety of planning and decision-making situations. This section illustrates some of the more frequently encountered applications of differential analysis. To focus on differential analysis concepts, we will continue with the **Uber** discussion introduced in the opening vignette of this module. For the purposes of our example, we assume a simplified financial model, which consists of variable costs based on number of miles driven and costs that are fixed in the short run. As Uber is primarily a technology company, other than driver fees, its costs are generally related to the processing, storage, and communication of information. Also, for this example, we assume that the entire amount of the customer fees collected by the drivers is categorized as revenue for Uber and the fees paid out to the drivers are categorized as variable driver fees.

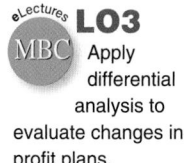

LO3
Apply differential analysis to evaluate changes in profit plans.

Multiple Changes in Profit Plans

Assume Uber collects an average of $45 for every 10 miles of customer rides. Variable costs per every 10 miles and fixed costs per month are as follows:

Variable Costs*		Fixed Costs per Month	
Driver fees	$35.00	Platform and cloud-based data storage	$ 40,000
Platform and cloud-based data storage	1.50	Mapping technology	75,000
Mapping technology	2.00	Advertising	5,000
Customer service	0.50	Total	$120,000
Total	$39.00		

*Per every 10 miles

    Assume the contribution margin per every 10 miles driven is $6 ($45 customer collection less $39 variable costs). Uber's hypothetical contribution income statement for April is presented in Exhibit 17.2. Assume the April operations are typical and monthly miles driven average 300,000 miles, with monthly profits averaging $60,000.

    Management wants to know the effect that each of the following three mutually exclusive alternatives would have on monthly profits.

1. The introduction of a bonus program. For every 500 miles a driver completes within a month, the driver receives an additional $25. The bonus program is expected to result in a 10% increase in miles per month and a bonus payout of $10,000 per month.

2. Increasing the cost of the rides to the customers by an average of $1 per every 10 miles. The average payout to the drivers will remain constant at $35 per every 10 miles. This should result in a decrease of 50,000 in monthly miles.

3. Decreasing the cost of the rides to the customers by an average of $1 per every 10 miles. The average payout to the drivers will remain constant at $35 per every 10 miles driven. This should result in an increase of 60,000 in monthly miles. Uber faces a constraint of driver availability. To encourage its drivers to work more, Uber is offering to pay an extra $1 for every 10 miles, after a driver completes 1,200 miles within a one-week period. Assume that 30,000 miles will be paid out at the higher rate.

It is possible to develop contribution income statements for each alternative and then determine the profit impact of the proposed change by comparing the new income with the current income. A more direct approach is to use differential analysis and focus on only those items that differ under each alternative.

Alternative 1	
Profit increase from increased miles (3,000* × $6)	$18,000
Profit decrease from bonus.	(10,000)
Increase in monthly profit	$ 8,000

*(300,000 × 10%) divided by 10

Alternative 2	
Profit decrease from reduced miles (5,000* × $6)	$(30,000)
Profit increase from increased price**.	25,000
Decrease in monthly profit	$ (5,000)

*50,000 divided by 10
**[(300,000 current miles − 50,000 lost miles) divided by 10] × $1

Alternative 3	
Profit increase from increase in miles (6,000* × $6).	$36,000
Profit decrease from reduced selling price (36,000** × $1)	(36,000)
Profit decrease from increased driver fees (3,000*** × $1)	($3,000)
Decrease in monthly profit	($3,000)

*60,000 divided by 10
**(300,000 current miles + 60,000 increased miles) divided by 10
***30,000 divided by 10

Alternatives 2 and 3 are undesirable because they would each result in a decrease in monthly profit. Because Alternative 1 results in an increase in monthly profit, it is preferred to both Alternatives 2 and 3.

Review 17-3 LO3

Epson produces color cartridges for inkjet printers. Suppose cartridges are sold to mail-order distributors for $4.80 each and that manufacturing and other costs are as follows:

Variable Costs per Unit		Fixed Costs per Month	
Direct materials.	$2.00	Factory overhead	$15,000
Direct labor.	0.20	Selling and administrative.	5,000
Factory overhead	0.25	Total	$20,000
Distribution	0.05		
Total	$2.50		

continued

continued from previous page

The variable distribution costs are for transportation to mail-order distributors. Also assume the current monthly production and sales volume is 15,000 and monthly capacity is 20,000 units.

Required

Determine the effect of the following independent situations on monthly profits.

a. A $1.50 increase in the unit selling price should result in an 1,800 unit decrease in monthly sales.

b. A $1.80 decrease in the unit selling price should result in a 6,000 unit increase in monthly sales. However, because of capacity constraints, the last 1,000 units would be produced during overtime, when the direct labor costs increase by 50%.   **Solution on p. 17-37.**

Special Orders

Assume that a not-for-profit is hosting a fundraising dinner, and it would like to offer its attendees Uber rides home from the event at a reduced rate of $40 for every 10 miles. The total expected miles related to the fundraiser are 3,000. Uber drivers will not be called to the site via the online app as the drivers will be ready and waiting at the event when it is over. Therefore, the mapping technology fees can be reduced to $1.50 per every 10 miles. Also assume that the driver fees will remain constant at $35 per every 10 miles. Uber has sufficient driver capacity to handle the event without reducing its rides to other customers. Uber's management wants to know the profit impact of accepting the offer. The following analysis focuses on those costs and revenues that will differ if the offer is accepted.

eLectures **LO4**
MBC Apply differential analysis to evaluate whether to accept a special order.

Increase in revenues (300* × $40)		$12,000
Increase in costs		
Driver fees (300* × $35)	$10,500	
Platform and cloud-based data storage (300* × $1.50)	450	
Mapping technology (300* × $1.50)	450	
Customer service (300* × $0.50)	150	11,550
Increase in profits		$ 450

*3,000 divided by 10

Accepting the offer will result in a profit increase of $450. Although this is not a significant increase, management might consider this to be a great marketing opportunity and a chance to convert the attendees into future customers.

If management were unaware of relevant cost concepts, they might be tempted to compare the special event price of $40 to the average cost per every 10 miles as developed from the accounting reports. Based on Uber's hypothetical April contribution income statement in Exhibit 17.2, the average cost per every 10 miles was $43, calculated as follows.

Total variable costs.	$1,170,000
Total fixed costs	120,000
Total costs	1,290,000
Total miles divided by 10 (300,000/10).	30,000
Average cost per every 10 miles	$ 43

Comparing the special event price of $40 per 10 miles to the average cost of $43, management might conclude the event would result in a loss of $3 per 10 miles.

It is apparent that the $43 figure encompasses variable costs of $39 per 10 miles (including irrelevant variable mapping technology costs of $0.50 per 10 miles) and irrelevant fixed costs of $120,000 spread over 3,000 miles. But remember, management may not have detailed cost information. To obtain appropriate information for decision-making purposes, management must ask its accounting staff for the specific information needed. Different configurations of cost information are provided for different purposes. In the absence of special instructions, the accounting staff might not supply relevant cost information.

Exhibit 17.2 ■ Contribution Income Statement		
UBER **Contribution Income Statement** **For the Month of April**		
Revenue (30,000* × $45.00)		$1,350,000
Less variable costs		
Driver fees (30,000* × $35.00)...........................	$1,050,000	
Platform and cloud-based data storage (30,000* × $1.50)...............	45,000	
Mapping technology (30,000* × $2.00).............................	60,000	
Customer service (30,000* × $0.50).............................	15,000	(1,170,000)
Contribution margin		180,000
Less fixed costs		
Platform and cloud-based data storage	40,000	
Mapping technology	75,000	
Advertising	5,000	(120,000)
Profit...		$ 60,000

*300,000 divided by 10

Importance of Time Span and Opportunity Costs

The special event is a one-time contract for 3,000 miles that will use current excess driver capacity. Because no special setups or technology are required to manage the event, it is appropriate to consider only variable costs in computing the event's profitability.

But what if the not-for-profit wanted Uber to sign a multiyear contract to provide 3,000 miles per month at $40 per every 10 miles? Under these circumstances, management would be well advised to reject the contract because there is a high probability that cost increases would make the order unprofitable in later years. At the very least, management should insist that a cost escalation clause be added to the agreement, specifying that the customer price would increase to cover any cost increases and detailing the cost computation.

Of more concern is the variable nature of all long-run costs. Given adequate time, management must replace fixed assets and may have to adjust the amount and quality of its equipment and technology. Accordingly, *in the long run, all costs (including costs classified as fixed in a given period) are relevant.* To remain in business in the long run, Uber must replace equipment, pay taxes, pay administrative salaries, and so forth. Consequently, management should consider *all costs,* fixed and variable, in evaluating a long-term contract.

Full costs include all costs, regardless of their behavior pattern or activity level. The average full cost per unit is sometimes used to approximate long-run variable costs. If accepting a long-term contract increases the monthly miles to 303,000, the average full cost per every 10 miles will be $42.97.

Driver fees	$35.00
Platform and cloud-based data storage	1.50
Mapping technology	2.00
Customer service support......................................	0.50
Platform and cloud-based data storage (40,000/30,300*)	1.32**
Mapping technology (75,000/30,300*)	2.48**
Advertising (5,000/30,300*)	0.17**
Average full cost per every 10 miles..........................	$42.97**

*303,000 divided by 10
**Rounded

In this case, the estimated long-run variable costs are $42.97 per every 10 miles. Many managers would say this is the minimum acceptable selling price, especially if the order extends over a long period of time.

Because Uber has excess productive driver capacity, no opportunity cost is associated with accepting the not-for-profit's one-time offer. There is no alternative use of the driving time related to the event, in the short run, so there is no opportunity cost.

But what if Uber was operating at driver capacity? In that case, accepting the special offer would require reducing regular miles. Assume hiring new drivers is not a possibility in the short run and there are safety concerns with having the current drivers driving too many miles. With an alternative use of the drivers' time, an opportunity cost is associated with using the drivers to drive for the fundraising event.

Every 10 miles driven at the event could otherwise generate a $6 contribution from regular customers. Accepting the special event would cause Uber to incur an opportunity cost of $1,800 for the contribution margin lost from foregoing rides to regular customers.

Lost fees to regular customers (3,000 miles/10)	300
Regular contribution margin per 10 miles.	× $6
Opportunity cost of accepting special event.	$1,800

Because this opportunity cost exceeds the $450 contribution derived from the special event, management might reject the special event. Accepting the event will reduce profits by $1,350 ($450 contribution – $1,800 opportunity cost). As discussed previously, there are also qualitative considerations. Even though there is a loss expected from accepting the special event, management might consider this a great marketing opportunity to reach out to new customers and decide that it is worthwhile to accept the order.

Qualitative Considerations

Although an analysis of cost and revenue information may indicate that a special order is profitable in the short run, management might still reject the order because of qualitative considerations. Any concerns regarding the order's impact on regular customers might lead management to reject the order even if there is excess capacity. If the order involves a special low price, regular customers might demand a similar price reduction and threaten to take their business elsewhere. Alternatively, management might accept the special order while operating at capacity if they believed there were long-term benefits associated with penetrating a new market. Legal factors must also be considered if the special order is from a buyer who competes with regular customers.

LO4 Review 17-4

Epson produces color cartridges for inkjet printers. Suppose cartridges are sold to mail-order distributors for $4.80 each and that manufacturing and other costs are as follows:

Variable Costs per Unit		Fixed Costs per Month	
Direct materials.	$2.00	Factory overhead	$15,000
Direct labor.	0.20	Selling and administrative.	5,000
Factory overhead	0.25	Total	$20,000
Distribution	0.05		
Total	$2.50		

The variable distribution costs are for transportation to mail-order distributors. Also assume the current monthly production and sales volume is 15,000 and monthly capacity is 20,000 units.

Required
Determine the effect of the following independent situations on monthly profits.

a. A Russian distributor has proposed to place a special, one-time order for 4,000 units next month at a reduced price of $4.00 per unit. The distributor would pay all transportation costs. There would be additional fixed selling and administrative costs of $500.00.

b. An Austrian distributor has proposed to place a special, one-time order for 8,000 units at a special price of $4.00 per unit. The distributor would pay all transportation costs. There would be additional fixed selling and administrative costs of $500.00. Assume overtime production is not possible.

Solution on p. 17-37.

Outsourcing Decisions (Make or Buy)

eLectures
MBC **LO5**
Apply
differential
analysis to
evaluate outsourcing
decisions.

One of the most common applications of relevant cost analysis involves the make-or-buy decision. Virtually any service, product, or component that can be produced or manufactured internally can also be acquired from an external source. The procurement of services, products, or components from an external source is called **outsourcing**. For example, the management of the bookstore at your college or university is likely outsourced to **Barnes and Noble** or **Follett**, and the dining facilities may be outsourced to **Compass Group North America** or **Aramark Corporation**. Similarly, **HP** and, more recently, **Samsung** actually manufacture very few of the components of their computers. Instead the manufacture of components is outsourced to other firms such as **Intel** for computer chips and **Seagate** for storage devices. Virtually all computer manufacturers, with the exception of **Apple**, outsource their operating systems to **Microsoft**.

Any time you call a customer support call center, the representative reached is likely to be working in a different country. A growing number of companies even outsource employees from employee leasing companies. In the past 25 years, outsourcing of goods and services has expanded exponentially with the emergence of well-trained, low-cost labor forces in China and India and other parts of the world.

As the above discussion reveals, the decision to outsource rather than to produce a service or product internally involves a vast array of qualitative issues. The quantitative issues surrounding the outsourcing (or make-or-buy) decision are often less challenging. To illustrate, we continue the Uber example. Suppose a technology firm, DataTech, offers Uber a one-year contract to manage all of Uber's data storage service at a cost of $15,000 per month. Uber is now faced with the decision to continue to supply the data storage service internally or outsource the technology to DataTech. An analysis of the decision reveals that if Uber accepts the offer, it will be able to reduce the following:

- Variable platform and data storage costs by $0.20 per 10 miles.

- Fixed platform and data storage costs by $5,000.

Business Insight ■ When Being Liked Is Worth the Money

Comcast wants to be loved. After years of being enthusiastically anchored to the bottom of customer satisfaction surveys, Comcast is changing strategies. Finally faced with competition from on-demand services such as Netflix, Hulu, and Amazon, Comcast has decided that it is time to court its customers. This initiative has two parts. First, the company has begun to improve customer service by redesigning physical locations to feel more welcoming and Apple-like. Second, it has developed a new app to help customers plan around service visits, tracking the technician's estimated time of arrival to make the visit convenient for customers.

The second part of this effort also takes a page from the Apple playbook: make Internet, TV, and home-security devices that people can connect with. Fraser Stirling, head of hardware development at Comcast, says, "we are genuinely trying to create an emotional experience, whether that's love, or whatever, like you have with your phone. We want people to be able to put something from Comcast in their study or their living room and people can look at it and go 'Oof, what is that? It's amazing.'"

Differential analysis helps a company like Comcast weigh the increased costs associated with customer satisfaction and hardware design against the forecasted loss of customers to on-demand entertainment. This sort of analysis helps companies deal with the changing realities of their markets. For years Comcast had significant market power and, thus, sought to deliver cable at the lowest possible cost; now facing competition, the company finds it profitable to invest in the customer's experience. Ultimately, it may be the answer to managerial accounting questions that drive increased satisfaction.

Source: Felix Gillette, "Can a Company You Hate Make a Cable Box You Love?" *Bloomberg Businessweek*, June 23, 2016.

A differential analysis of Uber's decision to supply storage service internally or to outsource it is presented in Exhibit 17.3. Continuing to provide the service internally has a net advantage of $4,000.

But what if the data storage capacity created by outsourcing to DataTech can be used to provide storage services to another company for $7,000 per month? In this case, the storage capacity has an alternative use, and the net cash flow from this alternative use is an opportunity cost of providing the service internally. Treating the revenue Uber will not receive if it continues to source data storage internally as an opportunity cost, the analysis in Exhibit 17.4 indicates that outsourcing now has a net advantage of $3,000.

Exhibit 17.3 ■ Differential Analysis of Outsourcing Decision

	Cost to Do Internally		Cost to Outsource	Difference (income effect of outsourcing)
Cost to outsource data storage			$15,000	$(15,000)
Cost to do internally				
Variable costs related to data storage ($0.20 × 30,000*) . . .	$ 6,000			6,000
Fixed costs related to data storage.	5,000			5,000
Total	$11,000		$15,000	$ (4,000)
Advantage of providing service internally.		$4,000		

*300,000 miles divided by 10

Exhibit 17.4 ■ Differential Analysis of of Outsourcing Decision with Opportunity Cost

	Cost to Do Internally		Cost to Outsource	Difference (income effect of outsourcing)
Cost to outsource data storage			$15,000	$(15,000)
Cost to do internally				
Variable costs related to data storage ($0.20 × 30,000*) . . .	$ 6,000			6,000
Fixed costs related to data storage.	5,000			5,000
Opportunity cost of lost subscription revenue.	7,000			7,000
Total	$18,000		$15,000	$ 3,000
Advantage of outsourcing.		$3,000		

*300,000 miles divided by 10

Although outsourcing has become widely accepted across virtually all industries, the results of outsourcing are not uniformly positive. Some companies that made a strong commitment to extensive outsourcing have discovered that there are many problems that can occur when they shift key processes and functions to other companies. It is usually easier to make major changes and to correct problems related to in-house functions and processes than for those outsourced to other companies, especially if they are located offshore. The following Business Insight discusses a peripheral issue in the aviation industry relating to outsourcing.

Business Insight ■ Outsourcing in the Airline Industry

In 2019, third-party contractors provided about 30% of airport ground and passenger services, up from 19% in 2001. But while wages paid by airlines have been rising since 2009, wages paid by those subcontractors have not kept pace. In fact, wages for wheelchair service, cleaning, catering, and even some baggage handling workers have remained stagnant.

Members of three unions (Communications Workers of America, Service Employees International Union, and Unite Here) spoke at a House of Representatives' aviation subcommittee hearing in early 2020, asking for more scrutiny of working conditions for low-paid service providers at airports and that airline companies be encouraged to verify subcontractor compliance with federal, state, and local labor laws.

If future legislation increases the cost of ground and passenger service outsourcing or if growth in the aviation industry results in a tight market for service workers, airline companies will need to reassess the cost of outsourcing and may need to consider hiring internally.

Source: Ted Reed, "Labor Movement Eyes 'Dark Corner of the Airline Industry,'" *Forbes*, January 15, 2020.

Even if outsourcing appears financially advantageous in the short run, management should not decide to outsource before considering a variety of qualitative risk factors. Is the outside supplier interested in developing a long-term relationship or merely attempting to use some temporarily idle capacity? If so, what will happen at the end of the contract period? What impact would a decision to outsource have on the morale of a company's employees? Will it have to rehire laid-off employees after the contract expires? Will the outside supplier meet delivery schedules? Does the supplied part meet quality standards? Will it continue to meet them? Organizations often manufacture products or provide services they can obtain elsewhere in order to control quality, to have an assured supply source, to avoid dealing with a potential competitor, or to maintain a core competency. Some of these issues are discussed in the Business Insight that follows.

Business Insight ■ Outsourcing Changes Cost Structure, Brings New Risks

Firms are finding that flexibility from outsourcing can come with significant costs, largely in holding the supplier to quality standards. Bert Ahill, who advises firms on outsourcing, feels that companies regularly forget the risks that they are exposing themselves to when outsourcing. Often firms forget to account for economic, political, and weather hazards that affect their international suppliers. Firms should take care to build redundancy into outsourced supply chains to control disruptions that could come from these sources.

Some firms are finding that the costs of monitoring outsourced contractors outweigh the benefits of outsourcing. Boston Scientific, a maker of medical devices, has been manufacturing its own batteries for 10 years. While companies like Boeing were making radical moves in the opposite direction, Boston Scientific found it more cost-effective to keep battery production in-house, as the quality and longevity of a battery implanted in a patient is of paramount importance. In addition to quality and stability, other supply chain issues arise with outsourcing. Taylor Guitars uses exotic woods in its products, and when concerns arose about the sustainability of its suppliers' practices, it chose to purchase a Cameroonian mill to improve sourcing. The organic soap maker Dr. Bronner's ran into similar issues with its palm oil supply, so it formed a company to manage sustainable sourcing of palm oil in Ghana.

Careful analysis of the costs and benefits of both outsourcing and vertical integration should be undertaken on an ongoing basis to make sure that the company chooses the correct supply chain.

Sources: Alexis Bateman, "Guest Voices: New Supplier Strategies Revive Important Corporate Questions," *Wall Street Journal*, March 7, 2016; and Ben DiPietro, "When Manufacturing Means Building Supply-Chain Resilience," *Wall Street Journal*, October 21, 2015.

The qualitative risk factors discussed above are often magnified when a company goes global, either as an outsourcing buyer or provider. Global outsourcing is often motivated by the desire to get projects completed "on time" and "within budget." In the following Research Insight, PricewaterhouseCoopers views outsourcing as a way to focus resources on operations that truly differentiate the firm.

Research Insight ■ Role of Outsourcing in Operations

A PricewaterhouseCoopers's Global Operations Survey offers a narrower view of the role of outsourcing in operations. Rather than recommending outsourcing as a way to change the firm's cost structure, PwC views outsourcing as a way to focus on operations that truly differentiate the firm. The PwC study divides a company's capabilities into four groups:

1. Differentiating capabilities,
2. Competitive necessities,
3. Basic capabilities, and
4. Other activities.

PwC recommends focusing resources on those activities where being best-in-category offers greatest returns (item 1). Investments in attention, staff, and capital should center on these differentiating operations. PwC recommends aggressive cost management and efficiency in activities that are required for participation in the market sector, where excellence in these areas offers no advantage, but is required for participation in a market (item 2). For example, consumers expect all banks to have excellent security; thus, banks should find ways to meet the excellent security standards with the greatest efficiency. PwC recommends outsourcing basic capabilities (item 3). As there is no return for excelling in these areas, they are the areas in which cost minimization is the best strategy. Most firms

continued

continued from previous page

outsource facilities maintenance and other operations that are unrelated to success in their sector but are required to function. All other activities that do not fit into the first three groups and deviate from the core business should be eliminated if possible (item 4).

Source: "2015 Global Operations Survey: Reimagining Operations," *PricewaterhouseCoopers*, 2015, p. 17. Link: http://operationssurvey.pwc.com/PwC-2015-Global-Operations-Survey.pdf

LO5 Review 17-5

Epson produces color cartridges for inkjet printers. Suppose cartridges are sold to mail-order distributors for $4.80 each and that manufacturing and other costs are as follows:

Variable Costs per Unit		Fixed Costs per Month	
Direct materials.	$2.00	Factory overhead	$15,000
Direct labor	0.20	Selling and administrative.	5,000
Factory overhead	0.25	Total	$20,000
Distribution	0.05		
Total	$2.50		

The variable distribution costs are for transportation to mail-order distributors. Also assume the current monthly production and sales volume is 15,000 and monthly capacity is 20,000 units.

Required
Determine the effect of the following situation on monthly profits.

A Mexican manufacturer has offered a one-year contract to supply ink for the cartridges at a cost of $1.00 per unit. If Epson accepts the offer, it will be able to reduce variable manufacturing costs by 40% and rent some of its factory space to another company for $1,000.00 per month.

Solution on p. 17-38.

Sell or Process Further

When a product is salable at various stages of completion, management must determine the product's most advantageous selling point. As each stage is completed, management must determine whether to sell the product then or to process it further. For example, petroleum companies have to determine how much crude oil to refine as diesel fuel and how much to process further as gasoline. We consider two types of sell or process further decisions: (1) for a single product and (2) for joint products.

LO6 Apply differential analysis to evaluate whether to sell or further process a product.

Single Product Decisions

Assume that Scandinavian Furniture Inc. manufactures modular wood furniture from precut and shaped wood. Although all units are salable before they are sanded and painted, Scandinavian Furniture Inc. sands and paints all units before they are sold. Management wishes to know if this is the optimal selling point.

A complete listing of unit costs and revenues for the alternative selling points for a low-end storage cabinet follows.

	Per Cabinet		
	Sell after Assembly	Sell after Painting	Difference (income effect of painting)
Selling price	$40	$75	$35
Assembly costs.	(25)	(25)	
Sanding and painting costs	—	(12)	(12)
Contribution margin	$15	$38	$23
Advantage of painting.		$23	

The sanding and painting operation has an additional contribution of $23 per unit. The storage cabinets should be sold after they are painted.

The assembly costs are the same under both alternatives. This illustrates that *all costs incurred prior to the decision point are irrelevant*. Given the existence of an assembled chair, the decision alternatives are to sell it now or to process it further. A differential analysis for the decision to sell or process further should include only revenues and the incremental costs of further processing as follows.

Increase in revenues		
Sell after painting	$75	
Sell after assembly	(40)	$35
Additional costs of sanding and painting		(12)
Advantage of sanding and painting		$23

The identical solution is obtained if the selling price without further processing is treated as an opportunity cost as follows.

Revenues after painting		$75
Additional costs of sanding and painting	$12	
Opportunity cost of not selling after assembly	40	(52)
Advantage of sanding and painting		$23

By processing a chair further, Scandinavian Furniture has foregone the opportunity to receive $40 from its sale. Since the chair is already assembled, and the cost of assembly is an irrelevant sunk cost, this $40 is the net cash inflow from the most desirable alternative; it is the opportunity cost of painting.

Joint Product Decisions

Two or more products simultaneously produced by a single process from a common set of inputs are called **joint products**. Joint products are often found in basic industries that process natural raw materials such as dairy, chemical, meat, petroleum, and wood products. In the petroleum industry, crude oil is refined into fuel oil, gasoline, kerosene, diesel, lubricating oil, and other products.

The point in the process where the joint products become separately identifiable is called the **split-off point**. Materials and conversion costs incurred prior to the split-off point are called **joint costs**. For external reporting purposes, a number of techniques are used to allocate joint costs among joint products. We do not discuss these techniques here (interested students should consult a cost accounting textbook), except to note that none of the methods provide information useful for determining what to do with a joint product once it is produced. Because joint costs are incurred prior to the decision point, they are sunk costs. Consequently, *joint costs are irrelevant to a decision to sell a joint product or to process it further*. The only relevant factors are the alternative costs and revenues subsequent to the split-off point.

Business Insight   ■   Product Mix Decisions in Consumer Electronics

The changing consumer electronics landscape is driving changes in product mix at companies like Microsoft Corporation, Apple Inc., and Dell Technologies, Inc.

Microsoft, long a software company, is expanding its hardware products, like Surface desktop and computers, and its cloud-based services like Azure. Revenue from Azure, a cloud computing platform that can be used for services such as analytics, virtual computing, storage, and networking, increased 72% in the year ending June 30, 2019.

Increases in sales of AirPods and Apple Watches were the primary contributors to the 41% increase in sales in Apple's Wearables, Home and Accessories segment during the year ended September 28, 2019. Sales of Apple Mac computers increased 2% during the same period.

Dell Technologies Inc., the third-largest PC manufacturer, is expanding its Mobile Connect software application. Users will now be able to drag photos, videos, and other files from their iPhone or Android handsets to their PC.

continued

continued from previous page

    The product mix decisions these companies are making rely on the decision relevance framework introduced in this chapter.

Sources: Mark Gurman, "Dell to Let Apple Users Control iPhones from Their Laptop," *Bloomberg Technology*, January 2, 2020. Dina Bass, "Microsoft Pushes Cloud Services to Retailers Anxious to Avoid Amazon," *Bloomberg Technology*, January 9, 2020. Microsoft Corporation Form 10-K for the year ended June 30, 2019. Apple Inc. Form 10-K for the year ended September 28, 2019.

LO6 Review 17-6

Epson produces color cartridges for inkjet printers. Suppose cartridges are sold to mail-order distributors for $4.80 each and that manufacturing and other costs are as follows:

Variable Costs per Unit		Fixed Costs per Month	
Direct materials.	$2.00	Factory overhead	$15,000
Direct labor.	0.20	Selling and administrative.	5,000
Factory overhead	0.25	Total	$20,000
Distribution	0.05		
Total	$2.50		

The variable distribution costs are for transportation to mail-order distributors. Also assume the current monthly production and sales volume is 15,000 and monthly capacity is 20,000 units.

Required
Determine the effect of the following situation on monthly profits.

    The cartridges are currently unpackaged; that is, they are sold in bulk. Individual packaging would increase costs by $0.10 per unit. However, the units could then be sold for $5.05.   **Solution on p. 17-38.**

Use of Limited Resources

All of us have experienced time as a limiting or constraining resource. With two exams the day after tomorrow and a paper due next week, our problem is how to allocate limited study time. The solution depends on our objectives, our current status (grades, knowledge, skill levels, and so forth), and available time. Given this information, we devise a work plan to best meet our objectives.

    Managers must also decide how to best use limited resources to accomplish organizational goals. A supermarket may lose sales because limited shelf space prevents stocking all available brands of soft drinks. A manufacturer may lose sales because limited machine hours or labor hours prevent filling all orders. Managers of for-profit organizations will likely find the problems of capacity constraints less troublesome than the problems of excess capacity; nonetheless, these problems are real. Ultimately, the problem often boils down to a product-mix decision, in which we must decide the mix of products or services we are going to offer our customers with the limited resources available to us.

    If the limited resource is not a core business activity, it may be appropriate to outsource additional units of the limited resource externally. For example, many organizations have a small legal staff to handle routine activities; if the internal staff becomes fully committed, the organization seeks outside legal counsel.

    The long-run solution to the problem of limited resources to perform core activities may be to expand capacity. However, this is usually not feasible in the short run. Economic models suggest that another solution is to reduce demand by increasing the price. Again, this may not be desirable. A hotel, for example, may want to maintain competitive prices. A manufacturer might want to maintain

eLectures MBC LO7 Allocate limited resources for purposes of maximizing short-run profit.

a long-run price to retain customer goodwill to avoid attracting competitors, or to prevent accusations of "price gouging."

Single Constraint

The allocation of limited resources should be made only after a careful consideration of many qualitative factors. The following rule provides a useful starting point in making short-run decisions of how to best use limited resources: *To achieve short-run profit maximization, a for-profit organization should allocate limited resources in a manner that maximizes the contribution per unit of the limited resource.* The application of this rule is illustrated in the following example.

Assume **Snap Fitness** offers three different personal training packages (A, B, and C) to its customers. These packages vary from a personalized nutrition and exercise training to a one-time consultation. Suppose a limitation of 120 labor hours per week prevents Snap from meeting the demand for its services. Information for the three service packages is as follows.

	A	B	C
Unit selling price	$100	$80	$50
Unit variable costs	(60)	(35)	(25)
Unit contribution margin	$ 40	$45	$25
Hours per unit	4	3	1

Package A has the highest selling price and Package B has the highest unit contribution margin. Package C is shown below to have the highest contribution per hour.

	A	B	C
Unit contribution margin	$40	$45	$25
Hours per unit	÷ 4	÷ 3	÷ 1
Contribution per hour	$10	$15	$25

Following the rule of maximizing the contribution per unit of a single constraining factor (labor hours), Snap should use its limited labor hours to sell Package C. As shown in the following analysis, any other plan would result in lower profits.

	A Highest Selling Price per Unit	B Highest Contribution per Unit	C Highest Contribution per Constraining Factor
Hours available	120	120	120
Hours per unit	÷ 4	÷ 3	÷ 1
Weekly production in units	30	40	120
Unit contribution margin	× $40	× $45	× $25
Total weekly contribution margin	$1,200	$1,800	$3,000

Despite this analysis, management may decide on a product mix that includes some units of A or B or both to satisfy the requests of some "good" customers or to offer a full product line. However, such decisions sacrifice short-run profits.

Multiple Constraints

Continuing our illustration, assume a second constraint; that is, the maximum weekly demand for C is only 90 units, although the company is capable of producing 120 units of C each week. In this case, the limited labor resource should first be used to satisfy the demand for Package C, with any remaining capacity going to produce Package B, which has the next highest contribution per unit of constraining factor. This allocation provides a total weekly contribution of $2,700 as follows.

Available hours.	120
Required for C (90 units × 1 hour)	(90)
Hours available for B	30
Labor hours per unit	÷ 3
Production of B in units.	10
Unit contribution margin of B	× $45
Contribution from B.	$ 450
Contribution from C ($25 per unit × 90 units).	2,250
Total weekly contribution margin	$2,700

When an organization has alternative uses for several limited resources, such as limited labor hours and limited space, the optimal use of those resources cannot be determined using the rule for short-run profit maximization. In these situations, techniques such as linear programming can be used to assist in determining the optimal mix of products or services.

Theory of Constraints

The **theory of constraints** states that every process has a bottleneck (constraining resource) and that production cannot take place faster than it is processed through that bottleneck. The goal of the theory of constraints is to maximize **throughput** (defined as sales revenue minus direct materials costs) in a constrained environment.[1] The theory has several implications for management.

- Management should identify the bottleneck. This is often difficult when several different products are produced in a facility containing many different production activities. One approach is to walk around and observe where inventory is building up in front of workstations. The bottleneck will likely have the largest piles of work that have been waiting for the longest time.

- Management should schedule production to maximize the efficient use of the bottleneck resource. Efficiently using the bottleneck resource might necessitate inspecting all units before they reach the bottleneck rather than after the units are completed. The bottleneck resource is too valuable to waste on units that may already be defective.

- Management should schedule production to avoid a buildup of inventory. Reducing inventory lowers the cost of inventory investments and the cost of carrying inventory. It also assists in improving quality by making it easier to identify quality problems that might otherwise be hidden in large piles of inventory. Reducing inventory will require a change in the attitude of managers who like to see machines and people constantly working. To avoid a buildup of inventory in front of the bottleneck, it may be necessary for people and equipment to remain idle until the bottleneck resource calls for additional input.

- Management should work to eliminate the bottleneck, perhaps by increasing the capacity of the bottleneck resource, redesigning products so they can be produced with less use of the bottleneck resource, rescheduling production procedures to substitute nonbottleneck resources, or outsourcing work performed by bottleneck resources.

The theory of constraints has implications for management accounting performance reports. Keeping people and equipment working on production full-time is often a goal of management. To support this goal, management accounting performance reports have traditionally highlighted underutilization as an unfavorable variance (see Module 23). This has encouraged managers to have people and equipment producing inventory, even if the inventory is not needed or cannot be further processed because of bottlenecks. The theory of constraints suggests that it is better to have

---

[1] *The Goal,* by Eliyah M. Goldratt and Jeff Cox, presents the concepts underlying the theory of constraints in the form of a novel.

nonbottleneck resources idle than it is to have them fully utilized. To support the theory of constraints, performance reports should

- Measure the utilization of bottleneck resources
- Measure factory throughput
- Not encourage the full utilization of nonbottleneck resources
- Discourage the buildup of excess inventory

While the theory of constraints is *similar* to our general rule for how to best use limited resources, it emphasizes throughput (selling price minus direct materials) rather than contribution (selling price minus variable costs) in allocating the limited resource. The exclusion of direct labor and variable manufacturing overhead yields larger unit margins, and it may affect resource allocations based on throughput rankings. The result will likely be a reduction in profits from those that could be achieved using our general rule for how to allocate limited resources. Although the theory of constraints has not been widely embraced by companies, many of its users are enthusiastic about its benefits.

Limitations of Decision Analysis Models

Analytical models, such as the relevant cost analysis model and applications presented in this module, are very useful in organizing information for purposes of determining the economics of a decision. However, it is important always to keep in mind that models do not make decisions—managers make decisions. The results of analytical models are an essential and necessary starting point in many decisions, but often there are other factors that weigh heavily on a decision that may cause the manager to go against the most economical alternative. There may be human resource, marketing, cultural, logistical, technological, or other factors that outweigh the analytics of a decision situation. It is in these situations where managers demonstrate leadership, problem-solving, and executive skill and potential, or the lack thereof.

Review 17-7 LO7

Assume that Innovative Components Inc. produces only three different types of injection-molded knobs. It produces the Pointer Knob, which is used for on/off devices, the Instrument Knob, which is used for precision adjustment, and the Star Knob, which is used for snowblowers and lawnmowers. The factory machine capacity is the company's constraining resource. It operates at 90% capacity and management wants to devote the unused capacity to one of the products. The following data represents the current operations:

	Pointer Knob	Instrument Knob	Star Knob
Per-case data:			
Sales price	$20	$22	$6
Variable cost	8	16	2
Contribution margin.	$12	$ 6	$4
Fixed costs*	6	2	1
Net income	$ 6	$ 4	$3

*Allocated on basis of machine hours at $1 per hour.

Required

Solution on p. 17-38. Which product should management produce with its extra capacity?

Guidance Answers

You Are the Vice President of Manufacturing

Pg. 17-5 This is a decision that has both economic and ethical dimensions. Economically, the cost of the old machine is a sunk cost, since the expenditure to acquire it has already been made. If it can be sold to another company to recover part of the initial cost, that amount would be relevant to the decision regarding the new technology. However, you should ignore the cost of the recently purchased machine and consider only the outlay costs that will differ between keeping the recently purchased machine and purchasing the new technology, plus any opportunity costs that may be involved with disposing of the existing machine and acquiring the new machine. From an ethical standpoint, managers are often hesitant to recommend an action that reflects poorly on their past decisions. The temptation is to try to justify the past decision. If you have evaluated all of the relevant costs and have considered all of the qualitative issues associated with upgrading the machine, these should be the basis for making your recommendation, not what it will do to your reputation with your superiors.

Questions

Q17-1. Distinguish between relevant and irrelevant costs.

Q17-2. In evaluating a cost reduction proposal, what three alternatives are available to management?

Q17-3. When are outlay costs relevant and when are they irrelevant?

Q17-4. Relate the manufacturing cost hierarchy discussed in Module 15 to the concept of relevant costs. Under what conditions would product-level costs be relevant?

Q17-5. Why is a differential analysis of relevant items preferred to a detailed listing of all costs and revenues associated with each alternative?

Q17-6. When are opportunity costs relevant to the evaluation of a special order?

Q17-7. Identify some important qualitative considerations in evaluating a decision to make or buy a part.

Q17-8. In a decision to sell or to process further, of what relevance are costs incurred prior to the decision point? Explain your answer.

Q17-9. How should limited resources be used to achieve short-run profit maximization?

Q17-10. What should performance reports do in support of the theory of constraints?

Assignments with the ⓜ logo in the margin are available in BusinessCourse.
See the Preface of the book for details.

Mini Exercises

M17-11. Relevant Cost Terms: Matching

Astel&Kern produces three different versions of high-quality portable digital music players, the A@ultima, A@futura, and A@norma. Assume Astel&Kern is evaluating a proposal that will result in doubling the production of A@futura and disontinuing the production of A@norma. The facilities currently used to produce A@norma will be devoted to the production of A@futura. Furthermore, additional machinery will be acquired to produce A@futura. The production of A@ultima will not be affected. All products have a positive contribution margin.

LO1
Astel&Kern

Homework
MBC

Required
Presented below are a number of phrases related to the proposal followed by a list of cost terms. For each phrase, select the most appropriate cost term. Each term is used only once.

Phrases
1. Cost of equipment to produce A@norma
2. Increased variable costs of A@futura
3. Property taxes on the new machinery
4. Revenues from the sale of A@ultima
5. Increased revenue from the sale of A@futura
6. Contribution margin of A@norma
7. Variable costs of A@ultima
8. Company president's salary

Cost terms
a. Opportunity cost
b. Sunk cost

    c. Irrelevant variable outlay cost
    d. Irrelevant fixed outlay cost
    e. Relevant variable outlay cost
    f. Relevant fixed outlay cost
    g. Relevant revenues
    h. Irrelevant revenues

LO1

Tapestry, Inc.
(TPR)

M17-12. Relevant Cost Terms: Matching

Assume **Coach**, owned by **Tapestry, Inc.**, produces and sells 4,000 specialty handbags per month and has the capacity to produce 5,000 units per month. Coach is evaluating a one-time, special order for 2,000 units from Bloomingdales. Accepting the order will increase variable manufacturing costs and certain fixed selling and administrative costs. It will also require the company to forego the sale of 1,000 units to regular customers.

Required
Presented below are a number of statements related to the proposal followed by a list of cost terms. For each statement, select the most appropriate cost term. Each term is used only once.

Statements
1. Increased revenues from special order
2. Lost contribution margin from foregone sales to regular customers
3. Revenues from 4,000 units sold to regular customers
4. Variable cost of 4,000 units sold to regular customers
5. Increase in fixed selling and administrative expenses
6. Cost of existing equipment used to produce special order
7. Salary paid to current supervisor who oversees manufacture of special order
8. Increased variable costs of special order

Cost terms
a. Irrelevant variable outlay cost
b. Irrelevant fixed outlay cost
c. Sunk cost
d. Relevant variable outlay cost
e. Relevant fixed outlay cost
f. Opportunity cost
g. Relevant revenues
h. Irrelevant revenues

LO1, 2

City of Hamilton
PJM Interconnection

M17-13. Identifying Relevant Costs and Revenues

The **City of Hamilton** operates a power plant on the Ohio River. The city uses some of this generated electricity to service Hamilton residents and sells the excess electricity to **PJM Interconnection**, manager of a wholesale electricity market serving nearby states. The city council is evaluating two alternative proposals:

- *Proposal A* calls for replacing the generators used in the plant with more efficient generators that will produce more electricity and have lower operating costs. The salvage value of the old generators is higher than their removal cost.
- *Proposal B* calls for raising the level of the dam to retain more water for generating power and increasing the force of water flowing through the dam. This will significantly increase the amount of electricity generated by the plant. Operating costs will not be affected.

Required
Presented are a number of cost and revenue items. Indicate in the appropriate columns whether each item is relevant or irrelevant to proposals A and B.

	Proposal A	Proposal B
1. Cost of new furniture for the city manager's office	_____	_____
2. Cost of old generators	_____	_____
3. Cost of new generators	_____	_____
4. Operating cost of old generators	_____	_____
5. Operating cost of new generators	_____	_____
6. The police chief's salary	_____	_____
7. Depreciation on old generators	_____	_____

continued

continued from previous page

	Proposal A	Proposal B
8. Salvage value of old generators		
9. Removal cost of old generators		
10. Cost of raising dam		
11. Maintenance costs of water plant		
12. Revenues from sale of electricity		

M17-14. Classifying Relevant and Irrelevant Items

The law firm of Greenberg Traurig LLP has been asked to represent a local client. All legal proceedings will be held out of town in Boston.

LO1
Greenberg Traurig
LLP

Homework
MBC

Required

The law firm's accountant has asked you to help determine the incremental cost of accepting this client. Classify each of the following items on the basis of their relationship to this engagement. Items may have multiple classifications.

	Relevant costs		Irrelevant costs	
	Opportunity	Outlay	Outlay	Sunk
1. The case will require three attorneys to stay four nights in a Boston hotel. The predicted hotel bill is $3,600.				
2. Greenberg Traurig LLP's professional staff is paid $2,000 per day for out-of-town assignments.				
3. Last year, depreciation on Greenberg Traurig LLP's Philadelphia's office was $25,000.				
4. Round-trip transportation to Boston is expected to cost $250 per person.				
5. The firm has recently accepted an engagement that will require several partners to spend two weeks in Chicago. The predicted out-of-pocket costs of this trip are $25,000.				
6. The firm has a maintenance contract on its computer equipment that will cost $2,200 next year.				
7. If the firm accepts the client and sends attorneys to Boston, it will have to decline a conflicting engagement in Miami that would have provided a net cash inflow of $15,000.				
8. The firm's variable overhead is $125 per client hour.				
9. The firm pays $900 per year for a subscription to a law journal.				
10. Last year the firm paid $22,500 to increase the insulation in its building.				

M17-15. Relevant Costs for Equipment Replacement Decision

Assume Urgent Care paid $42,000 for X-ray equipment four years ago. The equipment was expected to have a useful life of 10 years from the date of acquisition with annual operating costs of $25,000. Technological advances have made the machine purchased four years ago obsolete with a zero salvage value. An improved X-ray device incorporating the new technology is available at an initial cost of $50,000 and annual operating costs of $15,000. The new machine is expected to last only six years before it, too, is obsolete. Asked to analyze the financial aspects of replacing the obsolete but still functional machine, an Urgent Care accountant prepared the following analysis. After looking over these numbers, the company's manager rejected the proposal.

LO1, 2
Urgent Care

Homework
MBC

Six-year savings [($25,000 – $15,000) × 6]	$ 60,000
Cost of new machine	(50,000)
Undepreciated cost of old machine [($42,000/10) × 6]	25,200
Advantage (disadvantage) of replacement	$ 15,200

Required

Perform an analysis of relevant costs to determine whether the manager made the correct decision.

LO1, 2, 4
VideoSecu

M17-16. Special Order

VideoSecu produces wall mounts for flat panel television sets. Assume the forecasted income statement for next year is as follows.

VIDEOSECU Budgeted Income Statement For the Year	
Sales ($28 per unit)	$5,600,000
Cost of good sold ($19 per unit)	(3,800,000)
Gross profit	1,800,000
Selling expenses ($5 per unit)	(1,000,000)
Net income	$ 800,000

Additional Information

(1) Of the production costs and selling expenses, $1,520,000 and $750,000, respectively, are fixed.
(2) VideoSecu received a special order from a hospital supply company offering to buy 10,000 wall mounts for $15. If it accepts the order, there will be no additional fixed selling expenses, and there is currently sufficient excess capacity to fill the order. The company's sales manager argues for rejecting the order because "we are not in the business of paying $19 to make a product to sell for $15."

Required

Do you think the company should accept the special order? Should the decision be based only on the profitability of the sale, or are there other issues that VideoSecu should consider? Explain.

LO1, 2, 6
Beneteau

M17-17. Sell or Process Further

Assume **Beneteau** manufactures sailboat hulls at a cost of $7,500 per unit. The hulls are sold to boat-yards for $9,000. The company is evaluating the desirability of adding masts, sails, and rigging to the hulls prior to sale at an additional cost of $2,500. The completed sailboats could then be sold for $10,500 each.

Required

Determine whether the company should sell sailboat hulls or process them further into complete sailboats. Assume sales volume will not be affected.

Exercises

LO1, 2, 4
Full Belly Farm

E17-18. Special Order

Full Belly Farm grows organic vegetables and sells them to distributors and local restaurants after processing. Assume the farm's leading product for restaurant customers is a mixture of organic green salad ingredients prepared and ready to serve. The company sells a large bag to restaurants for $30. It calculates the variable cost per bag at $20 (including $1 for local delivery), and the average total cost per bag is $24. Growing conditions have been very good this season and Full Belly has extra capacity. A representative of a restaurant association in another city has offered to buy fresh salad stock from the company to augment its regular supply during an upcoming international festival. The restaurant association wants to buy 3,000 bags during the next month for $22 per bag. Delivery to restaurants in the other city will cost the company $0.75 per bag. It can meet most of the order with excess capacity but would sacrifice 200 bags of regular sales to fill this special order. Please assist Full Belly Farm's management by answering the following questions.

Required

a. Using differential analysis, what is the impact on profits of accepting this special order?
b. What nonquantitative issues should management consider before making a final decision?
c. How would the analysis change if the special order were for 3,000 bags per month for the next five years? (Assume there would be no loss of regular sales.)

E17-19. **Special Order**

Denny's, just off the San Bernardino Freeway in Pomona, California, specializes in a Super Slam breakfast selling for $7. Assume daily fixed costs are $1,575, and variable costs are $5 per meal. With a capacity of 750 meals per day, the restaurant serves an average of 700 meals each day.

LO1, 2, 4
Denny's (DENN)

Homework
MBC

Required

a. Determine the current average cost per meal.

b. A busload of 30 Girl Scouts stops on its way home from the San Bernardino National Forest. The leader offers to bring them in if the scouts can all be served a meal for a total of $195. The owner refuses, saying he would lose $0.75 per meal if he accepted this offer. How do you think the owner arrived at the $0.75 figure? Comment on the owner's reasoning.

c. A local businessman on a break overhears the conversation with the leader and offers the owner a one-year contract to feed 100 of the businessman's employees one meal each day at a special price of $5.50 per meal. Should the restaurant owner accept this offer? Why or why not?

E17-20. **Special Order: High-Low Cost Estimation**

Autoliv produces air bag systems that it sells to automobile manufacturers throughout the world. Assume the company has a capacity of 50 million units per year; it is currently producing at an annual rate of 40 million units. Autoliv has received an order from a Japanese manufacturer to purchase 100,000 units at $65 each. Budgeted costs for 40 million and 45 million units are as follows.

LO1, 2, 4
Autoliv (ALV)

Homework
MBC

(in thousands, except costs per unit)	40 Million Units	45 Million Units
Manufacturing costs		
Direct materials.	$ 560,000	$ 630,000
Direct labor	220,000	247,500
Factory overhead	1,780,000	1,822,500
Total	2,560,000	2,700,000
Selling and administrative.	1,120,000	1,125,000
Total	$3,680,000	$3,825,000
Costs per unit		
Manufacturing.	$64.00	$60.00
Selling and administrative.	28.00	25.00
Total	$92.00	$85.00

Sales to auto manufacturers are priced at $120 per unit, but the sales manager believes the company should aggressively seek the Japanese business even if it results in a loss of $20 per unit. She believes obtaining this order would open up several new markets for the company's product. The general manager commented that the company cannot tighten its belt to absorb the $2,000,000 loss ($20 × 100,000) it would incur if the order is accepted.

Required

a. Determine the financial implications of accepting the order. (*Hint:* Use the high-low method to determine variable costs per unit.)

b. How would your analysis differ if the company were operating at capacity? Determine the advantage or disadvantage of accepting the order under full-capacity circumstances.

E17-21. **Outsourcing (Make-or-Buy) Decision**

Assume a division of HP Inc. currently makes 50,000 circuit boards per year used in producing diagnostic electronic instruments at a cost of $50 per board, consisting of variable costs per unit of $35 and fixed costs per unit of $15. Further assume Sanmina Corporation offers to sell HP the 50,000 circuit boards for $50 each. If HP accepts this offer, the facilities currently used to make the boards could be rented to one of HP's suppliers for $75,000 per year. In addition, $8 per unit of the fixed overhead applied to the circuit boards would be totally eliminated.

LO1, 2, 5
HP Inc. (HPQ)
Sanmina Corp. (SANM)

Homework
MBC

Required

Should HP outsource this component from Sanmina Corporation? Support your answer with relevant cost calculations.

LO1, 2, 5
Coway

E17-22. Outsourcing (Make-or-Buy) Decision

Coway manufactures a line of room air purifiers. Assume that management is currently evaluating the possible production of an air purifier for automobiles. Based on an annual volume of 50,000 units, the predicted cost per unit of an auto air purifier follows.

Direct materials.	$ 2.50
Direct labor.	2.00
Factory overhead	12.00
Total	$16.50

These cost predictions include $450,000 in fixed factory overhead averaged over 50,000 units.

Also assume the completed air purifier units include a battery-operated electric motor, which Coway assembles with parts purchased from an outside vendor for $2.00 per motor. Mini Motor Company has offered to supply an assembled battery-operated motor at a cost of $5.25 per unit, with a minimum annual order of 5,000 units. If Coway accepts this offer, it will be able to reduce the variable labor and variable overhead costs of the auto air purifier by 50%.

Required

a. Determine whether Coway should continue to make the electric motor or outsource it from Mini Motor Company. (*Hint:* Analyze the relevant costs of making the "motors," not the entire air purifier.)

b. If it could otherwise rent the motor-assembly space for $50,000 per year, should it make or outsource this component?

c. What additional factors should it consider in deciding whether to make or outsource the electric motors?

LO1, 2, 5

E17-23. Make or Buy

Priya Rahavy, M.D., is a general practitioner whose offices are located in the Lake Forest Professional Building. In the past, Dr. Rahavy has operated her practice with a nurse, a receptionist/secretary, and a part-time bookkeeper. Dr. Rahavy, like many small-town physicians, has billed her patients and their insurance companies from her own office. The part-time bookkeeper, who works 20 hours per week, is employed exclusively for this purpose.

North Avenue Physician's Service Center has offered to take over all of Dr. Rahavy's billings and collections for an annual fee of $36,000. If Dr. Rahavy accepts this offer, she will no longer need the bookkeeper. The bookkeeper's wages and fringe benefits amount to $25 per hour, and the bookkeeper works 50 weeks per year. With all the billings and collections done elsewhere, Dr. Rahavy will have three additional hours available per week to see patients. She sees an average of four patients per hour at an average fee of $40 per visit. Dr. Rahavy's practice is expanding, and new patients often have to wait several weeks for an appointment. She has resisted expanding her office hours or working more than 50 weeks per year. Finally, if Dr. Rahavy signs on with the center, she will no longer need to rent a records storage facility for $250 per month.

Required

Conduct a relevant cost analysis to determine if it is profitable to outsource the bookkeeping.

LO1, 2, 6
Ecolab (ECL)

E17-24. Sell or Process Further

Ecolab produces cleaning and sanitizing chemicals for commercial markets. Assume the company processes raw material D into joint products E and F. Raw material D costs $8 per liter. It costs $150 to convert 100 liters of D into 60 liters of E and 40 liters of F. Product F can be sold immediately for $40 per liter or processed further into Product G at an additional cost of $12 per liter. Product G can then be sold for $55 per liter.

Required

Determine whether Product F should be sold or processed further into Product G.

LO7
Fender Musical
Instruments Corp.

E17-25. Limited Resources

Assume **Fender** produces only three guitars: the Stratocaster, Telecaster, and Jaguar. A limitation of 960 labor hours per week prevents Fender from meeting the sales demand for these products. Product information is as follows.

	Stratocaster	Telecaster	Jaguar
Unit selling price.	$1,200	$ 900	$1,400
Unit variable costs	(630)	(450)	(850)
Unit contribution margin	$ 570	$ 450	$ 550
Labor hours per unit	15	10	20

Required

a. Determine the weekly contribution from each product when total labor hours are allocated to the product with the highest
  1. Unit selling price.
  2. Unit contribution margin.
  3. Contribution per labor hour.
     (*Hint:* Each situation is independent of the others.)

b. What generalization can be made regarding the allocation of limited resources to achieve short-run profit maximization?

c. Determine the opportunity cost the company will incur if management requires the weekly production of 15 Jaguars. *Hint:* You want to maximize short-run profit. Think about which guitar is most profitable.

d. Give reasons why a company may not allocate resources in the most economical way in some situations.

E17-26. Limited Resources   LO7

Maria Pajet, a regional sales representative for UniTec Systems Inc., has been working about 60 hours per week calling on a total of 85 regular customers each month. Because of family and health considerations, she has decided to reduce her hours to a maximum of 160 per month. Unfortunately, this cutback will require Maria to turn away some of her regular customers or, at least, serve them less frequently than once a month. Maria has developed the following information to assist her in determining how to best allocate time.

	Customer Classification		
	Large Business	Small Business	Individual
Number of customers.	10	45	100
Average monthly sales per customer.	$ 4,000	$2,500	$ 1,000
Commission percentage.	5.0%	4.0%	3.0%
Hours per customer per monthly visit.	4.0	2.5	1.5

Required

a. Develop a monthly plan that indicates the number of customers Maria should call on in each classification to maximize her monthly sales commissions.

b. Determine the monthly commissions Maria will earn if she implements this plan.

c. Give one or two reasons why Maria might decide not to follow the conclusions of the above analysis entirely.

E17-27   Sell of Process Further   LO6

Rose Hill, a soybean farm in northern Minnesota, has a herd of 25 dairy cows. The cows produce approximately 1,400 gallons of milk per week. The farm currently sells all its milk to a nearby processor for $1.25 per gallon, a significant drop from the $2.00 per gallon they were able to charge five years ago. It costs $1.60 per gallon to produce the milk.

The owners of Rose Hill are deciding whether to sell the dairy cows or expand into the artisan cheese market. Both owners have prior cheese-making experience and they already have all the needed equipment.

It takes .8 gallons of milk to make a pound of cheese. Costs to produce a pound of cheese are expected to total $7 per pound. Artisan cheeses are currently selling for $10 per pound at farmer's markets and upscale groceries.

Required

a. How much incremental profit would Rose Hill recognize if half the milk each week was used to make cheese?

b. How much, in total, would Rose Hill earn each week if half the milk was used to make cheese and half was sold to the processor?

c. How much of the milk would need to be used to make cheese each week in order for Rose Hill to break even on its dairy operations assuming no cows were sold? (*Note:* Any milk not used to make cheese would still be sold to a processor.)

d. What other factors should the owners of Rose Hill consider when deciding whether to sell the dairy cows or expand into cheese-making?

Problems

LO1, 2, 3   **P17-28.** **Multiple Changes in Profit Plans**

In an attempt to improve profit performance, Anderson Company's management is considering a number of alternative actions. An October contribution income statement for Anderson Company follows.

ANDERSON COMPANY Contribution Income Statement For Month of October		
Sales (12,000 units × $75)		$900,000
Less variable costs		
Direct materials (12,000 units × $10)	$120,000	
Direct labor (12,000 units × $10)	120,000	
Variable factory overhead (12,000 units × $4)	48,000	
Selling and administrative (12,000 units × $2)	24,000	(312,000)
Contribution margin (12,000 units × $49)		588,000
Less fixed costs		
Factory overhead	360,000	
Selling and administrative	240,000	(600,000)
Net income (loss)		$ (12,000)

Required

Determine the effect of each of the following independent situations on monthly profit.

a. Purchasing automated assembly equipment, which should reduce direct labor costs by $4 per unit and increase variable overhead costs by $1 per unit and fixed factory overhead by $12,000 per month.

b. Reducing the selling price by $5 per unit. This should increase the monthly sales by 3,000 units. At this higher volume, additional equipment and salaried personnel would be required. This will increase fixed factory overhead by $4,000 per month and fixed selling and administrative costs by $1,800 per month.

c. Buying rather than manufacturing a component of Anderson's final product. This will increase direct materials costs by $5 per unit. However, direct labor will decline $3 per unit, variable factory overhead will decline $1 per unit, and fixed factory overhead will decline $25,000 per month.

d. Increasing the unit selling price by $5 per unit. This action should result in a 2,000-unit decrease in monthly sales.

e. Combining alternatives (*a*) and (*d*).

LO1, 2, 3   **P17-29.** **Multiple Changes in Profit Plans: Multiple Products**

Information on Guadalupe Ltd.'s three products follows:

	A	B	C
Unit sales per month.	1,500	1,200	2,000
Selling price per unit.	$20.00	$14.00	$30.00
Variable costs per unit	(22.00)	(10.00)	(18.00)
Unit contribution margin	$ (2.00)	$ 4.00	$12.00

Required

Determine the effect each of the following situations would have on monthly profits. Each situation should be evaluated independently of all others.

a. Product A is discontinued.

b. Product A is discontinued, and the subsequent loss of customers causes sales of Product B to decline by 150 units.

c. The selling price of A is increased to $25 with a sales decrease of 250 units.

d. The price of Product B is increased to $20 with a resulting sales decrease of 300 units. However, some of these customers shift to Product A; sales of Product A increase by 200 units.

e. Product A is discontinued, and the plant in which A was produced is used to produce D, a new product. Product D has a unit contribution margin of $2. Monthly sales of Product D are predicted to be 1,500 units.

f. The selling price of Product C is increased to $35, and the selling price of Product B is decreased to $10. Sales of C decline by 350 units, while sales of B increase by 400 units.

P17-30. Relevant Costs and Differential Analysis   LO1, 2

Cornerstone Bank paid $90,000 for a check-sorting machine 10 years ago this month. The machine had an estimated life of 15 years and annual operating costs of $40,000, excluding depreciation. Although management is pleased with the machine, recent technological advances have made check-sorting machines obsolete. Consequently, the machine now has a book value of $30,000, a remaining operating life of five years, and a salvage value of $0.

The manager of operations is evaluating a proposal to acquire check scanning equipment for all branches. The new equipment would cost $50,000 and reduce annual operating costs to $20,000, excluding depreciation. Because of expected technological improvements, the manager believes the new machine will have an economic life of four years and no salvage value at the end of that life. Prior to signing the papers authorizing the acquisition of the new machine, the president of the bank prepared the following analysis:

Six-year savings [($40,000 – $20,000) × 4 years]	$80,000
Cost of new machine	(50,000)
Loss on disposal of old machine	(30,000)
Advantage (disadvantage) of replacement	$ 0

After looking at these numbers, the manager rejected the proposal and commented that he was "tired of looking at marginal projects. This bank is in business to make a profit, not to break even. If you want to break even, go work for the government."

Required

a. Evaluate the president's analysis.

b. Prepare a differential analysis of six-year totals for the old and the new machines.

c. Speculate on some limitations of the model or other issues that might be a factor in making a final decision.

P17-31. Special Order   LO1, 2, 4
                                                                                                                        Razor USA

Razor USA produces a variety of electric scooters. Assume that Razor has just received an order from a customer (Pulse Cycles) for 500 Power Core scooters. The following price, based on cost plus a 60% markup, has been developed for the order:

Manufacturing costs	
Direct materials	$11,850
Direct labor	8,500
Factory overhead	15,800
Total	36,150
Markup (60%)	21,690
Selling price	$57,840

Pulse Cycles rejected this price and offered to purchase the 500 scooters at a price of $45,000. The following additional information is available:

• Razor has sufficient excess capacity to produce the scooters.

- Factory overhead is applied on the basis of direct labor dollars.
- Budgeted factory overhead is $8,000,000 for the current year. Of this amount, $6,000,000 is fixed. Of the $15,800 of factory overhead assigned to the Pulse Cycles order, only $3,950 is driven by the special order; $11,850 is a fixed cost.
- Selling and administrative expenses are budgeted as follows:

Fixed...	$3,000,000 per year
Variable	$10 per unit manufactured and sold

Required

a. The president of Razor wants to know if he should allow Pulse Cycles to have the scooters for $45,000. Determine the effect on profits of accepting Pulse Cycles' offer.

b. Briefly explain why certain costs should be omitted from the analysis in requirement (a).

c. Assume Razor is operating at capacity and could sell the 500 scooters at its regular markup.
   1. Determine the opportunity cost of accepting Pulse Cycles' offer.
   2. Determine the effect on profits of accepting Pulse Cycles' offer.

d. What other factors should Razor consider before deciding to accept the special order?

LO1, 2, 4   P17-32. Special Order

Every Halloween, Peterson's Ice Cream Shop offers a trick-or-treat package of 25 coupons for $20. The coupons are redeemable by children 12 years or under, for a single-scoop cone, with a limit of one coupon per child per visit. Coupon sales average 600 books per year. The printing costs are $75. A single-scoop cone of Peterson's ice cream normally sells for $2.00. The variable costs of a single-scoop cone are $1.50.

Required

a. Determine the loss if all coupons are redeemed without any other effect on sales.

b. Assume all coupons will not be redeemed. With regular sales unaffected, determine the coupon redemption rate at which Peterson's will break even on the offer.

c. Assuming regular sales are not affected and one additional single-scoop cone is sold at the regular price each time a coupon is redeemed, determine the coupon redemption rate at which Peterson's will break even on the offer.

d. Determine the profit or loss incurred on the offer if the coupon redemption rate is 60% and:
   1. One-fourth of the redeemed coupons have no effect on sales.
   2. One-fourth of the redeemed coupons result in additional sales of two single-scoop cones.
   3. One-fourth of the redeemed coupons result in additional sales of three single-scoop cones.
   4. One-fourth of the redeemed coupons come out of regular sales of single-scoop cones.

LO1, 2, 3, 4, 5   P17-33 Applications of Differential Analysis

Moscot

Moscot manufactures high-end sunglasses that it sells in retail shops and online for $310, on average. Assume the following represent manufacturing and other costs.

Variable Costs per Unit		Fixed Costs per Month	
Direct materials..................	$ 80	Factory overhead..................	$450,000
Direct labor.....................	50	Selling and administrative...........	375,000
Factory overhead................	35	Total	$825,000
Distribution	10		
Total	$175		

The variable distribution costs are for transportation to retail partners. Assume the current monthly production and sales volume is 15,000 units. Monthly capacity is 20,000 units.

Required

Determine the effect of each of the following independent situations on monthly profits.

a. A $50 increase in the unit selling price should result in a 2,000-unit decrease in monthly sales.

b. A 10% decrease in the unit selling price should result in a 6,000-unit increase in monthly sales. However, because of capacity constraints, the last 1,000 units would be produced during overtime with the direct labor costs increasing by 50%.

c. A British distributor has proposed to place a special, one-time order for 1,000 units at a reduced price of $250 per unit. The distributor would pay all transportation costs. There would be additional fixed selling and administrative costs of $750.

d. A Swiss distributor has proposed to place a special, one-time order for 6,000 units at a special price of $250 per unit. The distributor would pay all transportation costs. There would be additional fixed selling and administrative costs of $1,000. Assume overtime production is not possible.

e. Assume Moscat provides a designer case for each pair of sunglasses that it manufactures. A Chinese manufacturer has offered a one-year contract to supply the cases at a cost of $10 per unit. If Moscat accepts the offer, it will be able to reduce variable manufacturing costs by 5%, reduce fixed costs by $5,000, and rent out some freed-up space for $4,000 per month.

f. The glasses also come with a choice of lens tint. Assume that eliminating that option would reduce variable costs by $5 and eliminate $50,000 in fixed factory overhead. The selling price would likely have to decrease to $290 per unit.

P17-34. Applications of Differential Analysis   LO1, 2, 3, 4, 5

Adventure Expeditions offers guided back-country hiking/camping trips in British Columbia. Adventure provides a guide and all necessary food and equipment at a fee of $100 per person per day. Adventure currently provides an average of 600 guide-days per month in June, July, August, and September. Based on available equipment and staff, maximum capacity is 750 guide-days per month. Monthly variable and fixed operating costs (valued in Canadian dollars) are as follows.

Variable Costs per Guide-Day		Fixed Costs per Month	
Food	$ 6	Equipment rental	$10,000
Guide salary	20	Administration	12,000
Supplies	4	Advertising	2,500
Insurance	10	Total	$24,500
Total	$40		

Required

Determine the effect of each of the following situations on monthly profits. Each situation is to be evaluated independently of all others.

a. A $10 increase in the daily fee should result in a 100-unit decrease in monthly sales.

b. A $10 decrease in the daily fee should result in a 200-unit increase in monthly sales. However, because of capacity constraints, the last 50 guide-days would be provided by subcontracting to another firm at a cost of $50 per guide-day. (The $50 cost includes food, guides, supplies, and insurance.)

c. A French tour agency has proposed to place a special, one-time order for 100 guide-days at a reduced fee of $85 per guide-day. The agency would pay all insurance costs. There would be additional fixed administrative costs of $500.

d. An Italian tour agency has proposed to place a special, one-time order for 300 guide-days next month at a special fee of $80 per guide-day. The agency would pay all insurance costs. There would be additional fixed administrative costs of $500. Assume additional capacity beyond 800 guide-days is not available.

e. An Alberta outdoor supply company has offered to supply all necessary food and camping equipment at $7 per guide-day. This eliminates the current food costs and reduces the monthly equipment rental costs to $8,800.

f. Clients currently must carry a backpack and assist in camp activities such as cooking. Adventure is considering the addition of mules to carry all food and equipment and the hiring of college students to perform camp activities such as cooking. This will increase variable costs by $30 per guide-day and fixed costs by $5,000 per month. However, 600 full-service guide-days per month could now be sold at $150 each.

P17-35. Continue or Discontinue   LO1, 2

Westview Eye Clinic primarily performs three medical procedures: cataract removal, corneal implants, and laser keratotomy. At the end of the first quarter of this year, Dr. Rajan, president of Westview, expressed grave concern about the cataract sector because it had reported a loss of $150,000. He rationalized that "since the cataract market is losing $150,000, and the overall practice is making $300,000, if we eliminate the cataract market, our total profits will increase to $450,000."

Required

a. Is the president's analysis correct?

b. Will total profits increase if the cataract section is dropped?

c. Is it possible total profits will decline?

Management Applications

LO1, 2, 3   **MA17-36. Assessing the Impact of an Incentive Plan**[2]

Overview

Ladbrecks is a major department store with 50 retail outlets. The company's stores compete with outlets run by companies such as Nordstrom, Macy's, Bloomingdales, and Saks Fifth Avenue. During the early nineties the company decided that providing excellent customer service was the key ingredient for success in the retail industry. Therefore, during the mid 1990s the company implemented an incentive plan for its sales associates in 20 of its stores. Your job is to assess the financial impact of the plan and to provide a recommendation to management to continue or discontinue the plan based on your findings.

Incentives in Retail

The past decade has evidenced a concerted effort by many firms to empower and motivate employees to improve performance. A recent *New York Times* article reported that more and more firms are offering bonus plans to hourly workers. An Ernst and Young survey of the retail industry indicates that virtually all department stores currently offer incentive programs such as straight commissions, base salary plus commission, and quota bonus programs. Although these programs can add to payroll costs, the survey respondents indicated that they believe these plans have contributed to major improvements in customer service.

Company's Background

Ladbrecks was founded by members of the Ladbreck family in the 1880s. The first store opened under the name Ladbreck Dry Goods. Growth was fueled through acquisitions as the industry consolidated during the 1960s. Over this hundred-year period, sales associates were paid a fixed hourly wage. Raises were based on seniority. Sales associates were expected to be neat and courteous to customers. The advent of specialty stores and the stated intention of an upscale west coast retailer to begin opening stores in the Midwest concerned Ladbreck's management. Building on its history of excellence in customer service, the company initiated its performance-based incentive plan to support its stated firm-wide strategy of "customer emphasis" with "employee empowerment." Management expected it to result in further enhancement of customer service and, consequently, in an increase in sales generated at its stores.

Incentive Plan

The plan was implemented in stores sequentially as company managers intended to examine and evaluate the plan's impact on sales and profitability. Initially, the firm selected one store from a group of similar stores in the same general area to begin the implementation. By the end of 1994, 10 stores had implemented the plan. In 1995, 10 more stores implemented the plan, bringing the total to 20 out of a total of 50.

The performance-based incentive plan is best described as a bonus program. At the time of the plan's implementation, sales associates received little in the form of annual merit increases, and promotions were rare. The bonus payment became the only significant reward for high performance. Each week sales associates are paid a base hourly rate times hours worked. In addition, under the plan sales associates could increase their compensation by receiving a bonus at the end of each quarter. The contract provides sales-force personnel with a cash bonus only if the actual quarterly sales generated by the employee exceed a quarterly sales goal. Individualized pre-specified sales goals were established for each employee based only on the individual's base hourly rate, hours worked, and a multiplier (multiplier = 1/bonus rate). The bonus is computed as a fixed percentage of the excess sales (actual sales minus a pre-specified sales goal) by the employee in a quarter (see Exhibit 1).

$$\text{Employee's Bonus} = 0.08 \times (\text{Employee's actual sales for quarter} - \text{employee's targeted sales for quarter})$$

$$\text{Where employee's targeted sales for quarter} = \text{Employee's hourly wage} \times \text{Hours worked in quarter} \times 12.5$$

Senior managers regarded the incentive plan as a major change for the firm and its sales force. Management expected that the new incentive scheme would motivate many changes in employee behavior that would enhance customer service. Sales associates were now expected to build a client base to

---

[2] Written to illustrate the use of relevant costs and revenues for decision making. This example is based on an actual company's experience with implementing an incentive plan. The company name and the financial numbers and key ratios have been altered.

generate repeat sales. Actions consistent with this approach include developing and updating customer address lists (including details of their needs and preferences), writing thank you notes, and contacting customers about upcoming sales and new merchandise that matched their preferences.

Consultant's Task

Management decided to call you in to provide an independent assessment. While the company thought that sales had increased with the plan's implementation, the human resources department did not know exactly how to quantify the plan's impact on sales and expenses. It suspected that employee salaries, cost of goods sold, and inventory carrying costs, as well as sales, may have changed due to the plan's implementation. You, therefore, requested information on these financial variables.

Sales Analysis: Because each of the 20 stores implemented the plan at different dates, and store sales fluctuated greatly with the seasons and the economy, you could not simply plot store sales. Instead, for each of the 20 stores, you picked another Ladbreck store as a control and computed for 48 months the following series of monthly sales:[3]

$$\text{Percent Change in Sales} = \frac{[(\text{Plan Store Sales in Month t} \div \text{Plan Store Sales in Month t-24}) -}{(\text{Control Store Sales in Month t} \div \text{Control Store Sales in Month t-24})] \times 100}$$

The plan's implementation was denoted as month 25, so you had 24 months prior to the plan and 24 months after the plan. Averages were then taken for the 20 stores. If the control procedure worked, then you expected that the first 24 months of the series would fluctuate around zero. The actual results are reported in Figure 1, page 17-37. Month 25 is denoted as the rollout month, the month the incentive plan began.

Expense Analysis: You then plotted wage expense/sales, cost of goods sold/sales, and inventory turnover for the 20 stores for the 24 months preceding the plan and the first 24 months after plan implementation. After pulling out seasonal effects, these monthly series are presented in Figures 2, 3, and 4. If the plan has no impact on these expenses, then you would expect no dramatic change in the series around month 25.

Figure 2   plots (wage expense in month t/sales in month t)

Figure 3   plots (cost of goods sold in month t/sales in month t)

Figure 4   plots "annual" turnover computed as ($12 \times$ cost of goods sold in month t/inventory at beginning of month t)

> For example, if monthly cost of sales is $100 and the annual inventory turnover ratio is 4, it suggests a monthly turnover of 0.333 with the firm holding an average inventory of $300 throughout the year. (Note that a monthly inventory turnover of .333 implies an annual turnover of 4 (from 12×0.333).)

Financial Report for Store: A typical annual income statement for a pre-plan Ladbreck store before fixed charges, taxes, and incidentals looks as follows.

	Total	Percent
Sales.	10,000,000	100
Cost of goods sold	6,300,000	63
Gross profit.	3,700,000	37
Employee salaries	800,000	8
Profit before fixed charges	2,900,000	29

A store also has substantial charges for rent, management salaries, insurance, etc., but they are fixed with respect to the incentive plan.

Required

a. Suppose the goal of the firm is to now provide superior customer service by having the sales consultant identify and sell to the specific needs of the customer. What does this goal suggest about a change in managerial accounting and control systems?

b. Provide an estimate of the impact of the incentive plan on sales.

c. Did the sales impact occur all at once, or did it occur gradually?

---

[3] For instance, assume sales for plan store were $2,200 this January and $2,000 two Januarys ago. Also assume that sales in the control store were $4,400 this January and $4,000 two Januarys ago. Percent change = 2,200/2,000 − 4,400/4,000 = 0.

d. What is the impact of the incentive plan on wage expense as a percent of sales?

e. What is the impact of the incentive plan on cost of good sold as a percent of sales?

f. What is the impact of incentive plan on inventory turnover (turnover = cost of goods sold ÷ inventory)? [If sales go up, then stores are selling more goods; therefore, more goods need to be on the floor or those goods on floor need to turn over faster.]

g. What is the additional dollar amount of inventory that must be held?

h. Using the information on sales and expenses for a typical store, provide an analysis of the additional store profit contributed by the plan. Assume that it costs 10% a year to carry the added inventory.

i. Look at Exhibit 1, which provides a partial listing of employee pay for one small department within a store. Which "type" of employee is receiving the bonus?

j. Should the company keep the plan? Explain your estimate of the financial impact of the plan and also incorporate any nonfinancial information you feel is relevant in justifying your decision.

Exhibit 1 ■ Wages by subset of employees in Ladbreck's fashion department

Name	Years of Service	Hourly Wage Rate	Hours Worked in Quarter	Regular Pay	Actual Sales for Quarter	Bonus	Total Pay Quarter
BOB MARLEY	2	4.00	400	1,600	25,000	400	2,000
JIMI HENDRIX	16	7.50	440	3,300	41,000	0	3,300
MILLIE SMALL	24	9.99	440	4,396	40,000	0	4,396
AL GREEN	11	6.00	400	2,400	36,000	480	2,880
BOB DYLAN	4	5.00	400	2,000	30,000	400	2,400
JANIS JOPLIN	10	6.00	400	2,400	30,000	0	2,400
WILSON PICKETT	16	7.50	440	3,300	50,000	700	4,000
BRUCE SPRINGSTEEN	23	9.99	440	4,396	30,000	0	4,396
MICHIGAN & SMILEY	13	7.00	400	2,800	38,000	240	3,040
RICHIE FURAY	22	9.90	400	3,960	30,000	0	3,960
JOHN LENNON	5	5.00	400	2,000	34,000	720	2,720
JULIO IGLESIAS	4	5.00	480	2,400	46,000	1,280	3,680
TOMMY PETTY	11	6.00	400	2,400	36,000	480	2,880
JOAN BAEZ	21	9.90	400	3,960	40,000	0	3,960
BB KING	8	6.00	400	2,400	38,000	640	3,040
GLADYS KNIGHT	14	8.00	480	3,840	46,000	0	3,840
NEIL YOUNG	15	8.00	480	3,840	36,000	0	3,840
BO DIDDLEY	4	5.00	400	2,000	30,000	400	2,400

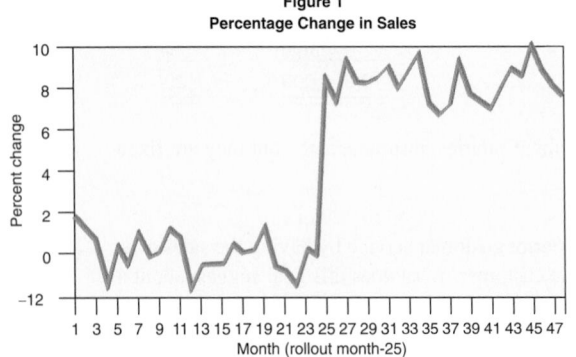

Figure 1
Percentage Change in Sales

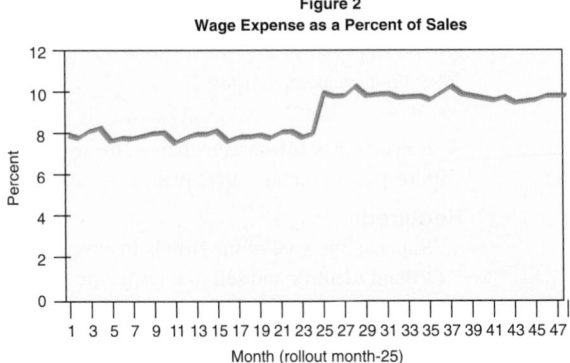

Figure 2
Wage Expense as a Percent of Sales

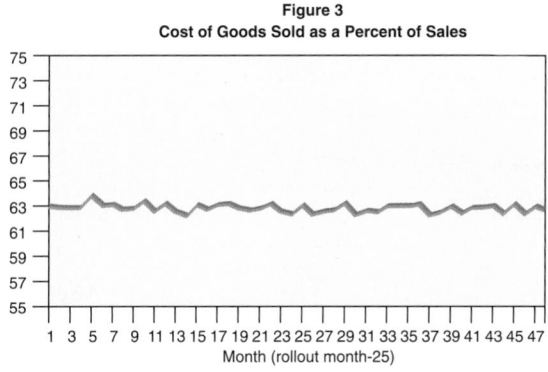

Figure 3
Cost of Goods Sold as a Percent of Sales

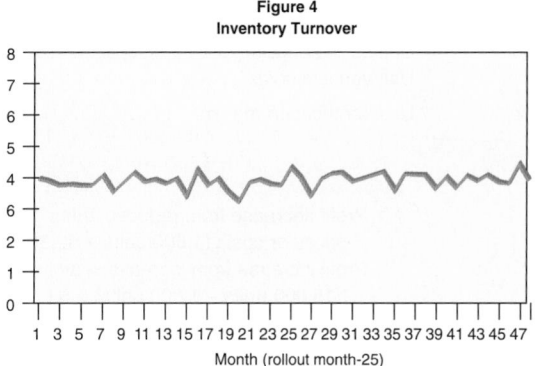

Figure 4
Inventory Turnover

Solutions to Review Problems

Review 17-1—Solution

Relevant Costs	Irrelevant Costs
Cost of machine	Building lease cost
Residual value of machine	Vice president's salary
Operating cost of machine	
Direct labor savings	
Cost of manager	
Opportunity cost of renting released space	

Review 17-2—Solution

a.

	Purchase Machine	Use Labor	Difference (in total cost of purchasing machine)
Cost of new machine	$1,000,000		$1,000,000
Residual value of machine	(100,000)		(100,000)
Operating cost of machine ($10,000 × 60 months)	600,000		600,000
Cost of direct laborers (5,000 clubs × $5 × 60 months)		$1,500,000	(1,500,000)
Cost of one manager ($6,000 × 60 months)		360,000	(360,000)
Rental value of freed-up space ($3,500 × 60 months)		210,000	(210,000)
Total costs	$1,500,000	$2,070,000	$ (570,000)
Advantage of purchasing machine	$570,000		

b. Even though the new machine would save estimated costs of $570,000 over the next five years, there are several qualitative questions that should be answered, including the following:
- Will the new machine provide the same quality product as the current workers?
- How important is it to have a cost structure that includes variable labor costs versus more fixed machine costs? If a business decline should occur, variable costs are often easier to eliminate than fixed costs.
- What is the expected effect on worker morale and community image of eliminating a significant number of jobs in the plant?
- How important is it for the sales staff to be able to promote the product as primarily handmade, versus machine made?

Review 17-3—Solution

Unit selling price	$4.80
Unit variable costs	(2.50)
Unit contribution margin	$2.30

a.

Profit decrease from reduced sales given no changes in prices or costs (1,800 units × $2.30)	$ (4,140)
Profit increase from increase in selling price [(15,000 units − 1,800 units) × $1.50]	19,800
Increase in monthly profit	$15,660

b.

Profit increase from increased sales given no changes in prices or costs (6,000 units × $2.30)	$13,800
Profit decrease from reduced selling price of all units [(15,000 units + 6,000 units) × $1.80]	(37,800)
Profit decrease from increased direct labor costs for the last 1,000 units [1,000 units × ($0.20 × 0.50)]	(100)
Decrease in monthly profit	$(24,100)

Review 17-4—Solution

a.

Increase in revenues (4,000 units × $4.00)		$16,000
Increase in costs		
Direct materials (4,000 units × $2.00)	$8,000	
Direct labor (4,000 units × $0.20)	800	
Factory overhead (4,000 units × $0.25)	1,000	
Selling and administrative	500	(10,300)
Increase in profits		$ 5,700

b.

Increase in revenues (8,000 units × $4.00)		$32,000
Increase in costs		
Direct materials (8,000 units × $2.00)	$16,000	
Direct labor (8,000 units × $0.20)	1,600	
Factory overhead (8,000 units × $0.25)	2,000	
Selling and administrative	500	
Opportunity cost of lost regular sales [(15,000 units + 8,000 units − 20,000 unit capacity) × $2.30]	6,900	(27,000)
Increase in profits		$ 5,000

Review 17-5—Solution

	Cost to Make	Cost to Buy	Difference (income effect of buying)
Cost to buy (15,000 units × $1.00)		$15,000	$(15,000)
Cost to make			
Direct materials			
(15,000 units × $2.00 × 0.40)	$12,000		12,000
Direct labor			
(15,000 units × $0.20 × 0.40)	1,200		1,200
Factory overhead			
(15,000 units × $0.25 × 0.40)	1,500		1,500
Opportunity cost	1,000		1,000
Totals	$15,700	$15,000	$ 700
Advantage of buying.		$700	

Review 17-6—Solution

Increase in revenues			
Package individually (15,000 units × $5.05)		$75,750	
Sell in bulk (15,000 units × $4.80)		(72,000)	$3,750
Additional packaging costs (15,000 units × $0.10).			(1,500)
Advantage of individual packaging.			$2,250

Review 17-7—Solution

Intuition suggests that the extra capacity should be devoted either to produce the Instrument Knob, which has the highest sales price, or the Pointer Knob, which has the highest per-unit contribution margin and net income. However, an analysis of the contribution margin of each product per unit of constraining factor reveals that the Star Knob should receive the extra capacity.

Note that fixed costs are allocated among products on the basis of machine hours—the constraining resource in our example. Furthermore, the unit allocations of fixed costs indicate that the Pointer Knob requires three times as many machine hours as the Instrument Knob and six times as many as the Star Knob. The contribution per unit of machine capacity for each product is as follows.

	Pointer Knob	Instrument Knob	Star Knob
Contribution margin per case	$12	$6	$4
Divided by units machine capacity required	6	2	1
Contribution margin per unit of machine capacity (the constraining resource)	$ 2	$3	$4

Use of the remaining capacity generates a greater contribution margin if devoted to the Star Knob.

Module 18

Product Costing: Job and Process Operations

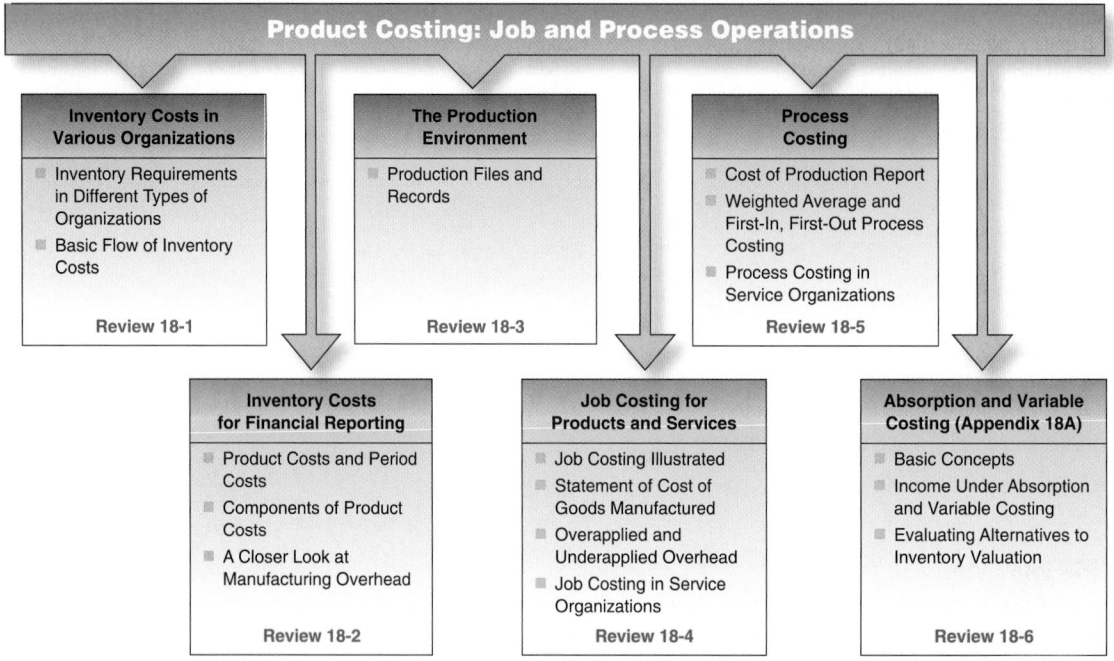

Product Costing: Job and Process Operations

Inventory Costs in Various Organizations
- Inventory Requirements in Different Types of Organizations
- Basic Flow of Inventory Costs

Review 18-1

The Production Environment
- Production Files and Records

Review 18-3

Process Costing
- Cost of Production Report
- Weighted Average and First-In, First-Out Process Costing
- Process Costing in Service Organizations

Review 18-5

Inventory Costs for Financial Reporting
- Product Costs and Period Costs
- Components of Product Costs
- A Closer Look at Manufacturing Overhead

Review 18-2

Job Costing for Products and Services
- Job Costing Illustrated
- Statement of Cost of Goods Manufactured
- Overapplied and Underapplied Overhead
- Job Costing in Service Organizations

Review 18-4

Absorption and Variable Costing (Appendix 18A)
- Basic Concepts
- Income Under Absorption and Variable Costing
- Evaluating Alternatives to Inventory Valuation

Review 18-6

PREVIEW   KSE

Merchandising firms such as ModCloth have one type of inventory—the goods purchased from suppliers that will be resold to customers. However, the inventory of a manufacturing firm such as South Korea's Samsung Electronics is more complicated. Let's consider Samsung's smartphones. First, there are several components used in the manufacturing process of a smartphone, including external cases, batteries, SIM cards, circuit boards, motherboards, speaker assemblies, cameras, flash memory, controller chips, and numerous other elements. Of these components, some are purchased from outside vendors, whereas others are made internally by Samsung. In fact, one of Samsung's competitive advantages is that it makes everything from chips to screens in its own factories, thereby controlling the processing time and technological know-how that goes into its smartphones. This allows the company to bring its products to market more quickly than its competitors, especially because its competitors often buy their components from Samsung. Clearly, Samsung will satisfy its own demand for the components before selling its output to its competitors.

Given that Samsung makes many of its smartphone components internally, the company will have something called raw materials inventory. These are materials that will be transformed during the manufacturing process to become smartphone components. Examples of Samsung's raw materials include steel, glass, chemicals, wood, papers, metals, and polycarbonates. However, Samsung purchases some components from external vendors, for example, chips for Galaxy S10s come from Broadcomm. These components are also considered raw materials inventory until they are requisitioned into the manufacturing process.

Half of Samsung's smartphones (120 million phones per year) are manufactured in two facilities in Vietnam. The other half are manufactured in a single plant in India. Within each factory, employees assemble smartphones at a three-sided workbench that has all the needed tools and raw materials within arm's reach. As raw materials are requisitioned into this part of the facility and direct labor and overhead are added to the raw materials to manufacture the smartphones, these costs are accumulated in another type of inventory called work-in-process inventory. When the smartphones are completed, they are transferred into a third type of inventory called finished goods, where they will await sale to a customer. This means that for manufacturing companies, the line item "inventory" on the balance sheet may be the sum of three types of inventory: raw materials inventory, work-in-process inventory, and finished goods inventory.

This module will illustrate how the costs of products and services flow through these inventory accounts and how we allocate costs to individual products or services based on those products' or services' consumption of the resources. Sometimes, this allocation is straightforward; for example, we can track the amount of raw materials or direct labor hours that go into a product or service. Other times, however, this allocation is more complicated.

Road Map

LO	Learning Objective | Topics	Page	eLecture	Guided Example	Assignments
18-1	**Describe inventory requirements and measurement issues for service, merchandising, and manufacturing organizations.** Inventory Requirements :: Flow of Inventory Costs	18-3	e18–1	Review 18-1	
18-2	**Explain the framework of inventory costing for financial reporting.** Product Costs and Period Costs :: Direct Material :: Direct Labor :: Manufacturing Overhead :: Predetermined Overhead Rates	18-4	e18–2	Review 18-2	14, 15, 21, 24, 25, 34, 35, 36, 37, 44, 45
18-3	**Describe the production environment as it relates to product costing systems.** Production Environment :: Production Files and Records	18-9	e18–3	Review 18-3	
18-4	**Explain the operation of a job costing system.** Basic Production Cost Flows :: Job Costing Illustrated :: Statement of Cost of Goods Manufactured :: Overapplied and Underapplied Overhead :: Job Costing in a Service Organization	18-11	e18–4	Review 18-4	16, 17, 21, 22, 23, 24, 26, 27, 33, 34, 35, 36, 37, 44, 45
18-5	**Explain the operation of a process costing system.** Cost of Production Report :: Weighted Average :: First-In, First-Out :: Process Costing in Service Organizations	18-20	e18–5	Review 18-5	16, 17, 18, 28, 29, 38, 39, 40
18-6	**Evaluate the differences between absorption and variable costing income (Appendix 18A).** Basic Concepts :: Income Under Absorption and Variable Costing :: Production Equals Sales :: Production Exceeds Sales :: Sales Exceed Production :: Evaluating Alternatives to Inventory Valuation	18-26	e18–6	Review 18-6	19, 20, 30, 31, 32, 41, 42, 43, 46

This module provides an overview of product costing systems and a framework for understanding costs in a production environment. It also examines aspects of the production environment that can affect product costing systems and discusses costing issues related to the production of physical products versus the production of services.

Inventory Costs in Various Organizations

LO1 Describe inventory requirements and measurement issues for service, merchandising, and manufacturing organizations.

Organizations can be classified as service, merchandising, or manufacturing. **Service organizations**, such as **SportClips** hair salons, **Shriners Hospitals for Children**, **The Cheesecake Factory** restaurants, and **Delta Air Lines**, perform services for others. **Merchandising organizations**, such as **Walmart**, **Urban Outfitters**, and **Best Buy**, buy and sell goods. **Manufacturing organizations**, such as **Garmin Ltd.**, **The Boston Beer Company**, and **Hershey**, process raw materials into finished products for sale to others.

Service organizations typically have a low percentage of their assets invested in inventory, which usually consists only of the supplies needed to facilitate their operations. In contrast, merchandising organizations usually have a high percentage of their assets invested in inventory. Their largest inventory investment is merchandise purchased for resale, but they also have supplies inventories.

Manufacturing organizations, like merchandisers, have a high percentage of their assets invested in inventories. However, rather than just one major inventory category, manufacturing organizations typically have three: raw materials, work-in-process, and finished goods. **Raw materials inventories** contain the physical ingredients and components that will be converted by machines and/or human labor into a finished product. **Work-in-process inventories** are the partially completed goods that are in the process of being converted into a finished product. **Finished goods inventories** are the completely manufactured products held for sale to customers. As of December 29, 2018, The Boston Beer Company reported the following current inventories:

Raw materials.	$44.7 million
Work-in-process.	8.3 million
Finished goods.	17.3 million
Total current inventory	$70.3 million

Manufacturing organizations also have supplies inventories used to facilitate production and selling and administrative activities. Exhibit 18.1 illustrates the flow of inventory costs in service, merchandising, and manufacturing organizations. In all three types of organizations, the financial accounting system initially records costs of inventories as assets; when they are eventually consumed or sold, inventory costs are recorded as expenses.

Most formal inventory costing systems are designed to provide information for general-purpose financial statements. Before the balance sheet and income statement are prepared, the cost of ending inventory and the cost of inventory sold or used during the period must be determined.

Review 18-1 LO1

Below is a list of asset accounts a company might maintain in its accounting records.

1. Office supplies inventory.
2. Merchandise inventory.
3. Finished goods inventory.
4. Manufacturing supplies inventory.

Required
For each of the above accounts, identify which type of organization—service, merchandising, or manufacturing—is most likely to maintain the account in its records. You may list more than one organization type if it is relevant. Discuss where each of the above asset accounts would be presented in the organization's financial statements. As each of the above asset accounts is eventually consumed or sold, identify how it would be presented in the organization's financial statements.

Solution on p. 18-46.

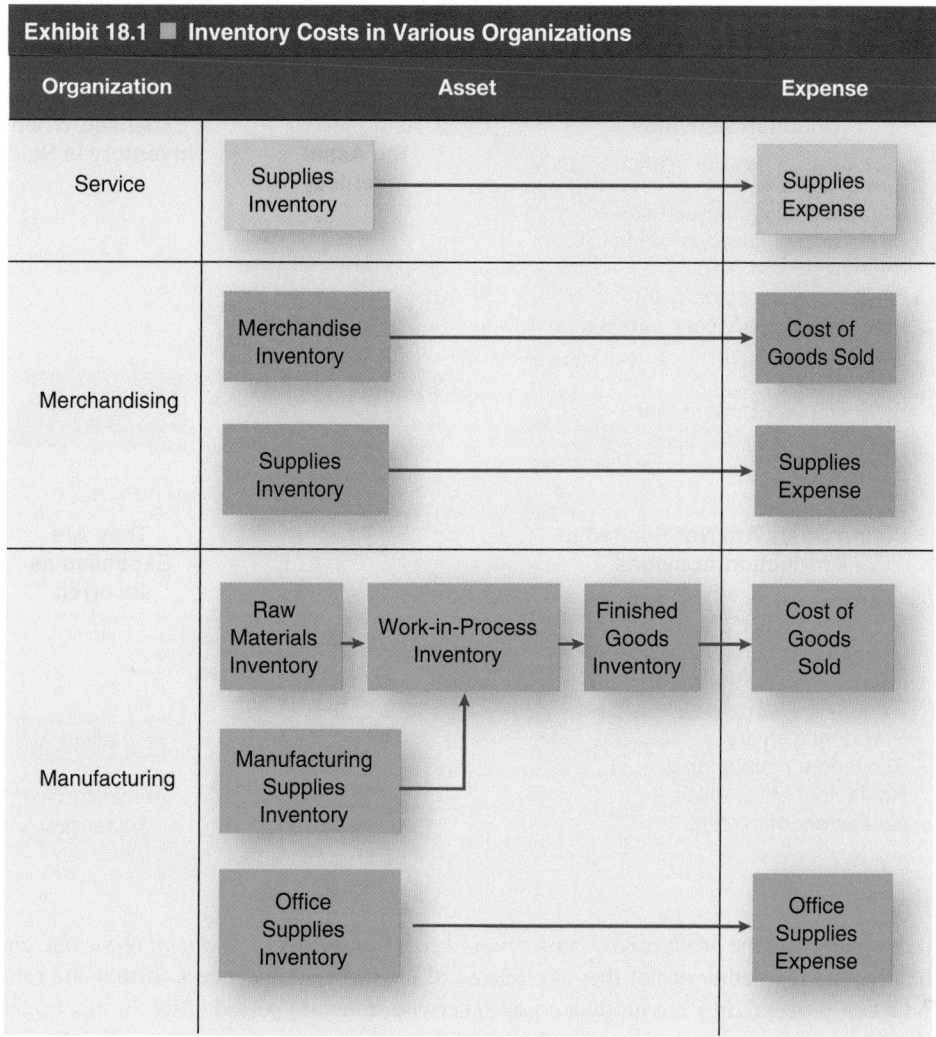

Exhibit 18.1 ■ Inventory Costs in Various Organizations

Inventory Costs for Financial Reporting

In financial reporting for manufacturing organizations, an important distinction is made between the cost of *producing* products and the cost of all other activities such as selling and administration.

LO2
Explain the framework of inventory costing for financial reporting.

Product Costs and Period Costs

For financial reporting, all costs incurred in the *manufacturing* of products are called **product costs**; these costs are carried in the accounts as an asset (inventory) until the product is sold, at which time they are recognized as an expense (cost of goods sold). Product costs include the costs of raw materials, production employee salaries and wages, and all other *manufacturing* costs incurred to transform raw materials into finished products. Costs that directly apply only to the income statement period (other than costs of goods sold) are called **period costs** and are recognized as expenses when incurred. Period costs include the president's salary, sales commissions, advertising costs, and all other *nonmanufacturing* costs. Product and period costs are illustrated in Exhibit 18.2.

Costs such as research and development, marketing, distribution, and customer service are important for strategic analyses; however, since these costs are not incurred in the production process, they are not product costs for *financial reporting purposes*. For *internal managerial purposes*, accountants and managers often use the term *product costing* to embrace all costs incurred in connection with a product or service throughout the value chain.

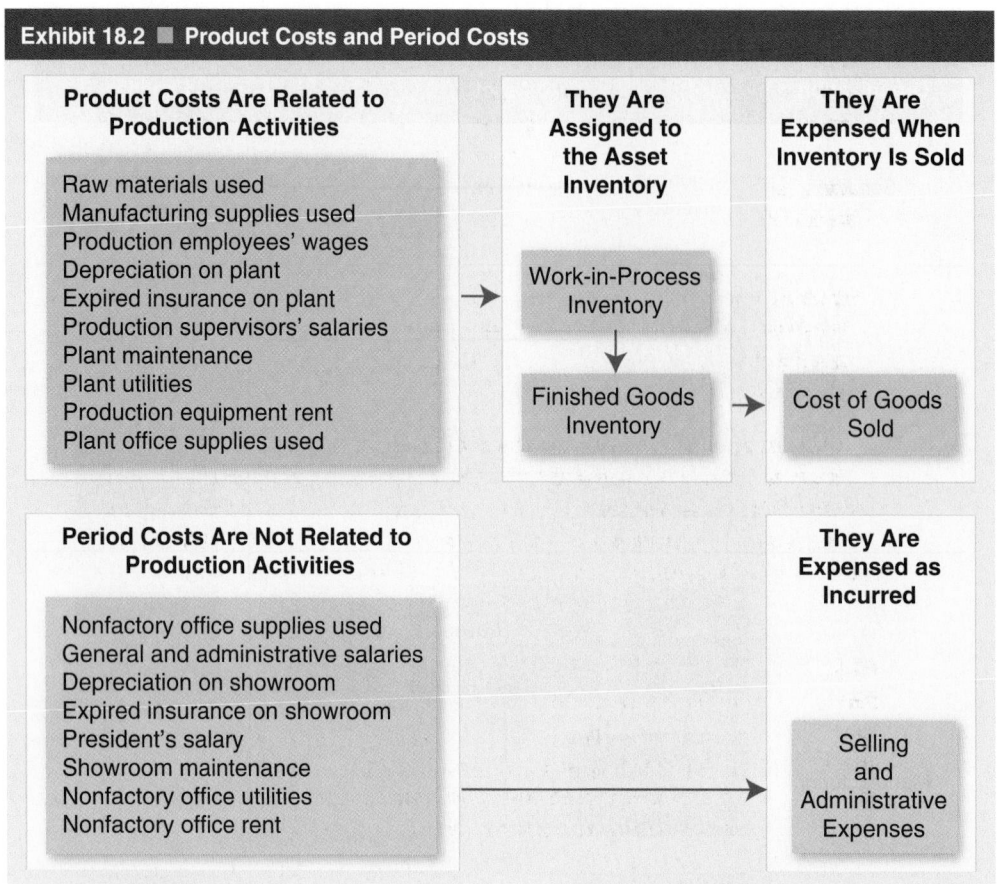

Exhibit 18.2 ■ Product Costs and Period Costs

To summarize, in the *product cost* versus *period cost* framework of *financial reporting,* costs are classified based on whether or not they are related to the production process. If they are related to the production process, they are product costs; otherwise, they are period costs. In this framework, costs that seem very similar may be treated quite differently. For example, note in Exhibit 18.2 that the expired cost of insurance on the *plant* is a *product cost,* but the expired cost of insurance on the *showroom* is a *period cost.* The reason is that the plant is used in production, but the showroom is not. This method of accounting for inventory that assigns all production costs to inventory is sometimes referred to as the **absorption cost** (or **full absorption cost**) method because all production costs are said to be fully absorbed into the cost of the product.

Three Components of Product Costs

The manufacture of even a simple product, such as a small wooden table, requires three basic ingredients: materials (wood), labor (the skill of a worker), and production facilities (a building to work in, a saw, and other tools). Corresponding to these three basic ingredients of any product are three basic categories of product costs: direct materials, direct labor, and manufacturing overhead.

Direct materials are the costs of the primary raw materials converted into finished goods. Examples of primary raw materials include iron ore to a steel mill, coiled aluminum to a manufacturer of aluminum siding, cow's milk to a dairy, logs to a sawmill, and lumber to a builder. The finished product of one firm may be the raw materials of another firm down the value chain. For example, rolled steel is a finished product of U.S. Steel, but it is the raw material of the Whirlpool Corporation for the manufacture of washers and dryers. **Direct labor** consists of wages earned by *production employees for the time they actually spend working on a product,* and **manufacturing overhead** includes all manufacturing costs other than direct materials and direct labor. (Manufacturing overhead is also called *factory overhead, burden, manufacturing burden,* and just *overhead.* Merchandising organizations occasionally refer to administrative costs as *overhead.*) **Conversion cost** consists of the combined costs of direct labor and manufacturing overhead incurred to convert raw materials into finished goods.

Examples of manufacturing overhead are manufacturing supplies, depreciation on manufacturing buildings and equipment, and the costs of plant taxes, insurance, maintenance, security, and utilities. Also included are production supervisors' salaries and all other manufacturing-related labor costs for employees who do not work directly on the product (such as maintenance, security, and janitorial personnel).

Just as raw materials, labor, and production facilities are combined to produce a finished product, direct materials costs, direct labor costs, and manufacturing overhead costs are accumulated to obtain the total cost of goods produced. Exhibit 18.3 illustrates that these product costs are accumulated in the general ledger in Work-in-Process Inventory (or just Work-in-Process) as production takes place and then are transferred to Finished Goods Inventory when production is completed. Product costs are finally assigned to Cost of Goods Sold when the finished goods are sold. (Account titles are capitalized to make it easier to determine when reference is being made to a physical item, such as work-in-process inventory, or to the account, Work-in-Process Inventory, in which costs assigned to the work-in-process inventory are accumulated.)

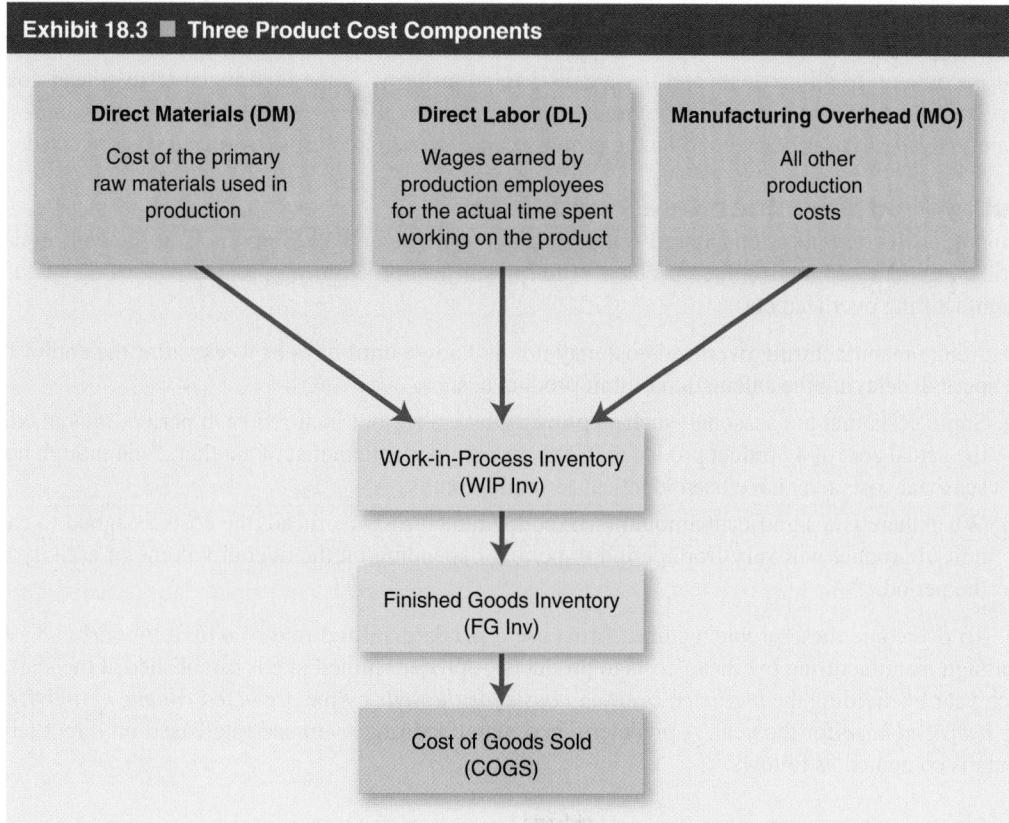

Exhibit 18.3 ■ Three Product Cost Components

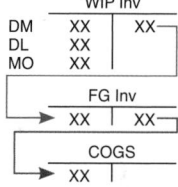

A Closer Look at Manufacturing Overhead

The biggest challenge in measuring the cost of a product is determining the amount of overhead incurred to produce it. Direct materials cost is driven by the number of raw materials units used; hence, its cost is simply the number of units of raw materials used multiplied by the related cost per unit. Direct labor cost is driven by the number of directly traceable labor hours worked on the product; so its cost is the number of direct labor hours used times the appropriate rate per hour. But what about manufacturing overhead? Manufacturing overhead often consists of dozens of different cost elements, potentially with many different cost drivers. Electricity cost is based on kilowatt-hours and water cost on gallons used; depreciation is usually measured in years of service and insurance in premium dollars per thousand dollars of coverage; and supervisors' salaries are a fixed amount per month.

Historically, accountants have believed that, even when possible, it is not cost effective to try to separately measure the cost incurred for each manufacturing overhead item to produce a unit of finished product. Instead of identifying separate cost drivers for each individual cost component in manufacturing overhead, all overhead costs for a department or plant are frequently placed in a cost pool and a single unit-level cost driver is used to assign (or apply) overhead to products.

If a company produced only one product, it would be simple to assign (or apply) overhead to the units produced because it would merely involve dividing total manufacturing overhead cost incurred by the number of units produced to get a cost per unit. For example, if total manufacturing overhead costs were $100,000 for a period when 20,000 units of product were produced, the overhead cost assigned to each unit would be $5.

Selecting a Basis (or Cost Driver) for Assigning Overhead

When multiple products are manufactured in the same facilities, using a simple average of manufacturing overhead cost per unit seldom provides a good estimate of the overhead costs incurred to produce each product. Units requiring extensive manufacturing activity will have too little cost assigned to them, while others requiring only a small amount of manufacturing effort will absorb too much cost. In these cases, units of production is not an appropriate cost driver for manufacturing overhead.

To solve this allocation problem, an overhead application base (or cost driver) other than number of units produced is used. The overhead application base selected is typically a unit-level activity that is common to all products and has a causal relationship with the incurrence of overhead costs. For example, *machine hours* may be used to assign manufacturing overhead costs if the *number of machine hours used* is believed to be the primary cause of manufacturing overhead cost incurred.

Using Predetermined Overhead Rates

Although some organizations assign actual manufacturing overhead to products at the end of each period (normally a month), three problems often result from measuring product cost using "actual" manufacturing overhead costs:

1. Actual manufacturing overhead cost may not be known until days or weeks after the end of the period, delaying the calculation of unit product cost.

2. Some costs that are seasonal, such as property taxes, are not incurred each period, thus making the actual cost of a product produced in one month greater than that of another, even though non-seasonal costs may have been identical for both months.

3. When there is a significant amount of fixed manufacturing overhead, the costs assigned to each unit of product will vary from period to period, depending on the overall volume of activity for the period.

To overcome these problems, most firms use a **predetermined manufacturing overhead rate** to assign manufacturing overhead costs to products. A predetermined rate is established at the start of each year by dividing the *predicted overhead costs for the year* by the *predicted volume of activity in the overhead base* for the year. A predetermined manufacturing overhead rate based on direct labor hours is computed as follows:

$$\text{Predetermined manufacturing overhead rate per direct labor hour} = \frac{\text{Predicted total manufacturing overhead cost for the year}}{\text{Predicted total direct labor hours for the year}}$$

If management believes machine hours is the major driver of manufacturing overhead, the denominator should be predicted machine hours.

Using a predetermined manufacturing overhead rate based on direct labor hours, we compute the assignment of overhead to Work-in-Process Inventory as follows:

$$\text{Manufacturing overhead applied to Work-in-Process Inventory} = \text{Actual direct labor hours} \times \text{Predetermined manufacturing overhead rate per direct labor hour}$$

To illustrate, assume that at the beginning of the current year, one of Garmin's plants predicted an activity level of 25,000 direct labor hours with manufacturing overhead totaling $187,500. Using this information, its predetermined overhead rate per direct labor hour for the year would have been computed as follows:

$$\text{Predetermined overhead rate} = \frac{\$187,500}{25,000 \text{ direct labor hours}}$$

$$= \$7.50 \text{ per direct labor hour}$$

If 2,000 direct labor hours were used in September of this year, the applied overhead for September would be $15,000, as shown here:

$$2,000 \times \$7.50 = \$15,000$$

When a predetermined rate is used, monthly variations between actual and applied manufacturing overhead are expected because of the seasonality in costs and the variations in monthly activity. Hence, in some months overhead will be "overapplied" as applied overhead exceeds actual overhead; in other months overhead will be "underapplied" as actual overhead exceeds applied overhead. If the beginning-of-the-year estimates are accurate for annual overhead costs and annual activity, monthly over- and underapplied amounts during the year should offset each other by the end of the year. Later in this module, we consider accounting for any over- or underapplied manufacturing overhead balance that may exist at the end of the year.

Changing Cost Structures Affect the Basis of Overhead Application

By using a single overhead rate, we assume that overhead costs are primarily caused by a single cost driver. Historically, a single plantwide overhead application rate based on direct labor hours was widely used when direct labor was the predominant cost factor in production, and manufacturing overhead costs were driven by the utilization of direct labor.

Changes in manufacturing processes have produced major shifts in the composition of conversion costs, resulting in significantly less direct labor and significantly more manufacturing overhead. An example of this shift is the automobile industry where firms such as Ford and Toyota have spent billions of dollars on robotics and other technologies, thereby reducing direct labor in the production process. In many cases, direct labor hours are no longer an appropriate basis for assigning manufacturing costs to products. In others, these changes mean there is no longer a single cost driver that is appropriate for assigning manufacturing overhead to products.

Although some companies continue to use a single manufacturing overhead rate because it is convenient, many companies no longer use this approach. Instead, they have adopted multiple overhead rates based on either major departments or activities within the organization. One method for using multiple overhead rates is activity-based costing, discussed in Module 19.

LO2 Review 18-2

Assume that the following predictions were made at the beginning of the year for one of the plants of Milliken & Company:

Total manufacturing overhead for the year.	$40,000,000
Total machine hours for the year	3,200,000

Actual results for February were as follows:

Manufacturing overhead.	$4,410,000
Machine hours	410,000

continued

continued from previous page

Required

a. Determine the predetermined overhead rate per machine hour for the current year.

b. Using the predetermined overhead rate per machine hour, determine the manufacturing overhead applied to Work-in-Process during February.

c. As of February 1, actual overhead was underapplied by $400,000. Determine the cumulative amount of any overapplied or underapplied overhead at the end of February.

Solution on p. 18-47.

The Production Environment

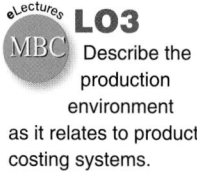
LO3
Describe the production environment as it relates to product costing systems.

Production personnel need to know the specific products to produce on specific machines on a daily or even hourly basis. The detailed scheduling of products on machines is performed by production scheduling personnel. Exactly how production is scheduled depends on whether process manufacturing or job production is used and whether production is in response to a specific customer sales order or for the company's inventory in anticipation of future sales.

In **process manufacturing**, production of identical units is on a *continuous* basis; a production facility may be devoted exclusively to one product or to a set of closely related products. Companies where you would likely find a process manufacturing environment include **Exxon Mobil** and **Procter & Gamble**. Process manufacturing is discussed later in this module.

In **job production**, also called **job order production**, products are manufactured in single units or in batches of identical units. Examples of single-unit jobs are found at **Schumacher Homes**, a builder of custom-designed homes, **Bechtel Corporation**, the largest commercial construction company in the U.S., and **Cray Inc.** (a subsidiary of **Hewlett Packard Enterprise**), which manufactures supercomputers. Examples of batches of identical units (multi-unit jobs) are found at **True Religion Brand Jeans**, a clothing manufacturer, and **Herman Miller**, a large producer of office chairs including the ergonomic Aeron model. Of course, the specific products included in different jobs or batches may vary considerably.

In a job production environment, when a customer's order is received, the marketing department forwards the order to production scheduling, where employees determine when and how the product is to be produced. Important scheduling considerations include the overall workload, raw materials availability, specific equipment or labor requirements, and the expected delivery date(s) of the finished product.

Important staff groups involved in production planning and control include engineering, scheduling, and accounting. Engineering is primarily concerned with determining how a product should be produced. Based on an engineering analysis and cost data, engineering personnel develop manufacturing specifications for each product. These manufacturing specifications are often summarized in two important documents: a bill of materials and an operations list. Each product's **bill of materials** specifies the kinds and quantities of raw materials required for one unit of product. The **operations list** (sometimes called an **activities list**) specifies the manufacturing operations and related times required for one unit or batch of product. The operations list should also include information on any machine setup time, movements between work areas, and other scheduled activities, such as quality inspections.

Scheduling personnel prepare a production order for each job. The **production order** contains a job's unique identification number and specifies such details as the quantity to be produced, raw materials requirements, manufacturing operations and other activities to be performed, and perhaps even the time when each manufacturing operation should be performed. In preparing a production order, scheduling personnel use the product's bill of materials and operations list to determine the materials, operations, and manufacturing times required for the job.

A **job cost sheet** is a document (usually an electronic document) used to accumulate the costs for a specific job. The job cost sheet serves as the basic record for recording actual progress on the job. As production takes place, the materials, labor, and machine resources utilized are recorded on the job cost sheet along with the related costs. When a job is completed, the final cost of the job is determined by totaling the costs on the job cost sheet.

Production Files and Records

Certain files in the cost system (typically in a computer database) provide the necessary detail for amounts maintained in total in the general ledger. For example, the raw materials inventory file contains separate records for each type of raw materials, indicating increases, decreases, and the available balance for both units and costs. Every time there is a change in the Raw Materials Inventory general ledger account, there must be an equal change in one or more individual inventory records. Therefore, at any given time, the total of the balances in the raw materials inventory file for all raw materials inventory items should equal the balance in the Raw Materials Inventory general ledger account. Because of this relationship between the raw materials inventory file and Raw Materials Inventory in the general ledger, Raw Materials Inventory is called a *control account* and the raw materials file of detailed records is called a *subsidiary ledger.* Other general ledger accounts related to the product cost system that have subsidiary files are Work-in-Process, Finished Goods Inventory, and Cost of Goods Sold.

Other records required to operate a job cost system include production orders, job cost sheets, materials requisition forms, and work tickets. Production orders and job cost sheets were previously discussed. The production order serves as authorization for production supervisors to obtain materials from the storeroom and to issue work orders to production employees, and the job cost sheet accumulates the cost of the job.

A **materials requisition form** indicates the type and quantity of each raw material issued to the factory. This form is used to record the transfer of responsibility for materials and to record materials changes on raw materials and job cost sheet records. The materials requisition form has a place to record the job number; the job cost sheet has a place to record the requisition number. If a question arises regarding the issuance of materials, the requisition number and job number provide a trail for tracing the destination and the source of the materials. The materials requisition form also identifies the materials warehouse employee who issued the materials and the production employee who received them.

A **work ticket** is used to record the time a job spends in a specific manufacturing operation. Each manufacturing operation performed on a job is documented by a work ticket. The completed work tickets for a job should correspond to the operations specified on the job production order. Time information on the work tickets is used by production scheduling or expediting personnel to determine whether the job is on schedule, and to assign costs to the job.

A production operation can involve a single employee, a group of employees, a machine, or even heating, cooling, or aging processes. When the operation involves a single employee, the rate recorded on the work ticket is simply the employee's wage rate. When it involves a group of employees, the rate is composed of the wage rates of all employees in the group. When the work involves a machine operation, the rate includes a charge for machine time, as well as the time of any machine operators. Other operations, such as heating, cooling, or aging, will also have a rate for each unit of time.

LO3 Review 18-3

Which term below (*a–f*) is best associated with the following statements?

a. Process costing
b. Job order costing
c. Production order
d. Job cost sheet
e. Materials requisition
f. Work ticket

____1. Authorization to production supervisors to obtain materials and issue work orders.
____2. The accounting system most likely used to capture the costs of the production of rolls of paper that are sold as finished goods to print newspaper companies.
____3. Accumulates the costs of the job.
____4. The accounting system used to capture the costs of the production of custom-built boats.
____5. Records the time a job spends in a specific manufacturing operation.
____6. Transfers responsibility for materials.

Solution on p. 18-47.

Job Costing for Products and Services

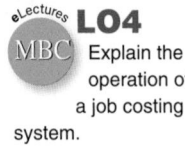

LO4
Explain the operation of a job costing system.

Exhibit 18.4 shows how inventory costs in a manufacturing organization flow in a logical pattern through the financial accounting system. Pay particular attention to the major inventory accounts (Raw Materials, Work-in-Process, and Finished Goods Inventory), Manufacturing Overhead, and the flow of costs through the inventory accounts. Each of the numbered items, representing a cost flow affecting an inventory account or Manufacturing Overhead, is explained here:

1. The costs of purchased raw materials and manufacturing supplies are recorded in Raw Materials and Manufacturing Supplies, respectively. An increase in Accounts Payable typically offsets these increases.

2. As primary raw materials are requisitioned to the factory, direct materials costs are transferred from Raw Materials to Work-in-Process.

3. Direct labor costs are assigned to Work-in-Process on the basis of the time devoted to processing raw materials. Indirect labor costs associated with production employees are initially assigned to Manufacturing Overhead.

4–6. Other production related costs are also assigned to Manufacturing Overhead. Other Payables represents the incurrence of a variety of costs such as repairs and maintenance, utilities, and property taxes.

7. Costs assigned to Manufacturing Overhead are periodically reassigned (applied) to Work-in-Process, preferably with the use of a predetermined overhead rate such as direct labor hours, machine hours, or some other cost assignment base.

8. When products are completed, their accumulated product costs are totaled on a job cost sheet and transferred from Work-in-Process to Finished Goods Inventory.

9. When the completed products are sold, their costs are transferred from Finished Goods Inventory to Cost of Goods Sold.

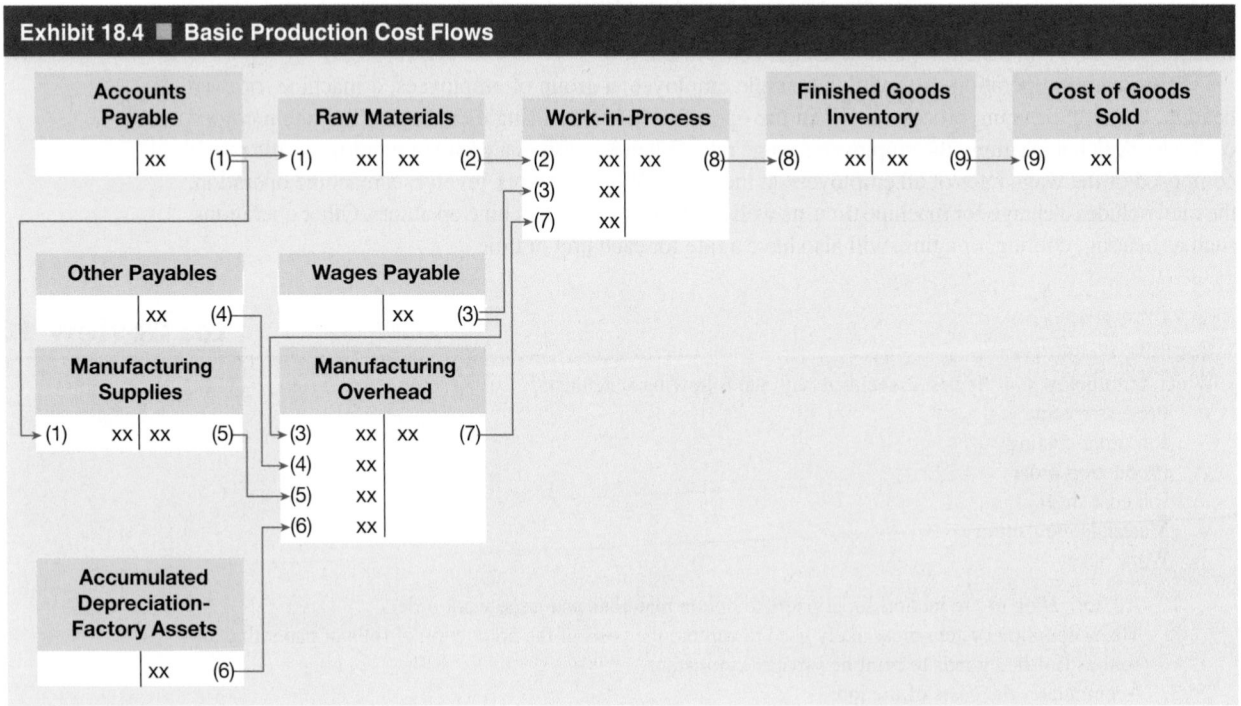

Exhibit 18.4 ■ Basic Production Cost Flows

Business Insight ■ Job Costing Illustration

Technological advances have increased product choices for customers. One dimension of product choice that has increased with technology is customization. From custom bicycle brands like Seven Cycles to made-to-order shirts like Proper Cloth, customization is an increasing trend in retail.

Take the fashion brand Frilly. Frilly is a contemporary clothing brand "meant to empower you and encourage you to embrace your own style." Customers can choose a design, then customize it by selecting cuts, fabrics, detailing, and more. Frilly claims that operating on a made-to-order model minimizes typical inventory issues that lead to pollution and waste. Of course customization demands a premium, and an accurate measure of costs is critical to any customization scheme. For example, different fabrics must be priced according to their cost, and more intricate stitching may result in upcharges for the customer.

Source: https://www.frilly.com/about-us

Job Costing Illustrated

Even though data are almost always processed with computerized systems, data processing procedures are best illustrated within the context of a paper-based manual system. Consider Frilly featured in the Business Insight box. Because variations in styles cause differences in costs, detailed records are kept concerning the costs assigned to specific jobs. Suppose raw materials consist of outer fabric, liner fabric, and thread.

Assume total inventory on August 1 included Raw Materials, $71,000; Work-in-Process, $109,900; and Finished Goods, $75,000. In addition there were manufacturing supplies of $1,600, consisting of various items such as thread, needles, sheers, and machine lubricant. The August 1 balance in Manufacturing Overhead was $0.

Raw Materials			
Description	**Quantity**	**Unit Cost**	**Total Cost**
Fabric..	3,000 square yards	$ 20	$60,000
Zippers...	100 cases	50	5,000
Buttons...	20 cases	150	3,000
Thread..	150 spool sets	20	3,000
Total..			$71,000

Manufacturing Supplies	
Item	**Total Cost**
Various..	$1,600

Work-in-Process	
Job	**Total Cost**
425...	$ 58,600
426...	51,300
Total..	$109,900

Finished Goods Inventory	
Job	**Total Cost**
424...	$75,000

To illustrate manufacturing cost flows in a job cost system, "T" accounts are presented in the margin for the cost system transactions for Frilly, for August. Each cost assignment is supported by documented information that is recorded in subsidiary cost system records. The hypothetical manufacturing cost transactions for Frilly for August are discussed here. The numbered jobs combine orders that share the same style choices.

RM Inv

BB	71,000		
(1)	30,000		

Mfg. Supplies

BB	1,600		
(1)	1,000		

Accounts Payable

		31,000	(1)

1. Raw materials and manufacturing supplies are purchased on account. The vendor's invoice totals $31,000, including $1,000 of manufacturing supplies and $30,000 of raw materials. The cost of the raw materials must be assigned to specific raw materials inventory records:

Fabric	850 square yards	× $ 20 =	$17,000
Zippers	140 cases	× $ 50 =	7,000
Buttons	40 cases	× $150 =	6,000
Total			$30,000

WIP Inv

BB	109,900		
(2)	54,300		

RM Inv

BB	71,000	54,300	(2)
(1)	30,000		

2. Materials needed to complete Jobs 425 and 426 are requisitioned. Two new jobs, 427 and 428, were also started and direct materials were requisitioned for them. A total of $54,300 of raw materials was requisitioned:

	Job 425	Job 426	Job 427	Job 428	Total
Fabric					
975 sq. yds. × $20			$19,500		$19,500
955 sq. yds. × $20				$19,100	19,100
Zippers					
52 cases × $50	$2,600				2,600
30 cases × $50		$1,500			1,500
43 cases × $50			2,150		2,150
20 cases × $50				1,000	1,000
Buttons					
12 cases × $150	1,800				1,800
12 cases × $150		1,800			1,800
11 cases × $150			1,650		1,650
14 cases × $150				2,100	2,100
Thread					
20 spool sets × $20.	400				400
15 spool sets × $20.		300			300
10 spool sets × $20.			200		200
10 spool sets × $20.				200	200
Total	$4,800	$3,600	$23,500	$22,400	$54,300

WIP Inv

BB	109,900		
(2)	54,300		
(3)	34,450		

MO

BB	–0–		
(3)	7,200		

Wages Payable

		41,650	(3)

3. Assume the August payroll liability was $41,650, including $34,450 for direct labor and $7,200 for indirect labor. Direct labor was assigned to the jobs as follows:

	Job 425	Job 426	Job 427	Job 428	Total
Direct labor hours	600	900	1,000	945	
Direct labor rate	× $10	× $10	× $10	× $10	
Total	$6,000	$9,000	$10,000	$9,450	$34,450

Note: The $7,200 of indirect labor costs is assigned to products as part of applied overhead.

MO

BB	–0–		
(3)	7,200		
(4)	950		
(5)	2,400		
(6)	3,230		

Mfg Supplies

BB	1,600	950	(4)
(1)	1,000		

Accum. Depr

		2,400	(5)

Other Payables

		3,230	(6)

4–6. In addition to indirect labor, suppose Frilly incurred the following manufacturing overhead costs:

Manufacturing Supplies	$ 950
Accumulated Depreciation—Factory Assets	2,400
Miscellaneous (Other Payables).	3,230

7. Assume manufacturing overhead is applied to jobs using a predetermined rate of $4 per direct labor hour. Assignments to individual jobs are as follows:

	Job 425	Job 426	Job 427	Job 428	Total
Labor hours	600	900	1,000	945	
Overhead rate per labor hour	× $4	× $4	× $4	× $4	
Total	$2,400	$3,600	$4,000	$3,780	$13,780

```
              MO
BB     -0- | 13,780  (7)
(3)  7,200 |
(4)    950 |
(5)  2,400 |
(6)  3,230 |

            WIP Inv
BB   109,900 |
(2)   54,300 |
(3)   34,450 |
(7)   13,780 |
```

8. Jobs 425, 426, and 427 are completed with the following costs:

	Job 425	Job 426	Job 427	Total
Beginning balance	$58,600	$51,300	$ 0	$109,900
Current costs				
Direct materials (entry 2).	4,800	3,600	23,500	31,900
Direct labor (entry 3).	6,000	9,000	10,000	25,000
Applied overhead (entry 7)	2,400	3,600	4,000	10,000
Total	$71,800	$67,500	$37,500	$176,800

```
             FG Inv
BB    75,000 |
(8)  176,800 |

             WIP Inv
BB   109,900 | 176,800  (8)
(2)   54,300 |
(3)   34,450 |
(7)   13,780 |
```

Additional analysis for the completed jobs indicates the following:

	Job 425	Job 426	Job 427
Total cost of job	$71,800	$67,500	$37,500
Units in job	÷ 1,200	÷ 900	÷ 500
Unit cost	$ 59.83	$ 75.00	$ 75.00

9. Jobs 424, 425, and 426 are delivered to customers for a sales price of $400,000. Determining the costs transferred from Finished Goods Inventory to Cost of Goods Sold requires summing the total cost of jobs sold:

```
            COGS
(9) 214,300 |

             FG Inv
BB    75,000 | 214,300  (9)
(8)  176,800 |
```

Job 424.	$ 75,000
Job 425.	71,800
Job 426.	67,500
Total	$214,300

At this point we can determine the gross profit on the completed jobs:

Sales.	$400,000
Cost of goods sold	(214,300)
Gross profit.	$185,700

If inventory were produced in anticipation of future sales rather than in response to specific customer orders, it is likely that not all units in a job would be sold at the same time. In this case, the unit cost information is used to determine the amount transferred from Finished Goods Inventory to Cost of Goods Sold.

Exhibit 18.5 shows the cost system records supporting the ending balances in the major inventory accounts and Cost of Goods Sold. Note the importance of the job cost sheets for determining cost transfers affecting Work-in-Process and Finished Goods Inventory. The job cost sheets are also used in determining the ending balances of these accounts.

Frilly's product costing system is adequate for determining the cost for each job for purposes of valuing ending inventories and cost of goods sold in its external financial statements. The costing system recognizes the differences in materials costs by carefully tracking each type of material as a separate

Exhibit 18.5 ■ General Ledger Accounts and Subsidiary Records for Inventory Categories and Cost of Goods Sold

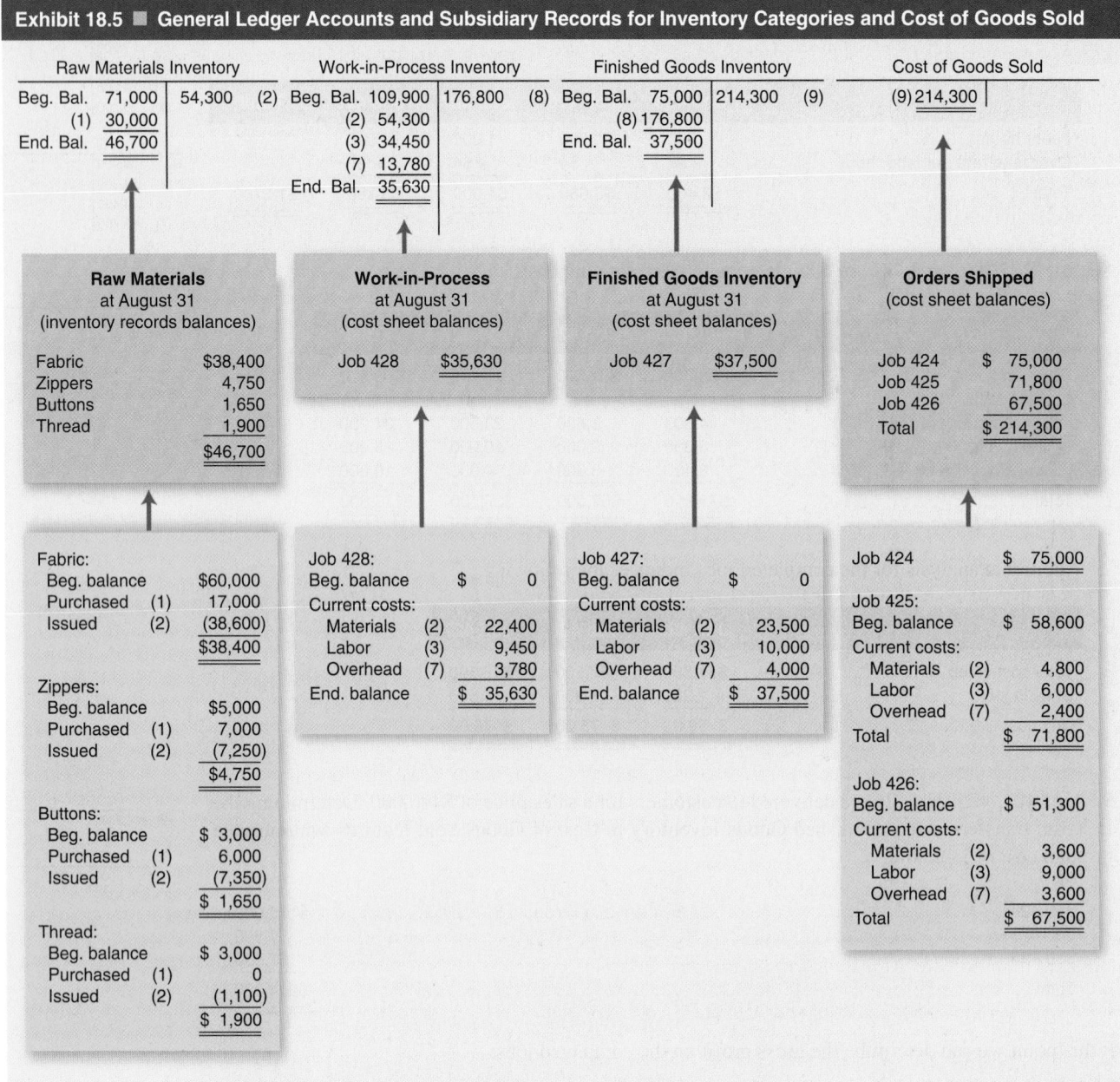

cost pool. Assuming all direct labor employees are paid the same rate, it is necessary to maintain only one labor cost pool. Although there are three distinct operations in making clothing (cutting, sewing, and finishing), the various styles likely require the same proportionate times on each operation. Hence, even with only one plantwide manufacturing overhead cost pool applied on the basis of direct labor hours, individual product costs are reasonably accurate.

Although Frilly's assumed costing system may be adequate for inventory costing for financial statement purposes, the data it routinely generates will not provide management with information for many management decisions. To evaluate product or customer profitability, management needs additional information concerning marketing, distributing, selling, and customer service costs, which are not included in the product cost system. The following Business Insight illustrates the importance of distribution costs in decision making at Coca-Cola.

Furthermore, the cost system does not provide information for decisions concerning individual operations, such as cutting. To answer questions regarding how best to perform operations, Frilly's accountants should perform a special cost study to obtain relevant activity-cost information.

> **Business Insight** ■ Coca-Cola Sheds Shipping and Production to Focus on Sales and Marketing
>
> For a global brand like Coca-Cola, distribution costs can become quite large and can distract the company from its core business. Coca-Cola has announced that it is overhauling its U.S. supply chain by selling both production and distribution portions of the business to partner companies. Coca-Cola will focus on selling and marketing drink concentrate to production partners and bottlers.
>
> This trend seems to be meaningful enough for logistics and distribution businesses to take note. FedEx and UPS have both announced acquisitions of logistics firms that offer supply chain tasks traditionally done in-house, such as processing returns and other distribution. In fact, Coyote Logistics, which UPS purchased in 2015, arranges shipping for 12,000 firms including beverage giant Heineken.
>
> Sources: Mike Esterl, "Coke Plans to Sell Nine U.S. Production Plants," *Wall Street Journal*, September 24, 2015; Laura Stevens, "FedEx Pays $1.4 Billion for GENCO," *Wall Street Journal*, March 19, 2015; and Laura Stevens, "UPS Agrees to Buy Coyote Logistics for $1.8 Billion," *Wall Street Journal*, July 31, 2015.

Statement of Cost of Goods Manufactured

The income statement for a merchandising organization normally includes a calculation of cost of goods sold as follows:

Sales.		$X,XXX
Less cost of goods sold		
Beginning inventory	$X,XXX	
Plus purchases	X,XXX	
Goods available for sale	X,XXX	
Less ending inventory	(X,XXX)	
Cost of goods sold		(X,XXX)
Gross profit		X,XXX
Less selling and administrative expenses		(X,XXX)
Net income		$X,XXX

Manufacturing organizations modify only one line of this income statement format, changing purchases to cost of goods manufactured. Since a manufacturer acquires finished goods from the factory, its cost of goods manufactured is the total cost transferred from Work-in-Process to Finished Goods Inventory during the period.

For internal reporting purposes, most companies prepare a separate **statement of cost of goods manufactured**, which summarizes the cost of goods completed and transferred into Finished Goods Inventory during the period. A hypothetical statement of cost of goods manufactured and an income statement for Frilly are presented in Exhibit 18.6 for August.

Exhibit 18.6 ■ Statement of Cost of Goods Manufactured and Income Statement

FRILLY Statement of Cost of Goods Manufactured August			
Current manufacturing costs			
Cost of materials placed in production			
Raw materials, 8/1	$ 71,000		
Purchases	30,000		
Total available	101,000		
Raw materials, 8/31	(46,700)	$ 54,300	
Direct labor		34,450	
Manufacturing overhead		13,780	$102,530
Work-in-process, 8/1			109,900
Total costs in process			212,430
Work-in-process, 8/31			(35,630)
Cost of goods manufactured			$176,800

continued

continued from previous page

Exhibit 18.6 ■ Statement of Cost of Goods Manufactured and Income Statement—continued

FRILLY
Income Statement
August

Sales.			$400,000
Cost of goods sold			
Finished goods inventory, 8/1	$ 75,000		
Cost of goods manufactured.	176,800		
Total goods available for sale	251,800		
Finished goods inventory, 8/31	(37,500)	214,300	
Gross profit.		185,700	
Selling and administrative expenses*		(90,000)	
Net income		$ 95,700	

* Selling and administrative expenses for Frilly are assumed to be $90,000.

Overapplied and Underapplied Overhead

In the Frilly example, assume that the predetermined manufacturing overhead rate of $4 per direct labor hour was based on predicted manufacturing overhead for the year of $100,000 and predicted direct labor hours of 25,000. Assume further that it was determined that the company actually incurred $100,000 in manufacturing overhead during the year and that actual direct labor hours for the year were 25,000, resulting in applied overhead of $100,000 (25,000 hours × $4). The activity in Manufacturing Overhead is summarized as follows:

Manufacturing Overhead	
Beginning balance	$ 0
Actual overhead	100,000
Total	100,000
Applied overhead	(100,000)
Ending balance.	$ 0

With identical amounts of actual and applied overhead, the ending balance in Manufacturing Overhead is zero. However, if either the actual overhead cost or the actual level of the production activity base differed from its predicted value, there would be a balance in Manufacturing Overhead representing overapplied or underapplied overhead.

Assume, for example, that the prediction of 25,000 direct labor hours was correct but that actual overhead cost was $105,000. In this case, Manufacturing Overhead shows a $5,000 positive balance, representing underapplied manufacturing overhead:

Manufacturing Overhead	
Beginning balance	$ 0
Actual overhead	105,000
Total	105,000
Applied overhead	(100,000)
Ending balance.	$ 5,000*

* Underapplied; actual exceeds applied.

If actual manufacturing overhead were only $98,000, Manufacturing Overhead would be overapplied and show a $2,000 negative balance.

If the *prediction* of total manufacturing overhead cost is not accurate, there will be an underapplied or overapplied balance in Manufacturing Overhead at the end of the year. A similar result occurs when the *predicted* activity level used in computing the predetermined rate differs from the actual activity level. It is not uncommon for such differences to occur. Predictions are exactly that—predictions.

Month-to-month balances in Manufacturing Overhead are usually allowed to accumulate during the year. In the absence of evidence to the contrary, it is assumed that such differences result from seasonal variations in production or costs or both. However, any year-end balance in Manufacturing Overhead must be eliminated.

Theoretically, the disposition of any year-end balance in Manufacturing Overhead should be accomplished in a manner that adjusts every account to what its balance would have been if an actual, rather than a predetermined, overhead rate had been used. This involves adjusting the ending balances in Work-in-Process, Finished Goods Inventory, and Cost of Goods Sold. Procedures to do this are examined in cost accounting textbooks.

In most situations, the simple procedure of treating the remaining overhead as an adjustment to Cost of Goods Sold is adequate. Unless there are large ending balances in inventories and a large year-end balance in Manufacturing Overhead, this simple procedure produces acceptable results. Underapplied overhead indicates that the assigned costs are less than the actual costs, understating Cost of Goods Sold. Hence, disposing of an underapplied balance in Manufacturing Overhead increases the balance in Cost of Goods Sold.

Manufacturing Overhead		
Beginning balance	$ 0	
Actual overhead	105,000	
Total	105,000	
Applied overhead	(100,000)	
Ending balance	$ 5,000*	← Increase Cost of Goods Sold

* Underapplied; actual exceeds applied.

Conversely, overapplied overhead indicates that the assigned costs are more than the actual costs, overstating Cost of Goods Sold. Hence, disposing of an overapplied balance in Manufacturing Overhead decreases Cost of Goods Sold.

Job Costing in Service Organizations

Service costing, the assignment of costs to services performed, uses job costing concepts to determine the cost of filling customer service orders in organizations such as automobile repair shops, charter

---

Business Insight   ■   The Versatility of Job Costing—A Perfect Fit for Designers

FNDR, an adviser to startups, helps entrepreneurs identify their values and beliefs through a series of meetings. "The result is an 'intentional narrative' that can guide future decisions." The company worked with the founder of Iris, a company that has developed software that makes sound more immersive and has plans to release meditation apps, synthesize its narrative into two words, 'Listen well' that have become part of their brand design.

A new approach to focus groups was developed by Juliet, a Toronto-based agency. Instead of using groups to evaluate an already developed advertising campaign, Juliet assembles a group of people with strong interests in or connections to a product a client wants to promote. An advertising campaign is then developed using input from the focus group. Juliet's "Real Talk" process has been used successfully by a subsidiary of Signet Jewelers to increase sales of engagement rings to male customers.

By tracking resources to jobs, these firms have the flexibility to accurately adapt the costing system to the structure of the work being done for the client.

Sources: Stephanie Mehta, "How Brand Consultancy FNDR helps Companies such as Snap and Glossier find their Voices," *Fast Company*, December 16, 2019. Jeff Beer, "This Ad Agency uses a Casting Agent to Create the Focus Group of the Future," *Fast Company*, November 5, 2019.

airlines, CPA firms, hospitals, and law firms. Many of these organizations bill clients on the basis of resources consumed. Consequently, they maintain detailed records for billing purposes. On the invoice sent to the client, the organization itemizes any materials consumed on the job at a selling price per unit, the labor hours worked on the job at a billing rate per hour, and the time special facilities were used at a billing rate per unit of time. Employees with different capabilities and experience often have different billing rates. In a CPA firm, for example, a partner or a senior manager has a higher billing rate than a staff accountant.

The prices and rates must be high enough to cover costs not assigned to specific jobs and to provide for a profit. To evaluate the contribution to common costs and profit from a job, a comparison must be made between the price charged the customer and the actual cost of the job. This is easily done when the actual cost of resources itemized on the customer's invoice is presented on a job cost sheet. A CPA firm, for example, should accumulate the actual hardware and software costs incurred in an accounting system installation for a client, along with the actual wages earned by employees while working on the job and any related travel costs. Comparing the total of these costs with the price charged, the client indicates the total contribution of the job to common costs and profit.

Although service organizations may identify costs with individual jobs for management accounting purposes, there is considerable variation in the way job cost information is presented in financial statements. Some organizations report the cost of jobs completed in their income statements using an account such as Cost of Services Provided. They use procedures similar to those outlined in Exhibit 18.6; the only major change involves replacing Cost of Goods Sold with Cost of Services Provided.

More often, however, service organizations do not formally establish detailed procedures to trace the flow of service costs. Instead, service job costs are left in their original cost categories such as materials expense, salaries and wages expense, travel expense, and so forth. Because all service costs are typically regarded as expenses rather than product costs, either procedure is acceptable for financial reporting. Regardless of the formal treatment of service costs in financial accounting records and statements, the managers of a well-run service organization need information regarding job cost and contribution. The previous Business Insight considers the importance of accurate cost estimation by service firms that focus on providing unique and customized service to each client.

All preceding examples of service costing involve situations in which the order is filled in response to a specific customer request. Job order costing can also be used to determine the cost of making services available even when the names of specific customers are not known in advance and the service is being provided on a speculative basis. A regularly scheduled airline flight, for example, could be regarded as a job. Management is interested in knowing the cost of the job in order to determine its profitability. This is but another example of the versatility of job order costing.

Managerial Decision ■ You Are the Chief Financial Officer

You have asked the accounting staff to provide you with cost information on each of the products manufactured by your company so you can conduct profitability analysis on each product. Accounting provided you with the costs that are used in the company's external financial statements. What additional information are you going to need before you can conduct a complete profitability analysis? [Answer p. 18-31]

Review 18-4 LO4

Stratasys, Ltd. is a manufacturer of 3D production systems. Assume that the company has a division that does custom prototypes for large clients. Production costs are accounted for using a job cost system. Suppose that at the beginning of June raw materials inventories totaled $7,000; manufacturing supplies amounted to $800; two jobs were in process—Job 225 with assigned costs of $13,750, and Job 226 with assigned costs of $1,800—and there were no finished goods inventories. There was no underapplied or overapplied manufacturing overhead on June 1. The following information summarized June manufacturing activities:

- Purchased raw materials costing $40,000 on account.
- Purchased manufacturing supplies costing $9,000 on account.

continued

continued from previous page

- Requisitioned materials needed to complete Job 226. Started two new jobs, 227 and 228, and requisitioned direct materials for them as follows:

Job 226.	$ 2,600
Job 227.	18,000
Job 228.	14,400
Total	$35,000

- Incurred June salaries and wages as follows:

Job 225 (500 hours × $10 per hour).	$ 5,000
Job 226 (1,500 hours × $10 per hour)	15,000
Job 227 (2,050 hours × $10 per hour)	20,500
Job 228 (800 hours × $10 per hour).	8,000
Total direct labor.	48,500
Indirect labor.	5,000
Total	$53,500

- Used manufacturing supplies costing $5,500.
- Recognized depreciation on factory fixed assets of $5,000.
- Incurred miscellaneous manufacturing overhead cost of $10,750 on account.
- Applied manufacturing overhead at the rate of $5 per direct labor hour.
- Completed Jobs 225, 226, and 227.
- Delivered Jobs 225 and 226 to customers.

Required

a. Prepare "T" accounts showing the flow of costs through the Work-in-Process, Finished Goods, and Cost of Goods Sold accounts.

b. Show the job cost details to support the June 30 balances in Work-in-Process, Finished Goods and Cost of Goods Sold.

c. Prepare a statement of cost of goods manufactured for June.

Solution on p. 18-47.

Process Costing

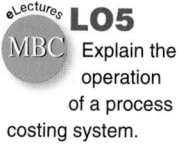

eLectures
MBC   **LO5**
Explain the operation of a process costing system.

A job costing system works well when products are made one at a time (building houses) or in batches of identical items (making blue jeans). However, if products are produced in a continuous manufacturing environment, where production does not have a distinct beginning and ending (refining fossil fuels such as gasoline or diesel, for example), companies usually use a process costing system.

In job costing, the unit cost is the total cost of the "job" divided by the units produced in the job. Costs are accumulated for each job on a job cost sheet, and those costs remain in Work-in-Process until the job is completed, regardless of how long the job is in progress. A multiple-unit job is not considered completed until all units in the job are finished. The cost is not determined until the job is completed, which will not necessarily coincide with the end of an accounting period. Large jobs (such as construction projects) and jobs started near the end of the period frequently overlap two or more accounting periods.

In process costing, the cost of a single unit is equal to the total product costs assigned to a "process" or "department" during the accounting period (frequently a month) divided by the number of units produced. Since goods in the beginning and ending work-in-process inventory are only partially processed during the period, it is necessary to determine the total production for the period in terms of the equivalent number of completed units. For example, if 300 units were started but were only 40% completed during the period, then the equivalent of 120 fully completed units (300 units × 0.40) was produced. The average cost per unit is computed as total product costs divided by the number of equivalent units produced.

A good example of a process costing environment involving continuous production is the soft drink bottling process. At Coca-Cola's bottling facility in Wakefield, England, more than 4,000 twelve-ounce cans and 3,200 varying sized bottles of Coca-Cola can be produced each minute in a continuous process. The process adds the ingredients (concentrate syrup, water, sweetener, and the carbonation agent) at various points in the process.

In a job cost system, job cost sheets are used to collect cost information for each and every job. In a process costing system, cost accumulation requires fewer records because each department's production is treated as the only job worked on during the period. In a department that has just one manufacturing process, process costing is particularly straightforward because the Work-in-Process account is, in effect, the departmental cost record. If a department has more than one manufacturing process, separate records should be maintained for each process.

Business Insight ■ 3D Printing Builds Customization into the Production Process

Breakthroughs in technology are making customization available to the masses with customization built in as part of the production process. In the past, bespoke (custom-made) suit makers and automakers often had a lot in common. There was a time when automakers like Bugatti, Duesenberg, and Roller would build custom automobiles as personalized as any suit from Savile Row, a renowned street in London with custom-tailored suit offerings. The customer paid a lot of money and the producer made the product substantially to order. Skilled craftsmen were tasked with producing the customizations one job at a time. Cost management in the presence of dramatic customization was only possible through job costing.

3D printing and other new technology has made customization less costly, and brings changes to cost management. The custom knit wear manufacturer Unmade uses proprietary software and programmable machines to produce unique sweaters and scarves for clients. While each garment is unique, the variation in cost due to customization is largely captured by conventional drivers like direct materials (yarn), direct labor (programming), and machine hours. In addition, this business model saves costs by allowing Unmade to hold very little inventory while still delivering to the customer within 10 days. Similar changes have come to auto manufacturing. Daihatsu Copen, a Toyota subsidiary, uses 3D printing to allow customers to customize portions of their cars. Local Motors, an Arizona automaker, is more aggressive in its use of 3D printing. Olli, its self-driving shuttle, is 80% 3D printed and holds eight seated passengers.

Sources: Michael Pooler, "Makers Follow the Techies to Create a 'Nurture' Space of Their Own," *Financial Times*, December 17, 2015; and "Print My Ride," *Economist*, June 23, 2016.

Cost of Production Report

To illustrate process costing procedures, consider Intel, which manufactures memory chips for microcomputers using sophisticated machinery. Assume each finished unit requires one unit of raw materials added at the beginning of the manufacturing process. Hypothetical production and cost data for the month of July for Intel are as follows:

July Production Data	
Units in process, beginning of period (75% converted)	4,000
Units started	36,000
Completed and transferred to finished goods	35,000
Units in process, end of period (20% converted)	5,000

July Cost Data	
Beginning work-in-process	
Materials costs	$ 16,000
Conversion costs	9,000
Total	$ 25,000

continued

continued from previous page

July Cost Data		
Current manufacturing costs		
Direct materials (36,000 × $4)		$144,000
Conversion costs		
Direct labor	$62,200	
Manufacturing overhead applied	46,700	108,900
Total		$252,900

Developing a cost of production report is a useful way of organizing and accounting for costs in a process costing environment. A **cost of production report**, which summarizes unit and cost data for each department or process for each period, consists of the following sections:

▪ Summary of units in process

▪ Equivalent units

▪ Total cost to be accounted for and cost per equivalent unit

▪ Accounting for total costs

The cost of production report for Intel is shown in Exhibit 18.7, and its four sections are discussed next.

Exhibit 18.7 ■ Cost of Production Report for Process Costing

INTEL
Cost of Production Report
For the Month Ending July 31

Summary of units in process

Beginning	4,000
Units started	36,000
In process	40,000
Completed	(35,000)
Ending	5,000

Equivalent units in process	Materials	Conversion
Units completed	35,000	35,000
Plus equivalent units in ending inventory	5,000	1,000*
Equivalent units in process	40,000	36,000

Total cost to be accounted for and cost per equivalent unit in process	Materials	Conversion	Total
Beginning work-in-process	$ 16,000	$ 9,000	$ 25,000
Current cost	144,000	108,900**	252,900
Total cost in process	$160,000	$117,900	$277,900
Equivalent units in process	÷ 40,000	÷ 36,000	
Cost per equivalent unit in process	$ 4.00	$ 3.275	$ 7.275
Accounting for total costs			
Transferred out (35,000 × $7.275)			$254,625
Ending work-in-process			
Materials (5,000 × $4.00)		$20,000	
Conversion (1,000 × $3.275)		3,275	23,275
Total cost accounted for			$277,900

* 5,000 units, 20% converted

** Includes direct labor of $62,200 and applied manufacturing overhead of $46,700

Summary of Units in Process

This section of the cost of production report provides a summary of all units in the department during the period—both from an input and an output perspective—regardless of their stage of completion. From an input perspective, total units in process during the period consisted of the following:

- Units in process at the beginning of the period, **plus**
- Units started during the period.

From an output perspective, these units in process during the period were either

- Completed and transferred out of the department, **or**
- Still on hand at the end of the period.

In the summary of units in process, all units are treated the same, regardless of the amount of processing that took place on them during the period. The objective here is to account for all discrete units of product in process at any time during the period. In the summary of units in process in Exhibit 18.7, suppose 40,000 individual units were in process, including 4,000 partially completed units in the beginning inventory and 36,000 new units started during the month. During the period, 35,000 units were completed, and the remaining 5,000 were still in process at the end of the month.

Equivalent Units in Process

This section of the report translates the number of units in process during the period into equivalent completed units of production. The term **equivalent completed units** refers to the number of completed units that is equal, in terms of production effort, to a given number of partially completed units. For example, 80 units for which 50% of the expected total processing cost has been incurred is the equivalent of 40 completed units (80×0.50).

Frequently, direct materials costs are incurred largely, if not entirely, at the beginning of the process, whereas direct labor and manufacturing overhead costs are added throughout the production process. If direct labor and manufacturing overhead costs are added to the process simultaneously, it is common to treat them jointly as conversion costs. Assume Intel adds all materials at the beginning of the process; all conversion costs are added evenly throughout the process. Therefore, separate computations are made for equivalent units of materials and equivalent units of conversion. Although the department worked on 40,000 units during the period, the total number of equivalent units in process with respect to conversion costs was only 36,000 units, consisting of 35,000 finished units plus 1,000 equivalent units in ending inventory (5,000 units 20% converted). Because all materials are added at the start of the process, 40,000 equivalent units (35,000 finished and 5,000 in process) were in process during the period with respect to materials costs.

Total Cost to Be Accounted for and Cost per Equivalent Unit in Process

This section of the report summarizes total costs in Work-in-Process during the period and calculates the cost per equivalent unit for materials, conversion, and in total. Total cost consists of the beginning Work-in-Process balance (if any) plus current costs incurred. For our Intel example, the total cost to be accounted for during July was $277,900, consisting of $25,000 in Work-in-Process at the beginning of the period plus current costs of $252,900 incurred in July. Exhibit 18.7 shows these amounts broken down between materials costs and conversion costs.

To compute cost per equivalent unit, total cost in process is divided by the equivalent units in process. This is done separately for materials cost and conversion cost. The total cost per equivalent unit is the sum of the unit costs for materials and conversion. Because the number of equivalent units in process was different for materials and conversion, it is not possible to get the total cost per unit by dividing total costs of $277,900 by some equivalent unit amount.

Accounting for Total Costs

This section shows the disposition of the total costs in process during the period divided between units completed (and sent to finished goods) and units still in process at the end of the period. As noted in the previous section, total cost in process is $277,900 and each equivalent unit in process has $4.00 of materials cost and $3.275 of conversion costs for a total of $7.275.

The first step in assigning total costs is to calculate the cost of units transferred out by multiplying the units completed during the period by the total cost per unit (35,000 units × $7.275). This assigns $254,625 of the total cost to units transferred out, leaving $23,275 ($277,900 − $254,625) to be assigned to ending Work-in-Process. To verify that $23,275 is the correct amount of cost remaining in ending Work-in-Process, the materials and conversion costs in ending Work-in-Process are calculated separately. Recall that the 5,000 units in process at the end of the period are 100% completed with materials costs, but only 20% completed with conversion costs. Therefore, in ending Work-in-Process, the materials cost component is $20,000 (5,000 × 1.00 × $4.00), the conversion cost component is $3,275 (5,000 × 0.20 × $3.275), and the total cost of ending Work-in-Process is $23,275 ($20,000 + $3,275).

The cost of production report summarizes manufacturing costs assigned to Work-in-Process during the period and provides information for determining the transfer of costs from Work-in-Process to Finished Goods Inventory. The supporting documents are similar to those previously illustrated for job costing, except that the single cost of production report replaces all the job cost sheets that flow through a department or process. The flow of costs through Work-in-Process is as follows:

Work-in-Process		
Beginning balance		$ 25,000
Current manufacturing costs		
Direct materials	$144,000	
Direct labor	62,200	
Applied overhead	46,700	252,900
Total		277,900
Cost of goods manufactured		(254,625)
Ending balance		$ 23,275

The reduction in Work-in-Process for the units completed during the period is determined in the cost of production report (see Exhibit 18.7). This amount is transferred to Finished Goods Inventory. The $23,275 ending balance in Work-in-Process is also determined in the cost of production report as the amount assigned to units in ending Work-in-Process.

Weighted Average and First-In, First-Out Process Costing

Because the costs of materials, labor, and overhead are constantly changing, unit costs are seldom exactly the same from period to period. Hence, if a unit is manufactured partially in one period and partially in the following period, its actual cost is seldom equal to the unit cost of units produced in either period.

In the cost of production report in Exhibit 18.7, we made no attempt to account separately for the completed units that came from beginning inventory and those that were started during the current period. The method illustrated in Exhibit 18.7 is called the **weighted average method**, and it simply spreads the combined beginning inventory cost and current manufacturing costs (for materials, labor, and overhead) over the units completed and those in ending inventory on an average basis. For example, the total cost in process for conversion ($117,900) included both beginning inventory cost and current costs; the 36,000 equivalent units in process for conversion included both units from beginning inventory and units started during the current period. Hence, the average cost per unit of $3.275 (or $117,900 ÷ 36,000) is a weighted average cost of the partially completed units in beginning inventory (prior period costs) and units started during the current period. It is not a precise cost per unit for the current period's production activity but an average cost that includes the cost of partially completed units in beginning inventory carried over from the previous period.

An alternative, more precise process costing method is the **first-in, first-out (FIFO) method**. It accounts for unit costs of beginning inventory units separately from those started during the current period. Under this method, the first costs incurred each period are assumed to have been used to complete the unfinished units carried over from the previous period. Hence, the cost of the beginning inventory is partially based on the prior period's unit costs and partially based on the current period's unit costs.

If unit costs are changing from period to period and beginning inventories are large in relation to total production for the period, the FIFO method is more accurate. However, with the current trend toward smaller inventories, the additional effort and cost of the FIFO method may not be justified. Detailed coverage of the FIFO method is included in cost accounting textbooks. Unless stated otherwise, weighted average process costing is used in module assignments.

Process Costing in Service Organizations

There are many applications of process costing for service organizations. Process costing in service organizations is similar to that in manufacturing organizations, the primary purpose being to assign costs to cost objects. Generally, the use of process costing techniques for service organizations is easier than for manufacturing organizations because the raw materials element is not necessary. The applications for the labor and overhead costs are similar, if not identical, to those of a manufacturing firm.

Process costing for services is similar to job costing for batches in that an average cost for similar or identical services is determined. There are important differences, though, between batch and process costing. In a batch environment, a discrete group of services is identified, but in a process environment, services are performed on a continuous basis. Batch costing accumulates the cost for a specific group of services as the batch moves through the various activities that make up the service. Process service costing measures the average cost of identical or similar services performed each period (each month) in a department. An example of batch service costing is determining the cost of registering a student at your college during the fall term registration period; an example of process service costing is determining the cost each month of processing a check by a bank. If continuously performed services involved multiple processes, the total cost of the service would be the sum of the costs for each process.

After it is determined that process costing would be appropriate for a service activity, the actual decision to use it is generally contingent on two important factors about the items being evaluated. First, is average cost per unit acceptable as an input item to the decision process? For some activities, the answer is obvious. For instance, tracking the actual cost of processing each check through a bank would probably not be as useful as determining the average cost of processing checks for a given period; therefore, average cost is acceptable. For other activities, the answer is more difficult to determine. Should the decision model include average cost per patient-day or actual cost per individual patient?

The second issue relates to the benefits versus the costs of the resulting information. Normally, it is easier to track and record the cost of an activity or process than it is to track and record the cost of each individual item in the activity. Often actual cost tracking is impossible for practical reasons (the actual cost of processing a check through a banking system, for example). Although process costing will not work in every situation, it has many applications in service organizations. As illustrated in this text, there are many possibilities for applying either job or process costing to activities in service organizations.

Review 18-5 LO5

SanDisk manufactures USB flash drives that are used in computing. Since there is little product differentiation between SanDisk's products, assume it uses a process costing system to determine inventory costs and that production and manufacturing cost data for one year are as follows:

Production Data (units)	
Units in process, beginning of period (60% converted)	3,000,000
Units started	27,000,000
Completed and transferred to finished goods	25,000,000
Units in process, end of period (30% converted)	5,000,000

continued

continued from previous page

Manufacturing Costs	
Work-in-Process, beginning of period (materials, $468,000; conversion, $252,000)	$ 720,000
Current manufacturing costs	
Raw materials transferred to processing	6,132,000
Direct labor for the period	1,550,000
Overhead applied for the period	3,498,000

Required

Prepare a cost of production report for SanDisk for the year.   Solution on p. 18-49.

Appendix 18A: Absorption and Variable Costing

Product costing for inventory valuation is the link between financial and managerial accounting. Product costing systems determine the cost-based valuation of the manufactured inventories used in making key financial accounting measurements (cost of goods sold and income on the income statement as well as inventory and total assets on the balance sheet). They also provide vital information to managers for setting prices, controlling costs, and evaluating management performance. The influence of financial accounting on product costing systems is apparent in the design of traditional job order and process costing systems. These systems reflect the requirement of financial accounting (i.e., generally accepted accounting principles) that all manufacturing costs be included in inventory valuations for external financial reporting purposes. In these systems, all other costs incurred, such as selling, general, and administrative costs, are treated as expenses of the period.

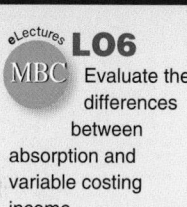

LO6 Evaluate the differences between absorption and variable costing income.

Basic Concepts

A debate exists over how to treat fixed manufacturing overhead costs in the valuation of inventory. The debate centers around whether fixed costs such as depreciation on manufacturing equipment should be considered an *inventoriable product cost* and treated as an asset cost until the inventory is sold, or as a *period cost* and recorded immediately as an operating expense. **Absorption costing** (also called **full costing**) treats fixed manufacturing overhead as a product cost, whereas **variable costing** (also called **direct costing**) treats it as a period cost. Therefore, fixed manufacturing overhead is recorded initially as an asset (inventory) under absorption costing but as an operating expense under variable costing.

> **Fixed manufacturing costs:**
>
> **Absorption costing** treats **fixed manufacturing costs** as **product costs**.
>
> **Variable costing** treats **fixed manufacturing costs** as **period costs**.

Since fixed product costs are eventually recorded as expenses under both variable and absorption costing by the time the inventory is sold, why does it matter whether fixed overhead is treated as a product cost or a period cost? It matters because the way it is treated affects the measurement of income for a particular period and the valuation assigned to inventory on the balance sheet at the end of the period. Because absorption costing presents fixed manufacturing overhead as a cost per unit rather than a total cost per period, management's perceptions of cost behavior, and decisions based on perceptions of cost behavior, may also be affected.

Inventory Valuations

To illustrate the difference in inventory valuations between absorption and variable costing, assume the following cost data for a single component of a **Trek** bicycle at a monthly volume of 4,000 units:

Direct materials.	$ 5	per unit
Direct labor	2	per unit
Variable manufacturing overhead.	3	per unit
Total variable cost.	$ 10	per unit
Fixed manufacturing overhead.	$8,000	per month

To determine the unit cost of inventory using absorption costing, an average fixed overhead cost per unit is calculated by dividing the monthly fixed manufacturing overhead by the monthly volume. Even though fixed manufacturing overhead is not a variable cost, under absorption costing it is applied to inventory on a per-unit basis, the same as variable costs. At a monthly volume of 4,000 units, Trek's total component inventory cost per unit is $10 under variable costing and $12 under absorption costing.

The $2 difference in total unit cost is attributed to the treatment of fixed overhead of $8,000 divided by 4,000 units. The difference in the total component inventory valuation on the balance sheet between absorption and variable costing is the number of units in ending inventory times $2. So if 1,000 units are on hand at the end of the month, they are valued at $12,000 if absorption costing is used but at only $10,000 with variable costing.

Income Under Absorption and Variable Costing

The income statement formats used for variable and absorption costing are not the same. One benefit of variable costing is that it separates costs into variable and fixed costs, making it possible to present the income statement in a contribution format. As illustrated in Module 16, in a contribution income statement, variable costs are subtracted from revenues to compute contribution margin; fixed costs are then subtracted from contribution margin to calculate profit, also called net income or earnings.

When absorption costing is used, the income statement is usually formatted using the functional format, which classifies costs based on cost function, such as manufacturing, selling, or administrative. The functional income statement, used for financial reporting, subtracts manufacturing costs (represented by cost of goods sold) from revenues to calculate gross profit; selling and administrative costs are then subtracted from gross profit to calculate profit or income.

The contribution format provides information for determining the contribution margin ratio, which is calculated as total contribution margin divided by total sales. It also provides the total amount of fixed costs. These are the primary items of data needed to determine the break-even point and to conduct other cost-volume-profit analysis (see Module 16).

Not only is the income statement format different for absorption and variable costing methods, but also as illustrated in the following hypothetical examples for Trek, the amount of income reported on the income statement might not be the same because of the difference in the treatment of fixed manufacturing overhead. The following additional information is assumed for the Trek component examples:

Selling price	$30	per unit
Variable selling and administrative expenses.	$3	per unit
Fixed selling and administrative expenses.	$10,000	per month

Production Equals Sales

Assume Trek has no component inventory on June 1. Production and sales for the third quarter of the fiscal year ending November 30 are:

Month	Production	Sales
June	3,200 units	3,200 units
July.	4,000 units	3,500 units
August	4,000 units	4,500 units
Third quarter.	11,200 units	11,200 units

Production and sales both total 11,200 units for the third quarter. A summary of unit production, sales, and inventory levels is presented in Exhibit 18A.1. Using previously presented costs and a selling price of $30 per unit, monthly contribution (variable costing) and functional (absorption costing) income statements are presented in Exhibit 18A.1 parts B and C. An analysis of fixed manufacturing overhead with absorption costing is presented in part D.

In June, with 3,200 units produced and sold all $8,000 of fixed manufacturing overhead is deducted as a period cost under variable costing and expensed as part of the cost of goods sold under absorption costing. Since no inventory remained, no costs were deferred.

Production Exceeds Sales

July production of 4,000 units exceeded sales of 3,500 units by 500 units. The ending inventory under variable costing consisted of only the variable cost of production, $5,000 (500 × $10). The entire $8,000 of fixed manufacturing overhead is deducted as a period cost.

Under absorption costing, in addition to the variable cost of production, a portion of the fixed manufacturing overhead is assigned to the ending inventory. As shown in the July column of Exhibit 18A.1, part D, absorption costing assigns $1,000 of the month's fixed manufacturing overhead to the July ending inventory and $7,000 to the cost of goods sold. Consequently, under absorption costing the July ending inventory is $1,000 higher, the July expenses are $1,000 lower, and the July net income is $1,000 higher than under variable costing.

Exhibit 18A.1 ■ Contribution (Variable Costing) and Functional (Absorption Costing) Income Statements with Variations in Production and Sales

	June (Production equals sales)	July (Production exceeds sales)	August (Sales exceed production)
A. Trek's Component: Summary of Unit Inventory Changes			
Beginning inventory	0	0	500
Production	3,200	4,000	4,000
Total available.	3,200	4,000	4,500
Sales.	(3,200)	(3,500)	(4,500)
Ending inventory.	0	500	0
B. Contribution (Variable Costing) Income Statements			
Sales ($30/unit)	$96,000	$105,000	$135,000
Less variable expenses			
Cost of goods sold ($10/unit)	32,000	35,000	45,000
Selling & admin. ($3/unit)	9,600	10,500	13,500
Total	(41,600)	(45,500)	(58,500)
Contribution margin	54,400	59,500	76,500
Less fixed expenses			
Manufacturing overhead	8,000	8,000	8,000
Selling & admin.	10,000	10,000	10,000
Total	(18,000)	(18,000)	(18,000)
Net income	$36,400	$ 41,500	$ 58,500
C. Functional (Absorption Costing) Income Statements			
Sales ($30/unit)	$96,000	$105,000	$135,000
Cost of goods sold (Part D.)	(40,000)	(42,000)	(54,000)
Gross profit.	56,000	63,000	81,000
Selling & admin. expenses			
Variable ($3/unit).	9,600	10,500	13,500
Fixed	10,000	10,000	10,000
Total	(19,600)	(20,500)	(23,500)
Net income	$36,400	$ 42,500	$ 57,500

continued

continued from previous page

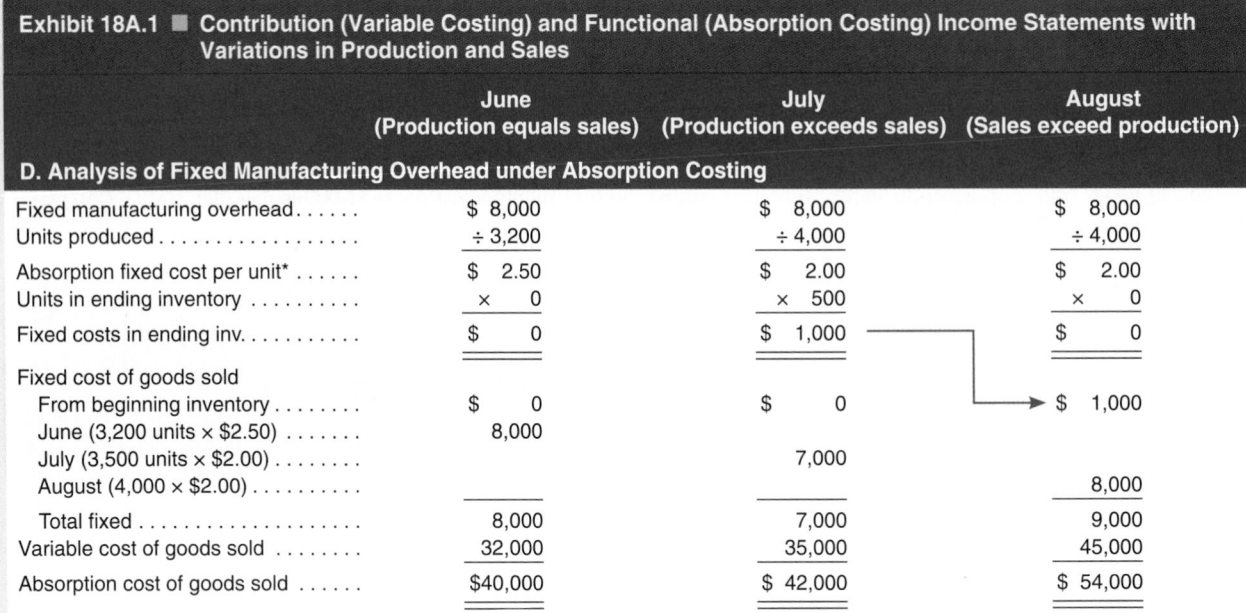

Exhibit 18A.1 ■ Contribution (Variable Costing) and Functional (Absorption Costing) Income Statements with Variations in Production and Sales

	June (Production equals sales)	July (Production exceeds sales)	August (Sales exceed production)
D. Analysis of Fixed Manufacturing Overhead under Absorption Costing			
Fixed manufacturing overhead......	$ 8,000	$ 8,000	$ 8,000
Units produced.................	÷ 3,200	÷ 4,000	÷ 4,000
Absorption fixed cost per unit*......	$ 2.50	$ 2.00	$ 2.00
Units in ending inventory..........	× 0	× 500	× 0
Fixed costs in ending inv...........	$ 0	$ 1,000	$ 0
Fixed cost of goods sold			
From beginning inventory........	$ 0	$ 0	$ 1,000
June (3,200 units × $2.50).......	8,000		
July (3,500 units × $2.00)........		7,000	
August (4,000 × $2.00).........			8,000
Total fixed..................	8,000	7,000	9,000
Variable cost of goods sold........	32,000	35,000	45,000
Absorption cost of goods sold	$40,000	$ 42,000	$ 54,000

* To simplify the illustration, the example does not use a predetermined overhead rate. If a predetermined overhead rate were used, an increase or decrease in the balance of Manufacturing Overhead is treated as an adjustment to ending inventory.

Sales Exceed Production

In August just the opposite of July's situation occurred: sales of 4,500 units exceeded production of 4,000 units by 500 units. The additional units came from the July production. There was no inventory remaining on August 31. Under variable costing all current manufacturing costs (August costs) are expensed either as the variable cost of goods sold or as part of the fixed expense. Additionally, the August variable cost of goods sold includes variable costs assigned the July ending inventory.

Under absorption costing all current month manufacturing costs are expensed as part of the cost of goods sold. Additionally, the cost of goods sold includes the variable and fixed costs assigned the July ending inventory. The inclusion of the July fixed costs caused absorption costing net income to be $1,000 lower than the corresponding variable costing amount.

The above relationships between absorption and variable costing are summarized in Exhibit 18A.2.

Exhibits 18A.1 and 18A.2 reveal several important relationships between absorption costing net income and variable costing net income, as well as the way net income responds to changes in sales and production under both methods.

Exhibit 18A.2 ■ Comparative Effects of Absorption and Variable Costing

Relationship between period production and sales	Effect on inventory costs	Effect on operating income	Explanation
Production = Sales	No change in inventory costs.	Absorption costing income = Variable costing income	All current fixed manufacturing costs are expensed under both absorption and variable costing.
Production > Sales	Absorption costing ending inventory increases more than variable costing inventory.	Absorption costing income > Variable costing income	Under absorption costing some current fixed manufacturing costs are assigned to ending inventory. Under variable costing all current fixed manufacturing costs are expensed.

continued

continued from previous page

Exhibit 18A.2 ■ Comparative Effects of Absorption and Variable Costing

Relationship between period production and sales	Effect on inventory costs	Effect on operating income	Explanation
Sales > Production	Absorption costing ending inventory declines more than variable costing inventory.	Absorption costing income < Variable costing income	Under absorption costing fixed manufacturing costs previously assigned to ending inventory are expensed along with current fixed manufacturing costs. Under variable costing only current fixed manufacturing costs are expensed.

For each period, the income differences between absorption and variable costing can be explained by analyzing the change in inventoried fixed manufacturing overhead under absorption costing net income. If fixed manufacturing cost per unit remains constant, the following relationship exists:

$$\begin{array}{ccccc} \textbf{Variable} & & \textbf{Increase (or minus decrease)} & & \textbf{Absorption} \\ \textbf{costing} & + & \textbf{in inventoried fixed} & = & \textbf{costing} \\ \textbf{net income} & & \textbf{manufacturing overhead} & & \textbf{net income} \end{array}$$

Using Trek's July information, the equation is as follows:

$$\$41,500 + (500 \times \$2.00) = \$42,500$$

For any given time period, regardless of length, if total units produced equals total units sold, net income is the same for absorption costing and variable costing, all other things being equal. Under absorption costing, all fixed manufacturing overhead is released as a product cost through cost of goods sold when inventory is sold. Under variable costing, all fixed manufacturing overhead is reported as a period cost and expensed in the period incurred. Consequently, over the life of a product, the income differences within periods are offset since they occur only because of the timing of the release of fixed manufacturing overhead to the income statement.

Evaluating Alternatives to Inventory Valuation

The issue in the variable costing debate is whether or not fixed manufacturing costs add value to products. Proponents of variable costing argue that these costs do not add value to a product. They believe that fixed costs are incurred to provide the capacity to produce during a given period, and these costs expire with the passage of time regardless of whether the related capacity was used. Variable manufacturing costs, on the other hand, are incurred only if production takes place. Consequently, these costs are properly assignable to the units produced.

Proponents of variable costing also argue that inventories have value only to the extent that they avoid the necessity of incurring costs in the future. Having inventory available for sale avoids the necessity of incurring some future variable costs, but the availability of finished goods inventory does not avoid the incurrence of future fixed manufacturing costs. Proponents conclude that inventories should be valued at their variable manufacturing cost, and fixed manufacturing costs should be expensed as incurred.

Opponents of variable costing argue that fixed manufacturing costs are incurred for only one purpose, namely, to manufacture the product. Because they are incurred to manufacture the product, they should be assigned to the product. It is also argued that in the long run all costs are variable. Consequently, by omitting fixed costs, variable costing understates long-run variable costs and misleads decision makers into underestimating true production costs.

On a pragmatic level, the central arguments for variable costing center around the fact that use of variable costing facilitates the development of contribution income statements and cost-volume-profit analysis. With costs accumulated on an absorption costing basis, contribution income statements are difficult to develop, and cost-volume-profit analysis becomes very complicated unless production and sales are equal.

The Research Insight below discusses recent inventory levels and how these might impact variable and absorption costing.

Research Insight ■ Inventory levels and Inventory Costing

Inventory levels are currently higher than they were prior to 2014. As of September 2019, the Total Business Inventories to Sales Ratio is 1.40, up 2.94 from the prior year. Inventories can build for a number of reasons including an economic slowdown (resulting in a reduction of sales); or, a positive economic outlook (resulting in aggressive inventory production). Increasing inventory levels create greater financial differences between absorption and variable costing methods. Using absorption costing, the building inventories will result in more fixed manufacturing costs sitting on the balance sheet. However, using variable costing will flow these fixed manufacturing costs through the income statement as an expense in the period of their production.

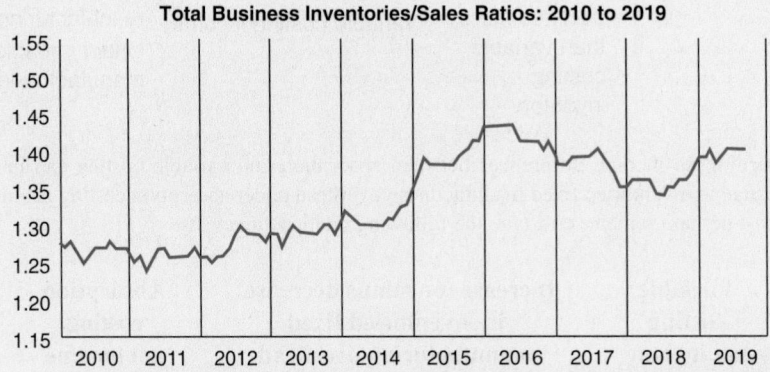

Total Business Inventories/Sales Ratios: 2010 to 2019

Source: U.S. Census Bureau, Manufacturing and Trade Inventories and Sales, October 16, 2019.
(Data adjusted for seasonal, holiday and trading day differences but not for price changes)

Review 18-6 LO6

Boxtel Inc. has a highly automated assembly line that uses very little direct labor. Therefore, direct labor is part of variable overhead. For October, assume that it incurred the following unit costs:

Direct materials.	$250
Variable overhead	220
Fixed overhead.	80

The 100 units of beginning inventory for October had an absorption costing value of $45,000 and a variable costing value of $38,000. For October, assume that Boxtel Inc. produced 500 units and sold 540 units.

Required

a. Compute Boxtel's October amount of ending inventory under both absorption and variable costing if the FIFO inventory method was used.

Solution on p. 18-49.   b. Compute Boxtel's October Cost of Goods Sold using both the variable and absorption costing methods.

Guidance Answers

You Are the Chief Financial Officer

Pg. 18-19 Inventory costs that are provided for financial statement purposes for external stockholders and lenders are required by generally accepted accounting principles to include only the manufacturing costs of the product for direct materials, direct labor, and manufacturing overhead. To conduct a complete profitability analysis, the CFO will need to gather data for all other costs that relate to the marketing, sales, and distribution of each product, as well as any costs related to providing service to customers who buy the products.

Questions

Q18-1. Distinguish among service, merchandising, and manufacturing organizations on the basis of the importance and complexity of inventory cost measurement.

Q18-2. Distinguish between product costing and service costing.

Q18-3. When is depreciation a product cost? When is depreciation a period cost?

Q18-4. What are the three major product cost elements?

Q18-5. How are predetermined overhead rates developed? Why are they widely used?

Q18-6. Briefly distinguish between process manufacturing and job order production. Provide examples of products typically produced under each system.

Q18-7. Briefly describe the role of engineering personnel and production scheduling personnel in the production planning process.

Q18-8. Identify the primary records involved in the operation of a job cost system.

Q18-9. Describe the flow of costs through the accounting system of a labor-intensive manufacturing organization.

Q18-10. Identify two reasons that a service organization should maintain detailed job cost information.

Q18-11. What are the four major elements of a cost of production report?

Q18-12. What are equivalent completed units?

Q18-13. Under what conditions will equivalent units in process be different for materials and conversion costs?

Assignments with the ⊚ logo in the margin are available in 𝓂𝓎 BusinessCourse.
See the Preface of the book for details.

Mini Exercises

M18-14. Classification of Product and Period Costs   **LO2**

Classify the following costs incurred by a manufacturer of golf clubs as product costs or period costs. Also classify the product costs as direct materials or conversion costs.

    a. Depreciation on computer in president's office
    b. Salaries of legal staff
    c. Graphite shafts
    d. Plant security department
    e. Electricity for the corporate office
    f. Rubber grips
    g. Golf club heads
    h. Wages paid assembly line maintenance workers
    i. Salary of corporate controller
    j. Subsidy of plant cafeteria
    k. Wages paid assembly line production workers
    l. National sales meeting in Orlando
    m. Overtime premium paid assembly line workers
    n. Advertising on national television
    o. Depreciation on assembly line

M18-15. Developing and Using a Predetermined Overhead Rate   **LO2**

Assume that the following predictions were made last year for one of the plants of **Milliken & Company**:

     Milliken & Company

Total manufacturing overhead for the year...	$15,000,000
Total machine hours for the year	1,200,000

Actual results for February were as follows:

Manufacturing overhead.	$1,238,500
Machine hours	98,500

Required

a. Determine the predetermined overhead rate per machine hour.
b. Using the predetermined overhead rate per machine hour, determine the manufacturing overhead applied to Work-in-Process during February.
c. As of February 1, actual overhead was overapplied by $35,000. Determine the cumulative amount of any overapplied or underapplied overhead at the end of February.

LO4, 5 **M18-16. Job Order Costing and Process Costing Applications**

For each of the following manufacturing situations, indicate whether job order or process costing is more appropriate and why.

a. Manufacturer of chocolate candy bars
b. Manufacturer of carbonated beverages
c. Manufacturer of high-quality men's suits
d. Manufacturer of subway cars
e. Printer of a variety of history books

LO4, 5 **M18-17. Job Order Costing and Process Costing Applications**

For each of the following situations, indicate whether job order or process costing is more appropriate and why.

a. Building contractor for residential dwellings
b. Manufacturer of nylon yarn (single weight) that it sells to fabric-making textile companies
c. Evening gown manufacturer that makes gowns in several different fabrics, colors, styles, and sizes
d. Hosiery mill that manufactures a one-size-fits-all product
e. Vehicle battery manufacturer that has just received an order for 400,000 identical batteries

LO5 **M18-18. Process Costing**

Snooz

Snooz makes a single model of its white noise sound machine. Assume the product is produced on a continuous basis in one department. All materials are added at the beginning of production. The total cost per equivalent unit in process in March was $56, consisting of $32 for materials and $24 for conversion. During the month, 12,000 units of product were transferred to finished goods inventory; on March 31, 5,000 units were in process, 10% converted. The company uses weighted average costing.

Required

a. Determine the cost of goods transferred to finished goods inventory.
b. Determine the cost of the ending work-in-process inventory.
c. What was the total cost of the beginning work-in-process inventory plus the current manufacturing costs?

LO6 **M18-19. Absorption and Variable Costing; Inventory Valuation**

Bondware Inc. has a highly automated assembly line that uses very little direct labor. Therefore, direct labor is part of variable overhead. For March, assume that it incurred the following unit costs:

Direct materials.	$450
Variable overhead	250
Fixed overhead.	550

The 1,200 units of beginning inventory for March had an absorption costing value of $1,500,000 and a variable costing value of $840,000. For March, assume that Bondware Inc. produced 3,000 units and sold 3,500 units.

Required

Compute Bondware's March amount of ending inventory under both absorption and variable costing if the FIFO inventory method was used.

LO6 **M18-20. Absorption and Variable Costing; Cost of Goods Sold**

Use data from Mini Exercise 18-19.

Required

Compute Bondware's March Cost of Goods Sold using both the variable and absorption costing methods.

E18-21. **Analyzing Activity in Inventory Accounts**

LO2, 4
Steger Designs

Steger Designs makes winter boots and moccasins at its factory in northern Minnesota. Assume the following represents data related to Steger operations last year:

Raw materials used	$400,000
Total manufacturing costs charged to production during the year (includes raw materials, direct labor, and manufacturing overhead applied at a rate of 200% of direct labor costs).	850,000
Cost of goods available for sale	958,000
Selling and general expenses	280,000

	Inventories	
	Beginning	**Ending**
Raw materials.	$110,000	$105,000
Work-in-process	75,000	92,000
Finished goods.	125,000	135,000

Required
Determine each of the following:
a. Cost of raw materials purchased
b. Direct labor costs charged to production
c. Cost of goods manufactured
d. Cost of goods sold

E18-22. **Statement of Cost of Goods Manufactured and Income Statement**

LO4

Information from the records of the Bridgeview Manufacturing Company for August follows:

Sales.	$250,000
Selling and administrative expenses	98,600
Purchases of raw materials	32,000
Direct labor.	22,000
Manufacturing overhead.	38,600

	Inventories	
	August 1	**August 31**
Raw materials.	$ 6,000	$ 6,500
Work-in-process	4,600	5,800
Finished goods.	12,000	15,000

Required
Prepare a statement of cost of goods manufactured and an income statement for August.

E18-23. **Statement of Cost of Goods Manufactured from Percent Relationships**

LO4

Information about Blue Line Products Company for the year ending December 31 follows:
• Sales equal $580,000.
• Direct materials used total $105,000.
• Manufacturing overhead is 200% of direct labor dollars.
• The beginning inventory of finished goods is 25% of the cost of goods sold.
• The ending inventory of finished goods is 1.5 times beginning inventory.
• The gross profit is 20% of sales.
• There is no beginning or ending work-in-process.

Required
Prepare a statement of cost of goods manufactured for the year. (*Hint:* Prepare an analysis of changes in Finished Goods Inventory.)

LO2, 4   **E18-24. Account Activity and Relationships**

	Case A	Case B	Case C	Case D
Sales.	$42,000	$ (b)	$82,500	$ (b)
Direct materials.	7,500	31,500	(f)	42,000
Direct labor.	3,000	(c)	15,000	(c)
Total direct costs.	(a)	48,000	(e)	60,000
Conversion cost	(b)	39,000	(g)	(g)
Manufacturing overhead.	4,000	(d)	7,500	(f)
Current manufacturing costs	(c)	(e)	71,250	158,000
Work-in-process, beginning	3,500	15,000	(d)	42,000
Work-in-process, ending.	2,500	(f)	15,750	(e)
Cost of goods manufactured	(d)	48,000	(c)	164,000
Finished goods inventory, beginning	4,500	12,000	5,250	24,000
Finished goods inventory, ending.	3,000	(g)	6,000	(d)
Cost of goods sold	(e)	52,500	(b)	160,000
Gross profit.	(f)	(a)	13,500	30,000
Selling and administrative expenses	10,000	22,500	(a)	(a)
Net income	(g)	33,000	9,000	12,000

Required

Each case is independent. Solve for missing data in alphabetical order. (*Hint:* Refer to Exhibit 18.6, p. 18-16 and the WIP table, p. 18-24.)

LO2   **E18-25. Developing and Using a Predetermined Overhead Rate: High-Low Cost Estimation**

For years, Mattoon Components Company has used an actual plantwide overhead rate and based its prices on cost plus a markup of 30%. Recently the marketing manager, Holly Adams, and the production manager, Sue Walsh, confronted the controller with a common problem. The marketing manager expressed a concern that Mattoon's prices seem to vary widely throughout the year. According to Adams, "It seems irrational to charge higher prices when business is bad and lower prices when business is good. While we get a lot of business during high-volume months because we charge less than our competitors, it is a waste of time to even call on customers during low-volume months because we are raising prices while our competitors are lowering them." Walsh also believed that it was "folly to be so pushed that we have to pay overtime in some months and then lay employees off in others." She commented, "While there are natural variations in customer demand, the accounting system seems to amplify this variation."

Required

a. Evaluate the arguments presented by Adams and Walsh. What suggestions do you have for improving the accounting and pricing procedures?

b. Assume that the Mattoon Components Company had the following total manufacturing overhead costs and direct labor hours in the last two years.

	Year 1	Year 2
Total manufacturing overhead	$325,000	$380,500
Direct labor hours.	34,000	40,000

Use the high-low method (see Module 15) to develop a cost-estimating equation for total manufacturing overhead.

c. Develop a predetermined rate for next year, assuming 35,000 direct labor hours are budgeted for next year.

d. Assume that the actual level of activity next year was 36,000 direct labor hours and that manufacturing overhead was $341,550. Determine the underapplied or overapplied manufacturing overhead at the end of the year.

e. Describe two ways of handling any underapplied or overapplied manufacturing overhead at the end of the year.

LO4   **E18-26. Manufacturing Cost Flows with Machine Hours Allocation**

On April 1, Telecom Manufacturing Company's beginning balances in manufacturing accounts and finished goods inventory were as follows:

Raw materials.	$35,000
Manufacturing supplies.	3,500
Work-in-process	12,000
Manufacturing overhead.	0
Finished goods	50,000

During April, Telecom Manufacturing completed the following manufacturing transactions:

1. Purchased raw materials costing $60,000 and manufacturing supplies costing $2,000 on account.
2. Requisitioned raw materials costing $52,000 to the factory.
3. Incurred direct labor costs of $18,000 and indirect labor costs of $6,500.
4. Used manufacturing supplies costing $3,800.
5. Recorded manufacturing depreciation of $11,000.
6. Miscellaneous payables for manufacturing overhead totaled $8,500.
7. Applied manufacturing overhead, based on 2,500 machine hours, at a predetermined rate of $10 per machine hour.
8. Completed jobs costing $90,500.
9. Finished goods costing $95,750 were sold.

Required

a. Prepare "T" accounts showing the flow of costs through all manufacturing accounts, Finished Goods Inventory, and Cost of Goods Sold.

b. Calculate the balances at the end of April for Work-in-Process Inventory and Finished Goods Inventory.

E18-27.   **Service Cost Flows**

LO4

Cutwater
Homework
MBC

Cutwater, an advertising agency with offices in San Francisco and New York, develops marketing campaigns for companies in the United States and overseas. To achieve cost control, assume Cutwater uses a job cost system similar to that found in a manufacturing organization. It uses some different account titles:

Account	Replaces
Jobs-in-Process	Work-in-Process
Job Supplies Inventory	Manufacturing Supplies Inventory
Cost of Jobs Completed	Cost of Goods Sold
Accumulated Depreciation, Agency Assets	Accumulated Depreciation, Factory Assets
Production Overhead	Manufacturing Overhead

Cutwater does not maintain Raw Materials or Finished Goods Inventory accounts. Materials, such as props needed for video shoots, are purchased as needed from outside sources and charged directly to Jobs-in-Process and the appropriate job. The April 1 balances were as follows:

Job Supplies Inventory	$ 10,000	
Jobs-in-Process	200,000	
Production Overhead	2,850	underapplied

During April, Cutwater completed the following production transactions:

1. Purchased job supplies costing $4,500 on account.
2. Purchased materials for specific jobs costing $150,000 on account.
3. Incurred direct labor costs of $225,000 and indirect labor costs of $155,000.
4. Used production supplies costing $2,200.
5. Recorded equipment depreciation of $12,000.
6. Incurred miscellaneous payables for production overhead of $78,000.
7. Applied production overhead at a predetermined rate of $100 per production hour, based on 2,500 production hours.
8. Completed jobs costing $622,000.

Required

a. Prepare "T" accounts showing the flow of costs through all service accounts and Cost of Jobs Completed.

b. Calculate the cost incurred as of the end of April for the incomplete jobs still in process.

LO5

Port Townsend Paper

E18-28. Cost of Production Report: No Beginning Inventories

Port Townsend Paper (PTPC) produces paper by blending recycled corrugated cardboard with other fibers. Assume the following represent production and cost data for October. There was no inventory on hand on October 1.

Units of product started in process during October	20,000 tons
Units completed and transferred to finished goods	19,000 tons
Machine hours operated	3,410
Direct materials costs incurred	$134,000
Direct labor costs incurred	$185,000

Raw materials are added at the beginning of the process for each unit of product produced, and labor and manufacturing overhead are added evenly throughout the manufacturing process. Manufacturing overhead is applied to Work-in-Process at the rate of $50 per machine hour. Units in process at the end of the period were 75% converted.

Required

Prepare a cost of production report for PTPC for October.

LO5

E18-29. Cost of Production Report: No Beginning Inventories

Howell Paving Company manufactures asphalt paving materials for highway construction through a one-step process in which all materials are added at the beginning of the process. During April, the company accumulated the following data in its process costing system:

Production data	
Work-in-process, 4/1	0 tons
Raw materials transferred to processing	35,000 tons
Work-in-process, 4/30 (60% converted)	5,000 tons
Cost data	
Raw materials transferred to processing	$440,000
Conversion costs	
Direct labor cost incurred	$95,000
Manufacturing overhead applied	?

Manufacturing overhead is applied at the rate of $15 per equivalent unit (ton) processed.

Required

Prepare a cost of production report for April.

LO6

The J.M. Smucker Company (SJM)

E18-30. Absorption and Variable Costing Comparisons: Production Equals Sales

Assume that Smuckers manufactures and sells 45,000 cases of peanut butter each quarter. The following data are available for the third quarter of the year.

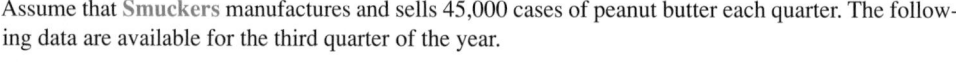

Total fixed manufacturing overhead	$ 675,000
Fixed selling and administrative expenses	1,225,000
Sales price per case	85
Direct materials per case	20
Direct labor per case	10
Variable manufacturing overhead per case	4

Required

a. Compute the cost per case under both absorption costing and variable costing.
b. Compute net income under both absorption costing and variable costing.
c. Reconcile any differences in income. Explain.

LO6

E18-31. Absorption and Variable Costing Income Statements: Production Exceeds Sales

Glenview Company sells its product at a unit price of $20. Unit manufacturing costs are direct materials, $5.00; direct labor, $2.00; and variable manufacturing overhead, $1.00. Total fixed manufacturing costs are $255,000 per year. Selling and administrative expenses are $1.00 per unit variable and $185,000 per year fixed. Though 60,000 units were produced during the year, only 54,000 units were sold. There was no beginning inventory.

Required

a. Prepare a functional income statement using absorption costing for the year.
b. Prepare a contribution income statement using variable costing for the year.

E18-32. **Absorption and Variable Costing Comparisons: Sales Exceed Production**   **LO6**

Wright Development purchases, develops, and sells commercial building sites. As the sites are sold, they are cleared at an average cost of $8,000 per site. Storm drains and driveways are also installed at an average cost of $10,000 per site. Selling costs are 6% of sales price. Administrative costs are $600,000 per year. Two years ago, the company bought 2,000 acres of land for $7,500,000 and divided it into 200 sites of equal size. During that year, 95 sites were sold at an average price of $150,000. Last year, the company purchased and developed another 2,000 acres, divided into 200 sites. The purchase price was again $7,500,000. Sales totaled 250 sites last year at an average price of $150,000.

Required

a. Prepare functional income statements using absorption costing for each of the two years.
b. Prepare contribution income statements using variable costing for each of the two years.

Problems

P18-33. **Cost of Goods Manufactured and Income Statement**   **LO4**

Following is information from the records of the Savoy Company for July.

Purchases	
Raw materials	$150,000
Manufacturing supplies	2,500
Office supplies	1,000
Sales	583,500
Administrative salaries	46,000
Direct labor	105,000
Production employees' fringe benefits*	10,500
Sales salaries and commissions	45,000
Production supervisors' salaries	10,000
Plant depreciation	12,000
Office depreciation	3,000
Plant maintenance	8,000
Plant utilities	7,500
Office utilities	2,500
Office maintenance	4,200
Production equipment rent	4,000
Office equipment rent	1,000

* Classified as manufacturing overhead

Inventories	July 1	July 31
Raw materials	$25,000	$28,000
Manufacturing supplies	4,000	3,500
Office supplies	1,500	1,000
Work-in-process	18,000	15,000
Finished goods	90,450	88,600

Required

Prepare a statement of cost of goods manufactured and an income statement. Actual overhead costs are assigned to products.

P18-34. **Cost of Goods Manufactured and Income Statement with Predetermined Overhead and Labor Cost Classifications**   **LO2, 4**

Assume information pertaining to Bauer Hockey for April of the current year follows.   Bauer Hockey, LLC

Sales	$745,500
Purchases	
Raw materials	225,000
Manufacturing supplies	12,000
Office supplies	2,200

continued

continued from previous page

Salaries (including fringe benefits)	
Administrative	102,600
Production supervisors	24,500
Sales	105,000
Depreciation	
Plant and machinery	24,000
Office and office equipment	8,000
Utilities	
Plant	15,000
Office	6,000

Inventories	April 1	April 30
Raw materials	$50,350	$52,500
Manufacturing supplies	6,200	7,400
Office supplies	1,800	1,500
Work-in-process	38,500	40,200
Finished goods	90,000	88,000

Additional information follows:
- Manufacturing overhead is applied to products at 125% of direct labor dollars.
- Employee base wages are $15 per hour.
- Employee fringe benefits amount to 20% of the base wage rate. They are classified as manufacturing overhead.
- During April, production employees worked 6,500 hours, including 5,200 regular hours and 400 overtime hours spent working on products. There were 900 indirect labor hours.
- Employees are paid a 50% overtime premium. Any overtime premium is treated as manufacturing overhead.

Required

a. Prepare a statement of cost of goods manufactured and an income statement for April.
b. Determine underapplied or overapplied overhead for April.
c. Recompute direct labor and actual manufacturing overhead assuming employee fringe benefits for direct labor hours are classified as direct labor.

LO2, 4
Custom Crate Engines

P18-35. Actual and Predetermined Overhead Rates

Custom Crate Engines assembles custom designed high-performance engines for classic American cars. Assume the following events occurred during the month of January:
- Materials costing $8,000 were purchased on account.
- Direct materials costing $6,000 were placed in process.
- A total of 450 direct labor hours was charged to individual jobs at a rate of $20 per hour.
- Overhead costs for the month were as follows:

Depreciation on building and equipment	$2,425
Indirect labor	2,700
Utilities	450
Property taxes on automotive shop	375
Insurance on building	350

- There were no jobs in process on January 1.
- On January 31, only one job (A06) was in process with materials costs of $1,800, direct labor charges of $1,000 for 50 direct labor hours, and applied overhead.
- The building and equipment were purchased before operations began and the insurance was prepaid. All other costs will be paid during the following month.

Note: Predetermined overhead rates are used throughout the module. An alternative is to accumulate actual overhead costs for the period in Manufacturing Overhead, and apply actual costs at the close of the period to all jobs in process during the period.

Required

a. Assuming Custom Crate assigned actual monthly overhead costs to jobs on the basis of actual monthly direct labor hours, prepare an analysis of the activity in Work-in-Process for the month of January.

b. Assuming Custom Crate uses a predetermined overhead rate of $15 per direct labor hour, prepare an analysis of Work-in-Process for the month of January. Describe the appropriate treatment of any overapplied or underapplied overhead for the month of January.

c. Assume that utilities and indirect labor are variable costs with respect to direct labor hours and that depreciation and property taxes are fixed costs. Predict the actual overhead rates for months when 250 and 750 direct labor hours are used. Assuming jobs similar to A06 were in process at the end of each month, determine the costs assigned to these jobs.

d. Why do you suppose predetermined overhead rates are preferred to actual overhead rates?

P18-36. Job Costing with Predetermined Overhead Rate

LO2, 4
Kubota Corporation
(KUBTY)

Kubota Corporation manufactures equipment in batches for inventory stock. Assume that Kubota's production costs are accounted for using a job cost system. At the beginning of April raw materials inventories totaled $9,350,000, manufacturing supplies amounted to $1,320,000, and finished goods inventories totaled $6,600,000. Two jobs were in process: Job 522 with assigned costs of $6,440,000 and Job 523 with assigned costs of $2,750,000. The following information summarizes April manufacturing activities:

- Purchased raw materials costing $27,500,000 on account.
- Purchased manufacturing supplies costing $3,300,000 on account.
- Requisitioned materials needed to complete Job 523. Started two new jobs, 524 and 525, and requisitioned direct materials for them.

Direct materials	
Job 523	$ 3,300,000
Job 524	14,190,000
Job 525	10,560,000
Total	$28,050,000

- Recorded April salaries and wages as follows:

Direct labor	
Job 522 (150,000 hours × $25 per hour)	$ 3,750,000
Job 523 (950,000 hours × $25 per hour)	23,750,000
Job 524 (1,350,000 hours × $25 per hour)	33,750,000
Job 525 (875,000 hours × $25 per hour)	21,875,000
Total direct labor	83,125,000
Indirect labor	7,100,000
Total	$90,225,000

- Used manufacturing supplies costing $2,475,000.
- Recognized depreciation on factory fixed assets of $5,800,000.
- Incurred miscellaneous manufacturing overhead costs of $7,250,000 on account.
- Applied manufacturing overhead at the rate of $6.25 per direct labor hour.
- Completed Jobs 522, 523, and 524.

Required

Prepare a complete analysis of all activity in Work-in-Process. Be sure to show the beginning and ending balances, all increases and decreases, and label each item. Provide support information on decreases with job cost sheets.

P18-37. Job Costing with Predetermined Overhead Rate

LO2, 4

SnoBlo Company manufactures a variety of gasoline-powered snow blowers for discount hardware and department stores. SnoBlo uses a job cost system and treats each customer's order as a separate job. The primary snow blower components (motors, chassis, and wheels) are purchased from three different suppliers under long-term contracts that call for the direct delivery of raw materials to the production floor as needed. When a customer's order is received, a raw materials purchase order is electronically placed with suppliers. The purchase order specifies the scheduled date that production is to begin as the delivery date for motors and chassis; the scheduled date production is to be completed is specified as the delivery date for the wheels. As a consequence, there are no raw materials inventories; raw materials are charged directly to Work-in-Process upon receipt. Upon completion, goods are shipped directly to customers rather than transferred to finished goods inventory. At the beginning of July SnoBlo had the following work-in-process inventories:

Job 365.	$ 40,000
Job 366.	29,800
Job 367.	30,600
Job 368.	17,000
Total	$117,400

During July, the following activities took place:
- Started Jobs 369, 370, and 371.
- Ordered and received the following raw materials for specified jobs:

Job	Motors	Chassis	Wheels	Total
366	$ 0	$ 0	$ 1,600	$ 1,600
367	0	0	2,400	2,400
368	0	0	3,050	3,050
369	28,000	10,000	2,100	40,100
370	18,000	7,000	1,800	26,800
371	17,000	7,200	0	24,200
Total	$63,000	$24,200	$10,950	$98,150

- Incurred July manufacturing payroll:

Direct labor	
Job 365.	$ 2,450
Job 366.	7,600
Job 367.	6,500
Job 368.	8,300
Job 369.	5,850
Job 370.	5,050
Job 371.	3,000
Total	38,750
Indirect labor.	6,850
Total	$45,600

- Incurred additional manufacturing overhead costs for July:

Manufacturing supplies purchased on account and used	$ 5,700
Depreciation on factory fixed assets.	11,800
Miscellaneous payables	9,500
Total	$27,000

- Applied manufacturing overhead using a predetermined rate based on predicted annual overhead of $405,000 and predicted annual direct labor of $450,000.
- Completed and shipped Jobs 365 through 370.

Required
Prepare a complete analysis of all activity in Work-in-Process. Be sure to show the beginning and ending balances, all increases and decreases, and label each item. Provide support information on decreases with job cost sheets.

P18-38. Weighted Average Process Costing

LO5

Minot Processing Company manufactures one product on a continuous basis in two departments, Processing and Finishing. All materials are added at the beginning of work on the product in the Processing Department. During November, the following events occurred in the Processing Department:

Units started	20,000 units
Units completed and transferred to Finishing Department	21,000 units

Costs assigned to processing	
Raw materials	$350,000
Manufacturing supplies used	25,000
Direct labor costs incurred	182,000
Supervisors' salaries	15,000
Other production labor costs	18,000
Depreciation on equipment	12,000
Other production costs	95,000

Additional information follows:

- Minot uses weighted average costing and applies manufacturing overhead to Work-in-Process at the rate of 90% of direct labor cost.
- Ending inventory in the Processing Department consists of 3,000 units that are one-fourth converted.
- Beginning inventory contained 4,000 units, one-half converted, with a cost of $57,950 ($34,000 for materials and $23,950 for conversion).

Required

a. Prepare a cost of production report for the Processing Department for November.

b. Prepare an analysis of all changes in Work-in-Process.

P18-39. Weighted Average Process Costing

LO5

JIF

The J.M. Smucker Company (SJM)

Assume that JIF, which is part of The J.M. Smucker Company, processes its only product, 12-ounce jars of peanut butter, in a single process and uses weighted average process costing to account for inventory costs. All materials are added at the beginning of production. Assume the following inventory, production, and cost data are provided for September:

Production data	
Beginning inventory (25% converted)	200,000 units
Units started	600,000 units
Ending inventory (75% converted)	225,000 units

Manufacturing costs	
Beginning inventory in process	
Materials cost	$182,000
Conversion cost	44,600
Raw materials cost added at beginning of process	578,000
Direct labor cost incurred	401,900
Manufacturing overhead applied	446,000

Required

a. Prepare a cost of production report for September.

b. Prepare a statement of cost of goods manufactured for September.

P18-40. Weighted Average Process Costing with Error Correction

LO5

Capital Manufacturing Company began operations on December 1. On December 31 a new accounting intern was assigned the task of calculating and costing ending inventories.

The intern estimated that the ending work-in-process inventory was 40% complete as to both materials and conversion, resulting in 6,000 equivalent units of materials and conversion. The ending work-in-process was then valued at $60,000, including $30,000 for materials and $30,000 for conversion. A subsequent review of the intern's work revealed that although the materials portion of the ending inventory was correctly estimated to be 40% complete, the units in ending inventory, on average, were only 25% complete as to conversion.

Required

a. Determine the number of units in the ending inventory.
b. How many equivalent units of conversion were in the ending inventory?
c. What cost per unit did the intern calculate for conversion?
d. Assuming 12,000 units were completed during the month of December, determine the correct cost per equivalent unit. (*Hint:* Find the total conversion costs in process.)
e. Determine the corrected cost of the ending inventory.
f. By how much was the cost of goods manufactured misstated as a result of the intern's error? Indicate whether the cost of goods manufactured was overstated or understated.

LO6   P18-41.   Absorption and Variable Costing Comparisons

Otabo

Otabo is a shoe manufacturer. Assume the company is concerned with changing to the variable costing method of inventory valuation for making internal decisions. Functional income statements using absorption costing for January and February follow.

OTABO Functional (Absorption Costing) Income Statements For January and February		
	January	**February**
Sales (10,000 units)	$800,000	$800,000
Cost of goods sold	(490,000)	(586,000)
Gross profit.	310,000	214,000
Selling and administrative expenses	(235,000)	(235,000)
Net operating income	$ 75,000	$ (21,000)

Production data follow.

Production units	12,000	8,000
Variable costs per unit	$25	$25
Fixed overhead costs	$288,000	$288,000

The preceding selling and administrative expenses include variable costs of $2 per unit sold.

Required

a. Compute the absorption cost per unit manufactured in January and February.
b. Explain why the net operating income for January was higher than the net operating income for February when the same number of units was sold in each month.
c. Prepare contribution income statements for both months using variable costing.
d. Reconcile the absorption costing and variable costing net operating income figures for each month. (Start with variable costing net operating income.)

LO6   P18-42.   Absorption and Variable Costing Comparisons

Red Arrow Blueberries manufactures blueberry jam. Because of bad weather, its blueberry crop was small. The following data have been gathered for the summer quarter of last year:

Beginning inventory (cases).	0
Cases produced	8,000
Cases sold	7,000
Sales price per case.	$115
Direct materials per case	$25
Direct labor per case	$40
Variable manufacturing overhead per case	$10
Total fixed manufacturing overhead	$192,000
Variable selling and administrative cost per case.	$2
Fixed selling and administrative cost	$38,000

Required

a. Prepare a functional income statement for the quarter using absorption costing.
b. Prepare a contribution income statement for the quarter using variable costing.
c. What is the value of ending inventory under absorption costing?
d. What is the value of ending inventory under variable costing?
e. Reconcile the difference in ending inventory under absorption costing and variable costing.

P18-43. **Variable and Absorption Costing with High-Low Cost Estimation and CVP Analysis Including**   **LO6**
Taxes
Presented are the Charger Company's functional income statements for January and February.

CHARGER COMPANY Functional (Absorption Costing) Income Statements For the Months of January and February		
	January	February
Production and sales	35,000	40,000
Sales Revenue	$2,450,000	$2,800,000
Cost of goods manufactured and sold	(1,470,000)	(1,540,000)
Gross profit	980,000	1,260,000
General and administrative expenses	(650,000)	(650,000)
Net operating income	330,000	610,000
Income taxes at 0.21	(69,300)	(128,100)
Net income after taxes	$ 260,700	$ 481,900

Required
a. Using the high-low method (see Module 15), develop a cost-estimating equation for total monthly manufacturing costs.
b. Determine Charger Company's monthly break-even point.
c. Determine the unit sales required to earn a monthly after-tax income of $600,000.
d. Prepare a January contribution income statement using variable costing.
e. If the January net income amounts differ using absorption and variable costing, explain why. If they are identical, explain why.

Management Applications

MA18-44. **Cost Data for Financial Reporting and Special Order Decisions**   **LO2, 4**
Harman Greeting Card Company produces a full range of greeting cards sold through pharmacies and   Walgreens Boots
department stores. Each card is designed by independent artists. A production master is then prepared   Alliance
for each design. The production master has an indefinite life. Product designs for popular cards are   (WBA)
deemed to be valuable assets. If a card sells well, many batches of the design will be manufactured
over a period of years. Hence, Harman Greeting maintains an inventory of production masters so
that cards may be periodically reissued. Cards are produced in batches that may vary by increments
of 1,000 units. An average batch consists of 10,000 cards. Producing a batch requires placing the
production master on the printing press, setting the press for the appropriate paper size, and making
other adjustments for colors and so forth. Following are facility-, product-, batch-, and unit-level cost
information:

Product design and production master per new card	$ 3,500
Batch setup (typically per 10,000 cards)	300
Materials per 1,000 cards	150
Conversion per 1,000 cards	200
Shipping (per batch)	15
Selling and administrative	
Companywide	306,000
Per product design marketed	675

Information from previous year:

Product designs and masters prepared for new cards	125
Product designs marketed	150
Batches manufactured	800
Cards manufactured and sold	8,000,000

Required

You may need to review materials in Module 17 to complete the requirements.

a. Describe how you would determine the cost of goods sold and the value of any ending inventory for financial reporting purposes. (No computations are required.)

b. You have just received an inquiry from **Walgreens** department stores to develop and manufacture 10 special designs for sale exclusively in Walgreens stores. The cards would be sold for $3.00 each, and Walgreens would pay Harman Greeting $0.70 per card. The initial order is for 30,000 cards of each design. If the cards sell well, Walgreens plans to place additional orders for these and other designs. Because of the preestablished sales relationship, no marketing costs would be associated with the cards sold to Walgreens. How would you evaluate the desirability of the Walgreens proposal?

c. Explain any differences between the costs considered in your answer to requirement (a) and the costs considered in your answer to requirement (b).

LO2, 4   **MA18-45. Continue or Discontinue: Plantwide Overhead with Labor- and Machine-Intensive Operations**

When Dart Products started operation five years ago, its only product was a radar detector known as the Bear Detector. The production system was simple, with Bear Detectors manually assembled from purchased components. With no ending work-in-process inventories, unit costs were calculated once a month by dividing current manufacturing costs by units produced.

Last year, Dart Products began to manufacture a second product, code-named the Lion Tamer. The production of Lion Tamers involves both machine-intensive fabrication and manual assembly. The introduction of the second product necessitated a change in the firm's simple accounting system. Dart Products now separately assigns direct material and direct labor costs to each product using information contained on materials requisitions and work tickets. Manufacturing overhead is accumulated in a single cost pool and assigned on the basis of direct labor hours, which is common to both products. Following are last year's financial results by product:

	Bear Detector	Lion Tamer
Sales		
Units	7,500	3,000
Dollars.......................	$ 750,000	$ 450,000
Cost of goods sold		
Direct materials................. $165,000		$ 97,500
Direct labor 281,250		90,000
Applied overhead 393,750		126,000
Total	(840,000)	(313,500)
Gross profit.....................	$ (90,000)	$ 136,500

Management is concerned about the mixed nature of last year's financial performance. It appears that the Lion Tamer is a roaring success. The only competition, the Nittney Company, has been selling a competing product for considerably more than Dart's Lion Tamer; this company is in financial difficulty and is likely to file for bankruptcy. The management of Dart Products attributes the Lion Tamer's success to excellent production management. Management is concerned, however, about the future of the Bear Detector and is likely to discontinue that product unless its profitability can be improved. You have been asked to help with this decision and have obtained the following information:

- The labor rate is $15 per hour.
- Dart has two separate production operations, fabrication and assembly. Bear Detectors undergo only assembly operations and require 2.5 assembly hours per unit. Lion Tamers undergo both fabrication and assembly and require 1.5 fabrication hours and 0.5 assembly hour per unit.
- The annual Fabricating Department overhead cost function is:

$$\$184,500 + \$6 \text{ (labor hours)}$$

- The annual Assembly Department overhead cost function is:

$$\$62,250 + \$12 \text{ (labor hours)}$$

Required

You may need to review materials in Modules 16 and 17 to complete this case. Evaluate the profitability of Dart's two products and make any recommendations you believe appropriate.

MA18-46. Absorption Costing and Performance Evaluation   **LO6**

On July 2, Maddon Financial acquired 90% of the outstanding stock of Kluber Industries in exchange for 2,000 shares of its own stock. Maddon Financial has a reputation as a "high flier" company that commands a high price-to-earnings ratio because its management team works wonders in improving the performance of ailing companies.

At the time of the acquisition, Kluber was producing and selling at an annual rate of 100,000 units per year. This is in line with the firm's average annual activity. Fifty thousand units were produced and sold during the first half of the year.

Immediately after the acquisition Maddon Financial installed its own management team and increased production to practical capacity. One-hundred thousand units were produced during the second half of the year.

At the end of the year, the new management declared another dramatic turnaround and a $100,000 cash dividend when the following set of income statements was issued:

KLUBER INDUSTRIES Income Statement For the first and second half of the year			
	First	Second	Total
Sales.	$2,800,000	$2,800,000	$5,600,000
Cost of goods sold*	(2,400,000)	(1,400,000)	(3,800,000)
Gross profit.	400,000	1,400,000	1,800,000
Selling and administrative expenses	(400,000)	(800,000)	(1,200,000)
Net income	$ 0	$ 600,000	$ 600,000

* Absorption costing with any underabsorbed or overabsorbed overhead written off as an adjustment to cost of goods sold. Kluber applies manufacturing overhead using a predetermined overhead rate based on predicted annual fixed overhead of $2,000,000 and annual production of 200,000 units.

Required

As the only representative of the minority interest on the board of directors, evaluate the performance of the new management team.

Solutions to Review Problems

Review 18-1—Solution

1. **Office supplies inventory**

   Each of the three types of organizations might include an office supplies inventory account on its balance sheet. Office supplies will typically be classified on the balance sheet as "other current asset." A manufacturing organization is most likely to have a supplies inventory account including the term "office" in order to distinguish it from manufacturing supplies. As the office supplies are consumed, they will move to the income statement and be classified as supply expense.

2. **Merchandise inventory**

   Merchandise inventory is an inventory account in the current asset section of the balance sheet of a merchandising company. As the inventory is sold, it moves to the income statement and is reported as a cost of goods sold expense.

3. **Finished goods inventory**

   Finished goods inventory is an inventory account in the current asset section of the balance sheet of a manufacturing company. As the inventory is sold, it moves to the income statement and is reported as a cost of goods sold expense.

4. **Work-in-process inventory**

   Work-in-process inventory is an inventory account in the current asset section of the balance sheet of a manufacturing company. As the work-in-process inventory is completed, it moves on to the finished goods inventory account in the current asset section of the balance sheet. Then, as discussed above, as the finished goods inventory is sold, it moves to the income statement and is reported as a cost of goods sold expense.

Review 18-2—Solution

a. Predetermined overhead rate per machine hour = $40,000,000/3,200,000 = $12.50
b. Applied overhead = $12.50 × 410,000 = $5,125,000
c. February overhead:

Actual	$4,410,000
Applied	(5,125,000)
Overapplied for February	(715,000)
Underapplied overhead, February 1.	400,000
Overapplied overhead, end of February.	$ (315,000)

Review 18-3—Solution

1. *c*: Production order
2. *a*: Process costing
3. *d*: Job cost sheet
4. *b*: Job order costing
5. *f*: Work ticket
6. *e*: Material requisition

Review 18-4—Solution

a.

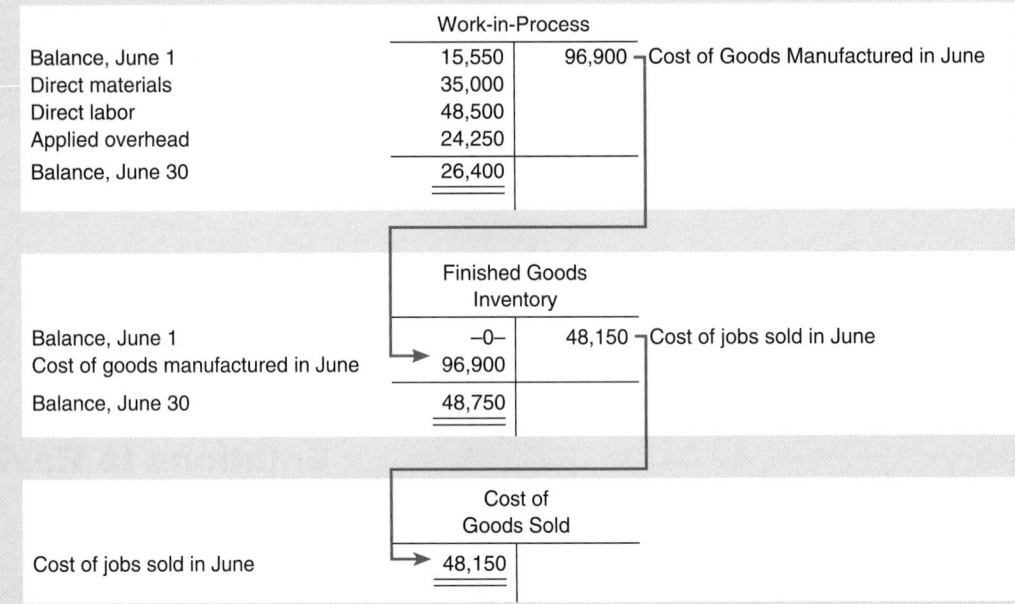

b. Job in Work-in-Process at June 30:

	Job 228
Direct materials.	$14,400
Direct labor	8,000
Applied overhead (800 × $5)	4,000
Total	$26,400

Job in Finished Goods at June 30:

	Job 227
Direct materials.	$18,000
Direct labor	20,500
Applied overhead (2,050 × $5)	10,250
Total	$48,750

Jobs sold in June:

	Job 225	Job 226	Total
Costs assigned from prior period	$13,750	$ 1,800	$15,550
June Costs: Direct materials	–0–	2,600	2,600
Direct labor	5,000	15,000	20,000
Applied overhead (500 & 1,500 × $5)	2,500	7,500	10,000
Total	$21,250	$26,900	$48,150

c. Statement of cost of goods manufactured for June:

STRATASYS LTD.
Statement of Cost of Goods Manufactured
June

Current manufacturing costs			
Cost of materials placed in production			
Raw materials, 6/1	$ 7,000 ^		
Purchases	40,000 ^		
Total available	47,000		
Raw materials, 6/30	(12,000)	$35,000 ^	
Direct labor		48,500	
Manufacturing overhead applied		24,250 *	$107,750
Work-in-process, 6/1			15,550 **
Total costs in process			123,300
Work-in-process, 6/30			(26,400) ***
Cost of goods manufactured			$ 96,900

*Manufacturing Overhead Applied

Job 225:	500 hrs. × $5 =	$ 2,500
Job 226:	1,500 hrs. × $5 =	$ 7,500
Job 227:	2,050 hrs. × $5 =	$10,250
Job 228:	800 hrs. × $5 =	$ 4,000
		$24,250

**Work-in-process, 6/1

Job 225:	$13,750^
Job 226:	$ 1,800^
	$15,550

***Work-in-process, 6/30 (see part b.)
^ Given

Review 18-5—Solution

SANDISK			
Cost of Production Report			
For the Year			
Summary of units in process			
Beginning	3,000,000		
Units started	27,000,000		
In process.	30,000,000		
Completed	(25,000,000)		
Ending	5,000,000		

Equivalent units in process	**Materials**	**Conversion**	
Units completed	25,000,000	25,000,000	
Plus equivalent units in ending inventory	5,000,000	1,500,000	
Equivalent units in process.	30,000,000	26,500,000	

Total costs to be accounted for and cost per equivalent unit in process	**Materials**	**Conversion**	**Total**
Work-in-Process, beginning	$ 468,000	$ 252,000	$ 720,000
Current cost	6,132,000	5,048,000	11,180,000
Total cost in process.	$ 6,600,000	$ 5,300,000	$11,900,000
Equivalent units in process.	÷ 30,000,000	÷26,500,000	
Cost per equivalent unit in process	$0.22	$0.20	$0.42
Accounting for total costs			
Transferred out (25,000,000 × $0.42).			$10,500,000
Work-in-Process, ending			
Materials (5,000,000 × $0.22).		$ 1,100,000	
Conversion (1,500,000 × $0.20)		300,000	1,400,000
Total cost accounted for			$11,900,000

Review 18-6—Solution

a.

Ending inventory = 100 BI + 500 PROD − 540 SOLD = 60	
Absorption costing	
Direct materials ($250 × 60)	$15,000
Variable overhead ($220 × 60)	13,200
Fixed overhead ($80 × 60)	4,800
Total	$33,000
Variable costing	
Direct materials ($250 × 60)	$15,000
Variable overhead ($220 × 60)	13,200
Total	$28,200

b.

Absorption costing		
Beginning inventory		$ 45,000
Production		
Direct materials (500 × $250)	$125,000	
Variable overhead (500 × $220)	110,000	
Fixed overhead (500 × $80)	40,000	275,000
Goods available for sale		320,000
Less ending inventory ($275,000/500 × 60)		33,000
Cost of goods sold		$287,000

Variable costing		
Beginning inventory		$ 38,000
Production		
Direct materials (500 × $250)	$125,000	
Variable overhead (500 × $220)	110,000	235,000
Goods available for sale		273,000
Less ending inventory ($235,000/500 × 60)		28,200
Cost of goods sold		$244,800

Module 19

Activity-Based Costing, Customer Profitability, and Activity-Based Management

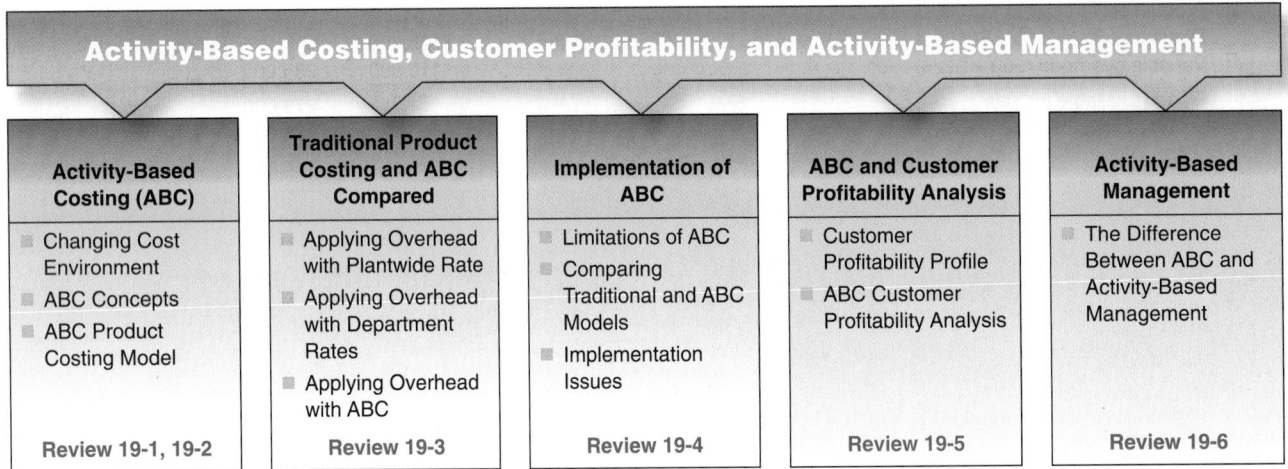

Activity-Based Costing, Customer Profitability, and Activity-Based Management				
Activity-Based Costing (ABC)	**Traditional Product Costing and ABC Compared**	**Implementation of ABC**	**ABC and Customer Profitability Analysis**	**Activity-Based Management**
■ Changing Cost Environment ■ ABC Concepts ■ ABC Product Costing Model	■ Applying Overhead with Plantwide Rate ■ Applying Overhead with Department Rates ■ Applying Overhead with ABC	■ Limitations of ABC ■ Comparing Traditional and ABC Models ■ Implementation Issues	■ Customer Profitability Profile ■ ABC Customer Profitability Analysis	■ The Difference Between ABC and Activity-Based Management
Review 19-1, 19-2	Review 19-3	Review 19-4	Review 19-5	Review 19-6

PREVIEW

UL

We learned in the last module that indirect product costs need to be allocated to units of products or services based on a cost driver—a measure of activity that causes that cost to increase. However, the choice of one activity driver over another may result in widely differing costs for the same unit. In this module, we will address which driver is the correct driver; in many instances, product costing will be improved if we incorporate multiple drivers into the computation, choosing the drivers based on the activities undertaken to produce the good or service.

Consider the Anglo-Dutch company **Unilever**, one of the largest fast moving consumer goods (FMCG) companies in the world. Over 2.5 billion people in over 190 countries use Unilever products each day. The company operates through three divisions. Unilever operational strategies differ for each division. Beauty & Personal Care has been successful in offering premium products in the high-growth segment of the industry. Expansion of products for emerging markets has been a successful strategy in the Home Care division. More than 58% of Unilever's overall revenues are from emerging markets with the strongest growth in Southeast Asia. Operations in Foods & Refreshments are consolidated—bringing more scale and allowing for faster response to changes in consumer demand.

Twenty-six of the company's brands qualified as Sustainable Living brands including B-Corp certified brands such as Ben & Jerry's, Seventh Generation, and Pukka Herbs. Certified B Corporations are businesses that meet high standards of social and environmental performance, public transparency, and legal accountability. In 2018, Sustainable Living brands grew 46% faster than other Unilever products and represented more than 70% of the company's growth.

Although still one of the top 10 global plastic polluters, the company recently adopted a "Less, Better, No" framework to transform its approach to plastic packaging. New ways of packaging and delivering products have reduced the amount of plastic used. Bottles made from recycled plastic are used in a variety of personal care products with a goal of at least 25% recycled plastic content in all packaging by 2025.

In 2019, Unilever committed to cutting its use of virgin plastic by 50% and to helping collect and process more plastic packaging than it sells by 2025. The company expects all plastic packaging to be fully reusable, recyclable, or compostable.

When we break down our costs by activity and then allocate those costs based on the set of activities a product or service consumes, we provide the basis by which a company such as Unilever can make broad strategic and operational changes to its business. This module will demonstrate how to develop and implement costing systems based on activity consumption, which will lead to better decision making regarding product, geographic, and customer selection.

Road Map

LO	Learning Objective | Topics	Page	eLecture	Guided Example	Assignments
19-1	**Explain the changes in the modern production environment that have affected cost structures.** Changing Cost Environment :: ABC Product Costing Model	19-3	e19-1	Review 19-1	23
19-2	**Outline the concept of activity-based costing and how it is applied.** Cost of Activities :: Cost Objects :: Two-Stage ABC Model	19-4	e19-2	Review 19-2	10, 11, 12, 13, 14, 15, 16, 17, 19, 21, 22, 24, 25, 28, 29, 30, 31, 33, 34, 35, 36
19-3	**Perform product costing using both traditional and activity- based costing methods.** Plantwide Rate :: Department Rates :: ABC Activity Rates	19-6	e19-3	Review 19-3	20, 21, 22, 23, 24, 25, 28, 29, 30, 31, 32, 36
19-4	**Compare activity-based costing to traditional methods. Assess implementation issues involved in activity-based costing systems.** Limitations of ABC :: Traditional vs. ABC Methods :: Implementation Issues	19-13	e19-4	Review 19-4	20, 21, 22, 23, 24, 25, 28, 29, 30, 31, 32, 35, 36
19-5	**Analyze customer profitability using activity-based costing.** Customer Profitability Profile :: Customer Profitability Analysis	19-16	e19-5	Review 19-5	14, 18, 26, 27, 33, 34
19-6	**Explain the difference between activity-based costing and activity-based management.** Maximizing Value	19-19	e19-6	Review 19-6	26, 31, 33, 34, 35, 36

Activity-Based Costing (ABC)

What are appropriate prices for our products and services? What are the current activities that contribute to our firm's costs? Does each of our activities add value for our customers? Which customers contribute the most to our profitability and which customers are unprofitable?

In a competitive business environment, it is imperative that a firm understand its costs in order to make good business decisions. It has become increasingly difficult to appropriately link overhead (indirect) costs to the products and services they support. In this module we will discuss some of the reasons behind the growing complexity of appropriately costing products and services and how activity-based costing can provide better information for decision making.

Changing Cost Environment

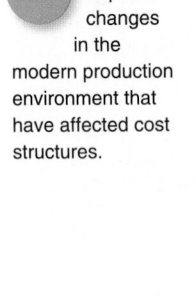

eLectures
MBC **LO1**
Explain the changes in the modern production environment that have affected cost structures.

As technology has advanced and competition has intensified over the last century, there has been a fundamental shift in manufacturing organizations from labor-intensive to automated assembly techniques. These changes have influenced the activities performed to meet customer needs and, consequently, the costs of producing goods and services.

At the beginning of the twentieth century, products had long life cycles, production procedures were relatively straightforward, production was labor based, and only a limited number of related products were produced in a single plant. It was said of the Model T Ford that "you could have any color you wanted, as long as it was black." The largest cost elements of most manufactured goods were the cost of raw materials and the wages paid to production employees. Manufacturing overhead was a relatively small portion of the overall cost of manufacturing products.

The twentieth century saw an accelerating shift from traditional labor-based activities to production procedures requiring large investments in automated equipment. In the past, production employees used equipment to assist them in performing their jobs. Now employees spend considerable time scheduling, setting up, maintaining, and moving materials to and from equipment. They spend relatively little time on actual production. The equipment does the work, and the employees keep it running efficiently. Increased complexity of production procedures and an increase in the variety of products produced in a single facility have also caused a shift toward more support personnel and fewer production employees. The result is a significant increase in manufacturing overhead as a percentage of total product cost. This change in the typical production cost structure over the past century is illustrated in Exhibit 19.1.

In the "low-tech," labor-intensive manufacturing environment, factors related to direct labor were often the primary drivers of manufacturing overhead costs; however, in today's "high-tech" automated environment there are many other factors that drive manufacturing overhead costs, and the specific set of cost drivers differs from organization to organization.

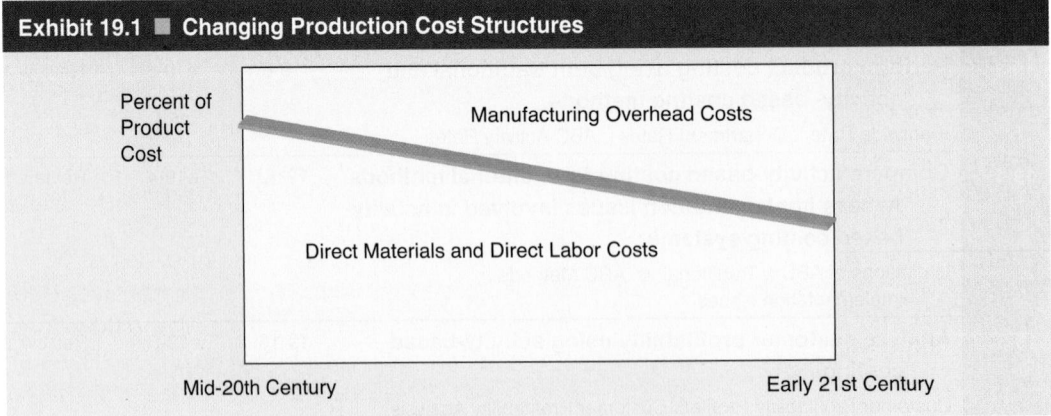

Exhibit 19.1 ■ Changing Production Cost Structures

Percent of Product Cost

Manufacturing Overhead Costs

Direct Materials and Direct Labor Costs

Mid-20th Century   Early 21st Century

The previous module on product costing illustrated a simplified traditional system for allocating manufacturing overhead to products using a single, volume-based cost driver, such as direct labor hours. The following section introduces activity-based costing, which recognizes the multiple activities that drive manufacturing overhead costs in today's production environment.

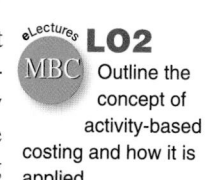

LO1 Review 19-1

In a competitive business environment, it is imperative that a firm understand its costs in order to make good business decisions. These decision might include: What are appropriate prices? What current activities contribute to a firm's costs? Which customers contribute the most to profitability?

Required
Discuss some of the factors in the U.S. economy that make it increasingly difficult to accurately assign costs to products and services.

Solution on p. 19-37.

Activity-Based Costing Concepts

The manufacturing overhead cost pool has been referred to as a "blob" of common costs. The constant growth of costs classified as overhead has forced us to search for increasingly detailed methods to analyze these costs. If overhead costs are low in comparison with other costs and if factories produce few products in large production runs, the use of an overhead rate based on direct labor hours or machine hours may be adequate. However, as the amount of overhead costs continues to grow, as manufacturing facilities produce a wider variety of products, and as competition intensifies, the inadequacies of a single overhead rate based on a single cost driver such as direct labor hours become evident.

eLectures LO2
MBC Outline the concept of activity-based costing and how it is applied.

Fortunately, advances in information technology and the declining costs of computerized information systems have facilitated the development and maintenance of increasingly detailed databases. The increased complexity of the production environment, coupled with faster and cheaper computing technology, gave rise to the emergence and development of activity-based costing during the 1980s and 1990s.

Activity-based costing (ABC) involves determining the cost of activities and tracing their costs to cost objects on the basis of the cost object's utilization of units of activity.

The concepts underlying ABC can be summarized in the following two statements and illustrations:

1. Activities performed to fill customer needs consume resources that cost money.

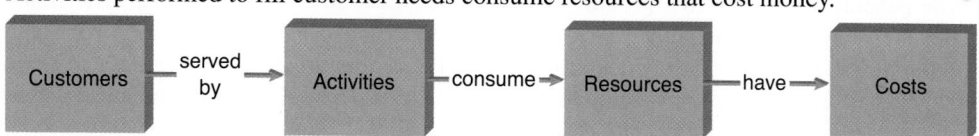

2. The cost of resources consumed by activities should be assigned to cost objects on the basis of the units of activity consumed by the cost object.

*Based on units of activity utilized by the cost object.

The cost object is typically a product or service provided to a customer. Depending on the information needs of decision makers, as we will discuss later in this module, the cost object might be the customer.

To summarize, activity-based costing is a system of analysis that identifies and measures the cost of key activities, and then traces these activity costs to products or other cost objects based on the quantity of activity consumed by the cost objects. ABC is based on the premise that activities drive costs and that costs should be assigned to products (or other cost objects) in proportion to the volume of activities they consume. Although activity cost analysis is most often associated with product costing, it offers many benefits for controlling and managing costs, as we will see later in this module. As the following Research Insight box explains, ABC was actually used first to improve cost management before it was used for product costing.

Research Insight ■ The History of ABC

ABC came to the forefront in the 1980s and 1990s; however, it was beginning to evolve as early as the 1960s when General Electric's (GE) finance and accounting staff attempted to improve the usefulness of accounting information in controlling ever-increasing indirect costs. The GE staff noted that indirect costs were often the result of "upstream" decisions, such as engineering design and change orders, which were made long before the costs were actually incurred. Frequently, the engineering department was not informed of the consequences their actions had on the other parts of the organization.

The second phase of the development of ABC was accomplished by business consultants, professors, and manufacturing companies during the 1970s and early 1980s. By generating more accurate cost and profitability measures for the various products offered by companies, these consultants and professors hoped to improve product cost information used in pricing and product mix decisions. ABC has since been extended to assess customer profitability.

In the late 1980s and 1990s, ABC was being promoted by many of the leading consulting firms, and it almost became a fad, much as TQM and JIT had become before it. Consequently, many companies that jumped on the ABC bandwagon early in its life later determined that it was not for them. Most of the companies that abandoned ABC probably adopted it initially for the wrong reasons.

Knowledge of the historical development of activity-based costing is important in order to clearly understand what ABC analysis was intended to accomplish, as well as what it was not intended to accomplish.

Source: Craig A. Latshaw and Teresa M. Cortese-Danile, "Activity-Based Costing: Usage and Pitfalls," *Review of Business*, Winter, 2002.

ABC Product Costing Model

Traditional costing considers the cost of a product to be its direct costs for materials and labor plus some allocated portion of factory overhead, using overhead rates typically based on direct labor or machine hours. Activity-based costing is based on the notion that companies incur costs because of the activities they conduct in pursuit of their goals and objectives. For example, various activities take place to produce a particular product, such as setting up, maintaining, or monitoring the machines to make the product, physically moving raw materials and work in process, and so forth. Each of these activities has a cost; therefore, the total cost of producing a product using ABC is the sum of the direct materials and direct labor costs of that product, plus the cost of other activities conducted to produce that product.

The general two-stage ABC product cost model is illustrated in Exhibit 19.2. The first stage includes the assignment of manufacturing overhead resource costs, such as indirect labor, depreciation, and utilities, to activity cost pools for the key activities identified. Typical activity cost pools in a manufacturing environment include pools for machine setup, material movement, and engineering. The second stage assigns those activity cost pools to products.

Notice in Exhibit 19.2 that direct product costs, such as direct materials and direct labor, are directly assigned to products and are excluded from the activity cost pools. Only indirect product costs (manufacturing overhead) are assigned to products via activity cost pools.

Probably the most critical step in ABC is identifying cost drivers. The activity cost driver for a particular cost (or cost pool) is the characteristic selected for measuring the quantity of the activity for a particular period of time. For example, if an activity cost pool is established for machine setup, it is necessary to select some basis for measuring the quantity of machine setup activity associated with the costs in the pool. The quantity of setup activity could be measured by the number of different times machines are set up to produce a different product, the amount of time used in completing machine setups, the number of staff working on setups, or some other measure. It is critical that the activity measure used has a logical causal relationship to the costs in the pool and that the quantity of the activity is highly correlated with the amount of cost in the pool. Statistical methods, such as regression analysis and correlation analysis, can be very useful in selecting activity cost drivers.

Once the total cost in the activity pool and the activity cost driver have been determined, the cost per unit of activity is calculated as the total cost divided by the total amount of activity. For example, if total costs assigned to the setup activity pool in July were $100,000 and 200 setups were completed in July, the cost per setup for the month would be $500. If during July machines were set up 10 times to make product JX2, the total setup cost that would be assigned to product JX2 would be $5,000 ($500 × 10).

Exhibit 19.2 ■ Two-Stage Activity-Based Costing Model

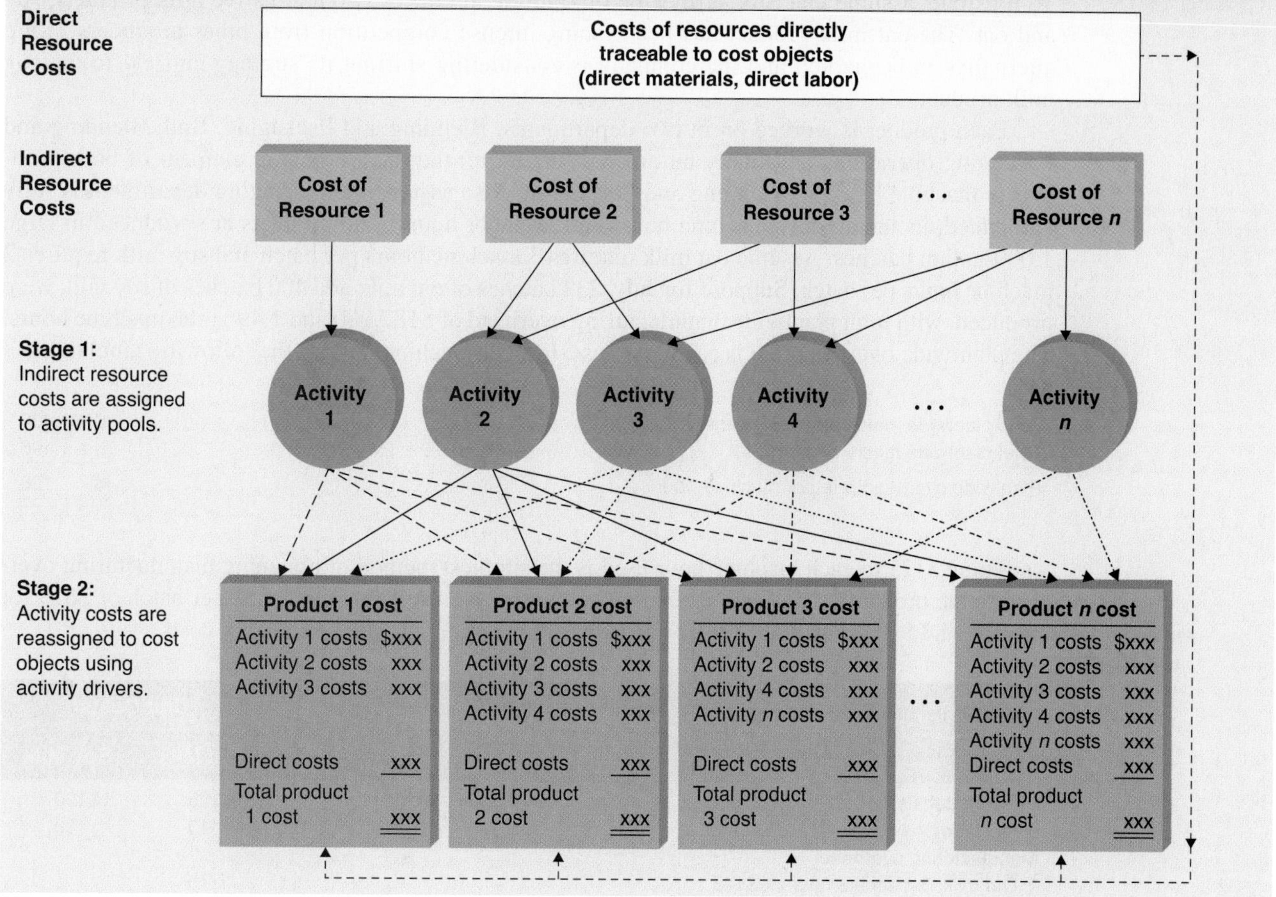

Direct Resource Costs	Costs of resources directly traceable to cost objects (direct materials, direct labor)

Indirect Resource Costs

Cost of Resource 1	Cost of Resource 2	Cost of Resource 3	. . .	Cost of Resource n

Stage 1: Indirect resource costs are assigned to activity pools.

Activity 1	Activity 2	Activity 3	Activity 4	. . .	Activity n

Stage 2: Activity costs are reassigned to cost objects using activity drivers.

Product 1 cost		**Product 2 cost**		**Product 3 cost**		**Product n cost**	
Activity 1 costs	$xxx	Activity 1 costs	$xxx	Activity 1 costs	$xxx	Activity 1 costs	$xxx
Activity 2 costs	xxx	Activity 2 costs	xxx	Activity 2 costs	xxx	Activity 2 costs	xxx
Activity 3 costs	xxx	Activity 3 costs	xxx	Activity 4 costs	xxx	Activity 3 costs	xxx
		Activity 4 costs	xxx	Activity n costs	xxx	Activity 4 costs	xxx
						Activity n costs	xxx
Direct costs	xxx	Direct costs	xxx	Direct costs	xxx	Direct costs	xxx
Total product 1 cost	xxx	Total product 2 cost	xxx	Total product 3 cost	xxx	Total product n cost	xxx

---

LO2 Review 19-2

Mobile Health Screening (MHS) offers onsite general health screening services for a flat rate of $35 per screening. MHS typically provides its services to businesses that offer fitness and health programs as a benefit to their employees. A representative of MHS arrives at a business early in the morning and sets up a room with the necessary equipment and supplies. MHS sees participating employees throughout the day and screens for basic health measures such as blood pressure, weight, blood screening, and health behaviors. MHS sends samples to an outside lab for testing. MHS then compiles the results of all the tests and provides employees access to their individual results via a logon identification and password on the website.

Required
Identify likely activities and related cost drivers that MHS might engage in throughout the processes of providing the health screening services.

Solution on p. 19-37.

Traditional Product Costing and ABC Compared

Recall that we assumed **Frilly** in Module 18 recognized manufacturing overhead using a plantwide manufacturing overhead rate of $4 per direct labor hour. It was assumed that each hour of labor worked on product caused $4 of manufacturing overhead to be incurred. In that case, all manufacturing costs were assumed to be driven by one factor, direct labor hours. As discussed at the beginning of this module, such an assumption is often not appropriate with modern methods of producing goods (or services) where manufacturing overhead is related to a diverse set of activities and cost drivers.

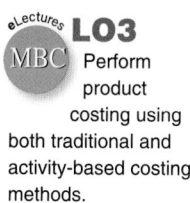

LO3 Perform product costing using both traditional and activity-based costing methods.

Applying Overhead with a Plantwide Rate

To illustrate, assume that Silk, a division of Danone, produces two alternative milk products, soy and oat. The oat milk product has been facing intense competition from other producers in the alternative milk market, and the company is considering shifting its strategy entirely to the soy milk product.

Each product is worked on in two departments, Blending and Packaging. Both Blending and Packaging operations are highly automated; therefore, the most common element of both products is machine hours in Blending and Packaging. Also assume the Packaging department is fully automated, incurring only machine hours and no labor hours. The products are produced in large 1,000-gallon batches. Assume oat milk requires 3 machine hours per batch and soy milk requires 2 machine hours per batch. Suppose for July, 232 batches of oat milk and 400 batches of soy milk were produced, with total plantwide manufacturing overhead of $187,000 and 1,496 total machine hours. The plantwide overhead rate is calculated as $125 per machine hour in the following tabulation.

Total plantwide manufacturing overhead	$187,000
Total plantwide machine hours	÷ 1,496
Plantwide overhead rate per machine hour	$ 125

Assigning $125 to each machine hour used is the simplest method of assigning manufacturing overhead to the products and, as the tabulation below shows, results in a total cost per batch of $610 for oat milk and $400 for soy milk after adding the direct materials and direct labor costs.

	Unit Costs	
	Oat Milk	**Soy Milk**
Direct materials	$125	$120
Direct labor	110	30
Manufacturing overhead		
Oat milk: 3 machine hours × $125	375	
Soy milk: 2 machine hours × $125		250
Total unit cost	$610	$400

A plantwide overhead allocation method is often used in situations where companies produce only one product in a plant, or where multiple products are very similar in regard to the use of activities, such as machine or labor hours, that drive most of the overhead costs. If multiple products are produced that consume varying levels of activities in multiple production departments, departmental overhead allocation rates will produce a more accurate allocation of overhead costs to the various products.

Applying Overhead with Department Rates

For Silk to establish separate overhead allocation rates for each of the two production departments, it is necessary first to assign the $187,000 of total overhead costs for the plant to the two production departments, some of which is directly assignable to the departments. For example, the departmental supervisors' salaries could be directly assignable to the departments. Other manufacturing overhead costs, such as support costs for maintenance, payroll, and so forth, are allocated to the production departments. Assume that after these allocations, the total costs assigned to the departments were $59,100 for Blending and $127,900 for Packaging.

The next step in the product costing process is to assign the departmental costs to the products. For this example, assume that the manufacturing process in the Blending Department is labor intensive, while the process in the Packaging Department is fully automated. Manufacturing overhead is applied to products as follows:

Department	Manufacturing Overhead Application Base
Blending	Direct labor hours
Packaging	Machine hours

During the month of July, 500 direct labor hours were worked in Blending. Packaging used 800 machine hours. Assume oat milk requires a total of 3 machine hours per batch with 1 of those hours incurred in Packaging. Soy milk requires a total of 2 machine hours per batch with 1.42 of those hours incurred in Packaging. The department manufacturing overhead rates based on actual costs for July and the total product costs using departmental overhead rates are calculated in the following tables:

Department manufacturing overhead rates for July	Blending	Packaging
Total department manufacturing overhead (direct department costs plus allocated costs)	$59,100	$127,900
Quantity of overhead application base		
Direct labor hours	÷ 500	
Machine hours		÷ 800
Department manufacturing overhead rates	$118.20	$159.875
	Per direct labor hour	Per machine hour

	Unit Costs per Batch	
Total costs per unit for July using department rates	Oat Milk	Soy Milk
Direct materials	$125	$120
Direct labor	110	30
Manufacturing overhead		
Blending: 1 labor hr. × $118.20	118	
0.67 labor hrs. × $118.20		79
Packaging: 1 machine hr. × $159.875	160	
1.42 machine hrs. × $159.875		227
Total costs	$513	$456

Allocating factory overhead costs based on department rates (rather than on a plantwide rate of $125 per machine hour) causes a shift in costs from oat to soy milk because oat milk's overhead activity is incurred evenly in both Blending and Packaging (1.00 hour each) while soy milk incurs more of its overhead activity in Packaging (1.42 hours versus 0.67 hour).

The per-unit costs with multiple allocations are substantially different from the per-unit costs when using plantwide rates and, in fact, show the cost of oat milk to be slightly below a competitor's bid of $525 that was offered to one of soy milk's customers. Assume that based on the plantwide rate, the cost of $610 for oat milk was higher than the competitor's price.

By creating separate manufacturing overhead cost allocation pools, allocation bases, and overhead application rates for Blending and Packaging, it is possible to recognize overhead cost differences in various products based on differences in Blending Department labor hours used and Packaging Department machine hours used for each product. In most multiproduct manufacturing environments, this approach represents a cost system improvement over using a single, plantwide overhead rate, and it reduces the likelihood of cost cross-subsidization, which occurs when one product is assigned too much cost as a result of another being assigned too little cost. While department overhead rates may improve product costing results for many organizations, and in fact may be satisfactory, this method does not attempt to reflect the actual activities used in producing the different product.

Applying Overhead with Activity-Based Costing

An even more precise method of measuring the cost of products than plantwide or departmental rates is the activity-based costing method. As stated earlier, activity-based costing involves determining the cost of activities associated with a particular cost object. ABC for product costing identifies and measures the cost of activities used to produce the various products and sums the cost of those activities to determine the cost of the products. The following Business Insight compares three key benefits regarding the accuracy of cost systems for ABC users and non-ABC users.

For Danone's Silk division, assume Blending and Packaging have overhead costs of $59,100 and $127,900, respectively. The overhead rates for each department were determined in the last section as $118.20 and $159.875, respectively, per relevant hour of use. The easiest way to assign these costs to products is by using one base and one rate for all products going through a given process (e.g., blending). However, different products typically use different amounts of resources from a given process and using the same base and overhead rate for all may distort the cost for some or all products.

Overhead costs in the Blending and Packaging departments consisted of two types of costs: direct department costs and allocated costs from other support departments. Direct department overhead costs are costs that are incurred directly by the department such as indirect labor, indirect materials, depreciation on equipment, supervisory wages, and so forth. Allocated support costs are costs allocated from other departments (specifically, engineering, support services, and building and grounds) that provide services to both Blending and Packaging. Danone's accountants determined that the *direct* department overhead costs in Blending were driven primarily by labor hours, whereas *direct* department overhead costs in Packaging were driven primarily by machine hours. It was also determined that each component of engineering, support services, and building and grounds represents a separate activity cost pool, and that these costs support both the Blending and Packaging Departments. Therefore, these costs should be assigned to the products based on specific cost drivers rather than a single department cost driver.

The following is a detailed analysis of overhead cost data for July's operations:

Overhead Activity	Total Activity Cost	Activity Cost Driver	Quantity of Activity	Unit Activity Rates
Direct departmental overhead costs				
Blending	$ 25,000	Labor hours	500	$ 50.00
Packaging.....................	105,000	Machine hours	800	$131.25
Common overhead costs				
Support Services				
Receiving.....................	14,000	Purchase orders.......	100	140.00
Inventory control	13,000	Units produced........	632	20.57
Engineering Resources				
Production setup	12,000	Production runs	20	600.00
Engineering and testing.........	8,000	Machine hours	1,496	5.35
Building and Grounds				
Maintenance, machines	4,000	Machine hours	1,496	2.67
Depreciation, machines.........	6,000	Units produced.......	632	9.49
Total	$187,000			

Business Insight ■ Key Benefits of Using ABC

A 2009 study of 348 manufacturing and service companies worldwide indicated that activity-based costing continues to provide strategic and operational benefits. Although the study showed that there has been a decline in ABC users since the 1990s, when it was first widely adopted, the following graphics from the study report support the conclusion that users of ABC have a higher level of confidence than non-ABC users that their cost system provides more accurate cost measurements.

Comparisons of ABC to Non-ABC Users on Three Key Benefits

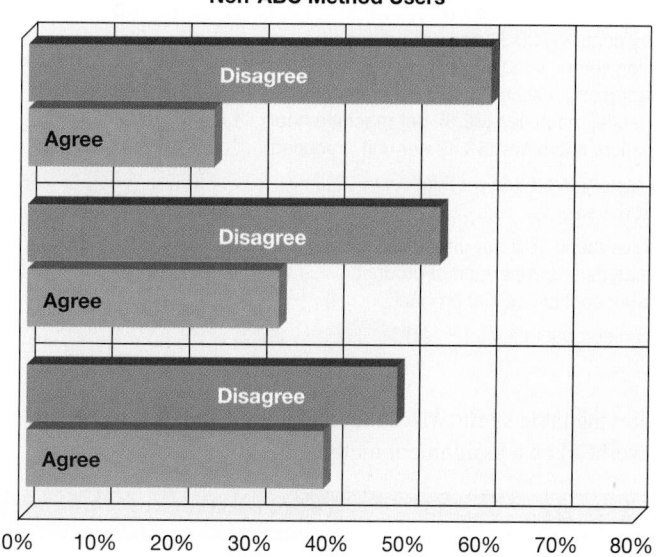

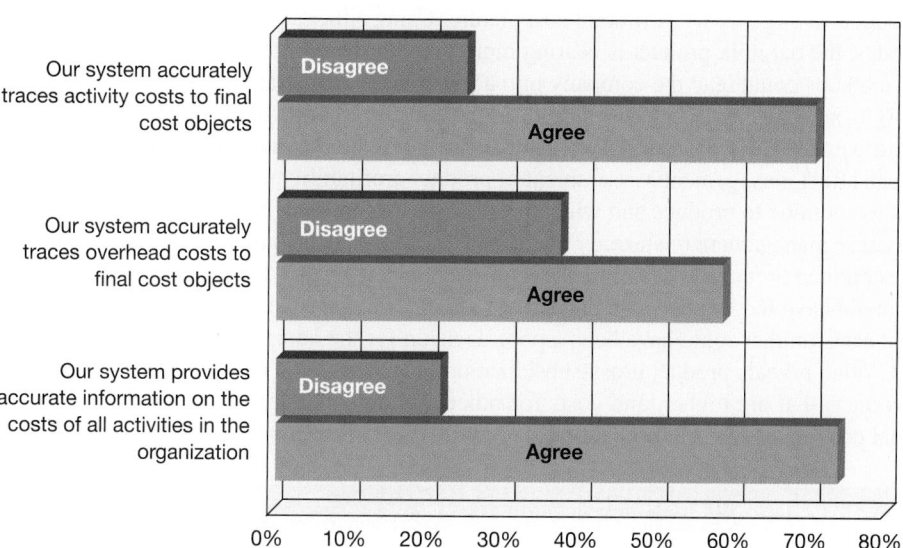

Source: William O. Stratton, Denis Desroches, Raef Lawson, and Toby Hatch, "Activity-Based Costing: Is It Still Relevant?" *Management Accounting Quarterly*, Spring 2009, Vol. 10, No. 3, pp. 31–40.

Suppose the amounts of activity attributed to oat and soy milk and the factory overhead cost per unit based on ABC costs are as follows:

Activity (cost per unit of driver activity)	Oat Milk Quantity of Activity	Oat Milk Cost of Activity	Soy Milk Quantity of Activity	Soy Milk Cost of Activity
Blending ($50.00 per labor hour)	232	$11,600	268	$ 13,400
Packaging ($131.25 per machine hour)	232	30,450	568	74,550
Receiving ($140.00 per order)	40	5,600	60	8,400
Inventory control ($20.57 per unit produced)	232	4,772	400	8,228
Production setup ($600.00 per run)	5	3,000	15	9,000
Engineering and testing ($5.35 per machine hour)	696	3,724	800	4,280
Maintenance, machines ($2.67 per machine hour)	696	1,858	800	2,136
Depreciation, machines ($9.49 per unit produced).	232	2,202*	400	3,796
Total factory overhead product cost		$63,206		$123,790
Units produced		÷ 232		÷ 400
Factory overhead cost per unit of product*		$ 272		$ 309
Direct materials cost per unit of product		125		120
Direct labor cost per unit of product		110		30
Total unit product cost using ABC		$ 507		$ 459

The following table summarizes the total product costs for Danone's two products using the three different overhead cost assignment methods:

	Oat Milk	Soy Milk
Plantwide overhead rate	$610	$400
Departmental overhead rates	513	456
ABC	507	459

ABC product costing reveals a different cost picture. Using either a plantwide overhead rate or departmental rates, the oat milk product is bearing more than its share of total overhead costs. Using either of these methods could lead the company into a potentially poor strategy of abandoning the oat milk market. With an actual per-batch cost of $507, rather than $513 or $610, the company clearly has more latitude to compete on price with other companies in this market and remain profitable. Inaccurate costing can affect management's assessment of product profitability and its decisions regarding which products to continue to produce and which products to discontinue. Flawed product costing information can cause management mistakenly to decide to keep products that are losing money, while deciding to discontinue products that are profitable. Using a plantwide or departmental overhead allocation method could have led Danone's management to shift its emphasis from the oat milk to the soy milk market, a decision that could have been a poor decision for the company.

ABC often reveals product cross-subsidization problems. This is when ABC produces costs for some products that are higher, and costs for other products that are lower, than costs produced by traditional costing methods. This is referred to as cross-subsidization.

Business Insight ■ ABC and Software-as-Service

Changes in distribution have altered the business model and cost structure of the software industry. When software was distributed on physical discs, both the business model and cost structure of the software industry were rather traditional, dominated by direct labor and shipping costs. With the rise of the Internet and cloud-based computing, the software industry's business model is changing rapidly. Oracle has been particularly aggressive in switching its business from traditional software-as-product to software-as-service (SAS) and platform-as-service. According to Oracle's annual report, cloud-based and license support service business represents 83% of total revenue in fiscal 2019, up from 81% in 2018. Total revenue was $32.6 billion for fiscal year 2019.

continued

continued from previous page

Providing SAS requires both production of the software product and ongoing hardware and networking support as the product is delivered and maintained on a subscription basis. Each customer will have different service needs and require different amounts of various services from storage to support, as well as added functionality to make the services meet their needs on an ongoing basis. ABC is particularly useful in this type of business where units sold offer a very incomplete picture of the costs of serving the client.

Source: Mamta Badkar and Eric Platt, "Oracle Tops the S&P 500 Leaderboard," *Financial Times*, March 20, 2015.

Managerial Decision ■ You Are the Controller

You have heard about companies that have adopted ABC and experienced significant differences in product costs compared with previous cost calculations using traditional costing methods. Consequently, you were surprised when your newly implemented ABC system provided product costs that were almost identical to those from the old costing system. You are, therefore, thinking about abandoning the ABC system, since it is quite costly to maintain. Should you abandon your ABC system? [Answer, p. 19-20]

LO3 Review 19-3

Assume that one of **Illinois Tool Works Inc's (ITW)** divisions has the following predicted indirect costs and cost drivers for the year for the given activity cost pools:

	Fabrication Department	Finishing Department	Cost Driver
Maintenance.	$ 20,000	$10,000	Machine hours
Materials handling	30,000	15,000	Material moves
Machine setups	70,000	5,000	Machine setups
Inspections	—	25,000	Inspection hours
	$120,000	$55,000	

The following activity predictions were also made for the year:

	Fabrication Department	Finishing Department
Machine hours	10,000	5,000
Materials moves	3,000	1,500
Machine setups	700	50
Inspection hours	—	1,000

It is assumed that the cost per unit of activity for a given activity does not vary between departments.

Suppose ITW's divisional manager is trying to evaluate the company's product mix strategy regarding two of its five product models, Cobra Latch and GrimLoc. The company has been using a plantwide overhead rate based on machine hours but is considering switching to either department rates or activity-based rates. The production manager has provided the following data for the production of a batch of 100 units for each of these models:

	Cobra Latch	GrimLoc
Direct materials cost.	$12,000	$18,000
Direct labor cost	$5,000	$4,000
Machine hours (Fabrication).	500	700
Machine hours (Finishing)	200	100
Materials moves	30	50
Machine setups	5	9
Inspection hours	30	60

continued

continued from previous page

Required

 a. Determine the cost of one unit each of Cobra Latch and GrimLoc, assuming a plantwide overhead rate is used based on total machine hours.
 b. Determine the cost of one unit of Cobra Latch and GrimLoc, assuming department overhead rates are used. Overhead is assigned based on machine hours in both departments.
 c. Determine the cost of one unit of Cobra Latch and GrimLoc, assuming activity-based overhead rates are used for maintenance, materials handling, machine setup, and inspection activities.

Solution on p. 19-37.

Implementation of ABC

Limitations of ABC Illustration

eLectures **LO4**

MBC Compare activity-based costing to traditional methods. Assess implementation issues involved in activity-based costing systems.

Several limitations of Danone's Silk division illustration should be mentioned. For the sake of simplicity, the example was limited to manufacturing cost considerations. A complete analysis would also require considerations of nonmanufacturing costs, such as marketing, distribution, and customer service, before a final determination of product profitability could be made. Finally, in calculating the activity cost per unit of activity, it is necessary to decide how to measure the total quantity of activity. For example, for the Silk division, the receiving cost per purchase order was calculated as $140.00 based on the actual quantity of 100 purchase orders for the period. Alternatively, the receiving cost could have been calculated based on **practical capacity**, which is the maximum possible volume of activity, while allowing for normal downtime for repairs and maintenance. If the plant has a practical capacity to prepare 140 purchase orders per period, the cost per purchase order based on the practical capacity is $100 per purchase order, or $14,000 ÷ 140. Using this overhead rate in costing product, only $10,000 would have been assigned to the two products, which required only 100 purchase orders, and the remaining $4,000 for the 40 purchase orders of excess (or idle) capacity not used would be written off as an operating expense of the period as underapplied overhead. Practical capacity is generally regarded as better than actual capacity for calculating activity costs because it does not hide the cost of idle capacity within product costs, and it gives a truer cost of the activities used to produce the product.

Comparing Traditional and Activity-Based Costing

Procedurally, ABC is not a new method for assigning costs to cost objects. Traditional costing systems have used a two-stage allocation model (similar to the ABC model) to assign costs to cost pools (such as departments) and subsequently assign those cost pools to products using an allocation base. In most traditional costing systems, overhead is assigned to one or more cost pools based on departments and functional characteristics (such as labor-related, machine-related, and space-related costs) and then reassigned to products using a general allocation base such as direct labor hours or machine hours. ABC is different in that it divides the overall manufacturing processes into activities. ABC accumulates costs in cost pools for the major activities and then assigns the costs of these activities to products or other cost objects that benefit from these activities. *Conceptually,* ABC is different because of the way it views the operations of the company; *procedurally,* it uses a methodology that has been around for a long time.

The challenge in using ABC is specifying the model; that is, determining how many activity pools should be established for a given cost measurement purpose, which costs should be assigned to each activity pool, and the appropriate activity driver for each pool. Specifying the model also includes determining the resource cost drivers for assigning indirect resource costs to the various activity cost pools.

When evaluating whether to implement an ABC model, management must weigh the value of more accurate information against the administrative efforts of producing it. This can be complicated by the fact that it is often more difficult to measure the benefits of a process than it is to measure tangible costs. Further, once a company makes the decision to implement an ABC system, it also needs to assess the level of accuracy it wants the system to provide. In his article, "Implementing Activity-Based Costing," Gary Cokins emphasizes that the "quest for perfection is expensive," and that a reasonable level of accuracy might be sufficient.[1]

Business Insight   ■   Batch Size Matters

Two trends are pushing American businesses to Maker's Row, a matchmaker for firms and factories in the United States. The rise of crowdfunding platforms like Kickstarter and IndieGogo has produced a large and growing number of small firms with a product and the cash required to produce it. Since these firms do not have the scale or resources to consider overseas production, they need local factories. At the same time, global manufacturing is shifting homeward. Large firms are trading lower labor costs and weaker regulatory environments at foreign plants for better supervision, more control, and lower shipping costs at U.S. plants. The crowdfunding and the "re-shoring" trends are both driving demand for domestic production, and Maker's Row is helping to match firms with factories that fit their needs.

According to Maker's Row cofounder Tanya Menendez, part of the problem with finding a factory is that the factory operators consider much of what they do to be a trade secret. Simple Internet searches yield little information of value, and even larger companies have difficulty finding the best option for their production. Maker's Row is a kind of online dating site for these manufacturers, allowing them to share information with potential clients and partners without making too much information public. By delivering information about factories to firms, Maker's Row helps firms make better production decisions about potential products.

Source: T.J. McCue, "80,000 Businesses Receive Manufacturing Help from Maker's Row," *Forbes*, September 3, 2015.

ABC Implementation Issues

The distortion in product costs for Danone's Silk division from using traditional cost systems based on plantwide or departmental rates, while hypothetical, is not uncommon. Studies have shown that distortions of this type occur regularly in traditional systems in which a significant variation exists in the volume and complexity of products and services produced.[2] Traditional systems tend to overcost high-volume, low-complexity products, and they tend to undercost low-volume, high-complexity products. These studies indicate that the typical amount of overcosting is up to 200% for high-volume products with low complexity and that the typical undercosting can be more than 1,000% for low-volume, highly complex products. In companies with a large number of different products, traditional costing can show that most products are profitable. After changing to ABC, however, these companies might find that 10% to 15% of the products are profitable while the remainder are unprofitable. Adopting ABC often leads to increased profits merely by changing the product mix to minimize the number of unprofitable products.

Most companies initially do not abandon their traditional cost system and move to a system that uses ABC for management and financial reporting purposes because financial statements must withstand the scrutiny of auditors and tax authorities. This scrutiny typically implies more demands on the cost accounting system for consistency, objectivity, and uniformity than required when the system is used only for management purposes. In addition, ABC systems must be built facility by facility rather than being embedded in a software program that can be used by all facilities within the company.[3] Often companies maintain traditional costing for external reporting purposes and ABC for pricing and other internal decision-making purposes.

Once an ABC system has been developed for a production facility, including an activities list (sometimes called an activities dictionary), identification of activity cost drivers, and calculation of cost per unit of driver activity, the activity costs of a current or proposed product can be readily determined. In ABC, as illustrated for Danone, manufacturing a product is viewed simply as the combination of activities selected to make it; therefore, the activity cost of a product or service is the sum of the costs of those activities. This approach to viewing a product enables management to evaluate the importance of each of the activities consumed in making a product. Possibly some activities can be eliminated or a lower cost activity substituted for a more costly one without reducing the quality or performance of the product.

---

[1] Gary Cokins, "Implementing Activity-Based Costing" (Institute of Management Accountants, 2014).

[2] Gary Cokins, Alan Stratton, and Jack Helbling, *An ABC Manager's Primer* (Montvale, NJ: Institute of Management Accountants, 1993).

[3] Robert S. Kaplan and Robin Cooper, *Cost and Effect* (Boston: Harvard Business School Press, 1998), p. 105.

In the 1980s, the Coca-Cola Company used ABC to determine that it was less costly—and thus, more profitable—to deliver soft drink concentrate to some fountain drink retailers (such as fast-food restaurants) in nonreturnable, disposable containers rather than in returnable stainless steel containers, which had been standard in the industry for many years.

Although an ABC system may be complex, it merely mirrors the complexity of an organization's design, manufacturing, and distribution systems. If a firm's products are diverse and its production and distribution procedures complex, the ABC system will also be complex; however, if its products are homogeneous and its production environment relatively simple, its ABC system should also be relatively simple. Even in highly complex manufacturing environments, ABC systems usually have no more than 10 to 20 cost pools. Many ABC experts in practice have observed that creating a large number of activity cost pools for a given costing application normally does not significantly improve cost accuracy above that of a smaller number of cost pools. As with any information system design, the costs of developing and maintaining the system must not exceed its benefits; hence, although adding more activity cost pools may result in some small amount of increased accuracy, it may be so small as not to be cost effective.

In addition to using ABC for product costing purposes, other important uses for ABC have also been found. One of the most useful applications for ABC discussed in the next section is in evaluating customer costs and distribution channel costs. Other applications include costing administrative functions such as processing accounts receivable or accounts payable; costing the process of hiring and training employees; and costing such menial tasks as processing a letter or copying a document. Any process, function, or activity performed in an organization, whether it is related to production, marketing and sales, finance and accounting, human resources, or even research and development, is a candidate for ABC analysis. In short, almost any cost object that has more than an insignificant amount of indirect costs can be more effectively measured using ABC.

Research Insight ■ A Time-Based Refinement of ABC for Health Care

ABC's complexity is both a strength and a weakness. To successfully implement ABC, an organization must be able to model and measure its production process in great detail. In industries such as health care this is all but impossible. Kaplan and his colleagues introduced a refinement to ABC in 2004 and tested its application to health care in 2011 with the help of several hospitals. Time-Driven Activity-Based Costing (TDABC) makes the patient and the diagnoses the unit of analysis. Rather than defining complex sets of activities and their rates, TDABC uses historical data to estimate two relationships—the cost of each resource used in treatment and the amount of time the patient spends with each resource.

These estimated relationships allow hospitals and other organizations to implement ABC without completely characterizing their activities. It also allows hospitals to determine which resources are particularly costly and focus on those resources for cost control. Thus, the benefits of ABC can be realized without the implementation issues discussed in this module. TDABC integrates easily with existing resource planning processes. The Mayo Clinic is a successful example of the benefits of TDABC implementation. It treats the TDABC process like it would any other improvement in medical care—as a scientific inquiry. It assembles a project team from every level of the organization and the group uses Kaplan's principles to estimate time/resource cost relationships. These relationships lead to experiments for improvement where they test the changes suggested in the TDABC process. Their findings are then shared with the whole organization.

Sources: Derek Haas, Richard Helmers, March Rucci, Meredith Brady, and Robert Kaplan, "The Mayo Clinic Model for Running a Value-Improvement Program," *Harvard Business Review*, October 22, 2015; Robert Kaplan and Michael Porter, "The Big Idea: How to Solve the Cost Crisis in Health Care," *Harvard Business Review*, September 2011; Alex Santana and Paulo Afonso, "Analysis of Studies on Time-Driven Activity Based Costing," *International Journal of Management Science & Technology Information* 15 (2015): 133–157.

Review 19-4 LO4

Refer to Review 19-3 on page 19-12 and review your unit cost calculations in parts *a*, *b*, and *c*.

Required

Based on your calculations, compare and contrast the unit costs of the Cobra Latch and GrimLoc using the plantwide, department, and activity-based rates to assign manufacturing overhead.

Solution on p. 19-39.

ABC and Customer Profitability Analysis

One of the most beneficial applications of activity-based costing is in the analysis of the profitability of customers. Companies that have a large number of diverse customers also usually have widely varied profits from serving those customers. Many companies never attempt to calculate the profit earned from individual customers. They merely assume that if they are selling products above their costs, and that overall the company is earning a profit, then each of the customers must be profitable. Unfortunately, the cost incurred to sell goods and services, and to provide service, to individual customers is not usually proportionate with the gross profits generated by those sales. Customers with high sales volume are not necessarily the most profitable. Profitability of individual customers depends on whether the gross profits from sales to those customers exceed the customer-specific costs of serving those customers. Some customers are simply more costly than others, and some may even be unprofitable, and the unprofitable customers are eating away at the total profits of the company. In an ideal world, only profitable customers would be retained, and unprofitable customers would be either converted to a profitable status or they would be dropped as customers.

eLectures **LO5**

MBC Analyze customer profitability using activity-based costing.

Customer Profitability Profile

If a company knows the amount of profits (or losses) generated by each of its customers, a **customer profitability profile** can be prepared similar to the one illustrated in Exhibit 19.3.

This hypothetical company has 350 customers and has current total profits of $5 million, but only 200 of its customers are profitable. Cumulative profits reach $7.5 million when the 200th customer is added to the graph, but the 201st through the 350th customers cause cumulative profits to decline to $5 million because they are unprofitable. Once a company has profitability data on each of its customers (or categories of customers), only then can it proceed to try to convert them to profitability, or seek to terminate the relationship with those customers. Just as we saw that ABC provided a model for producing more accurate product cost data, ABC is also a valuable tool for generating customer profitability data.

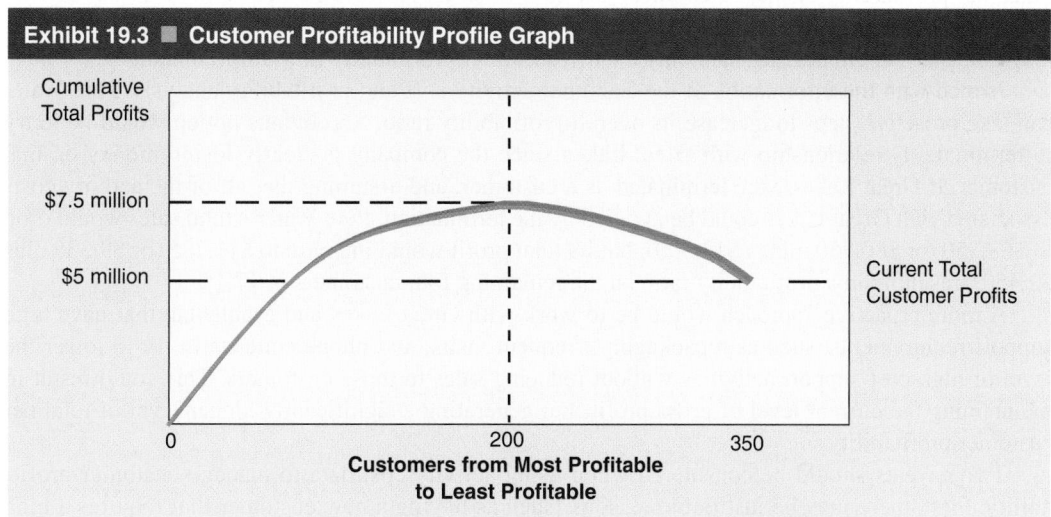

Exhibit 19.3 ■ Customer Profitability Profile Graph

ABC Customer Profitability Analysis Illustrated

Pure Water Company is a "green" company located in the Midwest that manufactures and sells all-natural compounds for purifying water distributed through large public water systems. The CEO and founder of Pure Water personally developed the compounds using natural materials obtained from remote regions of the world. He knows that he has a product that is far superior to the traditional processes based on synthetic chemicals that have been used for generations to purify water. After five years in business, Pure Water has built a solid and growing customer base, but it has to invest significant time and expense servicing customers, especially those who have recently embraced its approach to water purification. Some customers require a lot of "hand-holding" with frequent visits and telephone calls, and they tend to purchase frequently in small amounts, often requiring repackaging. Other customers require little attention and support, and many of them purchase in large amounts once a year.

Although the company is making money, there is concern that profits could be higher if sales and other customer-related costs could be decreased. Pure Water's accountant has decided to conduct a customer profitability analysis using activity-based costing. As a first step, she determined that there were five primary activities related to serving customers: visits of customers by sales representatives, remote contacts (phone, email, fax), processing and shipping of customer orders, repackaging, and billing and collection. After extensive analysis, including numerous interviews and statistical analyses of activity and cost data, the accountant determined the following cost drivers and cost per unit of activity for the five customer-related activities:

Activity	Activity Cost Driver	Cost per Unit of Driver Activity
Visits to customers	Visits	$800
Remote contacts	Number of contacts	75
Processing & shipping	Customer orders	450
Repackaging	Number of requests	250
Billing & collection	Invoices	90

After collecting activity driver data on each of these activities for its major customers, the accounting group prepared the customer activity cost and profitability analysis presented in Exhibit 19.4 for its five largest customers (in terms of sales dollars) in the order of greatest to least profit for the most recent year.

Since Pure Water is selling only one product to all of its customers, and has the same pricing policy for all customers, there is a constant 40% gross profit ratio across all customers, and the combined net profitability of these customers is 11.6% of sales. However, all customers are not equally profitable. The high level of support required by Manhattan and Great Lakes resulted in a net customer loss from sales to Great Lakes and only a 6.8% customer profitability ratio for Manhattan.

Armed with the information in the customer activity cost and profitability analysis, Pure Water can take proactive steps to increase its overall profitability ratio. An obvious option would be to try to terminate its relationship with Great Lakes since the company is clearly losing money on that customer. If Great Lakes were terminated as a customer, and assuming that all of the activity costs associated with Great Lakes could be avoided by the termination, Pure Water's total sales would drop to $68,750 (or $80,750 minus $12,000), but its total profit would increase to $11,785 (or $9,335 plus $2,450), resulting in a profitability ratio on the remaining four customers of 17.1%.

A more proactive approach would be to work with Great Lakes and Manhattan that have high support requirements, such as repackaging, frequent visits, and phone contacts to try to lower the level of high-cost support activities without reducing sales to those customers. This could result in maintaining the current level of gross profit, but generating a significantly higher level of total net customer profitability.

Two caveats should be considered when using activity cost data to manage customer profitability. First, there may be justifiable reasons (such as having a new customer that requires a high level of early-stage support, trying to penetrate a new geographic market, or existing relationships with other more profitable customers) for keeping customers that have lower profitability, or even customers that are not profitable. If so, these customers should be managed intensely to attempt to reduce the activities devoted to their support. Another caveat is that eliminating a customer may not immediately translate into an immediate reduction of activity costs. Some activity costs may not have a variable cost behavior pattern, and eliminating customers may merely create excess capacity in the short term. Of course, as stated previously, activity-based costing views virtually all costs

Exhibit 19.4 ■ Pure Water Company

Customer Activity Cost and Profitability Analysis

	Seattle Water District	Manhattan Water Authority	Great Lakes Utility	Gulf Coast Utilities	Consolidated Water, Inc.	Total
Customer Activity Cost Analysis						
Activity Cost Driver Data						
Visits to customers	3	5	4	1	1	
Remote contacts.	5	7	8	2	3	
Processing & shipping	3	3	5	4	1	
Repackaging.	0	2	3	0	0	
Billing & collection.	3	3	5	4	1	
Customer Activity Cost						
Visits to customers	$ 2,400	$ 4,000	$ 3,200	$ 800	$ 800	
Remote contacts.	375	525	600	150	225	
Processing & shipping	1,350	1,350	2,250	1,800	450	
Repackaging.	0	500	750	0	0	
Billing & collection.	270	270	450	360	90	
Total Activity Cost	$ 4,395	$ 6,645	$ 7,250	$ 3,110	$ 1,565	
Customer Profitability Analysis						
Customer sales.	$17,500	$20,000	$12,000	$15,000	$16,250	$80,750
Less cost of goods sold	10,500	12,000	7,200	9,000	9,750	48,450
Gross profit on sales.	7,000	8,000	4,800	6,000	6,500	32,300
Less activity costs.	4,395	6,645	7,250	3,110	1,565	22,965
Customer profitability	$ 2,605	$ 1,355	$ (2,450)	$ 2,890	$ 4,935	$ 9,335
Customer profitability ratio*.	14.9%	6.8%	(20.4%)	19.3%	30.4%	11.6%

* Customer profitability ÷ Sales

as variable in the longer term. As the following Business Insight illustrates, despite these limitations, customer profitability analysis can provide valuable information to help keep an organization focused on its most profitable customers. In the case of **General Growth Properties**, understanding its customer profitability profile allowed it to adjust its leasing strategy to meet the changing needs of the retail industry.

Business Insight ■ Activity-Based Costing Helps Malls Adapt

Zappos, a subsidiary of **Amazon.com**, has a unique management structure. Instead of a centralized, top-down corporate structure, Zappos operates in more of a marketplace system. Zappos "teams" (around 460 in early 2020) are operated like small businesses.

Each team is expected to manage its own profit-and-loss statement. Revenues are earned in most teams by selling their products to external customers or by selling their skills and services to other teams at market rates. Teams not focused on short-term profits, like research and development, are expected to fund their expenses through sponsorships from other teams.

Recently, the focus at Zappos has been to expand its offerings. CEO Tony Shieh said, "People can only wear so many shoes, the market is only so big." Employees are now being asked to consider possible services that Zappos could offer to entrepreneurs, similar to the way Amazon moved from selling books to selling just about everything to providing cloud computing services. Services could include anything from legal support to data analysis. Ideas that are considered promising receive $5,000 in seed funding as well as coaching and mentoring from Zappos employees.

The belief at Zappos is that encouraging "an entrepreneurial spirit and high degree of self-sovereignty" will result in revenue-producing or cost-cutting innovations that more than offset the costs related to self-direction and internal negotiations.

ABC can help Zappos teams analyze the relative profits of their current products and services and determine the profitability of new products and services.

Source: Aimee Growth, "Zappos Has Quietly Backed Away from Holacracy," *QUARTZ at WORK*, January 29, 2020.

Review 19-5 LO5

Suppose SAP is a systems design and implementation firm that serves five different types of customers. Assume SAP's design and installation projects are fairly standardized and routine; hence, the pricing is also standardized for all customers. While the company is profitable overall, the CFO thinks the net margins should be higher. She is concerned that customer support costs are eating up some of the margin and has decided to do a customer profitability analysis based on the five different types of customers to see if some of the customer groups may actually be less profitable than others. The following data for the most recent period have been collected to support the analysis.

Support Activity	Driver	Cost per Driver Unit
A. Minor systems maintenance	Hours on jobs	$160
B. Visits to customer	Number of visits	$300
C. Communication	Number of calls	$ 50

Customer Group	Activity A	Activity B	Activity C	Profit Before Support Costs
1......................	69	25	128	$80,000
2......................	141	42	205	85,000
3......................	74	19	99	83,000
4......................	61	28	106	90,000
5......................	136	39	189	78,000

Required

a. Calculate the customer profitability for each customer group taking into account the support activity required for each customer group.

b. Comment on the usefulness of this type of analysis. What reasonable actions might the company take as a result of this analysis?

Solution on p. 19-39.

Activity-Based Management

The Difference Between ABC and Activity-Based Management

eLectures LO6
MBC Explain the difference between activity-based costing and activity-based management.

Activity-based costing has been highly touted as a technique for improving the measurement of the cost and profitability of products, customers, and other cost objects. In the early development of ABC, it was discovered that a by-product of accurately measuring the cost using ABC is that management invariably gains a much better understanding of the processes and activities that are used to create cost objects, such as products. Although ABC could be justified on the basis of its value as a tool in helping produce more accurate cost measurements for various cost objects, its greatest potential value may be in its by-products. The access to ABC data enables managers to engage in **activity-based management (ABM)**, defined as the identification and selection of activities to maximize the value of the activities while minimizing their cost from the perspective of the final consumer. In other words, ABM is concerned with how to efficiently and effectively manage activities and processes to provide value to the final consumer.

Defining processes and identifying key activities helps management better understand the business and to evaluate whether activities being performed add value to the customer. ABM focuses managerial attention on what is most important among the activities performed to create value for customers.

A helpful analogy in understanding what ABC can do for a company is to compare a company's operations with a large retail store, such as a **Home Depot** store. In a Home Depot store there is a clearly marked price on each of the tens of thousands of individual items that customers may decide to purchase. Similarly, every activity that takes place in any organization has a cost that can be determined and that management can use to make a judgment about the activity's value. In an ideal world, a manager could walk through the business and evaluate the cost of every activity being performed—maybe thousands of different activities—and then decide which ones are worth the cost and which ones are not adding value. Since generating ABC data has a cost, management must decide which ABC data are likely to be useful and cost beneficial. Our discussion here is only an introduction to activity-based costing and some of its applications. As the following Research Insight points out, over the past quarter of a century, ABC has matured well beyond merely accurately measuring cost of products and customers. More advanced topics such as those shown in the graphic are covered in advanced managerial accounting (or cost accounting) courses.

Research Insight   ■   The Maturing of Activity-Based Costing

One of the leading thinkers and authors on the topic of activity-based costing over the past 25 years has been Peter B. B. Turney. He recently traced the evolution of ABC within the context of a product life cycle showing how ABC functionality has expanded since it was first introduced in the 1980s. As this graphic shows, ABC is now in its fourth generation, where it has become "an integral part of business performance management solutions, including profitability management, performance measurement, financial management, sustainability, and human capital management." In its current state of development, a single ABC model can support a number of needs, including historical cost measurement, resource planning, performance measurement, and other analyses.

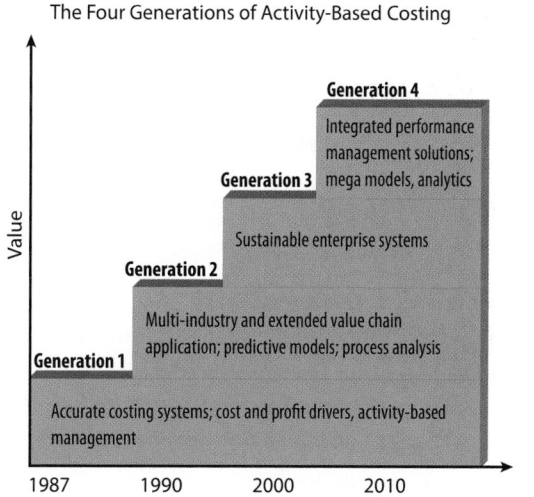

The Four Generations of Activity-Based Costing

Source: Peter B. B. Turney, "Activity-Based Costing: An Emerging Foundation for Performance Management," *Cost Management*, July/August 2010, pp. 33–42.

LO6 Review 19-6

Although ABC could be justified on the basis of its value as a tool in helping produce more accurate cost measurements for various cost objects, its greatest potential value may be in its by-products.

Required
Discuss the relationship between activity-based management and activity-based costing.

Solution on p. 19-39.

Guidance Answers

You Are the Controller
Pg. 19-12 It probably is not the right decision to abandon the ABC system because there are many benefits to using ABC other than just calculating product costs. Indeed, in cases where companies produce multiple products that are fairly homogeneous in terms of the use of resources, ABC may not produce more accurate costs than traditional methods; however, there are many uses of ABC information beyond just calculating the cost of products. Having detailed information about activities and their costs can significantly improve the management of those activities. Identifying key activities and measuring their costs often cause companies to seek more efficient processes, possibly considering outsourcing activities that are currently performed internally, or even looking for ways to eliminate activities altogether. Activity cost information can also be used to identify best practices within an organization, or to benchmark internal activity costs with other organizations.

Questions

Q19-1. Summarize the concepts underlying activity-based costing in two sentences.

Q19-2. What steps are required to implement the two-stage activity-based costing model?

Q19-3. Define activity cost pool, activity cost driver, and cost per unit of activity.

Q19-4. Name two possible activity cost drivers for each of the following activities: maintenance, materials movement, machine setup, inspection, materials purchases, and customer service.

Q19-5. What is the premise of activity-based costing for product costing purposes?

Q19-6. In what ways does ABC product costing differ from traditional product cost methods?

Q19-7. Explain why ABC often reveals existing product cost cross-subsidization problems.

Q19-8. How can ABC be used to improve customer profitability analysis?

Q19-9. Explain activity-based management and how it differs from activity-based costing.

Assignments with the ⓘ logo in the margin are available in BusinessCourse.
See the Preface of the book for details.

Mini Exercises

LO2

M19-10. Activities and Cost Drivers

For each of the following activities, select the most appropriate cost driver. Each cost driver may be used only once.

Activity	Cost Driver
1. Pay vendors	*a.* Number of different kinds of raw materials
2. Evaluate vendors	*b.* Number of classes offered
3. Inspect raw materials	*c.* Number of tables
4. Plan for purchases of raw materials	*d.* Number of employees
5. Packaging	*e.* Number of operating hours
6. Supervision	*f.* Number of units of raw materials received
7. Employee training	*g.* Number of moves
8. Clean tables	*h.* Number of vendors
9. Machine maintenance	*i.* Number of checks issued
10. Move in-process product from one workstation to the next	*j.* Number of customer orders

LO2

Southwest Airlines
(LUV)

M19-11. Developing a List of Activities for Baggage Handling at an Airport

Assume you have been asked to determine the activities involved in the baggage-handling process of Southwest Airlines' Chicago-Midway hub. Prior to conducting observations and interviews, you decide that a list of possible activities would help you to better observe key activities and ask meaningful questions.

Required

For incoming aircraft only, develop a sequential list of baggage-handling activities. Your list should contain between 8 and 10 activities.

LO2

University of Texas

M19-12. Stage 1 ABC at a College: Assigning Costs to Activities

Assume an accounting professor at the University of Texas devotes 60% of her time to teaching, 30% of her time to research and writing, and 10% of her time to service activities such as committee work and curriculum development. The professor teaches two semesters per year. During each semester, she teaches one section of an introductory financial accounting course (with a maximum enrollment of 60 students) and one section of a graduate financial accounting course (with a maximum enrollment of 30 students). Including course preparation, classroom instruction, and appointments with students, each course requires an equal amount of time. The accounting professor is paid $150,000 per year.

Required

Determine the activity cost of instruction per student in both the introductory and the graduate financial accounting courses.

M19-13. Stage 1 ABC for a Machine Shop: Assigning Costs to Activities

As the chief engineer of a small fabrication shop, Christine Sanders refers to herself as a "jack-of-all-trades." When an order for a new product comes in, Christine must do the following:

1. Design the product to meet customer requirements.
2. Prepare a bill of materials (a list of materials required to produce the product).
3. Prepare an operations list (a sequential list of the steps involved in manufacturing the product).

Each time the foundry manufactures a batch of the product, Christine must perform these activities:

1. Schedule the job.
2. Supervise the setup of machines that will work on the job.
3. Inspect the first unit produced to verify that it meets specifications.

Christine supervises the production employees who perform the actual work on individual units of product. She is also responsible for employee training, ensuring that production facilities are in proper operating condition, and attending professional meetings. Christine's estimates (in percent) of time spent on each of these activities last year are as follows:

Designing product.	15%
Preparing bills of materials.	5
Preparing operations lists.	9
Scheduling jobs.	12
Supervising setups.	6
Inspecting first units.	7
Supervising production.	25
Training employees.	8
Maintaining facility.	3
Attending professional meetings.	10
	100%

Required

Assuming Christine Sanders' salary is $115,000 per year, determine the dollar amount of her salary assigned to unit-, batch-, product-, and facility-level activities. (You may need to review Module 15 before answering this question.)

M19-14. Stage 2 ABC for a Wholesale Company

Charlie's Produce is a West Coast distributor of fresh produce. Assume the following information represents activity costs for the Los Angeles distribution center.

Activity	Cost per Unit of Activity Driver
Customer relations.	$110.00 per customer per month
Selling.	0.05 per sales dollar
Accounting.	7.50 per order
Warehousing.	0.60 per case shipped
Packing.	0.30 per case shipped
Shipping.	0.05 per pound shipped

The following information pertains to June operations for the Los Angeles distribution center of Charlie's Produce.

Number of orders.	3,220
Sales revenue.	$2,150,000
Cost of produce sold.	$1,405,000
Number of customers.	432
Cases shipped.	57,850
Pounds shipped.	1,250,000

Required

Determine the profitability of sales in the Los Angeles distribution center for June.

LO2

M19-15. Stage 2 ABC for Manufacturing: Reassigning Costs to Cost Objects

Woodland Corporation has developed the following activity cost information for its manufacturing activities:

Activity	Activity Cost
Machine setup	$120.00 per batch
Movement	15.00 per batch move
	0.10 per pound, per move
Drilling	6.00 per hole
Welding	4.00 per inch
Shaping	22.00 per hour
Assembly	18.00 per hour
Inspection	2.00 per unit

Filling an order for a batch of 125 fireplace inserts (each insert weighing 50 pounds) required the following:

- Four batch moves
- Three sets of inspections
- Drilling eight holes in each unit
- Completing 100 inches of welds on each unit
- Forty-five minutes of shaping for each unit
- One hour of assembly per unit

Required

Determine the activity cost of converting the raw materials into 125 fireplace inserts.

LO2

The Vollrath Company

M19-16. Two-Stage ABC for Manufacturing

Vollrath Manufacturing, a division of The Vollrath Company, manufactures restaurant equipment. Assume the company has determined the following activity cost pools and cost driver levels for the year:

Activity Cost Pool	Activity Cost	Activity Cost Driver
Machine setup	$750,000	18,750 setup hours
Material handling	121,600	3,800 tons of materials
Machine operation	552,500	16,250 machine hours

The following data are for the production of single batches of two products, Equipment Stands and Charbroilers during the month of August:

	Equipment Stands	Charbroilers
Units produced	100	50
Machine hours	8	25
Direct labor hours	400	1,200
Direct labor cost	$10,000	$30,000
Direct materials cost	$48,000	$125,000
Tons of materials	4	14
Setup hours	6	36

Required

Determine the unit costs of Equipment Stands and Charbroilers using ABC.

LO2

Sherwin-Williams (SHW)

M19-17. Two-Stage ABC for Manufacturing

Assume Sherwin-Williams, a large paint manufacturer, has determined the following activity cost pools and cost driver levels for the latest period:

Activity Cost Pool	Activity Cost	Activity Cost Driver
Machine setup	$210,000	3,500 setup hours
Material handling	468,000	6,500 material moves
Machine operation	1,026,270	12,670 machine hours

The following data are for the production of single batches of two of its products, Cashmere and Emerald:

	Cashmere	Emerald
Gallons produced	20,000	25,000
Direct labor hours	200	220
Machine hours	100	120
Direct labor cost	$5,000	$5,500
Direct materials cost	$282,940	$299,090
Setup hours	24	26
Material moves	35	40

Required
Determine the batch and unit costs per gallon of Cashmere and Emerald using ABC.

M19-18. Customer Profitability Analysis   **LO5**

Elite Services, Inc. provides residential painting services for three home building companies, Brookside, Edgewater, and Hillrose, and it uses a job costing system for determining the costs for completing each job. The job cost system does not capture any cost incurred by Elite for return touchups and refinishes after the homeowner occupies the home. Elite paints each house on a square footage contract price, which includes painting as well as all refinishes and touchups required after the homes are occupied. Each year, the company generates about one-third of its total revenues and gross profits from each of the three builders. The Elite owner has observed that the builders, however, require substantially different levels of support following the completion of jobs. The following data have been gathered:

Support Activity	Driver	Cost per Driver Unit
Major refinishes	Hours on jobs	$150
Touchups	Number of visits	$100
Communication	Number of calls	$ 30

Builder	Major Refinishes	Touchups	Communication
Brookside	120	260	900
Edgewater	70	205	530
Hillrose	80	220	590

Required
Assuming that each of the three customers produces gross profits of $150,000, calculate the profitability from each builder after taking into account the support activity required for each builder.

Exercises

E19-19. Two-Stage ABC for Manufacturing   **LO2**

Thornton Company has determined its activity cost pools and cost drivers to be the following:

Cost pools	
Setup	$ 55,000
Material handling	10,050
Machine operation	242,400
Packing	67,200
Total indirect manufacturing costs	$374,650

continued

continued from previous page

Cost drivers	
Setups	550
Material moves	670
Machine hours	20,200
Packing orders	1,400

One product made by Thornton, metal casements, used the following activities during the period to produce 500 units:

Setups	45
Material moves	112
Machine hours	2,400
Packing orders	195

Required

a. Calculate the cost per unit of activity for each activity cost pool for Thornton Company.

b. Calculate the manufacturing overhead cost per metal casement manufactured during the period.

LO3, 4   **E19-20.   Calculating Manufacturing Overhead Rates**

Windsor Company accumulated the following data from last year's operations.

Milling Department manufacturing overhead	$450,000
Finishing Department manufacturing overhead	$150,000
Machine hours used	
Milling Department	15,000 hours
Finishing Department	5,000 hours
Labor hours used	
Milling Department	2,000 hours
Finishing Department	2,000 hours

In the Milling department, grooves are cut into aluminum and steel rods using computer-controlled equipment. In the Finishing department, the rods are individually cleaned and polished.

Required

a. Calculate the plantwide manufacturing overhead rate using machine hours as the allocation base.

b. Calculate the plantwide manufacturing overhead rate using direct labor hours as the allocation base.

c. Calculate department overhead rates using machine hours in Milling and direct labor hours in Finishing as the allocation bases.

d. Calculate department overhead rates using direct labor hours in Milling and machine hours in Finishing as the allocation bases.

e. Which of these allocation systems seems to be the most appropriate? Explain.

LO2, 3, 4   **E19-21.   Calculating Activity-Based Costing Overhead Rates**

Assume that manufacturing overhead for Windsor Company in the previous exercise consisted of the following activities and costs:

Setup (2,500 setup hours)	$125,000
Production scheduling (150 batches)	75,000
Production engineering (20,000 machine hours)	265,000
Supervision (4,000 direct labor hours)	85,800
Machine maintenance (1,025 repair requests)	49,200
Total activity costs	$600,000

The following additional data were provided for Job 845:

Direct materials costs	$1,450
Direct labor cost (5 Milling direct labor hours; 15 Finishing direct labor hours)	$ 500
Setup hours	2 hours
Production scheduling	1 batch
Machine hours used (15 Milling machine hours; 5 Finishing machine hours)	20 hours
Machine maintenance	1 repair request

Required

a. Calculate the cost per unit of activity driver for each activity cost category.

b. Calculate the cost of Job 845 using ABC to assign the overhead costs.

c. Calculate the cost of Job 845 using the plantwide overhead rate based on machine hours calculated in the previous exercise.

d. Calculate the cost of Job 845 using a machine hour departmental overhead rate for the Milling Department and a direct labor hour overhead rate for the Finishing Department (see E19-20).

E19-22. Activity-Based Costing and Traditional Costs Compared

LO2, 3, 4
Conair Corporation

Cuisinart, a Conair Corporation, manufactures outdoor gas cookers and charcoal smokers. Assume that Cuisinart only makes a single model of each product and that the following information pertains to the total manufacturing costs for the products in the current month.

	Gas Cooker	Charcoal Smoker
Units.	4,000	3,500
Number of batches.	80	35
Number of machine hours	16,000	3,000
Direct materials.	$225,500	$108,500
Direct labor.	$100,683	$50,341

Manufacturing overhead follows:

Activity	Cost	Cost Driver
Materials acquisition and inspection.	$ 50,100	Amount of direct materials cost
Product assembly.	123,500	Number of machine hours
Scheduling	15,180	Number of batches
	$188,780	

Required

a. Determine the total and per-unit costs of manufacturing the Gas Cooker and Charcoal Smoker for the month, assuming all manufacturing overhead related to these two products is assigned on the basis of direct labor dollars.

b. Determine the total and per-unit costs of manufacturing the Gas Cooker and Charcoal Smoker for the month, assuming manufacturing overhead is assigned using activity-based costing.

E19-23. Activity-Based Costing Versus Traditional Costing

LO1, 3, 4

Refer to the previous exercise in E19-22 for Cuisinart.

Required

a. Comment on the differences between the solutions to requirements (a) and (b). Which is more accurate? What errors might managers make if all manufacturing overhead costs are assigned on the basis of direct labor dollars?

b. Cuisinart's manufacturing process has become increasingly automated over the past few years. Discuss how this will likely impact its ability to accurately measure product costs.

c. Comment on the adequacy of the preceding data to meet management's needs.

E19-24. Traditional Product Costing versus Activity-Based Costing

LO2, 3, 4
Panasonic Corporation (PCRFY)

Assume that Panasonic Corporation has determined its estimated total manufacturing overhead cost for one of its plants to be $436,000, consisting of the following activity cost pools for the current month:

Activity Centers	Activity Costs	Cost Drivers	Activity Level
Assembly setups	$124,000	Setup hours	4,000
Materials handling	57,000	Number of moves.	600
Assembly	225,000	Assembly hours	12,500
Maintenance.	30,000	Maintenance hours.	1,200
Total	$436,000		

Total direct labor hours used during the month were 16,000. Panasonic produces many different electronic products, including the following two products produced during the current month:

	Model X301	Model Z205
Units produced	2,000	2,000
Direct materials costs	$18,550	$18,550
Direct labor costs	$5,000	$5,000
Direct labor hours	200	200
Setup hours	30	60
Materials moves	75	150
Assembly hours	500	750
Maintenance hours	25	45

Required

a. Calculate the total per-unit cost of each model using direct labor hours to assign manufacturing overhead to products.

b. Calculate the total per-unit cost of each model using activity-based costing to assign manufacturing overhead to products.

c. Comment on the accuracy of the two methods for determining product costs.

d. Discuss some of the strategic implications of your answers to the previous requirements.

LO2, 3, 4

E19-25. Traditional Product Costing versus Activity-Based Costing

Ridgeland Inc. makes backpacks for large sporting goods chains that are sold under the customers' store brand names. The Accounting Department has identified the following overhead costs and cost drivers for next year:

Overhead Item	Expected Costs	Cost Driver	Maximum Quantity
Setup costs	$175,000	Number of setups	1,750
Ordering costs	120,000	Number of orders	15,000
Assembly	910,000	Number of machine hours	14,000
Finishing	208,000	Number of direct labor hours	104,000

The following data are for two recently completed jobs:

	Job 201	Job 202
Cost of direct materials	$12,000	$14,000
Cost of direct labor	$20,500	$40,000
Number of units completed	1,000	850
Number of setups	15	18
Number of orders	200	100
Number of machine hours	200	225
Number of direct labor hours	820	1,600

Required

a. Determine the unit cost for each job using a traditional plantwide overhead rate based on machine hours.

b. Determine the unit cost for each job using ABC. (Round answers to two decimal places.)

c. As the manager of Ridgeland, is there additional information that you would want to help you evaluate the pricing and profitability of Jobs 201 and 202?

d. Assuming the company has been using the method required in part a, how should management react to the findings in part b?

LO5, 6

E19-26. Customer Profitability Analysis

Leahy Inc. has 10 customers that account for all of its $1,472,000 of net income. Its activity-based costing system is able to assign all costs, except for $200,000 of general administrative costs, to key activities incurred in connection with serving its customers. A customer profitability analysis based on activity costing produced the following customer profits and losses:

Customer	#1	$ 350,000
	#2	262,000
	#3	(75,000)
	#4	240,000
	#5	50,000
	#6	375,000
	#7	(100,000)
	#8	325,000
	#9	225,000
	#10	(180,000)
Total		$1,472,000

Required
Prepare a customer profitability profile like the one in Exhibit 19.3.

E19-27. Customer Profitability Analysis LO5
Refer to the previous exercise E19-26 for Leahy Inc.

Required
a. If Leahy were to notify customers 3, 7, and 10 that it will no longer be able to provide them services in the future, will that increase company profits by $355,000? Why or why not?
b. What is the primary benefit of preparing a customer profitability analysis?

Problems

P19-28. Two-Stage ABC for Manufacturing with ABC Variances LO2, 3, 4
Meade Manufacturing developed the following activity cost pool information for its current year manufacturing activities:

	Budgeted Activity Cost	Activity Cost Driver at Practical Capacity
Purchasing and materials handling	$ 475,000	950,000 kilograms
Setup	225,000	1,500 setups
Machine operations	1,540,000	14,000 machine hours
First unit inspection	280,000	1,600 batches
Packaging	100,000	200,000 units

Actual production information for three of Meade's products during the year is as follows:

	Standard Product A	Standard Product B	Specialty Products
Units	35,000	15,000	10,000
Batches	140	50	400
Setups*	150	45	800
Machine hours	1,200	650	800
Kilograms of raw materials	175,000	65,000	95,000
Direct materials costs	$58,000	$44,350	$27,000
Direct labor costs	$95,500	$64,900	$45,000

* Some products require setups on two or more machines.

Required
a. Determine the unit cost of each product for Meade Manufacturing under activity-based costing.
b. Explain why the unit cost of the specialty products is so much higher than the unit cost of Standard Product A or Standard Product B.

LO2, 3, 4   **P19-29. ABC—A Service Application**

Grand Haven is a senior living community that offers a full range of services including independent living, assisted living, and skilled nursing care. The assisted living division provides residential space, meals, and medical services (MS) to its residents. The current costing system adds the cost of all of these services (space, meals, and MS) and divides by total resident days to get a cost per resident day. Recognizing that MS tends to vary significantly among the residents, Grand Haven's accountant recommended that an ABC system be designed to calculate more accurately the cost of MS provided to residents. She decided that residents should be classified into four categories (A, B, C, D) based on the level of services received, with group A representing the lowest level of service and D representing the highest level of service. Two cost drivers being considered for measuring MS costs are number of assistance calls and number of assistant contacts. A contact is registered each time an assistance professional provides medical services or aid to a resident. The accountant has gathered the following data for the most recent annual period:

Resident Classification	Annual Resident Days	Annual Assistance Hours	Number of Assistance Contacts
A	18,000	9,100	27,000
B	10,000	22,500	31,000
C	5,500	23,000	27,500
D	3,000	18,400	24,000
	36,500	73,000	109,500

Other data

Total cost of medical services for the period $4,927,500
Total cost of meals and residential space $2,591,500

Required (round answers to the nearest dollar):

a. Determine the total cost of a resident day using the current system.

b. Determine the ABC cost of a resident day for each category of residents using assistance hours as the cost driver for medical services and resident days as the cost driver for meals and residential space.

c. Determine the ABC cost of a resident day for each category of residents using assistance contacts as the cost driver for medical services and resident days as the cost driver for meals and residential space.

d. Which cost driver do you think provides the more accurate measure of the cost per day for a Grand Haven resident?

LO2, 3, 4
Molitor Financial
Group

P19-30. ABC Costing for a Service Organization

Molitor Financial Group is a full-service residential mortgage company in the Chicago area that operates in a very competitive market. Assume management is concerned about operating costs associated with processing mortgage applications and has decided to install an ABC costing system to help them get a handle on costs. Although labor hours seem to be the primary driver of the cost of processing a new mortgage, the labor cost for the different activities involved in processing new loans varies widely. The Accounting Department has provided the following data for the company's five major cost pools for the current year:

Activity Cost Pools		Activity Drivers	
Taking customer applications	$ 306,000	Time—assistant managers	3,600 hours
Conducting credit investigations	378,000	Time—credit managers	5,400 hours
Underwriting	405,000	Time—Underwriting Department	5,400 hours
Preparing loan packages	594,000	Time—Processing Department	10,800 hours
Closing loans	396,000	Time—Legal Department	3,600 hours
	$2,079,000		28,800 hours

During the year, the company processed and issued 900 new mortgages, two of which are summarized here with regard to activities used to process the mortgages:

	Loan 7023	Loan 8955
Application processing hours	2.00	4.00
Credit investigating hours	3.00	5.00
Underwriting hours	6.00	6.00
Processing hours	9.00	18.00
Legal hours	4.00	6.00
Total hours	24.00	39.00

Required

a. Determine the cost per unit of activity for each activity cost pool.

b. Determine the cost of processing loans 7023 and 8955.

c. Determine the cost of preparing loans 7023 and 8955 assuming that an average cost per hour for all activities is used.

d. Compare and discuss your answers to requirements (*b*) and (*c*).

P19-31. Activity-Based Costing in a Service Organization   LO2, 3, 4, 6

Banctronics Inc. has 10 automatic teller machines (ATMs) spread throughout the city maintained by the ATM Department. You have been assigned the task of determining the cost of operating each machine. Management will use the information you develop, along with other information pertaining to the volume and type of transactions at each machine, to evaluate the desirability of continuing to operate each machine and/or changing security arrangements for a particular machine.

The ATM Department consists of a total of six employees: a supervisor, a head cashier, two associate cashiers, and two maintenance personnel. The associate cashiers make between two and four daily trips to each machine to collect and replenish cash and to replenish supplies, deposit tickets, and so forth. Each machine contains a small computer that automatically summarizes and reports transactions to the head cashier. The head cashier reconciles the activities of the two associate cashiers to the computerized reports. The supervisor, who does not handle cash, reviews the reconciliation. When an automatic teller's computer, a customer, or a cashier reports a problem, the two maintenance employees and one cashier are dispatched immediately. The cashier removes all cash and transaction records, and the maintenance employees repair the machine.

Maintenance employees spend all of their time on maintenance-related activities. The associate cashiers spend approximately 25% of their time on maintenance-related activities and 75% on daily trips. The head cashier's time is divided, with 60% directly related to daily trips to each machine and 40% related to supervising cashiers on maintenance calls. The supervisor devotes 20% of the time to daily trips to each machine and 80% to the equal supervision of each employee. Cost information for a recent month follows:

Salaries	
Supervisor	$ 8,000
Head cashier	6,000
Other ($3,000 each for other cashiers; $3,500 each for maintenance employees)	13,000
Lease and operating costs	
Cashiers' service vehicle	2,400
Maintenance service vehicle	4,800
Office rent and utilities	12,000
Machine lease, space rent, and utilities ($2,000 each machine)	20,000
Total	$66,200

Related monthly activity information for this month follows:

Machine	Daily Trips	Maintenance Call Hours
1	40	22
2	50	20
3	40	18
4	80	20
5	40	22
6	80	18
7	80	24
8	30	14
9	20	16
10	40	16
Total	500	190

Additional information follows:
- The office is centrally located with about equal travel time to each machine.
- Maintenance hours include travel time.
- The cashiers' service vehicle is used exclusively for routine visits.
- The office space is divided equally between the supervisor and the head cashier.

Required

a. Determine the monthly operating costs of machines 7 and 8 when cost assignments are based on the number of machines.

b. Determine the activity cost of a routine trip and a maintenance hour for the month given. Round answers to the nearest cent.

c. Determine the operating costs assigned and reassigned to machines 7 and 8 when activity-based costing is used.

d. How can ABC cost information be used by Banctronics Inc. to improve the overall management of monthly operating costs?

LO3, 4 **P19-32.** **Product Costing: Plantwide Overhead versus Activity-Based Costing**

Sterling Industries produces machine parts as a contract provider for a large manufacturing company. Sterling produces two particular parts, shafts and gears. The competition is keen among contract producers, and Sterling's top management realizes how vulnerable its market is to cost-cutting competitors. Hence, having a very accurate understanding of costs is important to Sterling's survival.

Sterling's president, Sheila Hudson, has observed that the company's current cost to produce shafts is $23.35, and the current cost to produce gears is $14.30. She indicated to the controller that she suspects some problems with the cost system because Sterling is suddenly experiencing extraordinary competition on shafts, but it seems to have a virtual corner on the gears market. She is even considering dropping the shaft line and converting the company to a one-product manufacturer of gears. She asked the controller, George Coleman, to conduct a thorough cost study and to consider whether changes in the cost system are necessary. The controller collected the following data about the company's costs and various manufacturing activities for the most recent month:

	Shafts	Gears
Production units	50,000	18,000
Selling price	$34.95	$25.50
Overhead per unit (based on direct labor hours)	$12.50	$6.25
Materials and direct labor cost per unit	$10.85	$8.05
Number of production runs	20	30
Number of purchasing and receiving orders processed	50	98
Number of machine hours	43,000	6,500
Number of direct labor hours	25,000	4,500
Number of engineering hours	2,500	2,500
Number of material moves	62	33

The controller was able to summarize the company's total manufacturing overhead into the following pools:

Setup costs	$ 40,000
Machine costs	198,000
Purchasing and receiving costs	218,300
Engineering costs	209,000
Materials handling costs	72,200
Total	$737,500

Required

a. Calculate Sterling's current plantwide overhead rate based on direct labor hours.

b. Verify Sterling's calculation of overhead cost per unit of $12.50 for shafts and $6.25 for gears.

c. Calculate the manufacturing overhead cost per unit for shafts and gears using activity-based costing, assuming each of the five cost pools represents a separate activity pool. Use the most appropriate activity driver for assigning activity costs to the two products.

d. Comment on Sterling's current cost system and the reason the company is facing fierce competition for shafts but little competition for gears.

P19-33. Customer Profitability Analysis

LO2, 5, 6
Boeing (BA)
Airbus (AIR)

Remington Aeronautics LTD is a British aeronautics subcontract company that designs and manufactures electronic control systems for commercial airlines. The vast majority of all commercial aircraft are manufactured by **Boeing** in the U.S. and **Airbus** in Europe; however, there is a relatively small group of companies that manufacture narrow-body commercial jets. Assume for this exercise that Remington does contract work for the two major manufacturers plus three companies in the second tier.

Because competition is intense in the industry, Remington has always operated on a fairly thin 20% gross profit margin; hence, it is crucial that it manage nonmanufacturing overhead costs effectively in order to achieve an acceptable net profit margin. With declining profit margins in recent years, Remington Aeronautics' CEO, John Remington, has become concerned that the cost of obtaining contracts and maintaining relations with its five major customers may be getting out of hand. You have been hired to conduct a customer profitability analysis.

Remington Aeronautics' nonmanufacturing overhead consists of $2 million of general and administrative (G&A) expense (including, among other expenses, the CEO's salary and bonus and the cost of operating the company's corporate jet) and selling and customer support expenses of $3.15 million (including 5% sales commissions and $750,000 of additional costs).

The accounting staff determined that the $750,000 of additional selling and customer support expenses related to the following four activity cost pools:

Activity	Activity Cost Driver	Cost per Unit of Activity
1. Sales visits	Number of visit days	$1,000
2. Product adjustments	Number of adjustments	1,600
3. Phone and email contacts	Number of calls/contacts	100
4. Promotion and entertainment events	Number of events	3,000

Financial and activity data on the five customers follow (Sales and Gross Profit data in millions):

			Quantity of Sales and Support Activity			
Customer	Sales	Gross Profit	Activity 1	Activity 2	Activity 3	Activity 4
A	$19	$3.8	90	10	160	21
B	14	2.8	105	20	200	20
C	5	1.0	95	18	100	17
D	6	1.2	30	8	35	12
E	4	0.8	30	4	25	14
	$48	$9.6	350	60	520	84

In addition to the above, the sales staff used the corporate jet at a cost of $1,000 per hour for trips to customers as follows:

Customer A.	16 hours
Customer B.	32 hours
Customer C	8 hours
Customer D	0 hours
Customer E.	5 hours

The total cost of operating the airplane is included in general and administrative expense; none is included in selling and customer support costs.

Required

a. Prepare a customer profitability analysis for Remington Aeronautics that shows the gross profits less all expenses that can reasonably be assigned to the five customers.

b. Now assuming that the remaining general and administrative costs are assigned to the five customers based on relative sales dollars, calculate net profit for each customer.

c. Discuss the merits of the analysis in part a versus part b.

Management Applications

LO2, 5, 6   **MA19-34. Designing an ABC System for a Country Club**

The Reserve Club is a traditional private golf and country club that has three different categories of memberships: golf, tennis & swimming, and social. Golf members have access to all amenities and programs in the club, Tennis & Swimming members have access to all amenities and programs except use of the golf course, and Social members have access to only the social activities of the club, excluding golf, tennis, and swimming. All members have clubhouse privileges, including use of the bar and restaurant, which is operated by an outside contractor. During the past year, the average membership in each category, along with the number of club visits during the year, was:

	Members	Visits
Golf.	500	15,000
Tennis & Swimming	110	2,200
Social	250	5,000

Some members of the club have been complaining that heavy users of the club are not bearing their share of the costs through their membership fees. Dess Rosmond, General Manager of the Reserve Club, agrees that monthly fees paid by the various member groups should be based on the annual average amount of cost-related activities provided by the club for the three groups, and he intends to set fees on that basis for the coming year. The annual direct costs of operating the golf course, tennis courts, and swimming pool have been calculated by the club's controller as follows:

Golf course.	$1,250,000
Swimming pool.	75,000
Tennis courts	45,000

The operation of the bar and restaurant and all related costs, including depreciation on the bar and restaurant facilities, are excluded from this analysis. In addition to the above costs, the club incurs general overhead costs in the following amounts for the most recent (and typical) year:

General Ledger Overhead Accounts	Amounts
Indirect labor for the club management staff (the general manager, assistant general manager, membership manager, and club controller)	$375,000
Utilities (other than those directly related to golf, swimming, and tennis).	34,000
Website maintenance.	8,000
Postage	2,500
Computers and information systems maintenance	10,000
Clubhouse maintenance & depreciation.	32,000
Liability insurance.	6,000
Security contract.	15,000
	$482,500

Dess believes that the best way to assign most of the overhead costs to the three membership categories is with an activity-based system that recognizes four key activities that occur regularly in the club:

- Recruiting and providing orientation for new members
- Maintaining the membership roster and communicating with members
- Planning, scheduling, and managing club events
- Maintaining the financial records and reporting for the club

Required

a. Identify and explain which overhead costs can reasonably be assigned to one or more of the four key activities, and suggest a basis for making the assignment.

b. Identify a cost driver for each activity cost pool that would seem to be suitable for assigning the activity cost pool to the three membership categories.

c. Suggest a method for assigning any overhead costs to the three membership categories that cannot reasonably be assigned to activity pools.

d. Comment on the suitability of ABC to this cost assignment situation.

MA19-35. Product Costing: Department versus Activity-Based Costing for Overhead   LO2, 4, 6

Advertising Technologies, Inc. (ATI) specializes in providing both published and online advertising services for the business marketplace. The company monitors its costs based on the cost per column inch of published space printed in print advertising media and based on the cost per minute of online advertising time delivered on "The AD Line," a computer-based, online advertising service. ATI has one new competitor, Tel-a-Ad, in its local online advertising market; and with increased competition, ATI has seen a decline in sales of online advertising in recent years. ATI's president, Robert Beard, believes that predatory pricing by Tel-a-Ad has caused the problem. The following is a recent conversation between Robert and Jane Minnear, director of marketing for ATI.

Jane: I just received a call from one of our major customers concerning our advertising rates on "The AD Line" who said that a sales rep from another firm (it had to be Tel-a-Ad) had offered the same service at $1 per minute, which is $0.75 per minute less than our price.

Robert: It's costing about $1.40 per minute to produce that product. I don't see how they can afford to sell it so cheaply. I'm not convinced that we should meet the price. Perhaps the better strategy is to emphasize producing and selling more published ads, which we're more experienced with and where our margins are high and we have virtually no competition.

Jane: You may be right. Based on a recent survey of our customers, I think we can raise the price significantly for published advertising and still not lose business.

Robert: That sounds promising; however, before we make a major recommitment to publishing, let's explore other possible explanations. I want to know how our costs compare with our competitors. Maybe we could be more efficient and find a way to earn a good return on online advertising.

After this meeting, Robert and Jane requested an investigation of production costs and comparative efficiency of producing published versus online advertising services. The controller, Tim Gentry, indicated that ATI's efficiency was comparable to that of its competitors and prepared the following cost data:

	Published Advertising	Online Advertising
Estimated number of production units	100,000	5,000,000
Selling price	$210	$1.75
Direct product costs	$10,500,000	$2,500,000
Overhead allocation*	$5,100,000	$4,500,000
Overhead per unit.	$51	$0.90
Direct costs per unit	$105	$0.50
Number of customers.	90,000	12,500
Number of salesperson days	14,250	1,750
Number of art and design hours.	17,500	2,500
Number of creative services subcontract hours	50,000	12,500
Number of customer service calls	36,000	4,000

* Based on direct labor costs

Upon examining the data, Robert decided that he wanted to know more about the overhead costs since they were such a high proportion of total production costs. He was provided the following list of overhead costs and told that they were currently being assigned to products in proportion to direct labor costs.

Selling costs	$4,200,000
Visual and audio design costs	1,700,000
Creative services costs.	2,950,000
Customer service costs	750,000

Required

Using the data provided by the controller, prepare analyses to help Robert and Jane in making their decisions. (*Hint:* Prepare cost calculations for both product lines using ABC to see whether there is any significant difference in their unit costs.) Should ATI switch from the fast-growing, online advertising market back into the well-established published advertising market? Does the charge of predatory pricing seem valid? Why are customers likely to be willing to pay a higher price to get published services? Do traditional costing and activity-based costing lead to the same conclusions?

LO2, 3, 4, 6 **MA19-36. Unit-Level and Multiple-Level Cost Assignments with Decision Implications**

CarryAll Company[4] produces briefcases from leather, fabric, and synthetic materials in a single production department. The basic product is a standard briefcase made from leather and lined with fabric. CarryAll has a good reputation in the market because the standard briefcase is a high-quality item that has been produced for many years.

Last year, the company decided to expand its product line and produce specialty briefcases for special orders. These briefcases differ from the standard in that they vary in size, contain both leather and synthetic materials, and are imprinted with the buyer's logo (the standard briefcase is simply imprinted with the CarryAll name in small letters). The decision to use some synthetic materials in the briefcase was made to hold down the materials cost. To reduce the labor costs per unit, most of the cutting and stitching on the specialty briefcases is done by automated machines, which are used to a much lesser degree in the production of the standard briefcases. Because of these changes in the design and production of the specialty briefcases, CarryAll management believed that they would cost less to produce than the standard briefcases. However, because they are specialty items, they were priced slightly higher; standards are priced at $30 and specialty briefcases at $32.

After reviewing last month's results of operations, CarryAll's president became concerned about the profitability of the two product lines because the standard briefcase showed a loss while the specialty briefcase showed a greater profit margin than expected. The president is wondering whether the company should drop the standard briefcase and focus entirely on specialty items. Units and cost data for last month's operations as reported to the president are as follows:

---

[4] The CarryAll Company case, prepared by Professors Harold Roth and Imogene Posey, was originally published in the *Management Accounting Campus Report.*

	Standard	Specialty
Units produced	10,000	2,500
Direct materials		
Leather (1 sq. yd. × $15.00; ½ sq. yd. × $15.00)	$15.00	$ 7.50
Fabric (1 sq. yd. × $5.00; 1 sq. yd. × $5.00)	5.00	5.00
Synthetic		5.00
Total materials	20.00	17.50
Direct labor (½ hr. × $12.00, ¼ hr. × $12.00)	6.00	3.00
Manufacturing overhead (½ hr. × $8.98; ¼ hr. × $8.98)	4.49	2.25
Cost per unit	$30.49	$22.75

Factory overhead is applied on the basis of direct labor hours. The rate of $8.98 per direct labor hour was calculated by dividing the total overhead ($50,500) by the direct labor hours (5,625). As shown in the table, the cost of a standard briefcase is $0.49 higher than its $30 sales price; the specialty briefcase has a cost of only $22.75, for a gross profit per unit of $9.25. The problem with these costs is that they do not accurately reflect the activities involved in manufacturing each product. Determining the costs using ABC should provide better product costing data to help gauge the actual profitability of each product line.

The manufacturing overhead costs must be analyzed to determine the activities driving the costs. Assume that the following costs and cost drivers have been identified:

- The Purchasing Department's cost is $6,000. The major activity driving these costs is the number of purchase orders processed. During the month, the Purchasing Department prepared the following number of purchase orders for the materials indicated:

Leather	20
Fabric	30
Synthetic material	50

- The cost of receiving and inspecting materials is $7,500. These costs are driven by the number of deliveries. During the month, the following number of deliveries were made:

Leather	30
Fabric	40
Synthetic material	80

- Production line setup cost is $10,000. Setup activities involve changing the machines to produce the different types of briefcases. Each setup for production of the standard briefcases requires one hour; each setup for specialty briefcases requires two hours. Standard briefcases are produced in batches of 200, and specialty briefcases are produced in batches of 25. During the last month, there were 50 setups for the standard item and 100 setups for the specialty item.
- The cost of inspecting finished goods is $8,000. All briefcases are inspected to ensure that quality standards are met. However, the final inspection of standard briefcases takes very little time because the employees identify and correct quality problems as they do the hand cutting and stitching. A survey of the personnel responsible for inspecting the final products showed that 150 hours were spent on standard briefcases and 250 hours on specialty briefcases during the month.
- Equipment-related costs are $6,000. Equipment-related costs include repairs, depreciation, and utilities. Management has determined that a logical basis for assigning these costs to products is machine hours. A standard briefcase requires 1/2 hour of machine time, and a specialty briefcase requires 2 hours. Thus, during the last month, 5,000 hours of machine time relate to the standard line and 5,000 hours relate to the specialty line.
- Plant-related costs are $13,000. These costs include property taxes, insurance, administration, and others. For the purpose of determining average unit costs, they are to be assigned to products using machine hours.

Required

   a. Using activity-based costing concepts, what overhead costs should be assigned to the two products?

   b. What is the unit cost of each product using activity-based costing concepts?

   c. Reevaluate the president's concern about the profitability of the two product lines.

   d. Discuss the merits of activity-based management as it relates to CarryAll's ABC cost system.

Solutions to Review Problems

Review 19-1—Solution

Indirect expenses are displacing direct expenses. This may be attributed to the advancement of technology and equipment. It may also be largely related to an increase in the number of different types of products and services that companies offer. As companies move away from one simple product, the need for more indirect costs such as equipment design, changeover, and even the movement of products can increase. As the pool of indirect expenses becomes a more significant part of product costs, it is increasingly difficult yet important to come up with methods to reasonably assign indirect costs to products.

Review 19-2—Solution

Answers may vary but likely activities and related drivers might include:

- Reception and admission of participating employees/number of participating employees
- Consultations with physician/number of minutes of consultation services
- Administration of tests/number of tests
- Processing and distributing test results/number of participating employees
- Room setup/number of participating employees
- External lab processing/number of tests
- Technology support for website/number of participating employees

Review 19-3—Solution

a.

   Plantwide overhead rate = Total manufacturing overhead ÷ Total machine hours

$$= (\$120{,}000 + \$55{,}000) \div (10{,}000 + 5{,}000)$$

$$= \$175{,}000 \div 15{,}000$$

$$= \$11.67 \text{ per machine hour}$$

	Cobra Latch	GrimLoc
Product costs per unit		
Direct materials.	$12,000	$18,000
Direct labor	5,000	4,000
Manufacturing overhead		
700 machine hours × $11.67.	8,169	
800 machine hours × $11.67.		9,336
Total cost per batch	$25,169	$31,336
Number of units per batch.	÷ 100	÷ 100
Cost per unit.	$251.69	$313.36

b.

   Departmental overhead rates = Total departmental overhead ÷ Dept. allocation base

          Fabrication = $120,000 ÷ 10,000 machine hours

                    = $12 per machine hour

          Finishing = $55,000 ÷ 5,000 machine hours

                    = $11 per machine hour

	Cobra Latch	GrimLoc
Product costs per unit		
Direct materials.	$12,000	$18,000
Direct labor	5,000	4,000
Manufacturing overhead		
Fabrication Department		
500 machine hours × $12	6,000	
700 machine hours × $12		8,400
Finishing Department		
200 machine hours × $11	2,200	
100 machine hours × $11		1,100
Total cost per batch	$25,200	$31,500
Number of units per batch.	÷ 100	÷ 100
Cost per unit.	$252.00	$315.00

c.

$$\text{Activity-based overhead rates} = \text{Activity cost pool} \div \text{Activity cost driver}$$
$$\text{Maintenance} = \$30,000 \div 15,000 \text{ machine hours}$$
$$= \$2 \text{ per machine hour}$$
$$\text{Materials handling} = \$45,000 \div 4,500 \text{ materials moves}$$
$$= \$10 \text{ per materials move}$$
$$\text{Machine setups} = \$75,000 \div 750 \text{ setups}$$
$$= \$100 \text{ per machine setup}$$
$$\text{Inspections} = \$25,000 \div 1,000 \text{ inspection hours}$$
$$= \$25 \text{ per inspection hour}$$

	Cobra Latch	GrimLoc
Product costs per unit		
Direct materials.	$12,000	$18,000
Direct labor	5,000	4,000
Manufacturing overhead		
Maintenance activity		
700 machine hours × $2	1,400	
800 machine hours × $2		1,600
Materials handling activity		
30 materials moves × $10	300	
50 materials moves × $10		500
Machine setups activity		
5 machine setups × $100	500	
9 machine setups × $100		900
Inspections activity		
30 inspection hours × $25	750	
60 inspection hours × $25		1,500
Total cost per batch	$19,950	$26,500
Number of units per batch.	÷ 100	÷ 100
Cost per unit.	$199.50	$265.00

Review 19-4—Solution

Following is a summary of product costs for Cobra Latch and GrimLoc assigning overhead costs based on a plantwide rate, department rates, and activity-based rates:

	Cobra Latch	GrimLoc
Plantwide rate.	$251.69	$313.36
Department rates	$252.00	$315.00
Activity-based rates	$199.50	$265.00

Changing from a plantwide rate to department rates had little effect on unit costs because the department rates per machine hour are close to the plantwide rate per machine hour. Based on machine hours, both departments have similar cost structures.

When using activity-based rates, however, the cost of these two products drops dramatically because they use only a small portion (less than 2%) of the activities of setup (14 of 750) and materials moves (80 of 4,500). Neither a plantwide rate nor department rates recognize this fact, resulting in a large amount of cost cross-subsidization of other products by Cobra Latch and GrimLoc for these costs. Although this problem did not include cost analysis of the other three products, it shows that they are less profitable and that Cobra Latch and GrimLoc are much more profitable than management previously thought.

Review 19-5—Solution

a.   Activity A—Minor systems maintenance
       Activity B—Visits to customers
       Activity C—Communications via phone

Activity	1	2	3	4	5
A (@ $160)	$11,040	$22,560	$11,840	$ 9,760	$21,760
B (@ $300)	7,500	12,600	5,700	8,400	11,700
C (@ $50)	6,400	10,250	4,950	5,300	9,450
Total support costs	$24,940	$45,410	$22,490	$23,460	$42,910
Profit before support costs	80,000	85,000	83,000	90,000	78,000
Customer profits	$55,060	$39,590	$60,510	$66,540	$35,090
Ratio of support costs to profit before support costs	31%	53%	27%	26%	55%

b.   This analysis is beneficial to SAP because it shows that Groups 2 and 5 are outliers among the five customer groups in terms of support services required. Groups 2 and 5 are significantly larger consumers of activities for all three of the support activities. Note also that Group 4 customers are relatively light users of minor systems maintenance, and Group 3 are relatively light users of phone communications. Calculating the ratio of total support costs to profit before support costs provides additional insight into the relative profitability of the customer groups. All five customer groups are profitable; however, this analysis provides useful information for improving profits by working with Groups 2 and 5 to control support activities and related costs and attempt to bring their support costs in line with the other customer groups.

Review 19-6—Solution

Activity-based costing requires a company to understand, identify, and measure the activities it engages in in order to deliver its products or services. Activity-based management is the process of assessing those activities to make sure they align with companies' goals and objectives. It allows for a review of activities to identify which ones ultimately add value for its customers and can change or remove those activities that do not add value. It may also wish to make changes to activities that add value, to further a company's initiative. For example, Safety-Kleen is a subsidiary of Clean Harbors. Safety-Kleen states, "We are committed to continually examining our own operations to identify areas where we can reduce energy consumption, as well as determine innovative ways to drive enhancements across our entire network."[5] A firm is not in a position to do this effectively and profitably if it does not have a grasp of the costs and values of each of its activities.

---

[5] http://www.safety-kleen.com/about-us/sustainability

Additional Topics in
Product Costing

Module 20

Additional Topics in Product Costing

Additional Topics in Product Costing				
Production and Service Department Costs	**Service Department Cost Allocation**	**Lean Production and Just-in-Time Inventory Management**	**Performance Evaluation and Recordkeeping with Lean Production and JIT**	**Increased Focus on Data-Driven Decision Making**
▪ Direct and Indirect Department Costs	▪ Direct Method ▪ Step Method ▪ Linear Algebra Method ▪ Dual Rates	▪ Reducing Incoming Materials Inventory ▪ Reducing Work-in-Process Inventory ▪ Reducing Finished Goods Inventory	▪ Performance Evaluation ▪ Simplified Recordkeeping	▪ Changing Landscape of Managerial Accounting ▪ Risks Associated with Data-Driven Decision Making ▪ Skills Required of Managerial Accountants
Review 20-1	Review 20-2	Review 20-3	Review 20-4	Review 20-5

PREVIEW

AMZN

Whole Foods, a subsidiary of **Amazon.com, Inc.**, tried to shed its nickname "Whole Paycheck" for years without success. However, since being purchased by Amazon in 2017, attitudes about the company have improved, according to **YouGov**, a market research company. The main reasons for the change in perception? Expanded grocery delivery, online ordering, price cuts on selected items, and regular discounts for Amazon's Prime members.

To increase grocery delivery and online ordering volume, Whole Foods has been expanding, geographically, into areas previously unserved. Leasing and startup costs can be minimized by looking at sites previously occupied by struggling retailers like Sears and Kmart. These larger sites can also be used to accommodate Amazon delivery and pickup from online orders. Whole Foods now has over 500 retail locations. Although in-store revenue decreased slightly between 2018 and 2019, grocery deliveries in the fourth quarter of 2019 doubled from the same period in 2018.

To maintain profitability while cutting prices, Whole Foods has been moving away from local vendors and stocking larger national brands, including its own brand, 365 Everyday Value. Private labels typically have higher profit margins. 365 products are sold at Whole Foods and are one of the best-selling private label brands on Amazon.com.

A grocery operation has numerous support departments—areas that are necessary to the operation of the store, but not directly attributable to any one product or group of products. Examples of support departments include human resources, accounting, and custodial services. Whole Foods must develop a system of service cost allocation that will minimize distortions in profitability across grocery departments. The company must also operate as efficiently as possible; however, that efficiency shouldn't come at the expense of the quality that has become Whole Foods' bedrock.

The last, but perhaps most important factor for the company is its inventory management. Holding inventory is costly due to storage and insurance costs; and in the case of a grocer, perishable inventory is prone to spoilage and waste. This module discusses how companies such as Whole Foods assign the cost of their internal service departments to their products, and how they can benefit from adopting a lean operations philosophy in managing their inventory levels.

Road Map

LO	Learning Objective | Topics	Page	eLecture	Guided Example	Assignments
20-1	**Differentiate between production and service department costs and direct and indirect department costs.** Direct Department Costs :: Indirect Department Costs	20-3	e20-1	Review 20-1	
20-2	**Describe the allocation of service department costs under the direct, step, and linear algebra methods.** Direct Method :: Step Method :: Linear Algebra Method :: Dual Rates	20-4	e20-2	Review 20-2	17, 18, 19, 22, 23, 29, 30, 31, 32, 33, 34, 37
20-3	**Understand lean production and just-in-time inventory management.** Value Chain Approach to Inventory Management :: Just-in-Time :: Lean Production	20-10	e20-3	Review 20-3	20, 21, 24, 28, 35, 38, 39
20-4	**Explain how lean production and just-in-time affect performance evaluation and recordkeeping.** Dysfunctional Effects of Traditional Performance Measures :: Performance Measures under Lean and JIT :: Simplified Recordkeeping	20-13	e20-4	Review 20-4	20, 21, 24, 25, 26, 35, 36, 38, 39
20-5	**Evaluate ways in which the increasing availability of data might change the roles and responsibilities of managerial accountants.** Correlation vs Causation :: Technical Skills Gap	20-15	e20-6	Review 20-5	27

Production and Service Department Costs

eLectures
MBC
LO1
Differentiate between production and service department costs and direct and indirect department costs.

In Module 18, we discussed two basic methods (job order costing and process costing) for accumulating, measuring, and recording the costs of producing goods. In Module 19, we discussed both traditional and activity-based methods for assigning indirect costs to products. We now look in more detail at another aspect of assigning indirect costs.

In addition to *production* departments that actually perform work on a product, many companies have production *support* departments, such as payroll, human resources, information technology, security, and facilities, that provide support services for all of the production departments, and sometimes even for each other. These departments are typically called **service departments**. The cost of producing products, therefore, includes the costs incurred within production departments, as well as the cost of services received from service departments.

A **direct department cost** is a cost assigned directly to a department (production or service) when it is incurred. For a production department, direct department costs include both *direct* product costs (direct materials and direct labor) as well as *indirect* product costs (such as indirect labor and indirect materials) incurred directly in the department. An **indirect department cost** is a cost assigned to a department as a result of an indirect allocation, or reassignment, from another department, such as a service department.

The product costing system must include a policy for assigning to products the cost of services received from service departments. For companies that use a plantwide overhead rate, the costs of all service departments are added to the indirect product costs incurred within all of the producing departments to get total plantwide manufacturing overhead, which is then assigned to products using a single overhead rate based on a common factor such as direct labor hours. For companies that use departmental overhead rates, service department costs are allocated to the production departments that utilize their services, and the allocated service department costs are added to the indirect costs incurred within the department to arrive at total departmental overhead and allocation rates. Also, as illustrated in Module 19, service department costs may also be assigned to products using activity-based costing. As discussed in the following Business Insight, service department cost allocation can impact the amount of revenue received for some organizations.

Business Insight   ■   Cost Allocations in a Large University Setting

A major research university, such as Emory University, encounters numerous cost allocation situations where the cost allocation system can substantially impact the university's financial well-being. Two examples are (1) cost allocation of various overhead costs for purposes of billing governmental and private insurance systems for services rendered to patients in university hospitals and clinics, and (2) cost allocations for indirect costs when seeking research and other grants. Failing to properly allocate service department costs can result in large revenue losses to such organizations. During times of economic recession, it is even more important to accurately measure the indirect service costs that are being passed on to other organizations to ensure maximum cost recovery.

Review 20-1 LO1

GuidedExamples
MBC

Most companies have production support departments, such as payroll, human resources, and information technology that provide support services for multiple production departments. To create meaningful product and service cost information, the costs associated with support departments must be allocated to the ultimate products or services in a meaningful way.

Required

Discuss how a company using each of the product costing systems—plantwide overhead rate, department overhead rate, and activity-based costing—would handle the allocation of support department costs.

Solution on p. 20-27.

Service Department Cost Allocation

eLectures **LO2**
MBC Describe the
allocation
of service
department costs
under the direct, step,
and linear algebra
methods.

As discussed above, service departments (maintenance, administration, information technology, security, etc.) provide a wide range of support functions, primarily for one or more production departments. These departments, which are considered essential elements in the overall manufacturing process, do not work directly on the "product" but provide auxiliary support to the producing departments. In addition to providing support for the various producing departments, some service departments also provide services to *other service departments*. For example, the payroll and personnel departments typically provide services to all departments (producing and service), and engineering may provide services to only the producing departments. Services provided by one service department to other service departments are called **interdepartment services**.

To illustrate service department cost allocations, suppose the Dasani Division of The Coca-Cola Company has two producing departments, three service departments, and two products. The service departments and their respective service functions and cost allocation bases are as follows:

Department	Service Functions	Allocation Base
Support Services	Receiving and inventory control	Total amount of department capital investment
Engineering Resources	Production setup and engineering and testing	Number of employees
Building and Grounds	Machinery maintenance and depreciation	Amount of square footage occupied

Difficulty in choosing an allocation base for service department costs is not uncommon. For example, Dasani may have readily determined the appropriate allocation bases for the Engineering Resources and the Building and Grounds Departments but may have found the choice for Support Services to be less clear. Perhaps after conducting correlation studies, the most equitable base for allocating Support Services costs to other departments was determined to be total capital investment in the departments because they included expensive computer-tracking equipment, both manual and automated forklifts, and other material-moving equipment.

Assume direct department costs and allocation base information used to illustrate Dasani's July service department cost allocations are summarized as follows:

	Direct Department Costs	Number of Employees		Amount of Square Footage Occupied		Total Amount of Department Capital Investment	
Service departments							
Support Services.	$ 27,000	15	15%	4,000	8%	—	—
Engineering Resources. . . .	20,000	—	—	2,000	4	$ 45,000	8%
Building and Grounds	10,000	5	5	—	—	50,000	9
Producing departments							
Mixing	40,000*	24	24	11,000	22	180,000	33
Bottling	90,000*	56	56	33,000	66	270,000	50
	$187,000	100	100%	50,000	100%	$545,000	100%

*Direct department overhead

The preceding information omitted the amount of capital investment in the Support Services Department, the number of employees in the Engineering Resources Department, and the amount of square footage used by the Building and Grounds Department. These data were omitted because a department does not allocate costs to itself; it allocates costs only to the departments it serves.

The three methods commonly used for service department cost allocations—direct, step, and linear algebra—are discussed in this section. Each of these methods eventually results in all service department costs being assigned to the production departments. Once this is done, Dasani can then use either department overhead rates or activity-based costing to further assign the indirect costs that are accumulated in the producing departments to the actual products. If Dasani were to use a plant-wide overhead rate to allocate indirect costs, the service department costs would not be allocated to the producing departments; they would merely be added to the one plantwide indirect cost pool and allocated directly to the product using one plantwide overhead rate.

Direct Method

The **direct method** allocates all service department costs based only on the amount of services provided to the producing departments. Exhibit 20.1 shows the flow of costs using the direct method. All arrows depicting the cost flows extend directly from service departments to producing departments; under the direct method there are no cost allocations between the service departments.

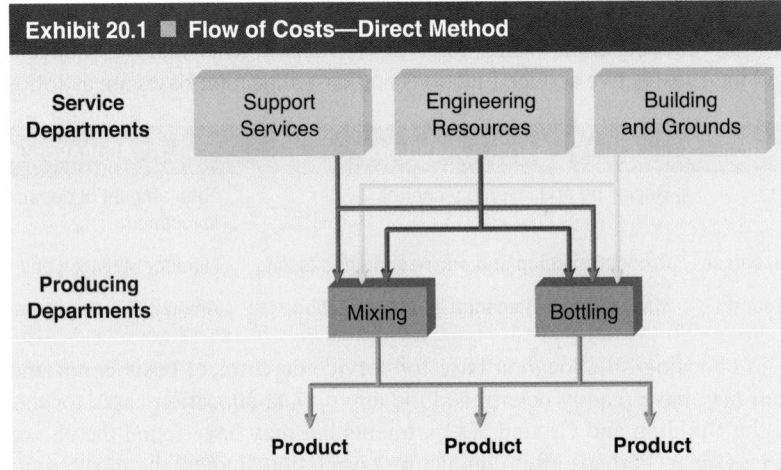

Exhibit 20.1 ■ Flow of Costs—Direct Method

Exhibit 20.2 shows the service department cost allocations for the direct method. Notice the allocation base used to allocate Engineering Resources costs; only the employees in the producing

Exhibit 20.2 ■ Service Department Cost Allocations—Direct Method

	Total	Mixing	Bottling
Support Services Department			
Allocation base (capital investment)	$450,000	$180,000	$270,000
Percent of total base.	100%	40%	60%
Cost allocations.	$ 27,000	$ 10,800	$ 16,200
Engineering Resources Department			
Allocation base (number of employees)	80	24	56
Percent of total base.	100%	30%	70%
Cost allocations.	$ 20,000	$ 6,000	$ 14,000
Building and Grounds Department			
Allocation base (square footage occupied). . .	44,000	11,000	33,000
Percent of total base.	100%	25%	75%
Cost allocations.	$ 10,000	$ 2,500	$ 7,500

Cost Allocation Summary

	Support Services	Engineering Resources	Building and Grounds	Mixing	Bottling	Total
Department cost before allocations	$27,000	$20,000	$10,000	$40,000	$ 90,000	$187,000
Cost allocations						
Support Services.	(27,000)			10,800	16,200	—
Engineering Resources.		(20,000)		6,000	14,000	—
Building and Grounds			(10,000)	2,500	7,500	—
Department costs after allocations	$ 0	$ 0	$ 0	$59,300	$127,700	$187,000

departments are considered in computing the allocation percentages—24 in Mixing and 56 in Bottling, for a total of 80 employees in the allocation base. Thirty percent (24 ÷ 80) of the producing department employees work in Mixing; therefore, 30% of Engineering Resources costs are allocated to Mixing. Applying the same reasoning, 70% of Engineering Resources costs are allocated to Bottling. Similar logic is followed in computing the cost allocations for Building and Grounds and Support Services.

The cost allocation summary at the bottom of Exhibit 20.2 shows that all service department costs have been allocated, decreasing the service department costs to zero and increasing the producing department overhead balances by the amounts of the respective allocations. Also, total costs are not affected by the allocations; the total of $187,000 was merely redistributed so that all costs are reassigned to the producing departments. Total department overhead costs of the producing departments after allocation of service costs are $59,300 for Mixing and $127,700 for Bottling.

The advantage of the direct method of allocating service department costs is that it is easy and convenient to use. Its primary disadvantage is that it does not recognize the costs for interdepartment services provided by one service department to another. Instead, any costs incurred to provide services to other service departments are passed directly to the producing departments. The step method improves on the allocation procedure by redirecting some of the costs to other service departments before they are finally allocated to the production departments.

Step Method

The **step method** gives partial recognition of interdepartmental services by using a methodology that allocates the service department costs *sequentially* both to the remaining service departments and the producing departments. Any indirect costs allocated to a service department in this process are added to that service department's direct costs to determine the total costs to allocate to the remaining departments. Through this procedure, all service department costs are assigned to the production departments and ultimately to the products.

To illustrate a problem that can result from using the direct method, assume that Prestige Company has two service departments, S1 and S2, and two producing departments, P1 and P2, that provide services as follows:

	Receiver of Services			
Provider of Services	**S1**	**S2**	**P1**	**P2**
S1.	0%	0%	70%	30%
S2.	50%	0%	25%	25%

If the direct method is used to allocate service department costs to the producing departments, S2 total costs will be allocated equally to the producing departments because they use the same amount of S2 services (25% each). Is this an equitable allocation of S2 costs? S2 actually provides half of its services to the other service department (S1), which, in turn, provides the majority of its services to P1. Assume that S2 has total direct department costs of $100,000. If the direct method is used to allocate service department costs, the entire $100,000 will be divided equally between the two producing departments, each being allocated $50,000, with no allocation to S1.

	S1	S2	P1	P2
Direct method allocation of S2 to P1 and P2	$0	$(100,000)	$50,000	$50,000

Consider the following alternative allocation of the $100,000 of S2 costs that takes into account interdepartment services. First, 25%, or $25,000, is allocated to each of the producing departments, and 50%, or $50,000, is allocated to S1. Next, the $50,000 allocated to S1 from S2 is reallocated to the producing departments in proportion to the amount of services provided to them by S1: 70% and 30%, respectively. In this scenario, the $100,000 of S2 costs is ultimately allocated $60,000 to P1 and $40,000 to P2 as follows:

	S1	S2	P1	P2
Step 1:				
Allocate S2 costs to S1, P1, and P2............	$50,000	$(100,000)	$25,000	$25,000
Step 2:				
Reallocate S1 costs to P1 and P2	(50,000)	0	35,000	15,000
Total allocation of S2 costs via step method	$ 0	$ 0	$60,000	$40,000

This calculation shows only the ultimate allocation of S2 costs. Of course, any S1 direct department costs would also have to be allocated to P1 and P2 on a 70:30 basis. If interdepartmental services are ignored, P1 is allocated only $50,000 of S2 costs; by considering interdepartmental services, P1 is allocated $60,000. Certainly, a more accurate measure of both the direct and indirect services received by P1 from S2 is $60,000, not $50,000.

As long as all producing departments use approximately the same percentage of services of each service department, the direct method provides a reasonably accurate cost assignment. In this example, the percentages of services used by the producing departments were quite different: 70% and 30% for S1, and 50% and 50% for S2. In such situations, the direct method can result in significantly different allocations.

The step method is illustrated graphically in Exhibit 20.3 for Dasani. Notice the sequence of the allocations: Engineering Resources, Support Services, and Building and Grounds.

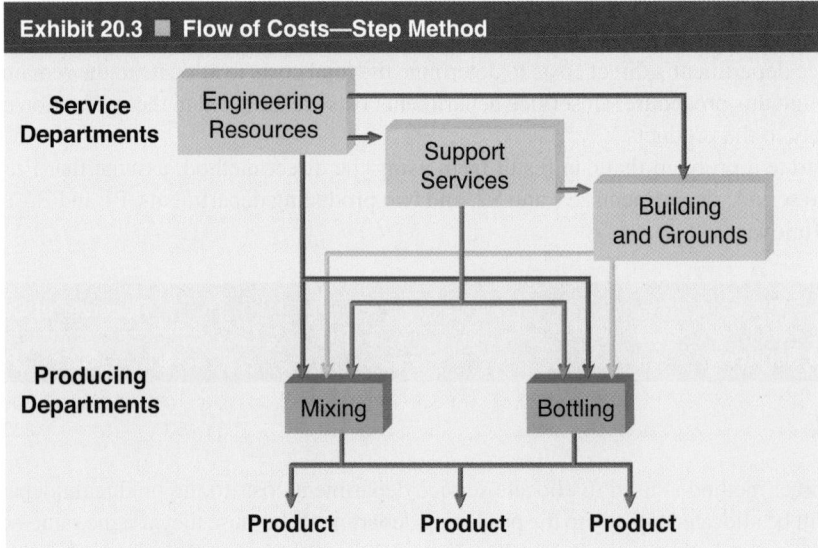

Exhibit 20.3 ■ Flow of Costs—Step Method

When using the step method, the sequence of allocation is typically based on the relative percentage of services provided to other service departments, with the largest provider of interdepartmental services allocated first and the smallest provider of interdepartmental services allocated last. For Dasani, Engineering Resources is allocated first because, of the three service departments, it provides the largest percentage (20%) of its services to other service departments: 15% to Support Services and 5% to Building and Grounds (see previous cost allocation data). Building and Grounds is allocated last because it provides the least amount (12%) of its services to other service departments: 8% to Support Services and 4% to Engineering Resources. The service department cost allocations for Dasani using the step method are shown in Exhibit 20.4.

Linear Algebra (Reciprocal) Method

The disadvantage of the step method is that it provides only partial recognition of interdepartmental services. For Dasani, the step method recognizes Engineering Resources services provided to the other two service departments; however, no services received by Engineering Resources from the other two departments are recognized. Similarly, services from Support Services to Building and Grounds are

Exhibit 20.4 ■ Service Department Cost Allocations—Step Method

	Total	Support Services	Building and Grounds	Mixing	Bottling
Engineering Resources Department					
Allocation base (number of employees)	100	15	5	24	56
Percent of total base.	100%	15%	5%	24%	56%
Cost allocations.	$20,000	$3,000	$1,000	$4,800	$11,200
Support Services Department					
Allocation base (capital investment)	$500,000		$50,000	$180,000	$270,000
Percent of total base.	100%		10%	36%	54%
Cost allocations.	$30,000		$3,000	$10,800	$16,200
Building and Grounds Department					
Allocation base (square footage occupied).	44,000			11,000	33,000
Percent of total base.	100%			25%	75%
Cost allocations.	$14,000			$3,500	$10,500

Cost Allocation Summary	Engineering Resources	Support Services	Building and Grounds	Mixing	Bottling	Total
Department costs before allocations	$ 20,000	$ 27,000	$ 10,000	$40,000	$ 90,000	$187,000
Cost allocations						
Engineering Resources.	(20,000)	3,000	1,000	4,800	11,200	—
Support Services.		(30,000)	3,000	10,800	16,200	—
Building and Grounds			(14,000)	3,500	10,500	—
Department costs after allocations	$ 0	$ 0	$ 0	$59,100	$127,900	$187,000

recognized, but not the reverse. To achieve the most mathematically accurate service department cost allocation, there should be full recognition of services between service departments as well as between service and producing departments. This requires using the linear algebra method, sometimes called the *reciprocal method*. The **linear algebra (reciprocal) method** uses a series of linear algebraic equations, which are solved simultaneously, to allocate service department costs both interdepartmentally and to the producing departments. This method is illustrated graphically in Exhibit 20.5 for a company that has two service departments and two producing departments. The cost allocation arrows run from each service department to the other service department as well as to the producing departments. Further discussion of this method can be found in cost accounting texts. Whether a company should use the direct method, step method, or linear algebra method depends on the extensiveness of interdepartmental services and how evenly services are used by the producing departments.

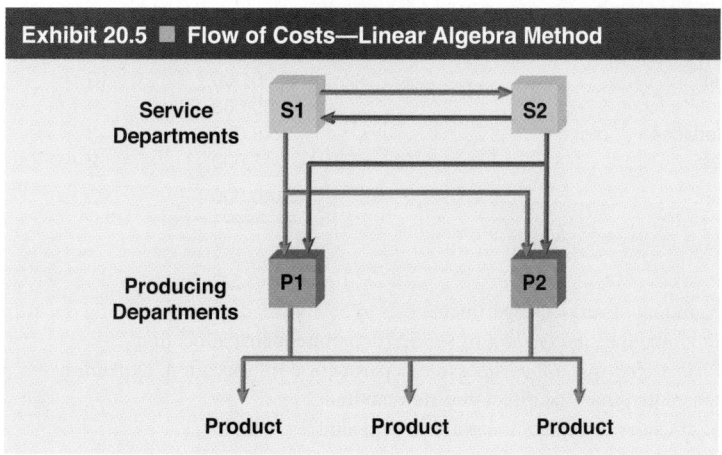

Exhibit 20.5 ■ Flow of Costs—Linear Algebra Method

> **Managerial Decision** ■ You Are the Controller
>
> As the person responsible for the product costing system, you are trying to decide which method is best to use in allocating service department costs to the producing departments and to the products. Some of the service departments provide services only to producing departments, whereas others provide services to both producing and service departments. You would like to use the method that provides reliable cost measurements, but without creating more costs than the benefits derived. Which method do you recommend? [Answer, p. 20-17]

Dual Rates

When allocating service department costs, it can be useful to provide separate allocations for fixed costs and variable costs. This will result in cost allocations that more accurately reflect the factors that drive costs. The capacity provided most often drives fixed costs, whereas some type of actual activity usually drives variable costs. Dual rates involve establishing separate bases for allocating fixed and variable costs. Dual rates may be used for one or all service departments, depending on the size and nature of the costs in each service department. They may also be used in conjunction with the direct, step, or linear algebra methods.

It is important to remember the relationship between capacity and cost when selecting the allocation method. Total variable costs change as activity changes. Fixed costs, however, are the same whether the activity is at or below capacity. Fixed costs should usually be allocated based on the relative capacity provided the benefiting department, while variable costs should be allocated on the basis of actual usage. The allocation methods and bases also may be different for variable and fixed costs.

Fixed costs based on capacity provided eliminates the possibility that the amount of the cost allocation to one department is affected by the level of services utilized by other departments. When fixed service department costs are allocated based on the capacity provided to the user department, managers of the user departments are charged for that capacity whether they use it or not, and their use of services has no effect on the amount of costs allocated to other departments. A benefit of this allocation system is that it reduces the temptation for managers to avoid or delay services to minimize fixed cost allocations to their departments. Dual rates are examined in more detail in most cost accounting texts.

Review 20-2 LO2

Suppose a **Buckle** retail store is organized into four departments: Women's Apparel, Men's Apparel, Administrative Services, and Facilities Services. The first two departments are the primary producing departments; the last two departments provide services to the producing departments as well as to each other. Top management has decided that, for internal reporting purposes, the cost of service department operations should be allocated to the producing departments. Administrative Services costs are allocated on the basis of the number of employees, and Facilities Services costs are allocated based on the amount of square footage of floor space occupied. Hypothetical data pertaining to the cost allocations for February are as follows:

Department	Direct Department Cost	Number of Employees	Square Footage Occupied
Women's Apparel	$ 60,000	15	15,000
Men's Apparel	50,000	9	7,500
Administrative Services	18,000	3	2,500
Facilities Services	12,000	2	1,000
Total	$140,000	29	26,000

Required

a. Determine the amount of service department costs to be allocated to the producing departments under both the *direct method* and the *step method* of service department cost allocation.

b. Discuss the *linear algebra method* of service department cost allocation, explaining circumstances when it should be considered over the direct and step methods.

Solution on p. 20-27. c. Should Buckle consider using the linear algebra method?

Lean Production and Just-in-Time Inventory Management

Previously, our discussions about inventories have centered around how to measure the cost of products. A related issue is how to manage the production process and physical inventory levels. Cost accounting textbooks, as well as operations management textbooks, usually discuss models that have been used for decades to determine the economic order quantities for products, given the particular level of inventory a company wants to maintain. Although these models are still relevant in many situations, managing the production process and inventory levels has changed dramatically for companies that have adopted a value chain approach to management. No longer do most managers consider only their company's strategies, goals, and objectives in deciding the characteristics and quantities of inventory that should be acquired or produced and maintained.

A value chain approach to inventory management requires that managers consider their suppliers' and customers' strategies, goals, and objectives as well if they hope to compete successfully in a global marketplace. Computer technology has affected the way inventories are manufactured and handled (using robotics, fully computerized manufacturing and product handling systems, bar code identification systems, etc.), and it is changing the way companies relate to other parties in the value chain. It has spawned worldwide use of alternative inventory production and management techniques and processes including just-in-time (JIT) inventory management and lean production methods.

Just-in-time (JIT) inventory management is a comprehensive inventory management philosophy that emerged in the 1970s that stresses policies, procedures, and attitudes by managers and other workers that result in the efficient production of high-quality goods while maintaining the minimum level of inventories. JIT is often described simply as an inventory model that maintains only the level of inventories required to meet current production and sales requirements, but it is, in reality, much more than that. The key elements of the JIT philosophy, which has come to be known as the "lean production" philosophy, include increased coordination throughout the value chain, reduced inventory, reduced production times, increased product quality, and increased employee involvement and empowerment.

In sum, the concept of a JIT/lean approach is that in a manufacturing environment, the customers pull the production through the system with customer orders. Instead of the business making the decisions of what and when to produce, the customer does. JIT/lean production is a system aimed at reducing or eliminating waste, increasing cost efficiency, and securing a competitive advantage. Accordingly, it emphasizes a nimble production process with small lot sizes, short setup and changeover times, effective and efficient quality controls, a minimum number of bottlenecks and backups, and maximum efficiency of people.

Reducing Incoming Materials Inventory

The JIT/lean approach to reducing incoming materials includes these elements:

1. Developing long-term relationships with a limited number of vendors.
2. Selecting vendors on the basis of service and material quality, as well as price.
3. Establishing procedures for key employees to order materials for current needs directly from approved vendors.
4. Accepting vendor deliveries directly to the shop floor, and only as needed.

When fully implemented, these steps minimize or eliminate many materials inventories. Sufficient materials would be on hand to meet only immediate needs, and the materials inventories in the manufacturing setting are located on the shop floor.

To achieve this reduction, it is apparent that vendors and buyers must work as a team and that key employees must be involved in decision making. The goal of the JIT approach to purchasing is not to shift materials carrying costs to vendors. A close, long-term working relationship between purchasers and vendors should be beneficial to both. Purchasers' scheduling information is provided to vendors so that vendors also can reduce inventories and minimize costs. Vendors are therefore able to manufacture small batches frequently, rather than manufacturing large batches infrequently. Further, vendors are more confident of future sales.

Business Insight ■ Costs of Mismanaged Inventories

Forever 21 was founded in 1984 by Do Won Chang and his wife, Jin Sook. In 2014, revenues were $4 billion. By 2016, the company operated over 700 stores in 44 countries. However, in September 2019, the company declared bankruptcy, and, in January 2020, Forever 21 asked a bankruptcy court to approve plans to sell "substantially" all of its assets to an unnamed buyer.

There is more than one reason for the company's decline, but inventory mismanagement was one of the primary factors.

The company ordered too much inventory one year, and too little the next. Excess inventory was sent to store managers who stacked boxes of clothes in dressing rooms and then ended up returning items to the distribution centers when styles changed. Inventory shortages required replacement stock to be shipped overnight to stores, which resulted in higher than usual shipping costs. Errors were also made in the choice of items sent to specific stores. For example, down coats were sent to all stores in late fall even though it was almost summer in South America.

In the end, Forever 21's failure to anticipate changes in the industry and manage its inventory appropriately contributed to the company's need to file bankruptcy.

Sources: Susan Berfield, Eliza Ronalds-Hannon, and Lauren Coleman-Lochner, "The Failure of the Forever 21 Empire," *Bloomberg Businessweek*, January 17, 2020.
Eliza Ronalds-Hannon, "Forever 21 Proposed Auction to Keep Fashion Chain in Business," *Bloomberg*, January 30, 2020.

Reducing Work-in-Process Inventory

Reducing the total time required to complete a process, or the **cycle time**, is the key to reducing work-in-process inventories and is central to a lean production approach. In a manufacturing organization, cycle time is composed of the time needed for setup, processing, movement, waiting, and inspection. **Setup time** is the time required to prepare equipment to produce a specific product, or to change from producing one product to another product. **Processing time** is the time spent working on units. **Movement time** is the time units spend moving between work or inspection stations. **Waiting time** is the time units spend in temporary storage waiting to be processed, moved, or inspected. **Inspection time** is the amount of time it takes units to be inspected. Of the five elements of cycle time, only processing time adds value to the product. Efforts to reduce cycle time are appropriate for both continuous and batch production.

Devising means of reducing setup times will directly reduce the cycle time for batch production and thus reduce setup costs. Setup times can also be reduced by shifting from batch to continuous production whenever practical. Rearranging the shop floor to eliminate unnecessary movements of materials can help reduce movement time for both continuous and batch production.

Many companies have created **quality circles**, which are groups of employees involved in production who have the authority, within certain parameters, to address and resolve quality problems as they occur, without seeking management approval. Giving employees more authority and responsibility for quality, including the right to stop production whenever quality problems are noted, can reduce the need for separate inspection time.

Waiting time can be reduced by moving from a materials push to a materials pull approach to production. Under a traditional **materials push system**, employees work to reduce the pile of inventory building up at their workstations. Workers at each station remove materials from an in-process storage area, complete their operation, and place the output in another in-process storage area. Hence, they *push* the work to the next workstation. The emphasis is on production efficiency at each station. In a push system, one of the functions of work-in-process inventory is to help make workstations independent of each other. Inventories are large enough to allow for variations in processing speeds, for discarding defective units without interrupting production, and for machine downtime.

Under a **materials pull system** (often called a **Kanban system**), employees at each station work to provide inventory for the next workstation only as needed. (*Kanban*, the Japanese word for *card*, is a system created in Japan that originally used cards to indicate that a department needed additional components.) The building of excess inventories is strictly prohibited. When the number of units in inventory reaches a specified limit, work at the station stops until workers at a subsequent station pull a unit from the in-process storage area. Hence, the *pull* of inventory by a subsequent station authorizes production to continue.

A pull, or Kanban, system's low inventory levels require a team effort. To avoid idle time, processing speeds must be balanced and equipment must be kept in good repair. Quality problems are identified immediately, and the low inventory levels require immediate correction of quality problems. To make a pull system work, management must accept the notion that it is better to have employees idle than to have them building excess inventory. A pull system also requires careful planning by management and active participation in decision making by employees. A lean production process involves minimizing cycle time, eliminating waste, producing inventory only as needed, and ensuring the highest level of quality and efficiency. To achieve these results on a continuing basis, there is a strong emphasis on continuous improvement programs (see Module 21).

Reducing Finished Goods Inventory

Finished goods inventory can be reduced by reducing cycle time and by better predicting customer demand for finished units. Lowering cycle times reduces the need for speculative inventories. If finished goods can be replenished quickly, the need diminishes for large inventory levels to satisfy customer needs and to provide for unanticipated fluctuations in customer orders. Anticipating customers' demand for goods can be improved by adopting a value chain approach to inventory management by which the manufacturer or supplier is working as a partner with its customers to meet their inventory needs. This frequently involves having online computer access to customers' inventory levels on a real-time basis and being able to synchronize changes in production with changes in customers' inventory levels as they occur.

Sharing this type of information obviously requires an enormous amount of mutual trust between a manufacturer or supplier and its customers, but it is becoming increasingly common among world-class organizations. An example of this type of vendor-customer relationship is the relationship between Procter & Gamble, one of the world's largest consumer products companies, and its largest customer, Walmart. By having access to Walmart's computer inventory system, Procter & Gamble is better able to determine and fill Walmart's specific needs for products, such as disposable diapers.

Business Insight   ■   Inventory Management and Supply Chain Risk

Toyota's just-in-time inventory system is central to the company's global manufacturing success; however, this system also creates vulnerabilities. Toyota keeps as little inventory on site as possible—it holds only several hours' worth of parts, working with suppliers to maintain a steady supply of parts for production. This lowers cost and increases quality control, as defects are noticed immediately. However, Toyota is vulnerable to events affecting its suppliers.

In 1997, a fire at a supplier halted Toyota's production for five days. A 2007 earthquake left the Toyota plants unscathed but still stopped production due to damage at the site of their supplier of piston rings. The massive 2011 earthquake affected 660 of Toyota's suppliers. Since 2011 Toyota has aggressively sought to manage this risk. While some earthquake risk is inherent in manufacturing in Japan, Toyota has worked with suppliers to diversify geographically. These measures should reduce the supply chain effects of future disasters.

Source: Yoko Kubota, "Japan Earthquakes Rattle Toyota's Vulnerable Supply Chain," *Wall Street Journal*, April 19, 2016.
Link: http://www.wsj.com/articles/japan-earthquakes-rattle-toyotas-supply-chain-1460986805

LO3 Review 20-3

1. An element of lean production and just-in-time inventory management.
2. An element of a traditional inventory model that focuses on a partial level of inventory that a company wants to maintain.
3. Cycle time.

Required

For each of the statements *a–f* below, identify which of the concepts listed in above is the most relevant. You can use each concept more than once.

_____ *a.*   Nimble production process with small lot sizes and short setup and changeover times.
_____ *b.*   Material push system.
_____ *c.*   Key to managing work-in-process inventories and central to a lean production approach.
_____ *d.*   Selecting venders on the basis of service and material quality, as well as price.
_____ *e.*   Accepting vendor deliveries directly to the shop floor, and only as needed.
_____ *f.*   Employees at each station work to provide inventory for the next workstation only as needed (Kanban system).

Solution on p. 20-29.

Performance Evaluation and Recordkeeping with Lean Production and JIT

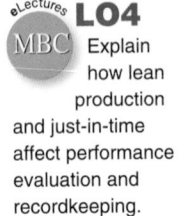

LO4
Explain how lean production and just-in-time affect performance evaluation and recordkeeping.

Movement toward a JIT/lean production philosophy requires changes in performance evaluation procedures and offers opportunities for significant reductions in recordkeeping costs. These changes are discussed in this section.

Performance Evaluation

JIT regards inventory as something to be eliminated. Hence, in a manufacturing organization, inventories are kept as small as possible. Under the JIT ideal, inventories do not exist because vendors deliver raw materials in small batches directly to the shop floor. JIT also strives to minimize, or eliminate, work-in-process inventory by minimizing the non-processing elements of cycle time and by having processing times as short as possible.

Dysfunctional Effects of Traditional Performance Measures

A potential conflict exists between the goals of JIT and lean production and those of traditional performance measures applied at the level of the department or cost center. Although lean production emphasizes overall efficiency, many traditional performance measures emphasize local (departmental) cost savings and local (departmental) efficiency. The following represent examples of cost and quality issues that may arise when management decisions are based solely on meeting departmental performance measures.

- To achieve quantity discounts and favorable prices, a purchasing agent might order excess inventory, thereby increasing subsequent storage, obsolescence, and handling costs.

- To obtain a low price, a purchasing agent might order from a supplier whose goods have not been certified as meeting quality specifications, thereby causing subsequent inspection, rework, and spoilage costs, and perhaps, dissatisfied customers further down the value chain.

- To avoid having idle employees and equipment, a supervisor might refuse to halt production to determine the cause of a quality problem, thereby increasing inspection, rework, and spoilage costs.

- To obtain low fixed costs per unit under absorption costing, a supervisor might produce in excess of current needs (preferably in long production runs), thereby causing subsequent increases in storage, obsolescence, and handling costs.

Performance Measures Under Lean Production and JIT

In accordance with the goal of eliminating inventory and reducing cycle time to processing time, JIT supportive performance measures emphasize inventory turnover, cycle time, and **cycle efficiency** (the ratio of value-added to non-value-added manufacturing activities).

When applied to a specific item of raw materials or finished goods, **inventory turnover** is computed as the annual demand in units divided by the average inventory in units:

$$\text{Inventory turnover (in units)} = \frac{\text{Annual demand in units}}{\text{Average inventory in units}}$$

Progress toward the goal of reducing inventory is measured by comparing successive inventory turnover ratios. Generally, the higher the inventory turnover, the better.

When measured with inventory dollars instead of inventory units, inventory turnover can be used as a measure of the organization's overall success in reducing inventory, or in increasing sales in relation to inventories. This financial measure can be derived directly from a firm's financial statements.

$$\text{Inventory turnover (in dollars)} = \frac{\text{Cost of goods sold}}{\text{Average inventory (in dollars)}}$$

Another ratio often used to monitor the effectiveness of inventory levels in retail organizations, such as Whole Foods or Macy's, is gross margin return on inventory investment (GMROI), calculated as follows:

$$\text{GMROI} = \frac{\text{Gross margin (in dollars)}}{\text{Average inventory (in dollars)}}$$

Cycle time is a measure of the total time required to produce one unit of a product:

$$\begin{array}{c}\text{Cycle} \\ \text{time}\end{array} = \begin{array}{c}\text{Setup} \\ \text{time}\end{array} + \begin{array}{c}\text{Processing} \\ \text{time}\end{array} + \begin{array}{c}\text{Movement} \\ \text{time}\end{array} + \begin{array}{c}\text{Waiting} \\ \text{time}\end{array} + \begin{array}{c}\text{Inspection} \\ \text{time}\end{array}$$

Under ideal circumstances, cycle time would consist of only processing time, and processing time would be as low as possible. Only processing time adds value to the product; hence, the time required for all other activities should be driven toward zero. The use of flexible manufacturing systems, properly sequencing jobs, and properly placing tools will minimize setup time. If the shop floor is optimally arranged, workers pass products directly from one workstation to the next. If production is optimally scheduled, inventory will not wait in temporary storage between workstations. If raw materials are of high quality and products are manufactured so that they always conform to specifications, separate inspection activities are not needed.

Cycle efficiency is computed as the ratio of processing time to total cycle time:

$$\text{Cycle efficiency} = \frac{\text{Processing time}}{\text{Cycle time}}$$

The highest cycle efficiency possible is always sought. If all non-value-added activities are eliminated, this ratio equals one.

Simplified Recordkeeping

Lean production and JIT enable significant reductions in the number of accounting transactions required for purchasing and production activities. This results in cost savings for bookkeeping activities and in shifting accounting resources from detailed bookkeeping to the development of more useful activity cost data.

Purchasing

In a traditional accounting system, every purchase results in the preparation of several documents. Additional documents are prepared for the issuance of raw materials to the factory. JIT, on the other hand, attempts to minimize inventory levels and stresses long-term relationships with a limited number of vendors who have demonstrated their ability to provide quality raw materials on a timely basis, as well as at a competitive price. Under a JIT inventory system, a company often has standing purchase orders for specified materials from specified vendors at specified prices. Production personnel are authorized to requisition materials directly from authorized vendors, who deliver limited quantities of materials as needed directly to the shop floor. Production personnel verify receipt of the raw materials. Periodically, each vendor sends an invoice for several shipments, which the company acknowledges and pays.

Product Costing

Another advantage of a lean production system is that it reduces the amount of detailed bookkeeping required for financial accounting purposes. If ending inventories are nonexistent, or so small that the costs assigned to them are insignificant in comparison with the costs assigned to Cost of Goods Sold, it makes little sense to track product costs through several inventory accounts. Instead of using a traditional product cost accounting system (as illustrated in Module 18), firms that have implemented JIT often use what is sometimes referred to as a backflush approach to accounting for product costs.

Under **backflush costing**, all costs of direct materials, direct labor, and manufacturing overhead are assigned as incurred to Cost of Goods Sold. If there are no inventories on hand at the end of the period, no additional steps are required. However, if there are inventories on hand at year-end, costs are backed out of Cost of Goods Sold and assigned to the appropriate inventory accounts. For a complete discussion of backflush costing, refer to a cost accounting text.

Also under a JIT inventory approach, many of the distinctions and arguments regarding absorption versus variable costing are moot (see Appendix 18A). If the quantity of inventory is insignificant, it matters little whether inventory cost includes only variable manufacturing costs or both variable and fixed manufacturing costs. Whether absorption or variable costing is used, the total cost assigned to inventory on the balance sheet will be small, and there is little difference in the amount of profit reported on the income statement.

As we discussed in previous modules, traditional product costing systems go to great lengths to calculate the materials, labor, and manufacturing overhead cost per unit for each unit produced. Overhead is typically assigned to inventory using a predetermined overhead rate based on an assumed volume-based driver such as direct labor hours or machine hours. If actual production is less than budgeted production, there will be underapplied overhead, which is usually written off as an expense of the period. To avoid this expense, managers are often motivated to overproduce product in order to ensure that all overhead is allocated to product. Also, by budgeting a large amount of produced units, fixed overhead cost is spread over more units, resulting in a lower cost per unit. Such overproduction is equivalent to a cardinal sin in a lean production company.

As we will see in Module 23, many companies also adopt standard cost systems where they account for product cost components on both an actual and budgeted cost basis, with variances between actual cost and standard (or allowed) costs reported on the internal performance reports as increased expenses if they are unfavorable and as a reduction of expenses if they are favorable. In such cases, managers are motivated to maximize favorable variances and minimize or eliminate unfavorable variances. Such systems of reporting often lead managers to actions that are contrary to the lean production philosophy.

Review 20-4 LO4

Assume Titleist is trying to decide which automated production line to use to produce its new Pro VI golf balls. Suppose the two best systems under consideration have the following estimated performance characteristics, based on minutes per 1,000 balls produced:

	System A	System B
Setup time	25	10
Movement time from start to finish	10	14
Waiting time	3	16
Inspection time	5	7
Processing time	40	30
Total time in minutes	83	77

Required

a. Determine the cycle time per batch for each system.

b. Determine the cycle efficiency for each system.

c. Which system do you recommend and why?

Solution on p. 20-29.   d. Assuming Titleist is a "lean" manufacturer, what improvements in the selected system is it likely to pursue?

Increased Focus on Data-Driven Decision Making

eLectures LO5
MBC Evaluate ways in which the increasing availability of data might change the responsibilities of managerial accountants.

Increased access to data is changing the landscape of managerial accounting. Business leaders should be able to increasingly rely on data to answer difficult questions. Which products or services are most profitable? What are the best prices to charge for our services? Which manufacturing process is the most efficient? When business leaders can rely on data to answer these types of questions, they can then focus efforts on understanding which questions to ask. What is our business's core competency? What is our organization's strategic position (as discussed in Module 14)? Which products or services should we offer, or in which markets should we compete?

In order to rely on data, it must be accurate and timely. Costing models such as ABC, step, and linear algebra can help provide more accurate information on product costs. However, the accuracy of this data relies on management choosing relevant activity cost pools and cost drivers, and reasonable additional assumptions. Further, employees throughout the organization must understand and support the costing model. The concept of GIGO (garbage in, garbage out) refers to the idea that incorrect information going into a system results in incorrect data coming out. The system does not magically fix the information.[1]

Even when analysts have reliable and timely data, there are risks associated with data-driven decision making. A common issue is the misunderstanding of correlation versus causation. The idea behind big data analytics is to uncover hidden patterns and correlation among activities, and then to use this information to make decisions and to predict outcomes.[2] Often, just because there is a high correlation between two events, it does not mean that one caused the other. Using this information to then extrapolate further outcomes will be inaccurate. An example often referenced to demonstrate this issue is the windmill. The faster the windmill rotates, the more wind can be observed. Can we conclude that windmills cause wind? As ice cream sales increase, the rate of drowning increases. Does ice cream consumption cause drowning? These examples make it fairly obvious that one event does not cause the other, even though they are correlated. However, as managers are inundated with data, it may not always be so easy to understand the distinction between correlation and causation, resulting in poor decision making.

As the environment changes in terms of the availability of managerial accounting information, so too do the skills required of managerial accountants. Exhibit 20.6 summarizes the research conducted by the IMA to better understand the talent gap between the skills business leaders perceive as important factors of success and the skills their finance teams possess.[3] Finance professionals seem to be reasonably prepared with the more traditional skills such as financial analysis; budgeting, planning, and forecasting; and operations analysis. However, a more significant talent gap exists related to data skills such as technological acumen; identifying key data trends; data mining and extraction; and statistical modeling and data analysis skills. The study also emphasizes that softer skills are also increasingly sought. Business leaders expect finance teams to be capable of using data to improve business performance through skills such as process improvement, strategic thinking and execution, adaptability to change, and communications.

Exhibit 20.6 ■ Technical Skills Gap			
	Important to Success	Possessed by Your Team	Talent Gap
Financial analysis	87%	69%	18%
Budgeting, planning, and forecasting	85%	63%	22%
Operational analysis	82%	54%	28%
Cost management	81%	61%	20%
Technological acumen	77%	50%	27%
Identifying key data trends	75%	46%	29%
Data mining and extraction	71%	43%	28%
Statistical modeling and data analysis	62%	35%	27%
Enterprise resource planning (ERP) systems	61%	40%	21%
Customer lifetime value (CLV)	55%	32%	23%

LO5 Review 20-5

Increased access to data can help business leaders make better and more timely decisions. This can also allow them to focus more of their efforts toward more strategic analysis and thinking. Even though there are many benefits to the increasing availability of data, there are also risks and concerns.

Required

Discuss some accompanying risks and concerns of growing access to big data.

Solution on p. 20-29.

[1] Rod Koch, "Big Data or Big Empathy," *Strategic Finance*, December 1, 2015.

[2] http://www.sas.com/en_us/insights/analytics/big-data-analytics.html

[3] Kip Krumweide, "Building a Team to Capitalize on the Promise of Big Data," *IMA*, January 2016.

Guidance Answers

You Are the Controller

Pg. 20-9 Designing any information processing system is a matter of weighing benefits with the costs of designing and operating the system. The same is true for a cost allocation system. Also, you have to decide how the cost information will be used. If it is used only for external financial reporting purposes, a high degree of precision may not be necessary. However, if it is used to determine the most profitable product mix, it may be crucial to have the most precise cost information. For the service departments that provide only services to producing departments and that receive no services from other service departments, a direct allocation method might be adequate. For departments that provide and/or receive interdepartmental services, you should consider using either a step or linear algebra approach to assigning costs. Whether you use a direct, step, or linear algebra approach, you will have to decide whether to assign the costs using a single volume-based cost driver (such as square footage or number of employees) or using multiple cost drivers that reflect the actual activities performed. In most cases, the ABC approach (discussed in Module 19) will give a higher level of precision, but at considerably greater cost.

Questions

Q20-1. Distinguish between the following sets of terms:
  a. Direct product costs and indirect product costs.
  b. Direct department costs and indirect department costs.

Q20-2. Define the terms direct cost and indirect cost.

Q20-3. Differentiate between cost assignment and cost allocation.

Q20-4. Explain how a cost item can be both a direct cost and an indirect cost.

Q20-5. What is the primary advantage of separately allocating fixed and variable indirect costs?

Q20-6. Define interdepartmental services.

Q20-7. To what extent are interdepartmental services recognized under the direct, step, and linear algebra methods of service department cost allocation?

Q20-8. Is it feasible to assign interdepartmental services to production departments using ABC?

Q20-9. Explain the concept of just-in-time inventory management.

Q20-10. What are the major elements of lean production?

Q20-11. What is the relationship between JIT and the lean production concept?

Q20-12. Explain how computer technology has affected the way companies approach JIT inventory management and lean production methods.

Q20-13. What elements of the JIT approach contribute to reducing materials inventories?

Q20-14. Define and identify the elements of cycle time. Which of these elements adds value to the product?

Q20-15. Explain briefly how JIT/lean production benefits organizations that take a value-chain approach to management.

Q20-16. Explain how traditional performance evaluation systems using standard costs conflict with the lean production concept.

Assignments with the ⓜ logo in the margin are available in Ḃusiness Course.
See the Preface of the book for details.

Mini Exercises

LO2

Genzink Steel

M20-17. Allocating Service Department Costs: Allocation Basis Alternatives
  Assume **Genzink Steel**, a metal fabrication company, has two producing departments, P1 and P2, and one service department, S1. Estimated overhead costs per month are as follows:

P1.	$2,000,000
P2.	750,000
S1.	1,000,000

Other data follow:

	P1	P2
Number of employees	50	30
Production capacity (units).	75,000	20,000
Space occupied (square feet).	57,600	22,400
Five-year average percent of S1's service output used	60%	40%

Required

a. For each of the following allocation bases, determine the total estimated overhead cost for P1 and P2 after allocating S1 cost to the producing departments.

  1. Number of employees
  2. Production capacity in units
  3. Space occupied
  4. Five-year average percentage of S1 services used
  5. Estimated overhead costs (Round your answer to the nearest dollar.)

b. For each of the five allocation bases, explain the circumstances (including examples) under which each allocation base might be most appropriately used to allocate service department cost in a manufacturing plant such as Genzink Steel. Also, discuss the advantages and disadvantages that might result from using each of the allocation bases.

M20-18. Indirect Cost Allocation: Direct Method

LO2

Charlie Manufacturing Company has two production departments, Melting and Molding. Direct general plant management and plant security costs benefit both production departments. Charlie allocates general plant management costs on the basis of the number of production employees and plant security costs on the basis of space occupied by the production departments using the direct method of overhead allocation. In November, the following overhead costs were recorded:

Melting Department overhead	$500,000
Molding Department overhead.	400,000
General plant management	200,000
Plant security	100,000

Other pertinent data follow:

	Melting	Molding
Number of employees	60	40
Space occupied (square feet).	20,000	80,000
Machine hours	1,056	3,200
Direct labor hours.	10,560	7,200

Required

a. Prepare a schedule allocating general plant management costs and plant security costs to the Melting and Molding Departments.

b. Determine the total departmental overhead costs for the Melting and Molding Departments.

c. Assuming the Melting Department uses machine hours and the Molding Department uses direct labor hours to apply overhead to production, calculate the overhead rate for each production department.

M20-19. Interdepartment Services: Direct Method

LO2

Wilhelm Manufacturing Company has five operating departments, two of which are producing departments (P1 and P2) and three of which are service departments (S1, S2, and S3). All costs of the service departments are allocated to the producing departments. The following table shows the distribution of services from the service departments.

Services provided from	Services Provided to				
	S1	**S2**	**S3**	**P1**	**P2**
S1..	—	10%	20%	28%	42%
S2..	5%	—	15%	52%	28%
S3..	7%	3%	—	27%	63%

The direct operating costs of the service departments are as follows:

S1..	$150,000
S2..	80,000
S3..	106,000

Required

Using the direct method, prepare a schedule allocating the service department costs to the producing departments.

LO3, 4

Tesla, Inc. (TSLA)

M20-20. Inventory Ratio Calculations

Tesla reported the following data for 2018 and 2019, in millions:

Inventory	
December 31, 2017	$ 2,067
December 31, 2018	2,264
December 31, 2019	3,113
Cost of automotive sales	
2018	$ 6,725
2019	13,686
Gross margin	
2018	$ 1,810
2019	3,946

Required

(round all calculations to two decimal places)

a. Calculate the inventory turnover ratio for 2018 and 2019.

b. Calculate the gross margin return on inventory investment for 2018 and 2019.

LO3, 4

Dell Technologies Inc. (DELL)

M20-21. Inventory Ratio Calculations

Dell Technologies reported the following data for 2018 and 2019 (in millions):

Inventory	
February 3, 2017...	$ 2,538
February 2, 2018...	2,678
February 1, 2019...	3,649
Cost of products sold	
Year ended February 2, 2018..	$51,433
Year ended February 1, 2019..	57,889
Gross margin	
Year ended February 2, 2018..	$ 9,818
Year ended February 1, 2019..	13,398

Required

(round all calculations to two decimal places)

a. Calculate the inventory turnover ratio for the years ended in February 2018 and February 2019.

b. Calculate the gross margin return on inventory investment for the years ended in February 2018 and February 2019.

E20-22. Interdepartment Services: Step Method

Refer to the data in Mini Exercise M20-19. Using the step method, prepare a schedule for Wilhelm Manufacturing Company allocating the service department costs to the producing departments. (Round calculations to the nearest dollar.)

LO2

E20-23. Interdepartment Services: Step Method

Assume that Wilson's, a department store in Massachusetts, allocates the costs of the Personnel and Payroll departments to three retail sales departments, Housewares, Clothing, and Toys. In addition to providing services to the operating departments, Personnel and Payroll provide services to each other. Wilson's allocates Personnel Department costs on the basis of the number of employees and Payroll Department costs on the basis of gross payroll. Cost and allocation information for June is as follows:

LO2
Wilson's Department Store

	Personnel	Payroll	Housewares	Clothing	Toys
Direct department cost	$25,000	$30,340	$50,174	$60,830	$45,156
Number of employees	3	5	12	20	10
Gross payroll	$12,960	$17,280	$36,000	$43,200	$34,560

Required

a. Determine the percentage of total Personnel Department services that was provided to the Payroll Department.

b. Determine the percentage of total Payroll Department services that was provided to the Personnel Department.

c. Prepare a schedule showing Personnel Department and Payroll Department cost allocations to the operating departments, assuming Wilson's uses the step method. (Round calculations to the nearest dollar.)

E20-24. Product Costing in a JIT/Lean Environment

Johanna Computer manufactures laptop computers under its own brand, but acquires all the components from outside vendors. No computers are assembled until the order is received online from customers, so there is no finished goods inventory. When an order is received, the bill of materials required to fill the order is prepared automatically and sent electronically to the various vendors. All components are received from vendors within three days and the completed order is shipped to the customer immediately when completed, usually on the same day the components are received from vendors. The number of units in process at the end of any day is negligible.

LO3, 4

The following data are provided for the most recent month of operations:

Actual components costs incurred	$1,200,000
Actual conversion costs incurred	$1,850,000
Units in process, beginning of month	0
Units started in process during the month	4,000
Units in process, end of month	0

Required

a. Assuming Johanna uses traditional cost accounting procedures:
   1. How much cost was charged to Work-in-Process during the month?
   2. How much cost was charged to cost of goods sold during the month?

b. Assuming Johanna is a lean production company and uses the backflush costing method:
   1. How much cost was charged to Work-in-Process during the month?
   2. How much cost was charged to cost of goods sold during the month?

E20-25. Inventory Management Metrics

Large retailers like Costco and Target typically use gross margin ratio (gross margin ÷ sales), inventory turnover (sometimes referred to as inventory turns), and gross margin return on investment (GMROI) to evaluate how well inventory has been managed. The goal is to maximize profits while minimizing

LO4
Costco (COST)
Target (TGT)

the investment in inventory. Below are data for four scenarios, a base scenario (A) followed by three modifications (B, C, and D) to the base scenario.

	Scenario A	Scenario B	Scenario C	Scenario D
Sales.	$50,000	$75,000	$60,000	$50,000
Cost of goods sold	35,000	35,000	30,000	35,000
Gross profit.	$15,000	$40,000	$30,000	$15,000
Average inventory.	$ 6,000	$ 6,000	$ 6,000	$ 4,000

Required
For each scenario calculate the gross margin percent, the inventory turnover, and GMROI.

LO4   E20-26.   Evaluating Inventory Management Metrics
Refer to E20-25.

Required
a. For Scenarios B through D, explain what change occurred relative to Scenario A to cause GMROI to change. For example, was the change in GMROI caused by a change in inventory turns, a change in gross margin percent, or by reducing inventory levels?
b. What general conclusions can be made from the calculations and observations regarding the factors that influence GMROI?

LO5   E20-27.   Technical Skills Gap
Katie Dempsey works as a recruiter, placing accounting and finance professionals. Katie's current project is to fill an open managerial accounting position at PepsiCo. Identify the technical skills that Katie will be looking for in the applicant's resume and application materials that will likely lead to success in the position. Do you think these skills will be difficult to find in candidates? If so, what are some ways PepsiCo might be able to develop these skills in-house?

LO3   E20-28.   Cycle Efficiency
Clarion Scooters, Inc. runs one 8-hour shift per day. Three different machines are used in the production of electric scooters, Clarion's sole product.

The operations manager at Clarion is looking at ways to be more efficient and has gathered the following information:

Manufacturing time per batch of 50 scooters	
Function	**Time**
Actual processing time on the machines for one batch of scooters	3.75 hours
Time spent moving a batch of scooters from one station to the next	2 hours
Time spent on quality control testing, per batch.	45 minutes
Time spent setting up equipment, for batch processing.	30 minutes

The operations manager also noted that, on average, there was about one hour of downtime per batch. (Downtime occurred when employees were unavailable to move or test the scooters.)

a. What is the cycle time per batch, in hours?
b. What is Clarion's cycle efficiency?
c. What are some practical steps Clarion could take to improve its efficiency?

Problems

LO2   P20-29.   Selecting Cost Allocation Bases and Direct Method Allocations
Seattle Company has three producing departments (P1, P2, and P3) for which direct department costs are accumulated. In January, the following indirect costs of operation were incurred.

Plant manager's salary and office expense	$20,500
Plant security	6,000
Plant nurse's salary and office expense	7,000
Factory depreciation (building)	20,000
Equipment depreciation	15,000
Machine maintenance	7,000
Plant cafeteria cost subsidy	5,000
	$80,500

The following additional data have been collected for the three producing departments:

	P1	P2	P3
Number of employees	20	30	10
Space occupied (square feet)	12,000	6,000	6,000
Direct labor hours	3,400	5,000	1,600
Machine hours	1,500	600	900
Number of nurse office visits	25	20	5

Required

a. Group the indirect cost items into cost pools based on their common basis for allocation. Identify the most appropriate allocation basis for each cost pool and determine the total January costs in the pool. (*Hint:* A cost pool may consist of one or more cost items.)

b. Allocate the cost pools directly to the three producing departments using the allocation bases selected in requirement (a).

c. How much indirect cost would be allocated to each producing department if Seattle Company were using a plantwide rate based on direct labor hours? Based on machine hours?

d. Comment on the benefits of allocating costs in pools compared with using a plantwide rate.

P20-30. Evaluating Allocation Bases and Direct Method Allocations   LO2

Brahtz Company has two service departments, Maintenance and Information Technology (IT), that serve two producing departments, Mixing and Packaging. The following data have been collected for these departments for the current year:

	IT	Maintenance	Mixing	Packaging
Direct department costs	$210,000	$185,000	$1,200,000	$550,000
Number of employees			40	20
Number of ethernet connections			50	30
Number of maintenance hours used			1,500	1,000
Number of maintenance orders			120	180

Required

a. Using the direct method, allocate the service department costs under the following independent assumptions:

   1. IT costs are allocated based on the number of employees, and Maintenance costs are allocated based on the number of maintenance hours used.

   2. IT costs are allocated based on the number of ethernet connections served, and Maintenance costs are allocated based on the number of maintenance orders.

b. Comment on the reasonableness of the bases used in the calculations in requirement (a). What considerations should determine which bases to use for allocating IT and Maintenance costs?

P20-31. Cost Reimbursement and Step Allocation Method   LO2

Hope Clinic is a not-for-profit outpatient facility that provides medical services to both fee-paying patients and low-income government-supported patients. Reimbursement from the government is based on total actual costs of services provided, including both direct costs of patient services and indirect operating costs. Patient services are provided through two producing departments, Medical Services and Ancillary Services (includes X-ray, therapy, etc.). In addition to the direct costs of these departments, the clinic incurs indirect costs in two service departments, Administration and Facilities. Administration costs are allocated first based on the number of full-time employees, and Facilities costs are then allocated based on space occupied. Costs and related data for the current month are as follows:

	Administration	Facilities	Medical Services	Ancillary Services
Direct costs........................	$65,000	$30,750	$745,700	$350,000
Number of employees	6	4	8	4
Amount of space occupied (square feet)	2,000	600	7,500	2,500
Number of patient visits	—	—	7,975	3,000

Required

a. Using the step method, prepare a schedule allocating the common service department costs to the producing departments.

b. Determine the amount to be reimbursed from the government for each low-income patient visit.

LO2 P20-32. Budgeted Service Department Cost Allocation: Pricing a New Product

Fit & Active Company is adding a new diet food concentrate called Body Fit & Healthy to its line of bodybuilding and exercise products. A plant is being built for manufacturing the new product. Management has decided to price the new product based on a 100% markup on total manufacturing costs. A direct cost budget for the new plant projects that direct department costs of $7,152,500 will be incurred in producing an expected normal output of 750,000 pounds of finished product. In addition, indirect costs for Administration and Technical Support will be shared by Body Fit & Healthy with the two exercise products divisions, Commercial Products and Retail Products. Budgeted annual data to be used in making the allocations are summarized here.

	Administration	Technical Support	Commercial Products	Retail Products	Body Fit & Healthy
Number of employees	10	4	70	60	20
Amount of technical support time (hours)	690	—	1,840	1,610	460

Direct costs are budgeted at $750,000 for the Administration Department and $500,000 for the Technical Support Department.

Required

a. Using the step method, determine the total direct and indirect costs of Body Fit & Healthy. (Administration costs are allocated based on number of employees; Technical Support costs are allocated based on technical support time.)

b. Determine the selling price per pound of Body Fit & Healthy. (Round calculations to the nearest cent.)

LO2 P20-33. Allocation and Responsibility Accounting

Timberland Company (TBL)

Assume that Timberland Company uses a responsibility accounting system for evaluating its managers, and that abbreviated performance reports for the company's three divisions for the month of March are as follows (amounts in thousands).

	Total	East	Central	West
Operating income before service department cost allocations	$480,000	$200,000	$170,000	$110,000
Less allocated costs:				
Information Technology................	(250,000)	(96,154)	(76,923)	(76,923)
Personnel	(160,000)	(71,111)	(53,333)	(35,556)
Division income	$ 70,000	$ 32,735	$ 39,744	$ (2,479)

The West Division manager is very disturbed over his performance report and recent rumors that his division may be closed because of its failure to report a profit in recent periods. He believes that the reported profit figures do not fairly present operating results because his division is being unfairly burdened with service department costs. He is particularly concerned over the amount of Information Technology costs charged to his division. He believes that it is inequitable for his division to be charged with one-third of the total cost when it is using only 20% of the services. He believes that the Personnel

Department's use of the Information Technology Department should also be considered in the cost allocations. Cost allocations were based on the following distributions of service provided:

| | | Services Receiver | | | |
Services Provider	Personnel	Computer Services	East	Central	West
Information Technology	35%	—	25%	20%	20%
Personnel	—	10%	40%	30%	20%

Required

a. What method is the company using to allocate Personnel and Information Technology costs?

b. Recompute the cost allocations using the step method. (Round calculations to the nearest dollar.)

c. Revise the performance reports to reflect the cost allocations computed in requirement (b).

d. Comment on the complaint of the West Division's manager.

P20-34. **Allocating Service Department Costs: Direct and Step Methods; Department and Plantwide Overhead Rates**   **LO2**

Assume that Brown Jordan, a manufacturer of fine casual outdoor furniture, allocates Human Resources Department costs to the producing departments (Cutting and Welding) based on number of employees; Facilities Department costs are allocated based on the amount of square footage occupied. Direct department costs, labor hours, and square footage data for the four departments for October are as follows:

     Brown Jordan

	Human Resources	Facilities	Cutting	Welding
Direct department overhead costs	$150,000	$450,000	$2,662,500	$1,102,500
Number of employees	12	20	60	90
Number of direct labor hours	—	—	12,000	15,000
Amount of square footage	15,000	4,500	225,000	75,000

Assume that two jobs, A1 and A2, were completed during October and that each job had direct materials costs of $3,000. Job A1 used 75 direct labor hours in the Cutting Department and 25 direct labor hours in the Welding Department. Job A2 used 25 direct labor hours in the Cutting Department and 75 direct labor hours in the Welding Department. The direct labor rate per hour, including benefits, is $50 in both departments.

Required

a. Find the cost of each job using a plantwide rate based on direct labor hours.

b. Find the cost of each job using department rates with *direct* service department cost allocation.

c. Find the cost of each job using department rates with *step* service department cost allocation.

d. Explain the differences in the costs computed in requirements (a)–(c) for each job. Which costing method is best for product pricing and profitability analysis?

P20-35. **JIT/Lean Production and Product Costing**   **LO3, 4**

Presented is information pertaining to the standard or budgeted unit cost of a product manufactured in a JIT/Lean Production environment at CNN Systems Inc.:

Direct materials.	$30
Conversion	60
Total	$90

All materials are added at the start of the production process. All raw materials purchases and conversion costs are directly assigned to Cost of Goods Sold. At the end of the period, costs are backed out and assigned to Raw Materials in Process (only for materials still in the plant) and Finished Goods Inventory (for materials and conversion costs for completed units). Costs assigned to inventories are based on the standard or budgeted cost multiplied by the number of units in inventory. Conversion costs are assigned to inventories only for fully converted units. Since inventory levels tend to be small in this JIT environment, partially completed units are assigned no conversion costs. CNN

Systems had no beginning inventories on August 1. During the month, it incurred the following manufacturing-related costs:

Purchase of raw materials on account	$500,000
Factory wages	100,000
Factory supervision salaries	25,000
Facilities costs	75,000
Factory supplies purchased	15,000
Depreciation	35,000

The end-of-month inventory included raw materials in process of 150 units and finished goods of 250 units. One hundred units of raw materials were 0% converted; the other 50 units averaged 40% converted.

Required

a. Calculate the total cost debited to Cost of Goods Sold during August.

b. Calculate the balances in Raw Materials in Process, Finished Goods Inventory, and Cost of Goods Sold at the end of August.

c. Assuming that August is a typical month, is it likely that using the company's shortcut backflush accounting procedures will produce misleading financial statements? Explain.

LO4   **P20-36.   Just-in-Time Performance Evaluation**

To control operations, Sirius Company makes extensive and exclusive use of financial performance reports for each department. Although all departments have been reporting favorable cost variances in most periods, management is perplexed by the firm's low overall return on investment. You have been asked to look into the matter. Believing the purchasing department is typical of the company's operations, you obtained the following information concerning the purchases of parts for a product it started producing five years ago:

Year	Purchase Price Variance	Quantity Used (units)	Average Inventory (units)
Year 1	$ 1,500 F	10,000	1,500
Year 2	10,500 F	15,000	2,500
Year 3	12,000 F	17,500	3,000
Year 4	20,000 U	12,500	2,500
Year 5	8,000 F	18,000	2,250
Current year	9,500 F	14,500	2,900

Required

a. Compute the inventory turnover for each year. What conclusions can be drawn from a yearly comparison of the purchase price variance and the inventory turnover?

b. Identify problems likely to be caused by evaluating purchasing only on the basis of the purchase price variance.

c. Offer whatever recommendations you believe appropriate.

LO2

Embassy Suites
Hilton Worldwide
(HLT)

P20-37.   Dual Allocation Approach and Charging for Services

Assume that the Maintenance Department of one of Embassy Suites, a Hilton Worldwide franchise properties, has fixed costs of $750,000 a year. It also incurs $75 in out-of-pocket expenses for every hour of work. During the year the Rooms Department used 35,000 maintenance hours. The Food and Beverage (F&B) Department used 15,000 maintenance hours. When the Maintenance Department was established, the Rooms and F&B departments estimated they would need 35,000 and 25,000 maintenance hours, respectively. It turns out F&B cut back on maintenance hours used to insure it would meet its budget.

Required

a. Calculate the amount of Maintenance Department costs to allocate to Rooms and F&B based entirely on actual usage.

b. Calculate the amount of Maintenance Department costs to allocate to Rooms and F&B using a dual allocation approach where fixed cost is allocated based on estimated capacity needed and variable cost is allocated based on actual usage.

c. Which of the two methods applied in parts *a* and *b* is more fair to the two departments?

d. Assume that the Maintenance Department allocates costs to the producing departments using a user charge. What amount would you suggest for the user charge? Is it a good idea to use a user charge for allocating costs?

Management Applications

MA20-38. Materials Push and Materials Pull Systems

LO3, 4

Data Storage Inc. produces three models of external storage devices for personal computers. Each model is produced on a separate assembly line. Production consists of several operations in separate work centers. Because of a high demand for Data's products, management is most interested in high-production volume and operating efficiency. Each work center is evaluated on the basis of its operating efficiency. To avoid idle time caused by defective units, variations in machine times, and machine breakdowns, significant inventories are maintained between each workstation.

At a recent administrative committee meeting, the director of research announced that the firm's engineers have made a dramatic breakthrough in designing a low-cost, read/write optical storage device. Data Storage's president is very enthusiastic, and the vice president of marketing wishes to add an assembly line for optical storage devices as soon as possible. The equipment necessary to manufacture the new product can be purchased and installed in less than 60 days. Unfortunately, all available plant space is currently devoted to the production of conventional storage devices, and expansion is not possible at the current plant location. It appears that adding the new product will require dropping a current product, relocating the entire operation, or manufacturing the optical storage devices at a separate location.

The vice president of marketing is opposed to dropping a current product. The vice president of finance is opposed to relocating the entire operation because of financing requirements and the associated financial risks. The vice president of production is opposed to splitting up production activities because of the loss of control and the added costs for various types of overhead.

Required

Explain how switching to a materials pull (Kanban) system can help solve Data Storage's space problems while improving quality and cycle time. Describe how a materials pull system works and the changes required in management attitude toward inventory and efficiency to make it work.

MA20-39. Product Costing Using Activity-Based Costing and Just-in-Time: A Value Chain Approach

LO3, 4

Wearwell Carpet Company is a small residential carpet manufacturer started by Don Stegall, a long-time engineer and manager in the carpet industry. Stegall began Wearwell in the early 1990s after learning about ABC, JIT, total quality management, and several other manufacturing concepts being used successfully in Japan and other parts of the world. Although it was a small company, he believed that with his many years of experience and by applying these advanced techniques, Wearwell could very quickly become a world-class competitor.

Stegall buys dyed carpet yarns for Wearwell from three different major yarn manufacturers with which he has done business for many years. He chose these companies because of their reputation for producing high-quality products and their state-of-the-art research and development departments. He has arranged for two carpet manufacturing companies to produce (tuft) all of his carpets on a contractual basis. Both companies have their own brands, but they also do contract work for other companies. For each manufacturer, Stegall had to agree to use the full output of one manufacturing production line at least one day per month. Each production line was dedicated to producing only one style of carpet, but each manufacturer had production lines capable of running each type of carpet that Wearwell sold.

Stegall signed a contract with a large transport company (CTC), which specializes in carpet-related shipping, to pick up and deliver yarn from the yarn plants to the tufting mills. This company will then deliver the finished product from the tufting mills to Wearwell's ten customers, which are carpet retailers in the ten largest residential building markets in the country. These retailers pay the shipping charges to have the carpets delivered to them. Wearwell maintains a small sales staff (which also doubles as a customer service staff) to deal with the retailers and occasionally with the end customers on quality problems that arise.

Wearwell started selling only one line of carpet, a medium-grade plush, but as new carpet styles were developed, it added two additional lines, a medium-grade berber carpet and a medium-grade textured carpet. Three colors are offered in each carpet style. By selling only medium grades with limited color choices, Stegall felt that he would reach a very large segment of the carpet market without having to deal with a large number of different products. As textured (trackless) carpets have become more popular, sales of plush have diminished substantially.

Required

a. Describe the value chain for Wearwell Carpet Company, and identify the parties who compose this value chain.

b. Identify and discuss the cost categories that would be included in the cost of the product for financial reporting purposes.

c. Identify and discuss the cost categories that would be included in the cost of the product for pricing and other management purposes.

d. Discuss some of the challenges that Stegall will have trying to apply JIT to regulate the levels of control at Wearwell. Suggest changes that might be necessary to make JIT work.

e. Does Wearwell seem to be an appropriate setting for implementing ABC? If so, what are likely to be the most important activities and related cost drivers?

Solutions to Review Problems

Review 20-1—Solution

Plantwide overhead rate—The costs of all service departments are added to the indirect product costs incurred within all the producing departments to get total plantwide manufacturing overhead, which is then assigned to products using a single overhead rate based on a common factor such as direct labor hours.

Department overhead rate—Service department costs are allocated to the production departments that use their services, and the allocated service department costs are added to the indirect costs incurred within the department to arrive at total department overhead and allocation rates.

Activity-based costing—Service department costs are assigned to activity cost pools; then the activity cost pools are assigned to the product based on an activity driver allocation rate.

Review 20-2—Solution

Service Department Cost Allocation

a. *Direct Method*

	Total	Women's	Men's
Administrative Services Department			
Allocation base (number of employees)	24	15	9
Percent of total base.	100%	62.5%	37.5%
Cost allocation	$18,000	$11,250	$6,750
Facilities Services Department			
Allocation base (square footage)	22,500	15,000	7,500
Percent of total base.	100%	66.7%	33.3%
Cost allocation	$12,000	$ 8,000	$4,000

Cost Allocation Summary	Administrative	Facilities	Women's	Men's	Total
Departmental costs before allocation	$18,000	$12,000	$60,000	$50,000	$140,000
Cost allocations					
Administrative	(18,000)	—	11,250	6,750	0
Facilities	—	(12,000)	8,000	4,000	0
Departmental costs after allocation.	$ 0	$ 0	$79,250	$60,750	$140,000

Step Method

Allocation Sequence		
	Administrative	**Facilities**
Allocation base	Number of employees	Amount of square footage
Total base for other service and producing departments (a)	26	25,000
Total base for other service departments (b)	2	2,500
Percent of total services provided to other service departments (b ÷ a)	7.7%	10.0%
Order of allocation	Second	First

Step Allocations				
	Total	**Administrative**	**Women's**	**Men's**
Facilities Services Department				
Allocation base (square footage)	25,000	2,500	15,000	7,500
Percent of total base.	100%	10%	60%	30%
Cost allocation	$12,000	$1,200	$ 7,200	$3,600
Administrative Services Department				
Allocation base (number of employees)	24	—	15	9
Percent of total base.	100%	—	62.5%	37.5%
Cost allocation ($18,000 + $1,200).	$19,200	—	$12,000	$7,200

Cost Allocation Summary					
	Facilities	**Administrative**	**Women's**	**Men's**	**Total**
Departmental costs before allocation	$12,000	$18,000	$60,000	$50,000	$140,000
Cost allocations					
Facilities	(12,000)	1,200	7,200	3,600	0
Administrative	—	(19,200)	12,000	7,200	0
Departmental costs after allocations.	$ 0	$ 0	$79,200	$60,800	$140,000

b. Another service department cost allocation method is the *linear algebra method*. This method simultaneously allocates service department costs both to other service departments and to the producing departments. It has an advantage over the *step method* in that it fully recognizes interdepartmental services.

c. If **Buckle** wants the most precise allocation of service department costs to the producing departments, considering both direct services and indirect services, it must use the linear algebra method of service department allocation. As indicated in the Allocation Sequence section of the step method in (*a*), Facilities provides 10% of its services to Administrative, and Administrative provides 7.7% of its services to Facilities. The step method recognized the Facilities services provided to Administrative, but it did not recognize the Administrative services provided to Facilities.

In this case, the producing departments are using approximately the same proportion of services from each of the service departments (60.0% to 62.5% for the Women's Department and 30.0% to 37.5% for the Men's Department). Hence, using a more precise measure of cost allocation is not likely to produce significantly different results, especially since the interdepartmental services are so close (7.7% versus 10.0%). Just as the step method allocation results were quite close to the direct method results, the linear method results would likely be quite close to both the direct and step method results. Use of the linear algebra method is not recommended in this case. On the basis of simplicity and convenience, the direct method is probably the best method for Buckle to use.

Review 20-3—Solution

  __1__   *a.*   Nimble production process with small lot sizes and short setup and changeover times.
  __2__   *b.*   Material push system.
  __3__   *c.*   Key to managing work-in-process inventories and central to a lean production approach.
  __1__   *d.*   Selecting venders on the basis of service and material quality, as well as price.
  __1__   *e.*   Accepting vendor deliveries directly to the shop floor, and only as needed.
  __1__   *f.*   Employees at each station work to provide inventory for the next workstation only as needed (Kanban system).

Review 20-4—Solution

a.   Cycle time is the total time required to produce one batch, including both value-added and non-value-added activities: System A = 83; System B = 77

b.   The cycle efficiency is the percent of total time used in value-added activities. In this case, only the processing time is adding value to the product. Cycle efficiency: System A = 40/83 = 0.48; System B = 30/77 = 0.39

c.   In selecting between A and B, the system with the higher efficiency would not likely be chosen because it has the longer total cycle time. Assuming both systems produce products of equal quality and characteristics, B is appealing because it requires one-fourth less processing time than A and offers greater opportunity for continuous improvement.

d.   In a lean environment, management and all employees involved will be seeking ways to reduce the cycle time while maintaining a high-quality product. For B, the most likely opportunity for significant reduction is to reduce the large amount of movement and waiting time. If these components of total cycle time can be reduced, B becomes even more attractive.

Review 20-5—Solution

Students will have a variety of answers. Here are a few possible responses.

1. The data must be timely and reliable. Incorrect or misleading data can result in bad information and lead to incorrect and poor decisions.
2. Softer skills such as communication, strategic thinking, and execution are also of growing importance as organizations focus more on the need to communicate and execute business strategies.
3. Analysts must be careful when drawing conclusions based on data. Often, events may seem to be linked when there may be no causal relationship driving the correlation. The cause may be inverted as in the windmill example. The machine does not cause the wind, but the wind causes the windmill to move. Or there may be additional factors to consider as in the ice cream/drowning relationship. The missing link here is that higher temperatures likely lead to more swimming and therefore, more drowning, and higher temperatures also lead to more ice cream consumption.

Module **21**

Pricing and Other Product Management Decisions

Pricing and Other Product Management Decisions			
Understanding the Value Chain	**The Pricing Decision**	**Target Costing**	**Other Costing Techniques**
▪ Usefulness of a Value Chain Perspective ▪ Value-Added and Value Chain Perspectives	▪ Economic Approaches to Pricing ▪ Cost-Based Approaches to Pricing	▪ Target Costing and Cost Management ▪ Target Costing and Design ▪ Target Costing and Product Life Cycles	▪ Continuous Improvement Costing ▪ Benchmarking
Review 21-1	Review 21-2	Review 21-3	Review 21-4, 21-5

PREVIEW   Roku Inc.

Roku, Inc. has been a dominant player in streaming media since 2008, when it introduced its first set-top streaming media device. The Roku Stick was introduced in 2012. Roku devices stream content from most major content providers (Netflix, Amazon Prime, Disney+, and Apple TV+, for example). The company also launched its own streaming channel in 2017, although the free Roku Channel includes no original content. Roku started selling its own branded smart TVs in 2014, manufactured by companies like Hitachi, Magnavox, and Sharp. All Roku products are built on the Roku OS. The company also licenses Roku OS to other television manufacturers and distributors.

In 2019, over 44% of all connected-TV viewing hours were streamed through Roku devices. By the end of 2019, Roku's software was embedded in one-third of all smart TVs sold in the U.S.

That's the good news. The bad news is that Roku has yet to report any profits from operations. However, its most lucrative business, advertising, has substantial upside. The television advertising market is around $70 billion annually. Over-the-top (OTT) advertising revenue (streamed through media devices) was about $4 billion in 2019. As consumers move from cable and satellite television to streamed content, advertising dollars are expected to move as well.

In an industry as dynamic and fast-moving as video streaming, staying competitive means continuing to grow and adapt as the technology and the market change. Roku's primary media device competitors are Apple's Apple TV, Alphabet's Google Chromecast, and Amazon's Fire TV. All three are actively pursuing the growing advertising revenues, and, although most content providers are currently allowing streaming on all media devices, that may change. CBS's decision to block Dish Network from retransmitting CBS stations in various markets, after a contract dispute, affected 3 million Dish subscribers. Although the situation was resolved, the sheer number of consumer options increases the risks to Roku.

Other companies are looking to limit the use of Roku devices. For example, Samsung sells more than a dozen smart TVs that don't use Roku's operating system, Amazon is exploring deals with smart TV manufacturers, and Comcast and AT&T are offering streaming devices to subscribers.

Given the fledgling industry's vast uncertainty, we must assume that product life-cycle stages will be abbreviated either from competition or regulation. To maximize its sales and profits in the short run, a company like Roku must compete on the functionality, quality, and continuous improvement of its products and services. The managerial tools discussed throughout this module are increasingly important for managers involved in the development, production, and marketing of products and services that compete in contested environments. A company that truly understands the value chain of its production and delivery systems will remain nimble and flexible in the face of a changing regulatory and competitive landscape.

Road Map

LO	Learning Objective | Topics	Page	eLecture	Guided Example	Assignments
21-1	**Explain the importance of the value chain in managing products and describe the key components of an organization's internal and external value chain.** Understanding the Value Chain :: Usefulness of the Value Chain :: Supplier-Buyer Partnerships :: Focus on Core Competencies :: Value Add	21-3	e21-1	Review 21-1	13, 14, 15, 16
21-2	**Distinguish between economic and cost-based approaches to pricing.** The Pricing Decision :: Economic Approach :: Cost-Based Approach :: Critique of Cost-Based Pricing	21-7	e21-2	Review 21-2	17, 18, 19, 21, 22, 23, 24, 25, 27, 31, 32, 33
21-3	**Explain target costing and discuss its acceptance in highly competitive industries.** Target Costing :: Cost Management :: Design for Production :: Benefits of Target Costing :: Managing Life-Cycle Costs	21-12	e21-3	Review 21-3	26, 28, 34
21-4	**Illustrate the relation between target costing and continuous improvement costing.** Kaizen Costing :: Continuous Improvement	21-17	e21-4	Review 21-4	29, 30
21-5	**Explain how benchmarking enhances quality management, continuous improvement, and process reengineering.** Benchmarking :: Setting Goals :: Six Steps	21-19	e21-5	Review 21-5	20

Strategic cost management techniques, such as *target costing* and *continuous improvement costing*, represent important concepts for product management professionals involved in the development, manufacture, and marketing of products and services. Virtually all such techniques are grounded in the notion of managing the value chain. This module examines pricing, the interrelation between price and cost, and the role of benchmarking in meeting customer needs at the lowest possible price.

We begin with a discussion of the value chain, followed by an overview of the pricing model economists use to explain price equilibrium. Given the limitations of this long-run equilibrium model for determining price of a product or service, we consider the widely used cost-plus approach to identifying initial prices. We then examine how intense competition (such as that for the green car market) has inverted the cost-plus pricing model into one that starts with an acceptable market price and subtracts a desired profit to determine a target cost. We also consider *life-cycle costs* from the perspectives of both the seller, who increasingly plans for all costs before production begins, and the buyer, who regards subsequent operating, maintenance, repair, and disposal costs as important as price. Finally, we consider how *benchmarking* can assist in improving competitiveness and profitability.

Understanding the Value Chain

eLectures
MBC **LO1** Explain the importance of the value chain in managing products and describe the key components of an organization's internal and external value chain.

The **value chain** for a product or service is the set of value-producing activities that stretches from basic raw materials to the final consumer. Each product or service has a distinct value chain, and all entities along the value chain depend on the final customer's perception of the value and cost of a product or service. It is the final customer who ultimately pays all costs and provides all profits to all organizations along the entire value chain. Consequently, *the goal of every organization is to maximize the value, while minimizing the cost, of a product or service to final customers.*

The value chain provides a viewpoint that encompasses all activities performed to deliver products and services to final customers. Depending on the needs of management, value chains are developed at varying levels of detail. Analyzing a value chain from the perspective of the final consumer requires working backward from the end product or service to the basic raw materials entering into the product or service. Analyzing a value chain from the viewpoint of an organization that is in the middle of a value chain requires working forward (downstream) to the final consumer and backward (upstream) to the source of raw materials. The paper industry provides a convenient context for illustrating the value chain concept.

Exhibit 21.1 presents the value chain for the paperboard cartons used to package beverages, such as Coca-Cola, Pepsi, or Evían products. The value chain is presented at three levels, with each successive level containing additional details. The first level depicts the various business entities in the value chain:

- Timber producers grow the pulp wood (usually pine) used as the basic input into paper products. Some paper companies, such as International Paper (the leading producer of paperboard), harvest much of their pulp wood from timberlands that they manage. Other companies, including Georgia Pacific, do not manage their own timberlands, but purchase pulp for their mills on the open market through pulp intermediaries.

- Pulp mills produce the kraft (unbleached) paper used to produce the paperboard. Companies such as International Paper and Georgia Pacific own pulp mills which produce the kraft paper. Other paperboard manufacturers can purchase pulp and kraft paper from companies such as Domtar.

- Paperboard manufacturers perform a laminating process of coating paperboard material used to produce beverage packages. The layers of coating give the top surface a high gloss finish that is water resistant and suitable for multicolor printing.

- The paperboard converter uses manufactured paperboard to print and produce the completed beverage packaging product, such as the cartons used to package the Diet Coca-Cola 12-pack.

- Beverage distributors, such as Coca-Cola Enterprises and Anheuser-Busch, purchase the completed paperboard packages from companies like Graphic Packaging to package their many different brands in various package sizes and shapes.

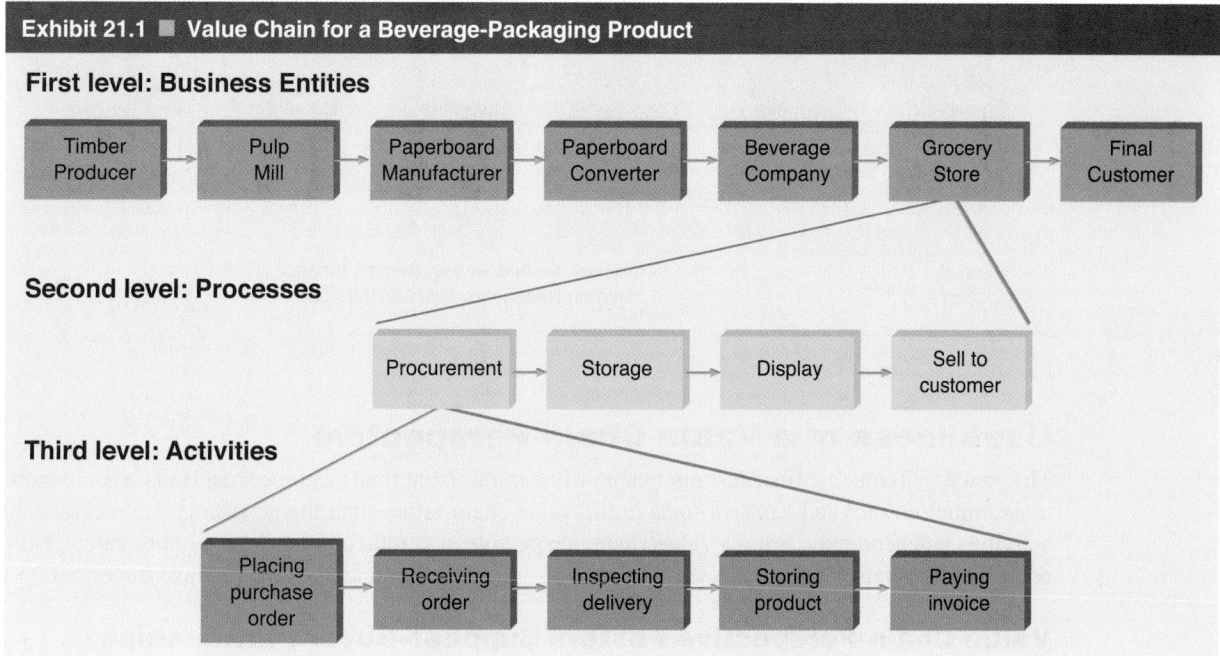

Exhibit 21.1 ■ Value Chain for a Beverage-Packaging Product

First level: Business Entities

Timber Producer → Pulp Mill → Paperboard Manufacturer → Paperboard Converter → Beverage Company → Grocery Store → Final Customer

Second level: Processes

Procurement → Storage → Display → Sell to customer

Third level: Activities

Placing purchase order → Receiving order → Inspecting delivery → Storing product → Paying invoice

- Grocery and convenience stores, such as **Publix** and **7-Eleven**, display and sell beverages packaged in the paperboard containers.

- The final customer purchases beverages packaged in paperboard packages and uses the packages to carry the beverages and to store them until consumed. The packages not only perform a transport and storage function but also serve as an advertising medium for the beverage company. The beverage company's advertising on the paperboard packages is intended to entice customers to purchase the beverage company's product and to help create a sense of satisfaction for the customer.

To better understand how business entities within the chain add value and incur costs, management might further refine the value chain into **processes**, collections of related activities intended to achieve a common purpose. The second level in Exhibit 21.1 represents major processes concerning the procurement and sale of Coca-Cola products by a grocery store. To simplify our illustration, we show only the processes for the grocery store related to the purchase and sale of Coca-Cola products packaged in paperboard packages. These processes include procuring Coca-Cola products from the bottling company, storing and displaying the product, and selling the product to the final consumer.

An **activity** is a unit of work. In the third level of Exhibit 21.1, the grocery store process to procure Coca-Cola products is further broken up into the following activities:

- *Placing* a purchase order for Coca-Cola products packaged in paperboard packages.

- *Receiving* delivery of the Coca-Cola products in paperboard packages.

- *Inspecting* the delivery to make sure it corresponds with the purchase order and to verify that the products are in good condition.

- *Storing* Coca-Cola products in paperboard packages until needed for display.

- *Paying* for Coca-Cola products acquired after the invoice arrives.

Each of the activities involved in procuring product from a vendor is described by a word ending with *ing*. This suggests that most work activities involve action. One way to think about the internal value chain for a particular company is provided in Exhibit 21.2 in terms of the basic components of the value chain that are found in most organizations. This generic model, first developed by Michael Porter, is a good starting point in identifying the internal value chain links for a particular organization.

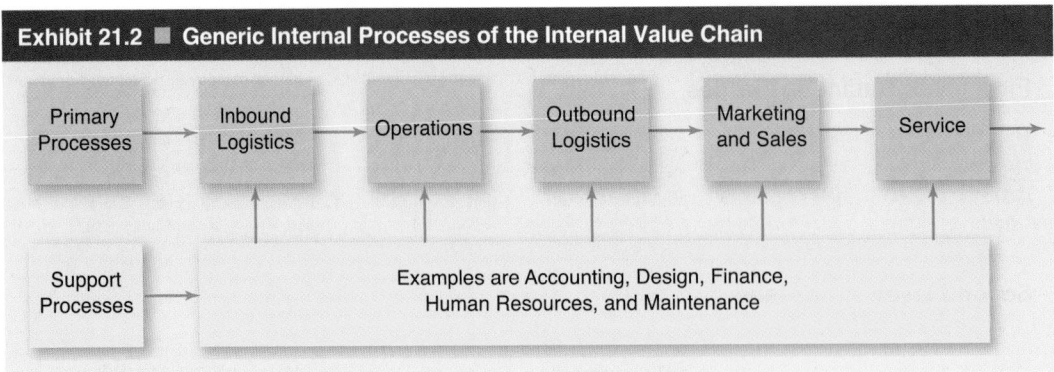

Exhibit 21.2 ■ Generic Internal Processes of the Internal Value Chain

Usefulness of a Value Chain Perspective

The goal of maximizing final customer value while minimizing final customer cost leads organizations to examine *internal* and *external links* in the value chain rather than the departments, processes, or activities independently. From a value chain perspective, it is total cost across the entire value chain, not the cost of individual businesses, departments, processes, or activities that is most important.

Value Chain Perspective Fosters Supplier–Buyer Partnerships

In the past, relationships between suppliers and buyers were often adversarial. Contact between suppliers and buyers was solely through the selling and purchasing departments. Suppliers attempted merely to meet purchasing contract specifications at the lowest possible cost. Buyers encouraged competition among suppliers with the primary—and often single—goal of obtaining the lowest purchase price.

As discussed in Module 20 with JIT and lean production, exploiting cost reduction and value-enhancing opportunities in the value chain has led many buyers and suppliers to view each other as partners rather than as adversaries. Buyers have reduced the number of suppliers they deal with, often developing long-term partnerships with a single supplier. Once they establish mutual trust, both proceed to share detailed information on internal operations and help each other solve problems. Partners work closely to examine mutual opportunities by studying their common value chain. Supplier engineers might determine that a minor relaxation in buyer specifications would significantly reduce supplier manufacturing costs with only minor increases in subsequent buyer processing costs. Working together, they determine how best to modify processes to reduce overall costs and share increased profits.

Companies such as Hewlett-Packard and Boeing involve suppliers in design, development, and manufacturing decisions. Motorola has even developed a survey asking suppliers to assess Motorola as a buyer. Among other questions, the survey asks sellers to evaluate Motorola's performance in helping suppliers to identify major cost drivers and to increase their profitability. These questions represent the concerns of a partner rather than those of an adversary. Michael Dell, at Dell Computers, stated that "rather than closely guarding our information databases, which took us years to develop, we used Internet browsers to essentially give that information to our customers and suppliers—bringing them into our business."[1] The following Business Insight box describes how General Motors is strengthening its relationships with its suppliers, in the hopes of working together to develop cost-cutting strategies.

On a smaller scale, the grocery store in Exhibit 21.1 should examine its external links. It may be willing to pay more for Coca-Cola products if the distributors cooperate to help reduce costs such as the following:

■ Making more frequent deliveries in small lots would reduce storage costs.

■ Being responsible for maintaining and changing the product displays would relieve store workers of these tasks.

■ Streamlining ordering and payment procedures would reduce bookkeeping costs.

---

[1] *Direct from Dell*, Michael Dell with Catherine Fredman, Harper Collins Publishers, 1999.
Also, see http://money.cnn.com/magazines/fortune/fortune500/2007/full_list/index.html

Business Insight ■ Cost Control: For Starters, Your Suppliers Don't Need to Hate You

General Motors is seeking to improve historically poor supplier relationships. The company's purchasing chief, Steve Kiefer, says that the company is now negotiating parts contracts that span two vehicle generations—up to a decade. North America's largest automaker hopes that this will give them access to both lower costs and advanced technology. Strengthening relationships with suppliers and then partnering on cost cutting is a new approach for GM. In the past, GM's suppliers saw the automaker's planning and cost-cutting processes as heavy handed, which made suppliers unwilling to give GM access to new technologies. Kiefer hopes that long-term commitments to suppliers will lead to more attention and productive partnerships for the company.

Source: Jeff Bennett, "GM Seeks Longer-Term Supplier Contracts in Bid to Cut Costs," *Wall Street Journal*, April 15, 2015.

If partnership arrangements with upstream suppliers enable the grocery store to reduce its total costs, the store can enhance or maintain its competitive position by reducing prices charged to its consumers. Remember that competitors are also striving to reduce costs and enhance their competitive position. Hence, failing to strive for improvements will likely result in reduced sales and profits.

Value Chain Perspective Fosters Focus on Core Competencies

Using value chain concepts, relationships with suppliers often begin to represent an extended family, allowing companies to focus on core competencies; this capability provides a distinct competitive advantage. In addition, a new breed of contract manufacturers, such as Sanmina has emerged. Sanmina promotes itself as an end-to-end solution. It partners with customers across a variety of industries to design and make complex optical, electronic, and mechanical products. This allows Sanmina's customers to focus on marketing and product development while Sanmina focuses on efficient, low-cost manufacturing.

Interestingly, because their facilities are available to all innovators with the necessary financing, the emergence of contract manufacturers may speed innovation. Toyota attributes much of its rapid growth and profitability to virtual integration with suppliers. **Virtual integration** is the use of information technology and partnership concepts to allow two or more entities along a value chain to act as if they were a single economic entity.

Business Insight ■ The Search for Little Chickens

More chicken is eaten in America than in any other country in the world; approximately 93.5 pounds per person according to the National Chicken Council. To meet demand, chicken producers have focused on raising bigger birds through improvements in breeding and nutrition. In the last hundred years, the average weight of broiler chickens has increased from 2.5 pounds to over 6 pounds.

When it comes to fast-food sandwiches, though, smaller is better. Smaller chicken breasts fit better on the sandwich and consumers prefer the juicier, more tender chicken from birds less than 4.25 pounds.

By 2019, demand for the smaller birds was beginning to outstrip supply. Popeyes dramatically under-forecasted consumer demand for its new chicken sandwich and ran out of chicken two weeks after its introduction in August. It took two months before the sandwich was available again.

McDonald's and Wendy's are both expected to introduce new chicken sandwiches and sales at Popeyes and Chick-fil-A remain strong. The companies with a value chain perspective are likely looking seriously at developing strong partnerships with top poultry producers.

Source: Leslie Patton and Lydia Mulvany, "Chick-fil-A's War with Popeyes Drains Little-Chicken Supply," *Bloomberg*, January 28, 2020.

Value-Added and Value Chain Perspectives

The value chain perspective is often contrasted with a value-added perspective. Under a value-added perspective, decision makers consider only the cost of resources to their organization and the selling price of products or services to their immediate customers. Using a value-added perspective, the goal is to maximize the value added (the difference between the selling price and costs) by the organization. To do this, the value-added perspective focuses primarily on internal activities and costs. Under a value chain perspective, the goal is to maximize value and minimize cost to final customers, often by developing linkages or partnerships with suppliers and customers.

Although initial efforts to enhance competitiveness might start with a value-added perspective, it is important to expand to a value chain perspective. World-class competitors utilize both a value-added and a value chain perspective. These firms always keep the final customer in mind and recognize that the profitability of each entity in the value chain depends on the overall value and cost of the products and services delivered to final customers.

The value-added perspective is the foundation of the make or buy (outsourcing) decision considered in Module 17. The key differences between the partnering decisions considered here and the make or buy decision in Module 17 concern time frame, perspective, and attitude. The make or buy decision is a stand-alone decision, often in the short run, that does not view vendors and customers as partners. In contrast, characteristics of the value chain perspective are as follows:

- Comprehensive
- Focused on the final customers
- Strategic
- Basis for partnerships between vendors and customers

Enhancing or maintaining a competitive position requires an understanding of the entire system used to develop and deliver value to final customers, including interactions among organizations along the value chain. All organizations in the value chain are in business together and should work together as partners rather than as adversaries.

Review 21-1 LO1

Peruse **Starbucks**' corporate website at https://www.starbucks.com. Think about the different processes that Starbucks likely conducts as a part of its business model.

Required
Using Michael Porter's generic model presented in Exhibit 21.2, identify probable elements of each of the primary processes in Starbucks' value chain (i.e., inbound logistics, operations, outbound logistics, marketing and sales, and service).

Solution on p. 21-27.

The Pricing Decision

LO2
Distinguish between economic and cost-based approaches to pricing.

Pricing products and services is one of the most important and complex decisions facing management. Pricing decisions directly affect the salability of individual products or services, as well as the profitability, and even the survival, of the organization. Many economists have spent their entire careers examining the foundations of pricing. To respond to the needs of pricing hundreds or thousands of individual items, managers have developed pricing guidelines that are typically based on costs. More recently, global competition has turned cost-based approaches upside down. Managers of world-class organizations increasingly start with a price that customers are willing to pay and then determine allowable costs.

Economic Approaches to Pricing

In economic models, the firm has a profit-maximizing goal and known cost and revenue functions. Typically, increases in sales quantity require reductions in selling prices, causing **marginal revenue** (the varying increment in total revenue derived from the sale of an additional unit) to decline as sales increase. Increases in production cause an increase in **marginal cost** (the varying increment in total cost required to produce and sell an additional unit of product). In economic models, profits are maximized at the sales volume at which marginal revenues equal marginal costs. Firms continue to produce as long as the marginal revenue derived from the sale of each additional unit exceeds the marginal cost of producing that unit.

Economic models provide a useful framework for considering pricing decisions. The ideal price is the one that will lead customers to purchase all units a firm can provide up to the point at which the last unit has a marginal cost exactly equal to its marginal revenue.

Despite their conceptual merit, economic models are seldom used for day-to-day pricing decisions. Perfect information and an indefinite time period are required to achieve equilibrium prices at which marginal revenues equal marginal costs. In the short run, most for-profit organizations attempt to achieve a target profit rather than a maximum profit. One reason for this is an inability to determine the single set of actions that will lead to profit maximization. Furthermore, managers are more apt to strive to satisfy a number of goals (such as profits for investors, job security for themselves and their employees, and being a "good" corporate citizen) than to strive for the maximization of a single profit goal. In any case, to maximize profits, a company's management would have to know the cost and revenue functions of every product the firm sells. For most firms, this information cannot be developed at a reasonable cost.

Cost-Based Approaches to Pricing

Although cost is not the only consideration in pricing, it has traditionally been the most important for several reasons.

- *Cost data are available.* When hundreds or thousands of different prices must be set in a short time, cost could be the only feasible basis for product pricing.

- *Cost-based prices are defensible.* Managers threatened by legal action or public scrutiny feel secure using cost-based prices. They can argue that prices are set in a manner that provides a "fair" profit.

- *Revenues must exceed costs if the firm is to remain in business.* In the long run, the selling price must exceed the full cost of each unit.

Cost-based pricing is illustrated in Exhibit 21.3. The process begins with market research to determine customer wants. If the product requires components to be designed and produced by vendors, the process of obtaining prices can be time consuming. When some costs, such as those fixed costs at the facility level, are not assigned to specific products, a markup is added to cover these costs. An

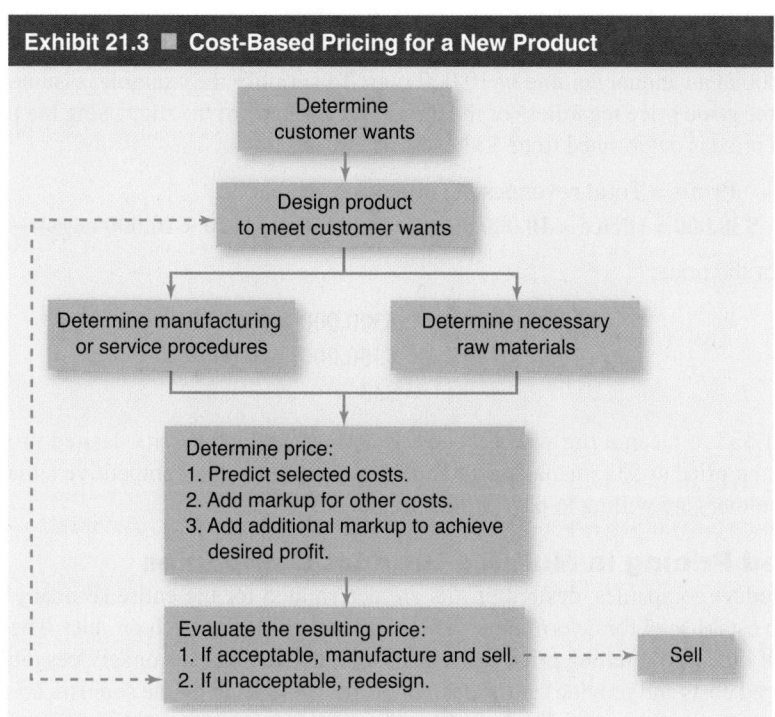

Exhibit 21.3 ■ Cost-Based Pricing for a New Product

Determine customer wants

Design product to meet customer wants

Determine manufacturing or service procedures

Determine necessary raw materials

Determine price:
1. Predict selected costs.
2. Add markup for other costs.
3. Add additional markup to achieve desired profit.

Evaluate the resulting price:
1. If acceptable, manufacture and sell.
2. If unacceptable, redesign.

Sell

additional markup is added to achieve a desired profit. The selling price is then set as the sum of the assigned costs, the markup to cover unassigned costs, and the markup to achieve the desired profit.

The proposed selling price should be evaluated with regard to competitive information and what customers are willing to pay. If the price is acceptable, the product or service is produced. If the price is too high, the product might be redesigned, manufacturing procedures might be changed, and different types of materials might be considered until either an acceptable price is achieved or it is determined that the product cannot be produced at an acceptable price. On the other hand, as the Business Insight below shows, the price can sometimes be a major driver of a company's growth.

Business Insight   ■   For a Better Price, Make a Better Product

While traditional media companies and advertising firms are struggling to adapt to the Internet age, Vice Media has cracked the code. Vice has found a way to connect with millennial viewers, born between 1980 and 2000. Vice Media's unique foothold in the millennial market allows the company to change the way ads are delivered and allows Vice to name its price.

Vice's partnership with A&E, called Viceland, airs on the A&E network but is not a part of traditional ad buys. Companies must pay a premium to access the Vice audience. For example, instead of a traditional spot on a website or before a BuzzFeed or YouTube video, Vice charges between $83,000 and $413,000 per episode to sponsor any one of its 70 original video series. Vice's advertising is often integrated into its content in a way that differs dramatically from traditional commercial-break or sidebar ads. Vice programs are marketed as being "produced with" the sponsor rather than simply showing an ad. By accessing a new group of consumers in new ways, Vice has changed the price the market will bear for its ads.

Sources: Mike Shields, "Vice, BuzzFeed Tread on Madison Avenue's Turf," *Wall Street Journal*, June 22, 2016.
Aaron Taube, "How Vice Media Will Make $500 Million This Year," *Business Insider*, June 21, 2014.
Jason Lynch, "Viceland Is Shaking Up TV Advertising by Running More Native Ads That Look Editorial," *ADWEEK*, March 1, 2016.
Jane Martinson, "The Virtues of Vice: How Punk Magazine Was Transformed into Media Giant," *The Guardian*, January 1, 2015.

Cost-Based Pricing in Single-Product Companies

Implementing cost-based pricing in a single-product company is straightforward if everything is known but the selling price. In this case, all known data are entered into the profit formula, which is then solved for the variable price. ServiceMaster provides residential and commercial cleaning and restoration services. Assume that a ServiceMaster location's annual fixed facility-level costs are $200,000 and the unit cost of cleaning a rug is $10. Suppose management desires to achieve an annual profit of $30,000 at an annual volume of 10,000 rugs. To simplify the example, assume that management charges the same price regardless of the type, size, or shape of the rug. Using the profit formula, the cost-based price is determined to be $33:

$$\text{Profit} = \text{Total revenues} - \text{Total costs}$$
$$\$30,000 = (\text{Price} \times 10,000 \text{ rugs}) - (\$200,000 + [\$10 \times 10,000 \text{ rugs}])$$

Solving for the price:

$$(\text{Price} \times 10,000) = \$300,000 + \$30,000$$
$$\text{Price} = \$330,000 \div 10,000$$
$$= \$33$$

A price of $33 to clean a rug will allow ServiceMaster to achieve its desired profit. However, before setting the price at $33, management should also evaluate the competitive situation and consider what customers are willing to pay for this service.

Cost-Based Pricing in Multiple-Product Companies

In multiple-product companies, desired profits are determined for the entire company, and standard procedures are established for determining the initial selling price of each product. These procedures typically specify the initial selling price as the costs assigned to products or services plus a markup to cover unassigned costs and provide for the desired profit. Depending on the sophistication of the organization's accounting system, possible cost bases in a manufacturing organization include markups based on a *combination of cost behavior and function*. The possible cost bases include the following:

■ Direct materials costs
■ Variable manufacturing costs
■ Total variable costs (manufacturing, selling, and administrative)
■ Full manufacturing costs

Regardless of the cost base, the general approach to developing a markup is to recognize that the markup must be large enough to provide for costs not included in the base plus the desired profit.

$$\text{Markup on cost base} = \frac{\text{Costs not included in the base} + \text{Desired profit}}{\text{Costs included in the base}}$$

First we illustrate a pricing decision with variable costs as the cost base; full manufacturing costs is the cost base in the second illustration.

1. When the markup is based on variable costs, it must be large enough to cover all fixed costs and the desired profit. Assume that the predicted annual variable and fixed costs for one of **Roku**'s divisions are are as follows:

Variable		Fixed	
Manufacturing.	$600,000	Manufacturing.	$300,000
Selling and administrative.	200,000	Selling and administrative.	100,000
Total	$800,000	Total	$400,000

Furthermore, assume that Roku's division has total assets of $1,250,000; management believes that an annual return of 16% on total assets is appropriate in Roku's industry. A 16% return translates into a desired annual profit of $200,000 ($1,250,000 × 0.16). Assuming all cost predictions are correct, obtaining a profit of $200,000 requires a 75% markup on variable costs:

$$\textbf{Markup on variable costs} \;=\; \frac{\$400,000 + \$200,000}{\$800,000}$$

$$=\quad 0.75$$

If the predicted variable costs for Product A1 are $12 per unit, the initial selling price for Product A1 is $21:

$$\textbf{Initial selling price} \;=\; \$12 + (\$12 \times 0.75)$$

$$=\quad \$21$$

2. When the markup is based on full manufacturing costs, it must be large enough to cover selling and administrative expenses and to provide for the desired profit. Again, it is necessary to determine the desired profit and predict all costs for the pricing period. The initial prices of individual products are then determined as their unit manufacturing costs plus the markup. For Roku, the markup on manufacturing costs would be 55.6%:

$$\textbf{Markup on manufacturing costs} \;=\; \frac{\$300,000 + \$200,000}{\$900,000}$$

$$=\quad 0.556$$

If the predicted manufacturing costs for Product B1 are $10, the initial selling price for Product B1 is $15.56:

$$\textbf{Initial selling price} \;=\; \$10 + (\$10 \times 0.556)$$

$$=\quad \$15.56$$

Cost-Based Pricing for Special Orders

Many organizations use cost-based pricing to bid on unique projects. If the project requires dedicated assets, the acquisition of new fixed assets, or an investment in employee training, the desired profit on the special order or project should allow for an adequate return on the dedicated assets or additional investment.

Critique of Cost-Based Pricing

Cost-based pricing has four major drawbacks:

1. Cost-based pricing requires accurate cost assignments. If costs are not accurately assigned, some products could be priced too high, losing market share to competitors; other products could be priced too low, gaining market share but being less profitable than anticipated.

2. The higher the portion of unassigned costs, the greater is the likelihood of over- or under-pricing individual products.

3. Cost-based pricing assumes that goods or services are relatively scarce and, generally, customers who want a product or service are willing to pay the price.

4. In a competitive environment, cost-based approaches increase the time and cost of bringing new products to market.

Cost-based pricing became the dominant approach to pricing during an era when products were relatively long-lived and there was relatively little competition. Also, these systems tend to focus on organizational units such as departments, plants, or divisions and not on activities or cost drivers. While easy to implement, reflecting the need to recover costs and earn a return on investment, and easily justified, cost-based prices might not be competitive. Competition puts intense downward pressure on prices and removes slack from pricing formulas. There is little margin for error in pricing. In a highly competitive market, small variations in pricing make significant differences in success.

Review 21-2 LO2

Assume that **Prince**, a tennis equipment manufacturer, has the following current year contribution income statement:

PRINCE Contribution Income Statement For Year Ended December		
Sales (100,000 units at $12 per unit)		$1,200,000
Less variable costs		
Manufacturing.	$300,000	
Selling and administrative.	150,000	(450,000)
Contribution margin		750,000
Less fixed costs		
Manufacturing.	400,000	
Selling and administrative.	200,000	(600,000)
Net income		$ 150,000

Assume Prince has total assets of $2,000,000, and management desires an annual return of 10% on total assets.

Required

a. Determine the dollar amount by which Prince exceeded or fell short of the desired annual rate of return for the year.

b. Given the current sales volume and cost structure, determine the unit selling price required to achieve an annual profit of $250,000.

continued

continued from previous page

   c. Assume that management wants to state the selling price as a percentage of variable manufacturing costs. Given your answer to requirement (*b*) and the current sales volume and cost structure, determine the selling price as a percentage of variable manufacturing costs.

   d. Restate your answer to requirement (*c*), dividing into two separate markup percentages:
     1. The markup on variable manufacturing costs required to cover unassigned costs.
     2. The additional markup on variable manufacturing costs required to achieve an annual profit of $250,000.

Solution on p. 21-27.

Target Costing

Economists argue that cost-based prices are not realistic, because in the real world prices are determined by the confluence of supply and demand. However, when a new product is introduced into the market for which there is no previously existing supply or demand, there has to be a starting point. As discussed above, cost has often been the baseline for determining initial selling prices. All too often, however, companies introduce new products into the market based on what the designers and engineers "think" the market wants (or based on inadequate market research), only to find out later that either the market does not want the product, or it is not willing to buy the new product at a price sufficient to cover its cost plus an acceptable profit to the producer. This often leads to costly redesign, or in many cases, complete abandonment of the product, typically resulting in substantial financial losses.

LO3 Explain target costing and discuss its acceptance in highly competitive industries.

   Toyota, which has pioneered many innovations in manufacturing systems, adopted and expanded price-based costing, referred to as target costing in the 1960s. Toyota determined that before a new product is introduced into the market, it must be able to be produced at a cost that will make it profitable when sold at a price acceptable to customers. The acceptable selling price to the marketplace determines the acceptable cost of producing the product.

Target Costing Is Proactive for Cost Management

Target costing starts with determining what customers are willing to pay for a product or service and then subtracts a desired profit on sales to determine the allowable, or target, cost of the product or service. This target cost is then communicated to a cross-functional team of employees representing such diverse areas as marketing, product design, manufacturing, and management accounting. Reflecting value chain concepts and the notion of partnerships up and down the value chain, suppliers of raw materials and components are often included in the teams. The target costing team is assigned the task of designing a product that meets customer price, function, and quality requirements while providing a desired profit. Its job is not completed until the target cost is met, or a determination is made that the product or service cannot be profitably introduced under the current circumstances. See Exhibit 21.4 for an overview of target costing.

   Although a formula can be used to determine a markup on cost, it is not possible to develop a formula indicating how to achieve a target cost. Hence, target costing is not a technique. It is more a philosophy or an approach to pricing and cost management. It takes a proactive approach to cost management, reflecting the belief that costs are best managed by decisions made during product development. This contrasts with the more passive cost-plus belief that costs result from design, procurement, and manufacture. Like the value chain, target costing helps orient employees toward the final customer and reinforces the notion that all departments within the organization and all organizations along the value chain must work together. Target costing also empowers employees who will be assigned the responsibility for carrying out activities necessary to deliver a product or service with the authority to determine what activities will be selected. Like process mapping, it helps employees to better understand their role in serving the customer. The following Research Insight discusses how target costing can improve margins for companies engaged in global sourcing.

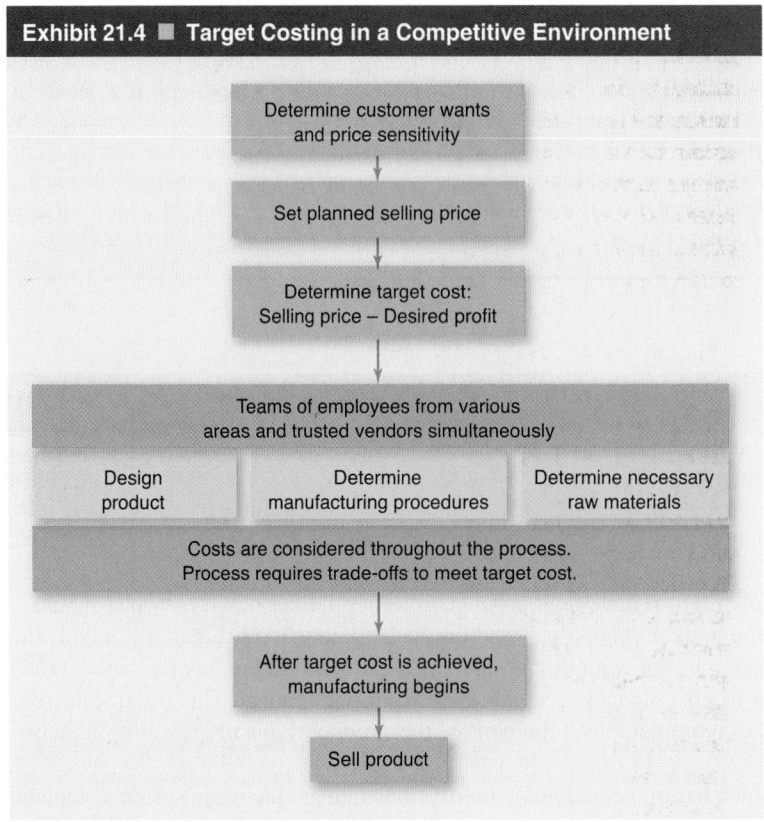

Exhibit 21.4 ■ Target Costing in a Competitive Environment

Determine customer wants
and price sensitivity

Set planned selling price

Determine target cost:
Selling price – Desired profit

Teams of employees from various
areas and trusted vendors simultaneously

| Design product | Determine manufacturing procedures | Determine necessary raw materials |

Costs are considered throughout the process.
Process requires trade-offs to meet target cost.

After target cost is achieved,
manufacturing begins

Sell product

Research Insight   ■   Target Costing and Global Sourcing

Creating and meeting cost targets in an age of global supply and distribution is fundamentally an information technology problem. Researchers with the Deloitte Consulting LLP Supply Chain Strategy Practice point to Toyota's response to the 2011 tsunami as an example of evolution toward modern supply chain management. Toyota's supply system now anticipates the impact of catastrophes on each part used in production. Parts are now designed to allow flexibility in sourcing. This focus is a shift from the optimization and cost minimization of the past. Toyota has adjusted its cost targets to build flexibility and durability into the supply chain, which requires data collection and analysis capabilities that are new for many organizations.

To meet these needs, Nordstrom Inc. has purchased a minority stake in the supply-chain software firm DS Co., a move specifically intended to help the retail giant manage inventories among its department stores, online business, and suppliers. This allows the company to maintain its traditional storefront business while also shipping directly from its suppliers to its online customers.

Information technology helps firms meet cost targets and manage inventories in a global marketplace.

Sources: Kelly Marchese and Bill Lam, "Anticipatory Supply Chains," Deloitte University Press, March 31, 2014. Loretta Chao, "Nordstrom Buys Stake in Software Firm," *Wall Street Journal*, July 8, 2016.

Target Costing Encourages Design for Production

In the absence of a target costing approach, design engineers are apt to focus on incorporating leading-edge technology and the maximum number of features in a product. Target costing keeps the customer's function, quality, and price requirements in the forefront at all times. If customers do not want leading-edge technology (which could be expensive and untested) and several product features, they will resist paying for them. Focusing on achieving a target cost keeps design engineers tuned in to the final customer.

Left on their own, design engineers might believe that their job ends when they design a product that meets the customer's functional requirements. The tendency is to simply pass on the design to manufacturing and let manufacturing determine how best to produce the product. Further down the line, if the product needs servicing, it becomes the service department's responsibility to determine how best to service the product. A target costing approach forces design engineers to explicitly consider the costs of manufacturing and servicing a product while it is being designed. This is known as **design for manufacture**.

Minor changes in design that do not affect the product's functioning can often produce dramatic savings in manufacturing and servicing costs. Examples of design for manufacture include the following:

- Using molded plastic parts to avoid assembling several small parts.
- Designing two parts that must be fit together so that joining them in the correct manner is obvious to assembly workers.
- Placing an access panel in the side of an appliance so service personnel can make repairs quickly.
- Using standard-size parts to reduce inventory requirements, to reduce the possibility of assembly personnel inserting the incorrect part, and to simplify the job of service personnel.
- Ensuring that tolerance requirements for parts that must fit together can be met with available equipment.
- Using manufacturing procedures that are common to other products.

The successful implementation of target costing requires employees from all involved disciplines to be familiar with costing concepts and the notions of value-added and non-value-added activities. When considering the manufacturing process, team members should minimize non-value-added activities such as movement, storage, inspection, and setup. They should also select the lowest-cost value-added activities that do the job properly.

Target Costing Reduces Time to Introduce Products

By designing a product to meet a target cost (rather than evaluating the marketability of a product at a cost-plus price and having to recycle the design through several departments), target costing reduces the time required to introduce new products. Involving vendors in target costing design teams makes the vendors aware of the necessity of meeting a target cost. This facilitates the concurrent engineering of components to be produced outside the organization and reduces the time required to obtain components.

Target Costing Requires Cost Information

Implementing target costing requires detailed information on the cost of alternative activities. This information allows decision makers to select design and manufacturing alternatives that best meet function and price requirements. Tables that contain detailed databases of cost information for various manufacturing variables are occasionally used in designing products and selecting processes to meet target costs.

Target Costing Requires Coordination

Limitations of target costing are employee and supplier attitudes and the many meetings required to coordinate product design and to select manufacturing processes. All people involved must have a basic understanding of the overall processes required to bring a product to market and an appreciation of the cost consequences of alternative actions. They must also respect, cooperate, and communicate with other team members and be willing to engage in a negotiation process involving trade-offs. Finally, they must understand that although the total time required to bring a new product to market can be reduced, the countless coordinating meetings could be quite intrusive on the individuals' otherwise orderly schedules. See Exhibit 21.5 for an evaluation of target costing.

This aspect of the process is even more difficult when suppliers must be brought in as part of the coordination process. This concept is frequently referred to as **chained target costing** because the supply chain's support is critical for the product to be both competitively priced and delivered to

> **Exhibit 21.5 ■ Pros and Cons of Target Costing**
>
> Pros
> - Takes proactive approach to cost management.
> - Orients organization toward customer.
> - Breaks down barriers between departments.
> - Enhances employee awareness and empowerment.
> - Fosters partnerships with suppliers.
> - Minimizes non-value-added activities.
> - Encourages selection of lowest-cost value-added activities.
> - Reduces time to market.
>
> Cons
> - To be effective, requires the development of detailed cost data.
> - Requires willingness to cooperate.
> - Requires many meetings for coordination.

the final customer in a timely manner. When multiple suppliers are required, the organization must obtain everyone's support or the process will probably not be successful due to gaps in the reliability of delivery, quality, and cost control. Each organization and unit must understand that if the product is not brought to market within the defined constraints, all will lose. They must make firm commitments for the project undertaken and to have faith that each participant will carry out whatever part of the supply chain it has promised to fulfill. Coordination across the supply chain is vital in the overall process of continuous improvement as discussed later in this module.

Target Costing Is Key for Products with Short Life Cycles

From a traditional marketing perspective, products with a relatively long life go through four distinct stages during their life cycle:

1. *Start-up.* Sales are low when a product is first introduced. Traditionally, initial selling prices are set high, and customers tend to be relatively affluent trendsetters.

2. *Growth.* Sales increase as the product gains acceptance. Traditionally, prices have remained high during this stage because of customer loyalty and the absence of competitive products.

3. *Maturity.* Sales level off as the product matures. Because of increased competition, pressure on prices is increasing; some price reductions could be necessary.

4. *Decline.* Sales decline as the product becomes obsolete. Significant price cuts could be required to sell remaining inventories.

Target costing is more important for products with a relatively short market life cycle. Products with a long life cycle present many opportunities to continuously improve design and manufacturing procedures that are not available when a product has a short life cycle. Hence, extra care must go into the initial planning for short-lived products. This is especially true when short product life cycles are combined with increased worldwide competition. It is important to introduce a product first and at a price that ensures rapid market penetration.

> **Business Insight   ■   Raise Prices or Cut Costs**
>
> When Britain decided to leave the European Union, the pound decreased in value. This created a problem for foreign companies selling products into the British market. The cost to make the product remained the same but the amount of money received from the sale decreased. To maintain the same profit margin, the importer had to either increase the price to Britain or decrease the cost.
>
> Researchers have found that, in general, companies are averse to increasing prices. Instead, the more common approach is to lower costs. After the drop in the British pound's value, many companies reduced costs by decreasin

continued

continued from previous page

the size of the item. Toilet rolls and toothpaste tubes became smaller. The Toblerone candy bar suddenly contained fewer peaks of chocolate.

This phenomenon is especially true during long periods of low inflation. If inflation has been high year after year, consumers are more willing to accept a price increase. If inflation has been low for a number of years, companies are more apt to redesign a product (reducing the size or the quality) to lower manufacturing costs rather than risk a price increase.

Source: The Economist Staff, "Prices For Many Goods Do Not Move the Way Economists Think They Should," *The Economist*, August 8, 2019.

Target Costing Helps Manage Life-Cycle Costs

An awareness of the impact of today's actions on tomorrow's costs underlies the notion of **life-cycle costs**, which include all costs associated with a product or service ranging from those incurred with the initial conception through design, preproduction, production, and after-production support.

The lower line in Exhibit 21.6 illustrates the cumulative expenditure of funds over the life of a product. For low-technology products with relatively long product lives, decisions committing the organization to spend money are made at approximately the same time the money is spent. However, for high-technology products with relatively short product lives, most of the critical decisions affecting cost, such as product design and the selection of manufacturing procedures, are made before production begins. The top line in Exhibit 21.6 represents decisions committing the organization to expenditures for a product.

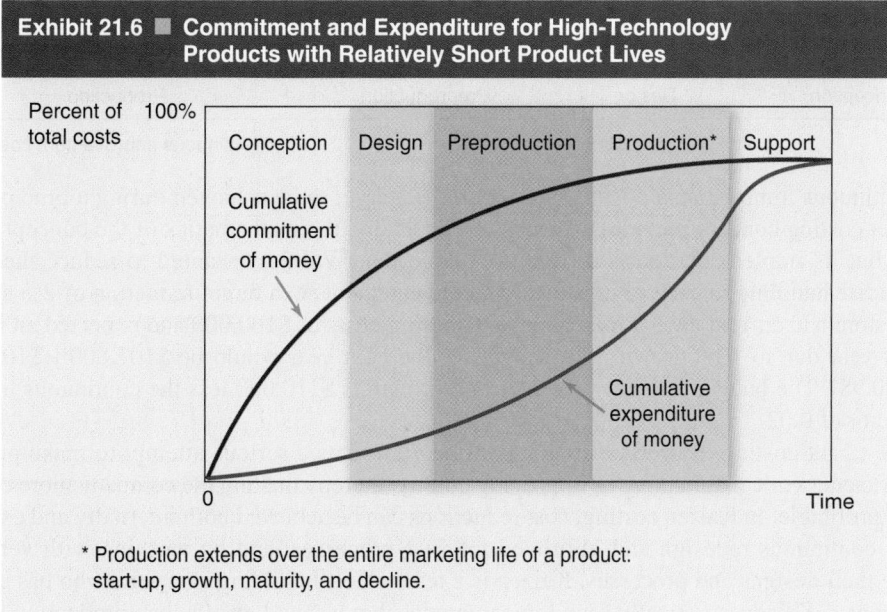

Exhibit 21.6 ■ Commitment and Expenditure for High-Technology Products with Relatively Short Product Lives

* Production extends over the entire marketing life of a product: start-up, growth, maturity, and decline.

Life-cycle cost concepts have also been usefully applied to low-technology issues, such as repair versus replace decisions. The New York State Throughway Authority uses life-cycle concepts to determine the point at which it is more expensive to repair than to replace bridges.

Managerial Decision ■ **You Are the Vice President of Product Development**

As head of new product development for your electronics company, you are concerned that so many of the ideas for new products coming from your research and development group are not succeeding in the market. Many recent attempts to take new products to market have failed, not because of technological deficiencies in the products, but because the market would not support the high prices for new products that were necessary to produce a satisfactory profit. What should you do to try to reverse this trend of new product failures? [Answer, p. 21-20]

Review 21-3 LO3

Chrysler has been conducting early-stage research on hydrogen-powered automobiles and is nearing the point where product development will soon begin. In order to determine the feasibility of the product, assume Chrysler has conducted marketing research that indicates that the price target for the product must be no more than $35,000 if it is to appeal to a large enough market segment to sell a minimum of 150,000 automobiles in the first year of production. The CFO has indicated that the new product must meet a 15% minimum profit margin requirement.

Required
a. Calculate the target cost per unit to produce the hydrogen-powered automobile.
b. How would Chrysler go about determining whether the target cost can be achieved?

Solution on p. 21-28.
c. What should Chrysler do if the estimated cost to produce the product exceeds the target cost?

Continuous Improvement Costing

eLectures **LO4**
Illustrate the relation between target costing and continuous improvement costing.

Continuous improvement (Kaizen) costing calls for establishing cost reduction targets for products or services that an organization is currently providing to customers. Developed in Japan, this approach to cost management is often referred to as *Kaizen costing. Kaizen* means "continuous improvement" in Japanese. Continuous improvement costing begins where target costing ends. Target costing takes a proactive approach to cost management during the conception, design, and preproduction stages of a product's life; continuous improvement costing takes a proactive approach to cost management during the production stage of a product's life:

Time

Conception	Design	Preproduction	Production
	Target costing		Continuous improvement costing

Continuous improvement costing adds a specific target to be achieved during a time period to the target costing concept previously discussed. Basically, the mathematics of the concept is quite simple, but its implementation is difficult. Assume that Walmart wanted to reduce the cost of merchandise handling in each of its stores, and management set a target reduction of 2% a year. If a given store had current annual merchandise handling costs of $100,000 and expected an increase the next year due to 10% growth, the budget for the next year would be $107,800 [($100,000 × 1.10) × 0.98]. The budget for next year based on growth is $110,000 less the continuous improvement factor of 0.02.

Like target costing, Kaizen costing should be viewed as a serious attempt to make processes more efficient, while maintaining or improving quality, thereby making the company more competitive and profitable. In Kaizen costing, cost reductions can be achieved both internally and externally through continuous redesign and improved internal processes, and by working with vendors to improve their designs and processes. Kaizen is a team effort involving everyone who has an influence on costs. Kaizen is typically found in companies that have adopted a lean production philosophy. The following Business Insight discusses Daisin's use of Kaizen to compete with Japanese suppliers for Toyota's business.

Business Insight ■ Thai Manufacturer Uses *Kaizen* to Compete

Thai auto component manufacturer Daisin uses the Japanese concept of *Kaizen*, or continual improvement, to compete with Japanese suppliers for Toyota's business. The firm was founded as a joint venture with Japanese brake parts maker Nissin Kogyo. Since the firm became independent in 2000, it has focused on developing production efficiency and quality control skills to rival other Toyota suppliers. To differentiate itself from other suppliers, the company has developed design capabilities. This allows Toyota to delegate important design steps to Daisin and to look to the supplier for design improvements. Daisin's efforts to differentiate fit with its effort to apply continuous improvement to costing. The firm's factory is designed to optimize use of time and space. The company produces jigs and molds

continued

continued from previous page

in-house so that it can improve production of these expensive and time-consuming tools. At the same time, bringing these tooling steps in-house makes its design focus possible. Daisin's application of Kaizen has helped it carve out a place in Toyota's highly competitive supply chain.

Source: Kohei Fujimura and Natsuko Katsuki, "Thai Car Parts Makers Muscle into Supply Chains, Venture Abroad," *Nikkei Asian Review*, December 31, 2015.

Successful companies use continuous improvement costing to avoid complacency. Competitors are constantly striving to win market share through better quality or lower prices. **Hewlett-Packard** studied **Epson** to determine its strengths and weaknesses. To fend off competition, prices and costs must be continuously reduced. To maintain its competitive position, Hewlett-Packard has reduced the list price of the basic inkjet printer from nearly $400 when first introduced to less than $50 today. This could not have been done without continuous reductions in costs.

The "Toyota Way" describes **Toyota's** method to set Kaizen cost reduction targets for each cost element, including purchased parts per car, direct materials per car, labor hours per car, and office utilities. Performance reports developed at the end of each month compare targeted and actual cost reductions. If actual cost reductions are more than the targeted cost reductions, the results are favorable; if the actual cost reductions are less than the targeted cost reductions, the results are unfavorable.

Because cost reduction targets are set before it is known how they will be achieved, continuous improvement costing can be stressful to employees. A critical element in motivating employee cooperation and teamwork in aggressive cost management techniques, such as target and continuous improvement costing, is to avoid using performance reports to place blame for failure. The proper response to an unfavorable performance report must be an offer of assistance to correct the failure.

LO4 Review 21-4

Patel Company does contract manufacturing of compact video cameras. At its Pacific plant, cost control has become a concern of management. The actual costs per unit for the last two years were as follows:

	Year 1	Year 2
Direct materials		
Plastic case.	$ 4.50	$ 4.40
Lens set	17.00	17.20
Electrical component set.	6.60	5.70
Film track	11.00	10.00
Direct labor.	32.00 (1.6 hours)	30.00 (1.5 hours)
Indirect manufacturing costs		
Variable.	7.50	7.10
Fixed.	3.00 (100,000 unit base)	2.85 (120,000 unit base)

The company manufactures all of the camera components except the lens sets, which it purchases from several vendors. The company has used target costing in the past but has not been able to meet the very competitive global pricing. Beginning in Year 2, the company implemented a continuous improvement program that requires cost reduction targets.

Required
If continuous improvement (Kaizen) costing sets a target of a 5% reduction of the Year 1 cost, how successful was the company in meeting its per unit cost reduction targets in Year 2? Support your answer with appropriate computations.

Solution on p. 21-28.

Benchmarking

When **Hewlett-Packard** studies **Epson** to identify Epson's strengths and weaknesses, each company is engaging in *benchmarking*, a practice that has been around for centuries. In recent years, however, as globalization and increased competitiveness have forced businesses to more aggressively compete on

LO5

Explain how benchmarking enhances quality management, continuous improvement, and process reengineering.

the bases of cost, quality, and service, benchmarking has become more formalized and open. No longer regarded as spying, **benchmarking** is now a systematic approach to identifying the best practices to help an organization take action to improve performance.

The formalization of benchmarking is largely attributed to a book written in the 1980s by Robert Camp of **Xerox**. Since then, many managers have come to believe that benchmarking is a requirement for success. Although benchmarking can focus on anything of interest, it typically deals with target costs for a product, service, or operation, customer satisfaction, quality, inventory levels, inventory turnover, cycle time, and productivity. Benchmarking initially focused on studying competitors, but benchmarking efforts have changed dramatically in recent years to include competitors, as well as companies in very different industries. For example, an electronics company like **Samsung** may benchmark its order fulfillment processes against **Amazon**, or a grocery company like the **Kroger Company** may benchmark its inventory management processes against an apparel company like **Gap**.

In considering how to go about benchmarking, an organization must be careful because it must consider nonfinancial limitations. No single numerical measurement can completely describe the performance of a complex device such as a microprocessor or a television camera, but benchmarks can be useful tools for comparing different products, components, and systems. The only totally accurate way to measure the performance of a given product is to test it against other products while performing the exact same activity. The following Business Insight box describes how **Intel Corporation** makes benchmarks available with some information on how to use them.

Business Insight ■ Intel Benchmarks Performance

Intel Corporation divides its benchmarks into two types, component and system. *Component benchmarks* measure the performance of specific parts of a computer system, such as a microprocessor or hard disk drive. *System benchmarks* typically measure the performance of the entire computer system. The performance obtained will almost certainly vary from benchmark performance for a number of reasons. First, individual components must usually be tested in a complete computer system, and it is not always possible to eliminate the considerable effects that differences in system design and configuration have on benchmark results. For instance, vendors sell systems with a wide variety of disk capabilities and speeds, system memory, and video and graphics capabilities, all of which influence how the system components perform in actual use. Differences in software, including operating systems and compilers, also affect component and system performance. Finally, benchmark tests are typically written to be exemplary for only a certain type of computer application, which might or might not be similar to what is being compared.

A benchmark is, at most, only one type of information that an organization might use during the purchasing or manufacturing process. To get a true picture of the performance of a component or system being considered, the organization should consult industry sources, publicly available research reports, and even government publications of related information.

Source: As described on the Intel website at: http://www.intel.com/content/www/us/en/benchmarks/resources-benchmark-limitations.html

---

Benchmarking provides measurements that are useful in setting goals. It can lead to dramatic innovations, and it can help overcome resistance to change. When presented with a major cost reduction target, employees often believe they are being asked to do the impossible. Benchmarking can be a psychological tool that helps overcome resistance to change by showing how others have already met the target.

Although each organization has its own approach to benchmarking, the following six steps are typical:

1. Decide what to benchmark.
2. Plan the benchmark project.
3. Understand your own performance.
4. Study others.
5. Learn from the data.
6. Take action.

In recent years, professional organizations, such as the Institute of Management Accountants, have set up clearinghouses for benchmark information or have performed benchmarking studies of interest to members as have certain corporations such as **Intel**.

Visit the website iSixSigma.com. iSixSigma provides information on the Lean Six Sigma process and training and tools for Six Sigma certifications. The website dedicates a page to understanding the purpose and use of benchmarking.

Required
Visit: https://www.isixsigma.com/methodology/benchmarking/understanding-purpose-and-use-benchmarking/.
Identify a few differences between benchmarking and competitor research.   Solution on p. 21-29.

Guidance Answers

You Are the Vice President of Product Development
Pg. 21-16 You should consider adopting target costing methods for new product development. Great product research ideas are successful only when they translate into products that can be produced and sold for an acceptable profit. Creating and producing new products before determining what the customer wants and is willing to pay often leads to failure. Target costing methods reverse this process by applying value chain concepts to bring customers and suppliers along the value chain together to produce a product only if it has features and a selling price that are acceptable to potential customers, and if its production costs allow the seller to make an acceptable profit.

Questions

Q21-1. What are the relationships among an organization's value chain, processes, and activities?

Q21-2. What should be the goal of every organization along the value chain?

Q21-3. Distinguish between the value-added perspective and the value chain perspective.

Q21-4. Why are economic models seldom used for day-to-day pricing decisions?

Q21-5. Identify three reasons that cost-based approaches to pricing have traditionally been important.

Q21-6. Identify four drawbacks to cost-based pricing.

Q21-7. How does target costing differ from cost-based pricing?

Q21-8. Why is cost-based pricing more a technique, and target costing is more a philosophy? Which approach takes a more proactive approach to cost management?

Q21-9. Distinguish between the marketing life cycles of products incorporating advanced technology (such as household electronic equipment) and those using more traditional technology (such as household paper products). Why would life-cycle costing be more important to a manufacturer of household electronic equipment than to a manufacturer of household paper products?

Q21-10. What is the relationship between target costing and continuous improvement (Kaizen) costing?

Q21-11. Distinguish between the seller's and the buyer's perspective of life-cycle costs.

Q21-12. What advantage is derived from benchmarking against firms other than competitors?

Assignments with the ⓜ logo in the margin are available in *my* BusinessCourse.
See the Preface of the book for details.

Mini Exercises

M21-13. Developing a Value Chain from the Perspective of the Final Customer   **LO1**
Prepare a value chain for bottled milk that was purchased for personal consumption at an on-campus cafeteria.

M21-14. Developing a Value Chain: Upstream and Downstream Entities   **LO1**
Prepare a value chain for a company that manufactures furniture. Clearly identify upstream and downstream entities in the value chain.

LO1

M21-15. Classifying Activities Using the Generic Internal Value Chain: Aluminum Cable Manufacturer

Using the generic internal value chain shown in Exhibit 21.2, classify each of the following activities of an aluminum cable manufacturer as inbound logistics, operations, outbound logistics, marketing and sales, service, or support.

a. Advertising in a construction magazine
b. Inspecting incoming aluminum ingots
c. Placing bar codes on coils of finished products
d. Borrowing money to finance a buildup of inventory
e. Hiring new employees
f. Heating aluminum ingots
g. Drawing wire from aluminum ingots
h. Coiling wire
i. Visiting a customer to determine the cause of cable breakage
j. Filing tax returns

LO1

M21-16. Classifying Activities Using the Generic Internal Value Chain: Cable TV Company

Using the generic internal value chain shown in Exhibit 21.2, classify each of the following activities of a cable television company as inbound logistics, operations, outbound logistics, marketing and sales, service, or support.

a. Installing coaxial cable in the apartment of a new customer
b. Repairing coaxial cable after a windstorm
c. Mailing brochures to prospective customers
d. Discussing a rate increase with members of a regulatory agency
e. Selling shares of stock in the company
f. Monitoring the quality of reception at the company's satellite downlink
g. Preparing financial statements
h. Visiting a customer to determine the cause of poor-quality television reception
i. Traveling to a conference to learn about technological changes affecting the industry
j. Replacing old routers with updated technology

LO2

Sue Bee Honey

M21-17. Product Pricing: Single Product

Sue Bee Honey is one of the largest processors of its product for the retail market. Assume that one of its plants has annual fixed costs totaling $16,317,500, of which $5,250,500 is for administrative and selling efforts. Sales are anticipated to be 950,000 cases a year. Variable costs for processing are $35 per case, and variable selling expenses are 10% of selling price. There are no variable administrative expenses.

Required

If the company desires a pretax profit of $9,000,000, what is the selling price per case?

LO2

Pinkberry

M21-18. Product Pricing: Single Product

Assume that you plan to open a Pinkberry franchise at a local shopping mall. Fixed operating costs for the year are projected to be $144,500. Variable costs per serving include the cost of the ice cream and cone, $1.50, and a franchise fee payable to Pinkberry, $0.20. A market analysis prepared by Pinkberry indicates that annual sales should total 130,000 servings.

Required

Determine the price you should charge for each serving to achieve a $125,000 pretax profit for the year.

LO2

M21-19. Product Pricing

A few years ago, Hotel Klingerhoffer, a large hotel chain, announced that because occupancy rates had declined during the previous quarter, it was raising room rates to cover the cost of its increase in vacant rooms. Although not referring to accounting or economics, several business journalists during the week following the announcement questioned the basis for the rate increases. One stated that "Hotel Klingerhoffer increases rates of vacant rooms."

Required

a. Did the journalist mean that vacant rooms would be more expensive? Explain.
b. Do you think Hotel Klingerhoffer's action to raise room rates was based on economics, accounting, or both?

LO5

M21-20. Benchmarking

Your company is developing a new product for the computer printer industry. You have talked to several material vendors about being able to supply quality components for the new product. The product designers are satisfied with the company's ability to make the product in the current facilities. Numerous potential customers also have been surveyed, and most have indicated a willingness to buy the product if the price is competitive.

Required

What are some means of benchmarking the development and production of your new product?

Exercises

E21-21. Product Pricing: Single Product

Presented is the current year contribution income statement of Grafton Products.

LO2

GRAFTON PRODUCTS Contribution Income Statement For Year Ended December 3		
Sales (15,000 units)		$2,625,000
Less variable costs		
Cost of goods sold	$1,275,000	
Selling and administrative.	150,000	(1,425,000)
Contribution margin		1,200,000
Less fixed costs		
Manufacturing overhead.	685,000	
Selling and administrative.	330,000	(1,015,000)
Net income		$ 185,000

Next year, Grafton expects an increase in variable manufacturing costs of $10 per unit and in fixed manufacturing costs of $30,000.

Required

a. If sales for next year remain at 15,000 units, what price should Grafton charge to obtain the same profit as last year?

b. Management believes that sales can be increased to 18,000 units if the selling price is lowered to $165. Is this action desirable? (Use the cost data from part a.)

c. After considering the expected increases in costs, what sales volume is needed to earn a pretax profit of $200,000 with a unit selling price of $165?

E21-22. Cost-Based Pricing and Markups with Variable Costs

Computer Consultants provides computerized inventory consulting. The office and computer expenses are $830,000 annually and are not assigned to specific jobs. The consulting hours available for the year total 18,000, and the average consulting hour has $40 of variable costs.

LO2

Required

a. If the company desires a profit of $250,000, what should it charge per hour?

b. What is the markup on variable costs if the desired profit is $322,000?

c. If the desired profit is $100,000, what is the markup on variable costs to cover (1) unassigned costs and (2) desired profit?

E21-23. Computing Markups

The predicted annual costs for Mighty Motors are as follows:

LO2

Manufacturing Costs		Selling and Administrative Costs	
Variable	$250,000	Variable	$250,000
Fixed.	350,000	Fixed.	550,000

Average total assets for the year are predicted to be $7,500,000.

Required

a. If management desires a 10% rate of return on total assets, what are the markup percentages based on total variable costs and based on total manufacturing costs?

b. If the company desires an 8% rate of return on total assets, what is the markup percentage on total manufacturing costs for (1) unassigned costs and (2) desired profit?

E21-24. Product Pricing: Two Products

Assume Verbatim, a subsidiary of CMC Magnetics, manufactures two products, CDs and DVDs, both on the same assembly lines and packaged 30 disks per pack. The predicted sales are 150,000 packs of CDs and 500,000 packs of DVDs. The predicted costs for the year are as follows:

	Variable Costs	Fixed Costs
Materials...	$4,000,000	$1,560,000
Other...	2,000,000	2,052,500

CDs use 25% of the materials costs and 10% of the other costs. DVDs use 75% of the materials costs and 90% of the other costs. The management of Verbatim desires an annual profit of $450,000.

Required

a. What price should Verbatim charge for each disk pack if management believes the DVDs sell for twice the price of the CDs?

b. What is the total profit per product using the selling prices determined in part a?

LO2 **E21-25. Product Pricing: Two Products**

Refer to the previous exercise, E21-24. Based on your calculations of the selling price and profit for CDs and DVDs, how should Verbatim evaluate the status of these two products? Should either CDs or DVDs be discontinued? What additional information does the management of Verbatim need in order to make an appropriate judgment on the future status of these two products?

E21-26. Target Costing

Assume Champion Power Equipment wants to develop a new log-splitting machine for rural home-owners. Market research has determined that the company could sell 7,500 log-splitting machines per year at a retail price of $1,200 each. An independent catalog company would handle sales for an annual fee of $12,000 plus $75 per unit sold. The cost of the raw materials required to produce the log-splitting machines amounts to $200 per unit.

Required

If company management desires a return equal to 30% of the final selling price, what is the target conversion and administrative cost per unit? *Hint*: The target unit cost will only or should only include conversion costs and remaining or additional sales and administrative costs.

Problems

LO2 **P21-27. Product Pricing: Two Products**

Macquarium Inc.

Macquarium Inc. provides computer-related services to its clients. Its two primary services are are Web page design (WPD) and Internet consulting services (ICS). Assume that Macquarium's management expects to earn a 35% annual return on the assets invested. Macquarium has invested $6 million since its opening. The annual costs for the coming year are expected to be as follows:

	Variable Costs	Fixed Costs
Consulting support..................................	$250,000	$1,750,000
Sales and administration	150,000	850,000

The two services expend about equal costs per hour, and the predicted hours for the coming year are 15,000 for WPD and 25,000 for ICS.

Required

a. If markup is based on variable costs, how much revenue must each service generate to provide the profit expected by corporate headquarters? What is the anticipated revenue per hour for each service? *Hint*: Start by determining the markup rate.

b. If the markup is based on total costs, how much revenue must each service generate to provide the expected profit?

c. Explain why answers in requirements (a) and (b) are either the same or different.

d. Comment on the advantages and disadvantages of using a cost-based pricing model.

P21-28. Target Costing

LO3
Ericsson (ERIC)

Ericsson is a large global company providing hardware, software, and related services for radio-access networks within mobile telecommunication systems. Assume that it is developing a new networking system for smaller, private telephone companies. To attract small companies, Ericsson must keep the price low without giving up too many of the features of larger networking systems. A marketing research study conducted on the company's behalf found that the price range must be $50,000 to $75,000. Management has determined a target price to be $65,000. The company's minimum profit percentage of sales is normally 15%, but the company is willing to reduce it to 12% to get the new product on the market. The fixed costs for the first year are anticipated to be $8,000,000. If sales reach 400 installed networks, the company needs to know how much it can spend on variable costs, which are primarily related to installation.

Required

a. What is the amount of total cost allowed if the 12% profit target is allowed and the 400 installations sales target is met? Show the amount for fixed and for variable costs.

b. What is the amount of total costs allowed if the 15% normal profit target is desired at the 400 installations sales target? Show the amount for fixed and for variable costs.

c. Discuss the advantages of using a target costing model versus using cost-based pricing.

P21-29. Continuous Improvement (Kaizen) Costing

LO4

Samira Company does contract manufacturing of compact video cameras. At its Pacific plant, cost control has become a concern of management. The actual costs per unit for the previous two years were as follows:

	Year 1		Year 2	
Direct materials				
Plastic case.	$ 5.10		$ 4.75	
Lens set	12.00		10.90	
Electrical component set.	8.30		7.00	
Film track	10.50		10.05	
Direct labor.	48.00	(1.6 hours)	45.00	(1.5 hours)
Indirect manufacturing costs				
Variable.	5.60		5.00	
Fixed.	16.00	(100,000 unit base)	12.75	(120,000 unit base)

The company manufactures all of the camera components except the lens sets, which it purchases from several vendors. The company has used target costing in the past but has not been able to meet the very competitive global pricing. Beginning in Year 2, the company implemented a continuous improvement program that requires cost reduction targets.

Required

a. If continuous improvement (Kaizen) costing sets a target of a 10% reduction of the first year cost base, how successful was the company in meeting the per unit cost reduction targets in the second year? Support your answer with appropriate computations.

b. Evaluate and discuss Samira's use of Kaizen costing.

P21-30. Continuous Improvement (Kaizen) Costing

LO4
General Electric
(GE)

Assume that GE Capital, a division of General Electric, has been displeased with the costs of servicing its consumer loans. Assume that it has decided to implement a Kaizen-based cost improvement program. For the current year, GE Capital incurred the following costs ($ millions):

Loan processing.	$12,500
Customer relations.	2,800
Printing, mailing, and postage	550

For the next two years, GE Capital expects an increase in consumer loans of 8% annually with related increases in costs.

Required

a. If the company has a continuous improvement goal of 4% each year, develop a budget for the next two years for the consumer loan department.

b. Identify some possible ways that GE Capital can achieve the Kaizen costing goal.

c. Discuss the potential benefits and limitations of GE's Kaizen costing model.

LO2   **P21-31.   Price Setting: Multiple Products**

Tech Com's predicted variable and fixed costs for next year are as follows:

	Variable Costs	Fixed Costs
Manufacturing.	$405,000	$ 424,200
Selling and administrative.	102,000	594,000
Total	$507,000	$1,018,200

Tech Com is a small company producing a wide variety of computer interface devices. Per-unit manufacturing cost information about one of these products, a high-capacity flash drive, is as follows:

Direct materials.	$8
Direct labor.	4
Manufacturing overhead	
Variable.	3
Fixed.	6
Total manufacturing costs.	$21

Variable selling and administrative costs for the flash drive are $4 per unit. Management has set a target profit for next year of $300,000 on the sale of the flash drive.

Required

a. Determine the markup percentage on variable costs required to earn the desired profit.

b. Use variable cost markup to determine a suggested selling price for the flash drive.

c. For the flash drive, break the markup on variable costs into separate parts for fixed costs and profit. Explain the significance of each part.

d. Determine the markup percentage on manufacturing costs required to earn the desired profit.

e. Use the manufacturing costs markup to determine a suggested selling price for the flash drive.

f. Evaluate the variable and the manufacturing cost approaches to determine the markup percentage.

LO2   **P21-32.   Price Setting: Multiple Products**

Pipestem Golf produces a wide variety of golfing equipment. In the past, product managers set prices using their professional judgment. Samuel Snead, the new controller, believes this practice has led to the significant underpricing of some products (with lost profits) and the significant overpricing of other products (with lost sales volume). You have been asked to assist Snead in developing a corporate approach to pricing. The output of your work should be a cost-based formula that can be used to develop initial selling prices for each product. Although product managers are allowed to adjust these prices to meet competition and to take advantage of market opportunities, they must explain such deviations in writing. The following cost information from the current year accounting records is available:

	Manufacturing Costs	Selling and Administrative Costs
Variable	$335,000	$ 55,000
Fixed.	245,000	365,000

During the year, Pipestem Golf reported earnings of $200,000. However, the controller believes that proper pricing should produce earnings of at least $250,000 on the same sales mix and unit volume. Accordingly, you are to use the preceding cost information and a target profit of $250,000 in developing a cost-based pricing formula. Selling and administrative expenses are not currently associated with individual products. However, you have obtained the following unit production cost information for the TW Irons:

Variable manufacturing costs	$145
Fixed manufacturing costs	105
Total	$250

Required

a. Determine the standard markup percentage for each of the following cost bases. Round answers to two decimal places.

1. Full costs, including fixed and variable manufacturing costs, and fixed and variable selling and administrative costs.
2. Manufacturing costs plus variable selling and administrative costs.
3. Manufacturing costs.
4. Variable costs.
5. Variable manufacturing costs.

b. Explain why the markup percentages become progressively larger from requirement (*a*), parts (1) through (5).

c. Determine the initial price of a set of TW Irons using the manufacturing cost markup and the variable manufacturing cost markup.

d. Do you believe the controller's approach to product pricing is reasonable? Why or why not?

Management Applications

MA21-33. Pricing Decision   **LO2**

Most utility poles carry electric and telephone lines. In areas served by cable television, they also carry television cables. However, cable television companies rarely own any utility poles. Instead, they pay utility companies a rental fee for the use of each pole on a yearly basis. The determination of the rental fee is a source of frequent disagreement between the pole owners and the cable television companies. In one situation, pole owners were arguing for a $10 annual rental fee per pole; this was the standard rate the electric and telephone companies charged each other for the use of poles.

"We object to that," stated the representative of the cable television company. "With two users, the $10 fee represents a rental fee for one-half the pole. This fee is too high because we only use about six inches of each 40-foot pole."

"You are forgetting federal safety regulations," responded a representative of the electric company. "They specify certain distances between different types of lines on a utility pole. Television cables must be a minimum of 40 inches below power lines and 12 inches above telephone lines. If your cable is added to the pole, the total capacity is reduced because this space cannot be used for anything else. Besides, we have an investment in the poles; you don't. We should be entitled to a fair return on this investment. Furthermore, speaking of fair, your company should pay the same rental fee that the telephone company pays us and we pay them. We do not intend to change this fee."

In response, the cable television company representative made two points. First, any fee represents incremental income to the pole owners because the cable company would pay all costs of moving existing lines. Second, because the electric and telephone companies both strive to own the same number of poles in a service area, their pole rental fees cancel themselves. Hence, the fee they charge each other is not relevant.

Required

Evaluate the arguments presented by the cable television and electric company representatives. What factors should be considered in determining a pole rental fee?

MA21-34. Target Costing   **LO3**

The president of Houston Electronics was pleased with the company's newest product, the HE Versatile CVD. The product is portable and can be attached to a computer to play or record computer programs or sound, attached to an amplifier to play or record music, or attached to a television to play or record TV programs. It can even be attached to a camcorder to record videos directly on compact disks rather than on tape. It also can be used with a headset to play or record sound. The proud president announced that this unique and innovative product would be an important factor in reestablishing the North American consumer electronics industry.

Based on development costs and predictions of sales volume, manufacturing costs, and distribution costs, the cost-based price of the HE Versatile CVD was determined to be $425. Following a market-skimming strategy, management set the initial selling price at $525. The marketing plan was to reduce the selling price by $50 during each of the first two years of the product's life to obtain the highest contribution possible from each market segment.

The initial sales of the HE Versatile CVD were strong, and Houston Electronics found itself adding second and third production shifts. Although these shifts were expensive, at a selling price of $525, the product had ample contribution margin to remain highly profitable. The president was talking with the company's major investors about the desirability of obtaining financing for a major plant expansion when the bad news arrived. A foreign company had announced that it would shortly introduce a similar product that would incorporate new design features and sell for only $350. The president was shocked. "Why," she remarked, "it costs us $375 to put a complete unit in the hands of customers."

Required

How could the foreign competitor profitably sell a similar product for less than the manufacturing costs to Houston Electronics? What advice do you have for the president concerning the HE Versatile CVD? What advice would you have to help the company avoid similar problems in the future?

Solutions to Review Problems

Review 21-1—Solution

Student answers will vary; possible responses include the following:

Inbound Logistics:
    Company-appointed buyers
    Unroasted coffee beans are brought in from growers in farming communities in key coffee-growing regions
    Starbucks roasting facilitates, storage sites, and regional distribution centers

Operations:
    Direct stores operated by company
    Licensed stores
    Stores add to customer value by offering free Wi-Fi and phone-charging stations

Outbound Logistics:
    Customers buy from company-operated and licensed stores
    Online sales for limited products are available
    Limited selection of products can be purchased in leading supermarket chains

Marketing and Sales:
    Traditionally Starbucks has relied on customer loyalty through customer service and high quality.
    As competition increases, it is increasing its budget for promotions, advertising, and public relations activities.

Service:
    Strives for customer loyalty through customer service and quality products. Its mission statement is, "To inspire and nurture the human spirit—one person, one cup and one neighborhood at a time."[2]

Review 21-2—Solution

a.

Desired annual profit ($2,000,000 × 0.10)	$200,000
Actual profit.	(150,000)
Amount actual profit fell short of achieving the desired return	$ 50,000

b.

Predicted costs		
Variable.	$450,000	
Fixed.	600,000	$1,050,000
Desired profit		250,000
Required revenue.		$1,300,000
Unit sales		÷ 100,000
Required unit selling price.		$ 13

c.

Variable manufacturing costs per unit ($300,000/100,000 units)	= $3
Selling price as a percent of variable manufacturing costs	= $13/3
	= 433⅓%
Markup as a percent of variable manufacturing costs ($10/$3)	= 333⅓%

[2] https://www.starbucks.com/about-us/company-information/mission-statement

d. Detail of markup on variable manufacturing costs:

1. Unassigned costs
Variable selling and administrative	$150,000	
Fixed costs	600,000	$750,000
Variable manufacturing costs		÷300,000
Markup on variable manufacturing costs to cover unassigned costs		250%

2. Desired profit
Desired profit	$250,000
Variable manufacturing costs	÷300,000
Additional markup on variable manufacturing costs to achieve desired profit ($250,000)	83⅓%

Review 21-3—Solution

a.

Total revenue (150,000 × $35,000)	$5,250,000,000
Required profit margin (15%)	−787,500,000
Total cost	$4,462,500,000
Number of units	÷ 150,000
Target cost per unit	$ 29,750

b. A new product such as an automobile is an extremely complex product with hundreds, if not thousands, of different components, involving many different vendors. Once Chrysler has determined what product features potential customers want, its engineers must determine how best to provide those features, working with vendors and potential vendors. The idea is to determine how best to provide the final product that the customers want at a cost that will provide a reasonable profit to Chrysler and its vendors.

c. Teams of engineers, accountants, designers, etc. from Chrysler and its vendors should work together to try to achieve the target cost. If initial cost estimates are too high, they should explore every possibility, including redesign of the product, using components from existing products, developing new production systems, etc. to meet the target cost. If it is finally determined that the target cannot be reached, then management has to decide if it is willing to go forward with the product with a lower than desired initial profit margin. In some cases, managers will proceed with the idea that additional cost savings will be found (using Kaizen costing methods) after the product is in production.

Review 21-4—Solution

Item	Year 1	× 95%	Year 2 Target	Year 2 Actual	Variance
Direct materials:					
Plastic case	$ 4.50	0.95	$ 4.275	$ 4.40	$0.125 U
Lens set	17.00	0.95	16.15	17.20	1.05 U
Electrical set	6.60	0.95	6.27	5.70	0.57 F
Film track	11.00	0.95	10.45	10.00	0.45 F
Direct labor	32.00	0.95	30.40	30.00	0.40 F
Indirect mfg:					
Variable costs	7.50	0.95	7.125	7.10	0.025 F
Fixed costs	3.00	0.95	2.85*	2.85	0.00*

*If 120,000 were used to adjust the Year 2 base, the target would be $2.375 [(100,000 × $3 × 0.95)/120,000], providing for a variance of $0.475 U ($2.375 − $2.85).

The company made progress during Year 2 with favorable variances for all components except cases and lens sets. The unfavorable lens items may require more consideration since they are vendor purchased. Maybe new vendors can be found, or current vendor contracts may be renegotiated.

    The fixed manufacturing costs also need attention. The total fixed costs increased from $300,000 (100,000 × $3) to $342,000 (120,000 × $2.85). If they are fixed, why did they increase? Did increased production or other factors cause the increase? If it was volume driven, maybe some of the costs are not fixed.

Review 21-5—Solution

Student responses will vary. According to iSixSigma.com, neither approach is superior to the other. Which approach to use will depend on an organization's available time and resources. A few of the differences identified by iSixSigma.com include the following:

Differences Between Benchmarking and Competitor Research	
Benchmarking	**Competitor Research**
Focuses on best practices	Focuses on performance measures
Strives for continuous improvement	Bandage or quick fix
Partnering to share information	Considered corporate spying by some
Needed to maintain a competitive edge	Simply a "nice to have"
Adapting based on customer needs after examination of the best	Attempting to mirror another company/process

Source: https://www.isixsigma.com/methodology/benchmarking/understanding-purpose-and-use-benchmarking/

Module 22

Operational Budgeting and Profit Planning

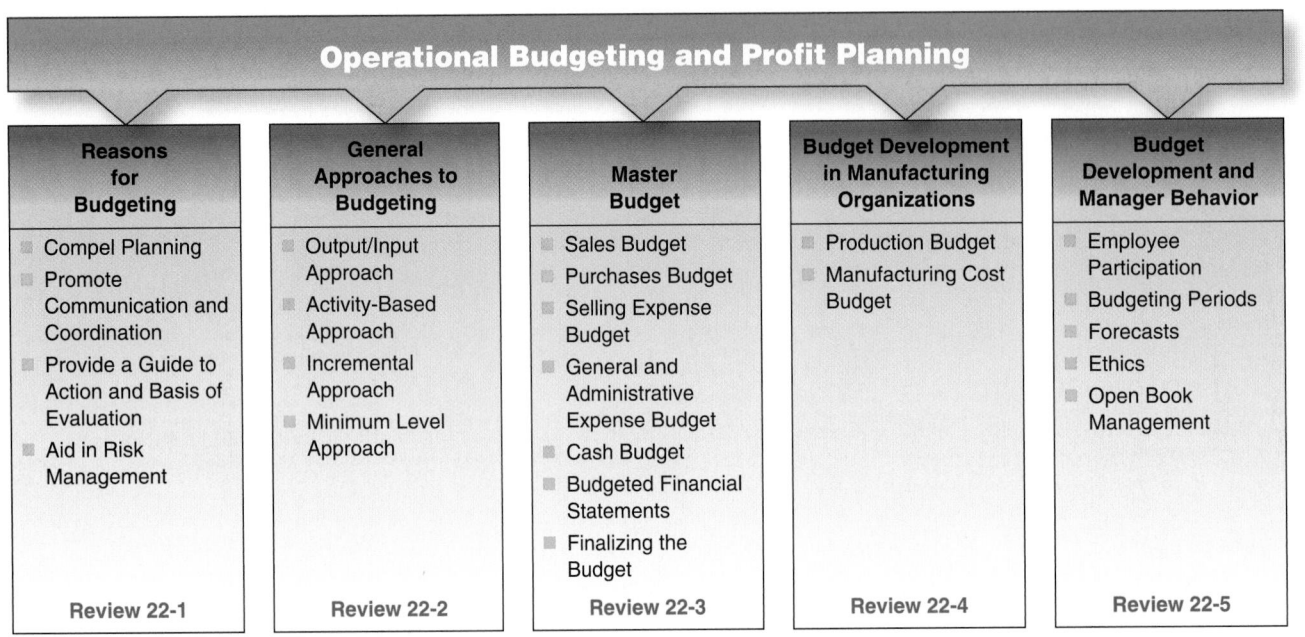

Operational Budgeting and Profit Planning				
Reasons for Budgeting	**General Approaches to Budgeting**	**Master Budget**	**Budget Development in Manufacturing Organizations**	**Budget Development and Manager Behavior**
▪ Compel Planning ▪ Promote Communication and Coordination ▪ Provide a Guide to Action and Basis of Evaluation ▪ Aid in Risk Management	▪ Output/Input Approach ▪ Activity-Based Approach ▪ Incremental Approach ▪ Minimum Level Approach	▪ Sales Budget ▪ Purchases Budget ▪ Selling Expense Budget ▪ General and Administrative Expense Budget ▪ Cash Budget ▪ Budgeted Financial Statements ▪ Finalizing the Budget	▪ Production Budget ▪ Manufacturing Cost Budget	▪ Employee Participation ▪ Budgeting Periods ▪ Forecasts ▪ Ethics ▪ Open Book Management
Review 22-1	Review 22-2	Review 22-3	Review 22-4	Review 22-5

PREVIEW   PINS

Every experienced executive knows that budgeting is the lifeblood of a business enterprise. It is the mechanism by which we plan the entity's operations for the upcoming year, or even decade. It's the way we quantitatively communicate those plans and coordinate the employees' efforts throughout the organization. The budget is unambiguous and unassailable; you either make your numbers or you don't, which makes the budget a valuable feedback loop by which to evaluate past operations. More importantly, preparing a budget alerts management ahead of time to the risks faced by the entity in the coming periods, whether those risks are a shortage of cash, too few or too many employees, or idle versus excess capacity.

Each period, most businesses prepare what is called a "master budget." The master budget covers every aspect of the financial (and often nonfinancial) operations. The first step in the master budget is to budget or forecast sales revenue. But how do you prepare a budget for a company that, until recently, generated zero revenue while experiencing explosive growth? Pinterest has over 320 million active users worldwide each month and has been valued at over $10 billion. Pinterest was founded in 2010 but didn't even have a revenue model until 2014. The company works with businesses to understand how Pinterest traffic can generate sales revenue for those businesses by advertising on Pinterest. The advertising fees paid by those companies exceeded $1 billion for the 12 months ended September 30, 2019.

From a budgeting perspective, Pinterest may need to prepare its sales budget using several what-if scenarios to help it determine the proper pricing for its advertisements. It will also to develop expense budgets for everything from labor to selling to general and administrative expenses. At the time of this writing, the company had grown to over 2,000 employees, including new hires from Facebook, Google, and Amazon.

Clearly, Pinterest is an evolving, dynamic company, but it will have to pay close attention to its budgeting to manage its cash flow and capital investments. The budgeting techniques discussed in this module will aid the manager in planning and managing the organization's revenues, costs, and other quantitative variables in the face of constantly changing business conditions.

Road Map

LO	Learning Objective | Topics	Page	eLecture	Guided Example	Assignments
22-1	**Discuss the importance of budgets.** Compel Planning :: Promote Communication and Coordination :: Guide to Action and Evaluation :: Risk Management	22-3	e22-1	Review 22-1	23
22-2	**Describe basic approaches to budgeting.** Output/Input :: Activity Based :: Incremental :: Minimum Level	22-4	e22-2	Review 22-2	17, 18, 23, 24, 25
22-3	**Explain the relationships among elements of a master budget and develop a basic budget.** Master Budget :: Sales Budget :: Purchases Budget :: Selling Expense Budget :: General and Administrative Expenses Budget :: Cash Budget :: Budgeted Financial Statements	22-7	e22-3	Review 22-3	19, 20, 26, 27, 28, 29, 30, 31, 32, 33, 36, 37, 38, 39, 40, 41, 42
22-4	**Explain and develop a basic manufacturing cost budget.** Production Budget :: Manufacturing Cost Budget	22-16	e22-4	Review 22-4	21, 22, 34, 35, 38, 39, 40, 41, 42
22-5	**Analyze the relationship between budget development and manager behavior.** Imposed Budget :: Participative Budget :: Budget Periods :: Forecasts :: Ethics :: Open Book Management	22-20	e22-5	Review 22-5	43, 44, 45, 46

A **budget** is a formal plan of action expressed in monetary terms. The purpose of this module is to examine the concepts, relationships, and procedures used in budgeting. Our emphasis is on **operating budgets**, which concern the development of detailed plans to guide operations throughout the budget period. We consider the reasons that organizations budget and alternative approaches to budget development. We also examine budget assembly and consider issues related to manager behavior and the budgeting process.

Reasons for Budgeting

LO1
Discuss the importance of budgets.

Operating managers frequently regard budgeting as a time-consuming task that diverts attention from current problems. Indeed, the development of an effective budget is a difficult job. It is also a necessary one. Organizations that do not plan are likely to wander aimlessly and ultimately succumb to the swirl of current events. The formal development of a budget helps to ensure both success and survival. As discussed below, budgeting compels planning; it improves communications and coordination among organizational elements; it provides a guide to action; and it provides a basis of performance evaluation. Budget models are also used to analyze and prepare for various business risks.

Compel Planning

Formal budgeting procedures require people to think about the future. Without the discipline of formal planning procedures, busy operating managers would not find time to plan. Immediate needs would consume all available time. Formal budgeting procedures, with specified deadlines, force managers to plan for the future by making the completion of the budget another immediate need. Budgeting moves an organization from an informal "reactive" style to a formal "proactive" style of management. As a result, management and other employees spend less time solving unanticipated problems and more time on positive measures and preventative actions.

Promote Communication and Coordination

When operating responsibilities are divided, it is difficult to synchronize activities. Production must know what marketing intends to sell. Purchasing and personnel must know the factory's material and labor requirements. The treasurer must plan to ensure the availability of the cash to support receivables, inventories, and capital expenditures. Budgeting forces the managers of these diverse functions to communicate their plans and coordinate their activities. It helps ensure that plans are feasible (Can purchasing obtain adequate inventories to support projected sales?) and that they are synchronized (Will inventory be available in advance of an advertising campaign?). The final version of the budget emerges after an extensive (often lengthy) process of communication and coordination.

Provide a Guide to Action and Basis of Evaluation

Once the budget has been finalized, the various operating managers know what is expected of them, and they can set about doing it. If employees do not have a guide to action, their efforts could be wasted on unproductive or even counterproductive activities.

After employees accept the budget as a guide to action, they can be held responsible for their portion of the budget. When results do not agree with plans, managers attempt to determine the cause of the divergence. This information is then used to adjust operations or to modify plans. More generally, budgeting is an important part of **management by exception**, whereby management directs attention only to those activities not proceeding according to plan. Without the budget, management might spend an inordinate amount of time seeking explanation of past activities and not enough time planning future activities.

Aid in Risk Management

The models used for budgeting are also used in managing risk. **Risk** is the danger that things will not go according to plan. Although some risk results from anticipated events having a positive impact, such as an increase in sales volume or selling prices, risk is more typically associated with events that have a negative impact, like a work stoppage at a key supplier, a fire, or hackers shutting down a retail website for an extended period of time.

Risk management (also called enterprise risk management) is the process of identifying, evaluating, and planning possible responses to risks that could impede an organization from achieving its plans. It also involves monitoring the sources of risk. An organization's budget model can be used to evaluate the financial impact of a risk and to determine, from a financial perspective, the best response to a risk. The following Research Insight summarizes a proposed approach to risk management. The performance evaluation procedures considered in Module 23, if completed on a timely basis, assist in monitoring risk.

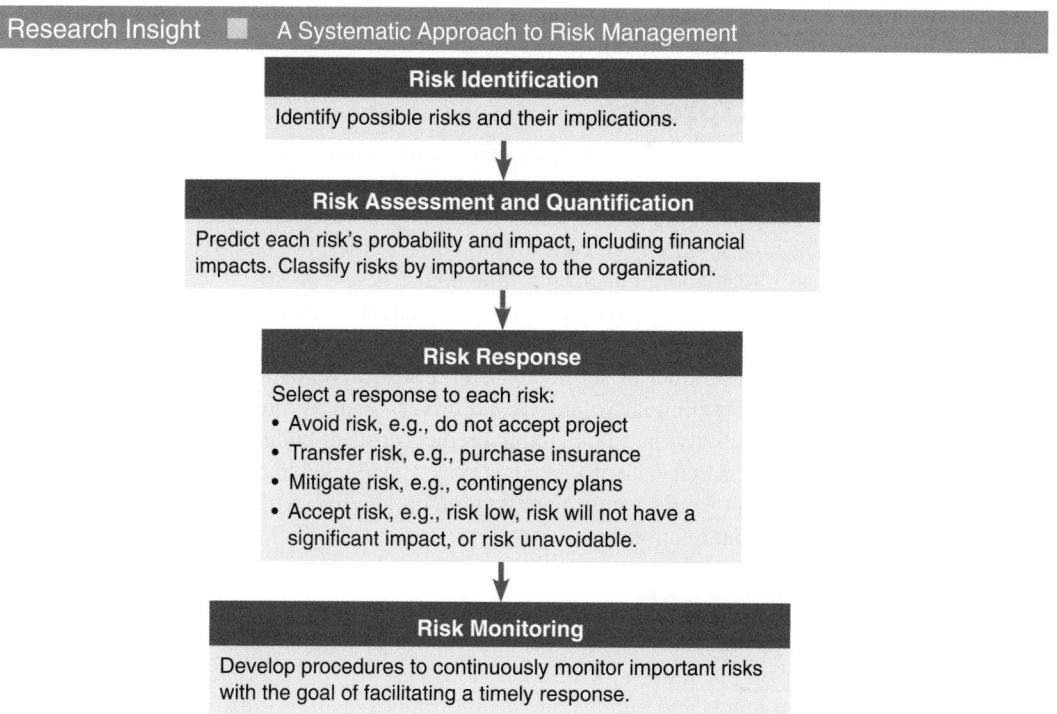

Research Insight ■ A Systematic Approach to Risk Management

Risk Identification
Identify possible risks and their implications.

Risk Assessment and Quantification
Predict each risk's probability and impact, including financial impacts. Classify risks by importance to the organization.

Risk Response
Select a response to each risk:
- Avoid risk, e.g., do not accept project
- Transfer risk, e.g., purchase insurance
- Mitigate risk, e.g., contingency plans
- Accept risk, e.g., risk low, risk will not have a significant impact, or risk unavoidable.

Risk Monitoring
Develop procedures to continuously monitor important risks with the goal of facilitating a timely response.

Source: Alan J. Chilcott, "Risk Management—A Developing Field of Study and Application," *Cost Engineering*, September 9, 2010, pp. 21–26; Neville Turbit, "Basics of Managing Risk," The Project Perfect White Paper Collection, www.projectperfect.com.au.

LO1 Review 22-1

Mark Fisher was recently hired as an intern at Mobile Innovations, a small manufacturer and seller of conveyer systems, which are used by other businesses in their manufacturing processes. After recently finishing a course in management accounting, Mark asks his manager if he can see a copy of the current year's operating budget. His manager replies that as a small business, they are too busy focusing on day-to-day operations to take the time to create a budget.

Required
Discuss some ways that an operating budget might benefit Mobile Innovations.

Solution on p. 22-37.

General Approaches to Budgeting

Before an organization can develop operating budgets, management must decide which approaches to budget planning will be used for the various revenue and expenditure activities and organizational units. Widely used planning approaches to budgeting include the output/input, activity-based, incremental, and minimum level approaches.

LO2 Describe basic approaches to budgeting.

Output/Input Approach

The **output/input approach** budgets physical inputs and costs as a function of planned unit-level activities. This approach is often used for service, merchandising, manufacturing, and distribution activities that have defined relationships between effort and accomplishment. If each unit produced requires 2 pounds of direct materials that cost $5 each, and the planned production volume is 25 units, the budgeted inputs and costs for direct materials are 50 pounds (25 units × 2 pounds per unit) and $250 (50 pounds × $5 per pound).

The budgeted inputs are a function of the planned outputs. The output/input approach starts with the planned outputs and works backward to budget the inputs. It is difficult to use this approach for costs that do not respond to changes in unit-level cost drivers.

Activity-Based Approach

The **activity-based approach** is a type of output/input method, but it reduces the distortions in the transformation through emphasis on the expected cost of the planned activities that will be consumed for a process, department, service, product, or other budget objective. Overhead costs are budgeted on the basis of the cost objective's anticipated consumption of activities, not based only on some broad-based cost driver such as direct labor hours or machine hours.

The amount of each activity cost driver used by each budget objective (for example, product or service) is determined and multiplied by the cost per unit of the activity cost driver. The result is an estimate of the costs of each product or service based on cost drivers such as assembly-line setup or inspections, as well as the traditional volume-based drivers such as direct labor hours or units of direct materials consumed. Activity-based budgeting predicts costs of budget objectives by adding all costs of the activity cost drivers that each product or service is budgeted to consume. In evaluating the proposed budget, management would focus their attention on identifying the optimal set of activities rather than just the output/input relationships.

Incremental Approach

The **incremental approach** budgets costs for a coming period as a dollar or percentage change from the amount budgeted for (or spent during) some previous period. This approach is often used when the relationships between inputs and outputs are weak or nonexistent. For example, it is difficult to establish a clear relationship between sales volume and advertising expenditures. Consequently, the budgeted amount of advertising for a future period is often based on the budgeted or actual advertising expenditures in a previous period. If budgeted advertising expenditures for last year were $200,000, the budgeted expenditures for this year would be some increment, say 5%, above $200,000. In evaluating the proposed current year budget, management would accept the $200,000 base and focus attention on justifying the increment.

The incremental approach is widely used in government and not-for-profit organizations. In seeking a budget appropriation, a manager using the incremental approach need only justify proposed expenditures in excess of the previous budget. The primary advantage of the incremental approach is that it simplifies the budget process by considering only the increments in the various budget items. A major disadvantage is that existing waste and inefficiencies could escalate year after year.

Minimum Level Approach

Using the **minimum level approach**, an organization establishes a base amount for budget items and requires explanation or justification for any budgeted amount above the minimum (base). This base is usually significantly less than the base used in the incremental approach. It likely is the minimum amount necessary to keep a program or organizational unit viable. For example, the corporate director of product development would need some basic amount to avoid canceling ongoing projects. Additional increments might also be included, first to support the current level of product development and second to undertake desirable new projects.

Some organizations, especially units of government, employ a variation of the minimum level approach, identified as zero-based budgeting. Under **zero-based budgeting** every dollar of expenditure must be justified. The essence of zero-based budgeting is breaking an organizational unit's total budget into program packages with related costs. Management then ranks all program packages on the basis of the perceived benefits in relation to their costs. Program packages are then funded for the budget period using this ranking. High-ranking packages are most likely to be funded and low-ranking packages are least likely to be funded.

Business Insight   ■   Budgeting for Uncertainty

As a firm builds its master budget, budgeting for uncertainty is essential. The financial struggles of Kodak can be seen as a cautionary tale for mature firms dealing with technological uncertainty. Kodak was decidedly ahead of the digital camera trend, creating its first prototype in the 1970s. Kodak's technology was foiled by its approach to uncertainty. Traditional approaches to long-term strategy and budgeting focus on forecasting trends and committing to the best single strategy. Kodak knew that the future of photography was digital but chose to bet on its core business rather than making risky investments in new products that would undermine its core.

Analysts at Bain and Company argue that firms should budget for a "range of futures," by

1. Deciding what uncertainties could affect the company. (The potential of digital photography is just such an uncertainty.)
2. Develop probable scenarios for the future. Consider the upsides and downsides of each scenario. (Kodak clearly knew that digital photography was a potential scenario.)
3. Match strategic plans to scenarios, balancing investment with flexibility to adjust to various states of the world.
4. Establish signals that trigger adoption of scenarios.

Though Kodak had the technology to adapt to the new market, the company was unable, or unwilling, to restructure its business accordingly. If the management team had agreed that they would shift toward digital cameras when digital had 15% market share, it would have been positioned to switch. By preparing for multiple uncertain futures and setting triggers, managers pre-commit to difficult decisions, and are prepared to be flexible.

General Electric's $200 million "multimodal" factory in Pune, India, is an example of this flexible scenario-based approach. Leadership was confident that four different businesses would need capacity in India, but the mix was uncertain. Rather than commit to a mix, GE built flexibility into the factory. The advanced facility they built is designed to switch between production of jet engines, locomotives, wind turbines, and water treatment equipment. Rather than committing to one business model, GE prepared for several possible scenarios. GE has since gone on to open other multimodal factories, including one in Vietnam in 2018.

Source: Martin Toner, Nikhil Ojha, Piet de Paepe, and Miguel Simoes de Melo, "A Strategy for Thriving in Uncertainty," *Bain Brief*, Bain & Company, August 12, 2015.

Budgeting for objectives is a variation on the minimum level approach that combines elements of activity-based and zero-based budgeting with a need to live within fixed financial constraints. The minimum level approach improves on the incremental approach by questioning the necessity for costs included in the base of the incremental approach, but it is very time-consuming. All three approaches are often used within the same organization. A pharmaceutical company might use the output/input or the activity-based approach to budget distribution expenditures, the incremental approach to budget administrative salaries, and the minimum level approach to budget research and development.

LO2 Review 22-2

To illustrate the various approaches to budgeting discussed above, assume that McNeil, a division of Johnson & Johnson, manufactures two products in institutional quantities, Regular Strength Tylenol and Tylenol Extra Strength. Suppose last period, McNeil produced 18,000 units of Regular and 45,000 units of Extra Strength at a total unit cost of $38 for Regular and $32 for Extra Strength. Also suppose that in the current period, overall costs are expected to rise about 3.5% over the last period. Assume estimated overhead costs of $408,500 for the next period include the cost of assembly-line setups, engineering and maintenance, and inspections. Total estimated assembly hours are 50,000 hours; therefore, the estimated overhead cost per assembly hour is $8.17. Other predicted data for the next period follow:

continued

continued from previous page

	Regular	Extra Strength
Direct materials (per unit)	$20.00	$14.50
Direct labor hours of assembly time (per unit)	0.5	0.8
Assembly labor cost (per hour)	$18	$18
Total estimated production (in units)	20,000	50,000
Total setup hours	1,000	1,500
Total engineering and maintenance hours	500	600
Total inspections	650	580
Setup cost (per setup hour)	$25	$25
Engineering and maintenance (per hour)	$35	$35
Inspection cost (per inspection)	$250	$250

Required

a. Calculate McNeil's budgeted cost per unit to produce Regular and Extra Strength Tylenol during the next period, assuming it uses an output/input approach and budgets overhead cost based only on assembly hours.

b. Repeat *a*, assuming McNeil uses an activity-based approach and budgets overhead cost based on budgeted activity costs.

c. Repeat *a*, assuming McNeil uses an incremental approach for budgeting overhead cost.

Solution on p. 22-38. d. Explain how the minimum level approach differs from the above methods.

Master Budget

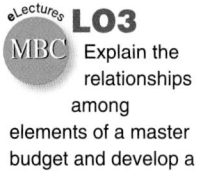

eLectures
MBC
LO3
Explain the relationships among elements of a master budget and develop a basic budget.

The culmination of the budgeting process is the preparation of a **master budget** for the entire organization that considers all interrelationships among organization units. The master budget groups together all budgets and supporting schedules and coordinates all financial and operational activities, placing them into an organization-wide set of budgets for a given time period.

Because it explicitly considers organizational interrelationships, the master budget is more complex than budgets developed for products, services, organization units, or specific processes. The elements of the master budget depend on the nature of the business, its products or services, processes and organization, and management needs.

A major goal of developing a master budget is to ensure the smooth functioning of a business throughout the budget period and the organization's operating cycle. As shown in Exhibit 22.1, the operating cycle involves the conversion of cash into other assets, which are intended to produce

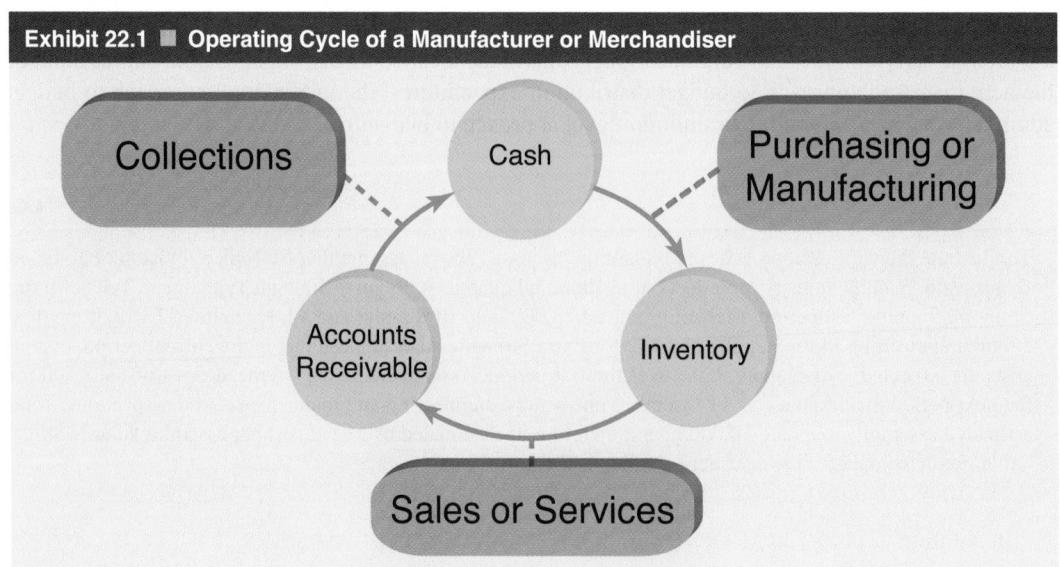

Exhibit 22.1 ■ Operating Cycle of a Manufacturer or Merchandiser

revenues in excess of their costs. The cycle generally follows a path from cash, to inventories, to receivables (via sales or services), and back to cash. There are, of course, intermediate processes such as the purchase or manufacture of inventories, payments of accounts payable, and the collection of receivables. The master budget is merely a detailed model of the firm's operating cycle that includes all internal processes.

Most for-profit organizations begin the budgeting process with the development of the sales budget and conclude with the development of budgeted financial statements. Exhibit 22.2 depicts the annual budget assembly process in a retail merchandising organization. Most of the budget data flow from sales toward cash and then toward the budgeted financial statements.

To illustrate the procedures involved in budget assembly, a hypothetical monthly budget for the second quarter of the year is developed for **REI**, a retail organization specializing in gear and apparel for outdoor and fitness activities. The assembly sequence follows the overview illustrated in Exhibit 22.2. Each element of the budget process in Exhibit 22.2 is illustrated in a separate exhibit. Because of the numerous elements in the budget process illustrated for REI, you will find it useful to refer to Exhibit 22.2 often.

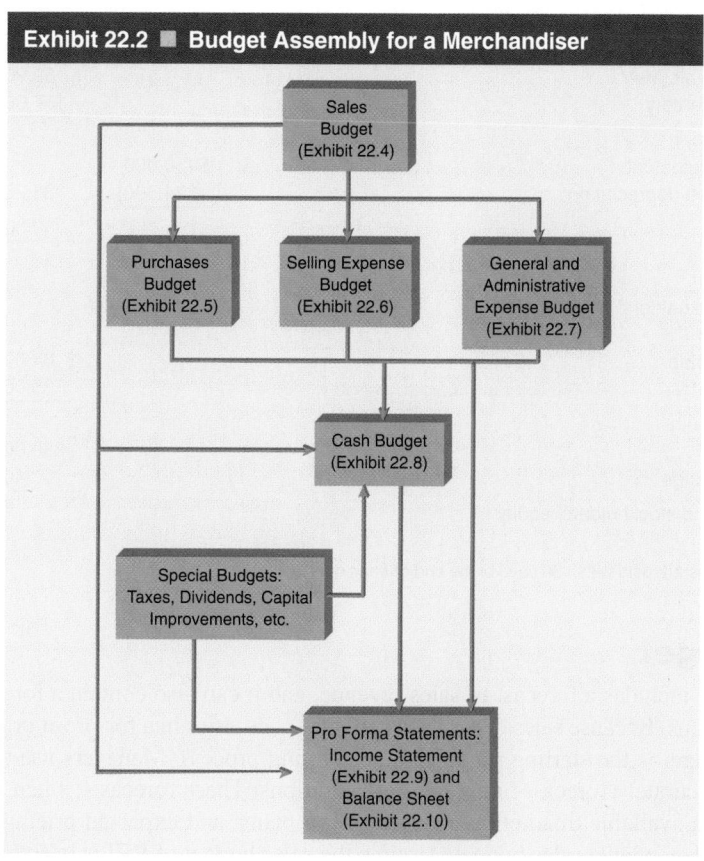

Exhibit 22.2 ■ Budget Assembly for a Merchandiser

The activities of a business can be summarized under three broad categories: operating activities, financing activities, and investing activities. To simplify the illustration, assume that REI engaged in no investing activities during the budget period and that the only anticipated financing activity is short-term borrowing. Normal profit-related activities performed in conducting the daily affairs of an organization are called **operating activities**. Assume the operating activities of REI include the following:

1. Purchasing inventory intended for sale.
2. Selling goods or services.
3. Purchasing and using goods and services classified as selling expenses.
4. Purchasing and using goods and services classified as general and administrative expenses.

In addition to preparing the budget for each operating activity, companies prepare a cash budget for cash receipts and disbursements related to their operating activities as well as for financing and

Operating activities

Activities related to generating business income.

Financing activities

Activities related to funding operations or expansion.

Investing activities

Activities related to buying and selling long-term assets and investments.

investing activities. The importance of cash planning makes this budget a vital part of the total budget process. Management must, for example, be aware in advance of the need to borrow and have some idea when borrowed funds can be repaid.

The hypothetical balance sheet for April 1, the start of the second quarter, is presented in Exhibit 22.3. It contains information used as a starting point in preparing the various budgets. To reduce complexity, we use the output/input approach to budget variable costs and assume that the budgets for other costs were previously developed using the incremental approach. Budgets to be prepared include those for sales, purchases, selling expense, general and administrative expense, and cash.

Beginning of the period balance sheet

The balance sheet at the beginning of the budgeted period contains information used as a starting point in preparing the various budgets.

Exhibit 22.3 ■ Initial Balance Sheet

REI
Balance Sheet
April 1

Assets			
Current assets			
Cash		$ 15,000	
Accounts receivable, net.		59,200	
Merchandise inventory		157,000	$231,200
Fixed assets			
Buildings and equipment.	$460,000		
Less accumulated depreciation	(124,800)	335,200	
Land		60,000	395,200
Total assets.			$626,400
Liabilities and Stockholders' Equity			
Current liabilities			
Accounts payable		$ 84,000	
Taxes payable*		35,000	$119,000
Stockholders' equity			
Capital stock		350,000	
Retained earnings		157,400	507,400
Total liabilities and stockholders' equity			$626,400

*Quarterly income taxes are paid within 30 days of the end of each quarter.

Sales Budget

The **sales budget** includes a forecast of sales revenue, and it can also contain a forecast of unit sales and sales collections. Because sales drive almost all other activities in a for-profit organization, developing a sales budget is the starting point in the budgeting process. Managers use the best available information to accurately forecast future market conditions. These forecasts, when considered along with merchandise available, marketing and promotion plans, and expected pricing policies, should lead to the most dependable sales budget. Assume the sales budget of REI is in Exhibit 22.4.

Sales budget

Developing a sales budget is the starting point in the budgeting process.

Exhibit 22.4 ■ Sales Budget

REI
Sales Budget
For the Second Quarter Ending June 30

	April	May	June	Quarter Total	July
Sales.	$190,000	$228,000	$250,000	$668,000	$309,000

The information in the sales budget along with predictions of the expected portion of cash sales and the timing of collections from credit sales are used to calculate cash receipts. In the event of a projected cash shortfall, management could consider ways to increase cash sales or to accelerate the collection of receipts from credit sales.

Purchases Budget

The **purchases budget** indicates the materials that must be acquired to meet sales needs and ending inventory requirements. It can be referred to as a merchandise budget if it contains only purchases of merchandise for sale. (For a manufacturer, the purchases budget would include raw materials costs.) The purchases budget, shown in Exhibit 22.5, includes only purchases of merchandise.

Exhibit 22.5 ■ Purchases Budget

REI Purchases Budget For the Second Quarter Ending June 30	April	May	June	Quarter Total	July
Budgeted sales (Exhibit 22.4).....	$190,000	$228,000	$250,000	$668,000	$309,000
Current cost of goods sold*......	$114,000	$136,800	$150,000	$400,800	
Desired ending inventory**.......	168,400	175,000	192,700	192,700	
Total needs..................	282,400	311,800	342,700	593,500	
Less beginning inventory***......	(157,000)	(168,400)	(175,000)	(157,000)	
Purchases...................	$125,400	$143,400	$167,700	$436,500	

> **Purchases budget**
>
> The purchases budget indicates the merchandise that must be acquired to meet sales needs and ending inventory requirements.

*Cost of goods sold is 60% of selling price
**Fifty percent of inventory required for next month's budgeted sales plus base inventory of $100,000.
  April: ($228,000 May sales × 0.60 cost × 0.50 desired ending inventory) + $100,000
  May: ($250,000 June sales × 0.60 cost × 0.50 desired ending inventory) + $100,000
  June :($309,000 July sales × 0.60 cost × 0.50 desired ending inventory) + $100,000
***Fifty percent of current month sales × 0.60 cost plus base inventory of $100,000. Note monthly beginning inventory.
  Same as previous month's ending inventory.

In reviewing REI's purchases budget, note the following:

- Because REI sells a wide variety of items, the purchases budget is expressed in terms of sales dollars, with the assumed cost of merchandise averaging 60% of the selling price. Management also keeps detailed records for budgeting the number of units of items carried. An organization that only sold a small number of items might present the sales budget in units as well as dollars.

- The budget assumes management desires to have 50% of the inventory needed to fill the following month's sales in stock at the end of the previous month.

- To provide for a possible delay in the receipt of inventory and to meet variations in customer demand, the budget assumes that REI maintains an additional base inventory of $100,000.

- The total inventory needs equal current sales plus desired ending inventory, including the base inventory.

- Budgeted purchases are computed as total inventory needs less the beginning inventory.

The information in the purchases budget and the information on expected timing of payments for purchases are used to budget cash disbursements for purchases. In the event of a projected cash shortfall, management can consider ways to delay the purchase of inventory or the payment for inventory purchases.

Selling Expense Budget

The **selling expense budget** presents the expenses the organization plans to incur in connection with sales and distribution. In the selling expense budget, Exhibit 22.6, the budgeted variable selling expenses are determined as a percentage of budgeted sales dollars. The budgeted fixed selling expenses are based on amounts obtained from the manager of the sales department. To simplify the presentation of the cash budget, the budget assumes REI pays its selling expenses in the month they are incurred.

Selling expense budget

The selling expense budget presents the expenses the organization plans to incur in connection with sales and distribution.

Exhibit 22.6 ■ Selling Expense Budget

REI
Selling Expense Budget
For the Second Quarter Ending June 30

	April	May	June	Quarter Total
Budgeted sales (Exhibit 22.4)................	$190,000	$228,000	$250,000	$668,000
Variable selling expenses				
Setup/Display (1% sales)	$ 1,900	$ 2,280	$ 2,500	$ 6,680
Commissions (2% sales)	3,800	4,560	5,000	13,360
Miscellaneous (1% sales).................	1,900	2,280	2,500	6,680
Total	7,600	9,120	10,000	26,720
Fixed selling expenses				
Advertising	2,250	2,250	2,250	6,750
Office...................................	1,250	1,250	1,250	3,750
Miscellaneous...........................	1,000	1,000	1,000	3,000
Total	4,500	4,500	4,500	13,500
Total selling expenses	$ 12,100	$ 13,620	$ 14,500	$ 40,220

General and Administrative Expense Budget

The **general and administrative expense budget** presents the expenses the organization plans to incur in connection with the general administration of the organization. Included are expenses for the accounting department, the computer center, and the president's office, for example. REI's assumed general and administrative expense budget is presented in Exhibit 22.7.

General and administrative expense budget

The general and administrative expense budget presents the expenses the organization plans to incur in connection with the general administration of the organization.

Exhibit 22.7 ■ General and Administrative Expense Budget

REI
General and Administrative Expense Budget
For the Second Quarter Ending June 30

	April	May	June	Quarter Total
General and administrative expenses				
Compensation.............................	$25,000	$25,000	$25,000	$75,000
Insurance	2,000	2,000	2,000	6,000
Depreciation	2,000	2,000	2,000	6,000
Utilities	3,000	3,000	3,000	9,000
Miscellaneous.............................	1,000	1,000	1,000	3,000
Total general and administrative expenses	$33,000	$33,000	$33,000	$99,000

The depreciation of $2,000 per month is a noncash item and is not carried forward to the cash budget. No variable general and administrative costs are included because most expenditures categorized as general and administrative are related to top-management operations that do not vary with unit-level cost drivers. To simplify the presentation of the cash budget, the budget assumes that general and administrative expenses, except depreciation, are paid in the month they are incurred.

Cash Budget

The **cash budget** summarizes all cash receipts and disbursements expected to occur during the budget period. Cash is critical to survival. Income is like food and cash is like water. Food is necessary to survive and prosper over time, but you can get along without food for a short period of time. You cannot survive very long without water. Hence, cash budgeting is very important, especially in a small business where cash receipts from sales lag purchases of inventory. As pointed out in the following Business Insight, cash budgets are also critical for managing the impact of changing customer preferences.

Budgeting within a large diversified multinational corporation is challenging when the business spans many markets and countries. Unilever operates segments across the globe with product lines from dairy to skin care, so the company must make sure it has the ability to invest in new products in these areas while insulating its performance from exchange rate fluctuations. In the first quarter of 2016, Unilever PCL posted an increase in both volume and price of sales but a 2% decrease in revenue. To limit its exposure to exchange rates, Unilever adopted strict cost controls and restructured its portfolio of brands to keep up with shifting demand.

Unilever's food business has been lagging behind other areas, especially personal care. Originally a Dutch margarine producer, Unilever is considering dropping the butter substitute altogether. Unilever is shifting resources to focus on men's skin and hair care as men are spending more time and money on their appearance and customers are returning to real butter. Rob Candelino, VP of hair care marketing at Unilever, says that "This generation of man—on all aspects of how they are taking care of themselves—is caring much more than previous generations." Therefore, the company is developing new products and has acquired the Dollar Shave Club, a low-cost direct provider of shaving supplies for men.

Careful cash budgeting is essential for Unilever in managing the impact of changing customer preferences and global economic fluctuations while still investing in continued growth.

Sources: Saabira Chaudhuri, "Unilever Sales Fall on Currencies, Offsetting Better Volume, Prices," *Wall Street Journal*, April 14, 2016. Sharon Terlep, "Dollar Shave Club's $1 Billion Deal: A Victory for Simplicity over Technology," *Wall Street Journal*, July 20, 2016. Elizabeth Holmes, "Young Men Are Obsessed with Their Hair" *Wall Street Journal*, March 1, 2016. Saabira Chaudhuri, "Will Margarine Become Toast at Unilever?" *Wall Street Journal*, January 19, 2016.

After it makes sales predictions, an organization uses information regarding credit terms, collections policy, and prior collection experience to develop a cash collections budget. Collections on sales normally include receipts from the current period's sales and collections from sales of prior periods. An allowance for bad debts, which reduces each period's collections, is also predicted. Other items often included are cash sales, sales discounts, allowances for volume discounts, and seasonal changes of sales prices and collections. REI's assumed cash budget is in Exhibit 22.8. Note the following important points:

■ Management estimates that one-half of all sales are for cash and the other half are on the company's credit card. (When sales are on bank credit cards, the collection is immediate, less any bank user fee; however, the budget assumes charges using REI's credit card are collected by the company from the customer.) Twenty-five percent of the credit card sales are collected in the month of sale, and 74% are collected in the following month. Bad debts are budgeted at 1% of credit sales. This resource flow is graphically illustrated as follows:

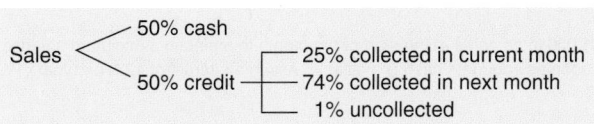

■ The budget assumes payments for purchases are made 20% in the month purchased and 80% in the next month.

■ Information on cash expenditures for selling expenses and for general and administrative expenses is based on budgets for these items. The monthly cash expenditures for general and administrative expenses are $31,000 rather than $33,000. The $2,000 difference relates to depreciation, which does not require use of cash.

■ The budget assumes REI's income taxes are determined on the basis of predicted taxable income following IRS rules. Estimated tax payments are made during the month following the end of each quarter. Hence, the taxes payable on April 1 are paid during April.

■ The cash budget shows cash operating deficiencies and surpluses expected to occur at the end of each month; this is used to plan for borrowing and loan payment.

■ The budget assumes the cash maintenance policy for REI specifies that a minimum balance of $15,000 is to be maintained.

Cash budget

The cash budget summarizes all cash receipts and disbursements expected to occur during the budget period.

Exhibit 22.8 ■ Cash Budget

REI
Cash Budget
For the Second Quarter Ending June 30

	April	May	June	Quarter Total
Budgeted sales (Exhibit 22.4)................	$190,000	$228,000	$250,000	$668,000
Cash balance, beginning	$ 15,000	$ 15,770	$ 44,850	$ 15,000
Collections on sales				
Cash sales (50% sales)	95,000	114,000	125,000	
Credit sales				
Current month (25% credit sales)	23,750	28,500	31,250	
Prior month (74% credit sales)	59,200*	70,300	84,360	
Total	177,950	212,800	240,610	631,360
Cash available for operations.................	192,950	228,570	285,460	646,360
Disbursements				
Purchases (Exhibit 22.5)				
Current month (20% purchases)............	25,080	28,680	33,540	
Prior month (80% purchases)	84,000**	100,320	114,720	
Total	109,080	129,000	148,260	386,340
Selling expenses (Exhibit 22.6)...............	12,100	13,620	14,500	40,220
General & Administrative Expenses				
(Exhibit 22.7, excluding depreciation)........	31,000	31,000	31,000	93,000
Taxes (Exhibit 22.3)	35,000			35,000
Total	(187,180)	(173,620)	(193,760)	(554,560)
Excess (deficiency) cash available over				
disbursements...........................	5,770	54,950	91,700	91,800
Short-term financing***				
New loans...............................	10,000			10,000
Repayments.............................		(10,000)		(10,000)
Interest	—	(100)	—	(100)
Net cash from financing	10,000	(10,100)	—	(100)
Cash balance, ending.......................	$ 15,770	$ 44,850	$ 91,700	$ 91,700

*April 1 accounts receivable.
**April 1 accounts payable.
***Loans are obtained in $1,000 increments at the start of the month to maintain a minimum balance of $15,000 at all times. Repayments are made as soon as adequate cash is available. Assume interest of 12% per year (1% per month) is paid when the loan is repaid.

- The budget assumes REI has a line of credit with a bank, with any interest on borrowed funds computed at the simple interest rate of 12.0% per year, or 1.0% per month. All necessary borrowing is assumed to occur at the start of each month in increments of $1,000. Repayments including interest are assumed to occur as soon as adequate cash is available.

- The cash budget indicates REI needs to borrow $10,000 in April. The $10,000 plus interest is repaid in May.

If REI had any cash disbursements for dividends or capital expenditures, they would be included in the cash budget. These items, along with information on income taxes, would be shown in special budgets.

Budgeted Financial Statements

The preparation of the master budget culminates in the preparation of budgeted financial statements. **Budgeted financial statements** are pro forma statements that reflect the "as-if" effects of the budgeted activities on the actual financial position of the organization. That is, the statements reflect the results of operations assuming all budget predictions are correct. Spreadsheets that permit the user to immediately determine the impact of any assumed changes facilitate developing budgeted financial statements. The budgeted income statement can follow the functional format traditionally used for financial accounting or the contribution format introduced in Module 16. In either case, the balance sheet amounts reflect the corresponding budgeted entries.

Exhibit 22.9 presents the budgeted income statement for the quarter ending June 30. If all predictions made in the operating budget are correct, REI will produce a net income of $51,540 for the quarter. Almost every item on the budgeted income statement comes from one of the budget schedules.

Exhibit 22.9 ■ Budgeted Income Statement

REI
Budgeted Income Statement
For the Second Quarter Ending June 30

Sales (Exhibit 22.4)		$668,000
Cost of goods sold*		
Beginning inventory (Exhibit 22.3)	$157,000	
Purchases (Exhibit 22.5)	436,500	
Cost of merchandise available	593,500	
Ending inventory (Exhibit 22.5)	(192,700)	(400,800)
Gross profit		267,200
Other expenses		
Bad debt (1% of credit sales)**	3,340	
Selling (Exhibit 22.6)	40,220	
General and administrative (Exhibit 22.7)	99,000	(142,560)
Income from operations		124,640
Interest expense (Exhibit 22.8)		(100)
Net income from operations		124,540
Allowance for income taxes***		(73,000)
Net income		$ 51,540

*Also computed at sales × 0.6
**$668,000 × 0.5 credit sales × 0.01 bad debts
***Provided by accounting

The budgeted balance sheet, presented in Exhibit 22.10 (page 22-15), shows REI's financial position as of June 30, assuming that all budget predictions are correct. Sources of the budgeted balance sheet data are included as part of the exhibit.

Finalizing the Budget

After studying the REI example, you might conclude that developing the master budget is a mechanical process. That is not the case. Understanding the basics of budget assembly is not the end; it is a tool to assist in efficient and effective budgeting. Before finalizing the budget, the following two questions must be addressed:

■ Is the proposed budget feasible?

■ Is the proposed budget acceptable?

To be feasible, the organization must be able to actually implement the proposed budget. Without the assumed line of credit, REI's budget is not feasible because the company would run out of cash sometime in April. Knowing this, management can take timely corrective action. Possible actions include obtaining equity financing, issuing long-term debt, reducing the amount of inventory on hand at the end of each quarter, or obtaining a line of credit. Other constraints that would make the budget infeasible include the availability of merchandise and, in the case of a manufacturing organization, production capacity.

Exhibit 22.10 ■ Budgeted Balance Sheet

REI
Balance Sheet
June 30

Assets
Current assets
Cash (Exhibit 22.8)	$ 91,700	
Accounts receivable, net*	92,500	
Merchandise inventory (Exhibits 22.5 and 22.9)	192,700	$376,900

Fixed assets
Buildings and equipment (Exhibit 22.3)	$460,000		
Less accumulated depreciation (Exhibit 22.3 plus depreciation Exhibit 22.7).	(130,800)	329,200	
Land (Exhibit 22.3)		60,000	389,200
Total assets			$766,100

Liabilities and Stockholders' Equity
Current liabilities
Accounts payable**	$134,160	
Taxes payable (Exhibit 22.9)	73,000	$207,160

Stockholders' equity
Capital stock (Exhibit 22.3)	350,000	
Retained earnings (Exhibit 22.3 plus net income Exhibit 22.9)	208,940	558,940
Total liabilities and stockholders' equity		$766,100

*June credit sales collected in July, $250,000 × 0.50 × 0.74.
**June purchases paid in July, $167,700 × 0.80.

Once management determines that the budget is feasible, they still need to determine if it is acceptable. To evaluate acceptability, management might consider various financial ratios, such as return on assets. They might compare the return provided by the proposed budget with past returns, industry averages, or some organizational goal.

Review 22-3 LO3

MBC

Budget for a Merchandising Organization

Bleu Mont Dairy is a wholesale distributor of artisan cheese and ice cream. Suppose the following information is available for April.

Estimated sales	
Cheese	160,000 hoops at $10 each
Ice cream	240,000 gallons at $5 each

Estimated costs	
Cheese	$8 per hoop
Ice cream	$2 per gallon

	Beginning	Ending
Desired inventories		
Cheese	10,000	12,000
Ice cream	4,000	5,000

continued

continued from previous page

Assumed financial information follows:

- Beginning cash balance is $400,000.
- Purchases of merchandise are paid 60% in the month of purchase and 40% in the following month. Purchases totaled $1,800,000 in March and are estimated to be $2,000,000 in May.
- Employee wages and salaries are paid for in the current month. Employee expenses for April totaled $156,000.
- Overhead expenses are paid in the next month. The accounts payable amount for these expenses from March is $80,000 and for May will be $90,000. April's overhead expenses total $80,000.
- Sales are on credit and are collected 70% in the current period and the remainder in the next period. March's sales were $3,000,000, and May's sales are estimated to be $3,200,000. Bad debts average 1% of sales.
- Selling and administrative expenses are paid monthly and total $450,000, including $40,000 of depreciation.
- All unit costs for April are the same as they were in March.

Required
Prepare the following for April:

a. Sales budget in dollars.
b. Purchases budget.
c. Cash budget.
d. Budgeted income statement.

Solution on p. 22-38.

Budget Development in Manufacturing Organizations

The importance of inventory in various organizations was introduced in Module 18 where Exhibit 18.1 (page 18-4) summarized inventory and related expense accounts for service, merchandising, and manufacturing organizations. Recall that service organizations usually have a low percentage of their assets invested in inventory, usually consisting of the supplies needed to facilitate operations. In contrast, merchandising organizations usually have a high percentage of their total assets invested in inventory, with the largest inventory investment in merchandise purchased for resale. The preceding illustration of the development of a master budget was for a merchandising organization. In this section, we will illustrate the the development of a master budget for a manufacturing organization. We will contrast the assembly of a budget for a merchandiser in Exhibit 22.2 with the assembly of a budget for a manufacturer in Exhibit 22.11 (page 21-17).

LO4 Explain and develop a basic manufacturing cost budget.

Production Budget

Because manufacturing organizations convert raw materials into finished goods that are sold to customers, there are additional steps in developing their master budget. The management of a manufacturing organization must determine the production volume required to support sales and finished goods ending inventory requirements (production budget). Then, based on available inventories or raw materials and the raw materials required for production, management develops a purchases budget.

Manufacturing Cost Budget

In addition to a selling expense budget and a general and administrative expense budget, management needs also to develop a manufacturing cost budget, which is similar in design to a statement of cost of goods manufactured (see Exhibit 18.6, page 18-16) except that it is prepared in advance of production rather than after production. Reflecting these additional steps, the cash budget includes payments for direct labor and manufacturing overhead, based on information in the manufacturing cost budget, and payments for purchases of raw materials based on the purchases budget. Note cash disbursements are for materials purchased rather than materials used in production.

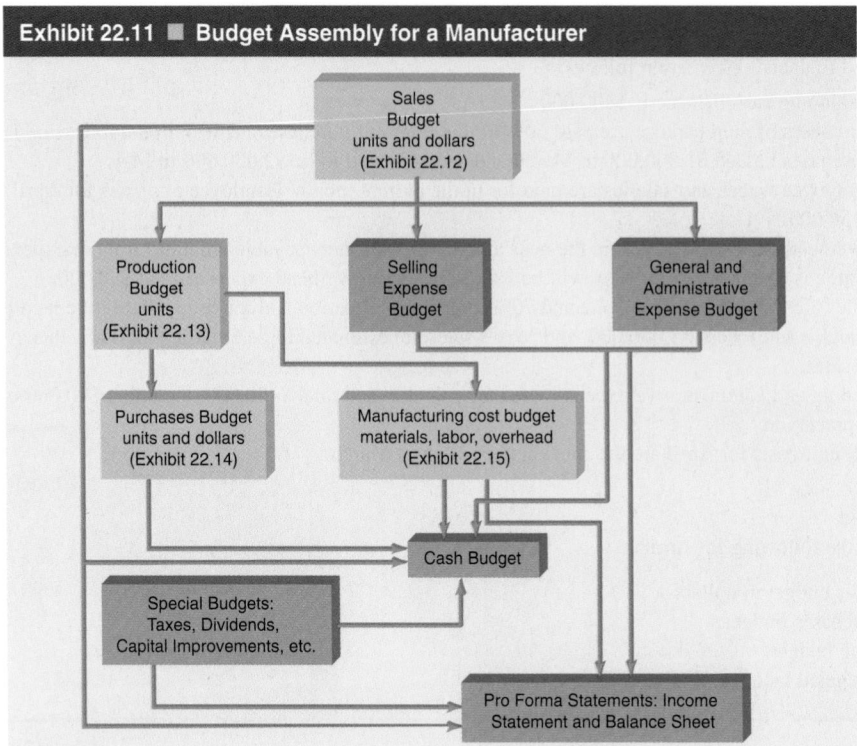

Exhibit 22.11 ■ Budget Assembly for a Manufacturer

Continuing our REI example, assume that management is considering the option of manufacturing a high-quality backpack, tentatively named the "Trekpack" as an alternative to purchasing a similar item from an outside vendor. Unit variable and monthly fixed cost estimates associated with the manufacture of Trekpacks follow:

Unit costs		
Direct materials		
Fabric: 2 square yards at $10 per yard	$20	
Hardware kits (buckles, straps, etc.)	5	$ 25
Direct labor 0.5 hours at $30 per hour		15
Variable overhead, per unit		8
Total variable costs per unit		$ 48
Fixed costs per month (rent, utilities, supervision)		$6,000

Because management anticipates an average monthly production volume of 500 Trekpacks, the average fixed cost per unit, a predetermined overhead rate, is $12 ($6,000/500).

For budgeting purposes, management uses a standard cost, a budget per unit of product, for valuing inventories and forecasting the cost of goods sold. The standard cost of a Trekpack is $60:

Direct materials	$25
Direct labor	15
Variable overhead	8
Fixed overhead	12
Standard cost	$60

Management, planning to introduce this new product in May, developed the sales budget shown in Exhibit 22.12. In this case, because unit information is necessary to determine production requirements, the sales budget is expressed in units as well as dollars.

Introducing Trekpacks in May requires some April production. To meet the initial sales requirement for the start of each month, management desires end-of-month inventories equal to 40% of the following month's budgeted sales. The sales budget and ending inventory plans, along with information on beginning inventories, are used to develop the production budget in Exhibit 22.13.

Manufacturing sales budget

Because unit information is necessary to determine production requirements, the sales budget is expressed in units as well as dollars.

Exhibit 22.12 ■ Sales Budget

REI
Sales Budget (Trekpacks)
For the Second Quarter Ending June 30

	April	May	June	Quarter Total	July
Sales—Units.	0	400	500	900	600
Sales—Dollars ($100 each)	0	$40,000	$50,000	$90,000	$60,000

Production budget

The sales budget and ending inventory plans, along with information on beginning inventories, are used to develop the production budget.

Exhibit 22.13 ■ Production Budget

REI
Production Budget (Trekpacks)
For the Second Quarter Ending June 30

	April	May	June	Quarter Total
Budgeted sales.	0	400	500	900
Desired ending inventory				
40% following month sales	160	200	240	240
Total requirements	160	600	740	1,140
Less beginning inventory	0	(160)	(200)	0
Budgeted production	160	440	540	1,140

The production budget, along with information on beginning inventories of raw materials and planned ending inventory levels (500 square yards of fabric and 200 kits), is then used to budget the purchases in Exhibit 22.14 for raw materials in units and dollars. The production budget, along with standard variable and predicted fixed cost information, is also used to develop the manufacturing cost budget in Exhibit 22.15.

Purchases budget

The production budget, along with information on beginning inventories of raw materials and planned ending inventory levels, is then used to budget the purchases for raw materials in units and dollars.

Exhibit 22.14 ■ Purchase Budget

REI
Purchases Budget
For the Second Quarter Ending June 30

	April	May	June	Quarter Total
Fabric				
Current needs (2 yards per unit).	320	880	1,080	2,280
Desired ending inventory (500 yards).	500	500	500	500
Total requirements	820	1,380	1,580	2,780
Less beginning inventory	(0)	(500)	(500)	(0)
Fabric purchases in yards.	820	880	1,080	2,780
Assembly kits				
Current needs (1 per unit).	160	440	540	1,140
Desired ending inventory (200 kits)	200	200	200	200
Total requirements	360	640	740	1,340
Less beginning inventory	(0)	(200)	(200)	(0)
Kit purchases in units	360	440	540	1,340
Purchases (Dollars)				
Fabric at $10 per yard.	$ 8,200	$ 8,800	$10,800	$27,800
Kits at $5 each	1,800	2,200	2,700	6,700
Total purchases in dollars.	$10,000	$11,000	$13,500	$34,500

Manufacturing cost budget

The production budget, along with standard variable and predicted fixed cost information, is also used to develop the manufacturing cost budget.

Exhibit 22.15 ■ Manufacturing Cost Budget

REI Manufacturing Cost Budget For the Second Quarter Ending June 30	April	May	June	Quarter Total
Direct materials				
Fabric used in production (production × 2 yards × $10)	$ 3,200	$ 8,800	$10,800	$22,800
Kits used in production (production × 1 kit × $5)	800	2,200	2,700	5,700
Total	4,000	11,000	13,500	28,500
Direct labor (production × 1/2 hour × $30)	2,400	6,600	8,100	17,100
Manufacturing overhead				
Variable ($8 per unit)	1,280	3,520	4,320	9,120
Fixed	6,000	6,000	6,000	18,000
Total	7,280	9,520	10,320	27,120
Total manufacturing costs.	$13,680	$27,120	$31,920	$72,720

Because it does not require the introduction of new concepts, the cash budget and the pro forma financial statements for REI with the manufacturing of Trekpacks are not presented. Keep in mind that the cash budget will include disbursements for purchases shown in Exhibit 22.14 and for direct labor, variable overhead, and fixed overhead shown in Exhibit 22.15. A pro forma functional income statement using absorption costing will include the predicted cost of goods sold for Trekpacks at a $60 standard cost per unit. A contribution income statement using variable costing would include the cost of goods sold for Trekpacks at a $48 standard cost per unit with all fixed manufacturing costs expensed in the period incurred. Finally, the pro forma balance sheet will include standard costs of any June raw materials (500 square yards at $10 per yard and 200 kits at $5 each), work in process (none), and finished goods. Any unpaid liabilities for purchases of raw materials, direct labor, and manufacturing overhead would also be shown under current liabilities. Note that completing the cash budget and the pro forma statements requires information on the timing of payments for the purchases of raw materials, direct labor, and manufacturing overhead.

Review 22-4 LO4

Budget for a Manufacturer

Assume DeWalt, a subsidiary of Stanley Black and Decker, manufactures and sells two industrial products in a single plant. Suppose a new manager wants to have quarterly budgets and has prepared the following information for the first quarter of the year:

Budgeted sales

Drills	60,000 at $100 each
Saws	40,000 at $125 each

Budgeted inventories

	Beginning	Ending
Drills, finished	20,000 units	25,000 units
Saws, finished	8,000 units	10,000 units
Metal, direct materials	32,000 pounds	36,000 pounds
Plastic, direct materials.	29,000 pounds	32,000 pounds
Handles, direct materials	6,000 each	7,000 each

continued

continued from previous page

Standard variable costs per unit

	Drills		Saws	
Direct materials				
Metal..............	5 pounds × $8.00	$40.00	4 pounds × $8.00	$32.00
Plastic.............	3 pounds × $5.00	15.00	3 pounds × $5.00	15.00
Handles............	1 handle × $3.00	3.00		
Total		58.00		47.00
Direct labor...........	2 labor hours × $12.00	24.00	3 labor hours × $16.00	48.00
Variable manufacturing				
Overhead	2 hours × $1.50	3.00	3 hours × $1.50	4.50
Total		$85.00		$99.50

Assume fixed manufacturing overhead is $214,000 per quarter (including noncash expenditures of $156,000) and is allocated on total units produced. Financial information follows:

- Beginning cash balance is $1,800,000.
- Sales are on credit and are collected 50% in the current period and the remainder in the next period. Last quarter's sales were $8,400,000. There are no bad debts.
- Purchases of direct materials and labor costs are paid for in the quarter acquired.
- Manufacturing overhead expenses are paid in the quarter incurred.
- Selling and administrative expenses are all fixed and are paid in the quarter incurred. They are budgeted at $340,000 per quarter, including $90,000 of depreciation.

Required
For the first quarter of the year, prepare the following:

a. Sales budget in dollars.
b. Production budget in units.
c. Purchases budget.
d. Manufacturing cost budget.

e. Cash budget.
f. Budgeted contribution income statement.
(*Hint:* See Module 16.)

Solution on p. 22-40.

Budget Development and Manager Behavior

Organizations are composed of individuals who perform a wide variety of activities in pursuit of the organization's goals. To accomplish these goals, management must recognize the effects that budgeting and performance evaluation methods have on the behavior of the organization's employees.

LO5

MBC Analyze the relationship between budget development and manager behavior.

Employee Participation

Budgeting should be used to promote productive employee behavior directed toward meeting the organization's goals. While no two organizations use exactly the same budgeting procedures, two approaches to employee involvement in budgeting represent possible end points on a continuum. These approaches are sometimes referred to as top-down and bottom-up methods.

With a **top-down** or **imposed budget**, top management identifies the primary goals and objectives for the organization and communicates them to lower management levels. Because relatively few people are involved in top-down budgeting, an imposed budget saves time. It also minimizes the slack that managers at lower organizational levels are sometimes prone to build into their budgets. However, this nonparticipative approach to budgeting can have undesirable motivational consequences. Personnel who do not participate in budget preparation might lack a commitment to achieve their part of the budget.

With a **bottom-up** or **participative budget**, managers at all levels—and in some cases, even nonmanagers—are involved in budget preparation. Budget proposals originate at the lowest level of management possible and are then integrated into the proposals for the next level, and so on, until the proposals reach the top level of management, which completes the budget.

Participation helps ensure that important issues are considered and that employees understand the importance of their roles in meeting the organization's goals. It also provides opportunities for problem solving and fosters employee commitment to agreed-upon goals. Hence, budget predictions are likely to be more accurate, and the people responsible for the budget are more likely to strive to accomplish its objectives. These self-imposed budgets reinforce the concept of participative management and should strengthen the overall budgeting process.

Participative approaches to budgeting have a few disadvantages. Because they require the involvement of many people, the preparation period is longer than that for an imposed budget. Another disadvantage is the tendency of some managers to intentionally understate revenues or overstate expenses to provide **budgetary slack**. A manager might do this to reduce his or her concern regarding unfavorable performance reviews or to make it easier to obtain favorable performance reviews. If a department consistently produces favorable variances (actual results versus budget) with little apparent effort, this might be a symptom of budgetary slack.

Budgetary slack
Cushion created in a budget to minimize risk that managers might fail to meet budgeted results.

Managerial Decision ■ **You Are the Chief Financial Officer**

As the CFO of a relatively new and fast-growing entrepreneurial enterprise, you and the other top managers have previously emphasized technical and marketing innovation and creativity over planning and budgeting. But now with growing competition and the maturing of the company's products, you recognized that a culture of better financial planning must be established if the company is to succeed in the long run. You feel that the financial staff has the best expertise and understanding of the business to prepare effective budgets, but you are concerned about the motivational effects of excluding the lower-level managers from the process and are seeking advice. [Answer, p. 22-23.]

Budgeting Periods

Although most organizations use a one-year budget period, some organizations budget for shorter or longer periods. In addition to fixed-length budget periods, two other types of budget periods commonly used are life-cycle budgeting and continuous budgeting.

When a fixed time period is not particularly relevant to planning, an organization can use **life-cycle budgeting**, which involves developing a budget for a project's entire life. An ice cream vendor at the beach might develop a budget for the season. A general contractor might budget costs for the entire (multiple-year) time required to construct a building.

Under **continuous budgeting**, the budget (sometimes called a **rolling budget**) is based on a moving time frame. For example, an organization on a continuous four-quarter budget system adds a quarter to the budget at the end of each quarter of operations, thereby always maintaining a budget for four quarters into the future. Under this system, plans for a full year into the future are always available, whereas under a fixed annual budget, operating plans for a full year ahead are available only at the beginning of the budget year. Because managers are constantly involved in this type of budgeting, the budget process becomes an active and integral part of the management process. Managers are forced to be future oriented throughout the year rather than just once each year.

Forecasts

Budget preparation requires the development of a variety of forecasts. The sales forecast is based on a variety of interrelated factors such as historical trends, product innovation, general economic conditions, industry conditions, and the organization's strategic position for competing on the basis of price, product differentiation, or market niche. Many organizations first determine the industry forecast for a given product or service and then extract from it their sales estimations.

Although the sales forecast is primary to most organizations, there are many other forecasts of varying importance that must be made, including (a) the collection period for sales on account, (b) percent of uncollectable sales on account, (c) cost of materials, supplies, utilities, and so forth, (d) employee turnover, (e) time required to perform activities, (f) interest rates, and (g) development time for new products or services.

> **Business Insight** ■ Developing Honesty in Budgeting
>
> Often the budgeting process involves soliciting information from mid-level managers, and honesty in this participative process is essential. Lower-level managers often have much better information about their sphere of the company's operations, but often these managers have financial incentives to misreport.
>
> Experiments by researchers at the University of Indiana and the University of Kentucky suggest that publishing rankings of division performance can eliminate these incentives. When mid-level managers are ranked by their department's contribution to firm performance, their budget reports become quite accurate. This result is independent of the manager's compensation structure. Firms who rely heavily on information from mid-level managers should be careful to construct incentive and recognition structures that encourage honest reporting.
>
> Source: Jason L. Brown, Joseph G. Fisher, Matthew Sooy, and Geoffrey B. Sprinkle, "The Effect of Rankings on Honesty in Budget Reporting," *Accounting, Organizations and Society*, 39, no. 4 (May 2014): 237–246. http://dx.doi.org/10.1016/j.aos.2014.03.001.

Ethics

Because most wrongful activities related to budgeting are unethical, rather than illegal, organizations often have difficulty dealing with them. However, when managers' actions cross the gray area between ethical and fraudulent behavior, organizations are not reluctant to dismiss employees or even pursue legal actions against them.

Although most managers have a natural inclination to be conservative in developing their budgets, at some level the blatant padding or building slack into the budget becomes unethical. In an extreme case, it might even be considered theft if an inordinate level of budgetary slack creates favorable performance variances that lead to significant bonuses or other financial gain for the manager. Another form of falsifying budgets occurs when managers include expense categories in their budgets that are not needed in their operations and subsequently use the funds to pad other budget categories. The deliberate falsification of budgets is unethical behavior and is grounds for dismissal in most organizations.

Ethical issues might also arise in the reporting of performance results, which usually compares actual data with budgeted data. Examples of unethical reporting of actual performance data include misclassification of expenses, overstating revenues or understating expenses, postponing or accelerating the recording of activities at the end of the accounting period, or creating fictitious activities.

Open Book Management

If an organization is to obtain the full benefit of budgeting, support for the budget must be obtained from employees at all levels. Many organizations, especially smaller ones, have used open book management to obtain employee support for the budget. **Open book management** involves sharing financial and related information with employees, teaching employees to understand financial numbers, encouraging employees to use the information in their work, and sharing financial results with employees, perhaps through a bonus program. The following Research Insight examines the success of open book management in small companies.

Properly used, an operating budget is an effective mechanism for motivating employees to higher levels of performance and productivity. Improperly developed and administered, budgets can foster feelings of animosity toward management and the budget process. Behavioral research has generally concluded that when employees participate in the preparation of budgets and believe that the budgets represent fair standards for evaluating their performance, they receive personal satisfaction from accomplishing the goals set in the budgets.

> **Research Insight** ■ Open Book Management Opens the Door to Profits
>
> Open book management has its roots at **Springfield Remanufacturing Corp.** (SRC). In the late 1970s, SRC was a subsidiary of **International Harvester** and was losing money. International Harvester sent a new plant manager, Jack Stack, to turn SRC around. Stack made SRC profitable by sharing information and using gamification techniques to improve firm performance. Stack's performance game is based on three principles:

continued

continued from previous page

1. Transparency: Make the business's goals and planning transparent; then continually educate employees about the plan.
2. Involvement: Involve employees in both planning and ownership.
3. Measurement: Create a "Critical Number," a measure of performance that the whole organization is invested in working toward.

The key to this approach is that all employees understand how their work fits into the larger success of the organization, and share the proceeds from success. In this context, sharing financial information with employees empowers them to find solutions to problems and inefficiencies throughout the organization.

This approach was so successful that in 1983 Stack and 12 employees bought SRC from International Harvester and have since grown the business to 1,200 employee-owners and 31 businesses, including a corporate training and education practice. The success of these practices extends far beyond SRC. Research by the McGill University Institute for Health and Social Policy finds that firms large and small are able to improve efficiency and profitability by following SRC's model.

Sources: Neil Amato, "Opening the Books, Growing the Business," *CGMA Magazine*, June 1, 2016.
Jody Heymann, with Magda Berrerra, "Profit at the Bottom of the Ladder," *Harvard Business School Press*, 2010.

Review 22-5 **LO5**

Items 1 though 4 represent manager behaviors related to operational budgeting.

1. Budgetary Slack
2. Participative Budget
3. Open Book Management
4. Life-Cycle Budgeting

Required
Identify the above term that most appropriately describes the scenarios below:

_____ *a.* The marketing department is asked to provide an estimate as to how much it will spend on print ads during the next fiscal year.

_____ *b.* The marketing department provides a budget amount for print ads for the next fiscal year that includes the expected expenditures plus 10% to account for uncertainty.

_____ *c.* Tristan Renken owns and operates a food truck that sells Mexican food along the beaches in Chicago. Tristan only operates the food truck during the summer and developed a budget to estimate how much he will make during the upcoming summer season.

_____ *d.* Top management hosts semi-annual meetings to discuss the budget and current performance vs. the budget. Management provides employees with tools to help gauge their own performance against the budgeted expectations.

Solution on p. 22-42.

Guidance Answers

You Are the Chief Financial Officer
Pg. 22-20 You seem to be leaning toward using a top-down approach to budgeting. While this method may produce an effective set of benchmarks for planning and evaluation, it does not maximize the benefits of budgeting. A key element in any effective budgeting system is that it must be embraced by the managers whose performance will be evaluated by it. If the budget is imposed from the top down, it is far less likely to be embraced by managers than if they have participated from the beginning of the budget development process. The most effective budgeting systems are those that are strongly embraced by managers at all levels, which is most readily achieved through a participative (bottom-up) approach.

Questions

Q22-1. What are the primary phases in the planning and control cycle?

Q22-2. Does budgeting require formal or informal planning? What are some advantages of this style of management?

Q22-3. Identify the advantages and disadvantages of the incremental approach to budgeting.

Q22-4. Explain the minimum level approach to budgeting.

Q22-5. How does activity-based budgeting predict a cost objective's budget?

Q22-6. Explain the continuous improvement concept of budgeting.

Q22-7. Which budget brings together all other budgets? How is this accomplished?

Q22-8. What budgets are normally used to support the cash budget? What is the net result of cash budget preparations?

Q22-9. Define *budgeted financial statements.*

Q22-10. Identify the two budgets that are part of the master budget of a manufacturing organization but not part of the master budget of a merchandising organization.

Q22-11. Contrast the top-down and bottom-up approaches to budget preparation.

Q22-12. Is budgetary slack a desirable feature? Can it be prevented? Why or why not?

Q22-13. Why are annual budgets not always desirable? What are some alternative budget periods?

Q22-14. Explain how continuous budgeting works.

Q22-15. In addition to the sales forecast, what forecasts are used in budgeting?

Q22-16. Why should motivational considerations be a part of budget planning and utilization? List several ways to motivate employees with budgets.

Assignments with the ⓜ logo in the margin are available in BusinessCourse.
See the Preface of the book for details.

Mini Exercises

M22-17. Output/Input Budget

LO2

Vinyard Clinic has the following resource input information available for a routine physical examination.
- Each exam normally requires 0.75 hours of examining room time, including
  - ○ 30 minutes of nursing services,
  - ○ 15 minutes of physician services.
- Each exam also utilizes one package of examination supplies costing $50 each.
- Including benefits, physicians earn $90/hour and nurses earn $35/hour.
- Variable overhead is budgeted at $15 per examining room hour and fixed overhead is budgeted at $8,000 per month.

Required

Prepare an output/input budget for October when 500 routine examinations are planned. Discuss some of the likely benefits to Vinyard Clinic of dedicating time to go through the budgeting process.

M22-18. Incremental Budget

LO2

Wood County uses an incremental approach to budgeting. The current year cash budget for the Wood County Department of Motor Vehicles is presented as follows:

Supplies	$ 12,000
Temporary and seasonal wages	32,000
Wages of full-time employees	200,000
Supervisor salaries	60,000
Rent	48,000
Insurance	16,000
Utilities	10,000
Miscellaneous.	9,600
Contingencies and equipment	25,000
Total	$412,600

Required

Prepare an incremental cash budget for next year, assuming the planned total budget increase is 3%. Budget details include a budget increment for salaries and wages of 3%, no change in rent, and 2.5% increases in the budget for supplies and miscellaneous. Utility companies have received approvals for rate increases amounting to 2% and insurance companies have announced an increase in premiums of 4%. (*Hint:* The Contingencies and equipment budget is a plug.)

LO3
Thunder Road Guitars

M22-19. Purchases Budget in Units and Dollars

Thunder Road Guitars specializes in vintage, used, and rare guitars. Assume budgeted sales for the first six months of the year are as follows:

Month	Unit Sales	Month	Unit Sales
January.....................	15	April	18
February....................	12	May........................	22
March	16	June	20

Beginning inventory for the year is 7 units. The budgeted inventory at the end of a month is 50% of units to be sold the following month. Purchase price per unit is $800.

Required

Prepare a purchases budget in units and dollars for each month, January through May.

LO3

M22-20. Cash Budget

Patrick's Retail Company is planning a cash budget for the next three months. Estimated sales revenue is as follows:

Month	Sales Revenue	Month	Sales Revenue
January................	$250,000	March	$400,000
February...............	350,000	April	375,000

All sales are on credit; 75% is collected during the month of sale, and 25% is collected during the next month. Cost of goods sold is 70% of sales. Payments for merchandise sold are made in the month following the month of sale. Operating expenses total $125,000 per month and are paid during the month incurred. The cash balance on February 1 is estimated to be $55,000.

Required

Prepare monthly cash budgets for February, March, and April.

LO4

M22-21. Production and Purchases Budgets in Units

At the end of business on June 30, the PE Rug Company had 35,000 square yards of rugs and 100,000 pounds of raw materials on hand. Budgeted sales for the third quarter are

Month	Sales
July..	50,000 sq. yards
August	35,000 sq. yards
September	42,000 sq. yards
October...	48,000 sq. yards

The PE Rug Company wants to have sufficient square yards of finished product on hand at the end of each month to meet 60% of the following month's budgeted sales and sufficient pounds of raw materials to meet 40% of the following month's production requirements. Seven pounds of raw materials are required to produce one square yard of carpeting.

Required

Prepare a production budget for the months of July, August, and September and a purchases budget in units for the months of July and August.

LO4
Carolina Table
Manufacturing

M22-22. Manufacturing Cost Budget

Assume Carolina Table, a furniture manufacturer located in South Carolina, produces a conference table with the following standard costs:

Unit costs		
Direct materials		
Wood: 24 square feet at $35......................................	$840	
Hardware kits (screws, etc.)	20	$ 860
Direct labor 0.75 hours at $40 per hour		30
Variable overhead, per unit...		25
Total variable costs per unit		$ 915
Fixed costs per month (rent, utilities, supervision)		$91,250

Management plans to produce 250 units in April.

Required

Prepare a manufacturing cost budget for April.

E22-23. **Activity-Based Budget**   LO1, 2

Highland Industries has the following budget information available for February:

Units manufactured	25,000
Factory administration	$145,000
Assembly	¼ hour per unit × $20
Direct materials.	3 pounds per unit × $6
Inspection	$40 per batch of 1,000 units
Manufacturing overhead.	$8 per unit
Product development	$50,000
Setup cost.	$100 per batch of 1,000 units

Required

a. Use activity-based costing to prepare a manufacturing cost budget for February. Clearly distinguish between unit, batch, and facility-level costs.

b. The operating managers at Highland Industries are concerned that the budgeting process is too time-consuming and diverts attention from their current day-to-day responsibilities. Discuss the reasons that Highland should continue budgeting.

E22-24. **Product and Department Budgets Using Activity-Based Approach**   LO2

The following data are from the general records of the Loading Department of Jonah Freight Company for November.

- Cleaning incoming trucks, 30 minutes.
- Obtaining and reviewing shipping documents for loading truck and instructing loaders, 15 minutes.
- Loading truck, 1 hour.
- Cleaning shipping dock and storage area after each loading, 15 minutes.
- Employees perform both cleaning and loading tasks and are currently averaging $25 per hour in wages and benefits.
- The supervisor spends 15% of her time overseeing the cleaning activities; 35% overseeing various loading activities; and the remainder of her time making general plans and managing the department. Her current salary is $6,000 per month.
- Other overhead of the department amounts to $12,000 per month, 30% for cleaning, 65% for loading, and 5% for adminstration.

Required

Prepare an activities budget for cleaning and loading in the Loading Department for November, assuming 20 working days and the loading of an average of 25 trucks per day.

E22-25. **Activity-Based Budgeting**   LO2
Mountain View Hospital

Assume Mountain View Hospital uses an activity-based budgeting approach for all costs except physician care. Some of the patients are treated in the emergency room as outpatients. Others are admitted to the hospital for additional tests and treatments. Its emergency room has three activity areas with cost drivers as follows:

1. *Reception*—paperwork of incoming patients. Cost driver is the number of forms completed.
2. *Treatment*—initial diagnosis and treatment of patients. Cost driver is the number of diagnoses treated.
3. *Cleaning*—general cleaning plus preparing treatment facilities for next patient. Cost driver is the number of people visiting the emergency room.

		Budgeted Amount of Cost Driver	
Activity Area	**Cost Driver Rates**	**Outpatients**	**Admitted Patients**
Reception	$ 20	9,200 forms	8,800 forms
Treatment	175	4,600 diagnoses	2,200 diagnoses
Cleaning	30	4,500 people	3,000 people

Required

a. Prepare the total budgeted cost for each activity.
b. How might you adjust the budget approach if you found that outpatients were kept in the emergency room for one hour on average while admitted patients remained for two hours?
c. What advantage does an activity-based approach have over the hospital's former budgeting method of basing the next year's budget on the last year's actual amount plus a percentage increase?

LO3
Honolulu Shirt Shop

E22-26. Sales Budget

Honolulu Shirt Shop has very seasonal sales. Assume that for next year management is trying to decide whether to establish a sales budget based on average sales or on sales estimated by quarter. The unit sales for next year are expected to be 5% higher than current year sales. Unit shirt sales by quarter for this year were as follows:

	Children's	Women's	Men's	Total
Winter quarter.	80	80	140	300
Spring quarter.	180	120	160	460
Summer quarter	500	600	260	1,360
Fall quarter.	120	160	160	440
Total	880	960	720	2,560

Children's T-shirts sell for $10 each, women's sell for $15, and men's sell for $18.

Required

Assuming a 5% increase in sales, prepare a sales budget for each quarter of the year using the following:
a. Average quarterly sales. (*Hint:* Winter quarter children's shirts are 231 [880 × 1.05 ÷ 4].)
b. Actual quarterly sales. (*Hint:* Winter quarter children's shirts are 84 [80 × 1.05].)
c. Suggest advantages of each method.

LO3

E22-27. Cash Budget & Short-Term Financing

Presented are partial October, November, and December cash budgets for Holiday Events:

HOLIDAY EVENTS Partial Cash Budgets				
	October	November	December	Total
Cash balance, beginning	$ 25,000	$?	$?	$?
Collections on sales	100,000	90,000	140,000	?
Cash available for operations	?	?	?	?
Disbursements for operations	(115,000)	(110,000)	(115,000)	?
Ending cash before borrowings or replacements	?	?	?	?
Short-term finance	?	?	?	?
New loans	?	?	?	?
Repayments	?	?	?	?
Interest	?	?	?	?
Cash balance, ending	$?	$?	$?	$?

Loans are obtained in increments of $1,000 at the start of each month to maintain a minimum end-of-month balance of $12,000. Interest is 1% simple interest (no compounding) per month, payable when a loan payment is made. Repayments are made as soon as possible, subject to the minimum end-of-month balance.

Required

Complete the short-term financing section of the cash budget.

LO3

E22-28. Purchases and Cash Budgets

On July 1, MTC Wholesalers had a cash balance of $125,000 and accounts payable of $160,000, and Inventory of $78,000. Actual sales for May and June, and budgeted sales for July, August, September, and October are

Month	Actual Sales	Month	Budgeted Sales
May......................	$250,000	July.......................	$260,000
June	225,000	August	240,000
		September	270,000
		October...................	275,000

All sales are on credit with 60% collected during the month of sale, 30% collected during the next month, and 10% collected during the second month following the month of sale. Cost of goods sold averages 60% of sales revenue. Ending inventory is one-half of the next month's predicted cost of sales. The other half of the merchandise is acquired during the month of sale. All purchases are paid for in the month after purchase. Operating costs are estimated at $95,000 each month and are paid during the month incurred.

Required
Prepare purchases and cash budgets for July, August, and September.

E22-29. Cash Receipts

LO3

The sales budget for Andrew Inc. is forecasted as follows:

Month	Sales Revenue
May..	$150,000
June	175,000
July...	160,000
August	200,000

To prepare a cash budget, the company must determine the budgeted cash collections from sales. Historically, the following trend has been established regarding cash collection of sales:

- 60% in the month of sale.
- 20% in the month following sale.
- 15% in the second month following sale.
- 5% uncollectible.

The company gives a 2% cash discount for payments made by customers during the month of sale. The accounts receivable balance on April 30 is $85,000, of which $25,000 represents uncollected March sales and $60,000 represents uncollected April sales. (*Hint:* For collections of March and April receivables, start by determining total sales for the month. Assume the normal sales pattern.)

Required
Prepare a schedule of budgeted cash collections from sales for May, June, and July. Include a three-month summary of estimated cash collections.

E22-30. Cash Disbursements

LO3
Stimson Lumber

Assume Stimson Lumber, headquartered in Portland, Oregon, is in the process of preparing its budget for next year. Cost of goods sold has been estimated at 60% of sales. Lumber purchases and payments are to be made during the month preceding the month of sale. Wages are estimated at 20% of sales and are paid during the month of sale. Other operating costs amounting to 5% of sales are to be paid in the month following the month of sale. Additionally, a monthly lease payment of $10,000 is paid for computer services. Sales revenue is forecast as follows:

Month	Sales Revenue
February...	$340,000
March	420,000
April	440,000
May..	520,000
June	480,000
July..	560,000

Required
Prepare a schedule of cash disbursements for April, May, and June.

LO3 **E22-31. Cash Disbursements**

Assume that Ringwood Manufacturing manages its cash flow from its home office. Ringwood controls cash disbursements by category and month. In setting its budget for the next six months, beginning in July, it used the following managerial guidelines:

Category	Guidelines
Purchases............	Pay 60% in current month and 40% in following month.
Payroll..............	Pay half in current and half in following month.
Loan payments........	Pay total amount due each month.

Predicted activity for selected months follow:

Category	May	June	July	August
Purchases...................................	$75,000	$80,000	$70,000	$85,000
Payroll......................................	45,000	40,000	50,000	45,000
Loan payments................................	15,000	15,000	15,000	15,000

Required

Prepare a schedule showing cash disbursements by account for July and August.

LO3 **E22-32. Budgeted Income Statement**

Quality Wool Company, a merchandising company, is developing its master budget for next year. The income statement for the current year is as follows:

QUALITY WOOL COMPANY	
Income Statement	
For Year Ending December 31	
Gross sales...	$1,200,000
Less uncollectible accounts	(26,000)
Collected sales......................................	1,174,000
Cost of goods sold	(780,000)
Profit before operating expense	394,000
Operating expenses (including $15,000 depreciation)...	(206,000)
Income before tax...................................	$ 188,000

The following are management's goals and forecasts for next year:

1. Selling prices will increase by 3%, and sales volume will increase by 5%.
2. The cost of merchandise will increase by 2%.
3. All operating expenses are fixed. Price increases for operating expenses will be 4%. The company uses straight-line depreciation.
4. The estimated uncollectibles are 2% of budgeted sales.

Required

Prepare a budgeted functional income statement for next year.

LO3 **E22-33. Budgeted Income Statement with CVP**

Barnes & Noble, Inc.

Assume **Barnes & Noble** is planning a budget for one of its stores. The estimate of sales revenue is $2,000,000 and of cost of goods sold is 70% of sales revenue. Depreciation on the office building and fixtures is budgeted at $36,000. Salaries and wages are budgeted at $375,000. Advertising has been budgeted at $12,000, and other operating costs should amount to $15,000. Income tax is estimated at 20% of operating income.

Required

a. Prepare a budgeted income statement for next year.
b. Assuming management desired an after-tax income of $150,000, determine the necessary sales volume.

E22-34. Production and Purchases Budgets

At the beginning of October, Comfy Cushions had 3,400 cushions and 8,500 pounds of raw materials on hand. Budgeted sales for the next three months are

Month	Sales
October..	11,000 cushions
November..	12,000 cushions
December..	10,000 cushions

Comfy Cushions wants to have sufficient raw materials on hand at the end of each month to meet 20% of the following month's production requirements and sufficient cushions on hand at the end of each month to meet 30% of the following month's budgeted sales. Four pounds of raw materials, at a standard cost of $1.10 per pound, are required to produce each cushion.

Required

a. Prepare a production budget for October and November.
b. Prepare a purchases budget in units and dollars for October.

E22-35. Production and Purchases Budgets

Advance Drainage Systems produces thermoplastic corrugated pipe. Assume budgeted unit sales for one of its products (a 12" by 20-ft pipe) over the next several months are

Month	Sales
September	3,000
October..	2,500
November..	1,500
December..	500

At the beginning of September, 850 units of finished goods were in inventory. During the final third of the year, as road construction declines, plans are to have an inventory of finished goods equal to 30% of the following month's sales. Each unit of finished goods requires 70 pounds of raw materials at a cost of $1.50 per pound. Management wishes to maintain month-end inventories of raw materials equal to 40% of the following month's needs. Sixty thousand pounds of raw materials were on hand at the start of September.

Required

a. Prepare a production budget for September, October, and November.
b. Prepare a purchases budget in units and dollars for September and October.

Problems

P22-36. Cash Budget

Assume all **Office Depot** stores do cash budgeting every quarter. One store is planning its cash needs for the third quarter of the year, and the following information is available to assist in preparing a cash budget. Budgeted income statements for July through October are as follows:

	July	August	September	October
Sales.............................	$45,000	$52,000	$60,000	$75,000
Cost of goods sold	23,500	25,500	30,500	35,000
Gross profit.......................	21,500	26,500	29,500	40,000
Less other expenses				
Selling.........................	6,000	8,000	8,500	10,500
Administrative	9,100	10,500	8,500	9,400
Total	(15,100)	(18,500)	(17,000)	(19,900)
Net income	$ 6,400	$ 8,000	$12,500	$20,100

Additional information follows:

1. Other expenses, which are paid monthly, include $3,500 of depreciation per month.
2. Sales are 44% for cash and 56% on credit.
3. Credit sales are collected 50% in the month of sale, 35% one month after sale, and 15% two months after sale. May sales were $40,000, and June sales were $42,000.
4. Merchandise is paid for 50% in the month of purchase; the remaining 50% is paid in the following month. Accounts payable for merchandise at June 30 totaled $12,000.
5. The store maintains its ending inventory levels at 30% of the cost of goods to be sold in the following month. The inventory at June 30 is $7,600.
6. An equipment note of $10,000 per month is being paid through August.
7. The store must maintain a cash balance of at least $10,000 at the end of each month. The cash balance on June 30 is $10,000.
8. The store can borrow from its bank as needed. Borrowings and repayments must be in multiples of $100. All borrowings take place at the beginning of a month, and all repayments are made at the end of a month. When the principal is repaid, interest on the repayment is also paid. The interest rate is 6% per year.

Required

a. Prepare a monthly schedule of budgeted operating cash receipts for July, August, and September.
b. Prepare a monthly purchases budget and a schedule of budgeted cash payments for purchases for July, August, and September.
c. Prepare a monthly cash budget for July, August, and September. Show borrowings from the store's bank and repayments to the bank as needed to maintain the minimum cash balance.

LO3   **P22-37. Cash Budget**

The Williams Supply Company sells for $50 one product that it purchases for $20. Budgeted sales in total dollars for the year are $3,000,000. The sales information needed for preparing the July budget follows:

Month	Sales Revenue
May.	$175,000
June	240,000
July	295,000
August	320,000

Account balances at July 1 include these:

Cash.	$125,000
Merchandise inventory	47,200
Accounts receivable (sales)	84,530
Accounts payable (purchases)	47,200

The company pays for one-half of its purchases in the month of purchase and the remainder in the following month. End-of-month inventory must be 40% of the budgeted sales in units for the next month. A 2% cash discount on sales is allowed if payment is made during the month of sale. Experience indicates that 60% of the billings will be collected during the month of sale, 25% in the following month, 12% in the second following month, and 3% will be uncollectible. Total budgeted selling and administrative expenses (excluding bad debts) for the fiscal year are estimated at $1,200,000, of which three-fourths is fixed expense (inclusive of a $36,000 annual depreciation charge). Fixed expenses are incurred evenly during the year. The other selling and administrative expenses vary with sales. Expenses are paid during the month incurred.

Required

a. Prepare a schedule of estimated cash collections for July.
b. Prepare a schedule of estimated July cash payments for purchases. *Hint:* Start by doing a purchase budget.
c. Prepare schedules of July selling and administrative expenses, separately identifying those requiring cash disbursements.
d. Prepare a schedule of cash receipts over disbursements assuming no equipment purchases or loan payments.

P22-38. Budgeting Purchases, Revenues, Expenses, and Cash in a Service Organization   **LO3, 4**

Wauconda Medical Center is located in a summer resort community. During the summer months (June through August), the center operates an outpatient clinic for the treatment of minor injuries and illnesses. The clinic is administered as a separate department within the hospital. It has its own staff and maintains its own financial records. All patients requiring extensive or intensive care are referred to other hospital departments.

An analysis of past operating data for the outpatient clinic reveals the following:

- Staff: Seven full-time employees with total monthly salaries of $42,000. On a monthly basis, one additional staff member is hired for every 500 budgeted patient visits in excess of 3,000, at a cost of $7,000 per month.
- Facilities: Monthly facility costs, including depreciation of $2,500, total $15,000.
- Supplies: The supplies expense averages $20 per patient visit. The center maintains an end-of-month supplies inventory equal to 10% of the predicted needs of the following month, with a minimum ending inventory of $4,000, which is also the desired inventory at the end of August.
- Additional variable patient costs, such as medications, are charged directly to the patient by the hospital pharmacy.
- Payments: All staff and maintenance expenses are paid in the month the cost is incurred. Supplies are purchased at cost directly from the hospital with an immediate transfer of cash from the clinic cash account to the hospital cash account.
- Collections: The average bill for services rendered is $75. Of the total bills, 40% are paid in cash at the time the service is rendered, 10% are never paid, and the remaining 50% are covered by insurance. In the past, insurance companies have disallowed 30% of the claims filed and paid the balance two months after services are rendered.
- May 30 status: At the end of May, the clinic had $15,000 in cash and supplies costing $5,000.

Budgeted patient visits for next summer are as follows:

Month	Patient Visits
June	3,000
July	3,500
August	4,500

Required

For the Wauconda Outpatient Clinic:

a. Prepare a supplies purchases budget for June, July, and August with a total column.
b. Prepare a revenue and expense budget for June, July, and August with a total column.
c. Prepare a cash budget for June, July, and August with a total column. (*Hint:* See requirement *d.*)
d. Is the cash budget for the annual summer outpatient clinic feasible? If not, make appropriate recommendations for management's consideration.

P22-39. Developing a Master Budget for a Merchandising Organization   **LO3, 4**

Assume Nordstrom prepares budgets quarterly. The following information is available for use in planning the second quarter budgets for one of its stores.

Nordstrom, Inc.
(JWN)

NORDSTROM Balance Sheet March 31			
(in thousands) **Assets**		**Liabilities and Stockholders' Equity**	
Cash	$ 2,525	Merchandise purchases payable	$ 2,400
Accounts receivable	2,040	Dividends payable	710
Inventory	3,400	Stockholders' equity	8,005
Prepaid insurance	150		
Fixtures	3,000		
Total assets	$11,115	Total liabilities and equity	$11,115

Actual and forecasted sales for selected months in the upcoming year are as follows:

Month (in thousands)	Sales Revenue
January.	$2,600
February.	2,700
March	3,000
April	3,600
May.	3,800
June	3,500
July.	3,200
August	4,000

Monthly operating expenses (in thousands) are as follows:

Wages and salaries	$750
Depreciation	75
Advertising	55
Other costs	350

Cash dividends for the store of $710 thousand are declared during the third month of each quarter and are paid during the first month of the following quarter. Operating expenses, except insurance, rent, and depreciation are paid as incurred. The prepaid insurance is for five more months. Cost of goods sold is equal to 60% of sales. Ending inventories are sufficient for 150% of the next month's cost of sales. Purchases during any given month are paid in full during the following month. Cash sales account for 50% of the revenue. Of the credit sales, 60% are collected in the next month and 40% are collected in the month after. Money can be borrowed and repaid in multiples of $100 thousand at an interest rate of 12% per year. The company desires a minimum cash balance of $2 million on the first of each month. At the time the principal is repaid, interest is paid on the portion of principal that is repaid. All borrowing is at the beginning of the month, and all repayment is at the end of the month. Money is never repaid at the end of the month it is borrowed.

Required

a. Prepare a purchases budget for each month of the second quarter ending June 30.

b. Prepare a cash receipts schedule for each month of the second quarter ending June 30. Do not include borrowings.

c. Prepare a cash disbursements schedule for each month of the second quarter ending June 30. Do not include repayments of borrowings.

d. Prepare a cash budget for each month of the second quarter ending June 30. Include budgeted borrowings and repayments.

e. Prepare an income statement for each month of the second quarter ending June 30.

f. Prepare a budgeted balance sheet as of June 30.

LO3, 4   **P22-40. Developing a Master Budget for a Manufacturing Organization**

Cubs Incorporated manufactures a product with a selling price of $75 per unit. Units and monthly cost data follow:

Variable	
Selling and administrative.	$ 3 per unit sold
Direct materials.	15 per unit manufactured
Direct labor	5 per unit manufactured
Variable manufacturing overhead.	7 per unit manufactured
Fixed	
Selling and administrative.	$160,000 per month
Manufacturing (including depreciation of $15,000).	150,000 per month

Cubs Inc. pays all bills in the month incurred. All sales are on account with 50% collected the month of sale and the balance collected the following month. There are no sales discounts or bad debts.

Cubs Inc. desires to maintain an ending finished goods inventory equal to 40% of the following month's sales and a raw materials inventory equal to 20% of the following month's production. January 1 inventories are in line with these policies.

Actual unit sales for December and budgeted unit sales for January, February, and March are as follows:

CUBS INCORPORATED Sales Budget For the Months of January, February, and March				
Month	December	January	February	March
Sales—Units....................	10,000	12,000	11,500	12,500
Sales—Dollars	$750,000	$900,000	$862,500	$937,500

Additional information:
- The January 1 beginning cash is projected as $10,000.
- For the purpose of operational budgeting, units in the January 1 inventory of finished goods are valued at variable manufacturing cost.
- Each unit of finished product requires one unit of raw materials.
- Cubs Inc. intends to pay a cash dividend of $15,000 in January

Required
a. A production budget for January and February.
b. A purchases budget in units for January.
c. A manufacturing cost budget for January.
d. A cash budget for January.
e. A budgeted contribution income statement for January.

P22-41. Risk Management in a Manufacturing Organization   LO3, 4

Required
Continuing problem P22-40, management is concerned that their supplier of raw materials will have a strike. Determine the budget implications if management plans to increase the January-end raw materials inventory to 150% of February's production needs. Offer any recommendations you believe appropriate.

P22-42. Developing a Master Budget for a Manufacturing Organization: Challenge Problem   LO3, 4

Electric Monkey Computer Accessories assembles a computer networking device from kits of imported components. You have been asked to develop a quarterly and annual operating budget and pro forma income statements for next year. You have obtained the following information:

		Units	Unit price	Total
Beginning-of-year balances				
Cash	$ 75,000			
Accounts receivable (previous quarter's sales).........	$245,000			
Raw materials...................................	950 kits			
Finished goods..................................	1,500 kits			
Accounts payable (materials)	$125,000			
Borrowed funds.................................	$ 30,000			
Desired end-of-year inventory balances				
Raw materials...................................	1,000 kits			
Finished goods..................................	1,600 kits			
Desired end-of-quarter balances				
Cash..	$ 30,000			
Raw materials as a portion of the following quarter's production	0.20			
Finished goods as a portion of the following quarter's sales................................	0.30			
Manufacturing costs				
Standard cost per unit		Units	Unit price	Total
Raw materials......................		1 kit	$75.00	$75.00
Direct labor hours at rate..........................		0.50 hour	$30.00	15.00
Variable overhead/labor hour		0.50 hour	$ 5.00	2.50
Total standard variable cost				$92.50

continued

continued from previous page

Fixed cost per quarter	
Cash	$110,000
Depreciation	15,000
Total	$125,000

Selling and administrative costs	
Variable cost per unit	$8.00
Fixed costs per quarter	
Cash	$150,000
Depreciation	7,500
Total	$157,500

Interest rate per quarter	0.015
Portion of sales collected	
Quarter of sale	0.70
Subsequent quarter	0.29
Bad debts	0.01

Portion of purchases paid	
Quarter of purchase	0.60
Subsequent quarter	0.40
Unit selling price	$225.00

Sales forecast				
Quarter	First	Second	Third	Fourth
Unit sales	4,400	4,600	4,500	4,800

Additional information

- All cash payments except purchases are made quarterly as incurred.
- All borrowings occur at the start of a quarter.
- All repayments on borrowings occur at the end of a quarter.
- At the time the principal is repaid, interest is paid on the portion of principal that is repaid.
- Borrowings and repayments may be made in any amount.

Required

a. A sales budget for each quarter and the year. (*Hint:* Use of spreadsheet software strongly recommended for this problem.)
b. A production budget for each quarter and the year.
c. A purchases budget for each quarter and the year.
d. A manufacturing cost budget for each quarter and the year.
e. A selling and administrative expense budget for each quarter and the year.
f. A cash budget for each quarter and the year.
g. A pro forma contribution income statement for each quarter and the year.

Management Applications

LO5   **MA23-43. Behavioral Implications of Budgeting**

Cindy Jones, controller of Systematic Designs, believes that effective budgeting greatly assists in meeting the organization's goals and objectives. She argues that the budget serves as a blueprint for the operating activities during each reporting period, making it an important control device. She believes that sound management evaluations can be based on the comparisons of performance and budgetary schedules and that employees respond more favorably when they participate in the budgetary process. Kevin Dobbs, treasurer of Systematic Designs, agrees that budgeting is essential for overall organization success, but he argues that human resources are too valuable to spend much time planning and preparing the budgetary process. He thinks that the roles people play in budgetary preparation are not important in the final analysis of a budget's effectiveness.

Required

Contrast the participative versus imposed budgeting concepts and indicate how the ideas of Jones and Dobbs fit the two categories.

MA23-44. Behavioral Considerations and Budgeting   **LO5**

Anthony Wagner, the controller in the Division of Transportation for the state, recognizes the importance of the budgetary process for planning, control, and motivation purposes. He believes that a properly implemented participative budgeting process for planning purposes and a management by exception reporting procedure based on that budget will motivate his subordinates to improve productivity within their particular departments. Based on this philosophy, Wagner has implemented the following budget procedures.

- An appropriation target figure is given to each department manager. This amount is the maximum funding that each department can expect to receive in the next fiscal year.
- Department managers develop their individual budgets within the following spending constraints as directed by the controller's staff.
    1. Expenditure requests cannot exceed the appropriation target.
    2. All fixed expenditures should be included in the budget; these should include items such as contracts and salaries at current levels.
    3. All government projects directed by higher authority should be included in the budget in their entirety.
- The controller consolidates the departmental budget requests from the various departments into one budget that is to be submitted for the entire division.
- Upon final budget approval by the legislature, the controller's staff allocates the appropriation to the various departments on instructions from the division manager. However, a specified percentage of each department's appropriation is held back in anticipation of potential budget cuts and special funding needs. The amount and use of this contingency fund are left to the discretion of the division manager.
- Each department is allowed to adjust its budget when necessary to operate within the reduced appropriation level. However, as stated in the original directive, specific projects authorized by higher authority must remain intact.
- The final budget is used as the basis of control for a management by exception form of reporting. Excessive expenditures by account for each department are highlighted on a monthly basis. Department managers are expected to account for all expenditures over budget. Fiscal responsibility is an important factor in the overall performance evaluation of department managers.

Wagner believes that his policy of allowing the department managers to participate in the budget process and then holding them accountable for their performance is essential, especially during these times of limited resources. He also believes that department managers will be positively motivated to increase the efficiency and effectiveness of their departments because they have provided input into the initial budgetary process and are required to justify any unfavorable performances.

Required

a. Explain the operational and behavioral benefits that generally are attributed to a participative budgeting process.

b. Identify deficiencies in Wagner's participative budgetary policy for planning and performance evaluation purposes. For each deficiency identified, recommend how the deficiency can be corrected.

(CMA Adapted)

MA23-45. Budgetary Slack with Ethical Considerations   **LO5**

Karen Bailey was promoted to department manager of a production unit in Parkway Industries three years ago. She enjoys her job except for the evaluation measures that are based on the department's budget. After three years of consistently poor annual evaluations based on a set annual budget, she has decided to improve the evaluation situation. At a recent budget meeting of junior-level managers, the topic of budgetary slack was discussed as a means to maintain some consistency in budgeting matters. As a result of this meeting, Bailey decided to take the following steps in preparing the upcoming year's budget:

1. Use the top quartile for all wage and salary categories.
2. Select the optimistic values for the estimated production ranges for the coming year. These are provided by the marketing department.
3. Use the average of the three months in the current year with poorest production efficiency as benchmarks of success for the coming year.
4. Base equipment charges (primarily depreciation) on replacement values furnished by the purchasing department.

5. Base other fixed costs on current cost plus an inflation rate estimated for the coming year.
6. Use the average of the 10 newly hired employees' performance as a basis of labor efficiency for the coming year.

Required

a. For each item on Bailey's list, explain whether it will create budgetary slack. Use numerical examples as necessary to illustrate.
b. Given the company's use of static budgets as one of the performance evaluation measures of its managers, can the managers justify the use of built-in budgetary slack?
c. What would you recommend as a means for Bailey to improve the budgeting situation in the company? Provide some specific examples of how the budgeting process might be improved.

LO5 **MA23-46. Budgetary Slack with Ethical Considerations**

Norton Company, a manufacturer of infant furniture and carriages, is in the initial stages of preparing the annual budget for next year. Scott Ford recently joined Norton's accounting staff and is interested to learn as much as possible about the company's budgeting process. During a recent lunch with Marge Atkins, sales manager, and Pete Granger, production manager, Ford initiated the following conversation:

Ford: Since I'm new around here and am going to be involved with the preparation of the annual budget, I'd be interested to learn how the two of you estimate sales and production numbers.

Atkins: We start out very methodically by looking at recent history, discussing what we know about current accounts, potential customers, and the general state of consumer spending. Then we add that usual dose of intuition to come up with the best forecast we can.

Granger: I usually take the sales projections as the basis for my projections. Of course, we have to make an estimate of what this year's closing inventories will be, which is sometimes difficult.

Ford: Why does that present a problem? There must have been an estimate of closing inventories in the budget for the current year.

Granger: Those numbers aren't always reliable since Marge makes some adjustments to the sales numbers before passing them on to me.

Ford: What kind of adjustments?

Atkins: Well, we don't want to fall short of the sales projections, so we generally give ourselves a little breathing room by lowering the initial sales projection anywhere from 5% to 10%.

Granger: So, you can see why this year's budget is not a very reliable starting point. We always have to adjust the projected production rates as the year progresses; of course, this changes the ending inventory estimates. By the way, we make similar adjustments to expenses by adding at least 10% to the estimates; I think everyone around here does the same thing.

Required

a. Marge Atkins and Pete Granger have described the use of budgetary slack.
   1. Explain why Atkins and Granger behave in this manner, and describe the benefits they expect to realize from the use of budgetary slack.
   2. Explain how the use of budgetary slack can adversely affect Atkins and Granger.
b. As a management accountant, Scott Ford believes that the behavior described by Marge Atkins and Pete Granger could be unethical and that he might have an obligation not to support this behavior. Explain why the use of budgetary slack could be unethical.

(CMA Adapted)

Solutions to Review Problems

Review 22-1—Solution

Operating managers frequently regard budgeting as a time-consuming task that diverts attention from current problems. The development of a budget can be difficult and time-consuming, although it is a necessary process. Organizations that plan will have a focus and their work and tasks will better support the organization's goals and objectives. Without a plan, although managers and employees might be busy, they may not be working on tasks that move their companies forward in a thoughtful way. The plan will allow them to more efficiently focus efforts on tasks that are productive toward the organization's goals. Generally, the budgeting process will compel planning; promote communication and coordination; provide a guide to action and a basis of evaluation; and act as an aid in risk management.

Review 22-2—Solution

a. Under the output/input approach, the output of units dictates the expected cost inputs. Here budgeted overhead costs are based on the number of budgeted assembly hours.

	Regular	Extra Strength
Direct materials (20,000 × $20)	$400,000	
(50,000 × $14.50)		$ 725,000
Direct assembly labor (20,000 × 0.5 × $18)	180,000	
(50,000 × 0.8 × $18)		720,000
Overhead (20,000 × 0.5 × $8.17)	81,700	
(50,000 × 0.8 × $8.17)		326,800
Total budgeted cost	$661,700	$1,771,800
Unit Cost	$33.085	$35.436

b. Under the activity-based approach, budgeted overhead costs are based on expected activities to produce the products, not only on assembly hours.

	Regular	Extra Strength
Direct materials (20,000 × $20)	$400,000	
(50,000 × $14.50)		$ 725,000
Direct assembly labor (20,000 × 0.5 × $18)	180,000	
(50,000 × 0.8 × $18)		720,000
Setup (1,000 hours × $25)	25,000	
(1,500 hours × $25)		37,500
Engineering and Maintenance (500 hours × $35)	17,500	
(600 hours × $35)		21,000
Inspections (650 inspections × $250)	162,500	
(580 inspections × $250)		145,000
Total budgeted cost	$785,000	$1,648,500
Unit cost	$39.25	$32.97

c. Under the incremental approach to budgeting, the cost per unit would be budgeted at last period's cost, plus an increment for expected additional costs in the current period. Based on last period's actual cost of $38 for Regular and $32 for Extra Strength, and using the 3.5% overall expected increase in costs, the current period's budgeted cost would be $39.33 for Regular and $33.12 for Extra Strength.

d. Under the minimum level approach, the company begins with either a zero or very low cost estimate, and then requires all additional costs beyond this minimum to be justified by the production managers. This approach forces managers to evaluate thoroughly all elements of cost each period.

Review 22-3—Solution

a.

BLEU MONT DAIRY Sales Budget For Month of April			
	Units	Price	Sales
Cheese	160,000	$10	$1,600,000
Ice cream	240,000	5	1,200,000
Total			$2,800,000

b.

BLEU MONT DAIRY
Purchases Budget
For Month of April

	Cheese	Ice Cream	Total
Units			
Sales needs	160,000	240,000	
Desired ending inventory	12,000	5,000	
Total	172,000	245,000	
Less beginning inventory	(10,000)	(4,000)	
Purchases	162,000	241,000	
Dollars			
Sales needs	$1,280,000	$480,000	
Desired ending inventory	96,000	10,000	
Total	1,376,000	490,000	
Less beginning inventory	(80,000)	(8,000)	
Purchases needed	$1,296,000	$482,000	$1,778,000

c.

BLEU MONT DAIRY
Cash Budget
For Month of April

Cash balance, beginning			$ 400,000
Collections on sales			
Current month's sales ($2,800,000 × 0.70)		$1,960,000	
Previous month's sales ($3,000,000 × 0.29)		870,000	2,830,000
Cash available from operations			3,230,000
Less budgeted disbursements			
March purchases ($1,800,000 × 0.40)		720,000	
April purchases ($1,778,000 × 0.60)		1,066,800	
Wages and salaries		156,000	
Overhead (March)		80,000	
Selling and administrative ($450,000 − $40,000 depreciation)		410,000	(2,432,800)
Cash balance, ending			$ 797,200

d.

BLEU MONT DAIRY
Budgeted Income Statement
For Month of April

Sales (sales budget)			$2,800,000
Allowance for bad debts			(28,000)
Net sales			2,772,000
Costs of merchandise sold			
Cheese (160,000 × $8)	$1,280,000		
Ice cream (240,000 × $2)	480,000	$1,760,000	
Wages and salaries	156,000		
Overhead	80,000		
Selling and administrative	450,000	686,000	(2,446,000)
Net income			$ 326,000

Review 22-4—Solution

a.

DEWALT Sales Budget For First Quarter	Units	Price	Sales
Drills	60,000	$100	$ 6,000,000
Saws	40,000	125	5,000,000
Total			$11,000,000

b.

DEWALT Production Budget For First Quarter	Drills	Saws
Budget sales	60,000	40,000
Plus desired ending inventory	25,000	10,000
Total inventory requirements	85,000	50,000
Less beginning inventory	(20,000)	(8,000)
Budgeted production	65,000	42,000

c.

DEWALT Purchases Budget For First Quarter	Drills	Saws	Total
Metal purchases			
Production units (production budget)	65,000	42,000	
Metal (pounds)	× 5	× 4	
Production needs (pounds)	325,000	168,000	493,000
Desired ending inventory (pounds)			36,000
Total metal needs (pounds)			529,000
Less beginning inventory (pounds)			(32,000)
Purchases needed (pounds)			497,000
Cost per pound			× $8
Total metal purchases			$3,976,000
Plastic purchases			
Production units (production budget)	65,000	42,000	107,000
Plastic (pounds)			× 3
Production needs (pounds)			321,000
Desired ending inventory (pounds)			32,000
Total plastic needs (pounds)			353,000
Less beginning inventory (pounds)			(29,000)
Purchases needed (pounds)			324,000
Cost per pound			× $5
Total plastic purchases			$1,620,000

continued

continued from previous page

DEWALT Purchases Budget For First Quarter			
	Drills	**Saws**	**Total**
Handle purchases			
Production units (production budget)	65,000		65,000
Handles.			× 1
Production needs			65,000
Desired ending inventory			7,000
Total handle needs			72,000
Less beginning inventory			(6,000)
Purchases needed			66,000
Cost per handle.			× $3
Total handle purchases			$198,000
Total purchases			
Metal.			$3,976,000
Plastic.			1,620,000
Handles.			198,000
Total purchases			$5,794,000

d.

DEWALT Manufacturing Cost Budget For First Quarter			
	Drills	**Saws**	**Total**
Direct materials			
Metal			
Production units (production budget)	65,000	42,000	
Metal per unit of product (pounds)	× 5	× 4	
Production needs for metal (pounds)	325,000	168,000	
Unit cost	× $8	× $8	
Cost of metal issued to production	$2,600,000	$1,344,000	$3,944,000
Plastic			
Production units (production budget)	65,000	42,000	
Plastic (pounds)	× 3	× 3	
Production needs for plastic (pounds)	195,000	126,000	
Unit cost	× $5	× $5	
Cost of plastic issued to production	$ 975,000	$ 630,000	1,605,000
Handles			
Production units (production budget)	65,000		
Handles.	× 1		
Production needs for handles.	65,000		
Unit cost	× $3		
Cost of handles issued to production	$ 195,000		195,000
Total			5,744,000
Direct labor			
Budgeted production.	65,000	42,000	
Direct labor hours per unit.	× 2	× 3	
Total direct labor hours	130,000	126,000	
Labor rate	× $12	× $16	
Labor expenditures.	$1,560,000	$2,016,000	3,576,000

continued

continued from previous page

DEWALT
Manufacturing Cost Budget
For First Quarter

	Drills	Saws	Total
Variable manufacturing overhead			
Direct labor hours	130,000	126,000	
Variable manufacturing overhead rate	× $1.50	× $1.50	
Total variable overhead	$ 195,000	$ 189,000	384,000
Fixed manufacturing overhead.			214,000
Total			$9,918,000

e.

DEWALT
Cash Budget
For First Quarter

Cash balance, beginning		$ 1,800,000
Collections on sales		
Current quarter's sales ($11,000,000 × 0.50)	$5,500,000	
Previous quarter's sales ($8,400,000 × 0.50)	4,200,000	9,700,000
Cash available from operations		11,500,000
Less budgeted disbursements		
Materials (purchases budget)	5,794,000	
Labor (manufacturing cost budget).	3,576,000	
Manufacturing overhead (manufacturing cost budget)		
([$384,000 + 214,000] − 156,000 noncash)	442,000	
Selling and administrative ($340,000 − $90,000 depreciation)		
	250,000	(10,062,000)
Cash balance, ending.		$ 1,438,000

f.

DEWALT
Contribution Income Statement
For First Quarter

Sales (sales budget).		$11,000,000
Less variable costs of goods sold		
Drills (60,000 × $85.00)	$5,100,000	
Saws (40,000 × $99.50)	3,980,000	(9,080,000)
Gross profit.		1,920,000
Less fixed costs		
Manufacturing overhead	214,000	
Selling and administrative expenses.	340,000	(554,000)
Net income		$ 1,366,000

Review 22-5—Solution

__2__ *a.* The marketing department is asked to provide an estimate as to how much it will spend on print ads during the next fiscal year.

__1__ *b.* The marketing department provides a budget amount for print ads for the next fiscal year that includes the expected expenditures plus 10% to account for uncertainty.

__4__ *c.* Tristan Renken owns and operates a food truck that sells Mexican food along the beaches in Chicago. Tristan only operates the food truck during the summer and developed a budget to estimate how much he will make during the upcoming summer season.

__3__ *d.* Top management hosts semi-annual meetings to discuss the budget and current performance vs. the budget. Management provides employees with tools to help gauge their own performance against the budgeted expectations.

Module 23

Standard Costs and Performance Reports

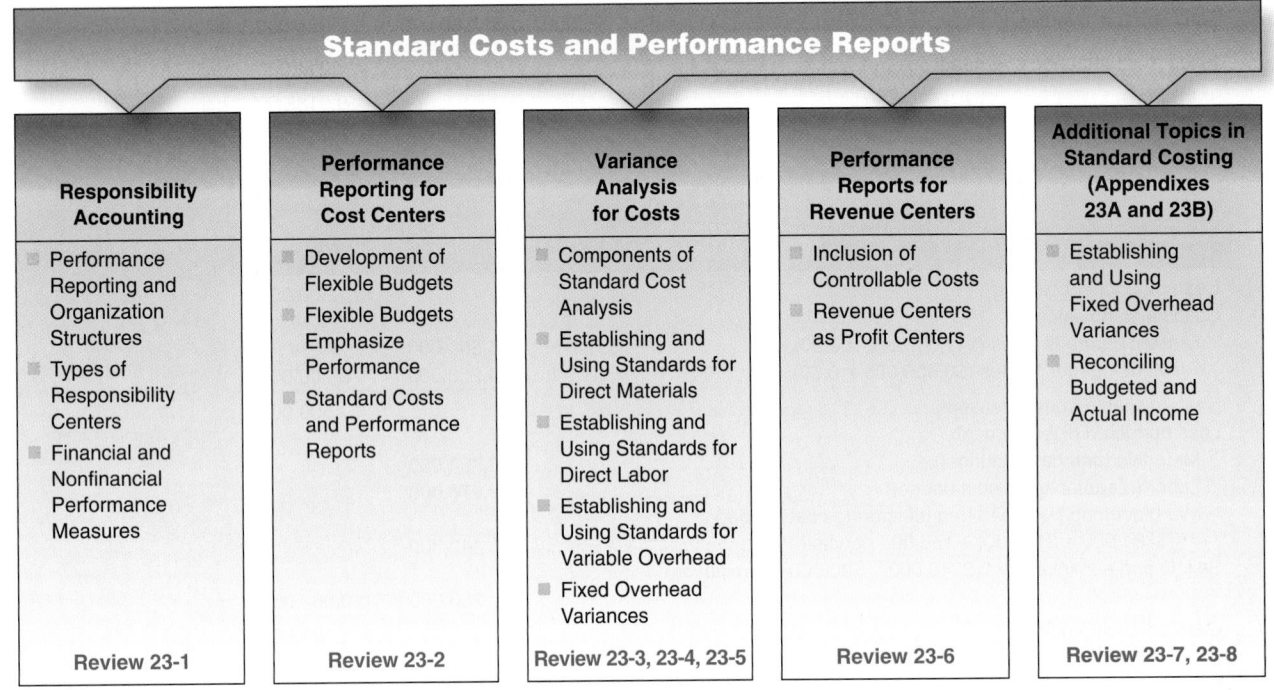

Standard Costs and Performance Reports				
Responsibility Accounting	**Performance Reporting for Cost Centers**	**Variance Analysis for Costs**	**Performance Reports for Revenue Centers**	**Additional Topics in Standard Costing (Appendixes 23A and 23B)**
▪ Performance Reporting and Organization Structures ▪ Types of Responsibility Centers ▪ Financial and Nonfinancial Performance Measures	▪ Development of Flexible Budgets ▪ Flexible Budgets Emphasize Performance ▪ Standard Costs and Performance Reports	▪ Components of Standard Cost Analysis ▪ Establishing and Using Standards for Direct Materials ▪ Establishing and Using Standards for Direct Labor ▪ Establishing and Using Standards for Variable Overhead ▪ Fixed Overhead Variances	▪ Inclusion of Controllable Costs ▪ Revenue Centers as Profit Centers	▪ Establishing and Using Fixed Overhead Variances ▪ Reconciling Budgeted and Actual Income
Review 23-1	Review 23-2	Review 23-3, 23-4, 23-5	Review 23-6	Review 23-7, 23-8

PREVIEW   LUV

In the last module, we discussed how budgeting was critical to planning within a business. But planning is only half of the story; at the end of the period, the operating results are compared to the budget. By evaluating the differences between the budgeted and the actual results, a manager can identify areas of the business that need attention. We call these differences *budget variances*, and a thorough analysis of these variances aids the manager in controlling the human and physical resources of the business.

To effectively control the business through variance analysis, it is important that the lines of responsibility are clearly defined among the managers. Managers (and the people who evaluate their results) need to understand who is responsible for revenues, costs, profits, capital investments, or some combination of those elements. This assignment of responsibility prevents managers from "passing the buck" when something goes wrong. Consider the case of Southwest Airlines, the Dallas, Texas–based airline, which completed a merger with Air Tran. When a structural shift such as a merger takes place, the lines of responsibility may be temporarily blurred. This can impede not only variance analysis, but also the integration of the merged entities.

While other airlines have bolstered revenue by charging fees for baggage, additional legroom, Wi-Fi, and changed flights, Southwest's strategy has been to offer passengers inexpensive and flexible flight arrangements with no hidden fees for baggage or other basic services. Inconsistencies between Southwest and Air Tran were prevalent in the merged business. Southwest permits customers to buy early boarding privileges, but Air Tran did not. Bags fly free on Southwest, but not on Air Tran. There is no business class on Southwest, whereas Air Tran passengers frequently received complementary upgrades to business class. The two reservation systems could not easily rebook passengers across the two airlines, and their frequent flier miles were not transferrable between the two airlines.

Even today, the merged airline is likely to encounter differences between expected and actual operating results. Some of the variances may relate to usage or efficiency, whereas others may relate to the dollar amount spent on a resource. For example, the airline could use more or less fuel than is expected and the price paid per gallon of fuel could differ from expectations. Flight personnel may work more or fewer hours than expected and scheduling issues may result in paying higher- or lower-than-average wages than expected for the number of hours worked. Variance analysis can be extended to issues such as bag handling, overbooking, and number of passenger complaints.

Even though mergers can decrease the level of competition within an industry, customers still have some choice of airlines available to them. Managers prefer timely notification of potential variances so they still have time to "right the ship" before the end of the reporting period. In this module, we focus on performance assessment and variance analysis.

Road Map

LO	Learning Objective | Topics	Page	eLecture	Guided Example	Assignments
23-1	**Explain responsibility accounting.** Management by Exception :: Performance Reporting :: Cost Center :: Profit Center :: Investment Center :: Financial and Nonfinancial Performance Measures	23-3	e23-1	Review 23-1	42, 44
23-2	**Differentiate between static and flexible budgets for performance reporting. Prepare a flexible budget.** Static Budget :: Flexible Budget :: Flexible Budget Variance :: Standard Cost	23-6	e23-2	Review 23-2	16, 25, 30, 35, 36, 40, 41, 43, 44
23-3	**Determine the components of standard cost variance analysis. Formulate and interpret direct materials cost variances.** Components of Standard Cost Analysis :: Direct Materials Price Variance :: Direct Materials Quantity Variance :: Interpreting Material Variances	23-9	e23-3	Review 23-3	17, 18, 27, 31, 32, 33, 34, 35, 36. 37. 40, 41, 44
23-4	**Formulate and interpret direct labor cost variances.** Direct Labor Rate Variance :: Direct Labor Efficiency Variance :: Interpreting Labor Variances	23-13	e23-4	Review 23-4	19, 20, 26, 27, 31, 32, 33, 34, 35, 36, 37, 40, 41, 44
23-5	**Formulate and interpret overhead cost variances.** Variable Overhead Spending Variance :: Variable Overhead Efficiency Variance :: Interpreting Variable Overhead Variances	23-15	e23-5	Review 23-5	21, 26, 27, 33, 34, 35, 36, 37, 40, 41, 44
23-6	**Calculate revenue variances and prepare a performance report for a revenue center.** Revenue Variance :: Sales Price Variance :: Sales Volume Variance :: Controllable Costs :: Net Sales Volume Variance	23-18	e23-6	Review 23-6	22, 28, 39, 40, 41
23-7	**Formulate and interpret fixed overhead cost variances (Appendix 23A).** Fixed Overhead Budget Variance :: Standard Fixed Overhead Rate	23-21	e23-7	Review 23-7	23, 29, 38, 40, 41
23-8	**Reconcile budgeted and actual income (Appendix 23B).** Contribution Format :: Assigning Variances to Responsibility Centers	23-23	e23-8	Review 23-8	29, 39, 40, 41, 45

Management accounting tools aid in the assessment of the performance of the firm as a whole and all of its various components. Feedback in the form of performance reports is essential if the benefits of budgeting and other types of planning are to be fully realized. To control current operations and to improve future operations, managers must know how actual results compare with the current budget. These performance reports should be prepared in accordance with the concept of **responsibility accounting**, which is the structuring of performance reports addressed to individual (or group) members of an organization to emphasize the factors they control.

This module focuses on responsibility accounting and performance assessment. We examine responsibility accounting and identify various types of responsibility centers. We then take a close look at performance assessment for cost centers and conclude by considering performance reports for revenue centers. Responsibility accounting for major business segments is considered in Module 24.

Responsibility Accounting

LO1
Explain responsibility accounting.

Performance reports that include comparisons of actual results with plans or budgets serve as assessment tools and attention-directors to help managers control activities. According to the concept of *management by exception,* the absence of significant differences indicates that activities are proceeding as planned, whereas the presence of significant differences indicates a need to either take corrective action or revise plans. These evaluations and actions are made within the framework of an organization's overall mission, goals, and strategies.

Responsibility accounting reports are customized to emphasize the activities of specific organizational units. For example, a performance report addressed to the head of a production department contains manufacturing costs controllable by the department head; it should not contain costs (such as advertising, sales commissions, or the president's salary) that the head of the production department cannot control. Including noncontrollable costs in the report distracts the manager's attention from the controllable costs, thereby diluting a manager's efforts to deal with controllable items.

If too much pressure is placed on managers to meet performance targets, they may take actions that are not in the best interest of the organization. The Business Insight that follows presents a classic example of such actions referred to as channel stuffing. The designers of an organization's responsibility accounting system need to be aware of the potential pressures that such a system can place on managers. The decision-making model of the organization should be such that managers are not influenced to make undesirable decisions just to receive bonuses or promotions.

Business Insight ■ Meeting Targets by Channel Stuffing

Good business requires good measurement, and GAAP requires measurement too. Financial accountants measure performance and communicate it to capital markets. Management accountants do the same for internal decision-making and stewardship. Bonuses are tied to these numbers, as are stock market performance and promotions. Where there are incentives for performance, there are incentives for unethical practices. Channel stuffing, as *Business Insider*'s Jim Edwards says, is the "oldest—and worst—trick in the book."

Channel stuffing occurs when a company ships more product to retailers than they need, and then books these increased shipments as sales. The immediate effect is that revenue goes up, but this technique almost always backfires. In the following period, the retailers have more than enough inventory, and revenues fall again. At this point the game is up, unless the company turns to more fraudulent methods. Often, firms will take the excess inventory back as sales returns and maintain the overshipping, thus increasing sales but also increasing return expense. This is a red flag for the SEC. Diageo, maker of Johnny Walker and Smirnoff, is being investigated by the SEC for just this impropriety. While it remains to be seen what action the SEC will take in this case, as not all channel stuffing amounts to fraud, it is important for firms to monitor this sort of behavior.

Source: "What Is Channel Stuffing and How Might It Affect Your Business?" PwC Fraud Academy Blog, May 12, 2016; Jim Edwards, "The SEC Wants to Know If Diageo Used the Oldest—and Worst—Trick in the Book to Fudge Its Numbers," *Business Insider*, July 24, 2015.

Performance Reporting and Organization Structures

Before implementing a responsibility accounting system, all areas of authority and responsibility within an organization must be clearly defined. Organization charts and other documents should be examined to determine an organization's authority and responsibility structure. **Organization structure** is the arrangement of lines of authority and responsibility within an organization. These structures vary widely. Some companies have functional-based structures along the lines of marketing, production, research, and so forth; others use products, services, customers, or geography as the basis of organization. When an attempt is made to implement a responsibility accounting system, management could find instances of overlapping duties, authority not commensurate with responsibility, and expenditures for which no one appears responsible. The identification and resolution of these problems can be a major benefit of implementing a responsibility accounting system.

Although performance reports can be developed for areas of responsibility as narrow as a single worker, the basic responsibility unit in most organizations begins with the department and progresses to division and corporate levels. In manufacturing plants, separate performance reports may be prepared for each production and service department, and then summarized into a performance report for all manufacturing activities. In large universities, reports may be prepared for individual departments such as history, philosophy, and English, and then summarized into a performance report of a college, such as Liberal Arts.

Types of Responsibility Centers

Based on the nature of their responsibility, responsibility centers can be classified as cost centers, revenue centers, profit centers, or investment centers.

Cost Center

A **cost center** manager is only responsible for costs; there is no revenue responsibility. A cost center can be as small as a segment of a department or large enough to include a major aspect of the organization, such as all manufacturing activities. Typical examples of cost centers include the following:

Organization	Cost Center
Manufacturing plant	Tooling department
	Assembly activities
Retail store	Inventory control function
	Maintenance department
Hospital	Radiology
	Emergency room
College	History department
	Registrar's office
City government	Public safety (police and fire)
	Road maintenance

Revenue Center

A **revenue center** manager is responsible for the generation of sales revenues. Even though the basic performance report of a revenue center emphasizes sales, revenue centers are likely to be assigned responsibility for the controllable costs they incur in generating revenues. If revenues and costs are evaluated separately, the center has dual responsibility as a revenue center and as a cost center. If controllable costs are deducted from revenues to obtain some bottom-line contribution, the center is, in fact, being treated more like a profit center than a revenue center.

Profit Center

A **profit center** manager is responsible for revenues, costs, and the resulting profits. A profit center could be an entire organization, but it is more frequently a segment of an organization such as a product line, marketing territory, or store. In the context of performance evaluation, the word "profit" does not necessarily refer to the bottom line of an income statement; instead, it likely refers to the profit center's contribution to common corporate costs and profit. Profit is computed as the center's revenues less all costs directly associated with operating the center. Having limited authority regarding the size of total assets, the profit center manager is not held responsible for the relationship between profits and assets. In recent years many hospitals have been treating critical care and clinical service departments as profit centers to encourage physician chiefs to manage their departments as small businesses. The following Research Insight examines some of the issues associated with this movement.

Research Insight   ■   **When Profit Centers Break Down**

Profit centers may be a poor fit for health care. In a 2008 article, Dr. David Young contends that there are four central problems with profit-based performance evaluation in hospitals:

1. Departments vary in their profitability for fundamental reasons unrelated to performance. Cardiovascular surgery will be more profitable than pediatrics due to the fundamental structure of health care rather than through performance.

2. Both transfer pricing and use of outside services are complicated, and in some cases impossible. It is impossible for the orthopedic surgery department to use outside radiology in some procedures, as that would require leaving the hospital.

3. The trend in health care is to integrate care across departments. For example, a trend in women's health is to integrate clinical and critical care seamlessly. This makes financially separating clinical and critical care both difficult and possibly counterproductive.

4. A focus on operating profit creates incentives for critical care departments not to treat low-income or uninsured patients.

Dr. Young's arguments are supported by a recent study of hospital profitability, which shows that hospital profitability is strongly determined by the market in which the hospital functions. Factors such as market power and the socio-economic status of patients are important determinants of profitability and are clearly out of the control of individual departments within the hospital.

Sources: David W. Young, "Profit Centers in Clinical Care Departments an Idea Whose Time Has Gone: A Case Can Be Made for Converting a Hospital's Clinical Care Departments from Profit Centers into Standard Expense Centers," *Healthcare Financial Management* (March 2008): 66+. Academic OneFile. Web. July 25, 2016.
G. Bai and G. F. Anderson, "A More Detailed Understanding of Factors Associated with Hospital Profitability," *Health Affairs*, Vol. 35, No. 5 (2016): pp. 889–897. DOI: 10.1377/hlthaff.2015.1193.
Harris Meyer, "Not-for-Profits Dominate Top-10 List of Hospitals with Biggest Surpluses," *Modern Healthcare*, May 2, 2016.

Investment Center

An **investment center** manager is responsible for the relationship between its profits and the total assets invested in the center. Investment center managers have a high degree of organization autonomy. In general, the management of an investment center is expected to earn a target profit per dollar invested. Investment center managers are evaluated on the basis of how well they use the total resources entrusted to their care to earn a profit. An investment center is the broadest and most inclusive type of responsibility center. Managers of these centers have more authority and responsibility than other managers and are primarily responsible for planning, organizing, and controlling firm activities. Because of their authority regarding the size of corporate assets, they are held responsible for the relationship between profits and assets. Investment centers are discussed further in Module 24.

Financial and Nonfinancial Performance Measures

This module's emphasis is on financial performance reports. Dollar-based financial reports have several advantages over other financial measures. Their "bottom line" impact is readily apparent. If actual fixed costs exceed budgeted fixed costs by $10,000, the before-tax income of an organization is $10,000 less than it would be without the extra fixed costs. Additionally, because dollars are additive and applicable to all organizational units, financial measures are easily summarized and reported up the organization chart.

It is important to keep in mind that although financial measures may indicate results are not in accordance with the budget, they do not indicate the root cause of financial deviations. The identification and analysis of the root cause of financial variances require asking questions and, frequently, the use of nonfinancial data. Managers and employees at lower levels of the organization are often better served by performance reports focusing on data directly related to their job, such as units processed or customers served per hour. Although financial performance is still critical to Southwest Airline's top management and still used to evaluate managers, aircraft, and routes, the focus for the evaluation should include customer satisfaction. Other examples of nonfinancial performance measures include defects per thousand units in a manufacturing plant, average and longest waiting time in a restaurant, nursing staff hours per patient day in a hospital, response time for a fire department, and customer satisfaction at a retail store or bank.

When organizations seek to improve financial performance beyond what is possible with current products, procedures, or services, the initial focus is most often on nonfinancial measures. Trader Joe's grocery stores might benchmark the length of their cash-register waiting times against Whole Foods'.

LO1 Review 23-1

Eli's Cheesecake is a family-owned business based out of Chicago, IL. Eli's operates its corporate office, bakery, retail store, and café from one location on the west side of the city and recently opened a Cheesecake Café at Chicago's O'Hare Airport.

Required
Peruse Eli's website at http://www.elicheesecake.com to become more familiar with the company. Listed below are likely reporting centers for Eli's. Identify the type of responsibility center that would most likely be assigned to each reporting center: (1) Cost Center; (2) Revenue Center; (3) Profit Center; or (4) Investment Center.

_____ Bakery
_____ Accounting department
_____ Product line—Original Plain Cheesecake
_____ Human resources department
_____ Cheesecake Café at O'Hare Airport

Solution on p. 23-38.

Performance Reporting for Cost Centers

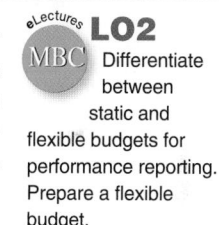

LO2 Differentiate between static and flexible budgets for performance reporting. Prepare a flexible budget.

Financial performance reports for cost centers include a comparison of actual and budgeted (or allowed) costs and identify the difference as a **variance**. *Allowed costs* in performance reports are the flexible budget amounts for the actual level of activity. The variance is favorable if actual costs are less than budgeted (or allowed) costs and unfavorable if actual costs are more than budgeted (or allowed) costs. These comparisons are made in total and individually for each type of controllable cost assigned to the cost center.

Development of Flexible Budgets

A budget that is based on a prediction of sales and production is called a **static budget**. The operating budget explained in Module 22 is a static budget. Budgets can also be set for a series of possible production and sales volumes, or budgets can be adjusted to a particular level of production after the fact. These budgets, based on cost-volume relationships, are called **flexible budgets**; they are used to determine what costs should be for a level of activity. For example, if the college cafeteria budgets $15,000 for food during April for 5,000 meals but provides 6,000 meals, the budget needs to be adjusted by the original food budget rate of $3 ($15,000/5,000 meals). If $17,500 was spent on food during the month, the analysis might appear as follows:

Budget Item	Actual	Budget	Difference
Static analysis			
Food.....................	$17,500	5,000 meals × $3 = $15,000	$2,500 over budget
Flexible analysis			
Food.....................	$17,500	6,000 meals × $3 = $18,000	$500 under budget

The cafeteria manager is better evaluated based on what actually happened with the flexible budget than with the static budget, especially if the manager had no control over how many student meals were requested.

For a complete example of a flexible budget, assume that Tumi, which produces high-quality bags, luggage, and accessories, produces only one product, a computer bag. Also assume Tumi has only three departments: production, sales, and administration. Focusing on the production department, the flexible budget cost-estimating equations for total monthly production costs of computer bags are based on the production standards for variable and fixed costs. The standards follow:

Variable costs
  Direct materials—2 pounds per bag at $5 per pound, or $10 per bag
  Direct labor—0.25 hour per bag at $24 per hour, or $6 per bag
  Variable overhead—2 pounds of direct material per bag at $4 per pound, or $8 per bag
Fixed costs—$52,000

If management plans to produce 10,000 computer bags in July, the budgeted manufacturing costs are $292,000:

TUMI Manufacturing Cost Budget For Month of July	
Manufacturing costs	
Variable costs	
Direct materials (10,000 bags × 2 pounds × $5)	$100,000
Direct labor (10,000 bags × 0.25 hours × $24)	60,000
Variable overhead (10,000 bags × 2 pounds × $4)	80,000
Fixed costs	52,000
Total	$292,000

Flexible Budgets Emphasize Performance

If actual production happened to equal budgeted production, the production department is evaluated by comparing the actual and budgeted costs. If production needs change, perhaps due to an unexpected increase or decrease in sales volume, the production department should attempt to make appropriate changes. When the actual production volume is anything other than the originally budgeted amount, the production department's financial responsibility for costs should be based on the actual level of production.

For the purpose of evaluating the financial performance of cost centers, a flexible budget is tailored, after the fact, to the actual level of activity. A **flexible budget variance** is computed for each cost as the difference between the actual cost and the flexible budget cost. Assume actual production for July totaled 11,000 bags rather than 10,000 bags. Examples of a performance report for July manufacturing costs based on static and flexible budgets are presented in Exhibit 23.1. When the production department's financial performance is evaluated using the static budget, the actual cost of producing 11,000 bags is compared to the budgeted cost of producing 10,000 bags. The result is a series of unfavorable static budget variances totaling $20,000.

When the production department's financial performance is evaluated by comparing actual costs with costs allowed in a flexible budget drawn up for the actual production volume, the results are mixed. Direct materials have a $2,000 favorable variance. Direct labor has a $4,000 unfavorable variance. The variable overhead variance is $7,000 favorable. The fixed overhead variance remains $1,000 unfavorable since the static and flexible fixed budgets stay the same. The net flexible budget variance is $4,000 favorable, a substantial change from the static variance of $20,000 unfavorable.

Flexible budget variances provide a much better indicator of performance than static budget variances that do not consider the increased level of production (11,000 bags rather than 10,000 bags). When production exceeds the planned level, the static budget variances are usually unfavorable. Likewise, when actual production is substantially below the planned level of activity, the static variances are usually favorable. While it is important to isolate and determine the cause of any variation between planned and actual production, the financial-based performance report is not the appropriate place to mix volume-created variances with those related to the actual production levels.

Exhibit 23.1 ■ Flexible Budgets and Performance Evaluation

TUMI
Production Department Performance Report
For Month of July

	Based on Static Budget			Based on Flexible Budget		
	Actual	Original Budget	Static Budget Variance	Actual	Flexible Budget*	Flexible Budget Variance
Volume	11,000	10,000		11,000	11,000	
Variable costs						
Direct materials.	$108,000	$100,000	$ 8,000 U	$108,000	$110,000	$2,000 F
Direct labor	70,000	60,000	10,000 U	70,000	66,000	4,000 U
Variable overhead. . .	81,000	80,000	1,000 U	81,000	88,000	7,000 F
Fixed costs	53,000	52,000	1,000 U	53,000	52,000	1,000 U
Totals	$312,000	$292,000	$20,000 U	$312,000	$316,000	$4,000 F

* Flexible budget manufacturing costs: (Actual level × Budgeted per bag cost)
Direct materials (11,000 bags × 2 pounds × $5)
Direct labor (11,000 bags × 0.25 labor hour × $24)
Variable overhead (11,000 bags × 2 pounds × $4)

Standard Costs and Performance Reports

A **standard cost** indicates what it should cost to provide an activity or produce one batch or unit of product under planned and efficient operating conditions. In a standard costing environment, the flexible budget is based on standard unit costs. Traditionally, standard costs have been developed from an engineering analysis or from an analysis of historical data adjusted for expected changes in the product, production technology, or costs. When standards are developed using historical data, management must be careful to ensure that past inefficiencies are excluded from current standards.

To obtain the full benefit of standard costs, the standards must be based on realistic expectations. Suppose the standard cost for direct labor for **Tumi** is $6.00 per bag (computed as 0.25 direct labor hours × $24 per hour). Some organizations intentionally set "tight" standards to motivate employees toward higher levels of production. The management of Tumi might set their standards for direct labor at 0.22 hours per bag rather than at the expected 0.25 hours per bag, hoping that employees will strive toward the lower time and, consequently, the lower cost of $5.28 ($24 × 0.22). The use of tight standards often causes planning and behavioral problems. Management expects them to result in unfavorable variances. Accordingly, tight standards should not be used to budget input requirements and cash flows because management expects to incur more labor costs than the standards allow. The use of tight standards can have undesirable behavioral effects if employees find that a second set of standards is used in the "real" budget or if they are constantly subject to unfavorable performance reports. These employees could come to distrust the entire budgeting and performance evaluation system, or they may quit trying to achieve any of the organization's standards.

Tight standards are more likely to occur in an imposed budget than in a participation budget. In a participation budget, the problem may be to avoid overstating the costs required to produce a product. Loose standards may fail to properly motivate employees and can make the company uncompetitive due to costs that are higher than competitors'.

LO2 Review 23-2

Suppose you receive the following performance report from the accounting department for your first month as plant manager for a new company. Your supervisor, the vice president of manufacturing, has concerns that the report does not provide an accurate picture of your performance in the area of cost control.

continued

continued from previous page

	Actual	Budgeted	Variance
Units	10,000	12,000	2,000 U
Costs			
Direct materials.	$ 299,000	$ 360,000	$ 61,000 F
Direct labor	345,500	432,000	86,500 F
Variable factory overhead.	180,000	216,000	36,000 F
Fixed factory overhead	375,000	360,000	15,000 U
Total costs	$1,199,500	$1,368,000	$168,500 F

Required

Solution on p. 23-38. Prepare a revised budget that better reflects your performance.

Variance Analysis for Costs

Components of Standard Cost Analysis

LO3
Determine the components of standard cost variance analysis. Formulate and interpret direct materials cost variances.

To use and interpret standard cost variances properly, managers must understand the processes and activities that drive costs. Cost variances are merely signals. They do not explain why costs differ from expectations. Underlying causes of variances must be investigated before final judgment is passed on the effectiveness and efficiency of an operation or activity.

Standard cost variance analysis is a systematic approach to examining flexible budget variances. Actual costs are determined from the organization's financial transactions. Flexible budget costs are determined by multiplying standard quantities allowed for the output times the standard price per unit. For a company using activity-based costing, each manufacturing activity could have its own standard costs that focus on underlying concepts and cost drivers, and companies even develop their own set of variances.

Standard cost variance analysis identifies the general causes of the total flexible budget variance by breaking it into separate price and quantity variances for each production component. Two possible reasons that actual cost could differ from flexible budget cost for a given amount of output produced are (1) a difference between actual and standard prices paid for the production components—the price variance—and (2) a difference between the actual quantity and the standard quantity allowed for the production components—the quantity variance. Variances have different names for different cost categories as follows:

Cost Category	Price Variance Name	Quantity Variance Name
Direct materials	Materials price variance	Materials quantity variance
Direct labor	Labor rate variance	Labor efficiency variance
Variable overhead	Variable overhead spending variance	Variable overhead efficiency variance

Fixed overhead is excluded from the unit standard costs because, within the relevant range of normal activity, it does not vary with the volume of production. To facilitate product costing, however, many organizations develop a standard fixed overhead cost per unit.

In the following sections, we analyze the flexible budget cost variances for materials, labor and variable overhead. Our illustration is based on the following hypothetical July activity and costs of **Tumi**'s production department.

TUMI Actual Manufacturing Costs For Month of July	
Actual bags completed.	11,000
Manufacturing costs	
Unit level costs	
Direct materials (24,000 pounds × $4.50).	$108,000
Direct labor (2,800 hours × $25.00)	70,000
Variable overhead.	81,000
Fixed overhead costs	53,000
Total	$312,000

Research Insight ■ When Are Variances Evidence of Fraud?

Standard cost variances can help firms hold managers and employees accountable for their work. Dr. Cecily Raiborn and her coauthors argue that variance analysis can also help strengthen internal controls, ultimately detecting fraud early and pointing to areas of the company that are weak. If purchasing managers are receiving kickbacks from suppliers, the behavior may show up in frequent, slightly unfavorable price variances. If employees are stealing materials for resale or personal use, the firm may see unfavorable materials variances.

This sort of data analysis for indicators of fraud is important enough for auditors that the Big Four auditing firms are developing tools to automate this process. KPMG recently partnered with IBM to use Watson's artificial intelligence engine to comb through financial data for just the sort of behaviors that will show up in the variances discussed here. EY (formerly Ernst & Young) has poured $400 million into its own tools for this analysis. Automating the data analysis allows all of the client's transactions to be considered, not just the top-level numbers that come out in variance analysis.

Such tools find patterns that raise suspicion, which can be variances or issues as simple as sales clustered just before the quarter end and expenses clustered just after. These tools do the work of combing through the firm's data for suspicious patterns, but it remains the job of management accountants and auditors to determine whether the patterns are operational or fraudulent.

Sources: Cecily Raiborn, Janet Butler, and Lucian Zelazny, "Standard Costing Variances: Potential Red Flags of Fraud?" *Cost Management*, 2013.
Michael Rapoport, "Auditing Firms Count on Technology for Backup," *Wall Street Journal*, March 7, 2016.

Note that detailed information on actual pounds and an actual rate is not provided for variable overhead. That is because variable overhead represents a pool of related costs driven by a number of factors rather than a single cost with a single driver. Although the basis used in budgeting variable overhead may, and should, have a high correlation with actual variable overhead, it is a surrogate for the multiple cost elements that comprise variable overhead. Issues related to variable overhead are discussed in greater detail later in this module.

Establishing and Using Standards for Direct Materials

The two basic elements contained in the standards for direct materials are the *standard price* and the *standard quantity*. Materials standards indicate how much an organization should pay for each input unit of direct materials and the quantity of direct materials it should use to produce one unit of output. The standard price per unit of direct materials should include all reasonable costs necessary to acquire the materials. These costs include the invoice price of materials, less planned discounts plus freight, insurance, special handling, and any other costs related to the acquisition of the materials. The standard quantity represents the number of units of raw materials allowed for the production of one unit of finished product. This amount should include the amount dictated by the physical characteristics of the process and the product, plus a reasonable allowance for normal spoilage, waste, and other inefficiencies. The quantity standard can be determined by engineering analysis, professional judgment, or by averaging the actual amount used for several periods. An average of actual past materials usage may not be a good standard because it could include excessive wastes and inefficiencies in the standard quantity.

Direct Materials Variances

The **materials price variance** is the difference between the actual materials cost and the standard cost of actual materials inputs. The **materials quantity variance** is the difference between the standard cost of actual materials inputs and the flexible budget cost for materials. The direct materials variances for Tumi follow.

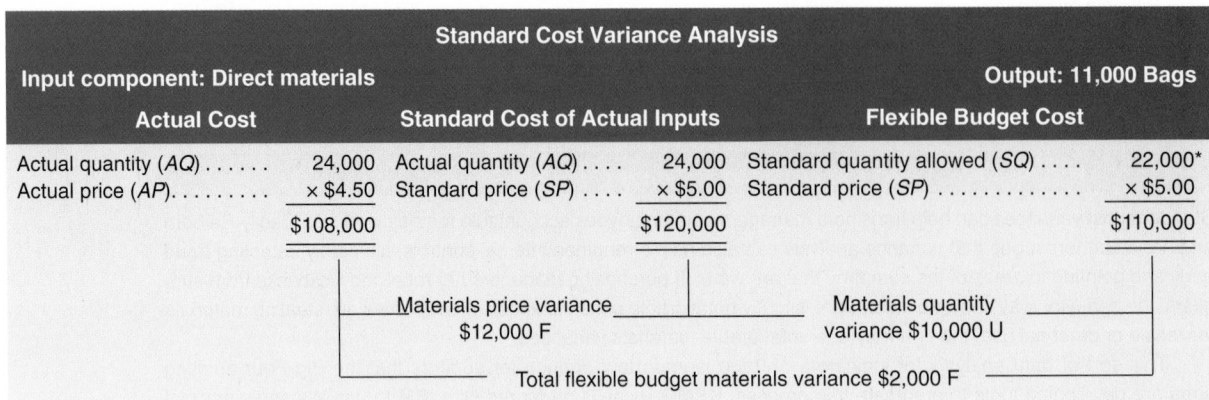

*11,000 bags × 2 pounds per bag

Tumi had a favorable materials price variance of $12,000 because the actual cost of materials used ($108,000) was less than the standard cost of actual materials used ($120,000). The price variance can also be computed using a formula approach as the actual quantity (AQ) used times the difference between the actual price (AP) and the standard price (SP). Tumi paid $0.50 per pound below the standard price for 24,000 pounds for a total savings of $12,000:

$$\text{Materials price variance} = \text{AQ(AP} - \text{SP)}$$
$$= 24{,}000(\$4.50 - \$5.00)$$
$$= 24{,}000 \times \$0.50$$
$$= \$12{,}000 \text{ F}$$

The unfavorable quantity variance of $10,000 occurred because the standard cost of actual materials used, $120,000 (24,000 × $5), was higher than the cost of materials allowed by the flexible budget, $110,000 (22,000 × $5). A total of 22,000 pounds of materials is allowed to produce 11,000 units of finished outputs. This is computed as 11,000 finished bags times 2.0 pounds of direct materials per bag. The materials quantity variance can also be computed using a formula approach as the standard price (SP) per pound times the difference between the number of pounds actually used (AQ) and the number of pounds allowed (SQ):

$$\text{Materials quantity variance} = \text{SP(AQ} - \text{SQ)}$$
$$= \$5(24{,}000 - 22{,}000)$$
$$= \$5 \times 2{,}000$$
$$= \$10{,}000 \text{ U}$$

Interpreting Materials Variances

As highlighted in the following two Business Insights, after computing variances, managers are in a better position to analyze their business's results and to make better and more relevant decisions. A *favorable materials price variance* indicates that the employee responsible for materials purchases paid less per unit than the price allowed by the standards. This could result from receiving discounts for purchasing more than the normal quantities, effective bargaining by the employee, purchasing substandard-quality materials, purchasing from a distress seller, or other factors. Ordinarily, when a favorable price variance is reported, the employee's performance is interpreted as favorable. However, if the favorable price variance results from the purchase of materials of lower than standard quality or from a purchase in more than desirable quantities, the employee's performance would be questionable. All large variances, including favorable variances, should be thoroughly investigated for causes and corrections.

Business Insight ■ Variance Analysis Helps Hospitals Understand Impact of Policy

To understand the impact of California's Hospital Fair Pricing Act (CHFPA), Professor Ge Bai of Washington and Lee University applied variance analysis to California hospitals' expense recovery data. Expense recovery is simply the rate at which the hospital is able to recover the costs of serving a patient by collecting from insurers.

The CHFPA stipulates that hospitals can only charge low-income, uninsured patients Medicare rates for services. The act also makes it more difficult to collect payment from these patients. Dr. Bai's study shows that the CHFPA decreases the rate of expense recovery from low-income patients and increases the share of these patients in the health-care system, consistent with the aims of the CHFPA. His study also shows that hospitals appear to be offsetting the cost of treating more low-income patients at lower rates by collecting more aggressively from both public programs and from private insurance companies.

Source: Ge Bai, "Applying Variance Analysis to Understand California Hospitals' Expense Recovery Status by Patient Groups," *Accounting Horizons* Vol. 30, No. 2 (June 2016): pp. 211–223.

An *unfavorable materials price variance* means that the purchasing employee paid more per unit for materials than the price allowed by the standards. This could be caused by failure to buy in sufficient quantities to receive normal discounts; purchase of higher-quality materials than called for in the product specifications; failure to place materials orders on a timely basis; failure to bargain for the best available prices; or other factors. An unfavorable variance does not always mean that the employee performed unfavorably. Many noncontrollable factors surround the purchasing function, including unanticipated price increases, the need to increase production to meet unanticipated sales, and supply chain problems such as a work stoppage at a vendor.

A *favorable materials quantity variance* means that the actual quantity of raw materials used was less than the quantity allowed for the units produced. This could result from factors such as less materials waste than allowed by the standards, better than expected machine efficiency, direct materials of higher quality than required by the standards, and more efficient use of direct materials by employees. An *unfavorable materials quantity variance* occurs when the quantity of raw materials used exceeds the quantity allowed for the units produced. This could result from incurring more waste than provided for in the standards, poorly maintained machinery requiring larger amounts of raw materials, raw materials of lower quality than required by the standards, or poorly trained employees who were unable to use the materials at the level of efficiency required by the standards.

Business Insight ■ Unfavorable Price Variance? Buy a Farm

Demand for organic ingredients is outpacing supply. Sales of organic food tripled from 2003 to 2013, and supply of some products is not keeping up. Not only are prices rising (unfavorable rate variance) but shortages are also interrupting supply chains for large food companies (unfavorable efficiency variance). In 2015, Nature's Path Foods Inc. decided that it had had enough. So it bought a 2,800-acre farm in Montana. Nature's Path had been dealing with supply shortages and unpredictable prices, once even importing ingredients from Sweden on very short notice. The company plans to invest $2 million each year in purchasing and converting farmland.

It turns out that changing a farm from conventional to organic requires a transition period that is tough for farmers. It takes between one and three years to transition a farm. During transition, the farm is using more costly organic practices, but farmers cannot sell their products as organic. Chipotle Mexican Grill Inc. and Pacific Foods of Oregon Inc. are trying to help farmers switch by offering financing and training. The maker of Garden of Eatin' corn chips, Hain Celestial Group Inc., is offering farmers long-term contracts to lock in corn supply and to help offset some of the risks farmers face.

When supply is erratic, companies may find that capital budgeting choices that include purchasing their suppliers make sense.

Source: Ilan Brat, "Hunger for Organic Foods Stretches Supply Chain," *Wall Street Journal*, April 3, 2015.

Review 23-3 LO3

Suppose the flexible budget performance report for **REI**'s camping chair product for March follows.

	Actual Costs	Flexible Budget Cost	Flexible Budget Variances
Output units	5,000	5,000	
Direct materials.	$104,125	$100,000	$ 4,125 U
Direct labor	82,400	75,000	7,400 U
Variable manufacturing overhead			
Category 1	31,000	30,000	1,000 U
Category 2	18,000	20,000	2,000 F
Fixed manufacturing overhead.	42,000	40,000	2,000 U
Total	$277,525	$265,000	$12,525 U

The standard unit cost for folding chairs follows:

Direct materials (4 pounds × $5.00 per pound)	$20
Direct labor (1.25 hours × $12.00 per hour)	15
Variable overhead, Category 1 (1.25 hours × $4.80)	6
Variable overhead, Category 2 ($4 per finished unit)	4
Total standard variable cost per unit.	$45

Actual cost of materials is based on 21,250 pounds of direct materials purchased and used at $4.90 per pound; actual cost of assembly is based on 7,000 labor hours. Variable overhead is applied on labor hours for Category 1 and finished units for Category 2.

Required

Solution on p. 23-39.   Calculate all standard cost variances for direct materials.

---

eLectures **LO4**

MBC   Formulate and interpret direct labor cost variances.

Establishing and Using Standards for Direct Labor

To evaluate management performance in controlling labor costs, it is necessary to determine the *standard labor rate* for each hour allowed and the *standard time allowed* to produce a unit. Setting labor rate standards can be quite simple or extremely complex. If all employees have the same wage rate, determining the standard cost is relatively easy: Simply adopt the normal wage rate as the standard labor rate. If there are variations in employee wage rates, the standard labor rate should be based on the expected mix of employee wage rates.

The standard labor time per unit can be determined by an engineering approach or an empirical observation approach. When using an engineering approach, industrial engineers ascertain the amount of time required to produce a unit of finished product by applying time and motion methods or other available techniques. Normal operating conditions are assumed in arriving at the labor standard. Therefore, allowances must be made for normal machine downtime, employee personal breaks, and so forth. Under the empirical approach, the average time required to produce a unit under normal operating conditions is used as a basis for the standard.

Direct Labor Variances

Using the general variance model that was used for materials, we can compute the labor rate and efficiency variances. The **labor rate variance** is the difference between the actual cost and the standard cost of actual labor inputs. The **labor efficiency variance** is the difference between the standard cost of actual inputs and the flexible budget cost for labor.

Tumi's labor standards provide for 0.25 hour of labor per bag produced at $24 per hour. During July, 2,800 hours were used at a cost of $25 per hour. Using these data, the labor rate (price) variance and labor efficiency (quantity) variance can be computed as shown in the following illustration.

Standard Cost Variance Analysis					
Input component: Direct labor				**Output: 11,000 Bags**	
Actual Cost		**Standard Cost of Actual Inputs**		**Flexible Budget Cost**	
Actual hours (*AH*)........	2,800	Actual hours (*AH*)......	2,800	Standard hours allowed (*SH*)......	2,750*
Actual rate (*AR*)	× $25	Standard rate (*SR*).....	× $24	Standard rate (*SR*).............	× $24
	$70,000		$67,200		$66,000
		Labor rate variance $2,800 U		Labor efficiency variance $1,200 U	
		Total flexible budget labor variance $4,000 U			

*11,000 bags × 0.25 hours per bag

The labor rate variance can also be computed in formula form as the actual number of hours used times the difference between the actual rate and the standard rate.

$$\textbf{Labor rate variance} = \textbf{AH(AR} - \textbf{SR)}$$
$$= \textbf{2,800(\$25} - \textbf{\$24)}$$
$$= \textbf{2,800} \times \textbf{\$1}$$
$$= \textbf{\$2,800 U}$$

This computation of the labor rate variance shows that the company paid $1 more than the standard rate for each of the 2,800 hours worked.

Since 11,000 units of product were finished during the period and 0.25 hour of labor was allowed for each bag, the total number of standard hours allowed was 2,750 (11,000 bags × 0.25 hour). The labor efficiency variance can also be computed as the standard rate times the difference between the actual labor hours and the standard hours allowed:

$$\textbf{Labor efficiency variance} = \textbf{SR(AH} - \textbf{SH)}$$
$$= \textbf{\$24(2,800} - \textbf{2,750)}$$
$$= \textbf{\$24} \times \textbf{50}$$
$$= \textbf{\$1,200 U}$$

Tumi's labor efficiency variance indicates that the company used 50 more labor hours than allowed. By itself, this inefficiency caused an unfavorable variance of $1,200.

Interpreting Labor Variances

The possible explanations for labor rate variances are rather limited. An *unfavorable labor rate variance* can be caused by the use of higher-paid laborers than the standards provided. An increase in wage rates not reflected in the standards can also cause an unfavorable labor rate variance. A *favorable labor rate variance* occurs if lower-paid workers were used or if actual wage rates declined.

Unfavorable labor efficiency variances occur when the actual labor hours exceed the number of hours allowed for the actual output. This could be caused by using poorly trained workers or poorly maintained machinery or by the use of low-quality materials. Low employee morale and generally poor working conditions could also adversely affect the efficiency.

Favorable labor efficiency variances occur when the actual labor hours are less than the number of hours allowed for the actual output. This above-normal efficiency can be caused by the company's use of higher-skilled (and higher-paid) workers, better machinery, or higher-quality raw materials than the standards require. High employee morale, improved job satisfaction, or generally improved working conditions could also account for the above-normal efficiency of the workers.

Review 23-4 LO4

Suppose the flexible budget performance report for **REI**'s camping chair product for March follows.

	Actual Costs	Flexible Budget Cost	Flexible Budget Variances
Output units	5,000	5,000	
Direct materials.................................	$104,125	$100,000	$ 4,125 U
Direct labor.....................................	82,400	75,000	7,400 U
Variable manufacturing overhead			
Category 1	31,000	30,000	1,000 U
Category 2	18,000	20,000	2,000 F
Fixed manufacturing overhead....................	42,000	40,000	2,000 U
Total	$277,525	$265,000	$12,525 U

The standard unit cost for folding chairs follows:

Direct materials (4 pounds × $5.00 per pound)	$20
Direct labor (1.25 hours × $12.00 per hour)...	15
Variable overhead, Category 1 (1.25 hours × $4.80)......................................	6
Variable overhead, Category 2 ($4 per finished unit).....................................	4
Total standard variable cost per unit..	$45

Actual cost of materials is based on 21,250 pounds of direct materials purchased and used at $4.90 per pound; actual cost of assembly is based on 7,000 labor hours. Variable overhead is applied on labor hours for Category 1 and finished units for Category 2.

Required

Solution on p. 23-39.   Calculate all standard cost variances for direct labor.

Establishing and Using Standards for Variable Overhead

eLectures **LO5**
MBC Formulate and interpret variable overhead cost variances.

The traditional unit-level approach to cost estimation, budgeting, and variance analysis separates overhead costs into fixed and variable elements. This separation is necessary because fixed costs are primarily driven by factors related to capacity and variable costs are primarily driven by factors related to volume.

Because it includes many heterogeneous costs, manufacturing overhead poses a unique problem in establishing standards for the standard quantity and the standard price of inputs. Direct materials have a natural physical measure of quantity such as tons, barrels, pounds, and liters. Similarly, labor or assembly is measurable in hours or minutes. However, no single quantity measure is common to all overhead items. Overhead is a cost group that can simultaneously include costs measurable in hours, pounds, liters, and kilowatts.

The most frequent approach to dealing with the problem of multiple quantity measures in variable manufacturing overhead is to use a single surrogate (or substitute) measure to represent the quantity of all items in a given group. Typical substitute measures include machine hours, units of finished product, direct labor hours, and direct labor dollars. The variable overhead standard is then stated in terms of this surrogate measure.

Variable Overhead Variances

The **variable overhead spending variance** is the difference between the actual variable overhead cost and the standard variable overhead cost for the actual inputs of the surrogate measure. The **variable overhead efficiency variance** is the difference between the standard variable overhead cost for the actual inputs of the surrogate measure and the flexible budget cost allowed for variable overhead based on outputs.

Assume for Tumi, the actual variable overhead in July was $81,000. This represents the actual cost of overhead items such as indirect materials and indirect labor. Pounds of materials is Tumi's surrogate measure for quantity for variable overhead allowed and used. This means that the standard costs allowed for variable overhead varies with the pounds of direct materials allowed. Hence the standard cost of actual inputs is calculated as actual pounds of direct materials (AQ) times the standard variable overhead rate per pound (SR):

$$\textbf{Standard cost of actual inputs} = (\textbf{AQ} \times \textbf{SR})$$
$$= 24{,}000 \times \$4$$
$$= \$96{,}000$$

The flexible budget cost for variable overhead allowed for the actual outputs is based on the 22,000 pounds of direct materials allowed (SQ) for the bags produced during the period (11,000 bags × 2 pounds). The allowed quantities are multiplied by the standard variable overhead rate (SR). The resulting variable overhead flexible budget cost is $88,000:

$$\textbf{Flexible budget cost} = (\textbf{SQ} \times \textbf{SR})$$
$$= 22{,}000 \times \$4$$
$$= \$88{,}000$$

Using these data, the variable overhead spending (price) variance and the variable overhead efficiency (quantity) variance follow.

Standard Cost Variance Analysis			
Input component: Variable overhead			**Output: 11,000 Bags**
Actual Cost	**Standard Cost of Actual Inputs**		**Flexible Budget Cost**
$81,000	Actual pounds (*AQ*) 24,000	Pounds allowed (*SQ*) 22,000*	
	Standard rate (*SR*) ..... × $4	Standard rate (*SR*) .... × $4	
	Total $96,000	Total $88,000	
	Variable overhead spending variance $15,000 F	Variable overhead efficiency variance $8,000 U	
	Total flexible budget variable overhead variance $7,000 F		

*11,000 bags × 2 lbs.

An alternative to the computation of the variable overhead effectiveness variance follows:

$$\textbf{Variable overhead efficiency variance} = \textbf{SR(AQ} - \textbf{SQ)}$$
$$= \$4(24{,}000 - 22{,}000)$$
$$= \$8{,}000 \ \textbf{U}$$

This approach emphasizes that the 2,000 extra pounds used should have increased variable overhead by $8,000 at the standard rate of $4 per pound.

Interpreting Variable Overhead Variances

A *favorable spending variance* encompasses all factors that cause actual expenditures to be less than the amount expected for the actual inputs of the measurement base, including consumption and payment. Conversely, an *unfavorable spending variance* results when the actual expenditures are more than expected for the inputs of the measurement base. This is caused by consuming more overhead items than expected, or by paying more than the expected amount for overhead items consumed, or by both. Thus, the term *spending variance* is used instead of *price variance*.

The key to understanding the variable overhead spending variance is recognizing that the amount of variable overhead cost allowed is determined by the level of the surrogate measurement base used. Any deviation from this spending budget causes a spending variance to occur.

The variable overhead efficiency variance measures the difference between the standard variable overhead cost for the actual quantity of the surrogate measurement base and the standard variable overhead cost for the allowed quantity of the surrogate measurement base. This variance measures the amount of variable overhead that should have been saved (or incurred) because of the efficient (or inefficient) use of the surrogate measurement base. It provides no information about the degree of efficiency in using variable overhead items such as indirect materials and indirect labor. This information is reflected in the spending variance.

Managerial Decision   ■   You Are the Vice President of Manufacturing

Your company has had a practice for many years of budgeting variable overhead costs based on direct labor hours. The managerial accountants have argued that if direct labor hours are controlled, variable overhead costs will take care of themselves since direct labor hours drive variable overhead costs. You (and your plant managers) have become very skeptical of this policy because in recent years variable overhead variances have been very erratic—sometimes being large favorable amounts and other times being large unfavorable amounts. You are beginning to plan for the coming budget year. How do you think you should budget variable overhead and evaluate managers who control these costs? [Answer, p. 23-25]

Fixed Overhead Variances

By definition, the quantity of goods and services purchased by fixed expenditures is not expected to change in proportion to short-run changes in the level of production. For example, in the short run, the production level does not affect the amount of depreciation on buildings, the number of fixed salaried employees, or the amount of real property subject to property taxes. Whether the organization produces 10,000 or 15,000 cases, the same quantity of fixed overhead is expected to be incurred, as long as the production level is within the relevant range of activity provided by the current fixed overhead items. Therefore, an efficiency variance is not computed for fixed overhead costs.

Even though the components of fixed overhead are not expected to be affected by the production activity level in the short run, the actual amount spent for fixed overhead items can differ from the amount budgeted. For example, higher than budgeted supervisors' salaries could be paid, there may be unanticipated increases in property taxes or insurance premiums, and the cost of leased facilities may increase. Fixed overhead costs in excess of the amount budgeted are reflected in the fixed overhead budget variance. The **fixed overhead budget variance** is, simply, the difference between budgeted and actual fixed overhead. Using the assumed fixed costs of Tumi as an example:

$$\textbf{Fixed overhead budget variance} = \textbf{Actual fixed overhead} - \textbf{Budgeted fixed overhead}$$
$$= \$53,000 - \$52,000$$
$$= \$1,000 \text{ U}$$

The fixed overhead budget variance is always the same as the total fixed overhead flexible budget variance. Because budgeted fixed overhead is the same for all outputs within the relevant range, the budget variance explains the total flexible budget variance between actual and allowed fixed overhead. Similar to variable overhead, fixed overhead variances can be caused by a combination of price and quantity factors. Fixed overhead variances are examined further in Appendix 23A.

Business Insight   ■   The Correct Diagnosis Is the Efficient Diagnosis

Misdiagnosis in the medical field is rampant. At its core, misdiagnosis is simply misidentifying a problem—a pathologist doesn't identify cancerous cells that exist, or a doctor may diagnose a patient as having cancer when, in fact, the patient does not. Second opinions of diagnoses raise questions in 25% of cases and prevent procedures that are costly for both the health-care system and the patient. On the other hand, second opinions can also catch missed diagnoses and help patients avoid costly convalescence. But getting a second opinion isn't always easy, especially in rural areas. Currently, lab samples must be physically transported across the country for diagnosis. GE is working with the US FDA to introduce a digital diagnosis system that allows samples to move more easily across the country for primary and secondary diagnoses. Getting the diagnosis right will have positive effects on both the patient's quality of life and medical bills and will yield better information for the hospital's budgeting process.

Sources: Laura Landro, "New Ways Doctors Reach Agreement on Patient Diagnoses," *Wall Street Journal*, June 9, 2015.

Suppose the flexible budget performance report for **REI**'s camping chair product for March follows.

	Actual Costs	Flexible Budget Cost	Flexible Budget Variances
Output units	5,000	5,000	
Direct materials.	$104,125	$100,000	$ 4,125 U
Direct labor.	82,400	75,000	7,400 U
Variable manufacturing overhead			
Category 1	31,000	30,000	1,000 U
Category 2	18,000	20,000	2,000 F
Fixed manufacturing overhead.	42,000	40,000	2,000 U
Total	$277,525	$265,000	$12,525 U

The standard unit cost for folding chairs follows:

Direct materials (4 pounds × $5.00 per pound)	$20
Direct labor (1.25 hours × $12.00 per hour)	15
Variable overhead, Category 1 (1.25 hours × $4.80)	6
Variable overhead, Category 2 ($4 per finished unit)	4
Total standard variable cost per unit.	$45

Actual cost of materials is based on 21,250 pounds of direct materials purchased and used at $4.90 per pound; actual cost of assembly is based on 7,000 labor hours. Variable overhead is applied on labor hours for Category 1 and finished units for Category 2.

Required
Calculate all standard cost variances for variable manufacturing overhead.

Solution on p. 23-39.

Performance Reports for Revenue Centers

The financial performance reports for revenue centers include a comparison of actual and budgeted revenues. Controllable costs can be deducted from revenues to obtain some bottom-line contribution margin. If the center is then evaluated on the basis of this contribution, it is being treated as a profit center.

LO6 Calculate revenue variances and prepare a performance report for a revenue center.

If the organization is to meet its budgeted profit goal for a period, with its budgeted fixed and variable costs, the organization's revenue centers must meet their original revenue budgets. Consequently, the original budget (a static budget) rather than a flexible budget is used to evaluate the financial performance of revenue centers.

Assume that Tumi's July sales budget called for the sale of 10,000 bags at $40.00 each. If Tumi actually sold 11,000 bags at $38.50 each, the total revenue variance is $23,500 favorable:

Actual revenues (11,000 × $38.50).	$423,500
Budgeted revenues (10,000 × $40)	(400,000)
Revenue variance.	$ 23,500 F

The **revenue variance** is the difference between the budgeted sales volume at the budgeted selling price and the actual sales volume at the actual selling price. Because Tumi's actual revenues exceeded budgeted revenues, the revenue variance is favorable. It can be presented as follows:

Revenue variance = (Actual volume × Actual price) – (Budgeted volume × Budgeted price)

The separate impact of changing prices and volume on revenue is analyzed with the sales price and sales volume variances. The **sales price variance** is computed as the change in selling price times the actual sales volume:

Sales price variance = (Actual selling price – Budgeted selling price) × Actual sales volume

For Tumi, the sales price variance for July follows:

$$\text{Sales price variance} = (\$38.50 - \$40.00) \times 11{,}000 \text{ bags}$$
$$= \$16{,}500 \text{ U}$$

The **sales volume variance** indicates the impact of the change in sales volume on revenues, assuming there was no change in selling price. The sales volume variance is computed as the difference between the actual and the budgeted sales volumes times the budgeted selling price:

Sales volume variance = (Actual sales volume – Budgeted sales volume) × Budgeted selling price

For Tumi, the sales volume variance for July follows:

$$\text{Sales volume variance} = (11{,}000 \text{ bags} - 10{,}000 \text{ bags}) \times \$40$$
$$= \$40{,}000 \text{ F}$$

The net of the sales price and the sales volume variances is equal to the revenue variance:

Sales price variance	$16,500 U
Sales volume variance	40,000 F
Revenue variance	$23,500 F

Interpretation of these variances is subjective. In this case, we could say that if the increase in sales volume had not been accompanied by a decline in selling price, revenues would have increased $40,000 instead of $23,500. The $1.50 per unit decline in selling price cost the company $16,500 in revenues. Alternatively, we might note that a $1.50 reduction in the unit selling price was more than offset by an increase in sales volume. An economic analysis could explain the relationship as volume being sensitive to price (price elasticity).

In any case, variances are merely signals that actual results are not proceeding according to plan. They help managers identify potential problems and opportunities. An investigation into their cause(s) could even indicate that a manager who received a favorable variance was doing a poor job, whereas a manager who received an unfavorable variance was doing an outstanding job. Consider Tumi's favorable revenue variance. This occurred because actual sales exceeded budgeted sales by 1,000 bags (10%), which on the surface indicates good performance. But what if the total market for the company's products exceeded the company's forecast by 15%? In this hypothetical case, Tumi's sales volume falls below its expected percentage share of the market; the favorable variance could occur (despite a poor marketing effort) because of strong customer demand that competitors could not fill.

Inclusion of Controllable Costs

Controllable costs should also be considered when evaluating the overall performance of revenue centers. A failure to consider costs could encourage uneconomic selling practices, such as excessive advertising and entertaining, and spending too much time on small accounts. The controllable costs of revenue centers include variable and fixed selling costs. These costs are sometimes further classified into order-getting and order-filling costs. **Order-getting costs** are incurred to obtain customers' orders (for example, advertising, salespersons' salaries and commissions, travel, telephone, and entertainment). **Order-filling costs** are distribution costs incurred to place finished goods in the hands of purchasers (for example, storing, packaging, and transportation).

The performance of a revenue center in controlling costs can be evaluated with the aid of a flexible budget drawn up for the actual level of activity. Assume that Tumi's July budget for the sales department calls for fixed costs of $10,000 and variable costs of $5 per bag sold. If the actual fixed and variable selling expenses for July are $9,500 and $65,000, respectively, the total cost variances assigned to the sales department, detailed in Exhibit 23.2, are $9,500 unfavorable. In evaluating the sales department's performance as both a cost center and a revenue center, management should consider these cost variances as well as the revenue variances. Although the revenue variances are based on the original budget, the cost variances are based on the flexible budget.

Exhibit 23.2 ■ Sales Department Performance Report for Controllable Costs

TUMI
Sales Department Performance Report for Controllable Costs
For Month of July

		Based on Flexible Budget	
	Actual	**Flexible Budget***	**Flexible Budget Variance**
Bags	11,000	11,000	
Selling expenses			
Variable	$65,000	$55,000	$10,000 U
Fixed	9,500	10,000	500 F
Total	$74,500	$65,000	$ 9,500 U

* Flexible budget formulas:
  Variable selling expenses ($5 per bag)
  Fixed selling expenses($10,000 per month)

Revenue Centers as Profit Centers

Even though we have computed revenue and cost variances for Tumi's sales department, we are still left with an incomplete picture of this revenue center's performance. Is the sales department's performance best represented by the $23,500 favorable revenue variance, by the $9,500 unfavorable cost variance, or by the net favorable variance of $14,000 ($23,500 F – $9,500 U)? Actually, it is inappropriate to attempt to obtain an overall measure of the sales department's performance by combining these separate revenue and selling cost variances. The combination of revenue and cost variances is appropriate only for a profit center; so far, we have left out one important cost that must be assigned to the sales department before it can be treated as a profit center. That cost is the *standard variable cost of goods sold.*

As a profit center, the sales department acquires units from the production department and sells them outside the firm. Its total responsibilities include revenues, the standard variable cost of goods sold, and actual selling expenses. The sales department is assigned the *standard,* rather than the *actual, variable cost of goods sold.* Because the sales department does not control production activities, it should not be assigned actual production costs. Doing so results in passing the production department's variances on to the sales department. Fixed manufacturing costs are not assigned to the sales department because short-run variations in sales volume do not normally affect the total amount of these costs.

To evaluate the sales department as a profit center, the net sales volume variance must be computed. The **net sales volume variance** indicates the impact of a change in sales volume on the contribution margin given the budgeted selling price *and* the standard variable costs. It is computed as the difference between the actual and the budgeted sales volumes times the budgeted unit contribution margin.

Net sales volume variance = (Actual volume – Budgeted volume) × Budgeted contribution margin

Using the $40 budgeted selling price, the standard variable manufacturing costs, and the standard variable selling expenses, the budgeted contribution margin is $11.00:

Sales		$40.00
Direct materials	$10.00	
Direct labor	6.00	
Variable manufacturing overhead	8.00	
Selling	5.00	(29.00)
Contribution margin		$11.00

The net sales volume variance is computed as follows:

$$\textbf{Net sales volume variance} = (11{,}000 - 10{,}000) \times \$11.00$$
$$= \$11{,}000 \textbf{ F}$$

As a profit center, the sales department has responsibility for the sales price variance, the net sales volume variance, and any cost variances associated with its operations. As shown in Exhibit 23.3, the sales department variances, as a profit center, net to $15,000 unfavorable:

Exhibit 23.3 ■ Sales Department Profit Center Performance Report
TUMI **Sales Department Profit Center Performance Report** **For Month of July**

Sales price variance.	$16,500 U
Net sales volume variance	11,000 F
Selling expense variance	9,500 U
Sales Department variances, net	$15,000 U

In an attempt to improve their overall performance, managers often commit themselves to unfavorable variances in some areas, believing that these variances will be more than offset by favorable variances in other areas. When the sales department is evaluated as a revenue center, the favorable sales volume variance more than offsets the price reductions and the higher selling expenses. The more complete evaluation of the sales department as a profit center (with a $15,000 unfavorable variance) gives a very different impression than the evaluation of the sales department as a pure revenue center (with a $23,500 favorable variance) or as a revenue center responsible only for its own direct costs with net favorable variances of $14,000, computed as $23,500 F minus $9,500 U. The performance reports of all the organization's responsibility centers are summarized to reconcile budgeted and actual income in Appendix 23B.

Review 23-6 LO6

Sales Variances Presented is information pertaining to an item sold by Winding Creek General Store:

	Actual	Budget
Unit sales	150	125
Unit selling price.	$26	$25
Unit standard variable costs	(20)	(20)
Unit contribution margin	$ 6	$ 5
Revenues	$3,900	$3,125
Standard variable costs	(3,000)	(2,500)
Contribution margin at standard costs	$ 900	$ 625

Required

Solution on p. 23-40.   Compute the revenue, sales price, and the sales volume variances.

Appendix 23A: Fixed Overhead Variances

eLectures **LO7**
Formulate and interpret fixed overhead cost variances.

By definition, the quantity of goods and services purchased by fixed expenditures is not expected to change in proportion to short-run changes in the level of production. For example, in the short run, the production level does not affect the amount of depreciation on buildings, the number of fixed salaried employees, or the amount of real property subject to property taxes.

Even though the components of fixed overhead are not expected to be affected by the production activity level in the short run, the actual amount spent for fixed overhead items can differ from the amount budgeted. For example, higher than budgeted supervisors' salaries could be paid, insurance premiums may increase unexpectedly, and price increases could cause the amounts paid for equipment to be higher than expected. Fixed overhead costs in excess of the amount budgeted are reflected in the fixed overhead budget variance. Tumi's fixed overhead budget variance was previously determined as

Fixed overhead budget variance = Actual fixed overhead − Budgeted fixed overhead

= $53,000 − $52,000

= $1,000 U

The fixed overhead budget variance is always the same as the total fixed overhead flexible budget variance. Because budgeted fixed overhead is the same for all outputs within the relevant range, the budget variance explains the total flexible budget variance between actual and allowed fixed overhead.

Recall that predetermined overhead rates are computed by dividing the predicted overhead costs for the period by the predicted activity of the period. The motivation for using a standard fixed overhead rate is the same as the motivation for using a predetermined overhead rate; namely, quicker product costing and assigning identical fixed costs to identical products, regardless of when they are produced during the year.

When a standard fixed overhead rate is used, total fixed overhead costs assigned to production behave as variable costs. As production increases, the total fixed overhead assigned to production increases. Because total budgeted fixed overhead does not vary, differences arise between budgeted and assigned fixed overhead, and managers often inquire about the cause of the differences.

The standard fixed overhead rate is computed as the budgeted fixed costs divided by some budgeted standard level of activity. Assume Tumi applies fixed manufacturing overhead on the basis of machine hours and that 0.40 machine hours are allowed to produce one computer bag. Further assume that the budgeted production is 10,000 computer bags per month, a level that allows 4,000 (10,000 × 0.40) machine hours. The standard fixed overhead rate per machine hour is $13.

Standard fixed overhead rate = Budgeted total fixed overhead ÷ Budgeted activity level

= $52,000 ÷ 4,000 hours

= $13 per machine hour

The total fixed overhead assigned to production is computed as the standard rate of $13 multiplied by the standard hours allowed for the units produced. Note that assigned fixed overhead cost equals budgeted fixed overhead only if the allowed activity equals the budgeted activity of 4,000 hours. If less than 4,000 hours are allowed, the fixed overhead assigned to production is less than the $52,000 budgeted; if more than 4,000 hours are allowed, the fixed overhead assigned to production is more than the amount budgeted.

Even though budgeted fixed overhead is not affected by production below or above 4,000 hours, the fixed overhead assigned to production increases at the rate of $13 per allowed machine hour. The difference between budgeted fixed overhead and fixed overhead assigned to production is called the **fixed overhead volume variance**. This variance is sometimes referred to as the **capacity variance**, a term that emphasizes the maximum output of an operation. The fixed overhead volume variance indicates neither good nor poor performance. Instead, it indicates the difference between the activity allowed for the actual output and the budget level used as the denominator in computing the standard fixed overhead rate.

To explain the difference between actual fixed overhead and fixed overhead assigned to production, two fixed overhead variances are computed: the fixed overhead budget variance and the fixed overhead volume variance. As previously explained, the fixed overhead budget variance represents the difference between actual fixed overhead and budgeted fixed overhead. The fixed overhead budget variance is caused by a combination of price and quantity factors related to the use of fixed overhead goods and services (e.g., depreciation, insurance, supervisors' salaries). The $1,000 unfavorable budget variance for Tumi was caused either by using higher quantities of fixed overhead goods and services, or by paying higher prices than expected for those items, or both.

The fixed overhead volume variance represents the difference between budgeted and assigned fixed overhead and is caused by a difference between the activity level allowed for the actual output and the budgeted activity used in computing the fixed overhead rate. Suppose for Tumi, actual July output of 11,000 bags resulted in 4,400 allowed machine hours and applied fixed overhead of $57,200 (11,000 bags × 0.40 hours × $13). The $5,200 favorable fixed overhead volume variance (budgeted costs of $52,000 minus applied costs of $57,200) indicates that the activity level allowed for the actual output was more than the budgeted activity level. As previously stated, this variance ordinarily cannot be used to control costs. If the budgeted activity is based on production capacity, an unfavorable variance alerts management that facilities are underutilized, and a favorable variance alerts management that facilities are utilized above their expectations. A summary standard cost variance analysis for fixed costs is shown on the following page.

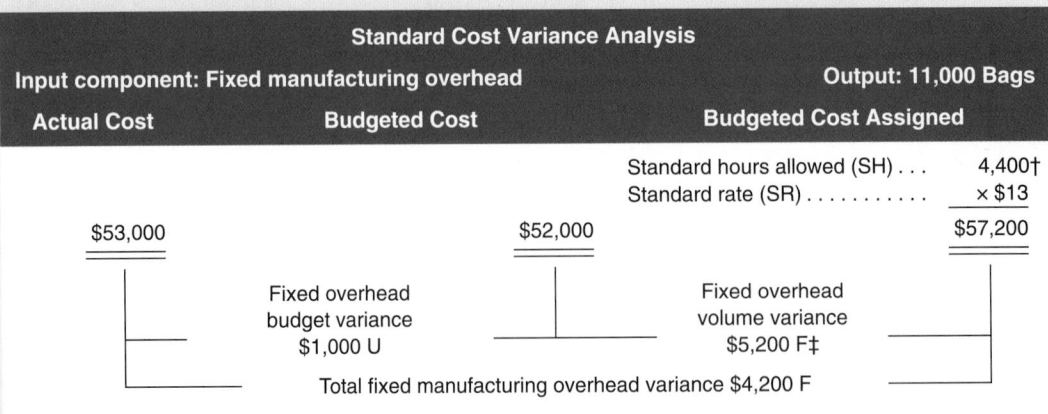

Standard Cost Variance Analysis		
Input component: Fixed manufacturing overhead		**Output: 11,000 Bags**
Actual Cost	**Budgeted Cost**	**Budgeted Cost Assigned**

		Standard hours allowed (SH) . . .	4,400†
		Standard rate (SR)	× $13
$53,000	$52,000		$57,200

Fixed overhead
budget variance
$1,000 U

Fixed overhead
volume variance
$5,200 F‡

Total fixed manufacturing overhead variance $4,200 F

†11,000 bags × 0.40
‡ Also computed as: (4,400 allowed hours – 4,000 budget hours) × $13 standard rate per hour

Review 23-7 LO7

Assume that Marathon Oil uses a standard cost system for each of its refineries. For the Texas City refinery, the monthly fixed overhead budget is $6,000,000 for a planned output of 2,000,000 barrels. For September, the actual fixed cost was $6,250,000 for 2,100,000 barrels.

Required
a. Determine the fixed overhead budget variance.
b. If fixed overhead is applied on a per-barrel basis, determine the volume variance.

Solution on p. 23-40.

Appendix 23B: Reconciling Budgeted and Actual Income

LO8
Reconcile
budgeted
and actual
income.

Using a contribution format, it is possible to reconcile the difference between budgeted and actual net income for an entire organization. This is done by assigning all costs and revenues to responsibility centers and summarizing the financial performance of each responsibility center. Tumi's budgeted and actual income statements, in a contribution format, for July are presented in Exhibit 23B.1.

Exhibit 23B.1 ■ Budgeted and Actual Income Statements: Contribution Format		
TUMI **Budgeted Income Statement** **For Month of July**		
Sales (10,000 bags × $40)		$400,000
Less variable costs		
Variable cost of goods sold		
Direct materials (10,000 bags × $10) $100,000		
Direct labor (10,000 bags × $6). 60,000		
Manufacturing overhead (10,000 bags × $8) 80,000	$240,000	
Selling (10,000 bags × $5)	50,000	(290,000)
Contribution margin		110,000
Less fixed costs		
Manufacturing overhead.	52,000	
Selling.	10,000	
Administrative	4,000	(66,000)
Budgeted net income		$ 44,000

continued

continued from previous page

Exhibit 23B.1 ■ Budgeted and Actual Income Statements: Contribution Format—continued

Actual Income Statement
For the Month of July

Sales (11,000 bags × $38.50).			$423,500
Less variable costs			
Variable cost of goods sold			
Direct materials	$108,000		
Direct labor	70,000		
Manufacturing overhead	81,000	$259,000	
Selling		65,000	(324,000)
Contribution margin			99,500
Less fixed costs			
Manufacturing overhead		53,000	
Selling		9,500	
Administrative		3,800	(66,300)
Net income			$ 33,200

We've assumed Tumi contains three responsibility centers: a production department, a sales department, and an administration department. Earlier in the module, we discussed both the production and the sales department variances. The sales department's variances in Exhibit 23.3 net to $15,000 U and the production department's variances in Exhibit 23.1 net to $4,000 F. Next, we assume that the administration department had a budgeted amount of $4,000 while the actual amount spent was $3,800. Because the administration department is a discretionary cost center, this variance of $200 ($3,800 actual – $4,000 budget) is best identified as being under budget. For consistency in the performance reports, however, it is labeled favorable. By assigning all variances to these three responsibility centers, the reconciliation of budgeted and actual income is as shown in Exhibit 23B.2.

Exhibit 23B.2 ■ Reconciliation of Budgeted and Actual Income

TUMI
Reconciliation of Budgeted and Actual Income
For Month of July

Budgeted net income	$44,000
Sales department variances (Exhibit 23.3)	15,000 U
Production department variances (Exhibit 23.1)	4,000 F
Administration department variances ($3,800 actual – $4,000 budgeted)	200 F
Actual net income	$33,200

LO8 Review 23-8

Midstate Supply Company has three responsibility centers: sales, production, and administration. The following information pertains to the November activities of Midstate Supply:

Budgeted contribution income	$18,000
Actual contribution income	27,000
Sales price variance	24,000 F
Sales volume variance	40,000 F
Net sales volume variance	6,000 F
Sales department variable expense variance	18,000 U
Sales department fixed expense variance	1,500 U
Administration department variances	500 F
Production department variances	2,000 U

Required

Prepare a reconciliation of budgeted and actual contribution income.

Solution on p. 23-40.

Guidance Answers

You Are the Vice President of Manufacturing

Pg. 23-17 It appears that direct labor hours may no longer be a reliable basis for budgeting variable overhead in your company. If actual variable overhead costs do not appear to correlate closely with direct labor hours, this could be an indication that the components of variable overhead have changed since direct labor hours was selected as the cost driver. Your cost accountants should consider other unit-level cost drivers for budgeting variable overhead costs. However, an activity-based costing method using multiple overhead cost pools with separate cost drivers might provide a more reliable basis for budgeting and controlling variable overhead costs.

Questions

Q23-1. What is responsibility accounting? Why should noncontrollable costs be excluded from performance reports prepared in accordance with responsibility accounting?

Q23-2. How can responsibility accounting lead to unethical practices?

Q23-3. Responsibility accounting reports must be expanded to include what nonfinancial areas? Give some examples of nonfinancial measures.

Q23-4. What is a cost center? Give some examples.

Q23-5. How is a cost center different from either an investment or a profit center?

Q23-6. What problems can result from the use of tight standards?

Q23-7. What is a standard cost variance, and what is the objective of variance analysis?

Q23-8. Standard cost variances can usually be broken down into two basic types of variances. Identify and describe these two types of variances.

Q23-9. Identify possible causes for (1) a favorable materials price variance; (2) an unfavorable materials price variance; (3) a favorable materials quantity variance; and (4) an unfavorable materials quantity variance.

Q23-10. How is standard labor time determined? Explain the two ways.

Q23-11. In the standard cost system, what is the appropriate treatment of a change in wage rates (per new labor union contract) that dominate the cost of labor?

Q23-12. Explain the difference between the revenue variance and the sales price variance.

Q23-13. Explain the net sales volume variance and list its components.

Q23-14. Explain the difference between how the *actual costs* and the *standard cost of actual inputs* are computed in variable overhead analysis.

Q23-15. Explain what the net sales volume variance measures.

Assignments with the ⓜ logo in the margin are available in BusinessCourse.
See the Preface of the book for details.

Mini Exercises

LO2   M23-16.   Flexible Budgets and Performance Evaluation

Presented is the January performance report for the Production Department of Nowwhat Company.

NOWWHAT COMPANY Production Department Performance Report For Month of January		
	Actual	**Budget**
Volume	50,000	46,000
Manufacturing costs		
Direct materials.	$130,500	$124,200
Direct labor	118,000	105,800
Variable overhead.	72,000	69,000
Fixed overhead.	252,000	250,000
Total	$572,500	$549,000

Required

a. Evaluate the performance report.

b. Prepare a more appropriate performance report. *Hint:* Start by determining the standard unit costs.

M23-17. Materials Variances

Dark Wind manufactures decorative weather vanes that have a standard materials cost of three pounds of raw materials at $4.00 per pound. During September 17,500 pounds of raw materials costing $4.25 per pound were used in making 6,000 weather vanes.

Required

Determine the materials price and quantity variances.

M23-18. Materials Variances

Assume that Pearle Vision uses standard costs to control the materials in its made-to-order sunglasses. The standards call for 3 ounces of material for each pair of lenses. The standard cost per ounce of material is $12. During July, the Santa Clara location produced 6,000 pairs of sunglasses and used 17,750 ounces of materials. The cost of the materials during July was $12.25 per ounce, and there were no beginning or ending inventories.

Required

a. Determine the flexible budget materials cost for the completion of the 6,000 pairs of glasses.

b. Determine the actual materials cost incurred for the completion of the 6,000 pairs of glasses and compute the total materials variance.

c. How much of the total variance was related to the price paid to purchase the materials?

d. How much of the difference between the answers to requirements (a) and (b) was related to the quantity of materials used?

M23-19. Direct Labor Variances

Advanced Micro Devices develops high-performing computing products. Assume one of its processors, Ryzen 7 Pro, has a standard labor time of 0.25 hours and a standard labor rate of $20 per hour. During February, the following activities pertaining to direct labor for Ryzen 7 Pro were recorded:

Direct labor hours used	64,000
Direct labor cost	$1,248,000
Units of Ryzen 7 Pro manufactured	250,000

Required

a. Determine the labor rate variance.

b. Determine the labor efficiency variance.

c. Determine the total flexible budget labor cost variance.

M23-20. Significance of Direct Labor Variances

The Tomorrow Company's April budget called for labor costs of $192,000. Because the actual labor costs were exactly $192,000, management concluded there were no labor variances.

Required

Comment on management's conclusion.

M23-21. Variable Overhead Variances

Assume that the best cost driver that Sony has for variable factory overhead in the assembly department is machine hours. During April, the company budgeted 585,000 machine hours and $4,972,500 for its Texas plant's assembly department. The actual variable overhead incurred was $5,002,500, which was related to 575,000 machine hours.

Required

a. Determine the variable overhead spending variance.

b. Determine the variable overhead efficiency variance.

M23-22. Sales Variances

Presented is information pertaining to an item sold by Wheeping Creek General Store:

	Actual	Budget
Unit sales	650	600
Unit selling price	$38	$40
Unit variable costs	31	32
Unit contribution margin	$7	$8
Revenues	$24,700	$24,000
Variable costs	20,150	19,200
Contribution margin at standard costs	$4,550	$4,800

Required

Compute the revenue, sales price, and the sales volume variances.

LO7

ExxonMobil (XOM)

M23-23. **Fixed Overhead Variances**

Assume that ExxonMobil uses a standard cost system for each of its refineries. For the Houston refinery, the monthly fixed overhead budget is $9,900,000 for a planned output of 6,000,000 barrels. For September, the actual fixed cost was $10,115,000 for 5,950,000 barrels.

Required

a. Determine the fixed overhead budget variance.
b. If fixed overhead is applied on a per-barrel basis, determine the volume variance.

LO8 **M23-24.** **Reconciling Budgeted and Actual Income**

Black Supply Company has three responsibility centers: sales, production, and administration. The following information pertains to the November activities of Black Supply:

Budgeted contribution income	$35,000
Actual contribution income	39,400
Sales price variance	13,000 U
Sales volume variance	15,000 F
Net sales volume variance	6,000 F
Sales department variable expense variance	2,600 U
Sales department fixed expense variance	500 F
Administration department variances	2,000 F
Production department variances	11,500 F

Required

Prepare a reconciliation of budgeted and actual contribution income.

Exercises

LO2 **E23-25.** **Elements of a Flexible Budget**

Presented are partial flexible cost budgets for various levels of output.

	Rate per Unit	Units		
		5,000	7,500	10,000
Direct materials	a.	$20,000	b.	c.
Direct labor	d.	e.	11,250	f.
Variable overhead	$2	g.	h.	i.
Fixed overhead		j.	k.	l.
Total		m.	n.	$140,000

Required

Solve for items "a" though "n."

E23-26. Elements of Labor and Variable Overhead Variances

LO4, 5

Chelsea Fabricating applies variable overhead to products on the basis of standard direct labor hours. Presented is selected information for last month when 25,000 units were produced.

	Direct Labor	Variable Overhead
Actual cost	a.	f.
Standard hours/unit	b.	b.
Actual hours (total)	12,000	12,000
Standard rate/hour	$25.00	$15.00
Actual rate	$25.50	
Flexible budget	$312,500	$187,500
Labor rate or variable overhead spending variance . . .	c.	g.
Efficiency variances	d.	h.
Total flexible budget variance	e.	$5,000 U

Required

Solve for items "a" through "h."

E23-27. Causes of Standard Cost Variances (Comprehensive)

LO3, 4, 5

Following are 10 unrelated situations that would ordinarily be expected to affect one or more standard cost variances:

1. A salaried production supervisor is given a raise, but no adjustment is made in the labor cost standards.
2. The materials purchasing manager gets a special reduced price on raw materials by purchasing a train carload. A warehouse had to be rented to accommodate the unusually large amount of raw materials. The rental fee was charged to Rent Expense, a fixed overhead item.
3. An unusually hot August caused the company to use 30,000 kilowatts more electricity than provided for in the variable overhead standards.
4. The local electric utility company raised the charge per kilowatt-hour. No adjustment was made in the variable overhead standards.
5. The plant manager traded in his leased company car for a new one in July, increasing the monthly lease payment by $85.
6. A machine malfunction on the assembly line (caused by using cheap and inferior raw materials) resulted in decreased output by the machine operator and higher than normal machine repair costs. Repairs are treated as variable overhead costs.
7. Two assembly workers retired after 20 years on the job. They were replaced by two young apprentices.
8. An announcement that vacation benefits had been increased resulted in improved employee morale. Consequently, raw materials pilferage and waste declined, and production efficiency increased. Employee benefits are charged to overhead.
9. The plant manager reclassified her secretary to administrative assistant and gave him an increase in salary.
10. A union contract agreement calling for an immediate 4% increase in production worker wages was signed. No changes were made in the standards.

Required

For each of these situations, indicate by letter which of the following standard cost variances would be affected. More than one variance will be affected in some cases.

a. Materials price variance.
b. Materials quantity variance.
c. Labor rate variance.
d. Labor efficiency variance.
e. Variable overhead spending variance.
f. Variable overhead efficiency variance.
g. Fixed overhead budget variance.

E23-28. Sales Variances

LO6

Casio Computer
Company, LTD.

Assume that **Casio Computer Company, LTD.** sells G-Shock for $50 during August as a back-to-school special. The normal selling price is $100. The standard variable cost for each device is $35.

Sales for August had been budgeted for 500,000 units nationwide; however, due to the uptick in the economy, sales came in at 525,000.

Required

Compute the revenue, sales price, sales volume, and net sales volume variances. *Hint:* Compute the variances using the normal selling price as the standard.

LO7   E23-29.   Fixed Overhead Variances

Petra Company uses standard costs for cost control and internal reporting. Fixed costs are budgeted at $125,000 per month at a normal operating level of 25,000 units of production output. During October, actual fixed costs were $122,000, and actual production output was 24,000 units.

Required

a. Determine the fixed overhead budget variance.
b. Assume that the company applied fixed overhead to production on a per-unit basis. Determine the fixed overhead volume variance.
c. Was the fixed overhead budget variance from requirement (*a*) affected because the company operated below the normal activity level of 25,000 units? Explain.
d. Explain the possible causes for the volume variance computed in requirement (*b*). How is reporting of the volume variance useful to management?

Problems

LO2   P23-30.   Multiple Product Performance Report

Case Products manufactures two models of DVD storage cases: regular and deluxe. Presented is standard cost information for each model:

Cost Components	Regular		Deluxe	
Direct materials				
Acrylic sheets	3 sheets × $12 =	$36.00	5 sheets × $12 =	$60.00
Assembly kit	=	5.00	=	5.00
Direct labor.	0.5 hour × $20 =	10.00	0.75 hours × $20 =	15.00
Variable overhead	0.5 labor hr. × $5 =	2.50	0.75 labor hrs. × $5 =	3.75
Total		$53.50		$83.75

Budgeted fixed manufacturing overhead is $46,000 per month. During July, the company produced 8,000 regular and 3,500 deluxe storage cases while incurring the following manufacturing costs:

Direct materials.	$561,300
Direct labor.	130,800
Variable overhead	34,625
Fixed overhead.	48,150
Total	$774,875

Required

Prepare a flexible budget performance report for the July manufacturing activities.

LO3, 4   P23-31.   Computation of Variable Cost Variances

The following information pertains to the standard costs and actual activity for Repine Company for September:

Standard cost per unit	
Direct materials.	3 units of material A × $8.00 per unit
	2 units of material B × $4.00 per unit
Direct labor	2 hours × $15.00 per hour
Activity for September	
Materials purchased	
Material A	7,000 units × $7.80 per unit
Material B	4,800 units × $4.50 per unit

continued

continued from previous page

Materials used
Material A	6,430 units
Material B	3,950 units
Direct labor used.	4,100 hours × $15.50 per hour
Production output	2,000 units

There were no beginning direct materials inventories.

Required

a. Determine the materials price and quantity variances.

b. Determine the labor rate and efficiency variances.

P23-32.   **Variance Computations and Explanations**

Tarptent manufactures camping tents from a lightweight synthetic fabric. Assume the company's two-person tent has a standard materials cost of $60, consisting of 4 yards of fabric at $15 per yard. The standards call for 1.5 hours of assembly at $20 per hour. The following data were recorded for October, the first month of operations:

Fabric purchased	6,500 yards × $14.50 per yard
Fabric used in production of 1,200 tents	4,850 yards
Direct labor used	1,850 hours × $19.50 per hour

Required

a. Compute all standard cost variances for materials and labor.

b. Give one possible reason for each of the preceding variances.

c. Determine the standard variable cost of the 1,200 tents produced, separated into direct materials and labor.

LO3, 4
Tarptent

P23-33.   **Determining Unit Costs, Variance Analysis, and Interpretation**

Nestlé, manufacturer of Purina Dog Chow, produces its product in 500-bag batches. Assume the standard batch consists of 10,000 pounds of direct materials at $0.25 per pound, 16 direct labor hours at $15 per hour, and variable overhead cost (based on machine hours) at the rate of $20 per hour with 10 machine hours per batch. The following variable costs were incurred for the last 500-bag batch produced:

Direct materials.	10,250 pounds costing $2,255 were purchased and used
Direct labor	15 hours costing $231
Variable overhead	$215
Machine hours used	9.5 hours

LO3, 4, 5
Nestlé (NESN)

Required

a. Determine the actual and standard variable costs per bag of dog food produced, separated into direct materials, direct labor, and variable overhead.

b. For the last 500-bag batch, determine the standard cost variances for direct materials, direct labor, and variable overhead.

c. Explain the possible causes for each of the variances determined in requirement (*b*).

P23-34.   **Computation of Variances and Other Missing Data**

The following data for Bernie Company pertain to the production of 1,000 units of Product X during December. Selected data items are omitted.

LO3, 4, 5

Direct materials (all materials purchased were used during period)
    Standard cost per unit: (a) pounds at $3.20 per pound
    Total actual cost: (b) pounds costing $10,626
    Standard cost allowed for units produced: $9,600
    Materials price variance: (c)
    Materials quantity variance: $704 U

continued

continued from previous page

Direct labor
   Standard cost: 2.5 hours at $12.00
   Actual cost per hour: $12.25
   Total actual cost: (d)
   Labor rate variance: (e)
   Labor efficiency variance: $144 F
Variable overhead
   Standard costs: (f) hours at $4.00 per direct labor hour
   Actual cost: $10,600
   Variable overhead spending variance: (g)
   Variable overhead efficiency variance: (h)

Required

Complete the missing amounts lettered (a) through (h).

LO2, 3, 4, 5   P23-35.   **Flexible Budgets and Performance Evaluation**

Kathy Vanderbosch, supervisor of housecleaning for Hotel Valhalla, was surprised by her summary performance report for March given below.

HOTEL VALHALLA Housekeeping Performance Report For the Month of March			
Actual	**Budget**	**Variance**	**%Variance**
$260,708	$252,000	$8,708 U	3.456% U

Kathy was disappointed. She thought she had done a good job controlling housekeeping labor and towel usage, but her performance report revealed an unfavorable variance of $8,708. She had been hoping for a bonus for her good work, but now expected a series of questions from her manager.

The cost budget for housekeeping is based on standard costs. At the beginning of a month, Kathy receives a report from Hotel Valhalla's Sales Department outlining the planned room activity for the month. Kathy then schedules labor and purchases using this information. The budget for the housekeeping was based on 8,000 room nights. Each room night is budgeted based on the following standards for various materials, labor, and overhead:

Shower supplies.........................	4 bottles @ $0.50 each
Towels*................................	1 @ $4.00
Laundry................................	8 lbs. @ $0.25 a lb.
Labor	¾ hour @ $15.00 an hour
VOH	$3.00 per labor hour
FOH	$10 a room night (based on 8,000 room nights)

*Replacements for towels evaluated by housekeeping as inappropriate for cleaning and reuse.

With 8,600 room nights sold, actual costs and usage for housekeeping during April were

$14,620 for 36,550 bottles of shower supplies.
$32,121 for 7,740 towels.
$20,898 for 69,660 lbs. of laundry.
$91,504 for 6,020 labor hours.
$19,565 in total VOH.
$82,000 in FOH.

Required

a. Develop a complete budget column for the above performance report presented to Kathy. Break it down by expense category. The following format, with additional lines for expense categories, is suggested:

Account	Actual	Budget	Variance
Shower Supplies.	$ 14,620	?	?
⋮	⋮	⋮	⋮
Total	$260,708	$252,000	$8,708 U

b. Evaluate the usefulness of the cost center performance report presented to Kathy.

c. Prepare a more logical performance report where standard allowed is based on actual output. Also, split each variance into its price/rate/spending and quantity/efficiency components (except fixed of course). The following format, with additional lines for expense categories, is suggested:

Account	Actual	Flexible Budget	Total Variance	Price/Rate/ Spending Variance	Quantity/ Efficiency Variance
Shower Supplies.	$ 14,620	?	?	?	?
⋮	⋮				
Total	$260,708	?	?		

d. Explain to Kathy's boss what your report suggests about Kathy's department performance.

e. Identify additional nonfinancial performance measures management might consider when evaluating the performance of the housekeeping department and Kathy as a manager.

P23-36. Flexible Budget Performance Evaluation with Process Costing   LO2, 3, 4, 5

The Evanston Company produces a single product on a continuous basis. During January, 2,000 units were completed. The July 31 ending work-in-process inventory contained 500 units, 50% complete as to materials and 25% complete as to conversion.

Evanston uses standard costs for planning and control. The following standard costs are based on a monthly volume of 2,000 equivalent units with fixed budgeted at $80,450 per month.

Direct materials [(3 square meters per unit × $12.00 per meter) × 2,000]	$72,000
Direct labor [(2 hours per unit × $22.00 per hour) × 2,000]	88,000
Variable overhead [(2 hours per unit × $5.00 per hour) × 2,000]	20,000
Fixed manufacturing overhead.	80,450

Actual July production costs were

Direct materials.	$ 80,525
Direct labor.	95,250
Manufacturing overhead.	101,165

Required

a. Determine the equivalent units of materials and conversion manufactured during July using the weighted average method.

b. Based on the July equivalent units of materials and conversion, prepare a July performance report for the Evanston Company. *Hint:* Combine variable and fixed manufacturing overhead data in the report.

c. Explain the treatment of overhead in the July performance report.

P23-37. Measuring the Effects of Decisions on Standard Cost Variances (Comprehensive)   LO3, 4, 5

The following five unrelated situations affect one or more standard cost variances for materials, labor (assembly), and overhead:

1. Sally Smith, a production worker, announced her intent to resign to accept another job paying $1.75 more per hour. To keep Sally, the production manager agreed to raise her salary from $12 to $14 per hour. Sally works an average of 175 regular hours per month.

2. At the beginning of the month, a supplier of a component used in our product notified us that, because of a minor design improvement, the price will be increased by 10% above the current standard price of $125 per unit. As a result of the improved design, we expect the number of defective components to decrease by 50 units per month. On average, 1,200 units of the component are purchased each month. Defective units are identified prior to use and are not returnable.

3. In an effort to meet a deadline on a rush order in Department A, the plant manager reassigned several higher-skilled workers from Department B, for a total of 360 labor hours. The average salary of the Department B workers was $2.15 more than the standard $11.00 per hour rate of the Department A workers. Since they were not accustomed to the work, the average Department B worker was able to produce only 24 units per hour instead of the standard 36 units per hour. (Consider only the effect on Department A labor variances.)

4. Robbie Wallace is an inspector who earns a base salary of $2,000 per month plus a piece rate of 40 cents per bundle inspected. His company accounts for inspection costs as manufacturing overhead. Because of a payroll department error in June, Robbie was paid $1,500 plus a piece rate of 60 cents per bundle. He received gross wages totaling $2,100. *Hints:* Robbie's compensation has both fixed and variable components.

5. The materials purchasing manager purchased 5,000 units of component K2X from a new source at a price $20 below the standard unit price of $200. These components turned out to be of extremely poor quality with defects occurring at three times the standard rate of 6%. The higher rate of defects reduced the output of workers (who earn $12 per hour) from 20 units per hour to 16 units per hour on the units containing the discount components. Each finished unit contains one K2X component. To appease the workers (who were irate at having to work with inferior components), the production manager agreed to pay the workers an additional $0.50 for each of the components (good and bad) in the discount batch. Variable manufacturing overhead is applied at the rate of $6.00 per direct labor hour. The defective units also caused a 25-hour increase in total machine hours. The actual cost of electricity to run the machines is $2.00 per hour.

Required

For each of the preceding situations, determine which standard cost variance(s) will be affected, and compute the amount of the effect for one month on each variance. Indicate whether the effect is favorable or unfavorable. Assume that the standards are not changed in response to these situations. (Round calculations to two decimal places.)

LO7   P23-38.   Fixed Overhead Budget and Volume Variance

Four-Leaf Clover Company assigns fixed overhead costs to inventory for external reporting purposes by using a predetermined standard overhead rate based on direct labor hours. The standard rate is based on a normal activity level of 30,000 standard allowed direct labor hours per year. There are five standard allowed hours for each unit of output. Budgeted fixed overhead costs are $420,000 per year. During the prior year, the company produced 5,800 units of output, and actual fixed costs were $425,000.

Required

a. Determine the standard fixed overhead rate used to assign fixed costs to inventory.
b. Determine the amount of fixed overhead assigned to inventory during the year.
c. Determine the fixed overhead budget variance.

LO6, 8   P23-39.   Profit Center Performance Report

Bach Tunes is a classical music retailer specializing in the Internet sale of MP3 albums of the works of J. S. Bach. Although prices vary with album popularity and file sizes, the albums sell for an average of $12 each and Bach Tunes pays a fixed royalty of $5.75 per MP3 album. With the exception of royalty fees, the operating costs of Bach Tunes are fixed. Presented are budgeted and actual income statements for the month of September.

BACH TUNES Budgeted and Actual Contribution Statements For Month of September		
	Actual	**Budget**
Unit sales	7,500	8,000
Unit selling price	$12.50	$12.00
Sales revenue.	$93,750	$96,000
Cost of goods sold	(43,125)	(46,000)
Gross profit.	50,625	50,000
Operating costs	(34,700)	(35,000)
Contribution to corporate costs and profits.	$15,925	$15,000

Required

Compute variances to assist in evaluating the performance of Bach Tunes as a profit center. What was the likely cause of the shortfall in sales revenue?

P23-40. Profit Center Performance Report

Falafel, Inc. operates fast-food restaurants in Washington, DC. Its main product is a serving of falafel that requires ground chick peas (direct material) and food preparation (direct labor). Assume the April budget for Falafel Inc.'s Georgetown restaurant was

LO2, 3, 4, 5, 6, 7, 8

Falafel, Inc.

- Sales 24,000 servings at $4.25 each
- Standard food cost of $0.50 per serving (1/4 pound @ $2.00 per pound)
- Standard direct labor of $0.60 per serving (1/25th hour @ $15.00 per hour)
- Fixed occupancy expenses (equipment and rent) of $7,500

Actual April performance of the Georgetown restaurant was

- Sales 26,000 servings at $4.50 each
- Food cost of $14,820 for 7,800 pounds
- Direct labor cost of $19,240 for 1,300 hours
- Fixed occupancy expenses of $7,200

In early May, the manager received the following financial performance report:

FALAFEL, INC.—GEORGETOWN Performance Report For the Month of April			
	Actual	**Budgeted**	**Variance**
Revenues.	$117,000	$102,000	$15,000 F
Food Cost.	(14,820)	(12,000)	2,820 U
Labor Cost	(19,240)	(14,400)	4,840 U
Occupancy	(7,200)	(7,500)	300 F
Profit.	$ 75,740	$ 68,100	$ 7,640 F

Required

a. Partition variance into variances for 1) selling price and net sales volume, 2) food variances for price and quantity, and 3) labor variances for rate and efficiency.

b. Using the results of your analysis, prepare an alternative reconciliation of budgeted and actual profit. Be sure to include the occupancy variance.

c. Explain why the total variances for sales, food, and labor in your reconciliation differ from those originally presented to the restaurant manager.

P23-41. Comprehensive Performance Report

Instant Computing is a contract manufacturer of laptop computers sold under brand named companies. Presented are Instant's budgeted and actual contribution income statements for October. The company has three responsibility centers: Production, Selling and Distribution, and Administration. Production and Administration are cost centers while Selling and Distribution is a profit center.

LO2, 3, 4, 5, 6, 7, 8

INSTANT COMPUTING Budgeted Contribution Income Statement For Month of October		
Sales (2,000 × $400)		$800,000
Less variable costs		
Variable cost of goods sold		
Direct materials (2,000 × $60).	$120,000	
Direct labor (2,000 × $40)	80,000	
Manufacturing overhead (2,000 × $20).	40,000	$240,000
Selling and Distribution (2,000 × $45).		90,000	(330,000)
Contribution margin		470,000

continued

continued from previous page

INSTANT COMPUTING Budgeted Contribution Income Statement For Month of October		
Less fixed costs		
Manufacturing overhead..............................	160,000	
Administrative..	125,000	
Selling and Distribution.............................	75,000	(360,000)
Net income..		$110,000

INSTANT COMPUTING Actual Contribution Income Statement For Month of October			
Sales (2,250 × $385)................................			$866,250
Less variable costs			
Cost of goods sold			
Direct materials.................................	$139,500		
Direct labor....................................	85,500		
Manufacturing overhead.........................	43,875	$268,875	
Selling and Distribution............................		105,750	(374,625)
Contribution margin................................			491,625
Less fixed costs			
Manufacturing overhead...........................		168,000	
Administrative....................................		135,000	
Selling and Distribution...........................		74,600	(377,600)
Net income (loss).................................			$114,025

Required
a. Prepare a performance report for Production that compares actual and allowed costs.
b. Prepare a performance report for Selling and Distribution that compares actual and allowed costs.
c. Determine the sales price and the net sales volume variances.
d. Prepare a report that summarizes the performance of Selling and Distribution.
e. Determine the amount by which Administration was over or under budget.
f. Prepare a report reconciling budgeted and actual net income. Your report should focus on the performance of each responsibility center.

Management Applications

LO1   **MA23-42. Discretionary Cost Center Performance Reports**

TruckMax had been extremely profitable, but the company has been hurt in recent years by competition and a failure to introduce new consumer products. Three years ago, Tom Lopez became head of Consumer Products Research (CPR) and began a number of product development projects. Under his leadership the group had good ideas that led to the introduction of several promising products. Nevertheless, when financial results for Lopez's second year were reviewed, CPR's report revealed large unfavorable variances leading management to criticize Lopez for poor cost control. Management was quite concerned about cost control because profits were low, and the company's cash budget indicated that additional borrowing would be required to cover out-of-pocket costs. Because of his inability to exert proper cost control, Lopez was relieved of his responsibilities last year, and Gabriella Garcia became head of Consumer Products Research. Garcia vowed to improve the performance of CPR and scaled back CPR's development activities to obtain favorable financial performance reports.

By the end of this year, the company had improved its market position, profitability, and cash position. At this time, the board of directors promoted Garcia to president, congratulating her for the contribution CPR made to the revitalization of the company, as well as her success in improving the financial performance of CPR. Garcia assured the board that the company's financial performance would improve even more in the future as she applied the same cost-reducing measures that had worked so well in CPR to the company as a whole.

Required

a. For the purpose of evaluating financial performance, what responsibility center classification should be given to the Consumer Products Research Department? What unique problems are associated with evaluating the financial performance of this type of responsibility center?

b. Compare the performances of Lopez and Garcia in the role as head of Consumer Products Research. Did Garcia do a much better job, thereby making her deserving of the promotion? Why or why not?

MA23-43. Developing Cost Standards for Materials and Labor   **LO2**

After several years of operating without a formal system of cost control, DeWalt Company, a tools manufacturer, has decided to implement a standard cost system. The system will first be established for the department that makes lug wrenches for automobile mechanics. The standard production batch size is 100 wrenches. The actual materials and labor required for eight randomly selected batches from last year's production are as follows:

Batch	Materials Used (in pounds)	Labor Used (in hours)
1	504.0	10.00
2	508.0	9.00
3	506.0	9.00
4	521.0	5.00
5	516.0	8.00
6	518.0	7.00
7	520.0	6.00
8	515.0	8.00
Average	513.5	7.75

Management has obtained the following recommendations concerning what the materials and labor quantity standards should be:

- The manufacturer of the equipment used in making the wrenches advertises in the toolmakers' trade journal that the machine the company uses can produce 100 wrenches with 500 pounds of direct materials and 5 labor hours. Company engineers believe the standards should be based on these facts.
- The accounting department believes more realistic standards would be 505 pounds and 5 hours.
- The production supervisor believes the standards should be 512 pounds and 7.75 hours.
- The production workers argue for standards of 522 pounds and 8 hours.

Required

a. State the arguments for and against each of the recommendations, as well as the probable effects of each recommendation on the quantity variance for materials and labor.

b. Which recommendation provides the best combination of cost control and motivation to the production workers? Explain.

MA23-44. Behavioral Effect of Standard Costs   **LO1, 2, 3, 4, 5**

Merit Inc. has used a standard cost system for evaluating the performance of its responsibility center managers for three years. Top management believes that standard costing has not produced the cost savings or increases in productivity and profits promised by the accounting department. Large unfavorable variances are consistently reported for most cost categories, and employee morale has fallen since the system was installed. To help pinpoint the problem with the system, top management asked for separate evaluations of the system by the plant manager, the controller, and the human resources director. Their responses are summarized here.

Plant Manager—The standards are unrealistic. They assume an ideal work environment that does not allow materials defects or errors by the workers or machines. Consequently, morale has gone down and productivity has declined. Standards should be based on expected actual prices and recent past averages for efficiency. Thus, if we improve over the past, we receive a favorable variance.

Controller—The goal of accounting reports is to measure performance against an absolute standard and the best approximation of that standard is ideal conditions. Cost standards should be comparable to "par" on a golf course. Just as the game of golf uses a handicap system to allow for differences in individual players' skills and scores, it could be necessary for management to interpret variances based on the circumstances that produced the variances. Accordingly, in one case, a given unfavorable variance could represent poor performance; in another case, it could represent good performance. The managers are just going to have to recognize these subtleties in standard cost systems and depend on upper management to be fair.

Human Resources Director—The key to employee productivity is employee satisfaction and a sense of accomplishment. A set of standards that can never be met denies managers of this vital motivator. The current standards would be appropriate in a laboratory with a controlled environment but not in the factory with its many variables. If we are to recapture our old "team spirit," we must give the managers a goal that they can achieve through hard work.

Required

Discuss the behavioral issues involved in Merit Inc.'s standard cost dilemma. Evaluate each of the three responses (pros and cons) and recommend a course of action.

LO8   MA23-45. Evaluating a Companywide Performance Report

Mr. Chandler, the production supervisor, bursts into your office, carrying the company's prior year performance report and thundering, "There is villainy here, sir! And I shall get to the bottom of it. I will not stop searching until I have found the answer! Why is Mr. Richards so down on my department? I thought we did a good job last year. But Richards claims my production people and I cost the company $31,500! I plead with you, sir, explain this performance report to me." Trying to calm Chandler, you take the report from him and ask to be left alone for 15 minutes. The report is as follows:

DICKENS COMPANY, LIMITED Performance Report For the Prior Year			
	Actual	**Budget**	**Variance**
Unit sales	9,000	7,500	
Sales	$526,500	$450,000	$ 76,500 F
Less manufacturing costs			
Direct materials	42,750	37,500	5,250 U
Direct labor	19,350	15,000	4,350 U
Manufacturing overhead	192,100	190,000*	2,100 U
Total	(254,200)	(242,500)	(11,700) U
Gross profit	272,300	207,500	64,800 F
Less selling and administrative expenses			
Selling (all fixed)	52,750	50,000	2,750 U
Administrative (all fixed)	54,785	50,000	4,785 U
Total	(107,535)	(100,000)	(7,535) U
Net income	$164,765	$107,500	$ 57,265 F
Performance summary			
Budgeted net income			$107,500
Sales department variances			
Sales revenue	$ 76,500 F		
Selling expenses	2,750 U	$ 73,750 F	
Administration department variances		4,785 U	
Production department variances		11,700 U	57,265 F
Actual net income			$164,765

*Includes fixed manufacturing overhead of $160,000.

Required

a. Evaluate the performance report. Is Mr. Richards correct, or is there "villainy here"?

b. Assume that the sales department is a profit center and that the production and administration departments are cost centers. Determine the responsibility of each for cost, revenue, and income variances, and prepare a report reconciling budgeted and actual net income. Your report should focus on the performance of each responsibility center.

Solutions to Review Problems

Review 23-1—Solution

There is some discretion as to how each of the reporting units below would be classified by Eli's. However, likely classifications would be as follows:

Bakery—Cost Center: In this case, the bakery is the "manufacturing facility." Typically, a manufacturing facility is a cost center. The bakery is responsible for producing high-quality products in the most cost-effective way possible.

Accounting—Cost Center

Product line/Original Plain Cheesecake—Profit Center: Typically, a product line is a profit center. The product manager of the Original Plain Cheesecake is likely responsible for the revenues, costs, and resulting profits of his or her product line. A product line is not typically an investment center as many of the production assets are shared with other products; therefore, any decisions regarding the overall bakery assets will be made at a higher level in the organization.

Human resources—Cost Center

Cheesecake Café at O'Hare Airport—Investment Center: The Café at O'Hare will have separate assets such as a display case, cash register, and refrigerators. It will be responsible for attractive displays and customer service. So it is likely that the Café will be evaluated based on its target profit per dollar invested.

Review 23-2—Solution

The performance report prepared by the accounting department was based on a "static" budget. A better basis for evaluating your performance is to compare actual performance with a flexible budget. By dividing the budgeted variable costs amounts by 12,000 units, the budgeted unit variable costs amounts can be determined as follows:

Direct materials cost	$360,000 ÷ 12,000 units = $30 per unit
Direct labor	$432,000 ÷ 12,000 units = $36 per unit
Variable factory overhead	$216,000 ÷ 12,000 units = $18 per unit

Using these budgeted unit values, a flexible budget can be prepared as follows:

	Actual	Flexible Budget	Variance
Units	10,000	10,000	
Costs			
Direct materials	$ 299,000	$ 300,000	$ 1,000 F
Direct labor	345,500	360,000	14,500 F
Variable factory overhead	180,000	180,000	
Fixed factory overhead	375,000	360,000	15,000 U
Total plant costs	$1,199,500	$1,200,000	$ 500 F

The plant did not produce the number of units originally budgeted. Therefore, from a cost control standpoint, a flexible budget is a better basis for evaluating performance because it compares the actual cost of producing 10,000 units with a budget also based on 10,000 units. Based on the flexible budget, your performance is still quite good; however, it is much less favorable than it appeared using a static budget.

Review 23-3—Solution

Standard Cost Variance Analysis		
Input component: Direct materials		**Output: 5,000 units**
Actual Cost	**Standard Cost of Actual Inputs**	**Flexible Budget Cost**

Actual quantity (AQ)	21,250	Actual quantity (AQ)	21,250	Standard quantity allowed (SQ)	20,000*
Actual price (AP).	× $4.90	Standard price (SP).	× $5.00	Standard price (SP).	× $5.00
	$104,125		$106,250		$100,000

Materials price variance $2,125 F

Materials quantity variance $6,250 U

Total flexible budget materials variance $4,125 U

*5,000 units × 4 pounds per unit produced

Review 23-4—Solution

Standard Cost Variance Analysis		
Input component: Direct labor		**Output: 5,000 units**
Actual Cost	**Standard Cost of Actual Inputs**	**Flexible Budget Cost**

$82,400	Actual hours (AH).	7,000	Standard hours allowed (SH)	6,250*
	Standard rate (SR)	× $12	Standard rate (SR)	× $12
		$84,000		$75,000

Labor rate variance $1,600 F

Labor efficiency variance $9,000 U

Total flexible budget labor variance $7,400 U

*5,000 units × 1.25 hours per unit

Review 23-5—Solution

Standard Cost Variance Analysis		
Input component: Variable overhead		**Output: 5,000 units**
Actual Costs	**Standard Cost of Actual Inputs**	**Flexible Budget Cost**

Category 1	$31,000	Actual labor hours.	7,000	Standard hours allowed	6,250
Category 2	18,000	Standard rate	× $4.80	Standard rate	× $4.80
Total	$49,000	Driver total.	$33,600	Driver total.	$30,000
		Finished units	5,000	Finished units	5,000
		Standard rate	× $4.00	Standard rate	× $4.00
		Driver total	$20,000	Driver total	$20,000
		Total	$53,600	Total	$50,000

Variable overhead spending variance $4,600 F

Variable overhead efficiency variance $3,600 U

Total flexible budget variable overhead variance $1,000 F

Review 23-6—Solution

Revenue variance	$= (AQ \times AP) - (BQ \times BP)$
	$= (150 \times \$26) - (125 \times \$25)$
	$= \$775$ F
Sales price variance	$= (AP - BP) \times AQ$
	$= (\$26 - \$25) \times 150$
	$= \$150$ F
Sales volume variance	$= (AQ - BQ) \times BP$
	$= (150 - 125) \times \$25$
	$= \$625$ F

Review 23-7—Solution

a.

Actual fixed overhead cost	$6,250,000
Budgeted fixed overhead cost	(6,000,000)
Fixed overhead budget variance	$ 250,000 U

b. Fixed overhead rate = $6,000,000/2,000,000 = $3.00/barrel

Budgeted fixed overhead cost	$6,000,000
Applied fixed overhead (2,100,000 × $3.00 barrels)	(6,300,000)
Volume variance	$ 300,000 F

Review 23-8—Solution

MIDSTATE SUPPLY COMPANY **Reconciliation of Budgeted and Actual Contribution Income** **For the Month of November**		
Budgeted income		$18,000
Sales department variances:		
Sales price variance	$24,000 F	
Net sales volume variance	6,000 F	
Variable expenses	18,000 U	
Fixed expenses	1,500 U	10,500 F
Administration department variances		500 F
Production department variances		2,000 U
Actual income		$27,000

Note: The important point is to leave out the sales volume variance and to properly consider the impact of favorable and unfavorable variances on income.

Module 24

Segment Reporting, Transfer Pricing, and Balanced Scorecard

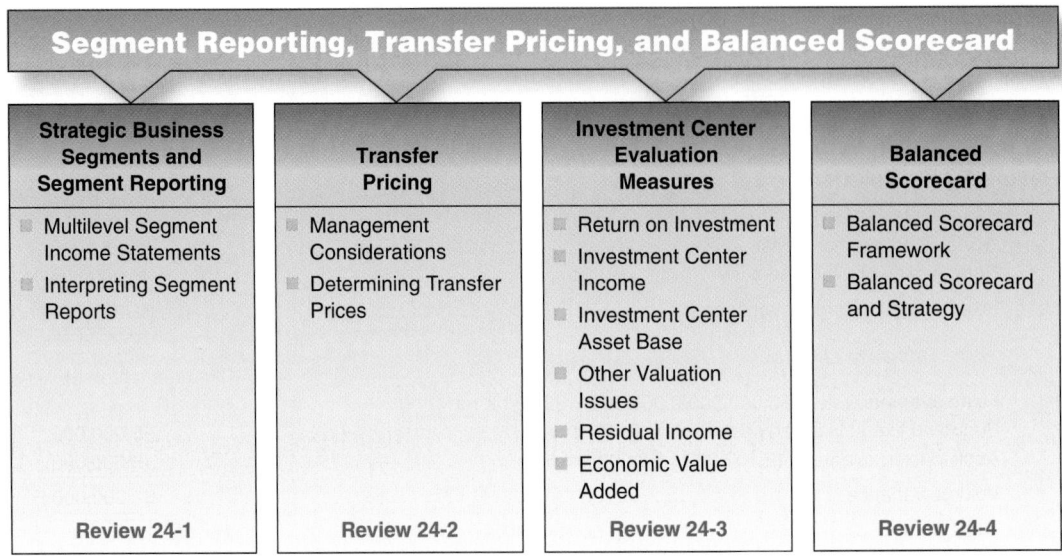

Segment Reporting, Transfer Pricing, and Balanced Scorecard			
Strategic Business Segments and Segment Reporting	**Transfer Pricing**	**Investment Center Evaluation Measures**	**Balanced Scorecard**
▪ Multilevel Segment Income Statements ▪ Interpreting Segment Reports	▪ Management Considerations ▪ Determining Transfer Prices	▪ Return on Investment ▪ Investment Center Income ▪ Investment Center Asset Base ▪ Other Valuation Issues ▪ Residual Income ▪ Economic Value Added	▪ Balanced Scorecard Framework ▪ Balanced Scorecard and Strategy
Review 24-1	Review 24-2	Review 24-3	Review 24-4

PREVIEW   VOW

On the shores of the Mittelland Canal, in the shadow of Wolfsburg Castle, stands the 70 million square-foot factory of Volkswagen (VW). Along with employing 60,500 workers, VW's presence is felt throughout the region from the Volkswagen Arena to the VW-owned Ritz Carlton to Autostadt, VW's sprawling theme park housing the most popular car museum in the world, the ZeitHaus. But VW's products go beyond its flagship brand to include Audi, Porsche, Lamborghini, Bentley, Bugatti, Ducati, SEAT, Skoda, MAN, Scania, and Volkswagen Commercial Vehicles, encompassing a total of 365 different vehicle models. VW also has manufacturing or assembly plants in 31 different countries in Europe, the Americas, Africa, and Asia.

Given the company's diversity by product line and geographic region, preparing the VW's financial and operating reports by segment assists VW managers in determining where the company should expand or contract its operations. However, the sheer complexity and volume of the company's business make the allocation of common costs across segments a difficult proposition.

One of VW's initiatives to manage the business across product and geographic lines is the introduction of modular tool-kit assemblies. This system allows the company to build all of its vehicles using four basic setups: a different tool kit for small, midsize, sports, or large/SUV vehicles. Doing this allows VW to standardize its engineering platforms and reduce inventory costs by using shared components wherever possible. With standardization comes an increase in transfers of components across product line and geographic divisions. However, what is the correct "price" to charge between internal divisions? The "selling" division would like to maximize its divisional performance by charging the highest price possible on the transfer, while the "buying" division would prefer to minimize its costs by paying the lowest price possible to the selling division. And each country in which VW manufactures and assembles its vehicles resides in a different tax jurisdiction such that the choice of a transfer price has real economic consequences for the overall corporate entity.

In this module, we will discuss performance measures that overcome the weaknesses of traditional performance ratios by taking into account leverage, taxation, level of investment, and the cost of accessing financial capital to make those investments.

Road Map

LO	Learning Objective | Topics	Page	eLecture	Guided Example	Assignments
24-1	**Define a strategic business segment, and prepare and use segment reports.** Strategic Business Segment :: Segment Reports :: Segment Margin	24-3	e24-1	Review 24-1	15, 16, 17, 31, 32, 33, 34
24-2	**Explain transfer pricing and assess alternative transfer-pricing methods.** Management Considerations :: Market Price :: Variable Costs :: Variable Costs Plus Opportunity Costs :: Absorption Cost Plus Markup :: Negotiated Prices :: Dual Prices	24-7	e24-2	Review 24-2	18, 19, 20, 24, 25, 26, 37, 38, 40, 41, 42
24-3	**Determine and contrast return on investment and residual income.** ROI :: Investment Center Income :: Investment Center Asset Base :: Valuation Issues :: Residual Income :: Economic Value Added	24-13	e24-3	Review 24-3	21, 22, 27, 28, 29, 35, 36, 37
24-4	**Describe the balanced scorecard as a comprehensive performance measurement system.** Balanced Scorecard Framework :: Balanced Scorecard Strategy	24-20	e24-4	Review 24-4	23, 30, 39

Organizations that maintain multiple product lines or that operate in several industries or in multiple markets often adopt a decentralized organization structure in which managers of major business units or strategic segments enjoy a high degree of autonomy. Examples of strategic business segments include the Porsche division of Volkswagen and the Asia Pacific Group of The Coca-Cola Company. Sometimes companies establish segments within segments such as at Coca-Cola, whose Asia Pacific Group has separate business units for individual countries (Japan, Korea, etc.). In organizations such as Volkswagen and Coca-Cola, upper management typically sets specific performance and profitability objectives for each segment and allows the manager of the segment the decision-making freedom to achieve those objectives.

This module explains the ways that an organization evaluates strategic business segments. It also considers transfer pricing and some of the problems that occur when one segment provides goods or services to another segment in the same organization.

Strategic Business Segments and Segment Reporting

LO1
Define a strategic business segment, and prepare and use segment reports.

A **strategic business segment** has its own mission and set of goals. Its mission influences the decisions that top managers make in both short-run and long-run situations. The organization structure dictates to a large extent the type of financial segment reporting and other measures used to evaluate the segment and its managers. In decentralized organizations, for example, the reporting units (typically called *divisions*) normally are quasi-independent companies, often having their own computer system, cost accounting system, and administrative and marketing staffs. With this type structure, top management monitors the segments to ensure that these independent units are functioning for the benefit of the entire organization.

Although segment reports are normally produced to coincide with managerial lines of responsibility, some companies also produce segment reports for smaller slices of the business that do not represent separate responsibility centers. These parts of the business are not significant enough to be identified as "strategic" business units as defined, but management could want information about them on a continuing basis.

For example, AT&T has four strategic business units: Communication, WarnerMedia, Latin America, and Xandr. Financial reports are prepared for each of these units. Within the WarnerMedia segment, AT&T can also prepare segment reports on a more detailed basis to determine the profitability of its smaller segments, such as Turner, Home Box Office, and Warner Bros. Most public companies are required to provide some segment information in their annual reports.

The point is that segment reporting is not constrained by lines of responsibility. A segment report can be prepared for any part of the business for which management believes more detailed information is useful in managing that portion of the business.

Business Insight ■ Strategic Segment Organization

Very few automakers have sold 10 million vehicles in a year. The first two were General Motors and Volkswagen, and both companies famously struggled after hitting the 10 million mark. Toyota's sales have been above 10 million vehicles for two years running, and the firm has had its struggles. Senior executives at Toyota have expressed concern that this scale of production, sales, and distribution is difficult to manage.

In order to remain nimble and competitive, Toyota has reorganized operations, shifting from a geographic organization to one based on product lines. Toyota President Akio Toyoda has said that as companies reach the 10 million milestone, reorganization is inevitable at all levels. "We can't talk about our future without finding new ways to do our jobs," Toyoda said. Analysts who cover the auto industry feel that this attitude is key to Toyota's ability to adjust more swiftly to challenges such as recalls and natural disasters.

One of the key ways that this new structure can help is by streamlining Toyota's product lines. Previously, Toyota modified the marketing and design of its vehicles to the target geography. The Vitz compact, sold in Japan, has a closely related model, the Yaris, sold only in Europe and the United States, while India has the Etios. What Japanese and American customers recognize as the Prius C is marketed in Europe as the Aqua. This geographical focus served Toyota well as it grew to its current size. Now there are gains to be had by simplifying the product lines, partially due to

continued

continued from previous page

the size of the company, but also due to the global familiarity with Toyota vehicles. All companies should be prepared to modify internal structures as the firm evolves.

Sources: Naomi Tajitsu, "Toyota Shakes Up Corporate Structure to Focus on Product Lines," *Reuters*, March 2, 2016. Yoko Kubota, "Toyota Plans Organizational Shake-Up," *Wall Street Journal*, February 29, 2016.

Segment reports are income statements for portions or segments of a business. Segment reporting is used primarily for internal purposes, although generally accepted accounting principles also require some disclosure of segment information for public corporations. Even though there are many different types of segment reports, at least three steps are basic to the preparation of all segment reports:

1. Identify the segments.
2. Assign direct costs to segments.
3. Allocate indirect costs to segments.

The format of segment income statements varies depending on the approach adopted by a company for reporting income statements internally. The income statement formats illustrated earlier in this text, including the functional format and the contribution format, can be used for segment reporting. Data availability can, however, dictate the format used. Regardless of the format adopted, it is essential that costs be separable into those directly traceable to the segments and those not directly traceable to segments. See Exhibit 24.1, below, for how the three steps above can be incorporated in the development of segment income.

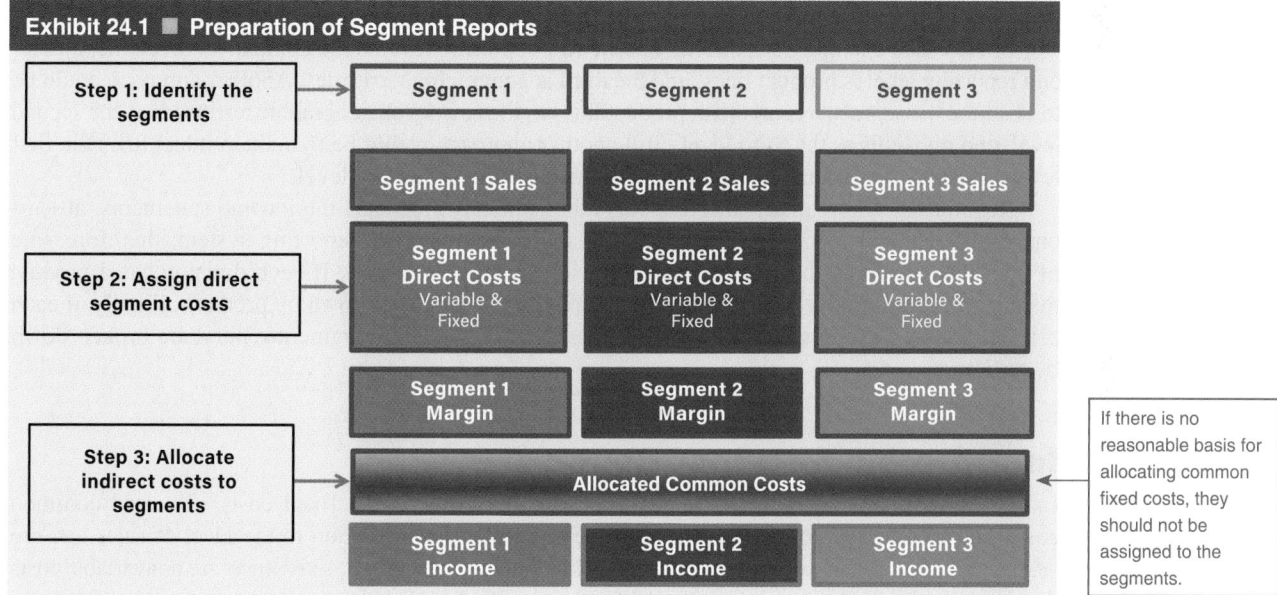

Exhibit 24.1 ■ Preparation of Segment Reports

Determining the segment reporting structure is often a more difficult decision than choosing the format for the segment income statements. Companies must decide whether to structure segment reporting along the lines of responsibility reporting, and whether segment reports will be prepared only on one level or on several levels.

For example, assume **Cisco** has two market divisions, three products, and two geographic territories. Suppose Cisco's two divisions include the National Division (serving large national accounts) and the Regional Division (serving smaller regional and local accounts). Further assume Cisco's three main product lines are switching, routing, and wireless. The company is organized into two geographic territories, United States and International. If Cisco were using only a single-level segment reporting approach for all three groupings, one report would show the total company income statement broken down into the two divisions, a second report would show the total company income statement broken down into the three products, and a third report would show the total company income statement broken down into the two geographic territories.

Multilevel Segment Income Statements

If top management of Cisco wants to know how much a particular product is contributing to the income of one of the two divisions or how much income a particular product in one of its two geographic territories contributes, it is necessary to prepare multilevel segment income statements. Since Cisco sells three products and operates through two divisions in two territories, many combinations of divisions, products, and territories could be used in structuring the company's multilevel segment reporting. The goal is not to slice and dice the revenue and cost data in as many ways as possible but to provide useful and meaningful information to management. Therefore, deciding what type of reporting structure is most useful in managing the company is important.

This decision will be constrained to a great extent by data availability and cost. If there were no data constraints, Cisco could look at the company's net income for every possible combination of division, product, and territory. The more data required to support a reporting system, however, the more costly it is to maintain the system, so management must determine the value and the cost of the additional information and make an appropriate cost-benefit judgment.

Panel A of Exhibit 24.2 illustrates hypothetical multilevel segment reporting for Cisco in which the first level shows the total company income statement segmented into the two market divisions, National Accounts and Regional Accounts. Panel B of Exhibit 24.2 shows a second-level report for Cisco in which the National Division's segment income statement is broken down into its three product lines, switching, routing, and wireless. Panel C then provides a third-level income statement for the National Division's switching product line sales in each of the company's two geographic territories, the U.S. and International territories. The example in Exhibit 24.2 shows only part of the segment reports for Cisco. The complete three-level set of segment reports would also break down the Regional Accounts Division into its product lines and all product lines for both divisions into geographic territories.

In the Cisco example in Exhibit 24.2, the first reporting level is the company's divisions, its second reporting level is product lines, and the third is geographic territories. Another approach could be to structure the segment reports with product lines as the first level, geographic territories as the second level, and divisions as the third level. Still another approach would be to make product lines the first level, divisions the second level, and geographic territories the third level.

Regardless of how many different ways the company segments the income statements, at least one set of segment reports follows the company's responsibility reporting system; therefore, one of the segment reports has the operating divisions as the first level. If each division has a product manager for each product, the division segment reports are broken down by products. Finally, if each product within each division has a territory manager, the product segment reports are broken down by territories.

Interpreting Segment Reports

Exhibit 24.2 reports costs in four categories: variable costs, direct fixed costs, allocated common costs, and unallocated common costs. Variable costs vary in proportion to the level of sales and are subtracted from sales in calculating contribution margin. **Direct segment fixed costs** are nonvariable costs directly traceable to the segments incurred for the specific benefit of the respective segments. **Segment margin** equals the contribution margin minus the direct segment fixed costs. For Cisco, segment margins are referred to as *division margins, product margins,* and *territory margins.* Segment margins represent the amount that a segment contributes directly to the company's profitability in the short run.

Common segment costs are incurred for the common benefit of all related segments shown on a segment income statement. In some cases, allocating some common costs is reasonable even though they cannot be directly traced to the various segments based on benefits received. For example, if segments share common space, allocating all space-related costs to the segments based on building space occupied could be appropriate. If there is no reasonable basis for allocating common costs, they should not be allocated to the segments. In Panel C of Exhibit 24.2, if advertising costs to promote the company's switching products on national television could not be reasonably allocated to the two geographic territories, they would be charged to the switching product line as an unallocated common cost, not to the individual territories.

Exhibit 24.2 ■ Multilevel Segment Reports

Panel A: First-Level Segment Report of Cisco—For Divisions

(in thousands)	Segments (Divisions)		Company Total
	National Accounts	Regional Accounts	
Sales.	$100,000	$ 200,000	$300,000
Less variable costs.	(55,000)	(95,000)	(150,000)
Contribution margin	45,000	105,000	150,000
Less direct fixed costs	(20,000)	(60,000)	(80,000)
Division margin.	25,000	45,000	70,000
Less allocated segment costs	(10,000)	(25,000)	(35,000)
Division income	$ 15,000	$ 20,000	35,000
Less unallocated common costs			(12,000)
Net income			$ 23,000

Panel B: Second-Level Segment Report of the National Division—For Products

(in thousands)	Segments (Products)			National Accounts Total
	Switching	Routing	Wireless	
Sales.	$30,000	$40,000	$30,000	$100,000
Less variable costs.	(15,000)	(19,000)	(21,000)	(55,000)
Contribution margin	15,000	21,000	9,000	45,000
Less direct fixed costs	(9,000)	(4,000)	(2,000)	(15,000)
Product margin.	6,000	17,000	7,000	30,000
Less allocated segment costs	(5,000)	(4,000)	(1,000)	(10,000)
Product income.	$ 1,000	$13,000	$ 6,000	20,000
Less unallocated common costs				(5,000)
National Division income				$ 15,000

> Common segment costs that are incurred for the common benefit of all related segments.

Panel C: Third-Level Segment Report of the Switching Product Line in the National Division—For Geographic Territories

(in thousands)	Segments (Territories)		Switching Total
	U.S.	International	
Sales.	$20,000	$10,000	$30,000
Less variable costs.	(11,000)	(4,000)	(15,000)
Contribution margin	9,000	6,000	15,000
Less direct fixed costs	(3,000)	(4,000)	(7,000)
Territory margin	6,000	2,000	8,000
Less allocated segment costs	(2,000)	(3,000)	(5,000)
Territory income	$ 4,000	$(1,000)	3,000
Less unallocated common costs			(2,000)
Switching income			$ 1,000

If some portion of common costs can be reasonably allocated to the segments, those allocated costs are subtracted from the segment margins to determine segment income. Hence, **segment income** represents all revenues of the segment minus all costs directly or indirectly charged to it.

To properly interpret segment income, we should ask whether segment income represents the amount by which net income of the company will change if that segment is discontinued. For example, if Cisco discontinues the wireless product line in the National Division, does this mean that Cisco's net income will decrease by $6 million? Also, does it mean that if the National Division stops selling switching products in the International territory, Cisco's net income will increase by $1 million?

The answer to these questions depends on whether the costs allocated to the segments are avoidable. **Avoidable common costs** are allocated common costs that eventually can be avoided (that is, can be eliminated) if a segment is discontinued. If all allocated common costs are avoidable, the effect of discontinuing the segment on corporate profitability equals the amount of segment income. In most cases, the short-term impact of discontinuing a segment equals the segment margin because allocated costs are capacity costs that cannot be adjusted in the short run. Over time, the company should be able to adjust capacity and eliminate some, or possibly all, of the allocated common costs or find productive uses for that capacity in other segments of the business. The unallocated common costs cannot be changed readily in the short term or the long term without causing major disruptions to the company and its strategy. Therefore, over the long term, the impact of discontinuing a segment should be, approximately, its segment income.

If Cisco discontinues selling switching products in the International territory (see Exhibit 24.2, Panel C), the short-term effect on the company's profits will probably be a $2 million reduction of profits, which equals the International territory's margin. The revenues and costs that make up the International territory margin would all be lost if switching sales were discontinued in the International territory, but the $3 million of common costs allocated to the International territory would continue, at least in the short term. Over the long term, however, after adjusting the capacity for selling this product in the International territory and eliminating the $3 million of allocated common costs, the effect of discontinuing switching products in the International territory on profits should be an increase of about $1 million, which is the amount of the segment loss for switching products in the International territory.

To summarize, generally, segment margin is relevant for measuring the short-term effects of decisions to continue or discontinue a segment; however, segment income is relevant for measuring the long-term effects of decisions to continue or discontinue.

Review 24-1 LO1

Refer to the Cisco example in Exhibit 24.2, Panel B. The following additional information is provided for the wireless product line in the National Division:

Sales—U.S. territory.	$12,000
Sales—International territory	18,000
Direct fixed cost—U.S. territory	500
Direct fixed cost—International territory	800
Allocated segment costs—U.S. territory.	200
Allocated segment costs—International territory	600

Required

a. Prepare a geographic territory segment report of the wireless product line in the National division. Assume variable costs are always the same percent of sales for wireless products.

b. Explain why the total of the Territory Margins for geographic segments of the wireless product line does not equal the product margin of the wireless product segment in Panel B of Exhibit 24.2.

Solution on p. 24-38.

Transfer Pricing

LO2
Explain transfer pricing and assess alternative transfer-pricing methods.

To determine whether each division is achieving its organizational objectives, managers must be accountable for the goods and services they acquire, both externally and internally. When goods or services are exchanged internally between segments of a decentralized organization, the way that the transferor and the transferee will report the transfer must be determined, either by negotiations between the two segments or by corporate policy. A **transfer price** is the internal value assigned a product or service that one division provides to another. The transfer price is recognized as revenue by the division providing goods or services and as expense (or cost) by the division receiving them. Transfer-pricing transactions normally occur between profit or investment centers rather than between cost centers of an organization;

however, managers often consider cost allocations between cost centers as a type of transfer price. The focus in this module is on transfers between responsibility centers that are evaluated based on profits.

Management Considerations

The desire of the selling and buying divisions of the same company to maximize their individual performance measures often creates transfer-pricing conflicts within an organization. Acting as independent units, divisions could take actions that are not in the best interest(s) of the organization as a whole. The three examples that follow illustrate the need for organizations to maintain a *corporate* profit-maximizing viewpoint while attempting to allow *divisional* autonomy and responsibility.

Suppose Sony Corporation has five divisions, some of which transfer products and product components to other Sony divisions. Suppose the Monitors and Displays (M&D) Division manufactures two products, Yokia Mount and PVMA. It sells Yokia Mount externally for $50 per unit and transfers PVMA to the Television Division for $60 per unit. The costs associated with the two products follow:

Monitors and Displays Division	Product	
	Yokia Mount	PVMA
Variable costs		
Direct materials.	$15	$14
Direct labor	5	10
Variable manufacturing overhead.	5	16
Selling.	4	0
Fixed costs		
Fixed manufacturing overhead	6	15
Total	$35	$55

An external company has just proposed to supply a PVMA substitute product to the Television Division at a price of $52. From the company's viewpoint, this is merely a make or buy decision. The relevant costs are the differential outlay costs of the alternative actions. Assuming that the fixed manufacturing costs of the M&D Division are unavoidable, the relevant costs of this proposal from the company's perspective are as follows:

Buy.		$52
Make		
Direct materials.	$14	
Direct labor	10	
Variable manufacturing overhead.	16	(40)
Difference.		$12

From the corporate viewpoint, the best decision is for the product to be transferred since the relevant cost is $40 rather than to buy it from an external source for $52. The decision for the Television Division management is basically one of cost minimization: Buy from the source that charges the lowest price. If the M&D Division is not willing to transfer PVMA at a price of $52 or less, the Television Division management could go to the external supplier to maximize the division's profits. (Although the Television Division's managers are concerned about the cost of PVMA, they are also concerned about the quality of the goods. If the $52 product does not meet its quality standards, the Television Division could decide to buy from the M&D Division at the higher price. For this discussion, assume that the internal and external products are identical; therefore, acting in its best interest, the Television Division purchases PVMA for $52 from the external source unless the M&D Division can match the price.)

Prior to Television's receipt of the external offer, the M&D Division had been transferring PVMA to the Television Division's for $60. The M&D Division must decide whether to reduce the contribution margin on its transfers of PVMA to the Television Division and, therefore, lower divisional profits or to try to find an alternative use for its resources. Of course, corporate management could intervene and require the internal transfer even though it would hurt M&D Division's profits.

As the second example, assume that the M&D Division has the option to sell an equivalent amount of PVMA externally for $60 per unit if the Television Division discontinues its transfers from the M&D Division. Now the decision for M&D's management is simple: Sell to the buyer willing to pay the most. From the corporate viewpoint, it is best for the M&D Division to sell to the external buyer for $60 and for Television to purchase from the external provider for $52.

To examine a slightly different transfer-pricing conflict, assume that the M&D Division can sell all the Yokia that it can produce (it is operating at capacity). Also assume that there is no external market for PVMA, but there is a one-to-one trade-off between the production of Yokia and PVMA, which use equal amounts of the M&D Division's limited capacity. (In other words, another Yokia can be made for every PVMA not made by the M&D Division.)

The corporation still regards this as a make or buy decision, but the costs of producing PVMA have changed. The cost of PVMA now includes an outlay cost and an opportunity cost. PVMA's opportunity cost is the net benefit foregone if the M&D Division's limited capacity is used to produce PVMA rather than Yokia:

Selling price of Yokia		$50
Outlay costs of Yokia		
Direct materials	$15	
Direct labor	5	
Variable manufacturing overhead	5	
Variable selling	4	(29)
Opportunity cost of making PVMA		$21

The outlay cost of PVMA is its variable cost of $40 ($14 + $10 + $16), as previously computed. Accordingly, the relevant costs in the make or buy decision are as follows.

Make		
Outlay cost of PVMA	$40	
Opportunity cost of PVMA	21	$61
Buy		$52

From the corporate viewpoint, the Television Division should purchase PVMA from the outside supplier for $52 because in this case it costs $61 to make the product. If there were no outside suppliers, the corporation's relevant cost of manufacturing PVMA would be $61. This is another way of saying that the Television Division should not acquire PVMA internally unless its revenues cover all outlay costs (including the $40 in the M&D Division) and provide a contribution of at least $21 ($61 − $40). From the corporate viewpoint, the relevant costs in make or buy decisions are the external price, the outlay costs to manufacture, and the opportunity cost to manufacture. The opportunity cost is zero if there is excess capacity.

The transfer of goods and services between divisions of a company located in different countries that have unequal tax structures often attracts the attention of the taxing authorities. Companies are sometimes accused of trying to minimize their total tax costs by setting transfer prices that shift profits from the division in the higher-tax-rate country to the division in the lower-tax-rate country. For example, assume that IBM has a division in Denmark that produces software that it sells to its systems division in the U.S. Denmark's corporate tax rate is about 50%; whereas, the U.S. rate is about 20%. By setting a transfer price at the lowest possible level, the profits of the Danish division will be less, and those of the American division will be higher, resulting in lower overall taxes for the company. The taxing authorities in the high-tax-rate country always insist that the transfer price for goods and services sold to divisions in other countries be at least as high as fair market value of the goods or services transferred out. The following Business Insight discusses a recent attempt by the IRS to collect taxes of more than $521 million from **Guidant Corp.** related to improper transfer prices.

Determining Transfer Prices

As illustrated, the transfer price of goods or services can be subject to much controversy. The most widely used and discussed transfer prices are covered in this section. Although a price must be agreed upon for each item or service transferred between divisions, the selection of the pricing method depends on many factors. The conditions surrounding the transfer determine which of the alternative methods discussed subsequently is selected.

Although no method is likely to be ideal, one must be selected if the profit or investment center concept is used. In considering each method, observe that each transfer results in a revenue entry on the supplier's books and a cost entry on the receiver's books. Transfers can be considered as sales by the supplier and as purchases by the receiver.

Market Price

When there is an existing market with established prices for an intermediate product and the transfer actions of the company will not affect prices, market prices are ideal transfer prices. If divisions are free to buy and sell outside the firm, the use of market prices preserves divisional autonomy and leads divisions to act in a manner that maximizes corporate goal congruence. Unfortunately, not all product transfers have equivalent external markets. Furthermore, the divisions should carefully evaluate whether the market price is competitive or controlled by one or two large companies. When substantial selling expenses are associated with outside sales, many firms specify the transfer price as market price less selling expenses. The internal sale may not require the incurrence of costs to get and fill the order.

To illustrate using the hypothetical Sony example, assume that product Yokia of the M&D Division can be sold competitively at $50 per unit or transferred to a third division, the Medical Equipment Division, for additional processing. Under most situations, the M&D Division will never sell Yokia for less than $50, and the Medical Equipment Division will likewise never pay more than $50 for it. However, if any variable expenses related to marketing and shipping can be eliminated by divisional transfers, these costs are generally subtracted from the competitive market price. In our illustration in which variable selling expenses are $4 for Yokia, the transfer price could be reduced to $46 ($50 − $4). A price between $46 and $50 would probably be better than either extreme price. To the extent that these transfer prices represent a nearly competitive situation, the profitability of each division can then be fairly evaluated.

Variable Costs

If excess capacity exists in the supplying division, establishing a transfer price equal to variable costs leads the purchasing division to act in a manner that is optimal from the corporation's viewpoint. The buying division has the corporation's variable cost as its own variable cost as it enters the external market. Unfortunately, establishing the transfer price at variable cost causes the supplying division to report zero profits or a loss equal to any fixed costs. If excess capacity does not exist, establishing a transfer price at variable cost would not lead to optimal action because the supplying division would have to forgo external sales that include a markup for fixed costs and profits. If PVMA could be sold externally for $60, the M&D Division would not want to transfer PVMA to the Television Division for a $40 transfer price based on the following variable costs:

Direct materials.	$14
Direct labor.	10
Variable manufacturing overhead.	16
Total variable costs.	$40

The M&D Division would much rather sell outside the company for $60, which covers variable costs and provides a profit contribution margin of $20:

Selling price of PVMA.	$60
Variable costs.	(40)
Contribution margin.	$20

Variable Costs Plus Opportunity Costs

From the organization's viewpoint, this is the optimal transfer price. Because all relevant costs are included in the transfer price, the purchasing division is led to act in a manner optimal for the overall company, whether or not excess capacity exists.

With excess capacity in the supplying division, the transfer price is the variable cost per unit. Without excess capacity, the transfer price is the sum of the variable and opportunity costs. Following this rule in the previous example, if the M&D Division had excess capacity, the transfer price of PVMA would be set at PVMA's variable costs of $40 per unit. At this transfer price, the Television Division would buy PVMA internally, rather than externally at $52 per unit. If the M&D Division cannot sell PVMA externally but can sell all the Yokia it can produce and is operating at capacity, the transfer price per unit would be set at $61, the sum of PVMA's variable and opportunity costs ($40 + $21). (Refer back two pages.) At this transfer price, the Television Division would buy PVMA externally for $52. In both situations, the management of the Television Division has acted in accordance with the organization's profit-maximizing goal.

There are two problems with this method. First, when the supplying division has excess capacity, establishing the transfer price at variable cost causes the supplying division to report zero profits or a loss equal to any fixed costs. Second, determining opportunity costs when the supplying division produces several products is difficult. If the problems with the previously mentioned transfer-pricing methods are too great, three other methods can be used: absorption cost plus markup, negotiated prices, and dual prices.

Absorption Cost Plus Markup

According to absorption costing, all variable and fixed manufacturing costs are product costs. Pricing internal transfers at absorption cost eliminates the supplying division's reported loss on each product that can occur using a variable cost transfer price. Absorption cost plus markup provides the supplying division a contribution toward unallocated costs. In "cost-plus" transfer pricing, "cost" should be defined as standard cost rather than as actual cost. This prevents the supplying division from passing on the cost of inefficient operations to other divisions, and it allows the buying division to know its cost in advance of purchase. Even though cost-plus transfer prices may not maximize company profits, they are widely used. Their popularity stems from several factors, including ease of implementation, justifiability, and perceived fairness. Once everyone agrees on absorption cost plus markup pricing rules, internal disputes are minimized.

Negotiated Prices

Negotiated transfer prices are used when the supplying and buying divisions independently agree on a price. As with market-based transfer prices, negotiated transfer prices are believed to preserve divisional autonomy. Negotiated transfer prices can lead to some suboptimal decisions, but this is regarded as a small price to pay for other benefits of decentralization. When they use negotiated transfer prices, some corporations establish arbitration procedures to help settle disputes between divisions. However, the existence of an arbitrator with any real or perceived authority reduces divisional autonomy.

Negotiated prices should have market prices as their ceiling and variable costs as their floor. Although frequently used when an external market for the product or component exists, the most common use of negotiated prices occurs when no identical-product external market exists. Negotiations could start with a floor price plus add-ons such as overhead and profit markups or with a ceiling price less adjustments for selling and administrative expenses and allowances for quantity discounts. When no identical-product external market exists, the market price for a similar completed product can be used, less the estimated cost of completing the product from the transfer stage to the completed stage.

Dual Prices

Dual prices exist when a company allows a difference in the supplier's and receiver's transfer prices for the same product. This method should minimize internal squabbles of division managers and problems of conflicting divisional and corporate goals. The supplier's transfer price normally approximates market price, which allows the selling division to show a "normal" profit on items that it transfers internally. The receiver's price is usually the internal cost of the product or service, calculated as variable cost plus opportunity cost. This ensures that the buying division will make an internal transfer when it is in the best interest of the company to do so.

In most cases, a market-based transfer price achieves the optimal outcome for both the divisions and the company as a whole. As discussed earlier, an exception occurs when a division is operating below full capacity and has no alternative use for its excess capacity. In this case, it is best for the company to have an internal transfer; therefore, to ensure that the receiving division makes an internal transfer, the company must require the internal transfer as long as its price does not exceed the established market rate. The only time an external price is more attractive when excess capacity exists is when the external price is below the variable cost of the providing internal division, and that scenario is highly unlikely.

A potential transfer-pricing problem exists when divisions exchange goods or services for which no established market exists. For example, suppose that a company is operating its information technology (IT) service department as a profit center that transfers services to other profit center departments using a cost-plus transfer price. If the departments using IT services can choose to use those services or to replicate them inside their departments, users might not make a decision that is best for the company. It could be best for the company to have all IT services come from the IT department, but other profit centers could believe that they can provide those services for themselves at lower cost. In this case, the company must decide how important it is to maintain the independence of its profit center. In the interest of maintaining a strong profit center philosophy, top management can decide that it is acceptable to suboptimize by allowing profit centers to provide IT services for themselves.

The ideal transfer-pricing arrangement is seldom the same for both the providing and receiving divisions for every situation. In these cases, what is good for one division is likely not to be good for the other division, resulting in no transfer, even though a transfer could achieve corporate goals. These conflicts are sometimes overcome by having a higher-ranking manager impose a transfer price and insist that a transfer be made. Managers in organizations that have a policy of decentralization, however, often regard these orders as undermining their autonomy. Therefore, the imposition of a price could solve the corporate profit optimization problem but create other problems regarding the company's organization strategy. Transfer pricing thus becomes a problem with no ideal solutions.

The previous discussion has focused on the challenges of establishing transfer prices that motivate managers to make decisions that are beneficial to their divisions as well as the overall company. However, research, discussed in the following Research Insight box, concluded that there are often price benefits when dealing with outside vendors, if the company has the option of acquiring the goods or services internally.

Research Insight ■ Transfer Pricing and External Competition

Researchers found that a firm can glean benefits from discussing transfer-pricing problems with external suppliers. Though transfer prices above marginal cost introduce interdivision coordination problems, they also reduce a firm's willingness to pay outside suppliers. Knowing that costly internal transfers will eat into demand, the supplier is more willing to set lower prices. Such supplier discounts can make decentralization worthwhile for the firm. The benefit of decentralization is shown to be robust in both downstream and upstream competition.

Source: Anil Arya and Brian Mittendorf, "Interacting Supply Chain Distortions: The Pricing of Internal Transfers and External Procurement," *The Accounting Review*, May 2007.

Review 24-2 LO2

University Poster Company has a Publication Division that is currently producing and selling 200,000 posters per year but has a capacity of 300,000 posters. The variable costs of each poster are $16, and the annual fixed costs are $1,350,000. The posters sell for $24 on the open market. The company's Retail Division wants to buy 100,000 posters at $13.50 each. The Publication Division manager refuses the order because the price is below variable cost. The Retail Division manager argues that the order should be accepted because it will lower the fixed cost per poster from $6.75 to $4.50.

Required

a. Should the Retail Division order be accepted? Why or why not?

b. From the viewpoints of the Publication Division and the company, should the order be accepted if the manager of the Retail Division intends to sell each print on the outside market for $44 after incurring additional costs of $10 per print?

Solution on p. 24-38.   c. What action should the company take, assuming it believes in divisional autonomy?

Investment Center Evaluation Measures

LO3
Determine and contrast return on investment and residual income.

Two of the most common measures of investment center performance, return on investment and residual income, are discussed in the following sections. Several supporting components of these measures that help clarify the applications are also presented. (Earlier in the book, we explained the advantages of separating operating and nonoperating items to compute sales, assets, income, and so forth. We can similarly separate operating and nonoperating items for performance measurement. In this case, all measures would be adjusted to yield operating sales, operating assets, operating income, and so forth. Then, the following analysis would apply to those operating metrics and would reflect the operating performance of each center.)

Return on Investment

Return on investment (ROI) is a measure of the earnings per dollar of investment. This assumes that financing decisions are made at the corporate level rather than the division level. Hence, the corporation's investment in the division equals the division's asset base. The return on investment of an investment center is computed by dividing the income of the center by its asset base (usually total assets):

$$\text{ROI} = \frac{\text{Investment center income}}{\text{Investment center asset base}}$$

ROI can be disaggregated into investment turnover times the return-on-sales ratio:

$$\text{ROI} = \text{Investment turnover} \times \text{Return-on-sales}$$

where

$$\text{Investment turnover} = \frac{\text{Sales}}{\text{Investment center asset base}}$$

and

$$\text{Return-on-sales} = \frac{\text{Investment center income}}{\text{Sales}}$$

When investment turnover is multiplied by return-on-sales, the product is the same as investment center income divided by investment center asset base:

$$ROI = \frac{Sales}{Investment\ center\ base} \times \frac{Investment\ center\ income}{Sales} = \frac{Investment\ center\ income}{Investment\ center\ asset\ base}$$

Once ROI has been computed, it is compared to some previously identified performance criteria. These include the investment center's previous ROI, overall company ROI, the ROI of similar divisions, or the ROI of nonaffiliated companies that operate in similar markets. The breakdown of ROI into investment turnover and return-on-sales is useful in determining the source of variance in overall performance.

To illustrate the computation and use of ROI, suppose the following information is available concerning the operations of Procter & Gamble Co. (P&G) (in thousands) for a single year:

Division	Asset Base	Sales	Divisional Income
Beauty	$8,000,000	$12,000,000	$1,440,000
Healthcare	4,000,000	8,000,000	960,000
Grooming	7,500,000	5,000,000	1,650,000
Fabric & Homecare....................	3,800,000	5,700,000	1,026,000

Using this information and the preceding equations, a set of performance measures is shown in Exhibit 24.3. To illustrate, the Beauty Division earned a return on its investment base of 18% ($1,440,000 ÷ $8,000,000), consisting of an investment turnover of 1.50 ($12,000,000 ÷ $8,000,000) and a return-on-sales of 0.12 ($1,440,000 ÷ $12,000,000). Using such an analysis, the company has three measurement criteria with which to evaluate the performance of the Beauty Division: (1) ROI, (2) investment turnover, and (3) return-on-sales.

Exhibit 24.3 ■ Performance Evaluation Data

PROCTER & GAMBLE CO.
Performance Measures
For Year Ending June 30

	Performance Measures		
	Investment Turnover ×	Return-on-Sales =	ROI
Operating unit			
Beauty.....................................	1.50	0.12	0.18
Healthcare..............................	2.00	0.12	0.24
Grooming	0.67	0.33	0.22
Fabric & Homecare.....................	1.50	0.18	0.27
Company performance criteria			
Projected minimums.....................	1.20	0.15	0.18

For the year, P&G chose to evaluate its divisions based on company ROI and its interrelated components of investment turnover and return-on-sales. Because each division is different in size, the company evaluation standard is not a simple average of the divisions but is based on desired relationships between assets, sales, and income.

Based on ROI, the Fabric & Homecare Division had the best performance, the Healthcare Division excelled in investment turnover, and the Grooming Division had the highest return-on-sales. From Exhibit 24.3, the Fabric & Homecare Division had the best year because it was the only division that exceeded each of the company's performance criteria. Each division equaled or exceeded the minimum ROI established by the company for the year, even though the component criteria of ROI were not always achieved.

To properly evaluate each division, the company should study the underlying components of ROI. For the Beauty Division, management would want to know why the minimum investment turnover was exceeded while the return-on-sales minimum was not. The Beauty Division could have incurred higher unit costs by producing inefficiently. As a result of inefficient production, the return-on-sales declined to a point below the minimum desired level. Evaluating a large operating division based on one financial indicator is difficult. Management should select several key indicators of performance when conducting periodic reviews of its operating segments.

A similar analysis of ROI and its components is useful for planning. In developing plans for the next year, management wants to know the possible effect of changes in the major elements of ROI for the Beauty Division. Sensitivity analysis can be used to predict the impact of changes in sales, the investment center asset base, or the investment center income.

Assuming the investment asset base is unchanged, a projected ROI can be determined for the Beauty Division for a sales goal of $16,000,000 and an income goal of $1,600,000:

$$\text{ROI} = \frac{\text{Sales}}{\text{Investment center asset base}} \times \frac{\text{Investment center income}}{\text{Sales}}$$

$$= \frac{\$16,000,000}{\$8,000,000} \times \frac{\$1,600,000}{\$16,000,000}$$

$$= 2.0 \times 0.10$$

$$= 0.20 \text{ or } 20\%$$

ROI increased from 18% to 20%, even though the return-on-sales decreased from 12% to 10%. The change in turnover from 1.5 to 2.0 more than offset the reduced return-on-sales.

Sensitivity analysis can involve changing only one factor or a combination of factors in the ROI model. When more than one factor is changed, it is important to analyze exactly how much change is caused by each factor.

Research Insight ■ Nonprofit Donations Decrease When Donors Believe Managers Are Overpaid

Over 1.4 million nonprofit organizations across the United States received more than $260 billion in donations during the year 2009. Yet with the weakening economy, contributors to nonprofit organizations are less willing to tolerate inflated salaries of the charity's executives. Specifically, donors decrease their contributions to the organization when the media reports an increase in executive compensation. On average, organizations that draw media coverage over executive compensation increases grow 15% less over the two years surrounding the media mention than their peer organizations. However, when this increase is reported on Form 990 for the Internal Revenue Service (IRS), only sophisticated donors reduce their contributions. Small donors may not know where to seek the compensation information out on their own, and larger donors have a greater stake in the stewardship of their donated funds. Among these larger donors, the study reports that contributions decrease by 3% for every $100,000 increase in executive compensation.

Source: Steven Balsam and Erica E. Harris, "The Impact of CEO Compensation on Nonprofit Donations," *The Accounting Review* 89, no. 2 (March 2014): 425–450.

Statistics such as ROI, investment turnover, and return-on-sales mean little by themselves. They take on meaning only when compared with an objective, a trend, another division, a competitor, or an industry average. Many businesses establish minimum ROIs for each of their divisions, expecting them to attain or exceed this minimum return. The salaries, bonuses, and promotions of division managers can be tied directly to their division's ROI. Without other evaluation techniques, managers often strive for ROI maximization, sometimes to the long-run detriment of the entire organization.

Investment Center Income

Despite the relevance and conceptual simplicity of ROI, a division's ROI cannot be determined until management decides how to measure divisional income and investment. Divisional income equals divisional revenues less divisional operating expenses. Determining divisional revenues is usually a relatively easy task since revenues are typically generated and recorded at the division level, but determining total operating expenses for divisions is more complicated. Because many expenses are incurred at the corporate level for the common benefit of the various operating divisions and to support corporate headquarters operations, the cost assignment issues discussed early in this module affect investment center income.

Direct division expenses are always included in division operating expenses, but there are conflicting viewpoints about how to deal with common corporate expenses. As stated earlier in this module, in corporate annual reports, many companies are required to provide segment revenues and expenses segmented by product lines, geographic territories, customer markets, and so on. Companies also show operating income for their various segments in their annual reports, but they include a category called *corporate* or *unallocated* for company expenses that cannot be reasonably allocated to the various segments. ("Unallocated" typically includes costs for corporate staffs, certain goodwill write-offs, and nonoperational gains and losses.) For example, the Toyota Motor Corporation's 2019 annual report includes the following breakdown of its operating income by segments (stated in millions of yen):

Japan	1,691,675 Yen
North America	114,515
Europe	124,868
Asia	457,489
Other (Central and South America, Oceania, Africa, and the Middle East)	91,110
Unallocated	(12,112)
Total operating income	2,467,545 Yen

For internal segment reporting, some companies do not allocate corporate costs that cannot be associated closely with individual segments. Other companies insist on allocating all common corporate costs to the operating divisions to emphasize that the company does not earn a profit until revenues have covered all costs. Some top managers believe that since only operating divisions produce revenues, they should also bear all costs, including corporate costs. These managers want to ensure that the sum of the division income for the various segments equals the total income for the company.

Division managers do not control corporate costs; therefore, these costs are seldom relevant in evaluating a division manager's performance. To deal with this conflict, some companies allocate some, or possibly all, common corporate costs in reporting segment operating income, but for ROI calculation purposes exclude allocated corporate costs that are not closely associated with the divisions. These companies include in the ROI calculation costs that represent an identifiable benefit to the divisions but not general corporate costs that provide no identifiable benefits to the divisions. In practice, the treatment of corporate costs for division performance evaluation varies widely.

Investment Center Asset Base

Because the primary purpose for computing ROI is to evaluate the effectiveness of a division's operating management in using the assets entrusted to them, most organizations define *investment* as the average total assets of a division during the evaluation period. For most companies, the *investment base* is defined as each division's operating assets. These normally include those assets held for productive use, such as accounts receivable, inventory, and plant and equipment. Nonproductive assets, such as land for a future plant site, are not included in the investment base of a division but in the investment base for the company.

General corporate assets allocated to divisions should not be included in their bases. Although the divisions might need additional administrative facilities if they were truly independent, they have no control over the headquarters' facilities. The joint nature and use of corporate facility-level expenses make any allocation arbitrary.

> The investment base can also be measured as operating assets less current operating liabilities (net operating assets). Operating liabilities are obligations directly related to normal business operations, such as accounts payable and accrued liabilities.

Other Valuation Issues

Once divisional investment and income have been operationally defined and ROI computations have been made, the significance of the resulting ratios can still be questioned. Return on investment can be overstated in terms of constant dollars because inflation and arbitrary inventory and depreciation procedures cause an undervaluation of the inventory and fixed assets included in the investment center asset base. Asset measurement is particularly troublesome if inventories are valued at last-in, first-out (LIFO) cost or if fixed assets were acquired many years ago. For example, a division manager could hesitate to replace an old, inefficient asset with a new, efficient one because the replacement could lower income and ROI through an increased investment base and increased depreciation.

To improve the comparability between divisions with old and new assets when computing ROI, some firms value assets at original cost rather than at net book value (cost less accumulated depreciation). This procedure does not reflect inflation, however. An old asset that cost $120,000 ten years ago is still being compared with an asset that costs $200,000 today. A better solution could be to value old assets at their replacement cost, although replacement costs are often difficult to determine.

Managerial Decision ■ **You Are the Division Vice President**

Division managers in your company are evaluated primarily based on division return on investment, and you recently received financial reports for your division for the most recent period and discovered that the ROI for your division was 14.5%; whereas, the target ROI for your division set by the CFO and the CEO was 15%. What action can you take to try to avoid missing your performance target for the next period? [Answer, p. 24-24]

Residual Income

Residual income is an often-mentioned alternative to ROI for measuring investment center performance. **Residual income** is the excess of investment center income over the minimum rate or dollar of return. The *minimum rate of return* represents the rate that can be earned on alternative investments of similar risks, which is the opportunity cost of the investment. The *minimum dollar return* is computed as a percentage of the investment center's asset base. When residual income is the primary basis of evaluation, the management of each investment center is encouraged to maximize residual income rather than ROI. (We can again measure assets, sales, income, and so forth, as excluding all nonoperating components; similarly, the investment base can be measured as operating assets less operating liabilities.)

To illustrate the computation, assume that a company requires a minimum return of 12% on each division's investment base. The residual income of a division with an annual net operating income of $2,000,000 and an investment base of $15,000,000 is $200,000 as computed here:

Division income	$2,000,000
Minimum return ($15,000,000 × 0.12)	(1,800,000)
Residual income	$ 200,000

Economic Value Added

A variation of residual income, referred to as **economic value added** or **EVA®**, is also often used as a basis for evaluating investment center performance. (The term EVA is a registered trademark of the financial consulting firm of Stern Stewart and Company.) EVA measures residual income earned on all funds committed long term to the organization by lenders (debt) or shareholders (equity). The key differences from the residual income approach, as discussed in the previous section, are the use of after-tax income and an organization's weighted average cost of capital. EVA can be calculated as follows:

Income after taxes – [(Total assets – Current liabilities) × Weighted average cost of capital]

Weighted average cost of capital is an average of the after-tax cost of all long-term borrowing and the cost of equity.[1] Economic value is added only if a division's taxable income exceeds its net cost of investing. (We can again measure assets, sales, income, and so forth, as excluding all nonoperating components; similarly, the net asset base can be measured as operating assets less operating liabilities.)

Using the preceding situation, assume that the company has a cost of capital of 10%, $1,800,000 in current liabilities, and a 30% tax rate. The economic value added is $80,000, computed as follows:

Division income after taxes ($2,000,000 × 0.70)	$1,400,000
Cost of capital employed [($15,000,000 – $1,800,000) × 0.10]	(1,320,000)
Economic value added	$ 80,000

---

[1] Weighted average cost of capital computations is covered in introductory corporate finance textbooks.

In calculating EVA, users often ignore any accounting principles that are viewed as distorting the measurement of wealth creation. In practice, EVA consultants have identified up to 150 different adjustments to GAAP income and equity that could be made to restore equity and income to their true economic values. Most companies use no more than about five adjustments (such as the capitalization of research and development cost, recognition of the market value of certain assets, and the elimination of goodwill write-offs).

EVA provides a good operational metric for assessing managers' performance in terms of maximizing the market value of the company over time. It is a model that can be used to guide managerial action. Companies that use EVA for evaluating performance use it in making a broad range of decisions such as evaluating capital expenditure proposals, adding or dropping a product line, or acquiring another company. Only alternatives that provide economic value are accepted. The following Business Insight box discusses how Whole Foods uses EVA to guide decisions about store locations.

Business Insight ■ Economic Value Added

One of the major puzzles facing the grocery industry is investing in new stores. Organic grocer Whole Foods Market uses economic value added (EVA) to guide its decisions about store locations. Whole Foods analyzes potential sites based on population density, income levels, and education levels. A prospective site is then studied in depth, considering sales projections and estimates of construction and operating costs. Before the company commits capital to a new store, the project must meet an EVA hurdle based on the company's cost of capital. This hurdle is generally positive EVA in under five years.

According to Joel Stern, CEO of Stern Stewart and Company (a consulting company), the EVA ethos pervades the entire Whole Foods Organization. Stern says that Whole Foods employees are trained to add value to every customer interaction. The practice is for employees to take customers to the items that they are looking for and to point out relevant specials on the way rather than simply giving directions.

Sources: "SEC Form 10-K, Whole Foods Market, Inc.," The Securities and Exchange Commission EDGAR SYSTEM, November 13, 2015, 6.
Joel Stern and Joseph Willett, "A Look Back at the Beginnings of EVA and Value-Based Management," *Journal of Applied Corporate Finance* 26, no. 1 (Winter 2014): 39–46.

Which Measure Is Best?

Many executives view residual income or EVA as a better measure of managers' performance than ROI. They believe that residual income and EVA encourage managers to make profitable investments that managers might reject if being measured exclusively by ROI.

To illustrate, assume that three divisions of Monsanto have an opportunity to make an investment of $100,000 that requires $10,000 of additional current liabilities and that will generate a return of 20%. The manager of the Chemical Division is evaluated using ROI, the manager of the Agriculture Division is evaluated using residual income, and the manager of the Nutrition Division is evaluated using economic value added. The current ROI of each division is 24%. Each division has a current income of $120,000, a minimum return of 18% on invested capital, and a cost of capital of 14%. If each division has a current investment base of $500,000, current liabilities of $40,000, and a tax rate of 30%, the effect of the proposed investment on each division's performance is as follows:

	Current	+	Proposed	=	Total
Chemical Division					
Investment center income/Asset base	$120,000		$ 20,000		$140,000
	$500,000		$100,000		$600,000
ROI	24%		20%		23.3%

continued

continued from previous page

	Current	+	Proposed	=	Total
Agriculture Division					
Asset base	$500,000		$100,000		$600,000
Investment center income	$120,000		$ 20,000		$140,000
Minimum return (0.18 × base)	(90,000)		(18,000)		(108,000)
Residual income	$ 30,000		$ 2,000		$ 32,000
Nutrition Division					
Assets	$500,000		$100,000		$600,000
Current liabilities	(40,000)		(10,000)		(50,000)
Evaluation base	$460,000		$ 90,000		$550,000
Investment center income	$120,000		$ 20,000		$140,000
Income taxes (30%)	(36,000)		(6,000)		(42,000)
Income after taxes	84,000		14,000		98,000
Cost of capital (0.14 × base)	(64,400)		(12,600)		(77,000)
Economic value added	$ 19,600		$ 1,400		$ 21,000

The Chemical Division manager will not want to make the new investment because it reduces the current ROI from 24% to 23.3%. This is true, even though the company's minimum return is only 18%. Not wanting to explain a decline in the division's ROI, the manager will probably reject the opportunity even though it could have benefited the company as a whole.

The Agriculture Division manager will probably be happy to accept the new project because it increases residual income by $2,000. Any investment that provides a return more than the required minimum of 18% will be acceptable to the Agriculture Division manager. Given a profit maximization goal for the organization, the residual income method is preferred over ROI evaluations because it encourages division managers to accept all projects with returns above the 18% cutoff. The same is true for the Nutrition Division manager, although the EVA increase is not as high as that of the residual income because it has a different base.

The primary disadvantage of the residual income and EVA methods as comparative evaluation tools is that they measure performance in absolute dollars rather than percentages. Although they can be used to compare period-to-period results of the same division or with similar-size divisions, they cannot be used effectively to compare the performance of divisions of substantially different sizes. For example, the residual income of a multimillion dollar sales division should be higher than that of a half-million-dollar sales division. Because most performance evaluations and comparisons are made between units or alternative investments of different sizes, ROI continues to be extensively used. The following Business Insight box discusses the changing role of IT as the need for data management and analysis grows.

Business Insight ■ Measuring the Value of an IT Project

Historically, a company's IT department has been a support department for the core business. According to research by The Hackett Group, the modern IT group has the opportunity to redefine its role as the need for data management and analysis grows. The issue facing leaders of IT departments is that traditional metrics for IT departments focus on minimizing costs. To redefine the role of the IT department, managers need to redefine the way department performance is measured. The Hackett Group recommends the use of key performance indicators (KPIs), developed with input from stakeholders across the organization, that focus on the transformative contribution of the IT department. In the past, IT supported the software and hardware that employees used to do their jobs. Now the IT group can support managers with information they can use to implement their strategic decisions.

Source: "IT Strives to Reinvent Itself Despite Budget Restrictions While Delivering Improved Information and Analytics," *The Hackett Group*, April 1, 2014.

LO3 Review 24-3

KBR Inc., a decentralized engineering and construction organization, has three divisions, Engineering, Construction, and Military. Assume corporate management desires a minimum return of 15% on its investments and has a 20% tax rate. Suppose the divisions' current results follow (in thousands):

Division	Income	Investment
Engineering	$30,000	$200,000
Construction	50,000	250,000
Military	22,000	100,000

The company is planning an expansion project next year that will cost $50,000,000 and return $9,000,000 per year.

Required

a. Compute the ROI for each division for the current year.
b. Compute the residual income for each division for the current year.
c. Rank the divisions according to their ROI and residual income.
d. Assume that other income and investments will remain unchanged. Determine the effect of the project by itself. What is the effect on ROI and residual income, if the new project is added to each division?   Solution on p. 24-39.

Balanced Scorecard

Although financial measures have been emphasized throughout this text, several sections stress that other measures, specifically qualitative measures, are important in evaluating managerial performance. This section examines one popular method of performance evaluation using *both* financial and nonfinancial information.

LO4 Describe the balanced scorecard as a comprehensive performance measurement system.

We might ask: why not use just financial measures? First, no single financial measure captures all performance aspects of an organization. More than one measure must be used. Second, financial measures have reporting time lags that could hinder timely decision making. Third, financial measures might not accurately capture the information needed for current decision making because of the delay that sometimes occurs between making financial investments and receiving their results. For example, building a new nuclear power plant can take several years with the investment in total assets increasing the entire time without generating any revenues.

Balanced Scorecard Framework

Comprehensive performance measurement systems are one suggested solution. The basic premise is to establish a set of diverse key performance indicators to monitor performance. The **balanced scorecard** is a performance measurement system that includes financial and operational measures related to a firm's goals and strategies. The balanced scorecard comprises several categories of measurements, the most common of which include the following:

- Financial
- Customer satisfaction
- Internal processes
- Innovation and learning

A balanced scorecard is usually a set of reports required of all common operating units in an organization. To facilitate the periodic evaluation of performance, a cover sheet (or sheets for a large operation) can be used to summarize the performance of each area using the established criteria for each category.

For example, Einstein Brothers might have a balanced scorecard that looks something like the one in Exhibit 24.4. This balanced scorecard uses four categories for evaluation and includes financial and nonfinancial information. Each category being monitored has information from the previous period and the standard related to the category. The report should always include the current period, at least one previous period, and some standard. Each store manager should attach documentation and an appropriate explanation as to the change in the measurements during the reporting period.

Exhibit 24.4 ■ Balanced Scorecard Illustration

	Standard	Prior Period	Current Period
Key financial indicators			
Cash flow	$ 25,000	$ 28,000	$ 21,000
Return on investment (ROI)	0.18	0.22	0.19
Sales	$4,400,000	$4,494,000	$4,342,000
Key customer indicators			
Average customers per hour	75	80	71
Number of customer complaints per period	22	21	17
Number of sales returns per period	10	8	5
Key operating indicators			
Bagels sold/produced per day ratio	0.96	0.93	0.91
Daily units lost (burned, dropped, etc.)	25	32	34
Employee turnover per period	0.10	0.07	0.00
Key growth and innovation indicators			
New products introduced during period	1	1	0
Products discontinued during period	1	1	1
Number of sales promotions	3	3	2
Special offers, discounts, etc.	4	5	3

In making assessments with the evaluation categories, it is important to consider both trailing and leading performance measures. *Trailing measures* look backward at historical data while *leading measures* provide some idea of what to expect currently or in the near future. For example, in the financial category, ROI is a trailing indicator while a budget of production units and costs for the next period is a leading indicator. In the customer category, the number of sales invoices per store might tell us whether each store is maintaining its customer base (a trailing indicator) while the number of product complaints per 1,000 invoices might be a leading indicator of customer satisfaction, quality control problems, and future sales.

The use of balanced scorecard systems to monitor and assess managerial and organizational performance is increasing worldwide. The following Business Insight discusses some of the complexities involved in the Department of Education's implementation of the College Scorecard.

Business Insight ■ Understanding Your Strategy: The First Step to a Balanced Scorecard

Since 2013, the Department of Education has been applying a modified version of the balanced scorecard to universities. The College Scorecard was developed to help prospective students evaluate universities before applying. Like all balanced scorecard approaches, the efficacy of the College Scorecard depends on how well what is measured reflects the underlying economics of the business or organization, which is reflected in both the praise and criticism of the College Scorecard. Proponents of the scorecard point to measurement of alumni debt and salaries as powerful reflections of important economic realities that prospective students should consider. Critics of the College Scorecard note that the data in the Scorecard does not allow students to compare themselves by major. A history major considering two schools can only compare average students at the two schools, not history majors at the two schools. Critics also point to the fact that the scorecard only considers full-time students who start and finish at the same school.

With all balanced scorecard approaches to performance evaluation, two essential considerations underpin success. First, the scorecard must be based on a clear understanding of the business activity. Second, the limitations of what can be measured should be carefully considered. Users of the scorecard approach must be careful to craft measurements that accurately reflect the underlying value creation process.

Sources: Peter McPherson and Andrew Kelly, "The College Scorecard Strikes Out," *Wall Street Journal*, March 16, 2015.
Jonathan Rothwell, "Understanding the College Scorecard," *Brookings*, September 28, 2015.

A balanced scorecard gives management a perspective of the organization's performance on a recurring set of criteria. Since each reporting unit knows what reports are expected, no one is surprised by changing monthly requests for data. Because the multiple perspectives provide management a broad analysis of the organization's performance, it allows them to determine how and where the goals and objectives are either being achieved or not achieved.

For most management teams, the balanced scorecard highlights trade-offs between measures. For example, a substantial increase in customer satisfaction can result in a short-run decrease in ROI because the extra effort to please customers is expensive, thereby reducing ROI. A balanced scorecard can be filtered down the organization with successively lower-level operating units having their own scorecards that mimic those of the higher-level units. This provides all levels of management an opportunity to evaluate operations from more than just a financial perspective.

Research Insight ■ A Picture May Be Worth a Higher Stock Price

In his book *The Winter of Our Discontent*, John Steinbeck wrote, "For the most part people are not curious except about themselves." Psychologists define narcissism as a sense of self-importance, uniqueness, entitlement, self-absorption, arrogance, and vanity. However, some of these same traits are correlated with leadership qualities. In a recent study, researchers investigate the link between CEO narcissism and financial performance, specifically, earnings per share (EPS) and stock price.

They measure CEO narcissism by examining the size and composition of the CEO's photograph in the annual report and components of the CEO's compensation package. They find that narcissistic managers are more likely to take actions that increase sales and production levels, such as extending lenient credit terms, offering sales discounts, and overproducing. There is no evidence that these same managers attempt to manage earnings through accrual-related actions.

Source: Kari Joseph Olsen, Kelsey Kay Dworkis, and S. Mark Young, "CEO Narcissism and Accounting: A Picture of Profits," *Journal of Management Accounting Research* 26, no. 2 (Fall 2014): 243–267.

As with all management tools and techniques, the use of the balanced scorecard must be incorporated with the other information sources within the organization. Just as the accounting information system cannot stand alone in managing a business, neither can the balanced scorecard. Some areas could need extensive accounting information in great detail to make the best possible decision while other areas need great detail in production or service integration to be at the right place at the right time. By using a multifaceted approach to managing, the organization should be able to better establish an operating strategy that coincides with its overall goals and objectives.

Balanced Scorecard and Strategy

When a balanced scorecard system is fully utilized to monitor and evaluate an organization's progress, it becomes a system for operationalizing the organization's strategy. Having a goal to maximize shareholder value or generate a certain income does not constitute a strategy. Maximizing shareholder value can be an overarching corporate goal, but it will not likely be realized without a well-developed strategy that identifies and establishes a balanced set of goals on various dimensions of performance.

A balanced scorecard can be the primary vehicle for translating strategy into action and establishing accountability for performance. The balanced scorecard identifies the areas of managerial action that are believed to be the drivers of corporate achievement. If the corporate goal is to increase ROI or residual income, the balanced scorecard should include key performance indicators that drive these measures.

An interesting parallel to the successful management of a company can be drawn by considering the key performance indicators the manager of a professional baseball team uses in setting goals and evaluating progress. The manager of the New York Yankees does not just tell his players and managers at the beginning of the baseball season that the team's goal is to win the World Series or even a certain number of ball games. The win-loss record is only one metric used to set goals and evaluate performance for a baseball team. The manager looks at many different drivers of success related to hitting, pitching, and fielding, including the earned-run averages of the pitchers, the batting and on-base averages of hitters, the number of errors per game by fielders, and the number of bases stolen by base runners. At the end of the season, the manager measures success not just by whether the Yankees won the World Series, but also by the batting average, number of home runs, and number of bases stolen by individual players, and whether or not a team member won a Golden Glove award or the Cy Young award. These are all measures by which to evaluate achievement and strategic accomplishment. By achieving the goals for each of these areas of the game, the win-loss ratio will take care of itself. If the win-loss results are not acceptable, then the manager adjusts his strategic goals with respect to the key performance indicators (or the manager is dismissed).

Like a baseball team, a company can use a balanced scorecard to develop performance metrics for managers from the top of the company to the lowest-level department. The scorecard becomes a vehicle for communicating the factors that are key to the success of managers, factors that upper management will monitor in evaluating the success of lower managers in carrying out the corporate strategy. To make balanced scorecards more user friendly, several companies use performance monitoring **dashboards**, which are computer-generated graphics that present scorecard results using graphics, some of which mimic the instrument displays on an automobile dashboard.

The following Business Insight provides an illustration of dashboard graphics.

Business Insight   ■   Balanced Scorecard Dashboard

Balanced scorecard dashboards provide information about an organization in an "at-a-glance" format. Many software companies now provide utilities for generating dashboards from SAP, Excel, QuickBooks, and other databases. The following is an example of a dashboard for Sonatica, a fictional company, designed by Dundas Dashboard for assessment of financial performance. The shaded tabs present financial information graphics for Sales and Support. Additional screens would provide performance data on other scorecard dimensions such as internal processes, customers, and innovation and growth.

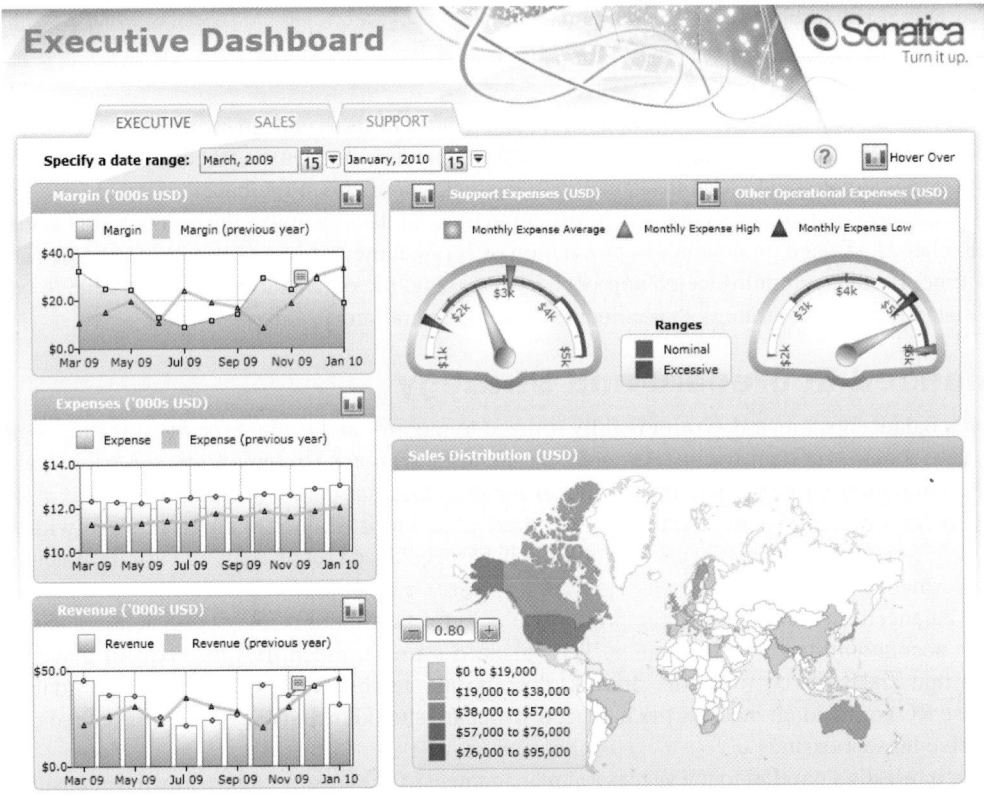

Source: *http://www.dashboardinsight.com/dashboards/live-dashboards/dundas-dashboard-v-2-0-demo.aspx*

Balanced Scorecard The following alphabetically ordered list of financial and nonfinancial performance metrics is provided for Northeast Inc.

Average call wait	Job offer acceptance rate	Net profit margin
Average customer survey rating	Market share	Number of complaints
Employee turnover ratio	New customer count	Number of defects reported
Expense as a % of revenue	New customer sales value	Service error rate
Expense variance %	New product acceptance rate	Time to market on new products
Fulfillment %	New product revenue	Unique repeat customer count
Headcount growth	New product ROI	Year-over-year revenue growth
Industry quality rating	Net profit	

Required

a. Assign the above metrics to the four balanced scorecard categories of (1) Financial Success, (2) Customer Satisfaction and Brand Improvement, (3) Business Process Improvement, (4) Learning and Growth of Motivated Workforce.

b. Comment on the use of balanced scorecard versus a single financial measure such as ROI or EVA.   Solution on p. 24-40.

Guidance Answers

You Are the Division Vice President

Pg. 24-17 ROI is primarily a measure of the profitability of a division's assets, which is in turn a measure of how effectively the investment in assets was used to generate sales, and how profitable those sales were. ROI is driven by investment (or asset) turnover (which is division sales divided by assets) and return on sales (which is division net income divided by division sales). Therefore, increasing ROI is similar to a simultaneous balancing act involving controlling sales, expenses, and asset investment. You can increase ROI by increasing sales more than expenses, while holding asset investment constant, or by other combinations of these three variables that ultimately increase ROI. If you adjust one of these variables, at the same time you must keep your eye on the other two variables or you may not achieve your goal of increasing ROI.

Questions

Q24-1. What is the relationship between segment reports and reports of operating results by product?

Q24-2. What is a business segment? How is it determined?

Q24-3. Can a company have more than one type of first-level statement in segment reporting?

Q24-4. Explain the relationships between any two levels of statements in segment reporting.

Q24-5. Distinguish between direct and indirect segment costs.

Q24-6. What types of information are needed before management should decide to drop a segment?

Q24-7. In what types of organizations and for what purpose are transfer prices used?

Q24-8. What problems arise when transfer pricing is used?

Q24-9. When do transfer prices lead to suboptimization? How can suboptimization be minimized? Can it be eliminated? Why or why not?

Q24-10. For what purpose do organizations use return on investment? Why is this measure preferred to net income?

Q24-11. What advantages do residual income and EVA have over ROI for segment evaluations?

Q24-12. Contrast the difference between residual income and EVA.

Q24-13. Explain how a balanced scorecard helps with the evaluation process of internal operations.

Q24-14. How can a balanced scorecard be used as a strategy implementation tool?

Assignments with the ⊚ logo in the margin are available in BusinessCourse.
See the Preface of the book for details.

Mini Exercises

LO1   **M24-15.**   **Multiple Levels of Segment Reporting**

Connect Inc. manufactures four different lines of computer devices: modems, routers, servers, and drives. Each of the product lines is produced in all of the company's three plants: Beckley, Huntington, and Charleston. Marketing efforts of the company are divided into five regions: East, West, South, North, and Central.

Required

a. Develop a reporting schematic that illustrates how the company might prepare single-level reports segmented on three different bases.

b. Develop a segment reporting schematic that has three different levels. Be sure to identify each segment's level. Briefly explain why you chose the primary-level segment.

LO1   **M24-16.**   **Income Statements Segmented by Territory**

Pentel of America, LTD

Assume **Pentel** has two product lines. The September income statements of each product line and the company are as follows:

PENTEL OF AMERICA, LTD Product Line and Company Income Statements For Month of September			
(in thousands)	Pens	Pencils	Total
Sales.	$60,000	$60,000	$120,000
Less variable expenses	(27,000)	(27,000)	(54,000)
Contribution margin	33,000	33,000	66,000
Less direct fixed expenses	(16,000)	(14,000)	(30,000)
Product margin	$17,000	$19,000	36,000
Less common fixed expenses			(15,500)
Net income			$20,500

Pens and pencils are sold in two sales regions, West and East, as follows:

(in thousands)	West	East
Pen sales	$35,000	$25,000
Pencil sales	20,000	40,000
Total sales	$55,000	$65,000

The common fixed expenses (in thousands) are traceable to each territory as follows:

West fixed expenses	$5,500
East fixed expenses	6,500
Home office administration fixed expenses	3,500
Total common fixed expenses	$15,500

The direct fixed expenses of pens, $16,000, and of pencils, $14,000, cannot be identified with either territory. The company's accountants were unable to allocate any of the common fixed expenses to the various segments.

Required

Prepare income statements segmented by territory for September, including a column for the entire firm.

LO1   **M24-17.**   **Income Statements Segmented by Products**

Francisco Consulting Firm provides three types of client services in three health-care-related industries. The income statement for July is as follows:

FRANCISCO CONSULTING FIRM Income Statement For Month of July		
Sales.		$820,000
Less variable costs.		(580,750)
Contribution margin		239,250
Less fixed expenses		
Service	$85,600	
Selling and administrative.	70,400	(156,000)
Net income.		$ 83,250

The sales, contribution margin ratios, and direct fixed expenses for the three types of services are as follows:

	Hospitals	Physicians	Nursing Care
Sales.	$340,000	$205,000	$275,000
Contribution margin ratio	25%	35%	30%
Direct fixed expenses of services.	$ 36,500	$ 8,500	$ 18,750
Allocated common fixed services expense.	$ 8,500	$ 2,500	$ 4,000

Required
Prepare income statements segmented by client categories. Include a column for the entire firm in the statement.

M24-18. **Internal or External Acquisitions: No Opportunity Costs**

The Van Division of Travel Vans Corporation has offered to purchase 48,000 wheels from the Wheel Division for $80 per wheel. At a normal volume of 320,000 wheels per year, production costs per wheel for the Wheel Division are as follows:

Direct materials.	$20
Direct labor.	12
Variable overhead	8
Fixed overhead.	25
Total	$65

The Wheel Division has been selling 320,000 wheels per year to outside buyers at $100 each. Capacity is 400,000 wheels per year. The Van Division has been buying wheels from outside suppliers at $95 per wheel.

Required
a. Should the Wheel Division manager accept the offer? Show computations.
b. From the standpoint of the company, will the internal sale be beneficial?

M24-19. **Transfer Prices at Full Cost with Excess Capacity: Divisional Viewpoint**

Karakomi Cameras Inc. has a Disposables Division that produces a camera that sells for $10 per unit in the open market. The cost of the product is $5.50 (variable manufacturing of $3.00, and fixed manufacturing of $2.50). Total fixed manufacturing costs are $100,000 at the normal annual production volume of 40,000 units. The Overseas Division has offered to buy 10,000 units at the full cost of $5.50. The Disposables Division has excess capacity, and the 10,000 units can be produced without interfering with the current outside sales of 40,000 units. The total fixed cost of the Disposables Division will not change.

Required
Explain whether the Disposables Division should accept or reject the offer. Show calculations.

M24-20. **Transfer Pricing with Excess Capacity: Divisional and Corporate Viewpoints**   **LO2**
Art.com
Assume Art.com has a Print Division that is currently producing 150,000 prints per year but has a capacity of 200,000 prints. The variable costs of each print are $30, and the annual fixed costs are $1,650,000. The prints sell for $44 in the open market. The company's Retail Division wants to buy 50,000 prints at $20 each. The Print Division manager refuses the order because the price is below

variable cost. The Retail Division manager argues that the order should be accepted because it will lower the fixed cost per print from $11 to $8.25.

Required

a. Should the Retail Division order be accepted? Why or why not?

b. From the viewpoints of the Print Division and the company, should the order be accepted if the manager of the Retail Division intends to sell each print in the outside market for $40 after incurring additional costs of $5 per print?

c. What action should the company take, assuming it believes in divisional autonomy?

LO3   **M24-21.**   **ROI and Residual Income: Impact of a New Investment**

The Stallion Division of Motortown Motors had an operating income of $805,000 and net assets of $3,500,000. Motortown Motors has a target rate of return of 20%.

Required

a. Compute the return on investment.

b. Compute the residual income.

c. The Stallion Division has an opportunity to increase operating income by $165,000 with an $800,000 investment in assets.

　　1. Compute the Stallion Division's return on investment if the project is undertaken. (Round your answer to three decimal places.)

　　2. Compute the Stallion Division's residual income if the project is undertaken.

LO3   **M24-22.**   **ROI: Fill in the Unknowns**

Provide the missing data in the following situations:

	Eastern Division	Western Division	Southern Division
Sales.	?	$8,000,000	?
Net operating income	$250,000	$ 600,000	$1,080,000
Operating assets	?	?	$3,000,000
Return on investment	20%	15%	?
Return on sales	5%	?	6%
Investment turnover	?	?	6

LO4   **M24-23.**   **Selection of Balanced Scorecard Items**

The Worldwide Auditors' Association is a professional association. Its current membership totals 65,400 worldwide. The association operates from a central headquarters in New Zealand but has local membership units throughout the world. The local units hold monthly meetings to discuss recent developments in accounting and to hear professional speakers on topics of interest. The association's journal, *Worldwide Auditor,* is published monthly with feature articles and topical interest areas. The association publishes books and reports and sponsors continuing education courses. A statement of revenues and expenses follows:

WORLDWIDE AUDITORS' ASSOCIATION Statement of Revenues and Expenses For Year Ending November 30		
($ in thousands)		
Revenues		$50,702
Expenses		
Salaries	$28,050	
Other personnel costs	5,872	
Occupancy costs	5,545	
Reimbursement to local units	2,536	
Other membership services	1,200	
Printing and paper	383	
Postage and shipping	165	
General and administrative	845	44,596
Excess of revenues over expenses		$ 6,106

Additional information follows:

- Membership dues are $480 per year, of which $100 is considered to cover a one-year subscription to the association's journal. Other benefits include membership in the association and unit affiliation.
- One-year subscriptions to *Worldwide Auditor* are sold to nonmembers for $120 each. A total of 10,000 of these subscriptions was sold. In addition to subscriptions, the journal generated $500,000 in advertising revenue. The cost per magazine was $50.
- A total of 30,000 technical reports was sold by the Books and Reports Department at an average unit selling price of $110. Average costs per publication were $36.
- The association offers a variety of continuing education courses to both members and nonmembers. During the year, the one-day course, which cost participants an average of $600 each, was attended by 25,600 people. A total of 3,800 people took two-day courses at a cost of $1,000 per person.
- General and administrative expenses include all other costs incurred by the corporate staff to operate the association.
- The organization has net capital assets of $87,230,000 and had an actual cost of capital of 6%.

Required

a. Give some examples of key financial performance indicators (no computations needed) that could be part of a balanced scorecard for the IAA.

b. Give some examples of key customer and operating performance indicators (no computations needed) that could be part of a balanced scorecard for IAA.

Exercises

E24-24. **Appropriate Transfer Prices: Opportunity Costs**

LO2

Olam International Limited

Olam International Limited sources and processes agricultural products including edible nuts and spices. Assume the company recently acquired a peanut-processing company that has a normal annual capacity of 180,000 bushels and that sold 125,000 bushels last year at a price of $35 per bushel. The purpose of the acquisition is to furnish peanuts for a new peanut butter plant, which needs 75,000 bushels of peanuts per year. It has been purchasing peanuts from suppliers at the market price. Production costs per bushel of the peanut-processing company are as follows:

Direct materials.	$9
Direct labor.	4
Variable overhead	2
Fixed overhead at normal capacity.	10
Total.	$25

Management is trying to decide what transfer price to use for sales from the newly acquired Peanut Division to the Peanut Butter Division. The manager of the Peanut Division argues that $35, the market price, is appropriate. The manager of the Peanut Butter Division argues that the cost price of $25 (or perhaps even less) should be used since fixed overhead costs should be recomputed. Any output of the Peanut Division up to 180,000 bushels that is not sold to the Peanut Butter Division could be sold to regular customers at $35 per bushel.

Required

a. Compute the annual gross profit for the Peanut Division using a transfer price of $35.

b. Compute the annual gross profit for the Peanut Division using a transfer price of $25.

c. What transfer price(s) will lead the manager of the Peanut Butter Division to act in a manner that will maximize company profits?

E24-25. **Negotiating a Transfer Price with Excess Capacity**

LO2

The Foundry Division of Findlay Pumps Inc. produces metal parts that are sold to the company's Assembly Division and to outside customers. Operating data for the Foundry Division for the current year are as follows:

	To the Assembly Division	To Outside Customers	Total
Sales			
600,000 parts × $8.00..................	$4,800,000		
400,000 parts × $9.00..................		$3,600,000	$8,400,000
Variable expenses at $3.75	(2,250,000)	(1,500,000)	(3,750,000)
Contribution margin	2,550,000	2,100,000	4,650,000
Fixed expenses*........................	(1,350,000)	(900,000)	(2,250,000)
Net income	$1,200,000	$1,200,000	$2,400,000

*Allocated on the basis of unit sales.

The Assembly Division has just received an offer from an outside supplier to supply parts at $5.50 each. The Foundry Division manager is not willing to meet the $5.50 price. She argues that it costs her $6.00 per part to produce and sell to the Assembly Division, so she would show no profit on the Assembly Division sales. Sales to outside customers are at a maximum, 400,000 parts.

Required
a. Verify the Foundry Division's $6 unit cost figure.
b. Should the Foundry Division meet the outside price of $5.50 for Assembly Division sales? Explain.
c. Could the Foundry Division meet the $5.50 price and still show a net profit for sales to the Assembly Division? Show computations.

LO2   E24-26.   Dual Transfer Pricing

The Athens Company has two divisions, Alpha and Delta. Delta Division produces a product at a variable cost of $12 per unit, and sells 200,000 units to outside customers at $20 per unit and 60,000 units to Alpha Division at variable cost plus 50%. Under the dual transfer price system, Alpha Division pays only the variable cost per unit. Delta Division's fixed costs are $575,000 per year. After further processing, Alpha sells the 60,000 units to outside customers at $40 per unit. Alpha has variable costs of $11 per unit, in addition to the costs from Delta Division. Alpha Division's annual fixed costs are $380,000. There are no beginning or ending inventories.

Required
a. Prepare the income statements for the two divisions and the company as a whole.
b. Why is the income for the company less than the sum of the profit figures shown on the income statements for the two divisions? Explain.

LO3   E24-27.   ROI and Residual Income: Basic Computations

Watkins Associated Industries

Watkins Associated Industries is a privately held conglomerate. Assume that the company uses return on investment and residual income as two of the evaluation tools for division managers. The company has a minimum desired rate of return on investment of 15%. Selected operating data for three of the divisions of the company follow.

	Trucking Division	Seafood Division	Construction Division
Sales...............	$6,450,000	$1,845,000	$5,200,000
Operating assets	3,750,000	580,000	1,750,000
Net operating income	525,000	116,000	385,000

Required
a. Compute the return on investment for each division. (Round answers to three decimal places.)
b. Compute the residual income for each division.

LO3   E24-28.   ROI and Residual Income: Assessing Performance
Refer to the computations in the previous exercise E24-27. Assess the performance of the division managers, basing your conclusions on ROI. Assess the performance of the division managers, basing your conclusions on residual income. Which manager is doing the best job?

LO3   E24-29.   ROI, Residual Income, and EVA with Different Bases

Envision Company has a target return on capital of 10%. In evaluating operations, management looks at book values (GAAP compliant) and current values. Current values reflect management's estimates of asset values. The following financial information is available for October ($ thousands):

	Software Division (Value Base)		Consulting Division (Value Base)		Venture Capital Division (Value Base)	
	Book	**Current**	**Book**	**Current**	**Book**	**Current**
Sales............	$200,000	$200,000	$450,000	$450,000	$625,000	$625,000
Pretax income......	35,000	37,200	37,000	38,500	63,000	43,200
Operating assets ...	250,000	310,000	185,000	175,000	700,000	720,000
Current liabilities....	30,000	30,000	20,000	20,000	65,000	65,000

Required

a. Compute the return on investment using both book and current values for each division. (Round answers to three decimal places.) For ROI calculations, Envision uses operating assets as the investment base.

b. Compute the residual income for both book and current values for each division.

c. Compute the economic value-added income for both book and current values for each division if the tax rate is 20% and the weighted average cost of capital is 8%.

d. Does book value or current value provide a better basis for performance evaluation? Which division do you consider the most successful?

E24-30.   **Balanced Scorecard Preparation**

The following information is in addition to that presented in exercise M24-23 for the Worldwide Auditors' Association. In the budget for the current year, the organization had set a membership goal of 75,000 members with the following anticipated results:

LO4

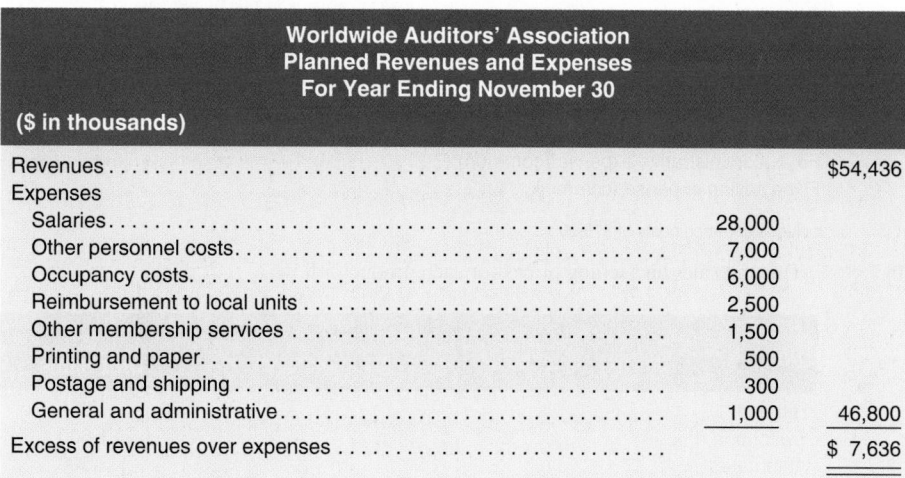

Worldwide Auditors' Association Planned Revenues and Expenses For Year Ending November 30		
($ in thousands)		
Revenues..		$54,436
Expenses		
Salaries..	28,000	
Other personnel costs...............................	7,000	
Occupancy costs....................................	6,000	
Reimbursement to local units	2,500	
Other membership services	1,500	
Printing and paper.................................	500	
Postage and shipping................................	300	
General and administrative............................	1,000	46,800
Excess of revenues over expenses		$ 7,636

Additional information follows:

- One-year subscriptions to *Worldwide Auditor* were anticipated to be 8,000 units.
- Advertising revenue was budgeted at $450,000. Each magazine was budgeted at a cost of $48.
- A total of 25,000 technical reports was anticipated at an average price of $100 with average costs of $36.
- The budgeted one-day courses had an anticipated attendance of 25,000 with an average fee of $600. The two-day courses had an anticipated attendance of 5,000 with an average fee of $1,000 per person.
- The organization began the year with net capital assets of $84,100,000 with a planned cost of capital of 6%.

Required

a. Prepare a balanced scorecard for IAA for November with calculated key performance indicators presented in two columns for planned performance and actual performance—include key financial, customer, and operating performance indicators.

b. Which of the evaluation areas you selected indicated success and which indicated failure?

c. Give some explanations of the successes and failures.

Problems

LO1 **P24-31.** **Multiple Segment Reports**

Worldwide Communications, Incorporated, sells telecommunication products throughout the world in three sales territories: Europe, Asia, and the Americas. For July, all $945,000 of administrative expense is traceable to the territories, except $200,000, which is common to all units and cannot be traced or allocated to the sales territories. The percentage of product line sales made in each of the sales territories and the assignment of traceable fixed expenses follow:

	Sales Territory			
	Europe	Asia	The Americas	Company
Handset sales.................	40%	35%	25%	100%
Switchboard sales	35%	35%	30%	100%
Automated switches sales	10%	15%	75%	100%
Fixed administrative expense......	$350,000	$275,000	$220,000	$845,000
Fixed selling expense...........	$155,000	$175,000	$550,000	$880,000

The manufacturing takes place in one large facility with three distinct manufacturing operations. Selected product-line cost data follow.

	Handset	Switchboard	Automated Switches	Company
Variable costs.....................	$ 15	$ 850	$ 1,950	
Depreciation and supervision..........	60,000	175,000	275,000	$ 585,000*
Other mfg. overhead (common)..				650,000
Fixed administrative expense (common)				1,045,000
Fixed selling expense (common)				880,000

*Includes common costs of $75,000

The unit sales and selling prices for each product follow.

	Unit Sales	Selling Price
Handset	6,500	$ 25
Switchboard	1,500	1,900
Automated	2,500	3,500

Required

a. Prepare an income statement for July segmented by product line. Include a column for the entire firm.

b. Prepare an income statement for July segmented by sales territory. Include a column for the entire firm.

c. Prepare an income statement for July by product line for The Americas sales territory. Include a column for the territory as a whole. Products are manufactured in a single facility. Although depreciation and supervision are allocated by product line, those costs are not allocated by territory.

d. Discuss the value of multilevel segment reporting as a managerial tool. Compare and contrast the benefits of the reports generated in parts a, b, and c.

LO1 **P24-32.** **Segment Reporting and Analysis**

The Essential Baking Company

The Essential Baking Company bakes artisan loaves, baguettes, and rolls and sells them in cities throughout the Northwest. Assume the following March income statement was prepared for the stores located in Seattle and Portland:

THE ESSENTIAL BAKING COMPANY Territory Income Statements For Month of March			
(in thousands)	Seattle	Portland	Total
Sales.	$8,400	$6,800	$15,200
Cost of goods sold	(4,796)	(3,894)	(8,690)
Gross profit.	3,604	2,906	6,510
Selling and administrative expenses	(2,755)	(2,155)	(4,910)
Net income.	$ 849	$ 751	$ 1,600

Sales and selected variable expense data are as follows:

	Products		
	Loaves	Baguettes	Rolls
Fixed baking expenses.	$ 565	$ 450	$410
Variable baking expenses as a percentage of sales	50%	50%	40%
Variable selling expenses as a percentage of sales.	10%	20%	20%
City of Seattle, sales (in thousands).	$3,800	$2,650	$1,950
City of Portland, sales (in thousands).	$3,250	$2,150	$1,400

The fixed selling expenses were $1,440 for March, of which $860 was a direct expense of the Seattle market and $580 was a direct expense of the Portland market. Fixed administrative expenses were $1,135, which management has decided not to allocate when using the contribution approach.

Required

a. Prepare a segment income statement showing the margin for each territory (city) for March. Include a column combining the two territories.

b. Prepare segment income statements showing the product margin for each product. Include a column for the combined products.

c. If the rolls line is dropped and fixed baking expenses do not change, what is the product margin for loaves and baguettes?

d. What other type of segmentation might be useful to The Essential Baking Company. Explain.

P24-33. **Segment Reporting and Analysis** LO1

Business Book Publishers, Inc. has prepared income statements segmented by divisions, but management is still uncertain about actual performance. Financial information for May is given as follows:

	Textbook Division	Professional Division	Company Total
Sales.	$150,000	$307,500	$457,500
Less variable expenses			
Manufacturing.	24,000	153,750	177,750
Selling and administrative.	7,500	15,375	22,875
Total.	(31,500)	(169,125)	(200,625)
Contribution margin	118,500	138,375	256,875
Less direct fixed expenses.	(15,000)	(150,000)	(165,000)
Net income.	$103,500	$ (11,625)	$ 91,875

Management is concerned about the Professional Division and requests additional analysis. Additional information regarding May operations of the Professional Division is as follows:

	Professional Division		
	Accounting Books Segment	**Executive Books Segment**	**Management Books Segment**
Sales...........................	$105,000	$105,000	$97,500
Variable manufacturing expenses as a percentage of sales............	60%	40%	50%
Other variable expenses as a percentage of sales............	5%	5%	5%
Direct fixed expenses................	$37,500	$55,100	$37,500
Allocated common fixed expenses......	$ 3,000	$ 1,500	$ 4,500

The professional accounting books are sold to auditors and controllers. The current information on these markets is as follows:

	Accounting Books Segment		
	Auditors Market	**Controllers Market**	**Total**
Sales...........................	$22,500	$82,500	$105,000
Variable manufacturing expenses as a percentage of sales............	60%	60%	—
Other variable expenses as a percentage of sales............	6%	6%	—
Direct fixed expenses................	$11,250	$22,500	$33,750
Allocated common fixed expenses.......	$ 1,125	$ 1,500	$ 2,625

Required

a. Prepare an income statement segmented by product for the Professional Division. Include a column for the division as a whole.

b. Prepare an income statement segmented by market for the Accounting Books Segment of the Professional Division.

c. Evaluate which Accounting Books Segment the Professional Division should keep or discontinue in the short run.

d. What is the correct long-run decision? Explain fully, including any possible risks associated with your recommendation.

LO1   **P24-34.   Segment Reports and Cost Allocations**

All Things Greek Inc. has three sales divisions. One of the key evaluation inputs for each division manager is the performance of his or her division based on division income. The division statements for August are as follows:

	Alpha	Beta	Gamma	Total
Sales.........................	$250,000	$300,000	$275,000	$825,000
Cost of sales....................	139,500	165,000	158,250	462,750
Division overhead...............	39,000	45,000	41,250	125,250
Division expenses...............	(178,500)	(210,000)	(199,500)	(588,000)
Division contribution.............	71,500	90,000	75,500	237,000
Corporate overhead.............	(41,000)	(49,000)	(45,000)	(135,000)
Division income	$ 30,500	$ 41,000	$ 30,500	$102,000

The Gamma manager is unhappy that his profitability is the same as that of the Alpha Division and 74% that of the Beta Division when his sales are halfway between these two divisions. The manager knows that his division must carry more product lines because of customer demands, and many of these additional product lines are not very profitable. He has not dropped these marginal product lines because of idle capacity; all of the products cover their own variable costs. After analyzing the product lines with the lowest profit margins, the divisional controller for Gamma provided the following to the manager:

Sales of marginal products.		$55,000
Cost of sales.	$34,100	
Avoidable fixed costs	13,500	47,600
Product margin.		$ 7,400

Although these products were 20% of Gamma's total sales, they contributed only about 10% of the division's profits. The controller also noted that the corporate overhead allocation was based on relative sales proportions and the allocation would decrease if the weak product line was dropped.

Required

a. Prepare a set of segment statements for August assuming that all facts remain the same except that Gamma's weak product lines are dropped and corporate overhead is allocated as follows: Alpha, $43,800; Beta, $52,600; and Gamma, $38,600. Does the Gamma Division appear better after this action? What will be the responses of the other two division managers?

b. Suggest improvements for All Things Greek's reporting process that will better reflect the actual operations of the divisions. Keep in mind the utilization of the reporting process to assist in the evaluation of the managers. What other changes could be made to improve the manager evaluation process?

P24-35. **ROI, Residual Income, and EVA: Impact of a New Investment**   **LO3**

EEG Inc. is a decentralized organization with four autonomous divisions. The divisions are evaluated on the basis of the change in their return on invested assets. Operating results in the Commercial Division for the year follow:

EEG INC.—COMMERCIAL DIVISION
Income Statement
For Year Ending December 31

Sales.	$3,000,000
Less variable expenses	(1,550,000)
Contribution margin	1,450,000
Less fixed expenses.	(1,200,000)
Net operating income	$ 250,000

Operating assets for the Commercial Division currently average $2,500,000. The Commercial Division can add a new product line for an investment of $400,000. Relevant data for the new product line are as follows:

Sales.	$625,000
Variable expenses (% of sales)	60%
Fixed expenses	$220,000
Increase in current liabilities.	$ 18,000

Required

a. Determine the effect on ROI of accepting the new product line. (Round calculations to three decimal places.)

b. If a return of 6% is the minimum that any division should earn and residual income is used to evaluate managers, would this encourage the division to accept the new product line? Explain and show computations.

c. If EVA is used to evaluate managers, should the new product line be accepted if the weighted average cost of capital is 6% and the income tax rate is 20%?

P24-36. **Valuing Investment Center Assets**   **LO3**

Six Flags Entertainment Corp operates theme parks in the United States, Mexico, and Europe. One of its first theme parks, Six Flags over Georgia, was built in the 1960s in Atlanta on a large tract of land that has appreciated enormously over the years. Although most of the rides and other attractions have a fairly short life, some of the major buildings that are still in use on the property have been fully depreciated since they were built. Assume that Six Flags over Georgia operates as an investment center with total assets that have a book value of $75 million and current liabilities of $5 million. Assume also that in the current year, this particular theme park had sales of $65 million and pretax division income of $12 million. The replacement cost of all the assets in this park is estimated to be $115 million. The company has a 20% tax rate and a target return of 10% and a cost of capital of 6%.

Required

a. Calculate the ROI, residual income, and EVA for Six Flags over Georgia using asset book value in the valuation basis for the investment center asset base.

b. Repeat requirement (a) using replacement cost as the investment center asset value.

c. Which valuation, accounting book value, or replacement cost do you think the company uses to evaluate the managers of its various theme parks? Discuss.

LO2, 3 **P24-37.** **Transfer Pricing with and without Capacity Constraints**

Elise Carpets Inc. has just acquired a new backing division that produces a rubber backing, which it sells for $3.75 per square yard. Sales are about 1 million square yards per year. Since the Backing Division has a capacity of 1.5 million square yards per year, top management is thinking that it might be wise for the company's Tufting Division to start purchasing from the newly acquired Backing Division. The Tufting Division now purchases 350,000 square yards per year from an outside supplier at a price of $3.50 per square yard. The current price is lower than the Backing division's $3.75 price as a result of the large quantity discounts. The Backing Division's cost per square yard follows.

Direct materials.	$1.25
Direct labor.	0.50
Variable overhead	0.15
Fixed overhead (1,000,000 level).	0.85
Total cost	$2.75

Required

a. If both divisions are to be treated as investment centers and their performance evaluated by the ROI formula, what transfer price would you recommend? Why?

b. If fixed costs are assumed not to change, determine the effect on corporate profits of making the backing.

c. Based on your transfer price, would you expect the ROI in the Backing Division to increase, decrease, or remain unchanged? Explain.

d. What would be the effect on the ROI of the Tufting Division using your transfer price? Explain.

e. Assume that the Backing Division is now selling 1.5 million square yards per year to retail outlets. What transfer price would you recommend? What will be the effect on corporate profits?

f. If the Backing Division is at capacity and decides to sell to the Tufting Division for $3.50 per square yard, what will be the effect on the company's profits?

LO2 **P24-38.** **Transfer Pricing and Special Orders**

Washington State Products has several manufacturing divisions. The Seattle Division produces a component part that is used in the manufacture of electronic equipment. The cost per part for July is as follows:

Variable cost.	$150
Fixed cost (at 3,000 units per month capacity).	90
Total cost per part.	$240

Some of Seattle Division's output is sold to outside manufacturers, and some is sold internally to the Redmond Division. The price per part is $375. The Redmond Division's cost and revenue structure follow.

Selling price per unit.		$1,500
Less variable costs per unit		
Cost of parts from the Seattle Division	$375	
Other variable costs	550	(925)
Contribution margin per unit.		575
Less fixed costs per unit (at 2,000 units per month).		(175)
Net income per unit		$ 400

The Redmond Division received a one-time order for 500 units. The buyer wants to pay only $750 per unit.

Required

a. From the perspective of the Redmond Division, should the $750 price be accepted? Explain.

b. If both divisions have excess capacity, would the Redmond Division's action benefit the company as a whole? Explain.

c. If the Redmond Division has excess capacity but the Seattle Division does not and can sell all of its parts to outside manufacturers, what would be the advantage or disadvantage of accepting the 500 unit order at the $750 price to the Redmond Division?

d. To make a decision that is in the best interest of the company, what transfer-pricing information does the Redmond Division need?

P24-39. Balanced Scorecard

LO4
JPMorgan Chase & Co.
(JPM)

Assume Chase Bank recently decided to adopt a balanced scorecard system of performance evaluation. Below is a list of primary performance goals for four major performance categories that have been identified by corporate management and the board of directors.

1. Financial Perspective—Maintain and grow the bank financially
   a. Increase customer deposits
   b. Manage financial risk
   c. Provide profits for the stockholders

2. Customer Perspective—Maintain and grow the customer base
   a. Increase customer satisfaction
   b. Increase number of depositors and customer retention
   c. Increase quality of deposits

3. Internal Perspective—Improve internal processes
   a. Achieve best practices for processing transactions
   b. Improve employee satisfaction
   c. Improve employee promotion opportunities

4. Learning and Innovation—Improve market differentiation
   a. Beat competitors in introducing new products
   b. Become first mover in establishing customer benefit for customers
   c. Become recognized as an innovator in the industry

Required

a. For each of the 12 goals above, suggest at least one measure of performance to measure the achievement of the goal.

b. At what level of the organization should the balanced scorecard be implemented as a means of evaluating performance? Explain.

Management Applications

MA24-40. Transfer Price Decisions

LO2
IBM Corporation (IBM)

The Consulting Division of IBM Corporation is often involved in assignments for which IBM computer equipment is sold as part of a systems installation. The Computer Equipment Division is frequently a vendor of the Consulting Division in cases for which the Consulting Division purchases the equipment from the Computer Equipment Division. The Consulting Division does not view itself as a sales arm of the Computer Equipment Division but as a strong competitor to the major consulting firms of information systems. The Consulting Division's goal is to maximize its profit contribution to the company, not necessarily to see how much IBM equipment it can sell. If the Consulting Division is truly an autonomous investment center, it has the freedom to purchase equipment from competing vendors if the consultants believe that a competitor's products serve the needs of a client better than the comparable IBM product in a particular situation.

Required

a. In this situation, should corporate management be concerned about whether the Consulting Division sells IBM products or those of other computer companies? Should the Consulting Division be required to sell only IBM products?

b. Discuss the transfer-pricing issues that both the Computer Equipment Division manager and the Consulting Division manager should consider. If top management does not have a policy on pricing transfers between these two divisions, what alternative transfer prices should the division managers consider?

c. What is your recommendation regarding how the managers of the Consulting and Computer Equipment Divisions can work together in a way that will benefit each of them individually and the company as a whole?

LO2 **MA24-41. Transfer Pricing at Absorption Cost**

The Injection Molding Division of Universal Sign Company produces molded parts that are sold to the Sign Division. This division uses the parts in constructing signs that are sold to various businesses. The Molding Division contains two operations, injection and finishing. The unit variable cost of materials and labor used in the injection operation is $150. The fixed injection overhead is $1,200,000 per year. Current production (20,000 units) is at full capacity. The variable cost of labor used in the finishing operation is $24 per part. The fixed overhead in this operation is $600,000 per year. The company uses an absorption-cost transfer price. The price data for each operation presented to the Sign Division by the Molding Division follow.

Injection		
Variable cost per unit	$150	
Fixed overhead cost per unit ($1,200,000 ÷ 40,000 units)	30	$180
Finishing		
Labor cost per unit	24	
Fixed overhead cost per unit ($600,000 ÷ 40,000 units)	15	39
Total cost per unit		$219

An outside company has offered to lease machinery to the Sign Division that would perform the finishing portion of the parts manufacturing for $400,000 per year. With the new machinery, the labor cost per part would remain at $24. If the Molding Division transfers the units for $180, the following analysis can be made:

Current process		
Finishing process costs (40,000 × $39)		$1,560,000
New process		
Machine rental cost per year.	$400,000	
Labor cost ($24 × 40,000 units)	960,000	1,360,000
Savings.		$ 200,000

The manager of the Sign Division wants approval to acquire the new machinery.

Required

a. How would you advise the company concerning the proposed lease?

b. How could the transfer-pricing system be modified or the transfer-pricing problem eliminated?

LO2 **MA24-42. Transfer Pricing Dispute**

MBR Inc. consists of three divisions that were formerly three independent manufacturing companies. Bader Corporation and Roper Company merged several years ago, and the merged corporation acquired Mitchell Company a year later. The name of the corporation was subsequently changed to MBR Inc., and each company became a separate division retaining the name of its former company.

The three divisions have operated as if they were still independent companies. Each division has its own sales force and production facilities. Each division management is responsible for sales, cost of operations, acquisition and financing of divisional assets, and working capital management. The corporate management of MBR evaluates the performance of the divisions and division management on the basis of return on investment.

Mitchell Division has just been awarded a contract for a product that uses a component manufactured by the Roper Division and also by outside suppliers. Mitchell used a cost figure of $3.80 for the component manufactured by Roper in preparing its bid for the new product. Roper supplied this cost figure in response to Mitchell's request for the average variable cost of the component; it represents the standard variable manufacturing cost and variable selling and distribution expenses.

Roper has an active sales force that is continually soliciting new prospects. Roper's regular selling price for the component Mitchell needs for the new product is $6.50. Sales of this component are expected to increase. The Roper management has indicated, however, that it could supply Mitchell the required quantities of the component at the regular selling price less variable selling and distribution expenses. Mitchell's management has responded by offering to pay standard variable manufacturing cost plus 20%.

The two divisions have been unable to agree on a transfer price. Corporate management has never established a transfer-pricing policy because interdivisional transactions have never occurred. As a compromise, the corporate vice president of finance suggested a price equal to the standard full manufacturing cost (i.e., no selling and distribution expenses) plus a 15% markup. The two division managers have also rejected this price because each considered it grossly unfair.

The unit cost structure for the Roper component and the three suggested prices follow.

Standard variable manufacturing cost	$3.20
Standard fixed manufacturing cost	1.20
Variable selling and distribution expenses	0.60
	$5.00
Regular selling price less variable selling and distribution expenses ($6.50 – $0.60)	$5.90
Standard full manufacturing cost plus 15% ($4.40 × 1.15)	$5.06
Variable manufacturing plus 20% ($3.20 × 1.20)	$3.84

Required

a. What should be the attitude of the Roper Division's management toward the three proposed prices?

b. Is the negotiation of a price between the Mitchell and Roper Divisions a satisfactory method of solving the transfer-pricing problem? Explain your answer.

c. Should the corporate management of MBR Inc. become involved in this transfer-price controversy? Explain your answer.

(CMA Adapted)

Solutions to Review Problems

Review 24-1—Solution

a.

	Segments (Territories)		
	U.S.	**International**	**Wireless Total**
Sales	$12,000	$18,000	$30,000
Less variable costs	(8,400)	(12,600)	(21,000)
Contribution margin	3,600	5,400	9,000
Less direct fixed costs	(500)	(800)	(1,300)
Territory margin	3,100	4,600	7,700
Less allocated segment costs	(200)	(600)	(800)
Territory income	$ 2,900	$ 4,000	6,900
Less unallocated common costs			(900)
Wireless income			$ 6,000

b. The Product Margin for the wireless product line in Panel B was $7,000 and reflected $2,000 of direct fixed costs that were attributable to that product line in the National Division. However, when the wireless product segment income statement is further segmented into geographic segments, only $1,300 of the $2,000 could be directly traced to the two geographic territories. Therefore, $700 of costs that were direct costs at the product segment level became common costs (either allocated or unallocated) at the territory segment level. This reflects the general notion that as segmentation is extended down to lower and lower levels, the total amount of common costs increases and direct costs decrease. Hence, segmentation rarely is extended to more than three levels.

Review 24-2—Solution

a. No.

	Current Sales	Proposed Sales
Selling price	$ 24.00	$ 13.50
Variable costs	(16.00)	(16.00)
Unit contribution margin	$ 8.00	$ (2.50)
Unit sales	× 200,000	× 100,000
Contribution margin	$1,600,000	$(250,000)

Currently, the division is making $250,000 on 100,000 posters ($1,600,000 − $1,350,000 fixed costs); but under the proposal, with a $250,000 negative contribution, it would revert to a break-even situation:

Current contribution margin		$1,600,000
Fixed costs	$1,350,000	
Loss on special order	250,000	(1,600,000)
Net income		$ 0

As a general rule, a project should never be undertaken if the contribution margin is negative.

b. What the Retail Division does with the posters after receiving them is of no concern to the Production Division. Hence, the Production Division would still object to a transfer price of $13.50. However, for the company, the proposal does have a contribution of $18 per unit ($44 − $16 − $10). Consequently, the order is desirable from the viewpoint of the company.

c. If the company believes in autonomous divisions, it should not require the Production Division to sell, nor should it dictate a higher transfer price. On the other hand, the company may want to create incentives to encourage (but not require) the two division managers to reach some compromise transfer price that would increase the contribution and profits of both divisions.

Review 24-3—Solution

a.
$$\text{Return on investment} = \frac{\text{Investment center income}}{\text{Investment center asset base}}$$

$$\text{Engineering Division} = \$30,000 \div \$200,000$$
$$= 0.15 \text{ or } 15\%$$

$$\text{Construction Division} = \$50,000 \div \$250,000$$
$$= 0.20 \text{ or } 20\%$$

$$\text{Military Division} = \$22,000 \div \$100,000$$
$$= 0.22 \text{ or } 22\%$$

b. $$\text{Residual income} = \text{Investment center income} − (\text{Investment center asset base} \times \text{Minimum return})$$
$$\text{Engineering Division} = \$30,000 − (0.15 \times \$200,000)$$
$$= \$0.00$$

$$\text{Construction Division} = \$50,000 − (0.15 \times \$250,000)$$
$$= \$12,500$$

$$\text{Military Division} = \$22,000 − (0.15 \times \$100,000)$$
$$= \$7,000$$

c. ROI ranks the Military Division first, the Construction Division second, and the Engineering Division third. Residual income ranks the Construction Division first, the Military Division second, and the Engineering Division third. Because the investments for each division are different, it is somewhat misleading to rank the divisions according to residual income. The Construction Division had the highest residual income, but it also had the largest investment. The Military Division's residual income was 56% of the Construction Division's income but only 40% of the investment of the Construction Division. This fact, along with the best ROI ranking, probably justifies the Military Division being evaluated as the best division of KBR.

d. Return on investment:

$$\text{Investment} = \$9,000 \div \$50,000$$
$$= 0.18 \text{ or } 18\%$$

$$\text{Engineering Division} = (\$30,000 + \$9,000) \div (\$200,000 + \$50,000)$$
$$= 0.156 \text{ or } 15.6\%$$

$$\text{Construction Division} = (\$50,000 + \$9,000) \div (\$250,000 + \$50,000)$$
$$= 0.1967 \text{ or } 19.67\%$$

$$\text{Military Division} = (\$22,000 + \$9,000) \div (\$100,000 + \$50,000)$$
$$= 0.2067 \text{ or } 20.67\%$$

ROI will increase for the Engineering Division but decrease for the Construction and Military Divisions, even though the project's ROI of 18% exceeds the company's minimum return of 15%.

Residual income:

$$\text{Engineering Division} = (\$30,000 + \$9,000) - [0.15 \times (\$200,000 + \$50,000)]$$
$$= \$1,500$$

$$\text{Construction Division} = (\$50,000 + \$9,000) - [0.15 \times (\$250,000 + \$50,000)]$$
$$= \$14,000$$

$$\text{Military Division} = (\$22,000 + \$9,000) - [0.15 \times (\$100,000 + \$50,000)]$$
$$= \$8,500$$

Because the project's ROI exceeds the company's minimum return, the residual income of all divisions will increase.

Review 24-4—Solution

a. Financial Success
   - Expense as a % of revenue
   - Expense variance %
   - New product ROI
   - Net profit
   - Net profit margin
   - Year-over-year revenue growth
   - New product revenue

   Customer Satisfaction and Brand Improvement
   - Number of complaints
   - Market share
   - Average customer survey rating
   - New customer count
   - New customer sales value
   - Unique repeat customer count

   Business Process Improvement
   - Average call wait
   - Service error rate
   - Fulfillment %
   - Industry quality rating
   - New product acceptance rate
   - Number of defects reported
   - Time to market on new products

   Learning and Growth of Motivated Workforce
   - Employee turnover ratio
   - Headcount growth
   - Job offer acceptance rate

   Note that some of the key performance indicators could be included in more than one category. For example New Product ROI is an indicator of the success of introducing new products, but it is also an indicator of financial success.

b. The balanced scorecard has been quite successful in helping companies to better focus managers' attention on the factors that drive ultimate success. If only a general performance metric such as ROI or EVA is used to evaluate performance, managers are left on their own to figure out for themselves the components of managerial performance that drive improvements in the overall indicator. Balanced scorecard provides a framework and structure for carefully thinking about the key performance indicators that drive ultimate success. Once top management has identified the key performance indicators with input from all levels, some or all of the indicators can be used to evaluate managers and employees throughout the organization.

Module 25

Capital Budgeting Decisions

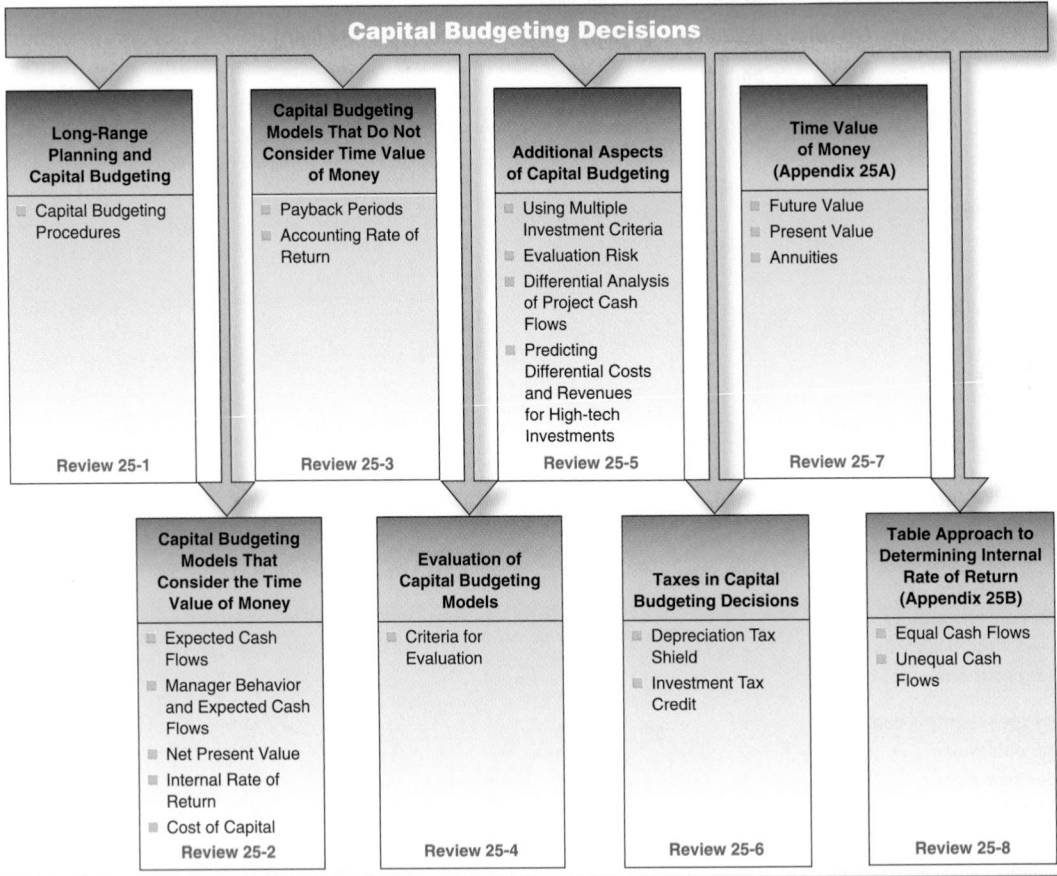

Capital Budgeting Decisions

Long-Range Planning and Capital Budgeting
- Capital Budgeting Procedures

Review 25-1

Capital Budgeting Models That Do Not Consider Time Value of Money
- Payback Periods
- Accounting Rate of Return

Review 25-3

Additional Aspects of Capital Budgeting
- Using Multiple Investment Criteria
- Evaluation Risk
- Differential Analysis of Project Cash Flows
- Predicting Differential Costs and Revenues for High-tech Investments

Review 25-5

Time Value of Money (Appendix 25A)
- Future Value
- Present Value
- Annuities

Review 25-7

Capital Budgeting Models That Consider the Time Value of Money
- Expected Cash Flows
- Manager Behavior and Expected Cash Flows
- Net Present Value
- Internal Rate of Return
- Cost of Capital

Review 25-2

Evaluation of Capital Budgeting Models
- Criteria for Evaluation

Review 25-4

Taxes in Capital Budgeting Decisions
- Depreciation Tax Shield
- Investment Tax Credit

Review 25-6

Table Approach to Determining Internal Rate of Return (Appendix 25B)
- Equal Cash Flows
- Unequal Cash Flows

Review 25-8

PREVIEW

AMZN

Seattle-based Amazon.com Inc. started out as an online bookseller in 1995 and quickly expanded its product offerings to DVDs, electronics, jewelry, apparel, and now a full spectrum of consumer goods. Amazon sells more goods online than all other Internet retailers, including Staples, Apple, Walmart, and Best Buy. Amazon's meteoric rise was no doubt fueled by well-chosen capital investments, including its website infrastructure that highlighted customer-centric features such as the first shopping carts, one-click buying, email purchase confirmations, and post-shipping follow-ups. Over the years Amazon has kept its prices low by leveraging its purchasing volume, thereby staving off its competition. To maintain its position, Amazon has forgone profits in favor of continual improvement of its business model. In an effort to gain more control over its fulfillment process, Amazon has invested billions of dollars in warehouses and inventory management information systems. As a result, Amazon has been able to offer expedited shipping on its orders since 2005. This program, called Amazon Prime, offers customers two-day shipping for an annual fee of $119.

Amazon is also beginning to open brick-and-mortar bookstore locations, including stores in Oregon, Washington, California, and New York. In 2017, Amazon made its first Prime Air drone delivery, testing its ability to make deliveries using drones. Amazon's management team needs to tread carefully in evaluating these new investments. Amazon's managers should be asking themselves these questions: How will these investments be financed, and at what cost can we raise the needed funds? What tax deductions or incentives might defray some of the costs of this investment? How long before the investment has been recouped through increased revenues? Does this estimate consider increases in operating costs? In other words, Amazon needs to determine which capital investments will have a positive effect on operating results.

This module will detail important tools that Amazon and managers can use to increase the probability that their capital investments will be sound.

Road Map

LO	Learning Objective | Topics	Page	eLecture	Guided Example	Assignments
25-1	**Explain the role of capital budgeting in long-range planning.** Capital Expenditures :: Capital Budgeting :: Long-Range Planning	25-3	e25-1	Review 25-1	41, 42
25-2	**Analyze capital budgeting decisions, using models such as net present value and internal rate of return, that consider the time value of money.** Expected Cash Flows :: Net Present Value :: Table Approach :: Spreadsheet Approach :: Internal Rate of Return :: Cost of Capital	25-6	e25-2	Review 25-2	13, 14, 15, 16, 20, 21, 22, 23, 25, 26, 27, 28, 29, 30, 31, 33, 34, 35, 36, 37, 39, 40, 41, 42
25-3	**Analyze capital budgeting decisions, using models such as payback period and accounting rate of return, that do not consider the time value of money.** Payback Period :: Accounting Rate of Return	25-11	e25-3	Review 25-3	17, 18, 19, 22, 23, 25, 26, 27, 28, 29, 31, 36, 38
25-4	**Evaluate the strengths and weaknesses of alternative capital budgeting models.** Strength and Weaknesses of Each Approach	25-14	e25-4	Review 25-4	28, 39
25-5	**Examine the impact of judgment, attitudes toward risk, and relevant cash flow information on capital budgeting decisions.** Evaluating Risk :: Differential Analysis :: High-Tech Investments	25-16	e25-5	Review 25-5	26, 27, 35, 36, 37, 38, 39, 40, 41, 42
25-6	**Determine the net present value of investment proposals with consideration of taxes.** Depreciation Tax Shield :: Investment Tax Credit	25-21	e25-6	Review 25-6	24, 30, 31, 32, 40
25-7	**Compute basic present value cash flow amounts (Appendix 25A).** Future Value :: Present Value :: Annuities :: Unequal Cash Flows :: Deferred Returns	25-23	e25-7	Review 25-7	13, 14
25-8	**Determine internal rate of return using present value tables (Appendix 25B).** Equal Cash Flows :: Unequal Cash Flows	25-29	e25-8	Review 25-8	15, 16, 20, 21, 22, 29, 39

LO1
Explain the role of capital budgeting in long-range planning.

Capital expenditures are investments of financial resources in projects to develop or introduce new products or services, to expand current production or service capacity, or to change current production or service facilities. Capital expenditures are made with the expectation that the new product, process, or service will generate future financial inflows that exceed the initial costs. Capital expenditure decisions affect structural cost drivers. They are made infrequently but once made are difficult to change. They commit the organization to the use of certain facilities and activities to satisfy customer needs. In making large capital expenditure decisions, such as for **Amazon**'s warehouse facilities, management is risking the future existence of the company.

Although capital expenditure decisions are fraught with risk, management accounting provides the concepts and tools needed to organize information and evaluate the alternatives. This systematic organization and analysis is the essence of capital budgeting. This module introduces important capital budgeting concepts and models, and it explains the proper use of accounting data in these models.

Capital budgeting is a process that involves identifying potentially desirable projects for capital expenditures, evaluating capital expenditure proposals, and selecting proposals that meet minimum criteria. A number of quantitative models are available to assist managers in evaluating capital expenditure proposals.

The best capital budgeting models are conceptually similar to the short-range planning models used in Modules 16 and 17. They all emphasize cash flows and focus on future costs (and revenues) that differ among decision alternatives. The major difference is that capital budgeting models involve cash flows over several years, whereas short-range planning models involve cash flows for a year or less. When the cash flows associated with a proposed activity extend over several years, an adjustment is necessary to make the cash flows comparable when they are expected to occur at different points in time.

The *time value of money concept* explains why monies received or paid at different points in time must be adjusted to comparable values. The time value of money is introduced in Appendix 25A at the end of this module.

Long-Range Planning and Capital Budgeting

Most organizations plan not only for operations in the current period but also for the longer term, perhaps 5, 10, or even 20 years in the future. Most planning beyond the next budget year is called *long-range planning.*

Increased uncertainty and business alternatives add to the difficulty of planning as the horizon lengthens. Even though long-range planning is difficult and involves uncertainties, management must make long-range planning and capital expenditure decisions. Capital expenditure decisions will be made. The question is: How will they be made? Will they be made on the basis of the best information available? Will care be taken to ensure that capital expenditure decisions are in line with the organization's long-range goals? Will the potential consequences, both positive and negative, of capital expenditures be considered? Will important alternative uses of the organization's limited financial resources be considered in a systematic manner? Will managers be held accountable for the capital expenditure programs they initiate? The alternative to a systematic approach to capital budgeting is the haphazard expenditure of resources on the basis of a hunch, immediate need, or persuasion—without accountability by the person(s) making the decisions.

The steps of an effective capital budgeting process are outlined in Exhibit 25.1. A basic requirement for a systematic approach to capital budgeting is a defined mission, a set of long-range goals, and a business strategy. These elements provide focus and boundaries that reduce the types of capital expenditure decisions management considers. If, for example, **Dunkin' Donuts**'s goal is to become the largest fast-food restaurant chain in North America, its management should not consider a proposal to purchase and operate a bus line.

A well-defined business strategy will likewise guide capital expenditure decisions. If **Cisco Systems** is following a strategy to obtain technological leadership, it might seriously consider a proposal to meet customer needs by investing in innovative production facilities but would not consider a proposal to purchase and refurbish used (but seemingly cost-efficient) equipment. The following Business Insight box identifies companies that focus capital budgeting decisions on the strategic goal of energy efficiency, and therefore, reducing expenses.

Exhibit 25.1 ■ Capital Budgeting Procedures

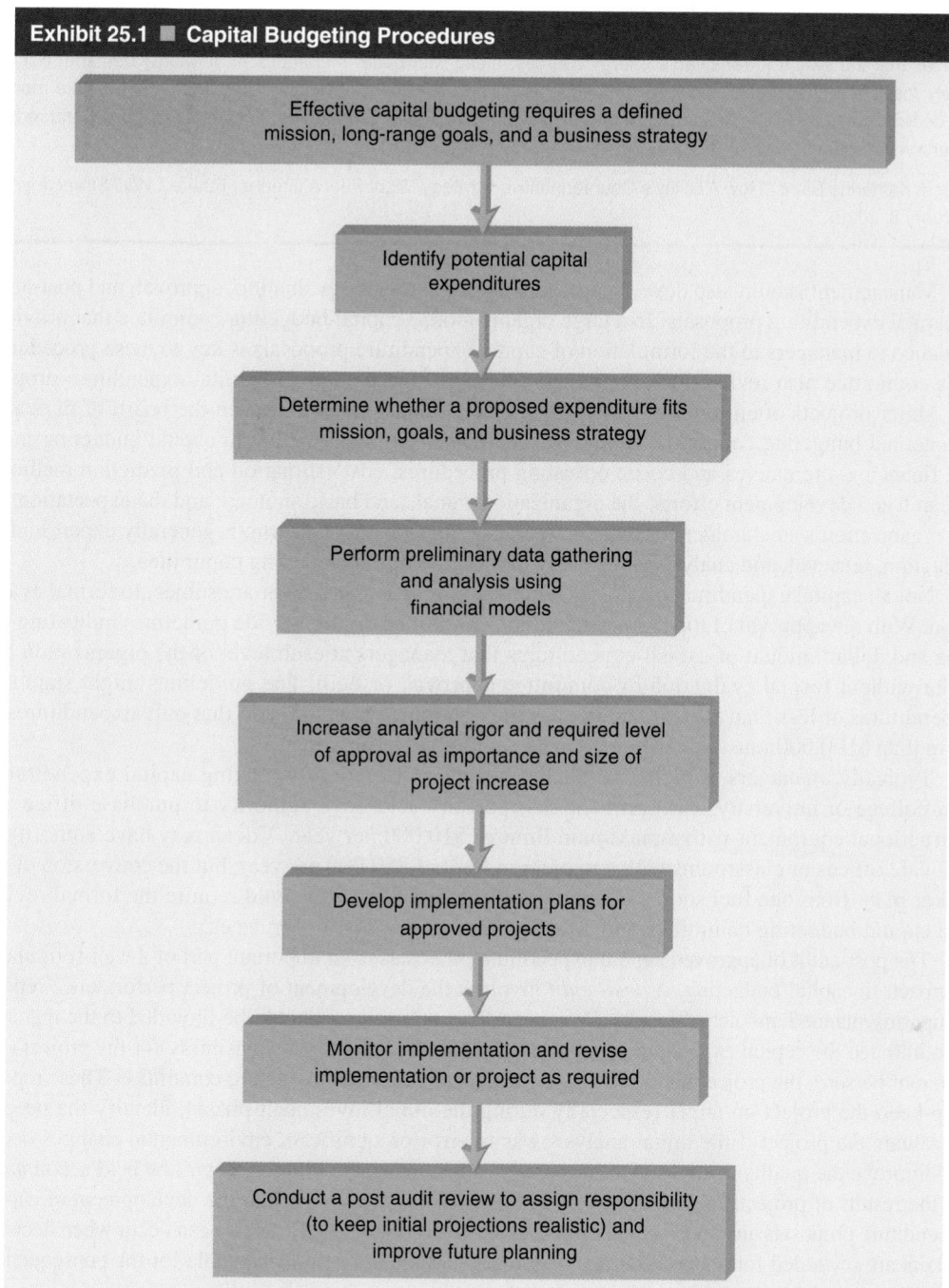

Effective capital budgeting requires a defined mission, long-range goals, and a business strategy

Identify potential capital expenditures

Determine whether a proposed expenditure fits mission, goals, and business strategy

Perform preliminary data gathering and analysis using financial models

Increase analytical rigor and required level of approval as importance and size of project increase

Develop implementation plans for approved projects

Monitor implementation and revise implementation or project as required

Conduct a post audit review to assign responsibility (to keep initial projections realistic) and improve future planning

Business Insight ■ Using the Capital Budget to Save Money

Consumers Energy, a public utility in Michigan serving 6.7 million people, has plans to spend $25 billion before 2030 to replace aging gas and electric equipment with solar panels, wind turbines, and large-scale battery storage units. When Consumers first started looking at renewable energy sources in 2016, its analysts forecasted decreases in solar prices of 30% over the next 20 years. But in the 18 months it took the company to complete the study, prices had already fallen 30%. The initial costs of solar and wind technologies were now competitive with the costs of natural gas plants. Because wind and sunlight are free, Consumers will be able to save hundreds of millions of dollars each year on fuel costs while reducing its carbon output by 90% over the levels in 2005. The company is also working to help customers reduce their consumption of electricity through the use of smart thermostats and smart meters. The focus on reducing consumption of Consumers' primary source of revenue may seem counterintuitive, but the company

continued

continued from previous page

believes that the switch to renewable energy sources, along with better management of energy demand, will ultimately result in higher profits. Most capital budget decisions are about deciding to spend money to make money. The decision by Consumers to budget for energy efficiency was about spending money to save money and reduce its carbon emissions.

Source: Katherine Blunt, "How A Utility's Counterintuitive Strategy Might Fuel A Greener Future," *Wall Street Journal*, February 8, 2020.

Management should also develop procedures for the review, evaluation, approval, and post-audit of capital expenditure proposals. In a large organization, a capital budgeting committee that provides guidance to managers in the formulation of capital expenditure proposals is key to these procedures. This committee also reviews, analyzes, and approves or rejects major capital expenditure proposals. Major projects often require the approval of top management and even the board of directors. The capital budgeting committee should include persons knowledgeable in capital budgeting models; financing alternatives and costs; operating procedures; cost estimation and prediction methods; research and development efforts; the organization's goals and basic strategy; and the expectations of the organization's stockholders or owners. A management accountant who is generally expert in data collection, retrieval, and analysis is normally part of the capital budgeting committee.

Not all capital expenditure proposals require committee approval or are subject to formal evaluation. With the approval of top management, the committee might provide guidelines indicating the type and dollar amount of capital expenditures that managers at each level of the organization can make without formal evaluation or committee approval, or both. The guidelines might state that expenditures of less than $20,000 do not require committee approval and that only expenditures of more than $100,000 must be evaluated using capital budgeting models.

Typically, managers at higher levels have greater discretion in making capital expenditures. In a college or university, a department chairperson could have authority to purchase office and instructional equipment with a maximum limit of $10,000 per year. A dean may have authority to renovate offices or classrooms with a maximum limit of $50,000 per year, but the conversion of the power plant from one fuel source to another at a cost of $400,000 could require the formal review of a capital budgeting committee and final approval of the board of trustees.

The post-audit of approved capital expenditure proposals is an important part of a well-formulated approach to capital budgeting. A *post-audit* involves the development of project performance reports comparing planned and actual results. Project performance reports should be provided to the manager who initiated the capital expenditure proposal, the manager assigned responsibility for the project (if a different person), the project manager's supervisor, and the capital budgeting committee. These reports help keep the project on target (especially during the initial investment phase), identify the need to reevaluate the project if the initial analysis was in error or significant environmental changes occur, and improve the quality of investment proposals. When managers know they will be held accountable for the results of projects they initiate, they are likely to put more care into the development of capital expenditure proposals and take a greater interest in approved projects. Problems can occur when decision makers are rewarded for undertaking major projects but are not held responsible for the consequences that occur several years later.

A post-audit review of approved projects also helps the capital budgeting committee do a better job in evaluating new proposals. The committee might learn how to adjust proposals for the biases of individual managers, learn of new factors that should be considered in evaluating proposals, and avoid the routine approval of projects that appear desirable by themselves but are related to larger projects that are not meeting management's expectations. As summarized in the Business Insight (on page 25-6), capital budgeting models play an important role in strategic decision making.

Managerial Decision ■   You Are the Vice President of Finance

You have recently accepted the position of VP of finance for a rapidly growing biotech company. Last year the company made capital expenditures of $10 million and you anticipate that annual capital expenditures will exceed $30 million in a couple of years. You believe it is time to develop a more formal approach to making capital expenditure decisions. Where do you begin? [Answer p. 25-30]

Business Insight ■ SodaStream and Pepsi, Partners Not Competitors

Consumer health concerns contributed to the steady decrease in sales of carbonated soft drinks over the last 20 years. Companies like PepsiCo, Coca-Cola, and Nestlé successfully responded by adding bottled water products to their product lines. Now, that business is threatened by consumer environmental concerns and soda makers are again looking for product alternatives. In 2015, PepsiCo partnered with SodaStream, an Israeli company that makes a countertop soda maker with a dizzying array of flavorings. Pepsi later purchased SodaStream in 2018. Pepsi also launched Drinkafinity in the United States in 2018. With Drinkafinity, consumers can infuse tap water with caffeine, vitamins, electrolytes, and flavors contained in pods that attach to a specially designed, reusable bottle. Pepsi's decision makers likely depend on net present value analysis in making decisions to add new products.

Source: Thomas Mulier and Corinne Gretler, "Coke, Pepsi, and Nestle Plan to Profit From Your Tap Water," *Bloomberg*, October 31, 2019.

LO1 Review 25-1

Below is a list of terms relevant to capital budgeting decisions.

1. Capital budgeting
2. Capital expenditures
3. Time value of money concept
4. Long-range planning
5. Post audit

Required

For each of the statements below, select the most relevant term from the above list. Each term above may be used more than once.

_____ *a.* Investment of financial resources with the expectation it will generate future financial inflows that exceed the initial cost.

_____ *b.* Process that involves identifying desirable projects, evaluating proposals, and selecting proposals that meet minimum criteria.

_____ *c.* Involves the development of project performance comparing planned and actual results.

_____ *d.* Concepts and tools that organize information and evaluate alternatives.

_____ *e.* Explains why monies received or paid at different points in time must be adjusted to comparable values.

_____ *f.* Requires an adjustment to make cash flows comparable when they are expected to occur at different points in time.

_____ *g.* Planning beyond the next budget year.

_____ *h.* Helps the capital budgeting committee do a better job in evaluating new proposals.

Solution on p. 25-42.

Capital Budgeting Models That Consider Time Value of Money

The capital budgeting models in this module have gained wide acceptance by for-profit and not-for-profit organizations. Our primary focus is on the *net present value* and the *internal rate of return models*, which are superior because they consider the time value of money. Later discussions will consider more traditional capital budgeting models, such as the payback period and the accounting rate of return that, while useful under certain circumstances, do not consider the time value of money. Although we briefly consider the cost of financing capital expenditures, we leave a detailed treatment of this topic, as well as a detailed examination of the sources of funds for financing investments, to books on financial management.

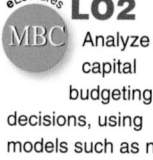

LO2 Analyze capital budgeting decisions, using models such as net present value and internal rate of return, that consider the time value of money.

Expected Cash Flows

The focus of capital budgeting models that consider the time value of money is on future cash receipts and future cash disbursements that differ under decision alternatives. It is often convenient to distinguish between the following three phases of a project's cash flows:

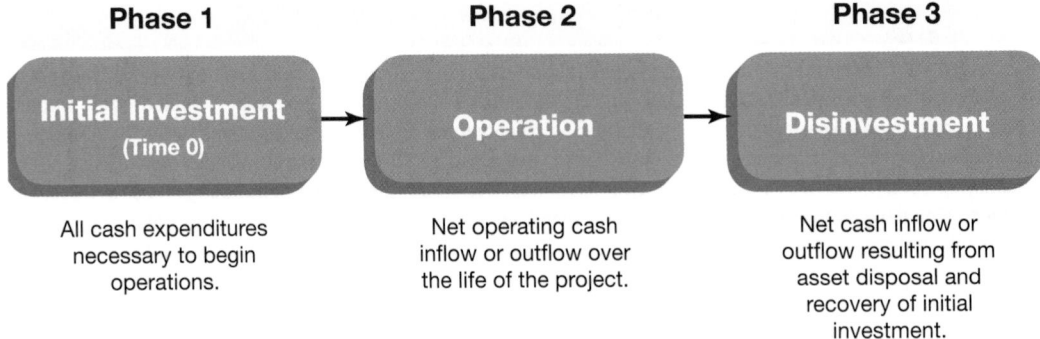

Phase 1	Phase 2	Phase 3
Initial Investment (Time 0)	**Operation**	**Disinvestment**
All cash expenditures necessary to begin operations.	Net operating cash inflow or outflow over the life of the project.	Net cash inflow or outflow resulting from asset disposal and recovery of initial investment.

All cash expenditures necessary to begin operations are classified as part of the project's *initial investment phase*. Expenditures to acquire property, plant, and equipment are part of the initial investment. Less obvious, but equally important, are expenditures to acquire working capital to purchase inventories and recruit and train employees. Although the initial investment phase often extends over many years, in our examples, we assume that the initial investment takes place at a single point in time.

Cash receipts from sales of goods or services, as well as normal cash expenditures for materials, labor, and other operating expenses, occur during the operation phase. The *operation phase* is typically broken down into one-year periods; for each period, operating cash expenditures are subtracted from operating cash receipts to determine the net operating cash inflow or outflow for the period.

The *disinvestment phase* occurs at the end of the project's life when assets are disposed of for their salvage value and any initial investment of working capital is recovered. Also included are any expenditures to dismantle facilities and dispose of waste. Although this phase might extend over many years, in our examples, we assume disinvestment takes place at a single point in time.

To illustrate the analysis of a project's cash flows, assume the management of Mobile Taqueria is considering a capital expenditure proposal to operate a new shop in a resort community. Each Mobile Taqueria is located in a specially constructed motor vehicle that moves on a regular schedule throughout the community it serves. The predicted cash flows associated with the project, which has an expected life of five years, are presented in Exhibit 25.2.

Exhibit 25.2 ■ Analysis of a Project's Predicted Cash Flows

Phase 1

Initial investment (at time 0)		
Vehicle and equipment		$ (90,554)
Inventories and other working capital		(4,000)
Total investment cash outflow		$ (94,554)

Phase 2

Operation (per year for 5 years)		
Sales		$ 175,000
Cash expenditures		
Food	$47,000	
Labor	65,000	
Supplies	9,000	
Fuel and utilities	8,000	
Advertising	4,000	
Miscellaneous	12,000	(145,000)
Net annual cash inflow		$ 30,000

Phase 3

Disinvestment (at the end of 5 years)	
Sale of vehicle and equipment	$ 8,000
Recovery of investment in inventories and other working capital	4,000
Total disinvestment cash inflow	$ 12,000

Manager Behavior and Expected Cash Flows

Accurately predicting the cash flows associated with a capital expenditure proposal is critical to properly evaluating the proposal. Managers might be overly optimistic with their predictions, and they are sometimes tempted to modify predictions to justify capital expenditures. Perhaps they are interested in personal rewards. They might also want to avoid a loss of prestige or employment for themselves or to keep a local facility operating for the benefit of current employees and the local economy. Unfortunately, if a major expenditure does not work out, not only the local plant but also the entire company could be forced out of business. For example, under pressure to increase current sales, automobile leasing companies could be tempted to overstate cash receipts during the disinvestment phase of a lease.

Net Present Value

A project's **net present value**, usually computed as of the time of the initial investment, is the present value of the project's net cash inflows from operations and disinvestment less the amount of the initial investment. Appendix 25A contains an introduction to the time value of money, including net present value fundamentals. In computing a project's net present value, the cash flows occurring at different points in time are adjusted for the time value of money using a **discount rate** that is the minimum rate of return required for the project to be acceptable. Projects with positive net present values (or values at least equal to zero) are acceptable, and projects with negative net present values are unacceptable. Two methods to compute net present value follow.

Table Approach

Assuming that management uses a 12% discount rate, the net present value of the proposed investment in a Mobile Taqueria is shown in Exhibit 25.3 (a) to be $20,398. Since the net present value is more than zero, the investment in the Mobile Taqueria is expected to be profitable, even when adjusted for the time value of money.

We can verify the amounts and computations in Exhibit 25.3. Start by tracing the cash flows back to Exhibit 25.2. Next, determine the 12% present value factors by referring to Exhibits 25A.1 and 25A.2 in Appendix 25A. The initial investment is assumed to occur at a single point in time (identified as time 0), the start of the project. In net present value computations, all cash flows are restated in terms of their value at time 0. Hence, time 0 cash flows have a present value factor of 1. To simplify computations, all other cash flows are assumed to occur at the end of years 1 through 5, even if they occurred during the year. Although further refinements could be made to adjust for cash flows occuring throughout each year, such adjustments are seldom necessary. Observe that net operating cash inflows are treated as an *annuity*, whereas cash flows for the initial investment and disinvestment are treated as *lump-sum amounts*. If net operating cash flows varied from year to year, we would treat each year's cash flow as a separate amount.

Spreadsheet Approach

Spreadsheet software contains functions that compute the present value of a series of cash flows. With this software, simply enter a column or row containing the net cash flows for each period and the appropriate formula. The discount rate of 0.12 is entered as part of the formula. Sample spreadsheet input to determine the net present value of the proposed investment in a Mobile Taqueria is shown on the left in Exhibit 25.3 (b). The spreadsheet output is shown on the right, in Exhibit 25.3 (b).

Two cautionary notes follow:

1. The spreadsheet formula for the net present value assumes that the first cash flow occurs at time "1," rather than at time "0." Hence, we cannot include the initial investment in the data set analyzed by the spreadsheet formula when computing the net present value. Instead, the initial investment is subtracted from the present value of future cash flows.

2. Arrange the cash flows subsequent to the initial investment from *top* to bottom in a column, or *left* to right in a row.

Exhibit 25.3 ■ Net Present Value of a Project's Predicted Cash Flows

(a) Table approach:

	Predicted Cash Inflows (outflows) (A)	Year(s) of Cash Flows (B)	12% Present Value Factor (C)	Present Value of Cash Flows (A) × (C)
Initial investment.................	$(94,554)	0	1.00000	$ (94,554)
Operation	30,000	1–5	3.60478	108,143
Disinvestment...................	12,000	5	0.56743	6,809
Net present value of all cash flows				$ 20,398

(b) Spreadsheet approach:

Input:

	A	B
1	Year of cash flow	Cash flow
2	1	$30,000
3	2	30,000
4	3	30,000
5	4	30,000
6	5	42,000
7	Present value	=NPV(0.12,B2:B6)
8	Initial investment at time 0	(94,554)
9	Net present value	=B7+B8

Output:

	A	B
1	Year of cash flow	Cash flow
2	1	$ 30,000
3	2	30,000
4	3	30,000
5	4	30,000
6	5	42,000
7	Present value	$114,952.41
8	Initial investment at time 0	(94,554.00)
9	Net present value	$ 20,398.41

Internal Rate of Return

The **internal rate of return (IRR)**, often called the **time-adjusted rate of return**, is the discount rate that equates the present value of a project's cash inflows with the present value of the project's cash outflows. Other ways to describe IRR include (1) the minimum rate that could be paid for the money invested in a project without losing money, and (2) the discount rate that results in a project's net present value equaling zero.

All practical applications of the IRR model use a calculator or spreadsheet. Thus, we illustrate determining an IRR with a spreadsheet. A table approach to determining a project's internal rate of return is illustrated in Appendix 25B of this module.

With spreadsheet software, simply enter a column or row containing the net cash flows for each period and the appropriate formula. Spreadsheet input for Mobile Taqueria's investment proposal is shown in Exhibit 25.4. The spreadsheet formula for the IRR assumes that the first cash flow occurs at time "0."

The spreadsheet approach requires an initial prediction or guess of the project's internal rate of return. Although the closeness of the prediction to the final solution affects computational speed, for textbook examples almost any number can be used. We use an initial estimate of 0.08 in all illustrations. Because the IRR formula assumes that the first cash flow occurs at time 0, the initial investment is included in the data analyzed by the IRR formula. Again, we must order the cash flows from top to bottom in a column or left to right in a row. As shown on the right column in Exhibit 25.4, the spreadsheet software computes the IRR as 20%.

The calculated internal rate of return is compared to the discount rate established by management to evaluate investment proposals. If the proposal's IRR is greater than or equal to the discount rate, the project is acceptable; if it is less than the discount rate, the project is unacceptable. Because Mobile Taqueria has a 12% discount rate, the project is acceptable using the IRR model.

Exhibit 25.4 ■ Spreadsheet Approach to Determining Internal Rate of Return

Input:

	A	B
	Year of cash flow	Cash flow
1	Year of cash flow	Cash flow
2	0	$(94,554)
3	1	30,000
4	2	30,000
5	3	30,000
6	4	30,000
7	5	42,000
8	IRR	=IRR(B2:B7,0.08)*

Output:

	A	B
	Year of cash flow	Cash flow
1	Year of cash flow	Cash flow
2	0	$(94,554)
3	1	30,000
4	2	30,000
5	3	30,000
6	4	30,000
7	5	42,000
8	IRR	0.20

*The formula is "=IRR(Input data range, guess)." The guess, which is any likely rate of return, is used as an initial starting point in determining the solution. We use 0.08 in all illustrations.

Although a project's IRR should be compared to the discount rate established by management, such a discount rate is often unknown. In these situations, computing the IRR still provides insights into a project's profitability.

Although a computer and appropriate software quickly and accurately perform tedious computations, computational ease increases the opportunity for inappropriate use. The ability to plug numbers into a computer or calculator and obtain an output labeled NPV or IRR could mislead the unwary into believing that capital budgeting models are easy to use. This is not true. Training and professional judgment are required to identify relevant costs, to implement procedures to obtain relevant cost information, and to make a good decision once results are available. Capital budgeting models are merely decision aids. Managers, not models, make the decisions. To better illustrate underlying concepts, all subsequent textbook illustrations use a table approach.

Cost of Capital

When discounting models are used to evaluate capital expenditure proposals, management must determine the discount rate (1) used to compute a proposal's net present value or (2) used as the standard for evaluating a proposal's IRR. An organization's cost of capital is often used as this discount rate.

The **cost of capital** is the average cost an organization pays to obtain the resources necessary to make investments. This average rate considers items such as the following:

■ Effective interest rate on debt (notes or bonds).

■ Effective dividend rate on preferred stock.

■ Discount rate that equates the present value of all dividends expected on common stock over the life of the organization to the current market value of the organization's common stock.

The cost of capital for a company that has no debt or preferred stock equals the cost of equity capital, computed as follows:

$$\text{Cost of equity capital} = \frac{\text{Current annual dividend per common share}}{\text{Current market price per common share}} + \frac{\text{Expected dividend}}{\text{growth rate}}$$

Procedures for determining the cost of capital for more complex capital structures are covered in finance books. Investing in a project that has an internal rate of return equal to the cost of capital should not affect the market value of the firm's securities. Investing in a project that has a return higher than the cost of capital should increase the market value of a firm's securities. If, however, a firm invests in a project that has a return less than the cost of capital, the market value of the firm's securities should fall.

The cost of capital is the minimum return acceptable for investment purposes. Any investment proposal not expected to yield this minimum rate should normally be rejected. Because of difficulties encountered in determining the cost of capital, many organizations adopt a discount rate or a target rate of return without complicated mathematical analysis.

Review 25-2 LO2

Consider the following investment proposal:

Initial investment	
Depreciable assets	$27,740
Working capital	3,000
Operations (per year for 4 years)	
Cash receipts	25,000
Cash expenditures	15,000
Disinvestment	
Salvage value of plant and equipment	2,000
Recovery of working capital	3,000

Required
Determine each of the following:

a. Net present value at a 10% discount rate.

Solution on p. 25-42. *b.* Internal rate of return. (Refer to Appendix 25B if using the table approach.)

Capital Budgeting Models That Do Not Consider Time Value of Money

eLectures **LO3**

Analyze capital budgeting decisions, using models such as payback period and accounting rate of return, that do not consider the time value of money.

Years ago, capital budgeting models that do not consider the time value of money were more widely used than discounting models. Although most large organizations use net present value or internal rate of return as their primary evaluation tool, currently they often use nondiscounting models as an initial screening device. Further, as discussed in the following Research Insight, nondiscounting models remain entrenched in small businesses. We consider two nondiscounting models, the *payback period* and the *accounting rate of return*.

Research Insight ■ Size and Education Matter in Capital Budgeting

A survey of small businesses (with an average of 10 employees) by Danielson and Scott shows that owners make capital expenditure decisions based on "gut feel" much more often than on other methods predicted by theory. Owners' gut feelings were followed by a payback period, then accounting rate of return—only a few firms reported using discounted cash flows. Danielson and Scott emphasize the following points:

1. Capital investments by small businesses tend not to be discretionary. The firm often either invests or goes out of business.
2. Use of a payback period increases with the formal education of the owner, and owners with advanced degrees are most likely to have a formal business plan and use discounted future cash flows.
3. Accounting rate of return is most common for firms that are planning to expand, or are required to provide financial information to banks.

Graham and Harvey surveyed Fortune 500 CFOs and CFOs of smaller members of the Financial Executives Institute. CFOs generally have advanced degrees in business, and 46% of these firms have sales over $1 billion. In this group most firms use multiple models for budgeting, and their use fits much more with the theory:

1. 76% use internal rate of return.
2. 75% use net present value.
3. More than 50% use a payback period.
4. About 20% use accounting rate of return.

Even in this sample, the smaller firms (sales under $100 million) are less likely to use net present value than larger firms. Follow-up research in Canada and Europe has confirmed that these results generalize beyond the United

continued

continued from previous page

States and the Fortune 500, with two additional insights. First, there is a long-term trend toward use of discounted cash flows in all firms, and second, the wealth of the firm's home nation also affects the sophistication of modeling.

Sources: Morris Danielson and Johnathan Scott, "The Capital Budgeting Decisions of Small Businesses," *Journal of Applied Finance* (Fall/Winter 2006): 46–56.

John Graham and Campbell Harvey, "The Theory and Practice of Corporate Finance: Evidence from the Field," *Journal of Financial Economics* (May–June 2001): 187–243.

Karim Bennouna, Geoffrey G. Meredith, and Teresa Marchant, "Improved Capital Budgeting Decision Making: Evidence from Canada," *Management Decision* 48, no. 2 (2010): 225–247.

Gyorgy Andor, Sunil K. Mohanty, and Tamas Toth, "Capital Budgeting Practices: A Survey of Central and Eastern European Firms," *Emerging Markets Review* 23 (June 2015): 148–172, http://dx.doi.org/10.1016/j.ememar.2015.04.002.

Payback Period

The **payback period** is the time required to recover the initial investment in a project from operations. The payback decision rule states that acceptable projects must have less than some maximum payback period designated by management. Payback emphasizes management's concern with liquidity and the need to minimize risk through a rapid recovery of the initial investment. It is frequently used for small expenditures having such obvious benefits that the use of more sophisticated capital budgeting models is not required or justified.

When a project is expected to have equal annual operating cash inflows, its payback period is computed as follows:

$$\text{Payback period} = \frac{\text{Initial investment}}{\text{Annual operating cash inflows}}$$

For Mobile Taqueria's investment proposal, outlined in Exhibit 25.2, the payback period is 3.15 years:

$$\text{Payback period} = \frac{\$94{,}554}{\$30{,}000}$$
$$= 3.15$$

Determining the payback period for a project having unequal cash flows is slightly more complicated. Assume that **Costco Wholesale** is evaluating a capital expenditure proposal that requires an initial investment of $50,000,000 and has the following expected net cash inflows:

Year	Net Cash Inflow
1	$15,000,000
2	25,000,000
3	40,000,000
4	20,000,000
5	10,000,000

To compute the payback period, we must determine the net unrecovered amount at the end of each year. In the year of full recovery, the net cash inflows are assumed to occur evenly and are prorated based on the unrecovered investment at the start of the year. Full recovery of Costco's investment proposal is expected to occur in Year 3:

Year	Net Cash Inflow	Unrecovered Investment
0	$ 0	$50,000,000
1	15,000,000	35,000,000
2	25,000,000	10,000,000
3	40,000,000	0

Therefore, $10,000,000 of $40,000,000 is needed in Year 3 to complete the recovery of the initial investment. This provides a proportion of 0.25 ($10,000,000 ÷ $40,000,000) and a payback period of 2.25 years (2 years plus 0.25 of Year 3). This project is acceptable if management specified a maximum payback period of three years. Because they occur after the payback period, the net cash inflows of Years 4 and 5 are ignored.

Accounting Rate of Return

The **accounting rate of return** is the average annual increase in net income that results from the acceptance of a capital expenditure proposal divided by either the initial investment or the average investment in the project. This method differs from other capital budgeting models in that it focuses on accounting income rather than on cash flow. In most capital budgeting applications, accounting net income is approximated as net cash inflow from operations minus expenses not requiring the use of cash, such as depreciation.

Consider Mobile Taqueria's capital expenditure proposal whose cash flows were outlined in Exhibit 25.2. The vehicle and equipment costs are $90,554 and have a disposal value of $8,000 at the end of five years, resulting in an average annual increase in net income of $13,489:

Annual net cash inflow from operations	$30,000
Less average annual depreciation [($90,554 − $8,000) ÷ 5]	(16,511)
Average annual increase in net income	$13,489

Considering the investment in inventories and other working capital, the initial investment is $94,554 ($90,554 + $4,000), and the *accounting rate of return on initial investment* is 14.27%:

$$\frac{\text{Accounting rate of return}}{\text{on initial investment}} = \frac{\text{Average annual increase in net income}}{\text{Initial investment}} = \frac{\$13,489}{\$94,554} = 0.1427$$

The average investment, computed as the initial investment plus the expected value of any disinvestment, all divided by 2, is $53,277 [($94,554 + $12,000) ÷ 2]. The *accounting rate of return on average investment* is 25.32%:

$$\frac{\text{Accounting rate of return}}{\text{on average investment}} = \frac{\text{Average annual increase in net income}}{\text{Average investment}} = \frac{\$13,489}{\$53,277} = 0.2532$$

When using the accounting rate of return, management specifies either the initial investment or average investment plus some minimum acceptable rate. Management rejects capital expenditure proposals with a lower accounting rate of return but accepts proposals with an accounting rate of return higher than or equal to the minimum.

Review 25-3 LO3

Consider the following investment proposal:

Initial investment		
	Depreciable assets	$27,740
	Working capital	3,000
Operations (per year for 4 years)		
	Cash receipts	25,000
	Cash expenditures	15,000
Disinvestment		
	Salvage value of plant and equipment	2,000
	Recovery of working capital	3,000

continued

continued from previous page

Required
Determine each of the following:

a. Payback period.
b. Accounting rate of return on initial investment and on average investment.

Solution on p. 25-43.

Evaluation of Capital Budgeting Models

As a single criterion for evaluating capital expenditure proposals, capital budgeting models that consider the time value of money are superior to models that do not consider it. The payback model concerns merely how long it takes to recover the initial investment from a project, yet investments are not made with the objective of merely getting the money back. Indeed, not investing has a payback period of 0. Investments are made to earn a profit. Hence, what happens after the payback period is more important than is the payback period itself. The payback period model, when used as the sole investment criterion, has a fatal flaw in that it fails to consider cash flows after the payback period. Despite this flaw, payback is a rough-and-ready approach to getting a handle on investment proposals. Sometimes a project is so attractive using payback that, when its life is considered, no further analysis is necessary.

For total life evaluations, the accounting rate of return is superior to the payback period because it does consider a capital expenditure proposal's profitability. Using the accounting rate of return, a project that merely returns the initial investment will have an average annual increase in net income of 0 and an accounting rate of return of 0. The problem with the accounting rate of return is that it fails to consider the timing of cash flows. It treats all cash flows within the life of an investment proposal equally despite the fact that cash flows occurring early in a project's life are more valuable than cash flows occurring late in a project's life. Early period cash flows can earn additional profits by being invested elsewhere. Consider the two investment proposals summarized in Exhibit 25.5. Both have an accounting rate of return of 5%, but Project A is superior to Project B because most of its cash flows occur in the first two years. Because of the timing of the cash flows when discounted at an annual rate of 10%, Project A has a net present value of $1,120 while Project B has a negative net present value of $(10,928).

LO4 Evaluate the strengths and weaknesses of alternative capital budgeting models.

Exhibit 25.5 ■ Evaluating Capital Budgeting Models with Differences in Cash Flow Timing

Accounting rate of return analysis of Projects A and B

	Project A	Project B
Predicted net cash inflow from operations		
Year 1	$ 50,000	$ 10,000
Year 2	50,000	10,000
Year 3	10,000	50,000
Year 4	10,000	50,000
Total	120,000	120,000
Total depreciation	(100,000)	(100,000)
Total net income	$ 20,000	$ 20,000
Project life	÷ 4 years	÷ 4 years
Average annual increase in net income	$ 5,000	$ 5,000
Initial investment	÷ 100,000	÷ 100,000
Accounting rate of return on initial investment	0.05	0.05

continued

continued from previous page

Exhibit 25.5 ■ Evaluating Capital Budgeting Models with Differences in Cash Flow Timing

Net present value analysis of Project A

	Predicted Cash Inflows (outflows)	Year(s) of Cash Flows	10% Present Value Factor	Present Value of Cash Flows
Initial investment.................	$(100,000)	0	1.00000	$(100,000)
Operation	50,000	1–2	1.73554	86,777
Operation	10,000	3–4	3.16987 – 1.73554	14,343
Net present value of all cash flows				$ 1,120

Net present value analysis of Project B

	Predicted Cash Inflows (outflows)	Year(s) of Cash Flows	10% Present Value Factor	Present Value of Cash Flows
Initial investment.................	$(100,000)	0	1.00000	$(100,000)
Operation	10,000	1–2	1.73554	17,355
Operation	50,000	3–4	3.16987 – 1.73554	71,717
Net present value of all cash flows				$ (10,928)

Business Insight ■ Patient Capital

In the UK, "patient capital" is outpacing traditional venture capital investment. Where venture capital (VC) groups expect returns after a fixed period, usually around 10 years, patient capital is characterized by willingness to wait and see. Of investments in new UK tech firms, 36% came from patient capital investors, while 34% came from traditional VCs. These two sources combined total just shy of $2 billion of funding.

Firms also use the patient capital principle to budget capital for activities such as research and development (R&D). The success of Corning's Gorilla Glass highlights what can go right with patient capital. Corning saw revenue from sales of Gorilla Glass, which was originally developed in the 1960s, go from $0 to $1 billion in 2007 when the glass was selected as the surface of the iPhone.

Because patient capital requires patient investors or owners, less established firms need to be creative to allow time for their investments to make good. Drugmaker Celator used a combination of quick returns from improving the delivery of existing leukemia drugs and funding from the Leukemia and Lymphoma Society to buy time while its revolutionary treatment for acute myeloid leukemia went through clinical trials. Now that the drug is widely used, investors' patience is being rewarded.

Sources: Muran Ahmed, "Patient Capital Overtakes VC for UK Tech Groups," *Financial Times*, November 1, 2015.
Martin Tillier, "Corning (GLW) and Coherent (COHR): Old Tech Companies Still Worth Investing In," *Nasdaq News*, January 8, 2014.
Brian Gormley, "Venture Investors in Celator Pharma Rewarded for Taking the Long View," *Wall Street Journal*, June 1, 2016.

The net present value and the internal rate of return models both consider the time value of money and project profitability. They almost always provide the same evaluation of individual projects whose acceptance or rejection will not affect other projects. An exception can occur when periods of net cash outflows are mixed with periods of net cash inflows. Under these circumstances, an investment proposal could have multiple internal rates of return. The net present value and the internal rate of return models, however, have two basic differences that often lead to differences in the evaluation of competing investment proposals:

1. The net present value model gives explicit consideration to investment size. The internal rate of return model does not.

2. The net present value model assumes that all net cash inflows are reinvested at the discount rate; the internal rate of return model assumes that all net cash inflows are reinvested at the project's internal rate of return.

When there is a difference in the size of competing investment proposals, and funds not invested in the accepted proposal can only be invested at the cost of capital, the net present value method is superior.

LO4 Review 25-4

Olive Theory Pizzeria is considering three different unrelated capital investments. Presented is information pertaining to each investment proposal.

	Proposal A	Proposal B	Proposal C
Initial investment.	$45,000	$45,000	$45,000
Cash flow from operations			
Year 1	40,000	22,500	45,000
Year 2	5,000	22,500	
Year 3	22,500	22,500	
Disinvestment			
Life (years)	3 years	3 years	1 year

Required
Determine each of the following:

a. Rank these investment proposals using the payback period, the accounting rate of return on initial investment, and the net present value criteria. Assume that the organization's cost of capital is 10%. Round all calculations to two decimal places.

b. Explain the difference in rankings. Which investment would you recommend?   **Solution on p. 25-44.**

Additional Aspects of Capital Budgeting

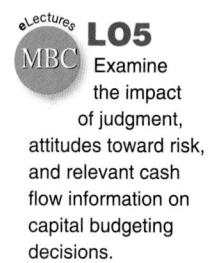

The capital budgeting models discussed do not make investment decisions. Rather, they help managers separate capital expenditure proposals that meet certain criteria from those that do not. Managers can then focus on those proposals that pass the initial screening.

LO5 Examine the impact of judgment, attitudes toward risk, and relevant cash flow information on capital budgeting decisions.

Using Multiple Investment Criteria

In performing this initial screening, management can use a single capital budgeting model or multiple models, including some we have not discussed. Management might specify that proposals must be in line with the organization's long-range goals and business strategy, have a maximum payback period of three years, have a positive net present value when discounted at 14%, and have an initial investment of less than $500,000. The maximum payback period might be intended to reduce risk, the present value criterion might be to ensure an adequate return to investors, and the maximum investment size might reflect the resources available for investment.

Nonquantitative factors such as market position, operational performance improvement, and strategy implementation often play a decisive role in management's final decision to accept or reject a capital expenditure proposal that has passed the initial screening. Also important at this point are top management's attitudes toward risk and financing alternatives, their confidence in the professional judgment of other managers making investment proposals, their beliefs about the future direction of the economy, and their evaluation of alternative investments. In the following sections, we will focus on evaluating risk, differential analysis of project cash flows, predicting differential costs and revenues for high-tech investments, and evaluating mutually exclusive investments.

Evaluating Risk

All capital expenditure proposals involve risk, including risk related to the following:

- Cost of the initial investment.
- Time required to complete the initial investment and begin operations.
- Whether the new facilities will operate as planned.
- Life of the facilities.
- Customers' demand for the product or service.
- Final selling price.
- Operating costs.
- Disposal values.

Projected cash flows (such as those summarized for the Mobile Taqueria proposal in Exhibit 25.2) are based on management's best predictions. Although these predictions are likely to reflect the professional judgment of economists, marketing personnel, engineers, and accountants, they are far from certain.

Many techniques have been developed to assist in the analysis of the risks inherent in capital budgeting. Suggested approaches include the following:

- *Adjust the discount rate for individual projects based on management's perception of the risks associated with a project.* A project perceived as being almost risk free might be evaluated using a discount rate of 12%; a project perceived as having moderate risk may be evaluated using a discount rate of 16%; and a project perceived as having high risk might be evaluated using a discount rate of 20%.

- *Compute several internal rates of return and/or net present values for a project.* For example, a project's net present value might be computed three times: first assuming the most optimistic projections of cash flows; second assuming the most likely projections of cash flows; and third assuming the most pessimistic projections of cash flows. The final decision is then based on management's attitudes toward risk. A project whose most likely outcome is highly profitable would probably be rejected if its pessimistic outcome might lead to bankruptcy.

- *Subject a capital expenditure proposal to sensitivity analysis*, a study of the responsiveness of a model's dependent variable(s) to changes in one or more of its independent variables. Management might want to know, for example, the minimum annual net cash inflows that will provide an internal rate of return of 12% with other cost and revenue projections being as expected.

Research Insight ■ Global Economic Changes Can Drive Capital Budgets

Global investment can shift due to factors far beyond the control of investors. The impact of the UK's decision to leave the European Union hit capital investment long before it officially hit the EU parliament. Investors, worried that their capital would be stuck in UK funds, pulled out quickly. This, coupled with a weakening British pound, slowed investment by domestic funds. Merger and acquisition (M&A) activity within the UK slowed, along with acquisition of foreign firms by UK firms. However, with the pound down and UK funds off the market, foreign firms found a window of relative affordability in the wake of the vote.

In the month following the vote, foreign companies closed 60 deals totaling $35 billion, compared to only $30 billion in the previous quarter. It is important to remember that capital budgeting decisions may depend directly on outside factors such as exchange rates and political processes around the globe.

Sources: Attracta Mooney, "Brexit 'Stampede' Out of UK Funds," *Financial Times*, July 24, 2016.
Pamela Barbaglia and Freya Berry, "Corporate Raiders Seek Brexit Bargains in Britain," *Reuters*, July 24, 2016.
Iain Macmillan, Siram Prakash, and Ian Stewart, "Impact of the EU Referendum on M&A Activity in the UK," *Deloitte*, June 2016.

Differential Analysis of Project Cash Flows

All previous examples assume that capital expenditure proposals produce additional net cash inflows, but this is not always the case. Units of government and not-for-profit organizations might provide services that do not produce any cash inflows. For-profit organizations might be required to make capital expenditures to maintain product quality or to bring facilities up to environmental or safety standards. In these situations, it is impossible to compute a project's payback period, accounting rate of return, or internal rate of return. It is possible, however, to compute the present value of all life-cycle costs associated with alternative ways of providing the service or meeting the environmental or safety standard. Here, the alternative with the smallest negative net present value is preferred.

Capital expenditure proposals to reduce operating costs by upgrading facilities might not provide any incremental cash inflows. Again, we can use a total cost approach and calculate the present value of the costs associated with each alternative, with the low-cost alternative being preferred. Alternatively, we can perform a differential analysis of cash flows and, treating any reduced operating costs as if they were cash inflows, compute the net present value or the internal rate of return of the cost reduction proposal. Recall from Module 17 that a relevant cost analysis focuses on the costs that differ under alternative actions. Once the differential amounts have been determined, they can be adjusted for the time value of money. To illustrate the differential approach, we consider an example introduced in Module 17.

Let's again assume Beats produces a variety of electronic components, including 10,000 units per year of a component used in wireless headsets. Further assume the machine currently used in manufacturing the headset components is two years old and has a remaining useful life of four years. It cost $90,000 and has an estimated salvage value of zero dollars at the end of its useful life. Its current book value (original cost less accumulated depreciation) is $60,000, but its current disposal value (resale value) is only $35,000.

Management is evaluating the desirability of replacing the machine with a new machine. The new machine costs $80,000, has a useful life of four years, and a predicted salvage value of zero dollars at the end of its useful life. Although the new machine has the same productive capacity as the old machine, its predicted operating costs are lower because it requires less electricity. Furthermore, because of a computer control system, the new machine will require less frequent and less expensive inspections and adjustments. Finally, the new machine requires less maintenance.

An analysis of the cash flows associated with this cost reduction proposal, separated into the three phases of the project's life, are presented in Exhibit 25.6. Because the proposal does not have a disposal value, this portion of the analysis could have been omitted. (A detailed explanation of the relevant costs included in this analysis is in Exhibit 17.1 and the accompanying Module 17

Exhibit 25.6 ■ Differential Analysis of Predicted Cash Flows

	One Year Totals		
	Keep Old Machine (A)	Replace with New Machine (B)	Difference (income effect of replacement) (A) – (B)
Initial investment			
Cost of new machine		$80,000	$(80,000)
Disposal value of old machine		(35,000)	35,000
Net initial investment.			$(45,000)
Annual operating cash savings			
Conversion			
Old machine (10,000 units × $5).	$50,000		
New machine (10,000 units × $4)		$40,000	$10,000
Inspection and adjustment			
Old machine (10 setups × $500 per setup)	5,000		
New machine (5 setups × $300 per setup)		1,500	3,500
Machine maintenance			
Old machine ($200 per month × 12 months)	2,400		
New machine ($200 per year).		200	2,200
Net annual cost savings			$15,700
Disinvestment at end of life			
Old machine	$ 0		
New machine		$ 0	

discussion of relevant costs.) Assuming that Beats has a discount rate of 12%, the proposal's net present value (computed in Exhibit 25.7) is $2,686, and the proposal is acceptable.

Exhibit 25.7 ■ Differential Analysis of Predicted Cash Flows

	Predicted Cash Inflows (outflows) (A)	Year(s) of Cash Flows (B)	12% Present Value Factor (C)	Present Value of Cash Flows (A) × (C)
Initial investment.................	$(45,000)	0	1.00000	$(45,000)
Operation	15,700	1–4	3.03735	47,686
Disinvestment..................	0	4	0.63552	0
Net present value of all cash flows...				$ 2,686

Predicting Differential Costs and Revenues for High-Tech Investments

Care must be taken when evaluating proposals for investments in technological innovations such as flexible manufacturing systems and computer integrated manufacturing. The three types of errors to consider are (1) investing in unnecessary or overly complex equipment, (2) overestimating cost saving, and (3) underestimating incremental sales.

Investing in Unnecessary or Overly Complex Equipment

A common error is to simply compare the cost associated with the current inefficient way of doing things with the predicted cost of performing the identical operations with more modern equipment. Although capital budgeting models might suggest that such investments are justifiable, the result could be the costly and rapid completion of non-value-added activities. Consider the following examples.

■ A company invests in an automated system to speed the movement of work in process between workstations without first evaluating the plant layout. The firm is still unable to compete with other companies having better organized plants that allow lower cycle times, lower work-in-process inventories, and lower manufacturing costs. Management should have evaluated the plant layout before investing in new equipment. They may have found that rearranging the factory floor would have reduced materials movement and eliminated the need for the investment.

■ A company invests in an automated warehouse to permit the rapid storage and retrieval of goods while competitors work to eliminate excess inventory. The firm is left with large inventories and a large investment in the automated warehouse while competitors, not having to earn a return on similar investments, are able to charge lower prices. Management should have evaluated the need for current inventory levels and perhaps shifted to a just-in-time approach to inventory management before considering the investment in an automated warehouse.

■ A company hires staff to perform quality inspections while competitors implement total quality management and seek to eliminate the need for quality inspections. While defective products or services are now identified before they affect customers, they still exist. Furthermore, the company has higher expenditures than competitors, resulting in a less competitive cost structure. The inspections might not have been needed if management had shifted from inspecting for conformance to an emphasis on "doing it right the first time."

■ A company invests in automated welding equipment to more efficiently produce printer casings while competitors simplify the product design and shift from welded to molded plastic casings. Although the cost of producing the welded casings might be lower, the company's cost structure is still not competitive.

All of these examples illustrate the limitations of capital budgeting models and the need for good judgment. *In the final analysis, managers, not models, make decisions.* Management must carefully evaluate the situations and determine whether they have considered the proper alternatives and all important cash flows.

Overestimating Cost Savings

When a number of activities drive manufacturing overhead costs, estimates of overhead cost savings based on a single activity cost driver can significantly overestimate cost savings. Assume, for example, that a company containing both machine-intensive and labor-intensive operations develops a cost-estimating equation for overhead with labor as the only independent variable. Because of this, all overhead costs are associated with labor. The predicted cost savings can be computed as the sum of predicted reductions in labor plus predicted reductions in overhead; the predicted reductions in overhead are computed as the overhead per direct labor dollar or labor hour multiplied by the predicted reduction in direct labor dollars or labor hours. Because a major portion of the overhead is driven by factors other than direct labor, reducing direct labor will not provide the predicted savings. Capital budgeting models might suggest that the investment is acceptable, but the models are based on inaccurate cost data.

Management should beware of overly simplistic computations of cost savings. This is an area in which management needs the assistance of well-trained management accountants and engineers.

Underestimating Incremental Sales or Cost Savings

In evaluating proposals for investments in new equipment, management often assumes that the baseline for comparison is the current sales level, but this might not be the case. If competitors are investing in equipment to better meet customer needs and to reduce costs, a failure to make similar investments might result in uncompetitive prices and declining, rather than steady, sales. Hence, the baseline for sales without the investment is overstated, and the incremental sales of the investment is understated. Not considering the likely decline in sales understates the incremental sales associated with the investment and biases the results against the proposed investment.

Investments in manufacturing technologies, such as flexible manufacturing systems (FMS) and computer integrated manufacturing (CIM), do more than simply allow the efficient production of current products. Flexible manufacturing systems are designed to easily adapt to changes in the type and quantity of the product being manufactured. In computer integrated manufacturing, companies can use computers to not only manage what equipment does but also manage the flow of materials and inventory levels. Such investments also make possible the rapid, low-cost switching to new products. The result is expanded sales opportunities.

Such investments might also produce cost savings further down the value chain, either within or outside the company. Beats' decision to acquire a new machine might have the unanticipated consequence of reducing customer warranty claims or increasing sales because customers are attracted to a higher-quality product.

Unfortunately, because such opportunities are difficult to quantify, they are often ignored in the evaluation of capital expenditure proposals. The solution to this dilemma involves the application of management's professional judgment, a willingness to take risks based on this professional judgment, and recognition that certain investments transcend capital budgeting models in that they involve strategic as well as long-range planning. At this level of planning, qualitative decisions concerning the nature of the organization are at least as important as quantified factors.

LO5 Review 25-5

Hilltop Ski Resort is considering making a capital investment in a new ski lift. Hilltop's finance team assessed the investment using the net present value model and predicts the ski lift will generate a positive net present value cash flow over the life of the asset.

Required
Identify and discuss additional factors that Hilltop's management should consider after the initial screening of the capital investment in the ski lift, before making a final evaluation of the investment.

Solution on p. 25-45.

Taxes in Capital Budgeting Decisions

To focus on capital budgeting concepts, we deferred consideration of the impact of taxes. Because income taxes affect cash flows and income, their consideration is important in evaluating investment proposals in for-profit organizations.

LO6
Determine the net present value of investment proposals with consideration of taxes.

The cost of investments in plant and equipment is not deducted from taxable revenues in determining taxable income and income taxes at the time of the initial investment. Instead, the amount of the initial investment is deducted as depreciation over the operating life of an asset. To illustrate the impact of taxes on cash flows, assume the following:

■ Revenues and operating cash receipts are the same each year.

■ Depreciation is the only noncash expense of an organization.

Depreciation Tax Shield

Depreciation does not require the use of cash (the funds were spent at the initial investment), but depreciation is said to provide a "tax shield" because it reduces cash payments for income taxes. The **depreciation tax shield** (the reduction in taxes due to the deductibility of depreciation from taxable revenues) is computed as follows:

> **Depreciation tax shield = Depreciation × Tax rate**

The value of the depreciation tax shield is illustrated using Mobile Taqueria's capital expenditure proposal summarized in Exhibit 25.2. Mobile Taqueria's annual straight-line depreciation of $16,511 is computed as the initial investment of $90,554 minus the predicted disposal value of $8,000, all divided by the predicted five-year life $16,511 [($90,554 – $8,000)/5]. With an assumed tax rate of 34%, the annual depreciation tax shield is $5,614 ($16,511 depreciation × 0.34 tax rate). The increase in annual cash flows provided by the depreciation tax shield is illustrated in Exhibit 25.8. Examine this exhibit, paying particular attention to the lines for depreciation, income taxes, and net annual cash flow.

Exhibit 25.8 ■ Effect of Depreciation on Taxes, Income, and Cash Flow

Annual Taxes and Income without Depreciation		Annual Taxes and Income with Depreciation	
Sales	$175,000	Sales	$175,000
Operating expenses (except depreciation)	(145,000)	Operating expenses (except depreciation)	(145,000)
Depreciation	0	Depreciation	(16,511)
Income before taxes without depreciation	30,000	Income before taxes with depreciation	13,489
Income taxes (34%)	(10,200)	Income taxes (34%)	(4,586)
Net income	$ 19,800	Net income	$ 8,903

Depreciation reduces income taxes by $5,614 ($10,200 taxes without depreciation – $4,586 taxes with depreciation). This is the amount of the depreciation tax shield.

Annual Taxes and Cash Flow without Depreciation		Annual Taxes and Cash Flow with Depreciation	
Sales	$175,000	Sales	$175,000
Operating expenses (except depreciation)	(145,000)	Operating expenses (except depreciation)	(145,000)
Income taxes	(10,200)	Income taxes	(4,586)
Net annual cash inflow	$ 19,800	Net annual cash inflow	$ 25,414

The deductibility of depreciation for tax purposes reduces cash payments for taxes, thus increasing the net cash flow by $5,614 ($25,414 with depreciation – $19,800 without depreciation). This is the amount of the depreciation tax shield.

The U.S. Tax Code contains guidelines concerning the depreciation of various types of assets. (Analysis of these guidelines is beyond the scope of this text.) Tax guidelines allow organizations a choice in tax depreciation procedures between straight-line depreciation and an accelerated depreciation method detailed in the Tax Code. Because of the time value of money, profitable businesses should usually select the tax depreciation procedure that provides the earliest depreciation. To illustrate the effect of accelerated depreciation on taxes and capital budgeting, we use double-declining balance depreciation rather than the accelerated method detailed in the Code. When making capital expenditure decisions, managers should, of course, refer to the most current version of the Tax Code to determine the specific depreciation guidelines in effect at that time.

Exhibits 12.9 and 12.10 illustrate the effect of two alternative depreciation procedures, straight-line and double-declining balance, on the net present value of Mobile Taqueria's proposed investment. The cash flows for this investment were presented in Exhibit 25.2, and the effect of taxes on the investment's annual cash flows were examined in Exhibit 25.8. Ignoring taxes, the investment was shown (in Exhibit 25.3) to have a positive net present value of $20,398 at a discount rate of 12%. With taxes, the investment has a positive net present value of $3,866 using straight-line depreciation and $6,082 using double-declining balance depreciation. Although taxes and cash flows are identical over the entire life of the project, the use of double-declining balance depreciation for taxes results in a higher net present value because it results in lower cash expenditures for taxes in the earlier years of an asset's life.

Exhibit 25.9 ■ Analysis of Capital Expenditures Including Tax Effects: Straight-Line Depreciation

	Predicted Cash Inflows (outflows) (A)	Year(s) of Cash Flows (B)	12% Present Value Factor (C)	Present Value of Cash Flows (A) × (C)
Initial investment				
Vehicle and equipment.	$(90,554)	0	1.00000	$ (90,554)
Inventory and other working capital	(4,000)	0	1.00000	(4,000)
Operations				
Annual taxable income without depreciation	30,000	1–5	3.60478	108,143
Taxes on income ($30,000 × 0.34).	(10,200)	1–5	3.60478	(36,769)
Depreciation tax shield*	5,614	1–5	3.60478	20,237
Disinvestment				
Sale of vehicle and equipment.	8,000	5	0.56743	4,539
Inventory and other working capital	4,000	5	0.56743	2,270
Net present value of all cash flows				$ 3,866

*Computation of depreciation tax shield:

Annual straight-line depreciation.	$16,511
Tax rate.	× 0.34
Depreciation tax shield	$ 5,614

Investment Tax Credit

From time to time, for the purpose of stimulating investment and economic growth, the U.S. federal government has implemented an investment tax credit. An **investment tax credit** reduces taxes in the year a new asset is placed in service by some stated percentage of the cost of the asset. In recent years tax credits, such as the credits for purchasing hybrid automobiles, have been used to stimulate investments that reduce the emission of greenhouses gases. Typically, this is done without reducing the depreciation base of the asset for tax purposes. An investment tax credit reduces cash payments for taxes and, hence, is treated as a cash inflow for capital budgeting purposes. This additional cash inflow increases the probability that a new asset will meet a taxpayer's capital expenditure criteria.

Exhibit 25.10 ■ Analysis of Capital Expenditures Including Tax Effects: DDB Depreciation

	Predicted Cash Inflows (outflows) (A)	Year(s) of Cash Flows (B)	12% Present Value Factor (C)	Present Value of Cash Flows (A) × (C)
Initial investment				
Vehicle and equipment	$(90,554)	0	1.00000	$ (90,554)
Inventory and other working capital	4,000	0	1.00000	(4,000)
Operations				
Annual taxable income without depreciation.	30,000	1–5	3.60478	108,143
Taxes on income ($30,000 × 0.34)	(10,200)	1–5	3.60478	(36,769)
Depreciation tax shield*				
Year 1	12,315	1	0.89286	10,996
Year 2	7,389	2	0.79719	5,890
Year 3	4,434	3	0.71178	3,156
Year 4	2,660	4	0.63552	1,690
Year 5	1,270	5	0.56743	721
Disinvestment				
Sale of vehicle and equipment	8,000	5	0.56743	4,539
Inventory and other working capital	4,000	5	0.56743	2,270
Net present value of all cash flows.				$ 6,082

*Computation of depreciation tax shield:

Year	Depreciation Base† (A)	Annual Rate (B)	Annual Depreciation (C) = (A) × (B)	Tax Rate (D)	Tax Shield (E) = (C) × (D)
1	$90,554	2/5	$36,222	0.34	$12,315
2	54,332	2/5	21,733	0.34	7,389
3	32,599	2/5	13,040	0.34	4,434
4	19,559	2/5	7,824	0.34	2,660
5	11,735	balance	3,735	0.34	1,270

†The depreciation base is reduced by the amount of all previous depreciation. The annual rate is twice the straight-line rate. For simplicity, we depreciated the remaining balance in the fifth year and did not switch to straight-line depreciation when the straight-line amount exceeds the double-declining balance amount. This would happen in the fourth year, when $19,559 ÷ 2 = $9,780. Although the depreciable base excludes the predicted disposal value of $8,000, under double-declining balance depreciation, an asset is only depreciated down to its disposal value. Hence, Year 5 depreciation is computed as the $11,735 depreciable base minus the $8,000 disposal value.

Review 25-6 LO6

Assume that Architecture Design is considering a proposal to change the company's manual design system to a computer-aided design system. The new system is expected to save 9,000 design hours per year; an operating cost savings of $45 per hour. The annual cash expenditures of operating the new system are estimated to be $200,000. The new system would require an initial investment of $550,000. The estimated life of this system is five years with no salvage value. The tax rate is 35%, and Architecture Design uses straight-line depreciation for tax purposes. Architecture Design has a cost of capital of 14%.

Required
a. Compute the annual after-tax cash flows related to the new design system.
b. Assume that management intends to use double declining balance depreciation with a switch to straight-line depreciation (applied to any undepreciated balance) starting in Year 4. Determine the project's net present value.

Solution on p. 25-45.

Appendix 25A: Time Value of Money

eLectures **LO7**
MBC Compute basic present value cash flow amounts.

When asked to choose between $500 today or an IOU for $500 to be paid one year later, rational decision makers choose the $500 today. Two reasons for this involve the *time value of money* and the *risk*. A dollar today is worth more than a dollar tomorrow or at some future time. Having a dollar provides flexibility. It can be spent, buried, or invested in a number of projects. If invested in a savings account, it will amount to more than one dollar at some future time because of the effect of interest. The interest paid by a bank (or borrower) for the use of money is analogous to the rent paid for the use of land, buildings, or equipment. Furthermore, we live in an uncertain world, and, for a variety of reasons, the possibility exists that an IOU might not be paid.

Future Value

Future value is the amount that a current sum of money earning a stated rate of interest will accumulate to at the end of a future period. Suppose we deposit $500 in a savings account at a financial institution that pays interest at the rate of 10% per year. At the end of the first year, the original deposit of $500 will total $550 ($500 × 1.10). If we leave the $550 for another year, the amount will increase to $605 ($550 × 1.10). It can be stated that $500 today has a future value in one year of $550, or conversely, that $550 one year from today has a present value of $500. Interest of $55 ($605 − $550) was earned in the second year, whereas interest of only $50 was earned in the first year. This happened because interest during the second year was earned on the principal plus interest from the first year ($550). When periodic interest is computed on principal plus prior periods' accumulated interest, the interest is said to be *compounded*. Compound interest is used throughout this text.

To determine future values at the end of one period (usually a year), multiply the beginning amount (present value) by 1 plus the interest rate. When multiple periods are involved, the future value is determined by repeatedly multiplying the beginning amount by 1 plus the interest rate for each period. When $500 is invested for two years at an interest rate of 10% per year, its future value is computed as $500 × 1.10 × 1.10. The following equation is used to figure future value:

$$fv = pv(1 + i)^n$$

where:

$$fv = \text{future value amount}$$
$$pv = \text{present value amount}$$
$$i = \text{interest rate per period}$$
$$n = \text{number of periods}$$

For our $500 deposit, the equation becomes:

$$fv \text{ of } \$500 = pv(1 + i)^n$$
$$= \$500(1 + 0.10)^2$$
$$= \$605$$

In a similar manner, once the interest rate and number of periods are known, the future value amount of any present value amount is easily determined.

Present Value

Present value is the current worth of a specified amount of money to be received at some future date at some interest rate. Solving for *pv* in the future value equation, the new present value equation is determined as follows:

$$pv = \frac{fv}{(1 + i)^n}$$

Using this equation, the present value of $8,800 to be received in one year, discounted at 10%, is computed as follows:

$$pv \text{ of } \$8,800 = \frac{\$8,800}{(1 + 0.10)^1}$$
$$= \frac{\$8,800}{(1.10)}$$
$$= \$8,000$$

Thus, when the discount rate is 10%, the present value of $8,800 to be received in one year is $8,000. The present value equation is often expressed as the future value amount times the present value of $1:

$$pv = fv_n \frac{\$1}{(1 + i)^n}$$

Using the equation for the present value of $1, the present value of $8,800 to be received in one year, discounted at 10%, is computed as follows:

$$\text{pv of } \$8{,}800 = \$8{,}800 \times \frac{\$1}{(1 + 0.10)^1}$$

$$= \$8{,}800 \times 0.90909$$

$$= \$8{,}000$$

The present value of \$8,800 two periods from now is \$7,273, computed as [\$8,800 ÷ (1.10)²] or [\$8,800 × \$1 ÷ (1.10)²].

If a calculator or computer with spreadsheet software is not available, present value computations can be done by hand. Tables, such as Exhibit 25A.1 for the present value of \$1 at various interest rates and time periods, can be used to simplify hand computations. Using the factors in Exhibit 25A.1, the present value of any future amount can be determined. For example, with an interest rate of 10%, the present value of the following future amounts to be received in one period are as follows:

Future Value Amount		Present Value Factor of $1		Present Value
$ 100	×	0.90909	=	$ 90.91
628	×	0.90909	=	570.91
4,285	×	0.90909	=	3,895.45
9,900	×	0.90909	=	8,999.99

To further illustrate the use of Exhibit 25A.1, consider the following application. Suppose Beats wants to invest its surplus cash at 12% to have \$10,000 to pay off a long-term note due at the end of five years. Exhibit 25A.1 shows that the present value factor of \$1, discounted at 12% per year for five years, is 0.56743. Multiplying \$10,000 by 0.56743, the present value is determined to be \$5,674:

$$\text{pv of } \$10{,}000 = \$10{,}000 \times \textbf{Present value factor for } \$1$$

$$= \$10{,}000 \times 0.56743$$

$$= \$5{,}674$$

Therefore, if Beats invests \$5,674 today, it will have \$10,000 available to pay off its note in five years.

Managers also use present value tables to make investment decisions. Assume that Monroe Company can make an investment that will provide a cash flow of \$12,000 at the end of eight years. If the company demands a rate of return of 14% per year, what is the most it will be willing to pay for this investment? From Exhibit 25A.1, we find that the present value factor for \$1, discounted at 14% per year for eight years, is 0.35056:

$$\text{pv of } \$12{,}000 = \$12{,}000 \times \textbf{Present value factor for } \$1$$

$$= \$12{,}000 \times 0.35056$$

$$= \$4{,}207$$

If the company demands an annual return of 14%, the most it would be willing to invest today is \$4,207.

Annuities

Not all investments provide a single sum of money. Many investments provide periodic cash flows called *annuities*. An **annuity** is a series of equal cash flows received or paid over equal intervals of time. Suppose that \$100 will be received at the end of each of the next three years. If the discount rate is 10%, the present value of this annuity can be determined by summing the present value of each receipt:

$$\text{Year 1 } \$100 \times \$1 \div (1 + 0.10)^1 = \$ \ 90.90$$

$$\text{Year 2 } \$100 \times \$1 \div (1 + 0.10)^2 = \ \ 82.65$$

$$\text{Year 3 } \$100 \times \$1 \div (1 + 0.10)^3 = \ \underline{\ \ 75.13}$$

$$\text{Total} \ldots \ldots \ldots \ldots \ldots \ldots \ldots \ \underline{\$248.68}$$

Alternatively, the following equation can be used to compute the present value of an annuity with cash flows at the end of each period:

$$pva = \frac{a}{i} \times \left[1 - \frac{1}{(1+i)^n} \right]$$

where:

pva = present value of an annuity (also called the annuity factor)
i = prevailing rate per period
n = number of periods
a = annuity amount

This equation was used to compute the factors presented in Exhibit 25A.2 for an annuity amount of $1. The present value of an annuity of $1 per period for three periods discounted at 10% per period is as follows:

$$pva \text{ of } \$1 = \frac{1}{0.10} + \left[1 - \frac{1}{(1+0.10)^3} \right]$$
$$= 2.48685$$

Using this factor, the present value of a $100 annuity can be computed as $100 × 2.48685, which yields $248.689. To determine the present value of an annuity of any amount, the annuity factor for $1 can be multiplied by the annuity amount.

To further illustrate the use of Exhibit 25A.2, assume that Red Kite Company is considering an investment in a piece of equipment that will produce net cash inflows of $2,000 at the end of each year for five years. If the company's desired rate of return is 12%, an investment of $7,210 will provide such a return:

$$pva \text{ of } \$2,000 = \$2,000 \times \begin{array}{l} \textbf{Present value for an annuity of \$1} \\ \textbf{for five periods discounted at 12\%} \end{array}$$
$$= \$2,000 \times \ 3.60478$$
$$= \$7,210$$

Here, the $2,000 annuity is multiplied by 3.60478, the factor for an annuity of $1 for five periods found in Exhibit 25A.2, discounted at 12% per period.

Another use of Exhibit 25A.2 is to determine the amount that must be received annually to provide a desired rate of return on an investment. Assume that Corning invests $33,550 in a piece of machinery and desires a return of the investment plus interest of 8% in equal year-end payments for 10 years. The minimum amount that must be received each year is determined by solving the equation for the present value of an annuity:

$$pva \ = \ a \times (pva \text{ of } \$1)$$

$$a \ = \ \frac{pva}{pva \text{ of } \$1}$$

From Exhibit 25A.2, we see that the 8% factor for 10 periods is 6.71008. Dividing the $33,550 investment by 6.71008, the required annuity is computed to be $5,000:

$$a = \frac{\$33,550}{6.71008}$$
$$= \$5,000$$

Unequal Cash Flows

Many investment situations do not produce equal periodic cash flows. When this occurs, the present value for each cash flow must be determined independently because the annuity table can be used only for equal periodic cash flows. Exhibit 25A.1 is used to determine the present value of each future amount separately. To illustrate, assume that the Atlanta Braves wish to acquire the contract of a popular baseball player who is known to attract large crowds. Management believes this player will return incremental cash flows to the team at the end of each of the next three years in the amounts of $2,500,000, $4,000,000, and $1,500,000. After three years, the player anticipates retiring. If the team's owners require a minimum return of 14% on their investment, how much would they be willing to pay for the player's contract?

Exhibit 25A.1 ■ Present Value of $1

$$\text{Present value of }\$1 = \frac{1}{(1+i)^n}$$

Discount rate (i)

Periods (n)	4%	6%	8%	10%	12%	14%	16%	18%	20%	22%	24%	26%	28%
1	0.96154	0.94340	0.92593	0.90909	0.89286	0.87719	0.86207	0.84746	0.83333	0.81967	0.80645	0.79365	0.78125
2	0.92456	0.89000	0.85734	0.82645	0.79719	0.76947	0.74316	0.71818	0.69444	0.67186	0.65036	0.62988	0.61035
3	0.88900	0.83962	0.79383	0.75131	0.71178	0.67497	0.64066	0.60863	0.57870	0.55071	0.52449	0.49991	0.47684
4	0.85480	0.79209	0.73503	0.68301	0.63552	0.59208	0.55229	0.51579	0.48225	0.45140	0.42297	0.39675	0.37253
5	0.82193	0.74726	0.68058	0.62092	0.56743	0.51937	0.47611	0.43711	0.40188	0.37000	0.34111	0.31488	0.29104
6	0.79031	0.70496	0.63017	0.56447	0.50663	0.45559	0.41044	0.37043	0.33490	0.30328	0.27509	0.24991	0.22737
7	0.75992	0.66506	0.58349	0.51316	0.45235	0.39964	0.35383	0.31393	0.27908	0.24859	0.22184	0.19834	0.17764
8	0.73069	0.62741	0.54027	0.46651	0.40388	0.35056	0.30503	0.26604	0.23257	0.20376	0.17891	0.15741	0.13878
9	0.70259	0.59190	0.50025	0.42410	0.36061	0.30751	0.26295	0.22546	0.19381	0.16702	0.14428	0.12493	0.10842
10	0.67556	0.55839	0.46319	0.38554	0.32197	0.26974	0.22668	0.19106	0.16151	0.13690	0.11635	0.09915	0.08470
11	0.64958	0.52679	0.42888	0.35049	0.28748	0.23662	0.19542	0.16192	0.13459	0.11221	0.09383	0.07869	0.06617
12	0.62460	0.49697	0.39711	0.31863	0.25668	0.20756	0.16846	0.13722	0.11216	0.09198	0.07567	0.06245	0.05170
13	0.60057	0.46884	0.36770	0.28966	0.22917	0.18207	0.14523	0.11629	0.09346	0.07539	0.06103	0.04957	0.04039
14	0.57748	0.44230	0.34046	0.26333	0.20462	0.15971	0.12520	0.09855	0.07789	0.06180	0.04921	0.03934	0.03155
15	0.55526	0.41727	0.31524	0.23939	0.18270	0.14010	0.10793	0.08352	0.06491	0.05065	0.03969	0.03122	0.02465
16	0.53391	0.39365	0.29189	0.21763	0.16312	0.12289	0.09304	0.07078	0.05409	0.04152	0.03201	0.02478	0.01926
17	0.51337	0.37136	0.27027	0.19784	0.14564	0.10780	0.08021	0.05998	0.04507	0.03403	0.02581	0.01967	0.01505
18	0.49363	0.35034	0.25025	0.17986	0.13004	0.09456	0.06914	0.05083	0.03756	0.02789	0.02082	0.01561	0.01175
19	0.47464	0.33051	0.23171	0.16351	0.11611	0.08295	0.05961	0.04308	0.03130	0.02286	0.01679	0.01239	0.00918
20	0.45639	0.31180	0.21455	0.14864	0.10367	0.07276	0.05139	0.03651	0.02608	0.01874	0.01354	0.00983	0.00717

Exhibit 25A.2 ■ Present Value of an Annuity of $1

$$\text{Present value of an annuity of }\$1 = \frac{1}{i} \times \left[1 - \frac{1}{(1+i)^n} \right]$$

Discount rate (i)

Periods (n)	4%	6%	8%	10%	12%	14%	16%	18%	20%	22%	24%	26%	28%
1	0.96154	0.94340	0.92593	0.90909	0.89286	0.87719	0.86207	0.84746	0.83333	0.81967	0.80645	0.79365	0.78125
2	1.88609	1.83339	1.78326	1.73554	1.69005	1.64666	1.60523	1.56564	1.52778	1.49153	1.45682	1.42353	1.39160
3	2.77509	2.67301	2.57710	2.48685	2.40183	2.32163	2.24589	2.17427	2.10648	2.04224	1.98130	1.92344	1.86844
4	3.62990	3.46511	3.31213	3.16987	3.03735	2.91371	2.79818	2.69006	2.58873	2.49364	2.40428	2.32019	2.24097
5	4.45182	4.21236	3.99271	3.79079	3.60478	3.43308	3.27429	3.12717	2.99061	2.86364	2.74538	2.63507	2.53201
6	5.24214	4.91732	4.62288	4.35526	4.11141	3.88867	3.68474	3.49760	3.32551	3.16692	3.02047	2.88498	2.75938
7	6.00205	5.58238	5.20637	4.86842	4.56376	4.28830	4.03857	3.81153	3.60459	3.41551	3.24232	3.08331	2.93702
8	6.73274	6.20979	5.74664	5.33493	4.96764	4.63886	4.34359	4.07757	3.83716	3.61927	3.42122	3.24073	3.07579
9	7.43533	6.80169	6.24689	5.75902	5.32825	4.94637	4.60654	4.30302	4.03097	3.78628	3.56550	3.36566	3.18421
10	8.11090	7.36009	6.71008	6.14457	5.65022	5.21612	4.83323	4.49409	4.19247	3.92318	3.68186	3.46481	3.26892
11	8.76048	7.88687	7.13896	6.49506	5.93770	5.45273	5.02864	4.65601	4.32706	4.03540	3.77569	3.54350	3.33509
12	9.38507	8.38384	7.53608	6.81369	6.19437	5.66029	5.19711	4.79322	4.43922	4.12737	3.85136	3.60595	3.38679
13	9.98565	8.85268	7.90378	7.10336	6.42355	5.84236	5.34233	4.90951	4.53268	4.20277	3.91239	3.65552	3.42718
14	10.56312	9.29498	8.24424	7.36669	6.62817	6.00207	5.46753	5.00806	4.61057	4.26456	3.96160	3.69485	3.45873
15	11.11839	9.71225	8.55948	7.60608	6.81086	6.14217	5.57546	5.09158	4.67547	4.31522	4.00129	3.72607	3.48339
16	11.65230	10.10590	8.85137	7.82371	6.97399	6.26506	5.66850	5.16235	4.72956	4.35673	4.03330	3.75085	3.50265
17	12.16567	10.47726	9.12164	8.02155	7.11963	6.37286	5.74870	5.22233	4.77463	4.39077	4.05911	3.77052	3.51769
18	12.65930	10.82760	9.37189	8.20141	7.24967	6.46742	5.81785	5.27316	4.81219	4.41866	4.07993	3.78613	3.52945
19	13.13394	11.15812	9.60360	8.36492	7.36578	6.55037	5.87746	5.31624	4.84350	4.44152	4.09672	3.79851	3.53863
20	13.59033	11.46992	9.81815	8.51356	7.46944	6.62313	5.92884	5.35275	4.86958	4.46027	4.11026	3.80834	3.54580

To solve this problem, it is necessary to determine the present value of the expected future cash flows. Here we use Exhibit 25A.1 to find the $1 present value factors at 14% for Periods 1, 2, and 3. The cash flows are then multiplied by these factors:

Year	Annual Cash Flow		Present Value of $1 at 14%		Present Value Amount
1	$2,500,000	×	0.87719	=	$2,192,975
2	4,000,000	×	0.76947	=	3,077,880
3	1,500,000	×	0.67497	=	1,012,455
Total					$6,283,310

The total present value of the cash flows for the three years, $6,283,310, represents the maximum amount the team would be willing to pay for the player's contract.

Deferred Returns

Many times, organizations make investments for which they receive no cash until several periods have passed. The present value of an investment discounted at 12% per year, which has a $2,000 return only at the end of Years 4, 5, and 6, can be determined as follows:

Year	Amount		Present Value of $1 at 12%		Present Value Amount
1	$ 0	×	0.89286	=	$ 0
2	0	×	0.79719	=	0
3	0	×	0.71178	=	0
4	2,000	×	0.63552	=	1,271
5	2,000	×	0.56743	=	1,135
6	2,000	×	0.50663	=	1,013
Total					$3,419

Computation of the present value of the deferred annuity can also be performed using the annuity tables if the cash flow amounts are equal for each period. The present value of an annuity for six years minus the present value of an annuity for three years yields the present value of an annuity for Years 4 through 6.

Present value of an annuity for 6 years at 12%: $2,000 × 4.11141 =		$8,223
Present value of an annuity for 3 years at 12%: 2,000 × 2.40183 =		(4,804)
Present value of the deferred annuity		$3,419

LO7 Review 25-7

Using the equations and tables in Appendix 25A of this module, determine the answers to each of the following independent situations:

a. The future value in two years of $2,000 deposited today in a savings account with interest compounded annually at 6%.

b. The present value of $8,000 to be received in four years, discounted at 12%.

c. The present value of an annuity of $2,000 per year for five years discounted at 14%.

d. An initial investment of $32,010 is to be returned in eight equal annual payments. Determine the amount of each payment if the interest rate is 12%.

e. A proposed investment will provide cash flows of $20,000, $8,000, and $6,000 at the end of Years 1, 2, and 3, respectively. Using a discount rate of 20%, determine the present value of these cash flows.

f. Find the present value of an investment that will pay $5,000 at the end of Years 10, 11, and 12. Use a discount rate of 14%.

Solution on p. 25-46.

Appendix 25B: Table Approach to Determining Internal Rate of Return

eLectures **LO8**

MBC Determine internal rate of return using present value tables.

We consider the use of present value tables to determine the internal rate of return of a series of cash flows with (1) equal net cash flows after the initial investment and (2) unequal net cash flows after the initial investment.

Equal Cash Inflows

An investment proposal's internal rate of return is easily determined when a single investment is followed by a series of equal annual net cash flows. The general relationship between the initial investment and the equal annual cash inflows is expressed as follows:

$$\text{Initial investment} = \text{Present value factor for an annuity of \$1} \times \text{Annual net cash inflow}$$

Solve for the appropriate present value factor as follows:

$$\text{Present value factor for an annuity of \$1} = \frac{\text{Initial investment}}{\text{Annual net cash inflows}}$$

Once the present value factor is calculated, use Exhibit 25A.2 and go across the row corresponding to the expected life of the project until a table factor equal to or closest to the project's computed present value factor is found. The corresponding percentage for the present value factor is the proposal's internal rate of return. If a table factor does not exactly equal the proposal's present value factor, a more accurate answer can be obtained by interpolation (which is not discussed in this text).

To illustrate, assume that Mobile Taqueria's proposed investment has a zero disinvestment value. Using all information in Exhibit 25.2 (except that for disinvestment), the proposal's present value factor is 3.15180:

$$\text{Present value factor for an annuity of \$1} = \frac{\text{Initial investment}}{\text{Annual net cash inflows}}$$

$$= \frac{\$94,554}{\$30,000}$$

$$= 3.15180$$

Using Exhibit 25A.2, go across the row for five periods; the closest table factor is 3.12717, which corresponds to an internal rate of return of 18%.

Unequal Cash Inflows

If periodic cash flows subsequent to the initial investment are unequal, the simple procedure of determining a present value factor and looking up the closest corresponding factor in Exhibit 25A.2 cannot be used. Instead, a trial-and-error approach must be used to determine the internal rate of return.

The first step is to select a discount rate estimated to be close to the proposal's IRR and to compute the proposal's net present value. If the resulting net present value is zero, the selected discount rate is the actual rate of return. However, it is unlikely that the first rate selected will be the proposal's IRR. If the computation results in a positive net present value, the actual IRR is higher than the initially selected rate. In this case, the next step is to compute the proposal's net present value using a higher rate. If the second computation produces a negative net present value, the actual IRR is less than the selected rate. Therefore, the actual IRR is between the first and the second rates. This trial-and-error approach continues until a discount rate is found that equates the proposal's cash inflows and outflows. For Mobile Taqueria's investment proposal outlined in Exhibit 25.2, the details of the trial-and-error approach are presented in Exhibit 25B.1.

In Exhibit 25B.1 the first rate produced a negative net present value, indicating that the proposal's IRR is less than 24%. To produce a positive net present value, a smaller rate was selected for the second trial. Since the second rate produced a positive net present value, the proposal's true IRR must be between 16% and 24%. The 20% rate selected for the third trial produced a net present value of $(13) which is approximately zero, indicating that this is the proposal's IRR.

Exhibit 25B.1 ■ Internal Rate of Return with Unequal Cash Flows

First trial with a 24% discount rate

	Predicted Cash Inflows (outflows) (A)	Year(s) of Cash Flows (B)	24% Present Value Factor (C)	Present Value of Cash Flows (A) × (C)
Initial investment.	$(94,554)	0	1.00000	$(94,554)
Operation	30,000	1–5	2.74538	82,361
Disinvestment.	12,000	5	0.34111	4,093
Net present value of all cash flows.				$ (8,100)

Second trial with a 16% discount rate

	Predicted Cash Inflows (outflows) (A)	Year(s) of Cash Flows (B)	16% Present Value Factor (C)	Present Value of Cash Flows (A) × (C)
Initial investment.	$(94,554)	0	1.00000	$(94,554)
Operation	30,000	1–5	3.27429	98,229
Disinvestment.	12,000	5	0.47611	5,713
Net present value of all cash flows.				$ 9,388

Third trial with a 20% discount rate

	Predicted Cash Inflows (outflows) (A)	Year(s) of Cash Flows (B)	20% Present Value Factor (C)	Present Value of Cash Flows (A) × (C)
Initial investment.	$(94,554)	0	1.00000	$(94,554)
Operation	30,000	1–5	2.99061	89,718
Disinvestment.	12,000	5	0.40188	4,823
Net present value of all cash flows.				$ (13)

LO8 Review 25-8

The internal rate of return is often referred to as the time-adjusted rate of return. It is the discount rate that equates the present value of a project's cash inflows with the present value of the project's cash outflows.

Required

a. Discuss the process, when using the table approach to determining internal rate of return, when the project involves equal cash flows.

b. Discuss the process, when using the table approach to determining the internal rate of return, when periodic cash flows subsequent to the initial investment are unequal.

Solution on p. 25-46.

Guidance Answers

You Are the Vice President of Finance

Pg. 25-5 There is no single correct response to this question. It is useful to start by learning how other companies in similar circumstances handle capital expenditure decisions. This might be done through personal contacts or through professional organizations, such as the Financial Executives Institute. Another starting point might be the formation of a small capital budgeting committee, which could be expanded as necessary once formal procedures were in place. Early tasks of the committee might include developing guidelines for the size of expenditures at various organizational levels subject to committee review and developing guidelines for the criteria used in formal reviews. You would want to ensure that the CEO is in agreement with these proposals. If the company has a board of directors, you would also want some mutual understanding of the board's role in the approval of capital expenditures. Finally, you would want to make clear the importance of a post-audit review.

Questions

Q25-1.   What is the relationship between long-range planning and capital budgeting?

Q25-2.   What tasks are often assigned to the capital budgeting committee?

Q25-3.   What purposes are served by a post-audit of approved capital expenditure proposals?

Q25-4.   Into what three phases are a project's cash flows organized?

Q25-5.   State three alternative definitions or descriptions of the internal rate of return.

Q25-6.   Why is the cost of capital an important concept when discounting models are used for capital budgeting?

Q25-7.   What weakness is inherent in the payback period when it is used as the sole investment criterion?

Q25-8.   What weakness is inherent in the accounting rate of return when it is used as an investment criterion?

Q25-9.   Why are the net present value and the internal rate of return models superior to the payback period and the accounting rate of return models?

Q25-10.   State two basic differences between the net present value and the internal rate of return models that often lead to differences in the evaluation of competing investment proposals.

Q25-11.   Identify several nonquantitative factors that are apt to play a decisive role in the final selection of projects for capital expenditures.

Q25-12.   In what way does depreciation affect the analysis of cash flows for a proposed capital expenditure?

Assignments with the ⬤ logo in the margin are available in BusinessCourse.
See the Preface of the book for details.

Mini Exercises

LO2, 7   **M25-13.**   **Time Value of Money: Basics**

Using the equations and tables in Appendix 25A of this module, determine the answers to each of the following independent situations:

    a. The future value in two years of $5,000 deposited today in a savings account with interest compounded annually at 4%.

    b. The present value of $15,000 to be received in four years, discounted at 10%.

    c. The present value of an annuity of $2,500 per year for five years discounted at 12%.

    d. An initial investment of $69,845 is to be returned in eight equal annual payments. Determine the amount of each payment if the interest rate is 8%.

    e. A proposed investment will provide cash flows of $20,000, $25,000, and $30,000 at the end of Years 1, 2, and 3, respectively. Using a discount rate of 6%, determine the present value of these cash flows.

    f. Find the present value of an investment that will pay $3,000 at the end of Years 10, 11, and 12. Use a discount rate of 8%.

LO2, 7   **M25-14.**   **Time Value of Money: Basics**

Using the equations and tables in Appendix 25A of this module, determine the answers to each of the following independent situations:

    a. The future value in three years of $8,900 invested today in a certificate of deposit with interest compounded annually at 6%.

    b. The present value of $12,000 to be received in five years, discounted at 6%.

    c. The present value of an annuity of $25,000 per year for four years discounted at 8%.

    d. An initial investment of $66,200 is to be returned in six equal annual payments. Determine the amount of each payment if the interest rate is 10%.

    e. A proposed investment will provide cash flows of $10,000, $7,500, and $5,000 at the end of Years 1, 2, and 3, respectively. Using a discount rate of 14%, determine the present value of these cash flows.

    f. Find the present value of an investment that will pay $15,000 at the end of Years 8, 9, and 10. Use a discount rate of 16%.

M25-15. **NPV and IRR: Equal Annual Net Cash Inflows**

LO2, 8

Kailey James Company is evaluating a capital expenditure proposal that requires an initial investment of $30,723, has predicted cash inflows of $5,000 per year for 10 years, and has no salvage value.

Required

a. Using a discount rate of 8%, determine the net present value of the investment proposal.
b. Determine the proposal's internal rate of return. (Refer to Appendix 25B if you use the table approach.)
c. What discount rate would produce a net present value of zero?

M25-16. **NPV and IRR: Equal Annual Net Cash Inflows**

LO2, 8

Spotify Technology
SA (SPOT)

Assume Spotify is evaluating a capital expenditure proposal that requires an initial investment of $294,800, has predicted cash inflows of $67,750 per year for six years, and has no salvage value.

Required

a. Using a discount rate of 12%, determine the net present value of the investment proposal.
b. Determine the proposal's internal rate of return. (Refer to Appendix 25B if you use the table approach.)
c. What discount rate would produce a net present value of zero?

M25-17. **Payback Period and Accounting Rate of Return: Equal Annual Operating Cash Flows without Disinvestment**

LO3

Juliana is considering an investment proposal with the following cash flows:

Initial investment—depreciable assets	$74,250
Net cash inflows from operations (per year for 5 years)	16,500
Disinvestment	0

Required

a. Determine the payback period.
b. Determine thxe accounting rate of return on initial investment.
c. Determine the accounting rate of return on average investment.

M25-18. **Payback Period and Accounting Rate of Return: Equal Annual Operating Cash Flows with Disinvestment**

LO3

Minn is considering an investment proposal with the following cash flows:

Initial investment—depreciable assets	$227,500
Net cash inflows from operations (per year for 10 years)	32,500
Disinvestment—depreciable assets	22,750

Required

a. Determine the payback period.
b. Determine the accounting rate of return on initial investment.
c. Determine the accounting rate of return on average investment.

M25-19. **Payback Period and Accounting Rate of Return: Equal Annual Operating Cash Flows with Disinvestment**

LO3

Roopali is considering an investment proposal with the following cash flows:

Initial investment—depreciable assets	$100,000
Initial investment—working capital	20,000
Net cash inflows from operations (per year for 5 years)	24,000
Disinvestment—depreciable assets	20,000
Disinvestment—working capital	20,000

Required

a. Determine the payback period.
b. Determine the accounting rate of return on initial investment.
c. Determine the accounting rate of return on average investment.

Exercises

LO2, 8
Goodrich Petroleum
Corporation
(GDP)

E25-20.   **NPV and IRR: Unequal Annual Net Cash Inflows**

Assume that Goodrich Petroleum Corporation is evaluating a capital expenditure proposal that has the following predicted cash flows:

Initial investment.	$(160,000)
Operation	
Year 1	42,000
Year 2	95,000
Year 3	65,000
Salvage.	0

Required

a. Using a discount rate of 10%, determine the net present value of the investment proposal.

b. Determine the proposal's internal rate of return. (Refer to Appendix 25B if you use the table approach.) *Hint:* You will need to use a trial-and-error approach.

LO2, 8

E25-21.   **NPV and IRR: Unequal Annual Net Cash Inflows**

Rocky Road Company is evaluating a capital expenditure proposal that has the following predicted cash flows:

Initial investment.	$(85,000)
Operation	
Year 1	30,500
Year 2	60,000
Year 3	31,000
Salvage.	0

Required

a. Using a discount rate of 12%, determine the net present value of the investment proposal.

b. Determine the proposal's internal rate of return. (Refer to Appendix 25B if you use the table approach.) *Hint:* You will need to use a trial-and-error approach.

LO2, 3, 8   **E25-22.**   **Payback Period, IRR, and Minimum Cash Flows**

The management of Mohawk Limited is currently evaluating the following investment proposal:

	Time 0	Year 1	Year 2	Year 3	Year 4
Initial investment.	$210,000	—	—	—	—
Net operating cash inflows	—	$70,000	$70,000	$70,000	$70,000

Required

a. Determine the proposal's payback period.

b. Determine the proposal's internal rate of return. (Refer to Appendix 25B if you use the table approach.)

c. Given the amount of the initial investment, determine the minimum annual net cash inflows required to obtain an internal rate of return of 14%.

LO2, 3   **E25-23.**   **Time-Adjusted Cost-Volume-Profit Analysis**

The Hershey
Company (HSY)

Assume The Hershey Company is considering the desirability of producing a new chocolate candy called Pleasure Bombs. Before purchasing the new equipment required to manufacture Pleasure Bombs, the company performed the following analysis:

Unit selling price.	$2.50
Variable manufacturing and selling costs.	(1.85)
Unit contribution margin	$0.65

continued

continued from previous page

Annual fixed costs	
Depreciation (straight-line for 5 years)	$ 62,000
Other (all cash)	48,500
Total	$110,500

Annual break-even sales volume = $110,500 ÷ $0.65 = 170,000 units

Because the expected annual sales volume is 200,000 units, Hershey decided to undertake the production of Pleasure Bombs. This required an immediate investment of $310,000 in equipment that has a life of four years and no salvage value. After four years, the production of Pleasure Bombs will be discontinued.

Required

a. Evaluate the analysis performed by the company.

b. If Hershey has a time value of money of 8%, should it make the investment with projected annual sales of 200,000 units?

c. Considering the time value of money, what annual unit sales volume is required to break even?

E25-24. Time-Adjusted Cost-Volume-Profit Analysis with Income Taxes

Assume the same facts as given in Exercise E25-23 for Hershey.

Required

With a 20% tax rate and a 8% time value of money, determine the annual unit sales required to break even on a time-adjusted basis. Assume straight-line depreciation is used to determine tax payments.

LO6

E25-25. Payback Period and IRR of a Cost Reduction Proposal—Differential Analysis

A light-emitting diode (LED) is a semiconductor diode that emits narrow-spectrum light. Although relatively expensive when compared to incandescent bulbs, they use significantly less energy and last six to ten times longer, with a slow decline in performance rather than an abrupt failure.

Metropolitan City currently has 40,000 incandescent bulbs in traffic lights at approximately 6,000 intersections. It is estimated that replacing all the incandescent bulbs with LEDs will cost $17.7 million. However, the investment is also estimated to save the city $4.42 million per year in energy costs.

Required

a. Determine the payback period of converting Metropolitan City traffic lights to LEDs.

b. If the average life of an incandescent streetlight is one year and the average life of an LED streetlight is seven years, should the city finance the investment in LEDs at an interest rate of 5% per year? Justify your answer.

LO2, 3

E25-26. Payback Period and NPV of a Cost Reduction Proposal—Differential Analysis

Hermione decided to purchase a new automobile. Being concerned about environmental issues, she is leaning toward the hybrid rather than the gasoline only model. Nevertheless, as a new business school graduate, she wants to determine if there is an economic justification for purchasing the hybrid, which costs $2,200 more than the regular model. She has determined that city/highway combined gas mileage of the hybrid and regular models are 40 and 30 miles per gallon respectively. Hermione anticipates she will travel an average of 15,000 miles per year for the next several years.

Required

a. Determine the payback period of the incremental investment if gasoline costs $2.60 per gallon.

b. Assuming that Hermione plans to keep the car about six years and does not believe there will be a trade-in premium associated with the hybrid model, determine the net present value of the incremental investment at 6% time value of money.

c. Determine the cost of gasoline required for a payback period of four years.

d. At $4.00 per gallon, determine the gas mileage required for a payback period of four years.

LO2, 3, 5

E25-27. Payback Period and NPV of Alternative Automobile Purchase

Wendy Li decided to purchase a new Honda Accord. Being concerned about environmental issues, she is leaning toward a Honda Accord Hybrid rather than the completely gasoline-powered LX model. Nevertheless, she wants to determine if there is an economic justification for purchasing the Hybrid, which costs $2,000 more than the LX. Based on a mix of city and highway driving, she predicts that the average gas mileage of each car is 48 MPG for the Hybrid and 30 MPG for the LX. Wendy also anticipates she will drive an average of 15,000 miles per year and that gasoline will cost an average of $2.50 per gallon over the next four years. She also plans to replace whichever car she purchases at the end of four years when the resale values of the Hybrid and the LX are predicted to be $12,500 and $9,000 respectively.

LO2, 3, 5

Required

a. Determine the payback period of the incremental investment associated with purchasing the Hybrid.

b. Determine the net present value of the incremental investment associated with purchasing the Hybrid at a 8% time value of money.

c. Determine the cost of gasoline required for a payback period of two and a half years on the incremental investment.

d. Identify other factors Wendy should consider before making her decision.

Problems

LO2, 3, 4   **P25-28.**   **Ranking Investment Proposals: Payback Period, Accounting Rate of Return, and Net Present Value**

Presented is information pertaining to the cash flows of three mutually exclusive investment proposals:

	Proposal A	Proposal B	Proposal C
Initial investment.	$100,000	$100,000	$100,000
Cash flow from operations			
Year 1	60,000	25,000	110,000
Year 2	40,000	40,000	—
Year 3	35,000	70,000	—
Disinvestment.	0	0	0
Life (years)	3 years	3 years	1 year

Required

a. Rank these investment proposals using the payback period, the accounting rate of return on initial investment, and the net present value criteria. Assume that the organization's cost of capital is 12% and that all investments are in depreciable assets. Round calculations to four decimal places.

b. Explain the difference in rankings. Which investment would you recommend?

LO2, 3, 8   **P25-29.**   **Cost Reduction Proposal: IRR, NPV, and Payback Period**

PA Chemical currently discharges liquid waste into Pittsburgh's municipal sewer system. However, the Pittsburgh municipal government has informed PA that a surcharge of $6 per thousand cubic liters will soon be imposed for the discharge of this waste. This has prompted management to evaluate the desirability of treating its own liquid waste.

A proposed system consists of three elements. The first is a retention basin, which would permit unusual discharges to be held and treated before entering the downstream system. The second is a continuous self-cleaning rotary filter required where solids are removed. The third is an automated neutralization process required where materials are added to control the alkalinity-acidity range.

The system is designed to process 700,000 liters a day. However, management anticipates that only about 350,000 liters of liquid waste would be processed in a normal workday. The company operates 300 days per year. The initial investment in the system would be $1,500,000, and annual operating costs are predicted to be $280,000. The system has a predicted useful life of 10 years and a salvage value of $100,000.

Required

a. Determine the project's net present value at a discount rate of 14%.

b. Determine the project's approximate internal rate of return. (Refer to Appendix 25B if you use the table approach.)

c. Determine the project's payback period.

LO2, 6   **P25-30.**   **NPV with Income Taxes: Straight-Line versus Accelerated Depreciation**

Carl William, Inc. is a conservatively managed boat company whose motto is, "The old ways are the good ways." Management has always used straight-line depreciation for tax and external reporting purposes. Although they are reluctant to change, they are aware of the impact of taxes on a project's profitability.

Required

For a typical $200,000 investment in equipment with a five-year life and no salvage value, determine the present value of the advantage resulting from the use of double-declining balance depreciation as opposed to straight-line depreciation. Assume an income tax rate of 21% and a discount rate of 20%. Also assume that there will be a switch from double-declining balance to straight-line depreciation in the fourth year.

P25-31.   **Payback Period and NPV: Taxes and Straight-Line Depreciation**

Assume that United Technologies Corporation is evaluating a proposal to change the company's manual design system to a computer-aided design (CAD) system. The proposed system is expected to save 12,000 design hours per year; an operating cost savings of $65 per hour. The annual cash expenditures of operating the CAD system are estimated to be $600,000. The CAD system requires an initial investment of $200,000. The estimated life of this system is five years with no salvage value. The tax rate is 21%, and United Technologies uses straight-line depreciation for tax purposes. United Technologies has a cost of capital of 14%.

Required
a. Compute the annual after-tax cash flows related to the CAD project.
b. Compute each of the following for the project:
   1. Payback period.
   2. Net present value.

P25-32.   **NPV: Taxes and Accelerated Depreciation**

Assume the same facts as given in P25-31, except that management intends to use double-declining balance depreciation with a switch to straight-line depreciation (applied to any undepreciated balance) starting in Year 4.

Required
Determine the project's net present value.

P25-33.   **NPV Total and Differential Analysis of Replacement Decision**

Assume Mitsubishi Chemical is evaluating a proposal to purchase a new compressor that would cost $200,000 and have a salvage value of $20,000 in five years. Mitsubishi's cost of capital is 16%. It would provide annual operating cash savings of $22,500, as follows:

	Old Compressor	New Compressor
Salaries.	$60,000	$75,000
Supplies	12,000	7,500
Utilities	23,000	15,000
Cleaning and maintenance.	35,000	10,000
Total cash expenditures	$130,000	$107,500

If the new compressor is purchased, Mitsubishi will sell the old compressor for its current salvage value of $60,000. If the new compressor is not purchased, the old compressor will be disposed of in five years at a predicted scrap value of $6,000. The old compressor's present book value is $85,000. If kept, the old compressor will require repairs one year from now predicted to cost $75,000.

Required
a. Use the total cost approach to evaluate the alternatives of keeping the old compressor and purchasing the new compressor. Indicate which alternative is preferred.
b. Use the differential cost approach to evaluate the desirability of purchasing the new compressor.

P25-34.   **NPV Total and Differential Analysis of Replacement Decision**

Assume Pinstripes Cleaning and Restoration, near Dallas, Texas, must either have a complete overhaul of its current dry-cleaning system or purchase a new one. Its cost of capital is 16%. The following cost projections have been developed:

	Old System	New System
Purchase cost (new).	$85,000	$90,000
Remaining book value	17,000	
Overhaul needed	25,000	
Annual cash operating costs	60,850	40,200
Current salvage value.	12,000	
Salvage value in 5 years	4,500	10,000

If Pinstripes keeps the old system, it will have to be overhauled immediately. With the overhaul, the old system will have a useful life of five more years.

Required

a. Use the total cost approach to evaluate the alternatives of keeping the old system and purchasing the new system. Indicate which alternative is preferred.

b. Use the differential cost approach to evaluate the desirability of purchasing the new system.

LO2, 5   P25-35.   NPV Differential Analysis of Replacement Decision

The management of Dusseldorf Manufacturing Company is currently evaluating a proposal to purchase a new, innovative drill press as a replacement for a less efficient piece of similar equipment, which would then be sold. The cost of the equipment, including delivery and installation, is $320,000. If the equipment is purchased, Dusseldorf will incur a $10,000 cost in removing the present equipment and revamping service facilities. The present equipment has a book value of $150,000 and a remaining useful life of 10 years. Because of new technical improvements that have made the present equipment obsolete, it now has a disposal value of only $70,500. Management has provided the following comparison of manufacturing costs:

	Present Equipment	New Equipment
Annual production (units)	500,000	500,000
Annual costs		
Direct labor (per unit)	$0.15	$0.08
Overhead		
Depreciation (10% of asset's book value).......	$15,000	$32,000
Other.....................................	$84,600	$42,500

Additional information follows:

- Management believes that if the current equipment is not replaced now, it will have to wait 10 years before replacement is justifiable.
- Both pieces of equipment are expected to have a negligible salvage value at the end of 10 years.
- Management expects to sell the entire annual production of 500,000 units.
- Dusseldorf's cost of capital is 14%.

Required

Evaluate the desirability of purchasing the new equipment.

Management Applications

LO2, 3, 5   MA25-36.   Payback, ARR, and IRR: Evaluating the Sale of Government Assets (Requires Spreadsheet)

Morgan Stanley
(MS)

In 2008 the City of Chicago agreed to lease 35,000 parking meters to a Morgan Stanley–led partnership for a one-time sum of $1.15 billion. The lease has been criticized as an example of "one-shot" deals arrived at behind closed doors to balance a current budget at the expense of future generations. Some have observed that deals such as this are akin to individuals using their retirement savings to meet current needs, instead of planning for the future. "These deals are rarely done under the light of public scrutiny," says Richard G. Little, director of the Keston Institute for Public Finance at the University of Southern California. "Often the facts come out long after the deal is done."

Since the lease was signed, helped by parking-fee hikes, the partnership has earned a profit before taxes and depreciation of $0.80 per dollar of revenue. In 2010, total revenues over the 75-year life of the lease were projected to be $11.6 billion.

Defending the city's action, Gene Saffold, Chicago's chief financial officer, stated that "The concession agreement was absolutely the best deal for Chicagoans. . . . The net present value of $11.6 billion in revenue over the life of the 75-year agreement is consistent with $1.15 billion.[1]

Required

Evaluate the 75-year lease and determine if the projected revenues are consistent with the initial investment. To simplify your analysis, assume equal revenues and operating costs in all periods, no investment

---

[1] "Windfall for Investors, A Loss for the Windy City," *Bloomberg Businessweek*, August 29, 2010, pp. 44-45; Ianthe Jeanne Dugan, "Facing Budget Gaps, Cities Sell Parking, Airports, Zoo," *Wall Street Journal*, August 23, 2010, pp. A1, A12.

required in working capital, and no salvage value at the end of the lease. Use a corporate tax rate of 34% (in effect in 2008) in your calculations. Suggested elements of your solution include the following:

a. Determine the payback period in the absence of taxes.
b. Determine the accounting rate of return on the initial investment in the absence of taxes.
c. Determine the accounting rate of return on the initial investment using 34% as the tax rate.
d. Determine the internal rate of return in the absence of taxes.
e. Determine the internal rate of return using 34% as the tax rate.
f. Summary of analysis and conclusions.

MA25-37. Determining Terms of Automobile Leases (Requires Spreadsheet)   **LO2, 5**

Avant-Garde Motor Company has asked you to develop lease terms for the firm's popular Avant-Garde Challenger, which has an average selling price (new) of $25,000. You know that leasing is attractive because it assists consumers in obtaining new vehicles with a small down payment and "reasonable" monthly payments. Market analysts have told you that to attract the widest number of young professionals, the Challenger must have an initial down payment of no more than $500, monthly payments of no more than $400, and lease terms of no more than five years. When the lease expires, Avant-Garde will sell the used Challengers at the automobile's resale market price at that time. It is difficult to predict the future price of the increasingly popular Challenger, but you have obtained the following information on the average resale prices of used Challengers:

Age	Resale Price
1 year	$21,000
2 years	18,000
3 years	17,000
4 years	15,500
5 years	13,000

Avant-Garde's cost of capital is 12% per year, or 1% per month.

Required

a. With the aid of spreadsheet software, develop a competitive and profitable lease payment program. Assuming a $500 down payment, calculate the program's monthly payments for two-, three-, four-, and five-year leases. Assume the down payment and the first lease payment are made immediately and that all subsequent lease payments are made at the start of the month. [*Hint:* Most software packages include a function such as the following: PMT (rate,nper,pv,fv,type), where rate = the time value of money; nper = the number of periods; pv = the present value; fv = the future value; and type = 0 (when the payment is at the end of the period) or 1 (when the payment is at the beginning of the period). For monthly payments, rate should be set at the annual rate divided by 12, and npr should be set at the number of months in the lease. Here, fv is the residual value.]
b. Reevaluate the lease program assuming a down payment of $1,000.
c. Reevaluate the lease program assuming a down payment of $500 and a $1,000 increase in residual values.
d. Reevaluate the lease program assuming a down payment of $1,000 and a $1,000 increase in residual values.
e. What is your final recommendation? What risks are associated with your recommendation? Are there any other actions to consider?

MA25-38. Evaluating Data and Using Payback Period for an Investment Proposal   **LO3, 5**

To determine the desirability of investing in a larger computer monitor (as opposed to the typical monitor that comes with a new personal computer), researchers developed an experiment testing the time required to perform a set of tasks. The tasks included the following:

- Setting up a meeting using electronic mail.
- Reviewing meeting requests.
- Checking an online schedule.
- Embedding a video file into a document.
- Searching a customer database to find a specific set of contracts.
- Copying a database into a spreadsheet.
- Modifying a slide presentation.

The researchers assumed this was a typical set of tasks performed by a manager. They determined that there was a 9% productivity gain using the larger monitor. One test manager commented that the largest productivity gain came from being able to have multiple applications open at the same time and from being able to view several files at once.

Required

Accepting the 9% productivity gain as accurate, what additional information is needed to determine the payback period of an investment in a larger monitor that is to be used by a manager? Make any necessary assumptions and obtain whatever data you can (perhaps from computer component advertisements) to determine the payback period for the proposed investment.

LO2, 4, 5, 8   **MA25-39. IRR and NPV with Performance Evaluation Conflict**

Pepperoni Pizza Company owns and operates fast-service pizza parlors throughout North America. The firm operates on a regional basis and provides almost complete autonomy to the manager of each region. Regional managers are responsible for long-range planning, capital expenditures, personnel policies, pricing, and so forth. Each year the performance of regional managers is evaluated by determining the accounting return on fixed assets in their regions; a return of 16% is expected. To determine this return, regional net income is divided by the book value of fixed assets at the start of the year. Managers of regions earning a return of more than 18% are identified for possible promotion, and managers of regions with a return of less than 14% are subject to replacement.

Mr. Light, with a degree in hotel and restaurant management, is the manager of the Northeast region. He is regarded as a "rising star" and will be considered for promotion during the next two years. Light has been with Pepperoni for a total of three years. During that period, the return on fixed assets in his region (the oldest in the firm) has increased dramatically. He is currently considering a proposal to open five new parlors in the Boston area. The total project involves an investment of $1,000,000 and will double the number of Pepperoni pizzas sold in the Northeast region to a total of 600,000 per year. At an average price of $9 each, total sales revenue will be $5,400,000.

The expenses of operating each of the new parlors include variable costs of $5 per pizza and fixed costs (excluding depreciation) of $175,000 per year. Because each of the new parlors has only a five-year life and no salvage value, yearly straight-line depreciation will be $40,000 [($1,000,000 ÷ 5 parlors) ÷ 5 years].

Required

a. Evaluate the desirability of the $1,000,000 investment in new pizza parlors by computing the internal rate of return and the net present value. Assume a time value of money of 16%. (Refer to Appendix 25B if you use the table approach.)

b. If Light is shrewd, will he approve the expansion? Why or why not? (Additional computations are suggested.)

LO2, 5, 6   **MA25-40. NPV and Project Reevaluation with Taxes, Straight-Line Depreciation**

Last year, the Bayside Chemical Company prepared the following analysis of an investment proposal for a new manufacturing facility:

	Predicted Cash Inflows (outflows) (A)	Year(s) of Cash Flows (B)	12% Present Value Factor (C)	Present Value of Cash Flows (A) × (C)
Initial investment				
Fixed assets	$(810,000)	0	1.00000	$ (810,000)
Working capital	(100,000)	0	1.00000	(100,000)
Operations				
Annual taxable income				
without depreciation	310,000	1–5	3.60478	1,117,482
Taxes on income ($310,000 × 0.21)	(65,100)	1–5	3.60478	(234,671)
Depreciation tax shield	34,020*	1–5	3.60478	122,635

continued

continued from previous page

	Predicted Cash Inflows (outflows) (A)	Year(s) of Cash Flows (B)	12% Present Value Factor (C)	Present Value of Cash Flows (A) × (C)
Disinvestment				
Site restoration	80,000	5	0.56743	(45,394)
Tax shield of restoration ($80,000 × 0.21)	16,800	5	0.56743	9,533
Working capital	100,000	5	0.56743	56,743
Net present value of all cash flows				$ 116,328

*Computation of depreciation tax shield:

Annual straight-line depreciation ($810,000 ÷ 5)	$162,000
Tax rate.	× 0.21
Depreciation tax shield	$ 34,020

Because the proposal had a positive net present value when discounted at Bayside's cost of capital of 12%, the project was approved; all investments were made at the end of the year. Shortly after production began this year, a government agency notified Bayside of required additional expenditures totaling $300,000 to bring the plant into compliance with new federal emission regulations. Bayside has the option either to comply with the regulations by the end of the year, or to sell the entire operation (fixed assets and working capital) for $350,000. The improvements will be depreciated over the remaining four-year life of the plant using straight-line depreciation. The cost of site restoration will not be affected by the improvements. If Bayside elects to sell the plant, any book loss can be treated as an offset against taxable income on other operations. This tax reduction is an additional cash benefit of selling.

Required

a. Should Bayside sell the plant or comply with the new federal regulations? To simplify calculations, assume that any additional improvements are paid for on the last day of the current year.

b. Would Bayside have accepted the proposal at the beginning of the year if it had been aware of the forthcoming federal regulations?

c. Do you have any suggestions that might increase the project's net present value? (No calculations are required.)

MA25-41. Post-Audit and Reevaluation of Investment Proposal: NPV   **LO1, 2, 5**

Anthony Company's capital budgeting committee is evaluating a capital expenditure proposal for the production of a high-definition television receiver to be sold as an add-on feature for personal computers. The proposal calls for an independent contractor to construct the necessary facilities by December 31 of the current year at a total cost of $350,000. Payment for all construction costs will be made on that date. An additional $75,000 in cash will also be made available on December 31 of the current year, for working capital to support sales and production activities.

Management anticipates that the receiver has a limited market life; there is a high probability that within six years all new PCs will have built-in high-definition receivers. Accordingly, the proposal specifies that production will cease after six years. The investment in working capital will be recovered on that date, and the production facilities will be sold for $80,000. Predicted net cash inflows from operations for the next six years are as follows:

20X1.	$125,000
20X2.	125,000
20X3.	125,000
20X4.	60,000
20X5.	60,000
20X6.	60,000

Anthony Company has a time value of money of 14%. For capital budgeting purposes, all cash flows are assumed to occur at the end of each year.

Required

a. Evaluate the capital expenditure proposal using the net present value method. Should Anthony accept the proposal?

b. Assume that the capital expenditure proposal is accepted, but construction delays caused by labor problems and difficulties in obtaining the necessary construction permits delay the completion of the project. Payments totaling $250,000 were made to the construction company on December 31 of the current year. However, completion is now scheduled for December 31, 20X1, and an additional $150,000 will be required to complete construction. If the project is continued, the additional $150,000 will be paid at the end of 20X1, and the plant will begin operations on January 1, 20X2.

Because of the cost overruns, the capital budgeting committee requests a reevaluation of the project, before agreeing to any additional expenditures. After much effort, the following revised predictions of net operating cash inflows are developed:

20X2	$150,000
20X3	125,000
20X4	60,000
20X5	60,000
20X6	60,000

The working capital investment and disinvestment and the plant salvage values have not changed, except that the cash for working capital would now be made available on December 31, 20X1. Use the net present value method to reevaluate the initial decision to accept the proposal. Given the information currently available about the project, should it have been accepted? (*Hint:* Determine the net present value as of December 31 of the current year assuming management has not committed Anthony to the proposal.)

c. Given the situation that exists in early 20X1, should management continue or cancel the project? Assume that the facilities have a current salvage value of $95,000. (*Hint:* Assume that the decision is being made on January 1, 20X1.)

LO1, 2, 5   **MA25-42. Post-Audit and Reevaluation of Investment Proposal: IRR**

Throughout his four years in college, Ronald King worked at the local Beef Burger Restaurant in College City. Although the working conditions were good and the pay was not bad, Ron believed he could do a much better job of managing the restaurant than the current owner-manager. In particular, Ron believed that the proper use of marketing campaigns and sales incentives, such as selling a second burger for a 25% discount, could increase annual sales by 40%.

Just before graduation Ron inherited $600,000 from his great uncle. He seriously considered buying the restaurant. It seemed like a good idea because he liked the town and its college atmosphere, knew the business, and always wanted to work for himself. He also knew that the current owner wanted to sell the restaurant and retire to Florida. As part of a small business management course, Ron developed the following income statement for the restaurant's prior year operations:

BEEF BURGER RESTAURANT: COLLEGE CITY Income Statement For Prior Year Ended December 31		
Sales		$495,000
Expenses		
Cost of food	$165,000	
Supplies	22,000	
Employee expenses	154,000	
Utilities	30,800	
Property taxes	22,000	
Insurance	11,000	
Advertising	8,800	
Depreciation	66,000	479,600
Net income		$ 15,400

Ron believed that the cost of food and supplies were all variable, the employee expenses and utilities were one-half variable and one-half fixed last year, and all other expenses were fixed. If Ron purchased the restaurant and followed through on his plans, he believed there would be a 40% increase in unit sales volume and all variable costs. Of the fixed costs, only advertising would increase by $10,000. The use of discounts and special promotions would, however, limit the increase in sales revenue to only 30% even though sales volume increased 40%.

Required

a. Determine
   1. The current annual net cash inflow.
   2. The predicted annual net cash inflow if Ron executes his plans and his assumptions are correct.

b. Ron believes his plan would produce equal net cash inflows during each of the next 15 years, the period remaining on a long-term lease for the land on which the restaurant is built. At the end of that time, the restaurant would have to be demolished at a predicted net cost of $88,000. Assuming Ron would otherwise invest the money in stock expected to yield 12%, determine the maximum amount he should pay for the restaurant.

c. Assume that Ron accepts an offer from the current owner to buy the restaurant for $450,000. Unfortunately, although the expected increase in sales volume does occur, customers make much more extensive use of the promotions than Ron had anticipated. As a result, total sales revenues are 8% below projections. Furthermore, to improve employee attitudes, Ron gave a 10% raise immediately after purchasing the restaurant. Reevaluate the initial decision using the actual sales revenue and the increase in labor costs, assuming conditions will remain unchanged over the remaining life of the project. Was the investment decision a wise one?

d. Ron can sell the restaurant to a large franchise operator for $350,000. Alternatively, he believes that additional annual marketing expenditures and changes in promotions costing $25,000 per year could bring the sales revenues up to their original projections, with no other changes in costs. Assume that Ron has just purchased the restaurant and his original assumptions remain unchanged; however, he immediately gave his employees a 10% raise. Should Ron sell the restaurant or keep it and make the additional expenditures?

Solutions to Review Problems

Review 25-1—Solution

a. **Capital expenditures**—Investment of financial resources with the expectation it will generate future financial inflows that exceed the initial cost.

b. **Capital budgeting**—Process that involves identifying desirable projects, evaluating proposals, and selecting proposals that meet minimum criteria.

c. **Post audit**—Involves the development of project performance comparing planned and actual results.

d. **Capital budgeting**—Concepts and tools that organize information and evaluate alternatives.

e. **Time value of money concept**—Explains why monies received or paid at different points in time must be adjusted to comparable values.

f. **Capital budgeting**—Requires an adjustment to make cash flows comparable when they are expected to occur at different points in time.

g. **Long-Range Planning**—Planning beyond the next budget year.

h. **Post Audit**—Helps the capital budgeting committee do a better job in evaluating new proposals.

Review 25-2—Solution

Basic computations:

Initial investment	
Depreciable assets	$(27,740)
Working capital	(3,000)
Total cash outflow	$(30,740)
Operation	
Cash receipts	$ 25,000
Cash expenditures	(15,000)
Net cash inflow	$ 10,000
Disinvestment	
Sale of depreciable assets	$ 2,000
Recovery of working capital	3,000
Total cash inflow	$ 5,000

a. Net present value at a 10% discount rate:

	Predicted Cash Inflows (outflows) (A)	Year(s) of Cash Flows (B)	10% Present Value Factor (C)	Present Value of Cash Flows (A) × (C)
Initial investment...........................	$(30,740)	0	1.00000	$(30,740)
Operation	10,000	1–4	3.16987	31,699
Disinvestment................................	5,000	4	0.68301	3,415
Net present value of all cash flows........................				$ 4,374

b. Internal rate of return:
Using a spreadsheet, the proposal's internal rate of return is readily determined to be 16%:

	A	B
1	Year of cash flow	Cash flow
2	0	$(30,740)
3	1	10,000
4	2	10,000
5	3	10,000
6	4	15,000
7	IRR	0.16

The table approach requires additional analysis. Because the proposal has a positive net present value when discounted at 10%, its internal rate of return must be higher than 10%. Through a trial-and-error approach, the internal rate of return is determined to be 16%.

	Predicted Cash Inflows (outflows) (A)	Year(s) of Cash Flows (B)	16% Present Value Factor (C)	Present Value of Cash Flows (A) × (C)
Initial investment........................	$(30,740)	0	1.00000	$(30,740)
Operation	10,000	1–4	2.79818	27,982
Disinvestment...........................	5,000	4	0.55229	2,761
Net present value of all cash flows............				$ 3

Review 25-3—Solution

Basic computations:

Initial investment	
Depreciable assets..	$27,740
Working capital...	3,000
Total...	$30,740

Operation	
Cash receipts	$25,000
Cash expenditures	(15,000)
Net cash inflow...	$10,000

Disinvestment	
Sale of depreciable assets	$ 2,000
Recovery of working capital	3,000
Total...	$ 5,000

a.   Payback period = $30,740 ÷ $10,000

                  = 3.074 years

b.   Accounting rate of return on initial and average investments:

Annual net cash inflow from operations	$10,000
Less average annual depreciation [($27,740 – $2,000) ÷ 4]	(6,435)
Average annual increase in net income	$ 3,565

$$\text{Average investment} = (\$30{,}740 + \$5{,}000) \div 2$$

$$= \$17{,}870$$

$$\frac{\text{Accounting rate of return on}}{\text{initial investment}} = \frac{\$\,3{,}565}{\$30{,}740}$$

$$= 0.1160 \text{ or } 11.6\%$$

$$\frac{\text{Accounting rate of return on}}{\text{average investment}} = \frac{\$\,3{,}565}{\$17{,}870}$$

$$= 0.1995 \text{ or } 19.95\%$$

Review 25-4—Solution

a.

	Proposal A	Proposal B	Proposal C
Payback period	2 years	2 years	1 year
Accounting rate of return			
Total increase in income before depreciation	$67,500	$67,500	$45,000
Total depreciation	(45,000)	(45,000)	(45,000)
Total increase in income	$22,500	$22,500	$0
Life in years.	÷ 3	÷ 3	÷ 1
Average annual increase in net income	$7,500	$7,500	$0
Initial investment.	÷45,000	÷45,000	÷45,000
Accounting rate of return	0.1667	0.1667	0.0

Net present value at 10%:

Year	Factor	Present Values		
1	0.90909	$36,363.60	$20,454.53	$40,909.05
2	0.82645	4,132.25	18,595.13	
3	0.75131	16,904.48	16,904.48	
Total		57,400.33	55,954.14	40,909.05
Initial investment.		(45,000.00)	(45,000.00)	(45,000.00)
Net present value		$12,400.33	$10,954.14	$ (4,090.95)

Rankings:

Payback	2–3	2–3	1
Accounting rate of return	1–2	1–2	3
Net present value	1	2	3

b.   While the accounting rate of return and the net present value criteria consider profitability, payback considers only the time required to recover the investment. Proposal C provides for the shortest payback; hence, it ranks first using the payback criterion even though Proposal C does not provide a profit.

      Proposals A and B have identical total cash flows over their lives; hence, they have identical accounting rates of return. However, the timing of their cash flows differs. Because Proposal A has higher early-period cash flows, its net present value is higher than that of Proposal B. Of the three criteria used, only net present value considers both profitability and the timing of cash flows.

Review 25-5—Solution

In making the final decision to accept or reject a capital expenditure proposal that has passed the initial screening, nonquantitative factors should also be considered. Very important at this point are management's attitudes toward risk and financing alternatives, their confidence in the professional judgment of managers making investment proposals, their beliefs about the future direction of the economy, and their evaluation of alternative investments.

Specific to Hilltop's investment decision, their management might consider factors such as the following:

- Will new models of the ski lift be available in the next few years that will be more efficient and/or safer?
- How is the economy and do they expect to be able to sustain the number of skiers that they have had in recent years?
- How likely is it that they will see a decline in customers?
- Are there any other revenue-generating uses for the space, such as snowmobile rentals, that might be a better alternative to skiing?

Review 25-6—Solution

a.

Operating cost savings (9,000 hours × $45)	$405,000
Operating costs of CAD/CAM system	(200,000)
Before-tax cash savings	205,000
Income taxes without tax shield at 35%	(71,750)
Depreciation tax shield [($550,000/5 years) × 0.35]	38,500
Relevant annual after-tax cash flows	$171,750

b.

	Predicted Cash Inflows (Outflows) (A)	Year(s) of Cash Flows (B)	14% Present Value Factor (C)	Present Value of Cash Flows (A) × (C)
Initial investment	$(550,000)	0	1.00000	$(550,000)
Operations				
Annual taxable income without depreciation	205,000	1–5	3.43308	703,781
Taxes on income ($205,000 × 0.35)	(71,750)	1–5	3.43308	(246,323)
Depreciation tax shield*				
Year 1	$77,000	1	0.87719	67,544
Year 2	46,200	2	0.76947	35,550
Year 3	27,720	3	0.67497	18,710
Year 4	20,790	4	0.59208	12,309
Year 5	20,790	5	0.51937	10,798
Net present value of all cash flows				$ 52,369

*Computation of depreciation tax shield†:

Year	Depreciation Base† (A)	Annual Rate (B)	Annual Depreciation (C) = (A) × (B)	Tax Rate (D)	Tax Shield (E) = (C) × (D)
1	$550,000	2/5	$220,000	0.35	$77,000
2	330,000	2/5	132,000	0.35	46,200
3	198,000	2/5	79,200	0.35	27,720
4	118,800	1/2	59,400	0.35	20,790
5	59,400	balance	59,400	0.35	20,790

† The depreciation base is reduced by the amount of any previous depreciation. The annual rate is twice the straight-line rate.

Review 25-7—Solution

a.
$$fv = pv(1 + r)^n$$
$$= \$2,000(1 + 0.06)^2$$
$$= \$2,247$$

or

$$\$2,000/0.89000 = \$2,247$$

b.
$$pv = \$8,000 \times 0.63552$$
$$= \$5,084$$

c.
$$pva = \$2,000 \times 3.43308$$
$$= \$6,866$$

d.
$$a = \$32,010/4.96764$$
$$= \$\ 6,444$$

e.

Year	Cash Flow		Present Value at 20%		Present Value Amount
1	$20,000	×	0.83333	=	$16,667
2	8,000	×	0.69444	=	5,556
3	6,000	×	0.57870	=	3,472
Total					$25,695

f.
Present value of an annuity for 12 years at 14% ($5,000 × 5.66029)	$28,301
Present value of an annuity for 9 years at 14% ($5,000 × 4.94637)	(24,732)
Present value of the deferred annuity	$ 3,569

or

$$\$5,000 \times (5.66029 - 4.94637) = \$3,570$$

Review 25-8—Solution

a. First solve for the appropriate present value factor using the equation:

Present value factor for an annuity of $1 = Initial investment/Annual net cash flows

Next, once the present value factor is calculated, use Exhibit 25A.2 and go across the row corresponding to the expected life of the project until a table factor equal to or closest to the project's computed present value factor is found. The corresponding percentage for the present value factor is the proposal's internal rate of return.

b. If periodic cash flows subsequent to the initial investment are unequal, a trial-and-error approach must be used to determine the internal rate of return. The first step is to select a discount rate estimated to be close to the proposal's IRR and to compute the proposal's net present value. If the resulting net present value is zero, the selected discount rate is the actual rate of return. However, it is unlikely that the first rate selected will be the proposal's IRR. If the computation results in a positive net present value, the actual IRR is higher than the initially selected rate. In this case, the next step is to compute the proposal's net present value using a higher rate. If the second computation produces a negative net present value, the actual IRR is less than the selected rate. Therefore, the actual IRR is between the first and the second rates. This trial-and-error approach continues until a discount rate is found that equates the proposal's cash inflows and outflows.

Appendix A—Compound Interest Tables

Table 1 ■ Present Value of Single Amount

$p = 1/(1 + i)^t$

Period	Interest Rate											
	0.01	0.02	0.03	0.04	0.05	0.06	0.07	0.08	0.09	0.10	0.11	0.12
1	0.99010	0.98039	0.97087	0.96154	0.95238	0.94340	0.93458	0.92593	0.91743	0.90909	0.90090	0.89286
2	0.98030	0.96117	0.94260	0.92456	0.90703	0.89000	0.87344	0.85734	0.84168	0.82645	0.81162	0.79719
3	0.97059	0.94232	0.91514	0.88900	0.86384	0.83962	0.81630	0.79383	0.77218	0.75131	0.73119	0.71178
4	0.96098	0.92385	0.88849	0.85480	0.82270	0.79209	0.76290	0.73503	0.70843	0.68301	0.65873	0.63552
5	0.95147	0.90573	0.86261	0.82193	0.78353	0.74726	0.71299	0.68058	0.64993	0.62092	0.59345	0.56743
6	0.94205	0.88797	0.83748	0.79031	0.74622	0.70496	0.66634	0.63017	0.59627	0.56447	0.53464	0.50663
7	0.93272	0.87056	0.81309	0.75992	0.71068	0.66506	0.62275	0.58349	0.54703	0.51316	0.48166	0.45235
8	0.92348	0.85349	0.78941	0.73069	0.67684	0.62741	0.58201	0.54027	0.50187	0.46651	0.43393	0.40388
9	0.91434	0.83676	0.76642	0.70259	0.64461	0.59190	0.54393	0.50025	0.46043	0.42410	0.39092	0.36061
10	0.90529	0.82035	0.74409	0.67556	0.61391	0.55839	0.50835	0.46319	0.42241	0.38554	0.35218	0.32197
11	0.89632	0.80426	0.72242	0.64958	0.58468	0.52679	0.47509	0.42888	0.38753	0.35049	0.31728	0.28748
12	0.88745	0.78849	0.70138	0.62460	0.55684	0.49697	0.44401	0.39711	0.35553	0.31863	0.28584	0.25668
13	0.87866	0.77303	0.68095	0.60057	0.53032	0.46884	0.41496	0.36770	0.32618	0.28966	0.25751	0.22917
14	0.86996	0.75788	0.66112	0.57748	0.50507	0.44230	0.38782	0.34046	0.29925	0.26333	0.23199	0.20462
15	0.86135	0.74301	0.64186	0.55526	0.48102	0.41727	0.36245	0.31524	0.27454	0.23939	0.20900	0.18270
16	0.85282	0.72845	0.62317	0.53391	0.45811	0.39365	0.33873	0.29189	0.25187	0.21763	0.18829	0.16312
17	0.84438	0.71416	0.60502	0.51337	0.43630	0.37136	0.31657	0.27027	0.23107	0.19784	0.16963	0.14564
18	0.83602	0.70016	0.58739	0.49363	0.41552	0.35034	0.29586	0.25025	0.21199	0.17986	0.15282	0.13004
19	0.82774	0.68643	0.57029	0.47464	0.39573	0.33051	0.27651	0.23171	0.19449	0.16351	0.13768	0.11611
20	0.81954	0.67297	0.55368	0.45639	0.37689	0.31180	0.25842	0.21455	0.17843	0.14864	0.12403	0.10367
21	0.81143	0.65978	0.53755	0.43883	0.35894	0.29416	0.24151	0.19866	0.16370	0.13513	0.11174	0.09256
22	0.80340	0.64684	0.52189	0.42196	0.34185	0.27751	0.22571	0.18394	0.15018	0.12285	0.10067	0.08264
23	0.79544	0.63416	0.50669	0.40573	0.32557	0.26180	0.21095	0.17032	0.13778	0.11168	0.09069	0.07379
24	0.78757	0.62172	0.49193	0.39012	0.31007	0.24698	0.19715	0.15770	0.12640	0.10153	0.08170	0.06588
25	0.77977	0.60953	0.47761	0.37512	0.29530	0.23300	0.18425	0.14602	0.11597	0.09230	0.07361	0.05882
30	0.74192	0.55207	0.41199	0.30832	0.23138	0.17411	0.13137	0.09938	0.07537	0.05731	0.04368	0.03338
35	0.70591	0.50003	0.35538	0.25342	0.18129	0.13011	0.09366	0.06763	0.04899	0.03558	0.02592	0.01894
40	0.67165	0.45289	0.30656	0.20829	0.14205	0.09722	0.06678	0.04603	0.03184	0.02209	0.01538	0.01075

Table 2 ■ Present Value of Ordinary Annuity

$p = \{1 - [1/(1 + i)^t]\}/i$

Period	Interest Rate											
	0.01	0.02	0.03	0.04	0.05	0.06	0.07	0.08	0.09	0.10	0.11	0.12
1	0.99010	0.98039	0.97087	0.96154	0.95238	0.94340	0.93458	0.92593	0.91743	0.90909	0.90090	0.89286
2	1.97040	1.94156	1.91347	1.88609	1.85941	1.83339	1.80802	1.78326	1.75911	1.73554	1.71252	1.69005
3	2.94099	2.88388	2.82861	2.77509	2.72325	2.67301	2.62432	2.57710	2.53129	2.48685	2.44371	2.40183
4	3.90197	3.80773	3.71710	3.62990	3.54595	3.46511	3.38721	3.31213	3.23972	3.16987	3.10245	3.03735
5	4.85343	4.71346	4.57971	4.45182	4.32948	4.21236	4.10020	3.99271	3.88965	3.79079	3.69590	3.60478
6	5.79548	5.60143	5.41719	5.24214	5.07569	4.91732	4.76654	4.62288	4.48592	4.35526	4.23054	4.11141
7	6.72819	6.47199	6.23028	6.00205	5.78637	5.58238	5.38929	5.20637	5.03295	4.86842	4.71220	4.56376
8	7.65168	7.32548	7.01969	6.73274	6.46321	6.20979	5.97130	5.74664	5.53482	5.33493	5.14612	4.96764
9	8.56602	8.16224	7.78611	7.43533	7.10782	6.80169	6.51523	6.24689	5.99525	5.75902	5.53705	5.32825
10	9.47130	8.98259	8.53020	8.11090	7.72173	7.36009	7.02358	6.71008	6.41766	6.14457	5.88923	5.65022
11	10.36763	9.78685	9.25262	8.76048	8.30641	7.88687	7.49867	7.13896	6.80519	6.49506	6.20652	5.93770
12	11.25508	10.57534	9.95400	9.38507	8.86325	8.38384	7.94269	7.53608	7.16073	6.81369	6.49236	6.19437
13	12.13374	11.34837	10.63496	9.98565	9.39357	8.85268	8.35765	7.90378	7.48690	7.10336	6.74987	6.42355
14	13.00370	12.10625	11.29607	10.56312	9.89864	9.29498	8.74547	8.24424	7.78615	7.36669	6.98187	6.62817
15	13.86505	12.84926	11.93794	11.11839	10.37966	9.71225	9.10791	8.55948	8.06069	7.60608	7.19087	6.81086
16	14.71787	13.57771	12.56110	11.65230	10.83777	10.10590	9.44665	8.85137	8.31256	7.82371	7.37916	6.97399
17	15.56225	14.29187	13.16612	12.16567	11.27407	10.47726	9.76322	9.12164	8.54363	8.02155	7.54879	7.11963
18	16.39827	14.99203	13.75351	12.65930	11.68959	10.82760	10.05909	9.37189	8.75563	8.20141	7.70162	7.24967
19	17.22601	15.67846	14.32380	13.13394	12.08532	11.15812	10.33560	9.60360	8.95011	8.36492	7.83929	7.36578
20	18.04555	16.35143	14.87747	13.59033	12.46221	11.46992	10.59401	9.81815	9.12855	8.51356	7.96333	7.46944
21	18.85698	17.01121	15.41502	14.02916	12.82115	11.76408	10.83553	10.01680	9.29224	8.64869	8.07507	7.56200
22	19.66038	17.65805	15.93692	14.45112	13.16300	12.04158	11.06124	10.20074	9.44243	8.77154	8.17574	7.64465
23	20.45582	18.29220	16.44361	14.85684	13.48857	12.30338	11.27219	10.37106	9.58021	8.88322	8.26643	7.71843
24	21.24339	18.91393	16.93554	15.24696	13.79864	12.55036	11.46933	10.52876	9.70661	8.98474	8.34814	7.78432
25	22.02316	19.52346	17.41315	15.62208	14.09394	12.78336	11.65358	10.67478	9.82258	9.07704	8.42174	7.84314
30	25.80771	22.39646	19.60044	17.29203	15.37245	13.76483	12.40904	11.25778	10.27365	9.42691	8.69379	8.05518
35	29.40858	24.99862	21.48722	18.66461	16.37419	14.49825	12.94767	11.65457	10.56682	9.64416	8.85524	8.17550
40	32.83469	27.35548	23.11477	19.79277	17.15909	15.04630	13.33171	11.92461	10.75736	9.77905	8.95105	8.24378

Table 3 ■ Future Value of Single Amount

$f = (1 + i)^t$

Period	0.01	0.02	0.03	0.04	0.05	0.06	0.07	0.08	0.09	0.10	0.11	0.12
1	1.01000	1.02000	1.03000	1.04000	1.05000	1.06000	1.07000	1.08000	1.09000	1.10000	1.11000	1.12000
2	1.02010	1.04040	1.06090	1.08160	1.10250	1.12360	1.14490	1.16640	1.18810	1.21000	1.23210	1.25440
3	1.03030	1.06121	1.09273	1.12486	1.15763	1.19102	1.22504	1.25971	1.29503	1.33100	1.36763	1.40493
4	1.04060	1.08243	1.12551	1.16986	1.21551	1.26248	1.31080	1.36049	1.41158	1.46410	1.51807	1.57352
5	1.05101	1.10408	1.15927	1.21665	1.27628	1.33823	1.40255	1.46933	1.53862	1.61051	1.68506	1.76234
6	1.06152	1.12616	1.19405	1.26532	1.34010	1.41852	1.50073	1.58687	1.67710	1.77156	1.87041	1.97382
7	1.07214	1.14869	1.22987	1.31593	1.40710	1.50363	1.60578	1.71382	1.82804	1.94872	2.07616	2.21068
8	1.08286	1.17166	1.26677	1.36857	1.47746	1.59385	1.71819	1.85093	1.99256	2.14359	2.30454	2.47596
9	1.09369	1.19509	1.30477	1.42331	1.55133	1.68948	1.83846	1.99900	2.17189	2.35795	2.55804	2.77308
10	1.10462	1.21899	1.34392	1.48024	1.62889	1.79085	1.96715	2.15892	2.36736	2.59374	2.83942	3.10585
11	1.11567	1.24337	1.38423	1.53945	1.71034	1.89830	2.10485	2.33164	2.58043	2.85312	3.15176	3.47855
12	1.12683	1.26824	1.42576	1.60103	1.79586	2.01220	2.25219	2.51817	2.81266	3.13843	3.49845	3.89598
13	1.13809	1.29361	1.46853	1.66507	1.88565	2.13293	2.40985	2.71962	3.06580	3.45227	3.88328	4.36349
14	1.14947	1.31948	1.51259	1.73168	1.97993	2.26090	2.57853	2.93719	3.34173	3.79750	4.31044	4.88711
15	1.16097	1.34587	1.55797	1.80094	2.07893	2.39656	2.75903	3.17217	3.64248	4.17725	4.78459	5.47357
16	1.17258	1.37279	1.60471	1.87298	2.18287	2.54035	2.95216	3.42594	3.97031	4.59497	5.31089	6.13039
17	1.18430	1.40024	1.65285	1.94790	2.29202	2.69277	3.15882	3.70002	4.32763	5.05447	5.89509	6.86604
18	1.19615	1.42825	1.70243	2.02582	2.40662	2.85434	3.37993	3.99602	4.71712	5.55992	6.54355	7.68997
19	1.20811	1.45681	1.75351	2.10685	2.52695	3.02560	3.61653	4.31570	5.14166	6.11591	7.26334	8.61276
20	1.22019	1.48595	1.80611	2.19112	2.65330	3.20714	3.86968	4.66096	5.60441	6.72750	8.06231	9.64629
21	1.23239	1.51567	1.86029	2.27877	2.78596	3.39956	4.14056	5.03383	6.10881	7.40025	8.94917	10.80385
22	1.24472	1.54598	1.91610	2.36992	2.92526	3.60354	4.43040	5.43654	6.65860	8.14027	9.93357	12.10031
23	1.25716	1.57690	1.97359	2.46472	3.07152	3.81975	4.74053	5.87146	7.25787	8.95430	11.02627	13.55235
24	1.26973	1.60844	2.03279	2.56330	3.22510	4.04893	5.07237	6.34118	7.91108	9.84973	12.23916	15.17863
25	1.28243	1.64061	2.09378	2.66584	3.38635	4.29187	5.42743	6.84848	8.62308	10.83471	13.58546	17.00006
30	1.34785	1.81136	2.42726	3.24340	4.32194	5.74349	7.61226	10.06266	13.26768	17.44940	22.89230	29.95992
35	1.41660	1.99989	2.81386	3.94609	5.51602	7.68609	10.67658	14.78534	20.41397	28.10244	38.57485	52.79962
40	1.48886	2.20804	3.26204	4.80102	7.03999	10.28572	14.97446	21.72452	31.40942	45.25926	65.00087	93.05097

Table 4 ■ Future Value of an Ordinary Annuity

$f = [(1 + i)^t - 1]/i$

Period	0.01	0.02	0.03	0.04	0.05	0.06	0.07	0.08	0.09	0.10	0.11	0.12
1	1.00000	1.00000	1.00000	1.00000	1.00000	1.00000	1.00000	1.00000	1.00000	1.00000	1.00000	1.00000
2	2.01000	2.02000	2.03000	2.04000	2.05000	2.06000	2.07000	2.08000	2.09000	2.10000	2.11000	2.12000
3	3.03010	3.06040	3.09090	3.12160	3.15250	3.18360	3.21490	3.24640	3.27810	3.31000	3.34210	3.37440
4	4.06040	4.12161	4.18363	4.24646	4.31013	4.37462	4.43994	4.50611	4.57313	4.64100	4.70973	4.77933
5	5.10101	5.20404	5.30914	5.41632	5.52563	5.63709	5.75074	5.86660	5.98471	6.10510	6.22780	6.35285
6	6.15202	6.30812	6.46841	6.63298	6.80191	6.97532	7.15329	7.33593	7.52333	7.71561	7.91286	8.11519
7	7.21354	7.43428	7.66246	7.89829	8.14201	8.39384	8.65402	8.92280	9.20043	9.48717	9.78327	10.08901
8	8.28567	8.58297	8.89234	9.21423	9.54911	9.89747	10.25980	10.63663	11.02847	11.43589	11.85943	12.29969
9	9.36853	9.75463	10.15911	10.58280	11.02656	11.49132	11.97799	12.48756	13.02104	13.57948	14.16397	14.77566
10	10.46221	10.94972	11.46388	12.00611	12.57789	13.18079	13.81645	14.48656	15.19293	15.93742	16.72201	17.54874
11	11.56683	12.16872	12.80780	13.48635	14.20679	14.97164	15.78360	16.64549	17.56029	18.53117	19.56143	20.65458
12	12.68250	13.41209	14.19203	15.02581	15.91713	16.86994	17.88845	18.97713	20.14072	21.38428	22.71319	24.13313
13	13.80933	14.68033	15.61779	16.62684	17.71298	18.88214	20.14064	21.49530	22.95338	24.52271	26.21164	28.02911
14	14.94742	15.97394	17.08632	18.29191	19.59863	21.01507	22.55049	24.21492	26.01919	27.97498	30.09492	32.39260
15	16.09690	17.29342	18.59891	20.02359	21.57856	23.27597	25.12902	27.15211	29.36092	31.77248	34.40536	37.27971
16	17.25786	18.63929	20.15688	21.82453	23.65749	25.67253	27.88805	30.32428	33.00340	35.94973	39.18995	42.75328
17	18.43044	20.01207	21.76159	23.69751	25.84037	28.21288	30.84022	33.75023	36.97370	40.54470	44.50084	48.88367
18	19.61475	21.41231	23.41444	25.64541	28.13238	30.90565	33.99903	37.45024	41.30134	45.59917	50.39594	55.74971
19	20.81090	22.84056	25.11687	27.67123	30.53900	33.75999	37.37896	41.44626	46.01846	51.15909	56.93949	63.43968
20	22.01900	24.29737	26.87037	29.77808	33.06595	36.78559	40.99549	45.76196	51.16012	57.27500	64.20283	72.05244
21	23.23919	25.78332	28.67649	31.96920	35.71925	39.99273	44.86518	50.42292	56.76453	64.00250	72.26514	81.69874
22	24.47159	27.29898	30.53678	34.24797	38.50521	43.39229	49.00574	55.45676	62.87334	71.40275	81.21431	92.50258
23	25.71630	28.84496	32.45288	36.61789	41.43048	46.99583	53.43614	60.89330	69.53194	79.54302	91.14788	104.60289
24	26.97346	30.42186	34.42647	39.08260	44.50200	50.81558	58.17667	66.76476	76.78981	88.49733	102.17415	118.15524
25	28.24320	32.03030	36.45926	41.64591	47.72710	54.86451	63.24904	73.10594	84.70090	98.34706	114.41331	133.33387
30	34.78489	40.56808	47.57542	56.08494	66.43885	79.05819	94.46079	113.28321	136.30754	164.49402	199.02088	241.33268
35	41.66028	49.99448	60.46208	73.65222	90.32031	111.43478	138.23688	172.31680	215.71075	271.02437	341.58955	431.66350
40	48.88637	60.40198	75.40126	95.02552	120.79977	154.76197	199.63511	259.05652	337.88245	442.59256	581.82607	767.09142

Appendix **B**
Chart of Accounts with Acronyms

Assets

Cash	Cash
MS	Marketable securities
AR	Accounts receivable
AU	Allowance for uncollectible accounts
INV	Inventory (or Inventories)
SUP	Supplies
PPD	Prepaid expenses
PPDA	Prepaid advertising
PPRNT	Prepaid rent
PPI	Prepaid insurance
PPE	Property, plant and equipment (PPE)
AD	Accumulated depreciation
INT	Intangible assets
DTA	Deferred tax assets
OA	Other assets
EMI	Equity method investments
ROU	Right-of-use asset (capitalized lease)
PA	Pension assets

Liabilities

NP	Notes payable
AP	Accounts payable
ACC	Accrued expenses
WP	Wages payable
SP	Salaries payable
RNTP	Rent payable
RSL	Restructuring liability
UP	Utilities payable
TP	Taxes payable
WRP	Warranty payable
IP	Interest payable
CMLTD	Current maturities of long-term debt
UR	Unearned (or deferred) revenues
DP	Dividends payable
LTD	Long-term debt
CLO	Capital lease obligations
DTL	Deferred tax liabilities
OL	Other liabilities
PL	Pension liability

Equity

EC	Earned capital
CS	Common stock
PS	Preferred stock
APIC	Additional paid-in capital
RE	Retained earnings
DIV	Dividends
TS	Treasury stock
AOCI	Accumulated other comprehensive income
DC	Deferred compensation expense
NCI	Noncontrolling interest
EQ	Total stockholders' equity
CI	Equity attributable to controlling interest

Revenues and Expenses

Sales	Sales
REV	Revenues
COGS	Cost of goods sold (or Cost of sales)
OE	Operating expenses
AE	Advertising expense
AIE	Asset impairment expense
BDE	Bad debts expense
DE	Depreciation expense
GN (LS)	Gain (loss)–operating
INSE	Insurance expense
PE	Pension expense
RDE	Research and development expense
RNTE	Rent expense
RSE	Restructuring expense
SE	Salaries expense
SUPE	Supplies expense
TE	Tax expense
UTE	Utilities expense
WE	Wages expense
WRE	Warranty expense
ONI (E)	Other nonoperating income (expense)
IE	Interest expense
II	Interest income
UG (UL)	Unrealized gain (loss)
DI	Dividend income (or revenue)
EI	Equity income (or revenue)
GN (LS)	Gain (loss)–nonoperating

Appendix C
Comprehensive Case

Harley-Davidson

Available for free download from the book's website in the Supplements section.

Index

A

A&E, 21-9
AB InBev/SABMiller, 9-14–9-15
Absorption costing, 18-5, 18-26, 24-11
  evaluating alternatives to inventory valuation, 18-30–18-31
  income under, 18-27
  inventory valuations, 18-26–18-27
  production equals sales, 18-27
  production exceeds sales, 18-28–18-29
  sales exceed production, 18-29–18-30
Accelerated depreciation method, 6-19
Accounting conservatism, 7-17
Accounting cycle, 3-17
  accounting adjustments
    accounting adjustments for Apple, 3-12–3-13
    accrued expenses, 3-11–3-12
    accrued revenues, 3-12
    prepaid expenses, 3-10
    types of, 3-9–3-10
    unearned revenues, 3-10–3-11
  closing books
    dividend account, 3-17
    expense and loss accounts, 3-17
    with journal entries, 3-16
    revenue and gain accounts, 3-16
    with template, 3-16
  financial statements, preparation
    balance sheet, 3-14–3-15
    income statement, 3-13–3-14
    statement of stockholders' equity, 3-15–3-16
  four-step, 3-3
  summary, 3-17–3-18
  transactions
    Apple, 3-6
    financial statement effects template, 3-6
    journal entry and T-account, 3-6–3-9
Accounting equation, 1-10
Accounting (fiscal) year, 1-9
Accounting information
  financial accounting, 14-3–14-4
  managerial accounting, 14-4–14-5
  strategic cost management, 14-5–14-6
Accounting rate of return, 25-11, 25-13
Accounts payable, 2-7, 11-13
Accounts payable turnover (APT), 6-15
Accounts receivable, 2-5, 11-12
  accounting for, 5-20
  aging analysis of, 5-19
  analysis of
    magnitude, 5-21–5-22
    quality, 5-22–5-24
Accounts receivable turnover, 5-21
Accruals, 3-9, 3-13
  accounting, 2-15, 3-9

anomaly, 11-22
Accrued expenses, 3-10, 3-11–3-12
Accrued liabilities, 2-7, 11-14
  contingent liabilities, accruals for, 7-5
    warranties, 7-5–7-7
  contractual liabilities, accruals for
    deferred revenue, 7-4–7-5
    wages payable, 7-4
  defined, 7-3–7-4
Accrued revenues, 3-10, 3-12
Accumulated depreciation, 6-19
  change in, 11-17
Accumulated other comprehensive income (AOCI), 2-10, 8-4, 8-5, 9-8, 9-24
  components
    employee benefit plans, 8-20
    foreign currency translation adjustments, 8-19
    gains and losses, 8-19, 8-20
  disclosures and interpretation, 8-20–8-22
Accumulated post-employment benefit obligation (APBO), 10-23
Acquired intangible assets, accounting for, 9-22
Acquisitions, 12-3
  impact of, 12-10
  and sale, 9-4–9-5
Activity, 14-17
  cost drivers, 14-19–14-20
    identifying, 15-18
  list, 18-9
  value chain and, 21-4
Activity-based approach, 22-5
Activity-based costing (ABC)
  and activity-based management, 19-19–19-20
  changing cost environment, 19-3–19-4
  concepts, 19-4
  and customer profitability analysis, 19-16–19-19
  history of, 19-5
  implementation of, 19-13–19-15
  limitations of illustration, 19-13
  product costing model, 19-5–19-6
  and software-as-service, 19-11–19-12
  traditional product costing and, 19-6
    overhead with activity-based costing, 19-9–19-13
    overhead with department rates, 19-7–19-9
    overhead with plantwide rate, 19-7
    traditional vs., 19-13–19-14
Activity-based management (ABM), 19-19–19-20
Actuarial adjustments, 10-15–10-16
Actuarial assumption, 10-19
Additional paid-in capital, 2-10, 8-5
Adjusted financial statements, 12-3
Adjustments, accounting
  accrued expenses, 3-11–3-12

accrued revenues, 3-12
  for Apple, 3-12–3-13
  prepaid expenses, 3-10
  types of, 3-9–3-10
  unearned revenues, 3-10–3-11
Aging analysis, 5-19
Air Tran, 23-1
Alamo, 15-11
Allocated common costs, 24-5
Allowance for uncollectible accounts, 5-20
Allowed costs, 23-6
Alphabet, 1-11, 1-12, 1-13, 5-18, 9-24–9-25, 21-1
  equity investments with control, 9-17–9-18
  investments in debt securities, 9-8–9-10
  passive investments in equity securities, 9-4–9-8
Altria Group Inc., 9-14, 9-26
Amazon, 4-33–4-34, 5-10, 14-4, 14-8, 16-4, 21-1, 21-19, 25-1–25-3
Amazon Prime, 25-1
American Airlines, 10-23–10-24, 10-38
American Apparel, 20-11
American Girl, 19-18
Amortization, 7-14, 7-31
  of debt, 7-31
  of deferred amounts, 10-19
  of discount, 7-31
  of intangible assets, 5-25
  of premium, 7-32
Amtrak, 14-20
Analyst reports, 2-25
Andersen, Arthur, 14-15
AngloAmerican, 16-20
Anheuser-Busch, 21-3
Annuity, 7-10, 25-8, 25-25–25-26
Anthropologie, 16-21–16-23
Apple Inc., 1-1, 1-13, 1-18, 1-19, 1-25, 2-4, 2-9, 3-5, 4-10, 14-18, 15-11, 16-16, 17-3, 17-13, 17-17, 21-1, 25-1
  accounting adjustments, 3-12–3-13
  accounting equation for, 3-3–3-4
  accrued expenses, 3-11–3-12
  accrued revenues, 3-12
  articulation of financial statements, 2-21
  audit report for, 1-31
  balance sheet, 1-10–1-11, 2-4, 3-14–3-15
    liabilities and equity sections of, 2-7
  closing books, accounting
    dividend account, 3-17
    expense and loss accounts, 3-17
    with journal entries, 3-16
    revenue and gain accounts, 3-16
    with template, 3-16
  Credit Suisse on, 1-5
  description of business, 2-23
  disclosure of loan covenants, 1-6
  financial statement effects template, 3-6, 3-7

Note: The letter "e" refers to an exhibit on the stated page, and the letter "n" indicates that the information is included in a footnote on the given page. For example, 11-3n1 means footnote 1 on page 11-3.

Apple Inc., *(continued)*
  fiscal year, 1-10
  income statement, 1-13, 2-13–2-14, 3-13–3-14
  journal entry and T-account, 3-6
  market value vs. book value, 2-11
  prepaid expenses, 3-10
  retained earnings reconciliation, 2-20
  retained earnings statement, 3-15
  statement of cash flows, 1-15–1-16, 2-19
  statement of stockholders' equity, 1-15, 2-17–2-18, 3-15–3-16
  transactions, 3-6, 3-8
  unearned revenues, 3-10–3-11
Aramark Corporation, 17-13
Architecture Design, 25-23
Artificial intelligence (AI), 14-13
Asset turnover (AT), 1-18, 4-6
Assets, 2-4
  balance sheet, 2-4
  current, 2-5
  long-term, 2-5
  measuring, 2-5–2-6
  sales, 6-20–6-21
  utilization, 6-15
  write-downs, 6-22, 6-24
Association for Financial Professionals (AFP), 16-4
AT&T, 4-34–4-35, 7-22, 10-19–10-20, 24-3
Atlanta Braves, 25-26
Atlassian, 14-19
Audit Committee, 1-32, 1-34
Audit report, 1-31–1-34
Australian Fortescue Metals Group, 16-20
Authorized shares, 8-3, 8-5, 8-7
Autozone, 8-25
Available-for-sale (AFS) debt securities, 9-8–9-10
Average cost (AC), 6-5–6-6, 15-8–15-9
Average days inventory outstanding (DIO). *See* Days inventory outstanding
Avoidable common costs, 24-7

B

Backflush costing, 20-14
Bain and Company, 22-6
Balance sheet, 11-3, 12-4
  accounts, computing cash flows from, 11-19–11-20
  analysis with operating focus, 4-14–4-15
    net nonoperating obligations, 4-17–4-18
    net operating assets, 4-15–4-17
    return on net operating assets, 4-15
  assets, 2-4–2-6
  defined benefit pension plan on, 10-12–10-13
  effects of inventory costing, 6-7
  financing activities, 1-12
  and flow of costs, 2-3–2-4
  forecasting, 12-12–12-16
  investing activities, 1-10–1-11
  lease accounting and, 10-6–10-7
  liabilities and equity, 2-6–2-13
  long-term debt, reporting, 7-13–7-14
  operating vs. nonoperating classification, 4-30
  preparation of, 3-14–3-15

  under IFRS, 2-18
Balanced scorecard
  framework, 24-20–24-22
  and strategy, 24-22–24-23
Bank of America, 16-22
Bargaining power, 1-7
  of buyers, 1-22
  of suppliers, 1-22
Barnes and Noble, 17-13
Barriers to entry, 1-24
Basic EPS, 8-24
Batch-level activity, 15-19
BDO, 1-31
Beats, 17-7, 25-18
Bechtel Corporation, 18-9
Bed Bath & Beyond, 25-6
Benchmark Paper Company, 16-6
Benchmarking, 21-3, 21-18–21-19
Benefits of disclosure, 1-7–1-8
Berkshire Hathaway, 8-24
Best Buy, 1-11, 1-12, 1-13, 16-22, 18-3, 25-1
BHP, 16-20
Big data, 14-12
Bill of materials, 18-9
Bill-and-hold arrangements, 5-6
Blaze Pizza, 15-21
Bleu Mont Dairy, 22-15–22-16
Blob of common costs, 19-4
Bloomberg U.S. Spin-Off Index, 9-36
BNSF Railway, 15-10
Board of directors, 8-4
Boeing, 5-7, 14-20, 17-14, 17-15, 21-5
Bond valuation, 7-27
Book value, 2-12, 7-15
Book value per share, 8-4
Boston Beer Company, The, 18-3
Boston Scientific Corporation, 4-3, 4-6, 17-15, 24-10
  common-size balance sheets, 4-39–4-40
  common-size income statements, 4-40
  current ratio, 4-36
  disaggregation of ROE, 4-7
  operating and nonoperating items
    balance sheet, 4-16
    income statement, 4-20
  return on net operating assets, 4-23
Bottom-up budget, 22-20
Break-even point
  cost-volume-profit graph, 16-11
  determining in units, 16-9–16-10
  income taxes, impact of, 16-13–16-15
  and profit planning, 16-10–16-11
  profit-volume graph, 16-11–16-13
Broadcomm, 18-1
BT Group plc, 8-26
Buckle, 20-9
Budget variances, 23-1
Budgetary slack, 22-21
Budgeted financial statements, 22-13–22-14
Budgeting, 22-3. *See also specific entries*
  activity-based approach, 22-5
  for communication and coordination, 22-3
  within consumer products giant, 22-12
  developing honesty in, 22-22
  development and manager behavior
    budgeting periods, 22-21

    employee participation, 22-20–22-21
    ethics, 22-22
    forecasts, 22-21–22-22
    open book management, 22-22–22-23
  development in manufacturing organizations
    manufacturing cost budget, 22-16–22-20
    production budget, 22-16
  guide to action and basis of evaluation, 22-3
  incremental approach, 22-5
  master budget, 22-7–22-9
    budgeted financial statements, 22-13–22-14
    cash budget, 22-11–22-13
    finalizing, 22-14–22-16
    general and administrative expense budget, 22-11
    purchases budget, 22-10
    sales budget, 22-9–22-10
    selling expense budget, 22-10–22-11
  minimum level approach, 22-5–22-6
  for objectives, 22-6
  output/input approach, 22-5
  periods, 22-21
  for planning, 22-3
  in risk management, 22-3–22-4
  for uncertainty, 22-6
Bugatti, 18-21
Burger King, 14-8
Business activities, 1-3–1-4
Business forces, 1-3
Business risk, 7-20
Business strategy, 1-3–1-4

C

Calendar-year, 1-9
California's Hospital Fair Pricing Act (CHFPA), 23-12
Capacity costs. *See* Committed fixed costs
Capacity variance, 23-22
Capital budgeting, 25-3
  additional aspects
    differential analysis of project cash flows, 25-17–25-19
    evaluating risk, 25-17
    multiple investment criteria, 25-16
    predicting differential costs and revenues for high-tech investments, 25-19–25-20
  evaluation of models, 25-14–25-16
  long-range planning and, 25-3–25-6
  models considering time value of money
    cost of capital, 25-10–25-11
    expected cash flows, 25-6–25-7
    internal rate of return, 25-9–25-10
    manager behavior and expected cash flows, 25-8
    net present value, 25-8–25-9
  models not considering time value of money, 25-11–25-12
    accounting rate of return, 25-13–25-14
    payback period, 25-12–25-13
  to save money, 25-4–25-5
  size and education matter in, 25-11–25-12
  table approach for internal rate of return
    equal cash inflows, 25-29
    unequal cash inflows, 25-29–25-30

Capital budgeting, *(continued)*
  taxes in, 25-20–25-21
    depreciation tax shield, 25-21–25-22
    investment tax credit, 25-22–25-23
  time value of money, 25-23–25-24
    annuities, 25-25–25-26
    deferred returns, 25-28
    future value, 25-24
    present value, 25-24–25-25, 25-27
    unequal cash flows, 25-26–25-28
Capital expenditures (CAPEX), 11-5, 12-12,
    6-18, 25-3, 25-18
  analysis of, 25-22–25-23
Capital IQ, 2-26
Capital leases, 10-9
Capital structure, maintaining, 12-16
Capitalization, 6-17–6-20
  lease
    using financial calculator, 10-33
    using present value tables, 10-34–10-35
Carnegie Steel Company, 14-8, 15-18
CarPrice, 14-4
Carrying value, 6-19
Cash, 2-5
Cash budget, 22-11–22-13. *See also* Budgeting
Cash conversion cycle, 2-9, 4-9, 6-16–6-17
Cash dividend
  disclosures, 8-16–8-17
  financial effects, 8-17–8-18
Cash equivalents, 11-3
Cash flow
  components, 11-21–11-22
  effects of inventory costing, 6-7–6-8
  equal, 25-29
  expected. *See* Expected cash flows
  from financing activities
    balance sheet accounts, 11-19–11-20
    Java House case illustration, 11-18–11-19
    liabilities and equity, 11-18
    supplemental disclosures for indirect
        method, 11-20–11-21
  foreign currency and, 5-16–5-17
  free cash flow, 11-28–11-29
  hedge, 9-30
  from investing activities
    Java House case illustration, 11-16–11-18
    noncash assets, 11-16
  net income vs., 11-22
  from operating activities, 11-9–11-10
    Java House case illustration, 11-11–11-16
    steps to compute net cash flow, 11-10–
        11-11
  patterns, 11-23–11-25
  ratio analysis of, 11-27–11-28
  statement of. *See also* Statement of cash
      flows
    direct method reporting for, 11-29–11-32
    financing activities, 11-8–11-9
    investing activities, 11-8
    operating activities, 11-5–11-7
    relation among financial statements,
        11-3–11-4
    structure, 11-4–11-5
    usefulness of, 11-25–11-27
  unequal, 25-29–25-30
Cash plug (plug), 12-15

Castlight Healthcare Inc., 15-16
Caterpillar Financial Services Corporation, 4-27,
    4-41
Caterpillar Inc. (CAT), 1-12, 4-27, 4-41, 6-7,
    6-9–6-10, 9-25–9-26
Caveat, 4-21
CBL & Associates Inc., 19-18
CBS Corporation, 9-35–9-36
Celadon Group Inc., 1-33
Celator, 25-15
CFA Institute, 9-31
Chained target costing, 21-14
Champion International, 15-11
Channel stuffing, 23-3
Charge-offs, 6-22
Chartists, 13-13
Cheesecake Factory, The, 18-3, 19-18
Chick-fil-A, 14-8
Chipotle Mexican Grill Inc., 14-8, 23-12
Christofle, 15-19
Chrysler, 21-17
Cigna, 15-16
Cisco Systems Inc., 1-11, 1-13, 1-19, 2-24, 9-29,
    25-4, 24-5–24-7
Closing books, accounting
  dividend account, 3-17
  expense and loss accounts, 3-17
  with journal entries, 3-16
  revenue and gain accounts, 3-16
  with template, 3-16
Closing process, 3-16
Coca-Cola Company, 5-24, 6-24, 8-9, 8-12,
    8-16, 8-21–8-22, 14-6–14-7, 18-15–18-16,
    18-21, 19-15, 20-4, 21-3–21-5, 24-3
Coco Froyo, 15-6
Codes of ethics, 14-15
Coefficient of determination, 15-15
Coffee Bean, 16-18
Cognitive technologies, 14-12–14-13
Colgate Palmolive, 1-11, 1-12, 1-14, 1-18, 4-21
Collateral, 7-21
Comcast, 1-11, 7-9, 7-13, 7-16, 7-22, 7-24,
    17-13
Committed fixed costs, 15-10
Committee of Sponsoring Organizations
    (COSO), 14-13
Common segment costs, 24-5
Common stock, 2-10, 8-3, 8-5, 8-7–8-8
  change in, 11-18
Common-size analysis, 2-16
Communication, budgeting and, 22-3
Company managers, 1-3
Compass Group North America, 17-13
Competitive advantage, 1-24–1-25
Competitive disadvantages, 1-8
Competitive environment, 1-22–1-23
Compound financial instruments, 8-23
Compounding, 7-25
Comprehensive performance measurement
    systems, 24-20
Computer integrated manufacturing (CIM), 25-20
Consignment sales, 5-6
Consolidation
  accounting, mechanics of, 9-19–9-22
  of foreign subsidiaries, 9-23–9-27
  reporting, limitations of, 9-27–9-28

Contingent liabilities, accruals for, 7-5
  warranties, 7-5–7-7
Continuous budgeting, 22-21
Continuous improvement costing, 21-3, 21-17–
    21-18
Contractual liabilities, accruals for
  deferred revenue, 7-4–7-5
  wages payable, 7-4
Contributed capital, 1-14, 2-10, 8-3
Contribution income statement, 16-7
  multi-level, 16-21–16-22
    variations in, 16-23
Contribution margin, 16-7
Contribution margin ratio, 16-8–16-9
Control account, 18-10
Control, equity investments with, 9-3, 9-4,
    9-17–9-18
  accounting for, 9-18–9-23
  consolidation of foreign subsidiaries,
      9-23–9-27
  limitations of consolidation reporting,
      9-27–9-28
Controllable costs, 23-19–23-20
Controlling, 14-10, 14-11
Controlling interest, 2-13, 4-5
Conversion cost, 18-5
Conversion option, 8-22
Conversion privileges, 8-6
Convertible securities
  disclosures and interpretation, 8-22–8-23
  financial effects, 8-23
  under IFRS, 8-23
Coors, 14-20
Core competencies, 21-6
Corning Inc., 8-6, 8-22, 25-15, 25-26
Corporate governance, 1-31, 14-15–14-16
  structure, 1-33
Corporate social responsibility, 14-16–14-17
Cost-based pricing, 21-8–21-9
  critique of, 21-11
  in multiple-product companies, 21-9–21-10
  in single-product companies, 21-9
  for special orders, 21-11
Cost behavior
  additional patterns, 15-8–15-10
  basic patterns, 15-3–15-5
  committed and discretionary fixed costs, 15-10
  factors affecting patterns, 15-5
  relevant range, 15-7–15-8
  total cost function, 15-6
Cost center, 23-4
  flexible budgets, 23-6–23-8
  standard costs and performance reports,
      23-8–23-9
Cost drivers, 14-17–14-18
  activity, 14-19–14-20
  alternative classifications, 15-18–15-19
    customer cost hierarchy, 15-20–15-21
    manufacturing cost hierarchy, 15-19–
        15-20
  analysis, 14-6
  identifying activity, 15-18
  organizational, 14-19
  profitability analysis with unit and nonunit,
      16-21–16-23
  structural, 14-18–14-19

Cost estimation
  changes in technology and prices, 15-17
  high-low, 15-11–15-13
  identifying activity cost drivers, 15-18
  least-squares regression, 15-14–15-17
  matching activity and costs, 15-17
  scatter diagrams, 15-13–15-14
Cost leader, 1-24
Cost of capital, 25-10–25-11
Cost of debt, 7-17
Cost of equity (Re), 13-8
Cost of goods sold (COGS), 1-13, 2-3, 6-3, 12-9
Cost of preferred stock (Rps), 13-8
Cost of production report, 18-21–18-24
Cost of sales, 1-13, 5-25
Cost prediction, 15-12
Cost reduction proposal, 17-4
Cost savings
  overestimating, 25-20
  underestimating, 25-20
Costco Wholesale, 16-11, 25-12
Costing methods, inventory, 6-3–6-4
  average cost, 6-5–6-6
  balance sheet effects, 6-7
  cash flow effects, 6-7–6-8
  financial statement effects of, 6-7–6-8
  first-in, first-out, 6-4–6-5
  income statement effects, 6-7
  last-in, first-out, 6-5
Costs of disclosure, 1-8
Cost-to-cost method, 5-7–5-8
Cost-to-cost reporting, 5-8–5-10
Cost-to-retail percentage, 6-6
Cost-volume-profit (CVP) analysis
  multiple-product
    break-even and target profit sales dollars, 16-15
    sales mix analysis, 16-15–16-18
  key assumptions, 16-3–16-4
  profit formula, 16-5–16-6
Cost-volume-profit graph, 16-11
Counterparty risk, 9-30
Coupon (contract or stated) rate, 7-9
Courts, 1-34
Covenants, 1-5, 4-35, 7-21
Coyote Logistics, 18-16
Cray Inc., 18-9
Credit analysis, 7-16–7-17
Credit facility, 1-6
Credit ratings, 1-21, 7-18–7-19
  and financial ratios, 7-19–7-21
  reasons for matter, 7-23–7-24
  Verizon, 7-21–7-23
Credit services, 2-26
Credit Suisse, 1-5
Creditors, 1-5–1-6
Cross-subsidization, 19-11
Crown Department Stores, 14-10–14-11
Cruise Automation, 14-18
Cumulative translation adjustment, 9-23–9-27
Current (nonoperating) assets, 2-5, 4-36, 11-5
Current (nonoperating) liabilities, 2-7–2-9, 4-36, 11-5
Current maturities of long-term debt, 2-7, 2-9, 7-8
Current operating assets, 11-10

  accounts receivable, 11-12
  inventory, 11-12–11-13
  prepaid expenses, 11-13
Current operating liabilities, 11-10
  accounts payable, 11-13
  accrued liabilities, 11-14
Current ratio, 4-36
Customer cost hierarchy, 15-20–15-21
Customer profitability analysis, 19-16–19-19
Customer profitability profile, 19-16
Customer-level activity, 15-20
Customers, 1-6
CVS, 1-13, 1-18, 7-15
Cycle efficiency, 20-13
Cycle time, 20-11

D

Daihatsu Copen, 18-21
Daimler Benz, 14-20
Daisin, 21-17
Danone, 19-7, 19-9, 19-11, 9-13–9-14
Darden Restaurants, 1-18
Dasani, 20-4
Dashboards, 24-23
Data analytics
  data visualization, 1-29–1-30
  importance of, 1-29
  types of, 1-29
Data services, 2-26
Data visualization, 1-29–1-30
Data-driven decision making, 20-15–20-16
Date of payment, 8-5
Date of record, 8-5
Days inventory outstanding, 6-13–6-15
Days payable outstanding (DPO), 6-15–6-16
Days sales outstanding (DSO), 5-21
Dean Foods Company, 6-21
Debt securities
  investments in
    available-for-sale, 9-8–9-10
    financial statement disclosures, 9-10–9-11
    held-to-maturity, 9-8
Debt, amortization of, 7-31
Decision analysis models, limitations of, 17-21
Decision making tools. *See under* Managerial accounting
Declaration date, 8-5
Deere & Company, 10-17–10-19, 10-23
Default, 7-18
Deferred returns, 25-28
Deferred tax assets
  expanded example of, 10-41
  expanded explanation of, 10-39–10-41
  reporting, 10-27–10-28
  rules for, 10-40
  timing differences create, 10-24–10-27
  valuation allowance for, 10-28
Deferred tax liabilities
  expanded explanation of, 10-39–10-41
  illustration of, 10-25
  reporting, 10-27–10-28
  rules for, 10-40
  timing differences create, 10-24–10-27
  valuation allowance for, 10-28
Defined benefit pension plan, 10-11
  on balance sheet, 10-12–10-13

  on income statement, 10-15–10-16
Defined contribution plan, 10-11
Dell Computers, 21-5
Deloitte, 1-31, 14-5, 14-13, 15-4–15-5, 21-13
Delta Airlines, 10-4, 14-4, 14-20, 18-3
  analysis issues relating to leases, 10-10
  leasing footnote disclosure from, 10-11
  new lease accounting standard, 10-8
Demand for information
  creditors and suppliers, 1-5–1-6
  customers and strategic partners, 1-6
  investment analysts and information intermediaries, 1-5
  managers and employees, 1-4–1-5
  regulators and tax agencies, 1-6–1-7
  stockholders and directors, 1-6
  voters and representatives, 1-7
Department manufacturing overhead rates, 19-7–19-9
Department of Education, 24-21
DePaul University, 16-3
Depreciation, 2-3, 6-17–6-20
  expense, 12-13–12-14
Depreciation tax shield, 25-21–25-22
Derivatives, 4-17, 9-29
  accounting for, 9-29–9-30
  analysis of, 9-30–9-31
Descriptive analytics, 1-29
Design by Structure Ltd., 18-18
Design for manufacture, 21-14
Deutsche Bank valuation, 13-14–13-25
DeWalt, 22-19–22-20
Diageo, 23-3
Diagnostic analytics, 1-29
Dick's Sporting Goods, 19-18
Differential analysis, 17-7–17-8
  multiple changes in profit plans, 17-8–17-10
  outsourcing decisions, 17-13–17-16
  of project cash flows, 25-17–25-19
  sell or process, 17-16–17-18
  special orders, 17-10–17-12
Differential costs, predicting, 25-19–25-20
Diluted EPS, 8-24
Direct costing. *See* Variable cost
Direct department cost, 20-3
Direct labor (DL), 6-3, 15-19, 16-5, 18-5–18-6
  standards for, 23-13–23-15
  variances, 23-13–23-14
    interpreting, 23-14–23-15
Direct materials (DM), 6-3, 15-19, 16-5, 18-5–18-6
  standards for, 23-10–23-11
  variances, 23-11
    interpreting, 23-11–23-13
Direct method, 11-9, 20-5–20-6
  reporting for statement of cash flows, 11-29–11-32
Direct segment fixed costs, 24-5
Directors, 1-6
Discontinued operations, 2-15–2-16, 4-17, 5-25, 5-28–5-31, 12-3
Discount, 7-11
  amortization of, 7-31
  rate, 10-15–10-16, 25-8
Discounted cash flow (DCF) model, 13-3
  advantages and disadvantages of, 13-13

Discounted cash flow (DCF) model, *(continued)*
  application of, 13-7
  illustrating, 13-6–13-8
  steps in applying, 13-6
  structure, 13-5–13-6
Discretionary fixed costs, 15-10
Disinvestment phase of cash flows, 25-7
Disney, 14-1
Disposal value, 17-5
Dissemination costs, 1-8
Divestitures, 12-3
  impact of, 12-11
Dividends, 8-5, 12-15
  in arrears, 8-18
  cash dividend disclosures, 8-16–8-17
  cash dividends financial effects, 8-17–8-18
  discount model, 13-3
  payout and yield, 8-17
  stock split in form of, 8-18–8-19
Division margins, 24-5
Divisions, 24-3
Dollar break-even point, 16-15
Domino's, 15-3
Domtar, 21-3
Door Dash, 14-8
Dr. Bronner's, 17-15
DS Co., 21-13
Dual prices, 24-12
Dual rates, 20-9
Duesenberg, 18-21
Dunedin LLP, 18-18
Dunkin Brands Group Inc., 16-4
Dunkin' Donuts, 25-4
DuPont analysis
  financial leverage, 4-4–4-6
  return on assets, 4-4

E

Earned capital, 1-14, 2-10, 8-3, 8-4–8-5
Earnings, 1-13
  and stock prices, 1-20
Earnings per share (EPS), 8-23–8-25
EarthLink, 9-27–9-28
Economic approaches to pricing, 21-7–21-8
Economic value added (EVA), 24-17–24-18
Effective cost of debt, 7-11–7-13
E.I. DuPont de Nemours and Company, 4-4
Einstein Brothers, 24-21
Eli's Cheesecake, 23-6
Employee benefit plans, 8-20
Employee participation, 22-20–22-21
Employee severance or relocation costs, 6-22,
  6-23
Employee share purchase plans, 8-13
Employee stock options, 8-13
Employee stock purchase plans (ESPP), 8-26
Employees, 1-4–1-5
Enron, 1-30, 1-34, 14-15
Enterprise risk management (ERM), 14-13. *See
  also* Risk, management
Envy, 16-19
Epson, 17-9–17-10, 17-12, 17-16, 17-18, 21-18
Equal cash inflows, 25-29
Equipment, 2-3
Equity, 1-10
  analyzing, 11-18

Equity carve-outs, 9-32–9-36
  analysis of, 9-36
  IPOs, 9-32
  sell-offs, 9-32
  spin-offs, 9-32
  split-offs, 9-32
Equity method accounting, 9-12, 9-14–9-17
Equity valuation models
  discounted cash flow model, 13-3
  dividend discount model, 13-3
  residual operating income model, 13-3
  valuation model inputs, 13-4–13-5
Equivalent completed units, 18-23
Ethics
  in budgeting, 22-22
  in managerial accounting, 14-13–14-15
    codes of ethics, 14-15
    corporate governance, 14-15–14-16
    sustainability accounting and corporate
      social responsibility, 14-16–14-17
Evían, 21-3
Expected cash flows, 25-6–25-7
  manager behavior and, 25-8
Expected return, 10-16
Expense recognition (matching) principle, 2-15,
  8-13
Expenses and losses
  deductions from income, 5-25
  discontinued operations, 5-28–5-31
  provision (benefit) for taxes on income, 5-28
  recognizing, 2-14–2-15
  research and development
    analysis of, 5-26–5-28
    R&D spending, 5-26
Express Scripts Inc., 8-23
Expresso Royale, 11-15–11-16
Extended protection plan contracts, 5-15
Exxon Mobil, 18-9
EY, 1-31, 14-17, 23-10

F

Face amount, 7-9
Facility-level activity, 15-19, 15-20
Factory overhead, 18-5
Fair value, 5-5
  accounting, 10-19–10-21
  disclosures, 7-15–7-16
  hedge, 9-30
  method, 9-5–9-6
Farmer Brothers, 11-27
Favorable labor efficiency variances, 23-14
Favorable labor rate variance, 23-14
Favorable materials price variance, 23-11
Favorable materials quantity variance, 23-12
Favorable spending variance, 23-16
FedEx, 10-13–10-14, 10-20, 10-21, 10-31,
  10-41, 16-22, 18-16
Film and television revenues and costs, 5-9
Finance leases, 10-3, 10-35–10-37
Financial accounting, 14-3–14-4
  accounting principles and governance
    audit report, 1-31–1-34
    financial accounting environment,
      1-30–1-31
    business activities, reporting on, 1-3–1-4
    financial statement. *See* Financial statement

    managerial accounting vs., 14-5
Financial Accounting Standards Board (FASB),
  1-8, 1-30
  financial statement presentation project, 3-19
Financial calculator, lease capitalization, 10-33
Financial flexibility, 11-25
Financial leverage (FLEV), 4-4–4-6, 4-24, 4-32,
  9-16
  analysis, 4-12–4-14
Financial planning and analysis (FP&A), 16-4
Financial ratios, 1-21
Financial reporting
  components of product costs, 18-5–18-6
  manufacturing overhead, 18-6–18-9
  product costs and period costs, 18-4–18-5
Financial risk, 7-20
Financial statement
  additional information sources
    analyst reports, 2-25
    credit services, 2-26
    data services, 2-26
    Form 8-K, 2-25
    Form 10-K, 2-22–2-24
    Form 20-F and Form 40-F, 2-24
  analysis of
    components of return on assets, 1-18–1-20
    financial statements relevancy, 1-20–1-21
    return on assets, 1-18
    return on equity, 1-20
  articulation of
    financial statement linkages, 2-20–2-22
    retained earnings reconciliation, 2-20
  balance sheet. *See* Balance sheet
  budgeted, 22-13–22-14
  and business analysis
    competitive advantage, 1-24–1-25
    competitive environment, 1-22–1-23
    SWOT analysis of business environment,
      1-23
  data analytics
    data visualization, 1-29–1-30
    importance of, 1-29
    types of, 1-29
  demand for information, 1-4–1-7
  Financial Accounting Standards Board
    presentation project, 3-19
  forecasting, 12-3–12-5
    balance sheet, 12-12–12-16
    building forecasts from bottom up,
      12-16–12-18
    company guidance, 12-5–12-7
    income statement, 12-8–12-12
    Morgan Stanley's report on Procter &
      Gamble, 12-23–12-30
    multiyear forecasting with target cash and
      new debt, 12-20–12-22
    parsimonious method for NOPAT and
      NOA, 12-22–12-23
    statement of cash flows, 12-19–12-20
  income statement. *See* Income statement
  international accounting standards, 1-8–1-9
  inventory costing, effects of, 6-7–6-8
    balance sheet, 6-7
    cash flow, 6-7–6-8
    income statement, 6-7
  LIFO reserve adjustments to, 6-9–6-10

Financial statement, *(continued)*
  linkages, 2-20–2-22
  preparation of
      balance sheet, 3-14–3-15
      income statement, 3-13–3-14
      statement of stockholders' equity,
          3-15–3-16
  return on assets and disaggregation, 4-6–4-8
      financial leverage analysis, 4-12–4-14
      productivity analysis, 4-9–4-12
      profitability analysis, 4-8–4-9
  return on equity, 4-3
      disaggregation, DuPont analysis, 4-4–4-6
  return on net operating assets, 4-23–4-25
      disaggregation into margin and turnover,
          4-25–4-29
  SEC filings, 1-26–2-28
  statement of cash flows. *See* Statement of
      cash flows
  statement of stockholders' equity. *See*
      Statement of stockholders' equity
  structure of, 1-9–1-10
      balance sheet, 1-10–1-12
      income statement, 1-13–1-14
      information beyond financial statements,
          1-16
      managerial choices in financial
          accounting, 1-17–1-18
      statement of cash flows, 1-15–1-16
      statement of stockholders' equity,
          1-14–1-15
  supply of information, 1-7–1-8
  for valuation
      assessment of valuation models, 13-12–
          13-13
      derivation of free cash flow formula,
          13-14
      Deutsche Bank valuation of Procter &
          Gamble, 13-14–13-25
      discounted cash flow model, 13-5–13-8
      equity valuation models, 13-3–13-5
      further considerations involving, 13-11–
          13-13
      residual operating income model,
          13-9–13-11
Financial statement effects template, 3-3–3-4,
      3-6, 3-7
Financing activities, 1-3, 1-12, 1-16, 11-3, 11-4,
      22-8
  cash flows from
      balance sheet accounts, 11-19–11-20
      Java House case illustration, 11-18–11-19
      liabilities and equity, 11-18
      supplemental disclosures for indirect
          method, 11-20–11-21
      preview, 11-8
Finished goods inventories, 18-3, 20-12
First Fuel, 25-4
First-in, first-out (FIFO), 6-4–6-5, 18-24–18-25
Fitch Ratings, 2-26, 7-18
Fixed costs, 15-3
  committed and discretionary, 15-10
Fixed manufacturing overhead, 16-5
Fixed overhead budget variance, 23-17
Fixed overhead variances, 23-17–23-18,
      23-21–23-23

Fixed overhead volume variance, 23-22
Fixed selling and administrative costs, 16-6
FIXthat4U, 15-8–15-9
Fleming's Prime Steakhouse, 14-17
Flexe Inc., 15-8
Flexible budgets, 23-6
  development of, 23-6–23-7
  emphasizing performance, 23-7–23-8
  variance, 23-7
Flexible manufacturing systems (FMS), 25-20
Flow of costs, balance sheet and, 2-3–2-4
Flow-based approach, 7-16
Follett, 17-13
Footnote disclosure
  key assumptions, 10-21–10-22
  for stock-based compensation, 8-15–8-16
  valuation implications of, 10-20
Ford Credit Corporation, 4-41
Ford Motor Company, 14-9, 18-8, 21-15
Forecasting, 12-3–12-5, 22-21–22-22
  adjusted financial statements, 12-3
  balance sheet, 12-12–12-16
  building forecasts from bottom up, 12-16–
      12-18
  company guidance, 12-5–12-7
  consistency and precision, 12-4–12-5
  income statement, 12-8–12-12
  mechanics, 12-4
  Morgan Stanley, 12-4
      report on Procter & Gamble, 12-23–12-30
  multiyear forecasting with target cash and
      new debt, 12-20–12-22
  order of financial statements, 12-3–12-4
  parsimonious method for NOPAT and NOA,
      12-22–12-23
  segment data, 12-16–12-18
  statement of cash flows, 12-19–12-20
Foreign currency, 5-3
  and cash flows, 5-16–5-17
  and future results, 5-17–5-18
  and income, 5-17
  revenue, expenses, and cash flow, effects on,
      5-15–5-16
  translation adjustments, 8-19
Foreign subsidiaries, consolidation of, 9-23–9-27
Form 10-K, 1-7, 2-22–2-24
Form 10-Q, 1-7
Form 20-F, 2-24
Form 40-F, 2-24
Form 8-K, 2-25
For-profit organizations, 14-7
  cost-volume-profit analysis, 16-3
Forward-looking predictions, 5-27
Franchises, 5-6
Free cash flow, 11-28–11-29
  definitions of, 13-6
  formula, derivation of, 13-14
Free cash flows to the firm (FCFF), 13-5
Fresh Market, 20-1
Frilly, 18-12–18-17, 19-6
Full absorption cost, 18-5
Full costing, 17-11. *See also* Absorption costing
Functional income statement, 16-7
Fundamental analysis, 1-6
Funded status, 10-12
Future value, 7-25, 25-24

  of annuity, 7-30
  concepts, 7-30
  of single amount, 7-30

G

Gains and losses, 11-10
  on asset dispositions and impairments, 12-3
  on bond repurchases, 7-15
  with no cash flow effects, 11-12
  pension, unrecognized
      accounting for, 10-37
      financial statement effects from, 10-37–
          10-38
      PBO assumptions and, 10-38–10-39
      sources of, 10-37
Game of Thrones, 14-1
Gap, 21-19
Garmin Ltd., 18-3, 18-8
General and administrative expense budget,
      22-11
General Electric (GE), 19-5, 22-6, 23-17
General Growth Properties Inc., 19-18
General Mills, 1-12, 12-6–12-7, 12-11–12-12,
      12-16, 12-18, 12-20, 12-22, 12-23, 13-8,
      13-11, 13-13
General Motors Co. (GM), 10-14, 14-9, 14-18,
      14-20, 21-5, 21-6, 24-3
Generally Accepted Accounting Principles
      (GAAP), 1-8, 1-30, 5-32
  vs. International Financial Reporting
      Standards
      accounts receivable, 5-35
      analyzing and interpreting financial
          statements, 4-29–4-30
      balance sheet, 2-26
      consolidation, 9-28–9-29
      current and long-term liabilities, 7-24
      equity method investment, 9-28
      financial accounting, 1-26
      income statement, 2-26
      income taxes, 10-33
      inventory, 6-27–6-28
      leases, 10-32
      passive investments, 9-28
      pensions, 10-32
      property, plant, and equipment, 6-28
      research and development, 5-35, 6-28
      restructuring, 6-28
      revenue recognition, 5-35
      stock transactions, dividends, and EPS,
          8-25–8-26
      transactions, adjustments, and financial
          statements, 3-18
      valuation, financial statements for, 13-14
Georgia Pacific, 21-3
Gift cards, 5-6
Gillette, 12-10
GlaxoSmithKline (GSK), 16-12
Goals, 14-7
  attainment, 14-9–14-10
GoDaddy Inc., 16-4
Goldman Sachs, 7-9
Goodwill, 9-21
Google, 9-13, 14-19, 25-4
Graphic Packaging, 21-3
Gresham Private Equity, 18-18

Gross margin, 12-9
Gross profit, 1-13, 4-25, 6-3
Gross profit analysis, 6-12–6-13
Gross profit margin (GPM), 2-16, 4-8–4-9, 6-12
Guidant Corp., 24-9, 24-10

H

H&M, 19-18
H&R Block, 14-20
Hackett Group, The, 24-19
Hain Celestial Group Inc., 23-12
Hallmark Cards, 16-16–16-17
Harley-Davidson Inc., 6-15, 7-6, 7-7, 9-29, 9-30, 14-19, 14-20
HealthMine Inc., 15-16
Heineken, 18-16
Heinz, 9-22
Held-to-maturity (HTM) debt securities, 9-8
Herman Miller, 18-9
Hershey Company, 9-24, 18-3
Hertz, 15-11
Hewlett-Packard 10bII, 10-33
Hewlett-Packard Enterprise Co. (HPE), 5-30–5-31, 18-9, 21-5, 21-18
High-low method of cost estimation, 15-11–15-13
High-tech investments, 25-19–25-20
Hilltop Ski Resort, 25-20
Historical costs, 2-5, 4-41
Home Depot, 1-18, 6-6, 6-8, 19-19
    analysis tools, 6-25
    cash conversion cycle, 6-16–6-17
    gross profit margin and related data for, 6-12–6-13
Honda, 21-6
Honeywell, 10-20
Horizon period, 13-6
Horizontal analysis, 4-38
Hornall Anderson, 18-18
HP Inc., 10-27, 10-41, 17-13

I

IBM, 10-20, 14-19, 15-21, 23-10
Ideal transfer-pricing arrangement, 24-12
Illinois Tool Works Inc. (ITW), 19-12
IM Flash Technologies LLC (IMFT), 9-17
Impairment, 6-21
Imposed budget, 22-20
Income statement, 1-13–1-14, 2-13–2-14, 11-3, 12-4
    analysis using contribution margin ratio, 16-8–16-9
    analysis with operating focus
        net nonoperating expense, 4-22–4-23
        nonoperating line items on, 4-19–4-22
        operating line items on, 4-19
    analyzing, 2-16–2-17
    budgeted and actual, 23-23
    contribution, 16-7
    defined benefit pension plan on, 10-15–10-16
    effects of inventory costing, 6-7
    forecasting, 12-8–12-12
    lease accounting and, 10-7–10-8
    long-term debt, reporting, 7-14

operating vs. nonoperating classification, 4-30–4-31
    preparation of, 3-13–3-14
    recognizing revenues and expenses, 2-14–2-15
    reporting of transitory items, 2-15–2-16
    functional, 16-7
    under IFRS, 2-18
Income taxes
    deferred taxes, expanded explanation of, 10-39–10-41
    disclosures for, 10-29–10-30
        analysis of, 10-30–10-32
    expense, 12-10
    impact of, 16-13–16-15
    timing differences create deferred tax assets and liabilities, 10-24–10-27
        reporting deferred tax assets and liabilities, 10-27–10-28
        valuation allowance for deferred tax assets, 10-28
Incoming materials inventory, 20-10–20-11
Incremental approach, 22-5
Indiana University, 15-11
IndieGogo, 19-14
Indirect department cost, 20-3
Indirect method, 11-9
    supplemental disclosures for, 11-20–11-21
Industry competition, 1-22
Information intermediaries, 1-5
Initial investment phase of cash flows, 25-7
Initial public offering (IPO), 8-5
Innovative Components Inc., 17-21
Inspection time, 20-11
Institute of Management Accountants (IMA), 14-4–14-5
In-store and on-line sales, 5-14
Intangible assets, 2-5, 12-14
Intel, 1-12, 1-13, 1-18, 1-19, 9-17, 9-27–9-28, 17-13, 18-21–18-22, 21-19
Intercorporate investments, 9-3–9-4
    debt securities
        available-for-sale, 9-8–9-10
        financial statement disclosures, 9-10–9-11
        held-to-maturity, 9-8
    derivatives
        accounting for, 9-29–9-30
        analysis of, 9-30–9-31
    equity carve-outs, 9-32–9-36
        analysis of, 9-36
    equity investments with control, 9-17–9-18
        accounting for investments with control, 9-18–9-23
        consolidation of foreign subsidiaries, 9-23–9-27
        limitations of consolidation reporting, 9-27–9-28
    equity investments with significant influence
        accounting for investments with significant influence, 9-12–9-14
        equity method accounting and ROE effects, 9-14–9-17
    passive investments in equity securities
        acquisition and sale, 9-4–9-5
        fair-value method, 9-5–9-6

initial adoption of new accounting rules, 9-7–9-10
    marketable equity securities, 9-6
    non-marketable equity securities, 9-6–9-7
Interdepartment services, 20-4
Interest cost, 10-15
Interest expense, 12-9–12-10
Internal consistency, 12-4–12-5
Internal control systems, 1-33, 14-15
Internal rate of return (IRR), 25-9–25-10
    models, 25-6
    table approach to, 25-29–25-30
Internal Revenue Code (IRC), 10-24
International Accounting Standards, 1-8–1-9
International Accounting Standards Board (IASB), 1-8
International Business Machines, 15-11
International Financial Reporting Standards (IFRS), 1-8
    balance sheet presentation and, 1-12
    vs. Generally Accepted Accounting Principles
        accounts receivable, 5-35
        analyzing and interpreting financial statements, 4-29–4-30
        balance sheet, 2-26
        consolidation, 9-28–9-29
        current and long-term liabilities, 7-24
        equity method investment, 9-28
        financial accounting, 1-26
        income statement, 2-26
        income taxes, 10-33
        inventory, 6-27–6-28
        leases, 10-32
        passive investments, 9-28
        pensions, 10-32
        property, plant, and equipment, 6-28
        research and development, 5-35, 6-28
        restructuring, 6-28
        revenue recognition, 5-35
        stock transactions, dividends, and EPS, 8-25–8-26
        transactions, adjustments, and financial statements, 3-18
        valuation, financial statements for, 13-14
    inventory measurement under, 6-11
    lease accounting under, 10-10
    pension funded status under, 10-15
    PPE valuation under, 6-21
    provisions and contingencies under, 7-7
International Harvester, 22-22
International Paper Company, 9-32, 21-3
Inventories, 2-3, 2-5, 11-12–11-13
    analysis tools
        cash conversion cycle, 6-16–6-17
        days inventory outstanding and inventory turnover, 6-13–6-15
        days payable outstanding, 6-15–6-16
        gross profit analysis, 6-12–6-13
    costing methods, 6-3–6-4
        average cost, 6-5–6-6
        balance sheet effects, 6-7
        cash flow effects, 6-7–6-8
        financial statement effects of, 6-7–6-8
        first-in, first-out, 6-4–6-5
        income statement effects, 6-7
        last-in, first-out, 6-5

Inventories, *(continued)*
  quality, 6-14–6-15
  reporting
    LIFO liquidations, 6-11
    LIFO reserve adjustments to financial
      statements, 6-9–6-10
    lower of cost or market, 6-8–6-9
  turnover, 6-13–6-15, 20-13
Inventory costs
  for financial reporting
    components of product costs, 18-5–18-6
    manufacturing overhead, 18-6–18-9
    product costs and period costs, 18-4–18-5
  in various organizations, 18-3–18-4
Investing activities, 1-3, 1-10–1-11, 1-15–1-16,
    11-3, 11-4, 22-8
  cash flows from
    Java House case illustration, 11-16–11-18
    noncash assets, 11-16
    preview, 11-8
Investing equals financing, 1-10
Investment analysts, 1-5
Investment center, 23-5
Investment center asset base, 24-16
Investment center evaluation measures, 24-18–
    24-20
  economic value added, 24-17–24-18
  investment center asset base, 24-16
  investment center income, 24-15–24-16
  other valuation issues, 24-16–24-17
  residual income, 24-17
  return on investment, 24-13–24-15
Investment center income, 24-15–24-16
Investment returns, 10-15, 10-16
Investment tax credit, 25-22–25-23
Investors and equity analysts, 1-3
Irrelevant costs, 17-3, 17-6
Issued shares, 8-3, 8-5, 8-7

J

Java House case illustration
  cash flow from financing activities
    common stock, change in, 11-18
    net cash from financing activities, 11-19
    retained earnings, change in, 11-18
  cash flow from investing activities
    accumulated depreciation, change in,
      11-17
    long-term investments, change in,
      11-16–11-17
    net cash from investing activities,
      11-17–11-18
    patent, 11-17
    PPE, change in, 11-17
  cash flow from operating activities
    accounts payable, 11-13
    accounts receivable, 11-12
    accrued liabilities, 11-14
    gains and losses with no cash flow
      effects, 11-12
    inventory, 11-12–11-13
    net cash from operating activities, 11-14
    prepaid expenses, 11-13
    revenues and expenses with no cash flow
      effects, 11-11–11-12
  financial data of, 11-10

for supplemental disclosures, 11-20–11-21
Job costing, 18-11–18-16
  overapplied and underapplied overhead,
    18-17–18-18
  in service organizations, 18-18–18-20
  sheet, 18-9
  statement of cost of goods manufactured,
    18-16–18-17
Job order production. *See* Job production
Job production, 18-9
Johnson & Johnson, 1-11, 1-13, 1-19, 22-6
  accounting for stock-based compensation,
    8-14–8-15
  AOCI disclosures and interpretation,
    8-20–8-21
  common stock, 8-7–8-8
  stockholders' equity
    accounts, 8-3–8-4
    statement of, 8-5–8-6
Joint costs, 17-17
Joint product, 17-17
Joint product decisions, 17-17–17-18
Journal entries, 3-5, 3-6
J.P. Morgan Chase, 15-16
Juniper Networks, 9-4, 9-5, 9-11
Just-in-time (JIT) inventory management,
    20-10–20-12

K

Kaizen costing. *See* Continuous improvement
    costing
Kanban system, 20-11
KBR Inc., 24-20
Kickstarter, 19-14
Kodak, 22-6
KPMG, 1-31, 23-10
Kraft, 9-22
Kraft Heinz Company, 9-22
Kroger Company, 6-6, 20-1, 21-19
Kubota, 6-10

L

Labor efficiency variance, 23-13
Labor rate variance, 23-13
La Brea Bakery, 18-18
Last-in, first-out (LIFO), 6-5
  liquidations, 6-11
  reserve adjustments to financial statements,
    6-9–6-10
Lattice method, 8-15
Lean production and just-in-time inventory
    management
  finished goods inventory, 20-12
  incoming materials inventory, 20-10–20-11
  performance measures under, 20-13–20-14
  work-in-process inventory, 20-11–20-12
Leases
  accounting, 10-5
    and balance sheet, 10-6–10-7
    and income statement, 10-7–10-8
    statement of cash flows, 10-8–10-9
  analysis issues relating to, 10-10–10-11
  capitalization
    using financial calculator, 10-33
    using present value tables, 10-34–10-35
  finance and operating leases, 10-35–10-37

Hewlett-Packard 10bII, 10-33
  imputed discount rate computation for, 10-7
  lessee reporting, 10-4–10-5
  liability, 10-6
  Microsoft Corporation, 10-4–10-5
  new lease reporting standard, 10-3–10-4
  summary, 10-9–10-10
  Texas Instruments BA II Plus, 10-33
Least-squares regression analysis, 15-14
  advantage of, 15-14–15-15
  managers, not mathematical models, are
    responsible, 15-15
  simple and multiple regression, 15-15–15-17
Lenders, 7-16
  and credit analysts, 1-3
Lessee, 10-3
  reporting, 10-4–10-5
Lessor, 10-3
Leukemia and Lymphoma Society, 25-15
Level of precision, 12-5
Levi Strauss, 5-11
  accounts receivable, 5-23–5-24
  balance sheet, 5-12
  income statement, 5-12
  sales allowances
    analysis of, 5-13
    reporting, 5-12
Liabilities, 1-10, 2-6–2-7
  analyzing, 11-18
  current, 2-7–2-9
  noncurrent, 2-9–2-10
  -to-equity ratio, 4-37–4-38
Licenses, 5-6
Life-cycle budgeting, 22-21
Life-cycle costs, 21-3
  management, 21-16–21-17
Line departments, 14-10
Linear algebra method, 20-7–20-9
Liquidity, 2-5, 7-20, 11-3
  analysis, 4-36
Litigation, 1-8
  expenses, 12-3
Local Motors, 18-21
Long-range planning, and capital budgeting,
    25-3–25-6
Long-term assets, 2-5
Long-term debt (LTD), 2-9, 12-14
  current maturities of, 7-8
  effective cost of debt, 7-11–7-13
  pricing, 7-9–7-10
    of bonds issued at discount, 7-10–7-11
    of bonds issued at par, 7-10
    of bonds issued at premium, 7-11
  reporting
    balance sheet, 7-13–7-14
    fair value disclosures, 7-15–7-16
    financial statement effects of bond
      repurchase, 7-14–7-15
    income statement, 7-14
Long-term investments, 2-5
  change in, 11-16–11-17
LookSmart, 9-17
Lowe's Companies Inc., 5-14–5-15, 6-17, 6-27,
    11-23
Lower of cost or market (LCM), 6-3, 6-8–6-9
Lump-sum, 7-10, 7-26

Lump-sum amounts, 25-8
Lyft, 5-33, 14-18

M

Macy's Inc., 1-13, 1-18, 6-20, 20-14
Magnitude, 5-21–5-22
Maker's Row, 19-14
Managed fixed costs. *See* Discretionary fixed
      costs
Management by exception, 22-3, 23-3
Management discussion and analysis (MD&A),
      2-23–2-24
Managerial accounting, 14-4–14-5
      accounting information
            financial accounting, 14-3–14-4
            managerial accounting, 14-4–14-5
            strategic cost management, 14-5–14-6
      changing environment of business
            big data and analysis, 14-12
            enterprise risk management, 14-13
            global competition and key dimensions,
                  14-12
            robotics and cognitive technologies,
                  14-12–14-13
      cost drivers, 14-17–14-18
            activity, 14-19–14-20
            organizational, 14-19
            structural, 14-18–14-19
      data-driven planning central to, 16-4
      defined, 14-3
      ethics in, 14-13–14-15
            codes of ethics, 14-15
            corporate governance, 14-15–14-16
            sustainability accounting and corporate
                  social responsibility, 14-16–14-17
      financial accounting vs., 14-5
      and goal attainment, 14-9–14-10
      mission and goals, 14-6–14-7
      planning, organizing, and controlling,
            14-10–14-11
      strategic position analysis, 14-7–14-9
Managers, 1-4–1-5
Manufacturing costs, 6-3, 18-4
      budget, 22-16–22-20
      hierarchy, 15-19–15-20
Manufacturing organizations, 18-3
Manufacturing overhead (MO), 6-3, 15-19,
      18-5–18-7
      changing cost structures, 18-8–18-9
      using predetermined overhead rates, 18-7–
            18-8
      selecting basis/cost driver for assigning, 18-7
Marathon Oil, 23-23
Margin of safety, 16-9
Marginal cost, 21-7
      of one unit, 15-7
Marginal revenue, 21-7
Market capitalization, 8-5, 8-8
Market price, 8-5, 24-10
Market value, 2-12
Market (yield or effective) rate, 7-9
Marketable equity securities, 9-6
Market-segment-level activity, 15-20
Market-to-book ratio, 2-12, 8-4
Markup pricing, 24-11
Master budget, 22-1, 22-7–22-9

budgeted financial statements, 22-13–22-14
cash budget, 22-11–22-13
finalizing, 22-14–22-16
general and administrative expense budget,
      22-11
purchases budget, 22-10
sales budget, 22-9–22-10
selling expense budget, 22-10–22-11
Materials price variance, 23-11
Materials pull system, 20-11
Materials push system, 20-11
Materials quantity variance, 23-11
Materials requisition form, 18-10
Mayo Clinic, 15-11, 19-15
McDonald's Corporation, 11-29, 14-8, 15-11
McNeil, 22-6–22-7
Measurability, 4-40
Mechanics of consolidation accounting, 9-19–
      9-22
Mercedes, 17-1
Merchandising organizations, 18-3
Merck & Co. Inc., 4-10–4-11, 5-34–5-35
Method of comparables model, 13-12
Metromile, 15-5
Metropolitan Life Insurance Co., 10-21
Michael Kors Holdings LTD, 9-29, 9-30
Microsoft Corporation, 2-13, 2-26, 5-4–5-5,
      5-15, 8-11–8-12, 9-11, 10-3–10-5, 14-19,
      15-11, 17-13, 17-17
      assets, 10-4
      financial statements, 2-22
      imputed discount rate computation for leases,
            10-7
      income statement, 2-17
      liabilities and stockholders' equity, 10-5
      statement of cash flows, 2-20
      statement of stockholders' equity, 2-18
Microsoft Excel, 15-14
Midas, 15-11
Midstate Supply Company, 23-24
Milliken & Company, 18-8–18-9
Minimum dollar return, 24-17
Minimum level approach, 22-5–22-6
Minimum rate of return, 24-17
Mission, 14-6–14-7
Mixed costs, 15-3
Mobile Health Screening (MHS), 19-6
Mobile Taqueria, 25-7–25-9, 25-12–25-13,
      25-17, 25-21–25-22
ModCloth, 18-1
Modified Accelerated Cost Recovery System
      (MACRS), 6-19, 10-25
Monsanto, 24-18–24-19
Moody's Investors Service, 1-21, 2-26, 7-18,
      7-24
Morgan Stanley, 12-17
      forecast report on Procter & Gamble, 12-23–
            12-30
      forecasting process, 12-4
Motorola, 21-5
Movement time, 20-11
MTV, 3-10
Multi-level contribution income statement,
      16-21–16-22
      variations in, 16-23
Multilevel segment income statements, 24-5

Multiple constraints, 17-19–17-20
Multiple-element-contracts, 5-6
Multiple investment criteria, 25-16
Multiple-product cost-volume-profit analysis
      break-even and target profit sales dollars,
            16-15
      sales mix analysis, 16-15–16-18
Multiple regression analysis, 15-15–15-16
Multiples model. *See* Method of comparables
      model

N

Nature's Path Foods Inc., 23-12
Negotiated transfer prices, 24-11–24-12
Net asset valuation model, 13-13
Net book value (NBV), 6-19, 10-39
Net cash
      from financing activities, 11-19
      flow, 11-10–11-11
      from investing activities, 11-17–11-18
Net income vs. cash flows, 11-22
Net nonoperating expense (NNE), 4-22–4-23,
      4-32
Net nonoperating expense percent (NNEP), 4-32
Net nonoperating obligations (NNO), 4-17–
      4-18, 4-32
Net operating asset (NOA), 4-15–4-17, 4-24,
      13-4, 13-11–13-12
      parsimonious method for forecasting,
            12-22–12-23
Net operating asset turnover (NOAT), 4-26–
      4-28, 9-16
Net operating profit after tax (NOPAT), 4-24,
      13-4, 13-11–13-12
      parsimonious method for forecasting,
            12-22–12-23
Net operating profit before tax (NOPBT), 4-24
Net operating profit margin (NOPM), 4-25–
      4-28, 9-16
Net present value, 25-6, 25-8–25-9
Net sales volume variance, 23-20
Net working capital, 2-8
Netgear Inc., 9-34–9-35
New lease reporting standard, 10-3–10-4
Nissan Motor Co., 21-6
Nissim Company, 9-18–9-21
Nissin Kogyo, 21-17
Noncapitalized costs, 4-41
Noncash assets, 11-16
Noncontrolling interest, 4-5, 8-8, 9-19–9-20
      income attributable to, 5-25
Noncurrent liabilities, 2-9–2-10
Nonmanufacturing costs, 18-4
Non-marketable equity securities, 9-6–9-7
Nonoperating assets, 4-17–4-18
Nonoperating expenses, 2-13
Nonoperating liabilities, 4-17
Nonowner financing, 1-10
Nonpension post-employment benefits, 10-23
Nonrefundable up-front fees, 5-6
Nordstrom Inc., 1-11, 1-13, 1-19, 19-18, 21-13
Normal balance, 3-4
North American Consumer Packaging, 9-32
Not-for-profit organizations, 14-7
      cost-volume-profit analysis, 16-3

O

Olive Theory Pizzeria, 25-16
Open book management, 22-22–22-23
Operating activities, 1-3, 1-15, 11-3, 11-4, 22-8
    cash flows from, 11-9–11-10
        Java House case illustration, 11-11–11-16
        steps to compute net cash flow, 11-10–
            11-11
    converting net income to net cash flow from,
        11-11
    preview, 11-5
Operating assets, 4-15
Operating budgets, 22-3
Operating cash flow to capital expenditures
    ratio, 11-27–11-28
Operating cash flow to current liabilities ratio,
    11-27
Operating (or cash) cycle, 2-8
Operating expenses, 2-13, 2-16
    margin, 4-9
Operating lease, 10-3, 10-35–10-37
    method, 10-9
    payments, present value of, 10-6
Operating leverage
    analysis of, 16-18–16-20
    ratio, 16-18
Operating liabilities, 4-15–4-16
Operating segment, 12-16
Operation phase of cash flows, 25-7
Operational budgeting and profit planning. See
    Budgeting
Operations list, 18-9
Opportunity costs, 17-5–17-6, 24-11
    differential analysis of outsourcing decision
        with, 17-14
    importance of, 17-11–17-12
Options, 7-21
Oracle, 19-11
Order-filling costs, 23-19
Order-getting costs, 23-19
Order-level activity, 15-20
Ordinary annuity, 7-26
Organization chart, 14-10, 14-11
Organization structures, 23-4
Organizational cost drivers, 14-19
Organizing, 14-10, 14-11
Other comprehensive income (OCI), 8-5, 8-20,
    9-25
Other long-term liabilities, 2-9
Other post-employment benefits (OPEB),
    10-23–10-24
Outlay costs, 17-4, 17-6
Output/input approach, 22-5
Outsourcing decisions, 17-13–17-16
Outstanding shares, 8-5, 8-8
Owner financing, 1-10

P

Pacific Foods of Oregon Inc., 23-12
Pads. See Accruals
Paid-in capital, 8-5
Panera Bread, 16-3
Par (face) value, 7-10, 8-3, 8-5, 8-7
Parsimonious model forecasts, 13-4
Participative budget, 22-20
Passive investments in equity securities, 9-3, 9-4

intercorporate investments
    acquisition and sale, 9-4–9-5
    fair-value method, 9-5–9-6
    initial adoption of new accounting rules,
        9-7–9-10
    marketable equity securities, 9-6
    non-marketable equity securities, 9-6–9-7
Patel Company, 21-18
Patent, 11-17
Patient capital, 25-15
Payback period, 25-11, 25-12–25-13
Penman Company, 9-18–9-21
Pension, 10-11–10-12
    amortization component of pension expense,
        10-37–10-39
    analysis implications, 10-22–10-23
    analysis issue, 10-13–10-15
    defined benefit pension plan
        on balance sheet, 10-12–10-13
        on income statement, 10-15–10-16
    fair value accounting for, 10-19–10-21
    footnote disclosure, 10-21–10-22
    other post-employment benefits, 10-23–10-24
    pension expense smoothing, 10-16–10-19
Pension expense
    amortization component of, 10-37–10-39
    smoothing, 10-16–10-19
Pension plan assets, 10-12, 10-17
    unexpected returns on, 10-19
PepsiCo Inc., 8-8, 9-31, 21-3, 25-
Performance evaluation
    financial and nonfinancial, 23-5–23-6
    under lean production and JIT, 20-13–20-14
    traditional, dysfunctional effects of, 20-13
Performance obligation, 5-4
Performance report, 14-9
    for cost centers
        flexible budgets, 23-6–23-8
        standard costs and performance reports,
            23-8–23-9
    and organization structures, 23-4
    for revenue centers, 23-18–23-19
        controllable costs inclusion, 23-19–23-20
        revenue centers as profit centers, 23-20–
            23-21
Period costs, 18-4–18-5
Periodic interest payments, 7-10
Permanent accounts, 2-3, 3-14
Pfizer, 5-3, 5-15–5-16, 5-33, 6-23
    accounts receivable, 5-19
    discontinued operations, 5-29
    expense and loss items, 5-25
    financial ratios, 5-22
    foreign currency
        and cash flows, 5-17
        and future results, 5-17–5-18
        and income, 5-17
    income statement, 5-3
    pro forma income reporting, 5-31–5-32
    R&D expense, 5-26–5-27
Pinterest, 22-1–22-2
Planning, 14-10, 14-11
Plant, property and equipment (PPE), 10-39–
    10-40, 12-12
    analysis of, 4-11–4-12
    analysis tools

PPE percent used up, 6-27
    PPE turnover, 6-25–6-26
    PPE useful life, 6-26
    capitalization and depreciation, 6-17–6-20
    change in, 11-17
    impairments, 6-21
    plant and equipment
        other depreciation methods, 6-19
        straight-line method, 6-18–6-19
    research and development facilities and
        equipment, 6-19–6-20
    restructuring costs
        analysis of, 6-23–6-24
        disclosure of, 6-22–6-23
    sales, 6-20–6-21
    turnover, 6-25–6-26
Plantwide overhead allocation method, 19-7
Political costs, 1-8
Porsche division of Volkswagen, 24-3
Post-audit, 25-5
Posting transactions, 3-4
Potential dilution, 8-13
Pottery Barn, 15-12
Practical capacity, 19-13
Predetermined manufacturing overhead rate,
    18-7
Predictive analytics, 1-29
Preferred stock, 2-10, 8-3, 8-4, 8-6–8-7
Premium, 7-11
    amortization of, 7-32
Prepaid advertising, 3-10
Prepaid expenses, 2-5, 3-10, 11-13
Preparation costs, 1-8
Prescriptive analytics, 1-29
Present value, 25-24–25-25, 25-27
    of annuity, 7-26–7-27
    concepts, 7-25
    of single amount, 7-25
    tables, lease capitalization, 10-34–10-35
Prestige Inc., 3-8–3-9, 3-13
Price gouging, 17-19
Price/cost, 14-12
PricewaterhouseCoopers, 17-15–17-16
Pricing, 7-9–7-10
    benchmarking, 21-18–21-19
    of bonds issued at discount, 7-10–7-11
    of bonds issued at par, 7-10
    of bonds issued at premium, 7-11
    continuous improvement costing, 21-17–
        21-18
    cost-based approaches to, 21-8–21-9
        critique of, 21-11
        in multiple-product companies, 21-9–
            21-10
        in single-product companies, 21-9
        for special orders, 21-11
    economic approaches to, 21-7–21-8
    target costing
        coordination, 21-14–21-15
        cost information, 21-14
        design for production, 21-13–21-14
        key for products with short life cycles,
            21-15–21-16
        life-cycle costs management, 21-16–
            21-17

Pricing, *(continued)*
  target costing, *(continued)*
    proactive for cost management, 21-12–21-13
    time to introduce products, 21-14
  value chain, 21-3–21-5
    core competencies, 21-6
    supplier–buyer partnerships, 21-5–21-6
    value-added and, 21-6–21-7
Primark, 14-1–14-3, 14-4
  mission statement for, 14-6
  strategic position analysis, 14-8
Prince, 21-11–21-12
Prior service costs, 10-37
Pro forma disclosure, 12-10
Pro forma income reporting
  disclosures and market assessments, 5-32–5-35
  Regulation G reconciliation, 5-31–5-32
  SEC warnings about pro forma numbers, 5-32
Process costing, 18-20–18-21
  cost of production report, 18-21–18-24
  process costing in service organizations, 18-25–18-26
  weighted average and first-in, first-out process costing, 18-24–18-25
Process manufacturing, 18-9
Processes, value chain and, 21-4
Processing time, 20-11
Procter & Gamble (P&G), 1-14, 18-9, 20-12, 24-14
  Deutsche Bank valuation of
    concluding observations of analyst report, 13-25
    qualitative and quantitative summary, 13-14–13-24
  forecasting, 13-4
    balance sheet, 12-12–12-16, 12-21
    guidance, 12-5–12-6
    income statement, 12-8–12-12, 12-21
    Morgan Stanley's report, 12-23–12-30
    parsimonious method of sales, NOPAT, and NOA, 12-23
    segment data, 12-16–12-18
    statement of cash flows, 12-19
  residual operating income model, 13-10
  weighted average cost of capital, 13-8
Product costing, 18-4–18-5, 20-14–20-15
  absorption and variable costing
    basic concepts, 18-26
    evaluating alternatives to inventory valuation, 18-30–18-31
    income under, 18-27
    inventory valuations, 18-26–18-27
    production equals sales, 18-27
    production exceeds sales, 18-28–18-29
    sales exceed production, 18-29–18-30
  components of, 18-5–18-6
  data-driven decision making, 20-15–20-16
  inventory costs
    for financial reporting, 18-4–18-9
    in various organizations, 18-3–18-4
  job costing, 18-11–18-16
    overapplied and underapplied overhead, 18-17–18-18

in service organizations, 18-18–18-20
  statement of cost of goods manufactured, 18-16–18-17
lean production and just-in-time inventory management
  finished goods inventory, 20-12
  incoming materials inventory, 20-10–20-11
  work-in-process inventory, 20-11–20-12
performance evaluation
  dysfunctional effects of traditional performance measures, 20-13
  performance measures under lean production and JIT, 20-13–20-14
process costing, 18-20–18-21
  cost of production report, 18-21–18-24
  process costing in service organizations, 18-25–18-26
  weighted average and first-in, first-out process costing, 18-24–18-25
production and service department costs, 20-3
production environment, 18-9
  production files and records, 18-10
service department costs allocation, 20-4–20-5
  direct method, 20-5–20-6
  dual rates, 20-9
  linear algebra (reciprocal) method, 20-7–20-9
  step method, 20-6–20-7
simplified recordkeeping
  product costing, 20-14–20-15
  purchasing, 20-14
Product differentiation, 1-24
Product margins, 24-5
Production budget, 22-16, 22-18
Production departments, 20-3
Production equals sales, 18-27
Production exceeds sales, 18-28–18-29
Production files and records, 18-10
Production order, 18-9
Productivity, 1-18
  analysis
    cash conversion cycle, 4-10–4-11
    plant, property and equipment, 4-11–4-12
    working capital, 4-9
Product-level activity, 15-19
Profit, 1-13
Profit center, 23-4–23-5
  revenue center as, 23-20–23-21
Profit margin (PM), 1-18, 4-6
Profit planning, 16-10–16-11
  operational budgeting and. *See* Budgeting
Profitability, 1-18
  analysis, 16-3
    gross profit margin, 4-8–4-9
    multi-level contribution income statement, 16-21–16-23
    operating expense margin, 4-9
    with unit and nonunit cost drivers, 16-21–16-23
Profit-volume graph, 16-11–16-13
Projected benefit obligation (PBO), 10-12, 10-17
Project-level activity, 15-21
Proper Cloth, 18-12

Prospective adoption, 10-3
Provision (benefit) for taxes on income, 5-25, 5-28
Public Company Accounting Oversight Board (PCAOB), 1-32
Publix, 21-4
Purchases budget, 22-10, 22-18
Purchasing, 20-14
Pure Water Company, 19-16–19-18
PwC, 1-31, 5-9

Q

Quaker, 18-18
Qualitative considerations, 17-12
Quality, 5-22–5-24, 14-12
Quality circles, 20-11
Quality of debt
  credit analysis, 7-16–7-17
  credit ratings, 7-18–7-19
    and financial ratios, 7-19–7-21
    reasons for matter, 7-23–7-24
    Verizon, 7-20–7-23
Quick ratio, 4-36–4-37

R

R&D spending, 5-26
Raj India Trading Co., 15-8
Ratio analysis, 11-27–11-28
Raw materials inventories, 18-3
Raytheon, 5-7
  cost-to-cost method, 5-7–5-8
  cost-to-cost reporting, 5-8–5-10
Razor USA, LLC, 16-1, 16-5, 16-19
  contribution income statement, 16-7
    with income taxes, 16-14
  functional income statement, 16-7
RBC Capital Markets, 2-25
Reasonable assurance, 1-32
Reciprocal method. *See* Linear algebra method
Regulation, 1-7
Regulation Fair Disclosure (FD), 1-8
Regulation G reconciliation, 5-31–5-32
Regulators, 1-6–1-7
REI, 22-8, 23-13, 23-15, 23-18
  balance sheet, 22-9, 22-15
  budgeted financial statements, 22-14
  cash budget, 22-13
  general and administrative expense budget, 22-11
  manufacturing cost budget, 22-19
  production budget, 22-18
  purchases budget, 22-10, 22-18
  sales budget, 22-9, 22-18
  selling expense budget, 22-11
Reinvested capital, 1-14
Relevant costs, 17-3–17-4, 17-6
  differential analysis of, 17-7–17-8
    multiple changes in profit plans, 17-8–17-10
    outsourcing decisions, 17-13–17-16
    sell or process, 17-16–17-18
    special orders, 17-10–17-12
  disposal and salvage values, 17-5
  future revenues, 17-4
  limited resources, use of, 17-18–17-19

Relevant costs, *(continued)*
  limited resources, use of, *(continued)*
    decision analysis models, limitations of, 17-21
    multiple constraints, 17-19–17-20
    single constraint, 17-19
    theory of constraints, 17-20–17-21
  opportunity costs, 17-5–17-6
  outlay costs, 17-4
  sunk costs
    causing ethical dilemmas, 17-5
    irrelevance of, 17-4–17-5
Relevant range, 15-7–15-8
Representatives, 1-7
Research and development (R&D)
  analysis of, 5-26–5-28
  R&D spending, 5-26
Residual claim, 8-5
Residual income, 24-17
Residual interest, 2-10
Residual operating income (ROPI) model, 13-3
  advantages and disadvantages of, 13-13
  illustrating, 13-10–13-11
  managerial insights from, 13-11–13-12
  steps in applying, 13-9–13-10
  structure, 13-9
Resources (assets), 1-10
Responsibility accounting, 23-3
  financial and nonfinancial performance measures, 23-5–23-6
  performance reporting and organization structures, 23-4
  responsibility centers
    cost center, 23-4
    investment center, 23-5
    profit center, 23-4–23-5
    revenue center, 23-4
Responsibility centers
  cost center, 23-4
  investment center, 23-5
  profit center, 23-4–23-5
  revenue center, 23-4
Restricted stock, 8-13
Restricted stock awards, 8-27
Restricted stock units (RSU), 8-13, 8-27
Restructuring cost, 5-25, 10-41
  analysis of, 6-23–6-24
  disclosure of, 6-22–6-23
  and managerial incentives, 6-24
Restructuring expenses, 12-3
Retail inventory method (RIM), 6-6
Retained earnings, 1-14, 2-6, 2-10, 2-11–2-13, 8-4, 12-14
  change in, 11-18
  reconciliation, 2-20
  statement, 3-15
Retroactive adoption, 10-3
Return on assets (ROA), 1-18, 4-4
  adjusted, 4-6
  components of, 1-18–1-20
  and disaggregation, 4-6–4-7
    financial leverage analysis, 4-12–4-14
    productivity analysis, 4-9–4-12
    profitability analysis, 4-8–4-9
Return on equity (ROE), 1-20, 4-3, 4-24, 9-14–9-17

accounts used to compute, 4-5
  disaggregation
    financial leverage, 4-4–4-6
    return on assets, 4-4. *See also* Return on assets
  nonoperating return, 4-31–4-32
    with noncontrolling interest, 4-34–4-35
    with substantial net nonoperating assets, 4-33–4-34
Return on invested capital (ROIC), 4-28
Return on investment (ROI), 24-13–24-15
Return on net operating assets (RNOA), 4-15, 4-23–4-25
  disaggregation into margin and turnover, 4-25–4-29
  vs. ROA, 4-23
Revenue, 17-4
  and expenses, with no cash flow effects, 11-10, 11-11–11-12
  for high-tech investments, 25-19–25-20
  recognizing, 2-14–2-15
  variance, 23-18
Revenue center, 23-4
  controllable costs inclusion, 23-19–23-20
  as profit centers, 23-20–23-21
Revenue recognition, 5-3–5-4
  complications of, 5-5–5-6
  foreign currency effects on, 5-15–5-18
  performance obligations satisfied over time, 5-7–5-11
  principle, 2-14
  rules, 5-4–5-5
  unearned (deferred), 5-14–5-15
Right of return, 5-6
Right-of-use asset, 10-6
Rio Tinto, 16-20
Risk, 22-3
  evaluating, 25-17
  management
    budgeting in, 22-3–22-4
    systematic approach to, 22-4
  premium, 7-17
Risk-free rate, 7-17
Rite Aid, 6-11
RJD Partners, 18-18
Robotic process automation (RPA), 14-12–14-13
Roku, 21-1, 21-10
Roller, 18-21
Rolling budget. *See* Continuous budgeting
Rolling Stones, 14-1
RSM, 1-31

S

S&P 500 Index, 4-3
Saks Fifth Avenue, 19-18
Sales allowances, 5-3
  accounting for, 5-11–5-12
  analysis of, 5-13–5-14
  reporting, 5-12
Sales budget, 22-9–22-10, 22-18
Sales dollar analysis, 16-17–16-18
Sales exceed production, 18-29–18-30
Sales mix, 16-4
  analysis, 16-15–16-16
    sales dollar, 16-17–16-18
    unit sales, 16-16–16-17

Sales price variance, 23-18
Sales volume variance, 23-19
Salvage value, 17-5
Salvation Army, 16-3
Samsung Electronics, 1-18, 1-25, 17-13, 18-1, 18-2, 21-19
SanDisk, 18-25–18-26
Sandstrom Partners, 18-18
Sanmina, 21-6
Santa Fe Railroad, 15-10
Sarbanes-Oxley Act of 2002 (SOX), 1-17, 14-15–14-16
Scandinavian Furniture Inc., 17-16
Scatter diagrams, 15-13–15-14
Schumacher Homes, 18-9
Seagate, 17-13
Sears, 19-18
Securities and Exchange Commission (SEC), 5-32
  enforcement actions, 1-33
  filings, 1-26–2-28
Segment data, 12-16–12-18
Segment income, 24-6
Segment margin, 24-5
Segment reporting, 24-4
  interpreting segment reports, 24-5–24-7
  preparation of segment reports, 24-4
  segment income statements, multilevel, 24-5
  strategic business segments and, 24-3–24-4
Self-liquidating, 4-15, 4-38
Selling expense budget, 22-10–22-11
Selling, general, and administrative expenses (SG&A), 1-13, 4-9, 5-25, 12-9
Semivariable costs. *See* Mixed costs
Sensitivity analysis, 12-21, 16-8
Service cost, 10-15, 18-18
Service departments, 20-3
  costs allocation, 20-4–20-5
    direct method, 20-5–20-6
    dual rates, 20-9
    linear algebra (reciprocal) method, 20-7–20-9
    step method, 20-6–20-8
Service organizations, 18-3
Service revenue, 5-15
ServiceMaster, 21-9
Setup time, 20-11
Seven Cycles, 18-12
7-Eleven, 21-4
Short-term debt, 2-7
  accounting for, 7-7–7-8
Short-term investments, 2-5
Shriners Hospitals for Children, 18-3
Significant influence, equity investments with, 9-3, 9-4
  accounting for, 9-12–9-14
  equity method accounting and ROE effects, 9-14–9-17
Silk, 19-7
Simon Property Group, 19-18
Simple regression analysis, 15-15–15-16
Simplified recordkeeping
  product costing, 20-14–20-15
  purchasing, 20-14
Single constraint, 17-19
Single payment, 7-10

Single product decisions, 17-16–17-17
Snap Fitness, 17-19
SodaStream, 25-6
Solo Cup Company, 16-8–16-9, 16-14–16-15
Solvency analysis, 4-37
Sony Corporation, 24-8–24-9
South32, 16-20
Southwest Airlines Inc., 1-11, 9-29, 9-30, 10-39,
    11-24, 14-8, 23-1, 23-6
Special orders, 17-10–17-12
    cost-based pricing for, 21-11
Spitz Inc., 5-7
Split-off point, 17-17
SportClips, 18-3
Spread, 4-32, 7-17
Spreadsheet approach, 25-8–25-9
    for internal rate of return, 25-10
Springfield Remanufacturing Corp. (SRC),
    22-22–22-23
Sprouts Farmers Markets, 20-1
Square, Inc., 15-1, 15-18
St. Jude Hospital, 14-20
Staff departments, 14-10
Stand-alone selling price (SSP), 5-5
Standard & Poor's (S&P), 2-26, 4-3, 5-21, 7-18,
    7-24
Standard costs
    analysis, components of, 23-9–23-10
    and performance reports, 23-8–23-9
    variance analysis, 23-9
Standard labor rate, 23-13
Standard price, 23-10
Standard quantity, 23-10
Standard time allowed, 23-13
Standard variable cost of goods sold, 23-20
Stanley Black and Decker, 22-19
Staples, 15-15, 16-3, 25-1
Starbucks, 11-5, 1-11, 1-12, 1-18, 11-27, 11-28,
    21-7
    adjustments for operating cash flow, 11-14–
        1-15
    financing activities, 11-19
    investing activities, 11-17
    statement of cash flows for, 11-6
Statement of cash flows, 1-15–1-16, 2-18–2-20,
    11-3
    direct method reporting for, 11-29–11-32
    financing activities, 11-8–11-9
    forecasting, 12-19–12-20
    investing activities, 11-8
    lease accounting and, 10-8–10-9
    operating activities, 11-5–11-7
    relation among financial statements, 11-3–
        11-4
    structure, 11-4–11-5
    usefulness of, 11-25–11-27
Statement of cost of goods manufactured,
    18-16–18-17
Statement of stockholders' equity, 1-14–1-15,
    2-17–2-18
    preparation of, 3-15–3-16
Static budget, 23-6
Step costs, 15-3
Step method, 20-6–20-8
Stern Stewart and Company, 24-18
Stock appreciation rights (SARs), 8-13, 8-28

Stock awards, 8-27
Stock-based compensation, 8-12
    accounting for, 8-14–8-15
    analysis implications, 8-28–8-29
    footnote disclosures for, 8-15–8-16
    interpretation of, 8-14–8-15
    plans
        analysis of, 8-13–8-14
        characteristics of, 8-13
        types of, 8-13
    reporting and analyzing
        employee stock purchase plans, 8-26
        stock appreciation rights, 8-28
        stock awards, 8-27
        stock options, 8-27
    summary of, 8-28
Stock issuance, 8-8–8-9
    and stock returns, 8-10
Stock options, 8-27
Stock repurchase, 8-10–8-12
Stock split, 8-5, 8-18
    in form of dividend, 8-18–8-19
Stock transactions
    stock issuance, 8-8–8-10
    stock repurchase, 8-10–8-12
Stockholders, 1-6
Stockholders' equity, 2-10–2-11
    accounts
        contributed capital, 8-3
        earned capital, 8-4–8-5
    common stock, 8-7–8-8
    preferred stock, 8-6–8-7
    statement of, 8-5–8-6. See also Statement of
        stockholders' equity
Stored-value cards, 5-15
Straight-line depreciation, 25-22
Straight-line method, 6-18–6-19
Stratasys, Ltd., 18-19–18-20
Strategic (business) plan, 1-3–1-4
Strategic alliances, 9-12
Strategic business segment, 24-3–24-4
Strategic cost management, 14-5–14-6
Strategic partners, 1-6
Strategic position analysis, 14-6, 14-7–14-9
Strategic segment organization, 24-3–24-4
Strategic thinking, 14-4
Strategy, 14-7
Structural cost drivers, 14-18–14-19
Stryker Corporation, 4-3, 4-5–4-6, 4-14, 4-18,
    4-22–4-23, 4-25, 4-29, 4-35, 4-41
Subsidiary ledger, 18-10
Subway, 15-5, 15-16–15-17
Sunk costs, 17-6
    causing ethical dilemmas, 17-5
    irrelevance of, 17-4–17-5
Supplier–buyer partnerships, 21-5–21-6
Suppliers, 1-5–1-6
Supply of information
    benefits of disclosure, 1-7–1-8
    costs of disclosure, 1-8
    International Accounting Standards, 1-8–1-9
Sustainability accounting, 14-16–14-17
SWOT analysis of business environment, 1-23

T

Table approach, 25-8

for determining internal rate of return,
    25-29–25-30
T-account, 3-4, 3-6–3-9
Takata Corp., 21-6
Target, 14-18, 16-3
Target Corporation, 1-13, 1-18, 10-35
Target costing, 21-3
    in competitive environment, 21-13
    coordination, 21-14–21-15
    cost information, 21-14
    design for production, 21-13–21-14
    and global sourcing, 21-13
    key for products with short life cycles,
        21-15–21-16
    life-cycle costs management, 21-16–21-17
    proactive for cost management, 21-12–21-13
    pros and cons of, 21-15
    time to introduce products, 21-14
Target dollar sales volume, 16-15
Tata Consultancy Services, 5-7
Tax Code, 25-22
Tax Cuts and Jobs Act, 10-30–10-31
Tax loss carryforwards, 10-27
Taxes. See also Income taxes
    agencies, 1-6–1-7
    in capital budgeting decisions, 25-20–25-21
        depreciation tax shield, 25-21–25-22
        investment tax credit, 25-22–25-23
    provision, 5-28
Taylor Guitars, 17-15
TaylorMade-Adidas Golf Company, 17-6, 17-8
Technicians, 13-13
TED, 14-6
Temporary accounts, 3-16
Terminal period, 13-6
Territory margins, 24-5
Tesla, 8-22, 11-24–11-25
Texas Instruments BA II Plus, 10-33
Theory of constraints, 17-20–17-21
Thomson Reuters Corporation, 2-26
Threat of entry, 1-22
Threat of substitution, 1-22
3M Company, 1-11, 1-14, 2-9
Throughput, 17-20
Tiffany & Co., 5-13–5-14, 9-29, 9-30
Time span and opportunity costs, 17-11–17-12
Time value of money, 25-3, 25-23–25-24
    annuities, 25-25–25-26
    bond valuation, 7-27
    capital budgeting models considering
        cost of capital, 25-10–25-11
        expected cash flows, 25-6–25-7
        internal rate of return, 25-9–25-10
        manager behavior and expected cash
            flows, 25-8
        net present value, 25-8–25-9
    capital budgeting models not considering,
        25-11–25-12
        accounting rate of return, 25-13–25-14
        payback period, 25-12–25-13
    computations using calculator, 7-28
    computations using Excel, 7-28–7-29
    deferred returns, 25-28
    future value, 25-24
        of annuity, 7-30
        concepts, 7-30

Time value of money, *(continued)*
  future value, *(continued)*
    of single amount, 7-30
    present value, 25-24–25-25, 25-27
      of annuity, 7-26–7-27
      concepts, 7-25
      of single amount, 7-25
      tables, 7-25–7-26
      unequal cash flows, 25-26–25-28
Time-adjusted rate of return. *See* Internal rate
  of return
Times interest earned, 4-38
Titleist, 20-15
TJX Companies Inc., 8-18
Top-down budget, 22-20
Toshiba, 14-14
Total costs, 15-8–15-9
  accounting for, 18-23–18-24
  function, 15-6
Toyota Motor Corporation, 18-8, 20-12, 21-6,
  21-13, 21-15, 21-18, 24-3, 24-16
Trade credit, 2-9
Trader Joe's, 23-6
Trading securities, 9-10–9-11
Trailing measures, 24-21
Transactions, accounting
  Apple, 3-6
  financial statement effects template, 3-6
  journal entry and T-account, 3-6–3-9
Transfer pricing, 24-7–24-8
  determination of
    absorption cost plus markup, 24-11
    dual prices, 24-12
    market price, 24-10
    negotiated prices, 24-11–24-12
    variable costs, 24-10–24-11
    variable costs plus opportunity costs,
      24-11
  management considerations, 24-8–24-10
Transitory items, reporting of, 2-15–2-16
Treasury shares, 8-5
Treasury stock, 2-10, 8-4, 8-7, 12-15
  companies increasingly choose retirement
    for, 8-11
  disclosures and interpretation, 8-11
  reissuing, 8-10–8-11
Trek, 18-26–18-27
Triple Bottom Line (TBL), 14-16
True Religion Brand Jeans, 18-9
Tumi, 23-13–23-14, 23-17
  flexible budgets and performance evaluation,
    23-8
  manufacturing cost budget, 23-7
  reconciling budgeted and actual income,
    23-23–23-24
  sales department performance report for
    controllable costs, 23-20–23-21
  sales department profit center performance
    report, 23-21
  standard cost variance analysis, 23-8–23-11
Twitter, 15-1
Two-step approach, 7-16

U

Uber, 5-33, 14-8, 17-1–17-2, 17-8–17-13
  contribution income statement, 17-10–17-11
Ultimate Revenues, 5-9
Unallocated common costs, 24-5
Unearned (deferred) revenue, 2-7, 3-10–3-11,
  5-3, 5-14–5-15, 7-4–7-5
Unequal cash flows, 25-26–25-28
Unequal cash inflows, 25-29–25-30
Unfavorable labor efficiency variances, 23-14
Unfavorable labor rate variance, 23-14
Unfavorable materials price variance, 23-12
Unfavorable materials quantity variance, 23-12
Unfavorable spending variance, 23-16
Unilever, 19-1–19-2, 22-12
Unit contribution margin, 16-8
Unit sales analysis, 16-16–16-17
United Way, 14-7
Unit-level activity, 15-19, 15-20
Units-of-production method, 6-19
University Poster Company, 24-13
Unmade, 18-21
Unusual income tax expense/benefit, 12-3
UPS, 10-20, 14-4, 18-16
Urban Outfitters, 18-3
U.S. Department of Defense, 15-21
U.S. Steel, 18-5

V

Valuation and qualifying accounts, 2-24
Valuation models. *See also specific models*
  inputs, 13-4–13-5
Value-added perspective, 21-6–21-7
Value chain, 21-3–21-5
  analysis, 14-6
  for beverage-packaging product, 21-4
  core competencies, 21-6
  supplier–buyer partnerships, 21-5–21-6
  value-added and, 21-6–21-7
Vanguard Group, The, 7-9
Variable cost, 15-3, 15-8–15-9, 18-26, 24-5,
  24-10–24-11
  evaluating alternatives to inventory valuation,
    18-30–18-31
  income under, 18-27
  inventory valuations, 18-26–18-27
  of one unit, 15-7
  plus opportunity costs, 24-11
  production equals sales, 18-27
  production exceeds sales, 18-28–18-29
  sales exceed production, 18-29–18-30
Variable interest entity (VIE), 9-18
Variable manufacturing overhead, 16-5
Variable overhead
  efficiency variance, 23-15
  spending variance, 23-15
  standards for, 23-15–23-17
  variances, 23-15–23-16
    interpreting, 23-16–23-17
Variable selling and administrative costs, 16-5
Variance analysis for costs
  fixed overhead variances, 23-17–23-18,
    23-21–23-23

reconciling budgeted and actual income,
  23-23–23-24
standard cost analysis, components of,
  23-9–23-10
standards for direct labor, 23-13–23-15
standards for direct materials, 23-10–23-13
standards for variable overhead, 23-15–23-17
Verizon Communications Inc., 9-29, 10-20
  accounting for short-term debt, 7-7–7-8
  accrued liabilities, 7-3–7-5
  amortization of discount, 7-31
  balance sheet reporting, 7-13–7-14
  credit ratings, 7-20–7-23
  effective cost of debt, 7-12
  loss on early extinguishment of debt, 7-14
Vertical analysis, 2-11, 4-38. *See also*
  Common-size analysis
Vesting period, 8-13
Vice Media, 21-9
Virtual integration, 21-6
Voice over Internet Protocol (VOIP), 15-17
Volkswagen (VW), 24-1, 24-3
Voters, 1-7

W

Wage inflation, 10-15
Wages payable, 7-4
Waiting time, 20-11
Wall Street Reform and Consumer Protection
  Act of 2010 (Dodd-Frank Act), 1-17
Walmart, 4-36, 15-16, 16-11, 18-3, 20-12, 21-17,
  25-1, 25-6
Walt Disney Company, 5-9
Weighted average cost of capital (WACC), 13-6,
  24-17
Weighted average method, 18-24–18-25
Wells Fargo (WFC), 8-18
WeWork, 5-33
Whirlpool Corporation, 18-5
Whistle-blowing, 14-14
Whole Foods Market, 16-3, 16-4, 20-1, 20-14,
  23-6, 24-18
Winding Creek General Store, 23-21
Work ticket, 18-10
Working capital, 4-9, 4-36
  accounts, 12-12
  management, 11-7
Work-in-process inventories, 18-3, 18-6,
  20-11–20-12
WorldCom Inc., 1-34, 5-33, 14-14
Write-offs, 6-22

X

Xerox, 21-19

Y

Years of benefit payments, 10-15
Yield, 8-6
YY, 14-9

Z

Zenith, 14-20
Zero-based budgeting, 22-5–22-6
Zoetis, 5-29